English Pronouncing Dictionary

English Pronouncing Dictionary

English Pronouncing Dictionary

Daniel Jones

FOURTEENTH EDITION EDITED BY
A. C. GIMSON

Revisions and Supplement by
SUSAN RAMSARAN

CAMBRIDGE
UNIVERSITY PRESS

Published by the Press Syndicate of the University of Cambridge
The Pitt Building, Trumpington Street, Cambridge CB2 1RP
40 West 20th Street, New York, NY 10011–4211, USA
10 Stamford Road, Oakleigh, Victoria 3166, Australia

First published by J. M. Dent & Sons 1917
Fourteenth edition 1977
Reprinted with Revisions and Supplement 1988
Reprinted 1989
First published by Cambridge University Press 1991
Reprinted 1992

Printed in Great Britain at the University Press, Cambridge

A catalogue record for this book is available from the British Library

ISBN 0 521 41568 3 hardback
ISBN 0 521 42586 7 paperback

CONTENTS

Contents

EDITOR'S PREFACE TO THE
FOURTEENTH EDITION

In the thirteenth edition (1967), I introduced certain changes in the
phonetic transcription as well as amendments to the pronunciations
recorded, with the aim of reflecting more faithfully the current state
of the style of speech on which the Dictionary had traditionally been
based. Now, sixty years after the first appearance of the Dictionary,
I have felt it necessary, while keeping the spirit of Daniel Jones's
original work, to undertake a revision more thoroughgoing than that
of any previous edition. As a result, the Introduction and most of the
Explanatory Notes have been rewritten. The Glossary of Phonetic
Terms, dating from 1963, has been omitted on the grounds that it
has become to some extent out of date and that there are, for those
interested in the more technical aspects of phonetic and phonological analysis, many textbooks which will supply their needs.
Moreover, it is intended that the terminology employed in the
introductory notes should be largely self-explanatory.

In addition, the definition of the speech model described has been
modified. Although the traditional term 'received pronunciation'
(RP) has been retained, I have thought it proper to widen its
application (see Introduction, §§ 1.0–1.5). It seems no longer
appropriate, at the end of the twentieth century, to define RP
speakers in the strict social terms used by Daniel Jones in 1917 and
in later editions of the Dictionary. The speech-style now recorded,
while retaining its underlying South-Eastern English characteristics,
is applicable to a wider sample of contemporary speakers, especially
those of the middle generations. Such a model will be of particular
relevance to foreign users of the Dictionary. As a result of this
relaxation of definition, the ordering of pronunciation variants has
frequently been modified and certain new variants have been
included.

I have also made changes in the phonetic symbolization of the
vowels and diphthongs (see Introduction, §§ 2.0–2.2), with a view
to underlining the essential qualitative differences between, for
instance, the vowels of 'beat' and 'bit' or those of 'fool' and 'full',
the traditional quantitative oppositions being often of lesser significance. The notation has also been simplified in three important

respects: the syllable-division of recent editions is, with one exception, no longer shown in the phonetic transcription, the syllable boundaries (and the associated implications for pronunciation) being invariably evident from the orthography or the sense; the distinction between the falling diphthongs previously shown as 'iə, uə' and the rising diphthongs ('ĭə, ŭə') has been abandoned, the occurrence of either being predictable by a simple rule given in the introductory notes (see Introduction, § 3.4(h) and Explanatory Notes, § 8); and the symbolization 'ɛə' for the diphthong in 'there' has been simplified to 'eə'. It is of course possible to predict many other variants of sound and stress pattern by general rule, but I have felt it unwise to forsake further the principle that all possible pronunciation information should be immediately available at the point of entry in the Dictionary, without requiring constant recourse to rules of varying complexity in the Introduction.

Some 1032 new words (806 ordinary [1] words; 226 proper [2] names and abbreviations) have been added, and 208 deleted (143; 65), a net increase of 824 words. The present edition thus records the pronunciation of some 59,664 words, comprising:

Ordinary words	44,548
Proper names and abbreviations	15,116

Throughout the years of my editorship of the Dictionary, I have been much indebted to correspondents and colleagues in Britain and many other parts of the world for their suggestions and corrections. All such comments have been taken into account in the compilation of this new edition, although, since the size of the Dictionary requires that only a selection from the possible English vocabulary items can be included, a large proportion of the many thousand new entries suggested have had to be rejected, usually because they are of rare or over-technical usage or because they seem likely to have but an ephemeral existence. Nevertheless, the compiler of a dictionary such as this relies heavily on the comments of its users, and I will always be grateful to receive them.

Of those who have helped me over the years, my especial gratitude is due to my colleague, Miss S. M. Ramsaran of University College,

---

[1] PUBLISHERS NOTE: The current edition contains more than 60,000 headwords and a total of more than 109,000 entries, printed in bold type. A single headword, for example 'steer', may contain several entries (steers, steering, steered, steerer/s, steerage, steersman, steersmen) and their pronunciations. The Dictionary provides more than 135,000 pronunciations for its 109,000 entries.

[2] 'Proper names' are defined as those entries written with a capital initial letter.

London, who gathered recorded material upon which the ordering of vowel variants in weak syllables has been largely based, who checked my revision of the entries and who helped in correcting the proofs; Mrs H. Wright and her colleagues of the BBC Pronunciation Unit who have been unstinting in giving me advice from their unique records; Mr Vincent Petti of Huddinge, Sweden, who has given me the benefit of his experience in lexicography as well as many suggestions concerning the addition and deletion of entries; Mr G. Walsh of Longman for many interesting discussions on problems of transcription; and Mr J. Windsor Lewis of the University of Leeds who has amassed invaluable information on the pronunciation usage of present-day BBC news-readers. I must thank, too, my colleagues in the Department of Phonetics and Linguistics, University College, London, who, with unfailing patience, have answered innumerable queries put to them at often inconvenient and unexpected moments.

1977   A. C. GIMSON

PREFACE TO THE REVISED EDITION

When Professor Gimson died suddenly in 1985 he was engaged in updating this Dictionary. Although he had envisaged that one day the work would devolve on me, we had no intention that it should be at this stage and I regret that it should be in such circumstances. Since I knew that he was preparing a supplement and since some updating was urgently needed, I have provided a supplement of about a thousand 'new' words, including such well-established items as 'aerobics', 'byte', 'cagoule', 'Ceefax', 'decaffeinated', 'logo', 'microwave', 'photon', 'reggae' and 'wok'. Keeping within strict limitations of space, I have not been able to make many of the additions that I would have liked. However, I have aimed at improving the consistency of coverage, for the first time including, for instance, every one of the chemical elements. Where existing page lay-out has allowed, I have managed to make several thousand alterations to pronunciation throughout the *Dictionary*, and I am grateful for helpful comments received from many colleagues, in particular Dr J. C. Wells. This, then, represents a thorough and detailed revision of the fourteenth edition which I hope will serve a useful purpose whilst the fifteenth is in preparation.

1987   SUSAN RAMSARAN
                                                   University College London

INTRODUCTION

1.0 The Pronunciation Model

1.1 In the first edition of this Dictionary (1917), Daniel Jones described the type of pronunciation recorded as 'that most usually heard in everyday speech in the families of Southern English persons whose menfolk have been educated at the great public boarding-schools'. Accordingly, he felt able to refer to his model as 'Public School Pronunciation' (PSP). In later editions, e.g. that of 1937, he added the remark that boys in boarding-schools tend to lose their markedly local peculiarities, whereas this is not the case for those in day-schools. He had by 1926, however, abandoned the term PSP in favour of 'received pronunciation' (RP). The type of speech he had in mind had for centuries been regarded as a kind of standard, having its base in the educated pronunciation of London and the Home Counties. Its use was not restricted to this region, however, being characteristic by the nineteenth century of upper-class speech throughout the country. Thus, though its base was a regional one, its occurrence was socially determined.

1.2 Such a definition of RP is hardly tenable today. Its regional base remains valid and it continues to have wide intelligibility throughout Britain (in a way that other regional forms do not)—one of the reasons why this type of pronunciation was originally adopted by the BBC for use by its news-readers. But in recent times, and especially in the last thirty years, the structure of British society has lost much of its earlier rigidity, so that it has become less easy to define a social class and, consequently, to correlate a certain type of pronunciation exclusively with one section of society. Because the whole population has, for nearly half a century, been exposed through broadcasting to RP in a way that was never the case before, it can safely be assumed that a much greater number of speakers, in more extensive layers of society, use RP or a style of pronunciation closely approximating to it. The result has been a certain dilution of the original concept of RP, a number of local variants formerly excluded by the definition having now to be admitted as of common and acceptable usage. Such an extended scope of usage is difficult to define. A specification in terms of a public boarding-school education is no longer valid, if only because the young are often influenced nowadays by other prestigious accents, e.g. Cockney or Mid-Atlantic, whatever their educational background. Nor can it be called simply 'educated' pronunciation, since not all educated speakers use it nor can all those who use it be safely described as 'educated'. If I have retained the traditional, though imprecise, term 'received pronunciation', it is because the label has such wide currency in books on present-day English and because it is a convenient name for an accent which remains generally acceptable and intelligible within Britain.

1.3   There are nevertheless two limiting factors which can be taken into account in defining the model. First, the pronunciation recorded in this Dictionary refers to usage current among speakers of the middle generations. Such a consideration is particularly relevant for foreign teachers and learners of English. So often, in general English dictionaries, the pronunciation given tends to be typical of the usage of an older generation, which must frequently be regarded as archaic or obsolescent. On the other hand, the speech of the young is likely at any time to be unstable, often reflecting transitory fashion. The extent to which new tendencies may be regarded as generally current among speakers of the middle generations has, in revising this Dictionary, been ascertained by consensus of opinion and by the analysis of recordings made by speakers of the relevant age groups, especially as regards certain crucial areas such as the type of vowel used in weak syllables (see Introduction, § 3.4(e)).

1.4   Secondly, certain bounds for the model are provided by the nature of the phonological system itself. Such constraints, apparently arbitrary, derive from the history of the model. They are concerned, in the first place, with the *number* of significantly oppositional sounds (phonemes) in the system. Thus, the model requires two significantly different vowels in pairs such as 'Sam' and 'psalm' or 'don' and 'dawn'. Next, the *incidence* of phonemes in words is generally determined (though there are a number of cases where alternatives exist). Thus, RP, in common with other accents, exploits the vowel opposition illustrated by the pair 'full, fool', the vowel of 'full' also occurring in the word 'book'; those accents which use the vowel of 'fool' in 'book' fall outside the definition. Or again, a feature of RP is that *r* is not pronounced before a following consonant or finally (except in the case of 'linking-*r*'—see

Introduction, § 3.13, and Explanatory Notes, § 14). Lastly, phonetic limits (i.e. concerning the specific quality of the sound) can be stated for the terms of the system. Thus, although RP and the local London accent oppose the diphthongs in 'bay' and 'buy', the qualitative realizations are different, the Cockney forms being sufficiently divergent to be unacceptable in RP.[1]

1.5   The following words illustrate the *sound oppositions* operating in the RP system:

(a) *Vowels*
     5 *long*: b*ea*n, b*ar*n, b*or*n, b*oo*n, b*ur*n
     7 *short*: p*i*t, p*e*t, p*a*t, p*u*tt, p*o*t, p*u*t, *a*noth*er*
     8 *diphthongs*: b*ay*, b*uy*, b*oy*, n*o*, n*ow*, p*eer*, p*air*, p*oor*

(b) *Consonants*
     6 *plosives*: *p*in, *b*in, *t*in, *d*in, *c*ome, gu*m*
     2 *affricates*: *ch*ain, *J*ane
     9 *fricatives*: *f*ine, *v*ine, *th*ink, *th*is, *s*eal, *z*eal, *sh*eep, mea*s*ure, *h*ow
     3 *nasals*: su*m*, su*n*, su*ng*
     1 *lateral*: *l*ight
     3 *approximants* or *semi-vowels*: *r*ight, *w*et, *y*et

2.0   The Notation [2]

2.1   The notation remains basically phonemic (i.e. one symbol is assigned to each significant sound), but a major change in this edition of the Dictionary concerns the symbolization of the vowels and diphthongs. RP vowels have traditionally been classified in pairs of long and short, e.g. those of 'b*ea*t, b*i*t'; 'f*oo*l, f*u*ll'; 'c*au*ght, c*o*t'; 'c*ar*t, c*a*t'; 'f*ore*word, for*war*d'. Accordingly, the vowels in the pairs are often differentiated in phonetic notation only by the presence or absence of ':' (the length mark), e.g. /bi:t, bit/,[3] etc. In previous editions of this Dictionary, only in the case of the pair

[1] For more detail concerning the RP system and its phonetic specification, see A. C. Gimson, *Introduction to the Pronunciation of English* (Edward Arnold), 2nd ed., 1970.

[2] The alphabet is that of the International Phonetic Association. (See the *Principles of the International Phonetic Association*, obtainable through booksellers or from the Department of Phonetics and Linguistics, University College, London.)

[3] In this Introduction, the symbols and transcribed words in the text are enclosed in / /, following the linguistic convention of showing phonemic notation in this way. In the Dictionary entries, however, the transcribed forms follow the orthographic version unenclosed, variants being shown in [ ]. (See Explanatory Notes, §3.)

'cart, cat' has the additional qualitative distinction been shown as /kɑːt, kæt/. I have thought it more realistic to show the differences of quality in all cases. Not only is the opposition of quality a strongly differentiating cue, but, in many cases, it is the only one of importance: thus, the so-called 'long' vowel in 'beat' is usually shorter than the so-called 'short' vowel in 'bid', and is only marginally (if at all) longer than the vowel in 'bit'. (See also Introduction, §§ 3.4 (a, b), for significant variations of vowel length.) It can reasonably be argued that to show features of both quality and quantity entails redundancy of notation, since either is predictable by rule from the other. The redundancy involved in the retention of the length mark (ː) has, however, seemed justifiable both for the sake of greater explicitness in a large number of oppositions and also in order to provide an additional differentiating cue between /i/ and /ɪ/, /u/ and /ʊ/, which may be confused in small print. The short vowel symbols are also appropriate to denote one element of the diphthongs.

2.2   The RP *vowels and diphthongs* are now transcribed as follows:

bean	barn	born	boon	burn
iː	ɑː	ɔː	uː	ɜː

pit	pet	pat	putt	pot	put	another
ɪ	e	æ	ʌ	ɒ	ʊ	ə

bay	buy	boy	no	now	peer	pair	poor	(pour)
eɪ	aɪ	ɔɪ	əʊ	aʊ	ɪə	eə	ʊə	ɔə

Note: In addition to the changes mentioned in § 2.1, the former /ɛə/ as in 'pair' has been simplified to /eə/ (see § 3.4(f)).

2.3   The RP *consonants* are transcribed, as in previous editions, as follows:

pin	bin	tin	din	come	gum	chain	Jane
p	b	t	d	k	g	tʃ	dʒ

fine	vine	think	this	seal	zeal	sheep	measure	how
f	v	θ	ð	s	z	ʃ	ʒ	h

sum	sun	sung	light	right	wet	yet
m	n	ŋ	l	r	w	j

2.4   The symbols used for *primary and secondary stress accent* (ˈ and ˌ) remain unchanged, but the conventions attached to them have been somewhat modified (see Introduction, § 3.17 et seq., and Explanatory Notes, §§ 6–9).

2.5   The sign for syllable division (-) has generally been omitted in this edition. Formerly, 'toe-strap' was transcribed as /'təu-stræp/ compared with 'toastrack' /'təust-ræk/. The situation of the syllable division (juncture) has implications for the duration and quality of the sounds involved: thus, in 'toe-strap' /əu/ is relatively long and /r/ is considerably devoiced (i.e. the vocal folds do not vibrate throughout most of the sound), whereas in 'toastrack' /əu/ is much reduced in length and there may be little devoicing of /r/. However, such divisions and their implications for pronunciation are generally evident from the orthography and from the meaningful segmentation (morpheme boundaries) of the word (see Introduction, § 3.24, for the special case of /t-ʃ/).

3.0   Characteristics of the Model

The following notes deal with topics of particular relevance to the interpretation of the Dictionary entries. For fuller information, readers are referred to the works recommended in the Selected Book List (p. xxxiii).

3.1   *Vowels and Diphthongs*

The phonetic (qualitative) characteristics may be described in terms of the conventional Cardinal Vowel diagram. This diagram, used in a simplified version in Figs. 1–3, was originally constructed by plotting the highest points of raising of the tongue during the production of vowel sounds.[1] The eight primary cardinal vowels (the relationship of which is shown by the numbers on Figs. 1–3) occupy the extreme peripheral positions, their qualities approximating to the following language values: 1—French 's*i*'; 2—French 'th*é*'; 3—French 'm*ê*me'; 4—French 'l*a*'; 5—French 'p*as*'; 6—German 'S*o*nne'; 7—French 'b*eau*'; 8—French 'd*oux*'. Essentially, the area assigned to an RP vowel or to the direction of movement shown for a diphthong on the diagram can be said to denote their auditory relationships with the cardinal vowels and with other English vowels.

---

[1] For more details concerning the selection of the cardinal vowels, readers are referred in particular to those works by Daniel Jones and A. C. Gimson in the Selected Book List (p. xxxiii).

3.2 *Vowels*

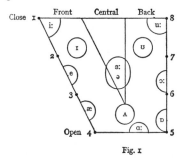

Fig. 1

3.3 *Diphthongs*

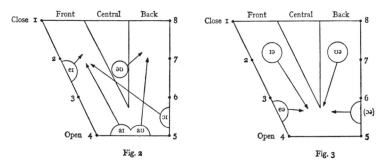

Fig. 2   Fig. 3

3.4

(a) The length of long vowels and diphthongs is very much reduced when they occur in syllables closed by the consonants /p, t, k, tʃ, f, θ, s, ʃ/. Thus, /iː/ in 'beat' has only about half the length of /iː/ in 'bead' or 'bee'; similarly, /eɪ/ in 'place' is much reduced in length compared with /eɪ/ in 'plays' or 'play'. In these cases, vowel duration provides a significant cue to meaning.

(b) The vowel /æ/, classified as a short vowel, is nevertheless generally lengthened by RP speakers before /b, d, g, dʒ, m, n/. Thus, /æ/ in 'bag' is considerably longer than /æ/ in 'back'.

(c) /ɜː/~/ə/. These two vowels are only rarely in opposition, e.g. 'forew*or*d' *v.* 'forw*ar*d' (/ə/ occurring essentially only in weak syllables), nor do they differ in quality to the extent of, for instance, /iː/ and /ɪ/. However, /ə/ can be either more open than /ɜː/, e.g. in a final position as in 'Chin*a*', or closer, e.g. adjacent to /k/, /g/ or /ŋ/ as in 'long *a*go'.

(d) The short vowels /ɪ, æ, ɒ, ʊ/ differ noticeably in quality from the long vowels traditionally paired with them (cf. their positions on Fig. 1). /e, æ, ʌ, ɒ/ do not occur in word final positions. As a consequence of this lack of oppositions, the quality of front vowel /ɪ/ in such a position is capable of considerable variation, often being lowered more than is shown in the diagram. However, there is a tendency among young RP speakers to use a closer variant, near to the quality of /iː/, in a final position, e.g. in a word such as 'happy'.

(e) In previous editions of the Dictionary, Daniel Jones remarked on the varying use of /ɪ/ or /ə/, e.g. in weak terminations such as '-less' and '-ness'. The trend towards /ə/ in weak syllables is now so firmly established among middle and young generation RP speakers that a number of changes in the ordering of pronunciation forms have been made in the present edition, particularly in the following cases:

'-ity', e.g. 'quality, capacity': /-ətɪ/ is generally more common than /-ɪtɪ/.

'-ate' (in nouns and adjectives), e.g. 'deliberate, fortunate, delicate, chocolate': /-ət/ is more common than /-ɪt/. In certain cases, e.g. 'magistrate, candidate', a form with /-eɪt/ is also common, and in a word such as 'nitrate' is the dominant form.

'-ess', e.g. 'hopeless, goodness': although /-ɪs/ remains the more common form for the middle generations, /-əs/ gains ground and is introduced as an acceptable variant. A form /-es/ is also heard occasionally in words of three or more syllables, e.g. 'happiness, penniless'. Similarly, when '-ess' denotes a feminine form, e.g. in 'duchess, waitress, mistress', /-ɪs/ remains a dominant pronunciation, with /-əs/ as an increasingly frequent variant; /-es/ is dominant in, for instance, 'heiress, hostess'.

'-et', e.g. 'sonnet, carpet, bonnet': is predominantly with /-ɪt/; /-ɪt/ is generally used after /k, g, tʃ, dʒ/, e.g. 'pocket, target, hatchet, budget'. However, in the endings '-let, -ret', e.g. 'bracelet, scarlet, toilet, claret, garret', /-ət/ is either dominant or a common variant.

'-ily', e.g. 'easily, happily, worthily': /-əlɪ/ gains ground, especially after /r/, e.g. 'angrily, primarily, extraordinarily', when it is the dominant form, and in certain words such as 'family'.

'-ace', e.g. 'palace, necklace, preface, populace': /ɪ/ and /ə/ are alternatives, with an increasing tendency to /ə/.

'-es, -ed', e.g. 'horses, waited': the /-ɪz, -ɪd/ forms remain dominant in RP, even among the young, despite the influence of the alternative /-əz, -əd/ characteristic of other types of English. The pairs 'boxes, boxers' and 'chatted, chattered' therefore retain the distinction based on /ɪ/ in the weak syllable of the first member of the pair and /ə/ in the second word.

In all other cases of weak terminations, /ɪ/ is retained as the vowel of first choice, though readers will note a number of cases where /ə/ has been introduced as a variant.

(f) The transcription /ɛə/, e.g. in 'there, pair', has been replaced by /eə/ for the sake of simplicity, with the convention that the first part of the diphthong is more open than the short vowel of 'pen', except when /eə/ results from the elision of /ɪ/ in the sequence /eɪə/, in which case /e/ may retain the closer quality typical of the first element of the diphthong /eɪ/.

(g) It is to be noted that, whenever the sequences /eɪ, aɪ, ɔɪ, əʊ, aʊ/ + /ə/ occur, the medial /ɪ/ or /ʊ/ may be elided, e.g. in 'player, fire, employer, slower, power'. This is especially true of /aɪ, aʊ/ + /ə/, which are sometimes reduced to a long open vowel, e.g. 'power' /pɑː/. However, the full disyllabic forms have been retained in the Dictionary entries, with the understanding that the reduced forms are common. The only case where /ɑː/ is recorded is that of 'our' which, being so often weak, is particularly liable to reduction.

(h) The treatment of /ɪə, ʊə/ has been simplified. In the most recent editions of the Dictionary, Daniel Jones introduced the distinction between falling diphthongs, where the prominence falls on the first element, e.g. in 'here, poor' (transcribed with /ɪə, ʊə/), and rising diphthongs in weak syllables, where the prominence is on the second element or where there may be said to be a syllable division between the two elements, e.g. in 'per*i*od, eas*i*er, gen*i*us, infl*ue*nce, resc*uer*' (transcribed with /ĭə, ŭə/). Although the phonetic distinction is real, I have thought it convenient to avoid the explicit notation of the rising diphthongs by the application of a general rule. Thus, all unstressed syllables containing /ɪə, ʊə/ are taken to have the pronunciation with a rising diphthong or with the variants /jə, wə/ or /ɪ-ə, ʊ-ə/. There are, however, a certain number of cases (some 60 for /ɪə/ and 100 for /ʊə/), previously carrying no stress in the Dictionary, where the falling diphthongs are used, e.g. 'reindeer, Shakespeare, contour, sinecure'. In these cases, the secondary stress sign ˌ has been used exceptionally to denote the necessity for a falling diphthongal pronunciation, e.g. /ˈreɪnˌdɪə, ˈʃeɪkˌspɪə, ˈkɒnˌtʊə, ˈsɪnɪˌkjʊə/. (See also Explanatory Notes, § 8.)

(i) The falling diphthong /ʊə/ is increasingly replaced by /ɔː/or /ɔə/. Thus, the most common form of 'sure' has /ɔː/, with a similar, though less conclusive, tendency being true for 'poor, moor, tour' and their derivatives. Rare words, such as 'gourd, dour', tend to retain /ʊə/ without a common /ɔː/ variant. The sequences /-jʊə/ are also strongly maintained, e.g. 'pure, cure, sewer', though in some cases with /ɔ:, ɔə/ variants. In addition, /ʊə/ is generally kept in derived forms such as 'fewer, doer' and also 'jewel, duel', where an alternative pronunciation with /u:ə/ is common.

(j) The form /ɔə/ is retained as a variant for /ɔ:/ in such words as 'pour, score' and for /ʊə/ (or /ɔ:/) in 'poor, sure'. Some RP speakers still use /ɔə/ to distinguish, for instance, 'pour' from 'paw' (/pɔə, pɔ:/), but this usage seems to be becoming increasingly rare. On the other hand, I have abandoned the variant /ɜ:/ for /ʊə, ɔ:/ or /ɔə/, e.g. in 'sure, pure, cure', which I introduced in the 1967 edition and which now seems to me too idiosyncratic to warrant inclusion.

(k) Some forms, such as /geəl/ for 'girl', I have deleted as archaic. Others, such as the use of /ɔ:/ in 'broth, cloth, cost, cross, cough, frost, froth, loss, off, often, soft, trough', have been retained but characterized as 'old-fashioned', while the /ɔ:/ variant in 'gone' has been deleted. I have also indicated the increasing dominance of /su:-/ over /sju:-/ in words like 'superstitious, suit'.

3.5 *Consonants*

3.6 The following table shows the system and general phonetic specification of the RP consonants:

TABLE OF ENGLISH CONSONANTS

	Bilabial	Labio-Dental	Dental	Alveolar	Post-Alveolar	Palato-Alveolar	Palatal	Velar	Glottal
Plosive	p b			t d				k g	
Affricate						tʃ dʒ			
Fricative		f v	θ ð	s z		ʃ ʒ		(x)	h
Nasal	m			n				ŋ	
Lateral				l					
Approximant or Semi-vowel	w				r		j		

Note: Where consonants appear in pairs, the one on the left is fortis (voiceless, i.e. typically without vibration of the vocal folds) and that on the right is lenis (often voiced, i.e. with vocal fold vibration, but always weaker in articulation than the fortis member of the pair). The presence of /x/ in ( ) denotes that the sound is optional.

3.7 It is to be noted that certain consonants have a restricted distribution. Thus, /ʒ/ occurs typically only in word medial positions; /ŋ/ occurs only in syllable final positions; /h, w, r, j/ occur only before a vowel.

3.8 /p, t, k/ are typically accompanied by aspiration (i.e. an interval of breath before the following vowel onset), especially when initial in a stressed syllable. Thus, 'pin' is distinguished from 'bin' very largely by the aspiration accompanying /p/. However, in the stressed syllable-initial sequences /sp-, st-, sk-/, /p, t, k/ lack such aspiration. Within a word, therefore, the situation of the stress accent in relation to such sequences will denote presence or absence of aspiration, e.g. the notation /əˈspaɪə/ for 'aspire' indicates that the /p/ is not aspirated. I have in many cases, including the word 'aspire' (formerly transcribed as /əsˈpaɪə/), found it necessary to shift the stress accent given in previous editions in order to denote or preclude aspiration of the plosive. Sometimes, such phonetic considerations over-ride traditional (etymological) syllable divisions, e.g. 'discover' transcribed as /dɪˈskʌvə/, whereas 'discolour' is retained as /dɪsˈkʌlə/. The criterion determining the separation of /s/ from /p, t, k/ appears to be the presence of an 'intuitively transparent morpheme boundary'[1] (i.e. a separation based on clearly felt sense units). There are, however, cases where usage regarding syllable division and the consequent presence or absence of aspiration cannot be easily determined, e.g. 'distasteful', where practice varies between speakers and according to the style of utterance.

3.9 Final syllabic /n/ is to be understood following /t, d, f, v, s, z, ʃ, ʒ/ as in 'cotton, sudden, often, oven, listen, dozen, ocean, vision'; in other sequences, e.g. 'open, broken', an intervening /ə/ is commonly heard. More freedom of choice as to the presence or absence of an /ə/ is recorded in the case of proper names, and also in such long words as 'metropolitan' where the sequence /-tən/ is frequently heard (see also Explanatory Notes, § 15).

---

[1] The term is used by Niels Davidsen-Nielsen, to whom I am much indebted for advice; see his article 'Syllabification in English words with medial *sp, st, sk*', *Journal of Phonetics*, vol. 2, no. 1 (1974).

3.10   Final syllabic /l/ is similarly to be understood following /p, b, t, d, k, g, f, v, θ, s, z, ʃ, m, n/ as in 'apple, trouble, cattle, medal, buckle, struggle, trifle, oval, Ethel, castle, hazel, bushel, camel, final', other sequences, e.g. in 'satchel, oral', often having an intervening /ə/ (see also Explanatory Notes, § 15).

3.11   The phoneme /l/ must be understood to have the following important allophones (i.e. variants predictable from their environment or their position in the word): a 'clear' /l/ (with a front vowel resonance) before a vowel or /j/, e.g. in 'leaf, million'; a 'dark' /l/ (with a back vowel resonance) finally, before a consonant and as a syllabic sound, e.g. in 'feel, help, middle'; and a partially or wholly voiceless /l/ (with little or no vibration of the vocal folds) following stressed /p, k/, e.g. 'please, clean'.

3.12   The phonemes /r, j, w/ are similarly devoiced following stressed /p, t, k/, e.g. in 'cry, pure, tune, cure, twist, quick'. In the case of /r/, some speakers use a 'one-tap' consonant, instead of the more usual frictionless approximant, when the sound occurs between vowels, e.g. in 'very, sorry, hurry'.

3.13   Many words ending in /-ə, -ɪə, -eə, -ʊə, -ɔə, -ɑː, -ɔː/, with an 'r' in the spelling, usually have a link with /r/ when followed by a word beginning with a vowel, particularly within a close-knit sense-group, e.g. 'father and mother, here and there, pair of, poor old, far off, pour out'. This potential link in connected speech is shown by *, e.g. 'father' /'fɑːðə*/. (Some speakers tend not to use such a link after the weak ending /-rə/, although the condition of an 'r' in the spelling exists, e.g. 'error of (judgment)' may be said as /'erə əv -/ rather than /'erər əv -/ or /'erɽ əv -/.) By analogy, it is common for an /r/ link to be used when there is no 'r' in the spelling—an 'intrusive' /r/, e.g. in connected speech, 'China/r/ and Japan'; within a word, 'draw/r/ing'. Although this usage has been common in South-Eastern England for at least two centuries, it can be regarded as optional and is not specifically indicated in the Dictionary entries (see also Explanatory Notes, § 14).

3.14   The sound /x/ is optional and is used only in the pronunciation of Scottish English words, e.g. 'loch' /lɒk/ or /lɒx/, 'Buchan' /'bʌkən/ or /'bʌxən/.

3.15   The pronunciation with /hw/ in the case of many words having 'wh' in the spelling, e.g. 'which, white, when', etc., must be regarded as increasingly rare among RP speakers. It is, however, retained as a variant because it may still be heard from some speakers, especially in more formal styles of speech.

3.16 The following features of consonant clusters are to be noted:

(a) It is to be understood that when a plosive is followed by another plosive or affricate, e.g. 'act' /ækt/, 'object' /əb'dʒekt/, the first plosive has no audible release. Similarly, there may be no audible release for plosives in final positions, e.g. in 'sit, bid'. Such features are not marked in the notation. (For the use of glottal closure with or in place of /p, t, k/ in certain positions, see the handbooks on English pronunciation recommended in the Selected Book List, p. xxxiii.)

(b) Certain consonants, especially /n/, may or may not assimilate to an adjacent consonant. Such variants within a word, depending on the style of utterance and on the habits of particular speakers, are only occasionally shown in the Dictionary. Thus, 'inconvenient' is given with both /ˌɪnk-/ and /ˌɪŋk-/. Often, assimilation within a word will depend upon the extent to which the word is felt as a compound, e.g. 'income' is treated as a simple word with the common form /'ɪŋk-/, whereas in 'incoming' the separateness of the elements is more strongly felt, resulting in a most frequent form with /'ɪnˌk-/. It should also be noted that in normal discourse isolate word final /n/ and /t, d, s, z/ are particularly liable to assimilation with the initial consonant of a following word, e.g. 'one more' /n → m/, 'that boy' /t → p/, 'this shop' /s → ʃ/, etc.

3.17 *Stress Accent*

3.18 *Primary Stress*
English polysyllabic words contain one or more syllables which are more prominent than their neighbours. This salience of syllables is achieved not only by stress (energy of articulation) but also by factors relating to pitch, length and inherent quality. In the Dictionary, the stress-marking takes into account both stress and pitch. Thus, the sign ' placed before a syllable, e.g. 'above' /ə'bʌv/, indicates that the syllable has primary (tonic) stress, with a potential associated pitch movement. When a word is said in isolation, the pitch change (tone) is likely to be falling; but when the word occurs within connected speech the type of movement will depend upon the

overall intonation of the utterance, the possibilities varying between falling, rising, combinations of fall and rise, or level.[1]

3.19 *Secondary Stress*

When more than one syllable in a word is stressed, stresses other than the primary must be regarded as secondary. These are marked with ˌ placed before the syllable, e.g. 'conversation' /ˌkɒnvə'seɪʃn/. Such secondary stresses may occur before the primary (pre-tonic), as in the example given, or following the primary (post-tonic). In the Dictionary, post-tonic secondary stresses are shown only in the case of polysyllabic second elements of compounds, e.g. 'season-ticket' /'siːzn ˌtɪkɪt/ (see Introduction, § 3.4(h), for the exceptional cases of /ɪə, ʊə/). Pre-tonic secondary stress may also have pitch prominence, especially when the syllable in question is strongly meaningful. Thus, in the word 'unprepared' /ˌʌnprɪ'peəd/, the syllable /ˌʌn-/ may have high or low pitch or even a pitch movement, but, unless some special contrastive meaning is intended, it remains subsidiary in prominence to /-'peəd/. The sign ˌ must therefore be taken to subsume subsidiary pitch variation. (In former editions, a word such as 'unprepared' was given the variants /ˌʌnprɪ'peəd/ and /'ʌnprɪ'peəd/, referring essentially to the pitch of the first syllable. The conventions attaching to the present system of stress-marking embrace the variants previously shown.)

3.20 A difficulty arises when it is a question of a possible secondary stress on a syllable immediately preceding the primary stress, e.g. in many words with the prefix 'un-' /ʌn-/. The decision in these cases is based as far as possible on the criterion of potential separability or contrastiveness, e.g. 'un-' in 'uncouth' is not separably meaningful and thus carries no secondary stress, whereas the prefix of 'uncork' would always seem to attract a secondary stress associated with meaning. In the majority of cases, however, usage may vary as to the presence or absence of secondary stress. In these cases, the alternatives are shown, e.g. 'uncertain' as either /ʌn'sɜːtn/ or /ˌʌn'sɜːtn/, the choice depending not only upon the significance placed on the negative weight of this particular prefix but also, when embedded in an extended utterance, on the preceding stress pattern.

3.21 It frequently happens that words carrying secondary and primary stress (especially compound adjectives) have a stress pattern in the citation or predicative forms which changes when

[1] For works on English intonation, see Selected Book List, p. xxxiii.

used attributively or within the general stress pattern of the context. Thus, 'afternoon' has the citation pattern /͵--'-/ which changes to /'---/ when followed by stressed 'tea'; similarly, 'good-looking' /͵-'--/ may change to /'-͵--/ when followed by stressed 'man'. Such variants are noted in the entries when relevant.

3.22   There is one exceptional case where the rule of only one sign ' per word has been relaxed. Many long polysyllabic words or compounds have two secondary stresses preceding the primary, e.g. 'cross-examination, decontamination, mispronunciation, intercontinental', etc. Of the two secondary stresses, the first is the stronger (while remaining subsidiary to the primary). It would have been possible to state a simple rule governing these cases, but, in order to be more explicit in the entries, I have chosen to use ' for the first secondary, e.g. 'cross-examination' /'krɒsɪɡ͵zæmɪ'neɪʃn/ with the convention that the first sign ' is subsidiary to the second '.

3.23   *Weak Forms*

A pronouncing dictionary is obliged, if it is not to enter into exhaustive complications, to record primarily the citation forms of words. Such a practice is nevertheless misleading as regards those words (grammatical items such as pronouns, conjunctions, prepositions, etc.) which invariably have a different pronunciation when unstressed in connected speech. An analysis of their occurrence in connected speech indicates clearly that the weakened form is overwhelmingly the most frequent. If I have persisted with the convention of previous editions, i.e. recording the pronunciation of, for example, 'and' as /ænd/ with variants /ənd, nd, ən, n/, it must be emphasized that the strong forms are typical only of the citation pronunciation and of the rarer stressed (contrastive) instances to be found in normal discourse.

3.24   *Syllable Division*

I have generally abandoned the use of - to show syllable division for the reasons given in Introduction, § 2.5. However, the mark has been retained in one case, viz. to signify the distinction between /tʃ/, e.g. in 'satchel' /'sætʃəl/ and the sequence /t/ + /ʃ/, e.g. in 'nutshell' /'nʌt-ʃel/, the /ʃ/ of the latter example being longer than the /ʃ/ element of the affricate in the first. This distinguishing mark is used in some 20 cases, e.g. 'courtship, pot-shot, Wiltshire', etc. In some other cases, e.g. 'profit-sharing' /'prɒfɪt͵ʃeərɪŋ/, the syllable division is indicated by the post-tonic secondary stress mark.

EXPLANATORY NOTES

[A † symbol in front of a headword indicates that additional derivatives and/or pronunciation variants are given in the Supplement to this Edition.]

The following notes explain how the entries are to be interpreted, within the conventions stated in the Introduction.

1. Simple Entries
A simple entry such as
> celluloid ˈseljʊlɔɪd

is to be taken to mean that, in the type of pronunciation referred to in the Introduction, §§ 1.1–5, and in a normal colloquial style of speech, the word **celluloid** is generally pronounced /ˈseljʊlɔɪd/, the decision being the result of the editor's observations.

2. The Use of Commas
An entry, for which two or more pronunciations are separated by commas, e.g.
> controversy ˈkɒntrəvɜːsɪ, kənˈtrɒvəsɪ

indicates that the two pronunciations appear to be equally common. Similarly, the entry
> Batho ˈbæθəʊ, ˈbeɪθəʊ

means that some people with this name pronounce /ˈbæθəʊ/, others /ˈbeɪθəʊ/.

3. The Use of [ ]
When variants are enclosed in [ ] as in
> dinastic dɪˈnæstɪk [daɪˈn-]

it is to be understood that there occur two or more pronunciations of the word, but that it has been judged that the forms enclosed in [ ], although widely used, are somewhat less common than the unenclosed form.

In an entry such as
> professional prəˈfeʃənl [prʊˈf-, -ʃnəl, -ʃn̩l, -ʃn̩l, -ʃənəl]

the last four variants denote different realizations of the final two syllables having little significance beyond that of individual choice or of style of speech.

When variants are given for different elements of the word, e.g.
> Australia ɒˈstreɪljə [ɔːˈs-, -lɪə]

the entry signifies that four possible forms occur: /ɒˈstreɪljə, ɒˈstreɪlɪə, ɔːˈstreɪljə, ɔːˈstreɪlɪə/.

4. Rare or Old-fashioned Pronunciations
Some pronunciations are characterized as *rarely* or *old-fashioned*. This comment is to be taken to mean either that the form in question is judged to have a relatively low frequency of occurrence or that it is a conservative form characteristic of the older generations, e.g.
> Persia ˈpɜːʃə [*rarely* ˈpɜːʒə]
> loss lɒs [*old-fashioned* lɔːs]

5. The Use of Italic Symbols
Many entries include pronunciations which contain an italic symbol, e.g.
> notation nəʊˈteɪʃn; contempt kənˈtem*p*t; strawberry ˈstrɔːb*ə*rɪ; conference ˈkɒnf*ə*rəns; territory ˈterɪt*ə*rɪ; regiment ˈred*ʒ*ɪmənt; Tibetan tɪˈbet*ə*n; engine en*d*ʒɪn.

The italicized symbol indicates that the sound is commonly omitted, the form with the sound elided being often characteristic of normal, familiar speech. Thus, the same speaker may use different pronunciations on different occasions.

In the case of potential elision of the medial vowel in a three-vowel sequence, e.g.

player 'pleɪə*

note should be taken of the comments in Introduction, §§ 3.4(f), (g).

6. Stress Accents ('), (ˌ)

Three degrees of stress accent are shown (see also Introduction, §§ 3.17–22):

(i) Primary (tonic) stress accent: ' placed before the syllable, e.g. **above** ə'bʌv; **under** 'ʌndə*; **afterwards** 'ɑːftəwədz.

(ii) Pre-tonic secondary stress accent: ˌ placed before the syllable, e.g. **conversation** ˌkɒnvə'seɪʃn; **undo** ˌʌn'duː; **consideration** kən,sɪdə'reɪʃn. *Note:* When more than one secondary stress precedes the primary, the first secondary is shown as ', e.g. **cross-examination** 'krɒsɪɡˌzæmɪ-'neɪʃn (see Introduction, § 3.22).

(iii) Post-tonic secondary stress accent: ˌ placed before the syllable, but used only in the polysyllabic second element of compounds, e.g. **season-ticket** 'siːzn,tɪkɪt (see Introduction, § 3.19).

(iv) Weak syllables: unmarked.

7. Stress Accent in Derived Words

(i) When the head-word is a monosyllable, and a termination for forming a derived word adds another syllable, it is to be understood that the derived word retains a primary stress on the root-syllable, e.g. in the entry

nine, -s, -fold naɪn, -z, -fəʊld

where **ninefold** has a primary stress on the first syllable.

(ii) In cases such as

ewe, -s; -lamb/s juː, -z; -'læm/z

it is to be understood that the form **ewe-lamb** is pronounced with two stressed syllables: /ˌjuː'læm/.

(iii) When a head-word is a compound of which the second separable element is a weak syllable, and a termination for forming a derived word adds yet another syllable, it is to be understood that the derived word has secondary stress on the first syllable of the second element, e.g. the entry

greenhou|se, -ses 'griːnhaʊ|s, -zɪz

implies that **greenhouses** is pronounced /'griːn,haʊzɪz/.

Exceptions to this rule are shown, e.g. the entry

tea-cup, -s; ful/s 'tiːkʌp, -s; -,fʊl/z

where the secondary stress is applied to **-ful** /'tiːkʌp,fʊl/.

8. Secondary Accent on /ɪə, ʊə/ (see also Introduction, § 3.4(h))

The convention adopted in the Dictionary is that /ɪə, ʊə/ are to be taken as falling diphthongs (i.e. with the prominence associated with the first element) when carrying primary or secondary accent. In a weak syllable, the diphthongs are rising or are realized as /jə, wə/ or are to be treated as disyllabic sequences, e.g. the entry **easier** is to be interpreted as having alternative pronunciations with /-zɪə*/ (rising diphthong), /-zjə*/, /-zɪ-ə*/ (disyllabic).

In some cases, where /ɪə, ʊə/ are falling but have not previously carried a stress mark, the secondary stress sign has been used exceptionally to indicate that they are falling, e.g.

reindeer 'reɪn,dɪə*; **contour** 'kɒn,tʊə*

9. Variations of Stress Accent (see also Introduction, § 3.21)

Variations in the stressing of the citation form resulting from the general stress pattern of the context (e.g. in the attributive use of adjectives) are shown usually by representing the syllables of the word in question by hyphens, e.g. the entry

Waterloo ˌwɔːtəˈluː [ˈ---]

is to be taken to mean that **Waterloo** before, for instance, **Road** or **Bridge** is likely to have the stress pattern /ˈ---/.

10. Variant Spellings

Square brackets [ ] are also used to show variant orthographic forms of the head-word, without implication as to the frequency of such forms, e.g. **organization [-isa-]**.

Where a spelling variant involves the presence or absence of a single letter, that letter is enclosed, when convenient, in round brackets ( ), e.g. **Ham(m)ond.**

When such variants would be widely separated in alphabetic order, such a device is not generally employed, e.g. **coloration** and **colouration** are shown separately.

11. Proper Names Identical with Ordinary Words

When a proper name is identical with an ordinary word in spelling and pro-nunciation, the fact is indicated by placing a capital letter in ( ) after the ordinary spelling of the word, e.g.

hay (H.) heɪ

When two proper names exist, one of which is identical in spelling and pronunciation with the singular and the other with the plural of an ordinary word, the one bracketed capital letter placed after the singular form is to be understood to apply also to the name having the plural form, e.g.

gibbon (G.), -s ˈɡɪbən, -z

implies that the proper names **Gibbon** and **Gibbons** are pronounced /ˈɡɪbən/ and /ˈɡɪbənz/.

Where, however, a name of plural form has a pronunciation different from that of the plural ordinary word, it is given a separate entry, e.g.

gillie (G.), -s ˈɡɪlɪ, -z
Gillies ˈɡɪlɪs

12. Words Grouped under Head-words

The pronunciations of all plurals of nouns are shown under the singulars; all comparatives and superlatives of adjectives and inflected forms of verbs are given under the simple words from which they are derived. Likewise nouns formed from other words by means of the terminations **-er, -ing, -ment, -or** or **-ness,** and adverbs formed by adding the termination **-ly,** will as a rule be found under the words from which they may be considered to be derived. Thus, **talker, meeting** (noun), **annulment** will be found under **talk, meet, annul.**

Other derivatives are also grouped under simple words, when no difficulty in finding them is caused thereby. Thus, **refractive** will be found under **refract, motherhood** and **motherless** under **mother.**

The derived forms of words are not as a rule written out in full, but the terminations to be added are each preceded by a hyphen and divided by a comma, or sometimes by a semicolon, from what preceded. Thus the entry

afford, -s, -ing, -ed əˈfɔːd, -z, -ɪŋ, -ɪd

is to be taken to mean that in RP the words **afford, affords, affording, afforded** are pronounced /əˈfɔːd, əˈfɔːdz, əˈfɔːdɪŋ, əˈfɔːdɪd/.

When the final part of the spelling of a head-word is not repeated before adding a termination, the part to be repeated is marked off by a vertical line | (see, for instance, **addendum, fade**). The same device is employed when the final part undergoes some alteration in pronunciation, though not in spelling, in an inflected form (see, for instance, **house, nocturnal,** where | precedes the **-se** and the **-al**).

Words not grammatically connected (especially proper names) are often similarly grouped together, with or without the use of the mark |, where no difficulty in finding the words is caused thereby. Thus the entry

Ruther|ford, -glen 'rʌðəfəd, -glen

is to be taken to mean that in RP **Rutherford** is pronounced /'rʌðəfəd/ and **Rutherglen** /'rʌðəglen/.

The mark / is often used to indicate derivatives of words grouped under a head-word. Thus the entry

elegan|ce, -t/ly 'elɪgən|s, -t/lɪ

is to be taken to mean that in RP the words **elegance, elegant, elegantly** are pronounced /'elɪgəns, 'elɪgənt, 'elɪgəntlɪ/.

When one or more derived words are grouped under a head-word as explained above, and a variant of the head-word is given, that variant is to be taken to apply to all the derived words in so far as this may be possible. Thus it is to be understood from the entry

Galt, -on gɔːlt [gɒlt], -ən

that **Galton** as well as **Galt** is subject to the variant pronunciation with /ɒ/.

13. Abbreviated Spellings
A certain number of common abbreviations, e.g. **Bros., Chas., cwt., E.C., q.v., V.I.P.,** are included and arranged in alphabetical order according to the letters composing them.

14. Linking /r/; Use of * (see also Introduction, § 3.13)
The sign * following final /-ə, -ɪə, -eə, -ʊə, -ɔə, -ɑː, -ɔː/ indicates a potential /r/ link (the spelling containing a letter 'r') before another word beginning with a vowel, especially within the same sense-group, e.g. **here** hɪə*, indicating that an /r/ link is normally used in such a phrase as **here and there**; similarly, **later** 'leɪtə*, which is likely to have an /r/ link in **later on**.

An 'intrusive' linking /r/ in other cases (with the above vowel endings but without the orthographic 'r') is frequently used by analogy but is not indicated in the Dictionary. Thus, intrusive /r/ sounds are commonly heard especially after /-ə, -ɪə/, e.g. **China**/r/ **and Japan, the idea**/r/ **of it,** or after /-ɑː/ in such a phrase as **Shah**/r/ **of Persia.** Native listeners tend to tolerate less easily an intrusive /r/ after /ɔː/, e.g. in phrases such as **law**/r/ **and order, I saw**/r/ **it.**

15. Syllabic Consonants (see also Introduction, §§ 3.9–10)
The fact that a consonant is syllabic (i.e. functions as a syllable without an accompanying vowel) is marked, by placing ˌ under the symbol, only where there might be ambiguity. Thus, the notation /'trævl/ for **travel** implies unambiguously that the /l/ is syllabic, whereas in the derived form **travelling** it is important to distinguish a three-syllable form /'trævlɪŋ/ from the alternative two-syllable /'trævlɪŋ/. Syllabic /n̩/ is also common, e.g. to distinguish the forms /'bʌtn̩ɪŋ/ and /'bʌtnɪŋ/ for **buttoning.** /r̩/ is used less frequently, e.g. to show the alternatives /'memər̩ɪ, 'memr̩ɪ, 'memrɪ/ for **memory.**

16. Strong and Weak Forms (see also Introduction, § 3.23)
The terms 'strong' and 'weak' refer to the alternative pronunciations possible for grammatical items in connected speech, the strong form being appropriate generally only when the items carry stress.[1] The citation form is obviously stressed and is given first in the Dictionary, but it must be noted that the weak form has a higher frequency of occurrence in connected speech.

---

[1] For more information concerning those cases where such items have a strong form, even when relatively unstressed, see my *Introduction to the Pronunciation of English*, op. cit., or other books given in the Selected Book List (p. xxxiii).

Explanatory Notes

17. Syllable Division (see also Introduction, §§ 2.5, 3.24)
The hyphen, placed between symbols, indicates a point of syllable division,
and is used only to distinguish the close-knit affricate /tʃ/ from the sequence
/t/ + /ʃ/, e.g. **satchel** /'sætʃəl/ as opposed to **nutshell** /'nʌt-ʃel/

18. Foreign Sounds
   (i) A number of foreign words and proper names are included in the
Dictionary. Many such personal and place names have an accepted anglicized
form. Other entries, especially ordinary words and phrases, may be anglicized
to a varying extent by English speakers or may be said with a pronunciation
identical to or approximating to the foreign pronunciation. Where there is no
single established English form, the foreign pronunciation is enclosed in ( ).
The languages thus treated include French, German, Italian, Spanish, Russian,
Hindi, North Welsh and, more occasionally, Scottish English, Hungarian and
Afrikaans. The transcription of such foreign words inevitably involves the
introduction of a number of non-English phonetic symbols (listed below) or the
use of symbols employed for English but with different values. For the precise
phonetic values to be assigned to symbols used for foreign words, readers are
recommended to refer to textbooks and pronouncing dictionaries concerned
with specific languages, of which the following are a selection:

French: L. E. Armstrong, *The Phonetics of French* (Bell, London); P. A. D.
   MacCarthy, *The Pronunciation of French* (Oxford University Press);
   A. Martinet and H. Walter, *Dictionnaire de la Prononciation Française dans
   son Usage Réel* (France Expansion).
German: P. A. D. MacCarthy, *The Pronunciation of German* (Oxford University
   Press); C. and P. Martens, *Phonetik der deutschen Sprache* (München);
   Duden: *Ausspracheworterbuch,* 1975.
Italian: P. Fiorelli, *Corso di pronunzia italiana* (Padova) and *Dizionario
   d'ortografia e di pronunzia* (Torino).
Spanish: W. Stirling, *The Pronunciation of Spanish* (Cambridge University
   Press); T. Navarro Tomás, *Manual de pronunciación española* (New York).
Russian: D. Jones and D. Ward, *The Phonetics of Russian* (Cambridge Uni-
   versity Press); B. A. Lapidus and S. V. Shevtsova, *A Russian-English
   Dictionary* (Moscow).
Hindi: A. H. Harley, *Colloquial Hindustani* (Kegan Paul); R. McGregor, *An
   Outline of Hindi Grammar* (Oxford University Press).
Welsh: J. Morris Jones, *A Welsh Grammar* (Oxford University Press).

   Brief information concerning the phonetic characteristics of these languages
may also be found in *The Principles of the International Phonetic Association*
(obtainable through booksellers or from the Secretary of the International
Phonetic Association, University College, London, WC1E 6BT).

   (ii) *Notes on the notation of foreign words*
No stress is marked in the transcription of French and Hindi, since these
languages make no use of lexically significant word-stress. It is to be understood that there is a certain increase of stress on the final syllables of polysyllabic French words, but that stress for special intensity may be applied to
other syllables. Similarly, no particular stress is associated with any syllables
of Hindi words, though there is generally prominence by length on /i, e, a, o, u/
and on /əy, əw/.

   For German, the short, more open /i, u/ vowels are denoted simply by 'i, u',
without the length mark ':' appropriate for the long, closer vowels.

   For Spanish, /b, d, g/ are commonly to be interpreted as having frictionless
continuant values, except when they follow a nasal consonant or when /d/
follows /l/, in which case they have plosive values. Thus, they have frictionless
continuant values in the Spanish renderings of **Oviedo** /o'bjedo/ or **Guadalquivir** /gwadaʹki'bir/, but /d/ has a plosive value in **Santander** /santan'der/
or **Calderon** /kalde'ron/.

xxviii

For Russian, the transcription is phonemic, except that the retracted variety of /i/ (a type of unrounded /u/ used after 'hard' consonants) is shown with 'ɨ', and the 'obscured' variety of /a/ (used in all unstressed positions except pretonic ones, and in initial positions when two unstressed syllables follow) is shown with 'ə'. Thus, **Kuibyshev** /ˈkujbɨʃɨf/ and **Ladoga** /ˈladəgə/; /a/ is, however, used in **Onega** /aˈnjegə/, where the first vowel, though unstressed, is pre-tonic; also in the first syllable of **Vladivostok** /vladjivaˈstok/, where the first syllable is followed by two weak syllables. The affricates and palatalized ('soft') consonants are represented digraphically, i.e. /ts, tʃ, pj, dj/, etc.

For Hindi, the transcription follows 'World Orthography', except that IPA 'ɟ' and 'j' replace 'j' and consonantal 'y'. It should be noted that Hindi /a/ is close to English RP /ɑː/ in quality; /i, e, o, u/ have approximately cardinal values nos. 1, 2, 7, 8 (see Introduction, § 3.1). The open varieties of /i, u/ are represented by 'y', 'w'. /ə/ is an obscure central vowel, resembling the more open quality of RP /ə/ when final. /əy, əw/ are only slightly diphthongal. /v/ is similar to English /v/ but without friction.

For Scottish, the open variety of /i/ is written with 'ɨ', though it may have a quality similar to that of RP /ɪ/, e.g. **Lerwick** /ˈlɛrwɨk/. /e, a, ɔ, o/ have approximately cardinal values nos. 2, 4, 6, 7, while /ɛ/ is similar to RP /e/. For Welsh, 'ɨ' denotes a central unrounded close vowel. /gw/ preceding /l/ or /r/ in Welsh words denotes a lip-rounded /g/; thus, **Gwrych** /gwrɨːx/ constitutes a single syllable. /hr/ indicates a voiceless /r/.

(iii) *Additional Symbols used for Foreign Sounds*

The additional symbols used in phonetic transcriptions of foreign or other unusual pronunciations are as follows:

ţ   'retroflex' /t/.

ḍ   'retroflex' /d/.

c   Hindi sound resembling English sound of **ch** (/tʃ/).

ɟ   Hindi sound resembling English sound of **j** (/dʒ/).

ɲ   French 'n mouillé' (sound of **gn** as in **signe**).

ṇ   'retroflex' /n/ (occurs only in Sanskrit words; it is used by Indian scholars, but ordinary Hindi speakers replace it by /n/).

ļ   voiceless /l/.

ṭ   'retroflex' /r/.

ɹ   'post-alveolar fricative', as in **draw;** also used to denote 'retroflex continuants', as in American pronunciation of **fur.**

ʎ   Italian sound of **gl** in **gli.**

ɼ   voiceless /r/.

ɸ   bi-labial /f/.

ṣ   'retroflex' /s/ (occurs only in Sanskrit words; it is used by Indian scholars, but ordinary Hindi speakers replace it by /ʃ/ or /s/.

ç   the sound of **ch** in German **ich.**

x   the sound of **ch** in Scottish **loch,** German **ach.**

ɣ   voiced consonant corresponding to /x/.

ɥ   the sound of **u** in French **nuit.**

ɛ   the sound of **ê** in French **même.**

y   normally the sound of **u** in French **lune.** For special use of /y/ in Hindi see above.

Explanatory Notes

  ø   the sound of **eu** in French **peu.**

  œ   the sound of **eu** in French **neuf.**

  ~   nasalization.

  Ɛ   the sound of **in** in French **vin.**

  æ̃   nasalized /æ/ in English version of French /ɛ̃/.

  ã   a nasalized /a/.

  ɑ̃   the sound of **an** in French **blanc.**

  ɔ̃   the sound of **on** in French **bon.**

  œ̃   the sound of **un** in French **brun.**

  ɨ   the North Welsh sound of **u** in **Llandudno** (/ɬanˈdɨdno/), Russian sound of ыı. Also used to denote ordinary 'open' /i/ in transcriptions of Scottish pronunciation.

  ɯ   'unrounded' /u/, a vowel resembling the Russian /ɨ/ (sound of ыı).

  ɐ   an 'open' variety of /ə/, as in Portuguese **para.**

  ʇ   alveolar or dental click (often used for English **tut**).

  ʖ   lateral click (the sound used for urging on a horse).

19. Extralinguistic Sounds
Some sounds, e.g. interjections and hesitation noises, are commonly used in English but fall outside the normal sound system. An attempt is made to represent such extralinguistic sounds by the use of the following symbols:

  ẙ   French /y/ but without voice.

  ə̃   nasalized /ə/.

  ʌ: a lengthened vowel similar in quality to RP /ʌ/.

  m̥   voiceless /m/.

  n̥   voiceless /n/.

20. Summary of Conventional Signs

  [ ]   encloses alternative pronunciations (Explanatory Notes, § 3). Also alternative spellings (Explanatory Notes, § 10).

  ( )   encloses alternative spellings (Explanatory Notes, §§ 10, 11). Also foreign pronunciations (Explanatory Notes, § 18).

  | marks off the part of word repeated in derivatives or other words grouped under a head-word (Explanatory Notes, § 12).

  —   (in association with ' or ˌ) denotes syllables (Explanatory Notes, § 9).

21. Abbreviations

abbrev.	means	abbreviation
accus.	,,	accusative
adj.	,,	adjective
adv.	,,	adverb
auxil.	,,	auxiliary
compar.	,,	comparative
conj.	,,	conjunction
cp.	,,	compare
demonstr.	,,	demonstrative
E.	,,	East

esp.	means	especially
fem.	,,	feminine, female
freq.	,,	frequent, frequently
Heb.	,,	Hebrew
Hung.	,,	Hungarian
interj.	,,	interjection
IPA	,,	International Phonetic Association
N.	,,	North
opp.	,,	as opposed to
p.	,,	past
partic.	,,	participle
plur.	,,	plural
Port.	,,	Portuguese
prep.	,,	preposition
pres.	,,	present
pron.	,,	pronoun
RP	,,	Received Southern English Pronunciation (see §§ 1.0–1.5 in the Introduction)
s.	,,	substantive (noun)
S.	,,	South
sing.	,,	singular
v.	,,	verb
W.	,,	West
WO	,,	'World Orthography'
zoolog.	,,	zoological

22. English Phonetic Symbols and Signs (see also Introduction and Explanatory Notes)

The following consonant letters have their usual English sound values:

p, b, t, d, k, m, n, l, r, f, v, s, z, h, w

Key-words for the remaining English sounds are:

Vowels and Diphthongs

i:	bean	ɪ	p*i*t	eɪ	b*a*y
ɑ:	b*a*rn	e	p*e*t	aɪ	b*uy*
ɔ:	b*o*rn	æ	p*a*t	ɔɪ	b*o*y
u:	b*oo*n	ʌ	p*u*tt	əʊ	n*o*
ɜ:	b*u*rn	ɒ	p*o*t	aʊ	n*ow*
		ʊ	p*u*t	ɪə	p*ee*r
		ə	*a*noth*er*	eə	p*air*
				ʊə	p*oor*

Note: ɔə also occurs as a variant of ɔ: (as in 'four') or of ʊə (as in 'poor');
* indicates a possible *r*-link before a following vowel.

Consonants

g	*g*ame	ŋ	lo*ng*	ʃ	*sh*ip
tʃ	*ch*ain	θ	*th*in	ʒ	mea*s*ure
dʒ	*J*ane	ð	*th*en	j	*y*es

Note: x occurs as a variant for k in Scottish words (as in 'loch');
subscript ˌ (as in l̩, ŋ̩) indicates a syllabic consonant;
a symbol in italic type indicates that the sound is often omitted.

Stress Accent
ˈ the following syllable carries primary (tonic) stress;
ˌ the following syllable carries secondary stress.

SELECTED BOOK LIST

The following books on British English pronunciation are recommended as a selection of works amplifying the information given in the introductory sections of this Dictionary.

G. Brown, *Listening to Spoken English* (Longman), 2nd ed., 1990.

E. Couper-Kuhlen, *An Introduction to English Prosody* (Edward Arnold), 1986.

A. Cruttenden, *Intonation* (Cambridge University Press), 1986.

D. Crystal, *Prosodic Systems and Intonation in English* (Cambridge University Press), 1969.

E.C. Fudge, *Stress in English Words* (Allen and Unwin), 1984.

A.C. Gimson, *An Introduction to the Pronunciation of English* (Edward Arnold), 4th ed., 1989.

A. Hughes and P. Trudgill, *English Accents and Dialects* (Edward Arnold), 2nd ed., 1987.

D. Jones, *An Outline of English Phonetics* (Cambridge University Press), 9th ed., 1975.

D. Jones, *The Pronunciation of English* (Cambridge University Press), definitive ed., 1972.

G.O. Knowles, *Patterns of Spoken English* (Longman), 1987.

C.W. Kreidler, *The Pronunciation of English* (Blackwell), 1989.

J.D. O'Connor, *Better English Pronunciation* (Cambridge University Press), 2nd ed., 1980.

G.E. Pointon, *BBC Pronouncing Dictionary of British Names* (Oxford University Press), 2nd ed., 1983.

P.J. Roach, *English Phonetics and Phonology* (Cambridge University Press), 2nd ed., 1991.

J.C. Wells, *Accents of English* (Cambridge University Press), 1982.

J.C. Wells, *Longman Pronunciation Dictionary* (Longman), 1990.

PUBLISHER'S NOTE: Selected Book List revised for 1991 reprinting of 14th edition.

A

A *(the letter)*, -'s eɪ, -z
a *(indefinite article)* eɪ *(strong form)*, ə *(weak form)*
aardvark, -s 'ɑːdvɑːk, -s
Aaron, -s 'eərən, -z
aback ə'bæk
Abaco *(in Bahamas)* 'æbəkəʊ
abacus, -es 'æbəkəs, -ɪz
Abadan *(in Iran)* ˌæbə'dɑːn [-'dæn]
Abaddon ə'bædən
abaft ə'bɑːft
abandon *(s.)* ə'bændən (abɑ̃dɔ̃)
abandon *(v.)*, -s, -ing, -ed/ly, -ment ə'bændən, -z, -ɪŋ, -d/lɪ, -mənt
abas|e, -es, -ing, -ement ə'beɪs, -ɪz, -ɪŋ, -t, -mənt
abash, -es, -ing, -ed ə'bæʃ, -ɪz, -ɪŋ, -t
abatab|le, -ly ə'beɪtəb|l, -lɪ
abat|e, -es, -ing, -ed, -ement/s ə'beɪt, -s, -ɪŋ, -ɪd, -mənt/s
abatis *(sing.)* 'æbətɪs [-tiː]
abatis *(plur.)* 'æbətiːz
abatises *(plur.)* 'æbətɪsɪz
abattis, -es ə'bætɪs, -ɪz
abattoir, -s 'æbətwɑː* [-twɔː*], -z
Abba 'æbə
abbac|y, -ies 'æbəs|ɪ, -ɪz
Abbas 'æbəs [-bæs]
abbé, -s 'æbeɪ (abe), -z
abbess, -es 'æbes [-bɪs], -ɪz
Abbeville *(in France)* 'æbviːl (abvil), *(in U.S.A.)* 'æbɪvɪl
abbey (A.), -s 'æbɪ, -z
abbot (A.), 'æbət, -s
Abbotsford 'æbətsfəd
abbotship, -s 'æbət-ʃɪp, -s
Abbott 'æbət
abbreviat|e, -es, -ing, -ed, -or/s ə'briːvɪeɪt [vjeɪt], -s, -ɪŋ, -ɪd, -ə*/z
abbreviation, -s əˌbriːvɪ'eɪʃn, -z
abbreviatory ə'briːvjətərɪ [-vɪət-, -vɪeɪt-]
abc, -'s ˌeɪbiː'siː, -z
Abdera æb'dɪərə
abdicant, -s 'æbdɪkənt, -s
abdicat|e, -es, -ing, -ed 'æbdɪkeɪt, -s, -ɪŋ, -ɪd
abdication, -s ˌæbdɪ'keɪʃn, -z
Abdiel 'æbdɪəl [-djəl]

abdomen, -s 'æbdəmen [æb'dəʊmen, -mɪn, -mən], -z
abdomin|al, -ally æb'dɒmɪn|l [əb-], -əlɪ
abduct, -s, -ing, -ed, -or/s əb'dʌkt [æb-], -s, -ɪŋ, -ɪd, -ə*/z
abduction, -s æb'dʌkʃn [əb-], -z
Abdulla, -s æb'dʌlə [əb-], -z
Abdy 'æbdɪ
Abe eɪb
abeam ə'biːm
abecedarian ˌeɪbiːsiː'deərɪən
A Becket ə'bekɪt
abed ə'bed
Abednego ˌæbed'niːgəʊ [ə'bednɪgəʊ]
Abel *(biblical name, English name)* 'eɪbəl, *(foreign name)* 'ɑːbəl, ɑː'bel
Abelard 'æbəlɑːd ['æbɪ-]
Abell 'eɪbəl
Abelmeholah ˌeɪbəlmɪ'həʊlə [-mə'h-]
Aberavon ˌæbə'rævən [-bə:'r-] *(Welsh* aber'avon)
Aberbrothock ˌæbə'brɒθək [-bɔː'b-]
   Note.—This place-name has to be pronounced ˌæbəbrə'θɒk [-bɔː:b-] in Southey's 'Inchcape Rock'.
Abercorn 'æbəkɔːn
Abercrombie [-by] 'æbəkrʌmbɪ [-krɒm-, ˌ--'--]
Aberdare ˌæbə'deə* *(Welsh* aber'daːr)
Aberdeen, -shire ˌæbə'diːn, -ʃə* [-ˌʃɪə*]
aberdevine, -s ˌæbədə'vaɪn, -z
Aberdonian, -s ˌæbə'dəʊnjən [-nɪən], -z
Aberdour ˌæbə'daʊə*
Aberdovey ˌæbə'dʌvɪ *(Welsh* aber'dəvi)
Abergavenny *(family name)* ˌæbə'genɪ, *(place)* ˌæbəgə'venɪ *(Welsh* aber-ga'veni)
Abergele ˌæbə'gelɪ *(Welsh* aber'gele)
Abernethy ˌæbə'neθɪ [*in the S. also* -'niːθɪ]
aberran|ce, -cy, -t æ'berən|s [ə'b-], -sɪ, -t
aberrat|e, -es, -ing, -ed 'æbəreɪt [-ber-], -s, -ɪŋ, -ɪd
aberration, -s ˌæbə'reɪʃn [-be'r-], -z
Abersychan ˌæbə'sɪkən *(Welsh* aber-'səxan)
Abert 'eɪbəːt

1

Abertillery ˌæbətɪ'leərɪ (*Welsh* abertə'leri)

Aberystwyth ˌæbə'rɪstwɪθ (*Welsh* aber'əstuɪθ)

abet, -s, -ting, -ted, -tor/s, -ment ə'bet, -s, -ɪŋ, -ɪd, -ə*/z, -mənt

abeyance ə'beɪəns

abhor, -s, -ring, -red, -rer/s əb'hɔ:*, -z, -rɪŋ, -d, -rə*/z

abhorren|ce, -t əb'hɒrən|s, -t

Abia (*biblical name*) ə'baɪə, (*city*) 'æbɪə

Abiathar ə'baɪəθə*

Abib 'eɪbɪb ['ɑ:bɪb]

abid|e, -es, -ing, abode ə'baɪd, -z, -ɪŋ, ə'bəʊd

abies 'æbɪi:z ['eɪb-]

abigail, -s 'æbɪgeɪl, -z

Abigail 'æbɪgeɪl [*with some Jews* ˌæbɪ'geɪl]

Abijah ə'baɪdʒə

Abilene (*in Syria*) ˌæbɪ'li:nɪ, (*in U.S.A.*) 'æbɪli:n

abilit|y, -ies ə'bɪlət|ɪ [-lɪt-], -ɪz

Abi|melech, -nadab ə'bɪ|mələk, -nədæb

Abingdon 'æbɪŋdən

Abinger 'æbɪndʒə*

ab initio ˌæbɪ'nɪʃɪəʊ [-'nɪtɪəʊ, -'nɪsɪəʊ]

Abinoam ə'bɪnəʊæm [*with some Jews* ˌæbɪ'nəʊəm]

abiogenesis ˌeɪbaɪəʊ'dʒenɪsɪs [-nəsɪs]

Abishai æ'bɪʃeraɪ [ə'b-, 'æbɪʃaɪ, ˌɑ:bɪ-'ʃeraɪ]

abject, -ly, -ness 'æbdʒekt, -lɪ, -nɪs [-nəs]

abjection æb'dʒekʃn

abjudicat|e, -es, -ing, -ed æb'dʒu:dɪkeɪt [əb-], -s, -ɪŋ, -ɪd

abjuration, -s ˌæbdʒʊə'reɪʃn, [-dʒɔə'r-, -dʒɔ:'r-], -z

abjur|e, -es, -ing, -ed, -er/s əb'dʒʊə* [æb-, -'dʒɔə*, -'dʒɔ:*], -z, -rɪŋ, -d, -rə*/z

ablation æb'leɪʃn [əb-]

ablatival ˌæblə'taɪvl

ablative (*s. adj.*), -s 'æblətɪv, -z

ablaut, -s 'æblaʊt ('aplaut), -s

ablaze ə'bleɪz

ab|le, -ler, -lest, -ly 'eɪb|l, -lə*, -lɪst, -lɪ

able-bodied ˌeɪbl'bɒdɪd ['eɪbl,b-]

ablution, -s ə'blu:ʃn, -z

abnegat|e, -es, -ing, -ed 'æbnɪgeɪt [-neg-], -s, -ɪŋ, -ɪd

abnegation, -s ˌæbnɪ'geɪʃn [-ne'g-], -z

Abner 'æbnə*

abnorm|al, -ally æb'nɔ:m|l [əb-, ˌæb'n-], -əlɪ

abnormalit|y, -ies ˌæbnɔ:'mælət|ɪ [-lɪt-], -ɪz

abnormit|y, -ies æb'nɔ:mət|ɪ [əb-, -mɪt-], -ɪz

aboard ə'bɔ:d [-'bɔəd]

abode (*s. v.*), -s ə'bəʊd, -z

abolish, -es, -ing, -ed, -er/s ə'bɒlɪʃ, -ɪz, -ɪŋ, -t, -ə*/z

abolition, -s ˌæbəʊ'lɪʃn [-bʊ'l-], -z

abolitioni|sm, -st/s ˌæbəʊ'lɪʃənɪ|zəm [-bʊ'l-, -ʃn̩ɪ-], -st/s

abominab|le, -ly, -leness ə'bɒmɪnəb|l [-mən-], -lɪ, -lnɪs [-nəs]

abominat|e, -es, -inɡ, -ed ə'bɒmɪneɪt, -s, -ɪŋ, -ɪd

abomination, -s ə,bɒmɪ'neɪʃn, -z

aborigin|al, -ally ˌæbə'rɪdʒən|l [-bɒ'r-, -dʒɪn-], -əlɪ

aborigines ˌæbə'rɪdʒəni:z [-bɒ'r-, -dʒɪ-]

abort, -s, -ing, -ed ə'bɔ:t, -s, -ɪŋ, -ɪd

abortion, -s, -ist/s ə'bɔ:ʃn, -s, -ɪst/s

abortive, -ly, -ness ə'bɔ:tɪv, -lɪ, -nɪs, [-nəs]

Aboukir ˌæbu:'kɪə* [ˌɑ:b-, -bʊ-]

abound, -s, -ing, -ed ə'baʊnd, -z, -ɪŋ, -ɪd

about ə'baʊt

above ə'bʌv

above-board ə,bʌv'bɔ:d [-'bɔəd, -'--]

above-mentioned ə,bʌv'menʃnd [*when attributive also* -'-,--]

abovo ˌæb'əʊvəʊ

abracadabra, -s ˌæbrəkə'dæbrə, -z

abrad|e, -es, -ing, -ed ə'breɪd, -z, -ɪŋ, -ɪd

Abraham 'eɪbrəhæm [-həm, *as a biblical name freq. also* 'ɑ:b-]

Abrahams 'eɪbrəhæmz

Abram 'eɪbrəm [-ræm, *as a biblical name freq. also* 'ɑ:b-]

abranchi|al, -ate æ'bræŋkɪ|əl, -eɪt [ə'br-]

abrasion, -s ə'breɪʒn, -z

abrasive ə'breɪsɪv

abraxus ə'bræksəs

abreac|t,-ts,-ting,-ted,-tion ˌæbrɪ'æk|t, -ts, -tɪŋ, -tɪd, -ʃn

abreast ə'brest

abridg|e, -es, -ing, -ed, -(e)ment/s ə'brɪdʒ, -ɪz, -ɪŋ, -d, -mənt/s

abroad ə'brɔ:d

abrogat|e, -es, -ing, -ed 'æbrəʊgeɪt [-rʊg-], -s, -ɪŋ, -ɪd

abrogation, -s ˌæbrəʊ'geɪʃn [-rʊ'g-], -z

A'Brook ə'brʊk

abrupt, -est, -ly, -ness ə'brʌpt, -ɪst, -lɪ, -nɪs [-nəs]

Abruzzi ə'brʊtsi: [-sɪ]

Absalom 'æbsələm

abscess, -es 'æbsɪs [-ses], -ɪz

2

absciss|a, -ae, -as æb'sɪs|ə [əb-], -i:, -əz
abscission, -s æb'sɪʒn [-sɪʃn], -z
abscond, -s, -ing, -ed əb'skɒnd [æb-],
  -z, -ɪŋ, -ɪd
absence, -s 'æbsəns, -ɪz
absent (adj.), -ly 'æbsənt, -lɪ
absent (v.), -s, -ing, -ed æb'sent [əb-],
  -s, -ɪŋ, -ɪd
absentee, -s, -ism ˌæbsən'ti: [-sen-], -z
  -ɪzəm
absent-minded, -ly, -ness ˌæbsənt-
  'maɪndɪd [also '--ˌ--, when attribu-
  tive], -lɪ, -nɪs [-nəs]
absinth(e) 'æbsɪnθ
absolute, -st, -ness 'æbsəlu:t [-slu:-,
  -lju:t], -ɪst, -nɪs [-nəs]
absolutely 'æbsəlu:tlɪ [-slu:-, -lju:-, also
  ˌ--'-]
  Note.—Some people use the form
  '---- meaning 'completely' and
  ˌ--'-- meaning 'certainly'.
absolution, -s ˌæbsə'lu:ʃn [-'lju:-], -z
absoluti|sm, -st/s 'æbsəlu:tɪ|zəm
  [-lju:-], -st/s
absolv|e, -es, -ing, -ed, -er/s əb'zɒlv,
  -z, -ɪŋ, -d, -ə*/z
absorb, -s, -ing/ly, -ed, -edly; -able;
  -ent/ly əb'sɔ:b [əb'zɔ:b], -z, -ɪŋ/lɪ, -d,
  -ɪdlɪ; -əbl; -ənt/lɪ
absorption əb'sɔ:pʃn [əb'zɔ:-]
absorptive əb'sɔ:ptɪv [əb'zɔ:-]
abstain, -s, -ing, -ed, -er/s əb'steɪn
  [æb-], -z, -ɪŋ, -d, -ə*/z
abstemious, -ly, -ness æb'sti:mjəs [əb-,
  -mɪəs], -lɪ, -nɪs [-nəs]
abstention, -s əb'stenʃn [æb-], -z
abstergent (s. adj.), -s əb'stɜ:dʒənt, -s
abstinen|ce, -t 'æbstɪnən|s, -t
abstract (s. adj.), -s, -ly, -ness 'æbs-
  trækt, -s, -lɪ [-'--], -nɪs [-nəs, -'--]
abstract (v.), -s, -ing, -ed/ly, -edness
  æb'strækt [əb-], -s, -ɪŋ, -ɪd/lɪ, -ɪdnɪs
  [-nəs]
abstraction, -s æb'strækʃn [əb-], -z
abstruse, -ly, -ness æb'stru:s [əb-], -lɪ,
  -nɪs [-nəs]
absurd, -est, -ly, -ness; -ity, -ities
  əb'sɜ:d, -ɪst, -lɪ, -nɪs [-nəs]; -ətɪ [-ɪtɪ],
  -ətɪz [-ɪtɪz]
Abu 'ɑ:bu:
Abukir ˌæbu:'kɪə* [ˌɑ:b-, -bu-]
abundan|ce, -t/ly ə'bʌndən|s, -t/lɪ
Abury 'eɪbərɪ
abuse (s.), -s ə'bju:s, -ɪz
abus|e (v.), -es, -ing, -ed, -er/s ə'bju:z,
  -ɪz, -ɪŋ, -d, -ə*/z
abusive, -ly, -ness ə'bju:sɪv, -lɪ, -nɪs
  [-nəs]

abut, -s, -ting, -ted, -ment/s; -tal
  ə'bʌt, -s, -ɪŋ, -ɪd, -mənt/s; -l
abutilon, -s ə'bju:tɪlən, -z
Abydos ə'baɪdɒs
abysm, -s ə'bɪzəm, -z
abysm|al, -ally ə'bɪzm|l, -əlɪ
abyss, -es ə'bɪs, -ɪz
Abyssinia, -n/s ˌæbɪ'sɪnjə [-bə's-, -nɪə],
  -n/z
acacia, -s ə'keɪʃə [-'keɪsjə], -z
academic, -al, -ally ˌækə'demɪk, -l, -əlɪ
academician, -s əˌkædə'mɪʃn [-de'm-,
  -dɪ'm-], -z
academ|y, -ies ə'kædəm|ɪ, -ɪz
Acadia, -n/s ə'keɪdjə [-dɪə], -n/z
acajou, -s 'ækəʒu:, -z
acanth|us, -i, -uses, -ine ə'kænθ|əs, -aɪ,
  -əsɪz, -aɪn
acatalectic æˌkætə'lektɪk [əˌk-]
acatalepsy æ'kætəlepsɪ [ə'k-]
acataleptic æˌkætə'leptɪk [əˌk-]
Accad 'ækæd
Accadia, -n/s ə'keɪdjə [-dɪə], -n/z
acced|e, -es, -ing, -ed, -er/s æk'si:d
  [ək-], -z, -ɪŋ, -ɪd, -ə*/z
accelerando æˌselə'rændəʊ [ək-,
  əˌtʃel-]
accelerat|e, -es, -ing, -ed ək'seləreɪt
  [æk-], -s, -ɪŋ, -ɪd
acceleration, -s ək,selə'reɪʃn [æk-], -z
accelerative ək'selərətɪv [æk-, -reɪt-]
accelerator, -s ək'seləreɪtə* [æk-], -z
accent (s.), -s 'æksent [-sənt], -s
accent (v.), -s, -ing, -ed æk'sent [ək-],
  -s, -ɪŋ, -ɪd
accentual, -ly æk'sentjʊəl [ək-, -tjwəl,
  -tjʊl, -tʃʊəl], -ɪ
accentuat|e, -es, -ing, -ed æk'sentjʊeɪt
  [ək-, -tʃʊeɪt], -s, -ɪŋ, -ɪd
accentuation, -s ækˌsentjʊ'eɪʃn [ək-,
  -tʃʊ-], -z
accept, -s, -ing, -ed, -er/s, -or/s ək'sept
  [æk-], -s, -ɪŋ, -ɪd, -ə*/z, -ə*/z
acceptability əkˌseptə'bɪlətɪ [æk-, -lɪt-]
acceptab|le, -ly, -leness ək'septəb|l
  [æk-], -lɪ, -lnɪs [-nəs]
acceptan|ce, -ces, -cy, -t/s ək'septən|s
  [æk-], -sɪz, -sɪ, -t/s
acceptation, -s ˌæksep'teɪʃn, -z
access 'ækses
accessar|y, -ies ək'sesər|ɪ [æk-], -ɪz
accessibility əkˌsesə'bɪlətɪ [æk-,
  ˌæksesə-, -sɪ'b-, -lɪt-]
accessible ək'sesəbl [æk-, -sɪb-]
accession, -s æk'seʃn [ək-], -z
accessit, -s æk'sesɪt [ək-], -s
accessor|y (s. adj.), -ies ək'sesər|ɪ [æk-],
  -ɪz

3

acciaccatura ə‚tʃækə'tʊərə
accidence 'æksɪdəns
accident, -s 'æksɪdənt, -s
accident|al, -ally ‚æksɪ'dent|l, -əlɪ [-l̩ɪ]
acclaim, -s, -ing, -ed ə'kleɪm, -z, -ɪŋ, -d
acclamation, -s ‚æklə'meɪʃn, -z
acclamatory ə'klæmətərɪ
acclimatation ə‚klaɪmə'teɪʃn
acclimation ‚æklaɪ'meɪʃn
acclimatization [-isa-] ə‚klaɪmətaɪ'zeɪʃn [-tɪ'z-]
acclimatiz|e [-is|e], -es, -ing, -ed ə'klaɪmətaɪz, -ɪz, -ɪŋ, -d
acclivit|y, -ies ə'klɪvət|ɪ [æ'k-, -vɪ-], -ɪz
accolade, -s 'ækəʊleɪd [-lɑ:d, ‚--'-], -z
accommodat|e, -es, -ing/ly, -ed, -or/s; -ive/ly ə'kɒmədeɪt, -s, -ɪŋ/lɪ, -ɪd, -ə*/z; -ɪv/lɪ
accommodation, -s ə‚kɒmə'deɪʃn, -z
accompaniment, -s ə'kʌmpənɪmənt, -s
accompanist, -s ə'kʌmpənɪst, -s
accompan|y, -ies, -ying, -ied, -ier/s; -yist/s ə'kʌmpən|ɪ, -ɪz, -ɪŋ, -ɪd, -ɪə*/z; -ɪɪst/s
accomplice, -s ə'kʌmplɪs [-'kɒm-], -ɪz
accomplish, -es, -ing, -ed, -ment/s ə'kʌmplɪʃ [-'kɒm-], -ɪz, -ɪŋ, -t, -mənt/s.
accord (s. v.), -s, -ing, -ed ə'kɔ:d, -z -ɪŋ, -ɪd
accordan|ce, -t ə'kɔ:dən|s, -t
according, -ly ə'kɔ:dɪŋ, -lɪ
accordion, -s ə'kɔ:djən [-dɪən], -z
accost, -s, -ing, -ed ə'kɒst, -s, -ɪŋ, -ɪd
accouchement, -s ə'ku:ʃmɑ̃:ŋ [-mɔ̃:ŋ, -mɒŋ] (akuʃmã), -z
accoucheur, -s ‚æku:'ʃɜ:* [ə'ku:ʃɜ:*] (akuʃœ:r), -z
accoucheuse, -s ‚æku:'ʃɜ:z (akuʃø:z), -ɪz
account (s. v.), -s, -ing, -ed ə'kaʊnt, -s, -ɪŋ, -ɪd
accountability ə‚kaʊntə'bɪlətɪ [-lɪt-]
accountab|le, -ly, -leness ə'kaʊntəb|l, -lɪ, -lnɪs [-nəs]
accountan|cy, -t/s ə'kaʊntən|sɪ, -t/s
account-book, -s ə'kaʊntbʊk, -s
accou|tre, -tres, -tring, -tred; -trement/s ə'ku:|tə*, -təz, -tərɪŋ [-trɪŋ], -təd; -təmənt/s [-trəmənt/s]
Accra (in Ghana) ə'krɑ: [æ'k-]
accredit, -s, -ing, -ed ə'kredɪt, -s, ɪŋ, -ɪd
accretion, -s æ'kri:ʃn [ə'k-], -z
accretive æ'kri:tɪv [ə'k-]
Accrington 'ækrɪŋtən
accru|e, -es, -ing, -ed ə'kru:, -z, -ɪŋ [ə'krʊɪŋ], -d

accumulat|e, -es, -ing, -ed, -or/s ə'kju:mjʊleɪt [-mjəl-], -s, -ɪŋ, -ɪd, -ə*/z
accumulation, -s ə‚kju:mjʊ'leɪʃn [-mjə'l-], -z
accumulative ə'kju:mjʊlətɪv [-mjəl-, -lert-]
accuracy 'ækjʊrəsɪ [-kjər-, -rɪsɪ]
accur|ate, -ately, -ateness 'ækjʊr|ət [-kjər-, -rɪt], -ətlɪ [-rtlɪ], -ətnɪs [-ɪtnɪs, -nəs]
accursed, -ly ə'kɜ:sɪd [ə'kɜ:st], -lɪ
accusal, -s ə'kju:zl, -z
accusation, -s ‚ækju:'zeɪʃn [-kjʊ-], -z
accusatival ə‚kju:zə'taɪvl
accusative (s. adj.), -s ə'kju:zətɪv, -z
accusatory ə'kju:zətərɪ
accus|e, -es, -ing/ly, -ed, -er/s ə'kju:z, -ɪz, -ɪŋ/lɪ, -d, -ə*/z
accustom, -s, -ing, -ed/ness ə'kʌstəm, -z, -ɪŋ, -d/nɪs [-nəs]
ace, -s eɪs, -ɪz
Aceldama ə'keldəmə [ə'sel-]
acerbity ə'sɜ:bətɪ [-bɪ-]
Acestes ə'sestɪ:z
acetate 'æsɪteɪt [-tɪt]
acetic ə'si:tɪk [æ's-, -'set-]
aceti|fy, -fies, -fying, -fied ə'setɪ|faɪ [æ's-], -faɪz, -faɪɪŋ, -faɪd
acetone 'æsɪtəʊn
acet|ose, -ous 'æsɪtəʊs, -əs
acetyl 'æsɪtɪl
acetylene ə'setɪli:n [æ's-, -təl-]
Achaea, -n/s ə'ki:ə [-'kɪə], -n/z
Achaia ə'kaɪə
Achates ə'keɪtɪ:z
ach|e (s.v.) (pain), -es, -ing, -ed, -er/s eɪk, -s, -ɪŋ, -t, -ə*/z
ache (letter H), -s eɪtʃ, -ɪz
Achernar (star) 'eɪkənɑ:*
Acheron 'ækərɒn [-rən]
Acheson 'ætʃɪsn
achiev|e, -es, -ing, -ed, -ement/s; -able ə'tʃi:v, -z, -ɪŋ, -d, -mənt/s; -əbl
Achil(l) 'ækɪl
Achilles ə'kɪli:z
Achille Serre ‚æʃɪl'seə* [-'ʃi:l-]
Achin ə'tʃi:n
Achish 'eɪkɪʃ
Achonry 'ækənrɪ
Achray ə'kreɪ [ə'xreɪ]
achromatic, -ally ‚ækrəʊ'mætɪk [-krʊ'm-], -əlɪ
achromatism ə'krəʊmətɪzəm [æ'k-, eɪ'k-]
achromatiz|e [-is|e], -es, -ing, -ed ə'krəʊmətaɪz [æ'k-], -ɪz, -ɪŋ, -d

acid (*s. adj.*), **-s, -est, -ly, -ness** 'æsɪd, -z, -ɪst, -lɪ, -nɪs [-nəs]
acidi|fy, -fies, -fying, -fied, -e ə'sɪdɪ|faɪ [æ's-], -faɪz, -faɪɪŋ, -faɪd, -k
acidity ə'sɪdətɪ [æ's-, -ɪtɪ]
acidiz|e [-is|e], **-es, -ing, -ed** 'æsɪdaɪz, -ɪz, -ɪŋ, -d
acidosis ˌæsɪ'dəʊsɪs
acidulat|e, -es, -ing, -ed ə'sɪdjʊleɪt [æ's-], -s, -ɪŋ, -ɪd
acidulous ə'sɪdjʊləs [æ's-]
Acis 'eɪsɪs
ack æk
ack-ack ˌæk'æk
Ackerman(n) 'ækəmən [-mæn]
acknowledg|e, -es, -ing, -ed, -(e)ment/s ; -eable ək'nɒlɪdʒ [æk-], -ɪz, -ɪŋ, -d, -mənt/s ; -əbl
   Note.—There is also a rare form -'nəʊl-.
Ackroyd 'ækrɔɪd
Acland 'æklənd
acme, -s 'ækmɪ, -z
acne 'æknɪ
Acol (*road in London, system of bridge playing*) 'ækəl
acolyte, -s 'ækəʊlaɪt, -s
Acomb 'eɪkəm
aconite, -s 'ækənaɪt, -s
acorn, -s ; -shell/s 'eɪkɔːn, -z ; -ʃel/z
acotyledon, -s æˌkɒtɪ'liːdən [əˌk-, ˌeɪkɒt-], -z
acoustic, -ally, -s ə'kuːstɪk [*old-fashioned* -'kaʊs-], -əlɪ, -s
acquaint, -s, -ing, -ed ; -ance/s ə'kweɪnt, -s, -ɪŋ, -ɪd ; -əns/ɪz
acquaintanceship, -s ə'kweɪntənʃɪp [-nsʃ-, -nʃʃ-], -s
acquest, -s æ'kwest [ə'k-], -s
acquiesc|e, -es, -ing, -ed ; -ence, -ent ˌækwɪ'es, -ɪz, -ɪŋ, -t ; -ns, -nt
acquir|e, -es, -ing, -ed, -ement/s ; -able ə'kwaɪə*, -z, -rɪŋ, -d, -mənt/s ; -rəbl
acquisition, -s ˌækwɪ'zɪʃn, -z
acquisitive, -ly, -ness ə'kwɪzɪtɪv [æ'k-, -zət-], -lɪ, -nɪs [-nəs]
acquit, -s, -ting, -ted; -tal/s; -tance ə'kwɪt, -s, -ɪŋ, -ɪd ; -l/z; -əns
acre (A.), -s ; -age/s 'eɪkə*, -z ; -rɪdʒ/ɪz
acrid, -ly, -ness 'ækrɪd, -lɪ, -nɪs [-nəs]
acridity æ'krɪdətɪ [ə'k-, -dɪ-]
acrimonious, -ly, -ness ˌækrɪ'məʊnjəs [-nɪəs], -lɪ, -nɪs [-nəs]
acrimon|y, -ies 'ækrɪmən|ɪ, ɪz
acritude 'ækrɪtjuːd
acrobat, -s ; -ism 'ækrəbæt, -s; -ɪzəm
acrobatic, -s, -ally ˌækrəʊ'bætɪk, -s, -əlɪ
acronym, -s 'ækrəʊnɪm, -z

acrophob|ia, -ic ˌækrəʊ'fəʊb|jə [-bɪə], -ɪk
acropolis, -es ə'krɒpəlɪs [-p|ɪs], -ɪz
across ə'krɒs [*old-fashioned* -'krɔːs]
acrostic, -s ə'krɒstɪk, -s
Acrux (*star*) 'eɪkrʌks
acrylic ə'krɪlɪk [æ'k-]
act (*s. v.*), **-s, -ing, -ed, -or/s** ækt, -s, -ɪŋ, -ɪd, -ə*/z
acta 'æktə
A.C.T.H. ˌeɪsiːtiː'eɪtʃ [ækθ]
actinic, -ly æk'tɪnɪk, -lɪ
actinium æk'tɪnɪəm [-njəm]
action, -s 'ækʃn, -z
actionable 'ækʃnəbl [-ʃnəb-, -ʃənəb-]
Actium 'æktɪəm [-tjəm]
activable 'æktɪvəbl
activat|e, -es, -ing, -ed, -or/s 'æktɪveɪt, -s, -ɪŋ, -ɪd, -ə*/z
active, -ly, -ness æktɪv, -lɪ, -nɪs [-nəs]
activ|ism, -ist/s 'æktɪv|ɪzəm, -ɪst/s
activit|y, -ies æk'tɪvət|ɪ [-vɪ-], -ɪz
Acton 'æktən
actor, -s 'æktə*, -z
actress, -es 'æktrɪs [-trəs, -tres], -ɪz
actual, -ly 'æktʃʊəl [-tjwəl, -tjʊl, -tjʊəl, -tʃwəl, -tʃʊl], -ɪ ['æktɪʃəlɪ]
actualit|y, -ies ˌæktʃʊ'ælət|ɪ [-tjʊ-, -lɪ-], -ɪz
actualiz|e [-is|e], **-es, -ing, -ed** 'æktʃʊəlaɪz [-tjwəl-, -tjʊəl-, -tʃwəl-], -ɪz, -ɪŋ, -d
actuarial ˌæktjʊ'eərɪəl [-tʃʊ-]
actuar|y, -ies 'æktjʊər|ɪ [-tjwər-, -tʃʊər-, -tʃwər-], -ɪz
actuate, -es, -ing, -ed 'æktjʊeɪt [-tʃʊ-], -s, -ɪŋ, -ɪd
actuation, -s ˌæktjʊ'eɪʃn [-tʃʊ-], -z
acuity ə'kjuːətɪ [-'kjʊ-, -ɪtɪ]
acumen 'ækjʊmən [ə'kjuːmən, -men]
acute, -r, -st, -ly, -ness ə'kjuːt, -ə*, -ɪst, -lɪ, -nɪs [-nəs]
A.D. ˌeɪ'diː [ˌænəʊ'dɒmɪnaɪ]
ad æd
Ada 'eɪdə
adage, -s 'ædɪdʒ, -ɪz
adagio, -s ə'dɑːdʒɪəʊ [-dʒəʊ], -z
Adair ə'deə*
Adalbert 'ædəlbɜːt
Adam 'ædəm
adamant 'ædəmənt
adamantine ˌædə'mæntaɪn
adamite (A.), -s 'ædəmaɪt, -s
Adams 'ædəmz
Adamson 'ædəmsn
Adamthwaite 'ædəmθweɪt
adapt, -s, -ing, -ed, -er/s, -ive ə'dæpt, -s, -ɪŋ, -ɪd, -ə*/z, -ɪv
adaptability əˌdæptə'bɪlətɪ [-lɪt-]

5

adaptable, -ness ə'dæptəbl, -nɪs [-nəs]
adaptation, -s ˌædæp'teɪʃn [-dəp-], -z
Adar 'eɪdɑ:*
Adare ə'deə*
Adastral ə'dæstrəl
Adcock 'ædkɒk
add, -s, -ing, -ed æd, -z, -ɪŋ, -ɪd
addend|um, -a ə'dend|əm [æ'd-], -ə
adder, -s; -'s-tongue, -wort 'ædə*, -z;
   -ztʌŋ, -wɜ:t
addict (s.), -s 'ædɪkt, -s
addict (v.) -s, -ing, -ed/ness, -ive ə'dɪkt,
   -s, -ɪŋ, -ɪd/nɪs [-nəs] -ɪv
addiction, -s ə'dɪkʃn, -z
Addington 'ædɪŋtən
Addis Ababa ˌædɪs'æbəbə [-'ɑ:b-]
Addiscombe 'ædɪskəm
Addison 'ædɪsn
addition, -s ə'dɪʃn, -z
addi|tional, -tionally ə'dɪ|ʃənl [-ʃnəl,
   -ʃn̩l, -ʃn̩l, -ʃənəl], -ʃn̩əlɪ [-ʃnəlɪ, -ʃn̩lɪ,
   -ʃn̩lɪ, -ʃənəlɪ]
additive, -s 'ædɪtɪv [-də-], -z
add|le (adj. v.), -les, -ling, -led 'æd|l, -lz,
   -lɪŋ [-lɪ̩ŋ], -ld
addle|headed,   -pated   'ædl|ˌhedɪd,
   -ˌpeɪtɪd [-'--]
Addlestone 'ædlstən
address (s. v.), -es, -ing, -ed ə'dres, -ɪz,
   -ɪŋ, -t
addressee, -s ˌædre'si:, -z
addressograph, -s ə'dresəʊɡrɑ:f [-ɡræf],
   -s
adduc|e, -es, -ing, -ed, -er/s; -ible
   ə'dju:s [æ'd-], -ɪz, -ɪŋ, -t, -ə*/z; -əbl
   [-ɪbl]
Adeane ə'di:n
Adel (in West Yorkshire) 'ædl
Adela (English name) 'ædɪlə, (foreign
   name) ə'deɪlə
Adelaide (in Australia) 'ædəleɪd [-dɪl-,
   -lɪd]. (Christian name, road in
   London) 'ædəleɪd [-dɪl-]
   Note. — The pronunciation in Aus-
      tralia is with -leɪd.
Adelina ˌædɪ'li:nə [-də'l-]
Adeline 'ædɪli:n [-dəl-, -laɪn]
Adelphi ə'delfɪ
Aden (in the Yemen) 'eɪdn, (in Grampian Region) 'ædn
adenoid, -s 'ædɪnɔɪd [-dən-], -z
adenoidal ˌædɪ'nɔɪdl [-də'n-]
adept (s.), -s 'ædept [ə'dept, æ'd-,
   rarely 'eɪdept], -s
adept (adj.) 'ædept [ə'd-, æ'd-]
adequacy 'ædɪkwəsɪ
adequate, -ly, -ness 'ædɪkwət [-ɪt], -lɪ
   [-ɪtlɪ], -nɪs [-nəs]

adher|e, -es, -ing, -ed, -er/s əd'hɪə*
   [æd-], -z, -rɪŋ, -d, -rə*/z
adheren|ce, -t/s əd'hɪərən|s [æd-], -t/s
adhesion, -s əd'hi:ʒn [æd-], -z
adhesive, -ly, -ness əd'hi:sɪv [æd-,
   -'hi:zɪv], -lɪ, -nɪs [-nəs]
ad hoc ˌæd'hɒk [-'həʊk]
Adie 'eɪdɪ
adieu, -s ə'dju:, -z
ad infinitum ˌæd ɪnfɪ'naɪtəm
adipocere ˌædɪpəʊ'sɪə*
adipose 'ædɪpəʊs
Adirondack, -s ˌædɪ'rɒndæk, -s
adit, -s 'ædɪt, -s
adjacen|cy, -t/ly ə'dʒeɪsən|sɪ, -t/lɪ
adjectiv|al, -ally ˌædʒek'taɪv|l [-dʒɪk-,
   -dʒək-], -əlɪ
adjective,   -s   'ædʒɪktɪv   [-dʒəkt-,
   -dʒekt-], -z
adjoin, -s, -ing, -ed ə'dʒɔɪn, -z, -ɪŋ, -d
adjourn, -s, -ing, -ed, -ment/s ə'dʒɜ:n,
   -z, -ɪŋ, -d, -mənt/s
adjudg|e, -es, -ing, -ed, -ment/s
   ə'dʒʌdʒ [æ'dʒ-], -ɪz, -ɪŋ, -d, -mənt/s
adjudicat|e, -es, -ing, -ed, -or/s ə'dʒu:-
   dɪkeɪt, -s, -ɪŋ, -ɪd, -ə*/z
adjudication, -s əˌdʒu:dɪ'keɪʃn, -z
adjunct,   -s,   -ly   'ædʒʌŋkt,   -s,   -lɪ
   [ə'dʒʌŋktlɪ]
adjuration, -s ˌædʒʊə'reɪʃn, -z
adjuratory ə'dʒʊərətərɪ
adjur|e, -es, -ing, -ed ə'dʒʊə*, -z, -rɪŋ,
   -d
adjus|t, -ts, -ting, -ted, -table, -tment/s
   ə'dʒʌs|t, -ts, -tɪŋ, -tɪd, -təbl,
   -tmənt/s
adjutage 'ædʒʊtɪdʒ [ə'dʒu:t-]
adjutan|cy, -t/s 'ædʒʊtən|sɪ [-dʒət-],
   -t/s
Adlai 'ædleɪ
Adler 'ædlə*, 'ɑ:dlə*
ad lib. ˌæd'lɪb
ad-man 'ædmæn
admass 'ædmæs
admeasur|e, -es, -ing, -ed, -ement/s
   æd'meʒə* [əd-], -z, -rɪŋ, -d, -mənt/s
administ|er, -ers, -ering, -ered əd-
   'mɪnɪst|ə*, -əz, -ərɪŋ, -əd
administr|able, -ant/s əd'mɪnɪstr|əbl,
   -ənt/s
administration, -s ədˌmɪnɪ'streɪʃn, -z
administrative əd'mɪnɪstrətɪv [-treɪt-]
administrator, -s, -ship/s əd'mɪnɪs-
   treɪtə*, -z, -ʃɪp/s
administratri|x, -xes, -ces əd'mɪnɪs-
   treɪtrɪ|ks, -ksɪz, -si:z
admirab|le, -ly, -leness 'ædmərəb|l, -lɪ,
   -lnɪs [-nəs]

admiral, -s 'ædmərəl, -z
admiralt|y, -ies 'ædmərəlt|ɪ, -ɪz
admiration ˌædmə'reɪʃn [-mɪ'r-]
admir|e, -es, -ing/ly, -ed, -er/s
əd'maɪə*, -z, -rɪŋ/lɪ, -d, -rə*/z
admissibility ədˌmɪsə'bɪlətɪ [-sɪ'b-, -lɪt-]
admissible əd'mɪsəbl [-sɪb-]
admission, -s əd'mɪʃn, -z
admit, -s, -ting, -ted/ly; -tance/s
əd'mɪt, -s, -ɪŋ, -ɪd/lɪ; -əns/ɪz
admix, -es, -ing, -ed; -ture/s æd'mɪks
[əd-], -ɪz, -ɪŋ, -t; -tʃə*/z
admonish, -es, -ing, -ed, -ment/s
əd'mɒnɪʃ, -ɪz, -ɪŋ, -t, -mənt/s
admonition, -s ˌædmɒʊ'nɪʃn, -z
admonitory əd'mɒnɪtərɪ [æd-]
ad nauseam ˌæd 'nɔ:zɪæm [-zɪəm]
ado ə'du:
adobe, -s ə'dəʊbɪ [ə'dəʊb], -z
adolescen|ce, -t/s ˌædəʊ'lesn|s, -t/s
Adolf (English name) 'ædɒlf, (German
name) 'ɑ:dɒlf ['æd-] ('a:dɔlf)
Adolphus ə'dɒlfəs
Adonais ˌædəʊ'neɪɪs
Adonijah ˌædəʊ'naɪdʒə
Adonis ə'dəʊnɪs
adopt, -s, -ing, -ed; -ive ə'dɒpt, -s, -ɪŋ,
-ɪd; -ɪv
adoption, -s ə'dɒpʃn, -z
adorab|le, -ly, -leness ə'dɔ:rəb|l, -lɪ,
-lnɪs [-nəs]
adoration, -s ˌædə'reɪʃn [-dɔ:'r-], -z
ador|e, -es, -ing/ly, -ed, -er/s ə'dɔ:*
[-'dɔə*], -z, -rɪŋ/lɪ, -d, -rə*/z
adorn, -s, -ing, -ed, -ment/s ə'dɔ:n,
-z, -ɪŋ, -d, -mənt/s
adrenal ə'dri:nl
adrenalin ə'drenəlɪn
Adria, -n 'eɪdrɪə, -n
Adrianople ˌeɪdrɪə'nəʊpl [ˌæd-]
Adriatic ˌeɪdrɪ'ætɪk [ˌæd-]
adrift ə'drɪft
adroit, -est, -ly, -ness ə'drɔɪt, -ɪst, -lɪ,
-nɪs [-nəs]
adsorb, -s, -ing, -ed æd'sɔ:b [əd-], -z,
-ɪŋ, -d
adsum 'ædsʌm [-sʊm, -səm]
adulation, -s ˌædjʊ'leɪʃn, -z
adulatory 'ædjʊleɪtərɪ [-lət-, ˌ—'—]
Adullam, -ite/s ə'dʌləm, -aɪt/s
adult (s. adj.), -s 'ædʌlt [ə'dʌlt], -s
adulterat|e, -es, -ing, -ed, -or/s
ə'dʌltəreɪt, -s, -ɪŋ, -ɪd, -ə*/z
adulteration, -s əˌdʌltə'reɪʃn, -z
adulter|er/s, -ess/es ə'dʌltər|ə*/z,
-ɪs/ɪz [-es/ɪz]
adulterous, -ly ə'dʌltərəs, -lɪ
adulter|y, -ies ə'dʌltər|ɪ, -ɪz

adumbrat|e, -es, -ing, -ed 'ædʌmbreɪt
[-dəm-], -s, -ɪŋ, -ɪd
adumbration, -s ˌædʌm'breɪʃn [-dəm-],
-z
ad valorem ˌædvə'lɔ:rem [-væ'l-, -rəm]
advanc|e (s. adj. v.), -es, -ing, -ed,
-ment/s əd'vɑ:ns, -ɪz, -ɪŋ, -t,
-mənt/s
advantage, -s əd'vɑ:ntɪdʒ, -ɪz
advantageous, -ly, -ness ˌædvən-
'teɪdʒəs [-vɑ:n-, -væn-], -lɪ, -nɪs
[-nəs]
adven|e, -es, -ing, -ed æd'vi:n [əd-], -z,
-ɪŋ, -d
advent (A.), -s 'ædvənt [-vent], -s
adventitious, -ly ˌædven'tɪʃəs [-vən-], -lɪ
advent|ure (s. v.), -ures, -uring, -ured,
-urer/s, -uress/es əd'ventʃ|ə*, -əz,
-ərɪŋ, -əd, -ərə*/z, -ərɪs [-res] /ɪz
adventuresome əd'ventʃəsəm
adventurous, -ly, -ness əd'ventʃərəs,
-lɪ, -nɪs [-nəs]
adverb, -s 'ædvɜ:b, -z
adverbial, -ly əd'vɜ:bjəl [æd-, -bɪəl], -ɪ
adversar|y, -ies 'ædvəsər|ɪ, -ɪz
†adversative əd'vɜ:sətɪv [æd-]
adverse, -ly 'ædvɜ:s, -lɪ [æd'vɜ:slɪ]
adversit|y, -ies əd'vɜ:sət|ɪ [-ɪt|ɪ], -ɪz
advert (advertisement), -s 'ædvɜ:t, -s
advert (v.), -s, -ing, -ed əd'vɜ:t [æd-], -s,
-ɪŋ, -ɪd
adverten|ce, -cy, -t/ly əd'vɜ:tən|s, -sɪ,
-t/lɪ
advertis|e, -es, -ing, -ed, -er/s 'ædvə-
taɪz, -ɪz, -ɪŋ, -d, -ə*/z
advertisement, -s   əd'vɜ:tɪsmənt
[-tɪzm-], -s
advice, -s əd'vaɪs, -ɪz
advisability ədˌvaɪzə'bɪlətɪ [-lɪt-]
advisab|le, -ly, -leness əd'vaɪzəb|l, -lɪ,
-lnɪs [-nəs]
advis|e, -es, -ing, -ed, -edly, -edness,
-er/s, -or/s; -ory əd'vaɪz, -ɪz, -ɪŋ,
-d, -ɪdlɪ, -ɪdnɪs [-nəs], -ə*/z, -ə*/z;
-ərɪ
advocacy 'ædvəkəsɪ [-vʊk-]
advocate (s.), -s 'ædvəkət [-vʊk-,
-keɪt, -kɪt], -s
advocat|e (v.), -es, -ing, -ed, -or/s
'ædvəkeɪt [-vʊk-], -s, -ɪŋ, -ɪd, -ə*/z
advocation ˌædvə'keɪʃn [-vʊ'k-]
advowson, -s əd'vaʊzn, -z
Adye 'eɪdɪ
adynamic ˌædaɪ'næmɪk [-dɪ'n-]
adz|e (s. v.), -es, -ing, -ed ædz, -ɪz, -ɪŋ,
-d

Aeacus 'i:əkəs
Aeaea i:'i:ə

7

aedile, -s ; -ship/s 'i:daɪl, -z; -ʃɪp/s
Aeetes i:'i:ti:z
Aegean i:'dʒi:ən [ɪ'dʒ-, -ɪən]
Aegeus 'i:dʒju:s [-dʒjəs, -dʒɪəs]
Aegina i:'dʒaɪnə [ɪ'dʒ-]
aegis 'i:dʒɪs
aegrotat, -s 'i:grəʊtæt ['aɪg-, i:'grəʊ-], -s
Aelfric 'ælfrɪk
Aemilius i:'mɪlɪəs [ɪ'm-, -ljəs]
Aeneas i:'ni:æs [ɪ'n-, 'i:nɪæs, -əs]
Aeneid, -s 'i:nɪɪd [-njɪd, ɪ'ni:ɪd], -z
Aeneus 'i:nju:s ['i:njəs, -nɪəs]
Aeolia, -n/s i:'əʊljə [ɪ'əʊ-, -lɪə], -n/z
Aeolic i:'ɒlɪk [ɪ'ɒ-]
Aeolus 'i:əʊləs ['ɪəʊ-]
aeon, -s 'i:ən ['i:ɒn], -z
aerat|e, -es, -ing, -ed, -or/s 'eɪəreɪt, -s,
    -ɪŋ, -ɪd, -ə*/z
aeration eɪə'reɪʃn
aerial (s. adj.), -s, -ly 'eərɪəl, -z, -ɪ
aerie, -s 'eərɪ ['ɪərɪ], -z
aeri|fy, -fies, -fying, -fied 'eərɪ|faɪ,
    -faɪz, -faɪŋ, -faɪd
aero 'eərəʊ
aerobatic|s ,eərəʊ'bætɪk|s
aerodrome, -s 'eərədrəʊm, -z
aerodynamic, -s ,eərəʊdaɪ'næmɪk
    [-dɪ'n-], -s
aerodyne, -s 'eərəʊdaɪn, -z
aerogram, -s 'eəgrəʊgræm, -z
aerolite, -s 'eərəʊlaɪt, -s
aerolith, -s 'eərəʊlɪθ, -s
aerological ,eərəʊ'lɒdʒɪkl
aerolog|ist/s, -y eə'rɒlədʒ|ɪst/s, -ɪ
aeronaut, -s 'eərənɔ:t, -s
aeronautic, -al, -s ,eərə'nɔ:tɪk, -l, -s
aerophone, -s 'eərəfəʊn, -z
aeroplane, -s 'eərəpleɪn, -z
aerosol, -s 'eərəʊsɒl, -z
aerospace 'eərəʊspeɪs
aerostat, -s 'eərəʊstæt, -s
aertex 'eəteks
aeruginous ɪə'ru:dʒɪnəs
aer|y (s.) (= aerie), -ies, 'eər|ɪ ['ɪər|ɪ],
    -ɪz
aery (adj.) 'eərɪ
Aeschines 'i:skɪni:z
Aeschylus 'i:skɪləs
Aesculapius ,i:skjʊ'leɪpjəs [-pɪəs]
Aesop 'i:sɒp
aesthete, -s 'i:sθi:t ['es-], -s
aesthetic, -al, -ally, -s i:s'θetɪk [ɪs-,
    es-], -l, -əlɪ, -s
aesthetici|sm, -st/s i:s'θetɪsɪ|zəm [ɪs-,
    es-], -st/s
aestival i:'staɪvl
Aethelstan 'æθəlstən
aether 'i:θə*

aetiolog|ist/s, -y ,i:tɪ'ɒlədʒ|ɪst/s, -ɪ
Aetna 'etnə
afar ə'fɑ:*
afeard ə'fɪəd
affability ,æfə'bɪlətɪ [-lɪt-]
affab|le, -ly, -leness 'æfəb|l, -lɪ, -lnɪs
    [-nəs]
affair, -s ə'feə*, -z
†affect, -s, -ing/ly, -ed/ly, -edness
    ə'fekt, -s, -ɪŋ/lɪ, -ɪd/lɪ, -ɪdnɪs [-nəs]
affectation, -s ,æfek'teɪʃn [-fɪk-], -z
affection, -s ə'fekʃn, -z
affectionate, -ly, -ness ə'fekʃnət [-ʃnət,
    -ʃənət, -nɪt], -lɪ, -nɪs [-nəs]
affective ə'fektɪv [æ'f-]
afferent 'æfərənt
affettuoso ə,fetjʊ'əʊzəʊ [æ,f-, -tʊ-]
affianc|e, -es, -ing, -ed ə'faɪəns, -ɪz, -ɪŋ,
    -t
affidavit, -s ,æfɪ'deɪvɪt, -s
affiliat|e, -es, -ing, -ed ə'fɪlɪeɪt, -s, -ɪŋ,
    -ɪd
affiliation, -s ə,fɪlɪ'eɪʃn, -z
affinit|y, -ies ə'fɪnət|ɪ [-ɪt|ɪ], -ɪz
affirm, -s, -ing, -ed ; -able ə'fɜ:m, -z, -ɪŋ,
    -d ; -əbl
affirmation, -s ,æfə'meɪʃn, -z
affirmative, -ly ə'fɜ:mətɪv, -lɪ
affirmatory ə'fɜ:mətərɪ
affix (s.), -es 'æfɪks, -ɪz
affix (v.), -es, -ing, -ed ə'fɪks [æ'f-], -ɪz,
    -ɪŋ, -t
afflatus ə'fleɪtəs
afflict, -s, -ing, -ed ; -ive ə'flɪkt, -s, -ɪŋ,
    -ɪd ; -ɪv
affliction, -s ə'flɪkʃn, -z
affluen|ce, -t/s, -tly 'æflʊən|s [-flwən-],
    -t/s, -tlɪ
afflux, -es 'æflʌks, -ɪz
afford, -s, -ing, -ed ə'fɔ:d, -z, -ɪŋ, -ɪd
afforest, -s, -ing, -ed æ'fɒrɪst [ə'f-], -s,
    -ɪŋ, -ɪd
afforestation, -s æ,fɒrɪ'steɪʃn [ə,f-,
    -re's-], -z
affranchis|e, -es, -ing, -ed ə'fræntʃaɪz
    [æ'f-], -ɪz, -ɪŋ, -d
affray, -s ə'freɪ, -z
affricate (s. adj.), -s 'æfrɪkət [-kɪt,
    -keɪt], -s
affricated 'æfrɪkeɪtɪd
affrication ,æfrɪ'keɪʃn
affricative (s. adj.), -s æ'frɪkətɪv [ə'f-],
    -z
affright, -s, -ing, -ed/ly ə'fraɪt, -s, -ɪŋ,
    -ɪd/lɪ
affront (s. v.), -s, -ing, -ed ə'frʌnt, -s,
    -ɪŋ, -ɪd
Afghan, -s 'æfgæn, -z

8

Afghanistan æf'gænɪstæn [-tən, -stɑ:n, æf͵gænɪ'stæn, æf͵gænɪ'stɑ:n]
aficionado ə͵fɪsjə'nɑ:dəʊ [-fɪʃ-] (afi-θjo'nado)
afield ə'fi:ld
afire ə'faɪə*
aflame ə'fleɪm
afloat ə'fləʊt
afoot ə'fʊt
afore, -said, -thought, -time ə'fɔ:* [-'fɔə*], -sed, -θɔ:t, -taɪm
aforementioned ə͵fɔ:'menʃənd [-͵fɔə-]
a fortiori 'eɪ͵fɔ:tɪ'ɔ:raɪ [-͵fɔ:ʃɪ-, 'ɑ:͵fɔ:-tɪ'ɔ:ri:]
afraid ə'freɪd
afreet, -s 'æfri:t, -s
afresh ə'freʃ
Afric 'æfrɪk
Africa, -n/s 'æfrɪkə, -n/z
Africander, -s ͵æfrɪ'kændə*, -z
Africanus ͵æfrɪ'kɑ:nəs [-'keɪn-]
Afridi, -s æ'fri:dɪ [ə'f-], -z
Afrikaans ͵æfrɪ'kɑ:ns
Afrikaner, -s ͵æfrɪ'kɑ:nə*, -z
afrit, -s 'æfri:t, -s
Afro-Asian, -s ͵æfrəʊ'eɪʃn [-'eɪʒn], -z
aft ɑ:ft
after 'ɑ:ftə*
after-birth, -s 'ɑ:ftəbə:θ, -s
after-care 'ɑ:ftəkeə*
after-crop, -s 'ɑ:ftəkrɒp, -s
afterglow, -s 'ɑ:ftəgləʊ, -z
after-guard, -s 'ɑ:ftəgɑ:d, -z
aftermath, -s 'ɑ:ftəmæθ [-mɑ:θ], -s
afternoon, -s ͵ɑ:ftə'nu:n [attributively 'ɑ:ftənu:n], -z
after-piece, -s 'ɑ:ftəpi:s, -ɪz
after-shave 'ɑ:ftəʃeɪv
afterthought, -s 'ɑ:ftəθɔ:t, -s
afterward, -s 'ɑ:ftəwəd, -z
Aga 'ɑ:gə
Agag 'eɪgæg
again, -st ə'gen [-'geɪn], -st
Agamemnon ͵ægə'memnən [-nəʊn, -nɒn]
agape (s.), **-s** 'ægəpi: [-pɪ, -peɪ], -z
agape (adj. adv.) ə'geɪp
agapemone ͵ægə'pi:mənɪ [-'pem-]
Agar 'eɪgɑ:*, 'eɪgə*
agaric (s.), **-s** 'ægərɪk [ə'gærɪk], -s
agaric (adj.) æ'gærɪk [ə'g-]
Agassiz (town in British Columbia) ͵ægə'si:
Agassizhorn ə'gæsɪhɔ:n
agate (stone), **-s** 'ægət [-gɪt], -s
Agate (surname) 'eɪgət, 'ægət, 'eɪgeɪt
Agatha 'ægəθə
Agathocles ə'gæθəʊkli:z

agave, -s ə'geɪvɪ ['æɡeɪv], -z
agaze ə'geɪz
age (s. v.), **-s, -ing, -d** (p. tense and partic.) eɪdʒ, -ɪz, -ɪŋ, -d
aged (adj.) (old) 'eɪdʒɪd, (of the age of) eɪdʒd
agedness 'eɪdʒɪdnɪs [-nəs]
ageless 'eɪdʒlɪs [-ləs]
agelong 'eɪdʒlɒŋ
agenc|y, -ies 'eɪdʒəns|ɪ, -ɪz
agend|a, -s ə'dʒendə, -z
agene 'eɪdʒi:n
Agenor ə'dʒi:nɔ:*
agent, -s 'eɪdʒənt, -s
agent provocateur 'æʒɑ̃:ŋ prə͵vɒkə'tɜ:* [-ɒŋ-] (aʒɑ̃ prɔvɔkatœ:r)
Ager 'eɪdʒə*
Agesilaus ə͵dʒesɪ'leɪəs
Aggie 'ægɪ
agglomerate (s. adj.), **-s** ə'glɒmərət [-rɪt, -reɪt], -s
agglomerat|e (v.), **-es, -ing, -ed** ə'glɒməreɪt, -s, -ɪŋ, -ɪd
agglomeration, -s ə͵glɒmə'reɪʃn, -z
agglutinate (adj.) ə'glu:tɪnət [-nɪt, -neɪt]
agglutinat|e (v.), **-es, -ing, -ed** ə'glu:-tɪneɪt, -s, -ɪŋ, -ɪd
agglutination, -s ə͵glu:tɪ'neɪʃn, -z
agglutinative ə'glu:tɪnətɪv [-neɪt-]
aggrandiz|e [-is|e], **-es, -ing, -ed** ə'grændaɪz ['ægrəndaɪz], -ɪz, -ɪŋ, -d
aggrandizement [-ise-] ə'grændɪzmənt
aggravat|e, -es, -ing/ly, -ed 'ægrəveɪt, -s, -ɪŋ/lɪ, -ɪd
aggravation, -s ͵ægrə'veɪʃn, -z
aggregate (s. adj.), **-s** 'ægrɪgət [-gɪt, -geɪt], -s
aggregat|e (v.), **-es, -ing, -ed** 'ægrɪgeɪt, -s, -ɪŋ, -ɪd
aggregation, -s ͵ægrɪ'geɪʃn, -z
aggress, -es, -ing, -ed, -or/s ə'gres [æ'g-], -ɪz, -ɪŋ, -t, -ə*/z
aggression, -s ə'greʃn [æ'g-], -z
aggressive, -ly, -ness ə'gresɪv [æ'g-], -lɪ, -nɪs [-nəs]
aggriev|e, -es, -ing, -ed ə'gri:v, -z, -ɪŋ, -d
Aggy 'ægɪ
aghast ə'gɑ:st
agile, -st, -ly, -ness 'ædʒaɪl, -ɪst, -lɪ, -nɪs [-nəs]
agility ə'dʒɪlətɪ [-ɪtɪ]
Agincourt 'ædʒɪnkɔ:t
agiotage 'ædʒətɪdʒ
agitat|e, -es, -ing, -ed, -or/s 'ædʒɪteɪt, -s, -ɪŋ, -ɪd, -ə*/z
agitation, -s ͵ædʒɪ'teɪʃn, -z

9

agitato ˌædʒɪˈtɑːtəʊ
Aglaia æˈglaɪə
aglow əˈgləʊ
agnail, -s ˈægneɪl, -z
agnate ˈægneɪt
agnation ægˈneɪʃn
Agnes ˈægnɪs
Agnew ˈægnjuː
agnomen, -s ægˈnəʊmen [ˌægˈn-], -z
agnostic, -s ægˈnɒstɪk [əg-], -s
agnosticism ægˈnɒstɪsɪzəm [əg-]
Agnus Dei, -s ˌægnəs ˈdeɪi: [-nʊs-, rarely -ˈdiːaɪ, sung ˌɑːnjəs-], -z
ago əˈgəʊ
agog əˈgɒg
agone əˈgɒn
Agonistes ˌægəʊˈnɪstiːz
agonistic, -ally, -s ˌægəʊˈnɪstɪk, -əlɪ, -s
agoniz|e [-is|e], -es, -ing/ly, -ed ˈægənaɪz, -ɪz, -ɪŋ/lɪ, -d
agon|y, -ies ˈægən|ɪ, -ɪz
agor|a, -ae, -as ˈægər|ə [-ɒr-], -iː, -əz
agoraphob|ia, -ic ˌægərəˈfəʊb|jə [-bɪə], -ɪk
agouti, -s əˈguːtɪ, -z
Agra ˈɑːgrə
agrarian, -s, -ism əˈgreərɪən [eɪˈg-], -z, -ɪzəm
agree, -s, -ing, -d əˈgriː, -z, -ɪŋ, -d
agreeab|le, -ly, -leness əˈgrɪəb|l, -lɪ, -lnɪs [-nəs]
agreement, -s əˈgriːmənt, -s
agrestic əˈgrestɪk [æˈg-]
Agricola əˈgrɪkəʊlə
agricultur|al, -alist/s ˌægrɪˈkʌltʃər|əl [-tʃʊr-], -əlɪst/s
agriculture ˈægrɪkʌltʃə*
agriculturist, -s ˌægrɪˈkʌltʃərɪst, -s
agrimony ˈægrɪmənɪ
Agrippa əˈgrɪpə
agronomics ˌægrəˈnɒmɪks
agronom|ist/s, -y əˈgrɒnəm|ɪst/s, -ɪ
aground əˈgraʊnd
ague, -s ˈeɪgjuː, -z
Aguecheek ˈeɪgjuːtʃiːk
Agutter əˈgʌtə*, ˈægətə*
ah ɑː
aha ɑːˈhɑː [əˈh-]
Ahab ˈeɪhæb
Ahasuerus əˌhæzjʊˈɪərəs [eɪˌhæz-, esp. by Jews]
Ahaz ˈeɪhæz
Ahaziah ˌeɪhəˈzaɪə
ahead əˈhed
aheap əˈhiːp
ahem mˈm̩m [m̩m, hm]
A'Hern ˈeɪhɜːn
Aherne əˈhɜːn

10

Ahijah əˈhaɪdʒə
Ahimelech əˈhɪmələk
Ahithophel əˈhɪθəʊfel
Ahmed ˈɑːmed
ahoy əˈhɔɪ
ahungered əˈhʌŋgəd
Ai ˈeɪaɪ [rarely eɪ, aɪ]
aid (s. v.), -s, -ing, -ed, -er/s eɪd, -z, -ɪŋ, -ɪd, -ə*/z
Aïda aɪˈiːdə
aide-de-camp, -s ˌeɪddəˈkãːŋ [-ˈkɔ̃:ŋ, -ˈkɒŋ] (ɛddəkɑ̃), -z
aides-de-camp ˌeɪdzdəˈkãːŋ [-kɔ̃:ŋ, -ˈkɒŋ] (ɛddəkɑ̃)
aigrette, -s ˈeɪgret [eɪˈgret], -s
aiguille, -s ˈeɪgwiːl [-wiː] (egɥiːj, ɛg-), -z
Aik|en, -in ˈeɪk|ɪn, -ɪn
ail, -s, -ing, -ed, -ment/s eɪl, -z, -ɪŋ, -d, -mənt/s
Aileen ˈeɪliːn
aileron, -s ˈeɪlərɒn, -z
Ailesbury ˈeɪlzbərɪ
Ailsa ˈeɪlsə
aim (s. v.), -s, -ing, -ed eɪm, -z, -ɪŋ, -d
aimless, -ly, -ness ˈeɪmlɪs [-ləs], -lɪ, -nɪs [-nəs]
Ainger ˈeɪndʒə*
Ainsl|ey, -ie ˈeɪnzl|ɪ, -ɪ
Ainsworth ˈeɪnzwɜːθ [-wəθ]
ain't eɪnt
Ainu, -s ˈaɪnuː, -z
air (s. v.), -s, -ing/s, -ed eə*, -z, -rɪŋ/z, -d
air-arm, -s ˈeərɑːm, -z
air-base, -s ˈeəbeɪs, -ɪz
air-ba|th, -ths ˈeəbɑː|θ [ˌeəˈb-], -ðz
air-bladder, -s ˈeəˌblædə*, -z
airborne ˈeəbɔːn [-bɔən]
air-brake, -s ˈeəbreɪk, -s
air-brick, -s ˈeəbrɪk, -s
air-carrier, -s ˈeəˌkærɪə*, -z
air-cell, -s ˈeəsel, -z
air-chamber, -s ˈeəˌtʃeɪmbə*, -z
air-condi|tion, -tions, -tioning, -tioned ˈeəkənˌdɪ|ʃn, -ʃnz, -ʃənɪŋ [-ʃn̩ɪŋ, -ʃnɪŋ], -ʃnd
air-cooled ˈeəkuːld
aircraft ˈeəkrɑːft
aircraft|man, -men ˈeəkrɑːft|mən, -mən
aircraft|woman, -women ˈeəkrɑːft|ˌwʊmən, -wɪmɪn
air-cushion, -s ˈeəˌkʊʃn [ˌeəˈk-, -ʃɪn], -z
Aird eəd
Airedale, -s ˈeədeɪl, -z
air-engine, -s ˈeəˌendʒɪn [ˈeəˌen-], -z
Airey ˈeərɪ
airfield, -s ˈeəfiːld, -z
airgraph, -s ˈeəgrɑːf [-græf], -s

air-gun, -s 'eəgʌn, -z
air-hole, -s 'eəhəul, -z
air-hostess, -es 'eə,həustɪs [-stes], -ɪz
airless 'eəlɪs [-ləs]
air-letter, -s 'eə,letə*, -z
Airlie 'eəlɪ
air-lift, -s, -ing, -ed 'eəlɪft, -s, -ɪŋ, -ɪd
airlin|e/s, -er/s 'eəlaɪn/z, -ə*/z
air-lock, -s 'eəlɒk, -s
air-mail, -s 'eəmeɪl, -z
air|man, -men 'eə|mən [-mæn], -men
[-mən]
air-minded 'eə,maɪndɪd
air-plane, -s 'eəpleɪn, -z
air-pocket, -s 'eə,pɒkɪt, -s
airport, -s 'eəpɔ:t, -s
air-pump, -s 'eəpʌmp, -s
air-raid, -s 'eəreɪd, -z
air-route, -s 'eəru:t, -s
air-shaft, -s 'eəʃɑ:ft, -s
airship, -s 'eəʃɪp, -s
air-sick 'eəsɪk
air-sickness 'eə,sɪknɪs [-nəs]
air-space 'eəspeɪs
air-strip, -s 'eəstrɪp, -s
air-terminal, -s 'eə,tɜ:mɪnl, -z
airtight 'eətaɪt
airway, -s 'eəweɪ, -z
airworth|y, -iness 'eə,wɜ:ð|ɪ, -ɪnɪs
[-ɪnəs]
air|y (A.), -ier, -iest, -ily, -iness 'eər|ɪ,
-ɪə*, -ɪɪst, -ɪnɪs [-ɪnəs], -əlɪ [-ɪlɪ]
Aisgill 'eɪsgɪl
Aislaby (in North Yorkshire) 'eɪzləbɪ
[locally 'eɪzlbɪ]
aisle, -s, -d aɪl, -z, -d
aitch (letter H), -es eɪtʃ, -ɪz
aitchbone, -s 'eɪtʃbəun, -z
Aitchison 'eɪtʃɪsn
Aith eɪθ
Aitken 'eɪtkɪn [-kən], 'eɪk-
Aix eɪks (ɛks)
Aix-la-Chapelle ,eɪksla:ʃæ'pel [-ʃə'p-]
(ɛksla ʃapɛl)
Aix-les-Bains ,eɪksleɪ'bæ̃:ŋ [-'bæŋ]
(ɛkslebɛ̃)
Ajaccio ə'jætʃɪəu [ə'dʒæsɪəu]
ajar ə'dʒɑ:*
Ajax, -es 'eɪdʒæks, -ɪz
ajutage 'ædʒutɪdʒ [ə'dʒu:t-]
Akaba 'ækəbə
Akbar 'ækbɑ:* ['ʌkbə*] (Hindi əkbər)
Akenside 'eɪkənsaɪd [-kɪn-]
Akerman 'ækəmən
Akers 'eɪkəz
akimbo ə'kɪmbəu
akin ə'kɪn
Akkad 'ækæd

Akond of Swat (former title of the
Wali of Swat territory in Pakistan)
ə,ku:ndəv'swɒt, (fancy name in poem
by Edward Lear) ,ækəndəv'swɒt
Akron 'ækrɒn [-rən]
Akroyd 'ækrɔɪd
Al æl
à la ɑ:lɑ: (ala)
Alabama ,ælə'bæmə [-'bɑ:mə]
alabaster ,ælə'bɑ:stə* [-'bæs-, '----]
Alabaster 'æləbɑ:stə*
à la carte ,ɑ:lɑ:'kɑ:t [,ælɑ:-, ,ælə-]
(alakart)
alack ə'læk
alackaday ə'lækədeɪ [-,--'-]
alacrity ə'lækrətɪ [-krɪtɪ]
Aladdin ə'lædɪn
Alamein 'æləmeɪn
à la mode ,ɑ:lɑ:'məud [,ælə'mɒd]
(alamɔd)
Alan 'ælən
Aland 'ɑ:lənd ['ɔ:l-]
aland (adv.) ə'lænd
alar 'eɪlə*
Alaric 'æləɪk
alarm (s. v.), -s, -ing/ly, -ed; -ist/s
ə'lɑ:m, -z, -ɪŋ/lɪ, -d; -ɪst/s
alarm-clock, -s ə'lɑ:mklɒk, -s
alarum, -s ə'leərəm [-'lɑ:r-, -'lær-], -z
alas ə'læs [-'lɑ:s]
Alaska ə'læskə
Alastair 'æləstə*
Alastor ə'læstɔ:* [æ'l-]
alate (winged) 'eɪleɪt
alb, -s ælb, -z
Alba 'ælbə
Alban 'ɔ:lbən ['ɒl-]
Albani æl'bɑ:nɪ
Albania, -n/s ælbeɪnjə [ɔ:l-, -nɪə],
-n/z
Albano ælbɑ:nəu
Albany (in London) 'ɔ:lbənɪ ['ɒl-, 'æl-],
(in Australia) 'æl-, (in U.S.A.) 'ɔ:l-
['ɒl-]
albatross, -es 'ælbətrɒs, -ɪz
albeit ɔ:l'bi:ɪt
Albemarle 'ælbəmɑ:l [-bɪm-]
Alberic 'ælbərɪk
albert (A.), -s 'ælbət, -s
Alberta ælbɜ:tə
albescen|ce, -t ælbesən|s, -t
Albigenses ,ælbɪ'gensi:z [-'dʒensi:z]
Albin 'ælbɪn
albinism 'ælbɪnɪzəm
albino, -s ælbi:nəu, -z
Albion 'ælbjən [-bɪən]
Albrecht 'ælbrekt ('albrɛçt)
Albright 'ɔ:lbraɪt ['ɒl-]

Albrighton 'ɔ:braɪtn ['ɔ:lb-, 'ɒlb-]
Albrow 'ɔ:lbraʊ
albugineous ˌælbju:'dʒɪnɪəs [-bjʊ-,
 -njəs]
Albula 'ælbjʊlə
album, -s 'ælbəm, -z
albumen 'ælbjʊmɪn [æl'bju:mɪn, -men,
 -mən]
albumin 'ælbjʊmɪn [æl'bju:mɪn]
albumin|oid/s, -ous æl'bju:mɪn|ɔɪd/z,
 -əs
albuminuria ˌælbju:mɪ'njʊərɪə [-bjʊ-]
alburnum, -s æl'bɜ:nəm, -z
Albury (surname, town in Australia)
 'ɔ:lbərɪ ['ɒl-]
Alcaeus æl'si:əs [-'sɪəs]
alcaic, -s æl'keɪɪk, -s
Alcatraz ˌælkə'træz
Alcazar (Spanish palace) ˌælkə'zɑ:,
 (al'kaθar), (music hall) æl'kæzə*
Alcester 'ɔ:lstə* ['ɒl-]
Alcestis æl'sestɪs
alchemic, -al æl'kemɪk, -l
alchem|ist/s, -y 'ælkəm|ɪst/s [-kɪm-], -ɪ
Alcibiades ˌælsɪ'baɪədi:z
Alcides æl'saɪdi:z
Alcinous æl'sɪnəʊəs
Alcmene ælk'mi:ni: [-nɪ]
Alcock 'ælkɒk, 'ɔ:lkɒk ['ɒl-]
alcohol, -s, -ism 'ælkəhɒl, -z, -ɪzəm
alcoholic ˌælkə'hɒlɪk
alcoholomet|er/s, -ry ˌælkəhɒ'lɒmɪt|-
 ə*/z [-mət|ə*/z], -rɪ
Alcoran ˌælkɒ'rɑ:n [-kɔ:'r-, -kə'r-]
Alcorn 'ɔ:lkɔ:n ['ɒl-]
Alcott 'ɔ:lkət ['ɒl-]
alcove, -s, -d 'ælkəʊv, -z, -d
Alcuin 'ælkwɪn
Alcyone æl'saɪənɪ
Aldborough (in North Yorkshire)
 'ɔ:ldbərə ['ɒl-, locally 'ɔ:brə]
Aldbury 'ɔ:ldbərɪ ['ɒl-]
Aldebaran æl'debərən [-ræn]
Aldeburgh 'ɔ:ldbərə ['ɒl-]
aldehyde, -s 'ældɪhaɪd, -z
Alden 'ɔ:ldən ['ɒl-]
Aldenham 'ɔ:ldnəm ['ɒl-, -dnəm]
alder (A.), -s 'ɔ:ldə* ['ɒl-], -z
alder|man (A.), -men, -manly 'ɔ:ldə-
 mən ['ɒl-], -mən, -mənlɪ
aldermanic ˌɔ:ldə'mænɪk [ˌɒl-]
aldern 'ɔ:ldən ['ɒl-, -dɜ:n]
Alderney 'ɔ:ldənɪ ['ɒl-]
Aldersgate 'ɔ:ldəzgeɪt ['ɒl-, -gɪt]
Aldershot 'ɔ:ldəʃɒt ['ɒl-]
Alderwasley ˌældəwəz'li:
Aldgate 'ɔ:ldgɪt ['ɒl-, -geɪt]
Aldine 'ɔ:ldaɪn ['ɒl-, -di:n]

Aldis 'ɔ:ldɪs ['ɒl-]
Aldous 'ɔ:ldəs ['ɒl-], 'ældəs
Aldred 'ɔ:ldrɪd ['ɒl-, -dred]
Aldrich 'ɔ:ldrɪtʃ ['ɒl-, -ɪdʒ]
Aldridge 'ɔ:ldrɪdʒ ['ɒl-]
Aldsworth 'ɔ:ldzwəθ ['ɒl-, -wɜ:θ]
Aldus 'ɔ:ldəs ['ɒl-, 'æl-]
Aldwych 'ɔ:ldwɪtʃ ['ɒl-]
ale (A.), -s eɪl, -z
†aleatory 'eɪlɪətərɪ [-ljə-]
Alec(k) 'ælɪk [-lek]
alehou|se, -ses 'eɪlhaʊ|s, -zɪz
Alemannic ˌælɪ'mænɪk [-le'm-]
alembic, -s ə'lembɪk, -s
Aleppo ə'lepəʊ
alert (s. adj.), -s, -est, -ly, -ness ə'lɜ:t,
 -s, -ɪst, -lɪ, -nɪs [-nəs]
Alessandria ˌælɪ'sændrɪə [-le's-, -'sɑ:n-]
Alethea ˌælə'θɪə
Aletsch 'ælɪtʃ ['ɑ:l-, -letʃ]
Aleutian ə'lu:ʃjən [-'lju:-, -ʃɪən, -ʃn]
A-level, -s 'eɪˌlevl, -z
alewi|fe, -ves 'eɪlwaɪ|f, -vz
Alexand|er, -ra, -ria, -rian/s ˌælɪg'zɑ:n-
 d|ə* [-leg-, -'zæn-, -k's-], -rə, -rɪə,
 -rɪən/z
Alexandrina ˌælɪgzɑ:n'dri:nə [-leg-,
 -zæn-, -ks-]
alexandrine, -s ˌælɪg'zændraɪn [-leg-,
 -'zɑ:n-, -k's-], -z
alexia eɪ'leksɪə [ə'l-, -sjə]
Alexis ə'leksɪs
alfalfa æl'fælfə
Alfonso æl'fɒnzəʊ [-nsəʊ]
Alford 'ɔ:lfəd ['ɒl-]
Alfred 'ælfrɪd
Alfreda æl'fri:də
Alfredian æl'fri:djən [-dɪən]
Alfree 'ɔ:lfrɪ ['ɒl-]
alfresco æl'freskəʊ
Alfreton 'ɔ:lfrɪtən ['ɒl-]
Alfric 'ælfrɪk
Alfriston (in Sussex) ɔ:l'frɪstən ['---,
 ɒl-, 'æl-]
al|ga, -gae 'æl|gə, -dʒi: [-gi:, -gaɪ]
algebra, -s 'ældʒɪbrə [-dʒə-], -z
algebraic, -al, -ally ˌældʒɪ'breɪk [-dʒə-],
 -l, -əlɪ
algebraist, -s ˌældʒɪ'breɪɪst [-dʒe-,
 '----], -s
Algeciras ˌældʒɪ'sɪərəs [-dʒə's-, -dʒe's-,
 -'saɪər-]
Alger 'ældʒə*
Algeria, -n/s æl'dʒɪərɪə, -n/z
Algernon 'ældʒənən
Algiers æl'dʒɪəz [rarely '-ˌ-]
Algoa æl'gəʊə
Algol 'ælgɒl

12

Algonquin ælˈgɒŋkwɪn [-kɪn]
algorithm, -s ˈælgərɪðəm, -z
algorithmic ˌælgəˈrɪðmɪk
Algy ˈældʒɪ
Alhambra ælˈhæmbrə [əl-]
alhambresque ˌælhæmˈbresk
alias, -es ˈeɪlɪəs [-ljəs, -lɪæs, -ljæs], -ɪz
Ali Baba ˌælɪˈbɑːbə [ˌɑːl-, ˈbɑːbɑː]
alibi, -s ˈælɪbaɪ, -z
Alicant ˈælɪkænt
Alicante, -s ˌælɪˈkæntɪ, -z
Alice ˈælɪs
Alicia əˈlɪʃɪə [-ʃjə, -ʃə]
Alick ˈælɪk
alien (s. adj. v.), **-s, -ing, -ed; -able, -age** ˈeɪljən [-lɪən], -z, -ɪŋ, -d; -əbl, -ɪdʒ
Aliena ˌælɪˈiːnə
alienat|e, -es, -ing, -ed, -or/s ˈeɪljəneɪt [-lɪən-], -s, -ɪŋ, -ɪd, -ə*/z
alienation, -s ˌeɪljəˈneɪʃn [-lɪəˈn-], -z
alienee, -s ˌeɪljəˈniː [ˌeɪlɪə-], -z
alieni|sm, -st/s ˈeɪljənɪzəm [-lɪən-], -st/s
alight (adj. v.), **-s, -ing, -ed** əˈlaɪt, -s, -ɪŋ, -ɪd
align, -s, -ing, -ed, -ment/s əˈlaɪn, -z, -ɪŋ, -d, -mənt/s
alike əˈlaɪk
aliment, -s ˈælɪmənt, -s
aliment|al, -ary ˌælɪˈmentl, -ərɪ
alimentation ˌælɪmenˈteɪʃn
alimon|y, -ies ˈælɪmən|ɪ, -ɪz
alin|e, -es, -ing, -ed əˈlaɪn, -z, -ɪŋ, -d
Aline æˈliːn [əˈl-], ˈælɪːn
alineation, -s əˌlɪnɪˈeɪʃn, -z
Alington ˈælɪŋtən
Ali Pasha ˌɑːlɪˈpɑːʃə [ˌæl-, -ˈpæʃə, *rarely* -pəˈʃɑː]
aliqu|ant, -ot ˈælɪkw|ənt, -ɒt
Alison ˈælɪsn
Alist|air, -er ˈælɪst|ə*, -ə*
alive əˈlaɪv
alizarin əˈlɪzərɪn
alkahest ˈælkəhest
alkalescen|ce, -cy, -t ˌælkəˈlesn|s, -sɪ, -t
alkali, -(e)s ˈælkəlaɪ, -z
alkali|fy, -fies, -fying, -fied ˈælkəlɪ|faɪ [ælˈkæl-], -faɪz, -faɪɪŋ, -faɪd
alkaline ˈælkəlaɪn
alkalinity ˌælkəˈlɪnətɪ [-rɪtɪ]
alkaloid, -s, -al ˈælkələɪd, -z, -l
Alkoran ˌælkɒˈrɑːn [-kɔːˈr-, -kəˈr-]
all ɔːl
Allah ˈælə [-lɑː]
Allahabad ˌæləhəˈbɑːd [-ˈbæd] (*Hindi* allahabad)
Allan ˈælən
Allan-a-Dale ˌælənəˈdeɪl

Allandale ˈæləndeɪl
Allard ˈælɑːd [-ləd]
Allardice ˈælədaɪs
allay, -s, -ing, -ed əˈleɪ, -z, -ɪŋ, -d
Allbright ˈɔːlbraɪt [ˈɒl-]
Allbutt ˈɔːlbət [ˈɒl-]
Allchin ˈɔːlʃɪn [ˈɒl-]
Allcorn ˈɔːlkɔːn [ˈɒl-]
Allcroft ˈɔːlkrɒft [ˈɒl-]
allegation, -s ˌælɪˈgeɪʃn [-leˈg-], -z
†**alleg|e, -es, -ing, -ed** əˈledʒ, -ɪz, -ɪŋ, -d
Alleghany ˈælɪgenɪ
Allegheny ˈælɪgenɪ
allegian|ce, -t əˈliːdʒən|s, -t
allegoric, -al, -ally ˌælɪˈgɒrɪk [-ləˈg-, -leˈg-], -l, -əlɪ
allegorist, -s ˈælɪgərɪst [-ləg-, -leg-], -s
allegoriz|e [-is|e), -es, -ing, -ed ˈælɪgəraɪz [-ləg-, -leg-], -ɪz, -ɪŋ, -d
allegor|y, -ies ˈælɪgər|ɪ [-ləg-, -leg-], -ɪz
allegretto, -s ˌælɪˈgretəʊ [-leˈg-], -z
allegro, -s əˈleɪgrəʊ [æˈl-, -ˈleg-, *rarely* ˈælɪgrəʊ], -z
Allegwash ˈælɪgwɒʃ
Allein(e) ˈælɪn
alleluia (A.), -s ˌælɪˈluːjə, -z
allemande, -s ˈæləmɑːnd [-mɔ̃ːnd, -mɑːnd, -mɒnd] (almɑ̃ːd), -z
Allen ˈælən [-lɪn]
Allenby ˈælənbɪ
Allendale ˈælɪndeɪl [-lən-]
Allentown ˈælɪntaʊn [-lən-]
allergic əˈlɜːdʒɪk
allerg|y, -ies ˈælədʒ|ɪ, -ɪz
Allerton ˈælətən
alleviat|e, -es, -ing, -ed, -or/s əˈliːvɪeɪt, [-vjeɪt], -s, -ɪŋ, -ɪd, -ə*/z
alleviation əˌliːvɪˈeɪʃn
alley, -s ˈælɪ, -z
Alleyn (*founder of Dulwich College*), ˈælɪn
Alleyne æˈliːn, ˈælɪn, ˈæleɪn
Alleynian, -s əˈleɪnjən [æˈl-, -nɪən], -z
All-Fools'-Day, -s ˌɔːlˈfuːlzdeɪ, -z
all-fours ˌɔːlˈfɔːz [-ˈfɔəz]
Allfrey ˈɔːlfrɪ [ˈɒl-]
all-hail ˌɔːlˈheɪl
All-Hallows ˌɔːlˈhæləʊz
Allhusen ælˈhjuːzn
alliance, -s əˈlaɪəns, -ɪz
Allies ˈælaɪz [əˈlaɪz]
alligator, -s ˈælɪgeɪtə*, -z
all-in ˌɔːlˈɪn ['-- *when attributive*]
allineation, -s əˌlɪnɪˈeɪʃn [æˌl-], -z
Allingham ˈælɪŋəm
Allison ˈælɪsn
alliterat|e, -es, -ing, -ed əˈlɪtəreɪt [æˈl-], -s, -ɪŋ, -ɪd

13

alliteration, -s əˌlɪtəˈreɪʃn [æˌl-], -z
alliterative əˈlɪtərətɪv [æˈl-, -reɪt-]
Allman ˈɔːlmən
Alloa ˈæləʊə
Allobroges əˈlɒbrədʒiːz [æˈl-, -brəʊdʒ-, ˌæləˈbrəʊdʒ-]
allocat|e, -es, -ing, -ed ˈæləʊkeɪt, -s, -ɪŋ, -ɪd
allocation, -s ˌæləʊˈkeɪʃn, -z
allochrone, -s ˈæləʊkrəʊn, -z
allocution, -s ˌæləʊˈkjuːʃn, -z
allodi|al/s, -um əˈləʊdj|əl/z [-dɪ|-], -əm
allomorph, -s ˈæləʊmɔːf, -s
Allon ˈælən
allopath, -s ˈæləʊpæθ, -s
allopathic ˌæləʊˈpæθɪk
allopath|ist/s, -y əˈlɒpəθ|ɪst/s [æˈl-], -ɪ
allophone, -s ˈæləʊfəʊn, -z
allophonic ˌæləʊˈfɒnɪk
allot, -s, -ting, -ted, -ment/s əˈlɒt, -s, -ɪŋ -ɪd, -mənt/s
allotone, -s ˈæləʊtəʊn, -z
†allotropic ˌæləʊˈtrɒpɪk
allotropy æˈlɒtrəpɪ [əˈl-]
all-out ˌɔːlˈaʊt [ˈ— when attributive]
allow, -s, -ing, -ed əˈlaʊ, -z, -ɪŋ, -d
allowab|le, -ly, -leness əˈlaʊəb|l, -lɪ, -lnɪs [-nəs]
allowanc|e (s. v.), -es, -ing, -ed əˈlaʊəns, -ɪz, -ɪŋ, -t
Alloway ˈæləweɪ [ˈæləʊeɪ]
alloy (mixture of metals), -s ˈælɔɪ [əˈlɔɪ], -z, (figurative sense) əˈlɔɪ
alloy (v.), -s, -ing, -ed əˈlɔɪ, -z, -ɪŋ, -d
Allpress ˈɔːlpres
all-round, -er/s ˌɔːlˈraʊnd [ˈ— when attributive], -ə*/z
All-Saints'-Day, -s ˌɔːlˈseɪntsdeɪ, -z
Allsop(p) ˈɔːlsɒp [ˈɒl-, -səp]
All-Souls'-Day, -s ˌɔːlˈsəʊlzdeɪ, -z
allspice ˈɔːlspaɪs
Allt (surname) ɔːlt
allud|e, -es, -ing, -ed əˈluːd [-ˈljuːd], -z, -ɪŋ, -ɪd
allur|e, -es, -ing/ly, -ed, -ement/s əˈljʊə* [-ˈlʊə*, -ˈljɔə*, -ˈljɔː*], -z, -rɪŋ/lɪ, -d, -mənt/s
allusion, -s əˈluːʒn [-ˈljuː-], -z
allusive, -ly, -ness əˈluːsɪv [-ˈljuː-], -lɪ, -nɪs [-nəs]
alluvi|al, -on/s, -um/s, -a əˈluːvj|əl [-ˈljuː-, -vɪ|əl], -ən/z, -əm/z, -ə
Allworth ˈɔːlwəθ [-wɜː|θ]
Allworthy ˈɔːl,wɜːðɪ
all|y (party to alliance), -ies ˈælaɪ [əˈlaɪ], -z
all|y (marble), -ies ˈæl|ɪ, -ɪz

all|y (v.), -ies, -ying, -ied əˈl|aɪ [æˈl-, ˈælaɪ], -aɪz, -aɪɪŋ, -aɪd [ˈælaɪd]
Note.—allied is generally pronounced ˈælaɪd when attributive.
Ally ˈælɪ
Alma ˈælmə
Almack ˈɔːlmæk [ˈɒl-]
almagest, -s ˈælmədʒest, -s
Alma Mater, -s ˌælməˈmɑːtə* [-ˈmeɪtə*, -z
almanac(k), -s ˈɔːlmənæk [ˈɒl-], -s
Almanzor ælˈmænzɔː* [-zə*]
Alma-Tadema ˌælməˈtædɪmə
Almeria, -s ˌælməˈrɪə, -z
Almesbury ˈɑːmzbərɪ
almight|y (A.), -ily, -iness ɔːlˈmaɪt|ɪ, -ɪlɪ [-əlɪ], -ɪnɪs [-nəs]
almner, -s ˈɑːmnə*, -z
almoi(g)n ˈælmɔɪn
Almon ˈælmən
almond (A.), -s ˈɑːmənd, -z
Almondbury (in West Yorkshire) ˈælmənd bərɪ, [ˈɑːmənd-, ˈɔːmbərɪ, ˈeɪm bərɪ]
Almondsbury ˈɑːməndzbərɪ
almoner, -s ˈɑːmənə* [ˈælm-], -z
almonr|y, -ies ˈɑːmənr|ɪ [ˈælm-], -ɪz
almost ˈɔːlməʊst [ˈɒl-, -məst]
Almroth ˈælmrəʊθ
alms ɑːmz
almsgiv|er/s, -ing ˈɑːmz,gɪv|ə*/z, -ɪŋ
almshou|se, -ses ˈɑːmzhaʊ|s, -zɪz
Alne (in North Yorkshire, Warwick-shire) ɔːn
Alnmouth ˈælnmaʊθ
Alnwick ˈænɪk
aloe, -s ˈæləʊ, -z
aloft əˈlɒft
alone, -ness əˈləʊn, -nɪs [-nəs]
along, -side əˈlɒŋ, (-ˌ-) -ˈsaɪd
aloof, -ness əˈluːf, -nɪs [-nəs]
Alor Star ˌælɔːˈstɑː*
aloud əˈlaʊd
Aloysius ˌæləʊˈɪʃəs [-ˈɪsɪəs]
alp (A.), -s ælp, -s
alpaca, -s ælˈpækə, -z
alpenhorn, -s ˈælpənhɔːn [-pɪn-], -z
alpenstock, -s ˈælpənstɒk [-pɪn-], -s
Alperton ˈælpətən
alpestrian ælˈpestrɪən
alpha, -s ˈælfə, -z
alphabet, -s ˈælfəbet [-bɪt], -s
†alphabetic, -al, -ally ˌælfəˈbetɪk, -l, -əlɪ
Alphaeus ælˈfiːəs [-ˈfɪəs]
Alphonso ælˈfɒnzəʊ [-nsəʊ]
alpine ˈælpaɪn
alpinist, -s ˈælpɪnɪst, -s

already ɔːlˈredɪ [ɒl-, ɔːˈredɪ, *also* '-,-- *when followed by a stress*]
Alresford 'ɔːlrɪsfəd [*locally* 'ɔːlsfəd]
Alsace ælˈsæs [-lˈzæs, '--] (alzas)
Alsager (*in Cheshire*) 'ɔːlsɪdʒə* [-sədʒ-], ɔːlˈseɪdʒə
Alsa|tia, -tian/s ælˈseɪ|ʃə [-ʃɪə, -ʃjə], -ʃən/z [-ʃɪən/z, -ʃjən/z]
also 'ɔːlsəʊ ['ɒl-]
Alsop(p) 'ɔːlsɒp ['ɒl-, -səp]
Alston 'ɔːlstən ['ɒl-]
alt ælt
Altai ælˈteɪaɪ [-ˈtaɪ]
Altaic ælˈteɪɪk
Altair ælˈteə* ['æltea*]
altar, -s 'ɔːltə* ['ɒl-], -z
altar|-cloth, -cloths 'ɔːltə|klɒθ ['ɒl-, *old-fashioned* -klɔːθ], -klɒθs [*old-fashioned* -klɔːðz, -klɔːθs]
altar-piece, -s 'ɔːltəpiːs ['ɒl-], -ɪz
altar-rail, -s 'ɔːltəreɪl ['ɒl-], -z
altazimuth, -s ælˈtæzɪməθ, -s
alt|er, -ers, -ering, -ered; -erable; -erant/s 'ɔːlt|ə* ['ɒl-], -əz, -ərɪŋ, -əd; -ərəbl; -ərənt/s
alteration, -s ˌɔːltəˈreɪʃn [ˌɒl-], -z
alterative 'ɔːltərətɪv ['ɒl-, -reɪt-]
altercat|e, -es, -ing, -ed 'ɔːltəkeɪt ['ɒl-], -s, -ɪŋ, -ɪd
altercation, -s ˌɔːltəˈkeɪʃn [ˌɒl-], -z
alter ego ˌæltərˈegəʊ [-təˈeg-, -ˈiːg-]
alternance, -s ɔːlˈtɜːnəns [ɒl-, *rarely* æl-], -ɪz
alternant, -s ɔːlˈtɜːnənt [ɒl-, *rarely* æl-], -s
alternate (*adj.*), -ly, -ness ɔːlˈtɜːnət [ɒl-, *rarely* æl-, -nɪt], -lɪ, -nɪs [-nəs]
alternat|e (*v.*), -es, -ing, -ed 'ɔːltəneɪt ['ɒl-, *rarely* 'æl-], -s, -ɪŋ, -ɪd
alternation, -s ˌɔːltəˈneɪʃn [ˌɒl-, *rarely* ˌæl-], -z
alternative (*s. adj.*), -s, -ly ɔːlˈtɜːnətɪv [ɒl-, *rarely* æl-], -z, -lɪ
Althorp 'ɔːlθɔːp ['ɒl-], 'ɔːltrəp ['ɒl-]
although ɔːlˈðəʊ [ɒl-]
altimeter, s 'æltɪmiːtə* ['ɔːl-], -z
altimetry ælˈtɪmɪtrɪ [*rarely* ɔːl-, ɒl-, -mətrɪ]
altissimo ælˈtɪsɪməʊ
altitude, -s 'æltɪtjuːd, -z
alto, -s 'æltəʊ [*rarely* 'ɑːl-], -z
altogether ˌɔːltəˈgeðə* [ˌɒl-, -tʊˈg-, *also sometimes* '--,-- *when attributive*]
Alton 'ɔːltən ['ɒl-]
Altona (*in Germany*) 'æltəʊnə, ('alto:na:), (*in U.S.A.*) ælˈtəʊnə
alto-relievo ˌæltəʊrɪˈliːvəʊ
alto-rilievo ˌæltəʊrɪlɪˈeɪvəʊ

Altrincham 'ɔːltrɪŋəm ['ɒl-]
altrui|sm, -st/s 'æltruɪ|zəm [-truː:-], -st/s
altruistic, -ally ˌæltruˈɪstɪk [-truː:-], -əlɪ
alum (A.), -s 'æləm, -z
alumina əˈluːmɪnə [æ'l-, -'lju:-]
aluminium ˌæljʊˈmɪnɪəm [-lju:-, -njəm]
aluminous əˈluːmɪnəs [æ'l-, -'lju:-]
alumn|a, -ae əˈlʌmn|ə, -iː
alumn|us, -i əˈlʌmn|əs, -aɪ
Alva 'ælvə
Alvar 'ælvɑː* [-və*]
Alvary 'ælvərɪ
Alvechurch 'ɔːlvtʃɜːtʃ
alveolar, -s æl'vɪələ* [ˌælvɪˈəʊlə*, 'ælvɪələ*], -z
alveole, -s 'ælvɪəʊl, -z
alveol|us, -i, -ate æl'vɪəl|əs [ˌælvɪˈəʊl-, 'ælvɪəl-], -aɪ [-iː], -ət [-ɪt, -eɪt]
Alverstone 'ɔːlvəstən ['ɒl-]
Alvescot 'ælvɪskɒt [-kət, *locally* 'ɔːlskət]
Alveston (*in Avon*) 'ælvɪstən
alway 'ɔːlweɪ
always 'ɔːlweɪz [-wəz, -wɪz]
Alwyn 'ælwɪn
alyssum 'ælɪsəm
a.m. ˌeɪˈem
am, æm (*strong form*), əm, m (*weak forms*)
Amabel 'æməbel
Amadis 'æmədɪs
amadou 'æmədu:
amain əˈmeɪn
Amalek 'æmələk
Amalekite, -s əˈmæləkaɪt, -s
Amalfi əˈmælfɪ [æ'm-]
†amalgam, -s əˈmælgəm, -z
amalgamation, -s əˌmælgəˈmeɪʃn, -z
Aman 'æmən
Amanda əˈmændə
amandine əˈmændaɪn
Amantia əˈmænʃɪə [-ʃjə]
amanuens|is, -es əˌmænjʊˈens|ɪs, -iːz
Amara əˈmɑːrə
amaranth, -s 'æmərænθ, -s
amaranthine ˌæməˈrænθaɪn
amaryllis (A.), -es ˌæməˈrɪlɪs, -ɪz
Amasa 'æməsə [əˈmeɪsə]
Amasis əˈmeɪsɪs
amass, -es, -ing, -ed əˈmæs, -ɪz, -ɪŋ, -t
Amata əˈmɜːtə
amateur, -s 'æmətə* [-tɜ:*, -tjʊə*, -tjɔə-, -tjɔ:*, -tʃə*, ˌæməˈtɜ:*], -z
amateurish, -ly, -ness ˌæməˈtɜːrɪʃ [-ˈtjʊər-, -ˈtjɔər-, -ˈtjɔ:r-, 'æmət-, -tʃə-], -lɪ, -nɪs [-nəs]
amateurism 'æmətərɪzəm [-tɜ:-, -tjə-, -tjʊə-, -tjɔə-, -tjɔ:-, -tʃə-]

15

Amati, -s ə'mɑːtɪ [æ'm-], -z
amative, -ness 'æmətɪv, -nɪs [-nəs]
amatol 'æmətɒl
amatory 'æmətərɪ
amaurosis ˌæmɔːˈrəʊsɪs
Amaury ə'mɔːrɪ, 'æmərɪ, 'eɪmərɪ
amaz|e, -es, -ing/ly, -ed, -edly, -edness,
 -ement/s ə'meɪz, -ɪz, -ɪŋ/lɪ, -d, -ɪdlɪ,
 -ɪdnɪs [-nəs], -mənt/s
Amaziah ˌæməˈzaɪə
amazon (A.), -s 'æməzən, -z
amazonian, ˌæməˈzəʊnjən [-nɪən]
ambage, -s 'æmbɪdʒ, æm'beɪdʒiːz
 ['æmbɪdʒɪz]
ambassador, -s æm'bæsədə* [-sɪd-], -z
ambassadorial æmˌbæsəˈdɔːrɪəl [ˌæmb-,
 -sɪ'd-]
ambassadress, -es æm'bæsədrɪs [-sɪd-,
 -dres], -ɪz
ambe, -s 'æmbɪ, -z
amber 'æmbə*
ambergris 'æmbəgriːs [-grɪs]
ambidexter, -s ˌæmbɪˈdekstə*, -z
ambidexterity ˌæmbɪdekˈsterətɪ [-ɪtɪ]
ambidextrous ˌæmbɪˈdekstrəs
ambience, -s 'æmbɪəns [-bjəns], -ɪz
ambient 'æmbɪənt [-bjənt]
ambiguit|y, -ies ˌæmbɪˈgjuːət|ɪ [-ˈgjʊə-,
 -ɪt|ɪ], -ɪz
ambiguous, -ly, -ness æm'bɪgjʊəs
 [-gjwəs], -lɪ, -nɪs [-nəs]
Ambiorix æm'baɪərɪks
ambit, -s 'æmbɪt, -s
ambition, -s æm'bɪʃn, -z
ambitious, -ly, -ness æm'bɪʃəs, -lɪ, -nɪs
 [-nəs]
ambivalen|ce, -t æm'bɪvələn|s [ˌæm-
 bɪ'veɪləns], -t [ˌæmbɪ'veɪlənt]
amb|le, -les, -ling, -led, -ler/s 'æmb|l,
 -lz, -lɪŋ [-lɪŋ], -ld, -lə*/z [-lə*/z]
Ambler 'æmblə*
Ambleside 'æmblsaɪd
amboyna (A.) æm'bɔɪnə
Ambree 'æmbrɪ
Ambrose 'æmbrəʊz [-əʊs]
ambrosia, -l, -lly, -n æm'brəʊzjə [-zɪə,
 -ʒjə, -ʒɪə, -ʒə], -l, -lɪ, -n
ambr|y, -ies 'æmbr|ɪ, -ɪz
ambs-ace 'eɪmzeɪs ['æm-]
ambulance, -s 'æmbjʊləns, -ɪz
ambulant 'æmbjʊlənt
ambulat|e, -es, -ing, -ed 'æmbjʊleɪt, -s,
 -ɪŋ, -ɪd
ambulation, -s ˌæmbjʊˈleɪʃn, -z
ambulator|y (s. adj.), -ies 'æmbjʊlə-
 tər|ɪ [-leɪt-, ˌæmbjʊˈleɪt-], -ɪz
ambuscad|e (s. v.), -es, -ing, -ed
 ˌæmbəsˈkeɪd, -z, -ɪŋ, -ɪd

ambush (s. v.), -es, -ing, -ed 'æmbʊʃ,
 -ɪz, -ɪŋ, -t
Amelia ə'miːljə [-lɪə]
ameliorat|e, -es, -ing, -ed ə'miːljəreɪt
 [-lɪər-, -lɪɔːr-, -ljɔːr-], -s, -ɪŋ, -ɪd
amelioration, -s əˌmiːljəˈreɪʃn [-lɪə'r-,
 -lɪɔː'r-, -ljɔː'r-], -z
ameliorative ə'miːljərətɪv [-lɪər-, -lɪɔːr-,
 -ljɔːr-, -reɪt-]
amen, -s ˌɑːˈmen, ˌeɪˈmen, -z
amenability əˌmiːnəˈbɪlətɪ [-lɪt-]
amenab|le, -ly, -leness ə'miːnəb|l, -lɪ,
 -lnɪs [-nəs]
Amen Corner ˌeɪmen 'kɔːnə*
amen|d, -ds, -ding, -ded, -dment/s
 ə'men|d, -dz, -dɪŋ, -dɪd, -dmənt/s
Amen House ˌeɪmen 'haʊs
amenit|y,-ies ə'miːnət|ɪ[-'men-, -ɪt|ɪ],-ɪz
amerc|e, -es, -ing, -ed, -ement/s
 ə'mɜːs, -ɪz, -ɪŋ, -t, -mənt/s
America, -n/s ə'merɪkə, -n/z
Americana əˌmerɪˈkɑːnə
americanism, -s ə'merɪkənɪzəm, -z
americanization [-isa-] əˌmerɪkənaɪ-
 'zeɪʃn [-nɪ'z-]
americaniz|e [-is|e], -es, -ing, -ed
 ə'merɪkənaɪz, -ɪz, -ɪŋ, -d
americium ˌæməˈrɪsɪəm [-sjəm, -ʃəm,
 -ʃjəm]
Amerindian, -s ˌæmərˈɪndjən [-dɪən], -z
Amersham 'æməʃəm
Amery 'eɪmərɪ
Ames, -bury eɪmz, -bərɪ
amethyst, -s 'æmɪθɪst [-məθ-, -meθ-], -s
amethystine ˌæmɪˈθɪstaɪn [-məˈθ-,
 -me'θ-]
Amharic æm'hærɪk
Amherst 'æməst, 'æmhɜːst
amiability ˌeɪmjəˈbɪlətɪ [-mɪə-, -lɪt-]
amiab|le, -ly, -leness 'eɪmjəb|l [-mɪə-],
 -lɪ, -lnɪs [-nəs]
Amias 'eɪmɪəs [-mjəs]
amicability ˌæmɪkəˈbɪlətɪ [-lɪt-]
amicab|le, -ly, -leness 'æmɪkəb|l, -lɪ,
 -lnɪs [-nəs]
amice, -s 'æmɪs, -ɪz
Amice 'eɪmɪs
amid ə'mɪd
Amidas 'æmɪdæs
amide, -s 'æmaɪd, -z
amidships ə'mɪdʃɪps
amidst ə'mɪdst [-ɪtst]
Amiel 'æmɪəl ['eɪm-, -mjəl]
Amiens (French city) 'æmjæ̃ːŋ [-mɪæ̃ːŋ,
 -mɪəŋ, -mɪənz, -mjənz] (amjɛ̃),
 (Shakespearian character) 'æmɪənz
 [-mjənz], (street in Dublin) 'eɪmjənz
 [-mɪənz]

Amies 'eɪmɪz
amir, -s ə'mɪə* [æ'm-, 'æˌmɪə*], -z
Amis 'eɪmɪs
amiss ə'mɪs
amity 'æmətɪ [-ɪtɪ]
Amlwch 'æmlʊk [-lʊx] (Welsh 'amlux)
Amman ə'mɑːn
ammeter, -s 'æmɪtə* [-mətə*], -z
Ammon 'æmən [-mɒn]
ammonia ə'məʊnjə [-nɪə]
ammoniac ə'məʊnɪæk [-njæk]
ammoniacal ˌæməʊ'naɪəkl
ammoniated ə'məʊnɪeɪtɪd [-njeɪ-]
ammonite (A.), -s 'æmənaɪt, -s
ammonium ə'məʊnjəm [-nɪəm]
ammunition ˌæmjʊ'nɪʃn
amnesia æm'niːzjə [-zɪə, -ʒjə, -ʒɪə, -ʒə]
amnest|y, -ies 'æmnəst|ɪ [-nɪs-, -nes-], -ɪz
Amnon 'æmnɒn
amoeb|a, -ae, -as, -ic ə'miːb|ə, -iː, -əz, -ɪk
amok ə'mɒk ['ɑːməʊ]
   Note.—'ɑːməʊ is the pronunciation used in Malaya.
among, -st ə'mʌŋ, -st [ə'mʌŋkst]
amontillado (A.) əˌmɒntɪ'lɑːdəʊ [-ɪ'ljɑː-]
Amoore 'eɪˌmʊə*
amoral ˌeɪ'mɒrəl [ə'm-, æ'm-]
amorist, -s 'æmərɪst, -s
Amorite, -s 'æməraɪt, -s
amorous, -ly, -ness 'æmərəs, -lɪ, -nɪs [-nəs]
amorpha, -s ə'mɔːfə, -z
amorph|ism, -ous ə'mɔːf|ɪzəm, -əs
amortization [-isa-], -s əˌmɔːtɪ'zeɪʃn, [ˌæmɔːt-, ˌæmət-, -taɪ-], -z
amortiz|e, -es, -ing, -ed ə'mɔːtaɪz [-tɪz], -ɪz, -ɪŋ, -d
Amory 'eɪmərɪ
Amos 'eɪmɒs
amount (s. v.), -s, -ing, -ed ə'maʊnt, -s, -ɪŋ, -ɪd
amour, -s ə'mʊə* [æ'm-], -z
amour-propre ˌæmʊə'prɒprə [-'prɒpə*] (amurprɔpr)
Amoy ə'mɔɪ
amp, -s, -erage æmp, -s, -ərɪdʒ
ampelopsis ˌæmpɪ'lɒpsɪs
ampère [-pere], -s 'æmpeə*, -z
Ampère 'æmpeə* (ɑ̃pɛːr)
ampersand, -s 'æmpəsænd, -z
amphibi|a, -an/s, -ous æm'fɪbɪ|ə [-bj|ə], -ən/z, -əs
amphibole (mineral) 'æmfɪbəʊl
amphibole (net), -s æm'fɪbəlɪ, -z
amphibology ˌæmfɪ'bɒlədʒɪ

amphibol|y, -ies æm'fɪbəl|ɪ, -ɪz
amphibrach, -s 'æmfɪbræk, -s
Amphictyon, -s æm'fɪktɪən [-tjən], -z
amphictyonic æmˌfɪktɪ'ɒnɪk
Amphimedon æm'fɪmɪdən [-dəʊn]
Amphion æm'faɪən
Amphipolis æm'fɪpəlɪs
amphiscian, -s æm'fɪʃɪən [-ʃjən], -z
amphitheatre, -s 'æmfɪˌθɪətə* [-θɪˌeɪtə*], -z
Amphitrite 'æmfɪtraɪtɪ
Amphitryon æm 'fɪtrɪən
amphor|a, ae, -as 'æmfər|ə, -iː, -əz
amphoric æm'fɒrɪk
amp|le, -ler, -lest, -ly, -leness 'æmp|l, -lə*, -lɪst, -lɪ, -lnɪs [-nəs]
amplification, -s ˌæmplɪfɪ'keɪʃn, -z
amplificatory 'æmplɪfɪkeɪtərɪ [ˌ---'---]
ampli|fy, -fies, -fying, -fied, -fier/s 'æmplɪ|faɪ, -faɪz, -faɪɪŋ, -faɪd, -faɪə*/z
amplitude, -s 'æmplɪtjuːd, -z
ampoule, -s 'æmpuːl, -z
Ampthill 'æmpθɪl
ampull|a, -ae æm'pʊl|ə, -iː
amputat|e, -es, -ing, -ed 'æmpjʊteɪt, -s, -ɪŋ, -ɪd
amputation, -s ˌæmpjʊ'teɪʃn, -z
Amram 'æmræm
Amritsar æm'rɪtsə* (Hindi əmrytsər)
Amsterdam ˌæmstə'dæm [-mps-, '--ˌ-]
amuck ə'mʌk
amulet, -s 'æmjʊlɪt [-let, -lət], -s
Amulree ˌæməl'riː
Amundsen 'ɑːmʊndsən [-mən-]
Amur ə'mʊə* [æ'm-, 'æˌmʊə*]
amus|e, -es, -ing/ly, -ingness, -ed, -ement/s ə'mjuːz, -ɪz, -ɪŋ/lɪ, -ɪŋnɪs [-nəs], -d, -mənt/s
Amy 'eɪmɪ
Amyas 'eɪmjəs [-mɪəs]
amygdal|in, -oid ə'mɪgdəl|ɪn [æ'm-], -ɔɪd
amytal 'æmɪtæl
an æn (strong form), ən, n (weak forms)
ana 'ɑːnə
anabapti|sm, -st/s ˌænə'bæptɪ|zəm, -st/s
anabaptistic ˌænəbæp'tɪstɪk
anabas|is, -es ə'næbəs|ɪs, -iːz
anabolism ə'næbəʊlɪzəm
anachronism, -s ə'nækərɪzəm, -z
anachron|ism/s, -ous/ly ə'nækrən|ɪzəm/z, -əs/lɪ
anachronistic əˌnækrə'nɪstɪk [-krɒ'n-]
anacoluth|on, -a ˌænəkəʊ'luːθ|ɒn [-næk-, -'lju:-, -θ|ən], -ə
anaconda, -s ˌænə'kɒndə, -z
Anacreon ə'nækrɪən
anacrus|is, -es ˌænə'kruːs|ɪs, -iːz

17

Anadin 'ænədɪn
anaemia ə'ni:mjə [æ'n-, -mɪə]
anaemic ə'ni:mɪk [æ'n-]
anaesthesia ˌænɪs'θi:zjə [-ni:s-, -nəs-, -zɪə, -ʒjə, -ʒɪə, -ʒə]
anaesthetic, -s, -ally ˌænɪs'θetɪk [-ni:s-, -nəs-], -s, -əlɪ
anaesthetist, -s æ'ni:sθətɪst [ə'n-, -θɪt-], -s
anaesthetiz|e [-is|e], **-es, -ing, -ed** æ'ni:sθətaɪz [ə'n-, -θɪt-], -ɪz, -ɪŋ, -d
anagogic, -s, -al, -ally ˌænə'gɒdʒɪk, -s, -l, -əlɪ
anagogy 'ænəgɒdʒɪ [-gɒgɪ, -gəʊdʒɪ]
anagram, -s 'ænəgræm, -z
anagrammatic, -al, -ally ˌænəgrə-'mætɪk, -l, -əlɪ
Anak 'eɪnæk [*rarely* 'ænæk]
Anakim 'ænəkɪm [*rarely* ə'nɑ:kɪm]
anal 'eɪnl
analects 'ænəlekts
analgesia ˌænæl'dʒi:zjə [ˌænəl-, -i:zɪə, -i:sjə, -i:sɪə]
analgesic ˌænæl'dʒi:sɪk [ˌænəl-, -'dʒesɪk]
analogic, -al, -ally ˌænə'lɒdʒɪk, -l, -əlɪ
analogist, -s ə'nælədʒɪst, -s
analogous, -ly, -ness ə'næləgəs, -lɪ, -nɪs [-nəs]
analog(ue), -s 'ænəlɒg, -z
analog|y, -ies ə'nælədʒ|ɪ, -ɪz
analphabetic, -al, -ally ˌænælfə'betɪk, -l, -əlɪ
analysable 'ænəlaɪzəbl
analys|e, -es, -ing, -ed 'ænəlaɪz, -ɪz, -ɪŋ, -d
analys|is, -es ə'næləs|ɪs [-lɪs-], -i:z
analyst, -s 'ænəlɪst. -s
analytic, -s, -al, -ally ˌænə'lɪtɪk, -s, -l, -əlɪ
anamorphosis ˌænə'mɔ:fəsɪs
anana, -s (*plur.*) ə'nɑ:nə, -z
ananas (*sing.*), **-es** ə'nɑ:nəs, -ɪz
Ananias ˌænə'naɪəs
anapaest, -s 'ænəpi:st [-pest], -s
anapaestic ˌænə'pi:stɪk [-'pest-]
anaphora, -s ə'næfərə, -z
anaphoric ˌænə'fɒrɪk
anarch, -s 'ænɑ:k, -s
anarchic, -al, -ally æ'nɑ:kɪk [ə'n-], -l, -əlɪ
anarch|ism, -ist/s, -y 'ænək|ɪzəm, -ɪst/s, -ɪ
Anastasia (*English Christian name*) ˌænə'steɪzjə [-zɪə], (*foreign name*) ˌænə'stɑ:z-
anastigmat, -s ə'næstɪgmæt [æ'n-], -s
anastomosis ˌænəstə'məʊsɪs [ˌænæs-]
anastrophe, -s ə'næstrəfɪ [æ'n-], -z

anathema, -s ə'næθəmə [-θɪm-], -z
anathematization [-isa-], **-s** əˌnæθə-mətaɪ'zeɪʃn [-θɪm-, -tɪ'z-], -z
anathematiz|e [-is|e], **-es, -ing, -ed** ə'næθəmətaɪz [-θɪm-], -ɪz, -ɪŋ, -d
Anatolia, -n/s ˌænə'təʊljə [-lɪə], -n/z
anatomic, -al, -ally ˌænə'tɒmɪk, -l, -əlɪ
anatomist, -s ə'nætəmɪst, -s
anatomiz|e [-is|e], **-es, -ing, -ed** ə'nætə-maɪz, -ɪz, -ɪŋ, -d
anatom|y, -ies ə'nætəm|ɪ, -ɪz
Anaxagoras ˌænæk'sægəræs [-rəs]
ancestor, -s 'ænsestə* [-sɪs-, -səs-], -z
ancestral æn'sestrəl
ancestress, -es 'ænsestrɪs [-sɪs-, -səs-, -tres, -trəs], -ɪz
ancestr|y, -ies 'ænsestr|ɪ [-sɪs-, -səs-], -ɪz
Anchises æŋ'kaɪsi:z [æn'k-]
Ancholme 'æŋkhəʊm
anchor (*s. v.*), **-s, -ing, -ed** 'æŋkə* [æŋkə*, -z, -rɪŋ, -d]
anchorage, -s 'æŋkərɪdʒ, -ɪz
anchoress, -es 'æŋkərɪs [-res], -ɪz
anchoret, -s 'æŋkəret [-rɪt], -s
anchorhold, -s 'æŋkəhəʊld, -z
anchorite, -s 'æŋkəraɪt [-kɒr-], -s
anchov|y, -ies 'æntʃəv|ɪ [æn'tʃəʊv-], -ɪz
anchylosis ˌæŋkaɪ'ləʊsɪs [ˌænk-]
ancient, -est, -ly, -s 'eɪnʃənt, -ɪst, -lɪ, -s
ancillary æn'sɪlərɪ
ancipit|al, -ous æn'sɪpɪt|l, -əs
Ancren Riwle ˌæŋkrɪn'rɪʊlɪ [-kren-, -krən-, -lə]
ancress, -es 'æŋkrɪs [-kres], -ɪz
Ancyra æn'saɪərə
and ænd (*strong form*), ənd, ən, nd, n, m, ŋ (*weak forms*)
Note.—The form m *only occurs next to* p *or* b, *and the form* ŋ *only occurs next to* k *or* g.
Andalusia ˌændə'lu:zjə [-u:zɪə, -u:ʒjə, -u:ʒɪə, -u:sjə, -u:sɪə, -u:ʃjə, -u:ʃɪə]
Andaman 'ændəmæn [-mən]
andante, -s æn'dæntɪ, -z
andantino ˌændæn'ti:nəʊ
Ander|sen, -son 'ændə|sn, -sn
Andes 'ændi:z
andiron, -s 'ændaɪən, -z
Andorra æn'dɔ:rə [-'dɒrə]
Andover 'ændəʊvə*
Andow (*surname*) 'ændaʊ
Andrade (*English surname*) 'ændreɪd
Andrassy æn'dræsɪ
Andreas 'ændrɪæs [-rəs]
Andrew 'ændru:
Andrewatha (*Cornish family*) æn-'dru:θə, (*Plymouth family*) æn-'dru:əθə, ˌændru:'ɒθə

Andrews 'ændru:z
Andria 'ændrɪə
Androcles 'ændrəʊkli:z
Androclus æn'drɒkləs
androgynous æn'drɒdʒɪnəs
android, -s 'ændrɔɪd, -z
Androm|ache, -eda æn'drɒm|əkɪ, -ɪdə
Andronicus (Byzantine emperors and
    other figures in ancient history)
    ˌændrə'naɪkəs [æn'drɒnɪkəs], (in
    Shakespeare's Titus Andronicus)
    æn'drɒnɪkəs
Andros 'ændrɒs
anecdotal ˌænek'dəʊtl [-nɪk-]
anecdote, -s 'ænɪkdəʊt [-nek-], -s
†anecdotic, -al, -ally ˌænek'dəʊtɪk [-nɪk-,
    -dɒt-], -l, -əlɪ
anechoic ˌænɪ'kəʊɪk
Anelay (surname) 'eɪnlɪ
anelectric, -s ˌænɪ'lektrɪk, -s
anelectrode, -s ˌænɪ'lektrəʊd, -z
anemomet|er/s, -ry ˌænɪ'mɒmɪt|ə*/z
    [-mət|ə*/z], -rɪ
anemometric ˌænɪməʊ'metrɪk
anemone, -s ə'nemənɪ, -z
anemoscope, -s ə'neməskəʊp, -s
anent ə'nent
aneroid, -s 'ænərɔɪd [-nɪr-], -z
aneurin 'ænjʊərɪn
Aneurin ə'naɪərɪn (Welsh a'nəirin)
aneurism, -s 'ænjʊərɪzəm, -z
anew ə'nju:
anfractuosity ˌænfræktjʊ'ɒsətɪ [-ɪtɪ]
Angear 'ænˌɡɪə*
angel (A.), -s 'eɪndʒəl, -z
Angela 'ændʒələ [-dʒɪl-]
Angeles 'ændʒɪli:z ['æŋɡɪl-, -əl-, -lɪz,
    -lɪs]
angelic, -al, -ally æn'dʒelɪk, -l, -əlɪ
angelica (A.) æn'dʒelɪkə
Angelina ˌændʒɪ'li:nə [-dʒe'l-, -dʒə'l-]
Angelo 'ændʒɪləʊ [-ələʊ]
angelus, -es 'ændʒələs [-dʒɪl-], -ɪz
anger (s. v.), -s, -ing, -ed 'æŋɡə*, -z
    -rɪŋ, -d
Angevin 'ændʒɪvɪn [-əvɪn]
Angier 'ænˌdʒɪə*
angina, -s æn'dʒaɪnə, -z
ang|le (s. v.) (A.), -les, -ling, -led, -ler/s
    'æŋɡ|l, -lz, -lɪŋ, -ld, -lə*/z
angledozer, -s 'æŋɡlˌdəʊzə*, -z
Angle|sea, -sey 'æŋɡl|sɪ [-si:], -sɪ
    [-si:]
Anglia, -n/s 'æŋɡlɪə [-ɡljə], -n/z
Anglic|an/s, -anism 'æŋɡlɪk|ən/z,
    -ənɪzəm
anglice 'æŋɡlɪsɪ
anglici|sm/s, -st/s 'æŋɡlɪsɪ|zəm/z, -st/s

anglicization [-isa-] ˌæŋɡlɪsaɪ'zeɪʃn
    [-sɪ'z-]
angliciz|e [-is|e], -es, -ing, -ed 'æŋɡlɪ-
    saɪz, -ɪz, -ɪŋ, -d
Anglo-French ˌæŋɡləʊ'frentʃ
anglomania ˌæŋɡləʊ'meɪnjə [-nɪə]
Anglo-Norman ˌæŋɡləʊ'nɔ:mən
anglophile, -s 'æŋɡləʊfaɪl, -z
anglophobe, -s 'æŋɡləʊfəʊb, -z
anglophobia ˌæŋɡləʊ'fəʊbjə [-bɪə]
Anglo-Saxon, -s ˌæŋɡləʊ'sæksən, -z
Anglo-Saxondom ˌæŋɡləʊ'sæksəndəm
Anglo-Saxonism, -s ˌæŋɡləʊ'sæk-
    sənɪzəm [-sŋɪ-], -z
Angmering 'æŋmərɪŋ
Angola æŋ'ɡəʊlə
Angora (old form of Ankara in Turkey)
    'æŋɡərə [æŋ'ɡɔ:rə]
Angora (cat, rabbit, cloth), -s æŋ'ɡɔ:rə,-z
Angostura ˌæŋɡə'stjʊərə [-ɡɒ's-,
    -'stjɔərə, -'stjɔ:rə, -'stʊərə, -'stɔərə,
    -'stɔ:rə]
angr|y, -ier, -iest, -ily, -iness 'æŋɡr|ɪ,
    -ɪə*, -ɪɪst, -əlɪ [-ɪlɪ], -ɪnɪs [-ɪnəs]
angst æŋst (aŋst)
angstrom, -s 'æŋstrəm, -z
anguine 'æŋɡwɪn
anguish, -ed 'æŋɡwɪʃ, -t
angular 'æŋɡjʊlə*
angularit|y, -ies ˌæŋɡjʊ'lærət|ɪ [-ɪt|ɪ], -ɪz
angulate 'æŋɡjʊleɪt [-lɪt, -lət]
angulated 'æŋɡjʊleɪtɪd
Angus 'æŋɡəs
Angustura ˌæŋɡə'stjʊərə [-'stjɔərə,
    -'stjɔ:rə, -'stʊərə, -'stɔərə, -'stɔ:rə]
anharmonic ˌænhɑ:'mɒnɪk
anhungered ən'hʌŋɡəd
anhydr|ide/s, -ite, -ous æn'haɪdr|aɪd/z,
    -aɪt, -əs
anil 'ænɪl
anile 'eɪnaɪl ['æn-]
aniline 'ænɪli:n [-lɪn, rarely -laɪn]
anility æ'nɪlətɪ [ə'n-, -ɪtɪ]
animadversion, -s ˌænɪmæd'vɜ:ʃn
    [-məd-], -z
animadvert, -s, -ing, -ed ˌænɪmæd'vɜ:t
    [-məd-], -s, -ɪŋ, -ɪd
animal, -s 'ænɪml [-nəm-], -z
animalcular ˌænɪ'mælkjʊlə*
animalcule, -s ˌænɪ'mælkju:l, -z
animalism 'ænɪməlɪzəm [-m|ɪ-]
animate (adj.) 'ænɪmət [-mɪt, -meɪt]
animat|e (v.), -es, -ing, -ed/ly, -or/s
    'ænɪmeɪt, -s, -ɪŋ, -ɪd/lɪ, -ə*/z
animation, -s ˌænɪ'meɪʃn
animism 'ænɪmɪzəm
animosit|y, -ies ˌænɪ'mɒsət|ɪ [-ɪt|ɪ], -ɪz
animus 'ænɪməs

19

anion, -s 'ænaɪən, -z
anise 'ænɪs
aniseed 'ænɪsi:d
anisette ˌænɪ'zet [-'set]
Anita ə'ni:tə
Anjou ɑ̃:ŋˈʒu: [ɒŋ-] (ɑ̃ʒu)
Ankara (in Turkey) 'æŋkərə
anker, -s 'æŋkə*, -z
ankh, -s æŋk, -s
ankle, -s 'æŋkl, -z
anklet, -s 'æŋklɪt [-lət], -s
Ann æn
anna (A.), -s 'ænə, -z
Annabel 'ænəbel
Annabella ˌænə'belə
Annagh æ'nɑ: ['ænɑ:]
Annakin 'ænəkɪn
annalist, -s 'ænəlɪst, -s
annals 'ænlz
Annaly 'ænəlɪ
Annam æn'æm ['ænæm]
Annamese ˌænə'mi:z
Annan, -dale 'ænən, -deɪl
Annapolis ə'næpəlɪs [æ'n-]
Annas 'ænæs [-nəs]
annatto ə'nætəʊ [æ'n-]
Anne æn
anneal, -s, -ing, -ed ə'ni:l, -z, -ɪŋ, -d
annelid, -s 'ænəlɪd, -z
Annesley 'ænzlɪ
annex(e) (s.), -es 'æneks, -ɪz
annex (v.), -es, -ing, -ed, -ment/s
  ə'neks [æ'n-], -ɪz, -ɪŋ, -t, -mənt/s
annexation, -s ˌænek'seɪʃn, -z
Annie 'ænɪ
annihilat|e, -es, -ing, -ed, -or/s ə'naɪə-
  leɪt [-'naɪl-, rarely 'ænɪəl-], -s, -ɪŋ,
  -ɪd, -ə*/z
annihilation, -s əˌnaɪə'leɪʃn [-ˌnaɪl'l-,
  rarely ˌænɪə'l-], -z
Anning 'ænɪŋ
Anniston 'ænɪstən
anniversar|y, -ies ˌænɪ'vɜ:sər|ɪ, -ɪz
Anno Domini ˌænəʊ'dɒmɪnaɪ
annotat|e, -es, -ing, -ed, -or/s, -ive
  'ænəʊteɪt, -s, -ɪŋ, -ɪd, -ə* /z, -ɪv
annotation, -s ˌænəʊ'teɪʃn, -z
announc|e, -es, -ing, -ed, -er/s,
  -ement/s ə'naʊns, -ɪz, -ɪŋ, -t, -ə*/z,
  -mənt/s
annoy, -s, -ing/ly, -ed; -ance/s ə'nɔɪ,
  -z, -ɪŋ/lɪ, -d; -əns/ɪz
annual (s. adj.), -s, -ly 'ænjʊəl [-njwəl,
  -njʊl], -z, -ɪ
annuit|y, -ies, -ant/s ə'nju:ɪt|ɪ [-'njʊ-,
  -ət|ɪ], -ɪz, -ənt/s
annul, -s, -ling, -led, -ment/s ə'nʌl, -z,
  -ɪŋ, -d, -mənt/s

annul|ar, -ate, -ated, -us/es, -i 'ænjʊl|ə*,
  -eɪt [-ɪt], -eɪtɪd, -əs/ɪz, -aɪ [-i:]
annulet, -s 'ænjʊlet [-lɪt, -lət], -s
annunciat|e, -es, -ing, -ed ə'nʌnsɪeɪt
  [-nsjeɪt, -nʃɪeɪt, -nʃjeɪt], -s, -ɪŋ, -ɪd
annunciation (A.), -s əˌnʌnsɪ'eɪʃn, -z
anode, -s 'ænəʊd, -z
anodyne, -s 'ænəʊdaɪn, -z
anoint, -s, -ing, -ed, -ment/s ə'nɔɪnt,
  -s, -ɪŋ, -ɪd, -mənt/s
anomalous, -ly ə'nɒmələs, -lɪ
anomal|y, -ies ə'nɒməl|ɪ, -ɪz
anon ə'nɒn
anonym, -s 'ænənɪm [-nɒn-], -z
anonymity ˌænə'nɪmətɪ [-nɒ'n-, -ɪtɪ]
anonymous, -ly ə'nɒnɪməs, -lɪ
anopheles ə'nɒfɪli:z [-fəl-]
anorak, -s 'ænəræk, -s
†anorex|ia, -ic ˌænə'reks|ɪə[-ksjə], -ɪk
another ə'nʌðə*
Anouilh 'ænu:i: [-u:ɪ] (anu:j)
Anrias 'ænrɪæs
Anselm 'ænselm
anserine 'ænsəraɪn
An|sley, -son 'æn|zlɪ, -sn
Ansonia æn'səʊnjə [-nɪə]
Ansted 'ænsted [-tɪd]
Anster 'ænstə*
Anstey 'ænstɪ
Anstruther 'ænstrʌðə*
answ|er (s. v.), -ers, -ering, -ered,
  -erer/s 'ɑ:ns|ə*, -əz, -ərɪŋ, -əd,
  -ərə*/z
answerab|le, -ly 'ɑ:nsərəb|l, -lɪ
ant, -s ænt, -s
antacid (s. adj.), -s ˌænt'æsɪd ['ænt,æ-],
  -z
Antaeus æn'ti:əs [-'tɪəs]
antagoni|sm/s, -st/s æn'tægənɪ|zəm/z,
  -st/s
antagonistic, -ally ænˌtægə'nɪstɪk
  [ˌ---'--], -əlɪ
antagoniz|e [-is|e], -es, -ing, -ed
  æn'tægənaɪz, -ɪz, -ɪŋ, -d
Antananarivo 'æntəˌnænə'ri:vəʊ
Antarctic æn'tɑ:ktɪk [ænt-, '-,--]
Antares æn'teəri:z
ant-bear, -s 'æntbeə*, -z
ant-eater, -s 'ænt,i:tə*, -z
anteceden|ce, -t/ly, -ts ˌæntɪ'si:dən|s
  ['æntɪˌs-], -t/lɪ, -ts
antechamber, -s 'æntɪˌtʃeɪmbə*, -z
antechapel, -s 'æntɪˌtʃæpl, -z
antedat|e, -es, -ing, -ed ˌæntɪ'deɪt ['---],
  -s, -ɪŋ, -ɪd
antediluvi|an/s, -al/ly ˌæntɪdɪ'lu:-
  vj|ən/z [-daɪ'l-, -'lju:-, -vɪ|ə-], -əl/ɪ
antelope, -s 'æntɪləʊp, -s

antemeridian ˌæntɪməˈrɪdɪən [-djən]
antenatal ˌæntɪˈneɪtl
antenn|a, -ae, -al, -ary ænˈten|ə, -iː, -l,
-ərɪ
Antenor ænˈtiːnɔ:*
antenuptial ˌæntɪˈnʌpʃl [-tʃəl]
antepenult, -s ˌæntɪpɪˈnʌlt [-peˈn-,
-pəˈn-], -s
antepenultimate, -s ˌæntɪpɪˈnʌltɪmət
[-peˈn-, -pəˈn-, -mɪt], -s
anteprandial ˌæntɪˈprændjəl [-dɪəl]
anterior, -ly, -ness ænˈtɪərɪə*, -lɪ, -nɪs
[-nəs]
anteroom, -s ˈæntɪrʊm [-ruːm], -z
Anthaea ænˈθɪə [-ˈθiːə, ˈænθɪə, ˈænθjə]
ant-heap, -s ˈænthiːp, -s
antheli|on/s, -a ænˈθiːlj|ən/z [-lɪ|ə-], -ə
anthelix, -es ænˈθiːlɪks [ˈænθɪlɪks], -ɪz
anthem, -s ˈænθəm [-θem], -z
anther, -s ˈænθə*, -z
anthill, -s ˈænthɪl, -z
anthological ˌænθəˈlɒdʒɪkl [-θəʊˈl-]
†antholog|y, -ies, -ist/s ænˈθɒlədʒ|ɪ, -ɪz,
-ɪst/s
Anthon ˈænθən
Anthony ˈæntənɪ, ˈænθənɪ
anthracic ænˈθræsɪk
anthracite ˈænθrəsaɪt
anthracitic ˌænθrəˈsɪtɪk
anthrax ˈænθræks
anthropocentric ˌænθrəʊpəʊˈsentrɪk
anthropoid (s. adj.), -s ˈænθrəʊpɔɪd
[ænˈθrəʊpɔɪd], -z
anthropoidal ˌænθrəʊˈpɔɪdl
anthropologic|al, -ally ˌænθrəpəˈlɒdʒ-
ɪk|l [-θrəʊp-], -əlɪ
anthropolog|ist/s, -y ˌænθrə'pɒlədʒ|-
ɪst/s [-θrəʊˈp-], -ɪ
anthropometric ˌænθrəʊpəʊˈmetrɪk
anthropometry ˌænθrəˈpɒmɪtrɪ[-θrəʊˈp-,
-mətrɪ, ˈænθrəʊpəʊmetrɪ]
anthropomorph|ic, -ism, -ist/s, -ous
ˌænθrəpəʊˈmɔːf|ɪk [-θrəʊp-], -ɪzəm,
-ɪst/s, -əs
anthropophagi ˌænθrəʊˈpɒfəgaɪ
[-fədʒaɪ]
anthropopha|gous, -gy ˌænθrəʊˈpɒ-
fə|gəs, -dʒɪ
anthroposoph|ist/s, -y ˌænθrəʊˈpɒsəf|-
ɪst/s, -ɪ
anti- ˈæntɪ-
Note.—Numerous compounds may be
formed by prefixing anti- to other
words. Those not entered below have
double stress.
anti-aircraft ˌæntɪˈeəkrɑːft
antibilious ˌæntɪˈbɪljəs [-lɪəs]
antibiotic (s. adj.), -s ˌæntɪbaɪˈɒtɪk, -s

antibod|y, -ies ˈæntɪˌbɒd|ɪ, -ɪz
antic, -s ˈæntɪk, -s
anticatholic, -s ˌæntɪˈkæθəlɪk [-ˈkɑː θ-,
-θlɪk], -s
Antichrist, -s ˈæntɪkraɪst, -s
antichristian, -s (opposing Christianity)
ˌæntɪˈkrɪstjən [-tɪən, -tʃən], (pertaining to Antichrist) ˈæntɪˌk-, -z
anticipant, -s ænˈtɪsɪpənt, -s
anticipat|e, -es, -ing, -ed; -ive/ly
ænˈtɪsɪpeɪt, -s, -ɪŋ, -ɪd; -ɪv/lɪ
anticipation, -s ænˌtɪsɪˈpeɪʃn [ˌæntɪ-],
-z
anticipator|y, -ily ænˈtɪsɪpeɪtər|ɪ
[-pət-, ˌæntɪsɪˈpeɪtər|ɪ], -əlɪ [-ɪlɪ]
anticiz|e [-is|e], -es, -ing, -ed ˈæntɪsaɪz,
-ɪz, -ɪŋ, -d
anticlerical ˌæntɪˈklerɪkl
anticlimax, -es ˌæntɪˈklaɪmæks [in contrast ˈæntɪˌklaɪmæks], -ɪz
anticyclone, -s ˌæntɪˈsaɪkloʊn [ˈæntɪˌs-],
-z
anticyclonic ˌæntɪsaɪˈklɒnɪk
anti-dazzle ˌæntɪˈdæzl
anti-depressant, -s ˌæntɪdɪˈpresnt, -s
antidotal ˈæntɪdəʊtl [ˌæntɪˈd-]
antidote, -s ˈæntɪdəʊt, -s
antifebrile ˌæntɪˈfiːbraɪl [-ˈfeb-]
anti-freeze ˈæntɪfriːz [ˌ--ˈ-]
Antigon|e, -us ænˈtɪgən|ɪ, -əs
Antigua ænˈtiːgə
anti|helix, -helixes, -helices ˌæntɪˈhiː-
lɪks, -ˈhiːlɪksɪz, -ˈhiːlɪsiːz [-helɪsiːz]
antihistamine ˌæntɪˈhɪstəmɪn [-miːn]
anti-icer, -s ˌæntɪˈaɪsə*, -z
Antilles ænˈtɪliːz
antilog|y, -ies ænˈtɪlədʒ|ɪ, -ɪz
antimacassar, -s ˌæntɪməˈkæsə*, -z
Antimachus ænˈtɪməkəs
antimonarchical ˌæntɪmɒˈnɑːkɪkl
[-məˈn-]
antimonarchist, -s ˌæntɪˈmɒnəkɪst, -s
antimonial, -s ˌæntɪˈməʊnjəl [-nɪəl], -z
antimonic ˌæntɪˈmɒnɪk
antimony ˈæntɪmənɪ [-ˈ---]
anti-national ˌæntɪˈnæʃənl [-ʃnəl, -ʃn̩,
-ʃn], -ʃənəl]
antinomic, -al, -ally ˌæntɪˈnɒmɪk, -l, -əlɪ
antinom|y, -ies ænˈtɪnəm|ɪ, -ɪz
Antinous ænˈtɪnəʊəs
Antioch ˈæntɪɒk [-tjɒk]
Antiochian, -s ˌæntɪˈəʊkjən [-kɪən], -z
Antiochus ænˈtaɪəkəs
Antioquia ˌæntɪəʊˈkiːə [-ɪə]
Antipas ˈæntɪpæs
Antipater ænˈtɪpətə*
antipathetic ˌæntɪpəˈθetɪk [-,--ˈ--]
antipath|y, -ies ænˈtɪpəθ|ɪ, -ɪz

anti-personnel ˌæntɪpɜːsəˈnel [-snˈel]
antiphlogistic ˌæntɪflɒʊˈdʒɪstɪk
antiphlogistine ˌæntɪflɒʊˈdʒɪstiːn
 [-flɒˈdʒ-, -tɪn]
antiphon, -s ˈæntɪfən [-fɒn], -z
antiphon|al/s, -er/s ænˈtɪfən|l/z, -ə*/z
antiphonic, -al, -ally ˌæntɪˈfɒnɪk, -l, -əlɪ
antiphon|y, -ies ænˈtɪfən|ɪ, -ɪz
antipodal ænˈtɪpədl
antipodean æn,tɪpəˈdiːən [ˌæntɪp-,
 -pəʊˈd-, -ˈdɪən]
antipodes ænˈtɪpədiːz
antipope, -s ˈæntɪpəʊp, -s
antipyretic, -s ˌæntɪpaɪˈretɪk [-paɪəˈr-,
 -pɪˈr-], -s
antipyrin ˌæntɪˈpaɪərɪn
antiquarian, -s -ism ˌæntɪˈkweərɪən, -z,
 -ɪzəm
antiquar|y, -ies ˈæntɪkwər|ɪ, -ɪz
antiquate (adj.) ˈæntɪkwɪt [-kweɪt]
antiquated ˈæntɪkweɪtɪd
antique (s. adj.), -s, -ly, -ness ænˈtiːk,
 -s, -lɪ, -nɪs [-nəs]
antiquit|y, -ies ænˈtɪkwət|ɪ [-kwɪt|ɪ], -ɪz
antirrhinum, -s ˌæntɪˈraɪnəm [-təˈr-], -z
antiscorbutic, -s ˌæntɪskɔːˈbjuːtɪk, -s
anti-semitic ˌæntɪsɪˈmɪtɪk [-sə-]
anti-semitism ˌæntɪˈsemɪtɪzəm [-mət-]
antisep|sis, -tic/s, -tically ˌæntɪˈsep|-
 sɪs, -tɪk/s, -tɪkəlɪ
antisocial ˌæntɪˈsəʊʃl
antisocialist, -s ˌæntɪˈsəʊʃəlɪst [-ʃɪ-], -s
antistrophe, -s ænˈtɪstrəfɪ, -z
antistrophic ˌæntɪˈstrɒfɪk
anti-tank ˌæntɪˈtæŋk
antithes|is, -es ænˈtɪθɪs|ɪs [-θəs-], -iːz
antithetic, -ally ˌæntɪˈθetɪk, -əlɪ
antitoxi|c, -n/s ˌæntɪˈtɒksɪ|k, -n/z
anti-trade, -s ˌæntɪˈtreɪd, -z
antiviral ˌæntɪˈvaɪərəl
anti-vivisection, -ist/s ˈæntɪ,vɪvɪˈsekʃn,
 -ɪst/s
antler, -s, -ed ˈæntlə*, -z, -d
ant-lion, -s ˈænt,laɪən, -z
Antoinette ˌæntwɑːˈnet [ˌ,ɑːn-, -twəˈn-]
 (ãtwanɛt)
Antonia ænˈtəʊnjə [-nɪə]
Antonine, -s ˈæntənaɪn, -z
Antoninus ˌæntəʊˈnaɪnəs
Antonio ænˈtəʊnɪəʊ [-njəʊ]
Antonius ænˈtəʊnjəs [-nɪəs]
Antony ˈæntənɪ
antonym, -s ˈæntəʊnɪm, -z
antonymy ænˈtɒnɪmɪ [-nəmɪ]
Antrim ˈæntrɪm
Antrobus ˈæntrəʊbəs
antr|um, -ums, -a ˈæntr|əm, -əmz, -ə
antrycide ˈæntrɪsaɪd

Antwerp ˈæntwɜːp
anus, -es ˈeɪnəs, -ɪz
anvil, -s ˈænvɪl, -z
Anwick ˈænɪk
anxiet|y, -ies æŋˈzaɪət|ɪ [-ŋgˈz-], -ɪz
anxious, -ly, -ness ˈæŋkʃəs, -lɪ, -nɪs
 [-nəs]
any ˈenɪ (normal form), ənɪ (occasional
 weak form), ŋɪ (occasional weak form
 after t or d)
anybody ˈenɪ,bɒdɪ [-bədɪ]
anyhow ˈenɪhaʊ
anyone ˈenɪwʌn [-wən]
anything ˈenɪθɪŋ
anyway ˈenɪweɪ
anywhere ˈenɪweə* [-hweə*]
anywise ˈenɪwaɪz
Anzac, -s ˈænzæk, -s
Aonia, -n/s eɪˈəʊnjə [-nɪə-], -n/z
aorist, -s ˈeərɪst [ˈeɪər-], -s
aort|a/s, -al, -ic eɪˈɔːt|ə/z, -l, -ɪk
Aosta ɑːˈɒstə
apace əˈpeɪs
Apache (American Indian), -s əˈpætʃɪ,
 -z
apache (ruffian), -s əˈpæʃ [æˈp-, -ˈpɑːʃ]
 (apaʃ), -ɪz
apart, -ness əˈpɑːt, -nɪs [-nəs]
apartheid əˈpɑːtheɪt [-eɪd, -aɪt, -teɪt,
 -taɪt, -taɪd] (Afrikaans aˈpartheɪt)
apartment, -s əˈpɑːtmənt, -s
apathetic, -al, -ally ˌæpəˈθetɪk, -l, -əlɪ
apath|y, -ies ˈæpəθ|ɪ, -ɪz
ap|e (s. v.), -es, -ing, -ed eɪp, -s, -ɪŋ, -t
apehood ˈeɪphʊd
Apelles əˈpeliːz
Apennines ˈæpɪnaɪnz [-pen-]
aperçu, -s ˌæpəːˈsjuː [-ˈsuː] (apɛrsy), -z
aperient, -s əˈpɪərɪənt, -s
aperitive, -s əˈperətɪv [-rɪt-], -z
aperture, -s ˈæpə,tjʊə* [-,tʃʊə*, -tʃə*],
 -z
aper|y, -ies ˈeɪpər|ɪ, -ɪz
apex, -es, -apices ˈeɪpeks, -ɪz, ˈeɪpɪsiːz
 [ˈæpɪsɪz]
aphasia əˈfeɪzjə [æˈf-, eɪˈf-, -zɪə, -ʒjə,
 -ʒɪə, -ʒə]
aphasic əˈfeɪzɪk
apheli|on, -a æˈfiːljlən [-lɪ|ən], -ə
apheresis æˈfɪərɪsɪs [əˈf-, -rəs-]
aphesis ˈæfɪsɪs [-fəs-]
aphid ˈeɪfɪd
aphidian, -s eɪˈfɪdɪən [æˈf-, -djən], -z
aph|is, -ides, -ises ˈeɪf|ɪs [ˈæf-], -ɪdiːz,
 -ɪsɪz
aphonia eɪˈfəʊnjə [æˈf-, əˈf-, -nɪə]
aphonic eɪˈfɒnɪk [æˈf-, əˈf-]
aphony ˈæfənɪ

aphori|sm/s, -st/s 'æfərɪ|zəm/z [-fɒr-], -st/s

aphoristic, -ally ˌæfəˈrɪstɪk [-fɒˈr-], -əlɪ

aphoriz|e [-is|e], -es, -ing, -ed, -er/s 'æfəraɪz [-fɒr-], -ɪz, -ɪŋ, -d, -ə*/z

aphrodis|iac/s, -ian ˌæfrəʊˈdɪz|ɪæk/s, -ɪən [-jən]

Aphrodite ˌæfrəʊˈdaɪtɪ

aphtha 'æfθə

apian 'eɪpjən [-pɪən]

apiarian, -s ˌeɪpɪˈeərɪən, -z

apiar|y, -ies, -ist/s 'eɪpjər|ɪ [-pɪər-], -ɪz, -ɪst/s

apic|al, -ally 'æpɪk|l ['eɪp-], -əlɪ

apices (plur. of apex) 'eɪpɪsiːz ['æp-]

apiculture 'eɪpɪkʌltʃə*

apiece əˈpiːs

apis (bee) 'eɪpɪs

Apis 'ɑːpɪs ['eɪpɪs]

apish, -ly, -ness 'eɪpɪʃ, -lɪ, -nɪs [-nəs]

aplomb əˈplɒm ['æplɔ̃ːŋ, -plɔ̃ːm] (aplɔ̃)

apocalyp|se/s (A.), -st/s, -t/s əˈpɒkə-lɪp|s/ɪz, -st/s, -t/s

apocalyptic|c, -st/s əˌpɒkəˈlɪptɪ|k, -st/s

apocopate (adj.) əˈpɒkəʊpɪt [-pət, -peɪt]

apocopat|e (v.), -es, -ing, -ed əˈpɒkəʊ-peɪt, -s, -ɪŋ, -ɪd

apocopation, -s əˌpɒkəʊˈpeɪʃn, -z

apocope, -s əˈpɒkəʊpɪ, -z

apocryph|a/s, -al əˈpɒkrɪf|ə/z, -l

apodeictic, -al, -ally ˌæpəʊˈdaɪktɪk, -l, -əlɪ

apodos|is, -es əˈpɒdəʊs|ɪs, -iːz

apogee, -s 'æpəʊdʒiː, -z

Apollinaris əˌpɒlɪˈneərɪs [-ˈnɑːr-]

Apollo əˈpɒləʊ

Apollodorus əˌpɒləˈdɔːrəs

Apolloni|a, -an, -us ˌæpəˈləʊnj|ə [-pɒˈl-, -nɪ|ə], -ən, -əs

Apollos əˈpɒlɒs

Apollyon əˈpɒljən [-lɪən]

apologetic, -al, -ally, -s əˌpɒləˈdʒetɪk, -l, -əlɪ, -s

apologist, -s əˈpɒlədʒɪst, -s

apologiz|e [-is|e], -es, -ing, -ed, -er/s əˈpɒlədʒaɪz, -ɪz, -ɪŋ, -d, -ə*/z

apologue, -s 'æpəlɒg [-pəʊl-, -ləʊg], -z

apolog|y, -ies əˈpɒlədʒ|ɪ, -ɪz

apophthegm, -s 'æpəʊθem, -z

apoplectic, -al, -ally ˌæpəʊˈplektɪk, -l, -əlɪ

apoplex|y, -ies 'æpəʊpleks|ɪ, -ɪz

aposiopes|is, -es ˌæpəʊsaɪəʊˈpiːs|ɪs, əˌpɒsɪəʊˈpiːsɪs, -iːz

apostas|y, -ies əˈpɒstəs|ɪ, -ɪz

apostate, -s əˈpɒsteɪt [-tɪt, -tət], -s

apostatic, -al ˌæpəʊˈstætɪk, -l

apostatiz|e [-is|e], -es, -ing, -ed əˈpɒstətaɪz, -ɪz, -ɪŋ, -d

a posteriori 'eɪpɒsˌterɪˈɔːraɪ [-ˌtɪər-, 'ɑːpɒsˌterɪˈɔːriː]

apostigmat, -s 'æpəʊstɪgmæt, -s

apostil, -s əˈpɒstɪl, -z

apostle, -s, -ship əˈpɒsl, -z, -ʃɪp

apostolate, -s əˈpɒstəʊlət [-lɪt, -leɪt], -s

apostolic, -al, -ally ˌæpəˈstɒlɪk, -l, -əlɪ

apostolicism ˌæpəˈstɒlɪsɪzəm

apostrophe, -s əˈpɒstrəfɪ, -z

apostrophiz|e [-is|e], -es, -ing, -ed əˈpɒstrəfaɪz, -ɪz, -ɪŋ, -d

apothecar|y, -ies əˈpɒθəkər|ɪ [-θɪk-], -ɪz

apotheos|is, -es əˌpɒθɪˈəʊs|ɪs [ˌæpəʊθ-], -iːz

apotheosiz|e [-is|e], -es, -ing, -ed əˈpɒθɪəʊsaɪz [-θɪəs-, ˌæpəʊˈθɪəʊsaɪz], -ɪz, -ɪŋ, -d

appal, -s, -ling/ly, -led əˈpɔːl, -z, -ɪŋ/lɪ, -d

Appalachian ˌæpəˈleɪtʃjən [-tʃɪən]

appanage, -s 'æpənɪdʒ, -ɪz

apparatus, -es ˌæpəˈreɪtəs, -ɪz

apparatus (alternative plur. of apparatus) ˌæpəˈreɪtəs

appar|el (s. v.), -els, -elling, -elled əˈpær|əl, -əlz, -əlɪŋ [-lɪŋ], -əld

apparent, -ly, -ness əˈpærənt [-ˈpeər-, -lɪ, -nɪs [-nəs]

apparition, -s ˌæpəˈrɪʃn, -z

apparitor, -s əˈpærɪtɔː* [-tə*], -z

appassionata (Beethoven sonata) əˌpæʃəˈnɑːtə [-ʃjə-, -sjə-, -sɪə-]

appeal (s. v.), -s, -ing/ly, -ingness, -ed, -er/s əˈpiːl, -z, -ɪŋ/lɪ, -ɪŋnɪs [-nəs], -d, -ə*/z

appear, -s, -ing, -ed, -er/s; -ance/s əˈpɪə*, -z, -rɪŋ, -d, -rə*/z; -rəns/ɪz

†appeas|e, -es, -ing/ly, -ed; -able əˈpiːz, -ɪz, -ɪŋ/lɪ, -d; -əbl

appellant, -s əˈpelənt, -s

appellate əˈpelət [æˈp-, -leɪt, -lɪt]

appellation, -s ˌæpəˈleɪʃn [-pɪˈl-, -peˈl-], -z

appellative, -ly, -ness əˈpelətɪv [æˈp-], -lɪ, -nɪs [-nəs]

append, -s, -ing, -ed; -age/s; -ant əˈpend, -z, -ɪŋ, -ɪd; -ɪdʒ/ɪz; -ənt

appendectomy ˌæpenˈdektəmɪ

appendicitis əˌpendɪˈsaɪtɪs [-də-]

append|ix, -ixes, -ices əˈpend|ɪks, -ɪksɪz, -ɪsiːz

appercep|tion, -tive ˌæpəˈsep|ʃn, -tɪv

appertain, -s, -ing, -ed ˌæpəˈteɪn, -z, -ɪŋ, -d

appertinent əˈpɜːtɪnənt [æˈp-]

appeten|ce, -cy, -t 'æpɪtən|s, -sɪ, -t

23

appetite, -s 'æpɪtaɪt, -s
appetiz|e, -es, -ing/ly, -ed, -er/s
'æpɪtaɪz, -ɪz, -ɪŋ/lɪ, -d, -ə*/z
Appi|an, -us 'æpɪ|ən [-pj|-], -əs
applaud, -s, -ing/ly, -ed, -er/s ə'plɔːd,
-z, -ɪŋ/lɪ, -ɪd, -ə*/z
applause ə'plɔːz
apple, -s; -blight 'æpl, -z; -blaɪt
apple-blossom 'æpl,blɒsəm
Appleby 'æplbɪ
apple-cart 'æplkɑːt
Appledore 'æpldɔː* [-dɔə*]
Appleford 'æplfəd
Applegate 'æplgeɪt [-gɪt]
apple|-pie/s, -sauce ˌæpl|'paɪ/z, -'sɔːs
Appleton 'æpltən
apple-tree, -s 'æpltriː, -z
appliable, -ness ə'plaɪəbl, -nɪs [-nəs]
appliance, -s ə'plaɪəns, -ɪz
applicability ˌæplɪkə'bɪlətɪ [ə,plɪk-, -lɪt-]
applicab|le, -ly, -leness 'æplɪkəb|l
[ə'plɪk-], -lɪ, -lnɪs [-nəs]
applicant, -s 'æplɪkənt, -s
applicate 'æplɪkət [-kɪt, -keɪt]
application, -s ˌæplɪ'keɪʃn, -z
appliqué, -s æ'pliːkeɪ [ə'p-] (aplike),
-z
appl|y, -ies, -ying, -ied ə'pl|aɪ, -aɪz,
-aɪŋ, -aɪd
appoggiatura, -s ə,pɒdʒə'tʊərə [-dʒə-,
-dʒɪə-, -'tjʊər-, -'tjɔər-, -'tjɔːr-], -z
appoint, -s, -ing, -ed, -ment/s ə'pɔɪnt,
-s, -ɪŋ, -ɪd, -mənt/s
appointee, -s əpɔɪn'tiː: [ˌæpɔɪn't-], -z
apport, -s, -ing, -ed ə'pɔːt, -s, -ɪŋ, -ɪd
apporti|on, -ons, -oning, -oned, -on-
ment/s ə'pɔː|ʃn, -ənz, -ʠɪŋ [-nɪŋ,
-ənɪŋ], -nd, -nmənt/s
appos|e, -es, -ing, -ed æ'pəʊz, -ɪz, -ɪŋ, -d
apposite, -ly, -ness 'æpəʊzɪt, -lɪ, -nɪs
[-nəs]
apposition, -s ˌæpəʊ'zɪʃn [-pʊ'z-], -z
appositional ˌæpəʊ'zɪʃənl [-pʊ'z-, -ʃnəl,
-ʃn̩l, -ʃnl, -ʃənəl]
apprais|e, -es, -ing, -ed, -er/s, -ement/s;
-able, -al/s ə'preɪz, -ɪz, -ɪŋ, -d, -ə*/z,
-mənt/s; -əbl, -l/z
appreciab|le, -ly, ə'priːʃəb|l [-ʃjəb-,
-ʃɪəb-], -lɪ
appreciat|e, -es, -ing/ly, -ed, -or/s
ə'priːʃɪeɪt [-ʃjeɪt, -iːsɪeɪt, -iːʃjeɪt], -s,
-ɪŋ/lɪ, -ɪd, -ə*/z
appreciation, -s ə,priːʃɪ'eɪʃn [-iːsɪ-], -z
appreciative, -ly, -ness ə'priːʃjətɪv
[-ʃɪət-, -ʃɪeɪt-], -lɪ, -nɪs [-nəs]
appreciatory ə'priːʃjətərɪ [-ʃɪət-, -ʃɪeɪt-]
apprehend, -s, -ing, -ed ˌæprɪ'hend, -z,
-ɪŋ, -ɪd

apprehensibility 'æprɪˌhensɪ'bɪlətɪ
[-sə'b-, -lɪt-]
apprehensible ˌæprɪ'hensəbl [-sɪb-]
apprehension, -s ˌæprɪ'henʃn, -z
apprehensive, -ly, -ness ˌæprɪ'hensɪv,
-lɪ, -nɪs [-nəs]
apprentic|e (s. v.), -es, -ing, -ed
ə'prentɪs, -ɪz, -ɪŋ, -t
apprenticeship, -s ə'prentɪʃɪp [-tɪsʃɪp,
-tɪʃʃɪp], -s
appris|e, -es, -ing, -ed ə'praɪz, -ɪz, -ɪŋ,
-d
appriz|e, -es, -ing, -ed, -er/s ə'praɪz,
-ɪz, -ɪŋ, -d, -ə*/z
appro 'æprəʊ
approach (s. v.), -es, -ing, -ed; -able
ə'prəʊtʃ, -ɪz, -ɪŋ, -t; -əbl
approachability ə,prəʊtʃə'bɪlətɪ [-lɪt-]
approbat|e, -es, -ing, -ed; -ive 'æprəʊ-
beɪt [-prʊb-], -s, -ɪŋ, -ɪd; -ɪv
approbation, -s ˌæprəʊ'beɪʃn [-prʊ'b-],
-z
approbatory ˌæprəʊ'beɪtərɪ
appro|priate (adj.), -priately, -priateness
ə'prəʊ|prɪət [-prɪt], -prɪətlɪ [-prɪtlɪ],
-prɪətnɪs [-prɪt-, -nəs]
appropriat|e (v.), -es, -ing, -ed, -or/s
ə'prəʊprɪeɪt, -s, -ɪŋ, -ɪd, -ə*/z
appropriation, -s ə,prəʊprɪ'eɪʃn, -z
approv|e, -es, -ing/ly, -ed, -er/s; -able,
-al/s ə'pruːv, -z, -ɪŋ/lɪ, -d, -ə*/z;
-əbl, -l/z
approximant, -s ə'prɒksɪmənt, -s
approximate (adj.), -ly ə'prɒksɪmət
[-mɪt], -lɪ [-mɪtlɪ]
approximat|e (v.), -es, -ing, -ed ə'prɒks-
ɪmeɪt, -s, -ɪŋ, -ɪd
approximation, -s ə,prɒksɪ'meɪʃn, -z
approximative ə'prɒksɪmətɪv
appui æ'pwiː [ə'p-] (apчi)
Appuldurcombe ˌæpldə'kuːm
appulse, -s æ'pʌls [ə'pʌls, 'æpʌls], -ɪz
appurtenan|ce, -ces, -t ə'pɜːtɪnən|s
[-tən-, -tnə-], -sɪz, -t
apricot, -s 'eɪprɪkɒt, -s
April, -s 'eɪprəl [-rɪl], -z
a priori ˌeɪpraɪ'ɔːraɪ [ˌɑːpriː'ɔːriː:, -rɪ'ɔː-]
apriority ˌeɪpraɪ'ɒrətɪ [-ɪtɪ]
apron, -s, -ed 'eɪprən, -z, -d
apron-string, -s 'eɪprənstrɪŋ, -z
apropos 'æprəpəʊ [ˌ--'-]
apse, -s æps, -ɪz
apsidal 'æpsɪdl
apsis, apsides 'æpsɪs, æp'saɪdiːz ['æp-
sɪdiːz]
Apsley 'æpslɪ
apt, -er, -est, -ly, -ness æpt, -ə*, -ɪst,
-lɪ, -nɪs [-nəs]

apter|al, -ous 'æptər|əl, -əs
apteryges æp'terɪdʒi:z
apteryx, -es 'æptərɪks, -ɪz
aptitude, -s 'æptɪtju:d, -z
Apulia, -n/s ə'pju:ljə [-lɪə], -n/z
apyretic ˌæpaɪ'retɪk [-paɪə'r-, -pɪ'r-]
aqua-fortis ˌækwə'fɔ:tɪs
aqua-lung, -s 'ækwəlʌŋ, -z
aquamarine, -s ˌækwəmə'ri:n, -z
aqua-plane, -s 'ækwəpleɪn, -z
aqua-regia ˌækwə'ri:dʒjə [-dʒɪə]
aquarell|e, -es; -ist/s ˌækwə'rel, -z; -ɪst/s
aquarist, -s 'ækwərɪst, -s
aquari|um, -ums, -a ə'kweərɪ|əm, -əmz, -ə
Aquari|us, -an/s ə'kweərɪ|əs, -ən/z
aquatic (s. adj.), -s ə'kwætɪk [-'kwɒt-], -s
aquatint, -s 'ækwətɪnt, -s
aquavit 'ækwəvɪt [-vi:t]
aqua-vitae ˌækwə'vaɪtɪ: [-tɪ, -'vi:taɪ]
aqueduct, -s 'ækwɪdʌkt [-kwəd-], -s
aqueous, -ly 'eɪkwɪəs ['æk-], -lɪ
Aquila 'ækwɪlə [as constellation also ə'kwɪlə]
aquilegia, -s ˌækwɪ'li:dʒjə [-dʒɪə], -z
aquiline 'ækwɪlaɪn
Aquinas ə'kwaɪnæs [æ'k-, -nəs]
Aquitaine ˌækwɪ'teɪn
Aquitania ˌækwɪ'teɪnjə [-nɪə]
Arab, -s, -ist/s 'ærəb, -z, -ɪst/s
Arabella ˌærə'belə
arabesque, -s, -d ˌærə'besk, -s, -t
Arabia, -n/s ə'reɪbjə [-bɪə], -n/z
Arabic (of Arabia) 'ærəbɪk, (name of ship) 'ærəbɪk [ə'ræb-]
arabis 'ærəbɪs
arable 'ærəbl ['eər-]
Araby 'ærəbɪ
Arachne ə'rækni
arachnid, -a, -s ə'ræknɪd, -ə, -z
arachnologist, -s ˌæræk'nɒlədʒɪst [-rək-], -s
Aragon 'ærəgən
aragonite ə'rægənaɪt
Aral 'ɑ:rəl ['eər-]
Aram (biblical name) 'eəræm [-rəm], (surname) 'eərəm
Aramai|c, -sm ˌærə'meɪɪ|k, -zəm
Aramean, -s ˌærə'mi:ən [-'mɪən], -z
Aramite, -s 'ærəmaɪt ['eəræm-, -rəm-], -s
Aran 'ærən
Ararat 'ærəræt
Araucania ˌærɔ:'keɪnjə [-nɪə]
araucaria, -s ˌærɔ:'keərɪə, -z
Arber 'ɑ:bə*

Arberry 'ɑ:bərɪ
arbiter, -s 'ɑ:bɪtə*, -z
arbitrage (arbitration) 'ɑ:bɪtrɪdʒ
arbitrage (of stocks, etc.) ˌɑ:bɪ'trɑ:ʒ ['ɑ:bɪtrɪdʒ]
arbitrament, -s ɑ:'bɪtrəmənt [-trɪm-], -s
arbitrar|y, -ily, -iness 'ɑ:bɪtrər|ɪ, -əlɪ [-ɪlɪ], -ɪnɪs [-ɪnəs]
arbitrat|e, -es, -ing, -ed, -or/s 'ɑ:bɪtreɪt, -s, -ɪŋ, -ɪd, -ə*/z
arbitration, -s ˌɑ:bɪ'treɪʃn, -z
arbitress, -es 'ɑ:bɪtrɪs [-tres], -ɪz
Arblay 'ɑ:bleɪ
arbor (tree) 'ɑ:bɔ:* [-bə*]
arbor (axle, arbour), -s 'ɑ:bə*, -z
Arbor 'ɑ:bə*
arboraceous ˌɑ:bə'reɪʃəs [-bɔ:'r-]
arbore|al, -ous ɑ:'bɔ:rɪ|əl, -əs
arborescen|ce, -t ˌɑ:bə'resn|s [-bɔ:'r-], -t
arboretum, -s ˌɑ:bə'ri:təm [-bɔ:'r-], -z
arboriculture 'ɑ:bərɪkʌltʃə* [-bɔ:r-]
arbor-vitae, -s ˌɑ:bə'vaɪtɪ [-ti:, -'vi:taɪ], -z
arbour, -s 'ɑ:bə*, -z
Arbroath ɑ:'brəʊθ
Arbuthnot(t) ɑ:'bʌθnət [ə'b-]
arbutus, -es ɑ:'bju:təs, -ɪz
arc (A.), -s, -(k)ing, -(k)ed ɑ:k, -s, -ɪŋ, -t
arcade, -s ɑ:'keɪd, -z
Arcadia, -n/s ɑ:'keɪdjə [-dɪə], -n/z
arcan|um, -a ɑ:'keɪn|əm, -ə
arch (s. v.), -es, -ing, -ed ɑ:tʃ, -ɪz, -ɪŋ, -t
arch (adj.), -est, -ly, -ness ɑ:tʃ, -ɪst, -lɪ, -nɪs [-nəs]
archaean ɑ:'ki:ən [-'kɪən]
archaeologic|al, -ally ˌɑ:kɪə'lɒdʒɪk|l [-kjə-], -əlɪ
archaeolog|ist/s, -y ˌɑ:kɪ'ɒlədʒ|ɪst/s, -ɪ
archaeopteryx, -es ˌɑ:kɪ'ɒptərɪks, -ɪz
archaic, -ally ɑ:'keɪɪk, -əlɪ
archaism, -s 'ɑ:keɪɪzəm, -z
archangel, -s 'ɑ:kˌeɪndʒəl [ˌɑ:k'eɪn-], -z
Archangel 'ɑ:kˌeɪndʒəl [ˌɑ:k'eɪn-]
archbishop, -s ˌɑ:tʃ'bɪʃəp [also '-ˌ-- according to sentence-stress], -s
archbishopric, -s ˌɑ:tʃ'bɪʃəprɪk, -s
Arch|bold, -dale 'ɑ:tʃ|bəʊld, -deɪl
archdeacon, -s ˌɑ:tʃ'di:kən [also '-ˌ-- according to sentence-stress], -s
archdeaconr|y, -ies ˌɑ:tʃ'di:kənr|ɪ, -ɪz
archdiocese, -s ˌɑ:tʃ'daɪəsɪs [-si:s], -ɪz
archducal ˌɑ:tʃ'dju:kl
archduchess, -es ˌɑ:tʃ'dʌtʃɪs, -ɪz
archduch|y, -ies ˌɑ:tʃ'dʌt|ʃɪ|ɪ, -ɪz
archduke, -s ˌɑ:tʃ'dju:k ['--], -s
archdukedom, -s ˌɑ:tʃ'dju:kdəm, -z
Archelaus ˌɑ:kɪ'leɪəs

25

arch-enem|y, -ies ˌɑːtʃˈenɪm|ɪ [-nəm-],
-ɪz
archer (A.), -s ˈɑːtʃə*, -z
archeress, -es ˈɑːtʃərɪs [-res], -ɪz
archery ˈɑːtʃərɪ
†archetype, -s ˈɑːkɪtaɪp, -s
arch-fiend (A.), -s ˌɑːtʃˈfiːnd, -z
arch-heretic, -s ˌɑːtʃˈherətɪk [-rɪt-], -s
Archibald ˈɑːtʃɪbɔːld [-bəld]
archidiacon|al, -ate ˌɑːkɪdaɪˈækən|l,
[-dɪˈæk-, -kn̩|l], -ət, [-eɪt]
Archie ˈɑːtʃɪ
archiepiscop|acy, -al, -ate ˌɑːkɪˈpɪs-
kəp|əsɪ [-kɪeˈp-], -l, -ɪt [-ət, -eɪt]
Archilochus ɑːˈkɪləkəs
Archimage ˈɑːkɪmeɪdʒ
archimandrite, -s ˌɑːkɪˈmændraɪt, -s
archimedean ˌɑːkɪˈmiːdjən [-dɪən,
ˌɑːkɪmiˈdiːən, -mɪ-, -ˈdɪən]
Archimedes ˌɑːkɪˈmiːdiːz
archipelago, -(e)s ˌɑːkɪˈpelɪgəʊ [-ləg-],
-z
archiphoneme, -s ˈɑːkɪˌfəʊniːm, -z
architect, -s ˈɑːkɪtekt, -s
architectonic, -s ˌɑːkɪtekˈtɒnɪk, -s
architec|tural, -turally ˌɑːkɪˈtek|tʃərəl
[-tʃʊrəl], -tʃərəlɪ [-tʃəʳlɪ, -tʃʊrəlɪ]
architecture ˈɑːkɪtektʃə*
architrave, -s, -d ˈɑːkɪtreɪv, -z, -d
archival ɑːˈkaɪvl
archive, -s ˈɑːkaɪv, -z
archivist, -s ˈɑːkɪvɪst, -s
archon, -s ˈɑːkən [-kɒn], -z
arch-prelate, -s ˌɑːtʃˈprelət [-lɪt], -s
arch-priest, -s ˌɑːtʃˈpriːst, -s
arch-traitor, -s ˌɑːtʃˈtreɪtə*, -z
archway (A.), -s ˈɑːtʃweɪ, -z
archwise ˈɑːtʃwaɪz
Archyll ˈɑːkɪl
Archytas ɑːˈkaɪtæs [-təs]
Arcite ˈɑːsaɪt
Arcot ɑːˈkɒt
arctic ˈɑːktɪk
Arcturus ɑːkˈtjʊərəs [-ˈtjɔər-, -ˈtjɔːr-]
arcuate ˈɑːkjʊɪt [-kjʊeɪt, -kjʊət]
arcuated ˈɑːkjʊeɪtɪd
Arcy ˈɑːsɪ
Ardagh ˈɑːdə [-dɑː]
Ardee ɑːˈdiː
Arden ˈɑːdn
arden|cy, -t/ly ˈɑːdn|sɪ, -t/lɪ
Ardennes ɑːˈden [-ˈdenz] (ardɛn)
Ardilaun ˌɑːdɪˈlɔːn
Arding ˈɑːdɪŋ
Ardingly (in West Sussex) ˈɑːdɪŋlaɪ
[ˌ--ˈ-]
Ardlamont ɑːdˈlæmənt
Ard|leigh, -ley ˈɑːd|lɪ, -lɪ

26

Ardoch ˈɑːdɒk [-ɒx]
ardour ˈɑːdə*
Ardrishaig ɑːˈdrɪʃɪg
Ardrossan ɑːˈdrɒsən
Arduin ˈɑːdwɪn
arduous, -ly, -ness ˈɑːdjʊəs [-djwəs],
-lɪ, -nɪs [-nəs]
Ardwick ˈɑːdwɪk
are (surface measure), -s ɑː*, -z
are (from be) ɑː* (strong form), ə*
(weak form), r (occasional weak form
before vowels)
area, -s ˈeərɪə, -z
areca, -s ˈærɪkə [æˈriːkə, əˈriːkə], -z
arena, -s əˈriːnə, -z
Arendt ˈærənt [ˈɑːr-]
aren't ɑːnt
areol|a, -as, -ae æˈrɪəʊl|ə [əˈr-], -əz, -iː
areomet|er/s, -ry ˌ æriˈɒmɪt|ə*/z [ˌeər-,
-mət|ə*/z], -rɪ
Areopagite, -s ˌæriˈɒpəgaɪt [-ədʒaɪt], -s
areopagitic, -a ˌæriɒpəˈdʒɪtɪk, -ə
Areopagus ˌæriˈɒpəgəs
Arequipa ˌæriˈkiːpə [-reˈk-] (areˈkipa)
Ares ˈeəriːz
arête, -s əˈret [æˈr-, -reɪt], (arɛːt), -s
Arete əˈriːti [æˈr-, -tɪ]
Arethusa ˌæriˈθjuːzə [-reˈθ-, -ˈθuːzə]
Argalus ˈɑːgələs
argand (A.), -s ˈɑːgænd [-gənd], -z
argent ˈɑːdʒənt
argentiferous ˌɑːdʒənˈtɪfərəs [-dʒenˈt-]
Argentina ˌɑːdʒənˈtiːnə [-dʒenˈt-]
argentine (A.) ˈɑːdʒəntaɪn
Argentinian ˌɑːdʒənˈtɪnɪən [-jən]
argil ˈɑːdʒɪl
argillaceous ˌɑːdʒɪˈleɪʃəs
Argive, -s ˈɑːgaɪv, -z
Argo ˈɑːgəʊ
argol ˈɑːgɒl
Argolis ˈɑːgəlɪs
argon ˈɑːgɒn [-gən]
Argonaut, -s ˈɑːgənɔːt, -s
Argonautic ˌɑːgəˈnɔːtɪk
Argos ˈɑːgɒs
argos|y, -ies ˈɑːgəs|ɪ, -ɪz
argot, -s ˈɑːgəʊ (argo), -z
arg|ue, -ues, -uing, -ued, -uer/s; -uable
ˈɑːg|juː, -juːz, -jʊɪŋ [-jwɪŋ], -juːd,
-jʊə*/z [-jwə*/z]; -jʊəbl [-jwəbl]
argument, -s ˈɑːgjʊmənt, -s
argumental ˌɑːgjʊˈmentl
argumentation, -s ˌɑːgjʊmenˈteɪʃn
[-mənˈt-], -z
argumentative, -ly, -ness ˌɑːgjʊˈmentə-
tɪv, -lɪ, -nɪs [-nəs]
argus (A.), -es ˈɑːgəs, -ɪz
Argyle ɑːˈgaɪl

Argyll ɑːˈgaɪl [*attributively also* 'ꟷ]
Argyllshire ɑːˈgaɪlʃə* [-ˌʃɪə*]
aria, -s ˈɑːrɪə, -z
Ariadne ˌærɪˈædnɪ
Arian, -s, -ism ˈeərɪən, -z, -ɪzəm
arianiz|e [-is|e]. -es, -ing, -ed ˈeərɪən-
aɪz, -ɪz, -ɪŋ, -d
arid, -ly, -ness ˈærɪd, -lɪ, -nɪs [-nəs]
aridity æˈrɪdətɪ [əˈr-, -dɪtɪ]
ariel (A.), -s ˈeərɪəl, -z
Aries (*constellation*) ˈeəriːz [ˈeərɪːz,
ˈæriːz]
arietta, -s ˌærɪˈetə, -z
aright əˈraɪt
Arimathaea ˌærɪməˈθɪə [-ˈθiːə]
Arion əˈraɪən [æˈr-]
arioso ˌɑːrɪˈəʊzəʊ [ˌær-]
Ariosto ˌærɪˈɒstəʊ
aris|e, -es, -ing, arose, arisen əˈraɪz,
-ɪz, -ɪŋ, əˈrəʊz, əˈrɪzn
Ariss ˈeərɪs
Aristaeus ˌærɪˈstiːəs [-ˈstɪəs]
Aristarch ˈærɪstɑːk
Aristarchus ˌærɪˈstɑːkəs
Aristides ˌærɪˈstaɪdiːz
aristocrac|y, -ies ˌærɪˈstɒkrəs|ɪ, -ɪz
aristocrat, -s ˈærɪstəkræt [æˈrɪs-, əˈrɪs-],
-s
aristocratic, -al, -ally ˌærɪstəˈkrætɪk,
-l, -əlɪ
aristocratism ˌærɪˈstɒkrətɪzəm
Aristogiton ˌærɪstəʊˈdʒaɪtn
Aristophanes ˌærɪˈstɒfəniːz [-fṇiːz]
aristophanic ˌærɪstəʊˈfænɪk [-tɒˈf-]
aristotelian, -s ˌærɪstɒˈtiːljən [-təʊˈt-,
-lɪən], -z
Aristotle ˈærɪstɒtl
Aristoxenus ˌærɪˈstɒksɪnəs [-sən-]
arithmetic (s.), -s əˈrɪθmətɪk [-mɪt-], -s
arithmetic (*adj.*), -al, -ally ˌærɪθ-
ˈmetɪk, -l, -əlɪ
arithmetician, -s əˌrɪθməˈtɪʃn [ˌærɪθ-,
-mɪˈt-], -z
Arius ˈeərɪəs [əˈraɪəs]
Arizona ˌærɪˈzəʊnə
ark (A.), -s ɑːk, -s
Arkansas (*state, city, river*) ˈɑːkənsɔː
[ɑːˈkænzəs]
Note.—*The most usual pronunciation
in U.S.A. appears to be* (ˈɑːkənsɔː),
but (ɑːˈkænzəs) *is also in use locally.*
Ark|low, -wright ˈɑːk|ləʊ, -raɪt
Arlberg ˈɑːlbɜːg
Arlington ˈɑːlɪŋtən
arm (s. v.), -s, -ing, -ed ɑːm, -z, -ɪŋ, -d
armada (A.), -s ɑːˈmɑːdə [*old-fashioned*
-ˈmeɪd-], -z
Armadale ˈɑːmədeɪl

armadillo, -s ˌɑːməˈdɪləʊ, -z
Armageddon ˌɑːməˈgedn
Armagh ɑːˈmɑː
armament, -s ˈɑːməmənt, -s
armature, -s ˈɑːməˌtjʊə* [-ˌtʃʊə*,
-tʃə*], -z
armchair, -s ˌɑːmˈtʃeə* [*also* 'ꟷ, *esp.
when followed by a stress*], -z
Armenia, -n/s ɑːˈmiːnjə [-nɪə], -n/z
Armes ɑːmz
Armfield ˈɑːmfiːld
armful, -s ˈɑːmfʊl, -z
armhole, -s ˈɑːmhəʊl, -z
armiger (A.), -s ˈɑːmɪdʒə*, -z
arm-in-arm ˌɑːmɪnˈɑːm
Arminian, -s ɑːˈmɪnɪən [-njən], -z
Armistead ˈɑːmɪsted [-tɪd]
armistice, -s ˈɑːmɪstɪs, -ɪz
Armitage ˈɑːmɪtɪdʒ
armless ˈɑːmlɪs [-ləs]
armlet, -s ˈɑːmlɪt [-lət], -s
armorial ɑːˈmɔːrɪəl
Armoric ɑːˈmɒrɪk
Armorica, -n/s ɑːˈmɒrɪkə, -n/z
armor|y, -ies = armour-
armour (A.), -s ˈɑːmə*, -z
armour-bearer, -s ˈɑːməˌbeərə*, -z
armourer, -s ˈɑːmərə*, -z
armour-plat|e, -es, -ing, -ed ˈɑːməpleɪt
[ˌɑːməˈp-], -s, -ɪŋ, -ɪd
armour|y, -ies ˈɑːmər|ɪ, -ɪz
armpit, -s ˈɑːmpɪt, -s
Armstead ˈɑːmsted [-stɪd]
Armstrong ˈɑːmstrɒŋ
arm|y, -ies ˈɑːm|ɪ, -ɪz
army-corps (*sing.*) ˈɑːmɪkɔː*, (*plur.*)
-kɔːz
Arnald ˈɑːnəld
Arne ɑːn
Arnhem ˈɑːnəm, ˈɑːnhem
arnica ˈɑːnɪkə
Arno ˈɑːnəʊ
Arnold, -son ˈɑːnəld, -sn
Arnot(t) ˈɑːnət [-nɒt]
Arolla əˈrɒlə
aroma, -s əˈrəʊmə, -z
aromatic (s. adj.), -s ˌærəʊˈmætɪk, -s
arose (*from* arise) əˈrəʊz
around əˈraʊnd
arous|e, -es, -ing, -ed; -al/s əˈraʊz, -ɪz,
-ɪŋ, -d; -l/z
arpeggio, -s ɑːˈpedʒɪəʊ, -z
arquebus, -es ˈɑːkwɪbəs, -ɪz
arquebusier, -s ˌɑːkwɪbəˈsɪə*, -z
arrack ˈærək
arrah ˈærə
arraign, -s, -ing, -ed, -er/s, -ment/s
əˈreɪn, -z, -ɪŋ, -d, -ə*/z, -mənt/s

27

Arran 'ærən
arrang|e, -es, -ing, -ed, -er/s, -ement/s
ə'reɪndʒ, -ɪz, -ɪŋ, -d, -ə*/z, -mənt/s
arrant, -ly 'ærənt, -lɪ
arras, -es 'ærəs, -ɪz
Arras (French town) 'ærəs (ɑrɑːs)
array (s. v.), -s, -ing, -ed ə'reɪ, -z, -ɪŋ, -d
arrear, -s, -age ə'rɪə*, -z, -rɪdʒ
arrest (s. v.), -s, -ing, -ed, -ment/s;
-able ə'rest, -s, -ɪŋ, -ɪd, -mənt/s; -əbl
arrestation, -s ˌære'steɪʃn, -z
Arrian 'ærɪən
arrière-ban, -s ˌærɪeə'bæn, -z
arrière pensée ˌærɪeə'pɑ̃ːnseɪ [-'pɒn-]
arris, -es 'ærɪs, -ɪz
arriv|e, -es, -ing, -ed; -al/s ə'raɪv, -z,
-ɪŋ, -d; -l/z
arriviste, -s ˌæriː'viːst, -s
arrogan|ce, -cy, -t/ly 'ærəgən|s [-rʊg-],
-sɪ, -t/lɪ
arrogat|e, -es, -ing, -ed 'ærəʊgeɪt
[-rʊg-], -s, -ɪŋ, -ɪd
arrogation, -s ˌærəʊ'geɪʃn [-rʊ'g-], -z
arrogative ə'rɒgətɪv
arrow, -s 'ærəʊ, -z
arrow-head, -s 'ærəʊhed, -z
Arrowpoint 'ærəʊpɔɪnt
arrowroot 'ærəʊruːt
Arrowsmith 'ærəʊsmɪθ
arrowy 'ærəʊɪ
Ars ɑːz
arse, -s ɑːs, -ɪz
arsenal, -s 'ɑːsənl [-sn̩l, -snl̩, -sɪnl], -z
arsenate, -s 'ɑːsənɪt [-sɪn-, -sn̩ɪt, -snɪt,
-ət, -eɪt], -s
arsenic (s.) 'ɑːsnɪk
arsenic (adj.), -al ɑː'senɪk, -l
arsenious ɑː'siːnjəs [-nɪəs]
arsenite 'ɑːsənaɪt [-sɪn-]
ars|is, -es 'ɑːs|ɪs, -iːz
arson 'ɑːsn
arsonist, -s 'ɑːsənɪst ['ɑːsnɪst], -s
art (s.), -s ɑːt, -s
art (from be) ɑːt (normal form), ət
(occasional weak form)
Artaxerxes ˌɑːtəg'zɜːksiːz ['ɑːt-,
-ək'sɜː-, -ə'zɜː-]
artefact, -s 'ɑːtɪfækt, -s
Artegal 'ɑːtɪgəl
Artemis 'ɑːtɪmɪs [-təm-]
Artemus 'ɑːtɪməs
arterial ɑː'tɪərɪəl
arterio-sclerosis ɑːˌtɪərɪəʊsklɪə'rəʊsɪs
[-sklɪə'r-, -sklɪ'r-, -sklə'r-]
arteritis ˌɑːtə'raɪtɪs
arter|y, -ies 'ɑːtər|ɪ, -ɪz
artesian ɑː'tiːzjən [-zɪən, -ʒən, -ʒɪən,
-ʒn]

art|ful, -fully, -fulness 'ɑːt|fʊl, -fəlɪ
[-fʊlɪ], -fʊlnɪs [-nəs]
arthritic (s. adj.), -s ɑː'θrɪtɪk, -s
arthritis ɑː'θraɪtɪs
Arthur 'ɑːθə*
Arthurian ɑː'θjʊərɪən [-jɔər-, -jɔːr-]
artichoke, -s 'ɑːtɪtʃəʊk, -s
artic|le (s. v.), -les, -ling, -led 'ɑːtɪk|l,
-lz, -lɪŋ, -ld
articular ɑː'tɪkjʊlə*
articulate (adj.), -ly, -ness ɑː'tɪkjʊlət
[-kjəl-, -lɪt], -lɪ, -nɪs [-nəs]
articulat|e (v.), -es, -ing, -ed, -or/s
ɑː'tɪkjʊleɪt [-kjəl-], -s, -ɪŋ, -ɪd, -ə*/z
articulation, -s ɑːˌtɪkjʊ'leɪʃn [-kjəl-],
-z
articulatory ɑː'tɪkjʊlətərɪ [-kjəl-, -leɪt-,
ɑːˌtɪkjʊ'leɪtərɪ]
artifact, -s 'ɑːtɪfækt, -s
artifice, -s 'ɑːtɪfɪs, -ɪz
artificer, -s ɑː'tɪfɪsə* ['----], -z
artifici|al, -ally, -alness ˌɑːtɪ'fɪʃ|l, -əlɪ
[-lɪ], -lnɪs [-nəs]
artificialit|y, -ies ˌɑːtɪfɪʃɪ'ælət|ɪ [-ɪt|ɪ],
-ɪz
artificializ|e [-is|e], -es, -ing, -ed
ˌɑːtɪ'fɪʃəlaɪz [-ʃlaɪz], -ɪz, -ɪŋ, -d
artiller|y, -ies, -ist/s ɑː'tɪlər|ɪ, -ɪz, -ɪst/s
artil|ery-|man, -men ɑː'tɪlərɪ|mən
[-mæn], -mən [-men]
artisan, -s ˌɑːtɪ'zæn ['---], -z
artist, -s 'ɑːtɪst, -s
artiste, -s ɑː'tiːst (artist), -s
artistic, -al, -ally ɑː'tɪstɪk, -l, -əlɪ
artistry 'ɑːtɪstrɪ
artless, -ly, -ness 'ɑːtlɪs [-ləs], -lɪ, -nɪs
[-nəs]
art-school, -s 'ɑːtskuːl, -z
arts|man, -men 'ɑːts|mæn, -men
arty 'ɑːtɪ
arum, -s 'eərəm, -z
Arun 'ærən
Arundel 'ærəndl
Arundell 'ærəndel [-dl]
Aryan, -s, -ism 'eərɪən ['ɑːr-], -z, -ɪzəm
arytenoid (s. adj.), -s ˌærɪ'tiːnɔɪd
[-rə't-], -z
as (s.), (coin), -es æs, -ɪz
as (conj.), æz (strong form), əz, z (weak
forms)
Asa (biblical name) 'eɪsə ['ɑːsə], (as
modern Christian name) 'eɪzə
asafoetida ˌæsə'fetɪdə [-'fiːt-]
Asaph 'æsəf
asbest|ic, -os, -ous æs'best|ɪk [əs-, æz-,
əz-], -ɒs [-əs], -əs
Ascalon 'æskəlɒn [-lən]
Ascanius æ'skeɪnjəs [-nɪəs]

28

ascend, -s, -ing, -ed, -er/s ə'send [æ's-], -z, -ɪŋ, -ɪd, -ə*/z
ascendan|ce, -cy, -t ə'sendən|s [æ's-], -sɪ, -t
ascen:den|ce, -cy, -t ə'sendən|s [æ's-], -sɪ, -t
ascension (A.), -s ə'senʃn, -z
ascensional ə'senʃənl [-ʃnəl, -ʃn̩l, -ʃn̩l, -ʃənəl]
Ascension-day, -s ə'senʃndeɪ, -z
ascent, -s ə'sent [æ's-], -s
ascertain, -s, -ing, -ed, -ment; -able ˌæsə'teɪn, -z, -ɪŋ, -d, -mənt; -əbl
ascetic (s. adj.), -al, -ally, -s ə'setɪk [æ's-], -l, -əlɪ, -s
asceticism ə'setɪsɪzəm [æ's-]
Ascham 'æskəm
ascian, -s 'æʃɪən [-ʃjən], -z
asclepiad, -s æ'skliːpɪæd [-pjæd, -pɪəd, -pjəd], -z
ascorbic ə'skɔːbɪk [æ's-]
Ascot, -s 'æskət, -s
ascrib|e, -es, -ing, -ed; -able ə'skraɪb, -z, -ɪŋ, -d; -əbl
ascription ə'skrɪpʃn [æs-]
asdic, -s 'æzdɪk, -s
asepsis ˌeɪ'sepsɪs [æ's-, ə's-]
aseptic (s. adj.), -s ˌeɪ'septɪk [æ's-, ə's-], -s
asexual ˌeɪ'sekʃʊəl [æ's-, ə's-, -ksjʊəl, -ksjwəl, -ksjʊl, -kʃwəl, -kʃʊl]
Asgard 'æsgɑːd
Asgill 'æsgɪl
ash (A.), -es æʃ, -ɪz
Asham 'æʃəm
asham|ed, -edly, -edness ə'ʃeɪm|d, -ɪdlɪ, -ɪdnɪs [-nəs]
Ashanti, -s ə'ʃæntɪ, -z
Ashbee 'æʃbɪ
Ashbourne 'æʃbɔːn [-bɔən, -bʊən, -bɜːn]
Ashburne 'æʃbɜːn
Ashbur|nham, ton 'æʃbɜː|nəm, -tn
Ash|bury, -by 'æʃ|bərɪ, -bɪ
Ashby - de - la - Zouch ˌæʃbɪdələ:'zuːʃ [-delə-]
Ashcombe 'æʃkəm
Ashdod 'æʃdɒd
Ashdown 'æʃdaʊn
Ashe æʃ
ashen 'æʃn
Asher 'æʃə*
asher|y, -ies 'æʃər|ɪ, ɪz
Ash|field, -ford 'æʃ|fiːld, -fəd
ash-heap, -s 'æʃhiːp, -s
Ashkelon 'æʃkɪlən [-kəl-, -lɒn]
Ashland 'æʃlənd
ashlar 'æʃlə*

Ash|ley, -mole 'æʃ|lɪ, -məʊl
Ashmolean æʃ'məʊljən [-lɪən]
Ashmore 'æʃmɔː* [-mɔə*]
Ashopton 'æʃəptən
ashore ə'ʃɔː* [-'ʃɔə*]
Ashover 'æʃəʊvə*
ash-pan, -s 'æʃpæn, -z
Ashtaroth 'æʃtərɒθ
Ashton 'æʃtən
Ashtoreth 'æʃtəreθ [-tɒr-]
ash-tray, -s 'æʃtreɪ, -z
Ash-Wednesday, -s ˌæʃ'wenzdɪ [-'wednz-, -deɪ], -z
Ash|well, -worth 'æʃ|wəl [-wel], -wɜːθ
ash|y, -ier, -iest, -iness 'æʃ|ɪ, -ɪə*, -ɪɪst, -ɪnɪs [-ɪnəs]
Asia 'eɪʃə ['eɪʒə]
Asian, -s 'eɪʃn ['eɪʃjən, 'eɪʃɪən, 'eɪsɪən, 'eɪsjən, 'eɪʒn, rarely 'eɪzɪən, 'eɪzjən], -z
Asiatic, -s ˌeɪʃɪ'ætɪk [ˌeɪsɪ-, ˌeɪʒɪ-], -s
aside (s. adv.), -s ə'saɪd, -z
asinine 'æsɪnaɪn
asininit|y, -ies ˌæsɪ'nɪnət|ɪ [-ɪt|ɪ], -ɪz
ask (s.) (newt), -s æsk, -s
ask (v.), -s, -ing, -ed ɑːsk, -s, -ɪŋ, -t [also ɑːst in familiar speech]
askance ə'skæns [-'kɑːns]
askant ə'skænt
Aske æsk
Askelon 'æskɪlən [-kəl-, -lɒn]
askew ə'skjuː
Askew 'æskjuː
Ask|rigg, -with 'æsk|rɪg, -wɪθ
aslant ə'slɑːnt
asleep ə'sliːp
Asmodeus æs'məʊdjəs [-dɪəs]
  Note.—The name must be pronounced ˌæsməʊ'diːəs in Milton's 'Paradise Lost', iv, 168.
Asoka ə'ʃəʊkə [ə'səʊ-] (Hindi əʃoka)
asp, -s æsp [ɑːsp], -s
asparagus ə'spærəgəs
Aspasia æ'speɪʒjə [-ʒɪə, -zjə, -zɪə]
aspect, -s 'æspekt, -s
aspectable ə'spektəbl
aspen, -s 'æspən ['ɑːs-, -pen, -pɪn], -z
asper 'æspə*
asperg|e, -es, -ing, -ed ə'spɜːdʒ [æ's-], -ɪz, -ɪŋ, -d
asperges (religious service) æ'spɜːdʒiːz [ə's-]
aspergill, -s 'æspədʒɪl, -z
asperit|y, -ies æ'sperət|ɪ [ə'sp-, -ɪt|ɪ], -ɪz
aspers|e, -es, -ing, -ed ə'spɜːs [æ's-], -ɪz -ɪŋ, -t
aspersion, -s ə'spɜːʃn [æ's-], -z
asphalt (s.), -s 'æsfælt, -s

asphalt (v.), -s, -ing, -ed 'æsfælt [æs'fælt], -s, -ɪŋ, -ɪd
asphaltic æs'fæltɪk
asphodel, -s 'æsfədel [-fɒd-], -z
asphyxia əs'fɪksɪə [æs-, -sjə]
asphyxiat|e, -es, -ing, -ed, -or/s əs-'fɪksɪeɪt [æs-], -s, -ɪŋ, -ɪd, -ə*/z
asphyxiation, -s əs,fɪksɪ'eɪʃn [æs-], -z
asphyx|y, -ies æs'fɪks|ɪ, -ɪz
aspic 'æspɪk
aspidistra, -s ,æspɪ'dɪstrə, -z
Aspinall 'æspɪnl [-nɔːl]
Aspinwall 'æspɪnwɔːl
aspirant, -s ə'spaɪərənt ['æspɪrənt], -s
aspirate (s. adj.), -s 'æspərət [-rɪt], -s
aspirat|e (v.), -es, -ing, -ed, -or/s 'æspəreɪt [-pɪr-], -s, -ɪŋ, -ɪd, -ə*/z
aspiration, -s ,æspə'reɪʃn [-pɪ'r-], -z
aspir|e, -es, -ing/ly, -ingness, -ed, -er/s ə'spaɪə*, -z, -rɪŋ/lɪ, -rɪŋnɪs [-nəs], -d, -rə*/z
aspirin, -s 'æspərɪn [-pɪr-], -z
aspirine, -s 'æspəriːn [-pɪr-], -z
asplenium, -s æ'spliːnjəm [ə's-, -nɪəm], -z
Asquith 'æskwɪθ
ass, -es æs [ɑːs, esp. as term of contempt], -ɪz
assagai, -s 'æsəgaɪ, -z
assai æ'saɪ
assail, -s, -ing, -ed; -able, -ant/s ə'seɪl, -z, -ɪŋ, -d; -əbl, -ənt/s
Assam æ'sæm ['æsæm]
Assamese ,æsə'miːz [-sæ'm-]
assassin, -s ə'sæsɪn, -z
assassinat|e, -es, -ing, -ed, -or/s ə'sæsɪneɪt [-sən-, -sŋeɪt], -s, -ɪŋ, -ɪd, -ə*/z
assassination, -s ə,sæsɪ'neɪʃn [-sə'n-], -z
assault (s. v.), -s, -ing, -ed, -er/s ə'sɔːlt [-'sɒlt], -s, -ɪŋ, -ɪd, -ə*/z
†assay (v.), -s, -ing, -ed, -er/s ə'seɪ [æ's-], -z, -ɪŋ, -d, -ə*/z
Assaye æ'seɪ
assay-master, -s ə'seɪ,mɑːstə* [æ's-, 'æseɪ-], -z
assay-office ə'seɪ,ɒfɪs [æ's-, 'æseɪ-]
Assche æʃ
assegai, -s 'æsəgaɪ [-sɪg-], -z
assemblage, -s ə'semblɪdʒ, -ɪz
assemb|le, -les, -ling, -led, -ler/s ə'semb|l, -lz, -lɪŋ, -ld, -lə*/z
assembl|y, -ies ə'sembl|ɪ, -ɪz
assembly-room, -s ə'semblɪrʊm [-ruːm], -z
assent (s. v.), -s, -ing/ly, -ed ə'sent [æ's-], -s, -ɪŋ/lɪ, -ɪd
Asser 'æsə*

assert, -s, -ing, -ed, -er/s, or/s; -able ə'sɜːt, -s, -ɪŋ, -ɪd, -ə*/z, -ə*/z; -əbl
assertion, -s ə'sɜːʃn, -z
assertive, -ly, -ness ə'sɜːtɪv, -lɪ, -nɪs [-nəs]
assess, -es, -ing, -ed, -or/s, -ment/s; -able ə'ses, -ɪz, -ɪŋ, -t, -ə*/z, -mənt/s; -əbl
asset, -s 'æset [-sɪt], -s
assever, -s, -ing, -ed æ'sevə* [ə's-], -z, -rɪŋ, -d
asseverat|e, -es, -ing/ly, -ed ə'sevəreɪt [æ's-], -s, -ɪŋ/lɪ, -ɪd
asseveration, -s ə,sevə'reɪʃn [æ,s-], -z
Assheton 'æʃtən
assibilated ə'sɪbɪleɪtɪd [æ's-, -bəl-]
assibilation, -s ə,sɪbɪ'leɪʃn [æ,s-, -bə'l-], -z
assiduit|y, -ies ,æsɪ'djuːət|ɪ [-'djʊ-, -ɪt|ɪ], -ɪz
assiduous, -ly, -ness ə'sɪdjʊəs [-djwəs], -lɪ, -nɪs [-nəs]
assign (s. v.), -s, -ing, -ed, -er/s, -ment/s; -able ə'saɪn, -z, -ɪŋ, -d, -ə*/z, -mənt/s; -əbl
assignat, -s ,æsɪn'jɑː (asiɲa), -z ['æsɪg-næt, -s]
assignation, -s ,æsɪg'neɪʃn, -z
assignee, -s ,æsɪ'niː [-saɪ'n-], -z
assimilat|e, -es, -ing, -ed ə'sɪmɪleɪt [-məl-], -s, -ɪŋ, -ɪd
assimilation, -s ə,sɪmɪ'leɪʃn [-mə'l-], -z
assimilative ə'sɪmɪlətɪv [-məl-, -leɪt-]
assimilatory ə'sɪmɪlətərɪ [-məl-, ə,sɪmɪ-'leɪtərɪ, -mə'l-]
Assiniboine ə'sɪnɪbɔɪn
Assisi ə'siːzɪ [æ's-]
assist, -s, -ing, -ed, -er/s ə'sɪst, -s, -ɪŋ, -ɪd, -ə*/z
assistan|ce/s, -t/s ə'sɪstən|s/ɪz, -t/s
Assiut æ'sjuːt
assiz|e, -es, -er/s ə'saɪz, -ɪz, -ə*/z
associable ə'səʊʃjəbl [-ʃɪə-, -ʃə-, -sjə-, -sɪə-]
associate (s.), -s ə'səʊʃɪət [-ʃɪt, -ʃjət, -ʃjɪt, -sɪt, -sjɪt, -sjət, -sɪət, -ʃɪeɪt, -s
associat|e (v.), -es, -ing, -ed ə'səʊʃɪeɪt [-əʊsɪ-, -əʊsj-, -ʃjeɪt], -s, -ɪŋ, -ɪd
association, -s ə,səʊsɪ'eɪʃn [-əʊʃɪ-], -z
associative ə'səʊʃjətɪv [-ʃɪət-, -ʃɪeɪt-, -ʃjeɪt-, -əʊsjət-, -əʊsɪət-, -əʊsɪeɪt-, -əʊsjeɪt-]
assoilzie (s. v.), -s, -ing, -d ə'sɔɪljɪ [-lɪ], -z, -ɪŋ, -d
assonan|ce/s, -t 'æsəʊnən|s/ɪz [-sŋə-], -t
assonat|e, -es, -ing, -ed 'æsəʊneɪt, -s, -ɪŋ, -ɪd

assort, -s, -ing, -ed, -ment/s ə'sɔːt, -s, -ɪŋ, -ɪd, -mənt/s
Assouan ˌæsʊ'æn [-'ɑːn, 'æsʊæn, -ɑːn, *esp. when attributive, as in* Assouan dam]
assuag|e, -es, -ing, -ed, -ement ə'sweɪdʒ, -ɪz, -ɪŋ, -d, -mənt
assum|e, -es, -ing/ly, -ed, -edly; -able, -ably ə'sjuːm [-'suːm], -z, -ɪŋ/lɪ, -d, -ɪdlɪ; -əbl, -əblɪ
assumpsit ə'sʌmpsɪt
assumption (A.), -s ə'sʌmpʃn, -z
assumptive ə'sʌmptɪv
assur|e, -es, -ing, -ed, -edly, -edness, -er/s; -ance/s ə'ʃɔː* [-'ʃɔə*, -'ʃʊə*], -z, -rɪŋ, -d, -rɪdlɪ, -dnɪs [-rɪdnɪs, -nəs], -rə*/z; -rəns/ɪz
Assynt 'æsɪnt
Assyria, -n/s ə'sɪrɪə, -n/z
assyriolog|ist/s, -y əˌsɪrɪ'ɒlədʒ|ɪst/s, -ɪ
Astarte æ'stɑːtɪ
astatine 'æstətiːn
Astbury 'æstbərɪ
aster, -s 'æstə* [*rarely* 'ɑːs-], -z
asterisk, -s 'æstərɪsk, -s
asterism, -s 'æstərɪzəm, -z
astern ə'stɜːn
asteroid, -s 'æstərɔɪd, -z
asthenia æs'θiːnjə [-nɪə, *rarely* ˌæsθɪ'naɪə]
asthenic, -al æs'θenɪk, -l
asthma 'æsmə [*rarely* 'æsθm-, 'æstm-]
asthmatic, -al, -ally, -s æs'mætɪk [*rarely* æsθ'm-, æst'm-, əs-], -l, -əlɪ, -s
Asti 'æsti: [-tɪ]
astigmatic ˌæstɪg'mætɪk
astigmatism ə'stɪgmətɪzəm [æ's-]
astir ə'stɜː*
Astle 'æsl, æstl
Astley 'æstlɪ
Aston 'æstən
astonish, -es, -ing/ly, -ed/ly, -ment ə'stɒnɪʃ, -ɪz, -ɪŋ/lɪ, -t/lɪ, -mənt
Astor 'æstə*, 'æstɔː*
Astoria æ'stɔːrɪə [ə's-]
astound, -s, -ing, -ed ə'staʊnd, -z, -ɪŋ, -ɪd
astraddle ə'strædl
astragal, -s 'æstrəgəl, -z
astrakhan (A.) ˌæstrə'kæn
astr|al, -ally 'æstr|əl, -əlɪ
astray ə'streɪ
astride ə'straɪd
astring|e, -es, -ing, -ed ə'strɪndʒ, -ɪz, -ɪŋ, -d
astringen|cy, -t/s, -tly ə'strɪndʒən|sɪ, -t/s, -tlɪ

astrolabe, -s 'æstrəʊleɪb, -z
astrologer, -s ə'strɒlədʒə*, -z
astrologic, -al, -ally ˌæstrə'lɒdʒɪk, -l, -əlɪ
astrolog|ist/s, -y ə'strɒlədʒ|ɪst/s, -ɪ
astromet|er/s, -ry æ'strɒmɪt|ə*/z [-mət|ə*/z] -rɪ
astronaut, -s 'æstrənɔːt, -s
astronomer, -s ə'strɒnəmə*, -z
astronomic, -al, -ally ˌæstrə'nɒmɪk, -l, -əlɪ
astronom|y, -ies ə'strɒnəm|ɪ, -ɪz
Astrophel 'æstrəʊfel
astrophysics ˌæstrəʊ'fɪzɪks
Asturias æ'stʊərɪæs [-'stjʊər, -'stjɔər-, -'stjɔːr-, -rɪəs]
astute, -r, -st, -ly, -ness ə'stjuːt [æ's-], -ə*, -ɪst, -lɪ, -nɪs [-nəs]
Astyanax ə'staɪənæks [æ's-]
Asuncion əˌsʊnsɪ'əʊn [-'ɒn]
asunder ə'sʌndə*
Aswan æs'wɑːn
asylum, -s ə'saɪləm, -z
asymmetric, -al, -ally ˌeɪsɪ'metrɪk [ˌæsɪ'm-], -l, -əlɪ
asymmetry eɪ'sɪmətrɪ [ˌæ'sɪm-, -mɪ-]
asymptote, -s 'æsɪmptəʊt, -s
asymptotic, -al, -ally ˌæsɪmp'tɒtɪk, -l, -əlɪ
asyndet|on, -a æ'sɪndɪt|ən [ə's-], -ə
At (*member of A.T.S.*), -s æt, -s
at (*prep.*) æt (*strong form*), ət (*weak form*)
Atalanta ˌætə'læntə
Atall 'ætɔːl
Ataturk 'ætətɜːk [ˌ--'-]
atavism 'ætəvɪzəm
atavistic ˌætə'vɪstɪk
ataxia ə'tæksɪə [æ't-, eɪ't-]
atax|y, -ies, -ic ə'tæks|ɪ, -ɪz, -ɪk
Atbara æt'bɑːrə
Atcheen ə'tʃiːn
Atchison 'ætʃɪsn, 'eɪtʃɪsn
Ate (s.) 'ɑːtɪ ['eɪtɪ]
ate (*from* eat) et [eɪt]
atelier, -s ə'telɪeɪ ['ætel-, 'ætəl-, -ljeɪ (atəlje], -z
Atfield 'ætfiːld
Athabasca ˌæθə'bæskə
Athaliah ˌæθə'laɪə
Athanase 'æθəneɪz
Athanasian ˌæθə'neɪʃn [-θn̩'eɪ-, -ʃjən, -ʃɪən, -sjən, -sɪən]
Athanasius ˌæθə'neɪʃəs [-θn̩'eɪ-, -ʃjəs, -ʃɪəs, -sjəs, -sɪəs]
Athawes (*surname*) 'æθɔːz
athei|sm, -st/s 'eɪθɪɪ|zəm [-θjɪ|-], -st/s
atheistic, -al, -ally ˌeɪθɪ'ɪstɪk, -l, -əlɪ

31

atheling (A.), -s 'æθəlɪŋ [-θɪl-], -z
Athelney 'æθəlnɪ
Athelstan 'æθəlstən (*Old English* 'æðəlstɑːn)
Athena ə'θiːnə
Athenaeum, -s ˌæθɪ'niːəm [-'nɪəm], -z
Athene ə'θiːni: [-nɪ]
Athenian, -s ə'θiːnjən [-nɪən], -z
Athenry ˌæθɪn'raɪ [-θən-]
Athens 'æθɪnz
Atherley 'æθəlɪ
Ather|ston, -ton 'æθə|stən, -tən
athirst ə'θɜːst
athlete, -s 'æθliːt, -s
athletic, -al, -ally, -s æθ'letɪk [əθ-], -l, -əlɪ, -s
athleticism æθ'letɪsɪzəm [əθ-]
Athlone æθ'ləʊn [*also* '-- *when attributive, as in* the Athlone Press]
Athlumney æθ'lʌmnɪ
Athole 'æθəl
Atholl 'æθəl
at home, -s ət'həʊm [ə'təʊm], -z
Athos 'æθɒs ['eɪθ-]
athwart ə'θwɔːt
Athy ə'θaɪ
Atkin|s, -son 'ætkɪn|z, -sn
Atlanta ət'læntə [æt'læn-, ə'tlæn-]
atlantean ˌætlæn'tiːən [-lən-, -'tɪən, ət'læntɪən, æt'læntɪən, ət'læntjən, æt'læntjən, ə'tlænt-]
Atlantes (*statues*) ət'lænti:z [æt'læn-, ə'tlæn-], (*in Ariosto's* '*Orlando Furioso*') ət'læntes [æt-]
Atlantic ət'læntɪk [ə'tlæn-]
Atlantis ət'læntɪs [æt'læn-, ə'tlæn-]
atlas, -es 'ætləs, -ɪz
Atlas 'ætləs [-læs]
atmometer, -s æt'mɒmɪtə* [-mətə*], -z
atmosphere, -s 'ætmə.sfɪə*, -z
atmospheric, -al, -ally, -s ˌætməs'ferɪk, -l, -əlɪ, -s
atoll, -s 'ætɒl [ə'tɒl], -z
atom, -s 'ætəm, -z
atomic ə'tɒmɪk
atomistic ˌætəʊ'mɪstɪk
atomization [-isa-] ˌætəʊmaɪ'zeɪʃn
atomiz|e [-is|e], -es, -ing, -ed, -er/s 'ætəʊmaɪz, -ɪz, -ɪŋ, -d, -ə*/z
†atonal eɪ'təʊnl [æ't-, ə't-]
aton|e, -es, -ing/ly, -ed, -er/s, -ment/s ə'təʊn, -z, -ɪŋ/lɪ, -d, -ə*/z, -mənt/s
atonic (s. adj.), -s eɪ'tɒnɪk [ə't-, æ't-], -s
atony 'ætənɪ
atrabilious ˌætrə'bɪljəs [-lɪəs]
Atreus 'eɪtrɪuːs [-truːs, -trjuːs, -trɪəs]
atri|um, -a 'eɪtrɪ|əm ['ɑːt-], -ə

atrocious, -ly, -ness ə'trəʊʃəs, -lɪ, -nɪs [-nəs]
atrocit|y, -ies ə'trɒsət|ɪ [-ɪt|ɪ], -ɪz
atrophic ə'trɒfɪk [æ't-]
atroph|y (s. v.), -ies, -ying, -ied 'ætrəf|ɪ [-trɒf-], -ɪz, -ɪŋ, -ɪd
atropine 'ætrəpɪn [-trʊp-, -piːn]
Atropos 'ætrəpɒs [-trʊp-]
attach, -es, -ing, -ed, -ment/s; -able ə'tætʃ, -ɪz, -ɪŋ, -t, -mənt/s; -əbl
attaché, -s ə'tæʃeɪ [æ't-] (ataʃe), -z
attaché-case, -s ə'tæʃɪkeɪs [-ʃeɪ-], -ɪz
attack (s. v.), -s, -ing, -ed, -er/s ə'tæk, -s, -ɪŋ, -t, -ə*/z
attain, -s, -ing, -ed, -ment/s; -able ə'teɪn, -z, -ɪŋ, -d, -mənt/s; -əbl
attainability əˌteɪnə'bɪlətɪ [-lɪt-]
attainder, -s ə'teɪndə*, -z
attaint (s. v.), -s, -ing, -ed ə'teɪnt, -s, -ɪŋ, -ɪd
attar 'ætə*
attemper, -s, -ing, -ed ə'tempə* [æ't-], -z, -rɪŋ, -d
attempt (s. v.), -s, -ing, -ed, -er/s; -able ə'tempt, -s, -ɪŋ, -ɪd, -ə*/z; -əbl
Attenborough 'ætnbrə [-bərə, -bʌrə]
attend, -s, -ing, -ed, -er/s; -ance/s, -ant/s ə'tend, -z, -ɪŋ, -ɪd, -ə*/z; -əns/ɪz, -ənt/s
attention, -s ə'tenʃn, -z
attentive, -ly, -ness ə'tentɪv, -lɪ, -nɪs [-nəs]
attenuate (adj.) ə'tenjʊɪt [-njʊət, -njʊeɪt]
attenuat|e (v.), -es, -ing, -ed ə'tenjʊeɪt, -s, -ɪŋ, -ɪd
attenuation, -s əˌtenjʊ'eɪʃn, -z
attenuator, -s ə'tenjʊeɪtə*, -z
Atter|bury, -cliffe 'ætə|bərɪ, -klɪf
attest (s. v.), -s, -ing, -ed, -or/s; -able ə'test, -s, -ɪŋ, -ɪd, -ə*/z; -əbl
attestation, -s ˌæte'steɪʃn, -z
Attfield 'ætfiːld
attic, -s 'ætɪk, -s
Attica 'ætɪkə
atticism, -s 'ætɪsɪzəm, -z
atticiz|e [-is|e], -es, -ing, -ed 'ætɪsaɪz, -ɪz, -ɪŋ, -d
Attila 'ætɪlə, ə'tɪlə
attir|e (s. v.), -es, -ing, -ed, -ement ə'taɪə*, -z, -rɪŋ, -d, -mənt
attitude, -s 'ætɪtjuːd, -z
attitudinal ˌætɪ'tjuːdɪnl
attitudinarian, -s ˌætɪtjuːdɪ'neərɪən, -z
attitudiniz|e [-is|e], -es, -ing, -ed, -er/s ˌætɪ'tjuːdɪnaɪz, -ɪz, -ɪŋ, -d, -ə*/z
Attleborough 'ætlbrə [-bərə, -bʌrə]
Attlee 'ætlɪ

Attock ə'tɒk (*Hindi* əʈək)
attorn, -s, -ing, -ed ə'tɜːn, -z, -ɪŋ, -d
attorney, -s; -ship/s ə'tɜːnɪ, -z; -ʃɪp/s
attorney-general ə,tɜːnɪ'dʒenrəl
attract, -s, -ing/ly, -ed, -or/s; -able
ə'trækt, -s, -ɪŋ/lɪ, -ɪd, -ə*/z; -əbl
attractability ə,træktə'bɪlətɪ [-lɪt-]
attraction, -s ə'trækʃn, -z
attractive, -ly, -ness ə'træktɪv, -lɪ, -nɪs
[-nəs]
attrahent ə'treɪrənt ['ætrəhənt, 'ætrɪənt]
attributable ə'trɪbjʊtəbl
attribute (s.), -s 'ætrɪbjuːt, -s
attrib|ute (v.), -utes, -uting, -uted
ə'trɪb|juːt, -juːts, -jʊtɪŋ, -jʊtɪd
attribution, -s ,ætrɪ'bjuːʃn, -z
attributive, -ly ə'trɪbjʊtɪv, -lɪ
Attride 'ætraɪd
attrition ə'trɪʃn [æ't-]
attun|e, -es, -ing, -ed ə'tjuːn [æ't-], -z,
-ɪŋ, -d
Attwood 'ætwʊd
At|water, -wood 'æt|,wɔːtə*, -wʊd
atypical ,eɪ'tɪpɪkl
aubade, -s əʊ'bɑːd, -z
auberge, -s əʊ'beəʒ ['əʊb-] (obɛrʒ), -ɪz
aubergine, -s 'əʊbəʒiːn [-dʒiːn, ,əʊbə-
'ʒiːn, ,əʊbə'dʒiːn, ,əʊbeə'ʒiːn]
(obɛrʒin), -z
Aubrey 'ɔːbrɪ
aubrietia, -s ɔː'briːʃə [-ʃɪə, -ʃjə], -z
auburn (A.) 'ɔːbən [-bɜːn]
Aucher 'ɔːkə*
Auchindachie ,ɔːkɪn'dækɪ [,ɔːxɪn'dæxɪ]
(*Scottish* ,ɔxɪn'daxɪ)
Auchinleck ,ɔːkɪn'lek ['---, ,ɔːx-] (*Scottish* ,ɔxɪn'lek)
Auchmuty ɔːk'mjuːtɪ
Auchtermuchty ,ɔːktə'mʌktɪ [,ɒktə-,
,ɔːxtə'mʌxtɪ, ,ɒxtə-] (*Scottish* ,ɔxtər-
'mʌxtɪ)
Auckland 'ɔːklənd
aucti|on (s. v.), -ons, -oning, -oned
'ɔːkʃ|n ['ɒk-], -nz, -ənɪŋ [-n̩ɪŋ], -nd
auctionary 'ɔːkʃənərɪ ['ɒk-, -ʃn̩ə-]
auctioneer, -s ,ɔːkʃə'nɪə* ['ɒk-, -ʃn̩'ɪə*],
-z
audacious, -ly, -ness ɔː'deɪʃəs, -lɪ, -nɪs
[-nəs]
audacit|y, -ies ɔː'dæsətɪ [-ɪt|ɪ], -ɪz
Auden 'ɔːdn [-dən]
Audi 'aʊdɪ ['ɔːdɪ]
audibility ,ɔːdɪ'bɪlətɪ [-də'b-, -lɪt-]
audib|le, -ly, -leness 'ɔːdəb|l [-dɪb-], -lɪ,
-lnɪs [-nəs]
audience, -s 'ɔːdjəns [-dɪəns], -ɪz
audiometer, -s ,ɔːdɪ'ɒmɪtə* [-mətə*], -z
audiometry ,ɔːdɪ'ɒmɪtrɪ [-mətrɪ]

audio-typ|ing, -ist/s 'ɔːdɪəʊ,taɪp|ɪŋ
['ɔːdjəʊ-], -ɪst/s
audio-visual ,ɔːdɪəʊ'vɪʒʊəl [-ʒwəl,
-zjʊəl, -zjwəl, -zjəl, -ʒʊl, -ʒl]
audiphone, -s 'ɔːdɪfəʊn, -z
audit (s. v.), -s, -ing, -ed, -or/s 'ɔːdɪt,
-s, -ɪŋ, -ɪd, -ə*/z
audition, -s ɔː'dɪʃn, -z
auditorium, -s ,ɔːdɪ'tɔːrɪəm, -z
auditorship, -s 'ɔːdɪtəʃɪp, -s
auditor|y (s. adj.), -ies 'ɔːdɪtər|ɪ, -ɪz
Aud|ley, -rey 'ɔːd|lɪ, -rɪ
au fait ,əʊ 'feɪ (o fɛ)
Augean ɔː'dʒiːən [-'dʒɪən]
Augeas ɔː'dʒiːæs ['ɔːdʒɪæs]
Augener (*music publisher*) 'aʊɡənə*
auger, -s 'ɔːɡə*, -z
Aughrim 'ɔːɡrɪm
aught ɔːt
augment (s.), -s 'ɔːɡmənt, -s
augment (v.). -s, -ing, -ed; -able
ɔːɡ'ment, -s, -ɪŋ, -ɪd; -əbl
augmentation, -s ,ɔːɡmen'teɪʃn
[-mən-], -z
augmentative ɔːɡ'mentətɪv
au gratin ,əʊ 'ɡrætæ̃ŋ [-tæŋ, -tæn]
(o ɡratɛ̃)
augur (s. v.), -s, -ing, -ed 'ɔːɡə*, -z,
-ɪŋ, -d
augural 'ɔːɡjʊrəl
augur|y, -ies 'ɔːɡjʊr|ɪ [-jər-], -ɪz
August (s.), -s 'ɔːɡəst, -s
august (adj.), -est, -ly, -ness ɔː'ɡʌst,
-ɪst, -lɪ, -nɪs [-nəs]
August|a, -an ɔː'ɡʌst|ə [ə'ɡ-], -ən
Augustine (*Saint*) ɔː'ɡʌstɪn [ə'ɡ-, *rarely* 'ɔːɡəstɪn]
Augustinian ,ɔːɡə'stɪnɪən [-njən]
Augustus ɔː'ɡʌstəs [ə'ɡ-]
auk, -s ɔːk, -s
aul|a, -ae 'ɔːl|ə ['aʊlə], -iː [-laɪ, -leɪ]
auld lang syne ,ɔːldlæŋ'saɪn
Ault ɔːlt
aumbr|y, -ies 'ɔːmbr|ɪ, -ɪz
Aumonier əʊ'mɒnɪeɪ [-'məʊn-, -njeɪ]
(omɔnje)
Aungier (*street in Dublin*) 'eɪndʒə*
aunt, -s; -ie/s ɑːnt, -s; -ɪ/z
au pair ,əʊ 'peə* (o pɛːr)
aura, -s 'ɔːrə, -z
aur|al, -ally 'ɔːr|əl, -əlɪ
aurate, -s 'ɔːreɪt [-rɪt], -s
aureate 'ɔːrɪɪt [-ɪeɪt, -ɪət]
Aureli|a, -an, -us ɔː'riːlj|ə [-lɪ|ə], -ən,
-əs
aureola -s ɔː'rɪəʊlə, -z
aureole, -s 'ɔːrɪəʊl, -z
aureomycin ,ɔːrɪəʊ'maɪsɪn

au revoir ˌəʊ rə'vwɑ:* [rɪ-] (o rəvwɑːr)
auric 'ɔːrɪk
auricle, -s 'ɔːrɪkl, -z
auricula, -s ə'rɪkjʊlə [ɔː'r-, ʊ'r-, -jələ],
-z
auricular, -ly ɔː'rɪkjʊlə*, -lɪ
auricul|ate, -ated ɔː'rɪkjʊl|ət [ʊ'r-, -ɪt,
-eɪt], -ertɪd
auriferous ɔː'rɪfərəs
Auriga ɔː'raɪgə
Aurignacian ˌɔːrɪg'neɪʃn [-ʃjən, -ʃrən]
aurist, -s 'ɔːrɪst, -s
aurochs, -es 'ɔːrɒks, -ɪz
auror|a (A.), -as, -al ɔː'rɔːr|ə [ə'r-], -əz,
-əl
auscultat|e, -es, -ing, -ed 'ɔːskəltert
['ɒs-, -kʌl-], -s, -ɪŋ, -ɪd
auscultation, -s ˌɔːskəl'teɪʃn [ˌɒs-,
-kʌl-], -z
auscultator, -s 'ɔːskəltertə* ['ɒs-, -kʌl-],
-z
auspice, -s 'ɔːspɪs ['ɒs-], -ɪz
auspicious, -ly, -ness ɔː'spɪʃəs [ɒ's-],
-lɪ, -nɪs
Aussie, -s 'ɒzɪ ['ɒsɪ], -z
Austell 'ɔːstəl ['ɒs-, local Cornish pronunciation 'ɔːsl]
Austen 'ɒstɪn ['ɔːs-]
Auster 'ɔːstə*
austere, -r, -st, -ly, -ness ɒ'stɪə* [ɔː's-],
-rə*, -rɪst, -lɪ, -nɪs [-nəs]
austerit|y, -ies ɒ'sterət|ɪ [ɔː's-, -ɪt|ɪ], -ɪz
Austerlitz 'ɔːstəlɪts
Austin, -s 'ɒstɪn ['ɔːs-], -z
austral 'ɔːstrəl
Australasia ˌɒstrə'leɪʒə [ˌɔːs-, -ʒɪə, -ʒə,
-zjə, -zɪə, -ʃjə, -ʃɪə, -ʃə]
Australasian, -s ˌɒstrə'leɪʒn [ˌɔːs-,
-ʒɪən, -zjən, -zɪən, -ʃjən, -ʃrən, -ʃn],
-z
Australia, -n/s ɒ'streɪljə [ɔː's-, -lɪə],
-n/z
Austria, -n/s 'ɒstrɪə ['ɔːs-], -n/z
Austro|-German, -Hungarian ˌɒstrəʊ|-
'dʒɜːmən [ˌɔːs-], -hʌŋ'geərɪən
authentic, -al, -ally ɔː'θentɪk, -l, -əlɪ
authenticat|e, -es, -ing, -ed ɔː'θentɪkert,
-s, -ɪŋ, -ɪd
authentication, -s ɔːˌθentɪ'keɪʃn, -z
authenticit|y, -ies ˌɔːθen'tɪsət|ɪ [-θən-,
-ɪt|ɪ], -ɪz
author, -s; -ess/es 'ɔːθə*, -z; -rɪs/ɪz
[-res/ɪz]
authoritarianism ɔːˌθɒrɪ'teərɪənɪzəm
[-ˌθɒrə-, -rjə-]
authoritative, -ly, -ness ɔː'θɒrɪtətɪv
[ɒ'θ-, ə'θ-, -'θɒrə-, -tert-], -lɪ, -nɪs
[-nəs]

authorit|y, -ies ɔː'θɒrət|ɪ [ɒ'θ-, ə'θ-,
-ɪt|ɪ], -ɪz
authorization [-isa-], -s ˌɔːθəraɪ'zeɪʃn
[-rɪ'z-], -z
authoriz|e [-is|e], -es, -ing, -ed; -able
'ɔːθəraɪz, -ɪz, -ɪŋ, -d; -əbl
authorship 'ɔːθəʃɪp
autism 'ɔːtɪzm
autistic ɔː'tɪstɪk
autobahn, -s 'ɔːtəʊbɑːn ['aʊt-], -z
autobiograph|er/s, -y, -ies ˌɔːtəʊbaɪ-
'ɒgrəf|ə*/z [-bɪ'ɒg-], -ɪ, -ɪz
autobiographic, -al, -ally 'ɔːtəʊˌbaɪəʊ-
'græfɪk, -l, -əlɪ
auto-car, -s 'ɔːtəʊkɑː:*, -z
autochthon, -s ɔː'tɒkθən ['ɔːtək-, -θɒn],
-z
autochthonous ɔː'tɒkθənəs [-θŋəs]
autocrac|y, ies ɔː'tɒkrəs|ɪ, -ɪz
autocrat, -s 'ɔːtəʊkræt, -s
autocratic, -al, -ally ˌɔːtəʊ'krætɪk, -l,
-əlɪ
auto-da-fé, -s ˌɔːtəʊdɑː'feɪ [ˌaʊt-], -z
autogiro [-gyro], -s ˌɔːtəʊ'dʒaɪərəʊ, -z
autograph, -s 'ɔːtəgrɑːf [-græf], -s
autographic, -al, -ally ˌɔːtəʊ'græfɪk, -l,
-əlɪ
autography ɔː'tɒgrəfɪ
autogyro, -s ˌɔːtəʊ'dʒaɪərəʊ, -z
Autolycus ɔː'tɒlɪkəs
automat 'ɔːtəʊmæt
automatic, -al, -ally ˌɔːtə'mætɪk, -l, -əlɪ
†automation ˌɔːtə'meɪʃn
automati|sm, -s/t/s ɔː'tɒmətɪ|zəm, -st/s
automat|ion, -ons, -a ɔː'tɒmət|ən, -ənz,
-ə
automobile, -s 'ɔːtəməʊbiːl [-tʊm-,
-mʊb-, ˌ—'-, ˌɔːtəʊ'məʊbiːl, -tʊ'm-]
autonomic ˌɔːtəʊ'nɒmɪk
autonom|ous, -y, -ies ɔː'tɒnəm|əs, -ɪ,
-ɪz
autonym, -s 'ɔːtənɪm, -z
auto-pilot, -s 'ɔːtəʊˌpaɪlət, -s
autops|y, -ies 'ɔːtəps|ɪ [-tɒp-, ɔː'tɒpsɪ],
-ɪz
auto-suggestion ˌɔːtəʊsə'dʒestʃən
[-eʃtʃən]
autotyp|e (s. v.), -es, -ing, -ed 'ɔːtəʊtaɪp,
-s, -ɪŋ, -t
autotypography ˌɔːtəʊtaɪ'pɒgrəfɪ
autumn, -s 'ɔːtəm, -z
autumn|al, -ally ɔː'tʌmn|əl [-l̩], -əlɪ
Auvergne əʊ'veən [-'vɜːn] (ovɛrŋ, ɔv-)
auxiliar|y (s. adj.), -ies ɔːg'zɪljər|ɪ
[ɔːk'sɪl-, ɒg'zɪl-, ɒk'sɪl-, -lɪər-], -ɪz
Ava 'ɑːvə, 'eɪvə
avail (s. v.), -s, -ing/ly, -ed ə'veɪl, -z,
-ɪŋ/lɪ, -d

availability ə‚veɪlə'bɪlətɪ [-lɪt-]
availab|le, -ly, -leness ə'veɪləb|l, -lɪ,
-lnɪs [-nəs]
avalanche, -s 'ævəlɑːntʃ [-lɔːntʃ], -ɪz
Avalon 'ævəlɒn
avant-courier,   -s   ‚ævɑ̃ːŋ'kʊrɪə*
[-vɔ̃ːŋ'k-, -vɑːŋ'k-, -vɒŋ'k-, -vɔːŋ-,
-vənt'k-], -z
avant-garde ‚ævɑ̃ːŋ'gɑːd [-vɔ̃ːŋ, -vɔːŋ,
-vɑːŋ, -vɒŋ, -vəŋ] (avɑ̃ gard)
avarice 'ævərɪs
avaricious, -ly, -ness ‚ævə'rɪʃəs, -lɪ, -nɪs
[-nəs]
avast ə'vɑːst
avatar,   -s   ‚ævə'tɑː:*   ['—]   (Hindi
əwtar), -z
avaunt ə'vɔːnt
ave (prayer), -s 'ɑːvɪ, -z
Avebury 'eɪvbərɪ
Aveling 'eɪvlɪŋ
Ave Maria (prayer), -s   ‚ɑːvɪmə'rɪə
[-'riːə], -z
Ave Maria Lane 'ɑːvɪmə‚rɪə'leɪn [for-
merly 'eɪvɪmə‚raɪə'leɪn]
aveng|e, -es, -ing, -ed, -er/s; -eful
ə'vendʒ, -ɪz, -ɪŋ, -d, -ə*/z; -fʊl
avengeress, -es ə'vendʒərɪs [-res], -ɪz
avenue, -s 'ævənjuː [-vɪn-], -z
aver, -s, -ring, -red, -ment/s ə'vɜː:*, -z,
-rɪŋ, -d, -mənt/s
averag|e, -es, -ing, -ed, -ely 'ævərɪdʒ,
-ɪz, -ɪŋ, -d, -lɪ
averruncat|e, -es, -ing, -ed ‚ævə'rʌŋkeɪt
[-vɪ'r-, -ve'r-], -s, -ɪŋ, -ɪd
averruncator, -s ‚ævə'rʌŋkeɪtə* [-vɪ'r-,
-ve'r-], -z
averse, -ly, -ness ə'vɜːs, -lɪ, -nɪs [-nəs]
aversion, -s ə'vɜːʃn [-ʒn], -z
avert, -s, -ing, -ed; -ible ə'vɜːt, -s, -ɪŋ,
-ɪd; -əbl [-ɪbl]
avertin ə'vɜːtɪn
Avery 'eɪvərɪ
Avesta ə'vestə
avian, -s 'eɪvjən [-vɪən], -z
aviar|ist/s, -y, -ies 'eɪvjər|ɪst/s [-vɪə-],
-ɪ, -ɪz
aviation ‚eɪvɪ'eɪʃn
aviator, -s 'eɪvɪeɪtə* [-vjeɪ-], -z
Avice (fem. name) 'eɪvɪs
Avicenna ‚ævɪ'senə
aviculture 'eɪvɪkʌltʃə*
avid, -ly 'ævɪd, -lɪ
avidity ə'vɪdətɪ [æ'v-, -ɪtɪ]
Aviemore ‚ævɪ'mɔː:* [-'mɔə*, '—]
Avilion æ'vɪlɪən [-ljən]
aviso, -s ə'vaɪzəʊ [-'viːz-], -z
Avoca ə'vəʊkə
avocado, -s ‚ævə'kɑːdəʊ, -z

avocation, -s ‚ævəʊ'keɪʃn, -z
avocet, -s 'ævəʊset, -s
Avoch ɔːk [ɔːx] (Scottish ɔx)
avoid, -s, -ing, -ed; -able, -ance/s
ə'vɔɪd, -z, -ɪŋ, -ɪd; -əbl, -əns/ɪz
avoirdupois ‚ævədə'pɔɪz
Avon (in Avon, etc.) 'eɪvən, (in Devon)
'ævən, (in the Grampian Region) ɑːn
Avondale 'eɪvəndeɪl
Avonmouth 'eɪvənmaʊθ [-məθ]
Avory 'eɪvərɪ
avouch, -es, -ing, -ed ə'vaʊtʃ, -ɪz, -ɪŋ,
-t
avow (s. v.), -s, -ing, -ed, -edly; -al/s
ə'vaʊ, -z, -ɪŋ, -d, -ɪdlɪ; -əl/z
avuncular ə'vʌŋkjʊlə*
await, -s, -ing, -ed ə'weɪt, -s, -ɪŋ, -ɪd
awak|e (adj. v.), -es, -ing, -ed, awoke
ə'weɪk, -s, -ɪŋ, -t, ə'wəʊk
awak|en, -ens, -ening, -ened, -enment/s
ə'weɪk|ən, -ənz, -nɪŋ [-ŋɪŋ, -ənɪŋ],
-ənd, -ənmənt/s
awakening (s.), -s ə'weɪknɪŋ, -z
award (s. v.), -s, -ing, -ed; -able ə'wɔːd,
-z, -ɪŋ, -ɪd; -əbl
aware, -ness ə'weə*, -nɪs [-nəs]
awash ə'wɒʃ
away ə'weɪ
aw|e (s. v.), (A.), -es, -ing, -ed ɔː, -z,
-ɪŋ, -d
awe-inspiring 'ɔːɪn‚spaɪərɪŋ
aweless, -ness 'ɔːlɪs [-ləs], -nɪs [-nəs]
awesome, -ness 'ɔːsəm, -nɪs [-nəs]
awe-stricken 'ɔː‚strɪkən
awe-struck 'ɔːstrʌk
awful, -ness (terrible) 'ɔːfʊl [-fl], -nɪs
[-nəs], (great, considerable) 'ɔːfl
awfully (terribly) 'ɔːfʊlɪ, (very) 'ɔːflɪ
awhile ə'waɪl [ə'hw-]
awkward, -est, -ly, -ness, -ish 'ɔːkwəd,
-ɪst, -lɪ, -nɪs [-nəs], -ɪʃ
awl, -s ɔːl, -z
awn, -s -ed ɔːn, -z, -d
awning, -s 'ɔːnɪŋ, -z
awoke (from awake) ə'wəʊk
awry ə'raɪ
axe, -s æks, -ɪz
axes (plur. of axis) 'æksiːz
Axholm(e) 'ækshəʊm [-səm]
axial, -ly 'æksɪəl [-sjəl], -ɪ
axil, -s 'æksɪl, -z
axill|a, -ae; -ar, -ary æk'sɪl|ə, -iː:; -ə*,
-ərɪ
axiom, -s 'æksɪəm [-sjəm], -z
axiomatic, -al, -ally ‚æksɪəʊ'mætɪk
[-sjəʊ'm-], -l, -əlɪ
ax|is, -es 'æks|ɪs, -iːz
axle, -s, -d 'æksl, -z, -d

35

axle-tree, -s 'æksltri:, -z
Axminster, -s 'æksmɪnstə*, -z
axolotl, -s ˌæksə'lɒtl, -z
ay (yes), -es aɪ, -z
ayah, -s 'aɪə ['ɑːjə], -z
aye (ever), eɪ
aye (yes), -s aɪ, -z
aye-aye (animal), -s 'aɪaɪ, -z
Ayer, -s eə*, -z
Ayerst 'aɪəst, 'erəst
Aylesbury 'eɪlzbərɪ
Aylesford 'eɪlzfəd [-lsf-]
Ayliffe 'eɪlɪf
Ayling 'eɪlɪŋ
Aylmer 'eɪlmə*
Aylsham 'eɪlʃəm
Aylward 'eɪlwəd
Aylwin 'eɪlwɪn
Aymer 'eɪmə*
Ayot 'erət
Ayr, -shire eə*, -ʃə* [-ˌʃɪə*]
Ayre, -s eə*, -z
Ayrton 'eətn

Ayscough 'æskə, 'æskju:, 'eɪskəf
Ayscue 'eɪskju:
Ayt|on, -oun 'eɪt|n, -n
azalea, -s ə'zeɪljə [-lɪə], -z
Azariah ˌæzə'raɪə .
Azaziel ə'zeɪzjəl [-zɪəl]
azimuth, -s 'æzɪməθ, -s
azoic ə'zəʊɪk [æ'z-]
Azores ə'zɔːz [-'zɔəz]
    Note.—It is customary to pronounce
    ə'zɔːrɪz (or ə'zɔərɪz orˌ -rez) in
    reciting Tennyson's poem 'The
    Revenge'.
azote ə'zəʊt [æ'z-, 'æzəʊt]
azotic ə'zɒtɪk [æ'z-]
Azov 'ɑːzɒv
Azrael 'æzreɪəl [-reɪl, -rɪəl]
Aztec, -s 'æztek, -s
azure 'æʒə* ['eɪʒ-, -ˌʒjʊə*, -ˌʒʊə*, -ʒjə*,
    -ˌzjʊə*]
azur|ine/s, -ite 'æʒʊr|aɪn/z ['æʒər-,
    'æˌʒʊər-, 'æʒjʊr-, 'æˌʒjʊər-, 'æzjʊr-,
    'æˌzjʊər-], -aɪt

B

B (the letter), -'s biː, -z
ba (note in Tonic Sol-fa), -s beɪ, -z
B.A. (British Airways, Bachelor of Arts) ˌbiːˈeɪ
baa (s. v.), -s, -ing, -ed bɑː, -z, -ɪŋ, -d
Baal 'beɪəl ['beɪæl, Jewish pronunciation bɑːl]
baa-lamb, -s 'bɑːlæm, -z
Baalim 'beɪəlɪm [Jewish pronunciation 'bɑːlɪm]
Baal Schem ˌbɑːlˈʃem
baas, -es bɑːs, -ɪz
Babbage 'bæbɪdʒ
babb|le, -les, -ling, -led, -ler/s, -lement/s 'bæb|l, -lz, -lɪŋ [-lɪŋ], -ld, -lə*/z [-lə*/z], -lmənt/s
Babcock 'bæbkɒk
babe, -s beɪb, -z
babel (B.), -s 'beɪbl, -z
Bab-el-Mandeb ˌbæbelˈmændeb
Babington 'bæbɪŋtən
baboo (B.), -s 'bɑːbuː, -z
baboon, -s bəˈbuːn, -z
babooner|y, -ies bəˈbuːnər|ɪ, -ɪz
babu (B.), -s 'bɑːbuː, -z
bab|y (B.), -ies 'beɪb|ɪ, -ɪz
baby-farmer, -s 'beɪbɪˌfɑːmə*, -z
babyhood 'beɪbɪhʊd
babyish, -ly, -ness 'beɪbɪʃ [-bjɪʃ], -lɪ, -nɪs [-nəs]
Babylon 'bæbɪlən [-lɒn]
Babylonia, -n/s ˌbæbɪˈləʊnjə [-nɪə], -n/z
baby-sit|ter/s, -ting 'beɪbɪˌsɪt|ə*/z, -ɪŋ
baccalaureate, -s ˌbækəˈlɔːrɪət [-rɪɪt], -s
baccara(t) 'bækərɑː [ˌbækəˈr-]
Bacchae 'bækiː
bacchanal, -s 'bækənl [-næl], -z
bacchanalia, -n/s ˌbækəˈneɪljə [-lɪə], -nz
bacchant, -s 'bækənt, -s
bacchante, -s bəˈkæntɪ, -z [bəˈkænt, -s]
bacchic 'bækɪk
Bacchus 'bækəs
Bacchylides bæˈkɪlɪdiːz [bəˈk-]
baccy 'bækɪ
Bach (English surname) beɪtʃ, bætʃ, (German composer) bɑːx [bɑːk](bax)
Bache beɪtʃ
bachelor (B.), -s ; -hood, -ship 'bætʃələ* [-tʃɪl-, -tʃlə*], -z; -hʊd, -ʃɪp

bacill|us, -i, -ary bəˈsɪl|əs, -aɪ, -ərɪ
back (s. v. adv.) (B.), -s, -ing, -ed, -er/s bæk, -s, -ɪŋ, -t, -ə*/z
backache, -s 'bækeɪk, -s
back-bencher, -s ˌbækˈbentʃə*, -z
backbit|e, -es, -ing, backbit, backbitten 'bækbaɪt, -s, -ɪŋ, 'bækbɪt, 'bækˌbɪtn
backbiter, -s 'bækˌbaɪtə*, -z
backboard, -s 'bækbɔːd [-bɔəd], -z
backbone, -s 'bækbəʊn, -z
backchat 'bæktʃæt
backdat|e, -es, -ing, -ed ˌbækˈdeɪt, -s, -ɪŋ, -ɪd
back-door, -s ˌbækˈdɔː* [-ˈdɔə*], -z
backfir|e, -es, -ing, -ed ˌbækˈfaɪə* ['--], -z, -rɪŋ, -d
backgammon 'bækˌgæmən [-'--]
background, -s 'bækgraʊnd, -z
back-hair ˌbækˈheə*
back-hand, -s, -ed, -er/s 'bækhænd [ˌbækˈh-], -z, -ɪd, -ə*/z
Backhouse 'bækhaʊs
backing (s.), -s 'bækɪŋ
backlash 'bæklæʃ
backless 'bæklɪs [-ləs]
backlog, -s 'bæklɒg, -z
back-pedal, -s, -ling, -led ˌbækˈpedl, -z, -lɪŋ [-ˈlɪŋ], -ld
back-room ˌbækˈruːm [-ˈrʊm, '--]
backsheesh [-shish] ˌbækˈʃiːʃ ['--]
backside, -s ˌbækˈsaɪd ['bæksaɪd], -z
backslid|e, -es, -ing, backslid, backslider/s ˌbækˈslaɪd ['--], -z, -ɪŋ, ˌbækˈslɪd, ˌbækˈslaɪdə* ['-ˌ--]/z
backstairs ˌbækˈsteəz ['--]
backstay, -s 'bæksteɪ, -z
backstitch, -es 'bækstɪtʃ, -ɪz
backstrap, -s 'bækstræp, -s
backward, -s, -ly, -ness 'bækwəd, -z, -lɪ, -nɪs [-nəs]
backwash, -es 'bækwɒʃ, -ɪz
backwater, -s 'bækˌwɔːtə*, -z
backwoods, -man, -men 'bækwʊdz, -mən, -mən
back-yard, -s ˌbækˈjɑːd, -z
bacon 'beɪkən [-kŋ]
Bacon 'beɪkən [-kn]
Baconian, -s beɪˈkəʊnjən [bəˈk-, -nɪən], -z

bacteriological bæk‚tɪərɪə'lɒdʒɪkl
 [‚---'---]
bacteriolog|ist/s, -y bæk‚tɪərɪ'ɒlədʒ|-
 ɪst/s [‚bæktɪərɪ'ɒ-], -ɪ
bacteri|um, -a, -al bæk'tɪərɪ|əm, -ə, -əl
Bactria, -n/s 'bæktrɪə, -n/z
Bacup 'beɪkəp
bad; bad|ly, -ness bæd; 'bæd|lɪ, -nɪs
 [-nəs]
Badajoz 'bædəhɒz (bada'xoθ)
Badam, -s 'bædəm, -z
Baddeley 'bædəlɪ, 'bædlɪ
baddish 'bædɪʃ
bade (from bid) bæd [beɪd]
Badel bə'del
Badely 'bædlɪ
Baden (in Germany) 'bɑːdn
Baden-Powell ‚beɪdn'pəʊəl [-'pəʊɪl,
 -'pəʊel, -'pəʊəl]
Bader (Scottish surname) 'bɑːdə*,
 'beɪdə*
badg|e (s. v.), -es, -ing, -ed bædʒ, -ɪz,
 -ɪŋ, -d
badger (s. v.) (B.), -s, -ing, -ed 'bædʒə*,
 -z, -rɪŋ, -d
badger-baiting 'bædʒə‚beɪtɪŋ
badger-dog, -s 'bædʒədɒg, -z
Badham, 'bædəm
badinage 'bædɪnɑːʒ [‚--'-] (badina:ʒ)
badminton (B.) 'bædmɪntən
Baeda 'biːdə
Baedeker, -s 'beɪdekə* [-dɪk-], -z
Baffin 'bæfɪn
baff|le (s. v.), -les, -ling, -led, -ler/s
 'bæf|l, -lz, -lɪŋ [-lɪŋ], -ld, -lə*/z
 [-lə*/z]
baffleboard, -s 'bæflbɔːd [-bɔəd], -z
bag (s.), -s bæg, -z
bag (v.), -s, -ging, -ged bæg, -z, -ɪŋ, -d
bagatelle, -s; -board/s ‚bægə'tel, -z;
 -bɔːd/z [-bɔəd/z]
Bagdad (in Iraq) ‚bæg'dæd ['--], (in
 Tasmania, Florida) 'bægdæd
Bagehot 'bædʒət
baggage, -s 'bægɪdʒ, -ɪz
baggage|man, -men 'bægɪdʒ|mæn
 [-mən], -men [-mən]
Baggallay 'bægəlɪ
bagg|y, -ier, -iest, -ily, -iness 'bæg|ɪ,
 -ɪə*, -ɪɪst, -ɪlɪ, -ɪnɪs [-ɪnəs]
Baghdad ‚bæg'dæd ['--]
Bagnall 'bægnəl [-nl̩, -nɔːl]
Bagnell 'bægnəl [-nl̩]
bagnio, -s 'bɑːnjəʊ [-nɪəʊ], -z
Bagot 'bægət
bagpipe, -s, -r/s 'bægpaɪp, -s, -ə*/z
Bagrie 'bægrɪ
Bagsh|aw(e), -ot 'bægʃ|ɔː, -ɒt

Bagworthy (in Devon) 'bædʒərɪ
bah bɑː
bahadur, -s bə'hɑːdə*, -z
Bahama, -s bə'hɑːmə, -z
Bahia bə'hiːə [-'hɪə]
Bahrein (-rain), -i bɑː'reɪn, -ɪ
Baiae 'baɪɪ
baignoire, -s 'beɪnwɑː* [-wɔː:*], -z
bail (s. v.), -s, -ing, -ed, -er/s; -able
 beɪl, -z, -ɪŋ, -d, -ə*/z; -əbl
bail-bond, -s 'beɪlbɒnd [‚beɪl'b-], -z
bailee, -s ‚beɪ'liː, -z
bailey (B.) 'beɪlɪ
Bailhache 'beɪlhæʃ
bailie (B.), -s 'beɪlɪ, -z
bailiff, -s 'beɪlɪf, -s
bailiwick, -s 'beɪlɪwɪk, -s
Baillieu 'beɪljuː
bailment, -s 'beɪlmənt, -s
Baily 'beɪlɪ
Bain, -es beɪn, -z
Bainbridge 'beɪnbrɪdʒ ['beɪmb-]
Baird beəd
bairn, -s beən, -z
bait (s. v.), -s, -ing, -ed beɪt, -s, -ɪŋ, -ɪd
baize, -s beɪz, -ɪz
bak|e, -es, -ing, -ed, -er/s beɪk, -s, -ɪŋ,
 -t, -ə*/z
bakehou|se, -ses 'beɪkhaʊ|s, -zɪz
bakelite 'beɪkəlaɪt
Baker 'beɪkə*
Bakerloo ‚beɪkə'luː
baker|y, -ies 'beɪkər|ɪ, -ɪz
baking-powder 'beɪkɪŋ‚paʊdə*
baksheesh ‚bæk'ʃiːʃ ['--]
Bala (in Wales) 'bælə (Welsh 'bala)
balaam (B.), -s 'beɪlæm [-ləm], -z
balaclava (B.), -s ‚bælə'klɑːvə, -z
Balakirev bə'lækɪrev [-'lɑːk-] (ba'la-
 kɪrjif)
balalaika, -s ‚bælə'laɪkə, -z
balanc|e (s. v.), -es, -ing, -ed 'bæləns,
 -ɪz, -ɪŋ, -t
balance-sheet, -s 'bælənsʃiːt [-nʃʃiːt,
 -nʃiːt], -s
Balbriggan bæl'brɪgən
Balbus 'bælbəs
Balcarres bæl'kærɪs
Balchin 'bɔːltʃɪn ['bɒl-]
balcon|y, -ies 'bælkən|ɪ, -ɪz
bald, -er, -est, -ly, -ness bɔːld, -ə*, -ɪst,
 -lɪ, -nɪs [-nəs]
baldachin [-quin], -s 'bɔːldəkɪn, -z
balderdash 'bɔːldədæʃ
bald-head, -s 'bɔːldhed, -z
bald-headed ‚bɔːld'hedɪd [also 'bɔːld‚h-
 when attributive]
Baldock 'bɔːldɒk

baldric—bandstand

baldric, -s 'bɔːldrɪk, -s
Baldry 'bɔːldrɪ
Baldwin 'bɔːldwɪn
bal|e (s. v.), -es, -ing, -ed beɪl, -z, -ɪŋ, -d
Bâle (in Switzerland) bɑːl
Balean (surname) 'bæ1ɪn
Balearic ˌbælɪ'ærɪk
baleen, -s bə'liːn [bæ'l-], -z
bale|ful, -fully, -fulness 'beɪl|fʊl, -fʊlɪ
[-fəlɪ], -fʊlnɪs [-nəs]
baler, -s 'beɪlə*, -z
Balfour 'bælfə* [-fɔː:*, -ˌfʊə*, -fɔə*]
Balgony bæl'gəʊnɪ
Balguy 'bɔːlgɪ
Balham 'bæləm
Baliol 'beɪljəl [-lɪəl]
balk (s. v.), -s, -ing, -ed bɔːk [bɔːlk], -s,
-ɪŋ, -t
Balkan, -s 'bɔːlkən ['bɒl-], -z
ball (B.), -s bɔːl, -z
ballad, -s 'bæləd, -z
ballade, -s bæ'lɑːd (balad), -z
Ballan|tine, -tyne 'bælən|taɪn, -taɪn
Ballarat, ˌbælə'ræt ['---]
Ballard 'bæləd, -lɑːd
ballast, -s 'bæləst, -s
Ballater 'bælətə*
ball-bearing, -s ˌbɔːl'beərɪŋ, -z
ball-cock, -s 'bɔːlkɒk, -s
Balleine (surname in Channel Islands)
bæ'len
ballerina, -s ˌbælə'riːnə, -z
ballet, -s 'bæleɪ [-lɪ], -z
ballet-dancer, -s 'bælɪˌdɑːnsə* [-leɪˌd-],
-z
ballet-girl, -s 'bælɪgɜːl [-leɪg-], -z
balletomane, -s 'bælɪtəʊmeɪn [-let-], -z
Balliol 'beɪljəl [-lɪəl]
ballistic, -s bə'lɪstɪk, -s
balloon, -s, -ist/s bə'luːn, -z, -ɪst/s
ballot (s. v.), -s, -ing, -ed ; -age 'bælət,
-s, -ɪŋ, -ɪd ; -ɪdʒ
ballot-box, -es 'bælətbɒks, -ɪz
ball-point, -s, -ed 'bɔːlpɔɪnt, -s, -ɪd
ball-proof 'bɔːlpruːf
ball-room, -s 'bɔːlrʊm [-ruːm], -z
bally 'bælɪ
Bally|castle, -mena, -money ˌbælɪ|-
'kɑːsl, -'miːnə, -'mʌnɪ
ballyhoo ˌbælɪ'huː
ballyrag, -s, -ging, -ged 'bælɪræg, -z,
-ɪŋ, -d
balm, -s bɑːm, -z
Balm(e) bɑːm
Balmoral bæl'mɒrəl
balm|y, -ier, -iest, -ily, -iness 'bɑːm|ɪ,
-ɪə* [-jə*], -ɪɪst [-jɪst], -ɪlɪ [-əlɪ],
-ɪnɪs [-ɪnəs]

Balniel bæl'niːl
Balogh 'bælɒg
baloney bə'ləʊnɪ
balsa 'bɒlsə ['bɔː:-]
balsam, -s 'bɔːlsəm ['bɒl-], -z
balsamic bɔːl'sæmɪk [bæl-, bɒl-]
Balta (in Ukraine) 'bæltə
Balthazar (in Shakespeare) ˌbælθə'zɑː:*
['---], (otherwise) bæl'θæzə*
Baltic 'bɔːltɪk ['bɒl-]
baltimore (B.), -s 'bɔːltɪmɔː:* ['bɒlt-,
-mɔə*], -z
Baluchistan bə'luːtʃɪstɑːn [-tæn, -ˌ--'-]
baluster, -s, -ed 'bæləstə*, -z, -d
balustrade, -s, ˌbælə'streɪd, -z
Baly 'beɪlɪ
Balzac 'bælzæk (balzak)
bamboo, -s bæm'buː:, -z
bambooz|le, -les, -ling, -led bæm'buːz|l,
-lz, -lɪŋ [-lɪŋ], -ld
Bamborough 'bæmbərə
Bam|field, -ford 'bæm|fiːld, -fəd
bamfooz|le, -les, -ling, -led bæm'fuːz|l,
-lz, -lɪŋ [-lɪŋ], -ld
Bamfyld 'bæmfiːld
ban (s. v.), -s, -ning, -ned bæn, -z, -ɪŋ,
-d
banal bə'nɑːl [bæ'n-, 'beɪnl]
Banal 'bænəl [-nl]
banalit|y, -ies bə'nælət|ɪ [bæ'n-, -ɪt|ɪ],
-ɪz
banana, -s bə'nɑːnə, -z
Banaras bə'nɑːrəs (Hindi vənarəsi)
Banbury 'bænbərɪ ['bæmbərɪ]
Banchory 'bæŋkərɪ
banco 'bæŋkəʊ
Bancroft 'bænkrɒft ['bæŋk-]
band (s.), -s bænd, -z
band (v.), -s, -ing, -ed bænd, -z, -ɪŋ,
-ɪd
bandag|e (s. v.), -es, -ing, -ed 'bændɪdʒ,
-ɪz, -ɪŋ, -d
bandana, -s bæn'dænə [-'dɑːnə], -z
bandanna, -s bæn'dænə, -z
bandbox, -es 'bændbɒks, -ɪz
bandeau, -x 'bændəʊ, -z
banderole, -s 'bændərəʊl, -z
bandicoot, -s 'bændɪkuːt, -s
bandit, -s, -ry 'bændɪt, -s, -rɪ
banditti bæn'dɪtɪ [-tiː]
bandmaster, -s 'bændˌmɑːstə*, -z
bandog, -s 'bændɒg, -s
bandoleer [-lier], -s ˌbændəʊ'lɪə*, -z
bandoline 'bændəʊliːn
bands|man, -men 'bændz|mən, -mən
[-men]
bandstand, -s 'bændstænd ['bænstænd],
-z

39

band|y (*adj. v.*), **-ier, -iest; -ies, -ying, -ied** 'bænd|ɪ, -ɪə* [-jə*], -ɪıst [-jɪst]; -ɪz, -ɪıŋ [-jɪŋ], -ıd
bandy-legged 'bændɪlegd [ˌ-'-]
bane, -s beın, -z
bane|ful, -fully, -fulness 'beın|fʊl, -fʊlɪ [-fəlɪ], -fʊlnɪs [-nəs]
Banff, -shire bæmf [bænf], -ʃə* [-ˌʃɪə*]
Banfield 'bænfi:ld
bang (*s. v.*), **-s, -ing, -ed, -er/s** bæŋ, -z, -ɪŋ, -d, -ə*/z
Bangalore ˌbæŋgə'lɔ:* [-'lɔə*]
Banger 'beınd͡ʒə*
Bangkok ˌbæŋ'kɒk ['--]
Bangladesh ˌbæŋglə'deʃ [ˌbʌŋ-, -'deıʃ]
bangle, -s, -d 'bæŋgl, -z, -d
Bangor (*in Wales*) 'bæŋgə* (*Welsh* 'baŋgor), (*in U.S.A.*) 'bæŋgɔ:*
Banham 'bænəm
banian, -s 'bænıən [-njən, -nıæn, -njæn], -z
banish, -es, -ing, -ed, -ment/s 'bænıʃ, -ɪz, -ɪŋ, -t, -mənt/s
banister, -s 'bænıstə*, -z
banjo, -s 'bænd͡ʒəʊ [-'-], -z
bank (*s. v.*), **-s, -ing, -ed, -er/s** bæŋk, -s, -ɪŋ, -t [bæŋt], -ə*/z
Bankes bæŋks
bank-holiday, -s ˌbæŋk'hɒlədɪ [-lɪd-, -deı]
bank-note, -s 'bæŋknəʊt, -s
bank-rate, -s 'bæŋkreɪt, -s
bankrupt, -s 'bæŋkrʌpt [-rəpt], -s
bankruptc|y, -ies 'bæŋkrəpts|ı [-krʌp-], -ız
Banks bæŋks
banksia, -s 'bæŋksıə [-sjə], -z
Bannatyne 'bænətaın
banner (B.), -s 'bænə*, -z
Bannerman 'bænəmən
Banning 'bænıŋ
Bannister 'bænıstə*
bannock, -s 'bænək, -s
Bannockburn 'bænəkbə:n
banns bænz
banquet (*s. v.*), **-s, -ing, -ed** 'bæŋkwıt, -s, -ıŋ, -ıd
banqueting-hall, -s 'bæŋkwıtıŋhɔ:l, -z
banquette, -s bæŋ'ket, -s
Banquo 'bæŋkwəʊ
banshee, -s bæn'ʃi: ['--], -z
bant, -s, -ing, -ed bænt, -s, -ıŋ, -ıd
bantam (B.), -s 'bæntəm, -z
banter (*s. v.*), **-s, -ing, -ed** 'bæntə*, -z, -rıŋ, -d
Banting 'bæntıŋ
bantling, -s 'bæntlıŋ, -z
Bantry 'bæntrı

Bantu ˌbæn'tu: [ˌbɑ:n't-, *also* '-- *according to sentence-stress*]
banyan, -s 'bænıən [-njən, -nıæn, -njæn], -z
baobab, -s 'beıəʊbæb, -z
baptism, -s 'bæptızəm, -z
baptism|al, -ally bæp'tızm|l, -əlı
baptist, -s 'bæptıst, -s
baptister|y, -ies 'bæptıstər|ı, -ız
baptistr|y, -ies 'bæptıstr|ı, -ız
baptiz|e, -es, -ing, -ed bæp'taız, -ız, -ıŋ, -d
bar (*s. v. prep.*), **-s, -ring, -red** bɑ:*, -z, -rıŋ, -d
Barabbas bə'ræbəs
Barak 'beəræk [-rək]
Barat 'bærət
barb (*s. v.*), **-s, -ing, -ed** bɑ:b, -z, -ıŋ, -d
Barbad|os, -ian bɑ:'beıd|ɒs [-əs, -əʊz], -ıən [-jən]
Barbara 'bɑ:bərə
barbarian, -s bɑ:'beərıən, -z
barbaric, -ally bɑ:'bærık, -lı
barbarism, -s 'bɑ:bərızəm, -z
barbarit|y, -ies bɑ:'bærət|ı [-ıt|ı], -ız
barbariz|e (-ise), -es, -ing, -ed 'bɑ:bə- raız, -ız, -ıŋ, -d
Barbarossa ˌbɑ:bə'rɒsə
barbarous, -ly, -ness 'bɑ:bərəs, -lı, -nıs [-nəs]
Barbary 'bɑ:bərı
barbate 'bɑ:beıt [-bıt]
barbated 'bɑ:beıtıd [bɑ:'beıtıd]
barbecu|e (*s. v.*), **-es, -ing, -ed** 'bɑ:bıkju:, -z, -ıŋ [-kjuıŋ], -d
barber (B.), -s 'bɑ:bə*, -z
barberr|y, -ies 'bɑ:bər|ı, -ız
barbette, -s bɑ:'bet, -s
barbican (B.), -s 'bɑ:bıkən, -z
Barbirolli ˌbɑ:bı'rɒlı
barbitone, -s 'bɑ:bıtəʊn, -z
barbiturate, -s bɑ:'bıtjʊrət [-rıt, -reıt], -s
barbituric ˌbɑ:bı'tjʊərık [-'tjɔər-, -'tjɔ:r-, ˌbɑ:'bıtjʊrık]
Barbour 'bɑ:bə*
Barca 'bɑ:kə
barcarolle, -s ˌbɑ:kə'rəʊl [-rɒl, '---], -z
Barcelona ˌbɑ:sı'ləʊnə [-sə'l-]
Barclay 'bɑ:klı [-leı]
Barcroft 'bɑ:krɒft
bard (B.), -s, -ic bɑ:d, -z, -ık
Bardell bɑ:'del, 'bɑ:dəl [-del, -dl]
Note.—In 'Pickwick' generally pronounced bɑ:'del.
bardolatry bɑ:'dɒlətrı
Bard|olph, -sley 'bɑ:d|ɒlf, -zlı
Bardswell 'bɑ:dzwəl [-wel]

Bardwell 'bɑːdwəl [-wel]
bare (*adj.*), **-r, -st, -ly, -ness** beə*, -rə*, -rɪst, -lɪ, -nɪs [-nəs]
bare (*archaic p. tense of* bear) beə*
bareback, -ed 'beəbæk, -t
Barebones 'beəbəʊnz
barefac|ed, -edly, -edness 'beəfeɪs|t, -tlɪ [-ɪdlɪ, -'--(-)], -tnɪs [-tnəs]
barefoot 'beəfʊt
barefooted ˌbeə'fʊtɪd ['-,--]
bare-headed ˌbeə'hedɪd ['-,--]
Bareilly bə'reɪlɪ (*Hindi* bərylli)
bare-legged ˌbeə'legd ['beəlegd, -'legɪd]
bare-necked ˌbeə'nekt ['-,--]
Barfield 'bɑːfiːld
bargain (*s. v.*), **-s, -ing, -ed, -er/s** 'bɑːgɪn, -z, -ɪŋ, -d, -ə*/z
barge, -s bɑːdʒ, -ɪz
bargee, -s bɑː'dʒiː: [ˌbɑː'dʒiː:], -z
barge|man, -men 'bɑːdʒ|mən [-mæn], -mən [-men]
bargepole, -s 'bɑːdʒpəʊl, -z
Barger 'bɑːdʒə*
Bargery 'bɑːdʒərɪ
Bargh bɑːdʒ, bɑːf
Bargrave 'bɑːgreɪv
Barham (*surname*) 'bærəm, 'bɑːrəm, (*in Kent*) 'bærəm
Baring 'beərɪŋ, 'bærɪŋ
baritone, -s 'bærɪtəʊn, -z
barium 'beərɪəm
Barjesus 'bɑːˌdʒiːzəs
bark (*s. v.*), **-s, -ing, -ed, -er/s** bɑːk, -s, -ɪŋ, -t, -ə*/z
Barker 'bɑːkə*
Barkston 'bɑːkstən
barley 'bɑːlɪ
barleycorn (**B.**), **-s** 'bɑːlɪkɔːn, -z
barley-sugar 'bɑːlɪˌʃʊgə* [ˌ--'--]
barley-water 'bɑːlɪˌwɔːtə*
Barlow(e) 'bɑːləʊ
barm bɑːm
barmaid, -s 'bɑːmeɪd, -z
bar|man, -men 'bɑː|mən [-mæn], -mən [-men]
Barmby 'bɑːmbɪ
Barmecide 'bɑːmɪsaɪd
Barmouth 'bɑːməθ
barm|y, -ier, -iest 'bɑːm|ɪ, -ɪə*, -ɪɪst
barn, -s bɑːn, -z
Barnab|as, -y 'bɑːnəb|əs [-æs], -ɪ
barnacle, -s 'bɑːnəkl, -z
Barnard 'bɑːnəd
Barnardiston ˌbɑːnə'dɪstən
Barnardo bɑː'nɑːdəʊ [bə'n-]
Barnby 'bɑːnbɪ
barn-door (*s.*), **-s** ˌbɑːn'dɔː* [-'dɔə*], -z
Barnea 'bɑːnɪə [bɑː'nɪə]

Barnes bɑːnz
Barnet(t) 'bɑːnɪt
Barney 'bɑːnɪ
Barnham 'bɑːnəm
Barnicott 'bɑːnɪkət [-kɒt]
Barnoldswick (*in Lancashire*) bɑː'nəʊldzwɪk
Barnsley 'bɑːnzlɪ
Barnstaple 'bɑːnstəpl [*locally* -əbl]
barnstormer, -s 'bɑːnˌstɔːmə*, -z
Barnum 'bɑːnəm
Baroda bə'rəʊdə (*Gujarati* vəḍodra)
barograph, -s 'bærəʊgrɑːf [-græf], -s
Barolong (*Botswana tribe*) ˌbɑːrəʊ'ləʊŋ [ˌbær-, -'lɒŋ]
baromet|er/s, -ry bə'rɒmɪt|ə*/z [-mət|ə*/z], -rɪ
barometric, -al, -ally ˌbærəʊ'metrɪk, -l, -əlɪ
baron (**B.**), **-s** 'bærən, -z
baron|age/s, -ess/es 'bærən|ɪdʒ/ɪz [-rn-], -ɪs/ɪz [-es/ɪz]
baronet, -s 'bærənɪt [-rnɪt, -et], -s
baronetage, -s 'bærənɪtɪdʒ [-rn-], -ɪz
baronetc|y, -ies 'bærənɪts|ɪ [-rn-, -et-], -ɪz
baronial bə'rəʊnjəl [-nɪəl]
baron|y, -ies 'bærən|ɪ [-rn-], -ɪz
baroque bə'rɒk [-'rəʊk]
barouche, -s bə'ruːʃ [bæ'r-], -ɪz
barque, -s bɑːk, -s
Barr bɑː:*
barrack (*s. v.*), **-s, -ing, -ed** 'bærək, -s, -ɪŋ, -t
Barraclough 'bærəklʌf
barracuda ˌbærə'kuːdə [-'kjuːdə]
barrage, -s 'bærɑːʒ [bæ'rɑːʒ, -rɑːdʒ], -ɪz
barratry 'bærətrɪ
Barrat(t) 'bærət
barrel, -s 'bærəl, -z
barrel-organ, -s 'bærəlˌɔːgən, -z
barr|en, -enest, -enly, -enness 'bær|ən, -ənɪst [-ɪst], -ənlɪ, -ənnɪs [-ənnəs]
Barrett 'bærət [-ret, -rɪt]
barricad|e (*s. v.*), **-es, -ing, -ed** ˌbærɪ'keɪd [-rə'k-, '---], -z, -ɪŋ, -ɪd
Barrie 'bærɪ
barrier (**B.**), **-s** 'bærɪə*, -z
barring 'bɑːrɪŋ
Barrington 'bærɪŋtən
barrister, -s 'bærɪstə*, -z
barrister-at-law, barristers-at-law ˌbærɪstərət'lɔː, ˌbærɪstəzət'lɔː
barristerial ˌbærɪ'stɪərɪəl
Barron 'bærən
barrow (**B.**), **-s** 'bærəʊ, -z
Barrow-in-Furness ˌbærəʊɪn'fɜːnɪs [-nes]

41

Barry 'bærɪ
Barrymore 'bærɪmɔ:* [-mɔə*]
bart. (B.), barts bɑ:t, -s
Bartelot 'bɑ:tɪlət [-lɒt]
bar-tender, -s 'bɑ:ˌtendə*, -z
barter (B.) (s. v.), -s, -ing, -ed 'bɑ:tə*,
  -z, -rɪŋ, -d
Bartholomew bɑ:'θɒləmju: [bə'θ-]
Bartimeus [-maeus] ˌbɑ:tɪ'mi:əs
  [-'mɪəs]
Bartle 'bɑ:tl
Bartlett 'bɑ:tlɪt
Bartók 'bɑ:tɒk
Bartolozzi ˌbɑ:tə'lɒtsɪ
Barton 'bɑ:tn
Bart's bɑ:ts
Baruch (biblical name) 'bɑ:rʊk ['beər-,
  -rək], (modern surname) bə'ru:k
Barugh (surname, place in South
  Yorkshire) bɑ:f
Barum 'beərəm
Barwick 'bærɪk
barysphere, -s 'bærɪˌsfɪə*, -z
barytone, -s = barit-
basal 'beɪsl
basalt 'bæsɔ:lt ['bæsəlt, bə'sɔ:lt, bə'sɒlt]
basaltic bə'sɔ:ltɪk [-'sɒl-]
basan 'bæzən
Basan 'beɪsæn
bascule, -s 'bæskju:l, -z
bas|e (s. adj. v.), -es; -er, -est, -ely,
  -eness; -ing, -ed beɪs, -ɪz; -ə*, -ɪst,
  -lɪ, -nɪs [-nəs]; -ɪŋ, -t
base-ball 'beɪsbɔ:l
base-born 'beɪsbɔ:n
basecourt, -s 'beɪskɔ:t [-kɔət], -s
Baseden 'beɪzdən
baseless, -ly, -ness 'beɪslɪs [-ləs], -lɪ,
  -nɪs [-nəs]
basement, -s 'beɪsmənt -s
bases (from base) 'beɪsɪz, (plur. of basis)
  'beɪsi:z
Basford (in Nottinghamshire) 'beɪsfəd,
  (in Staffordshire) 'bæsfəd
bash, -es, -ing, -ed bæʃ, -ɪz, -ɪŋ, -t
Basham (surname) 'bæʃəm
Bashan 'beɪʃæn
Bashford 'bæʃfəd
bash|ful, -fullest, -fully, -fulness 'bæʃ|-
  fʊl, -fʊlɪst [-fəlɪst, -flɪst], -fʊlɪ [-fəlɪ,
  -flɪ], -fʊlnɪs [-nəs]
basic (B.), -ally 'beɪsɪk, -əlɪ
basil (B.), bæzl [-zɪl]
basilica, -s, -n bə'zɪlɪkə [-'sɪl-], -z, -n
basilisk, -s 'bæzɪlɪsk [-z]ɪ-], -s
basin, -s 'beɪsn, -z
Basingstoke 'beɪzɪŋstəʊk
bas|is, -es 'beɪs|ɪs, -i:z

bask, -s, -ing, -ed bɑ:sk, -s, -ɪŋ, -t
Basker (surname) 'bɑ:skə*
Baskervill(e) 'bæskəvɪl
basket, -s -ful/s 'bɑ:skɪt, -s, -fʊl/z
basket-ball, 'bɑ:skɪtbɔ:l
basket-work 'bɑ:skɪtwɜ:k
Basle bɑ:l
basque (B.), -s bæsk [bɑ:sk], -s
Basra(h) 'bæzrə ['bʌzrə, 'bæsrə]
bas-relief, -s ˌbæsrɪ'li:f [ˌbɑ:r-, ˌbɑ:sr-,
  '--ˌ-], -s
bass (fish, fibre, beer) (B.) bæs
bass (in music), -es beɪs, -ɪz
Bassanio bə'sɑ:nɪəʊ [bæ's-, -njəʊ]
basset, -s 'bæsɪt, -s
basset-horn, -s 'bæsɪthɔ:n [ˌ--'-], -z
Basset(t) 'bæsɪt
bassinet(te), -s ˌbæsɪ'net, -s
basso, -s 'bæsəʊ, -z
bassoon, -s, -ist/s bə'su:n, -z, -ɪst/s
bass-wood 'bæswʊd
bast bæst
Bastable 'bæstəbl
bastard, -s, -y 'bɑ:stəd ['bæs-], -z, -ɪ
bastardiz|e [-is|e], -es, -ing, -ed 'bæst-
  ədaɪz ['bɑ:s-], -ɪz, -ɪŋ, -d
bast|e, -es, -ing, -ed beɪst, -s, -ɪŋ, -ɪd
bastille (B.), -s bæ'sti:l (basti:j), -z
bastinad|o (s. v.), -oes, -oing, -oed
  ˌbæstɪ'nɑ:d|əʊ [-'neɪd-], -əʊz, -əʊɪŋ,
  -əʊd
bastion, -s, -ed 'bæstɪən [-tjən], -z, -d
Basuto, -s bə'su:təʊ [bə'zu:-], -z
Basutoland bə'su:təʊlænd [bə'zu:-]
bat (s. v.), -s, -ting, -ted bæt, -s, -ɪŋ, -ɪd
Ba'taan bə'tɑ:n
Batavia bə'teɪvjə [-vɪə]
Batavier ˌbætə'vɪə*
batch, -es bætʃ, -ɪz
Batchel|ar, -or 'bætʃəl|ə* [-tʃɪl-], -ə*
bat|e (B.), -es, -ing, -ed beɪt, -s, -ɪŋ, -ɪd
Bate|man, -s, -son 'beɪt|mən, -s, -sən
Batey 'beɪtɪ
ba|th (s.) (B.), -ths bɑ:|θ, -ðz
bath (v.), -s, -ing, -ed bɑ:θ, -s, -ɪŋ, -t
bath-brick, -s 'bɑ:θbrɪk, -s
bath-chair, -s ˌbɑ:θ'tʃeə*, -z
bath|e (s. v.), -es, -ing, -ed, -er/s beɪð,
  -z, -ɪŋ, -d, -ə*/z
bathetic bə'θetɪk [bæ-]
Batho 'bæθəʊ, 'beɪθəʊ
bat-horse, -s 'bæthɔ:s, -ɪz
bathos 'beɪθɒs
bathrobe, -s 'bɑ:θrəʊb, -z
bathroom, -s 'bɑ:θrʊm [-ru:m], -z
Bathsheba bæθ'ʃi:bə ['bæθʃɪbə]
bath-stone 'bɑ:θstəʊn
Bathurst 'bæθɜ:st [-θəst]

42

bathyscaphe, -s 'bæθɪskæf, -s
bathysphere, -s 'bæθɪ,sfɪə*, -z
batik bə'ti:k ['bætɪk]
batiste bæ'ti:st [bə't-] (batist)
bat|man (military), -men 'bæt|mən, -mən
batman (oriental weight), -s 'bætmən, -z
baton, -s 'bætən [-tɒn, -tɔ:ŋ] (batɔ̃), -z
Baton Rouge ,bætən'ru:ʒ
batrachian, -s bə'treɪkjən [-kɪən], -z
bats bæts
bats|man, men 'bæts|mən, -mən
battalion, -s bə'tæljən, -z
battels 'bætlz
batt|en (s. v.), -ens, -ening, -ened 'bæt|n, -nz, -n̩ɪŋ [-nɪŋ], -nd
Battenberg 'bætnbə:g
batter (s. v.), -s, -ing, -ed 'bætə*, -z, -rɪŋ, -d
battering-ram, -s 'bætərɪŋræm, -z
Battersby 'bætəzbɪ
Battersea 'bætəsɪ
batter|y, -ies 'bætər|ɪ, -ɪz
batting (s.) 'bætɪŋ
Battishill 'bætɪʃɪl [-ʃl]
batt|le (s. v.) (B.), -les, -ling, -led 'bæt|l, -lz, -lŋ [-lɪŋ], -ld
battle-axe, -s 'bætlæks, -ɪz
battle-cruiser, -s 'bætl,kru:zə*, -z
battle-cr|y, -ies 'bætlkr|aɪ, -aɪz
battledore [-door], -s 'bætldɔ:* [-dɔə*], -z
battle-dress, -es 'bætldres, -ɪz
battlefield, -s 'bætlfi:ld, -z
battle-ground, -s 'bætlgraund, -z
battlement, -s, -ed 'bætlmənt, -s, -ɪd
battle-royal, -s ,bætl'rɔɪəl, -s
battleship, -s 'bætlʃɪp, -s
battue, -s bæ'tu: [-'tju:, '--] (baty), -z
Battye 'bætɪ
Batum ba:'tu:m
Baty 'beɪtɪ
bauble, -s 'bɔ:bl, -z
Baucis 'bɔ:sɪs
Bauer 'bauə*
Baugh bɔ:
Baughan bɔ:n
Baughurst 'bɔ:ghə:st
baulk (s. v.), -s, -ing, -ed bɔ:k [bɔ:lk], -s, -ɪŋ, -t
bauxite 'bɔ:ksaɪt
Bavaria, -n/s bə'veərɪə, -n/z
bawbee, -s ,bɔ:'bi:, -z
bawd, -s; -ry, -y bɔ:d, -z; -rɪ, -ɪ
bawdy-hou|se, -ses 'bɔ:dɪhau|s, -zɪz
bawl, -s, -ing, -ed, -er/s bɔ:l, -z, -ɪŋ, -d, -ə*/z

Bax bæks
Baxandall 'bæksəndɔ:l
Baxter 'bækstə*
bay (s. adj. v.) (B.), -s, -ing, -ed, beɪ, -z, -ɪŋ, -d
bayard (B.) (horse), -s 'berəd, -z
Bayard (surname) 'beɪa:d
Bayard (airship), -s beɪ'a:d ['beɪa:d, 'berəd] (baja:r), -z
Bayeux baɪ'jɜ: [baɪ'ɜ:, old-fashioned beɪ'ju:] (bajø)
bay-lea|f, -ves 'beɪli:|f, -vz
Bayl(e)y 'beɪlɪ
Bayliss 'beɪlɪs
Baynes beɪnz
bayonet, -s 'berənɪt [-nət, -net, ,berə'net], -s
Bayreuth 'baɪrɔɪt [-'-] (bai'rɔyt)
bay-rum ,beɪ'rʌm
bay-salt ,beɪ'sɔ:lt [-'sɒlt]
Bayswater 'beɪz,wɔ:tə*
bay-tree, -s 'beɪtri:, -z
bay-window, -s ,beɪ'wɪndəu, -z
bazaar, -s bə'za:*, -z
Bazalgette 'bæzəldʒɪt [-dʒet]
bazooka, -s bə'zu:kə, -z
B.B.C. ,bi:bi:'si:
B.C. ,bi:'si:
B.C.G. ,bi:si:'dʒi:
bdellium 'delɪəm [-ljəm]
be; being, been (s.) (strong form), bɪ (weak form); 'bi:ɪŋ, bi:n [bɪn]
Beacall 'bi:kɔ:l
beach (s. v.) (B.), -es, -ing, -ed bi:tʃ, -ɪz, -ɪŋ, -t
beachcomber (B.), -s 'bi:tʃ,kəumə*, -z
beachhead, -s 'bi:tʃhed, -z
beach-la-mar ,bi:tʃlə'ma:*
beachwear 'bi:tʃweə*
beachy (B.) 'bi:tʃɪ
beacon, -s 'bi:kən, -z
Beaconsfield (place in Buckinghamshire) 'bekənzfi:ld, (title of Benjamin Disraeli) 'bi:k-
bead, -s, -ing/s, -ed, -er/s bi:d, -z, -ɪŋ/z, -ɪd, -ə*/z
beadle (B.), -s 'bi:dl, -z
Beadnall 'bi:dnəl [-nl̩]
Beadon 'bi:dn
bead|y, -ier, -iest, -iness 'bi:d|ɪ, -ɪə*, -ɪɪst, -ɪnɪs [-məs]
beagle, -s 'bi:gl, -z
beak, -s, -ed bi:k, -s, -t
beaker, -s 'bi:kə*, -z
Beal(e) bi:l
beam (s. v.), -s, -ing, -ed bi:m, -z, -ɪŋ, -d
beam-ends ,bi:m'endz ['--]
beam-engine, -s 'bi:m,endʒɪn, -z

43

Beaminster 'bemɪnstə* [*locally also* 'bemɪstə*]
Note.—'biːm- *is sometimes heard from people unfamiliar with the place.*
Beamish 'biːmɪʃ
beam|y, -ily, -iness 'biːm|ɪ, -ɪlɪ [-əlɪ], -ɪnɪs [-ɪnəs]
bean, -s biːn, -z
beanfeast, -s, -er/s 'biːnfiːst, -s, -ə*/z
beano, -s 'biːnəʊ, -z
beanstalk, -s 'biːnstɔːk, -s
bear (*s. v.*), **-s, -ing/s, bore, born(e), bearer/s** beə*, -z, -rɪŋ/z, bɔː* [bɔə*], bɔːn, 'beərə*/z
bearab|le, -ly, -leness 'beərəb|l, -lɪ, -lnɪs [-lnəs]
bear-baiting 'beə‚beɪtɪŋ
beard (**B.**), **-s, -ed** bɪəd, -z, -ɪd
Beard|er, -sley 'bɪəd|ə*, -zlɪ
beardless 'bɪədlɪs [-ləs]
Beare bɪə*
bear-garden, -s 'beə‚ɡɑːdn, -z
bearing (*s.*), **-s** 'beərɪŋ, -z
bearing-rein, -s 'beərɪŋreɪn, -z
bearish, -ly, -ness 'beərɪʃ, -lɪ, -nɪs [-nəs]
Bearsden (*in Scotland*) beəz'den
bearskin, -s 'beəskɪn, -z
Bearsted 'bɜːsted, 'beəsted
Beasley 'biːzlɪ
beast, -s biːst, -s
beastl|y, -ier, -iest, -iness 'biːstl|ɪ, -ɪə* [-jə*], -ɪɪst [-jɪst], -ɪnɪs [-nəs]
beat (*s. v.*), **-s, -ing/s, -en, -er/s** biːt, -s, -ɪŋ/z, -n, -ə*/z
beatific, -al, -ally ‚biːə'tɪfɪk [bɪə't-], -l, -əlɪ
beatification, -s bi:‚ætɪfɪ'keɪʃn [bɪ‚æ-], -z
beati|fy, -fies, -fying, -fied biː'ætɪ|faɪ [bɪ'æ-], -faɪz, -faɪɪŋ, -faɪd
beatitude, -s biː'ætɪtjuːd [bɪ'æ-], -z
beatnik, -s 'biːtnɪk, -s
Beatri|ce, -x 'bɪətrɪ|s, -ks
Beatt|ie, -y 'biːt|ɪ, -ɪ
beau, -s bəʊ, -z
Beauchamp 'biːtʃəm
Beau|clerc, -clerk 'bəʊ|kleə*, -kleə*
Beaufort 'bəʊfət [-fɔːt]
Beaufoy 'bəʊfɔɪ
Beaujolais 'bəʊʒəleɪ [-ʒɒ-] (boʒɔlɛ)
Beaulieu (*in Hampshire*) 'bjuːlɪ
Beaumaris bəʊ'mærɪs [bjuː'm-] (*Welsh* biu'maris)
Beaumont 'bəʊmənt [-mɒnt]
Beaune bəʊn
beauteous, -ly, -ness 'bjuːtjəs [-tɪəs], -lɪ, -nɪs [-nəs]

beautician, -s bjuː'tɪʃn, -z
beautiful 'bjuːtəfʊl [-tɪf-]
beautifully 'bjuːtəflɪ [-tɪf-, -fʊlɪ, -fəlɪ]
beauti|fy, -fies, -fying, -fied, -fier/s 'bjuːtɪ|faɪ, -faɪz, -faɪɪŋ, -faɪd, -faɪə*/z
beaut|y, -ies 'bjuːt|ɪ, -ɪz
beauty-parlour, -s 'bjuːtɪpɑːlə*, -z
beauty-sleep 'bjuːtɪsliːp
beauty-spot, -s 'bjuːtɪspɒt, -s
Beav|an, -en 'bev|ən, -ən
beaver (**B.**), **-s** 'biːvə*, -z
Beaverbrook 'bɪːvəbrʊk
beaver|y, -ies 'biːvər|ɪ, -ɪz
Beavis 'biːvɪs
Beavon 'bevən
Beaworthy 'biː‚wɜːðɪ
Beazley 'biːzlɪ
becalm, -s, -ing, -ed bɪ'kɑːm [bə'k-], -z, -ɪŋ, -d
became (*from* **become**) bɪ'keɪm [bə'k-]
because bɪ'kɒz [bə'kɒz, bɪkəz, *rarely* bɪ'kɔːz, *colloquially also* kɒz, kəz]
Beccles 'beklz
Becher 'biːtʃə*
Bechstein, -s 'bekstaɪn, -z
Bechuana, -s, -land ‚betʃʊ'ɑːnə [be'tʃwɑː-], -z, -lænd
beck (**B.**), **-s** bek, -s
Becke bek
Beckenham 'bekənəm [-kŋəm, -knəm]
Becket(t) 'bekɪt
Beckles 'beklz
Beckley 'beklɪ
beck|on, -ons, -oning, -oned 'bek|ən, -əns, -ŋɪŋ [-ənɪŋ, -nɪŋ], -ənd
Beck|ton, -with 'bek|tən, -wɪθ
Becky 'bekɪ
becloud, -s, -ing, -ed bɪ'klaʊd [bə'k-], -z, -ɪŋ, -ɪd
becom|e, -es, -ing/ly, -ingness, became bɪ'kʌm [bə'k-], -z, -ɪŋ/lɪ, -ŋnɪs [-nəs], bɪ'keɪm [bə'k-]
Becontree 'bekəntriː
bed (*s. v.*), **-s, -ding, -ded** bed, -z, -ɪŋ, -ɪd
bedad bɪ'dæd [bə'd-]
Bedale (*North Yorkshire*) 'biːdl, 'biːdeɪl
Bedales 'biːdeɪlz
bedaub, -s, -ing, -ed bɪ'dɔːb [bə'd-], -z, -ɪŋ, -d
bedazz|le, -les, -ling, -led bɪ'dæz|l [bə-], -lz, -lɪŋ [-l̩ɪŋ], -ld
bedchamber, -s 'bed‚tʃeɪmbə*, -z
bedclothes 'bedkləʊðz [*old-fashioned* -kləʊz]
bedder, -s 'bedə*, -z
Beddgelert beð'gelət [-lɜːt] (*Welsh* be:ð'gelert)
bedding (*s.*) 'bedɪŋ

Beddoes 'bedəuz
Bede biːd
bedeck, -s, -ing, -ed bɪ'dek [bə'd-], -s, -ɪŋ, -t
Bedel 'biːdl, bɪ'del [bə'd-]
bedel(l), -s be'del [bɪ'd-, bə'd-], -z
bedev|il, -ils, -lling, -lled bɪ'dev|l [bə-], -lz, -lɪŋ [-lɪŋ], -ld
bedevilment bɪ'devlmənt [bə-]
bed|ew, -ews, -ewing, -ewed bɪ'd|juː [bə'd-], -juːz, -juːɪŋ [-jʊɪŋ], -juːd
bedfellow, -s 'bed,feləu, -z
Bedford, -shire 'bedfəd, -ʃə* [-,ʃɪə*]
bedim, -s, -ming, -med bɪ'dɪm [bə'd-], -z, -ɪŋ, -d
Bedivere 'bedɪ,vɪə*
bediz|en, -ens, -ening, -ened bɪ'daɪz|n [bə'd-, -'dɪz-], -nz, -nɪŋ, -nd
bedjacket, -s 'bed,dʒækɪt, -s
Bedlam 'bedləm
Bedlamite, -s 'bedləmaɪt, -s
bedlinen 'bed,lɪnɪn
bedmaker, -s 'bed,meɪkə*, -z
Bedouin, -s 'bedʊɪn, -z
bedpan, -s 'bedpæn, -z
bedplate, -s 'bedpleɪt, -s
bedpost, -s 'bedpəust, -s
bedragg|le, -les, -ling, -led bɪ'dræg|l [bə'd-], -lz, -lɪŋ [-lɪŋ], -ld
bed-ridden 'bed,rɪdn
bedrock, -s 'bedrɒk [,bed'rɒk], -s
bedroom, -s 'bedrʊm [-ruːm], -z
Bedruthan bɪ'drʌðən [bə'd-]
Beds. bedz
bedside 'bedsaɪd
bedsit, -s 'bedsɪt, -s
bedsitter, -s ,bed'sɪtə* ['-,--], -z
bed-sore, -s 'bedsɔː*, [-sɔə*], -z
bedspread, -s 'bedspred, -z
bedstead, -s 'bedsted [-stɪd], -z
bedstraw, -s 'bedstrɔː, -z
bedtime 'bedtaɪm
Bedwell 'bedwəl [-wel]
bee (B.), -s biː, -z
Beeby 'biːbɪ
beech (B.), -es, -en biːtʃ, -ɪz, -ən
Beecham 'biːtʃəm
Beecher 'biːtʃə*
Beeching 'biːtʃɪŋ
beechnut, -s 'biːtʃnʌt, -s
bee-eater, -s 'biː,iːtə*, -z
bee|f, -ves biː|f, -vz
beefburger, -s 'biːf,bɜːgə*, -z
beefeater, -s 'biːf,iːtə*, -z
beefsteak, -s biːf'steɪk [also '--], -s
beef-tea ,biːf'tiː
beef|y, -ier, -iest, -ily, -iness 'biːf|ɪ, -ɪə*, -ɪɪst, -ɪlɪ [-əlɪ], -ɪnɪs [-ɪnəs]

bee-hive, -s 'biːhaɪv, -z
bee-line, -s 'biːlaɪn [,biː'laɪn], -z
Beelzebub biː'elzɪbʌb [bɪ'el-]
been (from be) biːn [bɪn]
beer (B.), -s bɪə*, -z
Beerbohm 'bɪəbəum
beer-hou|se, -ses 'bɪəhaʊ|s, -zɪz
beer-money 'bɪə,mʌnɪ
Beersheba bɪə'ʃiːbə ['bɪəʃɪbə]
beer|y, -ier, -iest, -ily, -iness 'bɪər|ɪ, -ɪə*, -ɪɪst, -əlɪ [-ɪlɪ], -ɪnɪs [-ɪnəs]
Beesl(e)y 'biːzlɪ
bee-sting, -s 'biːstɪŋ, -z
beestings 'biːstɪŋz
beeswax 'biːzwæks
beeswing 'biːzwɪŋ
beet, -s biːt, -s
Beetham 'biːθəm
Beethoven (composer) 'beɪthəuvn, (London street) 'biːthəʊvn
†beet|le (s. v.), -les, -ling, -led 'biːt|l, -lz, -lɪŋ [-lɪŋ], -ld
Beeton 'biːtn
beetroot, -s 'biːtruːt, -s
beeves (plur. of beef) biːvz
be|fall, -falls, -falling, -fell, -fallen bɪ|'fɔːl [bə|-], -'fɔːlz, -fɔːlɪŋ, -'fel, -'fɔːlən
befit, -s, -ting/ly, -ted bɪ'fɪt [bə'f-], -s, -ɪŋ/lɪ, -ɪd
before bɪ'fɔː* [bə'f-, -'fɔə*]
beforehand bɪ'fɔːhænd [bə'f-, -'fɔəh-]
before - mentioned bɪ'fɔː,menʃnd [-'fɔə,m-, -,-'--]
beforetime bɪ'fɔːtaɪm [bə'f-, -'fɔət-]
befoul, -s, -ing, -ed bɪ'faʊl [bə'f-], -z, -ɪŋ, -d
befriend, -s, -ing, -ed bɪ'frend [bə'f-], -z -ɪŋ, -ɪd
beg, -s, -ging, -ged beg, -z, -ɪŋ, -d
begad bɪ'gæd [bə'g-]
began (from begin) bɪ'gæn [bə'g-]
be|get, -gets, -getting, -gat, -got, -gotten bɪ|'get [bə|-], -'gets, -'getɪŋ, -'gæt, -'gɒt, -'gɒtn
beggar, -s 'begə*, -z
beggarl|y, -iness 'begəl|ɪ, -ɪnɪs [-ɪnəs]
beggar-my-neighbour ,begəmɪ'neɪbə*
beggary 'begərɪ
Beggs begz
be|gin, -gins, -ginning/s, -gan, -gun, -ginner/s bɪ|'gɪn [bə|-], -'gɪnz, -'gɪnɪŋ/z, -'gæn, -'gʌn, -'gɪnə*/z
begone bɪ'gɒn [bə'g-]
begonia, -s bɪ'gəunjə [bə'g-, -nɪə], -z
begorra bɪ'gɒrə [bə'g-]
begot, -ten (from beget) bɪ'gɒt [bə'g-], -n

45

begrim|e, -es, -ing, -ed bɪˈgraɪm [bəˈg-], -z, -ɪŋ, -d

begrudge, -es, -ing, -ed bɪˈgrʌdʒ [bəˈg-], -ɪz, -ɪŋ, -d

beguil|e, -es, -ing, -ed bɪˈgaɪl [bəˈg-], -z, -ɪŋ, -d

Begum, -s ˈbeɪgəm [old-fashioned ˈbiːg-], -z

begun (from begin) bɪˈgʌn [bəˈg-]

behalf bɪˈhɑːf [bəˈh-]

Behar (surname) ˈbiːhɑ*, (former spelling of Bihar, q.v.) bɪˈhɑː*

behav|e, -es, -ing, -ed bɪˈheɪv [bəˈh-], -z, -ɪŋ, -d

behaviour, -s bɪˈheɪvjə* [bəˈh-], -z

behaviouri|sm, -st/s bɪˈheɪvjərɪ|zəm [bəˈh-], -st/s

behead, -s, -ing, -ed bɪˈhed [bəˈh-], -z, -ɪŋ, -ɪd

beheld (from behold) bɪˈheld [bəˈh-]

behemoth (B.) bɪˈhiːmɒθ [ˈbiːhɪməʊθ]

behest, -s bɪˈhest [bəˈh-], -s

behind, -hand bɪˈhaɪnd [bəˈh-], -hænd

be|hold, -holds, -holding, -held, -holder/s bɪ|ˈhəʊld [bə|-], -ˈhəʊldz, -ˈhəʊldɪŋ, -ˈheld, -ˈhəʊldə*/z

beholden bɪˈhəʊldən [bəˈh-]

behoof bɪˈhuːf [bəˈh-]

behov|e, -es, -ing, -ed bɪˈhəʊv [bəˈh-], -z, -ɪŋ, -d

Behrens (English name), ˈbeərənz

beige beɪʒ [beɪdʒ]

being (s.), -s ˈbiːɪŋ, -z

being (from be) ˈbiːɪŋ

Beira ˈbaɪərə (Port. ˈbeɪrɐ)

Beirut ˌbeɪˈruːt

Beit baɪt

Beith biːθ

bejan, -s ˈbiːdʒən, -z

bejewel, -s, -led, bejewelling bɪˈdʒuːəl [-ˈdʒʊəl, -ˈdʒuːl, -ˈdʒuːɪl, -ˈdʒʊɪl], -z, -d, bɪˈdʒuːəlɪŋ [bɪˈdʒʊəlɪŋ, bɪˈdʒuːɪlɪŋ, -ˈdʒʊɪlɪŋ]

bel, -s bel, -z

belab|our, -ours, -ouring, -oured bɪˈleɪb|ə* [bəˈl-], -əz, -ərɪŋ, -əd

belated, -ly, -ness bɪˈleɪtɪd [bəˈl-], -lɪ, -nɪs [-nəs]

belaud, -s, -ing, -ed bɪˈlɔːd [bəˈl-], -z, -ɪŋ, -ɪd

Belaugh ˈbiːlɔː

belay, -s, -ing, -ed bɪˈleɪ [bəˈl-], -z, -ɪŋ, -d

belch, -es, -ing, -ed, -er/s beltʃ [belʃ], -ɪz, -ɪŋ, -t, -ə*/z

Belcher ˈbeltʃə*, ˈbelʃə*

beldam(e), -s ˈbeldəm, -z

beleaguer, -s, -ing, -ed, -er/s bɪˈliːgə* [bəˈl-], -z, -rɪŋ, -d, -rə*/z

belemnite, -s ˈbeləmnaɪt, -s

Belfast ˌbelˈfɑːst [also ˈ--, esp. when attributive]

belfr|y, -ies ˈbelfr|ɪ, -ɪz

Belg|ian/s, -ic ˈbeldʒ|ən/z, -ɪk

Belgium ˈbeldʒəm

Belgrade ˌbelˈgreɪd

Belgrave ˈbelgreɪv

Belgravia, -n belˈgreɪvjə [-vɪə], -n

Belial ˈbiːljəl [-lɪəl]

bel|ie, -ies, -ying, -ied bɪˈl|aɪ [bəˈl-], -aɪz, -aɪɪŋ, -aɪd

belief, -s bɪˈliːf [bəˈl-], -s

believ|e, -es, -ing/ly, -ed, -er/s; -able bɪˈliːv [bəˈl-], -z, -ɪŋ/lɪ, -d, -ə*/z; -əbl

belike bɪˈlaɪk [bəˈl-]

Belinda bɪˈlɪndə [beˈl-, bəˈl-]

Belisha bɪˈliːʃə [beˈl-, bəˈl-]

belitt|le, -les, -ling, -led bɪˈlɪt|l [bəˈl-], -lz, -lɪŋ, [-lɪŋ], -ld

Belize beˈliːz [bəˈl-]

bell (s. v.) (B.), -s, -ing, -ed bel, -z, -ɪŋ, -d

Bella ˈbelə

belladonna ˌbeləˈdɒnə

Bellamy ˈbeləmɪ

Bellatrix (star) ˈbelətrɪks [beˈleɪtrɪks, bəˈleɪt-]

bell-buoy, -s ˈbelbɔɪ, -z

belle (B.), -s bel, -z

Belleisle beˈliːl

Belle Isle ˌbelˈaɪl

Bellerophon bəˈlerəfn [bɪˈl-]

belles lettres ˌbelˈletrə [-ˈletə*] (bɛlɛtr̩)

Bellevue ˌbelˈvju: [ˈbelvjuː]

Bellew ˈbelju:

bell-founder, -s ˈbel͵faʊndə*, -z

bell-glass, -es ˈbelglɑːs, -ɪz

bell-hanger, -s ˈbel͵hæŋə*, -z

bellicose, -ly ˈbelɪkəʊs, -lɪ

bellicosity ˌbelɪˈkɒsɪtɪ [-ɪtɪ]

belligerency bɪˈlɪdʒərənsɪ [beˈl-, bəˈl-, -dʒrən-]

belligerent, -s bɪˈlɪdʒərənt [beˈl-, bəˈl-, -dʒrənt], -s

Bellingham (in Northumberland) ˈbelɪndʒəm, (surname) ˈbelɪndʒəm, ˈbelɪŋəm, (S. London) ˈbelɪŋəm

bell|man, men ˈbel|mən [-mæn], -mən [-men]

bell-metal ˈbel͵metl

Belloc ˈbelɒk

Bellot ˈbelɒt

bellow, -s, -ing, -ed ˈbeləʊ, -z, -ɪŋ, -d

bellows (s.) ˈbeləʊz

Bellows ˈbeləʊz

bell-ringer, -s ˈbel͵rɪŋə*, -z

bell-rope, -s 'belrəup, -s
bell-shaped 'belʃeɪpt
bell-tent, -s 'beltent, -s
bell-tower, -s 'bel,tauə*, -z
bell-wether, -s 'bel,weðə*, -z
bell|y (s. v.), -ies, -ying, -ied 'bel|ɪ, -ɪz, -ɪŋ, -ɪd
belly-ache, -s 'belɪeɪk, -s
belly-band, -s 'belɪbænd, -z
bellyful, -s 'belɪful, -z
Belmont 'belmɒnt [-mənt]
Beloe 'biːləu
belong, -s, -ing/s, -ed bɪ'lɒŋ [bə'l-], -z, -ɪŋ/z, -d
beloved (used predicatively) bɪ'lʌvd [bə'l-], (used attributively or as noun) bɪ'lʌvd [bə'l-, -vɪd]
below bɪ'ləu [bə'l-]
Belsh|am, -aw 'belʃ|əm, -ɔː
Belshazzar bel'ʃæzə*
Belsize 'belsaɪz
Belstead 'belstɪd [-sted]
belt (B.), -s, -ed belt, -s, -ɪd
Belteshazzar ,beltɪ'ʃæzə*
belting, -s 'beltɪŋ, -z
Beltingham (in Northumberland) 'beltɪndʒəm
Belton 'beltən
Beluchistan bə'luːtʃɪstɑːn [bə'l-, bɪ'l-, -tæn, -,--'-]
belvedere (B.), -s 'belvɪ,dɪə* [-və-, ,belvɪ'd-], -z
Belvoir (castle) 'biːvə*, (in names of streets, etc.) 'belvwɔː* [-vɔɪə*, -vɔə*, -vɔː*]
bema, -s, -ta 'biːmə, -z, -tə
Beman 'biːmən
Bembridge 'bembrɪdʒ
Bemerton 'bemətən
bemoan, -s, -ing, -ed bɪ'məun [bə'm-], -z, -ɪŋ, -d
bemus|e, -es, -ing, -ed bɪ'mjuːz [bə'm-], -ɪz, -ɪŋ, -d
Ben ben
Benares (old form of Banaras, q.v.) bɪ'nɑːrɪz [be'n-, bə'n-]
Benbow 'benbəu
bench, -es benʧ, -ɪz
bencher, -s 'benʧə*, -z
bend (s. v.), -s, -ing, -ed, bent bend, -z, -ɪŋ, -ɪd, bent
beneath bɪ'niːθ [bə'n-]
Benedicite, -s ,benɪ'daɪsɪtɪ [,bene'diː-tʃɪtɪ, -ətɪ], -z
Benedick, -s 'benɪdɪk, -s
Benedict 'benɪdɪkt, 'benɪt
benedictine (liqueur), -s ,benɪ'dɪktiːn, -z

Benedictine (monk), -s ,benɪ'dɪktɪn [-taɪn], -z
Note.—Members of the Order pronounce -tɪn.
benediction, -s ,benɪ'dɪkʃn, -z
Benedictus, -es ,benɪ'dɪktəs [,bene-'dɪktʊs], -ɪz
benefaction, -s ,benɪ'fækʃn ['benɪf-], -z
benefactor, -s 'benɪfæktə* [,benɪ'f-], -z
benefactress, -es 'benɪfæktrɪs [,benɪ'f-, -tres], -ɪz
benefic bɪ'nefɪk
benefice, -s, -d 'benɪfɪs, -ɪz, -t
beneficen|ce, -t/ly bɪ'nefɪsən|s [bə'n-], -t/lɪ
benefici|al, -ally, -alness ,benɪ'fɪʃ|l, -əlɪ, -lnɪs [-nəs]
beneficiar|y, -ies ,benɪ'fɪʃər|ɪ [-ʃɪə-, -ʃjə-], -ɪz
benefit (s. v.), -s, -ing, -ed 'benɪfɪt, -s, -ɪŋ, -ɪd
Benelux 'benɪlʌks
Benenden 'benəndən
Bene't 'benɪt
Benet 'benɪt
Benét (American surname) be'neɪ
benevolen|ce, -t/ly bɪ'nevələn|s [bə'n-, -vl-, -vʊl-], -t/lɪ
Bengal ,ben'gɔːl [,ben'g-, occasionally also '-- when followed by a stress]
Bengali, -s ben'gɔːlɪ [ben'g-], -z
bengal-light, -s ,bengɔːl'laɪt [,beng-], -s
Benge (surname) bendʒ
Benger (food) 'bendʒə* ['beŋgə*]
Benham 'benəm
Benians 'benɪənz [-njənz]
benighted bɪ'naɪtɪd [bə'n-]
benign, -est, -ly bɪ'naɪn [bə'n-], -ɪst, -lɪ
benignan|cy, -t/ly bɪ'nɪgnən|sɪ [bə'n-], -t/lɪ
benignity bɪ'nɪgnətɪ [bə'n-, -ɪtɪ]
Benin be'nɪn [bɪ'n-, bə'n-]
benison, -s 'benɪzn [-ɪsn], -z
Benis(s)on 'benɪsn
Benjamin 'bendʒəmɪn [-mən]
Benjamite, -s 'bendʒəmaɪt, -s
Bennet(t) 'benɪt
Bennette be'net [bə'n-]
Ben Nevis ,ben'nevɪs
Bennington 'benɪŋtən
Benoliel ,benə'lɪəl [-'liːl]
Bensham (near Newcastle) 'benʃəm
Bensley 'benzlɪ
Benson 'bensn
bent (s.), -s bent, -s
bent (from bend) bent
Benten 'bentən
Bentham 'bentəm [-nθəm]

47

Bentinck (*surname*) 'bentɪŋk, *old-fashioned* 'bentɪk, (*as name of street*) 'bentɪŋk
Bentley, -s 'bentlɪ, -z
Benton 'bentən
benumb, -s, -ing, -ed bɪ'nʌm [bə'n-], -z, -ɪŋ, -d
benzedrine 'benzədri:n [-drɪn]
benzene [-zine] 'benzi:n [-'-]
benzoic ben'zəʊɪk ['benzəʊɪk]
benzoin 'benzəʊɪn
benzol 'benzɒl
benzoline 'benzəʊli:n
Beowulf 'beɪəʊwʊlf
bequea|th, -ths, -thing, -thed bɪ'kwi:|ð [bə'k-, -i:|θ], -ðz [-θs], -ðɪŋ, -ðd [-θt]
bequest, -s bɪ'kwest [bə'k-], -s
berat|e, -es, -ing, -ed bɪ'reɪt [bə-], -s, -ɪŋ, -ɪd
Berber, -s 'bɜːbə*, -z
berceuse beə'sɜːz [bɛrsø:z]
Bere bɪə*
Berea bə'rɪə [bɪ'r-]
bereav|e, -es, -ing, -ed, bereft bɪ'ri:v [bə'r-], -z, -ɪŋ, -d, bɪ'reft [bə'r-]
bereavement, -s bɪ'ri:vmənt [bə'r-], -s
bereft (*from* bereave) bɪ'reft [bə'r-]
Berengaria ˌberɪŋ'geərɪə [-reŋ-, -rəŋ-]
Berenice (*in ancient Egypt, etc.*) ˌberɪ-'naɪsi: [-sɪ], (*opera by Handel*) ˌberɪ'ni:tʃɪ
Beresford 'berɪzfəd [-ɪsf-]
beret, -s 'bereɪ ['berɪ], -z ['berɪt, -s]
berg, -s bɜːg, -z
bergamot, -s 'bɜːgəmɒt [-mət], -s
Bergen 'bɜːgən ['beəg-]
Berger (*English surname*) 'bɜːdʒə*
beriberi ˌberɪ'berɪ
Bering 'berɪŋ ['bɪər-, 'beər-]
Berkeleian bɑː'kli:ən [-'klɪən]
Berkeley (*in England*) 'bɑːklɪ [*rarely* 'bɜːk-], (*in U.S.A.*) 'bɜːklɪ
berkelium bɑː'ki:lɪəm [-ljəm, 'bɜːklɪəm]
Berkhamsted [-mpstead] 'bɜːkəmpstɪd [-sted, *less commonly* 'bɑːk-]
Note.—*The usual pronunciation is* 'bɜːk-, *but the form* 'bɑːk- *is used by some residents.*
Berks. bɑːks [*rarely* bɜːks]
Berkshire 'bɑːkʃə* [-ˌʃɪə*, *rarely* 'bɜːk-]
Berlin (*in Germany*) bɜː'lɪn [*occasionally also* '-- *when attributive*], (*surname*) 'bɜːlɪn, bɜː'lɪn, (*town in U.S.A.*) 'bɜːlɪn
Berlioz (*composer*) 'beəlɪəʊz ['bɜːl-] (bɛrljo:z)
Berlitz 'bɜːlɪts [-'-]
Bermondsey 'bɜːməndzɪ

Bermuda, -s bə'mju:də, -z
Bernard (*Christian name*) 'bɜːnəd, (*surname*) bɜː'nɑːd, 'bɜːnəd
Bern(e) bɜːn [beən]
Berners 'bɜːnəz
Bernese ˌbɜː'ni:z [*also* '-- *when attributive*]
Bernice (*biblical name*) bɜː'naɪsi: [-sɪ], (*modern Christian name*) 'bɜːnɪs, (*surname*) 'bɜːnɪs, bɜː'ni:s
Bernstein 'bɜːnstaɪn, -sti:n
Berowne bə'rəʊn
Berridge 'berɪdʒ
berr|y (B.), -ies 'ber|ɪ, -ɪz
bersaglieri ˌbeəsɑːlɪ'eərɪ: [-rɪ] (bersaʎ'ʎe:ri)
berserk, -s, -er/s bə'zɜːk [bɜː-, '-sɜːk], -s, -ə*/z
berth (*s.*), -s bɜːθ, -s [bɜːðz]
berth (*v.*), -s, -ing, -ed bɜːθ, -s, -ɪŋ, -t
Bertha 'bɜːθə
Berthold 'bɜːθəʊld
Bertie (*Christian name*) 'bɜːtɪ, (*surname*) 'bɑːtɪ, 'bɜːtɪ
Bertram 'bɜːtrəm
Berwick, -shire 'berɪk, -ʃə* [-ˌʃɪə*]
beryl (B.), -s 'berəl [-rɪl], -z
beryllium be'rɪlɪəm [bə'r-, -ljəm]
Besant 'besənt, 'bezənt, bɪ'zænt [bə'z-]
beseech, -es, -ing/ly, besought bɪ'si:tʃ [bə's-], -ɪz, -ɪŋ/lɪ, bɪ'sɔːt [bə's-]
beseem, -s, -ing, -ed bɪ'si:m [bə's-], -z, -ɪŋ, -d
beset, -s -ting bɪ'set [bə's-], -s, -ɪŋ
beshrew bɪ'ʃru: [bə'ʃ-]
beside, -s bɪ'saɪd [bə's-], -z
besieg|e, -es, -ing, -ed, -er/s bɪ'si:dʒ [bə's-], -ɪz, -ɪŋ, -d, -ə*/z
Besley 'bezlɪ
besmear, -s, -ing, -ed bɪ'smɪə* [bə's-], -z, -rɪŋ, -d
besmirch, -es, -ing, -ed bɪ'smɜːtʃ [bə's-], -ɪz, -ɪŋ, -t
besom, -s 'bi:zəm ['bɪz-], -z
besotted, -ly, -ness bɪ'sɒtɪd [bə's-], -lɪ, -nɪs [-nəs]
besought (*from* beseech) bɪ'sɔːt [bə's-]
bespang|le, -les, -ling, -led bɪ'spæŋg|l [bə's-], -lz, -lɪŋ [-l̩ŋ], -ld
bespatter, -s, -ing, -ed bɪ'spætə* [bə's-], -z, -rɪŋ, -d
bespeak, -s, -ing, bespoke, bespoken bɪ'spi:k [bə's-], -s, -ɪŋ, bɪ'spəʊk [bə's-], bɪ'spəʊkən [bə's-]
bespectacled bɪ'spektəkld [-tɪk-]
besprink|le, -les, -ling, -led bɪ'sprɪŋk|l [bə's-], -lz, -lɪŋ [-l̩ŋ], -ld
Bess bes

Bessarabia ˌbesəˈreɪbjə [-bɪə]
Bessborough ˈbezbrə
Bessemer ˈbesɪmə* [-səmə*]
Besses o' th' Barn ˌbesɪzəðˈbɑːn
Bessie ˈbesɪ
best (adj. adv. v.) (B.), -s, -ing, -ed best,
 -s, -ɪŋ, -ɪd
bestial, -ly, -ism ˈbestjəl [-tɪəl], -ɪ,
 -ɪzəm
bestialit|y, -ies ˌbestɪˈælət|ɪ [-ɪt|ɪ], -ɪz
bestiar|y, -ies ˈbestɪər|ɪ [-tjə-], -ɪz
bestir, -s, -ring, -red bɪˈstɜː* [bəˈs-], -z,
 -rɪŋ, -d
best|ow, -ows, -owing, -owed bɪˈst|əʊ
 [bəˈs-], -əʊz, -əʊɪŋ, -əʊd
bestowal, -s bɪˈstəʊəl [bəˈs-], -z
bestrid|e, -es, -ing, bestrode, bestridden
 bɪˈstraɪd [bəˈs-], -z, -ɪŋ, bɪˈstrəʊd
 [bəˈs-], bɪˈstrɪdn [bəˈs-]
Beswick ˈbezɪk
bet (s. v.) (B.), -s, -ting, -ted, -tor/s bet,
 -s, -ɪŋ, -ɪd, -ə*/z
beta, -s ˈbiːtə, -z
be|take, -takes, -taking, -took, -taken
 bɪ|ˈteɪk [bə-], -ˈteɪks, -ˈteɪkɪŋ, -ˈtʊk,
 -ˈteɪkən
betel, -nut/s ˈbiːtl, -nʌt/s
Betelgeuse ˌbiːtlˈʒɜːz [ˌbet-, ˈbetldʒuːz]
bête noire, -s ˌbeɪtˈnwɑː* [ˌbet-]
 (bɛːtnwaːr)
Bethany ˈbeθənɪ [-θŋɪ]
Bethel ˈbeθl [beˈθel]
 Note.—When used to denote a nonconformist chapel, the pronunciation is ˈbeθl.
Bethesda beˈθezdə [bɪˈθ-, bəˈθ-]
bethink, -s, -ing, bethought bɪˈθɪŋk
 [bəˈθ-], -s, -ɪŋ, bɪˈθɔːt [bəˈθ-]
Bethlehem ˈbeθlɪhem [-lɪəm, -ljəm]
Bethnal ˈbeθnəl
Bethphage ˈbeθfədʒɪ
Bethsaida beθˈseɪdə [-ˈsaɪdə]
Bethune (surname) ˈbiːtn, (in names of
 streets, etc.) beˈθjuːn [bɪˈθ-, bəˈθ-]
Béthune (French town) beˈθjuːn [bɪˈθ-,
 bəˈθ-, -ˈtjuːn, -ˈtuːn] (betyn)
betide bɪˈtaɪd [bəˈt-]
betimes bɪˈtaɪmz [bəˈt-]
Betjeman ˈbetʃəmən [-tjə-]
betok|en, -ens, -ening, -ened bɪˈtəʊk|ən
 [bəˈt-], -ənz, -ŋɪŋ [-ənɪŋ], -ənd
betony ˈbetənɪ
betook (from betake) bɪˈtʊk [bəˈt-]
betray, -s, -ing, -ed, -er/s bɪˈtreɪ
 [bəˈt-], -z, -ɪŋ, -d, -ə*/z [-ˈtreə*/z]
betrayal, -s bɪˈtreɪəl [bəˈt-, -ˈtreɪl], -z
betro|th, -ths, -thing, -thed bɪˈtrəʊ|ð
 [bəˈt-, əʊ|θ], -ðz [-θs], -ðɪŋ, -ðd [-θt]

betrothal, -s bɪˈtrəʊðl [bəˈt-], -z
Betsy ˈbetsɪ
Betteley ˈbetəlɪ
better (s. adj. v.), -s, -ing, -ed ˈbetə*, -z,
 -rɪŋ, -d
betterment ˈbetəmənt
betting, -s ˈbetɪŋ, -z
Bettws ˈbetəs (Welsh ˈbetus)
Bettws-y-Coed ˌbetəsɪˈkɔɪd [-tʊsɪ-,
 -təzɪ-, -ˈkəʊɪd] (Welsh ˈbetusəˈkoɪd)
Betty ˈbetɪ
between bɪˈtwiːn [bəˈt-]
betweentimes bɪˈtwiːntaɪmz [bəˈt-]
betwixt bɪˈtwɪkst [bəˈt-]
Beulah ˈbjuːlə
Beurle bɜːl
beurré (pear), -s ˈbjʊərɪ, -z
Beuthin ˈbjuːθɪn
Bevan ˈbevən
bev|el (s. v.), -els, -elling, -elled ˈbev|l,
 -lz, -lɪŋ [-əlɪŋ], -ld
Beven ˈbevən
beverage, -s ˈbevərɪdʒ, -ɪz
Beveridge ˈbevərɪdʒ
Beverley ˈbevəlɪ
Beves ˈbiːvɪs
Bevin ˈbevɪn
Bevis ˈbiːvɪs, ˈbevɪs
bev|y, -ies ˈbev|ɪ, -ɪz
bewail, -s, -ing, -ed bɪˈweɪl [bəˈw-], -z,
 -ɪŋ, -d
beware bɪˈweə* [bəˈw-]
Bewick(e) ˈbjuːɪk [ˈbjʊɪk]
bewild|er, -ers, -ering/ly, -ered,
 -erment/s bɪˈwɪld|ə* [bəˈw-], -əz,
 -ərɪŋ/lɪ, -əd, -əmənt/s
bewitch, -es, -ing/ly, -ed, -ment/s
 bɪˈwɪtʃ [bəˈw-], -ɪz, -ɪŋ/lɪ, -t, -mənt/s
Bewley ˈbjuːlɪ
bewrayeth bɪˈreɪθ [bəˈr-]
Bexhill ˌbeksˈhɪl
Bexley ˈbekslɪ
Bey, -s beɪ, -z
beyond bɪˈjɒnd [bɪˈɒnd]
Beyrout(h) (former spelling of Beirut)
 ˌbeɪˈruːt
Beyts beɪts
bezant, -s ˈbezənt, -s
bezel, -s ˈbezl, -z
bezique bɪˈziːk [beˈz-, bəˈz-]
bheest|y, -ies ˈbiːst|ɪ, -ɪz
Biarritz ˌbɪəˈrɪts [ˈ--] (bjarits)
bias (s. v.), -(s)es, -(s)ing, -(s)ed ˈbaɪəs,
 -ɪz, -ɪŋ, -t
biax|al, -ial baɪˈæks|l -rəl [-jəl]
bib, -s bɪb, -z
Bibby ˈbɪbɪ
Bible, -s ˈbaɪbl, -z

49

biblic|al, -ally 'bɪblɪk|l, -əlɪ
bibliograph|er/s, -y, -ies ˌbɪblɪ'ɒ-grəf|ə*/z, -ɪ, -ɪz
bibliolat|er/s, -ry ˌbɪblɪ'ɒlət|ə*/z, -rɪ
bibliomania ˌbɪblɪəʊ'meɪnjə [-nɪə]
bibliomaniac, -s ˌbɪblɪəʊ'meɪnɪæk [-njæk], -s
bibliophile, -s 'bɪblɪəʊfaɪl [-ljəf-], -z
bibulous 'bɪbjʊləs
bicarbonate, -s baɪ'kɑːbənət [ˌbaɪ'k-, -bnət, -bnət, -eɪt, -ɪt], -s
bice baɪs
Bice 'biːtʃɪ, baɪs
bicentenar|y (s. adj.), -ies ˌbaɪsen'tiː-nər|ɪ [-'ten-, baɪ'sentɪn-], -ɪz
bicentennial ˌbaɪsen'tenjəl [-nɪəl]
biceps, -es 'baɪseps, -ɪz
Bicester 'bɪstə*
bichloride ˌbaɪ'klɔːraɪd
bichromate ˌbaɪ'krəʊmeɪt [-mɪt]
bicker, -s, -ing/s, -ed, -er/s 'bɪkə*, -z, -rɪŋ/z, -d, -rə*/z
Bickerstaff 'bɪkəstɑːf
Bickersteth 'bɪkəsteθ [-stɪθ]
Bickerton 'bɪkətən
Bickford 'bɪkfəd
Bick|leigh, -ley 'bɪk|lɪ, -lɪ
Bicknell 'bɪknəl
bicuspid, -s ˌbaɪ'kʌspɪd [bɪ'k-], -z
bicyc|le (s. v.), -les, -ling, -led 'baɪsɪk|l [-səkl], -lz, -lɪŋ, -ld
bicyclist, -s 'baɪsɪklɪst [-sək-], -s
bid (s.), -s bɪd, -z
bid (v.) (at auction), -s, -ding, -der/s bɪd, -z, -ɪŋ, -ə*/z
bid (v.) (command), -s, -ding, bade, bidden bɪd, -z, -ɪŋ, bæd [beɪd], 'bɪdn
Bidder 'bɪdə*
Biddle 'bɪdl
Biddulph 'bɪdʌlf [-dəlf]
bid|e (B.), -es, -ing, -ed baɪd, -z, -ɪŋ, -ɪd
Bideford 'bɪdɪfəd
Biden 'baɪdn
bidet, -s 'biːdeɪ, -z (bidɛ)
biennial, -ly baɪ'enɪəl [-njəl], -ɪ
bier, -s bɪə*, -z
biff (s. v.), -s, -ing, -ed bɪf, -s, -ɪŋ, -t
bifocal (s. adj.), -s ˌbaɪ'fəʊkl, -z
bifurcat|e, -es, -ing, -ed 'baɪfəkeɪt [-fɜː-], -s, -ɪŋ, -ɪd
bifurcation, -s ˌbaɪfə'keɪʃn [-fɜː-], -z
big, -ger, -gest, -ness bɪg, -ə*, -ɪst, -nɪs [-nəs]
bigamist, -s 'bɪgəmɪst, -s
bigamous, -ly 'bɪgəməs, -lɪ
bigam|y, -ies 'bɪgəm|ɪ, -ɪz
Bigelow 'bɪgɪləʊ [-gəl-]
Bigge bɪg

biggish 'bɪgɪʃ
Big|gs, -ham bɪg|z, -əm
bight, -s baɪt, -s
Bignell 'bɪgnəl
Bigod 'baɪgɒd
bigot, -s, -ed; -ry 'bɪgət, -s, -ɪd; -rɪ
bigraph, -s 'baɪgrɑːf [-græf], -s
bigwig, -s 'bɪgwɪg, -z
Bihar bɪ'hɑː* (Hindi.byhar)
bijou, -s 'biːʒuː, -z
†bik|e (s. v.), -es, -ing, -ed baɪk, -s, -ɪŋ, -t
bikini (B.), -s bɪ'kiːnɪ [bə-], -z
bilabial (s. adj.), -s ˌbaɪ'leɪbjəl [-bɪəl], -z
bilater|al, -ally ˌbaɪ'lætər|əl, -əlɪ
Bilbao bɪl'bɑːəʊ [-'beɪəʊ]
bilberr|y, -ies 'bɪlbər|ɪ, -ɪz
Bilborough 'bɪlbərə
Bilbrough 'bɪlbrə
bile baɪl
bilg|e (s. v.), -es, -ing, -ed bɪldʒ, -ɪz, -ɪŋ, -d
bilge-pump, -s 'bɪldʒpʌmp, -s
bilge-water 'bɪldʒˌwɔːtə*
bilgy 'bɪldʒɪ
biliary 'bɪljərɪ [-lɪər-]
bilingual, -ism baɪ'lɪŋgwəl [ˌbaɪ'l-], -ɪzəm
bilious, -ly, -ness 'bɪljəs [-lɪəs], -lɪ, -nɪs [-nəs]
biliteral ˌbaɪ'lɪtərəl
bilk, -s, -ing, -ed bɪlk, -s, -ɪŋ, -t
bill (B.), -s bɪl, -z
Billerica 'bɪlrɪkə
Billericay ˌbɪlə'rɪkɪ
billet (s. v.), -s, -ing, -ed 'bɪlɪt, -s, -ɪŋ, -ɪd
billet-doux (sing.) ˌbɪleɪ'duː [-lɪ'd-], (plur.) -z
bill-hook, -s 'bɪlhʊk, -s
billiard, -s; -ball/s, -cue/s, -marker/s, -room/s, -table/s 'bɪljəd, -z; -bɔːl/z, -kjuː/z, -ˌmɑːkə*/z, -rʊm/z [-ruːm/z], -ˌteɪbl/z
Billing, -s, -hurst 'bɪlɪŋ, -z, -hɜːst
Billingsgate 'bɪlɪŋzgɪt [-geɪt]
Billington 'bɪlɪŋtən
billion, -s, -th/s 'bɪljən, -z, -θ/s
bill-of-fare, -s ˌbɪləv'feə* [-lə'feə*], -z
bill|ow, -ows, -owy 'bɪl|əʊ, -əʊz, -əʊɪ
bill-poster/s, -ing 'bɪlˌpəʊstə*, -ɪŋ
bill-stick|er/s, -ing 'bɪlˌstɪk|ə*/z, -ɪŋ
bill|y (B.), -ies 'bɪl|ɪ, -ɪz
billycock, -s 'bɪlɪkɒk, -s
billy-goat, -s 'bɪlɪgəʊt, -s
Bilston(e) 'bɪlstən
Bilton 'bɪltən
bimestrial ˌbaɪ'mestrɪəl

†**bimetalli|sm,** **-st/s** ˌbaɪˈmetəlɪ|zəm [-t]ɪ-], -st/s

bi-monthl|y, -ies ˌbaɪˈmʌnθl|ɪ, -ɪz

bin, -s bɪn, -z

binary ˈbaɪnərɪ

binaural ˌbaɪnˈɔːrəl [bɪn-]

bind (*s. v.*), **-s, -ing, bound, binder/s** baɪnd, -z, -ɪŋ, baʊnd, ˈbaɪndə*/z

bindweed ˈbaɪndwiːd

Binegar ˈbɪnɪgə*

binge, -s bɪndʒ, -ɪz

Bing|ham, -ley ˈbɪŋ|əm, -lɪ

bingo ˈbɪŋgəʊ

Bink(e)s bɪŋks

binnacle, -s ˈbɪnəkl, -z

Binn|ey, -ie ˈbɪn|ɪ, -ɪ

Binns bɪnz

binocle, -s ˈbɪnɒkl [ˈbaɪn-, -nəkl], -z

binocular (*s.*), **-s** bɪˈnɒkjʊlə* [ˌbaɪˈn-, -kjəl-], -z

binocular (*adj.*) ˌbaɪˈnɒkjʊlə* [bɪˈn-, -kjəl-]

binomial ˌbaɪˈnəʊmjəl [-mɪəl]

Binste(a)d ˈbɪnstɪd [-sted]

Binyon ˈbɪnjən

biochemist, -s, -ry ˌbaɪəʊˈkemɪst, -s, -rɪ

biogenesis ˌbaɪəʊˈdʒenɪsɪs [-nəsɪs]

biograph, -s ˈbaɪəʊgrɑːf [-græf], -s

biographer, -s baɪˈɒgrəfə* [bɪˈɒ-], -z

biographic, -al, -ally ˌbaɪəʊˈgræfɪk [ˌbɪəʊˈg-, brə'g-], -l, -əlɪ

biograph|y, -ies baɪˈɒgrəf|ɪ [bɪˈɒ-], -ɪz

biologic, -al, -ally ˌbaɪəʊˈlɒdʒɪk, -l, -əlɪ

biolog|ist/s, -y baɪˈɒlədʒ|ɪst/s, -ɪ

biometric/s, -al ˌbaɪəʊˈmetrɪk/s, -l

biometry baɪˈɒmɪtrɪ [-mətrɪ]

biophysic|s, -al ˌbaɪəʊˈfɪzɪk|s, -l

bioscope, -s ˈbaɪəskəʊp, -s

biosphere, -s ˈbaɪəʊˌsfɪə*, -z

biparous ˈbɪpərəs

bipartisan ˌbaɪpɑːtɪˈzæn [ˌ-ˈ—]

bipartite ˌbaɪˈpɑːtaɪt [ˈbaɪˌpɑːtaɪt]

biped, -s ˈbaɪped, -z

bipedal, -ism baɪˈpiːdl [-ˈped-], -ɪzəm

biplane, -s ˈbaɪpleɪn, -s

biquadratic (*s. adj.*), **-s** ˌbaɪkwɒˈdrætɪk [-kwəˈd-], -s

birch (*s. v.*) (**B.**), **-es, -ing, -ed** bɜːtʃ, -ɪz, -ɪŋ, -t

birchen ˈbɜːtʃən

Birchenough ˈbɜːtʃɪnʌf

bird (**B.**), **-s** bɜːd, -z

bird-cage, -s ˈbɜːdkeɪdʒ, -ɪz

bird-call, -s ˈbɜːdkɔːl, -z

bird-fancier, -s ˈbɜːdˌfænsɪə* [-sjə*], -z

birdie, -s ˈbɜːdɪ, -z

bird-lime ˈbɜːdlaɪm

bird-nest, -s, -ing, -ed ˈbɜːdnest, -s, -ɪŋ, -ɪd

birdseed ˈbɜːdsiːd

bird's-eye (*s. adj.*), **-s** ˈbɜːdzaɪ, -z

Birdseye ˈbɜːdzaɪ

bird's-nest (*s. v.*), **-s, -ing, -ed** ˈbɜːdznest, -s, -ɪŋ, -ɪd

bireme, -s ˈbaɪriːm [ˈbaɪər-], -z

biretta, -s bɪˈretə, -z

Birkbeck (*surname*) ˈbɜːbek, ˈbɜːkbek, (*college in London*) ˈbɜːkbek

Birkenhead (*in Merseyside*) ˈbɜːkənhed [*locally* ˌbɜːkənˈhed], (*Earl*) ˈbɜːkənhed

Birkett ˈbɜːkɪt

Birley ˈbɜːlɪ

Birling ˈbɜːlɪŋ

Birmingham ˈbɜːmɪŋəm

Birnam ˈbɜːnəm

biro, -s ˈbaɪərəʊ, -z

Biron (*modern surname*) ˈbaɪərən *Note.*—bɪˈruːn *in 'Love's Labour's Lost'.*

Birrell ˈbɪrəl

birth, -s bɜːθ, -s

birth-control ˈbɜːθkənˌtrəʊl

birthday, -s ˈbɜːθdeɪ [-dɪ], -z

birthmark, -s ˈbɜːθmɑːk, -s

birthplace, -s ˈbɜːθpleɪs, -ɪz

birth-rate, -s ˈbɜːθreɪt, -s

birthright, -s ˈbɜːθraɪt, -s

Birtwistle ˈbɜːtˌwɪsl

bis bɪs

Biscay ˈbɪskeɪ [-kɪ]

biscuit, -s ˈbɪskɪt, -s

bisect, -s, -ing, -ed, -or/s baɪˈsekt, -s, -ɪŋ, -ɪd, -ə*/z

bisection, -s ˌbaɪˈsekʃn, -z

bisexual ˌbaɪˈsekʃʊəl [-ksjʊəl, -ksjwəl, -ksjʊl, -kʃwəl, -kʃʊl]

bishop (**B.**), **-s; -ric/s** ˈbɪʃəp, -s; -rɪk/s

Bishopsgate ˈbɪʃəpsgeɪt [-gɪt]

Bishopst|oke, -on ˈbɪʃəpst|əʊk, -ən

Bishop's Stortford ˌbɪʃəpsˈstɔːfəd [-ɔːtf-]

Bisley, -s ˈbɪzlɪ, -z

Bismarck ˈbɪzmɑːk (ˈbismark)

bismuth ˈbɪzməθ

bison, -s ˈbaɪsn, -z

Bispham (*surname*) ˈbɪsfəm, ˈbɪspəm, (*place*) ˈbɪspəm

bisque, -s bɪsk, -s

Bisseker ˈbɪsɪkə*

Bissell ˈbɪsl

bissextile, -s bɪˈsekstaɪl, -z

bistour|y, -ies ˈbɪstʊr|ɪ [-tər-], -ɪz

bistre ˈbɪstə*

bistro(t), -s ˈbiːstrəʊ, -z (bistro)

51

bisulph|ate, -ite ˌbaɪˈsʌlf|eɪt [-fɪt], -aɪt
bisurated ˈbɪsjʊəreɪtɪd
bit, -s bɪt, -s
bit (*from* **bite**) bɪt
bitch, -es, -y, -iness bɪtʃ, -ɪz, -ɪ, -mɪs [-məs]
bit|e (*s. v.*), **-es, -ing, bit, bitten, biter/s** baɪt, -s, -ɪŋ, bɪt, ˈbɪtn, ˈbaɪtə*/z
Bithell bɪˈθel, ˈbɪθəl
Bithynia bɪˈθɪnɪə [baɪˈθ-, -njə]
bitter, -er, -est, -ly, -ness ˈbɪtə*, -rə*, -rɪst, -lɪ, -nɪs [-nəs]
bittern, -s ˈbɪtən [-tɜːn], -z
bitters ˈbɪtəz
bittersweet ˈbɪtəswiːt [ˌ--ˈ-]
bitumen, -s ˈbɪtjʊmɪn [ˈbɪtʃʊ-, -men, -mən, bɪˈtjuːm-], -z
bituminous bɪˈtjuːmɪnəs
bivalen|ce, -t ˈbaɪˌveɪlən|s [ˌbaɪˈv-], -t
bivalve, -s ˈbaɪvælv, -z
bivouac (*s. v.*), **-s, -king, -ked** ˈbɪvʊæk [-vwæk], -s, -ɪŋ, -t
bi-weekl|y (*s. adv.*), **-ies** ˌbaɪˈwiːkl|ɪ, -ɪz
bizarre bɪˈzɑː* (bizaːr)
Bizet ˈbiːzeɪ (bizɛ)
blab, -s, -bing, -bed, -ber/s blæb, -z, -ɪŋ, -d, -ə*/z
Blachford ˈblæʃfəd
black (*s. adj. v.*) (**B.**), **-s; -er, -est, -ish, -ly, -ness; -ing, -ed** blæk, -s; -ə*, -ɪst, -ɪʃ, -lɪ, -nɪs [-nəs]; -ɪŋ, -t
blackamoor, -s ˈblækəˌmʊə* [-mɔə*, -mɔː*], -z
blackball (*v.*), **-s, -ing, -ed** ˈblækbɔːl, -z, -ɪŋ, -d
blackbeetle, -s ˌblækˈbiːtl, -z
blackberr|y, -ies ˈblækbər|ɪ [-ˌber-], -ɪz
blackberrying ˈblækˌberɪŋ [-bər-]
blackbird, -s ˈblækbɜːd, -z
blackboard, -s ˈblækbɔːd [-bɔəd], -z
Blackburn(e) ˈblækbɜːn
blackcap, -s ˈblækkæp, -s
blackcock, -s ˈblækkɒk, -s
black-currant, -s ˌblækˈkʌrənt, -s
black-draught ˌblækˈdrɑːft
black|en, -ens, -ening, -ened ˈblæk|ən, -ənz, -ŋɪŋ [-ənɪŋ, -nɪŋ], -ənd
Blackett ˈblækɪt
black-eye, -s ˌblækˈaɪ, -z
black-eyed ˈblækaɪd [ˌ-ˈ-]
Blackford ˈblækfəd
Blackfriars ˌblækˈfraɪəz [ˈ--, *esp. when attributive*]
blackgame ˈblækgeɪm
blackguard, -s, -ly ˈblægɑːd [-gəd], -z, -lɪ
blackhead, -s ˈblækhed, -z

Blackheath ˌblækˈhiːθ [*also* ˈ--, *according to sentence-stress*]
Blackie ˈblækɪ, *in the N. also* ˈbleɪkɪ
blacking (*s.*), **-s** ˈblækɪŋ, -z
blacklead (*s. v.*), **-s, -ing, -ed** ˌblækˈled, -z, -ɪŋ, -ɪd
blackleg, -s ˈblækleg, -z
black-letter ˌblækˈletə* [ˈblækˌl-]
Blackley (*Manchester*) ˈbleɪklɪ, (*surname*) ˈblæklɪ
black-list (*s. v.*), **-s, -ing, -ed** ˈblæklɪst, -s, -ɪŋ, -ɪd
blackmail (*s. v.*), **-s, -ing, -ed, -er/s** ˈblækmeɪl, -z, -ɪŋ, -d, -ə*/z
Blackman ˈblækmən
Blackmoor ˈblækˌmɔ:* [-mɔə*, -mʊə*]
Blackmore ˈblækmɔ:* [-mɔə*]
black-out, -s ˈblækaʊt, -s
Blackpool ˈblækpu:l
Blackpudlian, -s ˌblækˈpʌdlɪən [-ljən], -z
Blackrock ˈblækrɒk
black-rod, -s ˌblækˈrɒd, -z
blacksmith, -s ˈblæksmɪθ, -s
Blackston(e) ˈblækstən
blackthorn, -s ˈblækθɔːn, -z
Blackwall ˈblækwɔːl
blackwater (**B.**) ˈblækˌwɔːtə*
Blackwell ˈblækwəl [-wel]
Blackwood (*surname*) ˈblækwʊd, (*place in Gwent*) ˌblækˈwʊd
bladder, -s ˈblædə*, -z
bladderwort, -s ˈblædəwɜːt, -s
blade, -s bleɪd, -z
blade-bone, -s ˈbleɪdbəʊn, -z
blaeberr|y, -ies ˈbleɪbər|ɪ, -ɪz
Blagrave ˈblægreɪv
Blagrove ˈbleɪgrəʊv
blah-blah ˌblɑːˈblɑː
Blaikie ˈbleɪkɪ
Blaikley ˈbleɪklɪ
blain, -s bleɪn, -z
Blair bleə*
Blair Atholl ˌbleər ˈæθl
Blairgowrie ˌbleəˈgaʊərɪ
Blake, -ney bleɪk, -nɪ
Blakiston ˈblækɪstən, ˈbleɪk-
blamab|le, -ly, -leness ˈbleɪməb|l, -lɪ, -lnɪs [-lnəs]
blam|e (*s. v.*), **-es, -ing, -ed** bleɪm, -z, -ɪŋ, -d
blameless, -ly, -ness ˈbleɪmlɪs [-ləs], -lɪ, -nɪs [-nəs]
blameworth|y, -iness ˈbleɪmˌwɜːð|ɪ, -ɪnɪs [-ɪnəs]
Blamires bləˈmaɪəz
Blanc (*Mont*) blɑ̃:ŋ [blɔ̃:ŋ, blɑːŋ, blɒŋ] (blɑ̃)
blanch, -es, -ing, -ed blɑːntʃ, -ɪz, -ɪŋ, -t

Blanchard 'blæntʃəd [-tʃɑ:d]
Blanche blɑ:ntʃ
blancmange, -s blə'mɒndʒ [-'mɔ̃:nʒ,
    -'mɔ:nʒ -'mɑ:nʒ], -ɪz
blanco 'blæŋkəʊ
bland (B.), -er, -est, -ly, -ness blænd,
    -ə*, -ɪst, -lɪ, -nɪs ['blænnɪs, -nəs]
Blandford 'blændfəd
blandish, -es, -ing, -ed, -ment/s 'blæn-
    dɪʃ, -ɪz, -ɪŋ, -t, -mənt/s
Blandy 'blændɪ
blank (s. adj. v.), -s; -er, -est, -ly, -ness;
    -ing, -ed blæŋk, -s; -ə*, -ɪst, -lɪ, -nɪs
    [-nəs]; -ɪŋ, -t
blanket (s. v.), -s, -ing, -ed 'blæŋkɪt, -s,
    -ɪŋ, -ɪd
Blankley 'blæŋklɪ
blank-verse ˌblæŋk'vɜ:s
Blantyre blæn'taɪə* (in Malawi '---)
blar|e (s. v.), -es, -ing, -ed bleə*, -z,
    -rɪŋ, -d
blarney (B.) 'blɑ:nɪ
blasé 'blɑ:zeɪ (blaze)
blasphem|e, -es, -ing/ly, -ed, -er/s
    blæs'fi:m [blɑ:s-], -z, -ɪŋ/lɪ, -d,
    -ə*/z
blasphemous, -ly 'blæsfəməs ['blɑ:s-,
    -fɪm-, -fm̩-], -lɪ
blasphem|y, -ies 'blæsfəm|ɪ ['blɑ:s-,
    -fɪm-, -fm̩-], -ɪz
blast (s. v.), -s, -ing, -ed blɑ:st, -s, -ɪŋ,
    -ɪd
blast-furnace, -s 'blɑ:stˌfɜ:nɪs [-nəs,
    ˌ-'--], -ɪz
blastoderm, -s 'blæstəʊdɜ:m, -z
blast-pipe, -s 'blɑ:stpaɪp, -s
blatan|cy, -t/ly 'bleɪtən|sɪ, -t/lɪ
Blatchford 'blætʃfəd
blather, -s, -ing, -ed 'blæðə*, -z, -rɪŋ, -d
Blawith (in Cumbria) 'blɑ:ɪθ, (road at
    Harrow) 'bleɪwɪθ
Blaydes bleɪdz
blaz|e (s. v.), -es, -ing, -ed bleɪz, -ɪz, -ɪŋ,
    -d
blazer, -s 'bleɪzə*, -z
Blazes 'bleɪzɪz
Blazey 'bleɪzɪ
blaz|on, -ons, -oning, -oned 'bleɪz|n [in
    original heraldic sense also 'blæz-],
    -nz, -nɪŋ [-ənɪŋ, -nɪŋ], -nd
bleach, -es, -ing, -ed bli:tʃ, -ɪz, -ɪŋ, -t
bleaching-powder 'bli:tʃɪŋˌpaʊdə*
bleak, -er, -est, -ly, -ness bli:k, -ə*, -ɪst,
    -lɪ, -nɪs [-nəs]
blear, -eyed blɪə*, -raɪd [ˌ-'-]
blear|y, -ier, -iest, -ily, -iness 'blɪər|ɪ,
    -ɪə*, -ɪɪst, -əlɪ [-ɪlɪ], -ɪnɪs [-məs]
bleat (s. v.), -s, -ing, -ed bli:t, -s, -ɪŋ, -ɪd

bleb, -s bleb, -z
bled bled
Bledisloe 'bledɪsləʊ
bleed, -s, -ing, bled bli:d, -z, -ɪŋ, bled
blemish (s. v.), -es, -ing, -ed 'blemɪʃ, -ɪz,
    -ɪŋ, -t
blench, -es, -ing, -ed blentʃ, -ɪz, -ɪŋ, -t
Blencowe blen'kəʊ
blend (s. v.), -s, -ing, -ed, -er/s blend,
    -z, -ɪŋ, -ɪd, -ə*/z
blende blend
Blenheim 'blenɪm [-nəm]
Blenkinsop 'bleŋkɪnsɒp
Blennerhassett ˌblenə'hæsɪt
Blériot, -s 'bleɪrɪəʊ ['blɪər-] (blerjo), -z
bless, -es, -ing, -ed (p. tense, p. partic.),
    blest bles, -ɪz, -ɪŋ, -t, blest
blessed (adj.), -ly, -ness 'blesɪd, -lɪ, -nɪs
    [-nəs]
blessing (s.), -s 'blesɪŋ, -z
blest (from bless) blest
Bletchley 'bletʃlɪ
bleth|er, -ers, -ering, -ered 'bleð|ə*, -əz,
    -ərɪŋ, -əd
blew (from blow) blu:
Blew|ett, -itt 'blu:|ɪt ['blʊɪt], -ɪt
Bligh blaɪ
blight (s. v.), -s, -ing, -ed blaɪt, -s, -ɪŋ,
    -ɪd
blighter, -s 'blaɪtə*, -z
Blighty 'blaɪtɪ
blimey 'blaɪmɪ
blimp, -s blɪmp, -s
blind (s. adj. v.), -er, -est, -ly, -ness;
    -s, -ing, -ed blaɪnd, -ə*, -ɪst, -lɪ, -nɪs
    ['blaɪnnɪs, -nəs]; -z, -ɪŋ, -ɪd
blindfold (adj. v.), -s, -ing, -ed 'blaɪnd-
    fəʊld, -z, -ɪŋ, -ɪd
blindman's-buff ˌblaɪndmænz'bʌf
blindworm, -s 'blaɪndwɜ:m, -z
blink (s. v.), -s, -ing, -ed blɪŋk, -s, -ɪŋ, -t
    [blɪŋt]
blinker, -s 'blɪŋkə*, -z
bliss (B.) blɪs
Blissett 'blɪsɪt
bliss|ful, -fully, -fulness 'blɪs|fʊl, -fʊlɪ
    [-fəlɪ], -fʊlnɪs [-nəs]
blist|er (s. v.), -ers, -ering, -ered
    'blɪst|ə*, -əz, -ərɪŋ, -əd
blithe, -r, -st, -ly, -ness blaɪð, -ə*, -ɪst,
    -lɪ, -nɪs [-nəs]
blith|er (v.), -ers, -ering, -ered, -erer/s
    'blɪð|ə*, -əz, -ərɪŋ, -əd, -ərə*/z
blithesome, -ly, -ness 'blaɪðsəm, -lɪ,
    -nɪs [-nəs]
blitz (s. v.), -es, -ing, -ed blɪts, -ɪz, -ɪŋ, -t
blitzkrieg, -s 'blɪtskri:g, -z
blizzard, -s 'blɪzəd, -z

53

bloat—bluish

bloat, -s, -ing, -ed/ness bləʊt, -s, -ɪŋ, -ɪd/nɪs [-nəs]
bloater, -s 'bləʊtə*, -z
blob, -s blɒb, -z
bloc, -s blɒk, -s
block (s. v.) (B.), -s, -ing, -ed, -er/s, -age/s blɒk, -s, -ɪŋ, -t, -ə*/z, -ɪdʒ/ɪz
blockad|e (s. v.), -es, -ing, -ed, -er/s blɒ'keɪd [blə'k-], -z, -ɪŋ, -ɪd, -ə*/z
blockbuster, -s 'blɒkbʌstə*, -z
blockhead, -s 'blɒkhed, -z
blockhou|se, -ses 'blɒkhaʊ|s, -zɪz
Bloemfontein 'bluːmfəntein [-fɒn-]
Blois blwɑ: [surname blɔɪs] (blwɑ, blwɑ)
bloke, -s bləʊk, -s
Blom (surname) blɒm
Blomefield 'bluːmfiːld
Blomfield 'blɒmfiːld, 'blʊm-, 'blʌm-, 'bluːm-
blond(e), -s blɒnd, -z
Blondel(l) 'blʌndl, 'blɒndl, blɒn'del
Blondin (French tight-rope walker) 'blɒndɪn (blɔ̃dɛ̃)
blood, -s blʌd, -z
bloodcurdling 'blʌd,kɜːdlɪŋ
blood-donor, -s 'blʌd,dəʊnə*, -z
blood-group, -s 'blʌdgruːp, -s
blood-guiltiness 'blʌd,gɪltɪnɪs [-nəs]
bloodheat 'blʌdhiːt
blood-horse, -s 'blʌdhɔːs, -ɪz
bloodhound, -s 'blʌdhaʊnd, -z
bloodless, -ly, -ness 'blʌdlɪs [-ləs], -lɪ, -nɪs [-nəs]
blood-money 'blʌd,mʌnɪ
bloodpoisoning 'blʌd,pɔɪznɪŋ [-znɪŋ]
blood-pressure 'blʌd,preʃə*
blood-red ,blʌd'red [also '— when attributive]
blood-relation, -s 'blʌdrɪ,leɪʃn [,-'—'—], -z
blood|shed, -shot 'blʌd|ʃed, -ʃɒt
bloodstain, -s, -ed 'blʌdsteɪn, -z, -d
blood-stone, -s 'blʌdstəʊn, -z
blood-sucker, -s 'blʌd,sʌkə*, -z
bloodthirst|y, -ier, -iest, -ily, -iness 'blʌd,θɜːst|ɪ, -ɪə* [-jə*], -ɪst [-jɪst], -ɪlɪ [-əlɪ], -ɪnɪs [-ɪnəs]
blood-vessel, -s 'blʌd,vesl, -z
blood|y, -ier, -iest, -ily, -iness 'blʌd|ɪ, -ɪə*, -ɪst, -ɪlɪ [-əlɪ], -ɪnɪs [-ɪnəs]
bloom (s. v.), -s, -ing, -ed bluːm, -z, -ɪŋ, -d
bloomer (B.), -s 'bluːmə*, -z
Bloomfield 'bluːmfiːld
Bloomsbury 'bluːmzbərɪ
Blore blɔː* [blɔə*]
blossom (s. v.) (B.), -s, -ing, -ed 'blɒsəm, -z, -ɪŋ, -d

blot (s. v.), -s, -ting, -ted blɒt, -s, -ɪŋ, -ɪd
blotch (s. v.), -es, -ing, -ed blɒtʃ, -ɪz, -ɪŋ, -t
blotch|y, -ier, -iest, -ily, -iness 'blɒtʃ|ɪ, -ɪə*, -ɪɪst, -ɪlɪ [-əlɪ], -ɪnɪs [-ɪnəs]
blotter, -s 'blɒtə*, -z
blotting-paper, -s 'blɒtɪŋ,peɪpə*, -z
blotto 'blɒtəʊ
Blougram 'bləʊgrəm ['blaʊ-]
Bloundelle 'blʌndl
Blount blʌnt
blouse, -s blaʊz, -ɪz
blow (s. v.) (B.), -s, -ing, blew, blow|n, -ed, -er/s bləʊ, -z, -ɪŋ, bluː, bləʊ|n, -d, -ə*/z
blow-fl|y, -ies 'bləʊflaɪ, -aɪz
blow-hole, -s 'bləʊhəʊl, -z
blow-lamp, -s 'bləʊlæmp, -s
blown (from blow) bləʊn
blow-out, -s 'bləʊaʊt, -s
blowpipe, -s 'bləʊpaɪp, -s
blow|y, -ier, -iest, -ily, -iness 'bləʊ|ɪ, -ɪə*, -ɪɪst, -ɪlɪ [-əlɪ], -ɪnɪs [-ɪnəs]
blowz|y, -ier, -iest, -iness 'blaʊz|ɪ, -ɪə*, -ɪɪst, -ɪnɪs [-ɪnəs]
Blox(h)am 'blɒksəm
blub, -s, -bing, -bed blʌb, -z, -ɪŋ, -d
blubber (s. v.), -s, -ing, -ed, -er/s 'blʌbə*, -z, -rɪŋ, -d, -rə*/z
bludg|eon (s. v.), -eons, -eoning, -eoned 'blʌdʒ|ən, -ənz, -ŋɪŋ [-ənɪŋ], -ənd
blue (s. adj. v.), -s; -r, -st; -ing, -d bluː, -z; -ə* [bluə*], -ɪst ['bluɪst]; -ɪŋ ['bluɪŋ], -d
Bluebeard 'bluː,bɪəd
bluebell, -s 'bluː:bel, -z
blueberr|y, -ies 'bluː:bər|ɪ, -ɪz [-,ber|ɪ, -ɪz]
blue-black ,bluː'blæk ['—]
blue-blooded ,bluː'blʌdɪd ['-,—]
blue-book, -s 'bluː:bʊk, -s
bluebottle, -s 'bluː:bɒtl, -z
blue-coat, -s 'bluː:kəʊt, -s
blue-devils ,bluː'devlz
blue-jacket, -s 'bluː:dʒækɪt, -s
blue-john 'bluː:dʒɒn
blue-light, -s 'bluː:laɪt, -s
blueness 'bluː:nɪs [-nəs]
blue-penc|il, -ils, -illing, -illed ,bluː'pens|l, -lz, -lɪŋ [-əlɪŋ], -ld
blue-print, -s 'bluː:prɪnt, -s
bluestocking, -s 'bluː:,stɒkɪŋ, -z
Bluett 'bluːɪt ['bluɪt]
bluey 'bluː:ɪ ['bluɪ]
bluff (s. adj. v.), -s; -er, -est, -ly, -ness; -ing, -ed blʌf, -s; -ə*, -ɪst, -lɪ, -nɪs [-nəs]; -ɪŋ, -t
bluish 'bluː:ɪʃ ['bluɪʃ]

54

Blundell 'blʌndl
blund|er (s. v.), -ers, -ering, -ered,
-erer/s 'blʌnd|ə*, -əz, -ərɪŋ, -əd,
-ərə*/z
blunderbuss, -es 'blʌndəbʌs, -ɪz
Blunn blʌn
blunt (adj. v.) (B.), -er, -est, -ly, -ness;
-s, -ing, -ed blʌnt, -ə*, -ɪst, -lɪ, -nɪs
[-nəs]; -s, -ɪŋ, -ɪd
blur, -s, -ing, -ed blɜ:*, -z, -rɪŋ, -d
blurb, -s blɜ:b, -z
blurt, -s, -ing, -ed blɜ:t, -s, -ɪŋ, -ɪd
blush (s. v.), -es, -ing/ly, -ed, -er/s
blʌʃ, -ɪz, -ɪŋ/lɪ, -t, -ə*/z
blust|er, -ers, -ering/ly, -ered, -erer/s
'blʌst|ə*, -əz, -ərɪŋ/lɪ, -əd, -ərə*/z
bluster|y, -iness 'blʌstər|ɪ, -ɪnɪs [-ɪnəs]
Bly blaɪ
Blyth blaɪ, blaɪθ, blaɪð
Blythborough 'blaɪbərə
Blythe blaɪð
Blyton 'blaɪtn
boa, -s 'bəʊə [bɔə, bɔ:], -z
Boadicea ˌbəʊədɪ'sɪə
Boag bəʊg
Boanas 'bəʊnəs
Boanerges ˌbəʊə'nɜ:dʒi:z
boar, -s bɔ:* [bɔə*], -z
board (s. v.), -s, -ing, -ed, -er/s bɔ:d
[bɔəd], -z, -ɪŋ, -ɪd, -ə*/z
boarding-hou|se, -ses 'bɔ:dɪŋhaʊ|s
['bɔəd-], -zɪz
boarding-school, -s 'bɔ:dɪŋsku:l
['bɔəd-], -z
boardroom, -s 'bɔ:drʊm [-ru:m], -z
board-school, -s 'bɔ:dsku:l ['bɔəd-], -z
board-wages ˌbɔ:d'weɪdʒɪz [ˌbɔəd-]
boar-hound, -s 'bɔ:haʊnd ['bɔəh-], -z
boarish 'bɔ:rɪʃ ['bɔər-]
Boas 'bəʊæz, 'bəʊəz
Boase bəʊz
boast (s. v.), -s, -ing, -ed, -er/s bəʊst, -s,
-ɪŋ, -ɪd, -ə*/z
boast|ful, -fully, -fulness 'bəʊst|fʊl,
-fʊlɪ [-fəlɪ], -fʊlnɪs [-nəs]
boat, -s; -er/s bəʊt, -s; -ə*/z
boat-hook, -s 'bəʊthʊk, -s
boat-hou|se, -ses 'bəʊthaʊ|s, -zɪz
boating 'bəʊtɪŋ
boat|man, -men 'bəʊt|mən, -mən
boat-race, -s 'bəʊtreɪs, -ɪz
boatswain, -s 'bəʊsn ['bəʊtsweɪn], -z
Boaz 'bəʊæz
bob (s. v.) (B.), -s, -bing, -bed bɒb, -z,
-ɪŋ, -d
bobbin, -s 'bɒbɪn, -z
bobbish, -ly, -ness 'bɒbɪʃ, -lɪ, -nɪs
[-nəs]

bobble, -s 'bɒbl, -z
bobb|y (B.), -ies 'bɒb|ɪ, -ɪz
bobbysox, -er/s 'bɒbɪsɒks, -ə*/z
bobolink, -s 'bɒbəlɪŋk [-bəʊl-], -s
bobsleigh, -s 'bɒbsleɪ, -z
bobstay, -s 'bɒbsteɪ, -z
bobtail, -s 'bɒbteɪl, -z
bob-wig, -s 'bɒb wɪg [ˌbɒb'wɪg], -z
Boccaccio bɒ'kɑ:tʃɪəʊ [bə'k-, -'kætʃ-,
-tʃjəʊ] (bo'kattʃo)
Bochaton 'bɒkətən
Bockett 'bɒkɪt
Bodd|ington, -y 'bɒd|ɪŋtən, -ɪ
bod|e (B.), -es, -ing, -ed bəʊd, -z, -ɪŋ,
-ɪd
bodega (B.), -s bəʊ'di:gə, -z
Bodey 'bəʊdɪ
Bodiam 'bəʊdjəm [-dɪəm]
bodice, -s 'bɒdɪs, -ɪz
Bodie 'bəʊdɪ
Bodilly bə'dɪlɪ [bɒ'd-, bəʊ'd-]
bodily 'bɒdɪlɪ [-əlɪ]
bodkin (B.), -s 'bɒdkɪn, -z
Bodleian 'bɒdlɪən [bɒd'li:ən, -'lɪən]
Bod|ley, -min 'bɒd|lɪ, -mɪn
bod|y, -ies 'bɒd|ɪ, -ɪz
bodyguard, -s 'bɒdɪgɑ:d, -z
body-snatcher, -s 'bɒdɪˌsnætʃə*, -z
Boeing 'bəʊɪŋ
Boeo|tia, -tian/s bɪ'əʊ|ʃɪə [-ʃɪə, -ʃə],
-ʃjən/z [-ʃɪən/z, -ʃn/z]
Boer, -s bɔ:* [bɔə*, 'bəʊə*, bʊə*], -z
Boethius bəʊ'i:θjəs [-θɪəs]
boffin (B.), -s 'bɒfɪn, -z
Bofors 'bəʊfəz
bog, -s bɒg, -z
bogey, -s 'bəʊgɪ, -z
bogey|man, -men 'bəʊgɪ|mæn, -men
bogg|le, -les, -ling, -led, -ler/s 'bɒg|l,
-lz, -lɪŋ [-lɪŋ], -ld, -lə*/z [-lə*/z]
bogg|y, -ier, -iest, -iness 'bɒg|ɪ, -ɪə*,
-ɪɪst, -ɪnɪs [-ɪnəs]
bogie, -s 'bəʊgɪ, -z
bogie-engine, -s 'bəʊgɪˌendʒɪn, -z
bogie-wheel, -s 'bəʊgɪwi:l [-ɪhw-], -z
Bognor 'bɒgnə*
bog-oak ˌbɒg'əʊk
Bogotá (in Colombia) ˌbɒgəʊ'tɑ:
[ˌbəʊg-]
Bogota (in New Jersey) bə'gəʊtə
bogus 'bəʊgəs
bog|y, -ies 'bəʊg|ɪ, -ɪz
bohea bəʊ'hi:
Bohemia, -n/s bəʊ'hi:mjə [-mɪə], -n/z
Bohn bəʊn
Bohun 'bəʊən, bu:n
Note.—bu:n in Shaw's 'You never
can tell'.

55

boil—bony

boil (s. v.), **-s, -ing, -ed, -er/s** bɔɪl, -z, -ɪŋ, -d, -ə*/z
boiling-point, **-s** 'bɔɪlɪŋpɔɪnt, -s
Bois bɔɪs
Boisragon 'bɒrəgən
boisterous, **-ly, -ness** 'bɔɪstərəs, -lɪ, -nɪs [-nəs]
Boivie (English surname) 'beɪvɪ
Bojador ˌbɒhə'dɔ:* [ˌbɒxə-]
Bokhara bəʊ'kɑːrə
Bolander 'bəʊlændə*
bolas, **-es** 'bəʊləs, -ɪz
bold, **-er, -est, -ly, -ness** bəʊld, -ə*, -ɪst, -lɪ, -nɪs [-nəs]
bold-face, **-d** 'bəʊldfeɪs, -t
Boldre 'bəʊldə*
bole, **-s** bəʊl, -z
bolero, **-s** (dance) bə'leərəʊ [bɒ'l-, -'lɪə-], (garment) 'bɒlərəʊ, -z
Boleyn 'bʊlɪn [bʊ'lɪn, bʊ'li:n]
Bolingbroke 'bɒlɪŋbrʊk [old-fashioned 'bʊl-]
Bolinger 'bəʊlɪndʒə* ['bɒl-]
Bolitho bə'laɪθəʊ [bɒ'l-]
Bolivar (S. American general) bɒ'li:vɑ:* (bo'libar), (places in U.S.A.) 'bɒlɪvə* [-vɑ:*]
Bolivia, **-n/s** bə'lɪvɪə [bɒ'l-, -vjə], -n/z
boll, **-s, -ed** bəʊl [bɒl], -z, -d
bollard, **-s** 'bɒlɑːd [-ləd], -z
Bolling 'bəʊlɪŋ
Bollinger (in U.S.A.) 'bɒlɪndʒə*
bolo, **-s** 'bəʊləʊ, -z
Bologna bə'ləʊnjə [-'lɒn-] (bo'loɲɲa)
bolometer, **-s** bəʊ'lɒmɪtə* [-mətə*], -z
boloney bə'ləʊnɪ
Bolshevi|k/s, **-st/s, -sm** 'bɒlʃɪvɪ|k/s [-ʃəv-, -ʃev-], -st/s, -zəm
bolshie, **-s** 'bɒlʃɪ, -z
Bolshoy bɒl'ʃɔɪ ['--]
bolshy 'bɒlʃɪ, -z
Bolsover (surname, street in London) 'bɒlsəvə* [-səʊvə*], (in Derbyshire) 'bəʊlzəʊvə*
bolst|er (s. v.), **-ers, -ering, -ered** 'bəʊlst|ə*, -əz, -ərɪŋ, -əd
bolt (s. v.) (B.), **-s, -ing, -ed** bəʊlt, -s, -ɪŋ, -ɪd
bolter (B.), **-s** 'bəʊltə*, -z
Bolton 'bəʊltən
bolt-upright ˌbəʊlt'ʌpraɪt
bolus, **-es** 'bəʊləs, -ɪz
bomb (s. v.), **-s, -ing, -ed** bɒm, -z, -ɪŋ, -d
bombard (s.), **-s** 'bɒmbɑːd, -z
bombard (v.), **-s, -ing, -ed, -ment/s** bɒm'bɑːd [bəm-], -z, -ɪŋ, -ɪd, -mənt/s
bombardier, **-s** ˌbɒmbə'dɪə* [ˌbʌm-, -bɑː'd-], -z

bombardon, **-s** bɒm'bɑːdn, -z
bombasine 'bɒmbəzi:n [-əsi:n, ˌ--'-]
bombast 'bɒmbæst
bombastic, **-ally** bɒm'bæstɪk, -lɪ
Bombay ˌbɒm'beɪ [also 'bɒmbeɪ when attributive]
bombe, **-s** bɔ̃:mb [bɒmb] (bɔ̃:b), -z
bomber, **-s** 'bɒmə*, -z
bomb-proof 'bɒmpru:f
bombshell, **-s** 'bɒmʃel, -z
Bompas 'bʌmpəs
bon bɒn (bɔ̃)
bona fid|e, **-es** ˌbəʊnə'faɪd|ɪ, -i:z [-ɪz]
bonanza, **-s** bəʊ'nænzə, -z
Bonapart|e, **-ist/s** 'bəʊnəpɑ:t, -ɪst/s
Bonar 'bɒnə*
bon-bon, **-s** 'bɒnbɒn ['bɒmbɒn, 'bɒmbɒŋ, bɔ̃:mbɔ̃:ŋ] (bɔ̃bɔ̃), -z
Bonchurch 'bɒntʃə:tʃ
bond (s. v.) (B.), **-s, -ing, -ed; -age** bɒnd, -z, -ɪŋ, -ɪd; -ɪdʒ
bond-holder, **-s** 'bɒnd,həʊldə*, -z
bondmaid, **-s** 'bɒndmeɪd, -z
bond|man, **-men** 'bɒnd|mən, -mən [-men]
bonds|man, **-men** 'bɒndz|mən, -mən [-men]
bonds|woman, **-women** 'bɒndz|-ˌwʊmən, -ˌwɪmɪn
bond|woman, **-women** 'bɒnd|ˌwʊmən, -ˌwɪmɪn
bon|e (s. v.), **-es, -ing, -ed** bəʊn, -z, -ɪŋ, -d
bone-ash 'bəʊnæʃ
Bonella bəʊ'nelə
bone-meal 'bəʊnmi:l
bone-setter, **-s** 'bəʊnˌsetə*, -z
bone-shaker, **-s** 'bəʊnˌʃeɪkə*, -z
Bo'ness ˌbəʊ'nes
bonfire, **-s** 'bɒnˌfaɪə*, -z
Bonham 'bɒnəm
bonhomie 'bɒnəmi: [-nɒm-, -mɪ]
Boniface 'bɒnɪfeɪs
Bonn bɒn
bonne-bouche, **-s** ˌbɒn'bu:ʃ (bɔnbuʃ), -ɪz
Bonner 'bɒnə*
bonnet (s. v.), **-s, -ing, -ed** 'bɒnɪt, -s, -ɪŋ, -ɪd
Bonnett 'bɒnɪt
bonn|y, **-ier, -iest, -ily, -iness** 'bɒn|ɪ, -ɪə*, -ɪɪst, -ɪlɪ [-əlɪ], -ɪnɪs [-ɪnəs]
bonsai 'bɒnsaɪ
Bonsor 'bɒnsə*
Bonthron 'bɒnθrən
bonus, **-es** 'bəʊnəs, -ɪz
bon|y, **-ier, -iest, -iness** 'bəʊn|ɪ, -ɪə* [-jə*], -ɪɪst [-jɪst], -ɪnɪs [-ɪnəs]

56

Bonython bə'naɪθən [bɒ'n-]
bonze, -s bɒnz, -ɪz
boo (*v. interj.*), **-s, -ing, -ed, -er/s** bu:,
-z, -ɪŋ, -d, -ə*/z
boob|y, -ies, -yish 'bu:b|ɪ, -ɪz, -ɪɪʃ [-jɪʃ]
booby-prize, -s 'bu:bɪpraɪz, -ɪz
booby-trap, -s 'bu:bɪtræp, -s
boodle (B.) 'bu:dl
Boog bəʊg
boogie-woogie 'bu:gɪˌwu:gɪ [ˌ--'--]
book (*s. v.*), **-s, -ing, -ed, -er/s** bʊk, -s,
-ɪŋ, -t, -ə*/z
bookable 'bʊkəbl
bookbind|er/s, -ing 'bʊkˌbaɪnd|ə*/z,
-ɪŋ
bookcase, -s 'bʊkkeɪs [*rarely* 'bʊkeɪs],
-ɪz
book-club, -s 'bʊkklʌb, -z
book-debt, -s 'bʊkdet, -s
Booker 'bʊkə*
bookie, -s 'bʊkɪ, -z
booking, -s 'bʊkɪŋ, -z
booking-office, -s 'bʊkɪŋˌɒfɪs, -ɪz
bookish, -ly, -ness 'bʊkɪʃ, -lɪ, -nɪs [-nəs]
book-keep|er/s, -ing 'bʊkˌki:p|ə*/z, -ɪŋ
bookland 'bʊklænd
book-learning 'bʊkˌlɜ:nɪŋ
booklet, -s 'bʊklɪt [-lət], -s
book-mak|er/s, -ing 'bʊkˌmeɪk|ə*/z,
-ɪŋ
book|man, men 'bʊk|mən, -mən
book-mark, -s 'bʊkmɑ:k, -s
book-muslin 'bʊkˌmʌzlɪn
bookplate, -s 'bʊkpleɪt, -s
book-post 'bʊkpəʊst
book-sell|er/s, -ing 'bʊkˌsel|ə*/z, -ɪŋ
book-shel|f, -ves 'bʊkʃel|f, -vz
book-shop, -s 'bʊkʃɒp, -s
book-stall, -s 'bʊkstɔ:l, -z
bookstand, -s 'bʊkstænd, -z
bookwork 'bʊkwɜ:k
bookworm, -s 'bʊkwɜ:m, -z
boom (*s. v.*), **-s, -ing, -ed** bu:m, -z, -ɪŋ,
-d
boomerang, -s 'bu:məræŋ, -z
boon, -s bu:n, -z
Boon(e) bu:n
boor, -s bʊə* [bɔ:*], -z
Boord bɜ:d
boorish, -ly, -ness 'bʊərɪʃ ['bɔ:r-], -lɪ,
-nɪs [-nəs]
Boosey 'bu:zɪ
boost (*s. v.*), **-s, -ing, -ed, -er/s** bu:st, -s,
-ɪŋ, -ɪd, -ə*/z
boot (*s. v.*) **(B.), -s, -ing, -ed** bu:t, -s, -ɪŋ,
-ɪd
bootblack, -s 'bu:tblæk, -s
bootee, -s 'bu:ti: [ˌ-'-], -z

Boötes bəʊ'əʊti:z
booth (B.), -s bu:ð, -z [bu:θ, -s]
Boothby 'bu:ðbɪ
Boothe bu:ð
bootjack, -s 'bu:tdʒæk, -s
bootlace, -s 'bu:tleɪs, -ɪz
Bootle 'bu:tl
bootlegg|er/s, -ing 'bu:tˌleg|ə*/z, -ɪŋ
bootless, -ly, -ness 'bu:tlɪs [-ləs], -lɪ,
-nɪs [-nəs]
boots (*hotel servant*) (*sing.*) bu:ts, (*plur.*)
bu:ts ['bu:tsɪz]
Boots bu:ts
boot-tree, -s 'bu:ttri:, -z
booty 'bu:tɪ
booz|e, -es, -ing, -ed, -er/s bu:z, -ɪz,
-ɪŋ, -d, -ə*/z
booz|y, -ier, -iest 'bu:z|ɪ, -ɪə* [-jə*],
-ɪɪst [-jɪst]
Bo-peep ˌbəʊ'pi:p
boracic bə'ræsɪk [bɒ'r-]
borage 'bɒrɪdʒ ['bʌr-]
borate, -s 'bɔ:reɪt [-rɪt], -s
borax 'bɔ:ræks
Bord bɔ:d
Bordeaux bɔ:'dəʊ (bɔrdo)
bord|er (*s. v.*), **-ers, -ering, -ered, -erer/s**
'bɔ:d|ə*, -əz, -ərɪŋ, -əd, -ərə*/z
borderland, -s 'bɔ:dəlænd, -z
borderline, -s 'bɔ:dəlaɪn, -z
bordure, -s 'bɔ:ˌdjʊə* [-djə*], -z
bor|e (*s. v.*), **-es, -ing, -ed, -er/s** bɔ:*
[bɔə*], -z, -rɪŋ, -d, -rə*/z
borealis ˌbɔ:rɪ'eɪlɪs [ˌbɒrɪ-]
Boreas 'bɒriæs ['bɔ:r-]
boredom 'bɔ:dəm ['bɔəd-]
Boreham 'bɔ:rəm ['bɔər-]
Borgia 'bɔ:dʒjə [-dʒɪə, -dʒə]
boric 'bɔ:rɪk ['bɒrɪk]
Boris 'bɒrɪs
Borland 'bɔ:lənd
born (*from* **bear,** *bring forth*) bɔ:n
borne (*from* **bear,** *carry*) bɔ:n
Borneo 'bɔ:nɪəʊ
boron 'bɔ:rɒn [-rən]
borough, -s 'bʌrə, -z
borough-English ˌbʌrə'ɪŋglɪʃ
borough-reeve, -s ˌbʌrə'ri:v, -z
borrow (B.), -s, -ing, -ed, -er/s 'bɒrəʊ,
-z, -ɪŋ, -d, -ə*/z
Borrowdale 'bɒrəʊdeɪl
Borstal 'bɔ:stl
borstch bɔ:ʃ [bɔ:stʃ, -ʃtʃ]
Borthwick 'bɔ:θwɪk
Borwick 'bɒrɪk
borzoi, -s 'bɔ:zɔɪ, -z
Bosanquet 'bəʊznket [-kɪt]
boscage, -s 'bɒskɪdʒ, -ɪz

Boscastle 'bɒsˌkɑːsl
Boscawen bɒs'kəʊən [-'kəʊm, -'kɔːm]
bosh bɒʃ
Bosham (in West Sussex) 'bɒzəm
['bɒsəm]
Note.—A new pronunciation 'bɒʃəm
is now heard.
Bosher 'bəʊʒə*
Bosinney bɒ'sɪnɪ [bə's-]
bosky 'bɒskɪ
Bosnia, -n/s 'bɒznɪə [-njə], -n/z
bosom, -s 'bʊzəm, -z
Bosphorus 'bɒsfərəs ['bɒspə-]
Bosporus 'bɒspərəs
boss (s. v.) (B.), -es, -ing, -ed bɒs, -ɪz,
-ɪŋ, -t
boss-eyed 'bɒsaɪd [ˌ-'-]
Bossiney bɒ'sɪnɪ [bə's-]
boss|y, -ier, -iest, -ily, -iness 'bɒs|ɪ, -ɪə*,
-ɪɪst, -ɪlɪ [-əlɪ], -ɪnɪs [-məs]
Bostock 'bɒstɒk
Boston 'bɒstən
Bostonian, -s bɒ'stəʊnjən [-nɪən], -z
bo'sun, -s 'bəʊsn, -z
Boswell 'bɒzwəl [-wel]
Bosworth 'bɒzwəθ [-wɜːθ]
botanic, -al, -ally bə'tænɪk [bɒ't-], -l,
-əlɪ
botanist, -s 'bɒtənɪst [-tn̩-], -s
botaniz|e [-is|e], -es, -ing, -ed 'bɒtənaɪz
[-tn̩aɪz], -ɪz, -ɪŋ, -d
botany 'bɒtənɪ [-tn̩ɪ]
botch (s. v.), -es, -ing, -ed, -er/s bɒtʃ,
-ɪz, -ɪŋ, -t, -ə*/z
both bəʊθ
Botha 'bəʊtə
Botham 'bɒdəm, 'bəʊθəm
both|er (s. v.), -ers, -ering, -ered
'bɒð|ə*, -əz, -ərɪŋ, -əd
botheration ˌbɒðə'reɪʃn
bothersome 'bɒðəsəm
Bothnia 'bɒθnɪə [-njə]
Bothwell 'bɒθwəl [-ɒθw-, -ɒ̃w-, -wel]
both|y, -ies 'bɒθ|ɪ, -ɪz
Botolph 'bɒtɒlf [-təlf]
Botswana bɒ'tswɑːnə [bə-]
Botticelli, -s ˌbɒtɪ'tʃelɪ, -z
bottine, -s bɒ'tiːn, -z
bott|le (s. v.), -les, -ling, -led, -ler/s
'bɒt|l, -lz, -lɪŋ [-lɪŋ], -ld, -lə*/z
[-lə*/z]
bottle-green 'bɒtlgriːn [ˌbɒtl'g-]
bottleneck, -s 'bɒtlnek, -s
bottle-nose, -s, -d 'bɒtlnəʊz, -ɪz, -d
bottle-wash|er/s, -ing 'bɒtlˌwɒʃ|ə*/z,
-ɪŋ
bottom (s. v.) (B.), -s, -ing, -ed 'bɒtəm,
-z, -ɪŋ, -d

Bottome (surname) bə'təʊm
bottomless 'bɒtəmlɪs [-ləs, -les]
Bottomley 'bɒtəmlɪ
bottomry 'bɒtəmrɪ
botulism 'bɒtjʊlɪzəm
Boucicault 'buːsɪkəʊ
Boudicca bəʊ'dɪkə [buː-]
boudoir, -s 'buːdwɑː* [-wɔː*], -z
bouffant 'buːfɑːŋ [-fɔːŋ, -fɒŋ]
Bougainville 'buːgənvɪl
bougainvillea, -s ˌbuːgən'vɪlɪə [-geɪn-,
-ljə], -z
bough, -s baʊ, -z
Boughey 'bəʊɪ
bought (from buy) bɔːt
Boughton 'bɔːtn, 'baʊtn
bougie, -s 'buːʒiː, -z
bouillabaisse 'buːjəbes [-beɪs, ˌ-'-]
(bujabɛs)
bouillon 'buːjɔ̃ːŋ [-jɒn] (bujɔ̃)
Boulby 'bəʊlbɪ
boulder, -s 'bəʊldə*, -z
boulevard, -s 'buːləvɑːd [-lɪv-, 'buːlvɑː*]
(bulvaːr), -z
Boulger 'bəʊldʒə*
Boulogne bʊ'lɔɪn [bə'l-, -'ləʊn] (bulɔɲ)
Boult bəʊlt
Boulter 'bəʊltə*
Boulton 'bəʊltən
Bouly 'buːlɪ, 'baʊlɪ
Boumphrey 'bʌmfrɪ
bounc|e (s. v. adj.), -es, -ing, -ed, -er/s,
-y baʊns, -ɪz, -ɪŋ, -t, -ə*/z, -ɪ
Bouncer 'baʊnsə*
bound (s. v.), -s, -ing, -ed baʊnd, -z, -ɪŋ,
-ɪd
bound (from bind) baʊnd
boundar|y, -ies 'baʊndər|ɪ, -ɪz
bounden 'baʊndən
bounder, -s 'baʊndə*, -z
boundless, -ly, -ness 'baʊndlɪs [-ləs],
-lɪ, -nɪs [-nəs]
bounteous, -ly, -ness 'baʊntɪəs [-tjəs],
-lɪ, -nɪs [-nəs]
bounti|ful, -fully, -fulness 'baʊntɪ|-
fʊl, -fʊlɪ [-fəlɪ], -fʊlnɪs [-nəs]
bount|y, -ies 'baʊnt|ɪ, -ɪz
bouquet, -s bʊ'keɪ [buː-, 'buː'keɪ, 'bʊ-,
bəʊ'keɪ], -z
Bourbon, -s 'bʊəbən [-bɒn] (burbɔ̃),
-z
bourbon (drink) 'bɜːbən ['bʊə-, -bɒn]
Bourchier English surname) 'baʊtʃə*
Bourdillon (English surname) bə'dɪljən,
bɔː'dɪljən [bɔə'd-], bɔː'dɪlən [bɔə'd-]
bourdon, -s 'bɔːdn ['bɔəd-, 'bʊəd-], -z
bourgeois (middle class) 'bɔːʒwɑː ['bʊəʒ-]
(burʒwa)

58

bourgeois (*printing type*) bɜ:ˈdʒɔɪs
bourgeoisie ˌbɔːʒwɑ:ˈzi: [ˌbʊəʒ-, -ʒwə'z-] (burʒwazi)
Bourke bɜ:k
bourn(e), -s bɔːn [bɔən, bʊən], -z
Bourne bɔːn [bɔən, bʊən], *as surname also* bɜːn
Bournemouth 'bɔːnməθ ['bɔən-, 'bʊən-, *rarely* -maʊθ]
Bournville 'bɔːnvɪl ['bɔən-, 'bʊən-]
bourrée, -s 'bʊreɪ (bure), -z
bourse, -s bʊəs, -ɪz
bous|e (*drink*), **-es, -ing, -ed** bu:z [baʊz], -ɪz, -ɪŋ, -d
bous|e (*nautical term*), **-es, -ing, -ed** baʊz, -ɪz, -ɪŋ, -d
Bousfield 'baʊsfiːld
boustrophedon ˌbaʊstrəˈfiːdən
bout, -s baʊt, -s
boutique, -s bu:ˈtiːk, -s (butik)
bouts-rimés ˌbuːˈriːmeɪ [-eɪz] (burime)
Bouverie 'bu:vərɪ
Bovey (*place*) 'bʌvɪ, (*surname*) 'bu:vɪ, 'bəʊvɪ, 'bʌvɪ
Bovill 'bəʊvɪl
bovine 'bəʊvaɪn
Bovingdon (*in Hertfordshire*) 'bʌvɪŋdən ['bɒv-]
Note.—Locally 'bʌv-.
Bovril 'bɒvrəl [-rɪl]
bow (*s.*) (*bending, fore end of ship*), **-s** baʊ, -z
bow (*s.*) (*for shooting, etc., knot*) (**B.**), **-s** bəʊ, -z
bow (*v.*) (*bend*), **-s, -ing, -ed** baʊ, -z, -ɪŋ, -d
bow (*v.*) (*in playing the violin, etc.*), **-s, -ing/s, -ed** bəʊ, -z, -ɪŋ/z, -d
Bowater (*surname*) 'bəʊˌwɔːtə*, 'baʊətə*
Bowden 'bəʊdn, 'baʊdn
Bowdler 'baʊdlə*
†**bowdlerization** [**-isa-**] ˌbaʊdləraɪˈzeɪʃn
bowdleriz|e [**-is|e**], **-es, -ing, -ed** 'baʊdləraɪz, -ɪz, -ɪŋ, -d
Bowdoin 'bəʊdn
bowel, -s 'baʊəl [-el, baʊl], -z
Bowen 'bəʊɪn
bower (**B.**), **-s** 'baʊə*, -z
Bowering 'baʊərɪŋ
bowery (**B.**) 'baʊərɪ
Bowes, -Lyon bəʊz, -'laɪən
Bowie (*Scottish surname*) 'baʊɪ
bowie-kni|fe, -ves 'bəʊɪnaɪ|f [ˌ-ˈ-], -vz
Bowker 'baʊkə*
bow-knot, -s 'bəʊnɒt [ˌbəʊ'n-], -s
bowl (*s. v.*), **-s, -ing, -ed, -er/s** bəʊl, -z, -ɪŋ, -d, -ə*/z

Bowland 'bəʊlənd
bow-legged 'bəʊlegd [-ˌlegɪd, ˌ-'-(-)]
bowler (**B.**), **-s** 'bəʊlə*, -z
Bowles bəʊlz
bowline, -s 'bəʊlɪn, -z
Bowling 'bəʊlɪŋ
bowling-green, -s 'bəʊlɪŋgriːn, -z
Bowlker 'bəʊkə*
bow|man (**B.**), **-men** 'bəʊ|mən, -mən [-men]
Bowmer 'bəʊmə*
Bown baʊn
Bowness bəʊ'nes [ˌbəʊ'nes]
Bowra 'baʊrə ['baʊərə]
Bowring 'baʊrɪŋ ['baʊər-]
Bowron 'baʊrən ['baʊər-]
bowshot, -s 'bəʊʃɒt, -s
bowsprit, -s 'bəʊsprɪt, -s
bowstring, -s 'bəʊstrɪŋ, -z
Bowtell bəʊ'tel
bow-tie, -s ˌbəʊ'taɪ ['--], -z
bow-window, -s ˌbəʊ'wɪndəʊ, -z
bow-wow, -s (*interj.*) ˌbaʊ'waʊ, (*s., dog*) 'baʊwaʊ, -z
Bowyer 'bəʊjə*
box (*s. v.*) (**B.**), **-es, -ing, -ed, -er/s** bɒks, -ɪz, -ɪŋ, -t, -ə*/z
box-bed, -s ˌbɒks'bed ['bɒksb-], -z
box-cloth 'bɒksklɒθ [*old-fashioned* -klɔːθ]
boxer (**B.**), **-s** 'bɒksə*, -z
Boxing-day, -s 'bɒksɪŋdeɪ, -z
boxing-glove, -s 'bɒksɪŋglʌv, -z
boxing-match, -es 'bɒksɪŋmætʃ, -ɪz
Boxmoor 'bɒksˌmʊə* [-mɔə*, -mɔː*, *also locally* -'-]
box-office, -s 'bɒksˌɒfɪs, -ɪz
box-room, -s 'bɒksrʊm [-ruːm], -z
boxwood 'bɒkswʊd
boy, -s bɔɪ, -z
Boyce bɔɪs
boycott (*s. v.*) (**B.**), **-s, -ing, -ed, -er/s** 'bɔɪkɒt [-kət], -s, -ɪŋ, -ɪd, -ə*/z
Boyd bɔɪd
Boyet (*Shakespearian character*) bɔɪ'et ['--]
boyhood, -s 'bɔɪhʊd, -z
boyish, -ly, -ness 'bɔɪʃ, -lɪ, -nɪs [-nəs]
Boy|le, -ne bɔɪ|l, -n
Boyton 'bɔɪtn
Boz bɒz [*rarely* bəʊz]
Note.—This pen-name of Charles Dickens was originally pronounced bəʊz, *but this pronunciation is not often heard now.*
Bozman 'bɒzmən
bra, -s brɑ:, -z
Brabant brə'bænt

59

Brabantio (*Shakespearian character*) brə'bæntɪəʊ [-nʃɪəʊ, -nʃjəʊ]
Brabazon 'bræbəzn
Brabourne (*place*) 'breɪbɔːn [-bɔən], (*family name*) 'breɪbən, -bɔːn [-bɔən]
brac|e (*s. v.*) (B.), -es, -ing, -ed breɪs, -ɪz, -ɪŋ, -t
bracelet, -s 'breɪslɪt [-lət], -s
brach, -es brætʃ, -ɪz
Bracher 'breɪtʃə*
brachial 'breɪkjəl [-kɪəl]
brachycephalic ˌbrækɪke'fælɪk [-kɪkɪ'f-, -kɪse'f-, -kɪsɪ'f-]
brack, -s bræk, -s
bracken 'brækən
Brackenbury 'brækənbərɪ
bracket (*s. v.*), -s, -ing, -ed 'brækɪt, -s, -ɪŋ, -ɪd
brackish, -ness 'brækɪʃ, -nɪs [-nəs]
Bracknell 'bræknəl [-nl̩]
brad, -s bræd, -z
bradawl, -s 'brædɔːl, -z
Bradbury 'brædbərɪ
Braddon 'brædn
Braden 'breɪdn
Brad|field, -ford 'bræd|fiːld, -fəd
Bradgate 'brædgɪt [-geɪt]
Brading 'breɪdɪŋ
Bradlaugh 'brædlɔː
Brad|law, -ley, -shaw 'bræd|lɔː, -lɪ, -ʃɔː
Bradwardine 'brædwədiːn
Brady 'breɪdɪ
brae, -s breɪ, -z
Braemar breɪ'mɑː* (*also* '— *when attributive*)
Braeriach ˌbreɪə'rɪək [-əx]
brag, -s, -ging/ly, -ged bræg, -z, -ɪŋ/lɪ, -d
Bragg bræg
braggadocio,   -s   ˌbrægə'dəʊtʃɪəʊ [-tʃjəʊ], -z
braggart, -s 'brægət [-gɑːt], -s
Braham 'breɪəm
Brahan brɔːn, brɑːn
Brahe (*Danish astronomer*) 'brɑːə ['brɑːhə, 'brɑːɪ, 'brɑːhɪ]
brahma (B.), -s 'brɑːmə, -z
Brahman, -s, -ism 'brɑːmən, -z, -ɪzəm
Brahmaputra ˌbrɑːmə'puːtrə (*Hindi* brəhməpwtrə)
Brahmin, -s, -ism 'brɑːmɪn, -z, -ɪzəm
brahminical brɑː'mɪnɪkl
Brahms brɑːmz (brɑːms)
braid (*s. v.*) (B.), -s, -ing, -ed breɪd, -z, -ɪŋ, -ɪd
brail, -s breɪl, -z
Braille (*writing for the blind*) breɪl
Brailsford 'breɪlsfəd

brain (B.), -s breɪn, -z
brain|-fag, -fever 'breɪn|fæg, -ˌfiːvə*
brainless, -ness 'breɪnlɪs [-ləs], -nɪs [-nəs]
brainsick 'breɪnsɪk
brainstorm, -s 'breɪnstɔːm, -z
Braintree 'breɪntriː [*locally* -trɪ]
brainwash, -es, -ing, -ed 'breɪnwɒʃ, -ɪz, -ɪŋ, -t
brainwave, -s 'breɪnweɪv, -z
brain|y, -ier, -iest 'breɪn|ɪ, -ɪə* [-jə*], -ɪɪst [-jɪst]
brais|e, -es, -ing, -ed breɪz, -ɪz, -ɪŋ, -d
Braithwaite 'breɪθweɪt
brake, (*s.*), -s breɪk, -s
Brakenridge 'brækənrɪdʒ
brake-van, -s 'breɪkvæn, -z
Bralsford 'brælsfəd
Bramah 'brɑːmə
Bramall 'bræmɔːl
bramble, -s; -bush/es 'bræmbl, -z; -bʊʃ/ɪz
brambly 'bræmblɪ
Bramley, -s 'bræmlɪ, -z
Brampton 'bræmptən
Bramwell 'bræmwəl [-wel]
bran bræn
brancard, -s 'bræŋkəd [-kɑːd], -z
branch (*s. v.*) (B.), -es, -ing, -ed brɑːntʃ, -ɪz, -ɪŋ, -t
bran|chia, -chiae 'bræŋ|kɪə, -kɪiː
branchiate 'bræŋkɪeɪt [-kɪt, -kɪət]
brand (*s. v.*) (B.), -s, -ing, -ed brænd, -z, -ɪŋ, -ɪd
Brandenburg 'brændənbɜːg
branding-iron, -s 'brændɪŋˌaɪən, -z
brandish, -es, -ing, -ed 'brændɪʃ, -ɪz, -ɪŋ, -t
brand-new ˌbrænd'njuː: ['--]
Brandon 'brændən
Brandram 'brændrəm
brand|y, -ies, -ied 'brænd|ɪ, -ɪz, -ɪd
brandy-snap, -s 'brændɪsnæp, -s
brank, -s bræŋk, -s
Branksome 'bræŋksəm
bran-mash ˌbræn'mæʃ
bran-pie, -s ˌbræn'paɪ, -z
Branson 'brænsn
Branston 'brænstən
brant, -s brænt, -s
Brant (*surname*) brɑːnt
brant|-goose, -geese ˌbrænt|'guːs, -'giːs
Braque brɑːk [bræk]
Brasenose 'breɪznəʊz
brash (*s. adj.*), -es bræʃ, -ɪz
brasier, -s 'breɪzjə* [-zɪə*, -ʒjə*, -ʒɪə*, -ʒə*], -z
Brasilia brə'zɪljə

brass, -es brɑ:s, -ɪz
brassard, -s 'bræsɑ:d [bræ'sɑ:d], -z
brass-band, -s ˌbrɑ:s'bænd, -z
brasserie, -s 'bræsərɪ, -z
Brassey 'bræsɪ
brass-founder, -s 'brɑ:sˌfaʊndə*, -z
brass-hat, -s ˌbrɑ:s'hæt ['--], -s
brassière, -s 'bræsɪə* [-sjə*, -sɪeə*,
'bræzɪə*, -zjə*], -z
brass|y [-|ie] (golf club), -ies 'brɑ:s|ɪ,
-ɪz
brass|y (adj.), -ier, -iest 'brɑ:s|ɪ, -ɪə*,
-ɪɪst
Brasted 'breɪstɪd ['bræ-]
brat, -s bræt, -s
Bratislava ˌbrætɪ'slɑ:və
bratt|le, -les, -ling, -led 'bræt|l, -lz,
-lɪŋ [-lɪŋ], -ld
Brattleboro 'brætlbərə
Braughing 'bræfɪŋ
Braun (English surname) brɔ:n
bravado, -(e)s brə'vɑ:dəʊ, -z
brav|e (adj. v.), -er, -est, -ely; -es, -ing,
-ed breɪv, -ə*, -ɪst, -lɪ; -z, -ɪŋ, -d
braver|y, -ies 'breɪvər|ɪ, -ɪz
Bravington 'brævɪŋtən
bravo (s. interj.), -(e)s ˌbrɑ:'vəʊ
[brɑ:'v-], -z
bravura brə'vʊərə [-'vjʊər-]
brawl (s. v.), -s, -ing, -ed, -er/s brɔ:l, -z,
-ɪŋ, -d, -ə*/z
brawn brɔ:n
Brawne brɔ:n
brawn|y, -ier, -iest, -iness 'brɔ:n|ɪ, -ɪə*
[-jə*], -ɪɪst [-jɪst], -ɪnɪs [-ɪnəs]
Braxton 'brækstən
braxy 'bræksɪ
bray (s. v.), (B.), -s, -ing, -ed breɪ, -z,
-ɪŋ, -d
Brayley 'breɪlɪ
braz|e, -es, -ing, -ed breɪz, -ɪz, -ɪŋ, -d
brazen, -ly, -ness 'breɪzn, -lɪ, -nɪs [-nəs]
brazen-faced 'breɪznfeɪst [ˌ--'-]
brazier, -s 'breɪzjə* [-zɪə*, -ʒjə*, -ʒɪə,
-ʒə*], -z
Brazier (surname) 'breɪʒə*
Brazil (country) brə'zɪl, (English surname) 'bræzɪl [-zl]
Brazilian, -s brə'zɪljən [-lɪən], -z
Brazil-nut, -s brə'zɪlnʌt, -s
breach (s. v.), -es, -ing, -ed bri:tʃ, -ɪz,
-ɪŋ, -t
bread, -s bred, -z
Breadalbane (Earl) brə'dɔ:lbən, (place)
brə'dælbən [-'dɔ:l-]
bread-basket, -s 'bredˌbɑ:skɪt, -s
breadcrumb, -s 'bredkrʌm, -z
bread-fruit 'bredfru:t

bread-stuff, -s 'bredstʌf, -s
breadth, -s bretθ [bredθ], -s
breadth|ways,   -wise   'bredθ|weɪz
['bretθ-], -waɪz
bread-winner, -s 'bredˌwɪnə*, -z
break (s. v.), -s, -ing, broke, broken
breɪk, -s, -ɪŋ, brəʊk, 'brəʊkən
breakable, -s 'breɪkəbl, -z
breakage, -s 'breɪkɪdʒ, -ɪz
break-away, -s 'breɪkəweɪ [ˌ--'-], -z
breakdown, -s 'breɪkdaʊn, -z
breaker, -s 'breɪkə*, -z
breakfast (s. v.), -s, -ing, -ed 'brekfəst,
-s, -ɪŋ, -ɪd
breakfast-set, -s 'brekfəstset, -s
break-neck 'breɪknek
Breakspear 'breɪkˌspɪə*
break-through, -s 'breɪkθru: [ˌ-'-], -z
break-up, -s 'breɪkʌp [ˌbreɪk'ʌp], -s
breakwater, -s 'breɪkˌwɔ:tə*, -z
bream (B.), -s bri:m, -z
Breamore 'bremə*
breast (s. v.), -s, -ing, -ed brest, -s, -ɪŋ,
-ɪd
breast-bone, -s 'brestbəʊn, -z
breast|-deep, -high ˌbrest|'di:p, -'haɪ
breast-plate, -s 'brestpleɪt, -s
breastsummer, -s 'bresəmə*, -z
breastwork, -s 'brestwɜ:k, -s
breath, -s breθ, -s
breathalys|e, -es, -ed, -ing, -er/s
'breθəlaɪz, -ɪz, -d, -ɪŋ, -ə*/z
breath|e, -es, -ing, -ed bri:ð, -z, -ɪŋ, -d
breathed (phonetic term) breθt [bri:ðd]
breather, -s 'bri:ðə*, -z
breath-group, -s 'breθgru:p, -s
breathiness 'breθɪnɪs [-nəs]
breathing-space, -s 'bri:ðɪŋspeɪs, -ɪz
breathless, -ly, -ness 'breθlɪs [-ləs], -lɪ,
-nɪs [-nəs]
breath|y, -ier, -iest 'breθ|ɪ, -ɪə*, -ɪɪst
Brebner 'brebnə*
Brechin (in Scotland) 'bri:kɪn ['bri:xɪn]
Breckenridge [-kin-] 'breknrɪdʒ
Brecknock, -shire 'breknɒk [-nək], -ʃə*
[-ˌʃɪə*]
Brecon 'brekən
bred (from breed) bred
Bredon 'bri:dən
bree bri:
breech (s.) (of a gun, etc.), -es, -ed bri:tʃ,
-ɪz, -t
breeches (garment) 'brɪtʃɪz
breeching, -s 'brɪtʃɪŋ, -z
breech-loader, -s 'bri:tʃˌləʊdə*, -z
breed (s. v.), -s, -ing, bred bri:d, -z, -ɪŋ,
bred
breeder, -s 'bri:də*, -z

breeder-reactor, -s 'briːdəri:ˌæktə* [-rɪˌækt-], -z
breeks briːks
breeze, -s briːz, -ɪz
breez|y, -ier, -iest, -ily, -iness 'briːz|ɪ, -ɪə* [-jə*], -ɪɪst [-jɪst], -ɪlɪ [-əlɪ], -ɪnɪs [-ɪnəs]
Breingan 'brɪŋən
Bremen 'breɪmən ('breːmən)
Brennan 'brenən
Brent brent
Brentford 'brentfəd
brent|-goose, -geese ˌbrent|'guːs, -'giːs
Brer brɜː* [breə*]
Brereton 'brɪətn
Breslau (now Wrocław) 'brezlaʊ ('brɛslaʊ)
Brest brest
brethren (archaic plur. of brother) 'breðrən [-rɪn]
Breton, -s 'bretən (brətɔ̃), -z
Bret(t) bret
Brettagh 'bretə
Bretwalda bret'wɔːldə ['bretˌw-, -ɒl-]
Breughel (Flemish artist) 'brɔɪgəl ['brɜːg-, 'bruːg-]
breve, -s briːv, -z
brevet (s. v.), -s, -ing, -ed 'brevɪt, -s, -ɪŋ, -ɪd
†breviar|y, -ies 'briːvjər|ɪ [-vɪə-], -ɪz
breviate, -s 'briːvɪɪt [-vjɪt, -ət], -s
brevier brə'vɪə* [brɪ'v-]
brevity 'brevətɪ [-ɪtɪ]
brew (s. v.) (B.), -s, -ing, -ed, -er/s bruː, -z, -ɪŋ ['bruɪŋ], -d, -ə*/z [bruə*/z]
Brewer 'bruːə* [bruə]
brewer|y, -ies 'bruər|ɪ ['bruːər-], -ɪz
Brewster 'bruːstə*
Brian 'braɪən
briar, -s 'braɪə*, -z
Briareus braɪ'eərɪəs
Briault 'briːəʊ
brib|e (s. v.), -es, -ing, -ed, -er/s braɪb, -z, -ɪŋ, -d, -ə*/z
briber|y, -ies 'braɪbər|ɪ, -ɪz
bric-à-brac 'brɪkəbræk
Brice braɪs
brick, -s brɪk, -s
brickbat, -s 'brɪkbæt, -s
brick-dust 'brɪkdʌst
brick-field, -s 'brɪkfiːld, -z
brick-kiln, -s 'brɪkkɪln [-kɪl], -z
   Note.—The pronunciation -kɪl is used chiefly by those concerned with the working of kilns.
bricklayer, -s 'brɪkˌleɪə*, -z
bricklaying 'brɪkˌleɪɪŋ
brickmak|er/s, -ing 'brɪkˌmeɪk|ə*/z, -ɪŋ

brickwork 'brɪkwɜːk
bridal 'braɪdl
bride, -s braɪd, -z
bride-chamber, -s 'braɪdˌtʃeɪmbə*, -z
bridegroom, -s 'braɪdgrʊm [-gruːm], -z
bridesmaid, -s 'braɪdzmeɪd, -z
brides|man, -men 'braɪdz|mən, -mən [-men]
Bridewell 'braɪdwəl [-wel]
bridg|e (s. v.) (B.), -es, -ing, -ed brɪdʒ, -ɪz, -ɪŋ, -d
bridgehead, -s 'brɪdʒhed, -z
Bridgenorth 'brɪdʒnɔːθ
Bridger 'brɪdʒə*
Bridgerule 'brɪdʒruːl
Bridges 'brɪdʒɪz
Bridget 'brɪdʒɪt
Bridgetown 'brɪdʒtaʊn
Bridgewater 'brɪdʒˌwɔːtə*
Bridgnorth 'brɪdʒnɔːθ
Bridgwater 'brɪdʒˌwɔːtə*
bridie (B.), -s 'braɪdɪ, -z
brid|le (s. v.), -les, -ling, -led 'braɪd|l, -lz, -lɪŋ [-lɪŋ], -ld
bridle-pa|th, -ths 'braɪdlpɑː|θ, -ðz
Bridlington 'brɪdlɪŋtən
bridoon, -s brɪ'duːn, -z
Bridport 'brɪdpɔːt
Bridson 'braɪdsn
brief (s. adj. v.), -s, -er, -est, -ly, -ness; -ing, -ed briːf, -s, -ə*, -ɪst, -lɪ, -nɪs [-nəs]; -ɪŋ, -t
briefcas|e, -es 'briːfkeɪs, -ɪz
briefless 'briːflɪs [-ləs]
brier, -s 'braɪə*, -z
Brierley 'braɪəlɪ
brig, -s brɪg, -z
brigade, -s brɪ'geɪd, -z
brigadier, -s ˌbrɪgə'dɪə* [attributively also '--ˌ-], -z
brigadier-general, -s 'brɪgəˌdɪə-'dʒenərəl, -z
brigand, -s, -age 'brɪgənd, -z, -ɪdʒ
brigantine, -s 'brɪgəntiːn [-taɪn], -z
Brigg, -s brɪg, -z
Brigham 'brɪgəm
bright (B.), -er, -est, -ly, -ness braɪt, -ə*, -ɪst, -lɪ, -nɪs [-nəs]
bright|en, -ens, -ening, -ened 'braɪt|n, -nz, -nɪŋ [-n̩ɪŋ], -nd
Brightlingsea 'braɪtlɪŋsiː
Brighton 'braɪtn
Brigid 'brɪdʒɪd
Brigstock(e) 'brɪgstɒk
brill (B.), -s brɪl, -z
brillian|ce, -cy 'brɪljən|s, -sɪ
brilliant (s. adj.), -s, -ly, -ness 'brɪljənt, -s, -lɪ, -nɪs [-nəs]

brilliantine 'brɪljənti:n [ˌ--'-]
brim (s. v.), -s, -ming, -med brɪm, -z, -ɪŋ, -d
brimful ˌbrɪm'fʊl ['--]
brimstone 'brɪmstəʊn
Brind brɪnd
Brindisi 'brɪndɪzɪ [-zi:]
brindle (B.), -s, -d 'brɪndl, -z, -d
brine braɪn
bring, -s, -ing, brought, bringer/s brɪŋ, -z, -ɪŋ, brɔ:t, 'brɪŋə*/z
brink, -s brɪŋk, -s
brinkmanship 'brɪŋkmənʃɪp
Brinsley 'brɪnzlɪ
Brinsmead, -s 'brɪnzmi:d, -z
brin|y, iness 'braɪn|ɪ, -ɪnɪs [-ɪnəs]
bri-nylon ˌbraɪ'naɪlən [-lɒn]
brio 'bri:əʊ ['briəʊ]
brioche, -s bri:'ɒʃ ['--, brɪ-, -əʊʃ] (brɪɔʃ), -ɪz
briquette, -s brɪ'ket, -s
Brisbane 'brɪzbən [-bem]
Note.—'brɪzbən is the pronunciation in Australia.

brisk, -er, -est, -ly, -ness brɪsk, -ə*, -ɪst, -lɪ, -nɪs [-nəs]
brisket, -s 'brɪskɪt, -s
brist|le (s. v.), -les, -ling, -led 'brɪs|l, -lz, -lɪŋ [-l̩ŋ], -ld
brist|ly, -liness 'brɪs|lɪ [-l̩ɪ], -lɪnɪs [-l̩nɪs, -ɪnəs]
Bristol 'brɪstl
Bristow(e) 'brɪstəʊ
Britain 'brɪtn [-tən]
Britannia brɪ'tænjə
Britannic, -a brɪ'tænɪk, -ə
briticism, -s 'brɪtɪsɪzəm, -z
British, -er/s 'brɪtɪʃ, -ə*/z
britishism, -s 'brɪtɪʃɪzəm, -z
Briton, -s 'brɪtn [-tən], -z
Brittain (surname) brɪ'teɪn, 'brɪtn [-tən]
Brittany 'brɪtənɪ [-tn̩ɪ]
Britten 'brɪtn [-tən]
britt|le, -ler, -lest, -leness 'brɪt|l, -l̩ə*, -l̩ɪst, -lnɪs [-nəs]
Britton 'brɪtən
Brixton 'brɪkstən
Brno 'bɜ:nəʊ, brə'nəʊ
broach, -es, -ing, -ed brəʊtʃ, -ɪz, -ɪŋ, -t
broad, -er, -est, -ly, -ness brɔ:d, -ə*, -ɪst, -lɪ, -nɪs [-nəs]
Broad, -s brɔ:d, -z
broad-arrow, -s ˌbrɔ:d'ærəʊ, -z
Broadbent 'brɔ:dbent
broadbrimmed ˌbrɔ:d'brɪmd [also '-- when attributive]

broadcast (s. adj. v.), -s, -ing, -er/s 'brɔ:dka:st, -s, -ɪŋ. -ə*/z
broadcloth 'brɔ:dklɒθ [old-fashioned -klɔ:θ]
broad|en, -ens, -ening, -ened 'brɔ:d|n, -nz, -n̩ɪŋ [-nɪŋ], -nd
broad-gauge 'brɔ:dgeɪdʒ
Broadhurst 'brɔ:dhɜ:st
broadloom 'brɔ:dlu:m
broad-minded ˌbrɔ:d'maɪndɪd ['-ˌ--]
broad-mindedness ˌbrɔ:d'maɪndɪdnɪs [-nəs]
Broadmoor 'brɔ:dˌmʊə* [-mɔə*, -mɔ:*]
broadsheet, -s 'brɔ:dʃi:t, -s
broadside, -s 'brɔ:dsaɪd, -z
Broadstairs 'brɔ:dsteəz
broadsword, -s 'brɔ:dsɔ:d [-sɔəd], -z
Broad|way, -wood/s 'brɔ:d|weɪ, -wʊd/z
Brobdingnag 'brɒbdɪŋnæg
Brobdingnagian, -s ˌbrɒbdɪŋ'nægɪən, -z
brocade, -s, -d brəʊ'keɪd [brʊ'k-], -z, -ɪd
brocard, -s 'brəʊkəd [-ka:d], -z
broc(c)oli 'brɒkəlɪ [also -laɪ, esp. in country districts]
brochure, -s 'brəʊʃə* [-ˌʃjʊə*, -ˌʃʊə*, brɒ'ʃjʊə*, brɒ'ʃʊə*, brə'ʃʊə*], -z
brock (B.), -s brɒk, -s
Brocken 'brɒkən
Brockenhurst 'brɒkənhɜ:st
Brocklehurst 'brɒklhɜ:st
Brock|ley, -man 'brɒk|lɪ, -mən
Brockwell 'brɒkwəl
Brod(e)rick 'brɒdrɪk
Brodie 'brəʊdɪ
brogue, -s brəʊg, -z
broil (s. v.), -s, -ing, -ed brɔɪl, -z, -ɪŋ, -d
brok|e (v.), -es, -ing, -ed brəʊk, -s, -ɪŋ, -t
broke (from break), -n/ly brəʊk, -ən/lɪ
Broke brʊk
broken-down ˌbrəʊkən'daʊn [also '-- when attributive]
broken-hearted ˌbrəʊkən'ha:tɪd ['-ˌ-- when attributive]
broken-winded ˌbrəʊkən'wɪndɪd
broker, -s; -age, -y 'brəʊkə*, -z; -rɪdʒ, -rɪ
broll|y, -ies 'brɒl|ɪ, -ɪz
Bromage 'brʌmɪdʒ
bromate, -s 'brəʊmeɪt [-mɪt], -s
brome (grass), -s brəʊm [rarely bru:m], -z
Brome (surname) bru:m
Bromham 'brɒməm
bromic 'brəʊmɪk
bromide, -s 'brəʊmaɪd, -z
bromine 'brəʊmi:n [-mɪn]

63

Bromley 'brɒmlɪ ['brʌm-]
Brompton 'brɒmptən ['brʌm-]
Bromsgrove 'brɒmzgrəʊv ['brʌm-]
Bromwich (in Castle Bromwich, district of Birmingham) 'brɒmɪdʒ ['brʌm-, -ɪtʃ], (in West Bromwich, West Midlands) 'brɒmɪdʒ ['brʌm-, -ɪtʃ], (surname) 'brʌmɪdʒ
bron|chia, -chiae 'brɒŋ|kɪə [-kjə], -kɪiː [-kjiː]
bronchial 'brɒŋkjəl [-kɪəl]
bronchitic brɒŋ'kɪtɪk [brɒn'k-]
bronchitis brɒŋ'kaɪtɪs [brɒn'k-, -təs]
broncho-pneumonia ˌbrɒŋkəʊnjuː-'məʊnjə [-njʊ'm-, -nɪə]
bronch|us, -i 'brɒŋk|əs, -aɪ
bronco, -s 'brɒŋkəʊ, -z
Brontë 'brɒntɪ [-teɪ]
brontosaur|us, -uses, -i ˌbrɒntə'sɔːr|əs -əsɪz, -aɪ
Bronx brɒŋks
bronz|e (s. v.), -es, -ing, -ed; -y brɒnz, -ɪz, -ɪŋ, -d; -ɪ
brooch, -es brəʊtʃ, -ɪz
brood (s. v.), -s, -ing, -ed bruːd, -z, -ɪŋ, -ɪd
brood|y, -ily, -iness 'bruːd|ɪ, -ɪlɪ [-əlɪ], -ɪnɪs [-ɪnəs]
brook (s. v.), -s, -ing, -ed brʊk, -s, -ɪŋ, -t
Brook(e), -s brʊk, -s
Brookfield 'brʊkfiːld
Brookland, -s 'brʊklənd, -z
brooklet, -s 'brʊklɪt [-lət], -s
Brookline 'brʊklaɪn
Brooklyn 'brʊklɪn
Brooksmith 'brʊksmɪθ
Brookwood 'brʊkwʊd
broom (shrub), -s bruːm [brʊm], -z
broom (for sweeping), -s bruːm [brʊm], -z
    Note.—Some people pronounce bruːm normally, but -brʊm when the word occurs unstressed as the second element of a compound.
Broom(e) bruːm
Broomfield 'bruːmfiːld ['brʊm-]
broomstick, -s 'bruːmstɪk ['brʊm-], -s
Bros. 'brʌðəz [sometimes facetiously brɒs, brɒz]
Brosnahan 'brɒznəhən ['brɒs-]
broth, -s brɒθ [old-fashioned brɔːθ, and in compounds], brɒθs [brɔːðz, brɔːθs]
brothel, -s 'brɒθl, -z
brother, -s 'brʌðə*, -z
brotherhood, -s 'brʌðəhʊd, -z
broth|er-in-law, -ers-in-law 'brʌð|ərɪn-lɔː, -əzɪnlɔː
brotherl|y, -iness 'brʌðəl|ɪ, -ɪnɪs [-ɪnəs]

Brough brʌf
brougham, -s 'bruːəm [brʊəm, old-fashioned bruːm], -z
Brougham brʊm [bruːm], 'bruːəm, 'brəʊəm
    Note.—The present baron pronounces brʊm.
Brougham and Vaux ˌbruːmən'vɔːks
brought (from bring) brɔːt
Broughton (in Northamptonshire) 'brautn, (all others in England) 'brɔːtn
Broughty 'brɔːtɪ
brow, -s brau, -z
browbeat, -s, -ing, -en 'braubiːt, -s, -ɪŋ, -n
brown (s. adj. v.) (B.), -s; -er, -est, -ness; -ing, -ed braun, -z; -ə*, -ɪst, -nɪs [-nəs]; -ɪŋ, -d
Browne braun
brownie, -s 'braunɪ, -z
browning (B.) 'braunɪŋ
brownish 'braunɪʃ
Brownrigg 'braunrɪg
Brownsmith 'braunsmɪθ
brows|e, -es, -ing, -ed brauz, -ɪz, -ɪŋ, -d
Browse brauz
Bruce, -smith bruːs, -smɪθ
Bruckner 'brʊknə*
Bruges bruːʒ (bry:ʒ)
bruin (B.), -s 'bruːɪn ['brʊɪn], -z
bruis|e (s. v.), -es, -ing, -ed, -er/s bruːz, -ɪz, -ɪŋ, -d, -ə*/z
bruit (s. v.), -s, -ing, -ed bruːt, -s, -ɪŋ,-ɪd
brume bruːm
Brummagem 'brʌmədʒəm
Brunei 'bruːnaɪ [-'-]
Brunel brʊ'nel [bruː'n-]
brunette, -s bruː'net [brʊ'n-] (brynɛt), -s
Brünnhilde brʊn'hɪldə ['brʊnˌh-] (bryn'hildə)
Brunswick 'brʌnzwɪk
brunt brʌnt
Brunton 'brʌntən
brush (s. v.), -es, -ing, -ed brʌʃ, -ɪz, -ɪŋ, -t
brushwood 'brʌʃwʊd
brusque, -ly, -ness bruːsk [brʊsk, brʌsk] (brysk), -lɪ, -nɪs [-nəs]
Brussels 'brʌslz
Brussels-sprouts ˌbrʌsl'sprauts
brut|al, -ally 'bruːt|l, -əlɪ [-ḷɪ]
brutalit|y, -ies bruː'tælət|ɪ [brʊ't-, -ɪt|ɪ], -ɪz
brutaliz|e [-is|e], -es, -ing, -ed 'bruːtə-laɪz [-tḷaɪz], -ɪz, -ɪŋ, -d
brute, -s bruːt, -s

brutish, -ly, -ness 'bru:tɪʃ, -lɪ, -nɪs [-nəs]
Brutnell 'bru:tnel [-nəl]
Bruton 'bru:tən
Brutus 'bru:təs
Bryan, -s, -t 'braɪən, -z, -t
Bryce braɪs
Brydson 'braɪdsn
Bryers 'braɪəz
Brynmawr (in Wales) brɪn'mauə* (Welsh brɪn'maur)
Bryn Mawr (in U.S.A.) brɪn'mɔ:*
Brynmor 'brɪnmɔ:* (Welsh 'brɪnmor)
bryony 'braɪənɪ
Bryson 'braɪsn
bubb|le (s. v.), -les, -ling, -led 'bʌb|l, -lz, -lɪŋ [-lɪŋ], -ld
bubble-and-squeak ˌbʌbləŋ'skwi:k
bubble-gum 'bʌblgʌm
bubbly 'bʌblɪ [-lɪ]
bubo, -es 'bju:bəu, -z
bubonic bju:'bɒnɪk [bjʊ-]
buccal 'bʌkəl
buccaneer, -s ˌbʌkə'nɪə*, -z
Buccleuch bə'klu:
Bucephalus bju:'sefələs [bjʊ-]
Buchan 'bʌkən ['bʌxən]
Buchanan bju:'kænən [bjʊ-]
Bucharest ˌbju:kə'rest [ˌbu:-, '---]
Buchel 'bju:ʃl
buck (s. v.) (B.), -s, -ing, -ed bʌk, -s, -ɪŋ, -t
buckboard, -s 'bʌkbɔ:d [-bɔəd], -z
bucket, -s 'bʌkɪt, -s
bucketful, -s 'bʌkɪtfʊl, -z
buckhorn 'bʌkhɔ:n
buckhound, -s 'bʊkhaʊnd, -z
Buckhurst 'bʌkhɜ:st ['bʌkə:st]
Buckingham, -shire 'bʌkɪŋəm, -ʃə* [-ˌʃɪə*]
Buckland 'bʌklənd
buck|le (s. v.) (B.), -les, -ling, -led 'bʌk|l, -lz, -lɪŋ [-lɪŋ], -ld
buckler, -s 'bʌklə*, -z
Buckley 'bʌklɪ
Buckmaster 'bʌkˌmɑ:stə*
Buckn|all, -ell 'bʌkn|əl [-l], -əl [-l]
Bucknill 'bʌknɪl
buck-passing 'bʌkˌpɑ:sɪŋ
buckram, -s 'bʌkrəm, -z
Bucks. bʌks
buckshee ˌbʌk'ʃi: ['--]
buckshot 'bʌkʃɒt
buckskin, -s, 'bʌkskɪn, -z
Buckston 'bʌkstən
buckwheat 'bʌkwi:t [-khw-]
bucolic, -al, -ally bju:'kɒlɪk [bjʊ-], -l, -əlɪ

bud (s. v.), -s, -ding, -ded bʌd, -z, -ɪŋ, -ɪd
Budapest ˌbju:də'pest [ˌbu:-]
Budd bʌd
Buddha 'bʊdə (Hindi bwddha)
Buddhi|c, -sm, -st/s 'bʊdɪ|k, -zəm, -st/s
buddleia, -s 'bʌdlɪə, -z
Bude bju:d
budg|e (B.), -es, -ing, -ed bʌdʒ, -ɪz, -ɪŋ, -d
budgerigar, -s 'bʌdʒərɪgɑ:*, -z
budget (s. v.), -s, -ing, -ed, -ary 'bʌdʒɪt, -s, -ɪŋ, -ɪd, -ərɪ
Budleigh 'bʌdlɪ
Buenos Aires ˌbwenəs'aɪərɪz [ˌbuɪn-, ˌbəuɪn-, ˌbəun-, -nə'zaɪərɪz, -nə'zeərɪz, -rɪs, -nə'zeəz] (ˌbwenos-'aires)
Buesst bju:st
buff bʌf
buffalo, -es 'bʌfələu [-fləu], -z
buffer, -s 'bʌfə*, -z
buffet (s.) (blow, sideboard), -s 'bʌfɪt, -s
buffet (s.) (refreshment), -s 'bʊfeɪ (byfɛ), -z
buffet (v.) (strike), -s, -ing, -ed 'bʌfɪt, -s, -ɪŋ, -ɪd
buffo, -s 'bʊfəu, -z
buffoon, -s bə'fu:n [bʌ'f-], -z
buffooner|y, -ies bə'fu:nər|ɪ [bʌ'f-], -ɪz
Buffs bʌfs
bug, -s, -ging, -ged bʌg, -z, -ɪŋ, -d
Bug (river) bu:g [bʌg]
bugaboo, -s 'bʌgəbu:, -z
Buganda bʊ'gændə
bugbear, -s 'bʌgbeə*, -z
bugger (s. v.), -s, -ing, -ed; -y 'bʌgə*, -z, -rɪŋ, -d; -rɪ
Buggs (surname) bju:gz, bʌgz
bugg|y, -ies 'bʌg|ɪ, -ɪz
bugle (B.), -s 'bju:gl, -z
bugler, -s 'bju:glə*, -z
bugloss 'bju:glɒs
buhl bu:l
Buick, -s 'bju:ɪk ['bjʊɪk], -s
build, -s, -ing, built, builder/s bɪld, -z, -ɪŋ, bɪlt, 'bɪldə*/z
build-up, -s 'bɪldʌp [ˌ-'-], -s
Builth bɪlθ
Buist bju:st
Bulawayo ˌbʊlə'weɪəu [-'waɪəu]
bulb, -s bʌlb, -z
bulbaceous bʌl'beɪʃəs
bulbous 'bʌlbəs
bulbul, -s 'bʊlbʊl, -z
Bulgar, -s 'bʌlgɑ:*, -z
Bulgaria, -n/s bʌl'geərɪə, -n/z
bulg|e (s. v.), -es, -ing, -ed bʌldʒ, -ɪz, -ɪŋ, -d

bulg|y, -iness 'bʌldʒ|ɪ, -ɪnɪs [-məs]
bulk (s. v.), -s, -ing, -ed bʌlk, -s, -ɪŋ, -t
bulkhead, -s 'bʌlkhed, -z
bulk|y, -ier, -iest, -ily, -iness 'bʌlk|ɪ, -ɪə* [-jə*], -ɪɪst [-jɪst], -ɪlɪ [-əlɪ], -ɪnɪs [-məs]
bull (s. v.) (B.), -s, -ing, -ed bʊl, -z, -ɪŋ, -d
bullace, -s 'bʊlɪs, -ɪz
Bullard 'bʊlɑ:d
bull-baiting 'bʊl,beɪtɪŋ
bull-cal|f, -ves ,bʊl'kɑ:|f ['bʊlkɑ:|f], -vz
bulldog, -s 'bʊldɒg, -z
bulldoz|e, -es, -ing, -ed, -er/s 'bʊldəʊz, -ɪz, -ɪŋ, -d, -ə*/z
Bulleid 'bʊli:d
Bull|en, -er 'bʊl|ɪn [-ən], -ə*
bullet, -s 'bʊlɪt, -s
bulletin, -s 'bʊlətɪn [-lɪt-], -z
bullet-proof 'bʊlɪtpru:f
bullfight, -s 'bʊlfaɪt, -s
bullfinch, -es 'bʊlfɪntʃ, -ɪz
bull-frog, -s 'bʊlfrɒg, -z
bullion, -ist/s 'bʊljən [-lɪən], -ɪst/s
bullish 'bʊlɪʃ
bullock (B.), -s 'bʊlək, -s
Bullokar 'bʊləkɑ:* [-lɒk-, -kə]
Bullough 'bʊləʊ
bull-ring, -s 'bʊlrɪŋ, -z
bull's-eye, -s 'bʊlzaɪ, -z
bull-terrier, -s ,bʊl'terɪə* [-rjə*], -z
bull|y (s. v.), -ies, -ying, -ied 'bʊl|ɪ, -ɪz, -ɪŋ, -ɪd
Bulmer 'bʊlmə*
bulrush, -es 'bʊlrʌʃ, -ɪz
Bulstrode 'bʊlstrəʊd, 'bʌl-
Bultitude 'bʊltɪtju:d
bulwark, -s 'bʊlwək [-wɜ:k], -s
Bulwer 'bʊlwə*
bum, -s bʌm, -z
bumble-bee, -s 'bʌmblbi:, -z
bumblepuppy 'bʌmbl,pʌpɪ
bumboat, -s 'bʌmbəʊt, -s
bumkin, -s 'bʌmkɪn [-mpk-], -z
bummaree, -s 'bʌmə'ri: ['---], -z
bummel 'bʊml ['bʌm-]
bump (s. v.), -s, -ing, -ed bʌmp, -s, -ɪŋ, -t [bʌmt]
bumper, -s 'bʌmpə*, -z
bumpkin, -s 'bʌmpkɪn, -z
bumptious, -ly, -ness 'bʌmpʃəs, -lɪ, -nɪs [-nəs]
Bumpus 'bʌmpəs
bump|y, -ier, -iest, -iness 'bʌmp|ɪ, -ɪə* [-jə*], -ɪɪst [-jɪst], -ɪnɪs [-məs]
bun, -s bʌn, -z

bunch (s. v.) (B.), -es, -ing, -ed bʌntʃ, -ɪz, -ɪŋ, -t
buncombe (B.) 'bʌŋkəm
bund|le (s. v.), -les, -ling, -led 'bʌnd|l, -lz, -lɪŋ [-lɪŋ], -ld
bung (s. v.), -s, -ing, -ed bʌŋ, -z, -ɪŋ, -d
bungaloid 'bʌŋgəlɔɪd
bungalow, -s 'bʌŋgələʊ [-glə̆ʊ], -z
Bungay 'bʌŋgɪ
Bunge 'bʌŋɪ
bung|le (s. v.), -les, -ling, -led, -ler/s 'bʌŋg|l, -lz, -lɪŋ [-lɪŋ], -ld, -lə*/z [-lə*/z]
bunion, -s 'bʌnjən, -z
bunk (s. v.), -s, -ing, -ed bʌŋk, -s, -ɪŋ, -t [bʌŋt]
bunker (s. v.) (B.), -s, -ing, -ed 'bʌŋkə*, -z, -rɪŋ, -d
bunkum 'bʌŋkəm
Bunnett 'bʌnɪt
bunn|y, -ies 'bʌn|ɪ, -ɪz
Bunsen 'bʊnsn ['bʌn-]
bunsen burner, -s ,bʌnsn'bɜ:nə*, -z
bunt, -s bʌnt, -s
bunting (B.), -s 'bʌntɪŋ, -z
buntline, -s 'bʌntlaɪn, -z
Bunyan 'bʌnjən
buoy (s. v.), -s, -ing, -ed bɔɪ, -z, -ɪŋ, -d
buoyan|cy, -t/ly 'bɔɪən|sɪ, -t/lɪ
bur, -s bɜ:*, -z
Burbage 'bɜ:bɪdʒ
Burberr|y, -ies 'bɜ:bər|ɪ, -ɪz
Burbey 'bɜ:bɪ
burb|le, -les, -ling, -led 'bɜ:b|l, -lz, -lɪŋ [-lɪŋ], -ld
Burbury 'bɜ:bərɪ
Burch, -ell bɜ:tʃ, -əl
burd|en, -ens, -ening, -ened 'bɜ:d|n, -nz, -nɪŋ [-nɪŋ], -nd
burdensome 'bɜ:dnsəm
Burdett bɜ:'det [bə-]
Burdett-Coutts ,bɜ:det'ku:ts [bɜ:,det-'ku:ts, bə-]
burdock, -s 'bɜ:dɒk, -s
Burdon 'bɜ:dn
bureau, -s 'bjʊərəʊ [bjʊə'rəʊ], -z
bureaucrac|y, -ies bjʊə'rɒkrəs|ɪ [bjə'r-, -'rəʊk-], -ɪz
bureaucrat, -s 'bjʊərəʊkræt, -s
bureaucratic ,bjʊərəʊ'krætɪk
burette, -s bjʊə'ret, -s
Burford 'bɜ:fəd
burg, -s bɜ:g, -z
Burgclere 'bɜ:kleə*
Burge, -s bɜ:dʒ, -ɪz
burgee, -s 'bɜ:dʒi: [-'-], -z
burge|on (s. v.), -ons, -oning, -oned 'bɜ:dʒ|ən, -ənz, -ənɪŋ [-nɪŋ], -ənd

66

burgess (**B.**), **-es** 'bɜːdʒɪs [-dʒes], -ɪz
burgh, **-s** 'bʌrə, -z
Burgh bɜːg, (*Baron*) 'bʌrə, (*Heath, in Surrey*) 'bʌrə, (*in Lincolnshire*) 'bʌrə, (*in Suffolk*) bɜːg ['bʌrə], (*Burgh-by-Sands*) brʌf
Burghclere 'bɜːkleə*
burgher, **-s** 'bɜːgə*, -z
Burghersh 'bɜːgəʃ
Burghley 'bɜːlɪ
Burgin 'bɜːgɪn, 'bɜːdʒɪn
burglar, **-s** 'bɜːglə*, -z
burglarious, **-ly** bɜː'gleərɪəs, -lɪ
burglar|y, **-ies** 'bɜːglər|ɪ, -ɪz
burg|le, **-les, -ling, -led** 'bɜːg|l, -lz, -lɪŋ [-lɪŋ], -ld
burgomaster, **-s** 'bɜːgəʊˌmɑːstə*, -z
Burgoyne 'bɜːgɔɪn, bɜː'gɔɪn
burgund|y (**B.**), **-ies** 'bɜːgənd|ɪ, -ɪz
burial, **-s**; **-ground/s, -place/s** 'berɪəl, -z; -graʊnd/z, -pleɪs/ɪz
burin, **-s** 'bjʊərɪn, -z
burk|e (**B.**), **-es, -ing, -ed** bɜːk, -s, -ɪŋ, -t
burlap 'bɜːlæp
Burleigh 'bɜːlɪ
burlesqu|e (*s. v.*), **-es, -ing, -ed** bɜː'lesk, -s, -ɪŋ, -t
Burley 'bɜːlɪ
Burlington 'bɜːlɪŋtən
burl|y (**B.**), **-ier, -iest, -iness** 'bɜːl|ɪ, -ɪə* [-jə*], -ɪɪst [-jɪst], -ɪnɪs [-ɪnəs]
Burma 'bɜːmə
Burman, **-s** 'bɜːmən, -z
Burmese ˌbɜː'miːz
burn (*s. v.*), **-s, -ing, -ed, burnt** bɜːn, -z, -ɪŋ, -d, bɜːnt
Burnaby 'bɜːnəbɪ
Burnand bɜː'nænd [bə-]
Burne,-Jones bɜːn, -'dʒəʊnz
burner, **-s** 'bɜːnə*. -z
burnet (**B.**), **-s** 'bɜːnɪt, -s
Burnett bɜː'net [bə-], 'bɜːnɪt
Burney 'bɜːnɪ
Burnham 'bɜːnəm
burning|-glass, **-glasses** 'bɜːnɪŋ|glɑːs, -ˌglɑːsɪz
burnish, **-es, -ing, -ed, -er/s** 'bɜːnɪʃ, -ɪz, -ɪŋ, -t, -ə*/z
Burnley 'bɜːnlɪ
burnous, **-es** bɜː'nuːs, -ɪz
burnouse, **-s** bɜː'nuːz, -ɪz
Burns bɜːnz
Burnside 'bɜːnsaɪd
burnt (*from* burn) bɜːnt
Burntisland bɜːnt'aɪlənd
burr (**B.**), **-s** bɜː*, -z
Burrell 'bʌrəl

Burrough(e)s 'bʌrəʊz
burr|ow (*s. v.*), **-ows, -owing, -owed** 'bʌr|əʊ, -əʊz, -əʊɪŋ, -əʊd
Burrows 'bʌrəʊz
bursar, **-s** 'bɜːsə*, -z
bursarship, **-s** 'bɜːsəʃɪp, -s
bursar|y, **-ies** 'bɜːsər|ɪ, -ɪz
Burslem 'bɜːzləm*
burst (*s. v.*), **-s, -ing** bɜːst, -s, -ɪŋ
Burt bɜːt
Burtchaell 'bɜːtʃəl
burthen, **-s** 'bɜːðn, -z
Burton 'bɜːtn
Burundi, **-an/s** bʊ'rʊndɪ, -ən/z
bur|y, **-ies, -ying, -ied** 'ber|ɪ, -ɪz, -ɪɪŋ, -ɪd
Bury (*place*) 'berɪ, (*surname*) 'bjʊərɪ, 'berɪ
burying-ground, **-s** 'berɪŋgraʊnd, -z
burying-place, **-s** 'berɪŋpleɪs, -ɪz
bus, **-es** bʌs, -ɪz
busb|y, **-ies** 'bʌzb|ɪ, -ɪz
bus-conductor, **-s** 'bʌskənˌdʌktə*, -z
bush (*s. v.*) (**B.**), **-es, -ing, -ed** bʊʃ, -ɪz, -ɪŋ, -t
bushel, **-s** 'bʊʃl, -z
Bushell 'bʊʃl
Bushey 'bʊʃɪ
Bushire bju:'ʃaɪə* [bjʊ-, bu:-]
bush|man (**B.**), **-men** 'bʊʃ|mən, -mən [-men]
Bushmills 'bʊʃmɪlz
Bushnell 'bʊʃnəl
bushranger, **-s** 'bʊʃˌreɪndʒə*, -z
bush|y (**B.**), **-ily, -iness** 'bʊʃ|ɪ, -ɪlɪ [-əlɪ], -ɪnɪs [-ɪnəs]
business (*profession, etc.*), **-es** 'bɪznɪs [-ŋɪs], -ɪz
business-like 'bɪznɪslaɪk
business-man, **-men** 'bɪznɪsmæn [-mən], -men [-mən]
busk (*s. v.*) (**B.**), **-s, -ing, -ed, -er/s** bʌsk, -s, -ɪŋ, -t, ə*/z
buskin, **-s, -ed** 'bʌskɪn, -z, -d
bus|-man, **-men** 'bʌs|mən [-mæn], -mən [-men]
Busoni bju:'səʊnɪ [bjʊ-, bʊ-, bu:-, -'zəʊ-]
buss (*s. v.*) (**B.**), **-es, -ing, -ed** bʌs, -ɪz, -ɪŋ, -t
bus-stop, **-s** 'bʌsstɒp, -s
bust (*s.*), **-s** bʌst, -s
bust (*s. v.*) (*burst*), **-s, -ing** bʌst, -s, -ɪŋ
bustard, **-s** 'bʌstəd, -z
buster (**B.**), **-s** 'bʌstə*, -z
bust|le (*s. v.*), **-les, -ling, -led** 'bʌs|l, -lz, -lɪŋ [-lɪŋ], -ld

67

Busvine 'bʌzvaın
bus|y, -ier, -iest, -ily 'bɪz|ɪ, -ɪə*, -ɪɪst, -ɪlɪ [-əlɪ]
busybod|y, -ies 'bɪzɪˌbɒd|ɪ, -ɪz
busyness (state of being busy) 'bɪzɪnɪs [-nəs]
Buszard 'bʌzəd
but bʌt (strong form), bət (weak form)
butane 'bjuːteın [-'-]
butcher (s. v.) (B.), -s, -ing, -ed 'butʃə*, -z, -ɪŋ, -d
butcher|y, -ies 'butʃər|ɪ, -ɪz
Bute bjuːt
butler (B.), -s 'bʌtlə*, -z
butler|age; -y, -ies 'bʌtlər|ɪdʒ; -ɪ, -ɪz
Butlin 'bʌtlɪn
butt (s. v.) (B.), -s, -ing, -ed bʌt, -s, -ɪŋ, -ɪd
Buttar bə'taː*
butt-end, -s ˌbʌt'end ['bʌtend], -z
butter, -s 'bʌtə*, -z
butter-boat, -s 'bʌtəbəut, -s
buttercup, -s 'bʌtəkʌp, -s
butter-dish, -es 'bʌtədɪʃ, -ɪz
Butterfield 'bʌtəfiːld
butter-fingers 'bʌtəˌfɪŋgəz
butterfl|y, -ies 'bʌtəfl|aı, -aız
Butterick 'bʌtərɪk
butter-kni|fe, -ves 'bʌtənaı|f, -vz
Butter|leigh, -ley 'bʌtə|lɪ, -lɪ
buttermilk 'bʌtəmɪlk
butternut, -s 'bʌtənʌt, -s
butterscotch 'bʌtəskɒtʃ [ˌbʌtə's-]
Butterwick 'bʌtərɪk, 'bʌtəwɪk
Butterworth 'bʌtəwəθ [-wɜ:θ]
butter|y (s. adj.), -ies 'bʌtər|ɪ, -ɪz
buttery-hatch, -es ˌbʌtərɪ'hætʃ, -ɪz
buttock, -s 'bʌtək, -s
butt|on (s. v.) (B.), -ons, -oning, -oned 'bʌt|n, -nz, -ŋɪŋ [-nɪŋ], -nd
button-hol|e (s. v.), -es, -ing, -ed 'bʌtnhəul, -z, -ɪŋ, -d
button-hook, -s 'bʌtnhuk, -s
buttress, -es 'bʌtrɪs [-rəs], -ɪz
butyric bju:'tɪrɪk [bjʊ't-]
buxom, -ness 'bʌksəm, -nɪs [-nəs]
Buxton 'bʌkstən

buy, -s, -ing, bought baı, -z, -ɪŋ, bɔ:t
buyable 'baıəbl
buyer, -s 'baıə*, -z
Buzfuz 'bʌzfʌz
buzz (s. v.), -es, -ing, -ed, -er/s bʌz, -ɪz, -ɪŋ, -d, -ə*/z
buzzard, -s 'bʌzəd, -z
by baı (normal form), bɪ, bə (occasional weak forms)
by-and-by ˌbaıənd'baı [-əm'b-]
Byard 'baıəd
Byas(s) 'baıəs
bye, -s baı, -z
bye-bye (sleep), -s 'baıbaı, -z
bye-bye (goodbye) ˌbaı'baı
bye-law, -s 'baılɔ:, -z
by-election, -s 'baıɪˌlekʃn, -z
Byends 'baıendz
Byers 'baıəz
Byfleet 'baıfli:t
bygone, -s 'baıgɒn, -z
by-law, -s 'baılɔ:, -z
Byles baılz
Byng bɪŋ
Bynoe 'baınəu
by-pass, -es 'baıpa:s, -ız
by-pa|th, -ths 'baıpa:|θ, -ðz
by-play 'baıpleı
by-product, -s 'baıˌprɒdʌkt [-dəkt], -s
Byrd bə:d
byre, -s 'baıə*, -z
Byrne bə:n
by-road, -s 'baırəud, -z
Byron 'baıərən
Byronic, -ally baı'rɒnɪk [ˌbaıə'r-], -əlɪ
Bysshe bɪʃ
byssus 'bɪsəs
bystander, -s 'baıˌstændə*, -z
by-street, -s 'baıstri:t, -s
Bythesea 'bɪðəsi:
by|way/s, -word/s 'baı|weı/z, -wɜ:d/z
Byzantian bɪ'zæntıən [baı'z-, -ntjən, -nʃıən, -nʃjən]
Byzantine bɪ'zæntaın [baı'z-, 'bɪzəntaın, -ti:n]
Byzantium bɪ'zæntıəm [baı'z-, -nʦjəm, -nʃıəm, -nʃjəm]

C

C (*the letter*), **-'s** si:, -z
cab, -s kæb, -z
cabal, -s kə'bæl, -z
Cabala kə'bɑ:lə [kæ'b-]
cabalistic, -al, -ally ˌkæbə'lɪstɪk, -l, -əlɪ
cabaret, -s 'kæbəreɪ, -z
cabbage, -s 'kæbɪdʒ, -ɪz
cabbage-rose, -s 'kæbɪdʒrəʊz, -ɪz
Cabbala kə'bɑ:lə [kæ'b-]
cabbalistic, -al, -ally ˌkæbə'lɪstɪk, -l, -əlɪ
cabb|y, -ies 'kæb|ɪ, -ɪz
Cabell 'kæbəl
caber, -s 'keɪbə*, -z
cabin, -s; -boy/s 'kæbɪn, -z; -bɔɪ/z
cabinet, -s; -maker/s 'kæbɪnɪt [-bən-, -bnɪt, -ət], -s; -ˌmeɪkə*/z
cab|le (*s. v.*), **-les, -ling, -led** 'keɪb|l, -lz, -lɪŋ [-lɪŋ], -ld
cablegram, -s 'keɪblgræm, -z
cab|man, -men 'kæb|mən, -mən [-men]
caboodle kə'bu:dl
caboose, -s kə'bu:s, -ɪz
cabot, -s 'kæbəʊ, -z
Cabot 'kæbət
cabotage 'kæbətɑ:ʒ [-tɪdʒ]
cabriole ˌkæbrɪ'əʊl
cab|-stand/s, -tout/s 'kæb|stænd/z, -taʊt/s
cacao kə'kɑ:əʊ [-'keɪəʊ]
cachalot, -s 'kæʃəlɒt, -s
cache, -s kæʃ, -ɪz
cachet, -s 'kæʃeɪ (kaʃɛ), -z
cachinnat|e, -es, -ing, -ed 'kækɪneɪt, -s, -ɪŋ, -ɪd
cachinnation ˌkækɪ'neɪʃn
cachou, -s 'kæʃu: [kæ'ʃu:, kə-], -z
cachucha, -s kə'tʃu:tʃə, -z
cacique, -s kæ'si:k [kə's-], -s
cack|le (*s. v.*), **-les, -ling, -led, -ler/s** 'kæk|l, -lz, -lɪŋ [-lɪŋ], -ld, -lə*/z [-lə*/z]
cacodyl 'kækəʊdaɪl [-dɪl]
cacoepy 'kækəʊepɪ
cacographic ˌkækəʊ'græfɪk
cacography kæ'kɒgrəfɪ [kə'k-]
cacology kæ'kɒlədʒɪ [kə'k-]
cacophonic, -al, -ally ˌkækəʊ'fɒnɪk, -l, -əlɪ

cacophonous kæ'kɒfənəs [kə'k-]
cacophon|y, -ies kæ'kɒfən|ɪ [kə'k-], -ɪz
cactus, -es, cacti 'kæktəs, -ɪz, 'kæktaɪ
cacuminal (*s. adj.*), **-s** kæ'kju:mɪnl [kə'k-], -z
cad, -s kæd, -z
cadast|ral, -re kə'dæst|rəl, -ə*
cadaver, -s kə'dɑ:və* [-'dæ-, -'deɪ-], -z
cadaveric kə'dævərɪk
cadaverous, -ness kə'dævərəs, -nɪs [-nəs]
Cad|bury, -by 'kæd|bərɪ, -bɪ
Caddell kə'del
caddice 'kædɪs
caddie, -s 'kædɪ, -z
caddis; -fly, -flies 'kædɪs; -flaɪ, -flaɪz
caddish, -ly, -ness 'kædɪʃ, -lɪ, -nɪs [-nəs]
cadd|y, -ies 'kæd|ɪ, -ɪz
cade (**C.**), **-s** keɪd, -z
Cadell 'kædl, kə'del
caden|ce/s, -cy 'keɪdən|s/ɪz, -sɪ
cadenza, -s kə'denzə, -z
Cader Idris ˌkædər'ɪdrɪs [-də'ɪ-]
cadet, -s kə'det, -s
cadet-corps (*sing.*) kə'detkɔ:*, (*plur.*) -z
cadetship, -s kə'det-ʃɪp, -s
cadg|e, -es, -ing, -ed, -er/s kædʒ, -ɪz, -ɪŋ, -d, -ə*/z
cadi, -s 'kɑ:dɪ ['keɪdɪ], -z
Cadillac, -s 'kædɪlæk ['kædlæk], -s
Cadiz (*in Spain*) kə'dɪz ['keɪdɪz] ('kadiθ), (*in Philippines*) 'kɑ:di:s, (*in U.S.A.*) 'kædɪz, 'keɪdɪz
Cadman 'kædmən
Cadmean kæd'mi:ən [-'mɪən, '---]
cadmium 'kædmɪəm [-mjəm]
Cadmus 'kædməs
Cadogan kə'dʌgən
cadre, -s 'kɑ:də* ['kɑ:drə, 'kædrɪ], 'kɑ:dəz ['kædrɪz]
caduce|us, -i kə'dju:sj|əs [-sɪ|əs, -fj|əs, -ʃɪ|əs], -aɪ
caec|um, -a 'si:k|əm, -ə
Caedmon 'kædmən
Caen (*French town*) kɑ̃:ŋ [kɔ̃:ŋ] (kɑ̃)
Caen (*in Caen stone*) keɪn
Caerleon kɑ:'li:ən [kə'l-, -'lɪən]
Caernarvon, -shire kə'nɑ:vən, -ʃə* [-ˌʃɪə*]

Caerphilly keə'fılı [kɑ:'f-, kəf-] (*Welsh*
  kar'fili, kair'fili)
Caesar, -s 'si:zə*, -z
Caesarea ˌsi:zə'rıə
Caesarean (*of Caesarea*) ˌsi:zə'rıən
caesarean (*of Caesar*) si:'zeərıən [sı'z-]
caesium 'si:zıəm [-zjəm]
caesura, -s sı'zjʊərə [si:'z-, -'zjɔər-,
  -'zjɔ:r-, -'ʒj-], -z
café, -s 'kæfeı ['kæfı] (kafe), -z
café chantant, -s ˌkæfeı'ʃɑ:ntɑ̃:ŋ [-'ʃɔ̃:n-
  tɔ̃:ŋ, -'ʃɑ:ntɑ:ŋ, -'ʃɒntɒŋ] (kafe-
  ʃɑ̃tɑ̃), -z
cafeteria, -s ˌkæfı'tıərıə [-fə't-], -z
caffeine 'kæfi:n [-fri:n, -feın]
cag|e (*s. v. adj.*), **-es, -ing, -ed, -ey** keıdʒ,
  -ız, -ıŋ, -d, -ı
cageling, -s 'keıdʒlıŋ, -z
Cagliari kæ'ljɑ:rı [ˌkælı'ɑ:-] ('kaʎʎari)
Cagliostro kæ'ljɒstrəʊ [ˌkælı'ɒ-]
Cahan (*surname*) kɑ:n
Cahill 'kɑ:hıl, 'keıhıl
Caiaphas 'kaıəfæs [-fəs]
Caillard (*English name*) 'keıləd, 'kaıɑ:d
Cain(e) keın
Cainite, -s 'keınaıt, -s
caique, -s kaı'i:k [kɑ:'i:k], **-s**
Cairene 'kaıəri:n
cairn, -s keən, -z
cairngorm (C.), -s ˌkeən'gɔ:m ['--], -z
Cairns keənz
Cairo (*in Egypt*) 'kaıərəʊ, (*in U.S.A.*)
  'keərəʊ
caisson, -s 'keısɒn [-sən, *sometimes in en-
  gineering* kə'su:n], -z
Caithness 'keıθnes [-nəs, ˌkeıθ'nes]
caitiff, -s 'keıtıf, -s
Caius (*Roman name, character in
  Shakespeare's 'Merry Wives'*) 'kaıəs,
  'keıəs, (*Cambridge College*) ki:z
cajol|e, -es, -ing, -ed, -er/s kə'dʒəʊl, -z
  -ıŋ, -d, -ə*/z
cajoler|y, -ies kə'dʒəʊlər|ı, -ız
Cajun 'keıdʒən
cak|e (*s. v.*), **-es, -ing, -ed ; -y** keık, -s,
  -ıŋ, -t; -ı
cakewalk, -s 'keıkwɔ:k, -s
Calabar ˌkælə'bɑ:* ['kæləb-]
calabash, -es 'kæləbæʃ, -ız
Calabria, -n/s kə'læbrıə [-'lɑ:b-, *old-
  fashioned* -'leıb-], -n/z
Calais 'kæleı ['kælı, *old-fashioned*
  'kælıs] (kalɛ)
calamine 'kæləmaın
calamitous, -ly, -ness kə'læmıtəs
  [-mət-], -lı, -nıs [-nəs]
calamit|y, -ies kə'læmət|ı [-ıt|ı], -ız
calamus 'kæləməs

calcareous, -ness kæl'keərıəs, -nıs
  [-nəs]
calceolaria, -s ˌkælsıə'leərıə [-sjə'l-], -z
calces (*plur. of* **calx**) 'kælsi:z
calciferous kæl'sıfərəs
calcification ˌkælsıfı'keıʃn
calci|fy, -fies, -fying, -fied 'kælsı|faı,
  -faız, -faıŋ, -faıd
calcimine 'kælsımaın
calcination ˌkælsı'neıʃn
calcin|e, -es, -ing, -ed 'kælsaın [-sın],
  -z, -ıŋ, -d
calcite 'kælsaıt
calcium 'kælsıəm [-sjəm]
Calcot (*near Reading*) 'kælkət
Calcott 'kɔ:lkət ['kɒl-]
calculable 'kælkjʊləbl [-kjəl-]
calculat|e, -es, -ing, -ed, -or/s 'kælkjʊ-
  leıt [-kjəl-], -s, -ıŋ, -ıd, -ə*/z
calculation, -s ˌkælkjʊ'leıʃn [-kjə'l-], -z
calculative 'kælkjʊlətıv [-kjəl-, -leıtıv]
calcul|us, -uses, -i 'kælkjʊl|əs [-kjəl-],
  -əsız, -aı
Calcutt (*surname*) 'kælkʌt
Calcutta kæl'kʌtə
Caldcleugh 'kɑ:ldklʌf
Caldecote (*in Hertfordshire*) 'kɔ:ldıkət
Caldecott 'kɔ:ldəkət ['kɒl-, -dık-]
Calder 'kɔ:ldə* ['kɒl-]
Calderara ˌkældə'rɑ:rə
Calderon (*English name*) 'kɔ:ldərən
  ['kɒl-, 'kæl-], (*Spanish name*) ˌkældə'rɒn (kalde'ron)
caldron, -s 'kɔ:ldrən ['kɒl-], -z
Caldwell 'kɔ:ldwəl ['kɒl-, -wel]
Caleb 'keıleb
Caledon 'kælıdən
Caledonia, -n/s ˌkælı'dəʊnjə [-nıə], -n/z
calefaction ˌkælı'fækʃn
calefactor|y, -ies ˌkælı'fæktər|ı, -ız
calendar, -s 'kælındə* [-lən-], -z
calend|er (*s. v.*), **-ers, -ering, -ered**
  'kælınd|ə* [-lən-], -əz, -ərıŋ, -əd
calends 'kælındz [-lendz, -ləndz]
calenture, -s 'kælən,tjʊə* [-ˌtʃʊə*,
  -tʃə*], -z
cal|f, -ves kɑ:|f, -vz
calf's-foot (*jelly*) 'kɑ:vzfʊt ['kɑ:fsfʊt]
calf-skin 'kɑ:fskın
Calgary 'kælgərı
Calhoun kæl'həʊn, kə'hu:n
Caliban 'kælıbæn [-bən]
calibrat|e, -es, -ing, -ed, -or/s 'kælı-
  breıt [-ləb-], -s, -ıŋ, -ıd, -ə*/z
calibration ˌkælı'breıʃn [-lə'b-]
calibre, -s 'kælıbə* [kə'li:bə*], -z
calicle, -s 'kælıkl, -z
calico, -(e)s 'kælıkəʊ, -z

Calicut ˈkælɪkət
calif = caliph
California, -n/s ˌkælɪˈfɔːnjə [-nɪə], -n/z
Caligula kəˈlɪgjʊlə
calipash ˈkælɪpæʃ
calipee ˈkælɪpiː [ˌkælɪˈpiː]
caliper, -s ˈkælɪpə*, -z
caliph, -s ˈkeɪlɪf, [ˈkæl-, ˈkɑːl-], -s
caliphate, -s ˈkælɪfeɪt [-fɪt, -fət], -s
Calippus kəˈlɪpəs
calisthenic, -s ˌkælɪsˈθenɪk, -s
calk (s. v.), -s, -ing, -ed kɔːk, -s, -ɪŋ, -t
calkin, -s ˈkælkɪn [ˈkɔːkɪn], -z
call (s. v.), -s, -ing, -ed, -er/s kɔːl, -z, -ɪŋ, -d, -ə*/z
Callaghan ˈkæləhən [-hæn], ˈkæləgən
Callander ˈkæləndə*
call|-boy/s, -girl/s ˈkɔːl|bɔɪ/z, -gɜːl/z
Callcott ˈkɔːlkət [ˈkɒl-]
Callender ˈkælmdə* [-lən-]
Caller ˈkælə*
Callicrates kəˈlɪkrətiːz [kæˈl-]
Callie ˈkɔːlɪ
calligraph|er/s, -ist/s, -y kəˈlɪgrəf|ə*/z [kæˈl-], -ɪst/s, -ɪ
calligraphic, -al, -ally ˌkælɪˈgræfɪk, -l, -əlɪ
calling (s.), -s ˈkɔːlɪŋ, -z
Calliope kəˈlaɪəpɪ [kæˈl-]
calliper, -s ˈkælɪpə*, -z
Callirrhoe kæˈlɪrəʊɪ: [kəˈl-, -əʊɪ]
Callisthenes kæˈlɪsθəniːz [kəˈl-]
callisthenic, -s ˌkælɪsˈθenɪk, -s
Callistratus kæˈlɪstrətəs [kəˈl-]
call-office, -s ˈkɔːlˌɒfɪs, -ɪz
callosit|y, -ies kæˈlɒsət|ɪ [kəˈl-, -ɪt|ɪ], -ɪz
callous, -ly, -ness ˈkæləs, -lɪ, -nɪs [-nəs]
call|ow (C.), -ower, -owest ˈkæl|əʊ, -əʊə*, -əʊɪst
calm (s. adj. v.), -s; -er, -est, -ly, -ness; -ing, -ed kɑːm, -z; -ə*, -ɪst, -lɪ, -nɪs [-nəs]; -ɪŋ, -d
calmative, -s ˈkælmətɪv [ˈkɑːm-], -z
Calne kɑːn
calomel ˈkæləʊmel
calor ˈkælə*
caloric kəˈlɒrɪk [ˈkælərɪk]
calorie, -s ˈkælərɪ, -z
calorific ˌkæləˈrɪfɪk [-lɔːˈr-, -lɒˈr-]
calorification kəˌlɒrɪfɪˈkeɪʃn [ˌkælər-, ˌkælɔːr-, ˌkælɒr-]
calorimet|er/s, -ry ˌkæləˈrɪmɪt|ə*/z [-lɔːˈr-, -lɒˈr-, -mət|ə*], -rɪ
calotte, -s kəˈlɒt, -s
caloyer, -s ˈkælɔɪə*, -z
Calpurnia kælˈpɜːnjə [-nɪə]
calque, -s kælk, -s
Calshot (in Hampshire) ˈkælʃɒt

Calthorpe (district in Birmingham) ˈkælθɔːp, (surname) ˈkɔːlθɔːp [ˈkɒl-], ˈkælθɔːp
Calton (Edinburgh) ˈkɔːltən, (Glasgow) ˈkɑːltən
caltrop, -s ˈkæltrəp, -s
calumet, -s ˈkæljʊmet, -s
calumniat|e, -es, -ing, -ed, -or/s kəˈlʌmnɪeɪt [-njeɪt], -s, -ɪŋ, -ɪd, -ə*/z
calumniation, -s kəˌlʌmnɪˈeɪʃn, -z
calumn|y, -ies ˈkæləmn|ɪ, -ɪz
calvar|y (C.), -ies ˈkælvər|ɪ, -ɪz
calv|e, -es, -ing, -ed kɑːv, -z, -ɪŋ, -d
Calverley (surname) ˈkælvəlɪ, (place in West Yorkshire) ˈkɑːvəlɪ [ˈkɔːvəlɪ]
Calvert ˈkælvɜːt [-vət], ˈkɔːlvət
calves'-foot ˈkɑːvzfʊt
Calvin, -ism, -ist/s ˈkælvɪn, -ɪzəm, -ɪst/s
calvinistic, -al, -ally ˌkælvɪˈnɪstɪk, -l, -əlɪ
cal|x, -ces, -xes kæl|ks, -siːz, -ksɪz
calycle, -s ˈkælɪkl, -z
Calydon ˈkælɪdən
caly|x, -ces, -xes ˈkeɪlɪ|ks [ˈkæl-], -siːz, -ksɪz
cam (C.), -s kæm, -z
Camalodunum ˌkæməˈləʊˈdjuːnəm
camaraderie ˌkæməˈrɑːdərɪ [-ˈræd-, -riː]
camarilla, -s ˌkæməˈrɪlə, -z
camber, -s ˈkæmbə*, -z
Camberley ˈkæmbəlɪ [-blɪ]
Camberwell ˈkæmbəwəl [-wel]
Cambodia, -n kæmˈbəʊdjə [-dɪə], -n
Camborne ˈkæmbɔːn [-bən]
Cambria, -n/s ˈkæmbrɪə, -n/z
cambric ˈkeɪmbrɪk
Cambridge ˈkeɪmbrɪdʒ
Cambridgeshire ˈkeɪmbrɪdʒ|ə* [-brɪdʒ,ʃɪə*, -brɪd,ʃɪə*, -brɪdʃə*]
Cambs. kæmbz
Cambyses kæmˈbaɪsiːz
Camden ˈkæmdən
came (from come) keɪm
camel, -s ˈkæml, -z
cameleer, -s ˌkæmɪˈlɪə* [-məˈl-], -z
Camelford ˈkæmlfəd
camellia, -s kəˈmiːljə [-ˈmel-, -lɪə], -z
camel|man, -men ˈkæml|mæn [-mən], -men [-mən]
camelopard, -s (giraffe) ˈkæmɪləpɑːd [kəˈmeləpɑːd, -ləʊp-], (facetiously applied to a person) ˌkæmlˈlepəd, -z
Camelot ˈkæmɪlɒt [-məl-]
Camembert ˈkæməmbeə* (kamãbɛːr)
cameo, -s ˈkæmɪəʊ, -z
camera, -s ˈkæmərə, -z
camera|-man, -men ˈkæmərə|mæn [-mən], -men

71

Cameron 'kæmərən
Cameronian, -s ˌkæmə'rəʊnjən [-nɪən], -z
Cameroon, -s ˌkæmə'ru:n ['---], -z
cami-knickers ˌkæmɪ'nɪkəz ['--ˌ--]
Camilla kə'mɪlə
camisole, -s 'kæmɪsəʊl, -z
Camlachie (Glasgow) kæm'læki [-'læxɪ]
camomile 'kæməʊmaɪl
camouflag|e (s. v.), -es, -ing, -ed 'kæməflɑːʒ [-mʊf, -ɑːdʒ], -ɪz, -ɪŋ, -d
Camoys kə'mɔɪz
camp (s. v.), -s, -ing, -ed, -er/s kæmp, -s, -ɪŋ, -t [kæmt], -ə*/z
Campagna kæm'pɑːnjə (kam'paɲɲa)
campaign (s. v.), -s, -ing, -ed, -er/s kæm'peɪn, -z, -ɪŋ, -d, -ə*/z
campanile, -s ˌkæmpə'niːlɪ, -z
campanolog|ist/s, -y ˌkæmpə'nɒlədʒ|ɪst/s, -ɪ
campanula, -s kəm'pænjʊlə [-njələ], -z
camp-bed, -s ˌkæmp'bed, -z
Campbell, -s 'kæmbl, -z
Campbellite, -s 'kæmbəlaɪt [-bl̩aɪt], -s
Campden 'kæmpdən
Campeachy kæm'piːtʃɪ
Camperdown 'kæmpədaʊn
camp-follower, -s 'kæmpˌfɒləʊə*, -z
camphor, -s, -ated 'kæmfə*, -z, -reɪtɪd
camphoric kæm'fɒrɪk
campion (C.) 'kæmpjən [-pɪən]
camp-stool, -s 'kæmpstuːl, -z
campus, -es 'kæmpəs, -ɪz
Camus 'kæmju: (kamy)
cam-wood 'kæmwʊd
can (s.), -s kæn, -z
can (auxil. v.) kæn (strong form), kən, kn, kŋ (weak forms)
    Note.—The form kŋ occurs only before words beginning with k or g.
can (v.) (put in cans), -s, -ning, -ned kæn, -z, -ɪŋ, -d
Cana 'keɪnə
Canaan 'keɪnən [-njən, -nɪən, Jewish pronunciation kə'neɪən]
Canaanite, -s 'keɪnənaɪt [-njən-, -nɪən-, Jewish pronunciation kə'neɪənaɪt], -s
Canada 'kænədə
Canadian, -s kə'neɪdjən [-dɪən], -z
canal, -s kə'næl, -z
canalization [-isa-] ˌkænəlaɪ'zeɪʃn [-nl̩aɪ-, -lɪ'z-]
canaliz|e [-is|e], -es, -ing, -ed 'kænəlaɪz [-nl̩aɪ-], -ɪz, -ɪŋ, -d
Cananite, -s 'kænənaɪt ['keɪn-], -s
canapé, -s 'kænəpeɪ, -z
canard, -s kæ'nɑːd [kə'nɑːd, 'kænɑːd] (kana:r), -z

Canarese ˌkænə'riːz
canar|y (C.), -ies kə'neər|ɪ, -ɪz
canasta kə'næstə
canaster, -s kə'næstə*, -z
Canberra 'kænbərə ['kæm-]
canc|el, -els, -elling, -elled 'kæns|l, -lz, -əlɪŋ [-lɪŋ, -lɪŋ], -ld
cancellation, -s ˌkænsə'leɪʃn [-se'leɪ-, -sɪ'leɪ-, -sl̩'eɪ-], -z
cancer (C.), -s 'kænsə*, -z
cancerous 'kænsərəs
Candace kæn'deɪsɪ
candelabr|a, -as, -um, ˌkændɪ'lɑːbr|ə [-də'l-, -'læb-, -'leɪb-], -əz, -əm
candescen|ce, -t kæn'desn|s, -t
Candia 'kændɪə [-djə]
candid, -ly, -ness 'kændɪd, -lɪ, -nɪs [-nəs]
Candida 'kændɪdə
candidate, -s 'kændɪdət [-deɪt, -dɪt], -s
candida|cy, -cies, -ture/s 'kændɪdə|sɪ, -sɪz, -tʃə*/z [-dɪtʃ-, -deɪtʃ-, -ˌtʃʊə*, -ˌtjʊə*]
candied 'kændɪd
candle, -s 'kændl, -z
candle-light 'kændllaɪt
Candlemas 'kændlməs [-mæs]
candlepower, -s 'kændlˌpaʊə*, -z
candlestick, -s 'kændlstɪk, -s
candlewick 'kændlwɪk
candour 'kændə*
cand|y (s. v.) (C.), -ies, -ying, -ied 'kænd|ɪ, -ɪz, -ɪŋ [-jɪŋ], -ɪd
candy-floss 'kændɪflɒs
candytuft 'kændɪtʌft
cane (C.), -s keɪn, -z
Canford 'kænfəd
canicular kə'nɪkjʊlə* [kæ'n-]
canine (s. adj.), -s 'keɪnaɪn ['kæn-], -z
Canis (constellation) 'keɪnɪs
canister, -s 'kænɪstə*, -s
canker (s. v.), -s, -ing, -ed 'kæŋkə*, -z, -rɪŋ, -d
cankerous 'kæŋkərəs
canna, -s 'kænə, -z
cannabis 'kænəbɪs
Cannan 'kænən
canner|y, -ies 'kænər|ɪ, -ɪz
cannibal, -s 'kænɪbl, -z
cannibalism 'kænɪbəlɪzəm [-bl̩-]
cannibalistic ˌkænɪbə'lɪstɪk
cannibaliz|e [-is|e], -es, -ing, -ed 'kænɪbəlaɪz [-bl̩aɪz], -ɪz, -ɪŋ, -d
cannikin, -s 'kænɪkɪn, -z
Cann|ing, -ock 'kæn|ɪŋ, -ək
cannon (C.), -s 'kænən, -z
cannonad|e (s. v.), -es, -ing, -ed ˌkænə'neɪd, -z, -ɪŋ, -ɪd
cannon-ball, -s 'kænənbɔːl, -z

cannoneer, -s ˌkænəˈnɪə*, -z
cannon-proof ˈkænənpruːf
cannonry ˈkænənrɪ
cannon-shot, -s ˈkænənʃɒt, -s
cannot ˈkænɒt [-nət]
  Note.—This word is usually contracted to kɑːnt. *See* can't.
cannula, -s ˈkænjʊlə, -z
cann|y, -ier, -iest, -ily, -iness ˈkæn|ɪ,
  -ɪə*, -ɪɪst, -ɪlɪ [-əlɪ], -ɪnɪs [-ɪnəs]
canoe (s. v.), -s, -ing, -d, -ist/s kəˈnuː:,
  -z, -ɪŋ [kəˈnʊɪŋ], -d, -ɪst/s
canon, -s ˈkænən, -z
cañon, -s ˈkænjən, -z
canoness, -es ˈkænənɪs [-nes], -ɪz
canonic, -al/s, -ally kəˈnɒnɪk, -l/z, -əlɪ
canonization [-isa-], -s ˌkænənaɪˈzeɪʃn
  [-nɪˈz-], -z
canoniz|e [-is|e], -es, -ing, -ed ˈkænə-
  naɪz, -ɪz, -ɪŋ, -d
canon|ry, -ies ˈkænənr|ɪ, -ɪz
Canopus kəˈnəʊpəs
canop|y, -ies ˈkænəp|ɪ, -ɪz
canst (*archaic form from* can) kænst
  (*strong form*), kənst (*weak form*)
cant (s. v.) (C.), -s, -ing, -ed, -er/s
  kænt, -s, -ɪŋ, -ɪd, -ə*/z
can't kɑːnt
Cantab. ˈkæntæb
cantabile kænˈtɑːbɪlɪ
Cantabrian kænˈteɪbrɪən
Cantabrigian, -s ˌkæntəˈbrɪdʒɪən
  [-dʒən], -z
cantaloup, -s ˈkæntəluːp, -s
cantankerous, -ly, -ness kænˈtæŋkərəs
  [kən-], -lɪ, -nɪs [-nəs]
cantata, -s kænˈtɑːtə [kən-], -z
cantatrice, -s ˈkæntətriːs, -ɪz
canteen, -s kænˈtiːn, -z
cant|er (s. v.), -ers, -ering, -ered
  ˈkænt|ə*, -əz, -ərɪŋ, -əd
Canterbury ˈkæntəbərɪ [-berɪ]
cantharides kænˈθærɪdiːz [kən-]
canticle, -s ˈkæntɪkl, -z
cantilever, -s ˈkæntɪliːvə*, -z
Cantire kænˈtaɪə*
Cantling ˈkæntlɪŋ
canto, -s ˈkæntəʊ, -z
canton (*Swiss state*) ˈkæntɒn [-ˈ-], (*in
  heraldry*) ˈkæntən, -z
Canton (*in China*) ˌkænˈtɒn, (*in Wales,
  surname*) ˈkæntən
canton (v.) (*divide into portions or
  districts*), -s, -ing, -ed kænˈtɒn, -z,
  -ɪŋ, -d
canton (v.) (*quarter soldiers*), -s, -ing,
  -ed; -ment/s kænˈtuːn [kən-], -z, -ɪŋ,
  -d; -mənt/s

cantonal ˈkæntənl [kænˈtɒnl]
Cantonese ˌkæntəˈniːz [-tɒˈn-]
cantor, -s ˈkæntɔː*, -z
cantoris kænˈtɔːrɪs
Cantuar. ˈkæntjʊɑ:*
Cantuarian ˌkæntjʊˈeərɪən
Canute kəˈnjuːt
canvas, -es ˈkænvəs, -ɪz
canvas-back, -s ˈkænvəsbæk, -s
canvass (s. v.), -es, -ing, -ed, -er/s
  ˈkænvəs, -ɪz, -ɪŋ, -t, -ə*/z
Canvey ˈkænvɪ
canyon, -s ˈkænjən [-nɪən], -z
canzone, -s kænˈtsəʊnɪ [-nˈzəʊ-], -z
canzonet, -s ˌkænzəʊˈnet, -s
caoutchouc ˈkaʊtʃʊk [-tʃuːk, -tʃuː]
cap (s. v.), -s, -ping, -ped kæp, -s, -ɪŋ, -t
capabilit|y, -ies ˌkeɪpəˈbɪlət|ɪ [-lɪt-], -ɪz
capab|le, -ly, -leness ˈkeɪpəb|l, -lɪ, -lnɪs
  [-nəs]
capacious, -ly, -ness kəˈpeɪʃəs, -lɪ, -nɪs
  [-nəs]
†capacitat|e, -es, -ing, -ed kəˈpæsɪteɪt, -s,
  -ɪŋ, -ɪd
capacit|y, -ies kəˈpæsət|ɪ [-ɪt|ɪ], -ɪz
cap-à-pie ˌkæpəˈpiː
caparis|on (s. v.), -ons, -oning, -oned
  kəˈpærɪs|n, -nz, -ṇɪŋ, -nd
cape (C.), -s keɪp, -s
Capel (*in Kent and Surrey*) ˈkeɪpl, (*in Wales*)
  ˈkæpl (*Welsh* ˈkapel)
Capel Curig ˌkæplˈkɪrɪg (*Welsh*
  ˌkapelˈkerig, -ˈkirɪg)
Capell ˈkeɪpəl
capel(l)et, -s ˈkæpələt [-lɪt], -s
cap|er (s. v.), -ers, -ering, -ered, -erer/s
  ˈkeɪp|ə*, -əz, -ərɪŋ, -əd, -ərə*/z
caper (*capercailzie*), -s ˈkæpə*, -z
capercailzie [-caillie], -s ˌkæpəˈkeɪlɪ
  [-ljɪ, -lzɪ], -z
Capernaum kəˈpɜːnjəm [-nɪəm]
Cape Town [Capetown] ˈkeɪptaʊn [ˌ-ˈ-]
capias, -es ˈkeɪpɪæs [-pjæs, -pjəs, -pɪəs],
  -ɪz
capillaire ˌkæpɪˈleə*
capillarity ˌkæpɪˈlærətɪ [-ɪtɪ]
capillary kəˈpɪlərɪ
capit|al (s. adj.), -als, -ally ˈkæpɪt|l, -lz,
  -lɪ [-l̩ɪ]
capitali|sm, -st/s ˈkæpɪtəlɪ|zəm
  [kəˈpɪt-, kæˈpɪt-, -tl̩-], -st/s
capitalization [-isa-], -s ˌkæpɪtəlaɪˈzeɪ-
  ʃn [kæˌp-, kə,p-, -tlaɪ-], -z
capitaliz|e [-is|e], -es, -ing, -ed ˈkæpɪtə-
  laɪz [kæˈp-, kəˈp-, -tl̩aɪz], -ɪz, -ɪŋ, -d
capitation, -s ˌkæpɪˈteɪʃn, -z
capitol (C.), -s ˈkæpɪtl, -z
capitolian ˌkæpɪˈtəʊljən [-lɪən]

capitoline kə'pɪtəʊlaɪn
capitular, -s kə'pɪtʃʊlə* [-'pɪtjʊ-], -z
capitular|y, -ies kə'pɪtʃʊlər|ɪ [-'pɪtjʊ-], -ɪz
capitulat|e, -es, -ing, -ed kə'pɪtʃʊleɪt [-'pɪtjʊ-], -s, -ɪŋ, -ɪd
capitulation kə,pɪtʃʊ'leɪʃn [-,pɪtjʊ-], -z
capitul|um, -a kə'pɪtʃʊl|əm [-tjʊl-], -ə
capon, -s 'keɪpən [-pɒn], -z
caporal (cigarette), -s ,kæpə'rɑ:l, -z
capot (s. v.), -s, -ting, -ted kə'pɒt, -s, -ɪŋ, -ɪd
capote, -s kə'pəʊt, -s
Cappado|cia, -cian/s ,kæpə'dəʊ|sjə [-sɪə, -ʃjə, -ʃɪə, -ʃə], -sjən/z [-sɪən/z, -ʃjən/z, -ʃɪən/z, -ʃn/z]
Capper 'kæpə*
Capri 'kæpri: ['kɑ:p-, -prɪ, kə'pri:] ('kɑ:pri)
capric 'kæprɪk
capriccio, -s kə'prɪtʃɪəʊ [-tʃjəʊ], -z
capriccioso kə,prɪtʃɪ'əʊzəʊ [-'əʊsəʊ]
caprice, -s kə'pri:s, -ɪz
capricious, -ly, -ness kə'prɪʃəs, -lɪ, -nɪs [-nəs]
Capricorn (constellation), -us 'kæprɪkɔ:n, ,kæprɪ'kɔ:nəs
capriol|e (s. v.), -es, -ing, -ed 'kæprɪəʊl, -z, -ɪŋ, -d
Capron 'keɪprən
capsicum 'kæpsɪkəm
capsiz|e, -es, -ing, -ed kæp'saɪz, -ɪz, -ɪŋ, -d
capstan, -s 'kæpstən, -z
capsular 'kæpsjʊlə*
capsule, -s 'kæpsju:l, -z
captain, -s 'kæptɪn, -z
captainc|y, -ies 'kæptɪns|ɪ, [-tən-], -ɪz
caption, -s 'kæpʃn, -z
captious, -ly, -ness 'kæpʃəs, -lɪ, -nɪs [-nəs]
captivat|e, -es, -ing, -ed 'kæptɪveɪt, -s, -ɪŋ, -ɪd
captive, -s 'kæptɪv, -z
captivit|y, -ies kæp'tɪvət|ɪ [-ɪt|ɪ], -ɪz
captor, -s 'kæptə* [-tɔ:*], -z
capt|ure (s. v.), -ures, -uring, -ured 'kæptʃ|ə*, -əz, -ərɪŋ, -əd
Capua (Italian town) 'kæpjʊə ['kɑ:pʊə] ('kɑ:pua)
capuche, -s kə'pu:ʃ, -ɪz
capuchin, -s 'kæpjʊtʃɪn [-ʊʃɪn], -z
Capulet 'kæpjʊlet [-lət, -lɪt]
car, -s kɑ:*, -z
carabineer, -s ,kærəbɪ'nɪə*, -z
caracal, -s 'kærəkæl, -z
Caracas kə'rækəs [-'rɑ:k-]
caracole, -s 'kærəkəʊl, -z

Caractacus kə'ræktəkəs
Caradoc kə'rædək
carafe, -s kə'ræf [-'rɑ:f], -s
caramel, -s 'kærəmel [-məl], -z
carapace, -s 'kærəpeɪs, -ɪz
carat, -s 'kærət, -s
Caratacus ,kærə'tɑ:kəs
caravan, -s 'kærəvæn [,kærə'v-], -z
caravanserai, -s ,kærə'vænsəraɪ [-reɪ, -rɪ], -z
caravanser|y, -ies ,kærə'vænsər|ɪ, -ɪz
caraway, -s 'kærəweɪ, -z
caraway-seed, -s 'kærəweɪsi:d, -z
Carbery 'kɑ:bərɪ
carbide, -s 'kɑ:baɪd, -z
carbine, -s 'kɑ:baɪn, -z
carbineer, -s ,kɑ:bɪ'nɪə*, -z
carbohydrate, -s ,kɑ:bəʊ'haɪdreɪt [-rɪt], -s
carbolic kɑ:'bɒlɪk [kə'b-]
carbon, -s 'kɑ:bən [-bn], -z
carbonaceous ,kɑ:bəʊ'neɪʃəs
carbonate, -s 'kɑ:bənɪt [-bn̩ɪt, -ət, -eɪt], -s
carbonated 'kɑ:bəneɪtɪd
carbonic kɑ:'bɒnɪk
carboniferous ,kɑ:bə'nɪfərəs
carbonization [-isa-] ,kɑ:bənaɪ'zeɪʃn [-bn̩aɪ-]
carboniz|e [-is|e], -es, -ing, -ed 'kɑ:bənaɪz, -ɪz, -ɪŋ, -d
carborundum ,kɑ:bə'rʌndəm
carboy, -s 'kɑ:bɔɪ, -z
carbuncle, -s 'kɑ:bʌŋkl, -z
carburet (s. v.), -s, -ting, -ted 'kɑ:bjʊret [-bər-, ,--'-], -s, -ɪŋ, -ɪd
carburett|er/s, -or/s ,kɑ:bə'ret|ə*/z [-bjʊr-, '----], -ə*/z
carcase, -s 'kɑ:kəs, -ɪz
carcass, -es 'kɑ:kəs, -ɪz
Carchemish 'kɑ:kɪmɪʃ [-kəm-]
carcinoma, -s ,kɑ:sɪ'nəʊmə, -z
card (s. v.), -s, -ing, -ed kɑ:d, -z, -ɪŋ, -ɪd
cardamom [-mum] 'kɑ:dəməm
cardboard 'kɑ:dbɔ:d [-bəəd]
card-case, -s 'kɑ:dkeɪs, -ɪz
Cardew 'kɑ:dju:
cardiac 'kɑ:dɪæk [-djæk]
cardiacal kɑ:'daɪəkl
Cardiff 'kɑ:dɪf
cardigan, -s 'kɑ:dɪgən, -z
Cardigan, -shire 'kɑ:dɪgən, -ʃə* [-,ʃɪə*]
cardinal (s. adj.), -s; -ship/s 'kɑ:dɪnl [-dn̩l, -dnl], -z; -ʃɪp/s
cardioid, -s 'kɑ:dɪɔɪd, -z
cardiolog|ist/s, -y ,kɑ:dɪ'ɒlədʒ|ɪst/s, -ɪ
cardiometer, -s ,kɑ:dɪ'ɒmɪt+ə* [-mətə*], -z

74

card-sharper, -s 'kɑːdˌʃɑːpə*, -z
card-table, -s 'kɑːdˌteɪbl, -z
Card|well, -y 'kɑːd|wəl [-wel], -ɪ
car|e (s. v.), -es, -ing, -ed, -er/s keə*, -z, -rɪŋ, -d, -rə*/z
careen, -s, -ing, -ed kə'riːn, -z, -ɪŋ, -d
career (s. v.), -s, -ing, -ed kə'rɪə*, -z, -rɪŋ, -d
careerist, -s kə'rɪərɪst, -s
care|ful, -fullest, -fully, -fulness 'keəfʊl, -flɪst [-flɪst, -fəlɪst, -fʊlɪst], -flɪ [-flɪ, -fəlɪ, -fʊlɪ], -fʊlnɪs [-nəs]
careless, -ly, -ness 'keəlɪs [-ləs], -lɪ, -nɪs [-nəs]
caress (s. v.), -es, -ing, -ed kə'res, -ɪz, -ɪŋ, -t
caret, -s 'kærət, -s
caretaker, -s 'keəˌteɪkə*, -z
Carew kə'ruː:, 'keərɪ, see also Pole Carew
careworn 'keəwɔːn
Carey 'keərɪ
Carfax 'kɑːfæks
car-ferr|y, -ies 'kɑːˌfer|ɪ, -ɪz
Cargill 'kɑːgɪl, kɑː'gɪl
cargo, -es 'kɑːgəʊ, -z
Caria 'keərɪə
Carib, -s 'kærɪb, -z
Caribbean ˌkærɪ'biːən [-'bɪən, kə'rɪbɪən]
Caribbees 'kærɪbiːz
caribou (C.), -s 'kærɪbuː:, -z
caricatur|e (s. v.), -es, -ing, -ed 'kærɪkəˌtjʊə* [-tjɔː:*, -tjɔə*, -ˌtʃʊə*, ˌ---'-, -tʃə*], -z, -rɪŋ, -d
caricaturist, -s 'kærɪkəˌtjʊərɪst [-tjɔː:-, -tjɔə-, -tjə-, -ˌtʃʊə-, -tʃə-, ˌ---'—], -s
caries 'keərɪːz [-riː:z]
carillon, -s 'kærɪljən [-lɒn, kə'rɪljən], -z
Carinthia kə'rɪnθɪə [-θjə]
carious 'keərɪəs
Carisbrooke 'kærɪsbrʊk [-ɪzb-]
Carl kɑːl
Carleton 'kɑːltən
Carlile kɑː'laɪl
Carlisle kɑː'laɪl [locally '--]
Carlist, -s 'kɑːlɪst, -s
Carlos 'kɑːlɒs
Carlovingian ˌkɑːləʊ'vɪndʒɪən [-dʒən, -dʒən]
Carlow 'kɑːləʊ
Carlsbad (K-) 'kɑːlzbæd
Carlsruhe (K-) 'kɑːlzˌruːə [-ˌrʊə]
Carlton 'kɑːltən
Carluke kɑː'luːk
Carlyle kɑː'laɪl [ˌkɑː'laɪl]
Carlyon kɑː'laɪən
car|man, -men 'kɑː|mən, -mən [-men]

Carmarthen, -shire kə'mɑːðn, -ʃə* [-ˌʃɪə*]
Carmel 'kɑːmel [-məl]
Carmelite, -s 'kɑːməlaɪt [-mɪl-, -mel-], -s
Carmen 'kɑːmen
Carmichael kɑː'maɪkl
carminative (s. adj.), -s 'kɑːmɪnətɪv, -z
carmine 'kɑːmaɪn
Carnaby 'kɑːnəbɪ
Carnac 'kɑːnæk
carnage 'kɑːnɪdʒ
Carnaghan 'kɑːnəgən
carn|al, -ally 'kɑːn|l, -əlɪ
carnality kɑː'nælətɪ [-ɪtɪ]
Carnarvon, old spelling of Caernarvon, q.v.
Carnatic kɑː'nætɪk
carnation, -s kɑː'neɪʃn, -z
Carnegie kɑː'negɪ, -'neɪgɪ, -'niː:gɪ
carnelian, -s kə'niːljən [kɑː:'n-, -lɪən], -z
Carnforth 'kɑːnfɔːθ
carnival, -s 'kɑːnɪvl, -z
carnivore, -s 'kɑːnɪvɔː:* [-vɔə*], -z
carnivorous kɑː'nɪvərəs
Carnochan 'kɑːnəkən [kɑː:'nɒ-, -xən]
Carnwath kɑːn'wɒθ, 'kɑːnwəθ
car|ol (s. v.) (C.), -ols, -olling, -olled 'kær|əl, -əlz, -əlɪŋ [-lɪŋ], -əld
Carolina ˌkærə'laɪnə
Caroline 'kærəlaɪn [-rlaɪn], less freq. -rəlɪn [-rlɪn]
carolus (C.), -es 'kærələs [-rləs], -ɪz
Carothers kə'rʌðəz
carotid, -s kə'rɒtɪd, -z
carous|e (s. v.), -es, -ing, -ed; -er/s; -al/s kə'raʊz, -ɪz, -ɪŋ, -d; -ə*/z; -l/z
car(r)ousel ˌkærə'sel [-ruː:'s-, -rʊ's-, -zel]
carp (s. v.), -s, -ing, -ed, -er/s kɑːp, -s, -ɪŋ, -t, -ə*/z
car-park, -s 'kɑːpɑːk, -s
Carpathian, -s kɑː'peɪθjən [-θɪən, -ðjən, -ðɪən], -z
carpel, -s 'kɑːpel, -z
Carpentaria ˌkɑːpən'teərɪə [-pen't-]
carpent|er (s. v.) (C.), -ers, -ering, -ered 'kɑːpənt|ə* [-pɪn-, -pn-], -əz, -ərɪŋ, -əd
carpentry 'kɑːpəntrɪ [-pɪn-, -pn-]
carpet (s. v.), -s, -ing, -ed 'kɑːpɪt, -s, -ɪŋ, -ɪd
carpet-bag, -s, -ging, -ger/s 'kɑːpɪtbæg, -z, -ɪŋ, -ə*/z
carpet-broom, -s 'kɑːpɪtbrʊm [-bruː:m], -z
carpet-sweeper, -s 'kɑːpɪtˌswiː:pə*, -z
Carpmael 'kɑːpmeɪl
Carr kɑː:*

carrag(h)een 'kærəgi:n
Carrara kə'rɑːrə
carraway, -s 'kærəweı, -z
Carrhae 'kæri:
carriage, -s 'kærɪdʒ, -ız
carriage-drive, -s 'kærɪdʒdraıv, -z
carriage-horse, -s 'kærɪdʒhɔːs, -ız
carriage-way 'kærɪdʒweı
carrick (C.) 'kærɪk
Carrickfergus ˌkærɪk'fɜːgəs
carrier-bag, -s 'kærɪəbæg, -z
Carrington 'kærɪŋtən
carrioca ˌkærɪ'əʊkə
carrion; -crow/s 'kærɪən; (ˌ--) -'krəʊ/z
Carrodus 'kærədəs
Carroll 'kærəl
carrot, -s, -y 'kærət, -s, -ı
Carruthers kə'rʌðəz
carr|y, -ies, -ying, -ied, -ier/s 'kær|ı,
 -ız, -ıŋ, -ıd, -ıə*/z
carry-cot, -s 'kærɪkɒt, -s
carryings-on ˌkærıŋz'ɒn
Carshalton kə'ʃɔːltən [kɑː'ʃ-, old-
 fashioned local pronunciations keıs-
 'hɔːltən, keıs'hɔːtn, keı'ʃɔːtn]
Carson 'kɑːsn
Carstairs 'kɑːsteəz
cart (s. v.) (C.), -s, -ing, -ed, -er/s;
 -age kɑːt, -s, -ıŋ, -ıd, -ə*/z; -ıdʒ
Carta 'kɑːtə
Cartagena ˌkɑːtə'dʒiːnə
carte (C.) kɑːt
carte blanche ˌkɑːt'blɑ̃ːnʃ [-'blɔ̃ːnʃ,
 -'blɑːnɪʃ, -'blɔːnʃ] (kartblɑ̃ːʃ)
carte-de-visite, -s ˌkɑːtdəvi:'ziːt [-vı'z-]
 (kartdəvizit), -s
cartel, -s (business combine) kɑː'tel,
 (other senses) kɑː'tel ['kɑːtl], -z
Carter 'kɑːtə*
Carteret (surname) 'kɑːtəret [-rɪt],
 (American place name) ˌkɑːtə'ret
Cartesian kɑː'tiːzjən [-zıən, -ʒjən,
 -ʒıən, -ʒn]
Carthage 'kɑːθɪdʒ
Carthaginian, -s ˌkɑːθə'dʒınıən [-njən],
 -z
cart-horse, -s 'kɑːthɔːs, -ız
Carthusian, -s kɑː'θjuːzjən [-'θuː:-,
 -zıən], -z
cartilage, -s 'kɑːtılɪdʒ [-təl-], -ız
cartilaginous ˌkɑːtı'lædʒınəs [-tə'l-,
 -dʒnəs]
cart-load, -s 'kɑːtləʊd, -z
Cartmel(e) 'kɑːtmel
cartograph|y, -er/s kɑː'tɒgrəf|ı, -ə*/z
cartomancy 'kɑːtəʊmænsı
carton, -s 'kɑːtən, -z
cartoon, -s, -ist/s kɑː'tuːn, -z, -ıst/s

cartouche, -s kɑː'tuːʃ, -ız
cartridge, -s 'kɑːtrıdʒ, -ız
cartridge-paper 'kɑːtrıdʒˌpeıpə*
cart-track, -s 'kɑːttræk, -s
cart-wheel, -s 'kɑːtwiːl [-thw-], -z
cartwright (C.), -s 'kɑːtraıt, -s
caruncle, -s 'kærəŋkl [kə'rʌŋkl], -z
Carus 'keərəs
Caruso kə'ruːzəʊ [-'ruːsəʊ]
Caruthers kə'rʌðəz
car|ve, -es, -ing, -ed, -er/s (C.) kɑːv, -z,
 -ıŋ, -d, -ə*/z
carving-kni|fe, -ves 'kɑːvıŋnaı|f, -vz
Carwardine 'kɑːwədiːn
Cary 'keərı
caryatid, -s, -es ˌkærı'ætıd, -z, -iːz
Caryll 'kærıl [-rəl]
Carysfort 'kærısfɔːt
Casabianca ˌkæsəbı'æŋkə [-æzə-, -'bjæ-]
Casablanca ˌkæsə'blæŋkə
Casanova ˌkæsə'nəʊvə [ˌkæzə-]
cascade, -s kæ'skeıd, -z
cascara, -s kæ'skɑːrə [kə's-], -z
cascarilla ˌkæskə'rılə
cas|e (s. v.) (C.), -es, -ing, -ed keıs, -ız,
 -ıŋ, -t
case-ending, -s 'keısˌendıŋ, -z
case-hardened 'keısˌhɑːdnd
casein 'keısiːn [-si:ın, -sıın]
case-kni|fe, -ves 'keısnaı|f, -vz
case-law 'keıslɔː
casemate, -s 'keısmeıt, -s
casement, -s 'keısmənt [old-fashioned
 'keızm-], -s
Casement 'keısmənt
casern, -s kə'zɜːn, -z
case-shot 'keısʃɒt ['keıʃʃɒt]
case-work, -er/s 'keıswɜːk, -ə*/z
Casey 'keısı
cash (s. v.), -es, -ing, -ed kæʃ, -ız, -ıŋ, -t
cash-account, -s ˌkæʃə'kaʊnt ['--ˌ-], -s
cash-book, -s 'kæʃbʊk, -s
cash-box, -es 'kæʃbɒks, -ız
cashew, -s 'kæʃuː [kə'ʃ-, kæ'ʃuː], -z
cashier (s.), -s kæ'ʃıə*, -z
cashier (v.), -s, -ing, -ed, -er/s kə'ʃıə*
 [kæ'ʃ-], -z, -ıŋ, -d, -rə*/z
cashmere (C.), -s kæʃ'mıə* [also '-ˌ-
 when attributive], -z
casing (s.), -s 'keısıŋ, -z
casino, -s kə'si:nəʊ [kə'zi:-], -z
cask (s. v.), -s, -ing, -ed kɑːsk, -s, -ıŋ, -t
casket, -s 'kɑːskıt, -s
Caslon 'kæzlən
Caspar 'kæspə* [-pɑː*]
Caspian 'kæspıən [-pjən]
casque, -s kæsk, -s
Cassandra kə'sændrə

cassation, -s kæˈseɪʃn [kəˈs-], -z
cassava kəˈsɑːvə
Cassel(l) ˈkæsl
casserole, -s ˈkæsərəʊl, -z
cassette, -s kəˈset [kæ-], -s
cassia ˈkæsɪə [-sjə]
Cassidy ˈkæsɪdɪ [-sədɪ]
Cassil(l)is ˈkæslz [ˈkɑːs-]
Cassio ˈkæsɪəʊ
Cassiopeia ˌkæsɪəʊˈpiːə [-ˈpɪə, *as name of constellation also* ˌkæsɪˈəʊpjə, -ˈəʊpɪə]
Cassius ˈkæsɪəs [-sjəs]
Cassivelaunus ˌkæsɪvɪˈlɔːnəs
cassock, -s, -ed ˈkæsək, -s, -t
cassowar|y, -ies ˈkæsəweər|ɪ [-wər-], -ɪz
cast (*s. v.*), -s, -ing kɑːst, -s, -ɪŋ
Castalia, -n/s kæˈsteɪljə [-lɪə], -n/z
castanet, -s ˌkæstəˈnet, -s
castaway, -s ˈkɑːstəweɪ, -z
caste, -s kɑːst, -s
castellated ˈkæstəleɪtɪd [-tɪl-, -tel-]
Castelnau (*road in S.W. London*) ˈkɑːslnɔː [-nəʊ]
caster, -s ˈkɑːstə*, -z
castigat|e, -es, -ing, -ed, -or/s ˈkæstɪgeɪt, -s, -ɪŋ, -ɪd, -ə*/z
castigation, -s ˌkæstɪˈgeɪʃn, -z
Castile kæˈstiːl
Castilian, -s kæˈstɪlɪən [kə-, -ljən], -z
casting (*s.*), -s ˈkɑːstɪŋ, -z
casting-net, -s ˈkɑːstɪŋnet, -s
casting-vote, -s ˌkɑːstɪŋˈvəʊt [ˈ---], -s
cast-iron ˌkɑːstˈaɪən [*also* ˈkɑːstˌaɪən *when attributive*]
castle, -s ˈkɑːsl, -z
Castlebar ˌkɑːslˈbɑː*
Castlenau (*engineering firm*) ˈkɑːslnɔː
Castlerea(gh) ˈkɑːslreɪ
Castleton ˈkɑːsltən
cast-off, -s ˈkɑːstɒf [*old-fashioned* ˈɔːf, *also* ˌ-ˈ-], -s
castor (C.), -s ˈkɑːstə*, -z
castor-oil ˌkɑːstərˈɔɪl [-təˈɔɪl]
castrametation ˌkæstrəmeˈteɪʃn [-mɪˈt-]
castrat|e, -es, -ing, -ed kæˈstreɪt [ˈkæstreɪt], -s, -ɪŋ, -ɪd
castration, -s kæˈstreɪʃn, -z
castrat|o, -i kæˈstrɑːt|əʊ, -iː
Castro ˈkæstrəʊ
casual, -ly ˈkæʒʊəl [-ʒjwəl, -ʒjʊl, -ʒjʊəl, -ʒwəl, -ʒʊl, -zjʊəl, -zjwəl, -zjʊl], -ɪ
casualt|y, -ies ˈkæʒʊəlt|ɪ [-ʒjwəl-, -ʒjʊl-, -ʒjʊəl-, -ʒwəl-, -ʒʊl-, -zjʊəl-, -zjwəl-, -zjʊl-], -ɪz
casuist, -s, -ry ˈkæzjʊɪst [ˈkæʒjʊ-, ˈkæʒʊ-], -s, -rɪ

casuistic, -al ˌkæzjʊˈɪstɪk [ˌkæʒjʊ-, ˌkæʒʊ-], -l
casus belli ˌkɑːsʊsˈbeli: [ˌkeɪsəsˈbelaɪ]
Caswell ˈkæzwəl [ˈwel]
cat, -s kæt, -s
cataclysm, -s ˈkætəklɪzəm, -z
catacomb, -s ˈkætəkuːm [-kəʊm], -z
catafalque, -s ˈkætəfælk, -s
Catalan, -s ˈkætələn [-lən], -z
catalectic ˌkætəˈlektɪk
cataleps|y, -ies ˈkætəleps|ɪ, -ɪz
cataleptic ˌkætəˈleptɪk
catalogu|e (*s. v.*), -es, -ing, -ed ˈkætəlɒg, -z, -ɪŋ, -d
Catalonia, -n/s ˌkætəˈləʊnjə [-nɪə], -n/z
catalpa, -s kəˈtælpə, -z
catalysis kəˈtæləsɪs [-lɪs-]
catalyst, -s ˈkætəlɪst, -s
catalytic ˌkætəˈlɪtɪk
catamaran, -s ˌkætəməˈræn, -z
Catania kəˈteɪnjə [-nɪə]
cataplasm, -s ˈkætəplæzəm, -z
catapult, -s ˈkætəpʌlt, -s
cataract, -s ˈkætərækt, -s
catarrh, -s, -al kəˈtɑː* [kæˈt-], -z, -rəl
catasta, -s kəˈtæstə, -z
catastas|is, -es kəˈtæstəs|ɪs, -iːz
catastrophe, -s kəˈtæstrəfɪ, -z
catastrophic ˌkætəˈstrɒfɪk
catawba (C.) kəˈtɔːbə
catbird, -s ˈkætbɜːd, -z
catboat, -s ˈkætbəʊt, -s
catcall, -s ˈkætkɔːl, -z
catch (*s. v.*), -es, -ing, caught, catcher/s kætʃ, -ɪz, -ɪŋ, kɔːt, ˈkætʃə*/z
catching (*adj.*) ˈkætʃɪŋ
catchpenn|y, -ies ˈkætʃˌpen|ɪ, -ɪz
catchpole, -s ˈkætʃpəʊl, -z
catchpoll, -s ˈkætʃpəʊl, -z
catchword, -s ˈkætʃwɜːd, -z
catch|y, -iness ˈkætʃ|ɪ, -ɪnɪs [-nəs]
Catcott ˈkætkət
catechetic, -al, -ally ˌkætɪˈketɪk [-teˈk-, -tək-], -l, -əlɪ
catechi|sm/s, -st/s ˈkætəkɪ|zəm/z [-tɪk-], -st/s
catechiz|e [-is|e], -es, -ing, -ed, -er/s ˈkætɪkaɪz [-tək-], -ɪz, -ɪŋ, -d, -ə*/z
catechu ˈkætɪtʃuː [-tə-]
catechumen, -s ˌkætɪˈkjuːmen [-təˈk-, -mɪn], -z
categoric|al -ally ˌkætəˈgɒrɪk|l [-teˈg-, -tɪˈg-], -əlɪ
categoriz|e [is|e], -es, -ing, -ed ˈkætəgəraɪz [-teg-, -tɪg-], -ɪz, -ɪŋ, -d
categor|y, -ies ˈkætəgər|ɪ [-teg-, -tɪg-], -ɪz
catena, -s kəˈtiːnə, -z

catenar|y, -ies kə'ti:nər|ɪ, -ɪz
catenat|e, -es, -ing, -ed 'kætɪneɪt [-tən-],
-s, -ɪŋ, -ɪd
catenation, -s ˌkætɪ'neɪʃn [-tə'n-], -z
cateniz|e [-is|e], -es, -ing, -ed 'kætɪnaɪz
[-tən-], -ɪz, -ɪŋ, -d
cat|er (C.), -ers, -ering, -ered, -erer/s
'keɪt|ə*, -əz, -ərɪŋ, -əd, -ərə*/z
cater-cousin, -s 'keɪtəˌkʌzn, -z
Caterham 'keɪtərəm
Caterina ˌkætə'ri:nə
caterpillar, -s 'kætəpɪlə*, -z
caterwaul (s. v.), -s, -ing, -ed 'kætəwɔ:l,
-z, -ɪŋ, -d
Catesby 'keɪtsbɪ
cat-eyed 'kætaɪd
catfish, -es 'kætfɪʃ, -ɪz
Catford 'kætfəd
catgut 'kætgʌt [-gət]
Catharine 'kæθərɪn
cathari|sm, -st|s 'kæθərɪ|zəm, -st/s
catharsis kə'θɑ:sɪs [kæ'θ-]
cathartic, -s kə'θɑ:tɪk [kæ'θ-], -s
Cathay kæ'θeɪ [kə'θ-]
Cathcart 'kæθkət [-kɑ:t], kæθ'kɑ:t
[kəθ-]
cathead, -s 'kæthed, -z
cathedra, -s kə'θi:drə [-'θed-], -z
cathedra (in phrase ex cathedra)
kə'θi:drə [kæ'tedrɑ:, kæ'θed-,
kə'ted-, kə'θed-]
cathedral, -s kə'θi:drəl, -z
Cather 'kæðə*
Catherine 'kæθərɪn
catherine-wheel, -s 'kæθərɪnwi:l
[-nhw-], -z
catheter, -s 'kæθɪtə* [-θət-], -z
cathetometer, -s ˌkæθɪ'tɒmɪtə* [-θə't-,
-mətə*], -z
cathode, -s 'kæθəʊd, -z
cat-hole, -s 'kæthəʊl, -z
catholic (C.), -s 'kæθəlɪk [-θ|ɪk, -θlɪk,
rarely 'kɑ:θ-], -s
catholicism kə'θɒləsɪzəm [-lɪs-]
catholicity ˌkæθəʊ'lɪsətɪ [-ɪtɪ]
catholiciz|e [-is|e], -es, -ing, -ed
kə'θɒləsaɪz, [-lɪs-], -ɪz, -ɪŋ, -d
Catiline 'kætɪlaɪn [-təl-]
cation, -s 'kætaɪən, -z
catkin, -s 'kætkɪn, -z
catlike 'kætlaɪk
catmint 'kætmɪnt
Cato 'keɪtəʊ
cat-o'-nine-tails ˌkætə'naɪnteɪlz
Cator 'keɪtə*
Catriona kə'trɪənə [kæ't-, -'tri:nə,
rarely ˌkætrɪ'əʊnə]
cat's-cradle 'kætsˌkreɪdl [ˌ-'--]

cat's-eye, -s 'kætsaɪ, -z
cat's-meat 'kætsmi:t
cat's-paw, -s 'kætspɔ:, -z
catsup, -s 'kætsəp ['kætʃəp, 'ketʃəp], -s
Cattanach 'kætənæk [-nɑ:x]
Cattegat 'kætɪgæt
Cattell kæ'tel [kə't-]
Cattermole 'kætəməʊl
cattish 'kætɪʃ
cattle 'kætl
cattle/-grid/s, -pen/s 'kætl/grɪd/z, -pen/z
cattle-show, -s 'kætlʃəʊ, -z
cattle-truck, -s 'kætltrʌk, -s
catt|y, -ier, -iest, -ily, -iness 'kæt|ɪ, -ɪə*,
-ɪɪst, -ɪlɪ [-əlɪ], -ɪnɪs [-ɪnəs]
Catullus kə'tʌləs
Caucasia kɔ:'keɪzjə [-zɪə, -ʒə, -ʒɪə, -ʒə]
Caucasian, -s kɔ:'keɪzjən [-eɪzɪən,
-eɪʒjən, -eɪʒɪən, -eɪʒn], -z
Caucasus 'kɔ:kəsəs
caucus, -es 'kɔ:kəs, -ɪz
caud|al, -ate 'kɔ:d|l, -eɪt
caudillo, -s kaʊ'dɪləʊ [-'dɪljəʊ], -z
Caudine 'kɔ:daɪn
caudle (C.) 'kɔ:dl
caught (from catch) kɔ:t
caul, -s kɔ:l, -z
cauldron, -s 'kɔ:ldrən ['kɒl-], -z
cauliflower, -s 'kɒlɪˌflaʊə*, -z
caulk, -s, -ing, -ed kɔ:k, -s, -ɪŋ, -t
caulker, -s 'kɔ:kə*, -z
caus|al, -ally 'kɔ:z|l, -əlɪ [-lɪ]
causality kɔ:'zælətɪ [-ɪtɪ]
causation kɔ:'zeɪʃn
causative, -ly 'kɔ:zətɪv, -lɪ
caus|e (s. v.), -es, -ing, -ed kɔ:z, -ɪz, -ɪŋ,
-d
cause célèbre ˌkɔ:z se'lebrə [ˌkəʊz-,
-leɪbrə] (ko:z selebr)
causeless, -ly 'kɔ:zlɪs [-ləs], -lɪ
causerie, -s 'kəʊzərɪ [-ri:] (kozri), -z
causeway, -s 'kɔ:zweɪ, -z
caustic, -al, -ally 'kɔ:stɪk ['kɒs-], -l,
-əlɪ
causticity kɔ:'stɪsətɪ [kɒ's-, -ɪtɪ]
cauterization [-isa-], -s ˌkɔ:təraɪ'zeɪʃn
[-rɪ'z-], -z
cauteriz|e [-is|e], -es, -ing, -ed 'kɔ:təraɪz,
-ɪz, -ɪŋ, -d
cauter|y, -ies 'kɔ:tər|ɪ, -ɪz
cauti|on (s. v.), -ons, -oning, -oned,
-oner/s 'kɔ:ʃ|n, -nz, -nɪŋ [-ənɪŋ,
-nɪŋ], -nd, -nə*/z [-ənə*/z, -nə*/z]
cautionary 'kɔ:ʃnərɪ [-ʃənə-, -ʃnə-]
caution-money 'kɔ:ʃnˌmʌnɪ
cautious, -ly, -ness 'kɔ:ʃəs, -lɪ, -nɪs
[-nəs]
cavalcade, -s ˌkævl'keɪd ['---], -z

cavalier, -s ˌkævəˈlɪə*, -z
Cavalleria Rusticana kəˌvælə'riːə-
ˌrʊstɪˈkɑːnə [ˌkævəl-, -ˈrɪə]
cavalr|y, -ies 'kævlr|ɪ, -ɪz
cavalry|man, -men 'kævlrɪ|mən
[-mæn], -mən [-men]
Cavan 'kævən
Cavanagh 'kævənə
Cavanaugh 'kævənɔː
cavatina, -s ˌkævəˈtiːnə, -z
cav|e (s. v.) (C.), -es, -ing, -ed keɪv, -z,
-ɪŋ, -d
cave (beware) 'keɪvɪ
caveat, -s 'kævɪæt ['keɪv-], -s
cave-dweller, -s 'keɪvˌdwelə*, -z
Cavell 'kævl, kə'vel
Note.—The family of Nurse Edith
Cavell pronounces 'kævl.
cave|man, -men 'keɪv|mæn, -men
Cavendish 'kævəndɪʃ
cavern, -s, -ous 'kævən [-vɜːn], -z, -əs
Caversham 'kævəʃəm
caviar(e) 'kævɪɑː* [ˌkævɪˈɑː*]
cavil (s. v.), -s, -ling, -led, -ler/s 'kævl
[-vɪl], -z, -ɪŋ, -d, -ə*/z
cavillation, -s ˌkævɪˈleɪʃn [-vəl-], -z
cavit|y, -ies 'kævət|ɪ [-ɪt|ɪ], -ɪz
cavort, -s, -ing, -ed kə'vɔːt, -s, -ɪŋ, -ɪd
cav|y, -ies 'keɪv|ɪ, -z
caw, -s, -ing, -ed kɔː, -z, -ɪŋ, -d
Caw|dor, -ley 'kɔː|də*, -lɪ
Cawnpore (old spelling of Kanpur)
kɔːnˈpɔː* [-ˈpɔə*] (Hindi kanpwr)
Cawse kɔːz
Caxton 'kækstən
cayenne (C.) keɪ'en [but 'keɪen in
Cayenne pepper]
Cayley 'keɪlɪ
cayman (C.), -s 'keɪmən, -z
Cearns keənz
ceas|e, -es, -ing, -ed siːs, -ɪz, -ɪŋ, -t
cease-fire ˌsiːsˈfaɪə* ['---]
ceaseless, -ly, -ness 'siːslɪs [-ləs], -lɪ,
-nɪs [-nəs]
Cecil (Christian name, surname) 'sesl
[-sɪl], 'sɪsl [-sɪl]
Note.—The family name of the Marquess of Exeter and that of the
Marquess of Salisbury is 'sɪsl [-sɪl].
Cecile (Christian name) 'sesɪl [-sl],
'sesiːl
Cecilia sɪ'sɪljə [sə's-, -'siː-, -lɪə]
Cecily 'sɪsɪlɪ [-əlɪ], 'sesɪlɪ [-əlɪ]
cedar, -s 'siːdə*, -z
ced|e, -es, -ing, -ed siːd, -z, -ɪŋ, -ɪd
cedilla, -s sɪ'dɪlə [sə-], -z
Cedric 'siːdrɪk, 'sedrɪk
ceil, -s, -ing, -ed siːl, -z, -ɪŋ, -d

ceilidh, -s 'keɪlɪ, -z
ceiling (s.), -s 'siːlɪŋ, -z
celadon 'selədɒn [-dən]
celandine, -s 'seləndaɪn, -z
celanese ˌseləˈniːz
Celebes se'liːbɪz [sɪ'l-]
celebrant, -s 'selɪbrənt, -s
celebrat|e, -es, -ing, -ed, -or/s 'selɪbreɪt,
-s, -ɪŋ, -ɪd, -ə*/z
celebration, -s ˌselɪˈbreɪʃn, -z
celebratory 'selɪbrətərɪ [-breɪt-, ˌselɪ-
ˈbreɪtərɪ]
celebrit|y, -ies sɪ'lebrət|ɪ [sə'l-, -ɪt|ɪ], -ɪz
celeriac 'selerɪæk [sə'l-, 'selərɪæk]
celerity sɪ'lerətɪ [sə'l-, -ɪtɪ]
celery 'selərɪ
celeste, -s sɪ'lest [sə'l-], -s
celestial (C.), -ly sɪ'lestjəl [sə'l-, -trəl],
-ɪ
celestine (mineral) 'selɪstaɪn
Celestine, -s 'selɪstaɪn [-ləs-, sɪ'lestaɪn,
sɪ'lestɪn, sə'l-], -z
Celia 'siːljə [-lɪə]
celibacy 'selɪbəsɪ
celibatarian, -s ˌselɪbəˈteərɪən, -z
celibate, -s 'selɪbət [-bɪt], -s
cell, -s sel, -z
cellar, -s; -age, -er/s 'selə*, -z; -rɪdʒ,
-rə*/z
cellaret, -s ˌseləˈret ['seləret], -s
cellarist, -s 'selərɪst, -s
cellar|man, -men 'selə|mən [-mæn],
-mən [-men]
cellist, -s 'tʃelɪst, -s
cello, -s 'tʃeləu, -z
cellophane 'seləʊfeɪn
cellular 'seljʊlə*
cellule, -s 'seljuːl, -z
celluloid 'seljʊlɔɪd
cellulose 'seljʊləus
Celsius 'selsɪəs [-sjəs]
celt, -s selt, -s
Celt, -s (as generally used) kelt [rarely
selt], (member of football team) selt, -s
Celtic (as generally used) 'keltɪk [rarely
'seltɪk], (in names of football team)
'seltɪk, (for Sea) 'keltɪk
Cely 'siːlɪ
cembalo, -s 'tʃembələu, -z
cement (s. v.), -s, -ing, -ed sɪ'ment
[sə'm-], -s, -ɪŋ, -ɪd
cementation, -s ˌsiːmen'teɪʃn, -z
cementium sɪ'menʃjəm [-ʃɪəm, -tɪəm]
cemeter|y, -ies 'semɪtr|ɪ [-ətr|ɪ], -ɪz
Cenci (poem by Shelley) 'tʃentʃɪ
Cenis sə'niː [se'n-] (səni)
cenobite, -s 'siːnəʊbaɪt, -s
cenotaph, -s 'senəʊtɑːf [-tæf], -s

cens|e, -es, -ing, -ed sens, -ız, -ıŋ, -t
censer, -s 'sensə*, -z
cens|or (s. v.), -ors, -oring, -ored
'sens|ə*, -əz, -ərıŋ, -əd
censorial, -ly sen'sɔ:rıəl, -ı
censorian sen'sɔ:rıən
censorious, -ly, -ness sen'sɔ:rıəs, -lı,
-nıs [-nəs]
censorship, -s 'sensəʃıp, -s
censurable 'senʃərəbl
censur|e (s. v.), -es, -ing, -ed 'senʃə*, -z,
-rıŋ, -d
census, -es 'sensəs, -ız
census-paper, -s 'sensəs₁peıpə*, -z
cent, -s sent, -s
centage 'sentıdʒ
cental, -s 'sentl, -z
centaur, -s 'sentɔ:*, -z
centaur|y, -ies 'sentɔ:r|ı, -ız
centenarian, -s ₁sentı'neərıən, -z
centenar|y, -ies sen'ti:nər|ı [-'ten-,
'sentınər|ı], -ız
centennial sen'tenjəl [-nıəl]
center (s. v.), -s, -ing, -ed 'sentə*, -z,
-rıŋ, -d
centesim|al, -ally, -o sen'tesım|l, -əlı,
-əʊ
centigrade 'sentıgreıd
centigramme, -s 'sentıgræm, -z
centilitre, -s 'sentı₁li:tə*, -z
centime, -s 'sɒnti:m ['sɑ̃:n-, 'sɔ̃:nt-,
'sɑ:nt-, 'sɔ:nt-] (sãtim), -z
centimetre, -s 'sentı₁mi:tə*, -z
centipede, -s 'sentıpi:d, -z
centner, -s 'sentnə* ('tsɛntnər), -z
cento, -s 'sentəʊ, -z
centr|al, -ally, -alism 'sentr|əl, -əlı,
-əlızəm
centrality sen'trælətı [-ıtı]
centralization [-isa-] ₁sentrəlaı'zeıʃn
[-trlaı'z-, -trəlı'z-, -trlı'z-]
centraliz|e [-is|e], -es, -ing, -ed, 'sentrə-
laız [-trl-], -ız, -ıŋ, -d
cent|re (s. v.), -res, -ring, -red 'sent|ə*,
-əz, -ərıŋ, -əd
centre-bit, -s 'sentəbıt, -s
centre-piece, -s 'sentəpi:s, -ız
centric, -al, -ally 'sentrık, -l, -əlı
†centrifugal sen'trıfjʊgl ['sentrıfju:g-,
₁sentrı'fju:g-]
centripetal sen'trıpıtl ['sentrıpi:t-,
₁sentrı'pi:t-]
centr|um, -a 'sentr|əm, -ə
centumvir, -s sen'tʌmvə:* [ken'tʊm-,
-və*], -z
centumvirate, -s sen'tʌmvırət [-vər-,
-ıt], -s
centuple 'sentjʊpl

centurion, -s sen'tjʊərıən [-'tjɔər-,
-'tjɔ:r-, -'tʃʊər-], -z
centur|y, -ies 'sentʃʊr|ı [-tjʊr-, -tʃər-,
'senʃər-], -ız
cephalic ke'fælık [kı'f-, se'f-, sı'f-]
cephalopod, -s 'sefələʊpɒd, -z
cephalopoda ₁sefə'lɒpədə
Cephas 'si:fæs
Cepheid, -s 'si:fııd, -z
Cepheus 'si:fju:s [-fjəs, -frəs]
ceramic, -s sı'ræmık [se'r-, sə'r-, kı'r-,
ke'r-, kə'r-], -s (experts tend to use
the forms with k-)
cerastes sı'ræsti:z [se'r-, sə'r-]
cerate, -s 'sıərıt [-reıt, -rət], -s
Cerberus 'sə:bərəs
cerca|ria, -riae sə:'keə|rıə, -rıi:
cer|e (s. v.), -es, -ing, -ed sıə*, -z, -rıŋ,
-d
cereal, -s 'sıərıəl, -z
cerebell|um, -ums, -a ₁serı'bel|əm,
-əmz, -ə
cerebos 'serıbɒs
cerebral (s. adj.), -s 'serıbrəl, -z
cerebration ₁serı'breıʃn
cerebr|um, -a 'serıbr|əm [sə'ri:-
br|əm], -ə
cere|-cloth, -cloths 'sıə|klɒθ [old-
fashioned -klɔ:θ], -klɒθs [-klɔ:ðz,
-klɔ:θs]
cerement, -s 'sıəmənt, -s
ceremonial (s. adj.), -s, -ly; -ism
₁serı'məʊnjəl [-rə'm-, -nıəl], -z, -ı;
-ızəm
ceremonious, -ly, -ness ₁serı'məʊnjəs
[-rə'm-, -nıəs], -lı, -nıs [-nəs]
ceremon|y, -ies 'serımən|ı [-rəm-], -ız
cereous 'sıərıəs
Ceres 'sıərı:z
cerif [ser-], -s 'serıf, -s
cerise sə'ri:z [sı'r-, -'ri:s]
ceroplastic ₁sıərəʊ'plæstık [-'plɑ:s-]
certain, -ly 'sə:tn [-tən, -tın], -lı
certaint|y, -ies 'sə:tnt|ı [-tən-, -tın-], -ız
certes 'sə:tız [sə:ts]
certifiabl|e, -ly ₁sə:tı'faıəb|l, -lı
certificate (s.), -es sə'tıfıkət [sə:'t-, -kıt],
-s
certificat|e (v.), -es, -ing, -ed sə'tıfıkeıt
[sə:'t-], -s, -ıŋ, -ıd [sə'tıfıkətıd,
-kıt-]
certification, -s (act of certifying) ₁sə:tı-
fı'keıʃn, (providing with a certificate)
₁sə:tıfı'keıʃn [sə₁t-], -z
certificatory sə'tıfıkətərı [sə:'t-, -keıt-]
certi|fy, -fies, -fying, -fied, -fier/s 'sə:-
tı|faı, -faız, -faıŋ, -faıd, -faıə*/z
certiorari, -s ₁sə:tıɔ:'reəraı [-tıə'r-], -z

certitude 'sɜːtɪtjuːd
cerulean sɪ'ruːljən [sɪə'r-, -lɪən]
cerumen sɪ'ruːmen
ceruse ['sɪəruːs [sɪ'ruːs, sə'r-]
Cervantes sɜː'væntɪz [-tiːz]
cervical sə'vaɪkl [sɜː'v-, 'sɜːvɪkl]
cervine 'sɜːvaɪn
cervi|x, -ces, -xes 'sɜːvɪ|ks, -siːz, -ksɪz
César 'seɪzaː* [-zə*] (seza:r)
Cesarewitch (Russian prince) sɪ'zaːrə-
vɪtʃ [-rɪv-], (race) sɪ'zærəwɪtʃ [-'zaːr-,
-rɪw-]
Cesario siːˈzɑːrɪəʊ [-'zær-]
cess, -es ses, -ɪz
cessation, -s se'seɪʃn [sɪ's-, sə's-], -z
cession, -s 'seʃn, -z
cessionar|y, -ies 'seʃənər|ɪ [-ʃɳər-], -ɪz
cesspit, -s 'sesprt, -s
cesspool, -s 'sespuːl, -z
Cestrian 'sestrɪən
cestui que trust, -s ˌsetɪkɪ'trʌst, -s
cestui que vie, -s ˌsetɪkɪ'viː, -z
cestuis que trust ˌsetɪzkɪ'trʌst
cestuis que vie ˌsetɪzkɪ'viː
cest|us, -i 'sest|əs, -aɪ
ceta|cea, -cean/s sɪ'teɪ|ʃjə [se't-, -ʃɪə,
-ʃə, -sjə, -sɪə], -ʃjən/z [-ʃɪən/z, -ʃn/z,
-sjən/z, -sɪən/z]
cetaceous sɪ'teɪʃjəs [se't-, -ʃɪəs, -ʃəs,
-sjəs, -sɪəs]
cetane 'siːteɪn
Cetewayo ketʃ'waɪəʊ [ˌketɪ'waɪəʊ,
-'waːjəʊ, old-fashioned ˌsetɪ'weɪəʊ]
(Zulu ʒetʃ'waːjo)
Cet(t)inje tse'tɪnjɪ [se't-]
Ceuta 'sjuːtə
Cévennes sɪ'ven [sə'v-, -enz] (sevεn)
Ceylon sɪ'lɒn
Ceylonese ˌselə'niːz [ˌsiː-]
Ceyx 'siːɪks
Cézanne seɪ'zæn [sɪ-, se-] (sezan)
cf. kəm'peə* [kən'fɜː*, ˌsiː'ef]
Chablis 'ʃæbliː [-blɪ] (ʃabli)
chaconne, -s ʃə'kɒn [ʃæ'k-] (ʃakɔn), -z
Chad, -ian/s tʃæd, -ɪən/z
Chadwick 'tʃædwɪk
chaf|e, -es, -ing, -ed tʃeɪf, -s, -ɪŋ, -t
chafer, -s 'tʃeɪfə*, -z
chaff (s. v.), -s, -ing/ly, -ed, -er/s tʃɑːf
[tʃæf], -s, -ɪŋ/lɪ, -t, -ə*/z
chaff-cutter, -s 'tʃɑːfˌkʌtə*, -z
chaffer (v.), -s, -ing, -ed 'tʃæfə*, -z,
-rɪŋ, -d
Chaffey 'tʃeɪfɪ
chaffinch, -es 'tʃæfɪntʃ, -ɪz
chaff|y, -iness 'tʃɑːf|ɪ, -ɪnɪs [-ɪnəs]
chafing-dish, -es 'tʃeɪfɪŋdɪʃ, -ɪz
chagrin (s.) 'ʃægrɪn

chagrin (v.), -s, -ing, -ed 'ʃægrɪn
[ʃə'griːn], -z, -ɪŋ, -d
Chaim haɪm (Heb. 'xajim, xa'jiːm)
chain (s. v.), -s, -ing, -ed tʃeɪn, -z, -ɪŋ, -d
chain-armour ˌtʃeɪn'ɑːmə* ['-ˌ--]
chain-bridge, -s ˌtʃeɪn'brɪdʒ ['--], -ɪz
chain-gang, -s 'tʃeɪngæŋ, -z
chainless 'tʃeɪnlɪs [-ləs]
chain-mail ˌtʃeɪn'meɪl ['--]
chainstitch 'tʃeɪnstɪtʃ
chain-stores 'tʃeɪnstɔːz [-stɔəz]
chainwork 'tʃeɪnwɜːk
chair (s. v.), -s, -ing, -ed tʃeə*, -z, -ɪŋ,
-d
chair-bed, -s 'tʃeəbed [ˌ-'-], -z
chair|man, -men 'tʃeə|mən, -mən
chairmanship, -s 'tʃeəmənʃɪp, -s
chaise, -s ʃeɪz, -ɪz
chaise-longue ˌʃeɪz'lɒŋ [ˌʃez-, -'lɒŋg,
-'lɔ̃ːŋg] (ʃεːzlɔ̃ːg)
Chalcedon 'kælsɪdən [-dn, -dɒn]
chalcedony kæl'sedənɪ
chalcedonyx, -es ˌkælsɪ'dɒnɪks, -ɪz
Chalcis 'kælsɪs
chalcography kæl'kɒgrəfɪ
Chaldaic kæl'deɪk
Chaldea, -n/s kæl'diːə [-'dɪə], -n/z
Chaldee, -s kæl'diː, -z
chaldron, -s 'tʃɔːldrən, -z
chalet, -s 'ʃæleɪ ['ʃælɪ] (ʃalε), -z
Chalfont (in Buckinghamshire)
'tʃælfənt [-fɒnt] [old-fashioned
'tʃɑːfənt]
Chaliapin ˌʃælɪ'ɑːpɪn (ʃa'ljapin)
chalice, -s, -d 'tʃælɪs, -ɪz, -t
chalk (s. v.) (C.), -s, -ing, -ed tʃɔːk, -s,
-ɪŋ, -t
Chalkis 'kælkɪs
chalk-pit, -s 'tʃɔːkpɪt, -s
chalk-stone, -s 'tʃɔːkstəʊn, -z
chalk|y, -ier, -iest, -ily, -iness 'tʃɔːk|ɪ,
-ɪə* [-jə*], -ɪɪst [-jɪst], -ɪlɪ [-əlɪ],
-ɪnɪs [-ɪnəs]
Challen 'tʃælɪn
challeng|e (s. v.), -es, -ing, -ed, -er/s
'tʃælɪndʒ [-əndʒ], -ɪz, -ɪŋ, -d, -ə*/z
Challenor 'tʃælɪnə*
challis 'ʃælɪs ['ʃælɪ]
Challoner 'tʃælənə*
Chalmers 'tʃɑːməz
Chaloner 'tʃælənə*
chalybeate kə'lɪbɪət [kæ'l-, -bjət, -ɪt]
Cham kæm
chamade, -s ʃə'mɑːd, -z
chamber, -s, -ed 'tʃeɪmbə*, -z, -d
Chamberlain 'tʃeɪmbəlɪn [-bˌlɪn, -lən],
-bələm
chamberlain, -s 'tʃeɪmbəlɪn [-bˌlɪn], -z

81

chamberlainship, -s 'tʃeɪmbəlɪnʃɪp
[-blɪn-], -s
chamber-maid, -s 'tʃeɪmbəmeɪd, -z
Chambers 'tʃeɪmbəz
chameleon, -s kə'miːljən [-lɪən], -s
chamfer, -s 'tʃæmfə* ['ʃæm-], -z
chamois (sing.) 'ʃæmwɑ: [-wɔ:] [in
chamois leather usually 'ʃæmɪ],
(plur.) -z
Chamonix 'ʃæmənɪ [-ni:]
champ, -s, -ing, -ed tʃæmp, -s, -ɪŋ, -t
[tʃæmt]
champagne, -s ˌʃæm'peɪn [also '-- when
attributive], -z
champaign, -s 'tʃæmpeɪn, -z
champerty 'tʃæmpə:tɪ [-pət-]
champignon, -s tʃæm'pɪnjən (ʃɑ̃piɲɔ̃),-z
champion (s. adj. v.) (C.), -s, -ing, -ed;
-ship/s 'tʃæmpjən, -z, -ɪŋ, -d; -ʃɪp/s
Champs Elysées ˌʃɑ̃:nze'liːzeɪ [ˌʃɒnz-,
ˌʃɔ̃:nz-, ˌʃɔ:nz-] (ʃɑ̃zelize)
chanc|e (s. v.), -es, -ing, -ed tʃɑːns, -ɪz,
-ɪŋ, -t
chancel, -s 'tʃɑːnsl, -z
chanceller|y, -ies 'tʃɑːnsələr|ɪ [-slə-,
-əlrɪ], -ɪz
chancellor (C.), -s; -ship/s 'tʃɑːnsələ*
[-slə*, -slə*, -sɪlə*], -z; -ʃɪp/s
chancer|y (C.), -ies 'tʃɑːnsər|ɪ, -ɪz
chanc|re, -roid 'ʃæŋk|ə*, -rɔɪd
chanc|y, -ier, -iest 'tʃɑːns|ɪ, -ɪə [-jə],
-ɪɪst [-jɪst]
chandelier, -s ˌʃændə'lɪə* [-dɪ'l-], -z
chandler (C.), -s 'tʃɑːndlə*, -z
Chandos 'tʃændɒs, 'tʃændɒs
Note.—Lord Chandos pronounces
'ʃæn-. Chandos Street in London is
generally pronounced with 'tʃ-.
chang|e (s. v.), -es, -ing, -ed, -er/s
tʃeɪndʒ, -ɪz, -ɪŋ, -d, -ə*/z
changeability ˌtʃeɪndʒə'bɪlətɪ [-lɪt-]
changeab|le, -ly, -leness 'tʃeɪndʒəb|l,
-lɪ, -lnɪs [-nəs]
changeless 'tʃeɪndʒlɪs [-ləs]
changeling, -s 'tʃeɪndʒlɪŋ, -z
chann|el (s. v.), -els, -elling, -elled
'tʃæn|l, -lz, -lɪŋ [-əlɪŋ], -ld
Channell 'tʃænl
Channing 'tʃænɪŋ
Channon 'tʃænən, 'ʃænən
chant (s. v.) (C.), -s, -ing, -ed, -er/s
tʃɑːnt, -s, -ɪŋ, -ɪd, -ə*/z
Chanter 'tʃɑːntə*
chanterelle, -s ˌtʃæntə'rel, -z
chanticleer, -s ˌtʃæntɪ'klɪə* [ˌtʃɑːnt-,
ˌʃæn-, ˌʃɑːn-, '---], -z
Chantilly ʃæn'tɪlɪ [ʃɑ̃:n't-, ʃɔ̃:n't-,
ʃɑːn't-, ʃɒn't-] (ʃɑ̃tiji)

Chantrey 'tʃɑːntrɪ
chantr|y, -ies 'tʃɑːntr|ɪ, -ɪz
chant|y, -ies 'tʃɑːnt|ɪ, -ɪz
chaos 'keɪɒs
chaotic, -ally keɪ'ɒtɪk, -lɪ
chap (s. v.), -s, -ping, -ped tʃæp, -s, -ɪŋ,
-t
chap-book, -s 'tʃæpbʊk, -s
chape, -s tʃeɪp, -s
chapel, -s 'tʃæpl, -z
Chapel - en - le - Frith ˌtʃæplənlə'frɪθ
[-plen-]
chapelr|y, -ies 'tʃæplr|ɪ, -ɪz
chaperon(e) (s. v.), -s, -ing, -ed; -age
'ʃæpərəʊn, -z, -ɪŋ, -d; -ɪdʒ
chapfallen 'tʃæpˌfɔːlən
chaplain, -s 'tʃæplɪn, -z
chaplainc|y, -ies 'tʃæplɪns|ɪ [-lən-], -ɪz
chaplet, -s 'tʃæplɪt [-lət, -let], -s
Chap|lin, -man 'tʃæp|lɪn, -mən
Chapp|ell, -le 'tʃæp|l, -l
chapter, -s 'tʃæptə*, -z
chapter-hou|se, -ses 'tʃæptəhaʊ|s, -zɪz
char (s. v.), -s, -ring, -red tʃɑː*, -z,
-rɪŋ, -d
char-à-banc, -s 'ʃærəbæŋ [-bɑ̃:ŋ, -bɔ̃:ŋ,
-bɒŋ] (ʃarabɑ̃, as if French), -s
character, -s 'kærəktə* [-rɪk-], -z
characteristic, -s, -al, -ally ˌkærək-
tə'rɪstɪk [-rɪk-], -s, -l, -əlɪ
characterization [-isa-], -s ˌkærəktərai-
'zeɪʃn [-rɪk-, -rɪ'z-], -z
characteriz|e [-is|e], -es, -ing, -ed
'kærəktəraɪz [-rɪk-], -ɪz, -ɪŋ, -d
charade, -s ʃə'rɑːd, -z
charcoal 'tʃɑːkəʊl
chard (C.) tʃɑːd
char|e, -es, -ing, -ed tʃeə*, -z, -rɪŋ, -d
charg|e (s. v.), -es, -ing, -ed tʃɑːdʒ, -ɪz,
-ɪŋ, -d
chargeab|le, -ly, -leness 'tʃɑːdʒəb|l, -lɪ,
-lnɪs [-nəs]
chargé(s) d'affaires (sing.) ˌʃɑːʒeɪ-
dæ'feə* [-də'f-] (ʃarʒedafɛːr), (plur.)
-z
charger, -s 'tʃɑːdʒə*, -z
Charig 'tʃærɪg
Charing Cross ˌtʃærɪŋ'krɒs [ˌtʃeər-,
old-fashioned -'krɔːs]
chariot, -s 'tʃærɪət, -s
charioteer, -s ˌtʃærɪə'tɪə*, -z
charisma kə'rɪzmə
charismatic ˌkærɪz'mætɪk
charitab|le, -ly, -leness 'tʃærətəb|l
[-rɪt-], -lɪ, -lnɪs [-nəs]
charit|y, -ies 'tʃærət|ɪ [-ɪt|ɪ], -ɪz
charivari, -s ˌʃɑːrɪ'vɑːrɪ, -z
charivaria ˌʃɑːrɪ'vɑːrɪə

charlad|y, -ies 'tʃɑːˌleɪd|ɪ, -ɪz
charlatan, -s 'ʃɑːlətən [-tæn], -z
charlatan|ism/s, -ry 'ʃɑːlətən|ɪzəm/z
  [-tn̩|-], -rɪ
Charlecote 'tʃɑːlkəʊt
Charlemagne 'ʃɑːləmeɪn [ˌ--'-, -'maɪn]
  (ʃarləmaɲ)
Charlemont 'tʃɑːlmənt ['tʃɑːlm-]
Charles tʃɑːlz
Charleston 'tʃɑːlstən
Charlestown 'tʃɑːlztaʊn
Charlesworth 'tʃɑːlzwɜːθ [-wəθ]
Charl|ey, -ie 'tʃɑːl|ɪ, -ɪ
charlock 'tʃɑːlɒk
charlotte (C.), -s 'ʃɑːlət, -s
Charlottenburg ʃɑː'lɒtnbɜːg
Charlton 'tʃɑːltən
charm (s. v.), -s, -ing/ly, -ed, -er/s
  tʃɑːm, -z, -ɪŋ/lɪ, -d, -ə*/z
Charmian 'tʃɑːmjən ['ʃɑː-, -mɪən]
charnel 'tʃɑːnl
charnel-hou|se, -ses 'tʃɑːnlhaʊ|s, -zɪz
Charnock 'tʃɑːnɒk [-nək]
Charon 'keərən [-rɒn]
Charrington 'tʃærɪŋtən
chart, -s tʃɑːt, -s
chart|er (s. v.), -ers, -ering, -ered,
  -erer/s 'tʃɑːt|ə*, -əz, -ərɪŋ, -əd,
  -ərə*/z
Charterhouse 'tʃɑːtəhaʊs
Charteris 'tʃɑːtəz, 'tʃɑːtərɪs
charter-part|y, -ies 'tʃɑːtəˌpɑːt|ɪ, -ɪz
charti|sm, -st/s 'tʃɑːtɪ|zəm, -st/s
Chartreuse, -s ʃɑː'trɜːz (ʃartrø:z), -ɪz
char|woman, -women 'tʃɑːˌ|wʊmən,
  -ˌwɪmɪn
char|y, -ier, -iest, -ily, -iness 'tʃeər|ɪ,
  -ɪə*, -ɪɪst, -əlɪ [-ɪlɪ], -ɪnɪs [-ɪnəs]
Charybdis kə'rɪbdɪs
Chas. tʃɑːlz [rarely tʃæs]
chas|e (s. v.) (C.), -es, -ing, -ed, -er/s
  tʃeɪs, -ɪz, -ɪŋ, -t, -ə*/z
chasm, -s 'kæzəm, -z
chasmy 'kæzmɪ [-zəmɪ]
chassé, -s 'ʃæseɪ (ʃase), -z
chasseur, -s ʃæ'sɜː* (ʃasœ:r), -z
chassis (sing.) 'ʃæsɪ [-si:], (plur.) 'ʃæsɪz
  [-si:z]
chaste, -ly, -ness tʃeɪst, -lɪ, -nɪs [-nəs]
chast|en, -ens, -ening, -ened 'tʃeɪs|n,
  -nz, -nɪŋ [-nɪŋ], -nd
chastis|e, -es, -ing, -ed, -er/s tʃæ'staɪz,
  -ɪz, -ɪŋ, -d, -ə*/z
chastisement, -s 'tʃæstɪzmənt [tʃæ-
  'staɪzmənt], -s
chastity 'tʃæstətɪ [-ɪtɪ]
Chastney 'tʃæsnɪ
chasuble, -s 'tʃæzjʊbl, -z

chat (s. v.), -s, -ting, -ted tʃæt, -s, -ɪŋ,
  -ɪd
Chataway 'tʃætəweɪ
château, -x 'ʃætəʊ (ʃato), -z
chatelain(e), -s 'ʃætəleɪn [-tɪl-], -z
Chater 'tʃeɪtə*
Chatham 'tʃætəm
Chatsworth 'tʃætswɜːθ [-wəθ]
chattel, -s 'tʃætl, -z
chatter, -s, -ing, -ed, -er/s 'tʃætə*, -z,
  -rɪŋ, -d, -rə*/z
chatterbox, -es 'tʃætəbɒks, -ɪz
Chatteris 'tʃætərɪs
Chatterton 'tʃætətən
Chatto 'tʃætəʊ
chatt|y, -ier, -iest, -ily, -iness 'tʃæt|ɪ,
  -ɪə*, -ɪɪst, -ɪlɪ [-əlɪ], -ɪnɪs [-ɪnəs]
Chaucer 'tʃɔːsə*
Chaucerian tʃɔː'sɪərɪən
chaudron, -s 'tʃɔːdrən, -z
chauffer, -s 'tʃɔːfə*, -z
chauffeur, -s 'ʃəʊfə* [ʃəʊ'fɜː*], -z
Chauncey 'tʃɔːnsɪ
chauvini|sm, -st/s 'ʃəʊvɪnɪ|zəm [-vən-],
  -st/s
chauvinistic ˌʃəʊvɪ'nɪstɪk [-və'n-]
Chawner 'tʃɔːnə*
Chaworth 'tʃɑːwɜːθ [-wəθ]
Chaytor 'tʃeɪtə*
cheap, -er, -est, -ly, -ness tʃiːp, -ə*, -ɪst,
  -lɪ, -nɪs [-nəs]
cheap|en, -ens, -ening, -ened 'tʃiːp|ən,
  -ənz, -ṇɪŋ [-nɪŋ], -ənd
cheap-jack, -s 'tʃiːpdʒæk, -s
Cheapside ˌtʃiːp'saɪd ['tʃiːpsaɪd]
cheat (s. v.), -s, -ing, -ed tʃiːt, -s, -ɪŋ,
  -ɪd
Cheatham 'tʃiːtəm
check (s. v. interj.), -s, -ing, -ed tʃek, -s,
  -ɪŋ, -t
checkers 'tʃekəz
checkmat|e (s. v. interj.), -es, -ing, -ed
  'tʃekmeɪt [tʃek'm-], -s, -ɪŋ, -ɪd
check-rein, -s 'tʃekreɪn [ˌtʃek'r-], -z
check-weigher, -s 'tʃekˌweɪə*, -z
Cheddar 'tʃedə*
cheek (s. v.), -s, -ing, -ed tʃiːk, -s, -ɪŋ, -t
cheekbone, -s 'tʃiːkbəʊn, -z
Cheeke tʃiːk
cheek|y, -ier, -iest, -ily, -iness 'tʃiːk|ɪ,
  -ɪə* [-jə*], -ɪɪst [-jɪst], -ɪlɪ [-əlɪ], -ɪnɪs
  [-ɪnəs]
cheep, -s, -ing, -ed tʃiːp, -s, -ɪŋ, -t
cheer (s. v.), -s, -ing, -ed tʃɪə*, -z, -rɪŋ,
  -d
cheer|ful, -fully, -fulness 'tʃɪə|fʊl, -fʊlɪ
  [-fəlɪ], -fʊlnɪs [-nəs]
cheerio ˌtʃɪərɪ'əʊ

cheerless, -ly, -ness 'tʃɪəlɪs [-ləs], -lɪ, -nɪs [-nəs]
cheer|y, -ier, -iest, -ily, -iness 'tʃɪər|ɪ, -ɪə*, -ɪɪst, -əlɪ [-ɪlɪ], -ɪnɪs [-ɪnəs]
Cheeryble 'tʃɪərɪbl
cheese, -s tʃiːz, -ɪz
cheeseburger, -s 'tʃiːzˌbɜːgə*, -z
cheesecake, -s 'tʃiːzkeɪk, -s
Cheeseman 'tʃiːzmən
cheesemonger, -s 'tʃiːzˌmʌŋgə*, -z
cheese-paring 'tʃiːzˌpeərɪŋ
Cheesewright 'tʃezraɪt
chees|y, -iness 'tʃiːz|ɪ, -ɪnɪs [-ɪnəs]
cheetah, -s 'tʃiːtə, -z
Cheetham 'tʃiːtəm
chef, -s ʃef, -s
chef-d'œuvre, -s ˌʃeɪ'dɜːvrə [-və*] (ʃɛdœːvr), -z
cheiromancy 'kaɪərəʊmænsɪ
Cheke tʃiːk
chel|a (claw), -ae 'kiːl|ə, -iː
chela (disciple), -s 'tʃeɪlə ['tʃiːlə], -z
Chelmsford 'tʃelmsfəd [old-fashioned local pronunciation 'tʃem-, 'tʃɒm-]
Chelsea 'tʃelsɪ
Cheltenham 'tʃeltnəm [-tŋəm]
chemic, -al, -ally, -als 'kemɪk, -l, -əlɪ, -lz
chemise, -s ʃə'miːz [ʃɪ'm-], -ɪz
chemisette, -s ˌʃemiː'zet [-mɪ'z-], -s
chemist, -s, -ry 'kemɪst, -s, -rɪ [-məstrɪ]
Chemnitz 'kemnɪts
Chemosh 'kiːmɒʃ
Chenevix 'ʃenəvɪks [-nɪv-], 'tʃen-
Cheney 'tʃiːnɪ, 'tʃeɪnɪ
Chenies (in Buckinghamshire) 'tʃeɪnɪz (street in London) 'tʃiːnɪz
chenille ʃə'niːl
Cheops 'kiːɒps
Chepstow 'tʃepstəʊ
cheque, -s tʃek, -s
cheque-book, -s 'tʃekbʊk, -s
chequer (s. v.), -s, -ing, -ed 'tʃekə*, -z, -rɪŋ, -d
Chequers 'tʃekəz
Cherbourg 'ʃeəˌbʊəg ['ʃɜːb-, -bɜːg] (ʃɛrbuːr)
cherish, -es, -ing, -ed 'tʃerɪʃ, -ɪz, -ɪŋ, -t
Cherith 'kɪərɪθ ['ker-]
Cherokee ˌtʃerə'kiː ['---]
cheroot, -s ʃə'ruːt [ʃɪ'r-], -s
cherr|y, -ies 'tʃer|ɪ, -ɪz
cherry-brand|y, -ies ˌtʃerɪ'brænd|ɪ, -ɪz
cherry-pie, -s ˌtʃerɪ'paɪ, -z
cherry-stone, -s 'tʃerɪstəʊn, -z
Chersonese 'kɜːsənɪːs, -niːz
Chertsey 'tʃɜːtsɪ
cherub, -s 'tʃerəb, -z
cherubic tʃe'ruːbɪk [tʃɪ'r-, tʃə'r-]

cherubim 'tʃerəbɪm [-rʊb-]
Cherubini ˌkerʊ'biːnɪ: [-rə'b-, -nɪ]
chervil 'tʃɜːvɪl
Cherwell (river, Lord) 'tʃɑːwəl
Chesapeake 'tʃesəpiːk
Chesebro(ugh) 'tʃiːzbrə
Chesham 'tʃeʃəm [old-fashioned local pronunciation 'tʃesəm]
Cheshire 'tʃeʃə* [-ˌʃɪə*]
Cheshunt 'tʃesnt
Chesney 'tʃesnɪ, 'tʃeznɪ
chess tʃes
chessboard, -s 'tʃesbɔːd [-bɔəd], -z
chess|-man, -men 'tʃes|mæn, -men
chest, -s, -ed tʃest, -s, -ɪd
Chester 'tʃestə*
chesterfield (C.), -s 'tʃestəfiːld, -z
Chester-le-Street ˌtʃestəlɪ'striːt
Chesterton 'tʃestətən [-tn]
chest-note, -s 'tʃestnəʊt, -s
chestnut, -s 'tʃesnʌt [-stn-, -nət], -s
Chetham 'tʃetəm
Chet|wode, -wynd 'tʃet|wʊd, -wɪnd
cheval-glass, -es ʃə'vælglɑːs, -ɪz
chevalier, -s ˌʃevə'lɪə*, -z
Chevalier (surname) ʃə'vælieɪ [ʃɪ'v-]
Chevening (in Kent) 'tʃiːvnɪŋ
Chevenix 'ʃevnɪks [-vən-]
cheveril 'ʃevərɪl [-rəl]
Cheves tʃiːvz
Cheviot (hills, sheep) 'tʃevɪət [-vjət, also 'tʃɪv-, 'tʃiːv- mostly by people accustomed to Scottish pronunciation], (cloth) 'tʃevɪət [-vjət]
Chevis 'tʃevɪs
Chevrolet 'ʃevrəʊleɪ [ˌ--'-]
chevron, -s 'ʃevrən, -z
chev|y (s. v.) (C.), -ies, -ying, -ied 'tʃev|ɪ, -ɪz, -ɪɪŋ, -ɪd
chew, -s, -ing, -ed tʃuː, -z, -ɪŋ ['tʃʊɪŋ], -d
chewing-gum 'tʃuːɪŋgʌm ['tʃʊɪŋ-]
Cheyenne ʃaɪ'æn [-'en]
Cheylesmore 'tʃaɪlzmɔː* [-mɔə*], 'tʃɪl-, 'tʃeɪl-
Cheyne 'tʃeɪnɪ, tʃeɪn
Note.—In Cheyne Walk some say 'tʃeɪnɪ and others tʃeɪn.
Cheyney 'tʃeɪnɪ
chianti (C.) kɪ'æntɪ
chiaroscuro kɪˌɑːrə'skʊərəʊ [-rɒ's-, -'skjʊə-]
chic ʃiːk [ʃɪk]
Chicago ʃɪ'kɑːgəʊ [tʃɪ-, also -'kɔːgəʊ in imitation of one American pronunciation]
chican|e (s. v.), -es, -ing, -ed, -er/s ʃɪ'keɪn [tʃɪ-], -z, -ɪŋ, -d, -ə*/z
chicaner|y, -ies ʃɪ'keɪnər|ɪ, -ɪz

Chichele 'tʃɪtʃɪlɪ
Chichester 'tʃɪtʃɪstə*
chi-chi 'ʃiːʃi
chick (C.), -s tʃɪk, -s
chickabidd|y, -ies 'tʃɪkə͵bɪd|ɪ, -ɪz
chicken, -s 'tʃɪkɪn, -z
chicken-feed 'tʃɪkɪnfiːd
chicken-hearted 'tʃɪkɪn͵hɑːtɪd [͵--'--]
chicken-pox 'tʃɪkɪnpɒks
chickweed 'tʃɪkwiːd
chicory 'tʃɪkərɪ
Chiddingly (in East Sussex) ͵tʃɪdɪŋ'laɪ
['---]
chid|e, -es, -ing, chid tʃaɪd, -z, -ɪŋ, tʃɪd
chief (s. adj.), -s, -ly tʃiːf, -s, -lɪ
chieftain, -s 'tʃiːftən [-tɪn], -z
chieftanc|y, -ies 'tʃiːftəns|ɪ [-tɪn-], -ɪz
Chiene ʃiːn
chiff-chaff, -s 'tʃɪf-tʃæf, -s
chiffon, -s 'ʃɪfɒn [-'-], -z
chiffonier, -s ͵ʃɪfə'nɪə*, -z
chignon, -s 'ʃiːnjɒn [-njɒŋ, -njɔ̃ːŋ, old
fashioned ʃɪ'nɒn], -z
chihuahua (dog), -s tʃɪ'wɑːwə [-wɑː], -z
chilblain, -s 'tʃɪlblem, -z
child (C.), -ren tʃaɪld, 'tʃɪldrən ['tʃʊldr-,
'tʃldr-]
child|bed, -birth 'tʃaɪld|bed, -bɜːθ
Childe tʃaɪld
Childermas 'tʃɪldəmæs [-məs]
Childers 'tʃɪldəz
childhood 'tʃaɪldhʊd
childish, -ly, -ness 'tʃaɪldɪʃ, -lɪ, -nɪs
[-nəs]
child|less, -like 'tʃaɪld|lɪs [-ləs], -laɪk
Chile [-ili] 'tʃɪlɪ
Chilean, -s 'tʃɪlɪən [-ljən], -z
chiliad, -s 'kɪlɪæd ['kaɪl-, -ljæd], -z
chilia|sm, -st/s 'kɪlɪæ|zəm, -st/s
chill (s. adj. v.), -s, -ing, -ed, -ness tʃɪl,
-z, -ɪŋ, -d, -nɪs [-nəs]
chilli, -s 'tʃɪlɪ, -z
Chillingham (in Northumberland)
'tʃɪlɪŋəm
Chillingworth 'tʃɪlɪŋwɜːθ [-wəθ]
Chillon 'ʃiːlɔ̃ːŋ ['ʃiːjɔ̃ːŋ, -ɔːŋ, old-
fashioned 'ʃɪlən, 'ʃɪlɒn, ʃɪ'lɒn] (ʃijɔ̃)
Note.—In reading Byron's 'Castle of
Chillon' it is usual to pronounce
'ʃɪlən or 'ʃɪlɒn.
chill|y, -ier, -iest, -iness 'tʃɪl|ɪ, -ɪə*,
-ɪɪst, -ɪnɪs [-ɪnəs]
Chiltern 'tʃɪltən
Chilton 'tʃɪltən
Chimborazo ͵tʃɪmbə'rɑːzəʊ [-bɒ'r-]
chim|e (s. v.), -es, -ing, -ed, -er/s tʃaɪm,
-z, -ɪŋ, -d, -ə*/z
chimera, -s kaɪ'mɪərə [kɪ'm-], -z

chimere, -s tʃɪ'mɪə* [ʃɪ-], -z
chimeric, -al, -ally kaɪ'merɪk [kɪ'm-],
-l, -əlɪ
chimney, -s 'tʃɪmnɪ, -z
chimney-corner, -s 'tʃɪmnɪ͵kɔːnə*, -z
chimney-piece, -s 'tʃɪmnɪpiːs, -ɪz
chimney-pot, -s 'tʃɪmnɪpɒt, -s
chimney-stack, -s 'tʃɪmnɪstæk, -s
chimney-sweep, -s 'tʃɪmnɪswiːp, -s
chimney-sweeper, -s 'tʃɪmnɪ͵swiːpə*, -z
chimpanzee, -s ͵tʃɪmpən'ziː [-pæn-], -z
chin, -s tʃɪn, -z
china (C.), 'tʃaɪnə
china-clay ͵tʃaɪnə'kleɪ
China|man, -men 'tʃaɪnə|mən, -mən
chinchilla, -s tʃɪn'tʃɪlə, -z
Chindau tʃɪn'daʊ ['--]
chin-deep ͵tʃɪn'diːp
Chindit 'tʃɪndɪt
chin|e (s.v.), -es, -ing, -ed tʃaɪn, -z, -ɪŋ, -d
Chinee, -s tʃaɪ'niː, -z
Chinese ͵tʃaɪ'niːz [also '-- according to
sentence-stress]
Chingford 'tʃɪŋfəd
chink, -s tʃɪŋk, -s
Chinnereth 'tʃɪnəreθ
Chinnock 'tʃɪnək
Chinnor 'tʃɪnə*
Chinook tʃɪ'nʊk [-'nuːk]
chintz, -es, -y tʃɪnts, -ɪz, -ɪ
Chios 'kaɪɒs
chip (s. v.), -s, -ping, -ped tʃɪp, -s, -ɪŋ, -t
chipboard 'tʃɪpbɔːd [-bɔəd]
chipmunk, -s 'tʃɪpmʌŋk, -s
chipolata, -s ͵tʃɪpə'lɑːtə, -z
Chipp, -endale, -enham tʃɪp, -əndeɪl,
-nəm [-ənəm]
Chippewa, -s 'tʃɪpɪwɑː [-wə], -z
Chipping 'tʃɪpɪŋ
chipp|y, -ier, -iest, -iness 'tʃɪp|ɪ, -ɪə*,
-ɪɪst, -ɪnɪs [-ɪnəs]
chirograph, -s 'kaɪərəʊgrɑːf ['kaɪr-,
-græf], -s
chirographer, -s ͵kaɪə'rɒgrəfə* [kaɪ'r-],
-z
chirographic ͵kaɪərəʊ'græfɪk [͵kaɪr-]
chirograph|ist/s, -y ͵kaɪə'rɒgrəf|ɪst/s
[kaɪ'r-], -ɪ
Chirol 'tʃɪrəl
chiromancer, -s 'kaɪərəʊmænsə*, -z
chiromancy 'kaɪərəʊmænsɪ ['kaɪr-]
Chiron (centaur) 'kaɪərən ['kaɪr-]
chiropod|ist/s, -y kɪ'rɒpəd|ɪst/s [ʃɪ'r-,
tʃɪ'r-, old-fashioned ͵kaɪə'r-], -ɪ
chirp (s. v.), -s, -ing, -ed; -y, -ier, -iest,
-ily, -iness tʃɜːp, -s, -ɪŋ, -t; -ɪ, -ɪə*
[-jə*], -ɪɪst [-jɪst], -ɪlɪ [-əlɪ], -ɪnɪs
[-ɪnəs]

Chirrol 'tʃɪrəl
chirrup (s. v.), -s, -ing, -ed 'tʃɪrəp, -s, -ɪŋ, -t
chis|el (s. v.), -els, -elling, -elled 'tʃɪz|l, -lz, -lɪŋ [-lɪŋ], -ld
Chisholm 'tʃɪzəm
Chislehurst 'tʃɪzlhɜ:st
Chiswick 'tʃɪzɪk
chit, -s tʃɪt, -s
chit-chat 'tʃɪttʃæt
chitin 'kaɪtɪn
Chittenden 'tʃɪtndən
Chitty 'tʃɪtɪ
chivalric 'ʃɪvlrɪk [old-fashioned 'tʃɪv-]
chivalrous, -ly, -ness 'ʃɪvlrəs [old-fashioned 'tʃɪv-], -lɪ, -nɪs [-nəs]
chivalry 'ʃɪvlrɪ [old-fashioned 'tʃɪv-]
chive, -s tʃaɪv, -z
Chivers 'tʃɪvəz
chiv|y (s. v.), -ies, -ying, -ied 'tʃɪv|ɪ, -ɪz, -ɪɪŋ, -ɪd
Chladni 'klædnɪ
chlamy|s, -des 'klæmɪ|s ['kleɪm-], -di:z
Chloe 'kləʊɪ
chloral 'klɔ:rəl
chlorate, -s 'klɔ:reɪt [-rɪt], -s
chloric 'klɔ:rɪk ['klɒr-]
chloride, -s 'klɔ:raɪd, -z
chlorinat|e, -es, -ing, -ed 'klɔ:rɪneɪt ['klɒr-], -s, -ɪŋ, -ɪd
chlorine 'klɔ:ri:n
Chloris 'klɔ:rɪs ['klɒr-]
chlorite, -s 'klɔ:raɪt, -s
chlorodyne 'klɒrədaɪn ['klɔ:r-]
chloroform (s. v.), -s, -ing, -ed 'klɒrəfɔ:m ['klɔ:r-], -z, -ɪŋ, -d
chloromycetin ˌklɔ:rəʊmaɪ'si:tɪn [ˌklɒr-]
chlorophyll 'klɒrəfɪl ['klɔ:r-]
chlorous 'klɔ:rəs
Choate tʃəʊt
chock, -s; -full tʃɒk, -s; -'fʊl
chock-a-block ˌtʃɒkə'blɒk
choke-damp 'tʃəʊkdæmp
chok|y, -ier, -iest, -iness 'tʃəʊk|ɪ, -ɪə*, [-jə*], -ɪɪst [-jɪst], -ɪnɪs [-ɪnəs]
Cholderton (near Salisbury) 'tʃəʊldətən [-tn]
choler 'kɒlə*

cholera 'kɒlərə
choleraic ˌkɒlə'reɪɪk
choleric 'kɒlərɪk [kɒ'lerɪk]
cholesterol kə'lestərɒl [kɒ-, -tɪər-, -rəl]
choliamb, -s 'kəʊlɪæmb, -z
choliambic ˌkəʊlɪ'æmbɪk
Cholmeley 'tʃʌmlɪ
Cholmondeley 'tʃʌmlɪ
Cholsey 'tʃəʊlzɪ
Cholmley 'tʃʌmlɪ
Chomolhari ˌtʃɒmɒl'hʌrɪ [ˌtʃəʊməl-'ha:rɪ]
Chomolungma ˌtʃəʊməʊ'lʊŋma:
choos|e, -es, -ing, chose, chosen, chooser/s tʃu:z, -ɪz, -ɪŋ, tʃəʊz, 'tʃəʊzn, 'tʃu:zə*/z
choos|y, -ier, -iest, -iness 'tʃu:z|ɪ, -ɪə* [-jə*], -ɪɪst [-jɪst], -ɪnɪs [-ɪnəs]
chop (s. v.), -s, -ping, -ped tʃɒp, -s, -ɪŋ, -t
chop-hou|se, -ses 'tʃɒphaʊ|s, -zɪz
Chopin 'ʃɒpæ:ŋ ['ʃəʊp-, -pæŋ] (ʃɔpɛ̃)
chopper, -s 'tʃɒpə*, -z
chopp|y, -ier, -iest, -ily, -iness 'tʃɒp|ɪ, -ɪə*, -ɪɪst, -ɪlɪ [-əlɪ], -ɪnɪs [-ɪnəs]
chop-stick, -s 'tʃɒpstɪk, -s
chop-suey ˌtʃɒp'su:ɪ [-'sju:ɪ, -'sʊɪ]
chor|al, -ally 'kɔ:r|əl ['kɒr-], -əlɪ
chorale, -s kɒ'ra:l [kə'r-, kɔ:'r-, -'ra:lɪ], -z
Chorazin kɒ'reɪzɪn [kə'r-]
chord, -s kɔ:d, -z
chordate 'kɔ:deɪt
chore, -s tʃɔ:* [tʃɔə*], -z
chorea kɒ'rɪə [kɔ:'r-]
choreg|us, -i kɒ'ri:g|əs [kɔ:'r-, kə'r-], -aɪ
choreographer, -s ˌkɒrɪ'ɒgrəfə* [ˌkɔ:r-], -z
choreographic ˌkɒrɪə'græfɪk [ˌkɔ:r-, -rɪəʊ'g-]
choreography ˌkɒrɪ'ɒgrəfɪ [ˌkɔ:r-]
choriamb, -s 'kɒrɪæmb ['kɔ:r-], -z
choriambic ˌkɒrɪ'æmbɪk [ˌkɔ:r-]
choric 'kɒrɪk
chorister, -s 'kɒrɪstə*, -z
Chorley 'tʃɔ:lɪ
chort|le, -les, -ling, -led 'tʃɔ:t|l, -lz, -lɪŋ [-lɪŋ], -ld
chorus (s. v.), -es, -ing, -ed 'kɔ:rəs, -ɪz, -ɪŋ, -t
chose (legal term), ʃəʊz
chose (from choose), -n tʃəʊz, -n
Chosen ˌtʃəʊ'sen
Chou-en-Lai ˌtʃəʊen'laɪ
chough, -s tʃʌf, -s
choux (pastry) ʃu:
chow, -s tʃaʊ, -z
chow-chow, -s ˌtʃaʊ'tʃaʊ ['--], -z
chowder, -s 'tʃaʊdə*, -z

Chowles tʃəʊlz
chrestomath|y, -ies kre'stɒməθ|ɪ, -ɪz
chrism 'krɪzəm
chrisom, -s 'krɪzəm, -z
Christ, -s kraɪst, -s
Christabel (Chrys-) 'krɪstəbel [-bəl]
Christchurch 'kraɪstʃɜːtʃ
Christ-cross-row, -s ˌkrɪskrɒs'rəʊ
[old-fashioned -krɔːs-], -z
Christdom 'kraɪstdəm
christ|en, -ens, -ening, -ened 'krɪs|n,
-nz, -n̩ɪŋ [-nɪŋ], -nd
Christendom 'krɪsndəm
christening, -s 'krɪsn̩ɪŋ [-nɪŋ], -z
Christi (in Corpus Christi) 'krɪstɪ
Christian, -s 'krɪstʃən [-tɪən, -tjən], -z
Christiana ˌkrɪstɪ'ɑːnə
Christiania ˌkrɪstɪ'ɑːnjə [-nɪə]
Christianism 'krɪstjənɪzəm [-trən-,
-tʃən-, -tʃn̩-]
Christianity ˌkrɪstɪ'ænətɪ [krɪ'stjæn-,
-ɪtɪ]
christianiz|e [-is|e], -es, -ing, -ed
'krɪstjənaɪz [-tɪən-, -tʃən-, -tʃn̩-], -ɪz,
-ɪŋ, -d
christianly 'krɪstʃənlɪ [-tɪən-, -tjən-]
Christian name, -s 'krɪstʃən neɪm
[-tjən], -z
Christie 'krɪstɪ
Christina krɪ'stiːnə
Christine 'krɪstiːn, krɪ'stiːn
Christlike 'kraɪstlaɪk
Christliness 'kraɪstlɪnɪs [-nəs]
Christmas, -es 'krɪsməs [-stm-], -ɪz
Christmas-box, -es 'krɪsməsbɒks
[-stm-], -ɪz
Christmas-card, -s 'krɪsməskɑːd
[-stm-], -z
Christmas-tree, -s 'krɪsməstriː [-stm-], -z
Christminster 'krɪstmɪnstə*
Christopher 'krɪstəfə*
Christopherson krɪ'stɒfəsn
Christy 'krɪstɪ
chromate, -s 'krəʊmeɪt [-mɪt], -s
chromatic, -ally krəʊ'mætɪk, -əlɪ
chrome krəʊm
chrom|ic, -ous 'krəʊm|ɪk, -əs
chromite, -s 'krəʊmaɪt, -s
chromium 'krəʊmɪəm [-mjəm]
chromium-plated ˌkrəʊmjəm'pleɪtɪd
[-mɪəm-, '--,--]
chromium-plating ˌkrəʊmjəm'pleɪtɪŋ
[-mɪəm-, '--,--]
chromolithograph, -s ˌkrəʊməʊ'lɪθəʊ-
grɑːf [-græf], -s
chromolithography ˌkrəʊməʊlɪ'θɒgrəfɪ
chromosome, -s 'krəʊməsəʊm, -z
chromosphere, -s 'krəʊməˌsfɪə*, -z

chromotype 'krəʊməʊtaɪp
chroneme, -s 'krəʊniːm, -z
chronemic krəʊ'niːmɪk
chronic, -al, -ally 'krɒnɪk, -l, -əlɪ
chronic|le (s. v.), -les, -ling, -led, -ler/s
'krɒnɪk|l, -lz, -lɪŋ, -ld, -lə*/z
chronogram, -s 'krɒnəʊgræm, -z
chronograph, -s 'krɒnəʊgrɑːf [-græf], -s
chronologic, -al, -ally ˌkrɒnə'lɒdʒɪk,
-l, -əlɪ
chronolog|ist/s, -y, -ies krə'nɒlədʒ|-
ɪst/s [krɒ'n-], -ɪ, -ɪz
chronomet|er/s, -ry krə'nɒmɪt|ə*/z
[-mət|ə*], -rɪ
chronometric, -al, -ally ˌkrɒnəʊ'metrɪk
-l, -əlɪ
chrysalis, -es, chrysalides 'krɪsəlɪs [-sɪl-,
-s|-], -ɪz, krɪ'sælɪdiːz
chrysanthemum, -s krɪ'sænθəməm
[-ɪ'zæ-, -θm-], -z
chryselephantine ˌkrɪselɪ'fæntaɪn
Chrysler, -s 'kraɪzlə*, -z
chrysolite, -s 'krɪsəʊlaɪt, -s
chrysoprase, -s 'krɪsəʊpreɪz, -ɪz
chrysoprasus, -es krɪ'sɒprəsəs, -ɪz
Chrysostom 'krɪsəstəm
chub, -s tʃʌb, -z
Chubb tʃʌb
chubb|y, -ier, -iest, -ily, -iness 'tʃʌb|ɪ,
-ɪə*, -ɪɪst, -ɪlɪ [-əlɪ], -ɪnɪs [-məs]
chuck (s. v.), -s, -ing, -ed tʃʌk, -s, -ɪŋ, -t
chucker-out, chuckers-out ˌtʃʌkər'aʊt
[-ə'aʊt], ˌtʃʌkəz'aʊt
chuck|le (s. v.), -les, -ling, -led 'tʃʌk|l,
-lz, -lɪŋ [-lɪŋ], -ld
Chudleigh 'tʃʌdlɪ
chuff, -s, -ed tʃʌf, -s, -t
Chuffey 'tʃʌfɪ
chug, -s, -ging, -ged tʃʌg, -z, -ɪŋ, -d
chukker, -s 'tʃʌkə*, -z
chum (s. v.), -s, -ming, -med tʃʌm, -z,
-ɪŋ, -d
Chumalhari ˌtʃʊməl'hʌrɪ [-'hɑːrɪ]
Chumbi 'tʃʊmbɪ
chumm|y, -ier, -iest, -ily, -iness 'tʃʌm|ɪ,
-ɪə*, -ɪɪst, -ɪlɪ [-əlɪ], -ɪnɪs [-məs]
chump, -s tʃʌmp, -s
Chungking ˌtʃʊŋ'kɪŋ [ˌtʃʌŋ-]
chunk, -s, -y tʃʌŋk, -s, -ɪ
Chunnel 'tʃʌnl
church, -es tʃɜːtʃ, -ɪz
Churchdown (near Gloucester) 'tʃɜːtʃ-
daʊn
Note.—There was until recently a
local pronunciation 'tʃəʊzn, which
is preserved as the name of a hill
near by, which is now written
Chosen.

87

church-goer, -s 'tʃɜːtʃˌgəʊə*, -z
Churchill 'tʃɜːtʃɪl
church|man (C.), -men 'tʃɜːtʃ|mən,
-mən
church-rate, -s 'tʃɜːtʃreɪt, -s
churchwarden, -s ˌtʃɜːtʃ'wɔːdn, -z
church|y, -ier, -iest, -ily, -iness 'tʃɜːtʃ|ɪ,
-ɪə*, -ɪɪst, -ɪlɪ [-əlɪ], -ɪnɪs [-məs]
churchyard, -s 'tʃɜːtʃjɑːd [ˌ-'-], -z
Churchyard (surname) 'tʃɜːtʃəd
churl, -s tʃɜːl, -z
churlish, -ly, -ness 'tʃɜːlɪʃ, -lɪ, -nɪs
[-nəs]
churn (s. v.), -s, -ing, -ed tʃɜːn, -z, -ɪŋ, -d
Churton 'tʃɜːtn
chute, -s ʃuːt, -s
Chute tʃuːt
Chuter 'tʃuːtə*
chutney [-nee], -s 'tʃʌtnɪ, -z
Chuzzlewit 'tʃʌzlwɪt
chyle kaɪl
chyme kaɪm
Cibber 'sɪbə*
cibori|um/s, -a sɪ'bɔːrɪ|əm/z, -ə
cicada, -s sɪ'kɑːdə [-'keɪd-], -z
cicala, -s sɪ'kɑːlə, -z
cicatrice, -s 'sɪkətrɪs, -ɪz
cicatrices (Latin plur. of cicatrix)
ˌsɪkə'traɪsiːz
cicatrix 'sɪkətrɪks
cicatriz|e [-is|e], -es, -ing, -ed 'sɪkətraɪz,
-ɪz, -ɪŋ, -d
Cicely 'sɪsɪlɪ [-əlɪ]
Cicero 'sɪsərəʊ
cicerone, -s ˌtʃɪtʃə'rəʊnɪ [ˌsɪsə'r-], -z
Ciceronian ˌsɪsə'rəʊnjən [-nɪən]
cicisbe|o, -i ˌtʃɪtʃɪz'beɪ|əʊ, -iː
C.I.D. ˌsiːaɪ'diː
cider, -s 'saɪdə*, -z
cider-cup, -s 'saɪdəkʌp [ˌsaɪdə'k-], -s
cigar, -s sɪ'gɑː*, -z
cigarette, -s ˌsɪgə'ret, -s
cigarette-holder, -s ˌsɪgə'retˌhəʊldə*, -z
cigar-shaped sɪ'gɑːʃeɪpt
cilia 'sɪlɪə [-ljə]
ciliary 'sɪlɪərɪ [-ljə-]
cilice, -s 'sɪlɪs, -ɪz
Cilicia saɪ'lɪʃɪə [sɪ'l-, -ʃjə, -sɪə, -sjə]
Cilla 'sɪlə
Cimabue ˌtʃɪməˈbuːɪ [ˌtʃiːm-, -'buːeɪ,
-'buɪ, -'bueɪ]
Cimmer|ian, -ii sɪ'mɪər|ɪən, -ɪaɪ
cinch, -es sɪntʃ, -ɪz
cinchona, -s sɪŋ'kəʊnə, -z
cinchonic sɪŋ'kɒnɪk
Cincinnati ˌsɪnsɪ'nætɪ [-'nɑːtɪ]
cincture, -s 'sɪŋktʃə* [-ˌtʃʊə*], -z
cinder, -s 'sɪndə*, -z

Cinderella ˌsɪndə'relə
cinder-pa|th, -ths 'sɪndəpɑː|θ, -ðz
cinder-sifter, -s 'sɪndəˌsɪftə*, -z
cinder-track, -s 'sɪndətræk, -s
cinecamera, -s 'sɪnɪˌkæmərə [ˌ-'---], -z
cinefilm, -s 'sɪnɪfɪlm, -z
cinema, -s 'sɪnəmə [-nɪ-, -mɑː], -z
cinemascope, -s 'sɪnəməskəʊp [-nɪm-],
-s
cinematic ˌsɪnɪ'mætɪk [ˌsɪnə-]
cinematograph, -s ˌsɪnə'mætəgrɑːf
[-nɪ'm-, -græf], -s
cinematographic ˌsɪnəmætə'græfɪk
[-nɪˌm-]
cinematography ˌsɪnəmə'tɒgrəfɪ [-nɪ-]
cinema verité ˌsɪnəməˈverɪteɪ
cine-projector, -s 'sɪnɪprəˌdʒektə*, -z
cinerama ˌsɪnə'rɑːmə [-nɪ-]
cineraria, -s ˌsɪnə'reərɪə, -z
cinerarium, -s ˌsɪnə'reərɪəm, -z
cinerary 'sɪnərərɪ
cineration ˌsɪnə'reɪʃn
Cingalese ˌsɪŋgə'liːz
cinnabar 'sɪnəbɑː*
cinnamon 'sɪnəmən
cinque (C.) sɪŋk
cinquefoil 'sɪŋkfɔɪl
Cinque Ports 'sɪŋkpɔːts
cinzano tʃɪn'zɑːnəʊ [sɪn'z-]
ciph|er (s. v.), -ers, -ering, -ered 'saɪf|ə*,
-əz, -ərɪŋ, -əd
cipher-key, -s 'saɪfəkiː, -z
Cipriani ˌsɪprɪ'ɑːnɪ
circa 'sɜːkə
circadian sɜː'keɪdɪən [sə'k-, -djən]
Circassia, -n/s sɜː'kæsɪə [-sjə, -ʃɪə, -ʃjə],
-n/z
Circe 'sɜːsɪ
circ|le (s. v.), -les, -ling, -led 'sɜːk|l, -lz,
-lɪŋ [-lɪŋ], -ld
circlet, -s 'sɜːklɪt [-lət], -s
circuit, -s, -ry 'sɜːkɪt, -s, -rɪ
circuitous, -ly, -ness sə'kjuːɪtəs [sɜː-,
-'kjʊɪ-], -lɪ, -nɪs [-nəs]
circular (s. adj.), -s 'sɜːkjʊlə* [-kjəl-], -z
circularity ˌsɜːkjʊ'lærətɪ [-kjə'l-, -ɪtɪ]
circulariz|e [-is|e], -es, -ing, -ed
'sɜːkjʊləraɪz [-kjəl-], -ɪz, -ɪŋ, -d
circulat|e, -es, -ing, -ed, -or/s 'sɜːkjʊ-
leɪt [-kjəl-], -s, -ɪŋ, -ɪd, -ə*/z
circulation, -s ˌsɜːkjʊ'leɪʃn [-kjə'l-], -z
circulatory ˌsɜːkjʊ'leɪtərɪ ['sɜːkjʊlətərɪ]
circumambient ˌsɜːkəm'æmbɪənt
[-bjənt]
circumambulat|e, -es, -ing, -ed ˌsɜːk-
əm'æmbjʊleɪt, -s, -ɪŋ, -ɪd
circumcis|e, -es, -ing, -ed 'sɜːkəmsaɪz,
-ɪz, -ɪŋ, -d

88

circumcision, -s ˌsɜːkəmˈsɪʒn, -z
circumference, -s səˈkʌmfərəns, -ɪz
circumferential səˌkʌmfəˈrenʃl
circumflex, -es ˈsɜːkəmfleks, -ɪz
circumlocution, -s ˌsɜːkəmləˈkjuːʃn, -z
circumlocutory ˌsɜːkəmˈlɒkjʊtəri
[-ləˈkjuːtəri]
circumnavigat|e, -es, -ing, -ed, -or/s
ˌsɜːkəmˈnævɪgeɪt, -s, -ɪŋ, -ɪd, -ə*/z
circumnavigation, -s ˈsɜːkəmˌnævɪ-
ˈgeɪʃn, -z
circumpolar ˌsɜːkəmˈpəʊlə*
circumscrib|e, -es, -ing, -ed ˈsɜːkəm-
skraɪb [ˌsɜːkəmˈskraɪb], -z, -ɪŋ, -d
circumscription, -s ˌsɜːkəmˈskrɪpʃn, -z
circumspect, -ly, -ness ˈsɜːkəmspekt,
-lɪ, -nɪs [-nəs]
circumspection ˌsɜːkəmˈspekʃn
circumstance, -s, -d ˈsɜːkəmstəns
[-stæns, -stɑːns], -ɪz, -t
circumstanti|al, -ally ˌsɜːkəmˈstænʃ|l,
-əlɪ
circumstantiality ˈsɜːkəmˌstænʃɪˈælətɪ
[-ɪtɪ]
circumstantiat|e, -es, -ing, -ed ˌsɜːkəm-
ˈstænʃɪeɪt [-ʃjeɪt], -s, -ɪŋ, -ɪd
circumvallation, -s ˌsɜːkəmvəˈleɪʃn
[-ˈvæ'l-], -z
circumvent, -s, -ing, -ed ˌsɜːkəmˈvent,
-s, -ɪŋ, -ɪd
circumvention, -s ˌsɜːkəmˈvenʃn, -z
circus, -es ˈsɜːkəs, -ɪz
Cirencester ˈsaɪərənsestə* [ˈsɪsɪtə*,
ˈsɪsɪstə*]
Note.—The pronunciation most
usually heard in the town is
ˈsaɪərənsestə* (or -stər with the
dialectal retroflex r). An older
pronunciation ˈsɪzɪtər may still be
heard in the country around.
Ciriax ˈsɪrɪæks
cirque, -s sɜːk [sɪək], -s
cirrhosis sɪˈrəʊsɪs
cirro-cumulus ˌsɪrəʊˈkjuːmjʊləs [-mjəl-]
cirro-stratus ˌsɪrəʊˈstrɑːtəs [-ˈstreɪt-]
cirrous ˈsɪrəs
cirrus ˈsɪrəs
Cisalpine sɪsˈælpaɪn
Cissie ˈsɪsɪ
cissoid, -s ˈsɪsɔɪd, -z
Cissy ˈsɪsɪ
cist, -s sɪst, -s
Cistercian, -s sɪˈstɜːʃn [-ʃɪən, -ʃjən], -z
cistern, -s ˈsɪstən, -z
cistus, -es ˈsɪstəs, -ɪz
citadel, -s ˈsɪtədəl [-tɪd-, -del], -z
citation, -s saɪˈteɪʃn [sɪˈt-], -z
citatory ˈsaɪtətəri [ˈsɪt-, saɪˈteɪtəri]

cit|e, -es, -ing, -ed saɪt, -s, -ɪŋ, -ɪd
cithar|a, -ae ˈsɪθər|ə, -iː
cither, -s ˈsɪθə*, -z
cithern, -s ˈsɪθən [-θɜːn, ˈsɪðən], -z
citizen, -s; -ry; -ship ˈsɪtɪzn, -z; -rɪ; -ʃɪp
citole, -s sɪˈtəʊl, -z
citrate, -s ˈsɪtreɪt [ˈsaɪt-, -trɪt], -s
citrated ˈsɪtreɪtɪd [ˈsaɪt-]
citric ˈsɪtrɪk
Citrine sɪˈtriːn
Citroën, -s ˈsɪtrəʊən [sɪˈt-, -əʊm, -əʊen,
ˈsɪtrən] (sitrɔen), -z
citron, -s ˈsɪtrən, -z
citr|ous, -us ˈsɪtr|əs, -əs
cittern, -s ˈsɪtɜːn [-tən], -z
cit|y, -ies ˈsɪt|ɪ, -ɪz
civet, -s ˈsɪvɪt, -s
civic, -s ˈsɪvɪk, -s
civ|il, -illy ˈsɪv|l [ˈsɪv|ɪl], -əlɪ [-ɪlɪ]
civilian, -s sɪˈvɪljən [-lɪən], -z
civilit|y, -ies sɪˈvɪlət|ɪ [-ɪt|ɪ], -ɪz
civilizable [-isa-] ˈsɪvɪlaɪzəbl
civilization [-isa-], -s ˌsɪvɪlaɪˈzeɪʃn
[-vəlaɪˈz-, -vlaɪˈz-, -vɪlɪˈz-, -vlɪˈz-], -z
civiliz|e [-is|e], -es, -ing, -ed ˈsɪvɪlaɪz
[-vəl-, -vl-], -ɪz, -ɪŋ, -d
civv|y, -ies ˈsɪv|ɪ, -ɪz
clack (s. v.), -s, -ing, -ed klæk, -s, -ɪŋ, -t
Clackmannan klækˈmænən
clack-valve, -s ˈklækvælv, -z
Clacton ˈklæktən
clad (from clothe) klæd
claim (s. v.), -s, -ing, -ed kleɪm, -z, -ɪŋ,
-d
claimant, -s ˈkleɪmənt, -s
claimer, -s ˈkleɪmə*, -z
clairaudien|ce, -t kleərˈɔːdjən|s [-dɪə-],
-t
clairvoyan|ce, -cy, -t/s, -te/s kleə-
ˈvɔɪən|s, -sɪ, -t/s, -t/s
clam, -s klæm, -z
clamant ˈkleɪmənt
clamb|er, -ers, -ering, -ered ˈklæmb|ə*,
-əz, -ərɪŋ, -əd
clamm|y, -ier, -iest, -ily, -iness ˈklæm|ɪ,
-ɪə*, -ɪɪst, -ɪlɪ [-əlɪ], -ɪnɪs [-ɪnəs]
clamorous, -ly, -ness ˈklæmərəs, -lɪ,
-nɪs [-nəs]
clamour (s. v.), -s, -ing, -ed ˈklæmə*, -z,
-rɪŋ, -d
clamp (s. v.), -s, -ing, -ed klæmp, -s, -ɪŋ,
-t [klæmt]
clan, -s klæn, -z
clandestine, -ly klænˈdestɪn [-taɪn,
ˈ---], -lɪ
clang (s. v.), -s, -ing, -ed klæŋ, -z, -ɪŋ, -d
clanger, -s ˈklæŋə*, -z
clangorous, -ly ˈklæŋgərəs [-ŋə-], -lɪ

clangour 'klæŋə* [-ŋgə*]
clank (s. v.), **-s, -ing, -ed** klæŋk, -s, -ɪŋ, -t [klæŋt]
Clanmaurice klæn'mɒrɪs
Clanmorris klæn'mɒrɪs
clannish, -ly, -ness 'klænɪʃ, -lɪ, -nɪs [-nəs]
Clanricarde klæn'rɪkəd ['klæn‚rɪkəd]
  *Note.—The second pronunciation
  may often be heard from residents in
  the neighbourhood of Clanricarde
  Gardens, London.*
clanship 'klænʃɪp
clans|man, -men 'klænz|mən, -mən
clap (s. v.), **-s, -ping, -ped** klæp, -s, -ɪŋ, -t
clapboard, -s 'klæpbɔːd [-bəd], -z
Clapham 'klæpəm [-pm]
clapper, -s 'klæpə*, -z
Clapton 'klæptən
clap-trap 'klæptræp
claque, -s klæk, -s
Clara 'kleərə
clarabella (C.), -s ‚klærə'belə, -z
Clare kleə*
Claremont 'kleəmɒnt [-mənt]
Clarence 'klærəns
Clarenc(i)eux 'klærənsuː [-sjuː]
clarendon (C.) 'klærəndən
claret, -s 'klærət [-ɪt], -s
claret-cup 'klærətkʌp [‚klærət'k-, -rɪt-]
Clarges (street) 'klɑːdʒɪz
Claridge, -'s 'klærɪdʒ, -ɪz
clarification ‚klærɪfɪ'keɪʃn
clari|fy, -fies, -fying, -fied, -fier/s 'klærɪ|faɪ, -faɪz, -faɪɪŋ, -faɪd, -faɪə*/z
Clarina klə'raɪnə
clarinet, -s ‚klærə'net [-rɪ-], -s
clarinettist, -s ‚klærə'netɪst [-rɪ-], -s
clarion, -s 'klærɪən, -z
Clarissa klə'rɪsə
clarity 'klærətɪ [-ɪtɪ]
Clark(e) klɑːk
clarkia, -s 'klɑːkjə [-kɪə], -z
Clarkson 'klɑːksn
clash (s. v.), **-es, -ing, -ed** klæʃ, -ɪz, -ɪŋ, -t
clasp (s. v.), **-s, -ing, -ed** klɑːsp, -s, -ɪŋ, -t
clasp-kni|fe, -ves 'klɑːspnaɪ|f, -vz
class, -es, -ing, -ed; -less klɑːs, -ɪz, -ɪŋ, -t; -lɪs [-ləs]
Classen 'klæsn
classic, -s, -al, -ally, -alness 'klæsɪk, -s, -l, -əlɪ, -əlnɪs [-nəs]
classicism, -s 'klæsɪsɪzm, -z
classicist, -s 'klæsɪsɪst, -s
classifiable 'klæsɪfaɪəbl [‚--'---]

classification, -s ‚klæsɪfɪ'keɪʃn, -z
classificatory ‚klæsɪfɪ'keɪtərɪ ['klæsɪfɪ-kətərɪ]
classi|fy, -fies, -fying, -fied, -fier/s 'klæsɪ|faɪ, -faɪz, -faɪɪŋ, -faɪd, -faɪə*/z
class|man, -men 'klɑːs|mæn [-mən], -men [-mən]
classroom, -s 'klɑːsrum [-ruːm], -z
class|y, -ier, -iest, -iness 'klɑːs|ɪ, -ɪə* [-jə*], -ɪɪst [-jɪst], -ɪnɪs [-ɪnəs]
clatter (s. v.), **-s, -ing, -ed** 'klætə*, -z, -rɪŋ, -d
Claud(e) klɔːd
Claudia, -n 'klɔː|djə [-dɪə], -n
Claudius 'klɔːdjəs [-dɪəs]
claus|e, -es; -al klɔːz, -ɪz, -l
claustral 'klɔːstrəl
claustrophob|ia, -ic ‚klɔːstrə'fəub|jə [-bɪə], -ɪk
clave (archaic p. of **cleave**) kleɪv
clavecin, -s 'klævɪsɪn, -z
Claverhouse 'kleɪvəhaus
clavichord, -s 'klævɪkɔːd, -z
clavicle, -s 'klævɪkl, -z
clavicular klə'vɪkjulə* [klæ'v-]
clavier (keyboard), **-s** 'klævɪə* [-vjə*], -z
clavier (instrument), **-s** klə'vɪə* ['klævɪə*, 'klævjə*], -z
claw (s. v.), **-s, -ing, -ed** klɔː, -z, -ɪŋ, -d
Claxton 'klækstən
clay (C.), -s kleɪ, -z
clayey 'kleɪɪ
Clayhanger 'kleɪ‚hæŋə*
claymore, -s 'kleɪmɔː* [-mɔə*], -z
Clayton 'kleɪtn
clean (s. adj. v.), **-s; -er, -est, -ly** (adv.), **-ness; -ing, -ed, -er/s** kliːn, -z; -ə*, -ɪst, -lɪ, -nɪs [-nəs]; -ɪŋ, -d, -ə*/z
clean-cut ‚kliːn'kʌt [also '-- when attributive]
clean|ly (adj.), **-ier, -iest, -iness** 'klenl|ɪ, -ɪə* [-jə*], -ɪɪst [-jɪst], -ɪnɪs [-ɪnəs]
cleans|e, -es, -ing, -ed, -er/s; -able klenz, -ɪz, -ɪŋ, -d, -ə*/z; -əbl
clean-up, -s ‚kliːn'ʌp ['--], -s
clear (adj. v.), **(C.), -er, -est, -ly, -ness; -s, -ing, -ed** klɪə*, -rə*, -rɪst, -lɪ, -nɪs [-nəs]; -z, -rɪŋ, -d
clearage 'klɪərɪdʒ
clearance, -s 'klɪərəns, -ɪz
clear-cut ‚klɪə'kʌt [also '-- when attributive]
clear-headed ‚klɪə'hedɪd [also '-‚-- when attributive]
clearing-hou|se, -ses 'klɪərɪŋhau|s, -zɪz
clear-sighted ‚klɪə'saɪtɪd [also '-‚-- when attributive]

clear-sighted|ly, -ness ˌklɪə'saɪtɪd|lɪ, -nɪs [-nəs]
clearstor|y, -ies 'klɪəstər|ɪ [-stɔːr-], -ɪz
clearway, -s 'klɪəweɪ, -z
cleat, -s kliːt, -s
Cleather 'kleðə*
cleavage, -s 'kliːvɪdʒ, -ɪz
cleav|e, -es, -ing, -ed, clove, cleft, cloven kliːv, -z, -ɪŋ, -d, kləʊv, kleft, 'kləʊvn
cleaver (C.), -s 'kliːvə*, -z
cleek (s. v.), -s, -ing, -ed kliːk, -s, -ɪŋ, -t
Cleethorpe, -s 'kliːθɔːp, -s
clef, -s klef, -s
cleft (s.), -s kleft, -s
cleft (from cleave) kleft
cleg -s kleg, -z
Clegg kleg
Cleishbotham 'kliːʃbɒðəm
clematis 'klemətɪs [klɪ'meɪtɪs, klə-'meɪt-, kle'meɪt-]
Clemence 'klemən s
clemen|cy, -t/ly 'klemən|sɪ, -t/lɪ
Clemens 'klemənz
Clement, -s 'klemənt, -s
Clementi klɪ'mentɪ [klə'm-]
Clementina ˌklemən'tiːnə
clementine (C.), -s 'klemənti:n [-taɪn], -z
clench, -es, -ing, -ed klentʃ, -ɪz, -ɪŋ, -t
Clendenin klen'denɪn
Cleo 'klɪəʊ ['kliː-, 'kleɪəʊ]
Cleobury (in Norfolk) 'klɪbərɪ ['kleb-]
Cleopatra klɪə'pætrə [ˌklɪəʊ'p-, -'pɑːt-]
clepsydr|a, -ae 'klepsɪdr|ə [klep's-], -iː
clerestor|y, -ies 'klɪəstɔːr|ɪ [-stər-], -ɪz
clergy 'klɜːdʒɪ
clergy|man, -men 'klɜːdʒɪ|mən, -mən
cleric (s. adj.), -s, -al/s, -ally 'klerɪk, -s, -l/z, -əlɪ
clerihew (C.) 'klerɪhjuː
clerk (C.), -s klɑːk, -s
Clerke klɑːk
Clerkenwell 'klɑːkənwel [-wəl]
clerkship, -s 'klɑːkʃɪp, -s
Clermont (towns in Ireland, village in Norfolk) 'kleəmɒnt [-mənt], (in U.S.A.) 'kleəmɒnt, 'klɜːmɒnt
Clery 'klɪərɪ
Clevedon 'kliːvdən
Cleveland 'kliːvlənd
clever, -er, -est, -ly, -ness, -ish 'klevə*, -rə*, -rɪst, -lɪ, -nɪs [-nəs], -rɪʃ
Cleverdon 'klevədən
Cleves kliːvz
clew (s. v.), -s, -ing, -ed kluː, -z, -ɪŋ ['kluɪŋ], -d
cliché, -s, -d 'kliːʃeɪ (kliʃe), -z, -d

click (s. v.), -s, -ing, -ed klɪk, -s, -ɪŋ, -t
client, -s 'klaɪənt, -s
clientèle, -s ˌkliːɒn'tel [-ɑ̃ːn't-, -ɔ̃ːn't-, -ɑːn't-, -ɒn't-, -'teɪl] (kliɑ̃tɛl), -z
cliff, -s klɪf, -s
cliff(e) klɪf
cliff-hanger, -s 'klɪfˌhæŋə*, -z
Clifford 'klɪfəd
cliffy 'klɪfɪ
clift, -s klɪft, -s
Clifton 'klɪftən
climacteric, -s klaɪ'mæktərɪk [ˌklaɪ-mæk'terɪk], -s
climacterical ˌklaɪmæk'terɪkl
climactic, -al, -ally klaɪ'mæktɪk, -l, -əlɪ
climate, -s 'klaɪmɪt [-mət], -s
climatic, -al, -ally klaɪ'mætɪk, -l, -əlɪ
climatolog|ist/s, -y ˌklaɪmə'tɒlədʒ|ɪst/s, -ɪ
climax, -es 'klaɪmæks, -ɪz
climb (s. v.), -s, -ing, -ed, -er/s; -able klaɪm, -z, -ɪŋ, -d, -ə*/z; -əbl
clime, -s klaɪm, -z
clinch (C.), -es, -ing, -ed, -er/s klɪntʃ, -ɪz, -ɪŋ, -t, -ə*/z
cline, -s klaɪm, -z
cling, -s, -ing, clung klɪŋ, -z, -ɪŋ, klʌŋ
clingy 'klɪŋɪ
clinic, -s, -al, -ally 'klɪnɪk, -s, -l, -əlɪ
clink (s. v.), -s, -ing, -ed klɪŋk, -s, -ɪŋ, -t [klɪŋt]
clinker, -s 'klɪŋkə*, -z
clinomet|er/s, -ry klaɪ'nɒmɪt|ə*/z [klɪ'n-, -mət|ə*/z], -rɪ
clinometric ˌklaɪnəʊ'metrɪk
Clinton 'klɪntən
Clio 'klaɪəʊ
clip, -s, -ping, -ped klɪp, -s, -ɪŋ, -t
clipper, -s 'klɪpə*, -z
clippie, -s 'klɪpɪ, -z
clipping (s. adj.), -s 'klɪpɪŋ, -z
clique, -s kliːk, -s
cliquish 'kliːkɪʃ
cliqu|y, -ier, -iest, -iness 'kliːk|ɪ, -ɪə* [-jə*], -ɪɪst [-jɪst], -ɪnɪs [-ɪnəs]
Clissold 'klɪsəld [-səʊld]
Clitheroe 'klɪðərəʊ
clitoris 'klɪtərɪs ['klaɪ-]
Clive klaɪv
Cliveden (in Berkshire) 'klɪvdən ['kliː-v-]
cloac|a/s, -ae kləʊ'eɪk|ə/z, -iː
cloacal kləʊ'eɪkl
cloak (s. v.) (C.), -s, -ing, -ed kləʊk, -s, -ɪŋ, -t
cloak-room, -s 'kləʊkrʊm [-ruːm], -z
Cloan kləʊn
cloche, -s klɒʃ [kləʊʃ], -ɪz

91

clock, -s klɒk, -s
clock-face, -s 'klɒkfeɪs, -ɪz
clock-maker, -s 'klɒk,meɪkə*, -z
clock|wise, -work 'klɒk|waɪz, -wɜ:k
clod, -s, -dy klɒd, -z, -ɪ
clodhopp|er/s, -ing 'klɒd,hɒp|ə*/z, -ɪŋ
Cloete kləʊ'i:tɪ, 'klu:tɪ
clog (s. v.), -s, -ging, -ged klɒg, -z, -ɪŋ, -d
clogg|y, -ier, -iest, -ily, -iness 'klɒg|ɪ, -ɪə*, -ɪɪst, -ɪlɪ [-əlɪ], -ɪnɪs [-ɪnəs]
Clogher 'klɒhə* ['klɒxə*], 'klɔ:ə*, klɔ:* [klɔə*]
cloist|er (s. v.), -ers, -ering, -ered 'klɔɪst|ə*, -əz, -ərɪŋ, -əd
cloistral 'klɔɪstrəl
Clonbrock klɒn'brɒk
Clonmel klɒn'mel ['klɒnmel]
Cloomber 'klu:mbə*
close (s.) (enclosure, yard), -s kləʊs, -ɪz
close (s.) (end), -s kləʊz, -ɪz
Close kləʊs
close (adj.), -r, -st, -ly, -ness kləʊs, -ə*, -ɪst, -lɪ, -nɪs [-nəs]
clos|e (v.), -es, -ing, -ed -er/s kləʊz, -ɪz, -ɪŋ, -d, -ə*/z
close-fisted ,kləʊs'fɪstɪd ['--- when attributive]
close-grained ,kləʊs'greɪnd ['-- when attributive]
close-hauled ,kləʊs'hɔ:ld
close-season, -s 'kləʊs,si:zn, -z
closet (s. v.), -s, -ing, -ed 'klɒzɪt, -s, -ɪŋ, -ɪd
close-time, -s 'kləʊstaɪm, -z
close-up (picture), -s 'kləʊsʌp [,-'-'], -s
closure, -s 'kləʊʒə*, -z
clot (s. v.), -s, -ting, -ted klɒt, -s, -ɪŋ, -ɪd
Cloten 'kləʊtn
cloth, -s klɒθ [old-fashioned klɔ:θ, and in compounds], klɒθs [klɒðz, klɔ:ðz, klɔ:θs] Note.—The plur. forms klɔ:ðz, klɔ:θs are only used by those who pronounce klɔ:θ in the sing.
cloth|e, -es, -ing, -ed, clad kləʊð, -z, -ɪŋ, -d, klæd
clothes (s.) kləʊðz [sometimes kləʊz]
clothes-basket, -s 'kləʊðz,bɑ:skɪt [sometimes 'kləʊz-], -s
clothes-brush, -es 'kləʊðzbrʌʃ [sometimes 'kləʊz-], -ɪz
clothes-horse, -s 'kləʊðzhɔ:s [sometimes 'kləʊz-], -ɪz
clothes-line, -s 'kləʊðzlaɪn [sometimes 'kləʊz-], -z
clothes-peg, -s 'kləʊðzpeg [sometimes 'kləʊz-], -z
clothier, -s 'kləʊðɪə* [-ðjə*], -z

clothing (s.) 'kləʊðɪŋ
Clotho 'kləʊθəʊ
cloth-yard, -s ,klɒθ'jɑ:d [,klɔ:θ-, also '-- when followed by a stress], -z
cloud (s. v.), -s, -ing, -ed klaʊd, -z, -ɪŋ, -ɪd
cloudberr|y, -ies 'klaʊd,ber|ɪ [-bər|ɪ], -ɪz
cloud-burst, -s 'klaʊdbɜ:st, -s
cloud-capt 'klaʊdkæpt
Cloudesley 'klaʊdzlɪ
cloudless, -ly, -ness 'klaʊdlɪs [-ləs], -lɪ, -nɪs [-nəs]
cloud|y, -ier, -iest, -ily, -iness 'klaʊd|ɪ, -ɪə* [-jə*], -ɪɪst [-jɪst], -ɪlɪ [-əlɪ], -ɪnɪs [-ɪnəs]
clough, -s klʌf, -s
Clough klʌf, klu:
Clouston 'klu:stən, 'klaʊstən
clout (s. v.), -s, -ing, -ed klaʊt, -s, -ɪŋ, -ɪd
clove (s.), -s kləʊv, -z
clove (from cleave), -n kləʊv, -n
Clovelly klə'velɪ
cloven-footed ,kləʊvn'fʊtɪd ['--,--]
clover, -s 'kləʊvə*, -z
Clovis 'kləʊvɪs
Clow (surname) kləʊ
Clowes (in Norfolk) klu:z, (surname) klaʊz, klu:z
clown, -s klaʊn, -z
clownish, -ly, -ness 'klaʊnɪʃ, -lɪ, -nɪs [-nəs]
cloy, -s, -ing, -ed klɔɪ, -z, -ɪŋ, -d
club (s. v.), -s, -bing, -bed klʌb, -z, -ɪŋ, -d
clubbable 'klʌbəbl
club-f|oot, -eet ,klʌb'f|ʊt ['--], -i:t
club-footed ,klʌb'fʊtɪd ['-,--]
club-hou|se, ses 'klʌbhaʊ|s [,-'-], -zɪz
clubland 'klʌblænd
club-law ,klʌb'lɔ: ['--]
club|man, -men 'klʌb|mən [-mæn], -mən [-men]
club-moss, -es ,klʌb'mɒs ['--], -ɪz
club-room, -s 'klʌbrʊm [-ru:m], -z
club-shaped 'klʌbʃeɪpt
cluck (s. v.), -s, -ing, -ed klʌk, -s, -ɪŋ, -t
clue, -s, -less klu:, -z, -lɪs [-ləs]
clump (s. v.), -s, -ing, -ed klʌmp, -s, -ɪŋ, -t [klʌmt]
clumpy 'klʌmpɪ
clums|y, -ier, -iest, -ily, -iness 'klʌmz|ɪ, -ɪə* [-jə*], -ɪɪst [-jɪst], -ɪlɪ [-əlɪ], -ɪnɪs [-ɪnəs]
clunch klʌntʃ
clung (from cling) klʌŋ
Cluse klu:z, klu:s

clust|er (s. v.), -ers, -ering, -ered
'klʌst|ə*, -əz, -ərɪŋ, -əd

clutch (s. v.), -es, -ing, -ed klʌtʃ, -ɪz,
-ɪŋ, -t

clutter, -s, -ing, -ed 'klʌtə*, -z, -rɪŋ, -d

Clutterbuck 'klʌtəbʌk

Clutton 'klʌtn

Clwyd 'klu:ɪd (Welsh kluɪd)

Clyde, -bank klaɪd, -bæŋk

Clymene 'klɪmɪnɪ [-mənɪ]

clyp|eus, -ei 'klɪp|ɪəs, -ɪaɪ

clyster, -s 'klɪstə*, -z

Clytemnestra ˌklaɪtɪm'nestrə [-ti:m-,
-tem-]

Clytie (nymph in Greek mythology)
'klɪtɪɪ ['klaɪti:], (modern Christian
name, chignon) 'klaɪtɪ [-ti:]

Cnidus 'naɪdəs ['kn-]

Cnut kə'nju:t

Co. kəʊ ['kʌmpənɪ]

coach (s. v.), -es, -ing, -ed kəʊtʃ, -ɪz, -ɪŋ,
-t

coach-horse, -s 'kəʊtʃhɔ:s, -ɪz

coach|man, -men 'kəʊtʃ|mən, -mən

coac|tion, -tive kəʊ'æk|ʃn, -tɪv

coadjacent ˌkəʊə'dʒeɪsnt

coadjutor, -s kəʊ'ædʒʊtə* [-dʒət-], -z

co-administrator, -s ˌkəʊəd'mɪnɪs-
treɪtə*, -z

coagulat|e, -es, -ing, -ed kəʊ'ægjʊleɪt
[-gjəl-], -s, -ɪŋ, -ɪd

coagulation, -s kəʊˌægjʊ'leɪʃn [-gjəl-], -z

coal (s. v.), -s, -ing, -ed kəʊl, -z, -ɪŋ, -d

coal-bed, -s 'kəʊlbed, -z

coal-black ˌkəʊl'blæk ['-- when attri-
butive]

coal-bunker, -s 'kəʊlˌbʌŋkə*, -z

coalesc|e, -es, -ing, -ed ˌkəʊə'les, -ɪz,
-ɪŋ, -t

coalescen|ce, -t ˌkəʊə'lesn|s, -t

coal|-face/s, -field/s 'kəʊl|feɪs/ɪz, -fi:ld/z

coal-gas 'kəʊlgæs [ˌ-'-]

coal-heaver, -s 'kəʊlˌhi:və*, -z

coal-hole, -s 'kəʊlhəʊl, -z

coal-hou|se, -ses 'kəʊlhaʊ|s, -zɪz

coaling-station, -s 'kəʊlɪŋˌsteɪʃn, -z

coalite 'kəʊlaɪt

coalition, -s ˌkəʊə'lɪʃn, -z

coal|man, -men 'kəʊl|mæn [-mən],
-men [-mən]

coal-measure, -s 'kəʊlˌmeʒə*, -z

coal-mine, -s 'kəʊlmaɪn, -z

coal-owner, -s 'kəʊlˌəʊnə*, -z

coal-pit, -s 'kəʊlpɪt, -s

coal-scuttle, -s 'kəʊlˌskʌtl, -z

coal-tar ˌkəʊl'tɑ:* ['--, esp. when
attributive]

coal-tit, -s 'kəʊltɪt, -s

coarse, -r, -st, -ly, -ness kɔ:s [kɔəs],
-ə*, -ɪst, -lɪ, -nɪs [-nəs]

coarse-grained 'kɔ:sgreɪnd ['kɔəs-]

coars|en, -ens, -ening, -ened 'kɔ:s|n
['kɔəs-], -nz, -nɪŋ [-nɪŋ], -nd

coast (s. v.), -s, -ing, -ed kəʊst, -s, -ɪŋ,
-ɪd

coaster, -s 'kəʊstə*, -z

coast-guard, -s 'kəʊstˌgɑ:d, -z

coast-line, -s 'kəʊstlaɪn, -z

coastwise 'kəʊstwaɪz

coat (s. v.), -s, -ing, -ed kəʊt, -s, -ɪŋ, -ɪd

Coatbridge 'kəʊtbrɪdʒ

coatee, -s 'kəʊti: [ˌkəʊ'ti:], -z

Coat(e)s kəʊts

coat-hanger, -s 'kəʊtˌhæŋə*, -z

coating, -s 'kəʊtɪŋ, -z

coat-of-arms, coats-of-arms ˌkəʊtəv-
'ɑ:mz, ˌkəʊtsəv'ɑ:mz

coax (s. v.), -es, -ing/ly, -ed, -er/s
kəʊks, -ɪz, -ɪŋ/lɪ, -t, -ə*/z

co-axial ˌkəʊ'æksɪəl [-sjəl]

cob, -s kɒb, -z

cobalt kəʊ'bɔ:lt [-'bɒlt, 'kəʊbɔ:lt]

Cobb, -ett kɒb, -ɪt

cobb|le (s. v.), -les, -ling, -led, -ler/s
'kɒb|l, -lz, -lɪŋ [-lɪŋ], -ld, -lə*/z

cobbler's-wax 'kɒbləzwæks

cobble-stone, -s 'kɒblstəʊn, -s

Cobbold 'kɒbəʊld [-bld]

Cobden 'kɒbdən

Cobh kəʊv

Cobham 'kɒbəm

Coblenz (K-) kəʊ'blents ['kəʊblents]

cob-nut, -s 'kɒbnʌt, -s

cobra, -s 'kəʊbrə ['kɒ-], -z

Coburg (K-), -s 'kəʊbɜ:g, -z

cobweb, -s 'kɒbweb, -z

coca 'kəʊkə

coca-cola ˌkəʊkə'kəʊlə

cocaine kəʊ'keɪn [kɒ'k-]

cocciferous kɒk'sɪfərəs

coc|cus, -ci 'kɒk|əs, -aɪ ['kɒksaɪ]

coccyx, -es 'kɒksɪks, -ɪz

Cochin (in India) 'kəʊtʃɪn [ˌkəʊ'tʃɪn]

Cochin-China ˌkɒtʃɪn'tʃaɪnə

cochineal 'kɒtʃɪni:l [ˌ--'-]

cochl|ea, -eas, -eae 'kɒkl|ɪə, -ɪəz, -ri:

Cochran 'kɒkrən

Cochrane 'kɒkrən [-rɪn]

cock (s. v.), -s, -ing, -ed kɒk, -s, -ɪŋ, -t

cockade, -s kɒ'keɪd, -z

cock-a-doodle-doo ˌkɒkədu:dl'du:

cock-a-hoop ˌkɒkə'hu:p ['---]

Cockaigne kɒ'keɪn [kə'k-]

cockalorum, -s ˌkɒkə'lɔ:rəm, -z

cockatoo, -s ˌkɒkə'tu:, -z

cockatrice, -s 'kɒkətraɪs [-trɪs], -ɪz

Cockburn 'kəʊbɜ:n [-bən]
cockchafer, -s 'kɒk,tʃeɪfə*, -z
Cockcroft 'kəʊkkrɒft, 'kɒkkrɒft
cock-cr|ow, -owing 'kɒkkr|əʊ, -əʊɪŋ
Cocke (place) kɒk, (surname) kəʊk, kɒk
Cockell 'kɒkl
cocker (C.), -s 'kɒkə*, -z
cockerel, -s 'kɒkərəl, -z
Cockerell 'kɒkərəl
Cockermouth 'kɒkəməθ [-maʊθ]
    Note.—Locally -məθ.
cock-eye, -d 'kɒkaɪ, -d [ˌ-'-]
cock-fight, -s, -ing 'kɒkfaɪt, -s, -ɪŋ
Cockfosters ˌkɒk'fɒstəz
cock-horse, -s ˌkɒk'hɔ:s ['--, also -'-
    when preceded by a stress], -ɪz
cock|le (s. v.) (C.), -les, -ling, -led
    'kɒk|l, -lz, -lɪŋ [-lɪŋ], -ld
cockleshell, -s 'kɒklʃel, -z
cockney (C.), -s 'kɒknɪ, -z
cockneyism, -s 'kɒknɪɪzəm [-njɪz-], -z
cock-pit, -s 'kɒkpɪt, -s
cockroach, -es 'kɒkrəʊtʃ, -ɪz
Cockroft 'kəʊkrɒft ['kɒk-]
cockscomb, -s 'kɒkskəʊm, -z
Cocksedge 'kɒksɪdʒ [-sedʒ], 'kɒsɪdʒ,
    'kəʊsɪdʒ
Cockshott 'kɒkʃɒt
cock-sh|y, -ies 'kɒkʃ|aɪ, -aɪz
Cockspur 'kɒkspɜ:* [-pə*]
cock-sure ˌkɒk'ʃɔ:* [-'ʃɔə*, -'ʃʊə*]
cocktail, -s 'kɒkteɪl, -z
Cockwood (in Devon) 'kɒkwʊd
    Note.—There exists also a local pro-
    nunciation 'kɒkʊd.
cock|y, -ier, -iest, -ily, -iness 'kɒk|ɪ,
    -ɪə*, -ɪɪst, -ɪlɪ [-əlɪ], -ɪnɪs [-ɪnəs]
cocky-leeky ˌkɒkɪ'li:kɪ
Cocles 'kɒkli:z
coco, -s 'kəʊkəʊ, -z
cocoa, -s 'kəʊkəʊ, -z
coco(a)nut, -s 'kəʊkənʌt, -s
cocoon, -s kə'ku:n [kɒ'k-], -z
cocotte, -s kɒ'kɒt [kəʊ-], -s
Cocytus kəʊ'saɪtəs
cod, -s kɒd, -z
Coddington 'kɒdɪŋtən
codd|le, -les, -ling, -led 'kɒd|l, -lz, -lɪŋ
    [-lɪŋ], -ld
†code (s.) -s kəʊd, -z
codeine 'kəʊdi:n [-dɪi:n]
cod|ex, -exes, -ices 'kəʊd|eks, -eksɪz,
    -ɪsi:z ['kɒdɪsi:z]
cod-fish|er/s, -ing 'kɒd,fɪʃ|ə*/z, -ɪŋ
cod-fisher|y, -ies 'kɒd,fɪʃər|ɪ, -ɪz
codger, -s 'kɒdʒə*, -z
codicil, -s 'kɒdɪsɪl ['kəʊd-], -z
codicillary ˌkɒdɪ'sɪlərɪ

Codicote 'kəʊdɪkəʊt
codification, -s ˌkəʊdɪfɪ'keɪʃn [ˌkɒd-], -z
codi|fy, -fies, -fying, -fied 'kəʊdɪ|faɪ
    ['kɒd-], -faɪz, -faɪɪŋ, -faɪd
codling, -s 'kɒdlɪŋ, -z
cod-liver-oil ˌkɒdlɪvər'ɔɪl [-və'ɔɪl]
codpiec|e, -es 'kɒdpi:s, -ɪz
Codrington 'kɒdrɪŋtən
Cody 'kəʊdɪ
Coe kəʊ
co-ed ˌkəʊ'ed
coeducation ˌkəʊedju:'keɪʃn [-dju-,
    -dʒu:-, -dʒʊ-]
coeducational ˌkəʊedju:'keɪʃənl [-dju-,
    -dʒu:-, -dʒʊ-, -ʃnəl, -ʃn̩l,
    -ʃnl̩, -ʃənəl]
coefficient, -s ˌkəʊɪ'fɪʃnt, -s
coelacanth, -s 'si:ləkænθ, -s
Coelesyria ˌsi:lɪ'sɪrɪə
coemption kəʊ'empʃn
coenobite, -s 'si:nəʊbaɪt, -s
coequ|al, -ally kəʊ'i:kw|əl, -əlɪ
coequality ˌkəʊi:'kwɒlətɪ [ˌkəʊɪ-, -rtɪ]
coerc|e, -es, -ing, -ed kəʊ'ɜ:s, -ɪz, -ɪŋ, -t
coercib|le, -ly kəʊ'ɜ:sɪb|l [-səb-], -lɪ
coercion kəʊ'ɜ:ʃn
coercionist, -s kəʊ'ɜ:ʃnɪst [-ʃənɪst], -s
coercive, -ly kəʊ'ɜ:sɪv, -lɪ
co-eternal ˌkəʊɪ'tɜ:nl [-i:'t-]
Cœur de Lion ˌkɜ:də'li:ɔ̃:ŋ [-'li:ɒŋ]
    (kœrdəljɔ̃)
coeval kəʊ'i:vl
co-executor, -s ˌkəʊɪg'zekjʊtə* [-eg-,
    -kjət-], -z
co-exist, -s, -ing, -ed ˌkəʊɪg'zɪst [-eg-],
    -s, -ɪŋ, -ɪd
co-existen|ce, -t ˌkəʊɪg'zɪstən|s [-eg-], -t
co-extend, -s, -ing, -ed ˌkəʊɪk'stend
    [-ek-], -z, -ɪŋ, -ɪd
co-extension, -s ˌkəʊɪk'stenʃn [-ek-], -z
co-extensive ˌkəʊɪk'stensɪv [-ek-]
coffee, -s 'kɒfɪ, -z
coffee-bar, -s 'kɒfɪbɑ:*, -z
coffee-bean, -s 'kɒfɪbi:n, -z
coffee-cup, -s 'kɒfɪkʌp, -s
coffee-hou|se, -ses 'kɒfɪhaʊ|s, -zɪz
coffee-mill, -s 'kɒfɪmɪl, -z
coffee-pot, -s 'kɒfɪpɒt, -s
coffee-room, -s 'kɒfɪrʊm [-ru:m], -z
coffer, -s 'kɒfə*, -z
coffin (s. v.) (C.), -s, -ing, -ed 'kɒfɪn, -z,
    -ɪŋ, -d
cog (s. v.), -s, -ging, -ged kɒg, -z, -ɪŋ, -d
cogen|ce, -cy, -t/ly 'kəʊdʒən|s, -sɪ, -t/lɪ
Coggeshall (in Essex) 'kɒgɪʃl, (sur-
    name) 'kɒgzɔ:l
Coggin 'kɒgɪn
Coghill 'kɒgɪl [-hɪl]

cogitat|e, -es, -ing, -ed, -or/s 'kɒdʒɪteɪt, -s, -ɪŋ, -ɪd, -ə*/z
cogitation, -s ˌkɒdʒɪ'teɪʃn, -z
cogitative 'kɒdʒɪtətɪv [-teɪt-]
cognac, -s 'kɒnjæk ['kəʊn-] (kɔɲak), -s
cognate (s. adj.), -s 'kɒgneɪt [-'-], -s
cognation kɒg'neɪʃn
cognition, -s kɒg'nɪʃn, -z
cognitive 'kɒgnɪtɪv [-nət-]
cognizable [-isa-] 'kɒgnɪzəbl ['kɒn-]
cognizan|ce [-isa-], -ces, -t 'kɒgnɪzən|s ['kɒn-], -sɪz, -t
cogniz|e [-is|e], -es, -ing, -ed kɒg'naɪz ['--], -ɪz, -ɪŋ, -d
cognomen, -s kɒg'nəʊmen, -z
cognominal kɒg'nəʊmɪnl [-'nɒm-]
cognoscent|e, -i ˌkɒnjəʊ'ʃent|ɪ [ˌkɒnəʊ-, ˌkɒgnəʊ-], -i: [-'i]
cognovit, -s kɒg'nəʊvɪt, -s
cogwheel, -s 'kɒgwi:l [-ghw-], -z
cohabit, -s, -ing, -ed kəʊ'hæbɪt, -s, -ɪŋ, -ɪd
cohabitant, -s kəʊ'hæbɪtənt, -s
cohabitation ˌkəʊhæbɪ'teɪʃn [kəʊˌhæ-]
co-heir, -s ˌkəʊ'eə* ['--], -z
co-heiress, -es ˌkəʊ'eərɪs [-res], -ɪz
Cohen 'kəʊɪn 'kəʊən
coher|e, -es, -ing, -ed kəʊ'hɪə*, -z, -rɪŋ, -d
coheren|ce, -cy, -t/ly kəʊ'hɪərən|s, -sɪ, -t/lɪ
cohesion kəʊ'hi:ʒn
cohesive, -ly, -ness kəʊ'hi:sɪv, -lɪ, -nɪs [-nəs]
Cohn kəʊn
Cohorn 'kəʊhɔ:n
cohort, -s 'kəʊhɔ:t, -s
coif (s. v.), -s, -ing, -ed kɔɪf, -s, -ɪŋ, -t
coiffé, -s, -ing, -d 'kwɑ:feɪ ['kwæf-, 'kwɒf-] (kwafe), -z, -ɪŋ, -d
coiffeur, -s kwɑ:'fɜ:* [kwæ'f-, kwɒ'f-] (kwafœ:r), -z
coiffure, -s kwɑ:'fjʊə* [kwæ'f-, kwɒ'f-] (kwafy:r), -z
coign, -s kɔɪn, -z
coil (s. v.), -s, -ing, -ed kɔɪl, -z, -ɪŋ, -d
Coimbra kəʊ'ɪmbrə
coin (s. v.), -s, -ing, -ed, -er/s kɔɪn, -z, -ɪŋ, -d, -ə*/z
coinage, -s 'kɔɪnɪdʒ, -ɪz
coincid|e, -es, -ing, -ed ˌkəʊɪn'saɪd, -z, -ɪŋ, -ɪd
coinciden|ce, -ces, -t/ly kəʊ'ɪnsɪdən|s, -sɪz, -t/lɪ
coincident|al, -ally kəʊˌɪnsɪ'dent|l [ˌkəʊɪn-], -əlɪ
co-inheritor, -s ˌkəʊɪn'herɪtə*, -z
coir 'kɔɪə*

coition kəʊ'ɪʃn
coitus 'kəʊɪtəs
coke kəʊk
Coke kəʊk, kʊk
   Note.—Members of the Essex family pronounce kʊk. So also the family name of the Earl of Leicester.
Coker 'kəʊkə*
col, -s kɒl, -z
Col. 'kɜ:nl
cola 'kəʊlə
colander, -s 'kʌləndə* ['kɒl-], -z
Colby 'kəʊlbɪ
Colchester 'kəʊltʃɪstə*
colchicum 'kɒltʃɪkəm [-lkɪ-]
Colchis 'kɒlkɪs
Colcleugh 'kəʊklku:
Colclough 'kəʊklɪ, 'kɒlklʌf, 'kəʊlklʌf
cold (s. adj.), -s, -er, -est, -ly, -ness kəʊld, -z, -ə*, -ɪst, -lɪ, -nɪs [-nəs]
cold-blooded, -ly, -ness ˌkəʊld'blʌdɪd ['-ˌ-- when attributive], -lɪ, -nɪs [-nəs]
cold-cream 'kəʊld kri:m
cold-hearted ˌkəʊld'hɑ:tɪd ['-ˌ--]
coldish 'kəʊldɪʃ
cold-shoulder, -s, -ing, -ed ˌkəʊld-'ʃəʊldə*, -z, -rɪŋ, -d
cold-storage ˌkəʊld'stɔ:rɪdʒ
Coldstream 'kəʊldstri:m
cole (C.), -s kəʊl, -z
Colebrook(e) 'kəʊlbrʊk
Coleby 'kəʊlbɪ
Coleclough 'kəʊlklaʊ
Coleford 'kəʊlfəd
Coleman 'kəʊlmən
Colenso kə'lenzəʊ
coleopter|a, -al ˌkɒlɪ'ɒptər|ə, -əl
Coleraine kəʊl'reɪn
Coleridge 'kəʊlərɪdʒ
Coles kəʊlz
coleslaw 'kəʊlslɔ:
Colet 'kɒlɪt
cole-tit, -s 'kəʊltɪt, -s
Colgate 'kəʊlgeɪt ['kɒl-, -gɪt]
colic, -ky 'kɒlɪk, -ɪ
Colin, -dale 'kɒlɪn, -deɪl
Coling 'kəʊlɪŋ
Coliseum ˌkɒlɪ'sɪəm [-lə-, -'si:əm]
colitis kɒ'laɪtɪs [kəʊ'l-]
collaborat|e, -es, -ing, -ed, -or/s kə'læbəreɪt [kɒ'l-], -s, -ɪŋ, -ɪd, -ə*/z
collaboration, -s kəˌlæbə'reɪʃn [kɒ,l-], -z
collage, -s 'kɒlɑ:ʒ [-'-, kə'-], -ɪz
collaps|e (s. v.), -es, -ing, -ed kə'læps, -ɪz, -ɪŋ, -t
collapsible kə'læpsəbl [-sɪb-]
collar (s. v.), -s, -ing, -ed 'kɒlə*, -z, -rɪŋ, -d

collar-bone, -s 'kɒləbəʊn, -z
Collard 'kɒləd
Collas 'kɒləs
collat|e, -es, -ing, -ed, -or/s kə'leɪt
 [kɒ'l-], -s, -ɪŋ, -ɪd, -ə*/z
collater|al/s, -ally kɒ'lætər|əl/z [kə'l-],
 -əlɪ
collation, -s kə'leɪʃn [kɒ'l-], -z
colleague, -s 'kɒli:ɡ, -z
collect (s.), -s 'kɒlekt [-lɪkt], -s
collect (v.), -s, -ing, -ed, -er/s kə'lekt,
 -s, -ɪŋ, -ɪd, -ə*/z
collectanea ˌkɒlek'tɑ:njə [-'teɪn-, -nɪə]
collected (adj.), -ly, -ness kə'lektɪd, -lɪ,
 -nɪs [-nəs]
collection, -s kə'lekʃn, -z
collective, -ly kə'lektɪv, -lɪ
collectivi|sm, -st/s kə'lektɪvɪ|zəm, -st/s
collector, -s kə'lektə*, -z
colleen, -s 'kɒli:n [in Ireland kɒ'li:n],
 -z
college, -s; -r/s 'kɒlɪdʒ, -ɪz; -ə*/z
collegian, -s kə'li:dʒən [kɒ'l-, -dʒɪən],
 -z
collegiate kə'li:dʒɪət [kɒ'l-, -dʒət,
 -dʒɪt, -dʒɪt]
Collen 'kɒlɪn
Colles 'kɒlɪs
collet (C.), -s 'kɒlɪt, -s
collid|e, -es, -ing, -ed kə'laɪd, -z, -ɪŋ, -ɪd
collie (C.), -s 'kɒlɪ, -z
collier (C.), -s 'kɒlɪə* [-ljə*], -z
collier|y, -ies 'kɒljər|ɪ [-lɪər|ɪ], -ɪz
collimat|e, -es, -ing, -ed 'kɒlɪmeɪt, -s,
 -ɪŋ, -ɪd
collimation ˌkɒlɪ'meɪʃn
collimator, -s 'kɒlɪmeɪtə*, -z
collinear kɒ'lɪnjə* [kə'l-, -nɪə*]
Collingham 'kɒlɪŋəm
Collingwood 'kɒlɪŋwʊd
Collin|s, -son 'kɒlɪn|z, -sn
Collis 'kɒlɪs
collision, -s kə'lɪʒn, -z
collocat|e, -es, -ing, -ed 'kɒləʊkeɪt, -s,
 -ɪŋ, -ɪd
collocation, -s ˌkɒləʊ'keɪʃn, -z
collodion kə'ləʊdjən [-dɪən]
colloid, -s 'kɒlɔɪd, -z
collop, -s 'kɒləp, -s
colloquial, -ly, -ism/s kə'ləʊkwɪəl
 [-kwjəl], -ɪ, -ɪzəm/z
colloquium kə'ləʊkwɪəm
colloqu|y, -ies 'kɒləkw|ɪ, -ɪz
collotype, -s 'kɒləʊtaɪp, -s
Colls kɒlz
collud|e, -es, -ing, -ed, -er/s kə'lu:d
 [kɒ'l-, -'lju:d], -z, -ɪŋ, -ɪd, -ə*/z
collusion, -s kə'lu:ʒn [-'lju:-], -z

collusive, -ly kə'lu:sɪv [-'lju:-], -lɪ
Collyns 'kɒlɪnz
collywobbles 'kɒlɪˌwɒblz
Colman 'kəʊlmən
Colmekill 'kəʊlmkɪl
Colnaghi kɒl'nɑ:ɡɪ
Colnbrook 'kəʊlnbrʊk ['kəʊn-]
Colne kəʊn, kəʊln
Colney 'kəʊnɪ
Cologne kə'ləʊn
Colombia, -n/s kə'lɒmbɪə [-'lʌm-, -bjə],
 -n/z
Colombo kə'lʌmbəʊ [-'lɒm-]
colon -s 'kəʊlən [-lɒn], -z
Colon kɒ'lɒn
colonel, -s; -cy, -cies, -ship/s 'kɜ:nl, -z;
 -sɪ, -sɪz, -ʃɪp/s
colonial (s. adj.), -s kə'ləʊnjəl [-nɪəl], -z
colonist, -s 'kɒlənɪst, -s
colonization [-isa-] ˌkɒlənaɪ'zeɪʃn
 [-nɪ'z-]
coloniz|e [-is|e], -es, -ing, -ed, -er/s
 'kɒlənaɪz, -ɪz, -ɪŋ, -d, -ə*/z
colonnade, -s ˌkɒlə'neɪd, -z
Colonus kə'ləʊnəs
colon|y, -ies 'kɒlən|ɪ [-lŋ|ɪ], -ɪz
colophon, -s 'kɒləfən [-fɒn], -z
Colorado ˌkɒlə'rɑ:dəʊ
colorant, -s 'kʌlərənt, -s
coloration ˌkʌlə'reɪʃn
coloratura ˌkɒlərə'tʊərə [-'tjʊər-]
colorific ˌkɒlə'rɪfɪk
coloss|al, -ally kə'lɒs|l, -əlɪ
Colosseum ˌkɒlə'sɪəm [-'si:əm]
Colossian, -s kə'lɒʃn [-ɒsɪən, -ɒsjən,
 -ɒʃɪən, -ɒʃjən], -z
coloss|us, -i kə'lɒs|əs, -aɪ
colour (s. v.), -s, -ing, -ed; -ist/s 'kʌlə*,
 -z, -rɪŋ, -d, -rɪst/s
colourab|le, -ly 'kʌlərəb|l, -lɪ
colouration ˌkʌlə'reɪʃn
colour-bar, -s 'kʌləbɑ:*, -z
colour-blin|d, -dness 'kʌləblaɪn|d
 [ˌkʌlə'b-], -dnɪs [-nəs]
colour|ful, -less 'kʌlə|fʊl, -lɪs [-ləs]
colour|man, -men 'kʌlə|mən [-mæn],
 -mən [-men]
colour-proc|ess, -esses 'kʌləˌprəʊs|es
 [rarely -ˌprɒs-], -esɪz [-ɪsɪz]
colour-sergeant, -s 'kʌləˌsɑ:dʒənt, -s
colporteur, -s 'kɒlˌpɔ:tə* [ˌkɒlpɔ:'tɜ:*],
 -z
Colquhoun kə'hu:n
Cols. 'kɜ:nlz
Colson 'kəʊlsn
Colston 'kəʊlstən
colt, -s kəʊlt, -s

coltsfoot, -s 'kəʊltsfʊt, -s
coluber, -s 'kɒljʊbə*, -z
colubrine 'kɒljʊbraɪn
Columba kə'lʌmbə
columbarium, -s ,kɒləm'beərɪəm, -z
Columbia, -n/s kə'lʌmbɪə [-bjə], -n/z
columbine, -s 'kɒləmbaɪn, -z
Columbus kə'lʌmbəs
column, -s, -ed 'kɒləm, -z, -d
column|al, -ar kə'lʌmn|l, -ə*
columnist, -s 'kɒləmnɪst [-əmɪst], -s
colure, -s kə'ljʊə*, -z
Colwyn 'kɒlwɪn
Colyton 'kɒlɪtn
colza 'kɒlzə
coma (deep sleep), -s 'kəʊmə, -z
com|a (tuft), -as, -ae 'kəʊm|ə, -əz, -iː
Coma Berenices 'kəʊmə ,berɪ'naɪsiːz
comatose 'kəʊmətəʊs
comb (s. v.), -s, -ing/s, -ed kəʊm, -z, -ɪŋ/z, -d
combat (s.), -s 'kɒmbæt ['kʌm-, -ət], -s
combat (v.), -s, -ing, -ed 'kɒmbæt ['kʌm-, -ət, kəm'bæt], -s, -ɪŋ, -ɪd
combatant, -s 'kɒmbətənt ['kʌm-], -s
combative, -ly, -ness 'kɒmbətɪv ['kʌm-], -lɪ, -nɪs [-nəs]
combe (C.), -s kuːm, -z
comber (combing machine), -s 'kəʊmə*, -z
comber (fish) (C.), -s 'kɒmbə*, -z
combination, -s; -room/s ,kɒmbɪ'neɪʃn, -z; -rʊm/z [-ruːm/z]
combinative 'kɒmbɪnətɪv [-neɪt-]
combinatory 'kɒmbɪnətərɪ [,kɒmbɪ'neɪtərɪ]
combine (s.), -s 'kɒmbaɪn [kəm'baɪn], -z
combin|e (v.), -es, -ing, -ed (join) kəm'baɪn, (harvest) 'kɒmbaɪn, -z, -ɪŋ, -d
combust, -er/s kəm'bʌst, -ə*/z
combustibility kəm,bʌstə'bɪlətɪ [-tɪ'b-, -lɪt-]
combustible, -ness kəm'bʌstəbl [-tɪb-], -nɪs [-nəs]
combustion, -s kəm'bʌstʃən, -z
com|e, -es, -ing, came kʌm, -z, -ɪŋ, keɪm
come-at-able ,kʌm'ætəbl
come-back, -s 'kʌmbæk, -s
comedian, -s kə'miːdjən [-dɪən], -z
comédienne, -s kə,miːdɪ'en [,kɒm-, kə,meɪd-] (kɔmedjɛn), -z
come-down, -s 'kʌmdaʊn [,-'-], -z
comed|y, -ies 'kɒməd|ɪ [-mɪdɪ], -ɪz
comel|y, -ier, -iest, -iness 'kʌml|ɪ, -ɪə* [-jə*], -ɪɪst [-jɪst], -ɪnɪs [-nəs]
Comenius kə'meɪnjəs [kɒ'm-, -nɪəs]
comestible, -s kə'mestɪbl [-əbl], -z

comet, -s; -ary 'kɒmɪt, -s; -ərɪ
comfit, -s 'kʌmfɪt ['kɒm-], -s
comfort (s. v.), -s, -ing, -ed, -er/s 'kʌmfət, -s, -ɪŋ, -ɪd, -ə*/z
comfortab|le, -ly 'kʌmfətəb|l, -lɪ
comforter (scarf), -s 'kʌmfətə*, -z
comfortless 'kʌmfətlɪs [-ləs]
comfrey 'kʌmfrɪ
comf|y, -ier, -iest, -ily, -iness 'kʌmf|ɪ -ɪə* [-jə*], -ɪɪst [-jɪst], -ɪlɪ [-əlɪ], -ɪnɪs [-nəs]
comic, -al, -ally, -alness 'kɒmɪk, -əl, -əlɪ, -əlnɪs [-nəs]
Comin 'kʌmɪn
Cominform 'kɒmɪnfɔːm [,-'-]
Comintern 'kɒmɪntɜːn [,-'-]
comity 'kɒmɪtɪ
comma, -s 'kɒmə, -z
Commager 'kɒmədʒə*
command (s. v.), -s, -ing/ly, -ed, -er/s kə'mɑːnd, -z, -ɪŋ/lɪ, -ɪd, -ə*/z
commandant, -s ,kɒmən'dænt [-'dɑːnt, '---], -s
commandantship, -s ,kɒmən'dænt-ʃɪp [-'dɑːnt-], -s
commandeer, -s, -ing, -ed ,kɒmən'dɪə*, -z, -rɪŋ, -d
commander-in-chief, commanders-in-chief kə,mɑːndərɪn'tʃiːf [-dəɪn-], kə,mɑːndəzɪn'tʃiːf
commandership, -s kə'mɑːndəʃɪp, -s
commandment, -s kə'mɑːndmənt, -s
commando, -(e)s kə'mɑːndəʊ, -z
comme-il-faut ,kɒmiːl'fəʊ (kɔmilfo)
commemorat|e, -es, -ing, -ed, -or/s kə'meməreɪt [-mʊr-], -s, -ɪŋ, -ɪd, -ə*/z
commemoration, -s kə,memə'reɪʃn [-mʊ'r-], -z
commemorative kə'memərətɪv [-mʊr-, -reɪt-]
commenc|e, -es, -ing, -ed, -ement/s kə'mens, -ɪz, -ɪŋ, -t, -mənt/s
commend, -s, -ing, -ed kə'mend, -z, -ɪŋ, -ɪd
commendab|le, -ly, -leness kə'mend-əb|l, -lɪ, -lnɪs [-nəs]
commendation, -s ,kɒmen'deɪʃn [-mən-], -z
†commendatory kə'mendətərɪ [kɒ'm-]
commensurability kə,menʃərə'bɪlətɪ [-sjər-, -sjʊr-, -ʃʊr-, -lɪt-]
commensurab|le, -ly, -leness kə'men-ʃərəb|l [-sjʊr-, -sjər-, -sjʊr-], -lɪ, -lnɪs [-nəs]
commensurate, -ly, -ness kə'menʃərət [-sjʊr-, -sjər-, -sjʊr-, -rɪt], -lɪ, -nɪs [-nəs]

97

comment (s.), **-s** 'kɒment, -s
comment (v.), **-s, -ing, -ed** 'kɒment
[-mənt, *rarely* kɒ'ment, kə'ment], -s,
-ɪŋ, -ɪd
commentar|y, **-ies** 'kɒməntər|ɪ, -ɪz
commentat|e, **-es, -ing, -ed, -or/s**
'kɒmənteɪt [-men-], -s, -ɪŋ, -ɪd, -ə*/z
commerce 'kɒmɜːs
commerci|al, **-ally** kə'mɜː∫|l, -əlɪ [-l̩ɪ]
commercialese kə‚mɜː∫ə'liːz [-∫l̩'iːz]
commerciali|sm, **-st/s** kə'mɜː∫əlɪ|zəm
[-∫lɪ-], -st/s
commerciality kə‚mɜː∫ɪ'ælətɪ [-ɪtɪ]
commercializ|e [-is|e], **-es, -ing, -ed**
kə'mɜː∫əlaɪz [-∫laɪz], -ɪz, -ɪŋ, -d
comminat|e, **-es, -ing, -ed** 'kɒmɪneɪt, -s,
-ɪŋ, -ɪd
commination, **-s** ‚kɒmɪ'neɪ∫n, -z
comminatory 'kɒmmətərɪ [-neɪt-]
comming|le, **-les, -ling, -led** kɒ'mɪŋg|l
[kəʊ'm-], -lz, -lɪŋ [-l̩ŋ], -ld
comminut|e, **-es, -ing, -ed** 'kɒmɪnjuːt,
-s, -ɪŋ, -ɪd
comminution ‚kɒmɪ'njuː∫n
commiserat|e, **-es, -ing, -ed** kə'mɪzəreɪt
[kɒ'm-], -s, -ɪŋ, -ɪd
commiseration kə‚mɪzə'reɪ∫n [kɒ‚m-]
commissar, **-s** 'kɒmɪsɑː [‚--'-'], -z
commissarial ‚kɒmɪ'seərɪəl
commissariat ‚kɒmɪ'seərɪət [-'sær-,
-rɪæt]
commissar|y, **-ies** 'kɒmɪsər|ɪ [kə'mɪs-],
-ɪz
commissi|on (s. v.), **-ons, -oning, -oned,
-oner/s** kə'mɪ∫|n, -nz, -n̩ɪŋ [-ənɪŋ],
-nd, -ŋə*/z [-ənə*/z, -nə*/z]
commission-agent, **-s** kə'mɪ∫n̩‚eɪdʒənt
-s
commissionaire, **-s** kə‚mɪ∫ə'neə*
[-∫n̩'eə*, -sjə'neə*], -z
commissure, **-s** 'kɒmɪ‚sjʊə* [-ɪ‚∫ʊə*], -z
commit, **-s, -ting, -ted, -ter/s, -ment/s**
kə'mɪt, -s, -ɪŋ, -ɪd, -ə*/z, -mənt/s
committal, **-s** kə'mɪtl, -z
committee (*council*), **-s** kə'mɪtɪ, -z
committee (*one committed*), **-s** ‚kɒmɪ'tiː,
-z
committor, **-s** ‚kɒmɪ'tɔː*, -z
commix, **-es, -ing, -ed** kɒ'mɪks, -ɪz, -ɪŋ,
-t
commode, **-s** kə'məʊd, -z
commodious, **-ly, -ness** kə'məʊdjəs
[-dɪəs], -lɪ, -nɪs [-nəs]
commodit|y, **-ies** kə'mɒdət|ɪ [-ɪt|ɪ], -ɪz
commodore, **-s** 'kɒmədɔː* [-dɔə*], -z
common (s. adj.), **-s ; -er, -est, -ly, -ness**
'kɒmən, -z; -ə*, -ɪst, -lɪ, -nɪs [-nəs]
commonage 'kɒmənɪdʒ

commonalt|y, **-ies** 'kɒmən̩t|ɪ [-nəl-],
-ɪz
Commondale 'kɒməndeɪl
commoner, **-s** 'kɒmənə*, -z
common law ‚kɒmən'lɔː ['---]
commonplace (s. adj.), **-s** 'kɒmənpleɪs,
-ɪz
common-room, **-s** 'kɒmənrʊm [-ruːm],
-z
commons (C.) 'kɒmənz
commonwealth, **-s** 'kɒmənwelθ, -s
commotion, **-s** kə'məʊ∫n, -z
communal, **-ly** 'kɒmjʊnl [kə'mjuːnl], -lɪ
commune (s.), **-s** 'kɒmjuːn, -z
commun|e (v.), **-es, -ing, -ed** kə'mjuːn
['kɒmjuːn], -z, -ɪŋ ['kɒmjʊnɪŋ], -d
communicab|le, **-ly, -leness** kə'mjuːnɪ-
kəb|l [-'mjʊn-], -lɪ, -lnɪs [-nəs]
communicant, **-s** kə'mjuːnɪkənt
[-'mjʊn-], -s
communicat|e, **-es, -ing, -ed, -or/s**
kə'mjuːnɪkeɪt [-'mjʊn-], -s, -ɪŋ, -ɪd,
-ə*/z
communication, **-s** kə‚mjuːnɪ'keɪ∫n
[-‚mjʊn-], -z
communicative, **-ness** kə'mjuːnɪkətɪv
[-'mjʊn-, -keɪt-], -nɪs [-nəs]
communion, **-s** kə'mjuːnjən [-nɪən], -z
communiqué, **-s** kə'mjuːnɪkeɪ [kɒ'm-,
-'mjʊn-] (kɔmynike), -z
communi|sm, **-st/s** 'kɒmjʊnɪ|zəm
[-mjuːn-, -mjən-], -st/s
communit|y, **-ies** kə'mjuːnət|ɪ [-ɪt|ɪ], -ɪz
commutability kə‚mjuːtə'bɪlətɪ [-lɪt-]
commutable kə'mjuːtəbl
commutation, **-s** ‚kɒmjuː'teɪ∫n [-mjʊ-],
-z
commutative, **-ly** kə'mjuːtətɪv ['kɒm-
juːteɪtɪv, -mjʊ-], -lɪ
commutat|e, **-es, -ing, -ed, -or/s**
'kɒmjuːteɪt [-mjʊ-], -s, -ɪŋ, -ɪd, -ə*/z
commut|e, **-es, -ing, -ed, -er/s** kə'mjuːt
[kɒ'm-], -s, -ɪŋ, -ɪd, -ə*/z
Como 'kəʊməʊ
Comont 'kəʊmɒnt
Comorin 'kɒmərɪn
comose 'kəʊməʊs
compact (s.), **-s** 'kɒmpækt, -s
†compact (adj. v.), **-er, -est, -ly, -ness; -s,
-ing, -ed** kəm'pækt, -ə*, -ɪst, -lɪ, -nɪs
[-nəs]; -s, -ɪŋ, -ɪd
companion, **-s, -ship** kəm'pænjən, -z,
-∫ɪp
companionable, **-ness** kəm'pænjənəbl,
-nɪs [-nəs]
companionate kəm'pænjənɪt [-nət]
companion-way, **-s** kəm'pænjənweɪ, -z
compan|y, **-ies** 'kʌmpən|ɪ, -ɪz

comparability ˌkɒmpərə'bɪlətɪ [-lɪt-]
comparab|le, -ly, -leness 'kɒmpərəb|l,
-lɪ, -lnɪs [-nəs]
comparative (s. adj.), **-s, -ly** kəm-
'pærətɪv, -z, -lɪ
compar|e (s. v.), **-es, -ing, -ed** kəm'peə*,
-z, -rɪŋ, -d
comparison, **-s** kəm'pærɪsn, -z
compartment, **-s** kəm'pɑːtmənt, -s
compartmentalization [-isa-] 'kɒm-
pɑːtˌmentlaɪ'zeɪʃn [-ɪz-]
compartmentaliz|e [-is|e], **-es, -ing, -ed**
ˌkɒmpɑːt'mentlaɪz, -ɪz, -ɪŋ, -d
compass (s. v.), **-es, -ing, -ed** 'kʌmpəs,
-ɪz, -ɪŋ, -t
compassion kəm'pæʃn
compassionate, **-ly, -ness** kəm'pæʃənət
[-ʃn̩ət, -ʃnət, -ɪt], -lɪ, -nɪs [-nəs]
compatibility kəmˌpætə'bɪlətɪ [-tɪ'b-,
-lɪt-]
compatib|le, **-ly, -leness** kəm'pætəb|l
[-tɪb-], -lɪ, -lnɪs [-nəs]
compatriot, **-s** kəm'pætrɪət [kɒm-], -s
compeer, **-s** kɒm'pɪə* ['kɒmˌpɪə*], -z
compel, **-s, -ling, -led; -lable** kəm'pel,
-z, -ɪŋ, -d; -əbl
compendious, **-ly, -ness** kəm'pendɪəs
[-djəs], -lɪ, -nɪs [-nəs]
compendium, **-s** kəm'pendɪəm [-djəm],
-z
compensat|e, **-es, -ing, -ed** 'kɒmpen-
seɪt [-pən-], -s, -ɪŋ, -ɪd
compensation, **-s** ˌkɒmpen'seɪʃn [-pən-],
-z
compensative kəm'pensətɪv ['kɒmpen-
seɪt-, 'kɒmpənseɪt-]
compensatory ˌkɒmpen'seɪtərɪ [kəm-
'pensətərɪ, 'kɒmpenseɪtərɪ, 'kɒmpən-
seɪtərɪ, ˌkɒmpən'seɪtərɪ]
comper|e (s. v.), **-es, -ing, -ed** 'kɒmpeə*,
-z, -rɪŋ, -d
compet|e, **-es, -ing, -ed** kəm'piːt, -s, -ɪŋ,
-ɪd
competen|ce, **-cy, -t/ly** 'kɒmpɪtən|s
[-pət-], -sɪ, -t/lɪ
competition, **-s** ˌkɒmpɪ'tɪʃn [-pə't-], -z
competitive kəm'petətɪv [-tɪt-]
competitor, **-s** kəm'petɪtə* [-tətə*], -z
compilation, **-s** ˌkɒmpɪ'leɪʃn [-paɪ'l-], -z
compil|e, **-es, -ing, -ed, -er/s** kəm'paɪl,
-z, -ɪŋ, -d, -ə*/z
complacen|ce, **-cy, -t/ly** kəm'pleɪsn|s,
-sɪ, -t/lɪ
complain, **-s, -ing, -ed, -er/s** kəm'pleɪn,
-z, -ɪŋ, -d, -ə*/z
complainant, **-s** kəm'pleɪnənt, -s
complaint, **-s** kəm'pleɪnt, -s
complaisan|ce, **-t/ly** kəm'pleɪzən|s, -t/lɪ

complement (s.), **-s** 'kɒmplɪmənt, -s
complement (v.), **-s, -ing, -ed** 'kɒm-
plɪment [ˌkɒmplɪ'ment], -s, -ɪŋ, -ɪd
complement|al, **-ary** ˌkɒmplɪ'ment|l,
-ərɪ
complet|e (adj. v.), **-est, -ely, -eness;
-es, -ing, -ed** kəm'pliːt, -ɪst, -lɪ, -nɪs
[-nəs]; -s, -ɪŋ, -ɪd
completion kəm'pliːʃn
†complex (s.) **-es** 'kɒmpleks, -ɪz
complexion, **-s, -ed** kəm'plekʃn, -z, -d
complexit|y, **-ies** kəm'pleksət|ɪ [kɒm-,
-ɪt|ɪ], -ɪz
complian|ce, **-ces, -t/ly** kəm'plaɪən|s,
-sɪz, -t/lɪ
complicat|e, **-es, -ing, -ed** 'kɒmplɪkeɪt,
-s, -ɪŋ, -ɪd
complication, **-s** ˌkɒmplɪ'keɪʃn, -z
complicity kəm'plɪsətɪ [kɒm-, -ɪtɪ]
compliment (s.), **-s** 'kɒmplɪmənt, -s
compliment (v.), **-s, -ing, -ed** 'kɒmplɪ-
ment [ˌkɒmplɪ'ment], -s, -ɪŋ, -ɪd
complimentar|y (s. adj.), **-ies, -ily**
ˌkɒmplɪ'mentər|ɪ, -ɪz, -əlɪ [-ɪlɪ]
complin, **-s** 'kɒmplɪn, -z
compline, **-s** 'kɒmplɪn [-laɪn], -z
compl|y, **-ies, -ying, -ied** kəm'pl|aɪ, -aɪz,
-aɪɪŋ, -aɪd
compo 'kɒmpəʊ
component, **-s** kəm'pəʊnənt, -s
comport, **-s, -ing, -ed, -ment** kəm'pɔːt,
-s, -ɪŋ, -ɪd, -mənt
compos|e, **-es, -ing, -ed, -er/s** kəm'pəʊz,
-ɪz, -ɪŋ, -d, -ə*/z
compos|ed (adj.), **-edly, -edness** kəm-
'pəʊz|d, -ɪdlɪ, -ɪdnɪs [-nəs]
composite, **-ly, -ness** 'kɒmpəzɪt [-sɪt,
-zaɪt, -saɪt], -lɪ, -nɪs [-nəs]
composition, **-s** ˌkɒmpə'zɪʃn, -z
compositor, **-s** kəm'pɒzɪtə*, -z
compost, **-s** 'kɒmpɒst, -s
composure kəm'pəʊʒə*
compote, **-s** 'kɒmpɒt [-pəʊt] (kɔ̃pɔt), -s
compound (s. adj.), **-s** 'kɒmpaʊnd, -z
compound (v.), **-s, -ing, -ed, -able**
kəm'paʊnd [kɒm-], -z, -ɪŋ, -ɪd, -əbl
comprehend, **-s, -ing, -ed** ˌkɒmprɪ-
'hend, -z, -ɪŋ, -ɪd
comprehensibility 'kɒmprɪˌhensə'bɪlətɪ
[-sɪ'b-, -lɪt-]
comprehensib|le, **-ly, -leness** ˌkɒmprɪ-
'hensəb|l [-sɪb-], -lɪ, -lnɪs [-nəs]
comprehension ˌkɒmprɪ'henʃn
comprehensive, **-ly, -ness** ˌkɒmprɪ'hensɪv, -lɪ, -nɪs [-nəs]
compress (s.), **-es** 'kɒmpres, -ɪz
compress (v.), **-es, -ing, -ed, -or/s**
kəm'pres, -ɪz, -ɪŋ, -t, -ə*/z

compressibility kəm‚presə'bɪlətɪ [-sɪ'b-, -lɪt-]

compressible, -ness kəm'presəbl [-sɪb-], -nɪs [-nəs]

compression, -s kəm'preʃn, -z

compressive kəm'presɪv

compris|e, -es, -ing, -ed; -able kəm-'praɪz, -ɪz, -ɪŋ, -d; -əbl

compromis|e (s. v.), -es, -ing/ly, -ed, -er/s 'kɒmprəmaɪz [-prʊm-], -ɪz, -ɪŋ/lɪ, -d, -ə*/z

comptometer, -s kɒmp'tɒmɪtə* [-mətə*], -z

Compton 'kɒmptən, 'kʌm-
Note.—As surname more often 'kʌm-; as place-name more often 'kɒm-; London street generally 'kɒm-.

comptroller, -s kən'trəʊlə*, -z

compulsion kəm'pʌlʃn

compuls|ive/ly, -ory, -orily kəm-'pʌls|ɪv/lɪ, -ərɪ, -ərəlɪ [-ərɪlɪ]

compunction kəm'pʌŋkʃn

compunctious kəm'pʌŋkʃəs

compurgation ‚kɒmpɜ:'geɪʃn

compurgator, -s 'kɒmpɜ:geɪtə*, -z

computable kəm'pju:təbl ['kɒmpjut-əbl]

computation, -s ‚kɒmpju:'teɪʃn [-pjʊ-], -z

computator, -s 'kɒmpju:teɪtə* [-pjʊ-], -z

comput|e, -es, -ing, -ed, -er/s kəm'pju:t, -s, -ɪŋ, -ɪd, -ə*/z

computerization [-isa-] kəm‚pju:təraɪ-'zeɪʃn [-rɪz-]

computeriz|e [-is|e], -es, -ing, -ed kəm'pju:təraɪz, -ɪz, -ɪŋ, -d

computist, -s kəm'pju:tɪst, -s

comrade, -s, -ship 'kɒmreɪd ['kɒmrɪd, 'kʌmrɪd], -z, -ʃɪp

Comte kɔ̃:nt [kɔ:nt] (kɔ̃:t)

comti|sm, -st/s 'kɔ̃:ntɪ|zəm ['kɔ:nt-], -st/s

Comus 'kəʊməs

Comyn 'kʌmɪn

con (s. v.), -s, -ning, -ned kɒn, -z, -ɪŋ, -d

Conan (personal name) 'kəʊnən, 'kɒnən, (place in Scotland) 'kɒnən
Note.—The members of the family of Sir Arthur Conan Doyle pronounce 'kəʊnən.

Conant 'kɒnənt

conation kəʊ'neɪʃn

conative 'kəʊnətɪv

concatenat|e, -es, -ing, -ed kən'kæt-meɪt [kɒn-], -s, -ɪŋ, -ɪd

concatenation, -s kən‚kætɪ'neɪʃn [kɒn-, ‚kɒnkæt-], -z

concave 'kɒŋkeɪv ['kɒnkeɪv, ‚kɒn'keɪv kɒn'k-]
Note.—The form kɒn'keɪv is not used attributively.

concavit|y, -ies kɒn'kævət|ɪ [kən-, -ɪt|ɪ], -ɪz

conceal, -s, -ing, -ed, -ment/s; -able kən'si:l, -z, -ɪŋ, -d, -mənt/s; -əbl

conced|e, -es, -ing, -ed kən'si:d, -z, -ɪŋ, -ɪd

conceit, -s kən'si:t, -s

conceited, -ly, -ness kən'si:tɪd, -lɪ, -nɪs [-nəs]

conceivab|le, -ly, -leness kən'si:vəb|l, -lɪ, -lnɪs [-nəs]

conceiv|e, -es, -ing, -ed kən'si:v, -z, -ɪŋ, -d

concent kən'sent [kɒn-]

concentrat|e, -es, -ing, -ed (s. v.), 'kɒn-səntreɪt [-sɪn-, -sen-], -s, -ɪŋ, -ɪd

concentration, -s ‚kɒnsən'treɪʃn [-sɪn-, -sen-], -z

concentrative 'kɒnsəntreɪtɪv [-sɪn-, -sen-]

concent|re, -res, -ring, -ering, -red kɒn'sent|ə*, -əz, -rɪŋ, -ərɪŋ, -əd

concentric, -ally kən'sentrɪk [kɒn-], -əlɪ

concept, -s 'kɒnsept, -s

conception, -s kən'sepʃn, -z

†conceptual kən'septʃʊəl [-tjwəl, -tjʊəl]

concern (s. v.), -s, -ing, -ed, -ment/s kən'sɜ:n, -z, -ɪŋ, -d, -mənt/s

concern|ed (adj.), -edly, -edness kən-'sɜ:n|d, -ɪdlɪ, -ɪdnɪs [-nəs]

concert (s.) (musical entertainment), -s 'kɒnsət, -s

concert (C.) (union), -s 'kɒnsɜ:t [-sət], -s

concert (v.), -s, -ing, -ed kən'sɜ:t, -s, -ɪŋ, -ɪd

concertante ‚kɒntʃə'tæntɪ [-tʃeə-, -teɪ]

concertina, -s ‚kɒnsə'ti:nə, -z

concerto, -s kən'tʃeətəʊ [-'tʃɜ:t-], -z

concession, -s kən'seʃn, -z

concessionaire, -s kən‚seʃə'neə* [-ʃn̩'eə*], -z

concessionary kən'seʃnərɪ [-ʃənə-]

concessive kən'sesɪv

conch, -s kɒntʃ, -ɪz [kɒŋk, -s]

concha, -s 'kɒŋkə, -z

conchoid, -s 'kɒŋkɔɪd, -z

concholog|ist/s, -y kɒŋ'kɒlədʒ|ɪst/s [kɒn'k], -ɪ

concierge, -s ‚kɒnsɪ'eəʒ [‚kɔ:ns-, ‚kɔ̃:ns-, '---] (kɔ̃sjɛrʒ), -ɪz

conciliat|e, -es, -ing, -ed, -or/s kən-'sɪlɪeɪt, -s, -ɪŋ, -ɪd, -ə*/z

conciliation kən‚sɪlɪ'eɪʃn

conciliative kən'sılıətıv [-ljət-, -lıeıt-]
conciliatory kən'sılıətərı [-ljə-, -lıeıtərı]
concise, -r, -st, -ly, -ness kən'saıs, -ə*, -ıst, -lı, -nıs [-nəs]
concision, -s kən'sıʒn, -z
conclave, -s 'kɒŋkleıv ['kɒnk-], -z
conclud|e, -es, -ing, -ed kən'klu:d [kəŋ'k-], -z, -ıŋ, -ıd
conclusion, -s kən'klu:ʒn [kəŋ'k-], -z
conclusive, -ly, -ness kən'klu:sıv [kəŋ'k-], -lı, -nıs [-nəs]
concoct, -s, -ing, -ed, -er/s kən'kɒkt [kɒŋ'k-], -s, -ıŋ, -ıd, -ə*/z
concoction, -s kən'kɒkʃn [kəŋ'k-], -z
concomitan|ce, -cy, -t/ly kən-'kɒmıtən|s, -sı, -t/lı
concord (s.), -s 'kɒŋkɔ:d ['kɒnk-], -z
concord (v.), -s, -ing, -ed kən'kɔ:d [kəŋ'k-], -z, -ıŋ, -ıd
concordan|ce, -ces, -t/ly kən'kɔ:dən|s [kəŋ'k-], -sız, -t/lı
concordat, -s kɒn'kɔ:dæt [kən'k-, kəŋ'k-], -s
concourse, -s 'kɒŋkɔ:s ['kɒnk-, -kɔəs], -ız
concrete (s. adj.) 'kɒŋkri:t ['kɒnk-]
concret|e (v.) (cover with concrete), -es, -ing, -ed 'kɒŋkri:t ['kɒnk-], -s, -ıŋ, -ıd
concret|e (v.) (coalesce, cause to coalesce), -es, -ing, -ed kən'kri:t [kəŋ'k-], -s, -ıŋ, -ıd
concrete|ly, -ness 'kɒŋkri:t|lı ['kɒnk-, kɒn'k-], -nıs [-nəs]
concretion, -s kən'kri:ʃn [kəŋ-, kɒn-], -z
concretiz|e [-is|e], -es, -ing, -ed 'kɒŋ-kri:taız ['kɒnk-, -krı-], -ız, -ıŋ, -d
concubinage kɒn'kju:bınıdʒ [kən-]
concubine, -s 'kɒŋkjʊbaın ['kɒnk-], -z
concupiscen|ce, -t kən'kju:pısən|s [‚kɒnkju:'p-, -kjʊ-], -t
concur, -s, -ring, -red kən'kɜ:* [kəŋ'k-], -z, -rıŋ, -d
concurren|ce, -cy, -t/ly kən'kʌrən|s [kəŋ'k-], -sı, -t/lı
concuss, -es, -ing, -ed kən'kʌs [kəŋ'k-], -ız, -ıŋ, -t
concussion, -s kən'kʌʃn [kəŋ'k-], -z
concyclic kɒn'saıklık [kən-]
condemn, -s, -ing, -ed; -able kən'dem, -z, -ıŋ, -d; -nəbl
condemnation, -s ‚kɒndem'neıʃn [-dəm-], -z
condemnatory kən'demnətərı [‚kɒn-dem'neıtərı, -dəm-]
condensation, -s ‚kɒnden'seıʃn [-dən-], -z

condens|e, -es, -ing, -ed; -able kən-'dens, -ız, -ıŋ, -t; -əbl
condenser, -s kən'densə*, -z
condescend, -s, -ing/ly, -ed ‚kɒndı'send, -z, -ıŋ/lı, -ıd
condescension ‚kɒndı'senʃn
condign, -ly, -ness kən'daın, -lı, -nıs [-nəs]
condiment, -s 'kɒndımənt, -s
conditi|on (s. v.), -ons, -oning, -oned kən'dıʃ|n, -nz, -ṇıŋ [-ənıŋ, -nıŋ], -nd
condi|tional, -tionally kən'dı|ʃənl [-ʃnəl, -ʃṇl, -ʃn̩l, -ʃənəl], -ʃṇəlı [-ʃnəlı, -ʃṇlı, -ʃn̩lı, -ʃənəlı]
condol|e, -es, -ing, -ed, -ement/s kən-'dəʊl, -z, -ıŋ, -d, -mənt/s
condolence, -s kən'dəʊləns ['kɒn-dələns], -ız
condolent kən'dəʊlənt
condom, -s 'kɒndəm [-dɒm], -z
condominium, -s ‚kɒndə'mınıəm [-njəm], -z
condonation, -s ‚kɒndəʊ'neıʃn, -z
condon|e, -es, -ing, -ed kən'dəʊn, -z, -ıŋ, -d
condor, -s 'kɒndɔ:* [-də*], -z
conduc|e, -es, -ing, -ed, -ement/s kən'dju:s, -ız, -ıŋ, -t, -mənt/s
conducive, -ly, -ness kən'dju:sıv, -lı, -nıs [-nəs]
conduct (s.), -s 'kɒndʌkt [-dəkt], -s
conduct (v.), -s, -ing, -ed, -or/s, -ance kən-'dʌkt, -s, -ıŋ, -ıd, -ə*/z, -əns
conductibility kən‚dʌktı'bılətı [-tə'b-, -lıt-]
conductible kən'dʌktəbl [-tıb-]
conduction kən'dʌkʃn
conductive kən'dʌktıv
conductivity ‚kɒndʌk'tıvətı [-dək-, -ıtı]
conductress, -es kən'dʌktrıs [-tres, -trəs], -ız
conduit, -s 'kɒndıt [old-fashioned 'kʌndıt, as an electrical term also 'kɒndjʊt and 'kɒndwıt], -s
Conduit (Street) 'kɒndıt ['kʌn-]
Condy 'kɒndı
condyle, -s 'kɒndıl [-daıl], -z
cone, -s kəʊn, -z
coney (C.), -s 'kəʊnı, -z
confab, -s 'kɒnfæb [kɒn'fæb], -z
confabulat|e, -es, -ing, -ed kən'fæbjʊ-leıt [kɒn-], -s, -ıŋ, -ıd
confabulation, -s kən‚fæbjʊ'leıʃn [kɒn-], -z
confect (s.), -s 'kɒnfekt, -s
confect (v.), -s, -ing, -ed kən'fekt, -s, -ıŋ, -ıd

101

confection—conglomerate

confecti|on (s. v.), -ons, -oning, -oned, -oner/s kən'fekʃ|n, -nz, -ŋɪŋ [-ənɪŋ], -nd, -nə*/z [-ŋə*/z, -ənə*/z]
confectionery kən'fekʃŋərɪ [-ʃənərɪ, -ʃnərɪ, -ʃənrɪ]
confederac|y, -ies kən'fedərəs|ɪ, -ɪz
confederate (s. adj.), -s kən'fedərət [-rɪt], -s
confederat|e (v.), -es, -ing, -ed kən-'fedəreɪt, -s, -ɪŋ, -ɪd
confederation, -s kən,fedə'reɪʃn, -z
confer, -s, -ring, -red; -rable; -ment, -ral kən'fɜ:*, -z, -rɪŋ, -d; -rəbl; -mənt, -rəl
conference, -s 'kɒnfərəns, -ɪz
confess, -es, -ing, -ed, -edly, -or/s kən'fes, -ɪz, -ɪŋ, -t, -ɪdlɪ, -ə*/z
Note.—Some Catholics pronounce confessor as 'kɒnfesə* or 'kɒn-fesɔ:* in the sense Father Confessor
confession, -s kən'feʃn, -z
confessional, -s kən'feʃənl [-ʃnəl, -ʃn̩l], -ʃn̩|, -ʃənəl], -z
confetti kən'fetɪ [kɒn-]
confidant(e), -s ,kɒnfɪ'dænt ['kɒnfɪ-dænt], -s
confid|e, -es, -ing/ly, -ed, -er/s kən-'faɪd, -z, -ɪŋ/lɪ, -ɪd, -ə*/z
confiden|ce, -ces, -t/ly 'kɒnfɪdən|s, -sɪz, -t/lɪ
confidenti|al, -ally ,kɒnfɪ'denʃ|l, -əlɪ
configuration, -s kən,fɪgə'reɪʃn [,kɒnfɪg-, -gjʊə'r-, -gjə'r-, -gjʊ'r-], -z
confine (s.) 'kɒnfaɪn, -z
confin|e (v.), -es, -ing, -ed, -ement/s kən'faɪn, -z, -ɪŋ, -d, -mənt/s
confirm, -s, -ing, -ed, -er/s kən'fɜ:m, -z, -ɪŋ, -d, -ə*/z
confirmation, -s ,kɒnfə'meɪʃn [-fm̩'eɪ-], -z
confirmat|ive, -ory kən'fɜ:mət|ɪv, -ərɪ
confiscable kɒn'fɪskəbl [kən-]
confiscat|e, -es, -ing, -ed, -or/s 'kɒn-fɪskeɪt, -s, -ɪŋ, -ɪd, -ə*/z
confiscation, -s ,kɒnfɪ'skeɪʃn, -z
confiscatory kən'fɪskətərɪ [kɒn'f-, 'kɒnfɪskeɪtərɪ, --'---]
confiserie, -s kɒn'fi:zərɪ [-rɪ], -z
confiteor, -s kɒn'fɪtɪɔ:* [kən-], -z
conflagration, -s ,kɒnflə'greɪʃn, -z
conflat|e, -es, -ing, -ed kən'fleɪt [kɒn-], -s, -ɪŋ, -ɪd
conflation kən'fleɪʃn [kɒn-]
conflict (s.), -s 'kɒnflɪkt, -s
conflict (v.), -s, -ing, -ed kən'flɪkt, -s, -ɪŋ, -ɪd
confluen|ce, -ces, -t/ly, -t/s 'kɒn-fluən|s [-flwən-], -sɪz, -t/lɪ, -t/s

conform, -s, -ing, -ed, -er/s kən'fɔ:m, -z, -ɪŋ, -d, -ə*/z
conformability kən,fɔ:mə'bɪlətɪ [-lɪt-]
conformab|le, -ly kən'fɔ:məb|l, -lɪ
conformation, -s ,kɒnfɔ:'meɪʃn [-fə'm-], -z
conformist, -s kən'fɔ:mɪst, -s
conformit|y, -ies kən'fɔ:mət|ɪ [-ɪt|ɪ], -ɪz
confound, -s, -ing, -ed/ly kən'faʊnd [as oath also ,kɒn'faʊnd], -z, -ɪŋ, -ɪd/lɪ
confraternit|y, -ies ,kɒnfrə'tɜ:nət|ɪ [-ɪt|ɪ], -ɪz
confrère, -s 'kɒnfreə* [kɔ̃frɛ:r], -z
confront, -s, -ing, -ed kən'frʌnt, -s, -ɪŋ, -ɪd
confrontation, -s ,kɒnfrʌn'teɪʃn [-frən-], -z
Confucian, -s kən'fju:ʃn, [-ʃɪən, -ʃjən], -z
Confuciani|sm, -st/s kən'fju:ʃənɪ|zəm [-ʃɪənɪ-, -ʃjənɪ-, -ʃnɪ-], -st/s
Confucius kən'fju:ʃəs [-ʃɪəs, -ʃjəs]
confus|e, -es, -ing/ly, -ed, -edly, -edness kən'fju:z, -ɪz, -ɪŋ/lɪ, -d, -ɪdlɪ, -ɪdnɪs [-nəs]
confusion, -s kən'fju:ʒn, -z
confutable kən'fju:təbl
confutation, -s ,kɒnfju:'teɪʃn [-fjʊ't-], -z
confut|e, -es, -ing, -ed kən'fju:t, -s, -ɪŋ, -ɪd
conga, -s 'kɒŋgə, -z
congé, -s 'kɔ̃:nʒeɪ ['kɔ:nʒ-, 'kɒnʒ-] (kɔ̃ʒe), -z
congeal, -s, -ing, -ed; -able kən'dʒi:l, -z, -ɪŋ, -d; -əbl
congee, -s 'kɒndʒi:, -z
congelation ,kɒndʒɪ'leɪʃn
congener, -s 'kɒndʒɪnə* [kən'dʒi:n-], -z
congenial, -ly kən'dʒi:njəl [-nɪəl], -ɪ
congeniality kən,dʒi:nɪ'ælətɪ [-ɪtɪ]
congenit|al, -ally kən'dʒenɪt|l [kɒn-], -əlɪ [-l̩ɪ]
conger, -s 'kɒŋgə*, -z
conger-eel, -s ,kɒŋgər'i:l [-gə'i:l], -z
congeries, -s kɒn'dʒɪərɪ:z [-'dʒɪərɪz, -'dʒɪə-rɪi:z, -'dʒerɪi:z, 'kɒndʒərɪz]
congest, -s, -ing, -ed; -ive kən'dʒest, -s, -ɪŋ, -ɪd; -ɪv
congestion, -s kən'dʒestʃən [-eʃtʃ-], -z
Congleton 'kɒŋgltən
conglobat|e (adj. v.), -es, -ing, -ed 'kɒŋgləʊbeɪt ['kɒŋg-], -s, -ɪŋ, -ɪd
conglobation ,kɒŋgləʊ'beɪʃn [,kɒŋg-]
conglomerate (s. adj.), -s kən'glɒmərət [kəŋ-, kɒn-, -ɪt], -s
conglomerat|e (v.), -es, -ing, -ed kən-'glɒməreɪt [kəŋ-, kɒn-], -s, -ɪŋ, -ɪd

conglomeration, -s kən̩ˌglɒmə'reɪʃn
[kəŋ-, kɒnˌglɒm-, ˌkɒŋglɒm-, ˌkɒŋ-
glɒm-], -z
Congo 'kɒŋgəʊ
Congolese ˌkɒŋgəʊ'li:z
congratulat|e, -es, -ing, -ed, -or/s kən-
'grætʃʊleɪt [kəŋ'g-, -tjʊl-, -tʃəl-], -s,
-ɪŋ, -ɪd, -ə*/z
congratulation, -s kən̩ˌgrætʃʊ'leɪʃn
[kəŋˌg-, -tjʊ'l-, -tʃə'l-], -z
congratulatory kən'grætʃʊlətərɪ [kəŋ'g-,
-tjʊl-, -tʃəl-, -leɪtərɪ, ---'---]
congregat|e, -es, -ing, -ed 'kɒŋgrɪgeɪt,
-s, -ɪŋ, -ɪd
congregation, -s ˌkɒŋgrɪ'geɪʃn, -z
congregational ˌkɒŋgrɪ'geɪʃənl [-ʃnəl,
-ʃn̩l, -ʃnl, -ʃənəl]
congregationali|sm, -st/s ˌkɒŋgrɪ'geɪ-
ʃnəlɪ|zəm [-ʃnəlɪ-, -ʃn̩lɪ-, -ʃnlɪ-,
-ʃənəlɪ-], -st/s
Congresbury 'kɒŋzbrɪ, 'ku:mzbərɪ
congress, -es 'kɒŋgres, -ɪz
congressional kəŋ'greʃənl [kɒŋ-, -ʃnəl,
-ʃn̩l, -ʃnl, -ʃənəl]
congress|man, -men 'kɒŋgres|mən,
-mən [-men]
Congreve 'kɒŋgri:v
congruen|ce/s, -cy, -cies, -t/ly 'kɒŋ-
grʊən|s/ɪz [-grwən-], -sɪ, -sɪz, -t/lɪ
congruit|y, -ies kɒŋ'gru:ət|ɪ [kən-,
kəŋ-, -'grʊ-, -ɪt|ɪ], -ɪz
congruous, -ly, -ness 'kɒŋgrʊəs
[-grwəs], -lɪ, -nɪs [-nəs]
conic, -s, -al, -ally, -alness 'kɒnɪk, -s,
-l, -əlɪ, -lnɪs [-nəs]
conifer, -s 'kɒnɪfə* ['kəʊn-], -z
coniferous kəʊ'nɪfərəs [kɒ-]
coniform 'kəʊnɪfɔ:m
Coningham 'kʌnɪŋəm
Conisbee 'kɒnɪsbɪ
Conisbrough 'kɒnɪsbrə, 'kʌn-
Coniston 'kɒnɪstən
conjecturable kən'dʒektʃərəbl
conjectur|al, -ally kən'dʒektʃər|əl
[-tʃʊr-], -əlɪ
conject|ure (s. v.), -ures, -uring, -ured
kən'dʒektʃ|ə*, -əz, -ərɪŋ, -əd
conjoin, -s, -ing, -ed kən'dʒɔɪn [kɒn-]
-z, -ɪŋ, -d
conjoint, -ly 'kɒndʒɔɪnt [ˌkɒn'dʒ-,
kən'dʒ-], -lɪ
conjug|al, -ally 'kɒndʒʊg|l [-dʒəg-],
-əlɪ
conjugality ˌkɒndʒʊ'gælətɪ [-ɪtɪ]
conjugate (s. adj), -s 'kɒndʒʊgɪt
[dʒəg-, -geɪt], -s
conjugat|e (v.), -es, -ing, -ed 'kɒndʒʊ-
geɪt [-dʒəg-], -s, -ɪŋ, -ɪd

conjugation, -s ˌkɒndʒʊ'geɪʃn [-dʒə'g-],
-z
†conjunct (adj.), -ly kən'dʒʌŋkt [ˌkɒn'dʒ-,
'kɒndʒ-], -lɪ
conjunction, -s kən'dʒʌŋkʃn, -z
conjunctiva ˌkɒndʒʌŋk'taɪvə
conjunctive, -ly kən'dʒʌŋktɪv, -lɪ
conjunctivitis kən̩ˌdʒʌŋktɪ'vaɪtɪs
conjuncture, -s kən'dʒʌŋktʃə*, -z
conjuration, -s ˌkɒndʒʊə'reɪʃn, -z
conjur|e (charge solemnly), -es, -ing, -ed
kən'dʒʊə*, -z, -rɪŋ, -d
conj|ure (invoke a spirit, do things as if
by magic), -ures, -uring, -ured,
-urer/s, -uror/s 'kʌndʒ|ə*, -əz, -ərɪŋ,
-əd, -ərə*/z, -ərə*/z
conk, -s kɒŋk, -s
conker, -s 'kɒŋkə*, -z
Conn. (1) = Connecticut, (2) = Connaught
Connally 'kɒnəlɪ
connate 'kɒneɪt
Connaught 'kɒnɔ:t
connect, -s, -ing, -ed/ly; -able, -or/s
kə'nekt, -s, -ɪŋ, -ɪd/lɪ; -əbl, -ə*/z
connectible kə'nektəbl [-tɪb-]
Connecticut kə'netɪkət
connection, -s kə'nekʃn, -z
connective (s. adj.), -s, -ly kə'nektɪv,
-z, -lɪ
Connemara ˌkɒnɪ'mɑ:rə [-nə'm-]
connexion, -s kə'nekʃn, -z
Connie 'kɒnɪ
conning-tower, -s 'kɒnɪŋˌtaʊə*, -z
connivance kə'naɪvəns
conniv|e, -es, -ing, -ed; -er/s kə'naɪv,
-z, -ɪŋ, -d; -ə*/z
connoisseur, -s ˌkɒnə'sɜ:* [ˌkɒnɪ-,
-'sʊə*, -'sjʊə*], -z
Connolly 'kɒnəlɪ
Connor 'kɒnə*
connotat|e, -es, -ing, -ed 'kɒnəʊteɪt, -s,
-ɪŋ, -ɪd
connotation, -s ˌkɒnəʊ'teɪʃn, -z
connotative 'kɒnəʊteɪtɪv [kə'nəʊtətɪv]
connot|e, -es, -ing, -ed kə'nəʊt [kɒ'n-],
-s, -ɪŋ, -ɪd
connubial, -ly kə'nju:bjəl [kɒ'n-, -bɪəl],
-ɪ
connubiality kəˌnju:bɪ'ælətɪ [kɒˌn-,
-ɪtɪ]
conoid, -s 'kəʊnɔɪd, -z
conoidal kəʊ'nɔɪdl
Conolly 'kɒnəlɪ
conqu|er, -ers, -ering, -ered, -eror/s;
-erable 'kɒŋk|ə*, -əz, -ərɪŋ, -əd,
-ərə*/z; -ərəbl
conquest (C.), -s 'kɒŋkwest, -s

conquistador, -s kɒnˈkwɪstədɔː*
[kɒŋˈk-, -ˌ—ˈ-], -z
Conrad ˈkɒnræd
consanguine kɒnˈsæŋgwɪn
consanguin|eous,-ity|ˌkɒnsæŋˈgwɪn|ɪəs,
-əti [-ɪti]
conscience, -s ˈkɒnʃəns, -ɪz
conscientious, -ly, -ness ˌkɒnʃɪˈenʃəs
[kɒnˈʃjen-], -lɪ, -nɪs [-nəs]
conscionab|le, -ly, -leness ˈkɒnʃnəb|l
[-ʃnə-, -ʃənə-], -lɪ, -lnɪs [-nəs]
conscious, -ly, -ness ˈkɒnʃəs, -lɪ, -nɪs
[-nəs]
conscrib|e, -es, -ing, -ed kənˈskraɪb, -z,
-ɪŋ, -d
conscript (s.), -s ˈkɒnskrɪpt, -s
conscript (v.), -s, -ing, -ed kənˈskrɪpt,
-s, -ɪŋ, -ɪd
conscription, -s kənˈskrɪpʃn, -z
consecrat|e, -es, -ing, -ed, -or/s ˈkɒnsɪ-
kreɪt, -s, -ɪŋ, -ɪd, -ə*/z
consecration, -s ˌkɒnsɪˈkreɪʃn, -z
consecutive, -ly, -ness kənˈsekjʊtɪv, -lɪ,
-nɪs [-nəs]
consensus kənˈsensəs [kɒn-]
consent (s. v.), -s, -ing, -ed kənˈsent, -s,
-ɪŋ, -ɪd
consequen|ce/s, -t/ly ˈkɒnsɪkwən|s/ɪz,
-t/lɪ
consequenti|al, -ally ˌkɒnsɪˈkwenʃ|l,
-əlɪ
conservable kənˈsɜːvəbl
conservanc|y, -ies kənˈsɜːvəns|ɪ, -ɪz
†conservation ˌkɒnsəˈveɪʃn
conservatism kənˈsɜːvətɪzəm
conservative, -s, -ly, -ness kənˈsɜːvətɪv,
-z, -lɪ, -nɪs [-nəs]
conservatoire, -s kənˈsɜːvətwɑː* [kɒn-,
-ˈseəv-, -twɔː*], -z
conservator (preserver), -s ˈkɒnsəveɪtə*,
-z
conservator (official guardian), -s kən-
ˈsɜːvətə*, -z
conservator|y, -ies kənˈsɜːvətr|ɪ, -ɪz
conserve (s.), -s kənˈsɜːv [ˈkɒnsɜːv], -z
conserv|e (v.), -es, -ing, -ed kənˈsɜːv, -z,
-ɪŋ, -d
consid|er, -ers, -ering, -ered kənˈsɪd|ə*,
-əz, -ərɪŋ, -əd
considerab|le, -ly, -leness kənˈsɪdər-
əb|l, -lɪ, -lnɪs [-nəs]
considerate, -ly, -ness kənˈsɪdərət [-ɪt],
-lɪ, -nɪs [-nəs]
consideration, -s kənˌsɪdəˈreɪʃn, -z
consign, -s, -ing, -ed, -er/s, -ment/s;
-able kənˈsaɪn, -z, -ɪŋ, -d, -ə*/z,
-mənt/s; -əbl
consignation ˌkɒnsaɪˈneɪʃn

consignee, -s ˌkɒnsaɪˈniː [-sɪˈniː], -z
consist, -s, -ing, -ed kənˈsɪst, -s, -ɪŋ, -ɪd
consisten|ce, -cy, -cies, -t/ly kən-
ˈsɪstən|s, -sɪ, -sɪz, -t/lɪ
consistorial ˌkɒnsɪˈstɔːrɪəl
consistor|y, -ies kənˈsɪstər|ɪ, -ɪz
consolable kənˈsəʊləbl
consolation, -s ˌkɒnsəˈleɪʃn [-sl̩ˈeɪʃ-,
-səʊ-], -z
consolatory kənˈsɒlətərɪ [-ˈsəʊl-]
console (s.), -s ˈkɒnsəʊl, -z
consol|e (v.), -es, -ing, -ed, -er/s kən-
ˈsəʊl, -z, -ɪŋ, -d, -ə*/z
consolidat|e, -es, -ing, -ed, -or/s; -ive
kənˈsɒlɪdeɪt, -s, -ɪŋ, -ɪd, -ə*/z; -ɪv
consolidation, -s kənˌsɒlɪˈdeɪʃn, -z
consols ˈkɒnsəlz [-sɒlz]
consommé kənˈsɒmeɪ [ˈkɒnsɒmeɪ]
(kɔ̃sɔme)
consonance, -s ˈkɒnsənəns [-sn̩ə-,
-snə-], -ɪz
consonant (s. adj.), -s, -ly ˈkɒnsənənt
[-snə-, -snə-], -s, -lɪ
consonant|al, -ally ˌkɒnsəˈnænt|l
[-sn̩ˈæ-], -əlɪ
consort (s.), -s ˈkɒnsɔːt, -s
consort (v.), -s, -ing, -ed kənˈsɔːt
[kɒnˈs-], -s, -ɪŋ, -ɪd
consortium, -s kənˈsɔːtjəm [-tɪəm], -z
conspectus, -es kənˈspektəs, -ɪz
conspicuous, -ly, -ness kənˈspɪkjʊəs
[-kjwəs], -lɪ, -nɪs [-nəs]
conspirac|y, -ies kənˈspɪrəs|ɪ, -ɪz
conspirator, -s kənˈspɪrətə* [-rɪt-], -z
conspiratorial kənˌspɪrəˈtɔːrɪəl
[ˌkɒnsp-, -rjəl]
conspir|e, -es, -ing, -ed, -er/s kən-
ˈspaɪə*, -z, -rɪŋ, -d, -rə*/z
constable, -s ˈkʌnstəbl [ˈkɒn-], -z
Constable (surname) ˈkʌnstəbl, in Scotland ˈkɒn-
constabular|y, -ies kənˈstæbjʊlər|ɪ, -ɪz
Constance ˈkɒnstəns
constancy ˈkɒnstənsɪ
constant (s. adj.), -s, -ly, -ness ˈkɒn-
stənt, -s, -lɪ, -nɪs [-nəs]
Constantine ˈkɒnstəntaɪn
Constantinople ˌkɒnstæntɪˈnəʊpl
constellation, -s ˌkɒnstəˈleɪʃn [-teˈl-,
-tɪˈl-], -z
consternat|e, -es, -ing, -ed ˈkɒnstəneɪt,
-s, -ɪŋ, -ɪd
consternation ˌkɒnstəˈneɪʃn
constipat|e, -es, -ing, -ed ˈkɒnstɪpeɪt, -s,
-ɪŋ, -ɪd
constipation ˌkɒnstɪˈpeɪʃn
constituen|cy, -cies, -t/s kənˈstɪtjʊən|sɪ
[-tjwən-, -tʃʊən-], -sɪz, -t/s

constitut|e, -es, -ing, -ed ˈkɒnstɪtjuːt, -s, -ɪŋ, -ɪd
constitution, -s ˌkɒnstɪˈtjuːʃn, -z
constitu|tional, -tionally ˌkɒnstɪˈtjuː|-ʃənl [-ʃnəl, -ʃn̩l, -ʃn̩l, -ʃənəl], -ʃn̩əlɪ [-ʃnəlɪ, -ʃn̩l̩ɪ, -ʃn̩l̩ɪ, -ʃənəlɪ]
constitutionali|sm, -st|s ˌkɒnstɪˈtjuː-ʃn̩əlɪ|zəm [-ʃnəlɪ-, -ʃn̩l̩ɪ-, -ʃn̩l̩ɪ-, -ʃənəlɪ-], -st/s
constitutionaliz|e [-is|e], -es, -ing, -ed ˌkɒnstɪˈtjuː:ʃn̩əlaɪz [-ʃnəl-, -ʃn̩l̩-, -ʃn̩l̩-, -ʃənəl-], -ɪz, -ɪŋ, -d
constitutive ˈkɒnstɪtjuːtɪv [kənˈstɪtjuː-, -tjʊt-]
constrain, -s, -ing, -ed, -edly; -able kənˈstreɪn, -z, -ɪŋ, -d, -ɪdlɪ; -əbl
constraint, -s kənˈstreɪnt, -s
constrict, -s, -ing, -ed, -or/s; -ive kənˈstrɪkt, -s, -ɪŋ, -ɪd, -ə*/z; -ɪv
constriction, -s kənˈstrɪkʃn, -z
†construct, -s, -ing, -ed, -or/s kənˈstrʌkt, -s, -ɪŋ, -ɪd, -ə*/z
construction, -s kənˈstrʌkʃn, -z
construc|tional, -tionally kənˈstrʌk|ʃənl [-ʃnəl, -ʃn̩l, -ʃn̩l, -ʃənəl], -ʃn̩əlɪ [-ʃnəlɪ, -ʃn̩l̩ɪ, -ʃn̩l̩ɪ, -ʃənəlɪ]
constructive, -ly, -ness kənˈstrʌktɪv, -lɪ, -nɪs [-nəs]
constr|ue (s. v.), -ues, -uing, -ued kənˈstr|uː [ˈkɒnst-], -uːz, -uːɪŋ [-ʊɪŋ], -uːd
consubstanti|al, -ally ˌkɒnsəbˈstænʃ|l [-bzˈt-, -ˈstɑːnʃ-], -əlɪ [-l̩ɪ]
consubstantiat|e, -es, -ing, -ed ˌkɒn-səbˈstænʃɪeɪt [-bzˈt-, -ˈstɑːnʃ-, -ʃjeɪt], -s, -ɪŋ, -ɪd
consubstantiation ˈkɒnsəbˌstænʃɪˈeɪʃn [-bzˌt-, -ˌstɑːnʃ-, -nsɪ-]
consul, -s; -ship/s ˈkɒnsəl, -z; -ʃɪp/s
consular ˈkɒnsjʊlə* [-sjəl-]
consulate, -s ˈkɒnsjʊlət [-sjəl-, -lɪt], -s
consult, -s, -ing, -ed kənˈsʌlt, -s, -ɪŋ, -ɪd
†consultant, -s kənˈsʌltənt, -s
consultation, -s ˌkɒnsəlˈteɪʃn [-sʌl-], -z
consultative kənˈsʌltətɪv
consultatory kənˈsʌltətərɪ [ˌkɒnsəl-ˈteɪtərɪ]
consultee, -s ˌkɒnsʌlˈtiː [-səl-], -z
consumable, -s kənˈsjuːməbl [-ˈsuː:-], -z
consum|e, -es, -ing, -ed, -er/s kən-ˈsjuːm [-ˈsuːm], -z, -ɪŋ, -d, -ə*/z
consummate (adj.), -ly kənˈsʌmɪt [-mət], -lɪ
consummat|e (v.), -es, -ing, -ed, -or/s ˈkɒnsəmeɪt [-sʌm-, -sjʊ-], -s, -ɪŋ, -ɪd, -ə*/z
consummation, -s ˌkɒnsəˈmeɪʃn [-sʌˈm-, -sjʊ-], -z

consummative ˈkɒnsəmeɪtɪv [-sʌm-, -sjʊ-, kənˈsʌmətɪv]
consumption kənˈsʌmpʃn
consumptive (s. adj.), -s, -ly, -ness kənˈsʌmptɪv, -z, -lɪ, -nɪs [-nəs]
contact (s. adj.), -s ˈkɒntækt, -s
contact (v.), -s, -ing, -ed ˈkɒntækt [kɒnˈtækt, kənˈtækt], -s, -ɪŋ, -ɪd
contagion, -s kənˈteɪdʒən [-dʒən, -dʒɪən], -z
contagious, -ly, -ness kənˈteɪdʒəs, -lɪ, -nɪs [-nəs]
contain, -s, -ing, -ed, -er/s; -able kənˈteɪn, -z, -ɪŋ, -d, -ə*/z; -əbl
contaminat|e, -es, -ing, -ed, -er/s kən-ˈtæmɪneɪt, -s, -ɪŋ, -ɪd, -ə*/z
contamination, -s kənˌtæmɪˈneɪʃn, -z
contaminative kənˈtæmɪnətɪv [-neɪt-]
contango, -s kənˈtæŋgəʊ [kɒn-], -z
contemn, -s, -ing, -ed, -er/s kənˈtem, -z, -ɪŋ, -d, -ə*/z [-nə*/z]
contemplat|e, -es, -ing, -ed, -or/s ˈkɒn-templeɪt [-təm-], -s, -ɪŋ, -ɪd, -ə*/z
contemplation, -s ˌkɒntemˈpleɪʃn [-təm-], -z
contemplative (pensive), -ly, -ness ˈkɒn-templeɪtɪv [-təm-, kənˈtemplət-], -lɪ, -nɪs [-nəs]
contemplative (of religious orders) kənˈtemplətɪv
contemporaneity kənˌtempərəˈniːətɪ [kɒn-, -ˈniːɪtɪ, -ˈnɪə-, -ˈnɪɪ-, -ˈneɪətɪ, -ˈneɪtɪ]
contemporaneous, -ly, -ness kənˌtem-pəˈreɪnjəs [kɒn-, -nɪəs], -lɪ, -nɪs [-nəs]
contemporar|y (s. adj.), -ies, -ily kən-ˈtempərər|ɪ, -ɪz, -əlɪ [-ɪlɪ]
contempt kənˈtempt
contemptibility kənˌtemptəˈbɪlətɪ [-tɪˈb-, -lɪt-]
contemptib|le, -ly, -leness kənˈtemp-təb|l [-tɪb-], -lɪ, -lnɪs [-nəs]
contemptuous, -ly, -ness kənˈtemp-tʃʊəs [-tjʊəs, -tjwəs], -lɪ, -nɪs [-nəs]
contend, -s, -ing, -ed, -er/s kənˈtend, -z, -ɪŋ, -ɪd, -ə*/z
content (s.) (what is contained) ˈkɒntent, (contentment) kənˈtent
content (adj. v.), -s, -ing, -ed/ly, -edness, -ment kənˈtent, -s, -ɪŋ, -ɪd/lɪ, -ɪdnɪs [-nəs], -mənt
contention, -s kənˈtenʃn, -z
contentious, -ly, -ness kənˈtenʃəs, -lɪ, -nɪs [-nəs]
contents (s.) ˈkɒntents [kənˈt-]
Note.—Always ˈkɒntents in **contents-bill**.

contermin|al, -ous kɒn'tɜ:mɪn|l [kən-], -əs

contest (s.), -s 'kɒntest, -s

contest (v.), -s, -ing, -ed; -able kən-'test, -s, -ɪŋ, -ɪd; -əbl

contestant, -s kən'testənt, -s

contestation, -s ˌkɒntes'teɪʃn, -z

context, -s 'kɒntekst, -s

contextual, -ly kɒn'tekstjʊəl [kən-, -tjwəl, -tjʊl, -tʃʊəl, -tʃwəl, -tʃʊl], -ɪ

contiguity ˌkɒntɪ'gju:ətɪ [-'gjʊ-, -ɪtɪ]

contiguous, -ly, -ness kən'tɪgjʊəs [kɒn-, -gjwəs], -lɪ, -nɪs [-nəs]

continen|ce, -cy 'kɒntɪnən|s, -sɪ

continent (s. adj.), -s, -ly 'kɒntɪnənt, -s, -lɪ

continental ˌkɒntɪ'nentl

contingen|ce, -cy, -cies kən'tɪndʒən|s, -sɪ, -sɪz

contingent (s. adj.), -s, -ly kən'tɪndʒənt, -s, -lɪ

continual, -ly kən'tɪnjʊəl [-njwəl, -njʊl], -ɪ

continuan|ce, -t/s kən'tɪnjʊən|s [-njwən-], -t/s

continuation, -s kənˌtɪnjʊ'eɪʃn, -z

continuative kən'tɪnjʊətɪv [-njwət-]

continuator, -s kən'tɪnjʊeɪtə*, -z

contin|ue, -ues, -uing, -ued, -uer/s kən'tɪn|ju: [-njʊ], -ju:z [-njʊz], -jʊɪŋ [-jwɪŋ], -ju:d [-jʊd], -jʊə*/z [-jwə*/z]

continuity ˌkɒntɪ'nju:ətɪ [-'njʊ-, -ɪtɪ]

continuo kən'tɪnjʊəʊ [-nʊəʊ]

continuous, -ly, -ness kən'tɪnjʊəs [-njwəs], -lɪ, -nɪs [-nəs]

continu|um, -a kən'tɪnjʊ|əm [-njw|əm], -ə

conto, -s 'kɒntəʊ, -z

contoid, -s 'kɒntɔɪd, -z

contort, -s, -ing, -ed kən'tɔ:t, -s, -ɪŋ, -ɪd

contortion, -s kən'tɔ:ʃn, -z

contortionist, -s kən'tɔ:ʃnɪst [-ʃənɪ-], -s

contour (s. v.), -s, -ing, -ed 'kɒnˌtʊə*, -z, -rɪŋ, -d

contra 'kɒntrə

contraband; -ist/s 'kɒntrəbænd; -ɪst/s

contrabass, -es ˌkɒntrə'beɪs ['---], -ɪz

contraception ˌkɒntrə'sepʃn

contraceptive, -s ˌkɒntrə'septɪv, -z

contract (s.), -s 'kɒntrækt, -s

contract (v.), -s, -ing, -ed, -or/s; -ive kən'trækt, -s, -ɪŋ, -ɪd, -ə*/z; -ɪv

contractibility kənˌtræktə'bɪlətɪ [-tɪ'b-, -lɪt-]

contractib|le, -ly, -leness kən'træktəb|l [-tɪb-], -lɪ, -lnɪs [-nəs]

contractile kən'træktaɪl

contraction, -s kən'trækʃn, -z

contractual kən'træktʃʊəl [-tjʊəl, -tjwəl, -tjʊl, -tʃwəl, -tʃʊl]

contradict, -s, -ing, -ed ˌkɒntrə'dɪkt, -s, -ɪŋ, -ɪd

contradiction, -s ˌkɒntrə'dɪkʃn, -z

contradictor|y, -ily, -ness ˌkɒntrə-'dɪktər|ɪ, -ɪlɪ [-əlɪ], -mɪs [-ɪnəs]

contradistinc|tion, -tive ˌkɒntrədɪ-'stɪŋk|ʃn, -tɪv

contradistinguish, -es, -ing, -ed ˌkɒntrədɪ'stɪŋgwɪʃ, -ɪz, -ɪŋ, -t

contralto, -s kən'træltəʊ [-'trɑ:l-], -z

contraposition ˌkɒntrəpə'zɪʃn [-pʊ'z-]

contraption, -s kən'træpʃn, -z

contrapuntal ˌkɒntrə'pʌntl

contrapuntist, -s 'kɒntrəpʌntɪst, -s

contrariant, -s kən'treərɪənt, -s

contrariety ˌkɒntrə'raɪətɪ [-aɪtɪ]

contrari|ness, -wise 'kɒntrərɪ|nɪs [kən-'treərɪ-, -nəs], -waɪz

contrar|y, -ies, -ily 'kɒntrər|ɪ [also kən'treər- in sense of 'obstinate'], -ɪz, -əlɪ [-ɪlɪ]

contrast (s.), -s 'kɒntrɑ:st, -s

contrast (v.), -s, -ing/ly, -ed kən'trɑ:st, -s, -ɪŋ/lɪ, -ɪd

contrastive kən'trɑ:stɪv

contraven|e, -es, -ing, -ed ˌkɒntrə'vi:n, -z, -ɪŋ, -d

contravention, -s ˌkɒntrə'venʃn, -z

contretemps (sing.) 'kɒntrətɑ̃:ŋ ['kɔ:nt-, 'kɔ̃:nt-, -tɔ̃:ŋ, -tɑ:ŋ, -tɒŋ] (kɔ̃trətɑ̃), (plur.) -z

contrib|ute, -utes, -uting, -uted, -utor/s kən'trɪb|ju:t ['kɒntrɪbju:t], -ju:ts, -jʊtɪŋ, -jʊtɪd, -jʊtə*/z

contribution, -s ˌkɒntrɪ'bju:ʃn, -z

contribut|ive, -ory kən'trɪbjʊt|ɪv, -ərɪ

contrite, -ly, -ness 'kɒntraɪt, -lɪ, -nɪs [-nəs]

contrition kən'trɪʃn

contrivance, -s kən'traɪvns, -ɪz

contriv|e, -es, -ing, -ed, -er/s kən'traɪv, -z, -ɪŋ, -ɪd, -ə*/z

control (s.), -s kən'trəʊl [in machinery also 'kɒntrəʊl], -z

control (v.), -s, -ling, -led, -ler/s; -lable kən'trəʊl, -z, -ɪŋ, -d, -ə*/z; -əbl

controversi|al, -ally ˌkɒntrə'vɜ:ʃ|l [-trʊ'v-], -əlɪ [-lɪ]

controversialist, -s ˌkɒntrə'vɜ:ʃəlɪst [-trʊ'v-, -ʃlɪ-], -s

controvers|y, -ies 'kɒntrəvɜ:s|ɪ [-trʊv-, -vəs-], kən'trɒvəs|ɪ, -ɪz

controvert, -s, -ing, -ed 'kɒntrəvɜ:t ['kɒntrʊv-, ˌ--'-], -s, -ɪŋ, -ɪd

controvertib|le, -ly ˌkɒntrə'vɜ:təb|l [ˌkɒntrʊ'v-, -tɪb-, '------], -lɪ
contumacious, -ly, -ness ˌkɒntju:-'meɪʃəs [-tjʊ-], -lɪ, -nɪs [-nəs]
contumacity ˌkɒntju:'mæsətɪ [-tjʊ-, -ɪtɪ]
contumacy 'kɒntjʊməsɪ
contumelious, -ly, -ness ˌkɒntju:'mi:-ljəs [-tjʊ-, -lɪəs], -lɪ, -nɪs [-nəs]
contumel|y, -ies 'kɒntju:ml|ɪ [-tjʊ-, 'kɒntjʊmɪl|ɪ, -əl|ɪ, kən'tju:mɪl|ɪ, -əl|ɪ], -ɪz
contus|e, -es, -ing, -ed kən'tju:z, -ɪz, -ɪŋ, -d
contusion, -s kən'tju:ʒn, -z
conundrum, -s kə'nʌndrəm, -z
conurbation, -s ˌkɒnɜ:'beɪʃn [-nə'b-], -z
convalesc|e, -es, -ing, -ed ˌkɒnvə'les, -ɪz, -ɪŋ, -t
convalescen|ce, -t/s ˌkɒnvə'lesn|s, -t/s
convection kən'vekʃn
convector, -s kən'vektə*, -z
convenance, -s 'kɔ̃:nvɑ̃:ns ['kɔ̃:ŋv-, 'kɔ:nv-, 'kɒnv-, -vm-, -nɔ̃:ns, -nɑ:ns] (kɔ̃vnɑ̃:s), -ɪz
conven|e, -es, -ing, -ed, -er/s kən'vi:n, -z, -ɪŋ, -d, -ə*/z
convenien|ce/s, -t/ly kən'vi:njən|s/ɪz [-nɪən-], -t/lɪ
convent, -s 'kɒnvənt [-vent], -s
conventicle, -s kən'ventɪkl, -z
convention, -s kən'venʃn, -z
conven|tional, -tionally kən'ven|ʃənl [-ʃnəl, -ʃn̩l, -ʃn̩l, -ʃənəl], -ʃnəlɪ [-ʃnəlɪ, -ʃn̩lɪ, -ʃn̩lɪ, -ʃənəlɪ]
conventionali|sm, -st/s kən'venʃn̩əlɪ|-zəm [-ʃnəl-, -ʃn̩l-, -ʃn̩l-, -ʃənəl-], -st/s
conventionalit|y, -ies kənˌvenʃə'nælət|ɪ [-ʃn̩'æl-, -ɪt|ɪ], -ɪz
conventionaliz|e [-is|e], -es, -ing, -ed kən'venʃn̩əlaɪz [-ʃnəl-, -ʃn̩l-, -ʃn̩l-, -ʃənəl-], -ɪz, -ɪŋ, -d
conventual, -s kən'ventjʊəl [-tjwəl, -tjʊl, -tʃʊəl, -tʃwəl, -tʃʊl], -z
converg|e, -es, -ing, -ed kən'vɜ:dʒ [kɒn-], -ɪz, -ɪŋ, -d
convergen|ce, -cy, -t/ly kən'vɜ:dʒən|s [kɒn-], -sɪ, -t/lɪ
conversable kən'vɜ:səbl
conversan|ce,   -cy kən'vɜ:sən|s ['kɒnvəs-], -sɪ
conversant, -ly kən'vɜ:sənt ['kɒnvəs-], -lɪ
conversation, -s ˌkɒnvə'seɪʃn, -z
conversa|tional, -tionally ˌkɒnvə'seɪ|-ʃənl [-ʃnəl, -ʃn̩l, -ʃn̩l, -ʃənəl], -ʃn̩əlɪ [-ʃnəlɪ, -ʃn̩lɪ, -ʃn̩lɪ, -ʃənəlɪ]

conversationalist, -s ˌkɒnvə'seɪʃn̩əlɪst [-ʃnəl-, -ʃn̩l-, -ʃn̩l-, -ʃənəl-], -s
conversazione, -s ˌkɒnvəsætsɪ'əʊnɪ, -z
converse (*s. adj.*), **-s, -ly** 'kɒnvɜ:s, -ɪz, -lɪ [ˌkɒn'vɜ:slɪ]
convers|e (*v.*), **-es, -ing, -ed** kən'vɜ:s, -ɪz, -ɪŋ, -t
conversion, -s kən'vɜ:ʃn, -z
convert (*s.*), **-s** 'kɒnvɜ:t, -s
convert (*v.*), **-s, -ing, -ed, -er/s** kən'vɜ:t, -s, -ɪŋ, -ɪd, -ə*/z
convertibility kənˌvɜ:tə'bɪlətɪ [-tɪ'b-, -lɪt-]
convertib|le, -ly kən'vɜ:təb|l [-tɪb-], -lɪ
convex, -ly kɒn'veks ['kɒnv-], -lɪ
Note.—The form kɒn'veks *is not used attributively.*
convexit|y, -ies kɒn'veksət|ɪ [kən-, -ɪt|ɪ], -ɪz
convey, -s, -ing, -ed, -er/s; -able kən'veɪ, -z, -ɪŋ, -d, -ə*/z [-'veə*/z]; -əbl [-'veəbl]
conveyance, -s kən'veɪəns, -ɪz
conveyanc|er/s, -ing kən'veɪəns|ə*/z, -ɪŋ
convict (*s.*), **-s** 'kɒnvɪkt, -s
convict (*v.*), **-s, -ing, -ed** kən'vɪkt, -s, -ɪŋ, -ɪd
conviction, -s kən'vɪkʃn, -z
convinc|e, -es, -ing/ly, -ed kən'vɪns, -ɪz, -ɪŋ/lɪ, -t
convincible kən'vɪnsəbl [-sɪb-]
convivial, -ly kən'vɪvɪəl [-vjəl], -ɪ
conviviality kənˌvɪvɪ'ælətɪ [-ɪtɪ]
convocation, -s ˌkɒnvəʊ'keɪʃn, -z
convok|e, -es, -ing, -ed kən'vəʊk, -s, -ɪŋ, -t
convolute, -d 'kɒnvəlu:t [-lju:t], -ɪd
convolution, -s ˌkɒnvə'lu:ʃn [-'lju:-], -z
convolv|e, -es, -ing, -ed kən'vɒlv, -z, -ɪŋ, -d
convolvul|us, -i, -uses kən'vɒlvjʊl|əs [-vjəl-], -aɪ, -əsɪz
convoy (*s. v.*), **-s, -ing, -ed** 'kɒnvɔɪ, -z, -ɪŋ, -d
convuls|e, -es, -ing, -ed; -ant kən'vʌls, -ɪz, -ɪŋ, -t; -ənt
convulsion, -s kən'vʌlʃn, -z
convulsionary kən'vʌlʃn̩ərɪ [-ʃənə-]
convulsive, -ly, -ness kən'vʌlsɪv, -lɪ, -nɪs [-nəs]
Conway 'kɒnweɪ
con|y, -ies 'kəʊn|ɪ, -ɪz
Conybeare 'kɒnɪˌbɪə*, 'kʌn-
Conyngham 'kʌnɪŋəm
coo (*s. v.*), **-es, -ing, -ed** ku:, -z, -ɪŋ, -d
Cooch ku:tʃ

107

cooee (s. v.), **-s, -ing, -d** 'ku:ɪ ['kʊ-, -i:], -z, -ɪŋ, -d

cook (s. v.), **-s, -ing, -ed, -er/s** kʊk, -s, -ɪŋ, -t, -ə*/z

Cook(e) kʊk

cookery; **-book/s** 'kʊkərɪ; -bʊk/s

cook-hou|se, **-ses** 'kʊkhaʊ|s, -zɪz

cookie, **-s** 'kʊkɪ, -z

cook-room, **-s** 'kʊkrʊm [-ru:m], -z

cook-shop, **-s** 'kʊkʃɒp, -s

cool (s. adj. v.), **-er, -est, -ly, -ness; -s, -ing, -ed, -er/s** ku:l, -ə*, -ɪst, -lɪ [-ɪ], -nɪs [-nəs]; -z, -ɪŋ, -d, -ə*/z

coolant, **-s** 'ku:lənt, -s

cool-headed ‚ku:l'hedɪd ['-‚-- when ˋ attributive]

Coolidge 'ku:lɪdʒ

coolie, **-s** 'ku:lɪ, -z

Cooling 'ku:lɪŋ

coom, **-s** ku:m, -z

coomb, **-s** ku:m, -z

Coomb(e) ku:m

Coomber 'ku:mbə*

Coombes ku:mz

coon, **-s; -song/s** ku:n, -z; -sɒŋ/z

coop (s. v.), **-s, -ing, -ed** ku:p, -s, -ɪŋ, -t

co-op, **-s** 'kəʊɒp, -s

cooper (s. v.) (C.), **-s, -ing, -ed** 'ku:pə*, -z, -rɪŋ, -d

cooperage, **-s** 'ku:pərɪdʒ, -ɪz

co-operat|e, **-es, -ing, -ed, -or/s** kəʊ-'ɒpəreɪt, -s, -ɪŋ, -ɪd, -ə*/z

co-operation, **-s** kəʊ‚ɒpə'reɪʃn [‚---'--], -z

co-operative (s. adj.), **-s** kəʊ'ɒpərətɪv, -z

coopery 'ku:pərɪ

Coopman 'ku:pmən

co-opt, **-s, -ing, -ed** kəʊ'ɒpt, -s, -ɪŋ, -ɪd

co-optation ‚kəʊɒp'teɪʃn

co-option kəʊ'ɒpʃn

co-ordinate (s. adj.), **-s, -ly, -ness** kəʊ'ɔ:dnət [-dɪnət, -dənət, -nɪt], -s, -lɪ, -nɪs [-nəs]

co-ordinat|e (v.), **-es, -ing, -ed, -er/s** kəʊ-'ɔ:dɪneɪt [-dn̩eɪt], -s, -ɪŋ, -ɪd, -ə*/z

co-ordination kəʊ‚ɔ:dɪ'neɪʃn [-dn̩'eɪ-]

co-ordinative kəʊ'ɔ:dɪnətɪv [-dnət-, -dɪneɪt-]

coot, **-s** ku:t, -s

Coote ku:t

co-ownership ‚kəʊ'əʊnəʃɪp

cop (s. v.), **-s, -ping, -ped** kɒp, -s, -ɪŋ, -t

copaiba kɒ'paɪbə [kəʊ'p-]

copal 'kəʊpəl [kəʊ'pæl]

coparcener, **-s** ‚kəʊ'pɑ:sənə* [-sɪn-], -z

copartner, **-s; -ship/s** ‚kəʊ'pɑ:tnə*, -z; -ʃɪp/s

108

cop|e (s. v.) (C.), **-es, -ing, -ed** kəʊp, -s, -ɪŋ, -t

copeck, **-s** 'kəʊpek ['kɒp-], -s

Copeland 'kəʊplənd

Copenhagen ‚kəʊpn'heɪgən [-pən-]

coper, **-s** 'kəʊpə*, -z

Copernic|an, **-us** kəʊ'pɜ:nɪk|ən, -əs

Cophetua kəʊ'fetjʊə [-tjwə]

coping (s.), **-s** 'kəʊpɪŋ, -z

coping-stone, **-s** 'kəʊpɪŋstəʊn, -z

copious, **-ly, -ness** 'kəʊpjəs [-pɪəs], -lɪ, -nɪs [-nəs]

Copland 'kɒplənd, 'kəʊplənd

Copleston 'kɒplstən

Copley 'kɒplɪ

Copp kɒp

Copped kɒpt

copper (s. v.), **-s, -ing, -ed** 'kɒpə*, -z, -rɪŋ, -d

copperas 'kɒpərəs

copper-bottomed ‚kɒpə'bɒtəmd [also 'kɒpə‚b- when attributive]

Copperfield 'kɒpəfi:ld

copper-plate 'kɒpəpleɪt [‚--'-]

copper-smith, **-s** 'kɒpəsmɪθ, -s

coppery 'kɒpərɪ

coppice, **-s, -ing, -ed** 'kɒpɪs, -ɪz, -ɪŋ, -t

copra 'kɒprə

copse, **-s** kɒps, -ɪz

Copt, **-s** kɒpt, -s

Copthall 'kɒptɔ:l [-thɔ:l]

Coptic 'kɒptɪk

copul|a, **-ae, -as** 'kɒpjʊl|ə, -i:, -əz

copulat|e, **-es, -ing, -ed** 'kɒpjʊleɪt, -s, -ɪŋ, -ɪd

copulation, **-s** ‚kɒpjʊ'leɪʃn, -z

copulat|ive, **-ory** 'kɒpjʊlət|ɪv [-leɪt-], -ərɪ

cop|y (s. v.), **-ies, -ying, -ied, -ier/s** 'kɒp|ɪ, -ɪz, -ɪɪŋ, -ɪd, -ɪə*/z

copy-book, **-s** 'kɒpɪbʊk, -s

copyhold, **-s, -er/s** 'kɒpɪhəʊld, -z, -ə*/z

copyist, **-s** 'kɒpɪɪst, -s

copyright (s. v.), **-s, -ing, -ed** 'kɒpɪraɪt, -s, -ɪŋ, -ɪd

coquet (s. v.), **-s, -ting, -ted** kɒ'ket [kəʊ'k-], -s, -ɪŋ, -ɪd

coquetr|y, **-ies** 'kɒkɪtr|ɪ ['kəʊk-, -ətrɪ], -ɪz

coquette (s.), **-s** kɒ'ket [kəʊ'k-], -s

coquettish, **-ly, -ness** kɒ'ketɪʃ [kəʊ'k-], -lɪ, -nɪs [-nəs]

cor, **-s** kɔ:*, -z

Cora 'kɔ:rə

cor(s) anglais ‚kɔ:r 'ɑ̃:ŋgleɪ [-'ɒŋg-]

coracle, **-s** 'kɒrəkl, -z

coral, **-s** 'kɒrəl, -z

corallaceous ‚kɒrə'leɪʃəs

corall|ine, **-ite** 'kɒrəl|aɪn [-r|-], -aɪt

coral-reef, -s 'kɒrəlriːf, -s
Coram 'kɔːrəm
coranto, -s kɒ'ræntəʊ [kə'r-], -z
corban 'kɔːbæn
corbel, -s 'kɔːbəl, -z
Corbett 'kɔːbɪt [-bet, -bət]
Corbishley 'kɔːbɪʃlɪ
Corbyn 'kɔːbɪn
Corcoran 'kɔːkərən
Corcyra kɔː'saɪərə
cord (s. v.), -s, -ing, -ed; -age kɔːd, -z,
    -ɪŋ, -ɪd; -ɪdʒ
Cordelia kɔː'diːljə [-lɪə]
cordelier (C.), -s ˌkɔːdɪ'lɪə*, -z
cordial (s. adj.), -s, -ly 'kɔːdjəl [-dɪəl],
    -z, -ɪ
cordialit|y, -ies ˌkɔːdɪ'ælət|ɪ [-ɪt|ɪ], -ɪz
cordillera (C.), ˌkɔːdɪ'ljeərə [-'leərə]
cording (s.) 'kɔːdɪŋ
cordite 'kɔːdaɪt
cor|don (s. v.), -dons, -doning, -doned
    'kɔː|dn [-dan], -dnz [-dənz], -dnɪŋ
    [-dənɪŋ], -dnd [-dənd]
cordon bleu ˌkɔːdɔ̃:mˈblɜː [-dɒn]
    (kɔrdɔ̃ blø)
Cordova, -n/s 'kɔːdəvə, -n/z
corduroy, -s 'kɔːdərɔɪ [-djʊr-, ˌ--'-], -z
cordwainer, -s 'kɔːdˌweɪnə*, -z
cor|e (s. v.), -es, -ing, -ed, -er/s kɔː:*
    [kɔə*], -z, -rɪŋ, -d, -rə*/z
co-regent, -s ˌkəʊˈriːdʒənt, -s
co-religionist, -s ˌkəʊrɪˈlɪdʒənɪst [-rə-,
    -dʒn̩-], -s
Corelli kə'relɪ [kɒ'r-]
co-respondent, -s ˌkəʊrɪˈspɒndənt
    ['kəʊrɪˌsp-], -s
corf, -s kɔːf, -s
Corfe kɔːf
Corfu kɔː'fuː [-'fjuː]
corgi (dog), -s 'kɔːgɪ, -z
coriaceous ˌkɒrɪ'eɪʃəs
coriander, -s ˌkɒrɪ'ændə*, -z
Corin 'kɒrɪn
Corinth 'kɒrɪnθ
Corinthian, -s kə'rɪnθɪən [kʊ'r-, -θjən],
    -z
Coriolanus ˌkɒrɪəʊ'leɪnəs
Corioles kə'raɪəliːz [kɒ'r-]
cork (s. v.), (C.), -s, -ing, -ed; -age
    kɔːk, -s, -ɪŋ, -t; -ɪdʒ
corker (C.), -s 'kɔːkə*, -z
Corkran 'kɔːkrən
cork-screw (s. v.), -s, -ing, -ed 'kɔːk-
    skruː:, -z, -ɪŋ [-ˌskrʊɪŋ], -d
corky 'kɔːkɪ
corm, -s kɔːm, -z
Cormac (king in Irish mythology)
    'kɜːmæk ['kɔːm-]

Cormack 'kɔːmæk
cormorant, -s 'kɔːmərənt, -s
corn (s. v.), -s, -ing, -ed kɔːn, -z, -ɪŋ, -d
Cornbury 'kɔːnbərɪ
corn-chandler, -s 'kɔːnˌtʃɑːndlə*, -z
corn-crake, -s 'kɔːnkreɪk, -s
cornea, -s, -l 'kɔːnɪə, -z, -l
Corneille kɔː'neɪ [·neɪl] (kɔrnɛ:j)
Cornelia kɔː'niːljə [-lɪə]
cornelian, -s kɔː'niːljən [kə'n-, -lɪən], -z
Cornelius kɔː'niːljəs [-lɪəs]
Cornell kɔː'nel [also 'kɔːnel when
    attributive]
Cornemuse 'kɔːnəmjuːz [-nɪ-]
corner (s. v.), -s, -ing, -ed 'kɔːnə*, -z,
    -rɪŋ, -d
corner-stone, -s 'kɔːnəstəʊn, -z
corner-wise 'kɔːnəwaɪz
cornet, -s 'kɔːnɪt, -s
corn-field, -s 'kɔːnfiːld, -z
cornflour 'kɔːnflaʊə*
corn-flower, -s 'kɔːnflaʊə*, -z
Cornhill ˌkɔːn'hɪl [also '-- according to
    sentence-stress]
cornice, -s 'kɔːnɪs, -ɪz
Cornish, -man, -men 'kɔːnɪʃ, -mən,
    -mən [-men]
cornopean, -s kə'nəʊpjən [kɔː'n-,
    -pɪən], -z
cornucopia, -s ˌkɔːnjʊ'kəʊpjə [-pɪə], -z
Cornwall 'kɔːnwəl [rarely -wɔːl]
Cornwallis kɔːn'wɒlɪs
corolla, -s kə'rɒlə, -z
corollar|y, -ies kə'rɒlər|ɪ, -ɪz
Coromandel ˌkɒrəʊ'mændl
coron|a, -ae, -as kə'rəʊn|ə, -iː, -əz
Corona (fem. name) 'kɒrənə
coronach (C.), -s 'kɒrənək [-nəx,
    -næk], -s
coronal (s.), -s 'kɒrənl, -z
coronal (adj.) (pertaining to the sun's
    corona) kə'rəʊnl, (medical, botanical
    and phonetic senses) 'kɒrənl
    [kə'rəʊnl]
coronary 'kɒrənərɪ
coronation, -s ˌkɒrə'neɪʃn [-rŋ̩'eɪ-], -z
Coronel 'kɒrənel
coroner, -s 'kɒrənə* [-rŋə*], -z
coronet, -s 'kɒrənɪt [-rŋ̩ɪt, -net, -nət],
    -s
coronis, -es kə'rəʊnɪs, -ɪz
corpor|al (s. adj.), -als, -ally 'kɔːpər|əl,
    -əlz, -əlɪ
corporality ˌkɔːpə'rælətɪ [-ɪtɪ]
corporate, -ly, -ness 'kɔːpərət [-rɪt], -lɪ,
    -nɪs [-nəs]
corporation, -s ˌkɔːpə'reɪʃn, -z
corporator, -s 'kɔːpəreɪtə*, -z

109

corporeal, -ly kɔː'pɔːrɪəl, -ɪ
corps (*sing.*) kɔː*, (*plur.*) kɔːz
corps de ballet ˌkɔːdə'bæleɪ [-lɪ]
(kɔːrdəbalɛ)
corps diplomatique 'kɔːˌdɪpləmæ'tiːk
(kɔːrdiplɔmatik)
corpse, -s kɔːps, -ɪz
corpulen|ce, -cy, -t 'kɔːpjʊlən|s, -sɪ, -t
corp|us, -era 'kɔːp|əs, -ərə
Corpus Christi ˌkɔːpəs'krɪstɪ
corpuscle, -s 'kɔːpʌsl [kɔː'pʌsl], -z
corpuscular kɔː'pʌskjʊlə*
corpuscule, -s kɔː'pʌskjuːl [-skjʊl], -z
corral, -s kə'rɑːl [kɒ'r-], -z
correct (*adj. v.*), -est, -ly, -ness; -s,
-ing, -ed, -or/s kə'rekt, -ɪst, -lɪ, -nɪs
[-nəs]; -s, -ɪŋ, -ɪd, -ə*/z
correction, -s kə'rekʃn, -z
correctional kə'rekʃənl [-ʃnəl, -ʃn̩l, -ʃn̩,
-ʃənəl]
correctitude kə'rektɪtjuːd
corrective, -s kə'rektɪv, -z
correlat|e, -es, -ing, -ed 'kɒrəleɪt [-rɪl-],
-s, -ɪŋ, -ɪd (*s. also* 'kɒrələt)
correlation, -s ˌkɒrə'leɪʃn [-rɪ'l-], -z
correlative, -ly, -ness kɒ'relətɪv [kə'r-,
-'relt-], -lɪ, -nɪs [-nəs]
correspond, -s, -ing/ly, -ed ˌkɒrɪ'spɒnd
[-rə's-], -z, -ɪŋ/lɪ, -ɪd
corresponden|ce/s, -t/s, -tly ˌkɒrɪ's-
pɒndən|s/ɪz [-rə's-], -t/s, -tlɪ
corridor, -s; -train/s 'kɒrɪdɔː* [-də*],
-z; -treɪn/z
corrie (C.) 'kɒrɪ
Corrientes ˌkɒrɪ'entes
corrigend|um, -a ˌkɒrɪ'dʒend|əm
[-ɪ'gen-], -ə
corrigible 'kɒrɪdʒəbl [-dʒɪb-]
corroborant, -s kə'rɒbərənt, -s
corroborat|e, -es, -ing, -ed, -or/s
kə'rɒbəreɪt, -s, -ɪŋ, -ɪd, -ə*/z
corroboration, -s kəˌrɒbə'reɪʃn, -z
corroborative kə'rɒbərətɪv [-bəreɪt-]
corroboratory kə'rɒbərətərɪ
corroboree, -s kə'rɒbərɪ [kɒ'r-, -riː],
-z
corrod|e, -es, -ing, -ed kə'rəʊd, -z, -ɪŋ,
-ɪd
corrodible kə'rəʊdəbl [-dɪb-]
corrosion, -s kə'rəʊʒn, -z
corrosive (*s. adj.*), -s, -ly, -ness kə-
'rəʊsɪv [-əʊzɪv], -z, -lɪ, -nɪs [-nəs]
corrugat|e, -es, -ing, -ed 'kɒrəgeɪt
[-rʊg-], -s, -ɪŋ, -ɪd
corrugation, -s ˌkɒrə'geɪʃn [-rʊ'g-], -z
corrupt (*adj. v.*), -est, -ly, -ness; -s,
-ing, -ed, -er/s kə'rʌpt, -ɪst, -lɪ, -nɪs
[-nəs]; -s, -ɪŋ, -ɪd, -ə*/z

corruptibility kəˌrʌptə'bɪlətɪ [-tɪ'b-,
-lɪt-]
corruptib|le, -ly, -leness kə'rʌptəb|l
[-tɪb-], -lɪ, -lnɪs [-nəs]
corruption, -s kə'rʌpʃn, -z
corruptive kə'rʌptɪv
corsage, -s kɔː'sɑːʒ ['kɔːsɑːʒ] (kɔrsaːʒ),
-ɪz
corsair, -s 'kɔːseə*, -z
corse, -s kɔːs, -ɪz
corselet, -s 'kɔːslɪt [-lət], -s
corset, -s, -ry 'kɔːsɪt, -s, -rɪ
Corsica, -n/s 'kɔːsɪkə, -n/z
corslet, -s 'kɔːslɪt [-lət], -s
cortège, -s kɔː'teɪʒ (kɔrtɛːʒ), -ɪz
Cortes 'kɔːtes [-tez] ('kortes)
cort|ex, -ices 'kɔːt|eks, -ɪsiːz
cortical 'kɔːtɪkl
cortisone 'kɔːtɪzəʊn
corundum kə'rʌndəm
Corunna kɒ'rʌnə [kə'r-]
coruscat|e, -es, -ing, -ed 'kɒrəskeɪt, -s,
-ɪŋ, -ɪd
coruscation, -s ˌkɒrə'skeɪʃn, -z
corvée, -s 'kɔːveɪ (kɔrve), -z
corvette, -s kɔː'vet, -s
Corwen 'kɔːwɪn [-wen]
corybant, -s, corybantes 'kɒrɪbænt, -s,
ˌkɒrɪ'bæntiːz
corybantic ˌkɒrɪ'bæntɪk
Corydon 'kɒrɪdən [-dɒn]
corymb 'kɒrɪmb
coryphae|us, -i ˌkɒrɪ'fiː|əs, -aɪ
coryphée 'kɒrɪfeɪ
Coryton 'kɒrɪtən
cos (C.) kɒs
cosaque, -s kɒ'zɑːk [kə'z-], -s
cosec 'kəʊsek
cosecant, -s ˌkəʊ'siːkənt, -s
Cosgrave 'kɒzgreɪv
cosh (*instrument*), -es kɒʃ, -ɪz
cosh (*mathematical term*) kɒʃ
Cosham (*in Hampshire*) 'kɒsəm
cosher (*feast, pamper*), -s, -ing, -ed
'kɒʃə*, -z, -rɪŋ, -d
cosher (=kosher) 'kəʊʃə* ['kɒʃ-]
Note.—*The Jewish pronunciation is
with* əʊ.
co-signator|y, -ies ˌkəʊ'sɪgnətər|ɪ, -ɪz
cosine, -s 'kəʊsaɪn, -z
cos-lettuce, -s ˌkɒs'letɪs ['kɒsˌl-, -təs],
-ɪz
cosmetic (*s. adj.*), -s, -al, -ally kɒz-
'metɪk, -s, -l, -əlɪ
cosmic, -al, -ally 'kɒzmɪk, -l, -əlɪ
cosmi|sm, -st/s 'kɒzmɪ|zəm, -st/s
cosmogonic, -al, -ally ˌkɒzməʊ'gɒnɪk,
-l, -əlɪ

cosmogon|ist/s, -y kɒz'mɒgən|ɪst/s, -ɪ
cosmograph|er/s, -y kɒz'mɒgrəf|ə*/z, -ɪ
cosmographic, -al, -ally ,kɒzməʊ'græfɪk -l, -əlɪ
cosmological ,kɒzməʊ'lɒdʒɪkl
cosmolog|ist/s, -y kɒz'mɒləd3|ɪst/s, -ɪ
cosmonaut, -s 'kɒzmənɔ:t, -s
cosmopolitan (s. adj.), -s ,kɒzmə-'pɒlɪtən [-lət-], -z
cosmopolitanism ,kɒzmə'pɒlɪtənɪzəm [-lət-, -tn̩ɪ-]
cosmopolite, -s kɒz'mɒpəlaɪt, -s
cosmos 'kɒzmɒs
Cossack, -s 'kɒsæk, -s
cosset (s. v.), -s, -ing, -ed 'kɒsɪt, -s, -ɪŋ, -ɪd
cost (s. v.), -s, -ing kɒst [old-fashioned kɔ:st], -s, -ɪŋ
Costa 'kɒstə
Costain kɒ'steɪn
costal 'kɒstl
costard (apple), -s 'kʌstəd ['kɒs-], -z
Costard (Shakespearian character) 'kɒstəd [-ta:d]
Costa Rica, -n/s ,kɒstə'ri:kə, -n/z
Costello (surname) kɒ'steləʊ [kə's-], 'kɒstələʊ
coster, -s; -monger/s 'kɒstə*, -z; -,mʌŋgə*/z
costive, -ly, -ness 'kɒstɪv, -lɪ, -nɪs [-nəs]
costl|y, -ier, -iest, -iness 'kɒstl|ɪ [old-fashioned 'kɔ:s-], -ɪə* [-jə*], -ɪɪst [-jɪst], -ɪnɪs [-ɪnəs]
costmary 'kɒstmeərɪ
costume (s.), -s 'kɒstju:m [kɒ'stju:m], -z
costum|e (v.), -es, -ing, -ed 'kɒstju:m [-'-], -z, -ɪŋ, -d
costumier, -s kɒ'stju:mɪə* [-mjə*], -z
Cosway, -s 'kɒzweɪ, -z
cos|y (s. adj.), -ies; -ier, -iest, -ily, -iness 'kəʊz|ɪ, -ɪz; -ɪə* [-jə*], -ɪɪst [-jɪst], -ɪlɪ [-əlɪ], -ɪnɪs [-ɪnəs]
cot, -s kɒt, -s
cot (mathematical term) kɒt
cotangent, -s ,kəʊ'tænd3ənt ['kəʊ,t-], -s
cot|e (s. v.), -es, -ing, -ed kəʊt, -s, -ɪŋ, -ɪd
co-tenant, -s ,kəʊ'tenənt, -s
coterie, -s 'kəʊtərɪ, -z
coterminous ,kəʊ'tɜ:mɪnəs
Cotgrave 'kɒtgreɪv
cotill(i)on, -s kə'tɪljən [kɒ't-], -z
Coton 'kəʊtn
cotoneaster, -s kə,təʊnɪ'æstə* [kɒ,t-], -z

Cotopaxi ,kɒtəʊ'pæksɪ
co-trustee, -s ,kəʊtrʌs'ti:, -z
Cotswold, -s 'kɒtswəʊld [-wəld], -z
Cotsworth 'kɒtzwɜ:θ [-wəθ]
cottage, -s; -r/s 'kɒtɪdʒ; -ɪz; -ə*/z
Cottam 'kɒtəm
Cottenham 'kɒtn̩əm ['kɒtnəm]
cotter (C.), -s 'kɒtə*, -z
Cotterell 'kɒtrəl
Cottesloe 'kɒtsləʊ
Cottian 'kɒtɪən [-tjən]
Cottingham 'kɒtɪŋəm
cott|on (s. v.) (C.), -ons, -oning, -oned 'kɒt|n, -nz, -n̩ɪŋ, -nd
cotton-grass 'kɒtngra:s
cotton-plant, -s 'kɒtnpla:nt, -s
cotton-seed 'kɒtnsi:d
cotton-spinner, -s 'kɒtn,spɪnə*, -z
cotton-tail, -s 'kɒtnteɪl, -z
cotton-wool ,kɒtn'wʊl
cottony 'kɒtn̩ɪ [-tənɪ]
cotyled|on/s, -onous ,kɒtɪ'li:d|ən/z, -ənəs [-n̩əs]
couch (s. v.), -es, -ing, -ed kaʊtʃ, -ɪz, -ɪŋ, -t
couch (grass) ku:tʃ, kaʊtʃ
Couch ku:tʃ
couchant 'kaʊtʃənt
couchée, -s 'ku:ʃeɪ (kuʃe), -z
couchette, -s ku:'ʃet, -s
Coué, -ism 'ku:eɪ, -ɪzəm
cougar, -s 'ku:gə*, -z
cough (s. v.), -s, -ing, -ed, -er/s kɒf [old-fashioned kɔ:f, and in compounds] -s, -ɪŋ, -t, -ə*/z
†Coughlan 'kɒglən, 'kɒklən ['kɒxlən]
Coughlin 'kɒglɪn, 'kɒklɪn ['kɒxlɪn]
could (from can) kʊd (strong form), kəd (weak form)
couldn't 'kʊdnt
coulisse, -s ku:'li:s [kʊ'l-], -ɪz
couloir, -s 'ku:lwa:* [-wɔ:*], -z
coulomb, -s 'ku:lɒm, -z
Coulsdon (in Greater London) 'kəʊlzdən, 'ku:l-
Note.—'kəʊl- is the traditional local pronunciation. People unfamiliar with the place generally pronounce 'ku:l-, as also do new residents in the district.
Coulson 'kəʊlsn, 'ku:lsn
coulter, -s 'kəʊltə*, -z
Coulton 'kəʊltən
council, -s 'kaʊnsl [-sɪl], -z
council-chamber, -s 'kaʊnsl,tʃeɪmbə* [-sɪl-], -z
councillor, -s 'kaʊnsələ* [-sɪlə*, -slə*, -slə*], -z

111

couns|el (*s. v.*), **-els, -elling, -elled,
-ellor/s** 'kaʊns|l, -lz, -lɪŋ [-əlɪŋ, -lɪŋ],
-ld, -lə*/z [-ələ*/z, -lə*/z]
count (*s. v.*), **-s, -ing, -ed** kaʊnt, -s, -ɪŋ,
-ɪd
count-down 'kaʊntdaʊn
countenanc|e (*s. v.*), **-es, -ing, -ed**
'kaʊntənəns [-tɪ-], -ɪz, -ɪŋ, -t
counter (*s. adj. v. adv.*), **-s, -ing, -ed**
'kaʊntə*, -z, -rɪŋ, -d
counteract, **-s, -ing, -ed** ˌkaʊntə'rækt,
[-tər'ækt, '---], -s, -ɪŋ, -ɪd
counteraction (*counteracting*), **-s** ˌkaʊntə'rækʃn [-tər'æk-], -z
counter-action '(*action by way of reply*),
-s 'kaʊntər,ækʃn [-tə,æk-], -z
counteractive, **-ly** ˌkaʊntə'ræktɪv
[-tər'æk-], -lɪ
counter-attack, **-s** 'kaʊntərə,tæk
[-təə,tæk], -s
counter-attraction, **-s** 'kaʊntərə,træk-
ʃn [-təə,træk-], -z
counterbalance (*s.*), **-s** 'kaʊntə,bæləns,
-ɪz
counterbalanc|e (*v.*), **-es, -ing, -ed**
ˌkaʊntə'bæləns, -ɪz, -ɪŋ, -t
counterblast, **-s** 'kaʊntəblɑːst, -s
counter-blow, **-s** 'kaʊntəbləʊ, -z
counter-charg|e (*s. v.*), **-es, -ing, -ed**
'kaʊntətʃɑːdʒ, -ɪz, -ɪŋ, -d
counter-claim (*s. v.*), **-s, -ing, -ed**
'kaʊntəkleɪm, -z, -ɪŋ, -d
counter-clockwise ˌkaʊntə'klɒkwaɪz
counter-espionage ˌkaʊntər'espjənɑːʒ
[-tə'e, -pɪən-, ,----'-, -nɪdʒ]
counterfeit (*s. v.*), **-s, -ing, -ed, -er/s**
'kaʊntəfɪt [-fiːt], -s, -ɪŋ, -ɪd, -ə*/z
counterfoil, **-s** 'kaʊntəfɔɪl, -z
counter-intelligence 'kaʊntərɪn,telɪ-
dʒəns [-təɪn-, ,---'---]
countermand (*s. v.*), **-s, -ing, -ed**
ˌkaʊntə'mɑːnd ['kaʊntəm-], -z, -ɪŋ,
-ɪd
counter-measure, **-s** 'kaʊntə,meʒə*, -z
counter-move, **-s** 'kaʊntəmuːv, -z
counterpane, **-s** 'kaʊntəpeɪn [-pɪn], -z
counterpart, **-s** 'kaʊntəpɑːt, -s
counter-plot, **-s** 'kaʊntəplɒt, -s
counterpoint 'kaʊntəpɔɪnt
counterpois|e (*s. v.*), **-es, -ing, -ed**
'kaʊntəpɔɪz, -ɪz, -ɪŋ, -d
counter-revolution, **-s** 'kaʊntərevə,luː-
ʃn [-v],uː-, -və,lju:-, ,----'--], -z
counterscarp, **-s** 'kaʊntəskɑːp, -s
countersign (*s.*), **-s** 'kaʊntəsaɪn, -z
countersign (*v.*), **-s, -ing, -ed** 'kaʊntəsaɪn [ˌkaʊntə's-], -z, -ɪŋ, -d
counterstroke, **-s** 'kaʊntəstrəʊk, -s

counter-tenor, **-s** ˌkaʊntə'tenə* ['-,--],
-z
countervail, **-s, -ing, -ed** 'kaʊntəveɪl
[,--'-], -z, -ɪŋ, -d
countess, **-es** 'kaʊntɪs [-tes], -ɪz
counting-hou|se, **-ses** 'kaʊntɪŋhaʊ|s,
-zɪz
countless 'kaʊntlɪs [-ləs]
countrified 'kʌntrɪfaɪd
countr|y, **-ies** 'kʌntr|ɪ, -ɪz
country-danc|e, **-es, -ing** ˌkʌntrɪ'dɑːns,
-ɪz, -ɪŋ
country-folk, **-s** 'kʌntrɪfəʊk, -s
country-hou|se, **-ses** ˌkʌntrɪ'haʊ|s, -zɪz
country|man, **-men** 'kʌntrɪ|mən, -mən
country-seat, **-s** ˌkʌntrɪ'siːt, -s
country-side 'kʌntrɪsaɪd [ˌ--'-]
country|woman, **-women** 'kʌntrɪ|-
ˌwʊmən, -,wɪmɪn
count|y, **-ies** 'kaʊnt|ɪ, -ɪz
coup, **-s** kuː, -z
coup d'état, **-s** ˌkuːdeɪ'tɑː [-de't-]
(kudeta), -z
coupé, **-s** 'kuːpeɪ (kupe), -z
Couper 'kuːpə*
Coupland 'kuːplənd
coup|le (*s. v.*), **-les, -ling, -led** 'kʌp|l,
-lz, -lɪŋ [-lɪŋ], -ld
coupler, **-s** 'kʌplə*, -z
couplet, **-s** 'kʌplɪt [-lət], -s
coupling (*s.*), **-s** 'kʌplɪŋ, -z
coupon, **-s** 'kuːpɒn, -z
courage (C.) 'kʌrɪdʒ
courageous, **-ly, -ness** kə'reɪdʒəs, -lɪ,
-nɪs [-nəs]
courante, **-s** kʊ'rɑ̃ːnt [-'rɔ̃ːnt, -'rɑːnt,
-'rænt] (kurɑ̃ːt), -s
courgette, **-s** kɔː'ʒet [ˌkʊə-], -s
courier, **-s** 'kʊrɪə* ['kʌ-], -z
Courland 'kʊələnd [-lænd]
cours|e (*s. v.*), **-es, -ing, -ed, -er/s** kɔːs
[kɔəs], -ɪz, -ɪŋ, -t, -ə*/z
court (*s. v.*), **-s, -ing, -ed** kɔːt [kɔət], -s,
-ɪŋ, -ɪd
Courtauld 'kɔːtəʊld, 'kɔːtəʊ
court-card, **-s** 'kɔːtkɑːd ['kɔət-], -z
court-dress, **-es** ˌkɔːt'dres [ˌkɔət-], -ɪz
Courtenay 'kɔːtnɪ ['kɔət-]
courteous, **-ly, -ness** 'kɜːtjəs ['kɔːt-,
'kɔət-, -tɪəs], -lɪ, -nɪs [-nəs]
courtesan, **-s** ˌkɔːtɪ'zæn [ˌkɔət-, ˌkʊə-,
'---], -z
courtes|y, **-ies** 'kɜːtɪs|ɪ ['kɔːt-, 'kɔət-,
-təs-], -ɪz
court-guide, **-s** 'kɔːtgaɪd ['kɔət-], -z
Courthope 'kɔːtəp ['kɔət-], -thəʊp
court-hou|se, **-ses** 'kɔːthaʊ|s ['kɔət-],
-zɪz

Courtice 'kɔːtɪs
courtier, -s 'kɔːtjə* ['kɔət-, -tɪə*], -z
courtl|y, -ier, -iest, -iness 'kɔːtl|ɪ
['kɔət-], -ɪə* [-jə*], -ɪɪst [-jɪst], -ɪnɪs
[-ɪnəs]
court-marti|al (s. v.), -als, -alling, -alled
ˌkɔːt'mɑːʃ|l [ˌkɔət-], -lz, -lɪŋ [-əlɪŋ],
-ld
Courtneidge 'kɔːtnɪdʒ ['kɔət-]
Courtney 'kɔːtnɪ ['kɔət-]
court-plaster ˌkɔːt'plɑːstə* [ˌkɔət-, '-ˌ--]
courtship, -s 'kɔːt-ʃɪp ['kɔət-], -s
courts-martial ˌkɔːts'mɑːʃl [ˌkɔəts-]
courtyard, -s 'kɔːtjɑːd ['kɔət-], -z
cousin, -s 'kʌzn, -z
Cousins 'kʌznz
Coutts kuːts
coutur|e, -ier/s kuː'tʊə* [kʊ-, -'tjʊə*],
-rɪeɪ [-rɪə*]/z
Couzens 'kʌznz
cove (C.), -s, kəʊv, -z
coven, -s 'kʌvn, -z
covenant (s. v.), -s, -ing, -ed, -er/s
'kʌvənənt [-vɪn-, -vn̩-], -s, -ɪŋ, -ɪd,
-ə*/z
Covent 'kɒvənt [old-fashioned 'kʌv-]
Coventry 'kɒvəntrɪ [rarely 'kʌv-]
cov|er (s.v.), -ers, -ering/s, -ered, -erage
'kʌv|ə*, -əz, -ərɪŋ/z, -əd, -ərɪdʒ
Coverack 'kɒvəræk ['kʌv-, -rək]
covercharg|e, -es 'kʌvətʃɑːdʒ, -ɪz
Coverdale 'kʌvədeɪl
coverlet, -s 'kʌvəlɪt [-lət], -s
Coverley 'kʌvəlɪ
Covernton 'kʌvəntən
cover-point, -s ˌkʌvə'pɔɪnt ['kʌvəp-], -s
covert (s.) (shelter, cloth), -s 'kʌvə*, -z
['kʌvət, -s]
Note.—See also wing-covert.
covert (adj.), -ly 'kʌvət, -lɪ
covert-coat, -s ˌkʌvət'kəʊt ['---, less
freq. 'kʌvəkəʊt], -s
coverture 'kʌvəˌtjʊə* [-ˌtʃʊə*]
covet, -s, -ing, -ed 'kʌvɪt [-vət], -s, -ɪŋ,
-ɪd
covetous, -ly, -ness 'kʌvɪtəs [-vət-], -lɪ,
-nɪs [-nəs]
covey (of birds), -s 'kʌvɪ, -z
covey (familiar diminutive of cove), -s
'kəʊvɪ, -z
Covington 'kʌvɪŋtən
cow (s. v.), -s, -ing, -ed kaʊ, -z, -ɪŋ, -d
Cowal 'kaʊəl
Cowan 'kaʊən
coward (C.), -s 'kaʊəd, -z
cowardice 'kaʊədɪs
cowardl|y, -iness 'kaʊədl|ɪ, -ɪnɪs [-ɪnəs]
cowbane 'kaʊbeɪn

cowboy, -s 'kaʊbɔɪ, -z
cow-catcher, -s 'kaʊˌkætʃə*, -z
Cowden (in Kent) 'kaʊdən [kaʊ'den]
Cowdenbeath ˌkaʊdn̩'biːθ
Cowdray 'kaʊdreɪ [-drɪ]
Cowdrey 'kaʊdrɪ
Cowen 'kaʊən ['kaʊɪn], 'kəʊən ['kəʊɪn]
cower, -s, -ing -ed 'kaʊə*, -z, -rɪŋ, -d
Cowes kaʊz
cowherd, -s 'kaʊhɜːd, -z
cowhide 'kaʊhaɪd
cow-hou|se, -ses 'kaʊhaʊ|s, -zɪz
Cowie 'kaʊɪ
cowl, -s kaʊl, -z
Cowley 'kaʊlɪ
cowlike 'kaʊlaɪk
cow|man, -men 'kaʊ|mən, -mən
Cowper 'kaʊpə*, 'kuːpə*
Note.—The poet called himself
'kuːpə*. 'kuːpə* is also the pronunciation in Cowper Powys
(ˌkuːpə* 'pəʊɪs) and Cowper-Black.
cow-pox 'kaʊpɒks
cow-puncher, -s 'kaʊˌpʌntʃə*, -z
cowr|ie [r|y], -ies 'kaʊr|ɪ ['kaʊər-], -ɪz
cowshed, -s 'kaʊʃed, -z
cowslip, -s 'kaʊslɪp, -s
Cowt|an, -on 'kaʊt|n, -n
cox (C.), -es kɒks, -ɪz
coxcomb, -s 'kɒkskəʊm, -z
coxswain, -s 'kɒkswein [nautical pronunciation 'kɒksn̩], -z
Coxtie 'kɒkstɪ
cox|y, -ier, -iest, -iness 'kɒks|ɪ, -ɪə*,
-ɪɪst, -ɪnɪs [-ɪnəs]
coy, -er, -est, -ly, -ness kɔɪ, -ə*, -ɪst, -lɪ,
-nɪs [-nəs]
coyish, -ly, -ness 'kɔɪʃ, -lɪ, -nɪs [-nəs]
coyote, -s kɔɪ'əʊtɪ, -z ['kɔɪəʊt, kɔɪ'əʊt,
-s]
coypu, -s 'kɔɪpuː [-pjuː], -z
Coysh kɔɪʃ
coz kʌz
coz|en, -ens, -ening, -ened, -ener/s
'kʌz|n, -nz, -nɪŋ, -nd, -nə*/z
Cozens 'kʌznz
crab, -s kræb, -z
crab-apple, -s 'kræbˌæpl, -z
Crabbe kræb
crabbed, -ly, -ness 'kræbɪd, -lɪ, -nɪs
[-nəs]
crabtree (C.), -s 'kræbtriː-, -z
crack (s. v.), -s, -ing, -ed kræk, -s, -ɪŋ, -t
crack-brain, -ed 'krækbreɪn, -d
Crackenthorpe 'krækənθɔːp
cracker, -s 'krækə*, -z
crack|le, -les, -ling, -led 'kræk|l, -lz, -lɪŋ
[-lɪŋ], -ld

113

crackling (s.) 'kræklɪŋ
crackly 'kræklɪ ['kræklɪ]
cracknel, -s 'kræknl [-nəl], -z
Cracknell 'kræknl [-nəl]
cracks|man, -men 'kræks|mən, -mən
Cracow 'krækɒv [-kɒf, -kaʊ, -kəʊ]
crad|le (s. v.), -les, -ling, -led 'kreɪd|l,
-lz, -lɪŋ [-lɪŋ], -ld
cradlesnatch, -ing, -er/s 'kreɪdlsnætʃ,
-ɪŋ, -ə*/z
Cradley 'kreɪdlɪ
craft, -s krɑːft, -s
crafts|man, -men, -manship 'krɑːfts|-
mən, -mən, -mənʃɪp
craft|y, -ier, -iest, -ily, -iness 'krɑːft|ɪ,
-ɪə* [-jə*], -ɪɪst [-jɪst], -ɪlɪ [-əlɪ], -ɪnɪs
[-ɪnəs]
crag, -s kræg, -z
Cragg kræg
cragg|y, -ier, -iest, -ily, -iness 'kræg|ɪ,
-ɪə*, -ɪɪst, -ɪlɪ [-əlɪ], -ɪnɪs [-ɪnəs]
crags|man, -men 'krægz|mən, -mən
[-men]
Craig, -ie kreɪg, -ɪ
Craigavon (Viscount) kreɪg'ævən
Craigenputtock ˌkreɪgən'pʌtək
Craik kreɪk
crak|e (s. v.), -es, -ing, -ed kreɪk, -s, -ɪŋ,
-t
cram (s. v.), -s, -ming, -med, -mer/s
kræm, -z, -ɪŋ, -d, -ə*/z
crambo 'kræmbəʊ
Cramer 'krɑːmə*, 'kreɪmə*
cram-full ˌkræm'fʊl [also '-- when
followed by a stress]
Cramlington 'kræmlɪŋtən
cramoisy 'kræmɔɪzɪ
cramp (s. v.) (C.), -s, -ing, -ed kræmp,
-s, -ɪŋ, -t [kræmt]
cramp-iron, -s 'kræmpˌaɪən, -z
crampon, -s 'kræmpɒn [-pən], -z
Crampton 'kræmptən
cran, -s kræn, -z
cranage 'kreɪnɪdʒ
Cranage (surname) 'krænɪdʒ
cranberr|y, -ies 'krænbər|ɪ, -ɪz
Cranborne 'krænbɔːn [-bɔən]
Cranbourn(e) 'krænbɔːn [-bɔən, -ˌbʊən]
Cranbrook 'krænbrʊk
cran|e (s. v.) (C.), -es, -ing, -ed kreɪn, -z,
-ɪŋ, -d
Cranford 'krænfəd
cranial 'kreɪnjəl [-nɪəl]
craniolog|ist/s, -y ˌkreɪnɪ'ɒlədʒ|ɪst/s, -ɪ
crani|um, -ums, -a 'kreɪnɪ|əm [-nɪ|əm],
-əmz, -ə
crank, -s, -shaft/s kræŋk, -s, -ʃɑːft/s
Crankshaw 'kræŋkʃɔː

crank|y, -ier, -iest, -ily, -iness 'kræŋk|ɪ,
-ɪə* [-jə*], -ɪɪst [-jɪst], -ɪlɪ [-əlɪ],
-ɪnɪs [-ɪnəs]
Cran|leigh, -ley, -mer 'kræn|lɪ, -lɪ, -mə*
crann|y, -ies, -ied 'kræn|ɪ, -ɪz, -ɪd
Cran|ston, -worth 'kræn|stən, -wɜːθ
[-wəθ]
crape, -s kreɪp, -s
crapulen|ce, -t/ly 'kræpjʊlən|s, -t/lɪ
crapulous 'kræpjʊləs
crash (s. v.), -es, -ing, -ed kræʃ, -ɪz, -ɪŋ,
-t
Crashaw 'kræʃɔː
crash-div|e (s. v.), -es, -ing, -ed 'kræʃ-
daɪv, -z, -ɪŋ, -d
crash-helmet, -s 'kræʃˌhelmɪt, -s
crash-land, -s, -ing, -ed 'kræʃlænd
[ˌ-'-], -z, -ɪŋ, -ɪd
crasis 'kreɪsɪs
crass, -er, -est, -ly, -ness kræs, -ə*, -ɪst,
-lɪ, -nɪs [-nəs]
crassitude 'kræsɪtjuːd
cratch, -es krætʃ, -ɪz
Cratchit 'krætʃɪt
crate, -s kreɪt, -s
crater, -s 'kreɪtə*, -z
Crathie 'kræθɪ
cravat, -s, -ted krə'væt, -s, -ɪd
crav|e, -es, -ing/s, -ed, -er/s kreɪv, -z,
-ɪŋ/z, -d, -ə*/z
craven (C.), -s, -ly 'kreɪvən, -z, -lɪ
craw, -s krɔː, -z
Crawcour 'krɔːkə*
crawfish, -es 'krɔːfɪʃ, -ɪz
Crawford 'krɔːfəd
crawl (s. v.), -s, -ing, -ed, -er/s krɔːl, -z,
-ɪŋ, -d, -ə*/z
Crawley 'krɔːlɪ
crawl|y, -ier, -iest, -iness 'krɔː|lɪ, -ɪə*
[-jə*], -ɪɪst [-jɪst], -ɪnɪs [-ɪnəs]
crayfish, -es 'kreɪfɪʃ, -ɪz
crayon, -s 'kreɪən ['kreɪɒn], -z
craze, -s, -d kreɪz, -ɪz, -d
craz|y, -ier, -iest, -ily, -iness 'kreɪz|ɪ,
-ɪə* [-jə*], -ɪɪst [-jɪst], -ɪlɪ [-əlɪ], -ɪnɪs
[-ɪnəs]
Creagh kreɪ
Creaghan 'kriːgən
creak (s. v.), -s, -ing, -ed kriːk, -s, -ɪŋ, -t
creak|y, -ier, -iest, -ily, -iness 'kriːk|ɪ,
-ɪə* [-jə*], -ɪɪst [-jɪst], -ɪlɪ [-əlɪ],
-ɪnɪs [-ɪnəs]
cream, -s kriːm, -z
cream-cheese, -s ˌkriːm'tʃiːz, -ɪz
cream-coloured 'kriːmˌkʌləd
creamer|y, -ies 'kriːmər|ɪ, -ɪz
cream-laid ˌkriːm'leɪd
cream-wove ˌkriːm'wəʊv

cream|y, -ier, -iest, -ily, -iness 'kri:m|ɪ, -ɪə* [-jə*], -ɪıst [-jɪst], -ɪlɪ [-əlɪ], -ɪnɪs [-ɪnəs]

creas|e (s. v.), -es, -ing, -ed kri:s, -ɪz, -ɪŋ, -t

Creas(e)y 'kri:sɪ

creasy (adj.) ᵗ'kri:sɪ

creat|e, -es, -ing, -ed kri:'eɪt [krɪ-], -s, -ɪŋ, -ɪd

creation (C.), -s kri:'eɪʃn [krɪ-], -z

creationi|sm, -st/s kri:'eɪʃɲɪ|zəm [krɪ-, -ʃənɪ-], -st/s

creative, -ly, -ness kri:'eɪtɪv [krɪ-], -lɪ, -nɪs [-nəs]

creativity ˌkri:eɪ'tɪvətɪ [ˌkrɪ-, ˌkrɪə-, -ɪtɪ]

creator (C.), -s, kri:'eɪtə* [krɪ-], -z

creature, -s 'kri:tʃə*, -z

crèche, -s kreɪʃ [kreʃ], -ɪz

Crécy 'kresɪ

credence 'kri:dəns

credential, -s krɪ'denʃl, -z

credibility ˌkredə'bɪlətɪ [-dɪ'b-, -lɪt-]

credib|le, -ly, -leness 'kredəb|l [-dɪb-], -lɪ, -lnɪs [-nəs]

credit (s. v.), -s, -ing, -ed, -or/s 'kredɪt, -s, -ɪŋ, -ɪd, -ə*/z

creditab|le, -ly, -leness 'kredɪtəb|l, -lɪ, -lnɪs [-nəs]

Crediton 'kredɪtn

credo, -s 'kri:dəʊ ['kreɪd-], -z

credulity krɪ'dju:lətɪ [krə'd-, kre'd-, -ɪtɪ]

credulous, -ly, -ness 'kredjʊləs, -lɪ, -nɪs [-dʒʊl-, -nəs]

creed (C.), -s kri:d, -z

creek, -s kri:k, -s

creel, -s kri:l, -z

creep, -s, -ing, crept kri:p, -s, -ɪŋ, krept

creeper, -s 'kri:pə*, -z

creep|y, -ier, -iest, -ily, -iness 'kri:p|ɪ, -ɪə* [-jə*], -ɪıst [-jɪst], -ɪlɪ [-əlɪ], -ɪnɪs [-ɪnəs]

Crees kri:s, kri:z

creese, -s kri:s, -ɪz

Creighton 'kraɪtn

cremat|e, -es, -ing, -ed, -or/s krɪ'meɪt [krə'm-], -s, -ɪŋ, -ɪd, -ə*/z

cremation, -s krɪ'meɪʃn [krə'm-], -z

crematori|al, -um/s, -a ˌkremə'tɔ:rɪ|əl, -əm/z, -ə

cremator|y, -ies 'kremətər|ɪ, -ɪz

crème - de - menthe ˌkreɪmdə'mɑːnt [-'mɔ:nt, -'mɒnt] (krɛːmdəmã:t)

Cremona krɪ'məʊnə [krə'm-]

crenate 'kri:neɪt

crenel(l)at|e, -es, -ing, -ed 'krenəleɪt [-nɪl-], -s, -ɪŋ, -ɪd

crenel(l)ation, -s ˌkrenə'leɪʃən [-nɪ'l-], -z

Creole, -s 'kri:əʊl ['krɪəʊl], -z

Creolian kri:'əʊljən [krɪ-, -lɪən]

creosote 'krɪəsəʊt ['kri:əs-]

crêpe, -s kreɪp, -s

crêpe de chine ˌkreɪpdə'ʃi:n (krɛpdəʃin)

crepitat|e, -es, -ing, -ed 'krepɪteɪt, -s, -ɪŋ, -ɪd

crepitation, -s ˌkrepɪ'teɪʃn, -z

crépon 'krepɔ̃:ŋ ['kreɪp-, -pɔ:ŋ, -pɒn] (krepɔ̃)

crept (from creep) krept

crepuscular krɪ'pʌskjʊlə* [kre'p-]

crepuscule 'krepəskju:l

Crerar 'krɪərə*

crescendo, -s krɪ'ʃendəʊ [krə'ʃ-], -z

crescent (moon, shape), -s 'kresnt [-eznt], -s

crescent (growing, when applied to objects other than the moon) 'kresnt

Crespigny (surname) 'krepɪnɪ, 'krepnɪ, 'krespɪnɪ, (in London streets) kre'spi:nɪ

cress, -es kres, -ɪz

Cressida 'kresɪdə

Cresswell 'krezwəl, -esw-

Cressy 'kresɪ

crest (s. v.), -s, -ing, -ed krest, -s, -ɪŋ, -ɪd

crestfallen 'krest.fɔ:lən

Creswick 'krezɪk

cretaceous krɪ'teɪʃəs [kre't-, -ʃjəs, -ʃɪəs]

Cretan, -s 'kri:tn, -z

Crete kri:t

Cretic, -s 'kri:tɪk, -s

cretin, -s 'kretɪn ['kri:t-], -z

cretinism 'kretɪnɪzəm ['kri:t-]

cretonne, -s 'kretɒn [kre'tɒn], -z

Creusa krɪ'u:zə [krɪ'ju:-]

crevasse, -s, -d krɪ'væs [krə'v-], -ɪz, -t

crevice, -s 'krevɪs, -ɪz

crew, -s kru:, -z

crew (from crow) kru:

crew-cut 'kru:kʌt

Crewe kru:

crewel, -s 'kru:əl ['krʊɪl, -ʊəl], -z

Crewkerne 'kru:kɜ:n ['krʊkən, rarely kru:'kɜ:n]

Crianlarich ˌkrɪən'lærɪk [-ɪx]

crib (s. v.), -s, -bing, -bed, -ber|s krɪb, -z, -ɪŋ, -d, -ə*/z

cribbage 'krɪbɪdʒ

cribbage - board, -s 'krɪbɪdʒbɔ:d [-bəəd], -z

Criccieth 'krɪkɪeθ [-kɪəθ, -kjəθ] (Welsh 'krikjeθ)

115

Crichel 'krɪtʃəl
Crichton 'kraɪtn
crick (s. v.), -s, -ing, -ed krɪk, -s, -ɪŋ, -t
cricket, -s, -er/s 'krɪkɪt, -s, -ə*/z
cricket-match, -es 'krɪkɪtmætʃ, -ɪz
cricklite 'krɪklaɪt
cricoid 'kraɪkɔɪd
cried (from cry) kraɪd
Crieff kri:f
crier, -s 'kraɪə*, -z
cries (from cry) kraɪz
crime, -s kraɪm, -z
Crimea, -n kraɪ'mɪə [krɪ'm-], -n
crimin|al/s, -ally 'krɪmɪn|l/z [-mən-], -əlɪ
criminality ˌkrɪmɪ'nælətɪ [-mə'n-, -ɪtɪ]
criminat|e, -es, -ing, -ed 'krɪmɪneɪt [-mən-], -s, -ɪŋ, -ɪd
crimination, -s ˌkrɪmɪ'neɪʃn [-mə'n-], -z
criminolog|ist/s, -y ˌkrɪmɪ'nɒlədʒ|ɪst/s [-mə'n-], -ɪ
crimp (adj. v.), -s, -ing, -ed krɪmp, -s, -ɪŋ, -t [krɪmt]
crimplene 'krɪmpli:n
crims|on (s. v. adj.), -ons, -oning, -oned 'krɪmz|n, -nz, -ŋɪŋ [-nɪŋ], -nd
crinal 'kraɪnl
cring|e (s. v.), -es, -ing, -ed, -er/s krɪndʒ, -ɪz, -ɪŋ, -d, -ə*/z
crink|le, -les, -ling, -led 'krɪŋk|l, -lz, -lɪŋ [-lɪŋ], -ld
crinkly 'krɪŋklɪ
crinoid, -s 'kraɪnɔɪd ['krɪn-], -z
crinoline (s.), -s 'krɪnəlɪn [-li:n, ˌkrɪnə-'li:n], -z
crinoline (adj.) 'krɪnəlɪn
Crippen 'krɪpɪn [-pən]
cripp|le (s. v.), -les, -ling, -led 'krɪp|l, -lz, -lɪŋ [-lɪŋ], -ld
Cripplegate 'krɪplgeɪt [-gɪt]
Crisfield 'krɪsfi:ld
cris|is, -es 'kraɪs|ɪs, -i:z
crisp (C.), -er, -est, -ly, -ness krɪsp, -ə*, -ɪst, -lɪ, -nɪs [-nəs]
crisp-bread 'krɪspbred
Crispin 'krɪspɪn
criss-cross 'krɪskrɒs [old-fashioned -krɔ:s]
criteri|on (C.), -ons, -a kraɪ'tɪərɪ|ən, -ənz, -ə
critic, -s, -al, -ally, -alness 'krɪtɪk, -s; -l, -əlɪ, -lnɪs [-nəs]
criticism, -s 'krɪtɪsɪzəm, -z
criticizable [-isa-] 'krɪtɪsaɪzəbl [ˌkrɪtɪ's-]
criticiz|e [-is|e], -es, -ing, -ed 'krɪtɪsaɪz, -ɪz, -ɪŋ, -d
critique, -s krɪ'ti:k, -s
Crittenden 'krɪtndən

croak (s. v.), -s, -ing/s, -ed, -er/s krəʊk, -s, -ɪŋ/z, -t, -ə*/z
croak|y, -ier, -iest, -ily, -iness 'krəʊk|ɪ, -ɪə* [-jə*], -ɪɪst [-jɪst], -ɪlɪ [-əlɪ], -ɪnɪs [-nəs]
Croat, -s 'krəʊæt [-ət], -s
Croatia krəʊ'eɪʃə [-ʃɪə, -ʃjə]
Croatian, -s krəʊ'eɪʃn [-ʃɪən, -ʃjən], -z
crochet (s. v.), -s, -ing, -ed 'krəʊʃeɪ [-ʃɪ], -z, -ɪŋ, -d
crochet-hook, -s 'krəʊʃɪhʊk [-ʃeɪh-], -s
crock, -s krɒk, -s
Crocker 'krɒkə*
crockery 'krɒkərɪ
crocket, -s 'krɒkɪt, -s
Crockett 'krɒkɪt
crocodile, -s 'krɒkədaɪl, -z
crocus, -es 'krəʊkəs, -ɪz
Croesus 'kri:səs
croft (C.), -s krɒft, -s
crofter, -s 'krɒftə*, -z
croissant, -s 'krwʌsɑ̃:ŋ ['krwɑ:-, -sɒŋ, -sɔ̃:ŋ], -z (krwɑsɑ̃)
Croker 'krəʊkə*
Cro-Magnon krəʊ'mænjɔ̃:ŋ (krɔmaɲɔ̃)
Cromarty 'krɒmətɪ
Crombie 'krɒmbɪ, 'krʌm-
Crome krəʊm
Cromer 'krəʊmə*
cromlech, -s 'krɒmlek, -s
Crommelin 'krʌmlɪn, 'krɒm-
Crompton 'krʌmptən, 'krɒm-
Cromwell 'krɒmwəl ['krʌm-, -wel]
Cromwellian krɒm'welɪən [krʌm-, -ljən]
crone, -s krəʊn, -z
Cronin 'krəʊnɪn
cron|y, -ies 'krəʊn|ɪ, -ɪz
crook (s. v.), -s, -ing, -ed (p. partic.) krʊk, -s, -ɪŋ, -t
Crookback 'krʊkbæk
crook-backed 'krʊkbækt
Crooke, -s krʊk, -s
crooked (adj.) (not straight), -er, -est, -ly, -ness 'krʊkɪd, -ə*, -ɪst, -lɪ, -nɪs [-nəs]
crooked (adj.) (having a crook) krʊkt
Croome kru:m
croon (s. v.), -s, -ing, -ed, -er/s kru:n, -z, -ɪŋ, -d, -ə*/z
crop (s. v.), -s, -ping, -ped krɒp, -s, -ɪŋ, -t
cropper, -s 'krɒpə*, -z
croquet (s. v.), -s, -ing, -ed 'krəʊkeɪ [-kɪ], -z, -ɪŋ, -d
croquette, -s krɒ'ket [krəʊ-], -s
crore, -s krɔ:* [krɔə*], -z
Crosby 'krɒzbɪ, 'krɒsbɪ

Crosfield 'krɒsfiːld [old-fashioned 'krɔːs-]
Croshaw 'krəʊʃɔː
crosier (C.), -s 'krəʊzjə* [-zɪə*, -ʒə*], -z
cross (s. adj. v.) (C.), -es; -er, -est, -ly, -ness; -ing, -ed krɒs [old-fashioned krɔːs, and in compounds], -ɪz; -ə*, -ɪst, -lɪ, -nɪs [-nəs]; -ɪŋ, -t
cross-action, -s 'krɒsˌækʃn ['krɔːs-], -z
cross-bar, -s 'krɒsbɑː* ['krɔːs-], -z
cross-beam, -s 'krɒsbiːm ['krɔːs-], -z
cross-bench, -es 'krɒsbentʃ ['krɔːs-], -ɪz
cross-bencher, -s 'krɒsˌbentʃə* ['krɔːs-, ˌ-'--], -z
crossbill, -s 'krɒsbɪl ['krɔːs-], -z
crossbones 'krɒsbəʊnz ['krɔːs-]
crossbow, -s 'krɒsbəʊ ['krɔːs-], -z
crossbred 'krɒsbred ['krɔːs-]
crossbreed, -s 'krɒsbriːd ['krɔːs-], -z
cross-bun, -s ˌkrɒs'bʌn [ˌkrɔːs-], -z
cross-country ˌkrɒs'kʌntrɪ [ˌkrɔːs-, '-ˌ-- when followed by a stress]
crosscut, -s 'krɒskʌt ['krɔːs-], -s
crosse, -s krɒs, -ɪz
Crosse krɒs [krɔːs]
cross-examination, -s 'krɒsɪgˌzæmɪ-'neɪʃn ['krɔːs-, -eg-], -z
cross-examin|e, -es, -ing, -ed, -er/s ˌkrɒsɪg'zæmɪn [ˌkrɔːs-, -eg-], -z, -ɪŋ, -d, -ə*/z
cross|-eyed, -grained 'krɒs|aɪd ['krɔːs-, ˌ-'-], -greɪnd
cross-fire 'krɒsˌfaɪə* ['krɔːs-]
crossing (s.), -s 'krɒsɪŋ ['krɔːs-], -z
crossing-sweeper, -s 'krɒsɪŋˌswiːpə* ['krɔːs-], -z
cross-jack, -s 'krɒsdʒæk ['krɔːs-], -s
cross-legged 'krɒslegd ['krɔːs-, ˌ-'-]
Cross|ley, -man 'krɒs|lɪ ['krɔːs-], -mən
crosspatch, -es 'krɒspætʃ ['krɔːs-], -ɪz
cross-purpose, -s ˌkrɒs'pɜː•pəs [ˌkrɔːs-], -ɪz
cross-questi|on, -ons, -oning, -oned ˌkrɒs'kwestʃ|ən [ˌkrɔːs-, -eʃtʃ-], -ənz, -ənɪŋ [-n̩ɪŋ], -ənd
cross-reference, -s ˌkrɒs'refərəns [ˌkrɔːs-], -ɪz
cross-road, -s 'krɒsrəʊd ['krɔːs-], -z
cross-row, -s 'krɒsrəʊ ['krɔːs-], -z
cross-section, -s ˌkrɒs'sekʃn [ˌkrɔːs-], -z
cross-stitch 'krɒsstɪtʃ ['krɔːs-]
crossway, -s 'krɒsweɪ ['krɔːs-], -z
cross-wise 'krɒswaɪz ['krɔːs-]
cross-word, -s 'krɒswɜːd ['krɔːswɜːd], -z
Crosthwaite 'krɒsθweɪt ['krɔːs-]
crotal|um, -a 'krɒtəl|əm, -ə

crotch (C.), -es krɒtʃ, -ɪz
crotchet, -s, -y, -iness 'krɒtʃɪt, -s, -ɪ, -ɪnɪs [-ɪnəs]
croton (C.), 'krəʊtən
crouch (C.), -es, -ing, -ed krautʃ, -ɪz, -ɪŋ, -t (village in Kent kruːtʃ)
croup, -s kruːp, -s
croupier, -s 'kruːpɪə* [-pjə*, -pɪeɪ] (krupje), -z
crow (s. v.), -s, -ing, -ed, crew krəʊ, -z, -ɪŋ, -d, kruː
crowbar, -s 'krəʊbɑː*, -z
crowd (s. v.), -s, -ing, -ed kraʊd, -z, -ɪŋ, -ɪd
Crowe krəʊ
crow-foot 'krəʊfʊt
Crow|hurst, -land, -ley 'krəʊ|hɜːst, -lənd, -lɪ
crown (s. v.), -s, -ing, -ed kraʊn, -z, -ɪŋ, -d
Crowndale 'kraʊndeɪl
crown-glass ˌkraʊn'glɑːs [in contrast '--]
crown-land, -s ˌkraʊn'lænd [in contrast '--], -z
crown-prince, -s ˌkraʊn'prɪns [also '-- when attributive], -ɪz
crow-quill, -s 'krəʊkwɪl, -z
crow's|-foot, -feet 'krəʊz|fʊt, -fiːt
crow's-nest, -s 'krəʊznest, -s
Crowte kraʊt
Crowther 'kraʊðə*
Croyd|en, -on 'krɔɪd|n, -n
crozier (C.), -s 'krəʊzjə* [-zɪə*, -ʒə*], -z
cruci|al, -ally 'kruːʃ|l [-ʃɪəl, -ʃjəl], -əlɪ
crucible, -s 'kruːsɪbl [-əbl], -z
crucifix, -es 'kruːsɪfɪks, -ɪz
crucifixion (C.), -s ˌkruːsɪ'fɪkʃn, -z
cruciform 'kruːsɪfɔːm
cruci|fy, -fies, -fying, -fied, -fier/s 'kruːsɪ|faɪ, -faɪz, -faɪɪŋ, -faɪd, -faɪə*/z
crude, -r, -st, -ly, -ness kruːd, -ə*, -ɪst, -lɪ, -nɪs [-nəs]
Cruden 'kruːdn [-dən]
crudit|y, -ies 'kruːdɪt|ɪ [-ət|ɪ], -ɪz
cruel, -ness kruəl ['kruːəl, 'kruɪl, 'kruːl, kruːl], -nɪs [-nəs]
cruel|ler, -lest, -ly 'kruəl|ə* ['kruːl-, 'kruɪl-, 'kruːəl-], -ɪst, -ɪ
cruelt|y, -ies 'kruəlt|ɪ ['kruːəl-, 'kruɪl-, 'kruːl-], -ɪz
cruet, -s; -stand/s 'kruːɪt ['kruɪt], -s; -stænd/z
Crui(c)kshank 'krʊkʃæŋk
cruis|e (s. v.), -es, -ing, -ed, -er/s kruːz, -ɪz, -ɪŋ, -d, -ə*/z

crumb (s. v.), -s, -ing, -ed krʌm, -z, -ɪŋ, -d

crumb-brush, -es 'krʌmbrʌʃ, -ɪz

crumb|le, -les, -ling, -led 'krʌmb|l, -lz, -lɪŋ, -ld

crumby 'krʌmɪ

Crummock 'krʌmək

crummy 'krʌmɪ

crump, -s, -ing, -ed krʌmp, -s, -ɪŋ, -t [krʌmt]

crumpet, -s 'krʌmpɪt, -s

crump|le, -les, -ling, -led 'krʌmp|l, -lz, -lɪŋ [-lɪŋ], -ld

crunch, -es, -ing, -ed, -y, -iness krʌntʃ, -ɪz, -ɪŋ, -t, -ɪ, -ɪnɪs [-nəs]

crupper, -s 'krʌpə*, -z

crusade, -s, -er/s kru:'seɪd, -z, -ə*/z

cruse, -s kru:z, -ɪz

crush (s. v.), -es, -ing, -ed, -er/s, -able krʌʃ, -ɪz, -ɪŋ, -t, -ə*/z, -əbl

crush-hat, -s ˌkrʌʃ'hæt, -s

crush-room, -s 'krʌʃrʊm [-ru:m], -z

Crusoe 'kru:səʊ ['kru:zəʊ]

crust, -s krʌst, -s

crusta|cea, -cean/s, -ceous krʌ'steɪ|ʃə [-ʃɪə, -ʃjə], -ʃn/z [-ʃɪən/z, -ʃjən/z], -ʃəs [-ʃɪəs, -ʃjəs]

crustate 'krʌsteɪt

crustated krʌ'steɪtɪd

crustation, -s krʌ'steɪʃn, -z

crusted 'krʌstɪd

crust|y, -ier, -iest, -ily, -iness 'krʌst|ɪ, -ɪə* [-jə*], -ɪɪst [-jɪst], -ɪlɪ [-əlɪ], -ɪnɪs [-ɪnəs]

crutch, -es, -ed krʌtʃ, -ɪz, -t

Crutched Friars ˌkrʌtʃɪd'fraɪəz [ˌkrʌtʃt-]

Cruttwell 'krʌtwəl

crux, -es krʌks, -ɪz

cr|y (s. v.), -ies, -ying, -ied, -ier/s kr|aɪ, -aɪz, -aɪɪŋ, -aɪd, -aɪə*/z

cry-bab|y, -ies 'kraɪˌbeɪb|ɪ, -ɪz

crypt, -s krɪpt, -s

cryptic, -al, -ally 'krɪptɪk, -l, -əlɪ

crypto, -s 'krɪptəʊ, -z

cryptogam, -s 'krɪptəʊgæm, -z

cryptogram, -s 'krɪptəʊgræm, -z

cryptograph, -s 'krɪptəʊgrɑːf [-græf], -s

cryptograph|er/s, -y krɪp'tɒgrəf|ə*/z, -ɪ

cryptology krɪp'tɒlədʒɪ

Crysell 'kraɪsl

crystal, -s 'krɪstl, -z

crystal-gaz|er/s, -ing 'krɪstlˌgeɪz|ə*/z, -ɪŋ

crystalline 'krɪstəlaɪn [-tˌlaɪn]

crystallizable [-isa-] 'krɪstəlaɪzəbl [-tˌlaɪ-]

crystallization [-isa-], -s ˌkrɪstəlaɪ-'zeɪʃn [-tˌlaɪ-], -z

crystalliz|e [-is|e], -es, -ing, -ed 'krɪs-təlaɪz [-tˌlaɪz], -ɪz, -ɪŋ, -d

crystallograph|er/s, -y ˌkrɪstə'lɒgrə-f|ə*/z, -ɪ

crystalloid, -s 'krɪstəlɔɪd, -z

C-spring, -s 'siːsprɪŋ, -z

cub (s. v.), -s, -bing, -bed kʌb, -z, -ɪŋ, -d

Cuba, -n/s 'kjuːbə, -n/z

cubage 'kjuːbɪdʒ

cubbish 'kʌbɪʃ

cubb|y, -ies 'kʌb|ɪ, -ɪz

cubby-hole, -s 'kʌbɪhəʊl, -z

cub|e (s. v.), -es, -ing, -ed kjuːb, -z, -ɪŋ, -d

cubic, -al, -ally 'kjuːbɪk, -l, -əlɪ

cubicle, -s 'kjuːbɪkl, -z

cub|ism, -ist/s 'kjuːb|ɪzəm, -ɪst/s

cubistic kjuː'bɪstɪk

cubit, -s, -al 'kjuːbɪt, -s, -l

Cubitt 'kjuːbɪt

cuboid, -s 'kjuːbɔɪd, -z

Cuchulinn 'kuːkʊlɪn ['kuːxʊ-]

Cuckfield 'kʊkfiːld

cucking-stool, -s 'kʌkɪŋstuːl, -z

Cuckmere 'kʊkˌmɪə*

cuckold (s. v.), -s, -ing, -ed 'kʌkəʊld [-kəld], -z, -ɪŋ, -ɪd

cuck|oo (s. v.), -oos, -ooing, -ooed 'kʊk|uː, -uːz, -uːɪŋ [-ʊɪŋ], -uːd

cuckoo (interj.) ˌkʊ'kuː: ['kʊkuː:]

cuckoo-clock, -s 'kʊkuːklɒk, -s

cuckoo-flower, -s 'kʊkuːˌflaʊə*, -z

cuckoo-pint, -s 'kʊkuːpaɪnt, -s

cuckoo-spit, -s 'kʊkuːspɪt, -s

cucumber, -s 'kjuːkʌmbə* ['kjʊkʌm-, 'kjuːkəm-], -z

cud, -s kʌd, -z

Cudahy 'kʌdəhɪ

cudd|le (s. v.), -les, -ling, -led, -ly 'kʌd|l, -lz, -lɪŋ [-lɪŋ], -ld, -lɪ

cudd|y, -ies 'kʌd|ɪ, -ɪz

cudg|el (s. v.), -els, -elling, -elled 'kʌdʒ|əl, -əlz, -lɪŋ [-əlɪŋ], -əld

Cudworth 'kʌdwəθ [-wɜːθ]

cue, -s kjuː, -z

Cufa 'kjuːfə

cuff (s. v.), -s, -ing, -ed kʌf, -s, -ɪŋ, -t

Cuffe kʌf

Cuffley 'kʌflɪ

Cufic 'kjuːfɪk

cui bono ˌkwiː'bɒnəʊ [ˌkuːɪ'bɒnəʊ, ˌkuːɪ'bəʊnəʊ]

cuirass, -es kwɪ'ræs, -ɪz

cuirassier, -s ˌkwɪə'sɪə*, -z

cuisine kwɪ'ziːn [kwiː'z-] (kɥizin)

118

cuisse, -s kwɪs, -ɪz
cul-de-sac, -s 'kʌldəsæk ['kʊl-, ‚--'-]
(kyldəsak, *pronounced as if French*),
-s
*Note.—The actual French pronun-
ciation is* kydsak *or* kytsak.
Culebra ku:'lebrə [kʊ'l-]
Culham 'kʌləm
culinary 'kʌlɪnərɪ [*old-fashioned* 'kju:l-]
cull, -s, -ing, -ed kʌl, -z, -ɪŋ, -d
Cull|en, -ey 'kʌl|ɪn, 'kʌl|ən, -ɪ
cullender, -s 'kʌlɪndə* [-lən-], -z
Cullinan 'kʌlɪnən [-næn]
Cullinnan kʌ'lɪnən [kə'l-]
Culloden kə'lɒdn [kʌ'l-, -'ləʊdn]
Cullompton kə'lʌmptən
culm, -s kʌlm, -z
Culme kʌlm
culminat|e, -es, -ing, -ed 'kʌlmɪneɪt, -s,
-ɪŋ, -ɪd
culmination, -s ‚kʌlmɪ'neɪʃn, -z
culotte, -s kju:'lɒt [kjʊ'l-] (kylɔt), -s
culpability ‚kʌlpə'bɪlətɪ [-lɪt-]
culpab|le, -ly, -leness 'kʌlpəb|l, -lɪ,
-lnɪs [-nəs]
culprit, -s 'kʌlprɪt, -s
Culross (*place in Scotland*) 'ku:rɒs
[-rəs], (*Scottish surname*) 'ku:rɒs
[-rəs], (*English surname*) 'kʌlrɒs,
(*street in London*) 'kʌlrɒs [kʌl'rɒs]
cult, -s kʌlt, -s
Culter (*in Scotland*) 'ku:tə*
cultivable 'kʌltɪvəbl
cultivat|e, -es, -ing, -ed, -or/s; -able
'kʌltɪveɪt, -s, -ɪŋ, -ɪd, -ə*/z; -əbl
cultivation ‚kʌltɪ'veɪʃn
Cults kʌlts
cultur|able, -al 'kʌltʃ|ər|əbl [-tʃʊr-], -əl
culture, -s, -d 'kʌltʃə*, -z, -d
culver, -s 'kʌlvə*, -z
culverin, -s 'kʌlvərɪn, -z
culvert, -s; -age 'kʌlvət, -s; -ɪdʒ
Culzean (*in Strathclyde*) kə'leɪn
cum kʌm
cumbent 'kʌmbənt
cumb|er, -ers, -ering, -ered, -erer/s
'kʌmb|ə*, -əz, -ərɪŋ, -əd, -ərə*/z
Cumberland 'kʌmbələnd [-blənd]
cumbersome, -ly, -ness 'kʌmbəsəm, -lɪ,
-nɪs [-nəs]
Cumbria, -n/s 'kʌmbrɪə, -n/z
cumbrous, -ly, -ness 'kʌmbrəs, -lɪ, -nɪs
[-nəs]
cumin 'kʌmɪn
cummerbund, -s 'kʌməbʌnd, -z
cummin 'kʌmɪn
Cumming, -s 'kʌmɪŋ, -z
Cummuskey (*surname*) 'kʌmskɪ

Cumnor 'kʌmnə*
cumulate (*adj.*) 'kju:mjʊlət [-mjəl-,
-lɪt, -leɪt]
cumulat|e (*v.*), -es, -ing, -ed 'kju:mjʊ-
leɪt [-mjəl-], -s, -ɪŋ, -ɪd
cumulation, -s ‚kju:mjʊ'leɪʃn [-mjə'l-],
-z
cumulative, -ly, -ness 'kju:mjʊlətɪv
[-mjəl-, -leɪt-], -lɪ, -nɪs [-nəs]
cumulus 'kju:mjʊləs [-mjəl-]
Cunard, -er/s kju:'nɑ:d [*also* '-- *when
attributive*], -ə*/z
cunctation, -s kʌŋk'teɪʃn, -z
cunctator, -s kʌŋk'teɪtə*, -z
Cund|all, -ell 'kʌnd|l, -l
cuneiform 'kju:nɪfɔ:m [-njɪf-, -nɪf-]
cuniform 'kju:nɪfɔ:m
Cunliffe 'kʌnlɪf
cunning (*s. adj.*), -est, -ly, -ness 'kʌnɪŋ,
-ɪst, -lɪ, -nɪs
Cunningham 'kʌnɪŋəm
cup (*s. v.*), -s, -ping, -ped kʌp, -s, -ɪŋ, -t
Cupar 'ku:pə*
cup-bearer, -s 'kʌp‚beərə*, -z
cupboard, -s 'kʌbəd, -z
cupboard-love 'kʌbədlʌv [‚kʌbəd'l-]
cupful, -s 'kʌpfʊl, -z
cupid (C.), -s 'kju:pɪd, -z
cupidity kju:'pɪdətɪ [kjʊ-, -ɪtɪ]
cupola, -s 'kju:pələ, -z
cupping-glass, -es 'kʌpɪŋglɑ:s, -ɪz
cupr|eous, -ic, -ous 'kju:pr|ɪəs, -ɪk, -əs
cupriferous kju:'prɪfərəs [kjʊ-]
cur, -s kɜ:*, -z
curability ‚kjʊərə'bɪlətɪ [‚kjɔər-, ‚kjɔ:r-,
-lɪt-]
curable 'kjʊərəbl ['kjɔər-, 'kjɔ:r-]
curaç|ao (C.), -oa (C.) ‚kjʊərə's|əʊ
[‚kjɔər-, ‚kjɔ:r-, '---, -'saʊ], -əʊə
curac|y, -ies 'kjʊərəs|ɪ ['kjɔər-, 'kjɔ:r-],
-ɪz
Curan 'kʌrən
curare kjʊ'rɑ:rɪ [‚kjʊə'r-]
curate, -s 'kjʊərət ['kjɔər-, 'kjɔ:r-,
-rɪt], -s
curative 'kjʊərətɪv ['kjɔər-, 'kjɔ:r-]
curator, -s; -ship/s ‚kjʊə'reɪtə* [kjʊ'r-,
kjɔə'r-, kjɔ:'r-], -z; -ʃɪp/s
curb (*s. v.*), -s, -ing, -ed kɜ:b, -z, -ɪŋ, -d
curbstone, -s 'kɜ:bstəʊn, -z
curd, -s kɜ:d, -z
curd|le, -les, -ling, -led 'kɜ:d|l, -lz, -lɪŋ
[-lɪŋ], -ld
curd|y, -ier, -iest, -iness 'kɜ:d|ɪ, -ɪə*
[-jə*], -ɪɪst [-jɪst], -ɪnɪs [-ɪnəs]
cur|e (*s. v.*), -es, -ing, -ed, -er/s kjʊə*
[kjɔə*, kjɔ:*], -z, -rɪŋ, -d, -rə*/z
curfew, -s 'kɜ:fju:, -z

119

cu|ria, -riae 'kjʊə|rɪə ['kjɔər-, 'kjɔːr-, 'kʊər-], -rɪi: ['kʊərɪaɪ]

curie, -s 'kjʊərɪ, -z

curio, -s 'kjʊərɪəʊ ['kjɔər-, 'kjɔːr-], -z

curiosit|y, -ies ˌkjʊərɪ'ɒsət|ɪ [ˌkjɔər-, ˌkjɔːr-, -ɪt|ɪ], -ɪz

curious, -ly, -ness 'kjʊərɪəs ['kjɔər-, 'kjɔːr-], -lɪ, -nɪs [-nəs]

curium 'kjʊərɪəm

curl (s. v.), -s, -ing, -ed, -er/s kɜːl, -z, -ɪŋ, -d, -ə*/z

curlew, -s 'kɜːlju: [-luː], -z

curling (s.) 'kɜːlɪŋ

curling-iron, -s 'kɜːlɪŋˌaɪən, -z

curling-stone, -s 'kɜːlɪŋstəʊn, -z

curling-tongs 'kɜːlɪŋtɒŋz

curl|y, -ier, -iest 'kɜːl|ɪ, -ɪə* [-jə*], -ɪɪst [-jɪst]

curmudgeon, -s kɜː'mʌdʒ*n [kə'm-], -z

curragh (C.), -s 'kʌrə, -z

Curran 'kʌr*n

currant, -s 'kʌr*nt, -s

currenc|y, -ies 'kʌr*ns|ɪ, -ɪz

current (s. adj.), -s, -ly, -ness 'kʌr*nt, -s, -lɪ, -nɪs [-nəs]

Currer 'kʌrə*

curricul|um, -a, -ar kə'rɪkjəl|əm [-kjʊl-], -ə, -ə*

curriculum vitae kəˌrɪkjələm'viːtaɪ [-kjʊl-]

Currie 'kʌrɪ

currish, -ly, -ness 'kɜːrɪʃ, -lɪ, -nɪs [-nəs]

curr|y (s. v.) (C.), -ies, -ying, -ied, -ier/s 'kʌr|ɪ, -ɪz, -ɪŋ, -ɪd, -ɪə*/z

curry-powder 'kʌrɪˌpaʊdə*

curs|e (s. v.), -es, -ing, -ed kɜːs, -ɪz, -ɪŋ, -t

cursed (adj.), -ly, -ness 'kɜːsɪd, -lɪ, -nɪs [-nəs]

cursive, -ly, -ness 'kɜːsɪv, -lɪ, -nɪs [-nəs]

Cursor Mundi ˌkɜːsɔː'mʊndi: [-'mʌndaɪ]

cursor|y, -ily, -iness 'kɜːsər|ɪ, -əlɪ [-ɪlɪ], -ɪnɪs [-ɪnəs]

cursus 'kɜːsəs

curt, -er, -est, -ly, -ness kɜːt, -ə*, -ɪst, -lɪ, -nɪs [-nəs]

curtail, -s, -ing, -ed, -ment/s kɜː'teɪl, -z, -ɪŋ, -d, -mənt/s

curtain, -s, -ed 'kɜːtn [-tən, -tɪn], -z, -d

curtain-raiser, -s 'kɜːtnˌreɪzə*, -z

curtesy 'kɜːtɪsɪ [-təsɪ]

Curti|ce, -s(s) 'kɜːtɪ|s, -s

curtsey (s. v.), -s, -ing, -ed 'kɜːtsɪ, -z, -ɪŋ [-jɪŋ], -d

curts|y (s. v.), -ies, -ying, -ied 'kɜːts|ɪ, -ɪz, -ɪŋ [-jɪŋ], -ɪd

curvaceous kɜː'veɪʃəs

curvation, -s kɜː'veɪʃn, -z

curvature, -s 'kɜːvətʃə* [-tjə*, -ˌtʃʊə*, -ˌtjʊə*], -z

curv|e (s. v.), -es, -ing, -ed kɜːv, -z, -ɪŋ, -d

curvet (s. v.), -s, -(t)ing, -(t)ed kɜː'vet, -s, -ɪŋ, -ɪd

curviline|al, -ar ˌkɜːvɪ'lɪnɪ|əl [-nj|əl], -ə*

curvital 'kɜːvɪtl

Curwen 'kɜːwɪn [-wən]

Curzon 'kɜːzn

Cusack 'kjuːsæk, 'kjuːzək

cushat, -s 'kʌʃət [-ʃæt], -s

Cushing 'kʊʃɪŋ

cushi|on (s. v.), -ons, -oning, -oned 'kʊʃ|n, -nz, -nɪŋ [-ənɪŋ], -nd

Cushny 'kʌʃnɪ

cushy 'kʊʃɪ

Cusins 'kjuːzɪnz

cusp, -s kʌsp, -s

cuspid, -or/s 'kʌspɪd, -ɔː*/z

cuss, -es kʌs, -ɪz

cussed, -ly, -ness 'kʌsɪd, -lɪ, -nɪs [-nəs]

Custance 'kʌstəns

custard, -s 'kʌstəd, -z

custard-apple, -s 'kʌstədˌæpl, -z

custodial kʌ'stəʊdjəl [-dɪəl]

custodian, -s kʌ'stəʊdjən [-dɪən], -z

custody 'kʌstədɪ

custom, -s 'kʌstəm, -z

customar|y, -ily, -iness 'kʌstəmər|ɪ, -əlɪ [-ɪlɪ], -ɪnɪs [-ɪnəs]

customer, -s 'kʌstəmə*, -z

custom-hou|se, -ses 'kʌstəmhaʊ|s, -zɪz

custos, custodes 'kʌstɒs, kʌ'stəʊdi:z

cut (s. v.), -s, -ting, -ter/s kʌt, -s, -ɪŋ, -ə*/z

cutaneous kju:'teɪnjəs [kjʊ-, -nɪəs]

cut-away 'kʌtəweɪ

Cutch kʌtʃ (Hindi kəch)

cutcherr|y, -ies kʌ'tʃer|ɪ [kə'tʃ-], -ɪz

cute, -r, -st, -ly, -ness kju:t, -ə*, -ɪst, -lɪ, -nɪs [-nəs]

Cutforth 'kʌtfɔːθ

Cuthbert, -son 'kʌθbət, -sn

cuticle, -s 'kjuːtɪkl, -z

cuticular kju:'tɪkjʊlə* [kjʊ-]

cutis 'kjuːtɪs

cutlass, -es 'kʌtləs, -ɪz

cutler, -s, -y 'kʌtlə*, -z, -rɪ

cutlet, -s 'kʌtlɪt [-lət], -s

cut-off, -s 'kʌtɒf [old-fashioned -ɔːf], -s

cut-out, -s 'kʌtaʊt, -s

Cuttell kə'tel

cutter, -s 'kʌtə*, -z

cut-throat, -s 'kʌtθrəʊt, -s

cutting (s.), -s 'kʌtɪŋ, -z

cuttle (**C.**), **-s**; **-bone** 'kʌtl, -z; -bəʊn
cuttle-fish, **-es** 'kʌtlfɪʃ, -ɪz
cutt|y, **-ies** 'kʌt|ɪ, -ɪz
cutwater, **-s** 'kʌt,wɔ:tə*, -z
cuvette, **-s** kju:'vet (kyvɛt), -s
Cuvier 'kju:vɪeɪ ['ku:-] (kyvje)
Cuxhaven 'kʊks,hɑ:vn (kuks'ha:fən)
Cuyp, **-s** kaɪp, -s
cwm, **-s** ku:m [kʊm] (*Welsh* kum), -z
cwt., cwts. 'hʌndrədweɪt [-drɪd-], -s
cyanate 'saɪəneɪt
cyanic saɪ'ænɪk
cyanide, **-s** 'saɪənaɪd, -z
cyanogen saɪ'ænədʒɪn [-dʒen]
cyanosis ,saɪə'nəʊsɪs
cybernetic, **-s** ,saɪbə'netɪk [-bɜ:'n-], -s
Cyclades 'sɪklədi:z
cyclamate, **-s** 'saɪkləmeɪt ['sɪk-], -s
cyclamen, **-s** 'sɪkləmən [-klɪm-], -z
cyc|le (*s. v.*), **-les, -ling, -led** 'saɪk|l, -lz, -lɪŋ, -ld
cyclic, **-al, -ally** 'saɪklɪk ['sɪk-], -l, -əlɪ
cyclist, **-s** 'saɪklɪst, -s
cyclograph, **-s** 'saɪkləʊgrɑ:f [-græf], -s
cycloid, **-s** 'saɪklɔɪd, -z
cycloidal saɪ'klɔɪdl
cyclometer, **-s** saɪ'klɒmɪtə* [-mətə*], -z
cyclone, **-s** 'saɪkləʊn, -z
cyclonic saɪ'klɒnɪk
cyclopaed|ia [-ped-], **-ias, -ic** ,saɪkləʊ-'pi:d|jə [-d|ɪə], -jəz [-ɪəz], -ɪk
cyclopean saɪ'kləʊpjən [-pɪən, ,saɪkləʊ-'pi:ən]
cyclops, cyclopes 'saɪklɒps, saɪ'kləʊpi:z
cyclorama, **-s** ,saɪklə'rɑ:mə, -z
cyclostyl|e (*s. v.*), **-es, -ing, -ed** 'saɪkləʊ-staɪl, -z, -ɪŋ, -d
cyclothymia ,saɪkləʊ'θaɪmɪə [-mjə]
cyclotron, **-s** 'saɪklətrɒn, -z
cyder, **-s** 'saɪdə*, -z
cygnet, **-s** 'sɪgnɪt [-nət], -s
Cygnus 'sɪgnəs
cylinder, **-s** 'sɪlɪndə*, -z
cylindric, **-al, -ally** sɪ'lɪndrɪk, -l, -əlɪ
cylindriform sɪ'lɪndrɪfɔ:m
cylindroid, **-s** 'sɪlɪndrɔɪd [sɪ'l-], -z
cyli|x, **-ces** 'saɪlɪ|ks, -si:z
cyma, **-s, -ta** 'saɪmə, -z, -tə
cymar, **-s** sɪ'mɑ:*, -z
cymbal, **-s** 'sɪmbl, -z

cymbal|o/s, **-um/s** 'sɪmbəl|əʊ/z, -əm/z
Cymbeline 'sɪmbɪli:n [-bəl-]
cyme, **-s** saɪm, -z
Cymr|ic, **-y** 'kɪmr|ɪk, -ɪ
Cynewulf 'kɪnɪwʊlf ['kɪnə-]
cynic (*s. adj.*), **-s, -al, -ally** 'sɪnɪk, -s, -l, -əlɪ
cynicism, **-s** 'sɪnɪsɪzəm, -z
cynocephalic ,saɪnəʊse'fælɪk [-ke'f-]
cynocephalous ,saɪnəʊ'sefələs [-'kef-]
cynosure, **-s** 'sɪnə,zjʊə* ['saɪn-, -ə,ʒjʊə*, -ə,ʒʊə*, -ə,sjʊə*, -ə,ʃʊə*], -z
Cynthi|a, **-us** 'sɪnθɪ|ə [-θj|ə], -əs
cyph|er (*s. v.*), **-ers, -ering, -ered** 'saɪf|ə*, -əz, -ərɪŋ, -əd
cy près ,si:'preɪ
cypress, **-es** 'saɪprəs [-prɪs], -ɪz
Cyprian, **-s** 'sɪprɪən, -z
Cypriot, **-s** 'sɪprɪət [-rɪɒt], -s
Cypriote, **-s** 'sɪprɪəʊt, -s
Cyprus 'saɪprəs
Cyrenaica ,saɪərə'neɪkə [-rɪ'n-, -'naɪkə]
Cyrene saɪ'ri:nɪ [,saɪə'r-]
Cyrenian saɪ'ri:njən [,saɪə'r-, sɪ'r-, -nɪən]
Cyrenius saɪ'ri:njəs [,saɪə'r-, -nɪəs]
Cyril 'sɪrəl [-rɪl]
Cyrille 'sɪrɪl, sɪ'ri:l
Cyrillic sɪ'rɪlɪk
Cyrus 'saɪərəs
cyst, **-s, -ic, -oid** sɪst, -s, -ɪk, -ɔɪd
cystitis sɪs'taɪtɪs
Cythera sɪ'θɪərə
Cytherean ,sɪθə'ri:ən [-'rɪən]
cytogenetics ,saɪtəʊdʒɪ'netɪks [-dʒe'n-, -dʒə'n-]
cytology saɪ'tɒlədʒɪ
czar (**C.**), **-s** zɑ:*, -z
czardas, **-es** 'tʃɑ:dæʃ ['zɑ:dæs, -dəs], -ɪz
czarevitch (**C.**), **-es** 'zɑ:rəvɪtʃ [-rɪv-], -ɪz
czarevna (**C.**), **-s** zɑ:'revnə, -z
czarina, **-s** zɑ:'ri:nə, -z
czarist, **-s** 'zɑ:rɪst, -s
Czech, **-s** tʃek, -s
Czechoslovak, **-s** ,tʃekəʊ'sləʊvæk, -s
Czechoslovakia, **-n** ,tʃekəʊsləʊ'vækɪə [-'vækjə, -'vɑ:kɪə, -'vɑ:kjə], -n
Czerny 'tʃɜ:nɪ ['zɜ:-]

D

D (*the letter*), **-'s** di:, -z
dab (*s. v.*), **-s, -bing, -bed, -ber/s** dæb,
  -z, -ɪŋ, -d, -ə*/z
dabb|le, -les, -ling, -led, -ler/s 'dæb|l,
  -lz, -lɪŋ [-lɪŋ], -ld, -lə*/z [-lə*/z]
dabchick, -s 'dæbtʃɪk, -s
da capo dɑː'kɑːpəʊ
dace deɪs
dachshund, -s 'dækshʊnd [-sənd], -z
Da|cia, -cian/s 'deɪ|sjə [-sɪə, -ʃjə, -ʃɪə,
  -ʃə], -sjən/z [-sɪən/z, -ʃjən/z, -ʃɪən/z,
  -ʃn/z]
dacoit, -s, -age də'kɔɪt, -s, -ɪdʒ
Dacre, -s 'deɪkə*, -z
dacron 'dækrɒn ['deɪ-]
dactyl, -s 'dæktɪl, -z
dactylic dæk'tɪlɪk
dactylogram, -s dæk'tɪləʊgræm ['----],
  -z
dactylography ˌdæktɪ'lɒgrəfɪ
dad, -s dæd, -z
Dada, -ism 'dɑːdɑː ['dɑːdə], -ɪzəm
Daddo 'dædəʊ
dadd|y, -ies 'dæd|ɪ, -ɪz
daddy-long-legs ˌdædɪ'lɒŋlegz
dado, -s 'deɪdəʊ, -z
Daedalus 'diːdələs
daemon, -s 'diːmən, -z
daemonic diː'mɒnɪk [dɪ-]
D'Aeth deɪθ
daffadowndill|y, -ies ˌdæfədaʊn'dɪl|ɪ,
  -ɪz
daffodil, -s 'dæfədɪl, -z
daft, -er, -est, -ly, -ness dɑːft, -ə*, -ɪst,
  -lɪ, -nɪs [-nəs]
dag, -s dæg, -z
dagger, -s 'dægə*, -z
Daggett 'dægɪt
dago, -(e)s 'deɪgəʊ, -z
dagoba, -s 'dɑːgəbə, -z
Dagobert 'dægəʊbɜ:t
Dagon 'deɪgɒn [-gən]
Dagonet 'dægənət [-nɪt]
daguerr(e)otype, -s də'gerəʊtaɪp, -s
D'Aguilar 'dægwɪlə*
dahlia, -s 'deɪljə [-ɪə], -z
Dahomey də'həʊmɪ
Dai daɪ
Daiches (*surname*) 'deɪʃɪz, 'deɪtʃɪz

Dáil Eireann ˌdɔɪl'eərən [ˌdaɪl-, *rarely*
  dɑːl-, ˌdɔːl-]
dail|y (*s. adj. adv.*), **-ies** 'deɪl|ɪ, -ɪz
Daimler (*car*), **-s** 'deɪmlə*, -z
Dain, -es deɪn, -z
Daintree 'deɪntriː [-trɪ]
daint|y (*s. adj.*), **-ies; -ier, -iest, -ily,
  -iness** 'deɪnt|ɪ, -ɪz; -ɪə* [-jə*], -ɪɪst
  [-jɪst], -ɪlɪ [-əlɪ], -ɪnɪs [-ɪnəs]
Dairen daɪ'ren
dair|y, -ies, -ying 'deər|ɪ, -ɪz, -ɪɪŋ
dairy-farm, -s 'deərɪfɑːm, -z
dairymaid, -s 'deərɪmeɪd, -z
dairy|man, -men 'deərɪ|mən [-mæn],
  -mən [-men]
dais, -es 'deɪs [deɪs], -ɪz
dais|y (**D.**), **-ies** 'deɪz|ɪ, -ɪz
daisy-chain, -s 'deɪzɪtʃeɪn, -z
Dakar 'dækɑː*, 'dækə*
Dakota, -s də'kəʊtə, -z
Dalai Lama, -s ˌdælaɪ'lɑːmə [ˌdɑːlaɪ-,
  də,laɪ-], -z
Dalbeattie dæl'biːtɪ
Dalbiac 'dɔːlbɪæk
Dalby 'dɔːlbɪ, 'dælbɪ
Daldy 'dældɪ
dale (**D.**), **-s** deɪl, -z
dales|man, -men 'deɪlz|mən [-mæn],
  -mən [-men]
Dalgleish dæl'gliːʃ
Dalhousie dæl'haʊzɪ
Dalila də'laɪlə
Dalkeith dæl'kiːθ
Dalkey (*suburb of Dublin*) 'dɔːkɪ
Dallam 'dæləm
Dallas 'dæləs
dalliance 'dælɪəns [-ljəns]
dall|y, -ies, -ying, -ied, -ier/s 'dæl|ɪ, -ɪz,
  -ɪɪŋ, -ɪd, -ɪə*/z
Dalmanutha ˌdælmə'nuːθə [-'njuː-]
Dalma|tia, -tian/s dæl'meɪ|ʃə [-ʃɪə,
  -ʃjə], -ʃn/z [-ʃɪən/z, -ʃjən/z]
Dalmeny dæl'menɪ
Dalnaspidal ˌdælnə'spɪdl
Dalny 'dælnɪ
Dalry dæl'raɪ
Dalrymple dæl'rɪmpl [dəl'r-], 'dælrɪmpl
  *Note.—The family name of the Earl
  of Stair is* dæl'r- [dəl'r-].

Dalston 'dɔːlstən ['dɒl-]

Dalton 'dɔːltən ['dɒl-]

Dalua dæ'luːə [də'l-]

Dalwhinnie dæl'wɪnɪ [-'hw-]

Daly 'deɪlɪ

Dalyell 'dæljəl, diː'el

Dalzell dæl'zel, diː'el

Dalziel 'dælzɪəl [-zjəl], 'dæljəl [-lɪəl], diː'el

Note.—The form diː'el *is chiefly used in Scotland.*

dam (*s. v.*), -s, -ming, -med dæm, -z, -ɪŋ, -d

damag|e, -es, -ing, -ed, -ingly 'dæmɪdʒ, -ɪz, -ɪŋ, -d, -ɪŋlɪ

Damaraland də'mɑːrəlænd ['dæmərə-]

Damaris 'dæmərɪs

damascene, -s 'dæməsiːn [ˌdæmə's-], -z

Damascus də'mæskəs [-'mɑːs-]

damask, -s 'dæməsk, -s

dame, -s deɪm, -z

Damien 'deɪmjən [-mɪən]

damn, -s, -ing, -ed dæm, -z, -ɪŋ, -d

damnab|le, -ly, -leness 'dæmnəb|l, -lɪ, -lnɪs [-nəs]

damnation, -s dæm'neɪʃn, -z

damnatory 'dæmnətərɪ

damni|fy, -fies, -fying, -fied 'dæmnɪ|faɪ, -faɪz, -faɪɪŋ, -faɪd

Damocles 'dæməkliːz

Damon 'deɪmən [-mɒn]

damosel, -s 'dæməʊzel [ˌ--'-], -z

damp (*s. adj. v.*), -er, -est, -ly, -ness, -ish; -s, -ing, -ed dæmp, -ə*, -ɪst, -lɪ, -nɪs [-nəs], -ɪʃ; -s, -ɪŋ, -t [dæmt]

damp-course, -s 'dæmpkɔːs [-kɔəs], -ɪz

damp|en, -ens, -ening, -ened 'dæmp|ən, -ənz, -nɪŋ [-ənɪŋ], -ənd

damper, -s 'dæmpə*, -z

Dampier 'dæmpjə* [-pɪə*, -ˌpɪə*]

damp-proof 'dæmppruːf

damsel, -s 'dæmzl, -z

damson, -s 'dæmzən, -z

dan (D.), -s dæn, -z

Dana (*personal name*) (*in U.S.A.*) 'deɪnə, (*in Canada*) 'dænə

Danaë 'dæneɪɪ [-niː:]

Danakil ˌdænə'kiːl

Danbury 'dænbərɪ

Danby 'dænbɪ

danc|e (*s. v.*), -es, -ing, -ed, -er/s dɑːns, -ɪz, -ɪŋ, -t, -ə*/z

Dance dɑːns, dæns

dance-music 'dɑːnsˌmjuːzɪk

Dancer (*surname*) 'dɑːnsə*

dancing-girl, -s 'dɑːnsɪŋgəːl, -z

dancing-master, -s 'dɑːnsɪŋˌmɑːstə*, -z

dancing-mistress, -es 'dɑːnsɪŋˌmɪstrɪs [-əs], -ɪz

Danckwerts 'dæŋkwɜːts

dandelion, -s 'dændɪlaɪən, -z

dandiacal dæn'daɪəkl

dandi|fy, -fies, -fying, -fied 'dændɪ|faɪ, -faɪz, -faɪɪŋ, -faɪd

dand|le, -les, -ling, -led 'dænd|l, -lz, -lɪŋ [-lɪŋ], -ld

dandr|iff, -uff 'dændr|ɪf, -ʌf [-əf]

dand|y, -ies; -yish, -yism 'dænd|ɪ, -ɪz; -ɪɪʃ [-jɪʃ], -ɪɪzəm

Dane, -s deɪn, -z

danegeld 'deɪmgeld

Dane|lagh, -law 'deɪn|lɔː, -lɔː

danger, -s 'deɪndʒə*, -z

Dangerfield 'deɪndʒəfiːld

dangerous, -ly, -ness 'deɪndʒərəs, -lɪ, -nɪs [-nəs]

danger-signal, -s 'deɪndʒəˌsɪgnl [-nəl], -z

dang|le (D.), -les, -ling, -led, -ler/s 'dæŋg|l, -lz, -lɪŋ [-lɪŋ], -ld, -lə*/z [-lə*/z]

Daniel(l), -s 'dænjəl, -z

Danish 'deɪnɪʃ

Danite, -s 'dænaɪt, -s

dank, -er, -est, -ly, -ness dæŋk, -ə*, -ɪst, -lɪ, -nɪs [-nəs]

Dannatt 'dænət

Dannemora ˌdænɪ'mɔːrə

Dannreuther 'dænrɔɪtə*

danseuse, -s dɑːn'sɜːz [dɑ̃ː*n*'s-, dɔ̃ː*n*'s-] (dɑ̃søːz), -ɪz

Dansville 'dænzvɪl

Dante 'dæntɪ ['dɑːn-, -teɪ]

Dantzic 'dæntsɪk

Danube 'dænjuːb

Danubian dæ'njuːbjən [də'n-, -bɪən]

Dan|vers, -ville 'dæn|vəz, -vɪl

Danzig 'dæntsɪg [-ɪk] ('dantsiç)

Daphn|e, -is 'dæfn|ɪ, -ɪs

dapper (D.), -est 'dæpə*, -rɪst

dappled 'dæpld

dapple-grey ˌdæpl'greɪ

darbies 'dɑːbɪz

Darbishire 'dɑːbɪʃə* [-ˌʃɪə*]

Darby 'dɑːbɪ

D'Arcy, Darcy 'dɑːsɪ

Dardanelles ˌdɑːdə'nelz [-dn̩'elz]

Dardani|a, -us dɑː'deɪnjə [-nɪ|ə], -əs

Dardanus 'dɑːdənəs

dar|e (D.), -es, -ing, -ed, durst deə*, -z, -rɪŋ, -d, dɜːst

dare-devil, -s 'deəˌdevl, -z

daren't deənt

Darenth 'dærənθ

Dares 'deərɪz

123

daresay ˌdeə'seɪ [also '-- according to sentence-stress]
Daresbury (Baron) 'dɑ:zbərɪ
Dar-es-Salaam ˌdɑ:ressə'lɑ:m
Darfield 'dɑ:fi:ld
Darfur 'dɑ:fə* [dɑ:'fɜ:*]
Dargue dɑ:g
Darien 'deərɪən, 'dær-
daring (adj.), -ly 'deərɪŋ, -lɪ
Darius də'raɪəs
Darjeeling dɑ:'dʒi:lɪŋ
dark, -er, -est, -ly, -ness dɑ:k, -ə*, -ɪst, -lɪ, -nɪs [-nəs]
dark|en, -ens, -ening, -ened 'dɑ:k|ən, -ənz, -nɪŋ [-ŋɪŋ, -ənɪŋ], -ənd
dark-haired ˌdɑ:k'heəd ['-- when attributive]
darkish 'dɑ:kɪʃ
darkling 'dɑ:klɪŋ
dark-room, -s 'dɑ:krʊm [-ru:m], -z
dark-skinned 'dɑ:kskɪnd [also ˌ-'- when not attributive]
darksome 'dɑ:ksəm
dark|y, -ies 'dɑ:k|ɪ, -ɪz
Darlaston 'dɑ:ləstən
Darley 'dɑ:lɪ
darling (D.), -s 'dɑ:lɪŋ, -z
Darlington 'dɑ:lɪŋtən
Darmady (surname) dɑ:'meɪdɪ
Darmstadt 'dɑ:mstæt ('dɑrmʃtat)
darn (s. v.), -s, -ing, -ed, -er/s dɑ:n, -z, -ɪŋ, -d, -ə*/z
darnel 'dɑ:nl
darning-needle, -s 'dɑ:nɪŋˌni:dl, -z
Darnley 'dɑ:nlɪ
Darracq 'dærək
Darrell 'dærəl
Darsie 'dɑ:sɪ
dart (s. v.) (D.), -s, -ing, -ed dɑ:t, -s,-ɪŋ, -ɪd
darter, -s 'dɑ:tə*, -z
Dartford 'dɑ:tfəd
Dartie 'dɑ:tɪ
Dartle 'dɑ:tl
Dartmoor 'dɑ:tmɔ:* [-mɔə*, -mʊə*]
Dartmouth 'dɑ:tməθ
Darton 'dɑ:tn
Darwen 'dɑ:wɪn
Darwin, -ism 'dɑ:wɪn, -ɪzəm
Darwinian dɑ:'wɪnɪən [-njən]
Daryll 'dærɪl
Dasent 'deɪsənt
dash (s. v.) (D.), -es, -ing, -ed, -er/s dæʃ, -ɪz, -ɪŋ, -t, -ə*/z
dash-board, -s 'dæʃbɔ:d [-bɔəd], -z
dashing (adj.), -ly 'dæʃɪŋ, -lɪ
Dashwood 'dæʃwʊd
dastard, -s 'dæstəd ['dɑ:s-], -z

dastardl|y (adj.), -iness 'dæstədl|ɪ ['dɑ:s-], -ɪnɪs [-ɪnəs]
data (plur. of datum) 'deɪtə ['dɑ:tə]
datar|y, -ies 'deɪtər|ɪ, -ɪz
Datch|ery, -et 'dætʃ|ərɪ, -ɪt
dat|e (s. v.), -es, -ing, -ed deɪt, -s, -ɪŋ, -ɪd
dateline, -s 'deɪtlaɪn, -z
date|palm/s, -tree/s 'deɪt|pɑ:m/z, -tri:/z
Dathan 'deɪθæn [-θən]
datival deɪ'taɪvl [də't-]
dative (s. adj.), -s 'deɪtɪv, -z
Datsun 'dætsən [-tsʊn]
dat|um, -a 'deɪt|əm ['dɑ:t-], -ə
daub (s. v.), -s, -ing, -ed, -er/s dɔ:b, -z, -ɪŋ, -d, -ə*/z
Daubeney 'dɔ:bənɪ
Daudet 'dəʊdeɪ (dodɛ)
daughter, -s 'dɔ:tə*, -z
daughter - in - law, daughters - in - law 'dɔ:tərɪnlɔ: [-təɪn-], 'dɔ:təzɪnlɔ:
daughterl|y, -iness 'dɔ:təl|ɪ, -ɪnɪs [-ɪnəs]
Daukes dɔ:ks
Daulis 'dɔ:lɪs
Daun dɔ:n
daunt (D.), -s, -ing, -ed dɔ:nt, -s, -ɪŋ, -ɪd
dauntless, -ly, -ness 'dɔ:ntlɪs [-ləs], -lɪ, -nɪs [-nəs]
dauphin (D.), -s 'dɔ:fɪn, -z
Dauphine 'dɔ:fɪn [-fi:n]
Dauphiné 'dəʊfmeɪ [-nɪ] (dofine)
dauphiness (D.), -es 'dɔ:fɪnɪs [-nes], -ɪz
Davenant 'dævɪnənt
davenport (D.), -s 'dævnpɔ:t [-vmp-], -s
Daventry 'dævəntrɪ [old-fashioned local pronunciation 'deɪntrɪ]
Davey 'deɪvɪ
David, -s 'deɪvɪd, -z
Davidge 'dævɪdʒ
Davidson 'deɪvɪdsn
Davies 'deɪvɪs
Davis 'deɪvɪs
Davison 'deɪvɪsn
davit, -s 'dævɪt, -s
Davos 'dɑ:vɒs [-vəʊs, dɑ:'vəʊs]
dav|y (D.), -ies 'deɪv|ɪ, -ɪz
davy-lamp, -s 'deɪvɪlæmp [ˌ--'-], -s
daw (D.), -s dɔ:, -z
dawd|le, -les, -ling, -led, -ler/s 'dɔ:d|l, -lz, -lɪŋ [-lɪŋ], -ld, -lə*/z [-lə*/z]
Dawdon 'dɔ:dn
Dawe, -s dɔ:, -z
Dawk|es, -ins 'dɔ:k|s, -ɪnz
Dawl|ey, -ish 'dɔ:l|ɪ, -ɪʃ
dawn (s. v.) (D.), -s, -ing, -ed dɔ:n, -z, -ɪŋ, -d
Dawson 'dɔ:sn
day (D.), -s deɪ, -z
day-boarder, -s 'deɪˌbɔ:də* [-ˌbɔəd-], -z

124

day-book, -s 'deɪbʊk, -s
day-boy, -s 'deɪbɔɪ, -z
daybreak, -s 'deɪbreɪk, -s
†day-dream (s.), -s 'deɪdriːm, -z
day-labour, -er/s 'deɪˌleɪbə* [ˌdeɪ'l-],
  -rə*/z
Daylesford 'deɪlzfəd [-lsf-]
daylight 'deɪlaɪt
daylight-saving 'deɪlaɪtˌseɪvɪŋ [ˌ--'--]
day-lil|y, -ies 'deɪˌlɪl|ɪ [ˌdeɪ'l-], -ɪz
day-nurser|y, -ies 'deɪˌnɜːsər|ɪ [ˌ-'---],
  -ɪz
day-school, -s 'deɪskuːl, -z
dayspring 'deɪsprɪŋ
day-star, -s 'deɪstɑː*, -z
day-time 'deɪtaɪm
Dayton 'deɪtn
Daytona deɪ'təʊnə
daywork 'deɪwɜːk
daz|e, -es, -ing, -ed, -edly deɪz, -ɪz, -ɪŋ,
  -d, -ɪdlɪ
dazz|le, -les, -ling/ly, -led 'dæz|l, -lz,
  -lɪŋ/lɪ [-lŋ/lɪ], -ld
D-day 'diːdeɪ
D.D.T. ˌdiːdiː'tiː
de (note in Tonic Sol-fa), -s diː, -z
deacon (D.), -s 'diːkən, -z
deaconess, -es ˌdiːkə'nes ['---, -nɪs], -ɪz
deacon|hood, -ry, -ries, -ship/s 'diːkən|-
  hʊd, -rɪ, -rɪz, -ʃɪp/s
dead ded
dead-alive ˌdedə'laɪv
dead-beat ˌded'biːt
dead-drunk ˌded'drʌŋk
dead|en, -ens, -ening, -ened 'ded|n,
  -nz, -ṇɪŋ [-nɪŋ], -nd
dead-eye (D.), -s 'dedaɪ, -z
deadhead, -s 'dedhed, -z
dead-heat, -s ˌded'hiːt ['--], -s
dead-letter, -s ˌded'letə*, -z
deadline, -s 'dedlaɪn, -z
deadlock, -s 'dedlɒk, -s
deadl|y, -ier, -iest, -iness 'dedl|ɪ, -ɪə*
  [-jə*], -ɪɪst [-jɪst], -ɪnɪs [-nəs]
dead-march, -es ded'mɑːtʃ ['--], -ɪz
dead-nettle, -s 'dedˌnetl [ˌ-'--], -z
dead-pan ˌded'pæn ['--]
dead-reckoning, -s ˌded'rekṇɪŋ [-kənɪŋ],
  -z
dead-set, -s ˌded'set ['--], -s
dead-wall, -s ˌded'wɔːl, -z
dead-water, -s 'dedˌwɔːtə*, -z
dead-weight, -s 'dedweɪt [ˌ-'-], -s
deaf, -er, -est, -ly, -ness def, -ə*, -ɪst,
  -lɪ, -nɪs [-nəs]
deaf-aid, -s 'defeɪd, -z
deaf|en, -ens, -ening, -ened 'def|n, -nz,
  -ṇɪŋ [-nɪŋ], -nd

deaf-mute, -s ˌdef'mjuːt, -s
Deakin 'diːkɪn
deal (s. v.) (D.), -s, -ing/s, dealt,
  dealer/s diːl, -z, -ɪŋ/z, delt, 'diːlə*/z
Dealtry (surname) 'dɔːltrɪ, 'dɪəltrɪ,
  (road in London) 'deltrɪ
dean, -s; -ship/s diːn, -z; -ʃɪp/s
Dean(e) diːn
deaner|y, -ies 'diːnər|ɪ, -ɪz
Deans diːnz
dear (s. adj. interj.), -s; -er, -est, -ly,
  -ness dɪə*, -z; -rə*, -rɪst, -lɪ, -nɪs
  [-nəs]
Dearmer 'dɪəmə*
dearth (D.), -s dɜːθ, -s
dear|y, -ies 'dɪər|ɪ, -ɪz
Dease diːs
death, -s deθ, -s
Death (surname) deɪθ, deθ, diːθ, diː'æθ
  [dɪ'æθ]
deathbed, -s 'deθbed, -z
death-bell, -s 'deθbel, -z
death-blow, -s 'deθbləʊ, -z
death-dut|y, -ies 'deθˌdjuːt|ɪ, -ɪz
death|less, -like 'deθ|lɪs [-ləs], -laɪk
death|ly, -lier, -liest, -liness 'deθ|lɪ, -lɪə*
  [-ljə*], -lɪɪst [-ljɪst], -lɪnɪs [-nəs]
death-mask, -s 'deθmɑːsk, -s
death-rate, -s 'deθreɪt, -s
death-rattle, -s 'deθˌrætl, -z
death's-head, -s 'deθshed, -z
death-trap, -s 'deθtræp, -s
death-warrant, -s 'deθˌwɒrənt, -s
death-watch 'deθwɒtʃ
débâcle, -s deɪ'bɑːkl [de'b-, dɪ'b-], -z
debar, -s, -ring, -red dɪ'bɑː*, -z, -rɪŋ,
  -d
debark, -s, -ing, -ed dɪ'bɑːk, -s, -ɪŋ, -t
debarkation, -s ˌdiːbɑː'keɪʃn, -z
debas|e, -es, -ing/ly, -ed, -ement
  dɪ'beɪs, -ɪz, -ɪŋ/lɪ, -t, -mənt
debatab|le, -ly dɪ'beɪtəb|l, -lɪ
debat|e (s. v.), -es, -ing, -ed, -er/s
  dɪ'beɪt, -s, -ɪŋ, -ɪd, -ə*/z
De Bathe də'bɑːθ
debauch (s. v.), -es, -ing, -ed, -er/s
  dɪ'bɔːtʃ, -ɪz, -ɪŋ, -t, -ə*/z
debauchee, -s ˌdebɔː'tʃiː [-ɔː'ʃiː], -z
debaucher|y, -ies dɪ'bɔːtʃər|ɪ, -ɪz
Debbitch 'debɪtʃ
Debeney 'debənɪ
Debenham 'debənəm [-bnəm, -bṇəm]
debenture, -s dɪ'bentʃə* [də'b-], -z
debile 'diːbaɪl
debilitat|e, -es, -ing, -ed dɪ'bɪlɪteɪt
  [-lət-], -s, -ɪŋ, -ɪd
debilitation dɪˌbɪlɪ'teɪʃn [-lə't-]
debility dɪ'bɪlətɪ [-ɪtɪ]

125

debit (s. v.), -s, -ing, -ed 'debɪt, -s, -ɪŋ, -ɪd
De Blaquiere də'blækɪə*
debonair, -ly, -ness ˌdebə'neə* [-bɒ'n-],
  -lɪ, -nɪs [-nəs]
Deborah 'debərə
debouch, -es, -ing, -ed, -ment dɪ'baʊtʃ
  [-'buː:ʃ], -ɪz, -ɪŋ, -t, -mənt
De Bourgh də'bɜ:g
De Bow də'bəʊ
Debrett də'bret [dɪ'b-]
debris 'deɪbri: ['deb-, -brɪ]
debt, -s det, -s
debtor, -s 'detə*, -z
debunk, -s, -ing, -ed ˌdi:'bʌŋk, -s, -ɪŋ,
  -t [-'bʌŋt]
De Bunsen də'bʊnsn
De Burgh də'bɜ:g
Debussy də'bu:si: [-'bʊs-, -'bju:s-, -sɪ]
  (dəbysi)
début, -s 'deɪbju: ['deb-, -bu:, -'-] (deby),
  -z
débutant, -s 'debju:tɑ̃:ŋ ['deɪb-, -bjʊ-,
  -tɑ:ŋ, -tɔ:ŋ, -tɒŋ] (debytɑ̃), -z
débutante, -s 'debju:tɑ:nt ['deɪb-,
  -bjʊ-, -tænt, -tɑ̃:nt, -tɒnt] (debytɑ̃:t),
  -s
decachord, -s 'dekəkɔ:d, -z
decade, -s 'dekeɪd [-kəd, -kɪd, dɪ'keɪd,
  de'keɪd], -z
decaden|ce, -cy, -t 'dekədən|s [dɪ'keɪd-,
  de'keɪd-], -sɪ, -t
decagon, -s 'dekəgən, -z
decagram(me), -s 'dekəgræm, -z
decalcification 'di:ˌkælsɪfɪ'keɪʃn
decalci|fy, -fies, -fying, -fied ˌdi:'kælsɪ|-
  faɪ, -faɪz, -faɪɪŋ, -faɪd
decalitre, -s 'dekəˌli:tə*, -z
Decalogue, -s 'dekəlɒg, -z
Decameron dɪ'kæmərən [de'k-]
decametre, -s 'dekəˌmi:tə*, -z
decamp, -s, -ing, -ed dɪ'kæmp [ˌdi:-], -s,
  -ɪŋ, -t [dɪ'kæmt]
decanal dɪ'keɪnl [de'k-]
decani dɪ'keɪnaɪ [de'k-]
decant, -s, -ing, -ed dɪ'kænt [ˌdi:-], -s,
  -ɪŋ, -ɪd
decantation, -s ˌdi:kæn'teɪʃn, -z
decanter, -s dɪ'kæntə*, -z
decapitat|e, -es, -ing, -ed dɪ'kæpɪteɪt
  [ˌdi:'k-], -s, -ɪŋ, -ɪd
decapitation, -s dɪˌkæpɪ'teɪʃn [di:ˌk-], -z
decapod, -s 'dekəpɒd, -z
Decapolis dɪ'kæpəlɪs [de'k-]
decarbonization [-isa-] di:ˌkɑ:bənaɪ-
  'zeɪʃn ['di:ˌkɑ:bənaɪ'z-, -bənɪ'z-,
  -bŋaɪ'z-, -bŋɪ'z-]
decarboniz|e [-is|e], -es, -ing, -ed ˌdi:-
  'kɑ:bənaɪz [-bŋaɪz], -ɪz, -ɪŋ, -d

decarburiz|e [-is|e], -es, -ing, -ed
  ˌdi:'kɑ:bjʊəraɪz, -ɪz, -ɪŋ, -d
decasyllabic ˌdekəsɪ'læbɪk
decasyllable, -s 'dekəsɪləbl, -z
decathlon, -s dɪ'kæθlɒn [de-, -lən], -z
decay (s. v.), -s, -ing, -ed dɪ'keɪ, -z, -ɪŋ,
  -d
Decca 'dekə
Deccan 'dekən [-kæn] (Hindi dəkhən)
deceas|e (s. v.), -es, -ing, -ed dɪ'si:s, -ɪz,
  -ɪŋ, -t
deceit, -s dɪ'si:t, -s
deceit|ful, -fully, -fulness dɪ'si:t|fʊl,
  -fʊlɪ [-fəlɪ], -fʊlnɪs [-nəs]
deceivable, -ness dɪ'si:vəbl, -nɪs [-nəs]
deceiv|e, -es, -ing, -ed, -er/s dɪ'si:v, -z,
  -ɪŋ, -d, -ə*/z
decelerat|e, -es, -ing, -ed ˌdi:'seləreɪt,
  -s, -ɪŋ, -ɪd
deceleration, -s 'di:ˌselə'reɪʃn [-ˌ-'-'-],
  -z
December, -s dɪ'sembə* [di:'s-], -z
decemvir, -s dɪ'semvə* [-vɜ:*], -z
decemvirate, -s dɪ'semvɪrət [-vər-, -rɪt],
  -s
decen|cy, -cies, -t/ly 'di:sn|sɪ, -sɪz,
  -t/lɪ
decennial dɪ'senjəl [de's-, di:'s-, -nɪəl]
decentralization [-isa-] di:ˌsentrəlaɪ-
  'zeɪʃn ['di:ˌsentrəlaɪ'z-, -trʃaɪ'z-,
  -trəlɪ'z-, -trʃɪ'z-]
decentraliz|e [-is|e], -es, -ing, -ed
  ˌdi:'sentrəlaɪz, -ɪz, -ɪŋ, -d
deception, -s dɪ'sepʃn, -z
deceptive, -ly, -ness dɪ'septɪv, -lɪ, -nɪs
  [-nəs]
decibel, -s 'desɪbel [-bəl, -bl], -z
decid|e, -es, -ing, -ed/ly, -er/s dɪ'saɪd,
  -z, -ɪŋ, -ɪd/lɪ, -ə*/z
deciduous, -ly, -ness dɪ'sɪdjʊəs [-sɪdʒʊ-,
  -djwəs], -lɪ, -nɪs [-nəs]
Decies 'di:ʃɪz
decigram(me), -s 'desɪgræm, -z
decilitre, -s 'desɪˌli:tə*, -z
decillion, -s dɪ'sɪljən [di:'s-], -z
decim|al, -als, -ally 'desɪm|l [-əm-],
  -lz, -əlɪ
decimaliz|e [-is|e], -es, -ing, -ed 'desɪ-
  məlaɪz [-səm-], -ɪz, -ɪŋ, -d
decimalization [-isation] ˌdesɪmələɪ-
  'zeɪʃn [-səm-, -mʃaɪ-, -ɪ'zeɪ-]
decimat|e, -es, -ing, -ed, -or/s 'desɪ-
  meɪt, -s, -ɪŋ, -ɪd, -ə*/z
decimation ˌdesɪ'meɪʃn
decimetre, -s 'desɪˌmi:tə*, -z
deciph|er, -ers, -ering, -ered dɪ'saɪf|ə*,
  -əz, -ərɪŋ, -əd
decipherable dɪ'saɪfərəbl

decision, -s dɪ'sɪʒn, -z
decisive, -ly, -ness dɪ'saɪsɪv [-aɪzɪv], -lɪ,
-nɪs [-nəs]
Decius 'diːʃjəs [-ʃɪəs, -sjəs, -sɪəs, 'dekɪəs,
'desɪəs]
deck (s. v.), -s, -ing, -ed, -er/s dek, -s,
-ɪŋ, -t, -ə*/z
deck-cabin, -s ˌdek'kæbɪn [also '-ˌ-- for
contrast], -z
deck-chair, -s 'dektʃeə* [ˌ-'-], -z
deck-hand, -s 'dekhænd, -z
deck-hou|se, -ses 'dekhaʊ|s, -zɪz
deckle, -s 'dekl, -z
deckle-edge, -d ˌdekl'edʒ ['dekḷedʒ], -d
deck-passenger, -s 'dekˌpæsɪndʒə*,
[-sən-], -z
declaim, -s, -ing, -ed, -er/s; -ant/s
dɪ'kleɪm, -z, -ɪŋ, -d, -ə*/z; -ənt/s
declamation, -s ˌdeklə'meɪʃn, -z
declamatory dɪ'klæmətərɪ
declarable dɪ'kleərəbl
declaration, -s ˌdeklə'reɪʃn, -z
declarat|ive/ly, -ory dɪ'klærət|ɪv/lɪ
[-'kleər-], -ərɪ
declar|e, -es, -ing, -ed, -er/s dɪ'kleə*,
-z, -ɪŋ, -d, -rə*/z
declass, -es, -ing, -ed ˌdi:'klɑːs [-'-], -ɪz,
-ɪŋ, -t
declension, -s dɪ'klenʃn, -z
declination, -s ˌdeklɪ'neɪʃn, -z
declin|e (s. v.), -es, -ing, -ed; -able
dɪ'klaɪn, -z, -ɪŋ, -d; -əbl
declinometer, -s ˌdeklɪ'nɒmɪtə*
[-mətə*], -z
declivitous, -ly, -ness dɪ'klɪvɪtəs, -lɪ,
-nɪs [-nəs]
declivit|y, -ies dɪ'klɪvət|ɪ [-ɪt|ɪ], -ɪz
declutch, -es, -ing, -ed ˌdi:'klʌtʃ
['di:klʌtʃ], -ɪz, -ɪŋ, -t
decoct, -s, -ing, -ed dɪ'kɒkt, -s, -ɪŋ, -ɪd
decoction, -s dɪ'kɒkʃn, -z
decod|e, -es, -ing, -ed ˌdi:'kəʊd, -z, -ɪŋ,
-ɪd
décolletage ˌdeɪkɒl'tɑːʒ [-'--]
(dekɔlta:ʒ)
décolleté(e) deɪ'kɒlteɪ [de'k-, dɪ'k-]
(dekɔlte)
decolo(u)rization [-isa-] di:ˌkʌləraɪ-
'zeɪʃn ['di:ˌk-]
decolo(u)riz|e [-is|e], -es, -ing, -ed
di:'kʌləraɪz, -ɪz, -ɪŋ, -d
decompos|e, -es, -ing, -ed; -able
ˌdi:kəm'pəʊz, -ɪz, -ɪŋ, -d; -əbl
decomposition, -s ˌdi:kɒmpə'zɪʃn, -z
decompound, -s, -ing, -ed ˌdi:kəm-
'paʊnd, -z, -ɪŋ, -ɪd
decompress, -es, -ing, -ed, -er/s
ˌdi:kəm'pres, -ɪz, -ɪŋ, -t, -ə*/z

decompression ˌdi:kəm'preʃn
deconsecrat|e, -es, -ing, -ed ˌdi:'kɒn-
sɪkreɪt, -s, -ɪŋ, -ɪd
deconsecration, -s 'di:ˌkɒnsɪ'kreɪʃn, -z
decontaminat|e, -es, -ing, -ed ˌdi:kən-
'tæmɪneɪt, -s, -ɪŋ, -ɪd
decontamination 'di:kənˌtæmɪ'neɪʃn
decontrol (s. v.), -s, -ling, -led ˌdi:kən-
'trəʊl, -z, -ɪŋ, -d
decor, -s 'deɪkɔ:* ['dekɔ:*, dɪ'kɔ:*], -z
decorat|e, -es, -ing, -ed, -or/s 'dekəreɪt,
-s, -ɪŋ, -ɪd, -ə*/z
decoration, -s ˌdekə'reɪʃn, -z
decorative, -ly, -ness 'dekərətɪv, -lɪ,
-nɪs [-nəs]
decorous, -ly, -ness 'dekərəs [old-
fashioned and poetical dɪ'kɔ:rəs], -lɪ,
-nɪs [-nəs]
decorum dɪ'kɔ:rəm
De Courcy də'kʊəsɪ [-'kɔəs-, -'kɔ:s-],
də'kɜːsɪ
decoy (v.), -s, -ing, -ed dɪ'kɔɪ, -z, -ɪŋ,
-d
decoy (s.), -s 'di:kɔɪ [dɪ'kɔɪ], -z
decoy-duck, -s dɪ'kɔɪdʌk [dɪˌkɔɪ'd-], -s
decrease (s.), -s 'di:kri:s [di:'kri:s,
dɪ'k-], -ɪz
decreas|e (v.), -es, -ing/ly, -ed di:'kri:s
[dɪ'k-, 'di:k-], -ɪz, -ɪŋ/lɪ, -t
decree (s. v.), -s, -ing, -d dɪ'kri:, -z, -ɪŋ,
-d
decree nisi dɪˌkri:'naɪsaɪ [-sɪ]
decrement, -s 'dekrɪmənt, -s
decrepit, -est, -ness; -ude dɪ'krepɪt,
-ɪst, -nɪs [-nəs]; -ju:d
decrepitation, -s dɪˌkrepɪ'teɪʃn, -z
decrescendo, -s ˌdi:krɪ'ʃendəʊ, -z
De Crespigny də'krepɪnɪ, də'krespɪnɪ
decrial, -s dɪ'kraɪəl, -z
decr|y, -ies, -ying, -ied, -ier/s dɪ'kraɪ,
-aɪz, -aɪɪŋ, -aɪd, -aɪə*/z
decumben|ce, -cy, -t/ly dɪ'kʌmbən|s,
-sɪ, -t/lɪ
decup|le (s. adj. v.), -les, -ling, -led
'dekjʊp|l, -lz, -lɪŋ, -ld
Dedan, -ite/s 'di:dən, -aɪt/s
Deddes 'dedɪs
Deddington 'dedɪŋtən
Dedham 'dedəm
dedicat|e, -es, -ing, -ed, -or/s 'dedɪkeɪt,
-s, -ɪŋ, -ɪd, -ə*/z
dedicatee, -s ˌdedɪkə'ti:, -z
dedication, -s ˌdedɪ'keɪʃn, -z
dedicatory 'dedɪkətərɪ [-keɪtərɪ, ˌdedɪ-
'keɪtərɪ]
de Dion, -s də'di:ən [-'dɪ-, -'di:ɔ̃:ŋ,
-'di:ɒŋ, -'di:ɒn] (dədjɔ̃), -z
Ded|lock, -man 'ded|lɒk, -mən

127

deduc|e, -es, -ing, -ed dɪˈdjuːs, -ɪz, -ɪŋ, -t

deducibility dɪˌdjuːsəˈbɪlətɪ [-sɪˈb-, -lɪt-]

deducible dɪˈdjuːsəbl [-sɪb-]

deduct, -s, -ing, -ed; -ive/ly; -ible dɪˈdʌkt, -s, -ɪŋ, -ɪd; -ɪv/lɪ; -əbl

deduction, -s dɪˈdʌkʃn, -z

Dee diː

deed, -s diːd, -z

Deedes diːdz

Deek(e)s diːks

deem, -s, -ing, -ed diːm, -z, -ɪŋ, -d

Deems diːmz

deemster, -s ˈdiːmstə*, -z

deep (*s. adj.*)**, -s, -er, -est, -ly, -ness** diːp, -s, -ə*, -ɪst, -lɪ, -nɪs [-nəs]

deep-drawn ˌdiːpˈdrɔːn [ˈ-- *when attributive*]

deep|en, -ens, -ening, -ened ˈdiːp|ən, -ənz, -ⁿɪŋ [-ənɪŋ, -nɪŋ], -ənd

deep-freeze ˌdiːpˈfriːz

deep-laid ˌdiːpˈleɪd [*also* ˈ-- *when attributive*]

deep-mouthed ˌdiːpˈmaʊðd [-ˈmaʊθt, ˈ-- *when attributive*]

deep-rooted ˌdiːpˈruːtɪd [*also* ˈ-ˌ-- *when attributive*]

deep-sea ˌdiːpˈsiː [*also* ˈ-- *when attributive*]

deep-seated ˌdiːpˈsiːtɪd [*also* ˈ-ˌ-- *when attributive*]

deer dɪə*

Deerfield ˈdɪəfiːld

deer-forest, -s ˈdɪəˌfɒrɪst, -s

deer-hound, -s ˈdɪəhaʊnd, -z

deer-park, -s ˈdɪəpɑːk, -s

deer-skin ˈdɪəskɪn

deer-stalk|ing, -er/s ˈdɪəˌstɔːk|ɪŋ, -ə*/z

de-escalat|e, -es, -ing, -ed diːˈeskəleɪt, -s, -ɪŋ, -ɪd

de-escalation ˌdiːeskəˈleɪʃn [-ˌ--ˈ--]

defac|e, -es, -ing, -ed, -er/s, -ement/s dɪˈfeɪs, -ɪz, -ɪŋ, -t, -ə*/z, -mənt/s

de facto deɪˈfæktəʊ [diːˈf-]

defalcat|e, -es, -ing, -ed ˈdiːfælkeɪt [diːˈfæl-, *rarely* ˈdiːfɔːl-], -s, -ɪŋ, -ɪd

defalcation, -s ˌdiːfælˈkeɪʃn [-fɔːl-], -z

defalcator, -s ˈdiːfælkeɪtə* [-fɔːl-], -z

defamation, -s ˌdefəˈmeɪʃn [ˌdiːfəˈm-], -z

defamatory dɪˈfæmətərɪ

defam|e, -es, -ing, -ed, -er/s dɪˈfeɪm, -z, -ɪŋ, -d, -ə*/z

default (*s. v.*)**, -s, -ing, -ed, -er/s** dɪˈfɔːlt [-ˈfɒlt], -s, -ɪŋ, -ɪd, -ə*/z

defeasance dɪˈfiːzns

defeasib|le, -ly, -leness dɪˈfiːzəbl [-zɪb-], -lɪ, -lnɪs [-nəs]

defeat (*s. v.*)**, -s, -ing, -ed** dɪˈfiːt, -s, -ɪŋ, -ɪd

defeati|sm, -st/s dɪˈfiːtɪ|zəm, -st/s

defect (*s.*)**, -s** ˈdiːfekt [dɪˈfekt], -s

defect (*v.*)**, -s, -ing, -ed, -or/s** dɪˈfekt, -s, -ɪŋ, -ɪd, -ə*/z

defection, -s dɪˈfekʃn, -z

defective, -ly, -ness dɪˈfektɪv, -lɪ, -nɪs [-nəs]

defence, -s dɪˈfens, -ɪz

defenceless, -ly, -ness dɪˈfenslɪs [-ləs, -les], -lɪ, -nɪs [-nəs]

defend, -s, -ing, -ed, -er/s dɪˈfend, -z, -ɪŋ, -ɪd, -ə*/z

defendant, -s dɪˈfendənt, -s

defensibility dɪˌfensɪˈbɪlətɪ [-səˈb-, -lɪt-]

defensib|le, -ly dɪˈfensəb|l [-sɪb-], -lɪ

defensive, -ly, -ness dɪˈfensɪv, -lɪ, -nɪs [-nəs]

defer, -s, -ring, -red, -rer/s dɪˈfɜː*, -z, -rɪŋ, -d, -rə*/z

deferen|ce, -t ˈdefərən|s, -t

deferenti|al, -ally ˌdefəˈren|ʃl, -əlɪ

defian|ce, -t/ly, -tness dɪˈfaɪən|s, -t/lɪ, -tnɪs [-nəs]

deficien|cy, -cies, -t/ly dɪˈfɪʃn|sɪ, -sɪz, -t/lɪ

deficit, -s ˈdefɪsɪt [ˈdiːf-, -fəs-, dɪˈfɪsɪt], -s

defilad|e (*s. v.*)**, -es, -ing, -ed** ˌdefɪˈleɪd, -z, -ɪŋ, -ɪd

defile (*s.*)**, -s** ˈdiːfaɪl [dɪˈfaɪl, diːˈf-], -z

defil|e (*v.*)**, -es, -ing, -ed, -er/s, -ement** dɪˈfaɪl, -z, -ɪŋ, -d, -ə*/z, -mənt

definable dɪˈfaɪnəbl

defin|e, -es, -ing, -ed, -er/s dɪˈfaɪn, -z, -ɪŋ, -d, -ə*/z

definite, -ly, -ness ˈdefɪnɪt [-fən-, -fnɪt, -fnɪt, -ət], -lɪ, -nɪs [-nəs]

definition, -s ˌdefɪˈnɪʃn [-fəˈn-, -fnˈɪʃ-], -z

definitive, -ly, -ness dɪˈfɪnɪtɪv [deˈf-, -ətɪv], -lɪ, -nɪs

deflagrat|e, -es, -ing, -ed, -or/s ˈdefləgreɪt [ˈdiːf-], -s, -ɪŋ, -ɪd, -ə*/z

deflagration, -s ˌdefləˈgreɪʃn [ˌdiːf-], -z

deflat|e, -es, -ing, -ed dɪˈfleɪt [ˌdiːˈf-], -s, -ɪŋ, -ɪd

deflation, -ary dɪˈfleɪʃn [ˌdiːˈf-], -ərɪ

deflect, -s, -ing, -ed, -or/s dɪˈflekt, -s, -ɪŋ, -ɪd, -ə*/z

deflection [-exion], -s dɪˈflekʃn, -z

defloration, -s ˌdiːflɔːˈreɪʃn [ˌdef-], -z

deflower, -s, -ing, -ed ˌdiːˈflaʊə* [dɪˈf-], -z, -rɪŋ, -d

Defoe dɪˈfəʊ [dəˈf-]

defoliat|e, -es, -ing, -ed ˌdiːˈfəʊlɪeɪt, -s, -ɪŋ, -ɪd

defoliation ˌdiːfəʊliˈeɪʃn [-ˌ--'--]
deforest, -s, -ing, -ed ˌdiːˈfɒrɪst, -s, -ɪŋ, -ɪd
deforestation diːˌfɒrɪˈsteɪʃn ['-ˌ--'--]
deform, -s, -ing, -ed, -er/s dɪˈfɔːm, -z, -ɪŋ, -d, -ə*/z
deformation, -s ˌdiːfɔːˈmeɪʃn, -z
deformit|y, -ies dɪˈfɔːmət|ɪ [-ɪt|ɪ], -ɪz
defraud, -s, -ing, -ed, -er/s dɪˈfrɔːd, -z, -ɪŋ, -ɪd, -ə*/z
defray, -s, -ing, -ed, -er/s, -ment dɪˈfreɪ, -z, -ɪŋ, -d, -ə*/z, -mənt
defrayal, -s dɪˈfreɪəl, -z
De Freitas dəˈfreɪtəs
defrock, -s, -ing, -ed ˌdiːˈfrɒk, -s, -ɪŋ, -t
de-frost, -s, -ing, -ed ˌdiːˈfrɒst [old-fashioned -'frɔːst], -s, -ɪŋ, -ɪd
deft, -er, -est, -ly, -ness deft, -ə*, -ɪst, -lɪ, -nɪs [-nəs]
defunct (s. adj.), -s dɪˈfʌŋkt, -s
defus|e, -es, -ing, -ed ˌdiːˈfjuːz [dɪ'f-], -ɪz, -ɪŋ, -d
def|y, -ies, -ying, -ied, -ier/s dɪˈf|aɪ, -aɪz, -aɪɪŋ, -aɪd, -aɪə*/z
Degas dəˈgɑː [ˈdeɪgɑː] (dəgɑ)
De Gaulle dəˈgəʊl (dəgoːl)
degauss, -es, -ing, -ed ˌdiːˈgaʊs, -ɪz, -ɪŋ, -t
degeneracy dɪˈdʒenərəsɪ
degenerate (adj.), -ly, -ness dɪˈdʒenərət [-rɪt], -lɪ, -nɪs [-nəs]
degenerat|e (v.), -es, -ing, -ed dɪˈdʒenəreɪt, -s, -ɪŋ, -ɪd
degeneration dɪˌdʒenəˈreɪʃn
degenerative dɪˈdʒenərətɪv [-nəreɪt-]
deglutinat|e, -es, -ing, -ed dɪˈgluːtɪneɪt, -s, -ɪŋ, -ɪd
deglutition ˌdiːgluːˈtɪʃn
degradation, -s ˌdegrəˈdeɪʃn, -z
degrad|e, -es, -ing/ly, -ed, -able dɪˈgreɪd, -z, -ɪŋ/lɪ, -ɪd, -əbl
degree, -s dɪˈgriː, -z
dehisc|e, -es, -ing, -ed; -ence, -ent dɪˈhɪs [diːˈh-], -ɪz, -ɪŋ, -t; -ns, -nt
Dehra Dun ˌdeɪrəˈduːn (Hindi dehra-dun)
dehumaniz|e [-is|e], -es, -ing, -ed ˌdiːˈhjuːmənaɪz, -ɪz, -ɪŋ, -d
dehydrat|e, -es, -ing, -ed ˌdiːˈhaɪdreɪt, -s, -ɪŋ, -ɪd
dehydration ˌdiːhaɪˈdreɪʃn
dehypnotiz|e [-is|e], -es, -ing, -ed ˌdiːˈhɪpnətaɪz, -ɪz, -ɪŋ, -d
de-ic|e, -es, -ing, -ed, -er/s ˌdiːˈaɪs, -ɪz, -ɪŋ, -t, -ə*/z
deicide, -s ˈdiːɪsaɪd [ˈdeɪɪs-], -z
dei|ctic, -xis ˈdaɪ|ktɪk, -ksɪs

deification, -s ˌdiːɪfɪˈkeɪʃn [ˌdeɪɪf-], -z
dei|fy, -fies, -fying, -fied ˈdiːɪ|faɪ [ˈdeɪɪ-], -faɪz, -faɪɪŋ, -faɪd
Deighton (surname) ˈdaɪtn, ˈdeɪtn, (place in North Yorkshire) ˈdiːtn
deign, -s, -ing, -ed deɪn, -z, -ɪŋ, -d
deipnosophist, -s daɪpˈnɒsəfɪst, -s
Deirdre ˈdɪədrɪ [-dreɪ]
dei|sm, -st/s ˈdiːɪ|zəm [ˈdeɪɪ-], -st/s
deistic, -al diːˈɪstɪk [deɪˈɪ-], -l
deit|y (D.), -ies ˈdiːɪt|ɪ [ˈdiːət-, ˈdɪət-, ˈdeɪt-, ˈdeɪət-], -ɪz
deject, -s, -ing, -ed/ly, -edness dɪˈdʒekt, -s, -ɪŋ, -ɪd/lɪ, -ɪdnɪs [-nəs]
dejection dɪˈdʒekʃn
déjeuner, -s ˈdeɪʒəneɪ [-ʒɑː-] (deʒøne, -ʒœne), -z
de jure ˌdeɪˈdʒʊərɪ [ˌdiːˈjʊərɪ, -reɪ]
Dekker ˈdekə*
de la Bère (English surname) ˌdeləˈbɪə*
Delagoa ˌdeləˈgəʊə [also ˈdeləg- in Delagoa Bay]
delaine dəˈleɪn [dɪ'l-]
Delamain ˈdeləmeɪn
De la Mare ˌdeləˈmeə*
Delamere ˈdeləˌmɪə*
De Lancey dəˈlɑːnsɪ
Deland ˈdiːlənd
Delan|e, -y dəˈleɪn [dɪ'l-], -ɪ
De la Pasture dəˈlæpətjə* [-ˌtjʊə*, -tʃə*]
De la Poer ˌdeləˈpʊə* [-ˈpɔə*, -ˈpɔː*]
De la Pole ˌdeləˈpəʊl
De la Rue ˈdeləruː [ˌdelə'r-]
De Laszlo dəˈlæsləʊ
de la Torre (English surname) ˌdeləˈtɔː*
Delaware ˈdeləweə*
De la Warr ˈdeləweə*
delay (s. v.), -s, -ing, -ed, -er/s dɪˈleɪ, -z, -ɪŋ, -d, -ə*/z
del credere delˈkredərɪ
dele ˈdiːliː [-lɪ]
delectab|le, -ly, -leness dɪˈlektəb|l, -lɪ, -lnɪs [-nəs]
delectation ˌdiːlekˈteɪʃn
delegac|y, -ies ˈdelɪgəs|ɪ, -ɪz
delegate (s.), -s ˈdelɪgət [-geɪt, -gɪt], -s
delegat|e (v.), -es, -ing, -ed ˈdelɪgeɪt, -s, -ɪŋ, -ɪd
delegation, -s ˌdelɪˈgeɪʃn, -z
delend|um, -a dɪˈlend|əm [diːˈl-], -ə
delet|e, -es, -ing, -ed dɪˈliːt [diːˈl-], -s, -ɪŋ, -ɪd
deleterious, -ly, -ness ˌdelɪˈtɪərɪəs [dɪl-, ˌdiːl-], -lɪ, -nɪs [-nəs]
deletion, -s dɪˈliːʃn [diːˈl-], -z
delf delf

129

Delft, -ware delft, -weə*
Delham 'deləm
Delhi 'delɪ
Delia, -n/s 'di:ljə [-lɪə], -n/z
deliber|ate (adj.), -ately, -ateness dɪ-
'lɪbər|ət [-ɪt], -ətlɪ [-ɪtlɪ], -ətnɪs [-ɪt-,
-nəs]
deliberat|e (v.), -es, -ing, -ed, -or/s
dɪ'lɪbəreɪt, -s, -ɪŋ, -ɪd, -ə*/z
deliberation, -s dɪ,lɪbə'reɪʃn, -z
deliberative, -ly dɪ'lɪbərətɪv, -lɪ
delicac|y, -ies 'delɪkəs|ɪ, -ɪz
delicate, -ly, -ness 'delɪkət [-kɪt], -lɪ,
-nɪs [-nəs]
delicatessen, -s ,delɪkə'tesn, -z
delicious, -ly, -ness dɪ'lɪʃəs, -lɪ, -nɪs
[-nəs]
delict, -s 'di:lɪkt, -s
delight (s. v.), -s, -ing, -ed/ly dɪ'laɪt, -s,
-ɪŋ, -ɪd/lɪ
delight|ful, -fully, -fulness dɪ'laɪt|fʊl,
-fəlɪ·[-fʊlɪ], -fʊlnɪs [-nəs]
delightsome dɪ'laɪtsəm
Delilah dɪ'laɪlə
delimit, -s, -ing, -ed di:'lɪmɪt [dɪ'l-], -s,
-ɪŋ, -ɪd
delimitation, -s dɪ,lɪmɪ'teɪʃn [,di:-
lɪmɪ't-], -z
delineat|e, -es, -ing, -ed, -or/s dɪ-
'lɪnɪeɪt, -s, -ɪŋ, -ɪd, -ə*/z
delineation, -s dɪ,lɪnɪ'eɪʃn, -z
delinquen|cy, -cies, -t/s dɪ'lɪŋkwən|sɪ,
-sɪz, -t/s
deliquesc|e, -es, -ing, -ed ,delɪ'kwes, -ɪz,
-ɪŋ, -t
deliquescen|ce, -t ,delɪ'kwesn|s, -t
delirious, -ly, -ness dɪ'lɪrɪəs [-'lɪər-], -lɪ,
-nɪs [-nəs]
delirium, -tremens dɪ'lɪrɪəm [-'lɪər-],
-'tri:menz [-'trem-]
De l'Isle (English name) də'laɪl
Delisle (French name) də'li:l (dəlil)
Delius 'di:ljəs [-lɪəs]
deliv|er, -ers, -ering, -ered, -erer/s
dɪ'lɪv|ə*, -əz, -ərɪŋ, -əd, -ərə*/z
deliverance, -s dɪ'lɪvərəns, -ɪz
deliver|y, -ies dɪ'lɪvər|ɪ, -ɪz
dell, -s del, -z
Delmar 'delmɑ:*, del'mɑ:*
Delos 'di:lɒs
de-lou|se, -ses, -sing, -sed ,di:'laʊ|s [-z],
-sɪz [-zɪz], -sɪŋ [-zɪŋ], -st [-zd]
Delphi (in Greece) 'delfaɪ [-fɪ], (city in
U.S.A.) 'delfaɪ
Delph|ian, -ic 'delf|ɪən [-jən], -ɪk
delphinium, -s del'fɪnɪəm [-njəm], -z
delta, -s 'deltə, -z
deltoid 'deltɔɪd

delud|e, -es, -ing, -ed, -er/s dɪ'lu:d
[-'lju:d], -z, -ɪŋ, -ɪd, -ə*/z
deluge (s. v.), -es, -ing, -ed 'delju:dʒ
[-ljʊdʒ], -ɪz, -ɪŋ, -d
delusion, -s dɪ'lu:ʒn [-'lju:-], -z
delusive, -ly, -ness dɪ'lu:sɪv [-'lju:-], -lɪ,
-nɪs [-nəs]
delusory dɪ'lu:sərɪ [-'lju:-, -u:zərɪ]
de luxe də'lʌks [dɪ-, -'lu:ks, -'lʊks]
delv|e, -es, -ing, -ed, -er/s delv, -z, -ɪŋ,
-d, -ə*/z
Delville 'delvɪl
demagnetization [-isa-], -s 'di:,mæg-
nɪtaɪ'zeɪʃn [di:,m-, -nət-], -z
demagnetiz|e [-is|e], -es, -ing, -ed
,di:'mægnɪtaɪz [di:'m-, -nət-], -ɪz,
-ɪŋ, -d
demagogic, -al ,demə'gɒgɪk [-'gɒdʒɪk],
-l
demagogue, -s 'demægɒg, -z
demagogy 'demægɒgɪ [-gɒdʒɪ]
demand (s. v.), -s, -ing, -ed dɪ'mɑ:nd,
-z, -ɪŋ, -ɪd
Demant dɪ'mænt [də'm-]
demarcat|e, -es, -ing, -ed 'di:mɑ:keɪt,
-s, -ɪŋ, -ɪd
demarcation ,di:mɑ:'keɪʃn
demarcative di:'mɑ:kətɪv
démarche, -s 'deɪmɑ:ʃ [-'-], -ɪz
Demas 'di:mæs
dematerializ|e [-is|e], -es, -ing, -ed
,di:mə'tɪərɪəlaɪz, -ɪz, -ɪŋ, -d
De Mauley də'mɔ:lɪ
demean, -s, -ing, -ed; -our/s dɪ'mi:n,
-z, -ɪŋ, -d; -ə*/z
dement, -s, -ing, -ed dɪ'ment, -s, -ɪŋ, -ɪd
dementia dɪ'menʃə [-ʃjə, -ʃɪə]
Demerara (district in Guyana) ,demə-
'rɑ:rə, (sugar from there) ,demə'reərə
demerit, -s di:'merɪt ['di:,m-], -s
demesne, -s dɪ'meɪn [də'm-, -'mi:n], -z
Demeter dɪ'mi:tə*
Demetrius dɪ'mi:trɪəs
demigod, -s 'demɪgɒd, -z
demijohn, -s 'demɪdʒɒn, -z
demilitariz|e [-is|e], -es, -ing, -ed
,di:'mɪlɪtəraɪz, -ɪz, -ɪŋ, -d
demilitarization [-isa-] 'di:,mɪlɪtəraɪ-
'zeɪʃn [di:,m-, -rɪ'z-]
demi-monde ,demɪ'mɔ̃:nd [-'mɔ:nd,
-'mɒnd, '---] (dəmimɔ̃:d)
demis|e (s. v.), -es, -ing, -ed dɪ'maɪz, -ɪz,
-ɪŋ, -d
demi-semiquaver, -s 'demɪsemɪ,kweɪ-
və*, -z
demission, -s dɪ'mɪʃn, -z
de-mist, -s, -ing, -ed, -er*/s ,di:'mɪst,
-s, -ɪŋ, -ɪd, -ə*/z

demiurge, -s 'di:mɪɜ:dʒ ['dem-], -ɪz
demo, -s 'deməʊ, -z
demob, -s, -bing, -bed ˌdiː'mɒb, -z, -ɪŋ, -d
demobilization [-isa-], -s 'di:ˌməʊbɪlaɪ-
'zeɪʃn [dɪˌməʊbɪlaɪ'z-, -lɪ'z-, -bəl-,
-bl̩-], -z
demobiliz|e [-is|e], -es, -ing, -ed di:-
'məʊbɪlaɪz [dɪ'm-, 'di:m-, -bəl-,
-bl̩aɪz], -ɪz, -ɪŋ, -d
democracy, -ies dɪ'mɒkrəs|ɪ, -ɪz
democrat, -s 'deməkræt [-mʊk-], -s
democratic, -al, -ally ˌdemə'krætɪk
[-mʊ'k-], -l, -əlɪ
democratization [-isa-] dɪˌmɒkrətaɪ-
'zeɪʃn [-tɪ'z-]
democratiz|e [-is|e], -es, -ing, -ed
dɪ'mɒkrətaɪz, -ɪz, -ɪŋ, -d
Democritus dɪ'mɒkrɪtəs
demogorgon, -s ˌdi:məʊ'gɔ:gən, -z
demographic ˌdeməʊ'græfɪk
demography di:'mɒgrəfɪ
Demoivre də'mɔɪvə* [dɪ'm-]
De Moleyns 'deməlɪ:nz [-mʊl-]
demolish, -es, -ing, -ed, -er/s dɪ'mɒlɪʃ,
-ɪz, -ɪŋ, -t, -ə*/z
demolition, -s ˌdemə'lɪʃn [ˌdi:m-,
-mʊ'l-], -z
demon, -s 'di:mən, -z
demonetization [-isa-] di:ˌmʌnɪtaɪ-
'zeɪʃn [-ˌmɒn-, -tɪ'z-]
demonetiz|e [-is|e], -es, -ing, -ed
ˌdi:'mʌnɪtaɪz [dɪ'm-, -'mɒn-], -ɪz, -ɪŋ,
-d
demoniac (s. adj.), -s dɪ'məʊnɪæk
[-njæk], -s
demoniac|al, -ally ˌdi:məʊ'naɪək|l
[-mʊ'n-], -əlɪ
demonic di:'mɒnɪk [dɪ'm-]
demoni|sm, -st/s 'di:mənɪ|zəm, -st/s
demonology ˌdi:mə'nɒlədʒɪ
demonstrability ˌdemənstrə'bɪlətɪ [dɪ-
ˌmɒns-, -lɪt-]
demonstrab|le, -ly 'demənstrəb|l
[dɪ'mɒn-], -lɪ
demonstrat|e, -es, -ing, -ed, -or/s
'demənstreɪt, -s, -ɪŋ, -ɪd, -ə*/z
demonstration, -s ˌdemən'streɪʃn, -z
demonstrative (s. adj.), -s, -ly, -ness
dɪ'mɒnstrətɪv, -z, -lɪ, -nɪs [-nəs]
demoralization [-isa-] dɪˌmɒrəlaɪ'zeɪʃn
[-rl̩aɪ'z-, -rəlɪ'z-, -rl̩ɪ'z-]
demoraliz|e [-is|e], -es, -ing, -ed dɪ-
'mɒrəlaɪz [-rl̩aɪz], -ɪz, -ɪŋ, -d
De Morgan də'mɔ:gən
de mortuis ˌdeɪ'mɔ:tjʊɪs [ˌdi:-, -tu:ɪs]
Demos 'di:mɒs
Demosthenes dɪ'mɒsθəni:z [də'm-,
-θɪn-]

demot|e, -es, -ing, -ed ˌdi:'məʊt [dɪ-],
-s, -ɪŋ, -ɪd
demotic dɪ'mɒtɪk [di:-]
demotion ˌdi:'məʊʃn [dɪ-]
Dempster 'dempstə*
demur (s. v.), -s, -ring, -red dɪ'mɜ:*, -z,
-rɪŋ, -d
demure, -r, -st, -ly, -ness dɪ'mjʊə*
[-'mjɔə*, -'mjɔ:*], -rə*, -rɪst, -lɪ, -nɪs
[-nəs]
demurrage dɪ'mʌrɪdʒ
demurrer (one who demurs), -s dɪ-
'mɜ:rə*, -z
demurrer (objection on ground of
irrelevance), -s dɪ'mʌrə*, -z
Demuth də'mu:θ
dem|y, -ies dɪ'm|aɪ [də'm-], -aɪz
demyship, -s dɪ'maɪʃɪp [də'm-], -s
den, -s den, -z
dena|rius, -rii dɪ'neə|rɪəs, -rɪaɪ [de-
'nɑ:rɪəs, de'nɑ:rɪi:]
denary 'di:nərɪ
denationalization [-isa-] 'di:ˌnæʃnəlaɪ-
'zeɪʃn [-ʃnəl-, -ʃn̩l-, -ʃnl̩-, -ʃənəl-,
-lɪ'z-]
denationaliz|e [-is|e], -es, -ing, -ed
ˌdi:'næʃnəlaɪz [-ʃnəl-, -ʃn̩l-, -ʃnl̩-,
-ʃənəl-], -ɪz, -ɪŋ, -d
denaturalization [-isa-] 'di:ˌnætʃrəlaɪ-
'zeɪʃn [-tʃʊr-, -tʃər-, -lɪ'z-]
denaturaliz|e [-is|e], -es, -ing, -ed ˌdi:-
'nætʃrəlaɪz [-tʃʊr-, -tʃər-], -ɪz, -ɪŋ, -d
Denbigh, -shire 'denbɪ, -ʃə* [-ˌʃɪə*]
Denby 'denbɪ
dendrology den'drɒlədʒɪ
dene (D.), -s di:n, -z
Deneb 'deneb
Denebola dɪ'nebələ [de'n-, də'n-]
dengue 'deŋgɪ
Denham 'denəm
Denholm(e) 'denəm
Denia, -s 'di:njə [-nɪə], -z
deniable dɪ'naɪəbl
denial, -s dɪ'naɪəl, -z
denier (coin), -s dɪ'nɪə* ['denɪə*], -z
denier (thickness of yarn) 'denɪə*
['denjə*, -nɪeɪ] (dənje)
denier (one who denies), -s dɪ'naɪə*, -z
denigrat|e, -es, -ing, -ed 'denɪgreɪt, -s,
-ɪŋ, -ɪd
denigration ˌdenɪ'greɪʃn
denim, -s 'denɪm, -z
Denis 'denɪs
Denise də'ni:z [de'n-]
Denison 'denɪsn
denizen, -s 'denɪzn, -z
Denman 'denmən
Denmark 'denmɑ:k

131

Dennehy 'denəhɪ, -hi:
Dennis 'denɪs
Denny, -s 'denɪ, -s
denominat|e, -es, -ing, -ed dɪ'nɒmɪneɪt,
-s, -ɪŋ, -ɪd
denomination, -s dɪˌnɒmɪ'neɪʃn, -z
denominational dɪˌnɒmɪ'neɪʃənl [-ʃnəl,
-ʃn̩, -ʃn̩, -ʃənəl]
denominationalism dɪˌnɒmɪ'neɪʃn̩əl-
ɪzəm [-ʃnəl-, -ʃn̩-, -ʃn̩-, -ʃənəl-]
denominative dɪ'nɒmɪnətɪv
denominator, -s dɪ'nɒmɪneɪtə*, -z
denotation, -s ˌdiːnəʊ'teɪʃn, -z
denot|e, -es, -ing, -ed dɪ'nəʊt, -s, -ɪŋ,
-ɪd
dénouement, -s deɪ'nuːmɑ̃:ŋ [-mɑːŋ,
-mɔ̃:ŋ, -mɒŋ] (denumɑ̃), -z
denounc|e, -es, -ing, -ed, -er/s,
-ement/s dɪ'naʊns, -ɪz, -ɪŋ, -t, -ə*/z,
-mənt/s
de novo ˌdeɪ'nəʊvəʊ [ˌdiː-]
dense, -r, -st, -ly, -ness dens, -ə*, -ɪst,
-lɪ, -nɪs [-nəs]
densit|y, -ies 'densət|ɪ [-ɪt|ɪ], -ɪz
dent (s. v.) (D.), -s, -ing, -ed dent, -s,
-ɪŋ, -ɪd
dental (s. adj.), -s 'dentl, -z
dentaliz|e [-is|e], -es, -ing, -ed 'dentə-
laɪz [-ntl̩-], -ɪz, -ɪŋ, -d
dentate 'denteɪt
dentated 'denteɪtɪd [den't-]
denticle, -s 'dentɪkl, -z
dentifrice, -s 'dentɪfrɪs, -ɪz
dentil, -s 'dentɪl, -z
dentilingual (s. adj.), -s ˌdentɪ'lɪŋgwəl,
-z
dentine 'dentiːn
dentist, -s, -ry 'dentɪst, -s, -rɪ
dentition den'tɪʃn
Denton 'dentən
denture, -s 'dentʃə*, -z
denudation, -s ˌdiːnjuː'deɪʃn [-njʊ-], -z
denud|e, -es, -ing, -ed dɪ'njuːd, -z, -ɪŋ,
-ɪd
denunciat|e, -es, -ing, -ed, -or/s
dɪ'nʌnsɪeɪt [-nsjeɪt, -nʃɪeɪt, -nʃjeɪt],
-s, -ɪŋ, -ɪd, -ə*/z
denunciation, -s dɪˌnʌnsɪ'eɪʃn, -z
denunciatory dɪ'nʌnsɪətərɪ [-nʃɪə-,
-nsjə-, dɪ'nʌnsɪeɪtərɪ, dɪ-
'nʌnʃɪeɪtərɪ]
Denver 'denvə*
den|y, -ies, -ying, -ied, -ier/s dɪ'n|aɪ,
-aɪz, -aɪɪŋ, -aɪd, -aɪə*/z
Denys 'denɪs
Denyse də'niːz [de'n-]
Denzil 'denzɪl
deodand, -s 'dɪəʊdænd, -z

deodar, -s 'dɪəʊdɑː*, -z
deodara, -s ˌdɪə'dɑːrə [dɪəʊ'd-, -'deərə],
-z
deodorant, -s diː'əʊdərənt [dɪ'əʊ-], -s
deodorization [-isa-], -s diːˌəʊdəraɪ-
'zeɪʃn [dɪˌəʊ-, -rɪ'z-], -z
deodoriz|e [-is|e], -es, -ing, -ed, -er/s
diː'əʊdəraɪz [dɪ'əʊ-], -ɪz, -ɪŋ, -d,
-ə*/z
deoxidization [-isa-], -s diːˌɒksɪdaɪ-
'zeɪʃn ['diː:ˌɒ-], -z
deoxidiz|e [-is|e], -es, -ing, -ed, -er/s
diː'ɒksɪdaɪz [ˌdiː'ɒ-], -ɪz, -ɪŋ, -d, -ə*/z
depart, -s, -ing, -ed dɪ'pɑːt, -s, -ɪŋ, -ɪd
department, -s dɪ'pɑːtmənt, -s
departmental ˌdiːpɑːt'mentl
departure, -s dɪ'pɑːtʃə*, -z
depast|ure, -ures, -uring, -ured diː-
'pɑːstʃ|ə*, -əz, -ərɪŋ, -əd
depauperiz|e [-is|e], -es, -ing, -ed
ˌdiː'pɔːpəraɪz, -ɪz, -ɪŋ, -d
depend, -s, -ing, -ed dɪ'pend, -z, -ɪŋ, -ɪd
dependable, -ness dɪ'pendəbl, -nɪs
[-nəs]
dependant, -s dɪ'pendənt, -s
dependen|ce, -cy, -cies, -t/s, -tly dɪ-
'pendən|s, -sɪ, -sɪz, -t/s, -tlɪ
Depere dɪ'prɪə* [də'p-]
Depew dɪ'pjuː [də'p-]
depict, -s, -ing, -ed dɪ'pɪkt, -s, -ɪŋ, -ɪd
depiction dɪ'pɪkʃn
depilat|e, -es, -ing, -ed 'depɪleɪt, -s, -ɪŋ,
-ɪd
depilatory dɪ'pɪlətərɪ [de'p-]
deplet|e, -es, -ing, -ed dɪ'pliːt [diː'p-],
-s, -ɪŋ, -ɪd
depletion, -s dɪ'pliːʃn [diː'p-], -z
deplet|ive, -ory dɪ'pliːt|ɪv [diː'p-], -ərɪ
deplorab|le, -ly, -leness dɪ'plɔːrəb|l
[-'plɔər-], -lɪ, -lnɪs [-nəs]
deplor|e, -es, -ing, -ed dɪ'plɔː* [-'plɔə*],
-z, -rɪŋ, -d
deploy, -s, -ing, -ed; -ment dɪ'plɔɪ, -z,
-ɪŋ, -d; -mənt
depolarization [-isa-] 'diːˌpəʊləraɪ'zeɪʃn
[-rɪ'z-]
depolariz|e [-is|e], -es, -ing, -ed ˌdiː-
'pəʊləraɪz, -ɪz, -ɪŋ, -d
deponent (s. adj.), -s dɪ'pəʊnənt, -s
depopulat|e, -es, -ing, -ed, -or/s ˌdiː-
'pɒpjʊleɪt, -s, -ɪŋ, -ɪd, -ə*/z
depopulation diːˌpɒpjʊ'leɪʃn ['-ˌ--'--]
deport, -s, -ing, -ed dɪ'pɔːt, -s, -ɪŋ, -ɪd
deportation, -s ˌdiːpɔː'teɪʃn, -z
deportment dɪ'pɔːtmənt
deposal, -s dɪ'pəʊzl, -z
depos|e, -es, -ing, -ed dɪ'pəʊz, -ɪz, -ɪŋ,
-d

132

deposit (s. v.), **-s, -ing, -ed, -or/s** dɪ-
'pɒzɪt, -s, -ɪŋ, -ɪd, -ə*/z
depositar|y, **-ies** dɪ'pɒzɪtər|ɪ, -ɪz
deposition, **-s** ˌdepə'zɪʃn [ˌdiːp-, -pʊ'z-],
-z
depositor|y, **-ies** dɪ'pɒzɪtər|ɪ, -ɪz
depot, **-s** 'depəʊ, -z
depravation ˌdeprə'veɪʃn
deprav|e, **-es, -ing, -ed, -edly, -edness**
dɪ'preɪv, -z, -ɪŋ, -d, -dlɪ [-ɪdlɪ], -dnɪs
[-ɪdnɪs, -nəs]
depravity dɪ'prævətɪ [-ɪtɪ]
deprecat|e, **-es, -ing/ly, -ed, -or/s**
'deprɪkeɪt [-prə-], -s, -ɪŋ/lɪ, -ɪd,
-ə*/z
deprecation, **-s** ˌdeprɪ'keɪʃn [-prə-], -z
deprecatory 'deprɪkətərɪ [-prə-, -keɪt-]
depreciat|e, **-es, -ing/ly, -ed, -or/s**
dɪ'priːʃɪeɪt [-ʃɪert, -sɪeɪt, -sjeɪt], -s,
-ɪŋ/lɪ, -ɪd, -ə*/z
depreciation dɪˌpriːʃɪ'eɪʃn [-sɪ'eɪ-]
depreciatory dɪ'priːʃjətərɪ [-ʃɪət-, -ʃət-,
-ʃɪeɪtərɪ]
depredat|e, **-es, -ing, -ed, -or/s** 'de-
prɪdeɪt [-prəd-], -s, -ɪŋ, -ɪd, -ə*/z
depredation, **-s** ˌdeprɪ'deɪʃn [-prə'd-], -z
depredatory dɪ'predətərɪ
depress, **-es, -ing/ly, -ed, -or/s, -ant/s**
dɪ'pres, -ɪz, -ɪŋ/lɪ, -t, -ə*/z, -ənt/s
depression, **-s** dɪ'preʃn, -z
depressive dɪ'presɪv
depressurization [-isation] diːˌpreʃəraɪ-
'zeɪʃn ['-ˌ---'--, -ərɪ'z-]
depressuriz|e [-is|e], **-es, -ing, -ed**
ˌdiː'preʃəraɪz, -ɪz, -ɪŋ, -d
deprivation, **-s** ˌdeprɪ'veɪʃn [ˌdiː-
praɪ'v-], -z
depriv|e, **-es, -ing, -ed** dɪ'praɪv, -z, -ɪŋ,
-d
Deptford 'detfəd ['depfəd]
depth, **-s** depθ, -s
depth-charge, **-s** 'depθtʃɑːdʒ, -ɪz
deputation, **-s** ˌdepjʊ'teɪʃn [-pjuː-], -z
deput|e, **-es, -ing, -ed** dɪ'pjuːt, -s, -ɪŋ,
-ɪd
deputiz|e [-is|e], **-es, -ing, -ed** 'de-
pjʊtaɪz, -ɪz, -ɪŋ, -d
deput|y, **-ies** 'depjʊt|ɪ, -ɪz
De Quincey də'kwɪnsɪ
derail, **-s, -ing, -ed, -ment/s** dɪ'reɪl
[ˌdiː'r-], -z, -ɪŋ, -d, -mənt/s
derang|e, **-es, -ing, -ed, -ement/s**
dɪ'reɪndʒ [də'r-], -ɪz, -ɪŋ, -d, -mənt/s
derat|e, **-es, -ing, -ed** ˌdiː'reɪt, -s, -ɪŋ,
-ɪd
de-ra|tion, **-tions, -tioning, -tioned**
ˌdiː'ræ|ʃn, -ʃnz, -ʃənɪŋ [-ʃn̩ɪŋ, -ʃnɪŋ],
-ʃnd

Derbe 'dɜːbɪ
Derby, **-shire** 'dɑːbɪ, -ʃə* [-ˌʃɪə*]
Note.—The form 'dɜːbɪ is also heard,
mainly from dialectal speakers.
Dereham 'dɪərəm
Derek 'derɪk
derelict (s. adj.), **-s** 'derəlɪkt [-rɪl-], -s
dereliction ˌderə'lɪkʃn [-rɪ'l-]
derequisi|tion, **-tions, -tioning, -tioned**
'diːˌrekwɪ'zɪ|ʃn, -ʃnz, -ʃənɪŋ [-ʃn̩ɪŋ,
-ʃnɪŋ], -ʃnd
D'Eresby 'drɪəzbɪ
De Reszke də'reskɪ
Derg(h) dɜːg
Derham 'derəm
derid|e, **-es, -ing/ly, -ed, -er/s** dɪ'raɪd
[də'r-], -z, -ɪŋ/lɪ, -ɪd, -ə*/z
de rigueur dərɪ'gɜː* (dərigœːr)
Dering 'dɪərɪŋ
derision dɪ'rɪʒn [də'r-]
derisive, **-ly, -ness** dɪ'raɪsɪv [də'r-,
-'raɪzɪv, -'rɪzɪv], -lɪ, -nɪs [-nəs]
derisory dɪ'raɪsərɪ [də'r-, -'raɪzərɪ]
derivation, **-s** ˌderɪ'veɪʃn, -z
derivative (s. adj.), **-s, -ly** dɪ'rɪvətɪv
[də'r-], -z, -lɪ
deriv|e, **-es, -ing, -ed; -able** dɪ'raɪv
[də'r-], -z, -ɪŋ, -d; -əbl
d'Erlanger (English surname) 'deə-
lɑ̃ːnʒeɪ [-lɔ̃ːn:-, -lɑːn:-]
derm, **-al** dɜːm, -l
dermatitis ˌdɜːmə'taɪtɪs
dermatolog|ist/s, **-y** ˌdɜːmə'tɒlədʒ|ɪst/s,
-ɪ
derogat|e, **-es, -ing, -ed** 'derəʊgeɪt, -s,
-ɪŋ, -ɪd
derogation ˌderəʊ'geɪʃn
derogator|y, **-ily, -iness** dɪ'rɒgətər|ɪ
[də'r-, -əlɪ [-ɪlɪ], -ɪnɪs [-ɪnəs]
De Rohan də'rəʊən
Deronda də'rɒndə [dɪ'r-]
De Ros də'ruːs
derrick (D.), **-s** 'derɪk, -s
derring-do ˌderɪŋ'duː
derringer (D.), **-s** 'derɪndʒə*, -z
Derry 'derɪ
De Rutzen də'rʌtsn
derv dɜːv
Derviche 'dɜːvɪtʃ
dervish (D.), **-es** 'dɜːvɪʃ, -ɪz
Derwent (river) 'dɜːwənt [-went, -wɪnt],
'dɑːw-
Derwentwater 'dɜːwəntˌwɔːtə* [-went-,
-wɪnt-]
De Salis də'sælɪs [dɪ's-], -'sɑːlɪs
Desart 'dezət
de Satgé də'sætdʒeɪ
Desbarres deɪ'bɑː*

133

Desborough 'dezbrə
descal|e, -es, -ing, -ed ˌdi:'skeɪl, -z, -ɪŋ,
-d
descant (s.), -s 'deskænt, -s
descant (v.), -s, -ing, -ed dɪ'skænt
[de's-], -s, -ɪŋ, -ɪd
Descartes deɪ'kɑːt ['deɪkɑːt] (dekart)
descend, -s, -ing, -ed, -er/s dɪ'send, -z,
-ɪŋ, -ɪd, -ə*/z
descendant (s. adj.), -s dɪ'sendənt, -s
descendent dɪ'sendənt
descent, -s dɪ'sent, -s
describ|e, -es, -ing, -ed, -er/s; -able
dɪ'skraɪb, -z, -ɪŋ, -d, -ə*/z; -əbl
description, -s dɪ'skrɪpʃn, -z
descriptive, -ly, -ness dɪ'skrɪptɪv, -lɪ,
-nɪs [-nəs]
descr|y, -ies, -ying, -ied dɪ'skr|aɪ, -aɪz,
-aɪɪŋ, -aɪd
Desdemona ˌdezdɪ'məʊnə
desecrat|e, -es, -ing, -ed, -or/s 'desɪ-
kreɪt, -s, -ɪŋ, -ɪd, -ə*/z
desecration, -s ˌdesɪ'kreɪʃn, -z
desegregat|e, -es, -ing, -ed ˌdi:'segrɪgeɪt
[-grə-], -s, -ɪŋ, -ɪd
desegregation ˌdi:segrɪ'geɪʃn [-grə-]
de Selincourt də'selɪnkɔːt [-lɪŋk-]
desensitiz|e [-is|e], -es, -ing, -ed ˌdi:-
'sensɪtaɪz, -ɪz, -ɪŋ, -d
desert (s.) (what is deserved), -s dɪ'zɜːt,
-s
desert (s. adj.) (wilderness, desolate), -s
'dezət, -s
desert (v.), -s, -ing, -ed, -er/s dɪ'zɜːt,
-s, -ɪŋ, -ɪd, -ə*/z
desertion, -s dɪ'zɜːʃn, -z
deserv|e, -es, -ing/ly, -ed, -edly dɪ'zɜːv,
-z, -ɪŋ/lɪ, -d, -ɪdlɪ
deshabille 'dezæbiːl [-zəb-]
déshabillé ˌdeɪzæ'biːeɪ [ˌdez-, -zə'b-,
-'biːleɪ] (dezabije)
desiccat|e, -es, -ing, -ed 'desɪkeɪt, -s, -ɪŋ,
-ɪd
desiccation ˌdesɪ'keɪʃn
desiccative de'sɪkətɪv [dɪ's-, 'desɪkətɪv]
desiderat|e, -es, -ing, -ed dɪ'zɪdəreɪt
[dɪ'sɪ-], -s, -ɪŋ, -ɪd
desideration, -s dɪˌzɪdə'reɪʃn [dɪˌsɪ-], -z
desiderative dɪ'zɪdərətɪv [dɪ'sɪ-]
desiderat|um, -a dɪˌzɪdə'rɑːt|əm [dɪˌsɪ-,
-'reɪt-], -ə
design (s. v.), -s, -ing, -ed, -edly, -er/s;
-able dɪ'zaɪn, -z, -ɪŋ, -d, -ɪdlɪ, -ə*/z;
-əbl
designate (adj.) 'dezɪgneɪt [-nɪt, -nət]
designat|e (v.), -es, -ing, -ed, -or/s
'dezɪgneɪt, -s, -ɪŋ, -ɪd, -ə*/z
designation, -s ˌdezɪg'neɪʃn, -z

desilveriz|e [-is|e], -es, -ing, -ed ˌdi:-
'sɪlvəraɪz, -ɪz, -ɪŋ, -d
desinence, -s 'desɪnəns, -ɪz
desirability dɪˌzaɪərə'bɪlətɪ [-lɪt-]
desirab|le, -ly, -leness dɪ'zaɪərəb|l, -lɪ,
-lnɪs [-nəs]
desir|e (s. v.), -es, -ing, -ed, -er/s
dɪ'zaɪə*, -z, -rɪŋ, -d, -rə*/z
Désirée (English name) deɪ'zɪəreɪ [de'z-]
desirous, -ly dɪ'zaɪərəs, -lɪ
desist, -s, -ing, -ed dɪ'zɪst [dɪ'sɪst], -s,
-ɪŋ, -ɪd
desistance dɪ'zɪstəns [dɪ'sɪs-]
desk, -s desk, -s
Deslys deɪ'liːs
Des Moines (in U.S.A.) dɪ'mɔɪn
[-'mɔɪnz]
Desmond 'dezmənd
desolate (adj.), -ly, -ness 'desələt [-sl-,
-ɪt], -lɪ, -nɪs [-nəs]
desolat|e (v.), -es, -ing, -ed, -or/s
'desəleɪt, -s, -ɪŋ, -ɪd, -ə*/z
desolation, -s ˌdesə'leɪʃn, -z
despair (s. v.), -s, -ing/ly, -ed dɪ'speə*,
-z, -rɪŋ/lɪ, -d
Despard 'despəd [-pɑːd]
despatch (s. v.), -es, -ing, -ed, -er/s
dɪ'spætʃ, -ɪz, -ɪŋ, -t, -ə*/z
despatch-boat, -s dɪ'spætʃbəʊt, -s
despatch-box, -es dɪ'spætʃbɒks, -ɪz
despatch-rider, -s dɪ'spætʃˌraɪdə*, -z
desperado, -es ˌdespə'rɑːdəʊ [-'reɪd-], -z
desperate, -ly, -ness 'despərət [-rɪt], -lɪ,
-nɪs [-nəs]
desperation ˌdespə'reɪʃn
despicability ˌdespɪkə'bɪlətɪ [dɪˌspɪk-,
-lɪt-]
despicab|le, -ly, -leness dɪ'spɪkəb|l
['despɪk-], -lɪ, -lnɪs [-nəs]
despis|e, -es, -ing, -ed, -er/s dɪ'spaɪz,
-ɪz, -ɪŋ, -d, -ə*/z
despite, -ful, -fully dɪ'spaɪt, -fʊl, -fʊlɪ
[-fəlɪ]
despoil, -s, -ing, -ed, -er/s dɪ'spɔɪl, -z,
-ɪŋ, -d, -ə*/z
despond (D.), -s, -ing/ly, -ed dɪ'spɒnd,
-z, -ɪŋ/lɪ, -ɪd
desponden|ce, -cy, -t/ly dɪ'spɒndən|s,
-sɪ, -t/lɪ
despot, -s 'despɒt [-pət], -s
despotic, -al, -ally, -alness de'spɒtɪk
[dɪ's-], -l, -əlɪ, -lnɪs [-nəs]
despotism, -s 'despətɪzəm, -z
dessert, -s dɪ'zɜːt, -s
dessert-kni|fe, -ves dɪ'zɜːtnaɪ|f, -vz
dessert-service, -s dɪ'zɜːtˌsɜːvɪs, -ɪz
dessert-spoon, -s dɪ'zɜːtspuːn, -z
destination, -s ˌdestɪ'neɪʃn, -z

destin|e, -es, -ing, -ed 'destɪn, -z, -ɪŋ, -d
destin|y, -ies 'destɪn|ɪ [-ən|ɪ], -ɪz
destitute, -ly, -ness 'destɪtjuːt, -lɪ, -nɪs
[-nəs]
destitution ˌdestɪ'tjuːʃn
destroy, -s, -ing, -ed, -er/s dɪ'strɔɪ, -z,
-ɪŋ, -d, -ə*/z
destructibility dɪˌstrʌktɪ'bɪlɪtɪ [-tə'b-,
-lɪt-]
destructible dɪ'strʌktəbl [-tɪb-]
destruction, -s dɪ'strʌkʃn, -z
destructive, -ly, -ness dɪ'strʌktɪv, -lɪ,
-nɪs [-nəs]
†destructor, -s dɪ'strʌktə*, -z
desuetude dɪ'sjuːɪtjuːd [-'sjʊɪ-, 'deswɪ-
tjuːd, 'diːswɪ-]
desultor|y, -ily, -iness 'desəltər|ɪ, -əlɪ
[-ɪlɪ] -ɪnɪs [-nəs]
Desvaux 'deɪvəʊ, deɪ'vəʊ, də'vəʊ
Des Vœux deɪ'vɜː
detach, -es, -ing, -ed, -edly, -ment/s;
-able dɪ'tætʃ, -ɪz, -ɪŋ, -t, -tlɪ [-ɪdlɪ],
-mənt/s; -əbl
detail (s. v.), -s, -ing, -ed 'diːteɪl
[dɪ'teɪl], -z, -ɪŋ, -d
detain, -s, -ing, -ed, -er/s dɪ'teɪn, -z,
-ɪŋ, -d, -ə*/z
detainee, -s ˌdiːteɪ'niː [dɪteɪ'niː], -z
detainer (legal term) dɪ'teɪnə*
detect, -s, -ing, -ed, -or/s; -able
dɪ'tekt, -s, -ɪŋ, -ɪd, -ə*/z; -əbl
detection, -s dɪ'tekʃn, -z
detective (s. adj.), -s dɪ'tektɪv, -z
detent, -s dɪ'tent, -s
détente deɪ'tãːnt [-aːnt, -ɔ̃ːnt, -ɒnt]
(detãːt)
detention, -s dɪ'tenʃn, -z
deter, -s, -ring, -red dɪ'tɜː*, -z, -rɪŋ, -d
Deterding 'detədɪŋ
detergent (s. adj.), -s dɪ'tɜːdʒənt, -s
deteriorat|e, -es, -ing, -ed dɪ'tɪərɪəreɪt,
-s, -ɪŋ, -ɪd
deterioration dɪˌtɪərɪə'reɪʃn
determinable dɪ'tɜːmɪnəbl
determinant (s. adj.), -s dɪ'tɜːmɪnənt, -s
determinate, -ly, -ness dɪ'tɜːmɪnət
[-ɪt], -lɪ, -nɪs [-nəs]
determination, -s dɪˌtɜːmɪ'neɪʃn, -z
determinative dɪ'tɜːmɪnətɪv
determin|e, -es, -ing, -ed/ly, -er/s
dɪ'tɜːmɪn, -z, -ɪŋ, -d/lɪ, -ə*/z
determini|sm, -st/s dɪ'tɜːmɪnɪ|zəm,
-st/s
deterrent (s. adj.), -s dɪ'terənt, -s
detest, -s, -ing, -ed dɪ'test, -s, -ɪŋ, -ɪd
detestab|le, -ly, -leness dɪ'testəb|l, -lɪ,
-lnɪs [-nəs]
detestation ˌdiːte'steɪʃn [dɪte'st-]

dethron|e, -es, -ing, -ed, -ement
dɪ'θrəʊn [ˌdiː-], -z, -ɪŋ, -d, -mənt
Detmold (surname) 'detməʊld, (German town) 'detməʊld ('detmɒlt)
detonat|e, -es, -ing, -ed, -or/s 'detə-
neɪt ['diːt-], -s, -ɪŋ, -ɪd, -ə*/z
detonation, -s ˌdetə'neɪʃn [ˌdiːt-], -z
détour, -s 'diːˌtʊə* ['deɪ-, deɪ'tʊə*,
dɪ't-] (detuːr), -z
detract, -s, -ing/ly, -ed, -or/s dɪ'trækt,
-s, -ɪŋ/lɪ, -ɪd, -ə*/z
detraction, -s dɪ'trækʃn, -z
detract|ive, -ory dɪ'trækt|ɪv, -ərɪ
detrain, -s, -ing, -ed ˌdiː'treɪn, -z, -ɪŋ, -d
de Trey də'treɪ
detriment, -s 'detrɪmənt, -s
detrimental ˌdetrɪ'mentl
detrition dɪ'trɪʃn
detritus dɪ'traɪtəs
Detroit də'trɔɪt [dɪ't-]
de trop (de trop) (dətro)
detruncat|e, -es, -ing, -ed ˌdiː'trʌŋkeɪt
['---], -s, -ɪŋ, -ɪd
detruncation, -s ˌdiːtrʌŋ'keɪʃn, -z
Dettol 'detɒl [-təl]
Deucalion djuː'keɪljən [djʊ-, -lɪən]
deuce, -s djuːs, -ɪz
deuc|ed, -edly djuːs|t ['djuːs|ɪd], -ɪdlɪ
deuterium djuː'tɪərɪəm [djʊ-]
deuteronomic ˌdjuːtərə'nɒmɪk
Deuteronomy ˌdjuːtə'rɒnəmɪ ['djuːtər-
ənəmɪ]
deutzia, -s 'djuːtsjə ['dɔɪts-, -sɪə], -z
deva, -s 'deɪvə ['diː'və] (Hindi deva), -z
de Valera dəvə'leərə [ˌdev-]
devaluation, -s ˌdiː'væljʊ'eɪʃn [dɪ-,
-ˌ--'--], -z
deval|ue, -ues, -uing, -ued ˌdiː'væl|juː
[-jʊ], -juːz [-jʊz], -jʊɪŋ [-jwɪŋ],
-juːd [-jʊd]
Devanagari ˌdeɪvə'nɑːgərɪ [ˌdev-]
Devant də'vænt [dɪ'v-]
devastat|e, -es, -ing, -ed 'devəsteɪt, -s,
-ɪŋ, -ɪd
devastation, -s ˌdevə'steɪʃn, -z
develop, -s, -ing, -ed, -er/s, -ment/s;
-able dɪ'veləp [də'v-], -s, -ɪŋ, -t,
-ə*/z, -mənt/s; -əbl
Devenish 'devnɪʃ [-vənɪʃ]
Deventer 'devəntə*
Deventhaugh 'devənthɔː
De Vere də'vɪə* [dɪ'v-]
Devereux 'devəruː, -ruːks
Deveron 'devərən
Devers (surname) 'diːvəz, 'devəz
Deverson 'devəsn
De Vesci də'vesɪ
deviant, -s 'diːvjənt [-vɪənt], -s

135

deviat|e, -es, -ing, -ed, -or/s 'diːvɪeɪt
[-vjeɪt], -s, -ɪŋ, -ɪd, -ə*/z
deviation, -s ˌdiːvɪ'eɪʃn, -z
deviation|ism, -ist/s ˌdiːvɪ'eɪʃən|ɪzəm
[-ʃn̩-], -ɪst/s
device, -s dɪ'vaɪs, -ɪz
dev|il (s. v.), -ils, -illing, -illed 'dev|l,
-lz, -lɪŋ [-lɪŋ], -ld
devil-fish, -es 'devlfɪʃ, -ɪz
devilish, -ly, -ness 'devlɪʃ [-vlɪʃ], -lɪ,
-nɪs [-nəs]
devil-may-care ˌdevlmeɪ'keə*
devilment, -s 'devlmənt, -s
devilr|y, -ies 'devlr|ɪ, -ɪz
devil-worship, -per/s 'devlˌwəːʃɪp,
-ə*/z
Devine də'vaɪn [dɪ'v-]
devious, -ly, -ness 'diːvjəs [-vɪəs], -lɪ,
-nɪs [-nəs]
devis|e, -es, -ing, -ed, -er/s; -able
dɪ'vaɪz, -ɪz, -ɪŋ, -d, -ə*/z; -əbl
devisee, -s ˌdevɪ'ziː [dɪvaɪ'ziː], -z
devisor, -s ˌdevɪ'zɔː* [dɪvaɪ'zɔː*,
dɪ'vaɪzɔː*], -z
devitalization [-isa-] diːˌvaɪtəlaɪ'zeɪʃn
['diːˌvaɪt-]
devitaliz|e [-is|e], -es, -ing, -ed ˌdiː-
'vaɪtəlaɪz [-t|aɪ-], -ɪz, -ɪŋ, -d
Devizes dɪ'vaɪzɪz
devocalization [-isa-], -s diːˌvəʊkəlaɪ-
'zeɪʃn ['diːˌvəʊkəlaɪ'z-, -k|aɪ-], -z
devocaliz|e [-is|e], -es, -ing, -ed ˌdiː-
'vəʊkəlaɪz [-k|aɪz], -ɪz, -ɪŋ, -d
devoic|e, -es, -ing, -ed ˌdiː'vɔɪs, -ɪz, -ɪŋ,
-t
devoid dɪ'vɔɪd
devolution, -s ˌdiːvə'luːʃn [ˌdev-,
-v|'uː-, -və'lju:-], -z
devolv|e, -es, -ing, -ed dɪ'vɒlv, -z, -ɪŋ,
-d
Devon, -shire 'devn, -ʃə* [-ˌʃɪə*]
Devonian, -s de'vəʊnjən [dɪ'v-, -nɪən],
-z
Devonport 'devnpɔːt [-vmp-]
devot|e, -es, -ing, -ed/ly, -edness
dɪ'vəʊt, -s, -ɪŋ, -ɪd/lɪ, -ɪdnɪs [-nəs]
devotee, -s ˌdevəʊ'tiː, -z
devotion, -s dɪ'vəʊʃn, -z
devo|tional, -tionally dɪ'vəʊ|ʃənl [-ʃnəl,
-ʃn̩l, -ʃnl, -ʃənəl], -ʃn̩əlɪ [-ʃnəlɪ, -ʃn̩lɪ,
-ʃn̩lɪ, -ʃənəlɪ]
devour, -s, -ing, -ed, -er/s dɪ'vaʊə*, -z,
-rɪŋ, -d, -rə*/z
devout, -er, -est, -ly, -ness dɪ'vaʊt, -ə*,
-ɪst, -lɪ, -nɪs [-nəs]
dew, -s djuː, -z
dewan, -s dɪ'wɑːn, -z
Dewar 'djuːə* [djʊə]

dewberr|y, -ies 'djuːber|ɪ [-bər-], -ɪz
dew-claw, -s 'djuːklɔː, -z
dew-drop, -s 'djuːdrɒp, -s
D'Ewes djuːz
De Wet də'vet [də'wet]
Dewey 'djuːɪ ['djʊɪ]
De Wiart (English name) də'waɪət
dewlap, -s 'djuːlæp, -s
dew-point, -s 'djuːpɔɪnt, -s
dew-pond, -s 'djuːpɒnd, -z
Dewsbury 'djuːzbərɪ
dew|y, -ness 'djuː|ɪ ['djʊ|ɪ], -ɪnɪs [-ɪnəs]
dexter (D.) 'dekstə*
dexterity dek'sterətɪ [-ɪtɪ]
dexterous, -ly, -ness 'dekstərəs, -lɪ, -nɪs
[-nəs]
dextrose 'dekstrəʊs
D'Eyncourt 'deɪnkəːt [-kɔːt]
De Zoete də'zuːt
dhobi, -(e)s 'dəʊbɪ (Hindi dhobi), -z
dhoti, -(e)s 'dəʊtɪ, -z
dhow, -s daʊ, -z
diabetes ˌdaɪə'biːtiːz [-ɪz, -ɪs]
diabetic, -s ˌdaɪə'betɪk [-'biːt-], -s
diabolic, -al, -ally ˌdaɪə'bɒlɪk, -l, -əlɪ
diabolism daɪ'æbəlɪzəm
diaboliz|e [-is|e], -es, -ing, -ed daɪ-
'æbəlaɪz, -ɪz, -ɪŋ, -d
diabolo dɪ'æbələʊ [-'ɑːb-]
diachronic ˌdaɪə'krɒnɪk
diaconal daɪ'ækənl
diaconate, -s daɪ'ækəneɪt [-nɪt, -nət], -s
diacritic (s. adj.), -s, -al ˌdaɪə'krɪtɪk, -s,
-l
diadem, -s 'daɪədem [-dəm], -z
diaeres|is, -es daɪ'erɪs|ɪs [daɪ'ɪər-,
-rəs-], -iːz
Diaghilev dɪ'ægɪlef
diagnos|e, -es, -ing, -ed 'daɪəgnəʊz
[ˌdaɪəg'n-], -ɪz, -ɪŋ, -d
diagnos|is, -es ˌdaɪəg'nəʊs|ɪs, -iːz
diagnostic (s. adj.), -s ˌdaɪəg'nɒstɪk, -s
diagon|al (s. adj.), -als, -ally daɪ'ægən|l,
-lz, -əlɪ [-l̩ɪ]
diagram, -s 'daɪəgræm, -z
diagrammatic, -al, -ally ˌdaɪəgrə-
'mætɪk, -l, -əlɪ
dial (s. v.), -s, -ling, -led 'daɪəl, -z,
'daɪəlɪŋ, 'daɪəld
dialect, -s 'daɪəlekt, -s
dialectal ˌdaɪə'lektl
dialectic, -s, -al, -ally ˌdaɪə'lektɪk, -s,
-l, -əlɪ
dialectician, -s ˌdaɪələk'tɪʃn, -z
dialectolog|ist/s, -y ˌdaɪəlek'tɒlədʒ|-
ɪst/s, -ɪ
diallage (figure of speech) daɪ'æləgɪ
[-lədʒɪ]

diallage (*mineral*) 'daɪəlɪdʒ
dialogi|sm, -st/s daɪ'æləʤɪ|zəm, -st/s
dialogue, -s 'daɪəlɒg, -z
dial-plate, -s 'daɪəlpleɪt, -s
dialys|is, -es daɪ'ælɪs|ɪs [-ləs-], -iːz
diamagnetic (s. adj.), -s, -ally ˌdaɪəmæg-
'netɪk [-məg-], -s, -əlɪ
diamagnetism ˌdaɪə'mægnɪtɪzəm [-nət-]
diamanté dɪə'mɒnteɪ [daɪə-, -mæntɪ]
diameter, -s daɪ'æmɪtə* [-mət-], -z
diametr|al, -ally daɪ'æmɪtr|əl, -əlɪ
diametric|al, -ally ˌdaɪə'metrɪk|l, -əlɪ
[-lɪ]
diamond, -s 'daɪəmənd, -z
diamond-field, -s 'daɪəmənd̸fiːld, -z
Diana daɪ'ænə
dianthus, -es daɪ'ænθəs, -ɪz
diapason, -s ˌdaɪə'peɪsn [-'peɪzn], -z
diaper, -s 'daɪəpə*, -z
diaphanous daɪ'æfənəs
diaphone, -s 'daɪəfəʊn, -z
diaphonic ˌdaɪə'fɒnɪk
diaphragm, -s 'daɪəfræm [-frəm], -z
diaphragmatic ˌdaɪəfræg'mætɪk [-frəg-]
diapositive, -s ˌdaɪə'pɒzɪtɪv [-zət-], -z
diarch|y, -ies 'daɪɑːk|ɪ, -ɪz
diarist, -s 'daɪərɪst, -s
diarrhoea ˌdaɪə'rɪə
diar|y, -ies 'daɪər|ɪ, -ɪz
Diaspora daɪ'æspərə
diastase 'daɪəsteɪs
diastole, -s daɪ'æstəlɪ, -z
diastolic ˌdaɪə'stɒlɪk
diatherm|ic, -ous ˌdaɪə'θɜːm|ɪk, -əs
diatom, -s 'daɪətəm [-tɒm], -z
diatonic, -ally ˌdaɪə'tɒnɪk, -əlɪ
diatribe, -s 'daɪətraɪb, -z
diazepam daɪ'æzɪpæm
dib (s. v.), -s, -bing, -bed, -ber/s dɪb, -z,
-ɪŋ, -d, -ə*/z
Dibb dɪb
dibb|le (s. v.), -les, -ling, -led, -ler/s
'dɪb|l, -lz, -lɪŋ [-lɪŋ], -ld, -lə*/z
[-lə*/z]
Dibdin 'dɪbdɪn
dicast, -s 'dɪkæst, -s
dice (plur. of die) daɪs
dic|e (v.), -es, -ing, -ed daɪs, -ɪz, -ɪŋ, -t
dice-box, -es 'daɪsbɒks, -ɪz
dicey (D.) 'daɪsɪ
dichloride, -s daɪ'klɔːraɪd, -z
dichotom|y, -ies daɪ'kɒtəm|ɪ [dɪ-], -ɪz
Dick dɪk
dickens (D.) 'dɪkɪnz
Dickensian dɪ'kenzɪən [-'kens- -jən]
Dicker 'dɪkə*
dickey, -s 'dɪkɪ, -z
Dickins 'dɪkɪnz

Dickinson 'dɪkɪnsn
Dicksee 'dɪksiː [-sɪ]
Dickson 'dɪksn
dick|y (D.), -ies 'dɪk|ɪ, -ɪz
dickybird, -s 'dɪkɪbɜːd, -z
dicotyledon, -s ˌdaɪkɒtɪ'liːdən [-tə'l-],
-z
dictaphone, -s 'dɪktəfəʊn, -z
dictate (s.), -s 'dɪkteɪt, -s
dictat|e (v.), -es, -ing, -ed, -or/s dɪk-
'teɪt, -s, -ɪŋ, -ɪd, -ə*/z
dictation, -s dɪk'teɪʃn, -z
dictatorial, -ly ˌdɪktə'tɔːrɪəl, -ɪ
dictatorship, -s dɪk'teɪtəʃɪp, -s
diction 'dɪkʃn
dictionar|y, -ies 'dɪkʃənr|ɪ [-ʃənər-], -ɪz
dict|um, -a, -ums 'dɪkt|əm, -ə, -əmz
did (from do) dɪd
Didache 'dɪdəkɪ [-kɪ]
didactic, -al, -ally dɪ'dæktɪk [daɪ'd-], -l,
-əlɪ
didacticism dɪ'dæktɪsɪzəm [daɪ'd-]
didapper, -s 'daɪdæpə*, -z
Didcot 'dɪdkət
didd|le, -les, -ling, -led, -ler/s 'dɪd|l, -lz,
-lɪŋ [-lɪŋ], -ld, -lə*/z [-lə*/z]
Diderot 'diːdərəʊ (didro)
didn't 'dɪdnt [also 'dɪdn when not final]
Dido 'daɪdəʊ
Didymus 'dɪdɪməs
die (s.) (stamp), -s daɪ, -z
die (s.) (cube), dice daɪ, daɪs
die (v.), -s, dying, died daɪ, -z, -ɪŋ, -d
dielectric (s. adj.), -s ˌdaɪɪ'lektrɪk, -s
Dieppe diː'ep [dɪ'ep] (djɛp)
dies (from die) daɪz
Diesel, -s 'diːzl, -z
die-sink, -er/s, -ing, 'daɪsɪŋk, -ə*/z, -ɪŋ
dies irae ˌdiːeɪz'ɪəraɪ [ˌdiːez-, ˌdiːes-,
-'ɪəreɪ, old-fashioned ˌdaɪiːz'aɪəriː]
dies|is, -es 'daɪɪs|ɪs ['daɪəs-], -iːz
dies non, -s ˌdaɪiːz'nɒn, -z
diet (s. v.), -s, -ing, -ed 'daɪət, -s, -ɪŋ, -ɪd
dietar|y (s. adj.), -ies 'daɪətər|ɪ ['daɪɪt-],
-ɪz
dietetic (s. adj.), -s, -al, -ally ˌdaɪə'tetɪk
[ˌdaɪɪt-], -s, -l, -əlɪ
dietitian [-ician], -s ˌdaɪə'tɪʃn
[ˌdaɪɪt-], -z
differ, -s, -ing, -ed 'dɪfə*, -z, -rɪŋ, -d
differen|ce, -ces, -t/ly 'dɪfrən|s
[-fərən-], -sɪz, -t/lɪ
differenti|al, -als, -ally ˌdɪfə'renʃ|l, -lz,
-əlɪ
differentiat|e, -es, -ing, -ed ˌdɪfə'ren-
ʃɪeɪt [-ʃjeɪt], -s, -ɪŋ, -ɪd
differentiation, -s ˌdɪfərenʃɪ'eɪʃn [-nsɪ-],
-z

137

difficult 'dɪfɪkəlt [-fək-]
difficult|y, -ies 'dɪfɪkəlt|ɪ [-fək-], -ɪz
diffiden|ce, -t/ly 'dɪfɪdən|s, -t/lɪ
diffract, -s, -ing, -ed dɪ'frækt, -s, -ɪŋ, -ɪd
diffraction dɪ'frækʃn
diffuse (adj.), -ly, -ness dɪ'fju:s, -lɪ, -nɪs
[-nəs]
diffus|e (v.), -es, -ing, -ed, -edly,
-edness, -er/s dɪ'fju:z, -ɪz, -ɪŋ, -d,
-ɪdlɪ, -ɪdnɪs [-nəs], -ə*/z
diffusibility dɪ,fju:zə'bɪlətɪ [-zɪ'b-, -lɪt-]
diffusible dɪ'fju:zəbl [-zɪb-]
diffusion dɪ'fju:ʒn
diffusive, -ly, -ness dɪ'fju:sɪv, -lɪ, -nɪs
[-nəs]
dig (s. v.), -s, -ging, -ged, dug dɪg, -z,
-ɪŋ, -d, dʌg
dig. (in phrase infra dig.) dɪg
digamma, -s daɪ'gæmə ['daɪgæmə], -z
Digby 'dɪgbɪ
digest (s.), -s 'daɪdʒest, -s
digest (v.), -s, -ing, -ed dɪ'dʒest
[daɪ'dʒ-], -s, -ɪŋ, -ɪd
digestibility dɪ,dʒestə'bɪlətɪ [daɪ,dʒ-,
-tɪ'b-, -lɪt-]
digestible dɪ'dʒestəbl [daɪ'dʒ-, -tɪb-]
digestion, -s dɪ'dʒestʃən [daɪ'dʒ-,
-eʃtʃ-], -z
digestive (s. adj.), -s, -ly, -ness dɪ'dʒes-
tɪv [daɪ'dʒ-], -z, -lɪ, -nɪs [-nəs]
digger, -s 'dɪgə*, -z
Digges dɪgz
diggings 'dɪgɪŋz
Diggle, -s 'dɪgl, -z
Diggory 'dɪgərɪ
dight daɪt
Dighton 'daɪtn
digit, -s; -al/s 'dɪdʒɪt, -s; -l/z
digitali|n, -s ,dɪdʒɪ'teɪlɪ|n, -s
digni|fy, -fies, -fying, -fied 'dɪgnɪ|faɪ,
-faɪz, -faɪɪŋ, -faɪd
dignitar|y, -ies 'dɪgnɪtər|ɪ, -ɪz
dignit|y, -ies 'dɪgnət|ɪ [-ɪt|ɪ], -ɪz
digraph, -s 'daɪgrɑːf [-græf], -s
digress, -es, -ing, -ed daɪ'gres [dɪ'g-],
-ɪz, -ɪŋ, -t
digression, -s daɪ'greʃn [dɪ'g-], -z
digressive, -ly, -ness daɪ'gresɪv [dɪ'g-],
-lɪ, -nɪs [-nəs]
digs (lodgings) dɪgz
Dijon 'di:ʒɔ̃ːŋ [-ʒɒŋ, -ʒɒn] (diʒɔ̃)
dik|e (s. v.), -es, -ing, -ed daɪk, -s, -ɪŋ, -t
diktat 'dɪktɑːt [-tæt]
dilapidat|e, -es, -ing, -ed dɪ'læpɪdeɪt, -s,
-ɪŋ, -ɪd
dilapidation, -s dɪ,læpɪ'deɪʃn, -z
dilatability daɪ,leɪtə'bɪlətɪ [dɪ,l-, -'bɪlɪt-]
dilatation, -s ,daɪleɪ'teɪʃn [-lət-], -z

dilat|e, -es, -ing, -ed, -er/s; -able
daɪ'leɪt [dɪ'l-], -s, -ɪŋ, -ɪd, -ə*/z; -əbl
dilation, -s daɪ'leɪʃn [dɪ'l-], -z
dilator|y, -ily, -iness 'dɪlətər|ɪ, -əlɪ [-ɪlɪ],
-ɪnɪs [-ɪnəs]
dilemma, -s dɪ'lemə [daɪ'l-], -z
dilettante, -s ,dɪlɪ'tæntɪ, -z
dilettantism ,dɪlɪ'tæntɪzəm
diligence 'dɪlɪdʒəns
diligent, -ly 'dɪlɪdʒənt, -lɪ
Dilke, -s dɪlk, -s
dill (D.), -s dɪl, -z
Dillon 'dɪlən
Dillwyn (English surname) 'dɪlɪn,
'dɪlwɪn
dilly-dall|y, -ies, -ying, -ied 'dɪlɪdæl|ɪ,
-ɪz, -ɪɪŋ, -ɪd
diluent (s. adj.), -s 'dɪljʊənt [-ljwənt], -s
dilut|e (adj. v.), -eness; -es, -ing, -ed
daɪ'lju:t [dɪ'l-, -'lu:t], -nɪs [-nəs]; -s,
-ɪŋ, -ɪd
dilutee, -s ,daɪlju:'ti: [-lu:'t-], -z
dilution, -s daɪ'lu:ʃn [dɪ'l-, -'lju:-], -z
diluvia|l, -n daɪ'lu:vjə|l [dɪ'l-, -'lju:-,
-vɪə-], -n
diluvi|um, -a daɪ'lu:vj|əm [dɪ'l-, -'lju:-,
-vɪ|əm], -ə
Dilwyn 'dɪlwɪn (Welsh 'dilwin)
Dilys 'dɪlɪs (Welsh 'dilɪs)
dim (adj. v.), -mer, -mest, -ly, -ness;
-s, -ming, -med dɪm, -ə*, -ɪst, -lɪ,
-nɪs [-nəs]; -z, -ɪŋ, -d
Diman 'daɪmən
dime, -s daɪm, -z
dimension, -s dɪ'menʃn [daɪ'm-], -z
dimensional dɪ'menʃənl [daɪ'm-, -ʃnəl,
ʃn̩l, -ʃnl, -ʃənəl]
dimeter, -s 'dɪmɪtə* [-mə-], -z
dimidiate (adj.) dɪ'mɪdɪət [-djət, -rt]
dimidiat|e (v.), -es, -ing, -ed dɪ'mɪdɪeɪt,
-s, -ɪŋ, -ɪd
dimidiation dɪ,mɪdɪ'eɪʃn
diminish, -es, -ing, -ed; -able dɪ'mɪnɪʃ,
-ɪz, -ɪŋ, -t; -əbl
diminuendo, -s dɪ,mɪnjʊ'endəʊ, -z
diminution, -s ,dɪmɪ'nju:ʃn, -z
diminutive, -ly, -ness dɪ'mɪnjʊtɪv, -lɪ,
-nɪs [-nəs]
dimity 'dɪmɪtɪ [-ətɪ]
Dimmesdale 'dɪmzdeɪl
dimmish 'dɪmɪʃ
dim-out, -s 'dɪmaʊt, -s
dimp|le (s. v.), -les, -ling, -led 'dɪmp|l,
-lz, -lɪŋ [-lɪŋ], -ld
dimply 'dɪmplɪ
Dimsdale 'dɪmzdeɪl
din (s. v.), -s, -ning, -ned dɪn, -z, -ɪŋ, -d
Dinah 'daɪnə

dinar, -s (*monetary unit in Yugoslavia*)
'di:nɑ:*, (*in Iran, Iraq, Jordan*)
'di:nɑ:* [di:'nɑ:*], -z
Dindigul 'dɪndɪgəl
din|e, -es, -ing, -ed, -er/s daɪn, -z, -ɪŋ,
-d, -ə*/z
Dinely (*surname*) 'dɪnlɪ
ding, -s, -ing, -ed dɪŋ, -z, -ɪŋ, -d
dingdong ˌdɪŋ'dɒŋ [*also* '— *according to
sentence-stress*]
dingey, -s 'dɪŋgɪ [-ŋɪ], -z
dingh|y, -ies 'dɪŋg|ɪ [-ŋ|ɪ], -ɪz
dingle (D.), -s 'dɪŋgl, -z
Dingley 'dɪŋlɪ
dingo, -s 'dɪŋgəʊ, -z
Dingwall 'dɪŋwɔ:l [-wəl]
ding|y (*adj.*) (*dirty, drab*), -ier, -iest,
-ily, -iness 'dɪndʒ|ɪ, -ɪə* [-jə*], -ɪɪst
[-jɪst], -ɪlɪ [-əlɪ], -ɪnɪs [-ɪnəs]
dining-car, -s 'daɪnɪŋkɑ:*, -z
dining-room, -s 'daɪnɪŋrʊm [-ru:m], -z
dining-table, -s 'daɪnɪŋˌteɪbl, -z
dink|y, -ier, -iest, -iness 'dɪŋk|ɪ, -ɪə*
[-jə*], -ɪɪst [-jɪst], -ɪnɪs [-ɪnəs]
Dinmont 'dɪnmɒnt [-mənt]
Dinneford 'dɪnɪfəd
dinner, -s 'dɪnə*, -z
dinner-bell, -s 'dɪnəbel, -z
dinner-hour, -s 'dɪnərˌaʊə* ['dɪnə-
ˌaʊə*], -z
dinner-jacket, -s 'dɪnəˌdʒækɪt, -s
dinner-part|y, -ies 'dɪnəˌpɑ:t|ɪ, -ɪz
dinner-plate, -s 'dɪnəpleɪt, -s
dinner-service, -s 'dɪnəˌsɜ:vɪs, -ɪz
dinner-set, -s 'dɪnəset, -s
dinner-table, -s 'dɪnəˌteɪbl, -z
dinner-time, -s 'dɪnətaɪm, -z
dinner-wagon, -s 'dɪnəˌwægən, -z
Dinocrates daɪ'nɒkrəti:z
Dinorah dɪ'nɔ:rə
dinosaur, -s 'daɪnəʊsɔ:*, -z
dinosaur|us, -i ˌdaɪnə'sɔ:r|əs, -aɪ
dinotheri|um, -a ˌdaɪnəʊ'θɪərɪ|əm, -ə
dint dɪnt
Dinwiddie dɪn'wɪdɪ
diocesan daɪ'ɒsɪsn [-səs-]
diocese, -s 'daɪəsɪs [-si:s, -si:z], -ɪz
Diocles 'daɪəkli:z
Diocletian ˌdaɪə'kli:ʃjən [-ʃɪən, -ʃn]
diode, -s 'daɪəʊd, -z
Diodorus ˌdaɪə'dɔ:rəs
Diogenes daɪ'ɒdʒɪni:z [-dʒən-]
Diomed 'daɪəmed
Diomede 'daɪəmi:d
Diomedes ˌdaɪə'mi:di:z
Dion (*Greek*) 'daɪən, (*French*) 'di:ən
['di:ɔ̃ŋ, 'di:ɒŋ, 'di:ɒn] (djɔ̃), (*in
D. Boucicault*) 'daɪən

Dionysia, -n ˌdaɪə'nɪzɪə [-zjə, -ʒɪə, -ʒjə,
-sɪə, -sjə], -n
Dionysius ˌdaɪə'nɪsɪəs [-sjəs]
Dionysus ˌdaɪə'naɪsəs
diopter, -s daɪ'ɒptə*, -z
dioptric daɪ'ɒptrɪk
Dior 'dɪɔ:* [dɪ'ɔ:*] (djɔ:r)
diorama, -s ˌdaɪə'rɑ:mə, -z
dioramic ˌdaɪə'ræmɪk
Diosy dɪ'əʊsɪ
dioxide, -s daɪ'ɒksaɪd [ˌdaɪ'ɒ-], -z
dip (*s. v.*), -s, -ping, -ped, -per/s dɪp, -s,
-ɪŋ, -t, -ə*/z
diphtheria dɪf'θɪərɪə [dɪp'θ-]
diphthong, -s 'dɪfθɒŋ ['dɪpθ-], -z
diphthong|al, -ally dɪf'θɒŋg|l [dɪp'θ-
-ɒŋ|l], -əlɪ
diphthongization [-isa-], -s ˌdɪfθɒŋ-
gaɪ'zeɪʃn [ˌdɪpθ-, -ɒŋaɪ-], -z
diphthongiz|e [-is|e], -es, -ing, -ed
'dɪfθɒŋgaɪz ['dɪpθ-, -ɒŋaɪ-], -ɪz, -ɪŋ, -d
diplodoc|us, -uses, -i dɪ'plɒdək|əs,
-əsɪz, -aɪ
diploma, -s dɪ'pləʊmə, -z
diplomacy dɪ'pləʊməsɪ
diplomat, -s 'dɪpləmæt [-plʊm-], -s
diplomatic (*s. adj.*), -s, -al, -ally ˌdɪ-
plə'mætɪk [-plʊ'm-], -s, -l, -əlɪ
diplomatist, -s dɪ'pləʊmətɪst, -s
diplomatiz|e [-is|e], -es, -ing, -ed
dɪ'pləʊmətaɪz, -ɪz, -ɪŋ, -d
dipole, -s 'daɪpəʊl, -z
dipper, -s 'dɪpə*, -z
Diprose 'dɪprəʊz
dipsomania ˌdɪpsəʊ'meɪnjə [-nɪə]
dipsomaniac (*s. adj.*), -s ˌdɪpsəʊ-
'meɪnɪæk [-njæk], -s
dipter|a, -al, -ous 'dɪptər|ə, -əl, -əs
diptych, -s 'dɪptɪk, -s
dire, -r, -st, -ness 'daɪə*, -rə*, -rɪst,
-nɪs [-nəs]
direct (*adj. v.*), -est, -ness; -s, -ing, -ed,
-or/s dɪ'rekt [də'r-, daɪ'r-, *occasionally* 'daɪrekt *when attributive adj.*],
-ɪst, -nɪs [-nəs]; -s, -ɪŋ, -ɪd, -ə*/z
direction, -s dɪ'rekʃn [də'r-, daɪ'r-], -z
directional dɪ'rekʃənl [də'r-, daɪ'r-,
-ʃnəl, -ʃn̩l, -ʃn̩l, -ʃənəl]
directive (*s. adj.*), -s dɪ'rektɪv [də'r-,
daɪ'r-], -z
directly dɪ'rektlɪ [də'r-, daɪ'r-, 'dreklɪ]
Note.—*The form* 'dreklɪ *is not used
in the sense of* '*in a straight
manner*'; *it is, however, freq. in the
sense of* '*at once*', *and still more
freq. in the sense of* '*as soon as*'.
directorate, -s dɪ'rektərət [də'r-, daɪ'r-,
-ɪt], -s

directorship, -s dɪ'rektəʃɪp [dəˈr-, daɪˈr-], -s

director|y, -ies dɪ'rektər|ɪ [dəˈr-, daɪˈr-], -ɪz

dire|ful, -fully, -fulness 'daɪə|fʊl, -fʊlɪ [-fəlɪ], -fʊlnɪs [-nəs]

dirge, -s dɜːdʒ, -ɪz

dirigible (s. adj.), -s 'dɪrɪdʒəbl [-dʒɪb-, dɪˈrɪdʒ-], -z

dirk (D.), -s dɜːk, -s

dirndl [-dle], -s 'dɜːndl, -z

dirt dɜːt

dirt-cheap ˌdɜːt'tʃiːp

dirt-track, -s 'dɜːttræk, -s

dirt|y (adj. v.), -ier, -iest, -ily, -iness; -ies, -ying, -ied 'dɜːt|ɪ, -ɪə* [-jə*], -ɪst [-jɪst], -ɪlɪ [-əlɪ], -ɪnɪs [-ɪnəs]; -ɪz, -ɪŋ [-jɪŋ], -ɪd

Dis dɪs

disabilit|y, -ies ˌdɪsə'bɪlət|ɪ [ˌdɪzə-, -lɪt-], -ɪz

disab|le, -les, -ling, -led, -lement dɪs-'eɪb|l [dɪ'zeɪ-], -lz, -lɪŋ [-|ɪŋ], -ld, -lmənt

disabus|e, -es, -ing, -ed ˌdɪsə'bjuːz, -ɪz, -ɪŋ, -d

disaccustom, -s, -ing, -ed ˌdɪsə'kʌstəm, -z, -ɪŋ, -d

disadvantage, -s, -d ˌdɪsəd'vɑːntɪdʒ, -ɪz, -d

disadvantageous, -ly, -ness ˌdɪsædvɑːn'teɪdʒəs ['dɪsˌædvɑːnˈt-, -vən-], -lɪ, -nɪs [-nəs]

disaffect, -s, -ing, -ed/ly, -edness ˌdɪsə'fekt, -s, -ɪŋ, -ɪd/lɪ, -ɪdnɪs [-nəs]

disaffection ˌdɪsə'fekʃn

disagree, -s, -ing, -d, -ment/s ˌdɪsə'griː, -z, -ɪŋ, -d, -mənt/s

disagreeab|le, -ly, -leness, -les ˌdɪsə'grɪəb|l, -lɪ, -lnɪs [-nəs], -lz

disallow, -s, -ing, -ed ˌdɪsə'laʊ, -z, -ɪŋ, -d

disallow|able, -ance ˌdɪsə'laʊ|əbl, -əns

disappear, -s, -ing, -ed ˌdɪsə'pɪə*, -z, -rɪŋ, -d

disappearance, -s ˌdɪsə'pɪərəns, -ɪz

disappoint, -s, -ing, -ed, -ment/s ˌdɪsə'pɔɪnt, -s, -ɪŋ, -ɪd, -mənt/s

disapprobation ˌdɪsæprəʊ'beɪʃn ['dɪsˌæprəʊ'b-, -prʊ'b-]

disapproval ˌdɪsə'pruːvl

disapprov|e, -es, -ing/ly, -ed ˌdɪsə'pruːv, -z, -ɪŋ/lɪ, -d

disarm, -s, -ing/ly, -ed dɪs'ɑːm [dɪ'zɑːm], -z, -ɪŋ/lɪ, -d

disarmament dɪs'ɑːməmənt [dɪ'zɑːm-]

disarrang|e, -es, -ing, -ed ˌdɪsə'reɪndʒ, -ɪz, -ɪŋ, -d

disarrangement, -s ˌdɪsə'reɪndʒmənt, -s

disarray (s. v.), -s, -ing, -ed ˌdɪsə'reɪ, -z, -ɪŋ, -d

disarticulat|e, -es, -ing, -ed ˌdɪsɑː-'tɪkjʊleɪt, -s, -ɪŋ, -ɪd

disarticulation 'dɪsɑːˌtɪkjʊ'leɪʃn

disaster, -s dɪ'zɑːstə*, -z

disastrous, -ly, -ness dɪ'zɑːstrəs, -lɪ, -nɪs [-nəs]

disavow, -s, -ing, -ed, -al ˌdɪsə'vaʊ, -z, -ɪŋ, -d, -əl

disband, -s, -ing, -ed, -ment dɪs'bænd, -z, -ɪŋ, -ɪd, -mənt [dɪs'bænmənt]

disbar, -s, -ring, -red dɪs'bɑː*, -z, -rɪŋ, -d

disbark, -s, -ing, -ed dɪs'bɑːk, -s, -ɪŋ, -t

disbelief ˌdɪsbɪ'liːf [-bə-, '---]

disbeliev|e, -es, -ing, -ed, -er/s ˌdɪsbɪ'liːv [-bə-], -z, -ɪŋ, -d, -ə*/z

disburs|e, -es, -ing, -ed, -ement/s dɪs-'bɜːs, -ɪz, -ɪŋ, -t, -mənt/s

disc, -s dɪsk, -s

discard (s.), -s 'dɪskɑːd [dɪ'skɑːd], -z

discard (v.), -s, -ing, -ed dɪ'skɑːd, -z, -ɪŋ, -ɪd

discern, -s, -ing, -ed, -er/s, -ment dɪ'sɜːn [dɪ'zɜːn], -z, -ɪŋ, -d, -ə*/z, -mənt

discernib|le, -ly, -leness dɪ'sɜːnəb|l [dɪ'zɜː-, -nɪb-], -lɪ, -lnɪs [-nəs]

discharge (s.), -s 'dɪstʃɑːdʒ [dɪs'tʃɑːdʒ], -ɪz

discharg|e (v.), -es, -ing, -ed, -er/s dɪs'tʃɑːdʒ, -ɪz, -ɪŋ, -d, -ə*/z

disciple, -s; -ship dɪ'saɪpl, -z; -ʃɪp

disciplinarian, -s ˌdɪsɪplɪ'neərɪən [-səp-], -z

disciplinary 'dɪsɪplɪnərɪ [ˌ--'---, -sə-, ˌdɪsɪ'plaɪ-]

disciplin|e (s. v.), -es, -ing, -ed 'dɪsɪplɪn [-səp-], -z, -ɪŋ, -d

disc-jockey, -s 'dɪskˌdʒɒkɪ, -z

disclaim, -s, -ing, -ed, -er/s dɪs'kleɪm, -z, -ɪŋ, -d, -ə*/z

disclos|e, -es, -ing, -ed dɪs'kləʊz, -ɪz, -ɪŋ, -d

disclosure, -s dɪs'kləʊʒə*, -z

discobol|us, -i dɪ'skɒbəl|əs [-b|l-], -aɪ

discolo(u)ration, -s dɪsˌkʌlə'reɪʃn [ˌdɪsk-], -z

discolour, -s, -ing, -ed dɪs'kʌlə*, -z, -rɪŋ, -d

discomfit, -s, -ing, -ed dɪs'kʌmfɪt, -s, -ɪŋ, -ɪd

discomfiture dɪs'kʌmfɪtʃə* [-fə-]

discomfort (s. v.), -s, -ing, -ed dɪs-'kʌmfət, -s, -ɪŋ, -ɪd

discompos|e, -es, -ing, -ed ˌdɪskəm-
'pəʊz, -ɪz, -ɪŋ, -d
discomposure ˌdɪskəm'pəʊʒə*
disconcert, -s, -ing, -ed ˌdɪskən'sɜːt, -s,
-ɪŋ, -ɪd
disconnect, -s, -ing, -ed ˌdɪskə'nekt, -s,
-ɪŋ, -ɪd
disconnection ˌdɪskə'nekʃn
disconsolate, -ly, -ness dɪs'kɒnsələt
[-lɪt], -lɪ, -nɪs [-nəs]
discontent, -ed, -edly, -edness ˌdɪskən'tent, -ɪd, -ɪdlɪ, -ɪdnɪs [-nəs]
discontinuance ˌdɪskən'tɪnjʊəns
[-njwəns]
discontin|ue, -ues, -uing, -ued
ˌdɪskən'tɪn|juː [-jʊ], -juːz [-jʊz],
-juːɪŋ [-jʊɪŋ, -jwɪŋ], -juːd [-jʊd]
discontinuit|y, -ies ˌdɪskɒntɪ'njuːət|ɪ
[-'njʊ-, -ɪt|ɪ, -ˌ--'---], -ɪz
discontinuous, -ly ˌdɪskən'tɪnjʊəs
[-njwəs], -lɪ
discord (s.), -s 'dɪskɔːd, -z
discord (v.), -s, -ing, -ed dɪ'skɔːd, -z, -ɪŋ,
-ɪd
discordan|ce, -cy, -t/ly dɪ'skɔːdən|s,
-sɪ, -t/lɪ
discothèque, -s 'dɪskəʊtek [-teɪk, ˌ--'-],
-s (diskɔtɛk)
discount (s.), -s 'dɪskaʊnt, -s
discount (v.), -s, -ing, -ed, -er/s 'dɪskaʊnt, dɪ'skaʊnt, -s, -ɪŋ, -ɪd, -ə*/z
discountenanc|e, -es, -ing, -ed
dɪ'skaʊntɪnəns [-tən-], -ɪz, -ɪŋ, -t
discourag|e, -es, -ing/ly, -ed, -ement/s
dɪ'skʌrɪdʒ, -ɪz, -ɪŋ/lɪ, -d, -mənt/s
discourse (s.), -s 'dɪskɔːs [dɪ'skɔːs,
-ɔəs], -ɪz
discours|e (v.), -es, -ing, -ed, -er/s
dɪ'skɔːs [-'kɔəs], -ɪz, -ɪŋ, -t, -ə*/z
discourteous, -ly, -ness dɪs'kɜːtjəs
[-'kɔːt-, -'kɔət-, -tɪəs], -lɪ, -nɪs [-nəs]
discourtesy dɪs'kɜːtɪsɪ [-'kɔːt-, -'kɔət-,
-təsɪ]
discov|er, -ers, -ering, -ered, -erer/s
dɪ'skʌv|ə*, -əz, -ərɪŋ, -əd, -ərə*/z
discoverable dɪ'skʌvərəbl
discovert dɪs'kʌvət
discover|y, -ies dɪ'skʌvər|ɪ, -ɪz
discredit, -s, -ing, -ed dɪs'kredɪt
[ˌdɪs'k-], -s, -ɪŋ, -ɪd
discreditab|le, -ly, -leness dɪs'kredɪt-
əb|l, -lɪ, -lnɪs [-nəs]
discreet, -est, -ly, -ness dɪ'skriːt, -ɪst,
-lɪ, -nɪs [-nəs]
discrepan|cy, -cies, -t dɪ'skrepən|sɪ,
-sɪz, -t
discrete, -ly, -ness dɪ'skriːt [also '--
when attributive], -lɪ, -nɪs [-nəs]

discretion, -s dɪ'skreʃn, -z
discre|tional, -tionally dɪ'skre|ʃənl
[-ʃnəl, -ʃn̩l, -ʃn̩l, -ʃənəl], -ʃn̩əlɪ
[-ʃnəlɪ, -ʃn̩lɪ, -ʃn̩lɪ, -ʃənəlɪ]
discretionar|y, -ily dɪ'skreʃn̩ər|ɪ
[-ʃənər-], -əlɪ [-ɪlɪ]
discriminate (adj.), -ly dɪ'skrɪmɪnət
[-ɪt], -lɪ
discriminat|e (v.), -es, -ing/ly, -ed dɪ-
'skrɪmɪneɪt, -s, -ɪŋ/lɪ, -ɪd
discrimination, -s dɪˌskrɪmɪ'neɪʃn, -z
discriminative, -ly dɪ'skrɪmɪnətɪv
[-neɪt-], -lɪ
discriminatory dɪ'skrɪmɪnətərɪ [dɪ-
ˌskrɪmɪ'neɪtərɪ]
discursion, -s dɪ'skɜːʃn, -z
discursive, -ly, -ness dɪ'skɜːsɪv, -lɪ, -nɪs
[-nəs]
discursory dɪ'skɜːsərɪ
disc|us, -i, -uses 'dɪsk|əs, -aɪ, -əsɪz
discuss, -es, -ing, -ed; -able; -ant/s
dɪ'skʌs, -ɪz, -ɪŋ, -t; -əbl; -ənt/s
discussion, -s dɪ'skʌʃn, -z
disdain (s. v.), -s, -ing, -ed dɪs'deɪn
[dɪz'd-], -z, -ɪŋ, -d
disdain|ful, -fully, -fulness dɪs'deɪn|fʊl
[dɪz'd-], -fʊlɪ [-fəlɪ], -fʊlnɪs [-nəs]
disease, -s, -d dɪ'ziːz, -ɪz, -d
disembark, -s, -ing, -ed ˌdɪsɪm'bɑːk
[-sem-], -s, -ɪŋ, -t
disembarkation, -s ˌdɪsembɑː'keɪʃn
[-sɪm-], -z
disembarkment, -s ˌdɪsɪm'bɑːkmənt
[-sem-], -s
disembarrass, -es, -ing, -ed ˌdɪsɪm-
'bærəs [-sem-], -ɪz, -ɪŋ, -t
disembarrassment, -s ˌdɪsɪm'bærəsmənt
[-sem-], -s
disembod|y, -ies, -ying, -ied ˌdɪsɪm-
'bɒd|ɪ [-sem-], -ɪz, -ɪŋ [-jɪŋ], -ɪd
disemb|owel, -owels, -owelling, -owelled
ˌdɪsɪm'b|aʊəl [-sem-, -aʊl], -aʊəlz,
-aʊəlɪŋ, -aʊəld [-aʊld]
disenchant, -s, -ing, -ed ˌdɪsɪn'tʃɑːnt
[-sen-], -s, -ɪŋ, -ɪd
disenchantment, -s ˌdɪsɪn'tʃɑːntmənt
[-sen-], -s
disencumb|er, -ers, -ering, -ered ˌdɪsɪn-
'kʌmb|ə* [-sen-], -əz, -ərɪŋ, -əd
disendow, -s, -ing, -ed ˌdɪsɪn'daʊ
[-sen-], -z, -ɪŋ, -d
disendowment ˌdɪsɪn'daʊmənt [-sen-]
disenfranchis|e, -es, -ing, -ed ˌdɪsɪn-
'fræntʃaɪz [-sen-], -ɪz, -ɪŋ, -d
disenfranchisement ˌdɪsɪn'fræntʃɪzmənt
[-sen-]
disengag|e, -es, -ing, -ed ˌdɪsɪn'geɪdʒ
[-sɪŋ'g-, -sen'g-], -ɪz, -ɪŋ, -d

141

disentail (s. v.), -s, -ing, -ed ˌdɪsɪn'teɪl [-sen-], -z, -ɪŋ, -d

disentang|le, -les, -ling, -led ˌdɪsɪn-'tæŋg|l [-sen-], -lz, -lɪŋ, [-lɪŋ], -ld

disentanglement ˌdɪsɪn'tæŋglmənt [-sen-]

disentit|le, -les, -ling, -led ˌdɪsɪn'taɪt|l [-sen-], -lz, -lɪŋ [-lɪŋ], -ld

disequilibrium ˌdɪsekwɪ'lɪbrɪəm

disestablish, -es, -ing, -ed ˌdɪsɪ'stæblɪʃ [-ses-], -ɪz, -ɪŋ, -t

disestablishment ˌdɪsɪ'stæblɪʃmənt [-ses-]

disfavour ˌdɪs'feɪvə* [dɪs'f-]

disfiguration, -s dɪsˌfɪgə'reɪʃn [ˌdɪsf-, -gjə-, -gjʊə-], -z

disfigur|e, -es, -ing, -ed, -ement/s dɪs-'fɪgə*, -z, -rɪŋ, -d, -mənt/s

disfranchis|e, -es, -ing, -ed ˌdɪs'fræn-tʃaɪz [dɪs'f-], -ɪz, -ɪŋ, -d

disfranchisement dɪs'fræntʃɪzmənt

disgorg|e, -es, -ing, -ed dɪs'gɔ:dʒ, -ɪz, -ɪŋ, -d

disgrac|e (s. v.), -es, -ing, -ed dɪs'greɪs [dɪz-], -ɪz, -ɪŋ, -t

disgrace|ful, -fully, -fulness dɪs'greɪs|fʊl [dɪz-], -fʊlɪ [-fəlɪ], -fʊlnɪs [-nəs]

disgruntled dɪs'grʌntld

disguis|e (s. v.), -es, -ing, -ed, -er/s dɪs'gaɪz [dɪz-], -ɪz, -ɪŋ, -d, -ə*/z

disgust (s. v.), -s, -ing/ly, -ed dɪs'gʌst [dɪz-], -s, -ɪŋ/lɪ, -ɪd

dish (s. v.), -es, -ing, -ed dɪʃ, -ɪz, -ɪŋ, -t

dishabille ˌdɪsæ'bi:l [-sə'b-]

disharmony ˌdɪs'hɑːmənɪ

dish|cloth, –cloths 'dɪʃ|klɒθ [old-fashioned -klɔ:θ], -klɒθs [-klɔ:ðz, -klɒ:θs]

dish-cover, -s 'dɪʃˌkʌvə*, -z

disheart|en, -ens, -ening, -ened dɪs-'hɑ:t|n, -nz, -nɪŋ [-ɳ̩ɪŋ], -nd

disherison dɪs'herɪzn [-ɪsn]

dishev|el, -els, -elling, -elled dɪ'ʃev|l, -lz, -lɪŋ [-lɪŋ], -ld

dishful, -s 'dɪʃfʊl, -z

dishonest, -ly dɪs'ɒnɪst [dɪ'zɒ-], -lɪ

dishonest|y, -ies dɪs'ɒnɪst|ɪ [dɪ'zɒ-, -əst|ɪ], -ɪz

dishonour (s. v.), -s, -ing, -ed, -er/s dɪs'ɒnə* [dɪ'zɒ-], -z, -rɪŋ, -d, -ə*/z

dishonourab|le, -ly, -leness dɪs'ɒnərəb|l [dɪ'zɒ-], -lɪ, -lnɪs [-nəs]

dishors|e,-es,-ing,-ed dɪs'hɔ:s, -ɪz, -ɪŋ,-t

dishwasher, -s 'dɪʃˌwɒʃə*, -z

dish-water 'dɪʃˌwɔ:tə*

disillusi|on (s. v.), -ons, -oning, -oned, -onment/s ˌdɪsɪ'lu:ʒ|n [-'lju:-], -nz, -ɳɪŋ [-ənɪŋ], -nd, -nmənt/s

disinclination ˌdɪsɪnklɪ'neɪʃn [-ɪŋk-, -ntl-, -lə'n-]

disinclin|e, -es, -ing, -ed ˌdɪsɪn'klaɪn [-ɪŋ'kl-, -ɪn'tl-], -z, -ɪŋ, -d

disinfect, -s, -ing, -ed ˌdɪsɪn'fekt, -s, -ɪŋ, -ɪd

disinfectant (s. adj.), -s ˌdɪsɪn'fektənt, -s

disinfection, -s ˌdɪsɪn'fekʃn, -z

disinfestation ˌdɪsɪnfe'steɪʃn

disinflation ˌdɪsɪn'fleɪʃn

disingenuous, -ly, -ness ˌdɪsɪn'dʒenjʊəs [-njwəs], -lɪ, -nɪs [-nəs]

disinherit, -s, -ing, -ed ˌdɪsɪn'herɪt, -ɪŋ, -ɪd

disinheritance ˌdɪsɪn'herɪtəns

disintegrable dɪs'ɪntɪgrəbl

disintegrat|e, -es, -ing, -ed, -or/s dɪs-'ɪntɪgreɪt, -s, -ɪŋ, -ɪd, -ə*/z

disintegration, -s dɪsˌɪntɪ'greɪʃn [ˌdɪsɪn-], -z

disinter, -s, -ring, -red ˌdɪsɪn'tɜ:*, -z, -rɪŋ, -d

disinterested, -ly, -ness dɪs'ɪntrəstɪd [ˌdɪs'ɪn-, -'ɪntərest-, -'ɪntrɪst-], -lɪ, -nɪs [-nəs]

disinterment, -s ˌdɪsɪn'tɜ:mənt -s

disjoin, -s, -ing, -ed dɪs'dʒɔɪn, -z, -ɪŋ, -d

disjoint, -s, -ing, -ed/ly, -edness dɪs-'dʒɔɪnt, -s, -ɪŋ, -ɪd/lɪ, -ɪdnɪs [-nəs]

disjunct 'dɪsdʒʌŋkt [-'-]

disjunction, -s dɪs'dʒʌŋkʃn, -z

disjunctive, -ly dɪs'dʒʌŋktɪv [ˌdɪs'dʒ-], -lɪ

disk, -s dɪsk, -s

dislik|e (s. v.), -es, -ing, -ed, -able dɪs-'laɪk, -s, -ɪŋ, -t, -əbl

Note.—The stress '- is, however, used in the expression likes and dislikes.

dislocat|e, -es, -ing, -ed 'dɪsləʊkeɪt, -s, -ɪŋ, -ɪd

dislocation, -s ˌdɪsləʊ'keɪʃn, -z

dislodg|e, -es, -ing, -ed, -(e)ment dɪs-'lɒdʒ, -ɪz, -ɪŋ, -d, -mənt

disloy|al, -ally, -alty ˌdɪs'lɔɪ|əl [dɪs'l-], -əlɪ, -əltɪ

dism|al, -ally, -alness 'dɪzm|əl, -əlɪ, -əlnɪs [-nəs]

dismant|le, -les, -ling, -led dɪs'mænt|l, -lz, -lɪŋ [-lɪŋ], -ld

dismast, -s, -ing, -ed ˌdɪs'mɑ:st, -s, -ɪŋ, -ɪd

dismay (s. v.), -s, -ing, -ed dɪs'meɪ [dɪz'm-], -z, -ɪŋ, -d

dismember, -s, -ing, -ed, -ment dɪs-'membə*, -z, -rɪŋ, [-brɪŋ], -d, -mənt

dismiss, -es, -ing, -ed dɪs'mɪs, -ɪz, -ɪŋ, -t

dismissal, -s dɪs'mɪsl, -z

dismount, -s, -ing, -ed ˌdɪsˈmaʊnt [dɪsˈm-], -s, -ɪŋ, -ɪd

Disney ˈdɪznɪ

disobedien|ce, -t/ly ˌdɪsəˈbi:djən|s [-dɪən-], -t/lɪ

disobey, -s, -ing, -ed ˌdɪsəˈbeɪ, -z, -ɪŋ, -d

disoblig|e, -es, -ing/ly, -ingness, -ed ˌdɪsəˈblaɪdʒ, -ɪz, -ɪŋ/lɪ, -ɪŋnɪs [-nəs], -d

disord|er (s. v.), **-ers, -ering, -ered** dɪsˈɔːd|ə* [dɪˈzɔː-], -əz, -ərɪŋ, -əd

disorder|ly, -liness dɪsˈɔːdə|lɪ [dɪˈzɔː-], -lɪnɪs [-nəs]

disorganization [-isa-] dɪsˌɔːgənaɪˈzeɪʃn [dɪˌzɔː-, ˌdɪsɔː-, -gn̩aɪˈz-, -gənɪˈz-, -gn̩ɪˈz-]

disorganiz|e [-is|e], **-es, -ing, -ed** dɪsˈɔːgənaɪz [dɪˈzɔː-, ˌdɪsˈɔː-, -gn̩aɪz], -ɪz, -ɪŋ, -d

disorientat|e, -es, -ing, -ed dɪsˈɔːrɪənteɪt [ˌdɪs-, -ˈɒr-, -rjə-, -rɪe-], -s, -ɪŋ, -ɪd

disorientation dɪsˌɔːrɪənˈteɪʃn [ˌ----ˈ--, -ɒr-, -rjə-, -rɪe-]

disown, -s, -ing, -ed dɪsˈəʊn [ˌdɪsˈəʊn], -z, -ɪŋ, -d

disparag|e, -es, -ing/ly, -ed, -er/s, -ement dɪˈspærɪdʒ, -ɪz, -ɪŋ/lɪ, -d, -ə*/z, -mənt

disparate (s. adj.), **-s** ˈdɪspərət [-rɪt, -reɪt], -s

disparity dɪˈspærətɪ [-rɪt]

dispassionate, -ly, -ness dɪsˈpæʃn̩ət [-ʃənət, -ʃnət, -rɪt], -lɪ, -nɪs [-nəs]

dispatch (s. v.), **-es, -ing, -ed, -er/s** dɪˈspætʃ, -ɪz, -ɪŋ, -t, -ə*/z

dispatch-boat, -s dɪˈspætʃbəʊt, -s

dispatch-box, -es dɪˈspætʃbɒks, -ɪz

dispatch-rider, -s dɪˈspætʃraɪdə*, -z

dispel, -s, -ling, -led dɪˈspel, -z, -ɪŋ, -d

dispensable dɪˈspensəbl

dispensar|y, -ies dɪˈspensər|ɪ, -ɪz

dispensation, -s ˌdɪspenˈseɪʃn [-pən-], -z

dispensator|y (s. adj.), **-ies** dɪˈspensətər|ɪ, -ɪz

dispens|e, -es, -ing, -ed, -er/s dɪˈspens, -ɪz, -ɪŋ, -t, -ə*/z

dispeop|le, -les, -ling, -led ˌdɪsˈpiːp|l, -lz, -lɪŋ [-lɪŋ], -ld

dispersal, -s dɪˈspɜːsl, -z

dispers|e, -es, -ing, -ed, -er/s, -ant/s dɪˈspɜːs, -ɪz, -ɪŋ, -t, -ə*/z, -ənt/s

dispersion, -s dɪˈspɜːʃn, -z

dispersive dɪˈspɜːsɪv

dispirit, -s, -ing, -ed/ly, -edness dɪˈspɪrɪt, -s, -ɪŋ, -ɪd/lɪ, -ɪdnɪs [-nəs]

displac|e, -es, -ing, -ed, -ement/s dɪsˈpleɪs, -ɪz, -ɪŋ, -t [also ˈdɪspleɪst when attributive], -mənt/s

display (s. v.), **-s, -ing, -ed, -er/s** dɪˈspleɪ, -z, -ɪŋ, -d, -ə*/z

displeas|e, -es, -ing/ly, -ingness, -ed dɪsˈpliːz, -ɪz, -ɪŋ/lɪ, -ɪŋnɪs [-nəs], -d

displeasure dɪsˈpleʒə*

disport, -s -ing, -ed dɪˈspɔːt, -s, -ɪŋ, -ɪd

dispos|e, -es, -ing, -ed, -er/s; -able, -al|s dɪˈspəʊz, -ɪz, -ɪŋ, -d, -ə*/z; -əbl, -l/z

disposition, -s ˌdɪspəˈzɪʃn [-pʊˈz-], -z

dispossess, -es, -ing, -ed ˌdɪspəˈzes [-pʊˈz-], -ɪz, -ɪŋ, -t

disproof ˌdɪsˈpruːf [-ˈ-]

disproportion, -ed ˌdɪsprəˈpɔːʃn [-prʊˈp-] -d [ˈ--,--]

dispropor|tional, -tionally ˌdɪsprəˈpɔː|-ʃənl [-prʊˈp-, -ʃnəl, -ʃn̩l, -ʃn̩l, -ʃənəl], -ʃn̩əlɪ [-ʃnəlɪ, -ʃn̩lɪ, -ʃn̩lɪ, -ʃənəlɪ]

disproportionate, -ly, -ness ˌdɪsprə-ˈpɔːʃnət [-prʊˈp-, -ʃn̩ət, -ʃənət; -nɪt], -lɪ, -nɪs [-nəs]

disproval dɪsˈpruːvl [ˌdɪsˈp-]

disprov|e, -es, -ing, -ed ˌdɪsˈpruːv [dɪsˈp-], -z, -ɪŋ, -d

disputable dɪˈspjuːtəbl [ˈdɪspjʊtəbl]

disputableness dɪˈspjuːtəblnɪs [-nəs]

disputant (s. adj.), **-s** dɪˈspjuːtənt [ˈdɪspjʊtənt], -s

disputation, -s ˌdɪspjuːˈteɪʃn [-pjʊ-], -z

disputatious, -ly, -ness ˌdɪspjuːˈteɪʃəs [-pjʊ], -lɪ, -nɪs [-nəs]

disputative dɪˈspjuːtətɪv

disput|e (s. v.), **-es, -ing, -ed, -er/s** dɪ-ˈspjuːt, -s, -ɪŋ, -ɪd, -ə*/z

Note.—The stress pattern ˈ-- is increasingly used for the noun.

disqualification, -s dɪsˌkwɒlɪfɪˈkeɪʃn [ˌdɪsk-], -z

disquali|fy, -fies, -fying, -fied dɪs-ˈkwɒlɪ|faɪ [ˌdɪsˈk-], -faɪz, -faɪɪŋ, -faɪd

disquiet (s. v.), **-s, -ing, -ed** dɪsˈkwaɪət, -s, -ɪŋ, -ɪd

disquietude dɪsˈkwaɪətjuːd [-ˈkwaɪt-]

disquisition, -s ˌdɪskwɪˈzɪʃn, -z

disquisitional ˌdɪskwɪˈzɪʃənl [-ʃnəl, -ʃn̩l, -ʃnl, -ʃənəl]

disquisitive dɪˈskwɪzətɪv [-zɪt-]

Disraeli dɪzˈreɪlɪ [dɪs-]

disregard (s. v.), **-s, -ing, -ed** ˌdɪsrɪˈgɑːd [-rəˈg-], -z, -ɪŋ, -ɪd

disregard|ful, -fully ˌdɪsrɪˈgɑːd|fʊl [-rəˈg-, -fʊlɪ [-fəlɪ]

disrepair ˌdɪsrɪˈpeə* [-rəˈp-]

disreputability dɪsˌrepjʊtəˈbɪlətɪ [-lɪt-]

disreputab|le, -ly, -leness dɪsˈrepjʊ-təb|l [-pjət-], -lɪ, -lnɪs [-nəs]

disrepute ˌdɪsrɪˈpjuːt [-rəˈp-]

disrespect ˌdɪsrɪˈspekt [-rəˈs-]

143

disrespect|ful, -fully, -fulness ˌdɪs-rɪ'spekt|fʊl [-rə's-], -fʊlɪ [-fəlɪ], -fʊlnɪs [-nəs]
disrob|e, -es, -ing, -ed ˌdɪs'rəʊb [dɪs'r-], -z, -ɪŋ, -d
disrupt, -s, -ing, -ed dɪs'rʌpt, -s, -ɪŋ, -ɪd
disruption, -s dɪs'rʌpʃn, -z
disruptive dɪs'rʌptɪv
Diss dɪs
dissatisfaction 'dɪsˌsætɪs'fækʃn [ˌdɪs-sæt-]
dissatisfactor|y, -ily, -iness 'dɪsˌsætɪs-'fæktər|ɪ [ˌdɪssæt-], -əlɪ [-ɪlɪ], -ɪnɪs [-nəs]
dissatis|fy, -fies, -fying, -fied ˌdɪs'sætɪs|faɪ [dɪs's-], -faɪz, -faɪɪŋ, -faɪd
dissect, -s, -ing, -ed, -or/s; -ible dɪ'sekt, -s, -ɪŋ, -ɪd, -ə*/z; -əbl [-ɪbl]
dissecting-room, -s dɪ'sektɪŋrʊm [-ru:m], -z
dissection, -s dɪ'sekʃn, -z
disseis|e, -es, -ing, -ed; -in/s dɪs'si:z, -ɪz, -ɪŋ, -d; -ɪn/z
dissemblance, -s dɪ'sembləns, -ɪz
dissemb|le, -les, -ling, -led, -ler/s dɪ'semb|l, -lz, -lɪŋ, -ld, -lə*/z
disseminat|e, -es, -ing, -ed, -or/s dɪ-'semɪneɪt, -s, -ɪŋ, -ɪd, -ə*/z
dissemination dɪˌsemɪ'neɪʃn
dissension, -s dɪ'senʃn, -z
dissent (s. v.), -s, -ing, -ed, -er/s dɪ'sent, -s, -ɪŋ, -ɪd, -ə*/z
dissentient, -s dɪ'senʃɪənt [-ʃjənt, -ʃənt], -s
dissertation, -s ˌdɪsə'teɪʃn, -z
disservice, -s ˌdɪs'sɜ:vɪs [dɪs's-], -ɪz
dissev|er, -ers, -ering, -ered, -erment; -erance dɪs'sev|ə*, -əz, -ərɪŋ, -əd, -əmənt; -ərəns
dissiden|ce, -t/s 'dɪsɪdən|s, -t/s
dissimilar, -ly ˌdɪ'sɪmɪlə*, [ˌdɪs's-, dɪ'sɪm-, -məl-], -lɪ
dissimilarit|y, -ies ˌdɪsɪmɪ'lærət|ɪ [ˌdɪss-, -mə-, -ɪt|ɪ], -ɪz
dissimilat|e, -es, -ing, -ed dɪ'sɪmɪleɪt [ˌdɪ's-, -mə-], -s, -ɪŋ, -ɪd
dissimilation, -s ˌdɪsɪmɪ'leɪʃn [dɪˌs-, -mə-], -z
dissimilitude ˌdɪsɪ'mɪlɪtju:d [ˌdɪss-]
dissimulat|e, -es, -ing, -ed, -or/s dɪ-'sɪmjʊleɪt, -s, -ɪŋ, -ɪd, -ə*/z
dissimulation, -s dɪˌsɪmjʊ'leɪʃn, -z
dissipat|e, -es, -ing, -ed; -ive 'dɪsɪpeɪt, -s, -ɪŋ, -ɪd; -ɪv
dissipation, -s ˌdɪsɪ'peɪʃn, -z
dissociable (separable) dɪ'səʊʃjəbl [-ʃɪəbl], (unsociable) dɪ'səʊʃəbl

dissociat|e, -es, -ing, -ed dɪ'səʊʃɪeɪt [-əʊʃjeɪt, -əʊsɪeɪt, -əʊsjeɪt], -s, -ɪŋ, -ɪd
dissociation dɪˌsəʊsɪ'eɪʃn [ˌdɪs-, -əʊʃɪ-]
dissolubility dɪˌsɒljʊ'bɪlətɪ [-lɪt-]
dissolub|le, -ly, -leness dɪ'sɒljʊb|l, -lɪ, -lnɪs [-nəs]
dissolute (s. adj.), -s, -ly, -ness 'dɪsəlu:t [-lju:t], -s, -lɪ, -nɪs [-nəs]
dissolution, -s ˌdɪsə'lu:ʃn [-'lju:-], -z
dissolvability dɪˌzɒlvə'bɪlətɪ [-lɪt-]
dissolv|e, -es, -ing, -ed; -able dɪ'zɒlv, -z, -ɪŋ, -d; -əbl
dissolvent (s. adj.), -s dɪ'zɒlvənt [dɪ'sɒ-], -s
dissonan|ce, -ces, -t/ly 'dɪsənən|s [-sn̩-], -sɪz, -t/lɪ
dissuad|e, -es, -ing, -ed dɪ'sweɪd, -z, -ɪŋ, -ɪd
dissuasion dɪ'sweɪʒn
dissuasive, -ly, -ness dɪ'sweɪsɪv; -lɪ, -nɪs [-nəs]
dissyll- = disyll-
dissymmetric ˌdɪsɪ'metrɪk [ˌdɪssɪ'm-]
dissymmetry ˌdɪ'sɪmɪtrɪ [ˌdɪs's-, dɪs's-, -mətrɪ]
distaff, -s 'dɪstɑːf, -s
distan|ce (s. v.), -es, -ing, -ed 'dɪstəns, -ɪz, -ɪŋ, -t
distant, -ly 'dɪstənt, -lɪ
distaste, -s ˌdɪs'teɪst [dɪs't-], -s
distaste|ful, -fully, -fulness dɪs'teɪst|fʊl [ˌdɪs't-], -fʊlɪ [-fəlɪ], -fʊlnɪs [-nəs]
distemp|er (s. v.), -ers, -ering, -ered dɪ'stemp|ə*, -əz, -ərɪŋ, -əd
distend, -s, -ing, -ed dɪ'stend, -z, -ɪŋ, -ɪd
distensible dɪ'stensəbl [-sɪb-]
distension dɪ'stenʃn
distich, -s, -ous 'dɪstɪk, -s, -əs
distil, -s, -ling, -led, -ler/s dɪ'stɪl, -z, -ɪŋ, -d, -ə*/z
distillate, -s 'dɪstɪlət [-leɪt, -lɪt], -s
distillation, -s ˌdɪstɪ'leɪʃn, -z
distillatory dɪ'stɪlətərɪ
distiller|y, -ies dɪ'stɪlər|ɪ, -ɪz
disti|nct, -nctest, -nctly, -nctness dɪ-'stɪ|ŋkt, -ŋktɪst, -ŋktlɪ [-ŋklɪ], -ŋktnɪs [-ŋknɪs, -nəs]
distinction, -s dɪ'stɪŋkʃn, -z
distinctive, -ly, -ness dɪ'stɪŋktɪv, -lɪ, -nɪs [-nəs]
distinguish, -es, -ing, -ed; -able, -ably dɪ'stɪŋgwɪʃ, -ɪz, -ɪŋ, -t; -əbl, -əblɪ
distoma, -s 'dɪstəʊmə, -z
distort, -s, -ing, -ed/ly, -edness dɪ'stɔːt, -s, -ɪŋ, -ɪd/lɪ, -ɪdnɪs [-nəs]
distortion, -s dɪ'stɔːʃn, -z
distract, -s, -ing, -ed/ly, -edness dɪ-'strækt, -s, -ɪŋ, -ɪd/lɪ, -ɪdnɪs [-nəs]
distraction, -s dɪ'strækʃn, -z

144

distrain, -s, -ing, -ed, -er/s; -able dɪ-
'streɪn, -z, -ɪŋ, -d, -ə*/z; -əbl
distrainee, -s ˌdɪstreɪ'niː, -z
distrainor, -s ˌdɪstreɪ'nɔː*, -z
distraint, -s dɪ'streɪnt, -s
distrait, -e dɪ'streɪ ['dɪstreɪ] (distrɛ), -t
distraught dɪ'strɔːt
distress (s. v.), -es, -ing/ly, -ed dɪ'stres,
-ɪz, -ɪŋ/lɪ, -t
distress|ful, -fully dɪ'stres|fʊl, -fʊlɪ
[-fəlɪ]
distributable dɪ'strɪbjʊtəbl
distribut|e, -es, -ing, -ed, -or/s dɪ-
'strɪbjuːt ['dɪstrɪbjuːt], -s, dɪ'strɪb-
jʊtɪŋ ['dɪstrɪbjuːtɪŋ], dɪ'strɪbjʊtɪd
['dɪstrɪbjuːtɪd], dɪ'strɪbjʊtə*/z ['dɪs-
trɪbjuːtə*/z]
distribution, -s ˌdɪstrɪ'bjuːʃn, -z
distributive, -ly dɪ'strɪbjʊtɪv, -lɪ
district, -s 'dɪstrɪkt, -s
distringas dɪ'strɪŋgæs [-gəs]
distrust (s. v.), -s, -ing, -ed dɪs'trʌst
[ˌdɪs't-], -s, -ɪŋ, -ɪd
distrust|ful, -fully, -fulness dɪs'trʌst|-
fʊl [ˌdɪs't-] -fʊlɪ [-fəlɪ], -fʊlnɪs [-nəs]
disturb, -s, -ing, -ed, -er/s dɪ'stɜːb, -z,
-ɪŋ, -d, -ə*/z
disturbance, -s dɪ'stɜːbəns, -ɪz
distyle, -s 'dɪstaɪl ['daɪstaɪl], -z
disulphate, -s daɪ'sʌlfeɪt [-fɪt], -s
disulphide, -s daɪ'sʌlfaɪd, -z
†disunion, -s ˌdɪs'juːnjən [dɪs'j-, -nɪən],
-z
disunit|e, -es, -ing, -ed ˌdɪsjuː'naɪt
[-jʊ'n-], -s, -ɪŋ, -ɪd
disuse (s.) ˌdɪs'juːs [dɪs'j-]
disus|e (v.), -es, -ing, -ed ˌdɪs'juːz
[dɪs'j-], -ɪz, -ɪŋ, -d [also 'dɪsjuːzd
when attributive]
disyllabic ˌdɪsɪ'læbɪk [ˌdaɪ-, '--,--]
disyllable, -s dɪ'sɪləbl [ˌdɪ's-, 'daɪˌs-], -z
ditch (s. v.), -es, -ing, -ed, -er/s dɪtʃ, -ɪz,
-ɪŋ, -t, -ə*/z
Ditchling 'dɪtʃlɪŋ
ditch-water 'dɪtʃˌwɔːtə*
dither, -s, -ing, -ed 'dɪðə*, -z, -rɪŋ, -d
dithyramb, -s 'dɪθɪræmb, -z
dithyramb|us, -i, -ic/s ˌdɪθɪ'ræmb|əs,
-aɪ, -ɪk/s
ditto, -s 'dɪtəʊ, -z
Ditton 'dɪtn
ditt|y, -ies 'dɪt|ɪ, -ɪz
diuretic (s. adj.), -s ˌdaɪjʊə'retɪk, -s
diurn|al (s. adj.), -als, -ally daɪ'ɜːn|l, -lz,
-əlɪ
diva, -s 'diːvə, -z
divagat|e, -es, -ing, -ed 'daɪvəgeɪt, -s,
-ɪŋ, -ɪd

divagation, -s ˌdaɪvə'geɪʃn, -z
divalent 'daɪˌveɪlənt [ˌdaɪ'v-]
divan, -s dɪ'væn [daɪ'v-, 'daɪvæn], -z
divaricat|e, -es, -ing, -ed daɪ'værɪkeɪt
[dɪ'v-], -s, -ɪŋ, -ɪd
divarication, -s daɪˌværɪ'keɪʃn [dɪˌv-], -z
div|e (s. v.), -es, -ing, -ed, -er/s daɪv, -z,
-ɪŋ, -d, -ə*/z
dive-bomb, -s, -ing, -ed, -er/s 'daɪv-
bɒm, -z, -ɪŋ, -d, -ə*/z
Diver 'daɪvə*
diverg|e, -es, -ing, -ed daɪ'vɜːdʒ [dɪ'v-],
-ɪz, -ɪŋ, -d
divergen|ce, -ces, -cy, -cies, -t/ly
daɪ'vɜːdʒən|s [dɪ'v-], -sɪz, -sɪ, -sɪz,
-t/lɪ
divers (adj.) 'daɪvəz [-ɜːz]
diverse, -ly daɪ'vɜːs ['daɪvɜːs], -lɪ
diversification, -s daɪˌvɜːsɪfɪ'keɪʃn [dɪ-],
-z
diversi|fy, -fies, -fying, -fied daɪ'vɜːsɪ|-
faɪ [dɪ-], -faɪz, -faɪɪŋ, -faɪd
diversion, -s, -ary, -ist daɪ'vɜːʃn [dɪ'v-],
-z, -ərɪ [-ʃən-], -ɪst [-ʃən-]
diversit|y, -ies daɪ'vɜːsət|ɪ [dɪ'v-, -ɪt|ɪ],
-ɪz
divert, -s, -ing/ly, -ed daɪ'vɜːt [dɪ'v-],
-s, -ɪŋ/lɪ, -ɪd
divertimento dɪˌvɜːtɪ'mentəʊ [-ˌveə-]
divertissement ˌdiːveə'tiːsmɑ̃ːŋ [-və-,
-vɜː-, -mɒŋ, -mɔ̃ːŋ] (divertismɑ̃)
Dives (rich man) 'daɪviːz, (surname)
daɪvz
divest, -s, -ing, -ed daɪ'vest [dɪ'v-], -s,
-ɪŋ, -ɪd
divestiture daɪ'vestɪtʃə* [dɪ'v-]
divid|e (s. v.), -es, -ing, -ed/ly, -er/s;
-able dɪ'vaɪd, -z, -ɪŋ, -ɪd/lɪ, -ə*/z;
-əbl
dividend, -s 'dɪvɪdend [-dənd], -z
dividend-warrant, -s 'dɪvɪdendˌwɒrənt
[-dənd-], -s
divination, -s ˌdɪvɪ'neɪʃn, -z
divine (s. adj.), -s, -r, -st, -ly, -ness
dɪ'vaɪn, -z, -ə*, -ɪst, -lɪ, -nɪs [-nəs]
divin|e (v.), -es, -ing, -ed, -er/s dɪ'vaɪn,
-z, -ɪŋ, -d, -ə*/z
diving-bell, -s 'daɪvɪŋbel, -z
diving-dress, -es 'daɪvɪŋdres, -ɪz
diving-rod, -s dɪ'vaɪnɪŋrɒd, -z
divinit|y, -ies dɪ'vɪnət|ɪ [-ɪt|ɪ], -ɪz
divisibility dɪˌvɪzɪ'bɪlətɪ [-zə'b-, -lɪt-]
divisib|le, -ly dɪ'vɪzəb|l [-zɪb-], -lɪ
division, -s dɪ'vɪʒn, -z
divisional dɪ'vɪʒənl [-ʒn̩], -ʒn̩l]
divisive, -ly, -ness dɪ'vaɪsɪv, -lɪ, -nɪs
[-nəs]
divisor, -s dɪ'vaɪzə*, -z

145

divorc|e (*s. v.*), **-es, -ing, -ed, -er/s,
-ement** dɪ'vɔːs, -ɪz, -ɪŋ, -t, -ə*/z,
-mənt
divorcée, -s dɪˌvɔː'siː: [ˌ--'-, -'--, dɪ-
vɔː'seɪ] (divorse), -z
divot, -s 'dɪvət, -s
divulg|e, -es, -ing, -ed daɪ'vʌldʒ [dɪ'v-],
-ɪz, -ɪŋ, -d
divulsion, -s daɪ'vʌlʃn [dɪ'v-], -z
diwan, -s dɪ'wɑːn, -z
Dix dɪks
Dixey 'dɪksɪ
Dixie 'dɪksɪ
Dixon 'dɪksn
Dixwell 'dɪkswəl [-wel]
diz|en, -ens, -ening, -ened 'daɪz|n, -nz,
-n̩ɪŋ, -nd
dizz|y (*adj. v.*), **-ier, -iest, -ily, -iness;
-ies, -ying, -ied** 'dɪz|ɪ, -ɪə*, -ɪɪst, -ɪlɪ
[-əlɪ], -ɪnɪs [-ɪnəs], -ɪz, -ɪŋ, -ɪd
Djakarta [Ja-] dʒə'kɑːtə
Djibouti dʒɪ'buːtɪ
djinn dʒɪn
Dnie|per, -ster '*d*niː|pə*, -stə*
do (*s.*) (*musical note*), **-s** dəʊ, -z
do (*s.*) (*swindle, entertainment*), **-s** duː, -z
do. 'dɪtəʊ
do (*v.*); **dost; doth; doeth; does; doing,
did, done, doer/s** duː (*strong form*),
dʊ (*weak form, also alternative strong
form before vowels*), də, d (*weak
forms*); dʌst (*strong form*), dəst
(*weak form*); dʌθ (*strong form*), dəθ
(*weak form*); 'duːɪθ ['dʊɪθ]; dʌz
(*strong form*), dəz, dz (*weak forms*);
'duːɪŋ ['dʊɪŋ], dɪd, dʌn, 'duːə*/z
[dʊə*/z]
Doane dəʊn
Dobb, -s dɒb, -z
dobbin (D.), -s 'dɒbɪn, -z
Dobell dəʊ'bel
Dobie 'dəʊbɪ
Dobrée 'dəʊbreɪ
Dobson 'dɒbsn
docent, -s 'dəʊsənt [dəʊ'sent], -s
Docet|ism, -ist/s dəʊ'siːt|ɪzəm, -ɪst/s
docile 'dəʊsaɪl ['dɒs-]
docility dəʊ'sɪlətɪ [-ɪtɪ]
dock (*s. v.*), **-s, -ing, -ed, -er/s; -age**
dɒk, -s, -ɪŋ, -t, -ə*/z; -ɪdʒ
Docker 'dɒkə*
docket (*s. v.*), **-s, -ing, -ed** 'dɒkɪt, -s, -ɪŋ,
-ɪd
dock-land 'dɒklænd
dockyard, -s 'dɒkjɑːd, -z
doct|or (*s. v.*), **-ors, -oring, -ored;
-orate/s, -orship/s** 'dɒkt|ə*, -əz,
-ərɪŋ, -əd; -ərət/s [-ərɪt/s], -əʃɪp/s

doctrinaire, -s ˌdɒktrɪ'neə*, -z
doctrin|al, -ally dɒk'traɪn|l ['dɒktrɪn-],
-əlɪ
doctrinarian, -s ˌdɒktrɪ'neərɪən, -z
doctrine, -s 'dɒktrɪn, -z
document (*s.*), **-s** 'dɒkjʊmənt, -s
document (*v.*), **-s, -ing, -ed** 'dɒkjʊment,
-s, -ɪŋ, -ɪd
documental ˌdɒkjʊ'mentl
documentar|y (*s. adj.*), **-ies** ˌdɒkjʊ'men-
tər|ɪ, -ɪz
documentation ˌdɒkjʊmen'teɪʃn
[-mən-]
Docwra 'dɒkrə
Dod(d), -s dɒd, -z
dodder (*s. v.*), **-s, -ing, -ed, -er/s, -y** 'dɒdə*,
-z, -rɪŋ, -d, -rə*/z, -rɪ
Doddington 'dɒdɪŋtən
Doddridge 'dɒdrɪdʒ
dodecagon, -s dəʊ'dekəgən, -z
dodecahedr|on, -ons, -a; -al ˌdəʊdekə-
'hiːdr|ən [-dɪk-, -'hed-, '---,--], -ənz,
-ə; -l
Dodecanese ˌdəʊdɪkə'niːz [-dek-]
dodg|e (*s. v.*), **(D.), -es, -ing, -ed, -er/s,
-y** dɒdʒ, -ɪz, -ɪŋ, -d, -ə*/z, -ɪ
Dodgson 'dɒdʒsn
Dodington 'dɒdɪŋtən
dodo (D.), -s 'dəʊdəʊ, -z
Dodona dəʊ'dəʊnə
Dodsley 'dɒdzlɪ
Dodson 'dɒdsn
Dodwell 'dɒdwəl [-wel]
doe (D.), -s dəʊ, -z
Doeg 'dəʊeg
doer, -s 'duːə* [dʊə*], -z
does (*from* do) dʌz (*strong form*), dəz,
dz (*weak forms*)
doeskin, -s 'dəʊskɪn, -z
doesn't 'dʌznt [*also* 'dʌzn *when not
final*]
doeth (*from* do) 'duːɪθ ['dʊɪθ]
doff, -s, -ing, -ed, -er/s dɒf, -s, -ɪŋ, -t,
-ə*/z
Dofort 'dəʊfɜːt
dog (*s. v.*), **-s, -ging, -ged** (*p. tense, p.
partic.*) dɒg, -z, -ɪŋ, -d
dog-bane 'dɒgbeɪn
Dogberry 'dɒgberɪ [-bərɪ]
dog-biscuit, -s 'dɒgˌbɪskɪt, -s
dog-cart, -s 'dɒgkɑːt, -s
dog-collar, -s 'dɒgˌkɒlə*, -z
dog-days 'dɒgdeɪz
doge, -s dəʊdʒ, -ɪz
dog-ear (*s. v.*), **-s, -ing, -ed** 'dɒgˌɪə*, -z,
-rɪŋ, -d
dogend, -s 'dɒgend, -z
dog-fancier, -s 'dɒgˌfænsɪə* [-sjɔ*], -z

146

dog-fight, -s ˈdɒgfaɪt, -s
dog-fish, -es ˈdɒgfɪʃ, -ɪz
dogged (adj.), -ly, -ness ˈdɒgɪd, -lɪ, -nɪs [-nəs]
dogger (D.), -s ˈdɒgə*, -z
doggerel ˈdɒgərəl [-rɪl]
Doggett ˈdɒgɪt
doggish, -ly, -ness ˈdɒgɪʃ, -lɪ, -nɪs [-nəs]
doggo ˈdɒgəʊ
doggrel ˈdɒgrəl
dogg|y (s. adj.), -ies ˈdɒg|ɪ, -ɪz
dog-headed ˈdɒgˌhedɪd
dog-kennel, -s ˈdɒgˌkenl, -z
dog-Latin ˌdɒgˈlætɪn [ˈ-ˌ--]
dogma, -s ˈdɒgmə, -z
dogmatic (s. adj.), -s, -al, -ally dɒgˈmætɪk, -s, -l, -əlɪ
dogmati|sm, -st/s ˈdɒgmətɪ|zəm, -st/s
dogmatiz|e [-is|e], -es, -ing, -ed, -er/s ˈdɒgmətaɪz, -ɪz, -ɪŋ, -d, -ə*/z
do-gooder, -s ˌduːˈgʊdə*, -z
dogpaddle ˈdɒgˌpædl
dog-rose, -s ˈdɒgrəʊz, -ɪz
dogsbod|y, -ies ˈdɒgzˌbɒd|ɪ, -ɪz
dog-skin ˈdɒgskɪn
dog-star ˈdɒgstɑː*
dog-tired ˌdɒgˈtaɪəd
dog|-tooth, -teeth ˈdɒg|tuːθ, -tiːθ
dog-watch, -es ˈdɒgwɒtʃ, -ɪz
dogwood ˈdɒgwʊd
doh (note in Tonic Sol-fa), -s dəʊ, -z
Doherty ˈdəʊətɪ, dəʊˈhɜːtɪ, ˈdɒhətɪ [ˈdɒxə-]
Dohnanyi dɒkˈnɑːnjiː [dɒxˈn-, -njɪ]
Dohoo ˈduːhuː
doil|y, -ies ˈdɔɪl|ɪ, -ɪz
doing, -s ˈduːɪŋ [ˈdʊɪŋ], -z
doit, -s dɔɪt, -s
do-it-yourself ˌduːɪtjɔːˈself [ˌdʊɪt-]
dolce ˈdɒltʃɪ [ˈdəʊl-] (ˈdoltʃe)
doldrum, -s ˈdɒldrəm, -z
dol|e (s. v.), -es, -ing, -ed dəʊl, -z, -ɪŋ, -d
dole|ful, -fully, -fulness ˈdəʊl|fʊl, -fʊlɪ [-fəlɪ], -fʊlnɪs [-nəs]
dolerite ˈdɒləraɪt
Dolgellau [Dolgelley] dɒlˈgeθlaɪ [-ˈgelaɪ, -lɪ] (Welsh dolˈgeɫa, -ɬaɨ)
dolichocephalic ˌdɒlɪkəʊseˈfælɪk [-sɪˈf-, -keˈf-, -kɪˈf-]
doll, -s dɒl, -z
dollar (D.), -s ˈdɒlə*, -z
Dollond ˈdɒlənd
dollop, -s ˈdɒləp, -s
doll's-hou|se, -ses ˈdɒlzhaʊ|s, -zɪz
doll|y (D.), -ies ˈdɒl|ɪ, -ɪz
dolman, -s ˈdɒlmən, -z
dolmen, -s ˈdɒlmen, -z

dolomite (D.), -s ˈdɒləmaɪt, -s
dolor ˈdɒlə* [ˈdəʊ-]
dolorous, -ly, -ness ˈdɒlərəs, -lɪ, -nɪs [-nəs]
dolour ˈdɒlə* [ˈdəʊ-]
dolphin, -s ˈdɒlfɪn, -z
dolt, -s dəʊlt, -s
doltish, -ly, -ness ˈdəʊltɪʃ, -lɪ, -nɪs [-nəs]
Dolton ˈdəʊltən
domain, -s dəʊˈmeɪn, -z
Dombey ˈdɒmbɪ
dome, -s, -d dəʊm, -z, -d
Domesday ˈduːmzdeɪ
domestic (s. adj.), -s, -ally dəʊˈmestɪk, -s, -əlɪ
domesticat|e, -es, -ing, -ed dəʊˈmestɪkeɪt, -s, -ɪŋ, -ɪd
domestication dəʊˌmestɪˈkeɪʃn
domesticity ˌdəʊmeˈstɪsətɪ [ˌdɒm-, -ɪtɪ]
domett (material) dəʊˈmet
Domett (surname) ˈdɒmɪt
domicil|e (s. v.), -es, -ing, -ed ˈdɒmɪsaɪl [ˈdəʊ-, -sɪl], -z, -ɪŋ, -d
domiciliary ˌdɒmɪˈsɪljərɪ [-lɪərɪ]
dominan|ce, -t/s, -tly ˈdɒmɪnən|s, -t/s, -tlɪ
dominat|e, -es, -ing, -ed, -or/s ˈdɒmɪneɪt, -s, -ɪŋ, -ɪd, -ə*/z
domination, -s ˌdɒmɪˈneɪʃn, -z
domineer, -s, -ing/ly, -ed ˌdɒmɪˈnɪə*, -z, -rɪŋ/lɪ, -d
Domingo dəʊˈmɪŋgəʊ [dɒˈm-]
Dominic ˈdɒmɪnɪk
Dominica (in the Leeward Islands) ˌdɒmɪˈniːkə [dəˈmɪnɪkə]
dominical dəˈmɪnɪkl [dɒˈm-]
Dominican (republic, religious order), -s dəˈmɪnɪkən [dɒˈm-], (of Dominica) ˌdɒmɪˈniːkən, -z
dominie, -s ˈdɒmɪnɪ, -z
dominion, -s dəˈmɪnjən [-nɪən], -z
domino, -es ˈdɒmɪnəʊ, -z
Domitian dəʊˈmɪʃɪən [dɒˈm-, -ʃjən, -ʃn]
Domvil(l)e ˈdʌmvɪl
don (s. v.) (D.), -s, -ning, -ned dɒn, -z, -ɪŋ, -d
dona(h), -s ˈdəʊnə, -z
Donaghadee ˌdɒnəkəˈdiː [-nəxə-]
Donalbain ˈdɒnlbeɪn
Donald, -son ˈdɒnld, -sn
Donat ˈdəʊnæt
donat|e, -es, -ing, -ed dəʊˈneɪt, -s, -ɪŋ, -ɪd
Donatello ˌdɒnəˈteləʊ
donation, -s dəʊˈneɪʃn, -z
Donatist, -s ˈdəʊnətɪst, -s

147

donative, -s 'dəʊnətɪv, -z
donator, -s dəʊ'neɪtə*, -z
donatory 'dəʊnətərɪ ['dɒn-, dəʊ'neɪ-]
Donatus dəʊ'neɪtəs
Don Carlos ˌdɒn'kɑːlɒs
Doncaster 'dɒŋkəstə*
done (from do) dʌn
Done dəʊn
donee, -s dəʊ'niː, -z
Donegal (place) 'dɒnɪgɔːl ['dʌn-, ˌ-ˈ-']
Note.—ˌdʌnɪ'gɔːl appears to be the
    most usual pronunciation in
    Ireland.
Donegall (Marquess) 'dɒnɪgɔːl
Donelson 'dɒnlsn
Doneraile 'dʌnəreɪl
Donetz dɒ'nets (da'njets)
donga, -s 'dɒŋgə, -z
Dongan 'dɒŋgən
Dönges (South African surname)
    'dɜːnjes
Don Giovanni ˌdɒndʒɪəʊ'vɑːnɪ [-'vænɪ]
    (dondʒo'vanni)
Dongola 'dɒŋgələ
Donington 'dʌnɪŋtən
Doniphan 'dɒnɪfən
Donizetti ˌdɒnɪ'zetɪ [-ɪ'dze-] (doni-
    'dzetti)
donjon, -s 'dɒndʒən ['dʌn-], -z
Don Juan ˌdɒn'dʒuːən [-'dʒʊən]
donkey, -s 'dɒŋkɪ, -z
donkey-engine, -s 'dɒŋkɪˌendʒɪn, -z
donna, -s 'dɒnə, -z
Donnan 'dɒnən
Donne dʌn, dɒn
Donnington 'dɒnɪŋtən
donnish 'dɒnɪʃ
Donnithorne 'dɒnɪθɔːn
Donnybrook 'dɒnɪbrʊk
Dono(g)hue 'dʌnəhuː, 'dɒn- [-hjuː]
Donohoe 'dʌnəhuː, 'dɒn-
donor, -s 'dəʊnə* [-nɔː*], -z
do-nothing, -s 'duːˌnʌθɪŋ, -z
Donough 'dɒnəʊ
Donoughmore 'dʌnəmɔː* [-mɔə*]
Donovan 'dɒnəvən
Don Pasquale ˌdɒnpæs'kwɑːlɪ
Don Quixote ˌdɒn'kwɪksət [-səʊt,
    -sɒt, ˌdɒnkɪ'həʊtɪ, -teɪ]
donship, -s 'dɒnʃɪp, -s
don't dəʊnt [also dəʊn when not final,
    also dəʊmp before the sounds p, b, m,
    and dəʊŋk before k, g]
    Note.—Weak forms dən, dn may
    sometimes be heard in the expression
    I don't know, and a weak form dəm
    in the expression I don't mind.
Doo, Doolittle duː, 'duːlɪtl̩

dood|le (s. v.), -les, -ling, -led, -ler/s
    'duːd|l̩, -lz, -lɪŋ [-l̩ŋ], -ld, -lə*/z
doodlebug, -s 'duːdlbʌg, -z
doom (s. v.), -s, -ing, -ed duːm, -z, -ɪŋ,
    -d
Doomsday 'duːmzdeɪ
Doon(e) duːn
door, -s dɔː* [dɔə*], -z
door-bell, -s 'dɔːbel ['dɔə-], -z
door-keeper, -s 'dɔːˌkiːpə* ['dɔə-], -z
door-knocker, -s 'dɔːˌnɒkə* ['dɔə-], -z
Doorly 'dʊəlɪ
door-mat, -s 'dɔːmæt ['dɔə-], -s
door-nail, -s 'dɔːneɪl ['dɔə-], -z
door-plate, -s 'dɔːpleɪt ['dɔə-], -s
door-post, -s 'dɔːpəʊst ['dɔə-], -s
doorstep, -s 'dɔːstep ['dɔə-], -s
doorway, -s 'dɔːweɪ ['dɔə-], -z
dop|e (s. v.), -es, -ing, -ed, -er/s, -ey dəʊp,
    -s, -ɪŋ, -t, -ə*/z, -ɪ
doppelganger 'dɒplˌgæŋə*
Dora 'dɔːrə
dorado, -s də'rɑːdəʊ [dɒ'r-], -z
Doran 'dɔːrən
Dorando də'rændəʊ [dɒ'r-]
Dorcas 'dɔːkəs [-kæs]
Dorchester 'dɔːtʃɪstə*
Dore dɔː* [dɔə*]
Doreen dɔː'riːn [dɒ'r-, də'r-, 'dɔːriːn]
Dorian (s. adj.), -s 'dɔːrɪən, -z
Doric 'dɒrɪk
Doricism, -s 'dɒrɪsɪzəm, -z
Doris (modern Christian name) 'dɒrɪs,
    (district and fem. name in Greek
    history) 'dɔːrɪs
Dorking 'dɔːkɪŋ
dorman|cy, -t 'dɔːmən|sɪ, -t
dormer-window, -s ˌdɔːmə'wɪndəʊ, -z
dormie 'dɔːmɪ
dormitor|y, -ies 'dɔːmətr|ɪ [-mɪtr|ɪ], -ɪz
dor|mouse, -mice 'dɔː|maʊs, -maɪs
dormy 'dɔːmɪ
Dornoch 'dɔːnɒk [-nək, -nɒx, -nəx]
Dornton 'dɔːntən
Dorothea ˌdɒrə'θɪə
Dorothy 'dɒrəθɪ
Dorr dɔː*
Dorrien 'dɒrɪən
Dorriforth 'dɒrɪfɔːθ
Dorrit 'dɒrɪt
dors|al, -ally 'dɔːs|l̩, -əlɪ
Dors|et, -etshire 'dɔːs|ɪt, -ɪt-ʃə* [-ɪt-ˌʃɪə*]
dor|y, -ies 'dɔːr|ɪ, -ɪz
dosage, -s 'dəʊsɪdʒ, -ɪz
dos|e (s. v.), -es, -ing, -ed dəʊs, -ɪz, -ɪŋ,
    -t
Dos Passos ˌdɒs'pæsɒs
doss, -es, -er/s dɒs, -ɪz, -ə*/z

dossal, -s 'dɒsl, -z
doss-hou|se, -ses 'dɒshaʊ|s, -zɪz
dossier, -s 'dɒsɪeɪ (dosje), -z
dost (from do) dʌst (strong form), dəst
(weak form)
Dostoievski ˌdɒstɔɪ'efskɪ
dot (s. v.), -s, -ting, -ted dɒt, -s, -ɪŋ, -ɪd
dotage 'dəʊtɪdʒ
dotard, -s 'dəʊtəd, -z
dot|e, -es, -ing/ly, -ed, -er/s dəʊt, -s,
-ɪŋ|lɪ, -ɪd, -ə*/z
doth (from do) dʌθ (strong form), dəθ
(weak form)
Dothan 'dəʊθæn [-θən]
Dotheboys Hall ˌdu:ðəbɔɪz'hɔ:l
dott(e)rel, -s 'dɒtrəl, -z
dottle, -s 'dɒtl, -z
dott|y, -ier, -iest, -ily, -iness 'dɒt|ɪ, -ɪə*,
-ɪɪst, -ɪlɪ [-əlɪ], -ɪnɪs [-ɪnəs]
Douai (French town) 'du:eɪ (dwe),
(school near Reading) 'daʊeɪ ['daʊɪ],
(version of Bible) 'daʊeɪ ['daʊɪ,
'du:eɪ]
douane, -s du:'ɑ:n [dʊ'ɑ:n], -z
doub|le (s. adj. v.), -ly, -leness; -les,
-ling, -led 'dʌb|l, -lɪ, -lnɪs [-nəs]; -lz,
-lɪŋ [-lɪŋ], -ld
double-barrelled 'dʌbl,bærəld [ˌ--'--]
double-bass, -es ˌdʌbl'beɪs, -ɪz
double-bedded 'dʌbl,bedɪd [ˌ--'--]
Doublebois 'dʌblbɔɪz
double-breasted ˌdʌbl'brestɪd ['--,--]
double-cross, -es, -ing, -ed ˌdʌbl'krɒs
[old-fashioned -'krɔ:s], -ɪz, -ɪŋ, -t
Doubleday 'dʌbldeɪ
double-deal|er/s, -ing ˌdʌbl'di:l|ə*/z
['--,--], -ɪŋ
double-decked 'dʌbldekt
double-decker, -s ˌdʌbl'dekə* ['--,--],
-z
double-dyed ˌdʌbl'daɪd [also '--- when
attributive]
double-edged ˌdʌbl'edʒd ['---]
double entendre ˌdu:b|ɑ̃:n'tɑ̃:ndrə
[-ɔ̃:n'tɔ̃:ndrə, -ɑ:n'tɑ:ndrə, -ɒn-
'tɒndrə] (dublɑ̃tɑ̃:dr, pronounced as
if French)
double-entry ˌdʌbl'entrɪ
double-faced 'dʌblfeɪst
double-first, -s ˌdʌbl'fɜ:st, -s
double-headed 'dʌbl,hedɪd
double-locked ˌdʌbl'lɒkt
double-minded ˌdʌbl'maɪndɪd ['--,--]
double-quick ˌdʌbl'kwɪk
double-stopping, -s ˌdʌbl'stɒpɪŋ, -z
double-stout ˌdʌbl'staʊt
doublet, -s 'dʌblɪt [-lət], -s
double-tongued ˌdʌbl'tʌŋd ['---]

doubloon, -s dʌ'blu:n, -z
doubt (s. v.), -s, -ing/ly, -ed, -er/s
daʊt, -s, -ɪŋ/lɪ, -ɪd, -ə*/z
doubt|ful, -fullest, -fully, -fulness
'daʊt|fʊl, -fʊlɪst [-fəlɪst], -fʊlɪ [-fəlɪ],
-fʊlnɪs [-nəs]
Doubting 'daʊtɪŋ
doubtless, -ly 'daʊtlɪs [-ləs], -lɪ
douch|e (s. v.), -es, -ing, -ed du:ʃ, -ɪz,
-ɪŋ, -t
Doudney 'daʊdnɪ, 'du:dnɪ, 'dju:dnɪ
Dougal(l) 'du:gəl
Dougan 'du:gən
dough dəʊ
Dougherty 'dəʊətɪ
doughfaced 'dəʊfeɪst
dough-nut, -s 'dəʊnʌt, -s
dought|y (D.), -ier, -iest, -ily, -iness
'daʊt|ɪ, -ɪə* [-jə*], -ɪɪst, [-jɪst], -ɪlɪ
[-əlɪ], -ɪnɪs [-ɪnəs]
dough|y, -ily, -iness 'dəʊ|ɪ, -ɪlɪ, -ɪnɪs
[-ɪnəs]
Douglas(s) 'dʌgləs
Douie 'dʊɪ ['du:ɪ], 'daʊɪ
douloureux (in tic d.) ˌdu:lə'rɜ: [-lu:'r-,
-lʊ'r-]
Doulton 'dəʊltən
dour, -ly, -ness dʊə*, -lɪ; -nɪs [-nəs]
Douro 'dʊərəʊ
Dousabel 'du:səbel
dous|e, -es, -ing, -ed daʊs, -ɪz, -ɪŋ, -t
Doust daʊst
Dousterswivel 'du:stəswɪvl
dove, -s dʌv, -z
Dove (surname, tributary of River
Trent), dʌv
dove-colour, -ed 'dʌv,kʌlə*, -d
dove-cot, -s 'dʌvkɒt, -s
dovecote, -s 'dʌvkəʊt [-kɒt], -s
Dovedale 'dʌvdeɪl
dove-like 'dʌvlaɪk
Dover 'dəʊvə*
dovetail (s. v.), -s, -ing, -ed 'dʌvteɪl, -z,
-ɪŋ, -d
Dovey (in Wales) 'dʌvɪ (Welsh 'dəvɪ)
Dow daʊ
dowager, -s 'daʊədʒə* ['daʊɪdʒ-], -z
Dowden 'daʊdn
dow|dy (s. adj.), -ies, -ier, -iest, -ily,
-iness 'daʊd|ɪ, -ɪz, -ɪə* [-jə*], -ɪɪst
[-jɪst], -ɪlɪ [-əlɪ], -ɪnɪs [-ɪnəs]
dowel (s. v.), -s, -ling, -led 'daʊəl
['daʊel], -z, -ɪŋ, -d
Dowell 'daʊəl [-ɪl, -el]
dower, -s; -less 'daʊə*, -z; -lɪs [-ləs]
Dowgate 'daʊgɪt [-geɪt]
Dowie 'daʊɪ
Dow Jones ˌdaʊ'dʒəʊnz

149

Dowland 'daʊlənd
dowlas (D.) 'daʊləs
Dowle daʊl
Dowler 'daʊlə*
down (s. adj. v. adv. prep. interj.), -s,
   -ing, -ed daʊn, -z, -ɪŋ, -d
Down, -shire daʊn, -ʃə* [-ˌʃɪə*]
down-bed, -s ˌdaʊn'bed [in contrast
   '--], -z
downcast 'daʊnkɑːst [ˌ-'-]
down-draught, -s 'daʊndrɑːft, -s
Downe, -s daʊn, -z
Downey 'daʊnɪ
downfall, -s 'daʊnfɔːl, -z
Downham 'daʊnəm
down-hearted ˌdaʊn'hɑːtɪd
downhill ˌdaʊn'hɪl [also '-- according to
   sentence-stress]
Downing 'daʊnɪŋ
downland (D.) 'daʊnlænd
down-market ˌdaʊn'mɑːkɪt
Downpatrick daʊn'pætrɪk
downpour, -s 'daʊnpɔː* [-pɔə*], -z
down-quilt, -s ˌdaʊn'kwɪlt [in contrast
   '--], -s
downright, -ness 'daʊnraɪt, -nɪs [-nəs]
downrush, -es 'daʊnrʌʃ, -ɪz
Downs daʊnz
Downside 'daʊnsaɪd
down-sitting ˌdaʊn'sɪtɪŋ ['daʊnˌs-]
downstage ˌdaʊn'steɪdʒ
downstairs ˌdaʊn'steəz [also '--
   according to sentence-stress]
downstream ˌdaʊn'striːm [in contrast
   '--]
Downton 'daʊntən
downtrodden 'daʊnˌtrɒdn
downward, -s 'daʊnwəd, -z
down|y, -ier, -iest 'daʊn|ɪ, -ɪə* [-jə*],
   -ɪɪst [-jɪst]
dowr|y, -ies 'daʊər|ɪ ['daʊr-], -ɪz
dows|e, -es, -ing, -ed, -er/s daʊz [daʊs],
   -ɪz, 'daʊzɪŋ ['daʊsɪŋ], daʊzd [daʊst],
   'daʊzə*/z ['daʊsə*/z]
Dowse daʊs
dowsing-rod, -s 'daʊzɪŋrɒd ['daʊsɪŋ-],
   -z
Dowson 'daʊsn
Dowton 'daʊtn
doxolog|y, -ies dɒk'sɒlədʒ|ɪ, -ɪz
doyen, -s dɔɪ'en ['dɔɪən, 'dɔɪen,
   'dwaɪæŋ] (dwajɛ̃), -z
Doyle dɔɪl
doyley, -s 'dɔɪlɪ, -z
D'Oyl(e)y 'dɔɪlɪ
doz|e (s. v.), -es, -ing, -ed, -er/s dəʊz,
   -ɪz, -ɪŋ, -d, -ə*/z
dozen, -s, -th 'dʌzn, -z, -θ

doz|y, -ier, -iest, -ily, -iness 'dəʊz|ɪ, -ɪə*
   [-jə*], -ɪɪst [-jɪst], -ɪlɪ [-əlɪ], -ɪnɪs
   [-ɪnəs]
Dr. 'dɒktə*, 'detə*
drab (s. adj.), -s dræb, -z
drabb|le, -les, -ling, -led 'dræb|l, -lz,
   -lɪŋ [-lɪŋ], -ld
dracaena, -s drə'siːnə, -z
Drachenfels 'drækənfelz [-fels]
   ('draxənfels)
drachm, -s dræm, -z
drachm|a, -as, -ae 'drækm|ə, -əz, -iː
Draco (Greek legislator) 'dreɪkəʊ, (English surname) 'drɑːkəʊ
Draconian drə'kəʊnjən [dreɪ'k-, -nɪən]
Dracula 'drækjʊlə
draff dræf [drɑːf]
draft (s. v.), -s, -ing, -ed, -er/s drɑːft, -s,
   -ɪŋ, -ɪd, -ə*/z
drafts|man, -men, -manship 'drɑːfts|-
   mən, -mən [-men], -mənʃɪp
drag (s. v.), -s, -ging, -ged dræg, -z, -ɪŋ,
   -d
Drage dreɪdʒ
dragg|le, -les, -ling, -led 'dræg|l, -lz,
   -lɪŋ [-lɪŋ], -ld
draggle-tail, -s, -ed 'dræglteɪl, -z, -d
drag-net, -s 'drægnet, -s
drago|man, -mans, -men 'drægəʊ|mən
   [-mæn], -mənz [-mænz], -mən [men]
dragon, -s 'drægən, -z
dragonet, -s 'drægənɪt [-net], -s
dragon-fl|y, -ies 'drægənfl|aɪ, -aɪz
dragon|ish, -like 'drægən|ɪʃ [-gn̩|-],
   -laɪk
dragonnade, -s ˌdrægə'neɪd, -z
dragon's-blood 'drægənzblʌd
dragoon, -s drə'guːn, -z
drain (s. v.), -s, -ing, -ed, -er/s; -able,
   -age dreɪn, -z, -ɪŋ, -d, -ə*/z; -əbl, -ɪdʒ
draining-board, -s 'dreɪnɪŋbɔːd [-bɔəd],
   -z
drain-pipe, -s 'dreɪnpaɪp, -s
drake (D.), -s dreɪk, -s
dram (s. v.), -s, -ming, -med dræm, -z,
   -ɪŋ, -d
drama, -s 'drɑːmə, -z
dramatic, -al, -ally, -s drə'mætɪk, -l,
   -əlɪ, -s
dramatis personae ˌdrɑːmətɪs pɜː-
   'səʊnaɪ [ˌdræmətɪspɜː'səʊniː, -pə's-]
dramatist, -s 'dræmətɪst, -s
dramatization [-isa-], -s ˌdræmətaɪ-
   'zeɪʃn [-tɪ'z-], -z
dramatiz|e [-is|e], -es, -ing, -ed; -able
   'dræmətaɪz, -ɪz, -ɪŋ, -d; -əbl
dramaturge, -s 'dræmətɜːdʒ, -ɪz
dramaturgic ˌdræmə'tɜːdʒɪk

drambuie dræm'bjuːɪ [-'bjʊɪ]
drank (from drink) dræŋk
drap|e, -es, -ing, -ed dreɪp, -s, -ɪŋ, -t
draper (D.), -s 'dreɪpə*, -z
draper|y, -ies 'dreɪpər|ɪ, -ɪz
Drapier 'dreɪpɪə* [-pjə*]
drastic, -ally 'dræstɪk ['drɑːs-], -əlɪ
drat dræt
draught, -s drɑːft, -s
draught-board, -s 'drɑːftbɔːd [-bɔəd],
   -z
draught-horse, -s 'drɑːfthɔːs, -ɪz
draught-net, -s 'drɑːftnet, -s
draughts|man (person who draws), -men
   'drɑːfts|mən, -mən
draughts|man (piece used in game of
   draughts), -men 'drɑːfts|mæn [-mən],
   -men [-mən]
draught|y, -ier, -iest, -ily, -iness
   'drɑːft|ɪ, -ɪə* [-jə*], -ɪɪst [-jɪst], -ɪlɪ
   [-əlɪ], -ɪnɪs [-ɪnəs]
Dravidian, -s drə'vɪdɪən [-djən], -z
draw (s. v.), -s, -ing, drew, drawn;
   drawable drɔː, -z, -ɪŋ, druː, drɔːn;
   'drɔːəbl
drawback, -s 'drɔːbæk, -s
drawbridge, -s 'drɔːbrɪdʒ, -ɪz
Drawcansir 'drɔːkænsə*
drawee, -s drɔː'iː, -z
drawer (person who draws), -s 'drɔːə*
   [drɔə*], -z
drawer (sliding box), -s drɔː* [drɔə*], -z
drawers (garment) drɔːz [drɔəz]
drawing-board, -s 'drɔːɪŋbɔːd [-bɔəd],
   -z
drawing-kni|fe, -ves 'drɔːɪŋnaɪ|f, -vz
drawing-master, -s 'drɔːɪŋˌmɑːstə*, -z
drawing-pen, -s 'drɔːɪŋpen, -z
drawing-pencil, -s 'drɔːɪŋˌpensl, -z
drawing-room, -s (room for drawing)
   'drɔːɪŋrʊm [-ruːm], (reception room)
   'drɔːɪŋrʊm ['drɔɪŋ-, -ruːm], -z
drawing-table, -s 'drɔːɪŋˌteɪbl, -z
drawl (s. v.), -s, -ing, -ed, -er/s drɔːl,
   -z, -ɪŋ, -d, -ə*/z
drawn (from draw) drɔːn
draw-well, -s 'drɔːwel, -z
Drax dræks
dray, -s dreɪ, -z
dray|man, -men 'dreɪ|mən [-mæn],
   -mən [-men]
Drayton 'dreɪtn
dread (s. v.), -s, -ing, -ed dred, -z, -ɪŋ,
   -ɪd
dread|ful, -fully, -fulness 'dred|fʊl,
   -fʊlɪ [-fəlɪ], -fʊlnɪs [-nəs]
dreadnought (D.), -s 'drednɔːt, -s

dream (s. v.), -s, -ing/ly, -ed, -t, -er/s
   driːm, -z, -ɪŋ/lɪ, dremt [drempt,
   rarely driːmd], dremt [-mpt],
   'driːmə*/z
dreamland 'driːmlænd
dreamless, -ly 'driːmlɪs [-ləs], -lɪ
dream|y, -ier, -iest, -ily, -iness 'driːm|ɪ,
   -ɪə* [-jə*], -ɪɪst [-jɪst], -ɪlɪ [-əlɪ], -ɪnɪs
   [-ɪnəs]
drear drɪə*
drear|y, -ier, -iest, -ily, -iness, -isome
   'drɪər|ɪ, -ɪə*, -ɪɪst, -əlɪ [-ɪlɪ], -ɪnɪs
   [-ɪnəs], -ɪsəm
dredg|e (s. v.), -es, -ing, -ed, -er/s
   dredʒ, -ɪz, -ɪŋ, -d, -ə*/z
dregg|y, -ily, -iness 'dreg|ɪ, -ɪlɪ [-əlɪ],
   -ɪnɪs [-ɪnəs]
dregs dregz
drench (s. v.), -es, -ing, -ed, -er/s
   drentʃ, -ɪz, -ɪŋ, -t, -ə*/z
Dresden 'drezdən ('dreːsdən)
dress (s. v.), -es, -ing, -ed, -er/s dres,
   -ɪz, -ɪŋ, -t, -ə*/z
dressage 'dresɑːʒ [-ɑːdʒ, rarely -sɪdʒ]
dress-circle, -s ˌdres'sɜːkl ['-ˌ--], -z
dress-coat, -s ˌdres'kəʊt, -s
dresser, -s 'dresə*, -z
dressing-case, -s 'dresɪŋkeɪs, -ɪz
dressing-down ˌdresɪŋ'daʊn
dressing-gown, -s 'dresɪŋgaʊn, -z
dressing-jacket, -s 'dresɪŋˌdʒækɪt, -s
dressing-room, -s 'dresɪŋrʊm [-ruːm],
   -z
dressing-table, -s 'dresɪŋˌteɪbl, -z
dressmak|er/s, -ing 'dresˌmeɪk|ə*/z, -ɪŋ
dress-suit, -s ˌdres'suːt [-'sjuːt], -s
dress|y, -ier, -iest, -ily, -iness 'dres|ɪ,
   -ɪə*, -ɪɪst, -ɪlɪ [-əlɪ], -ɪnɪs [-ɪnəs]
drew (from draw) druː
Drew, -s druː, -z
Dreyfus 'dreɪfəs, 'draɪf-
dribb|le (s. v.), -les, -ling, -led, -ler/s
   'drɪb|l, -lz, -lɪŋ, [-lɪŋ], -ld, -lə*/z
   [-lə*/z]
driblet, -s 'drɪblɪt [-lət], -s
dried (from dry v.) draɪd
drier (s. adj.), -s 'draɪə*, -z
dries (from dry v.) draɪz
driest 'draɪɪst
Driffield 'drɪfiːld
drift (s. v.), -s, -ing, -ed drɪft, -s, -ɪŋ, -ɪd
drift-ice 'drɪftaɪs
driftless 'drɪftlɪs [-ləs]
drift-wood 'drɪftwʊd
drifty 'drɪftɪ
drill (s. v.), -s, -ing, -ed drɪl, -z, -ɪŋ, -d
drill-sergeant, -s 'drɪlˌsɑːdʒənt, -s
drily (= dryly) 'draɪlɪ

151

drink (s. v.), -s, -ing, drank, drunk,
drinker/s drɪŋk, -s, -ɪŋ, dræŋk,
drʌŋk, 'drɪŋkə*/z
drinkable 'drɪŋkəbl
drinking-bout, -s 'drɪŋkɪŋbaʊt, -s
drinking-fountain, -s 'drɪŋkɪŋˌfaʊntɪn
[-tən], -z
drinking-horn, -s 'drɪŋkɪŋhɔ:n, -z
drinking-song, -s 'drɪŋkɪŋsɒŋ, -z
drinking-water 'drɪŋkɪŋˌwɔ:tə*
drink-offering, -s 'drɪŋkˌɒfərɪŋ, -z
Drinkwater 'drɪŋkˌwɔ:tə*
drip (s. v.), -s, -ping/s, -ped, -per/s drɪp,
-s, -ɪŋ/z, -t, -ə*/z
drip-dry ˌdrɪp'draɪ
dripping (melted fat) 'drɪpɪŋ
dripping-pan, -s 'drɪpɪŋpæn, -z
drip-stone, -s 'drɪpstəʊn, -z
drivable 'draɪvəbl
driv|e (s. v.), -es, -ing, drove, driven,
driver/s draɪv, -z, -ɪŋ, drəʊv, 'drɪvn,
'draɪvə*/z
driv|el (s. v.), -els, -elling, -elled,
-eller/s 'drɪv|l, -lz, -lɪŋ [-lɪŋ], -ld,
-lə*/z [-lə*/z]
Driver 'draɪvə*
driving-belt, -s 'draɪvɪŋbelt, -s
driving-iron, -s 'draɪvɪŋˌaɪən, -z
driving-licenc|e, -es 'draɪvɪŋˌlaɪsns, -ɪz
driving-wheel, -s 'draɪvɪŋwi:l [-ŋhw-],
-z
drizz|le (s. v.), -les, -ling, -led 'drɪz|l,
-lz, -lɪŋ [-lɪŋ], -ld
drizzly 'drɪzlɪ [-zlɪ]
Droeshout 'dru:shaʊt
Drogheda (place) 'drɒɪɪdə ['drɔ:ɪdə,
'drɔ:ədə, 'drɒhədə], (Earl) 'drɒɪɪdə
drogher, -s 'drəʊgə*, -z
Droitwich 'drɔɪtwɪtʃ [rarely 'drɔɪtɪtʃ]
droll, -er, -est, -y drəʊl, -ə*, -ɪst, -lɪ
['drəʊlɪ]
droller|y, -ies 'drəʊlər|ɪ, -ɪz
dromedar|y, -ies 'drɒmədər|ɪ ['drʌm-,
-mɪd-], -ɪz
Dromio 'drəʊmɪəʊ [-mjəʊ]
Dromore 'drəʊmɔ:* [-mɔə*]
dron|e (s. v.), -es, -ing, -ed drəʊn, -z,
-ɪŋ, -d
Dronfield 'drɒnfi:ld
drool, -s, -ing, -ed dru:l, -z, -ɪŋ, -d
droop, -s, -ing/ly, -ed dru:p, -s, -ɪŋ/lɪ,
-t
drop (s. v.), -s, -ping/s, -ped, -per/s
drɒp, -s, -ɪŋ/z, -t, -ə*/z
drop-curtain, -s 'drɒpˌkɜ:tn [-tən, -tɪn],
-z
drop-kick, -s 'drɒpkɪk, -s
droplet, -s 'drɒplɪt [-lət], -s

drop-out, -s 'drɒpaʊt, -s
drop-scene, -s 'drɒpsi:n, -z
dropsic|al, -ally, -alness 'drɒpsɪk|l, -əlɪ,
-lnɪs [-nəs]
dropsy 'drɒpsɪ
drosera 'drɒsərə
droshk|y, -ies 'drɒʃk|ɪ, -ɪz
drosometer, -s drɒ'sɒmɪtə* [-mətə*], -z
dross, -y drɒs, -ɪ
drought, -s, -y draʊt, -s, -ɪ
drove (s.), -s drəʊv, -z
drove (from drive) drəʊv
drover, -s 'drəʊvə*, -z
Drower, 'draʊə*
drown, -s, -ing, -ed draʊn, -z, -ɪŋ, -d
drows|e (s. v.), -es, -ing, -ed draʊz, -ɪz,
-ɪŋ, -d
drows|y, -ier, -iest, -ily, -iness 'draʊz|ɪ,
-ɪə* [-jə*], -ɪɪst [-jɪst], -ɪlɪ [-əlɪ], -ɪnɪs
[-ɪnəs]
Drs. 'dɒktəz
drub, -s, -bing, -bed drʌb, -z, -ɪŋ, -d
Druce dru:s
Drucker 'drʊkə*
drudg|e (s. v.), -es, -ing/ly, -ed drʌdʒ,
-ɪz, -ɪŋ/lɪ, -d
drudgery 'drʌdʒərɪ
drug (s. v.), -s, -ging, -ged drʌg, -z, -ɪŋ,
-d
drugget, -s 'drʌgɪt, -s
druggist, -s 'drʌgɪst, -s
druid, -s, -ess/es, -ism 'dru:ɪd ['drʊɪd],
-z, -ɪs/ɪz [-es/ɪz], -ɪzəm
druidic, -al dru:'ɪdɪk [drʊ-], -l
drum (s. v.), -s, -ming, -med, -mer/s
drʌm, -z, -ɪŋ, -d, -ə*/z
Drumclog drʌm'klɒg
drum-fire 'drʌmˌfaɪə*
drumhead, -s 'drʌmhed, -z
drum-major, -s ˌdrʌm'meɪdʒə*, -z
Drummond 'drʌmənd
drumstick, -s 'drʌmstɪk, -s
drunk (s. adj.), -s drʌŋk, -s
drunk (from drink) drʌŋk
drunkard, -s 'drʌŋkəd, -z
drunken, -ly, -ness 'drʌŋkən, -lɪ, -nɪs
[-nəs]
drupe, -s dru:p, -s
Drury 'drʊərɪ
druse (geological term), -s dru:z, -ɪz
Druse (surname) dru:z, dru:s
Druse (member of sect in Syria and Lebanon),
-s dru:z, -ɪz
Drusilla dru:'sɪlə [drʊ-]
dr|y (adj. v.), -ier, -iest, -yly, -yness;
-ies, -ying, -ied, -ier/s dr|aɪ, -aɪə*,
-aɪɪst, -aɪlɪ, -aɪnɪs [-nəs]; -aɪz, -aɪɪŋ,
-aɪd, -aɪə*/z

dryad, -s 'draɪəd ['draɪæd], -z
Dryasdust 'draɪəzdʌst
dry-bob, -s 'draɪbɒb, -z
Dryburgh 'draɪbərə
dry-clean, -s, -ing, -ed, -er/s ˌdraɪ'kli:n,
 -z, -ɪŋ, -d, -ə*/z
Dryden 'draɪdn
dry-dock (s. v.), -s, -ing, -ed ˌdraɪ'dɒk
 ['--], -s, -ɪŋ, -t
Dryfesdale 'draɪfsdeɪl
Dryhurst 'draɪhə:st
drying (from dry v.) 'draɪɪŋ
dryly 'draɪlɪ
dry-measure 'draɪˌmeʒə*
dryness 'draɪnɪs [-nəs]
dry-nurs|e (s. v.), -es, -ing, -ed ˌdraɪ-
 'nə:s, -ɪz, -ɪŋ, -t
dry-plate, -s ˌdraɪ'pleɪt ['--], -s
dry-point 'draɪpɔɪnt
dry-rot ˌdraɪ'rɒt
drysalter, s 'draɪˌsɔ:ltə* [-ˌsɒl-], -z
drysalter|y, -ies 'draɪˌsɔ:ltər|ɪ [-ˌsɒl-],
 -ɪz
Drysdale 'draɪzdeɪl
dryshod ˌdraɪ'ʃɒd ['--]
dual 'dju:əl [djʊəl]
duali|sm, -st/s 'dju:əlɪ|zm ['djʊəl-],
 -st/s
dualistic ˌdju:ə'lɪstɪk [ˌdjʊə'l-]
dualit|y, -ies dju:'ælət|ɪ [djʊ'æ-, -ɪt|ɪ],
 -ɪz
Duane du:'eɪn [dʊ'eɪn]
dub (s. v.), -s, -bing, -bed dʌb, -z, -ɪŋ,
 -d
dubbin 'dʌbɪn
Dubhe 'dʊbeɪ
dubiety dju:'baɪətɪ [djʊ-, -aɪtɪ]
dubious, -ly, -ness 'dju:bjəs [-bɪəs], -lɪ,
 -nɪs [-nəs]
dubitat|e, -es, -ing, -ed 'dju:bɪteɪt, -s,
 -ɪŋ, -ɪd
dubitation, -s ˌdju:bɪ'teɪʃn [djʊbɪ't-], -z
dubitative, -ly 'dju:bɪtətɪv [-teɪt-], -lɪ
Dublin 'dʌblɪn
Du Buisson (English name) 'dju:bɪsn
duc|al, -ally 'dju:k|l, -əlɪ
Du Cane djʊ'keɪn [dju:'k-]
ducat, -s 'dʌkət, -s
duce, -s 'du:tʃɪ, -z
Duchesne (English name) dju:'ʃeɪn,
 du:'ʃeɪn
duchess, -es 'dʌtʃɪs [-es], -ɪz
duch|y, -ies 'dʌtʃ|ɪ, -ɪz
Ducie 'dju:sɪ
duck (s. v.), -s, -ing, -ed dʌk, -s, -ɪŋ, -t
duck-bill, -s, -ed 'dʌkbɪl, -z, -d
duck-board, -s 'dʌkbɔ:d [-bɔəd], -z
duckling, -s 'dʌklɪŋ, -z

duck-pond, -s 'dʌkpɒnd, -z
duck's-egg, -s 'dʌkseg, -z
duck-shot 'dʌkʃɒt
duckweed 'dʌkwi:d
Duckworth 'dʌkwəθ [-wə:θ]
duck|y, -ies 'dʌk|ɪ, -ɪz
Du Croz (English surname) djʊ'krəʊ
 [dju:'k-]
duct, -s dʌkt, -s
ductile 'dʌktaɪl
ductility dʌk'tɪlətɪ [-ɪtɪ]
ductless 'dʌktlɪs [-ləs]
dud, -s dʌd, -z
Duddell dʌ'del, dju:'del [djʊ-]
Duddeston 'dʌdɪstən
Duddington 'dʌdɪŋtən
Duddon 'dʌdn
dude, -s dju:d, -z
Dudeney (surname) 'du:dnɪ, 'dju:dnɪ
dudgeon, -s 'dʌdʒən, -z
Dudhope 'dʌdəp
Dudley 'dʌdlɪ
dudu 'du:du:
due (s. adj.), -s dju:, -z
duel (s. v.), -s, -ling, -led, -ler/s; -list/s
 'dju:əl [djʊəl, -ɪl], -z, -ɪŋ, -d, -ə*/z;
 -ɪst/s
duenna, -s dju:'enə [djʊ'e-], -z
Duer 'dju:ə*
duet, -s dju:'et [djʊ'et], -s
duettino, -s ˌdju:e'ti:nəʊ [ˌdjʊe-] -z
duettist, -s dju:'etɪst [djʊ'e-], -s
duetto, -s dju:'etəʊ [djʊ'e-], -z
duff (D.) dʌf
duffel 'dʌfl
duffer, -s 'dʌfə*, -z
Dufferin 'dʌfərɪn
Duffield 'dʌfi:ld
duffle-coat, -s 'dʌflkəʊt, -s
Duffy 'dʌfɪ
dug (s.), -s dʌg, -z
dug (from dig) dʌg
Dugald 'du:gəld
Dugan 'du:gən
Dugdale 'dʌgdeɪl
dugong, -s 'du:gɒŋ ['dju:-], -z
dug-out (s.), -s 'dʌgaʊt, -s
dug-out (adj.) ˌdʌg'aʊt
Duguid 'dju:gɪd, 'du:gɪd
duiker, -s 'daɪkə*, -z
duke (D.), -s dju:k, -s
dukedom, -s 'dju:kdəm, -z
duker|y, -ies 'dju:kər|ɪ, -ɪz
Dukinfield 'dʌkɪnfi:ld
dulcamara ˌdʌlkə'mɑ:rə [-'meər-]
Dulce (Christian name) 'dʌlsɪ
dulcet 'dʌlsɪt
Dulcie 'dʌlsɪ

153

dulci|fy, -fies, -fying, -fied 'dʌlsɪ|faɪ, -faɪz, -faɪɪŋ, -faɪd
dulcimer, -s 'dʌlsɪmə*, -z
Dulcinea ˌdʌlsɪ'nɪə [dʌl'sɪnɪə]
dulia dju:'laɪə
dull (adj. v.), -er, -est, -y, -ness; -s, -ing, -ed dʌl, -ə*, -ɪst, -ɪ [-lɪ], -nɪs [-nəs]; -z, -ɪŋ, -d
dullard, -s 'dʌləd, -z
dull-brained, -eyed 'dʌl|breɪnd, -aɪd
Dulles 'dʌlɪs [-ləs]
dullish 'dʌlɪʃ
dulness (=dullness) 'dʌlnɪs [-nəs]
Duluth dju:'lu:θ [dʊ'l-]
Dulwich 'dʌlɪdʒ [-ɪtʃ]
duly 'dju:lɪ
Duma 'du:mə ['dju:-]
Dumain dju:'meɪn [djʊ-]
Dumaresq du:'merɪk [dʊ-]
Dumas 'dju:mɑ ['du:-] (dyma)
Du Maurier (English surname) dju:-'mɔːrɪeɪ [dʊ-, du:-, -'mɒr-]
Dumayne dju:'meɪn [djʊ'm-]
dumb (adj. v.), -ly, -ness; -s, -ing, -ed dʌm, -lɪ, -nɪs [-nəs]; -z, -ɪŋ, -d
Dumbarton dʌm'bɑːtn
dumb-bell, -s 'dʌmbel, -z
dumbfound, -s, -ing, -ed, -er/s dʌm-'faʊnd, -z, -ɪŋ, -ɪd, -ə*/z
Dumbiedikes 'dʌmbɪdaɪks
dumb-show, -s 'dʌmʃəʊ [ˌ-'-], -z
dumb-waiter, -s ˌdʌm'weɪtə*, -z
dumdum, -s 'dʌmdʌm, -z
Dumfries, -shire dʌm'fri:s [dəm-], -ʃə* [-ˌʃɪə*, dʌm'fri:ʃʃə*]
dumm|y (s. adj.), -ies 'dʌm|ɪ, -ɪz
Dumnorix 'dʌmnərɪks
dump, -s, -ing, -ed dʌmp, -s, -ɪŋ, -t [dʌmt]
Dumphreys 'dʌmfrɪz
dumpish, -ly, -ness 'dʌmpɪʃ, -lɪ, -nɪs [-nəs]
dumpling, -s 'dʌmplɪŋ, -z
dumps dʌmps
dump|y, -ier, -iest 'dʌmp|ɪ, -ɪə* [-jə*], -ɪɪst [-jɪst]
Dumville 'dʌmvɪl
dun (s. adj. v.), -s, -ning, -ned dʌn, -z, -ɪŋ, -d
Dunalley dʌ'nælɪ
Dunbar (place, surname) dʌn'bɑː*, 'dʌnbɑː*
Note.—In Scotland always -'-.
Dunblane dʌn'bleɪn
Duncan 'dʌŋkən ['dʌnk-]
Duncannon dʌn'kænən [dʌŋ'k-]
Duncansby 'dʌŋkənzbɪ ['dʌnk-]
dunce, -s dʌns, -ɪz

Dunciad 'dʌnsɪæd
Duncombe 'dʌnkəm ['dʌŋk-]
Dundalk dʌn'dɔːk [-'dɔːlk, also '— when attributive]
Dundas dʌn'dæs, 'dʌndæs
Dundee dʌn'di: [ˌdʌn'd-, also 'dʌnd- when attributive]
dunderhead, -s 'dʌndəhed, -z
Dundonald dʌn'dɒnld
dundrear|y (D.), -ies dʌn'drɪər|ɪ, -ɪz
Dundrennan dʌn'drenən
Dundrum dʌn'drʌm ['dʌndrəm]
dune, -s dju:n, -z
Dunedin (in New Zealand) dʌ'ni:dɪn [-dn]
Dunell djʊ'nel [dju:'n-]
Dunfermline dʌn'fɜːmlɪn [dʌm'f-]
dung dʌŋ
Dungannon dʌn'gænən [dʌŋ'g-]
dungaree, -s ˌdʌŋgə'ri:, -z
Dungarvan dʌn'gɑːvən [dʌŋ'g-]
Dungeness ˌdʌndʒɪ'nes, dʌndʒ'nes [-dʒə-]
dungeon, -s 'dʌndʒən, -z
dung-hill, -s 'dʌŋhɪl, -z
Dunglison 'dʌŋglɪsn
dungy 'dʌŋɪ
Dunhill 'dʌnhɪl
Dunholme 'dʌnəm
Dunkeld dʌn'keld [dʌŋ'k-]
Dunker, -s 'dʌŋkə*, -z
Dunkirk dʌn'kɜːk [ˌdʌn'kɜːk, dʌŋ'k-, ˌdʌŋ'k-]
Dun Laoghaire dʌn'lɪərɪ [less usually -'leərə]
Dunlap 'dʌnləp [-læp]
dunlin, -s 'dʌnlɪn, -z
Dunlop (surname) 'dʌnlɒp, dʌn'lɒp
Dunlop (tyre), -s 'dʌnlɒp, -s
Dunmail dʌn'meɪl
Dunmore dʌn'mɔː* [-'mɔə*], attributively also '--, as in D. Road
Dunmow 'dʌnməʊ
Dunn(e) dʌn
Dunning 'dʌnɪŋ
dunnock, -s 'dʌnək, -s
Dunnottar dʌ'nɒtə* [də'n-]
Dunraven dʌn'reɪvn
Dunrobin dʌn'rɒbɪn
Dunsany dʌn'seɪnɪ
Dunse dʌns
Dunsinane (in Tayside) dʌn'sɪnən
Note.—This name has to be pronounced 'dʌnsɪneɪn in Shakespeare's 'Macbeth'.
Dunstable 'dʌnstəbl
Dunstaffnage dʌn'stæfnɪdʒ [-'stɑːf-]
Dunst|an, -er, -on 'dʌnst|ən, -ə*, -ən

154

Dunton 'dʌntən
duo, -s 'dju:əʊ ['djʊəʊ], -z
duodecennial ˌdju:əʊdɪ'senjəl [ˌdjʊəʊ-, -nɪəl]
duodecimal, -s ˌdju:əʊ'desɪml [ˌdjʊəʊ-, djʊə'd-, -səm-], -z
duodecimo, -s ˌdju:əʊ'desɪməʊ [ˌdjʊəʊ-], -z
duodenal ˌdju:əʊ'di:nl [ˌdjʊəʊ-]
duodenary ˌdju:əʊ'di:nərɪ [ˌdjʊəʊ-]
duoden|um, -ums, -a ˌdju:əʊ'di:n|əm [ˌdjʊəʊ-], -əmz, -ə
duologue, -s 'dju:əlɒg ['dju:ə-], -z
Duparcq (*surname*) du:'pɑ:k [dju:-]
dup|e (*s. v.*), **-es, -ing, -ed** dju:p, -s, -ɪŋ, -t
dupery 'dju:pərɪ
Du Plat dju:'plɑ:
duple 'dju:pl
Dupleix (*governor in India*) dju:'pleɪks (dyplɛks), (*historian*) dju:'pleɪ (dyplɛ)
duplex 'dju:pleks
duplicate (*s. adj.*), **-s** 'dju:plɪkət [-ɪt], -s
duplicat|e (*v.*), **-es, -ing, -ed, -or/s** 'dju:-plɪkeɪt, -s, -ɪŋ, -ɪd, -ə*/z
duplication, -s ˌdju:plɪ'keɪʃn, -z
duplicature, -s 'dju:plɪkeɪtʃ|ə* ['dju:plɪkə,tjʊə*], -z
duplicity dju:'plɪsətɪ [djʊ-, -ɪtɪ]
dupl|y, -ies dju:'pl|aɪ [djʊ-], -aɪz
Dupont (*American surname*) 'dju:pɒnt
Duquesne (*French naval commander*) dju:'keɪn [djʊ-] (dykɛ:n), (*place in U.S.A.*) dju:'keɪn [djʊ-, du:'k-]
durability ˌdjʊərə'bɪlətɪ [ˌdjɔər-, ˌdjɔ:r-, -lɪt-]
durab|le, -ly, -leness 'djʊərəb|l ['djɔər-, 'djɔ:r-], -lɪ, -lnɪs [-nəs]
dural 'djʊərəl ['djɔə-, 'djɔ:-]
duralumin djʊə'ræljʊmɪn [djɔə'r-, djɔ:'r-]
duramen djʊə'reɪmen
durance 'djʊərəns
Durand djʊə'rænd
Durant djʊ'rɑ:nt, djʊ'rænt
duration, -s djʊə'reɪʃn [djɔə'r-, djɔ:'r-], -z
durative 'djʊərətɪv ['djɔər-, 'djɔ:r-]
Durban 'dɜ:bən
durbar, -s 'dɜ:bɑ:*, -z
Durbin 'dɜ:bɪn
Durden 'dɜ:dn
durdle, -s 'dɜ:dl, -z
Durell djʊə'rel
Dürer, -s 'djʊərə* ('dy:rər), -z
duress djʊə'res ['djʊəres, 'djʊərɪs]
Durham 'dʌrəm

during 'djʊərɪŋ ['djɔər-, 'djɔ:r-, 'dʒʊər-, 'dʒɔ:r-]
Durlacher də'lækə*
Durnford 'dɜ:nfəd
Durran dʌ'ræn [də'r-]
Durrant 'dʌrənt
Durrell 'dʌrəl
durst (*from* dare), **-n't** dɜ:st, 'dɜ:snt
Durward 'dɜ:wəd
Duse 'du:zɪ
dusk (*s. adj. v.*), **-s, -ing, -ed** dʌsk, -s, -ɪŋ, -t
dusk|y, -ier, -iest, -ily, -iness 'dʌsk|ɪ, -ɪə* [-ɪə*], -ɪɪst [-jɪst], -ɪlɪ [-əlɪ], -ɪnɪs [-ɪnəs]
dust (*s. v.*), **-s, -ing, -ed** dʌst, -s, -ɪŋ, -ɪd
dustbin, -s 'dʌstbɪn, -z
dust-cart, -s 'dʌstkɑ:t, -s
dust-coat, -s 'dʌstkəʊt, -s
dust-colour, -ed 'dʌst,kʌlə*, -d
duster, -s 'dʌstə*, -z
dusthole, -s 'dʌsthəʊl, -z
dust-jacket, -s 'dʌst,dʒækɪt, -s
dust|man, -men 'dʌst|mən, -mən
dust-pan, -s 'dʌstpæn, -z
dustproof 'dʌstpru:f
dust|y, -ier, -iest, -ily, -iness 'dʌst|ɪ, -ɪə* [-jə*], -ɪɪst [-jɪst], -ɪlɪ [-əlɪ], -ɪnɪs [-ɪnəs]
Dutch, -man, -men dʌtʃ, -mən, -mən
Dutch|woman, -women 'dʌtʃ|,wʊmən, -,wɪmɪn
duteous, -ly, -ness 'dju:tjəs [-tɪəs], -lɪ, -nɪs [-nəs]
Duthie 'dʌθɪ
Duthoit də'θɔɪt
dutiable 'dju:tjəbl [-tɪəb-]
duti|ful, -fully, -fulness 'dju:tɪ|fʊl, -fʊlɪ [-fəlɪ], -fʊlnɪs [-nəs]
Dutton 'dʌtn
dut|y, -ies 'dju:t|ɪ, -ɪz
duty-free ˌdju:tɪ'fri:
duumvir, -s dju:'ʌmvə* [djʊ'ʌ-, 'dju:əmv-, du:'ʊm-], -z
duumvirate, -s dju:'ʌmvɪrət [djʊ'ʌ-, -vər-, -rɪt], -s
duumviri (*alternative plur. of* duumvir) du:'ʊmvɪri: [dju:'ʌmvɪraɪ, djʊ'ʌ-, -vər-]
Duveen dju:'vi:n [djʊ-]
duvet, -s 'du:veɪ ['dju:-], -z
dux, -es dʌks, -ɪz
Duxbury 'dʌksbərɪ
D.V. (*deo volente*) ˌdi:'vi:
Dvorak [-řák] 'dvɔ:ʒɑ:k [-ɔ:rɑ:k, -æk]
dwale dweɪl
dwar|f (*s.*), **-s, -ves** dwɔ:|f, -s, -vz
dwarf (*v.*), **-s, -ing, -ed** dwɔ:f, -s, -ɪŋ, -t

155

dwarfish, -ly, -ness 'dwɔːfɪʃ, -lɪ, -nɪs [-nəs]

dwell, -s, -ing/s, dwelt, dweller/s dwel, -z, -ɪŋ/z, dwelt, 'dwelə*/z

dwelling-hou|se, -ses 'dwelɪŋhaʊ|s, -zɪz

dwelling-place, -s 'dwelɪŋpleɪs, -ɪz

Dwight dwaɪt

Dwina 'dviːnə ['dwiː-] (dvjiˈna)

dwind|le, -les, -ling, -led 'dwɪnd|l, -lz, -lɪŋ [-l̩ŋ], -ld

dyad, -s 'daɪæd ['daɪəd], -z

Dyak, -s 'daɪæk ['daɪək], -s

dyarch|y, -ies 'daɪɑːk|ɪ, -ɪz

Dyce daɪs

Dyche daɪtʃ

dye (s. v.), **-s, -ing, -d, -r/s** daɪ, -z, -ɪŋ, -d, 'daɪə*/z

Dyer 'daɪə*

dyestuff, -s 'daɪstʌf, -s

dye-wood 'daɪwʊd

dye-works 'daɪwɜːks

Dyfed 'dʌvɪd (Welsh 'dəved)

Dyffryn 'dʌfrɪn (Welsh 'dəfrɪn)

dying (from die v.) 'daɪɪŋ

dyk|e (s. v.), **-es, -ing, -ed** daɪk, -s, -ɪŋ, -t

Dyke, -s daɪk, -s

Dylan 'dɪlən (Welsh 'dəlan)

Dym|ock, -oke 'dɪm|ək, -ək

Dymon|d, -t 'daɪmən|d, -t

dynameter, -s daɪˈnæmɪtə* [dɪˈn-, -mətə*], -z

dynamic, -al, -ally, -s daɪˈnæmɪk [dɪˈn-], -l, -əlɪ, -s

dynamism 'daɪnəmɪzəm

dynamit|e (s. v.), **-es, -ing, -ed, -er/s** 'daɪnəmaɪt, -s, -ɪŋ, -ɪd, -ə*/z

dynamo, -s 'daɪnəməʊ, -z

dynamometer, -s ˌdaɪnəˈmɒmɪtə* [-mətə*], -z

dynamometric, -al ˌdaɪnəməʊˈmetrɪk, -l

dynast, -s 'dɪnəst ['dɪnæst, 'daɪnəst, 'daɪnæst], -s

dynastic dɪˈnæstɪk [daɪˈn-]

dynast|y, -ies 'dɪnəst|ɪ ['daɪn-], -ɪz

dynatron, -s 'daɪnətrɒn, -z

dyne, -s daɪn, -s

Dynevor 'dɪnɪvə*

Dysart 'daɪsət [-sɑːt, -zɑːt]

dysarthria dɪsˈɑːθrɪə

dyscrasia dɪsˈkreɪzjə [-zɪə, -ʒjə, -ʒɪə, -ʒə]

dysenteric ˌdɪsnˈterɪk [-sən-, -sen-]

dysentery 'dɪsntrɪ [-sən-]

dysfuncti|on (s. v.), **-ons, -oning, -oned** dɪsˈfʌŋkʃ|n, -nz, -nɪŋ [-ənɪŋ], -nd

dysgraphia dɪsˈɡræfɪə

dysgraphic dɪsˈɡræfɪk

dyslalia dɪsˈleɪlɪə [-ljə]

dyslexia dɪsˈleksɪə [-ksjə]

dyslexic dɪsˈleksɪk

Dyson 'daɪsn

dyspepsia dɪsˈpepsɪə [-sjə]

dyspeptic (s. adj.), **-s** dɪsˈpeptɪk, -s

dysphasia dɪsˈfeɪzjə [-zɪə, -ʒjə, -ʒɪə, -ʒə]

dysphasic, -s dɪsˈfeɪzɪk, -s

dysphonia dɪsˈfəʊnɪə [-njə]

dysphonic dɪsˈfɒnɪk

dyspnoea dɪsˈpniːə [-ˈpnɪə]

dysprosium dɪsˈprəʊzɪəm [-zjəm]

dysuria dɪsˈjʊərɪə [-rjə]

dystrophy 'dɪstrəfɪ

dziggetai, -s 'dzɪɡɪtaɪ, -z

E

E *(the letter)*, -'s iː, -z
each iːtʃ
Ead|ie, -y 'iːd|ɪ, -ɪ
eager, -ly, -ness 'iːgə*, -lɪ, -nɪs [-nəs]
eagle, -s 'iːgl, -z
eagle-eyed ˌiːgl'aɪd ['iːglaɪd]
Eaglefield 'iːglfiːld
Eaglehawk 'iːglhɔːk
eagle-owl, -s ˌiːgl'aʊl [*in contrast* '---], -z
eaglet, -s 'iːglɪt [-lət], -s
eagre, -s 'eɪgə* ['iːgə*], -z
Ealing 'iːlɪŋ
Eames iːmz, eɪmz
Eamon 'eɪmən
ear, -s ɪə*, -z
ear-ache 'ɪəreɪk
Eardley 'ɜːdlɪ
ear-drum, -s 'ɪədrʌm, -z
eared ɪəd
earl, -s; -dom/s ɜːl, -z; -dəm/z
Earl(e) ɜːl
earl-marshal, -s ˌɜːl'mɑːʃl, -z
Earl's Court ˌɜːlz'kɔːt
earl|y, -ier, -iest, -iness 'ɜːl|ɪ, -ɪə*
[-jə*], -ɪɪst [-jɪst], -ɪnɪs [-ɪnəs]
earmark *(s. v.)*, -s, -ing, -ed 'ɪəmɑːk, -s,
-ɪŋ, -t
earn (E.), -s, -ing, -ed ɜːn, -z, -ɪŋ, -d
[ɜːnt]
earnest *(s. adj.)*, -s, -ly, -ness 'ɜːnɪst, -s,
-lɪ, -nɪs [-nəs]
earnest-money, -s 'ɜːnɪstˌmʌnɪ, -z
earnings 'ɜːnɪŋz
Earp ɜːp
earphone, -s 'ɪəfəʊn, -z
earring, -s 'ɪərɪŋ, -s
Earsdon 'ɪəzdən
earshot 'ɪəʃɒt
earth *(s.)*, -s ɜːθ, -s [ɜːðz]
earth *(v.)*, -s, -ing, -ed ɜːθ, -s, -ɪŋ, -t
earth-board, -s 'ɜːθbɔːd [-bɔəd], -z
earth-born 'ɜːθbɔːn
earthbound 'ɜːθbaʊnd
earth-bred 'ɜːθbred
earth-closet, -s 'ɜːθˌklɒzɪt, -s
earthen, -ware 'ɜːθn, -weə*
earthiness 'ɜːθɪnɪs [-nəs]
earthl|y, -ier, -iest, -iness 'ɜːθl|ɪ, -ɪə*
[-jə*], -ɪɪst [-jɪst], -ɪnɪs [-ɪnəs]

earthly-minded, -ness ˌɜːθlɪ'maɪndɪd
['ɜːθlɪˌm-], -nɪs [-nəs]
earthquake, -s 'ɜːθkweɪk, -s
earthward 'ɜːθwəd
earthwork, -s 'ɜːθwɜːk, -s
earthworm, -s 'ɜːθwɜːm, -z
earthy 'ɜːθɪ
ear-trumpet, -s 'ɪəˌtrʌmpɪt, -s
ear-wax 'ɪəwæks
earwig, -s 'ɪəwɪg, -z
ear-witness, -es ˌɪə'wɪtnɪs ['-ˌ--, -nəs],
-ɪz
Easdale 'iːzdeɪl
eas|e *(s. v.)*, -es, -ing, -ed iːz, -ɪz, -ɪŋ, -d
Easebourne 'iːzbɔːn [-bɔən]
easel, -s 'iːzl, -z
easement, -s 'iːzmənt, -s
Easingwold 'iːzɪŋwəʊld
east (E.) iːst
Eastbourne 'iːstbɔːn [-bɔən]
Eastcheap 'iːsttʃiːp
East-end, -er/s ˌiːst'end, -ə*/z
Easter, -s, -tide 'iːstə*, -z, -taɪd
Easter-day, -s ˌiːstə'deɪ ['---], -z
easterly 'iːstəlɪ
eastern, -most 'iːstən [-tn], -məʊst
[-məst]
East Ham ˌiːst'hæm
Eastham 'iːsthəm
Easthampton ˌiːst'hæmptən
easting 'iːstɪŋ
Eastlake 'iːstleɪk
Eastleigh 'iːstliː [ˌiːst'liː]
Eastman 'iːstmən
east-north-east ˌiːstnɔːθ'iːst [*in nautical
usage* -nɔːr'iːst]
Easton 'iːstən
Eastport 'iːstpɔːt
east-south-east ˌiːstsaʊθ'iːst [*in
nautical usage also* -saʊ'iːst]
eastward, -ly, -s 'iːstwəd, -lɪ, -z
Eastwood 'iːstwʊd
eas|y, -ier, -iest, -ily, -iness 'iːz|ɪ, -ɪə*
[-jə*], -ɪɪst [-jɪst], -ɪlɪ [-əlɪ], -ɪnɪs [-nəs]
easy-chair, -s ˌiːzɪ'tʃeə* ['--ˌ-], -z
easygoing 'iːzɪˌgəʊɪŋ [ˌ--'--]
eat *(pres. tense)*, -s, -ing, ate, eat|en,
-er/s; -able/s iːt, -s, -ɪŋ, et [eɪt],
'iːt|n, -ə*/z; -əbl/z

157

eating-hou|se, -ses 'i:tɪŋhaʊ|s, -zɪz
Eaton 'i:tn
eau-de-Cologne ˌəʊdəkə'ləʊn [-dɪk-]
eau-de-vie ˌəʊdə'vi: (odvi)
eau-forte, eaux-fortes ˌəʊ'fɔ:t (ofort), -s
eave, -s (E.) i:v, -z
eavesdrop, -s, -ping, -ped, -per/s
  'i:vzdrɒp, -s, -ɪŋ, -t, -ə*/z
Ebal 'i:bæl [-bəl]
ebb (s. v.), -s, -ing, -ed eb, -z, -ɪŋ, -d
Ebbsfleet 'ebzfli:t
ebb-tide, -s ˌeb'taɪd ['--], -z
Ebbw 'ebu: (Welsh 'ebu)
Ebel e'bel, 'i:bl
Ebenezer ˌebɪ'ni:zə* [-bə-]
Ebionite, -s 'i:bjənaɪt [-bɪən-], -s
E-boat, -s 'i:bəʊt, -s
ebon, -ite 'ebən, -aɪt
ebony 'ebənɪ
Eboracum i:'bɒrəkəm [ɪ'b-]
ebriate 'i:brɪət [-ɪt]
ebriety i:'braɪətɪ [ɪ'b-, -ɪtɪ]
Ebrington 'ebrɪŋtən
Ebro 'i:brəʊ ['eb-] ('ebro)
ebullien|ce, -cy, -t ɪ'bʌljən|s [-'bʊl-,
  -lɪən-], -sɪ, -t
ebullition, -s ˌebə'lɪʃn [-bʊ'l-], -z
Ebury 'i:bərɪ
E.C. ˌi:'si:
écarté eɪ'kɑ:teɪ (ekarte)
Ecbatana ek'bætənə [ˌekbə'tɑ:nə]
Ecce Homo ˌeksɪ'həʊməʊ [ˌeker-,
  -'hɒməʊ]
eccentric (s. adj), -s, -al, -ally ɪk'sentrɪk [ek-], -s, -l, -əlɪ
eccentricit|y, -ies ˌeksen'trɪsət|ɪ [-sən-,
  -ɪt|ɪ], -ɪz
Ecclefechan ˌekl'fekən [-'fexən]
Eccles, -field 'eklz, -fi:ld
eccles|ia, -iast/s ɪ'kli:z|jə [-ɪə], -ɪæst/s
Ecclesiastes ɪˌkli:zɪ'æsti:z [-ɪ'ɑ:s-]
ecclesiastic (s. adj.), -s, -al, -ally
  ɪˌkli:zɪ'æstɪk [-ɪ'ɑ:s-], -s, -l, -əlɪ
ecclesiasticism ɪˌkli:zɪ'æstɪsɪzəm
  [-ɪ'ɑ:s-]
Ecclesiasticus ɪˌkli:zɪ'æstɪkəs [-ɪ'ɑ:s-]
Eccleston 'eklstən
echelon, -s, -ned 'eʃəlɒn ['eɪʃ-], -z, -d
echidn|a, -ae e'kɪdn|ə [ɪ'k-], -i:
echin|us, -i e'kaɪn|əs [ɪ'k-], -aɪ
echo (s. v.), -es, -ing, -ed 'ekəʊ, -z, -ɪŋ,
  -d
echoic e'kəʊɪk [ɪ'k-]
Echuca ɪ'tʃu:kə
Eckersl|e)y 'ekəzlɪ
Eck|ert, -ford 'ek|ət, -fəd
éclair, -s eɪ'kleə* [ɪ'k-, 'eɪkleə*], -z
eclampsia ɪ'klæmpsɪə [e'k-, -sjə]

éclat, -s 'eɪklɑ: [-'-] (ekla), -z
eclectic (s. adj.), -s, -al, -ally e'klektɪk
  [ɪ'klek-, i:'klek-], -s, -l, -əlɪ
eclecticism e'klektɪsɪzəm [ɪ'klek-,
  i:'klek-]
eclips|e (s. v.), -es, -ing, -ed ɪ'klɪps, -ɪz,
  -ɪŋ, -t
ecliptic, -s ɪ'klɪptɪk, -s
eclogue, -s 'eklɒg, -z
ecological ˌi:kə'lɒdʒɪkl [ˌek-]
ecolog|y, -ist/s i:'kɒləd|ʒ|ɪ [ɪ'k-, e'k-],
  -ɪst/s
economic, -al, -ally, -s ˌi:kə'nɒmɪk
  [ˌek-], -l, -əlɪ, -s
economist, -s ɪ'kɒnəmɪst [i:'k-], -s
economiz|e [-is|e], -es, -ing, -ed, -er/s
  ɪ'kɒnəmaɪz [i:'k-], -ɪz, -ɪŋ, -d, -ə*/z
econom|y, -ies ɪ'kɒnəm|ɪ [i:'k-], -ɪz
ecru 'eɪkru: [e'kru:]
ecstas|y, -ies 'ekstəs|ɪ, -ɪz
ecstatic, -al, -ally ɪk'stætɪk [ek-], -l,
  -əlɪ
ectoplasm 'ektəʊplæzəm
Ecuador 'ekwədɔ:* [ˌ--'-]
ecumenic, -al ˌi:kju:'menɪk [ˌek-, -kjʊ-],
  -l
ecumeni|sm, -st/s i:'kju:mənɪ|zəm
  [ɪ'kju:-], -st/s
eczema 'eksɪmə [-səm-, 'eksmə]
eczematous ek'semətəs [ek'zem-,
  ɪg'zem-, rarely ek'si:m-, ek'zi:m-]
edacious ɪ'deɪʃəs [i:'d-, e'd-]
Edam (cheese) 'i:dæm
Edda, -s 'edə, -z
Eddington 'edɪŋtən
edd|y (s. v.) (E.), -ies, -ying, -ied 'ed|ɪ,
  -ɪz, -ɪɪŋ, -ɪd
Eddystone 'edɪstən
Ede i:d
edelweiss 'eɪdlvaɪs
Eden, -bridge 'i:dn, -brɪdʒ
Edenfield (in Greater Manchester)
  'i:dnfi:ld
Edessa ɪ'desə
Edgar 'edgə*
Edgbaston 'edʒbəstən
Edgcumbe 'edʒkəm [-ku:m]
edg|e (s. v.) (E.), -es, -ing, -ed edʒ, -ɪz,
  -ɪŋ, -d
Edgecomb(e) 'edʒkəm
Edgecote 'edʒkəʊt [-kət]
Edgehill (name of a hill) ˌedʒ'hɪl, (sur-
  name) 'edʒhɪl
edgeless 'edʒlɪs [-ləs]
Edgerton 'edʒətən
edge|ways, -wise 'edʒ|weɪz, -waɪz
Edgeworth 'edʒwɜ:θ [-wəθ]
edging, -s 'edʒɪŋ, -z

Edgington 'edʒɪŋtən
Edgley 'edʒlɪ
Edgware (town) 'edʒweə*, (Road) 'edʒweə* [-wə*]
edgy 'edʒɪ
edibility ˌedɪ'bɪlətɪ [-də'b-, -lɪt-]
edible (s. adj.), -s, -ness 'edɪbl [-dəb-],
-z, -nɪs [-nəs]
edict, -s 'i:dɪkt, -s
Edie 'i:dɪ
edification ˌedɪfɪ'keɪʃn
edifice, -s 'edɪfɪs, -ɪz
edi|fy, -fies, -fying, -fied 'edɪ|faɪ, -faɪz,
-faɪɪŋ, -faɪd
edile, -s 'i:daɪl, -z
Edina ɪ'daɪnə [e'd-]
Edinburgh 'edɪnbərə ['edn-, -bʌrə]
Edington 'edɪŋtən
Edison 'edɪsn
Ediss 'i:dɪs, 'edɪs
edit, -s, -ing, -ed, -or/s 'edɪt, -s, -ɪŋ, -ɪd,
-ə*/z
Edith 'i:dɪθ
edition, -s ɪ'dɪʃn, -z
editorial (s. adj.), -s, -ly ˌedɪ'tɔ:rɪəl, -z,
-ɪ
editorship, -s 'edɪtəʃɪp, -s
Edmond, -s 'edmənd, -z
Edmonton 'edməntən
Edmund, -s 'edmənd, -z
Edna 'ednə
Edom, -ite/s 'i:dəm, -aɪt/s
Edridge 'edrɪdʒ
Edsall 'edsl
educability ˌedʒʊkə'bɪlətɪ [ˌedjʊ-, -lɪt-]
educable 'edʒʊkəbl ['edjʊ-]
educat|e, -es, -ing, -ed, -or/s 'edʒʊkeɪt
[-dʒu:-, -djʊ-, -dju:-], -s, -ɪŋ, -ɪd,
-ə*/z
education ˌedʒʊ'keɪʃn [-dʒu:-, -djʊ-,
-dju:-]
educa|tional, -tionally ˌedʒʊ'keɪʃǝnl
[-dʒu:-, -djʊ-, -dju:-, -ʃnǝl, -ʃn̩l,
-ʃn̩], -ʃǝnǝl], -ʃn̩ǝlɪ [-ʃnǝlɪ, -ʃn̩lɪ,
-ʃn̩lɪ, -ʃǝnǝlɪ]
educationalist, -s ˌedʒʊ'keɪʃn̩ǝlɪst
[-dʒu:-, -djʊ-, -dju:-, -ʃnǝl-, -ʃn̩l-,
-ʃn̩l-, -ʃǝnǝl-], -s
educationist, -s ˌedʒʊ'keɪʃnɪst [-dʒu:-,
-djʊ-, -dju:-, -ʃn̩ɪst, -ʃǝnɪst], -s
educative 'edʒʊkǝtɪv [-dʒu:-, -djʊ-,
-dju:-, -keɪt-]
educ|e, -es, -ing, -ed i:'dju:s [ɪ'd-], -ɪz,
-ɪŋ, -t
eduction, -s i:'dʌkʃn [ɪ'd-], -z
Edward, -(e)s 'edwǝd, -z
Edwardian (s. adj.), -s ed'wɔ:djǝn
[-dɪǝn], -z

Edwin, -stowe 'edwɪn, -stǝʊ
eel, -s i:l, -z
e'en i:n
e'er eǝ*
eer|ie, -y, -ily, -iness 'ɪǝr|ɪ, -ɪ, -ǝlɪ [-ɪlɪ],
-ɪnɪs [-ɪnǝs]
effac|e, -es, -ing, -ed, -ement; -eable
ɪ'feɪs [e'f-], -ɪz, -ɪŋ, -t, -mǝnt; -ǝbl
effect (s. v.), -s, -ing, -ed ɪ'fekt, -s, -ɪŋ,
-ɪd
effective, -s, -ly, -ness ɪ'fektɪv, -z, -lɪ,
-nɪs [-nǝs]
effectual, -ly ɪ'fektʃʊǝl [-tʃwǝl, -tʃʊl,
-tjʊǝl, -tjwǝl, -tjʊl], -ɪ
effectuality ɪˌfektjʊ'ælǝtɪ [-tʃʊ-, -ɪtɪ]
effectuat|e, -es, -ing, -ed ɪ'fektjʊeɪt
[-tʃʊ-], -s, -ɪŋ, -ɪd
effeminacy ɪ'femɪnǝsɪ [e'f-]
effeminate (adj.), -ly, -ness ɪ'femɪnǝt
[e'f-, -nɪt], -lɪ, -nɪs [-nǝs]
effeminat|e (v.), -es, -ing, -ed ɪ'femɪ-
neɪt [e'f-], -s, -ɪŋ, -ɪd
effendi e'fendɪ
efferent 'efǝrǝnt
effervesc|e, -es, -ing, -ed; -ence, -ent
ˌefǝ'ves, -ɪz, -ɪŋ, -t; -ns, -nt
effete ɪ'fi:t [e'f-]
efficacious, -ly, -ness efɪ'keɪʃǝs, -lɪ, -nɪs
[-nǝs]
efficacity ˌefɪ'kæsǝtɪ [-ɪtɪ]
efficacy 'efɪkǝsɪ
efficien|cy, -t/ly ɪ'fɪʃǝn|sɪ, -t/lɪ
Effie 'efɪ
effig|y, -ies 'efɪdʒ|ɪ [-fǝdʒ|ɪ], -ɪz
Effingham 'efɪŋǝm
effloresc|e, -es, -ing, -ed; -ence, -ent
ˌeflɔ:'res [-flɒ'r-, -flǝ'r-], -ɪz, -ɪŋ, -t;
-ns, -nt
effluen|ce, -t/s 'eflʊǝn|s [-flwǝn-], -t/s
effluvium ɪ'flu:vjǝm [e'f-, -vɪǝm]
efflux, -es 'eflʌks, -ɪz
effort, -s; -less 'efǝt, -s; -lɪs [-lǝs]
effronter|y, -ies ɪ'frʌntǝr|ɪ [e'f-], -ɪz
effulg|e, -es, -ing, -ed ɪ'fʌldʒ [e'f-], -ɪz,
-ɪŋ, -d
effulgen|ce, -t/ly ɪ'fʌldʒǝn|s [e'f-], -t/lɪ
effuse (adj.) ɪ'fju:s [e'f-]
effus|e (v.), -es, -ing, -ed ɪ'fju:z [e'f-],
-ɪz, -ɪŋ, -d
effusion, -s ɪ'fju:ʒn [e'f-], -z
effusive, -ly, -ness ɪ'fju:sɪv [e'f-], -lɪ,
-nɪs [-nǝs]
Efik 'efɪk
eft, -s eft, -s
e.g. ˌi:'dʒi: [fǝrɪg'zɑ:mpl]
egad i:'gæd
egalitarian, -ism ɪˌgælɪ'teǝrɪǝn, -ɪzǝm
Egan 'i:gǝn

159

Egbert 'egbɜːt [-bət]
Egeria iː'dʒɪərɪə [ɪ'dʒ-]
Egerton 'edʒətən
Egeus (in Greek mythology) 'iːdʒjuːs,
  (Shakespearian character) iː'dʒiːəs
  [ɪ'dʒ-]
egg (s. v.), -s, -ing, -ed, -er/s eg, -z, -ɪŋ,
  -d, -ə*/z
egg-cup, -s 'egkʌp, -s
Eggle|ton, -ston 'egl|tən, -stən
egg-plant, -s 'egplɑːnt, -s
egg-shaped 'egʃeɪpt
eggshell, -s 'egʃel, -z
egg-spoon, -s 'egspuːn, -z
Egham 'egəm
Eglamore 'egləmɔː* [-mɔə*]
eglantine (E.) 'egləntaɪn
Eglingham (in Northumberland)
  'eglɪndʒəm
Eglinton 'eglɪntən
Eglon 'eglɒn
Egmont 'egmɒnt [-mənt]
ego, -s 'egəʊ ['iːg-], -z
egocentric ˌegəʊ'sentrɪk [ˌiːg-]
egoi|sm, -st/s 'egəʊɪ|zəm, -st/s
egoistic, -al, -ally ˌegəʊ'ɪstɪk [ˌiːg-], -l,
  -əlɪ
Egon 'egən [-gɒn]
egoti|sm, -st/s 'egəʊtɪ|zəm ['iːg-],
  -st/s
egotistic, -al, -ally ˌegəʊ'tɪstɪk [ˌiːg-], -l,
  -əlɪ
egotiz|e [-is|e], -es, -ing, -ed 'egəʊtaɪz
  ['iːg-], -ɪz, -ɪŋ, -d
egregious, -ly, -ness i'griːdʒəs [-dʒjəs,
  -dʒɪəs], -lɪ, -nɪs [-nəs]
Egremont (in Merseyside, Cumbria)
  'egrəmənt [-grɪm-, -mɒnt]
egress, -es 'iːgres, -ɪz
egression, -s iː'greʃn [ɪ'g-], -z
egressive iː'gresɪv [ɪ'g-]
egret, -s 'iːgrɪt ['eg-, -ət, -et], -s
Egton 'egtən
Egypt 'iːdʒɪpt
Egyptian, -s ɪ'dʒɪpʃn, -z
egyptolog|ist/s, -y ˌiːdʒɪp'tɒlədʒ|ɪst/s,
  -ɪ
eh eɪ
eider, -s 'aɪdə*, -z
eiderdown, -s 'aɪdədaʊn, -z
eider-duck, -s ˌaɪdə'dʌk [in contrast
  '---], -s
eidograph, -s 'aɪdəʊgrɑːf [-græf], -s
eidol|on, -ons, -a aɪ'dəʊl|ɒn, -ɒnz, -ə
Eifel 'aɪfl
Eiffel Tower, -s ˌaɪfl'taʊə*, -z
Eiger 'aɪgə*
eight, -s, -some eɪt, -s, -səm

eighteen, -s, -th/s ˌeɪ'tiːn [also '--,
  according to sentence-stress], -z, -θ/s
eightfold 'eɪtfəʊld
eighth, -s, -ly eɪtθ, -s, -lɪ
eightieth, -s 'eɪtɪəθ [-tjəθ, -tɪɪθ, -tjɪθ], -s
eightish 'eɪtɪʃ
eight|pence, -penny 'eɪt|pəns, -pənɪ (see
  note under penny)
eight|y, -ies 'eɪt|ɪ, -ɪz
  Note.—In the N. of England often
  'eɪttɪ.
Eilean (near Inverness) 'iːlən
Eileen 'aɪliːn
Eiloart 'aɪləʊɑːt
Einstein 'aɪnstaɪn
Eire 'eərə
Eirene aɪ'riːnɪ [ˌaɪə'r-]
eirenicon, -s aɪ'riːnɪkɒn [ˌaɪə'r-, -'ren-],
  -z
Eisenhower 'aɪznˌhaʊə*
eisteddfod, -s [-au] aɪs'teðvɒd [-vəd]
  (Welsh əis'teðvod), -z [-aɪ] (-ai)
either 'aɪðə* ['iːðə*]
ejaculat|e, -es, -ing, -ed ɪ'dʒækjʊlert, -s,
  -ɪŋ, -ɪd
ejaculation, -s ɪˌdʒækjʊ'leɪʃn, -z
ejaculative ɪ'dʒækjʊlətɪv [-leɪt-]
ejaculatory ɪ'dʒækjʊlətərɪ [-leɪtərɪ]
eject (s.), -s 'iːdʒekt, -s
eject (v.), -s, -ing, -ed, -or/s; -ment/s
  ɪ'dʒekt [iː'dʒ-], -s, -ɪŋ, -ɪd, -ə*/z;
  -mənt/s
ejection, -s ɪ'dʒekʃn [iː'dʒ-], -z
ejective, -s ɪ'dʒektɪv [iː'dʒ-], -z
ek|e (v. adv.), -es, -ing, -ed iːk, -s, -ɪŋ, -t
Ekron 'ekrɒn
elabor|ate (adj.), -ately, -ateness
  ɪ'læbər|ət [-ɪt], -ətlɪ [-ɪtlɪ], -ətnɪs
  [-ɪt-, -nəs]
elaborat|e (v.), -es, -ing, -ed, -or/s
  ɪ'læbəreɪt, -s, -ɪŋ, -ɪd, -ə*/z
elaboration, -s ɪˌlæbə'reɪʃn, -z
elaborative ɪ'læbərətɪv [-reɪt-]
Elah 'iːlə
Elaine e'leɪn [ɪ'l-]
Elam, -ite/s 'iːləm, -aɪt/s
élan eɪ'lɑ̃ːŋ [-'lɔ̃ːŋ, -lɑːn] (elɑ̃)
eland (E.), -s 'iːlənd, -zˊ
elaps|e, -es, -ing, -ed ɪ'læps, -ɪz, -ɪŋ, -t
elastic, -s, -ally, -ate/d ɪ'læstɪk [-'lɑːs-],
  -s, -əlɪ, -eɪt/ɪd
elasticity ˌelæ'stɪsətɪ [ɪl-, ˌiːl-, -lə's-,
  -lɑː's-, -ɪtɪ]
Elastoplast ɪ'læstəʊplɑːst [iː'l-, e'l-,
  -plæst]
elat|e (adj. v.), -es, -ing, -ed/ly ɪ'leɪt, -s,
  -ɪŋ, -ɪd/lɪ
elation ɪ'leɪʃn

Elba 'elbə
Elbe elb
elbow (s. v.), -s, -ing, -ed 'elbəʊ, -z, -ɪŋ, -d
elbow-grease 'elbəʊgri:s
elbow-room 'elbəʊrʊm [-ru:m]
Elcho 'elkəʊ
elder (s. adj.), -s 'eldə*, -z
elder-berr|y, -ies 'eldə,ber|ɪ ['eldəbər-], -ɪz
elderl|y, -iness 'eldəl|ɪ, -ɪnɪs [-ɪnəs]
elder-wine ,eldə'waɪn ['---]
eldest 'eldɪst
Eldon 'eldən
El Dorado ,eldə'rɑːdəʊ [-dɒ'r-]
Eldred 'eldrɪd [-red]
Eldridge 'eldrɪdʒ
Eleanor 'elɪnə* [-lən-]
Eleanora ,elɪə'nɔːrə [-ljə-]
Eleazar ,elɪ'eɪzə*
elecampane, -s ,elɪkæm'peɪn, -z
elect (s. adj. v.), -s, -ing, -ed, -or/s; -ive/ly ɪ'lekt, -s, -ɪŋ, -ɪd, -ə*/z; -ɪv/lɪ
election, -s ɪ'lek∫n, -z
electioneer, -s, -ing, -ed, -er/s ɪ,lek∫ə'nɪə* [-∫n'ɪə*], -z, -rɪŋ, -d, -rə*/z
electoral ɪ'lektərəl
electorate, -s ɪ'lektərət [-ɪt], -s
Electra ɪ'lektrə
electric, -al, -ally ɪ'lektrɪk [ə'lek-], -l, -əlɪ
electrician, -s ,ɪlek'trɪ∫n [,elek-, ,i:lek-, ,elɪk-], -z
electricity ,ɪlek'trɪsətɪ [,elek-, ,i:lek-, ,elɪk-, -'trɪzə-, -'trɪzɪ-, -'trɪsɪ-]
electrification, -s ɪ,lektrɪfɪ'keɪ∫n, -z
electri|fy, -fies, -fying, -fied; -fiable ɪ'lektrɪ|faɪ, -faɪz, -faɪɪŋ, -faɪd; -faɪəbl
electro-biology ɪ,lektrəʊbaɪ'ɒlədʒɪ
electrocardio|gram/s, -graph/s ɪ,lektrəʊ'kɑːdɪəʊ|græm/z [-djəʊ-], -grɑːf/s [-græf/s]
electro-chemistry ɪ,lektrəʊ'kemɪstrɪ [-məstrɪ]
electrocut|e, -es, -ing, -ed ɪ'lektrəkju:t, -s, -ɪŋ, -ɪd
electrocution, -s ɪ,lektrə'kju:∫n, -z
electrode, -s ɪ'lektrəʊd, -z
electro-dynamic, -s ɪ,lektrəʊdaɪ'næmɪk [dɪ'n-], -s
electro-kinetics ɪ,lektrəʊkaɪ'netɪks
electrolier, -s ɪ,lektrəʊ'lɪə*, -z
electrolyz|e [-is|e], -es, -ing, -ed ɪ'lektrəʊlaɪz, -ɪz, -ɪŋ, -d
electrolys|is, -es, ,ɪlek'trɒləs|ɪs [,el-, ,i:l-, -lɪs-], -i:z
electrolyte, -s ɪ'lektrəʊlaɪt, -s
electrolytic ɪ,lektrəʊ'lɪtɪk

electro-magnet, -s, -ism ɪ,lektrəʊ'mæg-nɪt [ɪ'lektrəʊ,m-], -s, -ɪzəm
electro-magnetic ɪ,lektrəʊmæg'netɪk [-məg-]
electrometer, -s ,ɪlek'trɒmɪtə* [,el-, ,i:l-, -mətə*], -z
electromotive ɪ,lektrəʊ'məʊtɪv
electro-motor, -s ɪ,lektrəʊ'məʊtə* [ɪ'lektrəʊ,m-], -z
electron, -s ɪ'lektrɒn, -z
electronic, -s ,ɪlek'trɒnɪk [,el-, ,i:l-], -s
electrophone, -s ɪ'lektrəfəʊn, -z
electrophorus, -es ,ɪlek'trɒfərəs [,el-, ,i:l-], -ɪz
electroplat|e (s. v.), -es, -ing, -ed, -er/s ɪ'lektrəʊpleɪt [ɪ,lektrəʊ'p-], -s, -ɪŋ, -ɪd, -ə*/z
electro-polar ɪ,lektrəʊ'pəʊlə*
electro-positive ɪ,lektrəʊ'pɒzətɪv [-zɪt-]
electroscope, -s ɪ'lektrəskəʊp, -s
electrostatic, -s ɪ,lektrəʊ'stætɪk, -s
electro-therapeutic, -s ɪ,lektrəʊθerə-'pju:tɪk, -s
electro-therapy ɪ,lektrəʊ'θerəpɪ
electro-thermal ɪ,lektrəʊ'θɜːml
electrotype, -s ɪ'lektrəʊtaɪp, -s
electrum ɪ'lektrəm
electuar|y, -ies ɪ'lektjʊər|ɪ [-tjwər-], -ɪz
eleemosynary ,elɪiː'mɒsɪnərɪ [,elɪ:'m-, ,elɪ'm-, -'mɒzɪ-]
elegan|ce, -t/ly 'elɪgən|s, -t/lɪ
elegiac (s. adj.), -s, -al ,elɪ'dʒaɪək, -s, -l
elegist, -s 'elɪdʒɪst [-lədʒ-], -s
elegit ɪ'liːdʒɪt [e'l-]
elegiz|e [-is|e], -es, -ing, -ed 'elɪdʒaɪz [-lədʒ-], -ɪz, -ɪŋ, -d
eleg|y, -ies 'elɪdʒ|ɪ [-lədʒ-], -ɪz
element, -s 'elɪmənt [-ləm-], -s
element|al (s. adj.), -als, -ally ,elɪ-'ment|l [-lə'm-], -lz, -əlɪ
elementar|y, -ily, -iness ,elɪ'mentər|ɪ [-lə'm-], -əlɪ [-ɪlɪ], -ɪnɪs [-ɪnəs]
elemi 'elɪmɪ
elenchus ɪ'leŋkəs
Eleonora ,elɪə'nɔːrə [-ljə-]
elephant, -s 'elɪfənt [-ləf-], -s
elephantiasis ,elɪfən'taɪəsɪs [-ləf-, -fæn-]
elephantine ,elɪ'fæntaɪn [-lə'f-]
Eleusinian ,eljuː'sɪnɪən [-ljʊ-, -njən]
Eleusis e'ljuː:sɪs [ɪ'l-]
elevat|e, -es, -ing, -ed, -or/s; -ory 'elɪveɪt, -s, -ɪŋ, -ɪd, -ə*/z; -ərɪ
elevation, -s elɪ'veɪ∫n, -z
eleven, -s, -th/s ɪ'levn, -z, -θ/s
elevenish ɪ'levnɪ∫
eleven|pence, -penny ɪ'levn|pəns [-vm|p-], -pənɪ (see note under penny)

161

elevenses ɪ'levnzɪz

el|f, -ves el|f, -vz

elfin (s. adj.), -s 'elfɪn, -z

elfish 'elfɪʃ

elf|-land, -lock/s 'elf|lænd, -lɒk/s

Elfrida el'fri:də

Elgar 'elgə* [-gɑ:*]

Elgie 'eldʒɪ, 'elgɪ

Elgin 'elgɪn

Elham (in Kent) 'i:ləm

Eli 'i:laɪ

Elia 'i:ljə [-lɪə]

Eliab ɪ'laɪæb [e'l-, -'laɪəb]

Eliakim ɪ'laɪəkɪm [e'l-]

Elias ɪ'laɪəs [e'l-, -aɪæs]

Eliashow e'laɪəʃəʊ

Elibank 'elɪbæŋk

elicit, -s, -ing, -ed ɪ'lɪsɪt [e'l-], -s, -ɪŋ, -ɪd

elicitation ɪ,lɪsɪ'teɪʃn [e,l-]

elid|e, -es, -ing, -ed; -able ɪ'laɪd, -z, -ɪŋ, -ɪd; -əbl

Elie 'i:lɪ

Eliezer ,elɪ'i:zə*

eligibility ,elɪdʒə'bɪlətɪ [-dʒɪ'b-, -lɪt-]

eligib|le, -ly, -leness 'elɪdʒəb|l [-dʒɪb-], -lɪ, -lnɪs [-nəs]

Elihu ɪ'laɪhju: [e'l-]

Elijah ɪ'laɪdʒə

Eliman 'elɪmən

Elimelech ɪ'lɪmələk [e'l-]

eliminat|e, -es, -ing, -ed ɪ'lɪmɪneɪt [e'l-, -mən-], -s, -ɪŋ, -ɪd

elimination, -s, ɪ,lɪmɪ'neɪʃn [e,l-, -mə'n-], -z

Elinor 'elɪnə*

Eliot(t) 'eljət [-lɪət]

Eliphaz 'elɪfæz

Elis 'i:lɪs

Elisabeth ɪ'lɪzəbəθ

Elisha (prophet) ɪ'laɪʃə, (place in Northumberland) e'lɪʃə

elision, -s ɪ'lɪʒn, -z

Elissa ɪ'lɪsə

élite eɪ'li:t [ɪ'l-] (elit)

éliti|st, -sm eɪ'li:tɪ|st [ɪ'l-], -zəm

elixir, -s ɪ'lɪksə* [ė'l-], -z

Eliza ɪ'laɪzə

Elizabeth ɪ'lɪzəbəθ

Elizabethan, -s ɪ,lɪzə'bi:θn, -z

Elizabethian, -s ɪ,lɪzə'bi:θjən [-θɪən], -z

elk, -s elk, -s

Elkanah el'kɑ:nə [-'keɪn-]

Elkhart 'elkhɑ:t

Elkin 'elkɪn

Elkington 'elkɪŋtən

Elkins 'elkɪnz

ell, -s el, -z

Ella 'elə

Ellaline 'eləli:n

Ellam 'eləm

Elland, -un 'elənd, -ən

Ellangowan ,elən'gaʊən

Ellen, -borough 'elɪn, -bərə

Ellery 'elərɪ

Ellesmere 'elz,mɪə*

Ellet 'elɪt

Ellice 'elɪs

Ellicott 'elɪkət [-kɒt]

Elliman 'elɪmən

Ellingham (in Northumberland) 'elɪndʒəm, (surname) 'elŋəm

Elliot(t), -son 'eljət [-lɪət], -sn

ellipse, -s ɪ'lɪps, -ɪz

ellips|is, -es ɪ'lɪps|ɪs, -i:z

ellipsoid, -s ɪ'lɪpsɔɪd, -z

ellipsoidal ,elɪp'sɔɪdl [ɪlɪp's-]

elliptic, -al, -ally ɪ'lɪptɪk, -l, -əlɪ

ellipticity ,elɪp'tɪsətɪ [,ɪlɪp't-, -ɪtɪ]

Ellis, -on, -ton 'elɪs, -n, -tən

Ellsworth 'elzwз:θ [-wəθ]

Ellwood 'elwʊd

elm (E.), -s elm, -z

Elmes elmz

Elmhurst 'elmhз:st

Elmina el'mi:nə

Elmo 'elməʊ

Elmore 'elmɔ:* [-mɔə*]

Elmsley 'elmzlɪ

Elmwood 'elmwʊd

elocution ,elə'kju:ʃn

elocutionary ,elə'kju:ʃŋərɪ [-ʃənərɪ, -ʃnərɪ]

elocutionist, -s ,elə'kju:ʃŋɪst [-ʃənɪst, -ʃnɪst], -s

Elohim e'ləʊhɪm

Eloi i:'ləʊaɪ ['i:ləʊaɪ, 'i:lɔɪ]

Eloisa ,eləʊ'i:zə [-'i:sə]

elongat|e, -es, -ing, -ed 'i:lɒŋgeɪt, -s, -ɪŋ, -ɪd

elongation, -s ,i:lɒŋ'geɪʃn, -z

elop|e, -es, -ing, -ed, -ement/s ɪ'ləʊp, -s, -ɪŋ, -t, -mənt/s

eloquen|ce, -t/ly 'eləkwən|s, -t/lɪ

Elphin, -ston(e) 'elfɪn, -stən

Elsa (English name) 'elsə, (German name) 'elzə ('elza:)

else, -'s els, -ɪz

elsewhere ,els'weə* [-s'hw-]

Elsie 'elsɪ

Elsinore ,elsɪ'nɔ:* [-'nɔə*, '—]

Note.—The stressing ,--'- has to be used in Shakespeare's 'Hamlet'.

Elsmere 'elz,mɪə*

Elspeth 'elspəθ [-peθ]

Elstree 'elstri: ['elz-, -trɪ]

162

Elswick 'elsɪk, 'elzɪk, 'elzwɪk
*Note.—*Elswick *in Tyne and Wear is
locally* 'elsɪk *or* 'elzɪk.
Elsworthy 'elz‚wə:ðɪ
Eltham (*in S. London*) 'eltəm
Elton 'eltən
elucidat|e, -es, -ing, -ed, -or/s
ɪ'lu:sɪdeɪt [-'lju:-], -s, -ɪŋ, -ɪd, -ə*/z
elucidation, -s ɪ‚lu:sɪ'deɪʃn [-‚lju:-], -z
elucidative ɪ'lu:sɪdeɪtɪv [-'lju:-, -dət-]
elucidatory ɪ'lu:sɪdeɪtərɪ [-'lju:-]
elud|e, -es, -ing, -ed ɪ'lu:d [-'lju:d], -z,
-ɪŋ, -ɪd
elusion, -s ɪ'lu:ʒn [-'lju:-], -z
elusive, -ly, -ness ɪ'lu:sɪv [-'lju:-], -lɪ,
-nɪs [-nəs]
elusory ɪ'lu:sərɪ [-'lju:-]
elvan 'elvən
Elvedon (*in Suffolk*) 'elvdən ['eldən]
elver, -s 'elvə*, -z
elves (*plur. of* elf) elvz
Elv|ey, -in 'elvɪ|ɪ, -ɪn
Elvira el'vaɪərə, el'vɪərə
elvish 'elvɪʃ
Elwes 'elwɪz [-wez]
Ely 'i:lɪ
Elyot 'eljət [-lɪət]
Elysi|an, -um ɪ'lɪzɪ|ən [-zj|-], -əm
elzevir (E.) 'elzɪ‚vɪə* [-zə‚v-]
em, -s em, -z
'em (*weak form of* them) əm [m]
emaciat|e, -es, -ing, -ed ɪ'meɪʃɪeɪt [e'm-,
-'meɪʃjeɪt, -'meɪsɪeɪt, -'meɪsjeɪt,
-'mæsɪeɪt], -s, -ɪŋ, -ɪd
emaciation ɪ‚meɪsɪ'eɪʃn [e‚m-, -‚meɪʃɪ-,
-‚mæsɪ-]
emanat|e, -es, -ing, -ed; -ive 'eməneɪt
[*rarely* 'i:m-], -s, -ɪŋ, -ɪd; -ɪv
emanation, -s ‚emə'neɪʃn [*rarely*
‚i:m-], -z
emancipat|e, -s, -ing, -ed, -or/s
ɪ'mænsɪpeɪt [e'm-], -s, -ɪŋ, -ɪd, -ə*/z
emancipation, -s ɪ‚mænsɪ'peɪʃn [e‚m-],
-z
Emanuel ɪ'mænjʊəl [e'm-, -njwəl,
-njʊel]
emasculate (*adj.*) ɪ'mæskjʊlɪt [-lət]
emasculat|e (*v.*), -es, -ing, -ed, -or/s
ɪ'mæskjʊleɪt, -s, -ɪŋ, -ɪd, -ə*/z
emasculation, -s ɪ‚mæskjʊ'leɪʃn, -z
Emaus 'emɔ:s
embalm, -s, -ing, -ed, -er/s, -ment/s
ɪm'bɑ:m [em-], -z, -ɪŋ, -d, -ə*/z,
-mənt/s
embank, -s, -ing, -ed, -ment/s ɪm-
'bæŋk [em-], -s, -ɪŋ, -t [-'bæŋt],
-mənt/s
embarcation, -s ‚embɑ:'keɪʃn, -z

embargo (*s.*), -s em'bɑ:gəʊ [ɪm-], -z
embargo (*v.*), -es, -ing, -ed em'bɑ:gəʊ
[ɪm-], -z, -ɪŋ, -d
embark, -s, -ing, -ed ɪm'bɑ:k [em-], -s,
-ɪŋ, -t
embarkation, -s ‚embɑ:'keɪʃn, -z
embarrass, -es, -ing, -ed, -ment/s ɪm-
'bærəs [em-], -ɪz, -ɪŋ, -t, -mənt/s
embass|y, -ies 'embəs|ɪ, -ɪz
embatt|le, -les, -ling, -led ɪm'bæt|l
[em-], -lz, -lɪŋ [-lɪ̩ŋ], -ld
embay, -s, -ing, -ed ɪm'beɪ [em-], -z, -ɪŋ,
-d
embed, -s, -ding, -ded, -ment ɪm'bed
[em-], -z, -ɪŋ, -ɪd, -mənt
embellish, -es, -ing, -ed, -er/s, -ment/s
ɪm'belɪʃ, -ɪz, -ɪŋ, -t, -ə*/z, -mənt/s
ember, -s 'embə*, -z
Ember|-day/s, -week/s 'embə|deɪ/z,
-wi:k/s
embezz|le, -les, -ling, -led, -ler/s,
-lement/s ɪm'bez|l [em-], -lz, -lɪŋ
[-lɪ̩ŋ], -ld, -lə*/z [-lə*/z], -lmənt/s
embitter, -s, -ing, -ed, -er/s, -ment
ɪm'bɪtə* [em-], -z, -rɪŋ, -d, -rə*/z,
-mənt
emblaz|on, -ons, -oning, -oned,
-onment/s; -onry ɪm'bleɪz|n [em-],
-nz, -n̩ɪŋ [-nɪŋ], -nd, -nmənt/s; -nrɪ
emblem, -s 'embləm [-lem, -lɪm], -z
emblematic, -al, -ally ‚emblə'mætɪk
[-lɪ'm-], -l, -əlɪ
emblematiz|e [-is|e], -es, -ing, -ed
em'blemətaɪz ['emblem-], -ɪz, -ɪŋ, -d
emblement, -s 'emblmənt, -s
embod|y, -ies, -ying, -ied, -iment/s
ɪm'bɒd|ɪ [em-], -ɪz, -ɪŋ, -ɪd, -ɪmənt/s
embold|en, -ens, -ening, -ened ɪm-
'bəʊld|ən [em-], -ənz, -n̩ɪŋ [-nɪŋ],
-ənd
embolism, -s 'embəlɪzəm, -z
embonpoint‚ɔ̃:mbɔ̃:m'pwæ:ŋ [‚ɒmbɒm-,
-'pwɑ:ŋ, -'pwɒŋ, -'pwæŋ] (ãbɔ̃pwɛ̃)
embosom, -s, -ing, -ed ɪm'bʊzəm
[em-], -z, -ɪŋ, -d
emboss, -es, -ing, -ed, -er/s, -ment/s
ɪm'bɒs [em-], -ɪz, -ɪŋ, -t, -ə*/z,
-mənt/s
embouchure, -s 'ɑ:mbu:ʃʊə* ['ɒm-, ‚--'-,
-'ʃjʊə*] (ãbuʃy:r), -z
emb|owel, -owels, -owelling, -owelled
ɪm'b|aʊəl [em-, -aʊl], -aʊəlz, -aʊəlɪŋ,
-aʊəld [-aʊld]
embower, -s, -ing, -ed ɪm'baʊə* [em-],
-z, -rɪŋ, -d
embrac|e (*s. v.*), -es, -ing, -ed, -er/s,
-ement ɪm'breɪs [em-], -ɪz, -ɪŋ, -t,
-ə*/z, -mənt

163

embranchment, -s ɪmˈbrɑːntʃmənt [em-], -s

embrasure, -s ɪmˈbreɪʒə* [em-, -ˌʒjʊə, -ˌʒʊə*], -z

embrocat|e, -es, -ing, -ed ˈembrəʊkeɪt, -s, -ɪŋ, -ɪd

embrocation, -s ˌembrəʊˈkeɪʃn, -z

embroglio, -s emˈbrəʊljəʊ [ɪm-, -lɪəʊ], -z

embroid|er, -ers, -ering, -ered, -erer/s ɪmˈbrɔɪd|ə* [em-], -əz, -ərɪŋ, -əd, -ərə*/z

embroider|y, -ies ɪmˈbrɔɪdər|ɪ [em-], -ɪz

embroil, -s, -ing, -ed, -ment/s ɪmˈbrɔɪl [em-], -z, -ɪŋ, -d, -mənt/s

embryo, -s ˈembrɪəʊ, -z

embryolog|ist/s, -y ˌembrɪˈɒlədʒ|ɪst/s, -ɪ

embry|on, -ons, -a ˈembrɪ|ɒn [-ən], -ɒnz [-ənz], -ə

embryonic ˌembrɪˈɒnɪk

Embury ˈembərɪ

Emeer, -s eˈmɪə* [ɪˈm-, ˈeˌmɪə*], -z

Emeline ˈemɪliːn

emend, -s, -ing, -ed; -able ɪˈmend [iːˈm-], -z, -ɪŋ, -ɪd; -əbl

emendat|e, -es, -ing, -ed, -or/s ˈiːmendeɪt, -s, -ɪŋ, -ɪd, -ə*/z

emendation, -s ˌiːmenˈdeɪʃn, -z

emendatory ɪˈmendətərɪ [iːˈm-]

emerald, -s ˈemərəld [ˈemrəld], -z

emerg|e, -es, -ing, -ed ɪˈmɜːdʒ, -ɪz, -ɪŋ, -d

emergen|ce, -t/ly iːˈmɜːdʒən|s [ɪˈm-], -t/lɪ

emergenc|y, -ies ɪˈmɜːdʒəns|ɪ, -ɪz

emeritus ɪˈmerɪtəs [iːˈm-]

emersion, -s ɪˈmɜːʃn [iːˈm-], -z

Emerson ˈeməsn

emery (E.), -paper/s, -powder, -wheel/s ˈemərɪ, -ˌpeɪpə*/z, -ˌpaʊdə*, -wiːl/z [-hw-]

emesis ˈemɪsɪs

emetic (s. adj.), -s, -al, -ally ɪˈmetɪk, -s, -l, -əlɪ

émeute, -s eɪˈmɜːt (emøːt), -s

emigrant (s. adj.), -s ˈemɪɡrənt, -s

emigrate, -es, -ing, -ed, -or/s ˈemɪɡreɪt, -s, -ɪŋ, -ɪd, -ə*/z

emigration, -s ˌemɪˈɡreɪʃn, -z

emigratory ˈemɪɡrətərɪ [-ɡreɪt-]

émigré, -s ˈemɪɡreɪ, -z

Emilia ɪˈmɪlɪə [-ljə]

Emily ˈemɪlɪ [-məlɪ]

eminen|ce, -ces, -cy, -t/ly ˈemɪnən|s, -sɪz, -sɪ, -t/lɪ

Emir, -s eˈmɪə* [ɪˈm-, ˈeˌmɪə*], -z

emirate, -s eˈmɪərət [ɪˈm-, ˈeˌmɪər-, -rɪt, -reɪt], -s

emissar|y (s. adj.), -ies ˈemɪsər|ɪ, -ɪz

emission -s ɪˈmɪʃn [iːˈm-], -z

emissive ɪˈmɪsɪv [iːˈm-]

emit, -s, -ting, -ted, -ter/s ɪˈmɪt [iːˈm-], -s, -ɪŋ, -ɪd, -ə*/z

emitter-valve, -s ɪˈmɪtəvælv [iːˈm-], -z

Emley ˈemlɪ

Emma ˈemə

Emmanuel (biblical name) ɪˈmænjʊəl [eˈm, -jwəl, -jʊel], (Cambridge college) ɪˈmænjʊəl [-njʊl]

Emmaus eˈmeɪəs

Emmeline ˈemɪliːn

emmet (E.), -s ˈemɪt, -s

Emm|ie, -y ˈem|ɪ, -ɪ

emollient (s. adj.), -s ɪˈmɒlɪənt [eˈm-, -ljənt], -s

emolument, -s ɪˈmɒljʊmənt [eˈm-], -s

Emory ˈemərɪ

emotion, -s; -less ɪˈməʊʃn, -z; -lɪs [-ləs]

emo|tional, -tionally ɪˈməʊ|ʃənl [-ʃnəl, -ʃn̩l, -ʃnl, -ʃənəl], -ʃnəlɪ [-ʃnəlɪ, -ʃn̩lɪ, -ʃnlɪ, -ʃənəlɪ]

emotionalism ɪˈməʊʃnəlɪzəm [-ʃnəl-, -ʃn̩l-, -ʃnl-, -ʃənəl-]

emotive ɪˈməʊtɪv

empan|el, -els, -elling, -elled, -elment/s ɪmˈpæn|l [em-], -lz, -lɪŋ, -ld, -lmənt/s

†empathy ˈempəθɪ

Empedocles emˈpedəʊkliːz

emperor, -s ˈempərə*, -z

emphasis ˈemfəsɪs

emphasiz|e [-is|e], -es, -ing, -ed ˈemfəsaɪz, -ɪz, -ɪŋ, -d

emphatic, -al, -ally, -alness ɪmˈfætɪk [em-], -l, -əlɪ, -lnɪs [-nəs]

emphysema, -s ˌemfɪˈsiːmə, -z

empire, -s ˈempaɪə*, -z

empiric (s. adj.) -s, -al, -ally ɪmˈpɪrɪk [em-], -s, -l, -əlɪ

empirici|sm, -st/s ɪmˈpɪrɪsɪ|zəm [em-], -st/s

emplacement, -s ɪmˈpleɪsmənt [em-], -s

employ (s. v.), -s, -ing, -ed, -er/s, -ment/s; -able ɪmˈplɔɪ [em-], -z, -ɪŋ, -d, -ə*/z, -mənt/s; -əbl

employé, -s ɒmˈplɔɪeɪ [ɔ̃ːm-] (ɑ̃plwaje), -z

employee, -s ˌemplɔɪˈiː [emˈplɔɪː, ɪmˈplɔɪː], -z

emporium, -s emˈpɔːrɪəm [ɪmˈp-], -z

empower, -s, -ing, -ed ɪmˈpaʊə* [em-], -z, -rɪŋ, -d

164

empress, -es 'emprɪs [-rəs], -ɪz
Empson 'empsn
emption 'empʃn
empt|y (s. adj. v.), -ier, -iest, -ily,
-iness; -ies, -ying, -ied 'empti|ɪ, -ɪə*
[-jə*], -ɪɪst [-jɪst], -ɪlɪ [-əlɪ], -ɪnɪs
[-ɪnəs]; -ɪz, -ɪŋ [-jɪŋ], -ɪd
empty-handed ˌempti'hændɪd
empyema ˌempaɪ'iːmə
empyrea|l, -n ˌempaɪ'riːə|l [-pɪ'r-, -'rɪə|l,
em'pɪrɪə-], -n
Emsworth 'emzwəθ [-wɜ:θ]
emu, -s 'iːmjuː, -z
emulat|e, -es, -ing, -ed, -or/s 'emjʊleɪt,
-s, -ɪŋ, -ɪd, -ə*/z
emulation ˌemjʊ'leɪʃn
emulative 'emjʊlətɪv [-leɪt-]
emulous, -ly 'emjʊləs, -lɪ
emulsi|fy, -fies, -fying, -fied ɪ'mʌlsɪ|faɪ,
-faɪz, -faɪɪŋ, -faɪd
emulsion, -s ɪ'mʌlʃn, -z
emunctor|y (s. adj.), -ies ɪ'mʌŋktər|ɪ,
-ɪz
enab|le, -les, -ling, -led ɪ'neɪb|l [e'n-],
-lz, -lɪŋ [-lɪŋ], -ld
enact, -s, -ing, -ed, -or/s, -ment/s;
-ive ɪ'nækt [e'n-], -s, -ɪŋ, -ɪd, -ə*/z,
-mənt/s; -ɪv
enam|el (s. v.), -els, -elling, -elled,
-eller/s, -ellist/s ɪ'næm|l, -lz, -lɪŋ
[-əlɪŋ], -ld, -lə*/z [-ələ*/z], -lɪst/s
[-əlɪst/s]
enamour, -s, -ing, -ed ɪ'næmə* [e'n-],
-z, -rɪŋ, -d
Encaenia en'siːnjə [-nɪə]
encag|e, -es, -ing, -ed ɪn'keɪdʒ [ɪŋ-,
en-], -ɪz, -ɪŋ, -d
encamp, -s, -ing, -ed, -ment/s ɪn'kæmp
[ɪŋ-, en-], -s, -ɪŋ, -t [-'kæmt], -mənt/s
encas|e, -es, -ing, -ed, -ement/s ɪn'keɪs
[ɪŋ-, en-], -ɪz, -ɪŋ, -t, -mənt/s
encaustic (s. adj.), -s, -ally en'kɔːstɪk,
-s, -əlɪ
enceinte (s. adj.), -s ãːŋ'sæːnt
[ãːn'sæːnt, ɔːŋ'sæːnt, ɔːn'sæːnt,
aːn'sænt, ɒn'sænt] (ãsæ̃ːt), -s
Enceladus en'selədəs
encephalic ˌenkə'fælɪk [ˌenkɪ'f-, eŋk-,
ˌense'f-, ˌensɪ'f-]
encephalitis ˌenkefə'laɪtɪs [ˌenkɪf-,
en,kef-, eŋ,k-, ˌensef-, en,sef-]
encephalogram, -s en'sefələʊgræm
[ɪn's-, en'k-, eŋ'k-, ɪn'k-, ŋ'k-], -z
encephalograph, -s en'sefələʊgrɑːf
[ɪn's-, en'k-, eŋ'k-, ɪn'k-, ŋ'k-,
-græf], -s
enchain, -s, -ing, -ed, -ment ɪn'tʃeɪn
[en-], -z, -ɪŋ, -d, -mənt

enchant, -s, -ing, -ed, -er/s, -ress/es,
-ment/s ɪn'tʃɑːnt [en-], -s, -ɪŋ, -ɪd,
-ə*/z, -rɪs/ɪz, -mənt/s
enchiridion, -s ˌenkaɪə'rɪdɪən [ˌeŋk-,
-dɪɒn], -z
encirc|le, -les, -ling, -led, -lement/s
ɪn'sɜ:k|l [en-], -lz, -lɪŋ, -ld, -lmənt/s
Encke 'eŋkə
enclasp, -s, -ing, -ed ɪn'klɑːsp [ɪŋ-,
en-], -s, -ɪŋ, -t
enclave, -s 'enkleɪv ['eŋ-, -'-], -z
enclitic (s. adj.), -s, -ally ɪn'klɪtɪk [ɪŋ-,
en-], -s, -əlɪ
enclos|e, -es, -ing, -ed, -er/s ɪn'kləʊz
[ɪŋ-, en-], -ɪz, -ɪŋ, -d, -ə*/z
enclosure, -s ɪn'kləʊʒə* [ɪŋ-, en-, eŋ-], -z
encod|e, -es, -ing, -ed, -er/s en'kəʊd
[ˌen-, eŋ-, ɪŋ-], -z, -ɪŋ, -ɪd, -ə*/z
encom|iast/s, -ium/s en'kəʊm|ɪæst/s
[eŋ-], -jəm/z [-ɪəm/z]
encompass, -es, -ing, -ed ɪn'kʌmpəs
[ɪŋ-, en-], -ɪz, -ɪŋ, -t
encore (s. v.), -es, -ing, -ed 'ɒŋkɔ:* ['ɑ:ŋ-,
-kɔə*, -'-], -z, -rɪŋ, -d
encore (interj.) ɒŋ'kɔ:* [-'kɔə*]
encount|er (s. v.), -ers, -ering, -ered ɪn-
'kaʊnt|ə* [ɪŋ-, en-], -əz, -ərɪŋ, -əd
encourag|e, -es, -ing/ly, -ed, -er/s,
-ement/s ɪn'kʌrɪdʒ [ɪŋ-, en-], -ɪz,
-ɪŋ/lɪ, -d, -ə*/z, -mənt/s
encroach, -es, -ing/ly, -ed, -er/s,
-ment/s ɪn'krəʊtʃ [ɪŋ-, en-], -ɪz,
-ɪŋ/lɪ, -t, -ə*/z, -mənt/s
encrust, -s, -ing, -ed ɪn'krʌst [ɪŋ-, en-],
-s, -ɪŋ, -ɪd
encumb|er, -ers, -ering, -ered ɪn'kʌm-
b|ə* [ɪŋ-, en-], -əz, -ərɪŋ, -əd
encumbrance, -s ɪn'kʌmbrəns [ɪŋ-, en-],
-ɪz
encyclic, -s, -al/s ɪn'sɪklɪk [en-], -s,
-l/z
encyclop(a)edia, -s, -n ɪnˌsaɪkləʊ'piːdjə
[enˌsaɪk-, ˌensaɪk-, -klʊ'p-, -dɪə], -z,
-n
encyclop(a)edic, -al ɪnˌsaɪkləʊ'piːdɪk
[enˌsaɪk-, ˌensaɪk-, -klʊ'p-], -l
encyclop(a)ed|ism, -st/s ɪnˌsaɪkləʊ'piː-
dɪ|zəm [enˌsaɪk-, ˌensaɪk-,
-klʊ'p-], -st/s
end (s. v.), -s, -ing, -ed end, -z, -ɪŋ, -ɪd
endang|er, -ers, -ering, -ered, -erer/s,
-erment ɪn'deɪndʒ|ə* [en-], -əz, -ərɪŋ,
-əd, -ərə*/z, -əmənt
endear, -s, -ing, -ed, -ment ɪn'dɪə*
[en-], -z, -rɪŋ, -d, -mənt
endeav|our (s.v.), -ours, -ouring, -oured
ɪn'dev|ə*, -əz, -ərɪŋ, -əd
Endell 'endl

165

endemic (s. adj.), -s, -al, -ally, en-'demɪk, -s, -l, -əlɪ

Enderby 'endəbɪ

endermic, -al, -ally en'də:mɪk, -l, -əlɪ

Endicott 'endɪkət [-kɒt]

ending (s.), -s 'endɪŋ, -z

endive, -s 'endɪv, -z

endless, -ly, -ness 'endlɪs [-ləs], -lɪ, -nɪs [-nəs]

endlong 'endlɒŋ

endmost 'endməʊst

endocrine 'endəʊkraɪn

endogamy en'dɒgəmɪ

Endor 'endɔ:*

endors|e, -es, -ing, -ed, -er/s, -ement/s, -able ɪn'dɔ:s [en-], -ɪz, -ɪŋ, -t, -ə*/z, -mənt/s; -əbl

endorsee, -s ˌendɔ:'si:, -z

endow, -s, -ing, -ed, -ment/s ɪn'daʊ [en-], -z, -ɪŋ, -d, -mənt/s

endower, -s ɪn'daʊə* [en-], -z

end-product, -s 'endˌprɒdʌkt [-dəkt, ˌ-'—], -s

endu|e, -es, -ing, -ed ɪn'dju: [en-], -z, -ɪŋ [-'djʊŋ], -d

endurab|le, -ly, -leness ɪn'djʊərəb|l [en-, -'djɔər-, -'djɔ:r-], -lɪ, -lnɪs [-nəs]

endur|e, -es, -ing, -ed, -er/s; -ance ɪn'djʊə* [en-, -'djɔə*, -'djɔ:*], -z, -rɪŋ, -d, -rə*/z; -rəns

end|ways, -wise 'end|weɪz, -waɪz

Endymion en'dɪmɪən [-mjən]

Eneas i:'ni:æs [ɪ'n-, 'i:nɪæs, -əs]

Eneid 'i:nɪɪd [njɪd, ɪ'ni:ɪd]

enema, -s 'enɪmə ['enə-, ɪ'ni:mə], -z

enem|y, -ies 'enəm|ɪ [-nɪm-], -ɪz

energetic, -al, -ally ˌenə'dʒetɪk, -l, -əlɪ

energiz|e [-is|e], -es, -ing, -ed, -er/s 'enədʒaɪz, -ɪz, -ɪŋ, -d, -ə*/z

energumen, -s ˌenə:'gju:men, -z

energ|y, -ies 'enədʒ|ɪ, -ɪz

enervat|e, -es, -ing, -ed 'enə:veɪt [-nəv-], -s, -ɪŋ, -ɪd

enervation ˌenə:'veɪʃn [-nə'v-]

enfeeb|le, -les, -ling, -led, -lement ɪn-'fi:b|l [en-], -lz, -lɪŋ [-lŋ], -ld, -lmənt

enfeoff, -s, -ing, -ed, -ment/s ɪn'fi:f [en-, -'fef], -s, -ɪŋ, -t, -mənt/s

Enfield 'enfi:ld

enfilad|e (s. v.), -es, -ing, -ed ˌenfɪ'leɪd, -z, -ɪŋ, -ɪd

enfold, -s, -ing, -ed, -ment ɪn'fəʊld [en-], -z, -ɪŋ, -ɪd, -mənt

enforc|e, -es, -ing, -ed, -edly, -ement ɪn'fɔ:s [en-], -ɪz, -ɪŋ, -t, -ɪdlɪ, -mənt

enfranchis|e, -es, -ing, -ed ɪn'fræntʃaɪz [en-], -ɪz, -ɪŋ, -d

enfranchisement, -s ɪn'fræntʃɪzmənt [en-], -s

Engadine 'eŋgədi:n

engag|e, -es, -ing/ly, -ed, -er/s, -ement/s ɪn'geɪdʒ [ŋ-, en-], -ɪz, -ɪŋ/lɪ, -d, -ə*/z, -mənt/s

Engedi en'gi:dɪ [eŋ'g-, -'geđ-]

engend|er, -ers, -ering, -ered ɪn'dʒen-d|ə* [en-], -əz, -ərɪŋ, -əd

engin|e (s. v.), -es, -ing, -ed; -ery 'endʒɪn, -z, -ɪŋ, -d; -ərɪ

engine-driver, -s 'endʒɪnˌdraɪvə*, -z

engineer (s. v.), -s, -ing, -ed ˌen-dʒɪ'nɪə* [-dʒə-], -z, -rɪŋ, -d

engird, -s, -ing, -ed ɪn'gɜ:d [ɪŋ-, en-], -z, -ɪŋ, -ɪd

England, -er/s 'ɪŋglənd [-ŋl-, rarely 'eŋ-], -ə*/z

Engledow 'eŋgldaʊ

Engle|field, -wood 'eŋgl|fi:ld, -wʊd

English 'ɪŋglɪʃ [-ŋl-, rarely 'eŋ-]

english, -es, -ing, -ed 'ɪŋglɪʃ [-ŋl-, rarely 'eŋ-], -ɪz, -ɪŋ, -t

English|man, -men 'ɪŋglɪʃ|mən [-ŋl-, rarely 'eŋ-], -mən [-men]

Englishry 'ɪŋglɪʃrɪ [-ŋl-, rarely 'eŋ-]

English|woman, -women 'ɪŋglɪʃ|-ˌwʊmən [-ŋl-, rarely 'eŋ-], -ˌwɪmɪn

engraft, -s, -ing, -ed, -ment ɪn'grɑ:ft [ŋ-, en-], -s, -ɪŋ, -ɪd, -mənt

engrailed ɪn'greɪld [ŋ-, en-]

engrain, -s, -ing, -ed ɪn'greɪn [ŋ-, en-], -z, -ɪŋ, -d

engrav|e, -es, -ing/s, -ed, -er/s; -ery ɪn'greɪv [ŋ-, en-], -z, -ɪŋ/z, -d, -ə*/z; -ərɪ

engross, -es, -ing, -ed, -er/s, -ment/s ɪn'grəʊs [ŋ-, en-], -ɪz, -ɪŋ, -t, -ə*/z, -mənt/s

engulf, -s, -ing, -ed, -ment ɪn'gʌlf [ŋ-, en-], -s, -ɪŋ, -t, -mənt

enhan|ce, -es, -ing, -ed, -ement/s ɪn-'hɑ:ns [en-, -'hæns], -ɪz, -ɪŋ, -t, -mənt/s

enharmonic, -al, -ally ˌenhɑ:'mɒnɪk, -l, -əlɪ

Enid 'i:nɪd

enigma, -s ɪ'nɪgmə [e'n-], -z

enigmatic, -al, -ally ˌenɪg'mætɪk, -l, -əlɪ

enigmatist, -s ɪ'nɪgmətɪst [e'n-], -s

enigmatiz|e [-is|e], -es, -ing, -ed ɪ'nɪgmətaɪz [e'n-], -ɪz, -ɪŋ, -d

Enim 'i:nɪm

enjambment, -s ɪn'dʒæmbmənt [en-], -s

enjoin, -s, -ing, -ed, -er/s ɪn'dʒɔɪn [en-], -z, -ɪŋ, -d, -ə*/z

enjoy, -s, -ing, -ed, -er/s, -ment/s
ɪn'dʒɔɪ [en-], -z, -ɪŋ, -d, -ə*/z,
-mənt/s
enjoyab|le, -ly, -leness ɪn'dʒɔɪəb|l [en-],
-lɪ, -lnɪs [-nəs]
enkind|le, -les, -ling, -led ɪn'kɪnd|l
[en-], -lz, -lɪŋ, -ld
enlac|e, -es, -ing, -ed, -ement/s ɪn'leɪs
[en-], -ɪz, -ɪŋ, -t, -mənt/s
enlarg|e, -es, -ing, -ed, -er/s, -ement/s
ɪn'lɑːdʒ [en-], -ɪz, -ɪŋ, -d, -ə*/z,
-mənt/s
enlight|en, -ens, -ening, -ened,
-enment ɪn'laɪt|n [en-], -nz, -ŋɪŋ
[-nɪŋ], -nd, -nmənt
enlist, -s, -ing, -ed, -ment/s ɪn'lɪst [en-],
-s, -ɪŋ, -ɪd, -mənt/s
enliv|en, -ens, -ening, -ened, -ener/s
ɪn'laɪv|n [en-], -nz, -ŋɪŋ [-nɪŋ], -nd,
-ŋə*/z [-nə*/z]
en masse ɑ̃ː'mæs [ɔ̃ː'm-, ɑː'n-, ɒn-]
(ɑ̃mɑs)
enmesh, -es, -ing, -ed ɪn'meʃ [en-], -ɪz,
-ɪŋ, -t
enmit|y, -ies 'enmət|ɪ [-mɪt|-], -ɪz
Ennis 'enɪs
Enniscorthy ˌenɪs'kɔːθɪ
Enniskillen ˌenɪs'kɪlən [-lɪn]
Ennius 'enɪəs [-njəs]
ennob|le, -les, -ling, -led, -lement
ɪ'nəʊb|l [e'n-], -lz, -lɪŋ, -ld, -lmənt
ennui ɑ̃ː'nwiː [ɔ̃ː'n-, ɑː'n-, ɒ'n-, '--]
(ɑ̃nɥi)
Eno, -'s 'iːnəʊ, -z
Enoch 'iːnɒk
enormit|y, -ies ɪ'nɔːmət|ɪ [-ɪt|ɪ], -ɪz
enormous, -ly, -ness ɪ'nɔːməs, -lɪ, -nɪs
[-nəs]
Enos 'iːnɒs
enough ɪ'nʌf [ə'nʌf, ŋ'ʌf]
enounc|e, -es, -ing, -ed iː'naʊns [ɪ'n-],
-ɪz, -ɪŋ, -t
enow ɪ'naʊ
en passant ɑ̃ː'pæsɑ̃ːŋ [ɔ̃ː'mˈpæsɔ̃ːŋ,
ɑːm'pæsɑːŋ, ɒm'pæsɒŋ, -'pɑːs-, ˌ--'-]
(ɑ̃pasɑ̃)
enquir|e, -es, -ing, -ed, -er/s ɪn'kwaɪə*
[ɪŋ-, en-], -z, -rɪŋ, -d, -rə*/z
enquir|y, -ies ɪn'kwaɪər|ɪ [ɪŋ-, en-], -ɪz
enrag|e, -es, -ing, -ed ɪn'reɪdʒ [en-], -ɪz,
-ɪŋ, -d
enrapt ɪn'ræpt [en-]
enrapt|ure, -ures, -uring, -ured ɪn'ræp-
tʃ|ə* [en-], -əz, -ərɪŋ, -əd
enregist|er, -ers, -ering, -ered ɪn-
'redʒɪst|ə* [en-], -əz, -ərɪŋ, -əd
enrich, -es, -ing, -ed, -ment ɪn'rɪtʃ
[en-], -ɪz, -ɪŋ, -t, -mənt

enrob|e, -es, -ing, -ed ɪn'rəʊb [en-], -z,
-ɪŋ, -d
enrol, -s, -ling, -led, -ment/s ɪn'rəʊl
[en-], -z, -ɪŋ, -d, -mənt/s
en route ɑ̃ː'nˈruːt [ɔ̃ː'r-, ɑː'r-, ɒn'r-]
(ɑ̃rut)
en|s, -tia en|z, -ʃɪə [-ʃjə, -tɪə, -tjə]
ensample, -s en'sɑːmpl, -z
ensanguined ɪn'sæŋgwɪnd [en-]
ensconc|e, -es, -ing, -ed ɪn'skɒns [en-],
-ɪz, -ɪŋ, -t
ensemble, -s ɑ̃ː'nˈsɑː*mbl [ɔ̃ː'nˈsɔː*mbl,
ɑː'nˈsɑː*mbl, ɒn'sɒmbl] (ɑ̃sɑ̃ː*bl), -z
enshrin|e, -es, -ing, -ed, -ement ɪn-
'ʃraɪn [en-], -z, -ɪŋ, -d, -mənt
enshroud, -s, -ing, -ed ɪn'ʃraʊd [en-],
-z, -ɪŋ, -ɪd
ensign (flag), -s 'ensaɪn [in the navy
'ensn], -z
ensign (officer), -s; -cy, -cies, -ship/s
'ensaɪn, -z; -sɪ, -sɪz, -ʃɪp/s
ensign (v.), -s, -ing, -ed en'saɪn [ɪn-], -z,
-ɪŋ, -d
ensilage 'ensɪlɪdʒ
enslav|e, -es, -ing, -ed, -er/s, -ement
ɪn'sleɪv [en-], -z, -ɪŋ, -d, -ə*/z, -mənt
ensnar|e, -es, -ing, -ed, -er/s ɪn'sneə*
[en-], -z, -rɪŋ, -d, -rə*/z
ensoul, -s, -ing, -ed ɪn'səʊl [en-], -z, -ɪŋ,
-d
ensu|e, -es, -ing, -ed ɪn'sjuː [en-, -'suː],
-z, -ɪŋ [-'sjʊɪŋ, -'sʊɪŋ], -d
ensur|e, -es, -ing, -ed ɪn'ʃɔː* [en-,
-'ʃɔə*, -'ʃʊə*], -z, -rɪŋ, -d
entablature, -s en'tæblətʃə* [ɪn-, -blɪtʃ-,
-ˌtʃʊə*, -ˌtjʊə*], -z
entail (s. v.), -s, -ing, -ed, -er/s, -ment
ɪn'teɪl [en-], -z, -ɪŋ, -d, -ə*/z, -mənt
entang|le, -les, -ling, -led, -lement/s
ɪn'tæŋg|l [en-], -lz, -lɪŋ, -ld, -lmənt/s
entente, -s ɑ̃ː'nˈtɑ̃ːnt [ɔ̃ː'nˈtɔ̃ːnt,
ɑː'nˈtɑːnt, ɒn'tɒnt] (ɑ̃tɑ̃ːt), -s
ent|er, -ers, -ering, -ered, -erer/s
'ent|ə*, -əz, -ərɪŋ, -əd, -ərə*/z
enteric en'terɪk
enteritis ˌentə'raɪtɪs
enterology ˌentə'rɒlədʒɪ
enterotomy ˌentə'rɒtəmɪ
enterpris|e, -es, -ing/ly 'entəpraɪz, -ɪz,
-ɪŋ/lɪ
entertain, -s, -ing/ly, -ed, -er/s,
-ment/s ˌentə'teɪn, · -z, -ɪŋ/lɪ, -d,
-ə*/z, -mənt/s
enthral, -s, -ling, -led, -ment ɪn'θrɔːl
[en-], -z, -ɪŋ, -d, -mənt
enthrall = enthral
enthron|e, -es, -ing, -ed, -ement/s
ɪn'θrəʊn [en-], -z, -ɪŋ, -d, -mənt/s

enthus|e, -es, -ing, -ed ɪn'θjuːz [en-], -ɪz, -ɪŋ, -d

enthusia|sm, -st/s ɪn'θjuːzɪæ|zəm [en-, -'θuː-, -zjæ-], -st/s

enthusiastic, -al, -ally ɪn,θjuːzɪ'æstɪk [en-, -,θuː-, -ɪ'ɑːs-], -l, -əlɪ

entia (plur. of ens) 'enʃɪə [-ʃjə, -tɪə, -tjə]

entic|e, -es, -ing/ly, -ed, -er/s, -ement/s ɪn'taɪs [en-], -ɪz, -ɪŋ/lɪ, -t, -ə*/z, -mənt/s

entire, -ly, -ness ɪn'taɪə* [en-], -lɪ, -nɪs [-nəs]

entiret|y, -ies ɪn'taɪərət|ɪ [en-, ɪn'taɪət|ɪ], -ɪz

entit|le, -les, -ling, -led ɪn'taɪt|l [en-], -lz, -lɪŋ [-lɪŋ], -ld

entit|y, -ies 'entət|ɪ [-ɪt|ɪ], -ɪz

entomb, -s, -ing, -ed, -ment/s ɪn'tuːm [en-], -z, -ɪŋ, -d, -mənt/s

entomologic|al, -ally ,entəmə'lɒdʒɪk|l [-təʊməʊ'l], -əlɪ

entomolog|ist/s, -y ,entəʊ'mɒlədʒ|ɪst/s, -ɪ

entomologiz|e [-is|e], -es, -ing, -ed ,entəʊ'mɒlədʒaɪz, -ɪz, -ɪŋ, -d

entourage, -s ,ɒntʊ'rɑːʒ [,ɔ̃ːnt-, ,ɑ̃ːnt-, ,ɑːnt-, 'ɒn,tʊə'r-] (ɑ̃tuːrɑːʒ), -ɪz

entr'acte, -s 'ɒntrækt [ɒn'trækt, ɔ̃ːn't-, ɑ̃ːnt-, ɑːn't-] (ɑ̃trakt), -s

entrails 'entreɪlz

entrain, -s, -ing, -ed ɪn'treɪn [en-], -z, -ɪŋ, -d

entramm|el, -els, -elling, -elled ɪn'træm|l [en-], -lz, -lɪŋ [-əlɪŋ], -ld

entrance (s.) (entry, place of entry, etc.), -s 'entrəns, -ɪz

entranc|e (v.) (put in state of trance, delight), -es, -ing/ly, -ed, -ement/s ɪn'trɑːns [en-], -ɪz, -ɪŋ/lɪ, -t, -mənt/s

entrant (s. adj.), -s 'entrənt, -s

entrap, -s, -ping, -ped, -per/s, -ment ɪn'træp [en-], -s, -ɪŋ, -t, -ə*/z, -mənt

entreat, -s, -ing/ly, -ed, -ment ɪn'triːt [en-], -s, -ɪŋ/lɪ, -ɪd, -mənt

entreaty, -ies ɪn'triːt|ɪ [en-], -ɪz

entrecôte, -s 'ɒntrəkəʊt ['ɔ̃ːnt-, 'ɑ̃ːnt-, 'ɑːnt-] (ɑ̃trəkoːt), -s

entrée, -s 'ɒntreɪ ['ɔ̃ːnt-, 'ɑ̃ːnt-, 'ɑːnt-] (ɑ̃tre), -z

entremets (sing.) 'ɒntrəmeɪ ['ɔ̃ːnt-, 'ɑ̃ːnt-, 'ɑːnt-] (ɑ̃trəmɛ), (plur.) -z

entrench, -es, -ing, -ed, -ment/s ɪn'trentʃ [en-], -ɪz, -ɪŋ, -t, -mənt/s

entrenching-tool, -s ɪn'trentʃɪŋtuːl [en-] -z

entrepôt, -s 'ɒntrəpəʊ ['ɔ̃ːnt-, 'ɑ̃ːnt-, 'ɑːnt-] (ɑ̃trəpo), -z

entrepreneu|r, -rs, -rial ,ɒntrəprə'nɜː* [,ɔ̃ː:n-, ,ɑ̃:n-, ,ɑː:n-, -pre'n-] (ɑ̃trəprənœːr), -z, -rɪəl

entresol, -s 'ɒntrəsɒl ['ɔ̃ː:n-, 'ɑ̃:n-, 'ɑː:n-] (ɑ̃trəsɔl), -z

entropy 'entrəpɪ

entrust, -s, -ing, -ed ɪn'trʌst [en-], -s, -ɪŋ, -ɪd

entr|y, -ies 'entr|ɪ, -ɪz

entwin|e, -es, -ing, -ed ɪn'twaɪn [en-], -z, -ɪŋ, -d

entwist, -s, -ing, -ed ɪn'twɪst [en-], -s, -ɪŋ, -ɪd

enumerable ɪ'njuːmərəbl [iː'n-]

enumerat|e, -es, -ing, -ed, -or/s ɪ'njuː-məreɪt, -s, -ɪŋ, -ɪd, -ə*/z

enumeration, -s ɪ,njuːmə'reɪʃn, -z

enumerative ɪ'njuːmərətɪv [-reɪt-]

enunciable ɪ'nʌnʃɪəbl [-nʃjə-, -nsɪə-, -nsjə-]

enunciat|e, -es, -ing, -ed, -or/s ɪ'nʌn-sɪeɪt [-nʃɪeɪt, -nʃjeɪt], -s, -ɪŋ, -ɪd, -ə*/z

enunciation, -s ɪ,nʌnsɪ'eɪʃn, -z

enunciative ɪ'nʌnʃɪətɪv [-nʃjət- -nsɪət-, -nsjət-, -nʃɪeɪt-, -ʃjeɪt-, -nsɪeɪt-, -nsjeɪt-]

enur|e, -es, -ing, -ed ɪ'njʊə*, -z, -rɪŋ, -d

enuresis ,enjʊə'riːsɪs

envelop, -s, -ing, -ed, -ment/s ɪn-'veləp [en-], -s, -ɪŋ, -t, -mənt/s

envelope, -s 'envələʊp ['ɒn-, -vɪl-], -s

envenom, -s, -ing, -ed ɪn'venəm [en-], -z, -ɪŋ, -d

enviab|le, -ly, -leness 'envɪəb|l [-vjə-], -lɪ, -lnɪs [-nəs]

envious, -ly, -ness 'envɪəs [-vjəs], -lɪ, -nɪs [-nəs]

envir|on (v.), -ons, -oning, -oned, -onment/s ɪn'vaɪər|ən [en-], -ənz, -ənɪŋ [-ṇɪŋ], -ənd, -ənmənt/s

environmental ɪn,vaɪərən'mentl [en-]

environs (s.) ɪn'vaɪərənz ['envɪrənz, en'vaɪər-]

envisag|e, -es, -ing, -ed ɪn'vɪzɪdʒ [en-], -ɪz, -ɪŋ, -d

envoy, -s 'envɔɪ, -z

env|y (s. v.), -ies, -ying, -ied, -ier/s 'env|ɪ, -ɪz, -ɪɪŋ [-jɪŋ], -ɪd, -ɪə*/z [-jə*/z]

enwrap, -s, -ping, -ped ɪn'ræp [en-], -s, -ɪŋ, -t

enwreath|e, -es, -ing, -ed ɪn'riːð [en-], -z, -ɪŋ, -d

enzyme, -s 'enzaɪm, -z

eocene 'iːəʊsiːn ['ɪəʊ-]

Eochaidh 'jɒkeɪ ['jɒxeɪ]

Eoli- = Aeoli-

eolith, -s 'i:əʊlɪθ, -s
Eothen (title of book by Kinglake)
i:'əʊθen [ɪ'əʊ-, 'i:əʊθen, 'ɪəʊ-, -θn]
epact, -s 'i:pækt, -s
Epaminondas e,pæmɪ'nɒndæs [ɪ,p-]
eparch, -s; -y, -ies 'epɑːk, -s; -ɪ, -ɪz
epaulement, -s e'pɔːlmənt [ɪ'p-], -s
epaulet, -s 'epəʊlet [-pɔːl-, ,epə'let], -s
epenthes|is, -es e'penθɪs|ɪs [-θəs|-], -i:z
epenthetic ,epen'θetɪk
epergne, -s ɪ'pɜːn [e'peən], -z
epexegesis e,peksɪ'dʒi:sɪs
epexegetic, -al, -ally e,peksɪ'dʒetɪk, -l, -əlɪ
ephah, -s 'i:fə, -z
ephemer|a, -as, -al ɪ'femər|ə [e'f-, -'fi:m-], -əz, -əl
ephemeralit|y, -ies ɪ,femə'rælət|ɪ [e,f-, -,fi:m-, -ɪt|ɪ], -ɪz
ephemeris, ephemerides ɪ'femərɪs [e'f-, -'fi:m-], ,efɪ'merɪdi:z
ephemeron, -s ɪ'femərɒn [e'f-, -'fi:m-, -rən], -z
ephemerous ɪ'femərəs [e'f-, -'fi:m-]
Ephesian, -s ɪ'fi:ʒn [-i:ʒɪən, -i:ʒjən, -i:zjən, -i:zɪən], -z
Ephesus 'efəsəs [-fɪ-]
ephod, -s 'i:fɒd ['ef-], -z
Ephraim 'i:freɪɪm [-,frɪəm]
Ephrata 'efrətə
Ephron 'efrɒn ['i:f-]
epiblast, -s 'epɪblæst, -s
epic (s. adj.), -s 'epɪk, -s
epicene (s. adj.), -s 'episi:n, -z
epicentre, -s 'epɪsentə*, -z
Epicharmus ,epɪ'kɑːməs
epici|sm, -st/s 'epɪsɪ|zəm, -st/s
Epictetus ,epɪk'ti:təs
epicure, -s 'epɪ,kjʊə* [-kjɔə*, -kjɔ:*], -z
Epicurean, -s ,epɪkjʊə'ri:ən [-kjɔə'r-, -kjɔ:'r-, -'rɪən], -z
epicurism 'epɪkjʊərɪzəm [-kjɔər-, -kjɔ:r-]
Epicurus ,epɪ'kjʊərəs [-'kjɔər-, -'kjɔ:r-]
epicycle, -s 'epɪsaɪkl, -z
epicyclic ,epɪ'saɪklɪk [-'sɪk-]
epicycloid, -s ,epɪ'saɪklɔɪd, -z
Epidaurus ,epɪ'dɔ:rəs
epidemic (s. adj.), -s, -al, -ally ,epɪ'demɪk, -s, -l, -əlɪ
epiderm|al, -ic, -is, -oid ,epɪ'dɜ:m|l, -ɪk, -ɪs, -ɔɪd
epidiascope, -s ,epɪ'daɪəskəʊp, -s
epigene 'epɪdʒi:n
epigenesis ,epɪ'dʒenəsɪs [-ɪsɪs]
epiglott|al, -ic ,epɪ'glɒt|l ['epɪ,g-], -ɪk
epiglottis, -es ,epɪ'glɒtɪs ['epɪ,g-], -ɪz
epigone, -s 'epɪgəʊn, -z

Epigoni e'pɪgənaɪ [-ni:]
epigram, -s 'epɪgræm, -z
epigrammatic, -al, -ally ,epɪgrə'mætɪk, -l, -əlɪ
epigrammatist, -s ,epɪ'græmətɪst, -s
epigrammatiz|e [-is|e], -es, -ing, -ed ,epɪ'græmətaɪz, -ɪz, -ɪŋ, -d
epigraph, -s 'epɪgrɑ:f [-græf], -s
epigrapher, -s e'pɪgrəfə* [ɪ'p-], -z
epigraphic ,epɪ'græfɪk
epigraph|ist/s, -y e'pɪgrəf|ɪst/s [ɪ'p-], -ɪ
epilepsy 'epɪlepsɪ
epileptic (s. adj.), -s, -al ,epɪ'leptɪk, -s, -l
epilogic ,epɪ'lɒdʒɪk
epilogiz|e [-is|e], -es, -ing, -ed e'pɪləʊdʒaɪz [ɪ'p-], -ɪz, -ɪŋ, -d
epilogue, -s 'epɪlɒg, -z
Epimenides ,epɪ'menɪdi:z
Epinal 'epɪnl (epinal)
epiphan|y (E.), -ies ɪ'pɪfən|ɪ [e'p-, -fn̩|ɪ], -ɪz
Epipsychidion ,epɪsaɪ'kɪdɪɒn [-ɪpsaɪ-, -dɪən]
Epirus e'paɪrəs [ɪ'p-]
episcopac|y, -ies ɪ'pɪskəpəs|ɪ [e'p-], -ɪz
episcop|al, -ally ɪ'pɪskəp|l [e'p-], -əlɪ
episcopalian (s. adj.), -s, -ism ɪ,pɪskəʊ-'peɪljən [e,p-, -lɪən], -z, -ɪzəm
episcopate, -s ɪ'pɪskəʊpət [e'p-, -pɪt, -peɪt], -s
episcope, -s 'epɪskəʊp, -s
episcopiz|e [-is|e], -es, -ing, -ed ɪ'pɪskəʊpaɪz [e'p-], -ɪz, -ɪŋ, -d
episode, -s 'epɪsəʊd, -z
episodic, -al, -ally ,epɪ'sɒdɪk, -l, -əlɪ
epistemology e,pɪsti:'mɒlədʒɪ [ɪ,p-, -tɪ-, -tə-]
epistle, -s ɪ'pɪsl, -z
epistler, -s ɪ'pɪslə*, -z
epistolary ɪ'pɪstələrɪ [e'p-, -t|ərɪ]
epistoler, -s ɪ'pɪstələ* [e'p-], -z
epistoliz|e [-is|e], -es, -ing, -ed ɪ'pɪstəlaɪz [e'p-], -ɪz, -ɪŋ, -d
epistyle, -s 'epɪstaɪl, -z
epitaph, -s 'epɪtɑ:f [-tæf], -s
epithalami|um, -a, -ums ,epɪθə'leɪmj|əm [-mɪ-], -ə, -əmz
epithelium, -s ,epɪ'θi:ljəm [-lɪəm], -z
epithet, -s 'epɪθet [-θɪt], -s
epithetic ,epɪ'θetɪk
epitome, -s ɪ'pɪtəmɪ [e'p-], -z
epitomic, -al ,epɪ'tɒmɪk, -l
epitomist, -s ɪ'pɪtəmɪst [e'p-], -s
epitomiz|e [-is|e], -es, -ing, -ed, -er/s ɪ'pɪtəmaɪz [e'p-], -ɪz, -ɪŋ, -d, -ə*/z
epoch, -s 'i:pɒk [rarely 'ep-], -s
epochal 'epɒkl [i:'pɒk-]

169

epoch-making 'i:pɒk͵meɪkɪŋ
epode, -s 'epəʊd, -z
eponym, -s 'epəʊnɪm, -z
eponymous ɪ'pɒnɪməs [e'p-]
epopee, -s 'epəʊpi:, -z
epos, -es 'epɒs, -ɪz
Epping 'epɪŋ
Epps eps
epsilon, -s ep'saɪlən [-lɒn, 'epsɪlən,
  -lɒn], -z
Epsom 'epsəm
Epstein (sculptor) 'epstaɪn
Epworth 'epwɜ:θ [-wəθ]
equability ͵ekwə'bɪlətɪ [͵i:k-, -lɪt-]
equab|le, -ly, -leness 'ekwəb|l ['i:k-], -lɪ,
  -lnɪs [-nəs]
equ|al (s. adj. v.), -ally, -alness; -als,
  -alling, -alled 'i:kw|əl, -əlɪ, -əlnɪs
  [-nəs]; -əlz, -əlŋ, -əld
equalit|y, -ies ɪ'kwɒlət|ɪ [i:'k-, -ɪt|ɪ], -ɪz
equalization [-isa-], -s ͵i:kwəlaɪ'zeɪʃn
  [-lɪ'z-], -z
equaliz|e [-is|e], -es, -ing, -ed 'i:kwəlaɪz,
  -ɪz, -ɪŋ, -d
equanimity ͵ekwə'nɪmətɪ [͵i:k-, -ɪtɪ]
equanimous, -ly, -ness ɪ'kwænɪməs
  [i:'k-, e'k-], -lɪ, -nɪs [-nəs]
equat|e, -es, -ing, -ed; -able ɪ'kweɪt
  [i:'k-], -s. -ɪŋ, -ɪd; -əbl
equation, -s ɪ'kweɪʒn [-eɪʃn], -z
equator, -s ɪ'kweɪtə*, -z
equatorial (s. adj.), -s, -ly ͵ekwə'tɔ:rɪəl
  [͵i:k-], -z, -ɪ
equerr|y, -ies 'ekwər|ɪ, ɪ'kwer|ɪ, -ɪz
  Note.—The pronunciation at court is
  ɪ'kwerɪ.
equestrian (s. adj.), -s, -ism ɪ'kwes-
  trɪən [e'k-], -z, -ɪzəm
equestrienne, -s ɪ͵kwestrɪ'en [e͵k-], -z
equiangular ͵i:kwɪ'æŋgjʊlə*
equidistant, -ly ͵i:kwɪ'dɪstənt, -lɪ
equilateral ͵i:kwɪ'lætərəl
equilibrat|e, -es, -ing, -ed ͵i:kwɪ-
  'laɪbreɪt [-'lɪb-, i:'kwɪlɪb-, ɪ'k-], -s,
  -ɪŋ, -ɪd
equilibration ͵i:kwɪlaɪ'breɪʃn [͵i:kwɪ-
  lɪ'b-, i:͵kwɪlɪ'b-, ɪ͵k-]
equilibrist, -s i:'kwɪlɪbrɪst [ɪ'k-, ͵i:kwɪ-
  'lɪbrɪst], -s
equilibrium ͵i:kwɪ'lɪbrɪəm [͵ekw-]
equimultiple, -s ͵i:kwɪ'mʌltɪpl, -z
equine 'ekwaɪn ['i:k-]
equinoctial (s. adj.), -s ͵i:kwɪ'nɒkʃl
  [͵ek-], -z
equinox, -es 'i:kwɪnɒks ['ek-], -ɪz
equip, -s, -ping, -ped, -ment/s ɪ'kwɪp,
  -s, -ɪŋ, -t, -mənt/s
equipage, -s 'ekwɪpɪdʒ, -ɪz

equipois|e (s. v.), -es, -ing, -ed 'ekwɪ-
  pɔɪz ['i:k-], -ɪz, -ɪŋ, -d
equitab|le, -ly, -leness 'ekwɪtəb|l, -lɪ,
  -lnɪs [-nəs]
equitation ͵ekwɪ'teɪʃn
equit|y, -ies 'ekwət|ɪ [-ɪt|ɪ], -ɪz
equivalen|ce, -t/s, -tly ɪ'kwɪvələn|s
  [-vlə-], -t/s, -tlɪ
equivoc|al, -ally, -alness ɪ'kwɪvək|l
  [-vʊk-], -əlɪ, -əlnɪs [-nəs]
equivocat|e, -es, -ing, -ed, -or/s
  ɪ'kwɪvəkeɪt [-vʊk-], -s, -ɪŋ, -ɪd, -ə*/z
equivocation, -s ɪ͵kwɪvə'keɪʃn [-vʊ'k-],
  -z
equivoke [-voque], -s 'ekwɪvəʊk, -s
Equuleus e'kwʊlɪəs
er (interj.) ʌ:, ɜ:
era, -s 'ɪərə, -z
eradiat|e, -es, -ing, -ed ɪ'reɪdɪeɪt ͵[i:'r-,
  -djert], -s, -ɪŋ, -ɪd
eradiation ɪ͵reɪdɪ'eɪʃn [i:͵r-]
eradicable ɪ'rædɪkəbl
eradicat|e, -es, -ing, -ed ɪ'rædɪkeɪt, -s,
  -ɪŋ, -ɪd
eradication ɪ͵rædɪ'keɪʃn
eradicative ɪ'rædɪkətɪv [-keɪt-]
Erard, -s 'erɑːd (era:r), -z
eras|e, -es, -ing, -ed, -er/s, -ement;
  -able ɪ'reɪz, -ɪz, -ɪŋ, -d, -ə*/z, -mənt;
  -əbl
erasion, -s ɪ'reɪʒn, -z
Erasmian, -s, -ism ɪ'ræzmɪən [e'r-,
  -mjən], -z, -ɪzəm
Erasmus ɪ'ræzməs [e'r-]
Erastian, -s, -ism ɪ'ræstɪən [e'r-, -tjən],
  -z, -ɪzəm
Erastus ɪ'ræstəs [e'r-]
erasure, -s ɪ'reɪʒə*, -z
Erath ɪ'rɑ:θ [e'r-]
Erdington 'ɜ:dɪŋtən
ere eə*
Erebus 'erɪbəs
Erec 'ɪərek
Erechtheum ͵erek'θiːəm [-'θɪəm]
Erechtheus ɪ'rekθjuːs [e'r-, -θɪəs, -θjəs]
erect (adj. v.), -ly, -ness; -s, -ing, -ed;
  -ile ɪ'rekt, -lɪ, -nɪs [-nəs]; -s, -ɪŋ, -ɪd;
  -aɪl
erection, -s ɪ'rekʃn, -z
eremite, -s 'erɪmaɪt, -s
eremitic, -al erɪ'mɪtɪk, -l
Eretria, -n/s ɪ'retrɪə [e'r-], -n/z
erewhile eə'waɪl [-'hw-]
Erewhon 'erɪwɒn [-wən, -ɪhw-]
erg, -s ɜ:g, -z
ergo 'ɜ:gəʊ
ergon, -s 'ɜ:gɒn, -z
ergonic, -s, -ally ɜ:'gɒnɪk, -s, -əlɪ

ergonomics ˌɜːgəʊ'nɒmɪks
ergosterol ɜː'gɒstərɒl [-stɪər-]
ergot, -ism 'ɜːgət [-gɒt], -ɪzəm
eric (E.), -s 'erɪk, -s
erica (E.) 'erɪkə
ericaceous ˌerɪ'keɪʃəs
Erie 'ɪərɪ
Erin 'ɪərɪn
Eris 'erɪs
eristic, -s e'rɪstɪk, -s
Erith 'ɪərɪθ
Eritrea, -n/s ˌerɪ'treɪə [-'trɪə], -n/z
Erle ɜːl
erl-king, -s 'ɜːlkɪŋ [ˌɜːl'kɪŋ], -z
Erlynne 'ɜːlɪn
ermine, -s, -d 'ɜːmɪn, -z, -d
erne (E.), -s ɜːn, -z
Ernest 'ɜːnɪst
Ernle 'ɜːnlɪ
erod|e, -es, -ing, -ed ɪ'rəʊd [e'r-], -z, -ɪŋ, -ɪd
erogenous ɪ'rɒdʒɪnəs [e'r-, -dʒə-]
Eroica e'rəʊɪkə [ɪ'r-]
Eros 'ɪərɒs ['erɒs, also 'erəʊz]
erosion, -s ɪ'rəʊʒn [e'r-], -z
erosive ɪ'rəʊsɪv [e'r-]
erotic (s. adj.), -s ɪ'rɒtɪk [e'r-], -s
erotica ɪ'rɒtɪkə [e'r-]
eroticism ɪ'rɒtɪsɪzəm [e'r-]
err, -s, -ing, -ed ɜː:*, -z, -rɪŋ, -d
errand, -s 'erənd, -z
errand-boy, -s 'erəndbɔɪ, -z
errant, -ly, -ry 'erənt, -lɪ, -rɪ
erratic, -al, -ally ɪ'rætɪk [e'r-], -l, -əlɪ
errat|um, -a e'rɑː:t|əm [ɪ'r-, -'reɪt|-], -ə
Erroll 'erəl
erroneous, -ly, -ness ɪ'rəʊnjəs [e'r-, -nɪəs], -lɪ, -nɪs [-nəs]
error, -s 'erə*, -z
ersatz 'eəzæts ['ɜːsɑːts] (ɛr'zats)
Erse ɜːs
Erskine 'ɜːskɪn
erst ɜːst
erstwhile 'ɜːstwaɪl [-thw-]
erubescen|ce, -cy, -t ˌeruː'besn|s [-rʊ-], -sɪ, -t
eruct, -s, -ing, -ed ɪ'rʌkt [iː'r-], -s, -ɪŋ, -ɪd
eructat|e, -es, -ing, -ed ɪ'rʌkteɪt [iː'r-], -s, -ɪŋ, -ɪd
eructation, -s ˌiːrʌk'teɪʃn, -z
erudite, -ly, -ness 'eruːdaɪt [-rʊ-, -rjuː-, -rjʊ-], -lɪ, -nɪs [-nəs]
erudition ˌeruː'dɪʃn [-rʊ-, -rjuː-, -rjʊ-]
erupt, -s, -ing, -ed ɪ'rʌpt [e'r-], -s, -ɪŋ, -ɪd
eruption, -s ɪ'rʌpʃn [e'r-], -z
eruptive, -ly, -ness ɪ'rʌptɪv [e'r-], -lɪ, -nɪs [-nəs]

Ervine 'ɜːvɪn
erysipelas ˌerɪ'sɪpɪləs [-pəl-, -lɪs]
erythema ˌerɪ'θiːmə
Eryx 'erɪks
Erzerum 'eəzəruːm
Esau 'iːsɔː:
escalad|e (s. v.), -es, -ing, -ed ˌeskə'leɪd ['---], -z, -ɪŋ, -ɪd
escalat|e, -es, -ing, -ed 'eskəleɪt, -s, -ɪŋ, -ɪd
escalation ˌeskə'leɪʃn
escalator, -s 'eskəleɪtə*, -z
escallop, -ed ɪ'skɒləp [e's-], -t
escapade, -s ˌeskə'peɪd ['---], -z
escap|e (s. v.), -es, -ing, -ed, -ement/s ɪ'skeɪp [e's-], -s, -ɪŋ, -t, -mənt/s
escapi|sm, -st/s ɪ'skeɪpɪ|zəm [e's-], -st/s
escapologist, -s ˌeskeɪ'pɒlədʒɪst [-skə'p-], -s
escarp (s. v.), -s, -ing, -ed, -ment/s ɪ'skɑːp [e's-], -s, -ɪŋ, -t, -mənt/s
eschalot, -s 'eʃəlɒt [ˌeʃə'l-], -s
eschar, -s 'eskɑː*, -z
escharotic (s. adj.), -s ˌeskə'rɒtɪk, -s
eschatological ˌeskətə'lɒdʒɪkl [-kæt-]
eschatolog|ist/s, -y ˌeskə'tɒlədʒ|ɪst/s, -ɪ
escheat (s. v.), -s, -ing, -ed ɪs'tʃiːt [es-], -s, -ɪŋ, -ɪd
eschew, -s, -ing, -ed ɪs'tʃuː: [es-], -z, -ɪŋ [-'tʃʊɪŋ], -d
eschscholtzia, -s ɪs'kɒlʃə [ɪs'kɒltʃə, es'kɒltsɪə, es'kɒltsjə, e'ʃɒltsɪə, e'ʃɒltsjə], -z
Escombe 'eskəm
Escorial ˌeskɒrɪ'ɑːl [e'skɔːrɪəl]
escort (s.), -s 'eskɔːt, -s
escort (v.), -s, -ing, -ed ɪ'skɔːt [e's-], -s, -ɪŋ, -ɪd
Escow 'eskəʊ
escritoire, -s ˌeskriː'twɑː:* [-krɪ-, -'twɔː:*, '---] (ɛskritwaːr), -z
escudo, -s e'skuː:dəʊ, -z
esculent (s. adj.), -s 'eskjʊlənt, -s
Escurial e'skjʊərɪəl
escutcheon, -s ɪ'skʌtʃən [e's-], -z
Esdaile 'ezdeɪl
Esdraelon ˌezdreɪ'iːlɒn [-drə'iː-]
Esdras 'ezdræs [-rəs]
Esher 'iːʃə*
Esias ɪ'zaɪəs [e'z-, -æs]
Esk esk
Eskimo, -s 'eskɪməʊ, -z
Esmé 'ezmɪ
Esmeralda ˌezmə'rældə
Esmond(e) 'ezmənd
esophageal iːˌsɒfə'dʒiːəl [ɪ'sɒf-, -'dʒɪəl]
esopha|gus, -gi iː'sɒfə|gəs [ɪ's-], -gaɪ [-dʒaɪ]

171

esoteric, -al, -ally ˌesəʊˈterɪk [ˌiːs-], -l, -əlɪ

espalier (s. v.), -s, -ing, -ed ɪˈspæljə* [eˈs-, -lɪə*], -z, -rɪŋ, -d

esparto eˈspɑːtəʊ

especi|al, -ally ɪˈspeʃ|l [eˈs-], -əlɪ [-lɪ]

Esperant|ist/s, -o ˌespəˈrænt|ɪst/s [-peˈr-, -ˈrɑːn-], -əʊ

Espeut eˈspjuːt

espial ɪˈspaɪəl [eˈs-]

espionage ˈespɪənɑːdʒ [ˌespjəˈnɑːʒ, ˈespɪənɪdʒ, ˌespɪəˈnɑːʒ, eˈspaɪənɪdʒ, ɪˈspaɪənɪdʒ] (ˌespjɒnɑːʒ, pronounced as French espionnage)

esplanade, -s ˌespləˈneɪd [-ˈɑːd, ˈ---], -z

Esplanade (in Western Australia) ˈesplənɑːd

espous|e, -es, -ing, -ed, -er/s; -al/s ɪˈspaʊz [eˈs-], -ɪz, -ɪŋ, -d, -ə*/z; -l/z

espressivo ˌespreˈsiːvəʊ

espresso eˈspresəʊ [ɪˈs-]

esprit eˈspriː [ˈ--] (ɛspri)

esprit-de-corps eˌspriːdəˈkɔː* [ˌ---ˈ-] (ɛspridkɔːr)

esp|y, -ies, -ying, -ied ɪˈsp|aɪ [eˈs-], -aɪz, -aɪɪŋ, -aɪd

Espy ˈespɪ

Esq. ɪˈskwaɪə* [eˈs-]

Esquiline ˈeskwɪlaɪn

Esquimalt eˈskwaɪmɔːlt

Esquimau, -x ˈeskɪməʊ, -z

esquire, -s ɪˈskwaɪə* [eˈs-], -z

ess, -es es, -ɪz

essay (s.), -s; -ist/s ˈeseɪ [-sɪ], -z; -ɪst/s

essay (v.), -s, -ing, -ed, -er/s eˈseɪ [ˈeseɪ], -z, -ɪŋ, -d, -ə*/z

esse ˈesɪ

Essen ˈesn

essence, -s ˈesns, -ɪz

Essene, -s ˈesiːn [eˈsiːn], -z

essenti|al, -als, -ally, -alness ɪˈsenʃ|l [eˈs-], -lz, -əlɪ [-lɪ], -lnɪs [-nəs]

essentiality ɪˌsenʃɪˈælətɪ [eˌs-, -ɪtɪ]

Essex ˈesɪks

establish, -es, -ing, -ed, -er/s, -ment/s ɪˈstæblɪʃ [eˈs-], -ɪz, -ɪŋ, -t, -ə*/z, -mənt/s

estate, -s ɪˈsteɪt [eˈs-], -s

estate-car, -s ɪˈsteɪtkɑː* [eˈs-], -z

Estcourt ˈestkɔːt

Este ˈestɪ

esteem (s. v.), -s, -ing, -ed ɪˈstiːm [eˈs-], -z, -ɪŋ, -d

Estey ˈestɪ

Esther ˈestə*, ˈesθə*, esp. in the N.

esthet- = aesthet-

Esthonia, -n/s eˈstəʊnjə [esˈθəʊ-, -nɪə], -n/z

estimab|le, -ly, -leness ˈestɪməb|l, -lɪ, -lnɪs [-nəs]

estimate (s.), -s ˈestɪmət [-mɪt, -meɪt], -s

estimat|e (v.), -es, -ing, -ed, -or/s ˈestɪmeɪt, -s, -ɪŋ, -ɪd, -ə*/z

estimation ˌestɪˈmeɪʃn

estiv- = aestiv-

Estmere ˈestˌmɪə*

Estonia, -n/s eˈstəʊnjə [-nɪə], -n/z

estop, -s, -ping, -ped; -page, -pel/s ɪˈstɒp [eˈs-], -s, -ɪŋ, -t; -ɪdʒ, -l/z

estrade, -s eˈstrɑːd, -z

estrang|e, -es, -ing, -ed, -edness, -ement/s ɪˈstreɪndʒ [eˈs-], -ɪz, -ɪŋ, -d, -ɪdnɪs [-nəs], -mənt/s

estreat (s. v.), -s, -ing, -ed ɪˈstriːt [eˈs-], -s, -ɪŋ, -ɪd

estuar|y, -ies ˈestjʊər|ɪ [-tjwər-, -ˌtjʊər-, -tʃʊər-, -tʃwər-, -ˌtʃʊər-, -tjʊr-, -tʃʊr-], -ɪz

esurien|ce, -cy, -t ɪˈsjʊərɪən|s, -sɪ, -t

eta ˈiːtə

etacism ˈeɪtəsɪzəm

Etah ˈiːtə

Etain ˈeteɪn

Etamin ˈetəmɪn

etc. ɪtˈsetərə [et-, ət-]

etcetera, -s ɪtˈsetərə [et-, ət-], -z

etch, -es, -ing/s, -ed, -er/s etʃ, -ɪz, -ɪŋ/z, -t, -ə*/z

etern|al, -ally ɪˈtɜːn|l [iːˈt-], -əlɪ [-lɪ]

eternaliz|e [-is|e], -es, -ing, -ed ɪˈtɜː-nəlaɪz [iːˈt-, -n|aɪz], -ɪz, -ɪŋ, -d

eternit|y, -ies ɪˈtɜːnət|ɪ [iːˈt-, -ɪt|ɪ], -ɪz

etern|ize [-is|e], -es, -ing, -ed ɪˈtɜːnaɪz [iːˈt-], -ɪz, -ɪŋ, -d

Etesian ɪˈtiːʒjən [-ʒɪən, -ʒn]

Eteson ˈiːtsn

Ethbaal eθˈbeɪəl [usual Jewish pronunciation eθˈbɑːl]

Ethel, -bald, -bert ˈeθl, -bɔːld, -bɜːt

Ethelberta ˌeθlˈbɜːtə [ˈ--ˌ--]

Ethelburga ˌeθlˈbɜːgə [ˈ--ˌ--]

Ethel|red, -wulf ˈeθl|red, -wʊlf

ether, -s ˈiːθə*, -z

ethereal, -ly ɪˈθɪərɪəl [iːˈθ-], -ɪ

etherealiz|e [-is|e], -es, -ing, -ed ɪˈθɪərɪəlaɪz [iːˈθ-], -ɪz, -ɪŋ, -d

Etherege ˈeθərɪdʒ

etheric, -s -ally iːˈθerɪk [ɪˈθ-], -s, -əlɪ

Etherington ˈeðərɪŋtən

etheriz|e [-is|e], -es, -ing, -ed ˈiːθəraɪz, -ɪz, -ɪŋ, -d

ethic (s. adj.), -s, -al, -ally ˈeθɪk, -s, -l, -əlɪ

Ethiop, -s 'iːθɪɒp [-θjɒp], -s
Ethiopia, -n/s ˌiːθɪ'əʊpjə [-pɪə], -n/z
Ethiopic ˌiːθɪ'ɒpɪk [-ɪ'əʊp-]
ethnic, -al, -ally 'eθnɪk, -l, -əlɪ
ethnographer, -s eθ'nɒɡrəfə*, -z
ethnographic ˌeθnəʊ'ɡræfɪk
ethnography eθ'nɒɡrəfɪ
ethnologic, -al, -ally ˌeθnəʊ'lɒdʒɪk, -l, -əlɪ
ethnolog|ist/s, -y eθ'nɒlədʒ|ɪst/s, -ɪ
ethologic, -al ˌiːθəʊ'lɒdʒɪk, -l
etholog|ist/s, -y iː'θɒlədʒ|ɪst/s [ɪ'θ-], -ɪ
ethos 'iːθɒs
ethyl (commercial and general pronunciation) 'eθɪl, (chemists' pronunciation) 'iːθaɪl
ethylene 'eθɪliːn
etiolat|e, -es, -ing, -ed 'iːtɪəʊleɪt [-tɪəl-], -s, -ɪŋ, -ɪd
etiolog|ist/s, -y ˌiːtɪ'ɒlədʒ|ɪst/s, -ɪ
etiquette 'etɪket [-kət, ˌetɪ'ket]
Etna 'etnə
Eton 'iːtn
Etonian, -s iː'təʊnjən [ɪ't-, -nɪən], -z
Etruria, -n/s ɪ'trʊərɪə, -n/z
Etruscan, -s ɪ'trʌskən, -z
Ettrick 'etrɪk
Etty 'etɪ
étude(s) eɪ'tjuːd ['--] (etyd)
etui, -s e'twiː, -z
etymologic, -al, -ally ˌetɪmə'lɒdʒɪk, -l, -əlɪ
etymolog|ist/s, -y, -ies ˌetɪ'mɒlədʒ|ɪst/s, -ɪ, -ɪz
etymologiz|e [-is|e], -es, -ing, -ed ˌetɪ'mɒlədʒaɪz, -ɪz, -ɪŋ, -d
etymon, -s 'etɪmɒn, -z
Euboea juː'bɪə [jʊ'b-, -'biːə]
eucalyptus, -es ˌjuːkə'lɪptəs [jʊk-], -ɪz
Eucharist, -s 'juːkərɪst, -s
eucharistic, -al, -ally ˌjuːkə'rɪstɪk [jʊk-], -l, -əlɪ
euchre (s. v.), **-s, -ing, -d** 'juːkə*, -z, -rɪŋ, -d
Euclid, -s 'juːklɪd, -z
Euclidean juː'klɪdɪən [jʊ'k-, -djən]
eud(a)emoni|sm, -st/s juː'diːmənɪ|zəm [jʊ'd-], -st/s
eudiometer, -s ˌjuːdɪ'ɒmɪtə* [jʊd-, -mətə*], -z
Eudocia juː'dəʊʃjə [jʊ'd-, -ʃɪə, -sjə, -sɪə]
Eudora juː'dɔːrə [jʊ'd-]
Eudoxia juː'dɒksɪə [jʊ'd-, -sjə]
Eudoxus juː'dɒksəs [jʊ'd-]
Eugen (English name) 'juːdʒen [-dʒɪn, -dʒən], (German name) 'ɔɪɡən (ɔy'geːn)

Eugene (English name) juː'ʒeɪn, 'juːdʒiːn, juː'dʒiːn
Eugene Onegin ˌjuːdʒiːn ɒ'njeɪɡɪn (jiv'ɡenji a'njeɡin)
Eugénia juː'dʒiːnjə [jʊ'dʒ-, -'dʒeɪ-, -nɪə]
eugenic, -s juː'dʒenɪk [jʊ'dʒ-], -s
Eugénie (as English name) juː'ʒeɪnɪ, juː'ʒiːnɪ, juː'dʒiːnɪ
Eugenius juː'dʒiːnjəs [jʊ'dʒ-, -'dʒeɪ-, -nɪəs]
Eulalia juː'leɪljə [jʊ'l-, -lɪə]
Euler (English name) 'juːlə*, (German name) 'ɔɪlə* ('ɔylər)
eulogist, -s 'juːlədʒɪst, -s
eulogistic, -al, -ally ˌjuːlə'dʒɪstɪk, -l -əlɪ
eulogium, -s juː'ləʊdʒjəm [jʊ'l-, -dʒɪəm], -z
eulogiz|e [-is|e], -es, -ing, -ed 'juːlədʒaɪz, -ɪz, -ɪŋ, -d
eulog|y, -ies 'juːlədʒ|ɪ, -ɪz
Eumenides juː'menɪdiːz [jʊ'm-]
Eunice (modern Christian name) 'juːnɪs, (biblical name) juː'naɪsɪ [jʊ'n-]
eunuch, -s, -ism 'juːnək, -s, -ɪzəm
euonymus, -es juː'ɒnɪməs [jʊ'ɒ-], -ɪz
eupepsia juː'pepsɪə [-sjə]
eupeptic juː'peptɪk
Euphemia juː'fiːmjə [jʊ'f-, -mɪə]
euphemism, -s 'juːfəmɪzəm [-fɪ-], -z
euphemistic, -al, -ally ˌjuːfə'mɪstɪk [-fɪ-], -l, -əlɪ
euphemiz|e [-is|e], -es, -ing, -ed 'juː-fəmaɪz [-fɪ-], -ɪz, -ɪŋ, -d
euphonic, -al, -ally juː'fɒnɪk [jʊ'f-], -l, -əlɪ
euphonious, -ly juː'fəʊnjəs [jʊ'f-, -nɪəs], -lɪ
euphonium, -s juː'fəʊnjəm [jʊ'f-, -nɪəm], -z
euphoniz|e [-is|e], -es, -ing, -ed 'juː-fənaɪz [-fəʊn-, -fʊn-], -ɪz, -ɪŋ, -d
euphony 'juːfənɪ [-fɒn-]
euphoria juː'fɔːrɪə [jʊ'f-]
euphoric juː'fɒrɪk [jʊ-]
euphrasy 'juːfrəsɪ
Euphrates juː'freɪtiːz [jʊ'f-]
Euphronius juː'frəʊnjəs [jʊ'f-, -nɪəs]
Euphrosyne juː'frɒzɪnɪ [jʊ'f-]
Euphues 'juːfjuːiːz [-fjʊiːz]
euphui|sm/s, -st/s 'juːfjuːɪ|zəm/z [-fjʊɪ-], -st/s
euphuistic ˌjuːfjuː'ɪstɪk [-fjʊ'ɪ-]
Eurasian, -s jʊə'reɪʒjən [jɔə'r-, jɔː'r-, -eɪʒɪən, -eɪʒn, -eɪʃn], -z
Euratom jʊər'ætəm
eureka jʊə'riːkə

173

eurhythm|ic/s, -y ju:'rıðm|ık/s [jʊ'r-, ˌjʊə'r-, -'rıθm-], -ı
Euripides jʊə'rɪpɪdi:z
Euripus jʊə'raɪpəs
Europa jʊə'rəʊpə
Europe 'jʊərəp ['jɔ:r-]
European, -s ˌjʊərə'pi:ən [ˌjɔ:r-, -'pɪən], -z
europeaniz|e [-is|e], -es, -ing, -ed ˌjʊərə'pi:ənaɪz [ˌjɔ:r-, -'pɪən-], -ız,-ıŋ, -d
Eurovision 'jʊərəʊˌvɪʒn
Eurus 'jʊərəs
Eurydice jʊə'rɪdɪsi: [-sı]
Eurylochus jʊə'rɪləkəs
Eusebian, -s ju:'si:bjən [jʊ's-, -bɪən], -z
Eusebius ju:'si:bjəs [jʊ's-, -bɪəs]
Euskarian, -s ju:'skeərɪən, -z
Eustace 'ju:stəs [-tıs]
Eustachian ju:'steɪʃn [-ʃɪən, -ʃjən, rarely -'steɪkjən, -'steɪkɪən]
Eustachius ju:'steɪkjəs [-kɪəs]
Eustis 'ju:stıs
Euston 'ju:stən
Eutaw 'ju:tɔ:
Euterpe ju:'tɜ:pı [jʊ't-]
euthanasia ˌju:θə'neɪzjə [-eɪzɪə, -eɪʒjə, -eɪʒɪə, -eɪʒə]
Eutropius ju:'trəʊpjəs [jʊ't-, -pɪəs]
Euxine 'ju:ksaɪn
Eva 'i:və
evacuant (s. adj.), -s ı'vækjʊənt [i:'v-, -kjwənt], -s
evacuat|e, -es, -ing, -ed, -or/s ı'vækjʊeɪt [i:'v-], -s, -ıŋ, -ıd, -ə*/z
evacuation, -s ıˌvækjʊ'eɪʃn [i:ˌv-], -z
evacuee, -s ıˌvækju:'i: [i:ˌv-, -kjʊ'i:], -z
evad|e, -es, -ing, -ed, -er/s ı'veɪd, -z, -ıŋ, -ıd, -ə*/z
evaluat|e, -es, -ing, -ed ı'væljʊeɪt, -s, -ıŋ, -ıd
evaluation, -s ıˌvælju'eɪʃn, -z
Evan 'evən
Evander ı'vændə*
evanesc|e, -es, -ing, -ed ˌi:və'nes [ˌev-], -ız, -ıŋ, -t
evanescen|ce, -t/ly ˌi:və'nesn|s [ˌev-], -t/lı
evangel, -s ı'vændʒel [-dʒəl], -z
evangelic (s. adj.), -s, -al/s, -ally, -alism ˌi:væn'dʒelık [ˌev-, -vən-], -s, -l/z, -əlı, -əlızəm [-lız-]
Evangeline ı'vændʒıli:n [-dʒəl-, -dʒl-]
evangel|ism, -ist/s ı'vændʒəl|ızəm [-dʒıl-, -dʒl-], -ıst/s
evangelistic ıˌvændʒə'lıstık [-dʒı'l-, -dʒl'ıstık]

evangelization [-isa-] ıˌvændʒəlaɪ'zeɪʃn [-dʒıl-, -dʒl-, -lı'z-]
evangeliz|e [-is|e], -es, -ing, -ed ı'vændʒəlaɪz [-dʒıl-, -dʒl-], -ız, -ıŋ, -d
Evans 'evənz
Evanson 'evənsn
Evanston 'evənstən
Evansville 'evənzvıl
evaporable ı'væpərəbl
evaporat|e, -es, -ing, -ed, -or/s ı'væpəreıt, -s, -ıŋ, -ıd, -ə*/z
evaporation, -s ıˌvæpə'reıʃn, -z
evasion, -s ı'veıʒn, -z
evasive, -ly, -ness ı'veısıv, -lı, -nıs [-nəs]
eve (E.), -s, i:v, -z
Evele(i)gh 'i:vlı
Evelina ˌevı'li:nə
Eveline 'i:vlın, 'evlın, 'evıli:n
Evelyn 'i:vlın, 'evlın
ev|en (s. adj. v. adv.), -enly, -enness; -ens, -ening, -ened 'i:v|n, -nlı, -nnıs [-nəs]; -nz, -nıŋ [-ənıŋ], -nd
Evenden 'evəndən
evening (s.) (close of day), -s 'i:vnıŋ, -z
Evens 'evənz
evensong, -s 'i:vnsɒŋ, -z
†event, -s; -ful ı'vent, -s; -fʊl [-fəl]
eventide, -s 'i:vntaıd, -z
eventual, -ly ı'ventʃʊəl [-tjwəl, -tjʊəl, -tʃwəl, -tjʊl, -tʃʊl], -ı
eventualit|y, -ies ıˌventʃʊ'ælət|ı [-tjʊ-, -ıt|ı], -ız
eventuat|e, -es, -ing, -ed ı'ventʃʊeıt [-tjʊeıt], -s, -ıŋ, -ıd
ever 'evə*
Ever|ard, -est, -ett 'evər|ɑ:d, -ıst, -ıt
evergreen (s. adj.), -s 'evəgri:n, -z
Everitt 'evərıt
everlasting, -ly, -ness ˌevə'lɑ:stıŋ, -lı, -nıs [-nəs]
evermore ˌevə'mɔ:* [-'mɔə*, also sometimes '— when followed by a stress]
Evers 'evəz
Evershed 'evəʃed
eversion ı'vɜ:ʃn [i:'v-]
Eversley 'evəzlı
evert, -s, -ing, -ed ı'vɜ:t [i:'v-], -s, -ıŋ, -ıd
Everton 'evətən
every, -body 'evrı, -ˌbɒdı [-bədı]
everyday (adj.) 'evrıdeı [ˌ—'-]
Everyman 'evrımæn
everyone 'evrıwʌn
everything 'evrıθıŋ
everywhere 'evrıweə* [-ıhw-]
Evesham 'i:vʃəm [locally also 'i:vıʃəm]

Evett, -s 'evɪt, -s
evict, -s, -ing, -ed ɪ'vɪkt [iː'v-], -s, -ɪŋ, -ɪd
eviction, -s ɪ'vɪkʃn [iː'v-], -z
evidenc|e (s. v.), -es, -ing, -ed 'evɪdəns, -ɪz, -ɪŋ, -t
evident, -ly 'evɪdənt, -lɪ
evidenti|al, -ally ˌevɪ'denʃ|l, -əlɪ
evidentiary ˌevɪ'denʃərɪ
ev|il (s. adj.), -ils, -illy 'iːv|l [-ɪl], -lz [-ɪlz], -əlɪ [-ɪlɪ]
evil-doer, -s ˌiːvl'duːə* [ˌiːvɪl-, -'dʊə*, '--ˌ--], -z
evil-eye, -s, -d ˌiːvl̩'aɪ [ˌiːvɪl'aɪ], -z, -d
evil-minded, -ness ˌiːvl'maɪndɪd [ˌiːvɪl-, '--ˌ--], -nɪs [-nəs]
evil-speaking ˌiːvl'spiːkɪŋ [ˌiːvɪl-]
evinc|e, -es, -ing, -ed; -ive ɪ'vɪns, -ɪz, -ɪŋ, -t; -ɪv
evincib|le, -ly ɪ'vɪnsəb|l [-sɪb-], -lɪ
evirat|e, -es, -ing, -ed 'iːvɪreɪt ['ev-], -s, -ɪŋ, -ɪd
eviscerat|e, -es, -ing, -ed ɪ'vɪsəreɪt [iː'v-], -s, -ɪŋ, -ɪd
evisceration ɪˌvɪsə'reɪʃn [iːˌv-]
evocat|e, -es, -ing, -ed 'evəʊkeɪt ['iːv-], -s, -ɪŋ, -ɪd
evocation, -s ˌevəʊ'keɪʃn [ˌiːv-], -z
evocative ɪ'vɒkətɪv
evok|e, -es, -ing, -ed ɪ'vəʊk [iː'v-], -s, -ɪŋ, -t
evolute, -s 'iːvəluːt ['ev-, -ljuːt], -s
evolution, -s ˌiːvə'luːʃn [ˌev-, -'ljuː-], -z
evolutional ˌiːvə'luːʃənl [ˌev-, -'ljuː-, -ʃnəl, -ʃn̩l, -ʃnl, -ʃənəl]
evolutionary ɪ'vəˈluːʃnərɪ [ˌev-, -'ljuː-, -ʃṇərɪ, -ʃənərɪ]
evolutioni|sm, -st/s ˌiːvə'luːʃənɪ|zəm [ˌev-, -'ljuː-, -ʃn̩ɪ-], -st/s
evolv|e, -es, -ing, -ed; -able ɪ'vɒlv [iː'v-], -z, -ɪŋ, -d; -əbl
Evors 'iːvɔːz
evulsion, -s ɪ'vʌlʃn [iː'v-], -z
Ewart 'juːət, jʊət
Ewbank 'juːbæŋk
ewe, -s; -lamb/s juː-, -z; -læm/z
Ewell 'juːəl, jʊəl
Ewen 'juːən, 'jʊən [-ɪn]
ewe-neck, -s 'juːnek, -s
ewer, -s 'juːə* [jʊə*], -z
Ewing 'juːɪŋ, 'jʊɪŋ
ex eks
exacerbat|e, -es, -ing, -ed ɪg'zæsəbeɪt [ek'sæs-], -s, -ɪŋ, -ɪd
exacerbation, -s ɪgˌzæsə'beɪʃn [ekˌsæs-], -z

exact (adj. v.), -er, -est, -ly, -ness; -s, -ing, -ed, -er/s, -or/s ɪg'zækt [eg-], -ə*, -ɪst, -lɪ [ɪg'zæklɪ, 'gzæklɪ], -nɪs [-nəs] [ɪg'zæknɪs, -nəs]; -s, -ɪŋ, -ɪd, -ə*/z, -ə*/z
exaction, -s ɪg'zækʃn [eg-], -z
exactitude ɪg'zæktɪtjuːd [eg-]
exaggerat|e, -es, -ing, -ed, -or/s ɪg'zædʒəreɪt [eg-], -s, -ɪŋ, -ɪd, -ə*/z
exaggeration, -s ɪgˌzædʒə'reɪʃn [eg-], -z
exaggerative ɪg'zædʒərətɪv [eg-, -reɪt-]
exalt, -s, -ing, -ed/ly, -edness ɪg'zɔːlt [eg-, -'zɒlt], -s, -ɪŋ, -ɪd/lɪ, -ɪdnɪs [-nəs]
exaltation, -s ˌegzɔːl'teɪʃn [ˌeks-, -ɒl-], -z
exam, -s ɪg'zæm [eg-], -z
examen, -s eg'zeɪmen, -z
examination, -s ɪgˌzæmɪ'neɪʃn [eg-], -z
examin|e, -es, -ing, -ed, -er/s ɪg'zæmɪn [eg-], -z, -ɪŋ, -d, -ə*/z
examinee, -s ɪgˌzæmɪ'niː [eg-], -z
examp|le (s. v.), -les, -ling, -led ɪg'zɑːmp|l [eg-], -lz, -lɪŋ, -ld
exarch, -s; -ate/s 'eksɑːk, -s; -eɪt/s
exasperat|e, -es, -ing, -ed, -or/s ɪg'zæspəreɪt [eg-, -'zɑː-s], -s, -ɪŋ, -ɪd, -ə*/z
exasperation ɪgˌzæspə'reɪʃn [eg-, -ˌzɑːs-]
Excalibur eks'kælɪbə*
ex cathedra ˌekskæ'θiːdrə
excavat|e, -es, -ing, -ed, -or/s 'ekskəveɪt, -s, -ɪŋ, -ɪd, -ə*/z
excavation, -s ˌekskə'veɪʃn, -z
exceed, -s, -ing, -ed ɪk'siːd [ek-], -z, -ɪŋ, -ɪd
exceeding (adj.), -ly ɪk'siːdɪŋ [ek-], -lɪ
excel, -s, -ling, -led ɪk'sel [ek-], -z, -ɪŋ, -d
excellen|ce, -ces, -cy, -cies, -t/ly 'eksələn|s, -sɪz, -sɪ, -sɪz, -t/lɪ
excelsior ek'selsɪɔː* [ɪk-, -sɪə*, -sjə*]
except (v. prep. conj.), -s, -ing, -ed ɪk'sept [ek-], -s, -ɪŋ, -ɪd
exception, -s ɪk'sepʃn [ek-], -z
exceptionab|le, -ly, -leness ɪk'sepʃnəb|l [ek-, -ʃpə-, -ʃənə-], -lɪ, -lnɪs [-nəs]
excep|tional, -tionally ɪk'sep|ʃənl [ek-, -ʃnəl, -ʃn̩l, -ʃnl, -ʃənəl], -ʃnəlɪ [-ʃnəlɪ, -ʃn̩lɪ, -ʃnlɪ, -ʃənəlɪ]
excerpt (s.), -s 'eksɜːpt [ɪk'sɜːpt, ek's-], -s
excerpt (v.), -s, -ing, -ed ek'sɜːpt [ɪk-], -s, -ɪŋ, -ɪd
excerption, -s ek'sɜːpʃn [ɪk-], -z
excess (s. v.), -es, -ing, -ed ɪk'ses [ek-] (also 'ekses when noun is used attributively), -ɪz, -ɪŋ, -t

175

excessive, -ly, -ness ɪk'sesɪv [ek-], -lɪ, -nɪs [-nəs]

exchang|e (*s. v.*), **-es, -ing, -ed, -er/s; -eable** ɪks'tʃeɪndʒ [eks-], -ɪz, -ɪŋ, -d, -ə*/z; -əbl

exchangeability ɪks,tʃeɪndʒə'bɪlətɪ [eks-, -lɪt-]

exchangee, -s ,ekstʃeɪn'dʒiː [ɪks,tʃ-], -z

exchequer, -s ɪks'tʃekə* [eks-], -z

excisable ek'saɪzəbl [ɪk-]

excise (*s.*) (*tax*), **-man, -men** 'eksaɪz [ɪk's-, ek'saɪz], -mæn, -men

excis|e (*v.*) (*cut out*), **-es, -ing, -ed** ek'saɪz [ɪk-], -ɪz, -ɪŋ, -d

excision, -s ek'sɪʒn [ɪk-], -z

excitability ɪk,saɪtə'bɪlətɪ [ek-, -lɪt-]

excitant, -s 'eksɪtənt [ɪk'saɪtənt], -s

excitation, -s ,eksɪ'teɪʃn, -z

excitat|ive, -ory ek'saɪtət|ɪv [ɪk-], -ərɪ

excit|e, -es, -ing, -ed, -er/s, -ement/s; -able/ness ɪk'saɪt [ek-], -s, -ɪŋ, -ɪd, -ə*/z, -mənt/s; -əbl/nɪs [-nəs]

exclaim, -s, -ing, -ed ɪk'skleɪm [ek's-], -z, -ɪŋ, -d

exclamation, -s ,eksklə'meɪʃn, -z

exclamatory ek'sklæmətərɪ [ɪk's-]

exclud|e, -es, -ing, -ed ɪk'skluːd [ek's-], -z, -ɪŋ, -ɪd

exclusion, -s ɪk'skluːʒn [ek's-], -z

exclusionist, -s ɪk'skluːʒənɪst [ek's-, -ʒnɪst], -s

†**exclusive, -ly, -ness** ɪk'skluːsɪv [ek's-], -lɪ, -nɪs [-nəs]

excogitat|e, -es, -ing, -ed eks'kɒdʒɪteɪt [ɪks-], -s, -ɪŋ, -ɪd

excogitation, -s eks,kɒdʒɪ'teɪʃn [ɪks,kɒdʒ-, ,ekskɒdʒ-], -z

excommunicat|e, -es, -ing, -ed ,ekskə-'mjuːnɪkeɪt, -s, -ɪŋ, -ɪd

excommunication, -s 'ekskə,mjuːnɪ-'keɪʃn [-,mjʊn-], -z

excoriat|e, -es, -ing, -ed eks'kɔːrɪeɪt [ɪks-, -'kɒr-], -s, -ɪŋ, -ɪd

excoriation, -s eks,kɔːrɪ'eɪʃn [ɪks-, -,kɒr-], -z

excrement, -s 'ekskrɪmənt [-krəm-], -s

excremental ,ekskrɪ'mentl [-krə'm-]

excrementitious ,ekskrɪmen'tɪʃəs [-krəm-]

excrescen|ce, -ces, -t ɪk'skresn|s [ek's-], -sɪz, -t

excret|e, -es, -ing, -ed; -ive, -ory ɪk'skriːt [ek's-], -s, -ɪŋ, -ɪd; -ɪv, -ərɪ

excretion, -s ɪk'skriːʃn [ek's-], -z

excret|um, -a ɪk'skriːt|əm [ek's-], -ə

excruciat|e, -es, -ing/ly, -ed ɪk'skruː-ʃɪeɪt [ek's-, -ʃjeɪt], -s, -ɪŋ/lɪ, -ɪd

excruciation ɪk,skruː'ʃɪ'eɪʃn [ek,s-, -uːsɪ-]

exculpat|e, -es, -ing, -ed 'ekskʌlpeɪt, -s, -ɪŋ, -ɪd

exculpation ,ekskʌl'peɪʃn

exculpatory eks'kʌlpətərɪ ['ekskʌl-peɪtərɪ]

excurs|e, -es, -ing, -ed ɪk'skɜːs [ek's-], -ɪz, -ɪŋ, -t

excursion, -s ɪk'skɜːʃn [ek's-], -z

excursionist, -s ɪk'skɜːʃnɪst [ek's-, -ʃənɪst], -s

excursioniz|e [-is|e], -es, -ing, -ed ɪk'skɜːʃnaɪz [ek's-, -ʃənaɪz], -ɪz, -ɪŋ, -d

excursive, -ly, -ness ek'skɜːsɪv [ɪk's-], -lɪ, -nɪs [-nəs]

excursus, -es ek'skɜːsəs [ɪk's-], -ɪz

excusab|le, -ly, -leness ɪk'skjuːzəb|l [ek's-], -lɪ, -lnɪs [-nəs]

excusatory ɪk'skjuːzətərɪ [ek's-]

excuse (*s.*), **-s** ɪk'skjuːs [ek's-], -ɪz

excus|e (*v.*), **-es, -ing, -ed** ɪk'skjuːz [ek's-], -ɪz, -ɪŋ, -d

Exe eks

exeat, -s 'eksɪæt [-sjæt], -s

execrab|le, -ly, -leness 'eksɪkrəb|l, -lɪ, -lnɪs [-nəs]

execrat|e, -es, -ing, -ed 'eksɪkreɪt, -s, -ɪŋ, -ɪd

execration, -s ,eksɪ'kreɪʃn, -z

execrat|ive, -ively, -ory 'eksɪkreɪt|ɪv, -ɪvlɪ, -ərɪ

executant, -s ɪg'zekjʊtənt ['eg-], -s

execut|e, -es, -ing, -ed, -er/s; -able 'eksɪkjuːt, -s, -ɪŋ, -ɪd, -ə*/z; -əbl

execution, -s ,eksɪ'kjuːʃn, -z

executioner, -s ,eksɪ'kjuːʃnə* [-ʃŋə*, -ʃənə*], -z

executive (*s. adj.*), **-s, -ly** ɪg'zekjʊtɪv [eg-], -z, -lɪ

executor, -s; -ship/s ɪg'zekjʊtə* [eg-], -z; -ʃɪp/s

executory ɪg'zekjʊtərɪ [eg-]

executrix, -es ɪg'zekjʊtrɪks [eg-], -ɪz

exegesis ,eksɪ'dʒiːsɪs

exegetic, -al, -ally, -s ,eksɪ'dʒetɪk, -l, -əlɪ, -s

Exell 'eksl

exemplar, -s ɪg'zemplə* [eg-, -lɑː*], -z

exemplarity ,egzem'plærətɪ [-ɪtɪ]

exemplar|y, -ily, -iness ɪg'zemplər|ɪ [eg-], -əlɪ [-ɪlɪ], -ɪnɪs [-ɪnəs]

exemplification, -s ɪg,zemplɪfɪ'keɪʃn [eg-], -z

exempli|fy, -fies, -fying, -fied ɪg'zem-plɪ|faɪ [eg-], -faɪz, -faɪɪŋ, -faɪd

exempt (*adj. v.*), -s, -ing, -ed ɪɡ'zempt [eg-], -s, -ɪŋ, -ɪd
exemption, -s ɪɡ'zempʃn [eg-], -z
exequatur, -s ˌeksɪ'kweɪtə*, -z
exequies 'eksɪkwɪz
exercis|e (*s. v.*), -es, -ing, -ed, -er/s 'eksəsaɪz, -ɪz, -ɪŋ, -d, -ə*/z
exercitation eɡˌzɜːsɪ'teɪʃn [ɪɡ-]
exergue, -s ek'sɜːɡ ['eksɜːɡ], -z
exert, -s, -ing, -ed; -ive ɪɡ'zɜːt [eg-], -s, -ɪŋ, -ɪd; -ɪv
exertion, -s ɪɡ'zɜːʃn [eg-], -z
exes 'eksɪz
Exeter 'eksɪtə* [-sətə*]
exeunt 'eksɪʌnt [-sjʌnt, -sɪʊnt, -sɪənt, -sjənt]
exfoliat|e, -es, -ing, -ed eks'fəʊlɪeɪt [-ljeɪt], -s, -ɪŋ, -ɪd
exfoliation, -s eksˌfəʊlɪ'eɪʃn [ˌeksfəʊ-], -z
exhalant eks'heɪlənt [eg'zeɪ-]
exhalation, -s ˌekshə'leɪʃn [ˌeɡzə'l-], -z
exhal|e, -es, -ing, -ed eks'heɪl [ɪks-, eɡ'zeɪl], -z, -ɪŋ, -d
exhaust (*s. v.*), -s, -ing, -ed, -er/s; -ible, -less ɪɡ'zɔːst [eg-], -s, -ɪŋ, -ɪd, -ə*/z; -əbl [-ɪbl], -lɪs [-ləs]
exhaustion ɪɡ'zɔːstʃən [eg-]
exhaustive, -ly, -ness ɪɡ'zɔːstɪv [eg-], -lɪ, -nɪs [-nəs]
exhaust-pipe, -s ɪɡ'zɔːstpaɪp [eg-], -s
exhibit (*s.*), -s ɪɡ'zɪbɪt [eg'zɪb-, 'eɡzɪb-], -s
exhibit (*v.*), -s, -ing, -ed, -or/s; -ive, -ory ɪɡ'zɪbɪt [eg-], -s, -ɪŋ, -ɪd, -ə*/z; -ɪv, -ərɪ
exhibition, -s ˌeksɪ'bɪʃn, -z
exhibitioner, -s ˌeksɪ'bɪʃŋə* [-ʃənə*, -ʃnə*], -z
†exhibitionism ˌeksɪ'bɪʃŋɪzəm [-ʃənɪ-]
exhilarant, -s ɪɡ'zɪlərənt [eɡ'z-, ek's-], -s
exhilarat|e, -es, -ing, -ed ɪɡ'zɪləreɪt [eɡ'z-, ek's-], -s, -ɪŋ, -ɪd
exhilaration ɪɡˌzɪlə'reɪʃn [eɡˌz-, ekˌs-]
exhilarative ɪɡ'zɪlərətɪv [eɡ'z-, ek's-, -reɪt-]
exhort, -s, -ing, -ed ɪɡ'zɔːt [eg-], -s, -ɪŋ, -ɪd
exhortation, -s ˌeɡzɔː'teɪʃn [ˌeksɔː-], -z
exhortat|ive, -ory ɪɡ'zɔːtət|ɪv [eg-], -ərɪ
exhumation, -s ˌekshju:'meɪʃn, -z
exhum|e, -es, -ing, -ed, -er/s eks-'hju:m [ɪɡ'zju:m], -z, -ɪŋ, -d, -ə*/z
exigen|ce, -ces -t 'eksɪdʒən|s ['eɡzɪ-], -sɪz, -t

exigenc|y, -ies 'eksɪdʒəns|ɪ ['eɡzɪdʒ-, ɪɡ'zɪdʒ-, eɡ'zɪdʒ-, ek'sɪdʒ-], -ɪz
Note.—The form ɪɡ'zɪdʒənsɪ *is increasingly common.*
exiguity ˌeksɪ'ɡju:ətɪ [-'ɡjʊɪ-, -ɪtɪ]
exiguous, -ness eɡ'zɪɡjʊəs [ɪɡ'z-, ek's-, -ɡjwəs], -nɪs [-nəs]
exil|e (*s. v.*), -es, -ing, -ed 'eksaɪl ['eɡz-], -z, -ɪŋ, -d
exilic eɡ'zɪlɪk [ek's-]
exility eɡ'zɪlətɪ [ek's-, -ɪtɪ]
exist, -s, -ing, -ed ɪɡ'zɪst [eg-], -s, -ɪŋ, -ɪd
existen|ce, -ces, -t ɪɡ'zɪstən|s [eg-], -sɪz, -t
existential ˌeɡzɪ'stenʃl
existentiali|sm, -st/s ˌeɡzɪ'stenʃəlɪ|zəm [-ʃlɪ-], -st/s
exit, -s 'eksɪt ['eɡzɪt], -s
ex-libris eks'laɪbrɪs [-'liːb-]
Exmoor 'eksmɔː* [-mɔə*, -mʊə*]
Exmouth (*in Devon*) 'eksmaʊθ [-məθ], (*in Australia*) 'eksmaʊθ
Note.—Both pronunciations are heard locally at Exmouth in Devon.
exode, -s 'eksəʊd, -z
exodus (E.), -es 'eksədəs, -ɪz
ex officio ˌeksə'fɪʃɪəʊ [-sɒ'f-, -ʃjəʊ, -sɪəʊ, -sjəʊ]
exogam|ous, -y ek'sɒɡəm|əs, -ɪ
exon, -s 'eksɒn, -z
exonerat|e, -es, -ing, -ed ɪɡ'zɒnəreɪt [eg-], -s, -ɪŋ, -ɪd
exoneration ɪɡˌzɒnə'reɪʃn [eg-]
exonerative ɪɡ'zɒnərətɪv [eg-, -reɪt-]
exorbitan|ce, -cy, -t/ly ɪɡ'zɔːbɪtən|s [eg-], -sɪ, -t/lɪ
exorcis|e, -es, -ing, -ed 'eksɔːsaɪz ['eɡz-, -səsaɪz], -ɪz, -ɪŋ, -d
exorci|sm, -st/s 'eksɔːsɪ|zəm ['eɡz-, -səsɪ|zəm], -st/s
exordium, -s ek'sɔːdjəm [eɡ'z-, -dɪəm], -z
exoteric (*s. adj.*), -s, -al, -ally ˌeksəʊ-'terɪk, -s, -l, -əlɪ
exotic (*s. adj.*), -s, -a ɪɡ'zɒtɪk [ek's-, eɡ'z-], -s, -ə
expand, -s, -ing, -ed, -er/s ɪk'spænd [ek's-], -z, -ɪŋ, -ɪd, -ə*/z
expanse, -s ɪk'spæns [ek's-], -ɪz
expansibility ɪkˌspænsə'bɪlətɪ [ekˌsp-, -sɪ'b-, -lɪt-]
expansib|le, -ly, -leness ɪk'spænsəb|l [ek's-, -sɪb-], -lɪ, -lnɪs [-nəs]
expansile ɪk'spænsaɪl [ek's-]
expansion, -s ɪk'spænʃn [ek's-], -z
expansioni|sm, -st/s ɪk'spænʃənɪ|zəm [ek's-, -ʃŋɪ-], -st/s

expansive, -ly, -ness ɪk'spænsɪv [ek's-],
-lɪ, -nɪs [-nəs]
ex parte ˌeks'pɑːtɪ
expatiat|e, -es, -ing, -ed ek'speɪʃɪeɪt
[ɪk's-, -ʃjeɪt], -s, -ɪŋ, -ɪd
expatiation, -s ek,speɪʃɪ'eɪʃn [ɪkˌs-], -z
expatiat|ive, -ory ek'speɪʃjət|ɪv [ɪk's-,
-ʃɪət-, -ʃɪeɪt-], -ərɪ
expatriate (s. adj.), -s eks'pætrɪət [ɪks-,
-'peɪt-, -ɪɪt, -ɪeɪt], -s
expatriat|e (v), -es, -ing, -ed eks'pætrɪeɪt
[ɪks-, -'peɪt-], -s, -ɪŋ, -ɪd
expatriation eks,pætrɪ'eɪʃn [ɪks,pæt-,
-,peɪt-, ,ekspeɪt-, ,ekspæt-]
expect, -s, -ing, -ed, -er/s ɪk'spekt
[ek's-], -s, -ɪŋ, -ɪd, -ə*/z
expectan|ce, -cy, -cies, -t/ly ɪk'spek-
tən|s [ek's-], -sɪ, -sɪz, -t/lɪ
expectation, -s ˌekspek'teɪʃn, -z
expectorant (s. adj.), -s ɪk'spektərənt
[ek's-], -s
expectorat|e, -es, -ing, -ed ɪk'spektəreɪt
[ek's-], -s, -ɪŋ, -ɪd
expectoration ɪk,spektə'reɪʃn [ekˌs-]
expedien|ce, -cy, -t/s, -tly ɪk'spiːdjən|s
[ek's-, -dɪən-], -sɪ, -t/s, -tlɪ
expedit|e, -es, -ing, -ed 'ekspɪdaɪt
[-pəd-, -ped-], -s, -ɪŋ, -ɪd
expedition, -s ˌekspɪ'dɪʃn [-pə'd-], -z
expeditionary ˌekspɪ'dɪʃənərɪ [-pə'd-]
expeditious, -ly, -ness ˌekspɪ'dɪʃəs
[-pə'd-], -lɪ, -nɪs [-nəs]
expel, -s, -ling, -led; -lable ɪk'spel
[ek's-], -z, -ɪŋ, -d; -əbl
expend, -s, -ing, -ed ɪk'spend [ek's-], -z,
-ɪŋ, -ɪd
expendable (s. adj.), -s ɪk'spendəbl
[ek's-], -z
expenditure, -s ɪk'spendɪtʃə* [ek's-], -z
expense, -s ɪk'spens [ek's-], -ɪz
expensive, -ly, -ness ɪk'spensɪv [ek's-],
-lɪ, -nɪs [-nəs]
experienc|e (s. v.), -es, -ing, -ed ɪk'spɪə-
rɪəns [ek's-], -ɪz, -ɪŋ, -t
experiment (s.), -s ɪk'sperɪmənt [ek's-],
-s
experiment (v.), -s, -ing, -ed ɪk'sperɪ-
ment [ek's-], -s, -ɪŋ, -ɪd
experiment|al, -ally ekˌsperɪ'ment|l
[ɪkˌsper-, ˌeksper-], -əlɪ [-lɪ]
experimentali|sm, -st/s ekˌsperɪ'men-
təlɪ|zəm [ɪkˌsper-, ˌeksper-, -tlɪ-],
-st/s
experimentaliz|e [-is|e], -es, -ing, -ed
ekˌsperɪ'mentəlaɪz [ɪkˌsper-,
ˌeksper-, -tlaɪ-], -ɪz, -ɪŋ, -d
experimentation, -s ekˌsperɪmen'teɪʃn
[ɪkˌs-], -z

expert (s.), -s 'ekspɜːt, -s
expert (adj.), -est, -ly, -ness 'ekspɜːt
[also ek'spɜːt, ɪk'spɜːt, when not
attributive], -ɪst, -lɪ, -nɪs [-nəs]
expertise ˌekspɜː'tiːz [-pə't-]
expiable 'ekspɪəbl [-pjə-]
expiat|e, -es, -ing, -ed, -or/s 'ekspɪeɪt
[-pjeɪt], -s, -ɪŋ, -ɪd, -ə*/z
expiation, -s ˌekspɪ'eɪʃn, -z
expiatory 'ekspɪətərɪ [-pjət-, -pɪeɪt-]
expiration, -s ˌekspɪ'reɪʃn [-pə'r-,
-paɪə'r-], -z
expiratory ɪk'spaɪərətərɪ [ek's-]
expir|e, -es, -ing, -ed ɪk'spaɪə* [ek's-],
-z, -rɪŋ, -d
expiry ɪk'spaɪərɪ [ek's-]
explain, -s, -ing, -ed, -er/s; -able
ɪk'spleɪn [ek's-], -z, -ɪŋ, -d, -ə*/z;
-əbl
explanation, -s ˌeksplə'neɪʃn, -z
explanator|y, -ily, -iness ɪk'splænətər|ɪ
[ek's-, -nɪt-], -əlɪ [-ɪlɪ], -ɪnɪs [-nəs]
expletive (s. adj.), -s, -ly ɪk'spliːtɪv
[ek's-], -z, -lɪ
explicable ɪk'splɪkəbl ['eksplɪkəbl]
   Note.—The form with the stress on the
   second syllable has generally super-
   seded that with the stress on the
   first.
explicat|e, -es, -ing, -ed 'eksplɪkeɪt, -s,
-ɪŋ, -ɪd
explication, -s ˌeksplɪ'keɪʃn, -z
explicative ek'splɪkətɪv [ɪk's-, 'eksplɪ-
keɪtɪv]
explicatory ek'splɪkətərɪ [ɪk's-, 'eksplɪ-
keɪtərɪ, ˌeksplɪ'keɪt-]
explicit, -ly, -ness ɪk'splɪsɪt [ek's-], -lɪ,
-nɪs [-nəs]
explod|e, -es, -ing, -ed, -er/s ɪk'spləʊd
[ek's-], -z, -ɪŋ, -ɪd, -ə*/z
exploit (s.), -s 'eksplɔɪt, -s
exploit (v.), -s, -ing, -ed ɪk'splɔɪt [ek's-],
-s, -ɪŋ, -ɪd
exploitation ˌeksplɔɪ'teɪʃn
exploration, -s ˌeksplə'reɪʃn [-plɔː'r-], -z
explorat|ive, -ory ek'splɒrət|ɪv [ɪk's-,
-'plɔːr-, -'plɔər-], -ərɪ
explor|e, -es, -ing, -ed, -er/s ɪk'splɔː*
[ek's-, -'plɔə*], -z, -rɪŋ, -d, -rə*/z
explosion, -s ɪk'spləʊʒn [ek's-], -z
explosive (s. adj.), -s, -ly, -ness ɪk's-
pləʊsɪv [ek's-, -əʊzɪv], -z, -lɪ, -nɪs
[-nəs]
exponent, -s ɪk'spəʊnənt [ek's-], -s
exponential ˌekspəʊ'nenʃl
export (s.), -s 'ekspɔːt, -s
export (v.), -s, -ing, -ed, -er/s ɪk'spɔːt
[ek's-, 'ekspɔːt], -s, -ɪŋ, -ɪd, -ə*/z

exportable ɪk'spɔːtəbl [ek's-]
exportation ˌekspɔː'teɪʃn
exposal, -s ɪk'spəʊzl [ek's-], -z
expos|e, -es, -ing, -ed, -edness, -er/s ɪk'spəʊz [ek's-], -ɪz, -ɪŋ, -d, -dnɪs [-nəs], -ə*/z
exposé, -s ek'spəʊzeɪ (ɛkspoze), -z
exposition, -s ˌekspəʊ'zɪʃn [-pʊ'z-], -z
expositive ɪk'spɒzɪtɪv [ek's-, -zɒt-]
exposit|or/s, -ory ɪk'spɒzɪt|ə*/z [ek's-], -ərɪ
expostulat|e, -es, -ing, -ed, -or/s ɪk's-pɒstʃʊleɪt [ek's-, -tjʊ-], -s, -ɪŋ, -ɪd, -ə*/z
expostulation, -s ɪkˌspɒstʃʊ'leɪʃn [ekˌs-, -tjʊ-], -z
expostulative ɪk'spɒstʃʊlətɪv [ek's-, -tjʊ-, -leɪt-]
expostulatory ɪk'spɒstʃʊlətərɪ [ek's-, -tjʊ-, -leɪtərɪ]
exposure, -s ɪk'spəʊʒə* [ek's-], -z
expound, -s, -ing, -ed, -er/s ɪk'spaʊnd [ek's-], -z, -ɪŋ, -ɪd, -ə*/z
express (s. adj. v.), **-es; -ly, -ness; -ing, -ed** ɪk'spres [ek's-, 'ekspres *attributively*], -ɪz; -lɪ, -nɪs [-nəs]; -ɪŋ, -t
expressible ɪk'spresəbl [ek's-, -sɪb-]
expression, -s ɪk'spreʃn [ek's-], -z
expressional ɪk'spreʃənl [ek's-, -ʃn̩, -ʃnl̩]
expression|ism, -ist/s ɪk'spreʃn̩|ɪzəm [ek's-, -ʃən-], -ɪst/s
expressionistic ɪkˌspreʃə'nɪstɪk [ekˌs-, -ʃn̩'ɪs-]
expressionless ɪk'spreʃnlɪs [ek's-, -ləs]
expressive, -ly, -ness ɪk'spresɪv [ek's-], -lɪ, -nɪs [-nəs]
express|man, -men ɪk'spres|mæn [ek's-], -men
expropriat|e, -es, -ing, -ed, -or/s eks-'prəʊprɪeɪt, -s, -ɪŋ, -ɪd, -ə*/z
expropriation, -s eksˌprəʊprɪ'eɪʃn [ˌeksprəʊ-], -z
expugn, -s, -ing, -ed eks'pjuːn [ɪks-], -z, -ɪŋ, -d
expugnable eks'pʌgnəbl [ɪks-]
expulsion, -s ɪk'spʌlʃn [ek's-], -z
expulsive ɪk'spʌlsɪv [ek's-]
expung|e, -es, -ing, -ed ɪk'spʌndʒ [ek's-], -ɪz, -ɪŋ, -d
expurgat|e, -es, -ing, -ed, -or/s 'eks-pəgeɪt [-pɜː-], -s, -ɪŋ, -ɪd, -ə* /z
expurgation, -s ˌekspə'geɪʃn [-spɜː'g-], -z
expurgatorial ekˌspɜː'tɔːrɪəl [ˌekspɜː-]
expurgatory ek'spɜːgətərɪ

exquisite, -ly, -ness 'ekskwɪzɪt [ek-'skwɪzɪt, ɪk'skwɪzɪt], -lɪ, -nɪs [-nəs]
Note.—The forms ek'skwɪzɪt *and* ɪk'skwɪzɪt *are becoming very common.*
exscind, -s, -ing, -ed ek'sɪnd [ɪk-], -z, -ɪŋ, -ɪd
exsect, -s, -ing, -ed ek'sekt [ɪk-], -s, -ɪŋ, -ɪd
exsection, -s ek'sekʃn [ɪk-], -z
ex-service ˌeks'sɜːvɪs ['eksˌsɜːvɪs]
exsiccat|e, -es, -ing, -ed, -or/s 'eksɪkeɪt ['ekssɪ-], -s, -ɪŋ, -ɪd, -ə*/z
exsiccation ˌeksɪ'keɪʃn [ˌekssɪ-]
extant ek'stænt [ɪk'st-, 'ekstənt]
extemporaneous, -ly, -ness ekˌstem-pə'reɪnjəs [ˌekstem-, -pʊ'r-, -nɪəs], -lɪ, -nɪs [-nəs]
extemporary ɪk'stempərərɪ [ek's-]
extempore ek'stempərɪ [ɪk's-]
extemporization [-isa-], -s ekˌstem-pəraɪ'zeɪʃn [ɪkˌs-, -pʊr-], -z
extemporiz|e [-is|e], -es, -ing, -ed, -er/s ɪk'stempəraɪz [ek's-, -pʊr-], -ɪz, -ɪŋ, -d, -ə*/z
extend, -s, -ing, -ed ɪk'stend [ek's-], -z, -ɪŋ, -ɪd
extensibility ɪkˌstensə'bɪlətɪ [ekˌs-, -sɪ'b-, -lɪt-]
extensible ɪk'stensəbl [ek's-, -sɪb-]
extensile ek'stensaɪl [ɪk's-]
extension, -s ɪk'stenʃn [ek's-], -z
extensive, -ly, -ness ɪk'stensɪv [ek's-], -lɪ, -nɪs [-nəs]
extensor, -s ɪk'stensə* [ek's-], -z
extent, -s ɪk'stent [ek's-], -s
extenuat|e, -es, -ing/ly, -ed ɪk'sten-jʊeɪt [ek's-], -s, -ɪŋ/lɪ, -ɪd
extenuation, -s ɪkˌstenjʊ'eɪʃn [ek's-], -z
extenuative ɪk'stenjʊətɪv [ek's-, -jwət-, -jʊeɪt-]
extenuatory ɪk'stenjʊətərɪ [ek's-, -jwət-, -jʊeɪt-]
exterior (s. adj.), **-s, -ly** ɪk'stɪərɪə* [ek'st-], -z, -lɪ
exteriority ɪkˌstɪərɪ'ɒrətɪ [ˌekstɪə-, ekˌst-, -ɪtɪ]
exterioriz|e [-is|e], -es, -ing, -ed ɪk-'stɪərɪəraɪz [ek's-], -ɪz, -ɪŋ, -d
exterminable ɪk'stɜːmɪnəbl [ek's-]
exterminat|e, -es, -ing, -ed, -or/s ɪk-'stɜːmɪneɪt [ek's-], -s, -ɪŋ, -ɪd, -ə*/z
extermination, -s ɪkˌstɜːmɪ'neɪʃn [ekˌs-], -z
exterminative ɪk'stɜːmɪnətɪv [ek's-, -neɪt-]
exterminatory ɪk'stɜːmɪnətərɪ [ek's-, -neɪt-]

extern (*s. adj.*), **-s** ek'stɜːn, -z
extern|al (*s. adj.*), **-als, -ally** ɪk'stɜːn|l
['ekst-, ek'st-], -|z, -əlɪ [-|ɪ]
Note.—The form 'ekstɜːnl *is chiefly
used attributively, or when the word
is in contrast with* **internal.**
externali|sm, -st/s ɪk'stɜːnəlɪ|zəm
[-n|ɪ-, ek'st-], -st/s
externality ‚ekstɜː'nælətɪ [-ɪtɪ]
externalization [-**isa-**] ɪk‚stɜːnəlaɪ-
'zeɪʃn [ek‚st-, -n|aɪ-]
externaliz|e [-**is|e**], **-es, -ing, -ed** ɪk-
'stɜːnəlaɪz [ek'st-, -n|aɪz], -ɪz, -ɪŋ, -d
exterritorial 'eks‚terɪ'tɔːrɪəl
extinct ɪk'stɪŋ*k*t [ek's-]
extinction, -s ɪk'stɪŋ*k*ʃn [ek's-], -z
extinctive ɪk'stɪŋ*k*tɪv [ek's-]
**extinguish, -es, -ing, -ed, -er/s, -ment;
-able** ɪk'stɪŋgwɪʃ [ek's-], -ɪz, -ɪŋ, -t,
-ə*/z, -mənt; -əbl
extirpat|e, -es, -ing, -ed, -or/s 'eks-
təpeɪt [-tɜːp-], -s, -ɪŋ, -ɪd, -ə*/z
extirpation, -s ‚ekstə'peɪʃn [-tɜː'p-], -z
extol, -s, -ling, -led ɪk'stəʊl [ek's-,
-'tɒl], -z, -ɪŋ, -d
Exton 'ekstən
extort, -s, -ing, -ed,-er/s ɪk'stɔːt [ek's-],
-s, -ɪŋ, -ɪd, -ə*/z
extortion, -s ɪk'stɔːʃn [ek's-], -z
extortionate, -ly ɪk'stɔːʃŋət [ek's-,
-ʃənət, -ʃnət, -nɪt], -lɪ
extortioner, -s ɪk'stɔːʃŋə* [ek's-, -ʃənə*,
-ʃnə*], -z
extra (*s. adj. adv.*), **-s** 'ekstrə, -z
extract (*s.*), **-s** 'ekstrækt, -s
extract (*v.*), **-s, -ing, -ed, -or/s; -able,
-ive** ɪk'strækt [ek's-], -s, -ɪŋ, -ɪd,
-ə*/z; -əbl, -ɪv
extraction, -s ɪk'strækʃn [ek's-], -z
extra-curricular ‚ekstrəkə'rɪkjələ*
[-kjʊ-]
extradit|e, -es, -ing, -ed; -able 'ekstrə-
daɪt, -s, -ɪŋ, -ɪd; -əbl
extradition, -s ‚ekstrə'dɪʃn, -z
extrados, -es eks'treɪdɒs, -ɪz
extrajudici|al, -ally ‚ekstrədʒuː'dɪʃ|l
[-dʒʊ-], -əlɪ [-|ɪ]
extra-marital ‚ekstrə'mærɪtl
extramural ‚ekstrə'mjʊərəl [-'mjɔːr-,
-'mjɔː·r-]
extraneous, -ly ɪk'streɪmjəs [ek-, -nɪəs], -lɪ
extraordinar|y, -ily, -iness ɪk'strɔːdnr|ɪ
[ek'strɔː-, ‚ekstrə'ɔː-, -dɪnər|ɪ,
-dənər|ɪ], -əlɪ [-ɪlɪ], -ɪnɪs [-nəs]
extrapolat|e, -es, -ing, -ed ɪk'stræpəʊ-
leɪt [ek's-], -s, -ɪŋ, -ɪd
extrasensory ‚ekstrə'sensərɪ
extraterritorial 'ekstrə‚terɪ'tɔːrɪəl

extravagan|ce, -ces,-t/ly ɪk'strævəgən|s
[ek's-, -vɪg-], -sɪz, -t/lɪ
extravaganza, -s ek‚strævə'gænzə
[ɪk‚stræv-, ‚ekstræv-], -z
extravasat|e, -es, -ing, -ed ek'strævə-
seɪt [ɪk's-], -s, -ɪŋ, -ɪd
extravasation, -s ek‚strævə'seɪʃn
[‚ekstræv-], -z
extreme (*s. adj.*), **-s, -st, -ly, -ness**
ɪk'striːm [ek's-], -z, -ɪst, -lɪ, -nɪs
[-nəs]
Note.—Some Catholics pronounce
'ekstriːm *in* **extreme unction.**
extremi|sm, -st/s ɪk'striːmɪ|zəm [ek's-],
-st/s
extremit|y, -ies ɪk'stremət|ɪ [ek's-,
-ɪt|ɪ], -ɪz
extricable 'ekstrɪkəbl [ɪk'strɪkəbl, ek's-]
extricat|e, -es, -ing, -ed 'ekstrɪkeɪt, -s,
-ɪŋ, -ɪd
extrication ‚ekstrɪ'keɪʃn
extrinsic, -al, -ally ek'strɪnsɪk, -l, -əlɪ
extroversion ‚ekstrəʊ'vɜː·ʃn
extrovert, -s 'ekstrəʊvɜːt, -s
extrud|e, -es, -ing, -ed ɪk'struːd
[ek' s-], -z, -ɪŋ, -ɪd
extrusion, -s ɪk'struːʒn [ek's-], -z
extrus|ive, -ory ɪk'struːs|ɪv [ek's-],
-ərɪ
exuberan|ce, -cy, -t/ly ɪg'zjuːbərən|s
[eg-, -'zuː-], -sɪ, -t/lɪ
exuberat|e, -es, -ing, -ed ɪg'zjuːbəreɪt
[eg-, -'zuː-], -s, -ɪŋ, -ɪd
exudation, -s ‚eksjuː'deɪʃn [‚egz-], -z
exud|e, -es, -ing, -ed ɪg'zjuːd [eg'z-,
ek's-], -z, -ɪŋ, -ɪd
exult, -s, -ing/ly, -ed ɪg'zʌlt [eg-], -s,
-ɪŋ/lɪ, -ɪd
exultan|ce, -cy, -t/ly ɪg'zʌltən|s [eg-],
-sɪ, -t/lɪ
exultation ‚egzʌl'teɪʃn [‚eks-, -əl-]
exuviae ɪg'zjuːvɪiː [eg-, -'zuː-]
exuvial ɪg'zjuːvjəl [eg-, -'zuː-, -vɪəl]
exuviat|e, -es, -ing, -ed ɪg'zjuːvɪeɪt
[eg-, -'zuː-, -vjeɪt], -s, -ɪŋ, -ɪd
exuviation ɪg‚zjuːvɪ'eɪʃn [eg-, -‚zuː-]
ex voto ‚eks'vəʊtəʊ
Eyam 'iːəm
eyas, -es 'aɪəs, -ɪz
Eyck aɪk
eye (*s. v.*), **-s, -ing, -d** aɪ, -z, -ɪŋ, -d
Eye (*place*) aɪ
eye-ball, -s 'aɪbɔːl, -z
eye-bath, -s 'aɪbɑːθ, -s
eyebright 'aɪbraɪt
eyebrow, -s 'aɪbraʊ, -z
eyeglass, -es 'aɪglɑːs, -ɪz
eye-hole, -s 'aɪhəʊl, -z

eyelash, -es 'aɪlæʃ, -ɪz
eyeless 'aɪlɪs [-ləs]
eyelet, -s 'aɪlɪt [-lət], -s
eye-lid, -s 'aɪlɪd, -z
eyemark, -s 'aɪmɑːk, -s
Eyemouth 'aɪmaʊθ
eye-opener, -s 'aɪˌəʊpnə* [-pn̩ə*], -z
eye-piece, -s 'aɪpiːs, -ɪz
eye-rhyme, -s 'aɪraɪm, -z
eye-shadow 'aɪˌʃædəʊ
eyeshot 'aɪʃɒt
eyesight, -s 'aɪsaɪt, -s
eyesore, -s 'aɪsɔː* [-sɔə*], -z
eye-strain 'aɪstreɪn
eye|-tooth, -teeth 'aɪ|tuːθ, -tiːθ
eyewash 'aɪwɒʃ
eye-water 'aɪˌwɔːtə*

eye-witness, -es ˌaɪ'wɪtnɪs ['-ˌ--, -nəs],
    -ɪz
Eyles aɪlz
Eynsford 'eɪnsfəd
Eynsham (in Oxfordshire) 'eɪnʃəm
    [locally 'ensəm]
eyot, -s eɪt ['eɪət], -s
    Note.—The local pronunciation in
    the Thames valley is eɪt.
eyre (E.) eə*
eyr|ie, -y, -ies 'aɪər|ɪ ['ɪər-, 'eər-], -ɪ, -ɪz
Eyton (in Salop) 'aɪtn, (in Hereford
    and Worcester) 'eɪtn, (surname) 'aɪtn,
    'iːtn
Ezekiel ɪ'ziːkjəl [-kɪəl]
Eziongeber ˌiːzɪɒn'giːbə* [-zɪən-, -zjən-]
Ezra 'ezrə

F

F (*the letter*), -'s ef, -s
fa (*musical note*), -s fɑ:, -z
Fabel 'feɪbəl
Faber (*English name*) 'feɪbə*, (*German name*) 'fɑ:bə* ('fɑ:bər)
Fabian, -s, -ism 'feɪbjən [-bɪən], -z, -ɪzəm
Fa|bius, -bii 'feɪ|bjəs [-bɪəs], -bɪaɪ
fable, -s -d 'feɪbl, -z, -d
fabric, -s 'fæbrɪk, -s
fabricat|e, -es, -ing, -ed, -or/s 'fæbrɪkeɪt, -s, -ɪŋ, -ɪd, -ə*/z
fabrication, -s ˌfæbrɪ'keɪʃn, -z
Fabricius fə'brɪʃɪəs [-ʃjəs, -ʃəs]
fabulist, -s 'fæbjʊlɪst, -s
fabulous, -ly, -ness 'fæbjʊləs, -lɪ, -nɪs [-bjə-, -nəs]
Fabyan 'feɪbjən [-bɪən]
façade, -s fə'sɑ:d [fæ's-], -z
fac|e (s. v.), -es, -ing, -ed; -less feɪs, -ɪz, -ɪŋ, -t; -lɪs [-ləs]
face-ache 'feɪseɪk
face-lift 'feɪslɪft
facer, -s 'feɪsə*, -z
facet, -s, -ed 'fæsɪt ['feɪs-, -set], -s, -ɪd
facetiae fə'si:ʃɪi: [-ʃji:]
facetious, -ly, -ness fə'si:ʃəs, -lɪ, -nɪs [-nəs]
facia, -s 'feɪʃə, -z
faci|al, -ally 'feɪʃ|l [-ʃj|əl, -ʃɪ|əl], -əlɪ
facile 'fæsaɪl [-sɪl]
facilitat|e, -es, -ing, -ed fə'sɪlɪteɪt [-lət-], -s, -ɪŋ, -ɪd
facilitation fəˌsɪlɪ'teɪʃn [-lə't-]
facilit|y, -ies fə'sɪlət|ɪ [-lɪt-], -ɪz
facing (s.), -s 'feɪsɪŋ, -z
facsimile, -s fæk'sɪmɪlɪ [-əlɪ], -z
fact, -s fækt, -s
fact-finding 'fækt,faɪndɪŋ
faction, -s 'fækʃn, -z
factional 'fækʃənl [-ʃn̩l, -ʃnl̩]
factious, -ly, -ness 'fækʃəs, -lɪ, -nɪs [-nəs]
factitious, -ly, -ness fæk'tɪʃəs, -lɪ, -nɪs [-nəs]
factitive 'fæktɪtɪv
factor, -s; -age 'fæktə*, -z; -rɪdʒ
factorial fæk'tɔ:rɪəl
factor|y, -ies 'fæktər|ɪ, -ɪz
factotum, -s fæk'təʊtəm, -z

factual 'fæktʃʊəl [-tʃwəl, -tʃʊl, -tjʊəl, -tjwəl, -tjʊl]
facul|a, -ae 'fækjʊl|ə, -i:
facultative 'fækltətɪv [-teɪt-]
facult|y, -ies 'fæklt|ɪ, -ɪz
fad, -s fæd, -z
Faddiley 'fædɪlɪ
faddi|sh, -sm, -st/s 'fædɪ|ʃ, -zəm, -st/s
Faddle 'fædl
fadd|y, -ier, -iest, -ily, -iness 'fæd|ɪ, -ɪə*, -ɪɪst, -ɪlɪ [-əlɪ], -ɪnɪs [-ɪnəs]
fad|e, -es, -ing, -ed feɪd, -z, -ɪŋ, -ɪd
Fadladeen ˌfædlə'di:n
faeces 'fi:si:z
Faed feɪd
faerie [-ry] (F.) 'feɪərɪ
Faeroe, -s 'feərəʊ, -z
Faeroese ˌfeərəʊ'i:z
Fafner 'fɑ:fnə* ['fæf-] ('fɑ:fnər)
fag (s. v.), -s, -ging, -ged fæg, -z, -ɪŋ, -d
Fagan 'feɪgən
fag-end, -s ˌfæg'end ['--], -z
Fagg(e) fæg
Faggetter 'fægɪtə*
faggot, -s 'fægət, -s
Fagin 'feɪgɪn
fag-master, -s 'fægˌmɑ:stə*, -z
fagott|ist/s, -o/s, -i fə'gɒt|ɪst/s, -əʊ/z, -i:
fah (*note in Tonic Sol-fa*), -s fɑ:, -z
Fah|ey, -ie 'feɪ|ɪ, -i
Fahrenheit 'færənhaɪt ['fɑ:r-]
Fahy 'fɑ:ɪ
faience faɪ'ɑ:ns [feɪ-, -'ɔ̃:ns, -'ɑ:ns] (fajɑ̃:s)
fail (s. v.), -s, -ing/s, -ed feɪl, -z, -ɪŋ/z, -d
faille (*silk material*) feɪl
Failsworth 'feɪlzwɜ:θ [-wəθ]
failure, -s 'feɪljə*, -z
fain feɪn
Fainall 'feɪnɔ:l
faint (s. adj. v.), -s, -ly, -ness; -ing, -ed feɪnt, -s, -lɪ, -nɪs [-nəs]; -ɪŋ, -ɪd
faint-heart, -s 'feɪnthɑ:t, -s
faint-hearted, -ly, -ness ˌfeɪnt'hɑ:tɪd ['-,--], -lɪ, -nɪs [-nəs]
faintish 'feɪntɪʃ
Fainwell 'feɪnwel [-wəl]

fair (s. adj. adv.) (F.), -s, -er, -est, -ly,
-ness feə*, -z, -rə*, -ɪɪst, -lɪ, -nɪs
[-nəs]
Fairbairn, -s 'feəbeən, -z
Fairbank, -s 'feəbæŋk, -s
Fairbeard 'feə,bɪəd
Fairbrother 'feə,brʌðə*
Fairburn 'feəbɜ:n
Fairbury 'feəbərɪ
Fairchild 'feətʃaɪld
Fairclough 'feəklʌf
fair-do ,feə'du:
fair-faced ,feə'feɪst
Fairfax 'feəfæks
Fairfield 'feəfi:ld
Fairford 'feəfəd
fair-haired ,feə'heəd ['—, esp. when
attributive]
Fairhaven 'feə,heɪvn
Fairholme 'feəhəʊm
Fairholt 'feəhəʊlt
fairish 'feərɪʃ
Fairlegh 'feəlɪ
Fairleigh 'feəlɪ, -li:
Fairlight 'feəlaɪt
Fairman 'feəmən
fair-minded ,feə'maɪndɪd ['-,—]
Fairmont 'feəmənt [-mɒnt]
Fairmount 'feəmaʊnt
Fairport 'feəpɔ:t
Fairscribe 'feəskraɪb
Fairservice 'feə,sɜ:vɪs
fair-spoken ,feə'spəʊkən ['-,—]
Fairview 'feəvju:
fairway, -s 'feəweɪ, -z
fair-weather 'feə,weðə*
Fairweather 'feə,weðə*
fair|y (s. adj.), -ies 'feər|ɪ, -ɪz
fairy|land, -like 'feərɪ|lænd, -laɪk
fairy-ring, -s ,feərɪ'rɪŋ ['—], -z
fairy-tale, -s 'feərɪteɪl, -z
fait accompli ,feɪtə'kɒmpli: [,fet-,
-'kɔ:m-, ,—'-] (fɛtakɔ̃pli)
faith (F.), -s feɪθ, -s
faith|ful (F.), -fully, -fulness 'feɪθ|fʊl,
-fʊlɪ [-fəlɪ], -fʊlnɪs [-nəs]
Faithfull 'feɪθfʊl
faith-heal|er/s, -ing 'feɪθ,hi:l|ə*/z, -ɪŋ
faithless, -ly, -ness 'feɪθlɪs [-ləs], -lɪ,
-nɪs [-nəs]
Faithorne 'feɪθɔ:n
fak|e (s. v.), -es, -ing, -ed, -er/s feɪk, -s,
-ɪŋ, -t, -ə*/z
Fakenham 'feɪkŋəm [-knəm]
Fakes feɪks
fakir, -s; -ism 'feɪ,kɪə* ['fæ-, 'fɑ:-, -kə*,
fə'kɪə*], -z; -rɪzəm
Fal fæl

fa-la, -s fɑ:'lɑ:, -z
Falaba ,fælə'bɑ:
falcate, -d 'fælkeɪt, -ɪd
falchion, -s 'fɔ:ltʃən, -z
falcon, -s, -er/s 'fɔ:lkən ['fɒlk-, 'fɔ:k-],
-z, -ə*/z
Note.—'fɔ:k- is the usual pronuncia-
tion among those who practise the
sport of falconry.
Falconbridge 'fɔ:kənbrɪdʒ ['fɔ:lk-,
'fɒlk-]
Falconer 'fɔ:knə*, 'fɔ:lkənə* ['fɒlk-]
falconry 'fɔ:lkənrɪ ['fɒlk-, 'fɔ:k-] (see
note to falcon)
Falcy 'fælsɪ, 'fɔ:lsɪ
Falder 'fɔ:ldə* ['fɒl-]
falderal, -s ,fældə'ræl ['—], -z
faldstool, -s 'fɔ:ldstu:l, -z
Falerii fə'lɪərɪaɪ [fæ'l-, -rɪi:]
Falernian fə'lɜ:njən [-nɪən]
Falk fɔ:k
Falkenbridge 'fɔ:kənbrɪdʒ ['fɔ:lk-,
'fɒlk-]
Falkirk 'fɔ:lkɜ:k ['fɒlk-]
Falkland (Viscount) 'fɔ:klənd, (place in
Scotland) 'fɔ:lklənd ['fɒlk-], (islands)
'fɔ:klənd ['fɒlk-, 'fɔ:lk-]
Falkner 'fɔ:knə*
fall (s. v.), -s, -ing, fell, fallen fɔ:l, -z,
-ɪŋ, fel, 'fɔ:lən
fallacious, -ly, -ness fə'leɪʃəs, -lɪ, -nɪs
[-nəs]
fallac|y, -ies 'fæləs|ɪ, -ɪz
fal-lal, -s ,fæ'læl [,fæl'læl], -z
Faller 'fælə*
fallibility ,fælə'bɪlətɪ [-lɪ'b-, -lɪt-]
fallib|le, -ly, -leness 'fæləb|l [-lɪb-], -lɪ,
-nɪs [-nəs]
Fallod|en, -on 'fæləʊd|ən, -ən
Fallopian fə'ləʊpɪən [fæ-, -pjən]
fall-out 'fɔ:laʊt
fallow (s. adj. v.), -s, -ness; -ing, -ed
'fæləʊ, -z, -nɪs [-nəs]; -ɪŋ, -d
fallow-deer 'fæləʊ,dɪə* [,fæləʊ'd-]
Fallowfield 'fæləʊfi:ld
Fallows 'fæləʊz
Falmouth 'fælməθ
false, -r, -st, -ly, -ness fɔ:ls [fɒls], -ə*,
-ɪst, -lɪ, -nɪs [-nəs]
falsehood, -s 'fɔ:lshʊd ['fɒls-, -sʊd], -z
falsetto, -s fɔ:l'setəʊ [fɒl-], -z
Falshaw 'fɔ:lʃɔ: ['fɒl-]
falsification, -s ,fɔ:lsɪfɪ'keɪʃn [,fɒls-], -z
falsi|fy -fies, -fying, -fied, -fier/s
'fɔ:lsɪ|faɪ ['fɒls-], -faɪz, -faɪɪŋ, -faɪd,
-faɪə*/z
falsit|y, -ies 'fɔ:lsət|ɪ ['fɒls-, -ɪt|ɪ], -ɪz
Falstaff 'fɔ:lstɑ:f ['fɒl-]

183

Falstaffian fɔːlˈstɑːfjən [fɒl-, -fɪən]
falt|er (s. v.), **-ers, -ering/ly, -ered, -erer/s** ˈfɔːlt|əʳ [ˈfɒl-], -əz, -ərɪŋ/lɪ, -əd, -ərəʳ*/z
Famagusta ˌfæməˈɡʊstə [ˌfɑːm-]
fame, -d feɪm, -d
familiar (s. adj.), **-s, -ly** fəˈmɪljəʳ [-lɪəʳ], -z, -lɪ
familiarit|y, -ies fəˌmɪlɪˈærət|ɪ [-ɪt|ɪ], -ɪz
familiariz|e [-is|e], **-es, -ing, -ed** fəˈmɪljəraɪz [-lɪər-], -ɪz, -ɪŋ, -d
famil|y, -ies ˈfæməl|ɪ [-mɪl-], -ɪz
famine, -s ˈfæmɪn, -z
famish, -es, -ing, -ed ˈfæmɪʃ, -ɪz, -ɪŋ, -t
famous, -ly, -ness ˈfeɪməs, -lɪ, -nɪs [-nəs]
fan (s. v.) (**F.**), **-s, -ning, -ned** fæn, -z, -ɪŋ, -d
fanatic (s. adj.), **-s, -al, -ally** fəˈnætɪk [fɳˈæ-], -s, -l, -əlɪ
fanaticism fəˈnætɪsɪzəm [fɳˈæ-]
fanaticiz|e [-is|e], **-es, -ing, -ed** fəˈnætɪsaɪz [fɳˈæ-], -ɪz, -ɪŋ, -d
fanbelt, -s ˈfænbelt, -s
fanci|ful, -fully, -fulness ˈfænsɪ|fʊl, -fʊlɪ [-fəlɪ], -fʊlnɪs [-nəs]
Fancourt ˈfænkɔːt
fanc|y (s. adj. v.), **-ies, -ying, -ied, -er/s** ˈfæns|ɪ, -ɪz, -ɪɪŋ [-jɪŋ], -ɪd, -ɪəʳ*/z [-jəʳ/z]
fancy-dress, -es ˌfænsɪˈdres [also ˈ-- when attributive], -ɪz
fancy-free ˌfænsɪˈfriː
fancy-work ˈfænsɪwɜːk
fandango, -s fænˈdæŋɡəʊ, -z
fane (**F.**), **-s** feɪn, -z
Faneuil ˈfænl
fanfare, -s ˈfænfeəʳ*, -z
fanfaronade, -s ˌfænfærəˈnɑːd [-ˈneɪd], -z
fang (**F.**), **-s, -ed; -less** fæŋ, -z, -d; -lɪs [-ləs]
Faning ˈfeɪnɪŋ
fanlight, -s ˈfænlaɪt, -s
fanner, -s ˈfænəʳ*, -z
Fann|ick, -ing, -y ˈfæn|ɪk, -ɪŋ, -ɪ
Fanshawe ˈfænʃɔː
fantail, -s ˈfænteɪl, -z
fantasia, -s fænˈteɪzjə [-ˈtɑːz-, -zɪə, ˌfæntəˈzɪə, ˌfæntəˈsɪə], -z
fantastic, -al, -ally, -alness fænˈtæstɪk [fən-], -l, -əlɪ, -lnɪs [-nəs]
fantas|y, -ies ˈfæntəs|ɪ [-əz|ɪ], -ɪz
fantod, -s ˈfæntɒd, -z
far fɑː*
farad, -s ˈfærəd, -z
Faraday ˈfærədeɪ [-dɪ]
far-away (adj.) ˈfɑːrəweɪ [ˌ--ˈ-]

farce, -s fɑːs, -ɪz
farceur, -s fɑːˈsɜː:*, -z
farcic|al, -ally ˈfɑːsɪk|l, -əlɪ
farcy ˈfɑːsɪ
fardel, -s ˈfɑːdl, -z
Fardel ˈfɑːdel
far|e (s. v.), **-es, -ing, -ed** feəʳ*, -z, -rɪŋ, -d
Farebrother ˈfeəˌbrʌðəʳ*
Fareham ˈfeərəm
farewell, -s ˌfeəˈwel [ˈ-- according to sentence-stress], -z
Farewell ˈfeəwel [-wəl]
far-famed ˌfɑːˈfeɪmd [also ˈ-- when attributive]
far-fetched ˌfɑːˈfetʃt [also ˈ-- when attributive]
far-flung ˌfɑːˈflʌŋ [also ˈ-- when attributive]
Farg|o, -us ˈfɑːɡ|əʊ, -əs
Faribault ˈfærɪbəʊ
farina fəˈraɪnə [-ˈriːnə]
Farina fəˈriːnə
farinaceous ˌfærɪˈneɪʃəs
Faring|don, -ton ˈfærɪŋ|dən, -tən
farinose ˈfærɪnəʊs
Farjeon ˈfɑːdʒən
Far|leigh, -ley ˈfɑː|lɪ, -lɪ
farm (s. v.), **-s, -ing, -ed, -er/s** fɑːm, -z, -ɪŋ, -d, -əʳ*/z
Farm|an, -er ˈfɑːm|ən, -əʳ*
farmhou|se, -ses ˈfɑːmhaʊ|s, -zɪz
Farmington ˈfɑːmɪŋtən
farmland ˈfɑːmlænd [-lənd]
farmstead, -s ˈfɑːmsted, -z
farmyard, -s ˈfɑːmjɑːd [ˌ-ˈ-], -z
Farnaby ˈfɑːnəbɪ
Farnborough ˈfɑːnbərə
Farn(e) fɑːn
Farn|ham, -worth ˈfɑːn|əm, -wɜːθ
faro ˈfeərəʊ
Faroe ˈfeərəʊ
faroese ˌfeərəʊˈiːz
farouche fəˈruːʃ [fɑːˈr-, fæˈr-]
Farouk fəˈruːk
Farquhar ˈfɑːkwəʳ*, ˈfɑːkəʳ*
Farquharson ˈfɑːkəsn, ˈfɑːkwəsn
Farr fɑː*
farraginous fəˈreɪdʒɪnəs
farrago, -(e)s fəˈrɑːɡəʊ [-ˈreɪɡ-], -z
Farragut ˈfærəɡət
Farr|ant, -ar ˈfær|ənt, -əʳ*
Farr|en, -er ˈfær|ən, -əʳ*
far-reaching ˌfɑːˈriːtʃɪŋ [also ˈ-ˌ-- when attributive]
farrier, -s; -y, -ies ˈfærɪəʳ*, -z; -rɪ, -rɪz
Farring|don, -ford, -ton ˈfærɪŋ|dən, -fəd, -tən

farrow (s. v.) (F.), -s, -ing, -ed 'færəʊ, -z, -ɪŋ, -d
far-seeing ˌfɑː'siːɪŋ ['-ˌ--]
Farsi, -s ˌfɑː'siː, -z
far-sighted, -ness ˌfɑː'saɪtɪd, -nɪs [-nəs]
Farsley 'fɑːzlɪ
farth|er, -est 'fɑːð|ə*, -ɪst
farthing, -s 'fɑːðɪŋ, -z
farthingale, -s 'fɑːðɪŋɡeɪl, -z
Farwell 'fɑːwel [-wəl]
fasces 'fæsiːz
fascia, -s (medical term) 'fæʃɪə [-ʃjə, -ʃə], (other senses) 'feɪʃə [-ʃjə, -ʃɪə, also when referring to classical architecture 'feɪsjə], -z
fasciated 'fæʃɪeɪtɪd
fascicle, -s 'fæsɪkl, -z
fascicule, -s 'fæsɪkjuːl, -z
fascinat|e, -es, -ing/ly, -ed, -or/s 'fæsɪneɪt, -s, -ɪŋ/lɪ, -ɪd, -ə*/z
fascination, -s ˌfæsɪ'neɪʃn, -z
fascine, -s fæ'siːn [fə's-], -z
fascism 'fæʃɪzəm
Fascist, -s 'fæʃɪst, -s
Fascisti fæ'ʃɪsti: [fə'ʃ-]
fash, -es, -ing, -ed fæʃ, -ɪz, -ɪŋ, -t
fashi|on (s. v.), -ons, -oning, -oned, -oner/s 'fæʃ|n, -nz, -ṇɪŋ [-ənɪŋ], -nd, -ṇə*/z [-ənə*/z]
fashionab|le, -ly, -leness 'fæʃnəb|l [-ʃṇə-], -lɪ, -lnɪs [-nəs]
fashion-plate, -s 'fæʃnpleɪt, -s
Fasolt 'fɑːzɒlt ('fɑːzɔlt)
fast (s. adj. v. adv.), -s, -er, -est, -ness; -ing, -ed, -er/s fɑːst, -s, -ə*, -ɪst, -nɪs [-nəs]; -ɪŋ, -ɪd, -ə*/z
fast-day, -s 'fɑːstdeɪ, -z
fast|en, -ens, -ening, -ened 'fɑːs|n, -nz, -nɪŋ [-ṇɪŋ], -nd
fastener, -s 'fɑːsnə*, -z
fastening (s.) (contrivance for fastening), -s 'fɑːsnɪŋ, -z
fasti (F.) 'fæsti: [-taɪ]
fastidious, -ly, -ness fə'stɪdɪəs [fæ's-, -djəs], -lɪ, -nɪs [-nəs]
fastness, -es 'fɑːstnɪs [-nəs], -ɪz
Fastnet 'fɑːstnet [-nɪt]
fat (s. adj.), -ter, -test, -ness, -ted fæt, -ə*, -ɪst, -nɪs [-nəs], -ɪd
fat|al, -ally 'feɪt|l, -əlɪ [-t|ɪ]
fatali|sm, -st/s 'feɪtəlɪ|zəm [-t|ɪ-], -st/s
fatalistic ˌfeɪtə'lɪstɪk [-t|'ɪ-]
fatalit|y, -ies fə'tælət|ɪ [feɪ't-, -ɪt|ɪ], -ɪz
fate (F.), -s, -d feɪt, -s, -ɪd
fateful, -ly 'feɪtfʊl, -lɪ [-fəlɪ]
fathead, -s 'fæthed, -z
fath|er (s. v.), -ers, -ering, -ered 'fɑːð|ə*, -əz, -ərɪŋ, -əd

fatherhood 'fɑːðəhʊd
father - in - law, fathers - in - law 'fɑːðərɪnlɔː [-ðəɪn-], 'fɑːðəzɪnlɔː
fatherland, -s 'fɑːðəlænd, -z
fatherless 'fɑːðəlɪs [-ləs, -les]
fatherl|y, -iness 'fɑːðəl|ɪ, -ɪnɪs [-məs]
fathom (s. v.), -s, -ing, -ed; -able, -less 'fæðəm, -z, -ɪŋ, -d; -əbl, -lɪs [-ləs]
fathom-line, -s 'fæðəmlaɪn, -z
fatigu|e (s. v.), -es, -ing/ly, -ed fə'tiːɡ, -z, -ɪŋ/lɪ, -d
Fatima 'fætɪmə
fatling, -s 'fætlɪŋ, -z
fatt|en, -ens, -ening, -ened, -ener/s 'fæt|n, -nz, -ṇɪŋ [-nɪŋ], -nd, -ṇə*/z
fattish 'fætɪʃ
fatt|y (s. adj.), -ies, -ier, -iest, -iness 'fæt|ɪ, -ɪz, -ɪə*, -ɪɪst, -ɪnɪs [-məs]
fatuity fə'tjuːətɪ [fæ't-, -'tjʊ-, -ɪtɪ]
fatuous, -ly, -ness 'fætjʊəs [-tjwəs], -lɪ, -nɪs [-nəs]
faubourg,-s 'fəʊˌbʊəɡ [-bɜːɡ] (fobuːr),-z
faucal 'fɔːkl
fauces 'fɔːsiːz
faucet, -s 'fɔːsɪt, -s
Fauc|ett, -it 'fɔːs|ɪt, -ɪt
Faudel 'fɔːdl
faugh pφ: [fɔː]
Note.—This φ is often accompanied by vibration of the lips.
Faulconbridge 'fɔːkənbrɪdʒ ['fɔːlk-]
Faulds fəʊldz, fɔːldz
Faulhorn 'faʊlhɔːn
Faulk fɔːk
Faulkes fɔːks, fɔːlks
Faulkland 'fɔːklənd ['fɔːlk-]
Faulkner 'fɔːknə*
Faulks fəʊks
fault, -s fɔːlt [fɒlt], -s
faultfind|er/s, -ing 'fɔːltˌfaɪnd|ə*/z ['fɒlt-], -ɪŋ
faultless, -ly, -ness 'fɔːltlɪs ['fɒlt-, -ləs], -lɪ, -nɪs [-nəs]
fault|y, -ier, -iest, -ily, -iness 'fɔːlt|ɪ ['fɒlt-, -ɪə* [-jə*], -ɪɪst [-jɪst], -ɪlɪ [-əlɪ], -ɪnɪs [-məs]
faun, -s fɔːn, -z
fauna 'fɔːnə
Faunch fɔːntʃ
Faun|tleroy 'fɔːntlərɔɪ ['fɒnt-]
Faust faʊst
Faustina fɔː'stiːnə
Faustus 'fɔːstəs
fauteuil, -s 'fəʊtɜːɪ [fəʊ'tɜːɪ, -ɜːl] (fotœːj)
Faux fəʊ, fɔːks
faux pas (sing.) ˌfəʊ'pɑː, (plur.) ˌfəʊ'pɑːz

185

Favel (*surname*) 'feɪvəl
Faversham 'fævəʃəm
Favoni|an, -us fə'vəʊnj|ən [feɪ'v-, -nɪ|ən], -əs
fav|our (*s. v.*), -ours, -ouring, -oured, -ourer/s 'feɪv|ə*, -əz, -ərɪŋ, -əd, -ərə*/z
favourab|le, -ly, -leness 'feɪvərəb|l, -lɪ, -lnɪs [-nəs]
favourit|e, -es; -ism 'feɪvərɪt, -s; -ɪzəm
favourless 'feɪvəlɪs [-ləs]
Fawcett 'fɔːsɪt, 'fɒsɪt
Fawkes fɔːks
Fawkner 'fɔːknə*
Fawley 'fɔːlɪ
fawn (*s. adj. v.*), -s, -ing/ly, -ed, -er/s fɔːn, -z, -ɪŋ/lɪ, -d, -ə*/z
Fawssett 'fɔːsɪt
fay (F.), -s feɪ, -z
Fayette feɪ'et
Fayette City ˌfeɪet'sɪtɪ
Fayetteville 'feɪetvɪl
Faygate 'feɪgeɪt
Faza(c)kerley fə'zækəlɪ
F.B.I. ˌefbiː'aɪ
fe (*name of note in Tonic Sol-fa*), -(')s fiː, -z
fe (*syllable used in Tonic Sol-fa for counting a short note off the beat*) *generally* fɪ, *but the first* fe *in the sequence* ta fe tay fe *is sometimes sounded as* fə. *See* ta.
Feaist fiːst
fealty 'fiːəltɪ
fear (*s. v.*), -s, -ing, -ed fɪə*, -z, -rɪŋ, -d
Fearenside 'fɛːnsaɪd, 'fɪərənsaɪd
fear|ful, -fully, -fulness 'fɪə|fʊl, -fəlɪ [-fʊlɪ], -fʊlnɪs [-nəs]
Feargus 'fɜːgəs
fearless, -ly, -ness 'fɪəlɪs [-ləs], -lɪ, -nɪs [-nəs]
Fearn(e) fɜːn
Fearnside 'fɜːnsaɪd
Fearon 'fɪərən
fearsome, -ly, -ness 'fɪəsəm, -lɪ, -nɪs [-nəs]
feasibility ˌfiːzə'bɪlətɪ [-zɪ'b-, -lɪt-]
feasib|le, -ly, -leness 'fiːzəb|l [-zɪb-], -lɪ, -lnɪs [-nəs]
feast (*s. v.*), -s, -ing, -ed, -er/s fiːst, -s, -ɪŋ, -ɪd, -ə*/z
feat, -s fiːt, -s
feather (*s. v.*), -s, -ing, -ed feðə*, -z, -rɪŋ, -d
feather-bed, -s 'feðəbed [ˌ--'-'], -z
feather-brain, -s, -ed 'feðəbreɪn, -z, -d
feather-edge, -s 'feðəredʒ ['feðəedʒ, ˌ--'-], -ɪz

feather-head, -s, -ed 'feðəhed, -z, -ɪd
featherstitch (*s. v.*), -es, -ing, -ed 'feðəstɪtʃ, -ɪz, -ɪŋ, -t
Featherston 'feðəstən
Featherstone 'feðəstən [-stəʊn]
Featherstonehaugh 'feðəstənhɔː:, 'fænʃɔː: ['festənhɔː:, 'frəstənhɔː:]
featherweight, -s 'feðəweɪt, -s
feather|y, -iness 'feðər|ɪ, -ɪnɪs [-ɪnəs]
Featley 'fiːtlɪ
featly 'fiːtlɪ
featur|e (*s. v.*), -es, -ing, -ed; -eless 'fiːtʃə*, -z, -rɪŋ, -d; -lɪs [-ləs]
febrifuge, -s 'febrɪfjuːdʒ, -ɪz
febrile 'fiːbraɪl
February 'februərɪ [-rər-, -rʊr-, 'febjuərɪ]
fecit 'fiːsɪt ['feɪkɪt]
Feckenham 'fekŋəm [-kənəm]
feckless, -ly, -ness 'feklɪs [-ləs], -lɪ, -nɪs [-nəs]
feculen|ce, -t 'fekjʊlən|s, -t
fecund 'fiːkənd ['fek-, -kʌnd]
fecundat|e, -es, -ing, -ed 'fiːkəndeɪt ['fek-, -kʌn-], -s, -ɪŋ, -ɪd
fecundation ˌfiːkən'deɪʃn [ˌfek-, -kʌn-]
fecundity fɪ'kʌndətɪ [fiː:'k-, fe'k-, -ɪtɪ]
fed (*from* feed) fed
federal, -ly 'fedərəl, -ɪ
federali|sm, -st/s 'fedərəlɪ|zəm, -st/s
federate (*s. adj.*), -s 'fedərət [-rɪt, -reɪt], -s
federat|e (*v.*), -es, -ing, -ed 'fedəreɪt, -s, -ɪŋ, -ɪd
federation, -s ˌfedə'reɪʃn, -z
federative 'fedərətɪv [-reɪt-]
fed-up ˌfed'ʌp
fee (*s. v.*), -s, -ing, -d fiː:, -z, -ɪŋ, -d
feeb|le, -ler, -lest, -ly, -leness 'fiːb|l, -lə*, -lɪst, -lɪ, -lnɪs [-nəs]
feeble-minded, -ness ˌfiːbl'maɪndɪd ['--,--], -nɪs [-nəs]
feed (*s. v.*), -s, -ing, fed, feeder/s fiːd, -z, -ɪŋ, fed, 'fiːdə*/z
feed-back 'fiːdbæk
feeding-bottle, -s 'fiːdɪŋˌbɒtl, -z
feeding-cup, -s 'fiːdɪŋkʌp, -s
feed-pipe, -s 'fiːdpaɪp, -s
feed-tank, -s 'fiːdtæŋk, -s
fee-fo-fum 'fiː:ˌfəʊ'fʌm
Feeheny 'fiːnɪ, 'fɪənɪ
feel (*s. v.*), -s, -ing, felt fiː:l, -z, -ɪŋ, felt
feeler, -s 'fiː:lə*, -z
feeling (*s. adj.*), -s, -ly 'fiː:lɪŋ, -z, -lɪ
fee-simple, -s ˌfiː:'sɪmpl, -z
feet (*plur. of* foot) fiː:t
fee-tail ˌfiː:'teɪl

feign, -s, -ing, -ed, -edly, -edness feɪn, -z, -ɪŋ, -d, -ɪdlɪ, -ɪdnɪs [-nəs]
Feilden 'fiːldən
Feilding 'fiːldɪŋ
Feiling 'faɪlɪŋ
Feiller 'faɪlə*
feint (s. v.), -s, -ing, -ed feɪnt, -s, -ɪŋ, -ɪd
Feiron 'fɪərən
Feisal 'faɪsl ['feɪs-]
Feist fiːst
feldspar 'feldspɑː* ['felspɑː*]
Felicia fə'lɪsɪə [fe'l-, fɪ'l-, -sjə, -ʃɪə, -ʃjə]
felicitat|e, -es, -ing, -ed fə'lɪsɪteɪt [fe'l-, fɪ'l-], -s, -ɪŋ, -ɪd
felicitation, -s fə,lɪsɪ'teɪʃn [fe,l-, fɪ,l-], -z
felicitous, -ly, -ness fə'lɪsɪtəs [fe'l-, fɪ'l-], -lɪ, -nɪs [-nəs]
felicity (F.) fə'lɪsətɪ [fe'l-, fɪ'l-, -ɪtɪ]
feline (s. adj.), -s 'fiːlaɪn, -z
felinity fɪ'lɪnətɪ [fiː'l-, fə'l-, -ɪtɪ]
Felix, -stowe 'fiːlɪks, -təʊ
Felkin 'felkɪn
fell (s. adj. v.) (F.), -s, -ing, -ed, -er/s fel, -z, -ɪŋ, -d, -ə*/z
fell (from fall) fel
fellah, -s -een 'felə, -z, -hiːn [,felə'hiːn]
Felling 'felɪŋ
felloe, -s 'feləʊ, -z
fellow, -s 'feləʊ [colloquially also 'felə in sense of 'person'], -z
fellow|-citizen/s, -creature/s ,feləʊ|-'sɪtɪzn/z, -'kriːtʃə*/z
Fellowes 'feləʊz
fellow-feeling ,feləʊ'fiːlɪŋ
fellow|-man, -men ,feləʊ|'mæn, -'men
Fellows 'feləʊz
fellowship, -s 'feləʊʃɪp, -s
fellow-traveller, -s ,feləʊ'trævələ* [-vḷə*], -z
Felltham 'felθəm
felo de se ,fiːləʊdiː'siː [,fe-, -'seɪ]
felon, -s 'felən, -z
felonious, -ly, -ness fə'ləʊnjəs [fe'l-, fɪ'l-, -nɪəs], -lɪ, -nɪs [-nəs]
felon|y, -ies 'felən|ɪ, -ɪz
Felpham 'felpəm
felspar 'felspɑː*
Felste(a)d 'felstɪd [-ted]
felt (s.), -s felt, -s
felt (from feel) felt
Feltham (place) 'feltəm, (personal name) 'felθəm
felting, -s 'feltɪŋ, -z
felt-tip, -s ,felt'tɪp ['--], -s
Felton 'feltən
felucca, -s fe'lʌkə [fɪ'l-], -z
female (s. adj.), -s 'fiːmeɪl, -z

feme, -s fiːm [fem], -z
feminine, -ly, -ness 'femɪnɪn [-mənɪn], -lɪ, -nɪs [-nəs]
femininit|y, -ies ,femɪ'nɪnət|ɪ [-mə'n-, -ɪt|ɪ], -ɪz
femini|sm, -st/s 'femɪnɪ|zəm [-mən-], -st/s
feminiz|e [-is|e], -es, -ing, -ed 'femɪnaɪz [-mən-], -ɪz, -ɪŋ, -d
femora (alternative plur. of femur) 'femərə ['fiːm-]
femoral 'femərəl
femur, -s 'fiːmə*, -z
fen, -s (F.) fen, -z
fenc|e (s. v.), -es, -ing, -ed, -er/s; -eless fens, -ɪz, -ɪŋ, -t, -ə*/z; -lɪs [-ləs]
Fenchurch 'fentʃɜːtʃ
fend, -s, -ing, -ed fend, -z, -ɪŋ, -ɪd
fender, -s 'fendə*, -z
Fenella fɪ'nelə [fə'n-]
fenestr|a, -al fɪ'nestr|ə [fə'n-], -əl
fenestrat|e, -es, -ing, -ed fɪ'nestreɪt [fə-, 'fenɪstreɪt, 'fenə-], -s, -ɪŋ, -ɪd
fenestration, -s ,fenɪ'streɪʃn [-nə's-], -z
Fenham 'fenəm
Fenian, -s; -ism 'fiːnjən [-nɪən], -z; -ɪzəm
Fenimore 'fenɪmɔː* [-mɔə*]
Fenn fen
fennel 'fenl
Fennell 'fenl
Fennessy 'fenɪsɪ [-nəs-]
Fennimore 'fenɪmɔː* [-mɔə*]
fenny (F.) 'fenɪ
Fenton 'fentən
Fenwick (English surname) 'fenɪk [-wɪk] (American surname) 'fenwɪk, (places in Great Britain) 'fenɪk
Feodor 'fiːəʊdɔː* ['fɪ-]
Feodora ,fiːəʊ'dɔːrə [,fɪ-]
feoff (v.), -s, -ing, -ed, -er/s, -ment/s fiːf [fef], -s, -ɪŋ, -t, -ə*/z, -mənt/s
feoffee, -s fiː'fiː [fe'fiː], -z
feoffor, -s fiː'fɔː* [fe'fɔː*], -z
feral 'fɪərəl ['fer-]
Feramors 'ferəmɔːz
Ferdinand 'fɜːdɪnənd [-dṇənd]
feretor|y, -ies 'ferɪtər|ɪ, -ɪz
Fergus, -(s)on 'fɜːɡəs, -n
feria, -l 'fɪərɪə ['fer-], -l
ferine 'fɪəraɪn
Feringhee, -s fə'rɪŋɡɪ, -z
Fermanagh fə'mænə [fɜː-]
ferment (s.), -s 'fɜːment, -s
ferment (v.), -s, -ing, -ed; -able fə'ment [fɜː-], -s, -ɪŋ, -ɪd; -əbl
fermentation, -s ,fɜːmen'teɪʃn [-mən-], -z

187

fermentative, -ly, -ness fə'mentətɪv, -lɪ, -nɪs [-nəs]

Fermor 'fɜːmɔː*

Fermoy (near Cork) fɜː'mɔɪ, (street in London) 'fɜːmɔɪ

fern (F.), -s fɜːn, -z

Fernandez (Spanish navigator) fɜː'nændez [fə'n-], see also **Juan F.**

ferner|y, -ies 'fɜːnər|ɪ, -ɪz

Fernhough 'fɜːnhəʊ

Fernihough [-nyh-] 'fɜːnɪhʌf, -həʊ

ferny 'fɜːnɪ

ferocious, -ly, -ness fə'rəʊʃəs [fɪ'r-, fe'r-], -lɪ, -nɪs [-nəs]

ferocity fə'rɒsətɪ [fɪ'r-, fe'r-, -ɪtɪ]

Ferrand 'ferənd

Ferranti fə'ræntɪ [fɪ-, fe-]

Ferrar 'ferə*

ferrel (F.), -s 'ferəl, -z

ferreous 'ferɪəs

Ferrer, -s 'ferə*, -z

ferret (s. v.) (F.), -s, -ing, -ed 'ferɪt [-rət], -s, -ɪŋ, -ɪd

ferric 'ferɪk

Ferrier 'ferɪə*

Ferris, -burg 'ferɪs, -bɜːg

ferro-concrete ˌferəʊ'kɒŋkriːt [-'kɒnk-]

ferrotype, -s 'ferəʊtaɪp, -s

ferrous 'ferəs

ferruginous fe'ruːdʒɪnəs [fə'r-]

ferrule, -s 'feruːl [-rəl], -z
> Note.—'ferəl is the pronunciation used by those connected with the umbrella trade.

ferr|y (s. v.) (F.), -ies, -ying, -ied 'fer|ɪ, -ɪz, -ɪŋ, -ɪd

ferry-boat, -s 'ferɪbəʊt, -s

ferry|man, -men 'ferɪ|mən [-mæn], -mən [-men]

fertile, -ly 'fɜːtaɪl, -lɪ

fertility fə'tɪlətɪ [-ɪtɪ]

fertilization [-isa-] ˌfɜːtəlaɪ'zeɪʃn [-tɪl-, -lɪ'z-]

fertiliz|e [-is|e], -es, -ing, -ed, -er/s 'fɜːtəlaɪz [-tl-, -tɪl-], -ɪz, -ɪŋ, -d, -ə*/z

ferule, -s 'feruːl, -z

ferven|cy, -t/ly, -tness 'fɜːvən|sɪ, -t/lɪ, -tnɪs [-nəs]

fervid, -ly, -ness 'fɜːvɪd, -lɪ, -nɪs [-nəs]

fervour 'fɜːvə*

fescue, -s 'feskjuː, -z

fesse, -s fes, -ɪz

Fessenden 'fesndən

fest|al, -ally 'fest|l, -əlɪ

fest|er (s. v.), -ers, -ering, -ered 'fest|ə*, -əz, -ərɪŋ, -əd

Festiniog fe'stɪnɪɒg (Welsh fes'tinjog)

festival, -s 'festəvl [-tɪv-], -z

festive, -ly, -ness 'festɪv, -lɪ, -nɪs [-nəs]

festivit|y, -ies fe'stɪvət|ɪ [-ɪt|ɪ], -ɪz

festoon (s. v.), -s, -ing, -ed fe'stuːn, -z, -ɪŋ, -d

Festus 'festəs

fetch (s. v.), -es, -ing, -ed, -er/s fetʃ, -ɪz, -ɪŋ, -t, -ə*/z

fête, -s; -day/s feɪt, -s; -deɪ/z

fetid, -ly, -ness 'fetɪd ['fiːtɪd], -lɪ, -nɪs [-nəs]

fetish, -es; -ism, -ist/s 'fetɪʃ ['fiːtɪʃ], -ɪz; -ɪzəm, -ɪst/s

fetlock, -s, -ed 'fetlɒk, -s, -t

fetter (s. v.) (F.), -s, -ing, -ed 'fetə*, -z, -rɪŋ, -d

Fettes (place) 'fetɪs, (surname) 'fetɪs, 'fetɪz

Fettesian, -s fe'tiːzjən [-zɪən], -z

fett|le (s. v.), -les, -ling, -led 'fet|l, -lz, -lɪŋ, -ld

feu (s. v.), -s, -ing, -ed fjuː, -z, -ɪŋ ['fjʊɪŋ], -d

feud, -s; -al fjuːd, -z; -l

feudali|sm, -st/s 'fjuːdəlɪ|zəm [-dlɪ-], -st/s

feudality fjuː'dælətɪ [-ɪtɪ]

feudalization [-isa-] ˌfjuːdəlaɪ'zeɪʃn [-dlaɪ'z-, -dəlɪ'z-, -dlɪ'z-]

feudaliz|e [-is|e], -es, -ing, -ed 'fjuːdəlaɪz [-dlaɪz], -ɪz, -ɪŋ, -d

feudatory 'fjuːdətərɪ

feuilleton, -s 'fɜːɪtɔ̃ːŋ ['fɜːlt-, -tɒŋ] (fœjtɔ̃), -z

fever, -s, -ed 'fiːvə*, -z, -d

fever-heat 'fiːvəhiːt

feverish, -ly, -ness 'fiːvərɪʃ, -lɪ, -nɪs [-nəs]

Feversham 'fevəʃəm

few, -er, -est, -ness fjuː, -ə* [fjʊə*], -ɪst ['fjʊɪst], -nɪs [-nəs]

fey feɪ

fez (F.), -es fez, -ɪz

Fezzan fe'zaːn ['fezæn]

Ffitch fɪtʃ

Ffolliot 'fɒljət [-lɪət]

Ffoulkes fəʊks, fəʊlks, faʊks, fuːks

Ffrangcon 'fræŋkən

fiancé(e), -s fɪ'ɑ̃ːŋseɪ [fɪ'ɔ̃ːŋs-, fɪ'ɑːns-, fɪ'ɒns-, fɪ'ɒŋs-] (fjɑ̃se), -z

fiasco, -s fɪ'æskəʊ, -z

fiat (decree), -s 'faɪæt ['faɪət], -s

Fiat (car), -s fɪət ['fiːæt], -s

fib (s. v.), -s, -bing, -bed, -ber/s fɪb, -z, -ɪŋ, -d, -ə*/z

fibre, -s, -d; -less 'faɪbə*, -z, -d; -lɪs [-ləs]

fibreglass 'faɪbəglɑːs

fibriform 'faɪbrɪfɔːm

fibr|il/s, -in 'faɪbr|ɪl/z, -ɪn
fibrositis ˌfaɪbrəʊ'saɪtɪs
fibrous, -ly, -ness 'faɪbrəs, -lɪ, -nɪs [-nəs]
fibul|a, -as, -ae 'fɪbjʊl|ə, -əz, -i:
fichu, -s 'fi:ʃu: ['fɪʃ-, -ʃju:] (fiʃy), -z
fick|le, -ler, -lest, -ler·ess 'fɪk|l, -lə*,
  -lɪst, -lnɪs [-nəs]
fiction, -s 'fɪkʃn, z
fictional 'fɪkʃənl [-ʃnəl, -ʃn̩l̩, -ʃnl̩,
  -ʃənəl]
fictionist, -s 'fɪkʃənɪst [-ʃn̩ɪst], -s
fictitious, -ly, -ness fɪk'tɪʃəs, -lɪ, -nɪs
  [-nəs]
fictive 'fɪktɪv
fid, -s fɪd, -z
fidd|le (s. v.), -les, -ling, -led, -ler/s
  'fɪd|l, -lz, -lɪŋ [-lɪŋ], -ld, -lə*/z
  [-lə*/z]
fiddle-bow, -s 'fɪdlbəʊ, -z
fiddle-case, -s 'fɪdlkeɪs, -ɪz
fiddle-de-dee ˌfɪdldɪ'di:
fiddle-fadd|le (s. v. interj.), -les, -ling,
  -led 'fɪdlˌfæd|l, -lz, -lɪŋ, -ld
fiddlestick, -s 'fɪdlstɪk, -s
Fidele fɪ'di:lɪ
Fidelia fɪ'di:ljə [-lɪə]
Fidelio (opera) fɪ'deɪlɪəʊ [-ljəʊ]
fidelity fɪ'delətɪ [faɪ'd-, -ɪtɪ]
fidget (s. v.), -s, -ing, -ed 'fɪdʒɪt, -s, -ɪŋ,
  -ɪd
fidget|y, -ier, -iest, -ily, -iness 'fɪdʒɪt|ɪ
  [-ət|ɪ], -ɪə*, -ɪɪst, -ɪlɪ [-əlɪ], -ɪnɪs
  [-ɪnəs]
Fido 'faɪdəʊ
fiducial, -ly fɪ'dju:ʃjəl [-u:ʃɪəl, -u:sjəl,
  -u:sɪəl], -ɪ
fiduciar|y, -ies fɪ'dju:ʃjər|ɪ [-u:ʃɪə-,
  -u:ʃə-, -u:sjə-, -u:sɪə-], -ɪz
fie faɪ
fief, -s fi:f, -s
field (s. v.) (F.), -s, -ing, -ed, -er/s
  fi:ld, -z, -ɪŋ, -ɪd, -ə*/z
field-day, -s 'fi:lddeɪ, -z
Field|en, -er 'fi:ld|ən, -ə*
fieldfare, -s 'fi:ldfeə*, -z
field-glass, -es 'fi:ldgla:s, -ɪz
field-grey ˌfi:ld'greɪ
field-gun, -s 'fi:ldgʌn, -z
field-hospital, -s ˌfi:ld'hɒspɪtl, -z
field-ice 'fi:ldaɪs
Fielding 'fi:ldɪŋ
field-marshal, -s ˌfi:ld'mɑ:ʃl ['-'--], ˌ-z
field|-mouse, -mice 'fi:ld|maʊs, -maɪs
field-officer, -s 'fi:ld,ɒfɪsə*, -z
fields|man, -men 'fi:ldz|mən, -mən
  [-men]
field-telegraph,   -s   ˌfi:ld'telɪgrɑ:f
  [-græf], -s

field-telephone, -s ˌfi:ld'telɪfəʊn, -z
field-work, -s, -er/s 'fi:ldwɜ:k, -s, -ə*/z
Fieller 'faɪlə*
fiend (F.), -s fi:nd, -z
fiendish, -ly, -ness 'fi:ndɪʃ, -lɪ, -nɪs
  [-nəs]
Fiennes faɪnz
fierce, -r, -st, -ly, -ness fɪəs, -ə*, -ɪst, -lɪ,
  -nɪs [-nəs]
fier|y, -ily, -iness 'faɪər|ɪ, -əlɪ [-ɪlɪ] -ɪnɪs
  [-ɪnəs]
fif|e (s. v.), -es, -ing, -ed, -er/s faɪf, -s,
  -ɪŋ, -t, -ə*/z
Fife, -shire faɪf, -ʃə* [-ˌʃɪə*]
fife-major, -s ˌfaɪf'meɪdʒə*, -z
Fifield 'faɪfi:ld
fifteen, -s, -th/s ˌfɪf'ti:n [also 'fɪft-,
  fɪf't- according to sentence-stress], -z,
  -θ/s
fifth, -s, -ly fɪfθ [-ftθ], -s, -lɪ
fift|y, -ies, -ieth/s, -yfold 'fɪft|ɪ, -ɪz,
  -ɪəθ/s [-jəθ/s, -ɪɪθ/s, -jɪθ/s], -ɪfəʊld
fifty-fifty ˌfɪftɪ'fɪftɪ
fig (s. v.), -s, -ging, -ged fɪg, -z, -ɪŋ, -d
Figaro 'fɪgərəʊ (figaro)
Figg, -is fɪg, -ɪs
fight (s. v.), -s, -ing, fought, fighter/s
  faɪt, -s, -ɪŋ, fɔ:t, 'faɪtə*/z
fighting-cock, -s 'faɪtɪŋkɒk, -s
fig-lea|f, -ves 'fɪgli:|f, -vz
figment, -s 'fɪgmənt, -s
fig-tree, -s 'fɪgtri:, -z
figurability ˌfɪgjʊərə'bɪlətɪ [-gər-, -lɪt-]
figurable 'fɪgjʊərəbl [-gər-]
figurant, -s 'fɪgjʊrənt, -s
figurante (French fem. of figurant), -s
  ˌfɪgjʊ'rɑ̃:nt   [-'rɔ̃:nt,   -'rɑ:nt]
  (figyrɑ̃:t), -s
figurant|e (Italian form of figurant), -i
  ˌfɪgjʊ'rænt|ɪ, -i:
figuration, -s ˌfɪgə'reɪʃn [-gjə-, -gjʊ-],
  -z
figurative, -ly, -ness 'fɪgərətɪv [-gjər-,
  -gjʊr-], -lɪ, -nɪs [-nəs]
figur|e (s. v.), -es, -ing, -ed 'fɪgə*, -z,
  -rɪŋ, -d
figure-head, -s 'fɪgəhed, -z
figurine, -s 'fɪgəri:n [-gjʊr-, ˌ--'-], -z
Fiji ˌfi:'dʒi: ['--]
Fijian, -s ˌfi:'dʒi:ən, -z
filacer, -s 'fɪləsə*, -z
filament, -s 'fɪləmənt, -s
filamentous ˌfɪlə'mentəs
filature, -s 'fɪlətʃə* [-ˌtjʊə*, -tjə*,
  -ˌtʃʊə*], -z
filbert, -s 'fɪlbət, -s
filch, -es, -ing, -ed, -er/s fɪltʃ, -ɪz, -ɪŋ, -t,
  -ə*/z

189

Fildes faıldz
fill|e (s. v.), -es, -ing, -ed faıl, -z, -ıŋ, -d
filemot 'fılımɒt
Filey 'faılı
filial, -ly, -ness 'fıljəl [-lıəl], -ı, -nıs [-nəs]
filiation ˌfılı'eıʃn
filibeg, -s 'fılıbeg, -z
filibust|er (s. v.), -ers, -ering, -ered 'fılıbʌst|ə*, -əz, -ərıŋ, -əd
filigr|ane, -ee 'fılıgr|eın, -i:
filings 'faılıŋz
Filioque ˌfi:lı'əʊkwı [ˌfaıl-, ˌfıl-]
Filipino, -s ˌfılı'pi:nəʊ [-lə'p-], -z
Filkin, -s 'fılkın, -z
fill (s. v.), -s, -ing/s, -ed, -er/s fıl, -z, -ıŋ/z, -d, -ə*/z
fillet (s. v.), -s, -ing, -ed 'fılıt, -s, -ıŋ, -ıd
fillip (s. v.), -s, -ing, -ed 'fılıp, -s, -ıŋ, -t
Fillmore 'fılmɔ:* [-mɔə*]
fill|y, -ies 'fıl|ı, -ız
film, -s fılm, -z
film-actor, -s 'fılmˌæktə*, -z
filmland 'fılmlænd
film-star, -s 'fılmstɑ:*, -z
film|y, -ier, -iest, -ily, -iness 'fılm|ı, -ıə* [-jə*], -ııst [-jıst], -ılı [-əlı], -ınıs [-məs]
Filon (surname) 'faılən
filt|er (s. v.), -ers, -ering, -ered 'fılt|ə*, -əz, -ərıŋ, -əd
filter-paper, -s 'fıltəˌpeıpə*, -z
filter-tip, -s 'fıltətıp, -s
filth fılθ
filth|y, -ier, -iest, -ily, -iness 'fılθ|ı, -ıə* [-jə*], -ııst [-jıst], -ılı [-əlı], -ınıs [-məs]
filtrate (s.), -s 'fıltreıt [-rıt], -s
filtrat|e (v.), -es, -ing, -ed 'fıltreıt, -s, -ıŋ, -ıd
filtration, -s fıl'treıʃn, -z
fin, -s fın, -z
finable 'faınəbl
fin|al, -als, -ally 'faın|l, -lz, -əlı [-lı]
finale, -s fı'nɑ:lı, -z
finalist, -s 'faınəlıst [-nlıst], -s
finality faı'nælətı [-ıtı]
finaliz|e [-is|e], -es, -ing, -ed 'faınəlaız [-nlaız], -ız, -ıŋ, -d
financ|e (s. v.), -es, -ing, -ed faı'næns [fı'n-, 'faınæns], -ız, -ıŋ, -t
financi|al, -ally faı'nænʃ|l [fı'n-], -əlı
financier (s.), -s faı'nænsıə* [fı'n-, -sjə*], -z
finch (F.), -es fıntʃ, -ız
Finchale (Priory in Durham) 'fıŋkl
Finchampsted (in Berkshire) 'fıntʃəmsted [-tıd]

Finchley 'fıntʃlı
find (s. v.), -s, -ing/s, found, finder/s faınd, -z, -ıŋ/z, faʊnd, 'faındə*/z
Findlater 'fındlətə* [-leıtə*]
Findlay 'fındleı [-lı]
fin|e (s. adj. v.), -es; -er, -est, -ely, -eness; -ing, -ed faın, -z; -ə*, -ıst, -lı, -nıs [-nəs]; -ıŋ, -d
fine-draw, -s, -ing, -n, fine-drew ˌfaın'drɔ: ['--], -z, -ıŋ, -n, ˌfaın'dru: ['--]
finery 'faınərı
fine-spun ˌfaın'spʌn ['--]
finess|e (s. v.), -es, -ing, -ed fı'nes, -ız, -ıŋ, -t
Fingal (place) 'fıŋgəl
Fingall (Lord) fıŋ'gɔ:l
fing|er (s. v.), -ers, -ering/s, -ered 'fıŋg|ə*, -əz, -ərıŋ/z, -əd
finger-alphabet, -s 'fıŋgərˌælfəbet [-gəˌæl-, -bıt], -s
finger-board, -s 'fıŋgəbɔ:d [-bɔəd], -z
finger-bowl, -s 'fıŋgəbəʊl, -z
finger-breadth, -s 'fıŋgəbretθ [-bredθ], -s
finger-mark, -s 'fıŋgəmɑ:k, -s
finger-nail, -s 'fıŋgəneıl, -z
finger-plate, -s 'fıŋgəpleıt, -s
finger-post, -s 'fıŋgəpəʊst, -s
finger-print, -s 'fıŋgəprınt, -s
finger-stall, -s 'fıŋgəstɔ:l, -z
fingertip, -s 'fıŋgətıp, -s
Fingest (in Buckinghamshire) 'fındʒıst
finial, -s 'faınıəl ['fın-], -z
finic|al, -ally, -alness 'fınık|l, -əlı, -lnıs [-nəs]
finicking 'fınıkıŋ
finick|y, -ier, -iest, -ily, -iness 'fınık|ı, -ıə*, -ııst, -ılı [-əlı], -ınıs [-məs]
finikin 'fınıkın
finis 'fınıs ['fi:nıs, 'faınıs]
finish (s. v.), -es, -ing, -ed, -er/s 'fınıʃ, -ız, -ıŋ, -t, -ə*/z
Finisterre ˌfını'steə* ['---]
finite, -ly, -ness 'faınaıt, -lı, -nıs [-nəs]
finitude 'faınıtju:d
Finlaison 'fınlısn
Finland, -er/s 'fınlənd, -ə*/z
Finlay 'fınleı [-lı]
Finlayson 'fınlısn
Finley 'fınlı
Finn, -s fın, -z
Finnan 'fınən
Finney 'fını
Finn|ic, -ish 'fın|ık, -ıʃ
Finnon 'fınən
Finno-Ugri|an -c ˌfınəʊ'ju:grı|ən, -k
finny 'fını
Finsbury 'fınzbərı

Finsteraarhorn ˌfɪnstər'ɑːhɔːn
Finzean 'fɪŋən
Finzi 'fɪnzɪ
Fiona fɪ'əʊnə
fiord, -s fjɔːd [fɪ'ɔːd], -z
fiorin 'faɪərɪn
fir, -s fɜː*, -z
Firbank 'fɜːbæŋk
fir|e (s. v.), -es, -ing, -ed, -er/s 'faɪə*, -z, -rɪŋ, -d, -rə*/z
fire-alarm, -s 'faɪərəˌlɑːm ['faɪəəˌl-], -z
fire-arm, -s 'faɪərɑːm ['faɪəɑːm], -z
fireball, -s 'faɪəbɔːl, -z
fire-balloon, -s 'faɪəbəˌluːn, -z
fire-bomb, -s 'faɪəbɒm, -z
fire-box, -es 'faɪəbɒks, -ɪz
firebrand, -s 'faɪəbrænd, -z
fire-brick, -s 'faɪəbrɪk, -s
fire-brigade, -s 'faɪəbrɪˌɡeɪd, -z
fireclay 'faɪəkleɪ
fire-control, -s 'faɪəkənˌtrəʊl, -z
firecrest, -s 'faɪəkrest, -s
firedamp 'faɪədæmp
fire-dance, -s 'faɪədɑːns, -ɪz
fire-drill, -s 'faɪədrɪl, -z
fire-eat|er/s,   -ing   'faɪərˌiːt|ə*/z ['faɪəˌiːt-], -ɪŋ
fire-engine, -s 'faɪərˌendʒɪn ['faɪəˌen-], -z
fire-escape, -s 'faɪərɪˌskeɪp ['faɪəɪˌs-], -s
fire-extinguisher, -s 'faɪərɪkˌstɪŋgwɪʃə* ['faɪəɪkˌs-, -ekˌs-], -z
fire-fight|er/s, -ing 'faɪəˌfaɪt|ə*/z, -ɪŋ
firefl|y, -ies 'faɪəfl|aɪ, -aɪz
fire-guard, -s 'faɪəɡɑːd, -z
fire-hose, -s 'faɪəhəʊz, -ɪz
fire-insurance,   -s   'faɪərɪnˌʃɔːrəns ['faɪəɪn-, -ˌʃɔər-, -ˌʃʊər-], -ɪz
fire-iron, -s 'faɪərˌaɪən ['faɪəˌaɪən], -z
fire-light, -er/s 'faɪəlaɪt, -ə*/z
firelock, -s 'faɪəlɒk, -s
fire|man, -men 'faɪə|mən, -mən [-men]
fireplace, -s 'faɪəpleɪs, -ɪz
fire-plug, -s 'faɪəplʌɡ, -z
fire-power 'faɪəˌpaʊə*
fireproof 'faɪəpruːf
fire-screen, -s 'faɪəskriːn, -z
fire-ship, -s 'faɪəʃɪp, -s
fireside, -s 'faɪəsaɪd, -z
fire-stick, -s 'faɪəstɪk, -s
firestone 'faɪəstəʊn
fire-trap, -s 'faɪətræp, -s
fire-watch, -es, -ing, -ed, -er/s 'faɪəwɒtʃ, -ɪz, -ɪŋ, -t, -ə*/z
fire-water 'faɪəˌwɔːtə*
firewood 'faɪəwʊd
fireworks 'faɪəwɜːks
fire-worship, -per/s 'faɪəˌwɜːʃɪp, -ə*/z

firing, -line/s, -party, -parties, -point/s, -squad/s 'faɪərɪŋ, -laɪn/z, -ˌpɑːtɪ, -ˌpɑːtɪz, -pɔɪnt/s, -skwɒd/z
firkin, -s 'fɜːkɪn, -z
firm (s. adj.), -s, -er, -est, -ly, -ness fɜːm, -z, -ə*, -ɪst, -lɪ, -nɪs [-nəs]
firmament, -s 'fɜːməmənt, -s
firman, -s fɜː'mɑːn ['fɜːmɑːn, 'fɜːmən], -z
firr|y, -iness 'fɜːr|ɪ, -ɪnɪs [-nəs]
Firsby 'fɜːzbɪ
first, -ly fɜːst, -lɪ
firstborn 'fɜːstbɔːn
first-class ˌfɜːst'klɑːs [also '— when attributive]
first-fruit, -s 'fɜːstfruːt, -s
first-hand ˌfɜːst'hænd [also '— when attributive]
firstling, -s 'fɜːstlɪŋ, -z
firstly 'fɜːstlɪ
first-rate ˌfɜːst'reɪt [also '— when attributive]
firth (F.), -s fɜːθ, -s
fisc fɪsk
fiscal (s. adj.), -s 'fɪskl, -z
fish (s. v.) (F.), -es, -ing, -ed, -er/s fɪʃ, -ɪz, -ɪŋ, -t, -ə*/z
fish-ball, -s 'fɪʃbɔːl, -z
fishbone, -s 'fɪʃbəʊn, -z
fish-cake, -s 'fɪʃkeɪk, -s
fish-carver, -s 'fɪʃˌkɑːvə*, -z
fisher (F.), -s 'fɪʃə*, -z
fisher|man, -men 'fɪʃə|mən, -mən [-men]
fisher|y, -ies 'fɪʃər|ɪ, -ɪz
Fishguard 'fɪʃɡɑːd
fish-hook, -s 'fɪʃhʊk ['fɪʃʊk], -s
fishing-rod, -s 'fɪʃɪŋrɒd, -z
fishing-tackle 'fɪʃɪŋˌtækl
Fishkill 'fɪʃkɪl
fish-kni|fe, -ves 'fɪʃnaɪ|f, -vz
fishmonger, -s 'fɪʃˌmʌŋɡə*, -z
fishplate, -s 'fɪʃpleɪt, -s
fishpond, -s 'fɪʃpɒnd, -z
fish-sauce ˌfɪʃ'sɔːs
fish-slice, -s 'fɪʃslaɪs, -ɪz
fish-strainer, -s 'fɪʃˌstreɪnə*, -z
fishtail 'fɪʃteɪl
fish-torpedo, -es 'fɪʃtɔːˌpiːdəʊ, -z
Fishwick 'fɪʃwɪk
fishwi|fe, -ves 'fɪʃwaɪ|f, -vz
fish|woman, -women 'fɪʃ|ˌwʊmən, -ˌwɪmɪn
fish|y, -ier, -iest, -ily, -iness 'fɪʃ|ɪ, -ɪə*, -ɪɪst, -ɪlɪ [-əlɪ], -ɪnɪs [-nəs]
Fisk(e) fɪsk
Fison 'faɪsn
fissile 'fɪsaɪl

191

fission 'fɪʃn
fissionable 'fɪʃnəbl [-ʃənəbl]
fissiparous fɪ'sɪpərəs
fissure, -s, -d 'fɪʃə* [-ˌʃʊə*], -z, -d
fist, -s; -ic, -ical fɪst, -s; -ɪk, -ɪkl
fisticuff, -s 'fɪstɪkʌf, -s
fistul|a, -as, -ar, -ous 'fɪstjʊl|ə, -əz, -ə*, -əs
fit (s. adj. v.), -s, -ter, -test, -ly, -ness; -ting/ly, -ted, -ter/s fɪt, -s, -ə*, -ɪst, -lɪ, -nɪs [-nəs]; -ɪŋ/lɪ, -ɪd, -ə*/z
fitch (F.), -es fɪtʃ, -ɪz
Fitchburg 'fɪtʃbɜ:g
fitchew, -s 'fɪtʃu:, -z
fit|ful, -fully, -fulness 'fɪt|fʊl, -fʊlɪ [-fəlɪ], -fʊlnɪs [-nəs]
fitment, -s 'fɪtmənt, -s
fitting-out ˌfɪtɪŋ'aʊt
fitting-room, -s 'fɪtɪŋrʊm [-ru:m], -z
fitting-shop, -s 'fɪtɪŋʃɒp, -s
Fitzalan fɪts'ælən
Fitzcharles fɪts'tʃɑ:lz
Fitzclarence fɪts'klærəns
Fitzdottrel fɪts'dɒtrəl
Fitzgeorge fɪts'dʒɔ:dʒ
Fitzgerald fɪts'dʒerəld
Fitzgibbon fɪts'gɪbən
Fitzhardinge fɪts'hɑ:dɪŋ
Fitzharris fɪts'hærɪs
Fitzherbert fɪts'hɜ:bət
Fitzhugh fɪts'hju:
Fitzjames fɪts'dʒeɪmz [in James Fitzjames often -'fɪtsdʒ-]
Fitzjohn (surname) fɪts'dʒɒn
Fitzjohn's Avenue ˌfɪtsdʒɒnz'ævənju: [-vɪn-]
Fitzmaurice fɪts'mɒrɪs
Fitzpatrick fɪts'pætrɪk
Fitzroy (surname) fɪts'rɔɪ, (square and street in London) 'fɪtsrɔɪ
Fitzsimmons fɪts'sɪmənz
Fitzstephen fɪts'sti:vn
Fitzurse fɪts'ɜ:s
Fitzwalter fɪts'wɔ:ltə* [-'wɒl-]
Fitzwilliam fɪts'wɪljəm
Fitzwygram fɪts'waɪgrəm
five, -s -fold faɪv, -z, -fəʊld
five-ish 'faɪvɪʃ
fivepen|ce, -ny 'faɪfpən|s ['faɪvp-], -ɪ (see note under penny)
five-ply 'faɪvplaɪ [ˌ-'-]
fiver, -s 'faɪvə*, -z
fix (s. v.), -es, -ing, -ed, -edly, -edness, -er/s; -able, -ative fɪks, -ɪz, -ɪŋ, -t, -ɪdlɪ, -ɪdnɪs [-nəs], -ə*/z; -əbl, -ətɪv
†fixation fɪk'seɪʃn
fixity 'fɪksətɪ [-ɪtɪ]
fixture, -s 'fɪkstʃə*, -z

fizz (s. v.), -es, -ing, -ed, -er/s fɪz, -ɪz, -ɪŋ, -d, -ə*/z
fizz|le (s. v.), -les, -ling, -led 'fɪz|l, -lz, -lɪŋ [-lɪŋ], -ld
fizz|y, -ier, -iest, -iness 'fɪz|ɪ, -ɪə*, -ɪɪst, -ɪnɪs [-ɪnəs]
fjord, -s fjɔ:d, -z
flab flæb
flabbergast, -s, -ing, -ed 'flæbəgɑ:st, -s, -ɪŋ, -ɪd
flabb|y, -ier, -iest, -ily, -iness 'flæb|ɪ, -ɪə*, -ɪɪst, -ɪlɪ [-əlɪ], -ɪnɪs [-ɪnəs]
flaccid, -ly, -ness 'flæksɪd, -lɪ, -nɪs [-nəs, increasingly 'flæsɪd]
flaccidity flæk'sɪdətɪ [-ɪtɪ also flæ'sɪ-]
Flaccus 'flækəs
Fladgate 'flædgɪt [-geɪt]
flag (s. v.), -s, -ging, -ged flæg, -z, -ɪŋ, -d
flag-captain, -s ˌflæg'kæptɪn ['-ˌ--], -z
flag-day, -s 'flægdeɪ, -z
flagellant, -s 'flædʒələnt [-dʒɪ-, flə'dʒel-, flæ'dʒel-], -s
flagellat|e, -es, -ing, -ed, -or/s 'flædʒəleɪt [-dʒɪl-, -dʒel-], -s, -ɪŋ, -ɪd, -ə*/z
flagellation, -s ˌflædʒə'leɪʃn [-dʒɪ'l-, -dʒe'l-], -z
flagell|um, -a flə'dʒel|əm [flæ'dʒ-], -ə
flageolet, -s ˌflædʒəʊ'let ['---], -s
Flagg flæg
flaggy 'flægɪ
flagitious, -ly, -ness flə'dʒɪʃəs, -lɪ, -nɪs [-nəs]
flag-lieutenan|t, -ts, -cy, -cies ˌflæglef'tenən|t [-ləf't-], -ts, -sɪ, -sɪz (see note under lieutenancy)
flag-officer, -s 'flægˌɒfɪsə*, -z
flagon, -s 'flægən, -z
flagpole, -s 'flægpəʊl, -z
flagran|cy, -t/ly 'fleɪgrən|sɪ, -t/lɪ
flag|-ship/s, -staff/s 'flæg|ʃɪp/s, -stɑ:f/s
flagstone, -s 'flægstəʊn, -z
flag-wagging 'flægˌwægɪŋ
flag-waving 'flægˌweɪvɪŋ
Flaherty 'fleətɪ, 'flɑ:hətɪ, 'flæhətɪ
flail (s. v.), -s, -ing, -ed fleɪl, -z, -ɪŋ, -d
flair, -s fleə*, -z
flak flæk
flak|e (s. v.), -es, -ing, -ed fleɪk, -s, -ɪŋ, -t
flake-white ˌfleɪk'waɪt [-'hw-, in contrast '--]
flak|y, -ily, -iness 'fleɪk|ɪ, -ɪlɪ [-əlɪ], -ɪnɪs [-ɪnəs]
flam, -s flæm, -z
Flambard 'flæmbɑ:d [-bəd]
flambeau (F.), -s 'flæmbəʊ, -z
Flamborough 'flæmbərə
flamboyant flæm'bɔɪənt

flam|e (s. v.), -es, -ing, -ed fleɪm, -z, -ɪŋ, -d

flame-colour, -ed 'fleɪm‚kʌlə*, -d

flamen, -s 'fleɪmen, -z

flamenco flə'meŋkəʊ

flamingo, -(e)s flə'mɪŋgəʊ [flæ'm-], -z

Flaminius flə'mɪnɪəs [flæ'm-, -njəs]

Flammock 'flæmək

Flamstead 'flæmstɪd [-sted]

Flamsteed 'flæmstiːd

flamy 'fleɪmɪ

flan, -s flæn, -z

Flanders 'flɑːndəz

flange, -s, -d flændʒ, -ɪz, -d

flank (s. v.), -s, -ing, -ed, -er/s flæŋk, -s, -ɪŋ, -t [flæŋt], -ə*/z

flannel, -s, -led 'flænl, -z, -d

flannelette ‚flænl'et [-nə'let]

flannelly 'flænlɪ

flap (s. v.), -s, -ping, -ped flæp, -s, -ɪŋ, -t

flapdoodle 'flæp‚duːdl

flapjack, -s 'flæpdʒæk, -s

flapper, -s 'flæpə*, -z

flar|e (s. v.), -es, -ing/ly, -ed fleə*, -z, -rɪŋ/lɪ, -d

flare-pa|th, -ths 'fleəpɑː|θ, -ðz

flare-up, -s ‚fleər'ʌp ['--], -s

flash (s. adj. v.) (F.), -es, -ing, -ed, -er/s flæʃ, -ɪz, -ɪŋ, -t, -ə*/z

flashback, -s 'flæʃbæk, -s

flash-card, -s 'flæʃkɑːd, -z

flashlight, -s 'flæʃlaɪt, -s

flash-point, -s 'flæʃpɔɪnt, -s

flash|y, -ier, -iest, -ily, -iness 'flæʃ|ɪ, -ɪə*, -ɪɪst, -ɪlɪ [-əlɪ], -ɪnɪs [-ɪnəs]

flask, -s flɑːsk, -s

flasket, -s 'flɑːskɪt, -s

flat (s. adj.), -s, -ter, -test, -ly, -ness flæt, -s, -ə*, -ɪst, -lɪ, -nɪs [-nəs]

Flatbush 'flætbʊʃ

flatfish, -es 'flætfɪʃ, -ɪz

flatfoot 'flætfʊt

flat-footed ‚flæt'fʊtɪd ['-‚--]

flathead, -s 'flæthed, -z

flat-iron, -s 'flæt‚aɪən, -z

Flatland 'flætlænd

flatlet, -s 'flætlɪt [-lət], -s

flatt|en, -ens, -ening, -ened 'flæt|n, -nz, -nɪŋ [-nɪŋ], -nd

flatter, -s, -ing/ly, -ed, -er/s 'flætə*, -z, -rɪŋ/lɪ, -d, -rə*/z

flatter|y, -ies 'flætər|ɪ, -ɪz

flattish 'flætɪʃ

flatulen|ce, -cy, -t/ly 'flætjʊlən|s [-tʃʊ-], -sɪ, -t/lɪ

flatus, -es 'fleɪtəs, -ɪz

flat|ways, -wise 'flæt|weɪz, -waɪz

flaunt, -s, -ing/ly, -ed, -er/s flɔːnt, -s, -ɪŋ/lɪ, -ɪd, -ə*/z

flautist, -s 'flɔːtɪst, -s

Flavel 'flævəl

Flavell flə'vel, 'fleɪvəl

Flavi|a, -an, -us 'fleɪvj|ə [-vɪ|ə], -ən, -əs

flavorous 'fleɪvərəs

flav|our (s. v.), -ours, -ouring/s, -oured; -ourless 'fleɪv|ə*, -əz, -ərɪŋ/z, -əd; -əlɪs [-ləs]

flaw (s. v.), -s, -ing, -ed flɔː, -z, -ɪŋ, -d

flawless, -ly, -ness 'flɔːlɪs [-ləs], -lɪ, -nɪs [-nəs]

flax, -en flæks, -ən

Flaxman 'flæksmən

flaxy 'flæksɪ

flay, -s, -ing, -ed, -er/s fleɪ, -z, -ɪŋ, -d, -ə*/z

flea, -s fliː, -z

fleabane 'fliːbeɪn

flea|-bite/s, -bitten 'fliː|baɪt/s, -bɪtn

fleam, -s fliːm, -z

Fleance 'fliːəns [flɪəns]

Fleay fleɪ

flèche, -s fleɪʃ [fleʃ], -ɪz

fleck (s. v.), -s, -ing, -ed flek, -s, -ɪŋ, -t

Flecknoe 'fleknəʊ

flection, -s 'flekʃn, -z

flectional 'flekʃənl [-ʃnl, -ʃnl, -ʃənəl]

fled (from flee) fled

fledg|e, -es, -ing, -ed; -(e)ling/s fledʒ, -ɪz, -ɪŋ, -d; -lɪŋ/z

flee, -s, -ing, fled, fleer/s fliː, -z, -ɪŋ, fled, 'fliːə*/z

fleec|e (s. v.), -es, -ing, -ed, -er/s; -y, -iness fliːs, -ɪz, -ɪŋ, -t, -ə*/z; -ɪ, -ɪnɪs [-ɪnəs]

Fleeming 'flemɪŋ

fleer (sneer) (s. v.), -s, -ing, -ed flɪə*, -z, -rɪŋ, -d

fleet (s. adj. v.) (F.), -s; -er, -est, -ly, -ness; -ing/ly, -ed fliːt, -s; -ə*, -ɪst, -lɪ, -nɪs [-nəs]; -ɪŋ/lɪ, -ɪd

Fleet Street 'fliːtstriːt

Fleetwood 'fliːtwʊd

Fleming, -s, -ton 'flemɪŋ, -z, -tən

Flemish 'flemɪʃ

Flemming 'flemɪŋ

fiens|e, -es, -ing, -ed flenz, -ɪz, -ɪŋ, -d

flesh (s. v.), -es, -ing/s, -ed fleʃ, -ɪz, -ɪŋ/z, -t

flesh-colour, -ed 'fleʃ‚kʌlə*, -d

flesh-eat|er/s, -ing 'fleʃ‚iːt|ə*/z, -ɪŋ

flesh-hook, -s 'fleʃhʊk ['fleʃʊk], -s

fleshless 'fleʃlɪs [-ləs]

fleshl|y, -iness 'fleʃl|ɪ, -ɪnɪs [-ɪnəs]

flesh-pot, -s 'fleʃpɒt, -s

193

flesh-tint 'fleʃtɪnt
flesh-wound, -s 'fleʃwu:nd, -z
flesh|y, -iness 'fleʃ|ɪ, -ɪnɪs [-ɪnəs]
fletcher (F.), -s 'fletʃə*, -z
Flete fli:t
fleur-de-lis ˌflɜ:də'li: [-'li:s] (flœrdəlis)
Fleur de Lis (place in Gwent) ˌflɜ:də'li:
flew (from fly v.) flu:
flex (s. v.), -es, -ing, -ed fleks, -ɪz, -ɪŋ, -t
flexibility ˌfleksə'bɪlətɪ [-sɪ'b-, -lɪt-]
flexib|le, -ly, -leness 'fleksəb|l [-sɪb-],
   -lɪ, -lnɪs [-nəs]
flexion, -s 'flekʃn, -z
flexor, -s 'fleksə*, -z
flexure, -s 'flekʃə*, -z
flibbertigibbet, -s ˌflɪbətɪ'dʒɪbɪt, -s
flick (s. v.), -s, -ing, -ed flɪk, -s, -ɪŋ, -t
flicker (s. v.), -s, -ing, -ed 'flɪkə*, -z,
   -rɪŋ, -d
flick-kni|fe, -ves 'flɪknaɪ|f, -vz
flier, -s 'flaɪə*, -z
flight (F.), -s, -less flaɪt, -s, -lɪs [-ləs]
flight-deck, -s 'flaɪtdek, -s
flight-path, -s 'flaɪtpɑ:θ, -s [-pɑ:ðz]
flight|y, -ier, -iest, -ily, -iness 'flaɪt|ɪ,
   -ɪə* [-jə*], -ɪɪst [-jɪst], -ɪlɪ [-əlɪ], -ɪnɪs
   [-ɪnəs]
flim-flam, -s 'flɪmflæm, -z
Flimnap 'flɪmnæp
flims|y, -ier, -iest, -ily, -iness 'flɪmz|ɪ,
   -ɪə* [-jə*], -ɪɪst [-jɪst], -ɪlɪ [-əlɪ], -ɪnɪs
   [-ɪnəs]
flinch, -es, -ing/ly, -ed, -er/s flɪntʃ, -ɪz,
   -ɪŋ/lɪ, -t, -ə*/z
flinders (F.) 'flɪndəz
fling (s. v.), -s, -ing, flung flɪŋ, -z, -ɪŋ,
   flʌŋ
flint (F.), -s flɪnt, -s
flint-glass ˌflɪnt'glɑ:s ['--]
flint-lock, -s 'flɪntlɒk, -s
Flintshire 'flɪnt-ʃə* [-ˌʃɪə*]
flintstone 'flɪntstəʊn
Flintwinch 'flɪntwɪntʃ
flint|y, -ier, -iest, -ily, -iness 'flɪnt|ɪ,
   -ɪə* [-jə*], -ɪɪst [-jɪst], -ɪlɪ [-əlɪ], -ɪnɪs
   [-ɪnəs]
flip (s. v.), -s, -ping, -ped flɪp, -s, -ɪŋ, -t
flip-flap (s. adv.), -s 'flɪpflæp, -s
flippan|cy, -t/ly, -tness 'flɪpən|sɪ, -t/lɪ,
   -tnɪs [-nəs]
flipper, -s 'flɪpə*, -z
flirt (s. v.), -s, -ing/ly, -ed flɜ:t, -s,
   -ɪŋ/lɪ, -ɪd
flirtation, -s flɜ:'teɪʃn, -z
flirtatious flɜ:'teɪʃəs
flirty 'flɜ:tɪ
flit, -s, -ting, -ted flɪt, -s, -ɪŋ, -ɪd
flitch (F.), -es flɪtʃ, -ɪz

Flite flaɪt
flitter, -s, -ing, -ed 'flɪtə*, -z, -rɪŋ, -d
flitter|-mouse, -mice 'flɪtə|maʊs, -maɪs
Flixton 'flɪkstən
float (s. v.), -s, -ing, -ed, -er/s; -able,
   -age fləʊt, -s, -ɪŋ, -ɪd, -ə*/z; -əbl,
   -ɪdʒ
floatation fləʊ'teɪʃn
floating|-bridge/s, -dock/s ˌfləʊtɪŋ|-
   'brɪdʒ/ɪz, -'dɒk/s
float-stone, -s 'fləʊtstəʊn, -z
floccule, -s 'flɒkju:l, -z
flocculent 'flɒkjʊlənt
flock (s. v.), -s, -ing, -ed; -y flɒk, -s, -ɪŋ,
   -t; -ɪ
Flockton 'flɒktən
Flodden 'flɒdn
floe, -s fləʊ, -z
flog, -s, -ging/s, -ged flɒg, -z, -ɪŋ/z, -d
flood (s. v.) (F.), -s, -ing, -ed; -gate/s
   flʌd, -z, -ɪŋ, -ɪd; -geɪt/s
floodlight (s. v.), -s, -ing, floodlit
   'flʌdlaɪt, -s, -ɪŋ, 'flʌdlɪt
floodtide 'flʌdtaɪd
Flook flʊk
floor (s. v.), -s, -ing, -ed, -er/s flɔ:*
   [flɔə*], -z, -rɪŋ, -d, -rə*/z
floor|-cloth, -cloths 'flɔ:|klɒθ ['flɔə-],
   old-fashioned -klɔ:θ], -klɒθs [-klɔ:ðz,
   -klɔ:θs]
flop (s. v. adv. interj.), -s, -ping, -ped,
   -per/s flɒp, -s, -ɪŋ, -t, -ə*/z
flopp|y, -ier, -iest, -ily, -iness 'flɒp|ɪ,
   -ɪə*, -ɪɪst, -ɪlɪ [-əlɪ], -ɪnɪs [-ɪnəs]
flora (F.) 'flɔ:rə
floral 'flɔ:rəl ['flɒr-]
Floren|ce, -tine 'flɒrən|s, -taɪn
Flores 'flɔ:rɪz
florescen|ce, -t flɔ:'resn|s [flɒ'r-, flə'r-],
   -t
floret, -s 'flɔ:rɪt [-ret], -s
Florian 'flɔ:rɪən
floriat|e, -es, -ing, -ed 'flɔ:rɪeɪt, -s, -ɪŋ,
   -ɪd
floricultur|al, -ist/s ˌflɔ:rɪ'kʌltʃər|əl
   [ˌflɒr-, -tʃʊr-], -ɪst/s
floriculture 'flɔ:rɪkʌltʃə* ['flɒr-]
florid, -est, -ly, -ness 'flɒrɪd, -ɪst, -lɪ,
   -nɪs [-nəs]
Florida 'flɒrɪdə
floriferous flɔ:'rɪfərəs [flɒ'r-]
Florimel 'flɒrɪmel
florin, -s 'flɒrɪn, -z
Florinda flɔ:'rɪndə [flɒ'r-, flə'r-]
Florio 'flɔ:rɪəʊ
florist, -s 'flɒrɪst, -s
Florizel 'flɒrɪzel
Florrie 'flɒrɪ

floruit 'flɔːrʊɪt [-rjʊɪt]
Florus 'flɔːrəs
floss (F.), -y flɒs, -ɪ
Flossie 'flɒsɪ
floss-silk ˌflɒs'sɪlk
flotation, -s fləʊ'teɪʃn, -z
flotilla, -s fləʊ'tɪlə, -z
flotsam 'flɒtsəm
Floud flʌd
flounc|e (s. v.), -es, -ing, -ed flaʊns, -ɪz, -ɪŋ, -t
flound|er (s. v.), -ers, -ering, -ered 'flaʊnd|ə*, -əz, -ərɪŋ, -əd
flour (s. v.), -s, -ing, -ed 'flaʊə*, -z, -rɪŋ, -d
flourish (s. v.), -es, -ing/ly, -ed 'flʌrɪʃ, -ɪz, -ɪŋ/lɪ, -t
flour-mill, -s 'flaʊəmɪl, -z
floury 'flaʊərɪ
flout (s. v.), -s, -ing/ly, -ed flaʊt, -s, -ɪŋ/lɪ, -ɪd
fl|ow (s. v.), -ows, -owing/ly, -owingness, -owed fl|əʊ, -əʊz, -əʊɪŋ/lɪ, -əʊɪŋnɪs [-nəs], -əʊd
flower (s. v.) (F.), -s, -ing, -ed, -er/s 'flaʊə*, -z, -rɪŋ, -d, -rə*/z
flower-bearing 'flaʊəˌbeərɪŋ
flower|-bed/s, -bud/s 'flaʊə|bed/z, -bʌd/z
floweret, -s 'flaʊərɪt [-ret], -s
flower|-garden/s, -girl/s, -head/s 'flaʊə|ˌgɑːdn/z, -gɜːl/z, -hed/z
flowerless 'flaʊəlɪs [-ləs]
flower|-pot/s, -service/s, -stalk/s 'flaʊə|pɒt/s, -ˌsɜːvɪs/ɪz, -stɔːk/s
flowery 'flaʊərɪ
flown (from fly) fləʊn
Floy|d, -er flɔɪ|d, -ə*
'flu fluː
fluctuat|e, -es, -ing, -ed 'flʌktʃʊeɪt [-tjʊeɪt], -s, -ɪŋ, -ɪd
fluctuation, -s ˌflʌktʃʊ'eɪʃn [-tjʊ-], -z
Flud|d, -yer flʌd, -jə*
flue, -s fluː, -z
Fluellen fluː'elɪn [flʊ'e-]
fluen|cy, -t/ly, -tness 'fluːən|sɪ ['flʊən-], -t/lɪ, -tnɪs [-nəs]
flue-pipe, -s 'fluːpaɪp, -s
flue-work 'fluːwɜːk
fluff (s. v.), -s, -ing, -ed; -y, -ier, -iest, -iness flʌf, -s, -ɪŋ, -t; -ɪ, -ɪə*, -ɪɪst, -ɪnɪs [-ɪnəs]
fluid (s. adj.), -s 'fluːɪd ['flʊɪd], -z
fluidity fluː'ɪdətɪ [flʊ'ɪ-, -ɪtɪ]
fluk|e (s. v.), -es, -ing, -ed, -er/s; -y, -ier, -iest, -iness fluːk, -s, -ɪŋ, -t, -ə*/z; -ɪ, -ɪə* [-jə*], -ɪɪst [-jɪst], -ɪnɪs [-ɪnəs]

flume, -s fluːm, -z
flummery 'flʌmərɪ
flummox, -es, -ing, -ed 'flʌməks, -ɪz, -ɪŋ, -t
flung (from fling) flʌŋ
flunk (v.), -s, -ing, -ed flʌŋk, -s, -ɪŋ, -t
flunkey, -s; -ism 'flʌŋkɪ, -z; -ɪzəm
fluor 'fluːɔ:* ['flʊɔ:*, 'fluːə*, flʊə*]
fluorescen|ce, -t flɔː'resn|s [ˌflʊə'r-, ˌfluːɔ:'r-, ˌflʊɔː:-, ˌfluːɒ'r-, ˌflʊɒ-], -t
fluoric fluː'ɒrɪk
fluoridat|e, -es, -ing, -ed 'flɔːrɪdeɪt ['flʊər-], -s, -ɪŋ, -ɪd
fluoridation ˌflɔːrɪ'deɪʃn [ˌflʊər-, -raɪ-]
fluoride 'flɔːraɪd ['flʊər-]
fluoridization [-isa-] ˌflɔːrɪdaɪ'zeɪʃn [ˌflʊə-, -raɪd-, -dɪ-]
fluoridiz|e [-is|e-], -es, -ing, -ed 'flɔːrɪdaɪz ['flʊə-] -ɪz, -ɪŋ, -d
†fluor|ine, -ite 'flɔːr|iːn ['flʊər-, 'fluːər-], -aɪt
fluor-spar 'fluəspɑ:* ['fluːə-, 'fluːɔ:-]
flurr|y (s. v.), -ies, -ying, -ied 'flʌr|ɪ, -ɪz, -ɪɪŋ, -ɪd
flush (s. v.), -es, -ing, -ed flʌʃ, -ɪz, -ɪŋ, -t
flushing (F.), -s 'flʌʃɪŋ, -z
flust|er (s. v.), -ers, -ering, -ered 'flʌst|ə*, -əz, -ərɪŋ, -əd
flut|e (s. v.) (F.), -es, -ing, -ed; -ist/s; -y, -ier, -iest, -iness fluːt, -s, -ɪŋ, -ɪd; -ɪst/s; -ɪ, -ɪə* [-jə*], -ɪɪst [-jɪst], -ɪnɪs [-ɪnəs]
flutter (s. v.) (F.), -s, -ing, -ed, -er/s 'flʌtə*, -z, -rɪŋ, -d, -rə*/z
fluvial 'fluːvjəl [-vɪəl]
flux, -es flʌks, -ɪz
fluxion, -s 'flʌkʃn, -z
fluxional 'flʌkʃənl [-ʃn̩l, -ʃnl]
fl|y (s. v.) (all senses) (F.), -ies, -ying, flew, flown, flier/s fl|aɪ, -aɪz, -aɪɪŋ, fluː:, fləʊn, 'flaɪə*/z
flyable 'flaɪəbl
fly-blow, -s, -n 'flaɪbləʊ, -z, -n
fly-bomb, -s 'flaɪbɒm, -z
fly-button, -s 'flaɪbʌtn, -z
fly-by-night 'flaɪbaɪnaɪt
fly|-catcher/s, -fishing 'flaɪ|ˌkætʃə*/z, -ˌfɪʃɪŋ
flyer, -s 'flaɪə*, -z
flying-officer, -s 'flaɪɪŋˌɒfɪsə*, -z
fly-lea|f, -ves 'flaɪliː|f, -vz
fly-line, -s 'flaɪlaɪn, -z
Flyn|n, -t flɪn, -t
flyover, -s 'flaɪˌəʊvə*, -z
fly-paper, -s 'flaɪˌpeɪpə*, -z
fly-sheet, -s 'flaɪʃiːt, -s
fly-swatter, -s 'flaɪˌswɒtə*, -z
flyway, -s 'flaɪweɪ, -z

195

flywheel, -s 'flaɪwiːl [-hwiːl], -z
Foakes fəʊks
foal (s. v.), -s, -ing, -ed fəʊl, -z, -ɪŋ, -d
foam (s. v.), -s, -ing, -ed; -y, -iness
  fəʊm, -z, -ɪŋ, -d; -ɪ, -ɪnɪs [-nəs]
Foard fɔːd [fɔəd]
fob (s. v.), -s, -bing, -bed fɒb, -z, -ɪŋ, -d
focal 'fəʊkl
Fochabers 'fɒkəbəz ['fɒxə-]
Focke (surname) fɒk
fo'c'sle, -s 'fəʊksl, -z
fo|cus (s.), -ci 'fəʊ|kəs, -saɪ [-kiː]
focus (v.), -ses, -sing, -sed 'fəʊkəs, -ɪz,
  -ɪŋ, -t
fodder 'fɒdə*
foe, -s fəʊ, -z
foe|man, -men 'fəʊ|mən, -mən [-men]
foetal 'fiːtl
foetid, -ly, -ness 'fiːtɪd, -lɪ, -nɪs [-nəs]
foetus, -es 'fiːtəs, -ɪz
fog (s. v.), -s, -ging, -ged fɒg, -z, -ɪŋ, -d
fog-bank, -s 'fɒgbæŋk, -s
fog-bound 'fɒgbaʊnd
Fogerty 'fəʊgətɪ, 'fɒgətɪ
fogey, -s, -ish, -ism 'fəʊgɪ, -z, -ɪʃ, -ɪzəm
Fogg fɒg
fogg|y, -ier, -iest, -ily, -iness 'fɒg|ɪ,
  -ɪə*, -ɪɪst, -ɪlɪ [-əlɪ], -ɪnɪs [-ɪnəs]
fog-horn, -s 'fɒghɔːn, -z
fogram, -s 'fəʊgræm, -z
fog-signal, -s 'fɒg‚sɪgnl [-nəl], -z
fog|y, -ies 'fəʊg|ɪ, -ɪz
fogyi|sh, -sm 'fəʊgɪɪ|ʃ, -zəm
foible, -s 'fɔɪbl, -z
foil (s. v.), -s, -ing, -ed fɔɪl, -z, -ɪŋ, -d
foison, -s 'fɔɪzn, -z
foist, -s, -ing, -ed fɔɪst, -s, -ɪŋ, -ɪd
Foker 'fəʊkə*
fold (s. v.), -s, -ing, -ed, -er/s, -out/s fəʊld,
  -z, -ɪŋ, -ɪd, -ə*/z, -aʊt/s
Foley 'fəʊlɪ
Folgate 'fɒlgɪt [-geɪt]
Folger 'fəʊldʒə*
foli|age, -ar 'fəʊlɪ|ɪdʒ [-ljɪdʒ], -ə*
foliate (adj.) 'fəʊlɪət [-lɪɪt, -ljɪt, -lɪeɪt,
  -ljeɪt]
foliat|e (v.), -es, -ing, -ed 'fəʊlɪeɪt
  [-ljeɪt], -s, -ɪŋ, -ɪd
foliation, -s ‚fəʊlɪ'eɪʃn, -z
folio, -s 'fəʊlɪəʊ [-ljəʊ], -z
Foliot 'fɒlɪət [-ljət]
Foljambe 'fʊldʒəm
folk, -s, -sy fəʊk, -s, -sɪ
folk-dance, -s 'fəʊkdɑːns, -ɪz
Folkes fəʊlks, fuːks
Folkestone 'fəʊkstən
folklore 'fəʊklɔː* [-lɔə*]
folklorist, -s 'fəʊk‚lɔːrɪst, -s

folk-song, -s 'fəʊksɒŋ, -z
folk-tale, -s 'fəʊkteɪl, -z
Foll|en, -ett 'fɒl|ɪn [-ən], -ɪt
Follick 'fɒlɪk
follicle, -s 'fɒlɪkl, -z
Folliott 'fɒlɪət [-ljət]
foll|ow (s. v.), -ows, -owing/s, -owed,
  -ower/s 'fɒl|əʊ, -əʊz, -əʊɪŋ/z, -əʊd,
  -əʊə*/z
follow-my-leader ‚fɒləʊmɪ'liːdə*
follow-on, -s ‚fɒləʊ'ɒn, -z
follow-through, -s ‚fɒləʊ'θruː, -z
foll|y, -ies (F.) 'fɒl|ɪ, -ɪz
Fomalhaut 'fəʊmələʊt ['fɒməlhɔːt]
foment, -s, -ing, -ed, -er/s fəʊ'ment,
  -s, -ɪŋ, -ɪd, -ə*/z
fomentation, -s ‚fəʊmen'teɪʃn [-mən-],
  -z
fond, -er, -est, -ly, -ness fɒnd, -ə*, -ɪst,
  -lɪ, -nɪs ['fɒnnɪs, -nəs]
fond|le, -les, -ling, -led, -ler/s 'fɒnd|l,
  -lz, -lɪŋ, -ld, -lə*/z
font, -s -al fɒnt, -s, -l
Fontenoy 'fɒntənɔɪ [-tɪn-]
Fonteyn fɒn'teɪn
Fonthill 'fɒnthɪl
Foochow ‚fuː'tʃaʊ
food, -s; -less fuːd, -z, -lɪs [-ləs]
food-stuff, -s 'fuːdstʌf, -s
fool (s. v.), -s, -ing, -ed fuːl, -z, -ɪŋ, -d
fooler|y, -ies 'fuːlər|ɪ, -ɪz
fool-hard|y, -iest, -ily, -iness 'fuːl-
  ‚hɑːd|ɪ, -ɪɪst [-jɪst], -ɪlɪ [-əlɪ], -ɪnɪs
  [-ɪnəs]
foolish, -ly, -ness 'fuːlɪʃ, -lɪ, -nɪs [-nəs]
fool-proof 'fuːlpruːf
foolscap (cap), -s 'fuːlzkæp, -s
foolscap (paper size) 'fuːlskæp [-lzk-]
f|oot (s.), -eet f|ʊt, -iːt
foot (v.), -s, -ing, -ed fʊt, -s, -ɪŋ, -ɪd
football, -s, -er/s 'fʊtbɔːl, -z, -ə*/z
foot-ba|th, -ths 'fʊtbɑː|θ, -ðz
footboard, -s 'fʊtbɔːd [-bɔəd], -z
foot-bridge, -s 'fʊtbrɪdʒ, -ɪz
Foote fʊt
footer 'fʊtə*
foot|-fall/s,   -guard/s 'fʊt|fɔːl/z,
  -gɑːd/z
foot-fault (s. v.), -s, -ing, -ed 'fʊtfɔːlt
  [-fɒlt], -s, -ɪŋ, -ɪd
foothill, -s 'fʊthɪl, -z
foothold, -s 'fʊthəʊld, -z
footing (s.), -s 'fʊtɪŋ, -z
foot|le, -les, -ling, -led 'fuːt|l, -lz, -lɪŋ,
  -ld
foot-light, -s 'fʊtlaɪt, -s
foot|man, -men 'fʊt|mən, -mən
footmark, -s 'fʊtmɑːk, -s

footnote, -s 'futnəʊt, -s
footpad, -s 'futpæd, -z
foot-passenger, -s 'fut‚pæsɪndʒə*
[-əndʒə*], -z
footpa|th, -ths 'futpɑː|θ, -ðz
footplate, -s 'futpleɪt, -s
foot-pound, -s 'futpaʊnd, -z
foot-print, -s 'futprɪnt, -s
foot-pump, -s 'futpʌmp, -s
foot-race, -s 'futreɪs, -ɪz
foot-rule, -s 'futruːl, -z
Foots Cray ‚futs'kreɪ
foot-soldier, -s 'fut‚səʊldʒə* [rarely
-djə*], -z
footsore 'futsɔː* [-sɔə*]
footstep, -s 'futstep, -s
footstool, -s 'futstuːl, -s
foot-warmer, -s 'fut‚wɔːmə*, -z
footwear 'futweə*
fooz|le (s. v.) (F.), -les, -ling, -led, -ler/s
'fuːz|l, -lz, -lɪŋ [-lɪŋ], -ld, -lə*/z
[-lə*/z]
fop, -s fɒp, -s
fopper|y, -ies 'fɒpər|ɪ, -ɪz
Foppington 'fɒpɪŋtən
foppish, -ly, -ness 'fɒpɪʃ, -lɪ, -nɪs [-nəs]
for (prep. conj.) fɔː* (strong form), fɒr
(occasional strong form before vowels),
fə* (weak form), f (alternative weak
form before consonants), fr (alternative
weak form before vowels)
forag|e (s. v.), -es, -ing, -ed, -er/s
'fɒrɪdʒ, -ɪz, -ɪŋ, -d, -ə*/z
forasmuch fərəz'mʌtʃ [‚fɔːr-, ‚fɒr-]
foray (s. v.), -s, -ing, -ed 'fɒreɪ, -z, -ɪŋ,
-d
forbade (from forbid) fə'bæd [fɔː'b-,
-'beɪd]
forbear (s.) (ancestor), -s 'fɔːbeə*, -z
forbear (v.), -s, -ing/ly, forbore, for-
borne fɔː'beə*, -z, -rɪŋ/lɪ, fɔː'bɔː*
[-'bɔə*], fɔː'bɔːn
forbearance fɔː'beərəns
Forbes fɔːbz, 'fɔːbɪs
forbid, -s, -ding/ly, forbade, forbidden
fə'bɪd [fɔː'b-], -z, -ɪŋ/lɪ, fə'bæd
[fɔː'b-, -'beɪd], fə'bɪdn [fɔː'b-]
forbore (from forbear) fɔː'bɔː* [-'bɔə*]
forc|e (s. v.) (F.), -es, -ing, -ed, -edly,
-edness, -er/s fɔːs, -ɪz, -ɪŋ, -t, -ɪdlɪ,
-ɪdnɪs [-nəs], -ə*/z
force|ful, -fully, -fulness 'fɔːs|ful, -fulɪ
[-fəlɪ], -fulnɪs [-nəs]
force majeure ‚fɔːs mæ'ʒɜː* (fɔrs
maʒœːr)
force-meat 'fɔːsmiːt
forceps, -es 'fɔːseps [-sɪps], -ɪz
force-pump, -s 'fɔːspʌmp, -s

forcer, -s 'fɔːsə*, -z
forcib|le, -ly, -leness 'fɔːsəb|l [-sɪb-], -lɪ,
-lnɪs [-nəs]
forcing-frame, -s 'fɔːsɪŋfreɪm, -z
ford (s. v.), (F.), -s, -ing, -ed; -able
fɔːd, -z, -ɪŋ, -ɪd; -əbl
Fordcombe 'fɔːdkəm
Ford|e, -er, -ham, -ingbridge fɔːd, -ə*,
-əm, -ɪŋbrɪdʒ
fordone fɔː'dʌn
Fordoun 'fɔːdən [-dn]
Fordyce 'fɔːdaɪs
fore fɔː* [fɔə*]
forearm (s.), -s 'fɔːrɑːm ['fɔərɑːm,
'fɔːrɑːm, 'fɔərɑːm], -z
forearm (v.), -s, -ing, -ed fɔːr'ɑːm
[fɔər'ɑːm, fɔː'ɑːm, fɔə'ɑːm, ‚-'-], -z,
-ɪŋ, -d
forebod|e, -es, -ing/ly, -ed, -er/s
fɔː'bəʊd [fə'b-], -z, -ɪŋ/lɪ, -ɪd, -ə*/z
foreboding (s.), -s fɔː'bəʊdɪŋ [fə'b-], -z
forecabin, -s 'fɔː‚kæbɪn ['fɔə‚k-], -z
forecast (s.), -s 'fɔːkɑːst ['fɔə-], -s
forecast (v.), -s, -ing, -ed, -er/s
'fɔːkɑːst ['fɔəkɑːst, fɔː'kɑːst,
fɔə'kɑːst], -s, -ɪŋ, -ɪd, -ə*/z
forecastle, -s 'fəʊksl, -z
foreclos|e, -es, -ing, -ed fɔː'kləʊz, -ɪz,
-ɪŋ, -d
foreclosure, -s fɔː'kləʊʒə*, -z
forecourt, -s 'fɔːkɔːt ['fɔə-], -s
foredoom, -s, -ing, -ed fɔː'duːm, -z, -ɪŋ,
-d
fore-end, -s 'fɔːrend ['fɔərend, 'fɔːend,
'fɔəend], -z
fore|father/s, -finger/s 'fɔː|‚fɑːðə*/z
['fɔə|-], -‚fɪŋgə*/z
fore|-foot, -feet 'fɔː|fut ['fɔə-], -fiːt
forefront 'fɔːfrʌnt ['fɔə-]
fore|go, -goes, -going, -went, -gone,
-goer/s fɔː|'gəʊ, -'gəʊz, -'gəʊɪŋ,
-'went, -'gɒn [as adjective '--],
-'gəʊə*/z
foreground, -s 'fɔːgraʊnd ['fɔəg-], -z
forehand 'fɔːhænd ['fɔə-]
forehead, -s 'fɒrɪd [-red, 'fɔːhed,
'fɔəhed], -z
foreign, -er/s 'fɒrən [-rɪn], -ə*/z
forejudg|e, -es, -ing, -ed fɔː'dʒʌdʒ, -ɪz,
-ɪŋ, -d
fore|know, -knows, -knowing, -knew,
-known fɔː|'nəʊ, -'nəʊz, -'nəʊɪŋ,
-'njuː, -'nəʊn
foreknowledge ‚fɔː'nɒlɪdʒ [fɔː'n-]
forel 'fɒrəl
foreland (F.), -s 'fɔːlənd ['fɔəl-], -z
foreleg, -s 'fɔːleg ['fɔəl-], -z
forelock, -s 'fɔːlɒk ['fɔə-], -s

197

fore|man (F.), -men 'fɔː|mən ['fɔə-], -mən

foremast, -s 'fɔːmɑːst ['fɔə-, *nautical pronunciation* -məst], -s

foremost 'fɔːməʊst ['fɔə-, -məst]

forenoon, -s 'fɔːnuːn ['fɔə-, -'-], -z

forensic fə'rensɪk [fɒ'r-]

fore-ordain, -s, -ing, -ed ˌfɔːrɔː'deɪn [ˌˌfɔːɔː'd-, ˌfɔə-], -z, -ɪŋ, -d

forepart, -s 'fɔːpɑːt ['fɔə-], -s

fore|run, -runs, running, -ran fɔː|'rʌn [fɔə-], -'rʌnz, -'rʌnɪŋ, -'ræn

forerunner, -s 'fɔːˌrʌnə* ['fɔə-, ˌ-'--], -z

foresail, -s 'fɔːseɪl ['fɔə-, *nautical pronunciation* -sl], -z

fore|see, -sees, -seeing, -saw, -seen, -seeable fɔː|'siː [fɔə|-], -'siːz, ˌ-'siːɪŋ, -'sɔː, -'siːn, -'siːəbl [fə'siːəbl]

foreshad|ow, -ows, -owing, -owed, -ower/s fɔː'ʃæd|əʊ [fɔə-], -əʊz, -əʊɪŋ, -əʊd, -əʊə*/z

foreshore, -s 'fɔːʃɔː* ['fɔːʃɔə*, 'fɔəʃɔə*], -z

foreshort|en, -ens, -ening, -ened fɔː-'ʃɔːt|n [fɔə-], -nz, -nɪŋ [-nɪŋ], -nd

foreshow, -s, -ing, -ed, -n fɔː'ʃəʊ [fɔə-], -z, -ɪŋ, -d, -n

foresight, -s 'fɔːsaɪt ['fɔəsaɪt], -s

foreskin, -s 'fɔːskɪn ['fɔəskɪn], -z

forest (F.), -s 'fɒrɪst, -s

forestall, -s -ing, -ed, -er/s fɔː'stɔːl [fɔə-], -z, -ɪŋ, -d, -ə*/z

forester (F.), -s 'fɒrɪstə* [-rəstə*], -z

forest-land 'fɒrɪstlænd

forestry 'fɒrɪstrɪ [-rəstrɪ]

foretaste (s.), -s 'fɔːteɪst ['fɔə-], -s

foretast|e (v.), -es, -ing, -ed fɔː'teɪst [fɔə-], -s, -ɪŋ, -ɪd

fore|tell, -tells, -telling, -told, -teller/s fɔː|'tel [fɔə-], -'telz, -'telɪŋ, -'təʊld, -'telə*/z

forethought 'fɔːθɔːt ['fɔəθɔːt]

foretop, -s; -mast/s 'fɔːtɒp ['fɔət-, *nautical pronunciation* -təp], -s; -mɑːst/s

fore-topsail, -s 'fɔːtɒpseɪl ['fɔət-, *nautical pronunciation* -sl], -z

forever fə'revə*

forewarn, -s, -ing, -ed fɔː'wɔːn [fɔə-], -z, -ɪŋ, -d

forewent (*from* forego) fɔː'went [fɔə-]

fore|woman, -women 'fɔː|ˌwʊmən ['fɔə-], -ˌwɪmɪn

foreword, -s 'fɔːwɜːd ['fɔə-], -z

Forfar 'fɔːfə* ['fɔːfɑː*]

forfeit (s. v.), -s, -ing, -ed, -er/s; -able 'fɔːfɪt, -s, -ɪŋ, -ɪd, -ə*/z; -əbl

forfeiture, -s 'fɔːfɪtʃə*, -z

forfend, -s, -ing, -ed fɔː'fend, -z, -ɪŋ, -ɪd

forgather, -s, -ing, -ed fɔː'gæðə*, -z, -rɪŋ, -d

forgave (*from* forgive) fə'geɪv

forg|e (s. v.), -es, -ing, -ed, -er/s fɔːdʒ, -ɪz, -ɪŋ, -d, -ə*/z

forger|y, -ies 'fɔːdʒər|ɪ, -ɪz

for|get, -gets, -getting, -got, -gotten fə|'get, -'gets, -'getɪŋ, -'gɒt, -'gɒtn

forget|ful, -fully, -fulness fə'get|fʊl, -fʊlɪ [-fəlɪ], -fʊlnɪs [-nəs]

forget-me-not, -s fə'getmɪnɒt, -s

forgiv|e, -es, -ing, forgave, forgiv|en; -able, -eness fə'gɪv, -z, -ɪŋ, fə'geɪv, fə'gɪv|n; -əbl, -nɪs [-nəs]

for|go, -goes, -going, -went, -gone fɔː|'gəʊ, -'gəʊz, -'gəʊɪŋ, -'went, -'gɒn

forgot (*from* forget) fə'gɒt

Forington 'fɒrɪŋtən

fork (s. v.), -s, -ing, -ed fɔːk, -s, -ɪŋ, -t

forlorn, -ness fə'lɔːn, -nɪs [-nəs]

form (s. v.), -s, -ing, -ed, -er/s fɔːm, -z, -ɪŋ, -d, -ə*/z

form|al, -ally 'fɔːm|l, -əlɪ

formaldehyde fɔː'mældɪhaɪd

formalin 'fɔːməlɪn

†formali|sm, -st/s 'fɔːməlɪ|zəm [-ml̩-], -st/s

formalit|y, -ies fɔː'mælət|ɪ [-ɪt|ɪ], -ɪz

Forman 'fɔːmən

formant, -s 'fɔːmənt, -s

format (s. v.), -s, -ting, -ted, -ter/s 'fɔːmæt, -s, -ɪŋ, -ɪd, -ə*/z

formation, -s fɔː'meɪʃn, -z

formative 'fɔːmətɪv

forme, -s fɔːm, -z

former (*adj.*), -ly 'fɔːmə*, -lɪ

formic 'fɔːmɪk

formica fɔː'maɪkə [fə'm-]

formidab|le, -ly, -leness 'fɔːmɪdəb|l fɔː'mɪd-, fə'm-], -lɪ, -lnɪs [-nəs]

Formidable (*name of ship*) fɔː'mɪdəbl ['fɔːmɪd-]

formless, -ness 'fɔːmlɪs [-ləs], -nɪs [-nəs]

Formorian, -s fɔː'mɔːrɪən, -z

Formos|a, -an/s fɔː'məʊs|ə [-əʊz|ə], -n/z

Formosus fɔː'məʊsəs

†formul|a, -ae, -as 'fɔːmjʊl|ə [-jəl-], -iː, -əz

formular|y, -ies 'fɔːmjʊlər|ɪ [-jəl-], -ɪz

formulat|e, -es, -ing, -ed 'fɔːmjʊleɪt [-jəl-], -s, -ɪŋ, -ɪd

formulation, -s ˌfɔːmjʊ'leɪʃn [-jə'l-], -z

Forn|ax, -ey 'fɔːn|æks, -ɪ

fornicat|e, -es, -ing, -ed, -or/s 'fɔ:nɪ-
keɪt, -s, -ɪŋ, -ɪd, -ə*/z
fornication ˌfɔ:nɪ'keɪʃn
Forres 'fɒrɪs
Forrest, -er 'fɒrɪst, -ə*
for|sake, -sakes, -saking, -sook, -saken
fə|'seɪk [fɔ:'s-], -'seɪks, -'seɪkɪŋ,
-'sʊk, -'seɪkən
Forshaw 'fɔ:ʃɔ:
forsooth fə'su:θ [fɔ:'s-]
Forster 'fɔ:stə*
forswear, -s, -ing, forswore, forsworn
fɔ:'sweə*, -z, -rɪŋ, fɔ:'swɔ:* [-ɔə*],
fɔ:'swɔ:n
Forsyte, -ism 'fɔ:saɪt, -ɪzəm
Forsyth fɔ:'saɪθ
forsythia, -s fɔ:'saɪθjə [fə's-, -θɪə], -z
fort, -s fɔ:t, -s
fortalice, -s 'fɔ:təlɪs, -ɪz
forte (*strong point*), **-s** 'fɔ:teɪ [-tɪ, fɔ:t],
-z [fɔ:ts]
forte (*in music*), **-s** 'fɔ:tɪ, -z
Fortescue 'fɔ:tɪskju:
Forteviot fɔ:'ti:vjət [-vɪət]
forth (**F.**) fɔ:θ
forthcoming ˌfɔ:θ'kʌmɪŋ [*also* '-ˌ—
when attributive]
forthwith ˌfɔ:θ'wɪθ [-'wɪð]
Forties (*area in the North Sea*) 'fɔ:tɪz
fortieth, -s 'fɔ:tɪɪθ [-tjɪθ, -tɪəθ, -tjəθ],
-s
fortification, -s ˌfɔ:tɪfɪ'keɪʃn, -z
**forti|fy, -fies, -fying, -fied, -fier/s;
-fiable** 'fɔ:tɪ|faɪ, -faɪz, -faɪɪŋ, -faɪd,
-faɪə*/z; -faɪəbl
Fortinbras 'fɔ:tɪnbræs
fort|is (*phonetic term*), **-es** 'fɔ:t|ɪs, -i:z
[-eɪz]
fortissimo, -s fɔ:'tɪsɪməʊ, -z
fortitude 'fɔ:tɪtju:d
fortnight, -s 'fɔ:tnaɪt, -s
fortnightl|y (**F.**), **-ies** 'fɔ:tˌnaɪtl|ɪ [ˌ-'—],
-ɪz
Fortnum 'fɔ:tnəm
Fortran 'fɔ:træn
fortress, -es 'fɔ:trɪs [-trəs], -ɪz
fortuitous, -ly, -ness fɔ:'tju:ɪtəs [-'tjʊɪ-,
-ətəs], -lɪ, -nɪs [-nəs]
fortuit|y, -ies fɔ:'tju:ɪt|ɪ [-'tjʊɪ-, -ət|ɪ],
-ɪz
fortun|ate, -ately, -ateness 'fɔ:tʃn|ət,
[-tʃn̩|ət, -tʃən|ət, -ɪt], -ətlɪ [-ɪtlɪ],
-ətnɪs [-ɪt-, -nəs]
Fortunatus ˌfɔ:tju:'neɪtəs [-tjʊ-]
fortune, -s; -less 'fɔ:tʃu:n [-tʃən,
-tju:n], -z; -lɪs [-ləs]
Fortune (*surname*) 'fɔ:tju:n

fortune|-hunter/s, -teller/s 'fɔ:tʃən|-
ˌhʌntə*/z [-tʃu:n, -tju:n], -ˌtelə*/z
fort|y, -ies, -ieth/s, -yfold 'fɔ:t|ɪ, -ɪz,
-ɪəθ/s [-jəθ/s, -ɪɪθ/s, -jɪθ/s], -ɪfəʊld
forum, -s 'fɔ:rəm, -z
forward (*s. adj. v. interj.*), **-s, -ly, -ness,
-er, -est; -ing, -ed, -er/s** 'fɔ:wəd [*in
nautical use* 'fɒrəd], -z, -lɪ, -nɪs
[-nəs], -ə*, -ɪst; -ɪŋ, -ɪd, -ə*/z
forwent (*from* **forgo**) fɔ:'went
Fos|bery, -broke, -bury 'fɒz|bərɪ, -brʊk,
-bərɪ
Foss fɒs
fosse, -s fɒs, -ɪz
fossil, -s 'fɒsl [-sɪl], -z
fossiliferous ˌfɒsɪ'lɪfərəs
fossilization [**-isa-**] ˌfɒsɪlaɪ'zeɪʃn [-səl-,
-lɪ'z-]
fossiliz|e [**-is|e**], **-es, -ing, -ed** 'fɒsɪlaɪz
[-səl-], -ɪz, -ɪŋ, -d
fost|er (*s. v.*) (**F.**), **-ers, -ering, -ered,
-erer/s; -erage** 'fɒst|ə*, -əz, -ərɪŋ,
-əd, -ərə*/z; -ərɪdʒ
**foster|-brother/s, -child, -children,
-father/s, -mother/s, -sister/s**
'fɒstə|ˌbrʌðə*/z, -tʃaɪld, -ˌtʃɪldrən
[-ˌtʃʊld-], -ˌfɑ:ðə*/z, -ˌmʌðə*/z,
-ˌsɪstə*/z
fother, -s 'fɒðə*, -z
Fothergill 'fɒðəgɪl
Fothering|ay, -ham 'fɒðərɪŋ|geɪ, -əm
Fouberts 'fu:bə:ts
fought (*from* **fight**) fɔ:t
foul (*s. adj. v.*), **-s; -er, -est, -ly, -ness;
-ing, -ed** faʊl, -z; -ə*, -ɪst, -lɪ ['faʊlɪ],
-nɪs [-nəs]; -ɪŋ, -d
foulard 'fu:lɑ:* [-lɑ:d]
Foulden 'fəʊldən
Foulds fəʊldz
Foulerton 'fʊlətən
Foulger 'fu:ldʒə*, 'fu:lgə*
Foulis faʊlz
Foulkes fəʊks, faʊks
foul-mouthed 'faʊlmaʊðd [ˌ-'-]
foulness 'faʊlnɪs [-nəs]
Foulness ˌfaʊl'nes [*also* '— *according to
sentence-stress*]
foul-play ˌfaʊl'pleɪ
Foulsham (*in Norfolk*) 'fəʊlʃəm
foul-spoken 'faʊlˌspəʊkən [ˌ-'—]
found, -s, -ing, -ed, -er/s faʊnd, -z, -ɪŋ,
-ɪd, -ə*/z
found (*from* **find**) faʊnd
foundation, -s faʊn'deɪʃn, -z
foundationer, -s faʊn'deɪʃnə* [-ʃənə*,
-ʃnə*], -z
found|er, -ers, -ering, -ered 'faʊnd|ə*,
-əz, -ərɪŋ, -əd

foundling (F.), -s 'faʊndlɪŋ, -z
foundress, -es 'faʊndrɪs [-res], -ɪz
foundr|y, -ies 'faʊndr|ɪ, -ɪz
fount (*fountain, source*), -s faʊnt, -s
fount (*of type*), -s faʊnt [fɒnt], -s
Note.—*Those connected with the printing trade generally pronounce* fɒnt.

fountain (F.), -s 'faʊntɪn [-tən], -z
fountain-head, -s 'faʊntɪnhed [-tən-, ‚--'-], -z
fountain-pen, -s 'faʊntɪnpen [-tən-], -z
four, -s, -th/s, -thly fɔː* [fɔə*], -z, -θ/s, -θlɪ
four-cornered ‚fɔː'kɔːnəd [‚fɔə-, *also* '-‚-- *when attributive*]
four-dimensional ‚fɔːdɪ'menʃənl [‚fɔə-, -daɪ'm-, -ʃnəl, -ʃn̩l, -ʃnl, -ʃənəl]
fourfold 'fɔː‚fəʊld ['fɔə-]
four-footed ‚fɔː'fʊtɪd [‚fɔə-, *also* '-‚-- *when attributive*]
Fourier 'fʊrɪeɪ ['fʊrɪə*] (furje)
four-in-hand, -s ‚fɔːrɪn'hænd [‚fɔərɪn-, ‚fɔːrɪn-], -z
fourish 'fɔːrɪʃ ['fɔər-]
four-legged 'fɔːlegd ['fɔə-, ‚fɔː'legɪd]
fourpence 'fɔːpəns
fourpenny 'fɔːpənɪ [-pɲ̩ɪ, -pnɪ] (*see note under* penny)
four-ply 'fɔːplaɪ ['fɔə-, ‚-'-]
four-poster, -s ‚fɔː'pəʊstə* [‚fɔə-, -z
fourscore ‚fɔː'skɔː* [‚fɔə'skɔə*, *also* 'fɔːskɔː*, 'fɔəskɔə* *when immediately followed by a stress*]
four-sidedness ‚fɔː'saɪdɪdnɪs [‚fɔə's-, -nəs]
foursome, -s 'fɔːsəm ['fɔə-], -z
foursquare ‚fɔː'skweə* [‚fɔə'skweə*, '-‚-]
fourteen, -s, -th/s ‚fɔː'tiːn [‚fɔə-, *also* '--, -'- *according to sentence-stress*], -z, -θ/s
fourth, -s -ly fɔːθ [fɔəθ], -s, -lɪ
four-wheeler, -s ‚fɔː'wiːlə* [‚fɔə-, -'hw-], -z
Fowey fɔɪ ['fəʊɪ]
Fowke faʊk, fəʊk
Fowkes faʊks
fowl (s. v.), -s, -ing, -ed, -er/s faʊl, -z, -ɪŋ, -d, -ə*/z
Fowler 'faʊlə*
Fowles faʊlz
fowl-hou|se, -ses 'faʊlhaʊ|s, -zɪz
fowling|-net/s, -piece/s 'faʊlɪŋ|net/s, -piːs/ɪz
fowl-run, -s 'faʊlrʌn, -z
Fownes faʊnz

200

fox (s. v.) (F.), -es, -ing, -ed fɒks, -ɪz, -ɪŋ, -t
Foxboro' 'fɒksbərə
fox-brush, -es 'fɒksbrʌʃ, -ɪz
Foxcroft 'fɒkskrɒft
Foxfield 'fɒksfiːld
foxglove, -s 'fɒksglʌv, -z
foxhole, -s 'fɒkshəʊl, -z
foxhound, -s 'fɒkshaʊnd, -z
foxhunt, -s, -ing 'fɒkshʌnt, -s, -ɪŋ
foxterrier, -s ‚fɒks'terɪə*, -z
foxtrot, -s 'fɒkstrɒt, -s
Foxwell 'fɒkswəl [-wel]
fox|y, -ier, -iest, -ily, -iness 'fɒks|ɪ, -ɪə* [-jə*], -ɪɪst [-jɪst], -ɪlɪ [-əlɪ], -ɪnɪs [-ɪnəs]
foyer, -s 'fɔɪeɪ ['fɔɪə] (fwaje), -z
Foyers 'fɔɪəz
Foyle fɔɪl
fracas (*sing.*) 'frækɑː, (*plur.*) -z
Frackville 'frækvɪl
fraction, -s 'frækʃn, -z
fractional 'frækʃənl [-ʃnəl, -ʃn̩l, -ʃnl, -ʃənəl]
fractious, -ly, -ness 'frækʃəs, -lɪ, -nɪs [-nəs]
frac|ture (s. v.), -tures, -turing, -tured 'fræk|tʃə*, -tʃəz, -tʃərɪŋ, -tʃəd
Fradin 'freɪdɪn
fragile, -ly, -ness 'frædʒaɪl [*rarely* -dʒɪl], -lɪ, -nɪs [-nəs]
fragility frə'dʒɪlətɪ [fræ'dʒ-, -ɪtɪ]
fragment (s.), -s 'frægmənt, -s
fragment (v.), -s, -ing, -ed fræg'ment, -s, -ɪŋ, -ɪd
fragmental fræg'mentl
fragment|al|y, -ily, -iness 'frægmən-tər|ɪ [fræg'mentər|ɪ], -əlɪ [-ɪlɪ], -ɪnɪs [-ɪnəs]
fragmentation ‚frægmen'teɪʃn [-mən-]
fragran|ce, -cy, -t/ly, -tness 'freɪgrən|s, -sɪ, -t/lɪ, -tnɪs [-nəs]
frail, -er, -est, -ly, -ness freɪl, -ə*, -ɪst, -lɪ, -nɪs [-nəs]
frail|y, -ies 'freɪlt|ɪ, -ɪz
Fram fræm
fram|e (s. v.), -es, -ing, -ed, -er/s freɪm, -z, -ɪŋ, -d, -ə*/z
frame-up, -s 'freɪmʌp, -s
framework, -s 'freɪmwɜːk, -s
Framingham 'freɪmɪŋəm
Framlingham 'fræmlɪŋəm
Frampton 'fræmptən
franc, -s fræŋk, -s
France frɑːns
Frances 'frɑːnsɪs
Francesca fræn'seskə, fræn'tʃeskə
franchise, -s 'frænʧaɪz, -ɪz

franchisee, -s ˌfræntʃaɪˈziː, -z
Francie ˈfrɑːnsɪ
Francillon frænˈsɪlən
Francis ˈfrɑːnsɪs
Franciscan, -s frænˈsɪskən, -z
Francisco (*personal name*) frænˈsɪskəʊ,
  (*in* San Francisco) frənˈsɪskəʊ
Franck frɑ̃ːŋk [frɑːŋk, fræŋk] (frɑ̃ːk)
Franco-German ˌfræŋkəʊˈdʒɜːmən
francolin, -s ˈfræŋkəʊlɪn, -z
Franconia, -n fræŋˈkəʊnjə [-nɪə], -n
francophile, -s ˈfræŋkəʊfaɪl, -z
francophobe, -s ˈfræŋkəʊfəʊb, -z
frangibility ˌfrændʒɪˈbɪlətɪ [-dʒəˈb-,
  -lɪt-]
frangible, -ness ˈfrændʒɪbl [-dʒəb-], -nɪs
  [-nəs]
frank (*adj. v.*), -er, -est, -ly, -ness; -s,
  -ing, -ed fræŋk, -ə*, -ɪst, -lɪ, -nɪs
  [-nəs]; -s, -ɪŋ, -t [fræŋt]
Frank, -s fræŋk, -s
Frankau (*English surname*) ˈfræŋkəʊ
Frankenstein ˈfræŋkənstaɪn
Frankfort (-furt) ˈfræŋkfət [-fɔːt]
frankfurter, -s ˈfræŋkfɜːtə*, -z
frankincense ˈfræŋkɪnˌsens
Frankish ˈfræŋkɪʃ
Frankland ˈfræŋklənd
franklin (F.), -s ˈfræŋklɪn, -z
Franklyn ˈfræŋklɪn
frantic, -ally, -ness ˈfræntɪk, -əlɪ, -nɪs
  [-nəs]
Franz frænts
frap, -s, -ping, -ped fræp, -s, -ɪŋ, -t
frappé ˈfræpeɪ (frape)
Frascati fræˈskɑːtɪ
Fraser, -burgh ˈfreɪzə*, -bərə* [-bʌrə]
fratern|al, -ally frəˈtɜːn|l, -əlɪ
fraternit|y, -ies frəˈtɜːnət|ɪ [-ɪt|ɪ], -ɪz
fraternization [-isa-] ˌfrætənaɪˈzeɪʃn
  [-nɪˈz-]
fraterniz|e [-is|e], -es, -ing, -ed, -er/s
  ˈfrætənaɪz, -ɪz, -ɪŋ, -d, -ə*/z
fratricidal ˌfrætrɪˈsaɪdl [ˌfreɪt-]
fratricide, -s ˈfrætrɪsaɪd [ˈfreɪt-], -z
Fratton ˈfrætn
fraud, -s frɔːd, -z
fraudulen|ce, -t/ly ˈfrɔːdjʊlən|s, -t/lɪ
fraught frɔːt
fray (s. v.), -s, -ing, -ed freɪ, -z, -ɪŋ, -d
Frazer ˈfreɪzə*
frazil ˈfreɪzɪl
frazz|le (s. v.), -les, -ling, -led ˈfræz|l,
  -lz, -lɪŋ [-lɪŋ], -ld
freak, -s friːk, -s
Freake friːk
freakish, -ly, -ness ˈfriːkɪʃ, -lɪ, -nɪs
  [-nəs]

freak|y, -ier, -iest, -ily, -iness ˈfriːk|ɪ,
  -ɪə* [-jə*], -ɪɪst [-jɪst], -ɪlɪ [-əlɪ], -ɪnɪs
  [-ɪnəs]
Frean friːn
freck|le (s. v.), -les, -ling, -led ˈfrek|l,
  -lz, -lɪŋ [-lɪŋ], -ld
freckly ˈfreklɪ [-lɪ]
Frecknall ˈfreknɔːl [-nl]
Fred, -die, -dy fred, -ɪ, -ɪ
Frederic(k) ˈfredrɪk
Frederica ˌfredəˈriːkə
free (*adj. v.*), -r, -st, -ly; -s, -ing, -d,
  -r/s friː, -ə* [frɪə*], -ɪst, -lɪ; -z, -ɪŋ, -d,
  -ə*/z [frɪə*/z]
freebooter, -s ˈfriːˌbuːtə*, -z
free-born ˌfriːˈbɔːn [ˈ--, *esp. when*
  attributive]
freed|man, -men ˈfriːd|mæn [-mən],
  -men [-mən]
freedom, -s ˈfriːdəm, -z
free-for-all ˈfriːfərˌɔːl [ˌ-ˈ-]
free-hand (*adj.*) ˈfriːhænd
free-hearted, -ly, -ness ˌfriːˈhɑːtɪd, -lɪ,
  -nɪs [-nəs]
freehold, -s; -er/s ˈfriːhəʊld [ˈfriːəʊld],
  -z; -ə*/z
freelance, -s ˈfriːlɑːns [ˌ-ˈ-], -ɪz
Freeling ˈfriːlɪŋ
free|man (*of a city*), -men ˈfriː|mən,
  -mən, (*opposed to slave*) ˈfriː|mæn
  [-mən], -men [-mən]
Freeman ˈfriːmən
freemason, -s ˈfriːˌmeɪsn, -z
freemasonry ˈfriːˌmeɪsnrɪ [ˌfriːˈm-]
Freeport ˈfriːpɔːt
freesia, -s ˈfriːzjə [-zɪə, -ʒjə, -ʒɪə, -ʒə],
  -z
free-spoken ˌfriːˈspəʊkən [ˈ-ˌ--]
freestone ˈfriːstəʊn
freethinker, -s ˌfriːˈθɪŋkə*, -z
Freetown ˈfriːtaʊn
free-trade, -er/s ˌfriːˈtreɪd, -ə*/z
free-wheel (s. v.), -s, -ing, -ed ˌfriːˈwiːl
  [-ˈhw-, ˈ--], -z, -ɪŋ, -d
freewill ˌfriːˈwɪl [ˈ--]
freez|e, -es, -ing, froze, frozen, freezer/s
  friːz, -ɪz, -ɪŋ, frəʊz, ˈfrəʊzn, ˈfriːzə*/z
freeze-dr|y, -ies, -ying, -ied ˈfriːzdr|aɪ,
  -aɪz, -aɪɪŋ, -aɪd
freezing-mixture ˈfriːzɪŋˌmɪkstʃə*
freezing-point ˈfriːzɪŋpɔɪnt
Freiburg ˈfraɪbɜːg
freight (s. v.), -s, -ing, -ed, -er/s; -age
  freɪt, -s, -ɪŋ, -ɪd, -ə*/z; -ɪdʒ
Fremantle ˈfriːmæntl
fremitus ˈfremɪtəs
Fremont frɪˈmɒnt
French frentʃ

frenchi|fy, -fies, -fying, -fied 'frent∫ɪ|-
faɪ, -faɪz, -faɪŋ, -faɪd
French|man, -men 'frent∫|mən, -mən
french-polish (s. v.), -es, -ing, -ed, -er/s
,frent∫'pɒlɪ∫, -ɪz, -ɪŋ, -t, -ə*/z
French|woman, -women 'frent∫|-
,wʊmən, -,wɪmɪn
french|y, -ily, -iness 'frent∫|ɪ, -əlɪ
[-ɪlɪ], -ɪnɪs [-ɪnəs]
frenetic frə'netɪk [frɪ-, fre-]
frenz|y, -ies, -ied/ly 'frenz|ɪ, -ɪz, -ɪd/lɪ
frequen|ce, -cy, -cies 'fri:kwən|s, -sɪ,
-sɪz
frequent (adj.), -ly, -ness 'fri:kwənt, -lɪ,
-nɪs [-nəs]
frequent (v.), -s, -ing, -ed, -er/s frɪ-
'kwent [fri:'k-], -s, -ɪŋ, -ɪd, -ə*/z
frequentation ,fri:kwen'teɪ∫n
frequentative (s. adj.), -s frɪ'kwentətɪv,
-z
Frere frɪə*
fresco, -(e)s 'freskəʊ, -z
fresh, -er, -est, -ly, -ness fre∫, -ə*, -ɪst,
-lɪ, -nɪs [-nəs]
fresh|en, -ens, -ening, -ened 'fre∫|n,
-nz, -nɪŋ [-nɪŋ], -nd
fresher (s.), -s 'fre∫ə*, -z
freshet, -s 'fre∫ɪt, -s
fresh|man, -men 'fre∫|mən, -mən
freshwater (F.) 'fre∫,wɔ:tə*
Fresno 'freznəʊ
fret (s. v.), -s, -ting, -ted, -ter/s fret,
-s, -ɪŋ, -ɪd, -ə*/z
fret|ful, -fully, -fulness 'fret|fʊl, -fʊlɪ
[-fəlɪ], -fʊlnɪs [-nəs]
fret|saw/s, -work 'fret|sɔ:/z, -wɜ:k
Freud, -ian frɔɪd, -ɪən [-jən]
Frey (English surname) freɪ
Freyberg 'fraɪbɜ:g
Freyer frɪə*, 'fraɪə*
friability ,fraɪə'bɪlətɪ [-lɪt-]
friable, -ness 'fraɪəbl, -nɪs [-nəs]
friar, -s 'fraɪə*, -z
friar|y, -ies 'fraɪər|ɪ, -ɪz
fribb|le (s. v.), -les, -ling, -led, -ler/s
'frɪb|l, -lz, -lɪŋ [-lɪŋ], -ld, -lə*/z
[-lə*/z]
fricandeau, -x 'frɪkəndəʊ [-kɑ:n-]
(frikãdo), -z
fricassee (s.), -s 'frɪkəsi: [,--'-], -z
fricassee (v.), -s, -ing, -d ,frɪkə'si: ['---],
-z, -ɪŋ, -d
fricative (s. adj.), -s 'frɪkətɪv, -z
friction, -s; -less 'frɪk∫n, -z; -lɪs [-ləs,
-les]
frictional 'frɪk∫ənl [-∫n̩l, -∫n̩, -∫ənəl]
Friday, -s 'fraɪdɪ [-deɪ], -z
fridge, -s frɪdʒ, -ɪz

fried (from fry) fraɪd
friend, -s frend, -z
friendless, -ness 'frendlɪs [-ləs], -nɪs
[-nəs]
friendl|y, -ier, -iest, -iness 'frendl|ɪ,
-ɪə* [-jə*], -ɪɪst [-jɪst], -ɪnɪs [-ɪnəs]
Friendl|y, -ies 'frendl|ɪ, -ɪz
friendship, -s 'frend∫ɪp, -s
Friern 'fraɪən
fries (from fry) fraɪz
Fries fri:s [fri:z]
Friesian 'fri:zjən [-zɪən, -ʒən, -ʒɪən,
-ʒən]
Friesic 'fri:zɪk
Friesland, -er/s 'fri:zlənd [-lænd], -ə*/z
frieze (F.), -s fri:z, -ɪz
frigate, -s 'frɪgət [-gɪt], -s
fright (s. v.), -s, -ing, -ed fraɪt, -s, -ɪŋ,
-ɪd
fright|en, -ens, -ening, -ened 'fraɪt|n,
-nz, -nɪŋ [-nɪŋ], -nd
fright|ful, -fully, -fulness 'fraɪt|fʊl, -flɪ
[-fəlɪ, -fʊlɪ], -fʊlnɪs [-nəs]
frigid, -ly, -ness 'frɪdʒɪd, -lɪ, -nɪs [-nəs]
frigidity frɪ'dʒɪdətɪ [-ɪtɪ]
Friis fri:s
frill (s. v.), -s, -ing, -ed frɪl, -z, -ɪŋ, -d
frill|y, -ier, -iest 'frɪl|ɪ, -ɪə*, -ɪɪst
Frimley 'frɪmlɪ
fring|e (s. v.), -es, -ing, -ed; -eless, -y
frɪndʒ, -ɪz, -ɪŋ, -d; -lɪs [-ləs], -ɪ
fripper|y, -ies 'frɪpər|ɪ, -ɪz
frisette, -s frɪ'zet, -s
Frisian, -s 'frɪzɪən [-zjən, -ʒɪən, -ʒjən,
-ʒən], -z
frisk (s. v.), -s, -ing, -ed, -er/s frɪsk,
-s, -ɪŋ, -t, -ə*/z
frisket, -s 'frɪskɪt, -s
frisk|y, -ier, -iest, -ily, -ness 'frɪsk|ɪ,
-ɪə* [-jə*], -ɪɪst [-jɪst], -ɪlɪ [-əlɪ], -ɪnɪs
[-ɪnəs]
Friswell 'frɪzwəl [-wel]
frit (s. v.), -s, -ting, -ted frɪt, -s, -ɪŋ, -ɪd
frith (F.), -s frɪθ, -s
Frithsden (near Berkhamsted) 'fri:zdən
['frɪz-, 'frɪθsdən]
fritillar|y, -ies frɪ'tɪlər|ɪ, -ɪz
fritter (s. v.), -s, -ing, -ed 'frɪtə*, -z,
-rɪŋ, -d
Fritton 'frɪtn
Fritz frɪts
friv|ol, -ols, -ol(l)ing, -ol(l)ed 'frɪv|l,
-lz, -lɪŋ [-əlɪŋ], -ld
frivolit|y, -ies frɪ'vɒlət|ɪ [-ɪt|ɪ], -ɪz
frivolous, -ly, -ness 'frɪvələs [-vləs], -lɪ,
-nɪs [-nəs]
Frizell frɪ'zel
frizette, -s frɪ'zet, -s

Frizinghall 'fraɪzɪŋhɔ:l

Frizington 'frɪzɪŋtən

friz(z), **-es**, **-ing**, **-ed** frɪz, -ɪz, -ɪŋ, -d

frizz|le, **-les**, **-ling**, **-led** 'frɪz|l, -lz, -lɪŋ [-lɪŋ], -ld

frizzl|y, **-iness** 'frɪz|l|ɪ [-zl|ɪ], -ɪnɪs [-məs]

frizz|y, **-ier**, **-iest**, **-iness** 'frɪz|ɪ, -ɪə*, -ɪɪst, -ɪnɪs [-ɪnəs]

fro frəʊ

Frobisher 'frəʊbɪʃə*

frock, **-s** frɒk, -s

frock-coat, **-s**, **-ed** ˌfrɒk'kəʊt [*also* '-- *when followed by a stress*], -s, -ɪd

Froebel 'frəʊbl ['frə:bl] ('frø:bəl)

frog, **-s** frɒg, -z

frogg|y (*s. adj.*), **-ies** 'frɒg|ɪ, -ɪz

frog|man, **-men** 'frɒg|mən, -mən

frog-march, **-es**, **-ing**, **-ed** 'frɒgmɑ:tʃ, -ɪz, -ɪŋ, -t

Frogmore 'frɒgmɔ:* [-mɔə*]

frolic (*s. v.*), **-s**, **-king**, **-ked** 'frɒlɪk, -s, -ɪŋ, -t

frolicsome, **-ness** 'frɒlɪksəm, -nɪs [-nəs]

from frɒm (*strong form*), frəm, frm (*weak forms*)

Frome (*in Somerset*) fru:m

frond, **-s** frɒnd, -z

front (*s. adj. v.*), **-s**, **-ing**, **-ed** frʌnt, -s, -ɪŋ, -ɪd

frontage, **-s** 'frʌntɪdʒ, -ɪz

frontal (*s.*), **-s** 'frʌntl ['frɒn-], -z

frontal (*adj.*) 'frʌntl

frontier, **-s** 'frʌnˌtɪə* ['frɒn-, -tɪə*, -tjə*, frʌn'tɪə*], -z

frontispiece, **-s** 'frʌntɪspi:s ['frɒn-], -ɪz

front|less, **-let/s** 'frʌnt|lɪs [-ləs, -les], -lɪt/s [-lət/s]

frost (*s. v.*) (**F.**), **-s**, **-ing**, **-ed** frɒst [*old-fashioned* frɔ:st, *and in compounds*], -s, -ɪŋ, -ɪd

frost|bite/s, **-bitten**, **-bound** 'frɒst|-baɪt/s ['frɔ:st-], -ˌbɪtn, -baʊnd

frostwork 'frɒstwɜ:k ['frɔ:st-]

frost|y, **-ier**, **-iest**, **-ily**, **-iness** 'frɒst|ɪ ['frɔ:st-], -ɪə* [-jə*], -ɪɪst [-jɪst], -ɪlɪ [-əlɪ], -ɪnɪs [-ɪnəs]

froth (*s. v.*), **-s**, **-ing**, **-ed** frɒθ [*old-fashioned* frɔ:θ], -s, -ɪŋ, -t

Frothingham 'frɒðɪŋəm

froth|y, **-ier**, **-iest**, **-ily**, **-iness** 'frɒθ|ɪ ['frɔ:θ|ɪ], -ɪə*, -ɪɪst, -ɪlɪ [-əlɪ], -ɪnɪs [-ɪnəs]

Froud fru:d, fraʊd

Froude fru:d

frou-frou 'fru:fru:

froward, **-ly**, **-ness** 'frəʊəd, -lɪ, -nɪs [-nəs]

Frowde fru:d, fraʊd

frown (*s. v.*), **-s**, **-ing/ly**, **-ed** fraʊn, -z, -ɪŋ/lɪ, -d

frowst (*s. v.*), **-s**, **-ing**, **-ed**; **-y**, **-iness** fraʊst, -s, -ɪŋ, -ɪd; -ɪ, -ɪnɪs [-ɪnəs]

frowz|y, **-iness** 'fraʊz|ɪ, -ɪnɪs [-ɪnəs]

froze, **-n** (*from* **freeze**) frəʊz, -n

fructiferous frʌk'tɪfərəs

fructification ˌfrʌktɪfɪ'keɪʃn

fructi|fy, **-fies**, **-fying**, **-fied** 'frʌktɪ|faɪ, -faɪz, -faɪɪŋ, -faɪd

frug|al, **-ally**, **-alness** 'fru:g|l, -əlɪ, -lnɪs [-nəs]

frugality fru:'gælətɪ [frʊ'g-, -ɪtɪ]

fruit (*s. v.*), **-s**, **-ing**, **-ed**; **-age** fru:t, -s, -ɪŋ, -ɪd; -ɪdʒ

fruitarian, **-s** fru:'teərɪən, -z

fruiterer, **-s** 'fru:tərə*, -z

fruit|ful, **-fully**, **-fulness** 'fru:t|fʊl, -fʊlɪ [-fəlɪ], -fʊlnɪs [-nəs]

fruition fru:'ɪʃn [frʊ'ɪ-]

fruitless, **-ly**, **-ness** 'fru:tlɪs [-ləs], -lɪ, -nɪs [-nəs]

fruit-machine, **-s** 'fru:tməˌʃi:n, -z

fruit|y, **-ier**, **-iest**, **-iness** 'fru:t|ɪ, -ɪə*, -ɪɪst, -ɪnɪs [-ɪnəs]

frumenty 'fru:məntɪ

frump, **-s**; **-ish** frʌmp, -s; -ɪʃ

frustrat|e, **-es**, **-ing**, **-ed** frʌ'streɪt ['frʌstreɪt], -s, -ɪŋ, -ɪd

frustration frʌ'streɪʃn

frust|um, **-a**, **-ums** 'frʌst|əm, -ə, -əmz

fr|y (*s. v.*) (**F.**), **-ies**, **-ying**, **-ied** fr|aɪ, -aɪz, -aɪɪŋ, -aɪd

Frye fraɪ

Fuad 'fu:æd ['fʊæd]

fuchsia, **-s** 'fju:ʃə, -z

fuchsine 'fu:ksi:n [-sɪn]

fu|cus, **-ci** 'fju:|kəs, -saɪ

fudd|le (*s. v.*), **-les**, **-ling**, **-led**, **-ler/s** 'fʌd|l, -lz, -lɪŋ, -ld, -lə*/z

fudg|e (*s. v.*), **-es**, **-ing**, **-ed** fʌdʒ, -ɪz, -ɪŋ, -d

Fudge fju:dʒ, fʌdʒ

Fuehrer, **-s** 'fjʊərə* ['fjɔə-, 'fjɔ:-], -z

fuel, **-s** fjʊəl ['fju:əl, fju:l], -z

fug, **-s** fʌg, -z

fugacious, **-ly**, **-ness** fju:'geɪʃəs [fjʊ'g-], -lɪ, -nɪs [-nəs]

fugacity fju:'gæsətɪ [fjʊ'g-, -ɪtɪ]

fugal 'fju:gl

fugg|y, **-ier**, **-iest**, **-iness** 'fʌg|ɪ, -ɪə*, -ɪɪst, -ɪnɪs [-ɪnəs]

fugitive (*s. adj.*), **-s**, **-ly**, **-ness** 'fju:dʒə-tɪv [-dʒɪt-], -z, -lɪ, -nɪs [-nəs]

fugle|man, **-men** 'fju:glmæn [-mən], -men [-mən]

fugue, **-s** fju:g, -z

Fulcher 'fʊltʃə*

203

fulcr|um, -a, -ums 'fʊlkr|əm ['fʌl-],
-ə, -əmz
fulfil, -s, -ling, -led, -ler/s, -ment
fʊl'fɪl, -z, -ɪŋ, -d, -ə*/z, -mənt
Fulford 'fʊlfəd
fulgent, -ly 'fʌldʒənt, -lɪ
fulgurat|e, -es, -ing, -ed 'fʌlgjʊəreɪt, -s,
-ɪŋ, -ɪd
Fulham 'fʊləm
fuliginous, -ly fjuː'lɪdʒɪnəs, -lɪ
Fulke fʊlk
full, -er, -est, -y, -ness fʊl, -ə*, -ɪst, -ɪ,
-nɪs [-nəs]
full-back, -s 'fʊlbæk [ˌ-'-], -s
full-blooded ˌfʊl'blʌdɪd [also '-ˌ-- when
attributive]
full-blown ˌfʊl'bləʊn [also '-- when
attributive]
full-bodied ˌfʊl'bɒdɪd [also '-ˌ-- when
attributive]
fuller (F.), -s 'fʊlə*, -z
Fullerton 'fʊlətn
full-face ˌfʊl'feɪs ['--]
full-fledged ˌfʊl'fledʒd [also '-- when
attributive]
full-grown ˌfʊl'grəʊn [also '-- when
attributive]
full-length ˌfʊl'leŋkθ [also '-- when
attributive]
fulmar, -s 'fʊlmə* [-mɑː*], -z
Fulmer (in Buckinghamshire) 'fʊlmə*
fulminat|e, -es, -ing, -ed 'fʌlmɪneɪt, -s,
-ɪŋ, -ɪd
fulmination, -s ˌfʌlmɪ'neɪʃn, -z
fulness 'fʊlnɪs [-nəs]
fulsome, -ly, -ness 'fʊlsəm, -lɪ, -nɪs
[-nəs]
Fulton 'fʊltən
Fulvia 'fʌlvɪə [-vjə]
fulvous 'fʌlvəs
Fulwood 'fʊlwʊd
fumb|le, -les, -ling, -led, -ler/s 'fʌmb|l,
-lz, -lɪŋ, -ld, -lə*/z
fum|e (s. v.), **-es, -ing, -ed** fjuːm, -z, -ɪŋ,
-d
fumigat|e, -es, -ing, -ed, -or/s 'fjuːmɪ-
geɪt, -s, -ɪŋ, -ɪd, -ə*/z
fumigation, -s ˌfjuːmɪ'geɪʃn, -z
fun fʌn
funambulist,   **-s**   fjuː'næmbjʊlɪst
[fjʊ'n-], -s
Funchal fʊn'ʃɑːl
functi|on (s. v.), **-ons, -oning, -oned**
'fʌŋkʃ|n, -nz, -ŋɪŋ [-ənɪŋ], -nd
functional|ism,   -ly   'fʌŋkʃnəl|ɪzəm
[-ʃnļɪ-, -ʃənļɪ-, -ʃənəl-], -ɪ
functionar|y, -ies 'fʌŋkʃnər|ɪ [-ʃənər-,
-ʃnər-], -ɪz

fund (s. v.), **-s, -ing, -ed** fʌnd, -z, -ɪŋ, -ɪd
fundament, -s 'fʌndəmənt, -s
fundament|al (s. adj.), **-als,   -ally**
ˌfʌndə'ment|l, -lz, -əlɪ [-ļɪ]
fundamentali|sm, -st/s ˌfʌndə'ment-
əlɪ|zəm [-tļɪ-], -st/s
fundamentality ˌfʌndəmen'tælətɪ [-ɪtɪ]
fund-holder, -s 'fʌnd,həʊldə*, -z
fundless 'fʌndlɪs [-ləs, -les]
Fundy 'fʌndɪ
funeral, -s 'fjuːnərəl, -z
funereal fjuː'nɪərɪəl [fjʊ'n-]
funfair, -s 'fʌnfeə*, -z
fungible (s. adj.), **-s** 'fʌndʒɪbl [-dʒəbl],
-z
fungicide, -s 'fʌndʒɪsaɪd ['fʌŋgɪ-], -z
fung|us, -i, -uses; -oid, -ous, -usy
'fʌŋg|əs, -aɪ ['fʌndʒɪ, 'fʌndʒaɪ],
-əsɪz; -ɔɪd, -əs, -əsɪ
funicle, -s 'fjuːnɪkl, -z
funicular (s. adj.), **-s** fjuː'nɪkjʊlə*
[fjʊ'n-, fə'nɪk-, fŋ'ɪk-, -kjəl-], -z
funicul|us,   -i fjuː'nɪkjʊl|əs [fjʊ'n-,
-kjəl-], -aɪ
funk (s. v.) **(F.), -s, -ing, -ed** fʌŋk, -s,
-ɪŋ, -t [fʌŋt]
funkia, -s 'fʌŋkjə [-kɪə], -z
funk|y, -ier, -iest, -ily, -iness 'fʌŋk|ɪ,
-ɪə* [-jə*], -ɪɪst [-jɪst], -ɪlɪ [-əlɪ], -ɪnɪs
[-ɪnəs]
funnel, -s 'fʌnl, -z
funn|y, -ier, -iest, -ily, -iness 'fʌn|ɪ,
-ɪə*, -ɪɪst, -ɪlɪ [-əlɪ], -ɪnɪs [-ɪnəs]
funnybone, -s 'fʌnɪbəʊn, -z
fur (s. v.), **-s, -ring, -red** fɜ:*, -z, -rɪŋ, -d
Furbear 'fɜːbeə*
furbelow, -s 'fɜːbɪləʊ, -z
furbish, -es, -ing, -ed 'fɜːbɪʃ, -ɪz, -ɪŋ, -t
furcate (adj.) 'fɜːkeɪt [-kɪt, -kət]
furcat|e (v.), **-es, -ing, -ed** 'fɜːkeɪt
[fɜː'k-], -s, -ɪŋ, -ɪd
furcation, -s fɜː'keɪʃn, -z
furibund 'fjʊərɪbʌnd ['fjɔər-, 'fjɔːr-,
-bənd]
furioso (F.) ˌfjʊərɪ'əʊzəʊ [ˌfjɔər-, ˌfjɔːr-,
-'əʊsəʊ]
furious, -ly, -ness 'fjʊərɪəs ['fjɔər-,
'fjɔːr-], -lɪ, -nɪs [-nəs]
furl, -s, -ing, -ed fɜːl, -z, -ɪŋ, -d
furlong, -s 'fɜːlɒŋ, -z
furlough, -s 'fɜːləʊ, -z
furnace, -s 'fɜːnɪs [-nəs], -ɪz
Furneaux 'fɜːnəʊ
Furness 'fɜːnɪs [-nes]
Furneux (in Hertfordshire) 'fɜːnɪks
[-nuː, -nəʊ]
   Note.—'fɜːnɪks is the more usual
   local pronunciation.

furnish, -es, -ing/s, -ed, -er/s 'fɜːnɪʃ, -ɪz, -ɪŋ/z, -t, -ə*/z
furniture 'fɜːnɪtʃə*
Furnival(l) 'fɜːnɪvəl
furore (*admiration, craze*), **-s** fjʊə'rɔːrɪ ['fjʊərɔː*], -z
furore (*musical term*) fʊ'rɔːrɪ
furrier (*s.*), **-s** 'fʌrɪə*, -z
furrier|y, -ies 'fʌrɪər|ɪ, -ɪz
furr|ow (*s. v.*), **-ows, -owing, -owed; -owy** 'fʌr|əʊ, -əʊz, -əʊɪŋ, -əʊd; -əʊɪ
furr|y, -ier, -iest, -iness 'fɜːr|ɪ [*rarely* 'fʌr-], -ɪə*, -ɪɪst, -ɪnɪs [-ɪnəs]
furth|er (*adj. v. adv.*), **-ers, -ering, -ered, -erer/s** 'fɜːð|ə*, -əz, -ərɪŋ, -əd, -ərə*/z
furtherance 'fɜːðərəns
furthermore ˌfɜːðə'mɔː* [-'mɔə*]
furthermost 'fɜːðəməʊst
furthest 'fɜːðɪst
furtive, -ly, -ness 'fɜːtɪv, -lɪ, -nɪs [-nəs]
furuncle, -s 'fjʊərʌŋkl, -z
fur|y (F.), -ies 'fjʊər|ɪ ['fjɔər-, 'fjɔːr-], -ɪz
furze; -bush/es fɜːz; -bʊʃ/ɪz
Fusbos 'fʌzbɒs
fuscous 'fʌskəs
fus|e (*s. v.*), **-es, -ing, -ed** fjuːz, -ɪz, -ɪŋ, -d
fusee, -s fjuː'ziː, -z
fuselage, -s 'fjuːzəlɑːʒ [-zɪ-, -lɪdʒ], -ɪz
fusel-oil ˌfjuːzl'ɔɪl ['---]
fusibility ˌfjuːzə'bɪlətɪ [-zɪ'b-, -lɪt-]
fusible 'fjuːzəbl [-zɪb-]
fusil, -s 'fjuːzɪl, -z
fusile 'fjuːsaɪl [-uːzaɪl]
fusilier, -s ˌfjuːzə'lɪə* [-zɪ'lɪə*, -zl'ɪə*], -z
fusillade, -s ˌfjuːzə'leɪd [-zɪ'l-], -z

fusillade, -s ˌfjuːzɪ'leɪd [-zə'l-], -z
fusion, -s 'fjuːʒn, -z
fuss (*s. v.*), **-es, -ing, -ed, -er/s** fʌs, -ɪz, -ɪŋ, -t, -ə*/z
fuss-pot, -s 'fʌspɒt, -s
fuss|y, -ier, -iest, -ily, -iness 'fʌs|ɪ, -ɪə*, -ɪɪst, -ɪlɪ [-əlɪ], -ɪnɪs [-ɪnəs]
fustian 'fʌstɪən [-tjən]
fustic 'fʌstɪk
fustigat|e, -es, -ing, -ed 'fʌstɪɡeɪt, -s, -ɪŋ, -ɪd
fustigation, -s ˌfʌstɪ'ɡeɪʃn, -z
fust|y, -ier, -iest, -ily, -iness 'fʌst|ɪ, -ɪə* [-jə*], -ɪɪst [-jɪst], -ɪlɪ [-əlɪ], -ɪnɪs [-ɪnəs]
futhark 'fuːθɑːk
futile, -ly, -ness 'fjuːtaɪl, -lɪ, -nɪs [-nəs]
futilit|y, -ies fjuː'tɪlət|ɪ [fjʊ't-, -ɪt|ɪ], -ɪz
futtock, -s 'fʌtək, -s
future (*s. adj.*), **-s** 'fjuːtʃə*, -z
futurism 'fjuːtʃərɪzəm [-tʃʊr-]
futurist, -s 'fjuːtʃərɪst [-tʃʊr-], -s
futuristic, -ally ˌfjuːtʃə'rɪstɪk [-tʃʊ'r-, -tjə-, -tjʊ-], -lɪ
futurit|y, -ies fjuː'tjʊərət|ɪ [fjʊ'tj-, -'tjɔər-, -'tjɔːr-, -ɪt|ɪ], -ɪz
futurolog|ist/s, -y ˌfjuːtʃə'rɒlədʒ|ɪst/s, -ɪ
fuzz (*s. v.*), **-es, -ing, -ed** fʌz, -ɪz, -ɪŋ, -d
fuzzball, -s 'fʌzbɔːl, -z
fuzzbuzz, -es 'fʌzbʌz, -ɪz
fuzz|y, -ier, -iest, -ily, -iness 'fʌz|ɪ, -ɪə*, -ɪɪst, -ɪlɪ [-əlɪ], -ɪnɪs [-ɪnəs]
Fyf(f)e faɪf
Fyfield 'faɪfiːld
Fyne, -s faɪn, -z
Fyson 'faɪsn

G

G (*the letter*), -'s dʒiː, -z
gab (*s. v.*), -s, -bing, -bed gæb, -z, -ɪŋ, -d
Gabbatha ˈgæbəθə
Gabbitas ˈgæbɪtæs
gabb|le, -les, -ling, -led, -ler/s ˈgæb|l, -lz, -lɪŋ [-lŋ] -ld, -lə*/z [-lə*/z]
gaberdine, -s ˌgæbəˈdiːn [ˈ---], -z
gaberlunzie, -s ˌgæbəˈlʌnzɪ [ˈgæbəl-, -njɪ], -z
Gabii ˈgæbɪi: [-bɪaɪ]
gabion, -s ˈgeɪbjən [-bɪən], -z
gable, -s, -d ˈgeɪbl, -z, -d
gablet, -s ˈgeɪblɪt [-lət], -s
gable-window, -s ˌgeɪblˈwɪndəʊ, -z
Gabon gæˈbɒn [gə-, ˈgæbɔ̃ːŋ]
Gabonese ˌgæbɒˈniːz [-bə-]
Gaboon gəˈbuːn
Gabriel ˈgeɪbrɪəl
gab|y, -ies ˈgeɪb|ɪ, -ɪz
Gaby ˈgɑːbɪ
Gacrux (*star*) ˈgeɪkrʌks
gad (*s. v. interj.*) (G.), -s, -ding, -ded gæd, -z, -ɪŋ, -ɪd
gadabout, -s ˈgædəbaʊt, -s
Gadara ˈgædərə
Gadarene, -s ˌgædəˈriːn [ˈ---], -z
Gaddesden ˈgædzdən
Gade (*English river*) geɪd, (*Danish composer*) ˈgɑːdə
Gades ˈgeɪdiːz
gadfl|y, -ies ˈgædfl|aɪ, -aɪz
gadget, -s, -ry ˈgædʒɪt, -s, -rɪ
Gadhel, -s ˈgædel, -z
Gadhelic gæˈdelɪk [gəˈd-]
Gadite, -s ˈgædaɪt, -s
gadroon, -s gəˈdruːn, -z
Gads|by, -den, -hill ˈgædz|bɪ, -dən, -hɪl
gadwall, -s ˈgædwɔːl, -z
gadzooks ˌgædˈzuːks
Gael, -s geɪl, -z
Gaelic ˈgeɪlɪk [ˈgælɪk]
Gaetulia giːˈtjuːljə [dʒiː-, -lɪə]
gaff (*s. v.*), -s, -ing, -ed gæf, -s, -ɪŋ, -t
gaffe, -s gæf, -s
gaffer, -s ˈgæfə*, -z
Gaffney ˈgæfnɪ
gag (*s. v.*), -s, -ging, -ged gæg, -z, -ɪŋ, -d
gaga (*s. adj.*), -s ˈgɑːgɑː [ˈgæ-], -z

gag|e (*s. v.*) (G.), -es, -ing, -ed geɪdʒ, -ɪz, -ɪŋ, -d
gaggle, -s ˈgægl, -z
gaiet|y (G.), -ies ˈgeɪət|ɪ [ˈgeɪt-], -ɪz
gaily ˈgeɪlɪ
gain (*s. v.*), -s, -ing/s, -ed, -er/s; -able, -less geɪn, -z, -ɪŋ/z, -d, -ə*/z; -əbl, -lɪs [-ləs]
Gaines geɪnz
gain|ful, -fully, -fulness ˈgeɪn|fʊl, -fʊlɪ [-fəlɪ], -fʊlnɪs [-nəs]
gain|say, -says, -saying, -sayed, -said, -sayer/s ˌgeɪn|ˈseɪ, -ˈseɪz, -ˈseɪɪŋ, -ˈseɪd, -ˈseɪd [-ˈsed], -ˈseɪə*/z
Gainsborough, -s ˈgeɪnzbərə, -z
Gairdner ˈgeədnə*, ˈgɑːd-
Gairloch ˈgeəlɒk [-lɒx]
Gaisberg ˈgaɪzbəːg
Gaisford ˈgeɪsfəd
gait, -s geɪt, -s
gaiter, -s ˈgeɪtə*, -z
Gaitskell ˈgeɪtskəl [-kɪl]
Gaius ˈgaɪəs
gala, -s ˈgɑːlə [ˈgeɪl-], -z
Gala (*river*) ˈgɑːlə
galactic gəˈlæktɪk
Galahad ˈgæləhæd
Galan (*surname*) ˈgeɪlən
galantine, -s ˈgæləntiːn [ˌ--ˈ-], -z
Galapagos gəˈlæpəgəs [-gɒs]
Galapas ˈgæləpæs
Galashiels ˌgælæˈʃiːlz
Galata ˈgælətə
Galatea ˌgæləˈtɪə
Galatia gəˈleɪʃjə [-ʃɪə, -ʃə]
Galatian, -s gəˈleɪʃjən [-ʃɪən, -ʃn], -z
galax|y, -ies ˈgæləks|ɪ, -ɪz
Galba ˈgælbə
galbanum ˈgælbənəm
Galbraith gælˈbreɪθ
gale (G.), -s geɪl, -z
Galen ˈgeɪlɪn [-lən]
galena (G.) gəˈliːnə
galenic, -al gəˈlenɪk [geɪˈl-], -
Galerius gəˈlɪərɪəs
Galesburg ˈgeɪlzbəːg
Galicia, -n gəˈlɪʃɪə [-ʃjə, -sɪə, -sjə], -n
Galilean, -s ˌgælɪˈliːən [-ˈlɪən], -z
Galilee ˈgælɪliː

206

Galileo ˌgælɪˈleɪəʊ [-ˈliːəʊ]
galingale ˈgælɪŋgeɪl
Galion ˈgælɪən [-ljən]
galipot ˈgælɪpɒt
gall (s. v.), -s, -ing, -ed gɔːl, -z, -ɪŋ, -d
Gallagher ˈgæləhə* [-əxə*]
Gallaher ˈgæləhə*
gallant (s.), -s ˈgælənt [rarely gəˈlænt], -s
gallant (adj.) (brave), -ly, -ness ˈgælənt, -lɪ, -nɪs [-nəs]
gallant (adj.) (amorous), -ly, -ness ˈgælənt [gəˈlænt], -lɪ, -nɪs [-nəs]
gallantry ˈgæləntrɪ
Gallatin ˈgælətɪn
gall-bladder, -s ˈgɔːl͵blædə*, -z
galleon, -s ˈgælɪən [-ljən], -z
galler|y, -ies, -ied ˈgælər|ɪ, -ɪz, -ɪd
galley, -s ˈgælɪ, -z
galley-proof, -s ˈgælɪpruːf, -s
galley-slave, -s ˈgælɪsleɪv, -z
gall-fl|y, -ies ˈgɔːlfl|aɪ, -aɪz
Gallia ˈgælɪə
galliambic (s. adj.), -s ˌgælɪˈæmbɪk, -s
galliard, -s ˈgæljɑːd [-lɪɑːd, -əd], -z
gallic (G.) ˈgælɪk
Gallican (s. adj.), -s ˈgælɪkən, -z
gallice ˈgælɪsiː [-sɪ]
gallicism, -s ˈgælɪsɪzəm, -z
galliciz|e [-is|e], -es, -ing, -ed ˈgælɪsaɪz, -ɪz, -ɪŋ, -d
gallinaceous ˌgælɪˈneɪʃəs [-ʃjəs, -ʃɪəs]
Gallio ˈgælɪəʊ
galliot, -s ˈgælɪət, -s
Gallipoli gəˈlɪpəlɪ
Gallipolis (in U.S.A) ˌgælɪpəˈliːs
gallipot ˈgælɪpɒt, -s
gallivant, -s, -ing, -ed ˌgælɪˈvænt [ˈ---], -s, -ɪŋ, -ɪd
gall-nut, -s ˈgɔːlnʌt, -s
gallon, -s ˈgælən, -z
galloon gəˈluːn
gallop (s. v.), -s, -ing, -ed, -er/s ˈgæləp, -s, -ɪŋ, -t, -ə*/z
gallopade, -s ˌgæləˈpeɪd, -z
Gallovidian (s. adj.), -s ˌgæləʊˈvɪdɪən [-djən], -z
galloway (G.), -s ˈgæləweɪ [-lʊw-], -z
gallows ˈgæləʊz
gallows-bird, -s ˈgæləʊzbɜːd, -z
gall-stone, -s ˈgɔːlstəʊn, -z
Gallup ˈgæləp
Gallus ˈgæləs
galop, -s ˈgæləp [gæˈlɒp], -s
galore gəˈlɔː* [-ˈlɔə*]
galosh, -es gəˈlɒʃ, -ɪz
Galpin ˈgælpɪn
Galsham ˈgɔːlsəm [ˈgɒl-]

Galsworthy ˈgɔːlzwɜːðɪ, ˈgæl-
Note.—John Galsworthy, the author, is commonly called ˈgɔːlzwɜːðɪ.
Galt, -on gɔːlt [gɒlt], -ən
galumph, -s, -ing, -ed gəˈlʌmf, -s, -ɪŋ, -t
Galvani gælˈvɑːnɪ
galvanic gælˈvænɪk
galvanism ˈgælvənɪzəm [-vn̩-]
galvaniz|e [-is|e], -es, -ing, -ed, -er/s ˈgælvənaɪz [-vn̩aɪz], -ɪz, -ɪŋ, -d, -ə*/z
galvanometer, -s ˌgælvəˈnɒmɪtə* [-vn̩ˈɒ-, -mətə*], -z
Galvestone ˈgælvɪstən
Galway ˈgɔːlweɪ
Gama ˈgɑːmə
Gamage, -'s ˈgæmɪdʒ, -ɪz
Gamaliel gəˈmeɪljəl [-lɪəl, in Jewish usage also gəˈmɑːlɪəl, ˌgæməˈliːəl]
gamba, -s ˈgæmbə, -z
gambado (jump), -(e)s gæmˈbeɪdəʊ [-ˈbɑːd-], -z
gambadoes (leggings) gæmˈbeɪdəʊz
Gambetta gæmˈbetə
Gambia ˈgæmbɪə [-bjə]
gambier (substance used in dyeing) ˈgæm͵bɪə*
Gambier (surname) ˈgæm͵bɪə* [-bɪə*, -bjə*]
gambist, -s ˈgæmbɪst, -s
gambit, -s ˈgæmbɪt, -s
gamb|le (s. v.) (G.), -les, -ling, -led, -ler/s ˈgæmb|l̩, -lz, -lɪŋ, -ld, -lə*/z
gambling-hou|se, -ses ˈgæmblɪŋhaʊ|s, -zɪz
gamboge gæmˈbuːʒ [-ˈbəʊʒ]
gamb|ol (s. v.), -ols, -olling, -olled ˈgæmb|l̩, -lz, -lɪŋ [-əlɪŋ], -ld
gam|e (s. adj. v.), -es; -er, -est, -ely, -eness; -ing, -ed geɪm, -z; -ə*, -ɪst, -lɪ, -nɪs [-nəs]; -ɪŋ, -d
game|-bag/s, -cock/s, -keeper/s, -law/s, -licence/s ˈgeɪm|bæg/z, -kɒk/s, -͵kiːpə*/z, -lɔː/z, -͵laɪsns/ɪz
Game|lyn, -lin ˈgæmɪlɪn [-mlɪn]
games|-master/s, -mistress/es ˈgeɪmz|-͵mɑːstə*/z, -͵mɪstrɪs/ɪz [-trəs/ɪz]
gamester, -s ˈgeɪmstə*, -z
gaming|-house, -houses, -table/s ˈgeɪmɪŋ|haʊs, -͵haʊzɪz, -͵teɪbl/z
gamma, -s ˈgæmə, -z
Gammell ˈgæməl
gammer, -s ˈgæmə*, -z
gammon (s. v.), -s, -ing, -ed ˈgæmən, -z, -ɪŋ, -d
gamp (G.), -s gæmp, -s
gamut, -s ˈgæmət, -s
gam|y, -ier, -iest, -iness ˈgeɪm|ɪ, -ɪə* [-jə*], -ɪst [-jɪst], -ɪnɪs [-ɪnəs]

207

gander, -s 'gændə*, -z
Gandercleugh 'gændəklu:, -klu:x
Gandhi 'gændi: ['gɑ:n-, -dɪ] (Hindi
  gādhi)
Gandhi|ism, -ite/s 'gændɪ|ɪzəm, -aɪt/s
gang, -s; -er/s gæŋ, -z; -ə*/z
Ganges 'gændʒi:z
gangli|on, -a, -ons 'gæŋglɪ|ən, -ə, -ənz
gangren|e (s. v.), -es, -ing, -ed 'gæŋ-
  gri:n, -z, -ɪŋ, -d
gangrenous 'gæŋgrɪnəs
gangster, -s 'gæŋstə* [-ŋks-], -z
gangway, -s 'gæŋweɪ, -z
Gannel 'gænl
gannet, -s 'gænɪt, -s
Gannett 'gænɪt
gan(n)ister 'gænɪstə*
Gannon 'gænən
ganoid 'gænɔɪd
gantr|y, -ies 'gæntr|ɪ, -ɪz
Ganymede 'gænɪmi:d
gaol (s. v.), -s, -ing, -ed, -er/s dʒeɪl, -z,
  -ɪŋ, -d, -ə*/z
gaolbird, -s 'dʒeɪlbɜ:d, -z
gap, -s gæp, -s
gap|e (s. v.), -es, -ing, -ed, -er/s geɪp,
  -s, -ɪŋ, -t, -ə*/z
garag|e (s. v.), -es, -ing, -ed 'gærɑ:dʒ
  [-rɪdʒ, -rɑ:ʒ, occasionally gə'rɑ:dʒ,
  -ɑ:ʒ], -ɪz, -ɪŋ, -d
garb, -s, -ed gɑ:b, -z, -d
garbage 'gɑ:bɪdʒ
garb|le, -les, -ling, -led 'gɑ:b|l, -lz, -lɪŋ
  [-lɪŋ], -ld
Garbutt 'gɑ:bət
Garcia (English surname) 'gɑ:ʃjə [-ʃɪə],
  'gɑ:sjə [-sɪə]
gard|en (s. v.) (G.), -ens, -ening, -ened,
  -ener/s 'gɑ:d|n, -nz, -nɪŋ, -nd, -nə*/z
gardenia, -s gɑ:'di:njə [gə'd-, -nɪə],
  -z
garden-part|y, -ies 'gɑ:dn,pɑ:t|ɪ, -ɪz
Gard(i)ner 'gɑ:dnə*
garefowl, -s 'geəfaʊl, -z
Gareth 'gæreθ [-rəθ, -rɪθ] (Welsh
  'gareθ)
Garfield 'gɑ:fi:ld
garfish 'gɑ:fɪʃ
garganey, -s 'gɑ:gənɪ, -z
Gargantua gɑ:'gæntjʊə [-tjwə]
gargantuan gɑ:'gæntjʊən [-tjwən]
Gargery 'gɑ:dʒərɪ
garg|le (s. v.), -les, -ling/s, -led 'gɑ:g|l,
  -lz, -lɪŋ/z, -ld
gargoyle, -s 'gɑ:gɔɪl, -z
Garibaldi ,gærɪ'bɔ:ldɪ [-'bæl-]
Garioch (district in Scotland, surname)
  'gærɪɒk [-ɒx]

garish, -ly, -ness 'geərɪʃ ['gær-], -lɪ, -nɪs
  [-nəs]
garland (G.), -s 'gɑ:lənd, -z
garlic, -ky 'gɑ:lɪk, -ɪ
Garlick 'gɑ:lɪk
garment, -s, -ed 'gɑ:mənt, -s, -ɪd
garner (s. v.), -s, -ing, -ed 'gɑ:nə*, -z,
  -rɪŋ, -d
garnet, -s 'gɑ:nɪt, -s
Garn|et(t), -ham 'gɑ:n|ɪt, -əm
garnish (s. v.), -es, -ing, -ed, -ment/s
  'gɑ:nɪʃ, -ɪz, -ɪŋ, -t, -mənt/s
garnishee (s. v.), -s, -ing, -d ,gɑ:nɪ'ʃi:,
  -z, -ɪŋ, -d
garniture 'gɑ:nɪtʃə*
Garr|ard, -att 'gær|əd, -ət
Garraway 'gærəweɪ
garret, -s 'gærət [-rɪt], -s
Garr|et(t), -ick 'gær|ət [-rt], -ɪk
Garrioch (district in Scotland) 'gɪərɪ,
  (surname) 'gærɪək [-əx]
garris|on (s. v.) (G.), -ons, -oning, -oned
  'gærɪs|n, -nz, -nɪŋ [-ənɪŋ], -nd
Garr|od, -o(u)ld 'gær|əd, -əld
garrot, -s 'gærət, -s
garrott|e (s. v.), -es, -ing, -ed, -er/s
  gə'rɒt, -s, -ɪŋ, -ɪd, -ə*/z
garrulity gæ'ru:lətɪ [gə'r-, -'rju:-, -ɪtɪ]
garrulous, -ly, -ness 'gærələs [-rʊl-,
  -rjʊl-], -lɪ, -nɪs [-nəs]
Garston 'gɑ:stən
garter (s. v.), -s, -ing, -ed 'gɑ:tə*, -z,
  -rɪŋ, -d
garth (G.), -s gɑ:θ, -s
Garwood 'gɑ:wʊd
gas (s.), -es gæs, -ɪz
gas (v.), -ses, -sing, -sed gæs, -ɪz, -ɪŋ, -t
gas|-bag/s, -bracket/s, -burner/s 'gæs|-
  bæg/z, -,brækɪt/s, -,bɜ:nə*/z
Gascoigne 'gæskɔɪn
Gascon, -s 'gæskən, -z
gasconnad|e (s. v.), -es, -ing, -ed ,gæs-
  kə'neɪd, -z, -ɪŋ, -ɪd
Gascony 'gæskənɪ
Gascoyne 'gæskɔɪn
Gaselee 'geɪzli: [-lɪ]
gaselier, -s ,gæsə'lɪə*, -z
gas-engine, -s 'gæs,endʒɪn, -z
gaseous, -ness 'gæsjəs ['geɪ-, -sɪəs,
  -zjəs, -zɪəs, -ʃjəs, -ʃɪəs], -nɪs [-nəs]
gas-fire, -s 'gæs,faɪə* [,-'-], -z
gas|-fitter/s, -fixture/s 'gæs|,fɪtə*/z,
  -,fɪkstʃə*/z
gash (s. v.), -es, -ing, -ed gæʃ, -ɪz, -ɪŋ, -t
gas-helmet, -s 'gæs,helmɪt, -s
gasi|fy, -fies, -fying, -fied 'gæsɪ|faɪ
  ['geɪzɪ-], -faɪz, -faɪɪŋ, -faɪd
gas-jet, -s 'gæsdʒet, -s

Gaskell 'gæskəl [-kel]
gasket, -s 'gæskɪt, -s
gaskin (G.), -s 'gæskɪn, -z
gas-light 'gæslaɪt
gas-main -s 'gæsmeɪn, -z
gas|-man, -men 'gæs|mæn, -men
gas|-mantle/s, -mask/s 'gæs|ˌmæntl/z, -mɑːsk/s
gas-meter, -s 'gæsˌmiːtə*, -z
gasolene [-line] 'gæsəʊliːn
gasometer, -s gæ'sɒmɪtə* [gə'sɒ-, gə'zɒ-, -mətə*], -z
gasp (s. v.), -s, -ing, -ed gɑːsp, -s, -ɪŋ, -t
gas|-pipe/s, -ring/s 'gæs|paɪp/s, -rɪŋ/z
gas-stove, -s 'gæsstəʊv [ˌ-'-], -z
gass|y, -ier, -iest, -iness 'gæs|ɪ, -ɪə*, -ɪɪst, -ɪnɪs [-ɪnəs]
gasteropod, -s 'gæstərəpɒd, -z
gastric 'gæstrɪk
gastritis gæ'straɪtɪs
gastronome, -s 'gæstrənəʊm, -z
gastronomic, -al ˌgæstrə'nɒmɪk, -l
gastronom|ist/s, -y gæ'strɒnəm|ɪst/s, -ɪ
gasworks 'gæswɜːks
Gatacre 'gætəkə*
gat|e (s. v.), -es, -ing, -ed geɪt, -s, -ɪŋ, -ɪd
gâteau, -x[-s] 'gætəʊ, -z (gɑto)
gatecrash, -es, -ing, -ed, -er/s 'geɪt-kræʃ, -ɪz, -ɪŋ, -t, -ə*/z
gate|-fine/s, -house, -houses, -keeper/s 'geɪt|faɪn/z, -haʊs, -haʊzɪz, -kiːpə*/z
gate-legged 'geɪtlegd
gateless 'geɪtlɪs [-ləs]
gate|-money, -post/s 'geɪt|ˌmʌnɪ, -pəʊst/s
Gatenby 'geɪtnbɪ
Gater 'geɪtə*
Gates geɪts
Gateshead 'geɪtshed
gateway, -s 'geɪtweɪ, -z
Gath gæθ
gath|er (s. v.), -ers, -ering/s, -ered, -erer/s 'gæð|ə*, -əz, -ərɪŋ/z, -əd, -ərə*/z
Gathorne 'geɪθɔːn
Gat|ley, -ling 'gæt|lɪ, -lɪŋ
Gatty 'gætɪ
Gatwick 'gætwɪk
gauche gəʊʃ
gaucherie, -s 'gəʊʃəriː [-rɪ], -z
gaucho, -s 'gaʊtʃəʊ ['gɔːtʃ-], -z
gaud, -s gɔːd, -z
Gauden 'gɔːdn
gaud|y, -ier, -iest, -ily, -iness 'gɔːd|ɪ, -ɪə* [-jə*], -ɪɪst [-jɪst], -ɪlɪ [-əlɪ], -ɪnɪs [-ɪnəs]

gaug|e (s. v.), -es, -ing, -ed, -er/s; -eable geɪdʒ, -ɪz, -ɪŋ, -d, -ə*/z; -əbl
Gaul, -s, -ish gɔːl, -z, -ɪʃ
gauleiter, -s 'gaʊlaɪtə*, -z
Gauloise(s) (cigarette) 'gəʊlwɑːz [-'-] (golwa:z)
gaum (s. v.), -s, -ing, -ed gɔːm, -z, -ɪŋ, -d
Gaumont 'gəʊmɒnt [-mənt]
gaunt (G.), -er, -est, -ly, -ness gɔːnt, -ə*, -ɪst, -lɪ, -nɪs [-nəs]
gauntlet (G.), -s, -ed 'gɔːntlɪt [-lət], -s, -ɪd
Gauntlett 'gɔːntlɪt, 'gɑːn-
Gauss gaʊs
gauz|e, -es; -y, -iness gɔːz, -ɪz; -ɪ, -ɪnɪs [-ɪnəs]
gave (from give) geɪv
gavel, -s 'gævl, -z
gavelkind 'gævlkaɪnd [-kɪnd]
Gaveston 'gævɪstən
Gavey 'geɪvɪ
Gavin 'gævɪn
gavotte, -s gə'vɒt, -s
Gawain 'gɑːweɪn ['gæw-]
Gawith (surname) 'geɪwɪθ
gawk, -s gɔːk, -s
gawk|y, -ier, -iest, -iness 'gɔːk|ɪ, -ɪə*, -ɪɪst, -ɪnɪs [-ɪnəs]
gay (G.), -er, -est, gaily, gayness geɪ, -ə* [geə*], -ɪst, 'geɪlɪ, 'geɪnɪs [-nəs]
Gayn|ham, -or 'geɪn|əm, -ə*
Gaza (in Israel, formerly in Egypt) 'gɑːzə [in biblical use also 'geɪzə]
Gaza (Greek scholar) 'gɑːzə
gaz|e (s. v.), -es, -ing, -ed, -er/s geɪz, -ɪz, -ɪŋ, -d, -ə*/z
gazebo, -s gə'ziːbəʊ, -z
gazelle, -s gə'zel, -z
gazett|e (s. v.), -es, -ing, -ed gə'zet, -s, -ɪŋ, -ɪd
gazetteer, -s ˌgæzə'tɪə* [-zɪ't-], -z
gazogene 'gæzəʊdʒiːn
gazump, -s, -ing, -ed gə'zʌmp, -s, -ɪŋ, -t [-'zʌmt]
Geall giːl
gear (s. v.), -s, -ing, -ed gɪə*, -z, -rɪŋ, -d
gear|-box/es, -case/s 'gɪə|bɒks/ɪz, -keɪs/ɪz
Geare gɪə*
Geary 'gɪərɪ
Gebal 'giːbəl [-bæl]
Gebir 'dʒiːˌbɪə*
gecko, -s 'gekəʊ, -z
Ged ged
Geddes 'gedɪs
gee (s. v.) (G.), -s, -ing -d dʒiː, -z, -ɪŋ, -d
geegee, -s 'dʒiːdʒiː, -z

209

Geelong dʒɪˈlɒŋ [dʒəˈl-]
Geering ˈgɪərɪŋ
geese (plur. of goose) giːs
Geeson ˈdʒiːsn, ˈgiːsn
gee-up ˈdʒiːʌp
geezer, -s ˈgiːzə*, -z
Gehazi gɪˈheɪzaɪ [geˈh-, gəˈh-, -ˈheɪzɪ, -ˈhɑːzɪ]
Gehenna gɪˈhenə [gəˈh-]
Geierstein ˈgaɪəsťaɪn
Geiger ˈgaɪgə*
Geikie ˈgiːkɪ
geisha, -s ˈgeɪʃə, -z
gelatine ˌdʒeləˈtiːn [ˈ---, ˈdʒelətɪm]
gelatiniz|e [-is|e], -es, -ing, -ed dʒəˈlætɪnaɪz [dʒeˈl-, dʒɪˈl-, -tən-], -ɪz, -ɪŋ, -d
gelatinous dʒəˈlætɪnəs [dʒeˈl-, dʒɪˈl-, -tən-]
geld (adj. v.), -s, -ing, -ed geld, -z, -ɪŋ, -ɪd
gelding (s.), -s ˈgeldɪŋ, -z
gelid, -ly, -ness ˈdʒelɪd, -lɪ, -nɪs [-nəs]
gelignite ˈdʒelɪgnaɪt
Gell gel, dʒel
Gell|an, -er ˈgel|ən, -ə*
Gellatl(e)y ˈgelətlɪ, geˈlætlɪ, gəˈlætlɪ
gem, -s dʒem, -z
Gemara geˈmɑːrə [gɪˈm-]
geminat|e, -es, -ing, -ed ˈdʒemɪneɪt, -s, -ɪŋ, -ɪd
gemination ˌdʒemɪˈneɪʃn
Gemini (constellation) ˈdʒemmaɪ [-niː, -nɪ], (aircraft) ˈdʒemɪnɪ
Gemistus dʒeˈmɪstəs [dʒɪˈm-]
Gemmi ˈgemɪ
gemmiferous dʒeˈmɪfərəs
gemot, -s gɪˈməʊt [gəˈm-], -s
gemsbok, -s ˈgemzbɒk, -s
gemshorn, -s ˈgemzhɔːn, -z
gen dʒen
gendarme, -s ˈʒɑ̃ːndɑːm [ˈʒɔ̃ːnd-, ˈʒɑːnd-, ˈʒɒnd-] (ʒɑ̃darm)
gender (s. v.), -s, -ing, -ed ˈdʒendə*, -z, -rɪŋ, -d
gene (G.), -s dʒiːn, -z
genealogic|al, -ally ˌdʒiːnjəˈlɒdʒɪk|l [ˌdʒen-, -nɪə-], -əlɪ
genealog|ist/s, -y, -ies ˌdʒiːnɪˈælədʒ|-ɪst/s [ˌdʒen-], -ɪ, -ɪz
genera (plur. of genus) ˈdʒenərə
gener|al (s. adj.), -als, -ally ˈdʒenər|əl, -əlz, -əlɪ
generalissimo, -s ˌdʒenərəˈlɪsɪməʊ, -z
generalit|y, -ies ˌdʒenəˈrælət|ɪ [-ɪt|ɪ], -ɪz
generalization [-isa-], -s ˌdʒenərəlaɪˈzeɪʃn [-lɪˈz-], -z
generaliz|e [-is|e-], -es, -ing, -ed ; -able ˈdʒenərəlaɪz, -ɪz, -ɪŋ, -d; -əbl

generalship ˈdʒenərəlʃɪp
generat|e, -es, -ing, -ed, -or/s ˈdʒenə-reɪt, -s, -ɪŋ, -ɪd, -ə*/z
generation, -s ˌdʒenəˈreɪʃn, -z
generative ˈdʒenərətɪv [-reɪt-]
generator, -s ˈdʒenəreɪtə*, -z
generatri|x, -ces ˈdʒenəreɪtrɪ|ks, -siːz
generic, -ally dʒɪˈnerɪk [dʒəˈn-, dʒeˈn-], -əlɪ
generosity ˌdʒenəˈrɒsətɪ [-ɪtɪ]
generous, -ly, -ness ˈdʒenərəs, -lɪ, -nɪs [-nəs]
genesis ˈdʒenəsɪs [-nɪsɪs]
Genesis (book of the Bible) ˈdʒenəsɪs [-nɪsɪs, old-fashioned -sɪz]
Genesius dʒɪˈniːsjəs [dʒeˈn-, dʒəˈn-, -sɪəs]
Genesta dʒɪˈnestə [dʒeˈn-, dʒəˈn-]
genet, -s ˈdʒenɪt, -s
genetic, -s, -ally dʒɪˈnetɪk [dʒeˈn-, dʒəˈn-], -s, -əlɪ
geneticist, -s dʒɪˈnetɪsɪst [dʒe-, dʒə-], -s
Geneva, -n/s dʒɪˈniːvə [dʒəˈn-], -n/z
Genevieve (in Coleridge's poem 'Love') ˌdʒenəˈviːv, ˈdʒenɪviːv [-nəv-]
Geneviève (Saint) ˌʒenviˈeɪv (ʒənvjɛːv)
Genghis Khan ˌgeŋgɪs ˈkɑːn [ˌdʒe-, -gɪz-]
genial (amiable), -ly, -ness ˈdʒiːnjəl [-nɪəl], -ɪ, -nɪs [-nəs]
genial (of the chin) dʒɪˈnaɪəl
geniality ˌdʒiːnɪˈælətɪ [-ɪtɪ]
genie, -s ˈdʒiːnɪ, -z
genista, -s dʒɪˈnɪstə [dʒeˈn-, dʒəˈn-], -s
genital, -s ˈdʒenɪtl, -z
genitival ˌdʒenɪˈtaɪvl
genitive, -s ˈdʒenɪtɪv [-nət-], -z
ge|nius, -nii, -niuses ˈdʒiː|njəs [-nɪəs], -nɪaɪ, -njəsɪz [-nɪəsɪz]
Gennesare|t, -th gɪˈnezərɪ|t [geˈn-, gəˈn-, -re|t], -θ
Genoa ˈdʒenəʊə [dʒəˈnəʊə]
genocide ˈdʒenəʊsaɪd
Genoese ˌdʒenəʊˈiːz [also ˈdʒenəʊiːz when attributive]
genre ˈʒɑ̃ːŋrə [ˈʒɑːnrə, ˈʒɔ̃ːŋrə, ˈʒɑːŋrə, ˈʒɒŋrə] (ʒɑ̃ːr)
gen|s, -tes dʒen|z, -tiːz
Genseric ˈgensərɪk [ˈdʒen-]
Gensing ˈgenzɪŋ [-nsɪŋ]
gent, -s dʒent, -s
genteel, -ly, -ness dʒenˈtiːl [dʒən-], -lɪ, -nɪs [-nəs]
gentes (plur. of gens) ˈdʒentiːz
gentian, -s ˈdʒenʃɪən [-ʃjən, -ʃn], -z
gentile (G.), -s ˈdʒentaɪl, -z
gentian, -s ˈdʒenʃn [-ʃjən, -ʃɪən], -z
gent|le, -ler, -lest, -ly, -leness ˈdʒent|l, -lə*, -lɪst, -lɪ, -lnɪs [-nəs]

210

gentlefolk, -s ˈdʒentlfəʊk, -s
gentle|man, -men ˈdʒentl|mən, -mən [-men]
gentle|man-at-arms, -men-at-arms ˌdʒentl|mənət'ɑːmz, -mənət'ɑːmz [-men-]
gentlemanlike ˈdʒentlmənlaɪk
gentlemanl|y, -iness ˈdʒentlmənl|ɪ, -ɪnɪs [-ɪnəs]
gentle|woman,-women ˈdʒentl|ˌwʊmən, -ˌwɪmɪn
gentry (G.) ˈdʒentrɪ
genuflect, -s, -ing, -ed ˈdʒenjuːflekt [-njʊ-], -s, -ɪŋ, -ɪd
genuflection, -s ˌdʒenjuːˈflekʃn [-njʊ-], -z
genuine, -ly, -ness ˈdʒenjʊɪn, -lɪ, -nɪs [-nəs]
gen|us, -era ˈdʒiːn|əs [ˈdʒen|əs], ˈdʒenərə
Geo. dʒɔːdʒ
geocentric, -al, -ally ˌdʒiːəʊˈsentrɪk [ˌdʒɪ-], -l, -əlɪ
geode, -s ˈdʒiːəʊd [ˈdʒɪ-], -z
geodesic, -al ˌdʒiːəʊˈdesɪk [ˌdʒɪ-, -ˈdiːs-], -l
geod|esy, -ic dʒiˈɒd|ɪsɪ [dʒɪ-, -dəsɪ], -ɪk
Geoffr(e)y ˈdʒefrɪ
Geoghegan ˈɡeɪɡən, ˈɡəʊɡən
geographer, -s dʒiˈɒɡrəfə*, -z
geographic, -al, -ally dʒɪəˈɡræfɪk [dʒɪəʊˈɡ-], -l, -əlɪ
geograph|y, -ies dʒiˈɒɡrəf|ɪ [ˈdʒɒɡ-], -ɪz
geologic, -al, -ally ˌdʒɪəʊˈlɒdʒɪk, -l, -əlɪ
geolog|ist/s, -y dʒiˈɒlədʒ|ɪst/s, -ɪ
geologiz|e [-is|e], -es, -ing, -ed dʒiˈɒlə-dʒaɪz, -ɪz, -ɪŋ, -d
geomancy ˈdʒiːəʊmænsɪ
geometer, -s dʒiˈɒmɪtə* [-mətə*], -z
geometric, -al, -ally ˌdʒɪəʊˈmetrɪk, -l, -əlɪ
geometrician, -s ˌdʒɪəʊməˈtrɪʃn [dʒɪˌɒm-, -mɪˈt-], -z
geometr|y, -ies dʒiˈɒmətr|ɪ [ˈdʒɒm-, -mɪtr|ɪ], -ɪz
geophysic|al, -s ˌdʒiːəʊˈfɪzɪk|l [ˌdʒɪ-], -z
Geordie ˈdʒɔːdɪ
George, -s dʒɔːdʒ, -ɪz
georgette dʒɔːˈdʒet
Georgia, -n/s ˈdʒɔːdʒjə [-dʒɪə], -n/z
Georgiana ˌdʒɔːdʒɪˈɑːnə
georgic (G.), -s ˈdʒɔːdʒɪk, -s
Georgina dʒɔːˈdʒiːnə
Geraint ˈɡeraɪnt
Gerald ˈdʒerəld
Geraldine ˈdʒerəldiːn, -daɪn
    Note.—ˈdʒerəldaɪn in Coleridge's 'Christabel'.

geranium, -s dʒɪˈreɪmjəm [dʒəˈr-, -nɪəm], -z
Gerard (English name) ˈdʒerɑːd [ˈdʒerəd], dʒeˈrɑːd [dʒəˈrɑːd]
Gérard (French name) dʒeˈrɑːd (ʒerɑːr)
gerfalcon, -s ˈdʒɜː-ˌfɔːlkən [-ˌfɔːkən], -z
    Note.—Those who practise the sport of falconry pronounce -ˌfɔːk-.
Gergesene, -s ˈɡɜːɡɪsiːn [-ɡəs-, -ɡes-, ˌ--ˈ-], -z
geriatric, -s ˌdʒerɪˈætrɪk, -s
geriatrician, -s ˌdʒerɪəˈtrɪʃn, -z
geriatry ˈdʒerɪətrɪ [-ætrɪ]
Gerizim ɡeˈraɪzɪm [ɡəˈr-, -ˈriːzɪm, ˈɡerɪ-zɪm]
germ, -s dʒɜːm, -z
Germain (street) ˈdʒɜːmən [-meɪn]
German, -s ˈdʒɜːmən, -z
germander dʒɜːˈmændə* [dʒəˈm-]
germane dʒɜːˈmeɪn [ˈ--, dʒəˈm-]
Germanic dʒɜːˈmænɪk [dʒəˈm-]
germani|sm/s, -st/s ˈdʒɜːmənɪ|zəm/z, -st/s
germanization [-isa-] ˌdʒɜːmənaɪˈzeɪʃn
germaniz|e [-is|e], -es, -ing, -ed ˈdʒɜːmənaɪz, -ɪz, -ɪŋ, -d
Germany ˈdʒɜːmənɪ
germicide, -s ˈdʒɜːmɪsaɪd, -z
germinal ˈdʒɜːmɪnl
germinat|e, -es, -ing, -ed ˈdʒɜːmɪneɪt, -s, -ɪŋ, -ɪd
germination, -s ˌdʒɜːmɪˈneɪʃn, -z
Gerontius ɡəˈrɒntɪəs [ɡɪˈr-, ɡeˈr-, -ntjəs, -nʃɪəs, -nʃjəs, -nʃəs]
gerontolog|ist/s, -y ˌdʒerɒnˈtɒlədʒ|ɪst/s [ˌɡer-, -rən-], -ɪ
Gerrans ˈɡerənz
Gerrard ˈdʒerəd [-rɑːd], dʒeˈrɑːd [dʒəˈrɑːd]
Gerrard's Cross ˌdʒerədzˈkrɒs [-rɑːdz-, old-fashioned -ˈkrɔːs]
Gerry ˈɡerɪ, ˈdʒerɪ
gerrymand|er (s. v.), -ers, -ering, -ered ˈdʒerɪmænd|ə* [rarely ˈɡe-], -əz, -ərɪŋ, -əd
Gershwin ˈɡɜːʃwɪn
Gert|ie, -y ˈɡɜːt|ɪ, -ɪ
Gertrude ˈɡɜːtruːd
gerund, -s ˈdʒerənd [-rʌnd], -z
gerundive, -s dʒɪˈrʌndɪv [dʒeˈr-, dʒəˈr-], -z
Gervase ˈdʒɜːvəs
Geryon ˈɡerɪən
gesso ˈdʒesəʊ
gest, -s dʒest, -s
gestalt ɡəˈʃtælt [-ˈʃtɑːlt]
Gestapo ɡeˈstɑːpəʊ

gestat|e, -es, -ing, -ed dʒe'steɪt, -s, -ɪŋ, -ɪd

gestation dʒe'steɪʃn

gestatorial ˌdʒestə'tɔːrɪəl

gesticulat|e, -es, -ing, -ed, -or/s dʒe'stɪkjʊleɪt, -s, -ɪŋ, -ɪd, -ə*/z

gesticulation, -s dʒeˌstɪkjʊ'leɪʃn, -z

gesticulatory dʒe'stɪkjʊlətərɪ [-leɪt-]

gesture, -s 'dʒestʃə*, -z

get, -s, -ting, got get, -s, -ɪŋ, gɒt

Getae 'geɪtaɪ ['dʒiːtiː]

get-at-able get'ætəbl

get-away, -s 'getəweɪ, -z

Gethin 'geθɪn

Gethsemane geθ'semənɪ

get-rich-quick ˌgetrɪtʃ'kwɪk

Getty 'getɪ

Gettysburg 'getɪzbəːg

get-up, -s 'getʌp [ˌget'ʌp], -s

geum, -s 'dʒiːəm [dʒəm], -z

gewgaw, -s 'gjuːgɔː, -z

geyser (hot spring), -s 'gaɪzə* ['giːz-], -z Note.—In New Zealand the pronunciation is always 'gaɪzə*.

geyser (apparatus for heating water), -s 'giːzə* [in New Zealand 'gaɪzə*], -z

Ghana 'gɑːnə

Ghanaian, -s gɑː'neɪən, -z

ghastl|y, -ier, -iest, -iness 'gɑːstl|ɪ, -ɪə* [-jə*], -ɪst [-jɪst], -ɪnɪs [-ɪnəs]

Ghat, -s gɑːt [gɔːt], -s

ghee giː

Ghent gent

gherkin, -s 'gəːkɪn, -z

ghetto, -s 'getəʊ, -z

Ghibelline, -s 'gɪbɪlaɪn, -z

ghost, -s; -like gəʊst, -s; -laɪk

ghostl|y, -iness 'gəʊstl|ɪ, -ɪnɪs [-ɪnəs]

ghost-writer, -s 'gəʊstˌraɪtə*, -z

ghoul, -s; -ish guːl [gaʊl], -z; -ɪʃ

ghyll, -s gɪl, -z

G.I., -'s ˌdʒiː'aɪ [attributively '--], -z

giant, -s; -like 'dʒaɪənt, -s; -laɪk

giantess, -es 'dʒaɪəntes [-tɪs, dʒaɪən-'tes], -ɪz

Giaour 'dʒaʊə*

Gibb gɪb

gibber, -s, -ing, -ed 'dʒɪbə*, -z, -rɪŋ, -d

gibberish 'dʒɪbərɪʃ ['gɪb-]

gibbet (s. v.), -s, -ing, -ed 'dʒɪbɪt, -s, -ɪŋ, -ɪd

Gibbie 'dʒɪbɪ

gibbon (G.), -s 'gɪbən, -z

gibbosity gɪ'bɒsətɪ [-ɪtɪ]

gibbous, -ly, -ness 'gɪbəs, -lɪ, -nɪs [-nəs]

Gibbs gɪbz

gib|e (s. v.), -es, -ing/ly, -ed, -er/s dʒaɪb, -z, -ɪŋ/lɪ, -d, -ə*/z

Gibeah 'gɪbɪə

Gibeon 'gɪbɪən

giblet, -s 'dʒɪblɪt [-lət], -s

Giblett 'gɪblɪt

Gibraltar dʒɪ'brɔːltə* [-rɒl-]

Gibraltarian, -s ˌdʒɪbrɔːl'teərɪən [-rɒl-], -z

Gibson 'gɪbsn

gibus, -es 'dʒaɪbəs ['dʒɪb-], -ɪz

Gick dʒɪk

Gide ʒiːd (ʒid)

Gidding, -s 'gɪdɪŋ, -z

gidd|y (G.), -ier, -iest, -ily, -iness 'gɪd|ɪ, -ɪə*, -ɪst, -ɪlɪ [-əlɪ], -ɪnɪs [-ɪnəs]

giddy-headed 'gɪdɪˌhedɪd

Gidea 'gɪdɪə

Gideon 'gɪdɪən

Gielgud (English name) 'giːlgʊd

Gieve 'giːv

Giffard 'dʒɪfəd

Giffen 'gɪfɪn, 'dʒɪfɪn

Gifford (place near Haddington) 'gɪfəd, (surname) 'gɪfəd, 'dʒɪfəd

gift, -s, -ed gɪft, -s, -ɪd

gig, -s gɪg, -z

giga- 'gaɪgə- ['gɪgə-]

Gigadibs 'gɪgədɪbz

gigant|ean, -esque ˌdʒaɪgæn't|iːən [-ɪən], -esk

gigantic, -ally dʒaɪ'gæntɪk, -əlɪ

gigg|le (s. v.), -les, -ling, -led, -ler/s 'gɪg|l, -lz, -lɪŋ [-lɪŋ], -ld, -lə*/z [-lə*/z]

Gight (in Scotland) gɪkt [gɪxt]

Gigli 'dʒiːliː [-ljiː]

Giglio 'dʒiːlɪəʊ [-ljəʊ]

gigolo, -s 'ʒɪgələʊ ['dʒɪ-] -z

gigot, -s 'dʒɪgət, -s

gigue, -s ʒiːg [ʒɪg], -z

Gihon 'gaɪhɒn [in Jewish usage sometimes 'giːhəʊn]

gila (monster lizard), -s 'hiːlə, -z

Gilbert 'gɪlbət

Gilbertian gɪl'bəːtjən [-tɪən]

Gilbey 'gɪlbɪ

Gilboa gɪl'bəʊə

Gilchrist 'gɪlkrɪst

gild, -s, -ing, -ed, gilt, gilder/s gɪld, -z, -ɪŋ, -ɪd, gɪlt, 'gɪldə*/z

Gilder, -sleeve, -some 'gɪldə*, -sliːv, -səm

Gilding 'gɪldɪŋ

Gildredge 'gɪldrɪdʒ [-redʒ]

Gilead 'gɪlɪæd

Giles dʒaɪlz

Gilfil 'gɪlfɪl

Gilfillan gɪl'fɪlən

Gilford 'gɪlfəd

Gilgal 'gɪlgæl [-gɔ:l, *rarely* gɪl'gɔ:l]
Gilham 'gɪləm
Gilheney (*surname*) gɪ'li:nɪ
Gilheny gɪl'hi:nɪ
Gilkes dʒɪlks
gill (*respiratory organ, ravine*), **-s** gɪl, -z
gill (*measure*), **-s** dʒɪl, -z
Gill gɪl
    Note.—But dʒɪl *in* Jack and Gill (*now
    more usually written* Jack and Jill).
Gillam 'gɪləm
Gillard gɪ'lɑ:d, 'gɪlɑ:d, 'gɪləd
Gillen 'gɪlən
Gilleney (*surname*) 'gɪlənɪ
Gillespie gɪ'lespɪ
Gillett 'gɪlɪt, 'gɪlet, gɪ'let, dʒɪ'let
Gillette (*surname, razor*), **-s** dʒɪ'let, -s
Gilley 'gɪlɪ
Gilliam 'gɪlɪəm
Gillian 'dʒɪlɪən [-ljən], 'gɪl-
Gilliat 'gɪlɪət [-ljət]
Gillick 'gɪlɪk
gillie (G.), **-s** 'gɪlɪ, -z
Gillies 'gɪlɪs
Gilling, **-s** 'gɪlɪŋ, -z
Gillingham (*in Kent*) 'dʒɪlɪŋəm, (*in
    Dorset and Norfolk*) 'gɪl-, (*surname*)
    'gɪl-, 'dʒɪl-
Gillison 'gɪlɪsn
Gillmore 'gɪlmɔ:* [-mɔə*]
Gillott 'dʒɪlət, 'gɪlət
Gill|ow, -ray 'gɪl|əʊ, -reɪ
Gills gɪlz
Gillson 'dʒɪlsn
gillyflower, **-s** 'dʒɪlɪˌflaʊə*, -z
Gil|man, -mer, -more 'gɪl|mən, -mə*,
    -mɔ:* [-mɔə*]
Gilmour 'gɪlmə* [-mɔ:*, -mɔə*]
Gilpatrick gɪl'pætrɪk
Gilpin 'gɪlpɪn
Gilroy 'gɪlrɔɪ
Gilson 'dʒɪlsn, 'gɪlsn
gilt (*s.*) gɪlt
gilt-edged ˌgɪlt'edʒd [*also* '-- *when
    attributive*]
Gilwhite 'gɪlwaɪt ['gɪlhw-]
gimbal, **-s** 'dʒɪmbəl, -z
gimb|le, -les, -ling, -led 'gɪmb|l, -lz,
    -lɪŋ, -ld
Gimblett 'gɪmblɪt
gimcrack, **-s** 'dʒɪmkræk, -s
gimlet, **-s** 'gɪmlɪt [-lət], -s
gimmick, **-s** 'gɪmɪk, -s
gimp gɪmp
Gimson 'gɪmsn, 'dʒɪmsn
gin (*s.*) (*all senses*), **-s** dʒɪn, -z
Ginevra dʒɪ'nevrə
Gingell 'gɪndʒəl

ginger, **-s** 'dʒɪndʒə*, -z
ginger-ale ˌdʒɪndʒər'eɪl [-dʒə'eɪl]
gingerbeer, **-s** ˌdʒɪndʒə'bɪə*, -z
gingerbeer-bottle, **-s** ˌdʒɪndʒə'bɪəˌbɒtl,
    -z
gingerbread, **-s** 'dʒɪndʒəbred, -z
gingerly 'dʒɪndʒəlɪ
ginger-wine ˌdʒɪndʒə'waɪn
ginger|y, -iness 'dʒɪndʒər|ɪ, -ɪnɪs [-ɪnəs]
gingham, **-s** 'gɪŋəm, -z
gingival dʒɪn'dʒaɪvl
gingivitis ˌdʒɪndʒɪ'vaɪtɪs
gingko, **-s** 'gɪŋkəʊ, -z
Ginkel(l) 'gɪŋkəl
Ginn gɪn
gin-palace, **-s** 'dʒɪnˌpælɪs [-əs], -ɪz
Ginsberg 'gɪnzbɜ:g
ginseng 'dʒɪnseŋ
gin-shop, **-s** 'dʒɪnʃɒp, -s
gin-sling, **-s** ˌdʒɪn'slɪŋ, -z
Giovanni ˌdʒɪəʊ'vɑ:nɪ [dʒəʊ'v-, -'væn ɪ]
    (dʒo'vanni)
gip (*gipsy*), **-s** dʒɪp, -s
gip (*to clean fish*), **-s**, -ping, -ped gɪp, -s,
    -ɪŋ, -t
Gippsland 'gɪpslænd
gips|y, -ies 'dʒɪps|ɪ, -ɪz
giraffe, **-s** dʒɪ'rɑ:f [dʒə-, -'ræf], -s
Giralda dʒɪ'rældə
girandole, **-s** 'dʒɪrəndəʊl, -z
gird (*s. v.*), **-s**, -ing, -ed, girt gɜ:d, -z, -ɪŋ,
    -ɪd, gɜ:t
girder, **-s** 'gɜ:də*, -z
gird|le (*s. v.*), -les, -ling, -led 'gɜ:d|l, -lz,
    -lɪŋ [-lɪŋ], -ld
Girdlestone 'gɜ:dlstən
Girgashite, **-s** 'gɜ:gəʃaɪt, -s
Girgasite, **-s** 'gɜ:gəsaɪt, -s
girl, **-s**; -hood; -ish/ly, -ishness gɜ:l,
    -z; -hʊd; -ɪʃ/lɪ, -ɪʃnɪs [-nəs]
Giro 'dʒaɪərəʊ
Girondist, **-s** dʒɪ'rɒndɪst, -s
girt (*s.*), **-s** gɜ:t, -s
girt (*from* gird) gɜ:t
girth, **-s** gɜ:θ, -s
Girtin 'gɜ:tɪn
Girton 'gɜ:tn
Girtonian, **-s** gɜ:'təʊnjən [-nɪən], -z
Gisbourne 'gɪzbɔ:n [-bɔən]
Gissing 'gɪsɪŋ
gist, **-s** dʒɪst, -s
Gita 'gi:tə (*Hindi* gita)
Gitane(s) (*cigarette*) ʒi:'tɑ:n (ʒitan)
gittern, **-s** 'gɪtɜ:n, -z
Giuseppe dʒu:'sepɪ [dʒʊ's-] (dʒu'seppe)
giv|e, -es, -ing, gave, giv|en, -er/s gɪv,
    -z, -ɪŋ, geɪv, 'gɪv|n, -ə*/z
give-and-take ˌgɪvən'teɪk

213

Givenchy gɪ'ventʃɪ (ʒivãʃi)
Gizeh 'gi:zeɪ [-zə]
gizzard, -s 'gɪzəd, -z
glacé 'glæseɪ
glacial 'gleɪsjəl [-sɪəl, -ʃjəl, -ʃɪəl, -ʃl, 'glæsɪəl, 'glæsjəl]
glaciation ˌglæsɪ'eɪʃn [ˌgleɪs-]
glacier, -s 'glæsjə* ['gleɪs-, -sɪə*], -z
glacis (sing.) 'glæsɪs ['glæsɪ], (plur.) 'glæsɪz
glacises (alternative plur. of glacis) 'glæsɪsɪz
glad (adj.); glad|der, -dest, -ly, -ness glæd; 'glæd|ə*, -ɪst, -lɪ, -nɪs [-nəs]
glad (v.), -s, -ding, -ded glæd, -z, -ɪŋ, -ɪd
gladd|en, -ens, -ening, -ened 'glæd|n, -nz, -ŋɪŋ [-nɪŋ], -nd
glade, -s gleɪd, -z
gladiator, -s 'glædɪeɪtə*, -z
gladiatorial ˌglædɪə'tɔːrɪəl [-djə-]
gladiole, -s 'glædɪəʊl, -z
gladiol|us, -i ˌglædɪ'əʊl|əs ['glædɪəʊl-, 'glædɪəl-, rarely glə'daɪəl-], -aɪ
gladsome, -ly, -ness 'glædsəm, -lɪ, -nɪs [-nəs]
gladstone (G.), -s 'glædstən, -z
Gladstonian glæd'stəʊnjən [-nɪən]
Glad|win, -ys 'glæd|wɪn, -ɪs
glagolitic ˌglægəʊ'lɪtɪk
glair, -eous, -y gleə*, -rɪəs, -rɪ
Glaisdale (in North Yorkshire) 'gleɪz-deɪl [locally -dl]
Glaisher 'gleɪʃə*
glaive, -s gleɪv, -z
Glamis glɑːmz
Glamorgan, -shire glə'mɔːgən, -ʃə [-ˌʃɪə*]
glamorous, -ly 'glæmərəs, -lɪ
glamour 'glæmə*
glanc|e (s. v.), -es, -ing/ly, -ed glɑːns, -ɪz, -ɪŋ/lɪ, -t
gland, -s glænd, -z
glander|s, -ed 'glændə|z ['glɑː-], -d
glandiferous glæn'dɪfərəs
glandul|ar, -ous 'glændjʊl|ə* [-dʒələ*], -əs
glandule, -s 'glændjuːl, -z
Glanvill(e) 'glænvɪl
Glapthorne 'glæpθɔːn
glar|e (s. v.), -es, -ing/ly, -ingness, -ed gleə*, -z, -rɪŋ/lɪ, -rɪŋnɪs [-nəs], -d
Glarus 'glɑːrəs
Glasgow 'glɑːzgəʊ ['glɑːsg-, 'glɑːsk-, 'glæsg-, 'glæzg-, 'glæsk-]
glasier (G.), -s 'gleɪzjə* [-zɪə*, -ʒjə*, -ʒɪə*, -ʒə*], -z
Glasneven glɑːs'nevən
glass, -es glɑːs, -ɪz

glass-blow|er/s, -ing 'glɑːsˌbləʊ|ə*/z, -ɪŋ
Glasscock (surname) 'glɑːskɒk, -kəʊ
glass-cutter, -s 'glɑːsˌkʌtə*, -z
glassful, -s 'glɑːsfʊl, -z
glass-hou|se, -ses 'glɑːshaʊ|s, -zɪz
glass-paper 'glɑːsˌpeɪpə*
glassware 'glɑːsweə*
glass-work, -s 'glɑːswɜːk, -s
glasswort 'glɑːswɜːt
glass|y, -ier, -iest, -ily, -iness 'glɑːs|ɪ, -ɪə* [-jə*], -ɪɪst [-jɪst], -ɪlɪ [-əlɪ], -ɪnɪs [-nəs]
Glastonbury 'glæstənbərɪ ['glæsn-, 'glɑːs-]
Glaswegian, -s glæz'wiːdʒən [glɑːz-, glæs-, glɑːs-, -dʒɪən, -dʒən], -z
glaucoma, -tous glɔː'kəʊmə, -təs
glaucous 'glɔːkəs
Glave gleɪv
glaz|e (s. v.), -es, -ing, -ed, -er/s gleɪz, -ɪz, -ɪŋ, -d, -ə*/z
Glazebrook 'gleɪzbrʊk
glazier, -s 'gleɪzjə* [-zɪə, -ʒjə*, -ʒɪə* -ʒə*], -z
Glazunov 'glæzuːnɒf [-zʊ-, -nɒv] (gləzu'nof)
gleam (s. v.), -s, -ing, -ed ; -y gliːm, -z, -ɪŋ, -d, -ɪ
glean, -s, -ing/s, -ed, -er/s gliːn, -z, -ɪŋ/z, -d, -ə*/z
glebe, -s gliːb, -z
glee, -s gliː, -z
glee|ful, -fully, -fulness 'gliː|fʊl, -fʊlɪ [-fəlɪ], -fʊlnɪs [-nəs]
glee|man, -men 'gliː|mən [-mæn], -mən [-men]
glee-singer, -s 'gliːˌsɪŋə*, -z
Glegg gleg
Gleichen (English surname) 'glaɪkən
Glemsford 'glemsfəd
glen (G.), -s glen, -z
Glenallan glen'ælən
Glenalmond glen'ɑːmənd
Glenavon (in Northern Ireland) glen-'ævən
Glenavy (in Northern Ireland) glen-'eɪvɪ
Glencairn glen'keən
Glencoe glen'kəʊ
Glendale glen'deɪl, 'glendeɪl
Glendin(n)ing glen'dɪnɪŋ
Glendower glen'daʊə*
Glenelg glen'elg
Glenfinnan glen'fɪnən
glengarr|y (G.), -ies glen'gær|ɪ, -ɪz
Glenlivet glen'lɪvɪt
Glenmore glen'mɔː* [-'mɔə*]

Glenrothes glen'rɒθɪs
Glenwood 'glenwʊd
glib, -ber, -best, -ly, -ness glɪb, -ə*, -ɪst,
  -lɪ, -nɪs [-nəs]
glid|e (s. v.), -es, -ing/ly, -ed, -er/s
  glaɪd, -z, -ɪŋ/lɪ, -ɪd, -ə*/z
glimmer (s. v.), -s, -ing/s, -ingly, -ed
  'glɪmə*, -z, -rɪŋ/z, -rɪŋlɪ, -d
glimps|e (s. v.), -es, -ing, -ed glɪmps, -ɪz,
  -ɪŋ, -t
glint, -s, -ing, -ed glɪnt, -s, -ɪŋ, -ɪd
glissad|e (s. v.), -es, -ing, -ed glɪ'sɑːd
  [-'seɪd], -z, -ɪŋ, -ɪd
Glisson 'glɪsn
glist|en, -ens, -ening, -ened 'glɪs|n, -nz,
  -ṇɪŋ [-nɪŋ], -nd
glitt|er (s. v.), -ers, -ering/ly, -ered
  'glɪt|ə*, -əz, -ərɪŋ/lɪ, -əd
Gloag (surname) gləʊg
gloaming 'gləʊmɪŋ
gloat, -s, -ing, -ed gləʊt, -s, -ɪŋ, -ɪd
global 'gləʊbl
globe, -s gləʊb, -z
globe-trott|er/s, -ing 'gləʊb,trɒt|ə*/z,
  -ɪŋ
globose 'gləʊbəʊs [gləʊ'b-]
globosity gləʊ'bɒsətɪ [-ɪtɪ]
globous 'gləʊbəs
globular, -ly 'glɒbjʊlə*, -lɪ
globule, -s 'glɒbjuːl, -z
glockenspiel, -s 'glɒkənʃpiːl [-spiːl], -z
gloom (s. v.), -s, -ing, -ed gluːm, -z, -ɪŋ,
  -d
gloom|y, -ier, -iest, -ily, -iness 'gluːm|ɪ,
  -ɪə* [-jə*], -ɪɪst [-jɪst], -ɪlɪ [-əlɪ],
  -ɪnɪs [-ɪnəs]
Gloria, -s 'glɔːrɪə, -z
Gloriana ˌglɔːrɪ'ɑːnə
glorification ˌglɔːrɪfɪ'keɪʃn
glori|fy, -fies, -fying, -fied, -fier/s
  'glɔːrɪ|faɪ, -faɪz, -faɪɪŋ, -faɪd, -faɪə*/z
glorious, -ly, -ness 'glɔːrɪəs, -lɪ, -nɪs
  [-nəs]
glor|y (s. v.), -ies, -ying, -ied 'glɔːr|ɪ,
  -ɪz, -ɪɪŋ, -ɪd
glory-hole, -s 'glɔːrɪhəʊl, -z
Glos. glɒs
gloss (s. v.), -es, -ing, -ed, -er/s glɒs, -ɪz,
  -ɪŋ, -t, -ə*/z
glossarial glɒ'seərɪəl
glossar|ist/s, -y, -ies 'glɒsər|ɪst/s, -ɪ,
  -ɪz
glossematic, -s ˌglɒsɪ'mætɪk, -s
glossic 'glɒsɪk
glossograph|er/s, -y glɒ'sɒgrəf|ə*/z, -ɪ
glossological ˌglɒsəʊ'lɒdʒɪkl
glossolog|ist/s, -y glɒ'sɒlədʒ|ɪst/s, -ɪ
Glossop 'glɒsəp

gloss|y, -ier, -iest, -ily, -iness 'glɒs|ɪ,
  -ɪə*, -ɪɪst, -ɪlɪ [-əlɪ], -ɪnɪs [-ɪnəs]
Gloster 'glɒstə*
glottal 'glɒtl [rarely 'gləʊtl]
glottalic glɒ'tælɪk [glə-]
glottic 'glɒtɪk
glottis, -es 'glɒtɪs, -ɪz
glottology glɒ'tɒlədʒɪ
Gloucester,   -shire   'glɒstə*   [old-
  fashioned 'glɔːs-], -ʃə* [-ˌʃɪə*]
glove, -s, -d glʌv, -z, -d
glove-fight, -s 'glʌvfaɪt, -s
glover (G.), -s 'glʌvə*, -z
glove-stretcher, -s 'glʌvˌstretʃə*, -z
gl|ow (s. v.), -ows, -owing/ly, -owed
  gl|əʊ, -əʊz, -əʊɪŋ/lɪ, -əʊd
glower, -s, -ing, -ed 'glaʊə*, -z, -rɪŋ, -d
glow-worm, -s 'gləʊwɜːm, -z
gloxinia, -s glɒk'sɪnjə [-nɪə], -z
gloz|e (s. v.), -es, -ing, -ed gləʊz, -ɪz,
  -ɪŋ, -d
Glubbdubdrib ˌglʌbdʌb'drɪb
Gluck glʊk, gluːk
glucose 'gluːkəʊs [-əʊz]
†glu|e (s. v.), -es, -ing, -ed, -er/s gluː, -z,
  -ɪŋ ['gluɪŋ], -d, -ə*/z [gluə*/z]
glue-pot, -s 'gluːpɒt, -s
gluey, -ness 'gluːɪ ['gluɪ], -nɪs [-nəs]
gluish 'gluːɪʃ ['gluɪʃ]
glum, -mer, -mest, -ly, -ness glʌm,
  -ə*, -ɪst, -lɪ, -nɪs [-nəs]
glut (s. v.), -s, -ting, -ted glʌt, -s, -ɪŋ,
  -ɪd
glut|en, -in 'gluːt|ən [-|ɪn, -|n], -ɪn
glutinous, -ly, -ness 'gluːtɪnəs [-tən-],
  -lɪ, -nɪs [-nəs]
glutton, -s 'glʌtn, -z
gluttoniz|e [-is|e], -es, -ing, -ed 'glʌtṇ-
  aɪz [-tənaɪz], -ɪz, -ɪŋ, -d
gluttonous, -ly 'glʌtṇəs [-tənəs], -lɪ
gluttony 'glʌtṇɪ [-tənɪ]
glycerine 'glɪsəriːn [ˌglɪsə'riːn, 'glɪsərɪn]
glycerol 'glɪsərɒl
glycogen 'glaɪkəʊdʒen ['glɪk-, -dʒən]
glycol 'glaɪkɒl ['glɪk-, -kl]
Glyn glɪn
Glynde (in East Sussex) glaɪnd
Glyndebourne 'glaɪndbɔːn [-bɔən]
Glynis 'glɪnɪs
Glynne glɪn
glyph, -s glɪf, -s
glyptic 'glɪptɪk
glyptography glɪp'tɒgrəfɪ
G|-man, -men 'dʒiː|mæn, -men
gnaphalium næ'feɪljəm [nə'f-, -lɪəm]
gnar, -s, -ring, -red nɑː*, -z, -rɪŋ, -d
gnarl, -s, -ed nɑːl, -z, -d
gnash, -es, -ing, -ed næʃ, -ɪz, -ɪŋ, -t

gnat, -s næt, -s
gnathic 'næθɪk
gnaw, -s, -ing, -ed, -er/s nɔː, -z, -ɪŋ, -d, -ə*/z
gneiss naɪs [gn-]
gnome (goblin), -s nəʊm, -z
gnome (maxim), -s 'nəʊmiː, -z
gnomic, -al 'nəʊmɪk, -l
gnomish 'nəʊmɪʃ
gnomon, -s 'nəʊmɒn [-mən], -z
gnomonic, -al, -ally nəʊ'mɒnɪk, -l, -əlɪ
gnos|is, -es 'nəʊs|ɪs, -iːz
Gnossall (near Stafford) 'nəʊsl
gnostic (s. adj.), -s 'nɒstɪk, -s
gnosticism 'nɒstɪsɪzəm
gnu, -s nuː [njuː], -z
go (s. v.), -es, -ing, went, gone, goer/s gəʊ, -z, -ɪŋ, went, gɒn, 'gəʊə*/z
Goa 'gəʊə
Goad gəʊd, 'gəʊəd
goad (s. v.), -s, -ing, -ed gəʊd, -z, -ɪŋ, -ɪd
go-ahead 'gəʊəhed [,--'-]
goal, -s; -keeper/s, -post/s gəʊl, -z; -,kiːpə*/z, -pəʊst/s
Goanese ,gəʊə'niːz
goat, -s gəʊt, -s
goatee, -s gəʊ'tiː: [also '-- in goatee beard], -z
goat-herd, -s 'gəʊthɜːd, -z
Goathland 'gəʊθlənd
goatish 'gəʊtɪʃ
goat's-beard, -s 'gəʊts,bɪəd, -z
goat-sucker, -s 'gəʊt,sʌkə*, -z
gob, -s gɒb, -z
gobang gəʊ'bæŋ ['gəʊb-]
gobbet, -s 'gɒbɪt, -s
gobb|le, -les, -ling, -led, -ler/s 'gɒb|l, -lz, -lɪŋ [-lɪŋ], -ld, -lə*/z [-lə*/z]
Gobbo 'gɒbəʊ
Gobelin 'gəʊbəlɪn ['gɒbəlɪn] (gɔblɛ̃)
go-between, -s 'gəʊbɪ,twiːn [-bə-], -z
Gobi 'gəʊbɪ
goblet, -s 'gɒblɪt [-lət], -s
goblin, -s 'gɒblɪn, -z
gob|y, -ies 'gəʊb|ɪ, -ɪz
go-by 'gəʊbaɪ
go-cart, -s 'gəʊkɑːt, -s
god, -s gɒd, -z
God gɒd
Godalming 'gɒdlmɪŋ
god|child, -children 'gɒd|tʃaɪld, -,tʃɪl-drən [-,tʃʊldrən, -,tʃɪldrən]
Goddard 'gɒdəd, -dɑːd
god-daughter, -s 'gɒd,dɔːtə*, -z
goddess, -es 'gɒdɪs [-des], -ɪz
Goderich 'gəʊdrɪtʃ
godetia, -s gəʊ'diːʃə [-ʃjə, -ʃɪə], -z
godfather, -s 'gɒd,fɑːðə*, -z

god-fearing 'gɒd,fɪərɪŋ
god-forsaken 'gɒdfə,seɪkən
God|free, -frey 'gɒd|frɪ, -frɪ
god-given 'gɒd,gɪvn
godhead (G.), -s 'gɒdhed, -z
Godiva gəʊ'daɪvə
Godkin 'gɒdkɪn
godless, -ly, -ness 'gɒdlɪs [-ləs, -les], -lɪ, -nɪs [-nəs]
god|ly, -ier, -iest, -iness 'gɒdl|ɪ, -ɪə* [-jə*], -ɪɪst [-jɪst], -ɪnɪs [-nəs]
Godman (surname) 'gɒdmən
God-man (Christ) ,gɒd'mæn ['--]
Godmanchester 'gɒdmən,tʃestə*
godmother, -s 'gɒd,mʌðə*, -z
Godolphin gə'dɒlfɪn
godown, -s gəʊdaʊn, -z
godparent, -s 'gɒd,peərənt, -s
God's-acre, -s 'gɒdz,eɪkə*, -z
godsend, -s 'gɒdsend, -z
godson, -s 'gɒdsʌn, -z
god-speed ,gɒd'spiːd
godward (G.) 'gɒdwəd
Godwin 'gɒdwɪn
godwit, -s 'gɒdwɪt, -s
Goethe 'gɜːtə ('gøːtə)
Goff(e) gɒf
goffer, -s, -ing, -ed 'gəʊfə*, -z, -rɪŋ, -d
Gog, -s gɒg, -z
Gogarty 'gəʊgətɪ
gogg|le (s. v.), -les, -ling, -led 'gɒg|l, -lz, -lɪŋ [-lɪŋ], -ld
goggle-eyed 'gɒglaɪd [,--'-]
Gogmagog 'gɒgməgɒg
Gogo 'gəʊgəʊ
going|s, -s-on 'gəʊɪŋ|z, -z'ɒn
goitre, -s, -d 'gɔɪtə*, -z, -d
goitrous 'gɔɪtrəs
Golby 'gəʊlbɪ
Golconda gɒl'kɒndə
gold gəʊld
gold-beater, -s 'gəʊld,biːtə*, -z
goldcrest, -s 'gəʊldkrest, -s
gold-digger, -s 'gəʊld,dɪgə*, -z
gold-dust 'gəʊld,dʌst [,gəʊld'd-]
golden 'gəʊldən
goldeneye, -s 'gəʊldənaɪ, -z
goldfield, -s 'gəʊldfiːld, -z
goldfinch, -es 'gəʊldfɪntʃ, -ɪz
goldfish, -es 'gəʊldfɪʃ, -ɪz
goldilocks (G.) 'gəʊldɪlɒks
Golding 'gəʊldɪŋ
gold-lace ,gəʊld'leɪs
gold-leaf 'gəʊldliːf [,-'-]
gold-mine, -s 'gəʊldmaɪn, -z
Goldsborough 'gəʊldzbərə

Goldschmidt (*English name*) 'gəʊldʃmɪt
goldsmith (**G.**), **-s** 'gəʊldsmɪθ, -s
goldstick, **-s** 'gəʊldstɪk, -s
gold-wire ˌgəʊld'waɪə*
golf (*s. v.*), **-s, -ing, -ed, -er/s** gɒlf [*sometimes by players* gɒf], -s, -ɪŋ, -t, -ə*/z
golf|-club/s, **-links** 'gɒlf|klʌb/z [*sometimes by players* 'gɒf-], -lɪŋks
Golgotha 'gɒlgəθə
Goliath gəʊ'laɪəθ
Golightly (*surname*) gəʊ'laɪtlɪ
Gollancz gə'lænts, gɒ'lænts, 'gɒlənts ['gɒlæŋks, gɒ'læŋks]
golliwog, **-s** 'gɒlɪwɒg, -z
golly 'gɒlɪ
golosh, **-es** gə'lɒʃ, -ɪz
Golton 'gɒltən
Gomar, **-ist/s** 'gəʊmə*, -rɪst/s
Gomersal (*in West Yorkshire*) 'gɒməsəl
Gomes 'gəʊmez
Gomme gɒm
Gomorrah gə'mɒrə
Gomshall (*in Surrey*) 'gʌmʃl ['gɒm-]
gonad, **-s** 'gəʊnæd, -z
Gondibert 'gɒndɪbɜːt
gondola, **-s** 'gɒndələ, -z
gondolier, **-s** ˌgɒndə'lɪə*, -z
gone (*from* go) gɒn
Goneril 'gɒnərɪl
gonfalon, **-s** 'gɒnfələn, -z
gong, **-s** gɒŋ, -z
Gonin 'gəʊnɪn
goniometer, **-s** ˌgəʊnɪ'ɒmɪtə* [-mətə*], -z
gonorrhea ˌgɒnə'rɪə
Gonville 'gɒnvɪl
Gooch guːtʃ
good (*s. adj.*) (**G.**), **-s, -ness** gʊd, -z, -nɪs [-nəs]
good (*interj.*) gʊd
Good|ale, **-all, -body** 'gʊd|eɪl, -ɔːl, -ˌbɒdɪ
good-bye (*s.*), **-s** ˌgʊd'baɪ, -z
good-bye (*interj.*) ˌgʊd'baɪ
Goodchild 'gʊdtʃaɪld
good day ˌgʊd'deɪ
Goode gʊd
Goodell gʊ'del
Good|enough, **-eve** 'gʊd|ɪnʌf, -iːv
good evening ˌgʊd'iːvnɪŋ
Goodfellow 'gʊdˌfeləʊ
good-for-nothing (*s. adj.*), **-s** 'gʊdfəˌnʌθɪŋ [-fɪˌnʌθɪŋ, -fˌnʌθɪŋ], -z
Goodge guːdʒ [gʊdʒ]
Goodhart 'gʊdhɑːt
good-hearted ˌgʊd'hɑːtɪd ['-ˌ-- *when attributive*]

good-humoured, **-ly** ˌgʊd'hjuːməd [*old-fashioned* -'juː, '-ˌ-- *when attributive*], -lɪ
goodish 'gʊdɪʃ
Goodliffe 'gʊdlɪf
good-looking ˌgʊd'lʊkɪŋ [*also* '-ˌ-- *according to sentence-stress*]
goodl|y, **-ier, -iest, -iness** 'gʊdl|ɪ, -ɪə* [-jə*], -ɪɪst [-jɪst], -ɪnɪs [-ɪnəs]
good|man, **-men** 'gʊd|mæn, -men
Goodman 'gʊdmən
good morning ˌgʊd'mɔːnɪŋ
good morrow ˌgʊd'mɒrəʊ
good-natured, **-ly** ˌgʊd'neɪtʃəd ['-ˌ-- *when attributive*], -lɪ
goodness 'gʊdnɪs [-nəs]
good night ˌgʊd'naɪt
Good|rich, **-sir, -son** 'gʊd|rɪtʃ, -sə*, -sn
goods-train, **-s** 'gʊdztreɪn, -z
good-tempered, **-ly** ˌgʊd'tempəd ['-ˌ-- *when attributive*], -lɪ
goodwi|fe, **-ves** 'gʊdwaɪ|f, -vz
goodwill, **-s** ˌgʊd'wɪl, -z
Good|win, **-wood** 'gʊd|wɪn, -wʊd
good|y (**G.**), **-ier, -iest, -ily, -iness** 'gʊd|ɪ, -ɪə*, -ɪɪst, -ɪlɪ [-əlɪ], -ɪnɪs [-ɪnəs]
Good|year, **-yer** 'gʊd|jɪə* [-jə*, -jɜː*], -jə*
goof|y, **-ier, -iest, -ily, -iness** 'guːf|ɪ, -ɪə*, -ɪɪst, -ɪlɪ [-əlɪ], -ɪnɪs [-ɪnəs]
Googe guːdʒ [gʊdʒ]
Googie 'guːgɪ
googly 'guːglɪ
Goole guːl
goon, **-s** guːn, -z
Goonhilly ˌguːn'hɪlɪ
goop|y, **-ier, -iest, -ily, -iness** 'guːp|ɪ, -ɪə*, -ɪɪst, -ɪlɪ [-əlɪ], -ɪnɪs [-ɪnəs]
goosander, **-s** guː'sændə*, -z
g|oose (*bird*), **-eese** g|uːs, -iːs
goose (*tailor's iron*), **-s** guːs, -ɪz
gooseberr|y, **-ies; -y-fool** 'gʊzbər|ɪ, -ɪz; (ˌgʊzbr)-ɪ'fuːl
goose|-flesh, **-grass** 'guːs|fleʃ, -grɑːs
goose-quill, **-s** 'guːskwɪl, -z
goose-step 'guːsstep
goosey, **-s** 'guːsɪ, -z
gopher, **-s** 'gəʊfə*, -z
Gophir 'gəʊfə*
Gorbachev 'gɔːbətʃɒf [ˌ--'-]
Gorboduc 'gɔːbədʌk
Gordi|an, **-um** 'gɔːdj|ən [-dɪ|ən], -əm
Gordon 'gɔːdn
Gordonstoun 'gɔːdənstən
gor|e (*s. v.*) (**G.**), **-es, -ing, -ed** gɔː* [gɔə*], -z, -rɪŋ, -d
Gorell 'gɒrəl

217

gorg|e (s. v.), -es, -ing, -ed gɔːdʒ, -ɪz, -ɪŋ, -d

gorgeous, -ly, -ness 'gɔːdʒəs, -lɪ, -nɪs [-nəs]

Gorges 'gɔːdʒɪz

gorget, -s 'gɔːdʒɪt, -s

Gorgie 'gɔːgɪ

Gorgon, -s 'gɔːgən, -z

Gorgonzola, -s ˌgɔːgənˈzəʊlə, -z

Gorham 'gɔːrəm

gorilla, -s gəˈrɪlə [gʊˈr-], -z

Goring 'gɔːrɪŋ

Gorizia gɒˈrɪtsɪə [gəˈr-]

Gorleston 'gɔːlstən

gormandiz|e [-is|e], -es, -ing, -ed, -er/s 'gɔːməndaɪz, -ɪz, -ɪŋ, -d, -ə*/z

gormless 'gɔːmlɪs [-ləs]

Gornergrat 'gɔːnəgræt

Goronwy gəˈrɒnwɪ (Welsh goˈronui)

Gorringe 'gɒrɪndʒ

gorse gɔːs

Gorst gɔːst

Gorton 'gɔːtn

gor|y, -ier, -iest, -ily, -iness 'gɔːr|ɪ, -ɪə*, -ɪɪst, -əlɪ [-ɪlɪ], -ɪnɪs [-ɪnəs]

Goschen 'gəʊʃn

gosh gɒʃ

goshawk, -s 'gɒshɔːk, -s

Goshen 'gəʊʃn

gosling (G.), -s 'gɒzlɪŋ, -z

go-slow ˌgəʊˈsləʊ ['--]

gospel (G.), -s 'gɒspl [-pel], -z

gospeller, -s 'gɒspələ*, -z

Gosport 'gɒspɔːt

gossamer 'gɒsəmə*

Gosschalk 'gɒstʃɔːk

Goss(e) gɒs

gossip (s. v.), -s, -ing, -ed; -y 'gɒsɪp, -s, -ɪŋ, -t; -ɪ

got (from get) gɒt

Göteborg 'gɜːtəbɔːg (Swedish jøːtəˈbɔrj)

Goth, -s gɒθ, -s

Gotha (in Germany) 'gəʊθə ['gəʊtə] ('gɔːtaː), (old-fashioned English spelling of Göta in Sweden) 'gəʊtə

Gotham (in Nottinghamshire) 'gəʊtəm, (in New York) 'gəʊθəm, 'gɒθəm

Gothenburg 'gɒθənbɜːg ['gɒtn-]

Gothic 'gɒθɪk

gothicism, -s 'gɒθɪsɪzəm, -z

gothiciz|e [-is|e], -es, -ing, -ed 'gɒθɪsaɪz, -ɪz, -ɪŋ, -d

Gothland 'gɒθlənd

gotten (from get) 'gɒtn

gouache gʊˈɑːʃ [gwɑːˈʃ] (gwaʃ)

Gouda (Dutch town, cheese) 'gaʊdə

Goudie 'gaʊdɪ

goug|e (s. v.), -es, -ing, -ed gaʊdʒ [guːdʒ], -ɪz, -ɪŋ, -d

Gough gɒf

goulash, -es 'guːlæʃ [-lɑːʃ], -ɪz

Goulburn (place-name) 'gəʊlbɜːn, (sur-name) 'guːlbɜːn, 'gəʊlbən

Gould guːld

Goulden 'guːldən

Goulding 'guːldɪŋ

Gounod 'guːnəʊ (guno)

gourd, -s gʊəd, -z

Gourl|ay, -ey 'gʊəl|ɪ, -ɪ

gourmand, -s 'gʊəmənd (gurmɑ̃), -z

gourmet, -s 'gʊəmeɪ (gurmɛ), -z

gout, -y, -ily, -iness gaʊt, -ɪ, -ɪlɪ [-əlɪ], -ɪnɪs [-ɪnəs]

Govan 'gʌvən

Gover 'gəʊvə*

govern, -s, -ing, -ed; -able, -ance, -ess/es 'gʌvn, -z, -ɪŋ ['gʌvn̩ɪŋ], -d; -əbl ['gʌvn̩əbl], -əns ['gʌvn̩əns], -ɪs/ɪz ['gʌvn̩ɪs/ɪz]

government, -s 'gʌvnmənt [-vn̩mənt, -vənmənt, -vəmənt], -s

governmental ˌgʌvn'mentl

governor, -s 'gʌvənə* [-vn̩ə*, -vnə*], -z

governor-general, -s ˌgʌvənə'dʒenərəl [-vn̩ə-, -vnə-], -z

governorship, -s 'gʌvənəʃɪp [-vn̩ə-, -vnə-], -s

Govey 'gʌvɪ

Govier 'gəʊvɪə*

Gow gaʊ

Gowan 'gaʊən

Gowen 'gaʊən ['gaʊɪn]

Gower 'gaʊə*, gɔː* [gɔə*]

Note.—'gaʊə* is used in Gower Street and for the place in Wales. gɔː* [gɔə*] is the family name of the Duke of Sutherland; this pro-nunciation is also used in Leveson-Gower (q.v.).

Gowing 'gaʊɪŋ

gowk, -s gaʊk, -s

gown, -s, -ed gaʊn, -z, -d

gowns|man, -men 'gaʊnz|mən, -mən [-men]

Gowrie 'gaʊərɪ

Gozo 'gəʊzəʊ

G.P., -s ˌdʒiː'piː, -z

grab (s. v.), -s, -bing, -bed, -ber/s græb, -z, -ɪŋ, -d, -ə*/z

grabb|le, -les, -ling, -led 'græb|l, -lz, -lɪŋ [-lɪŋ], -ld

Grabham 'græbəm

Gracch|us, -i 'græk|əs, -i: [-aɪ]

grac|e (s. v.) (G.), -es, -ing, -ed greɪs, -ɪz, -ɪŋ, -t

218

Gracechurch 'greɪstʃɜːtʃ
grace|ful, -fully, -fulness 'greɪs|fʊl,
　-fʊlɪ [-fəlɪ], -fʊlnɪs [-nəs]
graceless, -ly, -ness 'greɪslɪs [-ləs], -lɪ,
　-nɪs [-nəs]
grace-note, -s 'greɪsnəʊt, -s
Gracie 'greɪsɪ
gracious, -ly, -ness 'greɪʃəs, -lɪ, -nɪs
　[-nəs]
grackle, -s 'grækl, -z
gradat|e, -es, -ing, -ed grə'deɪt, -s, -ɪŋ,
　-ɪd
gradation, -s grə'deɪʃn, -z
gradational grə'deɪʃənl [-ʃn̩l, -ʃn̩l,
　-ʃənəl]
grad|e (s. v.), -es, -ing, -ed greɪd, -z, -ɪŋ,
　-ɪd
Gradgrind 'grædgraɪnd
gradient, -s 'greɪdjənt [-dɪənt], -s
gradin, -s 'greɪdɪn, -z
gradual (s. adj.), -s, -ly 'grædʒʊəl
　[-dʒwəl, -dʒʊl, -djʊəl, -djwəl, -djʊl],
　-z, -ɪ
graduate (s.), -s 'grædʒʊət [-djʊət,
　-djʊɪt, -djʊeɪt, -dʒʊɪt], -s
graduat|e (v.), -es, -ing, -ed 'grædjʊeɪt
　[-dʒʊeɪt], -s, -ɪŋ, -ɪd
graduation, -s ˌgrædʒʊ'eɪʃn [-dju-], -z
graduator, -s 'grædjʊeɪtə*, -z
gradus, -es 'grædəs ['greɪd-], -ɪz
Grady 'greɪdɪ
Graeme greɪm, 'greɪəm
graffiti grə'fiːtɪ [græ-]
graft (s. v.), -s, -ing, -ed, -er/s grɑːft,
　-s, -ɪŋ, -ɪd, -ə*/z
Grafton 'grɑːftən
Graham(e) 'greɪəm
Grahamston 'greɪəmstən
Grahamstown 'greɪəmztaun
grail (G.), -s greɪl, -z
grain (s. v.), -s, -ing, -ed, -er/s; -y
　greɪn, -z, -ɪŋ, -d, -ə*/z; -ɪ
Grainger 'greɪndʒə*
gram, -s græm, -z
gramercy grə'mɜːsɪ
graminaceous ˌgræmɪ'neɪʃəs [ˌgreɪm-]
gramineous grə'mɪnɪəs [græ'm-, greɪ-,
　-njəs]
graminivorous ˌgræmɪ'nɪvərəs
grammalogue, -s 'græməlɒg, -z
grammar, -s 'græmə*, -z
grammar-school, -s 'græməskuːl, -z
grammarian, -s grə'meərɪən, -z
†grammatic, -al, -ally grə'mætɪk, -l, -əlɪ
grammaticiz|e [-is|e], -es, -ing, -ed
　grə'mætɪsaɪz, -ɪz, -ɪŋ, -d
gramme, -s græm, -z
gramophone, -s 'græməfəʊn, -z

Grampian, -s 'græmpjən [-pɪən], -z
grampus, -es 'græmpəs, -ɪz
Granada grə'nɑːdə (gra'nada)
granar|y, -ies 'grænər|ɪ, -ɪz
Granbury 'grænbərɪ
Granby 'grænbɪ
grand; grand|er, -est, -ly, -ness grænd;
　'grænd|ə*, -ɪst, -lɪ, -nɪs ['grænnɪs,
　-nəs]
grandam, -s 'grændæm, -z
grand-aunt, -s 'grændɑːnt, -s
grand|child, -children 'græn|tʃaɪld,
　-ˌtʃɪldrən [-ˌtʃʊldrən, -ˌtʃɪldrən]
granddad, -s 'grændæd [-ndd-], -z
granddaughter, -s 'græn,dɔːtə*
　[-nd,d-], -z
grand-duchess, -es ˌgrænd'dʌtʃɪs [also
　'grænd,d-, esp. when followed by a
　stress], -ɪz
grand-duke, -s ˌgrænd'djuːk [also
　'grænd-d-, esp. when followed by a
　stress], -s
grandee, -s græn'diː, -z
grandeur 'grændʒə* [-,djʊə*, -djə*]
grandfather, -s 'grænd,fɑːðə*, -z
Grandgent 'grændʒənt
grandiloquen|ce, -t/ly græn'dɪləkwən|s
　[-lʊk-], -t/lɪ
grandiose, -ly 'grændɪəus [-djəus,
　-dɪəuz, -djəuz], -lɪ
grandiosity ˌgrændɪ'ɒsətɪ [-ɪtɪ]
Grandison 'grændɪsn
grandma, -s 'grænmɑː, -z
grandmamma, -s 'grænmə,mɑː, -z
grandmother, -s 'græn,mʌðə* [-nd,m-],
　-z
grand-nephew, -s 'græn,nevjuː [-nd,n-,
　-,nefjuː, ,-'--], -z
grand-niece, -s 'grænniːs [-ndn-, ,-'-],
　-ɪz
grandpa, -s 'grænpɑː, -z
grandpapa, -s 'grænpə,pɑː, -z
grandparent, -s 'græn,peərənt [-nd,p-],
　-s
grandsire, -s 'græn,saɪə* [-nd,s-], -z
grandson, -s 'grænsʌn [-nds-], -z
grand-stand, -s 'grændstænd, -z
grand-uncle, -s 'grænd,ʌŋkl, -z
grange (G.), -s greɪndʒ, -ɪz
Grangemouth 'greɪndʒməθ [-maʊθ]
granger (G.), -s 'greɪndʒə*, -z
grangeriz|e [-is|e], -es, -ing, -ed 'greɪn-
　dʒəraɪz, -ɪz, -ɪŋ, -d
Grange|town, -ville 'greɪndʒ|taʊn, -vɪl
granite (G.), -s 'grænɪt, -s
granitic græ'nɪtɪk [grə'n-]
grann|y, -ies 'græn|ɪ, -ɪz
granolithic ˌgrænəʊ'lɪθɪk

219

grant (*s. v.*) (**G.**), **-s, -ing, -ed** grɑːnt, -s, -ɪŋ, -ɪd

grantee, -s grɑːn'tiː, -z

Grantham (*in Lincolnshire*) 'grænθəm [*rarely* 'græntəm], (*surname*) 'grænθəm

Grantie 'grɑːntɪ

Granton 'grɑːntən ['græn-]

grantor, -s grɑːn'tɔː*, -z

Grantown 'græntaʊn

granular, -y 'grænjʊlə* [-njəl-], -rɪ

granulat|e, -es, -ing, -ed 'grænjʊleɪt [-njəl-], -s, -ɪŋ, -ɪd

granulation, -s ˌgrænjʊ'leɪʃn [-njə'l-], -z

granule, -s 'grænjuːl, -z

granul|ite, -ous 'grænjʊl|aɪt [-njəl-], -əs

Granville 'grænvɪl

grape (**G.**), -s greɪp, -s

grape-cure, -s 'greɪpˌkjʊə* [-kjɔə*, -kjɔː*], -z

grape-fruit, -s 'greɪpfruːt, -s

grape-shot 'greɪpʃɒt

grape|-stone/s, -sugar, -vine/s 'greɪp|-stəʊn/z, -ˌʃʊgə*, -vaɪn/z

graph, -s grɑːf [græf], -s

graphic (**G.**), -s, -al, -ally 'græfɪk, -s, -l, -əlɪ

graphite 'græfaɪt ['greɪf-]

graphology græ'fɒlədʒɪ

graphometer, -s græ'fɒmɪtə* [-mətə*], -z

grapnel, -s 'græpnl, -z

grapp|le, -les, -ling, -led, -ler/s 'græp|l, -lz, -lɪŋ [-lɪŋ], -ld, -lə*/z [-lə*/z]

grappling-iron, -s 'græplɪŋˌaɪən [-plɪŋ-], -z

grapy 'greɪpɪ

Grasmere 'grɑːsˌmɪə*

grasp (*s. v.*), -s, -ing/ly, -ed, -er/s; -able grɑːsp, -s, -ɪŋ/lɪ, -t, -ə*/z; -əbl

grass (*s. v.*), -es, -ing, -ed grɑːs, -ɪz, -ɪŋ, -t

grass-cutter, -s 'grɑːsˌkʌtə*, -z

grass-green ˌgrɑːs'griːn ['grɑːsˌg-]

grasshopper, -s 'grɑːsˌhɒpə*, -z

grass-land 'grɑːslænd [-lənd]

grass-plot, -s ˌgrɑːs'plɒt ['--], -s

grass-root (*adj.*), -s (*s.*) ˌgrɑːs'ruːt ['-- *when attributive*], -s

grass-wid|ow/s, -ower/s ˌgrɑːs-'wɪd|əʊ/z, -əʊə*/z

grass|y, -ier, -iest 'grɑːs|ɪ, -ɪə* [-jə*], -ɪɪst [-jɪst]

grata (*in* persona grata) 'grɑːtə [*old-fashioned* 'greɪtə]

grat|e (*s. v.*), -es, -ing/ly, -ed, -er/s greɪt, -s, -ɪŋ/lɪ, -ɪd, -ə*/z

grate|ful, -fully, -fulness 'greɪt|fʊl, -fʊlɪ [-fəlɪ], -fʊlnɪs [-nəs]

Gratian 'greɪʃjən [-ʃɪən]

Gratiano (*Shakespearian character*) ˌgræʃɪ'ɑːnəʊ [ˌgrɑː-]

gratification, -s ˌgrætɪfɪ'keɪʃn, -z

grati|fy, -fies, -fying, -fied, -fier/s 'grætɪ|faɪ, -faɪz, -faɪɪŋ, -faɪd, -faɪə*/z

gratin 'grætæ̃ŋ [-tæn] (gratɛ̃)

grating (*s.*), -s 'greɪtɪŋ, -z

Gratiot (*in U.S.A.*) 'græʃɪət [-ʃjət, 'greɪʃ-]

gratis 'greɪtɪs ['grɑːtɪs, 'grætɪs]

gratitude 'grætɪtjuːd

Grattan 'grætn

gratuitous, -ly, -ness grə'tjuːɪtəs [-'tjʊɪ-], -lɪ, -nɪs [-nəs]

gratuit|y, -ies grə'tjuːət|ɪ [-'tjʊə-, -ɪt|ɪ], -ɪz

gravam|en, -ina grə'veɪm|en, -ɪnə

grave (*accent above a letter*) grɑːv

grav|e (*s. adj. v.*) (*other senses*), -es; -er, -est, -ely, -eness; -ing, -ed, -en, -er/s greɪv, -z; -ə*, -ɪst, -lɪ, -nɪs [-nəs]; -ɪŋ, -d, -n, -ə*/z

grave|-clothes, -digger/s 'greɪv|kləʊðz [*old-fashioned* -kləʊz], -ˌdɪgə*/z

grav|el (*s. v.*), -els, -elling, -elled, -elly 'græv|l, -lz, -lɪŋ [-əlɪŋ], -ld, -lɪ [-əlɪ]

gravel|-pit/s, -walk/s 'grævl|pɪt/s (ˌgrævl) -'wɔːk/s

graven (*from* grave v.) 'greɪvn

Graves (*surname*) greɪvz, (*wine*) grɑːv

Gravesend ˌgreɪvz'end [-v'zend]

grave|-stone/s, -yard/s 'greɪv|stəʊn/z, -jɑːd/z

graving-dock, -s 'greɪvɪŋdɒk, -s

gravitas 'grævɪtæs

gravitat|e, -es, -ing, -ed 'grævɪteɪt, -s, -ɪŋ, -ɪd

gravitation ˌgrævɪ'teɪʃn

gravity 'grævətɪ [-ɪtɪ]

gravure grə'vjʊə* [-'vjɔə*, -'vjɔː*]

grav|y, -ies 'greɪv|ɪ, -ɪz

gravy-spoon, -s 'greɪvɪspuːn, -z

gray (*s. adj.*) (**G.**), -s, -er, -est, -ness greɪ, -z, -ə* [greə*], -ɪst, 'greɪnɪs [-nəs]

graybeard, -s 'greɪˌbɪəd, -z

gray-eyed 'greɪaɪd [ˌ-'- *when not attributive*]

gray-haired ˌgreɪ'heəd ['-- *when attributive*]

gray-headed ˌgreɪ'hedɪd ['-ˌ-- *when attributive*]

grayish 'greɪɪʃ

grayling, -s 'greɪlɪŋ, -z

Grayson 'greɪsn

graystone 'greɪstəʊn
graz|e, -es, -ing, -ed greɪz, -ɪz, -ɪŋ, -d
grazier, -s 'greɪzjə* [-zɪə*, -ʒjə*, -ʒɪə*, -ʒə*], -z
grease (s.), -s griːs, -ɪz
greas|e (v.), -es, -ing, -ed, -er/s griːz [griːs], -ɪz ['griːsɪz], -ɪŋ ['griːsɪŋ], griːzd [griːst], -ə*/z
grease-paint 'griːspeɪnt
greaseproof 'griːspruːf
grease-trap, -s 'griːstræp, -s
greas|y, -ier, -iest, -ily, -iness 'griːz|ɪ ['griːs|ɪ], -ɪə* [-jə*], -ɪɪst [-jɪst], -ɪlɪ [-əlɪ], -ɪnɪs [-məs]
Note.—Some people use the forms 'griːsɪ and 'griːzɪ with a difference of meaning, 'griːsɪ having reference merely to the presence of grease and 'griːzɪ having reference to slipperiness caused by grease.
great, -er, -est, -ly, -ness greɪt, -ə*, -ɪst, -lɪ, -nɪs [-nəs]
great-aunt, -s ˌgreɪt'ɑːnt ['--], -s
great-coat, -s 'greɪtkəʊt, -s
great-grand|child, -children ˌgreɪt-'græn|tʃaɪld, -ˌtʃɪldrən [-ˌtʃʊldrən, -ˌtʃldrən]
great-granddaughter, -s ˌgreɪt'græn-ˌdɔːtə* [-nd,d-], -z
great-grandfather, -s ˌgreɪt'grænd-ˌfɑːðə*, -z
great-grandmother, -s ˌgreɪt'græn-ˌmʌðə* [-nd,m-], -z
great-grandparent, -s ˌgreɪt'grænd-ˌpeərənt, -s
great-grandson, -s ˌgreɪt'grænsʌn [-nds-], -z
Greatham (in Durham) 'griːtəm, (in Northamptonshire and West Sussex) 'gretəm
Greathead 'greɪthed
Greatheart 'greɪthɑːt
great-hearted ˌgreɪt'hɑːtɪd [also '-ˌ--, esp. when attributive]
Greatorex 'greɪtəreks
Greats greɪts
great-uncle, -s ˌgreɪt'ʌŋkl ['-ˌ--], -z
greave, -s griːv, -z
Greaves griːvz, greɪvz
grebe, -s griːb, -z
Grecian, -s 'griːʃn, -z
Grec|ism, -ize 'griːs|ɪzm, -aɪz
Greco-Roman ˌgrekəʊ'rəʊmən [ˌgriːk-]
Greece griːs
greed, -y, -ier, -iest, -ily, -iness griːd, -ɪ, -ɪə* [-jə*], -ɪɪst [-jɪst], -ɪlɪ [-əlɪ], -ɪnɪs [-məs]
Greek, -s griːk, -s

Greel(e)y 'griːlɪ
green (s. adj. v.), -s; -er, -est, -ly, -ness; -ing, -ed griːn, -z; -ə*, -ɪst, -lɪ, -nɪs [-nəs]; -ɪŋ, -d
Green(e) griːn
Greenall 'griːnɔːl
Greenaway 'griːnəweɪ
greenery 'griːnərɪ
green-eyed 'griːnaɪd [ˌ-'- when not attributive]
Greenfield 'griːnfiːld
greenfinch, -es 'griːnfɪntʃ, -ɪz
greenfly 'griːnflaɪ
Greenford 'griːnfəd
greengage, -s 'griːngeɪdʒ ['griːŋg-, also -'-, according to sentence-stress], -ɪz
greengrocer, -s 'griːnˌgrəʊsə* [-iːŋˌg-], -z
Greenhalgh 'griːnhælʃ, -hældʒ, -hɔː
Green|haulgh, -hill 'griːn|hɔː, -hɪl
Greenhithe 'griːnhaɪð
greenhou|se, -ses 'griːnhaʊ|s, -zɪz
greenish (G.), -ness 'griːnɪʃ, -nɪs [-nəs]
Greenland (country), -er/s 'griːnlənd [-lænd], -ə*/z
Greenland (surname) 'griːnlænd
Greenleaf 'griːnliːf
Greenock 'griːnək ['grɪn-, 'gren-]
Greenore griː'nɔː* [-'nɔə*]
Greenough 'griːnəʊ
Green|point, -port 'griːn|pɔɪnt, -pɔːt
green-room, -s 'griːnrʊm [-ruːm], -z
greensand 'griːnsænd
greenshank, -s 'griːnʃæŋk, -s
Greenslade 'griːnsleɪd
Greensleeves 'griːnsliːvz
greenstone 'griːnstəʊn
greensward 'griːnswɔːd
Green|ville, -well 'griːn|vɪl, -wəl [-wel]
Greenwich 'grenɪdʒ ['grɪn-, -ɪtʃ]
greenwood (G.), -s 'griːnwʊd, -z
greet (G.), -s, -ing/s, -ed griːt, -s, -ɪŋ/z, -ɪd
Greetland 'griːtlənd
Greg(g) greg
gregarious, -ly, -ness grɪ'geərɪəs [grə'g-, gre'g-], -lɪ, -nɪs [-nəs]
Gregorian, -s grɪ'gɔːrɪən [grə'g-, gre'g-]
Gregory, -powder 'gregərɪ, -ˌpaʊdə*
Greig greg
gremlin, -s 'gremlɪn, -z
Grenada grə'neɪdə [grɪ'n-, gre'n-]
grenade, -s grə'neɪd [grɪ'n-, gre'n-], -z
grenadier (G.), -s ˌgrenə'dɪə*, -z
grenadin(e) (textile), -s 'grenədɪn, -z

221

grenadine 'grenədi:n [ˌgrenə'di:n]
Grenadines ˌgrenə'di:nz
Grendel 'grendl
Gren|fell, -ville 'gren|fel [-fl], -vɪl
Gresham 'greʃəm
Gres|ley, -well 'grez|lɪ, -wəl
Greta (*English name*) 'gri:tə, 'gretə, 'greɪtə
Gretel (*German name*) 'gretl ('gre:təl)
Gretna 'gretnə
Greuze, -s grɜ:z (grø:z), -ɪz
Greville 'grevɪl [-vl]
grew (*from* **grow**) (**G.**) gru:
grey (*s. adj.*) (**G.**), **-s, -er, -est, -ness** greɪ, -z, -ə* [greə*], -ɪst, 'greɪnɪs [-nəs]
greybeard, -s 'greɪˌbɪəd, -z
greycoat (**G.**), **-s** 'greɪkəʊt, -s
grey-eyed 'greɪaɪd [ˌ-'- *when not attributive*]
grey-haired ˌgreɪ'heəd ['-- *when attributive*]
grey-headed ˌgreɪ'hedɪd ['-ˌ-- *when attributive*]
greyhound, -s 'greɪhaʊnd, -z
greyish 'greɪɪʃ
Grey|lock, son 'greɪ|lɒk, -sn
gribble (**G.**), **-s** 'grɪbl, -z
Grice graɪs
grid, -s grɪd, -z
griddle, -s 'grɪdl, -z
gridiron, -s 'grɪdˌaɪən, -z
Gridley 'grɪdlɪ
grief, -s gri:f, -z
Grieg (*Norwegian composer*) gri:g
Grierson 'grɪəsn
grievance, -s 'gri:vns, -ɪz
griev|e, -es, -ing, -ed, -er/s gri:v, -z, -ɪŋ, -d, -ə*/z
grievous, -ly, -ness 'gri:vəs, -lɪ, -nɪs [-nəs]
griffin (**G.**), **-s** 'grɪfɪn, -z
Griffith, -s 'grɪfɪθ, -s
grig, -s grɪg, -z
Grigg, -s grɪg, -z
Grildrig 'grɪldrɪg
grill (*s. v.*), **-s, -ing, -ed, -er/s** grɪl, -z, -ɪŋ, -d, -ə*/z
grillage, -s 'grɪlɪdʒ, -ɪz
grille, -s grɪl, -z
grill-room, -s 'grɪlrʊm [-ru:m], -z
grilse grɪls
grim, -mer, -mest, -ly, -ness grɪm, -ə*, -ɪst, -lɪ, -nɪs [-nəs]
grimac|e (*s. v.*), **-es, -ing, -ed** grɪ'meɪs ['grɪməs], -ɪz, -ɪŋ, -t
Grimald 'grɪməld
grimalkin, -s grɪ'mælkɪn [-'mɔ:l-], -z

grim|e (*s. v.*), **-es, -ing, -ed** graɪm, -z, -ɪŋ, -d
Grimes graɪmz
Grimm grɪm
Grimond 'grɪmənd
Grimsby 'grɪmzbɪ
Grimsel 'grɪmzl
Grim|shaw, -wig 'grɪm|ʃɔ:, -wɪg
grim|y, -ier, -iest, -ily, -iness 'graɪm|ɪ, -ɪə* [-jə*], -ɪɪst [-jɪst], -ɪlɪ [-əlɪ], -ɪnɪs [-nəs]
grin (*s. v.*), **-s, -ning, -ned** grɪn, -z, -ɪŋ, -d
grind (*s. v.*), **-s, -ing, ground, grinder/s** graɪnd, -z, -ɪŋ, graʊnd, 'graɪndə*/z
Grindal 'grɪndəl
Grindelwald 'grɪndlvɑ:ld
grindery 'graɪndərɪ
Grindon 'grɪndən
grindstone, -s 'graɪndstəʊn, -z
Grinnell grɪ'nel
Grinstead 'grɪnstɪd [-sted]
grip (*s. v.*), **-s, -ping, -ped** grɪp, -s, -ɪŋ, -t
grip|e (*s. v.*), **-es, -ing, -ed** graɪp, -s, -ɪŋ, -t
gripes (*s.*) graɪps
grippe grɪp [gri:p] (grip)
gripsack, -s 'grɪpsæk, -s
grisaille grɪ'zeɪl [gri:'zaɪ, grɪ-, -'zaɪl] (grizɑ:j)
Griscom 'grɪskəm
Griselda grɪ'zeldə
grisette, -s grɪ:'zet, -s
Grisewood 'graɪzwʊd
griskin 'grɪskɪn
grisl|y, -ier, -iest, -iness 'grɪzl|ɪ, -ɪə*, -ɪɪst, -ɪnɪs [-nəs]
Grisons 'gri:zɔ̃:ŋ [-zɔ:ŋ, -zɒŋ] (grizɔ̃)
grist grɪst
gristle 'grɪsl
gristly 'grɪsl|ɪ [-slɪ]
Griswold 'grɪzwəʊld
grit, -s; -stone grɪt, -s; -stəʊn
Gritton 'grɪtn
gritt|y, -ier, -iest, -ily, -iness 'grɪt|ɪ, -ɪə*, -ɪɪst, -ɪlɪ [-əlɪ], -ɪnɪs [-nəs]
Grizel grɪ'zel
grizzle, -d 'grɪzl, -d
grizzl|y (*s. adj.*), **-ies** 'grɪzl|ɪ, -ɪz
groan (*s. v.*), **-s, -ing/s, -ed** grəʊn, -z, -ɪŋ/z, -d
groat (*coin*), **-s** grəʊt, -s
groats (*grain*) grəʊts
Grobian, -s 'grəʊbjən [-bɪən], -z
grocer, -s 'grəʊsə*, -z
grocer|y, -ies 'grəʊsər|ɪ, -ɪz
Grocott 'grɒkət

Grocyn 'grəʊsɪn
grog grɒg
grogg|y, -ier, -iest, -ily, -iness 'grɒg|ɪ,
  -ɪə*, -ɪɪst, -ɪlɪ [-əlɪ], -ɪnɪs [-ɪnəs]
grogram 'grɒgrəm
grog-shop, -s 'grɒgʃɒp, -s
groin, -s grɔɪn, -z
gromwell 'grɒmwəl [-wel]
Grongar 'grɒŋgə*
groom (s. v.), -s, -ing, -ed gru:m
  [grʊm], -z, -ɪŋ, -d
grooms|man, -men 'gru:mz|mən,
  ['grʊmz-] -mən [-men]
groov|e (s. v.), -es, -ing, -ed gru:v, -z,
  -ɪŋ, -d
groov|y, -ier, -iest, -iness 'gru:v|ɪ, -ɪə*
  [-jə*], -ɪɪst [-jɪst], -ɪnɪs [-ɪnəs]
grop|e, -es, -ing/ly, -ed, -er/s grəʊp, -s,
  -ɪŋ/lɪ, -t, -ə*/z
Grosart 'grəʊzɑ:t
grosbeak, -s 'grəʊsbi:k ['grɒs-, 'grɒz-],
  -s
groschen 'grəʊʃn ['grɒʃ-]
Grose grəʊs, grəʊz
Grosmont (in North Yorkshire) 'grəʊ-
  mənt [-mɒnt, locally also 'grəʊs-
  mənt], (in Gwent) 'grɒsmənt
gross (s. adj.), -er, -est, -ly, -ness
  grəʊs, -ə*, -ɪst, -lɪ, -nɪs [-nəs]
Gross (surname) grɒs, grəʊs
Grossmith 'grəʊsmɪθ
Grosvenor 'grəʊvnə*
Grote grəʊt
grotesque, -ly, -ness grəʊ'tesk, -lɪ, -nɪs
  [-nəs]
grotto, -s 'grɒtəʊ, -z
ground (s. v.) (all senses), -s, -ing, -ed,
  -er/s graʊnd, -z, -ɪŋ, -ɪd, -ə*/z
ground (from grind) graʊnd
groundage 'graʊndɪdʒ
ground-ash ˌgraʊnd'æʃ
ground-bass, -es ˌgraʊnd'beɪs, -ɪz
groundcover 'graʊndˌkʌvə*
ground-floor ˌgraʊnd'flɔ:* [-'flɔə*]
ground-hog, -s ˌgraʊnd'hɒg ['--], -z
ground-ivy 'graʊndˌaɪvɪ [ˌ-'--]
groundless, -ly, -ness 'graʊndlɪs [-ləs],
  -lɪ, -nɪs [-nəs]
groundling, -s 'graʊndlɪŋ, -z
ground|-man, -men 'graʊnd|mæn
  [-mən], -men [-mən]
ground-nut, -s 'graʊndnʌt, -s
ground-plan, -s ˌgraʊnd'plæn ['--], -z
ground-rent, -s 'graʊndrent, -s
groundsel 'graʊnsl
grounds|man, -men 'graʊndz|mən
  [-mæn], -mən [-men]
ground-swell, -s 'graʊndswel, -z

groundwork 'graʊndwɜ:k
group (s. v.), -s, -ing/s, -ed gru:p, -s,
  -ɪŋ/z, -t
grous|e (s. v.) (G.), -es, -ing, -ed, -er/s
  graʊs, -ɪz, -ɪŋ, -t, -ə*/z
grove (G.), -s grəʊv, -z
grov|el, -els, -elling, -elled, -eller/s
  'grɒv|l ['grʌv-], -lz, -lɪŋ [-lɪŋ], -ld,
  -lə*/z [-lə*/z]
Grover 'grəʊvə*
gr|ow, -ows, -owing, grew, gr|own,
  -ower/s gr|əʊ, -əʊz, -əʊɪŋ, gru:,
  gr|əʊn, -əʊə*/z
growl (s. v.), -s, -ing, -ed, -er/s graʊl,
  -z, -ɪŋ, -d, -ə*/z
grown-up (s.), -s 'grəʊnʌp [ˌgrəʊn'ʌp],
  -s
grown-up (adj.) ˌgrəʊn'ʌp ['--]
growth, -s grəʊθ, -s
groyne, -s grɔɪn, -z
grub (s. v.), -s, -bing, -bed, -ber/s grʌb,
  -z, -ɪŋ, -d, -ə*/z
grubb|y, -ier, -iest, -iness 'grʌb|ɪ, -ɪə*,
  -ɪɪst, -ɪnɪs [-ɪnəs]
grudg|e (s. v.), -es, -ing/ly, -ed grʌdʒ,
  -ɪz, -ɪŋ/lɪ, -d
gruel grʊəl ['gru:əl]
gruelling (s. adj.), -s 'grʊəlɪŋ ['gru:əl-],
  -z
Gruenther (American surname)
  'grʌnθə*
gruesome, -ly, -ness 'gru:səm, -lɪ, -nɪs
  [-nəs]
gruff, -er, -est, -ly, -ness grʌf, -ə*, -ɪst,
  -lɪ, -nɪs [-nəs]
grumb|le, -les, -ling, -led, -ler/s
  'grʌmb|l, -lz, -lɪŋ, -ld, -lə*/z
grump|y, -ier, -iest, -ily, -iness
  'grʌmp|ɪ, -ɪə* [-jə*], -ɪɪst [-jɪst], -ɪlɪ
  [-əlɪ], -ɪnɪs [-ɪnəs]
Grundig 'grʊndɪg
Grundtvig (English surname) 'grʊntvɪg
Grundy 'grʌndɪ
grunt (s. v.), -s, -ing, -ed, -er/s grʌnt,
  -s, -ɪŋ, -ɪd, -ə*/z
Gruyère 'gru:jeə* [-jə*] (gryjɛ:r)
gryphon, -s 'grɪfn, -z
Guadalquivir ˌgwɑ:dəlkɪ'vɪə* [ˌgwɑ:-
  dl'kwɪvə*] (gwadalki'bir)
Guadeloupe ˌgwɑ:də'lu:p
Guaira 'gwaɪərə
guano, -s 'gwɑ:nəʊ [gju:'ɑ:nəʊ,
  gjʊ'ɑ:], -z
Guarani, -s ˌgwɑ:rə'ni:, -z
guarantee (s. v.), -s, -ing, -d ˌgærən'ti:,
  -z, -ɪŋ, -d
guarantor, -s ˌgærən'tɔ:* [gə'ræntɔ:*],
  -z

223

guarant|y, -ies 'gærənt|ɪ, -ɪz
guard (s. v.) (G.), -s, -ing, -ed/ly,
  -edness gɑːd, -z, -ɪŋ, -ɪd/lɪ, -ɪdnɪs
  [-nəs]
guardian (G.), -s; -ship 'gɑːdjən
  [-dɪən], -z; -ʃɪp
guardrail, -s 'gɑːdɾeɪl, -z
guard-room, -s 'gɑːdrʊm [-ruːm], -z
guard-ship, -s 'gɑːdʃɪp, -s
guards|man, -men 'gɑːdz|mən [-mæn],
  -mən [-men]
Guarner|i, -ius/es gwɑːˈnɪər|ɪ, -ɪəs/ɪz
Guatemala, -n/s ˌgwɑːtəˈmɑːlə [ˌgwæt-,
  -tɪ-], -n/z
guava, -s 'gwɑːvə, -z
Guayaquil ˌgwaɪəˈkiːl [-ˈkɪl]
Guayra (old-fashioned spelling of
  Guaira) 'gwaɪərə
Gubbins 'gʌbɪnz
gudgeon, -s 'gʌdʒən, -z
Gudrun 'gʊdruːn [gʊˈd-]
Gue gjuː
Guedalla gwɪˈdælə [gweˈd-, gwəˈd-]
guelder-rose, -s ˌgeldəˈrəʊz, -ɪz
Guelph gwelf
guerdon, -s 'gɜːdən, -z
guerilla gəˈrɪlə [gjə-]
guernsey (G.), -s 'gɜːnzɪ, -z
guerrilla, -s gəˈrɪlə [gjə-], -z
guess (s. v.), -es, -ing, -ed, -er/s; -able,
  -work ges, -ɪz, -ɪŋ, -t, -ə*/z; -əbl,
  -wɜːk
guest (G.), -s gest, -s
guest-chamber, -s 'gestˌtʃeɪmbə*, -z
guest-hou|se, -ses 'gesthaʊ|s, -zɪz
guest-night, -s 'gestnaɪt, -s
guest-room, -s 'gestrʊm [-ruːm], -z
guest-towel, -s 'gestˌtaʊəl [-taʊl], -z
guffaw (s. v.), -s, -ing, -ed gʌˈfɔː [gəˈf-],
  -z, -ɪŋ, -d
Guggenheim 'gʊgənhaɪm ['guː-]
Guggisberg (English surname) 'gʌgɪs-
  bəːg
Guiana gaɪˈænə [old-fashioned British
  pronunciation gɪˈɑːnə]
Guianese ˌgaɪəˈniːz
guid|e (s. v.), -es, -ing, -ed; -ance
  gaɪd, -z, -ɪŋ, -ɪd; -ns
guide-book, -s 'gaɪdbʊk, -s
guide-post, -s 'gaɪdpəʊst, -s
guide-rail, -s 'gaɪdreɪl, -z
guide-rope, -s 'gaɪdrəʊp, -s
Guido 'gwiːdəʊ
guidon, -s 'gaɪdən, -z
guild, -s gɪld, -z
Guildenstern 'gɪldənstɜːn
guilder, -s 'gɪldə*, -z
Guildford 'gɪlfəd

guildhall (G.), -s ˌgɪldˈhɔːl [also '--, esp.
  when attributive], -z
Guilding 'gɪldɪŋ
guile gaɪl
guile|ful, -fully, -fulness 'gaɪl|fʊl, -fʊlɪ
  [-fəlɪ], -fʊlnɪs [-nəs]
guileless, -ly, -ness 'gaɪllɪs [-ləs], -lɪ,
  -nɪs [-nəs]
Guilford 'gɪlfəd
Guillamore 'gɪləmɔː* [-mɔə*]
Guillebaud (English surname) 'giːlbəʊ,
  'gɪlɪbəʊ
guillemot, -s 'gɪlɪmɒt, -s
Guillim 'gwɪlɪm
guillotin|e (s. v.), -es, -ing, -ed ˌgɪləˈtiːn
  ['gɪlət-], -z, -ɪŋ, -d
  Note.—Some people use '--- for the
  noun and ˌ--'- for the verb.
guilt, -y, -ier, -iest, -ily, -iness gɪlt, -ɪ,
  -ɪə* [-jə*], -ɪɪst [-jɪst], -ɪlɪ [-əlɪ], -ɪnɪs
  [-ɪnəs]
guiltless, -ly, -ness 'gɪltlɪs [-ləs], -lɪ,
  -nɪs [-nəs]
guinea (G.), -s 'gɪnɪ, -z
guinea|-corn, -fowl/s, -pig/s 'gɪnɪ|-
  kɔːn, -faʊl/z, -pɪg/z
Guinevere ˌgwɪnɪˌvɪə* ['gɪn-]
Guinness 'gɪnɪs, gɪˈnes
  Note.—The beer is called 'gɪnɪs.
Guisborough (in Cleveland) 'gɪzbərə
guise, -s gaɪz, -ɪz
Guise giːz [gwiːz] (gɥiːz, giːz)
Guiseley 'gaɪzlɪ
guitar, -s gɪˈtɑː*, -z
guitarist, -s gɪˈtɑːrɪst, -s
Guiver 'gaɪvə*
Gujarat ˌguːdʒəˈrɑːt [ˌgʊdʒ-] (Hindi
  gwɪrat)
Gujarati ˌguːdʒəˈrɑːtɪ [ˌgʊdʒ-] (Hindi
  gwɪrati)
Gulbenkian gʊlˈbeŋkɪən [-kjən]
gulch (s. v.), -es gʌlʃ, -ɪz
gulden, -s 'gʊldən ['guː-l], -z
gules gjuːlz
gulf, -s; -y gʌlf, -s; -ɪ
gull (s. v.) (G.), -s, -ing, -ed gʌl, -z, -ɪŋ,
  -d
gull-catcher, -s 'gʌlˌkætʃə*, -z
guller|y, -ies 'gʌlər|ɪ, -ɪz
gullet, -s 'gʌlɪt [-lət], -s
gullibility ˌgʌləˈbɪlətɪ [-lɪˈb-, -lɪt-]
gullible 'gʌləbl [-lɪb-]
Gulliver 'gʌlɪvə*
gull|y (G.), -ies 'gʌl|ɪ, -ɪz
gulp (s. v.), -s, -ing, -ed gʌlp, -s, -ɪŋ, -t
gum (s. v.) (all senses), -s, -ming, -med,
  -mer/s gʌm, -z, -ɪŋ, -d, -ə*/z
gumboil, -s 'gʌmbɔɪl, -z

Gummere 'gʌmərɪ
Gummidge 'gʌmɪdʒ
gumm|y (s. adj.), -ies, -ier, -iest, -iness
  'gʌm|ɪ, -ɪz, -ɪə*, -ɪɪst, -ɪnɪs [-ɪnəs]
gumption 'gʌmpʃn
gum-tree, -s 'gʌmtri:, -z
gun (s. v.), -s, -ning, -ned, -ner/s gʌn,
  -z, -ɪŋ, -d, -ə*/z
gun|-barrel/s, -boat/s, -carriage/s,
  -case/s, -cotton 'gʌn|ˌbærəl/z,
  -bəʊt/s, -ˌkærɪdʒ/ɪz, -keɪs/ɪz, -ˌkɒtn
Gunby Hadath ˌgʌnbɪ'hædəθ
gun-drill 'gʌndrɪl
gun-fire 'gʌnˌfaɪə*
gun|man, -men 'gʌn|mən [-mæn],
  -mən [-men]
gun-metal 'gʌnˌmetl
gunnel, -s 'gʌnl, -z
Gunner 'gʌnə*
Gunnersbury 'gʌnəzbərɪ
gunnery 'gʌnərɪ
Gunning 'gʌnɪŋ
Gunnison 'gʌnɪsn
gunny 'gʌnɪ
gunpowder 'gʌnˌpaʊdə*
gun-room, -s 'gʌnrʊm [-ru:m], -z
gun-runn|er/s, -ing 'gʌnˌrʌn|ə*/z, -ɪŋ
gunshot, -s 'gʌnʃɒt, -s
gunsmith, -s 'gʌnsmɪθ, -s
gun-stock, -s 'gʌnstɒk, -s
Gunt|er, -ram 'gʌnt|ə*, -rəm
gunwale, -s 'gʌnl, -z
Gupta 'gʊptə (Hindi gwpta)
gurg|le (s. v.), -les, -ling, -led 'gɜ:g|l,
  -lz, -lɪŋ, -ld
Gurkha, -s 'gɜ:kə ['gʊək-], -z
Gurley 'gɜ:lɪ
Gurnall 'gɜ:nl
gurnard (G.), -s 'gɜ:nəd, -z
gurnet, -s 'gɜ:nɪt, -s
Gur|ney, -ton 'gɜ:|nɪ, -tn
guru, -s 'gʊru: ['gu:r-, 'gʊər-] (Hindi
  gwru), -z
Gus gʌs
gush (s. v.), -es, -ing/ly, -ed, -er/s gʌʃ,
  -ɪz, -ɪŋ/lɪ, -t, -ə*/z
Gushington 'gʌʃɪŋtən
gusset, -s 'gʌsɪt, -s
Guss|ie, -y 'gʌs|ɪ, -ɪ
gust, -s gʌst, -s
gustation gʌ'steɪʃn
gustatory 'gʌstətərɪ [gʌ'steɪtərɪ]
Gustavus gʊ'stɑ:vəs [gʌ's-]
gusto 'gʌstəʊ
gust|y, -ier, -iest, -ily, -iness 'gʌst|ɪ,
  -ɪə* [-jə*], -ɪɪst [-jɪst], -ɪlɪ [-əlɪ],
  -ɪnɪs [-ɪnəs]
gut (s. v.), -s, -ting, -ted gʌt, -s, -ɪŋ, -ɪd

Gutenberg 'gu:tnbɜ:g
Guthrie 'gʌθrɪ
gutta-percha ˌgʌtə'pɜ:tʃə
gutter (s. v.), -s, -ing, -ed 'gʌtə*, -z,
  -rɪŋ, -d
guttersnipe, -s 'gʌtəsnaɪp, -s
guttur|al (s. adj.), -als, -ally 'gʌtər|əl,
  -əlz, -əlɪ
guy (G.), -s gaɪ, -z
†Guyana gaɪ'ænə
Guyda (Christian name) 'gaɪdə
Guy Fawkes ˌgaɪ'fɔ:ks ['--]
Guysborough 'gaɪzbərə
Guzman (character in Kingsley's 'West-
  ward Ho!') 'gʌzmən ['gʊzm-, 'gʊθ-
  mɑ:n]
guzz|le, -les, -ling, -led, -ler/s 'gʌz|l,
  -lz, -lɪŋ [-lɪŋ], -ld, -lə*/z [-lə*/z]
Gwalia 'gwɑ:ljə [-lɪə]
Gwalior 'gwɑ:lɔ:* [-ljɔ:*] (Hindi
  gvalyər)
Gwatkin 'gwɒtkɪn
Gwen gwen
Gwendo|len, -line, -lyn 'gwendə|lɪn, -lɪn
  [-li:n], -lɪn
Gwent gwent
Gwinear 'gwɪnɪə*
Gwinnett gwɪ'net
Gwladys 'glædɪs (Welsh 'gwladɪs)
Gwrych gʊ'ri:k [-'ri:x] (Welsh gwri:x)
Gwydyr 'gwɪdɪə* [-də*] (Welsh 'gwɨdir)
Gwynedd 'gwɪnəð
gwyniad, -s 'gwɪnɪæd, -z
Gwyn(ne) gwɪn
gyb|e, -es, -ing, -ed dʒaɪb, -z, -ɪŋ, -d
Gye dʒaɪ, gaɪ
Gyges 'gaɪdʒi:z
Gyle (surname) gaɪl
gym dʒɪm
gymkhana, -s dʒɪm'kɑ:nə, -z
gymnasium, -s dʒɪm'neɪzjəm [-zɪəm],
  -z
gymnast, -s 'dʒɪmnæst, -s
gymnastic, -s, -al, -ally dʒɪm'næstɪk, -s,
  -l, -əlɪ
gymnosophist, -s dʒɪm'nɒsəfɪst, -s
Gympie 'gɪmpɪ
gynaecological ˌgaɪnəkə'lɒdʒɪkl [-nɪk-,
  -ni:k-]
gynaecolog|ist/s, -y ˌgaɪnə'kɒlədʒ|ɪst/s
  [-nɪ'k-, -ni:'k-], -ɪ
Gyngell 'gɪndʒəl
gyp, -s dʒɪp, -s
Gyp (nickname) dʒɪp, (French novelist) ʒi:p
  (ʒip)
gyps|eous, -ous 'dʒɪps|ɪəs [-jəs], -əs
gypsophila, -s dʒɪp'sɒfɪlə, -z
gypsum 'dʒɪpsəm

225

gyps|y, -ies 'dʒɪps|ɪ, -ɪz
gyrate (adj.) 'dʒaɪərət ['dʒaɪəreɪt, -rɪt]
gyrat|e (v.), -es, -ing, -ed ˌdʒaɪə'reɪt, -s, -ɪŋ, -ɪd
gyration, -s ˌdʒaɪə'reɪʃn, -z
gyratory 'dʒaɪərətərɪ [ˌdʒaɪə'reɪtərɪ]
gyr|e (s. v.), -es, -ing, -ed 'dʒaɪə*, -z, -rɪŋ, -d
gyre falcon, -s 'dʒɜː:ˌfɔːlkən [-ˌfɔːkən], -z
gyro-compass, -es 'dʒaɪərəuˌkʌmpəs, -ɪz

gyrodine, -s 'dʒaɪərəudaɪn, -z
gyromagnetic ˌdʒaɪrəumæg'netɪk [-məg-]
gyromancy 'dʒaɪərəumænsɪ
gyron, -s 'dʒaɪərən [-rɒn], -z
gyroscope, -s 'dʒaɪərəskəup ['gaɪə], -s
gyroscopic ˌdʒaɪərə'skɒpɪk [ˌgaɪə-]
gyrosin, -s 'dʒaɪərəuzɪn, -z
gyrostat, -s 'dʒaɪərəustæt ['gaɪə-], -s
gyrostatic, -s ˌdʒaɪərəu'stætɪk [ˌgaɪə-], -s
gyv|e, -es, -ing, -ed dʒaɪv, -z, -ɪŋ, -d

H

H (*the letter*), **-'s** eɪtʃ, -ɪz
ha hɑː
Haakon 'hɔːkɒn ['hɑːk-, -kən]
Haarlem 'hɑːləm [-lem]
Habakkuk 'hæbəkək [-kʌk, hə'bækək]
Habberton 'hæbətən
habeas corpus ˌheɪbjəs'kɔːpəs [-bɪəs-, -bɪæs-]
habendum hə'bendəm [hæ'b-]
haberdasher, -s, -y 'hæbədæʃə*, -z, -ɪɪ
habergeon, -s 'hæbədʒən, -z
Habershon 'hæbəʃn
habiliment, -s hə'bɪlɪmənt [hæ'b-, *also occasionally* ə'b- *when not initial*], -s
habilitat|e, -es, -ing, -ed, -or/s hə'bɪlɪteɪt [hæ'b-, -lə-], -s, -ɪɪ, -ɪd, -ə*/z
habilitation həˌbɪlɪ'teɪʃn [hæˌb-, -lə-]
Habington 'hæbɪɪtən
habit (*s. v.*), **-s, -ing, -ed** 'hæbɪt, -s, -ɪɪ, -ɪd
habitab|le, -ly, -leness 'hæbɪtəb|l, -lɪ, -lnɪs [-nəs]
habitant (*inhabitant*), **-s** 'hæbɪtənt, -s
habitant (*Canadian*), **-s** 'hæbɪtɔ̃ːɲ ['æb-, -tɒɲ] (abitɑ̃), -z
habitat, -s 'hæbɪtæt, -s
habitation, -s ˌhæbɪ'teɪʃn, -z
habitual, -ly hə'bɪtʃʊəl [hæ'b-, -tjwəl, -tjʊl, -tjʊəl, -tʃwəl, -tʃʊl], -ɪ
habituat|e, -es, -ing, -ed hə'bɪtʃʊeɪt [hæ'b-, -tjʊeɪt], -s, -ɪɪ, -ɪd
habitude, -s 'hæbɪtjuːd, -z
habitué, -s hə'bɪtjʊeɪ [hæ'b-, *also occasionally* ə'b- *when not initial*] (abitɥe), -z
Habsburg 'hæpsbɜːg
hachures hæ'ʃjʊə* [-'ʃʊə*]
hacienda, -s ˌhæsɪ'endə, -z
hack (*s. v.*) (**H.**), **-s, -ing, -ed, -er/s** hæk, -s, -ɪɪ, -t, -ə*/z
hackberr|y, -ies 'hækber|ɪ [-bər|ɪ], -ɪz
hacker|y, -ies 'hækər|ɪ, -ɪz
Hackett 'hækɪt
hack|le (*s. v.*), **-les, -ling, -led** 'hæk|l, -lz, -lɪɪ [-lɪɪ]
hackney (*s. v.*) (**H.**), **-s, -ing, -ed** 'hæknɪ, -z, -ɪɪ ['hæknjɪɪ], -d
hacksaw, -s 'hæksɔː, -z
hackwork 'hækwɜːk

had (*from* have) hæd (*strong form*), həd, əd, d (*weak forms*)
Hadad 'heɪdæd
Hadadezer ˌhæd ə'diːzə*
Hadar (*star*) 'heɪdɑː*
Hadath 'hædəθ
Haddington 'hædɪɲtən
haddock (**H.**), **-s** 'hædək, -s
Haddon 'hædn
had|e, -es, -ing, -ed heɪd, -z, -ɪɪ, -ɪd
Haden 'heɪdn
Hades 'heɪdiːz
Hadfield 'hædfiːld
hadji, -s 'hædʒiː, -z
Had|leigh, -ley, -low 'hæd|lɪ, -lɪ, -ləʊ
hadn't 'hædnt [*also* 'hædn *when not final*]
Hadow 'hædəʊ
Hadrian 'heɪdrɪən
hadst hædst (*strong form*), hədst, ədst (*weak forms*)
Hadubrand 'hædʊbrænd
haemal 'hiːml
haematite 'hiːmətaɪt ['hem-]
haemoglobin ˌhiːməʊ'gləʊbɪn
haemophili|a, -ac ˌhiːməʊ'fɪlɪ|ə, -æk
haemorrhage, -s 'hemərɪdʒ, -ɪz
haemorrhoid, -s 'hemərɔɪd, -z
Haes (*English surname*) heɪz
hafnium 'hæfnɪəm [-njəm]
haft, -s hɑːft, -s
hag, -s hæg, -s
Hagar (*biblical name*) 'heɪgɑː* [-gə*], (*modern personal name*) 'heɪgə*
Hagarene, -s 'hægəriːn [ˌ--'-, ˌheɪgɑː-'riːn], -z
Hagerstown 'heɪgəztaʊn
Haggada(h) hæ'gʌdə [-'gɒd-]
Haggai 'hægeɪaɪ [-gɪaɪ, -gaɪ, hæ'geɪaɪ]
haggard (**H.**), **-est** 'hægəd, -ɪst
Hagger, -ston 'hægə*, -stən
haggis, -es 'hægɪs, -ɪz
haggish, -ly, -ness 'hægɪʃ, -lɪ, -nɪs [-nəs]
hagg|le, -les, -ling, -led, -ler/s 'hæg|l, -lz, -lɪɪ [-lɪɪ], -ld, -lə*/z [-lə*/z]
hagio|grapher/s, -graphy ˌhægɪ-'ɒ|grəfə*/z, -grəfɪ
hagiolatry ˌhægɪ'ɒlətrɪ

227

hagiolog|ist/s, -y ˌhægɪˈɒlədʒ|ɪst/s, -ɪ
hagioscope, -s ˈhægɪəskəʊp [-gjəs-], -s
Hague heɪg
hag-weed ˈhægwiːd
ha-ha (interj.) hɑːˈhɑː [ˈ--]
ha-ha (sunken fence), -s ˈhɑːhɑː:, -z
Haifa ˈhaɪfə
Haig heɪg
Haigh heɪg, heɪ
hail (s. v. interj.), -s, -ing, -ed; -y heɪl,
-z, -ɪŋ, -d; -ɪ
Hailes heɪlz
Haile Selassie ˌhaɪlɪsɪˈlæsɪ [-səˈl-]
Haileybury ˈheɪlɪbərɪ
hail-fellow, -s ˈheɪlˌfeləʊ, -z
hail-fellow-well-met ˈheɪlˌfeləʊˌwel-
ˈmet
Hailsham ˈheɪlʃəm
hailstone, -s ˈheɪlstəʊn, -z
hailstorm, -s ˈheɪlstɔːm, -z
Hainan ˌhaɪˈnæn
Hainault (forest) ˈheɪnɔːt [-nɔːlt, -nɒlt]
Hainhault ˈheɪnɔːlt
hair, -s heə*, -z
hair-breadth, -s ˈheəbretθ [-bredθ], -s
hairbrush, -es ˈheəbrʌʃ, -ɪz
haircloth ˈheəklɒθ [old-fashioned -klɔːθ]
haircut, -s ˈheəkʌt, -s
haircutt|er/s, -ing ˈheəˌkʌt|ə*/z, -ɪŋ
hair-do, -s ˈheədu:, -z
hairdress|er/s, -ing ˈheəˌdresə*/z, -ɪŋ
hair-dye, -s ˈheədaɪ, -z
hairgrass ˈheəgrɑːs
hairgrip, -s ˈheəgrɪp, -s
hairless ˈheəlɪs [-ləs]
hair-line, -s ˈheəlaɪn, -z
hair-net, -s ˈheənet, -s
hair-oil ˈheərɔɪl [ˈheəɔɪl]
hairpiece, -s ˈheəpiːs, -ɪz
hairpin, -s ˈheəpɪn, -z
hair-raising ˈheəˌreɪzɪŋ
hair's-breadth, -s ˈheəzbretθ [-bredθ],
-s
hair-shirt, -s ˌheəˈʃɜːt [ˈ--], -s
hair-slide, -s ˈheəslaɪd, -z
hair-space, -s ˈheəspeɪs, -ɪz
hair-splitting ˈheəˌsplɪtɪŋ
hair-spring, -s ˈheəsprɪŋ, -z
hair-stroke, -s ˈheəstrəʊk, -s
hair|y, -ier, -iest, -ily, -iness ˈheər|ɪ,
-ɪə*, -ɪɪst, -əlɪ [-ɪlɪ], -ɪnɪs [-ɪnəs]
Haiti ˈheɪtɪ
Haitian, -s ˈheɪʃn [-ʃɪən, -ʃjən, ˈheɪtjən,
-tɪən], -z
hake, -s heɪk, -s
Hakluyt ˈhæklu:t
Hakodate ˌhækəʊˈdɑːtɪ
Hal hæl

Halakah hæˈlʌkə
halation, -s həˈleɪʃn [hæˈl-], -z
halberd, -s ˈhælbɜːd [ˈhɔːl-, -bəd], -z
halberdier, -s ˌhælbəˈdɪə*, -z
halcyon, -s ˈhælsɪən [-sjən], -z
Halcyone hælˈsaɪənɪ
Hald|ane, -on ˈhɔːld|eɪn [ˈhɒl-], -ən
hal|e (adj. v.) (H.), -er, -est; -es, -ing,
-ed heɪl, -ə*, -ɪst; -z, -ɪŋ, -d
Hales, -worth heɪlz, -wɜːθ
hal|f, -ves hɑː|f, -vz
    Note 1.—Words not entered below
    which are formed by prefixing half-
    to a partic. have double stress, e.g.
    half-done ˌhɑːfˈdʌn, half-ashamed
    ˌhɑːfəˈʃeɪmd, half-dressed ˌhɑːfˈ-
    ˈdrest.
    Note 2.—Half past, in half past ten,
    half past eleven, etc., is pro-
    nounced ˌhɑːpəs(t) by some:
    ˌhɑːpəs ˈten, ˌhɑːpəst ɪˈlevn, etc.
half a crown ˌhɑːfəˈkraʊn [also ˈ--
    according to sentence-stress]
half a dozen ˌhɑːfəˈdʌzn [also ˈ-ˌ--
    according to sentence-stress]
half and half ˌhɑːfənd'hɑːf
half-back, -s ˈhɑːfbæk, -s
half-baked ˌhɑːfˈbeɪkt [ˈ--]
half-binding ˈhɑːfˌbaɪndɪŋ
half-blood ˈhɑːfblʌd
half-bound ˌhɑːfˈbaʊnd [ˈ--]
half-bred ˈhɑːfbred
half|-breed/s, -brother/s, -caste/s
    ˈhɑːf|briːd/z, -ˌbrʌðə*/z, -kɑːst/s
half-crown, -s ˌhɑːfˈkraʊn, -z
half-dozen, -s ˌhɑːfˈdʌzn [also ˈ-ˌ--
    according to sentence-stress], -z
half-hardy ˌhɑːfˈhɑːdɪ [also ˈ-ˌ-- when
    attributive]
half-hearted ˌhɑːfˈhɑːtɪd [ˈ-ˌ--, esp.
    when attributive]
half-hearted|ly, -ness ˌhɑːfˈhɑːtɪd|lɪ,
    -nɪs [-nəs]
half-holiday, -s ˌhɑːfˈhɒlədeɪ [-lɪd-, -dɪ],
    -z
half-hose ˌhɑːfˈhəʊz [ˈ--]
half-hour, -s ˌhɑːfˈaʊə* [also ˈ--
    according to sentence-stress], -z
half-hourly ˌhɑːfˈaʊəlɪ
half-length, -s ˌhɑːfˈleŋθ [-ŋkθ, ˈ--], -s
half-mast ˌhɑːfˈmɑːst
half-measure, -s ˌhɑːfˈmeʒə* [ˈ-ˌ--], -z
half-moon, -s ˌhɑːfˈmuːn, -z
half-mourning ˌhɑːfˈmɔːnɪŋ [-ˈmɔən-]
half-nelson ˌhɑːfˈnelsn
Halford ˈhɔːlfəd [ˈhɒl-], ˈhæl-
half-pay ˌhɑːfˈpeɪ
halfpence (pre-decimalisation) ˈheɪpəns

228

halfpenn|y, -ies; -yworth/s 'heɪpn|ɪ
[-pn̩|ɪ, -pən|ɪ], -ɪz; -ɪwɜːθ/s [-wəθ/s,
'heɪpəθ/s] (*pre-decimalisation*)
Halfpenny 'hɑːfpenɪ [-pənɪ]
half-plate, -s 'hɑːfpleɪt, -s
half-price ˌhɑːf'praɪs [*also* '— *according
to sentence-stress*]
half-seas-over ˌhɑːfsiːz'əʊvə*
half-shift, -s ˌhɑːf'ʃɪft ['--], -s
half-sister, -s 'hɑːfˌsɪstə*, -z
half-size ˌhɑːf'saɪz [*also* '— *when
attributive*]
half-sovereign, -s ˌhɑːf'sɒvrɪn, -z
half-tide ˌhɑːf'taɪd ['--]
half-time, -r/s ˌhɑːf'taɪm, -ə*/z
half-tint, -s 'hɑːftɪnt, -s
half-tone, -s 'hɑːftəʊn, -z
half-tru|th, -ths 'hɑːftruː|θ, -ðz
half-volley, -s ˌhɑːf'vɒlɪ, -z
half-way ˌhɑːf'weɪ [*also* '— *according to
sentence-stress*]
half-witted ˌhɑːf'wɪtɪd [*also* '-ˌ-- *when
attributive*]
half-year, -s ˌhɑːf'jɪə* [-'jɜː*], -z
half-yearly ˌhɑːf'jɪəlɪ [-'jɜːlɪ]
Haliburton 'hælɪbɜːtn
halibut 'hælɪbət [-bʌt]
Halicarnassus ˌhælɪkɑː'næsəs
halidom 'hælɪdəm
Halidon 'hælɪdən
Halifax 'hælɪfæks
halitosis ˌhælɪ'təʊsɪs
Halkett 'hɔːlkɪt, 'hælkɪt, 'hækɪt
hall (H.), -s hɔːl, -z
Hallam 'hæləm
Hallé 'hæleɪ [-lɪ]
hallelujah (H.), -s ˌhælɪ'luːjə, -z
Haller 'hælə*
Halley 'hælɪ [*rarely* 'hɔːlɪ]
halliard = halyard
Halli|day, -well 'hælɪ|deɪ, -wəl [-wel]
hall-mark (s. v.), -s, -ing, -ed 'hɔːl-
mɑːk [ˌ-'-], -s, -ɪŋ, -t
hallo(a) hə'ləʊ [hæ'ləʊ]
halloo (s. v. interj.), -s, -ing, -ed hə'luː
[hæ'l-], -z, -ɪŋ, -d
hall|ow, -ows, -owing, -owed 'hæl|əʊ,
-əʊz, -əʊɪŋ, -əʊd
Hallowe'en ˌhæləʊ'iːn
Hallowmas, -es 'hæləʊmæs [-məs], -ɪz
Hallows 'hæləʊz
hall-stand, -s 'hɔːlstænd, -z
hallucination, -s həˌluː'sɪ'neɪʃn [-ˌljuː-],
-z
hallucinatory hə'luː'sɪnətərɪ [-'ljuː-,
həˌluː'sɪ'neɪtərɪ]
halm, -s hɑːm, -z
halma 'hælmə

halo (s.), -(e)s 'heɪləʊ, -z
hall|o (v.), -oes, -oing, -oed 'heɪl|əʊ,
-əʊz, -əʊɪŋ, -əʊd
Halpine 'hælpɪn
Hals (*Dutch artist*), -es hæls [hælz],
-ɪz
Halsbury 'hɔːlzbərɪ ['hɒl-]
Halsey 'hɔːlsɪ, 'hɔːlzɪ, 'hælzɪ
Halstead 'hɔːlsted ['hɒl-, -stɪd], 'hæl-
halt (s. adj. v.), -s, -ing/ly, -ed hɔːlt
[hɒlt], -s, -ɪŋ/lɪ, -ɪd
halter, -s 'hɔːltə* ['hɒl-], -z
halv|e, -es, -ing, -ed hɑːv, -z, -ɪŋ, -d
halves (*plur. of* half) hɑːvz
halyard, -s 'hæljəd, -z
Halys 'heɪlɪs
ham (H.), -s hæm, -z
hamadryad, -s ˌhæmə'draɪəd [-'draɪæd],
-z
Haman (*biblical name*) 'heɪmæn [-mən],
(*modern surname*) 'heɪmən
Hamar 'heɪmɑː*
Hamath 'heɪmæθ
Hamble, -den, -don, -ton 'hæmbl, -dən,
-dən, -tən
Hamblin 'hæmblɪn
Hambourg 'hæmbɔːg [-ˌbʊəg]
Hambro 'hæmbrəʊ [-brə]
Hamburg 'hæmbɜːg
hamburger, -s 'hæmbɜːgə*, -z
hamburg(h), -s 'hæmbɜːə, -z
Hamelin 'hæmɪlɪn
Hamerton 'hæmətən
ham-fisted ˌhæm'fɪstɪd
ham-handed ˌhæmˌhændɪd [ˌ-'--]
Hamilcar hæ'mɪlkɑː* [hə'm-, 'hæmɪl-]
Hamilton 'hæmɪltən [-məl-, -mɪl-]
Hamiltonian ˌhæml'təʊnjən [-məl-,
-mɪl-, -nɪən]
Hamish 'heɪmɪʃ
Hamite, -s 'hæmaɪt, -s
Hamitic hæ'mɪtɪk [hə'm-]
hamlet (H.), -s 'hæmlɪt [-lət], -s
Haml|ey, -in 'hæml|ɪ, -ɪn
hammam, -s 'hæmæm [-məm,
hə'mɑːm, 'hʌmʌm], -z
hammer (s. v.) (H.), -s, -ing, -ed
'hæmə*, -z, -rɪŋ, -d
hammer-blow, -s 'hæməbləʊ, -z
Hammerfest 'hæməfest
hammer-head, -s 'hæməhed, -z
Hammersmith 'hæməsmɪθ
hammock, -s 'hæmək, -s
Ham(m)ond 'hæmənd
Hammurabi ˌhæmʊ'rɑːbɪ
Hampden 'hæmpdən, 'hæmdən
hamper (s. v.), -s, -ing, -ed 'hæmpə*, -z,
-rɪŋ, -d

Hampshire 'hæmpʃə* [-ˌʃɪə*]
Hamp|stead, -ton 'hæmp|stɪd [-sted], -tən
Hamshaw 'hæmʃɔ:
hamster, -s 'hæmstə*, -z
hamstring (s. v.), -s, -ing, -ed, hamstrung 'hæmstrɪŋ, -z, -ɪŋ, -d, 'hæmstrʌŋ
hamza, -s 'hæmzə, -z
Han (Chinese dynasty) hæn
Hanan 'hænən
Hananiah ˌhænə'naɪə
Hanbury 'hænbərɪ
Hancock 'hænkɒk ['hæŋ-]
hand (s. v.) (H.), -s; hand|ing, -ed, -er/s hænd, -z; 'hænd|ɪŋ, -ɪd, -ə*/z
hand|-bag/s, -barrow/s, -bell/s, -bill/s, -book/s, -brake/s, -cart/s 'hænd|-bæg/z, -ˌbærəʊ/z, -bel/z, -bɪl/z, -bʊk/s, -breɪk/s, -kɑ:t/s
Handcock 'hændkɒk
handcuff (s. v.), -s, -ing, -ed 'hændkʌf ['hæŋk-], -s, -ɪŋ, -t
Handel 'hændl
Handelian hæn'di:ljən [-lɪən]
handful, -s hændfʊl, -z
hand-glass, -es 'hændglɑ:s, -ɪz
hand-grenade, -s 'hændgrəˌneɪd [-grɪˌn-, -greˌn-], -z
handgrip, -s 'hændgrɪp, -s
handhold, -s 'hændhəʊld, -z
handicap (s. v.), -s, -ping, -ped, -per/s 'hændɪkæp, -s, -ɪŋ, -t, -ə*/z
handi|craft/s, -work 'hændɪ|krɑ:ft/s, -wɜ:k
handkerchief, -s 'hæŋkətʃɪf [-tʃəf], -s
Note.—There exists also a pronunciation 'hæŋkətʃi:f with a plur. -tʃi:fs or -tʃi:vz.
hand|le (s. v.), -les, -ling, -led, -ler/s 'hænd|l, -lz, -lɪŋ [-lɪŋ], -ld, -lə*/z [-lə*/z]
handle-bar, -s 'hændlbɑ:*, -z
handless 'hændlɪs [-ləs]
Handley 'hændlɪ
hand|-line/s, -loom/s 'hænd|laɪn/z, -lu:m/z
hand-made ˌhænd'meɪd [also '— when attributive]
hand-maid, -s, -en/s 'hændmeɪd, -z, -n/z
hand-out, -s 'hændaʊt, -s
hand-rail, -s 'hændreɪl, -z
Hands hændz
hand-screen, -s 'hændskri:n, -z
handsel = hansel
handshake, -s 'hændʃeɪk, -s

handsome, -r, -st, -ly, -ness 'hænsəm [-ntsəm], -ə*, -ɪst, -lɪ, -nɪs [-nəs]
handwork 'hændwɜ:k
hand-worked ˌhænd'wɜ:kt ['—]
handwriting, -s 'hændˌraɪtɪŋ, -z
hand|y, -ier, -iest, -ily, -iness 'hænd|ɪ, -ɪə* [-jə*], -ɪɪst [-jɪst], -ɪlɪ [-əlɪ], -ɪnɪs [-ɪnəs]
handy-man, -men 'hændɪmæn [-mən], -men
hang, -s, -ing/s, -ed, hung, hanger/s hæŋ, -z, -ɪŋ/z, -d, hʌŋ, 'hæŋə*/z
hangar, -s 'hæŋə* [-ŋgə*], -z
hang-dog (s. adj.), -s 'hæŋdɒg, -z
Hanger 'hæŋə*
hanger-on, hangers-on ˌhæŋər'ɒn, ˌhæŋəz'ɒn
hang|man, -men 'hæŋ|mən, -mən
hang-nail, -s 'hæŋneɪl, -z
hang-over, -s 'hæŋˌəʊvə*, -z
hank, -s hæŋk, -s
hank|er, -ers, -ering, -ered 'hæŋk|ə*, -əz, -ərɪŋ, -əd
Hankow ˌhæn'kaʊ [ˌhæŋ'k-]
hank|y, -ies 'hæŋk|ɪ, -ɪz
hanky-panky ˌhæŋkɪ'pæŋkɪ ['—ˌ—]
Hanley 'hænlɪ
Hannah 'hænə
Hann|ay, -en 'hæn|eɪ, -ən
Hannibal 'hænɪbl
Hannington 'hænɪŋtən
Hanoi hæ'nɔɪ
Hanover 'hænəʊvə* (ha'no:fər)
Hanoverian, -s ˌhænəʊ'vɪərɪən, -z
Hansa 'hænsə [-nzə]
Hansard 'hænsɑ:d [-səd]
Hanse, -s hæns, -ɪz
Hanseatic ˌhænsɪ'ætɪk [-nzt-]
hans|el, -els, -elling, -elled 'hæns|l, -lz, -əlɪŋ [-lɪŋ], -ld
Hänsel (German name) 'hænsl ('henzəl)
Hans|ell, -on 'hæns|l, -n
hansom (H.), -s; -cab/s 'hænsəm, -z; -kæb/z
Hants hænts
Han|way, -well 'hæn|weɪ, -wəl [-wel]
hap (s. v.), -s, -ping, -ped hæp, -s, -ɪŋ, -t
haphazard ˌhæp'hæzəd
hapless, -ly, -ness 'hæplɪs [-ləs], -lɪ, -nɪs [-nəs]
haply 'hæplɪ
hap'orth, -s 'heɪpəθ, -s
happ|en, -ens, -ening/s -ened 'hæp|ən, -ənz, -ŋ̩ɪŋ/z [-ənɪŋ/z, -nɪŋ/z], -ənd
Happisburgh (in Norfolk) 'heɪzbərə
happ|y, -ier, -iest, -ily, -iness 'hæp|ɪ, -ɪə*, -ɪɪst, -ɪlɪ [-əlɪ], -ɪnɪs [-ɪnəs]

happy-go-lucky ˌhæpɪgəʊˈlʌkɪ [ˈ—ˌ—]
Hapsburg ˈhæpsbɜːg
hara-kiri ˌhærəˈkɪrɪ
harangu|e (s. v.), **-es, -ing, -ed, -er/s**
    həˈræŋ, -z, -ɪŋ, -d, -ə*/z
harass, -es, -ing, -ed, -er/s, -ment
    ˈhærəs, -ɪz, -ɪŋ, -t, -ə*/z, -mənt
Harben ˈhɑːbən
Harberton ˈhɑːbətən
harbinger, -s ˈhɑːbɪndʒə*, -z
Harborough ˈhɑːbərə
harb|our (s. v.), **-ours, -ouring, -oured,
    -ourer/s; -ourage, -ourless** ˈhɑːb|ə*,
    -əz, -ərɪŋ, -əd, -ərə*/z; -ərɪdʒ, -əlɪs
    [-ləs]
harbour-master, -s ˈhɑːbəˌmɑːstə*, -z
Harcourt ˈhɑːkət [-kɔːt]
hard (H.), **-er, -est, -ly, -ness** hɑːd, -ə*,
    -ɪst, -lɪ, -nɪs [-nəs]
hardbake (s.) ˈhɑːdbeɪk
hard-baked ˌhɑːdˈbeɪkt [ˈ—]
hard-bitten ˌhɑːdˈbɪtn [ˈ—]
hardboard ˈhɑːdbɔːd [-bɔəd]
hard-boiled ˌhɑːdˈbɔɪld [ˈ— when attri-
    butive]
Hardcastle ˈhɑːdˌkɑːsl
hard-earned ˌhɑːdˈɜːnd [also ˈ— when
    attributive]
hard|en (H.), **-ens, -ening, -ened**
    ˈhɑːd|n, -nz, -nɪŋ [-nɪŋ], -nd
hard-featured ˌhɑːdˈfiːtʃəd [ˈ-ˌ—]
hard-fought ˌhɑːdˈfɔːt [ˈ—]
hard-grained ˌhɑːdˈgreɪnd [ˈ—]
hard-headed ˌhɑːdˈhedɪd [also ˈ-ˌ—
    according to sentence-stress]
hard-hearted, -ly, -ness ˌhɑːdˈhɑːtɪd
    [also ˈ-ˌ— according to sentence-stress],
    -lɪ, -nɪs
Hardicanute ˈhɑːdɪkənjuːt [ˌhɑːdɪkəˈn-]
hardihood ˈhɑːdɪhʊd
Harding(e) ˈhɑːdɪŋ
hard|ish, -ly ˈhɑːd|ɪʃ, -lɪ
Hardres hɑːdz
Hardress ˈhɑːdres [-drɪs]
hardship, -s ˈhɑːdʃɪp, -s
hard-up ˌhɑːdˈʌp
hardware ˈhɑːdweə*
Hardwick(e) ˈhɑːdwɪk
hardwood ˈhɑːdwʊd
hard|y (H.), **-ier, -iest, -ily, -iness,
    -ihood** ˈhɑːd|ɪ, -ɪə* [-jə*], -ɪɪst [-jɪst],
    -ɪlɪ [-əlɪ], -ɪnɪs [-nəs], -ɪhʊd
hare (H.), **-s; -bell/s, -brained** heə*,
    -z; -bel/z, -breɪnd
harelip, -s -ped ˌheəˈlɪp [ˈ—], -s, -t
harem, -s ˈhɑːriːm [-rem, həˈriːm,
    hɑːˈriːm, ˈheərəm], -z
Harenc (surname) ˈhʌrɒŋ

hare's-foot ˈheəzfʊt
Harewood ˈhɑːwʊd, ˈheəwʊd
    Note.—The Earl of Harewood pro-
    nounces ˈhɑːwʊd, and his house is
    called ˌhɑːwʊd ˈhaʊs. The village
    in West Yorkshire is now gener-
    ally pronounced ˈheəwʊd, though
    ˈhɑːwʊd may sometimes be heard
    from very old people there. Other
    people with the surname **Harewood**
    pronounce ˈheəwʊd.
Har|ford, -graves ˈhɑː|fəd, -greɪvz
Hargreaves ˈhɑːgriːvz, -greɪvz
haricot, -s ˈhærɪkəʊ, -z
Haringey ˈhærɪŋgeɪ
Harington ˈhærɪŋtən
hark (v. interj.), **-s, -ing, -ed** hɑːk, -s,
    -ɪŋ, -t
Harlaw ˈhɑːlɔː [hɑːˈlɔː]
Harlech ˈhɑːlek [-lex]
Harleian hɑːˈliːən [-ˈlɪən, ˈhɑːlɪən, esp.
    when attributive]
Harlem ˈhɑːləm [-lem]
harlequin, -s ˈhɑːlɪkwɪn [-lək-], -z
harlequinade, -s ˌhɑːlɪkwɪˈneɪd [-lək-],
    -z
Harlesden ˈhɑːlzdən
Harley ˈhɑːlɪ
Harlock ˈhɑːlɒk
harlot, -s, -ry ˈhɑːlət, -s, -rɪ
Harlow(e) ˈhɑːləʊ
harm (s. v.), **-s, -ing, -ed** hɑːm, -z, -ɪŋ,
    -d
Harman ˈhɑːmən
Harmer ˈhɑːmə*
harm|ful, -fully, -fulness ˈhɑːm|fʊl,
    -fʊlɪ [-fəlɪ], -fʊlnɪs [-nəs]
harmless, -ly, -ness ˈhɑːmlɪs [-ləs], -lɪ,
    -nɪs [-nəs]
Harmonia hɑːˈməʊnjə [-nɪə]
harmonic (s. adj.), **-s, -al, -ally**
    hɑːˈmɒnɪk, -s, -l, -əlɪ
harmonic|a/s, -on/s hɑːˈmɒnɪk|ə/z,
    -ən/z
harmonious, -ly, -ness hɑːˈməʊnjəs
    [-nɪəs], -lɪ, -nɪs [-nəs]
harmonist, -s ˈhɑːmənɪst, -s
harmonium, -s hɑːˈməʊnjəm [-nɪəm],
    -z
harmonization [-isa-], **-s** ˌhɑːmənaɪ-
    ˈzeɪʃn, -z
harmoniz|e [-is|e], **-es, -ing, -ed, -er/s**
    ˈhɑːmənaɪz, -ɪz, -ɪŋ, -d, -ə*/z
harmon|y, -ies ˈhɑːmən|ɪ, -ɪz
Harmsworth ˈhɑːmzwəθ [-wɜː θ]
Harnack ˈhɑːnæk
harness (s. v.) (H.), **-es, -ing, -ed, -er/s**
    ˈhɑːnɪs, -ɪz, -ɪŋ, -t, -ə*/z

231

Harold ˈhærəld
Harosheth ˈhærəʊʃeθ
harp (s. v.), -s, -ing, -ed, -er/s hɑːp, -s, -ɪŋ, -t, -ə*/z
Harpenden ˈhɑːpəndən
Harper ˈhɑːpə*
Harpham ˈhɑːpəm
harpist, -s ˈhɑːpɪst, -s
Harpocration ˌhɑːpəʊˈkreɪʃjən [-ʃɪən]
harpoon (s. v.), -s, -ing, -ed, -er/s hɑːˈpuːn, -z, -ɪŋ, -d, -ə*/z
harpsichord, -s ˈhɑːpsɪkɔːd, -z
harp|y, -ies ˈhɑːp|ɪ, -ɪz
harquebus, -es ˈhɑːkwɪbəs, -ɪz
Harraden ˈhærədən [-den]
Harrap ˈhærəp
harridan, -s ˈhærɪdən, -z
Harrie ˈhærɪ
harrier, -s ˈhærɪə*, -z
Harr|ies, -iet ˈhær|ɪs, -ɪət
Harri|man, -ngton ˈhærɪ|mən, -ŋtən
Harriot ˈhærɪət
Harris, -on ˈhærɪs, -n
Harrisson ˈhærɪsn
Harrod, -s ˈhærəd, -z
Harrogate ˈhærəʊgɪt [-geɪt, -gət]
Harrop ˈhærəp
Harrovian, -s həˈrəʊvjən [hæˈr-, -vɪən], -z
harr|ow (s. v.) (H.), -ows, -owing/ly, -owed ˈhær|əʊ, -əʊz, -əʊɪŋ/lɪ, -əʊd
Harrowby ˈhærəʊbɪ
harr|y (H.), -ies, -ying, -ied ˈhær|ɪ, -ɪz, -ɪŋ, -ɪd
Harsant ˈhɑːsənt
harsh, -er, -est, -ly, -ness hɑːʃ, -ə*, -ɪst, -lɪ, -nɪs [-nəs]
hart (H.), -s hɑːt, -s
Harte hɑːt
hartebeest, -s ˈhɑːtɪbiːst [-təb-], -s
Hartford ˈhɑːtfəd
Harthan (surname) ˈhɑːðən, ˈhɑːθən
Hartington ˈhɑːtɪŋtən
Hartland ˈhɑːtlənd
Hartlepool ˈhɑːtlɪpuːl
Hartley ˈhɑːtlɪ
harts|horn (H.), -tongue/s ˈhɑːts|hɔːn, -tʌŋ/z
Hartz hɑːts
harum-scarum ˌheərəmˈskeərəm
Harun-al-Raschid hæˌruːnælræˈʃiːd [hɑːˌr-, —ˈ—, -ˈræʃɪd]
haruspex, haruspices həˈrʌspeks [ˈhærəspeks], həˈrʌspɪsiːz
Harvard ˈhɑːvəd [-vɑːd]
Harverson ˈhɑːvəsn
harvest (s. v.), -s, -ing, -ed, -er/s ˈhɑːvɪst, -s, -ɪŋ, -ɪd, -ə*/z

harvest-bug, -s ˈhɑːvɪstbʌg, -z
harvest-festival, -s ˌhɑːvɪstˈfestəvl [-tɪv-], -z
harvest-home ˌhɑːvɪstˈhəʊm
harvest|-man, -men; -moon/s ˈhɑːvɪst|-mæn, -men; -ˈmuːn/z
Harvey ˈhɑːvɪ
Harwich ˈhærɪdʒ [rarely -ɪtʃ]
Harwood ˈhɑːwʊd
Harz hɑːts
has (from have) hæz (strong form), həz, əz, z, s (weak forms)
Note.—In the auxil. verb, the form z is used only after words ending in a voiced sound other than z or ʒ; s is used only after words ending in a voiceless consonant other than s or ʃ.
Hasdrubal ˈhæzdrʊbl [-bæl]
Haselden ˈhæzldən
Hasemer ˈheɪzmə*
hash (s. v.), -es, -ing, -ed, -er/s hæʃ, -ɪz, -ɪŋ, -t, -ə*/z
hashish ˈhæʃiːʃ [-ʃɪʃ]
Haslam ˈhæzləm
Haslemere ˈheɪzlˌmɪə*
haslet ˈheɪzlɪt [-lət]
Haslett ˈheɪzlɪt [-lət], ˈhæzlɪt
Haslingden ˈhæzlɪŋdən
Hasluck ˈhæzlʌk [-lək]
hasn't ˈhæznt [also ˈhæzn when not final]
hasp (s. v.), -s, -ing, -ed hɑːsp [hæsp], -s, -ɪŋ, -t
Hassall ˈhæsl
Hassan (district in India) ˈhʌsən [ˈhæs-], (Arabic name) həˈsɑːn [ˈhæsən, ˈhʌsən]
hassock (H.), -s ˈhæsək, -s
hast (from have) (H.) hæst (strong form), həst, əst, st (weak forms)
hast|e (s. v.), -es, -ing, -ed heɪst, -s, -ɪŋ, -ɪd
hast|en, -ens, -ening, -ened ˈheɪs|n, -nz, -nɪŋ [-ṇɪŋ], -nd
Hastings ˈheɪstɪŋz
hast|y, -ier, -iest, -ily, -iness ˈheɪst|ɪ, -ɪə* [-jə*], -ɪɪst [-jɪst], -ɪlɪ [-əlɪ], -ɪnɪs [-ɪnəs]
hasty-pudding ˈheɪstɪˌpʊdɪŋ
hat, -s hæt, -s
hat-band, -s ˈhætbænd, -z
hat-box, -es ˈhætbɒks, -ɪz
hat-brush, -es ˈhætbrʌʃ, -ɪz
hatch (s. v.) (H.), -es, -ing, -ed hætʃ, -ɪz, -ɪŋ, -t
hatchet, -s ˈhætʃɪt, -s
hatchment, -s ˈhætʃmənt, -s
hatchway (H.), -s ˈhætʃweɪ, -z

hat|e (s. v.), -es, -ing, -ed, -er/s heɪt, -s, -ɪŋ, -ɪd, -ə*/z
hate|ful, -fully, -fulness 'heɪt|fʊl, -fʊlɪ [-fəlɪ], -fʊlnɪs [-nəs]
Hatfield 'hætfi:ld
hath (from have) hæθ (strong form), həθ, əθ (weak forms)
Hathaway 'hæθəweɪ
Hather|ell, -leigh, -ley 'hæðə|rəl, -lɪ [-li:], -lɪ
Hathersage 'hæðəsɪdʒ [-sedʒ]
Hatherton 'hæðətən
Hathorn(e) 'hɔ:θɔ:n
Hathway 'hæθweɪ
hatless 'hætlɪs [-ləs, -les]
hat-peg, -s 'hætpeg, -z
hat-pin, -s 'hætpɪn, -z
hat-rack, -s 'hætræk, -s
hatred 'heɪtrɪd
hat-stand, -s 'hætstænd, -z
hatter, -s 'hætə*, -z
Hatteras 'hætərəs
Hatt|o, -on 'hæt|əʊ, -n
hauberk, -s 'hɔ:bɜ:k, -s
haugh, -s hɔ:, -z
Haughton 'hɔ:tn
haught|y, -ier, -iest, -ily, -iness 'hɔ:t|ɪ, -ɪə* [-jə*], -ɪɪst [-jɪst], -ɪlɪ [-əlɪ], -ɪnɪs [-nəs]
haul (s. v.), -s, -ing, -ed; -age hɔ:l, -z, -ɪŋ, -d; -ɪdʒ
haulier, -s 'hɔ:ljə* [-lɪə*], -z
haulm, -s hɔ:m, -z
haunch, -es hɔ:ntʃ, -ɪz
haunt (s. v.), -s, -ing, -ed hɔ:nt, -s, -ɪŋ, -ɪd
Hausa, -s 'haʊsə ['haʊzə], -z
†hautboy, -s 'əʊbɔɪ ['həʊ-], -z
haute (couture) əʊt
hauteur əʊ'tɜ:* ['əʊtɜ:*] (otœ:r)
Havana, -s hə'vænə, -z
Havant 'hævənt
Havard 'hævɑ:d [-vəd]
have (one who has), -s hæv, -z
have (v.); hast; has; having; had hæv (strong form), həv, əv, v (weak forms); hæst (strong form), həst, əst, st (weak forms); hæz (strong form), həz, əz, z, s (weak forms); 'hævɪŋ; hæd (strong form), həd, əd, d (weak forms)
Note.—In the auxil. verb, the weak form z is used only after voiced sounds other than z and ʒ. The weak form s is used only after voiceless consonants other than s and ʃ.
Havell 'hævəl
Havelo(c)k 'hævlɒk [-lək]

haven, -s 'heɪvn, -z
have-not, -s 'hævnɒt, -s
haven't 'hævnt [also 'hævn when not final]
haver (v.) (talk nonsense), -s, -ing, -ed 'heɪvə*, -z, -ɪŋ, -d
Haverford, -west 'hævəfəd, -'west
Havergal 'hævəgəl
Haverhill 'heɪvərɪl
haversack, -s 'hævəsæk, -s
Haverstock 'hævəstɒk
Havill|ah, -and 'hævɪl|ə, -ənd
havoc 'hævək
Havre 'hɑ:vrə [-və*]
haw (s. v.), -s, -ing, -ed hɔ:, -z, -ɪŋ, -d
Hawaii hə'waɪɪ: [hɑ:'w-, -'wɑ:i:]
Hawaiian hə'waɪən [hɑ:'w-, -'waɪjən]
Haward 'heɪwəd, 'hɔ:əd, hɔ:d
Hawarden (in Clwyd) 'hɑ:dn ['hɔ:dn], (Viscount) 'heɪ,wɔ:dn, (town in U.S.A.) 'heɪ,wɑ:dn
Haweis 'hɔ:ɪs
Hawes hɔ:z
hawfinch, -es 'hɔ:fɪntʃ, -ɪz
haw-haw (s.), -s 'hɔ:hɔ:, -z (interj.) ,hɔ:'hɔ:
Hawick 'hɔ:ɪk [hɔɪk]
hawk (s. v.), -s, -ing, -ed, -er/s hɔ:k, -s, -ɪŋ, -t, -ə*/z
Hawke, -s hɔ:k, -s
hawk-eyed 'hɔ:kaɪd
Hawkins 'hɔ:kɪnz
hawkish 'hɔ:kɪʃ
Hawksley 'hɔ:kslɪ
hawkweed 'hɔ:kwi:d
Hawkwood 'hɔ:kwʊd
Hawley 'hɔ:lɪ
Haworth 'hɔ:əθ, 'hɔ:wəθ [-wɜ:θ], 'haʊəθ
hawse, -s; -hole/s, -pipe/s hɔ:z, -ɪz; -həʊl/z, -paɪp/s
hawser, -s 'hɔ:zə*, -z
hawthorn, -s 'hɔ:θɔ:n, -z
Hawthornden 'hɔ:θɔ:ndən
Hawthorne 'hɔ:θɔ:n
hay (H.) heɪ
hay-box, -es 'heɪbɒks, -ɪz
hay-cart, -s 'heɪkɑ:t, -s
haycock, -s 'heɪkɒk, -s
Haycock 'heɪkɒk
Hayd|en, -on 'heɪd|n, -n
Haydn (English surname) 'heɪdn, (Austrian composer) 'haɪdn
Hayes, -ford heɪz, -fəd
hay-fever 'heɪ,fi:və* [,-'—]
hay-field, -s 'heɪfi:ld, -z
hay-fork, -s 'heɪfɔ:k, -s
Hayhurst 'haɪəst, 'heɪhɜ:st

233

Hayles heɪlz
hay-loft 'heɪlɒft, -s
hay-mak|er/s, -ing 'heɪˌmeɪk|ə*/z, -ɪŋ
Haymarket 'heɪˌmɑːkɪt
Haynes heɪnz
hayrick, -s 'heɪrɪk, -s
Hays heɪz
haystack, -s 'heɪstæk, -s
Hayt|er, -or 'heɪt|ə*, -ə*
hayward (H.), -s 'heɪwəd, -z
haywire 'heɪwaɪə*
Hazael 'hæzeɪel ['heɪz-, -zeɪəl, hæ'z-, hə'z-]
hazard (s. v.) (H.), -s, -ing, -ed 'hæzəd, -z, -ɪŋ, -ɪd
hazardous, -ly, -ness 'hæzədəs, -lɪ, -nɪs [-nəs]
haz|e (s. v.), -es, -ing, -ed heɪz, -ɪz, -ɪŋ, -d
hazel, -s; -nut/s 'heɪzl, -z; -nʌt/s
Hazelhurst 'heɪzlhɜːst
Hazen 'heɪzn
Hazledean 'heɪzldiːn
Hazlett 'heɪzlɪt [-lət], 'hæzlɪt [-lət]
Hazlitt 'heɪzlɪt, 'hæzlɪt
    Note.—William Hazlitt, the essayist,
    called himself 'heɪzlɪt, and the
    present members of his family pro-
    nounce the name thus. He is, how-
    ever, commonly referred to as
    'hæzlɪt. In the Hazlitt Gallery in
    London the pronunciation is
    'hæzlɪt.
Hazor 'heɪzɔː*
haz|y, -ier, -iest, -ily, -iness 'heɪz|ɪ, -ɪə* [-jə*], -ɪɪst [-jɪst], -ɪlɪ [-əlɪ], -ɪnɪs [-nəs]
H-bomb, -s 'eɪtʃbɒm, -z
he hiː (normal form), hɪ (freq. weak form), iː, ɪ (weak forms when not initial)
head (s. v.) (H.), -s, -ing, -ed hed, -z, -ɪŋ, -ɪd
headach|e, -es, -y 'hedeɪk, -s, -ɪ
headband, -s 'hedbænd, -z
head|-cloth, -cloths 'hed|klɒθ [old-fashioned -klɔːθ], -klɒθs [-klɔːðz, -klɔːθs]
head-dress, -es 'heddres, -ɪz
header, -s 'hedə*, -z
head-first ˌhed'fɜːst
head-gear, -s 'hedˌgɪə*, -z
head-hunt|er/s, -ing 'hedˌhʌnt|ə*/z, -ɪŋ
heading, -s 'hedɪŋ, -z
Headingl(e)y 'hedɪŋlɪ
Headlam 'hedləm
headland, -s 'hedlənd, -z
headless 'hedlɪs [-ləs]

head-light, -s 'hedlaɪt, -s
headline, -s 'hedlaɪn, -z
headlong 'hedlɒŋ [ˌ-'-]
head|man, -men (of group of workers) ˌhed|'mæn ['hedmæn], -'men ['--], (of tribe) 'hed|mæn [-mən], -men [-mən]
head|-master/s, -mistress/es ˌhed|-'mɑːstə*/z, -'mɪstrɪs [-trəs]/ɪz
head-note, -s 'hednəut, -s
head-on ˌhed'ɒn ['--]
headphone, -s 'hedfəun, -z
headpiece, -s 'hedpiːs, -ɪz
headquarters ˌhed'kwɔːtəz ['---]
head-rest, -s 'hedrest, -s
head-room 'hedrum [-ruːm]
headset, -s 'hedset, -s
headship, -s 'hedʃɪp, -s
heads|man, -men 'hedz|mən, -mən
headstone (H.), -s 'hedstəun, -z
headstrong 'hedstrɒŋ
head-water, -s 'hedˌwɔːtə*, -z
headway, -s 'hedweɪ, -z
head-wind, -s 'hedwɪnd, -z
head-word, -s 'hedwɜːd, -z
head-work 'hedwɜːk
head|y, -ier, -iest, -ily, -iness 'hed|ɪ, -ɪə*, -ɪɪst, -ɪlɪ [-əlɪ], -ɪnɪs [-nəs]
Heagerty 'hegətɪ
heal (H.), -s, -ing, -ed, -er/s hiːl, -z, -ɪŋ, -d, -ə*/z
Healey 'hiːlɪ
health, -s helθ, -s
health|ful, -fully, -fulness 'helθ|ful, -fulɪ [-fəlɪ], -fulnɪs [-nəs]
health-giving 'helθˌgɪvɪŋ
health|y, -ier, -iest, -ily, -iness 'helθ|ɪ, -ɪə* [-jə*], -ɪɪst [-jɪst], -ɪlɪ [-əlɪ], -ɪnɪs [-nəs]
Healy 'hiːlɪ
Heanor (near Derby) 'hiːnə*
heap (s. v.), -s, -ing, -ed hiːp, -s, -ɪŋ, -t
hear, -s, -ing/s, heard, hearer/s hɪə*, -z, -ɪŋ/z, hɜːd, 'hɪərə*/z
heard (from hear) (H.) hɜːd
hear hear ˌhɪə'hɪə*
heark|en, -ens, -ening, -ened 'hɑːk|ən, -ənz, -nɪŋ [-ŋ̩ɪŋ, -ənɪŋ], -ənd
Hearn(e) hɜːn
hearsay 'hɪəseɪ
hearse, -s hɜːs, -ɪz
hearse|-cloth, -cloths 'hɜːs|klɒθ [old-fashioned -klɔːθ], -klɒθs [-klɔːðz, -klɔːθs]
Hearsey 'hɜːsɪ
Hearst hɜːst
heart, -s hɑːt, -s
heartache 'hɑːteɪk

heart-beat, -s 'hɑːtbiːt, -s
heart-blood 'hɑːtblʌd
heartbreak, -ing 'hɑːtbreɪk, -ɪŋ
heart-broken 'hɑːt,brəʊkən
heartburn, -ing/s 'hɑːtbɜːn, -ɪŋ/z
heart|en, -ens, -ening, -ened 'hɑːt|n,
-nz, -ɳɪŋ [-nɪŋ], -nd
heartfelt 'hɑːtfelt
hearth, -s; -brush/es, -rug/s, -stone/s
hɑːθ, -s; -brʌʃ/ɪz, -rʌg/z, -stəʊn/z
heartless, -ly, -ness 'hɑːtlɪs [-ləs], -lɪ,
-nɪs [-nəs]
heart-rending 'hɑːt,rendɪŋ
heart-searching, -s 'hɑːt,sɜːtʃɪŋ, -z
heart's-ease 'hɑːtsiːz
heart-shaped 'hɑːt-ʃeɪpt
heart-sick, -ness 'hɑːtsɪk, -nɪs [-nəs]
heartsore 'hɑːtsɔː* [-sɔə*]
heart-string, -s 'hɑːtstrɪŋ, -z
heart|y, -ier, -iest, -ily, -iness 'hɑːt|ɪ,
-ɪə* [-jə*], -ɪɪst [-jɪst], -ɪlɪ [-əlɪ], -ɪnɪs
[-ɪnəs]
heat (s. v.), -s, -ing, -ed, -er/s hiːt, -s,
-ɪŋ, -ɪd, -ə*/z
heath (H.), -s hiːθ, -s
Heathcoat 'hiːθkəʊt
Heathcote 'heθkət, 'hiːθkət
heathen (s. adj.), -s, -dom 'hiːðn, -z,
-dəm
heathenish, -ly, -ness 'hiːðənɪʃ [-ðɳɪʃ],
-lɪ, -nɪs [-nəs]
heathenism 'hiːðənɪzəm [-ðɳɪ-]
heatheniz|e [-is|e], -es, -ing, -ed
'hiːðənaɪz [-ðɳaɪz], -ɪz, -ɪŋ, -d
heather (H.), -s, -y 'heðə*, -z, -ɪɪ
heather-bell, -s 'heðəbel, -z
Heath|field, -man 'hiːθ|fiːld, -mən
heath|y, -ier, -iest 'hiːθ|ɪ, -ɪə* [-jə*],
-ɪɪst [-jɪst]
Heaton 'hiːtn
heat-spot, -s 'hiːtspɒt, -s
heat-stroke, -s 'hiːtstrəʊk, -s
heat-wave, -s 'hiːtweɪv, -z
heav|e (s. v.), -es, -ing, -ed, hove,
heaver/s hiːv, -z, -ɪŋ, -d, həʊv,
'hiːvə*/z
heaven, -s; -born 'hevn, -z; -bɔːn
heavenl|y, -iness 'hevnl|ɪ, -ɪnɪs [-ɪnəs]
heavenward, -s 'hevnwəd, -z
Heaviside 'hevɪsaɪd
heav|y, -ier, -iest, -ily, -iness 'hev|ɪ,
-ɪə* [-jə*], -ɪɪst [-jɪst], -ɪlɪ [-əlɪ], -ɪnɪs
[-ɪnəs]
heavy-handed ,hevɪ'hændɪd ['--,--]
heavy-hearted ,hevɪ'hɑːtɪd ['--,--]
heavy-laden ,hevɪ'leɪdn [also '--,-- when
attributive]
heavy-weight, -s 'hevɪweɪt, -s

Heazell 'hiːzəl
Hebden 'hebdən
hebdomad|al, -ary heb'dɒməd|l, -ərɪ
Hebe 'hiːbiː [-bɪ]
Heber 'hiːbə*
Heberden 'hebədən
Hebraic, -al, -ally hiː'breɪk [hɪ-,
he'b-], -l, -əlɪ
Hebrai|sm/s, -st/s 'hiːbreɪ|zəm/z,
-st/s
hebraiz|e [-is|e], -es, -ing, -ed
'hiːbreɪaɪz, -ɪz, -ɪŋ, -d
Hebrew, -s 'hiːbruː, -z
Hebrides 'hebrɪdiːz [-brəd-]
Hebron (biblical place-name) 'hebrɒn
['hiːb-], (modern surname) 'hebrən
[-rɒn]
Hecate 'hekətɪ [-tiː, in Shakespeare
sometimes 'hekət]
hecatomb, -s 'hekətuːm [-təʊm, -təm],
-z
heck|le, -les, -ling, -led, -ler/s 'hek|l,
-lz, -lɪŋ [-lɪŋ], -ld, -lə*/z [-lə*/z]
Hecla 'heklə
hectare, -s 'hekteə* [-tɑː*, -tə*] (ɛktaːr),
-z
hectic 'hektɪk
hectogramme, -s 'hektəʊgræm, -z
hectograph (s. v.), -s, -ing, -ed 'hektəʊ-
grɑːf [-græf], -s, -ɪŋ, -t
hectographic ,hektəʊ'græfɪk
hectolitre, -s 'hektəʊ,liːtə*, -z
hectometre, -s 'hektəʊ,miːtə*, -z
hector (s. v.) (H.), -s, -ing, -ed 'hektə*,
-z, -rɪŋ, -d
Hecuba 'hekjʊbə
Hecyra 'hekɪrə
hedera 'hedərə
Hedgcock 'hedʒkɒk
hedg|e (s. v.), -es, -ing, -ed, -er/s hedʒ,
-ɪz, -ɪŋ, -d, -ə*/z
hedgehog, -s 'hedʒhɒg, -z
hedgehop, -s, -ping, -ped 'hedʒhɒp, -s,
-ɪŋ, -t
Hedgeley 'hedʒlɪ
Hedger, -ley 'hedʒə*, -lɪ
hedgerow, -s 'hedʒrəʊ, -z
Hedges 'hedʒɪz
hedge-sparrow, -s 'hedʒ,spærəʊ, -z
Hedley 'hedlɪ
hedoni|sm, -st/s 'hiːdəʊnɪ|zəm ['hed-],
-st/s
hedonistic ,hiːdə'nɪstɪk [,hed-]
heed (s. v.), -s, -ing, -ed hiːd, -z, -ɪŋ, -ɪd
heed|ful, -fully, -fulness 'hiːd|fʊl, -fʊlɪ
[-fəlɪ], -fʊlnɪs [-nəs]
heedless, -ly, -ness 'hiːdlɪs [-ləs], -lɪ,
-nɪs [-nəs]

235

heehaw (s. v. interj.), -s, -ing, -ed
ˌhiːˈhɔː [ˈ--], -z, -ɪŋ, -d
heel (s. v.), -s, -ing, -ed hiːl, -z, -ɪŋ, -d
Heelas ˈhiːləs
Heep hiːp
Heffer ˈhefə*
heft|y, -ier, -iest, -ily, -iness ˈheft|ɪ,
-ɪə* [-jə*], -ɪɪst [-jɪst], -ɪlɪ [-əlɪ], -ɪnɪs
[-məs]
Hegarty ˈhegətɪ
Hegel ˈheɪgl (ˈheːgəl)
Hegelian heɪˈgiːljən [heˈg-, hɪˈg-, -lɪən]
hegemony hɪˈgemənɪ [hiː-, ˈhedʒɪm-,
ˈhegɪm-]
Hegira ˈhedʒɪrə [hɪˈdʒaɪərə, heˈdʒaɪərə]
he-goat, -s ˈhiːgəʊt, -s
Heidelberg ˈhaɪdlbəːg
Heidsieck ˈhaɪdsiːk [-sɪk]
heifer, -s ˈhefə*, -z
heigh heɪ
heigh-ho ˌheɪˈhəʊ
Heigho ˈheɪəʊ, ˈhaɪəʊ
height, -s haɪt, -s
height|en, -ens, -ening, -ened ˈhaɪt|n,
-nz, -n̩ɪŋ [-nɪŋ], -nd
Heighton ˈheɪtn
Heighway ˈhaɪweɪ
Heinekey ˈhaɪnɪkɪ
Heinemann ˈhaməmən [-mæn]
heinous, -ly, -ness ˈheɪnəs [ˈhiːn-], -lɪ,
-nɪs [-nəs]
Heinz haɪnts, haɪnz
heir, -s; -dom, -less eə*, -z; -dəm, -lɪs
[-ləs, -les]
heir-apparent, heirs-apparent ˌeərə-
ˈpærənt [ˌeəˈp-, -ˈpeər-], ˌeəzəˈp-
heir-at-law, heirs-at-law ˌeərətˈlɔː
[ˌeəət-], ˌeəzətˈlɔː
heiress, -es ˈeərɪs [-res, eəˈres], -ɪz
heirloom, -s ˈeəluːm, -z
heirship ˈeəʃɪp
Hekla ˈheklə
held (from hold) held
Helen ˈheln [-lən]
Helena ˈhelnə, heˈliːnə [-lənə, hɪˈl-,
həˈl-]
   Note.—ˈhelnə, ˈhelənə are the more
   usual pronunciations, except in the
   name of the island St. Helena (q.v.).
Helensburgh ˈhelnzbərə [-bʌrə]
Helenus ˈhelnəs
heliac ˈhiːlræk
heliac|al, -ally hɪˈlaɪək|l [hiː-, heˈl-],
-əlɪ
Heliades heˈlaɪədiːz
helianth|us, -i, -uses ˌhiːlɪˈænθ|əs [ˌhel-],
-aɪ, -əsɪz
helical ˈhelɪkl

Helicon ˈhelɪkən [-kɒn]
helicopter, -s ˈhelɪkɒptə*, -z
Heligoland ˈhelɪgəʊlænd
heliocentric, -al, -ally ˌhiːlɪəʊˈsentrɪk
[-ljəʊ-], -l, -əlɪ
Heliogabalus ˌhiːlɪəʊˈgæbələs [-ljəʊ-]
heliogram, -s ˈhiːlɪəʊgræm [-ljəʊg-], -z
heliograph, -s ˈhiːlɪəʊgrɑːf [-ljəʊg-,
-græf], -s
heliograph|er/s, -y ˌhiːlɪˈɒgrəf|ə*/z, -ɪ
heliographic, -al ˌhiːlɪəʊˈgræfɪk
[-ljəʊˈg-], -l
heliogravure, -s ˌhiːlɪəʊgrəˈvjʊə*, -z
heliometer, -s ˌhiːlɪˈɒmɪtə* [-mətə*], -z
Heliopolis ˌhiːlɪˈɒpəlɪs
Helios ˈhiːlɪɒs
helioscope, -s ˈhiːlɪəskəʊp [-ɪəs-], -s
heliostat, -s ˈhiːlɪəʊstæt [-ljəʊs-], -s
heliotrope, -s ˈheljətrəʊp [-lɪə-, ˈhiːl-],
-s
helium ˈhiːlɪəm [-ljəm]
heli|x, -xes, helices ˈhiːlɪ|ks, -ksɪz,
ˈhelɪsiːz [ˈhiːl-]
hell (H.), -s hel, -z
he'll (= he will) hiːl
Hellas ˈhelæs
hellebore ˈhelɪbɔː* [-bɔə*]
Hellene, -s ˈheliːn, -z
Hellenic heˈliːnɪk [-ˈlen-]
helleni|sm/s -st/s ˈhelɪnɪ|zəm/z, -st/s
hellenistic, -al, -ally ˌhelɪˈnɪstɪk, -l, -əlɪ
helleniz|e [-is|e], -es, -ing, -ed ˈhelɪnaɪz,
-ɪz, -ɪŋ, -d
Heller ˈhelə*
Hellespont ˈhelɪspɒnt
hell-fire ˌhelˈfaɪə* [ˈ-,--]
hell-gate, -s ˌhelˈgeɪt, -s
hell-hound, -s ˈhelhaʊnd, -z
Hellingly (in East Sussex) ˈhelŋlaɪ
hellish, -ly, -ness ˈhelɪʃ, -lɪ, -nɪs [-nəs]
hello həˈləʊ [he-]
hellward ˈhelwəd
helm, -s helm, -z
helmet, -s -ed ˈhelmɪt, -s, -ɪd
Helmholtz ˈhelmhəʊlts (ˈhɛlmhɔlts)
helminth, -s ˈhelmɪnθ, -s
Helmsley (in North Yorkshire) ˈhelmzlɪ
   [locally ˈhemz-]
helms-man, -men ˈhelmz|mən, -mən
   [-men]
helot, -s; -age, -ism, -ry ˈhelət, -s; -ɪdʒ,
-ɪzəm, -rɪ
help (s. v.), -s, -ing, -ed, -er/s help, -s,
-ɪŋ, -t, -ə*/z
help|ful, -fully, -fulness ˈhelp|fʊl, -fʊlɪ
[-fəlɪ], -fʊlnɪs [-nəs]
helpless, -ly, -ness ˈhelplɪs [-ləs], -lɪ,
-nɪs [-nəs]

236

helpmate, -s 'helpmeɪt, -s
helpmeet, -s 'helpmiːt, -s
Helps helps
Helsingfors 'helsɪŋfɔːz
Helsinki 'helsɪŋkɪ [-'--]
Helston(e) 'helstən
helter-skelter ˌheltə'skeltə*
helve, -s helv, -z
Helvellyn hel'velɪn
Helvetia, -n/s hel'viːʃjə [-ʃɪə], -n/z
Helvetic hel'vetɪk
Helvetius hel'viːʃjəs [-ʃɪəs] (ɛlvɛsjys)
Hely 'hiːlɪ
hem (s. v.), -s, -ming, -med hem, -z, -ɪŋ, -d
hem (interj.) m̩m [hm]
hemal 'hiːməl [-ml]
he|-man, -men 'hiː|mæn, -men
Hemans 'hemənz
hematite 'hiːmətaɪt ['hem-]
Hemel Hempstead ˌheml'hempstɪd
hemicycle, -s 'hemɪˌsaɪkl, -z
Heming 'hemɪŋ
hemisphere, -s 'hemɪˌsfɪə*, -z
hemispheric, -al ˌhemɪ'sferɪk, -l
hemistich, -s 'hemɪstɪk, -s
hemline, -s 'hemlaɪn, -z
hemlock, -s 'hemlɒk, -s
hemoglobin ˌhiːməʊ'gləʊbɪn
hemorrhage, -s 'hemərɪdʒ, -ɪz
hemorrhoid, -s 'hemərɔɪd, -z
hemp, -en; -seed hemp, -ən; -siːd
Hemp(e)l 'hempl
hem-stitch (s. v.), -es, -ing, -ed 'hemstɪtʃ, -ɪz, -ɪŋ, -t
Hemy 'hemɪ
hen, -s; -bane hen, -z; -beɪn
hence hens
hence|forth, -forward ˌhens|'fɔːθ, -'fɔːwəd
hench|man, -men 'hentʃ|mən, -mən
hen-coop, -s 'henkuːp, -s
hendecagon, -s hen'dekəgən, -z
hendecasyllabic, -s ˌhendekəsɪ'læbɪk, -s
hendecasyllable, -s 'hendekəˌsɪləbl, -z
Henderson 'hendəsn
hendiadys hen'daɪədɪs
Hendon 'hendən
Heneage 'henɪdʒ
Hengist 'heŋgɪst
Henley 'henlɪ
Henlopen hen'ləʊpən
henna 'henə
henner|y, -ies 'henər|ɪ, -ɪz
Henness(e)y 'henɪsɪ [-nəs-]
Henniker 'henɪkə*
Henning 'henɪŋ
henpeck, -s, -ing, -ed 'henpek, -s, -ɪŋ, -t

Henrietta ˌhenrɪ'etə
Henriques (English surname) hen'riːkɪz
hen-roost, -s 'henruːst, -s
Henry 'henrɪ
Hensen 'hensn
Hens|ley, -low(e) 'henz|lɪ, -ləʊ
Henson 'hensn
Henty 'hentɪ
hepatic hɪ'pætɪk [he'p-]
hepatica, -s hɪ'pætɪkə [he'p-], -z
hepatite 'hepətaɪt
hepatitis ˌhepə'taɪtɪs
Hepburn 'hebɜːn ['hepb-, -bən]
Hephaestus hɪ'fiːstəs [he'f-]
Hephzibah 'hefsɪbə ['heps-]
heptachord, -s 'heptəkɔːd, -z
heptad, -s 'heptæd, -z
heptaglot 'heptəglɒt
heptagon, -s 'heptəgən, -z
heptagonal hep'tægənl
heptahedr|on, -ons, -a; -al ˌheptə'hiː-dr|ən [-'hed-, 'heptə,h-], -ɒnz, -ə; -l
heptameron hep'tæmərən
heptarch, -s; -y, -ies 'heptɑːk, -s; -ɪ, -ɪz
Heptateuch 'heptətjuːk
Hepworth 'hepwɜːθ [-wəθ]
her hɜː* (normal form), hə* (freq. weak form), ɜː, ə (weak forms when not initial)
Heraclean ˌherə'kliːən [-'klɪən]
Heracles 'herəkliːz ['hɪər-]
Heraclitus ˌherə'klaɪtəs
herald (s. v.), -s, -ing, -ed; -ry 'herəld, -z, -ɪŋ, -ɪd; -rɪ
heraldic, -ally he'rældɪk [hɪ'r-, hə'r-], -əlɪ
Herapath (surname) 'herəpɑːθ
Herat he'ræt [hɪ'r-, hə'r-, -'rɑːt]
herb, -s; -age hɜːb, -z; -ɪdʒ
herbaceous hɜː'beɪʃəs [hə'b-]
herbal 'hɜːbl
†herbalist, -s 'hɜːbəlɪst [-blɪst], -s
herbarium, -s hɜː'beərɪəm, -z
Herbert 'hɜːbət
herbivorous hɜː'bɪvərəs [hə'b-]
herborist, -s 'hɜːbərɪst, -s
herboriz|e [-is|e], -es, -ing, -ed 'hɜː-bəraɪz, -ɪz, -ɪŋ, -d
Herculaneum ˌhɜːkjʊ'leɪnjəm [-nɪəm]
herculean ˌhɜːkjʊ'liːən [-'lɪən, hɜː-'kjuːljən, -'kjuːlɪən]
Hercules 'hɜːkjʊliːz
herd (s. v.) (H.), -s, -ing, -ed hɜːd, -z, -ɪŋ, -ɪd
Herdener 'hɜːdənə* [-dɪn-]
herd-instinct ˌhɜːd'ɪnstɪŋkt ['-,--]
herds|man, -men 'hɜːdz|mən, -mən
here hɪə*

237

hereabouts 'hɪərəˌbaʊts [ˌ–'-]
hereafter ˌhɪər'ɑ:ftə*
hereby ˌhɪə'baɪ [*also* '— *according to sentence-stress*]
hereditable hɪ'redɪtəbl [he'r-, hə'r-]
hereditament, -s ˌherɪ'dɪtəmənt [-rə'd-, -tɪm-], -s
hereditar|y, -ily, -iness hɪ'redɪtər|ɪ [he'r-, hə'r-], -əlɪ [-ɪlɪ], -ɪnɪs [-ɪnəs]
heredity hɪ'redətɪ [he'r-, hə'r-, -ɪtɪ]
Hereford, -shire 'herɪfəd, -ʃə* [-ˌʃɪə*]
herein ˌhɪər'ɪn
hereinafter ˌhɪərɪn'ɑ:ftə*
hereof ˌhɪər'ɒv [-'ɒf]
hereon ˌhɪər'ɒn
Herero, -s hə'reərəʊ [he'r-, -'rɪə-, 'hɪərərəʊ, 'her-], -z
heresiarch, -s he'ri:zɪɑ:k, -s
heres|y, -ies 'herəs|ɪ [-rɪs-], -ɪz
heretic (*s. adj.*), -s 'herətɪk [-rɪt-], -s
heretic|al, -ly hɪ'retɪk|l [hə'r-], -əlɪ
hereto ˌhɪə'tu:
heretofore ˌhɪətʊ'fɔ:* [-'fɔə*]
hereunder ˌhɪər'ʌndə*
hereunto ˌhɪərʌn'tu:
hereupon ˌhɪərə'pɒn
Hereward 'herɪwəd
herewith ˌhɪə'wɪð [-'wɪθ]
Herford 'hɜ:fəd, 'hɑ:fəd
heriot, -s 'herɪət, -s
herit|able, -age/s, -or/s 'herɪt|əbl, -ɪdʒ/ɪz, -ə*/z
Herkomer, -s 'hɜ:kəmə*, -z
Herlichy 'hɜ:lɪkɪ
Herlihy 'hɜ:lɪhɪ
Herman 'hɜ:mən
hermaphrodite, -s hə:'mæfrədaɪt [-frʊd-], -s
Hermes 'hɜ:mi:z
hermetic, -al, -ally hɜ:'metɪk, -l, -əlɪ
Hermia 'hɜ:mjə [-mɪə]
Hermione hə:'maɪənɪ [hə'm-]
hermit, -s 'hɜ:mɪt, -s
hermitage (H.), -s 'hɜ:mɪtɪdʒ, -ɪz
hermit-crab, -s 'hɜ:mɪtkræb [ˌ–'-], -z
hermitical hɜ:'mɪtɪkl
Hermocrates hɜ:'mɒkrəti:z
Hermogenes hɜ:'mɒdʒɪni:z [-dʒən-]
Hermon 'hɜ:mən
hern, -s hɜ:n, -z
Herne hɜ:n
hernia, -l 'hɜ:njə [-nɪə], -l
hero (H.), -es 'hɪərəʊ, -z
Herod 'herəd
Herodian, -s he'rəʊdjən [hɪ'r-, hə'r-, -dɪən], -z
Herodias he'rəʊdɪæs [hɪ'r-, hə'r-]
Herodotus he'rɒdətəs [hɪ'r-, hə'r-]

heroic, -s, -al, -ally hɪ'rəʊɪk [he'r-, hə'r-], -s, -l, -əlɪ
heroin 'herəʊɪn
heroi|ne, -nes, -sm 'herəʊɪ|n, -nz, -zəm
heron (H.), -s; -ry, -ries 'herən, -z; -rɪ, -rɪz
hero-worship 'hɪərəʊˌwɜ:ʃɪp
herpes 'hɜ:pi:z
Herr (*German title*) heə* (her)
Herr|ick, -ies 'her|ɪk, -ɪs
herring (H.), -s; -bone/s, -pond/s 'herɪŋ, -z; -bəʊn/z, -pɒnd/s
Herrnhuter, -s 'heənˌhu:tə* ['heərən-], -z
hers hɜ:z
Hersant 'hɜ:snt
Herschel(l) 'hɜ:ʃl
herself hə:'self [hə's-, *also* ɜ:'s-, ə's- *when not initial*]
Herstmonceux ˌhɜ:smən'zu: [-mɒn-, -'sju:, -'su:]
Hertford (*in England*), -shire 'hɑ:fəd ['hɑ:tf-], -ʃə* [-ˌʃɪə*]
Hertford (*in U.S.A.*) 'hɜ:tfəd
Herts. hɑ:ts [hɜ:ts]
Hertslet 'hɜ:tslɪt
Hertz, -ian hɜ:ts [heə-], -rən [-jən]
Hervey 'hɑ:vɪ, 'hɜ:vɪ
Herzegovina ˌheətsəgəʊ'vi:nə [ˌˌhɜ:ts-]
Herzog (*English surname*) 'hɜ:tsɒg
he's (= he is *or* he has) hi:z (*strong form*), hɪz, ɪz (*occasional weak forms*)
Hesba 'hezbə
Heseltine 'hesltaɪn
Hesiod 'hi:sɪɒd ['hes-, -jəd, -rəd]
hesitan|ce, -cy, -t/ly 'hezɪtən|s, -sɪ, -t/lɪ
hesitat|e, -es, -ing/ly, -ed 'hezɪteɪt, -s, -ɪŋ/lɪ, -ɪd
hesitation, -s ˌhezɪ'teɪʃn, -z
Hesketh 'heskɪθ [-keθ, -kəθ]
Hesper 'hespə*
Hesperian he'spɪərɪən
Hesperides he'sperɪdi:z
Hesperus 'hespərəs
Hess|e, -en 'hes|ɪ ['hesə, hes], -n
hessian (H.), -s 'hesɪən [-sjən], -z
Hester 'hestə*
Hesychius he'sɪkɪəs
heteroclite (*s. adj.*), -s 'hetərəʊklaɪt, -s
heterodox, -y 'hetərəʊdɒks, -ɪ
heterodyne 'hetərəʊdaɪn
heterogeneity ˌhetərəʊdʒɪ'ni:ətɪ [-dʒə'n-, -'ni:ɪtɪ, -'nɪətɪ]
heterogeneous, -ly, -ness ˌhetərəʊ'dʒi:njəs [-'dʒen-, -nɪəs], -lɪ, -nɪs [-nəs]
heterogenesis ˌhetərəʊ'dʒenɪsɪs [-'dʒenəsɪs]
heteronym|ous, -y ˌhetə'rɒnɪm|əs, -ɪ

hetero-sexual ˌhetərəʊ'sekʃʊəl [-ksjʊəl, -ksjwəl,-ksjʊl,-kʃwəl,-kʃʊl]
Hetherington 'heðərɪŋtən
Hetton-le-Hole ˌhetnlɪ'həʊl
Hetty 'hetɪ
Heugh (*place*) hjuːf, (*surname*) hjuː
heuristic hjʊə'rɪstɪk
Hever 'hiːvə*
hew, -s, -ing, -ed, -n, -er/s hjuː, -z, -ɪŋ ['hjʊɪŋ], -d, -n, -ə*/z [hjʊə*/z]
Hew|ard, -art, -etson, -ett, -itt 'hjuː|əd [hjʊəd], -ət, -ɪtsn, -ɪt, -ɪt
Hewke hjuːk
Hew|lett, -son 'hjuː|lɪt, -sn
hexachord, -s 'heksəkɔːd, -z
hexagon, -s 'heksəgən, -z
hexagon|al, -ally hek'sægən|l, -əlɪ
hexahedr|on, -ons, -a; -al ˌheksə'hedr|ən [-'hiːd-, 'heksə͵h-], -ənz, -ə; -əl
Hexam 'heksəm
hexameter, -s hek'sæmɪtə* [-mətə*], -z
Hexateuch 'heksətjuːk
Hexham 'heksəm
hey heɪ
Heycock 'heɪkɒk
heyday 'heɪdeɪ
Heyno 'heɪnəʊ
Heysham 'hiːʃəm
Heytesbury 'heɪtsbərɪ
Heywood 'heɪwʊd
Hezekiah ˌhezɪ'kaɪə
Hezlewood 'hezlwʊd
hi haɪ
hiatus, -es haɪ'eɪtəs, -ɪz
Hiawatha ˌhaɪə'wɒθə
Hibbert 'hɪbət [-bɜːt]
hibernal haɪ'bɜːnl
hibernat|e, -es, -ing, -ed 'haɪbəneɪt, -s, -ɪŋ, -ɪd
hibernation, -s ˌhaɪbə'neɪʃn, -z
Hibernia haɪ'bɜːnjə [-nɪə]
Hibernian (*s. adj.*), **-s** (*as ordinarily used*) haɪ'bɜːnjən [-nɪən], (*in name of football club*) hɪ'bɜːnjən [-nɪən], -z
Hibernicism, -s haɪ'bɜːnɪsɪzəm, -z
hibiscus hɪ'bɪskəs
hiccup [-ough] (*s. v.*), **-s, -ing, -ed** 'hɪkʌp, -s, -ɪŋ, -t
Hichens 'hɪtʃmz
Hickinbotham 'hɪkɪnbɒtəm
hickory (H.) 'hɪkərɪ
Hick|s, -son hɪk|s, -sn
hid (*from hide*) hɪd
hidalgo, -s hɪ'dælgəʊ, -z
hide (*s.*), **-s** haɪd, -z
hid|e (*conceal*), **-es, -ing/s, hid, hidden** haɪd, -z, -ɪŋ/z, hɪd, 'hɪdn

hid|e (*beat*), **-es, -ing/s, -ed** haɪd, -z, -ɪŋ/z, -ɪd
hidebound 'haɪdbaʊnd
hideous, -ly, -ness 'hɪdɪəs [-djəs], -lɪ, -nɪs [-nəs]
hiding-place, -s 'haɪdɪŋpleɪs, -ɪz
hie, -s, -ing, -d haɪ, -z, -ɪŋ, -d
Hierapolis ˌhaɪə'ræpəlɪs [-pʊl-]
hierarch, -s 'haɪərɑːk, -s
hierarchal ˌhaɪə'rɑːkl
hierarchic, -al, -ally ˌhaɪə'rɑːkɪk, -l, -əlɪ
hierarch|y, -ies 'haɪərɑːk|ɪ, -ɪz
hieratic ˌhaɪə'rætɪk
hieroglyph, -s 'haɪərəʊglɪf, -s
hieroglyphic (*s. adj.*), **-s, -al, -ally** ˌhaɪərəʊ'glɪfɪk, -s, -l, -əlɪ
Hieronymus ˌhaɪə'rɒnɪməs
hierophant, -s 'haɪərəʊfænt, -s
hi-fi 'haɪfaɪ [͵-'-]
Higginbotham 'hɪgɪnbɒtəm
Higgin|s, -son 'hɪgɪn|z, -sn
higg|le, -les, -ling, -led, -ler/s 'hɪg|l, -lz, -lɪŋ [-lɪŋ], -ld, -lə*/z [-lə*/z]
high, -er, -est haɪ, 'haɪə*, 'haɪɪst
Higham, -s 'haɪəm, -z
highborn 'haɪbɔːn
highbrow (*s. adj.*), **-s** 'haɪbraʊ, -z
high-chair, -s 'haɪtʃeə* [͵-'-], -z
high-church, -man, -men ͵haɪ'tʃɜːtʃ, -mən, -mən [-men]
high-day, -s 'haɪdeɪ, -z
high-falut|in, -ing ˌhaɪfə'luːt|ɪn, -ɪŋ
highflier [-flyer], **-s** ͵haɪ'flaɪə*, -z
highflown 'haɪfləʊn [͵-'-]
Highflyer 'haɪ͵flaɪə*
high-frequency ͵haɪ'friːkwənsɪ
Highgate 'haɪgɪt [-geɪt]
high-handed ͵haɪ'hændɪd [*also* '-͵— *when attributive*]
highland (H.), **-s; -er/s** 'haɪlənd, -z; -ə*/z
high-level ͵haɪ'levl [*also* '-͵— *when attributive*]
highlight (*s. v.*), **-s, -ing, -ed** 'haɪlaɪt, -s, -ɪŋ, -ɪd
highly (*in a high manner, very*) 'haɪlɪ
highly-strung ͵haɪlɪ'strʌŋ
high-minded ͵haɪ'maɪndɪd [*also* '-͵— *according to sentence-stress*]
high-mindedness ͵haɪ'maɪndɪdnɪs [-nəs]
high-necked ͵haɪ'nekt [*also* '— *when attributive*]
highness (*quality of being high*) 'haɪnɪs [-nəs]
Highness (*title*), **-es** 'haɪnɪs [-nəs], -ɪz
high-pitched ͵haɪ'pɪtʃt [*also* '— *when attributive*]

high-pressure ˌhaɪˈpreʃə* [also '-ˌ– when attributive]
high-priced ˌhaɪˈpraɪst [also '– when attributive]
high-priest, -s, -hood ˌhaɪˈpriːst, -s, -hʊd
high-principled ˌhaɪˈprɪnsəpld [-sɪp-]
high-rank|er/s, -ing 'haɪˌræŋk|ə*/z [ˌ-'–], -ɪŋ
high-road, -s 'haɪrəʊd, -z
high-school, -s 'haɪskuːl, -z
high-sounding 'haɪˌsaʊndɪŋ [also ˌ-'– when not attributive]
high-spirited ˌhaɪˈspɪrɪtɪd
high-stepper, -s ˌhaɪˈstepə* ['-ˌ–], -z
high-stepping 'haɪˌstepɪŋ
High Street 'haɪstriːt
Highton 'haɪtn
high-toned ˌhaɪˈtəʊnd ['–]
high-up, -s 'haɪʌp [ˌ-'-], -s
high-water ˌhaɪˈwɔːtə*
high-water-mark, -s ˌhaɪˈwɔːtəmɑːk, -s
highway, -s 'haɪweɪ, -z
highway-code ˌhaɪweɪˈkəʊd ['-ˌ-]
highway|man, -men 'haɪweɪ|mən, -mən
hijack (s. v.), -s, -ing, -ed, -er/s 'haɪdʒæk, -s, -ɪŋ, -t, -ə*/z
hik|e, -es, -ing, -ed, -er/s haɪk, -s, -ɪŋ, -t, -ə*/z
Hilaire (Belloc) 'hɪleə* [-'-]
hilarious, -ly, -ness hɪˈleərɪəs, -lɪ, -nɪs [-nəs]
hilarity hɪˈlærətɪ [-ɪtɪ]
Hilary 'hɪlərɪ
Hilda 'hɪldə
Hildebrand 'hɪldəbrænd
Hildegard(e) 'hɪldəgɑːd
hill (H.), -s hɪl, -z
Hillary 'hɪlərɪ
Hillborn 'hɪlbɔːn
Hillel 'hɪlel [-ləl]
hill-folk 'hɪlfəʊk
Hillhead hɪlˈhed ['–]
Note.—The pronunciation in Scotland is with -'-.
Hilliard 'hɪlɪəd [-ljəd, -lɪɑːd, -ljɑːd]
Hillingdon 'hɪlɪŋdən
hill|man, -men 'hɪl|mæn, -men
Hillman, -s 'hɪlmən -z
hillock, -s 'hɪlək, -s
Hillsboro 'hɪlzbərə [-bʌrə]
Note.—The local pronunciation in U.S.A. is with -ˌbʌrəʊ.
Hillsborough 'hɪlzbərə
hill-side, -s ˌhɪlˈsaɪd ['–], -z
Hillside ˌhɪlˈsaɪd ['–]
hill-top, -s ˌhɪlˈtɒp ['–], -s
Hilltop (name of road) 'hɪltɒp

hill|y, -ier, -iest, -iness 'hɪl|ɪ, -ɪə*, -ɪɪst, -ɪnɪs [-nəs]
Hillyard 'hɪljəd [-jɑːd]
hilt, -s, -ed hɪlt, -s, -ɪd
Hilton 'hɪltən
hilum, -s 'haɪləm, -z
Hilversum 'hɪlvəsʊm [-səm]
him hɪm (normal form), ɪm (freq. weak form)
Himalaya, -s, -n ˌhɪməˈleɪə [rarely hɪˈmɑːləjə, hɪˈmɑːljə, hɪˈmɑːlɪə], (Hindi hymaləjə), -z, -n
himself hɪmˈself [also ɪm- when not initial]
Himyaritic ˌhɪmjəˈrɪtɪk [-mɪə-]
Hinchcliffe 'hɪntʃklɪf
Hinchliffe 'hɪntʃlɪf
Hinckley 'hɪŋklɪ
hind (s. adj.) (H.), -s haɪnd, -z
Hinde haɪnd
Hindemith 'hɪndəmɪt [-mɪθ]
hinder (adj.), -most 'haɪndə*, -məʊst
hind|er (v.), -ers, -ering, -ered, -erer/s 'hɪnd|ə*, -əz, -ərɪŋ, -əd, -ərə*/z
Hinderwell 'hɪndəwel [-wəl]
Hindi 'hɪndi: (Hindi hyndi)
Hindle 'hɪndl
Hindley (surname) 'haɪndlɪ, 'hɪndlɪ, (town in Greater Manchester) 'hɪndlɪ
Hindlip 'hɪndlɪp
hindmost 'haɪndməʊst
hind-quarters ˌhaɪndˈkwɔːtəz ['-ˌ–]
hindrance, -s 'hɪndrəns, -ɪz
hindsight 'haɪndsaɪt
Hindu [-doo], -s ˌhɪnˈduː [also 'hɪnduː: when attributive], -z
Hinduism 'hɪnduːɪzəm [-dʊɪzəm, -'---]
Hindu-Kush ˌhɪnduːˈkuːʃ [-ˈkʊʃ]
Hindustan ˌhɪnduˈstɑːn [-ˈstæn]
Hindustani ˌhɪnduˈstɑːnɪ [-ˈstænɪ]
hing|e (s. v.), -es, -ing, -ed hɪndʒ, -ɪz, -ɪŋ, -d
Hingston 'hɪŋkstən
Hinkson 'hɪŋksn
hint (s. v.), -s, -ing, -ed hɪnt, -s, -ɪŋ, -ɪd
hinterland 'hɪntəlænd
Hinton 'hɪntən
Hiorns 'haɪənz
hip (s. v.), -s, -ping, -ped hɪp, -s, -ɪŋ, -t
hip-ba|th, -ths 'hɪpbɑː|θ, -ðz
hip-bone, -s 'hɪpbəʊn, -z
hip-joint, -s 'hɪpdʒɔɪnt, -s
Hipparchus hɪˈpɑːkəs
hipped hɪpt
hippety-hop, -pety ˌhɪpətɪˈhɒp, -ətɪ
Hippias 'hɪpɪæs
hippie, -s 'hɪpɪ, -z
hippish 'hɪpɪʃ

hippo, -s 'hɪpəʊ, -z
Hippocrates hɪ'pɒkrəti:z
hippocratic ˌhɪpəʊ'krætɪk
Hippocrene ˌhɪpəʊ'kri:ni: [-'kri:nɪ, *also in poetry* 'hɪpəʊkri:n]
Hippodamia ˌhɪpəʊdə'maɪə
hippodrome (H.), -s 'hɪpədrəʊm, -z
Hippolyt|a, -e, -us hɪ'pɒlɪt|ə, -i:, -əs
hippopotam|us, -uses, -i ˌhɪpə'pɒtəm|əs, -əsɪz, -aɪ
Hiram (*biblical name*) 'haɪərəm [-ræm], (*modern personal name*) 'haɪərəm, (*town in U.S.A.*) 'haɪərəm
hircine 'hɜ:saɪn
Hird hɜ:d
hir|e (*s. v.*), -es, -ing, -ed, -er/s; -eling/s 'haɪə*, -z, -rɪŋ, -d, -rə*/z; -lɪŋ/z
Hiroshima hɪ'rɒʃɪmə [ˌhɪrɒ'ʃi:mə]
Hirst hɜ:st
hirsute 'hɜ:sju:t [-'-]
his hɪz (*normal form*), ɪz (*freq. weak form when not initial*)
hispanic hɪ'spænɪk
hispanist, -s 'hɪspənɪst [-pæn-], -s
hiss (*s. v.*), -es, -ing, -ed, -er/s hɪs, -ɪz, -ɪŋ, -t, -ə*/z
hist s:t [hɪst]
histamine 'hɪstəmi:n [-mɪn]
histologic|al, -ally ˌhɪstə'lɒdʒɪk|l, -əlɪ
histolog|ist/s, -y hɪ'stɒlədʒ|ɪst/s, -ɪ
historian, -s hɪ'stɔ:rɪən [*also occasionally* ɪs- *when not initial, with* ən *as preceding indefinite article*], -z
historic, -al, -ally hɪ'stɒrɪk [*also occasionally* ɪs- *when not initial, with* ən *as preceding indefinite article*], -l, -əlɪ
historiograph|er/s, -y ˌhɪstɔ:rɪ-'ɒɡrəf|ə*/z [-tɒr-, -ˌ--'---], -ɪ
histor|y, -ies 'hɪstər|ɪ, -ɪz
Histriomastix ˌhɪstrɪəʊ'mæstɪks
histrionic, -al, -ally ˌhɪstrɪ'ɒnɪk, -l, -əlɪ
histrionism 'hɪstrɪənɪzəm
hit (*s. v.*), -s, -ting, -ter/s hɪt, -s, -ɪŋ, -ə*/z
hitch (*s. v.*), -es, -ing, -ed hɪtʃ, -ɪz, -ɪŋ, -t
Hitch|cock, -ens 'hɪtʃ|kɒk, -ɪnz
hitch-hik|e, -es, -ing, -ed, -er/s 'hɪtʃhaɪk, -s, -ɪŋ, -t, -ə*/z
Hitchin, -s 'hɪtʃɪn, -z
hither (H.) 'hɪðə*
hitherto ˌhɪðə'tu: [*also* '--- *according to sentence-stress*]
Hitler (*German name*) 'hɪtlə* ('hɪtlər)
Hitlerian hɪt'lɪərɪən
Hitlerism 'hɪtlərɪzəm
Hitlerite, -s 'hɪtləraɪt, -s
Hittite, -s 'hɪtaɪt, -s

hiv|e (*s. v.*), -es, -ing, -ed haɪv, -z, -ɪŋ, -d
hives (*disease*) haɪvz
Hivite, -s 'haɪvaɪt, -s
ho həʊ
Hoadl(e)y 'həʊdlɪ
Hoangho ˌhəʊæŋ'həʊ
hoar (H.) hɔ:* [hɔə*]
hoard (*s. v.*), -s, -ing, -ed, -er/s hɔ:d [hɔəd], -z, -ɪŋ, -ɪd, -ə*/z
hoarding (*s.*), -s 'hɔ:dɪŋ ['hɔəd-], -z
Hoare hɔ:* [hɔə*]
hoar-frost, -s ˌhɔ:'frɒst [ˌhɔə'f-, *old-fashioned* -'frɔ:st, '--], -s
hoarse, -r, -st, -ly, -ness hɔ:s [hɔəs], -ə*, -ɪst, -lɪ, -nɪs [-nəs]
hoar|y, -ier, -iest, -ily, -iness 'hɔ:r|ɪ ['hɔər-], -ɪə*, -ɪɪst, -əlɪ [-ɪlɪ], -ɪnɪs [-ɪnəs]
hoax (*s. v.*), -es, -ing, -ed, -er/s həʊks, -ɪz, -ɪŋ, -t, -ə*/z
hob, -s hɒb, -z
Hobart 'həʊbɑ:t
hobbadehoy, -s ˌhɒbədɪ'hɔɪ, -z
Hobbema, -s 'hɒbɪmə, -z
Hobbes hɒbz
hobb|le (*s. v.*), -les, -ling, -led, -ler/s 'hɒb|l, -lz, -lɪŋ [-lɪŋ], -ld, -lə*/z [-lə*/z]
hobbledehoy, -s ˌhɒbldɪ'hɔɪ, -z
Hobbs hɒbz
hobb|y, -ies 'hɒb|ɪ, -ɪz
hobby-horse, -s 'hɒbɪhɔ:s, -ɪz
Hobday 'hɒbdeɪ
hobgoblin, -s 'hɒbgɒblɪn [ˌ-'--], -z
Hobhouse 'hɒbhaʊs
hobnail, -s, -ed 'hɒbneɪl, -z, -d
hobnob (*s. v.*), -s, -bing, -bed 'hɒbnɒb [ˌ-'--], -z, -ɪŋ, -d
hobo, -s 'həʊbəʊ, -z
Hoboken 'həʊbəʊkən [-bək-]
Hobson 'hɒbsn
Hoby 'həʊbɪ
Hoccleve 'hɒkli:v
hochheimer 'hɒkhaɪmə* ['hɒxh-]
hock, -s hɒk, -s
hockey 'hɒkɪ
hockey-stick, -s 'hɒkɪstɪk, -s
Hock|in, -ing 'hɒk|ɪn, -ɪŋ
hocus-pocus ˌhəʊkəs'pəʊkəs
hod, -s hɒd, -z
Hodd|er, -esdon 'hɒd|ə*, -zdən
Hodge, -s hɒdʒ, -ɪz
hodge-podge 'hɒdʒpɒdʒ
Hodg|es, -kin/son 'hɒdʒ|ɪz, -kɪn/sn
Hodgson 'hɒdʒsn, *in N. of England also* 'hɒdʒən
hod|man, -men 'hɒd|mən, -mən [-men]
hodograph, -s 'hɒdəʊgrɑ:f [-græf], -s

241

hodometer, -s hɒ'dɒmɪtə* [-mətə*], -z
Hodson 'hɒdsn
hoe (s. v.), -s, -ing, -d, -r/s həʊ, -z, -ɪŋ, -d, -ə*/z
Hoe həʊ
Hoey hɔɪ, 'həʊɪ
hog, -s hɒg, -z
Hogan 'həʊgən
Hogarth 'həʊgɑ:θ
Hogarthian həʊ'gɑ:θjən [-θɪən]
Hogben 'hɒgbən [-ben]
Hogg hɒg
hogget (H.), -s 'hɒgɪt, -s
hoggish, -ly, -ness 'hɒgɪʃ, -lɪ, -nɪs [-nəs]
hogmanay 'hɒgməneɪ [ˌ—'-]
hogshead, -s 'hɒgzhed, -z
hogwash 'hɒgwɒʃ
Hogue həʊg
Hohenlinden ˌhəʊən'lɪndən
Hohenzollern, -s ˌhəʊən'zɒlən [ˌhəʊm-] (ˌho:ən'tsolərn), -z
hoi(c)k, -s, -ing, -ed hɔɪk, -s, -ɪŋ, -t
hoi polloi ˌhɔɪ'pɒlɔɪ [ˌhɔɪpə'lɔɪ]
hoist (s. v.), -s, -ing, -ed hɔɪst, -s, -ɪŋ, -ɪd
hoity-toity ˌhɔɪtɪ'tɔɪtɪ
hok(e)y-pok(e)y ˌhəʊkɪ'pəʊkɪ
hokum 'həʊkəm
Holbech 'hɒlbiːtʃ
Holbeck 'hɒlbek
Holbein, -s 'hɒlbaɪn, -z
Holborn (in London) 'həʊbən ['həʊlb-]
Holbrook(e) 'həʊlbrʊk, 'hɒl-
Holburn (near Aberdeen) 'hɒlbɜ:n ['həʊl-]
Holcroft 'həʊlkrɒft
hold (s. v.), -s, -ing, held, holder/s həʊld, -z, -ɪŋ, held, 'həʊldə*/z
hold-all, -s 'həʊldɔ:l, -z
Holden 'həʊldən
Holder 'həʊldə*
Holdfast, -s 'həʊldfɑ:st, -s
holding (s.), -s 'həʊldɪŋ, -z
Holdsworth 'həʊldzwɜ:θ [-wəθ]
hold-up, -s 'həʊldʌp, -s
hol|e (s. v.) (H.), -es, -ing, -ed həʊl, -z, -ɪŋ, -d
hole-and-corner ˌhəʊlənd'kɔ:nə*
Holford 'həʊlfəd
holiday, -s 'hɒlədeɪ [-lɪd-, -dɪ], -z
Holiday 'hɒlɪdeɪ
holiday-maker, -s 'hɒlədɪˌmeɪkə* [-lɪd-, -deɪ-], -z
Holies 'həʊlɪz
Holifield 'hɒlɪfi:ld
Holinshed 'hɒlɪnʃed
holism 'hɒlɪzm ['həʊ-]

Holkam 'həʊkəm
holland (H.), -s 'hɒlənd, -z
hollandaise ˌhɒlən'deɪz [also '— when attributive]
Hollander, -s 'hɒləndə*, -z
hollands 'hɒləndz
Holles 'hɒlɪs
Hollingsworth 'hɒlɪŋzwɜ:θ [-wəθ]
Hollins 'hɒlɪnz
holl|o, -oes, -oing, -oed 'hɒl|əʊ, -əʊz, -əʊɪŋ, -əʊd
Hollom 'hɒləm
holl|ow (s. adj. v.), -ows; -ower, -owest, -owly, -owness; -owing, -owed 'hɒl|əʊ, -əʊz; -əʊə*, -əʊɪst, -əʊlɪ, -əʊnɪs [-nəs]; -əʊɪŋ, -əʊd
Holloway 'hɒləweɪ [-lʊw-]
hollow-eyed 'hɒləʊaɪd [ˌ—'-]
holl|y (H.), -ies 'hɒl|ɪ, -ɪz
hollyhock, -s 'hɒlɪhɒk, -s
Hollywood 'hɒlɪwʊd
holm (H.), -s həʊm, -z
Holman 'həʊlmən
Holmby 'həʊmbɪ
Holmer 'həʊlmə*
Holmes, -dale həʊmz, -deɪl
holm-oak, -s ˌhəʊm'əʊk ['—], -s
holocaust, -s 'hɒləkɔ:st, -s
Holofernes ˌhɒləʊ'fɜ:ni:z
hologram, -s 'hɒləʊgræm, -z
holograph, -s 'hɒləʊgrɑ:f [-græf], -s
holography hɒ'lɒgrəfɪ
holpen (archaic p. partic. of help) 'həʊlpən, 'hɒlpən
Holroyd 'hɒlrɔɪd
Holst (Gustav Holst, musical composer) həʊlst
Holstein 'hɒlstaɪn
holster, -s, -ed 'həʊlstə*, -z, -d
holt (H.), -s həʊlt, -s
Holtby 'həʊltbɪ
Holtham (surname) 'həʊlθəm, 'hɒlθəm, 'həʊθəm
holus-bolus ˌhəʊləs'bəʊləs
hol|y (H.), -ier, -iest, -iness 'həʊl|ɪ, -ɪə* [-jə*], -ɪɪst [-jɪst], -ɪnɪs [-nəs]
Holycross 'həʊlɪkrɒs [old-fashioned -krɔ:s]
Holyhead 'hɒlɪhed
Holyoake 'həʊlɪəʊk
Holyrood 'hɒlɪru:d
holyston|e (s. v.), -es, -ing, -ed 'həʊlɪstəʊn, -z, -ɪŋ, -d
Holy-week 'həʊlɪwi:k
Holywell 'hɒlɪwəl [-wel]
homage; -r/s 'hɒmɪdʒ; -ə*/z
homburg (H.), -s 'hɒmbɜ:g, -z
home (s. adv.), -s həʊm, -z

Home həʊm, hjuːm
   Note.—hjuːm *in* **Milne-Home,**
   Douglas-Home, *and* **Baron Home of**
   the Hirsel.
home-bred ˌhəʊmˈbred [*also* ˈ— *when*
   attributive]
home-brewed ˌhəʊmˈbruːd [*also* ˈ—
   when attributive]
home-coming, -s ˈhəʊmˌkʌmɪŋ, -z
home-grown ˌhəʊmˈgrəʊn [*also* ˈ—
   when attributive]
homeland (H.), -s ˈhəʊmlænd, -z
homeless, -ness ˈhəʊmlɪs [-ləs], -nɪs
   [-nəs]
homelike ˈhəʊmlaɪk
homel|y, -ier, -iest, -iness ˈhəʊml|ɪ, -ɪə*,
   -ɪɪst, -ɪnɪs [-məs]
home-made ˌhəʊmˈmeɪd [*also* ˈ— *when*
   attributive]
Homer ˈhəʊmə*
Homeric (*relating to Homer*) həʊˈmerɪk,
   (*name of ship*) ˈhəʊmərɪk
Homerton ˈhɒmətən
homesick, -ness ˈhəʊmsɪk, -nɪs [-nəs]
homespun, -s ˈhəʊmspʌn, -z
homestead, -s ˈhəʊmsted [-stɪd], -z
home-thrust, -s ˌhəʊmˈθrʌst, -s
homeward, -s ˈhəʊmwəd, -z
homework ˈhəʊmwɜːk
Homfray ˈhʌmfrɪ
homicidal ˌhɒmɪˈsaɪdl [ˈ——, *esp. when*
   attributive]
homicide, -s ˈhɒmɪsaɪd, -z
Homildon ˈhɒmɪldən
homil|y, -ies ˈhɒmɪl|ɪ [-əl|ɪ], -ɪz
hominoid, -s ˈhɒmɪnɔɪd, -z
hominy ˈhɒmɪnɪ [-mənɪ]
homo ˈhəʊməʊ
homoeopath, -s ˈhəʊmjəʊpæθ [ˈhɒm-,
   -mɪəp-], -s
homoeopathic, -al, -ally ˌhəʊmjəʊ-
   ˈpæθɪk [ˌhɒm-, -mɪəʊˈp-], -l, -əlɪ
homoeopath|ist/s, -y ˌhəʊmɪˈɒpəθ|ɪst/s
   [ˌhɒm-], -ɪ
homogeneity ˌhɒməʊdʒeˈniːətɪ [ˌhəʊm-,
   -dʒə'n-, -dʒɪ'n-, -ˈniːɪtɪ, -ˈnɪətɪ]
homogeneous, -ly, -ness ˌhɒməʊˈdʒiː-
   njəs [ˌhəʊm-, -ˈdʒen-, -nɪəs], -lɪ, -nɪs
   [-nəs]
homogenize, -d hɒˈmɒdʒənaɪz [hə-], -d
homograph, -s ˈhɒməʊgrɑːf [-græf], -s
homographic ˌhɒməʊˈgræfɪk [ˌhəʊm-]
homologous hɒˈmɒləgəs [həʊˈm-]
homologue, -s ˈhɒməlɒg, -z
homology hɒˈmɒlədʒɪ [həʊˈm-]
homonym, -s ˈhɒməʊnɪm, -z
homonymous, -ly hɒˈmɒnɪməs
   [həʊˈm-], -lɪ

homonymy hɒˈmɒnɪmɪ [həʊˈm-,
   -nəmɪ]
homophone, -s ˈhɒməʊfəʊn, -z
homophon|ous, -y hɒˈmɒfən|əs
   [həʊˈm-], -ɪ
homorganic ˌhɒmɔːˈgænɪk [ˌhəʊ-]
homosexual, -ist/s ˌhɒməʊˈsekʃʊəl
   [ˌhəʊm-, -ksjʊəl, -ksjwəl, -ksjʊl,
   -kʃwəl, -kʃʊl], -ɪst/s
homosexuality ˌhɒməʊsekʃʊˈælətɪ
   [ˌhəʊm-, -ksjʊ-, -ɪtɪ]
hon. (H.) (*son of a peer, etc.*) ˈɒnərəbl,
   (*without salary*) ˈɒnərərɪ
Honda ˈhɒndə
Hondur|as, -an/s hɒnˈdjʊər|əs [-r|æs],
   -ən/z
hon|e (*s. v.*) **(H.), -es, -ing, -ed** həʊn,
   -z, -ɪŋ, -d
honest, -ly ; -y ˈɒnɪst, -lɪ; -ɪ [ˈɒnəstɪ]
honey, -ed ˈhʌnɪ, -d
honey-bag, -s ˈhʌnɪbæg, -z
honey-bee, -s ˈhʌnɪbiː, -z
Honeybourne ˈhʌnɪbɔːn [-bəən,
   -ˌbʊən]
honeycomb (H.), -s, -ed ˈhʌnɪkəʊm, -z,
   -d
honeydew ˈhʌnɪdjuː
honey-guide, -s ˈhʌnɪgaɪd, -z
honeymoon, -s ˈhʌnɪmuːn, -z
honeysucker, -s ˈhʌnɪˌsʌkə*, -z
honeysuckle, -s ˈhʌnɪˌsʌkl, -z
Hong Kong ˌhɒŋˈkɒŋ
Honiton ˈhɒnɪtn [*locally* ˈhʌn-]
Honolulu ˌhɒnəˈluːluː
Honor ˈɒnə*
honorarium, -s ˌɒnəˈreərɪəm [-ˈrɑːr-],
   -z
honorary ˈɒnərərɪ
honorific (*s. adj.*), **-s** ˌɒnəˈrɪfɪk, -s
Honorius həʊˈnɔːrɪəs [hɒˈn-]
honour (*s. v.*), **-s, -ing, -ed** ˈɒnə*, -z,
   -rɪŋ, -d
honourab|le, -ly, -leness ˈɒnərəb|l, -lɪ,
   -lnɪs [-nəs]
honours|-man, -men ˈɒnəz|mæn, -men
Honyman ˈhʌnɪmən
hood (*s. v.*) **(H.), -s, -ing, -ed ; -less**
   hʊd, -z, -ɪŋ, -ɪd ; -lɪs [-ləs]
hoodlum, -s ˈhuːdləm, -z
hoodwink, -s -ing, -ed ˈhʊdwɪŋk, -s,
   -ɪŋ, -t [-wɪŋt]
hoo|f (*s.*), **-fs, -ves** huː|f, -fs, -vz
hoof (*v.*), **-s, -ing, -ed** huːf, -s, -ɪŋ, -t
Hoog(h)ly ˈhuːglɪ
hook (*s. v.*) **(H.), -s, -ing, -ed, -er/s**
   hʊk, -s, -ɪŋ, -t, -ə*/z
hookah, -s ˈhʊkə [-kɑː], -z
Hooke, -r hʊk, -ə*

243

hook-nosed 'hʊknəʊzd
hook-up, -s 'hʊkʌp, -s
Hooley 'hu:lɪ
hooligan (H.), -s, -ism 'hu:lɪgən, -z, -ɪzəm
hoop (s. v.), -s, -ing, -ed hu:p, -s, -ɪŋ, -t
hooper (H.), -s 'hu:pə*, -z
hooping-cough 'hu:pɪŋkɒf [old-fashioned -kɔ:f]
hoop-la 'hu:plɑ: ['hʊp-]
hoopoe, -s 'hu:pu:, -z
†hooray hʊ'reɪ
hoot (s. v.), -s, -ing, -ed hu:t, -s, -ɪŋ, -ɪd
hooter, -s 'hu:tə*, -z
hoover (s. v.) (H.), -s, -ing, -ed 'hu:və*, -z, -rɪŋ, -d
hooves (from hoof) hu:vz
hop (s. v.), -s, -ping, -ped, -per/s hɒp, -s, -ɪŋ, -t, -ə*/z
Hopcraft 'hɒpkrɑ:ft
hop|e (s. v.) (H.), -es, -ing, -ed həʊp, -s, -ɪŋ, -t
hope|ful (H.), -fully, -fulness 'həʊp|fʊl, -fʊlɪ [-fəlɪ], -fʊlnɪs [-nəs]
hopeless, -ly, -ness 'həʊplɪs [-ləs], -lɪ, -nɪs [-nəs]
Hopetoun 'həʊptən, -taʊn
hop|-field/s, -garden/s 'hɒp|fi:ld/z, -,gɑ:dn/z
Hopkin|s, -son 'hɒpkɪn|z, -sn
hoplite, -s 'hɒplaɪt, -s
hop-manure 'hɒpmə,njʊə* [-,njɔ:*]
Hop-o'-my-thumb ,hɒpəmɪ'θʌm ['----]
hop-pick|er/s, -ing 'hɒp,pɪk|ə*/z, -ɪŋ
Hoppner, -s 'hɒpnə*, -z
hopscotch 'hɒpskɒtʃ
Hopton 'hɒptən
Hor hɔ:*
Horace 'hɒrɪs [-rəs]
Horatian hə'reɪʃn [hɒ'r-, -ʃɪən, -ʃjən]
Horatio hə'reɪʃɪəʊ [hɒ'r-, -ʃjəʊ]
Hora|tius, -tii hə'reɪʃ|əs [hɒ'r-, -ʃɪəs, -ʃjəs], -ʃɪaɪ
Horbury 'hɔ:bərɪ
horde, -s hɔ:d, -z
Horeb 'hɔ:reb
horehound 'hɔ:haʊnd ['hɒəh-]
horizon, -s hə'raɪzn [hʊ'r-, also occasionally ə'r-, ʊ'r- when not initial, with ən as preceding indefinite article], -z
horizont|al, -ally ,hɒrɪ'zɒnt|l, -əlɪ [-l̩ɪ]
Horlick, -s 'hɔ:lɪk, -s
†hormone, -s 'hɔ:məʊn, -z
horn (H.), -s hɔ:n, -z
hornbeam, -s 'hɔ:nbi:m, -z
hornbill, -s 'hɔ:nbɪl, -z
hornblende 'hɔ:nblend

hornbook, -s 'hɔ:nbʊk, -s
Horncastle 'hɔ:n,kɑ:sl
Horne hɔ:n
horned (poppy) 'hɔ:nɪd [-nd], (of cattle, birds, etc.) hɔ:nd, (poetically, as in horned moon) 'hɔ:nɪd
-horned -hɔ:nd
Hornell hɔ:'nel
Horner 'hɔ:nə*
hornet, -s 'hɔ:nɪt, -s
Horniman 'hɔ:nɪmən
hornpipe, -s 'hɔ:npaɪp, -s
Hornsey 'hɔ:nzɪ
hornwork, -s 'hɔ:nwɜ:k, -s
horn|y, -ier, -iest, -iness 'hɔ:n|ɪ, -ɪə* [-jə*], -ɪɪst [-jɪst], -ɪnɪs [-ɪnəs]
horny-handed 'hɔ:nɪ,hændɪd [,-'--]
horography hɒ'rɒgrəfɪ [hɔ:'r-]
horologe, -s 'hɒrəlɒdʒ ['hɔ:r-, -ləʊdʒ], -ɪz
horolog|er/s, -ist/s, -y hɒ'rɒlədʒ|ə*/z [hɔ:'r-], -ɪst/s, -ɪ
horological ,hɒrə'lɒdʒɪkl [,hɔ:r-]
horoscope, -s 'hɒrəskəʊp, -s
horoscopic ,hɒrə'skɒpɪk
horoscop|ist/s, -y hɒ'rɒskəp|ɪst/s [hə'r-], -ɪ
Horowitz 'hɒrəvɪts
horrib|le, -ly, -leness 'hɒrəb|l [-rɪb-], -lɪ, -lnɪs [-nəs]
horrid, -er, -est, -ly, -ness 'hɒrɪd, -ə*, -ɪst, -lɪ, -nɪs [-nəs]
horrific hɒ'rɪfɪk [hə-]
horri|fy, -fies, -fying, -fied 'hɒrɪ|faɪ, -faɪz, -faɪɪŋ, -faɪd
Horrocks, -es 'hɒrəks, -ɪz
horror, -s 'hɒrə*, -z
horror|-stricken, -struck 'hɒrə|,strɪkən, -strʌk
Horsa 'hɔ:sə
hors de combat ,hɔ:də'kɔ̃:mbɑ: [-'kɔ:m-, -'kɒm-] (ɔrdəkɔ̃ba)
hors-d'œuvre, -s ɔ:'dɜ:vrə [hɔ:'d-, ,-'-] (ɔrdœ:vr), -z
horse, -s, -d hɔ:s, -ɪz, -t
horseback 'hɔ:sbæk
horse-box, -es 'hɔ:sbɒks, -ɪz
horsebreaker, -s 'hɔ:s,breɪkə*, -z
horse-bus, -es 'hɔ:sbʌs, -ɪz
horse-chestnut, -s ,hɔ:s'tʃesnʌt [-nət, -stn-], -s
horse|-cloth, -cloths 'hɔ:s|klɒθ [old-fashioned -klɔ:θ], -klɒθs [-klɒ:ðz, -klɔ:θs]
horse-dealer, -s 'hɔ:s,di:lə*, -z
horse-doctor, -s 'hɔ:s,dɒktə*, -z
horseflesh 'hɔ:sfleʃ
horsefl|y, -ies 'hɔ:sfl|aɪ, -aɪz

Horse-guard, -s 'hɔːsgɑːd [ˌ-'-], -z
horse|-hair, -laugh/s 'hɔːs|heə*, -lɑːf/s
horse|man (H.), -men; -manship
'hɔːs|mən, -mən [-men]; -mənʃɪp
horse-marine, -s 'hɔːsməˌriːn, -z
horseplay 'hɔːspleɪ
horse-pond, -s 'hɔːspɒnd, -z
horse-power 'hɔːsˌpauə*
horse-rac|e, -es, -ing 'hɔːsreɪs, -ɪz, -ɪŋ
horse-radish, -es 'hɔːsˌrædɪʃ [ˌ-'--], -ɪz
horse-sense 'hɔːssens
horse-shoe, -s 'hɔːʃʃuː [ːhɔːsʃuː], -z
horse-show, -s 'hɔːʃʃəu [ːhɔːs-], -z
horsetail, -s 'hɔːsteɪl, -z
horse-train|er/s, -ing 'hɔːsˌtreɪn|ə*/z, -ɪŋ
horse-whip (s. v.), -s, -ping, -ped 'hɔːswɪp [ːhɔːshw-], -s, -ɪŋ, -t
horse|-woman, -women 'hɔːs|ˌwumən, -ˌwɪmɪn
Horsfall 'hɔːsfɔːl
Horsham 'hɔːʃəm
Horsley (surname, place-name) 'hɔːzlɪ, 'hɔːslɪ
Horsmonden (in Kent) ˌhɔːzmənˈden [old-fashioned local pronunciation ˌhɔːsnˈden]
hors|y, -ier, -iest, -ily, -iness 'hɔːs|ɪ, -ɪə* [-jə*], -ɪɪst [-jɪst], -ɪlɪ [-əlɪ], -ɪnɪs [-nəs]
hortat|ive, -ory 'hɔːtət|ɪv, -ərɪ
Hortensi|a, -us hɔːˈtensɪ|ə [-nsj|ə, -nʃɪ|ə, -nʃj|ə], -əs
horticultur|al, -ist/s ˌhɔːtɪˈkʌltʃər|əl [-tʃʊr-], -ɪst/s
horticulture 'hɔːtɪkʌltʃə*
Horton 'hɔːtn
Horwich 'hɒrɪtʃ
Hosack 'hɒsək
hosanna, -s həuˈzænə, -z
hose, -s həuz, -ɪz
Hosea həuˈzɪə
hose-pipe, -s 'həuzpaɪp, -s
hosier, -s, -y 'həuzɪə [-zjə*, -ʒə*, -ʒjə*, -ʒɪə*], -z, -rɪ
Hosier (surname) 'həuzjə* [-zɪə*]
Hosmer 'hɒzmə*
hospice, -s 'hɒspɪs, -ɪz
hospitab|le, -ly, -leness 'hɒspɪtəb|l [hə's-, 'hɒspɪt-], -lɪ, -lnɪs [-nəs]
hospital, -s 'hɒspɪtl, -z
hospitalit|y, -ies ˌhɒspɪˈtælət|ɪ [-ɪt|ɪ], -ɪz
hospital(l)er, -s 'hɒspɪtlə* [-tələ*], -z
host (H.), -s həust, -s
hostage, -s 'hɒstɪdʒ, -ɪz
hostel, -s; -ry, -ries 'hɒstl, -z; -rɪ, -rɪz
hostess, -es 'həustɪs [-tes], -ɪz
hostile, -ly 'hɒstaɪl, -lɪ

hostilit|y, -ies hɒˈstɪlət|ɪ [-lɪt-], -ɪz
hostler, -s 'ɒslə*, -z
hot (adj. v.), -ter, -test, -ly, -ness; -s, -ting, -ted hɒt, -ə*, -ɪst, -lɪ, -nɪs [-nəs]; -s, -ɪŋ, -ɪd
hotbed, -s 'hɒtbed, -z
hot-blooded ˌhɒtˈblʌdɪd ['-ˌ—]
Hotchkiss 'hɒtʃkɪs
hotch|pot, -potch 'hɒtʃ|pɒt, -pɒtʃ
hot-dog, -s ˌhɒtˈdɒg, -z
hotel, -s həuˈtel [əuˈt-], -z
Note.—Some use the form əuˈtel always; others use it occasionally when the word is not initial, with ən as preceding indefinite article.
hotelier, -s həuˈtelɪeɪ [-lɪə*], -z
Hotham (surname) 'hʌðəm
hothead, -s 'hɒthed, -z
hot-headed ˌhɒtˈhedɪd ['-ˌ—]
hothou|se, -ses 'hɒthau|s, -zɪz
hotpot, -s 'hɒtpɒt, -s
hotspur (H.), -s 'hɒtspɜː* [-spə*], -z
Hottentot, -s 'hɒtntɒt, -s
hot-water-bottle, -s ˌhɒtˈwɔːtəˌbɒtl, -z
Houdini huːˈdiːnɪ
hough (s. v.), -s, -ing, -ed hɒk, -s, -ɪŋ, -t
Hough hʌf, hɒf
Houghall (in Durham) 'hɒfl
Hougham (in Kent) 'hʌfəm
Houghton 'hɔːtn, 'hautn, 'həutn
Note.—'hɔːtn, 'hautn seem more usual when the word is a surname.
Houghton-le-Spring ˌhəutnlɪˈsprɪŋ [ˌhautn-]
Houltby 'həultbɪ
hound (s. v.), -s, -ing, -ed haund, -z, -ɪŋ, -ɪd
Houndsditch 'haundzdɪtʃ
Hounslow 'haunzləu
hour, -s, -ly 'auə*, -z, -lɪ
hourglass, -es 'auəglɑːs, -ɪz
hour-hand, -s 'auəhænd, -z
houri, -s 'huərɪ, -z
hou|se (s.) (H.), -ses hau|s, -zɪz
hous|e (v.), -es, -ing, -ed hauz, -ɪz, -ɪŋ, -d
house|-agent/s, -boat/s 'haus|ˌeɪdʒ-ənt/s, -bəut/s
house-break|er/s, -ing 'hausˌbreɪk|-ə*/z, -ɪŋ
house-dog, -s 'hausdɒg, -z
house-dut|y, -ies 'hausˌdjuːt|ɪ, -ɪz
housefather, -s 'hausˌfɑːðə*, -z
house-fl|y, -ies 'hausflaɪ, -aɪz
houseful, -s 'hausful, -z
household, -s; -er/s 'haushəuld, -z; -ə*/z

245

housekeep|er/s, -ing 'haʊs͵kiːp|ə*/z, -ɪŋ
House1 'haʊzl
house-leek, -s 'haʊsliːk, -s
houseless 'haʊslɪs [-ləs]
housemaid, -s 'haʊsmeɪd, -z
house|man, -men 'haʊsmən [-mæn], -mən [-men]
housemaster, -s 'haʊs͵mɑːstə*, -z
housemother, -s 'haʊs͵mʌðə*, -z
house-part|y, -ies 'haʊs͵pɑːt|ɪ, -ɪz
house-physician, -s 'haʊsfɪ͵zɪʃn [-fə-], -z
houseproud 'haʊspraʊd
house-room 'haʊsrʊm [-ruːm]
house-surgeon, -s 'haʊs͵sɜːdʒən, -z
house-to-house ͵haʊstə'haʊs
housetop, -s 'haʊstɒp, -s
house-warming, -s 'haʊs͵wɔːmɪŋ, -z
housewi|fe (woman), -ves 'haʊswaɪ|f, -vz
housewi|fe (needle-case), -fes, -ves 'hʌzɪ|f, -fs, -vz
housewifely 'haʊs͵waɪflɪ
housewifery 'haʊswɪfərɪ ['hʌzɪfrɪ]
house-work 'haʊswɜːk
Housman 'haʊsmən
Houston (English surname) 'huːstən, 'haʊs-, (Scottish surname) 'huːstən, (city in U.S.A.) 'hjuːstən
Houyhnhnm, -s 'hʊɪhnəm [hʊ'ɪnəm], -z
hove (from heave) (H.) həʊv
hov|el (s. v.), -els, -elling, -elled, -eller/s 'hɒv|l ['hʌv-], -lz, -lɪŋ [-əlɪŋ], -ld, -lə*/z [-ələ*/z]
Hovell (surname) 'həʊvl, 'hɒvl, həʊ'vel
Hovenden 'hɒvndən
hov|er, -ers, -ering, -ered 'hɒv|ə* ['hʌv-], -əz, -ərɪŋ, -əd
hovercraft 'hɒvəkrɑːft
hover-fl|y, -ies 'hɒvəfl|aɪ, -aɪz
Hovis 'həʊvɪs
how (H.) haʊ
Howard 'haʊəd
howbeit ͵haʊ'biːɪt
howdah, -s 'haʊdə, -z
how do you do ͵haʊdjʊ'duː: [-djə'd-, -dɪ'd-, -dʒʊ'd-, -dʒə'd-]
howdy-do, -s ͵haʊdɪ'duː:, -z
Howe haʊ
Howell, -s 'haʊəl, -z
however haʊ'evə*
   Note.—Variants 'haʊevə*, 'haʊəvə* are used by some people when the meaning is 'however that may be'.
Howick 'haʊɪk
How|ie, -itt 'haʊ|ɪ, -ɪt
howitzer, -s 'haʊɪtsə*, -z

howl (s. v.), -s, -ing, -ed haʊl, -z, -ɪŋ, -d
howler, -s 'haʊlə*, -z
Howley 'haʊlɪ
Howorth 'haʊəθ
Howse haʊz
howsoever ͵haʊsəʊ'evə*
Howson 'haʊsn
Howth (near Dublin) həʊθ
Hoxton 'hɒkstən
hoy (s. interj.) (H.), -s hɔɪ, -z
hoyden (H.), -s 'hɔɪdn, -z
Hoylake 'hɔɪleɪk
hub, -s hʌb, -z
Huback 'hjuːbæk
Hubback 'hʌbæk, -bək
Hubbard 'hʌbəd
hubble-bubble, -s 'hʌbl͵bʌbl, -z
hubbub, -s 'hʌbʌb [-bəb], -z
hubb|y, -ies 'hʌb|ɪ, -ɪz
hub-cap, -s 'hʌbkæp, -s
Hubert 'hjuːbət [-bɜːt]
huckaback, -s 'hʌkəbæk, -s
huckleberr|y (H.), -ies 'hʌklbər|ɪ [-͵ber|ɪ], -ɪz
Hucknall 'hʌknəl
huckster, -s 'hʌkstə*, -z
Huddersfield 'hʌdəzfiːld
hudd|le (s. v.), -les, -ling, -led 'hʌd|l, -lz, -lɪŋ [-lɪŋ], -ld
Hud(d)leston 'hʌdlstən
Hudibras 'hjuːdɪbræs
Hud|nott, -son 'hʌd|nɒt, -sn
hue, -s hjuː:, -z
hue and cry ͵hjuː:ən'kraɪ [-əŋ'k-]
Hueffer 'hefə*
huff (s. v.), -s, -ing, -ed hʌf, -s, -ɪŋ, -t
huffish, -ly, -ness 'hʌfɪʃ, -lɪ, -nɪs [-nəs]
huff|y, -ier, -iest, -ily, -iness 'hʌf|ɪ, -ɪə*, -ɪɪst, -ɪlɪ [-əlɪ], -ɪnɪs [-ɪnəs]
hug (s. v.), -s, -ging, -ged hʌg, -z, -ɪŋ, -d
Hugall 'hjuːgəl
huge, -r, -st, -ly, -ness hjuːdʒ, -ə*, -ɪst, -lɪ, -nɪs [-nəs]
Hugesson 'hjuːgɪsn
hugger-mugger 'hʌgə͵mʌgə*
Huggin, -s 'hʌgɪn, -z
Hugh, -es hjuː:, -z
Hughenden 'hjuːəndən ['hjʊən-]
Hugo (English name) 'hjuːgəʊ
Hugon 'hjuːgən [-gɒn]
Hugue|not, -nots 'hjuːgə|nəʊ [-nɒt], -nəʊz [-nɒts]
Huish 'hjuːɪʃ ['hjʊɪʃ]
Hulbert 'hʌlbət
hulk, -s, -ing, hʌlk, -s, -ɪŋ
hull (s. v.) (H.), -s, -ing, -ed hʌl, -z, -ɪŋ, -d
hullabaloo, -s ͵hʌləbə'luː:, -z

Hullah 'hʌlə
hullo hə'ləʊ [hʌ'l-]
Hulme hjuːm, huːm
Hulse hʌls
Hulsean hʌl'siːən [-'sɪən]
hum (s. v.), -s, -ming, -med hʌm, -z, -ɪŋ, -d
human, -ly 'hjuːmən, -lɪ
humane, -r, -st, -ly, -ness hjuː'meɪn [hjʊ-], -ə*, -ɪst, -lɪ, -nɪs [-nəs]
humani|sm, -st/s 'hjuːmənɪ|zəm, -st/s
humanistic ˌhjuːmə'nɪstɪk
humanitarian, -s, -ism hjuːˌmænɪ'teərɪən [hjuːˌ, ˌhjuːˌmæn-], -z, -ɪzəm
humanit|y, -ies hjuː'mænət|ɪ [hjʊ-, -ɪt|ɪ], -ɪz
humanization [-isa-] ˌhjuːmənaɪ'zeɪʃn
humaniz|e [-is|e], -es, -ing, -ed 'hjuːmənaɪz, -ɪz, -ɪŋ, -d
humankind ˌhjuːmən'kaɪnd
Humber, -s, -side 'hʌmbə*, -z, -saɪd
Humbert 'hʌmbət [-bɜːt]
humb|le (adj. v.), -ler, -lest, -ly, -leness; -les, -ling, -led 'hʌmb|l, -lə*, -lɪst, -lɪ, -lnɪs [-nəs]; -lz, -lɪŋ, -ld
humble-bee, -s 'hʌmblbiː, -z
humble-pie ˌhʌmbl'paɪ
Humboldt 'hʌmbəʊlt ['hʊm-] ('humbolt)
humbug (s. v.), -s, -ging, -ged 'hʌmbʌg, -z, -ɪŋ, -d
humdrum 'hʌmdrʌm
Hume hjuːm
humer|us, -i, -al 'hjuːmər|əs, -aɪ, -əl
Humian 'hjuːmjən [-mɪən]
humid, -ness 'hjuːmɪd, -nɪs [-nəs]
humidity hjuː'mɪdətɪ [hjʊ-, -ɪtɪ]
humiliat|e, -es, -ing, -ed hjuː'mɪlɪeɪt [hjʊ-], -s, -ɪŋ, -ɪd
humiliation, -s hjuːˌmɪlɪ'eɪʃn [hjʊ-, ˌhjuːmɪl-], -z
humility hjuː'mɪlətɪ [hjʊ-, -lɪt-]
humming-bird, -s 'hʌmɪŋbɜːd, -z
humming-top, -s 'hʌmɪŋtɒp, -s
hummock, -s, -ed; -y 'hʌmək, -s, -t; -ɪ
humor|al, -alism, -alist/s 'hjuːmər|əl, -əlɪzəm, -əlɪst/s
humoresque, -s ˌhjuːmə'resk, -s
humorist, -s 'hjuːmərɪst [old-fashioned 'juː-], -s
humoristic ˌhjuːmə'rɪstɪk [old-fashioned ˌjuː-]
humorous, -ly, -ness 'hjuːmərəs [old-fashioned 'juː-], -lɪ, -nɪs [-nəs]
humour (s. v.), -s, -ing, -ed 'hjuːmə* [old-fashioned 'juː-], -z, -rɪŋ, -d
humoursome, -ly, -ness 'hjuːməsəm [old-fashioned 'juː-], -lɪ, -nɪs [-nəs]

hump (s. v.), -s, -ing, -ed hʌmp, -s, -ɪŋ, -t [hʌmt]
humpback, -s, -ed 'hʌmpbæk, -s, -t
humph, m̩m, m̩mm̩, mm̩m, hə̃h [hʌmf]
Humphery 'hʌmfrɪ
Humphr(e)y, -s 'hʌmfrɪ, -z
Humpty-dumpty ˌhʌmptɪ'dʌmptɪ
hump|y, -ier, -iest, -iness 'hʌmp|ɪ, -ɪə* [-jə*], -ɪɪst [-jɪst], -ɪnɪs [-ɪnəs]
humus 'hjuːməs
Hun, -s hʌn, -z
hunch (s. v.), -es, -ing, -ed hʌntʃ, -ɪz, -ɪŋ, -t
hunchback, -s, -ed 'hʌntʃbæk, -s, -t
hundred, -s 'hʌndrəd [-drɪd], -z
hundredfold 'hʌndrədfəʊld [-drɪd-]
hundredth, -s 'hʌndrətθ [-drɪtθ, -drədθ, -drɪdθ], -s
hundredweight, -s 'hʌndrədweɪt [-drɪd-], -s
hung (from hang) hʌŋ
Hungarian, -s hʌŋ'geərɪən, -z
Hungary 'hʌŋgərɪ
hunger (s. v.), -s, -ing, -ed, -er/s 'hʌŋgə*, -z, -rɪŋ, -d, -rə*/z
Hungerford 'hʌŋgəfəd
hunger-strik|e (s. v.), -es, -ing, hunger-struck, hunger-striker/s 'hʌŋgəstraɪk, -s, -ɪŋ, 'hʌŋgəstrʌk, 'hʌŋgəˌstraɪkə*/z
hungr|y, -ier, -iest, -ily, -iness 'hʌŋgr|ɪ, -ɪə*, -ɪɪst, -əlɪ [-ɪlɪ], -ɪnɪs [-ɪnəs]
hunk, -s hʌŋk, -s
Hunn|ic, -ish 'hʌn|ɪk, -ɪʃ
Hunslet 'hʌnslɪt
Hunstanton hʌn'stæntən [locally 'hʌnstən]
Hunsworth 'hʌnzwəθ [-wɜː θ]
hunt (s. v.) (H.), -s, -ing, -ed, -er/s hʌnt, -s, -ɪŋ, -ɪd, -ə*/z
Hunter 'hʌntə*
Hunterian hʌn'tɪərɪən
hunting-box, -es 'hʌntɪŋbɒks, -ɪz
hunting-cap, -s 'hʌntɪŋkæp, -s
hunting-crop, -s 'hʌntɪŋkrɒp, -s
Huntingdon, -shire 'hʌntɪŋdən, -ʃə* [-ˌʃɪə*]
Huntingdonian, -s ˌhʌntɪŋ'dəʊnjən [-nɪən], -z
hunting-field, -s 'hʌntɪŋfiːld, -z
Huntingford 'hʌntɪŋfəd
hunting-ground, -s 'hʌntɪŋgraʊnd, -z
hunting-horn, -s 'hʌntɪŋhɔːn, -z
hunting-kni|fe, -ves 'hʌntɪŋnaɪ|f, -vz
hunting-song, -s 'hʌntɪŋsɒŋ, -z
Huntington 'hʌntɪŋtən
Huntl(e)y 'hʌntlɪ
Hunton 'hʌntən

247

huntress, -es 'hʌntrɪs [-trəs, -tres], -ɪz
Hunts. hʌnts
hunts|man, -men, -manship 'hʌnts|-
mən, -mən [-men], -mənʃɪp
Hunyadi 'hʊnjɑːdɪ ['hʌnj-, -'--]
Hurd hɜːd
hurd|le (s. v.), -les, -ling, -led 'hɜːd|l,
-lz, -lɪŋ [-lɪŋ], -ld
hurdle-race, -s 'hɜːdlreɪs, -ɪz
hurdy-gurd|y, -ies 'hɜːdɪˌɡɜːd|ɪ, -ɪz
Hurford 'hɜːfəd
hurl (s. v.), -s, -ing, -ed, -er/s hɜːl, -z,
-ɪŋ, -d, -ə*/z
hurley (H.), -s 'hɜːlɪ, -z
Hurlingham 'hɜːlɪŋəm
Hurlstone 'hɜːlstən
hurly-burly 'hɜːlɪˌbɜːlɪ [ˌ--'--]
Huron 'hjʊərən
hurrah (s. v.), -s, -ing, -ed hʊ'rɑː, -z,
-ɪŋ, -d
hurrah (interj.) hʊ'rɑː
hurray (s.), -s hʊ'reɪ, -z
hurray (interj.) hʊ'reɪ
hurricane, -s 'hʌrɪkən [-kɪn, -keɪn], -z
hurr|y (s. v.), -ies, -ying, -ied/ly, -ier/s
'hʌr|ɪ, -ɪz, -ɪɪŋ, -ɪd/lɪ, -ɪə*/z
hurry-scurry ˌhʌrɪ'skʌrɪ
hurst, -s hɜːst, -s
Hurstmonceux ˌhɜːsmən'zuː [-mɒn-,
ˌ-'sjuː, -'suː]
Hurstpierpoint ˌhɜːstpɪə'pɔɪnt
hurt (s. v.) (H.), -s, -ing hɜːt, -s, -ɪŋ
hurt|ful, -fully, -fulness 'hɜːt|fʊl, -fʊlɪ
[-fəlɪ], -fʊlnɪs [-nəs]
hurtle, -les, -ling, -led 'hɜːt|l, -lz, -lɪŋ,
-ld
husband (s. v.), -s, -ing, -ed 'hʌzbənd,
-z, -ɪŋ, -ɪd
husbandly 'hʌzbəndlɪ
husband|man, -men 'hʌzbənd|mən,
-mən [-men]
husbandry 'hʌzbəndrɪ
hush (s. v.), -es, -ing, -ed hʌʃ, -ɪz, -ɪŋ, -t
hush (interj.) ʃ: [hʌʃ]
hushaby 'hʌʃəbaɪ
Hushai 'hjuːʃeɪaɪ ['huː-, -ʃaɪ]
hush-hush ˌhʌʃ'hʌʃ ['--]
hush-money 'hʌʃˌmʌnɪ
husk, -s hʌsk, -s
Huskisson 'hʌskɪsn
husk|y, -ier, -iest, -ily, -iness 'hʌsk|ɪ,
-ɪə* [-jə*], -ɪɪst [-jɪst], -ɪlɪ [-əlɪ],
-ɪnɪs [-ɪnəs]
hussar, -s hʊ'zɑː:*, -z
Hussey 'hʌsɪ
Hussite, -s 'hʌsaɪt, -s
huss|y, -ies 'hʌs|ɪ ['hʌz|ɪ], -ɪz
Hussy 'hʌsɪ

hustings 'hʌstɪŋz
hust|le, -les, -ling, -led, -ler/s 'hʌs|l,
-lz, -lɪŋ [-lɪŋ], -ld, -lə*/z [-lə*/z]
hut, -s hʌt, -s
hutch, -es hʌtʃ, -ɪz
Hutch|eson, -ings 'hʌtʃ|ɪsn, -ɪŋz
Hutchinson 'hʌtʃɪnsn
Hutchinsonian, -s ˌhʌtʃɪn'səʊnjən
[-nɪən], -z
Hutchison 'hʌtʃɪsn
Huth, -waite huː:θ, -weɪt
hutment, -s 'hʌtmənt, -s
Hutton 'hʌtn
Hux|ley, -table 'hʌks|lɪ, -təbl
Huygens 'haɪɡənz
huzza (s. interj.), -s hʊ'zɑː: [hʌ'z-], -z
Hwang-ho ˌhwæŋ'həʊ
hyacinth (H.), -s 'haɪəsɪnθ, -s
hyacinthine ˌhaɪə'sɪnθaɪn
Hyades 'haɪədiːz
hyaena, -s haɪ'iːnə, -z
hyal|in(e), -ite, -oid 'haɪəl|ɪn, [-iːn,
-aɪn], -aɪt, -ɔɪd
Hyam, -son 'haɪəm, -sn
hybrid, -s; -ism 'haɪbrɪd, -z; -ɪzəm
hybridity haɪ'brɪdətɪ [-ɪtɪ]
hybridization [-isa-] ˌhaɪbrɪdaɪ'zeɪʃn
hybridiz|e [-is|e], -es, -ing, -ed, -er/s
'haɪbrɪdaɪz, -ɪz, -ɪŋ, -d, -ə*/z
Hydaspes haɪ'dæspiːz
Hyde haɪd
Hyde Park ˌhaɪd'pɑːk ['haɪdp- according to sentence-stress]
Hyderabad 'haɪdərəbæd [ˌhaɪdərə'b-]
(Hindi həydərabad)
hydra, -s 'haɪdrə, -z
hydrangea, -s haɪ'dreɪndʒə [-dʒə,
-dʒɪə], -z
hydrant, -s 'haɪdrənt, -s
hydrargyrum haɪ'drɑːdʒɪrəm
hydrate, -s 'haɪdreɪt [-rɪt], -s
hydraulic, -s haɪ'drɔːlɪk [-'drɒl-], -s
hydrazine 'haɪdrəziːn [-zɪn]
hydro, -s 'haɪdrəʊ, -z
hydrocarbon, -s ˌhaɪdrəʊ'kɑːbən
[-bɒn], -z
hydrocephalus ˌhaɪdrəʊ'sefələs
[-'kef-]
hydrochloric ˌhaɪdrəʊ'klɒrɪk [-'klɔː:r-,
also '--ˌ-- according to sentence-stress]
hydrodynamic, -al, -ally, -s ˌhaɪdrəʊ-
daɪ'næmɪk [-dɪ'n-], -l, -əlɪ, -s
hydrofoil, -s 'haɪdrəʊfɔɪl, -z
hydrogen 'haɪdrədʒən [-drɪdʒən,
-drədʒɪn]
hydrogenous haɪ'drɒdʒɪnəs [-dʒən-]
hydrograph|er/s, -y haɪ'drɒɡrəf|ə*/z,
-ɪ

hydrographic, -al, -ally ˌhaɪdrəʊ-
'græfɪk, -l, -əlɪ
hydro|logy, -lysis haɪ'drɒ|lədʒɪ, -lɪsɪs
[-ləsɪs]
hydromechanics ˌhaɪdrəʊmɪ'kænɪks
[-mə'k-]
hydrometer, -s haɪ'drɒmɪtə* [-mətə*],
-z
hydrometric, -al, -ally ˌhaɪdrəʊ'metrɪk,
-l, -əlɪ
hydrometry haɪ'drɒmətrɪ [-mɪtrɪ]
hydropathic (s. adj.), -s, -al, -ally ˌhaɪdrəʊ'pæθɪk, -s, -l, -əlɪ
hydropath|ist/s, -y haɪ'drɒpəθ|ɪst/s, -ɪ
hydrophilic ˌhaɪdrəʊ'fɪlɪk
hydrophobia ˌhaɪdrəʊ'fəʊbjə [-bɪə]
hydrophobic ˌhaɪdrəʊ'fəʊbɪk [-'fɒb-]
hydrophyte, -s 'haɪdrəʊfaɪt, -s
hydroplane, -s 'haɪdrəʊpleɪn, -z
hydroponic, -s ˌhaɪdrəʊ'pɒnɪk, -s
hydroquinone ˌhaɪdrəʊkwɪ'nəʊn
[-'kwaɪnəʊn, haɪ'drɒkɪnəʊn]
hydroscope, -s 'haɪdrəskəʊp, -s
hydrostat, -s 'haɪdrəʊstæt, -s
hydrostatic, -al, -ally, -s ˌhaɪdrəʊ-
'stætɪk, -l, -əlɪ, -s
hydro-therapy ˌhaɪdrəʊ'θerəpɪ
hydrous 'haɪdrəs
hydrox|ide/s, -yl haɪ'drɒks|aɪd/z, -ɪl
hyena, -s haɪ'iːnə, -z
Hygeia haɪ'dʒiːə [-'dʒɪə]
hygiene 'haɪdʒiːn
hygienic, -ally haɪ'dʒiːnɪk, -əlɪ
hygromet|er/s, -ry haɪ'grɒmɪt|ə*
[-mət|ə*]/z, -rɪ
hygrometric, -al, -ally ˌhaɪgrəʊ'metrɪk,
-l, -əlɪ
hygroscope, -s 'haɪgrəskəʊp, -s
Hyksos 'hɪksɒs
Hylas 'haɪlæs
Hylton 'hɪltən
Hyman 'haɪmən
hymen (H.), -s 'haɪmen, -z
hymene|al, -an ˌhaɪme'niː|əl [-mə'n-,
-'nɪəl], -ən
Hymettus haɪ'metəs
hymn (s. v.), -s, -ing, -ed hɪm, -z, -ɪŋ,
-d
hymnal, -s 'hɪmnəl, -z
hymnar|y, -ies 'hɪmnər|ɪ, -ɪz
hymn-book, -s 'hɪmbʊk, -s
hymnic 'hɪmnɪk
hymnody 'hɪmnəʊdɪ
hymnolog|ist/s, -y hɪm'nɒlədʒ|ɪst/s, -ɪ
Hyndley 'haɪndlɪ
Hyndman 'haɪndmən
hyoid 'haɪɔɪd
hyoscine 'haɪəʊsiːn

hypallage haɪ'pæləgɪ: [-gɪ, -lədʒɪ]
Hypatia haɪ'peɪʃjə [-ʃɪə, -ʃə]
hyperacute, -ness ˌhaɪpərə'kjuːt, -nɪs
[-nəs]
hyperbol|a, -ae, -as haɪ'pɜːbəl|ə, -iː, -əz
hyperbole, -s haɪ'pɜːbəlɪ, -z
hyperbolic, -al, -ally ˌhaɪpə'bɒlɪk, -l,
-əlɪ
hyperboli|sm, -st/s haɪ'pɜːbəlɪ|zəm,
-st/s
hyperboliz|e [-is|e], -es, -ing, -ed haɪ-
'pɜːbəlaɪz, -ɪz, -ɪŋ, -d
hyperboloid, -s haɪ'pɜːbəlɔɪd, -z
hyperborean, -s ˌhaɪpəbɔː'riːən [-pɜː-,
-'rɪən, -bɒ'riːən, -bɒ'rɪən, -'bɔːrɪən]
hypercritic|al, -ally ˌhaɪpə'krɪtɪk|l, -əlɪ
hypercriticism ˌhaɪpə'krɪtɪsɪzəm
hypercriticiz|e [-is|e], -es, -ing, -ed
ˌhaɪpə'krɪtɪsaɪz, -ɪz, -ɪŋ, -d
Hyperides ˌhaɪpə'raɪdiːz, haɪ'perɪdiːz
Hyperion haɪ'pɪərɪən [-'per-]
hypersensitive ˌhaɪpə'sensətɪv [-sɪtɪv]
hypertension ˌhaɪpə'tenʃn [-pɜː-]
hyper-thyroid, -ism ˌhaɪpə'θaɪrɔɪd
[-'θaɪər-], -ɪzəm
hypertroph|y, -ied haɪ'pɜːtrəʊf|ɪ, -ɪd
hyph|en (s. v.), -ens, -ening, -ened
'haɪf|n, -nz, -nɪŋ [-ənɪŋ], -nd
hyphenat|e, -es, -ing, -ed 'haɪfəneɪt
[-fn-, -fɪn-], -s, -ɪŋ, -ɪd
hypnosis hɪp'nəʊsɪs
hypnotic hɪp'nɒtɪk
hypnoti|sm, -st/s 'hɪpnətɪ|zəm, -st/s
hypnotization (-isa-) ˌhɪpnətaɪ'zeɪʃn
hypnotiz|e [-is|e], -es, -ing, -ed, -er/s
'hɪpnətaɪz, -ɪz, -ɪŋ, -d, -ə*/z
hypo 'haɪpəʊ
hypocaust, -s 'haɪpəʊkɔːst, -s
hypochond|ria, -riac/s ˌhaɪpəʊ'kɒnd|rɪə
[ˌhɪp-], -rɪæk/s
hypochondriacal ˌhaɪpəʊkɒn'draɪəkl
[ˌhɪp-, -kən-]
hypochondriasis ˌhaɪpəʊkɒn'draɪəsɪs
[ˌhɪp-, -kən-]
hypocris|y, -ies hɪ'pɒkrəs|ɪ [-krɪs-], -ɪz
hypocrite, -s 'hɪpəkrɪt [-pʊk-], -s
hypocritic|al, -ally ˌhɪpəʊ'krɪtɪk|l,
-əlɪ
hypocycloid, -s ˌhaɪpəʊ'saɪklɔɪd, -z
hypoderm|is, -ic ˌhaɪpəʊ'dɜːm|ɪs, -ɪk
hypophosphate, -s ˌhaɪpəʊ'fɒsfeɪt [-fɪt],
-s
hypostasis haɪ'pɒstəsɪs
hypostatiz|e [-is|e], -es, -ing, -ed
haɪ'pɒstətaɪz, -ɪz, -ɪŋ, -d
hypostyle 'haɪpəʊstaɪl
hyposulphite ˌhaɪpəʊ'sʌlfaɪt
hypotax|is, -es ˌhaɪpəʊ'tæks|ɪs ['--ˌ--],
-iːz

249

hypotension ˌhaɪpəʊ'tenʃn
hypotenuse, -s haɪ'pɒtənjuːz [-njuːs,
  -tnj-, -tɪn-], -ɪz
hypothalamus ˌhaɪpəʊ'θæləməs
hypothecat|e, -es, -ing, -ed haɪ'pɒθɪ-
  keɪt [-θə-], -s, -ɪŋ, -ɪd
hypothecation, -s haɪˌpɒθɪ'keɪʃn [-θə-],
  -z
hypothermia ˌhaɪpəʊ'θɜːmɪə [-mjə]
hypothes|is, -es haɪ'pɒθɪs|ɪs [-θəs-],
  -iːz
hypothetic, -al, -ally ˌhaɪpəʊ'θetɪk, -l,
  -əlɪ
hypothyroid, -ism ˌhaɪpəʊ'θaɪrɔɪd
  [-'θaɪər-], -ɪzəm

hypsomet|er/s, -ry hɪp'sɒmɪt|ə*
  [-mət|ə*]/z, -rɪ
hyrax, -es 'haɪəræks, -ɪz
Hyslop 'hɪzləp
hyson (H.), 'haɪsn
hyssop 'hɪsəp
hysterectom|y, -ies ˌhɪstə'rektəm|ɪ,
  -ɪz
hysteria hɪ'stɪərɪə
hysteric, -s, -al, -ally hɪ'sterɪk, -s, -l, -əlɪ
hysteron-proteron ˌhɪstərɒn'prɒtərɒn
  [-'prəʊ-]
hythe (H.), -s haɪð, -z
Hywel 'haʊəl

I

I (*the letter, pron.*), -'s aɪ, -z
Iacchus ɪ'ækəs [aɪ'æk-]
Iachimo ɪ'ækɪməʊ [aɪ'æk-]
Iago ɪ'ɑːgəʊ
Iain ɪən ['iːən]
iamb, -s 'aɪæmb, -z
iamb|ic/s, -us/es aɪ'æmb|ɪk/s, -əs/ɪz
Ian ɪən ['iːən]
I'Anson 'aɪənsn
Ianthe aɪ'ænθɪ
Iason 'aɪəsn
iatrogenic aɪˌætrəʊ'dʒenɪk [ˌ—'—]
Ibadan (*in Nigeria*) ɪ'bædən
Ibbertson 'ɪbətsn [-bəːt-]
Ibbetson 'ɪbɪtsn [-bət-]
Iberia, -n/s aɪ'bɪərɪə, -n/z
Iberus aɪ'bɪərəs
ibex, -es 'aɪbeks, -ɪz
ibidem 'ɪbɪdem [ɪ'baɪdem]
ibis, -es 'aɪbɪs, -ɪz
Ibrahim 'ɪbrəhiːm [ˌɪbrə'hiːm]
Ibrox 'aɪbrɒks
Ibsen 'ɪbsn
Icaria, -n ɪ'keərɪə [aɪ'k-], -n
Icarus 'ɪkərəs ['aɪk-]
ic|e (*s. v.*), -es, -ing, -ed aɪs, -ɪz, -ɪŋ, -t
ice-axe, -s 'aɪsæks, -ɪz
iceberg, -s 'aɪsbəːg, -z
ice-boat, -s 'aɪsbəʊt, -s
icebound 'aɪsbaʊnd
ice-breaker, -s 'aɪsˌbreɪkə*, -z
ice-cap, -s 'aɪskæp, -s
ice-cream, -s ˌaɪs'kriːm [*attributively* '—], -z
icefall, -s 'aɪsfɔːl, -z
ice|-field/s, -floe/s 'aɪs|fiːld/z, -fləʊ/z
ice-hockey 'aɪsˌhɒkɪ
ice-hou|se, -ses 'aɪshaʊ|s, -zɪz
Iceland 'aɪslənd
Icelander, -s 'aɪsləndə* [-lændə*], -z
Icelandic aɪs'lændɪk
iceloll|y, -ies ˌaɪs'lɒl|ɪ, -ɪz
ice|-man, -men 'aɪs|mæn [-mən], -men [-mən]
ice-pack, -s 'aɪspæk, -s
ice-pail, -s 'aɪspeɪl, -z
ice-spar ˌaɪs'spɑː* ['—]
Ichabod 'ɪkəbɒd ['ɪxə-]
ichneumon, -s ɪk'njuːmən, -z

ichnography ɪk'nɒgrəfɪ
ichor 'aɪkɔː*
ichthyolog|ist/s, -y ˌɪkθɪ'ɒlədʒ|ɪst/s, -ɪ
ichthyosaur|us, -i, -uses ˌɪkθɪə'sɔːr|əs [-θjə's-, -θɪəʊ-], -aɪ, -əsɪz
icicle, -s 'aɪsɪkl, -z
icing (*s.*) 'aɪsɪŋ
Icknield 'ɪkniːld
Ickornshaw 'ɪkɔːnʃɔː
Icolmkill ˌiːkɒlm'kɪl
icon, -s 'aɪkɒn [-kən], -z
iconic aɪ'kɒnɪk
Iconium aɪ'kəʊnjəm [-nɪəm]
iconoclasm aɪ'kɒnəʊklæzəm
iconoclast, -s aɪ'kɒnəʊklæst [-klɑːst], -s
iconoclastic, -ally aɪˌkɒnəʊ'klæstɪk, -lɪ
iconograph|er/s, -y ˌaɪkɒ'nɒgrəf|ə*/z [-kə'n-], -ɪ
iconoscope, -s aɪ'kɒnəskəʊp, -s
icosahedr|on, -ons, -a; -al ˌaɪkəsə-'hedr|ən [-kɒs-, -'hiːd-, '—ˌ—], -ənz, -ə; -əl
ictus, -es 'ɪktəs, -ɪz
ic|y, -ier, -iest, -ily, -iness 'aɪs|ɪ, -ɪə* [-jə*], -ɪɪst [-jɪst], -ɪlɪ [-əlɪ], -ɪnɪs [-məs]
id ɪd
I'd (= I would, I should, *or* I had) aɪd
Ida 'aɪdə
Idaho 'aɪdəhəʊ
Idalia, -n aɪ'deɪljə [-lɪə], -n
Iddesleigh 'ɪdzlɪ
Ide (*in Devon*) iːd
idea, -s aɪ'dɪə, -z
    Note.—The pronunciation 'aɪdɪə *is also sometimes heard, esp. when a stress immediately follows.*
ideal (*s.*), -s aɪ'dɪəl [-'diːəl, -'diːl], -z
ideal (*adj.*) aɪ'dɪəl [-'diːəl, -'diːl, '—, *esp. when attributive*]
ideal|ism, -ist/s aɪ'dɪəl|ɪzəm [aɪ'diːəl-, 'aɪdjəl-, 'aɪdɪəl-], -ɪst/s
idealistic, -ally aɪˌdɪə'lɪstɪk [aɪˌdiːə'l-, ˌaɪdjə'l-, ˌaɪdɪə'l-], -lɪ
ideality ˌaɪdɪ'ælətɪ [-ɪtɪ]
idealization [-isa-], -s aɪˌdɪəlaɪ'zeɪʃn [-ˌdiːəl-, -lɪ'z-, ˌ—'—], -z
idealiz|e [-is|e], -es, -ing, -ed, -er/s aɪ'dɪəlaɪz [-'diːəl-], -ɪz, -ɪŋ, -d, -ə*/z

251

ideally aɪ'dɪəlɪ [-'diːəlɪ]
idem 'aɪdem ['ɪdem]
Iden 'aɪdn
identic|al, -ally, -alness aɪ'dentɪk|l
  [ɪ'd-], -əlɪ, -lnɪs [-nəs]
identification, -s aɪ‚dentɪfɪ'keɪʃn [ɪ‚d-],
  -z
identi|fy, -fies, -fying, -fied, -fier/s;
  -fiable aɪ'dentɪ|faɪ [ɪ'd-], -faɪz, -faɪɪŋ,
  -faɪd, -faɪə*/z; -faɪəbl [-‚--'---]
identit|y, -ies aɪ'dentət|ɪ [ɪ'd-, -ɪt|ɪ], -ɪz
ideogram, -s 'ɪdɪəʊɡræm ['aɪd-], -z
ideograph, -s 'ɪdɪəʊɡrɑːf ['aɪd-, -ɡræf],
  -s
ideographic, -al, -ally ‚ɪdɪəʊ'ɡræfɪk
  [‚aɪd-], -l, -əlɪ
ideography ‚ɪdɪ'ɒɡrəfɪ [‚aɪd-]
ideological ‚aɪdɪə'lɒdʒɪkl [‚ɪd-]
ideolog|ist/s, -y, -ies ‚aɪdɪ'ɒlədʒ|ɪst/s
  [‚ɪd-], -ɪ, -ɪz
Ides aɪdz
idioc|y, -ies 'ɪdɪəs|ɪ ['ɪdjəs-], -ɪz
idiolect, -s 'ɪdɪəʊlekt, -s
idiom, -s 'ɪdɪəm ['ɪdjəm], -z
idiomatic, -al, -ally ‚ɪdɪə'mætɪk
  [‚ɪdjəʊ'm-, ‚ɪdɪʊ'm-, ‚ɪdjʊ'm-], -l,
  -əlɪ
idiosyncras|y, -ies ‚ɪdɪə'sɪŋkrəs|ɪ
  [-djə's-, -dɪʊ's-, -djʊ's-, -dɪəʊ's-,
  -djəʊ's-], -ɪz
idiosyncratic, -ally ‚ɪdɪəsɪŋ'krætɪk
  [‚ɪdɪəʊ-, ‚ɪdjəʊ-], -əlɪ
idiot, -s 'ɪdɪət ['ɪdjət], -s
idiotic, -al, -ally ‚ɪdɪ'ɒtɪk, -l, -əlɪ
idiotism, -s 'ɪdɪətɪzəm ['ɪdjət-], -z
Idist, -s 'iːdɪst, -s
id|le (adj. v.), -ly, -lest, -leness; -les,
  -ling, -led, -ler/s 'aɪd|l, -lɪ, -lɪst
  [-lɪst], -lnɪs [-nəs]; -lz, -lɪŋ, -ld, -lə*/z
Ido 'iːdəʊ
idol, -s 'aɪdl, -z
idolater, -s aɪ'dɒlətə*, -z
idolatress, -es aɪ'dɒlətrɪs [-trəs, -tres],
  -ɪz
idolatrous, -ly aɪ'dɒlətrəs, -lɪ
idolatr|y, -ies aɪ'dɒlətr|ɪ, -ɪz
idoli|sm, -st/s 'aɪdəlɪ|zəm [-dʒ|ɪ-], -st/s
idolization [-isa-] ‚aɪdəlaɪ'zeɪʃn [-dʒaɪ-]
idoliz|e [-is|e], -es, -ing, -ed, -er/s
  'aɪdəlaɪz [-dʒ|-], -ɪz, -ɪŋ, -d, -ə*/z
Idomeneus aɪ'dɒmɪnjuːs [ɪ'd-]
Idris 'ɪdrɪs ['aɪdrɪs]
Idumea ‚aɪdjuː'miːə [‚ɪd-, -djʊm-,
  -'mɪə]
idyll, -s 'ɪdɪl ['aɪd-], -z
idyllic ɪ'dɪlɪk [aɪ'd-]
idyllist, -s 'aɪdɪlɪst, -s
i.e. ‚aɪ'i: [‚ðæt'ɪz]

if ɪf
Ife (surname) aɪf, (town in Nigeria)
  'iːfeɪ
Iffley 'ɪflɪ
Ifor 'aɪvə*
I(g)bo, -s 'iːbəʊ, -z
Iggulden 'ɪɡldən
Ightham 'aɪtəm
igloo, -s 'ɪɡluː, -z
Igna|tian, -tius ɪɡ'neɪ|ʃn [-ʃɪən,
  -ʃjən], -ʃəs [-ʃɪəs, -ʃjəs]
igneous 'ɪɡnɪəs [-njəs]
ignis-fatuus ‚ɪɡnɪs'fætjʊəs [-tjwəs]
ignit|e, -es, -ing, -ed; -able ɪɡ'naɪt, -s,
  -ɪŋ, -ɪd; -əbl
ignition ɪɡ'nɪʃn
ignobility ‚ɪɡnəʊ'bɪlətɪ [-ɪtɪ]
ignob|le, -ly, -leness ɪɡ'nəʊb|l, -lɪ, -lnɪs
  [-nəs]
ignominious, -ly, -ness ‚ɪɡnəʊ'mɪnɪəs
  [-njəs], -lɪ, -nɪs [-nəs]
ignominy 'ɪɡnəmɪnɪ [-nɒm-, -mən-]
ignoramus, -es ‚ɪɡnə'reɪməs [-nʊ'r-], -ɪz
ignoran|ce, -t/ly 'ɪɡnərən|s [-nʊr-], -t/lɪ
ignor|e, -es, -ing, -ed ɪɡ'nɔː* [-'nɔə*],
  -z, -rɪŋ, -d
Igoe (surname) 'aɪɡəʊ
Igor 'iːɡɔː*
iguana, -s ɪ'ɡwɑːnə [‚ɪɡjʊ'ɑːnə], -z
iguanodon, -s ɪ'ɡwɑːnədɒn [‚ɪɡjʊ'ɑː-,
  -dən], -z
Ike aɪk
Ikey 'aɪkɪ
ikon, -s 'aɪkɒn [-kən], -z
Ilchester 'ɪltʃɪstə*
ilex, -es 'aɪleks, -ɪz
Ilford 'ɪlfəd
Ilfracombe 'ɪlfrəkuːm [‚ɪlfrə'k-]
iliac 'ɪlɪæk
Iliad 'ɪlɪəd ['ɪljəd, 'ɪlɪæd, 'ɪljæd]
Iliffe 'aɪlɪf
ili|um, -a 'ɪlɪ|əm ['ɪlj|əm], -ə
Ilium 'aɪlɪəm ['ɪl-, -ljəm]
ilk ɪlk
Ilkestone 'ɪlkɪstən [-kəs-]
Ilkley 'ɪlklɪ
ill, -ness/es ɪl, -nɪs [-nəs]/ɪz
I'll (= I will) aɪl
ill-advised ‚ɪləd'vaɪzd
illative ɪ'leɪtɪv
ill-bred ‚ɪl'bred [also '-- when attribu-
  tive]
ill-breeding ‚ɪl'briːdɪŋ
ill-conditioned ‚ɪlkən'dɪʃnd [also '--‚--
  when attributive]
illeg|al, -ally ɪ'liːɡ|l [‚ɪ'l-], -əlɪ
illegalit|y, -ies ‚ɪliː'ɡælət|ɪ [-lɪ'ɡ-, -ɪt|ɪ],
  -ɪz

252

illegibility ɪˌledʒɪˈbɪlətɪ [ˌ---ˈ---, -dʒəˈb-
-lɪt-]
illegib|le, -ly, -leness ɪˈledʒəb|l [ˌɪˈl-,
-dʒɪb-], -lɪ, -lnɪs [-nəs]
illegitimacy ˌɪlɪˈdʒɪtɪməsɪ [-ləˈdʒ-,
-təm-]
illegitimate, -ly ˌɪlɪˈdʒɪtɪmət [-ləˈdʒ-,
-təm-, -mɪt], -lɪ
ill-fated ˌɪlˈfeɪtɪd
ill-favoured, -ly, -ness ˌɪlˈfeɪvəd [also
'-ˌ— when attributive], -lɪ, -nɪs [-nəs]
ill-feeling ˌɪlˈfiːlɪŋ
ill-gotten ˌɪlˈgɒtn [also '-ˌ— when
attributive]
illiber|al, -ally ɪˈlɪbər|əl [ˌɪˈl-], -əlɪ
illiberality ɪˌlɪbəˈrælətɪ [ˌɪlɪbəˈr-, -ɪtɪ]
illicit, -ly, -ness ɪˈlɪsɪt [ˌɪˈl-], -lɪ, -nɪs
[-nəs]
illimitab|le, -ly, -leness ɪˈlɪmɪtəb|l [ˌɪˈl-],
-lɪ, -lnɪs [-nəs]
Illingworth ˈɪlɪŋwəθ [-wɜːθ]
Illinois ˌɪlɪˈnɔɪ [rarely -ˈnɔɪz]
illiteracy ɪˈlɪtərəsɪ [ˌɪˈl-]
illiterate (s. adj.), -s, -ly, -ness ɪˈlɪtərət
[ˌɪˈl-, -rɪt], -s, -lɪ, -nɪs [-nəs]
ill-judged ˌɪlˈdʒʌdʒd [also '-— when
attributive]
ill-looking 'ɪlˌlʊkɪŋ
ill-mannered ˌɪlˈmænəd
ill-nature ˌɪlˈneɪtʃə*
ill-natured, -ly ˌɪlˈneɪtʃəd [also '-ˌ—
when attributive], -lɪ
illness, -es 'ɪlnɪs [-nəs], -ɪz
Illogan ɪˈləʊgən, (Cornwall) ɪˈlʌgən
illogic|al, -ally, -alness ɪˈlɒdʒɪk|l [ˌɪˈl-],
-əlɪ, -lnɪs [-nəs]
illogicalit|y, -ies ˌɪlɒdʒɪˈkælət|ɪ [ɪˌl-,
-ɪt|ɪ], -ɪz
ill-omened ˌɪlˈəʊmend [-mənd, -mɪnd]
ill-starred ˌɪlˈstɑːd [also '-— when
attributive]
ill-tempered ˌɪlˈtempəd [also '-ˌ— when
attributive]
ill-timed ˌɪlˈtaɪmd [also '-— when
attributive]
ill-treat, -s, -ing, -ed, -ment ˌɪlˈtriːt
[ɪlˈt-], -s, -ɪŋ, -ɪd, -mənt
illum|e, -es, -ing, -ed ɪˈljuːm [ɪˈluːm],
-z, -ɪŋ, -d
illuminat|e, -es, -ing, -ed, -or/s ɪˈluː-
mɪneɪt [ɪˈlju:-], -s, -ɪŋ, -ɪd, -ə*/z
Illuminati ɪˌluːmɪˈnɑːtiː [old-fashioned
-ˈneɪtaɪ]
illumination, -s ɪˌluːmɪˈneɪʃn [ɪˌlju:-], -z
illuminative ɪˈluːmɪnətəv [ɪˈlju:-, -neɪt-]
illumin|e, -es, -ing, -ed ɪˈluːmɪn
[ɪˈlju:-], -z, -ɪŋ, -d
ill-usage ˌɪlˈjuːzɪdʒ [-ˈjuːs-]

ill-used ˌɪlˈjuːzd [also '-— according to
sentence-stress]
illusion, -s ɪˈluːʒn [ɪˈlju:-], -z
illusioni|sm, -st/s ɪˈluːʒənɪ|zəm [ɪˈlju:-,
-ʒɪ-], -st/s
illusive, -ly, -ness ɪˈluːsɪv [ɪˈlju:-], -lɪ,
-nɪs [-nəs]
illusor|y, -ily, -iness ɪˈluːsər|ɪ [ɪˈlju:-,
-uːzərɪ], -əlɪ [-ɪlɪ], -ɪnɪs [-ɪnəs]
illustrat|e, -es, -ing, -ed, -or/s 'ɪləs-
treɪt, -s, -ɪŋ, -ɪd, -ə*/z
illustration, -s ˌɪləˈstreɪʃn, -z
illustrative, -ly 'ɪləstrətɪv [-streɪt-,
rarely ɪˈlʌstrətɪv], -lɪ
illustrious, -ly, -ness ɪˈlʌstrɪəs, -lɪ, -nɪs
[-nəs]
ill-will ˌɪlˈwɪl
ill-wisher, -s ˌɪlˈwɪʃə* ['-ˌ--], -z
Illyria, -n/s ɪˈlɪrɪə, -n/z
Illyricum ɪˈlɪrɪkəm
Ilminster ˈɪlmɪnstə*
I'm (= I am) aɪm
imag|e (s. v.) (I.), -es, -ing, -ed 'ɪmɪdʒ,
-ɪz, -ɪŋ, -d
imagery 'ɪmɪdʒərɪ
image-worship 'ɪmɪdʒˌwɜːʃɪp
imaginab|le, -ly, -leness ɪˈmædʒɪnəb|l
[-dʒən-], -lɪ, -lnɪs [-nəs]
imaginar|y, -ily, -iness ɪˈmædʒɪnər|ɪ
[-dʒənər-], -əlɪ [-ɪlɪ], -ɪnɪs [-ɪnəs]
imagination, -s ɪˌmædʒɪˈneɪʃn [-dʒəˈn-],
-z
imaginative, -ly, -ness ɪˈmædʒɪnətɪv
[-dʒən-], -lɪ, -nɪs [-nəs]
imagin|e, -es, -ing/s, -ed, -er/s ɪˈmæ-
dʒɪn [-dʒən], -z, -ɪŋ/z, -d, -ə*/z
imago, -s, imagines (plur. of imago)
ɪˈmeɪgəʊ [ɪˈmɑːg-], -z, ɪˈmeɪdʒɪniːz
[ɪˈmɑːgɪneɪz]
imam, -s ɪˈmɑːm, -z
imbalance ˌɪmˈbæləns
imbecile, -s 'ɪmbɪsiːl [-bəs-, -saɪl], -z
imbecilit|y, -ies ˌɪmbɪˈsɪlət|ɪ [-bəˈs-,
-ɪt|ɪ], -ɪz
imbib|e, -es, -ing, -ed, -er/s ɪmˈbaɪb, -z,
-ɪŋ, -d, -ə*/z
imbroglio, -s ɪmˈbrəʊlɪəʊ [-ljəʊ], -z
imbru|e, -es, -ing, -ed ɪmˈbruː, -z, -ɪŋ
[ɪmˈbrʊɪŋ], -d
imbu|e, -es, -ing, -ed ɪmˈbjuː, -z, -ɪŋ
[ɪmˈbjʊɪŋ], -d
Imeson 'aɪmɪsn
imitability ˌɪmɪtəˈbɪlətɪ [-lɪt-]
imitable 'ɪmɪtəbl
imitat|e, -es, -ing, -ed, -or/s 'ɪmɪteɪt, -s,
-ɪŋ, -ɪd, -ə*/z
imitation, -s, -al ˌɪmɪˈteɪʃn, -z, -əl
[-ʃənəl]

253

imitative, -ly, -ness 'ɪmɪtətɪv [-teɪt-], -lɪ, -nɪs [-nəs]

immaculate, -ly, -ness ɪ'mækjʊlət [-lɪt], -lɪ, -nɪs [-nəs]

immanen|ce, -t 'ɪmənən|s, -t

Immanuel ɪ'mænjʊəl [-njwəl, -njʊl]

immaterial, -ly ˌɪmə'tɪərɪəl, -ɪ

immateriali|sm, -st/s ˌɪmə'tɪərɪəlɪ|zəm, -st/s

immateriality 'ɪməˌtɪərɪ'ælətɪ [-rtɪ]

immaterializ|e [-is|e], -es, -ing, -ed ˌɪmə'tɪərɪəlaɪz, -ɪz, -ɪŋ, -d

immature, -ly, -ness ˌɪmə'tjʊə* [-'tjɔə*, -'tjɔ:*, -'tʃʊə*, -'tʃɔ:*], -lɪ, -nɪs [-nəs]

immaturity ˌɪmə'tjʊərətɪ [-'tjɔər-, -'tjɔ:r-, -'tʃʊər-, -'tʃɔ:r-, -rtɪ]

immeasurable ɪ'meʒərəbl [ˌɪ'm-]

immeasurab|ly, -leness ɪ'meʒərəb|lɪ, -lnɪs [-nəs]

immediacy ɪ'mi:djəsɪ [-dɪəsɪ]

immediate, -ly ɪ'mi:djət [-dʒət, -dɪət, -dɪt, -djrt], -lɪ

immemorial, -ly ˌɪmɪ'mɔːrɪəl [-mə'm-], -ɪ

immense, -ly, -ness ɪ'mens, -lɪ, -nɪs [-nəs]

immensit|y, -ies ɪ'mensət|ɪ [-rt|ɪ], -ɪz

immers|e, -es, -ing, -ed ɪ'mɜːs, -ɪz, -ɪŋ, -t

immersion, -s ɪ'mɜːʃn, -z

immersion-heater, -s ɪ'mɜːʃnˌhiːtə*, -z

immigrant, -s 'ɪmɪgrənt, -s

immigrat|e, -es, -ing, -ed 'ɪmɪgreɪt, -s, -ɪŋ, -ɪd

immigration, -s ˌɪmɪ'greɪʃn, -z

imminen|ce, -t/ly 'ɪmɪnən|s, -t/lɪ

immobile ɪ'məʊbaɪl [-bi:l]

immobility ˌɪməʊ'bɪlətɪ [-lrt-]

immobilization [-isa-] ɪˌməʊbɪlaɪ'zeɪʃn [-bəl-, -lɪ'z-]

immobiliz|e [-is|e], -es, -ing, -ed ɪ'məʊbɪlaɪz [-bəl-], -ɪz, -ɪŋ, -d

immoderate, -ness ɪ'mɒdərət [ˌɪ'm-, -rrt], -nɪs [-nəs]

immoderately ɪ'mɒdərətlɪ [-rrt-]

immoderation ɪˌmɒdə'reɪʃn

immodest, -ly ɪ'mɒdɪst [ˌɪ'm-], -lɪ

immodesty ɪ'mɒdɪstɪ [ˌɪ'm-, -dəst-]

immolat|e, -es, -ing, -ed, -or/s 'ɪməʊleɪt, -s, -ɪŋ, -ɪd, -ə*/z

immolation, -s ˌɪməʊ'leɪʃn, -z

immor|al, -ally ɪ'mɒr|əl [ˌɪ'm-], -əlɪ [- lɪ]

immoralit|y, -ies ˌɪmə'rælət|ɪ [-mɒ'r-, -rt|ɪ], -ɪz

immort|al (s. adj.), -als, -ally ɪ'mɔ:t|l [ˌɪ'm-], -lz, -əlɪ [-lɪ]

immortality ˌɪmɔ:'tælətɪ [-rtɪ]

immortaliz|e [-is|e], -es, -ing, -ed ɪ'mɔ:təlaɪz [-tlaɪz], -ɪz, -ɪŋ, -d

immortelle, -s ˌɪmɔ:'tel, -z

immovability ɪˌmu:və'bɪlətɪ [ˌɪmu:v-, -lrt-]

immovab|le, -leness ɪ'mu:vəb|l [ˌɪ'm-], -lnɪs [-nəs]

immovably ɪ'mu:vəblɪ

immune ɪ'mju:n

immunit|y, -ies ɪ'mju:nət|ɪ [-rt|ɪ], -ɪz

immunization [-isa-] ˌɪmju:naɪ'zeɪʃn [-mjʊn-, -nɪ'z-]

immuniz|e [-is|e], -es, -ing, -ed 'ɪmju:naɪz [-mjʊn-], -ɪz, -ɪŋ, -d

immunolog|y, -ist/s ˌɪmju:n'ɒlədʒ|ɪ [-mjʊn-], -ɪst/s

immur|e, -es, -ing, -ed, -ement ɪ'mjʊə* [-'mjɔə*, -'mjɔ:*], -z, -rɪŋ, -d, -mənt

immutability ɪˌmju:tə'bɪlətɪ ['ɪˌm-, -lrt-]

immutab|le, -ly, -leness ɪ'mju:təb|l, -lɪ, -lnɪs [-nəs]

Imogen 'ɪməʊdʒən [-dʒen]

imp (s. v.), -s, -ing, -ed ɪmp, -s, -ɪŋ, -t [ɪmt]

impact (s.), -s 'ɪmpækt, -s

impact (v.), -s, -ing, -ed ɪm'pækt, -s, -ɪŋ, -ɪd

impair, -s, -ing, -ed ɪm'peə*, -z, -rɪŋ, -d

impairment ɪm'peəmənt

impal|e, -es, -ing, -ed, -ement ɪm'peɪl, -z, -ɪŋ, -d, -mənt

impalpab|le, -ly ɪm'pælpəb|l [ˌɪm'p-], -lɪ

imparisyllabic 'ɪmˌpærɪsɪ'læbɪk [-rəs-]

impart, -s, -ing, -ed ɪm'pɑ:t, -s, -ɪŋ, -ɪd

impartation ˌɪmpɑ:'teɪʃn

imparti|al, -ally, -alness ɪm'pɑ:ʃ|l [ˌɪm'p-], -əlɪ, -lnɪs [-nəs]

impartiality 'ɪmˌpɑ:ʃɪ'ælətɪ [ˌɪmpɑ:-, ɪmˌpɑ:-, -rtɪ]

impassability 'ɪmˌpɑ:sə'bɪlətɪ [-lrt-]

impassable ɪm'pɑ:səbl [ˌɪm'p-]

impasse, -s æm'pɑ:s ['--] (ɛ̃pɑ:s), -ɪz

impassible ɪm'pæsəbl [-sɪbl]

impassioned ɪm'pæʃnd

impassive, -ly, -ness ɪm'pæsɪv, -lɪ, -nɪs [-nəs]

impassivity ˌɪmpæ'sɪvətɪ [-rtɪ]

impatien|ce, -t/ly ɪm'peɪʃn|s, -t/lɪ

impeach, -es, -ing, -ed, -er/s, -ment/s; -able ɪm'pi:tʃ, -ɪz, -ɪŋ, -t, -ə*/z, -mənt/s; -əbl

impeccability ɪmˌpekə'bɪlətɪ [ˌɪmpek-, -lrt-]

impeccable ɪm'pekəbl

impecunious, -ness ˌɪmpɪ'kju:njəs [-nɪəs], -nɪs [-nəs]

impedance ɪm'pi:dəns

imped|e, -es, -ing, -ed ɪmˈpiːd, -z, -ɪŋ, -ɪd

impediment, -s ɪmˈpedɪmənt, -s
impedimenta ɪmˌpedɪˈmentə [ˌɪmped-]
impel, -s, -ling, -led, -ler/s; -lent ɪmˈpel, -z, -ɪŋ, -d, -ə*/z; -ənt
impend, -s, -ing, -ed ɪmˈpend, -z, -ɪŋ, -ɪd
impenetrability ɪmˌpenɪtrəˈbɪlətɪ [ˈɪmˌp-, -lɪt-]
impenetrab|le, -ly, -leness ɪmˈpenɪtrəb|l, -lɪ, -lnɪs [-nəs]
impeniten|ce, -t/ly ɪmˈpenɪtən|s [ˌɪmˈp-], -t/lɪ
imperative (s. adj.), -s, -ly, -ness ɪmˈperətɪv, -z, -lɪ, -nɪs [-nəs]
imperator, -s ˌɪmpəˈrɑːtɔː* [-ˈreɪtɔː*, -tə*], -z
imperatorial ɪmˌperəˈtɔːrɪəl [ˌɪmper-]
imperceptibility ˈɪmpəˌseptəˈbɪlətɪ [-tɪˈb-, -lɪt-]
imperceptib|le, -ly, -leness ˌɪmpəˈseptəb|l [-tɪb-], -lɪ, -lnɪs [-nəs]
imperfect (s. adj.), -s, -ly, -ness ɪmˈpəːfɪkt [ˌɪmˈp-], -s, -lɪ, -nɪs
imperfection, -s ˌɪmpəˈfekʃn, -z
imperforate ɪmˈpəːfərət [ˌɪmˈp-, -rɪt]
imperial (s. adj.), -s, -ly ɪmˈpɪərɪəl, -z, -ɪ
imperiali|sm -st/s ɪmˈpɪərɪəlɪ|zəm, -st/s
imper|il, -ils, -illing, -illed ɪmˈper|əl [-ɪl], -əlz [-ɪlz], -əlɪŋ [-ɪlɪŋ, -lɪŋ], -əld [-ɪld]
imperious, -ly, -ness ɪmˈpɪərɪəs, -lɪ, -nɪs [-nəs]
imperishability ɪmˌperɪʃəˈbɪlətɪ [ˈɪmˌp-, -lɪt-]
imperishab|le, -ly, -leness ɪmˈperɪʃəb|l [ˌɪmˈp-], -lɪ, -lnɪs [-nəs]
impermeability ɪmˌpəːmjəˈbɪlətɪ [ˈɪmˌp-, -mɪə-, -lɪt-]
impermeable, -ly, -leness ɪmˈpəːmjəb|l [ˌɪmˈp-, -mɪə-], -lɪ, -lnɪs [-nəs]
impers|onal, -onally ɪmˈpəːs|n̩l [ˌɪmˈp-, -n̩l, -ənl], -nəlɪ [-n̩əlɪ, -n̩lɪ, -nl̩ɪ, -ənl̩ɪ]
impersonality ɪmˌpəːsəˈnælətɪ [ˈɪmˌp-, -sn̩ˈæ-, -ɪtɪ]
impersonat|e, -es, -ing, -ed, -or/s ɪmˈpəːsənert [-sn̩ert], -s, -ɪŋ, -ɪd, -ə*/z
impersonation, -s ɪmˌpəːsəˈneɪʃn [-sn̩ˈeɪ-], -z
impertinen|ce (insolence, etc.), -t/ly ɪmˈpəːtɪnən|s [-tn̩ən-], -t/lɪ
impertinen|ce (irrelevance, etc.), -t/ly ɪmˈpəːtɪnən|s [ˌɪmˈp-], -t/lɪ
imperturbability ˈɪmpəˌtəːbəˈbɪlətɪ [-lɪt-]

imperturbab|le, -ly, -leness ˌɪmpə-ˈtəːbəb|l, -lɪ, -lnɪs [-nəs]
impervious, -ly, -ness ɪmˈpəːvjəs [ˌɪmˈp-, -vɪəs], -lɪ, -nɪs [-nəs]
impetigo ˌɪmpɪˈtaɪgəʊ [-pəˈt-, -peˈt-]
impetuosity ɪmˌpetjʊˈɒsətɪ [-ɪtɪ]
impetuous, -ly, -ness ɪmˈpetʃʊəs [-tjʊəs, -tjwəs], -lɪ, -nɪs [-nəs]
impetus ˈɪmpɪtəs [-pət-]
Impey ˈɪmpɪ
impiet|y, -ies ɪmˈpaɪət|ɪ [ˌɪmˈp-, -aɪt-], -ɪz
imping|e, -es, -ing, -ed, -ement/s ɪm-ˈpɪndʒ, -ɪz, -ɪŋ, -d, -mənt/s
impious, -ly, -ness ˈɪmpɪəs [-pjəs], -lɪ, -nɪs [-nəs]
impish, -ly, -ness ˈɪmpɪʃ, -lɪ, -nɪs [-nəs]
implacability ɪmˌplækəˈbɪlətɪ [ˈɪmˌplæk-, -ˌpleɪk-, -lɪt-]
implacab|le, -ly, -leness ɪmˈplækəb|l [-ˈpleɪk-], -lɪ, -lnɪs [-nəs]
implant (s.), -s ˈɪmplɑːnt, -s
implant (v.), -s, -ing, -ed, -er/s ɪm-ˈplɑːnt, -s, -ɪŋ, -ɪd, -ə*/z
implantation ˌɪmplɑːnˈteɪʃn [-plæn-]
implement (s.), -s ˈɪmplɪmənt [-plə-], -s
implement (v.), -s, -ing, -ed ˈɪmplɪ-ment [-plə-], -s, -ɪŋ, -ɪd
implementation ˌɪmplɪmenˈteɪʃn [-plə-]
implicate (s.) ˈɪmplɪkət [-kɪt, -keɪt]
implicat|e (v.), -es, -ing, -ed ˈɪmplɪkeɪt, -s, -ɪŋ, -ɪd
implication, -s ˌɪmplɪˈkeɪʃn, -z
implicative, -ly ɪmˈplɪkətɪv [ˈɪmplɪkeɪtɪv], -lɪ
implicit, -ly, -ness ɪmˈplɪsɪt, -lɪ, -nɪs [-nəs]
implod|e, -es, -ing, -ed ɪmˈpləʊd, -z, -ɪŋ, -ɪd
implor|e, -es, -ing/ly, -ed, -er/s ɪm-ˈplɔː* [-ˈplɔə*], -z, -ɪŋ/lɪ, -d, -rə*/z
implosion, -s ɪmˈpləʊʒn, -z
implosive (s. adj.), -s ɪmˈpləʊsɪv [ˌɪmˈp-, -əʊzɪ-], -z
impl|y, -ies, -ying, -ied, -iedly ɪmˈpl|aɪ, -aɪz, -aɪɪŋ, -aɪd, -aɪɪdlɪ
impolicy ɪmˈpɒləsɪ [ˌɪmˈp-, -lɪs-]
impolite, -ly, -ness ˌɪmpəˈlaɪt [-pəʊˈl-, -pʊˈl-], -lɪ, -nɪs [-nəs]
impolitic ɪmˈpɒlətɪk [ˌɪmˈp-, -lɪt-]
imponderable (s. adj.), -s ɪmˈpɒndərəbl, -z
import (s.), -s, ˈɪmpɔːt, -s
import (v.), -s, -ing, -ed, -er/s ɪmˈpɔːt [ˈɪmpɔːt], -s, -ɪŋ, -ɪd, -ə*/z
importable ɪmˈpɔːtəbl
importan|ce, -t/ly ɪmˈpɔːtn|s, -t/lɪ

255

importation, -s ˌɪmpɔːˈteɪʃn, -z
importunate, -ly, -ness ɪmˈpɔːtjʊnət
[-tʃʊ-, -tʃə-, -nɪt], -lɪ, -nɪs [-nəs]
importun|e, -es, -ing, -ed ɪmˈpɔːtjuːn
[-tʃuːn, ˌɪmpɔːˈtjuːn], -z, ɪmˈpɔːt-
jʊnɪŋ [-tʃʊnɪŋ, ˌɪmpɔːˈtjuːnɪŋ],
ɪmˈpɔːtjuːnd [-tʃuːnd, ˌɪmpɔːˈtjuːnd]
importunit|y, -ies ˌɪmpɔːˈtjuːnət|ɪ [-ɪt|ɪ],
-ɪz
impos|e, -es, -ing, -ed, -er/s; -able
ɪmˈpəʊz, -ɪz, -ɪŋ, -d, -ə*/z; -əbl
imposing (adj.), -ly, -ness ɪmˈpəʊzɪŋ, -lɪ
-nɪs [-nəs]
imposition, -s ˌɪmpəˈzɪʃn [-pʊˈz-], -z
impossibilit|y, -ies ɪmˌpɒsəˈbɪlət|ɪ
[ˌɪmpɒs-, -sɪˈb-, -lɪt-], -ɪz
impossib|le, -ly ɪmˈpɒsəb|l [-sɪb-], -lɪ
impost, -s ˈɪmpəʊst, -s
impos|tor/s, -ture/s ɪmˈpɒs|tə*/z
-tʃə*/z
impoten|ce, -cy, -t/ly ˈɪmpətən|s [-pʊt-],
-sɪ, -t/lɪ
impound, -s, -ing, -ed ɪmˈpaʊnd, -z,
-ɪŋ, -ɪd
impoverish, -es, -ing, -ed, -ment ɪm-
ˈpɒvərɪʃ, -ɪz, -ɪŋ, -t, -mənt
impracticability, -ies ɪmˌpræktɪkə-
ˈbɪlət|ɪ [ˈɪmˌpræktɪkəˈb-, -lɪt-], -ɪz
impracticab|le, -ly, -leness ɪmˈpræktɪk-
əb|l [ˌɪmˈp-], -lɪ, -lnɪs [-nəs]
imprecat|e, -es, -ing, -ed, -or/s ˈɪm-
prɪkeɪt, -s, -ɪŋ, -ɪd, -ə*/z
imprecation, -s ˌɪmprɪˈkeɪʃn, -z
imprecatory ˈɪmprɪkeɪtərɪ [ˌ--ˈ---,
ɪmˈprekətərɪ]
impregn, -s, -ing, -ed ɪmˈpriːn, -z, -ɪŋ,
-d
impregnability ɪmˌpregnəˈbɪlətɪ [-lɪt-]
impregnab|le, -ly ɪmˈpregnəb|l, -lɪ
impregnate (adj.) ɪmˈpregnɪt [-nət,
-neɪt]
impregnat|e (v.), -es, -ing, -ed ˈɪm-
pregneɪt [ɪmˈpregneɪt], -s, -ɪŋ, -ɪd
impregnation, -s ˌɪmpregˈneɪʃn, -z
impresario, -s ˌɪmprɪˈsɑːrɪəʊ [-prə's-,
-preˈs-, -ˈzɑː-], -z
impress (s.), -es ˈɪmpres, -ɪz
impress (v.), -es, -ing, -ed ɪmˈpres, -ɪz,
-ɪŋ, -t
impressibility ɪmˌpresɪˈbɪlətɪ [-səˈb-,
-lɪt-]
impressib|le, -ly, -leness ɪmˈpresəb|l
[-sɪb-], -lɪ, -lnɪs [-nəs]
impression, -s ɪmˈpreʃn, -z
impressionability ɪmˌpreʃnəˈbɪlətɪ
[-ʃənə-, -ʃnə-, -lɪt-]
impressionable ɪmˈpreʃnəbl [-ʃənə-,
-ʃnə-]

impressioni|sm, -st/s ɪmˈpreʃnɪ|zəm
[-ʃənɪ-], -st/s
impressionistic ɪmˌpreʃəˈnɪstɪk [-ʃŋ'ɪ-]
impressive, -ly, -ness ɪmˈpresɪv, -lɪ, -nɪs
[-nəs]
impressment, -s ɪmˈpresmənt, -s
imprest, -s ˈɪmprest, -s
imprimatur, -s ˌɪmprɪˈmeɪtə* [-praɪˈm-,
-ˈmɑːtə*, -ˌtʊə*], -z
imprimis ɪmˈpraɪmɪs
imprint (s.), -s ˈɪmprɪnt, -s
imprint (v.), -s, -ing, -ed ɪmˈprɪnt, -s,
-ɪŋ, -ɪd
impris|on, -ons, -oning, -oned,
-onment/s ɪmˈprɪz|n, -nz, -n̩ɪŋ, -nd,
-nmənt/s
improbabilit|y, -ies ɪmˌprɒbəˈbɪlət|ɪ
[ˈɪmˌprɒbəˈb-, -lɪt-], -ɪz
improbab|le, -ly ɪmˈprɒbəb|l [ˌɪmˈp-],
-lɪ
improbity ɪmˈprəʊbətɪ [ˌɪmˈp-, -ˈprɒb-,
-ɪtɪ]
impromptu, -s ɪmˈprɒmptjuː:, -z
improper, -ly ɪmˈprɒpə* [ˌɪmˈp-], -lɪ
impropriat|e, -es, -ing, -ed, -or/s ɪm-
ˈprəʊprɪeɪt, -s, -ɪŋ, -ɪd, -ə*/z
impropriation, -s ɪmˌprəʊprɪˈeɪʃn, -z
impropriet|y, -ies ˌɪmprəˈpraɪət|ɪ
[-prʊˈp-], -ɪz
improvability ɪmˌpruːvəˈbɪlətɪ [-lɪt-]
improvab|le, -ly, -leness ɪmˈpruːvəb|l,
-lɪ, -lnɪs [-nəs]
improv|e, -es, -ing, -ed, -er/s, -ement/s
ɪmˈpruːv, -z, -ɪŋ, -d, -ə*/z, -mənt/s
improviden|ce, -t/ly ɪmˈprɒvɪdən|s,
-t/lɪ
†improvisation, -s ˌɪmprəvaɪˈzeɪʃn
[-prʊv-, ˌɪmprɒvɪ'z-], -z
improvis|e, -es, -ing, -ed, -er/s ˈɪm-
prəvaɪz [-prʊv-], -ɪz, -ɪŋ, -d, -ə*/z
impruden|ce, -t/ly ɪmˈpruːdən|s
[ˌɪmˈp-], -t/lɪ
impuden|ce, -t/ly ˈɪmpjʊdən|s, -t/lɪ
impugn, -s, -ing, -ed, -er/s ɪmˈpjuːn, -z,
-ɪŋ, -d, -ə/*z
impuissan|ce, -t ɪmˈpjuːɪsn|s [-ˈpjʊɪ-],
-t
impulse, -s ˈɪmpʌls, -ɪz
impulsion, -s ɪmˈpʌlʃn, -z
impulsive, -ly, -ness ɪmˈpʌlsɪv, -lɪ, -nɪs
[-nəs]
impunity ɪmˈpjuːnətɪ [-ɪtɪ]
impur|e, -ely, -eness; -ity, -ities
ɪmˈpjʊə* [ˌɪmˈp-, -ˈpjɔə*, -ˈpjɔː*],
-lɪ, -nɪs [-nəs]; -rətɪ [-rɪtɪ], -rətɪz
[-rɪtɪz]
imputability ɪmˌpjuːtəˈbɪlətɪ [ˌɪmpjuːt-,
-lɪt-]

imputation, -s ˌɪmpjuːˈteɪʃn [-pjʊ-], -z
imput|e, -es, -ing, -ed, -er/s; -able
ɪmˈpjuːt, -s, -ɪŋ, -ɪd, -ə*/z; -əbl
Imr|ay, -e, -ie ˈɪmrˌeɪ, -ɪ, -ɪ
in ɪn
Ina ˈaɪnə
inability ˌɪnəˈbɪlətɪ [-lɪt-]
inaccessibility ˈɪnækˌsesəˈbɪlətɪ [-nək-,
-sɪˈb-, -lɪt-]
inaccessib|le, -ly, -leness ˌɪnækˈsesəb|l
[-nək-, -sɪb-], -lɪ, -lnɪs [-nəs]
inaccurac|y, -ies ɪnˈækjʊrəs|ɪ [ˌɪnˈæ-,
-kjər-, -rɪs-], -ɪz
inaccur|ate, -ately ɪnˈækjʊr|ət [ˌɪnˈæ-,
-kjər-, -rɪt], -ətlɪ [-ɪtlɪ]
inaction ɪnˈækʃn [ˌɪnˈæ-]
inactive, -ly ɪnˈæktɪv [ˌɪnˈæ-], -lɪ
inactivity ˌɪnækˈtɪvətɪ [-ɪtɪ]
inadequacy ɪnˈædɪkwəsɪ [ˌɪnˈæ-]
inadequate, -ly, -ness ɪnˈædɪkwət
[ˌɪnˈæ-, -kwɪt], -lɪ, -nɪs [-nəs]
inadmissibility ˈɪnədˌmɪsəˈbɪlətɪ [-sɪˈb-,
-lɪt-]
inadmissib|le, -ly ˌɪnədˈmɪsəb|l [-sɪb-],
-lɪ
inadverten|ce, -cy, -t/ly ˌɪnədˈvɜː-
tən|s, -sɪ, -t/lɪ
inadvisable ˌɪnədˈvaɪzəbl
inalienability ɪnˌeɪljənəˈbɪlətɪ [ˈɪnˌeɪ-,
-lɪən-, -lɪt-]
inalienable ɪnˈeɪljənəbl [ˌɪnˈeɪ-, -lɪən-]
inalienab|ly, -leness ɪnˈeɪljənəb|lɪ
[-lɪən-], -lnɪs [-nəs]
inamorata, -s ɪnˌæməˈrɑːtə [ˌɪnæ-,
-mɒˈr-], -z
inane, -ly, -ness ɪˈneɪn, -lɪ, -nɪs [-nəs]
inanimate, -ly, -ness ɪnˈænɪmət [ˌɪnˈæ-,
-mɪt], -lɪ, -nɪs [-nəs]
inanition ˌɪnəˈnɪʃn [-næˈn-]
inanit|y, -ies ɪˈnænət|ɪ [-ˈnem-, -ɪt|ɪ],
-ɪz
inappeasable ˌɪnəˈpiːzəbl
inapplicability ˈɪnˌæplɪkəˈbɪlətɪ [ˈɪn-
əˌplɪk-, -lɪt-]
inapplicable, -ness ɪnˈæplɪkəbl [ˌɪnˈæ-,
ˌɪnəˈplɪk-], -nɪs [-nəs]
inapposite, -ly ɪnˈæpəzɪt [ˌɪnˈæ-, -pʊz-],
-lɪ
inappreciab|le, -ly ˌɪnəˈpriːʃəb|l [-ʃjə-,
-ʃɪə-], -lɪ
inapproachab|le, -ly ˌɪnəˈprəʊtʃəb|l
-lɪ
inappropri|ate, -ately, -ateness ˌɪnə-
ˈprəʊprɪ|ət [-prɪ|ɪt], -ətlɪ [-ɪtlɪ], -ətnɪs
[-ɪt-, -nəs]
inapt, -ly, -ness ɪnˈæpt [ˌɪnˈæpt], -lɪ,
-nɪs [-nəs]
inaptitude ɪnˈæptɪtjuːd [ˌɪnˈæ-]

inarticulate, -ly, -ness ˌɪnɑːˈtɪkjʊlət
[-lɪt], -lɪ, -nɪs [-nəs]
inartistic, -al, -ally ˌɪnɑːˈtɪstɪk, -l, -əlɪ
inasmuch ˌɪnəzˈmʌtʃ
inattention ˌɪnəˈtenʃn
inattentive, -ly, -ness ˌɪnəˈtentɪv,
-lɪ, -nɪs [-nəs]
inaudibility ɪnˌɔːdəˈbɪlətɪ [ˈɪnˌɔːdəˈb-,
-dɪˈb-, -lɪt-]
inaudib|le, -ly, -leness ɪnˈɔːdəb|l [ˌɪnˈɔː-,
-dɪb-], -lɪ, -lnɪs [-nəs]
inaugural ɪˈnɔːgjʊrəl [-gjər-]
inaugurat|e, -es, -ing, -ed, -or/s ɪˈnɔː-
gjʊreɪt [-gjər-], -s, -ɪŋ, -ɪd, -ə*/z
inauguration, -s ɪˌnɔːgjʊˈreɪʃn [-gjəˈr-],
-z
inauspicious, -ly, -ness ˌɪnɔːˈspɪʃəs,
[-nɒˈs-], -lɪ, -nɪs
inborn ˌɪnˈbɔːn [also ˈɪnb- when attribu-
tive]
inbreath|e, -es, -ing, -ed ˌɪnˈbriːð, -z,
-ɪŋ, -d [also ˈɪnbriːðd when attribu-
tive]
inbreed, -s, -ing, inbred ˌɪnˈbriːd, -z,
-ɪŋ, ˌɪnˈbred [ˈɪnbred]
inbreeding (s.) ˈɪnˌbriːdɪŋ
Inca, -s ˈɪŋkə, -z
incalculability ɪnˌkælkjʊləˈbɪlətɪ [ˈɪn-
ˌkælkjʊləˈb-, (ˈ)ɪŋˌk-, -kjəl-, -lɪt-]
incalculable, -ness ɪnˈkælkjʊləbl [ˌɪnˈk-,
(ˌ)ɪŋˈk-, -kjəl-], -nɪs [-nəs]
incalculably ɪnˈkælkjʊləblɪ [ɪŋˈk-,
-kjəl-]
in camera ˌɪnˈkæmərə [ˌɪŋ-]
incandescen|ce -t ˌɪnkænˈdesn|s [ˌɪŋk-,
-kən-], -t
incantation, -s ˌɪnkænˈteɪʃn [ˌɪŋk-], -z
incapabilit|y, -ies ɪnˌkeɪpəˈbɪlət|ɪ
[ˈɪnˌkeɪpəˈb-, (ˈ)ɪŋˌk-, -lɪt-], -ɪz
incapable, -ness ɪnˈkeɪpəbl [ˌɪnˈk-,
(ˌ)ɪŋˈk-], -nɪs [-nəs]
incapacitat|e, -es, -ing, -ed ˌɪnkəˈpæsɪ-
teɪt [ˌɪŋk-, -sət-], -s, -ɪŋ, -ɪd
incapacitation ˈɪnkəˌpæsɪˈteɪʃn [ˈɪŋk-,
-səˈt-]
incapacit|y, -ies ˌɪnkəˈpæsət|ɪ [ˌɪŋk-,
-ɪt|ɪ], -ɪz
incarcerat|e, -es, -ing, -ed ɪnˈkɑːsəreɪt
[ɪŋˈk-], -s, -ɪŋ, -ɪd
incarceration, -s ɪnˌkɑːsəˈreɪʃn [ˌɪnkɑː-,
ɪŋˌk-, ˌɪŋk-], -z
incarnadine ɪnˈkɑːnədaɪn [ɪŋˈk-]
incarnate (adj.) ɪnˈkɑːneɪt [ɪŋˈk-, -nɪt]
incarnat|e (v.), -es, -ing, -ed ˈɪnkɑːneɪt
[ɪnˈkɑːneɪt, ˈɪŋk-, ɪŋˈk-], -s, -ɪŋ, -ɪd
incarnation (I.), -s ˌɪnkɑːˈneɪʃn [ˌɪŋk-],
-z
incaution ɪnˈkɔːʃn [ˌɪnˈk-, (ˌ)ɪŋˈk-]

incautious, -ly, -ness ɪnˈkɔːʃəs [ˌɪnˈk-, (ˌ)ɪŋ-], -lɪ, -nɪs [-nəs]

Ince ɪns

incendiar|ism, -y, -ies ɪnˈsendjər|ɪzəm [-dɪə-], -ɪ, -ɪz

incense (s.) ˈɪnsens

incens|e (v.) (enrage), -es, -ing, -ed ɪnˈsens, -ɪz, -ɪŋ, -t

incens|e (v.) (burn incense), -es, -ing, -ed ˈɪnsens, -ɪz, -ɪŋ, -t

incentive, -s ɪnˈsentɪv, -z

incept, -s, -ing, -ed, -or/s; -ive ɪnˈsept, -s, -ɪŋ, -ɪd, -ə*/z; -ɪv

inception, -s ɪnˈsepʃn, -z

incertitude ɪnˈsɜːtɪtjuːd [ˌɪnˈs-]

incessant, -ly ɪnˈsesnt, -lɪ

incest ˈɪnsest

incestuous, -ly, -ness ɪnˈsestjʊəs [-tjwəs], -lɪ, -nɪs [-nəs]

inch (s. v.) (I.), -es, -ing, -ed ɪntʃ, -ɪz, -ɪŋ, -t

Inch|bald, -cape, -colm, -iquin, -keith ˈɪntʃ|bɔːld, -keɪp, -kəm, -ɪkwɪn, -kiːθ

inchoate (adj.), -ly ˈɪnkəʊeɪt [ˈɪŋk-, -kəʊɪt, -ˈ--], -lɪ

inchoat|e (v.), -es, -ing, -ed ˈɪnkəʊeɪt [ˈɪŋk-], -s, -ɪŋ, -ɪd

inchoation ˌɪnkəʊˈeɪʃn [ˌɪŋk-]

inchoative ˈɪnkəʊeɪtɪv [ˈɪŋk-, ɪnˈkəʊətɪv, ɪŋˈkəʊətɪv]

Inchrye ɪntʃˈraɪ

inciden|ce, -t/s ˈɪnsɪdən|s, -t/s

incident|al, -ally, -alness ˌɪnsɪˈdent|l, -lɪ [-əlɪ], -lnɪs [-nəs]

incinerat|e, -es, -ing, -ed, -or/s ɪnˈsɪnəreɪt, -s, -ɪŋ, -ɪd, -ə*/z

incineration ɪnˌsɪnəˈreɪʃn

incipien|ce, -cy, -t/ly ɪnˈsɪprən|s [-pjən-], -sɪ, -t/lɪ

incis|e, -es, -ing, -ed, -or/s ɪnˈsaɪz, -ɪz, -ɪŋ, -d, -ə*/z

incision, -s ɪnˈsɪʒn, -z

incisive, -ly, -ness ɪnˈsaɪsɪv, -lɪ, -nɪs [-nəs]

incitation, -s ˌɪnsaɪˈteɪʃn [-sɪˈt-], -z

incit|e, -es, -ing/ly, -ed, -er/s, -ement/s ɪnˈsaɪt, -s, -ɪŋ/lɪ, -ɪd, -ə*/z, -mənt/s

incivilit|y, -ies ˌɪnsɪˈvɪlət|ɪ [-ɪt|ɪ], -ɪz

Incledon ˈɪŋkldən

inclemen|cy, -t/ly ɪnˈklemən|sɪ [ˌɪnˈk-, (ˌ)ɪŋˈk-], -t/lɪ

inclination, -s ˌɪnklɪˈneɪʃn [ˌɪŋkl-, -ləˈn-], -z

incline (s.), -s ɪnˈklaɪn [ɪŋˈkl-, ˈɪnklaɪn, ˈɪŋklaɪn], -z

inclin|e (v.), -es, -ing, -ed; -able ɪnˈklaɪn [ɪŋˈkl-], -z, -ɪŋ, -d; -əbl

inclos|e, -es, -ing, -ed ɪnˈkləʊz [ɪŋˈkl-], -ɪz, -ɪŋ, -d

inclosure, -s ɪnˈkləʊʒə* [ɪŋˈkl-], -z

includ|e, -es, -ing, -ed ɪnˈkluːd [ɪŋˈkl-], -z, -ɪŋ, -ɪd

inclusion, -s ɪnˈkluːʒn [ɪŋˈkl-], -z

inclusive, -ly ɪnˈkluːsɪv [ɪŋˈkl-, ˌ-ˈ--], -lɪ

incog. ɪnˈkɒg [ˌɪnˈk-, ɪŋˈk-, ˌɪŋˈk-]

incognito (s. adj. adv.), -s ˌɪnkɒgˈniːtəʊ [ɪnˈkɒgnɪtəʊ, ɪŋˈk-], -z

incoheren|ce -t/ly ˌɪnkəʊˈhɪərən|s [ˌɪŋk-], -t/lɪ

incombustibility ˈɪnkəmˌbʌstəˈbɪlətɪ [ˈɪŋk-, -tɪˈb-, -lɪt-]

incombustible, -ness ˌɪnkəmˈbʌstəbl [ˌɪŋk-, -tɪb-], -nɪs [-nəs]

income, -s ˈɪŋkʌm [ˈɪnk-, -kəm], -z

incomer, -s ˈɪnˌkʌmə*, -z

income-tax, -es ˈɪŋkəmtæks [ˈɪnk-, -kʌm-], -ɪz

incoming (s. adj.), -s ˈɪnˌkʌmɪŋ, -z

incommensurability ˈɪnkəˌmenʃərəˈbɪlətɪ [ˈɪŋk-, -ʃʊr-, -lɪt-]

incommensurab|le (s. adj.), -les, -ly, -leness ˌɪnkəˈmenʃərəb|l [ˌɪŋk-, -ʃʊr-], -lz, -lɪ, -lnɪs [-nəs]

incommensurate, -ly, -ness ˌɪnkəˈmenʃərət [ˌɪŋk-, -ʃʊr-, -rɪt], -lɪ, -nɪs [-nəs]

incommod|e, -es, -ing, -ed ˌɪnkəˈməʊd [ˌɪŋk-], -z, -ɪŋ, -ɪd

incommodious, -ly, -ness ˌɪnkəˈməʊdjəs [ˌɪŋk-, -dɪəs], -lɪ, -nɪs [-nəs]

incommunicab|le, -ly, -leness ˌɪnkəˈmjuːnɪkəb|l [ˌɪŋk-, -ˈmjʊn-], -lɪ, -lnɪs [-nəs]

incommunicado ˌɪnkəmjuːnɪˈkɑːdəʊ [ˌɪŋk-, -mjʊnɪ-, ˈ--ˌ-ˈ--]

incommutab|le, -ly, -leness ˌɪnkəˈmjuːtəb|l [ˌɪŋk-], -lɪ, -lnɪs [-nəs]

incomparability ɪnˌkɒmpərəˈbɪlətɪ [ɪŋˌk-, -lɪt-]

incomparab|le, -ly, -leness ɪnˈkɒmpərəb|l [ɪŋˈk-], -lɪ, -lnɪs [-nəs]

incompatibility ˈɪnkəmˌpætəˈbɪlətɪ [ˈɪŋk-, -tɪˈb-, -lɪt-]

incompatib|le, -ly, -leness ˌɪnkəmˈpætəb|l [ˌɪŋk-, -tɪb-], -lɪ, -lnɪs [-nəs]

incompeten|ce, -cy, -t/ly ɪnˈkɒmpɪtən|s [ˌɪnˈk-, (ˌ)ɪŋˈk-], -sɪ, -t/lɪ

incomplete, -ly, -ness ˌɪnkəmˈpliːt [ˌɪŋk-], -lɪ, -nɪs [-nəs]

incompletion ˌɪnkəmˈpliːʃn [ˌɪŋk]

incomprehensibility ɪnˌkɒmprɪhensəˈbɪlətɪ [ˈɪnˌkɒmprɪhensəˈb-, ɪŋˌk-, ˈɪŋˌk-, -sɪˈb-, -lɪt-]

incomprehensib|le, -ly, -leness ɪnˌkɒmprɪˈhensəb|l [ˈɪnˌkɒmprɪˈh-, ɪŋˌk-, ˈɪŋˌk-, -sɪb-], -lɪ, -lnɪs [-nəs]

incompressibility ˈmkəmˌpresəˈbɪlətɪ [ˈɪŋk-, -sɪˈb-, -lɪt-]

incompressible, -ness ˌmkəmˈpresəbl [ˌɪŋk-, -sɪb-], -nɪs [-nəs]

incomputable ˌmkəmˈpjuːtəbl [ˌɪŋkəmˈp-, mˈkɒmpjʊtəbl, ˌmˈkɒmpjʊt-, ɪŋˈkɒmpjʊt-, ˌɪŋˈkɒmpjʊt-]

inconceivability ˈmkənˌsiːvəˈbɪlətɪ [ˈɪŋk-, -lɪt-]

inconceivable, -ness ˌmkənˈsiːvəbl [ˌɪŋk-], -nɪs [-nəs]

inconceivably ˌmkənˈsiːvəblɪ [ˌɪŋk-]

inconclusive, -ly, -ness ˌmkənˈkluːsɪv [ˌɪŋk-, -kəŋˈk-], -lɪ, -nɪs [-nəs]

incongruit|y, -ies ˌmkɒŋˈgruːət|ɪ [ˌɪŋk-, -ˈgrʊ-, -rt|ɪ], -ɪz

incongruous, -ly, -nes mˈkɒŋgrʊəs [ɪŋˈk-, -grwəs], -lɪ, -nɪs [-nəs]

inconsequen|ce, -ces, -t/ly mˈkɒnsɪkwən|s [ɪŋˈk-], -sɪz, -t/lɪ

inconsequential, -ly ˌmkɒnsɪˈkwenʃl [ˌɪŋk-, -ˌ--ˈ--], -ɪ

inconsiderab|le, -ly, -leness ˌmkənˈsɪdərəb|l [ˌɪŋk-], -lɪ, -lnɪs [-nəs]

inconsiderate, -ly, -ness ˌmkənˈsɪdərət [ˌɪŋk-, -rɪt], -lɪ, -nɪs [-nəs]

inconsideration ˈmkənˌsɪdəˈreɪʃn [ˈɪŋk-]

inconsisten|cy, -cies, -t/ly ˌmkənˈsɪstən|sɪ [ˌɪŋk-], -sɪz, -t/lɪ

inconsolab|le, -ly, -leness ˌmkənˈsəʊləb|l [ˌɪŋk-], -lɪ, -lnɪs [-nəs]

inconspicuous, -ly, -ness ˌmkənˈspɪkjʊəs [ˌɪŋk-, -kjwəs], -lɪ, -nɪs [-nəs]

inconstan|cy, -t/ly mˈkɒnstən|sɪ [ˌmˈk-, ɪŋˈk-, ˌɪŋˈk-], -t/lɪ

incontestability ˈmkənˌtestəˈbɪlətɪ [ˈɪŋk-, -lɪt-]

incontestab|le, -ly ˌmkənˈtestəb|l [ˌɪŋk-], -lɪ

incontinen|ce, -t/ly mˈkɒntmən|s [ˌmˈk-, mˈk-, ɪŋˈk-], -t/lɪ

incontrollab|le, -ly ˌmkənˈtrəʊləb|l [ˌɪŋk-], -lɪ

incontrovertibility mˌkɒntrəvɜːtəˈbɪlətɪ [ˈmˌkɒntrəvɜːtəˈb-, ɪŋˌk-, ˈɪŋˌk-, -trʊv-, -tɪˈb-, -lɪt-]

incontrovertib|le, -ly ˌmkɒntrəˈvɜːtəb|l [ˌɪŋk-, -trʊv-, -trɪb-, -ˌ-ˈ---, -ˈ-----], -lɪ

inconvenienc|e (s. v.), **-es, -ing, -ed** ˌmkənˈviːnjəns [ˌɪŋk-, -nɪəns], -ɪz, -ɪŋ, -t

inconvenient, -ly ˌmkənˈviːnjənt [ˌɪŋk-, -nɪənt], -lɪ

inconvertibility ˈmkənˌvɜːtəˈbɪlətɪ [ˈɪŋk-, -tɪˈb-, -lɪt-]

inconvertib|le, -ly ˌmkənˈvɜːtəb|l [ˌɪŋk-, -tɪb-], -lɪ

incorporate (adj.) mˈkɔːpərət [ɪŋˈk-, -rɪt]

incorporat|e (v.), **-es, -ing, -ed** mˈkɔːpəreɪt [ɪŋˈk-], -s, -ɪŋ, -ɪd

incorporation, -s mˌkɔːpəˈreɪʃn [ɪŋˌk-], -z

incorporeal, -ly ˌmkɔːˈpɔːrɪəl [ˌɪŋk-], -ɪ

incorrect, -ly, -ness ˌmkəˈrekt [ˌɪŋk-], -lɪ, -nɪs [-nəs]

incorrigibility mˌkɒrɪdʒəˈbɪlətɪ [ɪŋˌk-, -dʒɪˈb-, -lɪt-]

incorrigib|le, -ly, -leness mˈkɒrɪdʒəb|l [ɪŋˈk-, -dʒɪb-], -lɪ, -lnɪs [-nəs]

incorruptibility ˈmkəˌrʌptəˈbɪlətɪ [ˈɪŋk-, -tɪˈb-, -lɪt-]

incorruptib|le, -ly, -leness ˌmkəˈrʌptəb|l [ˌɪŋk-, -tɪb-], -lɪ, -lnɪs [-nəs]

incorruption (when contrasted with corruption, as is usually the case) ˈmkəˌrʌpʃn [ˈɪŋk-], (when not so contrasted) ˌmkəˈr- [ˌɪŋk-]

increase (s.), **-s** ˈmkriːs [ˈɪŋkriːs, mˈkriːs], -ɪz

increas|e (v.), **-es, -ing/ly, -ed** mˈkriːs [ɪŋˈk-, ˈmkriːs, ˈɪŋkriːs], -ɪz, -ɪŋ/lɪ, -t

incredibility mˌkredɪˈbɪlətɪ [ɪŋˌk-, -dəˈb-, -lɪt-]

incredib|le, -ly, -leness mˈkredəb|l [ɪŋˈk-, -dɪb-], -lɪ, -lnɪs [-nəs]

incredulity ˌmkrɪˈdjuːlətɪ [ˌɪŋkrɪˈd-, -kreˈd-, -krəˈd-, -rtɪ]

incredulous, -ness mˈkredjʊləs [ɪŋˈk-, -dʒʊl-, -dʒəl-], -lɪ, -nɪs [-nəs]

increment, -s ˈmkrɪmənt [ˈɪŋk-, -krə-], -s

incremental ˌmkrɪˈmentl [ˌɪŋk-, -krə-]

incriminat|e, -es, -ing, -ed mˈkrɪmɪneɪt [ɪŋˈk-], -s, -ɪŋ, -ɪd

incrimination mˌkrɪmɪˈneɪʃn

incriminatory mˈkrɪmɪnətərɪ [ɪŋˈk-, -neɪtərɪ]

incrust, -s, -ing, -ed mˈkrʌst [ɪŋˈk-], -s, -ɪŋ, -ɪd

incrustation, -s ˌmkrʌsˈteɪʃn [ˌɪŋk-], -z

incubat|e, -es, -ing, -ed, -or/s; -ive, -ory ˈmkjʊbeɪt [ˈɪŋk-], -s, -ɪŋ, -ɪd, ə*/z; -ɪv, -ərɪ

incubation ˌmkjʊˈbeɪʃn [ˌɪŋk-]

incubus, -es ˈɪŋkjʊbəs [ˈmk-], -ɪz

inculcat|e, -es, -ing, -ed, -or/s ˈmkʌlkeɪt [ˈɪŋk-, -kəl-, mˈkʌlkeɪt, ɪŋˈkʌl-], -s, -ɪŋ, -ɪd, -ə*/z

inculcation ˌmkʌlˈkeɪʃn [ˌɪŋk-]

inculpat|e, -es, -ing, -ed ˈmkʌlpeɪt [ˈɪŋk-, mˈkʌlpeɪt, ɪŋˈk-], -s, -ɪŋ, -ɪd

inculpation ˌmkʌlˈpeɪʃn [ˌɪŋk-]

inculpatory mˈkʌlpətərɪ [ɪŋˈk-, ˈmkʌlpeɪtərɪ, ˈɪŋkʌlpeɪtərɪ]

259

incumben|cy, -cies, -t/s, -tly m'kʌm-
bən|sɪ [ɪŋ'k-], -sɪz, -t/s, -tlɪ
incunabula ˌɪnkjuːˈnæbjʊlə [ˌɪŋk-,
-kjʊ'n-]
incur, -s, -ring, -red; -able m'kɜː* [ɪŋ'k-],
-z, -rɪŋ, -d; -rəbl
incurability mˌkjʊərəˈbɪlətɪ [ˈmˌkjʊər-
ə'b-, ɪŋˌk-, 'ɪŋˌk-, -jɔər-, -jɔːr-,
-lɪt-]
incurab|le, -ly, -leness m'kjʊərəb|l
[ˌm'k-, ɪŋ'k-, ɪŋ'k-, -'kjɔər-, -'kjɔːr-],
-lɪ, -lnɪs [-nəs]
incurious m'kjʊərɪəs [ˌm'k-, ɪŋ'k-,
ˌɪŋ'k-, -'kjɔər-, -'kjɔːr-]
incursion, -s m'kɜːʃn [ɪŋ'k-, -'kɜːʒn], -z
incursive m'kɜːsɪv [ɪŋ'k-]
incurvat|e, -es, -ing, -ed 'mkɜːveɪt
['ɪŋk-], -s, -ɪŋ, -ɪd
incurvation ˌmkɜːˈveɪʃn [ˌɪŋk-]
incurv|e, -es, -ing, -ed ˌm'kɜːv [m'k-,
ɪŋ'k-], -z, -ɪŋ, -d [also 'mkɜːvd,
'ɪŋkɜːvd, esp. when attributive]
incus|e (s. adj. v.), -es, -ing, -ed m-
'kjuːz [ɪŋ'k-], -ɪz, -ɪŋ, -d
Ind (surname) ɪnd, (India) ɪnd [aɪnd]
Indaur m'dɔː* (Hindi yndəwr)
indebted, -ness m'detɪd, -nɪs [-nəs]
indecen|cy, -cies, -t/ly m'diːsn|sɪ
[ˌm'd-], -sɪz, -t/lɪ
indecipherable ˌmdɪˈsaɪfərəbl
indecision ˌmdɪˈsɪʒn
indecisive, -ly, -ness ˌmdɪˈsaɪsɪv -lɪ,
-nɪs [-nəs]
indeclinable (s. adj.), -s ˌmdɪˈklaɪnəbl,
-z
indecomposable 'mˌdiːkəmˈpəʊzəbl
indecorous, -ly, -ness m'dekərəs
[ˌm'd-], -lɪ, -nɪs [-nəs]
indecorum ˌmdɪˈkɔːrəm
indeed (adv.) m'diːd, (interj.) m'diːd
[ˌm'diːd]
indefatigable, -ness ˌmdɪˈfætɪgəbl, -nɪs
[-nəs]
indefatigably ˌmdɪˈfætɪgəblɪ
indefeasibility 'mdɪˌfiːzəˈbɪlətɪ [-zɪ'b-,
-lɪt-]
indefeasib|le, -ly ˌmdɪˈfiːzəb|l [-zɪb-], -lɪ
indefensibility 'mdɪˌfensəˈbɪlətɪ [-sɪ'b-,
-lɪt-]
indefensible ˌmdɪˈfensəbl [-sɪb-]
indefensibly ˌmdɪˈfensəblɪ [-sɪb-]
indefinable ˌmdɪˈfaɪnəbl
indefinably ˌmdɪˈfaɪnəblɪ
indefinite, -ly, -ness m'defɪnət [ˌm'd-,
-fənət, -fɪnət, -fnət, -ɪt], -lɪ, -nɪs
[-nəs]
indelibility mˌdelɪˈbɪlətɪ ['mˌdelɪ'b-,
-lə'b-, -lɪt-]

indelible m'deləbl [ˌm'd-, -lɪb-]
indelibly m'deləblɪ [-lɪb-]
indelicac|y, -ies m'delɪkəs|ɪ [ˌm'd-], -ɪz
indelicate, -ly m'delɪkət [ˌm'd-, -kɪt],
-lɪ
indemnification, -s mˌdemnɪfɪˈkeɪʃn, -z
indemni|fy, -fies, -fying, -fied m'dem-
nɪ|faɪ, -faɪz, -faɪɪŋ, -faɪd
indemnit|y, -ies m'demnət|ɪ [-ɪt|ɪ], -ɪz
indemonstrable m'demənstrəbl [ˌm'd-,
ˌmdɪ'mɒns-]
indent (s.), -s 'mdent [-'-], -s
indent (v.), -s, -ing, -ed m'dent, -s, -ɪŋ,
-ɪd
indentation, -s ˌmdenˈteɪʃn, -z
indenture, -s, -d m'dentʃə*, -z, -d
independen|ce, -cy ˌmdɪˈpendən|s, -sɪ
independent (s. adj.), -s, -ly ˌmdɪ-
'pendənt, -s, -lɪ
Inderwick 'mdəwɪk [-dɜː-]
indescribable ˌmdɪˈskraɪbəbl
indescribably ˌmdɪˈskraɪbəblɪ
indestructibility 'mdɪˌstrʌktəˈbɪlətɪ
[-tɪ'b-, -lɪt-]
indestructible, -ness ˌmdɪˈstrʌktəbl
[-tɪb-], -nɪs [-nəs]
indestructibly ˌmdɪˈstrʌktəblɪ [-tɪb-]
indeterminable, -ness ˌmdɪˈtɜːmɪnəbl,
-nɪs [-nəs]
indeterminacy ˌmdɪˈtɜːmɪnəsɪ
indeterminate, -ly, -ness ˌmdɪˈtɜːmɪnət
[-nɪt], -lɪ, -nɪs [-nəs]
indetermination 'mdɪˌtɜːmɪˈneɪʃn
ind|ex, -exes, -ices 'md|eks, -eksɪz,
-ɪsiːz
India, -n/s 'mdjə [-dɪə], -n/z
Indiana ˌmdɪˈænə [-'ɑːn-]
Indianapolis ˌmdɪəˈnæpəlɪs [-djə-,-pʊl-]
india-rubber, -s ˌmdjəˈrʌbə* [-dʒə-,
also '-,-,- according to sentence-
stress], -z
indicat|e, -es, -ing, -ed, -or/s 'mdɪkeɪt,
-s, -ɪŋ, -ɪd, -ə*/z
indication, -s ˌmdɪˈkeɪʃn, -z
indicative (s. adj.) (in grammar), -s, -ly
m'dɪkətɪv, -z, -lɪ
indicative (adj.) (pointing out), -ly m-
'dɪkətɪv ['mdɪkeɪtɪv], -lɪ
indicatory m'dɪkətərɪ ['mdɪkeɪtərɪ]
indict, -s, -ing, -ed, -er/s, -ment/s;
-able m'daɪt, -s, -ɪŋ, -ɪd, -ə*/z,
-mənt/s; -əbl
indiction, -s m'dɪkʃn, -z
Indies 'mdɪz
indifferen|ce, -cy, -t/ly m'dɪfrən|s
[-fərən-], -sɪ, -t/lɪ
indigen|ce, -t/ly 'mdɪdʒən|s, -t/lɪ
indigene, -s 'mdɪdʒiːn, -z

indigenous ɪn'dɪdʒɪnəs [-dʒɲəs, -dʒənəs]
indigestibility 'ɪndɪˌdʒestə'bɪlətɪ [-tɪ'b-, -lɪt-]
indigestible, -ness ˌɪndɪ'dʒestəbl [-tɪb-], -nɪs [-nəs]
indigestion ˌɪndɪ'dʒestʃən [-eʃtʃ-]
indignant, -ly ɪn'dɪgnənt, -lɪ
indignation ˌɪndɪg'neɪʃn
indignit|y, -ies ɪn'dɪgnət|ɪ [-ɪt|ɪ], -ɪz
indigo, -s 'ɪndɪgəʊ, -z
indirect, -ly, -ness ˌɪndɪ'rekt [-daɪ'r-, -də'r-], -lɪ, -nɪs [-nəs]
indiscernible ˌɪndɪ'sə:nəbl [-dɪ'zɜ:-, -nɪb-]
indisciplin|e, -able ɪn'dɪsɪplɪn [ˌɪn'd-, -səp-], -əbl
indiscreet, -ly, -ness ˌɪndɪ'skri:t, -lɪ, -nɪs [-nəs]
indiscretion, -s ˌɪndɪ'skreʃn, -z
indiscriminate, -ly ˌɪndɪ'skrɪmɪnət [-mən-, -nɪt], -lɪ
indiscrimination 'ɪndɪˌskrɪmɪ'neɪʃn [-mə'n-]
indispensability 'ɪndɪˌspensə'bɪlətɪ [-lɪt-]
indispensable, -ness ˌɪndɪ'spensəbl, -nɪs [-nəs]
indispos|e, -es, -ing, -ed ˌɪndɪ'spəʊz, -ɪz, -ɪŋ, -d
indisposition, -s ˌɪndɪspə'zɪʃn ['ɪn-ˌdɪspə'z-, -pʊ'z-], -z
indisputability ˌɪndɪspju:tə'bɪlətɪ [ɪn-ˌdɪspjʊtə'b-, -lɪt-]
indisputable, -ness ˌɪndɪ'spju:təbl [ɪn'dɪspjʊtəbl], -nɪs [-nəs]
indisputably ˌɪndɪ'spju:təblɪ [ɪn'dɪs-pjʊt-]
indissociable ˌɪndɪ'səʊʃjəbl [-ʃɪə-, -ʃə-]
indissolubility 'ɪndɪˌsɒljʊ'bɪlətɪ [ɪn-ˌdɪsɒljʊ'b-, -lɪt-]
indissoluble, -ness ˌɪndɪ'sɒljʊbl [ɪn'dɪsəl-], -nɪs [-nəs]
indissolubly ˌɪndɪ'sɒljʊblɪ [ɪn'dɪsəl-]
indistinct, -ly, -ness ˌɪndɪ'stɪŋkt -lɪ, -nɪs [-nəs]
indistinctive, -ly, -ness ˌɪndɪ'stɪŋktɪv, -lɪ, -nɪs [-nəs]
indistinguishab|le, -ly, -leness ˌɪndɪ-'stɪŋgwɪʃəb|l, -lɪ, -lnɪs [-nəs]
indit|e, -es, -ing, -ed, -er/s ɪn'daɪt, -s, -ɪŋ, -ɪd, -ə*/z
individual (s. adj.) -s, -ly ˌɪndɪ'vɪdʒʊəl [-djʊəl-, -djwəl, -djʊl, -dʒwəl-, -dʒʊl], -z, -ɪ
individuali|sm, -st/s ˌɪndɪ'vɪd-ʒʊəlɪ|zəm [-djʊəl-, -djwəl-, -djʊl-, -dʒwəl-, -dʒʊl-], -st/s
individualistic 'ɪndɪˌvɪdʒʊə'lɪstɪk [-djʊə'l-, -djwə'l-, -djʊ'l-, -dʒwə'l-, -dʒʊ'l-]

individualit|y, -ies 'ɪndɪˌvɪdʒʊ'ælət|ɪ [-ˌvɪdjʊ-, -ɪt|ɪ], -ɪz
individualization [-isa-] 'ɪndɪˌvɪdʒʊəlaɪ-'zeɪʃn [-djʊəl-, -djwəl-, -djʊl-, -dʒwəl-, -dʒʊl-, -lɪ'z-]
individualiz|e [is|e], -es, -ing, -ed ˌɪn-dɪ'vɪdʒʊəlaɪz [-djʊəl-, -djwəl-, -djʊl-, -dʒwəl-, -dʒʊl-], -ɪz, -ɪŋ, -d
†individuat|e, -es, -ing, -ed ˌɪndɪ-'vɪdʒʊeɪt, [-djʊ-], -s, -ɪŋ, -ɪd
indivisibility 'ɪndɪˌvɪzɪ'bɪlətɪ [-zə'b-, -lɪt-]
indivisib|le, -ly, -leness ˌɪndɪ'vɪzəb|l [-zɪb-], -lɪ, -lnɪs [-nəs]
Indo-China ˌɪndəʊ't ʃaɪnə
Indo-Chinese ˌɪndəʊtʃaɪ'ni:z
indocile ɪn'dəʊsaɪl [ˌɪn'd-, -'dɒs-]
indocility ˌɪndəʊ'sɪlətɪ [-ɪtɪ]
indoctrinat|e, -es, -ing, -ed ɪn'dɒk-trɪneɪt, -s, -ɪŋ, -ɪd
indoctrination ɪnˌdɒktrɪ'neɪʃn
Indo-European, -s 'ɪndəʊˌjʊərə'pi:ən [-ˌjɔər-, -ˌjɔ:r-, -'pɪən], -z
Indo-Germanic ˌɪndəʊdʒə'mænɪk [-dʒɜ:-]
indolen|ce, -t/ly 'ɪndələn|s [-dʊl-], -t/lɪ
indomitab|le, -ly ɪn'dɒmɪtəb|l, -lɪ
Indone|sia, -sian/s ˌɪndəʊ'ni:|zjə [-zɪə, -ʒə, -sjə, -sɪə, -ʃə], -zjən/z [-zɪən/z, -ʒn/z, -sjən/z, -sɪən/z, -ʃn/z]
indoor 'ɪndɔ:* [-dɔə*]
indoors ˌɪn'dɔ:z [-'dɔəz, also ɪn'd- when preceded by a stress]
Indore (former spelling of Indaur, q.v.) ɪn'dɔ:* [-'dɔə*]
indors|e, -es, -ing, -ed, -ement/s ɪn'dɔ:s, -ɪz, -ɪŋ, -t, -mənt/s
Indra 'ɪndrə
indraught, -s 'ɪndrɑ:ft, -s
indrawn ˌɪn'drɔ:n ['ɪndrɔ:n when attributive]
indubitable, -ness ɪn'dju:bɪtəbl, -nɪs [-nəs]
indubitably ɪn'dju:bɪtəblɪ
induc|e, -es, -ing, -ed, -er/s, -ement/s ɪn'dju:s, -ɪz, -ɪŋ, -t, -ə*/z, -mənt/s
induct, -s, -ing, -ed, -or/s ɪn'dʌkt, -s, -ɪŋ, -ɪd, -ə*/z
inductile ɪn'dʌktaɪl [ˌɪn'd-]
inductility ˌɪndʌk'tɪlətɪ [-ɪtɪ]
induction, -s ɪn'dʌkʃn, -z
induction-coil, -s ɪn'dʌkʃnkɔɪl, -z
inductive, -ly ɪn'dʌktɪv, -lɪ
indulg|e, -es, -ing, -ed, -er/s ɪn'dʌldʒ, -ɪz, -ɪŋ, -d, -ə*/z
indulgen|ce, -ces, -t/ly ɪn'dʌldʒən|s, -sɪz, -t/lɪ

indurat|e, -es, -ing, -ed 'ɪndjʊəreɪt [-jʊr-], -s, -ɪŋ, -ɪd
Indus 'ɪndəs
industrial, -ly ɪn'dʌstrɪəl, -ɪ
industriali|sm, -st/s ɪn'dʌstrɪəlɪ|zəm, -st/s
industrialization ɪn,dʌstrɪəlaɪ'zeɪʃn [-lɪ'z-]
industrializ|e, -es, -ing, -ed ɪn'dʌstrɪəlaɪz, -ɪz, -ɪŋ, -d
industrious, -ly ɪn'dʌstrɪəs, -lɪ
industr|y, -ies 'ɪndəstr|ɪ, -ɪz
indwel|l, -ls, -ling, -t ,ɪn'dwel [-'-], -z, -ɪŋ, -t
indweller, -s 'ɪn,dwelə*, -z
inebriate (s. adj.), **-s** ɪ'niːbrɪət [-brɪɪt, -brɪeɪt], -s
inebriat|e (v.), **-es, -ing, -ed** ɪ'niːbrɪeɪt, -s, -ɪŋ, -ɪd
inebriation ɪ,niːbrɪ'eɪʃn
inebriety ,mɪ'braɪətɪ [-nɪ'b-]
inedible ɪn'edɪbl [,ɪn'e-, -dəb-]
inedited ɪn'edɪtɪd [,ɪn'e-]
ineducable ɪn'edjʊkəbl [-dʒʊ-]
ineffab|le, -ly, -leness ɪn'efəb|l, -lɪ, -lnɪs [-nəs]
ineffaceable ,ɪnɪ'feɪsəbl
ineffaceably ,ɪnɪ'feɪsəblɪ
ineffective, -ly ,ɪnɪ'fektɪv, -lɪ
ineffectual, -ly, -ness ,ɪnɪ'fektʃʊəl [-tʃwəl, -tʃʊl, -tjʊəl, -tjwəl, -tjʊl], -ɪ, -nɪs [-nəs]
inefficacious, -ly ,ɪnefɪ'keɪʃəs, -lɪ
inefficacy ɪn'efɪkəsɪ [,ɪn'e-]
inefficien|cy, -t/ly ,ɪnɪ'fɪʃn|sɪ, -t/lɪ
inelastic ,ɪnɪ'læstɪk [-'lɑːs-]
inelasticity ,ɪnlæs'tɪsətɪ [,ɪniːlæs't-, -lɑːs-, -ɪtɪ]
inelegan|ce, -t/ly ɪn'elɪgən|s [,ɪn'e-], -t/lɪ
ineligibility ɪn,elɪdʒə'bɪlətɪ ['ɪn,elɪdʒə'b-, -dʒɪ'b-, -lɪt-]
ineligib|le, -ly ɪn'elɪdʒəb|l [,ɪn'e-, -dʒɪb-], -lɪ
ineluctable ,ɪnɪ'lʌktəbl
inept, -ly, -ness ɪ'nept [ɪn'ept], -lɪ, -nɪs [-nəs]
ineptitude ɪ'neptɪtjuːd [ɪn'ep-]
inequab|le, -ly ɪn'ekwəb|l [,ɪn-], -lɪ
inequalit|y, -ies ,ɪnɪ'kwɒlət|ɪ [-nɪː-, -ɪt|ɪ], -ɪz
inequitab|le, -ly ɪn'ekwɪtəb|l [,ɪn'e-], -lɪ
inequit|y, -ies ɪn'ekwət|ɪ [,ɪn'e-, -ɪt|ɪ], -ɪz
ineradicab|le, -ly ,ɪnɪ'rædɪkəb|l, -lɪ
inert, -ly, -ness ɪ'nɜːt, -lɪ, -nɪs [-nəs]
inertia ɪ'nɜːʃə [-ʃɪə, -ʃjə]

inescapable ,ɪnɪ'skeɪpəbl
inessential ,ɪnɪ'senʃl
inestimable ɪn'estɪməbl [,ɪn'e-]
inestimably ɪn'estɪməblɪ
inevitability ɪn,evɪtə'bɪlətɪ [ɪ,ne-, -lɪt-]
inevitable, -ness ɪn'evɪtəbl [,ɪn'e-, ɪ'ne-], -nɪs [-nəs]
inevitably ɪn'evɪtəblɪ [ɪ'ne-]
inexact, -ly, -ness ,ɪnɪg'zækt [-eg-], -lɪ, -nɪs [-nəs]
inexactitude, -s ,ɪnɪg'zæktɪtjuːd [-eg-], -z
inexcusable, -ness ,ɪnɪk'skjuːzəbl [-ek-], -nɪs [-nəs]
inexcusably ,ɪnɪk'skjuːzəblɪ [-ek-]
inexhaustibility 'ɪnɪg,zɔːstə'bɪlətɪ [-eg-, -tɪ'b-, -lɪtɪ]
inexhaustible ,ɪnɪg'zɔːstəbl [-eg-, -tɪb-]
inexhaustibly ,ɪnɪg'zɔːstəblɪ [-eg-, -tɪb-]
inexorability ɪn,eksərə'bɪlətɪ [-lɪt-]
inexorab|le, -ly, -leness ɪn'eksərəb|l, -lɪ, -lnɪs [-nəs]
inexpedien|cy, -t/ly ,ɪnɪk'spiːdjən|sɪ [-ek-, -dɪən-], -t/lɪ
inexpensive ,ɪnɪk'spensɪv [-ek-]
inexperience, -d ,ɪnɪk'spɪərɪəns [-ek-], -t
inexpert, -ness ɪn'ekspɜːt [,ɪn-, ,ɪnek'sp-, -nɪk'sp-], -nɪs [-nəs]
inexpiable, -ness ɪn'ekspɪəbl [,ɪn'e-, -pjə-], -nɪs [-nəs]
inexplicability ɪn,eksplɪkə'bɪlətɪ ['ɪn,eksplɪkə'b-, 'ɪnɪk,splɪkə'b-, 'ɪnek,s-plɪkə'b-, -lɪt-]
inexplicable, -ness ,ɪnɪk'splɪkəbl [ɪn'eksplɪkəbl], -nɪs [-nəs]
inexplicably ,ɪnɪk'splɪkəblɪ [ɪn'eksplɪk-əblɪ]
inexplicit ,ɪnɪk'splɪsɪt [-ek-]
inexplorable ,ɪnɪk'splɔːrəbl [-ek-]
inexpressible ,ɪnɪk'spresəbl [-ek-, -sɪb-]
inexpressibly ,ɪnɪk'spresəblɪ [-ek-, -sɪb-]
inexpressive, -ness ,ɪnɪk'spresɪv [-ek-], -nɪs [-nəs]
inexpugnable ,ɪnɪk'spʌgnəbl [-ek-]
inextensible ,ɪnɪk'stensəbl [-ek-, -sɪb-]
inextinguishable ,ɪnɪk'stɪŋgwɪʃəbl [-ek-]
inextinguishably ,ɪnɪk'stɪŋgwɪʃəblɪ [-ek-]
inextricable ɪn'ekstrɪkəbl [,ɪnɪk'strɪk-, ,ɪnek'strɪk-]
inextricably ɪn'ekstrɪkəblɪ [,ɪnɪk'strɪk-, ,ɪnek'strɪk-]
Inez 'iːnez
infallibility ɪn,fælə'bɪlətɪ [-lɪ'b-, -lɪt-]
infallib|le, -ly ɪn'fæləb|l [-lɪb-], -lɪ
infamous, -ly, -ness 'ɪnfəməs [-fɪ̩məs], -lɪ, -nɪs [-nəs]

infamy 'ɪnfəmɪ [-fm̩ɪ]
infancy 'ɪnfənsɪ
infant, -s 'ɪnfənt, -s
infanta, -s ɪn'fæntə, -z
infante, -s ɪn'fæntɪ, -z
infanticide, -s ɪn'fæntɪsaɪd, -z
infant|ile, -ine 'ɪnfənt|aɪl, -aɪn
infantilism ɪn'fæntɪlɪzəm
infantry, -man, -men 'ɪnfəntrɪ, -mən
[-mæn], -mən [-men]
infatuat|e, -es, -ing, -ed ɪn'fætjʊeɪt
[-'fætʃʊ-], -s, -ɪŋ, -ɪd
infatuation, -s ɪn,fætjʊ'eɪʃn [-,fætʃʊ-],
-z
infect, -s, -ing, -ed ɪn'fekt, -s, -ɪŋ, -ɪd
infection, -s ɪn'fekʃn, -z
infectious, -ly, -ness ɪn'fekʃəs, -lɪ, -nɪs
[-nəs]
infecundity ,ɪnfɪ'kʌndətɪ [-fiː'k-, -fe'k-,
-ɪtɪ]
infelicit|ous, -y ,ɪnfɪ'lɪsɪt|əs [-fe'l-,
-sət|əs], -ɪ
infer, -s, -ring, -red; -able ɪn'fɜ:*, -z,
-rɪŋ, -d; -rəbl
inference, -s 'ɪnfərəns, -ɪz
inferenti|al, -ally ,ɪnfə'renʃ|l, -əlɪ
inferior (s. adj.), -s ɪn'fɪərɪə* [,ɪn'f-],
-z
inferiority ɪn,fɪərɪ'ɒrətɪ [,ɪnfɪərɪ'ɒ-, -ɪtɪ]
infern|al (s. adj.), -als, -ally ɪn'fɜ:n|l,
-lz, -əlɪ [-l̩ɪ]
inferno, -s ɪn'fɜ:nəʊ, -z
Inferno ɪn'fɜ:nəʊ [-'feən-]
infertile ɪn'fɜ:taɪl [,ɪn'f-]
infertility ,ɪnfə'tɪlətɪ [-ɪtɪ]
infest, -s, -ing, -ed ɪn'fest, -s, -ɪŋ, -ɪd
infestation ,ɪnfe'steɪʃn
infidel, -s 'ɪnfɪdəl [-del], -z
infidelit|y, -ies ,ɪnfɪ'delət|ɪ [-faɪ'd-,
-ɪt|ɪ], -ɪz
in-fighting (s.) 'ɪn,faɪtɪŋ
infiltrat|e, -es, -ing, -ed 'ɪnfɪltreɪt [-'—],
-s, -ɪŋ, -ɪd
infiltration, -s ,ɪnfɪl'treɪʃn, -z
in fine ,ɪn'faɪnɪ [-'fiː-n-]
infinite (in non-technical sense), -ly, -ness
'ɪnfɪnət [-fən-, -fnət, -ɪt, in church
music also 'ɪnfɪnaɪt, 'ɪnfaɪnaɪt], -lɪ, -nɪs
[-nəs]
infinite (in grammar) ɪn'faɪnaɪt
infinite (in mathematics) 'ɪnfɪnət [-fən-,
-fnət, -ɪt, 'ɪn,faɪnaɪt]
infinitesim|al, -ally ,ɪnfɪnɪ'tesɪm|l,
[-nə't-], -əlɪ
infinitival ɪn,fɪnɪ'taɪvl [,ɪnfɪnɪ't-]
infinitive, -s, -ly ɪn'fɪnətɪv [-nɪt-], -z, -lɪ
infinitude, -s ɪn'fɪnɪtjuːd, -z
infinit|y, -ies ɪn'fɪnət|ɪ [-ɪt|ɪ], -ɪz

infirm, -ly ɪn'fɜ:m [,ɪn'fɜ:m], -lɪ
infirmar|y, -ies ɪn'fɜ:mər|ɪ [-mr|ɪ], -ɪz
infirmit|y, -ies ɪn'fɜ:mət|ɪ [-ɪt|ɪ], -ɪz
infix (s.), -es 'ɪnfɪks, -ɪz
infix (v.), -es, -ing, -ed ɪn'fɪks, -ɪz, -ɪŋ,
-t
inflam|e, -es, -ing, -ed ɪn'fleɪm, -z, -ɪŋ,
-d
inflammability ɪn,flæmə'bɪlətɪ [-lɪt-]
inflammable, -ness ɪn'flæməbl, -nɪs
[-nəs]
inflammation, -s ,ɪnflə'meɪʃn, -z
inflammatory ɪn'flæmətərɪ
inflat|e, -es, -ing, -ed, -or/s ɪn'fleɪt, -s,
-ɪŋ, -ɪd, -ə*/z
inflation, -s ɪn'fleɪʃn, -z
inflationary ɪn'fleɪʃŋərɪ [-ʃnərɪ, -ʃŋɪ,
-ʃənərɪ]
inflect, -s, -ing, -ed ɪn'flekt, -s, -ɪŋ, -ɪd
inflection, -s ɪn'flekʃn, -z
inflectional ɪn'flekʃənl [-ʃnəl, -ʃŋl̩, -ʃnl̩,
-ʃənəl]
inflective ɪn'flektɪv
inflexibility ɪn,fleksə'bɪlətɪ ['ɪn,fleks-
sə'b-, -sɪ'b-, -lɪt-]
inflexib|le, -ly, -leness ɪn'fleksəb|l
[-sɪb-], -lɪ, -lnɪs [-nəs]
inflexion, -s ɪn'flekʃn, -z
inflexional ɪn'flekʃənl [-ʃnəl, -ʃŋl̩, -ʃnl̩,
-ʃənəl]
inflict, -s, -ing, -ed ɪn'flɪkt, -s, -ɪŋ, -ɪd
infliction, -s ɪn'flɪkʃn, -z
inflow, -s 'ɪnfləʊ, -z
influenc|e (s. v.), -es, -ing, -ed 'ɪnflʊəns
[-flwəns], -ɪz, -ɪŋ, -t
influent, -s 'ɪnflʊənt [-flwənt], -s
influenti|al, -ally ,ɪnflʊ'enʃ|l, -əlɪ
influenza ,ɪnflʊ'enzə
influx, -es 'ɪnflʌks, -ɪz
influxion ɪn'flʌkʃn
inform, -s, -ing, -ed, -er/s ɪn'fɔ:m, -z,
-ɪŋ, -d, -ə*/z
inform|al, -ally ɪn'fɔ:m|l [,ɪn'f-], -əlɪ
informalit|y, -ies ,ɪnfɔ:'mælət|ɪ [-ɪt|ɪ], -ɪz
informant, -s ɪn'fɔ:mənt, -s
information, -s ,ɪnfə'meɪʃn [-fɔ:'m-], -z
informat|ive, -ory ɪn'fɔ:mət|ɪv, -ərɪ
infra 'ɪnfrə
infract, -s, -ing, -ed ɪn'frækt, -s, -ɪŋ, -ɪd
infraction, -s ɪn'frækʃn, -z
infralapsarian, -s ,ɪnfrəlæp'seərɪən, -z
infrangibility ɪn,frændʒɪ'bɪlətɪ ['ɪn-
,frændʒɪ'b-, -dʒə'b-, -lɪt-]
infrangible ɪn'frændʒɪbl [,ɪn'f-, -dʒəb-]
infra-red ,ɪnfrə'red
infra-structure, -s 'ɪnfrə,strʌktʃə*, -z
infrequen|cy, -t ɪn'friːkwən|sɪ [,ɪn'f-], -t
infrequently ɪn'friːkwəntlɪ

263

infring|e, -es, -ing, -ed, -er/s, -ement/s ɪnˈfrɪndʒ, -ɪz, -ɪŋ, -d, -ə*/z, -mənt/s

infuriat|e, -es, -ing/ly, -ed ɪnˈfjʊərɪeɪt [-ˈfjɔər-, -ˈfjɔːr-], -s, -ɪŋ/lɪ, -ɪd

infus|e, -es, -ing, -ed, -er/s ɪnˈfjuːz, -ɪz, -ɪŋ, -d, -ə*/z

infusible (capable of being infused) ɪnˈfjuːzəbl [-zɪb-]

infusible (not fusible) ɪnˈfjuːzəbl [ˌɪnˈf-, -zɪb-]

infusion, -s ɪnˈfjuːʒn, -z

infusoria, -l, -n ˌɪnfjuːˈzɔːrɪə [-ˈsɔː-], -l, -n

infusory ɪnˈfjuːzərɪ [-uːsə-]

Ingall ˈɪŋɡɔːl

Ingatestone ˈɪŋɡeɪtstəʊn [ˈɪŋɡ-]

ingathering, -s ˈɪnˌɡæðərɪŋ, -z

Inge ɪŋ, ɪndʒ

Ingelow ˈɪndʒɪləʊ

ingenious, -ly, -ness ɪnˈdʒiːnjəs [-nɪəs], -lɪ, -nɪs [-nəs]

ingénue, -s ˈ*ænʒ*eɪnjuː: [ˈænʒ-, ˌ--ˈ-] (ẽʒeny), -z

ingenuity ˌɪndʒɪˈnjuːətɪ [-dʒəˈn-, -ˈnjʊ-, -ɪtɪ]

ingenuous, -ly, -ness ɪnˈdʒenjʊəs [-njwəs], -lɪ, -nɪs [-nəs]

Ingersoll, -s ˈɪŋɡəsɒl, -z

Ingestre ˈɪŋɡestrɪ

Ingham ˈɪŋəm

ingle (I.), -s ˈɪŋɡl, -z

Ingle|borough, -by ˈɪŋɡl|bərə, -bɪ

ingle-nook, -s ˈɪŋɡlnʊk, -s

Inglewood ˈɪŋɡlwʊd

Inglis ˈɪŋɡlz, ˈɪŋɡlɪs

inglorious, -ly, -ness ɪnˈɡlɔːrəs [ˌɪnˈɡ-, ɪŋˈɡ-, ˌɪŋˈɡ-], -lɪ, -nɪs [-nəs]

ingoing ˈɪnˌɡəʊɪŋ

Ingold ˈɪŋɡəʊld

Ingoldsby ˈɪŋɡ*ə*ldzbɪ

ingot, -s ˈɪŋɡət [-ɡɒt], -s

Ingpen ˈɪnpen

Ingraham ˈɪŋɡrəhəm [-ɡrɪəm]

ingrain, -ed ˌɪnˈɡreɪn [also ˈ— according to sentence-stress], -d

Ingram ˈɪŋɡrəm

ingrate, -s ɪnˈɡreɪt [ˈ--], -s

ingratiat|e, -es, -ing, -ed ɪnˈɡreɪʃɪeɪt [-ʃjeɪt], -s, -ɪŋ, -ɪd

ingratitude ɪnˈɡrætɪtjuːd [ˌɪnˈɡ-, ɪŋˈɡ-, ˌɪŋˈɡ-]

Ingrebourne ˈɪŋɡrɪbɔːn [-bɔən]

ingredient, -s ɪnˈɡriːdjənt [ɪŋˈɡ-, -dɪənt], -s

ingress ˈɪnɡres [ˈɪŋɡ-]

ingressive ɪnˈɡresɪv

in|growing, -growth ˈɪn|ˌɡrəʊɪŋ, -ɡrəʊθ

inguinal ˈɪŋɡwɪnl

inhabit, -s, -ing, -ed, -er/s; -able, -ant/s ɪnˈhæbɪt, -s, -ɪŋ, -ɪd, -ə*/z; -əbl, -ənt/s

inhabitation ɪnˌhæbɪˈteɪʃn

inhalation, -s ˌɪnhəˈleɪʃn, -z

inhal|e, -es, -ing, -ed, -er/s, -ant/s ɪnˈheɪl, -z, -ɪŋ, -d, -ə*/z, -ənt/s

inharmonious, -ly, -ness ˌɪnhɑːˈməʊnjəs [-nɪəs], -lɪ, -nɪs [-nəs]

inher|e, -es, -ing, -ed ɪnˈhɪə*, -z, -rɪŋ, -d

inheren|ce, -cy, -t/ly ɪnˈhɪərən|s [-ˈher-], -sɪ, -t/lɪ

inherit, -s, -ing, -ed, -or/s; -able, -ance/s ɪnˈherɪt, -s, -ɪŋ, -ɪd, -ə*/z; -əbl, -əns/ɪz

inheritrix, -es ɪnˈherɪtrɪks, -ɪz

inhibit, -s, -ing, -ed, -or/s; -ory ɪnˈhɪbɪt, -s, -ɪŋ, -ɪd, -ə*/z; -ərɪ

inhibition, -s ˌɪnhɪˈbɪʃn, -z

inhospitab|le, -ly, -leness ˌɪnhɒˈspɪtəb|l [ˌɪnˈhɒs-, ɪnˈhɒs-], -lɪ, -lnɪs [-nəs]

inhospitality ˈɪnˌhɒspɪˈtælətɪ [-ɪtɪ]

inhuman, -ly ɪnˈhjuːmən [ˌɪnˈh-], -lɪ

inhumane, -ly ˌɪnhjuːˈmeɪn [-hjʊ-], -lɪ

inhumanit|y, -ies ˌɪnhjuːˈmænət|ɪ [-hjʊ-, -ɪt|ɪ], -ɪz

inhumation, -s ˌɪnhjuːˈmeɪʃn [-hjʊ-], -z

inhum|e, -es, -ing, -ed ɪnˈhjuːm, -z, -ɪŋ, -d

Inigo ˈɪnɪɡəʊ

inimic|al, -ally ɪˈnɪmɪk|l, -əlɪ

inimitability ɪˌnɪmɪtəˈbɪlətɪ [-lɪt-]

inimitab|le, -ly, -leness ɪˈnɪmɪtəb|l, -lɪ, -lnɪs [-nəs]

iniquitous, -ly ɪˈnɪkwɪtəs, -lɪ

iniquit|y, -ies ɪˈnɪkwət|ɪ [-ɪt|ɪ], -ɪz

initi|al (s. adj. v.), -als, -ally; -al(l)ing, -al(l)ed ɪˈnɪʃ|l, -lz, -əlɪ [-lɪ]; -əlɪŋ [-lɪŋ], -ld

initiate (s.), -s ɪˈnɪʃɪət [-ʃjət, -ʃɪeɪt, -ʃjeɪt, -ʃɪt, -ʃjɪt], -s

initiat|e (v.), -es, -ing, -ed, -or/s ɪˈnɪʃɪeɪt [-ʃjeɪt], -s, -ɪŋ, -ɪd, -ə*/z

initiation, -s ɪˌnɪʃɪˈeɪʃn, -z

initiative ɪˈnɪʃɪətɪv [-ʃjət-, -ʃət-]

initiatory ɪˈnɪʃɪətərɪ [-ʃjət-, -ʃɪeɪtərɪ]

initio (in ab initio) ɪˈnɪʃɪəʊ [-ˈnɪtɪəʊ, -ˈnɪsɪ-]

inject, -s, -ing, -ed, -or/s ɪnˈdʒekt, -s, -ɪŋ, -ɪd, -ə*/z

injection, -s ɪnˈdʒekʃn, -z

injudicious, -ly, -ness ˌɪndʒuːˈdɪʃəs [-dʒʊ-], -lɪ, -nɪs [-nəs]

injunction, -s ɪnˈdʒʌŋkʃn, -z

injurant, -s ˈɪndʒʊərənt [-dʒər-], -s

inj|ure, -ures, -uring, -ured, -urer/s ˈɪndʒ|ə*, -əz, -ərɪŋ, -əd, -ərə*/z

264

injurious, -ly, -ness ɪn'dʒʊərɪəs [-'dʒɔər-, -'dʒɔːr-], -lɪ, -nɪs [-nəs]
injur|y, -ies 'ɪndʒər|ɪ, -ɪz
injustice ɪn'dʒʌstɪs [ˌɪn'dʒ-]
ink (s. v.), -s, -ing, -ed, -er/s ɪŋk, -s, -ɪŋ, -t [ɪŋt], -ə*/z
ink-bottle, -s 'ɪŋk,bɒtl, -z
Inkerman 'ɪŋkəmən
ink-horn, -s 'ɪŋkhɔːn, -z
inking-roller, -s 'ɪŋkɪŋ,rəʊlə*, -z
inkling, -s 'ɪŋklɪŋ, -z
ink-pot, -s 'ɪŋkpɒt, -s
ink-stain, -s 'ɪŋksteɪn, -z
inkstand, -s 'ɪŋkstænd, -z
ink|y, -ier, -iest, -iness 'ɪŋk|ɪ, -ɪə* [-jə*], -ɪɪst [-jɪst], -ɪnɪs [-məs]
inland (s. adj.), -s 'ɪnlənd [-lænd], -z
inland (adv.) ɪn'lænd [ˌ-'-]
inlander, -s 'ɪnləndə*, -z
inlay (s.) 'ɪnleɪ
inlay (v.), -s, -ing, inlaid ˌɪn'leɪ, -z, -ɪŋ, ˌɪn'leɪd [also 'ɪnleɪd when attributive]
inlet, -s 'ɪnlet [-lɪt, -lət], -s
inly 'ɪnlɪ
Inman 'ɪnmən
inmate, -s 'ɪnmeɪt, -s
inmost 'ɪnməʊst [-məst]
inn, -s ɪn, -z
innate, -ly, -ness ˌɪ'neɪt ['--], -lɪ, -nɪs [-nəs]
innavigable ɪ'nævɪgəbl [ˌɪn'næ-]
inner, -most 'ɪnə*, -məʊst
innervat|e, -es, -ing, -ed 'ɪnɜːveɪt [ɪ'nɜːv-], -s, -ɪŋ, -ɪd
innervation ˌɪnɜː'veɪʃn
Innes(s) 'ɪnɪs
innings, -es 'ɪnɪŋz, -ɪz
Innisfail ˌɪnɪs'feɪl
Innisfree ˌɪnɪs'friː
innkeeper, -s 'ɪn,kiːpə*, -z
innocen|ce, -cy 'ɪnəsən|s [-nʊs-], -sɪ
innocent (s. adj.) (I.), -s, -ly 'ɪnəsnt [-nʊs-, -nəʊs-], -s, -lɪ
innocuous, -ly, -ness ɪ'nɒkjʊəs [-kjwəs], -lɪ, -nɪs [-nəs]
innominate ɪ'nɒmmət [-nɪt, -neɪt]
Innous 'ɪnəs
†innovat|e, -es, -ing, -ed, -or/s 'ɪnəʊveɪt, -s, -ɪŋ, -ɪd, -ə*/z
innovation, -s ˌɪnəʊ'veɪʃn, -z
innoxious, -ly, -ness ɪ'nɒkʃəs, -lɪ, -nɪs [-nəs]
Innsbruck 'ɪnzbrʊk (insbruk)
innuendo, -es ˌɪnjuː'endəʊ [-njʊ-], -z
innumerability ɪˌnjuːmərə'bɪlətɪ [-lɪt-]
innumerab|le, -ly, -leness ɪ'njuːmər-əb|l, -lɪ, -lnɪs [-nəs]

innutriti|on, -ous ˌɪnjuː'trɪʃ|n [-njʊ-], -əs
inobservan|ce, -t ˌɪnəb'zɜːvən|s, -t
inoccupation 'ɪnˌɒkjʊ'peɪʃn
inoculat|e, -es, -ing, -ed, -or/s ɪ'nɒkjʊ-leɪt, -s, -ɪŋ, -ɪd, -ə*/z
inoculation, -s ɪˌnɒkjʊ'leɪʃn, -z
inodorous ɪn'əʊdərəs [ˌɪn'əʊ-]
inoffensive, -ly, -ness ˌɪnə'fensɪv [-nʊ'f-], -lɪ, -nɪs [-nəs]
inofficious ˌɪnə'fɪʃəs [-nʊ'f-]
inoperable ɪn'ɒpərəbl
inoperative ɪn'ɒpərətɪv [ˌɪn'ɒ-]
inopportune, -ly ɪn'ɒpətjuːn [ˌɪn'ɒpət-, ˌɪnɒpə't-], -lɪ
inordinate, -ly, -ness ɪn'ɔːdmət [-dnət, -ɪt], -lɪ, -nɪs [-nəs]
inorganic, -ally ˌɪnɔː'gænɪk, -əlɪ
inosculat|e, -es, -ing, -ed ɪ'nɒskjʊleɪt, -s, -ɪŋ, -ɪd
inosculation ɪˌnɒskjʊ'leɪʃn
in-patient, -s 'ɪnˌpeɪʃnt, -s
input, -s 'ɪnpʊt ['ɪm-], -s
inquest, -s 'ɪnkwest ['ɪŋk-], -s
inquietude ɪn'kwaɪətjuːd [ɪŋ'k-, -aɪt-]
inquir|e, -es, -ing/ly, -ed, -er/s ɪn-'kwaɪə* [ɪŋ'k-], -z, -rɪŋ/lɪ, -d, -rə*/z
inquir|y, -ies ɪn'kwaɪər|ɪ [ɪŋ'k-], -ɪz
inquisition (I.), -s ˌɪnkwɪ'zɪʃn [ˌɪŋk-], -z
inquisitional ˌɪnkwɪ'zɪʃənl [ˌɪŋk-, -ʃnəl, -ʃn̩, -ʃnl̩, -ʃənəl]
inquisitive, -ly, -ness ɪn'kwɪzətɪv [ɪŋ'k-, -zɪt-], -lɪ, -nɪs [-nəs]
inquisitor, -s ɪn'kwɪzɪtə* [ɪŋ'k-], -z
inquisitorial, -ly ɪnˌkwɪzɪ'tɔːrɪəl [ɪŋˌk-, ˌɪnkwɪzɪ't-, ˌɪŋkwɪzɪ't-], -ɪ
inroad, -s 'ɪnrəʊd, -z
inrush, -es 'ɪnrʌʃ, -ɪz
insalubr|ious, -ity ˌɪnsə'luːbr|ɪəs .[-'ljuː-], -ətɪ [-ɪtɪ]
insane, -ly, -ness ɪn'seɪn, -lɪ, -nɪs [-nəs]
insanitar|y, -ily, -iness ɪn'sænɪtər|ɪ [ˌɪn's-, -nət-], -əlɪ [-ɪlɪ], -ɪnɪs [-məs]
insanity ɪn'sænətɪ [-ɪtɪ]
insatiability ɪnˌseɪʃjə'bɪlətɪ [-ʃɪə-, -ʃə-, -lɪt-]
insatiab|le, -ly, -leness ɪn'seɪʃəb|l [-ʃɪə-, -ʃjə-], -lɪ, -lnɪs [-nəs]
insatiate ɪn'seɪʃɪət [-ʃjət, -ʃɪt, -ʃɪt]
inscrib|e, -es, -ing, -ed, -er/s ɪn'skraɪb, -z, -ɪŋ, -d, -ə*/z
inscription, -s ɪn'skrɪpʃn, -z
inscrutability ɪnˌskruːtə'bɪlətɪ [ˌɪn-skruː-, -lɪt-]
inscrutab|le, -ly, -leness ɪn'skruːtəb|l, -lɪ, -lnɪs [-nəs]
insect, -s 'ɪnsekt, -s

insectarium, -s ˌɪnsekˈteərɪəm, -z

†insecticide, -s ɪnˈsektɪsaɪd, -z

insectivorous ˌɪnsekˈtɪvərəs

insecur|e, -ely, -ity ˌɪnsɪˈkjʊə*
[-ˈkjɔə*, -ˈkjɔː*], -lɪ, -rətɪ [-rɪtɪ]

inseminat|e, -es, -ing, -ed ɪnˈsemɪneɪt,
-s, -ɪŋ, -ɪd

insemination ɪnˌsemɪˈneɪʃn [ˌɪnsem-]

insensate, -ly, -ness ɪnˈsenseɪt [-sət,
-sɪt], -lɪ, -nɪs [-nəs]

insensibility ɪnˌsensəˈbɪlətɪ [ˌɪnsen-,
-sɪˈb-, -lɪt-]

insensib|le, -ly, -leness ɪnˈsensəb|l
[-sɪb-], -lɪ, -lnɪs [-nəs]

insensitive, -ness ɪnˈsensətɪv [ˌɪnˈs-,
-sɪt-], -nɪs [-nəs]

inseparability ɪnˌsepərəˈbɪlətɪ [ˈɪn-
ˌsepərəˈb-, -lɪt-]

inseparable ɪnˈsepərəbl [ˌɪnˈs-]

inseparab|ly, -leness ɪnˈsepərəb|lɪ, -lnɪs
[-nəs]

insert (s.), -s ˈɪnsɜːt, -s

insert (v.), -s, -ing, -ed ɪnˈsɜːt, -s, -ɪŋ,
-ɪd

insertion, -s ɪnˈsɜːʃn, -z

inset (s.), -s ˈɪnset, -s

inset (v.), -s, -ting ˌɪnˈset, -s, -ɪŋ

inseverable ɪnˈsevərəbl [ˌɪnˈs-]

inshore ˌɪnˈʃɔː* [-ˈʃɔə*, also ˈɪnʃ-
according to sentence-stress]

inside (s. adj. adv. prep.), -s ˌɪnˈsaɪd
[also ˈɪns-, ɪnˈs- according to sentence-
stress], -z

insider, -s ˌɪnˈsaɪdə* [also ɪnˈs- when
preceded by a stress], -z

insidious, -ly, -ness ɪnˈsɪdɪəs [-djəs], -lɪ,
-nɪs [-nəs]

insight ˈɪnsaɪt

insignia ɪnˈsɪgnɪə [-njə]

insignifican|ce, -cy, -t/ly ˌɪnsɪgˈnɪfɪ-
kən|s, -sɪ, -t/lɪ

insincere, -ly ˌɪnsɪnˈsɪə* [-sn̩ˈs-], -lɪ

insincerit|y, -ies ˌɪnsɪnˈserət|ɪ [-sn̩ˈs-,
-ɪt|ɪ], -ɪz

insinuat|e, -es, -ing/ly, -ed, -or/s ɪn-
ˈsɪnjʊeɪt, -s, -ɪŋ/lɪ, -ɪd, -ə*/z

insinuation, -s ɪnˌsɪnjʊˈeɪʃn, -z

insipid, -ly, -ness ɪnˈsɪpɪd, -lɪ, -nɪs
[-nəs]

insipidity ˌɪnsɪˈpɪdətɪ [-ɪtɪ]

insipien|ce, -t ɪnˈsɪpɪən|s [-pjə-], -t

insist, -s, -ing, -ed ɪnˈsɪst, -s, -ɪŋ, -ɪd

insisten|ce, -cy, -t/ly ɪnˈsɪstən|s, -sɪ,
-t/lɪ

Inskip ˈɪnskɪp

insobriety ˌɪnsəʊˈbraɪətɪ [-aɪtɪ]

insolation ˌɪnsəʊˈleɪʃn

insolen|ce, -t/ly ˈɪnsələn|s [-sʊl-], -t/lɪ

insolubility ɪnˌsɒljʊˈbɪlətɪ [ˈɪnˌsɒljʊˈb-,
-lɪt-]

insoluble, -ness ɪnˈsɒljʊbl [ˌɪnˈs-], -nɪs
[-nəs]

insolvable ɪnˈsɒlvəbl [ˌɪnˈs-]

insolven|cy, -t ɪnˈsɒlvən|sɪ [ˌɪnˈs-], -t

insomn|ia, -iac ɪnˈsɒmn|ɪə [-njə], -ɪæk

insomuch ˌɪnsəʊˈmʌtʃ

insouciance ɪnˈsuːsjəns [-sɪəns]
(ɛ̃susjɑ̃ːs)

insouciant ɪnˈsuːsjənt [-sɪənt] (ɛ̃susjɑ̃)

inspect, -s, -ing, -ed, -or/s ɪnˈspekt, -s,
-ɪŋ, -ɪd, -ə*/z

inspection, -s ɪnˈspekʃn, -z

inspectorate, -s ɪnˈspektərət [-rɪt], -s

inspectorship, -s ɪnˈspektəʃɪp, -s

inspectress, -es ɪnˈspektrɪs [-trəs], -ɪz

inspiration, -s ˌɪnspəˈreɪʃn [-spɪˈr-], -z

inspirational ˌɪnspəˈreɪʃənl [-spɪˈr-,
-ʃnəl, -ʃn̩l, -ʃnl, -ʃənəl]

inspirator, -s ˈɪnspəreɪtə* [-spɪr-], -z

inspiratory ɪnˈspaɪərətərɪ

inspir|e, -es, -ing/ly, -ed, -er/s ɪn-
ˈspaɪə*, -z, -rɪŋ/lɪ, -d, -rə*/z

inspirit, -s, -ing, -ed ɪnˈspɪrɪt, -s, -ɪŋ, -ɪd

inspissate ɪnˈspɪseɪt

inst. ɪnst, ˈɪnstənt

instability ˌɪnstəˈbɪlətɪ [-lɪt-]

install, -s, -ing, -ed ɪnˈstɔːl, -z, -ɪŋ, -d

installation, -s ˌɪnstəˈleɪʃn [-stɔːˈl-], -z

instalment, -s ɪnˈstɔːlmənt, -s

instanc|e (s. v.), -es, -ing, -ed ˈɪnstəns,
-ɪz, -ɪŋ, -t

instant (s. adj.), -s, -ly ˈɪnstənt, -s, -lɪ

instantaneous, -ly, -ness ˌɪnstənˈteɪmjəs
[-nɪəs], -lɪ, -nɪs [-nəs]

instanter ɪnˈstæntə*

instead ɪnˈsted

instep, -s ˈɪnstep, -s

instigat|e, -es, -ing, -ed, -or/s ˈɪnstɪgeɪt,
-s, -ɪŋ, -ɪd, -ə*/z

instigation, -s ˌɪnstɪˈgeɪʃn, -z

instil, -s, -ling, -led, -ment ɪnˈstɪl, -z,
-ɪŋ, -d, -mənt

instillation ˌɪnstɪˈleɪʃn

instinct (s.), -s ˈɪnstɪŋkt, -s

instinct (adj.) ɪnˈstɪŋkt

instinctive, -ly ɪnˈstɪŋktɪv, -lɪ

institut|e (s. v.), -es, -ing, -ed, -or/s
ˈɪnstɪtjuːt, -s, -ɪŋ, -ɪd, -ə*/z

institution, -s ˌɪnstɪˈtjuːʃn, -z

institutional ˌɪnstɪˈtjuːʃənl [-ʃnəl, -ʃn̩l,
-ʃnl, -ʃənəl]

instruct, -s, -ing, -ed, -or/s, -ress/es
ɪnˈstrʌkt, -s, -ɪŋ, -ɪd, -ə*/z, -rɪs/ɪz

instruction, -s ɪnˈstrʌkʃn, -z

instructional ɪnˈstrʌkʃənl [-ʃnəl, -ʃn̩l,
-ʃn̩l, -ʃənəl]

instructive, -ly, -ness ın'strʌktıv, -lı, -nıs [-nəs]

instrument, -s 'ınstrumənt [-trəm-], -s

instrument|al, -ally; -alist/s ‚ınstru-'ment|l [-trə'm-], -əlı [-|ı]; -əlıst/s [-lıst/s]

instrumentality ‚ınstrumen'tælətı [-trəm-, -mən-, -rtı]

instrumentation ‚ınstrumen'teıʃn [-trəm-, -mən-]

insubordinate ‚ınsə'bɔ:dɪ̩ət [-dənət, -dınət, -ıt]

insubordination 'ınsə‚bɔ:dı'neıʃn [-də'n-]

insubstantial ‚ınsəb'stænʃl [-bz't-, -stɑ:nʃ-]

insufferab|le, -ly ın'sʌfərəb|l, -lı

insufficien|cy, -t/ly ‚ınsə'fıʃn|sı, -t/lı

insular, -ly, -ism 'ınsjulə* [-sjəl-], -lı, -rızəm

insularity ‚ınsju'lærətı [-sjə'l-, -rtı]

insulat|e, -es, -ing, -ed, -or/s 'ınsju-leıt [-sjəl-], -s, -ıŋ, -ıd, -ə*/z

insulation ‚ınsju'leıʃn [-sjə'l-]

insulin 'ınsjulın

insult (s.), -s 'ınsʌlt, -s

insult (v.), -s, -ing/ly, -ed, -er/s ın'sʌlt, -s, -ıŋ/lı, -ıd, -ə*/z

insuperability ın‚su:pərə'bılətı ['ın-‚su:pərə'b-, -‚sju:-, -lıt-]

insuperable ın'su:pərəbl [‚ın's-, -'sju:-]

insuperably ın'su:pərəblı [-'sju:-]

insupportable, -ness ‚ınsə'pɔ:təbl, -nıs [-nəs]

insupportably ‚ınsə'pɔ:təblı

insuppressible ‚ınsə'presəbl [-sıb-]

insur|e, -es, -ing, -ed, -er/s; -able, -ance/s ın'ʃɔ:* [-'ʃɔə*, -'ʃuə*], -z, -rıŋ, -d, -rə*/z; -rəbl, -rəns/ız

insurgen|ce, -cy, -t/s ın'sɜ:dʒən/s, -sı, -t/s

insurmountability 'ınsə‚mauntə'bılətı [-lıt-]

insurmountable ‚ınsə'mauntəbl

insurrection, -s ‚ınsə'rekʃn, -z

insurrectional ‚ınsə'rekʃənl [-ʃnəl, -ʃn̩l, -ʃn̩], -ʃənəl]

insurrectionar|y (s. adj.), -ies ‚ınsə'rek-ʃn̩ər|ı [-ʃnə-, -ʃənə-], -ız

insurrectioni|sm, -st/s ‚ınsə'rekʃn̩ı|zəm [-ʃənı-], -st/s

insusceptibility 'ınsə‚septə'bılətı [-tı'b-, -lıt-]

insusceptible ‚ınsə'septəbl [-tıb-]

intact, -ness ın'tækt [‚ın't-], -nıs [-nəs]

intaglio, -s ın'tɑ:lıəu [-'tæl-, -ljəu], -z

intake 'ınteık

intangibility ın‚tændʒə'bılətı ['ın‚tæn-dʒə'b-, -dʒı'b-, -lıt-]

intangible, -ness ın'tændʒəbl [‚ın't-, -dʒıb-], -nıs [-nəs]

intangibly ın'tændʒəblı [-dʒıb-]

integer, -s 'ıntıdʒə*, -z

integral (s.), -s 'ıntıgrəl, -z

integral (adj.), -ly 'ıntıgrəl [ın'tegrəl], -ı Note.—As a mathematical term always 'ıntıgrəl.

integrat|e, -es, -ing, -ed 'ıntıgreıt, -s, -ıŋ, -ıd

integration, -s ‚ıntı'greıʃn, -z

integrity ın'tegrətı [-rtı]

integument, -s ın'tegjumənt, -s

intellect, -s 'ıntəlekt [-tıl-], -s

intellection ‚ıntə'lekʃn [-tı'l-]

intellective ‚ıntə'lektıv [-tı'l-]

intellectual, -ly ‚ıntə'lektjuəl [-tı'l-, -tjwəl, -tjul, -tʃuəl, -tʃwəl, -tʃul], -ı

intellectuali|sm, -st/s ‚ıntə'lektjuəlı|zəm [-tı'l-, -tjwəl-, -tjul-, -tʃuəl-, -tʃwəl-, -tʃul-], -st/s

intellectuality 'ıntə‚lektju'ælətı [-tı‚l-, -tʃu-, -ıtı]

intellectualiz|e [-is|e], -es, -ing, -ed ‚ıntə'lektjuəlaız [-tı'l-, -tjwəl-, -tjul-, -tʃuəl-, -tʃwəl-, -tʃul-], -ız, -ıŋ, -d

intelligen|ce, -ces, -t/ly, -cer/s ın-'telıdʒən|s, -sız, -t/lı, -sə*/z

intelligentsia ın‚telı'dʒentsıə [‚ınte-lı'dʒ-, -'gen-, -tsjə]

intelligibility ın‚telıdʒə'bılətı [-dʒı'b-, -lıt-]

intelligib|le, -ly, -leness ın'telıdʒəb|l [-dʒıb-], -lı, -lnıs [-nəs]

intemperance ın'tempərəns [‚ın't-]

intemperate, -ly, -ness ın'tempərət [‚ın't-, -rıt], -lı, -nıs [-nəs]

intend, -s, -ing, -ed ın'tend, -z, -ıŋ, -ıd

intendan|ce, -cy, -t/s ın'tendən|s, -sı, -t/s

intense, -r, -st, -ly, -ness ın'tens, -ə*, -ıst, -lı, -nıs [-nəs]

intensification, -s ın‚tensıfı'keıʃn, -z

intensi|fy, -fies, -fying, -fied, -fier/s ın'tensı|faı, -faız, -faıŋ, -faıd, -faıə*/z

intension ın'tenʃn

intensit|y, -ies ın'tensət|ı [-sıt-], -ız

intensive, -ly, -ness ın'tensıv, -lı, -nıs [-nəs]

intent (s. adj.), -s, -er, -est, -ly, -ness ın'tent, -s, -ə*, -ıst, -lı, -nıs [-nəs]

intention, -s, -ed ın'tenʃn, -z, -d

inten|tional, -tionally ın'ten|ʃənl [-ʃnəl, -ʃn̩l, -ʃn̩l, -ʃənəl], -ʃn̩əlı [-ʃnəlı, -ʃn̩lı, -ʃn̩ı, -ʃənəlı]

inter (v.), -s, -ring, -red ın'tɜ:*, -z, -rıŋ, -d

inter (*Latin prep.*, *in such phrases as* inter alia, inter se) 'ıntə*
interact (*s.*), **-s** 'ıntərækt, -s
interact (*v.*), **-s, -ing, -ed** ˌıntər'ækt [-tə'ækt], -s, -ıŋ, -ıd
interaction ˌıntər'ækʃn [-tə'æ-]
interactive ˌıntər'æktıv [-tə'æ-]
interblend, **-s, -ing, -ed** ˌıntə'blend, -z, -ıŋ, -ıd
inter|breed, **-breeds, -breeding, -bred** ˌıntə|'bri:d, -'bri:dz, -'bri:dıŋ, -'bred
intercalary ın'tɜ:kələrı [ˌıntə'kælərı]
intercalat|e, **-es, -ing, -ed** ın'tɜ:kəleıt, -s, -ıŋ, -ıd
intercalation, **-s** ın,tɜ:kə'leıʃn, -z
interced|e, **-es, -ing, -ed, -er/s** ˌıntə-'si:d, -z, -ıŋ, -ıd, -ə*/z
intercept (*s.*), **-s** 'ıntəsept, -s
intercept (*v.*), **-s, -ing, -ed, -er/s** ˌıntə-'sept, -s, -ıŋ, -ıd, -ə*/z
interception, **-s** ˌıntə'sepʃn, -z
interceptive ˌıntə'septıv
interceptor, **-s** ˌıntə'septə*, -z
intercession, **-s** ˌıntə'seʃn, -z
intercessional ˌıntə'seʃənl [-'ʃnəl, -'ʃn̩l, -ʃn̩l, -ʃənəl]
intercessor, **-s** ˌıntə'sesə* ['ıntəsesə*], -z
intercessory ˌıntə'sesərı
interchange (*s.*), **-s** 'ıntətʃeındʒ [ˌ--'-], -ız
interchang|e (*v.*), **-es, -ing, -ed** ˌıntə-'tʃeındʒ, -ız, -ıŋ, -d
interchangeability 'ıntə,tʃeındʒə'bılətı [-lıt-]
interchangeable, **-ness** ˌıntə'tʃeındʒ-əbl, -nıs [-nəs]
interchangeably ˌıntə'tʃeındʒəblı
intercollegiate ˌıntəkə'li:dʒıət [-kɒ'l-, -dʒət, -dʒıət, -dʒı't, -dʒırt]
intercolonial ˌıntəkə'ləunjəl [-nıəl]
intercom (*s.*), **-s** 'ıntəkɒm, -z
intercommunicat|e, **-es, -ing, -ed** ˌıntəkə'mju:nıkeıt [-'mjun-], -s, -ıŋ, -ıd
intercommunication 'ıntəkə,mju:nı-'keıʃn [-,mjun-]
intercommunion ˌıntəkə'mju:njən [-nıən]
intercommunity ˌıntəkə'mju:nətı [-rtı]
interconnect, **-s, -ing, -ed** ˌıntəkə'nekt, -s, -ıŋ, -ıd
interconnection, **-s** ˌıntəkə'nekʃn, -z
intercontinental 'ıntə,kɒntı'nentl
intercostal ˌıntə'kɒstl
intercourse 'ıntəkɔːs [-kɔəs]
intercurren|ce, **-t** ˌıntə'kʌrən|s, -t
interdental ˌıntə'dentl
interdependen|ce, **-t** ˌıntədı'pendən|s, -t

interdict (*s.*), **-s** 'ıntədıkt, -s
interdict (*v.*), **-s, -ing, -ed** ˌıntə'dıkt, -s, -ıŋ, -ıd
interdiction, **-s** ˌıntə'dıkʃn, -z
interest (*s. v*), **-s, -ing, -ed/ly** 'ıntrəst [-tərest, -trıst], -s, -ıŋ, -ıd/lı
interesting (*adj.*), **-ly** 'ıntrəstıŋ [-tərest-, -trıst-, ˌıntə'restıŋ], -lı
interfer|e, **-es, -ing, -ed, -er/s ; -ence/s** ˌıntə'fıə*, -z, -rıŋ, -d, -rə*/z ; -rəns/ız
interfus|e, **-es, -ing, -ed** ˌıntə'fju:z, -ız, -ıŋ, -d
interfusion ˌıntə'fju:ʒn
interglacial ˌıntə'gleısjəl [-sıəl, -ʃjəl, -ʃıəl, -ʃl, -'glæsıəl, -'glæsjəl]
interim 'ıntərım
interior (*s. adj.*), **-s, -ly** ın'tıərıə*, -z, -lı
interject, **-s, -ing, -ed, -or/s** ˌıntə-'dʒekt, -s, -ıŋ, -ıd, -ə*/z
interjection, **-s** ˌıntə'dʒekʃn, -z
interjec|tional, **-tionally** ˌıntə'dʒek|-ʃənl [-ʃnəl, -ʃn̩l, -ʃn̩l, -ʃənəl], -ʃnəlı [-ʃnəlı, -ʃn̩lı, -ʃn̩lı, -ʃənəlı]
interknit, **-s, -ting, -ted** ˌıntə'nıt, -s, -ıŋ, -ıd
interlac|e, **-es, -ing, -ed, -ement** ˌıntə-'leıs, -ız, -ıŋ, -t, -mənt
Interlaken 'ıntəlɑːkən
interlard, **-s, -ing, -ed** ˌıntə'lɑːd, -z, -ıŋ, -ıd
interlea|f, **-ves** 'ıntəli:|f, -vz
interleav|e, **-es, -ing, -ed** ˌıntə'li:v, -z, -ıŋ, -d
interlin|e, **-es, -ing, -ed** ˌıntə'laın, -z, -ıŋ, -d
interlinear ˌıntə'lınıə* [-njə*]
interlineation, **-s** 'ıntə,lını'eıʃn, -z
interlink, **-s, -ing, -ed** ˌıntə'lıŋk, -s, -ıŋ, -t [-'lıŋt]
interlock, **-s, -ing, -ed** ˌıntə'lɒk, -s, -ıŋ, -t
interlocution, **-s** ˌıntələʊ'kju:ʃn [-lɒ'k-], -z
interlocutor, **-s, -y** ˌıntə'lɒkjʊtə*, -z, -rı
interlop|e, **-es, -ing, -ed** ˌıntə'ləʊp, -s, -ıŋ, -t
interloper, **-s** 'ıntələʊpə* [ˌıntə'l-], -z
interlude, **-s** 'ıntəlu:d [-lju:d], -z
intermarriage, **-s** ˌıntə'mærıdʒ, -ız
intermarr|y, **-ies, -ying, -ied** ˌıntə-'mær|ı, -ız, -ıŋ, -ıd
intermedd|le, **-les, -ling, -led, -ler/s** ˌıntə'med|l, -lz, -l̩ıŋ [-lıŋ], -ld, -lə*/z [-lə*/z]
intermediar|y, **-ies** ˌıntə'mi:djər|ı [-dıər-], -ız
intermediate (*s. adj.*), **-s, -ly** ˌıntə-'mi:djət [-dıət, -dʒıt, -dı't], -s, -lı

interment, -s ɪnˈtɜːmənt, -s
intermezzo, -s ˌɪntəˈmetsəʊ [-ˈmedzəʊ]
(inter'meddzo), -z
interminable ɪnˈtɜːmɪnəbl [ˌɪnˈt-]
interminab|ly, -leness ɪnˈtɜːmɪnəb|lɪ,
-lnɪs [-nəs]
interming|le, -les, -ling, -led ˌɪntə-
ˈmɪŋg|l, -lz, -lɪŋ, -ld
intermission ˌɪntəˈmɪʃn
intermit, -s, -ting/ly, -ted ; -tent/ly ˌɪn-
təˈmɪt, -s, -ɪŋ/lɪ, -ɪd ; -ənt/lɪ
intermix, -es, -ing, -ed ˌɪntəˈmɪks, -ɪz,
-ɪŋ, -t
intermixture, -s ˌɪntəˈmɪkstʃə*, -z
intern (s.), -s ˈɪntɜːn [-ˈ-], -z
intern (v.), -s, -ing, -ed, -ment/s
ɪnˈtɜːn, -z, -ɪŋ, -d, -mənt/s
intern|al, -ally ɪnˈtɜːn|l [ˌɪnˈt-], -əlɪ [-lɪ]
interna|tional, -tionally ˌɪntəˈnæ|ʃənl
[-ʃnəl, -ʃn̩l, -ʃnl, -ʃənəl], -ʃnəlɪ [-ʃnəlɪ,
-ʃn̩lɪ, -ʃnlɪ, -ʃənəlɪ]
Internationale ˌɪntənæʃəˈnɑːl [-ʃɪəˈn-,
-ʃjəˈn-]
internationali|sm, -st/s ˌɪntəˈnæʃnəl-
ɪ|zəm [-ʃnəl-, -ʃn̩l-, -ʃnl-, -ʃənəl-],
-st/s
internationalization [-isa-] ˈɪntəˌnæʃ-
nəlaɪˈzeɪʃn [-ʃnəl-, -ʃn̩l-, -ʃnl-, -ʃənəl-,
-lɪˈz-]
internationaliz|e [-is|e], -es, -ing, -ed
ˌɪntəˈnæʃnəlaɪz [-ʃnəl-, -ʃn̩l-, -ʃnl-,
-ʃənəl-], -ɪz, -ɪŋ, -d
internecine ˌɪntəˈniːsaɪn [-tɜːˈn-]
internee, -s ˌɪntɜːˈniː, -z
interoceanic ˈɪntərˌəʊʃɪˈænɪk [-təˌəʊ-]
interpellant, -s ˌɪntəˈpelənt, -s
interpellat|e, -es, -ing, -ed ɪnˈtɜːpeleɪt
[-pəl-, -pɪl-], -s, -ɪŋ, -ɪd
interpellation, -s ɪnˌtɜːpeˈleɪʃn [-pəˈl-,
-pɪˈl-], -z
interpenetrat|e, -es, -ing, -ed ˌɪntə-
ˈpenɪtreɪt, -s, -ɪŋ, -ɪd
interpenetration ˈɪntəˌpenɪˈtreɪʃn
interplanetary ˌɪntəˈplænɪtərɪ [-nət-]
interplay ˈɪntəpleɪ [ˌ-ˈ-]
interpolat|e, -es, -ing, -ed, -or/s ɪn-
ˈtɜːpəʊleɪt [-pʊl-], -s, -ɪŋ, -ɪd, -ə*/z
interpolation, -s ɪnˌtɜːpəʊˈleɪʃn [-pʊˈl-],
-z
interposal, -s ˌɪntəˈpəʊzl, -z
interpos|e, -es, -ing, -ed, -er/s ˌɪntə-
ˈpəʊz, -ɪz, -ɪŋ, -d, -ə*/z
interposition, -s ɪnˌtɜːpəˈzɪʃn [ˌɪntə-,
-pʊˈz-], -z
interpret, -s, -ing, -ed, -er/s; -able
ɪnˈtɜːprɪt, -s, -ɪŋ, -ɪd, -ə*/z; -əbl
interpretation, -s ɪnˌtɜːprɪˈteɪʃn
[-prəˈt-], -z

interpretative, -ly ɪnˈtɜːprɪtətɪv [-prət-,
-teɪt-], -lɪ
interracial ˌɪntəˈreɪʃl [-ʃɪəl, -ʃjəl]
interregn|al, -um/s ˌɪntəˈregn|əl, -əm/z
interrelation, -s ˌɪntərɪˈleɪʃn, -z
interrogat|e, -es, -ing, -ed, -or/s ɪn-
ˈterəʊgeɪt [-rʊg-], -s, -ɪŋ, -ɪd, -ə*/z
interrogation, -s ɪnˌterəʊˈgeɪʃn [-rʊˈg-],
-z
interrogative (s. adj.), -s, -ly ˌɪntəˈrɒ-
gətɪv, -z, -lɪ
interrogator|y (s. adj.), -ies ˌɪntəˈrɒgə-
tər|ɪ, -ɪz
interrupt, -s, -ing, -ed, -er/s ˌɪntəˈrʌpt,
-s, -ɪŋ, -ɪd, -ə*/z
interruption, -s ˌɪntəˈrʌpʃn, -z
intersect, -s, -ing, -ed, -or/s ˌɪntəˈsekt,
-s, -ɪŋ, -ɪd, -ə*/z
intersection, -s ˌɪntəˈsekʃn, -z
interspac|e (s. v.), -es, -ing, -ed ˌɪntə-
ˈspeɪs, -ɪz, -ɪŋ, -t
interspers|e, -es, -ing, -ed ˌɪntəˈspɜːs,
-ɪz, -ɪŋ, -t
interspersion ˌɪntəˈspɜːʃn
interstellar ˌɪntəˈstelə* [also ˈɪntəˌs-
when attributive]
interstice, -s ɪnˈtɜːstɪs, -ɪz
intertribal ˌɪntəˈtraɪbl
intertwin|e, -es, -ing, -ed ˌɪntəˈtwaɪn,
-z, -ɪŋ, -d
intertwist, -s, -ing, -ed ˌɪntəˈtwɪst, -s,
-ɪŋ, -ɪd
interval, -s ˈɪntəvl, -z
interven|e, -es, -ing, -ed, -er/s ˌɪntə-
ˈviːn, -z, -ɪŋ, -d, -ə*/z
intervention, -s ˌɪntəˈvenʃn, -z
interview (s. v.), -s, -ing, -ed, -er/s
ˈɪntəvjuː, -z, -ɪŋ [-vjʊɪŋ], -d, -ə*/z
[-ˌvjʊə*/z]
intervocalic ˌɪntəvəʊˈkælɪk [-vʊˈk-]
interweav|e, -es, -ing, -ed, interwove, -n
ˌɪntəˈwiːv, -z, -ɪŋ, -d, ˌɪntəˈwəʊv, -n
intestac|y, -ies ɪnˈtestəs|ɪ, -ɪz
intestate (s. adj.), -s ɪnˈtesteɪt [-tɪt, -tət],
-s
intestinal ɪnˈtestɪnl [ˌɪntesˈtaɪnl]
intestine (s. adj.), -s ɪnˈtestɪn, -z
intimac|y, -ies ˈɪntɪməs|ɪ [-təm-], -ɪz
intimate (s. adj.), -s, -ly ˈɪntɪmət [-təm-,
-ɪt], -s, -lɪ
intimat|e (v.), -es, -ing, -ed ˈɪntɪmeɪt, -s,
-ɪŋ, -ɪd
intimation, -s ˌɪntɪˈmeɪʃn, -z
intimidat|e, -es, -ing, -ed, -or/s ɪnˈtɪ-
mɪdeɪt, -s, -ɪŋ, -ɪd, -ə*/z
intimidation ɪnˌtɪmɪˈdeɪʃn
intimity ɪnˈtɪmətɪ [-ɪtɪ]
intituled ɪnˈtɪtjuːld

into 'ɪntʊ ['ɪntuː], 'ɪntə
    Note.—The variant 'ɪntuː *occurs chiefly at the ends of sentences. The form* 'ɪntə *is used only before words beginning with a consonant.*

intolerab|le, -ly, -leness ɪn'tɒlərəb|l, -lɪ, -lnɪs [-nəs]

intoleran|ce, -t/ly ɪn'tɒlərən|s [ˌɪn't-], -t/lɪ

intonat|e, -es, -ing, -ed 'ɪntəʊneɪt, -s, -ɪŋ, -ɪd

intonation, -s ˌɪntəʊ'neɪʃn, -z

intonational ˌɪntəʊ'neɪʃənl [-ʃnəl, -ʃn̩l, -ʃn̩l, -ʃənəl]

inton|e, -es, -ing, -ed, -er/s ɪn'təʊn, -z, -ɪŋ, -d, -ə*/z

intoxicant (s. adj.), -s ɪn'tɒksɪkənt, -s

intoxicat|e, -es, -ing, -ed ɪn'tɒksɪkeɪt, -s, -ɪŋ, -ɪd

intoxication ɪnˌtɒksɪ'keɪʃn

intractability ɪnˌtræktə'bɪlətɪ ['ɪn-ˌtrækt-, -lɪt-]

intractab|le, -ly, -leness ɪn'træktəb|l, -lɪ, -lnɪs [-nəs]

intrados, -es ɪn'treɪdɒs, -ɪz

intramural ˌɪntrə'mjʊərəl [-'mjɔər-, -'mjɔːr-]

intransigen|t, -ce ɪn'trænsɪdʒən|t [-'trɑːnsɪ-, -'trænzɪ-, -'trɑːnzɪ-], -s

intransitive, -ly ɪn'trænsətɪv [ˌɪn't-, -'trɑːns-, -nzə-, -nsɪ-, -nzɪ-], -lɪ

intravenous ˌɪntrə'viːnəs

in-tray, -s 'ɪntreɪ, -z

intrench, -es, -ing, -ed, -ment/s ɪn-'trentʃ, -ɪz, -ɪŋ, -t, -mənt/s

intrepid, -ly ɪn'trepɪd, -lɪ

intrepidity ˌɪntrɪ'pɪdətɪ [-tre'p-, -rtɪ]

intricac|y, -ies 'ɪntrɪkəs|ɪ [ɪn'trɪk-], -ɪz

intricate, -ly, -ness 'ɪntrɪkət [ɪn'trɪk-, -krɪt], -lɪ, -nɪs [-nəs]

intrigu|e (s. v.), -es, -ing, -ed, -er/s ɪn-'triːg [also '— for noun], -z, -ɪŋ, -d, -ə*/z

intrinsic, -ally ɪn'trɪnsɪk [-nzɪk], -əlɪ

introduc|e, -es, -ing, -ed, -er/s ˌɪn-trə'djuːs [-trʊ'd-], -ɪz, -ɪŋ, -t, -ə*/z

introduction, -s ˌɪntrə'dʌkʃn [-trʊ'd-], -z

introduct|ive, -ory, -orily ˌɪntrə'dʌk-t|ɪv [-trʊ'd-], -ərɪ, -ərəlɪ [-ɪlɪ]

introit, -s 'ɪntrɔɪt ['ɪntrəʊɪt, ɪn'trəʊɪt], -s

intromission ˌɪntrəʊ'mɪʃn

intromit, -s, -ting, -ted ˌɪntrəʊ'mɪt, -s, -ɪŋ, -ɪd

introspect, -s, -ing, -ed ˌɪntrəʊ'spekt, -s, -ɪŋ, -ɪd

introspection ˌɪntrəʊ'spekʃn

introspective ˌɪntrəʊ'spektɪv

introversion ˌɪntrəʊ'vɜːʃn

introvert (s.), -s 'ɪntrəʊvɜːt, -s

introvert (v.), -s, -ing, -ed ˌɪntrəʊ'vɜːt, -s, -ɪŋ, -ɪd

intrud|e, -es, -ing, -ed, -er/s ɪn'truːd, -z, -ɪŋ, -ɪd, -ə*/z

intrusion, -s ɪn'truːʒn, -z

intrusive, -ly, -ness ɪn'truːsɪv, -lɪ, -nɪs [-nəs]

intuit, -s, -ing, -ed ɪn'tjuːɪt [-'tjʊɪt, 'ɪntjuːɪt, -tjʊɪt], -s, ɪn'tjuːɪtɪŋ [-'tjʊɪtɪŋ], ɪn'tjuːɪtɪd [-'tjʊɪtɪd]

intuition ˌɪntjuː'ɪʃn [-tjʊ'ɪ-]

intuitional ˌɪntjuː'ɪʃənl [-tjʊ'ɪ-, -ʃnəl, -ʃn̩l, -ʃn̩l, -ʃənəl]

intuitive, -ly, -ness ɪn'tjuːɪtɪv [-'tjʊɪ-, -'tjʊə-], -lɪ, -nɪs [-nəs]

intumescen|ce, -t ˌɪntjuː'mesn|s [-tjʊ-], -t

inundat|e, -es, -ing, -ed 'ɪnʌndeɪt [-nən-], -s, -ɪŋ, -ɪd

inundation, -s ˌɪnʌn'deɪʃn [-nən-], -z

inur|e, -es, -ing, -ed, -ement ɪ'njʊə* [-jɔə*, -jɔː*], -z, -rɪŋ, -d, -mənt

inutility ˌɪnjuː'tɪlətɪ [-jʊ't-, -rtɪ]

invad|e, -es, -ing, -ed, -er/s ɪn'veɪd, -z, -ɪŋ, -ɪd, -ə*/z

invalid (s. adj.) (infirm through illness, etc.), -s 'ɪnvəlɪd [-liːd], -z

invalid (adj.) (not valid) ɪn'vælɪd [ˌɪn'v-]

invalid (v.), -s, -ing, -ed 'ɪnvəliːd [ˌ,–'-], -z, -ɪŋ, -ɪd

invalidat|e, -es, -ing, -ed ɪn'vælɪdeɪt, -s, -ɪŋ, -ɪd

invalidation ɪnˌvælɪ'deɪʃn

invalidity ˌɪnvə'lɪdətɪ [-rtɪ]

invaluable ɪn'væljʊəbl [-ljwəb-, -ljʊb-]

invar ɪn'vɑː*

invariability ɪnˌveərɪə'bɪlətɪ ['ɪnˌveə-rɪə'b-, -lɪt-]

invariable ɪn'veərɪəbl [ˌɪn'v-]

invariab|ly, -leness ɪn'veərɪəb|lɪ, -lnɪs [-nəs]

invasion, -s ɪn'veɪʒn, -z

invasive ɪn'veɪsɪv

invective, -s ɪn'vektɪv, -z

inveigh, -s, -ing, -ed ɪn'veɪ, -z, -ɪŋ, -d

inveigl|e, -les, -ling, -led, -lement/s ɪn'veɪg|l [-'viːg-], -lz, -lɪŋ [-lɪŋ], -ld, -lmənt/s

invent, -s, -ing, -ed, -er/s, -or/s ɪn'vent, -s, -ɪŋ, -ɪd, -ə*/z, -ə*/z

invention, -s ɪn'venʃn, -z

inventive, -ly, -ness ɪn'ventɪv, -lɪ, -nɪs [-nəs]

inventor|y, -ies 'ɪnvəntr|ɪ, -ɪz

Inver|ary, -arity ˌɪnvə'r|eərɪ [-eərə],
-ærətɪ [-ɪtɪ]
Invercargill (in Scotland) ˌɪnvəkɑː'gɪl
[-'kɑːgɪl], (in New Zealand) ˌɪnvə'kɑː-
gɪl
Invergordon ˌɪnvə'gɔːdn
Inverkeithing ˌɪnvə'kiːðɪŋ
Inverlochy ˌɪnvə'lɒkɪ [-'lɒxɪ]
inverness (I.), -es ˌɪnvə'nes ['— when
attributive], -ɪz
Inverness-shire ˌɪnvə'nesʃə* [-'nes,ʃɪə*,
-'neʃ,ʃɪə*, -'neʃʃə*]
inverse (s. adj.), -s, -ly ˌɪn'vɜːs [ɪn'v-,
also '— when attributive], -ɪz, -lɪ
inversion, -s ɪn'vɜːʃn, -z
invert (s. adj.), -s 'ɪnvɜːt, -s
invert (v.), -s, -ing, -ed ɪn'vɜːt, -s, -ɪŋ,
-ɪd
invertebrata ɪnˌvɜːtɪ'brɑːtə [-'breɪtə,
'ɪnˌvɜːtɪ'b-]
invertebrate, -s ɪn'vɜːtɪbreɪt [ˌɪn'v-,
-brət, -brɪt], -s
Inverurie ˌɪnvə'rʊərɪ
invest, -s, -ing, -ed, -or/s ɪn'vest, -s,
-ɪŋ, -ɪd, -ə*/z
†investigat|e, -es, -ing, -ed, -or/s;
ɪn'vestɪgeɪt, -s, -ɪŋ, -ɪd, -ə*/z
investigatory ɪn'vestɪgeɪtərɪ [-ˌ--'---]
investigation, -s ɪnˌvestɪ'geɪʃn, -z
investiture, -s ɪn'vestɪtʃə* [-ˌtjʊə*],
-z
investment, -s ɪn'vesʈmənt, -s
inveteracy ɪn'vetərəsɪ
inveterate, -ly, -ness ɪn'vetərət [-rɪt],
-lɪ, -nɪs [-nəs]
invidious, -ly, -ness ɪn'vɪdɪəs [-djəs],
-lɪ, -nɪs [-nəs]
invigilat|e, -es, -ing, -ed, -or/s ɪn'vɪdʒɪ-
leɪt, -s, -ɪŋ, -ɪd, -ə*/z
invigilation, -s ɪnˌvɪdʒɪ'leɪʃn, -z
invigorat|e, -es, -ing, -ed, -or/s ɪn-
'vɪgəreɪt, -s, -ɪŋ, -ɪd, -ə*/z
invigoration ɪnˌvɪgə'reɪʃn
invincibility ɪnˌvɪnsɪ'bɪlətɪ [-sə'b-, -lɪt-]
invincib|le, -ly, -leness ɪn'vɪnsəb|l
[-sɪb-], -lɪ, -lnɪs [-nəs]
inviolability ɪnˌvaɪələ'bɪlətɪ ['ɪnˌvaɪəl-
ə'b-, -lɪt-]
inviolab|le, -ly, -leness ɪn'vaɪələb|l,
-lɪ, -lnɪs [-nəs]
inviolate, -ly, -ness ɪn'vaɪələt [-lɪt,
-leɪt], -lɪ, -nɪs
invisibility ɪnˌvɪzə'bɪlətɪ ['ɪnˌvɪzə'b-,
-zɪ'b-, -lɪt-]
invisible ɪn'vɪzəbl [ˌɪn'v-, -zɪb-]
invisib|ly, -leness ɪn'vɪzəb|lɪ [-zɪb-],
-lnɪs [-nəs]
invitation, -s ˌɪnvɪ'teɪʃn, -z

invit|e, -es, -ing/ly, -ingness, -ed, -er/s
ɪn'vaɪt, -s, -ɪŋ/lɪ, -ɪŋnɪs [-nəs], -ɪd,
-ə*/z
invocate, -s, -ing, -ed 'ɪnvəʊkeɪt, -s, -ɪŋ,
-ɪd
invocation, -s ˌɪnvəʊ'keɪʃn [-vʊ'k-], -z
invoic|e (s. v.), -es, -ing, -ed 'ɪnvɔɪs, -ɪz,
-ɪŋ, -t
invok|e, -es, -ing, -ed ɪn'vəʊk, -s, -ɪŋ, -t
involucre, -s 'ɪnvəluːkə* [-lju:-], -z
involuntar|y, -ily, -iness ɪn'vɒləntər|ɪ
[ˌɪn'v-, -pɪnt-], -əlɪ [-ɪlɪ], -ɪnɪs [-ɪnəs]
involute, -s, -d 'ɪnvəluːt [-lju:t], -s, -ɪd
involution, -s ˌɪnvə'lu:ʃn [-'lju:-], -z
involv|e, -es, -ing, -ed ɪn'vɒlv, -z, -ɪŋ,
-d
involvement ɪn'vɒlvmənt
invulnerability ɪnˌvʌlnərə'bɪlətɪ ['ɪn-
ˌvʌlnərə'b-, -lɪt-]
invulnerable ɪn'vʌlnərəbl [ˌɪn'v-]
invulnerab|ly, -leness ɪn'vʌlnərəb|lɪ,
-lnɪs [-nəs]
inward, -s, -ly, -ness 'ɪnwəd, -z, -lɪ,
-nɪs [-nəs]
Inwards 'ɪnwədz
inweav|e, -es, -ing, -ed, inwove, -n
ˌɪn'wiːv, -z, -ɪŋ, -d, ˌɪn'wəʊv, -n
Inwood 'ɪnwʊd
inwrought ˌɪn'rɔːt [also 'ɪnr- when
attributive]
io (I.), -s 'aɪəʊ, -z
iodate, -s, -d 'aɪəʊdeɪt, -s, -ɪd
iodic aɪ'ɒdɪk
iodide, -s 'aɪəʊdaɪd, -z
iodine 'aɪəʊdiːn ['aɪədaɪn]
iodiz|e [-is|e], -es, -ing, -ed 'aɪəʊdaɪz,
-ɪz, -ɪŋ, -d
iodoform aɪ'ɒdəfɔːm
Iolanthe ˌaɪəʊ'lænθɪ
Iolcus ɪ'ɒlkəs [aɪ'ɒl-]
iolite 'aɪəʊlaɪt
Iolo (Welsh Christian name) 'jəʊləʊ
(Welsh 'jolo)
ion (I.), -s 'aɪən ['aɪɒn], -z
Iona aɪ'əʊnə
Ionesco jɒ'neskəʊ [ˌɪɒ-, -sku:]
Ionia, -n/s aɪ'əʊnjə [-nɪə], -n/z
Ionic aɪ'ɒnɪk
ionization [-isa-] ˌaɪənaɪ'zeɪʃn
ioniz|e [-is|e], -es, -ing, -ed 'aɪənaɪz, -ɪz,
-ɪŋ, -d
ionosphere, -s aɪ'ɒnəˌsfɪə*, -z
iota, -s; -cism/s aɪ'əʊtə, -z; -sɪzəm/z
I O U, -s ˌaɪəʊ'juː, -z
Iowa 'aɪəʊə ['aɪəwə]
IPA ˌaɪpiː'eɪ
ipecacuanha ˌɪpɪkækjʊ'ænə ['ɪpɪ-
ˌkækjʊ'æ-, -'ɑːnə]

271

Iphicrates ɪˈfɪkrəti:z
Iphigenia ɪˌfɪdʒɪˈnaɪə [ˌɪfɪdʒ-]
Ipoh ˈiːpəʊ
ipso facto ˌɪpsəʊˈfæktəʊ
Ipswich ˈɪpswɪtʃ
Iquique ɪˈkiːkɪ
Ira ˈaɪərə
Irak, -i/s ɪˈrɑːk, -ɪ/z
Iran ɪˈrɑːn [ˌɪəˈrɑːn]
Iranian, -s ɪˈreɪnjən [aɪˈr-, ˌaɪəˈr-, -nɪən], -z
Iraq, -i/s ɪˈrɑːk, -ɪ/z
irascibility ɪˌræsəˈbɪlətɪ [aɪəˌr-, -sɪˈb-, -lɪt-]
irascib|le, -ly, -leness ɪˈræsəb|l [ˌaɪəˈr-, -sɪb|l], -lɪ, -lnɪs [-nəs]
irate aɪˈreɪt [ˌaɪəˈr-]
Irawadi ˌɪrəˈwɒdɪ
ire ˈaɪə*
Ire|dale, -dell ˈaɪə|deɪl, -del
ire|ful, -fully, -fulness ˈaɪə|fʊl, -fʊlɪ [-fəlɪ], -fʊlnɪs [-nəs]
Ireland ˈaɪələnd
Iremonger ˈaɪəˌmʌŋgə*
Irene aɪˈriːnɪ [ˌaɪəˈr-], in modern use also ˈaɪriːn [ˈaɪər-]
irenic, -al aɪˈriːnɪk [ˌaɪəˈr-, -ˈren-], -l
irenicon, -s aɪˈriːnɪkən [ˌaɪəˈr-, -ˈren-, -kɒn], z
Ireton ˈaɪətn
irian (pertaining to the iris) ˈaɪərɪən
Irian (New Guinea) ˈɪrɪən
iridescen|ce, -t ˌɪrɪˈdesn|s, -t
iridium ɪˈrɪdɪəm [ˌaɪəˈr-, aɪˈrɪd-, -djəm]
Irion ˈɪrɪən
iris (I.), -es ˈaɪərɪs, -ɪz
Irish; -ism/s ˈaɪərɪʃ; -ɪzəm/z
Irish|man, -men ˈaɪərɪʃ|mən, -mən [-men]
Irishry ˈaɪərɪʃrɪ
Irish|woman, -women ˈaɪərɪʃ|ˌwʊmən, -ˌwɪmɪn
irk, -s, -ing, -ed ɜːk, -s, -ɪŋ, -t
irksome, -ly, -ness ˈɜːksəm, -lɪ, -nɪs [-nəs]
Irkutsk ɜːˈkʊtsk [ɪəˈk-] (irˈkutsk)
iron (s. v.) (I.), -s, -ing, -ed ˈaɪən, -z, -ɪŋ, -d
ironbound ˈaɪənbaʊnd
ironclad, -s ˈaɪənklæd, -z
iron-found|er/s, -ry, -ries ˈaɪənˌfaʊnd|ə*/z, -rɪ, -rɪz
irongray [-grey] ˌaɪənˈgreɪ [also ˈ-- when attributive]
ironic, -al, -ally aɪˈrɒnɪk [ˌaɪəˈr-], -l, -əlɪ
ironing-board, -s ˈaɪənɪŋbɔːd [-bəəd], -z
ironmonger, -s ˈaɪənˌmʌŋgə*, -z

ironmongery ˈaɪənˌmʌŋgərɪ
ironmould ˈaɪənməʊld
ironside (I.), -s ˈaɪənsaɪd, -z
iron-stone ˈaɪənstəʊn
Ironton ˈaɪəntən
ironware ˈaɪənweə*
ironwood ˈaɪənwʊd
ironwork, -s ˈaɪənwɜːk, -s
iron|y (s.) (sarcasm, etc.), -ies ˈaɪərən|ɪ [-rn̩|-], -ɪz
irony (adj.) (like iron) ˈaɪənɪ
Iroquoian ˌɪrəʊˈkwɔɪən
Iroquois (sing.) ˈɪrəkwɔɪ [-kwɔɪz], (plur.) ˈɪrəkwɔɪz
irradian|ce, -cy, -t ɪˈreɪdjən|s [-dɪən-], -sɪ, -t
irradiat|e, -es, -ing, -ed ɪˈreɪdɪeɪt, -s, -ɪŋ, -ɪd
irradiation, -s ɪˌreɪdɪˈeɪʃn [ˌɪreɪ-], -z
irra|tional, -tionally ɪˈræ|ʃənl [ˌɪˈr-, -ʃnəl, -ʃn̩l, -ʃnl, -ʃənəl], -ʃnəlɪ [-ʃnəlɪ, -ʃn̩lɪ, -ʃnlɪ, -ʃənəlɪ]
irrationality ˌɪræʃəˈnælətɪ [ˈɪˌræʃəˈn-, -ʃn̩ˈæ-, -ɪtɪ]
irrebuttable ˌɪrɪˈbʌtəbl
irreceptive ˌɪrɪˈseptɪv
irreclaimable ˌɪrɪˈkleɪməbl
irreclaimably ˌɪrɪˈkleɪməblɪ
irrecognizable [-isa-] ɪˈrekəgnaɪzəbl [ˈɪˌrekəgˈn-]
irreconcilability ɪˌrekənsaɪləˈbɪlətɪ [ˈɪˌrekənsaɪlə'b-, -lɪt-]
irreconcilable, -ness ɪˈrekənsaɪləbl [ˈɪˌrekənˈs-], -nɪs [-nəs]
irreconcilably ɪˈrekənsaɪləblɪ [ˌɪrekən's-]
irrecoverable, -ness ˌɪrɪˈkʌvərəbl, -nɪs [-nəs]
irrecoverably ˌɪrɪˈkʌvərəblɪ
irredeemable, -ness ˌɪrɪˈdiːməbl, -nɪs [-nəs]
irredeemably ˌɪrɪˈdiːməblɪ
irredenti|sm, -st/s ˌɪrɪˈdentɪ|zəm, -st/s
irreducible, -ness ˌɪrɪˈdjuːsəbl [-sɪb-], -nɪs [-nəs]
irreducibly ˌɪrɪˈdjuːsəblɪ [-sɪb-]
irreformable ˌɪrɪˈfɔːməbl
irrefragability ɪˌrefrəgəˈbɪlətɪ [-lɪt-]
irrefragab|le, -ly, -leness ɪˈrefrəgəb|l, -lɪ, -lnɪs [-nəs]
irrefutability ɪˌrefjʊtəˈbɪlətɪ [ˈɪˌrefjʊtə'b-, ˈɪrɪˌfjuːtə'b-, -lɪt-]
irrefutable ɪˈrefjʊtəbl [ˌɪrɪˈfjuː-t-]
irrefutably ɪˈrefjʊtəblɪ [ˌɪrɪˈfjuː-t-]
irregular, -ly ɪˈregjʊlə* [-gjəl-], -lɪ
irregularit|y, -ies ɪˌregjʊˈlærət|ɪ [ˈɪˌregjʊˈl-, -gjəˈl-, -ɪt|ɪ], -ɪz
irrelevan|ce, -cy, -cies, -t/ly ɪˈreləvən|s [-lɪv-], -sɪ, -sɪz, -t/lɪ

272

irreligion ˌɪrɪˈlɪdʒən [-rəˈl-]
irreligious, -ly, -ness ˌɪrɪˈlɪdʒəs [-rəˈl-], -lɪ, -nɪs [-nəs]
irremediable ˌɪrɪˈmiːdjəbl [-dɪə-]
irremediably ˌɪrɪˈmiːdjəblɪ [-dɪə-]
irremovability ˈɪrɪˌmuːvəˈbɪlətɪ [-lɪt-]
irremovable ˌɪrɪˈmuːvəbl
irrepairable ˌɪrɪˈpeərəbl
irreparability ɪˌrepərəˈbɪlətɪ [ˈɪˌrep-ərəˈb-, -lɪt-]
irreparable, -ness ɪˈrepərəbl, -nɪs [-nəs]
irreparably ɪˈrepərəblɪ
irrepatriable ˌɪrɪˈpætrɪəbl
irreplaceable ˌɪrɪˈpleɪsəbl
irrepressible, -ness ˌɪrɪˈpresəbl [-sɪb-], -nɪs [-nəs]
irrepressibly ˌɪrɪˈpresəblɪ [-sɪb-]
irreproachability ˈɪrɪˌprəʊtʃəˈbɪlətɪ [-lɪt-]
irreproachable, -ness ˌɪrɪˈprəʊtʃəbl, -nɪs [-nəs]
irreproachably ˌɪrɪˈprəʊtʃəblɪ
irresistibility ˈɪrɪˌzɪstəˈbɪlətɪ [-tɪˈb-, -lɪt-]
irresistible, -ness ˌɪrɪˈzɪstəbl [-tɪb-], -nɪs [-nəs]
irresistibly ˌɪrɪˈzɪstəblɪ [-tɪb-]
irresoluble ɪˈrezəljʊbl
irresolute, -ly, -ness ɪˈrezəluːt [ˌɪˈr-, -zˌluːt, -zəljuːt], -lɪ, -nɪs [-nəs]
irresolution ˈɪˌrezəˈluːʃn [-zˌl ˈuː-, -zəˈljuː-]
irresolvability ˈɪrɪˌzɒlvəˈbɪlətɪ [-lɪt-]
irresolvable, -ness ˌɪrɪˈzɒlvəbl, -nɪs [-nəs]
irrespective, -ly ˌɪrɪˈspektɪv, -lɪ
irresponsibility ˈɪrɪˌspɒnsəˈbɪlətɪ [-sɪˈb-, -lɪt-]
irresponsible, -ly ˌɪrɪˈspɒnsəbl [-sɪb-], -lɪ
irresponsive, -ly, -ness ˌɪrɪˈspɒnsɪv, -lɪ, -nɪs [-nəs]
irrestrainable ˌɪrɪˈstreɪnəbl
irretentive ˌɪrɪˈtentɪv
irretrievability ˈɪrɪˌtriːvəˈbɪlətɪ [-lɪt-]
irretrievable ˌɪrɪˈtriːvəbl
irretrievably ˌɪrɪˈtriːvəblɪ
irreveren|ce, -t/ly ɪˈrevərən|s [ˌɪˈr-], -t/lɪ
irreversibility ˈɪrɪˌvɜːsəˈbɪlətɪ [-sɪˈb-, -lɪt-]
irreversible, -ness ˌɪrɪˈvɜːsəbl [-sɪb-], -nɪs [-nəs]
irrevocability ɪˌrevəkəˈbɪlətɪ [-vʊk-, -lɪt-]
irrevocable ɪˈrevəkəbl [-vʊk-], (when applied to letters of credit) ˌɪrɪˈvəʊkəbl
irrevocably ɪˈrevəkəblɪ [-vʊk-]

irrigable ˈɪrɪgəbl
irrigat|e, -es, -ing, -ed, -or/s ˈɪrɪgeɪt, -s, -ɪŋ, -ɪd, -ə*/z
irrigation, -s ˌɪrɪˈgeɪʃn, -z
irritability ˌɪrɪtəˈbɪlətɪ [-lɪt-]
irritab|le, -ly, -leness ˈɪrɪtəb|l, -lɪ, -lnɪs [-nəs]
irritant (s. adj.), -s ˈɪrɪtənt, -s
irritat|e, -es, -ing/ly, -ed; -ive ˈɪrɪteɪt, -s, -ɪŋ/lɪ, -ɪd; -ɪv
irritation, -s ˌɪrɪˈteɪʃn, -z
irrup|t, -ts, -ting, -ted, -tive/ly, -tion/s ɪˈrʌp|t, -ts, -tɪŋ, -tɪd, -tɪv/lɪ, -ʃn/z
Irv|ine, -ing ˈɜːv|ɪn [-vaɪn], -ɪŋ
Irving|ism, -ite/s ˈɜːvɪŋ|ɪzəm, -aɪt/s
Irwin ˈɜːwɪn
is (from be) ɪz (strong form), z, s (weak forms)
Note.—z is used only when the preceding word ends in a vowel or a voiced consonant other than z or ʒ. s is used only when the preceding word ends in a voiceless consonant other than s or ʃ.
Isaac, -s ˈaɪzək, -s
Isabel ˈɪzəbel
Isabella ˌɪzəˈbelə
Isaiah aɪˈzaɪə [old-fashioned -ˈzerə]
Isambard ˈɪzəmbɑːd
Isard ˈɪzɑːd
Iscariot ɪˈskærɪət
Ischia ˈɪskɪə [-kjə]
Iseult iːˈzuːlt [ɪˈz-, -ˈsuːlt]
Isham (surname) ˈaɪʃəm
Ishbosheth ˈɪʃbəʃeθ [-bɒʃ-, ɪʃˈbɒʃeθ, ɪʃˈbəʊʃeθ]
Isherwood ˈɪʃəwʊd
Ishmael ˈɪʃmeɪəl [-mɪəl, -mɪəl]
Ishmaelit|e, -es, -ish ˈɪʃˌmɪəlaɪt [-mɪəl-, -mjəl-, -merəl-, -məl-], -s, -ɪʃ
Ishtar ˈɪʃtɑː*
Isidore ˈɪzɪdɔː* [-zə-, -dɔə*]
Isidorian ˌɪzɪˈdɔːrɪən [-zəˈd-]
isinglass ˈaɪzɪŋglɑːs
Isis ˈaɪsɪs
Isla ˈaɪlə
Islam ˈɪzlɑːm [-læm, -ləm, ɪzˈlɑːm, ɪsˈl-]
islamic ɪzˈlæmɪk [ɪsˈl-]
Islam|ism, -ite/s ˈɪzləm|ɪzəm, -aɪt/s
island, -s, -er/s ˈaɪlənd, -z, -ə*/z
Islay ˈaɪleɪ [locally ˈaɪlə]
isle, -s aɪl, -z
islet, -s ˈaɪlɪt [-lət, -let], -s
Isleworth ˈaɪzlwəθ [-wɜː θ]
Islington ˈɪzlɪŋtən
Islip (archbishop) ˈɪzlɪp, (in Oxfordshire) ˈaɪslɪp
ism, -s ˈɪzəm, -z

Ismail ˌɪztnɑː'iːl [ˌɪsmɑː-, 'ɪzmaɪl, 'ɪzmeɪl]
Ismailia ˌɪzmaɪ'liːə [ˌɪsmaɪ-, -'lɪə]
Ismay 'ɪzmeɪ
isn't 'ɪznt [*also occasionally* 'ɪzn *when not final*]
isobar, -s 'aɪsəʊbɑː:*, -z
Isobel 'ɪzəbel [-zəʊb-]
isochromatic ˌaɪsəʊkrəʊ'mætɪk
isochron|al, -ism, -ous aɪ'sɒkrən|l, -ɪzəm, -əs
Isocrates aɪ'sɒkrəti:z
isogloss, -es 'aɪsəʊglɒs, -ɪz
isolate (*s.*), -s 'aɪsəʊleɪt [-lət], -s
isolat|e (*v.*), -es, -ing, -ed 'aɪsəleɪt [*rarely* 'aɪzəl-], -s, -ɪŋ, -ɪd
isolation ˌaɪsə'leɪʃn
isolationi|sm, -st/s ˌaɪsə'leɪʃn̩|zəm, -st/s
isolative 'aɪsələtɪv [-səleɪt-]
Isolda ɪ'zɒldə
Isolde ɪ'zɒldə (iː'zɒldə)
isomer, -s 'aɪsəmə*, -z
isomeric ˌaɪsəʊ'merɪk
isomer|ism, -ous aɪ'sɒmər|ɪzəm, -əs
isometric, -al, -ally ˌaɪsəʊ'metrɪk, -l, -əlɪ
isomorph, -s 'aɪsəʊmɔːf, -s
isomorph|ic, -ism, -ous ˌaɪsəʊ'mɔːf|ɪk, -ɪzəm, -əs
isophone, -s 'aɪsəʊfəʊn, -z
isosceles aɪ'sɒsɪliːz [-səl-, -s̩l-]
isotherm, -s 'aɪsəʊθɜːm, -z
isothermal ˌaɪsəʊ'θɜːml
isotope, -s 'aɪsəʊtəʊp, -s
isotopic ˌaɪsəʊ'tɒpɪk
isotype, -s 'aɪsəʊtaɪp, -s
Ispahan ˌɪspə'hɑːn [-'hæn]
Israel 'ɪzreɪəl [-ˌrɪəl, -rɪəl, *in formal reading also* -reɪel]
Israeli, -s ɪz'reɪlɪ, -z
Israelit|e, -es, -ish 'ɪz,rɪəlaɪt [-rɪəl-, -rəl-, -reɪəl-], -s, -ɪʃ
Issachar 'ɪsəkə* [-kɑː:*]
iss|ue (*s. v.*), -ues, -uing, -ued, -uer/s; -uable, -uance 'ɪʃ|uː [-'ɪsj|uː, -'ɪfj|uː], -uːz, -uːɪŋ [-uɪŋ], -uːd, -uːə* [-ʊə*]/z; -uːəbl [-ʊəbl], -uːəns [-ʊəns]
Istanbul ˌɪstæn'bʊl [-tɑːn-, -'buːl]
isthmian (I.) 'ɪsθmɪən [-stm-, -sm-, -mjən]
isthmus, -es 'ɪsməs [-sθm-, -stm-], -ɪz
istle 'ɪstlɪ
Istria 'ɪstrɪə
it ɪt
itacism 'iːtəsɪzəm
Italian (*s. adj.*), -s ɪ'tæljən, -z

italianate ɪ'tæljəneɪt [-nət, -nɪt]
italianism, -s ɪ'tæljənɪzəm, -z
italianiz|e [-is|e], -es, -ing, -ed ɪ'tæljən-aɪz, -ɪz, -ɪŋ, -d
italic (I.), -s ɪ'tælɪk, -s
italicization [-isa-] ɪˌtælɪsaɪ'zeɪʃn
italiciz|e [-is|e], -es, -ing, -ed ɪ'tælɪsaɪz, -ɪz, -ɪŋ, -d
Italy 'ɪtəlɪ ['ɪtlɪ]
itch (*s. v.*), -es, -ing, -ed ɪtʃ, -ɪz, -ɪŋ, -t
Itchen 'ɪtʃɪn
itch|y, -iness 'ɪtʃ|ɪ, -ɪnɪs [-ɪnəs]
item, -s 'aɪtəm [-tem, -tɪm], -z
itemiz|e [-is|e], -es, -ing, -ed 'aɪtəmaɪz, -ɪz, -ɪŋ, -d
iterat|e, -es, -ing, -ed 'ɪtəreɪt, -s, -ɪŋ, -ɪd
iteration ˌɪtə'reɪʃn
iterative 'ɪtərətɪv [-reɪt-]
Ithaca 'ɪθəkə
Ithamar 'ɪθəmɑː:* [-mə*]
Ithuriel ɪ'θjʊərɪəl
itineran|cy, -t/s ɪ'tɪnərən|sɪ [aɪ'ţ-], -t/s
itinerar|y, -ies aɪ'tɪnərər|ɪ [ɪ'ţ-], -ɪz
itinerat|e, -es, -ing, -ed ɪ'tɪnəreɪt [aɪ'ţ-], -s, -ɪŋ, -ɪd
its ɪts
it's (= it is) ɪts
itself ɪt'self
Iuca aɪ'juːkə
Ivan 'aɪvən
Ivanhoe 'aɪvənhəʊ
Ivanoff ɪ'vɑːnəf [iː'v-, -nɒf] (i'vanəf)
Ivatt, -s 'aɪvət [-væt], -s
I've (= I have) aɪv
Iveagh 'aɪvə
Ivens 'aɪvənz
Iver 'aɪvə*
Ives (*surname, and towns* St. Ives *in Cornwall and Cambridgeshire*) aɪvz, (*in Stevenson's 'St. Ives'*) iːvz
Ivey 'aɪvɪ
Ivimey 'aɪvɪmɪ
Ivone 'aɪvən
Ivor 'aɪvə*
ivor|y (*s. adj.*) (I.), -ies 'aɪvər|ɪ, -ɪz
ivory-black ˌaɪvərɪ'blæk
iv|y (I.), -ies, -ied 'aɪv|ɪ, -ɪz, -ɪd
Ivybridge 'aɪvɪbrɪdʒ
ixia, -s 'ɪksɪə [-sjə], -z
Ixion ɪk'saɪən
Iza 'aɪzə
Izaby (*surname*) 'ɪzəbɪ
Izal 'aɪzəl
izard, -s 'ɪzəd, -z
Izard 'aɪzɑːd, 'aɪzəd, 'ɪzəd
Izod 'aɪzəd
Izzard 'ɪzəd, 'ɪzɑːd

J

J (*the letter*), **-'s** dʒeɪ, -z
jab (*s. v.*), **-s, -bing, -bed** dʒæb, -z, -ɪŋ, -d
jabber (*s. v.*), **-s, -ing, -ed, -er/s** ˈdʒæbə*, -z, -rɪŋ, -d, -rə*/z
Jabberwock, -y ˈdʒæbəwɒk, -ɪ
Jabesh-gilead ˌdʒeɪbeʃˈgɪlɪæd [-lɪəd, -ljəd]
Jabez ˈdʒeɪbez [-bɪz]
Jabin ˈdʒeɪbɪn
jabiru, -s ˈdʒæbɪruː, -z
jaborandi ˌdʒæbəˈrændɪ [-bɔːˈr-]
jabot, -s ˈʒæbəʊ (ʒabo), -z
jacaranda ˌdʒækəˈrændə
Jachin ˈdʒeɪkɪn
jacinth, -s ˈdʒæsɪnθ [ˈdʒeɪs-], -s
jack (**J.**), **-s** dʒæk, -s
jackal, -s ˈdʒækɔːl [-kəl], -z
jackanapes, -es ˈdʒækəneɪps, -ɪz
jackass, -es ˈdʒækæs [-kɑːs], -ɪz
> *Note.*—ˈdʒækæs *is more usual for the animal and bird, but* ˈdʒækɑːs *is commoner when the word is used colloquially as a term of contempt.*

jack-boot, -s ˈdʒækbuːt [ˌdʒækˈb-], -s
jackdaw, -s ˈdʒækdɔː, -z
jacket, -s, -ed ˈdʒækɪt, -s, -ɪd
jack-in-office, jacks-in-office ˈdʒækɪn‚ɒfɪs, ˈdʒæksɪn‚ɒfɪs
jack-in-the-box, -es ˈdʒækɪnðəbɒks, -ɪz
jack-in-the-green, -s ˈdʒækɪnðəgriːn [ˌdʒækɪnðəˈg-], -z
jack-kni|fe, -ves ˈdʒæknaɪ|f, -vz
Jackman ˈdʒækmən
jack-of-all-trades ˌdʒækəvˈɔːltreɪdz
jack-o'-lantern, -s ˈdʒækəʊ‚læntən [ˌ--ˈ--], -z
jack-plane, -s ˈdʒækpleɪn, -z
jackpot, -s ˈdʒækpɒt, -s
jack-pudding, -s ˌdʒækˈpʊdɪŋ, -z
Jackson ˈdʒæksn
jack-tar, -s ˌdʒækˈtɑː* [ˈ--], -z
Jacob ˈdʒeɪkəb
Jacobean ˌdʒækəʊˈbiːən [-ˈbɪən]
Jacobi dʒəˈkəʊbɪ
jacobian (**J.**), **-s** dʒəˈkəʊbjən [-bɪən], -z
Jacobin, -s, -ism ˈdʒækəʊbɪn [-kʊb-], -z, -ɪzəm
Jacobit|e, -es, -ism ˈdʒækəʊbaɪt [-kʊb-], -s, -ɪzəm

Jacob|s, -son ˈdʒeɪkəb|z, -sn
Jacob's-ladder, -s ˌdʒeɪkəbzˈlædə*, -z
jacobus (**J.**), **-es** dʒəˈkəʊbəs, -ɪz
Jacoby dʒəˈkəʊbɪ, ˈdʒækəbɪ [-kʊb-]
Jacomb ˈdʒeɪkəm
Jacqueline ˈdʒækəlɪn [ˈʒæ-, -kliːn]
Jacques dʒeɪks
jactitation ˌdʒæktɪˈteɪʃn
jad|e (*s. v.*), **-es, -ing, -ed** dʒeɪd, -z, -ɪŋ, -ɪd
jaeger (**J.**), **-s** ˈjeɪgə*, -z
Jael ˈdʒeɪəl [dʒeɪl, ˈdʒeɪel]
Jaffa, -s ˈdʒæfə, -z
jag (*s. v.*), **-s, -ging, -ged** dʒæg, -z, -ɪŋ, -d
Jaggard ˈdʒægəd
jagged (*adj.*), **-ly, -ness** ˈdʒægɪd, -lɪ, -nɪs [-nəs]
jagger (**J.**), **-s** ˈdʒægə*, -z
jagg|y, -ier, -iest, -iness ˈdʒæg|ɪ, -ɪə*, -ɪɪst, -ɪnɪs [-məs]
Jago ˈdʒeɪgəʊ
jaguar (**J.**), **-s** ˈdʒægjuə* [-gwə*], -z
Jah dʒɑː [jɑː]
Jahaz ˈdʒeɪhæz
Jahveh ˈjɑːveɪ [ˌjɑːˈveɪ, ˈdʒɑːveɪ, ˈjɑːvə]
jail, -s dʒeɪl, -z
jailbird, -s ˈdʒeɪlbɜːd, -z
jailer, -s ˈdʒeɪlə*, -z
Jain, -s, -ism dʒaɪn [dʒeɪn], -z, -ɪzəm
Jaipur ˌdʒaɪˈpʊə* [-ˈpɔə*, -ˈpɔː*] (*Hindi*, ɟəypwr)
Jairus dʒeɪˈaɪərəs [ˈdʒaɪərəs]
Jalalabad dʒəˌlɑːləˈbɑːd [-ˈbæd] (*Hindi* ɟəlalabad)
jalap ˈdʒæləp
jalop|y, -ies dʒəˈlɒp|ɪ, -ɪz
jalousie, -s ˈʒæluːziː [-lʊz-, ˌʒæluːˈz-, -lʊˈz-], -z
jam (*s.*), **-s** dʒæm, -z
jam (*v.*) (*wedge, spread with jam*), **-s, -ming, -med** dʒæm, -z, -ɪŋ, -d
Jam (*Indian title*), **-s** dʒɑːm (*Hindi* ɟam), -z
Jamaica, -n/s dʒəˈmeɪkə, -n/z
jamb, -s dʒæm, -z
jamboree, -s ˌdʒæmbəˈriː [ˈ---], -z
James dʒeɪmz

275

Jameson (*surname*) 'dʒeɪmsn, 'dʒɪm-, 'dʒem-, -mɪsn
James's 'dʒeɪmzɪz
Jamia 'dʒʌmɪə ['dʒæm-] (*Hindi* ɟəmya)
Jamieson (*surname*) 'dʒeɪmɪsn, 'dʒæm-, 'dʒem-, 'dʒɪm-
jam-jar, -s 'dʒæmdʒɑ:*, -z
jamm|y, -ier, -iest, -iness 'dʒæm|ɪ, -ɪə*, -ɪɪst, -ɪnɪs [-ɪnəs]
jam-pot, -s 'dʒæmpɒt, -s
Jamrach 'dʒæmræk
Jamy 'dʒeɪmɪ
Jan dʒæn
Jane dʒeɪn
Janeiro dʒə'nɪərəʊ
Janet 'dʒænɪt
jang|le, -les, -ling, -led, -ler/s 'dʒæŋg|l, -lz, -lŋ [-lŋ], -ld, -lə*/z [-lə*/z]
Janiculum dʒæ'nɪkjʊləm [dʒə'n-]
janissar|y, -ies 'dʒænɪsər|ɪ, -ɪz
janitor, -s 'dʒænɪtə*, -z
Jan(n)ette dʒə'net
Jansen 'dʒænsn
Janseni|sm, -st/s 'dʒænsŋɪ|zəm [-sənɪ-], -st/s
Jantzen 'jæntsən ['dʒæn-]
Januarius ˌdʒænjʊ'eərɪəs
Januar|y, -ies 'dʒænjʊər|ɪ [-ˌnjʊər-, -njwər-, -njʊr-], -ɪz
Janus 'dʒeɪnəs
Jap, -s dʒæp, -s
japan (*s. v.*) (J.), -s, -ning, -ned, -ner/s dʒə'pæn, -z, -ɪŋ, -d, -ə*/z
Japanese ˌdʒæpə'ni:z [-pn̩'i:z]
jap|e (*s. v.*), -es, -ing, -ed dʒeɪp, -s, -ɪŋ, -t
Japhet 'dʒeɪfet
Japhetic dʒeɪ'fetɪk [dʒə'f-]
japonica, -s dʒə'pɒnɪkə, -z
Jaques dʒeɪks, dʒæks, (*Shakespearian character*) 'dʒeɪkwɪz
jar (*s. v.*), -s, -ring/ly, -red dʒɑ:*, -z, -rɪŋ/lɪ, -d
Jardine 'dʒɑ:di:n
jardinière, -s ˌʒɑ:dɪ'njeə* [ˌdʒɑ:-, -mɪ'eə*] (ʒardinjɛ:r), -z
jarful, -s 'dʒɑ:fʊl, -z
jargon, -s 'dʒɑ:gən, -z
jargonelle, -s ˌdʒɑ:gə'nel, -z
Jar|ley, -man 'dʒɑ:|lɪ, -mən
Jarr|att, -ett 'dʒær|ət, -ət [-ɪt]
Jarr|old, -ow 'dʒær|əld, -əʊ
jarvey, -s 'dʒɑ:vɪ, -z
Jarv|ie, -is 'dʒɑ:v|ɪ, -ɪs
Jas. dʒeɪmz [dʒæs]
jasey, -s 'dʒeɪzɪ, -z
Jasher 'dʒæʃə*
jasmine (J.) 'dʒæsmɪn [-æzm-]

Jason 'dʒeɪsn
jasper (J.), -s 'dʒæspə* [*rarely* 'dʒɑ:s-], -z
Jassy 'dʒæsɪ
jaundice, -d 'dʒɔ:ndɪs [*rarely* 'dʒɑ:n-], -t
jaunt (*s. v.*), -s, -ing, -ed dʒɔ:nt, -s, -ɪŋ, -ɪd
jaunt|y, -ier, -iest, -ily, -iness 'dʒɔ:nt|ɪ, -ɪə* [-jə*], -ɪɪst [-jɪst], -ɪlɪ [-əlɪ], -ɪnɪs [-ɪnəs]
Java 'dʒɑ:və
Javan (*of Java*) 'dʒɑ:vən, (*biblical name*) 'dʒeɪvæn
Javanese ˌdʒɑ:və'ni:z [*also* '— *when attributive*]
javelin (*spear*), -s 'dʒævlɪn [-vəlɪn], (J.) (*car, aeroplane*) 'dʒævəlɪn ['dʒævlɪn], -z
jaw (*s. v.*), -s, -ing, -ed dʒɔ:, -z, -ɪŋ, -d
jaw-bone, -s 'dʒɔ:bəʊn, -z
jaw-break|er/s, -ing 'dʒɔ:ˌbreɪk|ə*/z, -ɪŋ
Jaxartes dʒæk'sɑ:ti:z
jay (J.), -s dʒeɪ, -z
jazz dʒæz
jazz-band, -s 'dʒæzbænd, -z
Jeaffreson 'dʒefəsn
Jeakes dʒeɪks
jealous, -ly, -ness 'dʒeləs, -lɪ, -nɪs [-nəs]
jealous|y, -ies 'dʒeləs|ɪ, -ɪz
Jeames dʒi:mz
jean (*cotton fabric*) dʒeɪn
Jean dʒi:n
Jeaner 'dʒenə*
Jeanette dʒɪ'net [dʒə'n-]
jeans (*trousers*) (J.) dʒi:nz
Jebb dʒeb
Jebus 'dʒi:bəs
Jebusite, -s 'dʒebjʊzaɪt [-bju:z-], -s
Jedburgh 'dʒedbərə
Jeddah 'dʒedə
Jedediah ˌdʒedɪ'daɪə
jeep, -s dʒi:p, -s
jeer (*s. v.*), -s, -ing/ly, -ed, -er/s dʒɪə*, -z, -rɪŋ/lɪ, -d, -rə*/z
Jefferies 'dʒefrɪz
Jefferson 'dʒefəsn
Jeffery 'dʒefrɪ
Jeffrey, -s 'dʒefrɪ, -z
Jehoahaz dʒɪ'həʊəhæz [dʒə'h-]
Jehoash dʒɪ'həʊæʃ [dʒə'h-]
Jehoiachin dʒɪ'hɔɪəkɪn [dʒə'h-]
Jehoiada dʒɪ'hɔɪədə [dʒə'h-]
Jehoiakim dʒɪ'hɔɪəkɪm [dʒə'h-]
Jehonadab dʒɪ'hɒnədæb [dʒə'h-]
Jehoram dʒɪ'hɔ:rəm [dʒə'h-, -ræm]
Jehoshaphat dʒɪ'hɒʃəfæt [dʒə'h-]
Jehovah dʒɪ'həʊvə [dʒə'h-]

jehu (J.), -s 'dʒi:hju:, -z
jejune, -ly, -ness dʒɪ'dʒu:n, -lɪ, -nɪs [-nəs]
jejunum, -s dʒɪ'dʒu:nəm, -z
Jekyll (surname) 'dʒi:kɪl, 'dʒekɪl [-kəl]
Note.—In Jekyll and Hyde freq. pronounced 'dʒekɪl.
Jelf dʒelf
jell, -s, -ing, -ed dʒel, -z, -ɪŋ, -d
Jellicoe 'dʒelɪkəʊ
jell|y (s. v.), -ies, -ying, -ied 'dʒel|ɪ, -ɪz, -ɪŋ [-jɪŋ], -ɪd
jelly-bag, -s 'dʒelɪbæg, -z
Jellyby 'dʒelɪbɪ
jelly-fish, -es 'dʒelɪfɪʃ, -ɪz
jellygraph (s. v.), -s, -ing, -ed 'dʒelɪgrɑ:f [-græf], -s, -ɪŋ, -t
Jemima dʒɪ'maɪmə [dʒə'm-]
jemm|y, -ies 'dʒem|ɪ, -ɪz
Jena 'jeɪnə ('je:na:)
Jenkin, -s, -son 'dʒeŋkɪn ['dʒenk-], -z, -sn
Jenner 'dʒenə*
jennet, -s 'dʒenɪt, -s
Jennifer 'dʒenɪfə*
Jennings 'dʒenɪŋz
jenn|y (in machinery), -ies 'dʒen|ɪ, -ɪz
jenn|y (in billiards), -ies 'dʒɪn|ɪ ['dʒen-], -ɪz
Jenny 'dʒenɪ, 'dʒɪnɪ
Jensen (car), -s 'dʒensn, -z
jeopardiz|e [-is|e], -es, -ing, -ed 'dʒepədaɪz, -ɪz, -ɪŋ, -d
jeopardy 'dʒepədɪ
Jephthah 'dʒefθə
jerboa, -s dʒɜ:'bəʊə, -z
jeremiad, -s ˌdʒerɪ'maɪəd [-'maɪæd], -z
Jeremiah ˌdʒerɪ'maɪə [-rə'm-]
Jeremy 'dʒerɪmɪ [-rəmɪ]
Jericho 'dʒerɪkəʊ
jerk (s. v.), -s, -ing, -ed dʒɜ:k, -s, -ɪŋ, -t
jerkin, -s 'dʒɜ:kɪn, -z
jerk|y, -ier, -iest, -ily, -iness 'dʒɜ:k|ɪ, -ɪə* [-jə*], -ɪɪst [-jɪst], -ɪlɪ [-əlɪ], -ɪnɪs [-ɪnəs]
Jermyn 'dʒɜ:mɪn
jeroboam (J.), -s ˌdʒerə'bəʊəm, -z
Jerome (Saint) dʒə'rəʊm [dʒe'r-, dʒɪ'r-, rarely 'dʒerəm], (surname) dʒə'rəʊm [dʒe'r-, dʒɪ'r-], 'dʒerəm
Note.—Jerome K. Jerome, the author, pronounced dʒə'rəʊm.
Jerram 'dʒerəm
Jerrold 'dʒerəld
jerr|y (J.), -ies 'dʒer|ɪ, -ɪz
jerry-buil|d, -ds, -ding, -t, -der/s 'dʒerɪbɪl|d, -dz, -dɪŋ, -t, -də*/z
jersey (J.), -s 'dʒɜ:zɪ, -z

Jerubbaal ˌdʒerəb'beɪəl [Jewish pronunciation ˌdʒerə'bɑ:l]
Jerusalem dʒə'ru:sələm [dʒɪ'r-, -lem]
Jervaulx (in Yorkshire) 'dʒɜ:vəʊ ['dʒɑ:vəʊ]
Jervis 'dʒɑ:vɪs, 'dʒɜ:vɪs
Jervois 'dʒɜ:vɪs
Jespersen 'jespəsn
jess (s. v.) (J.), -es, -ing, -ed dʒes, -ɪz, -ɪŋ, -t
jessamine (J.) 'dʒesəmɪn
Jess|e, -el, -ica, -ie, -op 'dʒes|ɪ, -l, -ɪkə, -ɪ, -əp
jest (s. v.), -s, -ing/ly, -ed, -er/s dʒest, -s, -ɪŋ/lɪ, -ɪd, -ə*/z
Jeston 'dʒestən
Jesu 'dʒi:zju:
Jesuit, -s, -ism 'dʒezjʊɪt [-zʊɪt, -ʒʊɪt], -s, -ɪzəm
jesuitic, -al, -ally ˌdʒezjʊ'ɪtɪk [-zʊ'ɪt-, -ʒʊ'ɪt-], -l, -əlɪ
Jesus 'dʒi:zəs
jet (s. v.), -s, -ting, -ted dʒet, -s, -ɪŋ, -ɪd
jet-black ˌdʒet'blæk ['-- when attributive]
Jethro 'dʒeθrəʊ
jetsam 'dʒetsəm [-sæm]
jet-set, -ter/s 'dʒetset, -ə*/z
jettis|on (s. v.), -ons, -oning, -oned 'dʒetɪs|n [-tɪz|n], -nz, -n̩ɪŋ [-ən̩ɪŋ], -nd
jett|y (s. adj.), -ies 'dʒet|ɪ, -ɪz
jeu, -s dʒɜ: (ʒø), -z
Jeune dʒu:n
Jevons 'dʒevənz
Jew, -s dʒu:, -z
jewel (s. v.) (J.), -s, -led, jewelling 'dʒu:əl [dʒʊəl, dʒu:l], -z, -d, 'dʒu:əlɪŋ ['dʒʊəlɪŋ]
jewel-box, -es 'dʒu:əlbɒks ['dʒʊəl-, 'dʒu:l-], -ɪz
jewel-case, -s 'dʒu:əlkeɪs ['dʒʊəl-, 'dʒu:l-], -ɪz
jeweller, -s 'dʒu:ələ* ['dʒʊələ*], -z
jewellery 'dʒu:əlrɪ ['dʒʊəl-, 'dʒu:l-]
Jewess, -es 'dʒu:ɪs ['dʒʊɪs, 'dʒu:es, 'dʒʊes], -ɪz
Jewin 'dʒu:ɪn, 'dʒʊɪn
Jewish, -ly, -ness 'dʒu:ɪʃ ['dʒʊɪʃ], -lɪ, -nɪs [-nəs]
Jewry 'dʒʊərɪ
Jewsbury 'dʒu:zbərɪ
jew's-harp, -s ˌdʒu:z'hɑ:p, -s
Jeyes dʒeɪz
jezail dʒe'zeɪl
Jezebel 'dʒezəbl [-zɪb-, -bel]
Jezreel dʒez'ri:l
jib (s. v.), -s, -bing, -bed dʒɪb, -z, -ɪŋ, -d
jib-boom, -s ˌdʒɪb'bu:m, -z

277

jib|e (s. v.), -es, -ing, -ed dʒaɪb, -z, -ɪŋ, -d
jiff|y, -ies 'dʒɪf|ɪ, -ɪz
jig (s. v.), -s, -ging, -ged dʒɪg, -z, -ɪŋ, -d
jigger, -s 'dʒɪgə*, -z
jiggered 'dʒɪgəd
jiggery-pokery ˌdʒɪgərɪ'pəʊkərɪ
jigg|le (v.), -les, -ling, -led 'dʒɪg|l, -lz,
  -lɪŋ [-lɪŋ], -ld
jigsaw, -s 'dʒɪgsɔ:, -z
jihad dʒɪ'hɑ:d
Jill dʒɪl
jilt (s. v.), -s, -ing, -ed dʒɪlt, -s, -ɪŋ, -ɪd
Jim, -my dʒɪm, -ɪ
jimjams 'dʒɪmdʒæmz
jing|le (s. v.) (J.), -les, -ling, -led
  'dʒɪŋg|l, -lz, -lɪŋ, -ld
jingo (J.), -es 'dʒɪŋgəʊ, -z
jingoism 'dʒɪŋgəʊɪzəm
jink, -s, -ing, -ed dʒɪŋk, -s, -ɪŋ, -t
jinn, -s dʒɪn, -z
jinnee, -s dʒɪ'ni:, -z
jinrick|sha/s, -shaw/s ˌdʒɪn'rɪk|ʃə/z,
  -ʃɔ:/z
jinx, -es, -ing, -ed dʒɪŋks, -ɪz, -ɪŋ, -t
jitterbug (s.v.), -s, -ging, -ged 'dʒɪtəbʌg,
  -z, -ɪŋ, -d
jitters 'dʒɪtəz
jitter|y, -iness 'dʒɪtər|ɪ, -ɪnɪs [-məs]
jiujitsu dʒju:'dʒɪtsu: [dʒu:-]
jiv|e (s. v.), -es, -ing, -ed dʒaɪv, -z, -ɪŋ, -d
jo, -es dʒəʊ, -z
Joab 'dʒəʊæb
Joachim (violinist) 'jəʊəkɪm ('jo:axim)
Joan dʒəʊn
Joanna dʒəʊ'ænə
Joash 'dʒəʊæʃ
job (s. v.), -s, -bing, -bed, -ber/s; -bery
  dʒɒb, -z, -ɪŋ, -d, -ə*/z; -ərɪ
Job dʒəʊb
jobmaster, -s 'dʒɒb,mɑ:stə*, -z
Jobson 'dʒɒbsn, 'dʒəʊbsn
Jocasta dʒəʊ'kæstə
Jocelyn 'dʒɒslɪn
Jochebed 'dʒɒkəbed
Jock dʒɒk
jockey (s. v.), -s, -ing, -ed; -ship
  'dʒɒkɪ, -z, -ɪŋ, -d; -ʃɪp
Jockey Club 'dʒɒkɪklʌb
jockstrap, -s 'dʒɒkstræp, -s
jocose, -ly, -ness dʒəʊ'kəʊs, -lɪ, -nɪs
  [-nəs]
jocosity dʒəʊ'kɒsətɪ [-ɪtɪ]
jocular, -ly 'dʒɒkjʊlə* [-kjə-], -lɪ
jocularity ˌdʒɒkjʊ'lærətɪ [-kjə-, -ɪtɪ]
jocund, -ly, -ness 'dʒɒkənd ['dʒəʊk-,
  -kʌnd], -lɪ, -nɪs [-nəs]
jocundity dʒəʊ'kʌndətɪ [dʒɒ'k-, -ɪtɪ]
jod, -s jɒd, -z

jod|el, -els, -elling, -elled 'jəʊd|l ['jɒd-],
  -lz, -lɪŋ [-əlɪŋ], -ld
jodhpurs 'dʒɒdpəz [-pɜ:z, -ˌpʊəz]
Jodrell 'dʒɒdrəl
Joe dʒəʊ
Joel 'dʒəʊel ['dʒəʊəl, dʒəʊl]
Joey 'dʒəʊɪ
jog (s. v.), -s, -ging, -ged, -ger/s dʒɒg,
  -z, -ɪŋ, -d, -ə*/z
jogg|le (s. v.), -les, -ling, -led 'dʒɒg|l,
  -lz, -lɪŋ [-lɪŋ], -ld
jog-trot 'dʒɒgtrɒt [ˌ-'-]
johannes (coin), -es dʒəʊ'ænɪs, -ɪz
Johannes (personal name) jəʊ'hænɪs
Johannesburg dʒəʊ'hænɪsbɜ:g [-ɪzb-,
  -nəs-, -nəz-]
  Note.—There exists also a local pro-
  nunciation dʒəʊ'hɒnɪsbɜ:g, which is
  used by many English-speaking
  South Africans.
Johannine dʒəʊ'hænaɪn
Johannisburger jəʊ'hænɪsbɜ:gə*
John dʒɒn
john-dor|y, -ies ˌdʒɒn'dɔ:r|ɪ, -ɪz
Johnes dʒəʊnz, dʒɒnz
Johnian, -s 'dʒəʊnjən [-nɪən], -z
johnn|y (J.), -ies 'dʒɒn|ɪ, -ɪz
John o' Groat's ˌdʒɒnə'grəʊts
John|s, -son dʒɒn|z, -sn
Johnsonese ˌdʒɒnsə'ni:z [-sn̩'i:z]
Johnsonian dʒɒn'səʊnjən [-nɪən]
Johnston(e) 'dʒɒnstən, 'dʒɒnsn
Johore dʒəʊ'hɔ:*
join (s. v.), -s, -ing, -ed, -er/s; -ery
  dʒɔɪn, -z, -ɪŋ, -d, -ə*/z; -ərɪ
joint (s. adj. v.), -s, -ly; -ing, -ed, -er/s
  dʒɔɪnt, -s, -lɪ; -ɪŋ, -ɪd, -ə*/z
joint-stock 'dʒɔɪntstɒk
joint-tenan|cy, -cies, -t/s ˌdʒɔɪnt-
  'tenən|sɪ, -sɪz, -t/s
jointure, -s 'dʒɔɪntʃə*, -z
joist, -s dʒɔɪst, -s
jok|e (s. v.), -es, -ing/ly, -ed, -er/s
  dʒəʊk, -s, -ɪŋ/lɪ, -t, -ə*/z
Jolland 'dʒɒlənd
Jolliffe 'dʒɒlɪf
jollification, -s ˌdʒɒlɪfɪ'keɪʃn, -z
jolli|fy, -fies, -fying, -fied 'dʒɒlɪ|faɪ,
  -faɪz, -faɪɪŋ, -faɪd
jollit|y, -ies 'dʒɒlət|ɪ [-ɪt|ɪ], -ɪz
joll|y (J.), -ier, -iest, -ily, -iness 'dʒɒl|ɪ,
  -ɪə*, -ɪɪst, -ɪlɪ [-əlɪ], -ɪnɪs [-ɪnəs]
jollyboat, -s 'dʒɒlɪbəʊt, -s
jolt (s. v.), -s, -ing/ly, -ed dʒəʊlt, -s,
  -ɪŋ/lɪ, -ɪd
jolt|y, -ier, -iest, -ily, -iness 'dʒəʊlt|ɪ,
  -ɪə* [-jə*], -ɪɪst [-jɪst], -ɪlɪ [-əlɪ], -ɪnɪs
  [-ɪnəs]

Jolyon 'dʒəʊljən ['dʒɒl-]
Jon dʒɒn
Jonadab 'dʒɒnədæb
Jonah 'dʒəʊnə
Jonas 'dʒəʊnəs [-næs]
Jonathan 'dʒɒnəθən
Jones dʒəʊnz
jongleur, -s ʒɔ̃:ŋ'glə:* [ʒɔ:ŋ-, ʒɒŋ-] (ʒɔ̃-glœ:r), -z
jonquil, -s 'dʒɒŋkwɪl, -z
Jonson 'dʒɒnsn
Joppa 'dʒɒpə
Jopson 'dʒɒpsn
Joram 'dʒɔ:rəm [-ræm]
†Jordan, -s 'dʒɔ:dn, -z
jorum, -s 'dʒɔ:rəm, -z
joseph (J.), 'dʒəʊzɪf [-zəf], -s
Josephine 'dʒəʊzɪfi:n [-zəf-]
Josephus dʒəʊ'si:fəs
Josh dʒɒʃ
Joshua 'dʒɒʃwə [-ʃʊə, -ʃjʊə, -ʃjwə]
Josiah dʒəʊ'saɪə [-'zaɪə]
Josias dʒəʊ'saɪəs [-'zaɪəs]
joss, -es dʒɒs, -ɪz
joss-hou|se, -ses 'dʒɒshaʊ|s, -zɪz
joss-stick, -s 'dʒɒsstɪk, -s
Jost jəʊst
jost|le, -les, -ling, -led 'dʒɒs|l, -lz, -lɪŋ [-lɪŋ], -ld
jot (s. v.), -s, -ting/s, -ted dʒɒt, -s, -ɪŋ/z, -ɪd
jotation, -s jəʊ'teɪʃn, -z
joule, -s dʒu:l [dʒaʊl], -z
Joule (English surname) dʒu:l, dʒəʊl, dʒaʊl
journal, -s 'dʒɜ:nl, -z
journalese ˌdʒɜ:nə'li:z [-nl'i:z]
journali|sm, -st/s 'dʒɜ:nəlɪ|zəm [-nlɪ-], -st/s
journalistic ˌdʒɜ:nə'lɪstɪk [-nl'ɪ-]
journaliz|e [-is|e], -es, -ing, -ed 'dʒɜ:nəlaɪz [-nlaɪz], -ɪz, -ɪŋ, -d
journ|ey (s. v.), -eys, -eying/s, -eyed 'dʒɜ:n|ɪ, -ɪz, -ɪɪŋ/z [-jɪŋ/z], -ɪd
journey|man, -men 'dʒɜ:nɪ|mən, -mən
joust, -s dʒaʊst [dʒu:st], -s
Jove dʒəʊv
jovial, -ly, -ness 'dʒəʊvjəl [-vɪəl], -ɪ, -nɪs [-nəs]
joviality ˌdʒəʊvɪ'ælətɪ [-ɪtɪ]
Jowett 'dʒaʊɪt, 'dʒəʊɪt
   Note.—'dʒaʊɪt appears to be the commoner pronunciation.
Jowitt 'dʒaʊɪt, 'dʒəʊɪt
jowl, -s dʒaʊl, -z
joy (s. v.) (J.), -s, -ing, -ed dʒɔɪ, -z, -ɪŋ, -d
Joyce dʒɔɪs

joy|ful, -fullest, -fully, -fulness 'dʒɔɪ|fʊl, -fʊlɪst [-fəlɪst], -fʊlɪ [-fəlɪ], -fʊlnɪs [-nəs]
joyless, -ly, -ness 'dʒɔɪlɪs [-ləs], -lɪ, -nɪs [-nəs]
joyous, -ly, -ness 'dʒɔɪəs, -lɪ, -nɪs [-nəs]
joy-ride, -s 'dʒɔɪraɪd, -z
joy-stick, -s 'dʒɔɪstɪk, -s
jr. 'dʒu:njə* [-nɪə*]
Juan 'dʒu:ən [dʒʊən, hwɑ:n] (xwan)
Juan Fernandez (island) ˌdʒu:ənfə'nændez [ˌdʒʊən-]
Juanita (as English Christian name) dʒʊə'ni:tə [ˌdʒu:ə'n-], also hwə'ni:tə (approximation to the Spanish pronunciation xwa'nita)
Jubal 'dʒu:bəl [-bæl]
jubilant, -ly 'dʒu:bɪlənt, -lɪ
Jubilate (s.), -s ˌdʒu:bɪ'lɑ:tɪ [ˌju:bɪ'lɑ:tɪ, old-fashioned ˌdʒu:bɪ'leɪtɪ], -z
jubilat|e (v.), -es, -ing, -ed 'dʒu:bɪleɪt, -s, -ɪŋ, -ɪd
jubilation, -s ˌdʒu:bɪ'leɪʃn, -z
jubilee, -s 'dʒu:bɪlɪ: [-lɪ, ˌdʒu:bɪ'li:], -z
Judaea, -n/s dʒu:'dɪə [dʒʊ-, -'di:ə], -n/z
Judaeo- dʒu:'di:əʊ- [dʒʊ'd-] (following element also stressed)
Juda(h) 'dʒu:də
Judaic, -al, -ally dʒu:'deɪk [dʒʊ'd-], -l, -əlɪ
Judai|sm, -st/s 'dʒu:deɪɪ|zəm, -st/s
judaiz|e [-is|e], -es, -ing, -ed, -er/s 'dʒu:deraɪz, -ɪz, -ɪŋ, -d, -ə*/z
Judas, -es 'dʒu:dəs, -ɪz
Judd dʒʌd
Jude dʒu:d
Judea, -n/s dʒu:'dɪə [dʒʊ-, -'di:ə], -n/z
judg|e (s. v.) (J.), -es, -ing, -ed dʒʌdʒ, -ɪz, -ɪŋ, -d
judg(e)ment, -s ; -day/s, -hall/s, -seat/s 'dʒʌdʒmənt, -s; -deɪ/z, -hɔ:l/z, -si:t/s
judgeship, -s 'dʒʌdʒʃɪp [-dʃʃɪp, -dʃɪp], -s
judicature 'dʒu:dɪkətʃə* [dʒu:'dɪk-, dʒʊ'd-, -,tjʊə*]
judi|cial, -cially dʒu:'dɪ|ʃl [dʒʊ'd-], -ʃlɪ [-ʃlɪ]
judiciary dʒu:'dɪʃərɪ [dʒʊ'd-, -ʃjə, -ʃɪə-]
judicious, -ly, -ness dʒu:'dɪʃəs [dʒʊ'd-], -lɪ, -nɪs [-nəs]
Judith 'dʒu:dɪθ
judo 'dʒu:dəʊ
Judson 'dʒʌdsn
Judy 'dʒu:dɪ

279

jug—juxtapositional

jug (*s. v.*), **-s, -ging, -ged** dʒʌg, -z, -ɪŋ, -d
jugful, **-s** 'dʒʌgfʊl, -z
juggernaut (**J**), **-s** 'dʒʌgənɔːt, -s
juggins (**J.**), **-es** 'dʒʌgɪnz, -ɪz
jugg|le (*s. v.*), **-les, -ling, -led, -ler/s** 'dʒʌg|l, -lz, -lɪŋ [-lɪŋ], -ld, -lə*/z [-lə*/z]
jugglery 'dʒʌglərɪ
Jugoslav, **-s** ˌjuːgəʊ'slɑːv [-'slæv, *also* 'juːgəʊsl-, *esp. when attributive*], -z
Jugoslavia, **-n** ˌjuːgəʊ'slɑːvjə [-vɪə], -n
jugular 'dʒʌgjʊlə* [-gjə-, *rarely* 'dʒuːg-]
Jugurtha dʒʊ'gɜːθə [juː-]
juice, **-s; -less** dʒuːs, -ɪz; -lɪs [-les, -ləs]
juic|y, **-ier, -iest, -ily, -iness** 'dʒuːs|ɪ, -ɪə* [-jə*], -ɪɪst [-jɪst], -ɪlɪ [-əlɪ], -ɪnɪs [-məs]
jujitsu dʒuː'dʒɪtsuː
jujube, **-s** 'dʒuːdʒuːb, -z
juke-box, **-es** 'dʒuːkbɒks, -ɪz
Jukes dʒuːks
julep, **-s** 'dʒuːlɪp [-ləp], -s
Julia, **-n** 'dʒuːljə [-lɪə], -n
Juliana ˌdʒuːlɪ'ɑːnə, -'ænə
julienne ˌdʒuːlɪ'en [ˌʒuː-] (ʒyljɛn)
Juliet 'dʒuːljət [-lɪət, -ljet]
Julius 'dʒuːljəs [-lɪəs]
Jul|y, **-ies** dʒuː'l|aɪ [dʒʊ'laɪ], -aɪz
Julyan 'dʒuːljən
jumb|le (*s. v.*), **-les, -ling, -led; -le-sale/s** 'dʒʌmb|l, -lz, -lɪŋ, -ld; -lseɪl/z
Jumbl|y, **-ies** 'dʒʌmbl|ɪ, -ɪz
jumbo (**J.**), **-s** 'dʒʌmbəʊ, -z
Jumna 'dʒʌmnə (*Hindi* jəmnə)
†jump (*s. v.*), **-s, -ing, -ed, -er/s** dʒʌmp, -s, -ɪŋ, -t [dʒʌmt], -ə*/z
jun. 'dʒuːnjə* [-nɪə*]
junction, **-s** 'dʒʌŋkʃn, -z
juncture, **-s** 'dʒʌŋktʃə*, -z
June, **-s** dʒuːn, -z
Jungfrau 'jʊŋfraʊ
jungle, **-s** 'dʒʌŋgl, -z
jungle-fowl, **-s** 'dʒʌŋglfaʊl, -z
jungly 'dʒʌŋglɪ
junior, **-s** 'dʒuːnjə* [-nɪə*], -z
juniority ˌdʒuːnɪ'ɒrɪtɪ [-ɪtɪ]
juniper, **-s** 'dʒuːnɪpə* ['dʒʊn-], -z
Junius 'dʒuːnjəs [-nɪəs]
junk, **-s** dʒʌŋk, -s
junker (**J.**), **-s** 'jʊŋkə*, -z
junket, **-s, -ing** 'dʒʌŋkɪt, -s, -ɪŋ
junkie, **-s** 'dʒʌŋkɪ, -z
Juno 'dʒuːnəʊ
Junoesque ˌdʒuːnəʊ'esk
Junonian dʒuː'nəʊnjən [dʒʊ'n-, -nɪən]

junt|a/s, **-o/s** 'dʒʌnt|ə/z ['dʒʊ-], -əʊ/z
jupe, **-s** ʒuːp (ʒyp), -s
Jupiter 'dʒuːpɪtə* ['dʒʊp-]
jupon, **-s** 'ʒuːpɒn ['dʒuː:-, -pɔ̃ːŋ, -pɒŋ] (ʒypɔ̃), -z
Jura 'dʒʊərə
Jurassic dʒʊə'ræsɪk
jurat, **-s** 'dʒʊəræt, -s
juridic|al, **-ally** ˌdʒʊə'rɪdɪk|l [dʒʊ'r-], -əlɪ
jurisconsult, **-s** 'dʒʊərɪskən‚sʌlt, -s
jurisdiction, **-s** ˌdʒʊərɪs'dɪkʃn, -z
jurisdictional ˌdʒʊərɪs'dɪkʃənl [-ʃnəl, -ʃn̩l, -ʃnl, -ʃənəl]
jurisprudence ˌdʒʊərɪs'pruːdəns ['--‚--]
jurist, **-s** 'dʒʊərɪst, -s
juror, **-s** 'dʒʊərə*, -z
jur|y, **-ies** 'dʒʊər|ɪ, -ɪz
jury-box, **-es** 'dʒʊərɪbɒks, -ɪz
jury|man, **-men** 'dʒʊərɪ|mən, -mən [-men]
jury-mast, **-s** 'dʒʊərɪmɑːst [*nautical pronunciation* -məst], -s
just (*adj.*) (**J.**), **-er, -est, -ly, -ness** dʒʌst, -ə*, -ɪst, -lɪ, -nɪs [-nəs]
just (*adv.*) dʒʌst [*rarely* dʒest], *with some* dʒəst *even when stressed*
justice, **-s** 'dʒʌstɪs, -ɪz
justiciable dʒʌ'stɪʃɪəbl [-ʃjə-, -ʃə-]
justiciar, **-s** dʒʌ'stɪʃɪɑː* [-ɪsɪ-], -z
justiciar|y, **-ies** dʒʌ'stɪʃɪər|ɪ [-ɪʃjə-, -ɪʃə-, -ɪsɪə-, -ɪsjə-], -ɪz
justifiab|le, **-ly, -leness** 'dʒʌstɪfaɪəb|l [‚dʒʌstɪ'f-], -lɪ, -lnɪs [-nəs]
justification, **-s** ˌdʒʌstɪfɪ'keɪʃn, -z
justificat|ive, **-ory** 'dʒʌstɪfɪkeɪt|ɪv [-kət-], -ərɪ [‚dʒʌstɪfɪ'keɪtərɪ]
justi|fy, **-fies, -fying, -fied, -fier/s** 'dʒʌstɪ|faɪ, -faɪz, -faɪɪŋ, -faɪd, -faɪə*/z
Justin 'dʒʌstɪn
Justinian dʒʌ'stɪnɪən [-njən]
Justus 'dʒʌstəs
jut, **-s, -ting, -ted** dʒʌt, -s, -ɪŋ, -ɪd
Juta (*surname*) 'dʒuːtə
jute (**J.**), **-s** dʒuːt, -s
Jutland 'dʒʌtlənd
Juvenal 'dʒuːvənl [-vnl]
juvenescen|ce, **-t** ˌdʒuːvə'nesn|s [-vɪ'n-], -t
juvenile (*s. adj.*), **-s** 'dʒuːvənaɪl [-vɪn-], -z
juvenility ˌdʒuːvə'nɪlɪtɪ [-vɪ'n-, -ɪtɪ]
juxtapos|e, **-es, -ing, -ed** ˌdʒʌkstə'pəʊz ['---], -ɪz, -ɪŋ, -d
juxtaposition, **-s** ˌdʒʌkstəpə'zɪʃn [-pʊ'z-], -z
juxtapositional ˌdʒʌkstəpə'zɪʃənl [-pʊ'z-, -ʃnəl, -ʃn̩l, -ʃnl, -ʃənəl]

280

K

K (*the letter*), -'s keɪ, -z
Kaaba 'kɑːbə ['kɑːəbɑː]
Kabaka, -s kə'bɑːkə, -z
Kab(b)ala kə'bɑːlə [kæ'b-]
Kabul 'kɑːbl ['kɔː-, -bʊl]
Kabyle, -s kə'baɪl [kæ'b-, 'kæbiːl], -z
Kabylia kæ'bɪlɪə [kə'b-, -ljə]
Kaddish 'kædɪʃ
Kadesh-barnea ˌkeɪdeʃbɑː'nɪə [-'bɑːnɪə]
Kadmonite, -s 'kædmənaɪt [-mɒn-], -s
Kaffir, -s 'kæfə*, -z
Kafka, -esque 'kæfkə, -esk [--'-]
Kahn kɑːn
kailyard, -s 'keɪljɑːd, -z
Kaiser, -s 'kaɪzə*, -z
kakemono, -s ˌkækɪ'məʊnəʊ, -z
Kalat kə'lɑːt
kale keɪl
kaleidoscope, -s kə'laɪdəskəʊp, -s
kaleidoscopic kəˌlaɪdə'skɒpɪk
Kalends 'kælendz [-lɪndz, -ləndz]
Kalgoorlie kæl'ɡʊəlɪ
Kaliningrad kə'liːnɪŋɡræd [-ɡrɑːd]
Kalundborg 'kælənbɔːɡ
Kam|a, -ic 'kɑːm|ə, -ɪk
Kamasutra ˌkɑːmə'suːtrə
Kamerun ˌkæmə'ruːn ['---]
Kampala kæm'pɑːlə
kampong kæm'pɒŋ ['--]
kana (*Japanese syllabic writing*) 'kɑːnə
Kanarese ˌkænə'riːz
Kandahar ˌkændə'hɑː*
Kandy 'kændɪ
Kane keɪn
kangaroo, -s ˌkæŋɡə'ruː [*sometimes in Australia* '---], -z
Kanpur (*Cawnpore*) kɑːn'pʊə* (*Hindi* kanpwr)
Kansas 'kænzəs [-nsəs]
Kant kænt
Kantian 'kæntɪən [-tjən]
Kanti|sm, -st/s 'kæntɪ|zəm, -st/s
kaolin 'keɪəlɪn
kapok 'keɪpɒk
kappa 'kæpə
Karachi kə'rɑːtʃɪ (*Hindi* kəraci)
karate kə'rɑːtɪ [kæ'r-]
Karen, -s kə'ren, -z, (*girl's name*) 'kɑːrən, 'kærən

Karl kɑːl
Karlsbad 'kɑːlzbæd ('karlsbɑːt)
karm|a, -ik 'kɑːm|ə, -ɪk
  Note.—Some theosophists pronounce 'kɜːmə, 'kɜːmɪk, *thus distinguishing these words from* kama, kamic. 'kɜːmə *is an attempt at the Hindi pronunciation* kərma.
Karnak 'kɑːnæk
karroo, -s kə'ruː:, -z
Kars kɑːz
Kashgar 'kæʃɡɑː*
Kashmir ˌkæʃ'mɪə* [*also* '— *when attributive*]
Kaspar 'kæspə* [-pɑː:*]
Katakana ˌkætə'kɑːnə
Kate keɪt
Kater 'keɪtə*
Katharina ˌkæθə'riːnə
Katharine 'kæθərɪn
Katherine 'kæθərɪn
Kathie 'kæθɪ
Kathleen 'kæθliːn
Katie 'keɪtɪ
Katin (*surname*) 'keɪtɪn
Katisha 'kætɪʃɑː [-ʃə]
Katmandu ˌkætmæn'duː [ˌkɑːtmɑːn-] (*Hindi* kaʈhmāḍu)
Katrine 'kætrɪn
Kattegat ˌkætɪ'ɡæt ['---]
Katty 'kætɪ
katydid, -s 'keɪtɪdɪd, -z
Kaunda kɑː'ʊndə [kɑː'uːn-]
Kavanagh 'kævənə, kə'vænə
  Note.—In Ireland always 'kævənə.
Kay keɪ
kayak, -s 'kaɪæk, -s
Kaye, -s keɪ, -z
kea (*parrot*), -s 'keɪə, -z
Kean(e) kiːn
Kearn(e)y 'kɜːnɪ, 'kɑːnɪ
Kearsarge 'kɪəsɑːdʒ
Kearsley 'kɪəzlɪ [*locally* 'kɜːzlɪ]
Kearsney (*in Kent*) 'kɜːznɪ
Kearton 'kɪətn, 'kɜːtn
Keary 'kɪərɪ
Keating(e) 'kiːtɪŋ
Keats kiːts
Keble 'kiːbl

281

Kedah (*in Malaya*) 'kedə
Kedar 'kiːdɑː* [-də*]
Kedesh 'kiːdeʃ
kedg|e (*s. v.*), **-es, -ing, -ed** kedʒ, -ɪz, -ɪŋ, -d
kedgeree, -s ˌkedʒə'riː: ['—], -z
Kedleston 'kedlstən
Kedron 'kedrɒn ['kiːd-]
Keeble 'kiːbl
keel (*s. v.*), **-s, -ing, -ed** kiːl, -z, -ɪŋ, -d
keelhaul, -s, -ing, -ed 'kiːlhɔːl, -z, -ɪŋ, -d
keelson, -s 'kelsn ['kiːl-], -z
keen, -er, -est, -ly, -ness kiːn, -ə*, -ɪst, -lɪ, -nɪs [-nəs]
Keen(e) kiːn
keep (*s. v.*), **-s, -ing, kept, keeper/s** kiːp, -s, -ɪŋ, kept, 'kiːpə*/z
keepsake, -s 'kiːpseɪk, -s
Kefauver 'kiːˌfɔːvə* [-ˌfaʊvə*]
keg, -s keg, -z
Kegan 'kiːgən
Kehoe kjəʊ, 'kiːəʊ, 'kɪəʊ
Keig kiːg
Keighley (*place in West Yorkshire*) 'kiːθlɪ, (*surname*) 'kiːθlɪ, 'kiːlɪ, 'kaɪlɪ
Keightley 'kiːtlɪ, 'kaɪtlɪ
Keigwin 'kegwɪn
Keiller 'kiːlə*
Keir kɪə*
Keith kiːθ
Kekewich 'kekwɪtʃ [-wɪdʒ], 'kekɪwɪtʃ
Kelantan ke'læntən [kə'l-]
Kelat kɪ'læt
Kelland 'kelənd
Kellas 'kelæs
Kell(e)y 'kelɪ
Kellogg 'kelɒg
kelp kelp
kelpie, -s 'kelpɪ, -z
Kelsey 'kelsɪ, 'kelzɪ
Kelso 'kelsəʊ
kelson, -s 'kelsn, -z
Kelt, -s, -ic kelt, -s, -ɪk
kelvin (K.) 'kelvɪn
Kelway 'kelwɪ, -weɪ
Kemal (*Pasha*) ke'mɑːl [kə'm-]
Kemble 'kembl
kemp (K.) kemp
Kempenfelt 'kempənfelt
Kempis 'kempɪs
ken (*s. v.*) (K.), **-s, -ning, -ned** ken, -z, -ɪŋ, -d
Kend|al(l), -rick 'kend|l, -rɪk
Kenealy kɪ'niːlɪ [kə'n-, ke'n-]
Kenelm 'kenelm
Kenilworth 'kenəlwɜːθ [-nɪl-, -wəθ]
Kenite, -s 'kiːnaɪt, -s
Kenmare ken'meə*

Kenmore 'kenmɔː* [-mɔə*]
Kennaird kə'neəd [ke'n-]
Kennan 'kenən
Kennard ke'nɑːd [kə'n-]
Kennedy 'kenɪdɪ [-nədɪ]
kenn|el (K.) (*s. v.*), **-els, -elling, -elled** 'ken|l, -lz, -lɪŋ, -ld
Kennerley 'kenəlɪ
Kenn|et, -eth, -ey 'ken|ɪt, -ɪθ, -ɪ
Kenn|icot, -ington 'ken|ɪkət, -ɪŋtən
Kennish 'kenɪʃ
Kenny 'kenɪ
Kenrick 'kenrɪk
Kensal 'kensl
Kensington 'kenzɪŋtən
Kensit 'kenzɪt [-nsɪt]
Kent, -s, -ish kent, -s, -ɪʃ
Kentucky ken'tʌkɪ
Kenwood 'kenwʊd
Kenya 'kenjə ['kiːn-]
Note.—Both pronunciations are heard locally.
Kenyatta ken'jætə
Kenyon 'kenjən [-nɪən]
Keogh kjəʊ, 'kiːəʊ, 'kɪəʊ
Kepler 'keplə*
Keppel 'kepəl
kept (*from* keep) kept
Ker kɑː*, keə*, kɜː* (*in Scotland* kɛr)
Kerala (*in S. India*) 'kerələ
Kerans 'kerənz
keratin 'kerətɪn
keratitis ˌkerə'taɪtɪs
kerb, -s kɜːb, -z
kerbstone, -s 'kɜːbstəʊn, -z
kerchief, -s, -ed 'kɜːtʃɪf, -s, -t
Kerenhappuch ˌkɪəren'hæpʊk [ˌker-, -rən-, -pək]
Kergenwen kə'genwən
Kerguelen 'kɜːgɪlɪn [-gəl-]
Kerioth 'kɪərɪɒθ ['ker-]
Kerith 'kɪərɪθ ['ker-]
kermes 'kɜːmɪz [-miːz]
Kermit 'kɜːmɪt
kern (*s. v.*), **-s, -ing, -ed** kɜːn, -z, -ɪŋ, -d
Kernahan 'kɜːnəhən [-nɪən]
kernel, -s 'kɜːnl, -z
kerosene 'kerəsiːn [*also* ˌ—'-, *when not attributive*]
Kerr kɑː*, kɜː*
Kerry 'kerɪ
Kerse kɜːs
kersey (*s. v.*), **-s; -mere** 'kɜːzɪ, -z; -ˌmɪə*
Kesteven 'kestɪvən, ke'stiːvən [-'stɪv-]
kestrel, -s 'kestrəl, -z
Keswick 'kezɪk
ketch (K.), **-es** ketʃ, -ɪz
ketchup, -s 'ketʃəp, -s

Kettering 'ketərɪŋ
kettle (K.), -s 'ketl, -z
kettledrum, -s 'ketldrʌm, -z
Keturah ke'tjʊərə [kɪ't-, kə'tʊərə]
Keux kjuː
Kevin 'kevɪn
Kew kjuː
key (s. v.) (K.), -s, -ing, -ed kiː, -z, -ɪŋ, -d
keyboard, -s 'kiːbɔːd [-bɔəd], -z
Keyes kiːz, kaɪz
key-hole, -s 'kiːhəʊl, -z
Keymour 'kiːmə*
Keyne kiːn
Keynes (surname, place near Swindon) keɪnz
key-note, -s 'kiːnəʊt [ˌkiː'nəʊt], -s
key-ring, -s 'kiːrɪŋ, -z
Keyser 'kiːzə*, 'kaɪzə*
keystone, -s 'kiːstəʊn, -z
Keyte (surname) kiːt
Kezia kɪ'zaɪə [ke'z-]
khaki, -s 'kɑːkɪ [-kiː], -z
Khalif, -s 'keɪlɪf ['kæl-, 'kɑːl-], -s
Khalifa, -s kɑː'liːfə [kə'l-], -z
Khan kɑːn
Khanpur kɑːn'pʊə* ['--] (Hindi khanpwr)
Khart(o)um kɑː'tuːm
Khatmandu, incorrect spelling of Katmandu, q.v.
Khayyam kaɪ'ɑːm [kaɪ'jɑːm]
khedival kɪ'diːvl [ke'd-, kə'd-]
Khedive, -s kɪ'diːv [ke'd-, kə'd-], -z
khedivial kɪ'diːvjəl [ke'd-, kə'd-, -vɪəl]
Khelat (former spelling of Kalat) kə'lɑːt [kɪ'l-, ke'l-]
Khmer kmeə*
Khyber 'kaɪbə*
Kia Ora ˌkɪə'ɔːrə
kibbutz, -im kɪ'bʊts, kɪbʊ'tsiːm [-'--]
kibe, -s kaɪb, -z
kibosh 'kaɪbɒʃ
kick (s. v.), -s, -ing, -ed, -er/s kɪk, -s, -ɪŋ, -t, -ə*/z
kick-off, -s 'kɪkɒf [old-fashioned -'ɔːf, ˌ-'-], -s
kickshaw, -s 'kɪkʃɔː, -z
kid (s. v.), -s, -ding, -ded kɪd, -z, -ɪŋ, -ɪd
Kidd kɪd
Kidderminster 'kɪdəmɪnstə*
kiddle (K.), -s 'kɪdl, -z
kidd|y, -ies 'kɪd|ɪ, -ɪz
kid-glove (adj.) 'kɪdglʌv [ˌ-'-]
kidnap, -s, -ping, -ped, -per/s 'kɪdnæp, -s, -ɪŋ, -t, -ə*/z
kidney, -s; -bean/s 'kɪdnɪ, -z; -'biːn/z
Kidron 'kaɪdrɒn ['kɪd-]

Kieff 'kiːef ('kijif)
Kiel kiːl
kier (K.), -s kɪə*, -z
Kierkegaad 'kɪəkəgɔːd [-gɑːd]
Kiev 'kiːev [-ef] ('kijif)
Kikuyu kɪ'kuːjuː
Kilbowie kɪl'bəʊɪ
Kilburn 'kɪlbən [-bə:n]
Kilchurn kɪl'hɜːn [-'xɜːn]
Kildale 'kɪldeɪl
Kildare kɪl'deə*
kilderkin, -s 'kɪldəkɪn, -z
Kilham 'kɪləm
Kilimanjaro ˌkɪlɪmən'dʒɑːrəʊ
Kilkenny kɪl'kenɪ
kill (s. v.), -s, -ing, -ed, -er/s kɪl, -z, -ɪŋ, -d, -ə*/z
Killaloe ˌkɪlə'luː
Killarney kɪ'lɑːnɪ
Killearn kɪ'lɜːn
Killick 'kɪlɪk
Killiecrankie ˌkɪlɪ'kræŋkɪ
Killigrew 'kɪlɪgruː
Killin kɪ'lɪn
killjoy, -s 'kɪldʒɔɪ, -z
Killwick 'kɪlwɪk
Kilmacolm ˌkɪlmə'kəʊm
Kilmainham kɪl'meɪnəm
Kilmansegg 'kɪlmənseg
Kilmarnock kɪl'mɑːnək [-nɒk]
kiln, -s kɪln [kɪl], -z
   Note.—The pronunciation kɪl appears
   to be used only by those concerned
   with the working of kilns.
kilo, -s 'kiːləʊ, -z
kilocycle, -s 'kɪləʊˌsaɪkl, -z
kilogramme, -s 'kɪləʊgræm, -z
kilolitre, -s 'kɪləʊˌliːtə*, -z
kilometre [-meter], -s 'kɪləʊˌmiːtə* [kɪ'lɒmɪtə*, -mətə*], -z
kiloton, -s 'kɪləʊtʌn, -z
kilowatt, -s 'kɪləʊwɒt, -s
Kilpatrick kɪl'pætrɪk
Kilrush kɪl'rʌʃ
Kilsyth kɪl'saɪθ
kilt (s. v.), -s, -ing, -ed kɪlt, -s, -ɪŋ, -ɪd
Kilwarden kɪl'wɔːdn
Kim kɪm
Kimb|all, -erley 'kɪmb|l, -əlɪ
Kimbolton kɪm'bəʊltən
Kimmeridge 'kɪmərɪdʒ
Kimmins 'kɪmɪnz
kimono, -s kɪ'məʊnəʊ, -z
kin kɪn
kinaesthetic ˌkaɪniːs'θetɪk [ˌkɪn-, -nɪs-]
Kincardine kɪn'kɑːdɪn [kɪŋ'k-, -dn]
Kinchinjunga ˌkɪntʃɪn'dʒʌŋgə
kincob 'kɪŋkəb

283

kind (*s. adj.*), **-s, -er, -est, -ly, -ness/es** kaɪnd, -z, -ə*, -ɪst, -lɪ, -nɪs [ˈkaɪnnɪs, -nəs]/ɪz

kindergarten, -s ˈkɪndəˌgɑːtn, -z

kind-hearted, -ly, -ness ˌkaɪndˈhɑːtɪd [*also* '-ˌ-- *when attributive*], -lɪ, -nɪs [-nəs]

kind|le, -les, -ling, -led, -ler/s ˈkɪnd|l, -lz, -lɪŋ [-lɪŋ], -ld, -lə*/z [-lə*/z]

kindl|y, -ier, -iest, -iness ˈkaɪndl|ɪ, -ɪə* [-jə*], -ɪɪst [-jɪst], -ɪnɪs [-məs]

kindred ˈkɪndrɪd

kine kaɪn

kinema, -s ˈkɪnɪmə [-nəmə], -z

kinematic, -al, -s ˌkɪnɪˈmætɪk [ˌkaɪn-, -nəˈm-], -l, -s

kinematograph, -s ˌkɪnɪˈmætəʊgrɑːf [ˌkaɪn-, -nəˈm-, -græf], -s

kinesis kaɪˈniːsɪs [kɪˈn-]

kinesthetic ˌkaɪniːsˈθetɪk [ˌkɪn-, -nɪs-]

kinetic (*s. adj.*), **-s** kɪˈnetɪk [kaɪˈn-], -s

king (K.), -s kɪŋ, -z

king-at-arms, kings-at-arms ˌkɪŋət-ˈɑːmz, ˌkɪŋzətˈɑːmz

kingcraft ˈkɪŋkrɑːft

kingcup, -s ˈkɪŋkʌp, -s

kingdom (K.), -s ˈkɪŋdəm, -z

Kingdon ˈkɪŋdən

kingfisher, -s ˈkɪŋˌfɪʃə*, -z

King|horn, -lake ˈkɪŋ|hɔːn, -leɪk

kingless ˈkɪŋlɪs [-les, -ləs]

kinglet, -s ˈkɪŋlɪt [-lət], -s

kinglike ˈkɪŋlaɪk

kingl|y, -ier, -iest, -iness ˈkɪŋl|ɪ, -ɪə* [-jə*], -ɪɪst [-jɪst], -ɪnɪs [-məs]

king-maker (K.), -s ˈkɪŋˌmeɪkə*, -z

kingpin, -s ˈkɪŋpɪn [ˌ-ˈ-], -z

King's Bench ˌkɪŋzˈbenʧ

Kings|borough, -bury, -cote ˈkɪŋz|-bərə, -bərɪ, -kət [-kəʊt]

King's Counsel ˌkɪŋzˈkaʊnsl

kingship ˈkɪŋʃɪp

Kingsley ˈkɪŋzlɪ

Kings|man (*member of King's College*), **-men** ˈkɪŋz|mən [-mæn], -mən [-men]

Kingston(e) ˈkɪŋstən [-ŋks-]

Kingstown ˈkɪŋstən [-ŋks-, ˈkɪŋztaʊn]

Kingsway ˈkɪŋzweɪ

Kingussie kɪŋˈjuːsɪ

kink (*s. v.*), **-s, -ing, -ed** kɪŋk, -s, -ɪŋ, -t [kɪŋt]

kinkajou, -s ˈkɪŋkədʒuː, -z

kinless ˈkɪnlɪs [-les, -ləs]

Kinn|aird, -ear, -oull kɪˈn|eəd, -ɪə*, -uːl

kino ˈkiːnəʊ

Kinross kɪnˈrɒs

Kinsale kɪnˈseɪl

kinsfolk ˈkɪnzfəʊk

kinship ˈkɪnʃɪp

kins|man, -men ˈkɪnz|mən, -mən [-men]

kins|woman, -women ˈkɪnz|ˌwʊmən, -ˌwɪmɪn

Kintore kɪnˈtɔː* [-ˈtəə*]

Kintyre kɪnˈtaɪə*

Kinvig ˈkɪnvɪg

kiosk, -s ˈkiːɒsk [ˈkɪɒsk, kjɒsk, kɪˈɒsk], -s

kip, -s kɪp, -s

Kipling ˈkɪplɪŋ

kipper (*s. v.*), **-s, -ing, -ed** ˈkɪpə*, -z, -rɪŋ, -d

Kirby ˈkɜːbɪ

Kircaldie (*surname*) kɜːˈkɔːldɪ

Kirghiz ˈkɜːgɪz

Kirjathjearim ˌkɜːdʒæθˈdʒɪərɪm [ˌkɪrɪæθ-, -dʒɪˈɑːrɪm]
Note.—The pronunciation ˌkɜːdʒæθ- *is usual in the Church of England.* ˌkɪrɪæθ- *is a form used by some Jews.*

kirk, -s kɜːk, -s

Kirk(e) kɜːk

Kirkby (*surname*) ˈkɜːbɪ, ˈkɜːkbɪ, (*place*) ˈkɜːbɪ

Kirkcaldy (*place*) kɜːˈkɔːdɪ [-ˈkɔːldɪ], (*surname*) kɜːˈkɔːdɪ
Note.—The forms kɜːˈkædɪ *and* kɜːˈkɑːdɪ *may be heard occasionally. They are probably imitations of a local Scottish pronunciation* kərˈkadɨ.

Kirkcudbright kɜːˈkuːbrɪ [kəˈk-]

Kirk|dale, -ham ˈkɜːk|deɪl, -əm

Kirkland ˈkɜːklənd

Kirkman ˈkɜːkmən

Kirkness kɜːkˈnes

Kirkpatrick kɜːkˈpætrɪk

Kirkstall (*in West Yorkshire*) ˈkɜːkstɔːl

Kirkwall ˈkɜːkwɔːl

Kirriemuir ˌkɪrɪˈmjʊə* [-ˈmjɔə*, -ˈmjɔː*]

kirsch, -wasser kɪəʃ, -ˌvɑːsə* [-ˌvæsə*]

kirtle, -s ˈkɜːtl, -z

Kishon ˈkaɪʃɒn [*with some Jews* ˈkiːʃɒn]

kismet ˈkɪsmet [ˈkɪzmet]

kiss (*s. v.*), **-es, -ing, -ed** kɪs, -ɪz, -ɪŋ, -t

kissing-crust, -s ˈkɪsɪŋkrʌst, -s

Kissinger ˈkɪsɪndʒə* [-ŋə*]

kit, -s kɪt, -s

kit-bag, -s ˈkɪtbæg, -z

kitcat (K.), -s ˈkɪtkæt, -s

kitchen (K.), -s ˈkɪtʃɪn [-tʃən], -z

kitchener (K.), -s ˈkɪtʃɪnə* [-tʃən-], -z

kitchenette, -s ˌkɪtʃɪˈnet, -s

kitchen-garden, -s ˌkɪtʃɪnˈgɑːdn [ˈ--ˌ-, -tʃən-], -z

kitchen-maid, -s 'kɪtʃɪnmeɪd [-tʃən-], -z
kitchen-midden, -s ˌkɪtʃɪn'mɪdn [-tʃən-], -z
Kitch|in, -ing 'kɪtʃ|ɪn, -ɪŋ
kite, -s; -flying kaɪt, -s; -ˌflaɪɪŋ
kite-balloon, -s 'kaɪtbəˌluːn, -z
kith kɪθ
Kitson 'kɪtsn
kitten, -s 'kɪtn, -z
kittenish 'kɪtnɪʃ
kittiwake, -s 'kɪtɪweɪk, -s
kittle 'kɪtl
Kitto 'kɪtəʊ
Kittredge 'kɪtrɪdʒ
Kitts kɪts
Kittson 'kɪtsn
Kitty 'kɪtɪ
kiwi, -s 'kiːwiː [-wɪ], -z
Klaipeda 'klaɪpɪdə [-pedə]
klaxon, -s 'klæksn, -z
Kleenex 'kliːneks
kleptoma|nia, -niac/s ˌkleptəʊ'meɪ|njə [-nɪə], -nɪæk/s [-njæk/s]
Klondike 'klɒndaɪk
Kluge (English name) kluːdʒ
knack, -s næk, -s
knacker, -s 'nækə*, -z
knacker|y, -ies 'nækər|ɪ, -ɪz
knag, -s; -gy næg, -z; -ɪ
knap, -s, -ping, -ped, -per/s næp, -s, -ɪŋ, -t, -ə*/z
knapsack, -s 'næpsæk, -s
knar, -s nɑː*, -z
Knaresborough 'neəzbərə
knave, -s neɪv, -z
knaver|y, -ies 'neɪvər|ɪ, -ɪz
knavish, -ly, -ness 'neɪvɪʃ, -lɪ, -nɪs [-nəs]
knead, -s, -ing, -ed, -er/s niːd, -z, -ɪŋ, -ɪd, -ə*/z
kneading-trough, -s 'niːdɪŋtrɒf, -s
Note.—Some bakers pronounce -trau (plur. -trauz).
knee (s. v.), -s, -ing, -d niː, -z, -ɪŋ, -d
knee-breeches 'niːˌbrɪtʃɪz
knee-cap, -s 'niːkæp, -s
knee-deep ˌniː'diːp ['--]
knee-joint, -s 'niːdʒɔɪnt, -s
kneel, -s, -ing, -ed, knelt niːl, -z, -ɪŋ, -d, nelt
knell (s. v.), -s, -ing, -ed nel, -z, -ɪŋ, -d
Kneller, -s 'nelə*, -z
knelt (from kneel) nelt
Knesset 'kneset
knew (from know) njuː
knickerbocker (K.), -s 'nɪkəbɒkə*, -z
knickers 'nɪkəz
knick-knack, -s; -ery 'nɪknæk, -s; -ərɪ

kni|fe (s.), -ves naɪ|f, -vz
knif|e (v.), -es, -ing, -ed naɪf, -s, -ɪŋ, -t
knife-board, -s 'naɪfbɔːd [-bɔəd], -z
knife-edge, -s, -d 'naɪfedʒ, -ɪz, -d
knife-grind|er/s, -ing 'naɪfˌgraɪnd|ə*/z, -ɪŋ
knife-rest, -s 'naɪfrest
knife-tray, -s 'naɪftreɪ, -z
knight (s. v.) (K.), -s, -ing, -ed naɪt, -s, -ɪŋ, -ɪd
knightage 'naɪtɪdʒ
knight-bachelor, knights-bachelor ˌnaɪt'bætʃələ* [-tʃɪlə*], ˌnaɪts'b-
knight-errant, knights-errant ˌnaɪt-'erənt, ˌnaɪts'erənt
knighthood, -s 'naɪthʊd, -z
knight|ly, -ier, -iest, -iness 'naɪtl|ɪ, -ɪə* [jə*], -ɪɪst [-jɪst], -ɪnɪs [-ɪnəs]
Knighton 'naɪtn
Knightsbridge 'naɪtsbrɪdʒ
knight-service 'naɪtˌsɜːvɪs
knit, -s, -ting, -ted, -ter/s nɪt, -s, -ɪŋ, -ɪd, -ə*/z
knitting-machine, -s 'nɪtɪŋməˌʃiːn, -z
knitting-needle, -s 'nɪtɪŋˌniːdl, -z
knitwear 'nɪtweə*
knob, -s nɒb, -z
knobbly 'nɒbl|ɪ [-blɪ]
knobb|y, -ier, -iest, -iness 'nɒb|ɪ, -ɪə*, -ɪɪst, -ɪnɪs [-ɪnəs]
knock (s. v.), -s, -ing/s, -ed, -er/s nɒk, -s, -ɪŋ/z, -t, -ə*/z
knockabout, -s 'nɒkəbaʊt, -s
Knockbreda nɒk'briːdə
knock-down ˌnɒk'daʊn ['--]
knock-kneed ˌnɒk'niːd ['--]
knock-out, -s 'nɒkaʊt, -s
knock-up, -s 'nɒkʌp, -s
knoll, -s nəʊl, -z
Knoll|es, -ys nəʊl|z, -z
knop, -s nɒp, -s
Knossos 'knɒsɒs ['knəʊs-, -əs]
knot (s. v.), -s, -ting, -ted nɒt, -s, -ɪŋ, -ɪd
knot-grass 'nɒtgrɑːs
knott|y, -ier, -iest, -ily, -iness 'nɒt|ɪ, -ɪə*, -ɪɪst, -ɪlɪ [-əlɪ], -ɪnɪs [-ɪnəs]
knout (s. v.), -s, -ing, -ed naʊt, -s, -ɪŋ, -ɪd
know (s. v.), -s, -ing, knew, know|n, -er/s; -able nəʊ, -z, -ɪŋ, njuː; nəʊ|n, -ə/*z; -əbl
know-how 'nəʊhaʊ
knowing (adj.), -ly, -ness 'nəʊɪŋ, -lɪ, -nɪs [-nəs]
knowledge, -s 'nɒlɪdʒ, -ɪz
Knowles nəʊlz
know-nothing, -s 'nəʊˌnʌθɪŋ, -z
Knox nɒks

knuck|le (s. v.), -les, -ling, -led 'nʌk|l,
  -lz, -lɪŋ [-lɪŋ], -ld
knuckle-bone, -s 'nʌklbəʊn, -z
knuckleduster, -s 'nʌkl͵dʌstə*, -z
knuckle-joint, -s 'nʌkldʒɔɪnt, -s
knur(r), -s nɜ:*, -z
Knutsford 'nʌtsfəd
Knyvett 'nɪvɪt
koala, -s kəʊ'ɑ:lə, -z
Kobe 'kəʊbɪ
kobold, -s 'kɒbəʊld ['kəʊb-, -bld], -z
kodak, -s 'kəʊdæk, -s
Kodály 'kəʊdaɪ [-'-]
Kohathite, -s 'kəʊəθaɪt ['kəʊhə-], -s
Koh-i-noor 'kəʊɪ͵nʊə* [-nɔə*, -nɔ:*,
  ͵--'-]
kohl kəʊl
kohl-rabi ͵kəʊl'rɑ:bɪ
koine 'kɔɪni:
kola (K.) 'kəʊlə
Kolaba kə'lɑ:bə [kɒ'l-]
Kolnai (surname) 'kɒlnaɪ
Kongo 'kɒŋgəʊ
Königsberg 'kɜ:nɪgzbeəg   [-bɜ:g]
  ('kø:niçsberk, -berç)
Konrad 'kɒnræd
koodoo, -s 'ku:du:, -z
kookaburra, -s 'kʊkə͵bʌrə, -z
kopeck, -s 'kəʊpek ['kɒp-], -s
kopje, -s 'kɒpɪ, -z
Kops kɒps
Korah 'kɔ:rə
Koran kɒ'rɑ:n [kɔ:'r-, kʊ'r-, kə'r-]
koranic kɒ'rænɪk [kɔ:'r-, kʊ'r-, kə'r-]
Korea, -n/s kə'rɪə [kɒ'r-, kɔ:'r-], -n/z
Koreish 'kɔ:raɪʃ
kosher 'kəʊʃə* [occasionally 'kɒʃə* by
  non-Jews]
kotow (s. v.), -s, -ing, -ed ͵kəʊ'taʊ, -z,
  -ɪŋ, -d
Kough kjəʊ, kəʊ
koumiss 'ku:mɪs
Kowloon ͵kaʊ'lu:n
kowtow, -s, -ing, -ed ͵kaʊ'taʊ, -z, -ɪŋ,
  -d
kraal, -s krɑ:l [krɔ:l], -z
  Note.—Usually pronounced krɑ:l in
  England, but krɔ:l in South Africa.
krait, -s kraɪt, -s
Krakatoa ͵krækə'təʊə
kraken, -s 'krɑ:kən, -z
Krakow 'krækɒv [-kɒf, -kaʊ]
kremlin (K.), -s 'kremlɪn, -z
Kresge 'kresgɪ
kreutzer (K.), -s 'krɔɪtsə*, -z

krill krɪl
kris, -es kri:s, -ɪz
Krishna 'krɪʃnə
krone, -s 'krəʊnə, -z
Kronin 'krəʊnɪn
Krons(h)tadt 'krɒnʃtæt
Kruger 'kru:gə*
Krupp krʊp [krʌp]
krypton 'krɪptɒn
Kuala Kangsar ͵kwɑ:lə'kʌŋsə* [͵kwɒl-,
  -'kæŋ-]
Kuala Lumpur ͵kwɑ:lə'lʊm͵pʊə*
  [͵kwɒl-, -'lʌm-, -pə*]
Kublai Khan ͵kʊblaɪ'kɑ:n
kudos 'kju:dɒs
kudu, -s 'ku:du:, -z
Kuibyshev 'kwɪbɪʃev [-ʃef] ('kujbɪʃɪʃ)
Ku-Klux-Klan ͵kju:klʌks'klæn
kulak, -s 'ku:læk, -s
kultur kʊl'tʊə* (kul'tu:r)
Kumasi ku:'mæsɪ [kʊ'm-]
kümmel 'kʊməl ['kɪm-] ('kyməl)
kumquat, -s 'kʌmkwɒt [-kwæt], -s
kung-fu ͵kʊŋ'fu:
Kuomintang ͵kwəʊmɪn'tæŋ
Kup (surname) kʌp
Kurath (American surname) 'kjʊəræθ
Kurd, -s kɜ:d, -z
Kurdistan ͵kɜ:dɪ'stɑ:n [-'stæn]
Kuril, -s kʊ'ri:l, -z
Kurile (old spelling of Kuril), -s kʊ'ri:l,
  -z
kursaal, -s 'kʊəzɑ:l ['kʊəsɑ:l, 'kɜ:sɑ:l],
  -z
Kuwait kʊ'weɪt
Kuyper 'kaɪpə*
Kwantung ͵kwæn'tʌŋ
Kwoyu ͵kwəʊ'ju:
Kyd kɪd
Kyffin 'kʌfɪn
kyle (K.), -s kaɪl, -z
kylin, -s 'kaɪlɪn, -z
Kyllachy 'kaɪləkɪ [-əxɪ]
kyloe, -s 'kaɪləʊ, -z
kymo|graph, -s, -gram/s 'kaɪməʊ|grɑ:f
  [-græf], -s, -græm/z
kymographic ͵kaɪməʊ'græfɪk
Kynance 'kaɪnæns
Kynaston 'kɪnəstən
Kyoto 'kjəʊtəʊ [kɪ'əʊtəʊ]
kyrie, -s 'kɪrɪeɪ ['kɪəri:eɪ, 'kɪərɪɪ, 'kɪrɪɪ,
  rarely 'kaɪərɪ]
Kyrle kɜ:l
Kythe 'kaɪθɪ

L

L (*the letter*), **-'s** el, -z
la (*musical note*), **-s** lɑː, -z
la (*meaningless syllable used for singing a melody*) lɑː (*length of vowel is determined by the note sung*)
la (*interj.*) lɔː
laager, -s 'lɑːgə*, -z
Laban 'leɪbən [-bæn]
lab|el, -els, -elling, -elled 'leɪb|l, -lz, -l̩ɪŋ [-lɪŋ], -ld
labial (*s. adj.*), **-s, -ly** 'leɪbjəl [-bɪəl], -z, -ɪ
labialization [**-isa-**] ˌleɪbɪəlaɪ'zeɪʃn [-bjəl-, -lɪ'z-]
labializ|e [**-is|e**], **-es, -ing, -ed** 'leɪbɪəlaɪz [-bjəl-], -ɪz, -ɪŋ, -d
Labienus ˌlæbɪ'iːnəs
labile 'leɪbaɪl
labiodental (*s. adj.*), **-s** ˌleɪbɪəʊ'dentl [-bjəʊ-], -z
laborator|y, -ies lə'bɒrətər|ɪ ['læbərə-], -ɪz
laborious, -ly, -ness lə'bɔːrɪəs, -lɪ, -nɪs [-nəs]
Labouchere ˌlæbuː'ʃeə* ['læbuːʃeə*, -bʊ-]
lab|our, -ours, -ouring, -oured, -ourer/s 'leɪb|ə*, -əz, -ərɪŋ, -əd, -ərə*/z
labourite, -s 'leɪbəraɪt, -s
labour-saving 'leɪbəˌseɪvɪŋ
Labrador 'læbrədɔː*
Labuan lə'buːən [-'bʊən, 'læbjʊən]
laburnum, -s lə'bɜːnəm, -z
labyrinth, -s 'læbərɪnθ [-bɪr-], -s
labyrinth|ian, -ine ˌlæbə'rɪnθ|ɪən [-bɪ'r-, -jən], -aɪn
lac, -s læk, -s
Laccadive, -s 'lækədɪv, -z
lac|e (*s. v.*), **-es, -ing, -ed** leɪs, -ɪz, -ɪŋ, -t
Lacedaemon ˌlæsɪ'diːmən
Lacedaemonian, -s ˌlæsɪdɪ'məʊnjən [-nɪən], -z
lacerat|e (*v.*), **-es, -ing, -ed** 'læsəreɪt, -s, -ɪŋ, -ɪd
laceration, -s ˌlæsə'reɪʃn, -z
Lacert|a (*constellation*), **-ae** lə'sɜːt|ə, -iː
Lacey 'leɪsɪ
laches 'leɪtʃɪz ['lætʃɪz]
Lachesis 'lækɪsɪs

Lachish 'leɪkɪʃ
Lachlan 'læklən, 'lɒklən
lachrymal 'lækrɪml
lachrymatory 'lækrɪmətərɪ [-meɪtərɪ, ˌlækrɪ'meɪtərɪ]
lachrymose, -ly 'lækrɪməʊs, -lɪ
lack (*s. v.*), **-s, -ing, -ed** læk, -s, -ɪŋ, -t
lackadaisical ˌlækə'deɪzɪkl
lackaday 'lækədeɪ [ˌ--'-]
lackey (*s. v.*), **-s, -ing, -ed** 'lækɪ, -z, -ɪŋ, -d
lack-lustre 'lækˌlʌstə*
Lacon 'leɪkən
Laconia, -n/s lə'kəʊnjə [-nɪə], -n/z
laconic (**L.**), **-al, -ally** lə'kɒnɪk, -l, -əlɪ
lacquer (*s. v.*), **-s, -ing, -ed, -er/s** 'lækə*, -z, -rɪŋ, -d, -rə*/z
lacquey (*s. v.*), **-s, -ing, -ed** 'lækɪ, -z, -ɪŋ, -d
lacrosse lə'krɒs [lɑː'k-]
lactat|e, -es, -ing, -ed 'lækteɪt, -s, -ɪd
lactation læk'teɪʃn
lacteal 'læktɪəl [-tjəl]
lactic 'læktɪk
lactometer, -s læk'tɒmɪtə* [-mətə*], -z
lacun|a, -ae, -as lə'kjuːn|ə [læ'k-], -iː, -əz
lacustrine lə'kʌstraɪn [læ'k-, -trɪn]
Lacy 'leɪsɪ
lad, -s læd, -z
Ladakh (*in Kashmir*) lə'dɑːk [*old-fashioned* lə'dɔːk]
Ladbroke 'lædbrʊk
ladder, -s 'lædə*, -z
laddie, -s 'lædɪ, -z
lad|e, -es, -ing, -ed, -en leɪd, -z, -ɪŋ, -ɪd, -n
Ladefoged (*English surname*) 'lædɪfəʊgɪd
ladida(h) ˌlɑːdɪ'dɑː
ladies'|-man, -men 'leɪdɪz|mæn, -men
Ladislaus 'lædɪslɔːs
Ladislaw 'lædɪslɔː
ladl|e (*s. v.*), **-es, -ing, -led** 'leɪd|l, -lz, -l̩ɪŋ [-lɪŋ], -ld
ladleful, -s 'leɪdlfʊl, -z
Ladoga 'lædəʊgə ['lɑːd-, *old-fashioned* lə'dəʊgə] ('ladəgə)

287

ladrone (*Scottish term of reproach*), -s
  'lædrən, -z
ladrone (*highwayman in Spain, etc.*), -s
  lə'drəʊn, -z
Ladrone (*Islands*) lə'drəʊn
lad|y (L.), -ies 'leɪd|ɪ, -ɪz
ladybird, -s 'leɪdɪbɜːd, -z
lady-chapel, -s 'leɪdɪˌtʃæpl, -z
Ladyday, -s 'leɪdɪdeɪ, -z
lady-help, -s ˌleɪdɪ'help, -s
lady - in - waiting,   ladies - in - waiting
  ˌleɪdɪn'weɪtɪŋ   [-djɪn-],   ˌleɪdɪzɪn-
  'weɪtɪŋ
lady-killer, -s 'leɪdɪˌkɪlə*, -z
lady|like, -love/s, -ship/s 'leɪdɪ|laɪk,
  -lʌv/z, -ʃɪp/s
lady's-maid, -s 'leɪdɪzmeɪd, -z
Ladysmith 'leɪdɪsmɪθ
Laertes leɪ'ɜːtiːz
Laestrygones liːsˈtraɪgəniːz
Laetitia lɪ'tɪʃɪə [liːˈt-, -ʃjə, -ʃə]
Lafayette (*French   name*) ˌlɑːfaɪˈet
  (lafajet), (*in U.S.A.*) ˌlɑːfeɪˈet
Lafcadio læfˈkɑːdɪəʊ
Laffan 'læfən, lə'fæn
Laf(f)itte lɑːˈfiːt [læˈf-, lə'f-] (lafit)
lag (*s. v.*), -s, -ging, -ged, -ger/s læg,
  -z, -ɪŋ, -d, -ə*/z
lager (*beer*), -s 'lɑːgə*, -z
Lager (*English surname*) 'leɪgə*
laggard, -s 'lægəd, -z
lagoon, -s lə'guːn, -z
Lagos 'leɪgɒs
lah (*note in Tonic Sol-fa*), -s lɑː, -z
Lahore lə'hɔː* [lɑːˈh-, -'hɔə*]
laic, -al 'leɪk, -l
laid (*from* lay) leɪd
Laidlaw 'leɪdlɔː
lain (*from* lie) leɪn
Laing læŋ, leɪŋ
lair, -s leə*, -z
laird (L.), -s, -ship leəd, -z; -ʃɪp
laissez-faire ˌleɪseɪ'feə* (lɛsefɛːr)
laity 'leɪətɪ ['leɪtɪ]
Laius 'laɪəs ['leɪəs]
lake (L.), -s leɪk, -s
Lakeland 'leɪklænd [-lənd]
lakeside (L.) 'leɪksaɪd
lakh, -s lɑːk [læk] (*Hindi* lakh)
lak|y, -ier, -iest 'leɪk|ɪ, -ɪə*, -ɪɪst
Lalage 'læləgɪ [-gɪ, -ədʒɪ]
L'Allegro læ'leɪgrəʊ [-'leg-]
lam, -s, -ming, -med læm, -z, -ɪŋ, -d
lama (L.), -s 'lɑːmə, -z
lamaser|y, -ies 'lɑːməsər|ɪ ['læməs-,
  lə'mæs-], -ɪz
lamb (*s. v.*) (L.), -s, -ing, -ed læm, -z,
  -ɪŋ, -d

lambast|e, -es, -ing, -ed læm'beɪst, -s,
  -ɪŋ, -ɪd
lambda, -s 'læmdə, -z
lambdacism, -s 'læmdəsɪzəm, -z
lamben|cy, -t 'læmbən|sɪ, -t
Lambert 'læmbət
Lambeth 'læmbəθ
lambkin, -s 'læmkɪn [-mpk-], -z
lamblike 'læmlaɪk
lambrequin, -s 'læmbəkɪn [-brək-], -z
Lambretta læm'bretə
lambskin 'læmskɪn
lamb's-wool 'læmzwʊl
Lambton 'læmtən [-mpt-]
lam|e (*adj. v.*), -er, -est, -ely, -ness;
  -es, -ing, -ed leɪm, -ə*, -ɪst, -lɪ, -nɪs
  [-nəs]; -z, -ɪŋ, -d
Lamech 'leɪmek ['lɑːmek, 'lɑːmex]
lamell|a, -ae, -ar lə'mel|ə, -iː, -ə*
lament (*s. v.*), -s, -ing, -ed lə'ment, -s,
  -ɪŋ, -ɪd
lamentab|le, -ly 'læməntəb|l [-mɪn-,
  lə'mentəbl], -lɪ
lamentation, -s (L.) ˌlæmen'teɪʃn
  [-mən-, -mɪn-], -z
lamin|a, -ae, -as, -ar 'læmɪn|ə, -iː, -əz,
  -ə*
laminat|e, -es, -ing, -ed 'læmɪneɪt, -s,
  -ɪŋ, -ɪd
Lamington 'læmɪŋtən
Lammas, -tide 'læməs, -taɪd
lammergeier, -s 'læməgaɪə*, -z
Lammermoor   'læməmɔː*   [-mɔə*,
  -mʊə*, --'-]
Lamond 'læmənd
Lamont 'læmənt, (*in U.S.A.*) lə'mɒnt
lamp, -s læmp, -s
lampas (*silk material*) 'læmpəs
lampas (*swelling   in   horse's   mouth*)
  'læmpəz
lampblack 'læmpblæk [ˌlæmp'b-]
Lampet 'læmpɪt
Lampeter 'læmpɪtə*
Lampetie læm'petiː
lampion, -s 'læmpɪən [-pjən], -z
lamplight, -er/s 'læmplaɪt, -ə*/z
Lamplough 'læmpluː, -lʌf
Lamplugh 'læmpluː
lamp-oil 'læmpɔɪl
lampoon (*s. v.*), -s, -ing, -ed, -er/s
  læm'puːn, -z, -ɪŋ, -d, -ə*/z
lamp-post, -s 'læmppəʊst, -s
lamprey, -s 'læmprɪ, -z
lamp-shade, -s 'læmpʃeɪd, -z
Lampson 'læmpsn
Lanagan 'lænəgən
Lanark,   -shire   'lænək   [-nɑːk],   -ʃə*
  [-ˌʃɪə*]

Lancashire 'læŋkəʃə* [-kɪʃ-, -ˌʃɪə]
Lancaster 'læŋkəstə* [-kɪs-]
Lancasterian, -s ˌlæŋkæˈstɪərɪən
[-kəˈs-], -z
Lancastrian, -s læŋˈkæstrɪən, -z
lan|ce (s. v.) (L.), -es, -ing, -ed lɑːns,
-ɪz, -ɪŋ, -t
lance-corporal, -s ˌlɑːnsˈkɔːpərəl [ˈ-ˌ---],
-z
Lancelot 'lɑːnsəlɒt [-lət]
lancer, -s 'lɑːnsə*, -z
lancet (L.), -s 'lɑːnsɪt, -s
Lancing 'lɑːnsɪŋ
Lancs. læŋks
land (s. v.), -s, -ing, -ed lænd, -z, -ɪŋ, -ɪd
landau, -s 'lændɔː, -z
land-breeze, -s 'lændbriːz, -ɪz
Lander 'lændə*
land-force, -s 'lændfɔːs, -ɪz
landgrabb|er/s, -ing 'lændˌgræb|ə*/z,
-ɪŋ
landgrave, -s 'lændgreɪv, -z
landgravine, -s 'lændgrəviːn, -z
landholder, -s 'lændˌhəʊldə*, -z
landing (s.), -s; -net/s, -place/s,
-stage/s 'lændɪŋ, -z; -net/s, -pleɪs/ɪz,
-steɪdʒ/ɪz
landlad|y, -ies 'lænˌleɪd|ɪ [-nd,l-], -ɪz
landless 'lændlɪs [-ləs]
landlocked 'lændlɒkt
landlord, -s, -ism 'lænlɔːd [-ndl-], -z,
-ɪzəm
land-lubber, -s 'lændˌlʌbə*, -z
landmark, -s 'lændmɑːk, -s
land-mine, -s 'lændmaɪn, -z
Land|on, -or 'lænd|ən, -ɔː* [-ə*]
land-own|er/s, -ing 'lændˌəʊn|ə*/z,
-ɪŋ
landrail, -s 'lændreɪl, -z
land-rover, -s 'lændˌrəʊvə*, -z
landscape, -s 'lænskeɪp [-nds-, old-
fashioned -skɪp], -s
landscaper, -s 'lænˌskeɪpə* [-nd,s-], -z
Landseer, -s 'lænˌsɪə* [-nds-, -sjə*], -z
Land's End ˌlændzˈend
land|slide/s, -slip/s 'lænd|slaɪd/z,
-slɪp/s
lands|man, -men 'lændz|mən, -mən
land-tax, -es 'lændtæks, -ɪz
land|ward, -wind/s 'lænd|wəd, -wɪnd/z
landwehr 'lændveə*
lane (L.), -s leɪn, -z
Lanfranc 'lænfræŋk
Lang læŋ
Lang|baine, -bourne, -dale 'læŋ|beɪn,
-bɔːn [-bɔən], -deɪl
Langbarugh 'læŋbɑːf
Lang|ham, -holm 'læŋ|əm, -əm

Langhorne 'læŋhɔːn
Lang|land, -ley 'læŋ|lənd, -lɪ
Langmere 'læŋˌmɪə*
Lang|ridge, -rish(e) 'læŋg|rɪdʒ, -rɪʃ
Langside ˌlæŋˈsaɪd [ˈlæŋsaɪd]
lang-syne ˌlæŋˈsaɪn
Lang|ton, -try 'læŋ|tən, -trɪ
language, -s 'læŋgwɪdʒ, -ɪz
languid, -ly, -ness 'læŋgwɪd, -lɪ, -nɪs
[-nəs]
languish (L.), -es, -ing/ly, -ed, -ment
'læŋgwɪʃ, -ɪz, -ɪŋ/lɪ, -t, -mənt
languor, -ous 'læŋgə*, -rəs
Lanigan 'lænɪgən
lank, -er, -est, -ly, -ness læŋk, -ə*, -ɪst,
-lɪ, -nɪs [-nəs]
Lankester 'læŋkɪstə* [-kəs-]
lank|y, -ier, -iest, -ily, -iness 'læŋk|ɪ,
-ɪə* [-jə*], -ɪɪst [-jɪst], -ɪlɪ [-əlɪ],
-ɪnɪs [-ɪnəs]
lanoline 'lænəʊlɪn [-liːn]
Lansbury 'lænzbərɪ
Lansdown(e) 'lænzdaʊn
Lansing (in U.S.A.) 'lænsɪŋ
lantern, -s 'læntən, -z
lanyard, -s 'lænjəd [-jɑːd], -z
Laocoön leɪˈɒkəʊɒn [-əʊən]
Laodamia ˌleɪəʊdəˈmaɪə
Laodicea, -n/s ˌleɪəʊdɪˈsɪə, -n/z
Laois (formerly Laoighis) liːʃ
Laoise (formerly Laoighise) 'liːʃə
Laomedon leɪˈɒmɪdən
Laos 'lɑːɒs [laʊs, laʊz]
Laotian 'lɑːɒʃn ['laʊʃɪən, leɪˈəʊʃn]
Lao-tsze ˌlɑːəʊˈtseɪ [ˌlaʊ-, -ˈtsiː]
lap (s. v.), -s, -ping, -ped, -per/s læp, -s,
-ɪŋ, -t, -ə*/z
La Paz lɑːˈpæz (laˈpas)
lap-dog, -s 'læpdɒg, -z
lapel, -s ləˈpel [læˈpel], -z
lapful, -s 'læpfʊl, -z
lapidar|y (s. adj.), -ies 'læpɪdər|ɪ, -ɪz
lapis lazuli ˌlæpɪsˈlæzjʊlaɪ
Lapithae 'læpɪθiː
Lapland 'læplænd
Laplander, -s 'læplændə* [-lən-], -z
Lapp, -s, -ish læp, -s, -ɪʃ
lappet, -s, -ed 'læpɪt, -s, -ɪd
laps|e (s. v.), -es, -ing, -ed læps, -ɪz, -ɪŋ,
-t
lapsus linguae ˌlæpsəsˈlɪŋgwaɪ [old-
fashioned -gwiː]
Laput|a, -an/s ləˈpjuːt|ə, -ən/z
lapwing, -s 'læpwɪŋ, -z
lar, lares lɑː*, 'leərɪz ['lɑːreɪz]
Larbert 'lɑːbət
larboard 'lɑːbəd [-bɔːd, -bəəd]
larcenous, -ly 'lɑːsənəs [-sɪn-, -sn̩-], -lɪ

289

larcen|y, -ies 'lɑːsən|ɪ [-sn|ɪ, -sn̩|ɪ], -ɪz
larch, -es lɑːtʃ, -ɪz
lard (s. v.), -s, -ing, -ed lɑːd, -z, -ɪŋ, -ɪd
larder, -s 'lɑːdə*, -z
lares 'leəriːz ['lɑːreɪz]
largactil lɑːˈgæktɪl
large, -r, -st, -ly, -ness lɑːdʒ, -ə*, -ɪst, -lɪ, -nɪs [-nəs]
large-hearted, -ness ˌlɑːdʒˈhɑːtɪd ['-ˌ--], -nɪs [-nəs]
large-minded, -ness ˌlɑːdʒˈmaɪndɪd ['-ˌ--], -nɪs [-nəs]
Largen 'lɑːdʒən
largess(e), -es lɑːˈdʒes [-ˈʒes, 'lɑː-, -dʒɪs], -ɪz
larghetto (s. adv.), -s lɑːˈgetəʊ, -z
largish 'lɑːdʒɪʃ
largo (s. adv.), -s 'lɑːgəʊ, -z
lariat (s. v.), -s, -ing, -ed 'læriət, -s, -ɪŋ, -ɪd
lark (s. v.), -s, -ing, -ed lɑːk, -s, -ɪŋ, -t
Larkin, -s 'lɑːkɪn, -z
larkspur, -s 'lɑːkspɜː* [-spə*], -z
lark|y, -ier, -iest, -iness 'lɑːk|ɪ, -ɪə* [-jə*], -ɪɪst [-jɪst], -ɪnɪs [-nəs]
Larmor 'lɑːmɔː*
larrikin, -s 'lærɪkɪn, -z
Lars Porsena ˌlɑːzˈpɔːsɪnə
larum, -s 'lærəm, -z
larv|a, -ae, -al 'lɑːv|ə, -iː, -l
laryngal ləˈrɪŋgl [læ'r-, leə'r-]
laryngeal ˌlærɪnˈdʒiːəl [ˌleərɪnˈdʒ-, -ˈdʒɪəl, ləˈrɪndʒɪəl, ləˈrɪndʒjəl]
laryngectom|y, -ies ˌlærɪnˈdʒektəm|ɪ [ˌleər-, -ŋˈgek-], -ɪz
laryngitis ˌlærɪnˈdʒaɪtɪs [ˌleər-]
laryngolog|ist/s, -y ˌlærɪŋˈgɒlədʒ|ɪst/s [ˌleər-], -ɪ
laryngoscope, -s ləˈrɪŋgəskəʊp [læ'r-, leə'r-, 'lærɪŋg-, 'leərɪŋg-], -s
laryngoscopic ləˌrɪŋgəˈskɒpɪk [læˌr-, leəˌr-, ˌlærɪŋg-, ˌleərɪŋg-]
laryngoscop|ist/s, -y ˌlærɪŋˈgɒskəp|-ɪst/s [ˌleər-], -ɪ
larynx, -es 'lærɪŋks ['leər-], -ɪz
Lascar, -s 'læskə*, -z
Lascelles 'læslz
lascivious, -ly, -ness ləˈsɪvɪəs [-vjəs], -lɪ, -nɪs [-nəs]
laser, -s leɪzə*, -z
lash (s. v.), -es, -ing/s, -ed, -er/s læʃ, -ɪz, -ɪŋ/z, -t, -ə*/z
Lasham (in Hampshire) 'læʃəm (locally 'læsəm)
Las Palmas ˌlæsˈpælməs
lass, -es læs, -ɪz
Lassell læˈsel [ləˈs-]
lassie, -s 'læsɪ, -z

lassitude 'læsɪtjuːd
lasso (s.), -s læˈsuː [ləˈs-, 'læsəʊ], -z
lass|o (v.), -oes, -oing, -oed læ's|uː [ləˈs-], -uːz, -uːɪŋ [-ʊɪŋ], -uːd ['læs|əʊ, -əʊz, -əʊɪŋ, -əʊd]
last (s. adj. v.), -s, -ly, -ing/ly, -ed lɑːst, -s, -lɪ, -ɪŋ/lɪ, -ɪd
Las Vegas ˌlæsˈveɪgəs [ˌlɑːs-]
Latakia ˌlætəˈkɪə [-ˈkiːə]
latch (s. v.), -es, -ing, -ed lætʃ, -ɪz, -ɪŋ, -t
latchet, -s 'lætʃɪt, -s
latchkey, -s 'lætʃkiː, -z
late, -r, -st, -ly, -ness leɪt, -ə*, -ɪst, -lɪ, -nɪs [-nəs]
lateen ləˈtiːn
laten|cy, -t/ly 'leɪtən|sɪ, -t/lɪ
later|al (s. v.), -als, -ally 'lætər|əl, -əlz, -əlɪ
Lateran 'lætərən
latex 'leɪteks
lath, -s lɑːθ, -s [lɑːðz]
Latham 'leɪθəm, 'leɪðəm
    Note.—Generally 'leɪθəm in S. of England; always 'leɪðəm in N.
Lathbury 'læθbərɪ
lathe, -s leɪð, -z
lather (s. v.), -s, -ing, -ed 'lɑːðə* ['læð-], -z, -rɪŋ, -d
Lathom 'leɪθəm, 'leɪðəm
Lathrop 'leɪθrəp
lathy 'lɑːθɪ
Latimer 'lætɪmə*
Latin, -ate 'lætɪn, -eɪt
latini|sm/s, -st/s 'lætɪnɪ|zəm/z, -st/s
latinity ləˈtɪnətɪ [læ't-, -ɪtɪ]
latiniz|e [-is|e], -es, -ing, -ed 'lætɪnaɪz, -ɪz, -ɪŋ, -d
Latinus ləˈtaɪnəs
latish 'leɪtɪʃ
latitude, -s 'lætɪtjuːd, -z
latitudinal ˌlætɪˈtjuːdɪnl
latitudinarian, -s, -ism ˌlætɪtjuːdɪˈneərɪən, -z, -ɪzəm
Latium 'leɪʃjəm [-ʃəm]
latria ləˈtraɪə
latrine, -s ləˈtriːn, -z
latter, -ly 'lætə*, -lɪ
lattice, -s, -d 'lætɪs, -ɪz, -t
lattice-work 'lætɪswɜːk
Latvia, -n/s 'lætvɪə [-vjə], -n/z
laud (s. v.) (L.), -s, -ing, -ed lɔːd, -z, -ɪŋ, -ɪd
laudab|le, -ly, -leness 'lɔːdəb|l, -lɪ, -lnɪs [-nəs]
laudanum 'lɔːdənəm ['lɒd-, -dn-]
laudatory 'lɔːdətərɪ
Lauder, -dale 'lɔːdə*, -deɪl

laugh (*s. v.*), **-s, -ing/ly, -ed, -er/s** lɑːf, -s, -ɪŋ/lɪ, -t, -ə*/z

laughab|le, -ly, -leness 'lɑːfəb|l, -lɪ, -lnɪs [-nəs]

laughing-gas 'lɑːfɪŋgæs [ˌ-ˈ-]

laughing-stock, -s 'lɑːfɪŋstɒk, -s

Laughland 'lɒklənd [*in Scotland* 'lɔxlənd]

Laughlin 'lɒklɪn ['lɒxlɪn], 'lɒflɪn, 'lɑːflɪn

laughter 'lɑːftə*

Laughton 'lɔːtn

launce, -s lɑːns, -ɪz

Launce lɑːns, lɔːns

Launcelot 'lɑːnsəlɒt ['lɔːns-, -lət]

Launceston (*in Cornwall*) 'lɔːnstən [*locally* 'lɑːn-], (*in Tasmania*) 'lɔːnsəstən [*locally* 'lɒnsəstn]

launch (*s. v.*), **-es, -ing, -ed** lɔːntʃ [*rarely* lɑːntʃ], -ɪz, -ɪŋ, -t

laund|er, -ers, -ering, -ered 'lɔːnd|ə* [*rarely* 'lɑːn-], -əz, -ərɪŋ, -əd

laundress, -es 'lɔːndrɪs [*rarely* 'lɑːn-, -dres], -ɪz

laund(e)ret(te), -s ˌlɔːndəˈret [lɔːnˈdret], -s

laundr|y, -ies 'lɔːndr|ɪ [*rarely* 'lɑːn-], -ɪz

laundry-|maid/s, -man, -men 'lɔːndrɪ|-meɪd/z [*rarely* 'lɑːn-], -mən [-mæn], -mən [-men]

Laundy 'lɔːndɪ

Laura 'lɔːrə

laureate (*s. adj.*), **-s, -ship/s** 'lɔːrɪət ['lɒr-, -rɪɪt], -s, -ʃɪp/s

laureat|e (*v.*), **-es, -ing, -ed** 'lɔːrɪeɪt ['lɒr-], -s, -ɪŋ, -ɪd

laurel, -s, -led 'lɒrəl, -z, -d

Laurence 'lɒrəns

Laurie 'lɔːrɪ, 'lɒrɪ

Laurier (*English name*) 'lɒrɪə*, (*Canadian*) 'lɒrɪeɪ, 'lɒrɪə*

Lauriston 'lɒrɪstən

laurustinus, -es ˌlɒrəˈstaɪnəs, -ɪz

Lausanne ləʊˈzæn (lɔzan, lozan)

Lauterbrunnen 'laʊtəbrʊnən

lava 'lɑːvə

lavabo, -s (*ritual*) ləˈveɪbəʊ, (*basin*) ləˈveɪbəʊ ['lævəbəʊ], -z

lavage, -s læˈvɑːʒ [lə-, -ɑːdʒ], -ɪz

Lavater lɑːˈvɑːtə* ['lɑːvɑːtə*]

lavator|y, -ies 'lævətər|ɪ, -ɪz

lav|e, -es, -ing, -ed leɪv, -z, -ɪŋ, -d

lavender 'lævəndə* [-vɪn-]

Lavengro ləˈveŋgrəʊ

laver (L.), **-s** 'leɪvə* [*river* 'lɑːvə*], -z

Lavery 'leɪvərɪ, 'læv-

Lavington 'lævɪŋtən

Lavinia, -n ləˈvɪnɪə [-njə], -n

lavish (*adj. v.*), **-ly, -ness; -es, -ing, -ed** 'lævɪʃ, -lɪ, -nɪs [-nəs]; -ɪz, -ɪŋ, -t

law (L.), **-s** lɔː, -z

law|-abiding, -book/s 'lɔː|əˌbaɪdɪŋ, -bʊk/s

law-break|er/s, -ing 'lɔːˌbreɪk|ə*/z, -ɪŋ

Law|es, -ford lɔː|z, -fəd

law|ful, -fully, -fulness 'lɔː|fʊl, -fʊlɪ [-fəlɪ], -fʊlnɪs [-nəs]

law-giv|er/s, -ing 'lɔːˌgɪv|ə*/z, -ɪŋ

lawks lɔːks

lawless (L.), **-ly, -ness** 'lɔːlɪs [-ləs], -lɪ, -nɪs [-nəs]

law|-list/s, -lord/s 'lɔː|lɪst/s, -lɔːd/z

law-mak|er/s, -ing 'lɔːˌmeɪk|ə*/z, -ɪŋ

lawn, -s lɔːn, -z

lawn-mower, -s 'lɔːnˌməʊə*, -z

lawn-tennis ˌlɔːnˈtenɪs

Lawr|ance, -ence 'lɒr|əns [*rarely* 'lɔːr-], -əns

Lawrenson 'lɒrənsn

Lawrenson 'lɒrənsn

Lawrentian ləˈrenʃɪən, [lɒˈr-, -ʃjən, -ʃn]

law-suit, -s 'lɔːsuːt [-sjuːt], -s

Lawton 'lɔːtn

lawyer, -s 'lɔːjə* ['lɔɪə*], -z

lax, -er, -est, -ly, -ness læks, -ə*, -ɪst, -lɪ, -nɪs [-nəs]

laxative (*s. adj.*), **-s** 'læksətɪv, -z

laxity 'læksətɪ [-ɪtɪ]

lay (*s. adj. v.*), **-s, -ing, laid** leɪ, -z, -ɪŋ, leɪd

layabout, -s 'leɪəˌbaʊt, -s

Layamon 'laɪəmən [-mɒn] (*Middle English* 'lɑːjəmɒn)

Layard leəd

lay-brother, -s 'leɪˌbrʌðə* [ˌ-ˈ--], -z

lay-by, -s 'leɪbaɪ, -z

Laycock 'leɪkɒk

layer (*s.*), **-s** 'leə*, -z,

layer (*v.*), **-s, -ing, -ed** 'leə*, -z, -rɪŋ, -d

layette, -s leɪ'et, -s

lay-figure, -s ˌleɪˈfɪɡə*, -z

lay|man, -men 'leɪ|mən, -mən

lay-out, -s 'leɪaʊt, -s

lay-reader, -s ˌleɪˈriːdə* [ˈ-ˌ--], -z

Layton 'leɪtn

lazar, -s 'læzə*, -z

lazaretto, -s ˌlæzəˈretəʊ, -z

Lazarus 'læzərəs

laz|e, -es, -ing, -ed leɪz, -ɪz, -ɪŋ, -d

Lazenby 'leɪznbɪ

lazuli, -ite 'læzjʊl|aɪ, -aɪt

laz|y, -ier, -iest, -ily, -iness 'leɪz|ɪ, -ɪə* [-jə*], -ɪɪst [-jɪst], -ɪlɪ [-əlɪ], -ɪnɪs [-ɪnəs]

lazy-bones 'leɪzɪˌbəʊnz

lb., lbs., paʊnd, paʊndz
le (*note in Tonic Sol-fa*), -s liː, -z
lea (L.), -s liː, -z
leach (*s. v.*) (L.), -es, -ing, -ed liːtʃ, -ɪz, -ɪŋ, -t
Leachman 'liːtʃmən
Leacock 'liːkɒk
lead (*s. v.*) (*metal*), -s, -ing, -ed led, -z, -ɪŋ, -ɪd
lead (*s. v.*) (*to conduct, etc.*), -s, -ing, led liːd, -z, -ɪŋ, led
Lead (*surname*) liːd
leaden 'ledn
Leadenhall 'lednhɔːl
leader, -s; -ship 'liːdə*, -z; -ʃɪp
leaderette, -s ˌliːdə'ret, -s
lead-in, -s ˌliːd'ɪn ['--], -z
leading-rein, -s 'liːdɪŋreɪn, -z
leading-strings 'liːdɪŋstrɪŋz
lead-off, -s ˌliːd'ɒf [*old-fashioned* -'ɔːf], -s
lead-pencil, -s ˌled'pensl [-sɪl], -z
leads (*s.*) (*roofing*) ledz
leady (*like lead*) 'ledɪ
lea|f (*s.*), -ves liː|f, -vz
leaf (*v.*), -s, -ing, -ed liːf, -s, -ɪŋ, -t
leafless 'liːflɪs [-ləs]
leaflet, -s 'liːflɪt [-lət], -s
leaf-mould 'liːfməʊld
leaf|y, -ier, -iest, -iness 'liːf|ɪ, -ɪə* [-jə*], -ɪɪst [-jɪst], -ɪnɪs [-ɪnəs]
leagu|e (*s. v.*), -es, -ing, -ed liːg, -z, -ɪŋ, -d
leaguer (L.), -s 'liːgə*, -z
Leah lɪə
Leahy 'liːhɪ ['liːɪ]
leak (*s. v.*), -s, -ing, -ed; -age/s liːk, -s, -ɪŋ, -t; -ɪdʒ/ɪz
Leake liːk
Leakey 'liːkɪ
leak|y, -ier, -iest, -iness 'liːk|ɪ, -ɪə* [-jə*], -ɪɪst [-jɪst], -ɪnɪs [-ɪnəs]
leal liːl
Leamington 'lemɪŋtən
lean (*s. adj. v.*), -er, -est, -ly, -ness; -s, -ing, -ed, leant liːn, -ə*, -ɪst, -lɪ, -nɪs [-nəs]; -z, -ɪŋ, lent [liːnd], lent
Leander liː'ændə* [lɪ'æ-]
lean-to, -s 'liːntuː [ˌ-'-], -z
leap (*s. v.*), -s, -ing, -ed, leapt liːp, -s, -ɪŋ, lept [liːpt], lept
leaper, -s 'liːpə*, -z
leap-frog (*s. v.*), -s, -ging, -ged 'liːpfrɒg, -z, -ɪŋ, -d
leap-year, -s 'liːpˌjɪə:* [-jɜ:*], -z
Lear lɪə*
learn, -s, -ing, -ed, -t, -er/s lɜːn, -z, -ɪŋ, -t [-d], -t, -ə*/z

learned (*adj.*), -ly, -ness 'lɜːnɪd, -lɪ, -nɪs [-nəs]
Learney (*in Grampian*) 'leənɪ
leas|e (*s. v.*), -es, -ing, -ed liːs, -ɪz, -ɪŋ, -t
leasehold (*s. adj.*), -s; -er/s 'liːshəʊld, -z; -ə*/z
lease-|lend (*s. v.*), -lends, -lending, -lent ˌliːs|'lend, -'lendz, -'lendɪŋ, -'lent
leash (*s. v.*), -es, -ing, -ed liːʃ, -ɪz, -ɪŋ, -t
leasing (*telling lies*) 'liːsɪŋ
least, -ways, -wise liːst, -weɪz, -waɪz
leat, -s liːt, -s
Leatham 'liːθəm
Leathart 'liːθɑːt
leather (*s. v.*), -s, -ing, -ed 'leðə*, -z, -rɪŋ, -d
leatherette, ˌleðə'ret
Leatherhead 'leðəhed
leathern 'leðən
leath|ery, -eriness 'leð|ərɪ, -ərɪnɪs [-nəs]
Leathes liːðz
leave (*s.*), -s liːv, -z [*formerly, in the army also* liːf, -s]
leav|e (*v.*), -es, -ing/s, left liːv, -z, -ɪŋ/z, left
leaved liːvd
leav|en, -ens, -ening, -ened 'lev|n, -nz, -nɪŋ [-nɪŋ], -nd
Leavenworth 'levnwɜːθ [-wəθ]
leaves (*plur. of leaf*) liːvz
Leavis 'liːvɪs
Leavitt 'levɪt
Lebanese ˌlebə'niːz
Lebanon 'lebənən
Le Beau lə'bəʊ
Leburn 'liːbɜːn
lecher, -s 'letʃə*, -z
lecherous, -ly, -ness 'letʃərəs, -lɪ, -nɪs [-nəs]
lechery 'letʃərɪ
Lechlade 'letʃleɪd
Lechmere 'leʃˌmɪə*, 'letʃ-
Leckhampton 'lekˌhæmptən
Lecky 'lekɪ
Leconfield 'lekənfiːld
lectern, -s 'lektən [-tɜːn], -z
lection, -s 'lekʃn, -z
lectionar|y, -ies 'lekʃnər|ɪ [-ʃənər-, -ʃnər-], -ɪz
lector, -s 'lektɔː*, -z
lect|ure (*s. v.*), -ures, -uring, -ured, -urer/s; -ureship/s 'lektʃ|ə*, -əz, -ərɪŋ, -əd, -ərə*/z; -əʃɪp/s
led (*from lead* liːd) led
Leda 'liːdə
Ledbury 'ledbərɪ
ledge, -s ledʒ, -ɪz
ledger, -s 'ledʒə*, -z
ledger-line, -s 'ledʒəlaɪn, -z

Ledi 'ledɪ
Lediard 'ledɪəd [-dɪɑːd, -djəd]
Ledward 'ledwəd
Ledyard 'ledjəd
lee (L.), -s liː, -z
leech (L.), -es liːtʃ, -ɪz
Leeds liːdz
leek (L.), -s liːk, -s
leer (s. v.), -s, -ing/ly, -ed lɪə*, -z, -rɪŋ/lɪ, -d
Lees liːz
leet, -s liːt, -s
leeward 'liːwəd [nautical pronunciation 'luːəd, lʊəd, 'ljuːəd, ljʊəd]
Leeward (Islands) 'liːwəd
leeway 'liːweɪ
Lefanu (Le Fanu) 'lefənjuː [-fæn-], lə'fɑːnuː
Lefevre lə'fiːvə*, lə'feɪvə*, lə'fɛːvrə (as in French)
Note.—lə'fiːvə* in Sterne's 'Sentimental Journey'.
Lefroy lə'frɔɪ
left left
left-hand (adj.) 'lefthænd [ˌ-'-]
left-hand|ed, -edness, -er/s ˌleft-'hænd|ɪd, -ɪdnɪs [-nəs], -ə*/z
leftist, -s 'leftɪst, -s
left-off, -s ˌleft'ɒf [old-fashioned -'ɔːf, also '-- when attributive], -s
leftward, -s 'leftwəd, -z
leg (s. v.), -s, -ging, -ged leg, -z, -ɪŋ, -d
legac|y, -ies 'legəs|ɪ, -ɪz
leg|al, -ally 'liːg|l, -əlɪ
legalese ˌliːgə'liːz [-gl'iː-]
legali|sm, -st/s 'liːgəlɪ|zəm [-glɪ-], -st/s
legality liː'gælətɪ [lɪ'g-, -ɪtɪ]
legalization [-isa-] ˌliːgəlaɪ'zeɪʃn [-glaɪ-]
legaliz|e [-is|e], -es, -ing, -ed 'liːgəlaɪz [-glaɪz], -ɪz, -ɪŋ, -d
legate, -s 'legɪt [-gət, -geɪt], -s
legatee, -s ˌlegə'tiː, -z
legatine 'legətaɪn
legation, -s lɪ'geɪʃn [le'g-], -z
legatissimo ˌlegɑː'tɪsɪməʊ [-gə't-]
legato lə'gɑːtəʊ [lɪ'g-]
leg-bail, -s ˌleg'beɪl ['-- when in contrast with off-bail], -z
leg-bye, -s ˌleg'baɪ ['-- when in contrast with off-bye], -z
legend, -s 'ledʒənd, -z
legendary 'ledʒəndərɪ [-dʒɪn-]
Leger 'ledʒə*, see also St. Leger
legerdemain ˌledʒədə'meɪn
Leggatt 'legət
Legge leg
-legged -legd [-'legɪd]
Leggett, -er 'legɪt [-ət], -ə*

legging, -s 'legɪŋ, -z
leggy 'legɪ
Legh liː
leghorn (fowl), -s le'gɔːn [lɪ'g-, lə'g-], -z
leghorn (straw hat), -s 'leghɔːn [le'gɔːn, lɪ'gɔːn, lə'gɔːn], -z
Leghorn (place) ˌleg'hɔːn [also '-- according to sentence-stress]
legibility ˌledʒɪ'bɪlətɪ [-dʒə'b-, -lɪt-]
legib|le, -ly, -leness 'ledʒəb|l [-dʒɪb-], -lɪ, -lnɪs [-nəs]
legion (L.), -s 'liːdʒən, -z
legionar|y (s. adj.), -ies 'liːdʒənər|ɪ [-dʒnə-], -ɪz
legislat|e, -es, -ing, -ed, -or/s 'ledʒɪs-leɪt, -s, -ɪŋ, -ɪd, -ə*/z
legislation ˌledʒɪs'leɪʃn
legislative 'ledʒɪslətɪv [-leɪt-]
legislature, -s 'ledʒɪsleɪtʃə* [-lətʃə*, -ˌtjʊə*, -ˌtʃʊə*], -z
legist, -s 'liːdʒɪst, -s
legitimacy lɪ'dʒɪtɪməsɪ [lə-, -təm-]
legitimate (adj.), -ly, -ness lɪ'dʒɪtɪmət [lə-, -təm-, -mɪt], -lɪ, -nɪs [-nəs]
legitimat|e (v.), -es, -ing, -ed lɪ'dʒɪtɪ-meɪt [lə-, -təm-], -s, -ɪŋ, -ɪd
legitimation lɪˌdʒɪtɪ'meɪʃn [lə-, -tə'm-]
legitimatiz|e [-is|e], -es, -ing, -ed lɪ'dʒɪtɪmətaɪz [lə-, -təm-, -ɪz, -ɪŋ, -d
legitimist, -s lɪ'dʒɪtɪmɪst [lə-, -təm-], -s
legitimiz|e [-is|e], -es, -ing, -ed lɪ'dʒɪtɪ-maɪz [lə-, -təm-, -ɪz, -ɪŋ, -d
leg-pull, -s, -ing, -ed 'legpʊl, -z, -ɪŋ, -d
Legros (English surname) lə'grəʊ
legume, -s 'legjuːm, -z
leguminous le'gjuːmɪnəs [lɪ'g-]
Le Havre lə'hɑːvrə (lə ɑːvr)
Lehigh 'liːhaɪ
Lehmann 'leɪmən
lei 'leɪiː
Leicester, -shire 'lestə*, -ʃə* [-ˌʃɪə*]
Leics. (always said in full) 'lestəʃə* [-ˌʃɪə*]
Leiden (Dutch city) 'laɪdn ['leɪdn]
Leigh (surname) liː
Leigh (place-name) liː, laɪ
Note.—The places in Essex and Greater Manchester are liː; those in Surrey, Kent and Dorset are laɪ.
Leighton 'leɪtn
Leila 'liːlə
Leinster (Irish province) 'lenstə*, (Duke of) 'lɪnstə*, (square in London) 'lenstə*
Leipzig 'laɪpzɪg ('laiptsiç)
Leishman 'liːʃmən, 'lɪʃ-
leister, -s 'liːstə*, -z
Leister 'lestə*

293

Leiston (in Suffolk) 'leɪstən
leisure, -d, -ly, -liness 'leʒə*, -d, -lɪ,
-lɪnɪs [-nəs]
Leitch liːtʃ
Leith liːθ
leitmotif, -s 'laɪtməʊˌtiːf [ˌ-ˈ-], -s
Leitrim 'liːtrɪm
Leix (Irish county) liːʃ
Le Lacheur lə'læʃə*
Leland 'liːlənd
Lelean lə'liːn
Lely (portraitist) 'liːlɪ ['lɪlɪ]
leman, -s 'lemən, -z
Leman (lake) 'lemən ['liːmən, lɪ'mæn,
lə'mæn, lə'mãː]], (surname) 'lemən,
'liːmən, (street in London) 'lemən
[formerly lɪ'mæn]
Le Marchant lə'mɑːtʃənt
Lemare lə'meə*
Le May lə'meɪ
Lemberg 'lembɜːg
Lemesurier lə'meʒərə*
lemma, -s 'lemə, -z
lemming, -s 'lemɪŋ, -z
Lemnos 'lemnɒs
Lemoine lə'mɔɪn
lemon (L.), -s 'lemən, -z
lemonade, -s ˌlemə'neɪd, -z
lemon-coloured 'lemənˌkʌləd
lemon-drop, -s 'leməndrɒp, -s
lemon-juice 'leməndʒuːs
lemon-squash, -es ˌlemən'skwɒʃ, -ɪz
lemon-squeezer, -s 'lemənˌskwiːzə*, -z
lemon-yellow ˌlemən'jeləʊ
Lemuel 'lemjʊəl [-jʊel]
lemur, -s 'liːmə*, -z
Lena (personal name) 'liːnə, (Siberian
river) 'lenə ('ljenə)
lend, -s, -ing, lent, lender/s lend, -z,
-ɪŋ, lent, 'lendə*/z
lending-librar|y, -ies 'lendɪŋˌlaɪbrər|ɪ
[-brr|-], -ɪz
Le Neve lə'niːv
length, -s leŋθ [-ŋkθ], -s
length|en, -ens, -ening, -ened 'leŋθ|ən
[-ŋkθ-], -ənz, -ənɪŋ [-ŋɪŋ, -nɪŋ], -ənd
length|ways, -wise 'leŋθ|weɪz [-ŋkθ-],
-waɪz
length|y, -ier, -iest, -ily, -iness 'leŋθ|ɪ
[-ŋkθ-], -ɪə* [-jə*], -ɪɪst [-jɪst], -ɪlɪ
[-əlɪ], -ɪnɪs [-nəs]
lenien|ce, -cy, -t/ly 'liːnjən|s [-nɪən-],
-sɪ, -t/lɪ
Lenin 'lenɪn ['lemɪn] ('ljenjin)
Leningrad 'lenɪngræd [-grɑːd] (ljinjin-
'grat)
lenis, lenes 'liːnɪs ['lemɪs, 'lenɪs],
'liːneɪz ['lemeɪz, 'leniːz]

lenitive (s. adj.), -s 'lenɪtɪv, -z
lenity 'lenətɪ ['liːn-, -ɪtɪ]
Lennox 'lenəks
leno (L.) 'liːnəʊ
Lenoir (surname) lə'nwɑː*, (town in
U.S.A.) lə'nɔː:*
Lenore lə'nɔː:* [lɪ'n-, -'nɔə*]
Lenox 'lenəks
lens, -es lenz, -ɪz
lent (from lend) lent
Lent, -en lent, -ən
Lenthall (surname) 'lentɔːl, (place in
Yorkshire) 'lenθɔːl [-θəl]
lenticular len'tɪkjʊlə*
lentil, -s 'lentɪl [-tl], -z
lento 'lentəʊ
Lentulus 'lentjʊləs
Leo (constellation, name of popes)
'liːəʊ ['lɪəʊ]
Leofric 'leɪəʊfrɪk
Leominster 'lemstə* ['lemɪnstə*]
Leon 'liːən [lɪən]
Léon (as English name) 'leɪɒn ['leɪən]
Leonard, -s 'lenəd, -z
Leonardo, -s ˌliːəʊ'nɑːdəʊ [ˌlɪəʊ-], -z
Leonid, -s 'liːəʊnɪd ['lɪəʊ-], -z
Leonidas liː'ɒnɪdæs [lɪ'ɒ-]
leonine 'liːəʊnaɪn ['lɪəʊ-]
Leonora ˌliːə'nɔːrə [ˌlɪə-, ljə-]
Leontes liː'ɒntiːz [lɪ'ɒ-]
leopard,-s;-ess/es 'lepəd, -z; -ɪs[-es]/ɪz
Leopold 'lɪəpəʊld
leotard, -s 'liːəʊtɑːd ['lɪəʊ-], -z
Lepanto lɪ'pæntəʊ
Le Patourel lə'pætʊrəl [-tər-]
Lepel lə'pel
leper, -s 'lepə*, -z
lepidoptera ˌlepɪ'dɒptərə
Lepidus 'lepɪdəs
Le Play lə'pleɪ
Le Poer lə'pɔː:* [-'pɔə*, -'pʊə*]
Lepontine lɪ'pɒntaɪn [le'p-]
Leporis 'lepərɪs
leprechaun, -s 'leprəkɔːn [-prɪkɔːn,
-prəhɔːn, -prɪhɔːn], -z
leprosy 'leprəsɪ
leprous, -ly, -ness 'leprəs, -lɪ, -nɪs
[-nəs]
Lepsius 'lepsɪəs [-sjəs]
lept|on, -a 'lept|ɒn [-t|ən], -ə
Lepus (constellation) 'liːpəs ['lep-]
Le Queux lə'kjuː
Lereculey ˌlerɪ'kjuːlɪ
Lermontoff 'leəmɒntɒf ['leəməntəf]
('ljerməntəf)
Lerwick 'lɜː:wɪk [locally 'lerwɪk]
Lesbia, -n 'lezbɪə [-bjə], -n
Lesbos 'lezbɒs

294

Le Seelleur ləˈseɪlə*
lèse-majesté ˌleɪzˈmæʒesteɪ [-ˈmædʒ-, -ʒɪs-, -ʒəs-] (lɛːzmaʒeste)
lese-majesty ˌliːzˈmædʒɪstɪ [-dʒəs-]
lesion, -s ˈliːʒn, -z
Leslie, -ley ˈlezlɪ, in U.S.A. ˈleslɪ
Lesmahagow ˌlesməˈheɪgəʊ
Lesotho ləˈsuːtuː [-ˈsəʊ-, -təʊ]
less, -er les, -ə*
lessee, -s leˈsiː [ˌleˈsiː], -z
less|en, -ens, -ening, -ened ˈles|n, -nz, -nɪŋ [-nɪŋ], -nd
Lesseps leˈseps [ˈleseps]
Lessing ˈlesɪŋ
lesson, -s ˈlesn, -z
lessor, -s leˈsɔː* [ˌleˈsɔː*, ˈ--], -z
lest lest
Lestrade leˈstreɪd, -ˈstrɑːd
L'Estrange ləˈstreɪndʒ [leˈs-]
let (s. v.), **-s, -ting** let, -s, -ɪŋ
Letchworth ˈletʃwəθ [-wɜː:θ]
let-down, -s ˈletdaʊn [-ˈ-], -z
Lethaby ˈleθəbɪ
lethal ˈliːθl
lethargic, -al, -ally, -alness ləˈθɑːdʒɪk [lɪˈθ-, leˈθ-], -l, -əlɪ, -lnɪs [-nəs]
lethargy ˈleθədʒɪ
Lethe ˈliːθiː [-θɪ]
Letheby ˈleθəbɪ
Lethem ˈleθəm
Letitia lɪˈtɪʃə [lə-, -ʃjə, -ʃɪə]
Lett, -s let, -s
letter (s. v.), **-s, -ing, -ed** ˈletə*, -z, -rɪŋ, -d
letter-balance, -s ˈletəˌbæləns, -ɪz
letter-bomb, -s ˈletəbɒm, -z
letter-box, -es ˈletəbɒks, -ɪz
letterhead, -s ˈletəhed, -z
letter-perfect ˌletəˈpɜːfɪkt
letterpress ˈletəpres
letter-weight, -s ˈletəweɪt, -s
letter-writer, -s ˈletəˌraɪtə*, -z
Lettic ˈletɪk
Lettice ˈletɪs
Lettish ˈletɪʃ
Lettonian, -s leˈtəʊnjən [-nɪən], -z
Letts lets
lettuce, -s ˈletɪs [-təs], -ɪz
Letty ˈletɪ
Leuchars (place in Scotland) ˈluːkəz [ˈljuː-, -uːxəz] (Scottish ˈluxərz), (southern surname) ˈluːʃɑːz [ˈljuː-]
leucocyte, -s ˈluːkəʊsaɪt [ˈljuː-], -s
leucopathy luːˈkɒpəθɪ [lju:-]
leucotomy luːˈkɒtəmɪ [lju:-]
Leuctra ˈljuːktrə
leukaemia luːˈkiːmɪə [ljuː-, juː-, lʊ-, lə-, -mjə]

Levant (s.) (E. Mediterranean, leather) lɪˈvænt [ləˈv-]
levant (adj.) (opp. **couchant**) ˈlevənt
levant (v.) (abscond), **-s, -ing, -ed** lɪˈvænt [ləˈv-], -s, -ɪŋ, -ɪd
levanter (L.), **-s** lɪˈvæntə* [ləˈv-], -z
Levantine ˈlevəntaɪn [-vn-, -tiːn]
levee (royal reception), **-s** ˈlevɪ [-veɪ], -z
levee (embankment), **-s** ˈlevɪ [ləˈviː], -z
lev|el (s. adj. v.), **-els, -elness; -elling, -elled, -eller/s** ˈlev|l, -lz, -lnɪs [-nəs]; -lɪŋ [-əlɪŋ], -ld, -lə*/z [-ələ*/z]
level-crossing, -s ˌlevlˈkrɒsɪŋ [old-fashioned -ˈkrɔːs-], -z
level-headed ˌlevlˈhedɪd [also ˈ--ˌ-- when attributive]
Leven (loch) ˈliːvən, (Earl of) ˈliːvən, (surname) ˈlevən, ˈliːvən
lev|er (s. v.) (L.), **-ers, -ering, -ered; -erage** ˈliːv|ə*, -əz, -ərɪŋ, -əd; -ərɪdʒ
leveret, -s ˈlevərɪt [-rət], -s
Leverett ˈlevərɪt
Leverhulme ˈliːvəhjuːm
Leverkes (surname) ˈlevəkəs
Leveson (surname) ˈlevɪsn
Leveson-Gower ˌluːsnˈgɔː* [ˌljuː-, -ˈgəʊ*]
Levett ˈlevɪt
Levey ˈliːvɪ, ˈlevɪ
Levi ˈliːvaɪ
leviable ˈlevɪəbl
leviathan (L.), **-s** lɪˈvaɪəθn [ləˈv-], -z
Levin ˈlevɪn
Levine ləˈviːn
levirate ˈliːvɪrɪt [-rət]
Levis (in Quebec) ˈlevɪ
levitat|e, -es, -ing, -ed ˈlevɪteɪt, -s, -ɪŋ, -ɪd
levitation, -s ˌlevɪˈteɪʃn, -z
Levite, -s ˈliːvaɪt, -s
levitic, -al, -ally lɪˈvɪtɪk, -l, -əlɪ
Leviticus lɪˈvɪtɪkəs [lə-]
levit|y, -ies ˈlevət|ɪ [-ɪt|ɪ], -ɪz
lev|y (s. v.), **-ies, -ying, -ied, -ier/s** ˈlev|ɪ, -ɪz, -ɪɪŋ [-jɪŋ], -ɪd, -ɪə*/z [-jə*/z]
Levy (surname) ˈliːvɪ, ˈlevɪ, (American town) ˈliːvaɪ
lewd, -er, -est, -ly, -ness ljuːd [luːd], -ə*, -ɪst, -lɪ, -nɪs [-nəs]
Lew|es, -in ˈluː|ɪs [ˈlʊɪs, ˈljuː-, ˈljʊɪs], -ɪn
lewis (L.), **-es** ˈluːɪs [ˈlʊɪs, ˈljuːɪs, ˈljʊɪs], -ɪz
Lewisham ˈluːɪʃəm [ˈlʊɪ-, ˈljuːɪ-, ˈljʊɪ-]
Lewison ˈluːɪsn [ˈlʊɪ-, ˈljuːɪ-, ˈljʊɪ-]
Lewsey ˈljuːsɪ
lexic|al, -ally ˈleksɪk|l, -əlɪ

lexicograph|er/s, -y ˌleksɪ'kɒgrəf|ə*/z, -ɪ

lexicographic, -al ˌleksɪkəʊ'græfɪk, -l

lexicon, -s 'leksɪkən, -z

Lexington 'leksɪŋtən

ley (*land under grass*) leɪ

Ley li:

Leybourne (*in Kent*) 'leɪbɔːn [-bɔən]

Leyburn (*in North Yorkshire*) 'leɪbɜːn

Leycester 'lestə*

Leyden (*old-fashioned spelling of* Leiden, *q.v.*)

Leyden jar, -s ˌleɪdn'dʒɑ:*, -z

Leyland 'leɪlənd

Leys li:z

Leyshon 'leɪʃn

Leyton 'leɪtn

Lhasa 'lɑːsə ['læs-]

Lhuyd lɔɪd

li (*Chinese measure of length*) li:

liabilit|y, -ies ˌlaɪə'bɪlət|ɪ [-lɪt-], -ɪz

liable, -ness 'laɪəbl, -nɪs [-nəs]

liaison, -s lɪ'eɪzən [-zɒn, li:'eɪzɔ̃:ŋ] (ljɛzɔ̃), -z

Note.—In military use always -zən.

liais|e, -es, -ing, -ed lɪ'eɪz, -ɪz, -ɪŋ, -d

Liam lɪəm

liana lɪ'ɑːnə

liar, -s 'laɪə*, -z

Lias 'laɪəs

Liassic laɪ'æsɪk

Libanus 'lɪbənəs

libat|e, -es, -ing, -ed laɪ'beɪt, -s, -ɪŋ, -ɪd

libation, -s laɪ'beɪʃn [lɪ'b-], -z

lib|el, -els, -elling, -elled, -eller/s 'laɪb|l, -lz, -lɪŋ [-əlɪŋ], -ld, -lə*/z [-ələ*/z]

libellous, -ly 'laɪb|əs [-bələs], -lɪ

Liber 'laɪbə*

liber|al (*s. adj.*), -als, -ally 'lɪbər|əl, -əlz, -əlɪ

liberalism 'lɪbərəlɪzəm

liberality ˌlɪbə'rælətɪ [-ɪtɪ]

liberaliz|e [-is|e], -es, -ing, -ed 'lɪbərəl-aɪz, -ɪz, -ɪŋ, -d

liberat|e, -es, -ing, -ed, -or/s 'lɪbəreɪt, -s, -ɪŋ, -ɪd, -ə*/z

liberation ˌlɪbə'reɪʃn

Liberia, -n/s laɪ'bɪərɪə, -n/z

libertin|age, -ism 'lɪbətɪn|ɪdʒ, -ɪzəm

libertine, -s 'lɪbəti:n [-tɪn, -taɪn], -z

Liberton 'lɪbətn

libert|y (L.), -ies 'lɪbət|ɪ, -ɪz

libidinous, -ly, -ness lɪ'bɪdɪnəs, -lɪ, -nɪs [-nəs]

libido lɪ'bi:dəʊ [-'baɪd-, 'lɪbɪdəʊ]

libr|a (*pound*), -ae 'laɪbr|ə, -i: ['li:br|ə, -eɪ, -aɪ]

Libra (*constellation*) 'laɪbrə ['li:b-, 'lɪb-]

librarian, -s; -ship laɪ'breərɪən, -z; -ʃɪp

librar|y, -ies 'laɪbrər|ɪ [-bṛr|ɪ], -ɪz

libration, -s laɪ'breɪʃn, -z

librettist, -s lɪ'bretɪst, -s

librett|o, -os, -i lɪ'bret|əʊ, -əʊz, -ɪ [-i:]

Libya, -n/s 'lɪbɪə [-bjə], -n/z

lice (*plur. of* louse) laɪs

licence, -s, -d 'laɪsəns, -ɪz, -t

licens|e, -es, -ing, -ed, -er/s 'laɪsəns, -ɪz, -ɪŋ, -t, -ə*/z

licensee, -s ˌlaɪsən'si:, -z

licentiate, -s laɪ'senʃɪət [lɪ's-, -ʃjət, -ʃɪt, -ʃjɪt, -ʃət], -s

licentious, -ly, -ness laɪ'senʃəs, -lɪ, -nɪs [-nəs]

lichen, -s, -ed 'laɪkən [-kɪn, -ken, 'lɪtʃɪn], -z, -d

lichenous 'laɪkənəs ['lɪtʃ-, -kɪn-]

Lichfield 'lɪtʃfi:ld

lichgate, -s 'lɪtʃgeɪt, -s

Licini|an, -us laɪ'sɪnɪ|ən [lɪ's-, nj|-], -əs

licit 'lɪsɪt

lick (*s. v.*) (L.), -s, -ing/s, -ed, -er/s lɪk, -s, -ɪŋ/z, -t, -ə*/z

licorice 'lɪkərɪs

lictor, -s 'lɪktə* [-tɔ:*], -z

lid, -s lɪd, -z

Liddell 'lɪdl, lɪ'del

Lidd|esdale, -on 'lɪd|zdeɪl, -n

Lidell lɪ'del

Lidgate (*place near Newmarket*) 'lɪdgeɪt [-gɪt]

Lido, -s 'li:dəʊ, -z

lie (*s. v.*) (*falsehood, etc.*), lies, lying/ly, lied, liar/s laɪ, laɪz, 'laɪɪŋ/lɪ, laɪd, 'laɪə*/z

lie (*v.*) (*recline, etc.*), lies, lying, lay, lain, lier/s laɪ, laɪz, 'laɪɪŋ, leɪ, leɪn, 'laɪə*/z

lie-abed, -s 'laɪəbed, -z

Liebig 'li:bɪg

Liechtenstein 'lɪktənstaɪn ['lɪx-, 'li:-]

lief, -er li:f, -ə*

liege, -s li:dʒ, -ɪz

Liège lɪ'eɪʒ (ljɛ:ʒ)

liege|man, -men 'li:dʒmæn [-mən], -men [-mən]

lien, -s lɪən ['li:ən], -z

lieu lju: [lu:]

lieutenanc|y, -ies lef'tenənsɪ [ləf-], -ɪz

Note.—Until recently, the forms with lef't-, ləf't- *were used in the Army, whereas in the Navy alternative forms with* lə't-, le't-, lu:'t- *were current.*

lieutenant, -s lef'tenənt [ləf-], -s (see note under lieutenancy)

lieutenant-colonel, -s lef‚tenənt'kə:nl [ləf-], -z

lieutenant-commander, -s lef‚tenəntkə'mɑ:ndə* [ləf't-], -z (see note under lieutenancy)

lieutenant-general, -s lef‚tenənt-'dʒenərəl [ləf-], -z

lieutenant-governor, -s lef‚tenənt-'gʌvənə* [ləf-, -vn̩ə*, -vnə*], -z

li|fe, -ves laɪ|f, -vz

life-assurance, -s 'laɪfə‚ʃʊərəns [-‚ʃɔər-, -‚ʃɔːr-], -ɪz

life|-belt/s, -blood 'laɪf|belt/s, -blʌd

life-boat, -s 'laɪfbəʊt, -s

life-buoy, -s 'laɪfbɔɪ, -z

life-estate, -s ‚laɪfɪ'steɪt ['--‚-], -s

life-giving 'laɪf‚gɪvɪŋ

life-guard, -s 'laɪfgɑːd, -z

life-interest, -s ‚laɪf'ɪntrəst [-'ɪntərest, -rɪst], -s

life-jacket, -s 'laɪf‚dʒækɪt, -s

lifeless, -ly, -ness 'laɪflɪs [-ləs], -lɪ, -nɪs [-nəs]

lifelike 'laɪflaɪk

life-line, -s 'laɪflaɪn, -z

lifelong 'laɪflɒŋ [‚-'-]

life-preserver, -s 'laɪfprɪ‚zɜːvə*, -z

life-rent, -s 'laɪfrent, -s

life-saving 'laɪf‚seɪvɪŋ

life-sentence, -s 'laɪf‚sentəns [‚-'--], -ɪz

life-size 'laɪf'saɪz [also '-- according to sentence-stress]

life-tenan|cy, -cies, -t/s ‚laɪf'tenən|sɪ, -sɪz, -t/s

lifetime, -s 'laɪftaɪm, -z

life-work, -s ‚laɪf'wɜːk ['--], -s

Liff|ey, -ord 'lɪf|ɪ, -əd

lift (s. v.), -s, -ing, -ed, -er/s lɪft, -s, -ɪŋ, -ɪd, -ə*/z

lift-boy, -s 'lɪftbɔɪ, -z

lift|-man, -men 'lɪft|mæn, -men

lift-off 'lɪftɒf [old-fashioned -ɔːf]

ligament, -s 'lɪgəmənt, -s

ligament|al, -ous ‚lɪgə'ment|l, -əs

ligature, -s, -d 'lɪgətʃə* [-‚tʃʊə*, -‚tjʊə*], -z, -d

liger, -s 'laɪgə*, -z

Ligertwood 'lɪdʒətwʊd [-dʒə:t-]

light (s. adj. v.), -s; -er, -est, -ly, -ness; -ing, -ed, lit laɪt, -s; -ə*, -ɪst, -lɪ, -nɪs [-nəs]; -ɪŋ, -ɪd, lɪt

light|en, -ens, -ening, -ened 'laɪt|n, -nz, -n̩ɪŋ [-nɪŋ], -nd

lighter, -s 'laɪtə*, -z

lighterage 'laɪtərɪdʒ

lighter|man, -men 'laɪtə|mən, -mən

light-fingered 'laɪt‚fɪŋgəd [‚-'-‚--]

lightfoot (L.) 'laɪtfʊt

light-handed 'laɪt‚hændɪd [‚-'-‚--]

light-headed, -ly, -ness ‚laɪt'hedɪd [also '-‚-- when attributive], -lɪ, -nɪs [-nəs]

light-hearted, -ly, -ness ‚laɪt'hɑːtɪd [also '-‚-- when attributive], -lɪ, -nɪs [-nəs]

light-horse|man, -men ‚laɪt'hɔːs|mən, -mən

lighthou|se, -ses 'laɪthaʊ|s, -zɪz

lighthousekeeper, -s 'laɪthaʊs‚ki:pə*, -z

lightminded, -ly, -ness ‚laɪt'maɪndɪd [also '-‚-- when attributive], -lɪ, -nɪs [-nəs]

lightning, -s 'laɪtnɪŋ, -z

lightning-conductor, -s 'laɪtnɪŋkən-‚dʌktə*, -z

lightship, -s 'laɪt-ʃɪp, -s

lightsome, -ly, -ness 'laɪtsəm, -lɪ, -nɪs [-nəs]

light-spirited ‚laɪt'spɪrɪtɪd [-'spɪrət-]

light-wave, -s 'laɪtweɪv, -z

light-weight, -s 'laɪtweɪt, -s

ligneous 'lɪgnɪəs [-njəs]

lignite 'lɪgnaɪt

lignum 'lɪgnəm

Liguria, -n/s lɪ'gjʊərɪə [-'gjɔər-, -'gjɔːr-], -n/z

likable 'laɪkəbl

lik|e (s. adj. v.), -es, -ing, -ed laɪk, -s, -ɪŋ, -t

likel|y, -ier, -iest, -iness, -ihood 'laɪkl|ɪ, -ɪə* [-jə*], -ɪɪst [-jɪst], -ɪnɪs [-ɪnəs], -ɪhʊd

likeminded ‚laɪk'maɪndɪd ['-‚--]

lik|en, -ens, -ening, -ened 'laɪk|ən, -ənz, -n̩ɪŋ [-nɪŋ, -ənɪŋ], -ənd

likeness, -es 'laɪknɪs [-nəs], -ɪz

likewise 'laɪkwaɪz

liking, -s 'laɪkɪŋ, -z

lilac, -s 'laɪlək, -s

liliaceous ‚lɪlɪ'eɪʃəs

Lilia|n, -s 'lɪlɪə|n [-ljə-], -s

Lilith 'lɪlɪθ

Lill|a, -ey 'lɪl|ə, -ɪ

Lilliput 'lɪlɪpʌt [-pʊt, -pət]

lilliputian (L.), -s ‚lɪlɪ'pju:ʃn [-ʃɪən, -ʃjən], -z

Lilly, -white 'lɪlɪ, -waɪt [-hwaɪt]

lilt (s. v.), -s, -ing, -ed lɪlt, -s, -ɪŋ, -ɪd

lil|y (L.), -ies 'lɪl|ɪ, -ɪz

lily-white ‚lɪlɪ'waɪt [-ɪ'hw-, '--- when attributive]

Lima (in Peru) 'li:mə [old-fashioned 'laɪmə] (in U.S.A.) 'laɪmə

limb, -s, -ed lɪm, -z, -d

limber (s. adj.), -s 'lɪmbə*, -z

297

limbo (**L.**) 'lɪmbəʊ
lim|e (*s. v.*), **-es, -ing, -ed** laɪm, -z, -ɪŋ, -d
Limehouse 'laɪmhaʊs
lime-juice 'laɪmdʒuːs
limekiln, **-s** 'laɪmkɪln [-kɪl], -z
lime-light, **-s** 'laɪmlaɪt, -s
limen 'laɪmen
limerick (**L.**), **-s** 'lɪmərɪk, -s
lime|stone, **-tree/s** 'laɪm|stəʊn, -triː/z
limewash (*s. v.*), **-es, -ing, -ed** 'laɪmwɒʃ, -ɪz, -ɪŋ, -t
limewater 'laɪmˌwɔːtə*
liminal 'lɪmɪnl
limit (*s. v.*), **-s, -ing, -ed/ness; -able** 'lɪmɪt, -s, -ɪŋ, -ɪd/nɪs [-nəs]; -əbl
limitation, **-s** ˌlɪmɪ'teɪʃn, -z
limitless 'lɪmɪtlɪs [-ləs]
limitrophe 'lɪmɪtrəʊf
limn, **-s, -ing, -ed, -er/s** lɪm, -z, -ɪŋ [-nɪŋ], -d, -nə*/z
Limoges lɪ'məʊʒ (limɔːʒ)
limousine, **-s** 'lɪməziːn [-mʊz-, -muːz-, ˌ--'-], -z
limp (*s. adj. v.*), **-s; -er, -est, -ly, -ness; -ing/ly, -ed** lɪmp, -s; -ə*, -ɪst, -lɪ, -nɪs [-nəs]; -ɪŋ/lɪ, -t [lɪmt]
limpet, **-s** 'lɪmpɪt, -s
limpid, **-est, -ly, -ness** 'lɪmpɪd, -ɪst, -lɪ, -nɪs [-nəs]
limpidity lɪm'pɪdətɪ [-ɪtɪ]
Limpopo lɪm'pəʊpəʊ
limy 'laɪmɪ
Linacre 'lɪnəkə*
linage, **-s** 'laɪnɪdʒ, -ɪz
linchpin, **-s** 'lɪntʃpɪn, -z
Lincoln, **-shire** 'lɪŋkən, -ʃə* [-ˌʃɪə*]
Lincs. lɪŋks
Lind lɪnd
Lindbergh 'lɪndbɜːg
linden (**L.**), **-s** 'lɪndən, -z
Lindisfarne 'lɪndɪsfɑːn
Lindley 'lɪndlɪ
Lindon 'lɪndən
Lind|say, **-sey** 'lɪnd|zɪ, -zɪ
lin|e (*s. v.*) (**L.**), **-es, -ing, -ed** laɪn, -z, -ɪŋ, -d
lineage, **-s** 'lɪnɪɪdʒ [-njɪdʒ], -ɪz
lineal, **-ly** 'lɪnɪəl [-njəl], -ɪ
lineament, **-s** 'lɪnɪəmənt [-njə-], -s
linear, **-ly** 'lɪnɪə* [-njə*], -lɪ
lineation, **-s** ˌlɪnɪ'eɪʃn, -z
line-engraving, **-s** 'laɪnɪnˌgreɪvɪŋ [-ɪŋˌg-], -z
linen, **-s** 'lɪnɪn, -z
linen-draper, **-s, -y** 'lɪnɪnˌdreɪpə*, -z, -rɪ
liner, **-s** 'laɪnə*, -z
lines|man, **-men** 'laɪnz|mən, -mən [-men]

ling (**L.**), **-s** lɪŋ, -z
Ling|ay, **-en** 'lɪŋg|ɪ, -ən
ling|er, **-ers, -ering/ly, -ered, -erer/s** 'lɪŋg|ə*, -əz, -ərɪŋ/lɪ, -əd, -ərə*/z
lingerie 'læːnʒəriː ['lænʒ-, -rɪ] (lɛ̃ʒri)
lingo, **-s** 'lɪŋgəʊ, -z
lingua franca ˌlɪŋgwə'fræŋkə
lingu|al (*s. adj.*), **-als, -ally** 'lɪŋgw|əl, -əlz, -əlɪ
linguaphone (**L.**) 'lɪŋgwəfəʊn
linguist, **-s** 'lɪŋgwɪst, -s
linguistic, **-s, -al, -ally** lɪŋ'gwɪstɪk, -s, -l, -əlɪ
linguistician, **-s** ˌlɪŋgwɪ'stɪʃn, -z
linguo-dental ˌlɪŋgwəʊ'dentl
liniment, **-s** 'lɪnɪmənt [-nəm-], -s
lining (*s.*), **-s** 'laɪnɪŋ, -z
link (*s. v.*), **-s, -ing, -ed** lɪŋk, -s, -ɪŋ, -t [lɪŋt]
Linklater 'lɪŋkˌleɪtə*
links (*s.*) lɪŋks
Linley 'lɪnlɪ
Linlithgow lɪn'lɪθgəʊ
Linlithgowshire lɪn'lɪθgəʊʃə* [-ˌʃɪə*]
Linnae|an [-ne|-], **-us** lɪ'niː|ən [-'nɪən], -əs
linnet (**L.**), **-s** 'lɪnɪt, -s
lino, **-s** 'laɪnəʊ, -z
lino-cut, **-s** 'laɪnəʊkʌt, -s
linoleum, **-s** lɪ'nəʊljəm [-lɪəm], -z
linotype, **-s** 'laɪnəʊtaɪp, -s
linseed, **-oil** 'lɪnsiːd, -'ɔɪl
linsey-woolsey 'lɪnzɪ, -'wʊlzɪ
lint lɪnt
lintel, **-s** 'lɪntl, -z
Linthwaite 'lɪnθwət
Lint|on, **-ot(t)** 'lɪnt|ən, -ɒt
lion, **-s; -ess/es** 'laɪən, -z; -es/ɪz [-ɪs/ɪz, laɪə'nes/ɪz]
Lionel 'laɪənl
Lion-heart 'laɪənhɑːt
lion-hearted 'laɪənˌhɑːtɪd
lion-hunter, **-s** 'laɪənˌhʌntə*, -z
lioniz|e [-is|e], **-es, -ing, -ed** 'laɪənaɪz, -ɪz, -ɪŋ, -d
lion-like 'laɪənlaɪk
lion-tamer, **-s** 'laɪənˌteɪmə*, -z
lip (*s. v.*), **-s, -ping, -ped** lɪp, -s, -ɪŋ, -t
Lipari 'lɪpərɪ ('liːpari)
lipogram, **-s** 'lɪpəʊgræm, -z
Lippincott 'lɪpɪŋkət [-kɒt]
lip-reading 'lɪpˌriːdɪŋ
lip-salve, **-s** 'lɪpsælv [-sɑːlv], -z
Lipscomb(e) 'lɪpskəm
lip-service 'lɪpˌsɜːvɪs
lip-stick, **-s** 'lɪpstɪk, -s
Lipton 'lɪptən

liquefaction ˌlɪkwɪˈfækʃn
lique|fy, -fies, -fying, -fied, -fier/s;
 -fiable 'lɪkwɪ|faɪ, -faɪz, -faɪɪŋ, -faɪd,
 -faɪə*/z; -faɪəbl
liqueur, -s; -glass/es lɪˈkjʊə* [-ˈkjɔə*,
 -ˈkjɔː:*, -ˈkjɜ:*], -z; -glɑ:s/ɪz
liquid (s. adj.), -s, -est, -ly, -ness
 'lɪkwɪd, -z, -ɪst, -lɪ, -nɪs [-nəs]
liquidat|e, -es, -ing, -ed, -or/s 'lɪkwɪ-
 deɪt, -s, -ɪŋ, -ɪd, -ə*/z
liquidation, -s ˌlɪkwɪˈdeɪʃn, -z
liquidity lɪˈkwɪdətɪ [-ɪtɪ]
liquor (s. v.), -s, -ing, -ed 'lɪkə*, -z, -rɪŋ,
 -d
liquorice 'lɪkərɪs
lir|a, -as, -e 'lɪər|ə, -əz, -ɪ
Lisa 'li:zə, 'laɪzə
Lisb|et, -eth 'lɪzb|ɪt [-et, -ət], -əθ [-eθ,
 -ɪθ]
Lis|bon, -burn 'lɪz|bən, -bɜ:n
Liskeard lɪsˈkɑ:d
lisle (thread) laɪl
Lisle laɪl, li:l
 Note.—Baron Lisle pronounces laɪl.
Lismore (in Scotland and Ireland)
 lɪzˈmɔ:* [-ˈmɔə*], (in Australia)
 'lɪzmɔ:* [-mɔə*]
lisp (s. v.), -s, -ing/ly, -ed, -er/s lɪsp, -s,
 -ɪŋ/lɪ, -t, -ə*/z
lissome, -ness 'lɪsəm, -nɪs [-nəs]
Lisson 'lɪsn
list (s. v.), -s, -ing, -ed lɪst, -s, -ɪŋ, -ɪd
list|en, -ens, -ening, -ened, -ener/s
 'lɪs|n, -nz, -n̩ɪŋ [-nɪŋ], -nd, -n̩ə*/z
 [-nə*/z]
Lister 'lɪstə*
listerine 'lɪstəri:n
listless, -ly, -ness 'lɪstlɪs [-ləs], -lɪ, -nɪs
 [-nəs]
Liston 'lɪstən
Listowel lɪˈstəʊəl
Liszt lɪst
lit (from light) lɪt
litan|y, -ies 'lɪtən|ɪ [-tn̩|ɪ], -ɪz
Litchfield 'lɪtʃfi:ld
literacy 'lɪtərəsɪ
liter|al, -ally, -alness 'lɪtər|əl, -əlɪ,
 -əlnɪs [-nəs]
literali|sm, -st/s 'lɪtərəlɪ|zəm, -st/s
literality ˌlɪtəˈrælətɪ [-ɪtɪ]
literar|y, -ily, -iness 'lɪtərər|ɪ [-tr̩r|ɪ],
 -əlɪ [-ɪlɪ], -ɪnɪs [-nəs]
literate (s. adj.), -s 'lɪtərət [-rɪt], -s
literati ˌlɪtəˈrɑ:ti: [old-fashioned -'reɪtaɪ]
literatim ˌlɪtəˈrɑ:tɪm [-'reɪtɪm]
literature, -s 'lɪtərətʃə* [-rɪtʃə*,
 -ˌtjʊə*], -z
litharge 'lɪθɑ:dʒ

lithe, -r, -st, -ly, -ness laɪð, -ə*, -ɪst, -lɪ,
 -nɪs [-nəs]
Litheby 'lɪðɪbɪ [-ðəb-]
lither (supple) 'lɪðə*
lithesome, -ness 'laɪðsəm, -nɪs [-nəs]
Lithgow 'lɪθgəʊ
lithia 'lɪθɪə [-θjə]
lithic 'lɪθɪk
lithium 'lɪθɪəm [-θjəm]
litho, -s 'laɪθəʊ, -z
lithochromatic, -s ˌlɪθəʊkrəʊˈmætɪk, -s
lithograph (s. v.), -s, -ing, -ed 'lɪθəʊ-
 grɑ:f [-græf], -s, -ɪŋ, -t
 Note.—In printers' usage 'laɪθ-. So
 also with derived words (lithographer, etc.).
lithographer, -s lɪˈθɒgrəfə*, -z
lithographic, -al, -ally ˌlɪθəʊˈgræfɪk,
 -l, -əlɪ
lithography lɪˈθɒgrəfɪ
lithoprint (s. v.), -s, -ing, -ed 'lɪθəʊ-
 prɪnt, -s, -ɪŋ, -ɪd
lithosphere, -s 'lɪθəʊˌsfɪə*, -z
lithotyp|e (s. v.), -es, -ing, -ed, -er/s
 'lɪθəʊtaɪp, -s, -ɪŋ, -t, -ə*/z
Lithuania, -n/s ˌlɪθjuːˈeɪnjə [-θjʊ'eɪ-,
 -θu:-, -θʊ'eɪ-, -nɪə], -n/z
litigant, -s 'lɪtɪgənt, -s
litigat|e, -es, -ing, -ed 'lɪtɪgeɪt, -s, -ɪŋ,
 -ɪd
litigation, -s ˌlɪtɪˈgeɪʃn, -z
litigious, -ly, -ness lɪˈtɪdʒəs, -lɪ, -nɪs
 [-nəs]
litmus 'lɪtməs
litotes 'laɪtəʊti:z
litre, -s 'li:tə*, -z
Littel lɪˈtel
litter (s. v.), -s, -ing, -ed 'lɪtə*, -z, -rɪŋ, -d
litt|le (L.), -ler, -lest, -leness 'lɪt|l, -lə*,
 -lɪst, -lnɪs [-nəs]
Littlechild 'lɪtltʃaɪld
little-englander, -s ˌlɪtlˈɪŋgləndə*
 [rarely -'eŋg-], -z
little-go, -es 'lɪtlgəʊ, -z
Littlehampton 'lɪtlˌhæmptən [ˌ--'--]
Littlejohn 'lɪtldʒɒn
Littler 'lɪtlə*
Littleton 'lɪtltən
Litton 'lɪtn
littoral, -s 'lɪtərəl, -z
liturgic, -al, -ally lɪˈtɜ:dʒɪk, -l, -əlɪ
liturgist, -s 'lɪtədʒɪst [-tɜ:-], -s
liturg|y, -ies 'lɪtədʒ|ɪ [-tɜ:-], -ɪz
livable 'lɪvəbl
live (adj.) laɪv
liv|e (v.), -es, -ing, -ed, -er/s lɪv, -z, -ɪŋ,
 -d, -ə*/z
live-circuit, -s ˌlaɪvˈsɜ:kɪt, -s

livelihood, -s 'laɪvlɪhʊd, -z
livelong 'lɪvlɒŋ ['laɪv-]
livel|y, -ier, -iest, -iness 'laɪvl|ɪ, -ɪə*
[-jə*], -ɪɪst [-jɪst], -ɪnɪs [-ɪnəs]
liv|en, -ens, -ening, -ened 'laɪv|n [-ən],
-nz [-ənz], -ŋɪŋ [-nɪŋ, -ənɪŋ], -nd
[-ənd]
Livens 'lɪvənz
liver, -s, -ish 'lɪvə*, -z, -rɪʃ
live-rail, -s ˌlaɪv'reɪl, -z
Livermore 'lɪvəmɔː* [-mɔə*]
Liverpool 'lɪvəpuːl
Liverpudlian (s. adj.), -s ˌlɪvə'pʌdlɪən
[-ljən], -z
liver|y, -ies, -ied 'lɪvər|ɪ, -ɪz, -ɪd
livery|man, -men 'lɪvərɪ|mən, -mən
[-men]
livery-stable, -s 'lɪvərɪˌsteɪbl, -z
lives (plur. of life) laɪvz, (from live v.)
lɪvz
Livesey 'lɪvsɪ, 'lɪvzɪ
live-stock 'laɪvstɒk
Livia 'lɪvɪə [-vjə]
livid, -est, -ly, -ness 'lɪvɪd, -ɪst, -lɪ, -nɪs
[-nəs]
lividity lɪ'vɪdətɪ [-ɪtɪ]
living (s.), -s 'lɪvɪŋ, -z
living-room, -s 'lɪvɪŋrʊm [-ruːm], -z
living-space 'lɪvɪŋspeɪs
Livingston(e) 'lɪvɪŋstən
Livonia, -n/s lɪ'vəʊnjə [-nɪə], -n/z
Livy 'lɪvɪ
lixiviat|e, -es, -ing, -ed lɪk'sɪvɪeɪt, -s,
-ɪŋ, -ɪd
Liza 'laɪzə
lizard (L.), -s 'lɪzəd, -z
Lizzie 'lɪzɪ
llama (L.), -s 'lɑːmə, -z
Llanberis læn'berɪs [θlæn-] (Welsh
ɫan'beris)
†Llandaff 'lændəf (Welsh ɫan'daːv)
Llandeilo læn'daɪləʊ [θlæn-] (Welsh
ɫan'dəilo)
Llandovery læn'dʌvərɪ [θlæn-] (Welsh
ɫan'dəvri)
Llandrindod Wells læn,drɪndɒd'welz
[θlæn-] (Welsh ɫan,drindod'wels)
Llandudno læn'dɪdnəʊ [θlæn-, -'dʌd-]
(Welsh ɫan'didno)
Llanelli læ'neθlɪ [lə'n-, θlæn-, θlə'n-]
(Welsh ɫan'eɫi)
Llanfair 'lænfeə* ['θlæn-, -nvaɪə*]
(Welsh 'ɫanvair)
Llanfairfechan ˌlænfeə'fekən [ˌθlæn-,
-nvaɪə've-, -exən] (Welsh ɫanvair-
'vexan)
Llangattock læn'gætək [θlæn-] (Welsh
ɫan'gatok)

Llangollen læn'gɒθlən [θlæn-, -'gɒθlen]
(Welsh ɫan'goɫen)
Llanrwst læn'ruːst [θlæn-] (Welsh
ɫan'ruːst)
Llanuwchllyn læ'njuːklɪn [θlæ'n-,
-uːxlɪn] (Welsh ɫan'iuxɫin)
Llewellyn (English name) luː'elɪn
[lʊ'e-] (Welsh name) luː'elɪn [θluː-,
lʊ'e-, θlʊ'e-] (Welsh ɫe'welin)
Llewelyn luː'elɪn [θluː-, lʊ'e-, θlʊ'e-]
(Welsh 'ɫwelin, ɫe'welin)
Lloyd lɔɪd
Llywelyn lə'welɪn [θlə-] (Welsh
ɫə'welin)
lo ləʊ
load (s. v.), -s, -ing, -ed ləʊd, -z, -ɪŋ, -ɪd
load-shedding 'ləʊdˌʃedɪŋ
loadstone, -s 'ləʊdstəʊn, -z
loa|f (s.), -ves ləʊ|f, -vz
loaf (v.), -s, -ing, -ed, -er/s ləʊf, -s, -ɪŋ,
-t, -ə*/z
loaf-sugar 'ləʊfˌʃʊgə*
loam ləʊm
loam|y, -ier, -iest, -iness 'ləʊm|ɪ, -ɪə*
[-jə*], -ɪɪst [-jɪst], -ɪnɪs [-ɪnəs]
loan (s. v.), -s, -ing, -ed ləʊn, -z, -ɪŋ, -d
loan-collection, -s 'ləʊnkəˌlekʃn, -z
loan-office, -s 'ləʊnˌɒfɪs, -ɪz
loanword, -s 'ləʊnwɜːd, -z
loath (adj.), -ness ləʊθ, -nɪs [-nəs]
loath|e (v.), -es, -ing/ly, -ed ləʊð, -z,
-ɪŋ/lɪ, -d
loathl|y, -iness 'ləʊðl|ɪ, -ɪnɪs [-ɪnəs]
loathsome, -ly, -ness 'ləʊðsəm ['ləʊθs-],
-lɪ, -nɪs [-nəs]
loaves (plur. of loaf) ləʊvz
lob (s. v.) (L.), -s, -bing, -bed, -ber/s
lɒb, -z, -ɪŋ, -d, -ə*/z
lobb|y (s. v.), -ies, -ying, -ied 'lɒb|ɪ, -ɪz,
-ɪɪŋ [-jɪŋ], -ɪd
lobe, -s, -d ləʊb, -z, -d
lobelia, -s ləʊ'biːljə [-lɪə], -z
lobotomy ləʊ'bɒtəmɪ
lobster, -s 'lɒbstə*, -z
lobular 'lɒbjʊlə*
lobule, -s 'lɒbjuːl, -z
loc|al, -als, -ally 'ləʊk|l, -lz, -əlɪ [-lɪ]
locale, -s ləʊ'kɑːl, -z
locali|sm, -st/s 'ləʊkəlɪ|zəm [-klɪ-],
-st/s
localit|y, -ies ləʊ'kælət|ɪ [-ɪt|ɪ], -ɪz
localization [-isa-] ˌləʊkəlaɪ'zeɪʃn
[-klaɪ'z-, -kəlɪ'z-, -klɪ'z-]
localiz|e [-is|e], -es, -ing, -ed 'ləʊkəlaɪz
[-klaɪz], -ɪz, -ɪŋ, -d
Locarno ləʊ'kɑːnəʊ [lɒ'k-] (lo'karno)
locat|e, -es, -ing, -ed ləʊ'keɪt, -s, -ɪŋ, -ɪd
location, -s ləʊ'keɪʃn, -z

locative (s. adj.), -s 'lɒkətɪv, -z
loc. cit. ˌlɒk'sɪt [ˌlɒkəʊsɪ'tɑːtəʊ, old-fashioned ˌləʊkəʊsɪ'teɪtəʊ]
loch (L.), -s lɒx [lɒx], -s
Lochaber lɒ'kɑːbə* [-'kæb-, lɒ'x-]
Lochhead 'lɒkhed [in Scotland lɒx'hɛd]
Lochiel lɒ'kiːl [lɒ'xiːl]
Lochinvar ˌlɒkɪn'vɑː* [ˌlɒxɪn-]
Lochleven lɒx'liːvən [lɒx-]
Lochnagar ˌlɒxnə'gɑː* [ˌlɒxn-]
lock (s. v.) (L.), -s, -ing, -ed lɒk, -s, -ɪŋ, -t
Locke lɒk
locker (L.), -s 'lɒkə*, -z
Lockerbie 'lɒkəbɪ
locket, -s 'lɒkɪt, -s
lockgate, -s ˌlɒk'geɪt ['--], -s
Lockhart 'lɒkət, 'lɒkhɑːt
Note.—The Bruce-Lockhart family pronounce 'lɒkət (or in the Scottish manner 'lɒkərt).
Lockie 'lɒkɪ
lock-jaw 'lɒkdʒɔː
lock-keeper, -s 'lɒkˌkiːpə*, -z
lockout, -s 'lɒkaʊt, -s
Locksley 'lɒkslɪ
locksmith, -s 'lɒksmɪθ, -s
lockstitch, -es 'lɒkstɪtʃ, -ɪz
lock-up, -s 'lɒkʌp, -s
Lock|wood, -yer 'lɒk|wʊd, -jə*
locomotion ˌləʊkə'məʊʃn
locomotive (s. adj.), -s 'ləʊkəˌməʊtɪv [ˌləʊkə'm-], -z
locomotor (s.), -s 'ləʊkəˌməʊtə*, -z
locomotor (adj.) ˌləʊkə'məʊtə* ['--,--]
locoum, -s 'ləʊkəm [-kʊm], -z
Locria, -n/s 'ləʊkrɪə, -n/z
Locris 'ləʊkrɪs
locum, -s 'ləʊkəm, -z
locum-tenens ˌləʊkəm'tiːnenz [-'ten-]
locus, loci 'ləʊkəs ['lɒkəs], 'ləʊsaɪ ['ləʊkaɪ, 'lɒkiː]
locust, -s 'ləʊkəst, -s
locution, -s ləʊ'kjuːʃn [lɒ'k-], -z
locutor|y, -ies 'lɒkjʊtər|ɪ, -ɪz
lode, -s; -star/s, -stone/s ləʊd, -z; -stɑː*/z, -stəʊn/z
lodge (s. v.) (L.), -es, -ing/s, -ed, -er/s lɒdʒ, -ɪz, -ɪŋ/z, -d, -ə*/z
lodg(e)ment, -s 'lɒdʒmənt, -s
lodging-hou|se, -ses 'lɒdʒɪŋhaʊ|s, -zɪz
Lodore ləʊ'dɔː* [-'dɔə*]
Lodovico ˌlɒdəʊ'viːkəʊ
Lodowick 'lɒdəwɪk [-dəʊɪk]
Loe luː
Loeb lɜːb [ləʊb]
loess 'ləʊɪs [lɜːs]
Loewe (English surname) 'ləʊɪ

Lofoten ləʊ'fəʊtən ['ləʊˌfəʊtən]
loft (s. v.), -s, -ing, -ed, -er/s lɒft, -s, -ɪŋ, -ɪd, -ə*/z
Lofthouse 'lɒftəs [-thaus]
Loftus 'lɒftəs
loft|y, -ier, -iest, -ily, -iness 'lɒft|ɪ, -ɪə* [-jə*], -ɪɪst [-jɪst], -ɪlɪ [-əlɪ], -ɪnɪs [-ɪnəs]
log, -s lɒg, -z
Logan (personal name) 'ləʊgən
logan (L.) (rocking-stone), -s 'lɒgən, -z
loganberr|y, -ies 'ləʊgənbər|ɪ [-ˌber-], -ɪz
logarithm, -s 'lɒgərɪðəm [-ɪθəm], -z
logarithmic, -al, -ally ˌlɒgə'rɪðmɪk [-ɪθm-], -l, -əlɪ
log-book, -s 'lɒgbʊk, -s
log-cabin, -s 'lɒgˌkæbɪn, -z
loggerhead, -s 'lɒgəhed, -z
loggia, -s 'ləʊdʒə ['lɒ-, -dʒɪə, -dʒjə], -z
logging 'lɒgɪŋ
Logia 'lɒgɪə
logic, -al, -ally 'lɒdʒɪk, -l, -əlɪ
logician, -s ləʊ'dʒɪʃn [lɒ'dʒ-], -z
Logie 'ləʊgɪ
logistic, -al, -s ləʊ'dʒɪstɪk [lɒ'dʒ-], -l, -s
logogram, -s 'lɒgəʊgræm, -z
logograph, -s 'lɒgəʊgrɑːf [-græf], -s
logomach|ist/s, -y, -ies lɒ'gɒmək|ɪst/s, -ɪ, -ɪz
logopaedic, -s ˌlɒgəʊ'piːdɪk, -s
Log|os, -oi 'lɒg|ɒs, -ɔɪ
logotype, -s 'lɒgəʊtaɪp, -s
log-roll, -s, -ing, -ed, -er/s 'lɒgrəʊl, -z, -ɪŋ, -d, -ə*/z
Logue ləʊg
log-wood 'lɒgwʊd
Lohengrin 'ləʊɪngrɪn ['ləʊən-, -ŋg-] ('loːəngriːn)
loin, -s lɔɪn, -z
loin|-cloth, -cloths 'lɔɪn|klɒθ [old-fashioned -klɔːθ], -klɒθs [-klɔːðz, -klɒːθs]
Lois 'ləʊɪs
loit|er, -ers, -ering, -ered, -erer/s 'lɔɪt|ə*, -əz, -ərɪŋ, -əd, -ərə*/z
loll, -s, -ing, -ed, -er/s lɒl, -z, -ɪŋ, -d, -ə*/z
Lollard, -s 'lɒləd [-lɑːd], -z
lollipop, -s 'lɒlɪpɒp, -s
lollop, -s, -ing, -ed 'lɒləp, -s, -ɪŋ, -t
Lomax 'ləʊmæks [-məks]
Lombard, -s 'lɒmbəd [-bɑːd, old-fashioned 'lʌmbəd], -z
Lombardic lɒm'bɑːdɪk
Lombardy 'lɒmbədɪ [old-fashioned 'lʌm-]
Lomond 'ləʊmənd

Londesborough 'lɒnzbərə
London, -er/s, -ism/s 'lʌndən, -ə*/z, -ɪzəm/z
Londonderry (place) ˌlʌndən'derɪ [also '–,––]
Londonderry (Lord) 'lʌndəndərɪ [-derɪ]
lone ləʊn
lonel|y, -ier, -iest, -iness 'ləʊnl|ɪ, -ɪə* [-jə*], -ɪɪst [-jɪst], -ɪnɪs [-nəs]
lonesome, -ly, -ness 'ləʊnsəm, -lɪ, -nɪs [-nəs]
long (s. adj.) (L.), -s, -er, -est lɒŋ, -z, -gə*, -gɪst
long (v.), -s, -ing/ly, -ed, -er/s lɒŋ, -z, -ɪŋ/lɪ, -d, -ə*/z
longboat, -s 'lɒŋbəʊt, -s
long-bow (L.), -s 'lɒŋbəʊ, -z
long-drawn ˌlɒŋ'drɔːn [also '– when attributive]
long-drawn-out ˌlɒŋdrɔːn'aʊt
longeron, -s 'lɒndʒərən, -z
longeval lɒn'dʒiːvl
longevity lɒn'dʒevətɪ [-ɪtɪ]
Longfellow 'lɒŋˌfeləʊ
Longford 'lɒŋfəd
longhand 'lɒŋhænd
long-headed ˌlɒŋ'hedɪd ['–,–, esp. when attributive]
longing (s.), -s 'lɒŋɪŋ, -z
Longinus lɒn'dʒaɪnəs [lɒŋ'giːnəs]
longish 'lɒŋɪʃ
longitude, -s 'lɒndʒɪtjuːd [-ŋgɪ-], -z
longitudin|al, -ally ˌlɒndʒɪ'tjuːdɪn|l [-ŋgɪ-], -əlɪ [-lɪ]
Longland 'lɒŋlənd
Longleat 'lɒŋliːt
long-leg|ged, -s 'lɒŋleg|d [-ˌleg|ɪd, ˌ–'–'(-)], -z
long-lived ˌlɒŋ'lɪvd [also '– when attributive]
Longman, -s 'lɒŋmən, -z
long-off, -s ˌlɒŋ'ɒf [old-fashioned -'ɔːf], -s
long-on, -s ˌlɒŋ'ɒn, -z
long-range ˌlɒŋ'reɪndʒ [also '– when attributive]
Longridge 'lɒŋgrɪdʒ
Long|sdon, -shanks 'lɒŋ|zdən, -ʃæŋks
long-shore, -man, -men 'lɒŋʃɔː* [-ʃɔə*], -mən, -mən [-men]
long-sighted, -ness ˌlɒŋ'saɪtɪd ['–,–], -nɪs [-nəs]
Longstaff 'lɒŋstɑːf
long-stop, -s 'lɒŋstɒp, -s
long-suffering ˌlɒŋ'sʌfərɪŋ ['–,––]
long-tailed 'lɒŋteɪld
Longton 'lɒŋtən
Longus 'lɒŋgəs

long|ways, -wise 'lɒŋ|weɪz, -waɪz
long-winded, -ness ˌlɒŋ'wɪndɪd, -nɪs [-nəs]
Lonsdale 'lɒnzdeɪl
loo (s. v.) (L.), -es, -ing, -ed luː, -z, -ɪŋ, -d
loob|y, -ies 'luːb|ɪ, -ɪz
Looe luː
loofah, -s 'luːfə [-fɑː], -z
look (s. v.), -s, -ing, -ed, -er/s lʊk, -s, -ɪŋ, -t, -ə*/z
looker-on, lookers-on ˌlʊkər'ɒn, ˌlʊkəz'ɒn
looking-glass, -es 'lʊkɪŋglɑːs, -ɪz
look-out 'lʊkaʊt
loom, -s, -ing, -ed luːm, -z, -ɪŋ, -d
loon, -s luːn, -z
loon|y, -ies 'luːn|ɪ, -ɪz
loop (s. v.), -s, -ing, -ed luːp, -s, -ɪŋ, -t
loophole, -s, -d 'luːphəʊl, -z, -d
Loos (battlefield) ləʊs [luːs]
loos|e (s. adj. v.), -es; -er, -est, -ely, -eness; -ing, -ed luːs, -ɪz; -ə*, -ɪst, -lɪ, -nɪs [-nəs], -ɪŋ, -t
loos|en, -ens, -ening, -ened 'luːs|n, -nz, -n̩ɪŋ [-nɪŋ], -nd
loot (s. v.), -s, -ing, -ed, -er/s luːt, -s, -ɪŋ, -ɪd, -ə*/z
lop (s. v.), -s, -ping, -ped, -per/s lɒp, -s, -ɪŋ, -t, -ə*/z
lop|e (s. v.), -es, -ing, -ed ləʊp, -s, -ɪŋ, -t
lop-eared 'lɒpˌɪəd
Lopez 'ləʊpez
lopping (s.), -s 'lɒpɪŋ, -z
lop-sided, -ness ˌlɒp'saɪdɪd, -nɪs [-nəs]
loquacious, -ly, -ness ləʊ'kweɪʃəs [lɒ'k-], -lɪ, -nɪs [-nəs]
loquacity ləʊ'kwæsətɪ [lɒ'k-, -ɪtɪ]
lor lɔː*
Loraine lɒ'reɪn [lə'r-]
Loram 'lɔːrəm
lorcha, -s 'lɔːtʃə, -z
lord (s. v.) (L.), -s, -ing, -ed lɔːd, -z, -ɪŋ, -ɪd
  Note.—Lawyers addressing a judge in court sometimes pronounce my lord as mɪ'lʌd instead of the normal mɪ'lɔːd.
lordling, -s 'lɔːdlɪŋ, -z
lord|ly, -ier, -iest, -iness 'lɔːdl|ɪ, -ɪə* [-jə*], -ɪɪst [-jɪst], -ɪnɪs [-nəs]
Lord's-day, -s 'lɔːdzdeɪ, -z
lordship (L.), -s 'lɔːdʃɪp, -s
lore lɔː* [lɔə*]
Loreburn 'lɔːbɜːn ['lɔəb-]
Lorelei 'lɔːrəlaɪ ['lɒr-] (loːrə'laɪ)
Lorenzo lɒ'renzəʊ [lə'r-]

Loretto (*school*) lə'retəʊ [lɔ:r-]
lorgnette, -s lɔ:'njet (lɔrɲɛt), -s
Lorie 'lɒrɪ
lorimer (L.), -s 'lɒrɪmə*, -z
loris, -es 'lɔ:rɪs, -ɪz
lorn lɔ:n
Lorna 'lɔ:nə
Lorne lɔ:n
Lorraine lɒ'reɪn [lə'r-]
lorr|y, -ies 'lɒr|ɪ, -ɪz
lor|y, -ies 'lɔ:r|ɪ, -ɪz
losable 'lu:zəbl
Los Angeles lɒs'ændʒɪli:z [-'æŋgɪ-,
  -dʒəl-, -lɪz, -lɪs]
los|e, -es, -ing, lost, loser/s lu:z, -ɪz, -ɪŋ,
  lɒst [*old-fashioned* lɔ:st], 'lu:zə*/z
loss, -es lɒs [*old-fashioned* lɔ:s, *and in
  compounds*], -ɪz
loss-leader, -s ˌlɒs'li:də*, -z
lost (*from* lose) lɒst [lɔ:st]
Lostwithiel lɒst'wɪθɪəl [-θjəl]
lot (s. v.) (L.), -s, -ting, -ted lɒt, -s, -ɪŋ,
  -ɪd
loth ləʊθ
Lothair ləʊ'θeə*
Lothario ləʊ'θɑ:rɪəʊ [-'θeər-]
Lothbury 'ləʊθbərɪ ['lɒθ-]
Lothian 'ləʊðjən [-ðɪən]
lotion, -s 'ləʊʃn, -z
lotter|y, -ies 'lɒtər|ɪ, -ɪz
Lottie 'lɒtɪ
lotto 'lɒtəʊ
lotus, -es; -eater/s 'ləʊtəs, -ɪz; -ˌi:tə*/z
Lou lu:
loud, -er, -est, -ly, -ness laʊd, -ə*, -ɪst,
  -lɪ, -nɪs [-nəs]
loud-hailer, -s ˌlaʊd'heɪlə*, -z
Loud|on, -oun 'laʊd|n, -n
loud-speaker, -s ˌlaʊd'spi:kə*, -z
Loudwater 'laʊdˌwɔ:tə*
lough (*lake*), -s lɒk [lɒx], -s
Lough (*surname*) 'lʌf
Loughborough 'lʌfbərə
Loughlin 'lɒklɪn
Loughman 'lʌfmən
Loughrea lɒk'reɪ [lɒx'r-]
Loughton 'laʊtn
Louie 'lu:ɪ ['lʊɪ]
louis 'lu:ɪ ['lʊɪ], (*plur.*) -z
Louis (*English name*) 'lu:ɪ, 'lʊɪ, 'lu:ɪs,
  'lʊɪs, (*French name*) 'lu:ɪ, 'lu:i:, 'lʊɪ,
  'lʊi: (lwi)
Louisa lu:'i:zə [lʊ'i:-]
Louisburg 'lu:ɪsbə:g ['lʊɪs-]
louis-d'or, -s ˌlu:ɪ'dɔ:* [ˌlʊɪ-], -z
Louise (*English name*) lu:'i:z [lʊ'i:z]
Louisiana lu:ˌi:zɪ'ænə [lʊˌi:-, -'ɑ:nə]
Louisville 'lu:ɪvɪl ['lʊɪ-]

loung|e (s. v.), -es, -ing, -ed, -er/s
  laʊndʒ, -ɪz, -ɪŋ, -d, -ə*/z
lounge-lizard, -s 'laʊndʒˌlɪzəd, -z
Lounsbury 'laʊnzbərɪ
lour (s. v.), -s, -ing, -ed 'laʊə*, -z, -rɪŋ, -d
Lourdes lʊəd (lurd)
Lourenço Marques ləˌrensəʊ'mɑ:k
louse (s.), lice laʊs, laɪs
lous|e (v.), -es, -ing, -ed laʊz [laʊs], -ɪz,
  -ɪŋ, -d [laʊst]
lous|y, -ier, -iest, -ily, -iness 'laʊz|ɪ, -ɪə*
  [-jə*], -ɪɪst [-jɪst], -ɪlɪ [-əlɪ], -ɪnɪs
  [-ɪnəs]
lout (s. v.), -s, -ing, -ed laʊt, -s, -ɪŋ, -ɪd
Louth (*in Ireland*) laʊð, (*in Lincolnshire*) laʊθ
loutish, -ly, -ness 'laʊtɪʃ, -lɪ, -nɪs [-nəs]
Louvain 'lu:væ:ŋ [-veɪn, -væŋ] (luvẽ)
louver, -s 'lu:və*, -z
Louvre 'lu:vrə ['lu:və*] (lu:vr)
lovable, -ness 'lʌvəbl, -nɪs [-nəs]
Lovat 'lʌvət
lov|e (s. v.) (L.), -es, -ing/ly, -ed, -er/s
  lʌv, -z, -ɪŋ/lɪ, -d, -ə*/z
loveable, -ness 'lʌvəbl, -nɪs [-nəs]
love-affair, -s 'lʌvəˌfeə*, -z
lovebird, -s 'lʌvbɜ:d, -z
love|-child,   -children   'lʌv|tʃaɪld,
  -ˌtʃɪldrən [-ˌtʃʊldrən]
Loveday 'lʌvdeɪ
love-feast, -s 'lʌvfi:st, -s
Lovejoy 'lʌvdʒɔɪ
love-knot, -s 'lʌvnɒt, -s
Lovel(l) 'lʌvl
Lovelace 'lʌvleɪs
loveless 'lʌvlɪs [-ləs]
love-letter, -s 'lʌvˌletə*, -z
Lovell 'lʌvl
lovelorn 'lʌvlɔ:n
lovel|y (s. adj.), -ies, -ier, -iest, -iness
  'lʌvl|ɪ, -ɪz, -ɪə* [-jə*], -ɪɪst [-jɪst],
  -ɪnɪs [-ɪnəs]
love-making 'lʌvˌmeɪkɪŋ
love-match, -es 'lʌvmætʃ, -ɪz
love-potion, -s 'lʌvˌpəʊʃn, -z
lovesick 'lʌvsɪk
love-song, -s 'lʌvsɒŋ, -z
love-stor|y, -ies 'lʌvˌstɔ:r|ɪ, -ɪz
Lovett 'lʌvɪt
Loveys 'lʌvɪs
Lovibond 'lʌvɪbɒnd
Lovick 'lʌvɪk
loving-cup, -s 'lʌvɪŋkʌp [ˌ-'-], -s
loving-kindness,   -es   ˌlʌvɪŋ'kaɪndnɪs
  [-nəs], -ɪz
low (adj. v. adv.) (L.), -er, -est, -ness;
  -s, -ing, -ed ləʊ, -ə*, -ɪst, 'ləʊnɪs
  [-nəs]; -z, -ɪŋ, -d

303

low-born ˌləʊˈbɔːn [*also* 'ˈ—' *when attributive*]
low-bred ˌləʊˈbred [*also* 'ˈ—' *when attributive*]
low-brow 'ləʊbraʊ
low-church, -man, -men ˌləʊˈtʃɜːtʃ, -mən, -mən
low-down (*s. adj.*) 'ləʊdaʊn
Lowe ləʊ
Lowein (*surname*) 'ləʊɪn
Lowell 'ləʊəl ['ləʊel]
lower (*compar. of* low) 'ləʊə*
lower (*v.*) (*cause to descend*), -s, -ing, -ed 'ləʊə*, -z, -rɪŋ, -d
lower (*v.*) (*look threatening*), -s, -ing/ly, -ed 'laʊə*, -z, -rɪŋ/lɪ, -d
lower-case 'ləʊəkeɪs [ˌ—ˈ-]
lowermost 'ləʊəməʊst [-məst]
Lowery 'laʊərɪ
Lowes ləʊz
Lowestoft 'ləʊstɒft ['ləʊɪs-, -təft, *locally* 'ləʊstəf]
Lowick 'ləʊɪk
Lowis 'laʊɪs
lowland (L.), -s, -er/s 'ləʊlənd, -z, -ə*/z
low-life ˌləʊˈlaɪf ['ˈ—]
lowl|y, -ier, -iest, -iness 'ləʊl|ɪ, -ɪə* [-jə*], -ɪɪst [-jɪst], -ɪnɪs [-məs]
low-lying ˌləʊˈlaɪɪŋ ['-ˌ— *when attributive*]
Lowndes laʊndz
low-necked ˌləʊˈnekt [*also* 'ˈ—' *when attributive*]
Lowood 'ləʊwʊd
low-pressure ˌləʊˈpreʃə* [*also* 'ˈ-ˌ— *when attributive*]
Lowries 'laʊərɪz ['laʊr-]
Lowry 'laʊərɪ ['laʊrɪ]
Lowsley 'ləʊzlɪ
Lowson 'ləʊsn, 'laʊsn
low-spirited, -ly, -ness ˌləʊˈspɪrɪtɪd [-rət-], -lɪ, -nɪs [-nəs]
Lowth laʊθ
Lowther 'laʊðə*
Lowton 'ləʊtn
Lowville (*in U.S.A.*) 'laʊvɪl
Loxley 'lɒkslɪ
loy|al, -ally 'lɔɪ|əl, -əlɪ
loyalist, -s 'lɔɪəlɪst, -s
loyalt|y, -ies 'lɔɪəlt|ɪ, -ɪz
Loyd lɔɪd
Loyola lɔɪˈəʊlə ['lɔɪələ, 'lɔɪəʊlə]
lozenge, -s; -shaped 'lɒzɪndʒ [-zəndʒ], -ɪz; -ʃeɪpt
L. S. D. ˌeles'di:
Ltd. 'lɪmɪtɪd
lubber, -s 'lʌbə*, -z

lubberly 'lʌbəlɪ
Lubbock 'lʌbək
Lübeck 'luːbek ['ljuː-] ('lyːbek)
Lubin 'luːbɪn
lubricant, -s 'luːbrɪkənt ['ljuː-], -s
lubricat|e, -es, -ing, -ed, -or/s 'luːbrɪkeɪt ['ljuː-], -s, -ɪŋ, -ɪd, -ə*/z
lubrication, -s ˌluːbrɪˈkeɪʃn [ˌljuː-], -z
lubricity luːˈbrɪsətɪ [ljuː-, -ɪtɪ]
Lucan 'luːkən ['ljuː-]
Lucania luːˈkeɪnjə [ljuː-, -nɪə]
lucarne, -s luːˈkɑːn [ljuː-], -z
Lucas 'luːkəs ['ljuː-]
lucen|cy, -t 'luːsn|sɪ ['ljuː-], -t
Lucentio luːˈsenʃɪəʊ [ljuː-]
lucern(e) luːˈsɜːn [ljuː-'s-, lʊ's-, 'luːsɜːn]
Lucerne luːˈsɜːn [ljuː-'s-, lʊ's-]
Lucia 'luːsjə [-sɪə]
Lucian 'luːsjən [-sɪən, -ʃjən, -ʃɪən]
Luciana ˌluːsɪˈɑːnə
Lucianus ˌluːsɪˈɑːnəs [ˌljuː-, -sɪˈeɪn-]
lucid, -est, -ly, -ness 'luːsɪd ['ljuː-], -ɪst, -lɪ, -nɪs [-nəs]
lucidity luːˈsɪdətɪ [ljuː-, -ɪtɪ]
Lucie 'luːsɪ ['ljuː-]
lucifer (L.), -s 'luːsɪfə* ['ljuː-], -z
Lucilius luːˈsɪlɪəs [-ljəs]
Lucina luːˈsaɪnə [ljuː-, luːˈkiːnə]
Lucius 'luːsjəs [-sɪəs, -ʃjəs, -ʃɪəs]
luck (L.), -s lʌk, -s
luckless, -ly, -ness 'lʌklɪs [-ləs], -lɪ, -nɪs [-nəs]
Lucknow ˌlʌkˈnaʊ ['lʌkn-] (*Hindi* ləkhnəw)
luck|y, -ier, -iest, -ily, -iness 'lʌk|ɪ, -ɪə*, -ɪɪst, -ɪlɪ [-əlɪ], -ɪnɪs [-məs]
Lucock 'lʌkɒk
lucrative, -ly 'luːkrətɪv ['ljuː-], -lɪ
lucre 'luːkə* ['ljuː-]
Lucrece luːˈkriːs [ljuː-]
Lucreti|a, -us luːˈkriːʃ|ə [ljuː-'k-, lʊ'k-, ljuː'k-, -ʃɪ|ə, -ʃj|ə], -əs
lucubrat|e, -es, -ing, -ed 'luːkjuːbreɪt ['ljuː-, -kjʊ-], -s, -ɪŋ, -ɪd
lucubration, -s ˌluːkjuːˈbreɪʃn [ˌljuː-, -kjʊ-], -z
Lucullian luːˈkʌlɪən [ljuː-'k-, lʊ'k-, ljuː'k-, -ljən]
Lucullus luːˈkʌləs [ljuː-'k-, lʊ'k-, ljuː'k-]
Lucy 'luːsɪ
Lud lʌd
Ludgate 'lʌdgɪt [-geɪt, -gət]
ludicrous, -ly, -ness 'luːdɪkrəs ['ljuː-], -lɪ, -nɪs [-nəs]
Ludlow 'lʌdləʊ
ludo 'luːdəʊ
Ludovic 'luːdəvɪk

luff (*s. v.*) (**L.**), **-s, -ing, -ed** lʌf, -s, -ɪŋ, -t

lug (*s. v.*), **-s, -ging, -ged** lʌg, -z, -ɪŋ, -d

Lugano lu:'gɑ:nəʊ [lʊ'g-, lə'g-] (lu'ga:no)

Lugard lu:'gɑ:d, 'lu:gɑ:d

luggage 'lʌgɪdʒ

lugger, -s 'lʌgə*, -z

lugsail, -s 'lʌgseɪl [*nautical pronunciation* -sl], -z

lugubrious, -ly, -ness lu:'gu:brɪəs [lju:'g-, lʊ'g-, lə'g-, -'gju:-], -lɪ, -nɪs [-nəs]

lug-worm, -s 'lʌgwɜːm, -z

Luia 'lu:jə ['lu:ɪə]

Luke lu:k [lju:k]

lukewarm, -ly, -ness ˌlu:k'wɔːm [ˌlju:k-, '--], -lɪ, -nɪs [-nəs]

lull (*s. v.*), **-s, -ing, -ed** lʌl, -z, -ɪŋ, -d

lullab|y, -ies 'lʌləb|aɪ, -aɪz

lumbago lʌm'beɪgəʊ

lumbar 'lʌmbə*

lumb|er (*s. v.*), -ers, -ering, -ered -erer/s 'lʌmb|ə*, -əz, -ərɪŋ, -əd, -ərə*/z

lumber-room, -s 'lʌmbərʊm [-ru:m], -z

luminar|y, -ies 'lu:mɪnər|ɪ ['lju:-], -ɪz

luminiferous ˌlu:mɪ'nɪfərəs [ˌlju:-]

luminosity ˌlu:mɪ'nɒsətɪ [ˌlju:-, -ɪtɪ]

luminous, -ly, -ness 'lu:mɪnəs ['lju:-], -lɪ, -nɪs [-nəs]

Lumley 'lʌmlɪ

lummy 'lʌmɪ

lump (*s. v.*), **-s, -ing, -ed** lʌmp, -s, -ɪŋ, -t [lʌmt]

Lumphanan lʌm'fænən

lumpish, -ly, -ness 'lʌmpɪʃ, -lɪ, -nɪs [-nəs]

lump|y, -ier, -iest, -iness 'lʌmp|ɪ, -ɪə* [-jə*], -ɪɪst [-jɪst], -ɪnɪs [-ɪnəs]

lunacy 'lu:nəsɪ ['lju:-]

lunar 'lu:nə* ['lju:-]

lunate 'lu:neɪt ['lju:-, -nɪt]

lunated 'lu:neɪtɪd ['lju:-]

lunatic (*s. adj.*), **-s** 'lu:nətɪk, -s

lunation, -s lu:'neɪʃn [lju:'n-, lʊ'n-, ljʊ'n-], -z

Luncarty 'lʌŋkətɪ

lunch (*s. v.*), **-es, -ing, -ed** lʌntʃ, -ɪz, -ɪŋ, -t

luncheon, -s 'lʌntʃən, -z

Lund lʊnd

Lundy 'lʌndɪ

lune, -s lu:n [lju:n], -z

lunette, -s lu:'net [lju:'n-, lʊ'n-, ljʊ'n-], -s

lung, -s lʌŋ, -z

lung|e (*s. v.*), **-es, -ing, -ed** lʌndʒ, -ɪz, -ɪŋ, -d

lunged (*furnished with lungs*) lʌŋd, (*from* lunge) lʌndʒd

lung-fish, -es 'lʌŋfɪʃ, -ɪz

lunul|a, -ae 'lu:njʊl|ə ['lju:-], -i:

lunule, -s 'lu:nju:l ['lju:-], -z

Lupercal 'lu:pəkæl ['lju:-, -pɜ:-]

Lupercalia ˌlu:pə'keɪljə [ˌlju:-, -pɜ:'k-, -lɪə]

lupin(e) (*flower*), **-s** 'lu:pɪn ['lju:-], -z

lupine (*adj.*) (*wolfish*) 'lu:paɪn ['lju:-]

lupulin 'lu:pjʊlɪn ['lju:-]

lupus 'lu:pəs ['lju:-]

lurch (*s. v.*), **-es, -ing, -ed, -er/s** lɜ:tʃ, -ɪz, -ɪŋ, -t, -ə*/z

lur|e (*s. v.*), **-es, -ing, -ed** lʊə* [ljʊə*, ljɔə*, ljɔ:*], -z, -rɪŋ, -d

lurid, -ly, -ness 'lʊərɪd ['ljʊər-, 'ljɔər-, 'ljɔ:r-], -lɪ, -nɪs [-nəs]

lurk, -s, -ing, -ed, -er/s lɜ:k, -s, -ɪŋ, -t, -ə*/z

lurking-place, -s 'lɜ:kɪŋpleɪs, -ɪz

Lusaka lu:'sɑ:kə [lʊ's-]

Lusa|tia, -tian/s lu:'seɪ|ʃə [-ʃɪə, -ʃjə], -ʃn/z [-ʃɪən/z, -ʃjən/z]

luscious, -ly, -ness 'lʌʃəs, -lɪ, -nɪs [-nəs]

lush (**L.**) lʌʃ

Lushington 'lʌʃɪŋtən

Lusiad, -s 'lu:sɪæd ['lju:-], -z

Lusitania ˌlu:sɪ'teɪnjə [ˌlju:-, -nɪə]

lust (*s. v.*), **-s, -ing, -ed** lʌst, -s, -ɪŋ, -ɪd

lust|ful, -fully, -fulness 'lʌst|fʊl, -fʊlɪ [-fəlɪ], -fʊlnɪs [-nəs]

lustral 'lʌstrəl

lustration, -s lʌ'streɪʃn, -z

lustre, -s; -less 'lʌstə*, -z; -lɪs [-ləs]

lustrous, -ly, -ness 'lʌstrəs, -lɪ, -nɪs [-nəs]

lustr|um, -ums, -a 'lʌstr|əm, -əmz, -ə

lust|y, -ier, -iest, -ily, -iness 'lʌst|ɪ, -ɪə* [-jə*], -ɪɪst [-jɪst], -ɪlɪ [-əlɪ], -ɪnɪs [-ɪnəs]

lute, -s; -string/s lu:t [lju:t], -s; -strɪŋ/z

lutenist [-ta-], **-s** 'lu:tənɪst ['lju:-, -tnɪst], -s

Luth|er, -eran/s, -eranism, -erism 'lu:θ|ə* ['lju:-], -ərən/z, -ərənɪzəm, -ərɪzəm

Lutine (*bell at Lloyd's*) lu:'ti:n ['--]

lutist, -s 'lu:tɪst ['lju:-], -s

Luton 'lu:tn

Lutterworth 'lʌtəwəθ [-wɜ:θ]

Luttrell 'lʌtrəl

Lutwyche 'lʌtwɪtʃ

Lutyens (*English surname*) 'lʌtʃənz [-tjənz]

305

lux lʌks
luxe lʌks [luːks, lʊks] (lyks̓)
Luxemb(o)urg 'lʌksəmbəːg
Luxor 'lʌksɔː*
Luxulyan lʌk'sɪljən [-'sʌl-, -lrən]
luxurian|ce, -t/ly lʌg'ʒʊərɪən|s [ləg'zj-,
lʌk'sj-, lək'sj-, -jɔər-, -jɔːr-, lʌg-
'zjʊə-, ləg'ʒ-], -t/lɪ
luxuriat|e, -es, -ing, -ed lʌg'ʒʊərɪeɪt
[ləg'zj-, lʌk'sj-, lək'sj-, -jɔər-, -jɔːr-,
lʌg'zjʊə-, ləg'ʒ-], -s, -ɪŋ, -ɪd
luxurious, -ly, -ness lʌg'ʒʊərɪəs
[ləg'zj-, lʌk'sj-, lək'sj-, -jɔər-, -jɔːr-,
lʌg'zjʊə-, ləg'ʒ-], -lɪ, -nɪs
luxur|y, -ies 'lʌkʃər|ɪ [-kʃʊr-], -ɪz
Luzon luː'zɒn
Lyall 'laɪəl
lycée, -s 'liːseɪ (lise), -z
Lycett 'laɪsɪt [-set]
lyceum (L.), -s laɪ'sɪəm [-'siːəm], -z
lychee, -s ˌlaɪ'tʃiː ['--, 'lɪtʃiː, 'liː-], -z
lychgate, -s 'lɪtʃgeɪt, -s
lychnis 'lɪknɪs
Lycia, -n/s 'lɪsɪə [-sjə, -ʃɪə, -ʃjə], -n/z
Lycidas 'lɪsɪdæs
Lycoming laɪ'kɒmɪŋ
lycopodium, -s ˌlaɪkə'pəʊdjəm [-dɪəm],
-z
Lycurgus laɪ'kɜːgəs
Lydall 'laɪdl
Lydd lɪd
lyddite 'lɪdaɪt
Lydekker laɪ'dekə*
Lydgate (fifteenth-century poet) 'lɪdgeɪt
[-gɪt], (lane in Sheffield) 'lɪdʒɪt
Lydia, -n/s 'lɪdɪə [-djə], -n/z
Lydon 'laɪdn
lye (L.) laɪ
Lyell 'laɪəl
Lyghe laɪ
Lygon 'lɪgən
lying (from lie), -ly 'laɪɪŋ, -lɪ
lying-in ˌlaɪŋ'ɪn ['--- when attributive]
Lyly 'lɪlɪ

Lyme Regis ˌlaɪm'riːdʒɪs
Lymington 'lɪmɪŋtən
Lympany (surname) 'lɪmpənɪ
lymph, -s; -ous lɪmf, -s; -əs
lymphatic, -s lɪm'fætɪk, -s
lymphocyte, -s 'lɪmfəʊsaɪt, -s
Lympne lɪm
Lynam 'laɪnəm
lynch (L.), -es, -ing, -ed; -law lɪntʃ, -ɪz,
-ɪŋ, -t; -lɔː
Lynd|hurst, -on 'lɪnd|hɜːst, -ən
Lynmouth 'lɪnməθ
Lynn lɪn
Lynton 'lɪntən
lynx, -es lɪŋks, -ɪz
lynx-eyed 'lɪŋksaɪd
Lyon (surname) 'laɪən
Lyonesse ˌlaɪə'nes [ˌlaɪɒ'n-]
lyonnaise ˌlaɪə'neɪz (ljɔːnɛːz)
Lyons (English surname) 'laɪənz, (French
city) 'liːɔ̃ːŋ, 'laɪənz (or as French ljɔ̃)
Lyr|a (constellation), -ae 'laɪər|ə, -iː
lyrate 'laɪərɪt [-reɪt, -rət]
lyre, -s; -bird/s 'laɪə*, -z; -bɜːd/z
lyric (L.), -s, -al, -ally 'lɪrɪk, -s, -l, -əlɪ
lyricism 'lɪrɪsɪzəm
lyrist (player on the lyre), -s 'laɪərɪst
['lɪr-], -s
lyrist (lyric poet), -s 'lɪrɪst, -s
Lysaght 'laɪsət, 'laɪsɑːt
Lysander laɪ'sændə*
lysergic laɪ'sɜːdʒɪk [lɪ's-]
Lysias 'lɪsɪæs
Lysicrates laɪ'sɪkrəti:z
Lysippus laɪ'sɪpəs
Lysistrata laɪ'sɪstrətə
lysol 'laɪsɒl
Lystra 'lɪstrə
Lyte laɪt
Lytham 'lɪðəm
Lythe laɪð
Lyttelton 'lɪtltən
Lytton 'lɪtn
Lyveden 'lɪvdən

M

M (*the letter*), -'s em, -z
ma (*mother*), -s mɑ:, -z
ma (*note in Tonic Sol-fa*), -s mɔ:, -z
ma'am mæm [mɑ:m, məm, m]
    Note.—mɑ:m, *or alternatively* mæm,
    *is used in addressing members of
    the royal family.*
Maas (*English surname*) mɑ:z, (*river in
    Holland*) mɑ:s
Mab mæb
Mabel 'meɪbl
Mablethorpe 'meɪblθɔ:p
Mabley 'mæblɪ
Mabs mæbz
Mac mæk
macabre mə'kɑ:brə [mæ'k-, -bə*]
macadam mə'kædəm
MacAdam mə'kædəm, mək'ædəm
macadamization [-isa-] mə,kædəmaɪ-
    'zeɪʃn
macadamiz|e [-is|e], -es, -ing, -ed
    mə'kædəmaɪz, -ɪz, -ɪŋ, -d
MacAdoo ,mækə'du:, 'mækədu:
Macalister mə'kælɪstə*
McAll mə'kɔ:l
McAllister mə'kælɪstə*
McAloren ,mækə'lɔ:rən
McAlpine mə'kælpɪn, mə'kælpaɪn
Macan mə'kæn
MacAnnaly ;mækə'nælɪ
Macao mə'kau
McAra mə'kɑ:rə
macaroni ,mækə'rəunɪ
macaroon, -s ,mækə'ru:n ['— *when
    attributive*], -z
MacArthur mə'kɑ:θə*, mək'ɑ:θə*
macassar (M.); -oil mə'kæsə*; -r'ɔɪl
    [-ə'ɔɪl]
Macaulay mə'kɔ:lɪ
M(a)cAvoy 'mækəvɔɪ
macaw, -s mə'kɔ:, -z
Mc|Bain, -Bean mək|'beɪn, -'beɪn
Macbeth mək'beθ [mæk-]
    Note.—*In Scotland always* mək-.
McBride mək'braɪd
Maccabees 'mækəbi:z
Maccabeus ,mækə'bi:əs [-'bɪəs]
McCall [MacC-] mə'kɔ:l
McCallie mə'kɔ:lɪ

McCallum [MacC-] mə'kæləm
McCann mə'kæn
MacCarthy mə'kɑ:θɪ
McClellan mə'klelən
Macclesfield 'mæklzfi:ld [-lsf-]
McClintock mə'klɪntək [-tɒk]
McClure [M'Clure] mə'kluə*
McConochie mə'kɒnəkɪ [-əxɪ]
McCormick mə'kɔ:mɪk
McCorquodale mə'kɔ:kədeɪl
Mc|Crae, -Crea mə|'kreɪ, -'kreɪ
McCulloch mə'kʌlək [-ləx]
MacCumhail mə'ku:l
MacCunn mə'kʌn
MacDaire mək'dɑ:rə
MacDonald [Macd-] mək'dɒnəld [mæk-]
McDonald mək'dɒnəld
MacDonnell [Macd-] ,mækdə'nel, (*in
    Ireland*) mək'dɒnl
McDonough mək'dʌnə
MacDougal [Macd-] mək'du:gl [mæk-]
McDougall mək'du:gl
McDowell mək'dauəl [-el]
MacDuff mək'dʌf [mæk-]
    Note.—*In Scotland always* mək-.
mace, -s meɪs, -ɪz
McEachran mə'kekrən [-exr-]
Macedon 'mæsɪdən
Macedonia, -n/s ,mæsɪ'dəunjə [-nɪə],
    -n/z
McElderry 'mækldeɪɪ
McEldowney 'mækldaunɪ
MacElwain mə'kelweɪn, mək'el-,'mækl-
    weɪn
MacElwin mə'kelwɪn, mək'el-
macerat|e, -es, -ing, -ed 'mæsəreɪt, -s,
    -ɪŋ, -ɪd
McErlain 'mækələɪn
McEwen mə'kjuən [-ɪn]
McFadzean mək'fædjən
MacFarlane mək'fɑ:lɪn [-lən]
Macfarren mək'færən
Macfie mək'fi: [mæk-]
McGahey mə'gæhɪ [-'gæxɪ], mə'geɪɪ
McGee mə'gi:
MacGillicuddy (*Reeks*) mə'gɪlɪkʌdɪ,
    (*family name*) 'mæglɪkʌdɪ, 'mækɪlkʌdɪ
McGillivray mə'gɪlɪvrɪ [-'gɪlv-, -'glɪv-,
    -reɪ]

307

McGowan məˈgaʊən
McGrath məˈgrɑː
McGregor məˈgregə*
MacGregor [Macg-, M'G-] məˈgregə*
mach mæk [mɑːk, mɒk]
Machen ˈmeɪtʃən [-tʃɪn], ˈmækɪn
machete, -s məˈtʃetɪ [-ˈtʃeɪtɪ, -ʃetɪ], -z
Machiavelli ˌmækɪəˈvelɪ [-kjə-]
machiavellian ˌmækɪəˈveliən [-kjə-, -ljən]
machicolat|e, -es, -ing, -ed mæˈtʃɪkəʊleɪt [məˈtʃ-], -s, -ɪŋ, -ɪd
Machin ˈmeɪtʃɪn
machinat|e, -es, -ing, -or/s ˈmækɪneɪt [ˈmæʃ-], -s, -ɪŋ, -ɪd, -ə*/z
machination, -s ˌmækɪˈneɪʃn [ˌmæʃ-], -z
machin|e (s. v.), -es, -ing, -ed; -e-gun/s məˈʃiːn, -z, -ɪŋ, -d; -gʌn/z
machine-made məˈʃiːnmeɪd
machinery məˈʃiːnərɪ
machine-tool, -s məˈʃiːntuːl, -z
machinist, -s məˈʃiːnɪst, -s
McIlrath ˈmækɪlrɑːθ
MacIlwain ˈmæklweɪn
MacIlwraith [McI-] ˈmæklreɪθ, ˈmækɪl-
Macindoe ˈmækɪndu:
MacInn|es, -is məˈkɪn|ɪs, -ɪs
McIntosh ˈmækɪntɒʃ
MacIntyre ˈmækɪntaɪə*
Macirone ˌmætʃɪˈrəʊnɪ
MacIvor məˈkiːvə*, məˈkaɪvə*
Mack mæk
Mackay məˈkaɪ, məˈkeɪ
Note.—məˈkeɪ mainly in U.S.A.
McKeag məˈkiːg
McKee məˈkiː
McKenna məˈkenə
Mackenzie məˈkenzɪ
mackerel, -s ˈmækrəl, -z
Mackerras məˈkerəs
McKichan məˈkɪkən [-ˈkɪxən]
Mackie ˈmækɪ
McKie məˈkaɪ, məˈkiː
Mackin ˈmækɪn
Mackin|lay, -ley məˈkɪn|lɪ, -lɪ
McKinley məˈkɪnlɪ
mackintosh (M.), -es ˈmækɪntɒʃ, -ɪz
Mackmurdo mækˈmɜːdəʊ [mək-]
Mackowie [MacK-] məˈkaʊɪ
MacLachlan məˈklɒklən [-ˈklɒxlən], məˈklæklən [-ˈklæxlən]
MacLaglan məkˈlæglən
M(a)cl|aren, -aurin məˈkl|ærən, -ɔːrɪn
McLaughlin məˈklɒklɪn [-ɒxlɪn]
McLay məˈkleɪ
Macl|ean(e) (surname), -ear məˈkl|eɪn [-ˈkl|iːn], -ɪə*
McLean məˈkleɪn

MacLehose ˈmæklhəʊz
Macleod məˈklaʊd
McLeod məˈklaʊd
MacLiammoir məkˈlɪəmɔː:*
Maclise məˈkliːs
Macmahon məkˈmɑːən
MacManus məkˈmænəs, -ˈmɑːnəs, -ˈmeɪnəs
McMaster məkˈmɑːstə*
Macmillan məkˈmɪlən [mæk-]
Macmorran məkˈmɒrən [mæk-]
MacNab məkˈnæb
Macnaghten [McN-] məkˈnɔːtn
Macnamara ˌmæknəˈmɑːrə
MacNaught, -on məkˈnɔːt [mæk-], -n
MacNeice məkˈniːs
Mâcon (in France, wine) ˈmɑːkɔ̃:ŋ [ˈmæ-, -kɒn, -kən] (makɔ̃)
Macon (in U.S.A.) ˈmeɪkən
Maconchy məˈkɒŋkɪ
Maconochie məˈkɒnəkɪ [-əxɪ]
MacOuart məˈkjuːət [-ˈkjʊət]
McOutra məˈkuːtrə
Macpelah mækˈpiːlə
MacPherson [Macph-] məkˈfɜːsn [mæk-]
Macquarie məˈkwɒrɪ
Macquoid məˈkwɔɪd
Macready məˈkriːdɪ
macrocosm, -s ˈmækrəʊkɒzəm, -z
macron, -s ˈmækrɒn, -z
Macrow məˈkrəʊ
McShea məkˈʃeɪ
MacSwiney məkˈswiːnɪ [mæk-]
MacTavish məkˈtævɪʃ
macul|a, -ae ˈmækjʊl|ə, -iː
McVeagh məkˈveɪ
McVean məkˈveɪn
McVit(t)ie məkˈvɪtɪ
mad; mad|der, -dest, -ly, -ness mæd; ˈmæd|ə*, -ɪst, -lɪ, -nɪs [-nəs]
Madagascar ˌmædəˈgæskə*
madam ˈmædəm
madame (M.) ˈmædəm
Madan ˈmædən, ˈmeɪdn
madcap, -s ˈmædkæp, -s
Maddalo ˈmædəlɒ
madd|en (M.), -ens, -ening, -ened ˈmæd|n, -nz, -nɪŋ [-nɪŋ], -nd
madder (plant, colour), -s ˈmædə*, -z
madding ˈmædɪŋ
Maddox ˈmædəks
made (from make) meɪd
Madeira, -s məˈdɪərə, -z
Madeleine (English name) ˈmæd|ɪn [-dəlɪn, -eɪn]
Madeley (in Salop) ˈmeɪdlɪ
mademoiselle, -s ˌmædəm(w)əˈzel [ˌmæmwəˈzel] (madmwazɛl), -z

Madge mædʒ
madhou|se, -ses 'mædhaʊ|s, -zɪz
Madingley 'mædɪŋlɪ
Madison 'mædɪsn
mad|man, -men 'mæd|mən, -mən [-men]
Madoc 'mædək
Madonna, -s mə'dɒnə, -z
Madras mə'drɑːs [-'dræs]
madrepore, -s ˌmædrɪ'pɔː* [-'pɔə*], -z
Madrid mə'drɪd
madrigal, -s 'mædrɪgl, -z
madrigalist, -s 'mædrɪgəlɪst, -s
Madura (in S. India) 'mædjʊrə [-dʒʊ-, -dʊ-]
Maecenas miː'siːnæs [mɪ's-, maɪ's-, -nəs]
maelstrom 'meɪlstrɒm [-strəʊm]
maenad, -s 'miːnæd, -z
maestoso ˌmɑːeˈstəʊzəʊ [maɪ's-, -əʊsəʊ]
maestro, -s 'maɪstrəʊ [mɑː'estrəʊ], -z
Maeterlinck 'meɪtəlɪŋk ['mɑːt-]
Mae West, -s ˌmeɪ'west, -s
Mafeking 'mæfɪkɪŋ [-fə-]
maffick, -s, -ing, -ed 'mæfɪk, -s, -ɪŋ, -t
mafia 'mæfɪə ['mɑː-, -fjə]
mag (M.), -s mæg, -z
Magan 'meɪgən, mə'gæn
magazine, -s ˌmægə'ziːn [rarely '---], -z
    Note.—The stressing '--- is usual in
    the N. of England, but uncommon
    in the S.
Magdala 'mægdələ
magdalen, -s 'mægdəlɪn, -z
Magdalen (biblical name, modern Chris-
    tian name, Canadian islands) 'mæg-
    dəlɪn, (Oxford college and street)
    'mɔːdlɪn
Magdalene (biblical name) ˌmægdə'liːnɪ
    ['mægdəliːn, -lɪn], (modern Christian
    name) 'mægdəlɪn, (Cambridge college
    and street) 'mɔːdlɪn
Magdalenian ˌmægdə'liːnjən [-nɪən]
Magdeburg 'mægdəbɜːg [-dɪb-] ('mak-
    dəburk, -burç)
mage, -s meɪdʒ, -ɪz
Magee mə'giː
Magellan mə'gelən
magenta (M.) mə'dʒentə
Maggersfontein 'mɑːgəzˌfɒnteɪn ['---ˌ-]
Maggie 'mægɪ
Maggiore ˌmædʒɪ'ɔːrɪ [mæ'dʒɔːrɪ,
    mə'dʒɔːrɪ] (mad'dʒɔːre)
maggot, -s, -y 'mægət, -s, -ɪ
Maghull (near Liverpool) mə'gʌl
Magi 'meɪdʒaɪ [-gaɪ]
magic (s. adj.), -al, -ally 'mædʒɪk, -l, -əlɪ

magician, -s mə'dʒɪʃn, -z
magic-lantern, -s ˌmædʒɪk'læntən, -z
magilp mə'gɪlp
Maginot 'mæʒɪnəʊ ['mædʒɪ-] (maʒino)
magisterial, -ly ˌmædʒɪ'stɪərɪəl, -ɪ
magistrac|y, -ies 'mædʒɪstrəs|ɪ, -ɪz
magistral mə'dʒɪstrəl [mæ'dʒ-]
magistrate, -s 'mædʒɪstreɪt [-trɪt, -trət], -s
magistrature, -s 'mædʒɪstrətʃə*
    [-ˌtjʊə*, -ˌtʃʊə*], -z
Magna Carta ˌmægnə'kɑːtə
magnanimity ˌmægnə'nɪmətɪ [-ɪtɪ]
magnanimous, -ly mæg'nænɪməs
    [məg-], -lɪ
magnate, -s 'mægneɪt [-nɪt], -s
magnesia (substance) mæg'niːʃə [məg-,
    -ʃjə, -ʃɪə, -zjə, -zɪə, -ʒə]
Magnesia (city) mæg'niːzjə [-zɪə, -ʒjə,
    -ʒɪə, -ʃjə, -ʃɪə]
magnesium mæg'niːzɪəm [məg-, -zjəm,
    -sjəm, -sɪəm, -ʃjəm, -ʃɪəm]
magnet, -s 'mægnɪt, -s
magnetic, -al, -ally mæg'netɪk [məg-],
    -l, -əlɪ
magnetism 'mægnɪtɪzəm [-nət-]
magnetiz|e [-is|e], -es, -ing, -ed, -er/s
    'mægnɪtaɪz [-nət-], -ɪz, -ɪŋ, -d, -ə*/z
magneto, -s mæg'niːtəʊ [məg-], -z
magnetron, -s 'mægnɪtrɒn, -z
Magnificat, -s mæg'nɪfɪkæt [məg-], -s
magnification, -s ˌmægnɪfɪ'keɪʃn, -z
magnificen|ce, -t/ly mæg'nɪfɪsn|s
    [məg-], -t/lɪ
magnifico, -s mæg'nɪfɪkəʊ, -z
magni|fy, -fies, -fying, -fied, -fier/s;
    -fiable 'mægnɪ|faɪ, -faɪz, -faɪŋ, -faɪd,
    -faɪə*/z; -faɪəbl
magniloquen|ce, -t mæg'nɪləʊkwən|s, -t
magnitude, -s 'mægnɪtjuːd, -z
magnolia, -s mæg'nəʊljə [məg-, -lɪə], -z
magnum, -s 'mægnəm, -z
magnum bonum, -s ˌmægnəm'bəʊnəm
    [-'bɒn-], -z
magnum opus ˌmægnəm'əʊpəs [-'ɒpəs]
Magnus 'mægnəs
Magog 'meɪgɒg
magpie, -s 'mægpaɪ, -z
Magrath mə'grɑː
Magruder mə'gruːdə*
Maguiness mə'gɪnɪs [-nəs]
Maguire mə'gwaɪə*
Ma|gus, -gi 'meɪ|gəs, -dʒaɪ [-gaɪ]
Magyar, -s 'mægjɑː* [-gɪɑː*], -z
Mahaffy mə'hæfɪ
Mahan mə'hæn, mɑːn
Mahanaim ˌmeɪə'neɪɪm [usual Jewish
    pronunciation ˌmɑːhɑː'nɑːɪm]

309

Mahany 'mɑːnɪ
maharajah, -s ˌmɑːhəˈrɑːdʒə (*Hindi* məharaȷa), -z
maharanee, -s ˌmɑːhəˈrɑːni: (*Hindi* məharani), -z
mahatma, -s məˈhɑːtmə [-ˈhæt-] (*Hindi* məhatma), -z
Mahdi, -s 'mɑːdi: [-dɪ], -z
mah-jong(g) mɑːˈdʒɒŋ
Mahler 'mɑːlə*
mahl-stick, -s 'mɔːlstɪk, -s
Mahmud mɑːˈmuːd
mahogany məˈhɒgənɪ [-gn̩ɪ]
Mahomet (*prophet*) məˈhɒmɪt ['merə-met, 'merəmɪt], (*English surname*) 'merəmet [-mɪt]
Mahometan, -s məˈhɒmɪtən, -z
Mahommed məˈhɒmɪd [-med]
Mahommedan, -s məˈhɒmɪdən, -z
Mahon mɑːn, məˈhuːn, məˈhəʊn
Mahon(e)y 'mɑːənɪ ['mɑːnɪ]
mahout, -s məˈhaʊt, -s
Mahratta, -s məˈrætə, -z
maia 'maɪə
maid, -s meɪd, -z
Maida 'merdə
maidan (M.), -s maɪˈdɑːn, -z
maiden (*s. adj.*), -s, -ly; -hair/s 'meɪdn, -z, -lɪ; -heə*/z
Maidenhead 'merdnhed
maidenhood 'merdnhʊd
maiden-name, -s 'meɪdnneɪm, -z
maid-servant, -s 'meɪd,sɜːvənt, -s
Maidstone 'merdstən [-stəʊn]
maieutic meɪˈjuːtɪk [maɪˈj-]
mail (*s. v.*), -s, -ing, -ed meɪl, -z, -ɪŋ, -d
mail-bag, -s 'meɪlbæg, -z
mail-cart, -s 'meɪlkɑːt, -s
mail-coach, -es 'meɪlkəʊtʃ, -ɪz
Maillard (*surname*) 'meɪləd
mail-order 'meɪlˌɔːdə*
mail-train, -s 'meɪltreɪn, -z
maim, -s, -ing, -ed meɪm, -z, -ɪŋ, -d
main (*s. adj.*), -s, -ly meɪn, -z, -lɪ
Main (*German river*) maɪn [meɪn]
mainbrace, -s 'meɪnbreɪs, -ɪz
Maine meɪn
mainland 'meɪnlənd [-lænd]
mainmast, -s 'meɪnmɑːst [*nautical pronunciation* -məst], -s
mainsail, -s 'meɪnseɪl [*nautical pronunciation* -sl], -z
mainspring, -s 'meɪnsprɪŋ, -z
mainstay, -s 'meɪnsteɪ, -z
mainstream 'meɪnstriːm [ˌ-ˈ-]
maintain, -s, -ing, -ed, -er/s; -able meɪnˈteɪn [mən-, men-], -z, -ɪŋ, -d, -ə*/z; -əbl

maintenance 'meɪntənəns [-tɪn-, -tn̩əns, -tnəns]
Mainwaring 'mænərɪŋ, (*in Wales* 'meɪn-wərɪŋ)
Mainz maɪnts
Mais meɪz
Maisie 'meɪzɪ
maison(n)ette, -s ˌmeɪzəˈnet, -s
Maitland 'meɪtlənd
maître(s) d'hôtel ˌmetrədəʊˈtel [ˌmeɪt-] (mɛːtrə dɔtɛl)
maize meɪz
Majendie 'mædʒəndɪ
majestic (M.), -al, -ally məˈdʒestɪk, -l, -əlɪ
majest|y (M.), -ies 'mædʒəst|ɪ [-dʒɪs-], -ɪz
majolica məˈjɒlɪkə [məˈdʒɒl-]
major (*s. adj. v.*) (M.), -s, -ing, -ed 'meɪdʒə*, -z, -rɪŋ, -d
Majorca məˈdʒɔːkə [məˈjɔː-]
major-domo, -s ˌmeɪdʒəˈdəʊməʊ, -z
major-general, -s ˌmeɪdʒəˈdʒenərəl, -z
majorit|y, -ies məˈdʒɒrət|ɪ [-rɪt|-], -ɪz
Majuba məˈdʒuːbə
majuscule, -s 'mædʒəskjuːl, -z
mak|e (*s. v.*), -es, -ing, made, mak|er, -ers meɪk, -s, -ɪŋ, meɪd, 'meɪk|ə*, -əz
make-believe 'meɪkbɪˌliːv [-bəˌl-]
Makeham 'meɪkəm
Makepeace 'meɪkpiːs
Makerere məˈkerərɪ
makeshift, -s 'meɪkʃɪft, -s
make-up, -s 'meɪkʌp, -s
makeweight, -s 'meɪkweɪt, -s
Makins 'meɪkɪnz
Makower məˈkaʊə*
Malabar ˌmæləˈbɑː* [*also* 'mæləb- *when attributive*]
Malacca məˈlækə
Malachi 'mæləkaɪ
malachite 'mæləkaɪt
maladjusted ˌmæləˈdʒʌstɪd [*also* '-ˌ-- *when attributive*]
maladjustment, -s ˌmæləˈdʒʌstmənt, -s
maladministration 'mælədˌmɪnɪ'streɪʃn
maladroit, -ly, -ness ˌmæləˈdrɔɪt ['---], -lɪ, -nɪs [-nəs]
malad|y, -ies 'mæləd|ɪ, -ɪz
mala fide ˌmeɪləˈfaɪdɪ [ˌmæləˈfɪdɪ, -ˈfɪdeɪ]
Malaga 'mæləgə
Malagasy ˌmæləˈgæsɪ
malaise mæˈleɪz
Malan (*English surname*) 'mælən, (*South African name*) məˈlæn, məˈlɑːn
Malaprop 'mæləprɒp
malapropism, -s 'mæləprɒpɪzəm, -z

malapropos ˌmælˈæprəpəʊ [ˌ---'-]

malaria, -l, -n məˈleərɪə, -l, -n

Malawi, -an məˈlɑːwɪ, -ən

Malay (s. adj.), -s məˈleɪ, -z

Malaya, -n/s məˈleɪə, -n/z

Malayalam ˌmælɪˈɑːləm [-leɪˈɑː-, -ləˈjɑː-]

Malaysia məˈleɪzɪə [-zjə, -ʒɪə, -ʒə]

Malchus ˈmælkəs

Malcolm ˈmælkəm

malcontent, -s ˈmælkənˌtent, -s

Malden ˈmɔːldən [ˈmɒl-]

Maldive, -s ˈmɔːldɪv [ˈmɒl-], -z

Maldivian, -s mɔːlˈdɪvɪən [mɒl-, -vjən], -z

Maldon ˈmɔːldən [ˈmɒl-]

male, -s meɪl, -z

malediction, -s ˌmælɪˈdɪkʃn, -z

maledictory ˌmælɪˈdɪktərɪ

malefaction, -s ˌmælɪˈfækʃn, -z

malefactor, -s ˈmælɪfæktə*, -z

malefic məˈlefɪk

maleficent məˈlefɪsnt [mæˈl-]

Malet ˈmælɪt

malevolen|ce, -t/ly məˈlevələn|s [mæˈl-, -vlə-], -t/lɪ

malfeasance mælˈfiːzns

Malfi ˈmælfɪ

malformation, -s ˌmælfɔːˈmeɪʃn [-fəˈm-], -z

malfunction (s. v.), -s, -ing, -ed ˌmælˈfʌŋkʃn, -z, -ɪŋ, -d

Mali ˈmɑːlɪ

malic ˈmælɪk [ˈmeɪl-]

malice ˈmælɪs

malicious, -ly, -ness məˈlɪʃəs, -lɪ, -nɪs [-nəs]

malign (adj. v.), -ly; -s, -ing, -ed, -er/s məˈlaɪn, -lɪ; -z, -ɪŋ, -d, -ə*/z

malignan|cy, -t/ly məˈlɪgnən|sɪ, -t/lɪ

malignity məˈlɪgnətɪ [-ɪtɪ]

Malin (region of sea) ˈmælɪn

Malines mæˈliːn (malin)

malinger, -s, -ing, -ed, -er/s məˈlɪŋgə*, -z, -rɪŋ, -d, -rə*/z

Malins ˈmeɪlɪnz

malkin, -s ˈmɔːkɪn [ˈmɔːlk-], -z

Malkin ˈmælkɪn

mall, -s mɔːl [mæl], -z

Mall (in The Mall, Chiswick Mall) mæl, (in Pall Mall) mæl [mel]

mallard, -s ˈmælɑːd [-ləd], -z

malleability ˌmælɪəˈbɪlətɪ [-ljəˈb-, -ləˈb-, -lɪt-]

malleable, -ness ˈmælɪəbl [-ljə-, -lə-, -nɪs [-nəs]

mallet (M.), -s ˈmælɪt [-lət], -s

Malling (in Kent) ˈmɔːlɪŋ

Mallorca məˈljɔːkə [məˈlɔː-]

Mallory ˈmælərɪ

mallow (M.), -s ˈmæləʊ, -z

Malmaison, -s ˌmælˈmeɪzɔ̃ːŋ [-zɒn] (malmɛzɔ̃), -z

Malmesbury ˈmɑːmzbərɪ

malmsey (M.) ˈmɑːmzɪ

malnutrition ˌmælnjuːˈtrɪʃn [-njʊ-]

malodorant (s. adj.), -s mælˈəʊdərənt, -s

malodorous mælˈəʊdərəs

Malone məˈləʊn

Malory ˈmælərɪ

Malpas (near Truro) ˈməʊpəs, (in Cheshire) ˈmɔːlpəs [ˈmɔːpəs, ˈmælpəs]

Malplaquet ˈmælpləkeɪ

malpractice, -s ˌmælˈpræktɪs, -ɪz

malt (s. v.), -s, -ing, -ed mɔːlt [mɒlt], -s, -ɪŋ, -ɪd

Malta ˈmɔːltə [ˈmɒl-]

Maltese ˌmɔːlˈtiːz [ˌmɒl-, also '-- according to sentence-stress]

Malthus ˈmælθəs

Malthusian, -s, -ism mælˈθjuːzjən [-ˈθuː-, -zɪən], -z, -ɪzəm

Malton (in North Yorkshire) ˈmɔːltən [ˈmɒl-]

Maltravers mælˈtrævəz

maltreat, -s, -ing, -ed, -ment ˌmælˈtriːt, -s, -ɪŋ, -ɪd, -mənt

maltster, -s ˈmɔːltstə* [ˈmɒl-], -z

Malvern ˈmɔːlvən [ˈmɒl-, -vɜːn, locally also ˈmɔːvən]

malversation ˌmælvɜːˈseɪʃn

Malvolio mælˈvəʊljəʊ [-lɪəʊ]

Malyon ˈmæljən [-lɪən]

Mameluke, -s ˈmæmɪluːk [-ljuːk], -s

Mamie ˈmeɪmɪ

Mamilius məˈmɪlɪəs [mæˈm-, -ljəs]

mamma (mother), -s məˈmɑː, -z

mamm|a (milk-secreting organ), -ae ˈmæm|ə, -iː

mammal, -s ˈmæml, -z

mammalia, -n mæˈmeɪljə [məˈm-, -lɪə], -n

mammaliferous ˌmæməˈlɪfərəs

mammary ˈmæmərɪ

mammon (M.) ˈmæmən

mammoth, -s ˈmæməθ, -s

mamm|y, -ies ˈmæm|ɪ, -ɪz

man (s.) (M.), men mæn, men

man (v.), -s, -ning, -ned mæn, -z, -ɪŋ, -d

manac|le, -les, -ling, -led ˈmænək|l, -lz, -lɪŋ, -ld

manag|e, -es, -ing, -ed, -ement/s ˈmænɪdʒ, -ɪz, -ɪŋ, -d, -mənt/s

manageability ˌmænɪdʒəˈbɪlətɪ [-nədʒ-, -lɪt-]

manageab|le, -ly, -leness ˈmænɪdʒəb|l [-nədʒ-], -lɪ, -lnɪs [-nəs]

311

manager—manœuvre

manager, -s ˈmænɪdʒə* [-nədʒ-], -z
manageress, -es ˌmænɪdʒəˈres [-nədʒ-, ˈmænɪdʒəres], -ɪz
managerial ˌmænəˈdʒɪərɪəl
Manasseh məˈnæsɪ [-sə]
Manasses məˈnæsɪz [-siːz]
man-at-arms, men-at-arms mænət-ˈɑːmz, ˌmenətˈɑːmz
manatee (M.), -s ˌmænəˈtiː, -z
Manchester ˈmæntʃɪstə* [-tʃestə*, -tʃəstə*]
Manchu, -s ˌmænˈtʃuː [also ˈmæntʃuː: when attributive], -z
Manchukuo ˌmæntʃuːˈkwəʊ
Manchuria, -n/s mænˈtʃʊərɪə [-ˈtʃɔːr-, -ˈtʃɔːr-], -n/z
manciple, -s ˈmænsɪpl, -z
Mancunian, -s mæŋˈkjuːnjən [-nɪən], -z
Mandalay ˌmændəˈleɪ
mandamus, -es mænˈdeɪməs, -ɪz
mandarin, -s ˈmændərɪn, -z
mandate (s.), -s ˈmændeɪt [-dɪt], -s
mandat|e (v.), -es, -ing, -ed ˈmændeɪt [-ˈ-], -s, -ɪŋ, -ɪd
mandator|y (s. adj.), -ies ˈmændətər|ɪ [mænˈdeɪtər|ɪ], -ɪz
Mander (surname) ˈmɑːndə*, ˈmændə*
Mandeville ˈmændəvɪl [-dɪv-]
mandible, -s ˈmændɪbl [-dəbl], -z
mandolin, -s ˈmændəlɪn, -z
mandoline, -s ˌmændəˈliːn [ˈmændəli:n, ˈmændəlɪn], -z
mandragora mænˈdrægərə [mən-]
mandrake, -s ˈmændreɪk, -s
mandrill, -s ˈmændrɪl, -z
mane, -s, -d meɪn, -z, -d
man-eater, -s ˈmænˌiːtə*, -z
manège, -s mæˈneɪʒ [ˈmæneɪʒ], -ɪz
manes (ghosts) (M.) ˈmɑːneɪz [ˈmeɪniːz]
manet ˈmænet [old-fashioned ˈmeɪnet]
Manfred ˈmænfred [-frɪd]
man|ful, -fully, -fulness ˈmæn|fʊl, -fʊlɪ [-fəlɪ], -fʊlnɪs [-nəs]
manganese ˈmæŋgəniːz [ˌ-ˈ-]
manganic mæŋˈgænɪk
mange meɪndʒ
mangel-wurzel, -s ˈmæŋglˌwɜːzl [ˌ-ˈ-], -z
manger, -s ˈmeɪndʒə*, -z
mang|le, -les, -ling, -led ˈmæŋg|l, -lz, -lɪŋ [-l̩ɪŋ], -ld
mango, -es ˈmæŋgəʊ, -z
mangold, -s ˈmæŋgəld, -z
mangosteen, -s ˈmæŋgəʊstiːn, -z
mangrove, -s ˈmæŋgrəʊv, -z
mang|y, -ier, -iest, -ily, -iness ˈmeɪndʒ|ɪ, -ɪə* [-jə*], -ɪɪst [-jɪst], -ɪlɪ [-əlɪ], -ɪnɪs [-ɪnəs]

man-hand|le, -les, -ling, -led ˈmæn-ˌhænd|l [ˌ-ˈ--], -lz, -lɪŋ [-l̩ɪŋ], -ld
Manhattan mænˈhætn
manhole, -s ˈmænhəʊl, -z
manhood (M.) ˈmænhʊd
mania, -s ˈmeɪnjə [-nɪə], -z
maniac, -s ˈmeɪnɪæk [-njæk], -s
maniac|al, -ally məˈnaɪək|l, -əlɪ
manic-depressive ˌmænɪkdɪˈpresɪv
Manichean, -s ˌmænɪˈkiːən [-ˈkɪən], -z
manicur|e (s. v.), -es, -ing, -ed; -ist/s ˈmænɪˌkjʊə* [-kjəə*, -kjɔː*,] -z, -rɪŋ, -d; -rɪst/s
manifest (s. adj. v.), -ly; -s, -ing, -ed ˈmænɪfest, -lɪ; -s, -ɪŋ, -ɪd
manifestation, -s ˌmænɪfeˈsteɪʃn [-fəˈs-], -z
manifesto, -s ˌmænɪˈfestəʊ, -z
manifold, -ness ˈmænɪfəʊld [rarely ˈmen-], -nɪs [-nəs]
manikin, -s ˈmænɪkɪn, z
manil(l)a (M.), -s məˈnɪlə, -z
manioc ˈmænɪɒk
maniple, -s ˈmænɪpl, -z
manipulat|e, -es, -ing, -ed, -or/s məˈnɪpjʊleɪt [-pjəl-], -s, -ɪŋ, -ɪd, -ə*/z
manipulation, -s məˌnɪpjʊˈleɪʃn [-pjəˈl-], -z
manipulative məˈnɪpjʊlətɪv [-pjəl-]
Manitoba ˌmænɪˈtəʊbə
mankind (in general) mænˈkaɪnd, (when opp. womankind) ˈmænkaɪnd
Manley ˈmænlɪ
manlike ˈmænlaɪk
Manlius ˈmænlɪəs [-ljəs]
man|ly, -lier, -liest, -liness ˈmæn|lɪ, -lɪə* [-ljə*], -lɪɪst [-ljɪst], -lɪnɪs [-ɪnəs]
Mann mæn
manna ˈmænə
mannequin, -s ˈmænɪkɪn, -z
manner, -s, -ed; -ism/s ˈmænə*, -z, -d; -rɪzəm/z
manner|ly, -liness ˈmænə|lɪ, -lɪnɪs [-ɪnəs]
Manners ˈmænəz
Mannheim ˈmænhaɪm (ˈmanhaim)
mannikin, -s ˈmænɪkɪn, -z
Manning ˈmænɪŋ
mannish ˈmænɪʃ
Manns mænz
manny ˈmænɪ
Manoah məˈnəʊə
manœuvrability məˌnuːvrəˈbɪlətɪ [-vər-, -lɪt-]
manœuvrable məˈnuːvrəbl [-vər-]
manœuv|re, -res, -ring, -red, -rer/s məˈnuːv|ə*, -əz, -ərɪŋ, -əd, -ərə*/z

312

man-of-war, men-of-war ˌmænəvˈwɔː:*, ˌmenəvˈwɔː:*

manometer, -s məˈnɒmɪtə* [-mətə*], -z

manometric ˌmænəʊˈmetrɪk

manor, -s ˈmænə*, -z

manor-hou|se, -ses ˈmænəhaʊ|s, -zɪz

manorial məˈnɔːrɪəl [mæˈn-]

manostat, -s ˈmænəʊstæt, -s

manpower ˈmænˌpaʊə*

manqué ˈmãːŋkeɪ [ˈmɒŋ-] (mãke)

Manresa (town in Spain) mænˈreɪsə [-ˈreɪzə] (man'resa), (in names of streets, etc.) mænˈriːzə [-ˈriːsə]

Mansa ˈmænsə

manse, -s mæns, -ɪz

Mansel(l) ˈmænsl

Mansergh ˈmænsə*

Mansfield ˈmænsfiːld

mansion (M.), -s ˈmæn|ʃn, -z

mansion-hou|se (M.), -ses ˈmænʃn-haʊ|s, -zɪz

manslaughter ˈmænˌslɔːtə*

man-slayer, -s ˈmænˌsleɪə*, -z

mansuetude ˈmænswɪtjuːd

mantel, -s ˈmæntl, -z

mantel-board, -s ˈmæntlbɔːd [-bɔəd], -z

mantelpiece, -s ˈmæntlpiːs, -ɪz

mantelshel|f, -ves ˈmæntlʃel|f, -vz

mantilla, -s mænˈtɪlə, -z

Mantinea ˌmæntɪˈnɪə [-ˈniːə]

mantis, -es ˈmæntɪs, -ɪz

mant|le, -les, -ling, -led ˈmænt|l, -lz, -lɪŋ [-l̩ɪŋ], -ld

mantra, -s ˈmæntrə, -z

mantramistic ˌmæntrəˈmɪstɪk

mantrap, -s ˈmæntræp, -s

mantua (M.), -s ˈmæntjʊə [-tjwə, ˈmæntʊə], -z

manual (s. adj.), -s, -ly ˈmænjʊəl [-njwəl, -njʊl], -z, -ɪ

Manuel ˈmænjʊel [-njʊəl, -njwəl]

manufactor|y, -ies ˌmænjʊˈfæktər|ɪ, -ɪz

manufact|ure (s. v.), -ures, -uring, -ured, -urer/s ˌmænjʊˈfæktʃ|ə*, -əz, -ərɪŋ, -əd, -ərə*/z

manumission, -s ˌmænjʊˈmɪʃn, -z

manumit, -s, -ting, -ted ˌmænjʊˈmɪt, -s, -ɪŋ, -ɪd

manur|e (s. v.), -es, -ing, -ed məˈnjʊə* [-ˈnjɔə*, -ˈnjɔː:*], -z, -rɪŋ, -d

manuscript, -s ˈmænjʊskrɪpt [-njəs-], -s

Manutius məˈnjuːʃjəs [-ʃɪəs, -ʃəs]

Manwaring ˈmænərɪŋ

Manx, -man, -men mæŋks, -mən [-mæn], -mən [-men]

many ˈmenɪ

manysided ˌmenɪˈsaɪdɪd [also ˈ--ˌ-- when attributive]

manysidedness ˌmenɪˈsaɪdɪdnɪs [-nəs]

manzanilla ˌmænzəˈnɪlə [-ɪljə]

mao|ist/s, -ism ˈmaʊ|ɪst/s, -ɪzəm

Maori, -s ˈmaʊrɪ [ˈmɑ:ər-], -z

Mao Tse-tung ˌmaʊtseˈtʊŋ

map (s. v.), -s, -ping, -ped mæp, -s, -ɪŋ, -t

maple (M.), -s ˈmeɪpl, -z

Mapother ˈmeɪpɒðə*

Mappin ˈmæpɪn

maquillage ˌmækiːˈɑː:ʒ [-kɪˈɑ:ʒ] (makija:ʒ)

maquis ˈmæki: [ˈmɑ:k-] (maki)

mar (M.), -s, -ring, -red mɑ:*, -z, -rɪŋ, -d

marabou, -s ˈmærəbuː:, -z

maraschino (M.) ˌmærəˈski:nəʊ

Marathi, -s məˈrɑ:tɪ (Hindi məraṭhi), -z

marathon (M.) ˈmærəθn

maraud, -s, -ing, -ed, -er/s məˈrɔ:d, -z, -ɪŋ, -ɪd, -ə*/z

Marazion ˌmærəˈzaɪən

marble, -s, -d ˈmɑ:bl, -z, -d

Marburg (German town) ˈmɑ:ˌbʊəg [-bə:g] (ˈmarburk, -burç)

marcasite ˈmɑ:kəsaɪt

Marcel(le) mɑ:ˈsel [also ˈ-- when attributive]

Marcella mɑ:ˈselə

Marcellus mɑ:ˈseləs

march (s. v.) (M.), -es, -ing, -ed mɑ:tʃ, -ɪz, -ɪŋ, -t

Marchant ˈmɑ:tʃənt

Marchbank, -s ˈmɑ:tʃbæŋk, -s

Marchesi mɑ:ˈkeɪzɪ

marchioness, -es ˈmɑ:ʃənɪs [ˌmɑ:ʃəˈnes], -ɪz

Marchmont ˈmɑ:tʃmənt

marchpane ˈmɑ:tʃʃpeɪn

Marcia ˈmɑ:sjə [-sɪə]

Marco ˈmɑ:kəʊ

Marconi mɑ:ˈkəʊnɪ

marconigram, -s mɑ:ˈkəʊnɪgræm, -z

Marcus ˈmɑ:kəs

Marden (in Kent) ˈmɑ:dən [old-fashioned mɑ:ˈden]

mare, -s meə*, -z

Marengo məˈreŋgəʊ

mare's-nest, -s ˈmeəznest, -s

mare's-tail, -s ˈmeəzteɪl, -z

Margaret ˈmɑ:gərɪt

margarine ˌmɑ:dʒəˈriːn [ˌmɑ:gə-, ˈ---]

Margarita ˌmɑ:gəˈri:tə

Margate ˈmɑ:geɪt [-gɪt]

marge mɑ:dʒ

Margerison mɑ:ˈdʒerɪsn, ˈmɑ:dʒərɪsn

Margery ˈmɑ:dʒərɪ

Margetson ˈmɑ:dʒɪtsn, ˈmɑ:gɪtsn

313

Margetts 'mɑːgɪts
margin, -s 'mɑːdʒɪn, -z
margin|al, -ally 'mɑːdʒɪn|l, -əlɪ
marginalia ˌmɑːdʒɪ'neɪljə [-lɪə]
Margoliouth 'mɑːgəlju:θ
Margot 'mɑːgəʊ
margrave (M.), -s 'mɑːgreɪv, -z
margravine, -s 'mɑːgrəviːn, -z
marguerite (M.), -s ˌmɑːgə'riːt -s,
Margulies 'mɑːgʊlɪs
Marham (in Norfolk) 'mærəm ['mɑːr-]
    Note.—The pronunciation of the local
    residents is 'mærəm.
Marhamchurch 'mærəmtʃɜːtʃ
Maria (English name) mə'raɪə, mə'rɪə,
    (Latin name) mə'riːə [-'rɪə]
Marian 'meərɪən, 'mær-
Mariana (English name) ˌmeərɪ'ænə
    [ˌmær-], -'ɑːnə, (Spanish historian)
    ˌmɑːrɪ'ɑːnə (mari'ana)
Marie (Christian name) 'mɑːrɪ [-riː],
    mə'riː; (biscuits) 'mɑːrɪ [-riː]
Marienbad mə'riːənbɑːd [-'rɪən-, mɑː'r-]
    (mɑː'riːənbɑːt)
marigold (M.), -s 'mærɪgəʊld, -z
marijuana (-huana) ˌmærjuː'ɑːnə
    [-ruː'ɑːnə, -jʊ'ɑːnə, ˌmærɪ'wɑːnə,
    -ɪ'hwɑːnə, -ɪ'dʒwɑːnə]
Marilyn 'mærɪlɪn
marina (M.), -s mə'riːnə, -z
marinade ˌmærɪ'neɪd ['---]
marine (s. adj.), -s mə'riːn, -z
mariner, -s 'mærɪnə* [-rən-], -z
mariolatry ˌmeərɪ'ɒlətrɪ [ˌmær-]
Marion 'meərɪən, 'meər-
marionette, -s ˌmærɪə'net, -s
Marischal (college at Aberdeen) 'mɑːʃl
marish (s. adj.) (marsh, marshy), -es
    'mærɪʃ, -ɪz
marish (adj.) (like a mare) 'meərɪʃ
Marishes 'mærɪʃɪz
marital 'mærɪtl [mə'raɪtl]
maritime (M.) 'mærɪtaɪm
Marius 'meərɪəs, 'mærɪəs
marj [marge] mɑːdʒ
marjoram 'mɑːdʒərəm
Marjoribanks 'mɑːtʃbæŋks, 'mɑːʃb-
Marjor|ie, -y 'mɑːdʒər|ɪ, -ɪ
mark (s. v.) (M.), -s, -ing/s, -ed, -edly,
    -er/s mɑːk, -s, -ɪŋ/z, -t, -ɪdlɪ, -ə*/z
Markby 'mɑːkbɪ
market (s. v.) (M.), -s, -ing, -ed; -able
    'mɑːkɪt, -s, -ɪŋ, -ɪd; -əbl
marketability ˌmɑːkɪtə'bɪlətɪ [-ɪtɪ]
market-day, -s 'mɑːkɪtdeɪ, -z
marketeer, -s ˌmɑːkə'tɪə*, -z
market-garden, -s 'mɑːkɪtˌgɑːdn [ˌ--'--],
    -z

market-place, -s 'mɑːkɪtpleɪs, -ɪz
market-price, -s ˌmɑːkɪt'praɪs, -ɪz
market-town, -s 'mɑːkɪttaʊn, -z
Markham 'mɑːkəm
Marks mɑːks
marks|man, -men 'mɑːks|mən, -mən
    [-men]
marksmanship 'mɑːksmənʃɪp
marl mɑːl
Marlborough 'mɔːlbərə ['mɑːl-]
    Note.—'mɔːlbərə is the usual pro-
    nunciation of the name of the town
    in Wiltshire and of the family name.
    'mɑːl- is not infrequently heard in
    names of London streets. 'mɑːl- is
    also the form used for the name of
    the town in U.S.A. and the district
    in New Zealand.
Marlene (English name) 'mɑːliːn,
    mɑː'liːn, (German name) mɑː'leɪnə
    (mar'leːnə)
Marler 'mɑːlə*
Marl|ey, -ing 'mɑːl|ɪ, -ɪŋ
Marlow(e) 'mɑːləʊ
Marmaduke 'mɑːmədjuːk
marmalade, -s 'mɑːmleɪd [-mˌleɪd], -z
Marmion 'mɑːmjən [-mɪən]
marmite 'mɑːmaɪt [-miːt]
Marmora 'mɑːmərə
marmoset, -s 'mɑːməʊzet, -s
marmot, -s 'mɑːmət, -s
Marne mɑːn
Marner 'mɑːnə*
marocain 'mærəkeɪn
maroon (s. v.), -s, -ing, -ed mə'ruːn, -z,
    -ɪŋ, -d
Marquand 'mɑːkwənd
marque mɑːk
marquee, -s mɑː'kiː, -z
Marquesas mɑː'keɪsæs [-eɪzæs, -əs]
marquess [-quis], -es 'mɑːkwɪs, -ɪz
marquessate, -s 'mɑːkwɪsət [-ɪt], -s
marquet(e)ry 'mɑːkɪtrɪ [-ətrɪ]
marquisate, -s 'mɑːkwɪzət [-ɪt], -s
Marrakesh ˌmærə'keʃ [mə'rækeʃ]
marram 'mærəm
marriage, -s; -able 'mærɪdʒ, -ɪz; -əbl
marrow, -s, -y 'mærəʊ, -z, -ɪ
marrowbone, -s 'mærəʊbəʊn, -z
marrowfat, -s 'mærəʊfæt, -s
marr|y (v. interj.), -ies, -ying, -ied
    'mær|ɪ, -ɪz, -ɪɪŋ, -ɪd
Marryat 'mærɪət
Mars mɑːz
Marsala mɑː'sɑːlə
Marsden 'mɑːzdən
Marseillaise ˌmɑːseɪ'jeɪz [-seɪ'eɪz, -sə-
    'eɪz, -sl̩'eɪz] (marsɛjɛːz)

Marseilles mɑːˈseɪ [-ˈseɪlz]
marsh (M.), -es mɑːʃ, -ɪz
marsh|al (s. v.), -als, -alling, -alled
'mɑːʃ|l, -lz, -]ɪŋ [-əlɪŋ], -ld
Marshall 'mɑːʃl
marshalsea (M.) 'mɑːʃlsi: [-sɪ]
marsh|y, -ier, -iest, -iness 'mɑːʃ|ɪ, -ɪə*
[-jə*], -ɪɪst [-jɪst], -ɪnɪs [-ɪnəs]
Marsland 'mɑːzlənd
Marston 'mɑːstən
marsupial (s. adj.), -s mɑːˈsuːpjəl
[-ˈsjuː-, -pɪəl], -z
mart, -s mɑːt, -s
martel(l) mɑːˈtel
martello mɑːˈteləʊ
marten, -s 'mɑːtɪn, -z
Martha 'mɑːθə
marti|al (M.), -ally 'mɑːʃ|l, -əlɪ
Martian, -s 'mɑːʃn [-ʃɪən, -ʃjən], -z
martin (M.), -s 'mɑːtɪn, -z
Martineau 'mɑːtɪnəʊ
martinet, -s ˌmɑːtɪˈnet, -s
martini (M.), -s mɑːˈtiːnɪ, -z
Martinique ˌmɑːtɪˈniːk
Martinmas 'mɑːtɪnməs [-mæs]
martyr (s. v.) (M.), -s, -ing, -ed 'mɑːtə*,
-z, -rɪŋ, -d
martyrdom, -s 'mɑːtədəm, -z
martyriz|e [-is|e], -es, -ing, -ed 'mɑː-
təraɪz [-tɪr-], -ɪz, -ɪŋ, -d
marv|el (s. v.), -els, -elling, -elled
'mɑːv|l, -lz, -]ɪŋ [-əlɪŋ], -ld
Marvell 'mɑːvl
marvellous, -ly, -ness 'mɑːvələs, -lɪ,
-nɪs [-nəs]
Marx mɑːks
marxian 'mɑːksjən [-ɪən]
marxi|sm, -st/s 'mɑːksɪ|zəm, -st/s
Mary 'meərɪ
Maryborough 'meərɪbərə [-bʌrə]
Maryculter ˌmeərɪˈkuːtə*
Maryland 'meərɪlænd [-lənd, also 'merɪ-
lənd in imitation of American pro-
nunciation]
Marylebone (road, district (without St.))
'mærələbən [-bəʊn, 'mærəbən, 'mærɪ-
bən, 'mɑːlɪbən]
Mary-le-Bone (preceded by St. as in the
expressions Church of, Borough of
St. M.) ˌmeərɪləˈbəʊn
Maryport 'meərɪpɔːt
Marzials 'mɑːzjəlz [-zɪəlz]
marzipan ˌmɑːzɪˈpæn ['---]
Masai (African people, language)
'mɑːsaɪ
Masaryk 'mæsərɪk ['mæz-]
Mascagni mæˈskɑːnji: [-njɪ]
mascara mæˈskɑːrə

mascot, -s 'mæskət [-skɒt], -s
masculine (s. adj.), -s 'mæskjʊlɪn
['mɑːs-, -kjə-], -z
masculinity ˌmæskjʊˈlɪnətɪ [ˌmɑːs-,
-kjə-, -ɪtɪ]
Masefield 'meɪsfiːld ['meɪz-]
maser, -s 'meɪzə*, -z
mash (s. v.) (M.), -es, -ing, -ed mæʃ,
-ɪz, -ɪŋ, -t
Masham (in North Yorkshire) 'mæsəm,
(surname) 'mæsəm, 'mæʃəm
masher, -s 'mæʃə*, -z
mash|ie [-sh|y], -ies 'mæʃ|ɪ, -ɪz
Mashona, -land məˈʃɒnə [old-fashioned
-'ʃəʊn-], -lænd
Masie 'meɪzɪ
mask (s. v.), -s, -ing, -ed mɑːsk, -s, -ɪŋ,
-t
Maskell 'mæskl ['mɑːs-]
Maskelyne 'mæskɪlɪn [-kəl-]
Maslin 'mæzlɪn
masochi|sm, -st/s 'mæsəʊkɪ|zəm, -st/s
masochistic ˌmæsəʊˈkɪstɪk
mason (M.), -s 'meɪsn, -z
masonic məˈsɒnɪk
masonry 'meɪsnrɪ
masque, -s mɑːsk [mæsk], -s
masquerad|e (s. v.), -es, -ing, -ed, -er/s
ˌmæskəˈreɪd [ˌmɑːs-], -z, -ɪŋ, -ɪd,
-ə*/z
mass (s.) (quantity of matter), -es mæs,
-ɪz
mass (s.) (celebration of Eucharist) (M.),
-es mæs [mɑːs], -ɪz
mass (v.), -es, -ing, -ed mæs, -ɪz, -ɪŋ,
-t
Massachusetts ˌmæsəˈtʃuːsɪts [-səts]
massac|re (s. v.), -res, -ring, -red
'mæsək|ə* [-sɪk-], -əz, -ərɪŋ, -əd
massag|e (s. v.), -es, -ing, -ed 'mæsɑːʒ
[-ɑːdʒ], -ɪz, -ɪŋ, -d
mass-book, -s 'mæsbʊk ['mɑːs-], -s
Massenet 'mæsəneɪ (masnɛ)
masseur, -s mæˈsɜː* (masœːr), -z
masseuse, -s mæˈsɜːz (masøːz), -ɪz
massif, -s 'mæsiːf [-'-], -s
Massinger 'mæsɪndʒə*
massive, -ly, -ness 'mæsɪv, -lɪ, -nɪs
[-nəs]
mass-meeting, -s ˌmæsˈmiːtɪŋ ['-ˌ--], -z
Masson 'mæsn
Massowa məˈsəʊə
mass-produc|e (v.), -es, -ing; -ed 'mæs-
prəˌdjuːs [-prʊˌd-, ˌ--'-'], -ɪz, -ɪŋ, -t
mass-production ˌmæsprəˈdʌkʃn
[-prʊ'd-, '--ˌ--]
mass|y, -iness 'mæs|ɪ, -ɪnɪs [-ɪnəs]
mast (all senses), -s mɑːst, -s

315

mast|er (*s. v.*), **-ers, -ering, -ered** 'mɑːst|ə*, -əz, -ərɪŋ, -əd
master|ful, -fully, -fulness 'mɑːstə|fʊl, -fʊlɪ [-fəlɪ], -fʊlnɪs [-nəs]
master-hand, -s 'mɑːstəhænd, -z
master-key, -s 'mɑːstəkiː, -z
masterl|y, -iness 'mɑːstəl|ɪ, -ɪnɪs [-ɪnəs]
Masterman 'mɑːstəmən
masterpiece, -s 'mɑːstəpiːs, -ɪz
mastership, -s 'mɑːstəʃɪp, -s
master-stroke, -s 'mɑːstəstrəʊk, -s
mastery 'mɑːstərɪ
mast-head, -s 'mɑːsthed, -z
mastic 'mæstɪk
masticat|e, -es, -ing, -ed, -or/s 'mæstɪkeɪt, -s, -ɪŋ, -ɪd, -ə*/z
mastication ˌmæstɪ'keɪʃn
mastiff, -s 'mæstɪf ['mɑːs-], -s
mastitis mæ'staɪtɪs
mastodon, -s 'mæstədɒn [-dən], -z
mastoid, -s 'mæstɔɪd, -z
mastoidal mæ'stɔɪdl
Masurian mə'sjʊərɪən
mat (*s. v.*), **-s, -ting, -ted** mæt, -s, -ɪŋ, -ɪd
Matabele, -land ˌmætə'biːlɪ, -lænd
matador, -s 'mætədɔː*, -z
match (*s. v.*), **-es, -ing, -ed** mætʃ, -ɪz, -ɪŋ, -t
match-board 'mætʃbɔːd [-bəəd]
match-box, -es 'mætʃbɒks, -ɪz
matchless, -ly, -ness 'mætʃlɪs [-ləs], -lɪ, -nɪs [-nəs]
match-maker, -s 'mætʃˌmeɪkə*, -z
matchwood 'mætʃwʊd
mat|e (*s. v.*), **-es, -ing, -ed** meɪt, -s, -ɪŋ, -ɪd
mater, -s 'meɪtə*, -z
material (*s. adj.*), **-s, -ly** mə'tɪərɪəl, -z, -ɪ
materiali|sm, -st/s mə'tɪərɪəlɪ|zm, -st/s
materialistic məˌtɪərɪə'lɪstɪk
materialization [-isa-], -s məˌtɪərɪəlaɪ'zeɪʃn [-lɪ'z-], -z
materializ|e [-is|e], -es, -ing, -ed mə'tɪərɪəlaɪz, -ɪz, -ɪŋ, -d
materiel məˌtɪərɪ'el [mæˌt-]
matern|al, -ally mə'tɜːn|l, -əlɪ
maternity mə'tɜːnətɪ [-ɪtɪ]
mathematician, -s ˌmæθəmə'tɪʃn [-θɪm-], -z
mathematic|s, -al, -ally ˌmæθə'mætɪk|s [-θɪ'm-], -l, -əlɪ
Mather, -s 'meɪðə*, 'mæðə*, -z
Matheson 'mæθɪsn [-θəs-]
Mathew, -s 'mæθjuː, 'meɪθ-, -z
Mathias mə'θaɪəs
Mat(h)ilda mə'tɪldə
maths mæθs

matin, -s 'mætɪn, -z
matinée, -s 'mætɪneɪ, -z
Matlock 'mætlɒk
Maton 'meɪtn
Matravers mə'trævəz
matriarch, -y 'meɪtrɪɑːk, -ɪ
matriarchal ˌmeɪtrɪ'ɑːkl
matric mə'trɪk
matricide, -s 'mætrɪsaɪd ['meɪt-], -z
matriculat|e, -es, -ing, -ed mə'trɪkjʊleɪt [-kjə-], -s, -ɪŋ, -ɪd
matriculation, -s məˌtrɪkjʊ'leɪʃn [-kjə-], -z
matrilineal ˌmætrɪ'lɪnɪəl [-njəl]
matrimonial, -ly ˌmætrɪ'məʊnjəl [-nɪəl], -ɪ
matrimony 'mætrɪmənɪ
matri|x, -xes, -ces 'meɪtrɪ|ks ['mæt-], -ksɪz, -siːz
Note.—Doctors generally pronounce 'meɪt-. *Those connected with the printing trade pronounce* 'mæt-.
matron, -s; -hood, -ly 'meɪtrən, -z; -hʊd, -lɪ
matt mæt
matter (*s. v.*), **-s, -ing, -ed** 'mætə*, -z -rɪŋ, -d
Matterhorn 'mætəhɔːn
matter-of-fact ˌmætərəv'fækt
Matthes 'mæθəs
Matthew, -s 'mæθjuː, -z
Matthias mə'θaɪəs
Matthiessen 'mæθɪsn
matting (*s.*) 'mætɪŋ
mattins 'mætɪnz
mattock, -s 'mætək, -s
mattress, -es 'mætrɪs [-trəs], -ɪz
maturat|e, -es, -ing, -ed 'mætjʊreɪt [-tjə-, -tʃʊ-, -tʃə-], -s, -ɪŋ, -ɪd
maturation ˌmætjʊ'reɪʃn [-tjə-, -tʃʊ-, -tʃə-]
matur|e (*adj. v.*), **-ely, -eness, -ing, -ed; -ity** mə'tjʊə* [-'tjɔː*, -'tjɔː:*, -'tʃʊə*, -'tʃɔə*, -'tʃɔː*], -lɪ, -nɪs [-nəs]; -z, -rɪŋ, -d; -rətɪ [-rɪtɪ]
Maturin (*surname*) 'mætjʊrɪn [-tʃʊr-, -tʃər-]
matutinal ˌmætju'taɪnl [-tjʊ-, mə'tjuː-tɪnl]
matzos 'mɒtsəz ['mæt-, -əʊz]
maud (M.), -s mɔːd, -z
Maude mɔːd
maudlin 'mɔːdlɪn
Mauger 'meɪdʒə*
Maugha|m, -n mɔː|m, -n
maugre 'mɔːgə*
maul (*s. v.*), **-s, -ing, -ed** mɔːl, -z, -ɪŋ, -d
Mauleverer mɔː'levərə*

maulstick, -s 'mɔːlstɪk, -s
Mau-Mau 'maʊmaʊ [ˌ-'-]
maunder, -s, -ing, -ed 'mɔːndə*, -z, -rɪŋ, -d
maundy (M.) 'mɔːndɪ
Maunsell 'mænsl
Maureen 'mɔːriːn [mɔːˈriːn]
Mauretania ˌmɒrɪˈteɪnjə [ˌmɔːr-, -nɪə]
Maurice 'mɒrɪs
Mauritius məˈrɪʃəs [mʊˈr-, mɔːˈr-, mɒˈr-, -ʃjəs]
Mauser, -s 'maʊzə*, -z
mausoleum, -s ˌmɔːsəˈlɪəm [-'liːəm], -z
mauve, -s məʊv, -z
maverick 'mævərɪk
mavis (M.) 'meɪvɪs
Mavourneen məˈvʊəniːn [-ˈvɔːn-, -ˈvɔːn-]
maw, -s mɔː, -z
Mawer 'mɔːə* [mɔə*]
Mawhinny məˈwɪnɪ [-ˈhw-]
mawkish, -ly, -ness 'mɔːkɪʃ, -lɪ, -nɪs [-nəs]
Max mæks
maxi, -s 'mæksɪ, -z
maxill|a, -ae, -as, -ary mækˈsɪl|ə, -iː, -əz, -ərɪ
maxim (M.), -s 'mæksɪm, -z
maximal 'mæksɪml
Maximilian ˌmæksɪˈmɪljən [-lɪən]
†maxim|um, -a 'mæksɪm|əm, -ə
Maximus 'mæksɪməs
Maxse 'mæksɪ
Maxwell 'mækswəl [-wel]
may (auxil. v.) meɪ (normal form), me (occasional strong form before vowels)
May meɪ
Mayall 'meɪɔːl
maybe 'meɪbɪ: [ˌ-'-, -bɪ]
may-bug, -s 'meɪbʌg, -z
may-day (M.), -s 'meɪdeɪ, -z
Mayfair 'meɪfeə*
may-flower (M.), -s 'meɪˌflaʊə*, -z
may-fl|y, -ies 'meɪfl|aɪ, -aɪz
mayhap 'meɪhæp
mayhem 'meɪhem
Mayhew 'meɪhjuː
maying 'meɪɪŋ
Maynard 'meɪnəd [-nɑːd]
Maynooth məˈnuːθ
mayn't meɪnt [meɪŋt, meənt]
Maynwaring 'mænərɪŋ
Mayo, -s (in Ireland, surname) 'meɪəʊ, (American Indian) 'maɪəʊ, -z
mayonnaise, -s ˌmeɪəˈneɪz [rarely ˌmaɪəˈn, also '— when followed by a stress], -ɪz

mayor (M.), -s; -ess/es meə*, -z; -rɪs/ɪz [-res/ɪz, ˌ-'-]
mayoral, -ty 'meərəl, -tɪ
Mayou 'meɪuː
maypole, -s 'meɪpəʊl, -z
may-queen, -s ˌmeɪˈkwiːn ['meɪkwiːn], -z
mazda (M.), -s 'mæzdə, -z
maze, -s meɪz, -ɪz
Mazenod 'meɪznɒd
Mazin (surname) 'meɪzɪn
Mazo de la Roche ˌmeɪzəʊ dəlɑːˈrɒʃ
mazurka, -s məˈzɜːkə, -z
maz|y, -ier, -iest, -ily, -iness 'meɪz|ɪ, -ɪə* [-jə], -ɪɪst [-jɪst], -ɪlɪ [-əlɪ], -ɪnɪs [-ɪnəs]
me (note in Tonic Sol-fa), -s miː, -z
me (pron.) miː: (normal form), mɪ (freq. weak form)
mead (M.), -s miːd, -z
Meaden 'miːdn
meadow, -s, -y 'medəʊ, -z, -ɪ
meadow-grass 'medəʊgrɑːs
meadowsweet 'medəʊswiːt
Meagher mɑː*
meagre, -r, -st, -ly, -ness 'miːgə*, -rə*, -rɪst, -lɪ, -nɪs [-nəs]
Meaker 'miːkə*
meal, -s miːl, -z
mealie, -s 'miːlɪ, -z
mealtime, -s 'miːltaɪm, -z
meal|y, -ier, -iest, -iness 'miːl|ɪ, -ɪə* [-jə*], -ɪɪst [-jɪst], -ɪnɪs [-ɪnəs]
mealy-bug 'miːlɪbʌg
mealy-mouthed 'miːlɪmaʊðd [ˌ-'-]
mean (s. adj. v.), -s; -er, -est, -ly, -ness; -ing, meant miːn, -z; -ə*, -ɪst, -lɪ, -nɪs [-nəs]; -ɪŋ, ment
meander (s. v.) (M.), -s, -ing, -ed mɪˈændə* [miːˈæ-], -z, -rɪŋ, -d
meaning (s. adj.), -s, -ly 'miːnɪŋ, -z, -lɪ
meaningless 'miːnɪŋlɪs [-ləs]
means (s.) miːnz
meant (from mean) ment
meantime ˌmiːnˈtaɪm ['--]
meanwhile ˌmiːnˈwaɪl [-ˈhw-, '--]
Mearns mɜːnz, meənz [mɪənz]
Mears mɪəz
meas|les, -ly 'miːz|lz, -lɪ
measurab|le, -ly, -leness 'meʒərəb|l, -lɪ, -lnɪs [-nəs]
measur|e (s. v.), -es, -ing, -ed, -er/s; -ement/s; -eless 'meʒə*, -z, -rɪŋ, -d, -rə*/z; -mənt/s; -lɪs [-ləs]
meat, -s, -ball/s miːt, -s, -bɔːl/z
Meates miːts
Meath (Irish county) miːð [often pronounced miːθ by English people]

317

meatless 'mi:tlɪs [-ləs]
meat-offering, -s 'mi:t,ɒfərɪŋ, -z
meat-pie, -s ,mi:t'paɪ, -z
meat-safe, -s 'mi:tseɪf, -s
meatus, -es mɪ'eɪtəs [mi:'eɪ-], -ɪz
meat|y, -ier, -iest, -iness 'mi:t|ɪ, -ɪə*,
  -ɪɪst, -ɪnɪs [-nəs]
Mecca 'mekə
meccano (M.), -s mɪ'kɑ:nəʊ [me-, mə-],
  -z
mechanic, -s, -al, -ally mɪ'kænɪk [mə-],
  -s, -l, -əlɪ
mechanician, -s ,mekə'nɪʃn, -z
†mechanism, -s 'mekənɪzəm [-kn̩ɪ-],
  -z
mechanization [-isa-] ,mekənaɪ'zeɪʃn
  [-nɪ'z-]
mechaniz|e [-is|e], -es, -ing, -ed
  'mekənaɪz, -ɪz, -ɪŋ, -d
Mechlin 'meklɪn
Mecklenburg 'meklɪnbɜ:g [-lən-]
medal, -s 'medl, -z
medallion, -s mɪ'dæljən [me'd-, mə'd-],
  -z
medallist, -s 'medl|ɪst [-dəl-], -s
medd|le, -les, -ling, -led, -ler/s 'med|l,
  -lz, -lɪŋ [-lɪŋ], -ld, -lə*/z [-lə*/z]
meddlesome, -ness 'medlsəm, -nɪs
  [-nəs]
Mede, -s mi:d, -z
Medea mɪ'dɪə [mə'd, -'di:ə]
me|dia (phonetic term), -diae 'me|dɪə,
  -dɪi: [-dɪaɪ]
media (plur. of medium) 'mi:djə [-dɪə]
mediaeval= medieval
medial 'mi:djəl [-dɪəl]
median, -s 'mi:djən [-dɪən], -z
mediant, -s 'mi:djənt [-dɪənt], -s
mediate (adj.), -ly, -ness 'mi:dɪət [-djət,
  -djɪt, -dɪɪt], -lɪ, -nɪs [-nəs]
mediat|e (v.), -es, -ing, -ed 'mi:dɪeɪt, -s,
  -ɪŋ, -ɪd
mediation, -s ,mi:dɪ'eɪʃn, -z
mediator (M.), -s 'mi:dɪeɪtə*, -z
mediatorial ,mi:dɪə'tɔ:rɪəl [-djə-]
medic|al (s. adj.), -als, -ally 'medɪk|l,
  -lz, -əlɪ
medicament, -s mə'dɪkəmənt [mɪ'd-,
  me'd-, 'medɪk-], -s
medicat|e, -es, -ing, -ed 'medɪkeɪt, -s,
  -ɪŋ, -ɪd
medication ,medɪ'keɪʃn
Medicean ,medɪ'tʃi:ən [-'tʃɪən, -'si:ən,
  -'sɪən]
Medici 'medɪtʃi: [-tʃɪ, me'di:tʃi:]
  ('me:ditʃi)
medicin|al, -ally mə'dɪsɪn|l [mɪ'd-,
  me'd-, -sn̩|l]], -əlɪ [-l̩ɪ]

medicine, -s; -chest/s; -man, -men
  'medsɪn [-dɪsɪn, -dsən], -z; -tʃest/s;
  -mæn, -men
medico, -s 'medɪkəʊ, -z
mediev|al, -alism, -alist/s ,medɪ'i:v|l
  [me'di:v|l], -əlɪzəm [-l̩ɪzəm], -əlɪst/s
Medill mə'dɪl
Medina (in Arabia) me'di:nə [mɪ'd-],
  (in U.S.A.) me'daɪnə [mɪ'd-]
medinal 'medɪnl
mediocre ,mi:dɪ'əʊkə* [,med-, '——]
mediocrity ,mi:dɪ'ɒkrətɪ [,med-, -rɪtɪ]
meditat|e, -es, -ing, -ed 'medɪteɪt, -s,
  -ɪŋ, -ɪd
meditation, -s ,medɪ'teɪʃn, -z
meditative, -ly, -ness 'medɪtətɪv [-teɪt-],
  -lɪ, -nɪs [-nəs]
Mediterranean ,medɪtə'reɪnjən [-nɪən]
medi|um (s. adj.), -a, -ums 'mi:dj|əm
  [-dɪ|-], -ə, -əmz
mediumistic ,mi:djə'mɪstɪk [-dɪə-]
medlar, -s 'medlə*, -z
medley (M.), -s 'medlɪ, -z
Medlock 'medlɒk
Médoc, -s 'meɪdɒk ['med-, me'dɒk], -s
medulla, -s me'dʌlə [mɪ'd-], -z
Medusa mɪ'dju:zə [me'd-, mə'd-,
  -'dju:sə]
Medway 'medweɪ
Mee mi:
meed, -s mi:d, -z
meek (M.), -er, -est, -ly, -ness mi:k,
  -ə*, -ɪst, -lɪ, -nɪs [-nəs]
meerschaum, -s 'mɪəʃəm [-ʃaʊm], -z
Meerut 'mɪərət (Hindi merəth)
meet (s. adj. v.), -s, -ly, -ness; -ing/s,
  met mi:t, -s, -lɪ, -nɪs [-nəs]; -ɪŋ/z,
  met
meeting-hou|se, -ses 'mi:tɪŋhaʊ|s, -zɪz
meeting-place, -s 'mi:tɪŋpleɪs, -ɪz
Meg meg
mega- 'megə- [or ,megə- when main
  stress follows]
megacycle, -s 'megə,saɪkl, -z
megahertz 'megəhɜ:ts [-heəts]
megalithic ,megə'lɪθɪk
megalomania ,megələʊ'meɪnjə [-nɪə]
megalomaniac, -s ,megələʊ'meɪnɪæk
  [-njæk], -s
Megan 'megən
megaphone, -s 'megəfəʊn, -z
megatheri|um, -a ,megə'θɪərɪ|əm, -ə
megaton, -s 'megətʌn, -z
megawatt, -s 'megəwɒt, -s
megilp mə'gɪlp
megrim, -s 'mi:grɪm, -z
Meier 'maɪə*
Meighen (Canadian name) 'mi:ən

Meigs meɡz
Meikle 'miːkl
Meiklejohn 'mɪkldʒɒn
meiosis maɪ'əusɪs
Meistersinger, -s 'maɪstə,sɪŋə*, -z
melancholia ,melən'kəʊljə [-ləŋ'k-, -lɪə]
melancholic ,melən'kɒlɪk [-ləŋ'k-]
melancholy (s. adj.) 'melənkəlɪ [-ləŋk-, -kɒlɪ]
Melanchthon me'læŋkθɒn [mɪ'l-, -θən]
Melane|sia, -sian/s ,melə'niː|zjə [-zɪə, -ʒjə, -ʒɪə, -ʒə, -sjə, -sɪə, -ʃjə, -ʃɪə, -ʃə], -zjən/z [-zɪən/z, -ʒjən/z, -ʒɪən/z, -ʒn/z, -sjən/z, -sɪən/z, -ʃjən/z, -ʃɪən/z, -ʃn/z]
mélange, -s meɪ'lɑ̃ːnʒ [-'lɔ̃ːnʒ, '--] (melɑ̃ː3), -ɪz
Melanie 'melənɪ
mela|nin, -nism 'melə|nɪn, -nɪzəm
Melanthios me'lænθɪəs [-θɪɒs]
Melba 'melbə
Melbourne 'melbən [-bɔːn]
Note.—In Australia always 'melbən.
Melchett 'meltʃɪt
Melchizedek mel'kɪzədek
Melcombe 'melkəm
Meleager ,melɪ'eɪɡə*
mêlée, -s 'meleɪ ['meɪl-] (mɛle), -z
Melhuish 'melɪʃ, 'meljʊɪʃ [-lhjʊɪʃ]
melinite 'melɪnaɪt
Melita 'melɪtə
mellifluous me'lɪflʊəs [-flwəs]
Mellin 'melɪn
Mellor 'melə* [-lɔː*]
mellow (adj. v.), -er, -est, -ness; -s, -ing, -ed 'meləʊ, -ə*, -ɪst, -nɪs [-nəs]; -z, -ɪŋ, -d
melodic mɪ'lɒdɪk [me'l-, mə'l-]
melodious, -ly, -ness mɪ'ləʊdjəs [me'l-, mə'l-, -dɪəs], -lɪ, -nɪs [-nəs]
melodrama, -s 'meləʊ,drɑːmə [,--'--], -z
melodramatic ,meləʊdrə'mætɪk
melodramatist, -s ,meləʊ'dræmətɪst, -s
melod|y, -ies 'meləd|ɪ [-lʊd-], -ɪz
melon, -s 'melən, -z
Melos (island) 'miːlɒs ['mel-]
Melpomene mel'pɒmɪnɪ: [-mən-, -nɪ]
Melrose 'melrəʊz
melt, -s, -ing/ly, -ed melt, -s, -ɪŋ/lɪ, -ɪd
Mel|ton, -ville 'mel|tən, -vɪl*
member, -s; -ship/s 'membə, -z; -ʃɪp/s
membrane, -s 'membreɪn, -z
membraneous mem'breɪmjəs [-ɪəs]
membranous 'membrənəs
Memel 'meɪml
memento, -s mɪ'mentəʊ [me'm-, mə'm-], -z
Memnon 'memnɒn

memo, -s 'meməʊ ['miːməʊ], -z
memoir, -s 'memwɑː* [-wɔː*], -z
memorabilia ,memərə'bɪlɪə [-ljə]
memorab|le, -ly 'memərəb|l, -lɪ
memorand|um, -a, -ums ,memə'rænd|əm [-mʊ'r-, -mɾ'æ-], -ə, -əmz
memorial (s. adj.), -s mə'mɔːrɪəl [me'm-, mɪ'm-], -z
memorializ|e [-is|e], -es, -ing, -ed mə'mɔːrɪəlaɪz [me'm-, mɪ'm-], -ɪz, -ɪŋ, -d
memoriter mɪ'mɒrɪtə* [me'm-, mə'm-]
memoriz|e [-is|e], -es, -ing, -ed 'meməraɪz [-mʊr-, -mɾ-], -ɪz, -ɪŋ, -d
memor|y, -ies 'memər|ɪ [-mʊr-, -mɾ-, -mrɪ], -ɪz
Memphis 'memfɪs
memsahib, -s 'mem,sɑːhɪb [-sɑːb], -z
men (plur. of man) men
menac|e (s. v.), -es -ing/ly, -ed 'menəs [-nɪs], -ɪz, -ɪŋ/lɪ, -t
ménage, -s me'nɑːʒ [meɪ'n-] (menɑːʒ), -ɪz
menagerie, -s mɪ'nædʒərɪ [me'n-, mə'n-, -'nɑːdʒərɪ], -z
Menai (strait) 'menaɪ (Welsh 'menai)
Menander mɪ'nændə* [me'n-, mə'n-]
mend, -s, -ing, -ed, -er/s mend, -z, -ɪŋ, -ɪd, -ə*/z
mendacious, -ly men'deɪʃəs, -lɪ
mendacity men'dæsətɪ [-ɪtɪ]
Mendel 'mendl
mendelevium ,mendə'liːvɪəm [-vjəm]
Mendelian men'diːljən [-lɪən]
Mendelssohn (English surname) 'mendlsn, (German composer) 'mendlsn [-səʊn]
mendican|cy, -t/s 'mendɪkən|sɪ, -t/s
mendicity men'dɪsətɪ [-ɪtɪ]
Mendip, -s 'mendɪp, -s
Mendoza men'dəʊzə
mene 'miːnɪ
Menelaus ,menɪ'leɪəs
menhir, -s 'men,hɪə*, -z
menial (s. adj.), -s, -ly 'miːnjəl [-nɪəl], -z, -ɪ
meningitis ,menɪn'dʒaɪtɪs
Meno 'miːnəʊ
men-of-war (plur. of man-of-war) ,menəv'wɔː*
menopause 'menəʊpɔːz ['miːn-]
Menpes 'mempɪs ['menp-, -ɪz]
menses 'mensiːz
Menshevik, -s 'menʃəvɪk [-ʃɪv-], -s
menstrual 'menstrʊəl [-trwəl]
menstruat|e, -es, -ing, -ed 'menstrʊeɪt, -s, -ɪŋ, -ɪd
menstruation ,menstrʊ'eɪʃn

319

mensurability ˌmenʃʊrəˈbɪlətɪ [-ʃər-, -nsjʊr-, -lɪt-]
mensurable ˈmenʃʊrəbl [-ʃər-]
mensuration ˌmensjʊəˈreɪʃn [-sjʊˈr-]
ment|al, -ally ˈmentl|l, -əlɪ [-ļɪ]
mentalistic, -ally ˌmentəˈlɪstɪk [-tļˈɪs-, -əlɪ [-ļɪ]
mentalit|y, -ies menˈtælət|ɪ [-ɪt|ɪ], -ɪz
Menteith menˈtiːθ
menthol ˈmenθɒl [-θl]
menti|on (s. v.), -ons, -oning, -oned; -onable ˈmenʃ|n, -nz, -n̩ɪŋ [-nɪŋ, -ənɪŋ], -nd; -n̩əbl [-nəbl, -ənəbl]
Mentone menˈtəʊnɪ
mentor, -s ˈmentɔ:*, -z
menu, -s ˈmenjuː, -z
Menuhin (American violinist) ˈmenjʊɪn [-nʊhɪn, -nʊɪn]
Menzies ˈmenzɪz, ˈmenɪs, ˈmɪnɪs .
Note.—The former Prime Minister of Australia is ˈmenzɪz.
Meolse mels
Meopham ˈmepəm
Mepham ˈmefəm
Mephibosheth meˈfɪbəʃeθ [mɪˈf-, -bʊʃ-, among Jews also ˌmefɪˈbəʊʃeθ, -ˈbɒʃeθ]
Mephistophelean [-lian] ˌmefɪstəˈfiːljən [-tɒˈf-, -lɪən]
Mephistopheles ˌmefɪˈstɒfɪliːz [-fəl-, -fļ-]
mephitic meˈfɪtɪk [mɪˈf-]
mephitis meˈfaɪtɪs [mɪˈf-]
Mercadi mɜːˈkɑːdɪ
mercantile ˈmɜːkəntaɪl
mercantilism ˈmɜːkəntɪlɪzəm [-taɪl-]
Mercator mɜːˈkeɪtɔ:* [-tə*]
Mercedes (English fem. name) ˈmɜːsɪdiːz, (car) məˈseɪdiːz [mɜːˈs-]
mercenar|y (s. adj.), -ies ˈmɜːsɪnər|ɪ [-sn̩ə-, -snə-], -ɪz
mercer (M.), -s ˈmɜːsə*, -z
merceriz|e [-is|e], -es, -ing, -ed ˈmɜːsəraɪz, -ɪz, -ɪŋ, -d
merchandise ˈmɜːtʃəndaɪz
merchant, -s; -man, -men ˈmɜːtʃənt, -s; -mən, -mən [-men]
merchant-ship, -s ˈmɜːtʃənt-ʃɪp, -s
Merchison ˈmɜːkɪsn
Merchiston ˈmɜːkɪstən
Mercia, -n ˈmɜːsjə [-sɪə, -ʃjə, -ʃɪə], -n
merci|ful, -fully, -fulness ˈmɜːsɪ|fʊl, -fʊlɪ [-fəlɪ], -fʊlnɪs [-nəs]
merciless, -ly, -ness ˈmɜːsɪlɪs [-ləs], -lɪ, -nɪs [-nəs]
mercurial, -ly mɜːˈkjʊərɪəl [-ˈkjɔr-, -ˈkjɔ:r-], -ɪ
mercuric mɜːˈkjʊərɪk

mercurous ˈmɜːkjʊrəs
mercury (M.) ˈmɜːkjʊrɪ [-kjər-]
Mercutio mɜːˈkjuːʃjəʊ [-ʃɪəʊ]
merc|y (M.), -ies ˈmɜːs|ɪ, -ɪz
mercy-seat, -s ˈmɜːsɪsiːt, -s
mere (s. adj.), -s, -st, -ly mɪə*, -z, -rɪst, -lɪ
Meredith ˈmerədɪθ [-rɪd-], in Wales meˈredɪθ
meretricious, -ly, -ness ˌmerɪˈtrɪʃəs, -lɪ, -nɪs [-nəs]
merganser, -s mɜːˈɡænsə* [-zə*], -z
merg|e, -es, -ing, -ed mɜːdʒ, -ɪz, -ɪŋ, -d
merger, -s ˈmɜːdʒə*, -z
meridian, -s məˈrɪdɪən [mɪˈr-, -djən], -z
meridional məˈrɪdɪənl [mɪˈr-, -djən-]
meringue, -s məˈræŋ, -z
merino məˈriːnəʊ
Merioneth, -shire ˌmerɪˈɒnɪθ [-neθ, -nəθ] (Welsh meriˈoneθ), -ʃə* [-ˌʃɪə*]
merit (s. v.), -s, -ing, -ed ˈmerɪt, -s, -ɪŋ, -ɪd
meritocrac|y, -ies ˌmerɪˈtɒkrəs|ɪ, -ɪz
meritorious, -ly, -ness ˌmerɪˈtɔ:rɪəs, -lɪ, -nɪs [-nəs]
Merivale ˈmerɪveɪl
merlin (M.), -s ˈmɜːlɪn, -z
mermaid, -s ˈmɜːmeɪd, -z
mer|man, -men ˈmɜː|mæn, -men
Meroe ˈmerəʊɪ
Merope ˈmerəpɪ [-piː]
Merovingian ˌmerəʊˈvɪndʒɪən [-dʒjən]
Merrilies ˈmerɪlɪz
Merrimac ˈmerɪmæk
Merriman ˈmerɪmən
merriment ˈmerɪmənt
Merrivale ˈmerɪveɪl
merr|y (M.), -ier, -iest, -ily, -iness ˈmer|ɪ, -ɪə*, -ɪɪst, -əlɪ [-ɪlɪ], -ɪnɪs [-məs]
merry-andrew, -s ˌmerɪˈændruː, -z
merry-go-round, -s ˈmerɪɡəʊˌraʊnd, -z
merrymak|er/s, -ing ˈmerɪˌmeɪk|ə*/z, -ɪŋ
merrythought, -s ˈmerɪθɔ:t, -s
Merryweather ˈmerɪˌweðə*
Mersey, -side ˈmɜːzɪ, -saɪd
Merthyr ˈmɜːθə* (Welsh ˈmerθɪr)
Merthyr Tydfil ˌmɜːθəˈtɪdvɪl (Welsh ˌmerθɪrˈtɪdvɪl)
Merton ˈmɜːtn
mésalliance, -s meˈzælɪəns [meɪˈz-, -ljəns, -lɪɑ̃:ns, -lɪɔ̃:ns, -lɪɑːns] (mezaljɑ̃:s), -ɪz
mesdames ˈmeɪdæm (medam)
meseems mɪˈsiːmz
mesembryanthemum, -s mɪˌzembrɪˈænθɪməm [mə̯ˌz-, -θəm-], -z

mesh (*s. v.*), **-es, -ing, -ed** meʃ, -ɪz, -ɪŋ, -t

Meshach [-ak] 'miːʃæk

Meshed 'meʃed

mesial 'miːzjəl [-zɪəl]

Mesmer 'mezmə*

mesmeric mez'merɪk

mesmeri|sm, -st/s 'mezmərɪ|zəm [-mr̩-], -st/s

mesmeriz|e [-is|e], **-es, -ing, -ed, -er/s** 'mezməraɪz [-mr̩aɪz], -ɪz, -ɪŋ, -d, -ə*/z

mesne miːn

meson, -s 'miːzɒn ['mesɒn, 'miːsɒn], -z

Mesopotamia ˌmesəpə'teɪmjə [-mɪə]

mesotron, -s 'mesəʊtrɒn, -z

mesozoic ˌmesəʊ'zəʊɪk

mess (*s. v.*), **-es, -ing, -ed** mes, -ɪz, -ɪŋ, -t

message, -s 'mesɪdʒ, -ɪz

Messala me'sɑːlə

messenger, -s 'mesɪndʒə* [-sn̩-], -z

Messiah, -s mɪ'saɪə [me's-, mə's-], -z

messianic ˌmesɪ'ænɪk

Messina me'siːnə [mə's-, mɪ's-]

messmate, -s 'mesmeɪt, -s

Messrs. 'mesəz

messuage, -s 'meswɪdʒ [-sjʊɪdʒ], -ɪz

mess|y, -ier, -iest, -ily, -iness 'mes|ɪ, -ɪə*, -ɪɪst, -ɪlɪ [-əlɪ], -ɪnɪs [-məs]

Mestre 'mestrɪ

met (*from* meet) met

met|a, -ae (*column in Roman circus*) 'miːt|ə, -iː ['meɪt|ə, -aɪ]

meta- (*Greek prefix*) 'metə-, ˌmetə-

Meta (*Christian name*) 'miːtə

metabolic ˌmetə'bɒlɪk

metabolism me'tæbəlɪzəm [mɪ-, mə-, -bʊl-]

metacentre, -s 'metəˌsentə*, -z

metagalax|y, -ies 'metəˌɡæləks|ɪ, -ɪz

met|al (*s. v.*), **-als, -alling, -alled** 'met|l, -lz, -lɪŋ, -ld

metalanguage 'metəˌlæŋɡwɪdʒ

metallic mɪ'tælɪk [me't-, mə't-]

metalliferous ˌmetə'lɪfərəs

metallography ˌmetə'lɒɡrəfɪ

metalloid 'metəlɔɪd

metallurg|ist/s, -y me'tælədʒ|ɪst/s [mɪ't-, 'metələ:dʒ-, 'metlə:dʒ-], -ɪ

metamorphos|e, **-es, -ing, -ed** ˌmetə-'mɔːfəʊz, -ɪz, -ɪŋ, -d

metamorphos|is, -es (*plur.*) ˌmetə'mɔː-fəs|ɪs [ˌmetəmɔː'fəʊs-], -iːz

metaphor, -s 'metəfə* [-fɔː*], -z

metaphoric, -al, -ally ˌmetə'fɒrɪk, -l, -əlɪ

metaphysician, -s ˌmetəfɪ'zɪʃn, -z

metaphysic|s, -al, -ally ˌmetə'fɪzɪk|s, -l, -əlɪ

metaplasm 'metəplæzəm

metathes|is, -es me'tæθəs|ɪs [mɪ't-, mə't-, -θɪs-], -iːz

Metayers mɪ'teɪəz [mə't-]

Metcalfe (*surname*) 'metkɑːf [-kəf]

met|e, **-es, -ing, -ed** miːt, -s, -ɪŋ, -ɪd

Metellus mɪ'teləs [me't-]

metempsychosis ˌmetemsaɪ'kəʊsɪs [me ˌtem-, -sɪ'k-]

meteor, -s 'miːtɪɔː* [-tɪə*, -tjə*], -z

meteoric ˌmiːtɪ'ɒrɪk

meteorite, -s 'miːtɪjəraɪt [-tɪə-], -s

meteorologic, -al ˌmiːtɪjərə'lɒdʒɪk [-tɪə-], -l

meteorolog|ist/s, -y ˌmiːtɪjə'rɒlədʒ|ɪst/s [-tɪə-], -ɪ

meter, -s 'miːtə*, -z

meth, -s meθ, -s

methane 'miːθeɪn

metheglin me'θeɡlɪn [mɪ'θ-, mə'θ-]

methinks mɪ'θɪŋks

method, -s 'meθəd, -z

methodic, -al, -ally mɪ'θɒdɪk [me'θ-, mə'θ-], -l, -əlɪ

methodi|sm, -st/s 'meθədɪ|zəm, -st/s

methodological ˌmeθədə'lɒdʒɪkl

methodolog|y, -ies ˌmeθə'dɒlədʒ|ɪ, -ɪz

methought mɪ'θɔːt

Methuen (*surname*) 'meθjʊm [-θjʊən, -θjwən], (*American town*) mɪ'θjʊm [mə'θ-]

Methuselah mɪ'θjuːzələ [mə'θ-, -'θuː-]

Methven 'meθvən [-ven]

methyl (*commercial and general pronunciation*) 'meθɪl, (*chemists' pronunciation*) 'miːθaɪl

methylated 'meθɪleɪtɪd [-θ|eɪ-]

meticulous, -ly mɪ'tɪkjʊləs [me't-, mə-, -kjə-], -lɪ

métier, -s 'meɪtɪeɪ ['met-, -tjeɪ], -z (metje)

metonymy mɪ'tɒnɪmɪ [me't-, mə-, -nəmɪ]

metope, -s 'metəʊp, -s

metre, -s 'miːtə*, -z

metric, -al, ally 'metrɪk, -l, -əlɪ

metrication ˌmetrɪ'keɪʃn

metrics 'metrɪks

metrist, -s 'metrɪst, -s

Metroland 'metrəʊlænd

metronome, -s 'metrənəʊm [-trŋəʊm], -z

metronomic ˌmetrə'nɒmɪk

Metropole 'metrəpəʊl

metropolis, -es mɪ'trɒpəlɪs [me't-, mə't-, -p|ɪs], -ɪz

metropolitan (*s. adj.*), **-s** ˌmetrə'pɒlɪtən [-lət-], -z

mettle 'metl
Metz mets (*French* mɛs)
meuse (*track of hare*), -s mju:z, -ɪz
Meux mju:z, mju:ks, mju:
Mevagissey ˌmevə'gɪsɪ
mew (*s. v.*), -s, -ing, -ed mju:, -z, -ɪŋ
   ['mjuɪŋ], -d
mewl, -s, -ing, -ed mju:l, -z, -ɪŋ, -d
mews (*s.*) mju:z
Mexborough 'meksbərə
Mexic|an/s, -o 'meksɪk|ən/z, -əʊ
Meyer 'maɪə*
Meyerbeer (*composer*) 'maɪəˌbɪə*
Meynell 'menl, 'meɪnl
Meyrick 'merɪk, 'meɪrɪk
mezzanine, -s 'metsəni:n ['mez-], -z
mezzo-soprano, -s ˌmetsəʊsə'prɑ:nəʊ
   [ˌmedzəʊ-], -z
mezzotint, -s 'medzəʊtɪnt ['metsəʊ-], -s
Mgr., Mgrs. mɒn'si:njə*, -z
mi (*musical note*), -s mi:, -z
Miami maɪ'æmɪ
miaow, -s, -ing, -ed mi:'aʊ [mɪ'aʊ,
   mjaʊ], -z, -ɪŋ, -d
miasm|a, -as, -ata, -al mɪ'æzm|ə
   [maɪ'æ-], -əz, -ətə, -l
miasmatic ˌmɪəz'mætɪk [ˌmaɪæz-,
   ˌmaɪəz-]
mica 'maɪkə
micaceous maɪ'keɪʃəs
Micah 'maɪkə
Micaiah maɪ'kaɪə [mɪ'k-]
Micawber mɪ'kɔ:bə*
mice (*plur. of* mouse) maɪs
Michael 'maɪkl
Michaelmas, -es 'mɪklməs, -ɪz
Michelangelo ˌmaɪkəl'ændʒələʊ [-kl̩-,
   -dʒɪl-]
Micheldever 'mɪtʃəldevə*
Michelin, -s 'mɪʃlɪn ['mɪtʃəlɪn], -z
Michelle mi:'ʃel [mɪ'ʃ-]
Michelmore 'mɪtʃəlmɔː*
Michelson 'mɪtʃəlsn, 'mɪklsn
Michie 'mɪkɪ, *in Scotland also* 'mɪxɪ
Michigan 'mɪʃɪgən
Michmash 'mɪkmæʃ
microbe, -s 'maɪkrəʊb, -z
microcephalic ˌmaɪkrəʊke'fælɪk
   [-əʊkɪ'f-, -əʊse'f-, -əʊsɪ'f-]
microcephalous ˌmaɪkrəʊ'kefələs
   [-əʊ'sef-]
microcop|y, -ies 'maɪkrəʊˌkɒp|ɪ, -ɪz
microcosm, -s 'maɪkrəʊkɒzəm [-krʊk-],
   -z
microfilm, -s 'maɪkrəʊfɪlm, -z
micro-groove, -s 'maɪkrəʊgru:v, -z
micrometer, -s maɪ'krɒmɪtə* [-mətə*],
   -z

micron, -s 'maɪkrɒn [-rən], -z
micro-organism, -s ˌmaɪkrəʊ'ɔːgənɪzəm
   [-gnɪ-, '--ˌ----], -z
microphone, -s 'maɪkrəfəʊn, -z
microphonic ˌmaɪkrə'fɒnɪk
microscope, -s 'maɪkrəskəʊp [-krʊs-], -s
microscopic, -al, -ally ˌmaɪkrə'skɒpɪk
   [-krʊ's-], -l, -əlɪ
microscop|ist/s, -y maɪ'krɒskəp|ɪst/s,
   -ɪ
microwatt, -s 'maɪkrəʊwɒt, -s
micturat|e, -es, -ing, -ed 'mɪktjʊəreɪt,
   -s, -ɪŋ, -ɪd
micturition ˌmɪktjʊə'rɪʃn
mid mɪd
Midas 'maɪdæs [-dəs]
midday, -s 'mɪddeɪ [*also* ˌmɪd'd- *when
   not attributive*], -z
midden, -s 'mɪdn, -z
middle, -s 'mɪdl, -z
middle-aged ˌmɪdl'eɪdʒd [*also* '---, *esp.
   when attributive*]
middlebrow 'mɪdlbraʊ
middle-class ˌmɪdl'klɑːs [*also* '---, *esp.
   when attributive*]
middle|man, -men 'mɪdl|mæn, -men
Middlemarch 'mɪdlmɑːtʃ
Middlemast 'mɪdlmɑːst, -mæst
middlemost 'mɪdlməʊst
Middlesbrough 'mɪdlzbrə
Middlesex 'mɪdlseks
Middleton 'mɪdltən
middling 'mɪdlɪŋ [-dlɪŋ]
midd|y, -ies 'mɪd|ɪ, ɪz
midge, -s mɪdʒ, -ɪz
midget, -s 'mɪdʒɪt, -s
Midhurst 'mɪdhɜːst
midi, -s 'mɪdɪ, -z
Midian, -ite/s 'mɪdɪən [-djən], -aɪt/s
midland (M.), -s 'mɪdlənd, -z
Midlothian mɪd'ləʊðjən [-ðɪən]
midnight 'mɪdnaɪt
mid-off, -s ˌmɪd'ɒf [*old-fashioned* -'ɔːf],
   -s
mid-on ˌmɪd'ɒn, -z
midriff, -s 'mɪdrɪf, -s
midship|man, -men 'mɪdʃɪp|mən, -mən
midst mɪdst [mɪtst]
midsummer (M.) 'mɪdˌsʌmə* [-'--]
midway ˌmɪd'weɪ ['--]
Midway (*Island*) 'mɪdweɪ
midwi|fe, -ves 'mɪdwaɪ|f, -vz
midwifery 'mɪdwɪfərɪ [-'---]
midwinter ˌmɪd'wɪntə*
mien, -s mi:n, -z
Miers 'maɪəz
might (*s. v.*) maɪt
mightn't 'maɪtnt

might|y, -ier, -iest, -ily, -iness 'maɪt|ɪ,
-ɪə* [-jə*], -ɪıst [-ɪıst], -ɪlɪ [-əlɪ], -ɪnɪs
[-ɪnəs]
mignonette ,mɪnjə'net ['---]
migraine, -s 'miːgreɪn ['mɪg-, 'maɪ-], -z
migrant (s. adj.), -s 'maɪgrənt, -s
migrat|e, -es, -ing, -ed, -or/s maɪ'greɪt
['--], -s, -ɪŋ, -ɪd, -ə*/z
migration, -s maɪ'greɪʃn, -z
migratory 'maɪgrətərɪ [maɪ'greɪtərɪ]
Mikado, -s mɪ'kɑːdəʊ, -z
Mikardo mɪ'kɑːdəʊ
mike (M.), -s maɪk, -s
milady mɪ'leɪdɪ
Milan (in Italy) mɪ'læn [old-fashioned
'mɪlən]
Note.—'mɪlən is necessary for rhythm
in Shakespeare's 'The Tempest'.
Milan (in U.S.A.) 'maɪlən, (Serbian
king) 'miːlən
Milanese ,mɪlə'niːz
milch mɪltʃ [mɪlʃ]
mild, -er, -est, -ly, -ness maɪld, -ə*,
-ɪst, -lɪ, -nɪs [-nəs]
Mildenhall 'mɪldənhɔːl
mild|ew (s. v.), -ews, -ewing, -ewed
'mɪld|juː, -juːz, -juːɪŋ [-jʊɪŋ], -juːd
Mildmay 'maɪldmeɪ
Mildred 'mɪldrɪd [-red]
mile (M.), -s maɪl, -s
mileage, -s 'maɪlɪdʒ, -ɪz
mileometer, -s maɪ'lɒmɪtə* [-mətə*], -z
Miles maɪlz
Milesian, -s maɪ'liːzjən [mɪ'l-, -zɪən,
-ʒjən, -ʒɪən, -ʒn], -z
milestone, -s 'maɪlstəʊn, -z
Miletus mɪ'liːtəs [maɪ'l-]
milfoil, -s 'mɪlfɔɪl, -z
Milford 'mɪlfəd
Milhaud 'miːjəʊ (mijo)
milieu, -s 'miːljɜː [-'-, 'miːljə] (miljǿ), -z
militan|cy, -t/ly 'mɪlɪtən|sɪ [-lət-], -t/lɪ
militari|sm, -st/s 'mɪlɪtərɪ|zəm [-lət-],
-st/s
militarization [-isa-] ,mɪlɪtəraɪ'zeɪʃn
[-lət-, -rɪ'z-]
militariz|e [-is|e], -es, -ing, -ed 'mɪlɪ-
təraɪz [-lət-], -ɪz, -ɪŋ, -d
military 'mɪlɪtərɪ [-lət-]
militat|e, -es, -ing, -ed 'mɪlɪteɪt [-lət-],
-s, -ɪŋ, -d
militia, -man, -men mɪ'lɪʃə [mə'l-],
-mən, -mən [-men]
milk (s. v.), -s, -ing, -ed, -er/s mɪlk, -s,
-ɪŋ, -t, -ə*/z
milkmaid, -s 'mɪlkmeɪd, -z
milk|man, -men 'mɪlk|mən, -mən
[-men]

milk-shake, -s 'mɪlkʃeɪk, -s
milksop, -s 'mɪlksɒp, -s
milk-|tooth, -teeth 'mɪlk|tuːθ, -tiːθ
milk-white 'mɪlkwaɪt [-khw-]
milkwort, -s 'mɪlkwɜːt, -s
milk|y, -ier, -iest, -ily, -iness 'mɪlk|ɪ,
-ɪə* [-jə*], -ɪıst [-jɪst], -ɪlɪ [-əlɪ], -ɪnɪs
[-ɪnəs]
mill (s. v.) (M.), -s, -ing, -ed mɪl, -z, -ɪŋ, -d
Millais (sing.) 'mɪleɪ, (plur.) -z
Millard 'mɪləd, -lɑːd
Millbank 'mɪlbæŋk
mill-board 'mɪlbɔːd [-bəəd]
millenary mɪ'lenərɪ ['mɪlmənərɪ]
millenni|um, -ums, -a mɪ'lenɪ|əm
[-nj|əm], -əmz, -ə
millepede, -s 'mɪlɪpiːd, -z
miller (M.), -s 'mɪlə*, -z
millesimal mɪ'lesɪml
millet 'mɪlɪt
mill-hand, -s 'mɪlhænd, -z
milliard, -s 'mɪljɑːd [-lɪɑːd], -z
millibar, -s 'mɪlɪbɑː*, -z
Millicent 'mɪlɪsnt
milligram(me), -s 'mɪlɪgræm, -z
millimeter, -s 'mɪlɪ,miːtə*, -z
milliner, -s 'mɪlɪnə*, -z
millinery 'mɪlɪnərɪ
million, -s 'mɪljən, -z
millionaire, -s ,mɪljə'neə*, -z
millionairess, -es ,mɪljə'neərɪs [-res,
,mɪljəneə'res], -ɪz
millionfold 'mɪljənfəʊld
millionth, -s 'mɪljənθ, -s
Millom 'mɪləm
mill-pond, -s 'mɪlpɒnd, -z
Mills mɪlz
mill-stone, -s 'mɪlstəʊn, -z
Milltimber 'mɪl,tɪmbə*
Millwall 'mɪlwɔːl [-'-]
mill-wheel, -s 'mɪlwiːl ['mɪlhw-], -z
Miln mɪl
Milne mɪln, mɪl
Milne-Home ,mɪln'hjuːm
Milner 'mɪlnə*
Milnes mɪlz, mɪlnz
Milngavie mɪl'gaɪ
Milo 'maɪləʊ ['miː-]
milord, -s mɪ'lɔːd [-'lɔː*], -z
milreis (sing.) 'mɪlreɪs, (plur.) 'mɪlreɪs
[-reɪz]
Milton 'mɪltən
Miltonic mɪl'tɒnɪk
Milwaukee mɪl'wɔːkiː [-kɪ]
mime, -s maɪm, -z
mimeograph (s. v.), -s, -ing, -ed
'mɪmɪəgrɑːf [-mɪəʊg-, -græf], -s, -ɪŋ,
-t

mimetic mɪ'metɪk
mimic (s. adj. v.), -s, -king, -ked 'mɪmɪk, -s, -ɪŋ, -t
mimicry 'mɪmɪkrɪ
mimosa, -s mɪ'məuzə [-əusə], -z
mimulus, -es 'mɪmjʊləs, -ɪz
mina, -s 'maɪnə, -z
minaret, -s 'mɪnəret [ˌ-'-ˈ-], -s
minatory 'mɪnətərɪ ['maɪn-]
mince|e (s. v.), -s, -ing/ly, -ed mɪns, -ɪz, -ɪŋ/lɪ, -t
mincemeat 'mɪnsmiːt
mince-pie, -s ˌmɪns'paɪ, -z
Minch, -es, -in mɪntʃ, -ɪz, -ɪn
mind (s. v.), -s, -ing, -ed maɪnd, -z, -ɪŋ, -ɪd
mind|ful, -fully, -fulness 'maɪnd|fʊl, -fʊlɪ [-fəlɪ], -fʊlnɪs [-nəs]
mindless, -ly, -ness 'maɪndlɪs [-ləs], -lɪ, -nɪs [-nəs]
min|e (s. v.), -es, -ing, -ed, -er/s maɪn, -z, -ɪŋ, -d, -ə*/z
mine (pron.) maɪn
minefield, -s 'maɪnfiːld, -z
Minehead 'maɪnhed [ˌmaɪn'hed]
mine-layer, -s 'maɪnˌleɪə*, -z
mine-laying 'maɪnˌleɪɪŋ
mineral (s. adj.), -s 'mɪnərəl, -z
mineraliz|e [-is|e], -es, -ing, -ed 'mɪnərəlaɪz, -ɪz, -ɪŋ, -d
mineralogic|al, -ally ˌmɪnərə'lɒdʒɪk|l, -əlɪ
mineralog|ist/s, -y ˌmɪnə'rælədʒ|ɪst/s, -ɪ
Minerva mɪ'nɜːvə
minestrone ˌmɪnɪ'strəunɪ [-nə-]
mine-sweep|er/s, -ing 'maɪnˌswiːp|ə*/z, -ɪŋ
Minety 'maɪntɪ
minever 'mɪnɪvə*
Ming mɪŋ
ming|le, -les, -ling, -led 'mɪŋg|l, -lz, -lɪŋ [-lɪŋ], -ld
mingogram, -s 'mɪŋgəʊgræm ['mɪŋəʊ-], -z
mingograph, -s 'mɪŋgəʊgrɑːf ['mɪŋəʊ-, -græf], -s
ming|y, -ier, -iest 'mɪndʒ|ɪ, -ɪə* [-ə*], -ɪst [-jɪst]
miniature, -s 'mɪnətʃə* [-njətʃ-, -nɪtʃ-], -z
miniaturist, -s 'mɪnəˌtjʊərɪst [-njət-, -tʃər-, 'mɪnɪtʃərɪst], -s
mini-bus/es, -cab/s 'mɪnɪbʌs/ɪz, -kæb/z
mini-car, -s 'mɪnɪkɑː*, -z
minikin (s. adj.), -s 'mɪnɪkɪn, -z
minim (M.), -s 'mɪnɪm, -z
minimal 'mɪnɪml [-məl]

minimiz|e [-is|e], -es, -ing, -ed 'mɪnɪmaɪz, -ɪz, -ɪŋ, -d
minim|um, -a 'mɪnɪm|əm, -ə
mining 'maɪnɪŋ
minion, -s 'mɪnjən [-nɪən], -z
minish, -es, -ing, -ed 'mɪnɪʃ, -ɪz, -ɪŋ, -t
mini-skirt, -s 'mɪnɪskɜːt, -s
minist|er (s. v.), -ers, -ering, -ered 'mɪnɪst|ə* [-nəs-], -əz, -ərɪŋ, -əd
ministerial, -ly, -ist/s ˌmɪnɪ'stɪərɪəl [-nə's-], -ɪ, -ɪst/s
ministration, -s ˌmɪnɪ'streɪʃn [-nə's-], -z
ministr|y, -ies 'mɪnɪstr|ɪ [-nəs-], -ɪz
miniver (M.) 'mɪnɪvə*
mink mɪŋk
Minneapolis ˌmɪnɪ'æpəlɪs
Minne|haha, -sota ˌmɪnɪ|'hɑːhɑː, -'səʊtə
Minnesinger, -s 'mɪnɪˌsɪŋə*, -z
Minnie 'mɪnɪ
minnow, -s 'mɪnəʊ, -z
Minoan mɪ'nəʊən
minor (s. adj.), -s 'maɪnə*, -z
Minorca mɪ'nɔːkə
Minories 'mɪnərɪz
minorit|y, -ies maɪ'nɒrət|ɪ [mɪ'n-, mə'n-, -ɪt|ɪ], -ɪz
Minos 'maɪnɒs
Minotaur, -s 'maɪnətɔː*, -z
minster (M.), -s 'mɪnstə*, -z
minstrel, -s; -sy 'mɪnstrəl, -z; -sɪ
mint (s. v.), -s, -ing, -ed; -age mɪnt, -s, -ɪŋ, -ɪd; -ɪdʒ
Minto 'mɪntəʊ
mint-sauce ˌmɪnt'sɔːs
minuet, -s ˌmɪnjʊ'et, -s
minus (s. adj. prep.), -es 'maɪnəs, -ɪz
minuscule, -s 'mɪnəskjuːl [-nɪs-, mɪ'nʌskjuːl], -z
minute (very small), -st, -ly, -ness maɪ'njuːt [mɪ'n-], -ɪst, -lɪ, -nɪs [-nəs]
minute (s.) (division of time, angle, memorandum), -s 'mɪnɪt, -s
minut|e (v.), -es, -ing, -ed 'mɪnɪt, -s, -ɪŋ, -ɪd
minute-book, -s 'mɪnɪtbʊk, -s
minute-glass, -es 'mɪnɪtglɑːs, -ɪz
minute-gun, -s 'mɪnɪtgʌn, -z
minute-hand, -s 'mɪnɪthænd, -z
minutiae maɪ'njuːʃiː [mɪ'n-, -ʃjiː]
minx, -es mɪŋks, -ɪz
miocene 'maɪəʊsiːn
miracle, -s 'mɪrəkl [-rɪkl], -z
miraculous, -ly, -ness mɪ'rækjʊləs [mə'r-, -kjəl-], -lɪ, -nɪs [-nəs]
mirage, -s 'mɪrɑːʒ [-'-], -ɪz
Miranda mɪ'rændə
mire 'maɪə*

Miriam 'mɪrɪəm
mirror, -s, -ed 'mɪrə*, -z, -d
mirth mɜ:θ
mirth|ful, -fully, -fulness 'mɜ:θ|fʊl,
-fʊlɪ [-fəlɪ], -fʊlnɪs [-nəs]
mir|y, -ier, -iest, -iness 'maɪər|ɪ, -ɪə*,
-ɪɪst, -ɪnɪs [-ɪnəs]
Mirza 'mɜ:zə
misadventure, -s ˌmɪsəd'ventʃə*, -z
misalliance, -s ˌmɪsə'laɪəns, -ɪz
misanthrope, -s 'mɪsənθrəup ['mɪzən-],
-s
misanthropic, -al, -ally ˌmɪsən'θrɒpɪk
[ˌmɪzən-], -l, -əlɪ
misanthrop|ist/s, -y mɪ'sænθrəp|ɪst/s
[mɪ'zæ-, -θrʊp-], -ɪ
misapplication, -s 'mɪsˌæplɪ'keɪʃn, -z
misappl|y, -ies, -ying, -ied ˌmɪsə'pl|aɪ,
-aɪz, -aɪɪŋ, -aɪd
misapprehend, -s, -ing, -ed 'mɪsˌæprɪ-
'hend, -z, -ɪŋ, -ɪd
misapprehension, -s 'mɪsˌæprɪ'henʃn,
-z
misappropriat|e, -es, -ing, -ed ˌmɪsə-
'prəuprɪeɪt, -s, -ɪŋ, -ɪd
misappropriation, -s 'mɪsəˌprəuprɪ'eɪʃn,
-z
misbecoming ˌmɪsbɪ'kʌmɪŋ [-bə'k-]
misbegotten 'mɪsbɪˌgɒtn [ˌ--'--]
misbehav|e, -es, -ing, -ed; -iour ˌmɪs-
bɪ'heɪv [-bə'h-], -z, -ɪŋ, -d; -jə*
misbelief ˌmɪsbɪ'li:f [-bə'l-, '---]
misbeliev|e, -es, -ing, -ed, -er/s ˌmɪs-
bɪ'li:v [-bə'l-, '---], -z, -ɪŋ, -d, -ə*/z
miscalculat|e, -es, -ing, -ed ˌmɪs'kæl-
kjʊleɪt [-kjəl-], -s, -ɪŋ, -ɪd
miscalculation, -s 'mɪsˌkælkjʊ'leɪʃn
[-kjə'l-], -z
miscall, -s, -ing, -ed ˌmɪs'kɔ:l, -z, -ɪŋ,
-d
miscarr|y, -ies, -ying, -ied; -iage/s
ˌmɪs'kær|ɪ, -ɪz, -ɪɪŋ, -ɪd; -ɪdʒ/ɪz
miscegenation ˌmɪsɪdʒɪ'neɪʃn
miscellanea ˌmɪsə'leɪnɪə [-njə]
miscellaneous, -ly, -ness ˌmɪsə'leɪnjəs
[-sɪ'l-, -nɪəs], -lɪ, -nɪs [-nəs]
miscellan|y, -ies mɪ'selən|ɪ ['mɪsɪl-], -ɪz
mischance, -s mɪs'tʃɑ:ns ['mɪstʃɑ:ns],
-ɪz
mischief, -s 'mɪstʃɪf, -s
mischief-mak|er/s, -ing 'mɪstʃɪfˌmeɪk|-
ə*/z, -ɪŋ
mischievous, -ly, -ness 'mɪstʃɪvəs, -lɪ,
-nɪs [-nəs]
misconception, -s ˌmɪskən'sepʃn, -z
misconduct (s.) ˌmɪs'kɒndʌkt [-dəkt]
misconduct (v.), -s, -ing, -ed ˌmɪskən-
'dʌkt, -s, -ɪŋ, -ɪd

misconstruction, -s ˌmɪskən'strʌkʃn,
-z
misconstr|ue, -ues, -uing, -ued ˌmɪs-
kən'str|u: [-'kɒnst-], -u:z, -u:ɪŋ [-ʊɪŋ],
-u:d
miscount (s. v.), -s, -ing, -ed ˌmɪs'kaʊnt,
-s, -ɪŋ, -ɪd
miscreant, -s 'mɪskrɪənt, -s
miscu|e (s. v.), -es, -ing, -ed ˌmɪs'kju:,
-z, -ɪŋ [-'kjʊɪŋ], -d
misdeal (s. v.), -s, -ing, misdealt ˌmɪs-
'di:l, -z, -ɪŋ, ˌmɪs'delt
misdeed, -s ˌmɪs'di:d, -z
misdemean|ant/s, -our/s ˌmɪsdɪ'mi:n|-
ənt/s [-də'm-], -ə*/z
misdirect, -s, -ing, -ed ˌmɪsdɪ'rekt
[-də'r-, -daɪ'r-], -s, -ɪŋ, -ɪd
misdirection ˌmɪsdɪ'rekʃn [-də'r-,
-daɪ'r-]
misdoing, -s ˌmɪs'du:ɪŋ [-ʊɪŋ], -z
mise-en-scène ˌmi:zɑ̃:n'seɪn [-zɔ̃:n's-,
-zɒn's-, -sen] (mizɑ̃sɛ:n)
miser, -s maɪzə*, -z
miserab|le, -ly, -leness 'mɪzərəb|l, -lɪ,
-lnɪs [-nəs]
miserere, -s ˌmɪzə'rɪərɪ [-'reərɪ], -z
misericord, -s mɪ'zerɪkɔ:d ['mɪzərɪ-],
-z
miserl|y, -iness 'maɪzəl|ɪ, -ɪnɪs [-nəs]
miser|y, -ies 'mɪzər|ɪ [-zɹ̩-], -ɪz
misfeasance mɪs'fi:zəns
misfir|e (s. v.), -es, -ing, -ed ˌmɪs'faɪə*,
-z, -rɪŋ, -d
misfit, -s 'mɪsfɪt [ˌmɪs'f-], -s
misfortune, -s mɪs'fɔ:tʃu:n [-tʃən,
-tju:n], -z
misgiving, -s mɪs'gɪvɪŋ, -z
misgovern, -s, -ing, -ed, -ment ˌmɪs-
'gʌvən, -z, -ɪŋ, -d, -mənt
misguided, -ly ˌmɪs'gaɪdɪd, -lɪ
mishand|le, -les, -ling, -led ˌmɪs'hænd|l
-lz, -lɪŋ [-l̩ŋ], -ld
mishap, -s 'mɪshæp [mɪs'h-], -s
misinform, -s, -ing, -ed ˌmɪsɪn'fɔ:m, -z,
-ɪŋ, -d
misinterpret, -s, -ing, -ed ˌmɪsɪn'tɜ:prɪt,
-s, -ɪŋ, -ɪd
misinterpretation, -s 'mɪsɪnˌtɜ:prɪ'teɪʃn
[-prə't-], -z
misjudg|e, -es, -ing, -ed ˌmɪs'dʒʌdʒ,
-ɪz, -ɪŋ, -d
mis|lay, -lays, -laying, -laid ˌmɪs|'leɪ,
-'leɪz, -'leɪɪŋ, -'leɪd
mis|lead, -leads, -leading, -led ˌmɪs|-
'li:d, -'li:dz, -'li:dɪŋ, -'led
mismanag|e, -es, -ing, -ed, -ement
ˌmɪs'mænɪdʒ, -ɪz, -ɪŋ, -d, -mənt
misnomer, -s ˌmɪs'nəumə*, -z

325

misogam|ist/s, -y mɪˈsɒɡəm|ɪst/s [maɪˈs-], -ɪ

misogyn|ist/s, -y mɪˈsɒdʒɪn|ɪst/s [maɪˈs-, -ɒgɪ-, -ən|ɪst], -ɪ

misplac|e, -es, -ing, -ed, -ement ˌmɪsˈpleɪs, -ɪz, -ɪŋ, -t [also ˈmɪspleɪst when attributive], -mənt

misprint (s.), -s ˈmɪsprɪnt [also mɪsˈp- when preceded by a stress], -s

misprint (v.), -s, -ing, -ed ˌmɪsˈprɪnt, -s, -ɪŋ, -ɪd

misprision ˌmɪsˈprɪʒn

mispronounc|e, -es, -ing, -ed ˌmɪs-prəˈnaʊns [-prʊˈn-, -prɪˈaʊns], -ɪz, -ɪŋ, -t

mispronunciation, -s ˈmɪsprəˌnʌnsɪ-ˈeɪʃn [-prʊˌn-, -prɪˌʌn-], -z

misquotation, -s ˌmɪskwəʊˈteɪʃn, -z

misquot|e, -es, -ing, -ed ˌmɪsˈkwəʊt, -s, -ɪŋ, -ɪd

mis|read (pres.), -reads, -reading, -read (past) ˌmɪs|ˈriːd, -ˈriːdz, -ˈriːdɪŋ, -ˈred

misreport, -s, -ing, -ed ˌmɪsrɪˈpɔːt, -s, -ɪŋ, -ɪd

misrepresent, -s, -ing, -ed ˈmɪsˌreprɪ-ˈzent, -s, -ɪŋ, -ɪd

misrepresentation, -s ˈmɪsˌreprɪzen-ˈteɪʃn [-zən-], -z

misrule ˌmɪsˈruːl

miss (s. v.) (M.), -es, -ing, -ed mɪs, -ɪz, -ɪŋ, -t

missal, -s ˈmɪsl, -z

missel ˈmɪzl [ˈmɪsl]

Missenden ˈmɪsndən

misshapen ˌmɪsˈʃeɪpən [ˌmɪʃˈʃ-]

missile, -s ˈmɪsaɪl, -z

missing (adj.) ˈmɪsɪŋ

mission, -s ˈmɪʃn, -z

missionar|y, -ies ˈmɪʃnər|ɪ [-ʃnər-, -ʃn̩r-, -ʃənər-], -ɪz

missioner, -s ˈmɪʃnə* [-ʃənə*], -z

missis ˈmɪsɪz

Mississippi ˌmɪsɪˈsɪpɪ

missive (s. adj.), -s ˈmɪsɪv, -z

Missouri mɪˈzʊərɪ [mɪˈs-]
Note.—American pronunciation has -z-.

misspel|l, -ls, -ling/s, -led, -t ˌmɪsˈspel, -z, -ɪŋ/z, -t [-d], -t

misspen|d, -ds, -ding, -t ˌmɪsˈspen|d, -dz, -dɪŋ, -t [ˈ-- when attributive]

misstat|e, -es, -ing, -ed, -ement/s ˌmɪsˈsteɪt, -s, -ɪŋ, -ɪd, -mənt/s

missuit, -s, -ing, -ed ˌmɪsˈsuːt [-ˈsjuːt], -s, -ɪŋ, -ɪd

miss|y, -ies ˈmɪs|ɪ, -ɪz

mist, -s mɪst, -s

mistakable mɪsˈteɪkəbl

mis|take (s. v.), -takes, -taking, -took, -taken/ly mɪˈs|teɪk, -teɪks, -teɪkɪŋ, -tʊk, -teɪkən/lɪ

mister ˈmɪstə*

mistim|e, -es, -ing, -ed ˌmɪsˈtaɪm, -z, -ɪŋ, -d

mistletoe ˈmɪsltəʊ [ˈmɪzl-]

mistral, -s ˈmɪstrəl [mɪsˈtrɑːl] (mistral), -z

mistranslat|e, -es, -ing, -ed ˌmɪstræns-ˈleɪt [-trɑːns-, -trænz-, -trɑːnz-, -trəns-, -trənz-], -s, -ɪŋ, -ɪd

mistranslation, -s ˌmɪstrænsˈleɪʃn [-trɑːns-, -trænz-, -trɑːnz-, -trəns-, -trənz-], -z

mistress, -es ˈmɪstrɪs [-əs], -ɪz

mistrust (s. v.), -s, -ing, -ed ˌmɪsˈtrʌst, -s, -ɪŋ, -ɪd

mist|y, -ier, -iest, -ily, -iness ˈmɪst|ɪ, -ɪə* [-jə*], -ɪɪst [-jɪst], -ɪlɪ [-əlɪ], -ɪnɪs [-məs]

misunderst|and, -ands, -anding/s, -ood ˌmɪsʌndəˈst|ænd, -ændz, -ændɪŋ/z, -ʊd

misuse (s.) ˌmɪsˈjuːs [also ˈmɪsjuːs when followed by a stress]

misus|e (v.), -es, -ing, -ed ˌmɪsˈjuːz, -ɪz, -ɪŋ, -d

Mitch|am, -ell ˈmɪtʃ|əm, -l

mite, -s maɪt, -s

Mitford ˈmɪtfəd

Mithr|a, -as ˈmɪθr|ə, -æs

Mithridates ˌmɪθrɪˈdeɪtiːz [-θrə-]

mitigable ˈmɪtɪgəbl

mitigat|e, -es, -ing, -ed ˈmɪtɪgeɪt, -s, -ɪŋ, -ɪd

mitigation ˌmɪtɪˈgeɪʃn

mitosis maɪˈtəʊsɪs

mitrailleuse, -s ˌmɪtraɪˈəːz (mitrajøːz), -ɪz

mit|re (s. v.), -res, -ring, -red, -ral ˈmaɪt|ə*, -əz, -ərɪŋ, -əd, -rəl

mitten, -s ˈmɪtn, -z

Mitylene ˌmɪtɪˈliːnɪ

Mivart ˈmaɪvət [-vɑːt]

mix (s. v.), -es, -ing, -ed, -er/s mɪks, -ɪz, -ɪŋ, -t, -ə*/z

mixture, -s ˈmɪkstʃə*, -z

mix-up, -s ˈmɪksʌp, -s

Mizar (star) ˈmaɪzɑː* [-zə*]

Mizen ˈmɪzn

Mizpah ˈmɪzpə

mizzen, -s ˈmɪzn, -z

mizzen-mast, -s ˈmɪznmɑːst [nautical pronunciation -məst], -s

mizz|le, -les, -ling, -led ˈmɪz|l, -lz, -l̩ɪŋ [-lɪŋ], -ld

326

mnemonic (s. adj.), -s ni:'mɒnɪk [nɪ-, mn-], -s
Mnemosyne ni:'mɒzɪni: [mni:'m-, mnɪ'm-, -ɒsɪ-]
Moab 'məʊæb
Moabite, -s 'məʊəbaɪt, -s
moan (s. v.), -s, -ing/s, -ed məʊn, -z, -ɪŋ/z, -d
Moase məʊz
moat (s. v.) (M.), -s, -ing, -ed məʊt, -s, -ɪŋ, -ɪd
mob (s. v.), -s, -bing, -bed mɒb, -z, -ɪŋ, -d
Moberly 'məʊbəlɪ
mobile 'məʊbaɪl [-bi:l, -bɪl]
mobility məʊ'bɪlətɪ [-lɪt-]
mobilization [-isa-], -s ˌməʊbɪlaɪ'zeɪʃn [-bḷaɪ'z-, -bɪlɪ'z-, -bḷɪ'z-], -z
mobiliz|e [-is|e], -es, -ing, -ed 'məʊbɪlaɪz [-bḷaɪz], -ɪz, -ɪŋ, -d
moccasin, -s 'mɒkəsɪn, -z
mocha (coffee, leather, etc., from Mocha) 'mɒkə ['məʊkə]
Mocha (Arabian seaport) 'məʊkə ['mɒkə]
mock (adj. v.), -s, -ing/ly, -ed, -er/s mɒk, -s, -ɪŋ/lɪ, -t, -ə*/z
mocker|y, -ies 'mɒkər|ɪ, -ɪz
Mockett 'mɒkɪt
mocking-bird, -s 'mɒkɪŋbɜ:d, -z
mock-turtle ˌmɒk'tɜ:tl
mod|al, -ally 'məʊd|l, -əlɪ
modality məʊ'dælətɪ [-ɪtɪ]
mode, -s məʊd, -z
mod|el (s. v.), -els, -elling, -elled, -eller/s 'mɒd|l, -lz, -ḷɪŋ, -ld, -lə*/z
modena (colour) 'mɒdɪnə
Modena 'mɒdɪnə [mɒ'deɪnə, mə'd-, old-fashioned -'di:nə] ('mɔ:dena)
moderate (s. adj.), -s, -ly, -ness 'mɒdə-rət [-rɪt], -s, -lɪ, -nɪs [-nəs]
moderat|e (v.), -es, -ing, -ed, -or/s 'mɒdəreɪt, -s, -ɪŋ, -ɪd, -ə*/z
moderation, -s ˌmɒdə'reɪʃn, -z
moderato, -s ˌmɒdə'rɑ:təʊ, -z
modern (s. adj.), -s, -ly, -ness 'mɒdən, -z, -lɪ, -nɪs [-nəs]
moderni|sm, -st/s 'mɒdənɪ|zəm, -st/s
modernity mɒ'dɜ:nətɪ [məʊ'd-, -ɪtɪ]
modernization [-isa-] ˌmɒdənaɪ'zeɪʃn [-nɪ'z-]
moderniz|e [-is|e], -es, -ing, -ed 'mɒdə-naɪz, -ɪz, -ɪŋ, -d
modest, -ly, -y 'mɒdɪst, -lɪ, -ɪ
modicum, -s 'mɒdɪkəm, -z
modification, -s ˌmɒdɪfɪ'keɪʃn, -z
modi|fy, -fies, -fying, -fied, -fier/s; -fiable 'mɒdɪ|faɪ, -faɪz, -faɪɪŋ, -faɪd, -faɪə*/z; -faɪəbl

modish, -ly, -ness 'məʊdɪʃ, -lɪ, -nɪs [-nəs]
modiste, -s məʊ'di:st, -s
modulat|e, -es, -ing, -ed, -or/s 'mɒdjʊ-leɪt [-dʒʊ-], -s, -ɪŋ, -ɪd, -ə*/z
modulation, -s ˌmɒdjʊ'leɪʃn [-dʒʊ-], -z
module, -s 'mɒdju:l, -z
modul|us, -uses, -i 'mɒdjʊl|əs, -əsɪz, -aɪ
modus 'məʊdəs
modus operandi 'mɒdəsˌɒpə'rændi: ['məʊdəsˌɒpə'rændaɪ]
modus vivendi ˌmɒdəsvɪ'vendi: [-vi:'v-, ˌməʊdəsvɪ'vendaɪ]
Moeran 'mɔ:rən
Moesia 'mi:sjə [-sɪə, -ʃjə, -ʃɪə, -zjə, -zɪə, -ʒjə, -ʒɪə]
Moeso-gothic ˌmi:səʊ'gɒθɪk [ˌmi:zəʊ-]
Moffat 'mɒfət
Mogador ˌmɒgə'dɔ:*
Moggach 'mɒgək [-əx]
Mogul, -s 'məʊgl ['məʊgəl, -gʊl, -gʌl], -z
mohair 'məʊheə*
Mohammed məʊ'hæmed [-mɪd]
Mohammedan, -s məʊ'hæmɪdən, -z
Mohave məʊ'hɑ:vɪ
Mohawk, -s 'məʊhɔ:k, -s
Mohican, -s 'məʊɪkən, məʊ'hi:kən, -z
Mohun 'məʊən ['məʊhən], mu:n, mə'hʌn
moidore, -s 'mɔɪdɔ:* ['məʊɪd-, -dɔə*, mɔɪ'd-], -z
Note.—The stressing -'- has to be used in John Masefield's poem 'Cargoes'.
moiet|y, -ies 'mɔɪət|ɪ ['mɔɪɪt-], -ɪz
moil (s. v.), -s, -ing, -ed mɔɪl, -z, -ɪŋ, -d
Moir 'mɔɪə*
Moira 'mɔɪərə
moire, -s mwɑ:* [mwɔ:*] (mwa:r), -z
moiré 'mwɑ:reɪ ['mwɔ:r-] (mware)
moist, -er, -est, -ly, -ness mɔɪst, -ə*, -ɪst, -lɪ, -nɪs [-nəs]
moist|en, -ens, -ening, -ened 'mɔɪs|n, -nz, -ṇɪŋ [-nɪŋ], -nd
moistur|e, -izer/s 'mɔɪstʃə*, -raɪzə*/z
Moivre 'mɔɪvə*
Mojave (=Mohave) məʊ'hɑ:vɪ
moke, -s məʊk, -s
molar (s. adj.), -s 'məʊlə*, -z
molasses məʊ'læsɪz
molassine 'mɒləsi:n ['məʊl-]
mold=mould
Mold məʊld
Moldavia, -n mɒl'deɪvjə [-vɪə], -n
molder, moldy=mould-
mole, -s məʊl, -z
molecular məʊ'lekjʊlə* [mɒ'l-, -kjə-]

molecule, -s 'mɒlɪkjuːl ['məʊl-], -z
mole-hill, -s 'məʊlhɪl, -z
Molesey 'məʊlzɪ
mole-skin, -s 'məʊlskɪn, -z
molest, -s, -ing, -ed məʊ'lest, -s, -ɪŋ, -ɪd
molestation, -s ˌməʊle'steɪʃn, -z
Molesworth 'məʊlzwɜːθ [-wəθ]
Moleyns 'mʌlɪnz
Molière 'mɒliəɑ* ['məʊl-, -ljeə*]
(mɔljeːr)
mollification ˌmɒlɪfɪ'keɪʃn
molli|fy, -fies, -fying, -fied; -fiable
'mɒlɪ|faɪ, -faɪz, -faɪɪŋ, -faɪd; -faɪəbl
mollusc, -s 'mɒləsk [-lʌsk], -s
mollusc|an, -oid, -ous mɒ'lʌsk|ən
[mə'l-], -ɔɪd, -əs
moll|y (M.), -ies 'mɒl|ɪ, -ɪz
mollycodd|le, -les, -ling, -led 'mɒlɪ-
ˌkɒd|l, -lz, -lɪŋ [-lɪŋ], -ld
Moloch 'məʊlɒk
Molony mə'ləʊnɪ
Molotov 'mɒlətɒf
molten 'məʊltən
molto 'mɒltəʊ ('molto)
Molton 'məʊltən
moly 'məʊlɪ
molybdenum mə'lɪbdənəm [mɒ'l-,
ˌmɒlɪb'diːnəm]
Molyneux 'mɒlɪnjuːks, 'mʌlɪnjuːks,
'mɒlɪnjuː, 'mʌlɪnjuː
Mombasa mɒm'bæsə [-'bɑːsə]
moment, -s 'məʊmənt, -s
momentar|y, -ily, -iness 'məʊməntər|ɪ,
-əlɪ [-ɪlɪ], -ɪnɪs [-ɪnəs]
momentous, -ly, -ness məʊ'mentəs,
-lɪ, -nɪs [-nəs]
moment|um, -ums, -a məʊ'ment|əm,
-əmz, -ə
Momerie 'mʌmərɪ
Mon (language) məʊn
Mon. (abbrev. of Monmouthshire) mɒn
mona (M.), -s 'məʊnə, -z. (See also
Monna Lisa)
Monaco 'mɒnəkəʊ [-nɪk-]
monad, -s 'mɒnæd ['məʊn-], -z
monadic mɒ'nædɪk [məʊ'n-]
Monaghan 'mɒnəhən [-nəxən, -nəkən]
monarch, -s 'mɒnək, -s
monarch|al, -ic, -ical mɒ'nɑːk|l
[mə'n-], -ɪk, -ɪkl
monarchi|sm, -st/s 'mɒnəkɪ|zəm, -st/s
monarchiz|e [-is|e], -es, -ing, -ed 'mɒn-
əkaɪz, -ɪz, -ɪŋ, -d
monarch|y, -ies 'mɒnək|ɪ, -ɪz
monaster|y, -ies 'mɒnəstər|ɪ, -ɪz
monastic, -al,ً-ally mə'næstɪk [mɒ'n-],
-l, -əlɪ
monasticism mə'næstɪsɪzəm [mɒ'n-]

monaural ˌmɒn'ɔːrəl
Monck mʌŋk
Monckton 'mʌŋktən
Moncrieff mən'kriːf [mɒn-]
Mond (English name) mɒnd
Monday, -s 'mʌndɪ [-deɪ], -z
Monegasque ˌmɒnɪ'gæsk
†monetary 'mʌnɪtərɪ
monetiz|e [-is|e], -es, -ing, -ed 'mʌnɪ-
taɪz, -ɪz, -ɪŋ, -d
money (M.), -s, -ed 'mʌnɪ, -z, -d
money-box, -es 'mʌnɪbɒks, -ɪz
money-changer, -s 'mʌnɪˌtʃeɪndʒə*, -z
money-grubb|er/s, -ing 'mʌnɪˌgrʌb|-
ə*/z, -ɪŋ
money-lend|er/s, -ing 'mʌnɪˌlend|ə*/z,
-ɪŋ
money-market, -s 'mʌnɪˌmɑːkɪt, -s
money-order, -s 'mʌnɪˌɔːdə*, -z
Moneypenny 'mʌnɪˌpenɪ
money-spinner, -s 'mʌnɪˌspɪnə*, -z
monger, -s 'mʌŋgə*, -z
mongol (M.), -s, -oid 'mɒŋgəl [-gɒl], -z,
-ɔɪd
Mongolia, -n/s mɒŋ'gəʊljə [-lɪə], -n/z
mongoose, -s 'mɒŋguːs ['mʌŋ-], -ɪz
mongrel, -s 'mʌŋgrəl, -z
Monica 'mɒnɪkə
Monier 'mʌnɪə* ['mɒn-, -njə*]
moni|sm, -st/s 'mɒnɪ|zəm ['məʊn-], -st/s
monistic mɒ'nɪstɪk
monition, -s məʊ'nɪʃn [mɒ'n-], -z
monitor, -s; -ship/s 'mɒnɪtə*, -z; -ʃɪp/s
monitorial ˌmɒnɪ'tɔːrɪəl
monitory 'mɒnɪtərɪ
monk (M.), -s, -ish mʌŋk, -s, -ɪʃ
monkey, -s 'mʌŋkɪ, -z
monkey-engine, -s 'mʌŋkɪˌendʒɪn, -z
monkey-puzzle, -s 'mʌŋkɪˌpʌzl, -z
Monkhouse 'mʌŋkhaʊs
Monkton 'mʌŋktən
Monkwearmouth mʌŋk'wɪəmaʊθ
Monmouth, -shire 'mɒnməθ [rarely
'mʌn-], -ʃə* [-ˌʃɪə*]
Monna Lisa ˌmɒnə'liːzə (sometimes spelt
Mona and pronounced 'məʊnə)
mono (monotype), -s 'məʊnəʊ ['mɒnəʊ],
(in sound recording, opp. stereo)
'mɒnəʊ, -z
Monoceros mə'nɒsərɒs [mɒ'n-]
monochord, -s 'mɒnəʊkɔːd, -z
monochrome, -s 'mɒnəkrəʊm, -z
monocle, -s 'mɒnəkl [-nɒk-], -z
monocotyledon, -s 'mɒnəʊˌkɒtɪ'liːdən
[-ˌkɒtə-], -z
monod|y, -ies 'mɒnəd|ɪ, -ɪz
monogam|ist/s, -ous, -y mɒ'nɒgəm|-
ɪst/s [mə'n-], -əs, -ɪ

328

monoglot 'mɒnəglɒt

monogram, -s 'mɒnəgræm, -z

monograph, -s 'mɒnəgrɑːf [-græf],
-s

monolingual ˌmɒnəʊ'lɪŋgwəl

monolith, -s 'mɒnəʊlɪθ, -s

monolithic ˌmɒnəʊ'lɪθɪk

monologist, -s mɒ'nɒlədʒɪst, -s

monologiz|e [-is|e], -es, -ing, -ed, -er/s
mɒ'nɒlədʒaɪz, -ɪz, -ɪŋ, -d, -ə*/z

monologue, -s 'mɒnəlɒg [rarely -ləʊg],
-z

monoma|nia, -niac/s ˌmɒnəʊ'meɪ|njə
[-nɪə], -nɪæk/s

monophthong, -s 'mɒnəfθɒŋ, -z

monophthong|al, -ic, mɒnəf'θɒŋg|l, -ɪk

monophthongiz|e [-is|e], -es, -ing, -ed
'mɒnəfθɒŋgaɪz, -ɪz, -ɪŋ, -d

monoplane, -s 'mɒnəʊpleɪn, -z

Monopole 'mɒnəpəʊl

monopolism mə'nɒpəlɪzəm [-pˌlɪzəm]

monopolist, -s mə'nɒpəlɪst [-pˌlɪst], -s

monopolistic mə,nɒpə'lɪstɪk [-pˌ'ɪstɪk]

monopoliz|e [-is|e], -es, -ing, -ed, -er/s
mə'nɒpəlaɪz [-pˌaɪz], -ɪz, -ɪŋ, -d,
ə*/z

monopol|y, -ies mə'nɒpəl|ɪ [-pˌ|ɪ], -ɪz

monorail, -s 'mɒnəʊreɪl, -z

monosyllabic ˌmɒnəʊsɪ'læbɪk

monosyllable, -s 'mɒnəˌsɪləbl, -z

monothei|sm, -st/s 'mɒnəʊθiː,ɪ|zəm
['mɒnəʊˌθiː-], -st/s

monoton|e (s. v.), -es, -ing, -ed 'mɒnə-
təʊn, -z, -ɪŋ, -d

monotonic ˌmɒnə'tɒnɪk

monotonous, -ly mə'nɒtnəs [-tənəs], -lɪ

monotony mə'nɒtnɪ [-tənɪ]

monotype, -s 'mɒnəʊtaɪp, -s

monovalen|ce, -t ˌmɒnəʊ'veɪlən|s
['--,--], -t

monoxide, -s mɒ'nɒksaɪd [mə'n-],
-z

Monro(e) mən'rəʊ [mʌn'rəʊ], 'mʌnrəʊ

Mons mɒnz [mɔ̃:ns] (mɔ̃:s)

Monsarrat (surname) ˌmɒnsə'ræt

monseigneur, -s ˌmɒnsen'jɜ:*
(mɔ̃sɛɲœ:r), -z

Monserrat (Spanish general) ˌmɒnse'rɑːt
[-sə'r-]

monsieur (M.) mə'sjɜ:* (strong form)
(məsjø), məsjə* (weak form)

Monsignor mɒn'siːnjə*

Monson 'mʌnsn

monsoon, -s mɒn'suːn [mən-], -z

monster, -s 'mɒnstə*, -z

monstrance, -s 'mɒnstrəns, -ɪz

monstrosit|y, -ies mɒn'strɒsət|ɪ [mən-,
-ɪt|ɪ], -ɪz

monstrous, -ly, -ness 'mɒnstrəs, -lɪ,
-nɪs [-nəs]

montage, -s 'mɒntɑ:ʒ [mɒn'tɑ:ʒ, 'mɒn-
tɪdʒ], -ɪz

Montagu(e) 'mɒntəgju: [-tɪg-], 'mʌn-

Montaigne mɒn'teɪn

Montana (state of U.S.A.) mɒn'tænə
[-'tɑ:n-]

Mont Blanc ˌmɔ̃:m'blɑ̃:ŋ [-'blɔ̃:ŋ,
ˌmɒm'blɒŋ, ˌmɒn'blɒŋ] (mɔ̃blɑ̃)

montbretia, -s mɒn'briːʃə [mɒm'b-,
-ʃɪə, -ʃjə], -z

Mont Cenis ˌmɔ̃:nsə'niː [ˌmɒnt-] (mɔ̃sni)

monte (M.) 'mɒntɪ

Monte Carlo ˌmɒntɪ'kɑ:ləʊ

Montefiore ˌmɒntɪfɪ'ɔ:rɪ [-'fjɔ:rɪ]

monteith, -s mɒn'tiːθ, -s

Monteith mən'tiːθ [mɒn-]

Montenegr|o, -ian/s, -in/s ˌmɒntɪ'niː-
gr|əʊ [-'neɪg-], -ɪən/z, -ɪn/z

Monte Rosa ˌmɒntɪ'rəʊzə

Montesquieu ˌmɒnte'skju: [-'skjɜ:, '—]
(mɔ̃tɛskjø)

Montessori ˌmɒnte'sɔ:rɪ [-tɪ's-]

Montevideo ˌmɒntɪvɪ'deɪəʊ [old-
fashioned -'vɪdɪəʊ]

Montezuma ˌmɒntɪ'zuːmə

Montfort (Simon de Montfort) 'mɒntfət
[-fɔ:t]

Montgomerie mənt'gʌmərɪ [mɒnt-
'gɒm-, mənt'gɒm-]

Montgomery, -shire mənt'gʌmərɪ
[mɒnt'gɒm-, mənt'gɒm-] (Welsh
mont'gəmri), -ʃə* [-ˌʃɪə*]

month, -s, -ly mʌnθ, -s, -lɪ

Montmorency ˌmɒntmə'rensɪ

Montpelier (in U.S.A., London Street)
mɒnt'piːljə* [-lɪə*]

Montpellier (in France) mɔ̃:m'pelɪeɪ
[mɒnt'p-] (mɔ̃pəlje, -pɛlje), (in names
of streets, etc.) mɒnt'pelɪə* [mənt-,
-ljə*]

Montreal ˌmɒntrɪ'ɔ:l

Montreux mɒn'trɜ: (mɔ̃trø)

Montrose mɒn'trəʊz

Montserrat (island in West Indies)
ˌmɒntse'ræt [-sə'r-], (monastery in
Spain) -'rɑ:t

Monty 'mɒntɪ

monument, -s 'mɒnjʊmənt [-jəm-], -s

monument|al, -ally ˌmɒnjʊ'ment|l
[-jə'm-, -əlɪ [-ˌlɪ]

Monzie (in Tayside) mə'niː

moo, -s, -ing, -ed muː, -z, -ɪŋ, -d

mooch, -es, -ing, -ed muːtʃ, -ɪz, -ɪŋ,
-t

moo-cow, -s 'muːkaʊ, -z

mood, -s muːd, -z

mood|y (M.), -ier, -iest, -ily, -iness
'mu:d|ɪ, -ɪə* [-jə*], -ɪɪst [-jɪst], -ɪlɪ
[-əlɪ], -mɪs [-məs]
moon (s. v.) (M.), -s, -ing, -ed; -beam/s
mu:n, -z, -ɪŋ, -d; -bi:m/z
moon-cal|f, -ves 'mu:nkɑ:|f, -vz
moon|less, -light, -lit 'mu:n|lɪs [-ləs],
-laɪt, -lɪt
moonshine 'mu:nʃaɪn
moonstruck 'mu:nstrʌk
moonstone, -s 'mu:nstəʊn, -z
moony 'mu:nɪ
moor (s. v.) (M.), -s, -ing/s, -ed mɔ:* [mʊə*,
mʊə*], -z, -rɪŋ/z, -d
moor-cock, -s 'mɔ:kɒk ['mɔə-, 'mʊə-],
-z
Moore mʊə*, mɔ:*
Moorgate 'mɔ:geɪt ['mɔə-, 'mʊə-, -gɪt]
moorhen, -s 'mɔ:hen ['mɔə-, 'mʊə-], -z
mooring-mast, -s 'mɔ:rɪŋmɑːst ['mɔər-,
'mʊər-], -s
Moorish 'mʊərɪʃ ['mɔər-, 'mɔ:r-]
moorland, -s 'mɔ:lənd ['mɔəl-, 'mʊəl-,
-lænd], -z
Note.—The variant -lænd is not used
when the word is attributive.
moose, -s mu:s, -ɪz
moot (s. adj. v.), -s, -ing, -ed mu:t, -s
-ɪŋ, -ɪd
mop (s. v.), -s, -ping, -ped mɒp, -s, -ɪŋ,
-t
mop|e, -es, -ing/ly, -ed məʊp, -s, -ɪŋ/lɪ,
-t
moped (s.), -s 'məʊped, -z
mopish, -ly, -ness 'məʊpɪʃ, -lɪ, -nɪs
[-nəs]
moquette mɒ'ket [məʊ-]
mor|a, -ae, -as 'mɔ:r|ə, -i: [-aɪ], -əz
Morag 'mɔ:ræg
moraine, -s mɒ'reɪn [mə'r-], -z
mor|al (s. adj.), -als, -ally 'mɒr|əl, -əlz,
-əlɪ [-lɪ]
morale mɒ'rɑ:l [mə'r-]
moralist, -s 'mɒrəlɪst [-r|ɪst], -s
morality mə'rælətɪ [mɒ'r-, -ɪtɪ]
moraliz|e (-is|e), -es, -ing, -ed, -er/s
'mɒrəlaɪz [-r|aɪz], -ɪz, -ɪŋ, -d, -ə*/z
Moran 'mɔ:rən, 'mɒrən, mə'ræn
[mɒ'ræn]
Morant mə'rænt [mɒ'r-]
morass, -es mə'ræs [mɒ'r-], -ɪz
moratorium, -s ˌmɒrə'tɔ:rɪəm [ˌmɔ:r-],
-z
Moravia, -n/s mə'reɪvjə [mɒ'r-, -vɪə],
-n/z
†Moray, -shire 'mʌrɪ, -ʃə* [-ˌʃɪə*]
morbid, -est, -ly, -ness 'mɔ:bɪd, -ɪst, -lɪ,
-nɪs [-nəs]

morbidity mɔ:'bɪdətɪ [-ɪtɪ]
mordant (s. adj.), -s 'mɔ:dənt, -s
Mordecai ˌmɔ:dɪ'keraɪ
mordent, -s 'mɔ:dənt, -s
more (M.) mɔ:* [mɔə*]
Morea mɒ'rɪə [mə'r-, mɔ:'r-]
Morecambe 'mɔ:kəm
Moreen mɔ:'ri:n ['—]
morel (M.) mɒ'rel [mə'r-]
morello, -s mə'reləʊ [mɒ'r-], -z
moreover mɔ:'rəʊvə* [mə'r-]
mores 'mɔ:reɪz [-ri:z]
Moreton 'mɔ:tn
Morgan 'mɔ:gən
morganatic, -ally ˌmɔ:gə'nætɪk, -əlɪ
morgue, -s mɔ:g, -z
Moriah mɒ'raɪə [mɔ:'r-, mə'r-]
Moriarty ˌmɒrɪ'ɑ:tɪ
moribund 'mɒrɪbʌnd ['mɔ:r-, -bənd]
Morison 'mɒrɪsn
Morley 'mɔ:lɪ
Mormon, -s, -ism 'mɔ:mən, -z, -ɪzəm
morn, -s mɔ:n, -z
morning, -s 'mɔ:nɪŋ, -z
morning-coat, -s 'mɔ:nɪŋkəʊt [ˌ-'-'-], -s
morning-dress 'mɔ:nɪŋdres
morning-room, -s 'mɔ:nɪŋrʊm [-ru:m],
-z
morning-star, -s ˌmɔ:nɪŋ'stɑ:* ['—], -z
Mornington 'mɔ:nɪŋtən
morning-watch, -es ˌmɔ:nɪŋ'wɒtʃ, -ɪz
Moroccan, -s mə'rɒkən, -z
morocco (M.), -s mə'rɒkəʊ, -z
moron, -s 'mɔ:rɒn [-rən], -z
morose, -ly, -ness mə'rəʊs [mɒ'r-], -lɪ,
-nɪs [-nəs]
Morpeth 'mɔ:peθ [-pəθ]
morpheme, -s 'mɔ:fi:m, -z
morphemic mɔ:'fi:mɪk
Morpheus 'mɔ:fju:s [-fjəs, -fɪəs]
morph|ia, -ine 'mɔ:f|jə [-ɪə], -i:n
morphologic, -al, -ally ˌmɔ:fə'lɒdʒɪk, -l,
-əlɪ
morpholog|ist/s, -y mɔ:'fɒlədʒ|ɪst/s, -ɪ
morphophonemic ˌmɔ:fəʊfəʊ'ni:mɪk
morphophonology ˌmɔ:fəʊfəʊ'nɒlədʒɪ
Morphy 'mɔ:fɪ
Morrell 'mʌrəl, mə'rel
morris (M.), -es 'mɒrɪs, -ɪz
morris-dance, -s ˌmɒrɪs'dɑːns ['—], -ɪz
Morrison 'mɒrɪsn
morrow (M.), -s 'mɒrəʊ, -z
morse (M.), -s mɔ:s, -ɪz
morsel, -s 'mɔ:sl, -z
Morshead 'mɔ:zhed
mort, -s mɔ:t, -s
mort|al, -als, -ally 'mɔ:t|l, -lz, -əlɪ [-l̩ɪ]
mortalit|y (M.), -ies mɔ:'tælət|ɪ [-ɪt|ɪ], -ɪz

mortar, -s 'mɔ:tə*, -z
mortarboard, -s 'mɔ:təbɔ:d [-bɔəd], -z
mortgag|e (s. v.), -es, -ing, -ed 'mɔ:gɪdʒ, -ɪz, -ɪŋ, -d
mortgagee, -s ˌmɔ:gɪ'dʒi:, -z
mortgagor, -s ˌmɔ:gɪ'dʒɔ:*, -z
mortice, -s 'mɔ:tɪs, -ɪz
mortification, ˌmɔ:tɪfɪ'keɪʃn
morti|fy, -fies, -fying, -fied 'mɔ:tɪ|faɪ, -faɪz, -faɪɪŋ, -faɪd
Mortimer 'mɔ:tɪmə*
mortis|e (s. v.), -es, -ing, -ed 'mɔ:tɪs, -ɪz, -ɪŋ, -t
Mort|lake, -lock 'mɔ:t|leɪk, -lɒk
mortmain 'mɔ:tmeɪn
Morton 'mɔ:tn
mortuar|y, -ies 'mɔ:tʃʊər|ɪ [-tjwər-, -tjʊə-, -tjʊr-, -tʃjərɪ, -tʃərɪ], -ɪz
mosaic (s. adj.) (M.), -s məʊ'zeɪɪk, -s
Mosby 'mɒzbɪ
Moscow 'mɒskəʊ
Moseley 'məʊzlɪ
moselle (M.), -s məʊ'zel, -z
Moses 'məʊzɪz
Moslem, -s 'mɒzləm [-lem, 'mʊzlɪm], -z
Mosley 'mɒzlɪ, 'məʊzlɪ
mosque, -s mɒsk, -s
mosquit|o (M.), -oes, -oey; -o-net/s mə'ski:t|əʊ [mɒ's-], -əʊz, -əʊɪ; -əʊnet/s
moss (M.), -es mɒs, -ɪz
moss-grown 'mɒsgrəʊn
moss-rose, -s ˌmɒs'rəʊz ['--], -ɪz
moss|y, -ier, -iest, -iness 'mɒs|ɪ, -ɪə*, -ɪɪst, -ɪnɪs [-mɪs [-məs]
mos|t, -tly məʊs|t, -tlɪ
Mostyn 'mɒstɪn
Mosul 'məʊsəl
mot, -s məʊ, -z
mote, -s məʊt, -s
motel, -s məʊ'tel ['--], -z
motet, -s məʊ'tet, -s
moth, -s, -ball/s mɒθ, -s, -bɔ:l/z
moth-eaten 'mɒθˌi:tn
mother (s. v.), -s, -ing, -ed; -hood, -less 'mʌðə*, -z, -rɪŋ, -d; -hʊd, -lɪs [-ləs, -les]
mother-countr|y, -ies 'mʌðəˌkʌntr|ɪ [ˌ--'--], -ɪz
mother-in-law, -s 'mʌðərɪnlɔ:, -z
motherl|y, -iness 'mʌðəl|ɪ, '-ɪnɪs [-məs]
mother-of-pearl ˌmʌðərəv'pɜ:l
mothersill 'mʌðəsɪl
mothers-in-law (alternative plur. of mother-in-law) 'mʌðəzɪnlɔ:
motif, -s məʊ'ti:f ['--], -s

moti|on (s. v.), -ons, -oning, -oned; -onless 'məʊʃ|n, -nz, -ŋɪŋ [-ənɪŋ], -nd; -nlɪs [-ləs, -les]
motivat|e, -es, -ing, -ed 'məʊtɪveɪt, -s -ɪŋ, -ɪd
motivation ˌməʊtɪ'veɪʃn
motive (s. adj.), -s 'məʊtɪv, -z
mot juste ˌməʊ'ʒu:st (mɔʒyst)
motley (M.) 'mɒtlɪ
Motopo məʊ'təʊpəʊ
motor (s. adj. v.), -s, -ing, -ed 'məʊtə*, -z, -rɪŋ, -d
motor-bicycle, -s 'məʊtəˌbaɪsɪkl [-səkl], -z
motor-bike, -s 'məʊtəbaɪk, -s
motor-boat, -s 'məʊtəbəʊt, -s
motorcade, -s 'məʊtəkeɪd, -z
motor-car, -s 'məʊtəkɑ:*, -z
motor-cycle, -s 'məʊtəˌsaɪkl [ˌ--'--], -z
motor-cyclist, -s 'məʊtəsaɪklɪst, -s
motorist, -s 'məʊtərɪst, -s
motor-scooter, -s 'məʊtəˌsku:tə*, -z
motor-ship, -s 'məʊtəʃ:p, -s
motor-spirit 'məʊtəˌspɪrɪt [ˌ--'--]
motorway, -s 'məʊtəweɪ, -z
motory 'məʊtərɪ
Mott mɒt
Mottistone 'mɒtɪstən [-stəʊn]
mottle, -s, -d 'mɒtl, -z, -d
motto, -s 'mɒtəʊ, -z
Mottram 'mɒtrəm
Mouat 'məʊət
mouch, -es, -ing, -ed mu:tʃ, -ɪz, -ɪŋ, -t
mouf(f)lon, -s 'mu:flɒn, -z
Moughton 'məʊtn
moujik, -s 'mu:ʒɪk [-dʒɪk], -s
Mouland (surname) mu:'lænd [mʊ-]
mould (s. v.), -s, -ing/s, -ed məʊld, -z, -ɪŋ/z, -ɪd
mould|er, -ers, -ering, -ered 'məʊld|ə*, -əz, -ərɪŋ, -əd
mould|y, -ier, -iest, -iness 'məʊld|ɪ, -ɪə* [-jə*], -ɪɪst [-jɪst], -ɪnɪs [-məs]
Moule məʊl, mu:l
Moulmein maʊl'meɪn
Moulsford 'məʊlsfəd [-lzf-]
moult (s. v.), -s, -ing, -ed məʊlt, -s, -ɪŋ, -ɪd
Moulton 'məʊltən
Moultrie 'mɔ:ltrɪ, 'mu:trɪ
mound (M.), -s maʊnd, -z
Mounsey 'maʊnzɪ
mount (s. v.) (M.), -s, -ing, -ed maʊnt, -s, -ɪŋ, -ɪd
mountain, -s 'maʊntɪn [-tən], -z
mountain-ash, -es ˌmaʊntɪn'æʃ [-tən-], -ɪz

331

mountaineer, -s, -ing ˌmaʊntɪ'nɪə*
[-tə'n-], -z, -rɪŋ
mountainous 'maʊntɪnəs [-tən-]
mountant, -s 'maʊntənt, -s
Mountbatten maʊnt'bætn
mountebank, -s 'maʊntɪbæŋk, -s
Mountjoy maʊnt'dʒɔɪ, 'maʊntdʒɔɪ
Moura 'mʊərə
mourn, -s, -ing, -ed, -er/s mɔːn [mɔən,
rarely mʊən], -z, -ɪŋ, -d, -ə*/z
mourn|ful, -fully, -fulness 'mɔːn|fʊl
['mɔən-, rarely 'mʊən-], -fʊlɪ [-fəlɪ],
-fʊlnɪs [-nəs]
mouse (s.), mice maʊs, maɪs
mous|e (v.), -es, -ing, -ed maʊz, -ɪz, -ɪŋ,
-d [maʊs, -ɪz, -ɪŋ, -t]
mouse-hole, -s 'maʊshəʊl, -z
Mousehole (near Penzance) 'maʊzl
mouser, -s 'maʊzə* ['maʊsə*], -z
mouse-trap, -s 'maʊstræp, -s
*
Mousir muː'sɪə*
moussaka muː'sɑːkə
mousse muːs
mousseline 'muːslɪn [muːs'liːn]
moustache, -s mə'stɑːʃ [mʊs'-], -ɪz
mousy 'maʊsɪ
mou|th (s.), -ths maʊ|θ, -ðz
mouth (v.), -s, -ing, -ed maʊð, -z, -ɪŋ, -d
mouthful, -s 'maʊθfʊl, -z
mouth-organ, -s 'maʊθˌɔːgən, -z
mouthpiece, -s 'maʊθpiːs, -ɪz
mouth|y, -ier, -iest 'maʊð|ɪ, -ɪə* [-jə*],
-ɪɪst [-jɪst]
movability ˌmuːvə'bɪlətɪ [-lɪt-]
movable, -s, -ness 'muːvəbl, -z, -nɪs
[-nəs]
mov|e (s. v.), -es, -ing/ly, -ed, -er/s,
-ement/s muːv, -z, -ɪŋ/lɪ, -d, -ə*/z,
-mənt/s
movie, -s; -tone 'muːvɪ, -z; -təʊn
mow (s.) (stack), -s maʊ, -z
mow (s.) (grimace), -s maʊ, -z
mow (v.) (cut down), -s, -ing, -ed, -n,
-er/s məʊ, -z, -ɪŋ, -d, -n, -ə*/z
Mowatt 'maʊət, 'məʊət
Mowbray 'məʊbreɪ, -brɪ
Mowgli 'maʊglɪ
mowing-machine, -s 'məʊɪŋməˌʃiːn, -z
Mowll məʊl, muːl
Moxon 'mɒksn
moya (M.), -s 'mɔɪə, -z
Moyes mɔɪz
Moygashel (place) mɔɪ'gæʃl, (linen)
'mɔɪgəʃl
Moynihan 'mɔɪnjən [-nɪən]
Mozambique ˌməʊzæm'biːk [-zəm-]
Mozart 'məʊtsɑːt [old-fashioned
məʊ'zɑːt]

M.P. (member of Parliament) ˌem'piː
Mr. 'mɪstə*
Mrs. 'mɪsɪz
MS ˌem'es [em'es, 'mænjʊskrɪpt, -jəs-]
Ms. (used to avoid indicating a woman's
marital status; the pronunciation is unstable) mɪz, məz
MSS ˌemes'es ['mænjʊskrɪpts, -jəs-]
mu mjuː
much, -ly, -ness mʌtʃ, -lɪ, -nɪs [-nəs]
Muchalls 'mʌkəlz ['mʌxəlz]
mucilage, -s 'mjuːsɪlɪdʒ, -ɪz
mucilaginous ˌmjuːsɪ'lædʒɪnəs [-dʒənəs]
muck (s. v.), -s, -ing, -ed mʌk, -s, -ɪŋ,
-t
mucker (s. v.), -s, -ing, -ed 'mʌkə*, -z,
-rɪŋ, -d
muckrake, -s 'mʌkreɪk, -s
muck|y, -ier, -iest, -iness 'mʌk|ɪ, -ɪə*,
-ɪɪst, -ɪnɪs [-ɪnəs]
muc|ous, -us 'mjuːk|əs, -əs
mud, -s mʌd, -z
mud-ba|th, -ths 'mʌdbɑː|θ [ˌmʌd'b-],
-ðz
mudd|le (s. v.), -les, -ling, -led, -ler/s
'mʌd|l, -lz, -lɪŋ [-lɪŋ], -ld, -lə*/z
[-lə*/z]
muddleheaded 'mʌdlˌhedɪd [ˌ-'--]
mudd|y (adj. v.), -ier, -iest, -ily, -iness;
-ies, -ying, -ied 'mʌd|ɪ, -ɪə*, -ɪɪst, -ɪlɪ
[-əlɪ], -ɪnɪs [-ɪnəs]; -ɪz, -ɪɪŋ, -ɪd
Mud(d)eford 'mʌdɪfəd
mud-guard, -s 'mʌdgɑːd, -z
Mudie 'mjuːdɪ
mudlark, -s 'mʌdlɑːk, -s
muesli 'mjuːzlɪ
muezzin, -s muː'ezɪn [mʊ'e-], -z
muff (s. v.), -s, -ing, -ed mʌf, -s, -ɪŋ, -t
muffin, -s 'mʌfɪn, -z
muff|le, -les, -ling, -led 'mʌf|l, -lz, -lɪŋ
[-lɪŋ], -ld
muffler, -s 'mʌflə*, -z
mufti 'mʌftɪ
mug (s. v.), -s, -ging, -ged mʌg, -z, -ɪŋ,
-d
mugger, -s 'mʌgə*, -z
muggins, -es 'mʌgɪnz, -ɪz
Muggins 'mʌgɪnz, 'mjuːgɪnz
Muggleton 'mʌgltən
mugg|y, -ier, -iest, -iness 'mʌg|ɪ, -ɪə*,
-ɪɪst, -ɪnɪs [-ɪnəs]
mugwump, -s 'mʌgwʌmp, -s
Muir, -head mjʊə* [mjɔə*, mjɔː*], -hed
Mukden 'mʊkdən
Mukle 'mjuːklɪ
mulatto, -s mjuː'lætəʊ [mjʊ'l-], -z
mulberr|y, -ies 'mʌlbər|ɪ, -ɪz
Mulcaster 'mʌlkæstə*

mulch (s. v.), **-es, -ing, -ed** mʌltʃ, -ɪz, -ɪŋ, -t

mulct (s. v.), **-s, -ing, -ed** mʌlkt, -s, -ɪŋ, -ɪd

mule, **-s** mjuːl, -z

muleteer, **-s** ˌmjuːlɪˈtɪə* [-ləˈt-], -z

Mulgrave ˈmʌlɡreɪv

mulish, **-ly, -ness** ˈmjuːlɪʃ, -lɪ, -nɪs [-nəs]

mull (s. v.) (**M.**), **-s, -ing, -ed** mʌl, -z, -ɪŋ, -d

Mullah, **-s** ˈmʌlə [ˈmʊlə], -z

mullein, ˈmʌlɪn

mullet (**M.**), **-s** ˈmʌlɪt [-lət], -s

mulligatawny ˌmʌlɪɡəˈtɔːnɪ

Mullin|ar, **-er** ˈmʌlɪn|ə*, -ə*

Mullinger ˈmʌlɪndʒə*

mullion (**M.**), **-s, -ed** ˈmʌlɪən [-ljən], -z, -d

mullock ˈmʌlək

Mulready mʌlˈredɪ

multifarious, **-ly, -ness** ˌmʌltɪˈfeərɪəs, -lɪ, -nɪs [-nəs]

multiform ˈmʌltɪfɔːm

multilateral ˌmʌltɪˈlætərəl

multiliter|al, **-ally** ˌmʌltɪˈlɪtər|əl, -əlɪ

multi-millionaire, **-s** ˌmʌltɪmɪljəˈneə*, -z

multiple (s. adj.), **-s** ˈmʌltɪpl, -z

multiplex ˈmʌltɪpleks

multiplicand, **-s** ˌmʌltɪplɪˈkænd, -z

multiplication, **-s** ˌmʌltɪplɪˈkeɪʃn, -z

multiplicative ˌmʌltɪˈplɪkətɪv [ˈmʌltɪplɪkeɪtɪv]

multiplicator, **-s** ˈmʌltɪplɪkeɪtə*, -z

multiplicity ˌmʌltɪˈplɪsətɪ [-rtɪ]

multipl|y, **-ies, -ying, -ied, -ier/s** ˈmʌltɪpl|aɪ, -aɪz, -aɪɪŋ, -aɪd, -aɪə*/z

multi-purpose ˌmʌltɪˈpɜːpəs

multitude, **-s** ˈmʌltɪtjuːd, -z

multitudinous, **-ly, -ness** ˌmʌltɪˈtjuːdɪnəs [-dŋəs], -lɪ, -nɪs [-nəs]

multum in parvo ˌmʊltəmɪnˈpɑːvəʊ [ˌmʌl-]

mum mʌm

mumb|le, **-les, -ling/ly, -led, -ler/s** ˈmʌmb|l, -lz, -lɪŋ/lɪ, -ld, -lə*/z

Mumbles ˈmʌmblz

mumbo-jumbo ˌmʌmbəʊˈdʒʌmbəʊ

Mumm mʌm

mummer, **-s, -y** ˈmʌmə*, -z, -rɪ

mummification ˌmʌmɪfɪˈkeɪʃn

mummi|fy, **-fies, -fying, -fied** ˈmʌmɪ|faɪ, -faɪz, -faɪɪŋ, -faɪd

mumm|y, ies ˈmʌm|ɪ, -ɪz

mump, **-s, -ing, -ed** mʌmp, -s, -ɪŋ, -t [mʌmt]

mumpish, **-ly, -ness** ˈmʌmpɪʃ, -lɪ, -nɪs [-nəs]

mumps (s.) mʌmps

munch, **-es, -ing, -ed** mʌntʃ, -ɪz, -ɪŋ, -t

Munchausen mʌnˈtʃɔːzn [mʊnˈtʃaʊzn] (also as German **Münchhausen** ˈmynçˌhauzən)

mundane, **-ly** ˌmʌnˈdeɪn [ˈ--], -lɪ

Munich ˈmjuːnɪk

municipal mjuːˈnɪsɪpl [mjʊˈn-]

municipalit|y, **-ies** mjuːˌnɪsɪˈpælət|ɪ [mjʊˌn-, ˌmjuːnɪsɪˈp-, -ɪt|ɪ], -ɪz

municipaliz|e [-is|e], **-es, -ing, -ed** mjuːˈnɪsɪpəlaɪz [mjʊˈn-], -ɪz, -ɪŋ, -d

munificen|ce, **-t/ly** mjuːˈnɪfɪsn|s [mjʊˈn-], -t/lɪ

muniment, **-s** ˈmjuːnɪmənt, -s

munition, **-s** mjuːˈnɪʃn [mjʊˈn-], -z

Munro mʌnˈrəʊ [mən-], ˈmʌnrəʊ

Munsey ˈmʌnzɪ

Munster ˈmʌnstə*

muntjak, **-s** ˈmʌntdʒæk, -s

mural, **-s** ˈmjʊərəl [ˈmjɔːr-, ˈmjɔːr-], -z

Murchie ˈmɜːkɪ, in S. England also ˈmɜːtʃɪ

Murchison ˈmɜːtʃɪsn, ˈmɜːkɪsn

Murcott ˈmɜːkət

murd|er (s. v.), **-ers, -ering, -ered, -erer/s** ˈmɜːd|ə*, -əz, -ərɪŋ, -əd, -ərə*/z

murderess, **-es** ˈmɜːdərɪs [-res], -ɪz

murderous, **-ly** ˈmɜːdərəs, -lɪ

Murdoch ˈmɜːdɒk

Mure mjʊə* [mjɔə*, mjɔː*]

muriate ˈmjʊərɪət [ˈmjɔər-, ˈmjɔːr-, -rɪɪt, -rɪeɪt]

muriatic ˌmjʊərɪˈætɪk [ˌmjɔər-, ˌmjɔːr-, ˈ----]

Muriel ˈmjʊərɪəl [ˈmjɔər-, ˈmjɔːr-]

Murillo, **-s** mjʊəˈrɪləʊ [mjʊˈr-, -ljəʊ], -z

Murison ˈmjʊərɪsn [ˈmjɔər-, ˈmjɔːr-]

murk|y, **-ier, -iest, -ily, -iness** ˈmɜːk|ɪ, -ɪə* [-jə*], -ɪɪst [-jɪst], -ɪlɪ [-əlɪ], -ɪnɪs [-nəs]

murm|ur (s. v.), **-urs, -uring/ly, -ured, -urer/s** ˈmɜːm|ə*, -əz, -ərɪŋ/lɪ, -əd, -ərə*/z

murph|y (**M.**), **-ies** ˈmɜːf|ɪ, -ɪz

murrain ˈmʌrɪn [-reɪn]

Murray ˈmʌrɪ

Murree ˈmʌrɪ

Murrell ˈmʌrəl, mʌˈrel [məˈrel]

Murrie (surname) ˈmjʊərɪ

Murry ˈmʌrɪ

Murtagh ˈmɜːtə

Murtle ˈmɜːtl

Mus. Bac., **-'s** ˌmʌzˈbæk, -s

muscat (**M.**), **-s** ˈmʌskət [-kæt], -s

muscatel, **-s** ˌmʌskəˈtel, -z

Muschamp ˈmʌskəm

363

muscle, -s 'mʌsl, -z
muscle-bound 'mʌslbaʊnd
Muscovite, -s 'mʌskəʊvaɪt, -s
Muscovy 'mʌskəʊvɪ
muscular, -ly 'mʌskjʊlə* [-jəl-], -lɪ
muscularity ˌmʌskjʊ'lærətɪ [-jə'l-, -ɪtɪ]
Mus.D., -'s ˌmʌz'diː, -z
mus|e (s. v.) (M.), -es, -ing/ly, -ed
    mjuːz, -ɪz, -ɪŋ/lɪ, -d
musette, -s mjuː'zet [mjuː'z-], -s
museum, -s mjuː'zɪəm [mjuː'z-], -z
Musgrave 'mʌzgreɪv
mush (s. v.), -es, -ing, -ed mʌʃ, -ɪz, -ɪŋ,
    -t
mushroom, -s 'mʌʃrʊm [-ruːm], -z
mush|y -ier, -iest, -iness 'mʌʃ|ɪ, -ɪə*,
    -ɪɪst, -ɪnɪs [-ɪnəs]
music 'mjuːzɪk
musical (s.), -s 'mjuːzɪkl [ˌmjuːzɪ'kæl,
    -'kɑːl], -z
music|al (adj.), -ally, -alness 'mjuːzɪk|l,
    -əlɪ, -lnɪs [-nəs]
musical-box, -es 'mjuːzɪklbɒks, -ɪz
musicale, -s ˌmjuːzɪ'kæl [-'kɑːl], -z
music-hall, -s 'mjuːzɪkhɔːl, -z
musician, -s -ly, -ship mjuː'zɪʃn
    [mjʊ'z-], -z, -lɪ, -ʃɪp
musicolog|ist/s, -y ˌmjuːzɪ'kɒlədʒ|ɪst/s,
    -ɪ
music-stand, -s 'mjuːzɪkstænd, -z
music-stool, -s 'mjuːzɪkstuːl, -z
Musidor|a, -us ˌmjuːsɪ'dɔːr|ə, -əs
musk, -y mʌsk, -ɪ
musk-deer ˌmʌsk'dɪə* ['-ˌ-]
musket, -s; -ry 'mʌskɪt, -s; -rɪ
musketeer, -s ˌmʌskɪ'tɪə* [-kə't-], -z
Muskett 'mʌskɪt
musk-ox, -en 'mʌskɒks [ˌmʌsk'ɒks],
    -ən
musk-rat, -s 'mʌskræt [ˌmʌsk'ræt],
    -s
musk-rose, -s 'mʌskrəʊz [ˌ-'-], -ɪz
Muslim,-s 'mʊslɪm ['mʊzlɪm, 'mʌzlɪm],
    -z
muslin, -s 'mʌzlɪn, -z
musquash 'mʌskwɒʃ
mussel, -s 'mʌsl, -z
Musselburgh 'mʌslbərə [-bʌrə]
Mussolini ˌmʊsə'liːnɪ
Mussorgsky mʊ'sɔːgskɪ (mu'sorkskij,
    'musərkskij)
Mussulman, -s 'mʌslmən, -z
must (s. adj.) mʌst
must (v.) mʌst (strong form), məst, məs,
    mst, ms (weak forms)
mustang, -s 'mʌstæŋ, -z
Mustapha   (Turkish)   'mʊstəfə,
    (Egyptian) mʊ'stɑːfə

Mustapha   Kemal   ˌmʊstəfəke'mɑːl
    [-kɪ'm-]
mustard (M.) 'mʌstəd
mustard seed 'mʌstədsiːd
Mustel 'mʌstəl [-tl]
must|er (s. v.), -ers, -ering, -ered
    'mʌst|ə*, -əz, -ərɪŋ, -əd
mustn't 'mʌsnt [also occasionally 'mʌsn
    when not final]
must|y, -ier, -iest, -ily, -iness 'mʌst|ɪ,
    -ɪə* [-jə*], -ɪɪst [-jɪst], -ɪlɪ [-əlɪ], -ɪnɪs
    [-ɪnəs]
mutability ˌmjuːtə'bɪlətɪ [-lɪt-]
mutable 'mjuːtəbl
mutat|e, -es, -ing, -ed mjuː'teɪt, -s, -ɪŋ,
    -ɪd
mutation, -s mjuː'teɪʃn [mjʊ't-], -z
mutatis mutandis muːˌtɑːtɪsmuː'tændɪs
    [mjuːˌteɪtɪsmjuː'tændɪs, mjʊ't-]
mut|e (s. adj. v.), -es, -ely, -eness, -ing,
    -ed mjuːt, -s; -lɪ, -nɪs [-nəs]; -ɪŋ, -ɪd
mutilat|e, -es, -ing, -ed, -or/s 'mjuːtɪ-
    leɪt, -s, -ɪŋ, -ɪd, -ə*/z
mutilation, -s ˌmjuːtɪ'leɪʃn, -z
mutineer, -s ˌmjuːtɪ'nɪə* [-tə'n-], -z
mutinous, -ly, -ness 'mjuːtɪnəs [-tənəs,
    -tnəs], -lɪ, -nɪs [-nəs]
mutin|y (s. v.), -ies, -ying, -ied 'mjuː-
    tɪn|ɪ [-tə|n-, -tn-], -ɪz, -ɪɪŋ, -ɪd
mutism 'mjuːtɪzəm
mutt|er (s. v.), -ers, -ering/ly, -ered,
    -erer/s 'mʌt|ə*, -əz, -ərɪŋ/lɪ, -əd,
    -ərə*/z
mutton (M.); -chop/s 'mʌtn; -'tʃɒp/s
muttony 'mʌtn̩ɪ
mutual, -ly 'mjuːtʃʊəl [-tʃwəl, -tʃʊl,
    -tjʊəl, -tjwəl, -tjʊl] -ɪ
mutuality ˌmjuːtjʊ'ælətɪ [-tʃʊ-, -ɪtɪ]
muzz|le (s. v.), -les, -ling, -led 'mʌz|l,
    -lz, -l̩ɪŋ [-lɪŋ], -ld
muzzle-load|er/s, -ing 'mʌzlˌləʊd|ə*/z,
    -ɪŋ
muzz|y, -ier, -iest, -iness 'mʌz|ɪ, -ɪə*,
    -ɪɪst, -ɪnɪs [-ɪnəs]
my maɪ (normal form), mɪ (occas. weak
    form)
    Note.—Many people confine the use of mɪ
    to the special expression my lord (see
    lord) and occasionally (at Eton College)
    to the expressions my tutor and my
    dame. Some use mɪ in common idioms,
    such as never in my life, but not
    elsewhere.
Mycenae maɪ'siːniː [-nɪ]
Mycenaean ˌmaɪsə'niːən [-sɪ-, -siː-,
    -'nɪən]
mycolog|ist/s, -y maɪ'kɒlədʒ|ɪst/s, -ɪ
Myers 'maɪəz

Myerscough (*in Lancashire*) 'maɪəskəʊ
Myfanwy mə'vænwɪ (*Welsh* mə'vanwɨ)
myna(h), **-s** 'maɪnə, -z
mynheer, **-s** maɪn'hɪə* [-heə*], -z
Mynheer (*form of address in South Africa*) mə'nɪə* (*Afrikaans* mə'ne:r)
Mynott 'maɪnət
myope, **-s** 'maɪəʊp, -s
myopia maɪ'əʊpjə [-pɪə]
myopic maɪ'ɒpɪk
myosin 'maɪəʊsɪn
myosis maɪ'əʊsɪs
myosotis ˌmaɪəʊ'səʊtɪs
Myra 'maɪərə
myriad, **-s** 'mɪrɪəd, -z
myrmidon (**M.**), **-s** 'mɜːmɪdən [-dn, -dɒn], -z
myrrh mɜː*
Myrrha 'mɪrə
myrrhic 'mɜːrɪk ['mɪr-]
myrrhine 'mɜːraɪn ['mɪr-]
myrrhite 'mɜːraɪt ['mɪr-]
myrrhy 'mɜːrɪ
myrtle (**M.**), **-s** 'mɜːtl, -z
myself maɪ'self [mɪ's-, mə's-]

Mysia 'mɪsɪə [-sjə, -ʃɪə, -ʃjə]
Mysore maɪ'sɔ:* [-'sɔə*]
mysterious, **-ly**, **-ness** mɪ'stɪərɪəs, -lɪ, -nɪs [-nəs]
myster|y, **-ies** 'mɪstər|ɪ, -ɪz
mystic (*s. adj.*), **-s** 'mɪstɪk, -s
mystic|al, **-ally**, **-alness** 'mɪstɪk|l, -əlɪ, -lnɪs [-nəs]
mysticism 'mɪstɪsɪzəm
mystification ˌmɪstɪfɪ'keɪʃn
mysti|fy, **-fies**, **-fying**, **-fied** 'mɪstɪ|faɪ, -faɪz, -faɪɪŋ, -faɪd
mystique mɪ'sti:k
myth, **-s** mɪθ, -s
mythic, **-al**, **-ally** 'mɪθɪk, -l, -əlɪ
Mytholmroyd (*in West Yorkshire*) ˌmaɪðəm'rɔɪd
mythologic, **-al**, **-ally** ˌmɪθə'lɒdʒɪk [ˌmaɪθ-], -l, -əlɪ
patholog|ist/s, **-y**, **-ies** mɪ'θɒlədʒ|ɪst/s [maɪ'θ-], -ɪ, -ɪz
mythologiz|e [-is|e], **-es**, **-ing**, **-ed** mɪ'θɒlədʒaɪz [maɪ'θ-], -ɪz, -ɪŋ, -d
Mytilene ˌmɪtɪ'li:ni: [-nɪ]
myxomatosis ˌmɪksəʊmə'təʊsɪs

335

N

N (*the letter*), -'s en, -z
N.A.A.F.I. 'næfɪ
Naaman 'neɪəmən
Naas (*in Ireland*) neɪs
nab (*s. v.*), -s, -bing, -bed næb, -z, -ɪŋ, -d
Nabarro (*English surname*) nə'bɑːɪəʊ
Nablus 'nɑːbləs
nabob, -s 'neɪbɒb, -z
Nabokov nə'bəʊkɒf [næ-, nɑː-, 'næb-]
Naboth 'neɪbɒθ
nacelle, -s næ'sel, -z
nacre 'neɪkə*
nacreous 'neɪkrɪəs
nacrite 'neɪkraɪt
nacrous 'neɪkrəs
nadir, -s 'neɪˌdɪə* [-də*, 'næˌdɪə*], -z
nag (*s. v.*) (N.), -s, -ging, -ged, -ger/s næg, -z, -ɪŋ, -d, -ə*/z
Naga, -s; -land 'nɑːgə, -z; -lænd
Nagaina nə'gaɪnə
Nagari 'nɑːgərɪ
Nagasaki ˌnægə'sɑːkɪ [-'sæ-]
Nahum (*prophet*) 'neɪhəm [-hʌm], (*modern surname*) 'neɪəm
naiad, -s 'naɪæd, -z
nail (*s. v.*), -s, -ing, -ed neɪl, -z, -ɪŋ, -d
nail-brush, -es 'neɪlbrʌʃ, -ɪz
nail-scissors 'neɪlˌsɪzəz
Nain 'neɪɪn [neɪn]
Nairn(e) neən
Nairnshire 'neənʃə* [-ˌʃɪə*]
Nairobi naɪ'rəʊbɪ
Naish næʃ
naive, -ly, -ty naɪ'iːv [nɑː'iːv], -lɪ, -tɪ [-ətɪ, -ɪtɪ]
naïveté, nɑː'iːvteɪ [naɪ'iːv-] (naïfte)
naked, -ly, -ness 'neɪkɪd, -lɪ, -nɪs [-nəs]
naker, -s 'neɪkə* ['næ-], -z
namby-pamby ˌnæmbɪ'pæmbɪ
nam|e (*s. v.*), -es, -ing, -ed; -eless neɪm, -z, -ɪŋ, -d; -lɪs [-ləs]
namely 'neɪmlɪ
name-plate, -s 'neɪmpleɪt, -s
namesake, -s 'neɪmseɪk, -s
Namier 'neɪˌmɪə* [-mjə*, -mɪə*]
Nanaimo næ'naɪməʊ [nə'n-]
Nancy 'nænsɪ
nankeen næŋ'kiːn [næn'k-]

Nanki|n, -ng ˌnæn'kɪ|n [ˌnæŋ'k-, *also* '-- *when followed by a stress*], -ŋ
Nannie 'nænɪ
nann|y (N.), -ies 'næn|ɪ, -ɪz
Nansen 'nænsən
Nantucket næn'tʌkɪt
Nantwich (*in Cheshire*) 'næntwɪtʃ [*locally also* -waɪtʃ]
Naomi 'neɪəmɪ ['neɪəʊm-]
nap (*s. v.*), -s, -ping, -ped næp, -s, -ɪŋ, -t
napalm 'neɪpɑːm ['næp-]
nape, -s neɪp, -s
napery 'neɪpərɪ
Naphtali 'næftəlaɪ
naphtha, -lene, -line 'næfθə ['næpθ-], -liːn, -liːn
naphthol 'næfθɒl ['næpθ-]
Napier 'neɪpɪə* [-pjə*], nə'pɪə*
napierian nə'pɪərɪən [neɪ'p-]
napkin, -s; -ring/s 'næpkɪn, -z; -rɪŋ/z
Naples 'neɪplz
napoleon (N.), -s nə'pəʊljən [-lɪən], -z
napoleonic nəˌpəʊlɪ'ɒnɪk
napp|y, -ies 'næp|ɪ, -ɪz
Narbonne nɑː'bɒn (narbɔn)
narcissism 'nɑːsɪsɪzəm [-'---]
narcissistic ˌnɑːsɪ'sɪstɪk
narciss|us (N.), -uses, -i nɑː'sɪs|əs, -əsɪz, -aɪ
narcosis nɑː'kəʊsɪs
narcotic (*s. adj.*), -s nɑː'kɒtɪk, -s
narcoti|sm, -st/s 'nɑːkətɪ|zəm, -st/s
†nard nɑːd
†Nares neəz
narghile, -s 'nɑːgɪlɪ, -z
Narkunda nɑː'kʌndə (*Hindi* nərkwnɖa)
narrat|e, -es, -ing, -ed, -or/s nə'reɪt [næ'r-], -s, -ɪŋ, -ɪd, -ə*/z
narration, -s nə'reɪʃn [næ'r-], -z
narrative (*s. adj.*), -s 'nærətɪv, -z
narr|ow (*s. adj. v.*), -ows, -ower, -owest, -owly, -owness; -owing, -owed 'nær|əʊ, -əʊz, -əʊə*, -əʊɪst, -əʊlɪ, -əʊnɪs [-nəs]; -əʊɪŋ, -əʊd
narrow-gauge 'nærəʊgeɪdʒ
narrow-minded, -ly, -ness ˌnærəʊ'maɪndɪd ['--,--], -lɪ, -nɪs [-nəs]
narwhal, -s 'nɑːwəl, -z
nas|al (*s. adj.*), -als, -ally 'neɪz|l, -lz, -əlɪ

nasalism 'neɪzəlɪzəm [-z|ɪ-]
nasality neɪ'zælətɪ [nə'z-, -ɪtɪ]
nasalization [-isa-], **-s** ˌneɪzəlaɪ'zeɪʃn
[-z|aɪ'z-, -zəlɪ'z-, -z|ɪ'z-], **-z**
nasaliz|e [-is|e], **-es, -ing, -ed** 'neɪzəlaɪz
[-z|-], **-ɪz, -ɪŋ, -d**
nascent 'næsnt
Naseby 'neɪzbɪ
Nash, -ville næʃ, -vɪl
Nasmyth 'neɪzmɪθ [-eɪsm-], 'næzmɪθ
Nassau (*German province*) 'næsaʊ
('nasau), (*princely family*) 'næsɔ:
[-saʊ], (*in Bahamas and U.S.A.*)
'næsɔ:
nasturtium, -s nə'stɜ:ʃəm, -z
nast|y, -ier, -iest, -ily, -iness 'nɑ:st|ɪ,
-ɪə* [-jə*], -ɪɪst [-jɪst], -ɪlɪ [-əlɪ], -ɪnɪs
[-ɪnəs]
natal (*adj.*) 'neɪtl
Natal nə'tæl
natation nə'teɪʃn [neɪ-]
Nathan 'neɪθən [-θæn]
Nathaniel nə'θænjəl
nation, -s 'neɪʃn, -z
na|tional, -tionally 'næ|ʃənl [-ʃnəl, -ʃɳl̩,
-ʃɳl̩, -ʃənəl], -ʃɳəlɪ [-ʃnəlɪ, -ʃɳl̩ɪ, -ʃɳl̩ɪ,
-ʃənəlɪ]
nationali|sm, -st/s 'næʃɳəlɪ|zəm [-ʃnəl-,
-ʃɳl̩-, -ʃnl̩-, -ʃənəl-], -st/s
nationalistic ˌnæʃɳə'lɪstɪk [-ʃnə'lɪ-,
-ʃɳl̩'ɪ-, -ʃnl̩'ɪ-, -ʃənə'lɪ-]
nationalit|y, -ies ˌnæʃə'nælət|ɪ [-ʃɳ'æ-,
-ɪt|ɪ], -ɪz
nationalization [-isa-] ˌnæʃɳəlaɪ'zeɪʃn
[-ʃnəl-, -ʃɳl̩-, -ʃnl̩-, -ʃənəl-, -lɪ'z-]
nationaliz|e [-is|e], **-es, -ing, -ed**
'næʃɳəlaɪz [-ʃnəl-, -ʃɳl̩-, -ʃnl̩-,
-ʃənəl-], -ɪz, -ɪŋ, -d
native (*s. adj.*), **-s, -ly** 'neɪtɪv, -z, -lɪ
nativit|y (**N.**), **-ies** nə'tɪvət|ɪ [-ɪt|ɪ],
-ɪz
N.A.T.O. 'neɪtəʊ
natron 'neɪtrən [-rɒn]
natter (*s. v.*), **-s, -ing, -ed** 'nætə*, -z,
-rɪŋ, -d
natt|y, -ier, -iest, -ily, -iness 'næt|ɪ,
-ɪə*, -ɪɪst, -ɪlɪ [-əlɪ], -ɪnɪs [-ɪnəs]
natur|al (*s. adj.*), **-als, -ally, -alness**
'nætʃr|əl [-tʃʊr-, -tʃər-], -əlz, -əlɪ,
-əlnɪs [-nəs]
naturali|sm, -st/s 'nætʃrəlɪ|zəm [-tʃʊr-,
-tʃər-], -st/s
naturalistic ˌnætʃrə'lɪstɪk [-tʃʊr-, -tʃər-]
naturalization [-isa-] ˌnætʃrəlaɪ'zeɪʃn
[-tʃʊr-, -tʃər-, -lɪ'z-]
naturaliz|e [-is|e], **-es, -ing, -ed**
'nætʃrəlaɪz [-tʃʊr-, -tʃər-], -ɪz, -ɪŋ, -d
nature, -s, -d 'neɪtʃə*, -z, -d

naturi|sm, -st/s 'neɪtʃərɪ|zəm, -st/s
naught, -s nɔ:t, -s
naught|y, -ier, -iest, -ily, -iness 'nɔ:t|ɪ,
-ɪə* [-jə*], -ɪɪst [-jɪst], -ɪlɪ [-əlɪ], -ɪnɪs
[-ɪnəs]
nausea 'nɔ:sjə [-sɪə, -fjə, -fɪə, -zjə, -zɪə,
-ʒjə, -ʒɪə]
nauseat|e, -es, -ing, -ed 'nɔ:sɪeɪt [-sjeɪt,
-fɪeɪt, -fjeɪt, -zɪeɪt, -zjeɪt, -ʒɪeɪt,
-ʒjeɪt], -s, -ɪŋ, -ɪd
nauseous, -ly, -ness 'nɔ:sjəs [-sɪəs, -fjəs,
-fɪəs, -zjəs, -zɪəs, -ʒɪəs, -ʒjəs], -lɪ, -nɪs
[-nəs]
Nausicaa nɔ:'sɪkɪə [-keɪə]
nautch, -es nɔ:tʃ, -ɪz
nautic|al, -ally 'nɔ:tɪk|l, -əlɪ
nautilus, -es 'nɔ:tɪləs, -ɪz
naval 'neɪvl
Navarino ˌnævə'ri:nəʊ
Navarre nə'vɑ:* (nava:r)
nave, -s neɪv, -z
navel, -s 'neɪvl, -z
navicert, -s 'nævɪsɜ:t, -s
navigability ˌnævɪgə'bɪlətɪ [-lɪt-]
navigable, -ness 'nævɪgəbl, -nɪs [-nəs]
navigat|e, -es, -ing, -ed, -or/s 'nævɪ-
geɪt, -s, -ɪŋ, -ɪd, -ə*/z
navigation, -al ˌnævɪ'geɪʃn, -l [-ʃənl,
-ʃnəl]
navv|y, -ies 'næv|ɪ, -ɪz
nav|y, -ies 'neɪv|ɪ, -ɪz
nawab, -s nə'wɑ:b, -z
Nawanagar nə'wɑ:nəgə* (*Hindi*
nəvanəgər)
nay neɪ
Naylor 'neɪlə*
Nazarene, -s ˌnæzə'ri:n, -z
Nazareth 'næzərəθ [-rɪθ]
Nazarite, -s 'næzəraɪt, -s
naze (**N.**), **-s** neɪz, -ɪz
Nazeing 'neɪzɪŋ
Nazi, -s 'nɑ:tsɪ ['nɑ:zɪ], -z
nazism 'nɑ:tsɪzəm ['nɑ:zɪ-]
N.B. ˌen'bi: [ˌnəʊtə'bi:nɪ, -'benɪ]
N.E. ˌen'i: [ˌnɔ:θ'i:st]
ne (*in* ne plus ultra) neɪ [ni:]
Neaera ni:'ɪərə
Neagh neɪ
Neal(e) ni:l
Neanderthal nɪ'ændətɑ:l
neap (*s. adj.*), **-s** ni:p, -s
Neapolis nɪ'æpəlɪs
Neapolitan, -s nɪə'pɒlɪtən [ˌni:ə-, ˌnɪə-],
-z
near (*adj. v. adv. prep.*), **-er, -est, -ly,
-ness; -s, -ing, -ed** nɪə*, -rə*, -rɪst,
-lɪ, -nɪs [-nəs]; -z, -rɪŋ, -d
nearby (*adj.*) 'nɪəbaɪ [ˌ-'-]

337

nearside 'nɪəsaɪd

near-sighted, -ness ˌnɪə'saɪtɪd, -nɪs [-nəs]

Neasden 'niːzdən

neat, -er, -est, -ly, -ness niːt, -ə*, -ɪst, -lɪ, -nɪs [-nəs]

'neath niːθ

Neath niːθ

Neb|at, -o 'niːb|æt, -əʊ

Nebraska nɪ'bræskə [ne'b-, nə'b-]

Nebuchadnezzar ˌnebjʊkəd'nezə*

nebul|a, -ae, -as, -ar, -ous 'nebjʊl|ə, -iː, -əz, -ə*, -əs

nebulosity ˌnebjʊ'lɒsətɪ [-ɪtɪ]

necessarily 'nesəsərəlɪ [-sɪs-, -ser-, ˌnesə'serəlɪ, ˌnesɪ's-, -ɪlɪ]

necessar|y (s. adj.), -ies; -iness 'nesə-sər|ɪ [-sɪs-, -ser-], -ɪz; -ɪnɪs [-ɪnəs]

necessitat|e, -es, -ing, -ed nɪ'sesɪteɪt [ne's-, nə's-], -s, -ɪŋ, -ɪd

necessitous, -ly, -ness nɪ'sesɪtəs [ne's-, nə's-], -lɪ, -nɪs [-nəs]

necessit|y, -ies nɪ'sesət|ɪ [ne's-, nə's-, -ɪt|ɪ], -ɪz

neck, -s nek, -s

neckband, -s 'nekbænd, -z

neck|-cloth, -cloths 'nek|klɒθ [old-fashioned -klɔ:θ], -klɒθs [-klɔ:ðz, -klɔ:θs]

neckerchief, -s 'nekətʃɪf [-tʃiːf], -s

necklace, -s 'neklɪs [-ləs], -ɪz

necklet, -s 'neklɪt [-lət], -s

neck-line, -s 'neklaɪn, -z

neck-tie, -s 'nektaɪ, -z

neckwear 'nekweə*

necrolog|ist/s, -y, -ies ne'krɒlədʒ|ɪst/s [nɪ'k-], -ɪ, -ɪz

necromanc|er/s, -y 'nekrəʊmæns|ə*/z, -ɪ

necropolis, -es ne'krɒpəlɪs [nɪ'k-], -ɪz

necrosis ne'krəʊsɪs [nɪ'k-]

nectar 'nektə* [-tɑ:*]

nectarine, -s 'nektərɪn, -z

Nedd|y, -ies 'ned|ɪ, -ɪz

Neden 'niːdn

née neɪ

need (s. v.), -s, -ing, -ed niːd, -z, -ɪŋ, -ɪd

need|ful, -fully, -fulness 'niːd|fʊl, -fʊlɪ [-fəlɪ], -fʊlnɪs [-nəs]

Needham 'niːdəm

needle (N.), -s; -case/s, -ful/s, -shaped 'niːdl, -z; -keɪs/ɪz, -fʊl/z, -ʃeɪpt

needless, -ly, -ness 'niːdlɪs [-ləs], -lɪ, -nɪs [-nəs]

needle|woman, -women 'niːdl|ˌwʊmən, -ˌwɪmɪn

needlework 'niːdlwɜːk

needn't 'niːdnt [also occasionally 'niːdn when not final]

needs (adv.) niːdz

need|y, -ier, -iest, -ily, -iness 'niːd|ɪ, -ɪə* [-jə*], -ɪɪst [-jɪst], -ɪlɪ [-əlɪ], -ɪnɪs [-ɪnəs]

ne'er neə*

ne'er-do-well, -s 'neədu:ˌwel [-dʊ-], -z

nefarious, -ly, -ness nɪ'feərɪəs [ne'f-, nə'f-], -lɪ, -nɪs [-nəs]

†negation, -s nɪ'geɪʃn [ne'g-], -z

negativ|e (s. adj. v.), -es; -ely, -eness; -ing, -ed, -ism, -ist/s 'negətɪv, -z; -lɪ, -nɪs [-nəs]; -ɪŋ, -d, -ɪzəm, -ɪst/s

neglect (s. v.), -s, -ing, -ed, -er/s nɪ'glekt, -s, -ɪŋ, -ɪd, -ə*/z

neglect|ful, -fully, -fulness nɪ'glekt|fʊl, -fʊlɪ [-fəlɪ], -fʊlnɪs [-nəs]

négligé 'neglɪʒeɪ [-liːʒ-, --'-] (negliʒe)

negligen|ce, -ces, -t/ly 'neglɪdʒən|s, -sɪz, -t/lɪ

negligible 'neglɪdʒəbl [-dʒɪbl]

negotiability nɪˌgəʊʃjə'bɪlətɪ [-ʃɪə-, -ʃə-, -lɪt-]

negotiable nɪ'gəʊʃjəbl [-ʃɪə-, -ʃə-]

negotiat|e, -es, -ing, -ed, -or/s nɪ'gəʊʃɪ-eɪt [-ʃeɪt, -sɪeɪt, -sjeɪt], -s, -ɪŋ, -ɪd, -ə*/z

negotiation, -s nɪˌgəʊʃɪ'eɪʃn [-əʊsɪ-], -z

negress (N.), -es 'niːgrɪs [-gres], -ɪz

negrillo, -s ne'grɪləʊ [nɪ'g-], -z

Negri Sembilan ˌnegrɪsem'biːlən [-səm-]

negrito, -s ne'griːtəʊ [nɪ'g-], -z

negro (N.), -es 'niːgrəʊ, -z

negroid 'niːgrɔɪd

negus (N.) 'niːgəs

Nehemiah ˌniːɪ'maɪə [ˌniːhɪ'm-, ˌniːhə'm-, nɪə'm-]

Nehru 'neəru: [nɪə'm-]

neigh (s. v.), -s, -ing, -ed neɪ, -z, -ɪŋ, -d

neighb|our, -ours, -ouring, -ourly, -ourliness 'neɪb|ə*, -əz, -ərɪŋ, -əlɪ, -əlnɪs [-nəs]

neighbourhood, -s 'neɪbəhʊd [old-fashioned -bərʊd], -z

Neil(l) niːl

Neilson 'niːlsn

neither 'naɪðə* ['niːðə*]

Nellie [-ly] 'nelɪ

Nelson 'nelsn

nem. con. ˌnem'kɒn

Nemesis 'neməsɪs [-mɪs-]

Nemo 'niːməʊ

nemophila, -s nɪ'mɒfɪlə*, -z

Nen (river) nen

Nene (river) nen [niːn], (name of ship) niːn, (aero-engine) niːn

nenuphar, -s 'nenjʊfɑ:*, -z

neocolonialism ˌnɪəʊkəˈləʊnɪəlɪzəm [ˌniːəʊ-, -njəl-]
neo-latin ˌniːəʊˈlætɪn [ˌnɪəʊ-]
neolithic ˌniːəʊˈlɪθɪk [ˌnɪəʊ-]
neolog|ism/s, -ist/s, -y niːˈɒlədʒ|-ɪzəm/z [nɪˈD-], -ɪst/s, -ɪ
neologiz|e [-is|e], -es, -ing, -ed niː-ˈɒlədʒaɪz [nɪˈD-], -ɪz, -ɪŋ, -d
neon ˈniːɒn [non-chemists ˈniːən, nɪən]
neophyte, -s ˈniːəʊfaɪt [ˈnɪəʊ-], -s
Nepal nɪˈpɔːl [neˈp-, -ˈpɑːl]
Nepalese ˌnepəˈliːz [-pɔːˈl-]
nepenthe neˈpenθɪ [nɪˈp-]
neper, -s ˈniːpə*, -z
nephew, -s ˈnevju: [ˈnefj-, -jʊ], -z
nephritis nɪˈfraɪtɪs [nə-, ne-]
ne plus ultra ˌneɪplʊsˈʊltrɑː [-trə, ˌniːplʌsˈʌltrə]
Nepos ˈniːpɒs [ˈnep-]
nepotism ˈnepətɪzəm [-pɒt-]
Neptune ˈneptjuːn [-tʃuːn]
neptunian (N.) nepˈtjuːnjən [-nɪən]
neptunium nepˈtjuːnɪəm [-njəm]
Nereid, -s ˈnɪərɪɪd, -z
Nereus ˈnɪərjuːs [-rɪuːs, -rɪəs]
Neri ˈnɪərɪ
Nerissa nɪˈrɪsə [neˈr-, nəˈr-]
Nero ˈnɪərəʊ
nerv|e (s. v.), -es, -ing, -ed; -eless nɜːˈv, -z, -ɪŋ, -d; -lɪs [-ləs]
nerve-cell, -s ˈnɜːvsel, -z
nerve-centre, -s ˈnɜːvˌsentə*, -z
nerve-racking ˈnɜːvˌrækɪŋ
nervine ˈnɜːviːn
nervous, -ly, -ness ˈnɜːvəs, -lɪ, -nɪs [-nəs]
nerv|y, -ier, -iest, -ily, -iness ˈnɜːv|ɪ, -ɪə* [-jə*], -ɪɪst [-jɪst], -ɪlɪ [-əlɪ], -ɪnɪs [-ɪnəs]
Nesbit(t) ˈnezbɪt
nescience ˈnesɪəns [-sjəns]
Nesfield ˈnesfiːld
ness (N.), -es nes, -ɪz
nest (s. v.), -s, -ing, -ed nest, -s, -ɪŋ, -ɪd
Nesta ˈnestə
nest-egg, -s ˈnesteg, -z
nest|le, -les, -ling, -led ˈnes|l, -lz, -lɪŋ [-lɪŋ], -ld
Nestlé ˈnesl [ˈneslɪ]
nestling (s.) (young bird), -s ˈnestlɪŋ, -z
Nestor ˈnestɔː* [-tə*]
Nestorian, -s neˈstɔːrɪən, -z
net (s. v.), -s -ting, -ted net, -s, -ɪŋ, -ɪd
netball ˈnetbɔːl
nether, -most ˈneðə*, -məʊst [-məst]
Netherland, -s, -er/s ˈneðələnd [-ð|lənd], -z, -ə*/z

Netley ˈnetlɪ
Nettie ˈnetɪ
nett|le (s. v.), -les, -ling, -led ˈnet|l, -lz, -lɪŋ [-lɪŋ], -ld
Nettle|fold, -ship ˈnetl|fəʊld, -ʃɪp
nettlerash ˈnetlræʃ
net-work, -s ˈnetwɜːk, -s
Neuchâtel ˌnɜːʃæˈtel [-ʃəˈt-, ˈnɜːʃətel] (nœʃatɛl)
neume, -s njuːm, -z
neural ˈnjʊərəl
neuralg|ia, -ic ˌnjʊəˈrældʒ|ə [njəˈr-, njʊˈr-, njuːˈr-], -ɪk
neurasthenia ˌnjʊərəsˈθiːnjə [ˌnjuːr-, -nɪə]
neurasthenic (s. adj.), -s ˌnjʊərəs-ˈθenɪk [ˌnjuːr-], -s
neuritis ˌnjʊəˈraɪtɪs [njəˈr-, njʊˈr-, njuːˈr-]
neurological ˌnjʊərəˈlɒdʒɪkl [ˌnjuːr-]
neurolog|ist/s, -y ˌnjʊəˈrɒlədʒ|ɪst/s [njəˈr-, njʊˈr-, njuːˈr-], -ɪ
neuron, -s ˈnjʊərɒn, -z
neurone, -s ˈnjʊərəʊn, -z
neuros|is, -es ˌnjʊəˈrəʊs|ɪs [njəˈr-, njʊˈr-, njuːˈr-], -iːz
neurotic (s. adj.), -s ˌnjʊəˈrɒtɪk [njəˈr-, njʊˈr-, njuːˈr-], -s
neuter (s. adj.), -s ˈnjuːtə*, -z
neutr|al (s. adj.), -als, -ally ˈnjuːtr|əl, -əlz, -əlɪ
neutrality njuːˈtrælətɪ [njʊ-, -ɪtɪ]
neutralization [-isa-] ˌnjuːtrəlaɪˈzeɪʃn [-tr|əlˈɪz-, -trəlɪˈz-, -tr|ɪˈz-]
neutraliz|e [-is|e], -es, -ing, -ed ˈnjuː-trəlaɪz [-tr|aɪz], -ɪŋ, -ɪz, -d
neutron, -s ˈnjuːtrɒn [-trən], -z
Neva ˈneɪvə [old-fashioned ˈniːvə] (njiˈva)
Nevada nəˈvɑːdə [nɪˈv-, neˈv-]
Neve niːv
névé ˈneveɪ
never, -more ˈnevə*, -ˈmɔː* [-ˈmɔə*]
nevertheless ˌnevəðəˈles
Nevey ˈnevɪ
Nevil ˈnevɪl
Nevill(e) ˈnevɪl
Nevin, -son ˈnevɪn, -sn
Nevis (in Scotland) ˈnevɪs, (in West Indies) ˈniːvɪs
new, -er, -est, -ly, -ness njuː, -ə* [njʊə*], -ɪst [ˈnjuːɪst], -lɪ, -nɪs [-nəs]
Newark (in Nottinghamshire) ˈnjuːək [njʊək]
Newbiggin (place) ˈnjuːˌbɪgɪn, (surname) ˈnjuːˌbɪgɪn, njuːˈbɪgɪn
Newbol|d, -t ˈnjuːbəʊl|d, -t
newborn ˈnjuːbɔːn

New|burgh, -bury 'nju:|bərə, -bɛrɪ
Newcastle 'nju:,kɑ:sl
    Note.—Newcastle *in Tyne and Wear
    is locally* njʊ'kæsl.
Newcome, -s 'nju:kəm, -z
newcomer, -s 'nju:,kʌmə*, -z
Newdigate 'nju:dɪgɪt [-geɪt]
Newe nju:
newel, -s 'nju:əl [nju:l], -z
new-fangled 'nju:,fæŋgld [,-'--]
new-fashioned ,nju:'fæʃnd [*also* '-,--
    when attributive]
Newfoundland (*place*), -er/s 'nju:fəndlənd
    [-lænd, nju:'faʊndlənd, njʊ'f-,
    ,nju:fənd'lænd], -ə*/z
    Note.—,nju:fənd'lænd *is the local
    form; it is also the nautical pro-
    nunciation in England.*
Newfoundland (*dog*), -s nju:'faʊnd-
    lənd [njʊ'f-], -z
Newgate 'nju:gɪt [-geɪt]
Newham (*London borough*) 'nju:əm
    [njʊəm, *sometimes* 'nju:hæm, ,nju:-
    'hæm]
Newhaven 'nju:,heɪvn [-'--, njʊ'h-]
Newington 'nju:ɪŋtən ['njʊɪ-]
new-laid (*when attributive*) 'nju:leɪd,
    (*otherwise*) ,nju:'leɪd
New|man, -market 'nju:|mən, -,mɑ:kɪt
Newn|es, -ham nju:n|z, -əm
New Orleans ,nju:'ɔ:lɪənz [-ljənz, ,nju:-
    ɔ:'li:nz]
New|port, -quay 'nju:|pɔ:t, -ki:
New Quay ,nju:'ki:
Newry 'njʊərɪ
news nju:z
newsagent, -s 'nju:z,eɪdʒənt, -s
news-boy, -s 'nju:zbɔɪ, -z
newscast, -s, -ing, -er/s 'nju:zkɑ:st, -s,
    -ɪŋ, -ə*/z
news-letter, -s 'nju:z,letə*, -z
newsmonger, -s 'nju:z,mʌŋgə*, -z
New South Wales ,nju:saʊθ'weɪlz
newspaper, -s 'nju:s,peɪpə* ['nju:z,p-],
    -z
newsprint 'nju:zprɪnt
newsreel, -s 'nju:zri:l, -z
news-sheet, -s 'nju:zʃi:t [-u:ʒʃ-], -z
Newstead 'nju:stɪd [-sted]
newsvendor, -s 'nju:z,vendə* [-dɔ:*], -z
newsworthy 'nju:z,wɜ:ðɪ
newsy 'nju:zɪ
newt, -s nju:t, -s
newton (N.) 'nju:tn
Newtonian nju:'təʊnjən [-nɪən]
Newtown 'nju:taʊn
New York, -er/s ,nju:'jɔ:k [njʊ'j-],
    -ə*/z

New Zealand, -er/s ,nju:'zi:lənd[njʊ'z-],
    -ə*/z
next nekst [*often also* neks *when followed
    by a word beginning with a consonant*]
next of kin ,nekstəv'kɪn
nexus, -es 'neksəs, -ɪz
Ngaio (*authoress, suburb of Wellington,
    New Zealand*) 'naɪəʊ
Ngami ŋ'gɑ:mɪ ['ŋɑ:mɪ]
niacin 'naɪəsɪn
Niagara naɪ'ægərə [-grə]
nib, -s nɪb, -z
nibb|le (*s. v.*), -les, -ling, -led 'nɪb|l, -lz,
    -|ɪŋ [-lɪŋ], -ld
Nibelung, -s, -en 'ni:bəlʊŋ [-bɪl-], -z, -ən
niblick, -s 'nɪblɪk, -s
Nicaea naɪ'si:ə [-'sɪə]
Nicaragua, -n/s ,nɪkə'rægjʊə [-'rægjwə,
    -'rɑ:gwə], -n/z
nice, -r, -st, -ly, -ness naɪs, -ə*, -ɪst, -lɪ,
    -nɪs [-nəs]
Nice (*in France*) ni:s (nis)
Nicene ,naɪ'si:n [*sometimes also* 'naɪs-
    when attributive]
nicet|y, -ies 'naɪsət|ɪ [-sɪt-], -ɪz
niche, -s, -d nɪtʃ [ni:ʃ], -ɪz, -t
Nichol, -(l)s, -son 'nɪkl, -z, -sn
Nicholas 'nɪkələs [-kləs]
nick (*s. v.*) (N.),-s, -ing, -ed nɪk, -s, -ɪŋ, -t
nick|el (*s. v.*), -els, -elling, -elled 'nɪk|l,
    -lz, -|ɪŋ [-əlɪŋ], -ld
Nickleby 'nɪklbɪ
nick-nack, -s 'nɪknæk, -s
nicknam|e (*s. v.*), -es, -ing, -ed 'nɪk-
    neɪm, -z, -ɪŋ, -d
Nicobar 'nɪkəʊbɑ:*
Nicodemus ,nɪkəʊ'di:məs
Nicolas 'nɪkələs [-kləs]
Nicol, -(l) s, -son 'nɪkl, -z, -sn
Nicomachean ,naɪkɒmə'ki:ən [naɪ-
    ,kɒm-, -'krən]
Nicomachus naɪ'kɒməkəs
Nicosia ,nɪkəʊ'si:ə [-'sɪə]
nicotine 'nɪkəti:n [,--'-]
nicotinism 'nɪkəti:nɪzəm [-tɪn-]
niece, -s ni:s, -ɪz
Niersteiner 'nɪəstaɪnə*
Nietzsche 'ni:tʃə ('ni:tʃə)
Nigel 'naɪdʒəl
Niger (*river*) 'naɪdʒə*
Niger (*country*) ni:'ʒeə*
Nigeria, -n naɪ'dʒɪərɪə, -n
niggard, -s 'nɪgəd, -z
niggardl|y, -iness 'nɪgədl|ɪ, -ɪnɪs [-məs]
nigger, -s 'nɪgə*, -z
nigg|le, -les, -ling, -led 'nɪg|l, -lz, -|ɪŋ
    [-lɪŋ], -ld
niggl|y, -iness 'nɪgl|ɪ, -ɪnɪs [-məs]

nigh naɪ
night, -s naɪt, -s
night-bell, -s 'naɪtbel, -z
night-bird, -s 'naɪtbɜːd, -z
nightcap, -s 'naɪtkæp, -s
nightdress, -es 'naɪtdres, -ɪz
nightfall 'naɪtfɔːl
nightgown, -s 'naɪtgaʊn, -z
nightie, -s 'naɪtɪ, -z
nightingale (N.), -s 'naɪtɪŋgeɪl, -z
nightjar, -s 'naɪtdʒɑː*, -z
night|-light/s, -long 'naɪt|laɪt/s, -lɒŋ
nightly 'naɪtlɪ
nightmar|e, -es, -ish 'naɪtmeə*, -z, -rɪʃ
night-porter, -s 'naɪt,pɔːtə* [,ˈ--], -z
night-school, -s 'naɪtskuːl, -s
nightshade 'naɪt-ʃeɪd
nightshirt, -s 'naɪt-ʃɜːt, -s
night-time 'naɪttaɪm
night-walk|er/s, -ing 'naɪt,wɔːk|ə*/z, -ɪŋ
nightwatch, -es ,naɪt'wɒtʃ ['--], -ɪz
night-watch|man, -men ,naɪt'wɒtʃ|mən, -mən
night-work 'naɪtwɜːk
nihili|sm, -st/s 'naɪlɪ|zəm ['naɪhɪl-, 'naɪəl-], -st/s
Nijmegen 'naɪmeɪgən [-'--]
Nike 'naɪkiː
nil nɪl
nil desperandum ,nɪldespəˈrændəm
Nile naɪl
Nilgiri, -s 'nɪlgɪrɪ, -z
nilometer, -s naɪ'lɒmɪtə* [-mətə*], -z
Nilotic naɪ'lɒtɪk
nimb|le -ler, -lest, -ly, -leness 'nɪmb|l, -lə*, -lɪst, -lɪ, -lnɪs [-nəs]
nimb|us, -uses, -i 'nɪmb|əs, -əsɪz, -aɪ
Nimeguen 'naɪmeɪgən [-'--]
nimini-piminy ,nɪmɪnɪ'pɪmɪnɪ
Nimrod 'nɪmrɒd
Nina (Christian name) 'niːnə, 'naɪnə, (goddess) 'niːnə
nincompoop, -s 'nɪnkəmpuːp ['nɪŋk-], -s
nine, -s, -fold naɪn, -z, -fəʊld
ninepence, -s 'naɪnpəns ['naɪmp-] (see note under penny), -ɪz
ninepenny 'naɪnpənɪ ['naɪmp-]
ninepin, -s 'naɪnpɪn, -s
nineteen, -s, -th/s ,naɪn'tiːn [also '-- according to sentence-stress], -z, -θ/s
ninetieth, -s 'naɪntɪəθ [-tjəθ, -tɪɪθ, -tjɪθ], -s
ninet|y -ies 'naɪnt|ɪ, -ɪz
Nineveh 'nɪnɪvə [-nə-, -vɪ]
ninish 'naɪnɪʃ
ninn|y, -ies 'nɪn|ɪ, -ɪz

ninth, -s, -ly naɪnθ, -s, -lɪ
Ninus 'naɪnəs
Niobe 'naɪəʊbɪ
nip (s. v.), -s, -ping, -ped nɪp, -s, -ɪŋ, -t
nipper, -s 'nɪpə*, -z
nipple, -s 'nɪpl, -z
Nippon 'nɪpɒn
nipp|ly, -ier, -iest, -iness 'nɪp|ɪ, -ɪə*, -ɪɪst, -ɪnɪs [-məs]
Nirvana ,nɪə'vɑːnə [nɜː'v-] (Hindi nyrvaɳa)
Nisan 'naɪsæn [Jewish pronunciation 'nɪsɑːn]
Nisbet 'nɪzbɪt
Nish nɪʃ
nisi 'naɪsaɪ [-sɪ]
Nissen, -hut/s 'nɪsn, -hʌt/s
nitrate, -s 'naɪtreɪt [-trɪt], -s
nitre 'naɪtə*
nitr|ic, -ite/s 'naɪtr|ɪk, -aɪt/s
nitrogen 'naɪtrədʒən [-trɪdʒ-]
nitrogenous naɪ'trɒdʒɪnəs [-dʒən-, -dʒn-]
nitro-glycerine ,naɪtrəʊ'glɪsəriːn [-'glɪsərɪn, -glɪsə'riːn]
nitrous 'naɪtrəs
nitwit, -s 'nɪtwɪt, -s
Niven 'nɪvən
nix, -es nɪks, -ɪz
Nixey 'nɪksɪ
nixie, -s 'nɪksɪ, -z
Nixon 'nɪksən
Nizam, -s naɪ'zæm [naɪ'zɑːm, nɪ'zɑːm], -z
Nkrumah n'kruːmə,əŋ'kruː-mə [-'krʊ-]
no (s. interj.), -es nəʊ, -z
no (adj.) nəʊ (normal form), nə (in the expression no more do I (we, etc.))
no. (N.), nos. (N.) 'nʌmbə*, -z
Noah 'nəʊə [nɔə, nɔː]
Noakes nəʊks
nob, -s nɒb, -z
no-ball (s. v.), -s, -ing, -ed ,nəʊ'bɔːl, -z, -ɪŋ, -d
nobb|le, -les, -ling, -led 'nɒb|l, -lz, -|ɪŋ [-lɪŋ], -ld
nobb|y, -ier, -iest, -ily, -iness 'nɒb|ɪ, -ɪə*, -ɪɪst, -ɪlɪ [-əlɪ], -ɪnɪs [-məs]
Nobel (Swedish chemist) nəʊ'bel [also 'nəʊbel in Nobel prize]
nobilit|y, -ies nəʊ'bɪlət|ɪ [-lɪt-], -ɪz
nob|le (s. adj.) (N.), -les, -ler, -lest, -ly, -leness 'nəʊb|l, -z, -lə*, -lɪst, -lɪ, -lnɪs [-nəs]
noble|man, -men 'nəʊbl|mən, -mən
noble-minded, -ness ,nəʊbl'maɪndɪd [also '--,-- when attributive], -nɪs [-nəs]

341

noblesse nəʊ'bles

nobod|y, -ies 'nəʊbəd|ɪ [-,bɒd|ɪ], -ɪz

noctambul|ant, -ism, -ist/s nɒk'tæm-
bjʊl|ənt, -ɪzəm, -ɪst/s

nocturn|al, -ally nɒk'tɜ:n|l, -əlɪ

nocturn(e), -s 'nɒktɜ:n [,nɒk't-], -z

nod (s. v.) (N.), -s, -ding, -ded nɒd, -z,
-ɪŋ, -ɪd

nodal 'nəʊdl

noddle, -s 'nɒdl, -z

nodd|y, -ies 'nɒd|ɪ, -ɪz

node, -s nəʊd, -z

nodul|ar, -ous 'nɒdjʊl|ə*, -əs

nodule, -s 'nɒdju:l, -z

Noel (personal name) 'nəʊəl [-el, -ɪl],
(Christmas) nəʊ'el

noggin, -s 'nɒgɪn, -z

nohow 'nəʊhaʊ

nois|e (s. v.), -es, -ing, -ed nɔɪz, -ɪz, -ɪŋ,
-d

noiseless, -ly, -ness 'nɔɪzlɪs [-ləs], -lɪ,
-nɪs [-nəs]

noisette, -s nwɑ:'zet, -s

noisome, -ly, -ness 'nɔɪsəm, -lɪ, -nɪs
[-nəs]

nois|y, -ier, -iest, -ily, -iness 'nɔɪz|ɪ,
-ɪə* [-jə*], -ɪɪst [-jɪst], -ɪlɪ [-əlɪ], -ɪnɪs
[-ɪnəs]

Nokes nəʊks

Nokomis nəʊ'kəʊmɪs

nolens volens ,nəʊlenz'vəʊlenz

Noll nɒl

nomad, -s 'nəʊmæd [-məd, 'nɒmæd], -z

nomadic, -ally nəʊ'mædɪk [nɒ'm-], -əlɪ

no-man's-land 'nəʊmænzlænd

nom de plume, -s ,nɔ̃:mdə'plu:m [,nɒm-]
(nɔ̃dplym), -z

nomenclature, -s nəʊ'menklətʃə*
['nəʊmenklertʃə*, 'nəʊmənkleɪ-], -z

nomic 'nəʊmɪk ['nɒmɪk]

nomin|al, -ally 'nɒmɪn|l, -əlɪ

nominat|e, -es, -ing, -ed, -or/s 'nɒmɪ-
neɪt, -s, -ɪŋ, -ɪd, -ə*/z

nomination, -s ,nɒmɪ'neɪʃn, -z

nominative (s. adj.), -s 'nɒmɪnətɪv
[-mən-], -z

nominee, -s ,nɒmɪ'ni:, -z

non nɒn

non-acceptance ,nɒnək'septəns [-næk-]

nonage 'nəʊnɪdʒ ['nɒn-]

nonagenarian, -s ,nəʊnədʒɪ'neərɪən
[,nɒn-, -dʒə'n-], -z

non-appearance ,nɒnə'pɪərəns

nonary 'nəʊnərɪ

non-attendance ,nɒnə'tendəns

non-belligeren|cy, -t/s ,nɒnbə'lɪdʒər-
ən|sɪ [-be'l-, -bɪ'l-, -dʒrən-], -t/s

nonce, -word/s nɒns, -wɜ:d/z

non-certifiable ,nɒn'sɜ:tɪfaɪəbl ['nɒn-
,sɜ:tɪ'faɪ-]

nonchalan|ce, -t/ly 'nɒnʃələn|s, -t/lɪ

non-collegiate, -s ,nɒnkə'li:dʒɪət [-kɒ'l-,
-dʒjət, -dʒɪɪt-, -dʒɪɪt], -s

non-combatant, -s ,nɒn'kɒmbətənt
[-'kʌm-], -s

non-commissioned ,nɒnkə'mɪʃnd [also
'--,-- when attributive]

non-committal ,nɒnkə'mɪtl

non-compliance ,nɒnkəm'plaɪəns

non-conducting ,nɒnkən'dʌktɪŋ ['--,--]

non-conductor, -s 'nɒnkən,dʌktə*
[,--'--], -z

nonconformist, -s ,nɒnkən'fɔ:mɪst
[,nɒŋk-], -s

nonconformity ,nɒnkən'fɔ:mətɪ
[,nɒŋk-, -ɪtɪ]

non-contentious ,nɒnkən'tenʃəs

non-delivery ,nɒndɪ'lɪvərɪ

nondescript (s. adj.), -s 'nɒndɪskrɪpt, -s

none (s.) (church service), -s nəʊn, -z

none (adj. pron. adv.) nʌn

nonentit|y, -ies nɒ'nentət|ɪ [nə'n-, -ɪt|ɪ],
-ɪz

nones nəʊnz

non-essential, -s ,nɒnɪ'senʃl, -z

nonetheless ,nʌnðə'les ['---]

non-existen|ce, -t ,nɒnɪg'zɪstən|s [-eg-],
-t

non-feasance ,nɒn'fi:zəns

nonillion, -s nəʊ'nɪljən, -z

non-intervention 'nɒn,ɪntə'venʃn

nonjuror, -s ,nɒn'dʒʊərə* ['-,--], -z

non-member, -s 'nɒn,membə* [,-'--], -z

non-observance ,nɒnəb'zɜ:vəns

nonpareil 'nɒnpərəl [,nɒnpə'reɪl,
'nɒmprəl]

non-payment ,nɒn'peɪmənt

non-performance ,nɒnpə'fɔ:məns

nonplus, -ses, -sing, -sed ,nɒn'plʌs, -ɪz,
-ɪŋ, -t

non-resident, -s ,nɒn'rezɪdənt, -s

nonsense 'nɒnsəns

nonsensic|al, -ally, -alness nɒn'sen-
sɪk|l, -əlɪ, -lnɪs [-nəs]

non sequitur, -s ,nɒn'sekwɪtə*, -z

non-stop, -s, -ping ,nɒn'stɒp, -s, -ɪŋ

non(e)such, -es 'nʌnsʌtʃ, -ɪz

nonsuit (s. v.), -s, -ing, -ed ,nɒn'su:t
[-'sju:t], -s, -ɪŋ, -ɪd

non-user ,nɒn'ju:zə*

non-violen|t, -ce ,nɒn'vaɪələn|t, -s

noodle, -s 'nu:dl, -z

nook, -s nʊk, -s

noon, -s nu:n, -z

Noonan 'nu:nən

noonday 'nu:ndeɪ

no one 'nəʊwʌn
noontide 'nu:ntaɪd
noo|se (s. v.), -ses, -sing, -sed nu:|s
[nu:|z], -sɪz [-zɪz], -sɪŋ [-zɪŋ], -st [-zd]
nor nɔ:* (normal form), nə* (occasional
weak form)
Nora(h) 'nɔ:rə
Nordenfelt 'nɔ:dnfelt
Nordic 'nɔ:dɪk
Nore nɔ:* [nɔə*]
Norfolk 'nɔ:fək
Norgate 'nɔ:geɪt [-gɪt]
Norham 'nɒrəm ['nɔ:r-]
Norland 'nɔ:lənd
norm, -s nɔ:m, -z
norm|al, -ally 'nɔ:m|l, -əlɪ [-l̩ɪ]
normalcy 'nɔ:mlsɪ
normality nɔ:'mælətɪ [-ɪtɪ]
normalization [-isa-] ,nɔ:məlaɪ'zeɪʃn
[-m̩laɪ'z-, -məlɪ'z-, -m̩lɪ'z-]
normaliz|e [-is|e], -es, -ing, -ed 'nɔ:mə-
laɪz [-m̩laɪz], -ɪz, -ɪŋ, -d
Norman, -s 'nɔ:mən, -z
Normanby 'nɔ:mənbɪ
Normandy (in France) 'nɔ:məndɪ, (in
Surrey) 'nɔ:məndɪ [also locally
nɔ:'mændɪ]
Normanton 'nɔ:məntən
Norn, -s nɔ:n, -z
Norris 'nɒrɪs
Norroy, -s 'nɒrɔɪ, -z
Norse, -man, -men nɔ:s, -mən, -mən
[-men]
north (N.) nɔ:θ
Northallerton nɔ:'θælətən
Northampton, -shire nɔ:'θæmptən
[nɔ:θ'hæm-, locally nə'θæm-], -ʃə*
[-,ʃɪə*]
Northanger nɔ:'θæŋgə*
Northants. nɔ:'θænts
North|brook, -cliffe, -cote 'nɔ:θ|brʊk,
-klɪf, -kət [-kəʊt]
north-east ,nɔ:θ'i:st [nautical pronunciation nɔ:r'i:st, also '— according to
sentence-stress]
north-easter, -s ,nɔ:θ'i:stə* [in nautical
usage also nɔ:r'i:stə*], -z
north-easterly ,nɔ:θ'i:stəlɪ [in nautical
usage also nɔ:r'i:stəlɪ]
north-eastern ,nɔ:θ'i:stən
north-eastward, -s ,nɔ:θ'i:stwəd, -z
Northen 'nɔ:ðən
northerly 'nɔ:ðəlɪ
northern, -most 'nɔ:ðn, -məʊst [-məst]
northerner, -s 'nɔ:ðənə*, -z
North|field, -fleet 'nɔ:θ|fi:ld, -fli:t
northing 'nɔ:θɪŋ
Northland 'nɔ:θlənd

North|man, -men 'nɔ:θ|mən, -mən
[-men]
north-north-east ,nɔ:θnɔ:θ'i:st [nautical
pronunciation ,nɔ:nɔ:r'i:st]
north-north-west ,nɔ:θnɔ:θ'west [nauti-
cal pronunciation ,nɔ:nɔ:'west]
north-polar ,nɔ:θ'pəʊlə*
Northumberland nɔ:'θʌmbələnd [nə'θ-,
-bl̩ənd]
Northumbria, -n/s nɔ:'θʌmbrɪə, -n/z
northward, -s, -ly 'nɔ:θwəd, -z, -lɪ
north-west, -er/s, -erly ,nɔ:θ'west
[nautical pronunciation nɔ:'west, also
'— according to sentence-stress], -ə*/z,
-əlɪ
north-west|ern, -ward ,nɔ:θ'west|ən,
-wəd
North|wich, -wood 'nɔ:θ|wɪtʃ, -wʊd
Norton 'nɔ:tn
Norway 'nɔ:weɪ
Norwegian, -s nɔ:'wi:dʒən, -z
Norwich (in England) 'nɒrɪdʒ [-ɪtʃ], (in
U.S.A.) 'nɔ:wɪtʃ
Norwood 'nɔ:wʊd
nos. (N.) 'nʌmbəz
nos|e (s. v.), -es, -ing, -ed nəʊz, -ɪz, -ɪŋ,
-d
nose-bag, -s 'nəʊzbæg, -z
nose-div|e (s. v.), -es, -ing, -ed 'nəʊz-
daɪv, -z, -ɪŋ, -d
nosegay, -s 'nəʊzgeɪ, -z
nose-ring, -s 'nəʊzrɪŋ, -z
nosey 'nəʊzɪ
nostalg|ia, -ic, -ically nɒ'stældʒ|ə
[-jə, -ɪə], -ɪk, -ɪkəlɪ
Nostradamus ,nɒstrə'deɪməs
nostril, -s 'nɒstrəl [-ɪl], -z
nostrum, -s 'nɒstrəm, -z
nosy 'nəʊzɪ
not nɒt (normal form, nt, n (weak
forms used after auxil. verbs only)
nota bene ,nəʊtə'bi:nɪ [-'benɪ]
notabilit|y, -ies ,nəʊtə'bɪlət|ɪ [-ɪt-], -ɪz
notab|le, -ly, -leness 'nəʊtəb|l̩, -lɪ, -lnɪs
[-nəs]
notarial, -ly nəʊ'teərɪəl, -ɪ
notar|y, -ies 'nəʊtər|ɪ, -ɪz
notation, -s nəʊ'teɪʃn, -z
notch (s. v.), -es, -ing, -ed nɒtʃ, -ɪz, -ɪŋ,
-t
not|e (s. v.), -es, -ing, -ed nəʊt, -s, -ɪŋ,
-ɪd
note|-book/s, -paper, -worthy 'nəʊt|-
bʊk/s, -,peɪpə*, -,wɜ:ðɪ
nothing, -s, -ness 'nʌθɪŋ, -z, -nɪs [-nəs]
notic|e (s. v.), -es, -ing, -ed 'nəʊtɪs, -ɪz,
-ɪŋ, -t
noticeab|le, -ly 'nəʊtɪsəb|l̩, -lɪ

notice-board, -s 'nəʊtɪsbɔːd [-bɔəd], -z
notifiable 'nəʊtɪfaɪəbl [ˌnəʊtɪ'faɪ-]
notification, -s ˌnəʊtɪfɪ'keɪʃn, -z
noti|fy, -fies, -fying, -fied 'nəʊtɪ|faɪ,
  -faɪz, -faɪɪŋ, -faɪd
notion, -s 'nəʊʃn, -z
notional 'nəʊʃənl [-ʃnəl, -ʃn̩l, -ʃn̩,
  -ʃənəl]
notoriety ˌnəʊtə'raɪətɪ
notorious, -ly, -ness nəʊ'tɔːrɪəs, -lɪ, -nɪs
  [-nəs]
Notre Dame (English Catholic pronunciation) ˌnəʊtrə'dɑːm [ˌnɒt-]
  (notrədam) (American ˌnoʊtɪ'deɪm)
Nottingham, -shire 'nɒtɪŋəm, -ʃə*
  [-ˌʃɪə*]
Notting Hill ˌnɒtɪŋ'hɪl
Notts. nɒts
notwithstanding ˌnɒtwɪθ'stændɪŋ
  [-wɪð's-]
nougat, -s 'nuːgɑː ['nʌgət], 'nuːgɑːz
  ['nʌgəts]
nought, -s nɔːt, -s
noun, -s naʊn, -z
nourish, -es, -ing, -ed; -ment 'nʌrɪʃ, -ɪz,
  -ɪŋ, -t; -mənt
nous naʊs
nouveau riche ˌnuːvəʊ'riːʃ
Nova Scotia ˌnəʊvə'skəʊʃə
novel (s. adj.), -s 'nɒvl, -z
novelette, -s ˌnɒvə'let [-vɪ'let, -vl̩'et], -s
novelist, -s 'nɒvəlɪst [-vl̩ɪst], -s
Novello nə'veləʊ
novelt|y, -ies 'nɒvlt|ɪ, -ɪz
November, -s nəʊ'vembə*, -z
Novial (language) 'nəʊvjəl [-vɪəl]
novice, -s 'nɒvɪs, -ɪz
noviciate [-itiate], -s nəʊ'vɪʃɪət [nɒ'v-,
  -ʃɪeɪt, -ʃɪɪt], -s
novocaine 'nəʊvəʊkeɪn ['nɒv-]
now, -adays naʊ, -ədeɪz
Nowell (personal name) 'nəʊəl [-el],
  (Christmas) nəʊ'el
nowhere 'nəʊweə* ['nəʊhw-]
nowise 'nəʊwaɪz
Nox nɒks
noxious, -ly, -ness 'nɒkʃəs, -lɪ, -nɪs
  [-nəs]
noyau, -s 'nwaɪəʊ ['nwɔɪəʊ, 'nɔɪəʊ]
  (nwajo), -z
Noyes nɔɪz
nozzle, -s 'nɒzl, -z
-n't (= not) -nt
nu njuː
nuance, -s 'njuːɑːns ['njʊ-, -ãːns, -ɔ̃ːns,
  -'-] (nɥɑ̃ːs), -ɪz
nubble, -s 'nʌbl, -z
nubbly 'nʌbl̩ɪ

Nubia, -n/s 'njuːbjə [-bɪə], -n/z
nubile 'njuːbaɪl
nucl|eus, -ei, -eal, -ear, -eic 'njuːkl|ɪəs
  [-jəs], -ɪaɪ, -ɪəl [-jəl], -ɪə* [-jə*],
  -ɪɪk
nude (s. adj.), -s njuːd, -z
nudg|e (s. v.), -es, -ing, -ed nʌdʒ, -ɪz,
  -ɪŋ, -d
nudi|sm, -st/s 'njuːdɪ|zəm, -st/s
nudit|y, -ies 'njuːdət|ɪ [-ɪt|ɪ], -ɪz
Nuffield 'nʌfiːld
nugatory 'njuːgətərɪ [njuː'geɪtərɪ]
Nugent 'njuːdʒənt
nugget, -s 'nʌgɪt, -s
nuisance, -s 'njuːsns, -ɪz
null nʌl
nullah, -s 'nʌlə, -z
nullification ˌnʌlɪfɪ'keɪʃn
nulli|fy, -fies, -fying, -fied 'nʌlɪ|faɪ,
  -faɪz, -faɪɪŋ, -faɪd
nullit|y, -ies 'nʌlət|ɪ [-ɪt|ɪ], -ɪz
Numa Pompilius ˌnjuːməpɒm'pɪlɪəs
  [-ljəs]
numb (adj. v.), -ly, -ness; -s, -ing, -ed
  nʌm, -lɪ, -nɪs [-nəs]; -z, -ɪŋ, -d
numb|er (s. v.), -ers (N.), -ering, -ered;
  -erless 'nʌmb|ə*, -əz, -ərɪŋ, -əd; -əlɪs
  [-ləs]
numerable 'njuːmərəbl
numeral (s. adj.), -s 'njuːmərəl, -z
numerate 'njuːmərət [-rɪt]
numeration ˌnjuːmə'reɪʃn
numerative, -s 'njuːmərətɪv, -z
numerator, -s 'njuːməreɪtə*, -z
numeric|al, -ally njuː'merɪk|l [njʊ'm-],
  -əlɪ
numerous, -ly, -ness 'njuːmərəs, -lɪ,
  -nɪs [-nəs]
Numidia, -n/s njuː'mɪdɪə [njʊ'm-, -djə],
  -n/z
numismatic, -s, -ally ˌnjuːmɪz'mætɪk,
  -s, -əlɪ
numismatist, -s njuː'mɪzmətɪst
  [njʊ'm-], -s
numskull, -s 'nʌmskʌl, -z
nun (N.), -s nʌn, -z
Nunc Dimittis, -es ˌnʊŋkdɪ'mɪtɪs
  [ˌnʌŋk-, -daɪ'm-], -ɪz
nuncio, -s 'nʌnsɪəʊ [-ʃjəʊ, -ʃɪəʊ, -sjəʊ],
  -z
Nuneaton nʌn'iːtn
Nuneham 'njuːnəm
nunkey, -s 'nʌŋkɪ, -z
Nunn nʌn
nunner|y, -ies 'nʌnər|ɪ, -ɪz
nuptial, -s 'nʌpʃl ['nʌptʃəl], -z
Nuremberg 'njʊərəmbɜːg ['njɜːr-,
  'njɔːr-]

nurs|e (*s. v.*), **-es, -ing, -ed** nɜːs, -ɪz, -ɪŋ, -t

nurs(e)ling, -s 'nɜːslɪŋ, -z

nurse-maid, -s 'nɜːsmeɪd, -z

nurser|y, -ies 'nɜːsər|ɪ, -ɪz

nursery-maid, -s 'nɜːsrɪmeɪd, -z

nursery|man, -men 'nɜːsrɪ|mən, -mən

nurtur|e (*s. v.*), **-es, -ing, -ed** 'nɜːtʃə*, -z, -rɪŋ, -d

nut, -s nʌt, -s

nutant 'njuːtənt

nutat|e, -es, -ing, -ed njuː'teɪt, -s, -ɪŋ, -ɪd

nutation, -s njuː'teɪʃn, -z

nut-brown 'nʌtbraʊn [ˌ-'-]

nutcracker, -s 'nʌtˌkrækə*, -z

nuthatch, -es 'nʌthætʃ, -ɪz

nutmeg, -s 'nʌtmeg, -z

nutria 'njuːtrɪə

nutrient 'njuːtrɪənt

nutriment 'njuːtrɪmənt

nutrition, -al njuː'trɪʃn [njʊ'tr-], -l

nutritionist, -s njuː'trɪʃnɪst [-ʃənɪst, -ʃnɪst], -s

nutritious, -ly, -ness njuː'trɪʃəs [njʊ'tr-], -lɪ, -nɪs [-nəs]

nutritive 'njuːtrətɪv [-trɪt-]

nutshell, -s 'nʌt-ʃel, -z

Nuttall 'nʌtɔːl

Nutter 'nʌtə*

nutty 'nʌtɪ

nux vomica ˌnʌks'vɒmɪkə

nuzz|le, -es, -ing, -ed 'nʌz|l, -lz, -]ɪŋ [-lɪŋ], -ld

N.W. ˌen'dʌb|ju: [ˌnɔː'west]

Nyanja (*people, language*) 'njændʒə [nɪ'æn-]

Nyanza (*lake*) 'njænzə [nɪ'æn-, naɪ'æn-]

Nyasa (*lake*) naɪ'æsə [nɪ'æsə, 'njæsə]

Nyasaland naɪ'æsəlænd [nɪ'æs-, 'njæsəlænd]

Nyerere nje'reərɪ [njɪ-, njə-, nɪə-, -'rerɪ]

nylon 'naɪlɒn [-lən]

nymph, -s, -al nɪmf, -s, -l

nymphet nɪm'fet

nymph-like 'nɪmflaɪk

nympho, -s 'nɪmfəʊ, -z

nymphoman|ia, -iac/s ˌnɪmfəʊ'meɪn|ɪə [-jə], -ɪæk [-jæk]/s

nystagmus nɪ'stægməs

O

O (*the letter*), -'s [-es] əʊ, -z
O (*interj.*) əʊ
o' (*abbrev. of* of) ə (*weak form only*)
oaf, -s; -ish əʊf, -s; -ɪʃ
oak, -s əʊk, -s
oak-apple, -s 'əʊk,æpl, -z
oak-bark 'əʊkbɑːk
Oakeley 'əʊklɪ
oaken 'əʊkən
Oak|es, -ey əʊk|s, -ɪ
oak-gall, -s 'əʊkgɔːl, -z
Oakham 'əʊkəm
Oakhampton ,əʊk'hæmptən
Oakland, -s 'əʊklənd, -z
Oak|leigh, -ley 'əʊk|lɪ, -lɪ
oakling, -s 'əʊklɪŋ, -z
Oaks əʊks
oakum, -picking 'əʊkəm, -,pɪkɪŋ
Oakworth 'əʊkwəθ [-wɜːθ]
oar (*s. v.*), -s, -ing, -ed ɔː* [ɔə*], -z, -rɪŋ, -d
oars|man, -men 'ɔːz|mən ['ɔəz-], -mən
oas|is, -es əʊ'eɪs|ɪs, -iːz
oast, -s əʊst, -s
oast-hou|se, -ses 'əʊsthaʊ|s, -zɪz
oat, -s əʊt, -s
oatcake, -s 'əʊtkeɪk, -s
oaten 'əʊtn
Oates əʊts
oa|th, -ths əʊ|θ, -ðz [-θs]
oath-break|er/s, -ing 'əʊθ,breɪk|ə*/z, -ɪŋ
Oatlands 'əʊtləndz
oatmeal 'əʊtmiːl
Ob (*river in Siberia*) ɒb (opj)
Obadiah ,əʊbə'daɪə
Oban 'əʊbən
obbligato, -s ,ɒblɪ'gɑːtəʊ, -z
obduracy 'ɒbdjʊrəsɪ [-djə-]
obdurate, -ly, -ness 'ɒbdjʊrət [-djə-, -rɪt, -reɪt, ɒb'djʊərət, -rɪt], -lɪ, -nɪs [-nəs]
obduration ,ɒbdjʊə'reɪʃn [-djə'r-, -djɔə'r-, -djɔː'r-]
obeah 'əʊ,bɪə [-bɪə]
Obed 'əʊbed
Obededom ,əʊbed'iːdəm
obedien|ce, -t/ly ə'biːdjən|s [əʊ'b-, -dɪən-], -t/lɪ

O'Beirne əʊ'beən
obeisance, -s əʊ'beɪsəns, -ɪz
obelisk, -s 'ɒbəlɪsk [-bɪl-], -s
obelus, -es 'ɒbɪləs, -ɪz
Ober - Ammergau ,əʊbər'æməgaʊ [-bə'ræm-] (,oːbər'amərgaʊ)
Oberland 'əʊbəlænd
Oberlin (*in U.S.A.*) 'əʊbəlɪn
Oberon 'əʊbərən [-rɒn]
obes|e, -eness, -ity əʊ'biːs, -nɪs [-nəs], -ətɪ [-ɪtɪ]
obey, -s, -ing, -ed, -er/s ə'beɪ [əʊ'b-], -z, -ɪŋ, -d, -ə*/z [-ə*/z əʊ'beə*/z]
obfuscat|e, -es, -ing, -ed 'ɒbfʌskeɪt [-fəs-], -s, -ɪŋ, -ɪd
obfuscation, -s ,ɒbfʌ'skeɪʃn [-fə's-], -z
obi, -s 'əʊbɪ, -z
Obi (*river in Siberia*) 'əʊbɪ (opj)
Obion əʊ'baɪən
obit, -s 'ɒbɪt ['əʊbɪt], -s
obiter 'ɒbɪtə*
obituarist, -s ə'bɪtʃʊərɪst [ɒ'b-, -tjʊə-, -tjwər-, -tjər-, -tjʊr-], -s
obituar|y, -ies ə'bɪtʃʊər|ɪ [ɒ'b-, -tjʊə-, -tjwər-, -tjər-, -tjʊr-], -ɪz
object (*s.*), -s 'ɒbdʒɪkt [-dʒekt], -s
object (*v.*), -s, -ing, -ed, -or/s əb'dʒekt, -s, -ɪŋ, -ɪd, -ə*/z
object-glass, -es 'ɒbdʒɪktglɑːs [-dʒekt-], -ɪz
objecti|fy, -fies, -fying, -fied ɒb'dʒektɪ|faɪ [əb-], -faɪz, -faɪɪŋ, -faɪd
objection, -s əb'dʒekʃn, -z
objectionab|le, -ly əb'dʒekʃnəb|l [-ʃnəb-, -ʃənəb-], -lɪ
objective (*s.*), -s əb'dʒektɪv [ɒb-], -z
objective (*adj.*), -ly, -ness əb'dʒektɪv [ɒb'dʒ-], -lɪ, -nɪs [-nəs]
objectivism əb'dʒektɪvɪzəm [ɒb-]
objectivity ,ɒbdʒek'tɪvətɪ [-ɪtɪ]
objectless 'ɒbdʒɪktlɪs [-dʒekt-, -ləs]
object-lesson, -s 'ɒbdʒɪkt,lesn [-dʒekt-], -z
objet(s) d'art ,ɒbʒeɪ'dɑː* (ɔbʒeda:r)
objurgat|e, -es, -ing, -ed 'ɒbdʒəgeɪt [-dʒɜːg-], -s, -ɪŋ, -ɪd
objurgation, -s ,ɒbdʒə'geɪʃn [-dʒɜːg-], -z
objurgatory ɒb'dʒɜːgətərɪ [əb'dʒ-, 'ɒbdʒəgeɪtərɪ, -dʒɜːg-]

346

oblate (s.), **-s** 'ɒbleɪt, -s
oblate (adj.) 'ɒbleɪt [ɒ'bleɪt, əʊ'b-]
oblation, **-s** əʊ'bleɪʃn [ɒ'b-], -z
obligant, **-s** 'ɒblɪgənt, -s
obligation, **-s** ˌɒblɪ'geɪʃn, -z
obligato (s. adj.), **-s** ˌɒblɪ'gɑ:təʊ, -z
obligator|y, **-ily, -iness** ə'blɪgətər|ɪ
    [ɒ'b-, 'ɒblɪgətər-, 'ɒblɪgeɪtər-], -əlɪ
    [-ɪlɪ], -mɪs [-məs]
oblig|e, **-es, -ing/ly, -ingness, -ed**
    ə'blaɪdʒ, -ɪz, -ɪŋ/lɪ, -ɪŋnɪs [-nəs], -d
obligee, **-s** ˌɒblɪ'dʒi:, -z
obligor, **-s** ˌɒblɪ'gɔ:*, -z
oblique, **-ly, -ness** ə'bli:k [ɒ'b-, əʊ'b-],
    -lɪ, -nɪs [-nəs]
obliquit|y, **-ies** ə'blɪkwət|ɪ [ɒ'b-, əʊ'b-],
    -ɪt|ɪ], -ɪz
obliterat|e, **-es, -ing, -ed** ə'blɪtəreɪt
    [ɒ'b-], -s, -ɪŋ, -ɪd
obliteration, **-s** əˌblɪtə'reɪʃn [ɒˌb-], -z
oblivion ə'blɪvɪən [ɒ'b-, -vjən]
oblivious, **-ly, -ness** ə'blɪvɪəs [ɒ'b-,
    -vjəs], -lɪ, -nɪs [-nəs]
oblong (s. adj.), **-s** 'ɒblɒŋ, -z
obloquy 'ɒbləkwɪ
obnoxious, **-ly, -ness** əb'nɒkʃəs [ɒb-],
    -lɪ, -nɪs [-nəs]
Obock əʊ'bɒk ['əʊbɒk]
oboe, **-s** 'əʊbəʊ, -z
oboe d'amore ˌəʊbəʊdæ'mɔːreɪ [-də'm-]
oboist, **-s** 'əʊbəʊɪst, -s
obol, **-s** 'ɒbɒl [-bəl], -z
O'Brady əʊ'brɔ:dɪ [-'breɪ-]
O'Br|ien, **-yan** əʊ'br|aɪən, -aɪən
obscene, **-ly, -ness** əb'si:n [ɒb-], -lɪ, -nɪs
    [-nəs]
obscenit|y, **-ies** əb'senət|ɪ [ɒb-, -'si:n-,
    -ɪt|ɪ], -ɪz
obscurant (s. adj.) ɒb'skjʊərənt [əb-,
    -bz'k-]
obscurant|ism, **-ist/s** ˌɒbskjʊə'rænt|-
    ɪzəm [-bzk-, -kjʊ'r-, ɒb'skjʊərənt-,
    əb'skjʊərənt-, -bz'k-], -ɪst/s
obscuration, **-s** ˌɒbskjʊə'reɪʃn [-bzk-,
    -kjʊ'r-, -kjə'r-], -z
obscur|e (adj. v.), **-er, -est, -ely,
    -eness; -es, -ing, -ed** əb'skjʊə* [ɒb-,
    -bz'k-, -jɔə*, -jɔ:*], -rə*, -rɪst, -lɪ,
    -nɪs [-nəs]; -z, -ɪŋ, -d
obscurit|y, **-ies** əb'skjʊərət|ɪ[ɒb-, -bz'k-,
    -jɔər-, -jɔ:r-, -ɪt|ɪ], -ɪz
obsecration, **-s** ˌɒbsɪ'kreɪʃn [-se'k-], -z
obsequial ɒb'si:kwɪəl [əb-, -kwjəl]
obsequies 'ɒbsɪkwɪz [-sə-]
obsequious, **-ly, -ness** əb'si:kwɪəs [ɒb-,
    -kwjəs], -lɪ, -nɪs [-nəs]
observab|le, **-ly, -leness** əb'zɜ:vəb|l, -lɪ,
    -lnɪs [-nəs]

observan|ce, **-ces, -cy** əb'zɜ:vn|s, -sɪz,
    -sɪ
observant, **-ly** əb'zɜ:vnt, -lɪ
observation, **-s** ˌɒbzə'veɪʃn, -z
observa|tional, **-tionally** ˌɒbzə'veɪ|ʃənl
    [-ʃnəl, -ʃn̩, -ʃn̩, -ʃənəl], -ʃn̩əlɪ [-ʃnəlɪ,
    -ʃn̩lɪ, -ʃn̩lɪ, -ʃənəlɪ]
observator|y, **-ies** əb'zɜ:vətr|ɪ [-tər-],
    -ɪz
observ|e, **-es, -ing/ly, -ed, -er/s** əb'zɜ:v,
    -z, -ɪŋ/lɪ, -d, -ə*/z
obsess, **-es, -ing, -ed** əb'ses [ɒb-], -ɪz,
    -ɪŋ, -t
obsession, **-s, -al** əb'seʃn [ɒb-], **-s**, -l
    [-əl, -ʃənəl]
obsessive əb'sesɪv [ɒb-]
obsidian ɒb'sɪdɪən [-djən]
obsolescen|ce, **-t** ˌɒbsəʊ'lesn|s, -t
obsolete, **-ly, -ness** 'ɒbsəli:t [-s̩i:t,
    -sli:t], -lɪ, -nɪs [-nəs]
obstacle, **-s** 'ɒbstəkl [-bzt-, -tɪkl], **-z**
obstetric, **-al, -s** ɒb'stetrɪk [əb-, -bz't-],
    -l, -s
obstetrician, **-s** ˌɒbstə'trɪʃn [-bzt-, -te't,
    -tɪ't-], -z
obstinac|y, **-ies** 'ɒbstɪnəs|ɪ [-bzt-,
    -tənə-], -ɪz
obstinate, **-ly, -ness** 'ɒbstənət [-bzt-,
    -tɪn-, -nɪt], -lɪ, -nɪs [-nəs]
obstreperous, **-ly, -ness** əb'strepərəs
    [ɒb-, -bz't-], -lɪ, -nɪs [-nəs]
obstruct, **-s, -ing, -ed, -or/s** əb'strʌkt
    [-bz't-], -s, -ɪŋ, -ɪd, -ə*/z
obstruction, **-s** əb'strʌkʃn [-bz't-], **-z**
obstructionism əb'strʌkʃənɪzəm [-bz't-,
    -ʃn̩-]
obstructionist, **-s** əb'strʌkʃənɪst [-bz't-,
    -ʃn̩], -s
obstructive, **-ly, -ness** əb'strʌktɪv
    [-bz't-], -lɪ, -nɪs [-nəs]
obstruent (s. adj.), **-s** 'ɒbstrʊənt, **-s**
obtain, **-s, -ing, -ed, -er/s; -able**
    əb'teɪn, -z, -ɪŋ, -d, -ə*/z; -əbl
obtrud|e, **-es, -ing, -ed, -er/s** əb'tru:d
    [ɒb-], -z, -ɪŋ, -ɪd, -ə*/z
obtrusion, **-s** əb'tru:ʒn [ɒb-], -z
obtrusive, **-ly, -ness** əb'tru:sɪv [ɒb-], -lɪ,
    -nɪs [-nəs]
obturat|e, **-es, -ing, -ed, -or/s** 'ɒbtjʊə-
    reɪt [-tjʊr-], -s, -ɪŋ, -ɪd, -ə*/z
obturation, **-s** ˌɒbtjʊə'reɪʃn [-tjʊ'r-], -z
obtuse, **-ly, -ness** əb'tju:s [ɒb-], -lɪ, -nɪs
    [-nəs]
obverse (s. adj.), **-s** 'ɒbvɜ:s, -ɪz
obversely ɒb'vɜ:slɪ
obvert, **-s, -ing, -ed** ɒb'vɜ:t, -s, -ɪŋ, -ɪd
obviat|e, **-es, -ing, -ed** 'ɒbvɪeɪt [-vjeɪt],
    -s, -ɪŋ, -ɪd

obvious, -ly, -ness 'ɒbvɪəs [-vjəs], -lɪ, -nɪs [-nəs]
O'Byrne əʊ'bɜːn
O'Callaghan əʊ'kæləhən [-gən]
ocarina, -s ˌɒkə'riːnə, -z
O'Casey əʊ'keɪsɪ
Occam 'ɒkəm
occasi|on (s. v.), -ons, -oning, -oned ə'keɪʒ|n, -nz, -ṇɪŋ [-ənɪŋ, -nɪŋ], -nd
occa|sional, -sionally ə'keɪʒənl [-ʒnəl, -ʒṇl, -ʒṇl, -ʒənəl], -ʒṇəlɪ [-ʒnəlɪ, -ʒṇ̩lɪ, -ʒṇlɪ, -ʒənəlɪ]
occasionali|sm -st/s ə'keɪʒṇəlɪ|zəm [-ʒnəl-, -ʒṇl-, -ʒṇl-, -ʒənəl-], -st/s
occident (O.) 'ɒksɪdənt
occidental (s. adj.) (O.), -s ˌɒksɪ'dentl, -z
occidentali|sm, -st/s ˌɒksɪ'dentəlɪ|zəm [-tʃ̩ɪ-], -st/s
occidentaliz|e [-is|e], -es, -ing, -ed ˌɒksɪ'dentəlaɪz [-tʃ̩aɪz], -ɪz, -ɪŋ, -d
occipit|al, -ally ɒk'sɪpɪt|l, -əlɪ
occiput, -s 'ɒksɪpʌt [-pət], -s
Occleve 'ɒkliːv
occlud|e, -es, -ing, -ed ɒ'kluːd [ə'k-], -z, -ɪŋ, -ɪd
occlusion, -s ɒ'kluːʒn [ə'k-], -z
occlusive (s. adj.), -s ɒ'kluːsɪv [ə'k-], -z
occult (adj.), -ly, -ness ɒ'kʌlt [ə'k-, 'ɒkʌlt], -lɪ, -nɪs [-nəs]
occult (v.), -s, -ing, -ed ɒ'kʌlt [ə'k-], -s, -ɪŋ, -ɪd
occultation, -s ˌɒkəl'teɪʃn [-kʌl-], -z
occulti|sm, -st/s 'ɒkəltɪ|zəm ['ɒkʌl-, ɒ'kʌl-], -st/s
occupan|cy, -t/s 'ɒkjʊpən|sɪ [-kjə-], -t/s
occupation, -s ˌɒkjʊ'peɪʃn [-kjə-], -z
occupational ˌɒkjuː'peɪʃənl [-kjʊ-, -kjə-, -ʃnəl, -ʃṇl, -ʃn̩l, -ʃənəl]
occup|y, -ies, -ying, -ied, -ier/s 'ɒkjʊp|aɪ, -aɪz, -aɪɪŋ, -aɪd, -aɪə*/z
occur, -s, -ring, -red ə'kɜː:*, -z, -rɪŋ, -d
occurrence, -s ə'kʌrəns, -ɪz
ocean, -s 'əʊʃn, -z
Oceania, -n/s ˌəʊʃɪ'eɪnjə [-nɪə], -n/z
oceanic (O.) ˌəʊʃɪ'ænɪk [ˌəʊsɪ-]
Oceanica ˌəʊʃɪ'ænɪkə
oceanograph|er/s, -y ˌəʊʃə'nɒɡrəf|ə*/z [-ʃjə-, -ʃɪə-], -ɪ
oceanographic ˌəʊʃjənəʊ'ɡræfɪk [-ʃɪə-]
Oceanus əʊ'sɪənəs [əʊ'ʃɪə-]
ocell|us, -i əʊ'sel|əs, -aɪ [-iː]
ocelot, -s 'əʊsɪlɒt ['ɒs-, -sə-, -lət], -s
ochery 'əʊkərɪ
Ochill 'əʊkɪl ['əʊxɪl]
Ochiltree (in Scott's 'Antiquary') 'əʊkɪltriː: ['əʊxɪl-], (in U.S.A.) 'əʊkɪltriː:

och|re (s. v.), -res, -reing, -red 'əʊk|ə*, -əz, -ərɪŋ, -əd
ochreous 'əʊkrɪəs ['əʊkərəs]
ochry 'əʊkərɪ ['əʊkrɪ]
Ochterlony ˌɒktə'ləʊnɪ [ˌɒxt-]
Ock|ham, -ley 'ɒk|əm, -lɪ
Ocklynge 'ɒklɪndʒ
O'Clery əʊ'klɪərɪ
o'clock ə'klɒk
Ocmulgee əʊk'mʌlɡɪ
O'Con|nell, -(n)or əʊ'kɒn|l, -ə*
Ocracoke 'əʊkrəkəʊk
octagon, -s 'ɒktəgən, -z
octagonal ɒk'tægənl
octahedr|on, -ons, -a; -al ˌɒktə'hedr|ən [-'hiː d-, 'ɒktə ˌh-], -ənz, -ə; -əl
octane 'ɒkteɪn
octant, -s 'ɒktənt, -s
Octateuch 'ɒktətjuːk
octave (musical term), -s 'ɒktɪv [rarely -teɪv], -z
octave (ecclesiastical term), -s 'ɒkteɪv [-tɪv], -z
Octavia, -n ɒk'teɪvjə [-vɪə], -n
Octavius ɒk'teɪvjəs [-vɪəs]
octavo, -s ɒk'teɪvəʊ, -z
octennial ɒk'tenjəl [-nɪəl]
octet(te), -s ɒk'tet, -s
octillion, -s ɒk'tɪljən, -z
October, -s ɒk'təʊbə*, -z
octodecimo, -s ˌɒktəʊ'desɪməʊ, -z
octopus, -es 'ɒktəpəs, -ɪz
octoroon, -s ˌɒktə'ruːn, -z
octosyllabic ˌɒktəʊsɪ'læbɪk [-təs-]
octosyllable, -s 'ɒktəʊˌsɪləbl [-tə ˌs-], -z
octroi, -s 'ɒktrwɑ: (ɔktrwa), -z
octuple 'ɒktjuːpl [-tjʊpl]
ocular, -ly 'ɒkjʊlə* [-kjə-], -lɪ
oculist, -s 'ɒkjʊlɪst [-kjə-], -s
O'Curry əʊ'kʌrɪ
od (O.), -s ɒd, -z
odalisque, -s 'əʊdəlɪsk ['ɒd-], -s
O'Daly əʊ'deɪlɪ
Odam 'əʊdəm
odd, -er, -est, -ly, -ness ɒd, -ə*, -ɪst, -lɪ, -nɪs [-nəs]
Oddfellow, -s 'ɒdˌfeləʊ, -z
Oddie 'ɒdɪ
oddish 'ɒdɪʃ
oddit|y, -ies 'ɒdɪt|ɪ [-ət|ɪ], -ɪz
odd-looking 'ɒdˌlʊkɪŋ
oddment, -s 'ɒdmənt, -s
odds ɒdz
Oddy 'ɒdɪ
ode, -s əʊd, -z
O'Dea əʊ'deɪ

Odell əʊ'del
Odeon 'əʊdjən [-dɪən]
Oder 'əʊdə* ['oːdər]
Odessa əʊ'desə
Ode|um, -a, -ums əʊ'di:|əm [-'dɪəm, 'əʊdj|əm, 'əʊdɪ|əm], -ə, -əmz
Odgers 'ɒdʒəz
Odham 'ɒdəm
Odiham 'əʊdɪhəm
Odin 'əʊdɪn
odious, -ly, -ness 'əʊdjəs [-dɪəs], -lɪ, -nɪs [-nəs]
odium 'əʊdjəm [-dɪəm]
Odling 'ɒdlɪŋ
Odlum 'ɒdləm
Odo 'əʊdəʊ
Odoacer ˌɒdəʊ'eɪsə* [ˌəʊd-]
O'Doherty əʊ'dəʊətɪ, -'dɒhətɪ [-'dɒxə-]
odol 'əʊdɒl
odometer, -s əʊ'dɒmɪtə* [ɒ'd-, -mətə*], -z
O'Donnell əʊ'dɒnl
odontolog|ist/s, -y ˌɒdɒn'tɒlədʒ|ɪst/s, -ɪ
odoriferous, -ly, -ness ˌəʊdə'rɪfərəs [ˌɒd-], -lɪ, -nɪs [-nəs]
odorous, -ly, -ness 'əʊdərəs, -lɪ, -nɪs [-nəs]
odour, -s, -ed, -less 'əʊdə*, -z, -d, -lɪs [-ləs, -les]
O'Dowd əʊ'daʊd
odsbodikins ˌɒdz'bɒdɪkɪnz
O'Dwyer əʊ'dwaɪə*
Ody 'əʊdɪ
Odysseus ə'dɪsju:s [ɒ'd-, əʊ'd-, -sɪəs, -sjəs]
Odyssey 'ɒdɪsɪ
oecumenic, -al ˌiːkju:'menɪk [-kjʊ'm-], -l
oedema i:'di:mə [ɪ'd-]
oedematous i:'demətəs [ɪ'd-]
Oedipus 'i:dɪpəs
œillade, -s ɜ:'jɑːd (œjad), -z
Oeneus 'i:nju:s [-njəs, -nɪəs]
Oenomaus ˌi:nəʊ'meɪəs
Oenone i:'nəʊnɪ: [ɪ'n-, -nɪ]
o'er (*contracted form of* **over**) ɔə* [ɔː*, 'əʊə*]
oes (*plur. of* **O**) əʊz
oesophageal i:ˌsɒfə'dʒi:əl [ɪ,s-, -'dʒɪəl]
oesopha|gus, -gi, -guses ɪ'sɒfə|gəs [i:'s-, ə's-], -gaɪ [-dʒaɪ], -gəsɪz
oestrogen 'i:strəʊdʒən [-dʒen]
oestrus, -es 'i:strəs, -ɪz
Oettle 'ɜ:tlɪ
Oetzmann 'əʊtsmən
of ɒv (*strong form*), əv, v, f (*weak forms*)
Note.—*The form* f *occurs only before voiceless consonants.*

off ɒf [*old-fashioned* ɔːf, *and in compounds*]
Offa 'ɒfə
offal 'ɒfl
Offaly 'ɒfəlɪ
off-bail, -s ˌɒf'beɪl [ˌɔːf-, '--, *when in contrast with* **leg-bail**], -z
off-bye, -s ˌɒf'baɪ [ˌɔːf-, '--, *when in contrast with* **leg-bye**], -z ·
off-drive, -s 'ɒfdraɪv ['ɔːf-], -z
Offenbach 'ɒfənbɑːk
offence, -s, -less ə'fens, -ɪz, -lɪs [-ləs]
offend, -s, -ing, -ed -er/s ə'fend, -z, -ɪŋ, -ɪd, -ə*/z
offensive (*s. adj.*), **-s, -ly, -ness** ə'fensɪv [ɒ'f-], -z, -lɪ, -nɪs [-nəs]
off|er (*s. v.*), **-ers, -ering/s, -ered, -erer/s; -erable** 'ɒf|ə*, -əz, -ərɪŋ/z, -əd, -ərə*/z; -ərəbl
offertor|y, -ies 'ɒfətər|ɪ, -ɪz
off-hand ˌɒf'hænd [ˌɔːf'h-, *also* '-- *according to sentence-stress*]
off-handed ˌɒf'hændɪd [ˌɔːf-]
office, -s 'ɒfɪs, -ɪz
office-bearer, -s 'ɒfɪsˌbeərə*, -z
office-boy, -s 'ɒfɪsbɔɪ, -z
officer, -s 'ɒfɪsə*, -z
offici|al (*s. adj.*), **-als, -ally, -alism** ə'fɪʃ|l, -lz, -əlɪ [-lɪ], -əlɪzəm [-lɪzəm]
officialdom ə'fɪʃldəm
officialese əˌfɪʃə'li:z [əˌfɪʃ'i:z, ə'fɪʃəli:z, ə'fɪʃli:z]
officiat|e, -es, -ing, -ed ə'fɪʃɪeɪt, -s, -ɪŋ, -ɪd
officinal ˌɒfɪ'saɪnl [ɒ'fɪsml]
officious, -ly, -ness ə'fɪʃəs, -lɪ, -nɪs [-nəs]
offing, -s 'ɒfɪŋ ['ɔːf-], -z
offish 'ɒfɪʃ ['ɔːf-]
off-licenc|e, -s 'ɒfˌlaɪsns ['ɔːf-], -ɪz
Offor 'ɒfə*
off-print, -s 'ɒfprɪnt ['ɔːf-], -s
†**offset** (*s. v.*), **-s, -ting** 'ɒfset ['ɔːf-], -s, -ɪŋ
offshoot, -s 'ɒfʃu:t ['ɔːf-], -s
offside, -s ˌɒf'saɪd [ˌɔːf's-, '--, *when in contrast with* **on side**]
offspring, -s 'ɒfsprɪŋ ['ɔːf-], -z
off-the-record ˌɒfðə'rekɔːd [ˌɔːf-]
off-time 'ɒftaɪm ['ɔːf-, ˌ-'-]
O'Flaherty əʊ'fleətɪ [-'flæhətɪ, -'flɑːət-, -'flɑːt-]
O'Flynn əʊ'flɪn
oft ɒft [*old-fashioned* ɔːft]
often, -times 'ɒfn [*old-fashioned* 'ɔːf-, -fən, -ftən], -taɪmz
often|er, -est 'ɒfn̩|ə* ['ɔːf-, -fn|ə*, -fən|ə*, -ftən|ə*, -ftn̩|ə*, -ftn|ə*], -ɪst
ofttimes 'ɒfttaɪmz ['ɔːf-]
Og, -den ɒg, -dən

349

ogee, -s 'əʊdʒi: [əʊ'dʒi:], -z
Ogemaw 'əʊgɪmɔ:
og(h)am, -s 'ɒgəm, -z
og(h)amic ɒ'gæmɪk
Ogil|by, -vie, -vy 'əʊgl|bɪ, -vɪ, -vɪ
ogival əʊ'dʒaɪvl
ogive, -s 'əʊdʒaɪv [əʊ'dʒ-], -z
og|le (O.), -les, -ling, -led, -ler/s 'əʊg|l,
  -lz, -lɪŋ [-|ɪŋ], -ld, -lə*/z [-|ə*/z]
Ogle|by, -thorpe 'əʊgl|bɪ, -θɔ:p
Ogpu 'ɒgpu:
O'Grady əʊ'greɪdɪ
ogr|e, -es, -ish 'əʊgə*, -z, -rɪʃ
ogress, -es 'əʊgrɪs [-res], -ɪz
o'Groat ə'grəʊt
oh əʊ
O'Hagan əʊ'heɪgən
O'Halloran əʊ'hælərən
O'Hara əʊ'hɑ:rə
O'Hare əʊ'heə*
O'Hea əʊ'heɪ
Ohio əʊ'haɪəʊ
ohm (O.), -s əʊm, -z
oho əʊ'həʊ
oil (s. v.), -s, -ing, -ed, -er/s ɔɪl, -z, -ɪŋ,
  -d, -ə*/z
oil-box, -es 'ɔɪlbɒks, -ɪz
oil-burner, -s 'ɔɪl,bɜ:nə*, -z
oil-cake, -s 'ɔɪlkeɪk, -s
oil-can, -s 'ɔɪlkæn, -z
oil|cloth, -cloths 'ɔɪl|klɒθ [old-fashioned
  -klɔ:θ], -klɒθs [-klɔ:ðz, -klɔ:θs]
oil-colour, -s 'ɔɪl,kʌlə*, -z
oil-field, -s 'ɔɪlfi:ld, -z
oil-fuel 'ɔɪlfjʊəl [-,fju:əl, -fju:l]
oil|man, -men 'ɔɪl|mən [-mæn], -mən
  [-men]
oil-paint, -s; -ing/s ,ɔɪl'peɪnt ['--], -s;
  -ɪŋ/z
oil-rig, -s 'ɔɪlrɪg, -z
oil-silk 'ɔɪlsɪlk [,-'-]
oil-skin 'ɔɪlskɪn, -z
oil-slick, -s 'ɔɪlslɪk, -s
oil-stone, -s 'ɔɪlstəʊn, -z
oil-stove, -s 'ɔɪlstəʊv, -z
oil-well, -s 'ɔɪlwel, -z
oil|y, -ier, -iest, -iness 'ɔɪl|ɪ, -ɪə*
  [-jə*], -ɪɪst [-jɪst], -ɪnɪs [-məs]
ointment, -s 'ɔɪntmənt, -s
Oisin 'ɔɪzɪn
Oistrakh 'ɔɪstrɑ:k [-ɑ:x]
Ojai (in California) 'əʊhaɪ
Ojibway, -s əʊ'dʒɪbweɪ [ɒ'dʒ-], -z
O.K. ,əʊ'keɪ [əʊ'keɪ]
okapi, -s əʊ'kɑ:pɪ, -z
okay, -s, -ing, -ed ,əʊ'keɪ, -z, -ɪŋ, -d
O'Keef(f)e əʊ'ki:f
Okehampton ,əʊk'hæmptən

O'Kelly əʊ'kelɪ
Okhotsk əʊ'kɒtsk [ɒ'k-] (a'xotsk)
Okinawa ,ɒkɪ'nɑ:wə [,əʊk-]
Oklahoma ,əʊklə'həʊmə
Olav (Norwegian name) 'əʊləv [-læv]
Olave 'ɒlɪv [-ləv, -leɪv]
Olcott 'ɒlkət
old, -er, -est, -ness əʊld, -ə*, -ɪst, -nɪs
  [-nəs]
Oldbuck 'əʊldbʌk
Oldbury 'əʊldbərɪ
Oldcastle 'əʊld,kɑ:sl
old-clothes|man, -men ,əʊld'kləʊðz|-
  mæn [əʊld'k-, -mən, old-fashioned
  -'kləʊz-], -men [-mən]
olden 'əʊldən
Oldenburg 'əʊldənbɜ:g ('ɔldənburk,
  -burç)
old-fashioned ,əʊld'fæʃnd [also '-,-
  according to sentence-stress]
Oldfield 'əʊldfi:ld
old-fog(e)yish ,əʊld'fəʊgɪɪʃ [-gjɪʃ]
old-gentlemanly ,əʊld'dʒentlmənlɪ
Oldham 'əʊldəm
oldish 'əʊldɪʃ
old-maidish ,əʊld'meɪdɪʃ
Oldrey 'əʊldrɪ
old-time 'əʊldtaɪm
old-womanish ,əʊld'wʊmənɪʃ
old-world ,əʊld'wɜ:ld ['-- when attribu-
  tive]
oleaginous, -ness ,əʊlɪ'ædʒɪnəs, -nɪs
  [-nəs]
oleander (O.), -s ,əʊlɪ'ændə*, -z
O'Leary əʊ'lɪərɪ
oleaster, -s ,əʊlɪ'æstə*, -z
olefiant 'əʊlɪfaɪənt [əʊ'li:fɪənt, -'lef-]
oleograph, -s 'əʊlɪəʊgrɑ:f [-lɪəg-,
  -ljəʊg-, -græf], -s
oleography ,əʊlɪ'ɒgrəfɪ
oleomargarine   'əʊlɪəʊ,mɑ:dʒə'ri:n
  [-,mɑ:gə'r-, -'mɑ:dʒər-, -'mɑ:gər-]
O-level, -s 'əʊ,levl, -z
olfactory ɒl'fæktərɪ
Olga 'ɒlgə
olibanum ɒ'lɪbənəm [əʊ'l-]
Olifa(u)nt 'ɒlɪfənt
Oliffe 'ɒlɪf
oligarch, -s 'ɒlɪgɑ:k, -s
oligarchal 'ɒlɪgɑ:kl [,ɒlɪ'g-]
oligarchic ,ɒlɪ'gɑ:kɪk
oligarch|y, -ies 'ɒlɪgɑ:k|ɪ, -ɪz
oligocene ɒ'lɪgəʊsi:n ['----]
olio, -s 'əʊlɪəʊ [-ljəʊ], -z
Oliphant 'ɒlɪfənt
olivaceous ,ɒlɪ'veɪʃəs
olive (O.), -s; -branch/es, -coloured
  'ɒlɪv, -z; -brɑ:ntʃ/ɪz, -,kʌləd

olive oil ˌɒlɪvˈɔɪl
oliver (O.), -s ˈɒlɪvə*, -z
Oliverian ˌɒlɪˈvɪərɪən
Olivet ˈɒlɪvet [-vɪt]
olive|-tree/s, -wood ˈɒlɪv|triː/z, -wʊd
Olivia ɒˈlɪvɪə [əˈl-, əʊˈl-, -vjə]
Olivier (Lord) əˈlɪvɪeɪ [ɒˈl-]
olivine, -s ˌɒlɪˈviːn [ˈɒlɪv-], -z
olla podrida, -s ˌɒləpɒˈdriːdə [ˌɒljə-, -pəˈd-], -z
Ollendorf ˈɒləndɔːf [-lɪn-] (ˈɔləndɔrf)
Ollerton ˈɒlətən
Olley ˈɒlɪ
Olliffe ˈɒlɪf
Ollivant ˈɒlɪvənt [-vænt]
Olmstead ˈɒmsted
Olney (in Buckinghamshire) ˈəʊlnɪ [ˈəʊnɪ]
-olog|y, -ies -ˈɒlədʒ|ɪ, -ɪz
oloroso ˌɒləˈrəʊsəʊ [ˌəʊl-, -zəʊ]
Olver ˈɒlvə*
Olymp|ia, -iad/s, -ian, -ic/s, -us əʊˈlɪmp|ɪə [-jə], -ɪæd/z [-jæd/z], -ɪən [-jən], -ɪk/s, -əs
Olynth|iac/s, -us əʊˈlɪnθ|ɪæk/s [-jæk/s], -əs
Omagh ˈəʊmə, əʊˈmɑː
Omaha ˈəʊməhɑː
O'Malley əʊˈmælɪ, -ˈmeɪlɪ
Oman əʊˈmɑːn
Omar ˈəʊmɑː*
ombre ˈɒmbə*
ombudsman ˈɒmbʊdzmən [-mæn]
Omdurman ˌɒmdɔːˈmɑːn [ˈɒmdəmən]
O'Meara əʊˈmɑːrə, -ˈmɪərə
omega (O.), -s ˈəʊmɪgə [-meg-], -z
omelet(te), -s ˈɒmlɪt [-lət, -let], -s
omen, -s, -ed ˈəʊmen [-mən], -z, -d
omer (O.), -s ˈəʊmə*, -z
omicron, -s əʊˈmaɪkrən, -z
ominous, -ly, -ness ˈɒmɪnəs [ˈəʊm-], -lɪ, -nɪs [-nəs]
omissible əʊˈmɪsɪbl [-səb-]
omission, -s əˈmɪʃn [əʊˈm-], -z
omit, -s, -ting, -ted əˈmɪt [əʊˈm-], -s, -ɪŋ, -ɪd
Ommaney ˈɒmənɪ
omnibus, -es ˈɒmnɪbəs, -ɪz
omnifarious ˌɒmnɪˈfeərɪəs
omnipoten|ce, -t/ly ɒmˈnɪpətən|s, -t/lɪ
omnipresen|ce, -t ˌɒmnɪˈprezns, -t
omniscien|ce, -t/ly ɒmˈnɪsɪən|s [-sjən-, -ʃɪən-, -ʃjən-, -ʃn-], -t/lɪ
omnium, -s ˈɒmnɪəm [-njəm], -z
omnium gatherum, -s ˌɒmnɪəmˈgæðərəm [-njəm-], -z
omnivore, -s ˈɒmnɪvɔː*, -z
omnivorous, -ly ɒmˈnɪvərəs, -lɪ

Omond ˈəʊmənd
O'Morchoe əʊˈmʌrəʊ
omphalos ˈɒmfələs
Omri ˈɒmraɪ
Omsk ɒmsk
on (s. adj. adv. prep.) ɒn (normal form, strong and weak), ən, n (rare weak forms).
onager, -s ˈɒnəgə*, -z
Onan ˈəʊnæn [-nən]
Onassis əʊˈnæsɪs [ɒˈn-]
once wʌns
once-over ˈwʌnsˌəʊvə*
oncer, -s ˈwʌnsə*, -z
oncoming (s. adj.), -s ˈɒnˌkʌmɪŋ, -z
on-drive, -s ˈɒndraɪv, -z
one, -s wʌn, -z
O'Neal əʊˈniːl
one-eyed ˌwʌnˈaɪd [also ˈ-- when attributive]
Onega ɒˈnjegə [ɒˈnegə, əʊˈneɪgə, old-fashioned ˈəʊnɪgə] (ɑˈnjegə)
one-horse (adj.) ˌwʌnˈhɔːs [ˈ--]
O'Neil(l) əʊˈniːl
oneiromancy əʊˈnaɪərəʊmænsɪ
one-ish ˈwʌnɪʃ
one-legged ˌwʌnˈlegd [-ˈlegɪd, ˈ--(-)]
oneness ˈwʌnnɪs [-nəs]
one-off ˌwʌnˈɒf
oner, -s ˈwʌnə*, -z
onerous, -ly, -ness ˈɒnərəs [ˈəʊn-], -lɪ, -nɪs [-nəs]
oneself wʌnˈself
onesided, -ly, -ness ˌwʌnˈsaɪdɪd, -lɪ, -nɪs [-nəs]
Onesimus əʊˈnesɪməs
oneupmanship ˌwʌnˈʌpmənʃɪp [-ˈ---]
ongoing, -s ˈɒnˌgəʊɪŋ, -z
Onians əˈnaɪənz [əʊˈn-]
Onich (near Fort William) ˈəʊnɪk [-nɪx]
onion, -s, -y ˈʌnjən, -z, -ɪ
Onions ˈʌnjənz, əʊˈnaɪənz
onlook|er/s, -ing ˈɒnˌlʊk|ə*/z, -ɪŋ
only ˈəʊnlɪ
onomastic ˌɒnəʊˈmæstɪk
onomasticon, -s ˌɒnəʊˈmæstɪkən [-kɒn], -z
onomatolog|ist/s, -y ˌɒnəʊməˈtɒlədʒ|ɪst/s, -ɪ
onomato|poeia, -poeias, -poeic ˌɒnəʊmætəʊˈpiːə [ɒˌnɒmət-, əˌnɒmət-, -ˈpɪə], -ˈpiːəz [-ˈpɪəz], -ˈpiːɪk
Onoto, -s əʊˈnəʊtəʊ [ɒˈn-], -z
on|rush/es, -set/s, -slaught/s ˈɒn|ˌrʌʃ/ɪz, -set/s, -slɔːt/s
Onslow ˈɒnzləʊ
Ontario ɒnˈteərɪəʊ

351

onto 'ɒntu:, 'ɒntʊ, 'ɒntə
 Note.—The form 'ɒntə *is used only
  before words beginning with a
  consonant.*
ontogenesis ,ɒntəʊ'dʒenɪsɪs [-nəs-]
ontogenetic, -ally ,ɒntəʊdʒɪ'netɪk
 [-dʒə'n-], -əlɪ
ontogeny ɒn'tɒdʒɪnɪ [-dʒənɪ]
ontologic, -al, -ally ,ɒntəʊ'lɒdʒɪk, -l,
 -əlɪ
ontolog|ist/s, -y ɒn'tɒlədʒ|ɪst/s, -ɪ
onus 'əʊnəs
onward, -s 'ɒnwəd, -z
onyx, -es 'ɒnɪks ['əʊn-], -ɪz
oof u:f
oolite, -s 'əʊəlaɪt ['əʊəʊl-], -s
oolitic ,əʊə'lɪtɪk [,əʊəʊ'l-]
oolog|ist/s, -y əʊ'bləd ʒ|ɪst/s, -ɪ
Oolong 'u:lɒŋ [,u:'lɒŋ]
ooz|e (*s. v.*), **-es, -ing, -ed** u:z, -ɪz, -ɪŋ,
 -d
ooz|y, -ier, -iest, -ily, -iness 'u:z|ɪ, -ɪə*
 [-jə*], -ɪɪst [-jɪst], -ɪlɪ [-əlɪ], -ɪnɪs
 [-ɪnəs]
opacity əʊ'pæsətɪ [-ɪtɪ]
opal, -s 'əʊpl, -z
opalescen|ce, -t ,əʊpə'lesn|s, -t
opaline (*s.*), **-s** 'əʊpəli:n [-laɪn], -z
opaline (*adj.*) 'əʊpəlaɪn
opaque, -ly, -ness əʊ'peɪk, -lɪ, -nɪs
 [-nəs]
op. cit. ,ɒp'sɪt
op|e, -es, -ing, -ed əʊp, -s, -ɪŋ, -t
Opel 'əʊpl
op|en (*adj. v.*), **-ener, -enest, -enly,
 -enness; -ens, -ening, -ened, -ener/s**
 'əʊp|ən ['əʊp|m], -ṇə* [-ənə*, -nə*],
 -ṇɪst [-ənɪst, -nɪst], -ṇlɪ [-ənlɪ, -ṃlɪ],
 -ṇnɪs [-ənnɪs, -ṃnɪs, -nəs] ;-ənz [-mz],
 -nɪŋ [-ṇɪŋ], -ənd [-md], -nə*/z
 [-ṇə*/z]
open-air ,əʊpṇ'eə* [,əʊpən'eə*, '---]
opencast 'əʊpənkɑːst [-pn-]
open-eyed ,əʊpṇ'aɪd [,əʊpən'aɪd, '---]
open-handed ,əʊpṇ'hændɪd [-pən-,
 '--,-]
open - handedness ,əʊpṇ'hændɪdnɪs
 [-pən-, -nəs]
opening (*s.*), **-s** 'əʊpnɪŋ, -z
open-minded, -ly, -ness ,əʊpṇ'maɪndɪd
 [,əʊpən'm-, ,əʊpṃ'm-, '--,--], -lɪ, -nɪs
 [-nəs]
open-mouthed ,əʊpṇ'maʊðd [-pən'm-,
 -pṃ'm-, '---]
Openshaw 'əʊpənʃɔ:
open-work 'əʊpṇwɜːk [-pənw-, -pṃw-]

**opera, -s; -bouffe, -cloak/s, -glass/es,
 -hat/s, -house, -houses** 'ɒpərə, -z;
 -'bu:f, -kləʊk/s, -glɑːs/ɪz, -hæt/s,
 -haʊs, -,haʊzɪz
operant (*s. adj.*), **-s** 'ɒpərənt, -s
operat|e, -es, -ing, -ed, -or/s 'ɒpəreɪt,
 -s, -ɪŋ, -ɪd, -ə*/z
operatic, -s ,ɒpə'rætɪk, -s
operation, -s ,ɒpə'reɪʃn, -z
operational ,ɒpə'reɪʃənl [-ʃnəl, -ʃṇl,
 -ʃṇl, -ʃənəl]
operative (*s.*), **-s** 'ɒpərətɪv, -z
operative (*adj.*), **-ly, -ness** 'ɒpərətɪv
 ['ɒpəreɪtɪv], -lɪ, -nɪs [-nəs]
operetta, -s ,ɒpə'retə, -z
Ophelia ɒ'fi:ljə [əʊ'f-, -lɪə]
ophicleide, -s 'ɒfɪklaɪd, -z
ophidia, -n ɒ'fɪdɪə [əʊ'f-], -n
Ophir 'əʊfə* [*rarely* -,fɪə*]
Ophiuchus ɒ'fju:kəs
ophthalm|ia, -ic ɒf'θælm|ɪə [ɒp'θ-,
 -m|jə], -ɪk
ophthalmolog|ist/s, -y ,ɒfθæl'mɒlədʒ|-
 ɪst/s [,ɒpθ-], -ɪ
ophthalmoscope, -s ɒf'θælməskəʊp
 [ɒp'θ-], -s
ophthalmoscopy ,ɒfθæl'mɒskəpɪ [,ɒp-]
opiate, -s 'əʊpɪət [-pjət, -pɪɪt, -pjɪt,
 -pɪeɪt, -pjeɪt], -s
opiated 'əʊpɪeɪtɪd
Opie 'əʊpɪ
opin|e, -es, -ing, -ed əʊ'paɪn, -z, -ɪŋ,
 -d
opinion, -s; -ated ə'pɪnjən, -z; -eɪtɪd
opium; -den/s 'əʊpjəm [-pɪəm]; -den/z
opium-eater, -s 'əʊpjəm,i:tə* [-pɪəm-],
 -z
opodeldoc ,ɒpəʊ'deldɒk [-dək]
opopanax əʊ'pɒpənæks
Oporto əʊ'pɔːtəʊ (*Port.* u'portu)
opossum, -s ə'pɒsəm, -z
Oppenheim, -er 'ɒpənhaɪm, -ə*
oppidan (*s. adj.*), **-s** 'ɒpɪdən, -z
opponent, -s ə'pəʊnənt, -s
opportune, -ly, -ness 'ɒpətju:n [-tʃu:n,
 ,ɒpə'tju:n], -lɪ, -nɪs [-nəs]
opportuni|sm, -st/s 'ɒpətju:nɪ|zəm
 [-tjʊn-, -tʃu:n-, ,ɒpə'tju:n-], -st/s
opportunit|y, -ies ,ɒpə'tju:nət|ɪ [-'tjʊn-,
 -nɪt-, -'tju:ṇt|ɪ], -ɪz
oppos|e, -es, -ing, -ed, -er/s; -able
 ə'pəʊz, -ɪz, -ɪŋ, -d, -ə*/z; -əbl
opposite, -ly, -ness 'ɒpəzɪt [-əsɪt], -lɪ,
 -nɪs [-nəs]
opposition, -s ,ɒpə'zɪʃn [-pəʊ'z-], -z
oppress, -es, -ing, -ed, -or/s ə'pres, -ɪz,
 -ɪŋ, -t, -ə*/z
oppression, -s ə'preʃn, -z

oppressive, -ly, -ness ə'presɪv, -lɪ, -nɪs [-nəs]

opprobrious, -ly, -ness ə'prəubrɪəs [ɒ'p-], -lɪ, -nɪs [-nəs]

opprobrium ə'prəubrɪəm [ɒ'p-]

oppugn, -s, -ing, -ed, -er/s ə'pju:n [ɒ'p-], -z, -ɪŋ, -d, -ə*/z

oppugnan|cy, -t ɒ'pʌgnən|sɪ, -t

opt, -s, -ing, -ed ɒpt, -s, -ɪŋ, -ɪd

optative (s. adj.), -s 'ɒptətɪv [ɒp'teɪtɪv], -z

optic (s. v.), -s, -al, -ally 'ɒptɪk, -s, -l, -əlɪ

optician, -s ɒp'tɪʃn, -z

optim|al, -ally 'ɒptɪm|l, -əlɪ

optimate 'ɒptɪmət [-mɪt, -meɪt]

optimates ˌɒptɪ'meɪti:z

optime, -s 'ɒptɪmɪ, -z

optimi|sm, -st/s 'ɒptɪmɪ|zəm [-təm-], -st/s

optimistic, -al, -ally ˌɒptɪ'mɪstɪk [-tə'm-], -l, -əlɪ

optimum 'ɒptɪməm

option, -s 'ɒpʃn, -z

op|tional, -tionally 'ɒp|ʃənl [-ʃnəl, -ʃn̩l, -ʃnl, -ʃənəl], -ʃnəlɪ [-ʃnəlɪ, -ʃn̩lɪ, -ʃnlɪ, -ʃənəlɪ]

†optometric, -s ˌɒptəʊ'metrɪk, -s

opulen|ce, -t 'ɒpjʊlən|s [-pjə-], -t

opus 'əupəs ['ɒpəs]

opuscule, -s ɒ'pʌskju:l [əʊ'p-], -z

or (s.) ɔ:*

or (conj.) ɔ:* (normal form), ə* (occasional weak form)
Note.—The weak form is chiefly used in common phrases, such as two or three minutes.

orach|(e), -es 'ɒrɪtʃ, -ɪz

oracle, -s 'ɒrəkl [-rɪk-], -z

oracular, -ly, -ness ɒ'rækjʊlə* [ɔ:'r-, ə'r-, -kjə-], -lɪ, -nɪs [-nəs]

oracy 'ɔ:rəsɪ

or|al (s. adj.), -als, -ally 'ɔ:r|əl ['ɒr-], -əlz, -əlɪ [-l̩ɪ]

Oran ɔ:'rɑ:n [ɒ'r-, -'ræn]

orange (s. adj.) (O.), -s 'ɒrɪndʒ [-əndʒ], -ɪz

orangeade ˌɒrɪndʒ'eɪd [-əndʒ-]

orange-blossom, -s 'ɒrɪndʒˌblɒsəm [-əndʒ-], -z

orange-coloured 'ɒrɪndʒˌkʌləd [-əndʒ-]

orange-juice 'ɒrɪndʒdʒu:s [-əndʒ-]

Orange|man, -men 'ɒrɪndʒ|mən [-əndʒ-, -mæn], -mən [-men]

orange-peel 'ɒrɪndʒpi:l [-əndʒ-]

oranger|y, -ies 'ɒrɪndʒər|ɪ [-əndʒ-], -ɪz

orange-tree, -s 'ɒrɪndʒtri: [-əndʒ-], -z

orange-yellow ˌɒrɪndʒ'jeləʊ [-əndʒ-]

orang-outa|n/s, -ng/s ɔ:ˌræŋu:'tæ|n/z [ɒˌræŋ-, əˌræŋ-, -ʊ'tæ|n, -'tɑ:|n, ˌɒːrəŋ'u:tɑ:|n, -tæ|n], -ŋ/z

orat|e, -es, -ing, -ed ɔ:'reɪt [ɒ'r-, ə'r-], -s, -ɪŋ, -ɪd

oration, -s ɔ:'reɪʃn [ɒ'r-, ə'r-], -z

oratio obliqua ɒˌrɑ:tɪəʊ ɒ'bli:kwə [ɔ:ˌr-, əˌr-, ə'b-, old-fashioned əˌreɪʃɪəʊ ə'blaɪkwə]

orator, -s 'ɒrətə* [-rɪt-], -z

oratoric|al, -ally ˌɒrə'tɒrɪk|l, -əlɪ

oratorio, -s ˌɒrə'tɔ:rɪəʊ, -z

orator|y (O.), -ies 'ɒrətər|ɪ, -ɪz

orb (s. v.), -s, -ing, -ed ɔ:b, -z, -ɪŋ, -d

orbed (adj.) ɔ:bd [in poetry generally 'ɔ:bɪd]

orbicular, -ness ɔ:'bɪkjʊlə* [-kjə-], -nɪs [-nəs]

orbit, -s, -al 'ɔ:bɪt, -s, -l

orc, -s ɔ:k, -s

Orcadian, -s ɔ:'keɪdjən [-dɪən], -z

orchard (O.), -s 'ɔ:tʃəd, -z

Orchardson 'ɔ:tʃədsən

Orchehill 'ɔ:tʃɪl

orchestra, -s 'ɔ:kɪstrə [-kes-, -kəs-], -z

orchestral ɔ:'kestrəl

orchestrat|e, -es, -ing, -ed 'ɔ:kɪstreɪt [-kes-, -kəs-], -s, -ɪŋ, -ɪd

orchestration, -s ˌɔ:ke'streɪʃn [-kɪ's-, -kə's-], -z

orchestrion, -s ɔ:'kestrɪən, -z

orchid, -s 'ɔ:kɪd, -z

orchidaceous ˌɔ:kɪ'deɪʃəs

orchideous ɔ:'kɪdɪəs

orchil 'ɔ:tʃɪl

orchis, -es 'ɔ:kɪs, -ɪz

Orchy 'ɔ:kɪ ['ɔ:xɪ] (Scottish 'ɔrxɪ)

Orczy 'ɔ:ksɪ ['ɔ:tsɪ]

Ord ɔ:d

ordain, -s, -ing, -ed, -er/s ɔ:'deɪn, -z, -ɪŋ, -d, -ə*/z

Orde ɔ:d

ordeal, -s ɔ:'di:l [-'di:əl, -'dɪəl], -z

ord|er (s. v.), -ers, -ering, -ered; -erless 'ɔ:d|ə*, -əz, -ərɪŋ, -əd; -əlɪs [-ləs]

orderl|y (s. adj.), -ies, -iness 'ɔ:dəl|ɪ, -ɪz, -ɪnɪs [-ɪnəs]

ordinaire ˌɔ:dɪ'neə* ['ɔ:dɪneə*] (ɔrdinɛ:r)

ordinal (s. adj.), -s 'ɔ:dɪnl, -z

ordinance, -s 'ɔ:dɪnəns [-dn̩əns], -ɪz

ordinand, -s 'ɔ:dɪnænd [ˌ--'-], -z

ordinar|y (s. adj.), -ies, -ily 'ɔ:dnr|ɪ [-dɪnər-, -dənər-, -dnər-], -ɪz, -əlɪ [-ɪlɪ]

ordinate, -s 'ɔ:dnət [-dɪnət, -dɪnɪt], -s

ordination, -s ˌɔ:dɪ'neɪʃn, -z

ordnance 'ɔ:dnəns

ordure 'ɔ:ˌdjʊə* [-djwə*]

353

ore (O.), -s ɔː* [ɔə*], -z
oread, -s 'ɔːriæd, -z
Oreb 'ɔːreb
O'Regan əʊ'riːgən
Oregon 'ɒrɪgən [-gɒn]
O'|Reilly, -Rell əʊ|'raɪlɪ, -'rel
Orellana ˌɒre'lɑːnə [-rɪ'l-]
Orestes ɒ'restiːz [ɔː'r-, ə'r-]
Orford 'ɔːfəd
organ, -s; -blower/s, -builder/s, -case/s
'ɔːgən, -z; -ˌbləʊə*/z, -ˌbɪldə*/z,
-keɪs/ɪz
organd|y [-ie], -ies 'ɔːgənd|ɪ [ɔː'gæn-],
-ɪz
organ-grinder, -s 'ɔːgənˌgraɪndə*
['ɔːgŋˌg-], -z
organic, -al, -ally ɔː'gænɪk, -l, -əlɪ
organism, -s 'ɔːgənɪzəm [-gŋɪzəm], -z
organist, -s 'ɔːgənɪst [-gŋɪst], -s
organizability [-isa-] 'ɔːgəˌnaɪzə'bɪlətɪ
[-gŋˌaɪ-, -lɪt-]
organization [-isa-], -s ˌɔːgənaɪ'zeɪʃn
[-gŋaɪ'z-, -gənɪ'z-, -gŋɪ'z-], -z
organiz|e [-is|e], -es, -ing, -ed, -er/s;
-able 'ɔːgənaɪz [-gŋaɪz], -ɪz, -ɪŋ, -d,
-ə*/z; -əbl
organ-loft, -s 'ɔːgənlɒft, -s
organon, -s 'ɔːgənɒn, -z
organ-pipe, -s 'ɔːgənpaɪp, -s
organ-screen, -s 'ɔːgənskriːn, -z
organum, -s 'ɔːgənəm, -z
orgasm, -s 'ɔːgæzəm, -z
org|y, -ies 'ɔːdʒ|ɪ, -ɪz
Oriana ˌɒrɪ'ɑːnə [ˌɔːr-]
oriel (O.), -s 'ɔːrɪəl, -z
orient (s. adj.) (O.) 'ɔːrɪənt ['ɒr-]
orient (v.), -s, -ing, -ed 'ɔːrɪent ['ɒr-], -s,
-ɪŋ, -ɪd
oriental (s. adj.) (O.), -s ˌɔːrɪ'entl [ˌɒr-],
-z
orientali|sm, -st/s ˌɔːrɪ'entəlɪ|zəm
[ˌɒr-, -tʃɪ-], -st/s
orientaliz|e [-is|e], -es, -ing, -ed ˌɔːrɪ'en-
təlaɪz [ˌɒr-, -tʃaɪz], -ɪz, -ɪŋ, -d
orientat|e, -es, -ing, -ed 'ɔːrɪenteɪt
['ɒr-, -rɪən-, ˌɔːrɪ'enteɪt, ˌɒrɪ'en-], -s,
-ɪŋ, -ɪd
orientation, -s ˌɔːrɪen'teɪʃn [ˌɒr-, -rɪən-],
-z
orifice, -s 'ɒrɪfɪs, -ɪz
oriflamme, -s 'ɒrɪflæm, -z
Origen 'ɒrɪdʒen
origin, -s 'ɒrɪdʒɪn, -z
original (s. adj.), -s; -ness ə'rɪdʒənl
[ɒ'r-, -dʒɪnl, -dʒŋ̩, -dʒn̩l, -dʒənəl], -z;
-nɪs [-nəs]
originalit|y, -ies əˌrɪdʒə'nælət|ɪ [ɒˌr-
-dʒɪ'n-, -ɪt|ɪ], -ɪz

originally ə'rɪdʒənəlɪ [ɒ'r-, -dʒɪnəlɪ,
-dʒnəlɪ, -dʒŋ̩lɪ, -dʒn̩lɪ, -dʒŋ̩əlɪ]
originat|e, -es, -ing, -ed, -or/s; -ive
ə'rɪdʒəneɪt [ɒ'r-, -dʒɪn-], -s, -ɪŋ, -ɪd,
-ə*/z; -ɪv
origination əˌrɪdʒə'neɪʃn [ɒˌr- -dʒɪ'n-]
Orinoco ˌɒrɪ'nəʊkəʊ
oriole, -s 'ɔːrɪəʊl, -z
Orion ə'raɪən [ɒ'r-, ɔː'r-]
O'Riordan əʊ'rɪədən, -'raɪəd-
orison, -s 'ɒrɪzən, -z
Orissa ɒ'rɪsə [ɔː'r-, ə'r-]
Orkney, -s 'ɔːknɪ, -z
Orlando ɔː'lændəʊ
Orleanist, -s ɔː'lɪənɪst, -s
Orleans (in France) ɔː'lɪənz ['ɔːlɪənz,
'ɔːljənz] (ɔrleã), (in U.S.A.) 'ɔːlɪənz
[-ljənz, ɔː'liːnz]
Orlon 'ɔːlɒn
Orly 'ɔːlɪ (ɔrli)
Orm(e) ɔːm
Ormelie 'ɔːmɪlɪ
ormer, -s 'ɔːmə*, -z
Ormes, -by ɔːmz, -bɪ
Ormiston 'ɔːmɪstən
ormolu 'ɔːməʊluː [-ljuː] (ɔrmɔly,
pronounced as if French)
Ormond(e) 'ɔːmənd
Orms|by, -kirk 'ɔːmz|bɪ, -kɜːk
Ormulum 'ɔːmjʊləm
Ormuz 'ɔːmʌz
ornament (s.), -s 'ɔːnəmənt, -s
ornament (v.), -s, -ing, -ed 'ɔːnəment,
-s, -ɪŋ, -ɪd
ornament|al, -ally ˌɔːnə'ment|l, -əlɪ [-l̩ɪ]
ornamentation, -s ˌɔːnəmen'teɪʃn, -z
Ornan 'ɔːnæn
ornate, -ly, -ness ɔː'neɪt ['ɔːneɪt], -lɪ,
-nɪs [-nəs]
ornithologic|al, -ally ˌɔːnɪθə'lɒdʒɪk|l,
-əlɪ
ornitholog|ist/s, -y ˌɔːnɪ'θɒlədʒ|ɪst/s, -ɪ
orographic, -al ˌɒrəʊ'græfɪk [ˌɔːr-], -l
orography ɒ'rɒgrəfɪ [ɔː'r-]
orological ˌɒrə'lɒdʒɪkl [ˌɔːr-]
orology ɒ'rɒlədʒɪ [ɔː'r-]
Oronsay 'ɒrənseɪ [-nzeɪ]
Orontes ɒ'rɒntiːz [ə'r-]
Oroonoko ˌɒru'nəʊkəʊ
Orosius ə'rəʊsjəs [ɒ'r-, -sɪəs]
orotund 'ɒrəʊtʌnd ['ɔːr-]
O'Rourke əʊ'rɔːk
Orpah 'ɔːpə
orphan, -s 'ɔːfn, -z
orphanage, -s 'ɔːfənɪdʒ [-fŋ̩ɪ-], -ɪz
Orphean ɔː'fiːən [-'fɪən]
Orpheus 'ɔːfjuːs
orpiment 'ɔːpɪmənt

Orpington, -s 'ɔːpɪŋtən, -z
Orr ɔː*
Orrell 'ɒrəl
orrer|y (O.), -ies 'ɒrər|ɪ, -ɪz
orris 'ɒrɪs
Orrm, -in ɔːm, -ɪn
Orrock 'ɒrək
Orsino ɔː'siːnəʊ
Orson 'ɔːsn
Orth ɔːθ
orthochromatic ˌɔːθəʊkrəʊ'mætɪk
orthodonti|cs, -st/s ˌɔːθəʊ'dɒntɪ|ks, -st/s
orthodox, -ly 'ɔːθədɒks, -lɪ
orthodox|y, -ies 'ɔːθədɒks|ɪ, -ɪz
orthoepical ˌɔːθəʊ'epɪkl
orthoep|ist/s, -y 'ɔːθəʊep|ɪst/s [ɔː'θəʊɪp-, ˌɔːθəʊ'ep-], -ɪ
orthogonal ɔː'θɒgənl
orthographer, -s ɔː'θɒgrəfə*, -z
orthographic, -al, -ally ˌɔːθəʊ'græfɪk, -l, -əlɪ
orthograph|ist/s, -y ɔː'θɒgrəf|ɪst/s, -ɪ
orthopaedic [-ped-], -s ˌɔːθəʊ'piːdɪk, -s
orthopaedy [-ped-] 'ɔːθəʊpiːdɪ
orthopterous ɔː'θɒptərəs
orthoptic, -s ɔː'θɒptɪk, -s
Ortler 'ɔːtlə*
ortolan, -s 'ɔːtələn, -z
Orton 'ɔːtn
Orville 'ɔːvɪl
Orwell 'ɔːwəl [-wel]
oryx, -es 'ɒrɪks, -ɪz
Osage əʊ'seɪdʒ ['əʊseɪdʒ]
Osaka 'ɔːsəkə [əʊ'sɑːkə]
Osbaldiston(e) ˌɒzbəl'dɪstən
Osbert 'ɒzbət [-bɜːt]
Osborn(e) 'ɒzbən [-bɔːn]
Osbourne 'ɒzbən [-bɔːn]
Oscan, -s 'ɒskən, -z
Oscar, -s 'ɒskə*, -z
oscillat|e, -es, -ing, -ed, -or/s 'ɒsɪleɪt [-səl-], -s, -ɪŋ, -ɪd, -ə*/z
oscillation, -s ˌɒsɪ'leɪʃn [-sə'l-], -z
oscillatory 'ɒsɪlətərɪ [-leɪtərɪ]
oscillogram, -s ə'sɪləʊgræm [ɒ's-], -z
oscillograph, -s ə'sɪləʊgrɑːf [ɒ's-, -græf], -s
osculant 'ɒskjʊlənt
osculat|e, -es, -ing, -ed 'ɒskjʊleɪt, -s, -ɪŋ, -ɪd
osculation, -s ˌɒskjʊ'leɪʃn, -z
osculator|y (s.), -ies 'ɒskjʊlətər|ɪ, -ɪz
osculatory (adj.) 'ɒskjʊlətərɪ [-leɪtərɪ]
Osgood 'ɒzgʊd
O'Shaughnessy əʊ'ʃɔːnɪsɪ [-nəsɪ]
O'Shea əʊ'ʃeɪ

osier, -s 'əʊzɪə* ['əʊʒjə*, -ʒɪə*, 'əʊzjə*, -ʒə*], -z
Osirian, -s əʊ'saɪərɪən [ɒ's-], -z
Osiris əʊ'saɪərɪs [ɒ's-]
Osler 'əʊzlə*, 'əʊslə*
Oslo 'ɒzləʊ ['ɒsləʊ]
Osman ɒz'mɑːn [ɒs'mɑːn]
Osmanli, -s ɒz'mænlɪ [ɒs'm-, -'mɑːn-], -z
osmium 'ɒzmɪəm [-mjəm]
Osmond 'ɒzmənd
osmosis ɒz'məʊsɪs
osmotic ɒz'mɒtɪk
osmund (O.), -s 'ɒzmənd, -z
osmunda, -s ɒz'mʌndə, -z
Osnaburg(h) 'ɒznəbɜːg
osprey, -s 'ɒsprɪ ['ɒspreɪ], -z
Ospringe 'ɒsprɪndʒ
Ossa 'ɒsə
osseous 'ɒsɪəs [-sjəs]
Ossett 'ɒsɪt
Ossian 'ɒsɪən [-sjən]
Ossianic ˌɒsɪ'ænɪk
ossicle, -s 'ɒsɪkl, -z
ossification ˌɒsɪfɪ'keɪʃn
ossifrage, -s 'ɒsɪfrɪdʒ, -ɪz
ossi|fy, -fies, -fying, -fied 'ɒsɪ|faɪ, -faɪz, -faɪɪŋ, -faɪd
Ossory 'ɒsərɪ
ossuar|y, -ies 'ɒsjʊər|ɪ [-sjwə-], -ɪz
Ostend ɒ'stend
ostensibility ɒˌstensɪ'bɪlətɪ [-sə'b-, -lɪt-]
ostensib|le, -ly ɒ'stensəb|l [-sɪb-], -lɪ
ostentation ˌɒsten'teɪʃn [-tən-]
ostentatious, -ly, -ness ˌɒsten'teɪʃəs [-tən-], -lɪ, -nɪs [-nəs]
osteologic|al, -ally ˌɒstɪə'lɒdʒɪk|l [-tjə'l-, -tɪəʊ'l-], -əlɪ
osteolog|ist/s, -y ˌɒstɪ'ɒlədʒ|ɪst/s, -ɪ
osteopath, -s 'ɒstɪəpæθ [-tjəʊp-, -tɪəʊp-], -s
osteopathic ˌɒstɪə'pæθɪk [-tjəʊ'p-, -tɪəʊ'p-]
osteopath|ist/s, -y ˌɒstɪ'ɒpəθ|ɪst/s, -ɪ
Osterley 'ɒstəlɪ
Ostia 'ɒstɪə [-tjə]
ostiar|y, -ies 'ɒstɪər|ɪ [-tjə-], -ɪz
osti|um (O.), -a 'ɒstɪ|əm [-tj|əm], -ə
ostler, -s 'ɒslə*, -z
ostracism 'ɒstrəsɪzəm
ostraciz|e [-is|e], -es, -ing, -ed 'ɒstrə-saɪz, -ɪz, -ɪŋ, -d
ostrich, -es; -feather/s 'ɒstrɪtʃ [-ɪdʒ], -ɪz; -ˌfeðə*/z
Ostrogoth, -s 'ɒstrəʊgɒθ, -s
O'Sullivan əʊ'sʌlɪvən
Oswald 'ɒzwəld
Oswaldtwistle 'ɒzwəldtwɪsl

Oswego, -s ɒz'wi:gəʊ, -z
Oswestry 'ɒzwəstrɪ [-wɪs-, -wes-]
Otago (*in New Zealand*) əʊ'ta:gəʊ [ɒ't-]
Otaheite ˌəʊta:'heɪtɪ [-tə'h-]
otar|y, -ies 'əʊtər|ɪ, -ɪz
Ot|ford, -fried 'ɒt|fəd, -fri:d
Othello əʊ'θeləʊ [ɒ'θ-]
other, -s; -wise 'ʌðə*, -z; -waɪz
Othman ɒθ'ma:n
Othniel 'ɒθnɪəl [-njəl]
Otho 'əʊθəʊ
otiose, -ly, -ness 'əʊtɪəʊs [-tjəʊs, 'əʊʃɪəʊs, -ʃəʊs], -lɪ, -nɪs [-nəs]
otiosity ˌəʊtɪ'ɒsətɪ [ˌəʊʃɪ-, -ɪtɪ]
Otis 'əʊtɪs
otitis əʊ'taɪtɪs
Otley 'ɒtlɪ
otolaryngolog|y, -ist/s 'əʊtəʊˌlærɪŋ-'gɒlədʒ|ɪ [-ˌleər-], -ɪst/s
otolog|ist/s, -y əʊ'tɒlədʒ|ɪst/s, -ɪ
otoscope, -s 'əʊtəskəʊp, -s
Otranto ɒ'træntəʊ ['ɒtrəntəʊ] ('ɔ:tranto)
Otsego ɒt'si:gəʊ
Ottaw|a, -ay 'ɒtəw|ə, -eɪ
otter, -s 'ɒtə*, -z
Otterburn 'ɒtəbɜ:n
otter-hound, -s 'ɒtəhaʊnd, -z
Ott|ery, -ley 'ɒt|ərɪ, -lɪ
otto (O.) 'ɒtəʊ
ottoman (O.), -s 'ɒtəʊmən, -z
Ottoway 'ɒtəweɪ
Otway 'ɒtweɪ
oubliette, -s ˌu:blɪ'et, -s
Oubridge 'u:brɪdʒ
Oude aʊd
Oudenarde 'u:dəna:d [-dɪn-]
Oudh aʊd
Ough əʊ
Ougham 'əʊkəm
ought, -n't ɔ:t, -nt [*occasionally also* 'ɔ:tn *when not final*]
Oughter (*Lough*) 'u:ktə*
Oughterard ˌu:tə'ra:d
Oughton 'aʊtn, 'ɔ:tn
Oughtred 'ɔ:tred [-rɪd], 'u:t-, 'aʊt-
Ouida 'wi:də
ouija 'wi:dʒə [-dʒa:]
Ouin (*surname*) 'əʊɪn
Ould əʊld
Ouless 'u:lɪs [-les]
ounce, -s aʊns, -ɪz
Oundle 'aʊndl
our, -s 'aʊə* [a:*], -z
oursel|f, -ves ˌaʊə'sel|f [a:-], -vz
Oury 'aʊərɪ
Ouse u:z
ousel, -s 'u:zl, -z

Ouseley 'u:zlɪ
Ousey 'u:zɪ
Ousley (*in U.S.A.*) 'aʊslɪ
oust, -s, -ing, -ed, -er/s aʊst, -s, -ɪŋ, -ɪd, -ə*/z
Ouston 'aʊstən
out aʊt
out-and-out ˌaʊtnd'aʊt [ˌaʊtn̩'aʊt]
outback 'aʊtbæk
outbalanc|e, -es, -ing, -ed ˌaʊt'bæləns, -ɪz, -ɪŋ, -t
outbid, -s, -ding ˌaʊt'bɪd, -z, -ɪŋ
outboard 'aʊtbɔ:d [-bəəd]
outbound 'aʊtbaʊnd
outbrav|e, -es, -ing, -ed ˌaʊt'breɪv, -z, -ɪŋ, -d
out|break/s, -building/s, -burst/s 'aʊt|breɪk/s, -ˌbɪldɪŋ/z, -bɜ:st/s
outcast, -s 'aʊtka:st, -s
outcast|e (*s. adj. v.*), **-es, -ing, -ed** 'aʊt-ka:st, -s, -ɪŋ, -ɪd
outclass, -es, -ing, -ed ˌaʊt'kla:s, -ɪz, -ɪŋ, -t
out|come/s, -crop/s, -cry, -cries 'aʊt|-kʌm/z, -krɒp/s, -kraɪ, -kraɪz
outdar|e, -es, -ing, -ed ˌaʊt'deə*, -z, -rɪŋ, -d
outdistanc|e, -es, -ing, -ed ˌaʊt'dɪstəns, -ɪz, -ɪŋ, -t
out|do, -does, -doing, -did, -done ˌaʊt|'du:, -'dʌz, -'du:ɪŋ [-'dʊɪŋ], -'dɪd, -'dʌn
outdoor 'aʊtdɔ:* [-dəə*]
outdoors ˌaʊt'dɔ:z [-'dəəz]
outer, -most 'aʊtə*, -məʊst [-məst]
outerwear 'aʊtəweə*
outfac|e, -s, -ing, -ed ˌaʊt'feɪs, -ɪz, -ɪŋ, -t
outfall, -s 'aʊtfɔ:l, -z
outfield, -s, -er/s 'aʊtfi:ld, -z, -ə*/z
outfit (*s. v.*), **-s, -ting, -ted, -ter/s** 'aʊt-fɪt, -s, -ɪŋ, -ɪd, -ə*/z
outflank, -s, -ing, -ed ˌaʊt'flæŋk, -s, -ɪŋ, -t [-'flæŋt]
outflow (*s.*), **-s** 'aʊtfləʊ, -z
outfl|ow (*v.*), **-ows, -owing, -owed** ˌaʊt-'fl|əʊ, -əʊz, -əʊɪŋ, -əʊd
outgener|al, -als, -alling, -alled ˌaʊt-'dʒenər|əl, -əlz, -əlɪŋ, -əld
outgo (*s.*), **-es** 'aʊtgəʊ, -z
out|go (*v.*), **-goes, -going, -went, -gone** ˌaʊt|'gəʊ, -'gəʊz, -'gəʊɪŋ, -'went, -'gɒn
outgoer, -s 'aʊtˌgəʊə*, -z
outgoing (*s. adj.*), **-s** 'aʊtˌgəʊɪŋ, -z
outgrow (*s.*), **-s** 'aʊtgrəʊ, -z
out|grow (*v.*), **-grows, -growing, -grew, -grown** ˌaʊt|'grəʊ, -'grəʊz, -'grəʊɪŋ, -'gru:, -'grəʊn

356

outgrowth, -s 'aʊtgrəʊθ, -s
outguard, -s 'aʊtgɑːd, -z
out-herod, -s, -ing, -ed ˌaʊt'herəd, -z, -ɪŋ, -ɪd
outhou|se, -ses 'aʊthaʊ|s, -zɪz
Outhwaite 'uːθweɪt, 'əʊθweɪt, 'aʊθweɪt
Note.—More commonly 'uːθ-.
outing, -s 'aʊtɪŋ, -z
Outis 'aʊtɪs
Outlander, -s 'aʊtˌlændə*, -z
outlandish, -ly, -ness aʊt'lændɪʃ, -lɪ, -nɪs [-nəs]
outlast, -s, -ing, -ed ˌaʊt'lɑːst, -s, -ɪŋ, -ɪd
outlaw (s. v.), -s, -ing, -ed; -ry 'aʊtlɔː, -z, -ɪŋ, -d; -rɪ
outlay (s.), -s 'aʊtleɪ, -z
outlay (v.), -s, -ing, outlaid aʊt'leɪ, -z, -ɪŋ, aʊt'leɪd
outlet, -s 'aʊtlet [-lɪt], -s
outlier, -s 'aʊtˌlaɪə*, -z
outlin|e (s. v.), -es, -ing, -ed 'aʊtlaɪn, -z, -ɪŋ, -d
outliv|e, -es, -ing, -ed ˌaʊt'lɪv, -z, -ɪŋ, -d
outlook, -s 'aʊtlʊk, -s
outlying 'aʊtˌlaɪɪŋ
outmanœuv|re, -res, -ring, -red ˌaʊtmə'nuːv|ə*, -əz, -ərɪŋ, -əd
outmarch, -es, -ing, -ed ˌaʊt'mɑːtʃ, -ɪz, -ɪŋ, -t
outmatch, -es, -ing, -ed ˌaʊt'mætʃ, -ɪz, -ɪŋ, -t
outmoded ˌaʊt'məʊdɪd
outmost 'aʊtməʊst
outnumb|er, -ers, -ering, -ered ˌaʊt'nʌmb|ə*, -əz, -ərɪŋ, -əd
out-of-doors ˌaʊtəv'dɔːz [-'dɔəz]
out-of-the-way ˌaʊtəvðə'weɪ [-təð-]
outpac|e, -es, -ing, -ed ˌaʊt'peɪs, -ɪz, -ɪŋ, -t
outpatient, -s 'aʊtˌpeɪʃnt, -s
outplay, -s, -ing, -ed ˌaʊt'pleɪ, -z, -ɪŋ, -d
outport, -s 'aʊtpɔːt, -s
outpost, -s 'aʊtpəʊst, -s
outpour (s.), -s 'aʊtpɔː* [-pɔə*], -z
outpour (v.), -s, -ing, -ed ˌaʊt'pɔː* [-'pɔə*], -z, -rɪŋ, -d
outpouring (s.), -s 'aʊtˌpɔːrɪŋ [-ˌpɔər-], -z
output, -s 'aʊtpʊt, -s
outrag|e (s. v.), -es, -ing, -ed 'aʊtreɪdʒ [-rɪdʒ], -ɪz, -ɪŋ, -d
outrageous, -ly, -ness aʊt'reɪdʒəs, -lɪ, -nɪs [-nəs]
Outram 'uːtrəm
outrang|e, -es, -ing, -ed ˌaʊt'reɪndʒ, -ɪz, -ɪŋ, -d

outrank, -s, -ing, -ed aʊt'ræŋk, -s, -ɪŋ, -t
outré 'uːtreɪ (utre)
outreach (s.), -es 'aʊtriːtʃ, -ɪz
outreach (v.), -es, -ing, -ed ˌaʊt'riːtʃ, -ɪz, -ɪŋ, -t
Outred 'uːtrɪd [-red]
out|ride, -rides, -riding, -rode, -ridden ˌaʊt|'raɪd, -'raɪdz, -'raɪdɪŋ, -'rəʊd, -'rɪdn
outrider, -s 'aʊtˌraɪdə*, -z
outrigger, -s 'aʊtˌrɪgə*, -z
outright (adj.) 'aʊtraɪt, (adv.) aʊt'raɪt
outriv|al, -als, -alling, -alled ˌaʊt'raɪv|l, -lz, -lɪŋ [-əlɪŋ], -ld
out|run, -runs, -running, -ran ˌaʊt|'rʌn, -'rʌnz, -'rʌnɪŋ, -'ræn
outrush, -es 'aʊtrʌʃ, -ɪz
out|sell, -sells, -selling, -sold ˌaʊt|'sel, -'selz, -'selɪŋ, -'səʊld
outset, -s 'aʊtset, -s
out|shine, -shines, -shining, -shined, -shone ˌaʊt|'ʃaɪn, -'ʃaɪnz, -'ʃaɪnɪŋ, -'ʃaɪnd, -'ʃɒn
outside (s. adj. adv. prep.), -s ˌaʊt'saɪd ['-- according to sentence-stress], -z
outsider, -s ˌaʊt'saɪdə*, -z
outsize, -s, -d 'aʊtsaɪz, -ɪz, -d
outskirt, -s 'aʊtskɜːt, -s
Outspan, -s 'aʊtspæn, -z
outspan (v.), -s, -ning, -ned ˌaʊt'spæn, -z, -ɪŋ, -d
outspok|en, -enly, -enness ˌaʊt'spəʊk|ən, -ənlɪ [-ŋlɪ], -ənnɪs [-ŋnɪs, -nəs]
outspread ˌaʊt'spred ['-- according to sentence-stress]
outstanding (conspicuous, undone, remaining due) ˌaʊt'stændɪŋ, (sticking out (ears)) 'aʊtˌstændɪŋ
outstar|e, -es, -ing, -ed ˌaʊt'steə*, -z, -rɪŋ, -d
outstay, -s, -ing, -ed ˌaʊt'steɪ, -z, -ɪŋ, -d
outstretch, -es, -ing, -ed ˌaʊt'stretʃ, -ɪz, -ɪŋ, -t ['aʊtstretʃt when attributive]
outstrip, -s, -ping, -ped ˌaʊt'strɪp, -s, -ɪŋ, -t
outtop, -s, -ping, -ped ˌaʊt'tɒp, -s, -ɪŋ, -t
outv|ie, -ies, -ying, -ied ˌaʊt'v|aɪ, -aɪz, -aɪɪŋ, -aɪd
outvot|e, -es, -ing, -ed ˌaʊt'vəʊt, -s, -ɪŋ, -ɪd
out-voter (non-resident voter), -s 'aʊtˌvəʊtə*, -z
outwalk, -s, -ing, -ed ˌaʊt'wɔːk, -s, -ɪŋ, -t
outward, -s, -ly, -ness 'aʊtwəd, -z, -lɪ, -nɪs [-nəs]

357

outwear, -s, -ing, outworn ˌaʊtˈ
-z, -rɪŋ, ˌaʊtˈwɔːn [ˈaʊtwɔːn
attributive]
outweigh, -s, -ing, -ed ˌaʊtˈweɪ, -z
-d
outwent (*from* outgo) ˌaʊtˈwent
outwit, -s, -ting, -ted ˌaʊtˈwɪt, -s, -ɪŋ,
-ɪd
outwork (*s.*), **-s** ˈaʊtwɜːk, -s
outwork (*v.*), **-s, -ing, -ed** ˌaʊtˈwɜːk, -s,
-ɪŋ, -t
out-worker, -s ˈaʊtˌwɜːkə*, -z
outworn (*when attributive*) ˈaʊtwɔːn,
(*when not attributive*) ˌaʊtˈwɔːn
ouzel, -s ˈuːzl, -z
ouzo ˈuːzəʊ
ova (*plur. of* ovum) ˈəʊvə
ov|al (*s. adj.*), **-als, -ally** ˈəʊv|l, -lz, -əlɪ
ovaria|l, -n əʊˈveərɪə|l, -n
ovariotomy əʊˌveərɪˈɒtəmɪ [ˌəʊveə-]
ovar|y, -ies ˈəʊvər|ɪ, -ɪz
ovate (*s.*) (*Welsh title*), **-s** ˈɒvɪt, -s
ovate (*adj.*) (*egg-shaped*) ˈəʊveɪt [-vɪt]
ovation, -s əʊˈveɪʃn, -z
oven, -s; -bird/s; -ware ˈʌvn, -z;
-bɜːd/z; -weə*
over (*s. adj. prep.*), **-s** ˈəʊvə*, -z
Note—Compounds with over- *not entered
below have double stress, and their pro-
nunciation may be ascertained by refer-
ring to the simple words. Thus* **over-
eager, over-peopled** *are pro-
nounced* ˌəʊvərˈiːgə*, ˌəʊvəˈpiːpld.
*In all the compounds listed, the main
stress may shift to* ˈover *when another
stressed word follows.*
over-abundan|ce, -t ˌəʊvərəˈbʌndən|s,
-t
overact, -s, -ing, -ed ˌəʊvərˈækt
[ˌəʊvəˈækt], -s, -ɪŋ, -ɪd
overall (*s. adj.*) (**O.**), **-s** ˈəʊvərɔːl, -z
overall (*adv.*) ˌəʊvərˈɔːl
over-ambitious ˌəʊvəræmˈbɪʃəs
over-anxiety ˌəʊvəræŋˈzaɪətɪ [ˌəʊvəæŋ-]
over-anxious, -ly ˌəʊvərˈæŋkʃəs
[ˌəʊvəˈæ-], -lɪ
overarm ˈəʊvərɑːm
overaw|e, -es, -ing, -ed ˌəʊvərˈɔː
[ˌəʊvəˈɔː], -z, -ɪŋ, -d
overbalanc|e, -es, -ing, -ed ˌəʊvə-
ˈbæləns, -ɪz, -ɪŋ, -t
overbear, -s, -ing, overbore, overborne
ˌəʊvəˈbeə*, -z, -rɪŋ, ˌəʊvəˈbɔː*
[-ˈbɔə*], ˌəʊvəˈbɔːn
overbearing (*adj.*), **-ly, -ness** ˌəʊvə-
ˈbeərɪŋ, -lɪ, -nɪs [-nəs]
**over|blow, -blows, -blowing, -blew,
-blown** ˌəʊvə|ˈbləʊ, -ˈbləʊz, -ˈbləʊɪŋ,
-ˈbluː:, -ˈbləʊn]
overboard ˈəʊvəbɔːd [ˌəʊvəˈbɔːd, -bəd]
overboil, -s, -ing, -ed ˌəʊvəˈbɔɪl, -z, -ɪŋ,
-d
overbold, -ly ˌəʊvəˈbəʊld, -lɪ
overbrim, -s, -ming, -med ˌəʊvəˈbrɪm,
-z, -ɪŋ, -d
overbuil|d, -ds, -ding, -t ˌəʊvəˈbɪl|d,
-dz, -dɪŋ, -t
overburd|en, -ens, -ening, -ened ˌəʊvə-
ˈbɜːd|n, -nz, -ɳɪŋ [-nɪŋ], -nd
Overbury ˈəʊvəbərɪ
over-busy ˌəʊvəˈbɪzɪ
over-care|ful, -fully, -fulness ˌəʊvə-
ˈkeə|fʊl, -fʊlɪ [-fəlɪ], -fʊlnɪs [-nəs]
overcast ˈəʊvəkɑːst [ˌ--ˈ-]
over-cautious ˌəʊvəˈkɔːʃəs
overcharge (*s.*), **-s** ˌəʊvəˈtʃɑːdʒ [ˈ—],
-ɪz
overcharg|e (*v.*), **-es, -ing, -ed** ˌəʊvə-
ˈtʃɑːdʒ, -ɪz, -ɪŋ, -d
overcloud, -s, -ing, -ed ˌəʊvəˈklaʊd, -z,
-ɪŋ, -ɪd
overcoat, -s ˈəʊvəkəʊt, -s
over-colour (*s.*), **-s** ˈəʊvəˌkʌlə*, -z
over-colour (*v.*), **-s, -ing, -ed** ˌəʊvə-
ˈkʌlə*, -z, -rɪŋ, -d
over|come, -comes, -coming, -came
ˌəʊvə|ˈkʌm, -ˈkʌmz, -ˈkʌmɪŋ, -ˈkeɪm
over-confiden|ce, -t/ly ˌəʊvəˈkɒn-
fɪdən|s, -t/lɪ
over-cook, -s, -ing, -ed ˌəʊvəˈkʊk, -s,
-ɪŋ, -t
over-credulous ˌəʊvəˈkredjʊləs
overcrowd, -s, -ing, -ed ˌəʊvəˈkraʊd,
-z, -ɪŋ, -ɪd
over-develop, -s, -ing, -ed, -ment
ˌəʊvədɪˈveləp, -s, -ɪŋ, -t, -mənt
over|do, -does, -doing, -did, -done
ˌəʊvə|ˈduː:, -ˈdʌz, -ˈduːɪŋ [-ˈdʊɪŋ],
-ˈdɪd, -ˈdʌn
overdone (*over-cooked*) ˌəʊvəˈdʌn [ˈ—]
Overdone ˈəʊvədʌn
overdose (*s.*), **-s** ˈəʊvədəʊs [ˌ--ˈ-], -ɪz
overdos|e (*v.*), **-es, -ing, -ed** ˌəʊvəˈdəʊs,
-ɪz, -ɪŋ, -t
overdraft, -s ˈəʊvədrɑːft, -s
overdraught, -s ˈəʊvədrɑːft, -s
**over|draw, -draws, -drawing, -drew,
-drawn** ˌəʊvə|ˈdrɔː:, -ˈdrɔːz, -ˈdrɔːɪŋ,
-ˈdruː:, -ˈdrɔːn
overdress (*v.*), **-es, -ing, -ed** ˌəʊvəˈdres,
-ɪz, -ɪŋ, -t
overdress (*s.*), **-es** ˈəʊvədres, -ɪz
overdrive (*s.*) ˈəʊvədraɪv
over|drive (*v.*), **-drives, -driving, -drove,
-driven** ˌəʊvə|ˈdraɪv, -ˈdraɪvz,
-ˈdraɪvɪŋ, -ˈdrəʊv, -ˈdrɪvn

overdue ˌəʊvəˈdju: [also ˈ--- *according to sentence-stress*]

overeat, -s, -ing, -en, overate ˌəʊvərˈi:t [-vəˈi:t], -s, -ɪŋ, -n, ˌəʊvərˈet [-vəˈet, -vərˈeɪt, -vəˈeɪt]

overestimate (s.), -s ˌəʊvərˈestɪmət [ˌəʊvəˈes-, -ɪt], -s

overestimat|e (v.), -es, -ing, -ed ˌəʊvərˈestɪmeɪt [-vəˈes-], -s, -ɪŋ, -ɪd

over-estimation ˈəʊvərˌestɪˈmeɪʃn [-vəˌes-]

overexcit|e, -es, -ing, -ed, -ement ˌəʊvərɪkˈsaɪt [-vəɪk-, -ek-], -s, -ɪŋ, -ɪd, -mənt

overexert, -s, -ing, -ed ˌəʊvərɪgˈzɜ:t [-vəɪg-, -eg-], -s, -ɪŋ, -ɪd

overexertion ˌəʊvərɪgˈzɜ:ʃn [-vəɪg-, -eg-]

overexpos|e, -es, -ing, -ed ˌəʊvərɪkˈspəʊz [-vəɪk-, -ek-], -ɪz, -ɪŋ, -d

over-exposure ˌəʊvərɪkˈspəʊʒə* [-vəɪk-, -ek-]

overfatigu|e (s. v.), -es, -ing, -ed ˌəʊvəfəˈti:g, -z, -ɪŋ, -d

overfeed, -s, -ing, overfed ˌəʊvəˈfi:d, -z, -ɪŋ, ˌəʊvəˈfed

overflow (s.), -s ˈəʊvəfləʊ, -z

overfl|ow (v.), -ows, -owing, -owed ˌəʊvəˈfl|əʊ, -əʊz, -əʊɪŋ, -əʊd

over|-fond, -full ˌəʊvəˈ|fɒnd, -ˈfʊl

over-generalisation ˈəʊvəˌdʒenərəlaɪˈzeɪʃn [-lɪˈz-]

over|go, -goes, -going, -went, -gone ˌəʊvəˈ|gəʊ, -ˈgəʊz, -ˈgəʊɪŋ, -ˈwent, -ˈgɒn

overground ˈəʊvəgraʊnd [ˌ--ˈ-]

over|grow, -grows, -growing, -grew, -grown ˌəʊvəˈ|grəʊ, -ˈgrəʊz, -ˈgrəʊɪŋ, -ˈgru:, -ˈgrəʊn

overgrowth, -s ˈəʊvəgrəʊθ, -s

overhand (s. adj.), -s ˈəʊvəhænd, -z

overhang (s.), -s ˈəʊvəhæŋ, -z

over|hang (v.), -hangs, -hanging, -hung ˌəʊvəˈ|hæŋ, -ˈhæŋz, -ˈhæŋɪŋ, -ˈhʌŋ

over-hasty ˌəʊvəˈheɪstɪ

overhaul (s.), -s ˈəʊvəhɔ:l [ˌ--ˈ-], -z

overhaul (v.), -s, -ing, -ed ˌəʊvəˈhɔ:l, -z, -ɪŋ, -d

overhead (s. adj.), -s ˈəʊvəhed, -z

overhead (adv.) ˌəʊvəˈhed

overhear, -s, -ing, overheard ˌəʊvəˈhɪə*, -z, -rɪŋ, ˌəʊvəˈhɜ:d

overheat, -s, -ing, -ed ˌəʊvəˈhi:t, -s, -ɪŋ, -ɪd

over-impress|ed, -ive ˌəʊvərɪmˈpres|t, -ɪv

over-indulg|e, -es, -ing, -ed; -ence ˌəʊvərɪnˈdʌldʒ [-vəm-], -ɪz, -ɪŋ, -d; -əns

overjoy, -s, -ing, -ed ˌəʊvəˈdʒɔɪ, -z, -ɪŋ, -d

overkill (s.) ˈəʊvəkɪl

over-kind ˌəʊvəˈkaɪnd

overlad|e, -es, -ing, -ed, -en ˌəʊvəˈleɪd, -z, -ɪŋ, -ɪd, -n

overlaid ˌəʊvəˈleɪd

overland (adj.) ˈəʊvəlænd

overland (adv.) ˌəʊvəˈlænd [ˈ---]

overlap (s.), -s ˈəʊvəlæp, -s

overlap (v.), -s, -ping, -ped ˌəʊvəˈlæp, -s, -ɪŋ, -t

overlay (s.), -s ˈəʊvəleɪ, -z

overlay (v.), -s, -ing, overlaid ˌəʊvəˈleɪ, -z, -ɪŋ, ˌəʊvəˈleɪd

overleaf ˌəʊvəˈli:f

over|leap (leap over, leap too far), -leaps, -leaping, -leaped, -leapt ˌəʊvəˈ|li:p, -ˈli:ps, -ˈli:pɪŋ, -ˈlept [-ˈli:pt], -ˈlept

overload (s.), -s ˈəʊvələʊd, -z

overload (v.), -s, -ing, -ed ˌəʊvəˈləʊd, -z, -ɪŋ, -ɪd

overlong ˌəʊvəˈlɒŋ

overlook, -s, -ing, -ed ˌəʊvəˈlʊk, -s, -ɪŋ, -t

overlord, -s ˈəʊvələ:d, -z

overlying ˌəʊvəˈlaɪɪŋ

over|man, -men ˈəʊvə|mæn, -men

overmantel, -s ˈəʊvəˌmæntl, -z

overmast|er, -ers, -ering, -ered ˌəʊvəˈ|mɑ:st|ə*, -əz, -ərɪŋ, -əd

overmatch, -es, -ing, -ed ˌəʊvəˈmætʃ, -ɪz, -ɪŋ, -t

overmuch ˌəʊvəˈmʌtʃ [ˈ---]

over-nice ˌəʊvəˈnaɪs

overnight ˌəʊvəˈnaɪt [also ˈ--- *according to sentence-stress*]

overpass (s.), -es ˈəʊvəpɑ:s, -ɪz

overpass (v.), -es, -ing, -ed ˌəʊvəˈpɑ:s, -ɪz, -ɪŋ, -t

overpast (adj.) ˌəʊvəˈpɑ:st

over|pay, -pays, -paying, -paid, -payment/s ˌəʊvəˈ|peɪ, -ˈpeɪz, -ˈpeɪɪŋ, -ˈpeɪd, -ˈpeɪmənt/s

overplus, -es ˈəʊvəplʌs, -ɪz

overpopulat|e, -es, -ing, -ed ˌəʊvəˈpɒpjʊleɪt [-pjə-], -s, -ɪŋ, -ɪd

overpopulation ˈəʊvəˌpɒpjʊˈleɪʃn [-pjə-]

overpower, -s, -ing/ly, -ed ˌəʊvəˈpaʊə*, -z, -rɪŋ/lɪ, -d

overprint (s.), -s ˈəʊvəprɪnt, -s

overprint (v.), -s, -ing, -ed ˌəʊvəˈprɪnt [ˈ---], -s, -ɪŋ, -ɪd

overproduc|e, -es, -ing, -ed ˌəʊvəprəˈdju:s [-prʊˈd-], -ɪz, -ɪŋ, -t

overproduction ˌəʊvəprəˈdʌkʃn [-prʊˈd-]

overproud ˌəʊvəˈpraʊd

859

over-rate (s.), **-s**, (*cricket*) 'əʊvəreɪt, -s
overrat|e, **-es**, **-ing**, **-ed** ,əʊvə'reɪt, -s,
-ɪŋ, -ɪd
overreach (s.), **-es** 'əʊvəriːtʃ, -ɪz
overreach (v.), **-es**, **-ing**, **-ed** ,əʊvə'riːtʃ,
-ɪz, -ɪŋ, -t
overread (*pres. tense*), **-s**, **-ing**, **overread** (*p.*) ,əʊvə'riːd, -z, -ɪŋ, ,əʊvə'red
overrefin|e, **-es**, **-ing**, **-ed**, **-ement/s**
,əʊvərɪ'faɪn, -z, -ɪŋ, -d, -mənt/s
over|ride, **-rides**, **-riding**, **-rode**, **-ridden**
,əʊvə'raɪd, -'raɪdz, -'raɪdɪŋ, -'rəʊd,
-'rɪdn
overripe, **-ness** ,əʊvə'raɪp, -nɪs [-nəs]
overrip|en, **-ens**, **-ening**, **-ened** ,əʊvə-
'raɪp|n, -nz, -nɪŋ [-pɪŋ], -nd
overrul|e, **-es**, **-ing**, **-ed**, **-er/s** ,əʊvə-
'ruːl, -z, -ɪŋ, -d, -ə*/z
overrun, **-s**, **-ning**, **overran** ,əʊvə'rʌn,
-z, -ɪŋ, ,əʊvə'ræn
over-scrupulous, **-ly**, **-ness** ,əʊvə'skruː-
pjʊləs [-pjəl-], -lɪ, -nɪs [-nəs]
oversea, **-s** ,əʊvə'siː, -z
over|see, **-sees**, **-seeing**, **-saw**, **-seen**
,əʊvə|'siː, -'siːz, -'siːɪŋ, -'sɔː, -'siːn
overseer, **-s** 'əʊvə,sɪə* [-,siː-ə*], -z
overshad|ow, **-ows**, **-owing**, **-owed**
,əʊvə'ʃæd|əʊ, -əʊz, -əʊɪŋ, -əʊd
over-shoot, **-shoots**, **-shooting**, **-shot**
,əʊvə|'ʃuːt, -'ʃuːts, -'ʃuːtɪŋ, -'ʃɒt
oversight, **-s** 'əʊvəsaɪt, -s
oversize (s.), **-s**, **-d** ,əʊvə'saɪz, -ɪz, -d
overslaugh, **-s** 'əʊvəslɔː, -z
over|sleep, **-sleeps**, **-sleeping**, **-slept**
,əʊvə|'sliːp, -'sliːps, -'sliːpɪŋ, -'slept
oversoon ,əʊvə'suːn
overspen|d, **-ds**, **-ding**, **-t** ,əʊvə'spen|d,
-dz, -dɪŋ, -t
overspread, **-s**, **-ing** ,əʊvə'spred, -z, -ɪŋ
overstat|e, **-es**, **-ing**, **-ed** ,əʊvə'steɪt,
['---], -s, -ɪŋ, -ɪd
overstatement, **-s** ,əʊvə'steɪtmənt,
['--,--], -s
overstay, **-s**, **-ing**, **-ed** ,əʊvə'steɪ ['---],
-z, -ɪŋ, -d
overstep, **-s**, **-ping**, **-ped** ,əʊvə'step, -s,
-ɪŋ, -t
overstock, **-s**, **-ing**, **-ed** ,əʊvə'stɒk, -s,
-ɪŋ, -t
overstrain (s.) 'əʊvəstreɪn [,--'-]
overstrain (v.), **-s**, **-ing**, **-ed** ,əʊvə'streɪn,
-z, -ɪŋ, -d
Overstrand 'əʊvəstrænd
overstretch, **-es**, **-ing**, **-ed** ,əʊvə'stretʃ,
-ɪz, -ɪŋ, -t
overstrung (*in state of nervous tension*)
,əʊvə'strʌŋ
overstrung (*piano*) 'əʊvəstrʌŋ

oversubscrib|e, **-es**, **-ing**, **-ed** ,əʊvəsəb-
'skraɪb [-bz'k-], -z, -ɪŋ, -d
oversupp|ly, **-ies** ,əʊvəsə'pl|aɪ, -aɪz
overt, **-ly** 'əʊvɜːt [əʊ'vɜːt], -lɪ
over|take, **-takes**, **-taking**, **-took**, **-taken**
,əʊvə|'teɪk, -'teɪks, -'teɪkɪŋ, -'tʊk,
-'teɪkən [-'teɪkŋ]
overtask, **-s**, **-ing**, **-ed** ,əʊvə'tɑːsk, -s,
-ɪŋ, -t
overtax, **-es**, **-ing**, **-ed** ,əʊvə'tæks, -ɪz,
-ɪŋ, -t
overthrow (s.), **-s** 'əʊvəθrəʊ, -z
over|throw (v.), **-throws**, **-throwing**,
-threw, **-thrown** ,əʊvə|'θrəʊ, -'θrəʊz,
-'θrəʊɪŋ, -'θruː, -'θrəʊn
overthrust, **-s** 'əʊvəθrʌst, -s
overtilt, **-s**, **-ing**, **-ed** ,əʊvə'tɪlt, -s, -ɪŋ, -ɪd
overtime 'əʊvətaɪm
overtir|e, **-es**, **-ing**, **-ed** ,əʊvə'taɪə*, -z,
-ɪŋ, -d
Overton 'əʊvətən
overtone, **-s** 'əʊvətəʊn, -z
overtop, **-s**, **-ping**, **-ped** ,əʊvə'tɒp, -s,
-ɪŋ, -t
Overtoun 'əʊvətən
over-trump, **-s**, **-ing**, **-ed** ,əʊvə'trʌmp
-s, -ɪŋ, -t [-ʌmt]
overture, **-s** 'əʊvə,tjʊə* [-tjə*, -,tʃʊə*,
-tʃə*], -z
overturn (s.), **-s** 'əʊvətɜːn, -z
overturn (v.), **-s**, **-ing**, **-ed** ,əʊvə'tɜːn,
-z, -ɪŋ, -d
overval|ue, **-ues**, **-uing**, **-ued** ,əʊvə-
'væl|juː [-jʊ], -juːz [-jʊz], -jʊɪŋ
[-jwɪŋ], -juːd [-jʊd]
overview, **-s** 'əʊvəvjuː, -z
overweening ,əʊvə'wiːnɪŋ
overweight (s.), **-s** 'əʊvəweɪt, -s
over-weight (*adj.*) ,əʊvə'weɪt ['---]
overweight (v.), **-s**, **-ing**, **-ed** ,əʊvə'weɪt,
-s, -ɪŋ, -ɪd
overwhelm, **-s**, **-ing/ly**, **-ed** ,əʊvə'welm
[-'hwelm], -z, -ɪŋ/lɪ, -d
overwork (s.) (*extra work*) 'əʊvəwɜːk
overwork (s.) (*excessive work*) ,əʊvə-
'wɜːk
overwork (v.), **-s**, **-ing**, **-ed**, **-er/s**
,əʊvə'wɜːk, -s, -ɪŋ, -t, -ə*/z
overwrought ,əʊvə'rɔːt
Ovid (*Latin poet*) 'ɒvɪd, (*American
surname*) 'əʊvɪd
Ovidian ɒ'vɪdɪən [əʊ'v, -djən]
Oviedo ,ɒvɪ'eɪdəʊ (o'bjedo)
oviform 'əʊvɪfɔːm
ovine 'əʊvaɪn
Ovingdean 'ɒvɪŋdiːn
Ovingham (*in Northumberland*)
'ɒvɪndʒəm

Ovington (in North Yorkshire, street in London) 'ovɪŋtən, (in Norfolk, surname) 'əʊvɪŋtən
oviparous əʊ'vɪpərəs
Ovoca əʊ'vəʊkə
ovoid (s. adj.), -s 'əʊvɔɪd, -z
ovular 'ɒvjʊlə* ['əʊv-]
ovulation ˌɒvjʊ'leɪʃn [ˌəʊv-]
ovule, -s 'ɒvjuːl ['əʊv-], -z
ov|um, -a 'əʊv|əm, -ə
Owbridge 'əʊbrɪdʒ
ow|e, -es, -ing, -ed əʊ, -z, -ɪŋ, -d
Owego əʊ'wiːgəʊ
Owen, -s; -ite/s 'əʊɪn, -z; -aɪt/s
Ower 'aʊə*, 'əʊə*
Owers 'aʊəz
owing (from owe) 'əʊɪŋ
owl, -s aʊl, -z
owler|y, -ies 'aʊlər|ɪ, -ɪz
Owles əʊlz
owlet, -s 'aʊlɪt [-let, -lət], -s
Owlett 'aʊlɪt [-let]
owlish, -ly, -ness 'aʊlɪʃ, -lɪ, -nɪs [-nəs]
own, -s, -ing, -ed, -er/s əʊn, -z, -ɪŋ, -d, -ə*/z
owner-occupier, -s ˌəʊnər'ɒkjʊpaɪə*, -z
ownership 'əʊnəʃɪp
Owsley 'aʊzlɪ
Owyhe əʊ'waɪhiː
ox, -en ɒks, -ən
oxalate, -s 'ɒksəleɪt [-lɪt, -lət], -s
oxalic ɒk'sælɪk
oxalis ɒk'sɑːlɪs ['ɒksəlɪs]
oxbow, -s 'ɒksbəʊ, -z
Oxbridge 'ɒksbrɪdʒ
Oxbrow 'ɒksbraʊ
oxen (plur. of ox) 'ɒksn
Oxen|den, -ford 'ɒksn|dən, -fəd [-fɔːd]
Oxenham 'ɒksŋəm [-snəm]
Oxenhope 'ɒksnhəʊp
oxer, -s 'ɒksə*, -z
ox-eye, -s, -d 'ɒksaɪ, -z, -d
Oxfam 'ɒksfæm
Oxford, -shire 'ɒksfəd, -ʃə* [-ˌʃɪə*]
ox-hide, -s 'ɒkshaɪd, -z
oxidant, -s 'ɒksɪdənt, -s
oxidat|e, -es, -ing, -ed 'ɒksɪdeɪt, -s, -ɪŋ, -ɪd

oxidation ˌɒksɪ'deɪʃn
oxide, -s 'ɒksaɪd, -z
oxidization [-isa-] ˌɒksɪdaɪ'zeɪʃn [-dɪ'z-]
oxidiz|e [-is|e], -es, -ing, -ed, -er/s; -able 'ɒksɪdaɪz, -ɪz, -ɪŋ, -d, -ə*/z; -əbl
Oxley 'ɒkslɪ
oxlip, -s 'ɒkslɪp, -s
oxo 'ɒksəʊ
Oxon. 'ɒksən [-sɒn]
Oxonian, -s ɒk'səʊnjən [-nɪən], -z
Oxshott 'ɒkʃɒt
ox-tail, -s 'ɒksteɪl, -z
ox-tongue, -s 'ɒkstʌŋ, -z
Oxus 'ɒksəs
oxy-acetylene ˌɒksɪə'setɪliːn [-sɪæ's-, -təl-, -lɪn]
oxychloride, -s ˌɒksɪ'klɔːraɪd, -z
oxygen 'ɒksɪdʒən
oxygenat|e, -es, -ing, -ed ɒk'sɪdʒəneɪt ['ɒksɪ-, -dʒɪn-], -s, -ɪŋ, -ɪd
oxygenation ˌɒksɪdʒə'neɪʃn [ɒkˌsɪdʒ-, -dʒɪ'n-]
oxygenous ɒk'sɪdʒənəs [-dʒɪn-]
oxyhydrogen ˌɒksɪ'haɪdrədʒən [-drɪdʒ-]
oxymel 'ɒksɪmel
oxymoron, -s ˌɒksɪ'mɔːrɒn [-'mɔərˌ-, -rən], -z
oxytone (s. adj.), -s 'ɒksɪtəʊn, -z
oyer 'ɔɪə*
oyes əʊ'jes
oyez əʊ'jes ['əʊjes, 'əʊjez, əʊ'jez]
oyster (O.), -s; -bed/s, -bar/s 'ɔɪstə*, -z; -bed/z, -bɑː:*/z
oyster-catcher, -s 'ɔɪstəˌkætʃə*, -z
oyster-fisher|y, -ies 'ɔɪstəˌfɪʃər|ɪ, -ɪz
Oystermouth 'ɔɪstəmaʊθ
oyster-patt|y, -ies ˌɔɪstə'pæt|ɪ, -ɪz
oyster-shell, -s 'ɔɪstəʃel, -z
oz., ozs. aʊns, 'aʊnsɪz
Ozalid, -s 'ɒzəlɪd, -z
Ozanne əʊ'zæn
ozokerit(e) əʊ'zəʊkərɪt [ɒ'z-, ə'z-]
ozone 'əʊzəʊn [əʊ'zəʊn]
ozonic əʊ'zɒnɪk
ozoniferous ˌəʊzəʊ'nɪfərəs

P

P (*the letter*), -'s piː, -z
pa, -s pɑː, -z
pabulum ˈpæbjʊləm
pac|e (*s. v.*), -es, -ing, -ed, -er/s peɪs, -ɪz, -ɪŋ, -t, -ə*/z
pace (*prep.*) ˈpeɪsɪ
pace-maker, -s ˈpeɪsˌmeɪkə*, -z
pace-setter, -s ˈpeɪsˌsetə*, -z
Pachmann (*famous pianist*) ˈpɑːkmən [-mɑːn]
pachyderm, -s ˈpækɪdəːm, -z
pachydermat|a, -ous ˌpækɪˈdəːmət|ə, -əs
pacific (P.), -ally pəˈsɪfɪk, -əlɪ
pacification, -s ˌpæsɪfɪˈkeɪʃn, -z
pacificatory pəˈsɪfɪkətərɪ [pæˈs-, -keɪtərɪ, ˈpæsɪfɪkeɪtərɪ, ˌpæsɪfɪˈkeɪtərɪ]
pacificist, -s pəˈsɪfɪsɪst, -s
pacifism ˈpæsɪfɪzəm
pacifist, -s ˈpæsɪfɪst, -s
paci|fy, -fies, -fying, -fied, -fier/s ˈpæsɪ|faɪ, -faɪz, -faɪɪŋ, -faɪd, -faɪə*/z
pack, -s, -ing, -ed, -er/s pæk, -s, -ɪŋ, -t, -ə*/z
package, -s ˈpækɪdʒ, -ɪz
pack-animal, -s ˈpækˌænɪml [-nəml], -z
Packard ˈpækɑːd
Packer ˈpækə*
packet, -s ˈpækɪt, -s
packet-boat, -s ˈpækɪtbəʊt, -s
packhorse, -s ˈpækhɔːs, -ɪz
pack-ice ˈpækaɪs
packing|-case/s, -needle/s, -paper, -sheet/s ˈpækɪŋ|keɪs/ɪz, -ˌniːdl/z, -ˌpeɪpə*, -ʃiːt/s
pack|man, -men ˈpæk|mən, -mən
pack|-saddle/s, -thread ˈpæk|ˌsædl/z, -θred
pact, -s pækt, -s
pad (*s. v.*), -s, -ding, -ded pæd, -z, -ɪŋ, -ɪd
Paddington ˈpædɪŋtən
padd|le (*s. v.*), -les, -ling, -led, -ler/s ˈpæd|l, -lz, -lɪŋ [-lɪŋ], -ld, -lə*/z [-lə*/z]
paddle-board, -s ˈpædlbɔːd [-bɔəd], -z
paddle-box, -es ˈpædlbɒks, -ɪz
paddle-wheel, -s ˈpædlwiːl [-hwiːl], -z
paddock (P.), -s ˈpædək, -s

padd|y (P.), -ies ˈpæd|ɪ, -ɪz
Padella pəˈdelə
Paderewski (*famous pianist*) ˌpædəˈrev-skɪ [-ˈrefskɪ]
padlock (*s. v.*), -s, -ing, -ed ˈpædlɒk, -s, -ɪŋ, -t
Padraic Colum ˌpɑːdrɪkˈkɒləm
padre, -s ˈpɑːdrɪ, -z
padrone, -s pəˈdrəʊnɪ [pæˈd-], -z
Padstow ˈpædstəʊ
Padua, -n/s ˈpædjʊə [ˈpɑːdʊə], -n/z
paean, -s ˈpiːən, -z
paediatri- *see* pediatri-
paeon, -s ˈpiːən, -z
paeonic piːˈɒnɪk
paeony = peony
Paflagonia, -n/s ˌpæfləˈgəʊnjə [-nɪə], -n/z
pagan (*s. adj.*), -s ˈpeɪgən, -z
Pagani pəˈgɑːnɪ
Paganini ˌpægəˈniːnɪ [-nɪ]
paganism ˈpeɪgənɪzəm [-gnɪzəm]
paganiz|e [-is|e], -es, -ing, -ed ˈpeɪgən-aɪz, -ɪz, -ɪŋ, -d
pag|e (*s. v.*) (P.), -es, -ing, -ed peɪdʒ, -ɪz, -ɪŋ, -d
pageant, -s ˈpædʒənt, -s
pageantry ˈpædʒəntrɪ
Paget ˈpædʒɪt
paginal ˈpædʒɪnl [ˈpeɪdʒ-]
paginat|e, -es, -ing, -ed ˈpædʒɪneɪt [ˈpeɪdʒ-], -s, -ɪŋ, -ɪd
pagination, -s ˌpædʒɪˈneɪʃn [ˌpeɪdʒ-], -z
paging (*s.*) ˈpeɪdʒɪŋ
Pagliacci ˌpælɪˈɑːtʃɪ [-ˈætʃɪ]
pagoda, -s pəˈgəʊdə, -z
pah pɑː [pɑːh, pɸ]
Pahang pəˈhʌŋ [-ˈhæŋ]
   Note.—Usually pronounced pəˈhʌŋ *in Malaya.*
paid (*from* pay) peɪd
Paignton ˈpeɪntən
pail, -s; -ful/s peɪl, -z; -fʊl/z
paillasse, -s ˈpælɪæs [ˈpæljæs, ˌpælɪˈæs, pælˈjæs], -ɪz
paillette, -s pælˈjet [ˌpælɪˈet] (pajɛt), -s
pain (*s. v.*), -s, -ing, -ed peɪn, -z, -ɪŋ, -d
Pain(e) peɪn

362

pain|ful, -fully, -fulness 'peɪn|fʊl, -fʊlɪ [-fəlɪ], -fʊlnɪs [-nəs]
painless, -ly, -ness 'peɪnlɪs [-ləs], -lɪ, -nɪs [-nəs]
painstak|er/s 'peɪnz̩teɪk|ə*/z
painstaking, -ly 'peɪnz̩teɪkɪŋ, -lɪ
Painswick 'peɪnzwɪk
paint (s. v.), -s, -ing/s, -ed, -er/s; -able peɪnt, -s, -ɪŋ/z, -ɪd, -ə*/z; -əbl
paint|-box/es, -brush/es 'peɪnt|bɒks/ɪz, -brʌʃ/ɪz
Painter 'peɪntə*
paint|y, -ier, -iest 'peɪnt|ɪ, -ɪə*, -ɪɪst
pair (s. v.), -s, -ing, -ed peə*, -z, -rɪŋ, -d
pairing-time, -s 'peərɪŋtaɪm, -z
Paisley 'peɪzlɪ
pajamas pə'dʒɑːməz
Pakeman 'peɪkmən
Pakenham 'pæknəm [-kənəm]
Pakistan ˌpɑːkɪ'stɑːn [ˌpæk-, -'stæn]
Pakistani, -s ˌpɑːkɪ'stɑːnɪ [ˌpæk-], -z
pal, -s pæl, -z
palace, -s 'pælɪs [-ləs], -ɪz
paladin, -s 'pælədɪn, -z
palaeobotany ˌpælɪəʊ'bɒtənɪ [ˌpeɪl-, -tn̩ɪ]
palaeograph|er/s, -y ˌpælɪ'ɒɡrəf|ə*/z [ˌpeɪl-], -ɪ
palaeographic ˌpælɪəʊ'ɡræfɪk [ˌpeɪl-]
palaeolithic ˌpælɪəʊ'lɪθɪk [ˌpeɪl-]
palaeontological ˌpælɪɒntə'lɒdʒɪkl [ˌpeɪl-]
palaeontolog|ist/s, -y ˌpælɪɒn'tɒlədʒ|ɪst/s [ˌpeɪl-], -ɪ
palaeotype 'pælɪəʊtaɪp
Palaeozoic ˌpælɪəʊ'zəʊɪk [ˌpeɪl-]
palairet 'pælərɪt [-ret]
Palamedes ˌpælə'miːdiːz
Palamon 'pæləmən [-mɒn]
palanquin [-nkeen], -s ˌpælən'kiːn [-əŋ'k-], -z
palatab|le, -ly, -leness 'pælətəb|l [-lɪt-], -lɪ, -lnɪs [-nəs]
palatal (s. adj.), -s 'pælətl [pə'leɪtl], -z
palatalization [-isa-], -s ˌpælətəlaɪ'zeɪʃn [pəˌlæt-, pəˌleɪt-, -tʃaɪ'z-, -təlɪ'z-, -tʃɪ'z-], -z
palataliz|e [-is|e], -es, -ing, -ed 'pælətəlaɪz [pə'læt-, pə'leɪt-, -tʃaɪz], -ɪz, -ɪŋ, -d
palate, -s 'pælət [-lɪt], -s
palatial pə'leɪʃl [-ʃəl, -ʃɪəl]
palatinate (P.), -s pə'lætɪnət [-tn̩ət, -ɪt], -s
palatine (P.) 'pælətaɪn
palatogram, -s 'pælətəʊɡræm [pə'læt-], -z
palatography ˌpælə'tɒɡrəfɪ

palav|er (s. v.), -ers, -ering, -ered, -erer/s pə'lɑː|v|ə*, -əz, -ərɪŋ, -əd, -ərə*/z
pal|e (s. adj. v.), -er, -est, -ely, -eness; -es, -ing, -ed peɪl, -ə*, -ɪst, -lɪ, -nɪs [-nəs]; -z, -ɪŋ, -d
pale-face, -s 'peɪlfeɪs, -ɪz
paleo- see palaeo-
Palermo pə'lɜːməʊ [-leəm-] (pa'lɛrmo)
Palestine 'pæləstaɪn [-lɪs-, -les-]
Palestinian, -s ˌpælə'stɪnɪən [-lɪ's-, -le's-, -njən], -z
Palestrina ˌpæle'striːnə [-lɪs-, -ləs-]
paletot, -s 'pæltəʊ, -z
palette, -s; -knife, -knives 'pælət [-lɪt, -let], -s; -naɪf, -naɪvz
Paley 'peɪlɪ
Palfery 'pɔːlfərɪ ['pɒl-]
palfrey (P.), -s 'pɔːlfrɪ ['pɒl-], -z
Palgrave 'pɔːlɡreɪv, 'pæl-
Pali 'pɑːlɪ
palimpsest, -s 'pælɪmpsest, -s
Palin 'peɪlɪn
palindrome, -s 'pælɪndrəʊm, -z
paling (s.), -s 'peɪlɪŋ, -z
palingenesis ˌpælɪn'dʒenɪsɪs [-nəsɪs]
palinode, -s 'pælɪnəʊd, -z
palisad|e (s. v.), -es, -ing, -ed ˌpælɪ'seɪd, -z, -ɪŋ, -ɪd
palish 'peɪlɪʃ
Palk pɔːlk [pɒlk]
pall (s. v.), -s, -ing, -ed pɔːl, -z, -ɪŋ, -d
palladi|an (P.), -um/s pə'leɪdj|ən [-dɪ|ən], -əm/z
Pallas 'pælæs [-ləs]
pall-bearer, -s 'pɔːlˌbeərə*, -z
pallet, -s 'pælɪt [-lət], -s
palliasse, -s 'pælɪæs ['pæljæs, ˌpælɪ'æs, pæl'jæs], -ɪz
palliat|e, -es, -ing, -ed 'pælɪeɪt, -s, -ɪŋ, -ɪd
palliation ˌpælɪ'eɪʃn
palliative (s. adj.), -s 'pælɪətɪv [-ljət-], -z
pallid, -est, -ly, -ness 'pælɪd, -ɪst, -lɪ, -nɪs [-nəs]
Palliser 'pælɪsə*
pallium, -s 'pælɪəm, -z
Pall Mall ˌpæl'mæl [ˌpel'mel, also '—— according to sentence-stress]
pallor 'pælə*
palm (s. v.), -s, -ing, -ed pɑːm, -z, -ɪŋ, -d
palm|a (P.), -ar 'pælm|ə, -ə*
palmaceous pæl'meɪʃəs [-ʃəs, -ʃɪəs]
palmate 'pælmeɪt [-mɪt]
palmer (P.), -s 'pɑːmə*, -z
Palmerston 'pɑːməstən
palmhou|se, -ses 'pɑːmhaʊ|s, -zɪz
palmist, -s 'pɑːmɪst, -s

palmistry 'pɑːmɪstrɪ
palmitine, -s 'pælmɪtiːn [,pælmɪ't-], -z
palm-oil 'pɑːmɔɪl [,-'-]
Palm Sunday, -s ,pɑːm'sʌndɪ [-deɪ], -z
palm|y, -ier, -iest 'pɑːm|ɪ, -ɪə* [-jə*],
-ɪɪst [-jɪst]
palmyra (P.), -s pæl'maɪərə, -z
Palomar 'pæləʊmɑː:*
palpability ,pælpə'bɪlətɪ [-lɪt-]
palpab|le, -ly, -leness 'pælpəb|l, -lɪ, -lnɪs
[-nəs]
palpat|e, -es, -ing, -ed 'pælpeɪt, -s, -ɪŋ,
-ɪd
palpation pæl'peɪʃn
palpitat|e, -es, -ing, -ed 'pælpɪteɪt, -s,
-ɪŋ, -ɪd
palpitation, -s ,pælpɪ'teɪʃn, -z
palsgrave, -s 'pɔːlzgreɪv, -z
Palsgrave 'pɔːlzgreɪv, 'pælzgreɪv
pals|y, -ies, -ied 'pɔːlz|ɪ ['pɒl-], -ɪz, -ɪd
palt|er, -ers, -ering, -ered, -erer/s
'pɔːlt|ə* ['pɒl-], -əz, -ərɪŋ, -əd, -ərə*/z
paltr|y, -ier, -iest, -ily, -iness 'pɔːltr|ɪ
['pɒl-], -ɪə*, -ɪɪst, -əlɪ [-ɪlɪ], -ɪnɪs
[-ɪnəs]
pam (P.), -s pæm, -z
Pamela 'pæmələ [-mɪl-]
Pamir, -s pə'mɪə*, -z
Pampa (territory in South America), -s
'pæmpə, -z
pampas (grass) 'pæmpəs
pamp|er, -ers, -ering, -ered, -erer/s
'pæmp|ə*, -əz, -ərɪŋ, -əd, -ərə*/z
pamphlet, -s 'pæmflɪt [-lət], -s
pamphleteer, -s, -ing ,pæmflə'tɪə* [-lɪ-],
-z, -rɪŋ
Pamphylia, -n/s pæm'fɪlɪə [-ljə], -n/z
pan (P.), -s, -ning, -ned pæn, -z, -ɪŋ,
-d
panacea, -s ,pænə'sɪə [-'siːə], -z
panache, -s pə'næʃ [pæ'n-, -'nɑːʃ], -ɪz
panama (P.), -s 'pænəmɑː [,--'-], -z
Panamanian, -s ,pænə'meɪnjən [-nɪən],
-z
pan-american ,pænə'merɪkən
pan-anglican ,pæn'æŋglɪkən
panatella, -s ,pænə'telə, -z
pancake, -s 'pæŋkeɪk ['pænkeɪk], -s
panchayat, -s pʌn'tʃaɪət [pæn-, pən-,
-'tʃɑːjət], -s
panchromatic ,pænkrəʊ'mætɪk [,pæŋk-]
Pancras 'pæŋkrəs
pancreas, -es 'pæŋkrɪəs [-krɪæs], -ɪz
pancreatic ,pæŋkrɪ'ætɪk
panda, -s 'pændə, -z
Pandean pæn'diːən [-'dɪən]
pandect, -s 'pændekt, -s
pandemic (s. adj.), -s pæn'demɪk, -s

pandemonium, -s ,pændɪ'məʊnjəm
[-dəm-, -nɪəm], -z
pander (s. v.), -s, -ing, -ed 'pændə*, -z,
-rɪŋ, -d
pandora (P.), -s pæn'dɔːrə, -z
pan|e (s. v), -es, -ing, -ed peɪn, -z, -ɪŋ,
-d
panegyric (s. adj.), -s, -al ,pænɪ'dʒɪrɪk
[-nə'dʒ-], -s, -l
panegyrist, -s ,pænɪ'dʒɪrɪst [-nə-, '--,--],
-s
panegyriz|e [-is|e], -es, -ing, -ed
'pænɪdʒɪraɪz [-nə-], -ɪz, -ɪŋ, -d
†pan|el, -els, -elling/s, -elled 'pæn|l,
-lz, -lɪŋ/z [-əlɪŋ/z], -ld
panful, -s 'pænfʊl, -z
pang, -s pæŋ, -z
Pangbourne 'pæŋbɔːn [-,bʊən, -bɔən,
-bən]
pan-german ,pæn'dʒɜːmən
pan-germanic ,pændʒə'mænɪk
Pangloss 'pæŋglɒs
panhellenic ,pænhe'liːnɪk [-'len-]
panic, -s, -ky; -monger/s, -stricken
'pænɪk, -s, -ɪ; -,mʌŋgə*/z, -,strɪkən
pan-indian ,pæn'ɪndjən [-dɪən]
Panini 'pɑːnɪnɪ: [-nɪ] (Hindi paɳyni)
panjandrum, -s pæn'dʒændrəm [pən-],
-z
Pankhurst 'pæŋkhɜːst
pannage 'pænɪdʒ
pannier, -s 'pænɪə* [-njə*], -z
pannikin, -s 'pænɪkɪn, -z
Pannill 'pænɪl
panopl|y, -ies, -ied 'pænəpl|ɪ, -ɪz, -ɪd
panorama, -s ,pænə'rɑːmə, -z
panoramic ,pænə'ræmɪk [-'rɑːm-]
pan-pipe, -s 'pænpaɪp, -s
pan-slavism ,pæn'slɑːvɪzəm [-'slæv-]
pans|y (s. v.), -ies, -ying, -ied 'pænz|ɪ,
-ɪz, -ɪŋ, -ɪd
pant (s. v.), -s, -ing/ly, -ed pænt, -s,
-ɪŋ/lɪ, -ɪd
pantaloon, -s ,pæntə'luːn, -z
pantechnicon, -s pæn'teknɪkən, -z
panthei|sm, -st/s 'pænθiː|ɪzəm [-θɪɪzəm],
-st/s
pantheistic, -al ,pænθi:'ɪstɪk [-θɪ'ɪst-], -l
pantheon (P.), -s 'pænθɪən [pæn'θiːən,
-'θɪən], -z
panther, -s 'pænθə*, -z
panties 'pæntɪz
pantile, -s 'pæntaɪl, -z
pantisocrac|y, -ies ,pæntɪ'sɒkrəs|ɪ, -ɪz
pantograph, -s 'pæntəʊgrɑːf [-græf], -s
pantographic, -al ,pæntəʊ'græfɪk, -l
pantomime, -s; -ist/s 'pæntəmaɪm, -z;
-ɪst/s

pantomimic, -al, -ally ˌpæntəʊˈmɪmɪk, -l, -əlɪ

pantr|y, -ies ˈpæntr|ɪ, -ɪz

pants (s.) pænts

Panza ˈpænzə

panzer, -s ˈpæntsə* [ˈpænzə*], -z

pap, -s pæp, -s

papa, -s pəˈpɑː, -z

papac|y, -ies ˈpeɪpəs|ɪ, -ɪz

papal ˈpeɪpl

papali|sm, -st/s ˈpeɪpəlɪ|zəm [-pļɪ-], -st/s

papaliz|e [-is|e], -es, -ing, -ed ˈpeɪpəlaɪz [-pļaɪz], -ɪz, -ɪŋ, -d

papaver|ous, -aceous pəˈpeɪvər|əs, -eɪʃəs

papaw, -s pəˈpɔː [ˈpɔːpɔː]

papaya, -s pəˈpaɪə, -z

pap|er (s. v.), -ers, -ering, -ered, -erer/s ˈpeɪp|ə*, -əz, -ərɪŋ, -əd, -ərə*/z

paper-back, -s ˈpeɪpəbæk, -s

paper-case, -s ˈpeɪpəkeɪs, -ɪz

paper-chase, -s ˈpeɪpətʃeɪs, -ɪz

paper-clip, -s ˈpeɪpəklɪp, -s

paper-cutter, -s ˈpeɪpəˌkʌtə*, -z

paper-file, -s ˈpeɪpəfaɪl, -z

paper-hang|er/s, -ing ˈpeɪpəˌhæŋ|ə*/z, -ɪŋ

paper-kni|fe, -ves ˈpeɪpənaɪ|f, -vz

paper-maker, -s ˈpeɪpəˌmeɪkə*, -z

paper-mill, -s ˈpeɪpəmɪl, -z

paper-money ˈpeɪpəˌmʌnɪ

paper-nautilus, -es ˌpeɪpəˈnɔːtɪləs, -ɪz

paper-office, -s ˈpeɪpərˌɒfɪs [-pə,ɒf-], -ɪz

paper-weight, -s ˈpeɪpəweɪt, -s

Paphlagonia, -n/s ˌpæfləˈgəʊnjə [-nɪə], -n/z

Paphos (in Cyprus) (ancient city) ˈpeɪfɒs, (modern town) ˈpæfɒs

papier-mâché ˌpæpjeɪˈmæʃeɪ [-pɪeɪ-, -ˈmɑːʃeɪ] (papjemaʃe)

papill|a, -ae, -ar, -ary pəˈpɪl|ə, -i:, -ə*, -ərɪ

papist, -s ˈpeɪpɪst, -s

papistic, -al, -ally pəˈpɪstɪk [peɪˈp-], -l, -əlɪ

papistry ˈpeɪpɪstrɪ

papoose, -s pəˈpuːs, -ɪz

pappus (P.), -es ˈpæpəs, -ɪz

paprika ˈpæprɪkə [pəˈpriːkə]

Papua, -n/s ˈpɑːpʊə [pɑːˈpʊə, ˈpæpjʊə], -n/z

papyr|us, -i, -uses pəˈpaɪər|əs, -aɪ, -əsɪz

Papyrus (as name of a horse) ˈpæpɪrəs

par (P.) pɑː*

†para (coin) (P.), -s ˈpɑːrə, -z

parabas|is, -es pəˈræbəs|ɪs, -iːz

parable, -s ˈpærəbl, -z

parabola, -s pəˈræbələ, -z

parabolic, -al, -ally ˌpærəˈbɒlɪk, -l, -əlɪ

paraboloid, -s pəˈræbəlɔɪd, -z

Paracelsus ˌpærəˈselsəs

parachut|e (s. v.), -es, -ing, -ed, -er/s ˈpærəʃuːt [ˌ-ˈ-], -s, -ɪŋ, -ɪd, -ə*/z

parachutist, -s ˈpærəʃuːtɪst [ˌ-ˈ-], -s

Paraclete ˈpærəkliːt

parad|e (s. v.), -es, -ing, -ed pəˈreɪd, -z, -ɪŋ, -ɪd

parade-ground, -s pəˈreɪdgraʊnd, -z

paradigm, -s ˈpærədaɪm, -z

paradigmatic, -al, -ally ˌpærədɪgˈmætɪk, -l, -əlɪ

paradise (P.), -s ˈpærədaɪs, -ɪz

paradisiac ˌpærəˈdɪsɪæk [-ˈdɪzɪ-]

paradisiacal ˌpærədɪˈsaɪəkl [-dɪˈzaɪ-]

paradisic, -al ˌpærəˈdɪzɪk, -l

parados, -es ˈpærədɒs, -ɪz

paradox, -es ˈpærədɒks, -ɪz

paradoxic|al, -ally, -alness ˌpærəˈdɒk-sɪk|l, -əlɪ, -lnɪs [-nəs]

paraffin ˈpærəfɪn [-fiːn, ˌ-ˈ-]

paraffine ˈpærəfiːn

paragoge, -s ˌpærəˈgəʊdʒɪ, -z

paragogic ˌpærəˈgɒdʒɪk

paragon, -s ˈpærəgən, -z

paragraph (s. v.), -s, -ing, -ed ˈpærəgrɑːf [-græf], -s, -ɪŋ, -t

Paraguay ˈpærəgwaɪ [-gweɪ, ˌ-ˈgwaɪ]

Paraguayan ˌpærəˈgwaɪən [-ˈgweɪən]

parakeet, -s ˈpærəkiːt [ˌ-ˈ-], -s

paraldehyde pəˈrældɪhaɪd [-dəh-]

paralexia ˌpærəˈleksɪə [-sjə]

parallax, -es ˈpærəlæks [-rļæks], -ɪz

parallel (s. v.), -s, -ing, -ed; -ism ˈpærəlel [-rļel, -rələl, -rļəl], -z, -ɪŋ, -d; -ɪzəm

parallelepiped, -s ˌpærələˈlepɪped [-rļeˈl-, -rələˈl-, -rļəˈl-, ˈpærəˌleləˈparped, ˈpærļˌeləˈparp-], -z

parallelogram, -s ˌpærəˈleləʊgræm [-rļˈel-], -z

paralysant, -s ˈpærəlaɪznt [-rļaɪ-, pəˈræliznt], -s

paralys|e, -es, -ing, -ed ˈpærəlaɪz [-rļaɪz], -ɪz, -ɪŋ, -d

paralys|is, -es pəˈrælɪs|ɪs [-ləs-], -iːz

paralytic (s. adj.), -s ˌpærəˈlɪtɪk [-rļˈɪt-], -s

†parameter, -s pəˈræmɪtə* [-mətə*], -z

paramount, -ly ˈpærəmaʊnt, -lɪ

paramour, -s ˈpærəˌmʊə* [-mɔə*, -mɔː*], -z

paranoi|a, -ac ˌpærəˈnɔɪ|ə, -æk

paranoid ˈpærənɔɪd

parapet, -s, -ed ˈpærəpɪt [-pet], -s, -ɪd

paraphernalia ˌpærəfəˈneɪljə [-lɪə]

365

paraphras|e (s. v.), **-es**, **-ing**, **-ed** 'pærəfreɪz, -ɪz, -ɪŋ, -d
paraphrastic, **-ally** ˌpærə'fræstɪk, -əlɪ
parapleg|ia, **-ic** ˌpærə'pliːdʒ|ə, -ɪk
parapsychologic, **-al**, **-ally** 'pærəˌsaɪkə-'lɒdʒɪk ['pærəˌpsaɪ-], -l, -əlɪ
parapsycholog|ist/s, **-y** ˌpærəsaɪ-'kɒlədʒ|ɪst/s [ˌpærəpsaɪ-], -ɪ
parasang, **-s** 'pærəsæŋ, -z
parasite, **-s** 'pærəsaɪt, -s
parasitic, **-al**, **-ally**, **-alness** ˌpærə'sɪtɪk, -l, -əlɪ, -lnɪs [-nəs]
parasol, **-s** 'pærəsɒl [ˌ--'-], -z
parataxis ˌpærə'tæksɪs
paratroop, **-s**, **-er/s** 'pærətruːp, -s, -ə*/z
paratyphoid ˌpærə'taɪfɔɪd ['--ˌ--]
paravane, **-s** 'pærəveɪn, -z
parboil, **-s**, **-ing**, **-ed** 'pɑːbɔɪl, -z, -ɪŋ, -d
parc|el (s. v. adv.), **-els**, **-elling**, **-elled** 'pɑːs|l, -lz, -lɪŋ [-əlɪŋ], -ld
parch, **-es**, **-ing**, **-ed**, **-edness** pɑːtʃ, -ɪz, -ɪŋ, -t, -ɪdnɪs [-tnɪs, -nəs]
parchment (P.), **-s** 'pɑːtʃmənt, -s
pard, **-s** pɑːd, -z
Pardoe 'pɑːdəʊ
pard|on (s. v.), **-ons**, **-oning**, **-oned**, **-oner/s** 'pɑːd|n, -nz, -ŋɪŋ [-nɪŋ], -nd, -ṇə*/z [-nə*/z]
pardonab|le, **-ly**, **-leness** 'pɑːdṇəb|l [-dnə-], -lɪ, -lnɪs [-nəs]
par|e, **-es**, **-ing**, **-ed** peə*, -z, -rɪŋ, -d
paregoric ˌpærə'gɒrɪk [-rɪ'g-]
parent, **-s**; **-age** 'peərənt, -s; -ɪdʒ
parent|al, **-ally** pə'rent|l, -əlɪ
parenthes|is, **-es** pə'renθɪs|ɪs [-θəs-], -iːz
parenthetic, **-al**, **-ally** ˌpærən'θetɪk, -l, -əlɪ
parenthood 'peərənthʊd
parentless 'peərəntlɪs [-ləs]
parerg|on, **-a** pæ'rɜːg|ɒn, -ə
par excellence ˌpɑːr'eksəlɑ̃ːns [-sel-, -lɔ̃ːns, -lɑːns, -ləns] (parɛksɛlɑ̃ːs)
parget (s. v.), **-s**, **-ing**, **-ed** 'pɑːdʒɪt, -s, -ɪŋ, -ɪd
Pargiter 'pɑːdʒɪtə*
parhe|lion, **-lia** pɑː'hiː|ljən [-ljɒn, -lɪən, -lɪɒn], -ljə [-lɪə]
pariah, **-s** pə'raɪə ['pærɪə], -z
Parian, **-s** 'peərɪən, -z
parietal pə'raɪɪtl [-'raɪətl]
paring (s.), **-s** 'peərɪŋ, -z
Paris (French capital, Trojan prince) 'pærɪs
parish (P.), **-es** 'pærɪʃ, -ɪz
parishioner, **-s** pə'rɪʃənə* [-ʃṇə*, -ʃnə*], -z
Parisian, **-s** pə'rɪzjən [-zɪən, -ʒən, -ʒɪən, -ʒn], -z

parisyllabic ˌpærɪsɪ'læbɪk
parity 'pærətɪ [-ɪtɪ]
park (s. v.) (P.), **-s**, **-ing**, **-ed** pɑːk, -s, -ɪŋ, -t
Parke, **-r**, **-s** pɑːk, -ə*, -s
Parkestone 'pɑːkstən
Parkinson, **-ism** 'pɑːkɪnsn, -ɪzəm
Parkstone 'pɑːkstən
parlance 'pɑːləns
parley (s. v.) (P.), **-s**, **-ing**, **-ed** 'pɑːlɪ, -z, -ɪŋ, -d
parliament, **-s** 'pɑːləmənt[-lɪm-, -ljə-], -s
parliamentarian, **-s** ˌpɑːləmen'teərɪən [-lɪm-, -ljə-, -mən-], -z
parliamentary ˌpɑːlə'mentərɪ [-lɪ'm-, -ljə-]
parlour, **-s** 'pɑːlə*, -z
parlour-car, **-s** 'pɑːləkɑː*, -z
parlour-maid, **-s** 'pɑːləmeɪd, -z
parlous, **-ly** 'pɑːləs, -lɪ
Parma 'pɑːmə
Parmenter 'pɑːmɪntə* [-məntə*]
Parmesan ˌpɑːmɪ'zæn ['--- when attributive]
Parminter 'pɑːmɪntə*
Parmiter 'pɑːmɪtə*
Parnassian pɑː'næsɪən [-sjən]
Parnassus pɑː'næsəs
Parnell pɑː'nel, 'pɑːnəl
parnellism 'pɑːnelɪzəm [-nəl-]
parnellite, **-s** 'pɑːnelaɪt [-nəl-], -s
parochial, **-ly**; **-ism** pə'rəʊkjəl [-kɪəl], -ɪ; -ɪzəm
parodist, **-s** 'pærədɪst, -s
parod|y (s. v.), **-ies**, **-ying**, **-ied** 'pærəd|ɪ, -ɪz, -ɪŋ, -ɪd
parole pə'rəʊl
Parolles (Shakespearian character) pə'rɒlɪz [-lɪs, -liːz, -les, -lez]
Paros 'peərɒs
parotid, **-s** pə'rɒtɪd, -z
paroxysm, **-s** 'pærəksɪzəm, -z
paroxysmal ˌpærək'sɪzməl
paroxytone, **-s** pə'rɒksɪtəʊn [pæ'r-], -z
parozone 'pærəzəʊn
parquet, **-s** 'pɑːkeɪ [-kɪ], -z ['pɑːkɪt, -s]
parquetry 'pɑːkɪtrɪ
parr (P.) pɑː*
Parratt 'pærət
parricidal ˌpærɪ'saɪdl
parricide, **-s** 'pærɪsaɪd, -z
Parrish 'pærɪʃ
parrot (P.), **-s** 'pærət, -s
parr|y (s. v.) (P.), **-ies**, **-ying**, **-ied** 'pær|ɪ, -ɪz, -ɪŋ, -ɪd
pars|e, **-es**, **-ing**, **-ed** pɑːz, -ɪz, -ɪŋ, -d
Parsee, **-s** ˌpɑː'siː ['--], -z
Parsifal 'pɑːsɪfəl [-fɑːl, -fæl]

parsimonious, -ly, -ness ˌpɑːsɪ'məʊnjəs [-nɪəs], -lɪ, -nɪs [-nəs]
parsimony 'pɑːsɪmənɪ
parsley 'pɑːslɪ
parsnip, -s 'pɑːsnɪp, -z
parson, -s 'pɑːsn, -z
parsonage, -s 'pɑːsn̩ɪdʒ [-snɪ-], -ɪz
Parsons 'pɑːsnz
part (s. v.), -s, -ing, -ed pɑːt, -s, -ɪŋ, -ɪd
partak|e, -es, -ing, partook, partak|en, -er/s pɑː'teɪk, -s, -ɪŋ, pɑː'tʊk, pɑː'teɪk|ən, -ə*/z
parterre, -s pɑː'teə* (parte:r), -z
Parthenia pɑː'θiːnjə [-nɪə]
parthenogenesis ˌpɑːθɪnəʊ'dʒenɪsɪs [-'dʒenəsɪs]
Parthenon, -s 'pɑːθɪnən [-θən-, -θn̩-, -nɒn], -z
Parthenope pɑː'θenəpɪ
Parthia, -n/s 'pɑːθjə [-θɪə], -n/z
parti|al, -ally 'pɑːʃ|l, -əlɪ
partiality ˌpɑːʃɪ'ælətɪ [-ɪtɪ]
participant, -s pɑː'tɪsɪpənt [-səp-], -s
participat|e, -es, -ing, -ed, -or/s pɑː'tɪsɪpeɪt [-səp-], -s, -ɪŋ, -ɪd, -ə*/z
participation, -s pɑːˌtɪsɪ'peɪʃn [ˌpɑːtɪs-, -sə'p-], -z
participial, -ly ˌpɑːtɪ'sɪpɪəl [-pjəl], -ɪ
participle, -s 'pɑːtɪsɪpl, -z
particle, -s 'pɑːtɪkl, -z
particoloured 'pɑːtɪˌkʌləd
particular (s. adj.), -s, -ly pə'tɪkjʊlə* [-kjəl-], -z, -lɪ
particularit|y, -ies pəˌtɪkjʊ'lærət|ɪ [-kjə-, -ɪt|ɪ], -ɪz
particulariz|e [-is|e], -es, -ing, -ed pə'tɪkjʊləraɪz [-kjəl-], -ɪz, -ɪŋ, -d
parting (s.), -s 'pɑːtɪŋ, -z
Partington 'pɑːtɪŋtən
partisan, -s; -ship/s ˌpɑːtɪ'zæn ['---], -z; -ʃɪp/s
partite 'pɑːtaɪt
partiti|on (s. v.), -ons, -oning, -oned pɑː'tɪʃ|n [pə't-], -nz, -n̩ɪŋ [-ənɪŋ], -nd
partitive, -ly 'pɑːtɪtɪv, -lɪ
partly 'pɑːtlɪ
partner (s. v.), -s, -ing, -ed; -ship/s 'pɑːtnə*, -z, -rɪŋ, -d; -ʃɪp/s
Parton 'pɑːtn
partook (from partake) pɑː'tʊk
partridge (P.), -s 'pɑːtrɪdʒ, -ɪz
part-singing 'pɑːtˌsɪŋɪŋ
part-song, -s 'pɑːtsɒŋ, -z
parturition, -s ˌpɑːtjʊə'rɪʃn [-tjə'r-], -z
part|y, -ies 'pɑːt|ɪ, -ɪz
party|-man, -men 'pɑːtɪ|mæn, -men
party-spirit ˌpɑːtɪ'spɪrɪt
party-wall, -s 'pɑːtɪwɔːl [ˌ--'-], -z

parvenu, -s 'pɑːvənjuː: (parvəny), -z
pas (sing.) pɑː:, (plur.) -z
Pasadena ˌpæsə'diːnə
paschal 'pæskəl ['pɑːs-]
pas de deux ˌpɑːdə'dɜː:
pasha (P.), -s 'pɑːʃə ['pæʃə, pə'ʃɑː:], -z
paso doble ˌpæsəʊ'dəʊbleɪ
pasquinade, -s ˌpæskwɪ'neɪd, -z
pass (s. v.), -es, -ing, -ed, -er/s pɑːs, -ɪz, -ɪŋ, -t, -ə*/z
passab|le, -ly, -leness 'pɑːsəb|l, -lɪ, -lnɪs [-nəs]
passacaglia, -s ˌpæsə'kɑːljə [-lɪə], -z
passag|e (s. v.), -es, -ing, -ed 'pæsɪdʒ, -ɪz, -ɪŋ, -d
passant (in heraldry) 'pæsənt, (in chess) 'pæsɑ̃:ŋ ['pɑːs-, -sɔ̃:ŋ, -sɑːŋ, -sɒŋ] (pɑsɑ̃)
pass-book, -s 'pɑːsbʊk, -s
Passe (surname) pæs
passé(e) 'pæseɪ ['pɑːs-] (pɑse)
passenger, -s 'pæsɪndʒə* [-sən-], -z
passe-partout, -s ˌpæspə'tuː: [ˌpɑːs-, -pɑː'tuː:, '---] (pɑspartu), -z
passer (one who passes), -s 'pɑːsə*, -z
passer (sparrow), -es 'pæsə*, -riːz
passer-by, passers-by ˌpɑːsə'baɪ, ˌpɑːsəz'baɪ
passerine 'pæsəraɪn [-riːn]
Passfield 'pæsfiːld ['pɑːs-]
passibility ˌpæsɪ'bɪlətɪ [-lɪt-]
passible 'pæsɪbl
passim 'pæsɪm
passing-note, -s 'pɑːsɪŋnəʊt, -s
passion (P.), -s 'pæʃn, -z
passionate, -ly, -ness 'pæʃənət [-ʃn̩ət, -ʃnət, -nɪt], -lɪ, -nɪs [-nəs]
passion-flower, -s 'pæʃnˌflaʊə*, -z
passion-fruit, -s 'pæʃn̩fruːt, -s
passive, -ly, -ness 'pæsɪv, -lɪ, -nɪs [-nəs]
passivity pæ'sɪvətɪ [pə's-, -ɪtɪ]
pass-key, -s 'pɑːskiː:, -z
Passmore 'pɑːsmɔ:* ['pæs-, -mɔə*]
Passover, -s 'pɑːsˌəʊvə*, -z
passport, -s 'pɑːspɔːt, -s
pass-word, -s 'pɑːswɜːd, -z
past pɑːst
pasta 'pæstə ['pɑː-]
past|e (s. v.), -es, -ing, -ed peɪst, -s, -ɪŋ, -ɪd
paste-board 'peɪstbɔːd [-bɔəd]
pastel (coloured crayon, drawing made with this), -s pæ'stel ['pæstel, -təl, -tl], -z
pastel (attributive, as in pastel shade) 'pæstl [-təl, -tel, rarely pæs'tel]
pastelist, -s 'pæstəlɪst, -s
pastern, -s 'pæstɜːn [-tən], -z

367

Pasteur pæs'tɜ:* [pɑː-s-] (pastœ:r)
pasteurization [-isa-] ˌpɑːstʃəraɪ'zeɪʃn [ˌpæs-, -stjʊə-, -stjə-, -stə-]
pasteuriz|e [-is|e], -es, -ing, -ed 'pɑːstʃəraɪz ['pæs-, -stjʊə-, -stjə-, -stə-], -ɪz, -ɪŋ, -d
pastiche, -s pæ'stiːʃ ['pæstiːʃ], -ɪz
pastille, -s 'pæstəl [-stɪl, -stiːl, pæ'stiːl], -z
pastime, -s 'pɑːstaɪm, -z
past-master, -s ˌpɑːst'mɑːstə* ['-ˌ--], -z
Paston 'pæstən
pastor, -s 'pɑːstə*, -z
pastoral (s. adj.), -s 'pɑːstərəl ['pæs-], -z
pastorale, -s ˌpæstə'rɑːl [-'rɑːlɪ], -z
pastoralism 'pɑːstərəlɪzəm ['pæs-]
pastorate, -s 'pɑːstərət [-ɪt], -s
pastr|y, -ies 'peɪstr|ɪ, -ɪz
pastrycook, -s 'peɪstrɪkʊk, -s
pasturage 'pɑːstjʊrɪdʒ [-tjər-, -tʃər-]
pastur|e (s. v.), -es, -ing, -ed 'pɑːstʃə* -z, -rɪŋ, -d
past|y (s.), -ies 'pæst|ɪ [for the Cornish kind also 'pɑːs-], -ɪz
past|y (adj.), -ier, -iest, -ily, -iness 'peɪst|ɪ, -ɪə* [-jə*], -ɪɪst [-jɪst], -ɪlɪ [-əlɪ], -ɪnɪs [-ɪnəs]
pat (s. v. adv.) (P.), -s, -ting, -ted pæt, -s, -ɪŋ, -ɪd
pat-a-cake, -s 'pætəkeɪk, -s
Patagonia, -n/s ˌpætə'gəʊnjə [-nɪə], -n/z
Patara 'pætərə
patch, -es, -ing, -ed; -able, -work pætʃ, -ɪz, -ɪŋ, -t; -əbl, -wɜːk
patchouli 'pætʃʊlɪ [pə'tʃuːlɪ, -liː]
patch|y, -ier, -iest, -ily, -iness 'pætʃ|ɪ, -ɪə*, -ɪɪst, -ɪlɪ [-əlɪ], -ɪnɪs [-ɪnəs]
pate, -s peɪt, -s
pâté 'pæteɪ ['pɑː-, -tɪ] (pɑte)
Pateley 'peɪtlɪ
patell|a, -as, -ae, -ar pə'tel|ə, -əz, -iː, -ə*
paten, -s 'pætən, -z
patent (s. adj. v.), -s, -ing, -ed; -able 'peɪtənt ['pæt-], -s, -ɪŋ, -ɪd; -əbl
Note.—'pætənt seems the more usual in letters patent; otherwise 'peɪtənt seems the more usual.
patentee, -s ˌpeɪtən'tiː [ˌpæt-], -z
patent leather ˌpeɪtənt'leðə* [also 'peɪtəntˌl- when attributive]
patently 'peɪtəntlɪ
pater (P.), -s 'peɪtə*, -z
paterfamilias, -es ˌpeɪtəfə'mɪlɪæs [-lɪəs, -ljəs], -ɪz
patern|al, -ally, -alism pə'tɜːn|l, -əlɪ, -lɪzəm

paternity pə'tɜːnɪtɪ [-ɪtɪ]
Paternoster (Lord's Prayer), -s ˌpætə'nɒstə*, -z
Paternoster (Row) 'pætəˌnɒstə*
Paterson 'pætəsn
Pateshall 'pætəʃl [-tɪʃ-]
Patey 'peɪtɪ
pa|th, -ths pɑː|θ, -ðz
Pathan, -s pə'tɑːn (Hindi pəʈhan), -z
pathetic, -ally pə'θetɪk, -əlɪ
pathfinder (P.), -s 'pɑːθˌfaɪndə*, -z
pathless 'pɑːθlɪs [-ləs]
pathogen, -s 'pæθəʊdʒən [-dʒen], -z
pathogenic ˌpæθəʊ'dʒenɪk
pathogenesis ˌpæθəʊ'dʒenəsɪs [-nɪs-]
pathologic, -al, -ally ˌpæθə'lɒdʒɪk, -l, -əlɪ
patholog|ist/s, -y pə'θɒlədʒ|ɪst/s [pæ'θ-], -ɪ
pathos 'peɪθɒs
pathway, -s 'pɑːθweɪ, -z
patience (P.), -s 'peɪʃns, -ɪz
patient (s. adj.), -s, -ly 'peɪʃnt, -s, -lɪ
patina 'pætɪnə
patio, -s 'pætɪəʊ ['pɑːtɪəʊ, 'peɪtɪəʊ], -z
pâtisserie, -s pə'tiːsərɪ [pæ-], -z (pɑtisri)
Pat|man, -mos 'pæt|mən, -mɒs
Patmore 'pætmɔː* [-mɔə*]
Patna 'pætnə (Hindi pətna)
patois (sing.) 'pætwɑː [-wɔː] (patwa), (plur.) -z
Paton 'peɪtn
Patras pə'træs
patrial 'peɪtrɪəl
patriarch, -s 'peɪtrɪɑːk
patriarchal ˌpeɪtrɪ'ɑːkl
patriarchate, -s 'peɪtrɪɑːkɪt [-keɪt, -kət], -s
Patricia pə'trɪʃə [-ʃɪə, -ʃjə]
patrician, -s pə'trɪʃn, -z
patriciate pə'trɪʃɪət [-ʃjət, -ɪt, -ʃɪeɪt, -ʃjeɪt]
patricide 'pætrɪsaɪd ['peɪ-]
Patrick 'pætrɪk
patrimonial, -ly ˌpætrɪ'məʊnjəl [-nɪəl], -ɪ
patrimon|y, -ies 'pætrɪmən|ɪ, -ɪz
patriot, -s 'pætrɪət ['peɪt-], -s
patriotic, -ally ˌpætrɪ'ɒtɪk [ˌpeɪt-], -əlɪ
patriotism 'pætrɪətɪzəm ['peɪt-]
patristic pə'trɪstɪk
Patroclus pə'trɒkləs
patrol (s. v.), -s, -ling, -led; -man, -men pə'trəʊl, -z, -ɪŋ, -d; -mæn, -men
patron, -s 'peɪtrən ['pæt-], -z
patronage 'pætrənɪdʒ [-trɪnɪdʒ, rarely 'peɪt-]
patronal pə'trəʊnl [pæ't-]

patroness, -s 'peɪtrənɪs ['pæt-, -nes, -trn̩-, ˌpeɪtrə'nes], -ɪz
patroniz|e [-is|e], -es, -ing/ly, -ed, -er/s 'pætrənaɪz [-trn̩aɪz], -ɪz, -ɪŋ/lɪ, -d, -ə*/z
patronymic (*s. adj.*), **-s** ˌpætrə'nɪmɪk [-trn̩'ɪm-], -s
patroon, -s pə'truːn, -z
patten, -s 'pætn, -z
patter (*s. v.*), **-s, -ing, -ed, -er/s** 'pætə*, -z, -rɪŋ, -d, -rə*/z
Patterdale 'pætədeɪl
pattern, -s 'pætən [-tn], -z
Patterson 'pætəsn
Patteson 'pætɪsn [-təsn]
Pattison 'pætɪsn
Pattreiouex 'pætrɪəʊ
patt|y, -ies 'pæt|ɪ, -ɪz
paucity 'pɔːsətɪ [-ɪtɪ]
Paul, -'s pɔːl, -z
Pauline (*scholar of St. Paul's school*), **-s** 'pɔːlaɪn, -z
Pauline (*fem. name*) pɔː'liːn, 'pɔːliːn
Pauline (*adj.*) (*of St. Paul*) 'pɔːlaɪn
Paulinus pɔː'laɪnəs
Paulus 'pɔːləs
Pauncefote 'pɔːnsfʊt [-fət]
paunch, -es pɔːntʃ, -ɪz
pauper, -s 'pɔːpə*, -z
pauperism 'pɔːpərɪzəm
pauperization [-isa-] ˌpɔːpəraɪ'zeɪʃn [-rɪ'z-]
pauperiz|e [-is|e], -es, -ing, -ed 'pɔːpəraɪz, -ɪz, -ɪŋ, -d
Pausanias pɔː'seɪnɪæs [-njæs, -njəs, -nɪəs]
paus|e (*s. v.*), **-es, -ing, -ed** pɔːz, -ɪz, -ɪŋ, -d
pavan(e), -s 'pævən [pə'væn, -'vɑːn], -z
pav|e, -es, -ing, -ed, -er/s peɪv, -z, -ɪŋ, -d, -ə*/z
pavé, -s 'pæveɪ (pave), -z
pavement, -s 'peɪvmənt, -s
Pavia pə'viːə [pɑː'v-, -'vɪə] (pa'vi:a)
pavilion (*s. v.*), **-s, -ing, -ed** pə'vɪljən [-lɪən], -z, -ɪŋ, -d
paving-stone, -s 'peɪvɪŋstəʊn, -z
paviour, -s 'peɪvjə* [-vɪə*], -s
Pavitt 'pævɪt
Pavlov 'pævlɒv [-lɒf] ('pavləf)
Pavlova 'pævləvə ['pɑːv-, pæv'ləʊvə] ('pavləva)
paw (*s. v.*), **-s, -ing, -ed** pɔː, -z, -ɪŋ, -d
pawk|y, -ier, -iest, -ily, -iness 'pɔːk|ɪ, -ɪə* [-jə*], -ɪɪst [-jɪst], -ɪlɪ [-əlɪ], -ɪnɪs [-nəs]
pawl (*s. v.*), **-s, -ing, -ed** pɔːl, -z, -ɪŋ, -d
pawn (*s. v.*), **-s, -ing, -ed, -er/s** pɔːn, -z, -ɪŋ, -d, -ə*/z

pawnbrok|er/s, -ing 'pɔːnˌbrəʊk|ə*/z, -ɪŋ
pawnee (**P.**), **-s** ˌpɔː'niː, -z
pawnshop, -s 'pɔːnʃɒp, -s
pawn-ticket, -s 'pɔːnˌtɪkɪt, -s
pax (*s. interj.*), **-es** pæks, -ɪz
Paxton 'pækstən
pay (*s. v.*), **-s, -ing, paid, payer/s, payment/s** peɪ, -z, -ɪŋ, peɪd, 'peɪə*/z, 'peɪmənt/s
payable 'peɪəbl
P.A.Y.E. ˌpiːeɪwaɪ'iː
payee, -s peɪ'iː, -z
Payen-Payne ˌpeɪn'peɪn
paymaster, -s 'peɪˌmɑːstə*, -z
paynim 'peɪnɪm
Paynter 'peɪntə*
pay-roll, -s 'peɪrəʊl, -z
pay-sheet, -s 'peɪʃiːt, -s
pea, -s piː, -z
Peabody 'piːˌbɒdɪ
peace (**P.**), **-s** piːs, -ɪz
peaceab|le, -ly, -leness 'piːsəb|l, -lɪ, -lnɪs [-nəs]
peace|ful, -fully, -fulness 'piːs|fʊl, -fʊlɪ [-fəlɪ], -fʊlnɪs [-nəs]
peacemaker, -s 'piːsˌmeɪkə*, -z
peace-offering, -s 'piːsˌɒfərɪŋ, -z
Peacey 'piːsɪ
peach (*s. v.*), **-es, -ing, -ed, -er/s** piːtʃ, -ɪz, -ɪŋ, -t, -ə*/z
peach-colour, -ed 'piːtʃˌkʌlə*, -d
Peachey 'piːtʃɪ
pea-chick, -s 'piːtʃɪk, -s
peachy 'piːtʃɪ
peacock (**P.**), **-s** 'piːkɒk, -s
pea-fowl 'piːfaʊl
pea-green ˌpiː'griːn ['--, *esp. when attributive*]
peahen, -s 'piːhen [ˌ-'-], -z
pea-jacket, -s 'piːˌdʒækɪt, -s
peak (*s. v.*) (**P.**), **-s, -ing, -ed** piːk, -s, -ɪŋ, -t
peal (*s. v.*), **-s, -ing, -ed** piːl, -z, -ɪŋ, -d
Peall piːl
pean (*fur*) piːn
pean (= **paean**), **-s** 'piːən, -z
peanut, -s 'piːnʌt, -s
pear, -s peə*, -z
Pear (*surname*) pɪə*
Pearce pɪəs
Peard pɪəd
pearl (*s. v.*) (**P.**), **-s, -ing, -ed; -barley, -button/s** pɜːl, -z, -ɪŋ, -d; -'bɑːlɪ, -'bʌtn/z
pearl-diver, -s 'pɜːlˌdaɪvə*, -z
pearl-fisher|y, -ies 'pɜːlˌfɪʃər|ɪ, -ɪz
pearlies 'pɜːlɪz

369

pearly 'pɜːlɪ
pearmain 'pɜːmeɪn, 'peəmeɪn [-'-]
Pearman 'pɪəmən
Pears pɪəz, peəz
   Note.—peəz *in* Pears' *soap*; pɪəz *for singer.*
Pearsall 'pɪəsɔːl [-səl]
pear-shaped 'peəʃeɪpt
Pearson 'pɪəsn
Peart pɪət
Peary 'pɪərɪ
peasant, -s 'peznt, -s
peasantry 'pezntrɪ
peas(e)cod, -s 'piːzkɒd, -z
Peascod (*road at Windsor*) 'peskəd
pease (P.) piːz
Peaseblossom 'piːz,blɒsəm
pease-pudding ,piːz'pʊdɪŋ
pea-shooter, -s 'piː,ʃuːtə*, -z
pea-soup, -y piː'suːp, -ɪ
peat, -bog/s piːt, -bɒg/z
peat-moss 'piːtmɒs [,-'-]
peat|y, -ier, -iest, -iness 'piːt|ɪ, -ɪə* [-jə*], -ɪɪst [-jɪst], -ɪnɪs [-məs]
pebble, -s 'pebl, -z
pebbly 'peblɪ [-blɪ]
pecan, -s pɪ'kæn ['piːkən], -z
peccability ,pekə'bɪlətɪ [-lɪt-]
peccable 'pekəbl
peccadillo, -(e)s ,pekə'dɪləʊ, -z
peccant, -ly 'pekənt, -lɪ
peccar|y, -ies 'pekər|ɪ, -ɪz
peccavi pe'kɑːvi: [*old-fashioned* -'keɪvaɪ]
Pechey 'piːtʃɪ
Pechili 'petʃɪlɪ
peck (s. v.) (P.), -s, -ing, -ed, -er/s pek, -s, -ɪŋ, -t, -ə*/z
Peckham 'pekəm
peckish, -ly, -ness 'pekɪʃ, -lɪ, -nɪs [-nəs]
Peckitt 'pekɪt
Pecksniff 'peksnɪf
pectoral (s. adj.), -s 'pektərəl, -z
peculat|e, -es, -ing, -ed, -or/s 'pekjʊleɪt [-kjə-], -s, -ɪŋ, -ɪd, -ə*/z
peculation, -s ,pekjʊ'leɪʃn [-kjə-], -z
peculiar (s. adj.), -s, -ly pɪ'kjuːljə* [pə-, -lɪə*], -z, -lɪ
peculiarit|y, -ies pɪ,kjuːlɪ'ærət|ɪ [pə-, -ɪt|ɪ], -ɪz
peculium, -s pɪ'kjuːljəm [pə'k-, -lɪəm], -z
pecuniar|y, -ily pɪ'kjuːnjər|ɪ [-nɪə-], -əlɪ [-ɪlɪ]
pedagogic, -al ,pedə'gɒdʒɪk [-'gɒgɪk, -'gəʊdʒɪk], -l
pedagogue, -s 'pedəgɒg, -z
pedagogy 'pedəgɒdʒɪ [-gɒgɪ, -gəʊdʒɪ]

ped|al (s. v.), -als, -alling, -alled 'ped|l, -lz, -lɪŋ [-lɪŋ], -ld
pedal (adj.) (*pertaining to the foot*) 'piːdl ['pedl], (*in geometry*) 'pedl
pedant, -s 'pedənt, -s
pedantic, -al, -ally pɪ'dæntɪk [pə'd-, pe'd-], -l, -əlɪ
pedantism 'pedəntɪzəm [-dn-, pɪ'dænt-, pe'dænt-]
pedantr|y, -ies 'pedəntr|ɪ, -ɪz
pedd|le, -les, -ling, -led, -ler/s 'ped|l, -lz, -lɪŋ [-lɪŋ], -ld, -lə*/z
pederast, -s, -y 'pedəræst ['piː-], -s, -ɪ
pedestal, -s 'pedɪstl [-dəs-], -z
pedestrian (s. adj.), -s, -ism pɪ'destrɪən [pə'd-], -z, -ɪzəm
pedestrianiz|e [-is|e], -es, -ing, -ed pɪ'destrɪənaɪz [pə'd-], -ɪz, -ɪŋ, -d
pediatric, -s ,piːdɪ'ætrɪk, -s
pediatrician, -s ,piːdɪə'trɪʃn, -z
pedicle, -s 'pedɪkl, -z
pedicure, -s 'pedɪ,kjʊə* [-kjɔə*, -kjɔː*], -z
pedigree, -s, -d 'pedɪgriː, -z, -d
pediment, -s 'pedɪmənt, -s
pedimental ,pedɪ'mentl
pedimented 'pedɪmentɪd [-mənt-]
pedlar, -s 'pedlə*, -z
pedometer, -s pɪ'dɒmɪtə* [pe'd-, -mətə*], -z
Pedro 'peɪdrəʊ ['ped-, 'piːd-]
   Note.—*The pronunciation* 'piːdrəʊ *is generally used in Shakespeare's 'Much Ado.'*
peduncle, -s pɪ'dʌŋkl, -z
Peeb|les, -lesshire 'piːb|lz, -lzʃə* [-lʒʃə*, -lʃə*, -,ʃɪə*]
Peek piːk
peek|y, -ier, -iest 'piːk|ɪ, -ɪə*, -ɪɪst
peel (s. v.) (P.), -s, -ing/s, -ed piːl, -z, -ɪŋ/z, -d
peeler, -s 'piːlə*, -z
peep (s. v.) (P.), -s, -ing, -ed, -er/s piːp, -s, -ɪŋ, -t, -ə*/z
peep-bo 'piːpbəʊ
peep-hole, -s 'piːphəʊl, -z
peepshow, -s 'piːpʃəʊ, -z
peer (s. v.), -s, -ing, -ed pɪə*, -z, -rɪŋ, -d
peerage, -s 'pɪərɪdʒ, -ɪz
peeress, -es 'pɪərɪs [-res], -ɪz
peerless (P.), -ly, -ness 'pɪəlɪs [-ləs], -lɪ, -nɪs [-nəs]
peeved piːvd
peevish, -ly, -ness 'piːvɪʃ, -lɪ, -nɪs [-nəs]
peewit, -s 'piːwɪt, -s
peg (s. v.) (P.), -s, -ging, -ged peg, -z, -ɪŋ, -d
Pegasus 'pegəsəs

Pegeen pe'gi:n
Pegge peg
Peggotty 'pegətɪ
Peggy 'pegɪ
Pegr|am, -um 'pi:gr|əm, -əm
peg-top, -s 'pegtɒp [ˌ-'-], -s
peignoir, -s 'peɪnwɑ:* [-wɔ:*] (pɛɲwa:r),
    -z
Peile pi:l
Peiping ˌpeɪ'pɪŋ
Peirse pɪəz
pejorative pɪ'dʒɒrətɪv [pə-,'pi:dʒərətɪv]
Pek|in, -ing ˌpi:'k|ɪn, -ɪŋ
Pekinese ˌpi:kɪ'ni:z
Pekingese ˌpi:kɪŋ'i:z
pekoe 'pi:kəʊ
pelagic pe'lædʒɪk [pɪ'l-]
pelargonium, -s ˌpelə'gəʊnjəm [-nɪəm],
    -z
Pelasgian, -s pe'læzgɪən [pɪ'l-, -gjən], -z
pelasgic pe'læzgɪk [pɪ'l-, -zdʒɪk]
Peleg 'pi:leg [rarely 'pel-]
pelerine, -s 'peləri:n, -z
Peleus 'pi:lju:s [-ljəs, -lɪəs]
pelf pelf
Pelham 'peləm
Pelias 'pi:lɪæs [-lɪəs, 'pelɪæs]
pelican, -s 'pelɪkən, -z
pelisse, -s pe'li:s [pɪ'l-, pə'l-], -ɪz
pellet, -s 'pelɪt [-lət], -s
Pelley 'pelɪ
pellicle, -s 'pelɪkl, -z
Pellisier pə'lɪsɪeɪ [pe'l-, -sɪə*, -sjə*]
pell-mell ˌpel'mel
pellucid, -ly, -ness pe'lu:sɪd [pɪ'l-,
    -'lju:-], -lɪ, -nɪs [-nəs]
Pelly 'pelɪ
Pelman, -ism 'pelmən, -ɪzəm
pelmet, -s 'pelmɪt, -s
Peloponnese 'peləpəni:s [ˌ---'-]
Peloponnesian, -s ˌpeləpə'ni:ʃn [-ʃjən,
    -ʃɪən], -z
Peloponnesus ˌpeləpə'ni:səs
Pelops 'pi:lɒps
pelt (s. v.), -s, -ing, -ed pelt, -s, -ɪŋ, -ɪd
pelure pə'ljʊə* [pɪ'l-]
pelv|is, -ises, -es, -ic 'pelv|ɪs, -ɪsɪz, -i:z, -ɪk
Pemberton 'pembətən
Pembridge 'pembrɪdʒ
Pembroke, -shire 'pembrʊk, -ʃə* [-ˌʃɪə*]
Pemigewasset ˌpemɪgə'wɒsɪt
pemmican 'pemɪkən
pen (s. v.) (P.), -s, -ning, -ned pen, -z,
    -ɪŋ, -d
pen|al, -ally 'pi:n|l, -əlɪ
penaliz|e [-is|e], -es, -ing, -ed 'pi:nəlaɪz
    [-n̩aɪz], -ɪz, -ɪŋ, -d
penalt|y, -ies 'penlt|ɪ, -ɪz

penance, -s 'penəns, -ɪz
pen-and-ink ˌpenənd'ɪŋk
Penang pɪ'næŋ [pə'n-]
Penarth pe'nɑ:θ [pə'n-] (Welsh pen'arθ)
penates pe'nɑ:teɪz [pe'neɪti:z, pɪ'n-,
    pə'n-]
Penberthy 'penbəθɪ, 'penˌbɜ:θɪ, 'pen-
    ˌbɜ:ðɪ
pence (plur. of penny; see note under
    penny) pens
penchant, -s 'pɑ̃:ŋʃɑ̃:ŋ ['pɔ̃:ŋʃɔ̃:ŋ,
    'pɑ:ŋʃɑ:ŋ, 'pɒŋʃɒŋ] (pɑ̃ʃɑ̃), -z
penc|il (s. v.), -ils, -illing, -illed 'pens|l,
    -lz, -l̩ɪŋ [-əlɪŋ], -ld
pencil-case, -s 'penslkeɪs, -ɪz
pendant, -s 'pendənt, -s
Pendeen pen'di:n
penden|cy, -t 'pendən|sɪ, -t
Pendennis pen'denɪs
Pender 'pendə*
Pendine (in Wales) pen'daɪn (Welsh
    pen'daɪn)
pending 'pendɪŋ
Pendle|bury, -ton 'pendl̩|bərɪ, -tən
pendragon (P.), -s pen'drægən, -z
pendulous, -ly, -ness 'pendjʊləs [-dʒʊl-],
    -lɪ, -nɪs [-nəs]
pendulum, -s 'pendjʊləm [-djəl-, -dʒəl-],
    -z
Pendyce pen'daɪs
Penelope pə'neləpɪ [pɪ'n-]
penetrability ˌpenɪtrə'bɪlətɪ [-lɪt-]
penetrab|le, -ly, -leness 'penɪtrəb|l, -lɪ,
    -lnɪs [-nəs]
penetralia ˌpenɪ'treɪljə [-lɪə]
penetrat|e, -es, -ing/ly, -ed 'penɪtreɪt,
    -s, -ɪŋ/lɪ, -ɪd
penetration, -s ˌpenɪ'treɪʃn, -z
penetrative, -ly, -ness 'penɪtrətɪv
    [-treɪt-], -lɪ, -nɪs [-nəs]
Penfold 'penfəʊld
penful, -s 'penfʊl, -z
Penge pendʒ
penguin, -s 'peŋgwɪn, -z
pen-holder, -s 'penˌhəʊldə*, -z
penicillin ˌpenɪ'sɪlɪn
Penicuik 'penɪkʊk
peninsul|a (P.), -as, -ar pə'nɪnsjʊl|ə
    [pɪ'n-, pe'n-, ɪnfʊ-], əz, ə-*
penis, -es 'pi:nɪs, -ɪz
penitence 'penɪtəns
penitent (s. adj.), -s, -ly 'penɪtənt, -s, -lɪ
penitenti|al, -ally ˌpenɪ'tenʃ|l, -əlɪ
penitentiar|y, -ies ˌpenɪ'tenʃər|ɪ, -ɪz
penkni|fe, -ves 'pennaɪ|f, -vz
Penmaenmawr ˌpenmən'maʊə* [-'mɔ:*,
    -'mɔə*] (Welsh penmaen'maur,
    -mən-)

371

pen|man, -men 'pen|mən, -mən
penmanship 'penmənʃɪp
Penn pen
pen-name, -s 'penneɪm, -z
pennant (P.), -s 'penənt, -s
Pennefather 'penɪˌfɑːðə*, -ˌfeðə*
penniless 'penɪlɪs [-ləs, -les]
Pennine, -s 'penaɪn, -z
Pennington 'penɪŋtən
pennon, -s 'penən, -z
Pennsylvania ˌpensɪl'veɪnjə [-sl̩-, -nɪə]
penn|y (P.), -ies, pence 'pen|ɪ, -ɪz, pens
   Note.—Since decimalization of the currency, the pronunciation of compounds with
   penny, pence (now abbreviated to p)
   has been uncertain. Formerly, compounds from ½d to 11d invariably had
   -pənɪ, -pəns, e.g. see entries under halfpenny, fourpence, etc. With the
   extension of -pence compounds beyond
   11p, e.g. 12p, the reduced forms are
   falling out of use. Instead, the full forms
   'penɪ and pens, or commonly pi;, tend
   to be used, e.g. 4p ('fɔː'pəns) is ˌfɔː-
   'pens or -'piː:; 12p is ˌtwelv'pens or
   ˌ-'piː:. The plur. pens is also to be heard
   even in 1p.
penny-a-liner, -s ˌpenɪə'laɪnə* [-njə-],
   -z
penny-farthing, -s ˌpenɪ'fɑːðɪŋ, -z
penny-royal ˌpenɪ'rɔɪəl
pennyweight, -s 'penɪweɪt, -s
pennywort 'penɪwɜːt
pennyworth, -s 'penɪwəθ [-wɜː:θ,
   'penəθ], -s
Penobscot pe'nɒbskɒt [pə'n-]
penological ˌpiːnə'lɒdʒɪkl
penology piː'nɒlədʒɪ
Penrhyn 'penrɪn (Welsh 'penhrɪn, 'pen-
   drɪn)
Penrith (town in Cumbria) 'penrɪθ
   [pen'r-], (surname) 'penrɪθ
Penrose (surname) 'penrəʊz, pen'r-,
   (place in Cornwall) pen'rəʊz
Pensarn pen'sɑːn
penseroso ˌpensə'rəʊzəʊ
Penshurst 'penzhɜːst
pensi|on (s. v.) (monetary allowance,
   etc.), -ons, -oning, -oned 'penʃ|n, -nz,
   -ənɪŋ [-nɪŋ], -nd
pension (s.) (boarding-house, board), -s
   'pɑ̃:ŋsɪɔ̃:ŋ ['pɔ̃:ŋ-, 'pɑ:ŋsɪɔ:ŋ, 'pɑ:ns-,
   'pɒns-, -sjɔ̃:ŋ] (pɑ̃sjɔ̃), -z
pensioner, -s 'penʃənə* [-ʃŋə*, -ʃnə*],
   -z
pensionnaire, -s ˌpɑ̃:ŋsɪə'neə* [ˌpɔ̃:ŋs-,
   ˌpɑ:ns-, ˌpɒns-, -sjə-] (pɑ̃sjɔnɛːr),
   -z

pensive, -ly, -ness 'pensɪv, -lɪ, -nɪs [-nəs]
pent pent
pentad, -s 'pentæd, -z
pentagon (P.), -s 'pentəgən [-gɒn], -z
pentagon|al, -ally pen'tægən|l, -əlɪ
pentagram, -s 'pentəgræm, -z
pentahedr|on, -al ˌpentə'hiːdr|ɒn [-ən],
   -əl
pentamerous pen'tæmərəs
pentameter, -s pen'tæmɪtə* [-mətə*],
   -z
pentangle, -s 'pentˌæŋgl, -z
Pentateuch 'pentətjuːk
pentathlete, -s pen'tæθliːt, -s
pentathlon pen'tæθlɒn [-lən]
pentatonic ˌpentə'tɒnɪk
Pentecost, -s 'pentɪkɒst, -s
pentecostal ˌpentɪ'kɒstl
Penthesilea ˌpenθesɪ'liːə [-'lɪə]
penthou|se, -ses 'penthaʊ|s, -zɪz
Pentland, -s 'pentlənd, -z
Pentonville 'pentənvɪl
pentstemon, -s pent'stemən [-'stiːm-,
   'pentstɪmən], -z
pentyl 'pentaɪl [-tɪl]
penult, -s pe'nʌlt [pɪ'n-, pə'n-], -s
penultimate (s. adj.), -s pe'nʌltɪmət
   [pɪ'n-, pə'n-, -ɪt], -s
penumbr|a, -as, -ae, -al pɪ'nʌmbr|ə
   [pe'n-, pə'n-], -əz, -iː, -əl
penurious, -ly, -ness pɪ'njʊərɪəs [pe'n-,
   pə'n-], -lɪ, -nɪs [-nəs]
penury 'penjʊrɪ [-jʊərɪ]
pen-wiper, -s 'penˌwaɪpə*, -z
Penzance pen'zæns [pən-, locally pən-
   'zɑːns]
peon, -s (Indian servant) pjuːn ['piːən],
   (in U.S.A.) 'piːən, -z
peon|y, -ies 'pɪən|ɪ, -ɪz
peop|le (s. v.), -les, -ling, -led 'piːp|l, -lz,
   -lɪŋ [-lɪŋ], -ld
Peover 'piːvə*
pep, -talk 'pep, -tɔːk
Pepin 'pepɪn
pepper (s. v.) (P.), -s, -ing, -ed, -er/s
   'pepə*, -z, -rɪŋ, -d, -rə*/z
pepper-box, -es 'pepəbɒks, -ɪz
pepper-caster [-tor], -s 'pepəˌkɑːstə*, -z
pepper-corn, -s 'pepəkɔːn, -z
peppermint, -s 'pepəmɪnt [-mənt,
   'pepmɪnt, 'pepmənt], -s
pepper-pot, -s 'pepəpɒt, -s
pepper|y, -ily, -iness 'pepər|ɪ, -əlɪ [-ɪlɪ],
   -ɪnɪs [-məs]
pep|sin, -tic 'pep|sɪn, -tɪk
peptone, -s 'peptəʊn, -z
peptoniz|e [-is|e], -es, -ing, -ed 'pep-
   tənaɪz, -ɪz, -ɪŋ, -d

Pepys 'pepɪs, piːps, peps
Note.—The pronunciation in the family of the present Lord Cottenham is 'pepɪs. *Samuel Pepys is generally referred to as* piːps.

per pɜ:* *(strong form)*, pə* *(weak form)*
Pera 'pɪərə
peradventure pərəd'ventʃə* [ˌpɜːrəd'v-, ˌperə-]
Perak 'peərə ['pɪərə, pə'ræk, pɪ'r-, pe'r-]
Note.—Those who have lived in Malaya pronounce 'peərə *or* 'pɪərə.
perambulat|e, -es, -ing, -ed pə'ræmbjʊleɪt, -s, -ɪŋ, -ɪd
perambulation, -s pəˌræmbjʊ'leɪʃn, -z
perambulator, -s pə'ræmbjʊleɪtə* ['præm-], -z
per annum pər'ænəm
per capita pə'kæpɪtə [ˌpɜ:-]
perceivab|le, -ly pə'siːvəb|l [pɜ:'s-], -lɪ
perceiv|e, -es, -ing, -ed, -er/s pə'siːv, -z, -ɪŋ, -d, -ə*/z
per cent pə'sent
percentage, -s pə'sentɪdʒ, -ɪz
percept, -s 'pɜ:sept
perceptibility pəˌseptə'bɪlətɪ [-tɪ'b-, -lɪt-]
perceptib|le, -leness pə'septəb|l [-tɪb-], -lɪ, -lnɪs [-nəs]
perception, -s pə'sepʃn, -z
perceptive, -ly, -ness pə'septɪv, -lɪ, -nɪs [-nəs]
Perceval 'pɜːsɪvl
perch *(s. v.)*, **-es, -ing, -ed, -er/s** pɜ:tʃ, -ɪz, -ɪŋ, -t, -ə*/z
perchance pə'tʃɑ:ns [ˌpɜ:'tʃ-]
Percheron, -s 'pɜ:ʃərɒn (perʃərɔ̃), -z
percipien|ce, -t/s pə'sɪpɪən|s [-pjən-], -t/s
Percival 'pɜ:sɪvl
percolat|e, -es, -ing, -ed, -or/s 'pɜ:kəleɪt, -s, -ɪŋ, -ɪd, -ə*/z
percolation, -s ˌpɜ:kə'leɪʃn, -z
per contra ˌpɜ:'kɒntrə
percuss, -es, -ing, -ed pə'kʌs, -ɪz, -ɪŋ, -t
percussion, -s; -cap/s pə'kʌʃn, -z; -kæp/s
percussive pə'kʌsɪv
percutaneous, -ly ˌpɜ:kju:'teɪnjəs [-kjʊ't-, -nɪəs], -lɪ
Percy 'pɜ:sɪ
per diem ˌpɜ:'diːem [-'daɪem]
Perdita 'pɜ:dɪtə
perdition pə'dɪʃn
perdu(e) pɜ:'dju:
peregrin *(s. adj.)*, **-s** 'perɪgrɪn [-rəg-], -z
peregrinat|e, -es, -ing, -ed, -or/s 'perɪgrɪneɪt [-rəg-], -s, -ɪŋ, -ɪd, -ə*/z
peregrination, -s ˌperɪgrɪ'neɪʃn [-rəg-], -z

peregrine *(s. adj.)*, **-s** 'perɪgrɪn [-rəg-, -gri:n], -z
Peregrine *(personal name)* 'perɪgrɪn [-rəg-]
peremptor|y, -ily, -iness pə'remptər|ɪ [pɪ'rem-, 'perəm-], -əlɪ [-ɪlɪ], -ɪnɪs [-ɪnəs]
Note.—'perəm- *is more usual when the word is used as a legal term. Otherwise* pə'rem- *and* pɪ'rem- *are commoner.*
perennial *(s. adj.)*, **-s, -ly** pə'renjəl [pɪ'r-, -nɪəl], -z, -ɪ
perfec|t *(s. adj.)*, **-ts, -tly, -tness** 'pɜ:fɪk|t, -ts, -tlɪ, -tnɪs [-nəs]
perfect *(v.)*, **-s, -ing, -ed** pə'fekt [pɜ:'f-, 'pɜ:fɪkt], -s, -ɪŋ, -ɪd
perfectibility pəˌfektɪ'bɪlətɪ [pɜ:ˌf-, -tə'b-, -lɪt-]
perfectible pə'fektəbl [pɜ:'f-, -tɪb-]
perfection, -s, -ist/s pə'fekʃn, -z, -ɪst/s
perfective pə'fektɪv
perfervid pɜ:'fɜ:vɪd
perfidious, -ly, -ness pə'fɪdɪəs [pɜ:'f-, -djəs], -lɪ, -nɪs [-nəs]
perfid|y, -ies 'pɜ:fɪd|ɪ, -ɪz
perforable 'pɜ:fərəbl
perforate *(adj.)* 'pɜ:fərɪt [-rət]
perforat|e *(v.)*, **-es, -ing, -ed, -or/s** 'pɜ:fəreɪt, -s, -ɪŋ, -ɪd, -ə*/z
perforation, -s ˌpɜ:fə'reɪʃn, -z
perforce pə'fɔ:s [pɜ:'f-]
perform, -s, -ing, -ed, -er/s; -able, -ance/s pə'fɔ:m, -z, -ɪŋ, -d, -ə*/z; -əbl, -əns/ɪz
perfume *(s.)*, **-s** 'pɜ:fju:m, -z
perfum|e *(v.)*, **-es, -ing, -ed** pə'fju:m [pɜ:'f-, 'pɜ:f-], -z, -ɪŋ, -d
perfumed *(adj.)* 'pɜ:fju:md
perfum|er, -ers; -ery pə'fju:m|ə* [pɜ:'f-], -əz; -ərɪ
perfunctor|y, -ily, -iness pə'fʌŋktər|ɪ [pɜ:'f-], -əlɪ [-ɪlɪ], -ɪnɪs [-ɪnəs]
Perga, -mos 'pɜ:gə, -mɒs
Pergam|um, -us 'pɜ:gəm|əm, -əs
pergola, -s 'pɜ:gələ, -z
Pergolese ˌpɜ:gəʊ'leɪzɪ [ˌpeəg-]
Perham 'perəm
perhaps pə'hæps, præps
*Note.—*pə'hæps *is more usual in formal speech, and in colloquial when the word is said in isolation or used parenthetically (as˘ in* You know, perhaps, . . .). præps *is common in other situations, esp. initially (e.g. in* Perhaps we shall, Perhaps it is a mistake).
peri, -s 'pɪərɪ, -z
pericarditis ˌperɪkɑ:'daɪtɪs

pericardium, -s ˌperɪˈkɑːdjəm [-dɪəm], -z
pericarp, -s ˈperɪkɑːp, -s
Pericles ˈperɪkliːz
pericope pəˈrɪkəpɪ [pɪˈr-, peˈr-]
peridot, -s ˈperɪdɒt, -s
perigee, -s ˈperɪdʒiː, -z
periheli|on, -a ˌperɪˈhiːljǀən [-lɪǀən], -ə
peril, -s ˈperəl [-rɪl], -z
perilous, -ly, -ness ˈperələs [-rɪləs,
-rǀəs], -lɪ, -nɪs [-nəs]
Perim ˈperɪm
perimeter, -s pəˈrɪmɪtə* [pɪˈr-, peˈr-,
-mətə*], -z
period, -s ˈpɪərɪəd, -z
periodic ˌpɪərɪˈɒdɪk
periodic|al (s. adj.), -als, -ally ˌpɪərɪˈɒd-
ɪkǀl, -lz, -əlɪ
periodicit|y, -ies ˌpɪərɪəˈdɪsətǀɪ [-rɒˈd-,
-rtǀɪ], -ɪz
peripatetic, -ally ˌperɪpəˈtetɪk, -əlɪ
peripher|y, -ies, -al pəˈrɪfərǀɪ [pɪˈr-,
peˈr-], -ɪz, -əl
periphras|is, -es pəˈrɪfrəsǀɪs [pɪˈr-, peˈr-],
-iːz
periphrastic, -al, -ally ˌperɪˈfræstɪk, -l,
-əlɪ
periscope, -s ˈperɪskəup, -s
perish, -es, -ing/ly, -ed ˈperɪʃ, -ɪz, -ɪŋ/lɪ,
-t
perishability ˌperɪʃəˈbɪlətɪ [-lɪt-]
perishab|le, -ly, -leness ˈperɪʃəbǀl, -lɪ,
-lnɪs [-nəs]
perispomenon ˌperɪˈspəummən [-nɒn]
peristalsis ˌperɪˈstælsɪs
peristaltic ˌperɪˈstæltɪk
peristyle, -s ˈperɪstaɪl, -z
peritoneum, -s ˌperɪtəuˈniːəm [-ˈnɪəm],
-z
peritonitis ˌperɪtəuˈnaɪtɪs
Perivale ˈperɪveɪl
periwig, -s ˈperɪwɪg, -z
periwinkle, -s ˈperɪˌwɪŋkl, -z
Perizzite, -s ˈperɪzaɪt, -s
perj|ure, -ures, -uring, -ured, -urer/s
ˈpɜːdʒǀə*, -əz, -ərɪŋ, -əd, -ərə*/z
perjur|y, -ies ˈpɜːdʒərǀɪ, -ɪz
perk, -s, -ing, -ed pɜːk, -s, -ɪŋ, -t
Perkin, -s ˈpɜːkɪn, -z
perk|y, -ier, -iest, -ily, -iness ˈpɜːkǀɪ,
-ɪə* [-jə*], -ɪɪst [-jɪst], -ɪlɪ [-əlɪ], -ɪnɪs
[-ɪnəs]
Perlis ˈpɜːlɪs
perm, -s pɜːm, -z
permanenc|e, -es, -y, -ies ˈpɜːmənəns,
-ɪz, -ɪ, -ɪz
permanent, -ly ˈpɜːmənənt, -lɪ
permanganate pɜːˈmæŋgəneɪt [pəˈm-,
-nɪt, -nət]

permeability ˌpɜːmjəˈbɪlətɪ [-mɪə-, -lɪt-]
permeable ˈpɜːmjəbl [-mɪə-]
permeat|e, -es, -ing, -ed ˈpɜːmɪeɪt
[-mjet], -s, -ɪŋ, -ɪd
permeation ˌpɜːmɪˈeɪʃn
permissib|le, -ly, -leness pəˈmɪsəbǀl
[-sɪb-], -lɪ, -lnɪs [-nəs]
permission, -s pəˈmɪʃn, -z
permissive, -ly, -ness pəˈmɪsɪv, -lɪ, -nɪs
[-nəs]
permit (s.), -s ˈpɜːmɪt, -s
permit (v.), -s, -ting, -ted pəˈmɪt, -s, -ɪŋ,
-ɪd
permutation, -s ˌpɜːmjuːˈteɪʃn [-mjuˈt-],
-z
permut|e, -es, -ing, -ed; -able pəˈmjuːt,
-s, -ɪŋ, -ɪd; -əbl
Pernambuco ˌpɜːnæmˈbuːkəu [-nəm-]
pernicious, -ly, -ness pəˈnɪʃəs [pɜːˈn-],
-lɪ, -nɪs [-nəs]
pernicket|y, -iness pəˈnɪkətǀɪ [-ɪtǀɪ], -mɪs
[-ɪnəs]
perorat|e, -es, -ing, -ed ˈperəreɪt [-rɒr-],
-s, -ɪŋ, -ɪd
peroration, -s ˌperəˈreɪʃn [-rɒˈr-], -z
Perouse pəˈruːz [pɪˈr-, peˈr-]
Perowne pəˈrəun [pɪˈr-, peˈr-]
peroxide, -s pəˈrɒksaɪd, -z
perpend, -s, -ing, -ed pəˈpend, -z, -ɪŋ,
-ɪd
perpendicular (s. adj.), -s, -ly ˌpɜːpən-
ˈdɪkjulə* [ˌpɜːpmˈd-, -kjəl-], -z, -lɪ
perpendicularity ˈpɜːpənˌdɪkjuˈlærətɪ
[ˈpɜːpmˌd-, -kjəˈl-, -rtɪ]
perpetrat|e, -es, -ing, -ed, -or/s ˈpɜːpɪ-
treɪt [-pətr-], -s, -ɪŋ, -ɪd, -ə*/z
perpetration, -s ˌpɜːpɪˈtreɪʃn [-pəˈtr-], -z
perpetual, -ly pəˈpetʃuəl [-tʃwəl, -tʃul,
-tjuəl, -tjwəl, -tjul], -ɪ
perpetuat|e, -es, -ing, -ed pəˈpetʃueɪt
[pɜːˈp-, -ˈpetju-], -s, -ɪŋ, -ɪd
perpetuation, -s pəˌpetʃuˈeɪʃn [pɜːˌp-,
-ˌpetju-], -z
perpetuit|y, -ies ˌpɜːpɪˈtjuːətǀɪ [-pəˈt-,
-tju-, -rtǀɪ], -ɪz
perpetuum mobile pəˌpetʃuumˈməubɪleɪ
[pɜːˌp-, -ˌpetju-, -lɪ]
perplex, -es, -ing/ly, -ed, -edly, -edness
pəˈpleks, -ɪz, -ɪŋ/lɪ, -t, -ɪdlɪ [-tlɪ],
-ɪdnɪs [-tnɪs, -nəs]
perplexit|y, -ies pəˈpleksətǀɪ [-ɪtǀɪ], -ɪz
perquisite, -s ˈpɜːkwɪzɪt, -s
Perrault ˈperəu (peʀo)
Perrett ˈperɪt
Perrier ˈpereɪ [-rɪə*] (pɛʀje)
Perrin ˈperɪn
perr|y (P.), -ies ˈperǀɪ, -ɪz
Perse pɜːs

per se ˌpɜː'seɪ [-'siː]

persecut|e, -es, -ing, -ed, -or/s 'pɜːsɪkjuːt, -s, -ɪŋ, -ɪd, -ə*/z

persecution, -s ˌpɜːsɪ'kjuːʃn, -z

Persephone pɜː'sefənɪ [-fnɪ]

Persepolis pɜː'sepəlɪs

Perseus 'pɜːsjuːs [-sjəs, -sɪəs]

perseveration pəˌsevə'reɪʃn [pɜːˌs-]

persever|e, -es, -ing/ly, -ed; -ance ˌpɜːsɪ'vɪə*, -z, -rɪŋ/lɪ, -d; -rəns

Pershing 'pɜːʃɪŋ

Persi|a, -an/s 'pɜːʃ|ə [rarely 'pɜːʒ|ə], -n/z

persiflage 'pɜːsɪflɑːʒ [ˌpeəs-, ˌ--'-] (pɛrsiflaːʒ)

persimmon (P.), -s pə'sɪmən [pɜː's-], -z

persist, -s, -ing/ly, -ed pə'sɪst, -s, -ɪŋ/lɪ, -ɪd

persisten|ce, -cy pə'sɪstən|s, -sɪ

persistent, -ly pə'sɪstənt, -lɪ

person, -s 'pɜːsn, -z

person|a, -ae pə'səʊn|ə [pɜː's-], -iː [-aɪ]

persona (non) grata pəˌsəʊnə (nɒn) 'grɑːtə [pɜːˌs-, -'greɪtə]

personable 'pɜːsnəbl [-sənə-, -snə-]

personage, -s 'pɜːsnɪdʒ [-sənɪdʒ, -snɪdʒ], -ɪz

pers|onal, -onally 'pɜːs|nl̩ [-nl̩, -ənl̩], -nəlɪ [-nəlɪ, -nl̩ɪ, -nl̩ɪ, -ənl̩ɪ]

personalit|y, -ies ˌpɜːsə'nælət|ɪ [-sn̩'æ-, -ɪt|ɪ], -ɪz

personaliz|e [is|e], -es, -ing, -ed 'pɜːsn̩əlaɪz [-snəl-, -sn̩l̩-, -snl̩-, -sənəl-], -ɪz, -ɪŋ, -d

personalt|y, -ies 'pɜːsnl̩t|ɪ [-snəl-, -sən|-, -sn̩l̩-], -ɪz

personat|e, -es, -ing, -ed, -or/s 'pɜːsəneɪt [-sn̩eɪt], -s, -ɪŋ, -ɪd, -ə*/z

personation, -s ˌpɜːsə'neɪʃn [-sn̩'eɪ-], -s

personification, -s pəˌsɒnɪfɪ'keɪʃn [pɜːˌs-], -z

personi|fy, -fies, -fying, -fied pə'sɒnɪ|faɪ [pɜː's-], -faɪz, -faɪɪŋ, -faɪd

personnel, -s ˌpɜːsə'nel [-sn̩'el], -z

perspective (s. adj.), -s, -ly pə'spektɪv [pɜː's-], -z, -lɪ

perspex 'pɜːspeks

perspicacious, -ly, -ness ˌpɜːspɪ'keɪʃəs, -lɪ, -nɪs [-nəs]

perspicacity ˌpɜːspɪ'kæsətɪ [-ɪtɪ]

perspicuity ˌpɜːspɪ'kjuːətɪ [-kjʊ-, -ɪtɪ]

perspicuous, -ly, -ness pə'spɪkjuəs [pɜː's-, -kjwəs], -lɪ, -nɪs [-nəs]

perspiration ˌpɜːspə'reɪʃn

perspir|e, -es, -ing, -ed pə'spaɪə*, -z, -rɪŋ, -d

persuad|e, -es, -ing, -ed, -er/s pə'sweɪd, -z, -ɪŋ, -ɪd, -ə*/z

persuasion, -s pə'sweɪʒn, -z

persuasive, -ly, -ness pə'sweɪsɪv [-eɪzɪv], -lɪ, -nɪs [-nəs]

pert, -est, -ly, -ness pɜːt, -ɪst, -lɪ, -nɪs [-nəs]

pertain, -s, -ing, -ed pə'teɪn [pɜː't-], -z, -ɪŋ, -d

Perth, -shire pɜːθ, -ʃə* [-ˌʃɪə*]

pertinacious, -ly, -ness ˌpɜːtɪ'neɪʃəs, -lɪ, -nɪs [-nəs]

pertinacity ˌpɜːtɪ'næsətɪ [-ɪtɪ]

pertinen|ce, -cy, -t/ly 'pɜːtɪnən|s, -sɪ, -t/lɪ

perturb, -s, -ing, -ed, -er/s; -able pə'tɜːb [pɜː't-], -z, -ɪŋ, -d, -ə*/z; -əbl

perturbation, -s ˌpɜːtə'beɪʃn [-tɜː'b-], -z

Pertwee 'pɜːtwiː

Peru pə'ruː [pɪ'r-]

Perugia pə'ruːdʒə [pɪ'r-, pe'r-, -dʒɪə, -dʒjə] (pe'ruːdʒa)

Perugino ˌperuː'dʒiːnəʊ [-ruː'dʒ-] (peru-'dʒiːno)

peruke, -s pə'ruːk [pɪ'r-, pe'r-], -s

perusal, -s pə'ruːzl [pɪ'r-, pe'r-], -z

perus|e, -es, -ing, -ed, -er/s pə'ruːz [pɪ'r-, pe'r-], -ɪz, -ɪŋ, -d, -ə*/z

Peruvian, -s pə'ruːvjən [pɪ'r-, pe'r-, -vɪən], -z

pervad|e, -es, -ing, -ed pə'veɪd [pɜː'v-], -z, -ɪŋ, -ɪd

pervasion pə'veɪʒn [pɜː'v-]

pervasive pə'veɪsɪv [pɜː'v-]

perverse, -ly, -ness pə'vɜːs [pɜː'v-], -lɪ, -nɪs [-nəs]

perversion, -s pə'vɜːʃn [pɜː'v-], -z

perversity pə'vɜːsətɪ [pɜː'v-, -ɪtɪ]

pervert (s.), -s 'pɜːvɜːt, -s

pervert (v.), -s, -ing, -ed, -er/s pə'vɜːt [pɜː'v-], -s, -ɪŋ, -ɪd, -ə*/z

pervious, -ly, -ness 'pɜːvjəs [-vɪəs], -lɪ, -nɪs [-nəs]

Pescadores ˌpeskə'dɔːrɪz

peseta, -s pə'seɪtə [pɪ's-, -'setə] (pe'seta), -z

Peshawar pə'ʃɔːə* [pe'ʃ-, -'ʃaʊə*]

pesk|y, -ier, -iest, -ily, -iness 'pesk|ɪ, ɪə* [-jə*], -ɪɪst [-jɪst], -ɪlɪ [-əlɪ], -ɪnɪs [-ɪnəs]

peso, -s 'peɪsəʊ, -z

pessar|y, -ies 'pesər|ɪ, -ɪz

pessimi|sm, -st/s 'pesɪmɪ|zəm [-səm-], -st/s

pessimistic, -al, -ally ˌpesɪ'mɪstɪk [-sə'm-], -l, -əlɪ

pest (P.), -s pest, -s

Pestalozzi ˌpestə'lɒtsɪ (pesta'lɔttsi)

pest|er, -ers, -ering/ly, -ered, -erer/s 'pest|ə*, -əz, -ərɪŋ/lɪ, -əd, -ərə*/z

Pest(h) pest
pesticide, -s 'pestɪsaɪd, -z
pestiferous, -ly pe'stɪfərəs, -lɪ
pestilence, -s 'pestɪləns, -ɪz
pestilent, -ly 'pestɪlənt, -lɪ
pestilenti|al, -ally ˌpestɪ'lenʃ|l, -əlɪ
pe|stle (s. v.), -stles, -stling, -stled 'pe|sl
[-stl], -slz [-stlz], -s|ɪŋ [-slɪŋ, -st|ɪŋ,
-stlɪŋ], -sld [-stld]
pestolog|ist/s, -y pe'stɒlədʒ|ɪst/s, -ɪ
pet (s. v.), -s, -ting, -ted pet, -s, -ɪŋ, -ɪd
petal, -s, -(l)ed 'petl, -z, -d
petaline 'petəlaɪn
petard, -s pe'tɑːd [pɪ't-, pə't-], -z
Pete piːt
Peter 'piːtə*
Peterborough [-boro'] 'piːtəbrə [-bərə,
-bʌrə]
Peterculter 'piːtəkuːtə*
Peterhead ˌpiːtə'hed
Peters 'piːtəz
Petersburg 'piːtəzbɜːg
Petersfield 'piːtəzfiːld
petersham (P.), -s 'piːtəʃəm, -z
Pethick 'peθɪk
petite pə'tiːt
petiti|on (s. v.), -ons, -oning, -oned,
-oner/s pə'tɪʃ|n [pɪ't-], -nz, -ŋɪŋ
[-ənɪŋ, -nɪŋ], -nd, -ŋə*/z [-ənə*/z,
-nə*/z]
Peto 'piːtəʊ
Petrarch 'petrɑːk [old-fashioned 'piːt-]
Petre 'piːtə*
petrel, -s 'petrəl, -z
Petrie 'piːtrɪ
petrifaction ˌpetrɪ'fækʃn
petri|fy, -fies, -fying, -fied 'petrɪ|faɪ,
-faɪz, -faɪɪŋ, -faɪd
Petrograd 'petrəʊgræd [-grɑːd]
petr|ol (s. v.), -ols, -oling, -oled 'petr|əl
[-r|ɒl], -əlz [-ɒlz], -əlɪŋ [-l|ɪŋ, -ɒlɪŋ],
-əld [-ɒld]
petroleum pə'trəʊljəm [pɪ't-, -lɪəm]
Petruchio pɪ'truːkɪəʊ [pə't-, pe't-,
-kjəʊ, -tʃɪəʊ, -tʃjəʊ]
Pett pet
petticoat, -s, -ed 'petɪkəʊt, -s, -ɪd
pettifogg|er/s, -ery, -ing 'petɪfɒg|ə*/z,
-ərɪ, -ɪŋ
Pettigrew 'petɪgruː
pettish, -ly, -ness 'petɪʃ, -lɪ, -nɪs [-nəs]
Pettit 'petɪt
pettitoes 'petɪtəʊz
pett|y, -ier, -iest, -ily, -iness/es 'pet|ɪ,
-ɪə*, -ɪɪst, -ɪlɪ [-əlɪ], -ɪnɪs [-ɪnəs]/ɪz
Petula pə'tjuːlə [pɪ't-, pe't-]
petulan|ce, -cy 'petjʊlən|s [-tʃʊl-], -sɪ
petulant, -ly 'petjʊlənt [-tʃʊl-], -lɪ

Petulengro ˌpetjʊ'leŋgrəʊ [-tə'l-]
petunia, -s pə'tjuːnjə [pɪ't-, -nɪə], -z
Peugeot (car), -s 'pɜːʒəʊ (pøʒo), -z
Pevensey 'pevənzɪ
Peveril 'pevərɪl
pew, -s pjuː, -z
pew-holder, -s 'pjuːˌhəʊldə*, -z
pewit, -s 'piːwɪt, -s
pew|-opener/s, -rent/s 'pjuːˌəʊpnə*/z,
-rent/s
pewter, -s 'pjuːtə*, -z
Peynell 'peɪnl [-nel]
Peyton 'peɪtn
pfennig, -s 'pfenɪg ('pfɛniç), -z
Phaedo 'fiːdəʊ
Phaedr|a, -us 'fiːdr|ə, -əs
Phaer 'feɪə*
Phaethon 'feɪəθən ['feɪθ-]
phaeton, -s 'feɪtn, -z
phagocyte, -s 'fægəʊsaɪt, -s
phalange, -s 'fælændʒ, -ɪz
phalanges (alternative plur. of phalanx)
fæ'lændʒiːz [fə'l-]
phalangist (F.), -s fæ'lændʒɪst [fə-], -s
phalanster|y, -ies 'fælənstər|ɪ, -ɪz
phalanx, -es 'fælæŋks [rarely 'feɪl-], -ɪz
Phalaris 'fælərɪs
phalarope, -s 'fælərəʊp, -s
phallic 'fælɪk
phallicism 'fælɪsɪzəm
phallus, -es 'fæləs, -ɪz
phanerogam, -s 'fænərəʊgæm, -z
phanerogamic ˌfænərəʊ'gæmɪk
phanerogamous ˌfænə'rɒgəməs
phantasm, -s 'fæntæzəm, -z
phantasmagoria ˌfæntæzmə'gɒrɪə [-təz-,
-'gɔːr-]
phantasmagoric, -al ˌfæntæzmə'gɒrɪk,
-l [-təz-]
phantasm|al, -ally, -ic fæn'tæzm|l, -əlɪ,
-ɪk
phantom, -s 'fæntəm, -z
Pharamond 'færəmənd [-mɒnd]
Pharaoh, -s 'feərəʊ, -z
pharisaic, -al, -ally, -alness ˌfærɪ'seɪk
[-'zeɪk], -l, -əlɪ, -lnɪs [-nəs]
pharisaism 'færɪseɪɪzəm
pharisee (P.), -s 'færɪsɪ [-rəs-], -z
pharmaceutic, -al, -ally, -s ˌfɑːmə-
'sjuːtɪk [-'suː-, -'kjuː-], -l, -əlɪ, -s
pharmac|ist/s, -y, -ies 'fɑːməs|ɪst/s, -ɪ,
-ɪz
pharmacolog|ist/s, -y ˌfɑːmə'kɒlədʒ|-
ɪst/s, -ɪ
pharmacopoeia, -s, -l ˌfɑːməkə'piːə
[-kəʊ'p-, -'pɪə], -z, -l
Pharos 'feərɒs
Pharsalia fɑː'seɪljə [-lɪə]

pharyngal fə'rɪŋgl [fæˈr-, feəˈr-]
pharyngeal ˌfærɪn'dʒiːəl [ˌfeər-, -'dʒɪəl,
   fəˈrɪndʒɪəl,   fæ'rɪndʒ-,   feə'rɪndʒ-,
   -'rɪndʒjəl]
pharyngitis ˌfærɪn'dʒaɪtɪs [ˌfeər-]
pharynx, -es 'færɪŋks ['feər-], -ɪz
phase, -s feɪz, -ɪz
phas|is, -es 'feɪs|ɪs, -iːz
phatic 'fætɪk
Phayre (fem. Christian name) feə*
Ph.D., -'s ˌpiːertʃ'diː, -z
Phear feə*
pheasant, -s 'feznt, -s
Phebe 'fiːbɪ
Phelps felps
phenacetin fɪ'næsɪtɪn [fe'n-, fə'n-, -sət-]
Phenice fɪ'naɪsɪ [fiː'n-, -siː]
Pheni|cia, -cian/s fɪ'nɪ|ʃə [fiː'n-, -ʃjə,
   -ʃɪə, -sɪə, -sjə], -ʃn/z [-ʃjən/z, -ʃɪən/z,
   -sɪən/z, -sjən/z]
phenobarbitone ˌfiːnəʊ'bɑːbɪtəʊn
phenol 'fiːnɒl
phenolphthalein ˌfiːnɒl'fθælɪɪn
phenomen|on, -a, -al, -ally fə'nɒmɪn|ən
   [fɪ-], -ə, -l, -əlɪ
phew φː, ẏ̊ː, pẏ̊ː, ẏuː, ẏ̊ẏ̊ː [fjuː]
phi, -s faɪ, -z
phial, -s 'faɪəl, -z
Phidias 'fɪdɪæs ['faɪd-]
Philadelphia, -n/s ˌfɪlə'delfjə [-fɪə], -n/z
philander, -s, -ing, -ed, -er/s fɪ'lændə*,
   -z, -rɪŋ, -d, -rə*/z
philanthrope, -s 'fɪlənθrəʊp, -s
philanthropic, -al, -ally ˌfɪlən'θrɒpɪk, -l,
   -əlɪ
philanthrop|ist/s, -y fɪ'lænθrəp|ɪst/s, -ɪ
philatelic ˌfɪlə'telɪk [ˌfaɪl-]
philatel|ist/s, -y fɪ'lætəl|ɪst/s, -ɪ
Philbrick 'fɪlbrɪk
Philemon fɪ'liːmɒn [faɪ'l-, -mən]
philharmonic (s. adj.), -s ˌfɪlɑː'mɒnɪk
   [-lə'm-, -lhɑː'm-], -s
philhellene, -s fɪl'heliːn [ˈ-ˌ--], -z
philhellenic ˌfɪlhe'liːnɪk , [-'len-]
philhellenism fɪl'helɪnɪzəm
philibeg, -s 'fɪlɪbeg, -z
Philip, -pa 'fɪlɪp, -ə
Philippi fɪ'lɪpaɪ ['---]
Philippian, -s fɪ'lɪpɪən [-pjən], -z
Philippic, -s fɪ'lɪpɪk, -s
Philippine, -s 'fɪlɪpiːn [old-fashioned
   -paɪn], -z
Philip(p)s 'fɪlɪps
Philistia fɪ'lɪstjə [-tɪə]
philistine (P.), -s 'fɪlɪstaɪn [rarely -tɪn],
   -z
philistinism 'fɪlɪstɪnɪzəm
Phillimore 'fɪlɪmɔː* [-mɔə*]

Phillip(p)s 'fɪlɪps
Phillpot, -s 'fɪlpɒt, -s
phillumenist, -s fɪ'luːmənɪst [-'lju-], -s
Philoctetes ˌfɪlɒk'tiːtiːz [-lɒk-]
philologic, -al, -ally ˌfɪlə'lɒdʒɪk, -l, -əlɪ
philolog|ist/s, -y fɪ'lɒlədʒ|ɪst/s, -ɪ
Philomel, -s 'fɪləmel [-ləʊm-], -z
Philomela ˌfɪləʊ'miːlə
Philonous 'fɪləʊnaʊs
philosopher, -s fɪ'lɒsəfə* [fə-, -ɒzə-], -z
philosophic, -al, -ally ˌfɪlə'sɒfɪk [-ə'zɒ-],
   -l, -əlɪ
philosophi|sm, -st/s fɪ'lɒsəfɪ|zəm [fə-,
   -ɒzə-], -st/s
philosophiz|e [-is|e], -es, -ing, -ed
   fɪ'lɒsəfaɪz [fə-, -ɒzə-], -ɪz, -ɪŋ, -d
philosoph|y, -ies fɪ'lɒsəf|ɪ [fə-, -ɒzə-], -ɪz
Philostratus fɪ'lɒstrətəs
Philpot, -ts 'fɪlpɒt, -s
philtre [-ter], -s 'fɪltə*, -z
Phineas 'fɪnɪæs [-nɪəs]
Phinees 'fɪnɪəs [-nɪes]
Phinehas 'fɪnɪæs [-nɪəs]
Phip|ps, -son frɪp|s, -sn
phiz (P.) fɪz
Phizackerley fɪ'zækəlɪ
phlebitic flɪ'brtɪk [fliː'b-, fle'b-]
phlebitis flɪ'baɪtɪs [fliː'b-, fle'b-]
phlebotomy flɪ'bɒtəmɪ [fliː'b-, fle'b-]
Phlegethon 'flegɪθɒn [-θən]
phlegm, -s flem, -z
phlegmatic, -al, -ally fleg'mætɪk, -l, -əlɪ
phloem 'fləʊem
phlogistic flɒ'dʒɪstɪk [-ɒ'gɪ-]
phlogiston flɒ'dʒɪstən [-ɒ'gɪ-, -tɒn]
phlox, -es flɒks, -ɪz
phob|ia, -ias, -ic 'fəʊb|jə [-b|ɪə], -jəz
   [-ɪəz], -ɪk
Phocian, -s 'fəʊʃjən [-ʃɪən, -sjən, -sɪən],
   -z
Phocion 'fəʊsjən [-sɪən, -sɪɒn, -sjɒn]
Phocis 'fəʊsɪs
Phoeb|e, -us 'fiːb|ɪ, -əs
Phoeni|cia, -cian/s fɪ'nɪ|ʃə [fiː'n-,
   -ʃjə, -ʃɪə, -sɪə, -sjə], -ʃn/z [-ʃɪən/z,
   -ʃjən/z, -sɪən/z, -sjən/z]
phoenix (P.), -es 'fiːnɪks, -ɪz
phon, -s fɒn, -z
phonat|e, -es, -ing, -ed fəʊ'neɪt, -s, -ɪŋ,
   -ɪd
phonation fəʊ'neɪʃn
phonatory 'fəʊnətərɪ [fəʊ'neɪtərɪ]
phon|e (s. v.), -es, -ing, -ed fəʊn, -z, -ɪŋ,
   -d
phonematic, -s ˌfəʊnɪ'mætɪk [-niː-], -s
phoneme, -s 'fəʊniːm, -z
phonemic, -s fəʊ'niːmɪk, -s
phonemicist, -s fəʊ'niːmɪsɪst, -s

phonetic, -al, -ally, -s fəʊ'netɪk, -l, -əlɪ, -s

phonetician, -s ˌfəʊnɪ'tɪʃn [ˌfɒn-, -nə't-, -ne't-], -z

phoneticist, -s fəʊ'netɪsɪst, -s

phoneticiz|e [-is|e], -es, -ing, -ed fəʊ'netɪsaɪz, -ɪz, -ɪŋ, -d

phonetist, -s 'fəʊnɪtɪst [-net-], -s

phoney 'fəʊnɪ

phonic, -s 'fəʊnɪk ['fɒn-], -s

phonogram, -s 'fəʊnəgræm, -z

phonograph, -s 'fəʊnəgrɑːf [-græf], -s

phonographer, -s fəʊ'nɒgrəfə*, -z

phonographist, -s fəʊ'nɒgrəfɪst, -s

phonography fəʊ'nɒgrəfɪ

phonographic, -al, -ally ˌfəʊnə'græfɪk, -l, -əlɪ

phonologic|al, -ally ˌfəʊnə'lɒdʒɪk|l, -əlɪ

phonologist, -s fəʊ'nɒlədʒɪst, -s

phonolog|y, -ies fəʊ'nɒlədʒ|ɪ, -ɪz

phonotype, -s 'fəʊnəʊtaɪp, -s

phonotypy 'fəʊnəʊtaɪpɪ

phosgene 'fɒzdʒiːn ['fɒs-]

phosphate, -s 'fɒsfeɪt [-fɪt, -fət], -s

phosphite, -s 'fɒsfaɪt, -s

phosphoresc|e, -es, -ing, -ed; -ence, -ent ˌfɒsfə'res, -ɪz, -ɪŋ, -t; -ns, -nt

phosphoric fɒs'fɒrɪk

phosphor|ous, -us 'fɒsfər|əs, -əs

phossy 'fɒsɪ

photo, -s 'fəʊtəʊ, -z

photochrome, -s 'fəʊtəkrəʊm, -z

photo-cop|y, -ies 'fəʊtəʊˌkɒp|ɪ, -ɪz

photoelectric ˌfəʊtəʊɪ'lektrɪk (also '—ˌ— when attributive, e.g. cell)

photogenic ˌfəʊtəʊ'dʒenɪk [-'dʒiːn-]

photograph (s. v.), -s, -ing, -ed 'fəʊtəgrɑːf [-græf], -s, -ɪŋ, -t

photographer, -s fə'tɒgrəfə*, -z

photographic, -al, -ally ˌfəʊtə'græfɪk, -l, -əlɪ

photography fə'tɒgrəfɪ

photogravure, -s ˌfəʊtəgrə'vjʊə*, [-təʊg-, -'vjɔə*, -'vjɔ:*], -z

photosphere, -s 'fəʊtəʊˌsfɪə*, -z

photostat (s. v.), -s, -ting, -ted 'fəʊtəʊstæt, -s, -ɪŋ, -ɪd

photostatic ˌfəʊtəʊ'stætɪk

phrasal 'freɪzl

phras|e (s. v.), -es, -ing, -ed freɪz, -ɪz, -ɪŋ, -d

phrase-book, -s 'freɪzbʊk, -s

phrase-monger, -s 'freɪzˌmʌŋgə*, -z

phraseologic, -al, -ally ˌfreɪzɪə'lɒdʒɪk [-zjə-], -l, -əlɪ

phraseolog|y, -ies ˌfreɪzɪ'ɒlədʒ|ɪ, -ɪz

phrenetic, -al frɪ'netɪk [fre'n-, frə-], -l

phrenic 'frenɪk

phrenologic|al, -ally ˌfrenə'lɒdʒɪk|l, -əlɪ

phrenolog|ist/s, -y frɪ'nɒlədʒ|ɪst/s [fre'n-, frə-], -ɪ

Phrygia, -n/s 'frɪdʒɪə [-dʒjə], -n/z

Phryne 'fraɪniː

phthisic 'θaɪsɪk ['fθaɪ-, 'taɪ-]

phthisis 'θaɪsɪs ['fθaɪ-, 'taɪ-]

phut fʌt

phylacter|y, -ies frɪ'læktər|ɪ, -ɪz

Phyllis 'fɪlɪs

phylloxer|a, -ae, -as ˌfɪlɒk'sɪər|ə [frɪ'lɒk-sər|ə], -iː, -əz

physic (s. v.), -s, -king, -ked 'fɪzɪk, -s, -ɪŋ, -t

physic|al, -ally 'fɪzɪk|l, -əlɪ

physician, -s frɪ'zɪʃn, -z

physicist, -s 'fɪzɪsɪst, -s

physiognomic, -al, -ally ˌfɪzɪə'nɒmɪk [-zjə-], -l, -əlɪ

physiognomist, -s ˌfɪzɪ'ɒnəmɪst, -s

physiognom|y, -ies ˌfɪzɪ'ɒnəm|ɪ, -ɪz

physiography ˌfɪzɪ'ɒgrəfɪ

physiologic, -al, -ally ˌfɪzɪə'lɒdʒɪk [-zjə-], -l, -əlɪ

physiolog|ist/s, -y ˌfɪzɪ'ɒlədʒ|ɪst/s, -ɪ

physiophonic ˌfɪzɪəʊ'fəʊnɪk [-'fɒn-]

physiotherap|y, -ist/s ˌfɪzɪəʊ'θerəp|ɪ [-zjəʊ-], -ɪst/s

physique frɪ'ziːk [fiː'z-]

pi (s. adj.), -s paɪ, -z

piacere pɪə'tʃɪərɪ [ˌpi:ə-]

piacular paɪ'ækjʊlə*

piaff|e (s. v.), -es, -ing, -ed pɪ'æf [pjæf], -s, -ɪŋ, -t

pianissimo, -s pɪə'nɪsɪməʊ [ˌpɪæ'n-, pjɑ:'n, ˌpɪɑ:'n-, pjæ'n-, pjə'n-], -z

Note.—Among professional musicians pjɑ:'n-, ˌpɪɑ:'n-, pɪə'n- appear to be the most freq. used forms.

pianist, -s 'pɪənɪst ['pjænɪst, pɪ'æn-], -s

Note.—Professional musicians generally pronounce 'pɪənɪst.

piano (instrument), -s pɪ'ænəʊ ['pjæn-, 'pjɑ:n-, pɪ'ɑ:n-], -z

Note.—The forms 'pjɑ:n-, pɪ'ɑ:n-, are freq. among professional musicians.

piano (softly), -s 'pjɑ:nəʊ [pɪ'ɑ:-], -z

pianoforte, -s ˌpjænəʊ'fɔ:tɪ [ˌpjɑ:n-, pɪˌɑ:n-, '—ˌ—], -z

pianola, -s pɪə'nəʊlə [pjæ'n-, ˌpɪə'n-, ˌpɪæ'n-], -z

piano-organ, -s pɪ'ænəʊˌɔ:gən ['pjæn-, 'pjɑ:n-, pɪ'ɑ:n-], -z

piano-player, -s pɪ'ænəʊˌpleɪə* ['pjæn-, 'pjɑ:n-, pɪ'ɑ:n-], -z

piano-school, -s pɪ'ænəʊskuːl ['pjæn-, 'pjɑ:n-, pɪ'ɑ:n-], -z

piastre, -s pɪ'æstə* [pɪ'ɑ:s-], -z

piazza, -s pɪˈætsə [pɪˈɑːtsə] (ˈpjattsa), -z
pibroch, -s ˈpiːbrɒk [-ɒx], -s
pica ˈpaɪkə
picaninn|y, -ies ˌpɪkəˈnɪn|ɪ [ˈ----], -ɪz
Picardy ˈpɪkədɪ [-kɑːdɪ]
picaresque ˌpɪkəˈresk
picaroon (s. v.), -s, -ing, -ed ˌpɪkəˈruːn, -z, -ɪŋ, -d
Picasso pɪˈkæsəʊ
Piccadilly ˌpɪkəˈdɪlɪ [also ˈ--ˌ-- when followed by a stress]
piccalilli ˈpɪkəlɪlɪ [ˌ--ˈ--]
piccaninn|y, -ies ˌpɪkəˈnɪn|ɪ [ˈ----], -ɪz
piccolo, -s ˈpɪkələʊ, -z
pice paɪs
pick (s. v.), -s, -ing, -ed, -er/s pɪk, -s, -ɪŋ, -t, -ə*/z
pickaback ˈpɪkəbæk
pickaxe, -s ˈpɪkæks, -ɪz
pickerel, -s ˈpɪkərəl, -z
Pickering ˈpɪkərɪŋ
picket (s. v.), -s, -ing, -ed ˈpɪkɪt, -s, -ɪŋ, -ɪd
Pickford ˈpɪkfəd
picking (s.), -s ˈpɪkɪŋ, -z
pick|le (s. v.), -les (P.), -ling, -led ˈpɪk|l, -lz, -lɪŋ [-lɪŋ], -ld
picklock, -s ˈpɪklɒk, -s
pick-me-up, -s ˈpɪkmiːˌʌp [-mɪʌp], -s
pickpocket, -s ˈpɪkˌpɒkɪt, -s
pick-up (electric, truck), -s ˈpɪkʌp, -s
Pickwick ˈpɪkwɪk
Pickwickian pɪkˈwɪkɪən [-kjən]
picnic (s. v.), -s, -king, -ked, -ker/s ˈpɪknɪk, -s, -ɪŋ, -t, -ə*/z
picot, -s ˈpiːkəʊ [-ˈ-, pɪˈkəʊ]
picotee, -s ˌpɪkəˈtiː, -z
picquet (military term), -s ˈpɪkɪt, -s
picric ˈpɪkrɪk
Pict, -s pɪkt, -s
Pictish ˈpɪktɪʃ
pictograph, -s ˈpɪktəʊɡrɑːf [-ɡræf], -s
Picton ˈpɪktən
pictorial, -ly pɪkˈtɔːrəl, -ɪ
pict|ure (s. v.), -ures, -uring, -ured ˈpɪktʃ|ə*, -əz, -ərɪŋ, -əd
picture|-book/s, -card/s ˈpɪktʃə|bʊk/s, -kɑːd/z
picture-galler|y, -ies ˈpɪktʃəˌɡælər|ɪ, -ɪz
picture-hat, -s ˈpɪktʃəhæt, -s
picturesque, -ly, -ness ˌpɪktʃəˈresk, -lɪ, -nɪs [-nəs]
picture-writing ˈpɪktʃəˌraɪtɪŋ
pidgin ˈpɪdʒɪn
Pidsley ˈpɪdzlɪ
pie, -s paɪ, -z
Piears pɪəz
piebald ˈpaɪbɔːld

piec|e (s. v.), -es, -ing, -ed, -er/s piːs, -ɪz, -ɪŋ, -t, -ə*/z
piece-goods ˈpiːsɡʊdz
piecemeal ˈpiːsmiːl
piece-work ˈpiːswɜːk
pie-crust, -s ˈpaɪkrʌst, -s
pied, -ness paɪd, -nɪs [-nəs]
pied-à-terre ˌpjeɪdɑːˈteə* (pjetatɛːr)
Piedmont ˈpiːdmənt [-mɒnt]
Piedmontese ˌpiːdmənˈtiːz [-mɒn-]
pie|man, -men ˈpaɪ|mən, -mən [-men]
pier, -s pɪə*, -z
pierc|e (P.), -es, -ing, -ed, -er/s; -eable pɪəs, -ɪz, -ɪŋ, -t, -ə*/z; -əbl
pierglass, -es ˈpɪəɡlɑːs, -ɪz
Pierian paɪˈerɪən [paɪˈɪər-, pɪ-]
Pier|point, -pont ˈpɪə|pɔɪnt, -pɒnt [-pənt]
Pierrepont (English surname) ˈpɪəpɒnt [-pənt]
pierrot, -s ˈpɪərəʊ [ˈpjer-, ˈpjɪər-], -z
Pier|s, -son pɪə|z, -sn
pietà, -s ˌpɪeˈtɑː, -z
Pietermaritzburg ˌpiːtəˈmærɪtsbɜːɡ
pieti|sm, -st/s ˈpaɪətɪ|zəm [ˈpaɪt-], -st/s
piety ˈpaɪətɪ [ˈpaɪtɪ]
pif|fle (s. v.), -les, -ling, -led, -ler/s ˈpɪf|l, -lz, -lɪŋ [-lɪŋ], -ld, -lə*/z [-lə*/z]
pig (s. v.), -s, -ging, -ged pɪɡ, -z, -ɪŋ, -d
pigeon, -s ˈpɪdʒɪn [-dʒən], -z
pigeon-hol|e (s. v.), -es, -ing, -ed ˈpɪdʒɪnhəʊl [-dʒən-], -z, -ɪŋ, -d
pigger|y, -ies ˈpɪɡər|ɪ, -ɪz
piggish, -ly, -ness ˈpɪɡɪʃ, -lɪ, -nɪs [-nəs]
Piggott ˈpɪɡət
piggyback ˈpɪɡɪbæk
piggywig, -s ˈpɪɡɪwɪɡ, -z
pigheaded, -ly, -ness ˌpɪɡˈhedɪd [also ˈ-ˌ-- when attributive], -lɪ, -nɪs [-nəs]
pig-iron ˈpɪɡˌaɪən
piglet, -s ˈpɪɡlɪt [-lət], -s
pigment, -s ˈpɪɡmənt, -s
pigmentation ˌpɪɡmenˈteɪʃn [-mən-]
pigm|y, -ies ˈpɪɡm|ɪ, -ɪz
pignut, -s ˈpɪɡnʌt, -s
Pig|ott, -ou ˈpɪɡ|ət, -uː
pigskin, -s ˈpɪɡskɪn, -z
pig-sticking ˈpɪɡˌstɪkɪŋ
pig/sty, -sties, -swill ˈpɪɡ/staɪ, -staɪz, -swɪl
pigtail, -s ˈpɪɡteɪl, -z
pik|e (s. v.) (P.), -es, -ing, -ed paɪk, -s, -ɪŋ, -t
pikestaff, -s ˈpaɪkstɑːf, -s
pilaf(f), -s ˈpɪlæf [-ˈ-], -s
pilaster, -s pɪˈlæstə*, -z
Pilate ˈpaɪlət

379

Pilatus pɪˈlɑːtəs
pilau, -s pɪˈlaʊ, -z
Pilbrow ˈpɪlbraʊ
pilch (P.), -es pɪltʃ, -ɪz
pilchard, -s ˈpɪltʃəd, -z
pil|e (s. v.), -es, -ing, -ed paɪl, -z, -ɪŋ, -d
pileated ˈpaɪlɪertɪd
pile-driv|er/s, -ing ˈpaɪlˌdraɪv|ə*/z, -ɪŋ
pil|eus, -ei ˈpaɪl|ɪəs, -aɪ
pilf|er, -ers, -ering, -ered, -erer/s
  ˈpɪlf|ə*, -əz, -ərɪŋ, -əd, -ərə*/z
pilferage ˈpɪlfərɪdʒ
pilgrim, -s; -age/s ˈpɪlgrɪm, -z; -ɪdʒ/ɪz
piling (s.), -s ˈpaɪlɪŋ, -z
pill (s. v.), -s, -ing, -ed; -box/es pɪl, -z, -ɪŋ, -d; -bɒks/ɪz
pillag|e (s. v.), -es, -ing, -ed, -er/s
  ˈpɪlɪdʒ, -ɪz, -ɪŋ, -d, -ə*/z
pillar, -s, -ed ˈpɪlə*, -z, -d
pillar-box, -es ˈpɪləbɒks, -ɪz
pillion, -s ˈpɪljən [-lɪən], -z
pillor|y (s. v.), -ies, -ying, -ied ˈpɪlər|ɪ, -ɪz, -ɪŋ, -ɪd
pillow, -s, -y ˈpɪləʊ, -z, -ɪ
pillow-case, -s ˈpɪləʊkeɪs, -ɪz
pillow-slip, -s ˈpɪləʊslɪp, -s
Pillsbury ˈpɪlzbərɪ
pilocarpine ˌpaɪləʊˈkɑːpɪn [-paɪn]
pilot (s. v.), -s, -ing, -ed; -age ˈpaɪlət, -s, -ɪŋ, -ɪd; -ɪdʒ
pilot|-boat/s, -engine/s ˈpaɪlət|bəʊt/s, -ˌendʒɪn/z
pilot-light, -s ˈpaɪlətlaɪt, -s
Pilsener ˈpɪlznə* [-lsn-]
Piltdown ˈpɪltdaʊn
pilule, -s ˈpɪljuːl, -z
pimento pɪˈmentəʊ
Pimlico ˈpɪmlɪkəʊ
pimp (s. v.), -s, -ing, -ed pɪmp, -s, -ɪŋ, -t [pɪmt]
pimpernel, -s ˈpɪmpənel [-nl], -z
pimple, -s, -d ˈpɪmpl, -z, -d
pimpl|y, -iness ˈpɪmpl|ɪ, -ɪnɪs [-ɪnəs]
Pimpo ˈpɪmpəʊ
pin (s. v.), -s, -ning, -ned pɪn, -z, -ɪŋ, -d
pinafore (P.), -s ˈpɪnəfɔː* [-fɔə*], -z
pince-nez (sing.) ˌpæːˈnsˈneɪ [ˈpæns-, ˈpɪns-, ˈ--] (pɛ̃sne), (plur.) -z
pincer, -s ˈpɪnsə*, -z
pinch (s. v.), -es, -ing, -ed, -er/s pɪntʃ, -ɪz, -ɪŋ, -t, -ə*/z
pinchbeck, -s ˈpɪntʃbek, -s
Pinches ˈpɪntʃɪz
Pinckney ˈpɪŋknɪ
pincushion, -s ˈpɪnˌkʊʃn [ˈpɪŋˌk-], -z
Pindar ˈpɪndə*
Pindaric (s. adj.), -s pɪnˈdærɪk, -s
Pindus ˈpɪndəs

pin|e (s. v.), -es, -ing, -ed paɪn, -z, -ɪŋ, -d
pineapple, -s ˈpaɪnˌæpl, -z
pine-clad ˈpaɪnklæd
Pinel pɪˈnel
Pinero pɪˈnɪərəʊ
piner|y, -ies ˈpaɪnər|ɪ, -ɪz
ping (s. v. interj.), -s, -ing, -ed pɪŋ, -z, -ɪŋ, -d
pingpong ˈpɪŋpɒŋ
pinguid ˈpɪŋgwɪd
pinhole, -s ˈpɪnhəʊl, -z
pinion (s. v.), -s, -ing, -ed ˈpɪnjən [-nɪən], -z, -ɪŋ, -d
pink (s. adj. v.) (P.), -s, -ing, -ed pɪŋk, -s, -ɪŋ, -t [pɪŋt]
Pinkerton ˈpɪŋkətən
pink-eye, -d ˈpɪŋkaɪ, -d
pinkish ˈpɪŋkɪʃ
pink|y, -iness ˈpɪŋk|ɪ, -ɪnɪs [-ɪnəs]
pin-money ˈpɪnˌmʌnɪ
pinnace, -s ˈpɪnɪs [-nəs], -ɪz
pinnac|le (s. v.), -les, -ling, -led ˈpɪnək|l, -lz, -lɪŋ [-lɪŋ], -ld
pinnate ˈpɪneɪt [-nɪt]
pinner (P.), -s ˈpɪnə*, -z
Pinocchio pɪˈnɒkɪəʊ [-ˈnəʊ-, -kjəʊ] (piˈnɔkkjo)
pin-point, -s, -ing, -ed ˈpɪnpɔɪnt, -s, -ɪŋ, -ɪd
pin-prick, -s ˈpɪnprɪk, -s
pinstripe, -s ˈpɪnstraɪp, -s
pint, -s paɪnt, -s
pintado, -s pɪnˈtɑːdəʊ, -z
pintail, -s ˈpɪnteɪl, -z
Pinter ˈpɪntə*
pint-pot, -s ˌpaɪntˈpɒt [ˈ--], -s
pin-up, -s ˈpɪnʌp, -s
pinxit ˈpɪŋksɪt
pioneer (s. v.) (P.), -s, -ing, -ed ˌpaɪəˈnɪə*, -z, -rɪŋ, -d
pious, -ly, -ness ˈpaɪəs, -lɪ, -nɪs [-nəs]
pip (s. v.) (P.), -s, -ping, -ped pɪp, -s, -ɪŋ, -t
pip|e (s. v.) (P.), -es, -ing, -ed, -er/s paɪp, -s, -ɪŋ, -t, -ə*/z
pipeclay ˈpaɪpkleɪ
pipe-line, -s ˈpaɪplaɪn, -z
Piper ˈpaɪpə*
pipette, -s pɪˈpet, -s
piping (s. adj.) ˈpaɪpɪŋ
pipit, -s ˈpɪpɪt, -s
pipkin, -s ˈpɪpkɪn, -z
Pippa ˈpɪpə
pippin, -s ˈpɪpɪn, -z
pipp|y, -iness ˈpɪp|ɪ, -ɪnɪs [-ɪnəs]
pipsqueak, -s ˈpɪpskwiːk, -s
piquancy ˈpiːkənsɪ

piquant, -ly 'pi:kənt [-kɑ:nt], -lɪ
piqu|e (s. v.), -es, -ing, -ed pi:k, -s, -ɪŋ, -t
piqué (s. v.), -s, -ing, -d 'pi:keɪ (pike), -z, -ɪŋ, -d
piquet (group of men), -s 'pɪkɪt, -s
piquet (card game) pɪ'ket
pirac|y, -ies 'paɪərəs|ɪ ['pɪr-], -ɪz
Piraeus paɪ'rɪəs [-'ri:əs]
pirat|e (s. v.), -es, -ing, -ed 'paɪərət [-rɪt], -s, -ɪŋ, -ɪd
piratic|al, -ally paɪ'rætɪk|l [ˌpaɪə'r-], -əlɪ
Piratin pɪ'rætɪn
Pirbright 'pɜ:braɪt
Pirie 'pɪrɪ
pirouett|e (s. v.), -es, -ing, -ed ˌpɪru'et, -s, -ɪŋ, -ɪd
Pisa 'pi:zə
pis aller, -s ˌpi:z'æleɪ (pizale), -z
piscatorial ˌpɪskə'tɔ:rɪəl
piscatory 'pɪskətərɪ
piscean 'paɪsɪən [pɪ'si:ən, 'pɪsɪən, 'pɪsjən, 'pɪskɪən, 'pɪskjən]
Pisces (constellation) 'paɪsi:z ['pɪsi:z, 'pɪski:z]
pisciculture 'pɪsɪkʌltʃə*
piscina, -s pɪ'si:nə [-'saɪn-], -z
piscine (s., bathing pool), -s 'pɪsi:n [-'-'-], -z
piscine (adj., of fish) 'pɪsaɪn
Piscis Austrinus ˌpɪsɪsɒ'straɪnəs [ˌpɪskɪs-, -ɔ:'s-]
Pisgah 'pɪzgə [-gɑ:]
pish pɪʃ [pʃ]
Pisidia paɪ'sɪdɪə [-djə]
Pisistratus paɪ'sɪstrətəs [pɪ's-]
pismire, -s 'pɪsmaɪə*, -z
pistachio, -s pɪ'stɑ:ʃɪəʊ [-'stɑ:ʃjəʊ, -'stæʃ-, -'stætʃ-], -z
piste, -s pi:st, -s
pistil, -s 'pɪstɪl, -z
pistol, -s 'pɪstl, -z
pistole, -s pɪ'stəʊl ['--'], -z
piston, -s; -rod/s 'pɪstən, -z; -rɒd/z
pit (s. v.), -s, -ting, -ted pɪt, -s, -ɪŋ, -ɪd
pitapat ˌpɪtə'pæt ['pɪtəp-]
Pitcairn (surname) pɪt'keən, (island) pɪt'keən ['pɪtk-]
pitch (s. v.), -es, -ing, -ed pɪtʃ, -ɪz, -ɪŋ, -t
pitch-black ˌpɪtʃ'blæk
pitchblende 'pɪtʃblend
pitch-dark ˌpɪtʃ'dɑ:k
pitcher (P.), -s 'pɪtʃə*, -z
pitchfork (s. v.), -s, -ing, -ed 'pɪtʃfɔ:k, -s, -ɪŋ, -t
pitchpine, -s 'pɪtʃpaɪn, -z
pitch-pipe, -s 'pɪtʃpaɪp, -s
pitchy 'pɪtʃɪ

piteous, -ly, -ness 'pɪtɪəs [-tjəs], -lɪ, -nɪs [-nəs]
pitfall, -s 'pɪtfɔ:l, -z
Pitfodels pɪt'fɒdəlz
pith, -s -less pɪθ, -s, -lɪs [-ləs]
pithecanthrop|us, -i ˌpɪθɪkæn'θrəʊp|əs [ˌ--'---], -aɪ
pithead, -s 'pɪthed, -z
Pither 'paɪθə*, 'paɪðə*
pith|y, -ier, -iest, -ily, -iness 'pɪθ|ɪ, -ɪə*, -ɪɪst, -ɪlɪ [-əlɪ], -ɪnɪs [-ɪnəs]
pitiab|le, -ly, -leness 'pɪtɪəb|l [-tjə-], -lɪ, -lnɪs [-nəs]
piti|ful, -fully, -fulness 'pɪtɪ|fʊl, -fʊlɪ [-fəlɪ], -fʊlnɪs [-nəs]
pitiless, -ly, -ness 'pɪtɪlɪs [-ləs], -lɪ, -nɪs [-nəs]
Pitlochry pɪt'lɒkrɪ [-'lɒxrɪ]
pit|man (P.), -men 'pɪt|mən, -mən [-men]
piton, -s 'pi:tɒn [-tɔ̃:ŋ], -z
Pitt pɪt
pittance, -s 'pɪtəns, -ɪz
Pitts, -burg(h) pɪts, -bɜ:g
pituitary pɪ'tjʊɪtərɪ [-'tju:-, -ətərɪ]
pit|y (s. v.), -ies, -ying/ly, -ied 'pɪt|ɪ, -ɪz, -ɪɪŋ/lɪ, -ɪd
pityriasis ˌpɪtɪ'raɪəsɪs
Pius 'paɪəs
pivot (s. v.), -s, -ing, -ed 'pɪvət, -s, -ɪŋ, -ɪd
pivotal 'pɪvətl
pix|ie [-|y], -ies 'pɪks|ɪ, -ɪz
pizza, -s 'pi:tsə ['pɪtsə], -z
pizzicato, -s ˌpɪtsɪ'kɑ:təʊ, -z
placability ˌplækə'bɪlətɪ [ˌpleɪk-, -lɪt-]
placab|le, -ly, -leness 'plækəb|l ['pleɪk-], -lɪ, -lnɪs [-nəs]
placard (s. v.), -s, -ing, -ed 'plækɑ:d, -z, -ɪŋ, -ɪd
placat|e, -es, -ing, -ed plə'keɪt [pleɪ'k-], -s, -ɪŋ, -ɪd
placatory plə'keɪtərɪ [pleɪ'k-]
plac|e (s. v.), -es, -ing, -ed, -er/s pleɪs, -ɪz, -ɪŋ, -t, -ə*/z
placebo, -s plə'si:bəʊ [plæ's-], -z
place-kick, -s 'pleɪskɪk, -s
place|man, -men 'pleɪs|mən, -mən
placement 'pleɪsmənt
placenta plə'sentə
placet, -s 'pleɪset [-sɪt], -s
placid, -est, -ly, -ness 'plæsɪd, -ɪst, -lɪ, -nɪs [-nəs]
placidity plə'sɪdətɪ [plæ's-, -ɪtɪ]
placket, -s; -hole/s 'plækɪt, -s; -həʊl/z
plagal 'pleɪgəl
plage, -s plɑ:ʒ, -ɪz
plagiari|sm/s, -st/s 'pleɪdʒərɪ|zəm/z [-dʒɪə-, -dʒə-], -st/s

381

plagiarize—playful

plagiariz|e [-is|e], -es, -ing, -ed 'pleɪ-
dʒəraɪz [-dʒɪə-, -dʒə-], -ɪz, -ɪŋ, -d
plagiar|y, -ies 'pleɪdʒjər|ɪ [-dʒɪə-, -dʒə-],
-ɪz
plagu|e (s. v.), -es, -ing, -ed, -er/s pleɪg,
-z, -ɪŋ, -d, -ə*/z
plague-spot, -s 'pleɪgspɒt, -s
plagu|y, -ily, -iness 'pleɪg|ɪ, -ɪlɪ [-əlɪ],
-ɪnɪs [-nəs]
plaice pleɪs
plaid, -s, -ed plæd, -z, -ɪd
Plaid Cymru ˌplaɪd 'kʌmrɪ
plain (s. adj.), -s, -er, -est, -ly, -ness
pleɪn, -z, -ə*, -ɪst, -lɪ, -nɪs [-nəs]
plainsong 'pleɪnsɒŋ
plain-spoken ˌpleɪn'spəʊkən ['-ˌ--]
plaint, -s pleɪnt, -s
plaintiff, -s 'pleɪntɪf, -s
plaintive, -ly, -ness 'pleɪntɪv, -lɪ, -nɪs
[-nəs]
plaister, -s 'plɑːstə*, -z
Plaistow (in E. London) 'plæstəʊ
['plɑːs-]
Note.—The local pronunciation is
'plɑːstəʊ.
plait (s. v.), -s, -ing, -ed plæt, -s, -ɪŋ, -ɪd
plan (s. v.), -s, -ing, -ned, -ner/s plæn,
-z, -ɪŋ, -d, -ə*/z
planchet, -s 'plɑːntʃɪt, -s
planchette, -s plɑːn'ʃet [plɑ̃-n-, plɔ̃:n-,
plɒn-] (plɑ̃ʃet), -s
plan|e (s. v.), -es, -ing, -ed pleɪn, -z, -ɪŋ,
-d
planet, -s 'plænɪt, -s
planetari|um, -ums, -a ˌplænɪ'teərɪ|əm,
-əmz, -ə
planetary 'plænɪtərɪ
plane-tree, -s 'pleɪntri:, -z
plangent 'plændʒənt
planimeter, -s plæ'nɪmɪtə* [plə'n-,
-mətə*], -z
plank (s. v.), -s, -ing, -ed plæŋk, -s, -ɪŋ,
-t [plæŋt]
plankton 'plæŋtən [-tɒn]
plant (s. v.), -s, -ing, -ed, -er/s plɑːnt,
-s, -ɪŋ, -ɪd, -ə*/z
Plant (surname) plɑːnt
Plantagenet plæn'tædʒənɪt [-dʒɪn-,
-nət, -net]
plantain, -s 'plæntɪn ['plɑː-n-, -z
plantation, -s plæn'teɪʃn [plɑː-n-], -z
Plantin (type face) 'plæntɪn ['plɑː-nt-]
plaque, -s plɑːk [plæk], -s
plaquette, -s plæ'ket [plɑː'k-], -s
plash (s. v.), -es, -ing, -ed; -y plæʃ, -ɪz,
-ɪŋ, -t; -ɪ
plasm 'plæzəm
plasm|a, -ic 'plæzm|ə, -ɪk

Plassey 'plæsɪ
plast|er (s. v.), -ers, -ering, -ered, -erer/s
'plɑːst|ə*, -əz, -ərɪŋ, -əd, -ərə*/z
plastic, -s 'plæstɪk ['plɑːs-], -s
plasticine 'plæstɪsiːn ['plɑːs-]
plasticity plæ'stɪsətɪ [plɑː's-, -ɪtɪ]
plastographic ˌplæstəʊ'græfɪk [ˌplɑːst-]
plat (dish), -s plæt: (plɑ), -z
Plata 'plɑːtə
Plataea plə'tiːə [-'tɪə]
platan, -s 'plætən, -z
plat|e (s. v.), -es, -ing, -ed pleɪt, -s, -ɪŋ,
-ɪd
Plate (river in South America) pleɪt
plateau, -s [-x] 'plætəʊ [plæ'təʊ], -z
plate-basket, -s 'pleɪt,bɑːskɪt, -s
plateful, -s 'pleɪtfʊl, -s
plate-glass ˌpleɪt'glɑːs ['--]
plate-layer, -s 'pleɪt,leɪə*, -z
platen, -s 'plætən, -z
plate-powder 'pleɪt,paʊdə*
plate-rack, -s 'pleɪtræk, -s
platform (s. v.), -s, -ing, -ed 'plætfɔːm,
-z, -ɪŋ, -d
platiniz|e [-is|e], -es, -ing, -ed 'plætɪ-
naɪz [-tnaɪz], -ɪz, -ɪŋ, -d
platinotype, -s 'plætɪnəʊtaɪp [-tnəʊt-],
-s
platinum 'plætɪnəm [-tnəm]
platitude, -s 'plætɪtjuːd, -z
platitudinarian, -s ˌplætɪˌtjuːdɪ'neərɪən,
-z
platitudinous ˌplætɪ'tjuːdɪnəs
Plato 'pleɪtəʊ
platonic, -al, -ally plə'tɒnɪk [pleɪ't-], -l,
-əlɪ
platoni|sm/s, -st/s 'pleɪtəʊnɪ|zəm/z,
-st/s
platoon, -s plə'tuːn, -z
Platt, -s plæt, -s
platter, -s 'plætə*, -z
platypus, -es 'plætɪpəs, -ɪz
plaudit, -s 'plɔːdɪt, -s
plausibility ˌplɔːzə'bɪlətɪ [-zɪ'b-, -lɪt-]
plausib|le, -ly, -leness 'plɔːzəb|l [-zɪb-],
-lɪ, -lnɪs [-nəs]
Plautus 'plɔːtəs
play (s. v.), -s, -ing, -ed, -er/s pleɪ, -z,
-ɪŋ, -d, -ə*/z [pleə*/z]
playable 'pleɪəbl
play-actor, -s 'pleɪˌæktə*, -z
play-bill, -z 'pleɪbɪl, -z
play-boy, -s 'pleɪbɔɪ, -z
Player, -'s 'pleɪə*, -z
Playfair 'pleɪfeə*
playfellow, -s 'pleɪˌfeləʊ, -z
play|ful, -fully, -fulness 'pleɪ|fʊl, -fʊlɪ
[-fəlɪ], -fʊlnɪs [-nəs]

382

playgoer, -s 'pleɪˌgəuə*, -z
playground, -s 'pleɪgraund, -z
playhou|se, -ses 'pleɪhau|s, -zɪz
playing-field, -s 'pleɪŋfiːld, -z
playmate, -s 'pleɪmeɪt, -s
playpen, -s 'pleɪpen, -z
plaything, -s 'pleɪθɪŋ, -z
playtime, -s 'pleɪtaɪm, -z
playwright, -s 'pleɪraɪt, -s
plaza (P.), -s 'plɑːzə ['plæzə], -z
plea, -s pliː, -z
plead, -s, -ing/ly, -ed, -er/s pliːd, -z,
    -ɪŋ/lɪ, -ɪd, -ə*/z
pleading (s.), -s 'pliːdɪŋ, -z
pleasa(u)nce 'plezəns
pleasant, -er, -est, -ly, -ness 'pleznt,
    -ə*, -ɪst, -lɪ, -nɪs [-nəs]
pleasantr|y, -ies 'plezntr|ɪ, -ɪz
pleas|e, -es, -ing/ly, -ed pliːz, -ɪz,
    -ɪŋ/lɪ, -d
pleasurab|le, -ly, -leness 'pleʒərəb|l, -lɪ,
    -lnɪs [-nəs]
pleasure, -s 'pleʒə*, -z
pleasure-boat, -s 'pleʒəbəut, -s
pleasure-ground, -s 'pleʒəgraund, -z
pleat (s. v.), -s, -ing, -ed pliːt, -s, -ɪŋ, -ɪd
pleb, -s pleb, -z
plebeian (s. adj.), -s plɪ'biːən [-'brən], -z
plebiscite, -s 'plebɪsɪt [-bə-, -saɪt], -s
plectr|um/z, -a 'plektr|əm/z, -ə
pledg|e (s. v.), -es, -ing, -ed, -er/s
    pledʒ, -ɪz, -ɪŋ, -d, -ə*/z
Pleiad, -s, -es 'plaɪəd [old-fashioned
    'pliːəd, plɪəd, 'pleɪæd], -z, -iːz
pleistocene 'plaɪstəusiːn
plenar|y, -ily 'pliːnər|ɪ, -əlɪ [-ɪlɪ]
plenipotentiar|y (s. adj.), -ies ˌplenɪ-
    pəu'tenʃər|ɪ [-ʃɪər-, -ʃjər-], -ɪz
plenitude 'plenɪtjuːd
plenteous, -ly, -ness 'plentjəs [-tɪəs],
    -lɪ, -nɪs [-nəs]
plenti|ful, -fully, -fulness 'plentɪ|fʊl,
    -fʊlɪ [-fəlɪ], -fʊlnɪs [-nəs]
plenty 'plentɪ
plenum, -s 'pliːnəm, -z
pleonasm, -s 'plɪəunæzəm ['pliːəu-], -z
pleonastic, -al, -ally plɪəu'næstɪk
    [ˌpliːəu'n-], -l, -əlɪ
plesiosaur|us, -i, -uses ˌpliːsɪə'sɔːr|əs
    [-sjə's-, -sɪəu's-, '---], -aɪ, -əsɪz
plethora 'pleθərə
plethoric ple'θɒrɪk [plɪ'θ-]
pleur|a, -ae, -as, -al 'plʊər|ə, -iː, -əz, -əl
pleurisy 'plʊərəsɪ [-rɪs-]
pleuritic ˌplʊə'rɪtɪk
pleuro - pneumonia   ˌplʊərəunjʊ-
    'məunjə [-nju:-, -nɪə]
plexus, -es 'pleksəs, -ɪz

Pleyel, -s 'pleɪəl [-el], -z
pliability ˌplaɪə'bɪlətɪ [-lɪt-]
pliab|le, -ly, -leness 'plaɪəb|l, -lɪ, -lnɪs
    [-nəs]
pliancy 'plaɪənsɪ
pliant, -ly, -ness 'plaɪənt, -lɪ, -nɪs [-nəs]
pliers 'plaɪəz
plight (s. v.), -s, -ing, -ed plaɪt, -s, -ɪŋ,
    -ɪd
plimsoll (P.), -s 'plɪmsəl [-sɒl], -z
Plinlimmon plɪn'lɪmən
plinth, -s plɪnθ, -s
Pliny 'plɪnɪ
pliocene 'plaɪəusiːn
plod (s. v.), -s, -ding, -ded, -der/s plɒd,
    -z, -ɪŋ, -ɪd, -ə*/z
Plomer (surname) 'pluːmə* ['plʌmə*]
Plomley 'plʌmlɪ
plop (s. v. interj.), -s, -ping, -ped plɒp,
    -s, -ɪŋ, -t
plosion, -s 'pləuʒn, -z
plosive (s. adj.), -s 'pləusɪv [-əuzɪ-], -z
plot (s. v.), -s, -ting, -ted, -ter/s plɒt, -s,
    -ɪŋ, -ɪd, -ə*/z
plough (s. v.), -s, -ing, -ed, -er/s; -able;
    -boy/s, -man, -men plau, -z, -ɪŋ, -d,
    'plauə*/z, 'plauəbl; -bɔɪ/z, -mən,
    -mən [-men]
ploughshare, -s 'plauʃeə*, -z
plover, -s 'plʌvə*, -z
Plow|den, -man 'plau|dn, -mən
Plowright 'plauraɪt
ploy, -s 'plɔɪ, -z
pluck (s. v.), -s, -ing, -ed plʌk, -s, -ɪŋ, -t
Pluckley 'plʌklɪ
pluck|y, -ier, -iest, -ily, -iness 'plʌk|ɪ,
    -ɪə*, -ɪɪst, -ɪlɪ [-əlɪ], -ɪnɪs [-nəs]
plug (s. v.), -s, -ging, -ged plʌg, -z, -ɪŋ,
    -d
plum, -s plʌm, -z
plumage, -s 'pluːmɪdʒ, -ɪz
plumb (s. v.), -s, -ing, -ed, -er/s plʌm,
    -z, -ɪŋ, -d, -ə*/z
plumbago, -s plʌm'beɪgəu, -z
Plumbe plʌm
plumb-line, -s 'plʌmlaɪn, -z
plum|e (s. v.), -es, -ing, -ed pluːm, -z,
    -ɪŋ, -d
Plummer 'plʌmə*
plummet, -s 'plʌmɪt, -s
plummy 'plʌmɪ
plump (s. adj. v. adv. interj.), -s; -er,
    -est, -ly, -ness; -ing, -ed plʌmp, -s;
    -ə*, -ɪst, -lɪ, -nɪs [-nəs]; -ɪŋ, -t [plʌmt]
Plump|ton, -tre 'plʌmp|tən, -trɪ
plum-pudding, -s ˌplʌm'pudɪŋ, -z
Plumridge 'plʌmrɪdʒ
Plumstead 'plʌmstɪd [-ted]

plumy 'plu:mɪ
plund|er (s. v.), -ers, -ering, -ered, -erer/s; -erous 'plʌnd|ə*, -əz, -ərɪŋ, -əd, -ərə*/z, -ərəs
plung|e (s. v.), -es, -ing, -ed, -er/s plʌndʒ, -ɪz, -ɪŋ, -d, -ə*/z
Plunket(t) 'plʌŋkɪt
pluperfect, -s ˌplu:'pə:fɪkt ['-ˌ--], -s
plural (s. adj.), -s, -ly 'pluərəl ['plɔər-, 'plɔ:r-], -z, -ɪ
plurali|sm, -ist/s 'pluərəlɪ|zəm ['plɔər-, 'plɔ:r-, -rlɪ-], -st/s
pluralit|y, -ies ˌpluə'rælət|ɪ [-ɪt|ɪ], -ɪz
pluraliz|e [-is|e], -es, -ing, -ed 'pluərəlaɪz ['plɔər-, 'plɔ:r-, -rlaɪz], -ɪz, -ɪŋ, -d
plus, -(s)es plʌs, -ɪz
plus-fours ˌplʌs'fɔ:z [-'fɔəz]
plush, -es, -y plʌʃ, -ɪz, -ɪ
Plutarch 'plu:tɑ:k
Pluto 'plu:təʊ
plutocracy plu:'tɒkrəsɪ
plutocrat, -s 'plu:təʊkræt, -s
plutocratic ˌplu:təʊ'krætɪk
Plutonian plu:'təʊnjən [-nɪən]
Plutonic plu:'tɒnɪk
plutonium plu:'təʊnɪəm [-njəm]
pluvi|al, -ous 'plu:vj|əl [-vɪ|əl], -əs
pl|y (s. v.), -ies, -ying, -ied pl|aɪ, -aɪz, -aɪɪŋ, -aɪd
Plymouth 'plɪməθ
plywood 'plaɪwʊd
p.m. ˌpi:'em
pneumatic, -s, -al, -ally nju:'mætɪk [njʊ'm-], -s, -l, -əlɪ
pneumatolog|ist/s, -y ˌnju:mə'tɒlədʒ|-ɪst/s, -ɪ
pneumoconiosis ˌnju:məʊkəʊnɪ'əʊsɪs [-kɒn-]
pneumonia nju:'məʊnjə [njʊ'm-, -nɪə]
pneumonic nju:'mɒnɪk [njʊ'm-]
Pnompenh ˌnɒm'pen
Pnyx ᵽnɪks
po, -es pəʊ, -z
Po (Italian river) pəʊ
poach, -es, -ing, -ed, -er/s pəʊtʃ, -ɪz, -ɪŋ, -t, -ə*/z
pochard, -s 'pəʊtʃəd ['pɒtʃ-], -z
pock, -s, -ed pɒk, -s, -t
pocket (s. v.), -s, -ing, -ed; -able, -ful/s 'pɒkɪt, -s, -ɪŋ, -ɪd; -əbl, -fʊl/z
pocket-book, -s 'pɒkɪtbʊk, -s
pocket - handkerchief, -s ˌpɒkɪt-'hæŋkətʃɪf, -s (see note to handkerchief)
pocket-knif|e, -ves 'pɒkɪtnaɪ|f, -vz
pocket-money 'pɒkɪtˌmʌnɪ
Pocklington 'pɒklɪŋtən
pockmark, -s, -ed 'pɒkmɑ:k, -s, -t

poco 'pəʊkəʊ
Pocock 'pəʊkɒk
pococurante, -s ˌpəʊkəʊkjʊə'ræntɪ, -z
pod (s. v.), -s, -ding, -ded pɒd, -z, -ɪŋ, -ɪd
podagra pəʊ'dægrə [pɒ'd-, 'pɒdəgrə]
podg|y, -ier, -iest, -ily, -iness 'pɒdʒ|ɪ, -ɪə*, -ɪɪst, -ɪlɪ [-əlɪ], -ɪnɪs [-ɪnəs]
podi|um, -ums, -a 'pəʊdɪ|əm [-djəm], -əmz, -ə
Poe pəʊ
Poel 'pəʊel [-ɪl, -əl]
poem, -s 'pəʊɪm [-əm, -em], -z
poesy 'pəʊɪzɪ ['pəʊezɪ]
poet, -s 'pəʊɪt [-et], -s
poetaster, -s ˌpəʊɪ'tæstə* [ˌpəʊə't-], -z
poetess, -es 'pəʊɪtɪs ['pəʊət-, -tes], -ɪz
poetic, -al, -ally pəʊ'etɪk, -l, -əlɪ
poetiz|e [-is|e], -es, -ing, -ed, -er/s 'pəʊɪtaɪz ['pəʊət-], -ɪz, -ɪŋ, -d, -ə*/z
poetry 'pəʊɪtrɪ ['pəʊət-, rarely 'pɔɪt-]
Pogner (in Wagner's 'Die Meister-singer') 'pəʊgnə* ['pɔ:gnər)
pogrom, -s 'pɒgrəm [-grɒm, pə'grɒm], -z
poignan|cy, -t/ly 'pɔɪnjən|sɪ ['pɔɪnə-, 'pɔɪgnə-], t/lɪ
poinsettia pɔɪn'setɪə [-tjə]
point (s. v.), -s, -ing, -ed, -er/s pɔɪnt, -s, -ɪŋ, -ɪd, -ə*/z
point-blank ˌpɔɪnt'blæŋk [also '-- when attributive]
point-duty 'pɔɪntˌdju:tɪ
pointed (adj.), -ly, -ness 'pɔɪntɪd, -lɪ, -nɪs [-nəs]
pointillism 'pɔɪntɪlɪzəm ['pwænt-, 'pwænti:jɪzəm]
point-lace ˌpɔɪnt'leɪs ['--]
pointless, -ness 'pɔɪntlɪs [-ləs], -nɪs [-nəs]
points|man, -men 'pɔɪnts|mən, -mən [-men]
pois|e (s. v.), -es, -ing, -ed pɔɪz, -ɪz, -ɪŋ, -d
pois|on (s. v.), -ons, -oning, -oned, -oner/s 'pɔɪz|n, -nz, -ṇɪŋ [-nɪŋ], -nd, -ṇə*/z [-nə*/z]
poisonous, -ly, -ness 'pɔɪznəs [-zṇəs, -zənəs], -lɪ, -nɪs [-nəs]
Poitiers 'pwɑ:tjeɪ [pwɑ:'tjeɪ, old-fashioned pɔɪ'tɪəz] (pwatje)
pok|e (s. v.), -es, -ing, -ed pəʊk, -s, -ɪŋ, -t
poker, -s 'pəʊkə*, -z
pok|y, -ier, -iest, -ily, -iness 'pəʊk|ɪ, -ɪə* [-jə*], -ɪɪst [-jɪst], -ɪlɪ [-əlɪ], -ɪnɪs [-ɪnəs]
polacca, -s pəʊ'lækə [-lɑ:kə], -z
Poland 'pəʊlənd
polar (s. adj.), -s 'pəʊlə*, -z

Polaris (*star*) pəʊ'læɪɪs [-'lɑːr-, -'leər-; *the rocket and submarine are usually pronounced with* -'lɑːr-]
polariscope, -s pəʊ'læɪɪskəʊp, -s
polarity pəʊ'lærətɪ [-ɪtɪ]
polarization [**-isa-**] ˌpəʊlərɑɪ'zeɪʃn [-ɪɪ'z-]
polariz|e [**-is|e**], **-es, -ing, -ed, -er/s** 'pəʊləraɪz, -ɪz, -ɪŋ, -d, -ə*/z
polder, -s 'pɒldə* ['pəʊl-], -z
Poldhu 'pɒldjuː
pole, -s pəʊl, -z
Pole (*inhabitant of Poland*), **-s** pəʊl, -z
Pole (*surname*) pəʊl, puːl
Note.—puːl *in* **Pole Carew** (*q.v.*) *and* **Chandos Pole** (ˌʃændɒs'puːl).
pole|axe/s, -cat/s 'pəʊl|æks/ɪz, -kæt/s
Pole Carew ˌpuːl'keərɪ
polemic (*s. adj.*), **-s, -al, -ally** pə'lemɪk [pəʊ'l-, pɒ'l-], -s, -l, -əlɪ
pole-star, -s 'pəʊlstɑː:*, -z
Polhill 'pəʊlhɪl
polic|e (*s. v.*), **-es, -ing, -ed** pə'liːs [pʊ'l-], -ɪz, -ɪŋ, -t
police|man, -men pə'liːsmən [pl̩'iːs-, 'pliːs-, pʊ'l-], -mən
polic|y, -ies 'pɒləs|ɪ [-lɪs-], -ɪz
policy-holder, -s 'pɒləsɪˌhəʊldə* [-lɪs-], -z
polio 'pəʊlɪəʊ [-ljəʊ]
poliomyelitis ˌpəʊlɪəʊmaɪə'laɪtɪs [-ljəʊ-, -maɪˈl-, -maɪe'l-]
polish (*s. v.*), **-es, -ing, -ed, -er/s** 'pɒlɪʃ, -ɪz, -ɪŋ, -t, -ə*/z
Polish (*adj.*) (*of Poland*) 'pəʊlɪʃ
politburo 'pɒlɪtˌbjʊərəʊ
polite, -st, -ly, -ness pə'laɪt [pʊ'l-], -ɪst, -lɪ, -nɪs [-nəs]
politic, -s 'pɒlətɪk [-lɪt-], -s
politic|al, -ally pə'lɪtɪk|l [pʊ'l-, -tək-], -əlɪ
politician, -s ˌpɒlɪ'tɪʃn [-lə't-], -z
politiciz|e [**-cis|e**], **-es, -ing, -ed** pə'lɪtɪsaɪz, -ɪz, -ɪŋ, -d
polity 'pɒlətɪ [-ɪtɪ]
Polixenes pɒ'lɪksənɪːz [pə'l-, -sɪn-]
Polk pəʊk
polka, -s 'pɒlkə ['pəʊl-], -z
poll (*s. v.*) (*at elections*), **-s, -ing, -ed** pəʊl, -z, -ɪŋ, -d
poll (*s.*) (*parrot, student taking pass degree at Cambridge*) (**P.**), **-s** pɒl, -z
poll (*adj.*) (*hornless, cut, executed by one party*) pəʊl
pollard (*s. v.*) (**P.**), **-s, -ing, -ed** 'pɒləd [-lɑːd], -z, -ɪŋ, -ɪd
pollen (**P.**), **-s, -ing, -ed** 'pɒlən [-lɪn], -z, -ɪŋ, -d

pollinat|e, -es, -ing, -ed 'pɒləneɪt [-lɪn-], -s, -ɪŋ, -ɪd
pollination ˌpɒlɪ'neɪʃn [-lə'n-]
Pollock 'pɒlək
pollster, -s 'pəʊlstə*, -z
poll-tax, -es 'pəʊltæks, -ɪz
pollutant, -s pə'luːtənt [-'ljuː-], -s
pollut|e, -es, -ing, -ed, -er/s pə'luːt [-'ljuːt], -s, -ɪŋ, -ɪd, -ə*/z
pollution, -s pə'luːʃn [-'ljuː-], -z
Pollux 'pɒləks
Polly 'pɒlɪ
Polmont 'pəʊlmənt
polo 'pəʊləʊ
polonaise, -s ˌpɒlə'neɪz, -ɪz
Polonius pə'ləʊnjəs [pɒ'l-, -nɪəs]
polon|y, -ies pə'ləʊn|ɪ, -ɪz
Polson 'pəʊlsn
poltergeist, -s 'pɒltəgaɪst, -s
poltroon, -s; -ery pɒl'truːn, -z; -ərɪ
Polwarth (*in Borders Region*) 'pəʊlwəθ, (*surname*) 'pɒlwəθ
polyandrous ˌpɒlɪ'ændrəs
polyandry 'pɒlɪændrɪ [ˌpɒlɪ'æ-]
polyanthus, -es ˌpɒlɪ'ænθəs, -ɪz
Polybius pɒ'lɪbɪəs [pə'l-, -bjəs]
Polycarp 'pɒlɪkɑːp
Polycrates pɒ'lɪkrətiːz [pə'l-]
polyester ˌpɒlɪ'estə* ['----]
polyethylene ˌpɒlɪ'eθɪliːn [-θəl-]
polygam|ist/s, -y, -ous pə'lɪgəm|ɪst/s [pɒ'l-], -ɪ, -əs
polyglot (*s. adj.*), **-s** 'pɒlɪglɒt, -s
polygon, -s 'pɒlɪgən, -z
polygonal pɒ'lɪgənl [pə'l-]
polygonum pə'lɪgənəm
polyhedr|on, -ons, -a, -al ˌpɒlɪ'hiːdr|ən [-'hed-, 'pɒlɪˌh-], -ənz, -ə, -l
polymath, -s 'pɒlɪmæθ, -s
Polyne|sia, -sian/s ˌpɒlɪ'niː|zjə [-zɪə, -ʒə, -ʒɪə, -ʒə, -sjə, -sɪə, -ʃjə, -ʃɪə, -ʃə], -zjən/z [-zɪən/z, -ʒjən/z, -ʒɪən/z, -ʒn/z, -sjən/z, -sɪən/z, -ʃjən/z, -ʃɪən/z, -ʃn/z]
polynomial (*s. adj.*), **-s** ˌpɒlɪ'nəʊmjəl [-mɪəl], -z
polyp, -s, -ous 'pɒlɪp, -s, -əs
Polyphemus ˌpɒlɪ'fiːməs
polyphonic ˌpɒlɪ'fɒnɪk
polyphony pə'lɪfənɪ [pɒ'l-]
polypodium, -s ˌpɒlɪ'pəʊdjəm [-dɪəm], -z
polypody 'pɒlɪpədɪ
polyp|us, -uses, -i 'pɒlɪp|əs, -əsɪz, -aɪ
polysemous ˌpɒlɪ'siːməs [pə'lɪsɪməs, pɒ'l-]
polysemy ˌpɒlɪ'siːmɪ ['----, pə'lɪsɪmɪ]
polystyrene ˌpɒlɪ'staɪriːn

polysyllabic, -ally ˌpɒlɪsɪˈlæbɪk, -əlɪ
polysyllable, -s ˈpɒlɪˌsɪləbl, -z
polysynthesis ˌpɒlɪˈsɪnθəsɪs [-θɪs-]
polysynthetic ˌpɒlɪsɪnˈθetɪk
polytechnic (s. adj.), **-s** ˌpɒlɪˈteknɪk, -s
polythei|sm, -st/s ˈpɒlɪθiːɪ|zəm [ˌ--ˈ---, -θɪɪ|zəm], -st/s
polytheistic ˌpɒlɪθiːˈɪstɪk [-θɪˈɪstɪk]
polythene ˈpɒlɪθiːn
polyurethane ˌpɒlɪˈjʊərɪθeɪn [-rəθ-]
polyvinyl ˌpɒlɪˈvaɪnɪl [-nl]
Polyxen|a, -us pɒˈlɪksɪn|ə [pəˈl-, -sən-], -əs
Polzeath pɒlˈzeθ [-ˈziː:θ]
Note.—The local pronunciation is pɒlˈzɛ:θ.
pomace ˈpʌmɪs
pomade, -s pəˈmeɪd [pɒˈm-, -mɑː:d], -z
pomander, -s pəʊˈmændə*, -z
pomatum, -s pəʊˈmeɪtəm, -z
pome, -s pəʊm, -z
pomegranate,   -s ˈpɒmɪˌɡrænɪt [ˈpɒməˌɡ-, ˈpɒmˌɡ-], -s
pomelo, -s ˈpɒmɪləʊ, -z
Pomerania, -n/s ˌpɒməˈreɪnjə [-nɪə], -n/z
Pomeroy ˈpəʊmrɔɪ, ˈpɒmərɔɪ
pomfret (fish), **-s** ˈpɒmfrɪt, -s
Pomfret ˈpʌmfrɪt [ˈpɒm-]
pomfret cake, -s ˈpʌmfrɪtkeɪk [ˈpɒm-], -s
pommel, -s (s.) ˈpɒml, -z
pomm|el (v.), **-els, -elling, -elled** ˈpʌm|l [ˈpɒml], -l̩z, -l̩ɪŋ [-əlɪŋ], -l̩d
Pomona pəʊˈməʊnə
pomp, -s pɒmp, -s
pompadour (P.),   **-s** ˈpɒmpəˌdʊə* [ˈpɔ̃:mp-, ˈpɒ:mp-, -dɔə*, -dɔː:*] (pɔ̃padu:r), -z
Pompeian pɒmˈpiːən [-ˈpɪən]
Pompeii pɒmˈpeɪiː [ˈpɒmpɪaɪ, pɒm-ˈpiː:aɪ, -ˈpeɪɪ]
Pompey ˈpɒmpɪ
pompom, -s ˈpɒmpɒm, -z
pompon, -s ˈpɒmpɒn [-pɒŋ, ˈpɔ̃:mpɔ̃:ŋ] (pɔ̃pɔ̃), -z
pomposity pɒmˈpɒsətɪ [-ɪtɪ]
pompous, -ly, -ness ˈpɒmpəs, -lɪ, -nɪs [-nəs]
ponce, -s pɒns, -ɪz
poncho, -s ˈpɒntʃəʊ, -z
pond (s. v.) (P.), **-s, -ing, -ed** pɒnd, -z, -ɪŋ, -ɪd
pond|er, -ers, -ering/ly, -ered ˈpɒnd|ə*, -əz, -ərɪŋ/lɪ, -əd
ponderability ˌpɒndərəˈbɪlətɪ [-lɪt-]
ponderable, -ness ˈpɒndərəbl, -nɪs [-nəs]
ponderous, -ly, -ness ˈpɒndərəs, -lɪ, -nɪs [-nəs]

Ponders ˈpɒndəz
Pondicherry ˌpɒndɪˈtʃerɪ [-ɪˈʃe-]
pongee pɒnˈdʒiː: [pʌn-]
poniard (s. v.), **-s, -ing, -ed** ˈpɒnjəd [-jɑː:d], -z, -ɪŋ, -ɪd
Pons asinorum ˌpɒnzæsɪˈnɔː:rəm
Ponsonby ˈpʌnsnbɪ [ˈpɒn-]
Pontefract (in West Yorkshire) ˈpɒntɪfrækt
Note.—An old local pronunciation ˈpʌmfrɪt *is now obsolete. The pronunciation survives in* **pomfret cake** (q.v.).
pontifex (P.), **pontifices** ˈpɒntɪfeks, pɒnˈtɪfɪsiː:z
pontiff, -s ˈpɒntɪf, -s
pontific, -al/s, -ally; -ate/s pɒnˈtɪfɪk, -l/z, -əlɪ; -eɪt/s [-ɪt/s, -ət/s]
pontificat|e (v.), **-es, -ing, -ed** pɒn-ˈtɪfɪkeɪt, -s, -ɪŋ, -ɪd
Pontine ˈpɒntaɪn
Pontius ˈpɒntjəs [-ntɪəs, -ntʃjəs, -ntʃəs, -nʃjəs, -nʃəs]
pontoon, -s pɒnˈtuː:n, -z
Pontresina ˌpɒntrɪˈsiː:nə [-trəˈs-]
Pontus ˈpɒntəs
Pontypool ˌpɒntɪˈpuː:l (Welsh ˌpɒntə-ˈpuː:l)
Pontypridd ˌpɒntɪˈpriː:ð (Welsh ˌpɒntə-ˈpriː:ð)
pon|y, -ies, -ytail/s ˈpəʊn|ɪ, -ɪz, -ɪteɪl/z
pood, -s puː:d, -z
poodle, -s ˈpuː:dl, -z
pooh pʊ̯ [phuː:, puː:]
Pooh-Bah ˌpuːˈbɑː:
pooh-pooh, -s, -ing, -ed ˌpuːˈpuː:, -z, -ɪŋ [-ˈpʊɪŋ], -d
pool (s. v.), **-s, -ing, -ed** puː:l, -z, -ɪŋ, -d
Poole puː:l
Pooley ˈpuː:lɪ
poon, -s puː:n, -z
Poona ˈpuː:nə [-nɑː:] (Hindi puna; new designation **Pune** puné)
poop (s. v.), **-s, -ing, -ed** puː:p, -s, -ɪŋ, -t
poor, -er, -est, -ly, -ness pɔː:* [pɔə*, pʊə*], -rə*, -rɪst, -lɪ, -nɪs [-nəs]
poor-box, -es ˈpɔː:bɒks [ˈpɔə-, ˈpʊə-], -ɪz
Poore pʊə*
poor-hou|se,   -ses ˈpɔː:haʊ|s [ˈpɔə-, ˈpʊə-], -zɪz
poor-law ˈpɔː:lɔ: [ˈpɔə-, ˈpʊə-]
poorly ˈpɔː:lɪ [ˈpɔə-, ˈpʊə-]
pop (s. v. interj.), **-s, -ping, -ped, -per/s** pɒp, -s, -ɪŋ, -t, -ə*/z
pop-corn ˈpɒpkɔː:n
pope (P.), **-s; -dom/s** pəʊp, -s; -dəm/z
popery ˈpəʊpərɪ
pop-gun, -s ˈpɒpɡʌn, -z

Popham 'pɒpəm
popinjay, -s 'pɒpɪndʒeɪ, -z
popish, -ly, -ness 'pəʊpɪʃ, -lɪ, -nɪs [-nəs]
poplar (P.), -s 'pɒplə*, -z
poplin, -s 'pɒplɪn, -z
Popocatepetl 'pɒpəʊ,kætɪ'petl ['pəʊp-, -tə'p-] (*Aztec* po,poka'tepetl̩)
poppet, -s 'pɒpɪt, -s
popp|le, -les, -ling, -led 'pɒp|l̩, -lz, -l̩ɪŋ [-lɪŋ], -ld
popp|y (P.), -ies 'pɒp|ɪ, -ɪz
poppycock 'pɒpɪkɒk
poppy-head, -s 'pɒpɪhed, -z
populace 'pɒpjʊləs [-pjəl-, -lɪs]
popular, -ly 'pɒpjʊlə* [-pjəl-], -lɪ
popularity ,pɒpjʊ'lærətɪ [-pjə'l-, -ɪtɪ]
popularization ,pɒpjʊləraɪ'zeɪʃn [-pjəl-, -rɪ'z-]
populariz|e [-is|e], -es, -ing, -ed 'pɒpjʊləraɪz [-pjəl-], -ɪz, -ɪŋ, -d
populat|e, -es, -ing, -ed 'pɒpjʊleɪt [-pjəl-], -s, -ɪŋ, -ɪd
population, -s ,pɒpjʊ'leɪʃn [-pjə'l-], -z
populous, -ly, -ness 'pɒpjʊləs [-pjəl-], -lɪ, -nɪs [-nəs]
porage 'pɒrɪdʒ
porcelain, -s 'pɔːsəlɪn [-leɪn], -z
porch, -es pɔːtʃ, -ɪz
Porchester 'pɔːtʃɪstə* [-tʃəs-]
porcine 'pɔːsaɪn
porcupine, -s 'pɔːkjʊpaɪn, -z
por|e (s. v.), -es, -ing, -ed pɔː* [pɔə*], -z, -rɪŋ, -d
porgy (fish) 'pɔːdʒɪ
Porgy (name) 'pɔːgɪ
pork, -er/s, -y pɔːk, -ə*/z, -ɪ
pornographic ,pɔːnəʊ'græfɪk
pornography pɔː'nɒgrəfɪ
porosity pɔː'rɒsətɪ [-ɪtɪ]
porous, -ly, -ness 'pɔːrəs, -lɪ, -nɪs [-nəs]
porphyry (P.) 'pɔːfɪrɪ [-fərɪ]
porpoise, -s 'pɔːpəs, -ɪz
porridge 'pɒrɪdʒ
porringer, -s 'pɒrɪndʒə*, -z
Porsche pɔːʃ
Porsena 'pɔːsɪnə [-sən-]
Porson 'pɔːsn
port (s. v.), -s, -ing, -ed pɔːt, -s, -ɪŋ, -ɪd
portability ,pɔːtə'bɪlətɪ [-lɪt-]
portable, -ness 'pɔːtəbl, -nɪs [-nəs]
Portadown ,pɔːtə'daʊn
portage 'pɔːtɪdʒ
portal (P.), -s 'pɔːtl, -z
portamento, -s ,pɔːtə'mentəʊ, -z
portcullis, -es ,pɔːt'kʌlɪs, -ɪz
Porte pɔːt
portend, -s,-ing, -ed pɔː'tend, -z, -ɪŋ, -ɪd
portent, -s 'pɔːtent [-tənt], -s

portentous, -ly pɔː'tentəs, -lɪ
porter (P.), -s; -age 'pɔːtə*, -z; -rɪdʒ
Porteus 'pɔːtjəs [-tɪəs]
portfolio, -s ,pɔːt'fəʊljəʊ [-lɪəʊ], -z
porthole, -s 'pɔːthəʊl, -z
Portia 'pɔːʃə [-ʃɪə, -ʃjə]
portico, -s 'pɔːtɪkəʊ, -z
porti|on (s. v.), -ons, -oning, -oned 'pɔːʃ|n, -nz, -ŋɪŋ [-ənɪŋ], -nd
Portishead 'pɔːtɪshed
Portland 'pɔːtlənd
Portlaw ,pɔːt'lɔː
portl|y, -ier, -iest, -iness 'pɔːtl|ɪ, -ɪə* [-jə*], -ɪɪst [-jɪst], -ɪnɪs [-ɪnəs]
Portmadoc ,pɔːt'mædək (*Welsh* port-'madok)
Portman 'pɔːtmən
portmanteau, -s ,pɔːt'mæntəʊ, -z
Portobello ,pɔːtəʊ'beləʊ
Porto Rico ,pɔːtəʊ'riːkəʊ
portrait, -s; -ist/s 'pɔːtreɪt [-trɪt, -trət], -s; -ɪst/s
portraiture 'pɔːtrɪtʃə [-trətʃ-, -,tjʊə*]
portray, -s, -ing, -ed, -er/s pɔː'treɪ, -z, -ɪŋ, -d, -ə*/z [pɔː'treə*/z]
portrayal, -s pɔː'treɪəl [-'treɪl], -z
portreeve, -s 'pɔːtriːv, -z
Portrush ,pɔːt'rʌʃ
Port Said ,pɔːt'saɪd [*old-fashioned* -'seɪd]
Port Salut ,pɔːsə'luː: [-sæ-] (pɔrsaly)
Portsea 'pɔːtsɪ [-siː]
Portsmouth 'pɔːtsməθ
Portsoy ,pɔːt'sɔɪ
Portugal 'pɔːtʃʊgl [-tjʊ-]
Portuguese ,pɔːtʃʊ'giːz [-tjʊ-]
posaune, -s pə'zɔːn, -z
pos|e (s. v.), -es, -ing, -ed, -er/s pəʊz, -ɪz, -ɪŋ, -d, -ə*/z
Poseidon pɒ'saɪdən [pə's-]
poser (problem), -s 'pəʊzə*, -z
poseur, -s pəʊ'zɜː* (pozœːr), -z
posh pɒʃ
posit, -s, -ing, -ed 'pɒzɪt, -s, -ɪŋ, -ɪd
position, -s pə'zɪʃn [pʊ'z-], -z
positional pə'zɪʃənl [pʊ'z-, -ʃnəl, -ʃn̩l, -ʃnl, -ʃənəl]
positive (s. adj.), -s, -ly, -ness 'pɒzətɪv [-zɪt-], -z, -lɪ, -nɪs [-nəs]
positivi|sm, -st/s 'pɒzɪtɪvɪ|zəm [-zət-], -st/s
positron, -s 'pɒzɪtrɒn [-trən], -z
posse, -s 'pɒsɪ, -z
possess, -es, -ing, -ed, -or/s pə'zes [pʊ'z-], -ɪz, -ɪŋ, -t, -ə*/z
possession, -s pə'zeʃn [pʊ'z-], -z
possessive (s. adj.), -s, -ly, -ness pə'zesɪv [pʊ'z-], -z, -lɪ, -nɪs [-nəs]

possessory pə'zesərɪ [pʊ'z-]
posset 'pɒsɪt
possibilit|y, -ies ˌpɒsə'bɪlət|ɪ [-sɪ'b-, -lɪt-], -ɪz
possib|le, -ly 'pɒsəb|l [-sɪb-], -lɪ
possum, -s 'pɒsəm, -z
post (s. v.), **-s, -ing, -ed** pəʊst, -s, -ɪŋ, -ɪd
postage, -s 'pəʊstɪdʒ, -ɪz
postal 'pəʊstəl
postal-order (**P.O.**), **-s** 'pəʊstlˌɔːdə* (ˌpiː'əʊ), -z
post-bag, -s 'pəʊstbæg, -z
postcard, -s 'pəʊstkɑːd, -z
post-chaise, -s 'pəʊst-ʃeɪz [ˌ-'-], -ɪz
postdat|e, -es, -ing, -ed ˌpəʊst'deɪt ['--], -s, -ɪŋ, -ɪd
post-diluvian ˌpəʊstdɪ'luːvjən [-daɪ'l-, -'ljuː-, -vɪən]
poster, -s 'pəʊstə*, -z
poste restante ˌpəʊst'restɑːnt [-tɔ̃ːnt, -tɑ̃ːnt, -tɒnt, -tænt] (pɒstrɛstɑ̃ːt)
posterior, -ly pɒ'stɪərɪə*, -lɪ
posteriority pɒˌstɪərɪ'ɒrətɪ [ˌpɒstɪər-, -ɪtɪ]
posterit|y, -ies pɒ'sterət|ɪ [-ɪt|ɪ], -ɪz
postern, -s 'pɒstən ['pəʊs-, -tɜːn], -z
post-free ˌpəʊst'friː
Postgate 'pəʊstɡeɪt [-ɡɪt]
post-graduate ˌpəʊst'ɡrædʒʊət [-dʒʊɪt, -djʊət, -djʊɪt]
posthaste ˌpəʊst'heɪst
post|horn/s, -horse/s 'pəʊst|hɔːn/z, -hɔːs/ɪz
posthumous, -ly 'pɒstjʊməs, -lɪ
postiche, -s pɒ'stiːʃ ['--], -ɪz
postil, -s 'pɒstɪl, -z
postillion, -s pə'stɪljən [pɒ's-, -lɪən], -z
post-impressioni|sm, -st/s ˌpəʊstɪm-'preʃn̩ɪ|zəm [-ʃənɪ-], -st/s
Postlethwaite 'pɒslθweɪt
post|man, -men 'pəʊst|mən, -mən
postmark (s. v.), **-s, -ing, -ed** 'pəʊst-mɑːk, -s, -ɪŋ, -t
postmaster, -s 'pəʊstˌmɑːstə*, -z
post-meridian ˌpəʊstmə'rɪdɪən [-djən]
post-mistress, -es 'pəʊstˌmɪstrɪs [-trəs], -ɪz
post-mortem, -s ˌpəʊst'mɔːtem [-təm], -z
post-natal ˌpəʊst'neɪtl
post-office, -s 'pəʊst‚ɒfɪs, -ɪz
postpon|e (s. v.), **-es, -ing, -ed, -ement/s** ˌpəʊst'pəʊn [pəs'p-], -z, -ɪŋ, -d, -mənt/s
†**postposition, -s** ˌpəʊstpə'zɪʃn [-pʊ'z-, '-ˌ--], -z
postscript, -s 'pəʊsskrɪpt ['pəʊstskrɪpt], -s

post-tonic ˌpəʊst'tɒnɪk
post-town, -s 'pəʊsttaʊn, -z
postulant, -s 'pɒstjʊlənt, -s
postulate (s.), **-s** 'pɒstjʊlət [-lɪt, -leɪt], -s
postulat|e (v.), **-es, -ing, -ed** 'pɒstjʊleɪt, -s, -ɪŋ, -ɪd
postulation, -s ˌpɒstjʊ'leɪʃn, -z
postur|e (s. v.), **-es, -ing, -ed** 'pɒstʃə* [-ˌtjʊə*], -z, -rɪŋ, -d
post-war ˌpəʊst'wɔː* [also '— when attributive]
pos|y -ies 'pəʊz|ɪ, -ɪz
pot (s. v.), **-s, -ting, -ted, -er/s** pɒt, -s, -ɪŋ, -ɪd, -ə*/z
potable, -ness, -s 'pəʊtəbl, -nɪs [-nəs], -z
potage, -s pɒ'tɑːʒ ['pɒtɑːʒ] (pɔtaːʒ), -ɪz
potash, -water 'pɒtæʃ, -ˌwɔːtə*
potassium pə'tæsɪəm [-sjəm]
potation, -s pəʊ'teɪʃn, -z
potato, -es pə'teɪtəʊ, -z
pot-bellied, -y 'pɒtˌbelɪd [ˌ-'--], -ɪ
pot-boiler, -s 'pɒtˌbɔɪlə*, -z
poteen pɒ'tiːn [pəʊ-, -'tʃiːn]
Potemkin pə'temkɪn [pə'tjɒmkɪn]
poten|cy, -t/ly 'pəʊtən|sɪ, -t/lɪ
potentate, -s 'pəʊtənteɪt [-tɪt], -s
potenti|al (s. adj.), **-als, -ally** pəʊ'tenʃ|l [pʊ't-], -lz, -əlɪ
potentialit|y, -ies pəʊˌtenʃɪ'ælət|ɪ [pʊˌt-, -ɪt|ɪ], -ɪz
potentilla, -s ˌpəʊtən'tɪlə, -z
pother (s. v.), **-s, -ing, -ed** 'pɒðə*, -z, -rɪŋ, -d
pot-herb, -s 'pɒthɜːb, -z
pot-hole, -s, -er/s 'pɒthəʊl, -z, -ə*/z
pot-holing 'pɒtˌhəʊlɪŋ
pothook, -s 'pɒthʊk, -s
pothou|se, -ses 'pɒthaʊ|s, -zɪz
pot-hunter, -s 'pɒtˌhʌntə*, -z
potion, -s 'pəʊʃn, -z
Potiphar 'pɒtɪfə* [-fɑː*]
pot-luck ˌpɒt'lʌk
Potomac pə'təʊmək
Potosi (in Bolivia) ˌpɒtəʊ'siː, (in U.S.A.) pə'təʊsɪ
pot-pourri, -s ˌpəʊ'pʊərɪ [-riː, ˌpəʊpə'riː, -pʊ'r-] (popuri), -z
Potsdam 'pɒtsdæm
potsherd, -s 'pɒt-ʃɜːd, -z
pot-shot, -s 'pɒt-ʃɒt [ˌ-'-], -s
Pott pɒt
pottage 'pɒtɪdʒ
pott|er (s. v.) (**P.**), **-ers, -ering, -ered, -erer/s** 'pɒt|ə*, -əz, -ərɪŋ, -əd, -ərə*/z
potter|y, -ies (**P.**) 'pɒtər|ɪ, -ɪz
pottle, -s 'pɒtl, -z

pott|y, -ier, -iest, -iness 'pɒt|ɪ, -ɪə*, -ɪɪst, -ɪnɪs [-ɪnəs]
Pou (*French-Canadian name*) pju:
pouch (*s.*), -es pautʃ [*in the army also* pu:tʃ], -ɪz
pouch (*v.*), -es, -ing, -ed pautʃ, -ɪz, -ɪŋ, -t
pouf(fe), -s pu:f, -s
Poughill 'pɒfɪl
Poulett 'pɔ:lɪt [-let]
poulpe, -s pu:lp, -s
Poulson 'pəulsən ['pu:l-]
poult (*chicken*), -s pəult, -s
poult (*silk material*) pu:lt
poulter (P.), -s 'pəultə*, -z
poulterer, -s 'pəultərə*, -z
poultic|e (*s. v.*), -es, -ing, -ed 'pəultɪs, -ɪz, -ɪŋ, -t
Poultney 'pəultnɪ
Poulton 'pəultən
poultry, -man 'pəultrɪ, -mən
poultry-farm, -s, -ing, -er/s 'pəultrɪfɑ:m, -z, -ɪŋ, -ə*/z
poultry-yard, -s 'pəultrɪjɑ:d, -z
pounc|e (*s. v.*), -es, -ing, -ed pauns, -ɪz, -ɪŋ, -t
Pouncefoot 'paunsfut
pound (*s. v.*) (P.), -s, -ing, -ed, -er/s paund, -z, -ɪŋ, -ɪd, -ə*/z
poundage, -s 'paundɪdʒ, -ɪz
Pounds paundz
Pount(e)ney 'pauntnɪ
Poupart (*surname*) 'pəupɑ:t, 'pu:pɑ:t
Pouparts (*junction near Clapham Junction*) 'pu:pɑ:ts
pour (*s. v.*), -s, -ing, -ed, -er/s pɔ:* [pɔə*], -z, -ɪɪŋ, -d, -rə*/z
pourboire, -s 'puəbwa:* (purbwa:r), -z
pourparler, -s ˌpuə'pɑ:leɪ (purparle), -z
pout (*s. v.*), -s, -ing, -ed, -er/s paut, -s, -ɪŋ, -ɪd, -ə*/z
poverty 'pɒvətɪ
poverty-stricken 'pɒvətɪˌstrɪkən
Pow pau
P.O.W., -'s ˌpi:əu'dʌb|ju:, -z
powd|er (*s. v.*), -ers, -ering, -ered 'paud|ə*, -əz, -ərɪŋ, -əd
powder-magazine, -s 'paudəmægəˌzi:n, -z
powder-puff, -s 'paudəpʌf, -s
powder|y, -iness 'paudər|ɪ, -ɪnɪs [-məs]
Powell 'pəuəl [-ɪl, -el], 'pau-
power (P.), -s 'pauə*, -z
power-cut, -s 'pauəkʌt, -s
power|ful, -fully, -fulness 'pauə|ful, -fulɪ [-fəlɪ, -flɪ], -fulnɪs [-nəs]
power-hou|se, -ses 'pauəhau|s, -zɪz
powerless, -ly, -ness 'pauəlɪs [-ləs], -lɪ, -nɪs [-nəs]

Powerscourt (*family name*) 'pɔ:zkɔ:t
power-station, -s 'pauəˌsteɪʃn, -z
Powicke 'pəuɪk
Powis (*in Scotland*) 'pauɪs, (*surname*) 'pəuɪs, 'pauɪs, (*square in London*) 'pauɪs
Powles pəulz
Powlett 'pɔ:lɪt
Pownall 'paunl
Pownceby 'paunsbɪ
pow-wow (*s. v.*), -s, -ing, -ed 'pauwau, -z, -ɪŋ, -d
Powyke 'pəuɪk
Powys (*county in Wales, family name of Viscount Lilford*) 'pəuɪs, 'pauɪs
pox pɒks
Poynings 'pɔɪnɪŋz
Poynt|er, -on 'pɔɪnt|ə*, -ən
practicability ˌpræktɪkə'bɪlətɪ [-lɪt-]
practicab|le, -ly, -leness 'præktɪkəb|l, -lɪ, -lnɪs [-nəs]
practic|al, -alness 'præktɪk|l, -lnɪs [-nəs]
practicality ˌpræktɪ'kælətɪ [-rtɪ]
practically (*in a practical manner*) 'præktɪkəlɪ [-klɪ], (*very nearly*) 'præktɪklɪ [-kəlɪ]
practice, -s 'præktɪs, -ɪz
practician, -s præk'tɪʃn, -z
practis|e, -es, -ing, -ed, -er/s 'præktɪs, -ɪz, -ɪŋ, -t, -ə*/z
practitioner, -s præk'tɪʃnə* [prək-, -ʃənə*], -z
Praed preɪd
praenomen, -s ˌpri:'nəumen, -z
praepostor, -s ˌpri:'pɒstə*, -z
praesidium, -s prɪ'sɪdɪəm [prɪ'zɪd-, -djəm], -z
praetor, -s; -ship/s 'pri:tə* [-tɔ:*], -z; -ʃɪp/s
praetori|al, -an, -um/s, -a pri:'tɔ:rɪ|əl [prɪ-], -ən, -əm/z, -ə
pragmatic, -al, -ally præg'mætɪk, -l, -əlɪ
pragmati|sm, -st/s 'prægmətɪ|zəm, -st/s
Prague prɑ:g
prairie (P.), -s; -land 'preərɪ, -z; -lænd
prais|e (*s. v.*), -es, -ing, -ed, -er/s preɪz, -ɪz, -ɪŋ, -d, -ə*/z
praiseworth|y, -iness 'preɪzˌwɜ:ð|ɪ, -ɪnɪs [-nəs]
Prakrit 'prɑ:krɪt
praline, -s 'prɑ:li:n, -z
Prall prɔ:l
pram (*perambulator*), -s præm, -z
pram (*flat-bottomed boat*), -s prɑ:m, -z
pranc|e (P.), -es, -ing, -ed, -er/s prɑ:ns, -ɪz, -ɪŋ, -t, -ə*/z
prandial 'prændɪəl [-djəl]
prang (*s. v.*), -s, -ing, -ed præŋ, -z, -ɪŋ, -d

389

prank (s. v.), **-s, -ing, -ed** præŋk, -s, -ɪŋ, -t [præŋt]

prank|ish, **-some** 'præŋk|ɪʃ, -səm

prat|e (s. v.), **-es, -ing, -ed, -er/s** preɪt, -s, -ɪŋ, -ɪd, -ə*/z

pratincole, **-s** 'prætɪŋkəʊl, -z

pratique, **-s** 'præti:k [-tɪk, præ'ti:k], **-s**

Pratt præt

pratt|le (s. v.), **-les, -ling, -led, -ler/s** 'præt|l, -lz, -lɪŋ [-lɪŋ], -ld, -lə*/z [-lə*/z]

prawn, **-s** prɔ:n, -z

prax|is, **-es** 'præks|ɪs, -i:z

Praxiteles præk'sɪtəli:z [-tɪl-]

pray (P.), **-s, -ing, -ed** preɪ, -z, -ɪŋ, -d

prayer (one who prays), **-s** 'preɪə*, -z

prayer (supplication), **-s** preə*, -z

prayer-book, **-s** 'preəbʊk, -s

prayer|ful, **-fully, -fulness** 'preə|fʊl, -fʊlɪ [-fəlɪ], -fʊlnɪs [-nəs]

prayerless, **-ly, -ness** 'preəlɪs [-ləs], -lɪ, -nɪs [-nəs]

prayer-meeting, **-s** 'preə,mi:tɪŋ, **-z**

prayer-rug, **-s** 'preərʌg, -z

prayer-wheel, **-s** 'preəwi:l ['preəhw-], **-z**

preach (s. v.), **-es, -ing, -ed, -er/s** pri:tʃ, -ɪz, -ɪŋ, -t, -ə*/z

preachi|fy, **-fies, -fying, -fied** 'pri:tʃɪ|faɪ, -faɪz, -faɪɪŋ, -faɪd

pre-adamite ,pri:'ædəmaɪt

Preager 'preɪgə*

preamble, **-s** pri:'æmbl ['---, prɪ'æ-], -z

prearrang|e, **-es, -ing, -ed** ,pri:ə'reɪndʒ, -ɪz, -ɪŋ, -d

Prebble 'prebl

prebend, **-s** 'prebənd, **-z**

prebendar|y, **-ies** 'prebəndər|ɪ [-bmd-], -ɪz.

precarious, **-ly, -ness** prɪ'keərɪəs [prə'k-], -lɪ, -nɪs [-nəs]

precatory 'prekətərɪ

precaution, **-s** prɪ'kɔ:ʃn [prə'k-], -z

precautionary prɪ'kɔ:ʃṇərɪ [prə'k-, -ʃnə-, -ʃənə-]

preced|e, **-es, -ing, -ed** ,pri:'si:d [prɪ-], -z, -ɪŋ, -ɪd

preceden|ce, **-cy** 'presɪdən|s ['pri:-, prɪ'si:dən|s, ,pri:'s-] -sɪ

precedent (s.), **-s, -ed** 'presɪdənt ['pri:s-], -s, -ɪd

precedent (adj.), **-ly** prɪ'si:dənt ['presɪd-], -lɪ

precentor, **-s** ,pri:'sentə* [prɪ-], -z

precept, **-s** 'pri:sept, -s

preceptor, **-s** prɪ'septə*, -z

preceptor|y, **-ies** prɪ'septər|ɪ, -ɪz

preces 'pri:si:z

precession, **-s** prɪ'seʃn, -z

precinct, **-s** 'pri:sɪŋkt, **-s**

preciosity ,preʃɪ'ɒsətɪ [-esɪ-, -ɪtɪ]

precious, **-ly, -ness** 'preʃəs, -lɪ, -nɪs [-nəs]

precipice, **-s** 'presɪpɪs [-səp-], -ɪz

precipitan|ce, **-cy** prɪ'sɪpɪtən|s, -sɪ

precipitate (s.), **-s** prɪ'sɪpɪteɪt [prə's-, -tət, -tɪt], -s

precipitate (adj.), **-ly** prɪ'sɪpɪtət [prə's-, -tɪt], -lɪ

precipitat|e (v.), **-es, -ing, -ed** prɪ'sɪpɪteɪt [prə's-], -s, -ɪŋ, -ɪd

precipitation prɪ,sɪpɪ'teɪʃn [prə,s-]

precipitous, **-ly, -ness** prɪ'sɪpɪtəs [prə's-], -lɪ, -nɪs [-nəs]

précis (sing.) 'preɪsi: ['pres-], (plur.) **-z**

precise, **-ly, -ness** prɪ'saɪs [prə's-], -lɪ, -nɪs [-nəs]

precisian, **-s** prɪ'sɪʒn [prə's-], **-z**

precision prɪ'sɪʒn [prə's-]

preclud|e, **-es, -ing, -ed** prɪ'klu:d, **-z**, -ɪŋ, -ɪd

preclu|sion, **-sive** prɪ'klu:|ʒn, -sɪv

precocious, **-ly, -ness** prɪ'kəʊʃəs [prə'k-], -lɪ, -nɪs [-nəs]

precocity prɪ'kɒsətɪ [prə'k-, -ɪtɪ]

preconceiv|e, **-es, -ing, -ed** ,pri:kən'si:v, -z, -ɪŋ, -d [also 'pri:kənsi:vd when attributive]

preconception, **-s** ,pri:kən'sepʃn, **-z**

preconcert, **-s, -ing, -ed** ,pri:kən'sə:t, **-s**, -ɪŋ, -ɪd

precursor, **-s; -y** ,pri:'kə:sə* [prɪ-], **-z**; -rɪ

predation, **-s** prɪ'deɪʃn [pre'd-], -z

predator|y, **-ily, -iness** 'predətər|ɪ, -əlɪ [-ɪlɪ], -ɪnɪs [-ɪnəs]

predeceas|e, **-es, -ing, -ed** ,pri:dɪ'si:s, -ɪz, -ɪŋ, -t

predecessor, **-s** 'pri:dɪsesə* [,pri:dɪ's-], -z

predestinat|e, **-es, -ing, -ed** ,pri:-'destɪneɪt [prɪ-], -s, -ɪŋ, -ɪd

predestination pri:,destɪ'neɪʃn [prɪ'd-, 'pri:,destɪ'neɪʃn]

predestin|e, **-es, -ing, -ed** ,pri:'destɪn [prɪ'd-], -z, -ɪŋ, -d

predetermination 'pri:dɪ,tɜ:mɪ'neɪʃn

predetermin|e, **-es, -ing, -ed** ,pri:dɪ-'tɜ:mɪn, -z, -ɪŋ, -d

predicability ,predɪkə'bɪlətɪ [-lɪt-]

predicable 'predɪkəbl

predicament, **-s** prɪ'dɪkəmənt [prə'd-], -s

predicate (s.), **-s** 'predɪkət [-kɪt, -keɪt, 'pri:dɪkɪt, -kət], -s

predicat|e (v.), **-es, -ing, -ed** 'predɪkeɪt, -s, -ɪŋ, -ɪd

predication, **-s** ,predɪ'keɪʃn, -z

predicative, -ly prɪ'dɪkətɪv [prə'd-], -lɪ

predict, -s, -ing, -ed, -or/s; -able, -ably prɪ'dɪkt [prə'd-], -s, -ɪŋ, -ɪd, -ə*/z; -əbl, -əblɪ

prediction, -s prɪ'dɪkʃn [prə'd-], -z

predilection, -s ˌpriː'dɪ'lekʃn, -z

predispos|e, -es, -ing, -ed ˌpriː'dɪ'spəʊz -ɪz, -ɪŋ, -d

predisposition, -s 'priːˌdɪspə'zɪʃn [ˌpriː'dɪs-], -z

predominan|ce, -t/ly prɪ'dɒmɪnən|s [prə'd-], -t/lɪ

predominat|e, -es, -ing, -ed prɪ'dɒmɪneɪt [prə'd-], -s, -ɪŋ, -ɪd

predomination prɪˌdɒmɪ'neɪʃn [prəˌd-]

predorsal ˌpriː'dɔːsl

Preece priːs

pre-emin|ce, -t/ly ˌpriː'emɪnən|s [prɪ'em-], -t/lɪ

pre-empt, -s, -ing, -ed ˌpriː'empt [prɪ'em-], -s, -ɪŋ, -ɪd

pre-emption ˌpriː'empʃn [prɪ'em-]

pre-emptive ˌpriː'emptɪv [prɪ'em-]

preen, -s, -ing, -ed priːn, -z, -ɪŋ, -d

pre-exist, -s, -ing, -ed; -ence, -ent ˌpriːɪg'zɪst, -s, -ɪŋ, -ɪd; -əns, -ənt

prefab, -s 'priːfæb, -z

prefabricat|e, -es, -ing, -ed ˌpriː'fæbrɪkeɪt, -s, -ɪŋ, -ɪd

pre-fabrication 'priːˌfæbrɪ'keɪʃn [ˌ—'—, -ˌ—'—]

prefac|e (s. v.), -es, -ing, -ed 'prefɪs [-fəs], -ɪz, -ɪŋ, -t

prefatorial ˌprefə'tɔːrɪəl

prefatory 'prefətərɪ

prefect, -s 'priːfekt, -s

prefecture, -s 'priːfekˌtjʊə* [-ˌtʃʊə*, -tʃə*], -z

prefer, -s, -ring, -red prɪ'fɜː* [prə'f-], -z, -rɪŋ, -d

preferability ˌprefərə'bɪlətɪ [-lɪt-]

preferab|le, -ly, -leness 'prefərəb|l [rarely prɪ'fɜːr-, prə'fɜːr-], -lɪ, -lnɪs [-nəs]

preference, -s 'prefərəns, -ɪz

preferential ˌprefə'renʃl

preferment, -s prɪ'fɜːmənt [prə'f-], -s

prefix (s.), -es 'priːfɪks, -ɪz

prefix (v.), -es, -ing, -ed ˌpriː'fɪks ['priːfɪks], -ɪz, -ɪŋ, -t

pregnable 'pregnəbl

pregnan|cy, -t/ly 'pregnən|sɪ, -t/lɪ

prehensible prɪ'hensəbl [-sɪb-]

prehensile prɪ'hensaɪl [ˌpriː'h-]

prehistoric, -ally ˌpriːhɪ'stɒrɪk, -əlɪ [-lɪ]

pre-history ˌpriː'hɪstərɪ

prejudg|e, -es, -ing, -ed ˌpriː'dʒʌdʒ, -ɪz, -ɪŋ, -d

prejudic|e (s. v.), -es, -ing, -ed 'predʒʊdɪs [-dʒəd-], -ɪz, -ɪŋ, -t

prejudici|al, -ally ˌpredʒʊ'dɪʃ|l [-dʒə'd-], -əlɪ [-lɪ]

prelac|y, -ies 'preləs|ɪ, -ɪz

prelate, -s 'prelɪt [-lət], -s

preliminar|y, -ies, -ily prɪ'lɪmnər|ɪ [prə'l-, -'lɪmɪnr-, -mən-], -ɪz, -əlɪ [-ɪlɪ]

prelims (preliminary examination; introductory pages in book) 'priːlɪmz [ˌ-'-]

prelud|e (s. v.), -es, -ing, -ed 'prelju:d, -z, -ɪŋ ['preljʊdɪŋ], -ɪd ['preljʊdɪd]

premature, -ly, -ness 'premətjʊə* ['priːm-, -tjɔə*, -tjɔ:*, -ˌtʃʊə, ˌ--'-], -lɪ, -nɪs [-nəs]

premeditate, -es, -ing, -ed/ly ˌpriː'medɪteɪt [prɪ'm-], -s, -ɪŋ, -ɪd/lɪ

premeditation priːˌmedɪ'teɪʃn [prɪˌm-]

premier (s. adj.), -s; -ship/s 'premjə* [-mɪə*], -z; -ʃɪp/s

première, -s 'premɪeə*, -z

premise (s.), -s 'premɪs, -ɪz

premis|e (v.), -es, -ing, -ed prɪ'maɪz ['premɪs], -ɪz, -ɪŋ, prɪ'maɪzd ['premɪst]

premium, -s 'priːmjəm [-mɪəm], -z

premonition, -s ˌpreməʊ'nɪʃn [ˌpriːm-], -z

premonitor|y, -ily prɪ'mɒnɪtər|ɪ, -əlɪ [-ɪlɪ]

pre-natal ˌpriː'neɪtl

Prendergast 'prendəgɑːst, -gæst

prentice, -s 'prentɪs, -ɪz

Prenti|ce, -ss 'prentɪ|s, -s

preoccupation, -s priːˌɒkjʊ'peɪʃn [prɪˌɒk-, ˌpriːˈɒk-], -z

preoccup|y, -ies, -ying, -ied ˌpriː-'ɒkjʊp|aɪ [prɪ'ɒk-], -aɪz, -aɪɪŋ, -aɪd

preordain, -s, -ing, -ed ˌpriːɔː'deɪn, -z, -ɪŋ, -d

prep (s. adj.), -s prep, -s

prepaid (from prepay) ˌpriː'peɪd [also '— when attributive]

preparation, -s ˌprepə'reɪʃn, -z

preparative, -ly prɪ'pærətɪv [prə'p-], -lɪ

preparator|y, -ily prɪ'pærətər|ɪ [prə'p-], -əlɪ [-ɪlɪ]

prepar|e, -es, -ing, -ed, -edly, -edness, -er/s prɪ'peə* [prə'p-], -z, -rɪŋ, -d, -dlɪ [-rɪdlɪ], -dnɪs [-rɪdnɪs, -nəs], -rə*/z

prepay, -s, -ing, prepaid, prepayment/s ˌpriː'peɪ, -z, -ɪŋ, ˌpriː'peɪd [also '— when attributive], ˌpriː'peɪmənt/s

prepense, -ly prɪ'pens, -lɪ

preponderan|ce, -t/ly prɪ'pɒndərən|s [prə'p-], -t/lɪ

391

preponderat|e, -es, -ing/ly, -ed prɪ-
'pɒndərert [prə'p-], -s, -ɪŋ/lɪ, -ɪd
preponderation prɪ,pɒndə'reɪʃn [prə,p-]
prepos|e, -es, -ing, -ed ,priː'pəʊz, -ɪz,
-ɪŋ, -d
preposition, -s ,prepə'zɪʃn, -z
preposi|tional, -tionally ,prepə'zɪ|ʃənl
[-pʊ'z-, -ʃnəl, -ʃn̩l, -ʃn̩l, -ʃənəl], -ʃn̩əlɪ
[-ʃnəlɪ, -ʃn̩lɪ, -ʃn̩lɪ, -ʃənəlɪ]
prepositive prɪ'pɒzətɪv [-ɪtɪv]
prepossess, -es, -ing/ly, -ed ,priːpə'zes,
-ɪz, -ɪŋ/lɪ, -t
prepossession, -s ,priːpə'zeʃn, -z
preposterous, -ly, -ness prɪ'pɒstərəs
[prə'p-], -lɪ, -nɪs [-nəs]
prepuce, -s 'priːpjuːs, -ɪz
Pre-Raphaelite (s. adj.), -s ,priː'ræfəlaɪt
[-fɪl-, -f̩l-, -frəl-, -ferəl-], -s
prerequisite, -s ,priː'rekwɪzɪt, -s
prerogative (s. adj.), -s prɪ'rɒgətɪv
[prə'r-], -z
presage (s.), -s 'presɪdʒ, -ɪz
presag|e (v.), -es, -ing, -ed 'presɪdʒ
[prɪ'seɪdʒ], -ɪz, -ɪŋ, -d
presbyopia ,prezbɪ'əʊpjə [-pɪə]
presbyter, -s 'prezbɪtə*, -z
presbyterian, -s, -ism ,prezbɪ'tɪərɪən
[-bə't-], -z, -ɪzəm
presbyter|y, -ies 'prezbɪtər|ɪ, -ɪz
prescien|ce, -t/ly 'presɪən|s [-sjə-, -ʃɪə-,
-ʃjə-], -t/lɪ
Prescot(t) 'preskət
prescrib|e, -es, -ing, -ed, -er/s prɪ-
'skraɪb [prə'-], -z, -ɪŋ, -d, -ə*/z
prescript, -s 'priːskrɪpt, -s
prescription, -s prɪ'skrɪpʃn [prə's-], -z
prescriptive prɪ'skrɪptɪv [prə's-]
presence, -s 'prezns, -ɪz
present (s.) (ordinary senses), -s 'preznt
[-zənt], -s
present (s.) (military term), -s prɪ'zent
[prə'z-], -s
present (adj.), -ly 'preznt [-zənt], -lɪ
present (v.), -s, -ing, -ed, -ment prɪ'zent
[prə'z-], -s, -ɪŋ, -ɪd, -mənt
presentable, -ness prɪ'zentəbl [prə'z-],
-nɪs [-nəs]
presentation, -s ,prezən'teɪʃn [-zen-], -z
presentient prɪ'senʃɪənt [-ʃjənt, -ʃənt]
presentiment, -s prɪ'zentɪmənt [-ɪ'se-],
-s
presently 'prezntlɪ [-zənt-]
preservation, -s ,prezə'veɪʃn, -z
preservative (s. adj.), -s prɪ'zɜːvətɪv, -z
preserv|e (s. v.), -es, -ing, -ed, -er/s;
-able prɪ'zɜːv, -z, -ɪŋ, -d, -ə*/z; -əbl
presid|e, -es, -ing, -ed prɪ'zaɪd, -z, -ɪŋ,
-ɪd

presidenc|y, -ies 'prezɪdəns|ɪ, -ɪz
president, -s 'prezɪdənt, -s
presidential ,prezɪ'denʃl
presidium, -s prɪ'sɪdɪəm [prɪ'zɪd-,
-djəm], -z
press (s. v.), -es, -ing/ly, -ed, -er/s pres,
-ɪz, -ɪŋ/lɪ, -t, -ə*/z
press-agent, -s 'pres,eɪdʒənt, -s
press-conference, -s 'pres,kɒnfərəns, -ɪz
press-cutting, -s 'pres,kʌtɪŋ, -z
pressgang, -s 'presgæŋ, -z
pression 'preʃn
press|man, -men 'pres|mæn [-mən],
-mən [-men]
pressure, -s 'preʃə*, -z
pressure-cooker, -s 'preʃə,kʊkə*, -z
pressuriz|e [-is|e], -es, -ing, -ed
'preʃəraɪz, -ɪz, -ɪŋ, -d
Prestage 'prestɪdʒ
Prestatyn pre'stætɪn (Welsh pres'tatin)
Presteign pre'stiːn
prestidigitation 'prestɪ,dɪdʒɪ'teɪʃn
prestidigitator, -s ,prestɪ'dɪdʒɪteɪtə*, -z
prestige pre'stiːʒ
Prestige (surname) 'prestɪdʒ
prestigious pre'stɪdʒəs [prɪ-, prə-, -dʒɪəs]
prestissimo pre'stɪsɪməʊ
presto (P.), -s 'prestəʊ, -z
Preston 'prestən
Prestonpans ,prestən'pænz
Prestwich 'prestwɪtʃ
presum|e, -es, -ing/ly, -ed; -able, -ably
prɪ'zjuːm [prə'z-, -'zuːm], -z, -ɪŋ/lɪ,
-d; -əbl, -əblɪ
presumption, -s prɪ'zʌmpʃn [prə'z-], -z
presumptive, -ly prɪ'zʌmptɪv [prə'z-],
-lɪ
presumptuous, -ly, -ness prɪ'zʌmptʃʊəs
[prə'z-, -tʃwəs, -tjʊəs, -tjwəs], -lɪ,
-nɪs [-nəs]
presuppos|e, -es, -ing, -ed ,priːsə'pəʊz,
-ɪz, -ɪŋ, -d
presupposition, -s ,priːsʌpə'zɪʃn, -z
pretence, -s prɪ'tens [prə't-], -ɪz
pretend, -s, -ing, -ed, -er/s prɪ'tend
[prə't-], -z, -ɪŋ, -ɪd, -ə*/z
pretension, -s prɪ'tenʃn [prə't-], -z
pretentious, -ly, -ness prɪ'tenʃəs [prə't-],
-lɪ, -nɪs [-nəs]
preterite, -s 'pretərət [-rɪt], -s
preterito-present, -s priː,terɪtəʊ'preznt
[prɪ,t-, -zənt], -s
pretermission ,priːtə'mɪʃn
pretermit, -s, -ting, -ted ,priːtə'mɪt, -s,
-ɪŋ, -ɪd
preternatur|al, -ally, -alness ,priːtə-
'nætʃr|əl [-tʃʊr-, -tʃər-], -əlɪ, -əlnɪs
[-nəs]

pretext, -s 'pri:tekst, -s
pre-tonic ˌpri:'tɒnɪk
Pretori|a, -us prɪ'tɔ:rɪ|ə [prə't-], -əs
prett|y (*adj. adv.*), **-ier, -iest, -ily, -iness**
'prɪt|ɪ, -ɪə*, -ɪst, -ɪlɪ[-əlɪ], -ɪnɪs [-məs]
Pretty (*surname*) 'prɪtɪ, 'pretɪ
Pret(t)yman 'prɪtɪmən
pretty-pretty 'prɪtɪˌprɪtɪ
prevail, -s, -ing, -ed prɪ'veɪl [prə'v-], -z,
-ɪŋ, -d
prevalen|ce, -t/ly 'prevələn|s [-v]-], -t/lɪ
prevaricat|e, -es, -ing, -ed, -or/s prɪ-
'værɪkeɪt, -s, -ɪŋ, -ɪd, -ə*/z
prevarication, -s prɪˌværɪ'keɪʃn, -z
prevent (*hinder*), **-s, -ing, -ed, -er/s;**
-able prɪ'vent [prə'v-], -s, -ɪŋ, -ɪd,
-ə*/z; -əbl
prevent (*go before*), **-s, -ing, -ed** ˌprɪ:-
'vent [prɪ'v-], -s, -ɪŋ, -ɪd
preventability prɪˌ ventə'bɪlətɪ [prəˌv-,
-lɪt-]
preventative (*s. adj.*), **-s** prɪ'ventətɪv
[prə'v-], -z
prevention prɪ'venʃn [prə'v-]
preventive, -ly, -ness prɪ'ventɪv [prə'v-],
-lɪ, -nɪs [-nəs]
preview, -s 'pri:vju: [ˌ-'-], -z
previous, -ly, -ness 'pri:vjəs [-vɪəs], -lɪ,
-nɪs [-nəs]
prevision ˌprɪ:'vɪʒr [prɪ'v-]
Prevost (*English surname*) 'prevəʊ,
'prevəʊst, pre'vəʊ
pre-war ˌprɪ:'wɔ:* ['-- *when attributive*]
prey (*s. v.*), **-s, -ing, -ed** preɪ, -z, -ɪŋ, -d
Priam 'praɪəm [-æm]
priapism 'praɪəpɪzəm
priapus (**P.**), **-es** praɪ'eɪpəs, -ɪz
pric|e (*s. v.*) (**P.**), **-es, -ing, -ed** praɪs, -ɪz,
-ɪŋ, -t
priceless, -ness 'praɪslɪs [-ləs], -nɪs [-nəs]
prick (*s. v.*), **-s, -ing/s, -ed, -er/s** prɪk,
-s, -ɪŋ/z, -t, -ə*/z
prick|le (*s. v.*), **-les, -ling, -led** 'prɪk|l,
-lz, -lɪŋ [-lɪŋ], -ld
prickl|y, -iest, -iness 'prɪkl|ɪ [-k]|ɪ], -ɪst,
-ɪnɪs [-məs]
pride (**P.**) praɪd
Prideaux 'prɪdəʊ, 'pri:d-
Pridham 'prɪdəm
prie-dieu, -s ˌprɪ:'djɜ: ['--] (pridjǿ), -z
priest (**P.**), **-s; -craft, -hood, -like**
pri:st, -s; -krɑ:ft, -hʊd, -laɪk
priestess, -es 'pri:stɪs [-tes], -ɪz
Priestley 'pri:stlɪ
priestl|y, -iness 'pri:stl|ɪ, -ɪnɪs [-məs]
priest-ridden 'pri:stˌrɪdn
prig (*s. v.*), **-s, -ging, -ged, -ger/s; -gery**
prɪg, -z, -ɪŋ, -d, -ə*/z; -ərɪ

priggish, -ly, -ness 'prɪgɪʃ, -lɪ, -nɪs [-nəs]
prim (*adj. v.*) (**P.**), **-mer, -mest, -ly,**
-ness; -s, -ming, -med prɪm, -ə*, -ɪst,
-lɪ, -nɪs [-nəs]; -z, -ɪŋ, -d
primac|y, -ies 'praɪməs|ɪ, -ɪz
prima-donna, -s ˌpri:mə'dɒnə, -z
primaeval = **primeval**
prima facie ˌpraɪmə'feɪʃi: [-ʃɪ, -si:, -sɪ,
ʃɪi:, -sɪi:]
primage 'praɪmɪdʒ
primal 'praɪml
prim|ary (*s. adj.*), **-aries, -arily,**
-ariness 'praɪm|ərɪ, -ərɪz, -ərəlɪ [-ɪlɪ,
also praɪ'merəlɪ], -ərɪnɪs [-məs]
primate (*archbishop*), **-s** 'praɪmeɪt [-mɪt,
-mət], -s
primate (*higher mammal*), **-s** 'praɪmeɪt,
'praɪmeɪts [praɪ'meɪti:z]
primateship, -s 'praɪmət-ʃɪp [-mɪt-,
-meɪt-], -s
prim|e (*s. adj. v.*), **-es, -ing, -ed** praɪm,
-z, -ɪŋ, -d
primer (*he who or that which primes*), **-s**
'praɪmə*, -z
primer (*elementary book*), **-s** 'praɪmə*
['prɪm-], -z
primer (*printing type*) 'prɪmə*
primeval praɪ'mi:vl
primitive, -ly, -ness, -ism, -ist/s 'prɪmɪtɪv
[-mət-], -lɪ, -nɪs [-nəs], -ɪzəm, -ɪst/s
primogeniture ˌpraɪməʊ'dʒenɪtʃə*
[-ˌtʃʊə*, -ˌtjʊə*]
primordial praɪ'mɔ:djəl [-dɪəl]
primrose (**P.**), **-s** 'prɪmrəʊz, -ɪz
primula, -s 'prɪmjʊlə [-jələ], -z
primus, -es 'praɪməs, -ɪz
prince (**P.**), **-s; -dom/s, -like** prɪns, -ɪz;
-dəm/z, -laɪk
princel|y, -ier, -iest, -iness 'prɪnsl|ɪ,
-ɪə* [-jə*], -ɪst [-jɪst], -ɪnɪs [-məs]
princess, princesses prɪn'ses [*but* '--
when used attributively, also ˌ-'-],
prɪn'sesɪz
Prince|ton, -town 'prɪns|tən, -taʊn
princip|al (*s. adj.*), **-als, -ally, -alness**
'prɪnsəp|l [-sɪp-], -lz, -lɪ [-əlɪ], -lnɪs
[-nəs]
principalit|y, -ies ˌprɪnsɪ'pælət|ɪ [-ɪt|ɪ],
-ɪz
principalship, -s 'prɪnsəplʃɪp [-sɪp-],
-s
principate (*s.*), **-s** 'prɪnsɪpət [-pɪt, -peɪt],
-s
Principia prɪn'sɪpɪə [-pjə]
principle, -s, -d 'prɪnsəpl [-sɪp-], -z, -d
Pring prɪŋ
Pringle 'prɪŋgl
Prinsep 'prɪnsep

print (*s. v.*), -s, -ing/s, -ed, -er/s prɪnt, -s, -ɪŋ/z, -ɪd, -ə*/z

printable 'prɪntəbl

printing-machine, -s 'prɪntɪŋməˌʃiːn, -z

printing-office, -s 'prɪntɪŋˌɒfɪs, -ɪz

printing-press, -es 'prɪntɪŋˌpres, -ɪz

print-out 'prɪntaʊt

print-seller, -s 'prɪntˌselə*, -z

print-shop, -s 'prɪnt-ʃɒp, -s

prior (*s. adj.*) (**P.**), -s 'praɪə*, -z

prioress, -es 'praɪərɪs [-res], -ɪz

priorit|y, -ies praɪ'ɒrət|ɪ [-ɪt|ɪ], -ɪz

prior|y, -ies 'praɪər|ɪ, -ɪz

Priscian 'prɪʃɪən [-ʃjən]

Priscilla prɪ'sɪlə

pris|e (*s. v.*), -es, -ing, -ed praɪz, -ɪz, -ɪŋ, -d

prism, -s 'prɪzəm, -z

prismatic, -al, -ally prɪz'mætɪk, -l, -əlɪ

prison, -s 'prɪzn, -z

prisoner, -s 'prɪznə* [-znə*], -z

prison-hou|se, -ses 'prɪznhaʊ|s, -zɪz

pristine 'prɪstiːn [-taɪn]

Pritchard 'prɪtʃəd, -tʃɑːd

prithee 'prɪðɪ [-ðiː]

privacy 'prɪvəsɪ ['praɪv-]

private (*s. adj.*), -s, -ly, -ness 'praɪvɪt [-vət], -s, -lɪ, -nɪs [-nəs]

privateer, -s ˌpraɪvə'tɪə* [-vɪ't-], -z

privation, -s praɪ'veɪʃn, -z

privative, -ly 'prɪvətɪv, -lɪ

privet, -s 'prɪvɪt, -s

privilege, -s, -d 'prɪvɪlɪdʒ [-vəl-], -ɪz, -d

privity 'prɪvɪtɪ [-ɪtɪ]

priv|y (*s. adj.*), -ies, -ily 'prɪv|ɪ, -ɪz, -ɪlɪ [-əlɪ]

priz|e (*s. v.*), -es, -ing, -ed praɪz, -ɪz, -ɪŋ, -d

prize-fight, -s, -er/s 'praɪzfaɪt, -s, -ə*/z

prize|man, -men 'praɪz|mən, -mən [-men]

P.R.O. (*public relations officer*) ˌpiːɑːr'əʊ

pro (*s. prep.*), -s prəʊ, -z

probabilit|y, -ies ˌprɒbə'bɪlət|ɪ [-lɪt-], -ɪz

probab|le, -ly 'prɒbəb|l, -lɪ

probate, -s 'prəʊbeɪt [-bɪt], -s

probation, -s prə'beɪʃn [prəʊ'b-, prʊ'b-], -z

probationary prə'beɪʃn̩ərɪ [prəʊ'b-, prʊ'b-, -ʃnə-, -ʃənə-]

probationer, -s prə'beɪʃnə* [prəʊ'b-, prʊ'b-, -ʃn̩ə*, -ʃənə*], -z

probative 'prəʊbətɪv

prob|e (*s. v.*), -es, -ing, -ed prəʊb, -z, -ɪŋ, -d

probity 'prəʊbətɪ ['prɒb-, -ɪtɪ]

problem, -s 'prɒbləm [-lem, -lɪm], -z

problematic, -al, -ally ˌprɒblə'mætɪk [-blɪ'm-, -ble'm-], -l, -əlɪ

proboscis, -es prəʊ'bɒsɪs [prʊ'b-], -iːz

Prob|us, -yn 'prəʊb|əs, -ɪn

procedural prə'siːdʒərəl [prəʊ's-, prʊ's-, -djʊr-, -djər-]

procedure, -s prə'siːdʒə* [prəʊ's-, prʊ's-, -djə*], -z

proceed (*v.*), -s, -ing/s, -ed prə'siːd [prəʊ's-, prʊ's-], -z, -ɪŋ/z, -ɪd

proceeds (*s.*) 'prəʊsiːdz

proc|ess (*s.*), -esses 'prəʊs|es [*rarely* 'prɒs-, *also sometimes* -|ɪs, *esp. when followed by* **of**], -esɪz [-ɪsɪz]

process (*v.*) (*go in a procession*), -es, -ing, -ed prə'ses [prəʊ's-, prʊ's-], -ɪz, -ɪŋ, -t

process (*v.*) (*treat by a process*), -es, -ing, -ed, -or/s 'prəʊses, -ɪz ['prəʊsɪsɪz], -ɪŋ ['prəʊsɪsɪŋ], -t, -ə*/z

process-block, -s 'prəʊsesblɒk [-sɪs-], -s

procession, -s prə'seʃn [prʊ's-], -z

processional (*s. adj.*), -s prə'seʃənl [prʊ's-, -ʃnəl, -ʃn̩l, -ʃn̩l, -ʃənəl], -z

proclaim, -s, -ing, -ed, -er/s prə'kleɪm [prəʊ'k-, prʊ'k-], -z, -ɪŋ, -d, -ə*/z

proclamation, -s ˌprɒklə'meɪʃn, -z

proclitic (*s. adj.*), -s prəʊ'klɪtɪk, -s

proclivit|y, -ies prə'klɪvət|ɪ [prəʊ'k-, prʊ'k-, -ɪt|ɪ], -ɪz

proconsul, -s ˌprəʊ'kɒnsəl, -z

proconsul|ar, -ate/s ˌprəʊ'kɒnsjʊl|ə* [-sjəl-], -ət/s [-ɪt/s, -eɪt/s]

proconsulship, -s ˌprəʊ'kɒnsəlʃɪp, -s

procrastinat|e, -es, -ing, -ed, -or/s prəʊ'kræstɪneɪt [prʊ'k-], -s, -ɪŋ, -ɪd, -ə*/z

procrastination, -s prəʊˌkræstɪ'neɪʃn [prʊˌk-], -z

procreant 'prəʊkrɪənt

procreat|e, -es, -ing, -ed 'prəʊkrɪeɪt, -s, -ɪŋ, -ɪd

procreation ˌprəʊkrɪ'eɪʃn

procreative 'prəʊkrɪeɪtɪv

Procrust|es, -ean prəʊ'krʌst|iːz, -ɪən [-jən]

Procter 'prɒktə*

proctor (**P.**), -s 'prɒktə*, -z

proctorial prɒk'tɔːrɪəl

procumbent prəʊ'kʌmbənt

procuration, -s ˌprɒkjʊə'reɪʃn, -z

procurator, -s 'prɒkjʊəreɪtə*, -z

procur|e, -es, -ing, -ed, -er/s, -ess/es; -able prə'kjʊə* [prʊ'k-, -'kjɔə*, -'kjɔː*], -z, -rɪŋ, -d, -rə*/z, -rɪs/ɪz [-res/ɪz]; -rəbl

procurement prə'kjʊəmənt [prʊ-, -'kjɔə-, -'kjɔː-]

Procyon (*star*) 'prəʊsjən [-sɪən]
prod (*s. v.*), **-s, -ding, -ded** prɒd, -z, -ɪŋ, -ɪd
prodig|al (*s. adj.*), **-als, -ally, -alness** 'prɒdɪg|l, -lz, -əlɪ, -lnɪs [-nəs]
prodigality ˌprɒdɪ'gælətɪ [-ɪtɪ]
prodigaliz|e [**-is|ė**], **-es, -ing, -ed** 'prɒdɪgəlaɪz, -ɪz, -ɪŋ, -d
prodigious, -ly, -ness prə'dɪdʒəs [prʊ'd-], -lɪ, -nɪs [-nəs]
prodig|y, -ies 'prɒdɪdʒ|ɪ [-dədʒ|ɪ], -ɪz
produce (*s.*) 'prɒdjuːs [-dʒuːs]
produc|e (*v.*), **-es, -ing, -ed, -er/s** prə'djuːs [prʊ'd-], -ɪz, -ɪŋ, -t, -ə*/z
producible prə'djuːsəbl [prʊ'd-, -sɪb-]
product, -s 'prɒdʌkt [-dəkt], -s
production, -s prə'dʌkʃn [prʊ'd-], -z
productional prə'dʌkʃənl [prʊ'd-, -ʃnəl, -ʃn̩l, -ʃn̩l, -ʃənəl]
productive, -ly, -ness prə'dʌktɪv [prʊ'd-], -lɪ, -nɪs [-nəs]
productivity ˌprɒdʌk'tɪvətɪ [ˌprəʊd-, -dək-, -ɪtɪ]
proem, -s 'prəʊem, -z
profanation, -s ˌprɒfə'neɪʃn, -z
profan|e (*adj. v.*), **-er, -est, -ely, -eness; -es, -ing, -ed, -er/s** prə'feɪn [prʊ'f-], -ə*, -ɪst, -lɪ, -nɪs [-nəs]; -z, -ɪŋ, -d, -ə*/z
profanit|y, -ies prə'fænət|ɪ [prʊ'f-, -ɪt|ɪ], -ɪz
profess, -es, -ing, -ed, -edly, -er/s, -or/s prə'fes [prʊ'f-], -ɪz, -ɪŋ, -t, -ɪdlɪ, -ə*/z, -ə*/z
profession, -s prə'feʃn [prʊ'f-], -z
professional (*s. adj.*), **-s** prə'feʃənl [prʊ'f-, -ʃnəl, -ʃn̩l, -ʃn̩l, -ʃənəl], -z
professionalism prə'feʃn̩əlɪzəm [prʊ'f-, -ʃnəl-, -ʃn̩l-, -ʃn̩l-, -ʃənəl-]
professionally prə'feʃn̩əlɪ [prʊ'f-, -ʃnəlɪ, -ʃn̩lɪ, -ʃn̩lɪ, -ʃənəlɪ]
professor, -s; -ate/s, -ship/s prə'fesə* [prʊ'f-], -z; -rɪt/s [-rət/s], -ʃɪp/s
professorial, -ly ˌprɒfɪ'sɔːrɪəl [-fe's-, -fə's-], -ɪ
professoriate ˌprɒfɪ'sɔːrɪət [-fe's-, -fə's-, -rɪɪt]
proffer, -s, -ing, -ed, -er/s 'prɒfə*, -z, -rɪŋ, -d, -rə*/z
proficien|cy, -t/ly prə'fɪʃn|sɪ [prʊ'f-], -t/lɪ
profil|e (*s. v.*), **-es, -ing, -ed** 'prəʊfaɪl [*old-fashioned* -fiːl], -z, -ɪŋ, -d
profit (*s. v.*), **-s, -ing, -ed, -er/s** 'prɒfɪt, -s, -ɪŋ, -ɪd, -ə*/z
profitab|le, -ly, -leness 'prɒfɪtəb|l, -lɪ, -lnɪs [-nəs]

profiteer (*s. v.*), **-s, -ing, -ed** ˌprɒfɪ'tɪə* [-fə't-], -z, -rɪŋ, -d
profitless 'prɒfɪtlɪs [-ləs]
profit-sharing 'prɒfɪtˌʃeərɪŋ
profligacy 'prɒflɪgəsɪ
profligate (*s. adj.*), **-s, -ly, -ness** 'prɒflɪgət [-gɪt], -s, -lɪ, -nɪs [-nəs]
pro forma ˌprəʊ'fɔːmə
profoun|d, -der, -dest, -dly, -dness prə'faʊn|d [prʊ'f-], -də*, -dɪst, -dlɪ, -dnɪs [-nəs]
profundit|y, -ies prə'fʌndət|ɪ [prʊ'f-, -ɪt|ɪ], -ɪz
profuse, -st, -ly, -ness prə'fjuːs [prʊ'f-], -ɪst, -lɪ, -nɪs [-nəs]
profusion, -s prə'fjuːʒn [prʊ'f-], -z
prog (*s.v.*), **-s, -ging, -ged** prɒg, -z, -ɪŋ, -d
progenitor, -s prəʊ'dʒenɪtə*, -z
progeniture prəʊ'dʒenɪtʃə* [-ˌtjʊə*, -tjə*]
progen|y, -ies 'prɒdʒən|ɪ [-dʒɪn-], -ɪz
prognathic prɒg'næθɪk
prognathism 'prɒgnəθɪzəm [prɒg'næθ-]
prognathous prɒg'neɪθəs ['prɒgnəθəs]
prognos|is, -es prɒg'nəʊs|ɪs, -iːz
prognostic prɒg'nɒstɪk [prə'g-]
prognosticat|e, -es, -ing, -ed, -or/s prɒg'nɒstɪkeɪt [prəg-], -s, -ɪŋ, -ɪd, -ə*/z
prognostication, -s prəgˌnɒstɪ'keɪʃn [prɒg-], -z
program(me) (*s. v.*), **-s, -ing, -(e)d, -er/s** 'prəʊgræm, -z, -ɪŋ, -d, -ə*/z
progress (*s.*), **-es** 'prəʊgres [*rarely* 'prɒg-], -ɪz
progress (*v.*), **-es, -ing, -ed** prəʊ'gres [prʊ'g-], -ɪz, -ɪŋ, -t
progression, -s prəʊ'greʃn [prʊ'g-], -z
progressional prəʊ'greʃənl [prʊ'g-, -ʃnəl, -ʃn̩l, -ʃn̩l, -ʃənəl]
progressionist, -s prəʊ'greʃn̩ɪst [prʊ'g-, -ʃənɪst], -s
progressist, -s prəʊ'gresɪst [prʊ'g-], -s
progressive (*s. adj.*), **-s, -ly, -ness** prəʊ'gresɪv [prʊ'g-], -z, -lɪ, -nɪs [-nəs]
prohibit, -s, -ing, -ed, -or/s prə'hɪbɪt [prəʊ'h-, prʊ'h-], -s, -ɪŋ, -ɪd, -ə*/z
prohibition, -s ˌprəʊɪ'bɪʃn [ˌprəʊhɪ-], -z
prohibitioni|sm, -st/s ˌprəʊɪ'bɪʃn̩ɪ|zəm [ˌprəʊhɪ-, -ʃənɪ-], -st/s
prohibitive, -ly prə'hɪbətɪv [prəʊ'h-, prʊ'h-, -bɪt-], -lɪ
prohibitory prə'hɪbɪtərɪ [prəʊ'h-, prʊ'h-]
project (*s.*), **-s** 'prɒdʒekt [-dʒɪkt], -s
project (*v.*), **-s, -ing, -ed, -or/s** prə'dʒekt [prəʊ'dʒ-, prʊ'dʒ-], -s, -ɪŋ, -ɪd, -ə*/z

projectile (s.), **-s** prəʊˈdʒektaɪl [prʊ-, ˈprɒdʒektaɪl, -dʒɪk-], -z
projectile (adj.) prəʊˈdʒektaɪl [prʊˈdʒ-]
projection, -s, -ist/s prəˈdʒekʃn [prəʊˈdʒ-, prʊˈdʒ-], -z, -ɪst/s [-ʃənɪst/s]
projective, -ly prəˈdʒektɪv [prəʊˈdʒ-, prʊˈdʒ-], -lɪ
Prokofiev prəˈkɒfɪef
prolapse, -s ˈprəʊlæps, -ɪz
prolate ˈprəʊleɪt [prəʊˈleɪt]
prolegomen|on, -a ˌprəʊleˈgɒmɪn|ən [-lɪˈg-, -mən-, -|ɒn], -ə
proleps|is, -es prəʊˈleps|ɪs [-ˈliːp-], -iːz
proleptic, -ally prəʊˈleptɪk [-ˈliːp-], -əlɪ
proletarian (s. adj.), **-s, -ism** ˌprəʊlɪˈteərɪən [-leˈt-, -ləˈt-], -z, -ɪzəm
proletariat ˌprəʊlɪˈteərɪət [-leˈt-, -ləˈt-, -ɪæt]
proliferat|e, -es, -ing, -ed prəʊˈlɪfəreɪt, -s, -ɪŋ, -ɪd
proliferation prəʊˌlɪfəˈreɪʃn
prolific, -ness prəʊˈlɪfɪk [prʊˈl-], -nɪs [-nəs]
prolix ˈprəʊlɪks [prəʊˈlɪks]
prolixity prəʊˈlɪksətɪ [-ɪtɪ]
prolix|ly, -ness prəʊˈlɪks|lɪ [ˈprəʊlɪks-], -nɪs [-nəs]
prolocutor, -s prəʊˈlɒkjʊtə*, -z
prologu|e (s. v.), **-es, -ing, -ed** ˈprəʊlɒg [rarely -ləʊg], -z, -ɪŋ, -d
prolong, -s, -ing, -ed prəʊˈlɒŋ [prʊˈl-], -z, -ɪŋ, -d
prolongation, -s ˌprəʊlɒŋˈgeɪʃn [ˌprɒl-], -z
promenad|e (s. v.), **-es, -ing, -ed, -er/s** ˌprɒməˈnɑːd [-mɪˈn-], -z, -ɪŋ, -ɪd, -ə*/z
Note.—Also '--- *when attributive, as in* **promenade concert**. *There exists also a pronunciation* ˌprɒməˈneɪd [-mɪˈn-] *used chiefly in square dancing.*
Promethean prəˈmiːθjən [prəʊˈm-, prʊˈm-, -θɪən]
Prometheus prəˈmiːθjuːs [prəʊˈm-, prʊˈm-, -θjəs, -θɪəs]
prominence, -s ˈprɒmɪnəns [-mən-], -ɪz
prominent, -ly ˈprɒmɪnənt [-mən-], -lɪ
promiscuity ˌprɒmɪˈskjuːətɪ [-kjʊətɪ, -ɪtɪ]
promiscuous, -ly, -ness prəˈmɪskjʊəs [prʊˈm-, -kjwəs], -lɪ, -nɪs [-nəs]
promis|e (s. v.), **-es, -ing/ly, -ed, -er/s** ˈprɒmɪs, -ɪz, -ɪŋ/lɪ, -t, -ə*/z
promissory ˈprɒmɪsərɪ [prəˈmɪs-, prʊˈmɪs-]
promontor|y, -ies ˈprɒməntr|ɪ [-tər-], -ɪz

promot|e, -es, -ing, -ed, -er/s prəˈməʊt [prʊˈm-], -s, -ɪŋ, -ɪd, -ə*/z
promotion, -s prəˈməʊʃn [prʊˈm-], -z
promotive prəˈməʊtɪv [prʊˈm-]
prompt (s. adj. v.), **-s; -er, -est, -ly, -ness; -ing/s, -ed, -er/s** prɒmpt, -s; -ə*, -ɪst, -lɪ, -nɪs [-nəs]; -ɪŋ/z, -ɪd, -ə*/z
promptitude ˈprɒmptɪtjuːd
promulgat|e, -es, -ing, -ed, -or/s ˈprɒmlgeɪt [-mʌl-], -s, -ɪŋ, -ɪd, -ə*/z
promulgation, -s ˌprɒmlˈgeɪʃn [-mʌl-], -z
prone, -r, -st, -ly, -ness prəʊn, -ə*, -ɪst, -lɪ, -nɪs [-nəs]
prong (s. v.), **-s, -ing, -ed** prɒŋ, -z, -ɪŋ, -d
pronomin|al, -ally prəʊˈnɒmɪn|l [prʊˈn-], -əlɪ [-lɪ]
pronoun, -s ˈprəʊnaʊn, -z
pronounc|e, -es, -ing, -ed, -ed|y, -er/s, -ement/s; -eable/ness prəˈnaʊns [prʊˈn-, prɒˈnaʊns], -ɪz, -ɪŋ, -t, -tlɪ [-ɪdlɪ], -ə*/z, -mənt/s; -əbl/nɪs [-nəs]
pronunciamento, -s prəˌnʌnsɪəˈmentəʊ [prəʊˌn-, prʊˌn-, -sjə-, -ʃɪə-, -ʃjə-], -z
pronunciation, -s prəˌnʌnsɪˈeɪʃn [prʊˌn-, prɪnˌʌn-], -z
proof, -s; -less pruːf, -s; -lɪs [-ləs]
proof-read|er/s, -ing ˈpruːfˌriːd|ə*/z, -ɪŋ
prop (s. v.), **-s, -ping, -ped** prɒp, -s, -ɪŋ, -t
propaedeutic, -al, -s ˌprəʊpiːˈdjuːtɪk, -l, -s
propagand|a, -ist/s ˌprɒpəˈgænd|ə, -ɪst/s
propagandism ˌprɒpəˈgændɪzəm
propagat|e, -es, -ing, -ed, -or/s ˈprɒpəgeɪt, -s, -ɪŋ, -ɪd, -ə*/z
propagation ˌprɒpəˈgeɪʃn
propane ˈprəʊpeɪn
proparoxytone (s. adj.), **-s** ˌprəʊpəˈrɒksɪtəʊn [-tn], -z
propel, -s, -ling, -led, -ler/s; -lent/s prəˈpel [prʊˈp-], -z, -ɪŋ, -d, -ə*/z; -ənt/s
propensit|y, -ies prəˈpensət|ɪ [prəʊˈp-, prʊˈp-, -ɪt|ɪ], -ɪz
proper, -ly ˈprɒpə*, -lɪ [ˈprɒp|ɪ]
properispomen|on, -a ˈprəʊˌperɪˈspəʊmɪn|ən [-ˌɒn], -ə
Propertius prəʊˈpɜːʃəs [prʊˈp-, -ʃɪəs, -ʃjəs]
propert|y, -ies, -ied ˈprɒpət|ɪ, -ɪz, -ɪd
prophec|y, -ies ˈprɒfɪs|ɪ [-fəs|ɪ, -s|aɪ], -ɪz [-aɪz]

prophes|y, -ies, -ying, -ied, -ier/s 'prɒfɪs|aɪ [-fəs-], -aɪz, -aɪɪŋ, -aɪd, -aɪə*/z

prophet, -s 'prɒfɪt, -s

prophetess, -es 'prɒfɪtɪs [-tes], -ɪz

prophetic, -al, -ally prə'fetɪk [prəʊ'f-, prʊ'f-], -l, -əlɪ

Prophit 'prɒfɪt

prophylactic (s. adj.), -s ˌprɒfɪ'læktɪk, -s

prophylaxis ˌprɒfɪ'læksɪs

propinquity prə'pɪŋkwətɪ [prəʊ'p-, prʊ'p-, prɒ'p-, -ɪtɪ]

propitiat|e, -es, -ing, -ed, -or/s prə-'pɪʃɪeɪt [prʊ'p-], -s, -ɪŋ, -ɪd, -ə*/z

propitiation, -s prə,pɪʃɪ'eɪʃn [prʊ,p-], -z

propitiatory prə'pɪʃɪətərɪ [prʊ'p-, -ʃjə-tərɪ, -ʃətərɪ, -ʃɪeɪtərɪ]

propitious, -ly, -ness prə'pɪʃəs [prʊ'p-], -lɪ, -nɪs [-nəs]

proporti|on (s. v.), -ons, -oning, -oned prə'pɔ:ʃ|n [prʊ'p-], -nz, -ɳɪŋ [-nɪŋ, -ənɪŋ], -nd

proportionab|le, -ly prə'pɔ:ʃɳəb|l [prʊ'p-, -ʃnə-, -ʃənə-], -lɪ

propor|tional, -tionally prə'pɔ:ʃ|ənl [prʊ'p-, -ʃnəl, -ʃɳl̩, -ʃnl̩, -ʃənəl], -ʃɳəlɪ [-ʃnəlɪ, -ʃɳlɪ, -ʃnl̩ɪ, -ʃənəlɪ]

proportionality prə,pɔ:ʃə'nælətɪ [prʊ,p-, -ʃn̩'æ-, -ɪtɪ]

proportionate, -ly, -ness prə'pɔ:ʃnət [prʊ'p-, -ʃɳət, -ʃənət, -nɪt], -lɪ, -nɪs [-nəs]

propos|e, -es, -ing, -ed, -er/s; -al/s prə'pəʊz [prʊ'p-], -ɪz, -ɪŋ, -d, -ə*/z; -l/z

proposition, -s ˌprɒpə'zɪʃn, -z

propound, -s, -ing, -ed, -er/s prə'paʊnd [prʊ'p-], -z, -ɪŋ, -ɪd, -ə*/z

proprietary prə'praɪətərɪ [prʊ'p-]

proprietor, -s; -ship/s prə'praɪətə* [prʊ'p-], -z; -ʃɪp/s

proprietress, -es prə'praɪətrɪs [prʊ'p-, -tres], -ɪz

propriet|y, -ies prə'praɪət|ɪ [prʊ'p-], -ɪz

propriocep|tion, -tive ˌprəʊprɪəʊ'sep|ʃn, -tɪv

propul|sion, -sive prə'pʌl|ʃn [prʊ'p-], -sɪv

propylae|um (P.), -a ˌprɒpɪ'li:|əm [-'lɪ|əm], -ə

pro rata ˌprəʊ'rɑ:tə [-'reɪtə]

prorogation, -s ˌprəʊrə'geɪʃn [ˌprɒr-, -rəʊ'g-], -z

prorogu|e, -es, -ing, -ed prə'rəʊg [prəʊ'r-, prʊ'r-], -z, -ɪŋ, -d

prosaic, -al, -ally prəʊ'zeɪɪk, -l, -əlɪ, -nɪs [-nəs]

prosceni|um, -ums, -a prəʊ'si:nj|əm [-nɪ|əm], -əmz, -ə

proscrib|e, -es, -ing, -ed, -er/s prəʊ-'skraɪb, -z, -ɪŋ, -d, -ə*/z

proscription, -s prəʊ'skrɪpʃn, -z

proscriptive prəʊ'skrɪptɪv

pros|e (s. v.), -es, -ing, -ed, -er/s prəʊz, -ɪz, -ɪŋ, -d, -ə*/z

prosecut|e, -es, -ing, -ed, -or/s 'prɒsɪ-kju:t, -s, -ɪŋ, -ɪd, -ə*/z

prosecution, -s ˌprɒsɪ'kju:ʃn, -z

prosecutrix, -es 'prɒsɪˌkju:trɪks [ˌ--'--], -ɪz

proselyte, -s 'prɒsəlaɪt [-sɪl-], -s

proselytism 'prɒsəlɪtɪzəm [-sɪl-]

proselytiz|e [-is|e], -es, -ing, -ed 'prɒsəlɪtaɪz [-sɪl-], -ɪz, -ɪŋ, -d

Proserpina prə'sɜ:pɪnə [prɒ's-]

Proserpine 'prɒsəpaɪn

prosit 'prəʊzɪt ['prəʊsɪt, prəʊst]

prosodic, -al prə'sɒdɪk [prəʊ's-], -l

prosodist, -s 'prɒsədɪst, -s

prosod|y, -ies 'prɒsəd|ɪ, -ɪz

prospect (s.) (P.), -s 'prɒspekt, -s

prospect (v.), -s, -ing, -ed prə'spekt [prʊ's-, prɒ's-, 'prɒspekt], -s, -ɪŋ, -ɪd

prospective, -ly, -ness prə'spektɪv [prʊ's-, prɒ's-], -lɪ, -nɪs [-nəs]

prospector, -s prə'spektə* [prʊ's-, prɒ's-], -z

prospectus, -es prə'spektəs [prʊ's-], -ɪz

prosp|er, -ers, -ering, -ered 'prɒsp|ə*, -əz, -ərɪŋ, -əd

prosperity prɒ'sperətɪ [prəs-, -ɪtɪ]

Prospero 'prɒspərəʊ

prosperous, -ly, -ness 'prɒspərəs, -lɪ, -nɪs [-nəs]

prostate, -s 'prɒsteɪt [-tɪt], -s

prostatic prɒ'stætɪk

prosthesis 'prɒsθɪsɪs [-θəs-, prɒs'θi:sɪs]

prosthetic, -s prɒs'θetɪk, -s

prosthetist, -s prɒs'θi:tɪst [prəs-], -s

prostitut|e (s. v.), -es, -ing, -ed 'prɒstɪ-tju:t, -s, -ɪŋ, -ɪd

prostitution, -s ˌprɒstɪ'tju:ʃn, -z

prostrate (adj.) 'prɒstreɪt [-rɪt]

prostrat|e (v.), -es, -ing, -ed prɒ'streɪt [prəs-], -s, -ɪŋ, -ɪd

prostration, -s prɒ'streɪʃn [prəs-], -z

pros|y, -ier, -iest, -ily, -iness 'prəʊz|ɪ, -ɪə* [-jə*], -ɪɪst [-jɪst], -ɪlɪ [-əlɪ], -ɪnɪs [-ɪnəs]

protagonist, -s prəʊ'tægənɪst, -s

Protagoras prəʊ'tægərəs [-gɒr-, -rəs]

protas|is, -es 'prɒtəs|ɪs, -i:z

protean prəʊ'ti:ən ['prəʊtjən, 'prəʊtɪən]

397

protect—prude

protect, -s, -ing/ly, -ed, -or/s prə'tekt
[prʊ't-], -s, -ɪŋ/lɪ, -ɪd, -ə*/z
protection, -s prə'tekʃn [prʊ't-], -z
protectioni|sm, -st/s prə'tekʃənɪ|zəm
[prʊ't-, -ʃɲɪ-], -st/s
protective, -ly, -ness prə'tektɪv [prʊ't-],
-lɪ, -nɪs [-nəs]
protectorate, -s prə'tektərət [prʊ't-,
-rɪt], -s
protectress, -es prə'tektrɪs [prʊ't-,
-trəs], -ɪz
protégé(e), -s 'prɒtɪʒeɪ ['prəʊt-, -təʒ-,
-teʒ-, -teɪʒ-] (prɔteʒe), -z
proteid, -s 'prəʊti:d [-ti:ɪd, -tɪɪd], -z
protein 'prəʊti:n [-ti:ɪn, -tɪɪn]
pro tem ˌprəʊ'tem
protest (s.), -s 'prəʊtest, -s
protest (v.), -s, -ing/ly, -ed, -er/s
prə'test [prəʊ't-, prʊ't-, rarely 'prəʊ-
test], -s, -ɪŋ/lɪ, -ɪd, -ə*/z
protestant (P.), -s, -ism 'prɒtɪstənt
[-təs-], -s, -ɪzəm
protestantiz|e [-is|e], -es, -ing, -ed
'prɒtɪstəntaɪz [-təs-], -ɪz, -ɪŋ, -d
protestation, -s ˌprɒte'steɪʃn [ˌprəʊt-,
-tr'-, -tə's-], -z
Proteus 'prəʊtju:s [-tjəs, -tɪəs]
prothalami|on, -um ˌprəʊθə'leɪmɪ|ən
[-mjən], -əm [-mjəm]
Protheroe 'prɒðərəʊ
prothes|is, -es 'prɒθɪs|ɪs [-θəs-], -i:z
protium 'prəʊtjəm [-tɪəm]
protocol, -s 'prəʊtəkɒl [-təʊk-], -z
proton, -s 'prəʊtɒn, -z
protoplasm 'prəʊtəʊplæzəm
prototype, -s 'prəʊtəʊtaɪp, -s
protozo|ic, -on, -a ˌprəʊtəʊ'zəʊ|ɪk, -ən
[-ɒn], -ə
protract, -s, -ing, -ed/ly; -ile prə'trækt
[prʊ't-], -s, -ɪŋ, -ɪd/lɪ; -aɪl
protraction, -s prə'trækʃn [prʊ't-], -z
protractor, -s prə'træktə* [prʊ't-], -z
protrud|e, -es, -ing, -ed prə'tru:d
[prʊ't-], -z, -ɪŋ, -ɪd
protrusion, -s prə'tru:ʒn [prʊ't-], -z
protrusive, -ly, -ness prə'tru:sɪv [prʊ't-],
-lɪ, -nɪs [-nəs]
protuberan|ce/s, -t/ly prə'tju:bərən|s/ɪz
[prʊ't-], -t/lɪ
proud, -er, -est, -ly, -ness praʊd, -ə*,
-ɪst, -lɪ, -nɪs [-nəs]
Proust (French author) pru:st (prust)
proustian 'pru:stjən [-tɪən]
Prout praʊt
provab|le, -ly, -leness 'pru:vəb|l, -lɪ,
-lnɪs [-nəs]
prov|e, -es, -ing, -ed, -en, -er/s pru:v,
-z, -ɪŋ, -d, -n, -ə*/z

provenance 'prɒvənəns [-vɪn-]
Provençal ˌprɒvɑ̃:n'sɑ:l [-vɔ̃:n's-,
-vɑ:n's-, -vən's-] (prɔvɑ̃sal)
Provence prɒ'vɑ̃:ns [prəʊ'v-, -'vɔ̃:ns,
-'vɑ:ns] (prɔvɑ̃:s)
provender 'prɒvɪndə* [-vəndə*]
proverb, -s (P.) 'prɒvɜ:b, -z
proverbial, -ly prə'vɜ:bjəl [prʊ'v-,
-bɪəl], -ɪ
provid|e, -es, -ing, -ed, -er/s prə'vaɪd
[prʊ'v-], -z, -ɪŋ, -ɪd, -ə*/z
providen|ce (P.), -t/ly 'prɒvɪdən|s, -t/lɪ
providenti|al, -ally ˌprɒvɪ'denʃ|l, -əlɪ
province, -s 'prɒvɪns, -ɪz
provinci|al (s. adj.), -als, -ally prə'vɪnʃ|l
[prʊ'v-], -lz, -əlɪ
provincialism, -s prə'vɪnʃəlɪzəm [prʊ'v-,
-ʃlɪ-], -z
provinciality prəˌvɪnʃɪ'ælətɪ [prʊ'v-,
-rtɪ]
provincializ|e [-is|e], -es, -ing, -ed
prə'vɪnʃəlaɪz [prʊ'v-, -ʃlaɪz], -ɪz, -ɪŋ,
-d
provisi|on, -ons, -oning, -oned prə'vɪʒ|n
[prʊ'v-], -nz, -ɲɪŋ [-ənɪŋ], -nd
provi|sional, -sionally prə'vɪ|ʒnl
[prʊ'v-, -ʒnəl, -ʒɲl, -ʒnl, -ʒənəl],
-ʒnəlɪ [-ʒnəlɪ, -ʒnlɪ, -ʒɲlɪ, -ʒənəlɪ]
proviso, -(e)s prə'vaɪzəʊ [prəʊ'v-,
prʊ'v-], -z
provisor, -s prə'vaɪzə* [prʊ'v-], -z
provisor|y, -ily prə'vaɪzər|ɪ [prʊ'v-,
-əlɪ [-ɪlɪ]
provocation, -s ˌprɒvə'keɪʃn [-vəʊ'k-],
-z
provocative prə'vɒkətɪv [prəʊ'v-,
prʊ'v-]
provok|e, -es, -ing/ly, -ed, -er/s
prə'vəʊk [prʊ'v-], -s, -ɪŋ/lɪ, -t, -ə*/z
provost (civil and academic), -s 'prɒvəst,
-s
provost-marshal (military), -s prəˌvəʊ-
'mɑ:ʃl, -z
provostship, -s 'prɒvəst-ʃɪp, -s
prow, -s praʊ, -z
prowess 'praʊɪs [-es]
prowl (s. v.), -s, -ing, -ed, -er/s praʊl,
-z, -ɪŋ, -d, -ə*/z
Prowse praʊs, praʊz
prox. prɒks ['prɒksɪməʊ]
proxim|al, -ally 'prɒksɪm|l, -əlɪ
proximate, -ly 'prɒksɪmət [-ɪt], -lɪ
proxime accessit, -s ˌprɒksɪmɪæk'sesɪt
[-mɪək-], -s
proximit|y, -ies prɒk'sɪmət|ɪ [-ɪt|ɪ], -ɪz
proximo 'prɒksɪməʊ
prox|y, -ies 'prɒks|ɪ, -ɪz
prude, -s; -ry pru:d, -z; -ərɪ

pruden|ce (P.), -t/ly 'pru:dn|s, -t/lɪ
prudenti|al, -ally prʊ'denʃ|l [pru:'d-], -əlɪ
prudish, -ly 'pru:dɪʃ, -lɪ
prun|e (s. v.), -es, -ing, -ed pru:n, -z, -ɪŋ, -d
prunella (P.), -s prʊ'nelə [pru:'n-], -z
pruning-kni|fe, -ves 'pru:nɪŋnaɪ|f, -vz
prurien|ce, -t/ly 'prʊərɪən|s, -t/lɪ
Prussi|a, -an/s 'prʌʃ|ə, -n/z
prussiate, -s 'prʌʃɪət [-ʃjət, -ʃət, -ɪt], -s
prussic 'prʌsɪk
Prust prʌst
Pruth (tributary of the Danube) pru:t
pr|y, -ies, -ying/ly, -ied, -yer/s pr|aɪ, -aɪz, -aɪɪŋ/lɪ, -aɪd, 'praɪə*/z
Prynne prɪn
Przemysl 'pʃemɪsl
psalm (P.), -s; -ist/s sɑ:m, -z; -ɪst/s
psalmodic sæl'mɒdɪk
psalmod|ist/s, -y 'sælməd|ɪst/s ['sɑ:m-, -mʊd-], -ɪ
psalter, -s 'sɔ:ltə* ['sɒl-], -z
psalter|y, -ies 'sɔ:ltər|ɪ ['sɒl-], -ɪz
    Note.—In the following words begin-
    ning with ps-, the form with p is rare.
psepholog|ist/s, -y pse'fɒləd3|ɪst/s [psɪ-, psə-], -ɪ
†pseudo, -s 'psju:dəʊ, -z ['psu:dəʊ-]
    Note.—Compounds with pseudo- have
    double stress. Their pronunciation
    may be ascertained by referring to
    the simple words. Thus pseudo-
    classic is pronounced ˌpsju:dəʊ-
    'klæsɪk [ˌpsu:-].
pseudonym, -s 'psju:dənɪm ['psu:-], -z
pseudonymity ˌpsju:də'nɪmətɪ [ˌpsu:-, -ɪtɪ]
pseudonymous psju:'dɒnɪməs [psu:-]
pshaw (v.), -s, -ing, -ed pʃɔ: [ʃɔ:], -z, -ɪŋ, -d
pshaw (interj.) pɸ: [pʃɔ:]
psi psaɪ
psittacosis ˌpsɪtə'kəʊsɪs
psoriasis psɒ'raɪəsɪs [psɔ:'r-, psʊ'r-, psə'r-]
†psyche (s.) (P.), -s 'saɪkɪ [-ki:]
psychedelic ˌsaɪkɪ'delɪk [-kə'd-]
psychiatric, -al ˌsaɪkɪ'ætrɪk, -l
psychiatr|ist/s, -y saɪ'kaɪətr|ɪst/s [sɪ'k-, sə'k-], -ɪ
psychic, -al, -ally 'saɪkɪk ['psaɪk-], -l, -əlɪ [-|ɪ]
psychoanalys|e, -es, -ing, -ed ˌsaɪkəʊ-'ænəlaɪz [ˌpsaɪ-], -ɪz, -ɪŋ, -d
psychoanalysis ˌsaɪkəʊə'næləsɪs [ˌpsaɪ-, -lɪs-]

psychoanalyst, -s ˌsaɪkəʊ'ænəlɪst [ˌpsaɪ-], -s
psychologic, -al, -ally ˌsaɪkə'lɒd3ɪk [ˌpsaɪ-], -l, -əlɪ
psycholog|ist/s, -y saɪ'kɒləd3|ɪst/s [psaɪ-], -ɪ
psychologiz|e [-is|e], -es, -ing, -ed saɪ'kɒləd3aɪz [psaɪ-], -ɪz, -ɪŋ, -d
psychometric ˌsaɪkəʊ'metrɪk [ˌpsaɪ-]
psychometr|ist/s, -y saɪ'kɒmɪtr|ɪst/s [psaɪ-, -mət-], -ɪ
psychopath, -s 'saɪkəʊpæθ ['psaɪ-], -s
psychopathic ˌsaɪkəʊ'pæθɪk [ˌpsaɪ-]
psychophonic ˌsaɪkəʊ'fəʊnɪk [ˌpsaɪ-, -'fɒn-]
psychophysical ˌsaɪkəʊ'fɪzɪkl [ˌpsaɪ-]
psychos|is, -es saɪ'kəʊs|ɪs [psaɪ-], -i:z
psychosomatic ˌsaɪkəʊsəʊ'mætɪk [ˌpsaɪ-]
psychotherap|y, -ist/s ˌsaɪkəʊ'θerəp|ɪ [ˌpsaɪ-], -ɪst/s
psychotic saɪ'kɒtɪk [psaɪ-]
ptarmigan 'tɑ:mɪgən [-məg-]
pterodactyl, -s ˌpterəʊ'dæktɪl, -z
pterosaur, -s 'pterəʊsɔ:*, -z
ptisan, -s tɪ'zæn ['tɪzn], -z
P.T.O. ˌpi:ti:'əʊ
Ptolemai|c, -s ˌtɒlə'meɪ|k [-lɪ'm-], -s
Ptolem|y, -ies 'tɒləm|ɪ [-lɪm-], -ɪz
ptomaine 'təʊmeɪn [təʊ'meɪn]
pub, -s; -by pʌb, -z; -ɪ
puberty 'pju:bətɪ
pubescen|ce, -t pju:'besn|s [pjʊ'b-], -t
pubic 'pju:bɪk
public, -ly 'pʌblɪk, -lɪ
publican, -s 'pʌblɪkən, -z
publication, -s ˌpʌblɪ'keɪʃn, -z
public-hou|se, -ses ˌpʌblɪk'haʊ|s, -zɪz
publicist, -s 'pʌblɪsɪst, -s
publicity pʌb'lɪsətɪ [pə'blɪs-, -ɪtɪ]
publiciz|e, -es, -ing, -ed 'pʌblɪsaɪz, -ɪz, -ɪŋ, -d
public-relations ˌpʌblɪkrɪ'leɪʃnz
public-spirited ˌpʌblɪk'spɪrɪtɪd
publish, -es, -ing, -ed, -er/s 'pʌblɪʃ, -ɪz, -ɪŋ, -t, -ə*/z
Publius 'pʌblɪəs [-ljəs]
Puccini pu:'tʃi:nɪ [pʊ'tʃ-]
puce pju:s
puck (P.), -s pʌk, -s
pucker (s. v.), -s, -ing, -ed 'pʌkə*, -z, -rɪŋ, -d
pudding, -s 'pʊdɪŋ, -z
pudd|le (s. v.), -les, -ling, -led, -ler/s 'pʌd|l, -lz, -lɪŋ [-lɪŋ], -ld, -lə*/z [-lə*/z]
pudend|um, -a pju:'dend|əm, -ə
pudg|y, -ier, -iest 'pʌd3|ɪ, -ɪə*, -ɪɪst
Pudsey 'pʌd3ɪ [locally 'pʌdsɪ]

399

pueblo, -s 'pwebləʊ [pʊ'e-], -z
puerile, -ly 'pjʊəraɪl ['pjɔər-, 'pjɔːr-], -lɪ
puerilit|y, -ies pjʊə'rɪlət|ɪ [ˌpjʊə'r-, pjɔə'r-, pjɔː'r-, -ɪt|ɪ], -ɪz
puerperal pjuː'ɜːpərəl [pjʊ'ɜː-]
Puerto Ric|o, -an/s ˌpwɜːtəʊ'riːk|əʊ [ˌpweə-], -ən/z
puff (s. v.), -s, -ing, -ed, -er/s pʌf, -s, -ɪŋ, -t, -ə*/z
puff-ball, -s 'pʌfbɔːl, -z
puffin, -s 'pʌfɪn, -z
puff|y, -ier, -iest, -ily, -iness 'pʌf|ɪ, -ɪə*, -ɪɪst, -ɪlɪ [-əlɪ], -ɪnɪs [-məs]
pug, -s pʌg, -z
puggaree, -s 'pʌgərɪ, -z
Pugh pjuː
pugili|sm, -st/s 'pjuːdʒɪlɪ|zəm, -st/s
pugilistic, -ally ˌpjuːdʒɪ'lɪstɪk, -əlɪ
Pugin 'pjuːdʒɪn
pugnacious, -ly pʌg'neɪʃəs, -lɪ
pugnacity pʌg'næsətɪ [-ɪtɪ]
pug-nose, -s, -d 'pʌgnəʊz, -ɪz, -d
puisne 'pjuːnɪ
puissan|ce, -t 'pjuːɪsn|s ['pjuːɪ-, 'pwɪs-, sometimes in poetry pjuː'ɪs-, pjʊ'ɪs-], -t
puissance (in show-jumping) 'pwiːsɑːns [-sɑːns, -sɔ̃ːns, -sns]
puk|e, -es, -ing, -ed pjuːk, -s, -ɪŋ, -t
pukka 'pʌkə
pulchritude 'pʌlkrɪtjuːd
pul|e, -es, -ing, -ed pjuːl, -z, -ɪŋ, -d
Puleston (in Salop) 'pʊlɪstən [locally also 'pɪlsn]
Pulitzer (American publisher) 'pʊlɪtsə*, (prize at Columbia University) 'pjuː-lɪtsə*
pull (s. v.), -s, -ing, -ed, -er/s pʊl, -z, -ɪŋ, -d, -ə*/z
pullet, -s 'pʊlɪt [-lət], -s
pulley, -s 'pʊlɪ, -z
pullman (P.), -s; -car/s 'pʊlmən, -z; -kɑː*/z
pull-over, -s 'pʊl,əʊvə*, -z
pullulat|e, -es, -ing, -ed 'pʌljʊleɪt, -s, -ɪŋ, -ɪd
pullulation ˌpʌljʊ'leɪʃn
pull-up, -s 'pʊlʌp [ˌpʊl'ʌp], -s
pulmonary 'pʌlmənərɪ
pulmonic pʌl'mɒnɪk
pulp (s. v.), -s, -ing, -ed pʌlp, -s, -ɪŋ, -t
pulpi|fy, -fies, -fying, -fied 'pʌlpɪ|faɪ, -faɪz, -faɪɪŋ, -faɪd
pulpit, -s 'pʊlpɪt, -s
pulp|y, -ier, -iest, -iness 'pʌlp|ɪ, -ɪə* [-jə*], -ɪɪst [-jɪst], -ɪnɪs [-ɪnəs]
pulsar, -s 'pʌlsɑː* [-sə*], -z
pulsat|e, -es, -ing, -ed pʌl'seɪt ['pʌlseɪt], -s, -ɪŋ, -ɪd

pulsatile 'pʌlsətaɪl
pulsation, -s pʌl'seɪʃn, -z
pulsative 'pʌlsətɪv
pulsatory 'pʌlsətərɪ [pʌl'seɪtərɪ]
puls|e (s. v.), -es, -ing, -ed pʌls, -ɪz, -ɪŋ, -t
†Pulteney 'pʌltnɪ, 'pəʊltnɪ
pulverization [-isa-], -s ˌpʌlvəraɪ'zeɪʃn [-rɪ'z-], -z
pulveriz|e [-is|e], -es, -ing, -ed 'pʌlvər-aɪz, -ɪz, -ɪŋ, -d
puma, -s 'pjuːmə, -z
Pumblechook 'pʌmbltʃʊk
pumic|e (s. v.), -es, -ing, -ed 'pʌmɪs, -ɪz, -ɪŋ, -t
pumice-ston|e (s. v.), -es, -ing, -ed 'pʌmɪsstəʊn ['pʌmɪstəʊn], -z, -ɪŋ, -d
pumm|el, -els, -elling, -elled 'pʌm|l, -lz, -lɪŋ [-əlɪŋ], -ld
pump (s. v.), -s, -ing, -ed, -er/s pʌmp, -s, -ɪŋ, -t [pʌmt], -ə*/z
pumpernickel 'pʊmpənɪkl
pumpkin, -s 'pʌmpkɪn, -z
pun (s. v.), -s, -ning, -ned, -ner/s pʌn, -z, -ɪŋ, -d, -ə*/z
punch (s. v.) (P.), -es, -ing, -ed, -er/s pʌntʃ, -ɪz, -ɪŋ, -t, -ə*/z
punchbowl, -s 'pʌntʃbəʊl, -z
punch-drunk ˌpʌntʃ'drʌŋk ['--]
puncheon, -s 'pʌntʃən, -z
Punchinello ˌpʌntʃɪ'neləʊ
punch-ladle, -s 'pʌntʃ,leɪdl, -z
punctilio, -s pʌŋk'tɪlɪəʊ, -z
punctilious, -ly, -ness pʌŋk'tɪlɪəs [-ljəs], -lɪ, -nɪs [-nəs]
punctual, -ly 'pʌŋktʃʊəl [-tʃwəl, -tʃʊl, -tjʊəl, -tjwəl, -tjʊl], -ɪ
punctuality ˌpʌŋktʃʊ'ælətɪ [-tjʊ-, -ɪtɪ]
punctuat|e, -es, -ing, -ed, -or/s 'pʌŋktʃʊeɪt [-tjʊ-], -s, -ɪŋ, -ɪd, -ə*/z
punctuation, -s ˌpʌŋktʃʊ'eɪʃn [-tjʊ-], -z
punct|ure (s. v.), -ures, -uring, -ured 'pʌŋktʃ|ə*, -əz, -ərɪŋ, -əd
pundit, -s 'pʌndɪt (Hindi pəɳɖɪt), -s
pungen|cy, -t/ly 'pʌndʒən|sɪ, -t/lɪ
Punic 'pjuːnɪk
puniness 'pjuːnɪnɪs [-məs]
punish, -es, -ing/ly, -ed, -er/s; -able/ness 'pʌnɪʃ, -ɪz, -ɪŋ/lɪ, -t, -ə*/z, -mənt/s; -əbl/nɪs [-nəs]
punit|ive, -ory 'pjuːnət|ɪv [-nɪt|ɪv], -ərɪ
Punjab, -i ˌpʌn'dʒɑːb ['--], -i: [-ɪ]
punka(h), -s 'pʌŋkə, -z
punnet, -s 'pʌnɪt, -s
Punshon 'pʌnʃən
punster, -s 'pʌnstə*, -z
punt (s. v.), -s, -ing, -ed, -er/s pʌnt, -s, -ɪŋ, -ɪd, -ə*/z

pun|y, -ier, -iest, -iness 'pju:n|ɪ, -ɪə*
[-jə*], -ɪɪst [-jɪst], -mɪs [-məs]
pup (s. v.), -s, -ping, -ped pʌp, -s, -ɪŋ, -t
pup|a, -ae, -al 'pju:p|ə, -i:, -l
pupil, -s 'pju:pl [-pɪl], -z
pupil(l)age, -ary 'pju:pɪl|ɪdʒ, -ərɪ
puppet, -s 'pʌpɪt, -s
pupp|y, -ies 'pʌp|ɪ, -ɪz
Purbeck 'pɜ:bek
purblin|d, -dness 'pɜ:blaɪn|d, -dnɪs [-nəs]
Purcell 'pɜ:sel [-sl, -səl, pɜ:'sel]
purchas|e (s. v.), -es, -ing, -ed, -er/s;
-able 'pɜ:tʃəs [-tʃɪs], -ɪz, -ɪŋ, -t, -ə*/z;
-əbl
purdah 'pɜ:də [-dɑ:] (Hindi pərda)
Purd|ie, -ye 'pɜ:d|ɪ, -ɪ
pure, -r, -st, -ly, -ness pjʊə* [pjʊə*,
pjɔ:*], -rə*, -rɪst, -lɪ, -nɪs [-nəs]
purée, -s 'pjʊəreɪ ['pjɔər-, 'pjɔ:r-,
'pʊər-] (pyre), -z
purf|le, -les, -ling, -led 'pɜ:f|l, -lz, -lɪŋ
[-lɪŋ], -ld
purfling (s.), -s 'pɜ:flɪŋ, -z
purgation, -s pɜ:'geɪʃn, -z
purgative (s. adj.), -s 'pɜ:gətɪv, -z
purgatorial ‚pɜ:gə'tɔ:rɪəl
purgator|y (P.), -ies 'pɜ:gətər|ɪ, -ɪz
purg|e (s. v.), -es, -ing, -ed pɜ:dʒ, -ɪz,
-ɪŋ, -d
purification (P.), -s ‚pjʊərɪfɪ'keɪʃn
[‚pjɔər-, ‚pjɔ:r-], -z
purificatory 'pjʊərɪfɪkeɪtərɪ ['pjɔər-,
'pjɔ:r-, -kət-, ‚pjʊərɪfɪ'keɪtərɪ, ‚pjɔər-,
‚pjɔ:r-]
puri|fy, -fies, -fying, -fied, -fier/s
'pjʊərɪ|faɪ ['pjɔər-, 'pjɔ:r-], -faɪz,
-faɪŋ, -faɪd, -faɪə*/z
Purim 'pʊərɪm ['pjʊə-]
puri|sm, -st/s 'pjʊərɪ|zəm ['pjɔər-,
'pjɔ:r-], -st/s
puristic, -al ‚pjʊə'rɪstɪk [pjɔə'r-,
pjɔ:'r-], -l
purit|an (P.), -ans, -anism 'pjʊərɪt|ən
['pjɔər-, 'pjɔ:r-], -ənz, -ənɪzəm
[-nɪzəm]
puritanic, -al, -ally · ‚pjʊərɪ'tænɪk
[‚pjɔər-, ‚pjɔ:r-], -l, -əlɪ
purity 'pjʊərətɪ ['pjɔər-, 'pjɔ:r-, -rɪtɪ]
purl (s. v.), -s, -ing, -ed pɜ:l, -z, -ɪŋ, -d
Purley 'pɜ:lɪ
purlieu, -s 'pɜ:lju:, -z
purloin, -s, -ing, -ed pɜ:'lɔɪn ['pɜ:lɔɪn],
-z, -ɪŋ, -d
purloiner, -s pɜ:'lɔɪnə*, -z
purp|le (s. adj. v.), -ler, -lest; -les, -ling,
-led 'pɜ:p|l, -lə* [-lə*], -lɪst [-lɪst];
-lz, -lɪŋ [-lɪŋ], -ld
purplish 'pɜ:plɪʃ [-plɪʃ]

purport (s. v.), -s, -ing, -ed 'pɜ:pət
['pɜ:pɔ:t, pɜ:'pɔ:t, pə'pɔ:t], -s, -ɪŋ, -ɪd
purp|ose (s. v.), -oses, -osing, -osed
'pɜ:p|əs, -əsɪz, -əsɪŋ, -əst
purpose|ful, -fully, -fulness 'pɜ:pəs|fʊl,
-fʊlɪ [-fəlɪ], -fʊlnɪs [-nəs]
purposeless, -ly, -ness 'pɜ:pəslɪs [-ləs],
-lɪ, -nɪs [-nəs]
purposely 'pɜ:pəslɪ
purposive 'pɜ:pəsɪv
purr, -s, -ing, -ed pɜ:*, -z, -rɪŋ, -d
purs|e (s. v.), -es, -ing, -ed pɜ:s, -ɪz, -ɪŋ,
-t
purseful, -s 'pɜ:sfʊl, -z
purse-proud 'pɜ:spraʊd
purser, -s 'pɜ:sə*, -z
purse-string, -s 'pɜ:sstrɪŋ, -z
purslane 'pɜ:slɪn
pursuan|ce, -t/ly pə'sjʊən|s [-'sju:əns,
-'sʊ-, -'su:əns], -t/lɪ
purs|ue, -ues, -uing, -ued, -uer/s
pə'sj|u: [-'s|u:], -u:z, -u:ɪŋ [-ʊɪŋ],
-u:d, -u:ə*/z [-ʊə*/z]
pursuit, -s pə'sju:t [-'su:t], -s
pursuivant, -s 'pɜ:sɪvənt [old-fashioned
'pɜ:swɪ-], -s
purs|y, -iness 'pɜ:s|ɪ, -mɪs [-məs]
Purton 'pɜ:tn
purulen|cy, -t/ly 'pjʊərʊlən|sɪ [-rjʊ-],
-t/lɪ
Purv|er, -es 'pɜ:v|ə*, -ɪs
purvey, -s, -ing, -ed pə'veɪ [pɜ:'v-], -z,
-ɪŋ, -d
purvey|ance, -or/s pə'veɪ|əns [pɜ:'v-],
-ə*/z
purview, -s 'pɜ:vju:, -z
pus, -es pʌs, -ɪz
Pusey, -ite/s 'pju:zɪ, -aɪt/s
push (s. v.), -es, -ing/ly, -ed, -er/s pʊʃ,
-ɪz, -ɪŋ/lɪ, -t, -ə*/z
pushball 'pʊʃbɔ:l
push-bike, -s 'pʊʃbaɪk, -s
push-button, -s 'pʊʃ‚bʌtn, -z
push-car, -s 'pʊʃkɑ:*, -z
push-cart, -s 'pʊʃkɑ:t, -s
pushful, -ness 'pʊʃfʊl [-fl], -nɪs [-nəs]
Pushkin 'pʊʃkɪn
Pushtu 'pʌʃtu: [‚pʌʃ'tu:]
pusillanimity ‚pju:sɪlə'nɪmətɪ [-ju:zɪ-,
-læ'n-, -rtɪ]
pusillanimous, -ly, -ness ‚pju:sɪ'lænɪ-
məs [-ju:zɪ-, -nəməs], -lɪ, -nɪs [-nəs]
puss, -es pʊs, -ɪz
puss|y (cat), -ies 'pʊs|ɪ, -ɪz
pussyfoot, -s 'pʊsɪfʊt, -s
pustular 'pʌstjʊlə*
pustulat|e, -es, -ing, -ed 'pʌstjʊleɪt, -s,
-ɪŋ, -ɪd

pustulation, -s ˌpʌstjʊˈleɪʃn, -z
pustule, -s ˈpʌstjuːl, -z
pustulous ˈpʌstjʊləs
put (s.), (act of throwing a weight), -s
  pʊt, -s
put (v.) (place, move, throw), -s, -ting
  pʊt, -s, -ɪŋ
put(t) (s. v.) (at golf), -s, -ting, -ted
  -ter/s pʌt, -s, -ɪŋ, -ɪd, -ə*/z
putative ˈpjuːtətɪv
Puteoli pjuːˈtɪəlɪ [-ˈtɪəʊlɪ]
Putn|am, -ey ˈpʌtn|əm [-æm], -ɪ
putrefaction ˌpjuːtrɪˈfækʃn
putre|fy, -fies, -fying, -fied ˈpjuːtrɪ|faɪ,
  -faɪz, -faɪɪŋ, -faɪd
putrescenc|e, -t pjuːˈtresn|s, -t
putrid, -ly, -ness ˈpjuːtrɪd, -lɪ, -nɪs [-nəs]
putridity pjuːˈtrɪdətɪ [-ɪtɪ]
putsch, -es pʊtʃ, -ɪz
putt (s. v.) (P.), -s, -ing, -ed, -er/s pʌt,
  -s, -ɪŋ, -ɪd, -ə*/z
puttee, -s ˈpʌtɪ, -z
Puttenham ˈpʌtnəm
putter, -s ˈpʌtə*, -z
putti (pl. of putto) ˈpʊtɪ
Puttick ˈpʌtɪk
putting-green, -s ˈpʌtɪŋgriːn, -z
putt|o, -i ˈpʊt|əʊ, -ɪ
putt|y (s. v.), -ies, -ying, -ied ˈpʌt|ɪ, -ɪz,
  -ɪɪŋ, -ɪd
puzz|le, -les, -ling/ly, -led ˈpʌz|l, -lz,
  -lɪŋ/lɪ [-l̩ŋ/lɪ], -ld
puzzler, -s ˈpʌzlə* [-z̩lə*], -z
Pwllheli pʊθˈlelɪ [pʊlˈhelɪ]   (Welsh
  puːˈl̩ˈheli)
pyaemia paɪˈiːmjə [-mɪə]
Pybus ˈpaɪbəs
Pyddoke ˈpɪdək
Pye paɪ
pygmaean pɪgˈmiːən [-ˈmɪən]
Pygmalion pɪgˈmeɪljən [-lɪən]

pygm|y, -ies ˈpɪgm|ɪ, -ɪz
pyjama, -s pəˈdʒɑːmə [pɪˈdʒ-, old-
  fashioned paɪˈdʒ-], -z
Pyke paɪk
Pylades ˈpɪlədiːz
pylon, -s ˈpaɪlən, -z
pylorus paɪˈlɔːrəs
pyorrhoea ˌpaɪəˈrɪə
pyracantha ˌpaɪərəˈkænθə
pyramid (P.), -s ˈpɪrəmɪd, -z
pyramid|al, -ally pɪˈræmɪd|l, -əlɪ [-l̩ɪ]
Pyramus ˈpɪrəməs
pyre, -s ˈpaɪə*, -z
Pyrene paɪˈriːnɪ [ˌpaɪəˈr-]
Pyren|ean, -ees ˌpɪrəˈn|iːən [-rɪˈn-], -iːz
pyrethrum, -s paɪˈriːθrəm [ˌpaɪəˈr-], -z
pyretic paɪˈretɪk [ˌpaɪəˈr-, pɪˈr-]
pyriform (pear-shaped) ˈpɪrɪfɔːm
pyrites paɪˈraɪtiːz [ˌpaɪəˈr-, pɪˈr-, pəˈr-]
pyritic paɪˈrɪtɪk [ˌpaɪəˈr-]
pyro ˈpaɪərəʊ [ˈpaɪrəʊ]
pyrogallic ˌpaɪrəʊˈgælɪk [ˌpaɪər-]
pyromani|a, -ac ˌpaɪrəʊˈmeɪnɪ|ə [ˌpaɪər-,
  -njə], -æk [-njæk]
pyromet|er/s,   -ry   paɪˈrɒmɪt|ə*/z
  [ˌpaɪəˈr-, -mət|ə*], -rɪ
pyrometric, -al ˌpaɪrəʊˈmetrɪk [ˌpaɪər-],
  -l
pyrotechnic, -al, -ally, -s ˌpaɪrəʊˈteknɪk
  [ˌpaɪər-], -l, -əlɪ, -s
Pyrrh|a, -ic/s, -us ˈpɪr|ə, -ɪk/s, -əs
Pytchley ˈpaɪtʃlɪ
Pythagoras paɪˈθæɡəræs [-ɡɒr-, -rəs]
Pythagorean (s. adj.), -s paɪˌθæɡəˈrɪən
  [ˌpaɪθæɡ-, -ɡɒˈr-, -ˈriːən], -z
Pythian ˈpɪθɪən [-θjən]
Pythias ˈpɪθɪæs
python, -s ˈpaɪθn, -z
pythoness, -es ˈpaɪθənes [-nɪs], -ɪz
pythonic paɪˈθɒnɪk
pyx, -es pɪks, -ɪz

Q

Q (*the letter*) -'s kju:, -z
Qantas 'kwɒntəs [-tæs]
Q.C., -'s ˌkju:'si:, -z
q.e.d. ˌkju:i:'di:
q.e.f. ˌkju:i:'ef
q.t. ˌkju:'ti:
qua kwei [kwɑ:]
quack (*s. v.*), -s, -ing, -ed; -ery, -ish
    kwæk, -s, -ɪŋ, -t; -ərɪ, -ɪʃ
quad, -s kwɒd, -z
Quadragesima ˌkwɒdrə'dʒesɪmə
quadragesimal ˌkwɒdrə'dʒesɪml
quadrangle, -s 'kwɒdræŋgl [kwɒ'dræŋ-,
    kwə'dræŋ-], -z
quadrangular kwɒ'dræŋgjʊlə* [kwə'd-,
    -gjələ*]
quadrant, -s 'kwɒdrənt, -s
quadraphonic ˌkwɒdrə'fɒnɪk
quadrate (*s. adj.*), -s 'kwɒdrət [-rɪt,
    -reɪt], -s
quadrat|e (*v.*), -es, -ing, -ed kwɒ'dreɪt
    [kwə'd-], -s, -ɪŋ, -ɪd
quadratic (*s. adj.*), -s kwɒ'drætɪk
    [kwə'd-], -s
quadrature 'kwɒdrətʃə* [-rɪtʃ-, -ˌtjʊə*]
quadric (*s. adj.*), -s 'kwɒdrɪk, -s
quadriga, -s kwə'dri:gə [kwɒ'd-,
    -'draɪgə], -z
quadrilateral (*s. adj.*), -s ˌkwɒdrɪ-
    'lætərəl, -z
quadrilingual ˌkwɒdrɪ'lɪŋgwəl
quadrille, -s kwə'drɪl [*rarely* kə-], -z
quadrillion, -s kwɒ'drɪljən [kwə'd-],
    -z
quadrisyllabic ˌkwɒdrɪsɪ'læbɪk ['—ˌ—]
quadroon, -s kwɒ'dru:n [kwə'd-], -z
quadrumanous kwɒ'dru:mənəs [kwə'd-]
quadruped, -s 'kwɒdrʊped [-pɪd], -z
quadrup|le (*s. adj. v.*), -les, -ly; -ling,
    -led 'kwɒdrʊp|l [-dru:p-, kwɒ-
    'dru:p|l, kwə-], -lz, -lɪ; -lɪŋ, -ld
quadruplet, -s 'kwɒdrʊplɪt [-plet, -plət,
    kwɒ'dru:plɪt, -plət], -s
quadruplicate (*s. adj.*), -s kwɒ'dru:-
    plɪkət [kwə'd-, -kɪt, -keɪt], -s
quadruplicat|e (*v.*), -es, -ing, -ed kwɒ-
    'dru:plɪkeɪt [kwə'd-], -s, -ɪŋ, -ɪd
quaere 'kwɪərɪ
quaestor, -s 'kwi:stə* [-tɔ:*], -z

quaff, -s, -ing, -ed, -er/s kwɒf [kwɑ:f],
    -s, -ɪŋ, -t, -ə*/z
quag, -s kwæg [kwɒg], -z
quagga, -s 'kwægə, -z
Quaglino kwæg'li:nəʊ
quagmire, -s 'kwægmaɪə* ['kwɒg-], -z
quail (*s. v.*) (Q.), -s, -ing, -ed kweil, -z,
    -ɪŋ, -d
Quaile kweil
Quain kwein
quaint, -er, -est, -ly, -ness kweint, -ə*,
    -ɪst, -lɪ, -nɪs [-nəs]
quak|e (*s. v.*), -es, -ing, -ed kweik, -s,
    -ɪŋ, -t
Quaker, -s 'kweikə*, -z
qualification, -s ˌkwɒlɪfɪ'keɪʃn, -z
qualificative (*s. adj.*), -s 'kwɒlɪfɪkətɪv,
    -z
qualificatory ˌkwɒlɪfɪ'keɪtərɪ ['kwɒlɪ-
    fɪkətərɪ, -keɪtərɪ]
quali|fy, -fies, -fying, -fied, -fier/s
    'kwɒlɪ|faɪ, -faɪz, -faɪɪŋ, -faɪd, -faɪə*/z
qualitative, -ly 'kwɒlɪtətɪv [-teɪt-], -lɪ
qualit|y, -ies 'kwɒlət|ɪ [-ɪt|ɪ], -ɪz
qualm, -s kwɑ:m [kwɔ:m], -z
qualmish, -ly, -ness 'kwɑ:mɪʃ ['kwɔ:m-],
    -lɪ, -nɪs [-nəs]
Qualtrough 'kwɒltrəʊ
quandar|y, -ies 'kwɒndər|ɪ [*rarely*
    kwɒn'deər-], -ɪz
Quandary (*Peak*) 'kwɒndərɪ
Quant kwɒnt
quantic, -s 'kwɒntɪk, -s
quanti|fy, -fies, -fying, -fied, -fier/s,
    -fiable 'kwɒntɪ|faɪ, -faɪz, -faɪɪŋ, -faɪd,
    -faɪə*/z, -faɪəbl
quantitative, -ly 'kwɒntɪtətɪv [-teɪt-], -lɪ
quantit|y, -ies 'kwɒntət|ɪ [-ɪt|ɪ], -ɪz
Quantock (*in Somerset*) 'kwɒntək, (*in
    names of streets, etc., in London*)
    'kwɒntək [-tɒk]
quantum (*amount*) 'kwɒntəm, (*in Latin
    phrases*) 'kwæntəm ['kwɒn-]
quarantin|e (*s. v.*), -es, -ing, -ed
    'kwɒrənti:n [-taɪn, ˌ—'—], -z, -ɪŋ, -d
Quaritch 'kwɒrɪtʃ
Quarles kwɔ:lz
Quarmby 'kwɔ:mbɪ
Quarr kwɔ:*

403

quarr|el (*s. v.*), **-els, -elling, -elled, -eller/s** 'kwɒr|əl, -əlz, -əlɪŋ [-|ɪŋ], -əld, -ələ*/z [-|ə*/z]

quarrelsome, -ly, -ness 'kwɒrəlsəm, -lɪ, -nɪs [-nəs]

quarr|y (*s. v.*), **-ies, -ying, -ied** 'kwɒr|ɪ, -ɪz, -ɪɪŋ, -ɪd

quarry|man, -men 'kwɒrɪ|mən [-mæn], -mən [-men]

quart (*measure of capacity*), **-s** kwɔːt, -s

quart(e) (*s. v.*) (*in card games, fencing*), **-s, -ing, -ed** kɑːt, -s, -ɪŋ, -ɪd

quartan 'kwɔːtn [-tən]

quarter (*s. v.*), **-s, -ing/s, -ed; -age** 'kwɔːtə*, -z, -rɪŋ/z, -d; -rɪdʒ

quarter-day, -s 'kwɔːtədeɪ, -z

quarter-deck, -s 'kwɔːtədek, -s

quarterl|y (*s. adv.*), **-ies** 'kwɔːtəl|ɪ, -ɪz

Quartermaine 'kwɔːtəmeɪn

quartermaster, -s 'kwɔːtə,mɑːstə*, -z

quartern, -s 'kwɔːtən [-tn], -z

quarter-plate, -s 'kwɔːtəpleɪt, -s

quarter-tone, -s 'kwɔːtətəʊn, -z

quartet(te), -s kwɔː'tet, -s

quartic (*s. adj.*), **-s** 'kwɔːtɪk, -s

quartile, -s 'kwɔːtaɪl, -z

quarto, -s 'kwɔːtəʊ, -z

Quartus (**Q.**) 'kwɔːtəs

quartz kwɔːts

quasar 'kweɪzɑː*

quash, -es, -ing, -ed kwɒʃ, -ɪz, -ɪŋ, -t

quasi 'kweɪzaɪ [-saɪ, 'kwɑːzɪ, -ziː]

quassia 'kwɒʃə

quatercentenar|y,-ies ,kwætəsen'tiːnər|ɪ [,kwɔːt-, ,kwɒt-, ,kweɪt-, -'ten-, -'sentɪn-], -ɪz

Quatermain 'kwɔːtəmeɪn

quaternar|y (*s. adj.*), **-ies** kwə'tɜːnər|ɪ, -ɪz

quaternion, -s kwə'tɜːnjən [-nɪən], -z

quatorzain, -s kə'tɔːzeɪn [kæ'tɔː-, 'kætəzeɪn], -z

quatorze, -s kə'tɔːz, -ɪz

quatrain, -s 'kwɒtreɪn, -z

quatre-foil, -s 'kætrəfɔɪl [-təf-], -z

quatrillion, -s kwɒ'trɪljən [kwə't-], -z

quattrocento kwætrəʊ'tʃentəʊ

quav|er (*s. v.*), **-ers, -ering/ly, -ered** 'kweɪv|ə*, -əz, -ərɪŋ/lɪ, -əd

quay, -s; -age kiː, -z; -ɪdʒ

Quay (*place-name*) kiː, (*surname*) kweɪ

Quayle kweɪl

quean, -s kwiːn, -z

queas|y, -iness 'kwiːz|ɪ, -ɪnɪs [-ɪnəs]

Quebec kwɪ'bek [kwə'b-]

queen (*s. v.*), **-s, -ing, -ed** kwiːn, -z, -ɪŋ, -d

Queenborough 'kwiːnbərə

Queenie 'kwiːnɪ

queenlike 'kwiːnlaɪk

queenl|y, -ier, -iest, -iness 'kwiːnl|ɪ, -ɪə* [-jə*], -ɪɪst [-jɪst], -ɪnɪs [-ɪnəs]

Queens|berry, -bury, -ferry, -land, -town 'kwiːnz|bərɪ, -bərɪ, -,ferɪ, -lənd [-lænd], -taʊn

queer, -er, -est, -ly, -ness; -ish kwɪə*, -rə*, -rɪst, -lɪ, -nɪs [-nəs]; -rɪʃ

queerit|y, -ies 'kwɪərət|ɪ [-ɪt|ɪ], -ɪz

quell, -s, -ing, -ed, -er/s kwel, -z, -ɪŋ, -d, -ə*/z

quench, -es, -ing, -ed, -er/s; -able kwentʃ, -ɪz, -ɪŋ, -t, -ə*/z; -əbl

Quen(n)ell kwɪ'nel [kwə'n-], 'kwenl

quenelle, -s kə'nel [kɪ'n-], -z

Quentin 'kwentɪn

querist, -s 'kwɪərɪst, -s

quern, -s kwɜːn, -z

querulous, -ly, -ness 'kwerʊləs [-rjʊl-, -rəl-], -lɪ, -nɪs [-nəs]

quer|y (*s. v.*), **-ies, -ying, -ied** 'kwɪər|ɪ, -ɪz, -ɪɪŋ, -ɪd

Quesnel 'keɪnl

quest (*s. v.*), **-s, -ing, -ed** kwest, -s, -ɪŋ, -ɪd

questi|on (*s. v.*), **-ons, -oning/ly, -oned, -oner/s** 'kwestʃ|ən [-eʃtʃ-], -ənz, -ənɪŋ/lɪ [-ɲɪŋ/lɪ, -nɪŋ/lɪ], -ənd, -ənə*/z [-ɲə*/z, -nə*/z]

questionab|le, -ly, -leness 'kwestʃənəb|l [-eʃtʃ-, -tʃɲə-, -tʃnə-], -lɪ, -lnɪs [-nəs]

questionar|y (*s. adj.*), **-ies** 'kwestʃənər|ɪ [-tʃɲər-], ɪz

question-mark, -s 'kwestʃənmɑːk [-eʃtʃ-], -s

questionnaire, -s ,kwestʃə'neə* [,kwestjə-, ,kwestɪə-, ,kweʃtʃə-, ,kes-, '---], -z

Quetta 'kwetə

quetzal 'kwetsl

queue (*s. v.*), **-s, -ing, -d** kjuː, -z, -ɪŋ ['kjʊɪŋ], -d

queue-minded 'kjuː,maɪndɪd [,-'--]

Queux kjuː

Quex kweks

quibbl|e (*s. v.*), **-les, -ling, -led, -ler/s** 'kwɪb|l, -lz, -lɪŋ [-lɪŋ], -ld, -lə*/z [-lə*/z]

Quibell 'kwaɪbəl, 'kwɪbəl, kwɪ'bel
Note.—Baron Quibell of Scunthorpe pronounced 'kwaɪ-.

quick (*s. adj.*) (**Q.**), **-s, -er, -est, -ly, -ness** kwɪk, -s, -ə*, -ɪst, -lɪ, -nɪs [-nəs]

quick-change (*adj.*) 'kwɪktʃemdʒ [,-'-]

Quicke kwɪk

quick|en, -ens, -ening, -ened 'kwɪk|ən, -ənz, -ɲɪŋ [-ənɪŋ], -ənd

quick-fir|er/s, -ing 'kwɪk,faɪər|ə*/z,
-ɪŋ
quick|-freeze, -freezes, -freezing, -froze,
-frozen, -freezer/s 'kwɪk|fri:z [,-'-,
and in derived forms], -,fri:zɪz,
-,fri:zɪŋ, -frəʊz, -,frəʊzn, -,fri:zə*/z
quicklime 'kwɪklaɪm
Quickly 'kwɪklɪ
quickmarch ,kwɪk'mɑ:tʃ
quick|sand/s, -set 'kwɪk|sænd/z, -set
quicksilv|er (s. v.), -ers, -ering, -ered
'kwɪk,sɪlv|ə*, -əz, -ərɪŋ, -əd
quick-tempered ,kwɪk'tempəd ['-,--]
quick-witted, -ness ,kwɪk'wɪtɪd, -nɪs
[-nəs]
quid, -s kwɪd, -z
quidnunc, -s 'kwɪdnʌŋk, -s
quid pro quo, -s ,kwɪdprəʊ'kwəʊ, -z
quiescen|ce, -t/ly kwaɪ'esn|s, -t/lɪ
quiet (s. adj. v.), -er, -est, -ly, -ness;
-s, -ing, -ed 'kwaɪət, -ə*, -ɪst, -lɪ,
-nɪs [-nəs]; -s, -ɪŋ, -ɪd
quiet|en, -ens, -ening, -ened 'kwaɪət|n,
-nz, -ɳɪŋ [-nɪŋ], -nd
quieti|sm, -st/s 'kwaɪtɪ|zəm [-aɪət-],
-st/s
quietude 'kwaɪtju:d [-aɪət-]
quietus kwaɪ'i:təs [-'eɪtəs]
Quiggin 'kwɪgɪn
quill (s. v.), -s, -ing, -ed kwɪl, -z, -ɪŋ,
-d
Quilleash 'kwɪli:ʃ
Quiller-Couch ,kwɪlə'ku:tʃ
Quilliam 'kwɪljəm [-lɪəm]
Quilp kwɪlp
quilt (s. v.), -s, -ing, -ed kwɪlt, -s, -ɪŋ,
-ɪd
Quilter 'kwɪltə*
quin (Q.), -s kwɪn, -z
Quinault (surname) 'kwɪnlt [-nəlt,
-nɔ:lt]
quince (Q.), -s kwɪns, -ɪz
quincentenar|y, -ies ,kwɪnsen'ti:nər|ɪ
[-'ten-, kwɪn'sentɪn-], -ɪz
Quinc(e)y 'kwɪnsɪ
quincunx, -es 'kwɪnkʌŋks ['kwɪŋk-],
-ɪz
quindecagon, -s kwɪn'dekəgən, -z
quingentenar|y, -ies ,kwɪndʒen'ti:nər|ɪ
[-'ten-], -ɪz
quinine kwɪ'ni:n ['kwɪni:n]
Quinney 'kwɪnɪ
quinquagenarian, -s ,kwɪŋkwədʒɪ-
'neərɪən, -z
Quinquagesima ,kwɪŋkwə'dʒesɪmə
quinquennial kwɪŋ'kwenɪəl [-njəl]
quinquennium, -s kwɪŋ'kwenɪəm
[-njəm], -z

quinquereme, -s 'kwɪŋkwɪri:m [-kwər-],
-z
quinquina kwɪŋ'kwaɪnə
quinsy 'kwɪnzɪ
quint, -s (organ stop) kwɪnt, (in piquet)
kɪnt [kwɪnt, old-fashioned kent],
-s
quintain, -s 'kwɪntɪn, -z
quintal, -s 'kwɪntl, -z
quintessence kwɪn'tesns
quintet(te), -s kwɪn'tet, -s
quintic (s. adj.), -s 'kwɪntɪk, -s
Quintilian kwɪn'tɪljən [-lɪən]
quintillion, -s kwɪn'tɪljən, -z
Quintin 'kwɪntɪn
Quinton 'kwɪntən
quintup|le, -les, -ling, -led 'kwɪntjʊp|l
[-tju:p-, kwɪn'tju:pl], -lz, -lɪŋ, -ld
quintuplet, -s 'kwɪntjʊplɪt [-plet, -plət,
kwɪn'tju:plɪt, -plət], -s
quintus (Q.) 'kwɪntəs
quip, -s kwɪp, -s
quire, -s 'kwaɪə*, -z
Quirey (surname) (in England) 'kwaɪərɪ,
(in Ireland) 'kwɪərɪ
Quirinal 'kwɪrɪnəl
Quirinus kwɪ'raɪnəs
quirk (Q.), -s kwɜ:k, -s
quisling, -s 'kwɪzlɪŋ, -z
quit (adj. v.), -s, -ting, -ted kwɪt, -s, -ɪŋ,
-ɪd
quite kwaɪt
Quito 'ki:təʊ
quit-rent, -s 'kwɪtrent, -s
quits kwɪts
quittance, -s 'kwɪtəns, -ɪz
quiv|er (s. v.), -ers, -ering/ly, -ered
'kwɪv|ə*, -əz, -ərɪŋ/lɪ, -əd
qui vive ,ki:'vi:v
Quixote 'kwɪksət [-səʊt, kɪ'həʊtɪ]
(ki'xote)
quixotic, -ally kwɪk'sɒtɪk, -əlɪ
quiz (s. v.), -zes, -zing, -zed kwɪz, -ɪz,
-ɪŋ, -d
quizmaster, -s 'kwɪz,mɑ:stə*, -z
quizzic|al, -ally 'kwɪzɪk|l, -əlɪ
quod (s. v.), -s, -ding, -ded kwɒd, -z,
-ɪŋ, -ɪd
quodlibet, -s 'kwɒdlɪbet, -s
quoin (s. v.), -s, -ing, -ed kɔɪn [kwɔɪn],
-z, -ɪŋ, -d
quoit, -s kɔɪt [kwɔɪt], -s
quondam 'kwɒndæm [-dəm]
Quorn kwɔ:n
quorate 'kwɔ:reɪt [-rət, -rɪt]
quorum, -s 'kwɔ:rəm, -z
quota (s. v.), -s, -ing, -ed 'kwəʊtə, -z,
-ɪŋ [-ərɪŋ], -d

405

quotable 'kwəʊtəbl
quotation, -s kwəʊ'teɪʃn, -z
quot|e (s. v.), **-es, -ing, -ed** kwəʊt, -s,
  -ɪŋ, -ɪd
quoth, -a kwəʊθ, -ə
quotidian kwɒ'tɪdɪən [kwəʊ't-, -djən]

quotient, -s 'kwəʊʃnt, -s
quousque tandem kwəʊˌʊskwɪ'tændem
  [-ˌʌs-, -dəm]
Quy (in Cambridgeshire, surname) kwaɪ
q.v. ˌkjuː'viː [ˌwɪtʃ'siː, ˌkwɒd'vɪdeɪ,
  old-fashioned ˌkwɒd'vaɪdɪ]

R

R (*the letter*), -'s ɑ:*, -z
ra (*note in Tonic Sol-fa*), -s rɔ:, -z
Rabat (*in Morocco*) rə'bɑ:t
rabbet, -s 'ræbɪt, -s
rabbi, -s 'ræbaɪ, -z
rabbinic, -al, -ally rə'bɪnɪk [ræ'b-], -l, -əlɪ
rabbit, -s; -hole/s, -hutch/es 'ræbɪt, -s; -həʊl/z, -hʌtʃ/ɪz
rabbit-warren, -s 'ræbɪt͵wɒrən, -z
rabble, -s 'ræbl, -z
Rabelais 'ræbəleɪ (rablɛ)
Rabelaisian ͵ræbə'leɪzɪən [-zjən]
rabid, -est, -ly, -ness 'ræbɪd, -ɪst, -lɪ, -nɪs [-nəs]
rabies 'reɪbiː:z [-bɪz, -biːz, 'ræb-]
Rabin (*surname*) 'reɪbɪn
Rabindranath Tagore rə͵bɪndrənɑː:tə'gɔ:* [-'gɔə*] (*Bengali* robindrɔnath ṭhakur, *Hindi* rəbindrənath ṭhakwr)
Rabshakeh 'ræbʃɑːkɪ [-ʃəkɪ, -ʃəkə]
Raby 'reɪbɪ
raca 'rɑːkə
rac|e, -es, -ing, -ed, -er/s reɪs, -ɪz, -ɪŋ, -t, -ə*/z
race-course, -s 'reɪskɔ:s [-kɔəs], -ɪz
race-horse, -s 'reɪshɔ:s, -ɪz
race-meeting, -s 'reɪs͵miːtɪŋ, -z
Racheil 'reɪʃl
Rachel 'reɪtʃəl
rachitis ræ'kaɪtɪs [rə'k-]
Rachmaninoff ræk'mænɪnɒf (rax'manjinəf)
raci|al, -ally 'reɪʃ|l [-ʃɪ|əl, -ʃj|əl], -əlɪ
racialism 'reɪʃəlɪzəm [-ʃɪəl-, -ʃjəl-, -ʃl|ɪ-]
Racine (*English personal name*) rə'si:n, (*French author*) ræ'si:n (rasin)
rac|ism, -st/s 'reɪs|ɪzəm, -ɪst/s
rack (*s. v.*), -s, -ing, -ed ræk, -s, -ɪŋ, -t
racket (*s. v.*), -s, -ing, -ed; -y 'rækɪt, -s, -ɪŋ, -ɪd; -ɪ
racketeer, -s ͵rækə'tɪə* [-kɪ't-], -z
rack-rail, -s 'rækreɪl [͵-'-], -z
rack-rent, -s 'rækrent, -s
raconteur, -s ͵rækɒn'tɜ:* [-kɔ̃:n-] (rakɔ̃tœ:r), -z
racoon, -s rə'ku:n, -z
racquet, -s 'rækɪt, -s

rac|y, -ier, -iest, -ily, -iness 'reɪs|ɪ, -ɪə* [-jə*], -ɪɪst [-jɪst], -ɪlɪ [-əlɪ], -ɪnɪs [-ɪnəs]
rad (R.), -s ræd, -z
radar 'reɪdɑ:* [-də*]
Rad|cliffe, -ford 'ræd|klɪf, -fəd
radial, -ly 'reɪdjəl [-dɪəl], -ɪ
radian, -s 'reɪdjən [-dɪən], -z
radiance, -s 'reɪdjəns [-dɪəns], -ɪz
radiant (*s. adj.*), -s, -ly 'reɪdjənt [-dɪənt], -s, -lɪ
radiat|e (*v.*), -es, -ing, -ed 'reɪdɪeɪt [-djert], -s, -ɪŋ, -ɪd
radiation, -s ͵reɪdɪ'eɪʃn, -z
radiator, -s 'reɪdɪeɪtə* [-djertə*], -z
radic|al (*s. adj.*), -als, -ally, -alness; -alism 'rædɪk|l, -lz, -əlɪ [-l|ɪ], -lnɪs [-nəs]; -əlɪzəm [-l|ɪzəm]
radio (*s.*), -s 'reɪdɪəʊ [-djəʊ], -z
radi|o (*v.*), -o(e)s, -oing, -oed 'reɪdɪ|əʊ [-dj|əʊ], -əʊz, -əʊɪŋ, -əʊd
radio-active ͵reɪdɪəʊ'æktɪv [-djəʊ-]
radioactivity ͵reɪdɪəʊæk'tɪvətɪ [-djəʊ-, -ɪtɪ]
radiogenic ͵reɪdɪəʊ'dʒenɪk [-djəʊ-]
radiogram, -s 'reɪdɪəʊgræm [-djəʊg-], -z
radiograph, -s 'reɪdɪəʊgrɑ:f [-djəʊg-, -græf], -s
radiograph|y, -er/s ͵reɪdɪ'ɒgrəf|ɪ, -ə*/z
radiolocat|e, -es, -ing, -ed ͵reɪdɪəʊləʊ'keɪt [-djəʊ-], -s, -ɪŋ, -ɪd
radio-location ͵reɪdɪəʊləʊ'keɪʃn [-djəʊ-]
radiolog|ist/s, -y ͵reɪdɪ'ɒlədʒ|ɪst/s, -ɪ
radiometer, -s ͵reɪdɪ'ɒmɪtə* [-mətə*], -z
radiotelegram, -s ͵reɪdɪəʊ'telɪgræm [-djəʊ-], -z
radiotelephone, -s ͵reɪdɪəʊ'telɪfəʊn [-djəʊ-], -z
radiotherap|y, -ist/s ͵reɪdɪəʊ'θerəp|ɪ [-djəʊ-], -ɪst/s
radish, -es 'rædɪʃ, -ɪz
radium 'reɪdɪəm [-djəm]
ra|dius, -dii reɪ|dɪəs [-djəs], -dɪaɪ
radix, -es, radices 'reɪdɪks, -ɪz, 'reɪdɪsi:z
Radleian, -s ræd'li:ən [-'lɪən], -z
Radley 'rædlɪ
Radmall 'rædmɔ:l
Radnor, -shire 'rædnə* [-nɔ:*], -ʃə* [-͵ʃɪə*]

Rae reɪ
Raeburn, -s 'reɪbɜːn, -z
Raemakers 'rɑːmɑːkəz
Raf ræf
R.A.F. ˌɑːreɪ'ef
raffia 'ræfɪə [-fjə]
raffish 'ræfɪʃ
raff|le (s. v.), -les (R.), -ling, -led 'ræf|l,
-lz, -lɪŋ [-lɪŋ], -ld
raft (s. v.), -s, -ing, -ed rɑːft, -s, -ɪŋ, -ɪd
rafter, -s, -ed 'rɑːftə*, -z, -d
rag (s. v.), -s, -ging, -ged ræg, -z, -ɪŋ, -d
ragamuffin, -s 'rægə,mʌfɪn, -z
rag-and-bone|-man, -men ˌrægən-
'bəʊn|-mæn, -men
rag|le (s. v.), -es, -ing/ly, -ed reɪdʒ, -ɪz,
-ɪŋ/lɪ, -d
ragged (adj.), -er, -est, -ly, -ness 'rægɪd,
-ə*, -ɪst, -lɪ, -nɪs [-nəs]
Raglan 'ræglən
ragout, -s 'rægu:; -z
ragtag 'rægtæg
ragtime 'rægtaɪm
Rahab 'reɪhæb
Rahere rə'hɪə*
raid (s. v.), -s, -ing, -ed, -er/s reɪd, -z,
-ɪŋ, -ɪd, -ə*/z
Raikes reɪks
rail (s. v.), -s, -ing, -ed reɪl, -z, -ɪŋ, -d
railhead, -s 'reɪlhed, -z
railing, -s 'reɪlɪŋ, -z
railler|y, -ies 'reɪlər|ɪ, -ɪz
rail|road/s, -way/s 'reɪl|rəʊd/z, -weɪ/z
railway|man, -men 'reɪlweɪ|mən
[-mæn], -mən [-men]
raiment 'reɪmənt
rain (s. v.), -s, -ing, -ed; -less reɪn, -z,
-ɪŋ, -d; -lɪs [-ləs]
rainbow, -s 'reɪnbəʊ, -z
raincoat, -s 'reɪnkəʊt ['reɪŋk-], -s
raindrop, -s 'reɪndrɒp, -s
rainfall 'reɪnfɔːl
rain-gauge, -s 'reɪngeɪdʒ ['reɪŋg-], -ɪz
rainless 'reɪnlɪs [-ləs]
rainmak|er/s, -ing 'reɪn,meɪk|ə*/z, -ɪŋ
rainproof 'reɪnpruːf
rainstorm, -s 'reɪnstɔːm, -z
rainwater 'reɪn,wɔːtə*
rain|y, -ier, -iest, -iness 'reɪn|ɪ, -ɪə*
[-jə*], -ɪɪst [-jɪst], -ɪnɪs [-ɪnəs]
rais|e, -es, -ing, -ed reɪz, -ɪz, -ɪŋ, -d
raisin, -s 'reɪzn, -z
raison d'être ˌreɪzɔ̃:n'deɪtrə [-'detrə,
-zɒn'd-, -'deɪtə*] (rɛzɔ̃dɛːtr)
raj rɑːdʒ
rajah (R.), -s 'rɑːdʒə, -z
Rajasthani ˌrɑːdʒə'stɑːnɪ (Hindi raɪəs-
thani)

Rajput 'rɑːdʒpʊt (Hindi raɪpwt)
Rajputana ˌrɑːdʒpʊ'tɑːnə (Hindi raɪ-
pwtana)
rak|e (s. v.), -es, -ing, -ed reɪk, -s, -ɪŋ,
-t
rakish, -ly, -ness 'reɪkɪʃ, -lɪ, -nɪs [-nəs]
rale, -s rɑːl, -z
Rale(i)gh 'rɔːlɪ, 'rɑːlɪ, 'rælɪ
Note.—The family of the late Sir
Walter Raleigh pronounced 'rɔːlɪ.
Raleigh bicycles are generally called
'rælɪ. When used as the name of a
ship, the pronunciation is 'rælɪ.
rallentando, -s ˌrælen'tændəʊ [-lən-,
-lɪn-], -z
rall|y (s. v.), -ies, -ying, -ied 'ræl|ɪ, -ɪz,
-ɪŋ, -ɪd
Ralph (Christian name) reɪf, rælf
Ralph Cross (in North Yorkshire)
ˌrɑːlf'krɒs [ˌrælf-, old-fashioned
-'krɔːs]
Ralston 'rɔːlstən
ram (s. v.), -s, -ming, -med, -mer/s
ræm, -z, -ɪŋ, -d, -ə*/z
Ramadan ˌræmə'dæn [ˌrɑː-, -'dɑːn]
Rama(h) 'rɑːmə
Ramayana rɑː'maɪənə [-'mɑːjənə]
(Hindi ramajənə)
ramb|le (s. v.), -les, -ling, -led 'ræmb|l,
-lz, -lɪŋ [-lɪŋ], -ld
rambler (R.), -s 'ræmblə*, -z
rambling (adj.), -ly 'ræmblɪŋ, -lɪ
ramekin [-quin], -s 'ræmkɪn, -z
Rameses 'ræmɪsiːz [-məs-]
ramification, -s ˌræmɪfɪ'keɪʃn, -z
rami|fy, -fies, -fying, -fied 'ræmɪ|faɪ,
-faɪz, -faɪɪŋ, -faɪd
Ramillies 'ræmɪlɪz
Ramoth-Gilead ˌreɪmɒθ'gɪlɪæd [-məθ-,
-ljæd]
ramp (s. v.), -s, -ing, -ed ræmp, -s, -ɪŋ,
-t [ræmt]
rampag|e (s. v.), -es, -ing, -ed ræm-
'peɪdʒ, -ɪz, -ɪŋ, -d
rampageous, -ly, -ness ræm'peɪdʒəs, -lɪ,
-nɪs [-nəs]
rampan|cy, -t/ly 'ræmpən|sɪ, -t/lɪ
rampart, -s 'ræmpɑːt [-pət], -s
rampion, -s 'ræmpjən [-pɪən], -z
ramrod, -s 'ræmrɒd, -z
Ramsaran 'rɑːmsərən
Ramsay [-sey] 'ræmzɪ
Ramsden 'ræmzdən
Ramsgate 'ræmzgɪt [locally -geɪt]
ramshackle 'ræm,ʃækl [ˌ-'--]
ran (from run) ræn
rance ræns
Rance (surname) rɑːns

ranch (s. v.), -es, -ing, -ed, -er/s rɑːntʃ
[ræntʃ], -ɪz, -ɪŋ, -t, -ə*/z
rancid, -ness 'rænsɪd, -nɪs [-nəs]
rancidity ræn'sɪdətɪ [-ɪtɪ]
rancorous, -ly 'ræŋkərəs, -lɪ
rancour 'ræŋkə*
rand, -s rænd, -z
Rand (usual pronunciation in England)
rænd, (pronunciation of English-
speaking South Africans) rɑːnd, rɑːnt,
rɒnt (Afrikaans rɑnt)
Rand|all, -ell 'rænd|l, -l
Randolph 'rændɒlf [-dəlf]
random 'rændəm
randomization [-isa-] ˌrændəmaɪ'zeɪʃn
[-mɪ'z-]
randomiz|e [-is|e], -es, -ing, -ed 'rændə-
maɪz, -ɪz, -ɪŋ, -d
randy 'rændɪ
Ranee, -s 'rɑːniː [ˌ-'-], -z
Ranelagh 'rænɪlə, 'rænələ
rang (from ring) ræŋ
rang|e (s. v.), -es, -ing, -ed reɪndʒ, -ɪz,
-ɪŋ, -d
range-finder, -s 'reɪndʒˌfaɪndə*, -z
ranger (R.), -s 'reɪndʒə*, -z
Rangoon ræŋ'guːn
rank (s. adj. v.) (R.), -s; -er, -est, -ly,
-ness; -ing, -ed ræŋk, -s; -ə*, -ɪst, -lɪ,
-nɪs [-nəs]; -ɪŋ, -t [ræŋt]
Rankeillour ræŋ'kiːlə*
Rankin(e) 'ræŋkɪn
rank|le, -les, -ling, -led 'ræŋk|l, -lz, -lɪŋ,
[-lɪŋ], -ld
Rannoch 'rænək [-əx]
Rann of Cutch ˌrʌnəv'kʌtʃ [ˌræn-]
Ranoe 'rɑːnəʊ
ransack, -s, -ing, -ed, -er/s 'rænsæk, -s,
-ɪŋ, -t, -ə*/z
ransom (s. v.) (R.), -s, -ing, -ed, -er/s
'rænsəm, -z, -ɪŋ, -d, -ə*/z
Ransome 'rænsəm
rant (s. v.), -s, -ing/ly, -ed, -er/s rænt,
-s, -ɪŋ/lɪ, -ɪd, -ə*/z
ranuncul|us, -uses, -i rə'nʌŋkjʊl|əs
[-kjəl-], -əsɪz, -aɪ
Ranworth 'rænwɜːθ
rap (s. v.), -s, -ping, -ped ræp, -s, -ɪŋ, -t
rapacious, -ly, -ness rə'peɪʃəs, -lɪ, -nɪs
[-nəs]
rapacity rə'pæsətɪ [-ɪtɪ]
rap|e (s. v.), -es, -ing, -ed, -ist/s reɪp,
-s, -ɪŋ, -t, -ɪst/s
Raphael (angel) 'ræfeɪəl ['ræfɑːel,
'ræfeɪl, 'reɪfɪəl, and in Jewish usage
'reɪfl, 'ræfəel], (modern surname)
'reɪfl, 'ræfeɪl, (Italian artist) 'ræfeɪəl
[-frəl, -feɪl]

rapid, -est, -ly, -ness, -s 'ræpɪd, -ɪst, -lɪ,
-nɪs [-nəs], -z
rapidity rə'pɪdətɪ [ræ'p-, -ɪtɪ]
rapier, -s 'reɪpjə* [-pɪə*], -z
rapine 'ræpaɪn [-pɪn]
rapparee, -s ˌræpə'riː, -z
rapping, -s 'ræpɪŋ, -z
rapport ræ'pɔː* (rapɔːr)
rapporteur, -s ˌræpɔː'tɜː* (raportœːr), -z
rapprochement, -s ræ'prɒʃmɑ̃ːŋ [-mɔ̃ːŋ,
-mɑːŋ, -mɒŋ] (raprɔʃmɑ̃),
rapscallion, -s ræp'skæljən [-lɪən], -z
rapt ræpt
rapture, -s, -d 'ræptʃə*, -z, -d
rapturous, -ly 'ræptʃərəs, -lɪ
rara avis ˌrɑːrə'ævɪs [ˌreərə'eɪvɪs]
rare, -r, -st, -ly, -ness reə*, -rə*, -rɪst,
-lɪ, -nɪs [-nəs]
rarebit, -s 'reəbɪt ['ræbɪt], -s
rarefaction ˌreərɪ'fækʃn
rarefication ˌreərɪfɪ'keɪʃn
rare|fy, -fies, -fying, -fied 'reərɪ|faɪ,
-faɪz, -faɪɪŋ, -faɪd
rarit|y, -ies 'reərət|ɪ [-ɪt|ɪ], -ɪz
rascal, -s 'rɑːskəl, -z
rascalit|y, -ies rɑː'skælət|ɪ [-ɪt|ɪ], -ɪz
rascally 'rɑːskəlɪ [-klɪ]
ras|e, -es, -ing, -ed reɪz, -ɪz, -ɪŋ, -d
rash (s. adj.), -es; -er, -est, -ly, -ness
ræʃ, -ɪz; -ə*, -ɪst, -lɪ, -nɪs [-nəs]
rasher (s.), -s 'ræʃə*, -z
rasp (s. v.), -s, -ing, -ed rɑːsp, -s, -ɪŋ, -t
raspberr|y, -ies 'rɑːzbər|ɪ ['rɑːsb-], -ɪz
Rasputin ræ'spjuːtɪn ['-spuː-]
rasp|y, -iness 'rɑːsp|ɪ, -mɪs [-məs]
Rasselas 'ræsɪləs [-læs]
rat, -s, -ting, -ted ræt, -s, -ɪŋ, -ɪd
rata (tree), -s 'reɪtə, -z
rata (in pro rata) 'rɑːtə ['reɪtə]
ratability ˌreɪtə'bɪlətɪ [-lɪt-]
ratab|le, -ly 'reɪtəb|l, -lɪ
ratafia, -s ˌrætə'fɪə, -z
ratan, -s rə'tæn [ræ't-], -z
rataplan ˌrætə'plæn
ratatat ˌrætə'tæt
rat-catcher, -s 'ræt,kætʃə*, -z
ratchet, -s 'rætʃɪt, -s
Ratcliff(e) 'rætklɪf
rat|e (s. v.), -es, -ing, -ed reɪt, -s, -ɪŋ, -ɪd
rateab|le, -ly 'reɪtəb|l, -lɪ
ratel, -s 'reɪtel [-təl, -tl], -z
rate-payer, -s 'reɪt,peɪə*, -z
Rath ræθ
Rathbone 'ræθbəʊn [-bən]
rather 'rɑːðə* [as interj. also ˌrɑː'ðɜː*]
Rathfarnham ræθ'fɑːnəm
rat-hole, -s 'ræthəʊl, -z
ratification, -s ˌrætɪfɪ'keɪʃn, -z

409

rati|fy, -fies, -fying, -fied, -fier/s
ˈrætɪ|faɪ, -faɪz, -faɪɪŋ, -faɪd, -faɪə*/z
rating, -s ˈreɪtɪŋ, -z
ratio, -s ˈreɪʃɪəʊ [-ʃjəʊ], -z
ratiocinat|e, -es, -ing, -ed ˌrætɪˈɒsɪneɪt,
-s, -ɪŋ, -ɪd
ratiocination, -s ˌrætɪɒsɪˈneɪʃn [-tɪəʊs-],
-z
rati|on (s. v.), -ons, -oning, -oned
ˈræʃ|n, -nz, -n̩ɪŋ [-ənɪŋ, -nɪŋ], -nd
ra|tional, -tionally ˈræ|ʃənl [-ʃnəl, -ʃn̩l,
-ʃn̩], -ʃənəl], -ʃn̩əlɪ [-ʃnəlɪ-ʃn̩lɪ, -ʃn̩lɪ,
-ʃənəlɪ]
rationale, -s ˌræʃəˈnɑːl [-ʃɪəʊ'n-, -ʃjəˈn-,
-ˈnɑːlɪ], -z
rationali|sm, -st/s ˈræʃn̩əlɪ|zəm [-ʃnəl-,
-ʃn̩l-, -ʃnl-, -ʃənəl-], -st/s
rationalistic ˌræʃn̩əˈlɪstɪk [-ʃnəˈlɪ-,
-ʃn̩lˈɪ-, -ʃnlˈɪ-, -ʃənəˈlɪ-]
rationality ˌræʃəˈnælɪtɪ [-ʃn̩ˈæ-, -ɪtɪ]
rationalization [-isa-] ˌræʃn̩əlaɪˈzeɪʃn
[-ʃnəl-, -ʃn̩l-, -ʃnl-, -ʃənəl-, -lɪˈz-]
rationaliz|e [-is|e], -es, -ing, -ed
ˈræʃn̩əlaɪz [-ʃnəl-, -ʃn̩l-, -ʃnl-, -ʃənəl-],
-ɪz, -ɪŋ, -d
Ratisbon ˈrætɪzbɒn [-ɪsb-]
ratlin(e), -s ˈrætlɪn, -z
rat-race ˈrætreɪs
rat-tail, -ed ˈrætteɪl, -d
rattan, -s rəˈtæn [ræˈt-], -z
ratt|le (s. v.), -les, -ling, -led, -ler/s
ˈræt|l, -lz, -lɪŋ [-lɪŋ], -ld, -l̩ə*/z
[-lə*/z]
rattlesnake, -s ˈrætlsneɪk, -s
rat-trap, -s ˈrættræp, -s
raucous, -ly ˈrɔːkəs, -lɪ
ravag|e (s. v.), -es, -ing, -ed, -er/s
ˈrævɪdʒ, -ɪz, -ɪŋ, -d, -ə*/z
rav|e, -es, -ing/s, -ed reɪv, -z, -ɪŋ/z, -d
rav|el, -els, -elling, -elled ˈræv|l, -lz,
-lɪŋ [-əlɪŋ], -ld
Ravel (French composer) ræˈvel (ravɛl)
ravelin, -s ˈrævlɪn [-vəlɪn], -z
raven (s.) (R.), -s ˈreɪvn [-vən], -z
raven (v.), -s, -ing, -ed ˈrævn, -nz, -n̩ɪŋ
[-ənɪŋ], -nd
Ravening ˈreɪvnɪŋ
Ravenna rəˈvenə
ravenous, -ly, -ness ˈrævənəs [-vɪnəs,
-vn̩əs], -lɪ, -nɪs [-nəs]
Ravensbourne ˈreɪvnzbɔːn [-bəən]
ravin(e) (plunder) ˈrævɪn
ravine (deep valley), -s rəˈviːn, -z
raving (s. adj. adv.), -s ˈreɪvɪŋ, -z
ravish, -es, -ing/ly, -ed, -er/s, -ment
ˈrævɪʃ, -ɪz, -ɪŋ/lɪ, -t, -ə*/z, -mənt
raw, -er, -est, -ly, -ness rɔː, -ə*, -ɪst,
ˈrɔːlɪ, ˈrɔːnɪs [-nəs]

Rawalpindi ˌrɑːwəlˈpɪndɪ [ˌrɔːlˈp-]
Raw|don, -lings, -lins, -linson ˈrɔː|dn,
-lɪŋz, -lɪnz, -lɪnsn
ray (R.), -s; -less reɪ, -z; -lɪs [-ləs]
Ray|leigh, -ment, -mond, -ner, -nes
ˈreɪ|lɪ, -mənt, -mənd, -nə*, -nz
rayon ˈreɪɒn [ˈreɪən]
raz|e, -es, -ing, -ed reɪz, -ɪz, -ɪŋ, -d
razor, -s ˈreɪzə*, -z
razorbill, -s ˈreɪzəbɪl, -z
razor-blade, -s ˈreɪzəbleɪd, -z
razor-edge, -s ˈreɪzəredʒ [-zəedʒ, ˌ-ˈ-],
-ɪz
razor-shell, -s ˈreɪzəʃel, -z
Razzell rəˈzel
razzia, -s ˈræzɪə [-zjə], -z
razzle-dazzle ˈræzlˌdæzl [ˌ-ˈ-]
re (note in Tonic Sol-fa), -s reɪ [riː], -z
re (prep.) riː
re- (prefix denoting repetition) ˌriː-
  Note.—Compounds with this prefix
  not entered below have double stress.
  Thus restamp is ˌriːˈstæmp.
Rea reɪ, rɪə, riː:
  Note.—Baron Rea pronounces riː:.
reach (s. v.), -es, -ing, -ed riːtʃ, -ɪz, -ɪŋ,
-t
react, -s, -ing, -ed rɪˈækt [riː-], -s, -ɪŋ,
-ɪd
reaction, -s rɪˈækʃn [riː-], -z
reactionar|y (s. adj.), -ies rɪˈækʃnər|ɪ
[riː-, -ʃənə-, -ʃnə-], -ɪz
reactive, -ly rɪˈæktɪv [riː-], -lɪ
reactor, -s rɪˈæktə* [riː-], -z
read (pres. tense) (R.), -s, -ing riːd, -z,
-ɪŋ
read (p. tense) red
readability ˌriːdəˈbɪlətɪ [-lɪt-]
readab|le, -ly, -leness ˈriːdəb|l, -lɪ, -lnɪs
[-nəs]
re-address, -es, -ing, -ed ˌriːəˈdres, -ɪz,
-ɪŋ, -t
Reade riːd
reader, -s; -ship/s ˈriːdə*, -z; -ʃɪp/s
reading (s.), -s ˈriːdɪŋ, -z
Reading ˈredɪŋ
reading-desk, -s ˈriːdɪŋdesk, -s
reading-glass, -es ˈriːdɪŋglɑːs, -ɪz
reading-lamp, -s ˈriːdɪŋlæmp, -s
reading-room, -s ˈriːdɪŋrʊm [-ruːm], -z
readjus|t, -ts, -ting, -ted, -tment/s
ˌriːəˈdʒʌs|t, -ts, -tɪŋ, -tɪd, -tmənt/s
readmission, -s ˌriːədˈmɪʃn, -z
readmit, -s, -ting, -ted; -tance ˌriːəd-
ˈmɪt, -s, -ɪŋ, -ɪd; -əns
read|y, -ier, -iest, -ily, -iness ˈred|ɪ, -ɪə*
[-jə*], -ɪɪst [-jɪst], -ɪlɪ [-əlɪ], -ɪnɪs
[-ɪnəs]

ready-made ˌredɪˈmeɪd [ˈ--- *when attributive*]
reaffirm, -s, -ing, -ed ˌriːəˈfɜːm, -z, -ɪŋ,
-d
reagent, -s riːˈeɪdʒənt [rɪˈeɪ-], -s
real (*monetary unit*), -s reɪˈɑːl, -z
real (*adj.*), really rɪəl [ˈriːəl], ˈrɪəlɪ
reali|sm, -st/s ˈrɪəlɪ|zəm [ˈriːəl-], -st/s
realistic, -ally ˌrɪəˈlɪstɪk [ˌriːəˈl-, rɪəˈl-],
-əlɪ [-lɪ]
realit|y, -ies rɪˈælət|ɪ [riː-, -ɪt|ɪ], -ɪz
realization [-isa-], -s ˌrɪəlaɪˈzeɪʃn [-lɪˈz-],
-z
realiz|e [-is|e], -es, -ing, -ed; -able
ˈrɪəlaɪz, -ɪz, -ɪŋ, -d; -əbl [-ˈ---]
really ˈrɪəlɪ
realm, -s relm, -z
realty ˈrɪəltɪ [ˈriːəl-]
ream (*s. v.*), -s, -ing, -ed riːm, -z, -ɪŋ, -d
reamer, -s ˈriːmə*, -z
Rean ˈriːən
reap, -s, -ing, -ed, -er/s riːp, -s, -ɪŋ, -t,
-ə*/z
reappear, -s, -ing, -ed; -ance/s ˌriː-
əˈpɪə* [ˌrɪəˈp-, rɪəˈp-], -z, -rɪŋ, -d;
-rəns/ɪz
reapplication, -s ˈriːˌæplɪˈkeɪʃn, -z
reappl|y, -ies, -ying, -ied ˌriːəˈplaɪ, -aɪz,
-aɪɪŋ, -aɪd
reappoint, -s, -ing, -ed, -ment/s ˌriː-
əˈpɔɪnt [ˌrɪəˈp-, rɪəˈp-], -s, -ɪŋ, -ɪd,
-mənt/s
rear (*s. v.*), -s, -ing, -ed, -er/s rɪə*, -z, -rɪŋ, -d
rear-admiral, -s ˌrɪəˈædmərəl [ˌrɪərˈæd-],
-z
rear-guard, -s ˈrɪəɡɑːd, -z
rearm, -s, -ing, -ed ˌriːˈɑːm, -z, -ɪŋ, -d
rearmament rɪˈɑːməmənt [riːˈɑː-]
rearrang|e, -es, -ing, -ed, -ement/s
ˌriːəˈreɪndʒ [ˌrɪəˈr-, rɪəˈr-], -ɪz, -ɪŋ, -d,
-mənt/s
reas|on, -ons, -oning/s, -oned, -oner/s
ˈriːz|n, -nz, -n̩ɪŋ/z [-ən̩ɪŋ/z], -nd,
-n̩ə*/z [-ənə*/z]
reasonab|le, -ly, -leness ˈriːzn̩əb|l
[-znə-], -lɪ, -lnɪs [-nəs]
reassemb|le, -les, -ling, -led ˌriːəˈsemb|l
[ˌrɪəˈs-, rɪəˈs-], -lz, -lɪŋ, -ld
reassert, -s, -ing, -ed ˌriːəˈsɜːt [ˌrɪəˈs-],
-s, -ɪŋ, -ɪd
reassur|e, -es, -ing/ly, -ed; -ance
ˌriːəˈʃɔː* [ˌrɪə-, rɪə-, -ˈʃɔə*, -ˈʃʊə*], -z,
-rɪŋ/lɪ, -d; -rəns
Réaumur ˈreɪəˌmjʊə* [-mə*] (reomyːr)
Reay reɪ
rebarbative rɪˈbɑːbətɪv [rəˈb-]
rebate (*s.*) (*discount*), -s ˈriːbeɪt [rɪˈbeɪt],
-s

rebat|e (*v.*) (*heraldic term*), -es, -ing, -ed
ˈræbɪt, -s, -ɪŋ, -ɪd
Rebecca rɪˈbekə [rəˈb-]
rebec(k), -s ˈriːbek [ˈre-], -s
rebel (*s.*), -s ˈrebl, -z
rebel (*v.*), -s, -ling, -led rɪˈbel [rəˈb-], -z,
-ɪŋ, -d
rebellion, -s rɪˈbeljən [rəˈb-], -z
rebellious, -ly, -ness rɪˈbeljəs [rəˈb-], -lɪ,
-nɪs [-nəs]
re-bind, -s, -ing, re-bound ˌriːˈbaɪnd, -z,
-ɪŋ, ˌriːˈbaʊnd
rebirth, -s ˌriːˈbɜːθ, -s
reborn ˌriːˈbɔːn
rebound (*s.*), -s ˈriːbaʊnd [rɪˈbaʊnd,
ˌriːˈbaʊnd], -z
rebound (*adj.*) ˌriːˈbaʊnd
rebound (*v.*), -s, -ing, -ed rɪˈbaʊnd
[ˌriːˈb-], -z, -ɪŋ, -ɪd
rebuff (*s. v.*), -s, -ing, -ed rɪˈbʌf, -s, -ɪŋ,
-t
rebuil|d, -ds, -ding, -t ˌriːˈbɪl|d, -dz,
-dɪŋ, -t
rebuk|e (*s. v.*), -es, -ing/ly, -ed rɪˈbjuːk
[rəˈb-], -s, -ɪŋ/lɪ, -t
rebus, -es ˈriːbəs, -ɪz
rebut, -s, -ting, -ted rɪˈbʌt, -s, -ɪŋ, -ɪd
rebutt|able, -al/s, -er/s rɪˈbʌt|əbl, -l/z,
-ə*/z
recalcitrant (*s. adj.*), -s rɪˈkælsɪtrənt
[rəˈk-], -s
recall (*s. v.*), -s, -ing, -ed rɪˈkɔːl [rəˈk-,
also ˈriːkɔːl *as noun*], -z, -ɪŋ, -d
recant, -s, -ing, -ed rɪˈkænt, -s, -ɪŋ, -ɪd
recantation, -s ˌriːkænˈteɪʃn, -z
recapitulat|e, -es, -ing, -ed ˌriːkəˈpɪtjʊ-
leɪt, -s, -ɪŋ, -ɪd
recapitulation, -s ˈriːkəˌpɪtjʊˈleɪʃn, -z
recapitulatory ˌriːkəˈpɪtjʊlətərɪ [-leɪtərɪ]
recapt|ure (*s. v.*), -ures, -uring, -ured
ˌriːˈkæptʃ|ə*, -əz, -ərɪŋ, -əd
recast, -s, -ing ˌriːˈkɑːst, -s, -ɪŋ
recce (**R.**) ˈrekɪ
reced|e, -es, -ing, -ed rɪˈsiːd [riː-], -z,
-ɪŋ, -ɪd
receipt (*s. v.*), -s, -ing, -ed rɪˈsiːt [rəˈs-],
-s, -ɪŋ, -ɪd
receiv|e, -es, -ing, -ed, -er/s; -able
rɪˈsiːv [rəˈs-], -z, -ɪŋ, -d, -ə*/z; -əbl
recency ˈriːsnsɪ
recension, -s rɪˈsenʃn [rəˈs-], -z
recent, -ly ˈriːsnt, -lɪ
receptacle, -s rɪˈseptəkl [rəˈs-], -z
reception, -s rɪˈsepʃn [rəˈs-], -z
receptionist, -s rɪˈsepʃənɪst [rəˈs-, -ʃn̩ɪst,
-ʃnɪst], -s
receptive, -ness rɪˈseptɪv [rəˈs-], -nɪs
[-nəs]

411

receptivity ˌresep'trvətɪ [ˌriːs-, ˌrɪs-, -ɪtɪ]

recess, -es rɪ'ses [rəˈs-, 'riːses], -ɪz

recession, -s rɪˈseʃn [rəˈs-], -z

recessional, -s rɪˈseʃənl [rəˈs-, -ʃn̩l, -ʃnl̩, -ʃənəl], -z

Rechab 'riːkæb

recherché rəˈʃeəʃeɪ (rəʃɛrʃe)

re-christ|en, -ens, -ening, -ened ˌriːˈkrɪs|n, -nz, -n̩ɪŋ [-nɪŋ], -nd

recidivist, -s rɪˈsɪdɪvɪst, -s

recipe, -s 'resɪpɪ [-sə-, -piː], -z

recipient, -s rɪˈsɪpɪənt [rəˈs-, -pjənt], -s

reciproc|al (s. adj.), **-als, -ally, -alness** rɪˈsɪprək|l [rəˈs-, -prʊk-], -lz, -əlɪ, -lnɪs [-nəs]

reciprocat|e, -es, -ing, -ed rɪˈsɪprəkeɪt [rəˈs-, -prʊk-], -s, -ɪŋ, -ɪd

reciprocation rɪˌsɪprəˈkeɪʃn [rəˌs-, -prʊˈk-]

reciprocity ˌresɪˈprɒsətɪ [-ɪtɪ]

recital, -s rɪˈsaɪtl [rəˈs-], -z

recitation, -s ˌresɪˈteɪʃn, -z

recitative, -s ˌresɪtəˈtiːv, -z

recit|e, -es, -ing, -ed, -er/s rɪˈsaɪt [rəˈs-], -s, -ɪŋ, -ɪd, -ə*/z

reck, -s, -ing, -ed rek, -s, -ɪŋ, -t

reckless, -ly, -ness 'reklɪs [-ləs], -lɪ, -nɪs [-nəs]

reck|on, -ons, -oning/s, -oned, -oner/s 'rek|ən, -ənz, -n̩ɪŋ/z [-nɪŋ/z, -ənɪŋ/z], -ənd, -n̩ə*/z [-ənə*/z]

reclaim, -s, -ing, -ed rɪˈkleɪm [ˌriː-], -z, -ɪŋ, -d

reclaimable rɪˈkleɪməbl [ˌriː-]

reclamation, -s ˌreklə'meɪʃn, -z

reclin|e, -es, -ing, -ed rɪˈklaɪn [rəˈk-], -z, -ɪŋ, -d

recluse, -s rɪˈkluːs, -ɪz

recognition, -s ˌrekəg'nɪʃn, -z

recognizab|le [-isa-], -ly 'rekəgnaɪzəb|l [ˌrekəg'n-], -lɪ

recognizance [-isa-], -s rɪˈkɒgnɪzəns [rəˈk-, -'kɒnɪ-], -ɪz

recogniz|e [-is|e], -es, -ing, -ed 'rekəgnaɪz, -ɪz, -ɪŋ, -d

recoil (s.), **-s** 'riːkɔɪl [rɪˈkɔɪl], -z

recoil (v.), **-s, -ing, -ed** rɪˈkɔɪl [rəˈk-], -z, -ɪŋ, -d

recollect (remember), **-s, -ing, -ed** ˌrekəˈlekt [-kl̩ˈekt, '---], -s, -ɪŋ, -ɪd

recollect (regain (one's composure, etc.)), **-s, -ing, -ed** ˌrekəˈlekt [-kl̩ˈekt, ˌriːkə'lekt], -s, -ɪŋ, -ɪd

re-collect (collect over again), **-s, -ing, -ed** ˌriːkə'lekt, -s, -ɪŋ, -ɪd

recollection, -s ˌrekə'lekʃn [-kl̩'ek-], -z

recommenc|e, -es, -ing, -ed ˌriːkə'mens [ˌrekə'm-], -ɪz, -ɪŋ, -t

recommend, -s, -ing, -ed; -able ˌrekə'mend, -z, -ɪŋ, -ɪd; -əbl

recommendation, -s ˌrekəmen'deɪʃn [-km-, -mən-], -z

recompens|e (s. v.), **-es, -ing, -ed** 'rekəmpens [-km-], -ɪz, -ɪŋ, -t

recompos|e, -es, -ing, -ed ˌriːkəm'pəʊz, -ɪz, -ɪŋ, -d

reconcilab|le, -ly 'rekənsaɪləb|l [ˌrekən's-, -kn-], -lɪ

reconcil|e, -es, -ing, -ed, -er/s 'rekənsaɪl [-kn-], -z, -ɪŋ, -d, -ə*/z

reconciliation, -s ˌrekənsɪlɪ'eɪʃn [-kn-], -z

recondite 'rekəndaɪt [rɪˈkɒnd-, rəˈk-]

reconduct, -s, -ing, -ed ˌriːkən'dʌkt, -s, -ɪŋ, -ɪd

reconnaissance, -s rɪˈkɒnɪsəns [rəˈk-, -'kɒnəs-], -ɪz

reconnoit|re, -res, -ring, -red ˌrekə'nɔɪt|ə*, -əz, -ərɪŋ, -əd

reconqu|er, -ers, -ering, -ered ˌriːˈkɒŋk|ə*, -əz, -ərɪŋ, -əd

reconquest, -s ˌriːˈkɒŋkwest, -s

reconsid|er, -ers, -ering, -ered ˌriːkən'sɪd|ə* [-kn-], -əz, -ərɪŋ, -əd

reconsideration 'riːkənˌsɪdə'reɪʃn [-kn-]

reconstitut|e, -es, -ing, -ed ˌriːˈkɒnstɪtjuːt, -s, -ɪŋ, -ɪd

reconstitution, -s 'riːˌkɒnstɪ'tjuːʃn, -z

reconstruct, -s, -ing, -ed ˌriːkən'strʌkt [-kn-], -s, -ɪŋ, -ɪd

reconstruction, -s ˌriːkən'strʌkʃn [-kn-], -z

reconversion, -s ˌriːkən'vɜːʃn [-kn-], -z

reconvey, -s, -ing, -ed ˌriːkən'veɪ, -z, -ɪŋ, -d

record (s.), **-s** 'rekɔːd, -z

record (v.), **-s, -ing, -ed, -er/s; -able** rɪˈkɔːd [rəˈk-], -z, -ɪŋ, -ɪd, -ə*/z; -əbl

recorder (musical instrument), **-s** rɪˈkɔːdə* [rəˈk-], -z

record-player, -s 'rekɔːdˌpleɪə*, -z

recount (s.), **-s** 'riːkaʊnt [ˌriːˈkaʊnt], -s

recount (v.) (count again), **-s, -ing, -ed** ˌriːˈkaʊnt, -s, -ɪŋ, -ɪd

recount (v.) (narrate), **-s, -ing, -ed** rɪˈkaʊnt, -s, -ɪŋ, -ɪd

recoup, -s, -ing, -ed, -ment rɪˈkuːp, -s, -ɪŋ, -t, -mənt

recourse rɪˈkɔːs [rəˈk-, -'kɔəs]

recov|er (get back, come back to health, etc.), **-ers, -ering, -ered; -erable** rɪˈkʌv|ə* [rəˈk-], -əz, -ərɪŋ, -əd; -ərəbl

recover (cover again), **-s, -ing, -ed** ˌriːˈkʌvə*, -z, -ɪŋ, -d

recover|y, -ies rɪˈkʌvər|ɪ [rəˈk-], -ɪz

recreant (s. adj.), **-s, -ly** 'rekrɪənt, -s, -lɪ

recreat|e (*refresh*), **-es, -ing, -ed; -ive** 'rekrɪeɪt, -s, -ɪŋ, -ɪd; -ɪv
re-creat|e (*create anew*), **-es, -ing, -ed** ˌriːkriːˈeɪt [-krɪ-], -s, -ɪŋ, -ɪd
recreation (*refreshment, amusement*), **-s; -al** ˌrekrɪˈeɪʃn, -z; -əl
re-creation (*creating anew*), **-s** ˌriːkrɪˈeɪʃn, -z
recriminat|e, -es, -ing, -ed, -or/s rɪˈkrɪmɪneɪt [rəˈk-, -mən-], -s, -ɪŋ, -ɪd, -ə*/z
recrimination, -s rɪˌkrɪmɪˈneɪʃn [rəˌk-, -məˈn-], -z
recriminatory rɪˈkrɪmɪnətərɪ [rəˈk-, -mən-]
recross, -es, -ing, -ed ˌriːˈkrɒs [*old-fashioned* -ˈkrɔːs, *also* ˈriːk- *when contrasted with* **cross**], -ɪz, -ɪŋ, -t
recrudesc|e, -es, -ing, -ed ˌriːkruːˈdes [ˌrek-], -ɪz, -ɪŋ, -t
recrudescen|ce, -t ˌriːkruːˈdesn|s [ˌrek-], -t
recruit (*s. v.*), **-s, -ing, -ed, -er/s, -ment** rɪˈkruːt [rəˈk-], -s, -ɪŋ, -ɪd, -ə*/z, -mənt
rectal ˈrektəl [-tl]
rectangle, -s ˈrekˌtæŋgl [ˈrektˌæŋ-], -z
rectangular, -ly rekˈtæŋgjʊlə* [rektˈæŋ-, -gjəl-], -lɪ
rectification, -s ˌrektɪfɪˈkeɪʃn, -z
recti|fy, -fies, -fying, -fied, -fier/s; -fiable ˈrektɪ|faɪ, -faɪz, -faɪɪŋ, -faɪd, -faɪə*/z; -faɪəbl
rectiline|al, -ar ˌrektɪˈlɪnɪ|əl [-nj|əl], -ə*
rectitude ˈrektɪtjuːd
recto ˈrektəʊ
rector, -s; -ate/s, -ship/s ˈrektə*, -z; -rət/s [-rɪt/s], -ʃɪp/s
rectorial rekˈtɔːrɪəl
rector|y, -ies ˈrektər|ɪ, -ɪz
rect|um, -ums, -a ˈrekt|əm, -əmz, -ə
Reculver, -s rɪˈkʌlvə* [rəˈk-], -d
recumben|ce, -cy, -t/ly rɪˈkʌmbən|s [rəˈk-], -sɪ, -t/lɪ
†**recuperat|e, -es, -ing, -ed** rɪˈkuːpəreɪt [rəˈk-, -ˈkjuː-], -s, -ɪŋ, -ɪd
recuperation rɪˌkuːpəˈreɪʃn [rəˌk-, -ˌkjuː-]
recur, -s, -ring, -red rɪˈkɜː* [rəˈk-], -z, -rɪŋ [rɪˈkʌrɪŋ], -d
recurren|ce, -ces, -t/ly rɪˈkʌrən|s [rəˈk-], -sɪz, -t/lɪ
recursive (*s. adj.*), **-s** rɪˈkɜːsɪv [ˌriːˈk-], -z
recurv|e, -es, -ing, -ed ˌriːˈkɜːv, -z, -ɪŋ, -d
recusancy ˈrekjʊzənsɪ [rɪˈkjuː-, rə-ˈkjuː-]

recusant, -s ˈrekjʊzənt [rɪˈkjuːz-, rə-ˈkjuːz-], -s
re-cycl|e, -es, -ing, -ed ˌriːˈsaɪkl, -z, -ɪŋ, -d
red (*s. adj.*), **-s; -der, -dest, -ness** red, -z; -ə*, -ɪst, -nɪs [-nəs]
redact, -s, -ing, -ed, -or/s rɪˈdækt, -s, -ɪŋ, -ɪd, -ə*/z
redaction, -s rɪˈdækʃn, -z
redbreast, -s ˈredbrest, -s
redcap, -s ˈredkæp, -s
Redcliffe ˈredklɪf
redcoat, -s ˈredkəʊt, -s
Reddaway ˈredəweɪ
redd|en, -ens, -ening, -ened ˈred|n, -nz, -nɪŋ [-nɪŋ], -nd
Redding ˈredɪŋ
reddish, -ness ˈredɪʃ, -nɪs [-nəs]
Redditch ˈredɪtʃ
reddle ˈredl
redecorat|e, -es, -ing, -ed ˌriːˈdekəreɪt, -s, -ɪŋ, -ɪd
redeem, -s, -ing, -ed; -able rɪˈdiːm [rəˈd-], -z, -ɪŋ, -d; -əbl
redeemer (**R.**), **-s** rɪˈdiːmə* [rəˈd-], -z
redeliver, -s, -ing, -ed; -y ˌriːdɪˈlɪvə*, -z, -rɪŋ, -d; -rɪ
redemption (**R.**), **-s** rɪˈdempʃn [rəˈd-], -z
redemptive rɪˈdemptɪv [rəˈd-]
re-deploy, -s, -ing, -ed, -ment/s ˌriːdɪˈplɔɪ, -z, -ɪŋ, -d, -mənt/s
Red|fern, -field ˈred|fɜːn, -fiːld
Redgauntlet ˌredˈgɔːntlɪt [-lət]
Redgrave ˈredgreɪv
red-handed ˌredˈhændɪd
redhead (**R.**), **-s** ˈredhed, -z
Redheugh (*bridge in Newcastle upon Tyne*) ˈredjəf
Redhill ˌredˈhɪl [ˈ--]
red-hot ˌredˈhɒt
re|-dial, -dials, -dialling, -dialled ˌriː|ˈdaɪəl, -ˈdaɪəlz, -ˈdaɪəlɪŋ, -ˈdaɪəld
rediffus|e, -es, -ing, -ed ˌriːdɪˈfjuːz, -ɪz, -ɪŋ, -d
rediffusion ˌriːdɪˈfjuːʒn
redintegrat|e, -es, -ing, -ed reˈdɪntɪgreɪt [rɪˈd-], -s, -ɪŋ, -ɪd
redirect, -s, -ing, -ed ˌriːdɪˈrekt [-dəˈr-, -daɪˈr-], -s, -ɪŋ, -ɪd
rediscover, -s, -ing, -ed; -y ˌriːdɪˈskʌvə*, -z, -rɪŋ, -d; -rɪ
re|distribute, -distributes, -distributing, -distributed ˌriː|dɪˈstrɪbjuːt [-ˈdɪstrɪbjuːt], -dɪˈstrɪbjuːts [-ˈdɪstrɪbjuːts], -dɪˈstrɪbjʊtɪŋ [-ˈdɪstrɪbjuːtɪŋ], -dɪˈstrɪbjʊtɪd [-ˈdɪstrɪbjuːtɪd]
redistribution, -s ˈriːˌdɪstrɪˈbjuːʃn, -z

redivide—refill

redivid|e, -es, -ing, -ed ˌriːdɪˈvaɪd, -z,
-ɪŋ, -ɪd
redivivus ˌredɪˈvaɪvəs
red-letter ˌredˈletə*
Redmond ˈredmənd
re|-do, -does, -doing, -did, -done
ˌriːˈduː, -ˈdʌz, -ˈduːɪŋ [-ˈdʊɪŋ], -ˈdɪd,
-ˈdʌn
redolen|ce, -t ˈredələn|s [-dəʊl-], -t
redoub|le, -les, -ling, -led ˌriːˈdʌb|l
[rɪˈd-], -lz, -lɪŋ [-l̩ŋ], -ld
redoubt, -s; -able rɪˈdaʊt [rəˈd-], -s;
-əbl
redound, -s, -ing, -ed rɪˈdaʊnd [rəˈd-],
-z, -ɪŋ, -ɪd
redpole, -s ˈredpəʊl [-pɒl], -z
redraft, -s, -ing, -ed ˌriːˈdrɑːft, -s, -ɪŋ,
-ɪd
re-draw, -s, -ing, redrew, redrawn
ˌriːˈdrɔː, -z, -ɪŋ, ˌriːˈdruː, ˌriːˈdrɔːn
redress (s. v.) (amends, make amends
for), -es, -ing, -ed rɪˈdres [rəˈd-], -ɪz,
-ɪŋ, -t
redress (dress again), -es, -ing, -ed
ˌriːˈdres, -ɪz, -ɪŋ, -t
Redriff ˈredrɪf
Redruth ˈredruːθ, locally rɪˈdruːθ
redshank, -s ˈredʃæŋk, -s
redskin (R.), -s ˈredskɪn, -z
redstart, -s ˈredstɑːt, -s
red-tape ˌredˈteɪp
red-tapism ˌredˈteɪpɪzəm
reduc|e, -es, -ing, -ed, -er/s rɪˈdjuːs
[rəˈd-], -ɪz, -ɪŋ, -t, -ə*/z
reducibility rɪˌdjuːsəˈbɪlətɪ [rəˈd-, -sɪˈb-,
-lɪt-]
reducible rɪˈdjuːsəbl [rəˈd-, -sɪb-]
reduction, -s rɪˈdʌkʃn [rəˈd-], -z
redundan|ce, -cy, -cies, -t/ly rɪˈdʌnd-
ən|s [rəˈd-], -sɪ, -sɪz, -t/lɪ
redundantiz|e [-is|e], -es, -ing, -ed
rɪˈdʌndəntaɪz [rəˈd-], -ɪz, -ɪŋ, -d
reduplicat|e, -es, -ing, -ed rɪˈdjuːplɪkeɪt
[rəˈd-, -riː-], -s, -ɪŋ, -ɪd
reduplication, -s rɪˌdjuːplɪˈkeɪʃn [rəˈd-],
-z
reduplicative rɪˈdjuːplɪkətɪv [rəˈd-,
-keɪt-]
redwing, -s ˈredwɪŋ, -z
redwood (R.) ˈredwʊd
Reece riːs
re-ech|o, -oes, -oing, -oed riːˈek|əʊ
[rɪˈe-], -əʊz, -əʊɪŋ, -əʊd
reed (s. v.) (R.), -s, -ing, -ed riːd, -z, -ɪŋ,
-ɪd
re-edit, -s, -ing, -ed ˌriːˈedɪt, -s, -ɪŋ, -ɪd
re-edition, -s ˌriːɪˈdɪʃn, -z
reed-pipe, -s ˈriːdpaɪp, -s

re-educat|e, -es, -ing, -ed ˌriːˈedʒʊkeɪt
[riːˈed-, -djuː-, -djʊ-, -dʒuː-], -s, -ɪŋ,
-ɪd
re-education ˈriːˌedʒʊˈkeɪʃn [-djʊ-,
-dʒuː-, -djuː-]
reed-warbler, -s ˈriːdˌwɔːblə* [ˌ-ˈ--], -z
reed|y, -ier, -iest, -iness ˈriːd|ɪ, -ɪə*,
-ɪɪst, -mɪs [-ɪnəs]
reef (s. v.), -s, -ing, -ed riːf, -s, -ɪŋ, -t
reefer, -s ˈriːfə*, -z
reek (s. v.) -s (R.), -ing, -ed riːk, -s, -ɪŋ,
-t
Reekie ˈriːkɪ
reel (s. v.), -s, -ing, -ed riːl, -z, -ɪŋ, -d
re-elect, -s, -ing, -ed ˌriːɪˈlekt, -s, -ɪŋ, -ɪd
re-election, -s ˌriːɪˈlekʃn, -z
re-eligible ˌriːˈelɪdʒəbl [-dʒɪb-]
re-embark, -s, -ing, -ed ˌriːɪmˈbɑːk
[ˌriːem-], -s, -ɪŋ, -t
re-embarkation, -s ˈriːˌembɑːˈkeɪʃn, -z
re-enact, -s, -ing, -ed, -ment/s ˌriː-
ɪˈnækt [ˌriːeˈn-], -s, -ɪŋ, -ɪd, -mənt/s
re-engag|e, -es, -ing, -ed, -ement/s
ˌriːɪnˈgeɪdʒ [ˌriːen-], -ɪz, -ɪŋ, -d,
-mənt/s
re-enlist, -s, -ing, -ed ˌriːɪnˈlɪst [ˌriːen-],
-s, -ɪŋ, -ɪd
re-ent|er, -ers, -ering, -ered ˌriːˈent|ə*
[rɪˈen-], -əz, -ərɪŋ, -əd
re-entrant riːˈentrənt [rɪˈen-]
re-entr|y, -ies riːˈentr|ɪ [rɪˈen-], -ɪz
Rees riːs
Reese riːs
re-establish, -es, -ing, -ed, -ment
ˌriːɪˈstæblɪʃ [ˌriːeˈs-], -ɪz, -ɪŋ, -t, -mənt
re-examination, -s ˈriːɪgˌzæmɪˈneɪʃn
[ˈriːeg-, -məˈn-], -z
re-examin|e, -es, -ing, -ed ˌriːɪgˈzæmɪn
[ˌriːeg-], -z, -ɪŋ, -d
re-export (s.), -s ˈriːˈekspɔːt, -s
re-export (v.), -s, -ing, -ed ˌriːekˈspɔːt
[ˌriːɪkˈsp-], -s, -ɪŋ, -ɪd
re-fac|e, -es, -ing, -ed ˌriːˈfeɪs, -ɪz, -ɪŋ, -t
refashi|on, -ons, -oning, -oned ˌriː-
ˈfæʃ|n, -nz, -nɪŋ [-ənɪŋ], -nd
refection rɪˈfekʃn
refector|y, -ies rɪˈfektər|ɪ [rəˈf-, also
ˈrefɪkt-, esp. in monasteries], -ɪz
refer, -s, -ring, -red, -ral/s rɪˈfɜː* [rəˈf-],
-z, -rɪŋ, -d, -rəl/z
referable rɪˈfɜːrəbl [rəˈf-, ˈrefərəbl]
referee, -s ˌrefəˈriː:, -z
referen|ce/s, -t/s ˈrefrən|s/ɪz [-fər-], -t/s
referend|um, -ums, -a ˌrefəˈrend|əm,
-əmz, -ə
referential ˌrefəˈrenʃl
refill (s.), -s ˈriːfɪl [ˌriːˈfɪl], -z

414

refill (v.), -s, -ing, -ed ˌriːˈfɪl, -z, -ɪŋ, -d
refin|e, -es, -ing, -ed, -er/s, -ement/s rɪˈfaɪn [rəˈf-], -z, -ɪŋ, -d, -ə*/z, -mənt/s
refiner|y, -ies rɪˈfaɪnər|ɪ [rəˈf-], -ɪz
refit (s. v.), -s, -ting, -ted ˌriːˈfɪt (often '-- as noun), -s, -ɪŋ, -ɪd
reflat|e, -es, -ing, -ed ˌriːˈfleɪt, -s, -ɪŋ, -ɪd
†reflation riːˈfleɪʃn
reflect, -s, -ing/ly, -ed, -or/s rɪˈflekt [rəˈf-], -s, -ɪŋ/lɪ, -ɪd, -ə*/z
reflection, -s rɪˈflekʃn [rəˈf-], -z
reflective, -ly, -ness rɪˈflektɪv [rəˈf-], -lɪ, -nɪs [-nəs]
reflex (s. adj.), -es ˈriːfleks, -ɪz
reflexed rɪˈflekst [riːˈf-, ˈriːflekst]
reflexive rɪˈfleksɪv [rəˈf-]
refloat, -s, -ing, -ed ˌriːˈfləʊt, -s, -ɪŋ, -ɪd
refluent ˈreflʊənt [-flwənt]
reflux, -es ˈriːflʌks, -ɪz
re-foot, -s, -ing, -ed ˌriːˈfʊt, -s, -ɪŋ, -ɪd
reform (s. v.) (make better, become better, etc.), -s, -ing, -ed, -er/s; -able rɪˈfɔːm [rəˈf-], -z, -ɪŋ, -d, -ə*/z; -əbl
reform (v.) (form again), -s, -ing, -ed ˌriːˈfɔːm, -z, -ɪŋ, -d
reformation (R.), -s ˌrefəˈmeɪʃn [-fɔːˈm-], -z
reformative rɪˈfɔːmətɪv [rəˈf-]
reformator|y (s. adj.), -ies rɪˈfɔːmətər|ɪ [rəˈf-], -ɪz
reformist rɪˈfɔːmɪst [rəˈf-]
refract, -s, -ing, -ed, -or/s; -ive rɪˈfrækt [rəˈf-], -s, -ɪŋ, -ɪd, -ə*/z; -ɪv
refraction, -s rɪˈfrækʃn [rəˈf-], -z
refractor|y, -ily, -iness rɪˈfræktər|ɪ [rəˈf-], -əlɪ [-ɪlɪ], -ɪnɪs [-ɪnəs]
refrain (s. v.), -s, -ing, -ed rɪˈfreɪn [rəˈf-], -z, -ɪŋ, -d
refresh, -es, -ing/ly, -ingness, -ed, -er/s, -ment/s rɪˈfreʃ [rəˈf-], -ɪz, -ɪŋ/lɪ, -ɪŋnɪs [-nəs], -t, -ə*/z, -mənt/s
refrigerat|e, -es, -ing, -ed, -or/s rɪˈfrɪdʒəreɪt [rəˈf-], -s, -ɪŋ, -ɪd, -ə*/z
refrigeration rɪˌfrɪdʒəˈreɪʃn [rəˌf-]
reft reft
re-fuel, -s, -ling, -led ˌriːˈfjʊəl [-ˈfjuːəl, -ˈfjuːl], -z, -ɪŋ, -d
refuge, -s ˈrefjuːdʒ, -ɪz
refugee, -s ˌrefjuˈdʒiː [-fjuː-], -z
refulgen|ce, -t/ly rɪˈfʌldʒən|s [rəˈf-], -t/lɪ
refund (s.), -s ˈriːfʌnd, -z
refund (v.), -s, -ing, -ed riːˈfʌnd [ˌriːˈf-, rɪˈf-], -z, -ɪŋ, -ɪd
refurbish, -es, -ing, -ed ˌriːˈfɜːbɪʃ, -ɪz, -ɪŋ, -t

refurnish, -es, -ing, -ed ˌriːˈfɜːnɪʃ, -ɪz, -ɪŋ, -t
refusal, -s rɪˈfjuːzl [rəˈf-], -z
refuse (s. adj.) ˈrefjuːs
refus|e (v.), -es, -ing, -ed; -able rɪˈfjuːz [rəˈf-], -ɪz, -ɪŋ, -d; -əbl
refutability ˌrefjʊtəˈbɪlətɪ [rɪˌfjuːt-, rəˌfjuːt-, -lɪt-]
refutable ˈrefjʊtəbl [rɪˈfjuːt-, rəˈfjuːt-]
refutation, -s ˌrefjuːˈteɪʃn [-fjʊ-], -z
refut|e, -es, -ing, -ed rɪˈfjuːt [rəˈf-], -s, -ɪŋ, -ɪd
Reg (short for Reginald) redʒ
regain, -s, -ing, -ed rɪˈgeɪn [ˌriːˈg-], -z, -ɪŋ, -d
reg|al, -ally ˈriːg|l, -əlɪ
regal|e, -es, -ing, -ed rɪˈgeɪl, -z, -ɪŋ, -d
regalia rɪˈgeɪljə [rəˈg-, -lɪə]
Regan ˈriːgən
regard (s. v.), -s, -ing, -ed, -ant rɪˈgɑːd [rəˈg-], -z, -ɪŋ, -ɪd, -ənt
regardful rɪˈgɑːdfʊl [rəˈg-]
regardless, -ly, -ness rɪˈgɑːdlɪs [rəˈg-, -ləs], -lɪ, -nɪs [-nəs]
regatta, -s rɪˈgætə [rəˈg-], -z
regenc|y (R.), -ies ˈriːdʒəns|ɪ, -ɪz
regenerate (adj.) rɪˈdʒenərət [rəˈdʒ-, -rɪt, -reɪt]
regenerat|e (v.), -es, -ing, -ed rɪˈdʒenəreɪt [rəˈdʒ-, ˌriːˈdʒ-], -s, -ɪŋ, -ɪd
regeneration, -s rɪˌdʒenəˈreɪʃn [rəˌdʒ-, ˌriːdʒen-], -z
regent (R.), -s ˈriːdʒənt, -s
regentship, -s ˈriːdʒənt-ʃɪp, -s
Reggie ˈredʒɪ
Reggio ˈredʒɪəʊ (ˈreddʒo)
regicidal ˌredʒɪˈsaɪdl
regicide, -s ˈredʒɪsaɪd, -z
régie reɪˈʒiː [ˈreɪʒiː]
regil|d, -ds, -ding, -t ˌriːˈgɪl|d, -dz, -dɪŋ, -t
régime, -s reɪˈʒiːm [reˈʒ-, ˈ--] (reʒim), -z
regimen, -s ˈredʒɪmen, -z
regiment (s.), -s ˈredʒɪmənt, -s
regiment (v.), -s, -ing, -ed ˈredʒɪment [ˌ--ˈ-], -s, -ɪŋ, -ɪd
regimental (s. adj.), -s ˌredʒɪˈmentl [-dʒəˈm-], -z
regimentation ˌredʒɪmenˈteɪʃn [-mən-]
Regina rɪˈdʒaɪnə [rəˈdʒ-]
Reginald ˈredʒɪnld
region, -s ˈriːdʒən, -z
re|gional, -gionally ˈriː|dʒənl [-dʒənəl, -dʒn̩l, -dʒn̩l, -dʒənəl], -dʒnəlɪ [-dʒn̩lɪ, -dʒn̩lɪ, -dʒənəlɪ]
Regis ˈriːdʒɪs
regist|er (s. v.), -ers, -ering, -ered ˈredʒɪst|ə*, -əz, -ərɪŋ, -əd

415

registrant, -s 'redʒɪstrənt, -s
registrar, -s ˌredʒɪ'strɑː* ['---], -z
registrar|y, -ies 'redʒɪstrər|ɪ, -ɪz
registration, -s ˌredʒɪ'streɪʃn, -z
registr|y, -ies 'redʒɪstr|ɪ, -ɪz
Regius 'riːdʒjəs [-dʒɪəs, -dʒəs]
regn|al, -ant 'regn|əl, -ənt
regress (s.) 'riːgres
regress (v.), **-es, -ing, -ed** rɪ'gres [ˌriːˈg-], -ɪz, -ɪŋ, -t
regression, -s rɪ'greʃn [riːˈg-], -z
regressive, -ly rɪ'gresɪv [riːˈg-, ˌriːˈg-], -lɪ
regret (s. v.), **-s, -ting, -ted** rɪ'gret [rə'g-], -s, -ɪŋ, -ɪd
regret|ful, -fully rɪ'gret|fʊl [rə'g-], -fʊlɪ [-fəlɪ]
regrettab|le, -ly rɪ'gretəb|l [rə'g-], -lɪ
re-group, -s, -ing, -ed ˌriːˈgruːp, -s, -ɪŋ, -t
regular (s. adj.), **-s, -ly** 'regjʊlə* [-gjəl-], -z, -lɪ
regularity ˌregjʊ'lærətɪ [-gjə'l-, -ɪtɪ]
regularization [**-isa-**] ˌregjʊləraɪ'zeɪʃn [-gjəl-, -ɪ'z-]
regulariz|e [**-is|e**], **-es, -ing, -ed** 'regjʊ-ləraɪz [-gjəl-], -ɪz, -ɪŋ, -d
regulat|e, -es, -ing, -ed, -or/s 'regjʊleɪt [-gjəl-], -s, -ɪŋ, -ɪd, -ə*/z
regulation, -s ˌregjʊ'leɪʃn [-gjə'l-], -z
†**regulative** 'regjʊlətɪv [-gjəl-, -leɪt-]
regul|us (**R.**), **-i** 'regjʊl|əs [-gjəl-], -aɪ
regurgitat|e, -es, -ing, -ed rɪ'gɜːdʒɪteɪt [ˌriːˈg-], -s, -ɪŋ, -ɪd
rehabilitat|e, -es, -ing, -ed ˌriːə'bɪlɪteɪt [ˌriːhə-, ˌrɪə-], -s, -ɪŋ, -ɪd
rehabilitation, -s 'riːəˌbɪlɪ'teɪʃn ['riːhə-, 'rɪə-], -z
Rehan 'riːən, 'reɪən
re-hash (v.), **-es, -ing, -ed** ˌriːˈhæʃ, -ɪz, -ɪŋ, -t
re-hash (s.), **-es** 'riːhæʃ [ˌ-'-], -ɪz
rehear, -s, -ing, reheard ˌriːˈhɪə*, -z, -rɪŋ, ˌriːˈhɜːd
rehears|e, -es, -ing, -ed; -al/s rɪ'hɜːs [rə'h-], -ɪz, -ɪŋ, -t; -l/z
rehoboam (**R.**) ˌriːə'bəʊəm [ˌriːhə-, rɪə-]
re-hous|e, -es, -ing, -ed ˌriːˈhaʊz, -ɪz, -ɪŋ, -d
Reich raɪk [raɪx] (raiç)
Reichstag 'raɪkstɑːg [-tɑːk] ('raiçstaːk, -taːx)
Reid riːd
Reigate 'raɪgeɪt [-gɪt]
reign (s. v.), **-s, -ing, -ed** reɪn, -z, -ɪŋ, -d
Reigny (in Cumbria) 'reɪnɪ
Reikjavik 'reɪkjəviːk ['rek-, -vɪk]
Reilly 'raɪlɪ

reimburs|e, -es, -ing, -ed; -ement/s ˌriːɪm'bɜːs, -ɪz, -ɪŋ, -t; -mənt/s
reimport, -s, -ing, -ed ˌriːɪm'pɔːt, -s, -ɪŋ, -ɪd
reimpos|e, -es, -ing, -ed ˌriːɪm'pəʊz, -ɪz, -ɪŋ, -d
reimpression, -s ˌriːɪm'preʃn, -z
R(h)eims riːmz
rein (s. v.), **-s, -ing, -ed** reɪn, -z, -ɪŋ, -d
reincarnate (adj.) ˌriːɪn'kɑːneɪt [-nət, -nɪt]
reincarnat|e (v.), **-es, -ing, -ed** riːˈɪnkɑː-neɪt [ˌriːɪn'kɑːn-], -s, -ɪŋ, -ɪd
reincarnation, -s ˌriːɪnkɑːˈneɪʃn, -z
reindeer 'reɪn,dɪə*
reinforc|e, -es, -ing, -ed, -ement/s ˌriːɪn'fɔːs, -ɪz, -ɪŋ, -t, -mənt/s
reinstal|l, -ls, -ling, -led, -ment ˌriː-ɪn'stɔːl, -z, -ɪŋ, -d, -mənt
reinstat|e, -es, -ing, -ed, -ement ˌriːɪn-'steɪt, -s, -ɪŋ, -ɪd, -mənt
reinsur|e, -es, -ing, -ed; -ance/s ˌriː-ɪn'ʃɔː* [-'ʃɔə*, -'ʃʊə*], -z, -rɪŋ, -d; -rəns/ɪz
reintroduc|e, -es, -ing, -ed 'riː,ɪntrə-'djuːs [-trʊ'd-], -ɪz, -ɪŋ, -t
reintroduction 'riː,ɪntrə'dʌkʃn [-trʊ'd-]
reinvest, -s, -ing, -ed ˌriːɪn'vest, -s, -ɪŋ, -ɪd
reis (monetary unit) (sing.) reɪs, (plur.) reɪs [reɪz]
reiss|ue (s. v.), **-ues, -uing, -ued** ˌriː'ɪʃ|uː [-'ɪʃj|uː, -'ɪsj|uː], -uːz, -uːɪŋ [-ʊɪŋ], -uːd
reiterat|e, -es, -ing, -ed riː'ɪtəreɪt [rɪ'ɪt-], -s, -ɪŋ, -ɪd
reiteration riː,ɪtə'reɪʃn [rɪ,ɪ-]
reiterative riː'ɪtərətɪv [rɪ'ɪt-, -təreɪt-]
Reith riːθ
reject (s.), **-s** 'riːdʒekt, -s
reject (v.), **-s, -ing, -ed, -or/s** rɪ'dʒekt [rə'dʒ-], -s, -ɪŋ, -ɪd, -ə*/z
rejection, -s rɪ'dʒekʃn [rə'dʒ-], -z
rejoic|e, -es, -ing/ly, -ings, -ed rɪ'dʒɔɪs [rə'dʒ-], -ɪz, -ɪŋ/lɪ, -ɪŋz, -t
rejoin (answer), **-s, -ing, -ed** rɪ'dʒɔɪn [rə'dʒ-], -z, -ɪŋ, -d
rejoin (join again), **-s, -ing, -ed** ˌriː'dʒɔɪn [riː'dʒ-, rɪ'dʒ-], -z, -ɪŋ, -d
rejoinder, -s rɪ'dʒɔɪndə* [rə'dʒ-], -z
rejuvenat|e, -es, -ing, -ed rɪ'dʒuː-vəneɪt [-vɪn-], -s, -ɪŋ, -ɪd
rejuvenation rɪ,dʒuːvə'neɪʃn [rə'dʒ-, -vɪ'n-]
rejuvenesc|e, -es, -ing, -ed ˌriːdʒuːvə'nes [rɪ,dʒuː-, -vɪ'n-], -ɪz, -ɪŋ, -t
rejuvenescen|ce, -t ˌriːdʒuːvə'nesn|s [rɪ,dʒuː-, -vɪ'n-], -t

rekind|le, -les, -ling, -led ˌriːˈkɪnd|l, -lz, -lɪŋ [-l̩ŋ], -ld

re-lab|el, -els, -elling, -elled ˌriːˈleɪb|l, -lz, -lɪŋ [-lɪŋ], -ld

relaps|e (s. v.), -es, -ing, -ed rɪˈlæps [rəˈl-, also ˈriːlæps as noun], -ɪz, -ɪŋ, -t

†relat|e, -es, -ing, -ed, -er/s rɪˈleɪt [rəˈl-], -s, -ɪŋ, -ɪd, -ə*/z

relation, -s; -ship/s rɪˈleɪʃn [rəˈl-], -z; -ʃɪp/s

relatival ˌreləˈtaɪvl

relative (s. adj.), -s, -ly ˈrelətɪv, -z, -lɪ

relativity ˌreləˈtɪvɪtɪ [-ɪtɪ]

relax, -es, -ing, -ed; able, -ant/s rɪˈlæks [rəˈl-], -ɪz, -ɪŋ, -t; -əbl, -ənt/s

relaxation, -s ˌriːlækˈseɪʃn, -z

relay (s.) (fresh set of horses, relief gang), -s ˈriːleɪ [rɪˈleɪ], -z
   Note.—Always ˈriːleɪ in relay race, and in broadcasting.

relay (s.) (electrical apparatus), -s ˌriːˈleɪ [ˈ--], -z

relay (v.) (lay again), -s, -ing, relaid ˌriːˈleɪ, -z, -ɪŋ, ˌriːˈleɪd

relay (v.) (in broadcasting), -s, -ing, -ed riːˈleɪ [ˈriːleɪ], -z, -ɪŋ, -d

release (s.) (liberation, discharge), -s rɪˈliːs [rəˈl-], -ɪz

release (s.) (new lease), -s ˌriːˈliːs [ˈriːliːs], -ɪz

releas|e (v.), -es, -ing, -ed rɪˈliːs [rəˈl-], -ɪz, -ɪŋ, -t

relegat|e, -es, -ing, -ed ˈreligeɪt [-ləg-], -s, -ɪŋ, -ɪd

relegation ˌreliˈgeɪʃn [-ləˈg-]

relent, -s, -ing, -ed rɪˈlent [rəˈl-], -s, -ɪŋ, -ɪd

relentless, -ly, -ness rɪˈlentlɪs [rəˈl-, -ləs], -lɪ, -nɪs

re-let (s. v.), -s, -ting ˌriːˈlet, -s, -ɪŋ

relevan|ce, -cy, -t/ly ˈreləvən|s [-lɪv-], -sɪ, -t/lɪ

reliability rɪˌlaɪəˈbɪlətɪ [rəˌlaɪ-, -lɪt-]

reliab|le, -ly, -leness rɪˈlaɪəb|l [rəˈl-], -lɪ, -lnɪs [-nəs]

relian|ce, -t rɪˈlaɪən|s [rəˈl-], -t

relic, -s ˈrelɪk, -s

relict, -s ˈrelɪkt, -s

relief, -s rɪˈliːf [rəˈl-], -s

reliev|e, -es, -ing, -ed; -able rɪˈliːv [rəˈl-], -z, -ɪŋ, -d; -əbl

relievo rɪˈliːvəʊ

re|light, -lights, -lighting, -lighted, -lit ˌriː|ˈlaɪt, -ˈlaɪts, -ˈlaɪtɪŋ, -ˈlaɪtɪd, -ˈlɪt

religion, -s rɪˈlɪdʒən [rəˈl-], -z

religioni|sm, -st/s rɪˈlɪdʒənɪ|zəm [rəˈl-, -dʒn̩-], -st/s

religiosity rɪˌlɪdʒɪˈɒsətɪ [rəˌl-, -ɪtɪ]

religioso rɪˌlɪdʒɪˈəʊsəʊ [reˌl-, rəˌl-, -ˈəʊzəʊ]

religious, -ly, -ness rɪˈlɪdʒəs [rəˈl-], -lɪ, -nɪs [-nəs]

relin|e, -es, -ing, -ed ˌriːˈlaɪn, -z, -ɪŋ, -d

relinquish, -es, -ing, -ed, -ment rɪˈlɪŋkwɪʃ [rəˈl-], -ɪz, -ɪŋ, -t, -mənt

reliquar|y, -ies ˈrelɪkwər|ɪ, -ɪz

reliques (in Percy's Reliques) ˈrelɪks, (otherwise) rɪˈliːks [rəˈl-]

relish (s. v.), -es, -ing, -ed ˈrelɪʃ, -ɪz, -ɪŋ, -t

re-liv|e, -es, -ing, -ed ˌriːˈlɪv, -z, -ɪŋ, -d

reload, -s, -ing, -ed ˌriːˈləʊd, -z, -ɪŋ, -ɪd

reluctanc|e, -t/ly rɪˈlʌktən|s [rəˈl-], -t/lɪ

rel|y, -ies, -ying, -ied rɪˈl|aɪ [rəˈl-], -aɪz, -aɪɪŋ, -aɪd

remain, -s, -ing, -ed rɪˈmeɪn [rəˈm-], -z, -ɪŋ, -d

remainder, -s rɪˈmeɪndə* [rəˈm-], -z

re-make (s.), -s ˈriːmeɪk, -s

remak|e (v.), -es, -ing, remade ˌriːˈmeɪk, -s, -ɪŋ, ˌriːˈmeɪd

remand (s.), -s rɪˈmɑːnd [rəˈm-], -z

remand (v.), -s, -ing, -ed rɪˈmɑːnd [rəˈm-], -z, -ɪŋ, -ɪd

remark (s. v.) (notice, comment), -s, -ing, -ed rɪˈmɑːk [rəˈm-], -s, -ɪŋ, -t

re-mark (v.) (mark again), -s, -ing, -ed ˌriːˈmɑːk, -s, -ɪŋ, -t

remarkab|le, -ly, -leness rɪˈmɑːkəb|l [rəˈm-], -lɪ, -lnɪs [-nəs]

remarr|y, -ies, -ying, -ied; -iage/s ˌriːˈmær|ɪ, -ɪz, -ɪɪŋ, -ɪd; -ɪdʒ/ɪz

Rembrandt, -s ˈrembrænt [-rənt], -s

R.E.M.E. ˈriːmɪ

†remediable rɪˈmiːdjəbl [rəˈm-, -dɪəb-]

remedial rɪˈmiːdjəl [rəˈm-, -dɪəl]

remed|y (s. v.), -ies, -ying, -ied; -yless ˈremədǀɪ [-mɪd|ɪ], -ɪz, -ɪɪŋ, -ɪd; -ɪlɪs [-ləs]

rememb|er, -ers, -ering, -ered rɪˈmemb|ə* [rəˈm-], -əz, -ərɪŋ, -əd

remembrance, -s; -r/s rɪˈmembrəns [rəˈm-], -ɪz; -ə*/z

re-militariz|e [-is|e], -es, -ing, -ed ˌriːˈmɪlɪtəraɪz [-lət-], -ɪz, -ɪŋ, -d

remind, -s, -ing, -ed, -er/s rɪˈmaɪnd [rəˈm-], -z, -ɪŋ, -ɪd, -ə*/z

Remington, -s ˈremɪŋtən, -z

reminisc|e, -es, -ing, -ed ˌremɪˈnɪs [-məˈn-], -ɪz, -ɪŋ, -t

reminiscen|ce, -ces, -t ˌremɪˈnɪsn|s [-məˈn-], -sɪz, -t

remis|e (s. v.) (thrust in fencing; carriage, coach-house, etc.), -es, -ing, -ed rəˈmiːz [rɪˈm-], -ɪz, -ɪŋ, -d

417

remis|e (*s. v.*) (*surrender*), **-es, -ing, -ed**
rɪ'maɪz [rə'm-], -ɪz, -ɪŋ, -d
remiss, -ly, -ness rɪ'mɪs [rə'm-], -lɪ, -nɪs
[-nəs]
remission, -s rɪ'mɪʃn [rə'm-], -z
remit (*s.*), **-s** 'riːmɪt, -s
remit (*v.*), **-s, -ting, -ted, -ter/s** rɪ'mɪt
[rə'm-], -s, -ɪŋ, -ɪd, -ə*/z
remittal, -s rɪ'mɪtl [rə'm-], -z
remittance, -s rɪ'mɪtəns [rə'm-], -ɪz
remnant, -s 'remnənt, -s
remod|el, -els, -elling, -elled ˌriː'mɒd|l,
-lz, -lɪŋ, -ld
remonetiz|e [-is|e], **-es, -ing, -ed**
riː'mʌnɪtaɪz, -ɪz, -ɪŋ, -d
remonstran|ce, -ces, -t/ly rɪ'mɒnstrən|s
[rə'm-], -sɪz, -t/lɪ
remonstrat|e, -es, -ing, -ed 'remənstreɪt
[rɪ'mɒns-, rə'm-], -s, -ɪŋ, -ɪd
remorse rɪ'mɔːs [rə'm-]
remorse|ful, -fully rɪ'mɔːs|fʊl [rə'm-],
-fʊlɪ [-fəlɪ]
remorseless, -ly, -ness rɪ'mɔːslɪs [rə'm-,
-ləs], -lɪ, -nɪs [-nəs]
remote, -ly, -ness rɪ'məʊt [rə'm-], -lɪ,
-nɪs [-nəs]
remould, -s, -ing, -ed ˌriː'məʊld, -z, -ɪŋ,
-ɪd
re-mould (*s.*), **-s** 'riːməʊld, -z
remount (*s.*), **-s** 'riːmaʊnt [ˌ-'-], -s
remount (*v.*), **-s, -ing, -ed** ˌriː'maʊnt
[-'-], -s, -ɪŋ, -ɪd
removability rɪˌmuːvə'bɪlətɪ [rə,m-, -lɪt-]
removal, -s rɪ'muːvl [rə'm-], -z
remov|e (*s. v.*), **-es, -ing, -ed, -er/s;
-able** rɪ'muːv [rə'm-], -z, -ɪŋ, -d,
-ə*/z; -əbl
Remploy, -s 'remplɔɪ, -z
remunerat|e, -es, -ing, -ed rɪ'mjuːnəreɪt
[rə'm-, -'mjʊn-], -s, -ɪŋ, -ɪd
remuneration rɪˌmjuːnə'reɪʃn [rəˌm-,
-ˌmjʊn-]
remunerative rɪ'mjuːnərətɪv [rə'm-,
-'mjʊn-]
Remus 'riːməs
Renaissance rə'neɪsəns [rɪ'n-, 'rene-,
-sãːns, -sõːns, -sɑːns] (rənɛsãːs)
renal 'riːnl
renam|e, -es, -ing, -ed ˌriː'neɪm, -z, -ɪŋ,
-d
renascen|ce, -t rɪ'næsn|s [rə'n-], -t
Renault (*car*), **-s** 'renəʊ (rəno), -z
rend, -s, -ing, rent rend, -z, -ɪŋ, rent
rend|er, -ers, -ering/s, -ered 'rend|ə*,
-əz, -ərɪŋ/z, -əd
rendezvous (*sing.*) 'rɒndɪvuː [ˈrãːnd-,
'rõːnd-, 'rɑːnd-, -deɪv-] (rãdevu),
(*plur.*), -z

rendition, -s ren'dɪʃn, -z
renegade, -s 'renɪgeɪd, -z
reneg(u)|e (*s. v.*), **-es, -ing, -ed** rɪ'niːg
[rə'n-, -'neɪg], -z, -ɪŋ, -d
ren|ew, -ews, -ewing, -ewed; -ewable
rɪ'nj|uː [rə'n-], -uːz, -uːɪŋ [-ʊɪŋ],
-uːd; -uːəbl [-ʊəbl]
renewal, -s rɪ'njuːəl [rə'n-, -'njʊəl,
-'njuːl], -z
Renfrew, -shire 'renfruː, -ʃə* [-ˌʃɪə*]
renin 'riːnɪn
renn|et, -in 'ren|ɪt, -ɪn
Rennie 'renɪ
Reno 'riːnəʊ
Renoir rə'nwɑː* ['--, 're-] (rənwɑːr)
renounc|e, -es, -ing, -ed, -ement
rɪ'naʊns [rə'n-], -ɪz, -ɪŋ, -t, -mənt
renovat|e, -es, -ing, -ed, -or/s
'renəʊveɪt, -s, -ɪŋ, -ɪd, -ə*/z
renovation, -s ˌrenəʊ'veɪʃn, -z
renown, -ed rɪ'naʊn [rə'n-], -d
Renshaw 'renʃɔ:
rent (*s. v.*), **-s, -ing, -ed, -er/s** rent, -s,
-ɪŋ, -ɪd, -ə*/z
rent (*from* rend) rent
rental, -s 'rentl, -z
rent-free ˌrent'friː [*also* '-- *when attributive*]
rentier, -s 'rɒntɪeɪ (rãtje), -z
Rentoul rən'tuːl [ren-]
rent-roll, -s 'rentrəʊl, -z
renunciation, -s rɪˌnʌnsɪ'eɪʃn [rə,n-], -z
Renwick 'renwɪk, 'renɪk
reoccupation, -s 'riːˌɒkjʊ'peɪʃn [ˌrɒk-],
-z
reoccup|y, -ies, -ying, -ied ˌriː'ɒkjʊp|aɪ
[riː'ɒk-, rɪ'ɒk-], -aɪz, -aɪɪŋ, -aɪd
reop|en, -ens, -ening, -ened ˌriː'əʊp|ən
[riː'əʊ-, rɪ'əʊ-, -p|m], -ənz [-mz], -nɪŋ
[-ɳɪŋ], -ənd [-md]
reorganization [-isa-], **-s** 'riːˌɔːgənaɪ-
'zeɪʃn [riːˌɔː-, rɪˌɔː-, -gnaɪ'z-, -gənɪ'z-,
gn̩ɪ'z-], -z
reorganiz|e [-is|e], **-es, -ing, -ed**
ˌriː'ɔːgənaɪz [riː'ɔː-, rɪ'ɔː-, -gnaɪz], -ɪz,
-ɪŋ, -d
re-orientat|e, -es, -ing, -ed ˌriː'ɔːrɪenteɪt
[-'ɒr-, -rɪən-], -s, -ɪŋ, -ɪd
re-orientation 'riːˌɔːrɪen'teɪʃn [-ˌɒr-,
-rɪən-]
rep rep
repaid (*from* **repay,** *pay back*) riː'peɪd
[rɪ'p-, ˌriː'p-], (*from* **repay,** *pay a
second time*) ˌriː'peɪd
repair (*s. v.*), **-s, -ing, -ed, -er/s** rɪ'peə*
[rə'p-], -z, -rɪŋ, -d, -rə*/z
repairable rɪ'peərəbl [rə'p-]
reparability ˌrepərə'bɪlətɪ [-lɪt-]

reparable 'repǝrǝbl

reparation, -s ˌrepǝ'reɪʃn, -z

repartee ˌrepɑ:'ti:

repass, -es, -ing, -ed ˌri:'pɑ:s [also 'ri:pɑ:s when contrasted with pass], -ɪz, -ɪŋ, -t

repast, -s rɪ'pɑ:st [rǝ'p-], -s

repatriat|e, -es, -ing, -ed ri:'pætrɪeɪt [rɪ'p-, rarely -'peɪt-], -s, -ɪŋ, -ɪd

repatriation ˌri:pætrɪ'eɪʃn [rɪˌpætrɪ'eɪʃn]

re|pay (pay back), -pays, -paying, -paid ri:|'peɪ [rɪ|'peɪ, ˌri:|'peɪ], -'peɪz, -'peɪɪŋ, -'peɪd

re|pay (pay a second time), -pays, -paying, -paid ˌri:|'peɪ, -'peɪz, -'peɪɪŋ, -'peɪd

repayable ri:'peɪǝbl [rɪ'p-, ˌri:'p-]

repayment, -s ri:'peɪmǝnt [rɪ'p-, ˌri:'p-], -s

repeal (s. v.), -s, -ing, -ed rɪ'pi:l [rǝ'p-], -z, -ɪŋ, -d

repeat (s. v.), -s, -ing, -ed/ly, -er/s rɪ'pi:t [rǝ'p-], -s, -ɪŋ, -ɪd/lɪ, -ǝ*/z

repêchage 'repǝʃɑ:ʒ, ˌrepǝ'ʃɑ:ʒ

repel, -s, -ling, -led; -lent rɪ'pel [rǝ'p-], -z, -ɪŋ, -d; -ǝnt

repent, -s, -ing/ly, -ed rɪ'pent [rǝ'p-], -s, -ɪŋ/lɪ, -ɪd

repentan|ce, -ces, -t/ly rɪ'pentǝn|s [rǝ'p-], -sɪz, -t/lɪ

repeop|le, -les, -ling, -led ˌri:'pi:p|l, -lɪŋ [-lɪŋ], -ld

repercussion, -s ˌri:pǝ'kʌʃn [-pǝ:'k-], -z

repertoire, -s 'repǝtwɑ:* [-twɔ:*], -z

repertor|y, -ies 'repǝtǝr|ɪ, -ɪz

repetition, -s ˌrepɪ'tɪʃn [-pǝ't-], -z

repetitive rɪ'petǝtɪv [rǝ'p-, -tɪt-]

repin|e, -es, -ing, -ed rɪ'paɪn [rǝ'p-], -z, -ɪŋ, -d

repiqu|e (s. v.), -es, -ing, -ed ˌri:'pi:k [ri:'p-, also in contrast 'ri:pi:k], -s, -ɪŋ, -t

replac|e, -es, -ing, -ed, -ement/s rɪ'pleɪs [ri:'p-], -ɪz, -ɪŋ, -t, -mǝnt/s

replaceable rɪ'pleɪsǝbl [ri:'p-]

replant, -s, -ing, -ed ˌri:'plɑ:nt, -s, -ɪŋ, -ɪd

replay (s.), -s 'ri:pleɪ, -z

replay (v.), -s, -ing, -ed ˌri:'pleɪ, -z, -ɪŋ, -d

re-pleat, -s, -ing, -ed ˌri:'pli:t, -s, -ɪŋ, -ɪd

replenish, -es, -ing, -ed, -ment rɪ'plenɪʃ [rǝ'p-], -ɪz, -ɪŋ, -t, -mǝnt

replete, -ness rɪ'pli:t, -nɪs [-nǝs]

repletion rɪ'pli:ʃn

replevin rɪ'plevɪn [rǝ'p-]

†replica, -s 'replɪkǝ [rɪ'pli:kǝ, rǝ'pli:kǝ], -z

repl|y (s. v.), -ies, -ying, -ied rɪ'plɪ|aɪ [rǝ'p-], -aɪz, -aɪɪŋ, -aɪd

repoint, -s, -ing, -ed ˌri:'pɔɪnt, -s, -ɪŋ, -ɪd

repolish, -es, -ing, -ed ˌri:'pɒlɪʃ, -ɪz, -ɪŋ, -t

repopulat|e, -es, -ing, -ed ˌri:'pɒpjʊleɪt [ri:'p-, -pjǝl-], -s, -ɪŋ, -ɪd

report (s. v.), -s, -ing, -ed, -er/s rɪ'pɔ:t [rǝ'p-], -s, -ɪŋ, -ɪd, -ǝ*/z

reportage ˌrepɔ:'tɑ:ʒ ['---, rɪ'pɔ:tɪdʒ]

repos|e (s. v.), -es, -ing, -ed rɪ'pǝʊz [rǝ'p-], -ɪz, -ɪŋ, -d

repose|ful, -fully rɪ'pǝʊz|fʊl [rǝ'p-], -fʊlɪ [-fǝlɪ]

repositor|y, -ies rɪ'pɒzɪtǝr|ɪ [rǝ'p-], -ɪz

repoussé rǝ'pu:seɪ [rɪ'p-] (rǝpuse)

reprehend, -s, -ing, -ed ˌreprɪ'hend [-prǝ'h-], -z, -ɪŋ, -ɪd

reprehensib|le, -ly ˌreprɪ'hensǝb|l [-prǝ'h-, -sɪb-], -lɪ

reprehension ˌreprɪ'henʃn [-prǝ'h-]

represent, -s, -ing, -ed ˌreprɪ'zent [-prǝ'z-], -s, -ɪŋ, -ɪd

†representation, -s ˌreprɪzen'teɪʃn [-prǝz-, -zǝn-], -z

representative (s. adj.), -s, -ly ˌreprɪ'zentǝtɪv [-prǝ'z-], -z, -lɪ

repress, -es, -ing, -ed; -ible rɪ'pres [rǝ'p-], -ɪz, -ɪŋ, -t; -ǝbl [-ɪbl]

repression, -s rɪ'preʃn [rǝ'p-], -z

repressive rɪ'presɪv [rǝ'p-]

repriev|e (s. v.), -es, -ing, -ed rɪ'pri:v [rǝ'p-], -z, -ɪŋ, -d

reprimand (s.), -s 'reprɪmɑ:nd, -z

reprimand (v.), -s, -ing, -ed 'reprɪmɑ:nd [ˌreprɪ'm-], -z, -ɪŋ, -ɪd

reprint (s.), -s 'ri:prɪnt [ˌri:'prɪnt], -s

reprint (v.), -s, -ing, -ed ˌri:'prɪnt, -s, -ɪŋ, -ɪd

reprisal, -s rɪ'praɪzl [rǝ'p-], -z

reproach (s. v.), -es, -ing, -ed; -able rɪ'prǝʊtʃ [rǝ'p-], -ɪz, -ɪŋ, -t; -ǝbl

reproach|ful, -fully, -fulness rɪ'prǝʊtʃ|-fʊl [rǝ'p-], -fʊlɪ [-fǝlɪ], -fʊlnɪs [-nǝs]

reprobate (s. adj.), -s 'reprǝʊbeɪt [-prʊb-, -brt], -s

reprobat|e (v.), -es, -ing, -ed 'reprǝʊbeɪt [-prʊb-], -s, -ɪŋ, -ɪd

reprobation ˌreprǝʊ'beɪʃn [-prʊ'b-]

reproduc|e, -es, -ing, -ed, -er/s ˌri:prǝ'dju:s [-prʊ'd-], -ɪz, -ɪŋ, -t, -ǝ*/z

reproduction, -s ˌri:prǝ'dʌkʃn [-prʊ'd-], -z

reproductive, -ness ˌri:prǝ'dʌktɪv [-prʊ'd-], -nɪs [-nǝs]

reproof (s.), -s rɪ'pru:f [rǝ'p-], -s

re-proof (v.), -s, -ing, -ed ˌri:'pru:f, -s, -ɪŋ, -t

reproval, -s rɪ'pruːvl [rə'p-], -z
reprov|e, -es, -ing/ly, -ed, -er/s rɪ-'pruːv [rə'p-], -z, -ɪŋ/lɪ, -d, -ə*/z
reptile, -s 'reptaɪl, -z
reptilian (s. adj.), **-s** rep'tɪlɪən [-ljən], -z
Repton 'reptən
republic, -s rɪ'pʌblɪk [rə'p-], -s
republican, -s; -ism rɪ'pʌblɪkən [rə'p-], -z; -ɪzəm
republication, -s 'riː,pʌblɪ'keɪʃn, -z
republish, -es, -ing, -ed ,riː'pʌblɪʃ, -ɪz, -ɪŋ, -t
repudiat|e, -es, -ing, -ed, -er/s rɪ-'pjuːdɪeɪt [rə'p-], -s, -ɪŋ, -ɪd, -ə*/z
repudiation rɪ,pjuː'dɪ'eɪʃn [rə,p-]
repugnan|ce, -t/ly rɪ'pʌgnən|s [rə'p-], -t/lɪ
repuls|e (s. v.), **-es, -ing, -ed** rɪ'pʌls [rə'p-], -ɪz, -ɪŋ, -t
repulsion rɪ'pʌlʃn [rə'p-]
repulsive, -ly, -ness rɪ'pʌlsɪv [rə'p-], -lɪ, -nɪs [-nəs]
reputability ,repjʊtə'bɪlətɪ [-lɪt-]
reputab|le, -ly 'repjʊtəb|l, -lɪ
reputation, -s ,repjʊ'teɪʃn [-pjuː't-], -z
repute, -d, -dly rɪ'pjuːt [rə'p-], -ɪd, -ɪdlɪ
request (s. v.), **-s, -ing, -ed** rɪ'kwest [rə'k-], -s, -ɪŋ, -ɪd
requiem, -s 'rekwɪəm [-kwjəm, -kwɪem], -z
requir|e, -es, -ing, -ed, -ement/s rɪ'kwaɪə* [rə'k-], -z, -rɪŋ, -d, -mənt/s
requisite (s. adj.), **-s, -ly, -ness** 'rekwɪzɪt, -s, -lɪ, -nɪs [-nəs]
requisiti|on (s. v.), **-ons, -oning, -oned** ,rekwɪ'zɪʃ|n, -nz, -ŋɪŋ [-ənɪŋ], -nd
requit|e, -es, -ing, -ed; -al rɪ'kwaɪt [rə'k-], -s, -ɪŋ, -ɪd; -l
re-read (pres. tense), **-s, -ing, re-read** (p.) ,riː'riːd, -z, -ɪŋ, ,riː'red
reredos, -es 'rɪədɒs, -ɪz
resale (s.) ,riː'seɪl
resartus riː'sɑːtəs [rɪ's-]
rescind, -s, -ing, -ed rɪ'sɪnd [rə's-], -z, -ɪŋ, -ɪd
rescission rɪ'sɪʒn [rə's-]
rescript, -s 'riːskrɪpt, -s
resc|ue (s. v.), **-ues, -uing, -ued, -uer/s** 'resk|juː, -juːz, -jʊɪŋ [-juːɪŋ, -jwɪŋ], -juːd, -jʊə*/z [-jwə*/z]
research (s.), **-es** rɪ'sɜːtʃ [rə's-, 'riːsɜːtʃ], -ɪz
research (v.), **-es, -ing, -ed, -er/s** rɪ'sɜːtʃ [rə's-], -ɪz, -ɪŋ, -t, -ə*/z
reseat, -s, -ing, -ed ,riː'siːt, -s, -ɪŋ, -ɪd
resection, -s riː'sekʃn [rɪ's-], -z

reseda, -s (plant) 'resɪdə ['rezɪdə, rɪ'siːdə], (colour) 'resɪdə ['rezɪdə], -z
resell, -s, -ing, resold ,riː'sel, -z, -ɪŋ, ,riː'səʊld
resemblance, -s rɪ'zembləns [rə'z-], -ɪz
resemb|le, -les, -ling, -led rɪ'zemb|l [rə'z-], -lz, -lɪŋ [-l̩ŋ], -ld
resent, -s, -ing, -ed, -ment; -ful, -fully rɪ'zent, -s, -ɪŋ, -ɪd, -mənt; -fʊl, -fʊlɪ [-fəlɪ]
reservation, -s ,rezə'veɪʃn, -z
reserv|e (s. v.), **-es, -ing, -ed** rɪ'zɜːv [rə'z-], -z, -ɪŋ, -d
reservedly rɪ'zɜːvɪdlɪ [rə'z-]
reservist, -s rɪ'zɜːvɪst [rə'z-], -s
reservoir, -s 'rezəvwɑː* [-vwɔː*], -z
reset, -s, -ting/s ,riː'set, -s, -ɪŋ/z
reshap|e, -es, -ing, -ed riː'ʃeɪp, -s, -ɪŋ, -t
reship, -s, -ping, -ped, -ment/s ,riː'ʃɪp, -s, -ɪŋ, -t, -mənt/s
†**reshuff|le** (v.), **-les, -ling, -led** ,riː'ʃʌf|l, -lz, -lɪŋ, [-lɪŋ], -ld
resid|e, -es, -ing, -ed rɪ'zaɪd [rə'z-], -z, -ɪŋ, -ɪd
residence, -s 'rezɪdəns, -ɪz
residenc|y, -ies 'rezɪdəns|ɪ, -ɪz
resident, -s 'rezɪdənt, -s
residential ,rezɪ'denʃl
residual rɪ'zɪdjʊəl [rə'z-, -djwəl, -djʊl]
residuary rɪ'zɪdjʊərɪ [rə'z-, -djwərɪ, -djʊrɪ]
residue, -s 'rezɪdjuː, -z
residu|um, -a rɪ'zɪdjʊ|əm [rə'z-, -djw|əm], -ə
resign (give up), **-s, -ing, -ed, -edly** rɪ'zaɪn [rə'z-], -z, -ɪŋ, -d, -ɪdlɪ
re-sign (sign again), **-s, -ing, -ed** ,riː'saɪn, -z, -ɪŋ, -d
resignation, -s ,rezɪg'neɪʃn, -z
resilien|ce, -cy, -t rɪ'zɪlɪən|s [rə'zɪl-, rɪ'sɪl-, rə'sɪl-, -ljə-], -sɪ, -t
resin, -s; -ous 'rezɪn, -z; -əs
resist, -s, -ing, -ed rɪ'zɪst [rə'z-], -s, -ɪŋ, -ɪd
resistan|ce, -ces, -t rɪ'zɪstən|s [rə'z-], -sɪz, -t
resistless rɪ'zɪstlɪs [rə'z-, -ləs]
resol|e, -es, -ing, -ed ,riː'səʊl, -z, -ɪŋ, -d
resoluble rɪ'zɒljʊbl [rə'z-, 'rezəljʊbl]
resolute, -ly, -ness 'rezəluːt [-zl̩uːt, -zəljuːt], -lɪ, -nɪs [-nəs]
resolution, -s ,rezə'luːʃn [-zl̩'uː-, -zə'lju:-], -z
resolvability rɪ,zɒlvə'bɪlətɪ [rə,z-, -lɪt-]
resolv|e (s. v.), **-es, -ing, -ed; -able** rɪ'zɒlv [rə'z-], -z, -ɪŋ, -d; -əbl̩
resonan|ce, -ces, -t/ly 'rezənən|s [-zn̩ə-], -sɪz, -t/lɪ

resonator, -s 'rezəneɪtə* [-zn̩eɪ-], -z
resort (s. v.), -s, -ing, -ed rɪ'zɔːt [rə'z-],
-s, -ɪŋ, -ɪd
re-sort (sort out again), -s, -ing, -ed
‚riː'sɔːt, -s, -ɪŋ, -ɪd
resound, -s, -ing, -ed rɪ'zaʊnd [rə'z-], -z,
-ɪŋ, -ɪd
resource, -s; -ful, -fully, -fulness rɪ'sɔːs
[rə's-, -'zɔːs, -ɔəs], -ɪz; -fʊl, -fʊlɪ
[-fəlɪ], -fʊlnɪs [-nəs]
respect (s. v.), -s, -ing, -ed, -er/s
rɪ'spekt [rə's-], -s, -ɪŋ, -ɪd, -ə*/z
respectability rɪ‚spektə'bɪlətɪ [rə‚s-, -lɪt-]
respectab|le, -ly, -leness rɪ'spektəb|l
[rə's-], -lɪ, -lnɪs [-nəs]
respect|ful, -fully rɪ'spekt|fʊl [rə's-],
-fʊlɪ [-fəlɪ]
respecting (prep.) rɪ'spektɪŋ [rə's-]
respective, -ly rɪ'spektɪv [rə's-], -lɪ
Respighi re'spiːgɪ (re'spiːgi)
respirable 'respɪrəbl [rɪ'spaɪərəbl,
rə'spaɪər-]
respiration, -s ‚respə'reɪʃn [-pɪ'r-], -z
respirator, -s 'respəreɪtə* [-pɪr-], -z
respiratory rɪ'spaɪərətərɪ [re'sp-, rə'sp-,
-'spɪr-, 'respɪrətərɪ, 'respɪreɪtərɪ]
respir|e, -es, -ing, -ed rɪ'spaɪə* [rə's-],
-z, -rɪŋ, -d
respit|e (s. v.), -es, -ing, -ed 'respaɪt
[-pɪt], -s, -ɪŋ, -ɪd
resplenden|ce, -cy, -t/ly rɪ'splendən|s
[rə's-], -sɪ, -t/lɪ
respond, -s, -ing, -ed; -ent/s rɪ'spɒnd
[rə's-], -z, -ɪŋ, -ɪd; -ənt/s
response, -s rɪ'spɒns [rə's-], -ɪz
responsibilit|y, -ies rɪ‚spɒnsə'bɪlət|ɪ
[rə‚s-, -sɪ'b-, -lɪt-], -ɪz
responsib|le, -ly, -leness rɪ'spɒnsəb|l
[rə's-, -sɪb-], -lɪ, -lnɪs [-nəs]
responsions rɪ'spɒnʃnz [rə's-]
responsive, -ly, -ness rɪ'spɒnsɪv [rə's-],
-lɪ, -nɪs [-nəs]
rest (s. v.), -s, -ing, -ed rest, -s, -ɪŋ, -ɪd
restart, -s, -ing, -ed ‚riː'stɑːt, -s, -ɪŋ, -ɪd
restat|e, -es, -ing, -ed ‚riː'steɪt, -s, -ɪŋ,
-ɪd
re-statement, -s ‚riː'steɪtmənt, -s
restaurant, -s 'restərɔ̃ːŋ, [-rɑ̃ːŋ, -rɑːŋ,
-rɒŋ], -z, 'restərɒnt [-rɒnt, -rɑːnt], -s
restaurateur, -s ‚restɒrə'tɜː* [-tər-,
-tɔːr-] (restɔratœːr), -z
rest-cure, -s 'rest‚kjʊə* [-kjɔə*, -kjɔː*],
-z
rest|ful, -fully, -fulness 'rest|fʊl, -fʊlɪ
[-fəlɪ], -fʊlnɪs [-nəs]
rest-hou|se, -ses 'resthaʊ|s, -zɪz
resting-place, -s 'restɪŋpleɪs, -ɪz
restitution ‚restɪ'tjuːʃn

restive, -ly, -ness 'restɪv, -lɪ, -nɪs [-nəs]
restless, -ly, -ness 'restlɪs [-ləs], -lɪ, -nɪs
[-nəs]
restock, -s, -ing, -ed ‚riː'stɒk, -s, -ɪŋ, -t
restoration, -s ‚restə'reɪʃn [-tɔː'r-,
-tʊ'r-], -z
restorative (s. adj.), -s rɪ'stɒrətɪv [re's-,
rə's-, -'stɔːr-], -z
restor|e, -es, -ing, -ed, -er/s; -able
rɪ'stɔː* [rə's-, -'stɔə*], -z, -rɪŋ, -d,
-rə*/z; -rəbl
restrain (hold back), -s, -ing, -ed, -er/s
rɪ'streɪn [rə's-], -z, -ɪŋ, -d, -ə*/z
re-strain (strain again), -s, -ing, -ed
‚riː'streɪn, -z, -ɪŋ, -d
restraint, -s rɪ'streɪnt [rə's-], -s
restrict, -s, -ing, -ed; -ive rɪ'strɪkt
[rə's-], -s, -ɪŋ, -ɪd; -ɪv
restriction, -s rɪ'strɪkʃn [rə's-], -z
restrictionism rɪ'strɪkʃənɪzəm [rə's-,
-ʃn̩-]
result (s. v.), -s, -ing, -ed; -ant/s
rɪ'zʌlt [rə'z-], -s, -ɪŋ, -ɪd; -ənt/s
resultative rɪ'zʌltətɪv [rə'z-]
resum|e, -es, -ing, -ed rɪ'zjuːm [rə'z-,
-'zuːm], -z, -ɪŋ, -d
résumé, -s 'rezjuːmeɪ ['reɪz-, -zjʊm-,
-zuː-, -zʊm-, rɪ'zjuːmeɪ] (rezyme), -z
resumption, -s rɪ'zʌmpʃn [rə'z-], -z
re-surfac|e, -es, -ing, -ed ‚riː'sɜːfɪs
[-fəs], -ɪz, -ɪŋ, -t
resurrect, -s, -ing, -ed ‚rezə'rekt, -s, -ɪŋ,
-ɪd
resurrection (R.), -s ‚rezə'rekʃn, -z
resuscitat|e, -es, -ing, -ed rɪ'sʌsɪteɪt
[rə's-], -s, -ɪŋ, -ɪd
resuscitation, -s rɪ‚sʌsɪ'teɪʃn [rə‚s-], -z
retail (s. adj.) 'riːteɪl [riː't-]
retail (v. relate), -s, -ing, -ed, -er/s riː'teɪl
[rɪ't-, sell also '--], -z, -ɪŋ, -d, -ə*/z
retain, -s, -ing, -ed, -er/s rɪ'teɪn [rə't-],
-z, -ɪŋ, -d, -ə*/z
retake (s.), -s 'riːteɪk, -s
retak|e (v.), -es, -ing, retook, retaken
‚riː'teɪk [-'-], -s, -ɪŋ, ‚riː'tʊk [-'-],
‚riː'teɪkən [-'--]
retaliat|e, -es, -ing, -ed rɪ'tælɪeɪt [rə't-],
-s, -ɪŋ, -ɪd
retaliation rɪ‚tælɪ'eɪʃn [rə‚t-]
retaliatory rɪ'tælɪətərɪ [rə't-, -ljətərɪ,
-lɪeɪtərɪ, rɪ‚tælɪ'eɪtərɪ, rə‚t-]
Retallack rɪ'tælək [rə't-]
retard, -s, -ing, -ed rɪ'tɑːd [rə't-], -z,
-ɪŋ, -ɪd
retardation, -s ‚riːtɑː'deɪʃn, -z
retch, -es, -ing, -ed retʃ [riːtʃ], -ɪz, -ɪŋ, -t
retell, -s, -ing, retold ‚riː'tel, -z, -ɪŋ,
‚riː'təʊld

retention rɪˈtenʃn [rəˈt-]
retentive, -ly, -ness rɪˈtentɪv [rəˈt-], -lɪ, -nɪs [-nəs]
Retford ˈretfəd
reticen|ce, -t/ly ˈretɪsən|s, -t/lɪ
reticle, -s ˈretɪkl, -z
reticulate (adj.) rɪˈtɪkjʊlət [reˈt-, rəˈt-, -kjəl-, -lɪt, -leɪt]
reticulat|e (v.), -es, -ing, -ed rɪˈtɪkjʊleɪt [reˈt-, rəˈt-, -kjəl-], -s, -ɪŋ, -ɪd
reticulation, -s rɪˌtɪkjʊˈleɪʃn [reˌt-, rəˌt-, -kjəˈl-], -z
reticule, -s ˈretɪkjuːl, -z
retin|a, -as, -ae ˈretɪn|ə, -əz, -iː
retinue, -s ˈretɪnjuː, -z
retir|e, -es, -ing, -ed; -ement/s rɪˈtaɪə* [rəˈt-], -z, -rɪŋ, -d; -mənt/s
retold (from retell) ˌriːˈtəʊld
retort (s. v.), -s, -ing, -ed rɪˈtɔːt [rəˈt-], -s, -ɪŋ, -ɪd
retouch (s. v.), -es, -ing, -ed ˌriːˈtʌtʃ, -ɪz, -ɪŋ, -t
retrac|e, -es, -ing, -ed rɪˈtreɪs [ˌriːˈt-], -ɪz, -ɪŋ, -t
retract, -s, -ing, -ed, -or/s rɪˈtrækt [rəˈt-], -s, -ɪŋ, -ɪd, -ə*/z
retractable rɪˈtræktəbl [rəˈt-]
retractation ˌriːˈtrækˈteɪʃn
retraction, -s rɪˈtrækʃn [rəˈt-], -z
retranslat|e, -es, -ing, -ed ˌriːtrænsˈleɪt [-trɑːns-, -trænz-, -trɑːnz-, -trəns-, -trənz-], -s, -ɪŋ, -ɪd
retranslation, -s ˌriːtrænsˈleɪʃn [-trɑːns-, -trænz-, -trɑːnz-, -trəns-, -trənz-], -z
re-tread (tyres), -s ˈriːtred, -z
re|tread (v.), -treads, -treading, -trod ˌriːˈtred, -ˈtredz, -ˈtredɪŋ, -ˈtrɒd
retreat (s. v.), -s, -ing, -ed rɪˈtriːt [rəˈt-], -s, -ɪŋ, -ɪd
retrench, -es, -ing, -ed, -ment/s rɪˈtrentʃ [rəˈt-], -ɪz, -ɪŋ, -t, -mənt/s
retrial, -s ˌriːˈtraɪəl [ˈ--], -z
retribution ˌretrɪˈbjuːʃn
retribut|ive, -ory rɪˈtrɪbjʊt|ɪv [rəˈt-], -ərɪ
retrievab|le, -ly, -leness rɪˈtriːvəb|l [rəˈt-], -lɪ, -lnɪs [-nəs]
retrieval rɪˈtriːvl
retriev|e, -es, -ing, -ed, -er/s rɪˈtriːv [rəˈt-], -z, -ɪŋ, -d, -ə*/z
retrim, -s, -ming, -med ˌriːˈtrɪm, -z, -ɪŋ, -d
retroact, -s, -ing, -ed; -ive/ly ˌretrəʊˈækt [ˌriːt-], -s, -ɪŋ, -ɪd; -ɪv/lɪ
retroced|e, -es, -ing, -ed ˌretrəʊˈsiːd [ˌriːt-], -z, -ɪŋ, -ɪd
retrocession, -s ˌretrəʊˈseʃn [ˌriːt-], -z
retroflex, -ed ˈretrəʊfleks, -t

retroflexion ˌretrəʊˈflekʃn
retrograde ˈretrəʊɡreɪd
retrogress, -es, -ing, -ed, -ive/ly ˌretrəʊˈɡres [ˌriːt-], -ɪz, -ɪŋ, -t, -ɪv/lɪ
retrogression ˌretrəʊˈɡreʃn [ˌriːt-]
retro-rocket, -s ˈretrəʊˌrɒkɪt, -s
retrospect, -s ˈretrəʊspekt [ˈriːt-], -s
retrospection, -s ˌretrəʊˈspekʃn [ˌriːt-], -z
retrospective, -ly ˌretrəʊˈspektɪv [ˌriːt-], -lɪ
retroussé rəˈtruːseɪ [rɪˈt-] (rətruse)
retroversion, -s ˌretrəʊˈvɜːʃn [ˌriːt-], -z
retrovert (s.), -s ˈretrəʊvɜːt [ˈriːt-], -s
retrovert (v.), -s, -ing, -ed ˌretrəʊˈvɜːt [ˌriːt-], -s, -ɪŋ, -ɪd
retr|y, -ies, -ying, -ied ˌriːˈtr|aɪ, -aɪz, -aɪɪŋ, -aɪd
returf, -s, -ing, -ed ˌriːˈtɜːf, -s, -ɪŋ, -t
return (s. v.), -s, -ing, -ed; -able rɪˈtɜːn [rəˈt-], -z, -ɪŋ, -d; -əbl
Reuben ˈruːbɪn [-bən]
reunification, -s ˌriːjuːnɪfɪˈkeɪʃn [ˌriːjʊn-, rɪˌjuː-], -z
reunion, -s ˌriːˈjuːnjən [riːˈj-, -nɪən], -z
reunit|e, -es, -ing, -ed ˌriːjuːˈnaɪt [-jʊˈn-], -s, -ɪŋ, -ɪd
re-use (s.) ˌriːˈjuːs [ˈriːjuːs]
re-us|e (v.), -es, -ing, -ed ˌriːˈjuːz, -ɪz, -ɪŋ, -d [ˈriːjuːzd when attributive]
Reuter ˈrɔɪtə*
Rev. ˈrevərənd
rev (s. v.), -s, -ving, -ved rev, -z, -ɪŋ, -d
reveal, -s, -ing, -ed, -er/s; -able rɪˈviːl [rəˈv-], -z, -ɪŋ, -d, -ə*/z; -əbl
reveille, -s rɪˈvælɪ [rəˈv-, -ˈvel-], -z
revel|el (s. v.), -els, -elling, -elled, -eller/s ˈrevl|l, -lz, -lɪŋ, -ld, -lə*/z
revelation (R.), -s ˌrevəˈleɪʃn [-vlˈeɪ-, -vɪˈl-], -z
revelr|y, -ies ˈrevlr|ɪ, -ɪz
Revelstoke ˈrevəlstəʊk
revendication, -s rɪˌvendɪˈkeɪʃn [rəˌv-], -z
reveng|e (s. v.), -es, -ing, -ed rɪˈvendʒ [rəˈv-], -ɪz, -ɪŋ, -d
revenge|ful, -fully, -fulness rɪˈvendʒ|fʊl [rəˈv-], -fʊlɪ [-fəlɪ], -fʊlnɪs [-nəs]
revenue, -s ˈrevənjuː [-vɪn-, in old-fashioned legal usage rɪˈvenjuː, rəˈvenjuː], -z
   Note.—In Shakespeare both stressings occur, e.g. ˈ--- in 'Richard II', II. i. 226, and -ˈ- in 'The Tempest', I. ii. 98.
reverberat|e, -es, -ing, -ed, -or/s rɪˈvɜːbəreɪt [rəˈv-], -s, -ɪŋ, -ɪd, -ə*/z

reverberation, -s rɪ,vɜːbə'reɪʃn [rə,v-], -z

reverberatory rɪ'vɜːbərətərɪ [rə'v-, -reɪtərɪ]

rever|e (R.), -es, -ing, -ed rɪ'vɪə* [rə'v-], -z, -rɪŋ, -d

reverenc|e (s. v.), -es, -ing, -ed 'revərəns, -ɪz, -ɪŋ, -t

reverend (R.), -s 'revərənd, -z

reverent, -ly 'revərənt, -lɪ

reverential ,revə'renʃl

reverie, -s 'revərɪ, -z

revers (sing.) rɪ'vɪə* [rə'v-, -'veə*], (plur.) -z

reversal, -s rɪ'vɜːsl [rə'v-], -z

reverse (s.), -s rɪ'vɜːs [rə'v-, 'riːvɜːs], -ɪz

revers|e (v.), -es, -ing, -ed; -ely rɪ'vɜːs [rə'v-], -ɪz, -ɪŋ, -t; -lɪ

reversibility rɪ,vɜːsə'bɪlətɪ [rə,v-, -sɪ'b-, -lɪt-]

reversible rɪ'vɜːsəbl [rə'v-, -sɪb-]

reversion, -s rɪ'vɜːʃn [rə'v-], -z

reversionary rɪ'vɜːʃn̩ərɪ [rə'v-, -ʃnə-, -ʃənə-]

revert, -s, -ing, -ed rɪ'vɜːt [rə'v-], -s, -ɪŋ, -ɪd

revet, -s, -ting, -ted, -ment/s rɪ'vet [rə'v-], -s, -ɪŋ, -ɪd, -mənt/s

revictu|al, -als, -alling, -alled ,riː'vɪtl̩l, -lz, -l̩ɪŋ, -ld

revi|ew (s. v.), -ews, -ewing, -ewed, -ewer/s rɪ'vjuː [rə'v-], -uːz, -uːɪŋ [-ʊɪŋ], -uːd, -uːə*/z [-ʊə*/z]

revill|e, -es, -ing, -ed, -er/s rɪ'vaɪl [rə'v-], -z, -ɪŋ, -d, -ə*/z

Revillon (English surname) rə'vɪljən

revis|e (s. v.), -es, -ing, -ed, -er/s rɪ'vaɪz [rə'v-], -ɪz, -ɪŋ, -d, -ə*/z

revision, -s, -ist/s rɪ'vɪʒn [rə'v-], -z, -ɪst/s [-ʒənɪst/s]

revisit, -s, -ing, -ed ,riː'vɪzɪt, -s, -ɪŋ, -ɪd

revisualiz|e [-is|e], -es, -ing, -ed ,riː'vɪzjuəlaɪz [-zjwəl-, -zjʊl-, -ʒjʊəl-, -ʒjwəl-, -ʒʊəl-, -ʒwəl-, -ʒʊl-], -ɪz, -ɪŋ, -d

revitaliz|e [is|e], -es, -ing, -ed ,riː'vaɪtəlaɪz [-tl̩aɪz], -ɪz, -ɪŋ, -d

revival, -s rɪ'vaɪvl [rə'v-], -z

revivali|sm, -st/s rɪ'vaɪvəlɪ|zəm [rə'v-, -vl̩ɪ-], -st/s

reviv|e, -es, -ing, -ed rɪ'vaɪv [rə'v-], -z, -ɪŋ, -d

revivi|fy, -fies, -fying, -fied riː'vɪvɪ|faɪ [,riː'v-, rɪ'v-], -faɪz, -faɪɪŋ, -faɪd

reviviscence ,revɪ'vɪsns [,riː'vaɪ'v-, -səns]

revocability ,revəkə'bɪlətɪ [-vʊk-, -lɪt-]

revocable 'revəkəbl [-vʊk-], (when applied to letters of credit) rɪ'vəʊkəbl [rə'v-]

revocation, -s ,revə'keɪʃn [-vʊ'k-, -vəʊ'k-], -z

revok|e (s. v.), -es, -ing, -ed rɪ'vəʊk [rə'v-], -s, -ɪŋ, -t

revolt (s. v.), -s, -ing, -ed rɪ'vəʊlt [rə'v-], -s, -ɪŋ, -ɪd

revolution, -s ,revə'luːʃn [-vʊ'luː-, -vl̩'uː-, -və'ljuː-], -z

revolutionar|y (s. adj.), -ies ,revə'luː-ʃn̩ər|ɪ [-vʊ'luː-, -vl̩'uː-, -və'ljuː-, -ʃnər-, -ʃn̩r-, -ʃənər-], -ɪz

revolutionist, -s ,revə'luː-ʃn̩ɪst [-vʊ'luː-, -vl̩'uː-, -və'ljuː-, -ʃənɪst, -ʃn̩ɪst], -s

revolutioniz|e [-is|e], -es, -ing, -ed ,revə'luː-ʃn̩aɪz [-vʊ'luː-, -vl̩'uː-, -və'ljuː-, -ʃənaɪz, -ʃn̩aɪz], -ɪz, -ɪŋ, -d

revolv|e, -es, -ing, -ed rɪ'vɒlv [rə'v-], -z, -ɪŋ, -d

revolver, -s rɪ'vɒlvə* [rə'v-], -z

revue, -s rɪ'vjuː [rə'v-], -z

revulsion, -s rɪ'vʌlʃn [rə'v-], -z

reward (s. v.), -s, -ing, -ed rɪ'wɔːd [rə'w-], -z, -ɪŋ, -ɪd

reword, -s, -ing, -ed ,riː'wɜːd, -z, -ɪŋ, -ɪd

rewrit|e, -es, -ing, rewrote, rewritten ,riː'raɪt, -s, -ɪŋ, ,riː'rəʊt, ,riː'rɪtn

Rex reks

Reykjavik 'reɪkjəviːk ['rek-, -vɪk]

Reynaldo reɪ'nældəʊ

reynard, -s 'renɑːd ['reɪ-, -nəd], -z

Reynard 'renəd, 'renɑːd, 'remɑːd

Reynold, -s 'ren|d [-nəld], -z

Rhadamanthus ,rædə'mænθəs

Rhae|tia, -tian 'riː|ʃjə [-ʃɪə, -ʃə], -ʃjən [-ʃɪən, -ʃn]

Rhaetic 'riːtɪk

Rhaeto-Roman|ce, -ic ,riːtəʊrəʊ'mæn|s [-rʊ'm-], -ɪk

rhapsodic, -al, -ally ræp'sɒdɪk, -l, -əlɪ

rhapsodiz|e [-is|e], -es, -ing, -ed 'ræpsədaɪz, -ɪz, -ɪŋ, -d

rhapsod|y, -ies 'ræpsəd|ɪ, -ɪz

rhea (R.), -s rɪə ['riːə], -z

Rheims riːmz

Rheinallt 'raɪnælt (Welsh 'hrəmal̩t)

Rhenish 'riːnɪʃ ['ren-]

rheostat, -s 'rɪəʊstæt, -s

rhesus, -es 'riːsəs, -ɪz

rhetoric (s.) 'retərɪk

rhetoric|al, -ally rɪ'tɒrɪk|l [rə't-], -əlɪ

rhetorician, -s ,retə'rɪʃn [-tɒ'r-], -z

rheum ruːm

rheumatic, -s, -ky ruː'mætɪk [rʊ'm-], -s, -ɪ

rheumatism 'ruːmətɪzəm ['rʊm-]

423

rheumatoid 'ru:mətɔɪd ['rʊm-]
rheumatolog|y, -ist/s ˌru:mə'tɒlədʒ|ɪ [ˌrʊm-], -ɪst/s
Rhine, -land raɪn, -lænd [-lənd]
rhino, -s 'raɪnəʊ, -z
rhinoceros, -es raɪ'nɒsərəs, -ɪz
rhinolog|ist/s, -y raɪ'nɒlədʒ|ɪst/s, -ɪ
rhinoscope, -s 'raɪnəskəʊp, -s
rhinoscopy raɪ'nɒskəpɪ
rhizome, -s 'raɪzəʊm, -z
rho rəʊ
Rhoda 'rəʊdə
Rhode (biblical name) 'rəʊdɪ
Rhode (breed of fowls), -s rəʊd, -z
Rhode Island (state in U.S.A.) ˌrəʊd-'aɪlənd [rəʊ'daɪ-, 'rəʊdˌaɪlənd]
Note.—In U.S.A. the stress is ˌ-'--.
Rhode Island (breed of fowls), -s 'rəʊd-ˌaɪlənd, -z
Rhodes (Greek island, surname) rəʊdz
Rhode|sia, -sian rəʊ'di:|zjə [-zɪə, -zjə, -ʒɪə, -ʒə, -sjə, -sɪə, -ʃjə, -ʃɪə, -ʃə], -zjən [-zɪən, -ʒjən, -ʒɪən, -ʒn, -sjən, -sɪən, -ʃjən, -ʃɪən, -ʃn]
Rhodian, -s 'rəʊdjən [-dɪən], -z
rhodium 'rəʊdɪəm [-djəm]
rhododendron, -s ˌrəʊdə'dendrən [ˌrɒd-, -dɪ'd-], -z
rhodomontade = rodomontade
rhomb, -s rɒm, -z
rhomboid, -s 'rɒmbɔɪd, -z
rhombus, -es 'rɒmbəs, -ɪz
Rhondda 'rɒndə ['rɒnðə] (Welsh 'hrɔnða)
Rhone rəʊn
rhotacism 'rəʊtəsɪzəm
rhubarb 'ru:bɑ:b [old-fashioned -bəb]
Rhuddlan 'rɪðlən [-læn] (Welsh 'hrɪðlan)
rhumb, -s rʌm, -z
Rhyl rɪl (Welsh hrɪl)
rhym|e (s. v.), -es, -ing, -ed, -er/s raɪm, -z, -ɪŋ, -d, -ə*/z
rhymester, -s 'raɪmstə*, -z
Rhys (Welsh name) ri:s (Welsh hri:s), (family name of Baron Dynevor) raɪs
rhythm, -s 'rɪðəm ['rɪθəm], -z
rhythmic, -al, -ally 'rɪðmɪk ['rɪθm-], -l, -əlɪ
ria, -s 'ri:ə [rɪə], -z
Riach rɪək ['ri:ək, -əx]
Rialto rɪ'æltəʊ
rib (s. v.), -s, -bing, -bed rɪb, -z, -ɪŋ, -d
ribald (s. adj.), -s; -ry 'rɪbəld, -z; -rɪ
riband, -s 'rɪbənd, -z
ribbon, -s 'rɪbən, -z
riboflavin ˌraɪbəʊ'fleɪvɪn
Ribston, -s 'rɪbstən, -z
Rica 'ri:kə

Riccio 'rɪtʃɪəʊ
rice raɪs
Rice raɪs, ri:s
ricercata, -s ˌrɪtʃə:'kɑ:tə [-tʃeə'k-], -z
rich, -es, -er, -est, -ly, -ness rɪtʃ, -ɪz, -ə*, -ɪst, -lɪ, -nɪs [-nəs]
Richard, -s, -son 'rɪtʃəd, -z, -sn
Richelieu 'ri:ʃəljə: ['rɪ-, -lju:] (riʃəljø)
Riches 'rɪtʃɪz
Richey 'rɪtʃɪ
Richmond 'rɪtʃmənd
Richter, -scale 'rɪktə* ['rɪxt-], -skeɪl
rick, -s rɪk, -s
Rickard, -s 'rɪkɑ:d, -z
rickets 'rɪkɪts
Rickett 'rɪkɪt
ricket|y, -ier, -iest, -ily, -iness 'rɪkət|ɪ [-ɪt|ɪ], -ɪə*, -ɪɪst, -ɪlɪ [-əlɪ], -ɪnɪs [-ɪnəs]
Rickmansworth 'rɪkmənzwɜ:θ [-wəθ]
rickshaw, -s 'rɪkʃɔ:, -z
Rico 'ri:kəʊ
ricoch|et, -ets, -eting, -eted 'rɪkəʃ|eɪ [-kɒʃ-, -ʃ|et, ˌ--'-], -eɪz [-ets], -eɪɪŋ [-etɪŋ], -eɪd [-etɪd]
rictus 'rɪktəs
rid, -s, -ding rɪd, -z, -ɪŋ
riddance 'rɪdəns
Riddell 'rɪdl, rɪ'del
Ridding 'rɪdɪŋ
ridd|le (s. v.), -les, -ling, -led 'rɪd|l, -lz, -lɪŋ [-lɪŋ], -ld
rid|e, -es, -ing, rode, ridden raɪd, -z, -ɪŋ, rəʊd, 'rɪdn
Rideal rɪ'di:l
Ridealgh 'raɪdældʒ, 'rɪdɪælʃ
Ridehalgh 'raɪdhælʃ, 'rɪdɪhælʃ
rider (R.), -s; -less 'raɪdə*, -z; -lɪs [-ləs, -les]
ridge (R.), -s, -d rɪdʒ, -ɪz, -d
Ridg(e)way 'rɪdʒweɪ
ridicul|e (s. v.), -es, -ing, -ed 'rɪdɪkju:l, -z, -ɪŋ, -d
ridiculous, -ly, -ness rɪ'dɪkjʊləs [rə'd-, -kjəl-], -lɪ, -nɪs [-nəs]
Riding, -s, -hood 'raɪdɪŋ, -z, -hʊd
riding-habit, -s 'raɪdɪŋˌhæbɪt, -s
riding-master, -s 'raɪdɪŋˌmɑ:stə*, -z
riding-mistress, -es 'raɪdɪŋˌmɪstrɪs [-trəs], -ɪz
Rid|ley, -path 'rɪd|lɪ, -pɑ:θ
Ridout 'rɪdaʊt
Rienzi rɪ'entsɪ
Rievaulx (abbey in North Yorkshire) 'ri:vəʊ ['ri:vəʊz, 'rɪvəz]
Note.—'ri:vəʊ is the usual local pronunciation.
rife raɪf
riff-raff 'rɪfræf

rif|le (*s. v.*), -les, -ling, -led 'raɪf|l, -lz, -lɪŋ [-lɪŋ], -ld
rifle|man, -men 'raɪfl|mən [-mæn], -mən [-men]
rifle-range, -s 'raɪflreɪndʒ, -ɪz
rifle-shot, -s 'raɪflʃɒt, -s
rift (*s. v.*), -s, -ing, -ed rɪft, -s, -ɪŋ, -ɪd
rig (*s. v.*), -s, -ging, -ged rɪg, -z, -ɪŋ, -d
Riga 'ri:gə [*old-fashioned* 'raɪgə]
Rigby 'rɪgbɪ
Rigel (*star*) 'raɪgəl [*rarely* 'raɪdʒəl]
rigger, -s 'rɪgə*, -z
rigging (*s.*), -s 'rɪgɪŋ, -z
right (*s. adj. v. adv.*), -s, -ly, -ness; -ing, -ed raɪt, -s, -lɪ, -nɪs [-nəs]; -ɪŋ, -ɪd
rightabout 'raɪtəbaʊt
righteous, -ly, -ness 'raɪtʃəs [-tjəs], -lɪ, -nɪs [-nəs]
right|ful, -fully, -fulness 'raɪt|fʊl, -fʊlɪ [-fəlɪ], -fʊlnɪs [-nəs]
right-hand (*attributive adj.*) 'raɪthænd
right-handed ,raɪt'hændɪd ['-,--]
rightist, -s 'raɪtɪst, -s
right(h)o ,raɪt'əʊ
Rigi 'ri:gɪ
rigid, -ly, -ness 'rɪdʒɪd, -lɪ, -nɪs [-nəs]
rigidity rɪ'dʒɪdətɪ [-ɪtɪ]
rigmarole, -s 'rɪgmərəʊl, -z
Rigoletto ,rɪgə'letəʊ [-gəʊ'l-] (rigo-'letto)
rigor (*mortis*) 'raɪgɔ:* ['rɪgə*]
rigorous, -ly, -ness 'rɪgərəs, -lɪ, -nɪs [-nəs]
rigour, -s 'rɪgə*, -z
rig-out, -s 'rɪgaʊt [,-'-]
Rigveda ,rɪg'veɪdə
Rikki-Tiki-Tavi 'rɪkɪ,tɪkɪ'tɑ:vɪ
ril|e, -es, -ing, -ed raɪl, -z, -ɪŋ, -d
Riley 'raɪlɪ
rilievo ,rɪlɪ'eɪvəʊ
rill, -s rɪl, -z
rim, -s, -less rɪm, -z, -lɪs [-ləs]
Rimbault 'rɪmbəʊlt [*French poet* 'ræmbəʊ] (rɛbo)
rime, -s raɪm, -z
Rimmon 'rɪmən
Rimsky-Korsakov ,rɪmskɪ'kɔ:səkɒf [-ɒv] (,rjimskij'korsəkəf)
Rinaldo rɪ'næ1dəʊ
rind, -s raɪnd, -z
Rind rɪnd
rinderpest 'rɪndəpest
ring (*s. v.*) (*encircle, put a ring on, etc.*), -s, -ing, -ed rɪŋ, -z, -ɪŋ, -d
ring (*s. v.*) (*sound, etc.*), -s, -ing, rang, rung, ringer/s rɪŋ, -z, -ɪŋ, ræŋ, rʌŋ, 'rɪŋə*/z
ring-dove, -s 'rɪŋdʌv, -z

ring|leader/s, -let/s, -worm 'rɪŋ|-,li:də*/z, -lɪt/s [-lət/s], -wɜ:m
ring-road, -s 'rɪŋrəʊd, -z
Ringshall 'rɪŋʃəl
rink (*s. v.*), -s, -ing, -ed rɪŋk, -s, -ɪŋ, -t [rɪŋt]
rins|e, -es, -ing, -ed rɪns, -ɪz, -ɪŋ, -t
Rio 'ri:əʊ ['rɪəʊ]
Rio de Janeiro ,ri:əʊdədʒə'nɪərəʊ [,rɪəʊ-, -deɪ-]
Rio Grande (*in North America*) ,ri:əʊ-'grændɪ [,rɪəʊ-, -'grænd]
riot (*s. v.*), -s, -ing, -ed, -er/s 'raɪət, -s, -ɪŋ, -ɪd, -ə*/z
riotous, -ly, -ness 'raɪətəs, -lɪ, -nɪs [-nəs]
Riou 'rɪu: ['ri:u:]
rip, -s, -ping, -ped, -per/s rɪp, -s, -ɪŋ, -t, -ə*/z
riparian raɪ'peərɪən [rɪ'p-]
ripe, -r, -st, -ly, -ness raɪp, -ə*, -ɪst, -lɪ, -nɪs [-nəs]
rip|en, -ens, -ening, -ened 'raɪp|ən, -ənz, -ɪŋ [-nɪŋ], -ənd
ripieno ,rɪpɪ'eɪnəʊ
Ripley 'rɪplɪ
Ripman 'rɪpmən
Ripon 'rɪpən
ripost(e), -s rɪ'pɒst [-'pəʊst], -s
ripper, -s 'rɪpə*, -z
ripping (*adj.*), -est, -ly 'rɪpɪŋ, -ɪst, -lɪ
ripp|le, -les, -ling, -led 'rɪp|l, -lz, -lɪŋ [-lɪŋ], -ld
ripple-mark, -s 'rɪplmɑ:k, -s
ripply 'rɪplɪ [-plɪ]
ripuarian ,rɪpju:'eərɪən [-pjʊ'eə-]
Rip van Winkle ,rɪpvæn'wɪŋkl
Risboro' [-borough] 'rɪzbərə
ris|e (*s. v.*), -es, -ing, rose, risen raɪz, -ɪz, -ɪŋ, rəʊz, 'rɪzn
riser, -s 'raɪzə*, -z
risibility ,rɪzə'bɪlətɪ [,raɪz-, -zɪ-, -lɪt-]
risible 'rɪzəbl ['raɪz-, -ɪbl]
rising (*s.*), -s 'raɪzɪŋ, -z
risk (*s. v.*), -s, -ing, -ed rɪsk, -s, -ɪŋ, -t
risk|y, -ier, -iest, -iness 'rɪsk|ɪ, -ɪə* [-jə*], -ɪɪst [-jɪst], -ɪnɪs [-ɪnəs]
risotto, -s rɪ'zɒtəʊ [-'sɒ-], -z
risqué 'ri:skeɪ ['rɪs-] (riske)
rissole, -s 'rɪsəʊl [*old-fashioned* 'ri:s-], -z
Rita 'ri:tə
ritardando, -s ,rɪtɑ:'dændəʊ, -z
Ritchie 'rɪtʃɪ
rite, -s raɪt, -s
Ritson 'rɪtsn
ritual, -s 'rɪtʃʊəl [-tʃwəl, -tʃʊl, -tjʊəl, -tjwəl, -tjʊl], -z
†rituali|sm, -st/s 'rɪtʃʊəlɪ|zəm [tʃwəl-, -tʃʊl-, -tjʊəl, -tjwəl, -tjʊl], -st/s

425

ritualistic ‚rɪtʃʊəˈlɪstɪk [-tʃwəˈl-, -tjʊəˈl-, -tjwəˈl-]

riv|al (s. v.), -als, -alling, -alled ˈraɪv|l, -lz, -lɪŋ [-əlɪŋ], -ld

rivalr|y, -ies ˈraɪvlr|ɪ, -ɪz

riv|e, -es, -ing, -ed, riven raɪv, -z, -ɪŋ, -d, ˈrɪvən

river, -s (R.) ˈrɪvə*, -z

river-bank, -s ˈrɪvəbæŋk [‚--ˈ-], -s

river-basin, -s ˈrɪvə‚beɪsn, -z

river-bed, -s ˈrɪvəbed [‚--ˈ-], -z

riverside (R.) ˈrɪvəsaɪd

rivet, -s, -(t)ing, -(t)ed, -(t)er/s ˈrɪvɪt [-vət], -s, -ɪŋ, -ɪd, -ə*/z

Riviera ‚rɪvɪˈeərə

Rivington, -s ˈrɪvɪŋtən, -z

rivulet, -s ˈrɪvjʊlɪt [-let, -lət], -s

rix-dollar, -s ‚rɪksˈdɒlə* [ˈrɪks‚d-], -z

Rizzio ˈrɪtsɪəʊ

roach (R.) rəʊtʃ

road, -s rəʊd, -z

road-block, -s ˈrəʊdblɒk, -s

road-book, -s ˈrəʊdbʊk, -s

road-hog, -s ˈrəʊdhɒg, -z

road-hou|se, -ses ˈrəʊdhaʊ|s, -zɪz

road-mender, -s ˈrəʊd‚mendə*, -z

road-sense ˈrəʊdsens

roadshow, -s ˈrəʊdʃəʊ, -z

roadside ˈrəʊdsaɪd

roadstead, -s ˈrəʊdsted, -z

roadster, -s ˈrəʊdstə*, -z

road-test, -s ˈrəʊdtest, -s

roadway, -s ˈrəʊdweɪ, -z

roadworth|y, -iness ˈrəʊd‚wɜːð|ɪ, -ɪnɪs [-məs]

roam, -s, -ing, -ed rəʊm, -z, -ɪŋ, -d

roan (s. adj.) (R.), -s rəʊn, -z

Roanoke ‚rəʊəˈnəʊk

roar (s. v.), -s, -ing, -ed, -er/s rɔː* [rɔə*], -z, -rɪŋ, -d, -rə*/z

roast (s. v.), -s, -ing, -ed, -er/s rəʊst, -s, -ɪŋ, -ɪd, -ə*/z

roasting-jack, -s ˈrəʊstɪŋdʒæk, -s

rob (R.), -s, -bing, -bed, -ber/s rɒb, -z, -ɪŋ, -d, -ə*/z

Robb rɒb

robber|y, -ies ˈrɒbər|ɪ, -ɪz

Robbins ˈrɒbɪnz

rob|e (s. v.), -es, -ing, -ed rəʊb, -z, -ɪŋ, -d

Robens ˈrəʊbɪnz

Roberson ˈrəʊbəsn, ˈrɒbəsn

   Note.—In Roberson's medium *the usual pronunciation is* ˈrɒb-.

Robert, -s, -son ˈrɒbət, -s, -sn

Roberta rəˈbɜːtə [rɒˈb-, rəʊˈb-]

Robeson ˈrəʊbsn

Robespierre ˈrəʊbzpjeə* [-spjeə*] (rɔbɛspjɛːr)

426

robin, -s ˈrɒbɪn, -z

Robin, -son ˈrɒbɪn, -sn

Robina rɒˈbiːnə [rəʊˈb-]

Robins ˈrəʊbɪnz, ˈrɒbɪnz

Robinson ˈrɒbɪnsən

Roboam rəʊˈbəʊəm

robot, -s ˈrəʊbɒt [ˈrɒb-, -bət], -s

Robotham ˈrəʊbɒθəm

robotic, -s rəʊˈbɒtɪk [rɒˈb-], -s

Rob Roy ‚rɒbˈrɔɪ

Robsart ˈrɒbsɑːt

Robson ˈrɒbsn

robust, -ly, -ness rəʊˈbʌst, -lɪ, -nɪs [-nəs]

Rochdale ˈrɒtʃdeɪl

Roche rəʊtʃ, rəʊʃ, rɒʃ

Rochester ˈrɒtʃɪstə* [-tʃəstə*]

rochet, -s ˈrɒtʃɪt, -s

rock (s. v.) (R.), -s, -ing, -ed, -er/s rɒk, -s, -ɪŋ, -t, -ə*/z

rock-bottom ‚rɒkˈbɒtəm

rock-bound ˈrɒkbaʊnd

rockcake, -s ˈrɒkkeɪk, -s

Rockefeller ˈrɒkəfelə* [-kɪ-]

rocker|y, -ies ˈrɒkər|ɪ, -ɪz

rocket (s. v.), -s, -ing, -ed ˈrɒkɪt, -s, -ɪŋ, -ɪd

rocketry ˈrɒkɪtrɪ

rock-garden, -s ˈrɒk‚gɑːdn, -z

Rockies ˈrɒkɪz

rocking-chair, -s ˈrɒkɪŋtʃeə*, -z

Rockingham ˈrɒkɪŋəm

rocking-horse, -s ˈrɒkɪŋhɔːs, -ɪz

rocking-stone, -s ˈrɒkɪŋstəʊn, -z

rock 'n roll ‚rɒkənˈrəʊl

rock-plant, -s ˈrɒkplɑːnt, -s

rock-rose, -s ˈrɒkrəʊz, -ɪz

rock-salt ‚rɒkˈsɔːlt [-ˈsɒlt, ˈ--]

rock-salmon, -s ˈrɒkˈsæmən

Rockstro ˈrɒkstrəʊ

rockwork, -s ˈrɒkwɜːk, -s

rock|y, -ier, -iest, -iness ˈrɒk|ɪ, -ɪə*, -ɪɪst, -ɪnɪs [-məs]

rococo rəʊˈkəʊkəʊ

rod (R.), -s rɒd, -z

rode (from ride) rəʊd

rodent (s. adj.), -s ˈrəʊdənt, -s

rodeo, -s rəʊˈdeɪəʊ [ˈrəʊdɪəʊ], -z

Roderic(k) ˈrɒdərɪk

Rodgers ˈrɒdʒəz

Roding (several places in Essex) ˈrəʊdɪŋ [locally sometimes ˈruːdɪŋ, ˈruːðɪŋ]

Rod|ney, -way ˈrɒd|nɪ, -weɪ

rodomontad|e (s. v.), -es, -ing, -ed ‚rɒdəmɒnˈteɪd [-ˈtɑːd], -z, -ɪŋ, -ɪd

roe (R.), -s rəʊ, -z

roebuck (R.), -s ˈrəʊbʌk, -s

Roedean ˈrəʊdiːn

Roehampton rəʊˈhæmptən

Roentgen, see Röntgen
rogation (R.), -s rəʊˈgeɪʃn, -z
Roger, -s ˈrɒdʒə* [ˈrəʊdʒə*, esp.
  Scottish], -z
Roget ˈrɒʒeɪ
Rogozin rəˈgəʊzɪn [rɒˈg-]
rogue, -s rəʊg, -z
roguer|y, -ies ˈrəʊgər|ɪ, -ɪz
roguish, -ly, -ness ˈrəʊgɪʃ, -lɪ, -nɪs [-nəs]
roil, -s, -ing, -ed rɔɪl, -z, -ɪŋ, -d
roist|er, -ers, -ering, -ered, -erer/s
  ˈrɔɪst|ə*, -əz, -ərɪŋ, -əd, -ərə*/z
Rokeby ˈrəʊkbɪ
Roker ˈrəʊkə*
Roland ˈrəʊlənd
role, -s rəʊl, -z
roleplay, -ing ˈrəʊlpleɪ, -ɪŋ
Rolf(e) rɒlf, rəʊf
roll (s. v.), -s, -ing, -ed, -er/s rəʊl, -z,
  -ɪŋ, -d, -ə*/z
roll-back, -s ˈrəʊlbæk, -s
roll-bar, -s ˈrəʊlbɑ:*, -z
roll-call, -s ˈrəʊlkɔːl, -z
roller-skat|e (s. v.), -es, -ing, -ed ˈrəʊlə-
  skeɪt [ˌ--ˈ-], -s, -ɪŋ, -ɪd
roller-towel, -s ˈrəʊləˌtaʊəl [ˌ--ˈ--], -z
Rolleston ˈrəʊlstən
rollick, -s, -ing, -ed ˈrɒlɪk, -s, -ɪŋ, -t
rolling-pin, -s ˈrəʊlɪŋpɪn, -z
rolling-stock, -s ˈrəʊlɪŋstɒk, -s
Rollo ˈrɒləʊ
Rolls rəʊlz
Rolls-Royce, -s ˌrəʊlzˈrɔɪs, -ɪz
roll-top, -s ˈrəʊltɒp, -s
roly-pol|y, -ies ˌrəʊlɪˈpəʊl|ɪ, -ɪz
Romagna rəʊˈmɑːnjə (roˈmaɲɲa)
Romaic rəʊˈmeɪɪk
Roman, -s ˈrəʊmən, -z
romanc|e (s. v.) (R.), -es, -ing, -ed,
  -er/s rəʊˈmæns [rʊˈm-, s. also
  ˈrəʊmæns], -ɪz, -ɪŋ, -t -ə*/z
Romanes (surname) rəʊˈmɑːnɪz (gipsy
  language) ˈrɒmənes
romanesque ˌrəʊməˈnesk
Romania (Ru-), -n/s ruːˈmeɪnjə [rʊˈm-,
  rə-, -nɪə], -n/z
Romanic rəʊˈmænɪk
romani|sm, -st/s ˈrəʊmənɪ|zəm, -st/s
romanization [-isa-], -s ˌrəʊmənaɪ-
  ˈzeɪʃn, -z
romaniz|e [-is|e], -es, -ing, -ed ˈrəʊ-
  mənaɪz, -ɪz, -ɪŋ, -d
Romansch rəʊˈmænʃ
romantic, -ally rəʊˈmæntɪk, -əlɪ
romantici|sm, -st/s rəʊˈmæntɪsɪ|zəm,
  -st/s
Roman|y, -ies ˈrɒmən|ɪ [ˈrəʊm-], -ɪz
romaunt, -s rəʊˈmɔːnt, -s

Rome rəʊm
Romeike rəʊˈmiːkɪ
Romeo ˈrəʊmɪəʊ [-mjəʊ]
Romford ˈrɒmfəd [old-fashioned ˈrʌm-]
romic (R.) ˈrəʊmɪk
Romish ˈrəʊmɪʃ
Romney, -s ˈrɒmnɪ [ˈrʌm-], -z
Romola ˈrɒmələ
romp (s. v.), -s, -ing, -ed rɒmp, -s, -ɪŋ, -t
  [rɒmt]
romper, -s ˈrɒmpə*, -z
Romsey ˈrʌmzɪ
Romulus ˈrɒmjʊləs
Ronald, -shay ˈrɒnld, -ʃeɪ
Ronan ˈrəʊnən
rondeau, -s ˈrɒndəʊ, -z
rondel, -s ˈrɒndl, -z
rondo, -s ˈrɒndəʊ, -z
roneo (s. v.), -s, -ing, -ed ˈrəʊnɪəʊ
  [-njəʊ], -z, -ɪŋ, -d
Roney ˈrəʊnɪ
Rongbuk ˈrɒŋbʊk
Ronson ˈrɒnsən
Rontgen ˈrɒntjən [-tgən]
Röntgen ˈrɒntjən [ˈrʌnt-, ˈrɜːnt-, -tgən]
röntgenogram, -s rɒntˈgenəgræm
  [rʌnt-, rɜːnt-, ˈrɒntjənəg-, ˈrʌnt-
  jənəg-, ˈrɜːntjənəg-], -z
Ronuk ˈrɒnək
rood, -s ruːd, -z
rood-loft, -s ˈruːdlɒft, -s
rood-screen, -s ˈruːdskriːn, -z
roo|f (s.), -fs, -ves ruː|f, -fs, -vz
roof (v.), -s, -ing, -ed ruːf, -s, -ɪŋ, -t
roof-garden, -s ˈruːfˌgɑːdn, -z
rook (s. v.), -s, -ing, -ed rʊk, -s, -ɪŋ, -t
rooker|y, -ies ˈrʊkər|ɪ, -ɪz
rookie, -s ˈrʊkɪ, -z
room, -s ruːm [rʊm], -z
Room ruːm
-roomed -ruːmd [-rʊmd]
roomful, -s ˈruːmfʊl [ˈrʊm-], -z
Rooms ruːmz
room|y, -ier, -iest, -ily, -iness ˈruːm|ɪ
  [ˈrʊm-], -ɪə*, -ɪɪst, -ɪlɪ [-əlɪ], -ɪnɪs
  [-nəs]
Roosevelt (American surname) ˈrəʊzəvelt [ˈruːsvelt]
  Note.—ˈrəʊzəvelt is the pronunciation used in the families of the late
  presidents of the U.S.A. In England this name is often pronounced
  ˈruːsvelt.
roost (s. v.), -s, -ing, -ed, -er/s ruːst, -s
  -ɪŋ, -ɪd, -ə*/z
root (s. v.) (R.), -s, -ing, -ed; -less, -y
  ruːt, -s, -ɪŋ, -ɪd; -lɪs [-ləs], -ɪ
Rootham ˈruːtəm

427

rop|e (s. v.), -es, -ing, -ed rəup, -s, -ıŋ, -t
rope-dancer, -s 'rəup‚dɑ:nsə*, -z
Roper 'rəupə*
rope-trick, -s 'rəuptrık, -s
rope-walker, -s 'rəup‚wɔ:kə*, -z
Ropner 'rɒpnə*
Roquefort, -s 'rɒkfɔ:* (rɔkfɔ:r), -z
roquet (s. v.), -s, -ing, -ed 'rəukı [-keı],
  -z, -ıŋ, -d
Rorke rɔ:k
Rosa 'rəuzə
rosace, -s 'rəuzeıs, -ız
rosaceous rəu'zeıʃəs
Rosalba rəu'zælbə
Rosalie 'rəuzəlı, 'rɒzəlı
Rosalind 'rɒzəlınd
Rosaline (Shakespearian character)
  'rɒzəlaın
Rosamond 'rɒzəmənd
rosarium, -s rəu'zeərıəm, -z
rosar|y, -ies 'rəuzər|ı, -ız
Roscius 'rɒʃıəs [-ʃjəs]
Roscoe 'rɒskəu
Roscommon rɒs'kɒmən
rose (R.), -s rəuz, -ız
rose (from rise) rəuz
roseate 'rəuzıət [-zjət, -zııt, -zjıt]
Rosebery 'rəuzbərı
rose-bud, -s 'rəuzbʌd, -z
rose-bush, -es 'rəuzbuʃ, -ız
rose-colour 'rəuz‚kʌlə*
rose-garden, -s 'rəuz‚gɑ:dn, -z
Rosehaugh 'rəuzhɔ:
rose-lea|f, -ves 'rəuzli:|f, -vz
rosemar|y (R.), -ies 'rəuzmər|ı, -ız
Rosencrantz 'rəuzənkrænts
roseola rəu'zi:ələ [-'zıə-]
rose-pink ‚rəuz'pıŋk
rose-red ‚rəuz'red
rose-tree, -s 'rəuztri:, -z
Rosetta rəu'zetə
rosette, -s rəu'zet, -s
rose-water 'rəuz‚wɔ:tə*
rosewood 'rəuzwud
Rosherville 'rɒʃəvıl
Rosicrucian, -s ‚rəuzı'kru:ʃn [‚rɒz-,
  -ʃıən, -ʃjən], -z
Rosier 'rəu‚zıə* [-zıə*, -zjə*]
rosin 'rɒzın
Rosina rəu'zi:nə
Roslin 'rɒzlın
Ross rɒs
Rossall 'rɒsəl
Rosse, -r rɒs, -ə*
Rossetti rɒ'setı [rə's-, -'zetı]
Rossini rɒ'si:nı [rə's-, -ni:] (ros'si:ni)
Rosslare 'rɒsleə*, rɒs'leə*
Rosslyn 'rɒslın

Ross-shire 'rɒsʃə* ['rɒʃʃə*, -‚ʃıə*]
roster, -s 'rɒstə* ['rəus-], -z
Rostrevor rɒs'trevə*
rostrum, -s 'rɒstrəm, -z
ros|y (R.), -ier, -iest, -ily, -iness 'rəuz|ı,
  -ıə* [-jə*], -ııst [-jıst], -ılı [-əlı], -ınıs
  [-ınəs]
Rosyth rɒ'saıθ [rə's-]
rot (s. v.), -s, -ting, -ted, -ter/s rɒt, -s,
  -ıŋ, -ıd, -ə*/z
rota, -s 'rəutə, -z
rotar|y (s. adj.), -ies 'rəutər|ı, -ız
rotatable rəu'teıtəbl
rotat|e, -es, -ing, -ed, -or/s rəu'teıt, -s,
  -ıŋ, -ıd, -ə*/z
rotation, -s rəu'teıʃn, -z
rotatory 'rəutətərı [rəu'teıtərı]
rote rəut
Rothamsted 'rɒθəmsted
Rothenstein (English surname) 'rəuθən-
  staın, 'rəutən-, 'rɒθən-
Rothera 'rɒθərə
Rother|ham, -hithe 'rɒðə|rəm, -haıð
Rothermere 'rɒðə‚mıə*
Rotherston 'rɒðəstən
Rotherwick 'rɒðərık, -ðəwık
Rothes 'rɒθıs
Rothesay 'rɒθsı [-seı]
Rothschild (English surname) 'rɒθʃaıld,
  'rɒstʃ-, 'rɒθstʃ-
rotor, -s 'rəutə*, -z
rott|en, -enest, -enly, -enness 'rɒt|n,
  -nıst, -nlı, -nnıs [-nnəs]
rottenstone 'rɒtnstəun
rotter, -s 'rɒtə*, -z
Rotterdam ‚rɒtə'dæm ['---]
Rottingdean 'rɒtıŋdi:n
rotund, -ity, -ness rəu'tʌnd, -ətı [-ıtı],
  -nıs [-nəs]
rotunda (R.), -s rəu'tʌndə, -z
rouble, -s 'ru:bl, -z
roué, -s 'ru:eı ['rueı], -z
Rouen 'ru:ɑ̃:ŋ [-ɔ̃:ŋ, -ɑːŋ, -ɒŋ] (rwɑ̃)
roug|e (s. v.), -es, -ing, -ed ru:ʒ, -ız, -ıŋ,
  -d
rough (s. adj. v.), -s; -er, -est, -ly, -ness;
  -ing, -ed rʌf, -s; -ə*, -ıst, -lı, -nıs
  [-nəs]; -ıŋ, -t
roughage 'rʌfıdʒ
rough-cast 'rʌfkɑ:st
rough-hew, -s, -ing, -ed, -n ‚rʌf'hju:,
  -z, -ıŋ [-'hjuıŋ], -d, -n
roughish 'rʌfıʃ
rough-rider, -s 'rʌf‚raıdə*, -z
rough-shod 'rʌfʃɒd
rough-spoken ‚rʌf'spəukən [also '--‚--
  when attributive]
Rough Tor (in Cornwall) ‚rəu'tɔ:*

roulade, -s ruːˈlɑːd, -z
roulette ruːˈlet [rʊˈl-]
Ro(u)mania, -n/s ruːˈmeɪnjə [rʊˈm-, -nɪə], -n/z
Roumelia ruːˈmiːljə [rʊˈm-, -lɪə]
rounceval, -s ˈraʊnsɪvl, -z
round (*s. adj. v. adv. prep.*), **-s; -er, -est, -ly, -ness, -ish; -ing, -ed** raʊnd, -z; -ə*, -ɪst, -lɪ, -nɪs [-aʊnnɪs, -nəs], -ɪʃ; -ɪŋ, -ɪd
roundabout (*s. adj.*), **-s** ˈraʊndəbaʊt, -s
roundel, -s ˈraʊndl, -z
roundelay, -s ˈraʊndɪleɪ, -z
rounders ˈraʊndəz
roundhand ˈraʊndhænd
Roundhead, -s ˈraʊndhed, -z
roundish ˈraʊndɪʃ
round-shouldered ˌraʊndˈʃəʊldəd [ˈ-ˌ--]
rounds|man, -men ˈraʊndzmən, -mən
round-the-clock ˈraʊndðəklɒk [ˌ--ˈ-]
round-up, -s ˈraʊndʌp [ˌ-ˈ-], -s
Rourke rɔːk
Rous raʊs
rous|e, -es, -ing/ly, -ed raʊz, -ɪz, -ɪŋ/lɪ, -d
Rouse raʊs, ruːs
Rousseau ˈruːsəʊ (ruso)
Roussin ˈrʊsɪn
rout (*s. v.*), **-s, -ing, -ed** raʊt, -s, -ɪŋ, -ɪd
route, -s ruːt, -s
route-march, -es ˈruːtmɑːtʃ [ˈraʊt-], -ɪz
Routh raʊθ
routine, -s ruːˈtiːn [rʊˈt-], -z
Routledge ˈraʊtlɪdʒ [-ledʒ], ˈrʌt-
Routley ˈraʊtlɪ
rov|e, -es, -ing, -ed, -er/s rəʊv, -z, -ɪŋ, -d, -ə*/z
Rover, -s ˈrəʊvə*, -z
row (*s.*) (*number of persons or things in a line*), **-s** rəʊ, -z
row (*s.*) (*excursion in a rowing-boat*), **-s** rəʊ, -z
row (*s.*) (*disturbance*), **-s** raʊ, -z
row (*v.*) (*propel boat with oars*), **-s, -ing, -ed** rəʊ, -z, -ɪŋ, -d
row (*v.*) (*quarrel*), **-s, -ing, -ed** raʊ, -z, -ɪŋ, -d
Rowallan rəʊˈælən
rowan (*tree*), **-s** ˈraʊən [ˈrəʊən], -z
Note.—More commonly ˈraʊən *in Scotland.*
Rowan (*surname*) ˈrəʊən, ˈraʊən
Rowant (*in Oxfordshire*) ˈraʊənt
row-boat, -s ˈrəʊbəʊt, -s
row-de-dow [**rowdydow**], **-s** ˌraʊdɪˈdaʊ, -z
Rowden ˈraʊdn
rowd|y (*s. adj.*), **-ies, -ier, -iest, -ily, -iness, -yism** ˈraʊd|ɪ, -ɪz, -ɪə* [-jə*], -ɪɪst [-jɪst], -ɪlɪ [-əlɪ], -ɪnɪs [-ɪnəs], -ɪɪzəm
Rowe rəʊ
Rowed ˈrəʊɪd
rowel, -s ˈraʊəl, -z
Rowell ˈraʊəl, ˈrəʊəl
Rowena rəʊˈiːnə
rower (*one who rows a boat*), **-s** ˈrəʊə*, -z
rowing-boat, -s ˈrəʊɪŋbəʊt, -s
Rowland, -s ˈrəʊlənd, -z
Rowles rəʊlz
Rowley ˈrəʊlɪ
rowlock, -s ˈrɒlək [ˈrəʊlɒk, ˈrʌlək], -s
Rowney ˈrəʊnɪ, ˈraʊnɪ
Rowntree ˈraʊntriː
Rowridge ˈraʊrɪdʒ
Rowse raʊs
Rowton ˈraʊtn, ˈrɔːtn
Roxburgh(e) ˈrɒksbərə
Roy rɔɪ
roy|al, -ally ˈrɔɪ|əl, -əlɪ
royali|sm, -st/s ˈrɔɪəlɪ|zəm, -st/s
royalt|y, -ies ˈrɔɪəlt|ɪ, -ɪz
Royce rɔɪs
Royston ˈrɔɪstən
Ruabon ruːˈæbən [rʊˈæ-] (*Welsh* riuˈabon)
rub (*s. v.*), **-s, -bing, -bed** rʌb, -z, -ɪŋ, -d
Rubáiyát ˈruːbaɪjæt [ˌ--ˈ-, -jɑːt]
rubato, -s rʊˈbɑːtəʊ [ruːˈb-], -z
rubber, -s -y ˈrʌbə*, -z, -rɪ
rubbish, -y ˈrʌbɪʃ, -ɪ
rubb|le, -ly ˈrʌb|l, -lɪ
Rubbra ˈrʌbrə
rubefacient ˌruːbɪˈfeɪʃjənt [-ʃɪənt]
rubella rʊˈbelə [ruːˈb-]
Rubens ˈruːbɪnz [-bənz, -benz]
rubeola rʊˈbiːəʊlə [ruːˈb-, -ˈbɪələ]
Rubicon ˈruːbɪkən [-kɒn]
rubicund ˈruːbɪkənd
rubidium ruːˈbɪdɪəm [rʊˈb-, -djəm]
Rubinstein (*pianist*) ˈruːbɪnstaɪn [-bən-]
rubric, -s ˈruːbrɪk, -s
rub|y (**R.**), **-ies** ˈruːb|ɪ, -ɪz
ruch|e, -es, -ing ruːʃ, -ɪz, -ɪŋ
ruck rʌk
rucksack, -s ˈrʌksæk [ˈrʊk-], -s
ruction, -s ˈrʌkʃn, -z
rudd (**R.**), **-s** rʌd, -z
rudder, -s, -less ˈrʌdə*, -z, -lɪs [-ləs]
Ruddigore ˈrʌdɪgɔː* [-gɔə*]
rudd|le (*s. v.*), **-les, -ling, -led** ˈrʌd|l, -lz, -lɪŋ, -ld
rudd|y, -ier, -iest, -ily, -iness ˈrʌd|ɪ, -ɪə* [-jə*], -ɪɪst [-jɪst], -ɪlɪ [-əlɪ], -ɪnɪs [-ɪnəs]

rude, -r, -st, -ly, -ness ruːd, -ə*, -ɪst, -lɪ, -nɪs [-nəs]
Rudge, -s rʌdʒ, -ɪz
rudiment, -s 'ruːdɪmənt, -s
rudiment|al, -ary ˌruːdɪ'ment|l, -ərɪ
Rudmose 'rʌdməʊz
Rudol|f, -ph 'ruːdɒl|f, -f
Rudyard 'rʌdjəd [-jɑːd]
Rudyard (Staffs.) 'rʌdʒəd
rue (s. v.), -s, -ing, -d ruː, -z, -ɪŋ ['rʊɪŋ], -d
rue|ful, -fully, -fulness 'ruː|fʊl, -fʊlɪ [-fəlɪ], -fʊlnɪs [-nəs]
ruff (s. v.), -s, -ing, -ed rʌf, -s, -ɪŋ, -t
ruffian, -s, -ly; -ism 'rʌfjən [-fɪən], -z, -lɪ; -ɪzəm
ruff|le (s. v.), -les, -ling, -led 'rʌf|l, -lz, -lɪŋ [-lɪŋ], -ld
Rufus 'ruːfəs
rug, -s rʌg, -z
Rugbeian, -s rʌg'biːən [-'bɪən], -z
Rugby 'rʌgbɪ
Rugeley 'ruːdʒlɪ ['ruːʒlɪ]
rugged, -ly, -ness 'rʌgɪd, -lɪ, -nɪs [-nəs]
rugger 'rʌgə*
Ruhr rʊə*
ruin (s. v.), -s, -ing, -ed 'rʊɪn ['ruːɪn], -z, -ɪŋ, -d
ruination rʊɪ'neɪʃn [ˌruːɪ'n-]
ruinous, -ly, -ness 'rʊɪnəs ['ruːɪn-], -lɪ, -nɪs
Ruislip (in Greater London) 'raɪslɪp ['raɪzl-]
Ruiz ruː'iːθ [rʊ'iːθ]
rul|e (s. v.), -es, -ing, -ed, -er/s ruːl, -z, -ɪŋ, -d, -ə*/z
ruling (s.), -s 'ruːlɪŋ, -z
rum (s. adj.), -mer, -mest rʌm, -ə*, -ɪst
Rumania (Ro-), -n/s ruː'meɪnjə [rʊ'm-, -nɪə], -n/z
rumba, -s 'rʌmbə, -z
rumb|le (s. v.), -les, -ling/s, -led 'rʌmb|l, -lz, -lɪŋ/z, -ld
Rumbold 'rʌmbəʊld
rumbustious rʌm'bʌstɪəs [-tjəs, -tʃəs]
Rumelia ruː'miːljə [rʊ'm-, -lɪə]
Rumford 'rʌmfəd
ruminant (s. adj.), -s 'ruːmɪnənt, -s
ruminat|e, -es, -ing, -ed 'ruːmɪneɪt, -s, -ɪŋ, -ɪd
rumination, -s ˌruːmɪ'neɪʃn, -z
ruminative 'ruːmɪnətɪv [-neɪt-]
rummag|e (s. v.), -es, -ing, -ed 'rʌmɪdʒ, -ɪz, -ɪŋ, -d
rumm|y (s. adj.), -ier, -iest, -ily, -iness 'rʌm|ɪ, -ɪə*, -ɪɪst, -ɪlɪ [-əlɪ], -ɪnɪs [-ɪnəs]

rumour, -s, -ed 'ruːmə*, -z, -d
rumour-mong|er, -ers, -ering 'ruːmə-ˌmʌŋg|ə*, -əz, -ərɪŋ
rump, -s rʌmp, -s
rump|le, -les, -ling, -led 'rʌmp|l, -lz, -lɪŋ [-lɪŋ], -ld
rumpus, -es 'rʌmpəs, -ɪz
rum-runner, -s 'rʌmˌrʌnə*, -z
run (s. v.), -s, -ning, ran rʌn, -z, -ɪŋ, ræn
runabout, -s 'rʌnəbaʊt, -s
runagate, -s 'rʌnəgeɪt, -s
runaway (s. adj.), -s 'rʌnəweɪ, -z
Runciman 'rʌnsɪmən
Runcorn 'rʌŋkɔːn
run-down, -s 'rʌndaʊn, -z
rune (R.), -s ruːn, -z
rung (s.), -s rʌŋ, -z
rung (from ring) rʌŋ
runic (R.) 'ruːnɪk
runnel, -s 'rʌnl, -z
runner, -s 'rʌnə*, -z
runner-up, runners-up ˌrʌnər'ʌp, ˌrʌnəz'ʌp
running-board, -s 'rʌnɪŋbɔːd [-bɔəd], -z
Runnymede 'rʌnɪmiːd
runt, -s rʌnt, -s
Runton 'rʌntən
runway, -s 'rʌnweɪ, -z
Runyon 'rʌnjən
rupee, -s ruː'piː [rʊ'p-], -z
Rupert 'ruːpət
rupt|ure (s. v.), -ures, -uring, -ured 'rʌptʃ|ə*, -əz, -ərɪŋ, -əd
rur|al, -ally 'rʊər|əl, -əlɪ
ruridecanal ˌrʊərɪdɪ'keɪnl [-'dekənl]
Ruritania, -n ˌrʊərɪ'teɪnjə [-nɪə], -n
ruse, -s ruːz, -ɪz
rusé 'ruːzeɪ (ryze)
rush (s. v.), -es, -ing, -ed, -er/s rʌʃ, -ɪz, -ɪŋ, -t, -ə*/z
Rushforth 'rʌʃfɔːθ
rush-hour, -s 'rʌʃˌaʊə*, -z
rush|light/s, -like 'rʌʃ|laɪt/s, -laɪk
Rushmere 'rʌʃmɪə*
Rusholme (near Manchester) 'rʌʃəm ['rʌʃhəʊm]
Rushton 'rʌʃtən
Rushworth 'rʌʃwɜːθ
rushy 'rʌʃɪ
rusk (R.), -s rʌsk, -s
Ruskin 'rʌskɪn
Rusper 'rʌspə*
Russell 'rʌsl
russet (s. adj.), -s, -y 'rʌsɪt, -s, -ɪ
Russi|a, -an/s 'rʌʃ|ə, -n/z
russianism, -s 'rʌʃənɪzəm [-ʃnɪ-], -z
russianiz|e (-is|e], -es, -ing, -ed 'rʌʃənaɪz [-ʃnaɪz], -ɪz, -ɪŋ, -d

430

rust (*s. v.*), **-s, -ing, -ed** rʌst, -s, -ɪŋ, -ɪd
rustic (*s. adj.*), **-s, -ally** 'rʌstɪk, -s, -əlɪ
rusticat|e, -es, -ing, -ed 'rʌstɪkeɪt, -s, -ɪŋ, -ɪd
rustication ˌrʌstɪ'keɪʃn
rusticity rʌ'stɪsətɪ [-ɪtɪ]
rust|le (*s. v.*), **-les, -ling, -led, -ler/s** 'rʌs|l, -lz, -lɪŋ [-l̩ɪŋ], -ld, -lə*/z
Rustum 'rʌstəm
rust|y, -ier, -iest, -iness 'rʌst|ɪ, -ɪə* [-jə*], -ɪɪst [-jɪst], -ɪnɪs [-məs]
Ruswarp (*near Whitby*) 'rʌsəp [-zəp, -zwɔːp]
rut, -s, -ted rʌt, -s, -ɪd
Rutgers 'rʌtgəz
ruth (**R.**) ruːθ
Ruthenian, -s ruː'θiːnjən [rʊ'θ-, -nɪən], -z
ruthenium ruː'θiːnɪəm [-njəm]
Ruther|ford, -glen 'rʌðə|fəd, -glen
Ruthin 'rɪθɪn ['ruːθɪn] (*Welsh* 'hrɨθɨn)
ruthless, -ly, -ness 'ruːθlɪs [-ləs], -lɪ, -nɪs [-nəs]
Ruthrieston 'rʌðrɪstən

Ruthven (*personal name*) 'ruːθvən, 'rɪvən, (*place in Tayside Region*) 'rɪvən, (*place in Grampian Region, loch in Highland Region*) 'rʌθvən
  Note.—Baron Ruthven is 'rɪvən.
Ruthwell 'rʌθwəl [*locally* 'rɪðəl]
Rutland, -shire 'rʌtlənd, -ʃə* [-ˌʃɪə*]
Rutter 'rʌtə*
rutt|y, -ier, -iest, -iness 'rʌt|ɪ, -ɪə*, -ɪɪst, -ɪnɪs [-məs]
Ruy Lopez ˌruːɪ'ləʊpez
Ruysdael 'raɪzdɑːl
Ruyter 'raɪtə*
Rwanda rʊ'ændə [ruː'æ-, 'rwændə]
Ryan 'raɪən
Rydal 'raɪdl
Ryde raɪd
rye (**R.**), **-bread, -grass** raɪ, -bred, -grɑːs
Ryle raɪl
Rylstone 'rɪlstən [-stəʊn]
Ryman 'raɪmən
ryot, -s 'raɪət, -s
Ryswick 'rɪzwɪk
Ryvita raɪ'viːtə

S

S (*the letter*), **-'s** es, -ız
Saab (*car*) sɑ:b
Saba (*in Arabia*) 'sɑ:bə, (*in West Indies*) 'sæbə
Sabaean sə'bi:ən [sæ'b-, -'bɪən]
Sabaoth sæ'beɪɒθ [sə'b-, 'sæbeɪɒθ, -əθ]
sabbatarian, -s, -ism ˌsæbə'teərɪən, -z, -ɪzəm
Sabbath, -s 'sæbəθ, -s
sabbatical sə'bætɪkl
Sabin (*surname*) 'seɪbɪn, 'sæbɪn
Sabine (*Italian people*), **-s** 'sæbaɪn, -z
Sabine (*surname*) 'sæbaɪn, 'sæbɪn, 'seɪbɪn
Sabine (*river, lake, pass*) sə'bi:n [sæ'b-]
sable (*s. adj.*), **-s** 'seɪbl, -z
sabot, -s 'sæbəʊ, -z
sabotag|e (*s. v.*), **-es, -ing, -ed** 'sæbətɑ:ʒ [-tɑ:dʒ], -ız, -ıŋ, -d
saboteur, -s ˌsæbə'tɜ:* ['---], -z
sab|re (*s. v.*), **-res, -ring, -red** 'seɪb|ə*, -əz, -ərıŋ, -əd
sabretache, -s 'sæbətæʃ, -ız
sabre-toothed 'seɪbətu:θt [-tu:ðd]
sabulous 'sæbjʊləs
sac, -s sæk, -s
saccade, -s sæ'kɑ:d, -z
saccharine (*s.*) 'sækərın [-ri:n, -raɪn]
saccharine (*adj.*) 'sækəraɪn [-ri:n]
sacerdot|al, -ally ˌsæsə'dəʊt|l, -əlɪ
sachem, -s 'seɪtʃəm [-tʃem], -z
sachet, -s 'sæʃeɪ, -z
Sacheverell sə'ʃevərəl
sack (*s. v.*), **-s, -ing, -ed, -er/s** sæk, -s, -ıŋ, -t, -ə*/z
sackbut, -s 'sækbʌt [-bət], -s
sackful, -s 'sækfʊl, -z
sacking (*s.*) 'sækıŋ
Sackville 'sækvɪl
sacral 'seɪkrəl
sacrament, -s 'sækrəmənt [-krım-], -s
sacramental ˌsækrə'mentl [-krı'm-]
Sacramento ˌsækrə'mentəʊ
sacred, -ly, -ness 'seɪkrɪd, -lı, -nıs [-nəs]
sacrific|e (*s. v.*), **-es, -ing, -ed** 'sækrıfaɪs, -ız, -ıŋ, -t
sacrifici|al, -ally ˌsækrı'fıʃ|l, -əlı
sacrilege 'sækrılıdʒ [-krə-]

sacrilegious ˌsækrı'lıdʒəs [-krə-, -'lıdʒjəs, -'lıdʒɪəs, *rarely* -'li:dʒ-]
sacristan, -s 'sækrıstən, -z
sacrist|y, -ies 'sækrıst|ı, -ız
sacrosanct 'sækrəʊsæŋkt
sacr|um, -a 'seɪkr|əm ['sæ-], -ə
sad, -der, -dest, -ly, -ness sæd, -ə*, -ıst, -lı, -nıs [-nəs]
sadd|en, -ens, -ening, -ened 'sæd|n, -nz, -ŋıŋ [-nıŋ], -nd
sadd|le, -les, -ling, -led 'sæd|l, -lz, -lıŋ [-lıŋ], -ld
saddleback (**S.**) 'sædlbæk
saddlebag, -s 'sædlbæg, -z
saddle-horse, -s 'sædlhɔ:s, -ız
saddler, -s; -y 'sædlə*, -z; -rı
Sadducee, -s 'sædjʊsi:, -z
Sade sɑ:d
Sadie 'seɪdı
sadi|sm, -st/s 'seɪdı|zəm, -st/s
sadistic sə'dıstık [sæ'd-]
Sadleir 'sædlə*
Sadler 'sædlə*
Sadowa 'sɑ:dəʊə*
safari, -s sə'fɑ:rı, -z
safe (*s. adj.*), **-s; -r, -st, -ly, -ness** seɪf, -s; -ə*, -ıst, -lı, -nıs [-nəs]
safe-conduct, -s ˌseɪf'kɒndʌkt [-dəkt], -s
safe-deposit, -s 'seɪfdı,pɒzıt, -s
safeguard (*s. v.*), **-s, -ing, -ed** 'seɪfgɑ:d, -z, -ıŋ, -ıd
safe-keeping ˌseɪf'ki:pıŋ
safety 'seɪftı
safety-bolt, -s 'seɪftıbəʊlt, -s
safety-catch, -es 'seɪftıkætʃ, -ız
safety-curtain, -s 'seɪftı,kɜ:tn [-tən, -tın], -z
safety-lamp, -s 'seɪftılæmp, -s
safety-lock, -s 'seɪftılɒk, -s
safety-match, -es 'seɪftımætʃ, -ız
safety-pin, -s 'seɪftıpın, -s
safety-razor, -s 'seɪftı,reɪzə*, -z
safety-valve, -s 'seɪftıvælv, -z
Saffell sə'fel
saffron (**S.**) 'sæfrən
sag (*s. v.*), **-s, -ging, -ged** sæg, -z, -ıŋ, -d
saga, -s 'sɑ:gə, -z

432

sagacious, -ly, -ness sə'geɪʃəs, -lɪ, -nɪs [-nəs]
sagacity sə'gæsətɪ [-ɪtɪ]
sage (*s. adj.*) **(S.), -s, -ly, -ness** seɪdʒ, -ɪz, -lɪ, -nɪs [-nəs]
sagitt|a, -ae sə'dʒɪt|ə, -i: [-aɪ]
Sagitta (*constellation*) sə'gɪtə [sə'dʒɪ-]
sagittal 'sædʒɪtl
Sagittarian, -s ˌsædʒɪ'teərɪən, -z
Sagittarius (*constellation*) ˌsædʒɪ'teərɪəs [ˌsægɪ-, -'tɑːrɪəs]
sago 'seɪgəʊ
Sahara sə'hɑːrə
sahib (S.), -s sɑːb ['sɑː*h*ɪb], -z
said (*from* **say**) sed (*normal form*), səd (*occasional weak form*)
Said (*in* **Port Said**) saɪd [*old-fashioned* seɪd]
sail (*s. v.*), **-s, -ing/s, -ed, -er/s, -or/s** seɪl, -z, -ɪŋ/z, -d, -ə*/z, -ə*/z
sailor|man, -men 'seɪlə|mæn, -men
sailplane, -s 'seɪlpleɪn, -z
sainfoin 'sænfɔɪn ['seɪn-]
Sainsbury 'seɪnzbərɪ
saint (S.), -s seɪnt (*strong form*), -s, sənt, sɪnt, snt (*weak forms*)
St. Abb's snt'æbz [sənt-, sɪnt-]
St. Agnes snt'ægnɪs [sənt-, sɪnt-]
St. Alban, -'s snt'ɔːlbən [sənt-, sɪnt-, -'ɒl-], -z
St. Aldate's (*street in Oxford*) snt'ɔːldeɪts [sənt-, sɪnt-, -'ɒl-, -dɪts, *old-fashioned* -'əʊldz]
St. Ambrose snt'æmbrəʊz [sənt-, sɪnt-, -əʊs]
St. Andrew, -s snt'ændru: [sənt-, sɪnt-], -z
St. Anne snt'æn [sənt-, sɪnt-]
St. Anthony snt'æntənɪ [sənt-, sɪnt-]
St. Asaph snt'æsəf [sənt-, sɪnt-]
St. Augustine səntɔ:'gʌstɪn [sɪnt-, ˌsent-, ˌseɪnt-, -tə'g-, *rarely* sənt-'ɔ:gəstɪn, sɪnt'ɔ:gəstɪn]
St. Austell snt'ɔ:stl [sənt-, sɪnt-, *locally* -'ɔ:sl]
St. Bartholomew, -'s sən*t*bɑ:'θɒləmju: [sɪn*t*-, -bə'θ-], -z
St. Bees sn*t*'bi:z [sən*t*-, sɪn*t*-]
St. Bernard, -s sn*t*'bə:nəd [sən*t*-, sɪn*t*-], -z
St. Blaize sn*t*'bleɪz [sən*t*-, sɪn*t*-]
St. Blazey sn*t*'bleɪzɪ [sən*t*-, sɪn*t*-]
St. Bride's sn*t*'braɪdz [sən*t*-, sɪn*t*-]
St. Catherine [-thar-], -'s sn*t*'kæθərɪn [sən*t*-, sɪn*t*-, sŋ'k-], -z
St. Cecilia səntsɪ'sɪljə [sɪnt-, -lɪə]
St. Christopher sn*t*'krɪstəfə* [sən*t*-, sɪn*t*-, sŋ'k-]

St. Clair (*surname*) 'sɪŋkleə* ['sɪnk-], (*place in U.S.A.*) snt'kleə* [sən*t*-, sɪn*t*-]
St. Columb sn*t*'kɒləm [sən*t*-, sɪn*t*-]
St. David, -'s sn*t*'deɪvɪd [sən*t*-, sɪn*t*-], -z
St. Edmunds snt'edməndz [sənt-, sɪnt-]
St. Elian snt'i:ljən [sənt-, sɪnt-, -lɪən]
St. Elias səntɪ'laɪəs [sɪnt-, -'laɪæs]
St. Elmo snt'elməʊ [sənt-, sɪnt-]
St. Francis snt'frɑ:nsɪs [sənt-, sɪnt-]
St. Gall sn*t*'gæl [sən*t*-, sɪn*t*-, -'gɑ:l, -'gɔ:l]
St. Galmier sn'gælmɪeɪ [sŋ'g-, sən*t*'g-, sɪn*t*'g-, -mjeɪ] (sẽgalmje)
St. George, -'s sn*t*'dʒɔ:dʒ [sən*t*-, sɪn*t*-], -ɪz
St. Giles, -'s sn*t*'dʒaɪlz [sən*t*-, sɪn*t*-], -ɪz
St. Gotthard sn*t*'gɒtəd [sən*t*-, sɪn*t*-]
St. Helena (*Saint*) snt'helɪnə [sənt-, sɪnt-], (*island*) ˌsentɪ'li:nə [sənt-, -ə'l-]
St. Helen's snt'helɪnz [sənt-, sɪnt-, -lənz]
St. Helier, -'s snt'heljə* [sənt-, sɪnt-, -lɪə*], -z
St. Ives snt'aɪvz [sənt-, sɪnt-]
St. James, -'s sn*t*'dʒeɪmz [sən*t*-, sɪn*t*-], -ɪz
St. Joan sn*t*'dʒəʊn [sən*t*-, sɪn*t*-]
St. John, -'s (*Saint, place*) sn*t*'dʒɒn [sən*t*-, sɪn*t*-], -z, (*surname*) 'sɪndʒən
St. Joseph sn*t*'dʒəʊzɪf [sən*t*-, sɪn*t*-, -zəf]
St. Kilda sn*t*'kɪldə [sən*t*-, sɪn*t*-]
St. Kitts sn*t*'kɪts [sən*t*-, sɪn*t*-]
St. Lawrence snt'lɒrəns [sənt-, sɪnt-]
St. Leger (*surname*) snt'ledʒə* [sənt-, sɪnt-], 'selɪndʒə*, (*race*) snt'ledʒə* [sənt-, sɪnt-]
Note.—Most people bearing this name (including the Irish families) pronounce snt'ledʒə* [sənt-, sɪnt-]. *But there are members of the Doncaster family who pronounce* 'selɪndʒə*.
St. Legers snt'ledʒəz [sənt-, sɪnt-]
St. Leonards snt'lenədz [sənt-, sɪnt-]
St. Levan snt'levən [sənt-, sɪnt-]
saintlike 'seɪntlaɪk
St. Louis (*city in U.S.A.*) snt'luɪs [sənt-, sɪnt-, -'lu:ɪs], (*places in Canada*) -'luɪ [-'lu:ɪ, -ɪs]
St. Lucia snt'lu:ʃə [sənt-, sɪnt-, *rarely* -ʃjə, -ʃɪə, -sjə, -sɪə]
St. Ludger snt'lu:dʒə* [sənt-, sɪnt-]
St. Luke snt'lu:k [sənt-, sɪnt-]
saintl|y, -ier, -iest, -iness 'seɪntl|ɪ, -ɪə* [-jə*], -ɪɪst [-jɪst], -ɪnɪs [-nəs]

433

St. Malo snt'mɑːləʊ [sənt-, smt-] (sēmalo)

St. Margaret, -'s snt'mɑːgərɪt [sənt-, smt-], -s

St. Mark snt'mɑːk [sənt-, smt-]

St. Martin, -'s snt'mɑːtɪn [sənt-, smt-], -z

St. Martin's le Grand snt,mɑːtɪnzlə-'grænd [sənt-, smt-]

St. Mary, -'s snt'meərɪ [sənt-, smt-], -z

St. Mary Axe snt,meərɪ'æks [sənt-, smt-]
  Note.—The old form ,sɪmərɪ'æks has to be used in Gilbert and Sullivan's opera 'The Sorcerer'.

St. Marylebone snt'mærələbən [sənt-, smt-]
  Note.—See also **Marylebone**.

St. Mary-le-Bow snt,meərɪlə'bəʊ [sənt-, smt-]

St. Matthew snt'mæθju: [sənt-, smt-]

St. Maur (surname) 'siːmɔː* [-mɔə*]

St. Mawes snt'mɔːz [sənt-, smt-]

St. Michael, -'s snt'maɪkl [sənt-, smt-], -z

St. Moritz ,sænmə'rɪts [snɪ'mɒrɪts, sənt-, smɪ-]

St. Neots (in Cambridgeshire) snt'niːts [sənt-, smt-, -'niːəts]

St. Nicholas snt'nɪkələs [sənt-, smt-, -kləs]

St. Olaves (in Suffolk) snt'ɒlɪvz [sənt-, smt-, -ləvz]

St. Olave's (hospital in London) snt-'ɒlɪvz [sənt-, smt-, -ləvz]

St. Osyth (in Essex) snt'əʊzɪθ [sənt-, smt-, -'əʊsɪθ]

St. Pancras snt'pæŋkrəs [sənt-, smt-, sm'pæŋkrəs]

St. Patrick snt'pætrɪk [sənt-, smt-]

St. Paul, -'s snt'pɔːl [sənt-, smt-], -z

St. Peter, -'s, -sburg snt'piːtə* [sənt-, smt-], -z, -zbɜːg

St. Regis snt'riːdʒɪs [sənt-, smt-]

St. Ronan snt'rəʊnən [sənt-, smt-]

Saint-Saëns sæ̃'sɑ̃ːŋs [sæŋ-, -'sɑːns, -'sɔ̃ːŋs] (sɛ̃sɑ̃ːs)

St. Salvator's (college) sntsæl'veɪtəz [sənt-, smt-]

Saintsbury 'seɪntsbərɪ

St. Simon snt'saɪmən [sənt-, smt-]

St. Swithin snt'swɪðɪn

St. Thomas, -'s snt'tɒməs [sənt-, smt-], -ɪz

St. Vincent snt'vɪnsənt [sənt-, smt-]

St. Vitus, -'s snt'vaɪtəs [sənt-, smt-], -ɪz

saith (from say) seθ [seɪθ]

sake, -s seɪk, -s

saké (Japanese wine) 'sɑːkɪ

Saki 'sɑːkɪ

salaam (s. v.), **-s, -ing, -ed** sə'lɑːm, -z, -ɪŋ, -d

salacious, -ly, -ness sə'leɪʃəs, -lɪ, -nɪs [-nəs]

salacity sə'læsətɪ [-rtɪ]

salad, -s 'sæləd, -z

Saladin 'sælədɪn

Salamanca ,sælə'mæŋkə

salamander, -s 'sælə,mændə* [-,mɑːn-], -z

salami sə'lɑːmɪ [-miː]

Salamis 'sæləmɪs

sal-ammoniac ,sælə'məʊnɪæk [-njæk]

salar|y, -ies, -ied 'sælər|ɪ, -ɪz, -ɪd

Salcombe (in Devon) 'sɔːlkəm ['sɒl-]

sale (S.), -s seɪl, -z

sal(e)ability ,seɪlə'bɪlətɪ [-lɪt-]

sal(e)able 'seɪləbl

Salem 'seɪlem [-ləm]

Salesbury 'seɪlzbərɪ

sales|man, -men 'seɪlz|mən, -mən [-men]

salesmanship 'seɪlzmənʃɪp

salesroom, -s 'seɪlzrʊm [-ruːm], -z

Salford 'sɔːlfəd ['sɒl-]

Salian, -s 'seɪljən [-lɪən], -z

Salic 'sælɪk

salicional, -s sə'lɪʃənl [-ʃn̩, -ʃnl, -ʃənəl], -z

salicylate sæ'lɪsɪleɪt [sə'l-]

salicylic ,sælɪ'sɪlɪk

salient (s. adj.), **-s** 'seɪljənt [-lɪənt], -s

saline 'seɪlaɪn ['sæl-]

Saline (in Fife) 'sælɪn, (in U.S.A.) sə'liːn

Salinger 'sælɪndʒə* ['seɪ-]

salinity sə'lɪnətɪ [-rtɪ]

Salisbury 'sɔːlzbərɪ ['sɒlz-]

saliva sə'laɪvə [sl̩'aɪ-]

salivary 'sælɪvərɪ [sə'laɪvərɪ, sl̩'aɪv-]

sallet, -s 'sælɪt [-lət], -s

sallow (s. adj.), **-s, -y, -ness** 'sæləʊ, -z, -ɪ, -nɪs [-nəs]

Sallust 'sæləst

sall|y (s. v.) **(S.), -ies, -ying, -ied** 'sæl|ɪ, -ɪz, -ɪŋ, -ɪd

sally-lunn, -s ,sælɪ'lʌn, -z

salmi, -s 'sælmɪ [-miː], -z

salmon 'sæmən

Salmon (surname) 'sæmən, 'sælmən, 'sɑːmən, (river, etc., in Canada and U.S.A.) 'sæmən, (biblical name) 'sælmɒn [-mən]

salmonella ,sælmə'nelə

Salome sə'ləʊmɪ [sl̩'əʊ-]

salon, -s 'sælɔ̃ːŋ [-lɒn] (salɔ̃), -z

Salonica (*modern town*) sə'lɒnɪkə [*old-fashioned* ˌsælə'niːkə], (*in Greek history*) ˌsælə'naɪkə
saloon, -s sə'luːn [sl̩'uːn], -z
Salop 'sæləp
Salopian, -s sə'ləʊpjən [sl̩'əʊ-, -pɪən], -z
Salpeter (*English name*) 'sælpiːtə*
salpiglossis ˌsælpɪ'glɒsɪs
Salsette sɔːl'set [sɒl-]
salsify 'sælsɪfaɪ [-fɪ]
salt (*s. adj. v.*) (**S.**), **-s; -er, -est, -ly, -ness, -ish; -ing, -ed, -er/s** sɔːlt [sɒlt], -s; -ə*, -ɪst, -lɪ, -nɪs [-nəs], -ɪʃ; -ɪŋ, -ɪd, -ə*/z
saltant 'sæltənt ['sɔːl-, 'sɒl-]
Saltash 'sɔːltæʃ ['sɒlt-]
saltation sæl'teɪʃn
salt-cellar, -s 'sɔːltˌselə* ['sɒlt-], -z
Salter, -ton 'sɔːltə* ['sɒl-], -tən
Saltfleetby 'sɔːltˌfliːtbɪ ['sɒlt-, *locally also* 'sɒləbɪ]
Salting 'sɔːltɪŋ ['sɒl-]
saltire, -s 'sɔːltaɪə* ['sæl-], -z
Saltmarsh 'sɔːltmɑːʃ ['sɒlt-]
Saltoun 'sɔːltən ['sɒlt-]
saltpetre ˌsɔːlt'piːtə* [ˌsɒlt-, '---]
saltspoon, -s 'sɔːltspuːn ['sɒlt-], -z
salt|y, -ier, -iest, -iness 'sɔːlt|ɪ ['sɒl-], -ɪə* [-jə*], -ɪɪst [-jɪst], -ɪnɪs [-ɪnəs]
salubrious, -ly, -ness sə'luːbrɪəs [sl̩'u-:, sə'ljuː-], -lɪ, -nɪs [-nəs]
salubrity sə'luːbrətɪ [sl̩'u-:, sə'ljuː-, -ɪtɪ]
Salusbury (*surname*) 'sɔːlzbərɪ
Salut (*in Port Salut*) sə'luː (saly)
Salutaris ˌsælju:'teərɪs [-ljʊ't-, -'tɑːr-]
salutary 'sæljʊtərɪ
salutation, -s ˌsælju:'teɪʃn [-ljʊ't-], -z
salut|e (*s. v.*), **-es, -ing, -ed** sə'luːt [sl̩'u:t, sə'ljuːt], -s, -ɪŋ, -ɪd
salvable 'sælvəbl
Salvador 'sælvədɔ:* [ˌsælvə'dɔ:*]
salvag|e (*s. v.*), **-es, -ing, -ed** 'sælvɪdʒ, -ɪz, -ɪŋ, -d
salvarsan 'sælvəsən [-sæn]
salvation, -s sæl'veɪʃn -z
salvationi|sm, -st/s sæl'veɪʃn̩ɪ|zəm [-ʃənɪ-], -st/s
salv|e (*s. v.*) (*anoint, soothe, etc.*), **-es, -ing, -ed** sælv [sɑːv], -z, -ɪŋ, -d
salv|e (*save ship, cargo*), **-es, -ing, -ed** sælv, -z, -ɪŋ, -d
Salve (*Catholic antiphon*), **-s** 'sælvɪ, -z
salver, -s 'sælvə*, -z
salvia, -s 'sælvɪə [-vjə], -z
Salviati ˌsælvɪ'ɑːtɪ
salvo, -es 'sælvəʊ, -z
sal volatile ˌsælvə'lætəlɪ [-vəʊ'l-, -vʊ'l-, -tlɪ]

Salyut sə'ljuːt ['sælju:t]
Salzburg 'sæltsbɜ:g ['sɑːl-] ('zaltsburk, -burç)
Sam sæm
Samantha sə'mænθə
Samaria sə'meərɪə [sm̩'eə-]
Samaritan, -s sə'mærɪtən [sm̩'æ-], -z
Samarkand ˌsæmɑː'kænd [-mə'k-]
same, -ness seɪm, -nɪs [-nəs]
samite 'sæmaɪt ['seɪm-]
Sammy 'sæmɪ
samnite, -s 'sæmnaɪt, -s
Samoa, -n/s sə'məʊə [sɑː'm-], -n/z
Samos 'seɪmɒs
Samothrace 'sæməʊθreɪs
Samothracian, -s ˌsæməʊ'θreɪʃn [-ʃɪən, -ʃjən], -z
samovar, -s 'sæməvɑ:* [ˌ--'-] (səma-'var), -z
Samoyed, -s (*people*) ˌsæmɔɪ'ed, (*dog*) sə'mɔɪed, -z
sampan, -s 'sæmpæn, -z
samphire 'sæmfaɪə*
samp|le (*s. v.*), **-les, -ling, -led** 'sɑːmp|l, -lz, -lɪŋ [-l̩ŋ], -ld
sampler, -s 'sɑːmplə*, -z
Sampson 'sæmpsn
Samson 'sæmsn [-mps-]
Samuda sə'mjuːdə
Samuel, -s 'sæmjʊəl [-mjwəl, -mjʊl], -z
samurai, -s 'sæmʊraɪ [-mjʊ-], -z
sanatorium, -s ˌsænə'tɔ:rɪəm, -z
sanatory 'sænətərɪ
Sancho Panza ˌsæntʃəʊ'pænzə [-kəʊ-]
sanctification ˌsæŋktɪfɪ'keɪʃn
sancti|fy, -fies, -fying, -fied 'sæŋktɪ|faɪ, -faɪz, -faɪɪŋ, -faɪd
sanctimonious, -ly, -ness ˌsæŋktɪ'məʊnjəs [-nɪəs], -lɪ, -nɪs [-nəs]
sancti|on (*s. v.*), **-ons, -oning, -oned** 'sæŋkʃ|n, -nz, -ṇɪŋ [-ənɪŋ], -nd
sanctity 'sæŋktətɪ [-ɪtɪ]
sanctuar|y, -ies 'sæŋktʃʊər|ɪ [-tʃwər-, -tjʊr-, -tjʊərɪ, -tjwərɪ, -tʃərɪ], -ɪz
sanctum, -s 'sæŋktəm, -z
Sanctus, -es 'sæŋktəs, -ɪz
sand sænd
sandal, -s; -wood 'sændl, -z; -wʊd
Sandbach 'sændbætʃ
sandbag, -s 'sændbæg, -z
sandbank, -s 'sændbæŋk, -s
sandboy, -s 'sændbɔɪ, -z
sanderling, -s 'sændəlɪŋ, -z
Sander|s, -son 'sɑːndə|z, -sn
Sanderstead 'sɑːndəsted [-stɪd]
sandfl|y, -ies 'sændfl|aɪ, -aɪz
Sand|ford, -gate 'sæn|fəd, -gɪt [-geɪt]

435

sandhi 'sændi: ['sʌn-, -dhi:] (Hindi səndhi)
sandhopper, -s 'sænd₁hɒpə*, -z
Sandhurst 'sændhɜːst
Sandling 'sændlɪŋ
sand|man, -men 'sænd|mæn, -men
San Domingo ₁sændə'mɪŋgəʊ [-dəʊ'm-, -dɒ'm-]
Sandown 'sændaʊn
sand-pap|er (s. v.), -ers, -ering, -ered 'sænd₁peɪp|ə*, -əz, -ərɪŋ, -əd
sandpiper, -s 'sænd₁paɪpə*, -z
Sandra 'sændrə ['sɑː-n-]
Sandringham 'sændrɪŋəm
sandstone 'sændstəʊn
sandstorm, -s 'sændstɔːm, -z
sandwi|ch (s. v.), -ches, -ching, -ched 'sænwɪ|dʒ [-tʃ], -dʒɪz [-tʃɪz], -dʒɪŋ [-tʃɪŋ], -dʒd [-tʃt]
    Note.—Some people use -tʃ in the uninflected form and -dʒ- in the inflected forms of this word.
Sandwich (in Kent) 'sænwɪtʃ [-ndw-, -wɪdʒ, old-fashioned 'sænɪdʒ]
sandwich|man, -men 'sænwɪdʒ|mæn [-ɪtʃ-], -men
sand|y (S.), -ier, -iest, -iness 'sænd|ɪ, -ɪə* [-jə*], -ɪɪst [-jɪst], -ɪnɪs [-məs]
Sandys sændz
sane, -r, -st, -ly, -ness seɪn, -ə*, -ɪst, -lɪ, -nɪs [-nəs]
Sanford 'sænfəd
sanforiz|e [-is|e], -es, -ing, -ed 'sænfəraɪz, -ɪz, -ɪŋ, -d
San Francisco ₁sænfrən'sɪskəʊ
sang (from sing) sæŋ
Sanger 'sæŋgə*, 'sæŋə*
sang-froid ₁sɑː'ɲ'frwɑː [₁sɔ̃:ŋ-, ₁sɑ:ŋ-, ₁sɒŋ-, ₁sæŋ-, -'frwɔ:] (sɑ̃frwɑ)
sanguinar|y, -ily, -iness 'sæŋgwɪnər|ɪ, -əlɪ [-ɪlɪ], -ɪnɪs [-məs]
sanguine, -ly, -ness 'sæŋgwɪn, -lɪ, -nɪs [-nəs]
sanguineous sæŋ'gwɪnɪəs [-njəs]
Sanhedri|m, -n 'sænɪdrɪ|m [-ned-, -nəd-, Jewish pronunciation sæn'hed-], -n
sanitar|y, -ily, -iness 'sænɪtər|ɪ, -əlɪ [-ɪlɪ], -ɪnɪs [-məs]
sanitation ₁sænɪ'teɪʃn
sanity 'sænətɪ [-ɪtɪ]
sank (from sink) sæŋk
Sankey 'sæŋkɪ
San Marinese ₁sænmærɪ'niːz
San Marino ₁sænmə'riːnəʊ
Sanquhar 'sæŋkə*
San Remo ₁sæn'reɪməʊ [-'riːm-]
sans (English word) sænz, (in French phrases) sɑ̃:ŋ [sɔ̃:ŋ] (sɑ̃)

Sanscrit, see Sanskrit
sanserif ₁sæn'serɪf
Sanskrit 'sænskrɪt
sanskritic sæn'skrɪtɪk
sanskritiz|e [-is|e], -es, -ing, -ed 'sænskrɪtaɪz, -ɪz, -ɪŋ, -d
Santa Claus 'sæntəklɔːz [₁--'-]
Santa Cruz ₁sæntə'kruːz
Santa Fé ₁sæntə'feɪ
Santander ₁sæntən'deə* [₁₁sæntæn'deə*, sæn'tændə*] (santan'der)
Santayana ₁sæntə'jɑːnə
Santiago ₁sæntɪ'ɑːgəʊ
Santley 'sæntlɪ
Saône səʊn (soːn)
sap (s. v.), -s, -ping, -ped, -per/s sæp, -s, -ɪŋ, -t, -ə*/z
Sapele (place in Nigeria) 'sæpɪlɪ, (mahogany from that district) sə'piːlɪ
sapien|ce, -t/ly 'seɪpjən|s [-pɪən-], -t/lɪ
Sapir (American linguist) sə'pɪə*
sapless 'sæplɪs [-ləs]
sapling, -s 'sæplɪŋ, -z
saponaceous ₁sæpəʊ'neɪʃəs
sapper, -s 'sæpə*, -z
Sapphic, -s 'sæfɪk, -s
Sapphira sə'faɪərə [sæ'f-]
sapphire, -s 'sæfaɪə*, -z
Sappho 'sæfəʊ
sapp|y, -iness 'sæp|ɪ, -ɪnɪs [-məs]
saprogenic ₁sæprəʊ'dʒenɪk
saprophyte, -s 'sæprəʊfaɪt, -s
Sapt sæpt
saraband, -s 'særəbænd, -z
Saracen, -s 'særəsn [-sɪn, -sen], -z
Saracenic ₁særə'senɪk
Saragossa ₁særə'gɒsə
Sarah 'seərə
sarai (inn), -s sə'raɪ [sɑː'raɪ], -z
Sarai (wife of Abram) 'seəreɪaɪ [-raɪ]
Sarajevo ₁særə'jeɪvəʊ
Sarasate ₁særə'sɑːtɪ
Saratoga ₁særə'təʊgə
Sarawak sə'rɑːwɔk [-wæk, -wə]
Sarawakian, -s ₁særə'wækɪən, -z
sarcasm, -s 'sɑːkæzəm, -z
sarcastic, -ally sɑː'kæstɪk, -əlɪ
sarcoma, -s, -ta sɑː'kəʊmə, -z, -tə
sarcopha|gus, -guses, -gi sɑː'kɒfə|gəs, -gəsɪz, -gaɪ [-dʒaɪ]
Sardanapalus ₁sɑːdə'næpələs [-nə-'pɑːləs]
sardine (fish), -s sɑː'diːn ['--], -z
sardine (stone) 'sɑːdaɪn
Sardinia, -n/s sɑː'dɪnjə [-nɪə], -n/z
Sardis 'sɑːdɪs
sardius, -es 'sɑːdɪəs [-djəs], -ɪz
sardonic, -ally sɑː'dɒnɪk, -əlɪ

sardonyx, -es ˈsɑːdənɪks [ˈsɑːd,ɒn-, -ˈ--], -ɪz
Sarepta səˈreptə
Sargant ˈsɑːdʒənt
sargasso (S.), -(e)s sɑːˈgæsəʊ, -z
Sargeant ˈsɑːdʒənt
Sargent, -s ˈsɑːdʒənt, -s
sari, -s ˈsɑːrɪ [-riː] (Hindi saṛi), -z
Sark sɑːk
Sarma|tia, -tian/s sɑːˈmeɪ|ʃjə [-ʃɪə, -ʃə], -ʃjən/z [-ʃɪən/z, -ʃn/z]
sarong, -s səˈrɒŋ [ˈsɑːr-, ˈsær-], -z
Saroyan səˈrɔɪən
sarsaparilla ˌsɑːsəpəˈrɪlə
sarsenet ˈsɑːsnɪt [-net]
Sartor ˈsɑːtɔː*
sartorial sɑːˈtɔːrɪəl
Sarum ˈseərəm
sash, -es sæʃ, -ɪz
Saskatchewan səsˈkætʃɪwən [sæs-, -wɒn]
sassafras, -es ˈsæsəfræs, -ɪz
Sassanian sæˈseɪnjən [-nɪən]
Sassenach, -s ˈsæsənæk [-nək, -nəx], -s
Sassoon səˈsuːn
sat (from sit) sæt
Satan ˈseɪtən [old-fashioned ˈsæt-]
satanic, -ally səˈtænɪk [seɪˈt-], -əlɪ
satchel, -s ˈsætʃəl, -z
sat|e, -es, -ing, -ed seɪt, -s, -ɪŋ, -ɪd
sateen, -s sæˈtiːn [səˈt-], -z
satellite, -s ˈsætəlaɪt [-tɪl-, -tʃ-], -s
satiable ˈseɪʃjəbl [-ʃɪə-, -ʃə-]
satiat|e, -es, -ing, -ed ˈseɪʃɪeɪt [-ʃjeɪt], -s, -ɪŋ, -ɪd
satiation ˌseɪʃɪˈeɪʃn
satiety səˈtaɪətɪ [-aɪtɪ, ˈseɪʃjətɪ, ˈseɪʃɪətɪ]
satin, -s, -y ˈsætɪn, -z, -ɪ
satinette ˌsætɪˈnet
satin-wood ˈsætɪnwʊd
satire, -s ˈsætaɪə*, -z
satiric|al, -ally, -alness səˈtɪrək|l [-rɪ-], -əlɪ, -lnɪs [-nəs]
satirist, -s ˈsætərɪst [-tɪr-], -s
satiriz|e [-is|e], -es, -ing, -ed ˈsætəraɪz [-tɪr-], -ɪz, -ɪŋ, -d
satisfaction ˌsætɪsˈfækʃn
satisfactor|y, -ily, -iness ˌsætɪsˈfæktər|ɪ, -əlɪ [-ɪlɪ], -ɪnɪs [-ɪnəs]
satis|fy, -fies, -fying, -fied ˈsætɪs|faɪ, -faɪz, -faɪɪŋ, -faɪd
Satow ˈsɑːtəʊ
satrap, -s; -y, -ies ˈsætrəp [-træp], -s; -ɪ, -ɪz
Satsuma ˌsætˈsuːmə [ˈsætsʊmə]
saturat|e, -es, -ing, -ed ˈsætʃəreɪt [-tʃʊr-, -tjʊr-], -s, -ɪŋ, -ɪd
saturation ˌsætʃəˈreɪʃn [-tʃʊˈr-, -tjʊˈr-]

Saturday, -s ˈsætədɪ [-deɪ], -z
Saturn ˈsætən [-tɜːn]
saturnalia (S.) ˌsætəˈneɪljə [-tɜːˈn-, -lɪə]
saturnian sæˈtɜːnjən [səˈt-, -nɪən]
saturnine ˈsætənaɪn
satyr, -s ˈsætə*, -z
satyric səˈtɪrɪk
sauce, -s sɔːs, -ɪz
sauce-boat, -s ˈsɔːsbəʊt, -s
saucepan, -s ˈsɔːspən, -z
saucer, -s ˈsɔːsə*, -z
sauce-tureen, -s ˈsɔːstəˌriːn [-tʊˌr-, -tjʊˌr-], -z
Sauchiehall ˌsɔːkɪˈhɔːl [ˌsɒk-, ˈ---] (Scottish ˌsɔxɪˈhɒl)
sauc|y, -ier, -iest, -ily, -iness ˈsɔːs|ɪ, -ɪə* [-jə*], -ɪɪst [-jɪst], -ɪlɪ [-əlɪ], -ɪnɪs [-nəs]
Saudi Arabia ˌsaʊdɪəˈreɪbɪə [ˌsɔː-, -bjə]
sauerkraut ˈsaʊəkraʊt (ˈzauərkraut)
Saul sɔːl
Sault St. Marie (in Ontario) ˌsuːseɪntməˈriː
sauna ˈsɔːnə [ˈsaʊnə]
Saunder|s, -son ˈsɔːndə|z, ˈsɑːndə|z, -sn
saunt|er, -ers, -ering, -ered ˈsɔːnt|ə*, -əz, -ərɪŋ, -əd
saurian, -s ˈsɔːrɪən, -z
sausage, -s ˈsɒsɪdʒ, -ɪz
Sausmarez ˈsɒmərɪz [-rez]
sauté, -s ˈsəʊteɪ, -z
Sauterne, -s səʊˈtɜːn [-ˈteən], -z
Sauvage (English surname) ˈsævɪdʒ, səʊˈvɑːʒ
savage (s. adj.) (S.), -s, -st, -ly, -ness; -ry ˈsævɪdʒ, -ɪz, -ɪst, -lɪ, -nɪs [-nəs]; -ərɪ
savanna(h) (S.), -s səˈvænə, -z
savant, -s ˈsævənt, -s
sav|e (s. v. prep. conj.), -es, -ing, -ed seɪv, -z, -ɪŋ, -d
saveloy, -s ˈsævəlɔɪ [-vɪl-, ˌ--ˈ-]
Savels (surname) ˈsævəlz
Savernake ˈsævənæk
Savile ˈsævɪl [-vl]
saving (s. adj. prep.), -s ˈseɪvɪŋ, -z
saviour (S.), -s ˈseɪvjə*, -z
savoir faire ˌsævwɑːˈfeə* [-vwɔː-] (savwarfɛːr)
Savonarola ˌsævənəˈrəʊlə [-vnə-]
savory (S.) ˈseɪvərɪ
sav|our (s. v.), -ours, -ouring, -oured; -ourless ˈseɪv|ə*, -əz, -ərɪŋ, -əd; -əlɪs [-ləs]
savour|y (s. adj.), -ies, -ily, -iness ˈseɪvər|ɪ, -ɪz, -əlɪ [-ɪlɪ], -ɪnɪs [-nəs]
savoy (S.), -s səˈvɔɪ, -z
Savoyard, -s səˈvɔɪɑːd [ˌsævɔɪˈɑːd], -z

437

savvy 'sævɪ
saw (s. v.), **-s, -ing, -ed, -n** sɔː, -z, -ɪŋ,
-d, -n
saw (from see) sɔː
sawbones, -es 'sɔːbəʊnz, -ɪz
Sawbridgeworth 'sɔːbrɪdʒwɜ:θ
sawder 'sɔːdə*
sawdust 'sɔːdʌst
sawfish 'sɔːfɪʃ
Sawney, -s 'sɔːnɪ, -z
sawyer (S.), **-s** 'sɔːjə*, -z
Saxe - Coburg - Gotha (')sæks,kəʊbɜ:g-
'gəʊθə [-'gəʊtə]
saxhorn, -s 'sækshɔːn, -z
saxifrage, -s 'sæksɪfrɪdʒ [-freɪdʒ, -freɪʒ],
-ɪz
Saxon, -s 'sæksn, -z
Saxone (shoe company) sæk'səʊn [also
'sæksəʊn when attributive]
Saxony 'sæksn̩ɪ [-sənɪ, -snɪ]
saxophone, -s 'sæksəfəʊn, -z
saxophonist, -s sæk'sɒfənɪst ['sæksə-
fəʊnɪst], -s
Note.—Professional saxophone players use the first pronunciation.
say (s. v.); says; saying/s; said seɪ; sez
(normal form), səz (occasional weak
form); 'seɪŋ/z; sed (normal form),
səd (occasional weak form)
Sayce seɪs
Saye and Sele ,seɪən'si:l
Sayer, -s 'seɪə*, -z
'sblood zblʌd
scab, -s, -by, -biness skæb, -z, -ɪ, -ɪnɪs
[-məs]
scabbard, -s 'skæbəd, -z
scabies 'skeɪbiːz [-bjiːz, -bɪiːz]
scabious, -es 'skeɪbjəs [-bɪəs], -ɪz
scabrous 'skeɪbrəs
Scafell ,skɔː'fel [also 'skɔːfel, according
to sentence-stress]
scaffold, -s 'skæfəʊld [-fəld], -z
scaffolding, -s 'skæfəldɪŋ, -z
Scala 'skɑːlə
scalable 'skeɪləbl
scald (s. v.), **-s, -ing, ed** skɔːld, -z, -ɪŋ,
-ɪd
scall|e (s. v.), **-es, -ing, -ed, -ar** skeɪl, -z,
-ɪŋ, -d, -ə*
scalene 'skeɪliːn [skeɪ'liːn, skæ'liːn]
Scaliger 'skælɪdʒə*
scallion, -s 'skæljən [-lɪən], -z
scallop (s. v.), **-s, -ing, -ed** 'skɒləp, -s,
-ɪŋ, -t
scallop-shell, -s 'skɒləpʃel, -z
scallywag, -s 'skælɪwæg, -z
scalp (s. v.), **-s, -ing, -ed** skælp, -s, -ɪŋ, -t
scalpel, -s 'skælpəl, -z

scal|ly, -ier, -iest, -iness 'skeɪl|ɪ, -ɪə*
[-jə*], -ɪɪst [-jɪst], -ɪnɪs [-məs]
Scammell 'skæməl
scamp (s. v.), **-s, -ing, -ed** skæmp, -s,
-ɪŋ, -t [skæmt]
scamp|er (s. v.), **-ers, -ering, -ered**
'skæmp|ə*, -əz, -ərɪŋ, -əd
scampi 'skæmpɪ
scan, -s, -ning, -ned skæn, -z, -ɪŋ, -d
scandal, -s 'skændl, -z
scandalization [-isa-] ,skændəlaɪ'zeɪʃn
[-dlaɪ-]
scandaliz|e [-is|e], **-es, -ing, -ed**
'skændəlaɪz [-dlaɪz], -ɪz, -ɪŋ, -d
scandalmong|er, **-ers, -ering** 'skændl-
,mʌŋg|ə*, -əz, -ərɪŋ
scandalous, -ly, -ness 'skændələs [-dləs],
-lɪ, -nɪs [-nəs]
scandent 'skændənt
Scandinavia, -n/s ,skændɪ'neɪvjə
[-dən-, -vɪə], -n/z
Scan|lan, -lon 'skæn|lən, -lən
scansion, -s 'skænʃn, -z
scant, -ly skænt, -lɪ
scant|ly, -ier, -iest, -ily, -iness 'skænt|ɪ,
-ɪə* [-jə*], -ɪɪst [-jɪst], -ɪlɪ [-əlɪ], -ɪnɪs
[-nəs]
Scapa Flow ,skæpə'fləʊ
scape, -s; -goat/s, -grace/s skeɪp, -s;
-gəʊt/s, -greɪs/ɪz
scapul|a, -as, -ae, -ar 'skæpjʊl|ə, -əz,
-iː, -ə*
scar (s. v.) (S.), **-s, -ring, -red** skɑː*, -z,
-rɪŋ, -d
scarab, -s 'skærəb, -z
scarab|aeus, -aeuses, -aei ,skærə'b|iːəs
[-'brəs], -iːəsɪz [-ɪəsɪz], -iːaɪ
scaramouch, -es 'skærəmuːtʃ [-muːʃ,
-maʊtʃ], -ɪz
Scarborough [-boro'] 'skɑːbrə [-bərə]
Scarbrough 'skɑːbrə
scarc|e, -er, -est, -ely, -eness; -ity
skeəs, -ə*, -ɪst, -lɪ, -nɪs [-nəs]; -ətɪ
[-ɪtɪ]
scar|e (s. v.), **-es, -ing, -ed** skeə*, -z,
-rɪŋ, -d
scarecrow, -s 'skeəkrəʊ, -z
scaremong|er, **-ers, -ering** 'skeə-
,mʌŋg|ə*, -əz, -ərɪŋ
scar|f (s.), **-ves, -fs** skɑː:|f, -vz, -fs
scarf (v.), **-s, -ing, -ed** skɑːf, -s, -ɪŋ, -t
scarf-pin, -s 'skɑːfpɪn, -z
scarification ,skærɪfɪ'keɪʃn [,skeər-]
scari|fy, -fies, -fying, -fied 'skærɪ|faɪ
['skeər-], -faɪz, -faɪŋ, -faɪd
scarlatina ,skɑːlə'tiːnə [-lɪ't-]
Scarlatti skɑː'lætɪ (skar'latti)
scarlet 'skɑːlət [-lɪt]

scarp (*s. v.*), **-s, -ing, -ed** skɑːp, -s, -ɪŋ, -t
scarves (*plur. of* scarf) skɑːvz
Scase skeɪs
scath|e, **-es, -ing/ly, -ed; -eless** skeɪð,
-z, -ɪŋ/lɪ, -d; -lɪs [-ləs]
scatt|er (*s. v.*), **-ers, -ering, -ered, -erer/s**
'skæt|ə*, -əz, -ərɪŋ, -əd, -ərə*/z
scatterbrain, **-s, -ed** 'skætəbreɪn, -z, -d
scaup, **-s** skɔːp, -s
scaveng|e, **-es, -ing, -ed, -er/s** 'skæv-
ɪndʒ [-vəndʒ], -ɪz, -ɪŋ, -d, -ə*/z
Scawen 'skɔːɪn ['skɔːən]
Scawfell ˌskɔː'fel [*also* 'skɔːfel *according
to sentence-stress*]
scean dhu, **-s** ˌskiːən'duː [ˌskɪə-], -z
Sceats skiːts
scena, **-s** 'ʃeɪnə, -z
scenario, **-s** sɪ'nɑːrɪəʊ [se'n-, sə'n-], -z
scenarist, **-s** 'siːnərɪst, -s
scene, **-s** siːn, -z
scene-paint|er/s, **-ing** 'siːnˌpeɪnt|ə*/z,
-ɪŋ
scenery 'siːnərɪ
scene-shifter, **-s** 'siːnˌʃɪftə*, -z
scenic, **-ally** 'siːnɪk ['sen-], -əlɪ
scent (*s. v.*), **-s, -ing, -ed** sent, -s, -ɪŋ,
-ɪd
scent-bag, **-s** 'sentbæg, -z
scent-bottle, **-s** 'sentˌbɒtl, -z
sceptic (*s. adj.*), **-s, -al, -ally** 'skeptɪk, -s,
-l, -əlɪ
scepticism 'skeptɪsɪzəm
sceptre, **-s, -d** 'septə*, -z, -d
schedul|e (*s. v.*), **-es, -ing, -ed** 'ʃedjuːl
['ʃedʒuːl, 'skeː-, -dʒl], -z, -ɪŋ, -d
Scheherazade ʃɪˌhɪərə'zɑːdə [ʃə,h-,
-ˌher-, -dɪ]
Scheldt skelt [ʃelt]
schema, **-s, -ta** 'skiːmə, -z, -tə
schematic, **-ally** skɪ'mætɪk [ski:'m-], -əlɪ
schem|e (*s. v.*), **-es, -ing/ly, -ed, -er/s**
skiːm, -z, -ɪŋ/lɪ, -d, -ə*/z
Schenectady skɪ'nektədɪ
scherzando skeət'sændəʊ [skɜ:t-]
scherzo, **-s** 'skeətsəʊ ['skɜ:t-], -z
Schiedam skɪ'dæm ['--]
Schiehallion ʃɪ'hæljən [-lɪən]
Schiller 'ʃɪlə* (ʃilər)
Schipperke, **-s** 'ʃɪpəkɪ ['skɪ-], -z ['ʃɪpək,
-s]
schism, **-s** 'sɪzəm ['skɪ-], -z
schismatic, **-al** sɪz'mætɪk [skɪ-], -l
schist, **-s, -ose** ʃɪst, -s, -əʊs
schizoid 'skɪtsɔɪd
schizophrenia ˌskɪtsəʊ'friːnjə [ˌskɪdzəʊ-,
-nɪə]
schizophrenic, **-s** ˌskɪtsəʊ'frenɪk
[ˌskɪdzəʊ-], -s

Schleswig 'ʃlezvɪg [-zwɪg] ('ʃleːsvɪç)
schnap(p)s ʃnæps
Schofield 'skəʊfiːld
scholar, **-s, -ly** 'skɒlə*, -z, -lɪ
scholarship, **-s** 'skɒləʃɪp, -s
scholastic, **-ally** skə'læstɪk [skɒ'l-], -əlɪ
scholasticism skə'læstɪsɪzəm [skɒ'l-]
Scholes skəʊlz
scholiast, **-s** 'skəʊlɪæst, -s
scho|lium, **-lia** 'skəʊ|lɪəm [-lɪəm], -ljə
[-lɪə]
Scholl (*surname*) ʃɒl, ʃəʊl, skɒl
school (*s. v.*), **-s, -ing, -ed** skuːl, -z, -ɪŋ,
-d
school-book, **-s** 'skuːlbʊk, -s
schoolboy, **-s** 'skuːlbɔɪ, -z
schoolfellow, **-s** 'skuːlˌfeləʊ, -z
schoolgirl, **-s** 'skuːlgɜːl, -z
schoolhous|e, **-ses** 'skuːlhaʊ|s, -zɪz
school|man, **-men** 'skuːl|mən [-mæn],
-mən [-men]
school-marm, **-s** 'skuːlmɑːm, -z
schoolmaster, **-s** 'skuːlˌmɑːstə*, -z
schoolmate, **-s** 'skuːlmeɪt, -s
schoolmistress, **-es** 'skuːlˌmɪstrɪs [-trəs],
-ɪz
schoolroom, **-s** 'skuːlrʊm [-ruːm], -z
school-teacher, **-s** 'skuːlˌtiːtʃə*, -z
school-time 'skuːltaɪm
schooner, **-s** 'skuːnə*, -z
Schopenhauer 'ʃəʊpənhaʊə* ['ʃɒp-]
('ʃoːpənhauər)
schottische, **-s** ʃɒ'tiːʃ [ʃə't-], -ɪz
Schreiner 'ʃraɪnə*
Schubert 'ʃuːbət [-bɜːt]
Schumann 'ʃuːmən [-mæn, -mɑːn]
schwa, **-s** ʃwɑː, -z
Schwabe (*English surname*) ʃwɑːb
Schwann (*English surname*) ʃwɒn
Schweppe, **-s** ʃwep, -s
sciagram, **-s** 'skaɪəgræm ['saɪə-], -z
sciagraph, **-s** 'skaɪəgrɑːf ['saɪə-, -græf],
-s
sciatic, **-a** saɪ'ætɪk, -ə
science, **-s** 'saɪəns, -ɪz
scientific, **-ally** ˌsaɪən'tɪfɪk, -əlɪ
scientist, **-s** 'saɪəntɪst, -s
scilicet 'saɪlɪset ['sɪl-]
Scillonian, **-s** sɪ'ləʊnjən [-nɪən], -z
Scill|y, **-ies** 'sɪl|ɪ, -ɪz
scimitar, **-s** 'sɪmɪtə* [-mətə*], -z
scintilla sɪn'tɪlə
scintillat|e, **-es, -ing, -ed** 'sɪntɪleɪt
[-təl-], -s, -ɪŋ, -ɪd
scintillation, **-s** ˌsɪntɪ'leɪʃn [-tə'l-], -z
scioli|sm, **-st/s** 'saɪəʊlɪ|zəm, -st/s
scion, **-s** 'saɪən, -z
Scipio 'skɪpɪəʊ ['sɪ-]

439

scire facias ˌsaɪərɪ'feɪʃɪæs [-ʃjæs, -ʃjəs, -ʃɪəs]
scirrhous 'sɪrəs
scirrh|us, -i 'sɪr|əs, -aɪ
scission, -s 'sɪʒn ['sɪʃn], -z
scissors 'sɪzəz
scleros|is, -es sklə'rəus|ɪs [sklɪ'r-, skle'r-, sklɪə'r-], -i:z
sclerotic sklə'rɒtɪk [sklɪ'r-, skle'r-, sklɪə'r-]
scoff, -s, -ing/ly, -ed, -er/s skɒf, -s, -ɪŋ/lɪ, -t, -ə*/z
Scofield 'skəʊfi:ld
scold, -s, -ing/s, -ed skəʊld, -z, -ɪŋ/z, -ɪd
scoliosis ˌskɒlɪ'əʊsɪs
scollop (s. v.), -s, -ing, -ed 'skɒləp, -s, -ɪŋ, -t
sconc|e (s. v.), -es, -ing, -ed skɒns, -ɪz, -ɪŋ, -t
scone, -s skɒn [skəʊn], -z
Scone (in Scotland) sku:n
scoop (s. v.), -s, -ing, -ed, -er/s sku:p, -s, -ɪŋ, -t, -ə*/z
scoot (s. v.), -s, -ing, -ed sku:t, -s, -ɪŋ, -ɪd
scooter, -s 'sku:tə*, -z
scope, -s skəʊp, -s
scorbutic skɔ:'bju:tɪk
scorch (s. v.), -es, -ing/ly, -ed, -er/s skɔ:tʃ, -ɪz, -ɪŋ/lɪ, -t, -ə*/z
scor|e (s. v.), -es, -ing, -ed, -er/s skɔ:* [skɔə*], -z, -rɪŋ, -d, -rə*/z
scoria 'skɔ:rɪə ['skɒr-]
scoriaceous ˌskɔ:rɪ'eɪʃəs [ˌskɒr-]
scorn (s. v.), -s, -ing, -ed skɔ:n, -z, -ɪŋ, -d
scorn|ful, -fully, -fulness 'skɔ:n|fʊl, -fʊlɪ [-fəlɪ], -fʊlnɪs [-nəs]
Scorpio (constellation) 'skɔ:pɪəʊ [-pjəʊ]
scorpion, -s 'skɔ:pjən [-pɪən], -z
scot (S.), -s skɒt, -s
scotch (s. v.) (S.), -es, -ing, -ed skɒtʃ, -ɪz, -ɪŋ, -t
Scotch|man, -men 'skɒtʃ|mən, -mən
Scotch|woman, -women 'skɒtʃ|ˌwʊmən, -ˌwɪmɪn
scoter, -s 'skəʊtə*, -z
scot-free ˌskɒt'fri:
Scotia 'skəʊʃə
Scotland 'skɒtlənd
Scots (adj.) skɒts
Scots|man, -men 'skɒts|mən, -mən
Scots|woman, -women 'skɒts|ˌwʊmən, -ˌwɪmɪn
Scott skɒt
scottice 'skɒtɪsɪ [-si:]
scotticism, -s 'skɒtɪsɪzəm, -z

scotticiz|e [-is|e], -es, -ing, -ed 'skɒtɪsaɪz, -ɪz, -ɪŋ, -d
Scottish 'skɒtɪʃ
scoundr|el, -els, -elly 'skaʊndr|əl, -əlz, -əlɪ [-ˌlɪ]
scour (s. v.), -s, -ing, -ed 'skaʊə*, -z, -rɪŋ, -d
scourg|e (s. v.), -es, -ing, -ed skɜ:dʒ, -ɪz, -ɪŋ, -d
scout (s. v.), -s, -ing, -ed, -er/s skaʊt, -s, -ɪŋ, -ɪd, -ə*/z
scoutmaster, -s 'skaʊtˌmɑ:stə*, -z
scow, -s skaʊ, -z
Scowen 'skəʊən [-m]
scowl (s. v.), -s, -ing/ly, -ed skaʊl, -z, -ɪŋ/lɪ, -d
scrabb|le, -les, -ling, -led 'skræb|l, -lz, -ⱡɪŋ [-lɪŋ], -ld
scrag (s. v.), -s, -ging, -ged; -gy, -gier, -giest, -gily, -giness skræg, -z, -ɪŋ, -d; -ɪ, -ɪə*, -ɪɪst, -ɪlɪ [-əlɪ], -ɪnɪs [-məs]
scrag-end ˌskræg'end
scramb|le (s. v.), -les, -ling, -led 'skræmb|l, -lz, -lɪŋ, [-lɪŋ], -ld
scrap (s. v.), -s, -ping, -ped; -py, -pier, -piest, -pily, -piness skræp, -s, -ɪŋ, -t; -ɪ, -ɪə*, -ɪɪst, -ɪlɪ [-əlɪ], -ɪnɪs [-məs]
scrap|e (s. v.), -es, -ing/s, -ed, -er/s skreɪp, -s, -ɪŋ/z, -t, -ə*/z
scrap|y, -ier, -iest, -ily, -iness 'skreɪp|ɪ, -ɪə* [-jə*], -ɪɪst [-jɪst], -ɪlɪ [-əlɪ], -ɪnɪs [-məs]
scratch (s. v.), -es, -ing, -ed; -y, -ier, -iest, -ily, -iness skrætʃ, -ɪz, -ɪŋ, -t; -ɪ, -ɪə*, -ɪɪst, -ɪlɪ [-əlɪ], -ɪnɪs [-məs]
scrawl (s. v.), -s, -ing, -ed; -y, -ier, -iest, -ily, -iness skrɔ:l, -z, -ɪŋ, -d; -ɪ, -ɪə* [-jə*], -ɪɪst [-jɪst], -ɪnɪs [-məs]
scrawn|y, -ier, -iest 'skrɔ:n|ɪ, -ɪə*, -ɪɪst
scray, -s skreɪ, -z
scream (s. v.), -s, -ing, -ed, -er/s; -y, -ier, -iest, -ily, -iness skri:m, -z, -ɪŋ, -d, -ə*/z; -ɪ, -ɪə* [-jə*], -ɪlɪ [-əlɪ], -ɪnɪs [-məs]
scree, -s skri:, -z
screech (s. v.), -es, -ing, -ed, -er/s skri:tʃ, -ɪz, -ɪŋ, -t, -ə*/z
screech-owl, -s 'skri:tʃaʊl, -z
screed, -s skri:d, -z
screen (s. v.), -s, -ing, -ed skri:n, -z, -ɪŋ, -d
screen-play, -s 'skri:npleɪ, -z
screen-writer, -s 'skri:nˌraɪtə*, -z
screw (s. v.), -s, -ing, -ed skru:, -z, -ɪŋ ['skruɪŋ], -d
screw-cap, -s 'skru:kæp, -s
screwdriver, -s 'skru:ˌdraɪvə*, -z
screw-top, -s 'skru:tɒp, -s

Scriabin 'skrɪəbɪn [skrɪ'æbɪn] ('skrjabjin)
scribal 'skraɪbl
scribb|le (*s. v.*), **-les, -ling, -led, -ler/s** 'skrɪb|l, -lz, -lɪŋ [-lɪŋ], -ld, -lə*/z [-lə*/z]
scribbling-paper 'skrɪblɪŋ,peɪpə* [-blɪŋ-]
scribe, -s skraɪb, -z
Scriblerus skrɪb'lɪərəs
Scribner ,skrɪbnə*
scrim skrɪm
scrimmage, -s 'skrɪmɪdʒ, -ɪz
scrimp, -s, -ing, -ed skrɪmp, -s, -ɪŋ, -t [skrɪmt]
scrimshaw (*s. v.*), **-s, -ing, -ed** 'skrɪmʃɔ:, -z, -ɪŋ, -d
scrip, -s skrɪp, -s
scripsit 'skrɪpsɪt
script (*s. v.*), **-s, -ing, -ed, -er/s** skrɪpt, -s, -ɪŋ, -ɪd, -ə*/z
scriptor|ium, -iums, -ia skrɪp'tɔ:r|ɪəm, -ɪəmz, -ɪə
scriptur|al, -ally 'skrɪptʃər|əl [-tʃʊr-], -əlɪ
scripture (S.), -s 'skrɪptʃə*, -z
script-writer, -s 'skrɪpt,raɪtə*, -z
Scriven 'skrɪvən
scrivener (S.), -s 'skrɪvnə*, -z
scrofula 'skrɒfjʊlə
scrofulous, -ly, -ness 'skrɒfjʊləs, -lɪ, -nɪs [-nəs]
scroll, -s skrəʊl, -z
Scrooge skru:dʒ
Scrooope skru:p
Scrope skru:p, skrəʊp
scrot|um/s, -a, -al 'skrəʊt|əm/z, -ə, -l
scroung|e, -es, -ing, -ed skraʊndʒ, -ɪz, -ɪŋ, -d
scrub (*s. v.*), **-s, -bing, -bed; -by, -bier, -biest, -bily, -biness** skrʌb, -z, -ɪŋ, -d; -ɪ, -ɪə*, -ɪɪst, -ɪlɪ [-əlɪ], -ɪnɪs [-nəs]
scruff, -s skrʌf, -s
scruff|y, -ily 'skrʌf|ɪ, -ɪlɪ [-əlɪ]
scrum, -s skrʌm, -z
scrummage, -s 'skrʌmɪdʒ, -ɪz
scrumptious 'skrʌmpʃəs [-mptʃəs]
scrunch, -es, -ing, -ed skrʌntʃ, -ɪz, -ɪŋ, -t
scrup|le (*s. v.*), **-les, -ling, -led** 'skru:p|l, -lz, -lɪŋ [-lɪŋ], -ld
scrupulosity ,skru:pjʊ'lɒsətɪ [-ɪtɪ]
scrupulous, -ly, -ness 'skru:pjʊləs [-pjəl-], -lɪ, -nɪs [-nəs]
scrutator, -s skru:'teɪtə*, -z
scrutineer, -s ,skru:tɪ'nɪə* [-tə'n-], -z
scrutiniz|e (-is|e), -es, -ing, -ed 'skru:tɪnaɪz [-tənaɪz, -tn̩aɪz], -ɪz, -ɪŋ, -d
scrutin|y, -ies 'skru:tɪn|ɪ [-tən|ɪ, -tn̩|ɪ], -ɪz

scr|y, -ies, -ying, -ied skr|aɪ, -aɪz, -aɪɪŋ, -aɪd
Scrymgeour 'skrɪmdʒə*
Scrymsour 'skrɪmsə*
scud (*s. v.*), **-s, -ding, -ded** skʌd, -z, -ɪŋ, -ɪd
Scudamore 'skju:dəmɔ:* [-mɔə*]
scudo, -s 'sku:dəʊ, -z
scuff, -s, -ing, -ed skʌf, -s, -ɪŋ, -t
scuff|le (*s. v.*), **-les, -ling, -led** 'skʌf|l, -lz, -lɪŋ [-lɪŋ], -ld
scull (*s. v.*), **-s, -ing, -ed, -er/s** skʌl, -z, -ɪŋ, -d, -ə*/z
sculler|y, -ies 'skʌlər|ɪ [-lr|ɪ], -ɪz
scullery-maid, -s 'skʌlərɪmeɪd [-lrɪ-], -z
scullion, -s 'skʌljən [-lɪən], -z
sculpsit 'skʌlpsɪt
sculpt, -s, -ing, -ed skʌlpt, -s, -ɪŋ, -ɪd
sculptor, -s 'skʌlptə*, -z
sculptur|e (*s. v.*), **-es, -ing, -ed** 'skʌlptʃə*, -z, -rɪŋ ['skʌlptʃrɪŋ], -d
scum (*s. v.*), **-s, -ming, -med; -my** skʌm, -z, -ɪŋ, -d; -ɪ
Scunthorpe 'skʌnθɔ:p
scupper, -s 'skʌpə*, -z
scurf, -y, -iness skɜ:f, -ɪ, -ɪnɪs [-nəs]
scurrility skʌ'rɪlətɪ [skə'r-, -ɪtɪ]
scurrilous, -ly, -ness 'skʌrələs [-rɪl-], -lɪ, -nɪs [-nəs]
scurr|y (*s. v.*), **-ies, -ying, -ied** 'skʌr|ɪ, -ɪz, -ɪŋ, -ɪd
scurv|y (*s. adj.*), **-ier, -iest, -ily, -iness** 'skɜ:v|ɪ, -ɪə* [-jə*], -ɪɪst [-jɪst], -ɪlɪ [-əlɪ], -ɪnɪs [-məs]
Scutari 'sku:tərɪ [sku:'tɑ:rɪ, skʊ't-]
scutcheon, -s 'skʌtʃən, -z
scutt|le (*s. v.*), **-les, -ling, -led** 'skʌt|l, -lz, -lɪŋ [-lɪŋ], -ld
scut|um, -ums, -a 'skju:t|əm, -əmz, -ə
Scylla 'sɪlə
scyth|e (*s. v.*), **-es, -ing, -ed** saɪð, -z, -ɪŋ, -d
Scythia, -n/s 'sɪðɪə ['sɪθ-, -jə], -n/z
'sdeath zdeθ
se (*note in Tonic Sol-fa*), **-s** si:, -z
sea, -s si:, -z
sea-bird, -s 'si:bɜ:d, -z
seaboard 'si:bɔ:d [-bəəd]
sea-borne 'si:bɔ:n [-bəən]
sea-breeze, -s ,si:'bri:z ['si:bri:z], -ɪz
Seabright 'si:braɪt
sea-captain, -s 'si:,kæptɪn [-tən], -z
sea-coast, -s ,si:'kəʊst ['--], -s
sea-cow, -s 'si:kaʊ, -z
sea-dog, -s 'si:dɒg, -z
sea-elephant, -s 'si:,elɪfənt [-ləf-, ,-'---], -s
seafar|er/s, -ing 'si:,feər|ə*/z, -ɪŋ

441

sea-fog, -s 'siːfɒg, -z
Seaford (in East Sussex) 'siːfəd [-fɔːd]
Seaforth, -s 'siːfɔːθ, -s
Seager 'siːgə*
Seago 'siːgəʊ
sea-going 'siːˌgəʊɪŋ
sea-green ˌsiːˈgriːn ['--]
sea-gull, -s 'siːgʌl, -z
seakale 'siːkeɪl [ˌsiːˈkeɪl]
seal (s. v.), -s, -ing, -ed, -er/s, -ant/s siːl,
    -z, -ɪŋ, -d, -ə*/z, -ənt/s
sealing-wax 'siːlɪŋwæks
sea-lion, -s 'siːˌlaɪən, -z
sealskin, -s 'siːlskɪn, -z
Sealyham, -s 'siːlɪəm, -z
seam (s. v.), -s, -ing, -ed; -less siːm, -z,
    -ɪŋ, -d; -lɪs [-ləs]
sea|man (S.), -men, -manship 'siːˌmən,
    -mən [-men], -mənʃɪp
Seamas 'ʃeɪməs
sea-mew, -s 'siːmjuː, -z
sea-monster, -s 'siːˌmɒnstə*, -z
seamstress, -es 'semstrɪs ['siːm-,
    -mps-, -strəs], -ɪz
Seamus 'ʃeɪməs
seamy 'siːmɪ
Sean ʃɔːn
seance, -s 'seɪɑ̃ːns [-ɔ̃ːns, -ɑːns, -ɒns]
    (seɑ̃ːs), -ɪz
sea-pink ˌsiːˈpɪŋk
seaplane, -s 'siːpleɪn, -z
seaport, -s 'siːpɔːt, -s
sea-power 'siːˌpaʊə*
sear, -s, -ing, -ed sɪə*, -z, -rɪŋ, -d
search (s. v.), -es, -ing/ly, -ed, -er/s
    sɜːtʃ, -ɪz, -ɪŋ/lɪ, -t, -ə*/z
searchlight, -s 'sɜːtʃlaɪt, -s
search-part|y, -ies 'sɜːtʃˌpɑːt|ɪ, -ɪz
search-warrant, -s 'sɜːtʃˌwɒrənt, -s
Searle sɜːl
seascape, -s 'siːskeɪp, -s
sea-serpent, -s 'siːˌsɜːpənt, -s
seashore(s) 'siːˈʃɔː* [-ˈʃəə*, ˌ-ˈ-]
seasick, -ness 'siːsɪk, -nɪs [-nəs]
seaside 'siːsaɪd [ˌ-ˈ-]
seas|on (s. v.), -ons, -oning, -oned
    'siːz|n, -nz, -n̩ɪŋ [-nɪŋ], -nd
seasonab|le, -ly, -leness 'siːzn̩əb|l
    [-znə-], -lɪ, -lnɪs [-nəs]
seasonal 'siːzənl [-zn̩l̩, -znl̩]
seasoning (s.), -s 'siːzn̩ɪŋ [-znɪŋ], -z
season-ticket, -s 'siːzn̩ˌtɪkɪt [ˌ--ˈ--], -s
seat (s. v.), -s, -ing, -ed siːt, -s, -ɪŋ, -ɪd
seat-belt, -s 'siːtbelt, -s
S.E.A.T.O. 'siːtəʊ
Seaton 'siːtn
sea-trout 'siːtraʊt
Seattle sɪˈætl

sea-urchin, -s 'siːˌɜːtʃɪn [ˌ-ˈ--], -z
sea-wall, -s ˌsiːˈwɔːl ['--], -z
seaward 'siːwəd
sea-water 'siːˌwɔːtə*
seaweed 'siːwiːd
seaworth|y, -iness 'siːˌwɜːð|ɪ, -mɪs [-məs]
sebaceous sɪˈbeɪʃəs [se'b-]
Sebastian sɪˈbæstjən [se'b-, sə'b-, -tɪən]
Sebastopol sɪˈbæstəpl [se'b-, sə'b-, -pɒl]
seborrhea ˌsebəˈriːə [-ˈrɪə]
sec sek
secant, -s 'siːkənt, -s
secateurs ˌsekəˈtɜːz ['sekətɜːz, -təz]
seced|e, -es, -ing, -ed, -er/s sɪˈsiːd
    [siː's-], -z, -ɪŋ, -ɪd, -ə*/z
secession, -s sɪˈseʃn, -z
secessionist, -s sɪˈseʃn̩ɪst [-ʃənɪst], -s
seclud|e, -es, -ing, -ed sɪˈkluːd, -z, -ɪŋ,
    -ɪd
seclusion sɪˈkluːʒn
second (s. adj. v.) (ordinary senses), -s;
    -ly; -ing, -ed, -er/s 'sekənd, -z; -lɪ;
    -ɪŋ, -ɪd, -ə*/z
second (to release for temporary service),
    -s, -ing, -ed sɪˈkɒnd [sə'k-], -z, -ɪŋ,
    -ɪd
secondar|y (s. adj.), -ies, -ily 'sekəndər|ɪ,
    -ɪz, -əlɪ [-ɪlɪ]
second-class ˌsekəndˈklɑːs [also '—
    when attributive]
second hand (of clock or watch), -s
    'sekəndhænd, -z
second-hand (adj.) ˌsekəndˈhænd [when
    attributive '—]
Secondi (town in Ghana) ˌsekənˈdiː,
    (surname) sɪˈkɒndɪ [sə'k-]
secondment sɪˈkɒndmənt [sə'k-]
secondo, -s seˈkɒndəʊ [sɪ'k-], -z
second-rate ˌsekəndˈreɪt [also '— when
    attributive]
second-rater, -s ˌsekəndˈreɪtə*, -z
secrecy 'siːkrəsɪ [-krɪs-]
secret (s. adj.), -s, -ly 'siːkrɪt [-krət], -s,
    -lɪ
secretarial ˌsekrəˈteərɪəl [-krɪ't-]
secretariat, -s ˌsekrəˈteərɪət [-krɪ't-,
    -ræt], -s
secretar|y, -ies; -yship/s 'sekrətr|ɪ,
    [-krɪt-, -ter|ɪ], -ɪz; -ɪʃɪp/s
secret|e, -es, -ing, -ed sɪˈkriːt [siː'k-],
    -s, -ɪŋ, -ɪd
secretion, -s sɪˈkriːʃn [siː'k-], -z
secretive, -ly, -ness 'siːkrətɪv [-krɪ-,
    sɪˈkriːtɪv], -lɪ, -nɪs [-nəs]
Secrett 'siːkrɪt
sect, -s sekt, -s
sectarian (s. adj.), -s, -ism sekˈteərɪən,
    -z, -ɪzəm

442

sectar|y, -ies 'sektər|ɪ, -ɪz
section, -s 'sekʃn, -z
sec|tional, -tionally 'sek|ʃənl [-ʃnəl,
-ʃn̩], -ʃnl̩, -ʃənəl], -ʃn̩əlɪ [-ʃnəlɪ, -ʃn̩lɪ,
-ʃn̩lɪ, -ʃənəlɪ]
sector, -s 'sektə*, -z
secular, -ly 'sekjʊlə* [-kjəl-], -lɪ
seculari|sm, -st/s 'sekjʊlərɪ|zəm [-kjəl-],
-st/s
secularity ‚sekjʊ'lærətɪ [-kjə'l-, -rtɪ]
secularization [-isa-] ‚sekjʊləraɪ'zeɪʃn
[-kjəl-, -rɪ'z-]
seculariz|e [-is|e], -es, -ing, -ed
'sekjʊləraɪz [-kjəl-], -ɪz, -ɪŋ, -d
secur|e (adj. v.), -er, -est, -ely; -es,
-ing, -ed; -able sɪ'kjʊə* [sə'k-,
-'kjɔə*, -'kjɔ:*], -rə*, -rɪst, -lɪ; -z,
-rɪŋ, -d; -rəbl
securit|y, -ies sɪ'kjʊərət|ɪ [sə'k-,
-'kjɔər-, 'kjɔ:r-, -rt|ɪ], -ɪz
Sedan sɪ'dæn [sə'd-]
sedan-chair, -s sɪ'dænt∫eə* [sə'd-, -‚-'-],
-z
sedate, -ly, -ness sɪ'deɪt, -lɪ, -nɪs [-nəs]
†sedative (s. adj.), -s 'sedətɪv, -z
Sedbergh (public school) 'sedbə* [-bə:g],
(name of town) 'sedbə*
Sedd|ing, -on 'sed|ɪŋ, -n
sedentar|y, -ily, -iness 'sedntər|ɪ, -əlɪ
[-ɪlɪ], -ɪnɪs [-məs]
sedge, -s sedʒ, -ɪz
Sedge|field, -moor 'sedʒ|fi:ld, -mɔ:*
[-mɔə*, -mʊə*]
sedge-warbler, -s 'sedʒ‚wɔ:blə* [‚-'--], -z
Sedgley 'sedʒlɪ
Sedgwick 'sedʒwɪk
sedil|e, -ia se'daɪl|ɪ [sɪ'd-], -jə [-ɪə,
-'dɪljə, -'dɪlɪə]
sediment, -s 'sedɪmənt, -s
sedimentary ‚sedɪ'mentərɪ
sedition, -s sɪ'dɪʃn [sə'd-], -z
seditious, -ly, -ness sɪ'dɪʃəs [sə'd-], -lɪ,
-nɪs [-nəs]
Sedlescombe 'sedlskəm
Sedley 'sedlɪ
seduc|e, -es, -ing, -ed, -er/s, -ement/s
sɪ'dju:s, -ɪz, -ɪŋ, -t, -ə*/z, -mənt/s
seduction, -s sɪ'dʌkʃn, -z
seductive, -ly, -ness sɪ'dʌktɪv, -lɪ, -nɪs
[-nəs]
sedulous, -ly, -ness 'sedjʊləs [-dʒʊl-],
-lɪ, -nɪs [-nəs]
sedum, -s 'si:dəm, -z
see (s. v.) (S.), -s, -ing, saw, seen si:, -z,
-ɪŋ, sɔ:, si:n
seed (s. v.), -s, -ing, -ed si:d, -z, -ɪŋ, -ɪd
seed-cake 'si:dkeɪk
seedless 'si:dlɪs [-ləs]

seedling, -s 'si:dlɪŋ, -z
seed-pearl, -s ‚si:d'pə:l ['--], -z
seed-potato, -es 'si:dpə‚teɪtəʊ [‚--'--], -z
seeds|man, -men 'si:dz|mən, -mən
[-men]
seed-time, -s 'si:dtaɪm, -z
seed|y, -ier, -iest, -ily, -iness 'si:d|ɪ, -ɪə*
[-jə*], -ɪɪst [-jɪst], -ɪlɪ [-əlɪ], -ɪnɪs
[-məs]
seek, -s, -ing, sought, seeker/s si:k, -s,
-ɪŋ, sɔ:t, 'si:kə*/z
Seel(e)y 'si:lɪ
seem, -s, -ing/ly, -ed si:m, -z, -ɪŋ/lɪ, -d
seeml|y, -ier, -iest, -iness 'si:ml|ɪ, -ɪə*
[-jə*], -ɪɪst [-jɪst], -mɪs [-məs]
seen (from see) si:n
seep, -s, -ing, -ed si:p, -s, -ɪŋ, -t
seepage 'si:pɪdʒ
seer (one who sees), -s 'si:ə* [sɪə*], -z
seer (Indian weight), -s sɪə*, -z
seersucker 'sɪə‚sʌkə*
seesaw (s. v.), -s, -ing, -ed 'si:sɔ:
[‚si:'sɔ:], -z, -ɪŋ, -d
seeth|e, -es, -ing, -ed si:ð, -z, -ɪŋ, -d
segment (s.), -s 'segmənt, -s
segment (v.), -s, -ing, -ed seg'ment ['--,
səg'm-], -s, -ɪŋ, -ɪd
segmental seg'mentl [səg'm-]
segregate (adj.) 'segrɪgət [-geɪt, -gɪt]
segregat|e (v.), -es, -ing, -ed 'segrɪgeɪt,
-s, -ɪŋ, -ɪd
segregation ‚segrɪ'geɪʃn
Seidlitz 'sedlɪts
Seigel 'si:gəl
seignior, -s 'seɪnjə* [-nɪə*, rarely 'si:n-],
-z
Seignior (surname) 'si:njə*
seignior|y, -ies 'seɪnjər|ɪ [-nɪər-, rarely
'si:n-], -ɪz
seine (net), -s seɪn, -z
Seine (river in France) seɪn (sɛn, sɛ:n)
seis|ed, -in/s si:z|d, -ɪn/z
seismic 'saɪzmɪk
seismograph, -s 'saɪzməgrɑ:f [-məʊg-,
-græf], -s
seismograph|er/s, -y saɪz'mɒgrəf|ə*/z,
-ɪ
seismographic ‚saɪzmə'græfɪk [-məʊ'g-]
seismologic|al, -ally ‚saɪzmə'lɒdʒɪk|l
[-məʊ'l-], -əlɪ
seismolog|ist/s, -y saɪz'mɒlədʒ|ɪst/s, -ɪ
seismometer, -s saɪz'mɒmɪtə* [-mətə*],
-z
seizable 'si:zəbl
seiz|e, -es, -ing, -ed si:z, -ɪz, -ɪŋ, -d
seizin, -s 'si:zɪn, -z
seizure, -s 'si:ʒə*, -z
sejant 'si:dʒənt

443

Sejanus sɪ'dʒeməs [se'dʒ-]
selah, -s 'si:lə, -z
Selangor sə'læŋə* [-ŋɔ:*]
Sel|borne, -by 'sel|bɔ:n [-bən], -bɪ
Selden 'seldən
seldom 'seldəm
select (adj. v.), -ness; -s, -ing, -ed,
  -or/s; -ive/ly sɪ'lekt [sə'l-], -nɪs
  [-nəs]; -s, -ɪŋ, -ɪd, -ə*/z; -ɪv/lɪ
selection, -s sɪ'lekʃn [sə'l-], -z
selective sɪ'lektɪv [sə'l-]
selectivity ˌsɪlek'trvətɪ [ˌsel-, -ɪtɪ]
Selena sɪ'li:nə [sə'l-]
selenite (substance) 'selmart
Selenite (inhabitant of moon), -s
  sɪ'li:nart [sə'l-], -s
selenium sɪ'li:nɪəm [sə'l-, -njəm]
Seleucia, -n/s sɪ'lju:ʃjə [sə'l-, -'lu:-, -ʃɪə,
  -sjə, -sɪə], -n/z
Seleucid, -s sɪ'lju:sɪd [se'l-, -'lu:-], -z
Seleucus sɪ'lju:kəs [se'l-, -'lu:-]
sel|f, -ves sel|f, -vz
  Note.—Most compounds with self-
  have double stress, e.g. self-com-
  placent ˌselfkəm'pleɪsənt, self-con-
  fidence ˌself'kɒnfɪdəns, self-sup-
  porting ˌselfsə'pɔ:tɪŋ. Only a few of
  the most important are given below.
self-centred ˌself'sentəd
self-command ˌselfkə'mɑ:nd
self-conscious, -ness ˌself'kɒnʃəs, -nɪs
  [-nəs]
self-contained ˌselfkən'teɪnd
self-control, -led ˌselfkən'trəʊl, -d
self-deception ˌselfdɪ'sepʃn
self-defence ˌselfdɪ'fens
self-denial ˌselfdɪ'naɪəl
self-denying ˌselfdɪ'naɪɪŋ
self-determination 'selfdɪˌtɜ:mɪ'neɪʃn
self-employed ˌselfɪm'plɔɪd [-em-]
self-esteem ˌselfɪ'sti:m [-ə's-]
self-evident ˌself'evɪdənt
self-explanatory ˌselfɪk'splænətərɪ
  [-ek's-, -nrt-]
self-governing ˌself'gʌvənɪŋ [-vnrŋ]
self-government ˌself'gʌvnmənt
  [-vrmmənt, -vənmənt, -vəmənt]
self-heal 'selfhi:l
self-importan|ce, -t ˌselfɪm'pɔ:tən|s, -t
self-indulgen|ce, -t ˌselfɪn'dʌldʒən|s, -t
self-interest ˌself'ɪntrɪst [-tərest, -trəst]
selfish, -ly, -ness 'selfɪʃ, -lɪ, -nɪs [-nəs]
selfless 'selflɪs [-ləs]
self-made ˌself'meɪd [also '-- when
  attributive]
self-pity ˌself'pɪtɪ
self-possessed ˌselfpə'zest [-pʊ'z-]
self-possession ˌselfpə'zeʃn

self-preservation 'selfˌprezə'veɪʃn
self-relian|ce, -t ˌselfrɪ'laɪən|s [-rə'l-], -t
self-respect ˌselfrɪ'spekt [-rə's-]
self-respecting ˌselfrɪ'spektɪŋ [-rə's-]
self-restraint ˌselfrɪ'streɪnt
Selfridge 'selfrɪdʒ
self-righteous ˌself'raɪtʃəs [-tjəs]
self-rule ˌself'ru:l
self-sacrifice ˌself'sækrɪfaɪs
selfsame 'selfseɪm
self-satisfaction 'selfˌsætɪs'fækʃn
self-satisfied ˌself'sætɪsfaɪd
self-service ˌself'sɜ:vɪs
self-starter, -s ˌself'stɑ:tə*, -z
self-styled ˌself'staɪld ['selfstaɪld]
self-sufficien|cy, -t ˌselfsə'fɪʃn|sɪ, -t
self-taught ˌself'tɔ:t
self-will, -ed ˌself'wɪl, -d
self-winding ˌself'waɪndɪŋ ['self-
  ˌwaɪndɪŋ]
Selkirk 'selkɜ:k
sell (s. v.) (S.), -s, -ing, sold, seller/s
  sel, -z, -ɪŋ, səʊld, 'selə*/z
Sellar 'selə*
Sellers 'seləz
Selous sə'lu:
Selsey 'selsɪ
Seltzer, -s 'seltsə*, -z
selvage, -s 'selvɪdʒ, -ɪz
selvedge, -s 'selvɪdʒ, -ɪz
selves (plur. of self) selvz
Selwyn 'selwɪn
semantic, -s, -ally sɪ'mæntɪk [se'm-,
  sə'm-, si:'m-], -s, -əlɪ
semanticism sɪ'mæntɪsɪzəm [se'm-,
  sə'm-, si:'m-]
semanticiz|e [-is|e], -es, -ing, -ed
  sɪ'mæntɪsaɪz [se'm-, sə'm-, -si:'m-],
  -ɪz, -ɪŋ, -d
semaphore, -s 'seməfɔ:* [-fɔə*], -z
semaphoric, -ally ˌsemə'fɒrɪk, -əlɪ
semasiology sɪˌmeɪsɪ'ɒlədʒɪ [seˌm-,
  sə,m-, -eɪzɪ-]
sematology ˌsemə'tɒlədʒɪ [ˌsi:m-]
semblance, -s 'sembləns, -ɪz
semé 'semeɪ
Semele 'semɪlɪ
semen 'si:men [-mən]
semester, -s sɪ'mestə* [sə'm-], -z
semi- 'semɪ-
  Note.—Numerous compounds may be
  formed by prefixing semi- to other
  words. Compounds not entered below
  have double stress, i.e. a stress on
  semi- and the stress of the simple
  word. Examples: semi-detached
  ˌsemɪdɪ'tætʃt, semi-official ˌsemɪə-
  'fɪʃl, semi-tropical ˌsemɪ'trɒpɪkl.

semibreve, -s 'semɪbriːv, -z
semicircle, -s 'semɪ,sɜːkl, -z
semicircular ,semɪ'sɜːkjʊlə* [-kjəl-]
semicolon, -s ,semɪ'kəʊlən ['semɪ,k-, -lɒn], -z
semi-final, -s ,semɪ'faɪnl, -z
seminal 'semɪnl ['siːm-]
seminar, -s 'semɪnɑː* [,ˌ-'-], -z
seminar|y, -ies, -ist/s 'semɪnər|ɪ, -ɪz, -ɪst/s
Seminole, -s 'semɪnəʊl, -z
semiology ,semɪ'ɒlədʒɪ [,ˌsiːm-]
semiotic, -s ,semɪ'ɒtɪk [,ˌsiːm-], -s
semi-precious 'semɪ,preʃəs [,ˌ--'--]
semiquaver, -s 'semɪ,kweɪvə*, -z
Semiramide ,semɪ'rɑːmɪdɪ
Semiramis se'mɪrəmɪs [sɪ'm-]
Semite, -s 'siːmaɪt ['sem-], -s
Semitic sɪ'mɪtɪk [se'm-, sə'm-]
semitism 'semɪtɪzəm
semitone, -s 'semɪtəʊn, -z
semivowel, -s 'semɪ,vaʊəl [,semɪ'v-, -el], -z
semolina ,semə'liːnə [-mʊ'l-]
Semon (surname) 'siːmən
sempervivum ,sempə'viːvəm
Sempill 'sempl
sempiternal ,sempɪ'tɜːnl
semplice 'semplɪtʃɪ
sempre 'semprɪ
sempstress, -es 'sempstrɪs [-strəs], -ɪz
sen sen
senary 'siːnərɪ
senate (S.), -s 'senɪt [-nət], -s
senator, -s 'senətə* [-nɪt-], -z
senatorial, -ly ,senə'tɔːrɪəl, -ɪ
senatus se'neɪtəs [sɪ'n-, -'nɑː-]
send, -s, -ing, sent, sender/s send, -z, -ɪŋ, sent, 'sendə*/z
send-off, -s 'sendɒf [old-fashioned -ɔːf], -s
Seneca 'senɪkə
Senegal ,senɪ'gɔːl
Senegalese ,senɪgə'liːz [-gɔː'l-]
Senegambia ,senɪ'gæmbɪə [-bjə]
senescen|ce, -t sɪ'nesn|s [se'n-, sə'n-], -t
seneschal, -s 'senɪʃl, -z
senile 'siːnaɪl
senility sɪ'nɪlətɪ [sə'n-, se'n-, -ɪtɪ]
senior (s. adj.) (S.), -s 'siːnjə* [-nɪə*], -z
seniorit|y, -ies ,siːnɪ'ɒrət|ɪ [-ɪt|ɪ], -ɪz
Senlac 'senlæk
senna 'senə
Sennacherib se'nækərɪb [sɪ'n-, sə'n-]
sennet 'senɪt [-nət]
sennight, -s 'senaɪt, -s
señor se'njɔː*
sensation, -s sen'seɪʃn [sən-, sn-], -z

sensa|tional, -tionally sen'seɪʃənl [sən-, -ʃnəl, -ʃnl, -ʃnl, -ʃənəl], -ʃnəlɪ [-ʃnəlɪ, -ʃnlɪ, -ʃnlɪ, -ʃənəlɪ]
sensationali|sm, -st/s sen'seɪʃnəlɪ|zəm [sən-, -ʃnəl-, -ʃnl-, -ʃnl-, -ʃənəl-], -st/s
sense, -s sens, -ɪz
senseless, -ly, -ness 'senslɪs [-ləs], -lɪ, -nɪs [-nəs]
sensibility ,sensɪ'bɪlətɪ [-sə'b-, -lɪt-]
sensib|le, -ly 'sensəb|l [-sɪb-], -lɪ
sensitive (s. adj.), -s, -ly, -ness 'sensɪtɪv [-sət-], -z, -lɪ, -nɪs [-nəs]
sensitivity ,sensɪ'tɪvətɪ [-sə't-, -ɪtɪ]
sensitization [-isa-] ,sensɪtaɪ'zeɪʃn [-sət-]
sensitiz|e [-is|e], -es, -ing, -ed 'sensɪtaɪz [-sət-], -ɪz, -ɪŋ, -d
sensorial sen'sɔːrɪəl
sensor|y, -ily 'sensər|ɪ, -əlɪ [-ɪlɪ]
sensual, -ly, -ness, -ism, -ist/s 'sensjʊəl [-sjwəl, -sjʊl, -ʃʊəl, -ʃwəl, -ʃʊl], -ɪ, -nɪs [-nəs], -ɪzəm, -ɪst/s
sensuality ,sensjʊ'ælətɪ [,senʃʊ-, -ɪtɪ]
sensuous, -ly, -ness 'sensjʊəs [-sjwəs, -ʃʊəs, -ʃwəs], -lɪ, -nɪs [-nəs]
sent (from send) sent
sentenc|e (s. v.), -es, -ing, -ed 'sentəns, -ɪz, -ɪŋ, -t
sententious, -ly, -ness sen'tenʃəs [sən-], -lɪ, -nɪs [-nəs]
sentience 'senʃəns [-ʃɪəns, -ʃjəns]
sentient, -ly 'senʃnt [-ʃɪənt, -ʃjənt], -lɪ
sentiment, -s 'sentɪmənt, -s
sentiment|al, -ally, -alism ,sentɪ'ment|l, -əlɪ [-lɪ], -əlɪzəm [-lɪzəm]
sentimentality ,sentɪmen'tælətɪ [-mən-, -ɪtɪ]
sentimentalization [-isa-] ,sentɪmentlaɪ-'zeɪʃn [-təl-, -tlɪ'z-, sentɪ,ment-]
sentimentaliz|e [-is|e], -es, -ing, -ed ,sentɪ'mentlaɪz [-təl-] -ɪz, -ɪŋ, -d
sentinel, -s 'sentɪnl, -z
sentr|y, -ies 'sentr|ɪ, -ɪz
sentry-box, -es 'sentrɪbɒks, -ɪz
sentry-go 'sentrɪgəʊ
senza 'sentsə
Seoul səʊl
sepal, -s 'sepəl ['siːp-], -z
separability ,sepərə'bɪlətɪ [-lɪt-]
separab|le, -ly, -leness 'sepərəb|l, -lɪ -lnɪs [-lnəs]
separ|ate (adj.), -ately, -ateness 'sepr|ət [-pər-, -rɪt], -ətlɪ [-rtlɪ], -ətnɪs [-rtnɪs, -nəs]
separat|e (v.), -es, -ing, -ed, -or/s 'sepəreɪt, -s, -ɪŋ, -ɪd, -ə*/z
separation, -s ,sepə'reɪʃn, -z
separati|sm, -st/s 'sepərətɪ|zəm, -st/s

445

Sephardi|c, -m sə'fɑ:dɪ|k [se'f-], -m
sepia 'si:pjə
sepoy, -s 'si:pɔɪ, -z
sepsis 'sepsɪs
September, -s sep'tembə* [səp-, sɪp-], -z
septennial sep'tenjəl [-nɪəl]
septet(te), -s sep'tet, -s
septic 'septɪk
septicaemia ˌseptɪ'si:mɪə [-mjə]
septillion, -s sep'tɪljən, -z
septime, -s 'septi:m, -z
septuagenarian, -s ˌseptjʊədʒɪ'neərɪən [-tjwə-, -dʒə'n-], -z
Septuagesima ˌseptjʊə'dʒesɪmə [-tjwə-]
Septuagint 'septjʊədʒɪnt [-tjwə-]
sept|um, -ums, -a 'sept|əm, -əmz, -ə
septuple 'septjʊpl
sepulchral sɪ'pʌlkrəl [se'p-, sə'p-]
sepulchre, -s 'sepəlkə*, -z
sepulture 'sepəltʃə* [-ˌtjʊə*]
sequacious sɪ'kweɪʃəs [se'k-, sə'k-]
sequel, -s 'si:kwəl, -z
sequel|a, -ae sɪ'kwi:l|ə [sə'k-], -i:
sequence, -s 'si:kwəns, -ɪz
sequenti|al, -ally sɪ'kwenʃ|l, -əlɪ
sequest|er, -ers, -ering, -ered sɪ'kwest|ə* [sə'k-], -əz, -ərɪŋ, -əd
sequestrat|e, -es, -ing, -ed sɪ'kwestreɪt ['si:kw-], -s, -ɪŋ, -ɪd
sequestration, -s ˌsi:kwe'streɪʃn [ˌsek-], -z
sequin, -s 'si:kwɪn, -z
sequoia, -s sɪ'kwɔɪə [se'k-], -z
serac, -s 'seræk, -s
seraglio, -s se'rɑ:lɪəʊ [sɪ'r-, sə'r-, -ljəʊ], -z
serai, -s se'raɪ [sə'r-], -z
seraph (S.), -s, -im 'serəf, -s, -ɪm
seraphic, -al, -ally se'ræfɪk [sɪ'r-, sə'r-], -l, -əlɪ
Serapis 'serəpɪs
Serb, -s, -ia, -ian/s sɜ:b, -z, -jə [-ɪə], -jən/z [-ɪən/z]
Serbo-Croat, -s ˌsɜ:bəʊ'krəʊæt, -s
Serbo-Croatian, -s ˌsɜ:bəʊkrəʊ'eɪʃn
Serbonian sɜ:'bəʊnjən [-nɪən]
sere (s. adj.), **-s** sɪə*, -z
Seremban sə'rembən
serenad|e (s. v.), **-es, -ing, -ed** ˌserə'neɪd [-rɪ'n-], -z, -ɪŋ, -ɪd
serenata, -s ˌserə'nɑ:tə [-rɪ'n-], -z
serendipity ˌserən'dɪpətɪ [-ren-, -ɪtɪ]
serene, -st, -ly sɪ'ri:n [sə'r-], -ɪst, -lɪ
serenity sɪ'renətɪ [sə'r-, -ɪtɪ]
serf, -s, -dom sɜ:f, -s, -dəm
serge (S.), -s sɜ:dʒ, -ɪz
sergeant (S.), -s 'sɑ:dʒənt, -s

sergeant-major, -s ˌsɑ:dʒənt'meɪdʒə*, -z
serial (s. adj.), **-s** 'sɪərɪəl, -z
seriatim ˌsɪərɪ'eɪtɪm [ˌser-, -'ɑ:tɪm]
series 'sɪəri:z [-rɪz, rarely -rɪi:z]
serif [cer-], **-s** 'serɪf, -s
serin, -s 'serɪn, -z
seringa, -s sɪ'rɪŋgə [sə'r-], -z
Seringapatam səˌrɪŋgəpə'tɑ:m [sɪˌr-, -'tæm]
serio-comic ˌsɪərɪəʊ'kɒmɪk
serious, -ly, -ness 'sɪərɪəs, -lɪ, -nɪs [-nəs]
serjeant (S.), -s 'sɑ:dʒənt, -s
Serjeantson 'sɑ:dʒəntsn
sermon, -s 'sɜ:mən, -z
sermonette, -s ˌsɜ:mə'net, -s
sermoniz|e [-is|e], **-es, -ing, -ed** 'sɜ:mənaɪz, -ɪz, -ɪŋ, -d
serous 'sɪərəs
Serpell 'sɜ:pl
Serpens (constellation) 'sɜ:penz
serpent, -s 'sɜ:pənt, -s
serpentine (s. adj.) **(S.)** 'sɜ:pəntaɪn
serrate (adj.) 'sereɪt [-rɪt, -rət]
serrated sɪ'reɪtɪd [sə'r-, se'r-]
serration, -s sɪ'reɪʃn [sə'r-, se'r-], -z
serried 'serɪd
serum, -s 'sɪərəm, -z
servant, -s 'sɜ:vənt, -s
servant-girl, -s 'sɜ:vəntgɜ:l, -z
serv|e (s. v.), **-es, -ing/s, -ed, -er/s** sɜ:v, -z, -ɪŋ/z, -d, -ə*/z
servic|e (s. v.) **(S.), -es, -ing, -ed** 'sɜ:vɪs, -ɪz, -ɪŋ, -t
serviceability ˌsɜ:vɪsə'bɪlətɪ [-lɪt-]
serviceab|le, -ly, -leness 'sɜ:vɪsəb|l, -lɪ, -lnɪs [-nəs]
serviette ˌsɜ:vɪ'et [sɜ:'vjet], -s
servile, -ly 'sɜ:vaɪl, -lɪ
servility sɜ:'vɪlətɪ [-lɪt-]
serving-spoon, -s 'sɜ:vɪŋspu:n, -z
servitor, -s 'sɜ:vɪtə*, -z
servitude 'sɜ:vɪtju:d
sesame (S.), -s 'sesəmɪ, -z
sesquialtera, -s ˌseskwɪ'æltərə, -z
sesquicentennial ˌseskwɪsen'tenɪəl [-sən-, -njəl]
sesquipedalian ˌseskwɪpɪ'deɪljən [-pe'd-, -lɪən]
session, -s 'seʃn, -z
sessional (s. adj.), **-s** 'seʃənl [-ʃnəl, -ʃn̩l, -ʃn̩l, -ʃənəl], -z
sesterce, -s 'sestɜ:s, -ɪz ['sestəsɪz]
sester|tium, -tia se'stɜ:|tjəm [-tɪəm, -ʃjəm, -ʃɪəm], -tjə [-tɪə, -ʃjə, -ʃɪə]
sestet, -s ses'tet, -s
set (s. v.), **-s, -ting** set, -s, -ɪŋ
set-back, -s 'setbæk, -s

Setebos 'setɪbɒs
Seth seθ
set-off, -s ˌset'ɒf [old-fashioned -'ɔːf], -s
seton (S.), -s 'siːtn, -z
set-square, -s 'setskweə*, -z
settee, -s se'tiː, -z
setter, -s 'setə*, -z
setting (s.), -s 'setɪŋ, -z
sett|le (s. v.), -les, -ling, -led, -ler/s, -lement/s 'set|l, -lz, -l̩ŋ [-lɪŋ], -ld, -lə*/z [-lə*/z], -lmənt/s
set-to ˌset'tuː ['--]
set-up, -s 'setʌp, -s
Seurat 'sɜːrɑː (sœra)
seven, -s, -th/s, -thly; -fold 'sevn, -z, -θ/s, -θlɪ; -fəʊld
sevenish 'sevn̩ɪʃ ['sevənɪʃ]
Sevenoaks 'sevn̩əʊks [-vnəʊ-]
seven|pence, -penny 'sevn|pəns [-vm|p-], -pənɪ (see note under penny)
seventeen, -s, -th/s, -thly ˌsevn'tiːn ['-- according to sentence-stress], -z, -θ/s, -θlɪ
sevent|ly, -ies, -ieth/s 'sevnt|ɪ, -ɪz, -ɪəθ/s [-jɪθ/s, -ɪɪθ/s, -jəθ/s]
sever, -s, -ing, -ed; -able, -ance 'sevə*, -z, -rɪŋ, -d; -rəbl, -rəns
sever|al, -ally 'sevr|əl, -əlɪ
severe, -r, -st, -ly, -ness sɪ'vɪə* [sə'v-], -rə*, -rɪst, -lɪ, -nɪs [-nəs]
severit|y, -ies sɪ'verət|ɪ [sə'v-, -ɪt|ɪ], -ɪz
Severn 'sevən [-vn]
Severus sɪ'vɪərəs [sə'v-]
Sevier 'sevɪə* [-vjə*]
Seville sə'vɪl [se'v-, sɪ'v-, 'sevɪl, 'sevl]
Sèvres 'servrə [-və*] (sɛːvr)
sew, -s, -ing, -ed, -n səʊ, -z, -ɪŋ, -d, -n
sewage 'suːɪdʒ ['sʊɪdʒ, 'sjuː-, 'sjʊɪ-]
Sewanee sə'wɒnɪ
Seward 'siːwəd
Sewell 'sjuːəl [sjʊəl]
sewer (one who sews), -s 'səʊə*, -z
sewer (drain), -s sʊə* [sjʊə*], -z
sewerage 'sʊərɪdʒ ['sjʊ-]
sewer-gas 'sʊəgæs ['sjʊ-]
sewing-machine, -s 'səʊɪŋmə.ʃiːn, -z
sewing|-woman, -women 'səʊɪŋ|-ˌwʊmən, -ˌwɪmɪn
sex, -es, -less seks, -ɪz, -lɪs [-ləs]
sexagenarian, -s ˌseksədʒɪ'neərɪən [-dʒə'n-], -z
Sexagesi|ma, -mal ˌseksə'dʒesɪ|mə, -ml
sex-appeal 'seksə.piːl
sext(e) sekst
sextan 'sekstən
sextant, -s 'sekstənt, -s

sextet(te), -s seks'tet, -s
sextillion, -s seks'tɪljən, -z
sexto, -s 'sekstəʊ, -z
sextodecimo, -s ˌsekstəʊ'desɪməʊ, -z
sexton, -s 'sekstən, -z
sextuple 'sekstjʊpl
sexual, -ly 'seksjʊəl [-ksjʊəl, -ksjwəl, -ksjʊl, -kʃwəl, -kʃʊl], -ɪ
sexuality ˌseksjʊ'ælətɪ [-ksjʊ-, -ɪtɪ]
sex|y, -ier, -iest, -ily, -iness 'seks|ɪ, -ɪə*, -ɪɪst, -ɪlɪ, -ɪnɪs [-məs]
Seychelle, -s seɪ'ʃel, -z
Seymour 'siːmɔː* [-mɔə*, -mə*], 'seɪm-
Note.—'seɪm- chiefly in families of Scottish origin.
Seys seɪs
sforzando sfɔːt'sændəʊ
sgeandhu ˌskiːən'duː [ˌskɪən-]
shabb|y, -ier, -iest, -ily, -iness 'ʃæb|ɪ, -ɪə*, -ɪɪst, -ɪlɪ [-əlɪ], -ɪnɪs [-məs]
shack|le (s. v.) (S.), -les, -ling, -led 'ʃæk|l, -lz, -l̩ŋ [-lɪŋ], -ld
Shackleton 'ʃækltən
Shadbolt 'ʃædbəʊlt
shaddock (S.) 'ʃædək
shad|e (s. v.), -es, -ing, -ed; -eless ʃeɪd, -z, -ɪŋ, -ɪd; -lɪs [-ləs]
shadoof, -s ʃə'duːf [ʃæ'd-], -s
shad|ow (s. v.), -ows, -owing, -owed; -owy, -owiness 'ʃæd|əʊ, -əʊz, -əʊɪŋ, -əʊd; -əʊɪ, -əʊɪnɪs [-məs]
shadowless 'ʃædəʊlɪs [-ləs]
Shadrach [-ak] 'ʃeɪdræk ['ʃæd-]
Note.—Some Jews pronounce 'ʃædrɑːx.
Shadwell 'ʃædwəl [-wel]
shad|y, -ier, -iest, -ily, -iness 'ʃeɪd|ɪ, -ɪə* [-jə*], -ɪɪst [-jɪst], -ɪlɪ [-əlɪ], -ɪnɪs [-məs]
shaft, -s ʃɑːft, -s
Shaftesbury 'ʃɑːftsbərɪ
shag, -s ʃæg, -z
shagg|y, -ier, -iest, -ily, -iness 'ʃæg|ɪ, -ɪə*, -ɪɪst, -ɪlɪ [-əlɪ], -ɪnɪs [-məs]
shagreen ʃæ'griːn [ʃə'g-]
shah (S.), -s ʃɑː, -z
Shairp ʃeəp, ʃɑːp
shak|e (s. v.), -es, -ing, shook, shak|en, -er/s ʃeɪk, -s, -ɪŋ, ʃʊk, 'ʃeɪk|ən, -ə*/z
shakedown, -s 'ʃeɪkdaʊn [also -'- when preceded by a stress], -s
Shak(e)spear(e) 'ʃeɪk.spɪə*
Shak(e)spearian ʃeɪk'spɪərɪən
Shak(e)speariana 'ʃeɪk.spɪərɪ'ɑːnə [ʃeɪk-ˌspɪər-]
shake-up, -s 'ʃeɪkʌp [also -'- when preceded by a stress], -s
shako, -s 'ʃækəʊ, -z

447

shak|y, -ier, -iest, -ily, -iness 'ʃeɪk|ɪ, -ɪə* [-jə*], -ɪɪst [-jɪst], -ɪlɪ [-əlɪ], -ɪnɪs [-məs]
Shalders 'ʃɔːldəz
shale ʃeɪl
shall ʃæl (*strong form*), ʃəl, ʃl, ʃə, ʃ (*weak forms*)
  Note.—The forms ʃə, ʃ, are chiefly used when we or be follows.
shallop, -s 'ʃæləp, -s
shallot (S.), -s ʃə'lɒt, -s
shall|ow (*s. adj. v.*) (S.), -ows, -ower, -owest, -owness, -owly 'ʃæl|əʊ, -əʊz, -əʊə*, -əʊɪst, -əʊnɪs [-nəs], -əʊlɪ
shalt (*from* shall) ʃælt (*strong form*), ʃəlt, ʃlt (*weak forms*)
shal|y, -iness 'ʃeɪl|ɪ, -ɪnɪs [-məs]
sham (*s. v.*), -s, -ming, -med, -mer/s ʃæm, -z, -ɪŋ, -d, -ə*/z
shaman, -s, -ism 'ʃæmən, -z, -ɪzəm
shamb|le, -les, -ling, -led 'ʃæmb|l, -lz, -lɪŋ, -ld
shambles (*s.*) 'ʃæmblz
sham|e (*s. v.*), -es, -ing, -ed ʃeɪm, -z, -ɪŋ, -d
shamefaced ˌʃeɪm'feɪst ['-- *when attributive*]
shamefacedly ˌʃeɪm'feɪstlɪ [-sɪdlɪ, '-ˌ--]
shamefacedness 'ʃeɪmˌfeɪstnɪs [-sɪdnɪs, -nəs, ˌ-'---]
shame|ful, -fully, -fulness 'ʃeɪm|fʊl, -fʊlɪ [-fəlɪ], -fʊlnɪs [-nəs]
shameless, -ly, -ness 'ʃeɪmlɪs [-ləs], -lɪ, -nɪs [-nəs]
shammy 'ʃæmɪ
shampoo (*s.*), -s ʃæm'puː [ˌʃæm-], -z
shampoo (*v.*), -(e)s, -ing, -ed ʃæm'puː [ˌʃæm-], -z, -ɪŋ [-'pʊɪŋ], -d
shamrock (S.) 'ʃæmrɒk
Shan (*state, language*) ʃɑːn
shandy (S.) 'ʃændɪ
Shane ʃɑːn, ʃɔːn, ʃeɪn
shanghai (S.), -s, -ing, -ed ˌʃæŋ'haɪ, -z, -ɪŋ, -d
Shangri La ˌʃæŋgrɪ'lɑː
shank, -s ʃæŋk, -s
Shanklin 'ʃæŋklɪn
Shanks ʃæŋks
Shannon 'ʃænən
shan't ʃɑːnt
shantung (*silk material*) ˌʃæn'tʌŋ
Shantung ˌʃæn'dʌŋ [-'tʌŋ, -'dʊŋ, -'tʊŋ]
shant|y, -ies 'ʃænt|ɪ, -ɪz
shanty-town, -s 'ʃæntɪtaʊn, -z
shap|e (*s. v.*), -es, -ing, -ed ʃeɪp, -s, -ɪŋ, -t
S.H.A.P.E. ʃeɪp
shapeless, -ness 'ʃeɪplɪs [-ləs], -nɪs [-nəs]

shapel|y, -ier, -iest, -iness 'ʃeɪpl|ɪ, -ɪə*, -ɪɪst, -ɪnɪs [-nəs]
Shapiro ʃə'pɪərəʊ
shard, -s ʃɑːd, -z
shar|e (*s. v.*), -es, -ing, -ed ʃeə*, -z, -rɪŋ, -d
shareholder, -s 'ʃeəˌhəʊldə*, -z
share-out, -s 'ʃeəraʊt [ˌ-'-], -s
shark, -s ʃɑːk, -s
sharkskin 'ʃɑːkskɪn
Sharon 'ʃærən ['ʃɑː-, 'ʃeə-, '-rɒn]
sharp (*s. adj. adv.*) (S.), -s; -er, -est, -ly, -ness ʃɑːp, -s; -ə*, -ɪst, -lɪ, -nɪs [-nəs]
Sharpe ʃɑːp
sharp|en, -ens, -ening, -ened 'ʃɑːp|ən, -ənz; -nɪŋ [-ṇɪŋ], -ənd
sharpener, -s 'ʃɑːpnə*, -z
sharper (*s.*), -s 'ʃɑːpə*, -z
Sharples 'ʃɑːplz
sharp-set ˌʃɑːp'set
sharpshooter, -s 'ʃɑːpˌʃuːtə*, -z
sharp-sighted ˌʃɑːp'saɪtɪd
sharp-witted ˌʃɑːp'wɪtɪd
Shasta (*in California*) 'ʃæstə
shatter, -s, -ing, -ed 'ʃætə*, -z, -rɪŋ, -d
Shaughnessy 'ʃɔːnəsɪ, ʃɒknəsɪ
Shaula (*star*) 'ʃəʊlə
Shaun ʃɔːn
shav|e (*s. v.*), -es, -ing/s, -ed ʃeɪv, -z, -ɪŋ/z, -d
shaven 'ʃeɪvn
shaver, -s 'ʃeɪvə*, -z
Shavian 'ʃeɪvjən [-vɪən]
shaving-brush, -es 'ʃeɪvɪŋbrʌʃ, -ɪz
shaving-stick, -s 'ʃeɪvɪŋstɪk, -s
shaw (S.), -s ʃɔː, -z
shawl, -s ʃɔːl, -z
shawm, -s ʃɔːm, -z
shay, -s ʃeɪ, -z
she ʃiː (*normal form*), ʃɪ (*freq. weak form*)
shea, -s ʃɪə ['ʃiːə, ʃiː], -z
Shea ʃeɪ
shea|f, -ves ʃiː|f, -vz
Sheaffer 'ʃeɪfə*
shear (*s. v.*), -s, -ing, -ed, shorn ʃɪə*, -z, -rɪŋ, -d, ʃɔːn
Sheard ʃeəd, ʃɪəd, ʃɜːd
shearer (S.), -s 'ʃɪərə*, -z
Shearman 'ʃɪəmən, 'ʃɜːmən
Shearme ʃɜːm
Shearn ʃɪən, ʃɜːn
shears (S.) ʃɪəz
Shearson 'ʃɪəsn
shearwater, -s 'ʃɪəˌwɔːtə*, -z
shea|th, -ths ʃiː|θ, -ðz [-θs]
sheath|e, -es, -ing, -ed ʃiː|ð, -z, -ɪŋ, -d
sheaves (*plur. of* sheaf) ʃiːvz

Sheba 'ʃiːbə
she-bear, -s 'ʃiːbeə*, -z
shebeen, -s ʃɪ'biːn [ʃe'b-], -z
she-cat, -s 'ʃiːkæt, -s
Shechem 'ʃiːkem [*among Jews also* 'ʃekem, ʃə'xem]
shed (*s. v.*), -s, -ding ʃed, -z, -ɪŋ
she-devil, -s 'ʃiːˌdevl [ˌ-'--], -z
Shee ʃiː
sheen (S.) ʃiːn
sheen|y (*s. adj.*), -ies 'ʃiːn|ɪ, -ɪz
sheep ʃiːp
sheep-dip 'ʃiːpdɪp
sheep-dog, -s 'ʃiːpdɒg, -z
sheep-fold, -s 'ʃiːpfəʊld, -z
sheepish, -ly, -ness 'ʃiːpɪʃ, -lɪ, -nɪs [-nəs]
sheep-pen, -s 'ʃiːppen, -z
sheep-run, -s 'ʃiːprʌn, -z
Sheepshanks 'ʃiːpʃæŋks
sheep-shearing 'ʃiːpˌʃɪərɪŋ
sheepskin, -s 'ʃiːpskɪn, -z
sheer (*s. adj. v. adv.*), -s, -ing, -ed ʃɪə*, -z, -rɪŋ, -d
Sheerness ˌʃɪə'nes [*also* '-- *according to sentence-stress*]
sheet, -s, -ing ʃiːt, -s, -ɪŋ
sheet-anchor, -s 'ʃiːtˌæŋkə*, -z
sheet-iron 'ʃiːtˌaɪən
sheet-lightning 'ʃiːtˌlaɪtnɪŋ
Sheffield 'ʃefiːld [*locally* -fɪld]
she-goat, -s 'ʃiːgəʊt [*also* ˌʃiː'g- *when preceded by a stress*], -s
sheik(h), -s ʃeɪk [ʃiːk, ʃek, ʃex], -s
Sheila 'ʃiːlə
shekel, -s 'ʃekl, -z
Shekinah ʃe'kaɪnə [ʃɪ'k-]
Shelagh 'ʃiːlə
Sheldon 'ʃeldən
Sheldonian ʃel'dəʊnjən [-nɪən]
sheldrake, -s 'ʃeldreɪk, -s
shelduck, -s 'ʃeldʌk, -s
shel|f, -ves ʃel|f, -vz
shell (*s. v.*), -s, -ing, -ed ʃel, -z, -ɪŋ, -d
shellac (*s. v.*), -s, -king, -ked ʃə'læk [ʃe'l-, 'ʃelæk], -s, -ɪŋ, -t
Shelley 'ʃelɪ
shell-fish 'ʃelfɪʃ
shell-proof 'ʃelpruːf
Shelmerdine 'ʃelmədiːn
shelt|er (*s. v.*), -ers, -ering, -ered; -erless 'ʃelt|ə*, -əz, -ərɪŋ, -əd; -əlɪs [-ləs]
shelv|e, -es, -ing, -ed ʃelv, -z, -ɪŋ, -d
shelves (*plur. of* shelf, *3rd sing. pres. of* shelve) ʃelvz
Shem ʃem
Shemeld 'ʃeməld
shemozzle, -s ʃɪ'mɒzl, -z
Shenandoah ˌʃenən'dəʊə

Shennan 'ʃenən
Shenstone 'ʃenstən
she-oak, -s 'ʃiːəʊk [ˌ-'-], -s
shepherd (*s. v.*) (S.), -s, -ing, -ed 'ʃepəd, -z, -ɪŋ, -ɪd
shepherdess, -es ˌʃepə'des ['ʃepədɪs, -des], -ɪz
Shepp|ard, -ey 'ʃep|əd, -ɪ
Sheraton 'ʃerətən
sherbet 'ʃɜːbət
Sherborne 'ʃɜːbən [-bɔːn]
Sherbrooke 'ʃɜːbrʊk
sherd, -s ʃɜːd, -z
Shere ʃɪə*
Sheridan 'ʃerɪdn
sheriff, -s 'ʃerɪf, -s
Sherlock 'ʃɜːlɒk
Sherman 'ʃɜːmən
Sherriff 'ʃerɪf
sherr|y, -ies 'ʃer|ɪ, -ɪz
Sherwood 'ʃɜːwʊd
she's (=she is *or* she has) ʃiːz (*normal form*), ʃɪz (*occasional weak form*)
Shetland, -s, -er/s 'ʃetlənd, -z, -ə*/z
shew, -s, -ing, -ed, -n ʃəʊ, -z, -ɪŋ, -d, -n
shewbread 'ʃəʊbred
Shewell ʃʊəl ['ʃuːəl]
shewn (*from* shew) ʃəʊn
she-wol|f, -ves 'ʃiːwʊl|f [ˌ-'-], -vz
Shewry 'ʃʊərɪ
shibboleth (S.), -s 'ʃɪbəleθ [-bəʊl-], -s
shield (*s. v.*) (S.), -s, -ing, -ed ʃiːld, -z, -ɪŋ, -ɪd
shieling, -s 'ʃiːlɪŋ, -z
shift (*s. v.*), -s, -ing, -ed ʃɪft, -s, -ɪŋ, -ɪd
shiftless 'ʃɪftlɪs [-ləs]
shift|y, -ier, -iest, -ily, -iness 'ʃɪft|ɪ, -ɪə* [-jə*], -ɪɪst [-jɪst], -ɪlɪ [-əlɪ], -ɪnɪs [-məs]
shikaree, -s ʃɪ'kɑːrɪ [-'kær-], -z
Shillan ʃɪ'læn
shillela(g)h (S.), -s ʃɪ'leɪlə [-lɪ], -z
Shilleto [-lito] 'ʃɪlɪtəʊ
shilling, -s; -sworth 'ʃɪlɪŋ, -z; -zwɜːθ [-wəθ]
shilly-shall|y (*s. v.*), -ies, -ying, -ied 'ʃɪlɪˌʃæl|ɪ, -ɪz, -ɪɪŋ [-jɪŋ], -ɪd
Shiloh 'ʃaɪləʊ
shimmer (*s. v.*), -s, -ing, -ed 'ʃɪmə*, -z, -rɪŋ, -d
shin (*s. v.*), -s, -ning, -ned ʃɪn, -z, -ɪŋ, -d
shin-bone, -s 'ʃɪnbəʊn, -z
shind|y, -ies, -dig/s 'ʃɪnd|ɪ, -ɪz, -dɪg/z
shin|e (*s. v.*), -es, -ing, -ed, shone ʃaɪn, -z, -ɪŋ, -d, ʃɒn
shingle, -s 'ʃɪŋgl, -z
shingly 'ʃɪŋglɪ

449

Shint|o, -oism, -oist/s 'ʃɪnt|əʊ, -əʊɪzəm,
-əʊɪst/s

shin|y, -ier, -iest, -iness 'ʃaɪn|ɪ, -ɪə*
[-jə*], -ɪɪst [-jɪst], -ɪnɪs [-məs]

ship (s. v.), -s, -ping, -ped, -per/s ʃɪp, -s,
-ɪŋ, -t, -ə*/z

shipboard 'ʃɪpbɔːd [-bɔəd]

ship-build|er/s, -ing 'ʃɪp‚bɪld|ə*/z, -ɪŋ

Shiplake 'ʃɪpleɪk

Shipley 'ʃɪplɪ

shipload, -s 'ʃɪpləʊd, -z

ship-master, -s 'ʃɪp‚mɑːstə*, -z

shipmate, -s 'ʃɪpmeɪt, -s

shipment, -s 'ʃɪpmənt, -s

ship-money 'ʃɪp‚mʌnɪ

ship-owner, -s 'ʃɪp‚əʊnə*, -z

shipshape 'ʃɪpʃeɪp

Shipton 'ʃɪptən

ship-way, -s 'ʃɪpweɪ, -z

shipwreck (s. v.), -s, -ing, -ed 'ʃɪprek,
-s, -ɪŋ, -t

shipwright (S.), -s 'ʃɪpraɪt, -s

shipyard, -s 'ʃɪpjɑːd, -z

Shiraz ‚ʃɪə'rɑːz

shire, -s 'ʃaɪə*, -z

-shire (suffix) -ʃə* [-‚ʃɪə*]

shirk (s. v.), -s, -ing, -ed, -er/s ʃɜːk, -s,
-ɪŋ, -t, -ə*/z

Shirley 'ʃɜːlɪ

shirt, -ing/s; -collar/s; -sleeves; -tails
ʃɜːt, -s, -ɪŋ/z; -‚kɒlə*/z; -sliːvz; -teɪlz

shirt-front, -s 'ʃɜːtfrʌnt, -s

shirty 'ʃɜːtɪ

Shishak 'ʃaɪʃæk [-ʃək, rarely 'ʃɪʃ-]

Shiva 'ʃiːvə ['ʃɪvə] (Hindi ʃyva)

shiv|er, -ers, -ering/ly, -ered 'ʃɪv|ə*,
-əz, -ərɪŋ/lɪ, -əd

shiver|y, -iness 'ʃɪvər|ɪ, -ɪnɪs [-məs]

shoal, -s ʃəʊl, -z

shock (s. v.), -s, -ing/ly, -ed, -er/s ʃɒk,
-s, -ɪŋ/lɪ, -t, -ə*/z

shockhead, -s, -ed 'ʃɒkhed, -z, -ɪd

shod (from shoe v.) ʃɒd

shodd|y, -ier, -iest, -ily, -iness 'ʃɒd|ɪ,
-ɪə*, -ɪɪst, -ɪlɪ [-əlɪ], -ɪnɪs [-məs]

shoe (s. v.), -s, -ing, shod ʃuː, -z, -ɪŋ
['ʃʊɪŋ], ʃɒd

shoeblack, -s 'ʃuːblæk, -s

Shoeburyness ‚ʃuːbərɪ'nes

shoehorn, -s 'ʃuːhɔːn, -z

shoe-lace, -s 'ʃuːleɪs, -ɪz

shoe-leather 'ʃuː‚leðə*

shoeless 'ʃuːlɪs [-ləs]

shoe-maker, -s 'ʃuː‚meɪkə*, -z

Shona (language) 'ʃɒnə ['ʃəʊnə]

shone (from shine) ʃɒn

shoo (v. interj.), -s, -ing, -ed ʃuː, -z, -ɪŋ,
-d

shook (from shake) ʃʊk

Shoolbred 'ʃuːlbred

shoot (s. v.), -s, -ing, shot ʃuːt, -s, -ɪŋ,
ʃɒt

shooter (S.), -s 'ʃuːtə*, -z

shooting-box, -es 'ʃuːtɪŋbɒks, -ɪz

shooting-galler|y, -ies 'ʃuːtɪŋ‚gælər|ɪ,
-ɪz

shop (s. v.), -s, -ping, -ped ʃɒp, -s, -ɪŋ, -t

shop-assistant, -s 'ʃɒpə‚sɪstənt, -s

shop-floor ‚ʃɒp'flɔː* [-'flɔə*]

shop-girl, -s 'ʃɒpɜːl, -z

shopkeeper, -s 'ʃɒp‚kiːpə*, -z

shop-lift|er/s, -ing 'ʃɒp‚lɪft|ə*/z, -ɪŋ

shop|man, -men 'ʃɒp|mən, -mən [-men]

shoppy 'ʃɒpɪ

shop-soiled ‚ʃɒp'sɔɪld ['--]

shop-steward, -s ‚ʃɒp'stjʊəd [-'stjuːəd,
'-‚-(-)], -z

shop-walker, -s 'ʃɒp‚wɔːkə*, -z

shop-window, -s ‚ʃɒp'wɪndəʊ, -z

shore, -s ʃɔː* [ʃɔə*], -z

Shore|ditch, -ham 'ʃɔː|dɪtʃ ['ʃɔə-], -rəm

shoreward 'ʃɔːwəd ['ʃɔə-]

shorn (from shear) ʃɔːn

Shorncliffe 'ʃɔːnklɪf

short (s. adj.) (S.), -s; -er, -est, -ly, -ness
ʃɔːt, -s; -ə*, -ɪst, -lɪ, -nɪs [-nəs]

shortage, -s 'ʃɔːtɪdʒ, -ɪz

shortbread, -s 'ʃɔːtbred, -z

shortcake, -s 'ʃɔːtkeɪk, -s

short-circuit (s. v.), -s, -ing, -ed ‚ʃɔːt-
'sɜːkɪt, -s, -ɪŋ, -ɪd

shortcoming, -s ‚ʃɔːt'kʌmɪŋ ['-‚--], -z

short-dated ‚ʃɔːt'deɪtɪd

short-eared 'ʃɔːt‚ɪəd

short|en, -ens, -ening, -ened 'ʃɔːt|n, -nz,
-nɪŋ [-ŋɪŋ], -nd

shortfall, -s 'ʃɔːtfɔːl, -z

shorthand 'ʃɔːthænd

short-handed ‚ʃɔːt'hændɪd

shorthorn, -s 'ʃɔːthɔːn, -z

short-lived ‚ʃɔːt'lɪvd [also '-- when
attributive]

short-sighted, -ly, -ness ‚ʃɔːt'saɪtɪd, -lɪ,
-nɪs [-nəs]

short-tempered ‚ʃɔːt'tempəd [also '-‚--
when attributive]

short-term 'ʃɔːttɜːm [‚-'-]

short-winded ‚ʃɔːt'wɪndɪd

Shostakovich ‚ʃɒstə'kəʊvɪtʃ

shot, -s ʃɒt, -s

shot-gun, -s 'ʃɒtgʌn, -z

shough, -s ʃʌf, -s

should ʃʊd (strong form), ʃəd, ʃd, ʃt
(weak forms)
  Note.—The form ʃt occurs only before
  voiceless consonants.

450

should|er (*s. v.*), **-ers, -ering, -ered**
ˈʃəʊld|ə*, -əz, -ərɪŋ, -əd
shoulder-blade, -s ˈʃəʊldəbleɪd, -z
shoulder-strap, -s ˈʃəʊldəstræp, -s
shouldn't ˈʃʊdnt
shout (*s. v.*), **-s, -ing, -ed** ʃaʊt, -s, -ɪŋ, -ɪd
shov|e (*s. v.*), **-es, -ing, -ed** ʃʌv, -z, -ɪŋ, -d
Shove (*surname*) ʃəʊv
shov|el (*s. v.*) (**S.**), **-els, -elling, -elled,
-eller/s; -elful/s** ˈʃʌv|l, -lz, -lɪŋ [-lɪŋ], -ld, -lə*/z [-lə*/z]; -lfʊl/z
show (*s. v.*), **-s, -ing, -ed, -n** ʃəʊ, -z, -ɪŋ, -d, -n
show-business ˈʃəʊˌbɪznɪs
show-case, -s ˈʃəʊkeɪs, -ɪz
show-down, -s ˈʃəʊdaʊn, -z
shower (*one who shows*), **-s** ˈʃəʊə*, -z
shower (*s. v.*) (*fall of rain, etc.*), **-s, -ing,
-ed; -y** ˈʃaʊə*, -z, -rɪŋ, -d; -rɪ
shower-ba|th, -ths ˈʃaʊəbɑː|θ, -ðz
showjump, -s, -ing; -er/s ˈʃəʊdʒʌmp, -s, -ɪŋ, -ə*/z
show|man, -men ˈʃəʊ|mən, -mən [-men]
showmanship ˈʃəʊmənʃɪp
shown (*from* show) ʃəʊn
showpiece, -s ˈʃəʊpiːs, -ɪz
show-place, -s ˈʃəʊpleɪs, -ɪz
show-room, -s ˈʃəʊrʊm [-ruːm], -z
show|y, -ier, -iest, -ily, -iness ˈʃəʊ|ɪ, -ɪə*, -ɪɪst, -ɪlɪ [-əlɪ], -ɪnɪs [-ɪnəs]
shrank (*from* shrink) ʃræŋk
shrapnel ˈʃræpnl̩ [-nəl]
shred (*s. v.*), **-s, -ding, -ded** ʃred, -z, -ɪŋ, -ɪd
shrew, -s ʃruː, -z
shrewd, -er, -est, -ly, -ness ʃruːd, -ə*, -ɪst, -lɪ, -nɪs [-nəs]
shrewish, -ly, -ness ˈʃruːɪʃ, -lɪ, -nɪs [-nəs]
Shrewsbury ˈʃrəʊzbərɪ [ˈʃruːz-]
Note.—ˈʃrəʊ- *is the pronunciation
used by those connected with Shrewsbury School and by many residents
in the neighbourhood.*
shriek (*s. v.*), **-s, -ing, -ed** ʃriːk, -s, -ɪŋ, -t
shrievalt|y, -ies ˈʃriːvlt|ɪ, -ɪz
shrift ʃrɪft
shrike, -s ʃraɪk, -s
shrill, -er, -est, -y, -ness ʃrɪl, -ə*, -ɪst, -ɪ [-lɪ], -nɪs [-nəs]
shrimp, -s, -ing, -er/s ʃrɪmp, -s, -ɪŋ, -ə*/z
shrine, -s ʃraɪn, -z
shrink, -s, -ing/ly, shrank, shrunk,
shrunken ʃrɪŋk, -s, -ɪŋ/lɪ, ʃræŋk, ʃrʌŋk, ˈʃrʌŋkən
shrinkage ˈʃrɪŋkɪdʒ

shriv|e (**S.**), **-es, -ing, shrove, shriven**
ʃraɪv, -z, -ɪŋ, ʃrəʊv, ˈʃrɪvn
shriv|el, -els, -elling, -elled ˈʃrɪv|l, -lz, -lɪŋ [-lɪŋ], -ld
Shropshire ˈʃrɒpʃə* [-ˌʃɪə*]
shroud (*s. v.*), **-s, -ing, -ed; -less** ʃraʊd, -z, -ɪŋ, -ɪd; -lɪs [-ləs]
Shrove ʃrəʊv
shrub, -s ʃrʌb, -z
shrubber|y, -ies ˈʃrʌbər|ɪ, -ɪz
shrubby ˈʃrʌbɪ
shrug (*s. v.*), **-s, -ging, -ged** ʃrʌg, -z, -ɪŋ, -d
shrunk (*from* shrink), **-en** ʃrʌŋk, -ən
Shubrook ˈʃuːbrʊk
shuck, -s ʃʌk, -s
Shuckburgh ˈʃʌkbrə
shudder, -s, -ing, -ed ˈʃʌd|ə*, -z, -rɪŋ, -d
shuff|le, -les, -ling, -led, -ler/s ˈʃʌf|l, -lz, -lɪŋ [-lɪŋ], -ld, -lə*/z [-lə*/z]
shuffle-board, -s ˈʃʌflbɔːd [-bɔəd], -z
shun, -s, -ning, -ned ʃʌn, -z, -ɪŋ, -d
shunt (*s. v.*), **-s, -ing, -ed, -er/s** ʃʌnt, -s, -ɪŋ, -ɪd, -ə*/z
shut, -s, -ting ʃʌt, -s, -ɪŋ
Shute ʃuːt
Shutte ʃuːt
shutter, -s, -ing, -ed ˈʃʌtə*, -z, -rɪŋ, -d
shuttle, -s; -cock/s ˈʃʌtl, -z; -kɒk/s
sh|y (*s. adj. v.*), **-ies, -yer, -yest, -yly,
-yness; -ying, -ied** ʃ|aɪ, -aɪz; -aɪə*, -aɪnst, -aɪlɪ, -aɪnɪs [-nəs]; -aɪɪŋ, -aɪd
Shylock ˈʃaɪlɒk
si (*musical note*) siː
Siam ˌsaɪˈæm [ˈsaɪæm]
Siamese ˌsaɪəˈmiːz
Sibelius sɪˈbeɪlɪəs [-ljəs]
Siberia, -n/s saɪˈbɪərɪə, -n/z
sibilan|ce, -t/s ˈsɪbɪlən|s, -t/s
sibilation, -s ˌsɪbɪˈleɪʃn, -z
Sible (*in Essex*) ˈsɪbl
Sibley ˈsɪblɪ
sibling, -s ˈsɪblɪŋ, -z
Sibun ˈsaɪbən
sibyl (**S.**), **-s** ˈsɪbəl [-bɪl], -z
sibylline ˈsɪbəlaɪn [-bɪl-, sɪˈbɪlaɪn]
sic sɪk
sice, -s saɪs, -ɪz
Sichel ˈsɪtʃəl
Sichem ˈsaɪkem
Sicilian, -s sɪˈsɪljən [-lɪən], -z
siciliano, -s sɪˌsɪlɪˈɑːnəʊ [sɪˌtʃɪ-, ˌ—ˈ—], -z
Sicil|y, -ies ˈsɪsɪl|ɪ [-səl|ɪ], -ɪz
sick, -er, -est, -ness sɪk, -ə*, -ɪst, -nɪs [-nəs]
sick-bed, -s ˈsɪkbed, -z

451

sick|en, -ens, -ening (*adj. v.*), -ened, -ener/s 'sɪk|ən, -ənz, -nɪŋ [-ənɪŋ], -nd, -ŋə*/z [-nə*/z]
sickish 'sɪkɪʃ
sickle, -s 'sɪkl, -z
sick|-leave, -list/s 'sɪkliːv, -lɪst/s
sickl|y, -ier, -iest, -iness 'sɪkl|ɪ, -ɪə*, -ɪɪst, -ɪnɪs [-məs]
sickness 'sɪknɪs [-nəs]
sick-nurse, -s 'sɪknəːs, -ɪz
sick-room, -s 'sɪkrʊm [-ruːm], -z
Siddeley 'sɪdəlɪ
Siddons 'sɪdnz
sid|e (*s. v.*), -es, -ing, -ed saɪd, -z, -ɪŋ, -ɪd
sideboard, -s 'saɪdbɔːd [-bɔəd], -z
Sidebotham 'saɪd,bɒtəm
side-car, -s 'saɪdkɑː*, -z
sidelight, -s 'saɪdlaɪt, -s
side-line, -s 'saɪdlaɪn, -z
sidelong 'saɪdlɒŋ
sidereal saɪ'dɪərɪəl
siderite 'saɪdəraɪt
Sidery 'saɪdərɪ
side-saddle, -s 'saɪd,sædl,-z
side-show, -s 'saɪdʃəʊ, -z
side-slip (*s. v.*), -s, -ping, -ped 'saɪdslɪp, -s, -ɪŋ, -t
sides|man, -men 'saɪdz|mən, -mən [-men]
side|stroke, -step 'saɪd|strəʊk, -step
side-track (*s. v.*), -s, -ing, -ed 'saɪdtræk, -s, -ɪŋ, -t
side-walk, -s 'saɪdwɔːk, -s
sideways 'saɪdweɪz
Sidgwick 'sɪdʒwɪk
siding (*s.*), -s 'saɪdɪŋ, -z
sid|le, -les, -ling, -led 'saɪd|l, -lz, -lɪŋ [-lɪŋ], -ld
Sid|mouth, -ney 'sɪd|məθ, -nɪ
Sidon 'saɪdn [-dɒn]
Sidonian, -s saɪ'dəʊnjən [-nɪən], -z
Sidonie sɪ'dəʊnɪ
siege, -s siːdʒ, -ɪz
Siegfried 'siːgfriːd ('ziːkfriːt)
Sieglinde siːg'lɪndə (ziːk'lində)
Siegmund 'siːgmʊnd [-mənd] ('ziːkmunt)
Siemens 'siːmənz
sienna sɪ'enə
Sien(n)a sɪ'enə
Sien(n)ese ˌsɪe'niːz [ˌsɪə'n-]
sierra (S.), -s sɪ'erə ['sɪərə], -z
Sierra Leone sɪˌerəlɪ'əʊn [ˌsɪər-, -'əʊnɪ]
siesta, -s sɪ'estə, -z
siev|e (*s. v.*), -es, -ing, -ed sɪv, -z, -ɪŋ, -d
sift, -s, -ing, -ed, -er/s sɪft, -s, -ɪŋ, -ɪd, -ə*/z
sigh (*s. v.*), -s, -ing, -ed saɪ, -z, -ɪŋ, -d

sight (*s. v.*), -s, -ing, -ed; -less saɪt, -s, -ɪŋ, -ɪd; -lɪs [-ləs]
sightl|y, -iness 'saɪtl|ɪ, -ɪnɪs [-məs]
sight-read|er/s, -ing 'saɪt,riːd|ə*/z, -ɪŋ
sight-seeing 'saɪt,siːɪŋ
sightseer, -s 'saɪt,siːə* ['saɪt,sɪə*], -z
Sigismond [-mund] 'sɪgɪsmənd
sigma, -s 'sɪgmə, -z
sign (*s. v.*), -s, -ing, -ed saɪn, -z, -ɪŋ, -d
sign|al (*s. adj. v.*), -als; -ally; -alling, -alled, -aller/s 'sɪgn|l [-əl]; -lɪ [-əlɪ]; -əlɪ; -lɪŋ [-əlɪŋ], -ld [-əld], -ələ*/z
signal-box, -es 'sɪgnl̩bɒks [-nəl-], -ɪz
signaliz|e [-is|e], -es, -ing, -ed 'sɪgnəlaɪz, -ɪz, -ɪŋ, -d
signal|man, -men 'sɪgnl̩|mən [-nəl|-, -mæn], -mən [-men]
signator|y, -ies 'sɪgnətər|ɪ, -ɪz
signature, -s 'sɪgnətʃə* [-nɪtʃ-], -z
signboard, -s 'saɪnbɔːd [-bɔəd], -z
signeme, -s 'sɪgniːm, -z
signet, -s 'sɪgnɪt, -s
signet-ring, -s 'sɪgnɪtrɪŋ, -z
significan|ce, -t/ly sɪg'nɪfɪkən|s, -t/lɪ
signification ˌsɪgnɪfɪ'keɪʃn
significative sɪg'nɪfɪkətɪv [-keɪt-]
signi|fy, -fies, -fying, -fied 'sɪgnɪ|faɪ, -faɪz, -faɪɪŋ, -faɪd
Signior 'siːnjɔː*
signor (S.), -s 'siːnjɔː* (sɪn'nor), -z
sign-paint|er/s, -ing 'saɪn,peɪnt|ə*/z, -ɪŋ
sign-post, -s 'saɪnpəʊst, -s
Sigurd (*English Christian name*) 'siːgəːd, (*Scandinavian name*) 'sɪˌgʊəd [-gəːd]
Sikes saɪks
Sikh, -s siːk (*Hindi* sikh), -s
Sikkim 'sɪkɪm
silage 'saɪlɪdʒ
Silas 'saɪləs [-læs]
Silchester 'sɪltʃɪstə*
silenc|e (*s. v.*), -es, -ing, -ed 'saɪləns, -ɪz, -ɪŋ, -t
silencer, -s 'saɪlənsə*, -z
silent, -ly 'saɪlənt, -lɪ
Silenus saɪ'liːnəs
Silesia saɪ'liːzjə [sɪ'l-, -zɪə, -ʒjə, -ʒɪə, -ʒə, -sjə, -sɪə, -ʃjə, -ʃɪə, -ʃə]
Silesian, -s saɪ'liːzjən [sɪ'l-, -zɪən, -ʒjən, -ʒɪən, -ʒn, -sjən, -sɪən, -ʃjən, -ʃɪən, -ʃn], -z
silex 'saɪleks
silhouette, -s ˌsɪluː'et [-lʊ'et, '---], -s
silic|a, -ate, -ated 'sɪlɪk|ə, -ɪt [-eɪt, -ət], -eɪtɪd
silicon 'sɪlɪkən
silicone 'sɪlɪkəʊn
silicosis ˌsɪlɪ'kəʊsɪs

silicotic (s. adj.), -s ˌsılıˈkɒtık, -s
silk, -s, -en sılk, -s, -ən
silkworm, -s ˈsılkwɜːm, -z
silk|y, -ier, -iest, -iness ˈsılk|ı, -ıə*
[-jə*], -ııst [-jıst], -ınıs [-ınəs]
sill, -s (S.) sıl, -z
sillabub ˈsıləbʌb [-bəb]
Sillence ˈsaıləns
Sillery ˈsılərı
Sillitoe ˈsılıtəʊ
sill|y (s. adj.), -ies; -ier, -iest, -ily, -iness
ˈsıl|ı, -ız; -ıə*, -ııst, -ılı [-əlı], -ınıs
[-ınəs]
silo, -s ˈsaıləʊ, -z
Siloam saıˈləʊəm [-ˈləʊæm]
silt (s. v.), -s, -ing, -ed; -y sılt, -s, -ıŋ,
-ıd; -ı
Silurian saıˈlʊərıən [sıˈl-, -ˈljʊə-,
-ˈljɔər-, -ˈljɔːr-]
Silva ˈsılvə
silvan ˈsılvən
Silvanus sılˈveınəs
silv|er (s. v.), -ers, -ering, -ered; -ery,
-eriness ˈsılv|ə*, -əz, -ərıŋ, -əd; -ərı,
-ərınıs [-ınəs]
silverfish ˈsılvəfıʃ
silver-gilt ˌsılvəˈgılt [also ˈ--- when
attributive]
silver-plate ˌsılvəˈpleıt
silverside, -s ˈsılvəsaıd, -z
silversmith, -s ˈsılvəsmıθ, -s
Silvertown, -s ˈsılvətaʊn, -z
Silvester sılˈvestə*
Silvia ˈsılvıə [-vjə]
Simca ˈsımkə
Simenon ˈsiːmənɔ̃ːŋ [-nɒn] (simnɔ̃)
Simeon ˈsımıən [-mjən]
simian (s. adj.), -s ˈsımıən [-mjən], -z
similar, -ly ˈsımılə* [-mələ*], -lı
similarit|y, -ies ˌsımıˈlærət|ı [-məˈl-,
-ıt|ı], -ız
simile, -s ˈsımılı, -z
similitude, -s sıˈmılıtjuːd, -z
Simla ˈsımlə
simmer, -s, -ing, -ed ˈsımə*, -z, -rıŋ, -d
Simmon(d)s ˈsımənz
simnel (S.), -s ˈsımnl̩ [-nəl], -z
Simon ˈsaımən, as surname also sıˈməʊn
Simond ˈsaımənd, ˈsımənd
Simonds (Lord) ˈsıməndz
simoniacal ˌsaıməˈnaıəkl [-məʊˈn-]
simony ˈsaımənı
simoom, -s sıˈmuːm, -z
simper (s. v.), -s, -ing, -ed ˈsımpə*, -z,
-rıŋ, -d
Simpkin, -s, -son ˈsımpkın, -z, -sn
simp|le, -les, -ler, -lest, -ly, -leness
ˈsımp|l̩, -lz, -lə*, -lıst, -lı, -lnıs [-nəs]

simplehearted ˌsımplˈhɑːtıd [ˈ--,--]
simple-minded ˌsımplˈmaındıd [also
ˈ--,-- when attributive]
simpleton, -s ˈsımpltən, -z
simplicity sımˈplısətı [-ıtı]
simplification, -s ˌsımplıfıˈkeıʃn, -z
simpli|fy, -fies, -fying, -fied ˈsımplı|faı,
-faız, -faııŋ, -faıd
Simplon ˈsæmplɔ̃ːŋ [ˈsæmp-, ˈsımplən]
(sɛ̃plɔ̃)
simply ˈsımplı
Simpson ˈsımpsn
Sims sımz
Simson ˈsımsn [-mps-]
simulacr|um, -a ˌsımjʊˈleıkr|əm, -ə
simulat|e, -es, -ing, -ed, -er/s ˈsım-
jʊleıt, -s -ıŋ, -ıd, -ə*/z
simulation, -s ˌsımjʊˈleıʃn, -z
simultaneity ˌsıməltəˈnıətı [ˌsaım-,
-mʊl-, -ˈniːrtı, -ˈniːətı, -ˈneıtı, -neıətı]
simultaneous, -ly, -ness ˌsıməlˈteınjəs
[ˌsaım-, -mʊl-, -nıəs], -lı, -nıs [-nəs]
sin (s. v.), -s, -ning, -ned, -ner/s sın, -z,
-ıŋ, -d, -ə*/z
sin (in trigonometry) saın
Sinai ˈsaınaı [-neıaı, -nıaı]
sinapism, -s ˈsınəpızəm, -z
Sinatra sıˈnɑːtrə
Sinbad ˈsınbæd
since sıns
sincere, -r, -st, -ly, -ness sınˈsıə* [sn-],
-rə*, -rıst, -lı, -nıs [-nəs]
sincerity sınˈserətı [sn-, -ıtı]
sinciput, -s ˈsınsıpʌt [-pət], -s
Sinclair ˈsıŋkleə* [ˈsınk-], ˈsıŋklə*
Sind sınd
Sindbad ˈsınbæd [-ndb-]
Sindh sınd (Hindi syndh)
Sindhi ˈsındı: [-dı] (Hindi syndhi)
Sindlesham ˈsındlʃəm
sine, -s saın, -z
sinecure, -s ˈsaınıˌkjʊə* [ˈsın-, -kjɔə*,
-kjɔː*], -z
sine die ˌsaınıˈdaıı: [-ˈdan, ˌsınıˈdiːeı]
Sinel ˈsınəl
sine qua non, -s ˌsaınıkweıˈnɒn [ˌsını-
kwɑːˈnəʊn], -z
sinew, -s ˈsınjuː, -z
sinewy ˈsınjuːı [-njʊı]
sin|ful, -fully, -fulness ˈsın|fʊl, -fʊlı
[-fəlı], -fʊlnıs [-nəs]
sing, -s, -ing, sang, sung, singer/s sıŋ,
-z, -ıŋ, sæŋ, sʌŋ, ˈsıŋə*/z
singable ˈsıŋəbl
Singapore ˌsıŋəˈpɔː* [ˌsıŋgə-,-ˈpɔə*]
singe, -s, -ing, -d sındʒ, -ız, -ıŋ, -d
Singer ˈsıŋə*, ˈsıŋgə*
Singhalese ˌsıŋhəˈliːz [ˌsıŋgəˈl-]

453

singing-master, -s 'sɪŋɪŋ‚mɑ:stə*, -z
sing|le, -ly, -leness 'sɪŋg|l, -lɪ, -lnɪs
[-nəs]
single-handed ‚sɪŋgl'hændɪd
singlehearted, -ly, -ness ‚sɪŋgl'hɑ:tɪd
['--‚--], -lɪ, -nɪs [-nəs]
single-minded ‚sɪŋgl'maɪndɪd ['--‚--]
singlestick, -s 'sɪŋglstɪk, -s
singlet, -s 'sɪŋglɪt [-lət], -s
singleton (S.), -s 'sɪŋgltən, -z
singly 'sɪŋglɪ
singsong (s. adj.), -s 'sɪŋsɒŋ, -z
singular (s. adj.), -s, -ly 'sɪŋgjʊlə*
[-gjəl-], -z, -lɪ
singularit|y, -ies ‚sɪŋgjʊ'lærət|ɪ [-gjə'l-,
-ɪt|ɪ], -ɪz
sinh (in trigonometry) ʃaɪn [sɪnɪʃ]
Sinhalese ‚sɪŋhə'li:z [‚sɪnhə'l-, ‚sɪnə'l-]
Sinim 'sɪnɪm ['saɪn-]
sinister 'sɪnɪstə*
sinistr|al, -ally 'sɪnɪstr|əl, -əlɪ
sink (s. v.), -s, -ing, sank, sunk, sunken,
sink|er/s; -able sɪŋk, -s, -ɪŋ, sæŋk,
sʌŋk, 'sʌŋkən, 'sɪŋk|ə*/z; -əbl
sinless, -ly, -ness 'sɪnlɪs [-ləs], -lɪ, -nɪs
[-nəs]
sinner, -s 'sɪnə*, -z
Sinnett 'sɪnɪt, sɪ'net
Sinn Fein, -er/s ‚ʃɪn'feɪn [‚sɪn-], -ə*/z
sinologue, -s 'sɪnəlɒg ['saɪ-, -ləʊg], -z
sinolog|y, -ist saɪ'nɒlədʒ|ɪ [sɪ'n-], -ɪst
sinuosit|y, -ies ‚sɪnjʊ'ɒsət|ɪ [-ɪt|ɪ], -ɪz
sinuous 'sɪnjʊəs [-njwəs]
sinus, -es 'saɪnəs, -ɪz
sinusitis ‚saɪnə'saɪtɪs
sinusoid, -s 'saɪnəsɔɪd, -z
Siobhan ʃɪ'vɔ:n [ʃə'v-]
Sion 'saɪən ['zaɪən]
Sioux (sing.) su:, (plur.) su:z
sip (s. v.), -s, -ping, -ped sɪp, -s, -ɪŋ, -t
siph|on (s. v.), -ons, -oning, -oned
'saɪf|n, -nz, -ənɪŋ [-nɪŋ], -nd
sir, -s sɜ:*, -z (strong form), sə* (weak
form)
Sirach 'saɪəræk
sirdar (S.), -s 'sɜ:dɑ:*, -z
sir|e (s. v.), -es, -ing, -ed 'saɪə*, -z, -rɪŋ,
-d
siren, -s 'saɪərən [-rɪn], -z
Sirion 'sɪrɪən
Sirius (star) 'sɪrɪəs [rarely 'saɪər-]
sirloin, -s 'sɜ:lɔɪn, -z
sirocco, -s sɪ'rɒkəʊ, -z
sirrah 'sɪrə
sisal 'saɪsl [old-fashioned 'sɪsl]
Sisal (Mexican port) sɪ'sɑ:l (si'sal)
Sisam 'saɪsəm
Sisera 'sɪsərə

siskin (S.), -s 'sɪskɪn, -z
sisson (S.) 'sɪsn
siss|y, -ies 'sɪs|ɪ, -ɪz
sister, -s; -ly 'sɪstə*, -z; -lɪ
sisterhood, -s 'sɪstəhʊd, -z
sister-in-law, sisters-in-law 'sɪstərɪnlɔ:,
'sɪstəzɪnlɔ:
Sistine 'sɪsti:n [-taɪn]
sistrum, -s 'sɪstrəm, -z
Sisum 'saɪsəm
Sisyphean ‚sɪsɪ'fi:ən [-'fɪən]
Sisyphus 'sɪsɪfəs
sit, -s, -ting/s, sat, sitter/s sɪt, -s, -ɪŋ/z,
sæt, 'sɪtə*/z
sitar sɪ'tɑ:
sit-down (s.) 'sɪtdaʊn
site, -s saɪt, -s
sit-in, -s 'sɪtɪn, -z
sitter-in, sitters-in ‚sɪtər'ɪn, ‚sɪtəz'ɪn
Sittingbourne 'sɪtɪŋbɔ:n [-bɔən]
situate (adj.) 'sɪtjʊert [-tʃʊert, -tjʊrt,
-tʃʊrt, -ʊət]
situat|e (v.), -es, -ing, -ed 'sɪtjʊert
[-tʃʊ-], -s, -ɪŋ, -ɪd
situation, -s ‚sɪtjʊ'eɪʃn [-tʃʊ-], -z
Sitwell 'sɪtwəl [-wel]
Siva 'ʃi:və ['si:v-, 'sɪv-, 'ʃɪv-] (Hindi
ʃyva)
Sivyer (surname) 'sɪvɪə* [-vjə*]
Siward 'sju:əd [sjʊəd]
six, -es; -fold sɪks, -ɪz; -fəʊld
sixain, -s 'sɪkseɪn, -z
sixer, -s 'sɪksə*, -z
six-foot (adj.) 'sɪksfʊt
six-footer, -s ‚sɪks'fʊtə*, -z
sixish 'sɪksɪʃ
six|pence, -pences, -penny 'sɪks|pəns,
-pənsɪz, -pənɪ (see note under penny)
six-shooter, -s ‚sɪks'ʃu:tə* [‚sɪkʃ'ʃ-], -z
sixte sɪkst
sixteen, -s, -th/s, -thly ‚sɪks'ti:n ['--
according to sentence-stress], -z, -θ/s,
-θlɪ
sixteenmo [16mo] sɪks'ti:nməʊ
sixth, -s, -ly sɪksθ [-kstθ], -s, -lɪ
Sixtus 'sɪkstəs
sixt|y, -ies, -ieth/s 'sɪkstɪ, -ɪz, -ɪəθ/s
[-jəθ/s, -ɪɪθ/s, -jɪθ/s]
sizar, -s; -ship/s 'saɪzə*, -z; -ʃɪp/s
siz|e (s. v.), -es, -ing, -ed saɪz, -ɪz, -ɪŋ, -d
siz(e)able 'saɪzəbl
sizz|le, -les, -ling, -led 'sɪz|l, -lz, -lɪŋ
[-lɪŋ], -ld
sjambok (s. v.), -s, -ing, -ed 'ʃæmbɒk,
-s, -ɪŋ, -t
Skagerrak 'skægəræk
skat|e (s. v.), -es, -ing, -ed, -er/s skeɪt,
-s, -ɪŋ, -ɪd, -ə*/z

skating-rink, -s 'skeɪtɪŋrɪŋk, -s
skean dhu, -s ˌski:ən'du: [ˌskɪən-], -z
Skeat ski:t
skedadd|le, -les, -ling, -led skɪ'dæd|l,
 -lz, -l̩ɪŋ [-lɪŋ], -ld
Skeggs skegz
Skegness ˌskeg'nes ['-- *according to
 sentence-stress*]
skein, -s skeɪn, -z
skeletal 'skelɪtl [-lət-, skə'li:tl]
skeleton, -s 'skelɪtn, -z
skelter 'skeltə*
Skelton 'skeltən
sketch (s. v.), -es, -ing, -ed; -able sketʃ,
 -ɪz, -ɪŋ, -t; -əbl
sketch-book, -s 'sketʃbʊk, -s
Sketchley 'sketʃlɪ
sketch|y, -ier, -iest, -ily, -iness 'sketʃ|ɪ,
 -ɪə*, -ɪɪst, -ɪlɪ [-əlɪ], -ɪnɪs [-ɪnəs]
skew (s. adj.), -s skju:, -z
skewer (s. v.), -s, -ing, -ed skjʊə*, -z,
 -rɪŋ, -d
Skey ski:
ski (s. v.), -s, -ing, -'d [ski-ed] ski:, -z,
 -ɪŋ, -d
skiagram, -s 'skaɪəgræm, -z
skiagraph, -s 'skaɪəgrɑ:f [-græf], -s
Skibo 'ski:bəʊ
ski-borne 'ski:bɔ:n [-bɔən]
skid, -s, -ding, -ded skɪd, -z, -ɪŋ, -ɪd
Skiddaw 'skɪdɔ: [*locally* -də]
skier (one who skis), -s 'ski:ə*, -z
skiff, -s skɪf, -s
skiffle 'skɪfl
ski-jump, -s 'ski:dʒʌmp, -s
skil|ful, -fully, -fulness 'skɪl|fʊl, -fʊlɪ
 [-fəlɪ], -fʊlnɪs [-nəs]
skill, -s, -ed skɪl, -z, -d
skilly 'skɪlɪ
skim, -s, -ming, -med, -mer/s skɪm, -z,
 -ɪŋ, -d, -ə*/z
skim-milk ˌskɪm'mɪlk ['--]
skimp, -s, -ing/ly, -ed; -y, -ier, -iest,
 -iness skɪmp, -s, -ɪŋ/lɪ, -t [skɪmt]; -ɪ,
 -ɪə* [-jə*], -ɪɪst [-jɪst], -ɪnɪs [-ɪnəs]
skin (s. v.), -s, -ning, -ned skɪn, -z, -ɪŋ,
 -d
skin-deep ˌskɪn'di:p ['--]
skin-div|e, -es, -ing, -ed, -er/s 'skɪn-
 daɪv, -z, -ɪŋ, -d, -ə*/z
skinflint, -s 'skɪnflɪnt, -s
skinhead, -s 'skɪnhed, -z
skinner (S.), -s 'skɪnə*, -z
skinn|y, -ier, -iest, -iness 'skɪn|ɪ, -ɪə*,
 -ɪɪst, -ɪnɪs [-ɪnəs]
skip (s. v.), -s, -ping, -ped skɪp, -s, -ɪŋ, -t
skipper, -s 'skɪpə*, -z
skipping-rope, -s 'skɪpɪŋrəʊp, -s

Skipton 'skɪptən
skirmish (s. v.), -es, -ing, -ed, -er/s
 'skɜ:mɪʃ, -ɪz, -ɪŋ, -t, -ə*/z
skirt (s. v.), -s, -ing/s, -ed skɜ:t, -s,
 -ɪŋ/z, -ɪd
skirt-danc|er/s, -ing 'skɜ:t̩dɑ:ns|ə*/z,
 -ɪŋ
skirting-board, -s 'skɜ:tɪŋbɔ:d [-bɔəd],
 -z
skit, -s skɪt, -s
ski-troops 'ski:tru:ps
skittish, -ly, -ness 'skɪtɪʃ, -lɪ, -nɪs
 [-nəs]
skittle, -s 'skɪtl, -z
skiv|e, -es, -ing, -ed, -er/s skaɪv, -z, -ɪŋ,
 -d, -ə*/z
skivv|y, -ies 'skɪv|ɪ, -ɪz
Skrimshire 'skrɪmʃə*
Skrine skri:n
skua, -s 'skju:ə [skjʊə], -z
skulduggery skʌl'dʌgərɪ
skulk, -s, -ing, -ed skʌlk, -s, -ɪŋ, -t
skull, -s skʌl, -z
skull-cap, -s 'skʌlkæp, -s
skunk, -s skʌŋk, -s
sk|y (s. v.), -ies, -ying, -ied, -ier/s sk|aɪ,
 -aɪz, -aɪŋ, -aɪd, -aɪə*/z
sky-blue ˌskaɪ'blu: [*also* '-- when attri-
 butive]
Skye skaɪ
skydiv|er/s, -ing 'skaɪˌdaɪv|ə*/z, -ɪŋ
sky-high ˌskaɪ'haɪ
skyjack (s. v.), -s, -ing, -ed, -er/s
 'skaɪdʒæk, -s, -ɪŋ, -t, -ə*/z
skylark (s. v.), -s, -ing, -ed 'skaɪlɑ:k, -s,
 -ɪŋ, -t
skylight, -s 'skaɪlaɪt, -s
sky-line, -s 'skaɪlaɪn, -z
sky-rocket (s. v.), -s, -ing, -ed 'skaɪ-
 ˌrɒkɪt, -s, -ɪŋ, -ɪd
skyscape, -s 'skaɪskeɪp, -s
skyscraper, -s 'skaɪˌskreɪpə*, -z
skyward, -s 'skaɪwəd, -z
sky-writing 'skaɪˌraɪtɪŋ
slab (s. v.), -s, -bing, -bed slæb, -z, -ɪŋ,
 -d
slack (s. adj. v.), -s; -er, -est, -ly, -ness;
 -ing, -ed, -er/s slæk, -s; -ə*, -ɪst, -lɪ,
 -nɪs [-nəs]; -ɪŋ, -t, -ə*/z
slack|en, -ens, -ening, -ened 'slæk|ən,
 -ənz, -ŋɪŋ [-nɪŋ, -ənɪŋ], -ənd
Slade sleɪd
slag, -gy slæg, -ɪ
slain (from slay) sleɪn
Slaithwaite 'slæθwət [-weɪt, *locally also*
 'slaʊɪt]
slak|e, -es, -ing, -ed sleɪk, -s, -ɪŋ, -t
slalom, -s 'slɑ:ləm ['sleɪl-], -z

455

slam—slipper

slam (*s. v.*), **-s, -ming, -med** slæm, -z, -ıŋ, -d

sland|er (*s. v.*), **-ers, -ering, -ered, -erer/s** 'slɑːnd|ə*, -əz, -ərıŋ, -əd, -ərə*/z

slanderous, -ly, -ness 'slɑːndərəs, -lı, -nıs [-nəs]

slang (*s. v.*), **-s, -ing, -ed; -y, -ier, -iest, -ily, -iness** slæŋ, -z, -ıŋ, -d; -ı, -ıə*, -ııst, -ılı [-əlı], -ınıs [-ınəs]

slant (*s. adj. v.*), **-s, -ing/ly, -ed** slɑːnt, -s, -ıŋ/lı, -ıd

slantwise 'slɑːntwaız

slap (*s. v. adv.*), **-s, -ping, -ped** slæp, -s, -ıŋ, -t

slap-bang ˌslæp'bæŋ

slapdash 'slæpdæʃ

slap-stick, -s 'slæpstık, -s

slap-up (*adj.*) 'slæpʌp [ˌ-'-]

slash (*s. v.*), **-es, -ing, -ed** slæʃ, -ız, -ıŋ, -t

slat, -s slæt, -s

slat|e (*s. v.*), **-es, -ing, -ed, -er/s** sleıt, -s, -ıŋ, -ıd, -ə*/z

slate-coloured 'sleıtˌkʌləd

slate-grey ˌsleıt'greı

slate-pencil, -s ˌsleıt'pensl, -z

Slater 'sleıtə*

slattern, -s, -ly, -liness 'slætən [-tɜːn], -z, -lı, -lınıs [-nəs]

slaty 'sleıtı

slaught|er (*s. v.*) (S.), **-ers, -ering, -ered, -erer/s; -erous/ly** 'slɔːt|ə*, -əz, -ərıŋ, -əd, -ərə*/z, -ərəs/lı

slaughterhou|se, -ses 'slɔːtəhaʊ|s, -zız

Slav, -s slɑːv [*rarely* slæv], -z

slav|e (*s. v.*), **-es, -ing, -ed, -er/s** sleıv, -z, -ıŋ, -d, -ə*/z

slave-driv|er/s, -ing 'sleıvˌdraıv|ə*/z, -ıŋ

slave-owner, -s 'sleıvˌəʊnə*, -z

slaver (*slave-trader*), -s 'sleıvə*, -z

slaver (*s. v.*) (*slobber*), **-s, -ing, -ed** 'slævə* ['sleıvə*], -z, -rıŋ, -d

slavery 'sleıvərı

slave-ship, -s 'sleıvʃıp, -s

slave-trade, -r/s 'sleıvtreıd, -ə*/z

slavey, -s 'sleıvı ['slævı], -z

Slavic 'slɑːvık ['slæv-]

slavish, -ly, -ness 'sleıvıʃ, -lı, -nıs [-nəs]

Slavonic slə'vɒnık [slæ'v-, slɑː'v-]

slay, -s, -ing, slew, slain, slayer/s sleı, -z, -ıŋ, sluː, sleın, 'sleıə*/z

Slazenger 'slæzəndʒə*

sledg|e (*s. v.*), **-es, -ing, -ed** sledʒ, -ız, -ıŋ, -d

sledge-hammer, -s 'sledʒˌhæmə*, -z

sleek, -er, -est, -ly, -ness sliːk, -ə*, -ıst, -lı, -nıs [-nəs]

sleep (*s. v.*), **-s, -ing, slept** sliːp, -s, -ıŋ, slept

sleeper, -s 'sliːpə*, -z

sleeping-bag, -s 'sliːpıŋbæg, -z

sleeping-car, -s 'sliːpıŋkɑː*, -z

sleeping-draught, -s 'sliːpıŋdrɑːft, -s

sleeping-pill, -s 'sliːpıŋpıl, -z

sleepless, -ly, -ness 'sliːplıs [-ləs], -lı, -nıs [-nəs]

sleepwalk|er/s, -ing 'sliːpˌwɔːk|ə*/z, -ıŋ

sleep|y, -ier, -iest, -ily, -iness 'sliːp|ı, -ıə* [-jə*], -ııst [-jıst], -ılı [-əlı], -ınıs [-ınəs]

sleepyhead, -s 'sliːpıhed, -z

sleet (*s. v.*), **-s, -ing, -ed; -y, -iness** sliːt, -s, -ıŋ, -ıd; -ı, -ınıs [-ınəs]

sleeve, -s, -d; -less sliːv, -z, -d; -lıs [-ləs]

sleigh (*s. v.*), **-s, -ing, -ed** sleı, -z, -ıŋ, -d

sleight (S.) slaıt

Sleights (*in North Yorkshire*) slaıts

slender, -er, -est, -ly, -ness 'slendə*, -rə*, -rıst, -lı, -nıs [-nəs]

slept (*from* sleep) slept

sleuth (*s. v.*), **-s, -ing, -ed** sluː:θ [slju:θ], -s, -ıŋ, -t

sleuth-hound, -s 'sluː:θhaʊnd ['slju:θ-], -z

slew (*from* slay) sluː:

slic|e (*s. v.*), **-es, -ing, -ed, -er/s** slaıs, -ız, -ıŋ, -t, -ə*/z

slick, -er, -est, -ly, -ness slık, -ə*, -ıst, -lı, -nıs [-nəs]

slid (*from* slide) slıd

slid|e (*s. v.*), **-es, -ing, slid** slaıd, -z, -ıŋ, slıd

slide-rule, -s 'slaıdruː:l, -z

slide-valve, -s 'slaıdvælv, -z

slight (*s. adj. v.*), **-s; -er, -est, -ly, -ness; -ing/ly, -ed** slaıt, -s; -ə*, -ıst, -lı, -nıs [-nəs]; -ıŋ/lı, -ıd

slightish 'slaıtıʃ

Sligo 'slaıgəʊ

slim (*adj. v.*) (S.), **-mer, -mest, -ly, -ness; -s, -ming, -med** slım, -ə*, -ıst, -lı, -nıs [-nəs]; -z, -ıŋ, -d

slim|e (*s. v.*), **-es, -ing, -ed** slaım, -z, -ıŋ, -d

slim|y, -ier, -iest, -ily, -iness 'slaım|ı, -ıə* [-jə*], -ııst [-jıst], -ılı [-əlı], -ınıs [-ınəs]

sling (*s. v.*), **-s, -ing, slung** slıŋ, -z, -ıŋ, slʌŋ

slink, -s, -ing, slunk slıŋk, -s, -ıŋ, slʌŋk

slip (*s. v.*), **-s, -ping, -ped** slıp, -s, -ıŋ, -t

slip-knot, -s 'slıpnɒt, -s

slipover, -s 'slıpˌəʊvə*, -z

slipper, -s, -ed 'slıpə*, -z, -d

slipper|y, -ier, -iest, -ily, -iness 'slɪpər|ɪ, -ɪə*, -ɪɪst, -əlɪ [-ɪlɪ], -ɪnɪs [-ɪnəs]

slipp|y, -ier, -iest, -iness 'slɪp|ɪ, -ɪə*, -ɪɪst, -ɪnɪs [-nəs]

slipshod 'slɪpʃɒd

slipstream, -s 'slɪpstriːm, -z

slipware 'slɪpweə*

slipway, -s 'slɪpweɪ, -z

slit (s. v.), -s, -ting slɪt, -s, -ɪŋ

slith|er, -ers, -ering, -ered; -ery 'slɪð|ə*, -əz, -ərɪŋ, -əd; -ərɪ

sliver (s. v.), -s, -ing, -ed 'slɪvə* ['slaɪv-], -z, -rɪŋ, -d

Sloan(e) sləʊn

slobber (s. v.), -s, -ing, -ed 'slɒbə*, -z, -rɪŋ, -d

slobber|y, -iness 'slɒbər|ɪ, -ɪnɪs [-ɪnəs]

Slocombe 'sləʊkəm

Slocum 'sləʊkəm

sloe, -s sləʊ, -z

slog (s. v.), -s, -ging, -ged, -ger/s slɒg, -z, -ɪŋ, -d, -ə*/z

slogan, -s 'sləʊgən, -z

sloid slɔɪd

sloop, -s sluːp, -s

slop (s. v.), -s, -ping, -ped slɒp, -s, -ɪŋ, -t

slop-basin, -s 'slɒp,beɪsn, -z

slop|e (s. v.), -es, -ing/ly, -ed, -er/s sləʊp, -s, -ɪŋ/lɪ, -t, -ə*/z

Sloper 'sləʊpə*

slop-pail, -s 'slɒppeɪl, -z

slopp|y, -ier, -iest, -ily, -iness 'slɒp|ɪ, -ɪə*, -ɪɪst, -ɪlɪ [-əlɪ], -ɪnɪs [-ɪnəs]

slosh (s. v.), -es, -ing, -ed; -y, -ier, -iest, -iness slɒʃ, -ɪz, -ɪŋ, -t; -ɪ, -ɪə*, -ɪɪst, -ɪnɪs [-ɪnəs]

slot (s. v.), -s, -ting, -ted slɒt, -s, -ɪŋ, -ɪd

sloth, -s sləʊθ, -s

sloth|ful, -fully, -fulness 'sləʊθ|fʊl, -fʊlɪ [-fəlɪ], -fʊlnɪs [-nəs]

slot-machine, -s 'slɒtmə,ʃiːn, -z

slouch (s. v.), -es, -ing/ly, -ed slaʊtʃ, -ɪz, -ɪŋ/lɪ, -t

slouch-hat, -s ˌslaʊtʃ'hæt, -s

slough (bog), -s, -y slaʊ, -z, -ɪ

slough (skin of snake), -s slʌf, -s

slough (v.) (cast off skin), -s, -ing, -ed slʌf, -s, -ɪŋ, -t

Slough slaʊ

Slovak, -s 'sləʊvæk, -s

Slovakia sləʊ'vækɪə [-'vækjə, -'vɑːkɪə, -'vɑːkjə, rarely -'veɪkɪə, -'veɪkjə]

sloven, -s 'slʌvn, -z

Slovene, -s 'sləʊviːn [sləʊ'viːn], -z

Slovenian, -s sləʊ'viːnjən [-nɪən], -z

slovenl|y, -iness 'slʌvnl|ɪ, -ɪnɪs [-ɪnəs]

slow (adj. v.), -er, -est, -ly, -ness; -s, -ing, -ed sləʊ, -ə*, -ɪst, 'sləʊlɪ, 'sləʊnɪs [-nəs], -z, -ɪŋ, -d

slow-coach, -es 'sləʊkəʊtʃ, -ɪz

slow-motion ˌsləʊ'məʊʃn

slow-worm, -s 'sləʊwɜːm, -z

sludge slʌdʒ

slug, -s slʌg, -z

sluggard, -s 'slʌgəd, -z

sluggish, -ly, -ness 'slʌgɪʃ, -lɪ, -nɪs [-nəs]

sluic|e (s. v.), -es, -ing, -ed sluːs, -ɪz, -ɪŋ, -t

sluice-gate, -s 'sluːsgeɪt [ˌ-'-], -s

slum (s. v.), -s, -ming, -med, -mer/s slʌm, -z, -ɪŋ, -d, -ə*/z

slumb|er (s. v.), -ers, -ering, -ered, -erer/s; -erless 'slʌmb|ə*, -əz, -ərɪŋ, -əd, -ərə*/z; -əlɪs [-ləs]

slumland 'slʌmlænd

slumm|y, -ier, -iest, -iness 'slʌm|ɪ, -ɪə*, -ɪɪst, -ɪnɪs [-ɪnəs]

slump (s. v.), -s, -ing, -ed slʌmp, -s, -ɪŋ, -t [slʌmt]

slung (from sling) slʌŋ

slunk (from slink) slʌŋk

slur (s. v.), -s, -ring, -red slɜː*, -z, -rɪŋ, -d

slush, -y, -ier, -iest, -iness slʌʃ, -ɪ, -ɪə*, -ɪɪst, -ɪnɪs [-ɪnəs]

slut, -s slʌt, -s

sluttish, -ly, -ness 'slʌtɪʃ, -lɪ, -nɪs [-nəs]

Sluys slɔɪs

sly, -er, -est, -ly, -ness slaɪ, 'slaɪə*, 'slaɪɪst, 'slaɪlɪ, 'slaɪnɪs [-nəs]

slyboots 'slaɪbuːts

smack (s. v.), -s, -ing/s, -ed smæk, -s, -ɪŋ/z, -t

Smale smeɪl

small (s. adj. adv.) (S.), -s; -er, -est, -ness; -ish smɔːl, -z; -ə*, -ɪst, -nɪs [-nəs]; -ɪʃ

smallage 'smɔːlɪdʒ

Smalley 'smɔːlɪ

smallfry 'smɔːlfraɪ

small-hold|er/s, -ing/s 'smɔːl,həʊld|-ə*/z [ˌ-'--], -ɪŋ/z

smallpox 'smɔːlpɒks

small-talk 'smɔːltɔːk

Smallwood 'smɔːlwʊd

smalt smɔːlt [smɒlt]

smarm (s. v.), -s, -ing, -ed; -y, -iness smɑːm, -z, -ɪŋ, -d; -ɪ, -ɪnɪs [-ɪnəs]

smart (s. adj. v.) (S.), -s; -er, -est, -ly, -ness; -ing, -ed smɑːt, -s; -ə*, -ɪst, -lɪ, -nɪs [-nəs]; -ɪŋ, -ɪd

smart|en, -ens, -ening, -ened 'smɑːt|n, -nz, -ɲɪŋ [-nɪŋ], -nd

457

smartish 'smɑːtıʃ
smash (s. v.), **-es, -ing, -ed, -er/s** smæʃ,
  -ız, -ıŋ, -t, -ə*/z
smash-and-grab ˌsmæʃn'græb ['---]
smatter|er/s, -ing/s 'smætər|ə*/z, -ıŋ/z
smear (s. v.), **-s, -ing, -ed; -y, -iness**
  smıə*, -z, -rıŋ, -d; -rı, -rınıs [-nəs]
Smeaton 'smiːtn
Smeeth (Kent) smiːð
smel|l (s. v.), **-ls, -ling, -t** smel, -z, -ıŋ, -t
smelling-salts 'smelıŋsɔːlts [-sɒlts]
smell|y, -ier, -iest, -iness 'smel|ı, -ıə*,
  -ııst, -ınıs [-ınəs]
smelt (s. v.), **-s, -ing, -ed** smelt, -s, -ıŋ,
  -ıd
Smetana 'smetənə
Smethwick 'smeðık
smew, -s smjuː, -z
Smieton 'smiːtn
Smike smaık
smilax, -es 'smaılæks, -ız
smil|e (s. v.), **-es (S.), -ing/ly, -ed** smaıl,
  -z, -ıŋ/lı, -d
Smiley 'smaılı
Smillie 'smaılı
smirch (s. v.), **-es, -ing, -ed** smɜːtʃ, -ız,
  -ıŋ, -t
smirk (s. v.), **-s, -ing, -ed, -er/s; -y**
  smɜːk, -s, -ıŋ, -t, -ə*/z; -ı
Smirke smɜːk
smit (from smite) smıt
smit|e, **-es, -ing, smote, smit, smitten,
  smiter/s** smaıt, -s, -ıŋ, sməut, smıt,
  'smıtn, 'smaıtə*/z
smith (S.), **-s** smıθ, -s
Smith|ells, -er/s 'smıð|əlz, -ə*/z
smithereens ˌsmıðə'riːnz
Smithfield 'smıθfiːld
Smithson 'smıθsn
Smithsonian smıθ'səunjən [-nıən]
smith|y, -ies 'smıð|ı ['smıθ|ı], -ız
smitten (from smite) 'smıtn
smock (s. v.), **-s, -ing, -ed** smɒk, -s, -ıŋ,
  -t
smock-frock, -s 'smɒkfrɒk, -s
smog smɒg
smokable, -s 'sməukəbl, -z
smok|e (s. v.), **-es, -ing, -ed, -er/s**
  sməuk, -s, -ıŋ, -t, -ə*/z
smoke-ball, -s 'sməukbɔːl, -z
smoke-bomb, -s 'sməukbɒm, -z
smokeless 'sməuklıs [-ləs]
smoke-room, -s 'sməukrum [-ruːm], -z
smoke-screen, -s 'sməukskriːn, -z
smoke-stack, -s 'sməukstæk, -s
Smokies 'sməukız
smoking-carriage, -s 'sməukıŋˌkærıdʒ,
  -ız

smoking-compartment, -s 'sməukıŋ-
  kəmˌpɑːtmənt, -s
smoking-concert, -s 'sməukıŋˌkɒnsət, -s
smoking-jacket, -s 'sməukıŋˌdʒækıt, -s
smoking-room, -s 'sməukıŋˌrum
  [-ˌruːm], -z
smok|y, -ier, -iest, -ily, -iness 'sməuk|ı,
  -ıə* [-jə*], -ııst [-jıst], -ılı [-əlı], -ınıs
  [-ınəs]
Smollett 'smɒlıt
smolt sməult
smooth (adj.), **-er, -est, -ly, -ness**
  smuːð, -ə*, -ıst, -lı, -nıs [-nəs]
smooth|(e) (v.), **-(e)s, -ing, -ed** smuːð,
  -z, -ıŋ, -d
smoothbore 'smuːðbɔː* [-bɔə]
smooth-faced 'smuːðfeıst [ˌ-'-]
smooth-spoken ˌsmuːð'spəukən
smorgasbord 'smɔːgəsbɔːd [-bɔəd]
smote (from smite) sməut
smoth|er, -ers, -ering, -ered 'smʌð|ə*,
  -əz, -ərıŋ, -əd
smould|er, -ers, -ering, -ered 'sməuld|-
  ə*, -əz, -ərıŋ, -əd
smudg|e (s. v.), **-es, -ing, -ed; -y, -ier,
  -iest, -ily, -iness** smʌdʒ, -ız, -ıŋ, -d;
  -ı, -ıə*, -ııst, -ılı [-əlı], -ınıs [-ınəs]
smug (s. adj.), **-s, -ly, -ness** smʌg, -z,
  -lı, -nıs [-nəs]
smugg|le, -les, -ling, -led 'smʌg|l, -lz,
  -lıŋ [-ļıŋ], -ld
smuggler, -s 'smʌglə*, -z
smut, **-s; -ty, -tier, -tiest, -tily, -tiness**
  smʌt, -s; -ı, -ıə*, -ııst, -ılı [-əlı], -ınıs
  [-ınəs]
Smyrna 'smɜːnə
Smyth smıθ, smaıθ
Smythe smaıð, smaıθ
snack, -s snæk, -s
snack-bar, -s 'snækbɑː*, -z
Snaefell ˌsneı'fel
snaff|le (s. v.), **-les, -ling, -led** 'snæf|l,
  -lz, -ļıŋ [-lıŋ], -ld
snag, -s snæg, -z
Snagge snæg
snail, **-s; -like** sneıl, -z; -laık
snake, -s sneık, -s
snake-charmer, -s 'sneık,tʃɑːmə*, -z
snak|y, -iness 'sneık|ı, -ınıs [-ınəs]
snap (s. v.), **-s, -ping, -ped** snæp, -s, -ıŋ,
  -t
snapdragon, -s 'snæpˌdrægən, -z
snappish, -ly, -ness 'snæpıʃ, -lı, -nıs
  [-nəs]
snapp|y, -ier, -iest, -ily, -iness 'snæp|ı,
  -ıə*, -ııst, -ılı [-əlı], -ınıs [-ınəs]
snapshot (s. v.), **-s, -ting, -ted** 'snæpʃɒt,
  -s, -ıŋ, -ıd

snar|e (s. v.), -es, -ing, -ed sneə*, -z, -rɪŋ, -d
snark, -s snɑːk, -s
snarl (s. v.), -s, -ing, -ed snɑːl, -z, -ɪŋ, -d
snatch (s. v.), -es, -ing, -ed, -er/s snætʃ, -ɪz, -ɪŋ, -t, -ə*/z
snatch|y, -ier, -iest, -ily 'snætʃ|ɪ, -ɪə*, -ɪɪst, -ɪlɪ [-əlɪ]
sneak (s. v.), -s, -ing/ly, -ed; -y, -ier, -iest, -ily, -iness sniːk, -s, -ɪŋ/lɪ, -t; -ɪ, -ɪə* [-jə*], -ɪɪst [-jɪst], -ɪlɪ [-əlɪ], -ɪnɪs [-ɪnəs]
sneakers 'sniːkəz
sneak-raid, -s, -ing, -er/s 'sniːkreɪd, -z, -ɪŋ, -ə*/z
sneer (s. v.), -s, -ing/ly, -ed snɪə*, -z, -rɪŋ/lɪ, -d
sneez|e (s. v.), -es, -ing, -ed sniːz, -ɪz, -ɪŋ, -d
Sneffels 'snefəlz
Snelgrove 'snelgrəʊv
snell (S.), -s snel, -z
Snewin 'snjuːɪn ['snjʊm]
Sneyd (in Staffordshire) sniːd
Sneyd-Kinnersley ˌsniːd'kɪnəslɪ
snick (s. v.), -s, -ing, -ed snɪk, -s, -ɪŋ, -t
snickersnee, -s ˌsnɪkə'sniː, -z
snide snaɪd
sniff (s. v.), -s, -ing, -ed; -y, -ier, -iest, -ily, -iness snɪf, -s, -ɪŋ, -t; -ɪ, -ɪə*, -ɪɪst, -ɪlɪ [-əlɪ], -ɪnɪs [-ɪnəs]
snigger (s. v.), -s, -ing, -ed 'snɪgə*, -z, -rɪŋ, -d
snip, -s, -ping, -ped, -per/s snɪp, -s, -ɪŋ, -t, -ə*/z
snip|e (s. v.), -es, -ing, -ed, -er/s snaɪp, -s, -ɪŋ, -t, -ə*/z
snippet, -s; -y 'snɪpɪt, -s; -ɪ
sniv|el, -els, -elling, -elled, -eller/s 'snɪv|l, -lz, -lɪŋ, -ld, -lə*/z
snob, -s; -bery, -bism snɒb, -z; -ərɪ, -ɪzəm
snobbish, -ly, -ness 'snɒbɪʃ, -lɪ, -nɪs [-nəs]
Snodgrass 'snɒdgrɑːs
snood, -s, -ed snuːd [snʊd], -z, -ɪd
snook [snoek] (fish), -s snuːk, -s
snook (gesture), -s snuːk [snʊk], -s
snooker 'snuːkə*
snoop, -s, -ing, -ed, -er/s snuːp, -s, -ɪŋ, -t, -ə*/z
snoot|y, -ily, -iness 'snuːt|ɪ, -ɪlɪ [-əlɪ], -ɪnɪs [-ɪnəs]
snooz|e (s. v.), -es, -ing, -ed snuːz, -ɪz, -ɪŋ, -d
snor|e (s. v.), -es, -ing, -ed, -er/s snɔː* [snɔə*], -z, -rɪŋ, -d, -rə*/z
snorkel, -s 'snɔːkl, -z

snort (s. v.), -s, -ing, -ed snɔːt, -s, -ɪŋ, -ɪd
snorter, -s 'snɔːtə*, -z
snort|y, -ier, -iest, -ily, -iness 'snɔːt|ɪ, -ɪə*, -ɪɪst, -ɪlɪ [-əlɪ], -ɪnɪs [-ɪnəs]
snot, -ty snɒt, -ɪ
snout (S.), -s snaʊt, -s
snow (s. v.) (S.), -s, -ing, -ed snəʊ, -z, -ɪŋ, -d
snowball, -s, -ing 'snəʊbɔːl, -z, -ɪŋ
snow-blindness 'snəʊˌblaɪndnɪs [-nəs]
snow-boot, -s 'snəʊbuːt, -s
snow-bound 'snəʊbaʊnd
snow-cap, -s, -ped 'snəʊkæp, -s, -t
snowcat, -s 'snəʊkæt, -s
Snow|den, -don 'snəʊ|dn, -dn
Snowdonia snəʊ'dəʊnjə [-nɪə]
snow-drift, -s 'snəʊdrɪft, -s
snowdrop, -s 'snəʊdrɒp, -s
snowfall, -s 'snəʊfɔːl, -z
snow-field, -s 'snəʊfiːld, -z
snowflake, -s 'snəʊfleɪk, -s
snow-line, -s 'snəʊlaɪn, -z
snow|-man, -men 'snəʊ|mæn, -men
snow-plough, -s 'snəʊplaʊ, -z
snow-shoe, -s 'snəʊʃuː, -z
snowstorm, -s 'snəʊstɔːm, -z
snow-white ˌsnəʊ'waɪt [-'hwaɪt, '--]
snow|y, -ily, -iness 'snəʊ|ɪ, -ɪlɪ [-əlɪ], -ɪnɪs [-ɪnəs]
snub (s. adj. v.), -s, -bing, -bed snʌb, -z, -ɪŋ, -d
snub-nosed 'snʌbnəʊzd [ˌ-'-]
snuff (s. v.), -s, -ing, -ed, -er/s snʌf, -s, -ɪŋ, -t, -ə*/z
snuff-box, -es 'snʌfbɒks, -ɪz
snuff-coloured 'snʌfˌkʌləd
snuff|le, -les, -ling, -led, -ler/s 'snʌf|l, -lz, -lɪŋ [-lɪŋ], -ld, -lə*/z [-lə*/z]
snug, -ger, -gest, -ly, -ness snʌg, -ə*, -ɪst, -lɪ, -nɪs [-nəs]
snugger|y, -ies 'snʌgər|ɪ, -ɪz
snugg|le, -les, -ling, -led 'snʌg|l, -lz, -lɪŋ [-lɪŋ], -ld
so səʊ (normal form), sə (occasional weak form)
soak (s. v.), -s, -ing, -ed səʊk, -s, -ɪŋ, -t
Soames səʊmz
so-and-so 'səʊənsəʊ
Soane, -s səʊn, -z
soap (s. v.), -s, -ing, -ed; -y, -ier, -iest, -ily, -iness səʊp, -s, -ɪŋ, -t; -ɪ, -ɪə* [-jə*], -ɪɪst [-jɪst], -ɪlɪ [-əlɪ], -ɪnɪs [-ɪnəs]
soap-bubble, -s 'səʊpˌbʌbl, -z
soapstone 'səʊpstəʊn
soapsuds 'səʊpsʌdz
soar, -s, -ing, -ed sɔː* [sɔə*], -z, -rɪŋ, -d
Soares səʊ'ɑːrɪz

459

sob (s. v.), -s, -bing, -bed sɒb, -z, -ɪŋ, -d
sober, -er, -est, -ly, -ness; -s, -ing/ly, -ed
ˈsəʊbə*, -rə*, -rɪst, -lɪ, -nɪs [-nəs]; -z,
-rɪŋ/lɪ, -d
sobriety səʊˈbraɪətɪ
sobriquet, -s ˈsəʊbrɪkeɪ, -z
sob-stuff ˈsɒbstʌf
socage ˈsɒkɪdʒ
so-called ˌsəʊˈkɔːld [ˈ-- according to
sentence-stress]
soccer ˈsɒkə*
sociability ˌsəʊʃəˈbɪlətɪ [-lɪt-]
sociab|le, -ly, -leness ˈsəʊʃəb|l, -lɪ, -lnɪs
[-nəs]
soci|al, -ally ˈsəʊʃ|l, -əlɪ [-l̩ɪ]
sociali|sm, -st/s ˈsəʊʃəlɪ|zəm [-ʃlɪ-], -st/s
socialistic ˌsəʊʃəˈlɪstɪk [-ʃlˈɪ-]
socialite, -s ˈsəʊʃəlaɪt [-ʃlaɪt], -s
socialization [-isa-] ˌsəʊʃəlaɪˈzeɪʃn
[-ʃlaɪ-]
socializ|e [-is|e], -es, -ing, -ed ˈsəʊʃəlaɪz
[-ʃlaɪz], -ɪz, -ɪŋ, -d
societ|y (S.), -ies, -al səˈsaɪət|ɪ, -ɪz, -l
Socinian, -s səʊˈsɪnɪən [-njən], -z
socinianism səʊˈsɪnɪənɪzəm [-njən-]
Socinus səʊˈsaɪnəs
sociologic|al, -ally ˌsəʊsjəˈlɒdʒɪk|l [-sɪə-,
-ʃjə-, -ʃɪə-], -əlɪ
sociolog|ist/s, -y ˌsəʊsɪˈɒlədʒ|ɪst/s, -ɪ
sock, -s sɒk, -s
socket, -s, -ed ˈsɒkɪt, -s, -ɪd
Socotra səʊˈkəʊtrə [sɒˈk-]
Socrates ˈsɒkrətiːz [ˈsəʊk-]
socratic, -ally sɒˈkrætɪk [səʊˈk-], -əlɪ
sod, -s sɒd, -z
soda, -s ˈsəʊdə, -z
soda-fountain, -s ˈsəʊdəˌfaʊntɪn [-tən],
-z
sodalit|y, -ies səʊˈdælət|ɪ [-ɪt|ɪ], -ɪz
soda-siphon, -s ˈsəʊdəˌsaɪfn, -z
soda-water ˈsəʊdəˌwɔːtə*
sodd|en (adj. v.), -enness; -ens, -ening,
-ened ˈsɒd|n, -nnɪs [-nnəs]; -nz, -n̩ɪŋ,
-nd
sodium ˈsəʊdɪəm [-djəm]
Sodom ˈsɒdəm
sodom|y, -ite/s ˈsɒdəm|ɪ, -aɪt/s
Sodor ˈsəʊdə*
soever səʊˈevə*
sofa, -s ˈsəʊfə, -z
Sofala səʊˈfɑːlə
Soffe (surname) səʊf
soffit, -s ˈsɒfɪt, -s
Sofia (in Bulgaria) ˈsəʊfjə [ˈsəʊfɪə,
ˈsɒfɪə, səʊˈfiːə, old-fashioned səˈfaɪə]
soft (s. adj.), -s; -er, -est, -ly, -ness sɒft
[old-fashioned sɔːft, and in com-
pounds], -s; -ə*, -ɪst, -lɪ, -nɪs [-nəs]

soft|en, -ens, -ening, -ened ˈsɒf|n
[ˈsɔːf-], -nz, -nɪŋ [-n̩ɪŋ], -nd
softener, -s ˈsɒfnə* [ˈsɔːf-, -fnə*], -z
soft-headed ˈsɒftˌhedɪd [ˈsɔːft-, ˌ-ˈ--]
soft-hearted ˌsɒftˈhɑːtɪd [ˌsɔːft-, also
ˈ-ˌ--, when attributive]
softish ˈsɒftɪʃ [ˈsɔːft-]
soft-ped|al (v.), -als, -alling, -alled
ˌsɒftˈped|l [ˌsɔːft-], -lz, -l̩ɪŋ, -ld
soft-spoken ˈsɒftˌspəʊkən [ˈsɔːft-, ˌ-ˈ--]
sogg|y, -ier, -iest, -iness ˈsɒg|ɪ, -ɪə*,
-nɪst, -ɪnɪs [-nəs]
soh (note in Tonic Sol-fa), -s səʊ, -z
Soho ˈsəʊhəʊ [səʊˈhəʊ]
Sohrab ˈsɒhræb
soi-disant ˌswɑːdiːˈzɑ̃ːŋ [-ˈzɒŋ, ˌ-ˈ--]
(swadizã)
soil (s. v.), -s, -ing, -ed sɔɪl, -z, -ɪŋ, -d
soil-pipe, -s ˈsɔɪlpaɪp, -s
soirée, -s ˈswɑːreɪ [ˈswɒr-] (sware), -z
sojourn (s. v.), -s, -ing, -ed, -er/s
ˈsɒdʒɜːn [ˈsʌdʒ-, -dʒən], -z, -ɪŋ, -d,
-ə*/z
sol (S.), -s sɒl, -z
sola ˈsəʊlə
solac|e (s. v.), -es, -ing, -ed ˈsɒləs [-lɪs],
-ɪz, -ɪŋ, -t
solamen, -s səʊˈleɪmen, -z
solanum səʊˈleɪnəm [-ˈlɑːnəm]
solar ˈsəʊlə*
solarium, -s səʊˈleərɪəm, -z
solati|um, -ums, -a səʊˈleɪʃj|əm [-ʃɪ-],
-əmz, -ə
sold (from sell) səʊld
sold|er (s. v.), -ers, -ering, -ered ˈsɒld|ə*
[ˈsɔːd-, -sɒd-, ˈsəʊld-], -əz, -ərɪŋ, -əd
soldier, -s, -ing; -y ˈsəʊldʒə* [rarely
-djə*], -z, -rɪŋ; -rɪ
soldierly ˈsəʊldʒəlɪ [rarely -djə-]
sold|o, -i ˈsɒld|əʊ, -iː
sol|e (s. adj. v.) (S.), -es; -ely; -ing, -ed
səʊl, -z; -lɪ; -ɪŋ, -d
solecism, -s ˈsɒlɪsɪzəm [-les-, -ləs-], -z
solemn, -ly ˈsɒləm, -lɪ
solemnity səˈlemnətɪ [sɒˈl-, -ɪtɪ]
solemnization [-isa-], -s ˌsɒləmnaɪˈzeɪʃn
[-nɪˈz-], -z
solemniz|e [-is|e], -es, -ing, -ed ˈsɒləm-
naɪz, -ɪz, -ɪŋ, -d
solenoid, -s ˈsəʊlənɔɪd [ˈsɒlɪ-, -lɪn-], -z
Solent ˈsəʊlənt
sol-fa (S.) ˌsɒlˈfɑː
solfegg|io, -i sɒlˈfedʒ|ɪəʊ, -iː
solferino (S.) ˌsɒlfəˈriːnəʊ
solicit, -s, -ing, -ed səˈlɪsɪt, -s, -ɪŋ, -ɪd
solicitation, -s səˌlɪsɪˈteɪʃn, -z
solicitor, -s səˈlɪsɪtə* [sl̩ˈɪs-, -sətə*], -z
solicitous, -ly səˈlɪsɪtəs, -lɪ

solicitude səˈlɪsɪtjuːd
solid (s. adj.), -s; -est, -ly, -ness ˈsɒlɪd,
  -z; -ɪst, -lɪ, -nɪs [-nəs]
solidarity ˌsɒlɪˈdærətɪ [-ɪtɪ]
solidifiable səˈlɪdɪfaɪəbl [sɒˈl-]
solidification səˌlɪdɪfɪˈkeɪʃn [sɒˌl-]
solidi|fy, -fies, -fying, -fied səˈlɪdɪ|faɪ
  [sɒˈl-], -faɪz, -faɪɪŋ, -faɪd
solidity səˈlɪdətɪ [sɒˈl-], -ɪtɪ]
solid|us, -i ˈsɒlɪd|əs, -aɪ [-iː]
Solihull ˌsəʊlɪˈhʌl
soliloquiz|e [-is|e], -es, -ing, -ed səˈlɪlə-
  kwaɪz [sɒˈl-], -ɪz, -ɪŋ, -d
soliloqu|y, -ies səˈlɪləkwɪ [sɒˈl-], -ɪz
solipsism ˈsɒlɪpsɪzəm [ˈsəʊ-]
solitaire, -s ˌsɒlɪˈteə* [ˈ---], -z
solitar|y (s. adj.), -ies; -ily, -iness
  ˈsɒlɪtər|ɪ [-lət-], -ɪz; -əlɪ [-ɪlɪ], -ɪnɪs
  [-nəs]
solitude, -s ˈsɒlɪtjuːd, -z
Sollas ˈsɒləs
Solloway ˈsɒləweɪ [-lʊw-]
solo, -s ˈsəʊləʊ, -z
soloist, -s ˈsəʊləʊɪst, -s
Solomon ˈsɒləmən
Solon ˈsəʊlɒn [-lən]
so-long ˌsəʊˈlɒŋ [sə-l-]
solstice, -s ˈsɒlstɪs, -ɪz
solubility ˌsɒljʊˈbɪlətɪ [-lɪt-]
soluble ˈsɒljʊbl
solus ˈsəʊləs
solution, -s səˈluːʃn [s]ˈuː-, səˈljuː-], -z
solvability ˌsɒlvəˈbɪlətɪ [-lɪt-]
solv|e, -es, -ing, -ed; -able sɒlv, -z, -ɪŋ,
  -d; -əbl
solven|cy, -t ˈsɒlvən|sɪ, -t
Solway ˈsɒlweɪ
Solzhenitsyn ˌsɒlʒəˈnɪtsɪn
Somal|i, -ia, -is, -iland səʊˈmɑːl|ɪ, -ɪə
  [-jə], -ɪz, -ɪlænd
somatic səʊˈmætɪk
sombre, -st, -ly, -ness ˈsɒmbə*, -rɪst,
  -lɪ, -nɪs [-nəs]
sombrero, -s sɒmˈbreərəʊ [-ˈbrɪər-], -z
some sʌm (strong form), səm, sm (weak
  forms)
somebody ˈsʌmbədɪ [-ˌbɒdɪ, -bdɪ]
somehow ˈsʌmhaʊ [occasionally ˈsʌmaʊ
  in quick speech]
someone ˈsʌmwʌn
Somers ˈsʌməz
somersault, -s ˈsʌməsɔːlt [-sɒlt], -s
Somerset, -shire ˈsʌməsɪt [-set], -ʃə*
  [-ˌʃɪə*]
Somerton ˈsʌmətn
Somervell ˈsʌməvɪl [-vel]
Somerville ˈsʌməvɪl
something ˈsʌmθɪŋ [-mpθ-]

sometime ˈsʌmtaɪm
sometimes ˈsʌmtaɪmz
somewhat ˈsʌmwɒt [-mhw-]
somewhere ˈsʌmweə* [-mhw-]
Somme sɒm
somnambuli|sm, -st/s sɒmˈnæmbjʊ-
  lɪ|zəm, -st/s
somniferous sɒmˈnɪfərəs
somnolen|ce, -t/ly ˈsɒmnələn|s [-nʊl-,
  -nəʊl-], -t/lɪ
son (S.), -s sʌn, -z
sonagram, -s ˈsəʊnəgræm, -z
sonagraph, -s ˈsəʊnəgrɑːf [-græf], -s
sonalator, -s ˈsəʊnəlertə*, -z
sonant (s. adj.), -s ˈsəʊnənt, -s
sonar ˈsəʊnɑː*
sonata, -s səˈnɑːtə [sŋˈɑːtə], -z
sonatina, -s ˌsɒnəˈtiːnə, -z
song, -s sɒŋ, -z
song-bird, -s ˈsɒŋbɜːd, -z
song-book, -s ˈsɒŋbʊk, -s
songster, -s ˈsɒŋstə*, -z
song-thrush, -es ˈsɒŋθrʌʃ, -ɪz
song-writ|er/s, -ing ˈsɒŋˌraɪt|ə*/z, -ɪŋ
Sonia ˈsɒnɪə [-njə, ˈsəʊ-]
sonic ˈsɒnɪk
son-in-law, sons-in-law ˈsʌnɪnlɔː,
  ˈsʌnzɪnlɔː
sonnet, -s ˈsɒnɪt, -s
sonneteer (s. v.), -s, -ing, -ed ˌsɒnɪˈtɪə*
  [-nəˈt-], -z, -rɪŋ, -d
Sonning (near Reading) ˈsɒnɪŋ [ˈsʌn-]
sonn|y, -ies ˈsʌn|ɪ, -ɪz
sonometer, -s səʊˈnɒmɪtə* [-mətə*], -z
sonorant, -s ˈsɒnərənt [ˈsəʊ-], -s
sonorit|y, -ies səˈnɒrət|ɪ [səʊˈn-, -rɪt|ɪ],
  -ɪz
sonorous, -ly ˈsɒnərəs [səˈnɔːrəs,
  səʊˈn-], -lɪ
sonship ˈsʌnʃɪp
soon, -er, -est suːn [rarely sʊn], -ə*, -ɪst
soot; -y, -ier, -iest, -iness sʊt; -ɪ, -ɪə*,
  -ɪɪst, -ɪnɪs [-ɪnəs]
sooth suːθ
sooth|e, -es, -ing/ly, -ed suːð, -z, -ɪŋ/lɪ,
  -d
soothsayer, -s ˈsuːθˌseɪə* [ˈsuːˌð-], -z
sop (s. v.), -s, -ping, -ped sɒp, -s, -ɪŋ, -t
soph, -s sɒf, -s
Sophia səʊˈfaɪə
Sophie ˈsəʊfɪ
sophi|sm/s, -st/s ˈsɒfɪ|zəm/z, -st/s
sophister, -s ˈsɒfɪstə*, -z
sophistic, -al, -ally səˈfɪstɪk [səʊˈf-], -l,
  -əlɪ
sophisticat|e, -es, -ing, -ed səˈfɪstɪkeɪt,
  -s, -ɪŋ, -ɪd
sophistication səˌfɪstɪˈkeɪʃn

461

sophistr|y, -ies 'spfɪstr|ɪ, -ɪz
Sophoclean ˌspfə'kli:ən [-'klɪən]
Sophocles 'spfəkli:z
sophomore, -s 'spfəmɔ:* [-mɔə*], -z
Sophy 'səʊfɪ
soporific ˌsppə'rɪfɪk [ˌsəʊp-]
sopp|y, -ier, -iest, -iness 'spp|ɪ, -ɪə*, -ɪɪst, -ɪnɪs [-ɪnəs]
sopranino, -s ˌspprə'ni:nəʊ, -z
sopran|o, -os, -i sə'prɑ:n|əʊ, -əʊz, -i:
Sopwith, -s 'sppwɪθ, -s
sorbet 'sɔ:beɪ [-bət, -bɪt]
Sorbonne sɔ:'bpn (sɔrbɔn)
sorcer|y, -ies; -er/s; -ess/es 'sɔ:sər|ɪ, -ɪz; -ə*/z; -ɪs/ɪz [-es/ɪz]
sordid, -ly, -ness 'sɔ:dɪd, -lɪ, -nɪs [-nəs]
sordin|o, -i sɔ:'di:n|əʊ, -i:
sore (s. adj. adv.), -s; -r, -st, -ly, -ness sɔ:* [sɔə*], -z; -rə*, -rɪst, -lɪ, -nɪs [-nəs]
soroptimist, -s sɔ:'rpptɪmɪst [-təm-], -s
sororit|y, -ies sə'rprət|ɪ [sp'r-, sɔ:'r-, -ɪt|ɪ], -ɪz
sorosis (S.) sə'rəʊsɪs [sp'r-, sɔ:'r-]
sorrel 'sprəl
sorr|ow (s. v.), -ows, -owing/ly, -owed, -ower/s 'spr|əʊ, -əʊz, -əʊɪŋ/lɪ, -əʊd, -əʊə*/z
sorrow|ful, -fully, -fulness 'sprəʊ|fʊl [-rʊ|f-], -flɪ [-fəlɪ, -fʊlɪ], -fʊlnɪs [-nəs]
sorr|y, -ier, -iest, -ily, -iness 'spr|ɪ, -ɪə*, -ɪɪst, -əlɪ [-ɪlɪ], -ɪnɪs [-ɪnəs]
sort (s. v.), -s, -ing, -ed, -er/s sɔ:t, -s, -ɪŋ, -ɪd, -ə*/z
sortie, -s 'sɔ:ti: [-tɪ], -z
sortilege 'sɔ:tɪlɪdʒ
so-so 'səʊsəʊ [-'-]
sostenuto ˌspstə'nu:təʊ [-tɪ'n-, -'nju:-]
Sosthenes 'spsθəni:z [-θɪn-]
sot, -s spt, -s
Sotheby 'sʌðəbɪ ['spð-]
Sothern 'sʌðən
sottish, -ly, -ness 'sptɪʃ, -lɪ, -nɪs [-nəs]
sotto voce ˌsptəʊ'vəʊtʃɪ (ˌsotto'vo:tʃe)
sou, -s su:, -z
soubrette, -s su:'bret [sʊ'b-], -s
souchong ˌsu:'tʃpŋ [-'ʃpŋ, '--]
souffle (murmur), -s 'su:fl, -z
soufflé, -s 'su:fleɪ, -z
sough (s. v.), -s, -ing, -ed saʊ, -z, -ɪŋ, -d [sʌf, -s, -ɪŋ, -t]
sought (from seek) sɔ:t
soul, -s səʊl, -z
Soulbury 'səʊlbərɪ
soul|ful, -fully, -fulness 'səʊl|fʊl [-fl], -fʊlɪ [-fəlɪ, -flɪ], -fʊlnɪs [-flnɪs, -nəs]
soulless, -ly, -ness 'səʊllɪs [-ləs], -lɪ, -nɪs [-nəs]

sound (s. adj. v. adv.), -s; -er, -est, -ly, -ness; -ing/s, -ed saʊnd, -z; -ə*, -ɪst, -lɪ, -nɪs ['saʊnnɪs, -nəs]; -ɪŋ/z, -ɪd
sound-board, -s 'saʊndbɔ:d [-bɔəd], -z
sound-box, -es 'saʊndbpks, -ɪz
sound-effect, -s 'saʊndɪˌfekt, -s
soundless 'saʊndlɪs [-ləs]
soundproof, -ing 'saʊndpru:f, -ɪŋ
sound-track, -s 'saʊndtræk, -s
sound-wave, -s 'saʊndweɪv, -z
soup, -s; -y su:p, -s; -ɪ
soupçon, -s 'su:psɔ̃:ŋ [-spŋ, -spn] (supsɔ̃)
soup-kitchen, -s 'su:pˌkɪtʃɪn, -z
soup-plate, -s 'su:ppleɪt, -s
soup-tureen, -s 'su:ptəˌri:n [-tʊ,r-, -tjʊ,r-], -z
sour (adj. v.), -er, -est, -ly, -ness; -s, -ing, -ed 'saʊə*, -rə*, -rɪst, -lɪ, -nɪs [-nəs], -z, -rɪŋ, -d
source, -s sɔ:s [sɔəs], -ɪz
sourdine, -s ˌsʊə'di:n, -z
Sousa (American composer) 'su:zə
sous|e, -es, -ing, -ed saʊs, -ɪz, -ɪŋ, -t
soutane, -s su:'tɑ:n, -z
Souter 'su:tə*
south (s. adj. adv.) (S.) saʊθ
sou|th (v.), -ths, -thing, -thed saʊ|ð [-θ], -ðz [-θs], -ðɪŋ [-θɪŋ], -ðd [-θt]
Southall 'saʊðɔ:l ['saʊðɔ:l]
Southampton saʊθ'æmptən [saʊθ'hæ-, saʊ'θ-, sə'θæ-]
Southdown 'saʊθdaʊn
south-east ˌsaʊθ'i:st [in nautical usage also saʊ'i:st, also '-- according to sentence-stress]
south-easter, -s ˌsaʊθ'i:stə*, -z
south-easterly ˌsaʊθ'i:stəlɪ
south-eastern ˌsaʊθ'i:stən
south-eastward, -s ˌsaʊθ'i:stwəd, -z
Southend ˌsaʊθ'end [also '-- according to sentence-stress]
souther|ly, -n, -ner/s, -nmost 'sʌðə|lɪ, -n, -nə*/z, -nməʊst [-nməst]
southernwood 'sʌðənwʊd
Southey 'saʊðɪ, 'sʌðɪ
Southon 'saʊðən
south-paw, -s 'saʊθpɔ:, -z
Southport 'saʊθpɔ:t
southron, -s 'sʌðrən, -z
Southsea 'saʊθsi: [-sɪ]
south-south-east ˌsaʊθsaʊθ'i:st [in nautical usage also ˌsaʊsaʊ'i:st]
south-south-west ˌsaʊθsaʊθ'west [nautical pronunciation ˌsaʊsaʊ'west]
southward, -s, -ly 'saʊθwəd, -z, -lɪ
Southwark 'sʌðək, 'saʊθwək

Southwell (*surname*) 'saʊθwəl, 'saʊθwel, 'sʌðl, (*cathedral town in Nottinghamshire*) 'saʊθwəl [*locally* 'sʌðl]
Note.—Viscount Southwell is 'sʌðl.
south-west ˌsaʊθ'west [*nautical pronunciation* saʊ'west, *also* '-- *according to sentence-stress*]
south-wester (*wind*), **-s** ˌsaʊθ'westə* [*in nautical usage also* saʊ'westə*], -z
south-westerly ˌsaʊθ'westəlɪ [*nautical pronunciation* saʊ'w-]
south-western ˌsaʊθ'westən
south-westward, -s ˌsaʊθ'westwəd, -z
South|wick, -wold 'saʊθ|wɪk, -wəʊld
Soutter 'suːtə*
souvenir, -s ˌsuːvə'nɪə* [-vɪn-, '--ˌ-], -z
sou'wester (*hat*), **-s** saʊ'westə*, -z
Souza 'suːzə
sovereign (*s. adj.*), **-s** 'sɒvrɪn, -z
sovereignty 'sɒvrəntɪ [-rɪn-]
soviet (**S.**), **-s; -ism** 'səʊvɪət ['sɒv-, -vjət, -vjet, səʊ'vjet, sɒ'vjet], -s; -ɪzəm
sovran 'sɒvrən
sow (*s.*) (*fem. pig, block of iron, trough for molten iron*), **-s** saʊ, -z
sow (*v.*) (*plant seed*), **-s, -ing, -ed, -n, -er/s** səʊ, -z, -ɪŋ, -d, -n, -ə*/z
Sowerby (*in North Yorkshire*) 'saʊəbɪ, (*in West Yorkshire*) 'səʊəbɪ ['saʊəbɪ], (*surname*) 'səʊəbɪ, 'saʊəbɪ
Sowry 'saʊərɪ
soy sɔɪ
soya 'sɔɪə
Soyuz 'sɔːjʊz [sə'juːz]
spa, -s spɑː, -z
Spa spɑː
spac|e (*s. v.*), **-es, -ing, -ed** speɪs, -ɪz, -ɪŋ, -t
space-bar, -s 'speɪsbɑː*, -z
space-craft, -s 'speɪskrɑːft, -s
space|-ship/s, -shot/s 'speɪʃ|ʃɪp/s, -ʃɒt/s
space-suit, -s 'speɪssuːt [-sjuːt], -s
space-time ˌspeɪs'taɪm
space-walk 'speɪswɔːk
spacious, -ly, -ness 'speɪʃəs, -lɪ, -nɪs [-nəs]
spade, -s; -ful/s speɪd, -z; -fʊl/z
spade-work 'speɪdwɜːk
spaghetti spə'getɪ [spɑː'g-]
spahi, -s 'spɑːhiː ['spɑːiː], -z
Spain speɪn
spake (*archaic p. tense of* **speak**) speɪk
Spalding 'spɔːldɪŋ ['spɒl-]
spall (*s. v.*), **-s, -ing, -ed** spɔːl, -z, -ɪŋ, -d
spam spæm

span (*s. v.*), **-s, -ning, -ned** spæn, -z, -ɪŋ, -d
spandrel, -s 'spændrəl, -z
spang|le (*s. v.*), **-les, -ling, -led** 'spæŋg|l, -lz, -lɪŋ [-ˌlɪŋ], -ld
Spaniard, -s 'spænjəd, -z
spaniel, -s 'spænjəl, -z
Spanish 'spænɪʃ
spank (*s. v.*), **-s, -ing, -ed, -er/s** spæŋk, -s, -ɪŋ, -t [spæŋt], -ə*/z
spanking (*s. adj.*), **-s** 'spæŋkɪŋ, -z
spanner, -s 'spænə*, -z
spar (*s. v.*), **-s, -ring, -red** spɑː*, -z, -rɪŋ, -d
spar|e (*adj. v.*), **-ely, -eness; -es, -ing/ly, -ed** speə*, -lɪ, -nɪs [-nəs]; -z, -rɪŋ/lɪ, -d
spark (*s. v.*) (**S.**), **-s, -ing, -ed** spɑːk, -s, -ɪŋ, -t
sparking-plug, -s 'spɑːkɪŋplʌg, -z
spark|le (*s. v.*), **-les, -ling, -led** 'spɑːk|l, -lz, -lɪŋ, -ld
sparkl|et/s, -er/s 'spɑːkl|ɪt/s [-lət], -ə*/z
spark-plug, -s 'spɑːkplʌg, -z
sparring-match, -es 'spɑːrɪŋmætʃ, -ɪz
sparrow, -s 'spærəʊ, -z
sparrowhawk, -s 'spærəʊhɔːk, -s
sparse, -ly, -ness spɑːs, -lɪ, -nɪs [-nəs]
Spart|a, -an/s 'spɑːt|ə, -ən/z
spasm, -s 'spæzəm, -z
spasmodic, -ally spæz'mɒdɪk, -əlɪ
spastic (*s. adj.*), **-s** 'spæstɪk, -s
spat (*s.*), **-s** spæt, -s
spat (*from* spit) spæt
spatchcock (*s. v.*), **-s, -ing, -ed** 'spætʃkɒk, -s, -ɪŋ, -t
spate, -s speɪt, -s
spati|al, -ally 'speɪʃ|l [-ʃj|əl, -ʃɪ|əl], -əlɪ
spatter (*s. v.*), **-s, -ing, -ed** 'spætə*, -z, -rɪŋ, -d
spatul|a, -ae, -as 'spætjʊl|ə, -iː, -əz
spatulate (*adj.*) 'spætjʊlət [-lɪt, -leɪt]
spavin 'spævɪn
spawn (*s. v.*), **-s, -ing, -ed** spɔːn, -z, -ɪŋ, -d
Speaight speɪt
speak, -s, -ing, spoke, spoken, speaker/s spiːk, -s, -ɪŋ, spəʊk, 'spəʊkən, 'spiːkə*/z
speak-eas|y, -ies 'spiːk,iːz|ɪ, -ɪz
speaking-trumpet, -s 'spiːkɪŋ,trʌmpɪt, -s
speaking-tube, -s 'spiːkɪŋtjuːb, -z
Spean spɪən ['spiːən]
spear (*s. v.*), **-s, -ing, -ed** spɪə*, -z, -rɪŋ, -d
spear-head, -s 'spɪəhed, -z
spear|man (**S.**), **-men** 'spɪə|mən, -mən [-men]

spearmint 'spɪəmɪnt
spec spek
speci|al (*s. adj.*), **-als, -ally** 'speʃ|l, -lz,
  -əlɪ [-l̩ɪ, -lɪ]
speciali|sm, -st/s 'speʃəlɪ|zəm [-ʃlɪ-,
  -ʃlɪ-], -st/s
specialit|y, -ies ˌspeʃɪ'ælət|ɪ [-ɪt|ɪ], -ɪz
specialization [-isa-] ˌspeʃəlaɪ'zeɪʃn
  [-ʃlaɪ'z-, -ʃəlɪ'z-, -ʃlɪ'z-]
specializ|e [-is|e], **-es, -ing, -ed** 'speʃəl-
  aɪz [-ʃlaɪz], -ɪz, -ɪŋ, -d
specialt|y, -ies 'speʃlt|ɪ, -ɪz
specie 'spi:ʃi: [-ʃɪ]
species 'spi:ʃi:z [-ʃɪz]
specific (*s. adj.*), **-s; -ally** spə'sɪfɪk
  [spɪ's-], -s; -əlɪ
specification, -s ˌspesɪfɪ'keɪʃn, -z
specificity ˌspesɪ'fɪsətɪ [-ɪtɪ]
speci|fy, -fies, -fying, -fied; -fiable
  'spesɪ|faɪ, -faɪz, -faɪɪŋ, -faɪd; -faɪəbl
specimen, -s 'spesɪmən [-mɪn], -z
specious, -ly, -ness 'spi:ʃəs, -lɪ, -nɪs
  [-nəs]
speck, -s, -ed spek, -s, -t
speckle, -s, -d 'spekl, -z, -d
speckless 'speklɪs [-ləs]
spectacle, -s, -d 'spektəkl [-tɪk-], -z,
  -d
spectacular, -ly spek'tækjʊlə* [-kjələ*],
  -lɪ
spectator (**S.**), **-s** spek'teɪtə*, -z
spectral 'spektrəl
spectre, -s 'spektə*, -z
spectrogram, -s 'spektrəʊgræm, -z
spectrograph, -s 'spektrəʊgrɑ:f [-græf],
  -s
spectrographic ˌspektrəʊ'græfɪk
spectrography spek'trɒgrəfɪ
spectrometer, -s spek'trɒmɪtə* [-mətə*],
  -z
spectroscope, -s 'spektrəskəʊp, -s
spectroscopic, -al, -ally ˌspektrə'skɒpɪk,
  -l, -əlɪ
spectroscop|ist/s, -y spek'trɒskəp|ɪst/s,
  -ɪ
spectr|um, -a, -ums 'spektr|əm, -ə, -əmz
speculat|e, -es, -ing, -ed, -or/s 'spekjʊ-
  leɪt [-kjəl-], -s, -ɪŋ, -ɪd, -ə*/z
speculation, -s ˌspekjʊ'leɪʃn [-kjə'l-], -z
speculative, -ly, -ness 'spekjʊlətɪv
  [-kjəl-, -leɪt-], -lɪ, -nɪs [-nəs]
specul|um, -a, -ar 'spekjʊl|əm, -ə, -ə*
sped (*from* **speed**) sped
speech, -es spi:tʃ, -ɪz
speech-day, -s 'spi:tʃdeɪ, -z
speechification, -s ˌspi:tʃɪfɪ'keɪʃn, -z
speechi|fy, -fies, -fying, -fied, -fier/s
  'spi:tʃɪ|faɪ, -faɪz, -faɪɪŋ, -faɪd, -faɪə*/z

speechless, -ly, -ness 'spi:tʃlɪs [-ləs], -lɪ,
  -nɪs [-nəs]
speech-sound, -s 'spi:tʃsaʊnd, -s
speed (*s. v.*) (**S.**), **-s, -ing, -ed, sped; -y,
  -ier, -iest, -ily, -iness** spi:d, -z, -ɪŋ,
  -ɪd, sped; -ɪ, -ɪə* [-jə*], -ɪɪst [-jɪst],
  -ɪlɪ [-əlɪ], -ɪnɪs [-ɪnəs]
speed-cop, -s 'spi:dkɒp, -s
speed-limit, -s 'spi:dˌlɪmɪt, -s
speed-merchant, -s 'spi:dˌmɜ:tʃənt, -s
speedometer, -s spɪ'dɒmɪtə* [spi:'d-,
  -mətə*], -z
speedway, -s 'spi:dweɪ, -z
speedwell (**S.**), **-s** 'spi:dwel [-wəl], -z
Speen spi:n
Speigal 'spi:gəl
Speight speɪt
Speirs spɪəz
speiss spaɪs
speleolog|y, **-ist/s** ˌspi:lɪ'ɒlədʒ|ɪ,
  [spe-], -ɪst/s
spel|l (*s. v.*), **-ls, -ling/s, -led, -t, -ler/s**
  spel, -z, -ɪŋ/z, -t [-d], -t, -ə*/z
spellbound 'spelbaʊnd
spelt (*from* **spell**) spelt
spelt|er (*s. v.*), **-ers, -ering, -ered**
  'spelt|ə*, -əz, -ərɪŋ, -əd
spence (**S.**), **-s** spens, -ɪz
spencer (**S.**), **-s** 'spensə*, -z
spen|d, -ds, -ding, -t, -der/s spen|d, -dz,
  -dɪŋ, -t, -də*/z
Spender 'spendə*
spendthrift, -s 'spendθrɪft, -s
Spens spenz
Spenser 'spensə*
Spenserian spen'sɪərɪən
spent (*from* **spend**) spent
sperm, -s spɜ:m, -z
spermaceti ˌspɜ:mə'setɪ [-'si:t-]
spermatoz|oon, -oa ˌspɜ:mətəʊ'z|əʊɒn
  [-əʊən], -əʊə
sperm-whale, -s 'spɜ:mweɪl [-hw-], -z
spew, -s, -ing, -ed spju:, -z, -ɪŋ ['spjʊɪŋ],
  -d
Spey speɪ
Spezia (*Italian port*) 'spetsɪə [-tsjə,
  -dzɪə, -dzjə]
Spezzia (*Greek island*) 'spetsɪə [-tsjə]
sphagnum 'sfægnəm
sphene (*jewel*), **-s** spi:n [sf-], -z
sphere, -s sfɪə*, -z
spheric, -s, -al, -ally 'sferɪk, -s, -l, -əlɪ
spheroid, -s 'sfɪərɔɪd, -z
spheroidal ˌsfɪə'rɔɪdl [sfe'r-]
spherometer, -s ˌsfɪə'rɒmɪtə* [-mətə*],
  -z
spherule, -s 'sferju:l [-ru:l], -z
sphincter, -s 'sfɪŋktə*, -z
sphinx, -es; -like sfɪŋks, -ɪz; -laɪk

Spica (*star*) 'spaɪkə
spic|e (*s. v.*) (**S.**), -es, -ing, -ed; -y, -ier,
　-iest, -ily, -iness spaɪs, -ɪz, -ɪŋ, -t; -ɪ,
　-ɪə* [-jə*], -ɪɪst [-jɪst], -ɪlɪ [-əlɪ], -ɪnɪs
　[-məs]
spick spɪk
spicule, -s 'spaɪkju:l ['spɪk-], -z
spider, -s; -y 'spaɪdə*, -z; -rɪ
Spiers spɪəz, 'spaɪəz
spiff|ing/ly, -y 'spɪf|ɪŋ/lɪ, -ɪ
spigot, -s 'spɪgət, -s
spik|e (*s. v.*), -es, -ing, -ed spaɪk, -s, -ɪŋ,
　-t
spikenard 'spaɪknɑːd
Spikins 'spaɪkɪnz
spik|y, -ier, -iest, -iness 'spaɪk|ɪ, -ɪə*,
　-ɪɪst, -ɪnɪs [-məs]
spill|l (*s. v.*), -ls, -ling, -led, -t spɪl, -z,
　-ɪŋ, -d, -t
spiller (**S.**), -s 'spɪlə*, -z
spillikins 'spɪlɪkɪnz
Spilling 'spɪlɪŋ
spilt (*from* spill) spɪlt
spin (*s. v.*), -s, -ning, span, spun,
　spinner/s spɪn, -z, -ɪŋ, spæn, spʌn,
　'spɪnə*/z
spina bifida ˌspaɪnə'bɪfɪdə
spinach 'spɪnɪdʒ [-ɪtʃ]
spinal 'spaɪnl
spind|le, -les, -ly 'spɪnd|l, -lz, -lɪ
spindle|-legged, -shaped 'spɪndl|legd,
　-ʃeɪpt
spindrift 'spɪndrɪft
spin-dr|y (*s. v.*), -ies, -ying, -ied, -ier/s
　ˌspɪn'dr|aɪ ['--], -aɪz, -aɪɪŋ, -aɪd,
　-aɪə*/z
spine, -s, -d; -less spaɪn, -z, -d; -lɪs
　[-ləs]
spinel spɪ'nel
spinet, -s spɪ'net ['spɪnet, 'spɪnɪt], -s
Spink spɪŋk
spinney, -s 'spɪnɪ, -z
spinning-wheel, -s 'spɪnɪŋwi:l [-hwi:l],
　-z
spin|ose, -ous 'spaɪn|əʊs, -əs
Spinoza spɪ'nəʊzə
spinster, -s; -hood 'spɪnstə*, -z; -hʊd
spiny 'spaɪnɪ
Spion Kop ˌspaɪən'kɒp
spiraea, -s spaɪ'rɪə [-'ri:ə], -z
spir|al (*s. adj.*), -als, -ally 'spaɪər|əl,
　-əlz, -əlɪ
spirant (*s. adj.*), -s 'spaɪərənt, -s
spire, -s, -d 'spaɪə*, -z, -d
spirit, -s, -ed, -edly, -edness 'spɪrɪt, -s,
　-ɪd, -ɪdlɪ, -ɪdnɪs [-nəs]
spirit-gum 'spɪrɪtgʌm
spiritism 'spɪrɪtɪzəm

spirit-lamp, -s 'spɪrɪtlæmp, -s
spiritless, -ly, -ness 'spɪrɪtlɪs [-ləs], -lɪ,
　-nɪs [-nəs]
spirit-level, -s 'spɪrɪtˌlevl, -z
spirit-rapping, -s 'spɪrɪtˌræpɪŋ, -z
spirit-stove, -s 'spɪrɪtstəʊv, -z
spiritual, -ly 'spɪrɪtʃʊəl [-tʃwəl, -tʃʊl,
　-tjʊəl, -tjwəl, -tjʊl], -ɪ
spirituali|sm, -st/s 'spɪrɪtʃʊəlɪ|zəm
　[-tʃwəl-, -tʃʊl-, -tjʊəl, -tjwəl-, -tjʊl-],
　-st/s
spiritualistic ˌspɪrɪtʃʊə'lɪstɪk [-tʃwə'l-,
　-tʃʊ'l-, -tjʊə'l-, -tjwə'l-, -tjʊ'l-]
spiritualit|y, -ies ˌspɪrɪtʃʊ'ælət|ɪ
　[-tjʊ-, -ɪt|ɪ], -ɪz
spirituous 'spɪrɪtʃʊəs [-tʃwəs, -tjʊəs,
　-tjwəs]
spiritus 'spɪrɪtəs ['spaɪər-]
spirometer, -s ˌspaɪə'rɒmɪtə* [-mətə*],
　-z
spirt (*s. v.*), -s, -ing, -ed spɜːt; -s, -ɪŋ,
　-ɪd
spit (*s. v.*) (*eject saliva, etc.*), -s, -ting,
　spat spɪt, -s, -ɪŋ, spæt
spit (*s. v.*) (*for roasting, etc.*), -s, -ting,
　-ted spɪt, -s, -ɪŋ, -ɪd
Spitalfields 'spɪtlfi:ldz
spit|e (*s. v.*), -es, -ing, -ed; -eful, -efully,
　-efulness spaɪt, -s, -ɪŋ, -ɪd; -fʊl, -fʊlɪ
　[-fəlɪ], -fʊlnɪs [-nəs]
spitfire (**S.**), -s 'spɪtˌfaɪə*, -z
Spithead ˌspɪt'hed ['-- *according to
　sentence-stress*]
Spitsbergen 'spɪtsˌbɜːgən [ˌ-'--]
spittle 'spɪtl
spittoon, -s spɪ'tu:n, -z
spiv, -s; -vy spɪv, -z; -ɪ
splash (*s. v.*), -es, -ing, -ed, -er/s splæʃ,
　-ɪz, -ɪŋ, -t, -ə*/z
splash-board, -s 'splæʃbɔːd [-bɔəd], -z
splash|y, -iness 'splæʃ|ɪ, -ɪnɪs [-məs]
splatter, -s, -ing, -ed 'splætə*, -z, -rɪŋ,
　-d
splay (*s. v.*), -s, -ing, -ed spleɪ, -z, -ɪŋ, -d
spleen, -s; -ful, -fully, -ish, -ishly; -y
　spli:n, -z; -fʊl, -fʊlɪ [-fəlɪ], -ɪʃ, -ɪʃlɪ; -ɪ
splendid, -ly, -ness 'splendɪd, -lɪ, -nɪs
　[-nəs]
splendiferous splen'dɪfərəs
splendour, -s 'splendə*, -z
splenetic (*s. adj.*), -s, -ally splɪ'netɪk, -s,
　-əlɪ
splic|e (*s. v.*), -es, -ing, -ed splaɪs, -ɪz,
　-ɪŋ, -t
splint (*s. v.*), -s, -ing, -ed splɪnt, -s, -ɪŋ,
　-ɪd
splinter, -s; -y 'splɪntə*, -z; -rɪ
split (*s. v.*), -s, -ting splɪt, -s, -ɪŋ

465

splodd|y, -ier, -iest, -iness, -ily 'splɒd|ɪ, -ɪə*, -ɪɪst, -ɪnɪs [-ɪnəs], -ɪlɪ [-əlɪ]

splodg|e, -es splɒdʒ, -ɪz

splodg|y, -ier, -iest, -iness 'splɒdʒ|ɪ, -ɪə* [-jə*], -ɪɪst [-jɪst], -ɪnɪs [-məs]

splotch, -es, -y splɒtʃ, -ɪz, -ɪ

splutter (s. v.), **-s, -ing, -ed** 'splʌtə*, -z, -rɪŋ, -d

Spode spəʊd

Spofforth 'spɒfəθ [-fɔːθ]

Spohr spɔː* [spɔə*] (ʃpoːr)

spoil (s. v.), **-s, -ing, -ed, -t, -er/s; -age** spɔɪl, -z, -ɪŋ, -t, [-d], -t, -ə*/z; -ɪdʒ

spoil-sport, -s 'spɔɪlspɔːt, -s

spoke (s.), **-s** spəʊk, -s

spoke, -n (from **speak**) spəʊk, -ən

spokes|man, -men 'spəʊks|mən, -mən

spokes|woman, -women 'spəʊks|-ˌwʊmən, -ˌwɪmɪn

spoliation ˌspəʊlɪ'eɪʃn

spoliator, -s 'spəʊlɪeɪtə*, -z

spondaic spɒn'deɪɪk

spondee, -s 'spɒndiː [-dɪ], -z

spong|e (s. v.), **-es, -(e)ing, -ed, -er/s** spʌndʒ, -ɪz, -ɪŋ, -d, -ə*/z

sponge|-cake/s, -finger/s 'spʌndʒ|-keɪk/s, -ˌfɪŋgə*/z

spong|y, -ier, -iest, -iness 'spʌndʒ|ɪ, -ɪə* [-jə*], -ɪɪst [-jɪst], -ɪnɪs [-ɪnəs]

sponson, -s 'spɒnsn, -z

sponsor (s. v.), **-s, -ing, -ed; -ship** 'spɒnsə*, -z, -rɪŋ, -d; -ʃɪp

spontaneity ˌspɒntə'neɪətɪ [-'nɪətɪ, -'niːətɪ, -'niːɪtɪ]

spontaneous, -ly, -ness spɒn'teɪnjəs [spən-, -nɪəs], -lɪ, -nɪs [-nəs]

spoof (s. v.), **-s, -ing, -ed** spuːf, -s, -ɪŋ, -t

spook, -s, -ing, -ed; -ish, -y, -iness spuːk, -s, -ɪŋ, -t; -ɪʃ, -ɪ, -ɪnɪs [-ɪnəs]

spool (s. v.), **-s, -ing, -ed** spuːl, -z, -ɪŋ, -d

spoon (s.v.), **-s, -ing, -ed** spuːn, -z, -ɪŋ, -d

spoonbill, -s 'spuːnbɪl, -z

Spooner 'spuːnə*

spoonerism, -s 'spuːnərɪzəm, -z

spoon|-feed, -feeds, -feeding, -fed 'spuːn|fiːd, -ˌfiːdz, -ˌfiːdɪŋ, -fed

spoonful, -s 'spuːnfʊl, -z

spoon|y, -ier, -iest, -ily, -iness 'spuːn|ɪ, -ɪə*, -ɪɪst, -ɪlɪ [-əlɪ], -ɪnɪs [-ɪnəs]

spoor, -s spɔː* [spɔə*, spʊə*], -z

Sporades 'spɒrədiːz

sporadic, -ally spə'rædɪk [spɒ'r-], -əlɪ

spore, -s spɔː* [spɔə*], -z

sporran, -s 'spɒrən, -z

sport (s. v.), **-s, -ing, -ed** spɔːt, -s, -ɪŋ, -ɪd

sportive, -ly, -ness 'spɔːtɪv, -lɪ, -nɪs [-nəs]

sports|man, -men 'spɔːts|mən, -mən

sports|manlike, -manship, -woman, -women 'spɔːts|mənlaɪk, -mənʃɪp, -wʊmən, -wɪmɪn

spot (s. v.), **-s, -ting, -ted** spɒt, -s, -ɪŋ, -ɪd

spotless, -ly, -ness 'spɒtlɪs [-ləs], -lɪ, -nɪs [-nəs]

spotlight, -s 'spɒtlaɪt, -s

Spottiswoode 'spɒtɪzwʊd ['spɒtɪswʊd], 'spɒtswʊd

spott|y, -ier, -iest, -iness 'spɒt|ɪ, -ɪə*, -ɪɪst, -ɪnɪs [-ɪnəs]

spouse, -s spaʊz [spaʊs], -ɪz

spout (s. v.), **-s, -ing, -ed, -er/s** spaʊt, -s, -ɪŋ, -ɪd, -ə*/z

Spragge spræg

Sprague spreɪg

sprain (s.v.), **-s, -ing, -ed** spreɪn, -z, -ɪŋ, -d

sprang (from **spring**) spræŋ

Sprange spreɪndʒ

Sprangle 'spræŋgl

sprat (S.), **-s** spræt, -s

Spratt spræt

sprawl (s. v.), **-s, -ing, -ed, -er/s** sprɔːl, -z, -ɪŋ, -d, -ə*/z

sprawl|y, -ier, -iest, -iness 'sprɔːl|ɪ, -ɪə* [-jə*], -ɪɪst [-jɪst], -ɪnɪs [-ɪnəs]

spray (s. v.), **-s, -ing, -ed; -ey** spreɪ, -z, -ɪŋ, -d; -ɪ

spread (s. v.), **-s, -ing, -er/s** spred, -z, -ɪŋ, -ə*/z

spread-eagl|e, -es, -ing, -ed ˌspred'iːgl, -z, -ɪŋ [-lɪŋ], -d

spree, -s spriː, -z

sprig, -s sprɪg, -z

Sprigg sprɪg

sprightl|y, -ier, -iest, -iness 'spraɪtl|ɪ, -ɪə* [-jə*], -ɪɪst [-jɪst], -ɪnɪs [-ɪnəs]

Sprigings 'sprɪgɪŋz

spring (s. v.), **-s, -ing, sprang, sprung, springer/s** sprɪŋ, -z, -ɪŋ, spræŋ, sprʌŋ, 'sprɪŋə*/z

spring-balance, -s ˌsprɪŋ'bæləns ['-ˌ--], -ɪz

spring-board, -s 'sprɪŋbɔːd [-bɔəd], -z

springbok, -s 'sprɪŋbɒk, -s

springe, -s sprɪndʒ, -ɪz

Springell 'sprɪŋəl, 'sprɪŋgəl

Springfield 'sprɪŋfiːld

spring-gun, -s 'sprɪŋgʌn, -z

springlike 'sprɪŋlaɪk

Springpark 'sprɪŋpɑːk

springtime 'sprɪŋtaɪm

spring|y, -ier, -iest, -ily, -iness 'sprɪŋ|ɪ, -ɪə*, -ɪɪst, -ɪlɪ [-əlɪ], -ɪnɪs [-ɪnəs]

sprink|le (s. v.), **-les, -ling, -led, -ler/s** 'sprɪŋk|l, -lz, -lɪŋ [-l̩ɪŋ], -ld, -lə*/z [-l̩ə*/z]

sprinkling (s.), **-s** 'sprɪŋklɪŋ, -z
sprint (s. v.), **-s, -ing, -ed, -er/s** sprɪnt,
-s, -ɪŋ, -ɪd, -ə*/z
sprit, **-s** sprɪt, -s
sprite, **-s** spraɪt, -s
spritsail, **-s** 'sprɪtsl [-seɪl], -z
sprocket, **-s** 'sprɒkɪt, -s
Sproule sprəʊl
sprout (s. v.), **-s, -ing, -ed** spraʊt, -s,
-ɪŋ, -ɪd
spruce (s. adj.), **-s; -r, -st, -ly, -ness**
spru:s, -ɪz; -ə*, -ɪst, -lɪ, -nɪs [-nəs]
sprue, **-s** spru:, -z
sprung (from spring) sprʌŋ
Sprunt sprʌnt
spry (S.), **-er, -est, -ness** spraɪ, 'spraɪə*,
'spraɪɪst, 'spraɪnɪs [-nəs]
spud, **-s** spʌd, -z
spu|e, **-es, -ing, -ed** spju:, -z, -ɪŋ
['spjʊɪŋ], -d
spum|e, **-es, -ing, -ed** spju:m, -z, -ɪŋ,
-d
spun (from spin) spʌn
spunk; **-y, -ier, -iest** spʌŋk; -ɪ, -ɪə*, -ɪɪst
spur (s. v.), **-s, -ring, -red** spɜ:*, -z, -rɪŋ,
-d
Spurgeon 'spɜ:dʒən
spurious, **-ly, -ness** 'spjʊərɪəs [-jɔər-,
-jɔ:r-], -lɪ, -nɪs [-nəs]
spurn (S.), **-s, -ing, -ed** spɜ:n, -z, -ɪŋ,
-d
Spurr spɜ:*
Spurrier (surname) 'spʌrɪə*
spurt (s. v.), **-s, -ing, -ed** spɜ:t, -s, -ɪŋ, -ɪd
sputnik, **-s** 'spʊtnɪk ['spʌt-], -s
sputter (s. v.), **-s, -ing, -ed, -er/s**
'spʌtə*, -z, -rɪŋ, -d, -rə*/z
sputum 'spju:təm
sp|y (s. v.), **-ies, -ying, -ied** sp|aɪ, -aɪz,
-aɪɪŋ, -aɪd
spy-glass, **-es** 'spaɪglɑ:s, -ɪz
squab (s. adj.), **-s** skwɒb, -z
squabb|le (s. v.), **-les, -ling, -led, -ler/s**
'skwɒb|l, -lz, -lɪŋ [-lɪŋ], -ld, -lə*/z
[-lə*/z]
squad, **-s** skwɒd, -z
squadron, **-s** 'skwɒdrən, -z
squalid, **-est, -ly, -ness** 'skwɒlɪd, -ɪst, -lɪ,
-nɪs [-nəs]
squall (s. v.), **-s, -ing, -ed; -y** skwɔ:l, -z,
-ɪŋ, -d; -ɪ
squaloid 'skweɪlɔɪd
squalor 'skwɒlə*
squam|a, **-ae** 'skweɪm|ə, -i:
squam|ose, **-ous** 'skweɪm|əʊs, -əs
squand|er, **-ers, -ering, -ered, -erer/s**
'skwɒnd|ə*, -əz, -ərɪŋ, -əd, -ərə*/z
squandermania ˌskwɒndə'meɪnjə [-nɪə]

squar|e (s. adj. v. adv.), **-es; -er, -est,
-ely, -eness; -ing, -ed** skweə*, -z;
-rə*, -rɪst, -lɪ, -nɪs [-nəs]; -rɪŋ, -d
squaredanc|e, **-es, -ing** 'skweədɑ:ns,
-ɪz, -ɪŋ
square-jawed ˌskweə'dʒɔ:d ['-- when
attributive]
squarish 'skweərɪʃ
squash (s. v.), **-es, -ing, -ed** skwɒʃ, -ɪz,
-ɪŋ, -t
squash-hat, **-s** ˌskwɒʃ'hæt, -s
squash|y, **-ier, -iest, -iness** 'skwɒʃ|ɪ,
-ɪə*, -ɪɪst, -ɪnɪs [-ɪnəs]
squat (s. adj. v.), **-s, -ting, -ted, -ter/s**
skwɒt, -s, -ɪŋ, -ɪd, -ə*/z
squaw, **-s** skwɔ:, -z
squawk (s. v.), **-s, -ing, -ed** skwɔ:k, -s,
-ɪŋ, -t
squeak (s. v.), **-s, -ing, -ed, -er/s** skwi:k,
-s, -ɪŋ, -t, -ə*/z
squeak|y, **-ier, -iest, -ily, -ness** 'skwi:k|ɪ,
-ɪə* [-jə*], -ɪɪst [-jɪst], -ɪlɪ [-əlɪ], -ɪnɪs
[-ɪnəs]
squeal (s. v.), **-s, -ing, -ed, -er/s** skwi:l,
-z, -ɪŋ, -d, -ə*/z
squeamish, **-ly, -ness** 'skwi:mɪʃ, -lɪ, -nɪs
[-nəs]
squeegee (s. v.), **-s, -ing, -d** ˌskwi:'dʒi:
['--], -z, -ɪŋ, -d
Squeers skwɪəz
squeez|e (s. v.), **-es, -ing, -ed, -er/s;
-able** skwi:z, -ɪz, -ɪŋ, -d, -ə*/z; -əbl
squegger, **-s** 'skwegə*, -z
squelch (s. v.), **-es, -ing, -ed** skweltʃ, -ɪz,
-ɪŋ, -t
squib, **-s** skwɪb, -z
squid, **-s** skwɪd, -z
squiff|y, **-ier, -iest** 'skwɪf|ɪ, -ɪə*, -ɪɪst
squigg|le (s. v.), **-les, -ling, -led** 'skwɪg|l,
-lz, -lɪŋ [-lɪŋ], -ld
squilgee (s. v.), **-s, -ing, -d** ˌskwɪl'dʒi:,
-z, -ɪŋ, -d
squill, **-s** skwɪl, -z
squint (s. v.), **-s, -ing, -ed** skwɪnt, -s, -ɪŋ,
-ɪd
squint-eyed 'skwɪntaɪd
squire (S.), **-s** 'skwaɪə*, -z
squirearchy 'skwaɪərɑ:kɪ
squireen, **-s** ˌskwaɪə'ri:n, -z
squirm (s. v.), **-s, -ing, -ed** skwɜ:m, -z, -ɪŋ, -d
squirrel, **-s** 'skwɪrəl, -z
squirt (s. v.), **-s, -ing, -ed** skwɜ:t, -s, -ɪŋ,
-ɪd
squish (s. v.), **-es, -ing, -ed** skwɪʃ, -ɪz,
-ɪŋ, -t
Sri Lanka ˌsri:'læŋkə
Srinagar sri:'nʌgə* [srɪ'n-, -'nɑ:g-,
'sri:nəgə*] (Hindi syrɪnəgər)

s.s. ˌes'es ['eses, 'sti:mʃɪp]
St. (=Saint) sənt, sɪnt, snt [rarely sent, semt]
Note.—Names beginning with St. are entered after saint.
stab (s. v.), -s, -bing, -bed stæb, -z, -ɪŋ, -d
Stabat Mater, -s ˌstɑ:bæt'mɑ:tə* [-bət-], -z
stability stə'bɪlətɪ [-lɪt-]
stabilization [-isa-] ˌsteɪbəlaɪ'zeɪʃn [ˌstæb-, -bɪl-, -bl̩-, -lɪ'z-]
stabiliz|e [-is|e], -es, -ing, -ed, -er/s 'steɪbəlaɪz ['stæb-, -bɪl-, -bl̩-], -ɪz, -ɪŋ, -d, -ə*/z
stab|le (s. adj. v.), -les; -ly, -leness; -ling, -led 'steɪb|l, -lz; -lɪ, -lnɪs [-nəs]; -lɪŋ [-l̩ŋ], -ld
stable-boy, -s 'steɪblbɔɪ, -z
stable|man, -men 'steɪbl|mən [-mæn], -mən [-men]
stabling (s.) 'steɪblɪŋ
stablish, -es, -ing, -ed 'stæblɪʃ, -ɪz, -ɪŋ, -t
staccato, -s stə'kɑ:təʊ, -z
Stac(e)y 'steɪsɪ
stack (s. v.), -s, -ing, -ed stæk, -s, -ɪŋ, -t
stadi|um, -ums, -a 'steɪdj|əm [-dɪ|-], -əmz, -ə
staff (s. v.), -s, -ing, -ed stɑ:f, -s, -ɪŋ, -t
Staffa 'stæfə
Stafford, -shire 'stæfəd, -ʃə* [-ˌʃɪə*]
Staffs. stæfs
stag, -s stæg, -z
stag|e (s. v.), -es, -ing, -ed steɪdʒ, -ɪz, -ɪŋ, -d
stage-craft 'steɪdʒkrɑ:ft
stage-effect, -s 'steɪdʒɪˌfekt, -s
stage-manag|e, -es, -ing, -ed, -er/s ˌsteɪdʒ'mænɪdʒ ['-ˌ-], -ɪz, -ɪŋ, -d, -ə*/z [-nədʒə*/z]
stager, -s 'steɪdʒə, -z
stage-struck 'steɪdʒstrʌk
stagger (s. v.), -s, -ing, -ed, -er/s 'stægə*, -z, -rɪŋ, -d, -rə*/z
staghound, -s 'stæghaʊnd, -z
stag-hunting 'stægˌhʌntɪŋ
Stagirite, -s 'stædʒɪraɪt, -s
stagnan|cy, -t/ly 'stægnən|sɪ, -t/lɪ
stagnat|e, -es, -ing, -ed stæg'neɪt ['--], -s, -ɪŋ, -ɪd
stagnation stæg'neɪʃn
stag|ly, -ier, -iest, -ily, -iness 'steɪdʒ|ɪ, -ɪə* [-jə*], -ɪɪst [-jɪst], -ɪlɪ [-əlɪ], -ɪnɪs [-nəs]
staid, -ly, -ness steɪd, -lɪ, -nɪs [-nəs]
stain (s. v.), -s, -ing, -ed, -er/s steɪn, -z, -ɪŋ, -d, -ə*/z

Stainer (English name) 'steɪnə*, (German name) 'staɪnə* ('ʃtaɪnər)
Staines steɪnz
stainless, -ly, -ness 'steɪnlɪs [-ləs], -lɪ, -nɪs [-nəs]
stair, -s steə*, -z
stair-carpet, -s 'steəˌkɑ:pɪt, -s
staircase, -s 'steəkeɪs, -ɪz
stair-rod, -s 'steərɒd, -z
stairway, -s 'steəweɪ, -z
Staithes steɪðz
stak|e (s. v.), -es, -ing, -ed steɪk, -s, -ɪŋ, -t
stake-holder, -s 'steɪkˌhəʊldə*, -z
stalactite, -s 'stæləktaɪt, -s
stalagmite, -s 'stæləgmaɪt, -s
Stalbridge 'stɔ:lbrɪdʒ ['stɒl-]
stale, -r, -st, -ly, -ness steɪl, -ə*, -ɪst, -lɪ, -nɪs [-nəs]
stalemat|e (s. v.), -es, -ing, -ed 'steɪlmeɪt [ˌ-'-], -s, -ɪŋ, -ɪd
Stalin 'stɑ:lɪn ['stæl-] ('staljin)
Stalingrad 'stɑ:lɪngræd ['stæl-, -grɑ:d] (stəljin'grat)
stalinism 'stɑ:lɪnɪzəm ['stæl-]
stalk (s. v.), -s, -ing, -ed, -er/s; -y stɔ:k, -s, -ɪŋ, -t, -ə*/z; -ɪ
stalking-horse, -s 'stɔ:kɪŋhɔ:s, -ɪz
Stalky 'stɔ:kɪ
stall (s. v.), -s, -ing, -ed; -age stɔ:l, -z, -ɪŋ, -d; -ɪdʒ
stallion, -s 'stæljən, -z
stalwart (s. adj.), -s, -ly, -ness 'stɔ:lwət ['stɒl-, -wɑ:t], -s, -lɪ, -nɪs [-nəs]
Stalybridge 'steɪlɪbrɪdʒ
Stamboul stæm'bu:l
stamen, -s 'steɪmen [-mən], -z
Stamford, -ham 'stæmfəd, -əm
stamina 'stæmɪnə [-mənə]
stammer (s. v.), -s, -ing, -ed, -er/s 'stæmə*, -z, -rɪŋ, -d, -rə*/z
stamp (s. v.) (S.), -s, -ing, -ed, -er/s stæmp, -s, -ɪŋ, -t [stæmt], -ə*/z
stamp-album, -s 'stæmpˌælbəm, -z
stamp-collection, -s 'stæmpkəˌlekʃn, -z
stamp-collector, -s 'stæmpkəˌlektə*, -z
stamp-dut|y, -ies 'stæmpˌdju:t|ɪ, -ɪz
stamped|e (s. v.), -es, -ing, -ed stæm'pi:d, -z, -ɪŋ, -ɪd
stamp-machine, -s 'stæmpməˌʃi:n, -z
stance, -s stæns [stɑ:ns], -ɪz
stanch, -es, -ing, -ed stɑ:ntʃ, -ɪz, -ɪŋ, -t
stanchion, -s 'stɑ:nʃn, -z
stand (s. v.), -s, -ing, stood stænd, -z, -ɪŋ, stʊd
standard, -s 'stændəd, -z
standardization [-isa-] ˌstændədaɪ'zeɪʃn [-dɪ'z-]

standardiz|e [-is|e], -es, -ing, -ed
'stændədaɪz, -ɪz, -ɪŋ, -d
standard-lamp, -s 'stændədlæmp [ˌ--'-],
-s
stand-by, -s 'stændbaɪ ['stæmbaɪ], -z
stand-in, -s 'stændɪn [ˌ-'-], -z
standing (s.), -s 'stændɪŋ, -z
standish (S.), -es 'stændɪʃ, -ɪz
standoffish ˌstænd'ɒfɪʃ [old-fashioned
-'ɔːf-]
standpoint, -s 'stændpɔɪnt ['stæm-
pɔɪnt], -s
standstill, -s 'stændstɪl, -z
stand-to 'stændtuː [ˌ-'-]
stand-up (adj.) 'stændʌp
Stan|field, -ford 'stæn|fiːld, -fəd
stanhope (S.), -s 'stænəp, -s
staniel, -s 'stænjəl [-nɪəl], -z
Stanis|las, -aus 'stænɪsl|əs [-ɑːs], -ɔːs
stank (from stink) stæŋk
Stanley 'stænlɪ
stannar|y, -ies 'stænər|ɪ, -ɪz
stann|ic, -ous 'stæn|ɪk, -əs
Stansfield 'stænzfiːld [-nsf-]
Stanton 'stæntən, 'stɑːn-
stanza, -s 'stænzə, -z
stapl|e (S.) (s. v.), -es, -ing, -ed, -er/s
'steɪpl, -z, -ɪŋ, -d, -ə*/z
Stapleton 'steɪpltən
Stapley 'stæplɪ, 'steɪplɪ
star (s. v.), -s, -ring, -red stɑː*, -z, -rɪŋ,
-d
starboard 'stɑːbəd [-bɔːd, -bɔəd]
Note.—The nautical pronunciation is
'stɑːbəd.
starch (s. v.), -es, -ing, -ed; -y, -ier,
-iest, -iness stɑːtʃ, -ɪz, -ɪŋ, -t; -ɪ, -ɪə*,
-ɪɪst, -ɪnɪs [-nəs]
stardom 'stɑːdəm
star|e (s. v.), -es, -ing/ly, -ed, -er/s
steə*, -z, -rɪŋ/lɪ, -d, -rə*/z
starfish, -es 'stɑːfɪʃ, -ɪz
star-gaz|er/s, -ing 'stɑːˌgeɪz|ə*/z, -ɪŋ
stark (S.), -ly, -ness stɑːk, -lɪ, -nɪs [-nəs]
starland 'stɑːlænd
star|less, -light, -lit 'stɑː|lɪs [-ləs], -laɪt,
-lɪt
starlet, -s 'stɑːlɪt [-lət], -s
starling (S.), -s 'stɑːlɪŋ, -z
Starr stɑː*
starr|y, -iness 'stɑːr|ɪ, -ɪnɪs [-nəs]
starry-eyed ˌstɑːrɪ'aɪd ['--- *when attributive*]
start (s. v.) (S.), -s, -ing, -ed, -er/s
stɑːt, -s, -ɪŋ, -ɪd, -ə*/z
starting-point, -s 'stɑːtɪŋpɔɪnt, -s
start|le, -les, -ling, -led, -ler/s 'stɑːt|l,
-lz, -lɪŋ, -ld, -lə*/z

starvation stɑː'veɪʃn
starv|e, -es, -ing, -ed; -eling/s stɑːv, -z,
-ɪŋ, -d; -lɪŋ/z
stat|e (s. v.), -es, -ing, -ed, -ement/s
steɪt, -s, -ɪŋ, -ɪd, -mənt/s
statecraft 'steɪtkrɑːft
statel|y, -ier, -iest, -iness 'steɪtl|ɪ, -ɪə*
[-jə*], -ɪɪst [-jɪst], -ɪnɪs [-nəs]
stateroom, -s 'steɪtrum [-ruːm], -z
states|man, -men 'steɪts|mən, -mən
statesman|like, -ly, -ship 'steɪtsmən|-
laɪk, -lɪ, -ʃɪp
Statham 'steɪθəm, 'steɪðəm
static, -s, -al, -ally 'stætɪk, -s, -l, -əlɪ
statice (plant), -s 'stætɪs, -ɪz ['stætɪsɪ, -z]
stati|on (s. v.), -ons, -oning, -oned
'steɪʃ|n, -nz, -ŋɪŋ [-nɪŋ], -nd
stationar|y, -ily, -iness 'steɪʃnər|ɪ
[-ʃnər-, -ʃŋr-, -ʃənər-], -əlɪ [-ɪlɪ], -ɪnɪs
[-nəs]
stationer, -s 'steɪʃnə* [-ʃŋə*], -z
stationery 'steɪʃŋərɪ [-ʃnər-, -ʃŋr-,
-ʃənər-]
station-master, -s 'steɪʃnˌmɑːstə*, -z
station-wag(g)on, -s 'steɪʃnˌwægən, -z
statism 'steɪtɪzəm
statist, -s 'steɪtɪst, -s
statistic, -s, -al, -ally stə'tɪstɪk [stæ't-],
-s, -l, -əlɪ
statistician, -s ˌstætɪ'stɪʃn, -z
statuary 'stætʃʊərɪ [-tʃwərɪ, -tʃʊrɪ,
-tjʊərɪ, -tjwərɪ, -tjʊrɪ]
statue, -s 'stætʃuː [-tjuː], -z
statuesque ˌstætjʊ'esk [-tʃʊ'e-]
statuette, -s ˌstætjʊ'et [-tʃʊ'e-], -s
stature 'stætʃə*, -z
status, -es 'steɪtəs, -ɪz
status quo ˌsteɪtəs'kwəʊ [ˌstæt-]
statute, -s 'stætjuːt [-tʃuːt], -s
statute-book, -s 'stætjuːtbʊk [-tʃuːt-], -s
statutory 'stætjʊtərɪ [-tʃʊt-]
staunch, -er, -est, -ly, -ness stɔːntʃ
[stɑːn-], -ə*, -ɪst, -lɪ, -nɪs [-nəs]
Staunton (English surname) 'stɔːntən,
'stɑːn-, (towns in U.S.A.) 'stæntən
Stavanger stə'væŋə*
stav|e (s. v.), -es, -ing, -ed, stove steɪv,
-z, -ɪŋ, -d, stəʊv
stay (s. v.), -s, -ing, -ed, -er/s steɪ, -z,
-ɪŋ, -d, -ə*/z [steə*/z]
stay-at-home 'steɪəθəʊm
stay-in 'steɪɪn [ˌ-'-]
staysail, -s 'steɪseɪl [nautical pronunciation 'steɪsl], -z
Steabben 'stebən
stead (S.) sted
steadfast, -ly, -ness 'stedfɑːst [-fəst],
-lɪ, -nɪs [-nəs]

stead|y, -ier, -iest, -ily, -iness; -ies,
-ying, -ied 'sted|ɪ, -ɪə*, -ɪɪst, -ɪlɪ [-əlɪ],
-ɪnɪs [-ɪnəs]; -ɪz, -ɪɪŋ, -ɪd

steak, -s steɪk, -s

steakhou|se, -ses 'steɪkhaʊ|s, -zɪz

steal (s. v.), -s, -ing, stole, stolen,
stealer/s stiːl, -z, -ɪŋ, stəʊl, 'stəʊlən,
'stiːlə*/z

stealth, -y, -ier, -iest, -ily, -iness stelθ,
-ɪ, -ɪə* [-jə*],· -ɪɪst [-jɪst], -ɪlɪ [-əlɪ],
-ɪnɪs [-ɪnəs]

steam (s. v.), -s, -ing, -ed, -er/s; -y,
-iness stiːm, -z, -ɪŋ, -d, -ə*/z; -ɪ, -ɪnɪs
[-ɪnəs]

steamboat, -s 'stiːmbəʊt, -s

steam-engine, -s 'stiːm,endʒɪn, -z

steam-hammer, -s 'stiːm,hæmə*, -z

steam-power 'stiːm,paʊə*

steam-roller, -s 'stiːm,rəʊlə* [ˌ-'--], -z

steamship, -s 'stiːmʃɪp, -s

stearic stɪ'ærɪk

stearin 'stɪərɪn

Stearn(e), -s stɜːn, -z

steatite 'stɪətaɪt

steatolysis stɪə'tɒləsɪs [-lɪs-]

steatopy|gia, -gous ˌstɪətəʊ'paɪ|dʒɪə
[-dʒɪə], -gəs

Stedman 'stedmən

steed, -s stiːd, -z

steel (s. v.), -s, -ing, -ed; -y, -ier, -iest,
-iness stiːl, -z, -ɪŋ, -d; -ɪ, -ɪə* [-jə*],
-ɪɪst [-jɪst], -ɪnɪs [-ɪnəs]

Steele stiːl

steel-plated ˌstiːl'pleɪtɪd ['-ˌ--]

steelyard, -s 'stiːljɑːd ['stɪljɑːd, 'stɪljəd],
-z

steenbok, -s 'stiːnbɒk ['steɪn-], -s

steep (s. adj. v.), -s; -er, -est, -ly, -ness;
-ing, -ed stiːp, -s; -ə*, -ɪst, -lɪ, -nɪs
[-nəs]; -ɪŋ, -t

steep|en, -ens, -ening, -ened 'stiːp|ən,
-ənz, -nɪŋ [-nɪŋ], -ənd

steeple, -s, -d; -chase/s, -jack/s 'stiːpl,
-z, -d; -tʃeɪs/ɪz, -dʒæk/s

steer (s. v.), -s, -ing, -ed, -er/s; -age;
-sman, -smen stɪə*, -z, -rɪŋ, -d,
-rə*/z; -rɪdʒ; -zmən, -zmən [-zmen]

steering-gear 'stɪərɪŋ,gɪə*

steering-wheel, -s 'stɪərɪŋwiːl[-ŋhw-], -z

steev|e (s. v.), -es, -ing, -ed stiːv, -z, -ɪŋ,
-d

Steevens 'stiːvnz

Stein (English name), -itz staɪn, -ɪts

Steinbeck 'staɪnbek

steinbock, -s 'staɪnbɒk, -s

Steinway, -s 'staɪnweɪ, -z

stell|e, -ae 'stiːl|ɪ [-iː], -iː

Stella, -land 'stelə, -lænd

stellar 'stelə*

stem (s. v.), -s, -ming, -med stem, -z,
-ɪŋ, -d

stemma, -ta 'stemə, -tə

stemple, -s 'stempl, -z

Sten sten

stench, -es stentʃ, -ɪz

stenc|il, -ils, -illing, -illed 'stens|l [-ɪl],
-lz [-ɪlz], -lɪŋ [-ɪlɪŋ], -ld [-ɪld]

sten-gun, -s 'stengʌn, -z

stenograph, -s 'stenəgrɑːf [-nəʊg-,
-græf], -s

stenograph|er/s, -y stə'nɒgrəf|ə*/z
[ste'n-], -ɪ

stenotyp|e, -ing 'stenəʊtaɪp, -ɪŋ

Stent stent

stentorian sten'tɔːrɪən

step (s. v.), -s, -ping, -ped, -per/s step,
-s, -ɪŋ, -t, -ə*/z

step-aunt, -s 'stepɑːnt, -s

step-brother, -s 'step,brʌðə*, -z

step|-child, -children 'step|tʃaɪld,
-,tʃɪldrən [-,tʃʊldrən]

step-dance, -s 'stepdɑːns, -ɪz

step-daughter, -s 'step,dɔːtə*, -z

step-father, -s 'step,fɑːðə*, -z

Stephano 'stefənəʊ

stephanotis ˌstefə'nəʊtɪs

Stephany (-ie) 'stefənɪ

Stephen, -s, -son 'stiːvn, -z, -sn

step-ladder, -s 'step,lædə*, -z

step-mother, -s 'step,mʌðə*, -z

Stepney 'stepnɪ

steppe, -s step, -s

stepping-stone, -s 'stepɪŋstəʊn, -z

step-sister, -s 'step,sɪstə*, -z

step-son, -s 'stepsʌn, -z

step-uncle, -s 'step,ʌŋkl, -z

stereo, -s 'stɪərɪəʊ ['stɪər-], -z

stereophonic ˌstɪərɪəʊ'fɒnɪk [ˌstɪə-]

stereophony ˌstɪərɪ'ɒfənɪ [ˌstɪə-]

stereopticon, -s ˌstɪərɪ'ɒptɪkən [ˌstɪər-],
-z

stereoscope, -s 'stɪərɪəskəʊp ['stɪər-],
-s

stereoscopic, -al, -ally ˌstɪərɪə'skɒpɪk
[ˌstɪər-], -l, -əlɪ

stereoscopy ˌstɪərɪ'ɒskəpɪ [ˌstɪər-]

stereotyp|e (s. v.), -es, -ing, -ed, -er/s;
-y 'stɪərɪətaɪp ['ster-, -rɪəʊt-], -s, -ɪŋ,
-t, -ə*/z; -ɪ

sterile 'steraɪl

sterility stə'rɪlətɪ [ste'r-, -ɪtɪ]

sterilization [-isa-], -s ˌsterəlaɪ'zeɪʃn
[-rɪl-, -lɪ'z-], -z

steriliz|e [-is|e], -es, -ing, -ed, -er/s
'sterəlaɪz [-rɪl-], -ɪz, -ɪŋ, -d, -ə*/z

sterling 'stɜːlɪŋ

stern (s.) (of ship), **-s**; **-most** stɜːn, -z;
-məʊst [-məst]
stern (adj.), **-er**, **-est**, **-ly**, **-ness** stɜːn,
-ə*, -ɪst, -lɪ, -nɪs [-nəs]
Sterne stɜːn
stern|um, **-ums**, **-a** 'stɜːn|əm, -əmz, -ə
steroid, **-s** 'stɪərɔɪd ['ste-], -z
stertorous, **-ly**, **-ness** 'stɜːtərəs, -lɪ, -nɪs
[-nəs]
stet stet
stethoscope, **-s** 'steθəskəʊp, -s
stethoscopic, **-al**, **-ally** ˌsteθə'skɒpɪk, -l,
-əlɪ
stethoscopy ste'θɒskəpɪ
stetson (S.) 'stetsn
Steve stiːv
stevedore, **-s** 'stiːvədɔː* [-vɪd-], -z
Stevenage 'stiːvnɪdʒ [-vənɪdʒ]
Steven|s, **-son** 'stiːvn|z, -sn
stew (s. v.), **-s**, **-ing**, **-ed** stjuː, -z, -ɪŋ
['stjʊɪŋ], -d
steward (S.), **-s**; **-ess/es**; **-ship/s** stjʊəd
['stjuːəd], -z; -ɪs/ɪz [ˌstjʊə'des/ɪz];
-ʃɪp/s
Stewart stjʊət ['stjuːət]
stew-pan, **-s** 'stjuːpæn, -z
Steyne stiːn
Steyning 'stenɪŋ
stg. 'stɜːlɪŋ
stichomythia, **-s** ˌstɪkəʊ'mɪθɪə [-θjə], -z
stick (s. v.), **-s**, **-ing**, **stuck**, **sticker/s**
stɪk, -s, -ɪŋ, stʌk, 'stɪkə*/z
stick-in-the-mud, **-s** 'stɪkɪnðəmʌd, -z
stickjaw, **-s** 'stɪkdʒɔː, -z
stickleback, **-s** 'stɪklbæk, -s
stickler, **-s** 'stɪklə*, -z
stick-up (s. adj.), **-s** 'stɪkʌp, -s
stick|y, **-ier**, **-iest**, **-ily**, **-iness** 'stɪk|ɪ,
-ɪə*, -ɪɪst, -ɪlɪ [-əlɪ], -ɪnɪs [-ɪnəs]
stiff, **-er**, **-est**, **-ly**, **-ness** stɪf, -ə*, -ɪst,
-lɪ, -nɪs [-nəs]
stiff|en, **-ens**, **-ening**, **-ened** 'stɪf|n, -nz,
-ɲɪŋ [-nɪŋ], -nd
Stiffkey (in Norfolk) 'stɪfkɪ: [-kɪ, old-
fashioned local pronunciation 'stjuːkɪ]
stiff-necked ˌstɪf'nekt [also '--, esp.
when attributive]
stif|le, **-les**, **-ling/ly**, **-led** 'staɪf|l, -lz,
-lɪŋ/lɪ, -ld
Stiggins 'stɪgɪnz
stigma, **-s**, **-ta**, **-tism** 'stɪgmə, -z, -tə,
-tɪzəm
stigmatic stɪg'mætɪk
stigmatization [-isa-] ˌstɪgmətaɪ'zeɪʃn
[-tɪ'z-]
stigmatiz|e [-is|e], **-es**, **-ing**, **-ed** 'stɪg-
mətaɪz, -ɪz, -ɪŋ, -d
stile, **-s** staɪl, -z

stiletto (s.), **-(e)s** stɪ'letəʊ, -z
stilett|o (v.), **-oes**, **-oing**, **-oed** stɪ'let|əʊ,
-əʊz, -əʊɪŋ, -əʊd
still (s. adj. v. adv.) (S.), **-s**; **-er**, **-est**,
-ness; **-ing**, **-ed**, **-ly** stɪl, -z; -ə*, -ɪst, -nɪs
[-nəs]; -ɪŋ, -d, -lɪ
still-born 'stɪlbɔːn
still-life ˌstɪl'laɪf ['--]
still-room, **-s** 'stɪlrʊm [-ruːm], -z
stilly (adj.) 'stɪlɪ
stilt, **-s**, **-ed/ly**, **-edness** stɪlt, -s, -ɪd/lɪ,
-ɪdnɪs [-nəs]
Stilton, **-s** 'stɪltən, -z
stimulant, **-s** 'stɪmjʊlənt [-mjəl-], -s
stimulat|e, **-es**, **-ing**, **-ed**, **-or/s** 'stɪmjʊ-
leɪt [-mjəl-], -s, -ɪŋ, -ɪd, -ə*/z
stimulation, **-s** ˌstɪmjʊ'leɪʃn [-mjə'l-], -z
stimulative 'stɪmjʊlətɪv [-mjəl-, -leɪt-]
stimul|us, **-i** 'stɪmjʊl|əs [-mjəl-], -aɪ [-iː]
stim|y (s. v.), **-ies**, **-ying**, **-ied** 'staɪm|ɪ,
-ɪz, -ɪɪŋ, -ɪd
sting (s. v.), **-s**, **-ing**, **stung**, **stinger/s**
stɪŋ, -z, -ɪŋ, stʌŋ, 'stɪŋə*/z
stinging-nettle, **-s** 'stɪŋɪŋˌnetl, -z
stingo 'stɪŋgəʊ
sting|y, **-ier**, **-iest**, **-ily**, **-iness** 'stɪndʒ|ɪ,
-ɪə* [-jə*], -ɪɪst [-jɪst], -ɪlɪ [-əlɪ], -ɪnɪs
[-ɪnəs]
stink (s. v.), **-s**, **-ing**, **stank**, **stunk** stɪŋk,
-s, -ɪŋ, stæŋk, stʌŋk
stinker, **-s** 'stɪŋkə*, -z
stink-pot, **-s** 'stɪŋkpɒt, -s
stint (s. v.), **-s**, **-ing**, **-ed** stɪnt, -s, -ɪŋ, -ɪd
stipend, **-s** 'staɪpend [-pənd], -z
stipendiar|y (s. adj.), **-ies** staɪ'pendjər|ɪ
[stɪ'p-, -dɪə-], -ɪz
stipp|le, **-les**, **-ling**, **-led** 'stɪp|l, -lz, -lɪŋ
[-lɪŋ], -ld
stipulat|e, **-es**, **-ing**, **-ed**, **-or/s** 'stɪpjʊ-
leɪt [-pjəl-], -s, -ɪŋ, -ɪd, -ə*/z
stipulation, **-s** ˌstɪpjʊ'leɪʃn [-pjə'l-], -z
stipule, **-s** 'stɪpjuːl, -z
stir (s. v.), **-s**, **-ring**, **-red**, **-rer/s** stɜː*, -z,
-rɪŋ, -d, -rə*/z
Stirling 'stɜːlɪŋ
stirp|s, **-es** stɜːp|s, -iːz [-eɪz]
stirrup, **-s** 'stɪrəp, -s
stirrup-pump, **-s** 'stɪrəppʌmp, -s
stitch (s. v.), **-es**, **-ing**, **-ed** stɪtʃ, -ɪz, -ɪŋ,
-t
stith|y, **-ies** 'stɪðɪ|ɪ, -ɪz
stiver, **-s** 'staɪvə*, -z
stoat, **-s** stəʊt, -s
Stobart 'stəʊbɑːt
stochastic stɒ'kæstɪk [stə-]
stock (s. v.), **-s**, **-ing**, **-ed** stɒk, -s, -ɪŋ, -t
stockad|e (s. v.), **-es**, **-ing**, **-ed** stɒ'keɪd,
-z, -ɪŋ, -ɪd

stock-book, -s 'stɒkbʊk, -s
stock-breeder, -s 'stɒk‚briːdə*, -z
stockbrok|er/s, -ing 'stɒk‚brəʊk|ə*/z,
-ɪŋ
Stock Exchange 'stɒkɪks‚tʃeɪndʒ
stock-farm, -s 'stɒkfɑːm, -z
stockfish 'stɒkfɪʃ
stockholder, -s 'stɒk‚həʊldə*, -z
Stockholm 'stɒkhəʊm
stockinet ‚stɒkɪ'net
stocking (s.), -s, -ed 'stɒkɪŋ, -z, -d
stock-in-trade ‚stɒkɪn'treɪd
stockjobber, -s 'stɒk‚dʒɒbə*, -z
stock-market, -s 'stɒk‚mɑːkɪt, -s
stockpil|e (s. v.), -es, -ing, -ed 'stɒkpaɪl,
-z, -ɪŋ, -d
Stockport 'stɒkpɔːt
stock-pot, -s 'stɒkpɒt, -s
stock-raising 'stɒk‚reɪzɪŋ
stock-still ‚stɒk'stɪl
stock-taking 'stɒk‚teɪkɪŋ
Stock|ton, -well 'stɒk|tən, -wəl [-wel]
stock|y, -ier, -iest, -iness 'stɒk|ɪ, -ɪə*,
-ɪɪst, -ɪnɪs [-məs]
Stoddar|d, -t 'stɒdə|d, -t [-dɑːt]
stodg|e (s. v.), -es, -ing, -ed; -y, -ier,
-iest, -iness stɒdʒ, -ɪz, -ɪŋ, -d; -ɪ, -ɪə*,
-ɪɪst, -ɪnɪs [-məs]
stoep, -s stuːp, -s
Stogumber (in Somerset) stəʊ'gʌmbə*,
(character in Shaw's 'Saint Joan')
'stɒgəmbə*
stoic (S.), -s, -al, -ally 'stəʊɪk, -s, -l, -əlɪ
stoicism (S.) 'stəʊɪsɪzəm
stok|e (S.), -es, -ing, -ed, -er/s stəʊk, -s,
-ɪŋ, -t, -ə*/z
Stoke Courcy [Stogursey] stəʊ'gɜːzɪ
Stoke d'Abernon ‚stəʊk'dæbənən
stokehold, -s 'stəʊkhəʊld, -z
stokehole, -s 'stəʊkhəʊl, -z
Stoke Poges ‚stəʊk'pəʊdʒɪz
stole (S.), -s stəʊl, -z
stole (from steal), -n stəʊl, -ən
stolid, -est, -ly 'stɒlɪd, -ɪst, -lɪ
stolidity stɒ'lɪdətɪ [stə'l-, -rtɪ]
Stoll (surname) stəʊl, stɒl
stomach (s. v.), -s, -ing, -ed 'stʌmək, -s,
-ɪŋ, -t
stomach-ache, -s 'stʌməkeɪk, -s
stomacher, -s 'stʌməkə* [old-fashioned
-ətʃə*, -ədʒə*], -z
stomachic stəʊ'mækɪk [stɒ-]
stomatitis ‚stəʊmə'tartɪs [‚stɒ-]
stomatoscope, -s stəʊ'mætəskəʊp [stɒ-],
-s
ston|e (s. v.) (S.), -es, -ing, -ed stəʊn, -z,
-ɪŋ, -d
stone-blind ‚stəʊn'blaɪnd

stone-breaker, -s 'stəʊn‚breɪkə*, -z
stone-cast, -s 'stəʊnkɑːst, -s
stonechat, -s 'stəʊntʃæt, -s
stone-cold ‚stəʊn'kəʊld
stonecrop, -s 'stəʊnkrɒp, -s
stone-cutter, -s 'stəʊn‚kʌtə*, -z
stone-dead ‚stəʊn'ded
stone-deaf ‚stəʊn'def
stone-fruit 'stəʊnfruːt
Stonehaven stəʊn'heɪvn
Stonehenge ‚stəʊn'hendʒ [also '--
according to sentence-stress]
Stonehouse 'stəʊnhaʊs
stonemason, -s 'stəʊn‚meɪsn, -z
stonewall, -s, -ing, -ed, -er/s ‚stəʊn-
'wɔːl, -z, -ɪŋ, -d, -ə*/z
stone-ware 'stəʊnweə*
stone-work 'stəʊnwɜːk
Stoney 'stəʊnɪ
ston|y (adj. adv.), -ier, -iest, -ily, -iness
'stəʊn|ɪ, -ɪə* [-ɪə*], -ɪɪst [-ɪɪst], -ɪlɪ
[-əlɪ], -ɪnɪs [-məs]
stony-hearted 'stəʊnɪ‚hɑːtɪd [‚--'--]
stood (from stand) stʊd
stoog|e (s. v.), -es, -ing, -ed stuːdʒ, -ɪz,
-ɪŋ, -d
stook, -s stʊk [stuːk], -s
stool, -s stuːl, -z
stoop (s. v.), -s, -ing, -ed, -er/s stuːp, -s,
-ɪŋ, -t, -ə*/z
stop (s. v.), -s, -ping, -ped, -per/s stɒp,
-s, -ɪŋ, -t, -ə*/z
stop|-cock/s, -gap/s 'stɒp|kɒk/s,
-gæp/s
Stopford 'stɒpfəd
stop-go ‚stɒp'gəʊ
Stopher 'stəʊfə*
stoppage, -s 'stɒpɪdʒ, -ɪz
stopover (s.), -s 'stɒp‚əʊvə*, -z
stopper, -s 'stɒpə*, -z
stop-watch, -es 'stɒpwɒtʃ, -ɪz
storage 'stɔːrɪdʒ ['stɒə-]
storage-heater, -s 'stɔːrɪdʒ‚hiːtə*
['stɒə-], -z
stor|e (s. v.), -es, -ing, -ed; -able stɔː*
[stɒə*], -z, -ɪŋ, -d; -rəbl
store-hou|se, -ses 'stɔːhaʊ|s ['stɒə-], -zɪz
store-keeper, -s 'stɔː‚kiːpə* ['stɒə-],
-z
store-room, -s 'stɔːrʊm ['stɒərʊm,
-ruːm], -z
storey (S.), -s, -ed 'stɔːrɪ, -z, -d
storiated 'stɔːrɪeɪtɪd
stork, -s stɔːk, -s
storm (s. v.) (S.), -s, -ing, -ed stɔːm, -z,
-ɪŋ, -d
storm-bound 'stɔːmbaʊnd
storm-centre, -s 'stɔːm‚sentə*, -z

storm-cloud, -s 'stɔːmklaʊd, -z
Stormont 'stɔːmənt [-mɒnt]
Stormonth (surname) 'stɔːmʌnθ [-mənθ]
storm-tossed 'stɔːmtɒst [old-fashioned
-tɔːst]
storm-trooper, -s 'stɔːm‚truːpə*, -z
storm|y, -ier, -iest, -ily, -iness 'stɔːm|ɪ,
-ɪə* [-jə*], -ɪɪst [-jɪst], -ɪlɪ [-əlɪ], -ɪnɪs
[-məs]
Stornoway 'stɔːnəweɪ [-nʊw-]
Storr, -s stɔː*, -z
Stortford (in Hertfordshire) 'stɔːfəd
[-ɔːtf-]
Storthing 'stɔːtɪŋ
stor|y (S.), -ies 'stɔːr|ɪ, -ɪz
story-book, -s 'stɔːrɪbʊk, -s
story-tell|er/s, -ing 'stɔːrɪ‚tel|ə*/z, -ɪŋ
Stothard 'stɒðəd
Stoughton (in West Sussex, Leicestershire) 'stəʊtn, (in Somerset) 'stɔːtn,
(in Surrey) 'staʊtn, (surname) 'stɔːtn,
'staʊtn, 'stəʊtn
Note.—'stəʊtn in Hodder & Stoughton, the publishers.
stoup, -s stuːp, -s
Stour (in Suffolk, Essex) stʊə*, (in
Kent) stʊə* [rarely 'staʊə*], (in
Hampshire) 'staʊə*, stʊə*, (in War-
wickshire) 'staʊə*, 'stəʊə*, (in Dorset)
'staʊə*
Stourbridge 'staʊəbrɪdʒ
Stourmouth (in Kent) 'staʊəmaʊθ
[rarely 'stʊəmaʊθ]
Stourton (in Wiltshire, surname) 'stɜːtn
stout (s. adj.), -s; -er, -est, -ly, -ness
staʊt, -s; -ə*, -ɪst, -lɪ, -nɪs [-nəs]
stout-hearted, -ly, -ness ‚staʊt'hɑːtɪd
['-‚-- when attributive], -lɪ, -nɪs [-nəs]
stoutish 'staʊtɪʃ
stove (s.), -s stəʊv, -z
stove (from stave) stəʊv
stove-pipe, -s 'stəʊvpaɪp, -s
Stovold 'stɒvəʊld
stow (S.), -s, -ing, -ed; -age stəʊ, -z,
-ɪŋ, -d; -ɪdʒ
stowaway, -s 'stəʊəweɪ [-əʊʊweɪ], -z
Stowe stəʊ
Stowers 'staʊəz
Stowey (in Somerset) 'stəʊɪ
Strabane strə'bæn
strabismus strə'bɪzməs [stræ'b-]
Strabo 'streɪbəʊ
Strabolgi strə'bəʊgɪ
Strachan strɔːn, 'strækən
Strachey 'streɪtʃɪ
Strad, -s stræd, -z
stradd|le (s. v.), -les, -ling, -led 'stræd|l,
-lz, -lɪŋ [-lɪŋ], -ld

Stradivarius, -es ‚strædɪ'veərɪəs
[-'vɑːr-], -ɪz
straf|(e) (s. v.), -(e)s, -ing/s, -ed strɑːf
[streɪf], -s, -ɪŋ/z, -t
Strafford 'stræfəd
stragg|le, -les, -ling, -led, -ler/s; -ly,
-liness 'stræg|l, -lz, -lɪŋ [-lɪŋ], -ld,
-lə*/z [-lə*/z]; -lɪ [-lɪ], -lɪnɪs [-lɪnɪs,
-nəs]
Strahan strɔːn, strɑːn
straight (adj. adv.), -er, -est, -ness
streɪt, -ə*, -ɪst, -nɪs [-nəs]
straight-edge, -s 'streɪtedʒ, 'streɪt‚edʒɪz
straight|en, -ens, -ening, -ened 'streɪt|n,
-nz, -nɪŋ [-nɪŋ], -nd
straightforward, -ly, -ness ‚streɪt-
'fɔːwəd, -lɪ, -nɪs [-nəs]
straightway 'streɪtweɪ
strain (s. v.) (S.), -s, -ing, -ed, -er/s
streɪn, -z, -ɪŋ, -d, -ə*/z
strait, -s (S.), -ened streɪt, -s, -nd
strait-jacket, -s 'streɪt‚dʒækɪt, -s
strait-laced ‚streɪt'leɪst
strait-waistcoat, -s ‚streɪt'weɪskəʊt
[-stk-, old-fashioned -'weskət, '-‚--],
-s
Straker 'streɪkə*
strand (s. v.) (S.), -s; -ing, -ed strænd,
-z; -ɪŋ, -ɪd
strange (S.), -r (adj.), -st, -ly, -ness
streɪndʒ, -ə*, -ɪst, -lɪ, -nɪs [-nəs]
stranger (s.), -s 'streɪndʒə*, -z
Strangeways 'streɪndʒweɪz
strang|le, -les, -ling, -led 'stræŋg|l, -lz,
-lɪŋ, -ld
strangle-hold, -s 'stræŋglhəʊld, -z
strangulat|e, -es, -ing, -ed 'stræŋgjʊ-
leɪt [-gjəl-], -s, -ɪŋ, -ɪd
strangulation, -s ‚stræŋgjʊ'leɪʃn
[-gjə'l-], -z
Strangways 'stræŋweɪz
Stranraer stræn'rɑː* [-'rɑː‚ə*]
strap (s. v.), -s, -ping, -ped, -per/s
stræp, -s, -ɪŋ, -t, -ə*/z
strap|hang, -hangs, -hanging, -hung,
-hanger/s 'stræp|hæŋ, -hæŋz,
-‚hæŋɪŋ, -hʌŋ, -‚hæŋə*/z
strapless 'stræplɪs [-ləs]
Stras(s)b(o)urg 'stræzbɜːg
strata (plur. of stratum) 'strɑːtə
[-reɪt-]
stratagem, -s 'strætədʒəm [-tɪdʒ-,
-dʒɪm, -dʒem], -z
strategic, -al, -ally strə'tiːdʒɪk [stræ't-,
-'tedʒ-], -l, -əlɪ
strateg|ist/s, -y 'strætɪdʒ|ɪst/s [-tədʒ-],
-ɪ
Stratford 'strætfəd

473

Stratford-atte-Bowe 'strætfəd,ætɪ'bəʊɪ [-ætə'bəʊə]

Stratford-on-Avon ,strætfədɒn'eɪvn

strath, -s stræθ, -s

Strathaven 'streɪvən

Strathavon stræθ'ɑːn

Strathclyde stræθ'klaɪd

Strathcona stræθ'kəʊnə

Strathearn stræθ'ɜːn

Strathmore stræθ'mɔː:* [-'mɔə*]

Strathpeffer stræθ'pefə*

strathspey (S.), -s stræθ'speɪ, -z

stratification ,strætɪfɪ'keɪʃn

strati|fy, -fies, -fying, -fied 'strætɪ|faɪ, -faɪz, -faɪɪŋ, -faɪd

stratocruiser, -s 'strætəʊ,kruːzə*, -z

Straton 'strætn

stratosphere, -s 'strætəʊ,sfɪə* ['strɑːt-, old-fashioned 'streɪt-], -z

stratospheric ,strætəʊ'sferɪk [,strɑːt-, old-fashioned ,streɪt-]

Stratton 'strætn

strat|um, -a 'strɑːt|əm [-reɪt-], -ə

stratus 'streɪtəs [-rɑːt-]

Straus(s) straʊs

Stravinsky strə'vɪnskɪ (strɑ'vjinskij)

straw, -s, -y strɔː, -z, -ɪ

strawberr|y (S.), -ies 'strɔːbər|ɪ, -ɪz

stray (s. adj. v.) (S.), -s, -ing, -ed streɪ, -z, -ɪŋ, -d

streak (s. v.), -s, -ing, -ed; -y, -ier, -iest, -iness 'striːk, -s, -ɪŋ, -t; -ɪ, -ɪə* [-jə*], -ɪɪst [-jɪst], -ɪnɪs [-məs]

stream (s. v.), -s, -ing, -ed, -er/s striːm, -z, -ɪŋ, -d, -ə*/z

streamlet, -s 'striːmlɪt [-lət], -s

streamlin|e (s. v.), -es, -ing, -ed 'striːmlaɪn, -z, -ɪŋ, -d

Streatfeild 'stretfiːld

Streatfield 'stretfiːld

Streatham 'stretəm

Streatley 'striːtlɪ

street (S.), -s striːt, -s

strength, -s streŋθ [-ŋkθ], -s

strength|en, -ens, -ening, -ened, -ener/s 'streŋθ|n [-ŋkθ-], -nz, -ənɪŋ [-ŋɪŋ, -nɪŋ], -nd, -ənə*/z [-ŋə*/z, -nə*/z]

strenuous, -ly, -ness 'strenjʊəs [-njwəs], -lɪ, -nɪs [-nəs]

streptococcal ,streptəʊ'kɒkl

streptococc|us, -i ,streptəʊ'kɒk|əs, -aɪ

streptomycin ,streptəʊ'maɪsɪn

stress (s. v.), -es, -ing, -ed stres, -ɪz, -ɪŋ, -t

stress-group, -s 'stresɡruːp, -s

stressless 'streslɪs [-ləs]

stretch (s. v.), -es, -ing, -ed, -er/s, -y stretʃ, -ɪz, -ɪŋ, -t, -ə*/z, -ɪ

Strevens 'strevənz

strew, -s, -ing, -ed, -n struː, -z, -ɪŋ ['strʊɪŋ], -d, -n

stri|a, -ae 'straɪ|ə, -iː

striate (adj.) 'straɪɪt [-aɪeɪt]

striated straɪ'eɪtɪd

striation, -s straɪ'eɪʃn, -z

stricken (from strike) 'strɪkən

Strickland 'strɪklənd

strict, -er, -est, -ly, -ness strɪkt, -ə*, -ɪst, -lɪ ['strɪklɪ], -nɪs ['strɪknɪs, -nəs]

stricture, -s 'strɪktʃə*, -z

strid|e (s. v.), -es, -ing, strode, stridden straɪd, -z, -ɪŋ, strəʊd, 'strɪdn

strident, -ly 'straɪdnt, -lɪ

strife straɪf

strigil, -s 'strɪdʒɪl, -z

strik|e (s. v.), -es, -ing/ly, struck, stricken, striker/s straɪk, -s, -ɪŋ/lɪ, strʌk, 'strɪkən, 'straɪkə*/z

strike-break|er/s, -ing 'straɪk,breɪk|-ə*/z, -ɪŋ

strike-pay 'straɪkpeɪ

Strindberg 'strɪndbɜːɡ ('strind,berj)

string (s. v.), -s, -ing, -ed, strung, stringer/s strɪŋ, -z, -ɪŋ, -d, strʌŋ, 'strɪŋə*/z

stringen|cy, -t/ly 'strɪndʒən|sɪ, -t/lɪ

stringendo strɪn'dʒendəʊ

Stringer 'strɪŋə*

string|y, -ier, -iest, -iness 'strɪŋ|ɪ, -ɪə*, -ɪɪst, -ɪnɪs [-məs]

strip (s. v.), -s, -ping, -ped, -per/s strɪp, -s, -ɪŋ, -t, -ə*/z

strip|e (s. v.), -es, -ing, -ed; -y, -iness straɪp, -s, -ɪŋ, -t; -ɪ, -ɪnɪs [-məs]

stripling, -s 'strɪplɪŋ, -z

striptease 'strɪptiːz

striv|e, -es, -ing/s, strove, striven, striver/s straɪv, -z, -ɪŋ/z, strəʊv, 'strɪvn, 'straɪvə*/z

strobilion, -s strəʊ'bɪlɪən [-ljən], -z

strobolion, -s strəʊ'bəʊljən [-lɪən], -z

stroboscope, -s 'strəʊbəskəʊp ['strɒb-], -s

stroboscopic ,strəʊbəʊ'skɒpɪk [,strɒ-]

stroboscopy strəʊ'bɒskəpɪ [strɒ'b-]

strode (from stride) strəʊd

strok|e (s. v.), -es, -ing, -ed strəʊk, -s, -ɪŋ, -t

stroll (s. v.), -s, -ing, -ed, -er/s strəʊl, -z, -ɪŋ, -d, -ə*/z

Stromboli 'strɒmbəlɪ [-bʊl-, -bəʊl-, strɒm'bəʊlɪ] ('stromboli)

strong (S.), -er, -est, -ly, -ish strɒŋ, -ɡə*, -ɡɪst, -lɪ, -ɪʃ

strong-box, -es 'strɒŋbɒks, -ɪz

stronghold, -s 'strɒŋhəʊld, -z

474

strong-minded ˌstrɒŋ'maɪndɪd [also '-ˌ-- when attributive]

strong-mindedness ˌstrɒŋ'maɪndɪdnɪs [-nəs]

strong-room, -s 'strɒŋrʊm [-ruːm], -z

stron|tia, -tian, -tium 'strɒn|ʃɪə [-ʃjə, -ʃə, -tɪə, -tjə], -ʃɪən [-ʃjən, -ʃn, -tɪən, -tjən], -tɪəm [-tjəm, rarely -ʃɪəm, -ʃjəm, -ʃəm]

Strood struːd

strop (s. v.), -s, -ping, -ped, -py strɒp, -s, -ɪŋ, -t, -ɪ

strophe, -s 'strəʊfɪ ['strɒf-], -z

strophic 'strɒfɪk

Stroud straʊd (sometimes struːd as a surname)

strove (from strive) strəʊv

strow, -s, -ing, -ed, -n strəʊ, -z, -ɪŋ, -d, -n

struck (from strike) strʌk

structur|al, -ally 'strʌktʃər|əl [-tʃʊr-], -əlɪ

structural|ism, -ist/s 'strʌktʃərəl|ɪzm [-tʃʊr-], -ɪst/s

structure, -s 'strʌktʃə*, -z

strugg|le (s. v.), -les, -ling, -led, -ler/s 'strʌg|l, -lz, -lɪŋ [-l̩ɪŋ], -ld, -lə*/z [-l̩ə*/z]

strum (s. v.), -s, -ming, -med, -mer/s strʌm, -z, -ɪŋ, -d, -ə*/z

strumpet, -s 'strʌmpɪt, -s

strung (from string) strʌŋ

strut (s. v.), -s, -ting, -ted strʌt, -s, -ɪŋ, -ɪd

Struthers 'strʌðəz

Strutt strʌt

Struwwelpeter (English) 'struː|əlˌpiːtə* strychnine 'strɪkniːn

Stuart, -s stjʊət ['stjuːət], -s

stub, -s; -by, -bier, -biest, -biness stʌb, -z; -ɪ, -ɪə*, -ɪɪst, -ɪnɪs [-ɪnəs]

stubb|le, -ly 'stʌb|l, -lɪ [-lɪ]

stubborn, -er, -est, -ly, -ness 'stʌbən, -ə*, -ɪst, -lɪ, -nɪs [-nəs]

Stubbs stʌbz

stucco (s.), -(e)s 'stʌkəʊ, -z

stucco (v.), -es, -ing, -ed 'stʌkəʊ, -z, -ɪŋ, -d

stuck (from stick) stʌk

stuck-up ˌstʌk'ʌp [also '-- according to sentence-stress]

Stucley 'stjuːklɪ

stud (s. v.), -s, -ding, -ded stʌd, -z, -ɪŋ, -ɪd

studding-sail, -s 'stʌdɪŋseɪl [nautical pronunciation 'stʌnsl], -z

Studebaker 'stuːdəbeɪkə*

student, -s 'stjuːdnt, -s

studentship, -s 'stjuːdnt-ʃɪp, -s

studio, -s 'stjuːdɪəʊ [-djəʊ], -z

studious, -ly, -ness 'stjuːdjəs [-dɪəs], -lɪ, -nɪs [-nəs]

stud|y (s. v.), -ies, -ying, -ied 'stʌd|ɪ, -ɪz, -ɪɪŋ, -ɪd

stuff (s. v.), -s, -ing, -ed; -y, -ier, -iest, -iness stʌf, -s, -ɪŋ, -t; -ɪ, -ɪə*, -ɪɪst, -ɪnɪs [-ɪnəs]

stuffing (s.), -s 'stʌfɪŋ, -z

stultification ˌstʌltɪfɪ'keɪʃn

stulti|fy, -fies, -fying, -fied 'stʌltɪ|faɪ, -faɪz, -faɪɪŋ, -faɪd

stum stʌm

stumb|le (s. v.), -les, -ling, -led, -ler/s 'stʌmb|l, -lz, -lɪŋ, -ld, -lə*/z

stumbling-block, -s 'stʌmblɪŋblɒk, -s

stump (s. v.), -s, -ing, -ed; -y, -ier, -iest, -iness stʌmp, -s, -ɪŋ, -t [stʌmt]; -ɪ, -ɪə* [-jə*], -ɪɪst [-jɪst], -ɪnɪs [-ɪnəs]

stun, -s, -ning/ly, -ned stʌn, -z, -ɪŋ/lɪ, -d

stung (from sting) stʌŋ

stunk (from stink) stʌŋk

stunner, -s 'stʌnə*, -z

stunt (s. v.), -s, -ing, -ed stʌnt, -s, -ɪŋ, -ɪd

stupe, -s stjuːp, -s

stupefaction ˌstjuːpɪ'fækʃn [ˌstjʊpɪ'f-]

stupe|fy, -fies, -fying, -fied 'stjuːpɪ|faɪ ['stjʊp-], -faɪz, -faɪɪŋ, -faɪd

stupendous, -ly, -ness stjuː'pendəs [stjʊ'p-], -lɪ, -nɪs [-nəs]

stupid (s. adj.), -s, -er, -est, -ly, -ness 'stjuːpɪd ['stjʊp-, rarely 'stʊp-], -z, -ə*, -ɪst, -lɪ, -nɪs [-nəs]

stupidit|y, -ies stjuː'pɪdət|ɪ [stjʊ'p-, -ɪt|ɪ], -ɪz

stupor 'stjuːpə*

Sturdee 'stɜːdɪ

sturd|y, -ier, -iest, -ily, -iness 'stɜːd|ɪ, -ɪə* [-jə*], -ɪɪst [-jɪst], -ɪlɪ [-əlɪ], -ɪnɪs [-ɪnəs]

sturgeon, -s 'stɜːdʒən, -z

Sturtevant 'stɜːtɪvənt [-vænt]

stutter (s. v.), -s, -ing, -ed, -er/s 'stʌtə*, -z, -rɪŋ, -d, -rə*/z

Stuttgart 'stʊtgɑːt ('ʃtutgart)

Stuyvesant 'staɪvəsənt

st|y, -ies st|aɪ, -aɪz

Styche staɪtʃ

stye, -s staɪ, -z

Stygian 'stɪdʒɪən [-dʒən]

styl|e (s. v.), -es, -ing, -ed staɪl, -z, -ɪŋ, -d

stylet, -s 'staɪlɪt [-lət], -s

stylish, -ly, -ness 'staɪlɪʃ, -lɪ, -nɪs [-nəs]

stylist, -s 'staɪlɪst, -s

stylistic, -s staɪ'lɪstɪk, -s

475

stylite, -s 'staɪlaɪt, -s
Stylites (*Simeon S.*) staɪ'laɪti:z
stylization [-isa-] ˌstaɪlaɪ'zeɪʃn [-lɪ'z-]
stylize [-ise], -d 'staɪlaɪz, -d
stylograph, -s 'staɪləʊgrɑ:f [-græf], -s
stylographic ˌstaɪləʊ'græfɪk
styl|us, -uses, -i 'staɪl|əs, -əsɪz, -aɪ
stymie = stimy
styptic 'stɪptɪk
styrax, -es 'staɪəræks ['staɪr-], -ɪz
Styria, -n/s 'stɪrɪə, -n/z
Styx stɪks
suable 'sju:əbl ['sjuəbl]
Suaki|m, -n su:'ɑ:kɪ|m [sʊ'ɑ:-], -n
suasion 'sweɪʒn
suave, -r, -st, -ly, -ness swɑ:v [*old-fashioned* sweɪv], -ə*, -ɪst, -lɪ, -nɪs
[-nəs]
suavity 'swɑ:vətɪ ['sweɪv-, 'swæv-, -ɪtɪ]
sub (*s. prep.*), -s sʌb, -z
subacid ˌsʌb'æsɪd
subalpine ˌsʌb'ælpaɪn
subaltern, -s 'sʌbltən, -z
sub-bass, -es ˌsʌb'beɪs, -ɪz
subclass, -es 'sʌbklɑ:s, -ɪz
subclassification, -s 'sʌbˌklæsɪfɪ'keɪʃn
[ˈ-ˌ---ˌ--], -z
subclassi|fy, -fies, -fying, -fied ˌsʌb-'klæsɪ|faɪ, -faɪz, -faɪɪŋ, -faɪd
subcommittee, -s 'sʌbkəˌmɪtɪ, -z
subconscious, -ly, -ness sʌb'kɒnʃəs, -lɪ, -nɪs [-nəs]
subcutaneous ˌsʌbkju:'teɪnjəs [-kjʊ't-, -nɪəs]
subdean, -s ˌsʌb'di:n, -z
subdivid|e, -es, -ing, -ed ˌsʌbdɪ'vaɪd [ˈ--ˌ-], -z, -ɪŋ, -ɪd
subdivision, -s 'sʌbdɪˌvɪʒn [ˌ--'--], -z
subdominant, -s ˌsʌb'dɒmɪnənt, -s
subdual, -s səb'dju:əl [-'djʊəl], -z
subd|ue, -ues, -uing, -ued, -uer/s, -uable səb'd|ju:, -ju:z, -ju:ɪŋ [-jʊɪŋ], -ju:d, -ju:ə*/z [-jʊə*/z]; -ju:əbl [-jʊəbl]
sub-edit, -s, -ing, -ed ˌsʌb'edɪt, -s, -ɪŋ, -ɪd
sub-editor, -s; -ship/s ˌsʌb'edɪtə* [ˈ-ˌ---], -z; -ʃɪp/s
sub-famil|y, -ies ˌsʌb,fæməl|ɪ [-mɪl-], -ɪz
subfusc 'sʌbfʌsk
subgroup, -s 'sʌbgru:p, -s
sub-heading, -s 'sʌbˌhedɪŋ [ˌ-'--], -z
sub-human (*s. adj.*), -s ˌsʌb'hju:mən, -z
subjacent sʌb'dʒeɪsənt [səb-]
subject (*s. adj.*), -s 'sʌbdʒɪkt [-dʒekt], -s
subject (*v.*), -s, -ing, -ed səb'dʒekt [sʌb'dʒekt, *less commonly* 'sʌbdʒɪkt, 'sʌbdʒekt], -s, -ɪŋ, -ɪd

subjection səb'dʒekʃn
subjective, -ly, -ness səb'dʒektɪv [sʌb'dʒ-, ˌsʌb'dʒ-], -lɪ, -nɪs [-nəs]
subjectivism səb'dʒektɪvɪzəm [sʌb-]
subjectivity ˌsʌbdʒek'tɪvətɪ [-ɪtɪ]
subject-matter 'sʌbdʒɪktˌmætə*
subjoin, -s, -ing, -ed ˌsʌb'dʒɔɪn, -z, -ɪŋ, -d
sub judice ˌsʌb'dʒu:dɪsɪ [ˌsʊb'ju:dɪkɪ]
subjugat|e, -es, -ing, -ed, -or/s 'sʌb-dʒʊgeɪt [-dʒəg-], -s, -ɪŋ, -ɪd, -ə*/z
subjugation ˌsʌbdʒʊ'geɪʃn [-dʒə'g-]
subjunctive (*s. adj.*), -s səb'dʒʌŋktɪv, -z
sublease, -s ˌsʌb'li:s ['sʌbli:s], -ɪz
subless|ee/s, -or/s ˌsʌble's|i:/z, -ɔ:*/z
sublet, -s, -ting ˌsʌb'let, -s, -ɪŋ
sub-librarian, -s ˌsʌblaɪ'breərɪən, -z
sub-lieutenan|t/s, -cy, -cies ˌsʌblef-'tenən|t/s [-ləf't-]; -sɪ, -sɪz (*see note under* lieutenancy)
sublimate (*s.*), -s 'sʌblɪmət [-mɪt, -meɪt], -s
sublimat|e (*v.*), -es, -ing, -ed 'sʌblɪmeɪt, -s, -ɪŋ, -ɪd
sublimation ˌsʌblɪ'meɪʃn
sublim|e (*s. adj. v.*), -er, -est, -ely, -eness; -es, -ing, -ed sə'blaɪm, -ə*, -ɪst, -lɪ, -nɪs [-nəs]; -z, -ɪŋ, -d
subliminal ˌsʌb'lɪmɪnl [səb-, -mən-]
sublimity sə'blɪmətɪ [-ɪtɪ]
submachine-gun, -s ˌsʌbmə'ʃi:ngʌn [-'ʃi:ˌŋgʌn], -z
†submarin|e (*s. adj. v.*), -es, -ing, -ed ˌsʌbmə'ri:n ['sʌbməri:n], -z, -ɪŋ, -d
submerg|e, -es, -ing, -ed; -ence səb-'mɜ:dʒ [sʌb-], -ɪz, -ɪŋ, -d; -əns
submersible (*s. adj.*), -s səb'mɜ:səbl [sʌb-, -sɪbl], -z
submersion, -s səb'mɜ:ʃn [sʌb-], -z
submission, -s səb'mɪʃn, -z
submissive, -ly, -ness səb'mɪsɪv, -lɪ, -nɪs [-nəs]
submit, -s, -ting, -ted səb'mɪt, -s, -ɪŋ, -ɪd
submultiple, -s ˌsʌb'mʌltɪpl, -z
sub-normal ˌsʌb'nɔ:ml [*in contrast* '-ˌ--]
suboctave, -s 'sʌb,ɒktɪv, -z
subordinate (*s. adj.*), -s; -ly sə'bɔ:dɲət [-dənət, -dɪnət, -dnət, -ɪt], -s; -lɪ
subordinat|e (*v.*), -es, -ing, -ed sə'bɔ:-dɪneɪt, -s, -ɪŋ, -ɪd
subordination səˌbɔ:dɪ'neɪʃn
subordinative sə'bɔ:dɪnətɪv [-dɲ-, -dən-]
suborn, -s, -ing, -ed, -er/s sʌ'bɔ:n [sə'b-], -z, -ɪŋ, -d, -ə*/z
subornation ˌsʌbɔ:'neɪʃn
subpoena (*s. v.*), -s, -ing, -ed səb'pi:nə [ˌsʌb'p-, sə'p-], -z, -ɪŋ [-nərɪŋ], -d

sub-prefect, -s ˌsʌb'priːfekt [*in contrast* '-ˌ--], -s
subrogation ˌsʌbrəʊ'geɪʃn
sub rosa ˌsʌb'rəʊzə
subscrib|e, -es, -ing, -ed, -er/s səb-'skraɪb [-bz'k-], -z, -ɪŋ, -d, -ə*/z
subscript 'sʌbskrɪpt [-bzk-]
subscription, -s səb'skrɪpʃn [-bz'k-], -z
sub-section, -s 'sʌbˌsekʃn, -z
subsequent, -ly 'sʌbsɪkwənt, -lɪ
subserv|e, -es, -ing, -ed səb'sɜːv [sʌb-], -z, -ɪŋ, -d
subservien|ce, -cy, -t/ly səb'sɜːvjən|s [sʌb-, -vɪən-], -sɪ, -t/lɪ
subsid|e, -es, -ing, -ed səb'saɪd, -z, -ɪŋ, -ɪd
subsidence, -s səb'saɪdns ['sʌbsɪd-], -ɪz
subsidiar|y (*s. adj.*), -ies, -ily səb'sɪdjər|ɪ [-dɪə-], -ɪz, -ɪlɪ [-ɪlɪ]
subsidiz|e [-is|e], -es, -ing, -ed 'sʌb-sɪdaɪz [-səd-], -ɪz, -ɪŋ, -d
subsid|y, -ies 'sʌbsɪd|ɪ [-səd|ɪ], -ɪz
subsist, -s, -ing, -ed; -ence səb'sɪst, -s, -ɪŋ, -ɪd; -əns
subsoil, -s 'sʌbsɔɪl, -z
sub-species 'sʌbˌspiːʃiːz [-ʃɪz]
substance, -s 'sʌbstəns [-bzt-], -ɪz
substanti|al, -ally, -alness səb'stænʃ|l [-bz't-, -staːnʃ-], -əlɪ [-lɪ, -lɪ], -lnɪs [-nəs]
substantiality səbˌstænʃɪ'ælətɪ [-bzˌt-, -staːnʃ-, -ɪtɪ]
substantiat|e, -es, -ing, -ed səb'stæn-ʃɪeɪt [-bz't-, -staːnʃ-, -ʃjeɪt, -nsɪ-], -s, -ɪŋ, -ɪd
substantiation səbˌstænʃɪ'eɪʃn [-bzˌt-, -staːnʃ-, -nsɪ-]
substantival ˌsʌbstən'taɪvl [-bzt-]
substantive (*s.*), -s 'sʌbstəntɪv [-bzt-], -z
substantive (*adj.*), -ly, -ness 'sʌbstəntɪv [-bzt-, səb'stæn-], -lɪ, -nɪs [-nəs]
Note.—Generally səb'stæntɪv *when applied to* rank, pay, *etc.*
substitut|e (*s. v.*), -es, -ing, -ed 'sʌb-stɪtjuːt [-bzt-], -s, -ɪŋ, -ɪd
substitution, -s ˌsʌbstɪ'tjuːʃn [-bzt-], -z
substitu|tional, -tionally ˌsʌbstɪ'tjuː|ʃənl [-bzt-, -ʃnəl, -ʃpl, -ʃnl, -ʃənəl], -ʃpəlɪ [-ʃnəlɪ, -ʃplɪ, -ʃnlɪ, -ʃənəlɪ]
substitutive 'sʌbstɪtjuːtɪv [-bzt-]
substratosphere, -s ˌsʌb'strætəˌsfɪə* [-'straːt-, *rarely* -'streɪt-, -təʊs-], -z
substrat|um, -a ˌsʌb'straːt|əm [-reɪt-, '-ˌ--], -ə
substructure, -s 'sʌbˌstrʌktʃə*, -z
subsum|e, -es, -ing, -ed səb'sjuːm, -z, -ɪŋ, -d
subtangent, -s ˌsʌb'tændʒənt, -s
subtenan|cy, -t/s ˌsʌb'tenən|sɪ, -t/s

subtend, -s, -ing, -ed səb'tend, -z, -ɪŋ, -ɪd
subterfuge, -s 'sʌbtəfjuːdʒ, -ɪz
subterranean ˌsʌbtə'reɪnjən [-nɪən]
subterraneous ˌsʌbtə'reɪnjəs [-nɪəs]
subtil(e) 'sʌtl
subtility sʌb'tɪlətɪ [-ɪtɪ]
subtiliz|e [-is|e], -es, -ing, -ed 'sʌtɪlaɪz [-tlaɪz], -ɪz, -ɪŋ, -d
subtilty 'sʌtltɪ [-tɪltɪ]
sub-title, -s 'sʌbˌtaɪtl [ˌ-'--], -z
subt|le, -ler, -lest, -ly, -leness 'sʌt|l, -lə* [-lə*], -lɪst [-lɪst], -lɪ, -lnɪs [-nəs]
subtlet|y, -ies 'sʌtlt|ɪ, -ɪz
subtopia sʌb'təʊpɪə [-pjə]
subtract, -s, -ing, -ed səb'trækt, -s, -ɪŋ, -ɪd
subtraction, -s səb'trækʃn, -z
subtrahend, -s 'sʌbtrəhend, -z
subtropical ˌsʌb'trɒpɪkl
suburb, -s 'sʌbɜːb [-bəb], -z
suburban sə'bɜːbən
suburbaniz|e [-is|e], -es, -ing, -ed sə'bɜːbənaɪz, -ɪz, -ɪŋ, -d
suburbia sə'bɜːbɪə [-bjə]
subvariet|y, -ies 'sʌbvəˌraɪət|ɪ, -ɪz
subvention, -s səb'venʃn [sʌb-], -z
subver|sion, -sive səb'vɜː|ʃn [sʌb-], -sɪv
subvert, -s, -ing, -ed sʌb'vɜːt [səb-], -s, -ɪŋ, -ɪd
subway, -s 'sʌbweɪ, -z
succeed, -s, -ing, -ed sək'siːd, -z, -ɪŋ, -ɪd
succentor, -s sək'sentə* [sʌk-], -z
success, -es; -ful, -fully sək'ses, -ɪz; -fʊl, -fʊlɪ [-fəlɪ]
succession, -s sək'seʃn, -z
successive, -ly sək'sesɪv, -lɪ
successor, -s sək'sesə*, -z
succinct, -ly, -ness sək'sɪŋkt [sʌk-], -lɪ, -nɪs [-nəs]
succory 'sʌkərɪ
succotash 'sʌkətæʃ
Succoth 'sʌkəs, su'kɒt
succour (*s. v.*), -s, -ing, -ed 'sʌkə*, -z, -rɪŋ, -d
succub|a, -ae, -us, -i 'sʌkjʊb|ə, -iː, -əs, -aɪ
succulen|ce, -t/ly 'sʌkjʊlən|s [-kjəl-], -t/lɪ
succumb, -s, -ing, -ed sə'kʌm, -z, -ɪŋ, -d
succursal, -s sʌ'kɜːsl, -z
such sʌtʃ (*normal form*), sətʃ (*occasional weak form*)
such-and-such 'sʌtʃənsʌtʃ
suchlike 'sʌtʃlaɪk
suck (*s. v.*), -s, -ing, -ed, -er/s sʌk, -s, -ɪŋ, -t, -ə*/z
sucking-pig, -s 'sʌkɪŋpɪg, -z

477

suck|le (*s. v.*), **-les, -ling, -led** 'sʌk|l, -lz, -lɪŋ [-lɪŋ], -ld
suckling (*s.*), **-s** 'sʌklɪŋ, -z
suction 'sʌkʃn
Suda 'suːdə
Sudan suːˈdɑːn [suˈdɑ-, -ˈdæn]
Sudanese ˌsuːdəˈniːz [*also* '— *when attributive*]
Sudanic suːˈdænɪk [suˈd-]
sudarium (*s. adj.*), **-s** suːˈdeərɪəm [sju-, sjuː-, su-], -z
sudatory 'suːdətərɪ ['sjuː-]
Sudbury 'sʌdbərɪ
sudd sʌd
sudd|en, **-enest, -enly, -enness** 'sʌd|n, -nɪst, -nlɪ, -nnɪs [-nnəs]
Sudeley 'sjuːdlɪ
sudorific (*s. adj.*), **-s** ˌsuːdəˈrɪfɪk [ˌsjuː-, -dɒˈr-], -s
suds sʌdz
sue (**S.**), **sues, suing, sued** suː [sjuː], suːz [sjuːz], 'suːɪŋ ['suɪŋ, 'sjuːɪŋ, 'sjuɪŋ], suːd [sjuːd]
suède sweɪd [sɥɛːd]
suet, **-y** 'suɪt ['sjuɪt, 'suːɪt, 'sjuːɪt], -ɪ
Suetonius swiːˈtəunjəs [swɪˈt-, -nɪəs]
Suez 'suːɪz ['sjuːɪz, 'suːɪz, 'sjuːɪz]
suff|er, **-ers, -ering/s, -ered, -erer/s; -erable, -erance** 'sʌf|ə*, -əz, -ərɪŋ/z, -əd, -ərə*/z; -ərəbl, -ərəns
suffic|e, **-es, -ing, -ed** səˈfaɪs, -ɪz, -ɪŋ, -t
sufficien|cy, **-t/ly** səˈfɪʃn|sɪ, -t/lɪ
suffix (*s.*), **-es** 'sʌfɪks, -ɪz
suffix (*v.*), **-es, -ing, -ed** 'sʌfɪks [-'-], -ɪz, -ɪŋ, -t
suffocat|e, **-es, -ing/ly, -ed** 'sʌfəkeɪt, -s, -ɪŋ/lɪ, -d
suffocation ˌsʌfəˈkeɪʃn
Suffolk 'sʌfək
suffragan (*s. adj.*), **-s** 'sʌfrəgən, -z
suffrage, **-s** 'sʌfrɪdʒ, -ɪz
suffragette, **-s** ˌsʌfrəˈdʒet, -s
suffragist, **-s** 'sʌfrədʒɪst, -s
suffus|e, **-es, -ing, -ed** səˈfjuːz [sʌˈf-], -ɪz, -ɪŋ, -d
suffusion, **-s** səˈfjuːʒn [sʌˈf-], -z
sufi, **-s; -sm** 'suːfɪ, -z; -zəm
sugar (*s. v.*), **-s, -ing, -ed** 'ʃʊgə*, -z, -rɪŋ, -d
sugar-basin, **-s** 'ʃʊgəˌbeɪsn, -z
sugar-cane, **-s** 'ʃʊgəkeɪn, -z
sugarloa|f, **-ves** 'ʃʊgələu|f, -vz
sugar-plum, **-s** 'ʃʊgəplʌm, -z
sugar-refiner, **-s** 'ʃʊgərɪˌfaɪnə*, -z
sugar-refiner|y, **-ies** 'ʃʊgərɪˌfaɪnər|ɪ, -ɪz
sugar-tongs 'ʃʊgətɒŋz
sugar|y, **-iest, -iness** 'ʃʊgər|ɪ, -ɪɪst, -ɪnɪs [-ɪnəs]

suggest, **-s, -ing, -ed** səˈdʒest, -s, -ɪŋ, -ɪd
suggestion, **-s** səˈdʒestʃən [-eʃtʃ-], -z
suggestive, **-ly, -ness** səˈdʒestɪv, -lɪ, -nɪs [-nəs]
suicidal suɪˈsaɪdl [ˌsuːɪ-, sjuɪ-, ˌsjuːɪ-, '----]
suicide, **-s** 'suɪsaɪd ['suːɪ-, 'sjuɪ-, 'sjuːɪ-], -z
sui generis ˌsjuaɪˈdʒenərɪs [ˌsuː-, ˌsjuː-, ˌsuː-, -iːˈgen-]
sui juris ˌsjuaɪˈdʒuərɪs [ˌsuː-, ˌsjuː-, ˌsuː, -ˈdʒɔər-, -ˈdʒɔːr-, -iːˈjuərɪs]
Suirdale 'ʃɜːdl [-dəl]
suit (*s. v.*), **-s, -ing/s, -ed, -or/s** suːt [sjuːt], -s, -ɪŋ/z, -ɪd, -ə*/z
suitability ˌsuːtəˈbɪlətɪ [ˌsjuː-, -lɪt-]
suitab|le, **-ly, -leness** 'suːtəb|l ['sjuː-], -lɪ, -lnɪs [-nəs]
suit-case, **-s** 'suːtkeɪs ['sjuːt-], -ɪz
suite, **-s** swiːt, -s
sukiyaki ˌsukɪˈjækɪ
sulcal 'sʌlkəl [-kl]
sulcate 'sʌlkeɪt [-kɪt, -kət]
sulcalization [-isa-] ˌsʌlkəlaɪˈzeɪʃn
sulcaliz|e [-is|e], **-es, -ing, -ed** 'sʌlkəlaɪz, -ɪz, -ɪŋ, -d
Suleiman ˌsuleɪˈmɑːn ['---]
Suliman ˌsulɪˈmɑːn ['---]
sulk (*s. v.*), **-s, -ing, -ed; -y, -ier, -iest, -ily, -iness** sʌlk, -s, -ɪŋ, -t; -ɪ, -ɪə* [-jə*], -ɪɪst [-jɪst], -ɪlɪ [-əlɪ], -ɪnɪs [-ɪnəs]
Sulla 'sʌlə ['sulə]
sullen, **-est, -ly, -ness** 'sʌlən, -ɪst, -lɪ, -nɪs [-nəs]
Sullivan 'sʌlɪvən
sull|y (**S.**), **-ies, -ying, -ied** 'sʌl|ɪ, -ɪz, -ɪɪŋ, -ɪd
sulphanilamide ˌsʌlfəˈnɪləmaɪd
sulphate, **-s** 'sʌlfeɪt [-fɪt, -fət], -s
sulphi|de/s, **-te/s** 'sʌlfaɪ|d/z, -t/s
sulphonamide, **-s** sʌlˈfɒnəmaɪd, -z
sulphur 'sʌlfə*
sulphureous sʌlˈfjuərɪəs [-ˈfjɔər-, -ˈfjɔːr-]
sulphuretted 'sʌlfjuretɪd [-fər-]
sulphuric sʌlˈfjuərɪk [-ˈfjɔər-, -ˈfjɔːr-]
sulphurous 'sʌlfərəs [-fjʊr-]
sulphury 'sʌlfərɪ
sultan (**S.**), **-s** 'sʌltən, -z
sultana (*kind of raisin*), **-s** səlˈtɑːnə [sʌl-], -z
Sultana (*Sultan's wife, mother, etc.*), **-s** sʌlˈtɑːnə, -z
sultanate, **-s** 'sʌltənət [-neɪt, -nɪt], -s
sultr|y, **-ier, -iest, -ily, -iness** 'sʌltr|ɪ, -ɪə*, -ɪɪst, -əlɪ [-ɪlɪ], -ɪnɪs [-ɪnəs]
sum (*s. v.*), **-s, -ming, -med** sʌm, -z, -ɪŋ, -d

sumach, -s 'ʃuːmæk ['sjuː-, 'suː-], -s
Sumatra su'maːtrə [sjʊ-, suː-, sjuː-]
Sumerian suː'mɪərɪən [sjuː-, sʊ'm-,
sjʊ'm-]
summariz|e [is|e], -es, -ing, -ed
'sʌməraɪz, -ɪz, -ɪŋ, -d
summar|y (s. adj.), -ies, -ily, -iness
'sʌmər|ɪ, -ɪz, -əlɪ [-ɪlɪ], -ɪnɪs [-ɪnəs]
summation, -s sʌ'meɪʃn, -z
summer, -s; -like 'sʌmə*, -z; -laɪk
Summerfield, -s 'sʌməfiːld, -z
summerhou|se, -ses 'sʌməhaʊ|s, -zɪz
summertime 'sʌmətaɪm
Summerville 'sʌməvɪl
summery 'sʌmərɪ
summing-up, summings-up ˌsʌmɪŋ'ʌp,
ˌsʌmɪŋz'ʌp
summit, -s 'sʌmɪt, -s
summon, -s, -ing, -ed, -er/s 'sʌmən, -z,
-ɪŋ, -d, -ə*/z
summons (s. v.), -es, -ing, -ed 'sʌmənz,
-ɪz, -ɪŋ, -d
Sumner 'sʌmnə*
sump, -s sʌmp, -s
sumpter (S.), -s 'sʌmptə*, -z
sumptuary 'sʌmptjʊərɪ [-tjwərɪ, -tjʊrɪ,
-tʃʊərɪ, -tʃwərɪ, -tʃʊrɪ]
sumptuous, -ly, -ness 'sʌmptʃʊəs
[-tʃwəs, -tjʊəs, -tjwəs], -lɪ, -nɪs [-nəs]
Sumsion 'sʌmʃn
Sumurun ˌsʊmʊ'ruːn
sun (s. v.), -s, -ning, -ned sʌn, -z, -ɪŋ, -d
sun-ba|th, -ths 'sʌnbɑː|θ, -ðz
sun-bath|e, -es, -ing, -ed, -er/s 'sʌn-
beɪð, -z, -ɪŋ, -d, -ə*/z
sunbeam (S.), -s 'sʌnbiːm, -z
sunblind, -s 'sʌnblaɪnd, -z
sun-bonnet, -s 'sʌn,bɒnɪt, -s
sunburn, -s, -t 'sʌnbɜːn, -z, -t
Sunbury 'sʌnbərɪ
Sunda 'sʌndə
sundae, -s 'sʌndeɪ, -z
Sundanese ˌsʌndə'niːz
Sunday, -s 'sʌndɪ [-deɪ], -z
sunder, -s, -ing, -ed 'sʌndə*, -z, -rɪŋ, -d
Sunderland 'sʌndələnd
sundial, -s 'sʌndaɪəl, -z
sundown 'sʌndaʊn
sun-dried 'sʌndraɪd
sundr|y, -ies 'sʌndr|ɪ, -ɪz
sun-fish 'sʌnfɪʃ
sunflower, -s 'sʌn,flaʊə*, -z
sung (from sing) sʌŋ
Sung (Chinese dynasty) sʊŋ [sʌŋ]
sun|-glasses, -hat/s 'sʌŋglɑː|sɪz, -hæt/s
sun-helmet, -s 'sʌn,helmɪt [ˌ-'--], -s
sunk (from sink) sʌŋk
sunken (from sink) 'sʌŋkən

sunlamp, -s 'sʌnlæmp, -s
sun|less, -light, -like 'sʌn|lɪs [-ləs], -laɪt,
-laɪk
Sunningdale 'sʌnɪŋdeɪl
sunn|y, -ier, -iest, -iness 'sʌn|ɪ, -ɪə*,
-ɪɪst, -ɪnɪs [-ɪnəs]
Sunnyside 'sʌnɪsaɪd
sunproof 'sʌnpruːf
sunrise, -s 'sʌnraɪz, -ɪz
sunset, -s 'sʌnset, -s
sunshade, -s 'sʌnʃeɪd, -z
sunshin|e, -y 'sʌnʃaɪn, -ɪ
sun-spot, -s 'sʌnspɒt, -s
sunstroke, -s 'sʌnstrəʊk, -s
suntan, -s, -ned 'sʌntæn, -z, -d
sun-trap, -s 'sʌntræp, -s
sun-worship, -per/s 'sʌn,wɜːʃɪp, -ə*/z
sup (s. v.), -s, -ping, -ped sʌp, -s, -ɪŋ, -t
super (s. adj.), -s 'suːpə* ['sjuː-], -z
superab|le, -ly, -leness 'suːpərəb|l
['sjuː-], -lɪ, -lnɪs [-nəs]
superabundan|ce, -t/ly ˌsuːpərə'bʌnd-
ən|s [ˌsjuː-], -t/lɪ
superadd, -s, -ing, -ed ˌsuːpər'æd
[ˌsjuː-], -z, -ɪŋ, -ɪd
superannuat|e, -es, -ing, -ed ˌsuːpə-
'rænjʊeɪt [ˌsjuːpə'r-, sjʊpə'r-,
sʊpə'r-], -s, -ɪŋ, -ɪd
superannuation, -s 'suːpəˌrænjʊ'eɪʃn
['sjuː-], -z
superb, -ly, -ness suː'pɜːb [sjuː-, sʊ-,
sjʊ-], -lɪ, -nɪs [-nəs]
superbus (extra large bus), -es 'suːpəbʌs
['sjuː-], -ɪz
Superbus sjuː'pɜːbəs [suː-, sjʊ-, sʊ-]
supercargo, -es 'suːpəˌkɑːgəʊ ['sjuː-], -z
supercharg|e (s. v.), -es, -ing, -ed
'suːpətʃɑːdʒ ['sjuː-], -ɪz, -ɪŋ, -d
supercilious, -ly, -ness ˌsuːpə'sɪlɪəs
[ˌsjuːpə's-, sjʊpə's-, sʊpə's-, -ljəs], -lɪ,
-nɪs [-nəs]
supererogation 'suːpərˌerə'geɪʃn ['sjuː-,
-rəʊ'g-]
supererogatory ˌsuːpəre'rɒgətərɪ [ˌsjuː-,
-rɪ'r-]
superfici|al, -ally, -alness ˌsuːpə'fɪʃ|l
[ˌsjuːpə'f-, sjʊpə'f-, sʊpə'f-], -əlɪ [-lɪ],
-lnɪs [-nəs]
superficialit|y, -ies 'suːpəˌfɪʃɪ'æləti|ɪ
['sjuː-, -ɪt|ɪ], -ɪz
superficies ˌsuːpə'fɪʃiːz [ˌsjuːpə'f-,
sjʊpə'f-, sʊpə'f-, -ʃiːz]
superfine ˌsuːpə'faɪn [ˌsjuː-, '---]
superfluit|y, -ies ˌsuːpə'fluət|ɪ [ˌsjuː-
pə'f-, sjʊpə'f-, sʊpə'f-, -ɪt|ɪ], -ɪz
superfluous, -ly, -ness suː'pɜːfluəs
[sjuː-, sʊ-, sjʊ-, -flwəs], -lɪ, -nɪs [-nəs]
superglottal ˌsuːpə'glɒtl [ˌsjuː-, '--ˌ--]

479

superhet, -s 'su:pəhet ['sju:-], -s
superheterodyne, -s ˌsu:pə'hetərədaɪn [ˌsju:-, -rəʊd-], -z
superhuman, -ly ˌsu:pə'hju:mən [ˌsju:-], -lɪ
superimpos|e, -es, -ing, -ed ˌsu:pər-ɪm'pəʊz [ˌsju:-], -ɪz, -ɪŋ, -d
superintend, -s, -ing, -ed; -ence, -ent/s ˌsu:pərɪn'tend [ˌsju:-], -z, -ɪŋ, -ɪd; -əns, -ənt/s
superior (s. adj.), -s su:'pɪərɪə* [sju:'p-, sʊ'p-, sjʊ'p-, sə'p-], -z
superiorit|y, -ies su:ˌpɪərɪ'ɒrət|ɪ [sju:-, sʊˌp-, sjʊˌp-, səˌp-, -ɪt|ɪ], -ɪz
superlative (s. adj.), -s, -ly, -ness su:'pə:lətɪv [sju:-, sʊ'p-, sjʊ'p-, -'pə:|tɪv], -z, -lɪ, -nɪs [-nəs]
super|man, -men 'su:pə|mæn ['sju:-], -men
supermarket, -s 'su:pəˌmɑ:kɪt['sju:-], -s
supernal su:'pə:nl [sju:-, sʊ'p-, sjʊ'p-]
supernatur|al, -ally ˌsu:pə'næt∫r|əl [ˌsju:pə'n-, sjʊpə'n-, sʊpə'n-, -t∫ʊr-, -t∫ər-], -əlɪ
supernormal ˌsu:pə'nɔ:ml [ˌsju:-]
supernumerar|y (s. adj.), -ies ˌsu:pə-'nju:mərər|ɪ [ˌsju:-], -ɪz
superoctave, -s 'su:pərˌɒktɪv ['sju:-], -z
superpos|e, -es, -ing, -ed ˌsu:pə'pəʊz [ˌsju:-], -ɪz, -ɪŋ, -d
superposition, -s ˌsu:pəpə'zɪ∫n [ˌsju:-, -pʊ'z-], -z
superpriorit|y, -ies ˌsu:pəpraɪ'ɒrət|ɪ [ˌsju:-, -ɪt|ɪ], -ɪz
superscrib|e, -es, -ing, -ed ˌsu:pə'skraɪb [ˌsju:-, '---], -z, -ɪŋ, -d
superscript 'su:pəskrɪpt ['sju:-]
superscription, -s ˌsu:pə'skrɪp∫n [ˌsju:pə's-, sjʊpə's-, sʊpə's-], -z
supersed|e, -es, -ing, -ed ˌsu:pə'si:d [ˌsju:pə's-, sjʊpə's-, sʊpə's-], -z, -ɪŋ, -ɪd
supersession ˌsu:pə'se∫n [ˌsju:pə's-, sjʊpə's-, sʊpə's-]
supersonic ˌsu:pə'sɒnɪk [ˌsju:-, also '--ˌ-- when attributive]
superstition, -s ˌsu:pə'stɪ∫n [ˌsju:pə's-, sjʊpə's-, sʊpə's-], -z
superstitious, -ly, -ness ˌsu:pə'stɪ∫əs [ˌsju:pə's-, sjʊpə's-, sʊpə's-], -lɪ, -nɪs [-nəs]
superstructure, -s 'su:pəˌstrʌkt∫ə* ['sju:-], -z
super-submarine, -s ˌsu:pə'sʌbməri:n [ˌsju:-], -z
supertax, -es 'su:pətæks ['sju:-], -ɪz
supertonic, -s ˌsu:pə'tɒnɪk [ˌsju:-, in contrast '--ˌ-], -s

superven|e, -es, -ing, -ed ˌsu:pə'vi:n [ˌsju:pə'v-, sjʊpə'v-, sʊpə'v-], -z, -ɪŋ, -d
supervis|e, -es, -ing, -ed, -or/s 'su:pə-vaɪz ['sju:-, ˌsju:pə'v-, ˌsu:pə'v-, sjʊpə'v-, sʊpə'v-], -ɪz, -ɪŋ, -d, -ə*/z
supervision, -s ˌsu:pə'vɪʒn [ˌsju:pə'v-, sjʊpə'v-, sʊpə'v-], -z
supervisory 'su:pəvaɪzərɪ ['sju:-, ˌsju:-pə'v-, ˌsu:pə'v-, sjʊpə'v-, sʊpə'v-]
supine (s.), -s 'su:paɪn ['sju:-], -z
supine (adj.), -ly, -ness su:'paɪn [sju:'p-, '--], -lɪ, -nɪs [-nəs]
supper, -s, -less 'sʌpə*, -z, -lɪs [-ləs]
supplant, -s, -ing, -ed, -er/s sə'plɑ:nt, -s, -ɪŋ, -ɪd, -ə*/z
suppl|e, -eness, -ly 'sʌp|l, -lnɪs [-nəs], -lɪ [-lɪ]
supplement (s.), -s 'sʌplɪmənt, -s
supplement (v.), -s, -ing, -ed 'sʌplɪment [ˌ--'-], -s, -ɪŋ, -ɪd
supplement|al, -ary ˌsʌplɪ'ment|l, -ərɪ
supplementation ˌsʌplɪmen'teɪ∫n
suppliant (s. adj.), -s, -ly 'sʌplɪənt [-pljənt], -s, -lɪ
supplicant, -s 'sʌplɪkənt, -s
supplicat|e, -es, -ing/ly, -ed 'sʌplɪkeɪt, -s, -ɪŋ/lɪ, -ɪd
supplication, -s ˌsʌplɪ'keɪ∫n, -z
supplicatory 'sʌplɪkətərɪ [-keɪtərɪ]
suppl|y (s. v.), -ies, -ying, -ied, -ier/s sə'pl|aɪ, -aɪz, -aɪɪŋ, -aɪd, -aɪə*/z
support (s. v.), -s, -ing, -ed, -er/s; -able, -ably sə'pɔ:t, -s, -ɪŋ, -ɪd, -ə*/z; -əbl, -əblɪ
supportive sə'pɔ:tɪv
suppos|e, -es, -ing, -ed sə'pəʊz [spəʊz], -ɪz, -ɪŋ, -d
supposedly sə'pəʊzɪdlɪ
supposition, -s ˌsʌpə'zɪ∫n [-pʊ'z-], -z
supposi|tional, -tionally ˌsʌpə'zɪ|∫ənl [-pʊ'z-, -∫nəl, -∫n̩l, -∫nl̩, -∫ənəl], -∫n̩əlɪ [-∫nəlɪ, -∫n̩lɪ, -∫nlɪ, -∫ənəlɪ]
supposititious, -ly, -ness sə,pɒzɪ'tɪ∫əs, -lɪ, -nɪs [-nəs]
suppositor|y, -ies sə'pɒzɪtər|ɪ, -ɪz
suppress, -es, -ing, -ed, -or/s; -ible sə'pres, -ɪz, -ɪŋ, -t, -ə*/z; -əbl [-ɪbl]
suppression, -s sə'pre∫n, -z
suppurat|e, -es, -ing, -ed 'sʌpjʊəreɪt, -s, -ɪŋ, -ɪd
suppuration, -s ˌsʌpjʊə'reɪ∫n, -z
supra (in vide s.) 'su:prə ['sju:-]
supradental ˌsu:prə'dentl [ˌsju:-]
supra-national ˌsu:prə'næ∫ənl [ˌsju:-, -∫nəl, -∫n̩l, -∫nl, -∫ənəl]
suprarenal ˌsu:prə'ri:nl [ˌsju:-, '--ˌ--]

480

suprasegmental ˌsuːprəsegˈmentl
[ˌsjuː-]
supremac|y, -ies suˈpreməsɪ [sjʊˈp-,
sjuːˈp-, suːˈp-], -ɪz
supreme, -ly, -ness suˈpriːm [suːˈp-,
sjʊˈp-, sjuːˈp-], -lɪ, -nɪs [-nəs]
sura, -s ˈsuərə, -z
surah ˈsjuərə
surat (cotton fabric) suˈræt
Surat ˈsuərət [ˈsuːrət, suˈrɑːt, suˈræt]
(Hindi surət)
Surbiton ˈsɜːbɪtn
surceas|e (s. v.), **-es, -ing, -ed** sɜːˈsiːs,
-ɪz, -ɪŋ, -t
surcharge (s.), **-s** ˈsɜːtʃɑːdʒ [ˌsɜːˈtʃ-],
-ɪz
surcharg|e (v.), **-es, -ing, -ed** sɜːˈtʃɑːdʒ
[ˈ--], -ɪz, -ɪŋ, -d
surcingle, -s ˈsɜːsɪŋgl, -z
surcoat, -s ˈsɜːkəʊt, -s
surd (s. adj.), **-s; -ity** sɜːd, -z; -ətɪ [-ɪtɪ]
sure (adj. adv.), **-r, -st, -ly, -ness; -footed**
ʃɔː* [ʃɔə*, ʃʊə*], -rə*, -rɪst, -lɪ [ˈʃʊəlɪ,
ˈʃəəlɪ], -nɪs [ˈʃʊənɪs, ˈʃɔənɪs, -nəs];
-ˈfʊtɪd.
suret|y, -ies; -yship/s ˈʃɔːrətɪ [ˈʃʊə-,
ˈʃɔə-, ˈʃʊət-], -ɪz; -ɪʃɪp/s
surf sɜːf
surfac|e (s. v.), **-es, -ing, -ed** ˈsɜːfɪs
[-fəs], -ɪz, -ɪŋ, -t
surf-bathing ˈsɜːfˌbeɪðɪŋ
surfboard, -s ˈsɜːfbɔːd [-bɔːəd], -z
surf-boat, -s ˈsɜːfbəʊt, -s
surfeit (s. v.), **-s, -ing, -ed** ˈsɜːfɪt, -s, -ɪŋ,
-ɪd
surfing sɜːfɪŋ
surf-riding ˈsɜːfˌraɪdɪŋ
surg|e (s. v.), **-es, -ing, -ed** sɜːdʒ, -ɪz,
-ɪŋ, -d
surgeon, -s ˈsɜːdʒən, -z
surger|y, -ies ˈsɜːdʒərɪ, -ɪz
surgic|al, -ally ˈsɜːdʒɪkl, -əlɪ
Surinam ˌsʊərɪˈnæm
surl|y, -ier, -iest, -ily, -iness ˈsɜːlɪ, -ɪə*
[-jə*], -ɪɪst [-jɪst], -ɪlɪ [-əlɪ], -ɪnɪs
[-ɪnəs]
surmise (s.), **-s** ˈsɜːmaɪz [sɜːˈmaɪz,
səˈm-], -ɪz
surmis|e (v.), **-es, -ing, -ed** sɜːˈmaɪz
[ˈ--, səˈm-], -ɪz, -ɪŋ, -d
surmount, -s, -ing, -ed; -able sɜː-
ˈmaʊnt [səˈm-], -s, -ɪŋ, -ɪd; -əbl
surnam|e (s. v.), **-es, -ing, -ed** ˈsɜːneɪm,
-z, -ɪŋ, -d
surpass, -es, -ing/ly, -ed; -able səˈpɑːs
[sɜːˈp-], -ɪz, -ɪŋ/lɪ, -t; -əbl
surplice, -s, -d ˈsɜːplɪs [-pləs], -ɪz, -t
surplus, -es; -age ˈsɜːpləs, -ɪz; -ɪdʒ

surpris|e (s. v.), **-es, -ing/ly, -ed, -edly**
səˈpraɪz, -ɪz, -ɪŋ/lɪ, -d, -ɪdlɪ
†**surreali|sm, -st/s** səˈrɪəlɪ|zəm [sjʊ-,
sʊ-], -st/s
surrend|er (s. v.), **-ers, -ering, -ered**
səˈrend|ə*, -əz, -ərɪŋ, -əd
surreptitious, -ly ˌsʌrəpˈtɪʃəs [-rɪp-,
-rep-], -lɪ
Surrey ˈsʌrɪ
surrogate, -s ˈsʌrəgeɪt [-rʊg-, -gɪt,
-gət], -s
surround (s. v.), **-s, -ing/s, -ed** səˈraʊnd,
-z, -ɪŋ/z, -ɪd
surtax, -es ˈsɜːtæks, -ɪz
Surtees ˈsɜːtiːz
surtout, -s ˈsɜːtuː [ˌ-ˈ-], -z
surveillance sɜːˈveɪləns [səˈv-]
survey (s.), **-s** ˈsɜːveɪ [ˌ-ˈ-], -z
survey (v.), **-s, -ing, -ed** səˈveɪ [sɜːˈveɪ],
-z, -ɪŋ, -d
surveyor, -s səˈveɪə*, -z
surviv|e, -es, -ing, -ed, -or/s; -al/s
səˈvaɪv, -z, -ɪŋ, -d, -ə*/z; -l/z
Susan ˈsuːzn
Susanna suːˈzænə [sʊˈz-]
susceptibilit|y, -ies səˌseptəˈbɪlətɪ
[-tɪˈb-, -lɪt-], -ɪz
susceptib|le, -ly səˈseptəb|l [-tɪb-], -lɪ
susceptive səˈseptɪv
suspect (s. adj.), **-s** ˈsʌspekt, -s
suspect (v.), **-s, -ing, -ed** səˈspekt, -s,
-ɪŋ, -ɪd
suspend, -s, -ing, -ed, -er/s səˈspend, -z,
-ɪŋ, -ɪd, -ə*/z
suspens|e, -ible səˈspens, -əbl [-ɪbl]
suspensibility səˌspensɪˈbɪlətɪ [-sə'b-,
-lɪt-]
suspension, -s səˈspenʃn, -z
suspens|ive, -ory səˈspens|ɪv, -ərɪ
suspicion, -s səˈspɪʃn, -z
suspicious, -ly, -ness səˈspɪʃəs, -lɪ, -nɪs
[-nəs]
Sussams ˈsʌsəmz
Sussex ˈsʌsɪks
sustain, -s, -ing, -ed, -er/s; -able
səˈsteɪn, -z, -ɪŋ, -d, -ə*/z; -əbl
sustenance ˈsʌstɪnəns [-tən-, -tnəns]
sustentation ˌsʌstenˈteɪʃn [-tən-]
susurration, -s ˌsuːsəˈreɪʃn [ˌsjuː-], -z
Sutherland ˈsʌðələnd
Sutlej ˈsʌtlɪdʒ [-ledʒ] (Hindi sətlwɪ)
sutler, -s ˈsʌtlə*, -z
Sutro ˈsuːtrəʊ
suttee, -s ˈsʌtiː [sʌˈtiː] (Hindi səti),
-z
Sutton ˈsʌtn
suture, -s ˈsuːtʃə* [-tjə*], -z
suzerain, -s ˈsuːzərem [ˈsjuː-], -z

481

suzeraint|y, -ies 'suːzəreɪnt|ɪ ['sjuː-, -rən-], -ɪz

svarabhakti ˌsvʌrə'bʌktɪ [ˌsvɑːr-, -'bæk-, -tiː] (*Hindi* svərəbhəkti)

svelte svelt

Svengali sveŋ'gɑːlɪ

Sverdlov 'sveədlɒv [-lɒf, -ləf] ('svjerdləf)

Sverdlovsk 'sveədlɒvsk [-ləvsk, -ləfsk] ('svjerdləfsk)

swab (*s. v.*), -s, -bing, -bed, -ber/s swɒb, -z, -ɪŋ, -d, -ə*/z

Swabia, -n/s 'sweɪbjə [-bɪə], -n/z

swaddl|e, -les, -ling, -led 'swɒd|l, -lz, -lɪŋ [-lɪŋ], -ld

swaddling-clothes 'swɒdlɪŋkləʊðz [-d|ɪ-, *old-fashioned* -kləʊz]

Swadling 'swɒdlɪŋ

Swaffer 'swɒfə*

swag swæg

swag|le (*s. v.*), -es, -ing, -ed sweɪdʒ, -ɪz, -ɪŋ, -d

swagg|ler (*s. v.*), -ers, -ering/ly, -ered, -erer/s 'swæg|ə*, -əz, -ərɪŋ/lɪ, -əd, -ərə*/z

Swahili, -s swɑː'hiːlɪ [swə'h-], -z

swain (S.), -s sweɪn, -z

swall|ow (*s. v.*), -ows, -owing, -owed 'swɒl|əʊ, -əʊz, -əʊɪŋ, -əʊd

swallow-tail, -s, -ed 'swɒləʊteɪl, -z, -d

swam (*from* swim) swæm

Swami, -s 'swɑːmɪ (*Hindi* svami), -z

swamp (*s. v.*), -s, -ing, -ed; -y, -ier, -iest, -iness swɒmp, -s, -ɪŋ, -t [swɒmt]; -ɪ, -ɪə* [-jə*], -ɪɪst [-jɪst], -ɪnɪs [-məs]

swan, -s swɒn, -z

Swanage 'swɒnɪdʒ

Swanee 'swɒnɪ

swank; -y, -ier, -iest, -ily, -iness swæŋk; -ɪ, -ɪə* [-jə*], -ɪɪst [-jɪst], -ɪlɪ [-əlɪ], -ɪnɪs [-məs]

swan-like 'swɒnlaɪk

swanner|y, -ies 'swɒnər|ɪ, -ɪz

swan's-down 'swɒnzdaʊn

Swansea (*in Wales*) 'swɒnzɪ, (*in Tasmania*) 'swɒnsɪ [-siː]

swan-song, -s 'swɒnsɒŋ, -z

swan-upping 'swɒnˌʌpɪŋ

Swanwick 'swɒnɪk

swap (*s. v.*), -s, -ping, -ped swɒp, -s, -ɪŋ, -t

swaraj, -ist/s swə'rɑːdʒ [swɑː'r-] (*Hindi* svəraj), -ɪst/s

sward, -s swɔːd, -z

swarf swɔːf

swarm (*s. v.*), -s, -ing, -ed swɔːm, -z, -ɪŋ, -d

swart swɔːt

swarth|y, -ier, -iest, -ily, -iness 'swɔːð|ɪ [-ɔːθ|ɪ], -ɪə* [-jə*], -ɪɪst [-jɪst], -ɪlɪ [-əlɪ], -mɪs [-məs]

swash, -es, -ing, -ed; -buckler/s swɒʃ, -ɪz, -ɪŋ, -t; -ˌbʌklə*/z

swastika, -s 'swɒstɪkə, -z

swat, -s, -ting, -ted, -ter/s swɒt, -s, -ɪŋ, -ɪd, -ə*/z

swath, -s swɔːθ, -s [swɔːðz]

swath|e, -es, -ing, -ed sweɪð, -z, -ɪŋ, -d

Swatow 'swɒtaʊ

sway (*s. v.*), -s, -ing, -ed sweɪ, -z, -ɪŋ, -d

Swaziland 'swɑːzɪlænd

swear (*s. v.*), -s, -ing, swore, sworn, swearer/s sweə*, -z, -rɪŋ, swɔː* [swɔə*], swɔːn, 'sweərə*/z

swear-word, -s 'sweəwɜːd, -z

sweat (*s. v.*), -s, -ing, -ed, -er/s, -y, -iness swet, -s, -ɪŋ, -ɪd, -ə*/z; -ɪ, -ɪnɪs [-məs]

swede (S.), -s swiːd, -z

Sweden, -borg 'swiːdn, -bɔːg

Swedenborgian, -s ˌswiːdn'bɔːdʒən [-dʒɪən], -z

Swedish 'swiːdɪʃ

Sweeney 'swiːnɪ

sweep (*s. v.*), -s, -ing, swept, sweeper/s swiːp, -s, -ɪŋ, swept, 'swiːpə*/z

sweeping (*s. adj.*), -s 'swiːpɪŋ, -z

sweepstake, -s 'swiːpsteɪk, -s

sweet (*s. adj.*) (S.), -s; -er, -est, -ly, -ness swiːt, -s; -ə*, -ɪst, -lɪ, -nɪs [-nəs]

sweetbread, -s 'swiːtbred, -z

sweet-brier [-briar], -s ˌswiːt'braɪə*, -z

sweet|en, -ens, -ening, -ened, -ener/s 'swiːt|n, -nz, -nɪŋ [-ɲɪŋ], -nd, -nə*/z [-ɲə*/z]

sweetheart, -s 'swiːthɑːt, -s

sweeting (S.), -s 'swiːtɪŋ, -z

sweetish 'swiːtɪʃ

sweetmeat, -s 'swiːtmiːt, -s

sweet-scented ˌswiːt'sentɪd ['-ˌ—]

sweet-tempered ˌswiːt'tempəd ['-ˌ—]

sweet-william, -s ˌswiːt'wɪljəm, -z

sweet|y, -ies 'swiːt|ɪ, -ɪz

swell (*s. v.*), -s, -ing/s, -ed, swollen swel, -z, -ɪŋ/z, -d, 'swəʊlən

swell-box, -es 'swelbɒks, -ɪz

swelt|er, -ers, -ering/ly, -ered 'swelt|ə*, -əz, -ərɪŋ/lɪ, -əd

swept (*from* sweep) swept

swerv|e (*s. v.*), -es, -ing, -ed swɜːv, -z, -ɪŋ, -d

Swete swiːt

Swettenham 'swetɲəm

swift (*s. adj. adv.*) (S.), -s; -er, -est, -ly, -ness swɪft, -s; -ə*, -ɪst, -lɪ, -nɪs [-nəs]

swift-footed ˌswɪft'fʊtɪd ['-ˌ—]

Swiftsure 'swɪftʃɔː* [-ʃɔə*, -ʃʊə*]
swig (s. v.), -s, -ging, -ged swɪg, -z, -ɪŋ, -d
swill (s. v.), -s, -ing, -ed swɪl, -z, -ɪŋ, -d
swim (s. v.), -s, -ming/ly, swam, swum, swimmer/s swɪm, -z, -ɪŋ/lɪ, swæm, swʌm, 'swɪmə*/z
swimming-ba|th, -ths 'swɪmɪŋbɑː|θ, -ðz
swimming-pool, -s 'swɪmɪŋpuːl, -z
swim-suit, -s 'swɪmsuːt [-sjuːt], -s
Swinburne 'swɪnbɜːn [-bən]
swind|le, -les, -ling, -led, -ler/s 'swɪnd|l, -lz, -lɪŋ, -ld, -lə*/z
Swindon 'swɪndən
swine, -herd/s swaɪn, -hɜːd/z
swing (s. v.), -s, -ing, swung swɪŋ, -z, -ɪŋ, swʌŋ
swing-boat, -s 'swɪŋbəʊt, -s
swinge, -s, -ing, -d swɪndʒ, -ɪz, -ɪŋ, -d
swingeing (adj.) 'swɪndʒɪŋ
swing|le (s. v.), -les, -ling, -led 'swɪŋg|l, -lz, -lɪŋ, -ld
swinish, -ness 'swaɪnɪʃ, -nɪs [-nəs]
swip|e (s. v.), -es, -ing, -ed, -er/s swaɪp, -s, -ɪŋ, -t, -ə*/z
swirl (s. v.), -s, -ing, -ed swɜːl, -z, -ɪŋ, -d
swish (s. v.), -es, -ing, -ed swɪʃ, -ɪz, -ɪŋ, -t
Swiss swɪs
switch (s. v.), -es, -ing, -ed swɪtʃ, -ɪz, -ɪŋ, -t
switchback, -s 'swɪtʃbæk, -s
switch-board, -s 'swɪtʃbɔːd [-bɔəd], -z
Swithin 'swɪðɪn [-θɪn]
Switzerland 'swɪtsələnd
swiv|el (s. v.), -els, -elling, -elled 'swɪv|l, -lz, -lɪŋ [-lɪŋ], -ld
swizz|le (s. v.), -les, -ling, -led, -ler/s, -stick/s 'swɪz|l, -lz, -lɪŋ [-lɪŋ], -ld, -lə*/z [-lə*/z], -stɪk/s
swollen (from swell) 'swəʊlən
swoon (s. v.), -s, -ing, -ed swuːn, -z, -ɪŋ, -d
swoop (s. v.), -s, -ing, -ed swuːp, -s, -ɪŋ, -t
swop (s. v.), -s, -ping, -ped swɒp, -s, -ɪŋ, -t
sword, -s sɔːd [sɔəd], -z
sword-bearer, -s 'sɔːd,beərə* ['sɔəd-], -z
sword-belt, -s 'sɔːdbelt ['sɔəd-], -s
sword-dance, -s 'sɔːddɑːns ['sɔəd-], -ɪz
Sworder 'sɔːdə*
swordfish 'sɔːdfɪʃ ['sɔəd-]
swords|man, -men 'sɔːdz|mən ['sɔədz-], -mən
swore (from swear) swɔː* [swɔə*]
sworn (from swear) swɔːn

swot (s. v.), -s, -ting, -ted, -ter/s swɒt, -s, -ɪŋ, -ɪd, -ə*/z
swum (from swim) swʌm
swung (from swing) swʌŋ
Sybaris 'sɪbərɪs
sybarite, -s 'sɪbəraɪt, -s
sybaritic ,sɪbə'rɪtɪk
Sybil 'sɪbɪl [-bəl]
sycamore (S.), -s 'sɪkəmɔː* [-mɔə*], -z
syce, -s saɪs, -ɪz
sycophancy 'sɪkəfənsɪ [-kʊf-, -fænsɪ]
sycophant, -s 'sɪkəfænt [-kʊf-, -fənt], -s
sycophantic ,sɪkəʊ'fæntɪk
Sycorax 'sɪkəræks
Sydenham 'sɪdnəm [-dnəm]
Sydney 'sɪdnɪ
Syed 'saɪed ['saɪəd]
syenite 'saɪənaɪt ['saɪɪn-]
Sygrove 'saɪgrəʊv
Sykes saɪks
syllabar|y, -ies 'sɪləbər|ɪ, -ɪz
syllabic, -ally sɪ'læbɪk, -əlɪ
syllabicat|e, -es, -ing, -ed sɪ'læbɪkeɪt, -s, -ɪŋ, -ɪd
syllabication sɪ,læbɪ'keɪʃn
syllabicity ,sɪlə'bɪsətɪ [-ɪtɪ]
syllabification sɪ,læbɪfɪ'keɪʃn
syllabi|fy, -fies, -fying, -fied sɪ'læbɪ|faɪ, -faɪz, -faɪɪŋ, -faɪd
syllable, -s 'sɪləbl, -z
syllabub 'sɪləbʌb
syllabus, -es 'sɪləbəs, -ɪz
syllogism, -s 'sɪlədʒɪzəm [-ləʊdʒ-], -z
syllogistic, -ally ,sɪlə'dʒɪstɪk [-ləʊ'dʒ-], -əlɪ
syllogiz|e (-is|e), -es, -ing, -ed 'sɪlədʒaɪz [-ləʊdʒ-], -ɪz, -ɪŋ, -d
sylph, -s sɪlf, -s
Sylva 'sɪlvə
sylvan 'sɪlvən
Sylvester sɪl'vestə*
Sylvia 'sɪlvɪə [-vjə]
symbiosis ,sɪmbɪ'əʊsɪs [-baɪ'əʊ-]
symbol, -s 'sɪmbl, -z
symbolic, -al, -ally sɪm'bɒlɪk, -l, -əlɪ
†symbolism 'sɪmbəlɪzəm [-bʊl-, -bl-]
symbolization [-isa-] ,sɪmbəlaɪ'zeɪʃn [-bʊl-, -blaɪ'z-, -bəlɪ'z-, -blɪ'z-]
symboliz|e (-is|e), -es, -ing, -ed 'sɪmbəlaɪz [-bʊl-, -bl-], -ɪz, -ɪŋ, -d
Syme saɪm
Symington 'saɪmɪŋtən, 'sɪm-
symmetric, -al, -ally, -alness sɪ'metrɪk, -l, -əlɪ, -lnɪs [-nəs]
symmetry 'sɪmətrɪ [-mɪtrɪ]
Symond 'saɪmənd
Symonds (surname) 'saɪməndz, 'sɪm-
Symonds Yat ,sɪməndz'jæt

Symons 'saɪmənz, 'sɪm-
sympathetic, -al, -ally ˌsɪmpə'θetɪk, -l, -əlɪ
sympathiz|e [is|e], -es, -ing, -ed, -er/s 'sɪmpəθaɪz, -ɪz, -ɪŋ, -d, -ə*/z
sympath|y, -ies 'sɪmpəθ|ɪ, -ɪz
symphonic sɪm'fɒnɪk
symphon|y, -ies 'sɪmfən|ɪ, -ɪz
symposi|um, -ums, -a sɪm'pəʊzj|əm [-'pɒz-, -zɪ|əm], -əmz, -ə
symptom, -s 'sɪmptəm [-tɪm], -z
symptomatic ˌsɪmptə'mætɪk [-tɪ'm-]
synaer = syner-
synaesthesia ˌsɪnɪs'θiːzjə [-niːs-, -nəs-, -zɪə, -ʒjə, -ʒə]
synagogue, -s 'sɪnəgɒg, -z
synaloepha ˌsɪnə'liːfə
synapse 'saɪnæps [sɪ'næps, 'sɪnæps]
sync sɪŋk
synchromesh, -es ˌsɪŋkrəʊ'meʃ ['---], -ɪz
synchronic sɪŋ'krɒnɪk [sɪn'k-]
synchronism 'sɪŋkrənɪzəm [-krʊn-]
synchronistic ˌsɪŋkrə'nɪstɪk [-krʊ'n-]·
synchronization [-isa-], -s ˌsɪŋkrənaɪ'zeɪʃn [-krʊn-, -nɪ'z-], -z
synchroniz|e [-is|e], -es, -ing, -ed 'sɪŋkrənaɪz [-krʊn-], -ɪz, -ɪŋ, -d
synchronous, -ly, -ness 'sɪŋkrənəs [-krʊn-], -lɪ, -nɪs [-nəs]
synchrony 'sɪŋkrənɪ [-krʊn-]
synchrotron, -s 'sɪŋkrəʊtrɒn, -z
syncopat|e, -es, -ing, -ed 'sɪŋkəpeɪt [-kəʊp-, -kʊp-], -s, -ɪŋ, -ɪd
syncopation, -s ˌsɪŋkə'peɪʃn [-kəʊ'p-, -kʊ'p-], -z
syncope 'sɪŋkəpɪ [-kʊp-]
syncretic sɪŋ'kriːtɪk [sɪn'k-, -'kret-]
syncretism 'sɪŋkrɪtɪzəm
syndesis sɪn'diːsɪs
syndetic sɪn'detɪk
syndic, -s 'sɪndɪk, -s
syndicali|sm, -st/s 'sɪndɪkəlɪ|zəm [-k]ɪ-], -st/s
syndicate (s.), -s 'sɪndɪkət [-kɪt], -s
syndicat|e (v.), -es, -ing, -ed 'sɪndɪkeɪt, -s, -ɪŋ, -ɪd
syndication ˌsɪndɪ'keɪʃn
syndrome, -s 'sɪndrəʊm [-drəmɪ, -drəʊmɪ], -z
syne saɪn
synecdoche sɪ'nekdəkɪ
syneres|is, -es sɪ'nɪərəs|ɪs [-rɪs-], -iːz
synergism 'sɪnədʒɪzəm
synergy 'sɪnədʒɪ
Synge sɪŋ

synod, -s, -al 'sɪnəd [-nɒd], -z, -l
synodic, -al, -ally sɪ'nɒdɪk, -l, -əlɪ
synonym, -s 'sɪnənɪm [-nɒn-, -nʊn-], -z
synonymous, -ly sɪ'nɒnɪməs [-nəm-], -lɪ
synonymy sɪ'nɒnɪmɪ [-nəmɪ]
synops|is, -es sɪ'nɒps|ɪs, -iːz
synoptic, -s, -al, -ally sɪ'nɒptɪk, -s, -l, -əlɪ
synovia, -l saɪ'nəʊvɪə [sɪ'n-, -vjə], -l
synovitis ˌsaɪnəʊ'vaɪtɪs [ˌsɪn-]
syntactic, -al, -ally sɪn'tæktɪk, -l, -əlɪ
syntagm, -s 'sɪntæm, -z
syntagmatic ˌsɪntæg'mætɪk
syntax, -es 'sɪntæks, -ɪz
synthes|is, -es sɪnθəs|ɪs [-θɪs-], -iːz
synthesiz|e [-is|e], -es, -ing, -ed, -er/s 'sɪnθəsaɪz [-θɪs-], -ɪz, -ɪŋ, -d, -ə*/z
synthetic, -s, -al, -ally sɪn'θetɪk, -s, -l, -əlɪ
synthetist, -s 'sɪnθɪtɪst [-θət-], -s
synthetiz|e [-is|e], -es, -ing, -ed 'sɪnθɪtaɪz [-θət-], -ɪz, -ɪŋ, -d
syphilis 'sɪfɪlɪs [-fəl-]
syphilitic ˌsɪfɪ'lɪtɪk [-fə'l-]
syph|on (s. v.), -ons, -oning, -oned 'saɪf|n, -nz, -ənɪŋ [-n̩ɪŋ], -nd
Syracusan ˌsaɪərə'kjuːzən
Syracuse (in classical history) 'saɪərəkjuːz, (modern town in Sicily) ˌsaɪərəkjuːz ['sɪr-], (town in U.S.A.) 'sɪrəkjuːs
syren, -s 'saɪərən [-rɪn], -z
Syria, -n/s 'sɪrɪə, -n/z
Syriac 'sɪrɪæk
syringa, -s sɪ'rɪŋgə, -z
syring|e (s. v.), -es, -ing, -ed 'sɪrɪndʒ [-'-], -ɪz, -ɪŋ, -d
syrinx (all senses), -es 'sɪrɪŋks, -ɪz
syrophoenician ˌsaɪərəʊfɪ'nɪ|n [-fiː'n-, -ʃjən, -ʃɪən, -sɪən, -sjən]
syrt|is (S.), -es 'sɜːt|ɪs, -iːz
syrup, -s; -y 'sɪrəp, -s; -ɪ
systaltic sɪ'stæltɪk
system, -s 'sɪstəm [-tɪm], -z
systematic, -ally ˌsɪstə'mætɪk [-tɪ'm-], -əlɪ
systematization [-isa-] ˌsɪstɪmətaɪ'zeɪʃn [-təm-, -tɪ'z-]
systematiz|e [-is|e], -es, -ing, -ed, -er/s 'sɪstɪmətaɪz [-təm-], -ɪz, -ɪŋ, -d, -ə*/z
systemic sɪ'stemɪk [-'stiː'mɪk]
systole 'sɪstəlɪ
systolic sɪ'stɒlɪk
syzyg|y, -ies 'sɪzɪdʒ|ɪ, -ɪz

T

T (*the letter*), **-'s** tiː, -z
ta (*Tonic Sol-fa name for diminished seventh from the tonic*), **-s** tɔː, -z
ta (*syllable used in Tonic Sol-fa for counting time*) *generally* taː, *but* tæ *in the sequence* **ta fe tay fe**, *q.v.*
ta (*thank you*) taː
Taal taːl
tab, -s tæb, -z
tabard (**T.**), **-s** 'tæbəd [-baːd], -z
tabb|y, -ies 'tæb|ɪ, -ɪz
taberdar, -s 'tæbədaː* [-də*], -z
tabernacle, -s 'tæbənækl, -z
Taberner təˈbɜːnə*
tabes 'teɪbiːz
Tabitha 'tæbɪθə
tablature, -s 'tæblətʃə* [-blɪtʃ-, -ˌtjʊə*], -z
tab|le (*s. v.*) (**T.**), **-les, -ling, -led** 'teɪb|l, -lz, -lɪŋ [-ˌlɪŋ], -ld
tableau, -s 'tæbləʊ, -z
table-|cloth, -cloths 'teɪbl|klɒθ [*old-fashioned* -klɔːθ], -klɒθs [-klɔːðz, -klɔːθs]
table d'hôte ˌtaːblˈdəʊt
table-kni|fe, -ves 'teɪblnaɪ|f, -vz
table-land, -s 'teɪbllænd, -z
table-linen 'teɪblˌlɪnɪn
tablespoon, -s 'teɪblspuːn, -z
tablespoonful, -s 'teɪblˌspuːnfʊl ['---ˌ-], -z
tablet, -s 'tæblɪt [-lət], -s
table-tennis 'teɪblˌtenɪs
table-turning 'teɪblˌtɜːnɪŋ
tableware 'teɪblweə*
tabloid, -s 'tæblɔɪd, -z
taboo (*s.*), **-s** təˈbuː, -z
taboo (*v.*), **-(e)s, -ing, -ed** təˈbuː, -z, -ɪŋ [təˈbʊɪŋ], -d
tabor, -s 'teɪbə* [-bɔː*], -z
Tabor (*Mount*) 'teɪbɔː* [-bə*]
tabouret, -s 'tæbərɪt [-bʊr-, -ret], -s
tabul|a, -ae 'tæbjʊl|ə, -iː
tabular 'tæbjʊlə* [-bjəl-]
tabulat|e, -es, -ing, -ed, -or/s 'tæbjʊleɪt [-bjəl-], -s, -ɪŋ, -ɪd, -ə*/z
tabulation, -s ˌtæbjʊˈleɪʃn [-bjə'l-], -z
tacet 'teɪset ['tæs-, -sɪt]
tache, -s taːʃ [tæʃ], -ɪz

tachism 'tæʃɪzəm
tachograph, -s 'tækəʊgraːf [-græf], -s
tachometer, -s tæˈkɒmɪtə* [-mətə*], -z
tachycardia ˌtækɪˈkaːdɪə [-djə]
tachygraph|er/s, -y tæˈkɪgrəf|ə*/z, -ɪ
tacit, -ly, -ness 'tæsɪt, -lɪ, -nɪs [-nəs]
taciturn, -ly 'tæsɪtɜːn, -lɪ
taciturnity ˌtæsɪˈtɜːnətɪ [-ɪtɪ]
Tacitus 'tæsɪtəs
tack (*s. v.*), **-s, -ing, -ed** tæk, -s, -ɪŋ, -t
tack|le (*s. v.*), **-les, -ling, -led, -ler/s** 'tæk|l [*nautical often* 'teɪkl], -lz, -lɪŋ [-lɪŋ], -ld, -lə*/z [-lə*/z]
tacky 'tækɪ
Tacon 'teɪkən
tact tækt
tact|ful, -fully, -fulness 'tækt|fʊl, -fʊlɪ [-fəlɪ], -fʊlnɪs [-nəs]
tactic, -s, -al, -ally 'tæktɪk, -s, -l, -əlɪ
tactician, -s tækˈtɪʃn, -z
tactile 'tæktaɪl
tactless, -ly, -ness 'tæktlɪs [-ləs], -lɪ, -nɪs [-nəs]
tactual, -ly 'tæktjʊəl [-tjwəl, -tjʊl, -tʃʊəl, -tʃʊl], -ɪ
Tadcaster 'tædkæstə* [-kəs-]
Tadema 'tædɪmə
Tadhg taɪg
tadpole, -s 'tædpəʊl, -z
tael, -s teɪl ['teɪəl], -z
ta'en (*dialectal for* **taken**) teɪn
ta fe tay fe (*syllables used in Tonic Sol-fa for counting four in a bar*) 'tæfɪˌtefɪ [-fəˌt-]
Taff tæf
taffeta 'tæfɪtə [-fətə]
taffrail, -s 'tæfreɪl [-frɪl, -frəl], -z
Taff|y, -ies 'tæf|ɪ, -ɪz
taft, -s, -ing, -ed taːft [tæft], -s, -ɪŋ, -ɪd
Taft (*surname*) tæft, taːft, (*town in Iran*) taːft
tag (*s. v.*), **-s, -ging, -ged** tæg, -z, -ɪŋ, -d
Tagalog təˈgaːlɒg [-ləg]
tagetes tæˈdʒiːtiːz
tagliatelle ˌtæljəˈtelɪ
Tagore təˈgɔː* [-ˈgɔə*] (*Bengali* ʈhakur)
Tagus 'teɪgəs
Tahi|ti, -tian taːˈhiː|tɪ [təˈh-], -ʃn

tail (*s. v.*), **-s, -ing, -ed; -less** teɪl, -z, -ɪŋ, -d; -lɪs [-ləs]

tail-back, **-s** 'teɪlbæk, -s

tail-coat, **-s** ˌteɪl'kəʊt [*in contrast* '--], -s

tail-end, **-s** ˌteɪl'end ['teɪlend], -z

tailor (*s. v.*), **-s, -ing, -ed** 'teɪlə*, -z, -rɪŋ, -d

tailoress, **-es** ˌteɪlə'res ['teɪləres], -ɪz

tailor-made (*s. adj.*), **-s** 'teɪləmeɪd [*often* ˌ--'- *for predicative adj.*], -z

tailpiece, **-s** 'teɪlpiːs, -ɪz

tail-spin, **-s** 'teɪlspɪn, -z

Taine tem (tɛːn)

taint (*s. v.*), **-s, -ing, -ed; -less** teɪnt, -s, -ɪŋ, -ɪd; -lɪs [-ləs]

Taiping (*in Malaysia*) ˌtaɪ'pɪŋ

Tait teɪt

Taiwan ˌtaɪ'wɑːn [-'wæn]

Taj Mahal ˌtɑːdʒmə'hɑːl [-'hʌl] (*Hindi* tɑɪməhəl)

tak|e, **-es, -ing,** took, tak|en, **-er/s** teɪk, -s, -ɪŋ, tʊk, 'teɪk|ən [-ŋ], -ə*/z

takeaway (*s.*), **-s** 'teɪkəˌweɪ, -z

take-off, **-s** 'teɪkɒf [*old-fashioned* -ɔːf, ˌ-'-], -s

take-over, **-s** 'teɪkˌəʊvə*, -z

take-up, **-s** 'teɪkʌp, -s

taking (*s. adj.*), **-s, -ly, -ness** 'teɪkɪŋ, -z, -lɪ, -nɪs [-nəs]

Talbot (*surname*) 'tɔːlbət ['tɒl-], (*place*) 'tɔːlbət ['tɒl-], 'tælbət
Note.—Both pronunciations are current at Port Talbot *in Wales.*

talc tælk

talcum, -powder 'tælkəm, -ˌpaʊdə*

tale, **-s** teɪl, -z

tale-bearer, **-s** 'teɪlˌbeərə*, -z

talent, **-s, -ed, -less** 'tælənt, -s, -ɪd, -lɪs [-ləs]

tales (*for completing a jury*) 'teɪliːz

tales|man (*person summoned to complete a jury*), **-men** 'teɪliːz|mən [-lz-, -mæn], -mən [-men]

tale-teller, **-s** 'teɪlˌtelə*, -z

Talfourd 'tælfəd

Taliesin ˌtælɪ'esɪn (*Welsh* tal'jesɪn)

talisman, **-s** 'tælɪzmən [-ɪsm-], -z

talk (*s. v.*), **-s, -ing, -ed, -er/s** tɔːk, -s, -ɪŋ, -t, -ə*/z

talkative, **-ly, -ness** 'tɔːkətɪv, -lɪ, -nɪs [-nəs]

talkback (*s.*), **-s** 'tɔːkbæk, -s

talkie, **-s** 'tɔːkɪ, -z

talking-to, **-s** 'tɔːkɪŋtuː:, -z

tall, **-er, -est, -ness** tɔːl, -ə*, -ɪst, -nɪs [-nəs]

tallage 'tælɪdʒ

tallboy, **-s** 'tɔːlbɔɪ, -z

Tallis 'tælɪs

tall|ow, **-owy** 'tæl|əʊ, -əʊɪ

tall|y (*s. v.*), **-ies, -ying, -ied** 'tæl|ɪ, -ɪz, -ɪɪŋ, -ɪd

tally-ho (**T.**), **-s** ˌtælɪ'həʊ, -z

tally|man, **-men** 'tælɪ|mən, -mən [-men]

Talman 'tɔːlmən

Talmud 'tælmʊd [-məd, -mʌd]

talmudic, **-al** tæl'mʊdɪk [-'mʌd-, -'mjuːd-], -l

talon, **-s** 'tælən, -z

tam(e)ability ˌteɪmə'bɪlətɪ [-lɪt-]

tam(e)able 'teɪməbl

Tamaqua tə'mɑːkwə

Tamar (*river in W. of England*) 'teɪmə*, (*biblical name*) 'teɪmɑː* [-mə*]

tamarind, **-s** 'tæmərɪnd, -z

tamarisk, **-s** 'tæmərɪsk, -s

tamber, **-s** 'tæmbə*, -z

tambour, **-s** 'tæm,bʊə* [-bʊə*, -bɔː*, -bə*], -z

tambourine, **-s** ˌtæmbə'riːn, -z

Tamburlaine 'tæmbəlem

tam|e (*adj. v.*), **-er, -est, -ely, -eness; -es, -ing, -ed, -er/s** teɪm, -ə*, -ɪst, -lɪ, -nɪs [-nəs]; -z, -ɪŋ, -d, -ə*/z

Tamerlane 'tæmələm

Tamil, **-s** 'tæmɪl [-ml], -z

Tammany 'tæmənɪ

Tammerfors 'tæməfɔːz

Tamora 'tæmərə

tam-o'-shanter (**T.**), **-s** ˌtæmə'ʃæntə*, -z

tamp, **-s, -ing, -ed** tæmp, -s, -ɪŋ, -t [tæmt]

tamp|er, **-ers, -ering, -ered** 'tæmp|ə*, -əz, -ərɪŋ, -əd

tampon, **-s** 'tæmpɒn [-pən], -z

Tamworth 'tæmwəθ [-wɜː:θ]

tan (*s. adj. v.*), **-s, -ning, -ned, -ner/s** tæn, -z, -ɪŋ, -d, -ə*/z

Tancred 'tæŋkred [-rɪd]

tandem, **-s** 'tændəm [-dem], -z

Tanfield 'tænfiːld

tang, **-s** tæŋ, -z

Tang (*Chinese dynasty*) tæŋ

Tanganyika ˌtæŋgə'njiːkə [-gæn-]

tangent, **-s** 'tændʒənt, -s

tangenti|al, **-ally** tæn'dʒenʃ|l [-entʃ-], -əlɪ

tangerine, **-s** ˌtændʒə'riːn ['---], -z

tangibility ˌtændʒə'bɪlətɪ [-dʒɪ'b-, -lɪt-]

tangib|le, **-ly, -leness** 'tændʒəb|l [-dʒɪb-], -lɪ, -lnɪs [-nəs]

Tangier tæn'dʒɪə* ['--]

tang|le (*s. v.*), **-les, -ling, -led** 'tæŋg|l, -lz, -lɪŋ [-lɪŋ], -ld

Tanglewood 'tæŋglwʊd

tangly 'tæŋglɪ

tango, -s 'tæŋgəu, -z
tang|y, -ier, -iest 'tæŋ|ɪ, -ɪə*, -ɪɪst
Tangye 'tæŋgɪ
tanh (mathematical term) θæn [tæntʃ]
tank, -s; -age, -er/s tæŋk, -s; -ɪdʒ, -ə*/z
tankard, -s 'tæŋkəd, -z
tanner (T.), -s 'tænə*, -z
tanner|y, -ies 'tænər|ɪ, -ɪz
Tannhäuser 'tæn,hɔɪzə* ('tan,hɔyzər)
tanni|c, -n 'tænɪ|k, -n
Tannoy 'tænɔɪ
Tanqueray 'tæŋkərɪ
tansy 'tænzɪ
tantalization [-isa-], -s ,tæntəlaɪ'zeɪʃn,
-z
tantaliz|e [-is|e], -es, -ing/ly, -ed, -er/s
'tæntəlaɪz, -ɪz, -ɪŋ/lɪ, -d, -ə*/z
tantalum, -s 'tæntələm, -z
tantalus (T.), -es 'tæntələs, -ɪz
tantamount 'tæntəmaunt
tantiv|y, -ies tæn'tɪv|ɪ, -ɪz
tanto 'tæntəu
tantrum, -s 'tæntrəm, -z
Tanzania, -n/s ,tænzə'nɪə [rarely
tæn'zeɪnɪə, -njə], -n/z
Taoi|sm, -st/s 'tɑːɔʊɪ|zəm ['taʊɪ-], -st/s
tap (s. v.), -s, -ping, -ped tæp, -s, -ɪŋ, -t
tap-danc|e, -es, -ing, -ed, -er/s 'tæp-
dɑːns, -ɪz, -ɪŋ, -t, -ə*/z
tap|e (s. v.) (T.), -es, -ing, -ed teɪp, -s,
-ɪŋ, -t
tape-machine, -s 'teɪpmə,ʃiːn, -z
tape-measure, -s 'teɪp,meʒə*, -z
taper (s. v.), -s, -ing, -ed 'teɪpə*, -z,
-rɪŋ, -d
tape-record|er/s, -ing/s 'teɪp-
rɪ,kɔːd|ə*/z, -ɪŋ/z
tapestr|y, -ies 'tæpɪstr|ɪ [-pəs-], -ɪz
tapeworm, -s 'teɪpwɜːm, -z
tapioca ,tæpɪ'əʊkə
tapir, -s 'teɪpə* [-,pɪə*, rarely 'tæp-],
-z
tapis 'tæpiː [-pɪ] (tapi)
Tapling 'tæplɪŋ
Tappertit 'tæpətɪt
tappet, -s 'tæpɪt, -s
tap-room, -s 'tæprum [-ruːm], -z
tap-root, -s 'tæpruːt, -s
tapster, -s 'tæpstə*, -z
tar (s. v.), -s, -ring, -red tɑː:*, -z, -rɪŋ,
-d
tar(r)adiddle, -s 'tærədɪdl, -z
tarantella, -s ,tærən'telə, -z
Taranto tə'ræntəu ['tɑːrəntəu]
('ta:ranto)
tarantula, -s tə'ræntjulə [-tjələ, -tʃələ], - z
taraxacum tə'ræksəkəm
tar-brush, -es 'tɑː:brʌʃ, -ɪz

tard|y, -ier, -iest, -ily, -iness 'tɑːd|ɪ,
-ɪə* [-jə*], -ɪɪst [-jɪst], -ɪlɪ [-əlɪ], -ɪnɪs
[-məs]
tare, -s teə*, -z
Tarentaise ,tærən'teɪz (tarɑ̆tɛːz)
Tarentum tə'rentəm
target, -s, -ing, -ed 'tɑː:gɪt, -s, -ɪŋ, -ɪd
targeteer, -s ,tɑː:gɪ'tɪə* [-gə't-], -z
tariff, -s 'tærɪf, -s
Tarkington 'tɑː:kɪŋtən
Tarleton 'tɑː:ltən, 'tɑː:lətən
tarmac, -s 'tɑː:mæk, -s
tarn, -s tɑː:n, -z
tarnish, -es, -ing, -ed 'tɑː:nɪʃ, -ɪz, -ɪŋ,
-t
tarot, -s 'tærəu, -z
tarpan, -z 'tɑː:pæn, -z
tarpaulin, -s tɑː:'pɔːlɪn, -z
Tarpeian tɑː:'piːən [-'pɪən]
tarpon, -s 'tɑː:pɒn, -z
Tarquin, -s 'tɑː:kwɪn, -z
Tarquin|ius, -ii tɑː:'kwɪn|ɪəs [-jəs], -ɪaɪ
[-iː]
tarragon 'tærəgən
Tarragona ,tærə'gəunə
Tarring (surname) 'tærɪŋ
tarrock, -s 'tærək, -s
tarry (adj.) (tarred, like tar) 'tɑː:rɪ
tarr|y (v.) (wait), -ies, -ying, -ied, -ier/s
'tær|ɪ, -ɪz, -ɪŋ, -ɪd, -ɪə*/z
Tarshish 'tɑː:ʃɪʃ
Tarsus 'tɑː:səs
tart (s. adj.), -s, -ly, -ness tɑː:t, -s, -lɪ,
-nɪs [-nəs]
tartan, -s 'tɑː:tən, -z
tartar (T.), -s 'tɑː:tə*, -z
tartaric tɑː:'tærɪk
Tartar|us, -y 'tɑː:tər|əs, -ɪ
tartlet, -s 'tɑː:tlɪt [-lət], -s
Tarzan 'tɑː:zən [-zæn]
Tashken|d, -t tæʃ'ken|d, -t
task (s. v.), -s, -ing, -ed tɑːsk, -s, -ɪŋ,
-t
Tasker 'tæskə*
taskmaster, -s 'tɑːsk,mɑːstə*, -z
task-mistress, -es 'tɑːsk,mɪstrɪs [-trəs],
-ɪz
Tasman 'tæzmən
Tasmania, -n/s tæz'meɪmjə [-nɪə], -n/z
Tass tæs
tassel, -s, -led 'tæsl, -z, -d
Tasso 'tæsəu
tast|e (s. v.), -es, -ing, -ed, -er/s teɪst,
-s, -ɪŋ, -ɪd, -ə*/z
taste|ful, -fully, -fulness 'teɪst|ful, -fulɪ
[-fəlɪ], -fulnɪs [-nəs]
tasteless, -ly, -ness 'teɪstlɪs [-ləs], -lɪ,
-nɪs [-nəs]

487

tast|y, -ier, -iest, -ily, -iness 'teɪst|ɪ, -ɪə*
[-jə*], -ɪɪst [-jɪst], -ɪlɪ [-əlɪ], -ɪnɪs
[-ɪnəs]
tat (s. v.), -s, -ting, -ted tæt, -s, -ɪŋ, -ɪd
ta-ta ˌtæˈtɑː
Tatar, -s 'tɑːtə*, -z
ta tay fe (syllables used in Tonic Sol-fa
for counting time) 'tɑːtefɪ
Tate teɪt
Tatham 'teɪθəm
Tatiana ˌtætɪˈɑːnə
tatler (T.), -s 'tætlə*, -z
tatter, -s, -ed 'tætə*, -z, -d
tatterdemalion ˌtætədəˈmeɪljən [-dɪˈm-,
-lɪən]
Tattersall, -s 'tætəsɔːl [-sl], -z
tatt|le (s. v.), -les, -ling, -led, -ler/s
'tætl, -lz, -lɪŋ [-lɪŋ], -ld, -lə*/z
[-lə*/z]
tatt|oo (s. v.) (all senses), -oo(e)s, -ooing,
-ooed, -ooer/s tə'tu: [tæˈt-], -uːz,
-uːɪŋ [-ʊɪŋ], -uːd, -uːə*/z [-ʊə*/z]
tau taʊ
Tauchnitz 'taʊknɪts ('tauxnits)
taught (from teach) tɔːt
taunt, -s, -ing/ly, -ed, -er/s tɔːnt, -s,
-ɪŋ/lɪ, -ɪd, -ə*/z
Taunton (in Somerset) 'tɔːntən [locally
'tɑːn-]
Taurus (constellation) 'tɔːrəs
taut, -ness tɔːt, -nɪs [-nəs]
tautologic, -al, -ally ˌtɔːtəˈlɒdʒɪk, -l, -əlɪ
tautologism, -s tɔːˈtɒlədʒɪzəm, -z
tautologiz|e [-is|e], -es, -ing, -ed
tɔːˈtɒlədʒaɪz, -ɪz, -ɪŋ, -d
tautologous tɔːˈtɒləɡəs
tautolog|y, -ies tɔːˈtɒlədʒ|ɪ, -ɪz
Tautpheus tɔːtˈfiːəs
tavern, -s 'tævən, -z
Tavistock 'tævɪstɒk
taw (s. v.), -s, -ing, -ed tɔː, -z, -ɪŋ, -d
tawdr|y, -ier, -iest, -ily, -iness 'tɔːdr|ɪ,
-ɪə*, -ɪɪst, -əlɪ [-ɪlɪ], -ɪnɪs [-ɪnəs]
Tawell 'tɔːəl
tawn|y, -ier, -iest, -iness 'tɔːn|ɪ, -ɪə*
[-jə*], -ɪɪst [-jɪst], -ɪnɪs [-ɪnəs]
tax (s. v.), -es, -ing, -ed tæks, -ɪz, -ɪŋ, -t
taxability ˌtæksəˈbɪlətɪ [-lɪt-]
taxable, -ness 'tæksəbl, -nɪs [-nəs]
taxation, -s tækˈseɪʃn, -z
tax-collector, -s 'tækskəˌlektə*, -z
tax-free ˌtæksˈfriː ['--]
tax-gatherer, -s 'tæksˌɡæðərə*, -z
taxi (s.), -s 'tæksɪ, -z
tax|i (v.), -ies, -ying, -ied 'tæks|ɪ, -ɪz,
-ɪɪŋ, -ɪd
taxi-cab, -s 'tæksɪkæb, -z
taxiderm|al, -ic ˌtæksɪˈdɜːm|l, -ɪk

taxidermist, -s 'tæksɪdɜːmɪst [ˌ--ˈ--,
tækˈsɪdəmɪst], -s
taxidermy 'tæksɪdɜːmɪ
taximeter, -s 'tæksɪˌmiːtə*, -z
taxis (T.) 'tæksɪs
taxonomic, -ally ˌtæksəʊˈnɒmɪk, -əlɪ
taxonom|ist/s, -y tækˈsɒnəmɪst/s, -ɪ
tax-payer, -s 'tæksˌpeɪə*, -z
tay (syllable used in Tonic Sol-fa in
counting time) generally teɪ, but te in
the sequence tay fe, q.v.
Tay, -side teɪ, -saɪd
tay fe (syllables used in Tonic Sol-fa in
counting time) 'tefɪ, ˌtefɪ, see ta fe
tay fe
Taylor 'teɪlə*
Taylorian teɪˈlɔːrɪən
Taymouth 'teɪmaʊθ [-məθ]
T.B. ˌtiːˈbiː
Tchad tʃæd
Tchaikovsky (Russian composer)
tʃaɪˈkɒfskɪ [-ˈkɒvskɪ] (tʃijˈkofskij)
Tcherkasy tʃɜːˈkæsɪ
Tcherkessian, -s tʃɜːˈkesɪən [-sjən], -z
tchick (s. v.), -s, -ing, -ed tʃɪk, -s, -ɪŋ,
-t
tchick (interj.) ♭ [tʃɪk]
te (Tonic sol-fa name for leading-note),
-s tiː, -z
tea, -s tiː, -z
tea-cadd|y, -ies 'tiːˌkæd|ɪ, -ɪz
tea-cake, -s 'tiːkeɪk, -s
teach, -es, -ing/s, taught, teacher/s
tiːtʃ, -ɪz, -ɪŋ/z, tɔːt, 'tiːtʃə*/z
teachability ˌtiːtʃəˈbɪlətɪ [-lɪt-]
teachable, -ness 'tiːtʃəbl, -nɪs [-nəs]
tea-chest, -s 'tiːtʃest, -s
teach-in, -s 'tiːtʃɪn, -z
tea-|cloth, -cloths 'tiːˌklɒθ [old-
fashioned -klɔːθ], -klɒθs [-klɔːðz,
-klɔːθs]
tea-cup, -s; -ful/s 'tiːkʌp, -s; -ˌfʊl/z
tea-fight, -s 'tiːfaɪt, -s
tea-garden, -s 'tiːˌɡɑːdn, -z
tea-gown, -s 'tiːɡaʊn, -z
Teague, -s tiːɡ, -z
tea-hou|se, -ses 'tiːhaʊ|s, -zɪz
teak tiːk
tea-kettle, -s 'tiːˌketl, -z
teal tiːl
tea-lea|f, -ves 'tiːliː|f, -vz
team (s. v.), -s, -ing, -ed tiːm, -z, -ɪŋ, -d
teamster, -s 'tiːmstə*, -z
team-work 'tiːmwɜːk
tea-part|y, -ies 'tiːˌpɑːt|ɪ, -ɪz
tea-pot, -s 'tiːpɒt, -s
teapoy, -s 'tiːpɔɪ, -z
tear (s.) (fluid from the eye), -s tɪə*, -z

tear (*s. v.*) (*pull apart, rend, rush, a rent, etc.*), **-s, -ing, tore, torn** teə*, -z, -rɪŋ, tɔː* [tɔə*], tɔːn
tear-drop, -s 'tɪədrɒp, -s
tear|ful, -fully, -fulness 'tɪə|fʊl, -fʊlɪ [-fəlɪ], -fʊlnɪs [-nəs]
tear-gas 'tɪəgæs
tearless 'tɪəlɪs [-ləs]
tea-room, -s 'tiːrʊm [-ruːm], -z
tea-rose, -s 'tiːrəʊz, -ɪz
tear-stained 'tɪəsteɪnd
teas|e (*s. v.*), **-es, -ing/ly, -ed, -er/s** tiːz, -ɪz, -ɪŋ/lɪ, -d, -ə*/z
teas|el (*s. v.*), **-els, -eling, -eled** 'tiːz|l, -lz, -əlɪŋ [-lɪŋ], -ld
tea-service, -s 'tiː,sɜːvɪs, -ɪz
tea-set, -s 'tiːset, -s
tea-shop, -s 'tiːʃɒp, -s
teaspoon, -s 'tiːspuːn, -z
teaspoonful, -s 'tiːspuːn,fʊl [-spʊn-], -z
tea-strainer, -s 'tiː,streɪnə*, -z
teat, -s tiːt, -s
tea-table, -s 'tiː,teɪbl, -z
tea-things 'tiːθɪŋz
tea-time 'tiːtaɪm
tea-tray, -s 'tiːtreɪ, -z
tea-urn, -s 'tiːɜːn, -z
Teazle 'tiːzl
Tebay 'tiːbeɪ
tec, -s tek, -s
technetium tek'niːsɪəm, [-sjəm]
technic, -s 'teknɪk, -s
technic|al, -ally, -alness 'teknɪk|l, -əlɪ [-lɪ], -lnɪs [-nəs]
technicalit|y, -ies ,teknɪ'kælət|ɪ [-ɪt|ɪ], -ɪz
technician, -s tek'nɪʃn, -z
technicolor 'teknɪ,kʌlə*
technique, -s tek'niːk ['--], -s
technocrat, -s 'teknəʊkræt, -s
technologic, -al ,teknə'lɒdʒɪk, -l
technolog|ist/s, -y tek'nɒlədʒ|ɪst/s, -ɪ
tech|y, -ier, -iest, -ily, -iness 'tetʃ|ɪ, -ɪə*, -ɪɪst, -ɪlɪ [-əlɪ], -ɪnɪs [-ɪnəs]
Teck tek
ted (**T.**), **-s, -ding, -ded, -der/s** ted, -z, -ɪŋ, -ɪd, -ə*/z
Teddington 'tedɪŋtən
Teddy 'tedɪ
Te Deum, -s ,tiː'diːəm [-'dɪəm, ,teɪ-'deɪʊm], -z
tedious, -ly, -ness 'tiːdjəs [-dɪəs], -lɪ, -nɪs [-nəs]
tedium 'tiːdjəm [-dɪəm]
tee (*s. v.*), **-s, -ing, -d** tiː, -z, -ɪŋ, -d
Teed tiːd
teem, -s, -ing, -ed tiːm, -z, -ɪŋ, -d
teen, -s tiːn, -z

teenag|er/s, -ed 'tiːn,eɪdʒ|ə*/z, -d
teen|y, -iest 'tiːn|ɪ, -ɪɪst [-jɪst]
Tees, -dale tiːz, -deɪl
teeshirt, -s 'tiːʃɜːt, -s
tee-square, -s 'tiːskweə* [,tiː's-], -z
teeter, -s, -ing, -ed 'tiːtə*, -z, -rɪŋ, -d
Teetgen 'tiːdʒən
teeth (*pl. of* **tooth**) tiːθ
teeth|e, -es, -ing, -ed tiːð, -z, -ɪŋ, -d
teetot|al, -alism tiː'təʊt|l ['---], -lɪzəm [-əlɪzəm]
teetotaller, -s tiː'təʊtlə* ['---, -tl̩ə*], -z
teetotum, -s ,tiː'təʊtʌm ['tiː'təʊtʌm, tiː'təʊtəm], -z
tegument, -s 'tegjʊmənt, -s
Teheran ,tɪə'rɑːn [,tehə'r-, ,teɪə'r-]
Teign (*in Devon*) tɪn [tiːn]
Teignbridge 'tɪnbrɪdʒ
Teignmouth 'tɪnməθ [*locally also* 'tɪŋməθ]
Teignton 'teɪntən
tekel 'tiːkel [-kəl]
telamon (**T.**), **-s** 'teləmən [-mɒn], -z
telautograph, -s te'lɔːtəgrɑːf [-græf], -s
tele, -s 'telɪ, -z
telecast (*s. v.*), **-s, -ing, -ed, -er/s** 'telɪkɑːst, -s, -ɪŋ, -ɪd, -ə*/z
tele-cine ,telɪ'sɪnɪ
telecommunication, -s 'telɪkə,mjuːnɪ-'keɪʃn, -z
telefilm, -s 'telɪfɪlm, -z
telegenic ,telɪ'dʒenɪk
telegram, -s 'telɪgræm, -z
telegraph (*s. v.*), **-s, -ing, -ed** 'telɪgrɑːf [-græf], -s, -ɪŋ, -t
telegrapher, -s tɪ'legrəfə* [te'l-, tə'l-], -z
telegraphese ,telɪgrɑː'fiːz [-græ'f-, -grə'f-]
telegraphic, -ally ,telɪ'græfɪk, -əlɪ
telegraphist, -s tɪ'legrəfɪst [te'l-, tə'l-], -s
telegraph-|line/s, -pole/s, -post/s, -wire/s 'telɪgrɑː|f|laɪn/z [-græf-], -pəʊl/z, -pəʊst/s, -,waɪə*/z
telegraphy tɪ'legrəfɪ [te'l-, tə'l-]
Telemachus tɪ'leməkəs [te'l-, tə'l-]
telemark (*s. v.*), **-s, -ing, -ed** 'telɪmɑːk [-ləm-], -s, -ɪŋ, -t
telemeter (*s. v.*), **-s, -ing, -ed** 'telɪmiːtə*, -z, -rɪŋ, -d
telemetric ,telɪ'metrɪk [-'miːt-]
telemetry tɪ'lemɪtrɪ [-mətrɪ]
teleological ,telɪə'lɒdʒɪkl [,tiːl-, -ljə-]
teleology ,telɪ'ɒlədʒɪ [,tiːl-]
telepathic, -ally ,telɪ'pæθɪk, -əlɪ
telepath|ist/s, -y tɪ'lepəθ|ɪst/s [te'l-, tə'l-], -ɪ
telepathiz|e [-is|e], **-es, -ing, -ed** tɪ'lepəθaɪz [te'l-, tə'l-], -ɪz, -ɪŋ, -d

489

telephon|e (*s. v.*), **-es, -ing, -ed, -er/s**
'telɪfəʊn, -z, -ɪŋ, -d, -ə*/z
telephonee, **-s** ˌtelɪfəʊˈniː, -z
telephonic, **-ally** ˌtelɪˈfɒnɪk, -əlɪ
telephonist, **-s** tɪˈlefənɪst [te'l-, tə'l-], -s
telephony tɪˈlefənɪ [te'l-, tə'l-]
telephoto, **-s** ˌtelɪˈfəʊtəʊ ['--ˌ-- *when attributive*], -z
telephotograph, **-s** ˌtelɪˈfəʊtəgrɑːf [-grɑːf], -s
telephotography ˌtelɪfəˈtɒgrəfɪ
teleprinter, **-s** 'telɪˌprɪntə*, -z
teleprompter, **-s** 'telɪˌprɒmptə*, -z
telerecord (*s.*), **-s** 'telɪˌrekɔːd, -z
telerecord (*v.*), **-s, -ing/s, -ed** 'telɪrɪˌkɔːd [-rəˌk-, ˌ--'-], -z, -ɪŋ/z, -ɪd
telescop|e (*s. v.*), **-es, -ing, -ed** 'telɪskəʊp, -s, -ɪŋ, -t
telescopic, **-ally** ˌtelɪˈskɒpɪk, -əlɪ
telescop|ist/s, **-y** tɪˈleskəp|ɪst/s [te'l-, tə'l-], -ɪ
telescreen, **-s** 'telɪskriːn, -z
teletype, **-s** 'telɪtaɪp, -s
teletypesetter, **-s** ˌtelɪˈtaɪpˌsetə*, -z
teleview, **-s, -ing, -ed, -er/s** 'telɪvjuː, -z, -ɪŋ [-ˌvjʊɪŋ], -d, -ə*/z [-ˌvjʊə*/z]
televis|e, **-es, -ing, -ed** 'telɪvaɪz, -ɪz, -ɪŋ, -d
television 'telɪˌvɪʒn [ˌ--'--]
televisor, **-s** 'telɪvaɪzə*, -z
telex 'teleks
tell (**T.**), **-s, -ing, told, teller/s** tel, -z, -ɪŋ, təʊld, 'telə*/z
telling (*adj.*), **-ly** 'telɪŋ, -lɪ
telltale, **-s** 'telteɪl, -z
tellurium te'ljʊərɪəm [-jɔər-, -jɔːr-]
tell|y, **-ies** 'tel|ɪ, -ɪz
Telstar 'telstɑː*
Telugu 'telǝguː [-lʊg-, ˌ--'-]
Teme tiːm
Téméraire ˌteməˈreə* (temerɛːr)
temerity tɪˈmerətɪ [te'm-, tə'm-, -ɪtɪ]
Tempe 'tempɪ
temp|er (*s. v.*), **-ers, -ering, -ered, -erer/s** 'temp|ə*, -əz, -ərɪŋ, -əd, -ərə*/z
tempera 'tempərə
temperable 'tempərəbl
temperament, **-s** 'tempərəmənt, -s
temperament|al, **-ally** ˌtempərə'ment|l, -əlɪ [-ļɪ]
temperance 'tempərəns
temperate, **-ly, -ness** 'tempərət [-rɪt], -lɪ, -nɪs [-nəs]
temperature, **-s** 'temprətʃə* [-pər-, -rɪtʃ-], -z
temperedly 'tempədlɪ
Temperley 'tempəlɪ

tempest (**T.**), **-s** 'tempɪst, -s
tempestuous, **-ly, -ness** tem'pestjʊəs [təm-, -tjwəs], -lɪ, -nɪs [-nəs]
Templar, **-s** 'templə*, -z
temple (**T.**), **-s** 'templ, -z
templet, **-s** 'templɪt [-lət], -s
Templeton 'templtən
temp|o, **-os, -i** 'temp|əʊ, -əʊz, -iː
tempor|al, **-ally** 'tempər|əl, -əlɪ
temporality ˌtempə'rælətɪ [-rtɪ]
temporar|y (*s. adj.*), **-ies, -ily, -iness** 'tempərər|ɪ [-prər-], -ɪz, -əlɪ [-ɪlɪ], -ɪnɪs [-məs]
temporization [-isa-] ˌtempəraɪ'zeɪʃn
temporiz|e [-is|e], **-es, -ing/ly, -ed, -er/s** 'tempəraɪz, -ɪz, -ɪŋ/lɪ, -d, -ə*/z
tempt, **-s, -ing, -ed, -er/s** tempt, -s, -ɪŋ, -ɪd, -ə*/z
temptation, **-s** tempˈteɪʃn, -z
tempting (*adj.*), **-ly, -ness** 'temptɪŋ, -lɪ, -nɪs [-nəs]
ten, **-s, -th, -ths, -thly** ten, -z, -θ, -θs, -θlɪ
tenability ˌtenəˈbɪlətɪ [ˌtiː-, -lɪt-]
tenable, **-ness** 'tenəbl ['tiː-], -nɪs [-nəs]
tenacious, **-ly, -ness** tɪˈneɪʃəs [te'n-, tə'n-], -lɪ, -nɪs [-nəs]
tenacity tɪˈnæsətɪ [te'n-, tə'n-, -ɪtɪ]
tenanc|y, **-ies** 'tenəns|ɪ, -ɪz
tenant, **-s** 'tenənt, -s
tenant|able, **-less, -ry** 'tenənt|əbl, -lɪs [-ləs], -rɪ
Ten|bury, **-by** 'ten|bərɪ, -bɪ
tench tenʃ [-ntʃ]
tend, **-s, -ing, -ed** tend, -z, -ɪŋ, -ɪd
tendencious [-ntious] ten'denʃəs
tendenc|y, **-ies** 'tendəns|ɪ, -ɪz
tend|er (*s. adj. v.*), **-ers, -erer, -erest, -erly, -erness; -ering, -ered** 'tend|ə*, -əz, -ərə*, -ərɪst, -əlɪ, -ənɪs [-nəs]; -ərɪŋ, -əd
tenderfoot, **-s** 'tendəfʊt, -s
tender-hearted, **-ly, -ness** ˌtendəˈhɑːtɪd ['tendə,h-], -lɪ, -nɪs [-nəs]
tenderloin, **-s** 'tendəlɔɪn, -z
tendon, **-s** 'tendən, -z
tendril, **-s** 'tendrəl [-drɪl], -z
tenebrae 'tenɪbriː
tenebrous 'tenɪbrəs
tenement, **-s** 'tenəmənt [-nɪm-]ˌ, -s
Tenerif(f)e ˌtenəˈriːf
tenet, **-s** 'tenɪt ['tiːn-, -net], -s
tenfold 'tenfəʊld
Teniers 'tenɪəz [-njəz]
tenish 'tenɪʃ
Tenison 'tenɪsn
Tennant 'tenənt
tenner, **-s** 'tenə*, -z

Tennessee ˌtenə'si: [-nɪ's-]
Tenniel 'tenjəl [-nɪəl]
tennis, -ball/s 'tenɪs, -bɔːl/z
tennis-court, -s 'tenɪskɔːt [-kɔət], -s
tennis-racket, -s 'tenɪsˌrækɪt, -s
Tennyson 'tenɪsn
tenon, -s 'tenən, -z
tenor, -s 'tenə*, -z
tenour 'tenə*
ten|pence, -penny 'ten|pəns, -pənɪ (see note under penny)
tense (s. adj.), -s, -r, -st, -ly, -ness tens, -ɪz, -ə*, -ɪst, -lɪ, -nɪs [-nəs]
tensile 'tensaɪl
tension, -s 'tenʃn, -z
tensity 'tensətɪ [-ɪtɪ]
tensor, -s 'tensə*, -z
tent (s. v.), -s, -ing, -ed tent, -s, -ɪŋ, -ɪd
tentacle, -s 'tentəkl [-tɪk-], -z
tentacular ten'tækjʊlə* [-kjələ*]
tentative (s. adj.), -s, -ly 'tentətɪv, -z, -lɪ
tenter, -s 'tentə*, -z
Tenterden 'tentədən
tenter-hook, -s 'tentəhʊk, -s
tenth, -s, -ly tenθ, -s, -lɪ
tent-pegging 'tentˌpegɪŋ
tenu|is, -es 'tenjʊ|ɪs, -iːz [-eɪz]
tenuity te'njuːətɪ [tə'n-, tɪ'n-, -'njʊ-, -ɪtɪ]
tenuous 'tenjʊəs [-njwəs]
tenure, -s 'teˌnjʊə* [-njə*], -z
tepee, -s 'tiːpiː, -z
tepid, -est, -ly, -ness 'tepɪd, -ɪst, -lɪ, -nɪs [-nəs]
tepidity te'pɪdətɪ [-ɪtɪ]
ter (three times) tɜː*
Ter (river in Essex) tɑː*
Terah 'tɪərə [rarely 'terə]
teraph, -im 'terəf, -ɪm
terbium 'tɜːbɪəm [-bjəm]
tercel, -s 'tɜːsl, -z
tercentenar|y (s. adj.), -ies ˌtɜːsen'tiːnər|ɪ [-'ten-, tɜː'sentɪn-], -ɪz
tercentennial ˌtɜːsen'tenjəl [-nɪəl]
tercet, -s 'tɜːsɪt [-set], -s
terebene 'terəbiːn [-rɪb-]
terebinth, -s 'terəbɪmθ [-rɪb-], -s
terebinthine ˌterə'bɪmθaɪm [-rɪ'b-]
Terence 'terəns
Teresa tə'riːzə [tɪ'r-, te'r-]
tergiversat|e, -es, -ing, -ed 'tɜːdʒɪvɜː:-sert, -s, -ɪŋ, -ɪd
tergiversation ˌtɜːdʒɪvɜː:'seɪʃn
Terling (in Essex) 'tɑːlɪŋ ['tɜːl-]
term, -s tɜːm, -z
termagant (s. adj.), -s 'tɜːməgənt, -s
terminable, -ness 'tɜːmɪnəbl, -nɪs [-nəs]
terminal (s. adj.), -s 'tɜːmɪnl, -z

terminat|e, -es, -ing, -ed, -or/s 'tɜː:-mɪnert, -s, -ɪŋ, -ɪd, -ə*/z
termination, -s ˌtɜːmɪ'neɪʃn, -z
terminative, -ly 'tɜːmɪnətɪv [-neɪt-], -lɪ
terminer 'tɜːmɪnə*
terminologic|al, -ally ˌtɜːmɪnə'lɒdʒɪk|l, -əlɪ
terminolog|y, -ies ˌtɜːmɪ'nɒlədʒ|ɪ, -ɪz
termin|us, -i, -uses 'tɜːmɪn|əs, -aɪ, -əsɪz
termite, -s 'tɜːmaɪt, -s
tern, -s tɜːn, -z
ternary 'tɜːnərɪ
Ternate (island) tɜː'nɑːtɪ
terner|y, -ies 'tɜːnər|ɪ, -ɪz
Terpsichore tɜːp'sɪkərɪ
Terpsichorean ˌtɜːpsɪkə'riːən [-kɒ'r-, -'rɪən]
terra 'terə
terrac|e (s. v.), -es, -ing, -ed 'terəs [-rɪs], -ɪz, -ɪŋ, -t
terra-cotta ˌterə'kɒtə
Terra del Fuegian, -s ˌterədelfʊ'iːdʒən [-dʒɪən, -dʒjən], -z
Terra del Fuego ˌterədelfʊ'eɪgəʊ [-'fweɪ-]
terra firma ˌterə'fɜːmə
terrain, -s te'reɪn [tɪ-, tə-, 'tereɪn], -z
terra incognita ˌterəɪŋ'kɒgnɪtə
terramycin ˌterə'maɪsɪn
terrapin, -s 'terəpɪn, -z
terrestrial (s. adj.), -s, -ly, -ness tə'res-trɪəl [te'r-, tɪ'r-], -z, -ɪ, -nɪs [-nəs]
terret, -s 'terɪt, -s
terrib|le, -ly, -leness 'terəb|l [-rɪb-], -lɪ, -lnɪs [-nəs]
terrier, -s 'terɪə*, -z
terrific, -ally tə'rɪfɪk [tɪ'r-], -əlɪ
terri|fy, -fies, -fying, -fied 'terɪ|faɪ, -faɪz, -faɪŋ, -faɪd
territorial (s. adj.), -s, -ly, ˌterə'tɔːrɪəl [-rɪ't-], -z, -ɪ
territorializ|e [-is|e], -es, -ing, -ed ˌterə'tɔːrɪəlaɪz [-rɪ't-], -ɪz, -ɪŋ, -d
territor|y, -ies 'terətər|ɪ [-rɪt-], -ɪz
terror, -s 'terə*, -z
terrori|sm, -st/s 'terərɪ|zəm, -st/s
terrorization [-isa-] ˌterəraɪ'zeɪʃn [-rɪ'z-]
terroriz|e [-is|e], -es, -ing, -ed, -er/s 'terəraɪz, -ɪz, -ɪŋ, -d, -ə*/z
Terry 'terɪ
terse, -r, -st, -ly, -ness tɜːs, -ə*, -ɪst, -lɪ, -nɪs [-nəs]
tertian 'tɜːʃn [-ʃjən, -ʃɪən]
tertiary 'tɜːʃərɪ [-ʃjə-, -ʃɪə-]
Tertis 'tɜːtɪs
tertium quid ˌtɜːtjəm'kwɪd [ˌtɜːtɪəm-, ˌtɜːʃjəm-, ˌtɜːʃɪəm-]
Tertius (as English name) 'tɜːʃjəs [-ʃɪəs]

491

Tertullian tɜ:'tʌlɪən [-ljən]
terylene 'terəli:n [-rɪ-]
terzetto, -s tɜ:t'setəʊ [teət-], -z
Tesla 'teslə
tessaract, -s 'tesərækt, -s
tessellat|e, -es, -ing, -ed 'tesəleɪt [-sɪl-], -s, -ɪŋ, -ɪd
tessellation ˌtesə'leɪʃn [-sɪ'l-]
tessitura ˌtesɪ'tʊərə
test (s. v.) (T.), -s, -ing, -ed; -able test, -s, -ɪŋ, -ɪd; -əbl
testac|ean, -eous te'steɪʃ|n [-jən, -ɪən], -əs [-jəs, -ɪəs]
testament (T.), -s 'testəmənt, -s
testament|al, -ary, -arily ˌtestə'ment|l, -ərɪ, -ərəlɪ [-ɪlɪ]
testamur, -s te'steɪmə*, -z
testate, -s 'testeɪt [-tɪt], -s
testation, -s te'steɪʃn, -z
testator, -s te'steɪtə*, -z
testatri|x, -ces, -xes te'steɪtrɪ|ks, -si:z, -ksɪz
tester, -s 'testə*, -z
testicle, -s 'testɪkl, -z
testicular te'stɪkjʊlə* [-kjələ*]
testification, -s ˌtestɪfɪ'keɪʃn, -z
testi|fy, -fies, -fying, -fied, -fier/s 'testɪ|faɪ, -faɪz, -faɪɪŋ, -faɪd, -faɪə*/z
testimonial, -s ˌtestɪ'məʊnjəl [-nɪəl], -z
testimonializ|e [-is|e], -es, -ing, -ed ˌtestɪ'məʊnjəlaɪz [-nɪəl-], -ɪz, -ɪŋ, -d
testimon|y, -ies 'testɪmən|ɪ, -ɪz
Teston (Kent) 'ti:sən
testosterone te'stɒstərəʊn
test-tube, -s 'tesʔtju:b, -z
testud|o, -os, -ines te'stju:d|əʊ [-'stu:-], -əʊz, te'stju:dɪni:z [te'stu:dɪneɪz]
test|y, -ier, -iest, -ily, -iness 'test|ɪ, -ɪə* [-jə*], -ɪɪst [-jɪst], -ɪlɪ [-əlɪ], -ɪnɪs [-ɪnəs]
tetan|us, -y 'tetən|əs [-tn̩-], -ɪ
tetch|y, -ier, -iest, -ily, -iness 'tetʃ|ɪ, -ɪə*, -ɪɪst, -ɪlɪ [-əlɪ], -ɪnɪs [-ɪnəs]
tête-à-tête, -s ˌteɪtɑ:'teɪt, -s
tether (s. v.), -s, -ing, -ed 'teðə*, -z, -rɪŋ, -d
tetrachord, -s 'tetrəkɔ:d, -z
tetrad, -s 'tetræd [-rəd], -z
tetragon, -s 'tetrəgən, -z
tetrahedr|on, -ons, -a; -al ˌtetrə'hedr|ən [-'hi:d-], 'tetrə,h-], -ənz, -ə; -əl
tetralog|y, -ies te'træləʤ|ɪ [tə't-], -ɪz
tetrameter, -s te'træmɪtə* [-mətə*], -z
tetrarch, -s; -y, -ies 'tetrɑ:k ['ti:t-], -s; -ɪ, -ɪz
tetrasyllabic ˌtetrəsɪ'læbɪk
tetrasyllable, -s 'tetrə,sɪləbl [ˌ-'—'—], -z
tetter 'tetə*

Teucer 'tju:sə*
Teutoburgian ˌtju:təʊ'bɜ:gjən [-gɪən]
Teuton, -s 'tju:tən, -z
Teutonic tju:'tɒnɪk [tjʊ't-]
teutonization [-isa-] ˌtju:tənaɪ'zeɪʃn [-tn̩aɪ'z-, -tənɪ'z-, -tn̩ɪ'z-]
teutoniz|e [-is|e], -es, -ing, -ed 'tju:tən-aɪz [-tn̩aɪz], -ɪz, -ɪŋ, -d
Teviot (river) 'ti:vjət [-vɪət], (Lord) 'tevɪət [-vjət]
Teviotdale 'ti:vjətdeɪl [-vɪət-]
Tewfik 'tju:fɪk
Tewin 'tju:ɪn ['tjʊɪn]
Tewkesbury 'tju:ksbərɪ
Texan 'teksən
Texas 'teksəs [-sæs]
Texel 'teksl
text, -s tekst, -s
text-book, -s 'teksʔbʊk, -s
textile, -s 'tekstaɪl, -z
textual, -ly 'tekstjʊəl [-tjwəl, -tjʊl], -ɪ
texture, -s 'tekstʃə*, -z
Teynham (Baron, place in Kent) 'tenəm
Thackeray 'θækərɪ
Thackley 'θæklɪ
Thaddeus θæ'di:əs [-'dɪəs]
Thai, -s, -land taɪ, -z, -lænd [-lənd]
thalamus 'θæləməs
Thalben 'θælbən, 'θɔ:lbən
thaler, -s 'tɑ:lə*, -z
Thales 'θeɪli:z
Thalia, -n θə'laɪə, -n
thalidomide θə'lɪdəmaɪd [θæ'l-]
thallium 'θælɪəm [-ljəm]
Thame (in Oxfordshire) teɪm
Thames (in England, Canada, New Zealand) temz, (in Connecticut) θeɪmz [temz]
than ðæn (strong form), ðən, ðn̩ (weak forms)
Note.—The strong form is normally used only when the word is said in isolation.
thane (T.), -s θeɪn, -z
Thanet 'θænɪt
thank (s. v.), -s, -ing, -ed, -er/s θæŋk, -s, -ɪŋ, -t [θæŋt], -ə*/z
Note.—The interjection Thank you (normally 'θæŋkjʊ) has several other forms, the chief of which are 'hæŋkjʊ, 'ŋkjʊ, 'kkjʊ. The first k of 'kkjʊ has no sound, but the speaker feels the stress to be there.
thank|ful, -fully, -fulness 'θæŋk|fʊl, -fʊlɪ [-fəlɪ], -fʊlnɪs [-nəs]
thankless, -ly, -ness 'θæŋklɪs [-ləs], -lɪ, -nɪs [-nəs]
thank-offering, -s 'θæŋk,ɒfərɪŋ, -z

492

thanksgiving, -s 'θæŋks,gɪvɪŋ [ˌ-'--], -z
thankworth|y, -iness 'θæŋk,wɜːð|ɪ, -ɪnɪs
[-nəs]
that (adj., demonstr. pron., adv.) ðæt
that (relative pron.) ðæt (strong form),
ðət, ðt (weak forms)
Note.—The strong form is seldom
used, except in very deliberate
speech or when the word is said in
isolation.
that (conj.) ðæt (strong form), ðət (weak
form)
Note.—The strong form is rarely used.
thatch (s. v.), -es, -ing, -ed, -er/s θætʃ,
-ɪz, -ɪŋ, -t, -ə*/z
Thatcher 'θætʃə*
thaumaturge, -s 'θɔːmətɜːdʒ, -ɪz
thaumaturgic ˌθɔːmə'tɜːdʒɪk
thaumaturg|ist/s, -y 'θɔːmətɜːdʒ|ɪst/s,
-ɪ
thaw (s. v.), -s, -ing, -ed θɔː, -z, -ɪŋ, -d
the ðiː (strong form, also sometimes used
as a weak form before vowels), ðɪ
(weak form before vowels), ðə, ð (weak
forms before consonants)
Thea θɪə, 'θiːə
theatre, -s θɪ'etə* ['θɪətə*], -z
theatre-goer, -s θɪ'etə,gəʊə* ['θɪət-], -z
theatre-land θɪ'etəlænd ['θɪət-]
theatric|al, -als, -ally, -alness θɪ'ætrɪk|l
['θjæ-], -lz, -əlɪ, -lnɪs [-nəs]
theatricality θɪ,ætrɪ'kælətɪ [-ɪtɪ]
Thebaid 'θiːbeɪd
Theban, -s 'θiːbən, -z
Thebes θiːbz
thee (accus. of thou) ðiː (normal form),
ðɪ (occasional weak form)
theft, -s θeft, -s
thegn, -s θeɪn, -z
their ðeə* (normal form), ðər (occasional
weak form when a vowel follows)
theirs ðeəz
thei|sm, -st/s 'θiːɪ|zəm, -st/s
theistic, -al θiː'ɪstɪk, -l
Thelma 'θelmə
Thelusson (surname) 'teləsn
them ðem (strong form), ðəm, ðm (weak
forms), əm, m (occasional weak forms)
thematic θɪ'mætɪk
theme, -s θiːm, -z
Themistocles θɪ'mɪstəkliːz [θeˈmˈ-,
θəˈmˈ-]
themselves ðəmˈselvz
then ðen
thence ðens
thenceforth ˌðensˈfɔːθ
thenceforward ˌðensˈfɔːwəd
Theo 'θiːəʊ, 'θɪəʊ

Theobald 'θɪəbɔːld [formerly 'θɪbəld,
'tɪbəld]
Theobalds (in Hertfordshire) 'tɪbldz
['θɪəbɔːldz], (road in London)
'θɪəbɔːldz [formerly 'tɪbldz]
theocrac|y, -ies θɪ'ɒkrəs|ɪ, -ɪz
theocratic, -al θɪə'krætɪk [ˌθɪəʊ'k-], -l
Theocritus θɪ'ɒkrɪtəs
theodicy θɪ'ɒdɪsɪ
theodolite, -s θɪ'ɒdəlaɪt, -s
Theodora ˌθɪə'dɔːrə [ˌθiː:ə-]
Theodore 'θɪədɔː:* [-dɔə*]
Theodoric θɪ'ɒdərɪk
Theodosi|a, -us θɪə'dəʊsj|ə [ˌθɪə'd-,
-sɪ|ə], -əs
theologian, -s θɪə'ləʊdʒən [ˌθɪə'l-,
-dʒɪən, -dʒjən], -z
theologic, -al, -ally θɪə'lɒdʒɪk [ˌθɪə'l-],
-l, -əlɪ
theolog|ist/s, -y θɪ'ɒlədʒ|ɪst/s, -ɪ
theologiz|e [-is|e], -es, -ing, -ed θɪ'ɒlə-
dʒaɪz, -ɪz, -ɪŋ, -d
Theophilus θɪ'ɒfɪləs
Theophrastus θɪə'fræstəs [ˌθɪəʊ'f-]
theorem, -s 'θɪərəm [-rem, -rɪm], -z
theoretic, -al, -ally θɪə'retɪk [ˌθɪə'r-], -l,
-əlɪ
theoretician, -s ˌθɪərə'tɪʃn [-rɪ't-, -re't-],
-z
theorist, -s 'θɪərɪst, -s
theoriz|e [-is|e], -es, -ing, -ed, -er/s
'θɪəraɪz, -ɪz, -ɪŋ, -d, -ə*/z
theor|y, -ies 'θɪər|ɪ, -ɪz
theosophic, -al, -ally θɪə'sɒfɪk [ˌθɪə's-,
ˌθiːə's-], -l, -əlɪ
theosoph|ism, -ist/s, -y θɪ'ɒsəf|ɪzəm
[θiː:'ɒ-], -ɪst/s, -ɪ
theosophiz|e [-is|e], -es, -ing, -ed
θɪ'ɒsəfaɪz [θiː:'ɒ-], -ɪz, -ɪŋ, -d
Thera 'θɪərə
therapeutic, -s, -ally ˌθerə'pjuːtɪk, -s,
-əlɪ
therapeutist, -s ˌθerə'pjuːtɪst, -s
therap|ist/s, -y 'θerəp|ɪst/s, -ɪ
there ðeə* (normal form), ðə* (weak
form), ðr (alternative weak form before
vowels)
Note.—The weak forms occur only when
there is used existentially as in there
is, there are, there was, there
won't be, etc. The form ðeə* is also
used in such expressions.
thereabouts 'ðeərəbaʊts [ˌðeərə'b-]
Note.—The form ˌðeərə'baʊts is
always used in the expression there
or thereabouts.
thereafter ˌðeər'ɑːftə*
thereat ˌðeər'æt

thereby ˌðeə'baɪ ['— *according to sentence-stress*]
therefor ˌðeə'fɔ:*
therefore 'ðeəfɔ:* [-fɔə*]
therefrom ˌðeə'frɒm
therein ˌðeər'ɪn [*occasionally* '—]
thereinafter ˌðeərɪn'ɑ:ftə*
thereof ˌðeər'ɒv
thereon ˌðeər'ɒn
there's (= **there is, there has**) ðeəz (*strong form*), ðəz (*weak form*)
Theresa tɪ'ri:zə [tə'r-]
thereto ˌðeə'tu:
thereunto ˌðeər'ʌntu: [-tʊ, ˌðeərʌn'tu:]
thereupon ˌðeərə'pɒn ['—]
therewith ˌðeə'wɪð [-'wɪθ]
therewithal ˌðeəwɪ'ðɔ:l ['— *when used as noun*]
therm, -s θɜ:m, -z
therm|al, -ally 'θɜ:m|l, -əlɪ
thermic, -ally 'θɜ:mɪk, -əlɪ
Thermidor 'θɜ:mɪdɔ:*
thermionic, -s ˌθɜ:mɪ'ɒnɪk, -s
thermit 'θɜ:mɪt
thermodynamic, -s ˌθɜ:məʊdaɪ'næmɪk [-dɪ'n-], -s
thermogene 'θɜ:məʊdʒi:n
thermograph, -s 'θɜ:məʊgrɑ:f [-græf], -s
thermometer, -s θə'mɒmɪtə* [-mətə*], -z
thermometric, -al, -ally ˌθɜ:məʊ'metrɪk [-mʊ'm-], -l, -əlɪ
thermopile, -s 'θɜ:məʊpaɪl, -z
thermoplastic (*s. adj.*), **-s** ˌθɜ:məʊ'plæstɪk, -s
Thermopylae θɜ:'mɒpɪli: [θə'm-]
thermos, -es 'θɜ:mɒs [-məs], -ɪz
thermostat, -s 'θɜ:məʊstæt, -s
thermostatic ˌθɜ:məʊ'stætɪk
Thersites θɜ:'saɪti:z
thesaur|us, -i, -uses θɪ'sɔ:r|əs [θi:'s-, θə's-], -aɪ, -əsɪz
these (*plur. of* **this**) ði:z
Theseus (*in Greek legend*) 'θi:sju:s [-sjəs, -sɪəs], (*Shakespearian character, and as name of ship*) 'θi:sjəs [-sɪəs]
Thesiger 'θesɪdʒə*
thes|is (*dissertation*), **-es** 'θi:s|ɪs, -i:z
thesis (*metrical term*) 'θesɪs ['θi:s-]
Thespian 'θespɪən [-pjən]
Thespis 'θespɪs
Thessalian, -s θe'seɪljən [-lɪən], -z
Thessalonian, -s ˌθesə'ləʊnjən [-nɪən], -z
Thessalonica ˌθesələ'naɪkə [-'ni:kə]
Thessaly 'θesəlɪ
theta, -s 'θi:tə, -z
Thetis (*Greek*) 'θetɪs, (*otherwise*) 'θi:tɪs
theurgic, -al θi:'ɜ:dʒɪk [θɪ'ɜ:-], -l

theurg|ist/s, -y 'θi:ɜ:dʒ|ɪst/s, -ɪ
thews θju:z
they ðeɪ (*normal form*), ðe (*not infrequent as weak form, esp. before vowels*)
—— *Note.*—ðe *occurs as a strong form in the single expression* **they are,** *when* **are** *has its weak form* ə*. **They are** *in this case is also written* **they're.**
Theydon Bois ˌθeɪdn'bɔɪz
thiamin(e) 'θaɪəmi:n [-mɪn]
thias|us, -i 'θaɪəs|əs, -aɪ
thick (*s. adj. adv.*), **-er, -est, -ly, -ness/es** θɪk, -ə*, -ɪst, -lɪ, -nɪs [-nəs]/ɪz
thick|en, -ens, -ening, -ened 'θɪk|ən, -ənz, -nɪŋ [-ənɪŋ, -nɪŋ], -ənd
thicket, -s 'θɪkɪt, -s
thick-headed ˌθɪk'hedɪd [*also* '-ˌ— *when attributive*]
thickish 'θɪkɪʃ
thick-set ˌθɪk'set ['— *when attributive*]
thick-skinned ˌθɪk'skɪnd ['— *when attributive*]
thick-skulled ˌθɪk'skʌld ['— *when attributive*]
thick-witted ˌθɪk'wɪtɪd [*also* '-ˌ— *when attributive*]
thie|f, -ves θi:|f, -vz
thiev|e, -es, -ing, -ed; -ery θi:v, -z, -ɪŋ, -d; -ərɪ
thievish, -ly, -ness 'θi:vɪʃ, -lɪ, -nɪs [-nəs]
thigh, -s θaɪ, -z; -bəʊn/z
thill, -s θɪl, -z
thimble, -s; -ful/s 'θɪmbl, -z; -fʊl/z
thimblerig (*s. v.*), **-s, -ging, -ged** 'θɪmblrɪg, -z, -ɪŋ, -d
thin (*adj. v.*), **-ner, -nest, -ly, -ness; -s, -ning, -ned** θɪn, -ə*, -ɪst, -lɪ, -nɪs [-nəs]; -z, -ɪŋ, -d
thine ðaɪn
thing, -s θɪŋ, -z
thingam|y, -ies 'θɪŋəm|ɪ, -ɪz
thingumabob, -s 'θɪŋəmɪbɒb [-məb-], -z
thingumajig, -s 'θɪŋəmɪdʒɪg [-mədʒ-], -z
thingumm|y, -ies 'θɪŋəm|ɪ, -ɪz
think, -s, -ing, thought, thinker/s θɪŋk, -s, -ɪŋ, θɔ:t, 'θɪŋkə*/z
thinkable 'θɪŋkəbl
Thinn θɪn
thinnish 'θɪnɪʃ
thin-skinned ˌθɪn'skɪnd ['— *when attributive*]
third (*s. adj.*), **-s, -ly** θɜ:d, -z, -lɪ
third-rate ˌθɜ:d'reɪt [*also* '— *when attributive*]
Thirsk θɜ:sk
thirst (*s. v.*), **-s, -ing, -ed** θɜ:st, -s, -ɪŋ, -ɪd

494

thirst|y, -ier, -iest, -ily, -iness 'θɜːst|ɪ,
-ɪə* [-jə*], -ɪɪst [-jɪst], -ɪlɪ [-əlɪ], -ɪnɪs
[-ɪnəs]
thirteen, -s, -th/s, -thly ˌθɜː'tiːn ['--
according to sentence-stress], -z, -θ/s,
-θlɪ
thirt|y, -ies, -ieth/s, -iethly, -yfold
'θɜːt|ɪ, -ɪz, -ɪəθ/s [-jəθ/s, -ɪɪθ/s, -jɪθ/s],
-ɪəθlɪ [-jəθlɪ, -ɪɪθlɪ, -jɪθlɪ], -ɪfəuld
this ðɪs
Note.—*Some use a weak form* ðəs *in*
this morning (afternoon, evening).
Thisbe 'θɪzbɪ
Thiselton 'θɪsltən
thistle, -s 'θɪsl, -z
thistle-down 'θɪsldaun
thistly 'θɪsl|ɪ [-slɪ]
thither, -ward 'ðɪðə*, -wəd [-wɔːd]
tho' ðəu
thole, -s θəul, -z
Thom tɒm
Thomas 'tɒməs
Thomond (*in Ireland*) 'θəumənd
Thompson 'tɒmpsn
Thompstone 'tɒmpstəun
Thomson 'tɒmsn [-mpsn]
thong, -s θɒŋ, -z
Thor θɔː*
thoracic θɔː'ræsɪk [θɒ'r-, θə'r-]
thorax, -es 'θɔːræks, -ɪz
Thoreau (*American writer*) 'θɔːrəu
thorium 'θɔːrɪəm
thorn, -s θɔːn, -z
Thornaby 'θɔːnəbɪ
thornbush, -es 'θɔːnbuʃ, -ɪz
Thorne θɔːn
Thorneycroft 'θɔːnɪkrɒft
Thornhill 'θɔːnhɪl
thornless 'θɔːnlɪs [-ləs]
Thornton 'θɔːntən
thorn|y, -ier, -iest, -ily, -iness 'θɔːn|ɪ,
-ɪə* [-jə*], -ɪɪst [-jɪst], -ɪlɪ [-əlɪ], -ɪnɪs
[-ɪnəs]
Thorold 'θɒrəld, 'θʌrəld
thorough, -ly, -ness 'θʌrə, -lɪ, -nɪs [-nəs]
thorough-bass ˌθʌrə'beɪs
thorough-bred, -s 'θʌrəbred, -z
thoroughfare, -s 'θʌrəfeə*, -z
thoroughgoing 'θʌrəˌgəuɪŋ [ˌ--'--]
thorough-paced 'θʌrəpeɪst
thorp(e) (T.), -s θɔːp, -s
Thor(r)owgood 'θʌrəgud
those (*plur. of* that) ðəuz
thou ðau
though ðəu
thought (*s.*), -s θɔːt, -s
thought (*from* think) θɔːt

thought|ful, -fully, -fulness 'θɔːt|ful,
-fulɪ [-fəlɪ], -fulnɪs [-nəs]
thoughtless, -ly, -ness 'θɔːtlɪs [-ləs], -lɪ,
-nɪs [-nəs]
thought-read|er/s, -ing 'θɔːtˌriːd|ə*/z,
-ɪŋ
thought-wave, -s 'θɔːtweɪv, -z
Thouless 'θauləs [-lɪs]
thousan|d, -ds, -dth/s, -dfold 'θauzn|d,
-dz, -tθ/s, -dfəuld
Thrace θreɪs
Thracian, -s 'θreɪʃn [-ʃɪən, -ʃjən], -z
thraldom 'θrɔːldəm
thrall (*s. v.*), -s, -ing, -ed θrɔːl, -z, -ɪŋ, -d
thrash, -es, -ing, -ed, -er/s θræʃ, -ɪz, -ɪŋ,
-t, -ə*/z
thread (*s. v.*), -s, -ing, -ed; -bare θred,
-z, -ɪŋ, -ɪd; -beə*
Threadneedle (*street*) ˌθred'niːdl ['-ˌ--]
thread|y, -iness 'θred|ɪ, -ɪnɪs [-nəs]
threat, -s θret, -s
threat|en, -ens, -ening/ly, -ened 'θret|n,
-nz, -nɪŋ/lɪ [-nɪŋ/lɪ], -nd
three, -s θriː, -z
three-cornered ˌθriː'kɔːnəd ['-ˌ-- *when
attributive*]
three-decker, -s ˌθriː'dekə*, -z
three-dimensional ˌθriːdɪ'menʃənl
[-daɪ'm-, -ˌnəl, -ʃn̩l, -ʃnl, -ʃənəl]
threefold 'θriːfəuld
threeish 'θriːɪʃ
three-legged ˌθriː'legd ['-- *when attributive,* ˌθriː'legɪd]
three|pence, -pences, -penny 'θre|pəns
['θrɪ|p-, 'θrʌ|p-, 'θru|p-], -pənsɪz,
-pənɪ [-pn̩ɪ, -pnɪ] (*see note under*
penny)
three-ply 'θriːplaɪ [ˌ-'-]
three-quarter, -s ˌθriː'kwɔːtə* ['-ˌ--
according to sentence-stress], -z
threescore ˌθriː'skɔː* [-kɔə*, '-- *when
followed by a stress*]
threesome, -s 'θriːsəm, -z
threnod|y, -ies 'θrenəd|ɪ ['θriːn-,
-nəud-], -ɪz
thresh, -es, -ing, -ed, -er/s θreʃ, -ɪz, -ɪŋ,
-t, -ə*/z
threshing-floor, -s 'θreʃɪŋflɔː* [-flɔə*],
-z
threshold, -s 'θreʃhəuld, -z
threw (*from* throw) θru:
thrice θraɪs
thrift θrɪft
thriftless, -ly, -ness 'θrɪftlɪs [-ləs], -lɪ,
-nɪs [-nəs]
thrift|y, -ier, -iest, -ily, -iness 'θrɪft|ɪ,
-ɪə* [-jə*], -ɪɪst [-jɪst], -ɪlɪ [-əlɪ], -ɪnɪs
[-ɪnəs]

thrill (*s. v.*), **-s, -ing/ly, -ed** θrɪl, -z, -ɪŋ/lɪ, -d

thriller, **-s** 'θrɪlə*, -z

Thring θrɪŋ

thriv|e, **-es, -ing/ly, -ed, throve, thriven** θraɪv, -z, -ɪŋ/lɪ, -d, θrəʊv, 'θrɪvn

thro' θru:

throat, **-s, -ed** θrəʊt, -s, -ɪd

throat|y, **-ier, -iest, -ily, -iness** 'θrəʊt|ɪ, -ɪə* [-jə*], -ɪɪst [-jɪst], -ɪlɪ [-əlɪ], -ɪnɪs [-ɪnəs]

throb (*s. v.*), **-s, -bing/ly, -bed** θrɒb, -z, -ɪŋ/lɪ, -d

throe, **-s** θrəʊ, -z

Throgmorton θrɒg'mɔ:tn ['-ˌ--]

thrombosis θrɒm'bəʊsɪs

thrombus 'θrɒmbəs

thron|e (*s. v.*), **-es, -ing, -ed** θrəʊn, -z, -ɪŋ, -d

throneless 'θrəʊnlɪs [-ləs]

throng (*s. v.*), **-s, -ing, -ed** θrɒŋ, -z, -ɪŋ, -d

throstle, **-s** 'θrɒsl, -z

thrott|le (*s. v.*), **-les, -ling, -led** 'θrɒt|l, -lz, -ɭɪŋ [-lɪŋ], -ld

through, **-ly, -ness** θru:, -lɪ, -nɪs [-nəs]

Througham (*place*) 'θrʌfəm

throughout θru:'aʊt [θrʊ'aʊt]

throughput, **-s** 'θru:pʊt, -s

throve (*from* thrive) θrəʊv

throw (*s. v.*), **-s, -ing, threw, throw|n, -er/s** θrəʊ, -z, -ɪŋ, θru:, θrəʊ|n, -ə*/z

throw-back, **-s** 'θrəʊbæk, -s

thrum (*s. v.*), **-s, -ming, -med** θrʌm, -z, -ɪŋ, -d

thrush, **-es** θrʌʃ, -ɪz

thrust (*s. v.*), **-s, -ing** θrʌst, -s, -ɪŋ

Thucydides θju:'sɪdɪdi:z [θjʊ's-, -dəd-]

thud (*s. v.*), **-s, -ding, -ded** θʌd, -z, -ɪŋ, -ɪd

thug, **-s** θʌg (*Hindi* ʈhəg), -z

thuggery 'θʌgərɪ

Thuillier 'twɪljə* [-lɪə*]

Thule 'θju:lɪ [-lɪ]

thulium 'θu:lɪəm [-ljəm]

thumb (*s. v.*), **-s, -ing, -ed** θʌm, -z, -ɪŋ, -d

thumb-mark, **-s** 'θʌmmɑ:k, -s

thumbscrew, **-s** 'θʌmskru:, -z

thumbstall, **-s** 'θʌmstɔ:l, -z

thumbtack, **-s** 'θʌmtæk, -s

thummim 'θʌmɪm [*in Jewish usage also* 'θʊm- *and* 'tʊm-]

thump (*s. v.*), **-s, -ing, -ed, -er/s** θʌmp, -s, -ɪŋ, -t [θʌmt], -ə*/z

Thun tu:n

thund|er, **-ers, -ering/ly, -ered, -erer/s** 'θʌnd|ə*, -əz, -ərɪŋ/lɪ, -əd, -ərə*/z

thunderbolt, **-s** 'θʌndəbəʊlt, -s

thunder-clap, **-s** 'θʌndəklæp, -s

thunderous, **-ly** 'θʌndərəs, -lɪ

thunder-storm, **-s** 'θʌndəstɔ:m, -z

thunderstruck 'θʌndəstrʌk

thund|ery, **-eriness** 'θʌnd|ərɪ, -ərɪnɪs [-nəs]

thurible, **-s** 'θjʊərɪbl, -z

Thuringia, **-n/s** θjʊə'rɪndʒɪə [tʊə'r-, -dʒə, -ɪŋgjə], -n/z

Thurloe 'θɜ:ləʊ

Thurlow 'θɜ:ləʊ

Thurn tɜ:n

Thuron (*English surname*) tʊ'rɒn [ˌtʊə'r-, tə'r-]

Thursday, **-s** 'θɜ:zdɪ [-deɪ], -z

Thurso 'θɜ:səʊ ['θɜ:zəʊ] (*Scottish* 'θʌrzo)

Thurston 'θɜ:stən

thus, **-ness** ðʌs, -nɪs [-nəs]

thwack (*s. v.*), **-s, -ing, -ed** θwæk, -s, -ɪŋ, -t

thwaite (**T.**), **-s** θweɪt, -s

thwart (*of a boat*), **-s** θwɔ:t [*in nautical usage also* θɒ:t], -s

thwart (*v.*), **-s, -ing, -ed** θwɔ:t, -s, -ɪŋ, -ɪd

thy ðaɪ

Thyatira ˌθaɪə'taɪərə

thyme, **-s** taɪm, -z

thymol 'θaɪmɒl ['taɪmɒl]

thymus, **-es** 'θaɪməs, -ɪz

thymy 'taɪmɪ

Thynne θɪn

thyroid (*s. adj.*), **-s** 'θaɪrɔɪd ['θaɪər-], -z

thyroxin θaɪ'rɒksɪn

Thyrsis 'θɜ:sɪs

thyself ðaɪ'self

tiara, **-s, -ed** tɪ'ɑ:rə, -z, -d

Tibbitts 'tɪbɪts

Tibbs tɪbz

Tiber 'taɪbə*

Tiberias taɪ'bɪərɪæs [-rɪəs]

Tiberius taɪ'bɪərɪəs

Tibet tɪ'bet

Tibetan, **-s** tɪ'betən, -s

tib|ia, **-iae, -ias** 'tɪb|ɪə ['taɪb-, -bjə], -ɪi:, -ɪəz

Tibullus tɪ'bʌləs [-'bʊl-]

tic tɪk

tic douloureux ˌtɪkdu:lə'rɜ: (tik dulurø)

tic|e (*s. v.*), **-es, -ing, -ed** taɪs, -ɪz, -ɪŋ, -t

Ticehurst 'taɪshɜ:st

Tichborne 'tɪtʃbɔ:n [-bɔən, -bən]

Ticino tɪ'tʃi:nəʊ (ti'tʃi:no)

tick (*s. v.*), **-s, -ing, -ed, -er/s** tɪk, -s, -ɪŋ, -t, -ə*/z

ticket (*s. v.*), **-s, -ing, -ed** 'tɪkɪt, -s, -ɪŋ, -ed

ticking (*s.*), **-s** 'tɪkɪŋ, -z

tick|le, -les, -ling, -led, -ler/s 'tɪk|l, -lz, -lɪŋ [-lɪŋ], -ld, -lə*/z [-lə*/z]

Tickler 'tɪklə*

ticklish, -ly, -ness 'tɪk|ɪʃ [-lɪʃ], -lɪ, -nɪs [-nəs]

tickly 'tɪk|ɪ [-klɪ]

tick-tack, -s 'tɪktæk, -s

tidal 'taɪdl

tidbit, -s 'tɪdbɪt, -s

tiddledywinks 'tɪdldɪwɪŋks

tiddlywinks 'tɪd|ɪwɪŋks [-dlɪ-]

tid|e (s. v.), -es, -ing, -ed taɪd, -z, -ɪŋ, -ɪd

tide-waiter, -s 'taɪd,weɪtə*, -z

tide|water, -way 'taɪd|,wɔːtə*, -weɪ

tidings 'taɪdɪŋz

tid|y (s. adj. v.), -ies; -ier, -iest, -ily, -iness; -ying, -ied 'taɪd|ɪ, -ɪz; -ɪə* [-jə*], -ɪɪst [-jɪst], -ɪlɪ [-əlɪ], -ɪnɪs [-məs]; -ɪŋ [-jɪŋ], -ɪd

tie (s. v.), ties, tying, tied taɪ, taɪz, 'taɪɪŋ, taɪd

tie-break, -s, -er/s 'taɪbreɪk, -s, -ə*/z

Tien-tsin ,tjen'tsɪn

tier (one who ties), -s 'taɪə*, -z

tier (set of seats in theatre, etc.), -s tɪə*, -z

tierce (in music, in fencing, cash), -s tɪəs, -ɪz

tierce (in cards), -s tɜːs [tɪəs], -ɪz

tiercel, -s 'tɜːsl, -z

Tierra del Fuego tɪ,erədel'fweɪgəʊ [,tjerə-, -fʊ'eɪ-]

tiff (s. v.), -s, -ing, -ed tɪf, -s, -ɪŋ, -t

tiffany 'tɪfənɪ

tiffin, -s 'tɪfɪn, -z

Tiflis 'tɪflɪs

tig, -s tɪg, -z

tige, -s tiːʒ, -ɪz

tiger, -s 'taɪgə*, -z

tiger-cat, -s 'taɪgəkæt, -s

tigerish 'taɪgərɪʃ

tiger-lil|y, -ies 'taɪgə,lɪl|ɪ, -ɪz

tiger-moth, -s 'taɪgəmɒθ, -s

Tighe taɪ

tight, -er, -est, -ly, -ness taɪt, -ə*, -ɪst, -lɪ, -nɪs [-nəs]

tight|en, -ens, -ening, -ened, -ener/s 'taɪt|n, -nz, -nɪŋ [-nɪŋ], -nd, -nə*/z [-nə*/z]

tight-fisted ,taɪt'fɪstɪd ['-,-- when attributive]

tights taɪts

Tiglath-pileser ,tɪglæθpaɪ'liːzə* [-pɪ'l-]

tigon, -s 'taɪgən, -z

tigress, -es 'taɪgrɪs [-gres], -ɪz

Tigris 'taɪgrɪs

tike, -s taɪk, -s

tilbur|y (T.), -ies 'tɪlbər|ɪ, -ɪz

tilde, -s 'tɪldə ['tɪldɪ, tɪld], -z

til|e (s. v.), -es, -ing, -ed taɪl, -z, -ɪŋ, -d

Tilehurst 'taɪlhɜːst

tiler, -s 'taɪlə*, -z

tiler|y, -ies 'taɪlər|ɪ, -ɪz

till (s. v. prep. conj.), -s, -ing, -ed, -er/s; -able, -age tɪl, -z, -ɪŋ, -d, -ə*/z; -əbl, -ɪdʒ

tiller (of rudder), -s 'tɪlə*, -z

Tilley 'tɪlɪ

Tilling, -s 'tɪlɪŋ, -z

Tillotson 'tɪlətsn

Tilly 'tɪlɪ

tilt (s. v.), -s, -ing, -ed, -er/s tɪlt, -s, -ɪŋ, -ɪd, -ə*/z

tilth tɪlθ

tilt-yard, -s 'tɪltjɑːd, -z

Timaeus taɪ'miːəs [tɪ'm-, -'mɪəs]

timbal, -s 'tɪmbl, -z

timbale, -s tæm'bɑːl ['tɪmbl] (tɛ̃bal), -z

timber, -s, -ing, -ed 'tɪmbə*, -z, -rɪŋ, -d

timbre, -s 'tæ̃mbrə ['tæm-, -bə*, 'tɪmbə*] (tɛ̃ːbr), -z

timbrel, -s 'tɪmbrəl, -z

Timb|uctoo [-uktu] ,tɪmbʌk'tuː [-bək-]

tim|e (s. v.), -es, -ing, -ed, -er/s taɪm, -z, -ɪŋ, -d, -ə*/z

time-base, -s 'taɪmbeɪs, -ɪz

time-bomb, -s 'taɪmbɒm, -z

time-expired 'taɪmɪk,spaɪəd [-mek-]

time-honoured 'taɪm,ɒnəd [,-'--]

timekeeper, -s 'taɪm,kiːpə*, -z

timeless 'taɪmlɪs [-ləs]

time-lock, -s 'taɪmlɒk, -s

timel|y, -ier, -iest, -iness 'taɪml|ɪ, -ɪə*, -ɪɪst, -ɪnɪs [-məs]

timeous 'taɪməs

timepiece, -s 'taɪmpiːs, -ɪz

Times taɪmz

time-saving 'taɪm,seɪvɪŋ

time-serv|er/s, -ing 'taɪm,sɜːv|ə*/z, -ɪŋ

time-sheet, -s 'taɪmʃiːt, -s

time-switch, -es 'taɪmswɪtʃ, -ɪz

time-table, -s 'taɪm,teɪbl, -z

time-work 'taɪmwɜːk

timid, -est, -ly, -ness 'tɪmɪd, -ɪst, -lɪ, -nɪs [-nəs]

timidity tɪ'mɪdətɪ [-ɪtɪ]

Timon 'taɪmən [-mɒn]

Timor 'tiːmɔː*

timorous, -ly, -ness 'tɪmərəs, -lɪ, -nɪs [-nəs]

Timotheus tɪ'məʊθjəs [-θɪəs]

timothy (T.), -grass 'tɪməθɪ, -grɑːs

timpan|o, -i 'tɪmpən|əʊ, -ɪ [-iː]

Timpson 'tɪmpsn

tin (s. v.), -s, -ning, -ned tɪn, -z, -ɪŋ, -d

tinctorial tɪŋk'tɔːrɪəl

tinctur|e (s. v.), **-es, -ing, -ed** 'tɪŋktʃə*, -z, -rɪŋ, -d
Tindal(e) 'tɪndl
Tindall 'tɪndl
tinder; -box/es 'tɪndə*; -bɒks/ɪz
tine, -s taɪn, -z
tinfoil ˌtɪn'fɔɪl ['--]
ting|e (s. v.), **-es, -(e)ing, -ed** tɪndʒ, -ɪz, -ɪŋ, -d
Tingey 'tɪŋɡɪ
ting|le (s. v.), **-les, -ling, -led** 'tɪŋɡ|l, -lz, -lɪŋ [-l̩ŋ], -ld
tink|er (s. v.), **-ers, -ering, -ered** 'tɪŋk|ə*, -əz, -ərɪŋ, -əd
tink|le (s. v.), **-les, -ling/s, -led, -ler/s** 'tɪŋk|l, -lz, -lɪŋ/z, -ld, -lə*/z
Tinnevelly tɪ'nevəlɪ, ˌtɪnɪ'velɪ
tinnitus tɪ'naɪtəs ['tɪnɪtəs]
tinny 'tɪnɪ
tin-opener, **-s** 'tɪnˌəʊpnə* [-pn̩ə*], -z
Tin Pan Alley ˌtɪnpæn'ælɪ
tin-plate 'tɪnpleɪt [ˌ-'-]
tinsel 'tɪnsl
tint (s. v.), **-s, -ing, -ed, -er/s** tɪnt, -s, -ɪŋ, -ɪd, -ə*/z
Tintagel tɪn'tædʒəl
Tintern 'tɪntən [-tɜːn]
tintinnabulation, **-s** 'tɪntɪˌnæbjʊ'leɪʃn, -z
tintinnabul|um, **-a, -ar, -ary, -ous** ˌtɪntɪ'næbjʊl|əm, -ə, -ə*, -ərɪ, -əs
Tintoretto, **-s** ˌtɪntə'retəʊ [-tɒ'r-], -z
tin|y, **-ier, -iest, -iness** 'taɪn|ɪ, -ɪə* [-jə*], -ɪɪst [-jɪst], -ɪnɪs [-məs]
tip (s. v.), **-s, -ping, -ped** tɪp, -s, -ɪŋ, -t
tipcat 'tɪpkæt
Tippell 'tɪpəl
Tipperary ˌtɪpə'reərɪ
tippet, **-s** 'tɪpɪt, -s
Tippett 'tɪpɪt
tipp|le, **-les, -ling, -led, -ler/s** 'tɪp|l, -lz, -l̩ŋ [-lɪŋ], -ld, -lə*/z [-lə*/z]
tipstaff, **-s** 'tɪpstɑːf, -s
tipster, **-s** 'tɪpstə*, -z
tips|y, **-ier, -iest, -ily, -iness** 'tɪps|ɪ, -ɪə* [-jə*], -ɪɪst [-jɪst], -ɪlɪ [-əlɪ], -ɪnɪs [-məs]
tipsy-cake 'tɪpsɪkeɪk
tiptoe 'tɪptəʊ [ˌ-'-]
tiptop (s. adj.), ˌtɪp'tɒp ['--]
tirade, **-s** taɪ'reɪd [tɪ'reɪd, tɪ'rɑːd], -z
tirailleur, **-s** ˌtɪraɪ'ɜː* [-aɪ'jɜː*, -aɪ'lɜː*] (tirajœːr), -z
tirasse, **-s** tɪ'ræs, -ɪz
tir|e (s. v.), **-es, -ing, -ed/ly, -edness** 'taɪə*, -z, -rɪŋ, -d/lɪ, -dnɪs [-nəs]
tireless, **-ly, -ness** 'taɪəlɪs [-ləs], -lɪ, -nɪs [-nəs]

Tiresias taɪ'riːsɪæs [ˌtaɪə'r-, -'res-, -sɪəs, -sjəs]
tiresome, **-ly, -ness** 'taɪəsəm, -lɪ, -nɪs [-nəs]
tiro, **-s** 'taɪərəʊ ['taɪrəʊ], -z
Tirzah 'tɜːzə
'tis tɪz
tisane, **-s** tiː'zæn [tɪ'z-], -z
Tishbite, **-s** 'tɪʃbaɪt, -s
Tissaphernes ˌtɪsə'fɜːniːz
tissue, **-s** 'tɪʃuː: ['tɪsjuː:, 'tɪʃjuː:], -z
tit, **-s** tɪt, -s
Titan, **-s** 'taɪtən, -z
Titania tɪ'tɑːnjə [tɪ'tem-, taɪ'tem-, -nɪə]
titanic (T.) taɪ'tænɪk [tɪ't-]
titanium tɪ'temɪəm [taɪ't-, -njəm]
titbit, **-s** 'tɪtbɪt, -s
tith|e (s. v.), **-es, -ing, -ed** taɪð, -z, -ɪŋ, -d
tithing (s.), **-s** 'taɪðɪŋ, -z
Titian, **-s** 'tɪʃn [-ʃjən, -ʃɪən], -z
titillat|e, **-es, -ing, -ed** 'tɪtɪleɪt, -s, -ɪŋ, -ɪd
titillation, **-s** ˌtɪtɪ'leɪʃn, -z
titivat|e, **-es, -ing, -ed** 'tɪtɪveɪt, -s, -ɪŋ, -ɪd
titivation, **-s** ˌtɪtɪ'veɪʃn, -z
title, **-s, -d; -less** 'taɪtl, -z, -d; -lɪs [-ləs]
titling (stamping a title), **-s** 'taɪtlɪŋ, -z
Titlis 'tɪtlɪs
tit|mouse, **-mice** 'tɪt|maʊs, -maɪs
Tito 'tiːtəʊ
titter (s. v.), **-s, -ing, -ed, -er/s** 'tɪtə*, -z, -rɪŋ, -d, -rə*/z
tittle, **-s** 'tɪtl, -z
tittle-tattle 'tɪtlˌtætl
titular (s. adj.), **-s, -ly** 'tɪtjʊlə* [-jəl-], -z, -lɪ
titular|y (s. adj.), **-ies** 'tɪtjʊlər|ɪ [-jəl-], -ɪz
Titus 'taɪtəs
Tiverton 'tɪvətən
Tivoli 'tɪvəlɪ
Tivy (surname) 'taɪvɪ
Tizard 'tɪzəd
tmesis 'tmiːsɪs
T.N.T. ˌtiːen'tiː:
to (adv.) tuː:
to (prep.) tuː: (strong form, also occasionally used as weak form, esp. in final position), tʊ (weak form, also used as strong form before vowels), tə (weak form used before consonants only), t (occasional weak form before consonants)
toad, **-s** təʊd, -z
toad-flax 'təʊdflæks
toad-in-the-hole ˌtəʊdmðə'həʊl
toadstool, **-s** 'təʊdstuː:l, -z

toad|y (*s. v.*), **-ies, -ying, -ied** 'təʊd|ɪ, -ɪz, -ɪɪŋ [-jɪŋ], -ɪd
to-and-fro ˌtuːən'frəʊ [ˌtʊən-}
toast (*s. v.*), **-s, -ing, -ed, -er/s** təʊst, -s, -ɪŋ, -ɪd, -ə*/z
toasting-fork, **-s** 'təʊstɪŋfɔːk, -s
toast-master, **-s** 'təʊstˌmɑːstə*, -z
toast-rack, **-s** 'təʊstræk, -s
tobacco, **-s** tə'bækəʊ, -z
tobacconist, **-s** tə'bækənɪst [-kn̩-], -s
tobacco-pouch, **-es** tə'bækəʊpaʊtʃ, -ɪz
†Tobago təʊ'beɪgəʊ
Tobias tə'baɪəs [təʊ'b-]
Tobi|n, **-t** 'təʊbɪ|n, -t
tobogg|an (*s. v.*), **-ans, -aning, -aned, -aner/s** tə'bɒg|ən, -ənz, -ənɪŋ [-n̩ɪŋ], -ənd, -ənə*/z [-n̩ə*/z]
tob|y (**T.**), **-ies** 'təʊb|ɪ, -ɪz
toccata, **-s** tə'kɑːtə [tɒ'k-], -z
Tocharian tɒ'keərɪən [təʊ-, -'kɑː-]
toco 'təʊkəʊ
tocsin, **-s** 'tɒksɪn, -z
tod (**T.**), **-s** tɒd, -z
today tə'deɪ [tʊ'd-]
Todd tɒd
todd|le, **-les, -ling, -led, -ler/s** 'tɒd|l, -lz, -l̩ɪŋ [-lɪŋ], -ld, -lə*/z [-lə*/z]
toddy 'tɒdɪ
Todhunter 'tɒdˌhʌntə* ['tɒdʰəntə*]
Todmorden 'tɒdmədən ['tɒdˌmɔːdn]
to-do, **-s** tə'duː [tʊ'd-], -z
toe (*s. v.*), **-s, -ing, -d** təʊ, -z, -ɪŋ, -d
toe-cap, **-s** 'təʊkæp, -s
toe-nail, **-s** 'təʊneɪl, -z
toe-strap, **-s** 'təʊstræp, -s
toff, **-s** tɒf, -s
toffee 'tɒfɪ
tog (*s. v.*), **-s, -ging, -ged** tɒg, -z, -ɪŋ, -d
toga, **-s, -ed** 'təʊgə, -z, -d
together, **-ness** tə'geðə* [tʊ'g-], -nɪs [-nəs]
toggery 'tɒgərɪ
toggle, **-s, -d** 'tɒgl, -z, -d
Togo, **-land** 'təʊgəʊ, -lænd
toil (*s. v.*), **-s, -ing, -ed, -er/s** tɔɪl, -z, -ɪŋ, -d, -ə*/z
toile, **-s** twɑːl [twɔːl] (twal), -z
toilet, **-s** 'tɔɪlɪt [-lət], -s
toilet-cover, **-s** 'tɔɪlɪtˌkʌvə* [-lət-], -z
toilet-paper 'tɔɪlɪtˌpeɪpə* [-lət-]
toilet-powder, **-s** 'tɔɪlɪtˌpaʊdə* [-lət-], -z
toiletr|y, **-ies** 'tɔɪlɪtr|ɪ [-lətr|ɪ], -ɪz
toilet-set, **-s** 'tɔɪlɪtset [-lət-], -s
toilet-table, **-s** 'tɔɪlɪtˌteɪbl [-lət-], -z
toilet-water 'tɔɪlɪtˌwɔːtə* [-lət-]
toilette, **-s** twɑː'let (twalɛt), -s
toilsome, **-ly, -ness** 'tɔɪlsəm, -lɪ, -nɪs [-nəs]

toilworn 'tɔɪlwɔːn
tokay (**T.**) təʊ'keɪ [təʊ'kaɪ, 'təʊkaɪ, tɒ'kaɪ] (*Hung.* 'toːkɒj)
token, **-s, -ism** 'təʊkən, -z, -ɪzəm
Tokharian tɒ'keərɪən [təʊ'k-, -'kɑː-]
Tokley 'təʊklɪ
Tokyo [-kio] 'təʊkjəʊ [-kɪəʊ]
Toland 'təʊlənd
tolbooth, **-s** 'tɒlbuːθ, -s ['təʊl-, -buːð, -z]
told (*from* tell) təʊld
toledo (*blade*), **-s** tə'liːdəʊ [tɒ'l-], -z
Toledo (*in Spain*) tɒ'leɪdəʊ [tə'l-, -'liːd-] (to'ledo), (*in U.S.A.*) tə'liːdəʊ
tolerability ˌtɒlərə'bɪlətɪ [-lɪt-]
tolerab|le, **-ly, -leness** 'tɒlərəb|l, -lɪ, -lnɪs [-nəs]
toleran|ce, **-t/ly** 'tɒlərən|s, -t/lɪ
tolerat|e, **-es, -ing, -ed** 'tɒləreɪt, -s, -ɪŋ, -ɪd
toleration ˌtɒlə'reɪʃn
Tolkien 'tɒlkiːn [tɒl'kiːn]
toll (*s. v.*), **-s, -ing, -ed, -er/s** təʊl, -z, -ɪŋ, -d, -ə*/z
toll-booth, **-s** 'tɒlbuːθ, -s ['təʊl-, -buːð,-z]
Tollemache 'tɒlmæʃ, -mɑːʃ
Tollesbury 'təʊlzbərɪ
Tolleshunt (*in Essex*) 'təʊlzhʌnt
toll-gate, **-s** 'təʊlgeɪt, -s
toll-hou|se, -ses 'təʊlhaʊ|s, -zɪz
Tolstoy 'tɒlstɔɪ (tal'stoj)
Toltec, **-s** 'tɒltek, -s
tolu (**T.**) təʊ'luː [tə'ljuː]
tom (**T.**), **-s** tɒm, -z
tomahawk (*s. v.*), **-s, -ing, -ed** 'tɒməhɔːk, -s, -ɪŋ, -t
toman, **-s** təʊ'mɑːn, -z
tomato, **-es** tə'mɑːtəʊ, -z
tomb, **-s** tuːm, -z
tombola, **-s** tɒm'bəʊlə, -z
tomboy, **-s** 'tɒmbɔɪ, -z
tombstone, **-s** 'tuːmstəʊn, -z
tomcat, **-s** 'tɒmkæt [ˌ-'-], -s
tome, **-s** təʊm, -z
Tomelty 'tʌməltɪ
tomfool, **-s** ˌtɒm'fuːl, -z
tomfoolery tɒm'fuːlərɪ
Tomintoul ˌtɒmɪn'taʊl
tomm|y (**T.**), **-ies** 'tɒm|ɪ, -ɪz
tommy-gun, **-s** 'tɒmɪgʌn, -z
tommy-rot 'tɒmɪrɒt [ˌ-'-]
tomogram, **-s** 'təʊməgræm ['tɒm-], -z
tomography tə'mɒgrəfɪ
tomorrow tə'mɒrəʊ [tʊ'm-]
   Note.—Variants with final -rə *or* -rʊ *are often used in the expressions* **tomorrow morning, tomorrow night,** *and with* -rʊ *in* **tomorrow afternoon, tomorrow evening.**

499

Tompion 'tɒmpjən [-prən]
Tompkins 'tɒmɸkɪnz
Tomsk tɒmsk (tomsk)
tomtit, -s 'tɒmtɪt [ˌtɒm't-], -s
tom-tom, -s 'tɒmtɒm, -z
ton (weight), -s tʌn, -z
ton (fashion) formerly tɔ̃:ŋ (tɔ̃)
tonal 'təʊnl
tonalit|y, -ies təʊ'nælət|ɪ [-rt|ɪ], -ɪz
Tonbridge 'tʌnbrɪdʒ ['tʌmb-]
ton|e (s. v.), -es, -ing, -ed təʊn, -z, -ɪŋ, -d
toneless 'təʊnlɪs [-ləs]
tonematic, -s ˌtəʊnɪ'mætɪk, -s
toneme, -s 'təʊni:m, -z
tonemic, -s təʊ'ni:mɪk, -s
tonetic, -s təʊ'netɪk, -s
tonga (cart, medicinal bark), -s 'tɒŋgə, -z
Tonga (Friendly Islands), -n/s 'tɒŋə [-ŋgə], -n/z
Tonga (East Africa), -s, -n 'tɒŋgə, -z, -n
Tongking ˌtɒŋ'kɪŋ
tongs tɒŋz
tongue, -s, -d; -less tʌŋ, -z, -d; -lɪs [-ləs]
tongue-tied 'tʌŋtaɪd
tongue-twister, -s 'tʌŋˌtwɪstə*, -z
tonic (s. adj.), -s 'tɒnɪk, -s
tonicity təʊ'nɪsətɪ [-rtɪ]
tonic-solfa [Tonic Sol-fa] ˌtɒnɪksɒl'fɑː
tonight tə'naɪt [tʊ'n-]
tonnage, -s 'tʌnɪdʒ, -ɪz
tonological ˌtəʊnə'lɒdʒɪkl
tonology təʊ'nɒlədʒɪ
tonsil, -s 'tɒnsl [-sɪl], -z
tonsillectom|y, -ies ˌtɒnsɪ'lektəm|ɪ [-sə'l-, -sl'e-], -ɪz
tonsil(l)itis ˌtɒnsɪ'laɪtɪs [-sl'aɪ-]
tonsorial tɒn'sɔːrɪəl
tonsure, -s, -d 'tɒnʃə* [-ˌʃʊə*, -ˌsjʊə*], -z, -d
tontine tɒn'ti:n ['tɒnti:n]
tony (T.) 'təʊnɪ
Tonypandy ˌtɒnɪ'pændɪ (Welsh tonə-'pandɪ)
too tu:
toodle-oo ˌtu:dl'u:
took (from take) tʊk
Tooke tʊk
tool (s. v.), -s, -ing, -ed tu:l, -z, -ɪŋ, -d
tool-box, -es 'tu:lbɒks, -ɪz
tool-chest, -s 'tu:ltʃest, -s
Toole tu:l
Tooley 'tu:lɪ
toot (s. v.), -s, -ing, -ed, -er/s tu:t, -s, -ɪŋ, -ɪd, -ə*/z
tooth (s.), teeth tu:θ, ti:θ
tooth (v.), -s, -ing, -ed tu:θ, -s, -ɪŋ, -t
toothache 'tu:θeɪk
toothbrush, -es 'tu:θbrʌʃ, -ɪz

toothcomb (s. v.), -s, -ing, -ed 'tu:θkəʊm, -z, -ɪŋ, -d
toothed (having teeth) tu:θt [tu:ðd]
toothless 'tu:θlɪs [-ləs]
toothpaste, -s 'tu:θpeɪst, -s
toothpick, -s 'tu:θpɪk, -s
tooth-powder, -s 'tu:θˌpaʊdə*, -z
toothsome, -ly, -ness 'tu:θsəm, -lɪ, -nɪs [-nəs]
toot|le, -les, -ling, -led 'tu:t|l, -lz, -lɪŋ [-lɪŋ], -ld
top (s. v.), -s, -ping, -ped tɒp, -s, -ɪŋ, -t
topaz, -es 'təʊpæz, -ɪz
top-boot, -s ˌtɒp'bu:t, -s
top-coat, -s 'tɒpkəʊt, -s
top-dressing ˌtɒp'dresɪŋ ['-ˌ--]
top|e (s. v.), -es, -ing, -ed, -er/s təʊp, -s, -ɪŋ, -t, -ə*/z
Topeka təʊ'pi:kə
topflight 'tɒpflaɪt
top-gallant ˌtɒp'gælənt [nautical pronunciation tə'gælənt]
Topham 'tɒpəm
top-hat, -s ˌtɒp'hæt, -s
top-heav|y, -iness ˌtɒp'hev|ɪ, -ɪnɪs [-məs]
Tophet 'təʊfet
top-hole ˌtɒp'həʊl
topi (topee), -s 'təʊpɪ, -z
topiary 'təʊpjərɪ [-prə-]
topic, -s, -al, -ally 'tɒpɪk, -s, -l, -əlɪ
topicalit|y, -ies ˌtɒpɪ'kælət|ɪ [-rt|ɪ], -ɪz
topknot, -s 'tɒpnɒt, -s
Toplady 'tɒpˌleɪdɪ
topless 'tɒplɪs [-ləs]
topmast, -s 'tɒpmɑːst [-məst], -s
topmost 'tɒpməʊst [-məst]
topnotch ˌtɒp'nɒtʃ
topograph|er/s, -y tə'pɒgrəf|ə*/z [tɒ'p-, təʊ'p-], -ɪ
topographic, -al, -ally ˌtɒpə'græfɪk [ˌtəʊp-, -pəʊ'g-], -l, -əlɪ
toponymy tɒ'pɒnɪmɪ [tə'p-, -nəmɪ]
topper, -s 'tɒpə*, -z
topping (s. adj.), -s, -ly 'tɒpɪŋ, -z, -lɪ
topp|le, -les, -ling, -led 'tɒp|l, -lz, -lɪŋ [-lɪŋ], -ld
topsail, -s 'tɒpsl [-seɪl], -z
Topsham (near Exeter) 'tɒpsəm
topsyturv|y, -ily, -yness, -ydom ˌtɒpsɪ-'tɜ:v|ɪ, -ɪlɪ [-əlɪ], -ɪnɪs [-ɪnəs], -ɪdəm
toque, -s təʊk, -s
tor, -s tɔ:*, -z
Torah 'tɔ:rə [with some Jews 'təʊrɑ:, təʊ'rɑ:]
Torbay ˌtɔ:'beɪ [also '-- when attributive]
torch, -es tɔ:tʃ, -ɪz
torchlight, -s 'tɔ:tʃlaɪt, -s

torchon 'tɔːʃn [-ʃɒn] (tɔrʃɔ̃)
tore (*from* tear) tɔː* [tɔə*]
toreador, -s 'tɒrɪədɔː*, -z
toric 'tɒrɪk
torment (*s.*), -s 'tɔːment [-mənt], -s
torment (*v.*), -s, -ing/ly, -ed, -or/s
   tɔː'ment, -s, -ɪŋ/lɪ, -ɪd, -ə*/z
torn (*from* tear) tɔːn
tornado, -es tɔː'neɪdəʊ, -z
Toronto tə'rɒntəʊ
torped|o (*s. v.*), -oes, -oing, -oed
   tɔː'piːd|əʊ, -əʊz, -əʊɪŋ, -əʊd
torpedo|-boat/s, -net/s, -tube/s tɔː-
   'piːdəʊ|bəʊt/s, -net/s, -tjuːb/z
Torpenhow (*in Cumbria*) 'tɔːpənhaʊ
   [*also very commonly* trə'penə *locally,
   and sometimes* tɔː'penəʊ]
Torphichen tɔː'fɪkən [-'fɪxən]
Torphins tɔː'fɪnz
torpid, -s, -ly, -ness 'tɔːpɪd, -z, -lɪ, -nɪs
   [-nəs]
torpidity tɔː'pɪdətɪ [-ɪtɪ]
torpor, -s 'tɔːpə*, -z
Torquay ˌtɔː'kiː
torque, -s tɔːk, -s
Torquemada (*Spanish inquisitor*)
   ˌtɔːkɪ'mɑːdə [-ke'm-, -kwɪ'm-,
   -kwe'm-] (torke'mada)
torrefaction ˌtɒrɪ'fækʃn
torre|fy, -fies, -fying, -fied 'tɒrɪ|faɪ,
   -faɪz, -faɪɪŋ, -faɪd
torrent, -s 'tɒrənt, -s
torrenti|al, -ally tə'renʃ|l [tɒ'r-], -əlɪ
torrentiality təˌrenʃɪ'ælətɪ [tɒˌr-, -ɪtɪ]
Torres 'tɒrɪs [-ɪz]
Torricell|i, -ian ˌtɒrɪ'tʃel|ɪ, -ɪən [-jən]
torrid, -ness 'tɒrɪd, -nɪs [-nəs]
Torrington 'tɒrɪŋtən
torsion 'tɔːʃn
torso, -s 'tɔːsəʊ, -z
tort, -s tɔːt, -s
tortilla tɔː'tiːjə [-'tɪlə]
tortious 'tɔːʃəs
tortoise, -s 'tɔːtəs, -ɪz
tortoiseshell 'tɔːtəʃel [-təʃʃel]
tortuosity ˌtɔːtʃʊ'ɒsətɪ [-tjʊ-, -ɪtɪ]
tortuous, -ly, -ness 'tɔːtʃʊəs [-tʃwəs,
   -tjʊəs, -tjwəs], -lɪ, -nɪs [-nəs]
tor|ture (*s. v.*), -tures, -turing/ly,
   -tured, -turer/s 'tɔː|tʃə*, -tʃəz,
   -tʃərɪŋ/lɪ, -tʃəd, -tʃərə*/z
torturous 'tɔːtʃərəs
tor|y (T.), -ies, -yism 'tɔːr|ɪ, -ɪz, -ɪzəm
Tosberry 'tɒsbərɪ
Toscanini ˌtɒskə'niːnɪ (toska'niːni)
tosh tɒʃ
toss (*s. v.*), -es, -ing, -ed tɒs [*old-
   fashioned* tɔːs], -ɪz, -ɪŋ, -t

toss-up, -s 'tɒsʌp [ˌ-'-], -s
tot (*s. v.*), -s, -ting, -ted tɒt, -s, -ɪŋ, -ɪd
tot|al (*s. adj. v.*) (T.), -als, -ally; -alling,
   -alled 'təʊt|l, -lz, -l̩ɪ [-əlɪ]; -l̩ɪŋ [-əlɪŋ],
   -ld
totalizator [-isa-], -s 'təʊtəlaɪzeɪtə*
   [-tl̩aɪ-], -z
totalitarian, -ism ˌtəʊtælɪ'teərɪən
   [təʊ,t-], -ɪzəm
totality təʊ'tælətɪ [-ɪtɪ]
totaliz|e [-is|e], -es, -ing, -ed, -er/s
   'təʊtəlaɪz [-tl̩aɪz], -ɪz, -ɪŋ, -d, -ə*/z
tote, -s təʊt, -s
totem, -s; -ism 'təʊtəm, -z; -ɪzəm
t'other 'tʌðə*
Tothill 'tɒthɪl ['tɒtɪl]
Totland 'tɒtlənd
Totnes 'tɒtnɪs [-nes]
Tottenham 'tɒtnəm [-tn̩əm]
totter, -s, -ing/ly, -ed, -er/s, -y 'tɒtə*,
   -z, -rɪŋ/lɪ, -d, -rə*/z, -rɪ
Totteridge 'tɒtərɪdʒ
toucan, -s 'tuːkən [-kæn], -z
touch (*s. v.*), -es, -ing, -ed tʌtʃ, -ɪz, -ɪŋ, -t
touchable 'tʌtʃəbl
touch-and-go ˌtʌtʃən'gəʊ [-əŋ'gəʊ]
touch-down 'tʌtʃdaʊn
touché 'tuːʃeɪ
touching (*adj. prep.*), -ly, -ness 'tʌtʃɪŋ,
   -lɪ, -nɪs [-nəs]
touch-line, -s 'tʌtʃlaɪn, -z
touch-paper 'tʌtʃˌpeɪpə*
touchstone (T.), -s 'tʌtʃstəʊn, -z
touchwood 'tʌtʃwʊd
touch|y, -ier, -iest, -ily, -iness 'tʌtʃ|ɪ,
   -ɪə*, -ɪɪst, -ɪlɪ [-əlɪ], -ɪnɪs [-nəs]
tough (*s. adj.*), -s, -er, -est, -ly, -ness
   tʌf, -s, -ə*, -ɪst, -lɪ, -nɪs [-nəs]
tough|en, -ens, -ening, -ened 'tʌf|n, -nz,
   -n̩ɪŋ [-nɪŋ], -nd
toughish 'tʌfɪʃ
Toulmin 'tuːlmɪn
Toulon tuː'lɔ̃ːŋ ['-lɒn, -'lɒŋ] (tulɔ̃)
Toulouse tuː'luːz (tuluːz)
toupée, -s 'tuːpeɪ, -z
tour (*s. v.*), -s, -ing, -ed tʊə* [tɔə*,
   tɔː*], -z, -rɪŋ, -d
Touraine tʊ'reɪn
tourbillon, -s ˌtʊə'bɪljən [tə:'b-,
   'tʊəbɪlən, 'tɜːbɪlən], -z
tour de force, -s ˌtʊədə'fɔːs, -ɪz
tourist, -s 'tʊərɪst ['tɔər-, 'tɔːr-], -s
Tourle tɜːl
tourmal|in/s, -ine/s 'tʊəməl|ɪn/z
   ['tɜːm-], -iːn/z
tournament, -s 'tɔːnəmənt ['tɔːn-,
   'tʊən-, 'tɜːn-], -s
tournedos 'tʊənədəʊ ['tɜː-] (turnədo)

501

Tourneur (*English surname*) 'tɜːnə*
tourney, -s 'tʊənɪ ['tɔən-, 'tɔːn-], -z
tourniquet, -s 'tʊənɪkeɪ ['tɔən-, 'tɔːn-, 'tɜːn-], -z
tournure, -s 'tʊə͵njʊə* ['tɜːn-, *also* -'-] (turny:r), -z
Tours (*French town*) tʊə* (tuːr), (*English musical composer*) tʊəz
tous|le, -les, -ling, -led 'taʊz|l, -lz, -lɪŋ, -ld
tout (*s. v.*), **-s, -ing, -ed** taʊt, -s, -ɪŋ, -ɪd
Tout (*in* Belle Tout *in East Sussex*) tuːt, (*surname*) taʊt
Tovey 'təʊvɪ, 'tʌvɪ
tow (*s. v.*), **-s, -ing, -ed** təʊ, -z, -ɪŋ, -d
toward (*adj.*), **-ly, -ness** 'təʊəd, -lɪ, -nɪs [-nəs]
toward (*prep.*), **-s** tə'wɔːd [tʊ'wɔːd, twɔːd, tɔːd, təd], -z
Towcester 'təʊstə*
towel, -s 'taʊəl [taʊl], -z
towel-horse, -s 'taʊəlhɔːs, -ɪz
towelling, -s 'taʊəlɪŋ, -z
tower (*one who tows*), **-s** 'təʊə*, -z
tower (*s. v.*) (*tall building, etc.*), **-s, -ing, -ed** 'taʊə*, -z, -rɪŋ, -d
Towle təʊl
Towler 'taʊlə*
town, -s taʊn, -z
Towne taʊn
townee, -s taʊ'niː ['--], -z
town|ish, -y 'taʊn|ɪʃ, -ɪ
townscape, -s 'taʊnskeɪp, -s
Townsend 'taʊnzend
townsfolk 'taʊnzfəʊk
Townshend 'taʊnzend
township, -s 'taʊnʃɪp, -s
towns|man, -men 'taʊnz|mən, -mən [-men]
townspeople 'taʊnz͵piːpl
tow-pa|th, -ths 'təʊpɑː|θ, -ðz
tow-rope, -s 'təʊrəʊp, -z
Towton 'taʊtn
Towyn 'taʊɪn (*Welsh* 'təʊɪn)
toxaemia tɒk'siːmɪə [-mjə]
toxic, -al, -ally 'tɒksɪk, -l, -əlɪ
toxicity tɒk'sɪsətɪ [-ɪtɪ]
toxicolog|ist/s, -y ͵tɒksɪ'kɒlədʒ|ɪst/s, -ɪ
toxin, -s 'tɒksɪn, -z
toxophilite, -s tɒk'sɒfɪlaɪt [-fəl-], -s
Toxteth 'tɒksteθ [-təθ]
toy (*s. v.*), **-s, -ing, -ed** tɔɪ, -z, -ɪŋ, -d
Toye tɔɪ
toyes, -es tɔɪz, -ɪz
Toynbee 'tɔɪnbɪ
Toyota tɔɪ'jəʊtə [tɔː'j-]
toy-shop, -s 'tɔɪʃɒp, -s
Tozer 'təʊzə*

trac|e (*s. v.*), **-es, -ing, -ed, -er/s** treɪs, -ɪz, -ɪŋ, -t, -ə*/z
traceab|le, -ly, -leness 'treɪsəb|l, -lɪ, -lnɪs [-nəs]
trace-element, -s 'treɪs͵elɪmənt [-͵eləm-], -s
tracer-bullet, -s 'treɪsə͵bʊlɪt, -s
tracer|y, -ies 'treɪsər|ɪ, -ɪz
trachea, -s, -l, -n trə'kiːə [-'kɪə], -z, -l, -n
tracheae (*alternative plur. of* **trachea**) trə'kiːiː [-'kiːaɪ]
tracheotomy ͵trækɪ'ɒtəmɪ
trachoma trə'kəʊmə [træ'k-]
tracing (*s.*), **-s** 'treɪsɪŋ, -z
tracing-paper 'treɪsɪŋ͵peɪpə*
track (*s. v.*), **-s, -ing, -ed, -er/s** træk, -s, -ɪŋ, -t, -ə*/z
trackless, -ly, -ness 'træklɪs [-ləs], -lɪ, -nɪs [-nəs]
tract, -s trækt, -s
tractability ͵træktə'bɪlətɪ [-lɪt-]
tractab|le, -ly, -leness 'træktəb|l, -lɪ, -lnɪs [-nəs]
tractarian, -s, -ism træk'teərɪən, -z, -ɪzəm
tractate, -s 'trækteɪt, -s
tractile 'træktaɪl
traction 'trækʃn
traction-engine, -s 'trækʃṇ͵endʒɪn, -z
tractor, -s 'træktə*, -z
Tracy 'treɪsɪ
trad|e (*s. v.*), **-es, -ing, -ed, -er/s** treɪd, -z, -ɪŋ, -ɪd, -ə*/z
trade-mark, -s 'treɪdmɑːk, -s
trade-name, -s 'treɪdneɪm, -z
tradesfolk 'treɪdzfəʊk
trades|man, -men 'treɪdz|mən, -mən
tradespeople 'treɪdz͵piːpl
trade(s)-union, -s ͵treɪd(z)'juːnjən [-nɪən], -z
trade-wind, -s 'treɪdwɪnd, -z
tradition, -s trə'dɪʃn, -z
tradi|tional, -tionally trə'dɪ|ʃənl [-ʃnəl, -ʃn̩l, -ʃnl, -ʃənəl], -ʃnəlɪ [-ʃnəlɪ, -ʃn̩lɪ, -ʃnlɪ, -ʃənəlɪ]
traditionalism trə'dɪʃnəlɪzəm [-ʃnəlɪ-, -ʃn̩lɪ-, -ʃnlɪ-, -ʃənəlɪ-]
traduc|e, -es, -ing, -ed, -er/s, -ement trə'djuːs, -ɪz, -ɪŋ, -t, -ə*/z, -mənt
Trafalgar (*in Spain*) trə'fælgə* [*archaic and poetical* ͵træfl'gɑː*], (*Square*) trə'fælgə*, (*Viscount*) trə'fælgə* [͵træfl'gɑː*], (*House near Salisbury*) ͵træfl'gɑː*
Note.—The present Lord Nelson pronounces the family name as trə'fælgə*. *Previous holders of the title pronounced* ͵træfl'gɑː*.

traffic (s. v.), -s, -king, -ked, -ker/s 'træfɪk, -s, -ɪŋ, -t, -ə*/z
trafficator, -s 'træfɪkeɪtə*, -z
traffic-jam, -s 'træfɪkdʒæm, -z
traffic-warden, -s 'træfɪk‚wɔːdn, -z
tragacanth 'trægəkænθ
tragedian, -s trə'dʒiːdjən [-dɪən], -z
traged|y, -ies 'trædʒəd|ɪ [-dʒɪd|ɪ], -ɪz
Trager 'treɪgə*
tragic, -al, -ally, -alness 'trædʒɪk, -l, -əlɪ, -lnɪs [-nəs]
tragi-comed|y, -ies ‚trædʒɪ'kɒməd|ɪ [-mɪd|ɪ], -ɪz
tragi-comic, -al, -ally ‚trædʒɪ'kɒmɪk, -l, -əlɪ
tragus, -es 'treɪgəs, -ɪz
Traherne trə'hɜːn
trail (s. v.), -s, -ing, -ed, -er/s treɪl, -z, -ɪŋ, -d, -ə*/z
train (s. v.), -s, -ing/s, -ed, -er/s treɪn, -z, -ɪŋ/z, -d, -ə*/z
train-band, -s 'treɪnbænd, -z
train-bearer, -s 'treɪn‚beərə*, -z
trainee, -s treɪ'niː, -z
train-ferr|y, -ies 'treɪn‚fer|ɪ, -ɪz
training-ship, -s 'treɪnɪŋʃɪp, -s
train-oil 'treɪnɔɪl
train-sick 'treɪnsɪk
traips|e, -es, -ing, -ed treɪps, -ɪz, -ɪŋ, -t
trait, -s treɪ, -z [treɪt, -s]
traitor, -s 'treɪtə*, -z
traitorous, -ly, -ness 'treɪtərəs, -lɪ, -nɪs [-nəs]
traitress, -es 'treɪtrɪs [-trəs, -tres], -ɪz
Trajan 'treɪdʒən
trajector|y, -ies trə'dʒektər|ɪ ['trædʒɪktər|ɪ, -dʒək-], -ɪz
Tralee trə'liː
tram, -s træm, -z
tramcar, -s 'træmkɑː*, -z
tram-line, -s 'træmlaɪn, -z
tramm|el (s. v.), -els, -elling, -elled 'træm|l, -lz, -əlɪŋ [-l̩ɪŋ], -ld
tramp (s. v.), -s, -ing, -ed, -er/s træmp, -s, -ɪŋ, -t [træmt], -ə*/z
tramp|le, -les, -ling, -led, -ler/s 'træmp|l, -lz, -lɪŋ [-l̩ɪŋ], -ld, -lə*/z [-l̩ə*/z]
trampolin(e) 'træmpəliːn [-lɪn], -z
tramway, -s 'træmweɪ, -z
trance, -s trɑːns, -ɪz
tranquil, -ly, -ness 'træŋkwɪl, -ɪ, -nɪs [-nəs]
tranquillity træŋ'kwɪlətɪ [-ɪtɪ]
tranquillization [-isa-] ‚træŋkwɪlaɪ'zeɪʃn
tranquilliz|e [-is|e], -es, -ing/ly, -ed, -er/s 'træŋkwɪlaɪz, -ɪz, -ɪŋ/lɪ, -d, -ə*/z

transact, -s, -ing, -ed, -or/s træn'zækt [trɑː-, trən-, -n'sækt], -s, -ɪŋ, -ɪd, -ə*/z
transaction, -s træn'zækʃn [trɑː-, trən- -n'sæk-], -z
transalpine ‚trænz'ælpaɪn [‚trɑː-]
transatlantic ‚trænzət'læntɪk [‚trɑː-, -zə'tlæn-, -zæt'læn-, -zæ'tlæn-]
Transbaikalia ‚trænzbaɪ'kɑːljə [‚trɑː-, -lɪə]
Transcaspian ‚trænz'kæspjən [‚trɑː-, -pɪən]
transcend, -s, -ing, -ed træn'send [trɑː-], -z, -ɪŋ, -ɪd
transcenden|ce, -cy, -t/ly træn'sendən|s [trɑː-], -sɪ, -t/lɪ
transcendent|al, -ally ‚trænsen'dent|l [‚trɑː-, -sən-], -əlɪ [-l̩ɪ]
transcendentali|sm, -st/s ‚trænsen-'dentəlɪ|zəm [‚trɑː-, -sən-, -tl̩ɪ-], -st/s
transcontinental 'trænz‚kɒntɪ'nentl ['trɑː-nz-]
transcrib|e, -es, -ing, -ed, -er/s træn-'skraɪb [trɑː-], -z, -ɪŋ, -d, -ə*/z
transcript, -s 'trænskrɪpt ['trɑː-], -s
transcription, -s træn'skrɪpʃn [trɑː-], -z
transducer, -s trænz'djuːsə* [trɑː-, -ns-], -z
transept, -s 'trænsept ['trɑː-], -s
transfer (s.), -s 'trænsfɜː* ['trɑː-], -z
transfer (v.), -s, -ring, -red, -rer/s træns'fɜː* [trɑː-], -z, -rɪŋ, -d, -rə*/z
transferability træns‚fɜːrə'bɪlətɪ [trɑː-ns-, ‚trænsfərə'b-, ‚trɑː-nsfərə'b-, -lɪt-]
transferable træns'fɜːrəbl [trɑː-ns'fɜːrə-, 'trænsfərə-, 'trɑː-nsfərə-]
transferee, -s ‚trænsfɜː'riː [‚trɑː-], -z
transference, -s 'trænsfərəns ['trɑː-ns-fər-, træns'fɜːr-, trɑː-ns'fɜːr-], -ɪz
transfiguration (T.), -s ‚trænsfɪgə'reɪʃn [‚trɑː-nsf-, ‚træns‚f-, trɑː-ns‚f-, -gjʊə'r-, -gjə'r-, -gjʊ'r-], -z
transfigur|e, -es, -ing, -ed, -ement/s træns'fɪgə* [trɑː-], -z, -rɪŋ, -d, -mənt/s
transfix, -es, -ing, -ed træns'fɪks [trɑː-], -ɪz, -ɪŋ, -t
transfixion, -s træns'fɪkʃn [trɑː-], -z
transform, -s, -ing, -ed, -er/s; -able træns'fɔːm [trɑː-], -z, -ɪŋ, -d, -ə*/z; -əbl
†transformation, -s ‚trænsfə'meɪʃn [‚trɑː-, -fɔː'm-], -z
transfus|e, -es, -ing, -ed, -er/s træns-'fjuːz [trɑː-], -ɪz, -ɪŋ, -d, -ə*/z
transfusible træns'fjuːzəbl [trɑː-n-, -zɪb-]

503

transfusion, -s træns'fju:ʒn [trɑ:n-], -z

transgress, -es, -ing, -ed, -or/s træns-'gres [trɑ:n-, -nz'g-], -ɪz, -ɪŋ, -t, -ə*/z

transgression, -s træns'greʃn [trɑ:n-, -nz'g-], -z

transien|ce, -cy, -t/ly, -tness 'trænzɪən|s ['trɑ:n-, -nzjən-, -nʒɪən-, -nʒjən-, -nsɪən-, -nsjən-, -nʃɪən-, -nʃjən-], -sɪ, -t/lɪ, -tnɪs [-nəs]

transilient træn'sɪlɪənt [trɑ:n-, -ljənt]

transistor, -s, -ized [-ised] træn'sɪstə* [trɑ:n-, -n'z-], -z, -raɪzd

transit, -s 'trænsɪt ['trɑ:nsɪt, 'trænzɪt, 'trɑ:nzɪt], -s

transition, -s træn'sɪʒn [trɑ:n-, trən-, -n'zɪʃn], -z

tran|sitional, -sitionally træn|'sɪʒənl [trɑ:n-, trən-, -'sɪʒnəl, -'sɪʒnˌl, -'sɪʒnˌl, -'sɪʒənəl, -'zɪʃənl, -'zɪʃnəl, -'zɪʃnˌl, -'zɪʃnˌl, -'zɪʃənəl], -'sɪʒnəlɪ [-'sɪʒnəlɪ, -'sɪʒnˌlɪ, -'sɪʒnəlɪ, -'zɪʃnəlɪ, -'zɪʃnˌlɪ, -'zɪʃnˌlɪ, -'zɪʃənəlɪ]

transitive, -ly, -ness 'trænsətɪv ['trɑ:n-, -nzə-, -nsɪ-, -nzɪ-], -lɪ, -nɪs [-nəs]

transitor|y, -ily, -iness 'trænsɪtər|ɪ ['trɑ:n-, -nzɪ-, -sət-, -zət-], -əlɪ [-ɪlɪ], -ɪnɪs [-məs]

Transjordan ˌtrænz'dʒɔ:dn [ˌtrɑ:n-]

Transjordania, -n/s ˌtrænzdʒɔ:'demjə [ˌtrɑ:n-, -nɪə], -n/z

Transkei ˌtræns'kaɪ [ˌtrɑ:ns-, ˌtrænz-, ˌtrɑ:nz-]

translat|e, -es, -ing, -ed, -or/s; -able træns'leɪt [trɑ:ns-, trænz-, trɑ:nz-, trəns-, trənz-], -s, -ɪŋ, -ɪd, -ə*/z; -əbl

translation, -s træns'leɪʃn [trɑ:ns-, trænz-, trɑ:nz-, trəns-, trənz-], -z

transliterat|e, -es, -ing, -ed, -or/s trænz'lɪtəreɪt [trɑ:n-, -ns'l-], -s, -ɪŋ, -ɪd, -ə*/z

transliteration, -s ˌtrænzlɪtə'reɪʃn [ˌtrɑ:n-, -nsl-, -ˌ--'--], -z

translucen|ce, -cy, -t/ly trænz'lu:sn|s [trɑ:n-, -ns'l-, -'lju:-], -sɪ, -t/lɪ

transmigrat|e, -es, -ing, -ed, -or/s ˌtrænzmaɪ'greɪt [ˌtrɑ:n-, -nsm-, -'--], -s, -ɪŋ, -ɪd, -ə*/z

transmigration, -s ˌtrænzmaɪ'greɪʃn [ˌtrɑ:n-, -nsm-], -z

transmissibility trænz,mɪsə'bɪlətɪ [trɑ:n-, -ns,m-, -sɪ'b-, -lɪt-, ˌ---'---]

transmissible trænz'mɪsəbl [trɑ:n-, -ns'm-, -sɪb-]

transmission, -s trænz'mɪʃn [trɑ:n-, -ns'm-], -z

transmit, -s, -ting, -ted, -ter/s trænz-'mɪt [trɑ:n-, -ns'm-], -s, -ɪŋ, -ɪd, -ə*/z

transmittal, -s trænz'mɪtl [trɑ:n-, -ns'm-], -z

transmittance, -s trænz'mɪtəns [trɑ:n-, -ns'm-], -ɪz

transmogrification ˌtrænzmɒgrɪfɪ'keɪʃn [ˌtrɑ:n-, -nsm-, -ˌ---'---]

transmogri|fy, -fies, -fying, -fied trænz-'mɒgrɪ|faɪ [trɑ:n-, -ns'm-], -faɪz, -faɪɪŋ, -faɪd

transmutability trænz,mju:tə'bɪlətɪ [trɑ:nz,m-, -ns,m-, -lɪt-, ˌ---'---]

transmutation, -s ˌtrænzmju:'teɪʃn [ˌtrɑ:n-, -nsm-, -mjʊ't-], -z

transmut|e, -es, -ing, -ed, -er/s; -able trænz'mju:t [trɑ:n-, -ns'm-], -s, -ɪŋ, -ɪd, -ə*/z; -əbl

transoceanic 'trænz,əʊʃɪ'ænɪk [-,əʊsɪ-]

transom, -s 'trænsəm, -z

transparenc|y, -ies træns'pærəns|ɪ [trɑ:n-, trən-, -nz'p-, -'peər-], -ɪz

transparent, -ly, -ness træns'pærənt [trɑ:n-, trən-, -nz'p-, -'peər-], -lɪ, -nɪs [-nəs]

transpir|e, -es, -ing, -ed træn'spaɪə* [trɑ:n-], -z, -rɪŋ, -d

transplant, -s, -ing, -ed; -able træns-'plɑ:nt [trɑ:n-], -s, -ɪŋ, -ɪd; -əbl

transplant (s.), -s 'trænsplɑ:nt ['trɑ:n-], -s

transplantation, -s ˌtrænsplɑ:n'teɪʃn [ˌtrɑ:n-], -z

transpontine ˌtrænz'pɒntaɪn

transport (s.), -s 'trænspɔ:t ['trɑ:n-], -s

transport (v.), -s, -ing, -ed; -able træn'spɔ:t [trɑ:n-], -s, -ɪŋ, -ɪd; -əbl

transportability træn,spɔ:tə'bɪlətɪ [trɑ:n-, -lɪt-, ˌ---'---]

transportation, -s ˌtrænspɔ:'teɪʃn [ˌtrɑ:n-], -z

transporter, -s træn'spɔ:tə* [trɑ:n-], -z

transpos|e, -es, -ing, -ed, -er/s; -able, -al/s træns'pəʊz [trɑ:n-], -ɪz, -ɪŋ, -d, -ə*/z; -əbl, -l/z

transposition, -s ˌtrænspə'zɪʃn [ˌtrɑ:n-, -pʊ'z-], -z

trans-ship, -s. -ping, -ped, -ment/s træns'ʃɪp [trɑ:n-, -nʃ'ʃ-, -nz'ʃ-, -nʒ'ʃ-, træn'ʃ-, trɑ:n'ʃ-], -s, -ɪŋ, -t, -mənt/s

Trans - Siberian ˌtrænzsaɪ'bɪərɪən [ˌtrɑ:n-]

transubstantiat|e, -es, -ing, -ed ˌtræn-səb'stænʃɪeɪt [ˌtrɑ:n-, -bz't-, -ʃɪeɪt, -sɪeɪt], -s, -ɪŋ, -ɪd

transubstantiation, -s 'trænsəb,stænʃɪ'eɪʃn ['trɑ:n-, -bz,t-, -nsɪ-], -z

Transvaal 'trænzvɑ:l ['trɑ:n-, -nsv-, ˌ-'-]

Transvaaler, -s 'trænz‚vɑːlə* ['trɑːn-, -nsv-, ‚-'--], -z
transversal, -s trænz'vɜːsl [trɑːn-], -z
transverse 'trænzvɜːs ['trɑːn-, *also* ‚-'-, *esp. when not attributive*]
transversely ‚trænz'vɜːslɪ [‚trɑːn-, '-‚--]
transvesticism trænz'vestɪsɪzəm [trɑːn-]
transvestite, -s trænz'vestaɪt [trɑːn-], -s
Transylvania, -n ‚trænsɪl'veɪnjə [‚trɑːn-, -nɪə], -n
tranter, -s 'træntə*, -z
trap (*s. v.*), **-s, -ping/s, -ped, -per/s** træp, -s, -ɪŋ/z, -t, -ə*/z
trap-door, -s ‚træp'dɔː:* [-'dɔə*], -z
trapes (*v.*), **-es, -ing, -ed** treɪps, -ɪz, -ɪŋ, -t
trapeze, -s trə'piːz, -ɪz
trapezium, -s trə'piːzjəm [-zɪəm], -z
trapezoid, -s 'træpɪzɔɪd, -z
Trappist, -s 'træpɪst, -s
trapply, -iness 'træp|ɪ, -mɪs [-məs]
Traprain trə'preɪn
trapse, *see* **traipse, trapes**
Traquair trə'kweə*
trash (*s. v.*), **-es, -ing, -ed** træʃ, -ɪz, -ɪŋ, -t
trashly, -ier, -iest, -iness 'træʃ|ɪ, -ɪə*, -ɪɪst, -ɪnɪs [-məs]
Trasimene 'træzɪmiːn
trauma, -s 'trɔːmə ['traʊ-], -z
traumatic trɔː'mætɪk [traʊ'm-]
trav|ail (*s. v.*), **-ails, -ailing, -ailed** 'træv|eɪl [trə'veɪl], -eɪlz, -eɪlɪŋ, -eɪld
Travancore ‚trævəŋ'kɔː:* [-'kɔə*]
trav |el (*s. v.*), **-els, -elling, -elled, -eller/s** 'træv|l, -lz, -lɪŋ [-|lɪŋ], -ld, -lə*/z [-|ə*/z]
travelator, -s 'trævəleɪtə*, -z
travelogue, -s 'trævəlɒg [-ləʊg], -z
Travers 'trævəz
travers|e (*s. adj. v.*), **-es, -ing, -ed** 'trævəs [trə'vɜːs], -ɪz, -ɪŋ, -t
travestly (*s. v.*), **-ies, -ying, -ied** 'trævəst|ɪ [-vɪs-], -ɪz, -ɪɪŋ, -ɪd
Traviata ‚trævɪ'ɑːtə
Travis 'trævɪs
trawl (*s. v.*), **-s, -ing, -ed** trɔːl, -z, -ɪŋ, -d
trawler, -s 'trɔːlə*, -z
tray, -s treɪ, -z
Traylee, -s treɪ'liː:, -z
treacherous, -ly, -ness 'tretʃərəs, -lɪ, -nɪs [-nəs]
treacherly, -ies 'tretʃər|ɪ, -ɪz
treacle, -s 'triːkl, -z
treacly, -liness 'triːk|lɪ [-lɪ], -|mɪs [-lmɪs, -nəs]
tread (*s. v.*), **-s, -ing, trod, trodden, treader/s** tred, -z, -ɪŋ, trɒd, 'trɒdn, 'tredə*/z

treadle, -s 'tredl, -z
treadmill, -s 'tredmɪl, -z
Treanor 'tremə*
treason, -s 'triːzn, -z
treasonab|le, -ly, -leness 'triːznəb|l [-znə-, -zənə-], -lɪ, -lnɪs [-nəs]
treasonous 'triːznəs [-znəs, -zənəs]
treas|ure (*s. v.*), **-ures, -uring, -ured** 'treʒ|ə*, -əz, -ərɪŋ, -əd
treasure-hou|se, -ses 'treʒəhaʊ|s, -zɪz
treasurer, -s 'treʒərə*, -z
treasurership, -s 'treʒərəʃɪp, -s
treasure-trove 'treʒətrəʊv
treasurly, -ies 'treʒər|ɪ, -ɪz
treat (*s. v.*), **-s, -ing, -ed, -ment/s** triːt, -s, -ɪŋ, -ɪd, -mənt/s
treatise, -s 'triːtɪz [-tɪs], -ɪz
treatly, -ies 'triːt|ɪ, -ɪz
Trebarwith trɪ'bɑːwɪθ [trə'b-]
Trebizond 'trebɪzɒnd
treb|le (*s. adj. v.*), **-les, -ly; -ling, -led** 'treb|l, -lz, -lɪ, -|lɪŋ [-lɪŋ], -ld
Tredegar trɪ'diːgə* [trə'd-] (*Welsh* tre'degar)
Tredennick trɪ'denɪk [trə'd-]
tree (*s. v.*) (**T.**), **-s, -ing, -d** triː, -z, -ɪŋ, -d
tree-creeper, -s 'triː‚kriːpə*, -z
tree-fern, -s 'triːfɜːn, -z
treeless 'triːlɪs [-ləs]
trefoil, -s 'trefɔɪl ['triːf-, trɪ'f-], -z
Trefor 'trevə* (*Welsh* 'trevor)
Trefriw 'trevrɪu: (*Welsh* 'trevriu)
Trefusis trɪ'fjuːsɪs [trə'f-]
Tregaskis trɪ'gæskɪs [trə'g-]
Tregear (*surname, place in Cornwall*) trɪ'gɪə* [trə'g-]
Tregoning trɪ'gɒnɪŋ [trə'g-]
Treherne trɪ'hɜːn [trə'h-]
trek (*s. v.*), **-s, -king, -ked, -ker/s** trek, -s, -ɪŋ, -t, -ə*/z
Trelawn(e)y trɪ'lɔːnɪ [trə'l-]
Treleaven trɪ'levən [trə'l-]
trellis, -es, -ed 'trelɪs, -ɪz, -t
trellis-work 'trelɪswɜːk
Treloar trɪ'ləʊə* [trə'l-], -'ləə*
Tremadoc trɪ'mædək [trə'm-]
Tremayne trɪ'meɪn [trə'm-]
tremb|le, -les, -ling/ly, -led, -ler/s 'tremb|l, -lz, -lɪŋ/lɪ, -ld, -lə*/z
trembly 'tremblɪ
tremendous, -ly, -ness trɪ'mendəs [trə'm-], -lɪ, -nɪs [-nəs]
Tremills 'tremlz
tremolo, -s 'tremələʊ, -z
Tremont trɪ'mɒnt [trə'm-]
tremor, -s 'tremə*, -z
Tremoutha trɪ'maʊðə [trə'm-]

505

tremulant, -s 'tremjʊlənt [-mjə-], -s
tremulous, -ly, -ness 'tremjʊləs [-mjə-],
-lɪ, -nɪs [-nəs]
trench (s. v.) (T.), -es, -ing, -ed, -er/s
trentʃ, -ɪz, -ɪŋ, -t, -ə*/z
trenchan|cy, -t/ly 'trentʃən|sɪ, -t/lɪ
Trenchard 'trentʃɑːd [-tʃəd]
trencher, -s 'trentʃə*, -z
trend (s. v.), -s, -ing, -ed trend, -z, -ɪŋ,
-ɪd
trend|y, -ies 'trend|ɪ, -ɪz
Trent trent
Trentham 'trentəm
trepan (s. v.), -s, -ning, -ned trɪ'pæn
[trə'p-], -z, -ɪŋ, -d
trephin|e (s. v.), -es, -ing, -ed trɪ'fiːn
[tre'f-, trə'f-, -'fam], -z, -ɪŋ, -d
trepidation ˌtrepɪ'deɪʃn
Treshinish trɪ'ʃɪnɪʃ [trə'ʃ-]
Tresilian trɪ'sɪlɪən [trə's-, -ljən]
Tresmeer 'trez.mɪə*
trespass (s. v.), -es, -ing, -ed, -er/s
'trespəs, -ɪz, -ɪŋ, -t, -ə*/z
tress, -es, -ed; -y tres, -ɪz, -t; -ɪ
trestle, -s 'tresl, -z
Trethewy trɪ'θjuː ɪ [trə'θ-, -'θjʊɪ]
Trethowan trɪ'θəʊən [trə'θ-], -'θaʊən,
-'θɔːən
Trevaldwyn trɪ'vɔːldwɪn [trə'v-]
Trevaskis trɪ'væskɪs [trə'v-]
Trevelga trɪ'velgə [trə'v-]
Trevelyan trɪ'vɪljən [trə'v-], -'veljən
Treves triːvz
Trevethick trɪ'veθɪk [trə'v-]
Trevigue trɪ'viːg [trə'v-]
Trevisa (John of) trɪ'viːsə [trə'v-]
Trevithick 'trevɪθɪk
Trevor 'trevə* (Welsh 'trevor)
Trew truː
Trewavas trɪ'wɒvəs [trə'w-]
Trewin trɪ'wɪn [trə'w-]
trews truːz
trey, -s treɪ, -z
triable 'traɪəbl
triad, -s 'traɪæd ['traɪəd], -z
trial, -s 'traɪəl, -z
trialogue, -s 'traɪəlɒg, -z
triangle, -s, -d 'traɪæŋgl, -z, -d
triangular, -ly traɪ'æŋgjʊlə* [trɪ-,
-gjəl-], -lɪ
triangularity traɪˌæŋgjʊ'lærətɪ [trɪ-,
ˌtraɪæŋ-, -gjə'l-, -rtɪ]
triangulat|e, -es, -ing, -ed traɪ'æŋg-
jʊleɪt [trɪ-, -gjəl-], -s, -ɪŋ, -ɪd
triangulation traɪˌæŋgjʊ'leɪʃn [trɪ-,
ˌtraɪæŋ-, -gjə'l-]
Triangulum traɪ'æŋgjʊləm [-gjəl-]
triassic traɪ'æsɪk

trib|al, -ally, -alism 'traɪb|l, -əlɪ, -əlɪzəm
[-ˌlɪzəm]
tribe, -s traɪb, -z
tribes|man, -men 'traɪbz|mən, -mən
[-men]
tribrach, -s 'trɪbræk, -s
tribrachic trɪ'brækɪk
tribulation, -s ˌtrɪbjʊ'leɪʃn, -z
tribunal, -s traɪ'bjuːnl [trɪ'b-], -z
tribunate, -s 'trɪbjʊneɪt [-nɪt, -nət], -s
tribune, -s 'trɪbjuːn, -z
tributar|y (s. adj.), -ies 'trɪbjʊtər|ɪ, -ɪz
tribute, -s 'trɪbjuːt, -s
tricar, -s 'traɪkɑː:*, -z
trice traɪs
tricel 'traɪsel
triceps, -es 'traɪseps, -ɪz
trichin|a, -ae, -as trɪ'kaɪn|ə, -iː, -əz
Trichinopoli [-ly] ˌtrɪtʃɪ'nɒpəlɪ
trichinosis ˌtrɪkɪ'nəʊsɪs [-kə'n-]
trichord (s. adj.), -s 'traɪkɔːd, -z
trichosis trɪ'kəʊsɪs
trichotomy trɪ'kɒtəmɪ
trick (s. v.), -s, -ing, -ed, -er/s trɪk, -s,
-ɪŋ, -t, -ə*/z
tricker|y, -ies 'trɪkər|ɪ, -ɪz
trickish, -ly, -ness 'trɪkɪʃ, -lɪ, -nɪs [-nəs]
trick|le (s. v.), -les, -ling, -led 'trɪk|l, -lz,
-lɪŋ [-lɪŋ], -ld
trickle-charger, -s 'trɪkl,tʃɑːdʒə*, -z
trickly 'trɪk|lɪ [-klɪ]
trickster, -s 'trɪkstə*, -z
trick|y, -ier, -iest, -ily, -iness 'trɪk|ɪ,
-ɪə*, -ɪɪst, -ɪlɪ [-əlɪ], -ɪnɪs [-ɪnəs]
tricolo(u)r, -s 'trɪkələ* ['traɪ,kʌlə*], -z
tricoloured 'traɪ,kʌləd
tricot, -s 'triːkəʊ ['trɪk-] (triko), -z
tricyc|le (s. v.), -les, -ling, -led 'traɪsɪk|l
[-səkl], -lz, -lɪŋ, -ld
trident, -s 'traɪdnt, -s
Tridentine trɪ'dentaɪn [traɪ-, -tiːn]
tried (from try) traɪd
triennial, -ly traɪ'enjəl [-nɪəl], -ɪ
trier, -s 'traɪə*, -z
trierarch, -s; -y, -ies 'traɪərɑːk, -s; -ɪ,
-ɪz
tries (from try) traɪz
Trieste triː'est [trɪ'e-, -'estɪ] (trɪ'ɛste)
trifid 'traɪfɪd
trif|le (s. v.), -les, -ling, -led, -ler/s
'traɪf|l, -lz, -lɪŋ [-lɪŋ], -ld, -lə*/z
[-lə*/z]
trifling (adj.), -ly, -ness 'traɪflɪŋ, -lɪ, -nɪs
[-nəs]
trifolium, -s traɪ'fəʊljəm [-lɪəm], -z
trifori|um, -a, -ums traɪ'fɔːrɪ|əm, -ə,
-əmz
trig (s. v.), -s, -ging, -ged trɪg, -z, -ɪŋ, -d

trigam|ist/s, -ous, -y 'trɪgəm|ɪst/s, -əs, -ɪ

trigger, -s 'trɪgə*, -z

triglyph, -s 'traɪglɪf ['trɪg-], -s

trigon, -s 'traɪgən, -z

trigonometric, -al, -ally ˌtrɪgənə'metrɪk [-nəʊ'm-], -l, -əlɪ

trigonometr|y, -ies ˌtrɪgə'nɒmətr|ɪ [-mɪt-], -ɪz

trigraph, -s 'traɪgrɑːf [-græf], -s

trilater|al, -ally, -alness ˌtraɪ'lætər|əl, -əlɪ, -əlnɪs [-nəs]

trilb|y (T.), -ies 'trɪlb|ɪ, -ɪz

trilingual ˌtraɪ'lɪŋgwəl

triliteral ˌtraɪ'lɪtərəl

trill (s. v.), -s, -ing, -ed trɪl, -z, -ɪŋ, -d

trillion, -s, -th/s 'trɪljən, -z, -θ/s

trilobite, -s 'traɪləʊbaɪt, -s

trilog|y, -ies 'trɪlədʒ|ɪ, -ɪz

trim (s. adj. v.) (T.), -mer, -mest, -ly, -ness; -s, -ming/s, -med, -mer/s trɪm, -ə*, -ɪst, -lɪ, -nɪs [-nəs]; -z, -ɪŋ/z, -d, -ə*/z

trimaran, -s 'traɪməræn [ˌ-ˈ-], -z

Trimble 'trɪmbl

trimeter, -s 'trɪmɪtə [-mətə*], -z

Trincomalee ˌtrɪŋkəʊmə'liː

Trinculo 'trɪŋkjʊləʊ

Trinder 'trɪndə*

trine (T.) traɪn

Tring trɪŋ

tringle, -s 'trɪŋgl, -z

Trinidad 'trɪnɪdæd [ˌ-ˈ-]

Trinidadian, -s ˌtrɪnɪ'dædɪən [-'deɪ-, -djən], -z

trinitarian (T.), -s, -ism ˌtrɪnɪ'teərɪən, -z, -ɪzəm

trinitrotoluene traɪˌnaɪtrəʊ'tɒljʊiːn ['traɪˌnaɪ-]

trinit|y (T.), -ies 'trɪnɪt|ɪ [-ɪt|ɪ], -ɪz

trinket, -s 'trɪŋkɪt, -s

trinomial traɪ'nəʊmjəl [-mɪəl]

trio, -s 'triːəʊ ['trɪəʊ], -z

triode, -s 'traɪəʊd, -z

triolet, -s 'triːəʊlet ['trɪəʊ-, 'traɪəʊ-, -lɪt, -lət], -s

trip (s. v.), -s, -ping/ly, -ped, -per/s trɪp, -s, -ɪŋ/lɪ, -t, -ə*/z

tripartite, -ly ˌtraɪ'pɑːtaɪt ['-ˌ-], -lɪ

tripe, -s traɪp, -s

triphibious traɪ'fɪbɪəs [-bjəs]

triphthong, -s 'trɪfθɒŋ [-ɪpθ-], -z

triphthongal trɪf'θɒŋgl [-ɪp'θ-]

triplane, -s 'traɪpleɪn, -s

trip|le (adj. v.), -ly; -les, -ling, -led 'trɪp|l, -lɪ; -lz, -lɪŋ [-lɪŋ], -ld

triplet, -s 'trɪplɪt [-lət], -s

triplex 'trɪpleks

triplicate (adj.) 'trɪplɪkət [-kɪt]

triplicat|e (v.), -es, -ing, -ed 'trɪplɪkeɪt, -s, -ɪŋ, -ɪd

tripod, -s 'traɪpɒd, -z

tripoli (T.) 'trɪpəlɪ [-pʊl-]

Tripolis 'trɪpəlɪs [-pʊl-]

Tripolitania ˌtrɪpɒlɪ'teɪmjə [-ˌ-ˈ--, -pəl-, -nɪə]

tripos, -es 'traɪpɒs, -ɪz

triptych, -s 'trɪptɪk, -s

trireme, -s 'traɪriːm ['traɪər-], -z

Trisagion trɪ'sægɪɒn [-gɪən]

trisect, -s, -ing, -ed, -or/s traɪ'sekt, -s, -ɪŋ, -ɪd, -ə*/z

trisection, -s traɪ'sekʃn, -z

Tristan (personal name) 'trɪstən [-tæn]

Tristan da Cunha ˌtrɪstəndə'kuːnə [-njə]

Tristram 'trɪstrəm [-ræm]

trisyllabic, -al, -ally ˌtraɪsɪ'læbɪk [ˌtrɪsɪ-], -l, -əlɪ

trisyllable, -s ˌtraɪ'sɪləbl [ˌtrɪ's-, '-ˌ---], -z

trite, -r, -st, -ly, -ness traɪt, -ə*, -ɪst, -lɪ, -nɪs [-nəs]

tritium 'trɪtɪəm [-tjəm]

triton (T.), -s 'traɪtn, -z

triton (physics), -s 'traɪtɒn [-tn], -z

tritone, -s 'traɪtəʊn, -z

Tritonia traɪ'təʊnjə [-nɪə]

triumph (s. v.), -s, -ing, -ed, -er/s 'traɪəmf [-ʌmf], -s, -ɪŋ, -t, -ə*/z

triumphal traɪ'ʌmfl

triumphant, -ly traɪ'ʌmfənt, -lɪ

triumvir, -s trɪ'ʌmvə* [trɪ'ʊm-, traɪ'ʌm-, 'traɪəm-, -vɜː*]

triumvirate, -s traɪ'ʌmvɪrət [-vər-, -rt], -s

triumviri (alternative plur. of triumvir) trɪ'ʊmvɪriː: [traɪ'ʌmvɪraɪ, -vər-]

triune 'traɪjuːn

trivet, -s 'trɪvɪt, -s

trivia 'trɪvɪə [-vjə]

trivial, -ly, -ness 'trɪvɪəl [-vjəl], -ɪ, -nɪs [-nəs]

trivialit|y, -ies ˌtrɪvɪ'ælət|ɪ [-ɪt|ɪ], -ɪz

trivializ|e [-is|e], -es, -ing, -ed 'trɪvɪəlaɪz [-vjəl-], -ɪz, -ɪŋ, -d

trivium 'trɪvɪəm

Trixie 'trɪksɪ

trizonal ˌtraɪ'zəʊnl [-nəl]

Trizone 'traɪzəʊn

Troa|d, -s 'trəʊæ|d, -z

Trocadero ˌtrɒkə'dɪərəʊ

trochaic trəʊ'keɪɪk [trɒ-]

troche (lozenge), -s trəʊʃ, -ɪz

trochee, -s 'trəʊkiː [-kɪ], -z

trod, -den (from tread) trɒd, -n

troglodyte, -s 'trɒglədaɪt [-ləʊd-], -s

507

troika, -s ˈtrɔɪkə, -z
Troilus ˈtrəʊɪləs [ˈtrɔɪl-]
Trojan, -s ˈtrəʊdʒən, -z
troll (s.), -s trəʊl [trɒl], -z
troll (v.), -s, -ing, -ed trəʊl, -z, -ɪŋ, -d
trolley, -s ˈtrɒlɪ, -z
trolley-bus, -es ˈtrɒlɪbʌs, -ɪz
trollop, -s ˈtrɒləp, -s
Trollope ˈtrɒləp
tromba, -s ˈtrɒmbə, -z
trombone, -s trɒmˈbəʊn, -z
trombonist, -s trɒmˈbəʊnɪst, -s
trompe l'œil, -s ˌtrɒmpˈlɔɪ, -z
Trondheim ˈtrɒnhaɪm [-ndh-]
Trondhjem (old name of Trondheim)
  ˈtrɒnjəm
troop (s. v.), -s, -ing, -ed truːp, -s, -ɪŋ, -t
troop-carrier, -s ˈtruːpˌkærɪə*, -z
trooper, -s ˈtruːpə*, -z
troop-ship, -s ˈtruːpʃɪp, -s
troop-train, -s ˈtruːptreɪn, -z
trope, -s trəʊp, -s
trophic ˈtrɒfɪk
troph|y, -ies ˈtrəʊf|ɪ, -ɪz
tropic, -s, -al, -ally ˈtrɒpɪk, -s, -l, -əlɪ
troppo ˈtrɒpəʊ [ˈtrɒppo]
Trossachs ˈtrɒsəks [-sæks, -səxs]
trot (s. v.), -s, -ting, -ted, -ter/s trɒt, -s,
  -ɪŋ, -ɪd, -ə*/z
troth trəʊθ [trɒθ]
Trotsky, -ist/s ˈtrɒtskɪ, -ɪst/s
Trott, -er trɒt, -ə*
Trottiscliffe (Kent) ˈtrɒslɪ
troubadour, -s ˈtruːbədɔː* [-dɔə*,
  -dʊə*], -z
troub|le (s. v.), -les, -ling, -led, -ler/s
  ˈtrʌb|l, -lz, -lɪŋ [-l̩ɪŋ], -ld, -lə*/z
  [-l̩ə*/z]
troublesome, -ly, -ness ˈtrʌblsəm, -lɪ,
  -nɪs [-nəs]
troublous ˈtrʌbləs
Troubridge ˈtruːbrɪdʒ
trough, -s trɒf [old-fashioned trɔːf, and
  in compounds], -s
  Note.—Some bakers pronounce trʊ,
  -z.
Troughton ˈtrautn
trounc|e, -es, -ing/s, -ed traʊns, -ɪz,
  -ɪŋ/z, -t
Troup truːp
troupe, -s truːp, -s
Trousdell ˈtruːzdel [-dəl, -dl]
trousering, -s ˈtrauzərɪŋ, -z
trousers ˈtrauzəz
trousseau, -s ˈtruːsəʊ, -z
trout traʊt
trout|let/s, -ling/s ˈtraʊt|lɪt/s [-lət/s],
  -lɪŋ/z

Trouton ˈtraʊtn
trove trəʊv
trover ˈtrəʊvə*
trow trəʊ [traʊ]
Trowbridge (in Wiltshire) ˈtrəʊbrɪdʒ
trow|el (s. v.), -els, -elling, -elled
  ˈtraʊ|əl [-el], -əlz [-elz], -əlɪŋ [-elɪŋ],
  -əld [-eld]
Trowell ˈtrəʊəl, ˈtraʊəl
trowsers ˈtrauzəz
troy (T.) trɔɪ
truancy ˈtruːənsɪ [ˈtruənsɪ]
truant, -s ˈtruːənt [truənt], -s
trubeniz|e [-is|e], -es, -ing, -ed ˈtruː-
  bənaɪz [-bɪn-], -ɪz, -ɪŋ, -d
Trübner ˈtruːbnə* (ˈtryːbnər)
truce, -s truːs, -ɪz
trucial ˈtruːʃl [-sjəl, -sɪəl]
truck (s. v.), -s, -ing, -ed; -age trʌk, -s,
  -ɪŋ, -t; -ɪdʒ
truck|le, -les, -ling, -led ˈtrʌk|l, -lz, -lɪŋ
  [-l̩ɪŋ], -ld
truckler, -s ˈtrʌklə*, -z
truculen|ce, -cy, -t/ly ˈtrʌkjʊlən|s
  [-kjəl-], -sɪ, -t/lɪ
trudg|e (s. v.), -es, -ing, -ed trʌdʒ, -ɪz,
  -ɪŋ, -d
trudg|en (s. v.) (T.), -ens, -ening, -ened
  ˈtrʌdʒ|ən, -ənz, -ənɪŋ [-n̩ɪŋ], -ənd
Trudgian ˈtrʌdʒɪən [-dʒən]
Trudy ˈtruːdɪ
tr|ue (T.), -uer, -uest, -uly, -ueness
  tr|uː, -uːə* [-ʊə*], -uːɪst [-ʊɪst],
  ˈtruːlɪ, ˈtruːnɪs [-nəs]
Truefitt ˈtruːfɪt
true-hearted ˌtruːˈhɑːtɪd [ˈ-ˌ--]
truffle, -s, -d ˈtrʌfl, -z, -d
trug, -s trʌg, -z
truism, -s ˈtruːɪzəm [ˈtrʊɪ-], -z
truly ˈtruːlɪ
Tru(e)man ˈtruːmən
trump (s. v.), -s, -ing, -ed trʌmp, -s, -ɪŋ,
  -t [trʌmt]
trump-card, -s ˌtrʌmpˈkɑːd [in contrast
  ˈ--], -z
Trumper ˈtrʌmpə*
trumpery ˈtrʌmpərɪ
trumpet (s. v.), -s, -ing/s, -ed, -er/s
  ˈtrʌmpɪt, -s, -ɪŋ/z, -ɪd, -ə*/z
trumpet-call, -s ˈtrʌmpɪtkɔːl, -z
trumpet-shaped ˈtrʌmpɪt-ʃeɪpt
truncat|e, -es, -ing, -ed trʌŋˈkeɪt
  [ˈtrʌŋk-], -s, -ɪŋ, -ɪd
truncation, -s trʌŋˈkeɪʃn, -z
truncheon, -s, -ed ˈtrʌntʃən, -z, -d
trund|le (s. v.), -les, -ling, -led ˈtrʌnd|l,
  -lz, -lɪŋ [-l̩ɪŋ], -ld
trunk, -s; -ful/s trʌŋk, -s; -fʊl/z

trunk-hose ˌtrʌŋkˈhəʊz
trunk-line, -s ˈtrʌŋklaɪm, -z
trunnion, -s, -ed ˈtrʌnjən [-nɪən], -z, -d
Truro ˈtrʊərəʊ
Truscott ˈtrʊskət
Truslove ˈtrʌslʌv
truss (*s. v.*), **-es, -ing, -ed** trʌs, -ɪz, -ɪŋ, -t
trust (*s. v.*), **-s, -ing/ly, -ed, -er/s** trʌst, -s, -ɪŋ/lɪ, -ɪd, -ə*/z
trustee, -s ˌtrʌsˈtiː, -z
trusteeship, -s ˌtrʌsˈtiːʃɪp, -s
trust|ful, -fully, -fulness ˈtrʌst|fʊl, -fʊlɪ [-fəlɪ], -fʊlnɪs [-nəs]
trustworth|y, -iness ˈtrʌstˌwɜːð|ɪ, -ɪnɪs [-məs]
trust|y, -ier, -iest, -ily, -iness ˈtrʌst|ɪ, -ɪə* [-jə*], -ɪɪst [-jɪst], -ɪlɪ [-əlɪ], -ɪnɪs [-məs]
tru|th, -ths truː|θ, -ðz [-θs]
truth|ful, -fully, -fulness ˈtruː|θfʊl, -fʊlɪ [-fəlɪ], -fʊlnɪs [-nəs]
tr|y (*s. v.*), **-ies, -ying, -ied, -ier/s** tr|aɪ, -aɪz, -aɪɪŋ, -aɪd, -aɪə*/z
Tryon ˈtraɪən
try-on, -s ˈtraɪɒn, -z
try-out, -s ˈtraɪaʊt, -s
trypanosome, -s ˈtrɪpənəsəʊm, -z
trypanosomiasis ˌtrɪpənəʊsəʊˈmaɪəsɪs
tryst (*s. v.*), **-s, -ing, -ed** trɪst [traɪst], -s, -ɪŋ, -ɪd
Trystan ˈtrɪstæn [-tən]
Tsar, -s zɑː* [tsɑː*], -z
Tsarevitch, -es ˈzɑːrəvɪtʃ [ˈtsɑː-, -rɪv-], -ɪz
Tsarina, -s zɑːˈriːnə [tsɑː-], -z
tsarist, -s ˈzɑːrɪst [ˈtsɑː-], -s
tsetse ˈtsetsɪ [ˈtetsɪ]
T-square, -s ˈtiːskweə*, -z
T.T. ˌtiːˈtiː [ˈ--, *esp. when attributive*]
tub (*s. v.*), **-s, -bing, -bed** tʌb, -z, -ɪŋ, -d
tuba, -s ˈtjuːbə, -z
Tubal ˈtjuːbəl [*rarely* -bæl]
tubb|y, -ier, -iest, -iness ˈtʌb|ɪ, -ɪə*, -ɪɪst, -ɪnɪs [-məs]
tube, -s tjuːb, -z
tubeless ˈtjuːblɪs [-ləs]
tuber, -s ˈtjuːbə*, -z
tubercle, -s ˈtjuːbəkl [-bɜːkl], -z
tubercular tjuːˈbɜːkjʊlə* [tjʊˈb-, -kjəl-]
tuberculariz|e [-is|e], -es, -ing, -ed tjuːˈbɜːkjʊləraɪz [tjʊˈb-, -kjəl-], -ɪz, -ɪŋ, -d
tuberculization [-isa-] tjuːˌbɜːkjʊlaɪˈzeɪʃn [tjʊˌb-, -kjəl-, -lɪˈz-]
tuberculiz|e [-is|e], -es, -ing, -ed tjuːˈbɜːkjʊlaɪz [tjʊˈb-, -kjəl-], -ɪz, -ɪŋ, -d

tuberculosis tjuːˌbɜːkjʊˈləʊsɪs [tjʊˌb-, -kjəˈl-]
tuberculous tjuːˈbɜːkjʊləs [tjʊˈb-, -kjəl-]
tuberose (*s.*) ˈtjuːbərəʊz
tuberose (*adj.*) ˈtjuːbərəʊs
tuberous ˈtjuːbərəs
tubful, -s ˈtʌbfʊl, -z
tubiform ˈtjuːbɪfɔːm
tubing, -s ˈtjuːbɪŋ, -z
tubular ˈtjuːbjʊlə* [-bjəl-]
tubule, -s ˈtjuːbjuːl, -z
tuck (*s. v.*) (**T.**), **-s, -ing, -ed** tʌk, -s, -ɪŋ, -t
tucker (**T.**), **-s** ˈtʌkə*, -z
tuck-shop, -s ˈtʌkʃɒp, -s
Tucson (*in U.S.A.*) tuːˈsɒn [ˈtuːsɒn]
Tudor, -s ˈtjuːdə*, -z
Tuesday, -s ˈtjuːzdɪ [-deɪ], -z
tufa ˈtjuːfə
Tufnell ˈtʌfnl̩ [-nəl]
tuft (*s. v.*), **-s, -ing, -ed** tʌft, -s, -ɪŋ, -ɪd
tuft|y, -ier, -iest, -iness ˈtʌft|ɪ, -ɪə* [-jə*], -ɪɪst [-jɪst], -ɪnɪs [-məs]
tug (*s. v.*), **-s, -ging, -ged, -ger/s** tʌg, -z, -ɪŋ, -d, -ə*/z
tug-of-war, -s ˌtʌgəvˈwɔː*, -z
tugs-of-war (*alternative plur. of* **tug-of-war**) ˌtʌgzəvˈwɔː*
Tuileries ˈtwiːlərɪ [-rɪ] (tɥilri)
tuition, -s tjuːˈɪʃn [tjʊˈɪ-], -z
tuitionary tjuːˈɪʃn̩ərɪ [tjʊˈɪ-, -ʃnərɪ, -ʃn̩rɪ, -ʃənərɪ]
Tuke tjuːk
tulip, -s ˈtjuːlɪp, -s
tulle, -s tjuːl (tyl), -z
Tullibardine ˌtʌlɪˈbɑːdɪn
Tullichewan ˌtʌlɪˈkjuːən [-ɪˈxj-, -jʊən]
Tulloch ˈtʌlək [-əx]
Tulloh ˈtʌləʊ
Tulse tʌls
tumb|le (*s. v.*), **-les, -ling, -led** ˈtʌmb|l, -lz, -lɪŋ, -ld
tumble-down (*adj.*) ˈtʌmbldaʊn
tumbler, -s; -ful/s ˈtʌmblə*, -z; -fʊl/z
tumbl|y, -iness ˈtʌmbl|ɪ, -ɪnɪs [-məs]
tumbrel, -s ˈtʌmbrəl, -z
tumbril, -s ˈtʌmbrɪl, -z
tumefaction ˌtjuːmɪˈfækʃn
tume|fy, -fies, -fying, -fied ˈtjuːmɪ|faɪ, -faɪz, -faɪɪŋ, -faɪd
tumescen|ce, -t tjuːˈmesn̩|s [tjʊˈm-], -t
tumid, -ly, -ness ˈtjuːmɪd, -lɪ, -nɪs [-nəs]
tumidity tjuːˈmɪdətɪ [tjʊˈm-, -ɪtɪ]
tumm|y, -ies ˈtʌm|ɪ, -ɪz
tumour, -s ˈtjuːmə*, -z
tum-tum, -s ˈtʌmtʌm, -z
tumular, -y ˈtjuːmjʊlə*, -rɪ
tumult, -s ˈtjuːmʌlt [-məlt], -s

509

tumultuous—tut

tumultuous, -ly, -ness tjuːˈmʌltjʊəs [tjʊˈm-, -tjwəs], -lɪ, -nɪs [-nəs]
tumul|us, -i, -uses ˈtjuːmjʊl|əs, -aɪ, -əsɪz
tun (s. v.), -s, -ning, -ned tʌn, -z, -ɪŋ, -d
tuna, -s ˈtuːnə [ˈtjuː-], -z
Tunbridge ˈtʌnbrɪdʒ [ˈtʌmb-]
tundra, -s ˈtʌndrə, -z
tun|e (s. v.), -es, -ing, -ed, -er/s tjuːn, -z, -ɪŋ, -d, -ə*/z
tune|ful, -fullest, -fully, -fulness ˈtjuːn|fʊl, -fʊlɪst [-fəlɪst], -fʊlɪ [-fəlɪ], -fʊlnɪs [-nəs]
tuneless ˈtjuːnlɪs [-ləs]
Tun(g)ku, -s ˈtʊŋkuː, -z
tungsten ˈtʌŋstən [-ten, -tɪn]
tunic, -s ˈtjuːnɪk, -s
tunicle, -s ˈtjuːnɪkl, -z
tuning-fork, -s ˈtjuːnɪŋfɔːk, -s
Tunis ˈtjuːnɪs
Tunisia, -n/s tjuːˈnɪzɪə [tjʊˈn-, -zjə, -sɪə, -sjə], -n/z
Tunnard ˈtʌnəd
tunn|el, -els, -elling, -elled ˈtʌn|l, -lz, -lɪŋ [-əlɪŋ], -ld
tunny ˈtʌnɪ
Tuohy ˈtuːɪ, ˈtuːhɪ
Tupman ˈtʌpmən
tuppence, -s ˈtʌpəns [-pns, -pms], -ɪz (see note under penny)
tuppeny ˈtʌpnɪ [-pnɪ, -pənɪ]
tu quoque, -s ˌtjuːˈkwəʊkwɪ, -z
Turandot (operas by Puccini and Busoni) ˈtʊərəndɒt [ˈtjʊə-, -dəʊ]
Turania, -n/s ˌtjʊəˈreɪmjə [tjʊˈr-, -nɪə], -n/z
turban, -s, -ed ˈtɜːbən, -z, -d
turbid, -ly, -ness ˈtɜːbɪd, -lɪ, -nɪs [-nəs]
turbidity tɜːˈbɪdətɪ [-ɪtɪ]
turbine, -s ˈtɜːbaɪn [-bɪn], -z
turbo-jet, -s ˌtɜːbəʊˈdʒet [ˈ—-], -s
turbo-prop, -s ˌtɜːbəʊˈprɒp [ˈ—], -s
turbot, -s ˈtɜːbət, -s
turbulen|ce, -cy, -t/ly ˈtɜːbjʊlən|s [-bjəl-], -sɪ, -t/lɪ
Turcoman, -s ˈtɜːkəmən [-mæn, -mɑːn], -z
tureen, -s təˈriːn [tʊˈr-, tjʊˈr-, tjəˈr-], -z
tur|f (s.), -fs, -ves tɜː|f, -fs, -vz
turf (v.), -s, -ing, -ed tɜːf, -s, -ɪŋ, -t
turf|y, -ier, -iest, -iness ˈtɜːf|ɪ, -ɪə*, -ɪɪst, -ɪnɪs [-nəs]
Turgenev tɜːˈgeɪnjev [ˌtʊəˈg-, -njef, -njɪf, -nev, -nəv] (tur'genjif)
turgescen|ce, -t tɜːˈdʒesn|s, -t
turgid, -ly, -ness ˈtɜːdʒɪd, -lɪ, -nɪs [-nəs]
turgidity tɜːˈdʒɪdətɪ [-ɪtɪ]
Turin tjʊˈrɪn [ˌtjʊəˈr-]

Turk, -s tɜːk, -s
Turkestan ˌtɜːkɪˈstɑːn [-ˈstæn]
turkey (T.), -s ˈtɜːkɪ, -z
turkey-cock, -s ˈtɜːkɪkɒk, -s
Turki ˈtɜːkiː
Turkic ˈtɜːkɪk
Turkish ˈtɜːkɪʃ
Turkoman, -s ˈtɜːkəmən [-mæn, -mɑːn], -z
turmeric ˈtɜːmərɪk
turmoil, -s ˈtɜːmɔɪl, -z
turn (s. v.), -s, -ing, -ed tɜːn, -z, -ɪŋ, -d
Turnbull ˈtɜːnbʊl
turn|coat/s, -cock/s ˈtɜːn|kəʊt/s [ˈtɜːŋk-], -kɒk/s
turner (T.), -s ˈtɜːnə*, -z
turnery ˈtɜːnərɪ
Turnham ˈtɜːnəm
Turnhouse ˈtɜːnhaʊs
turning (s.), -s ˈtɜːnɪŋ, -z
turning-point, -s ˈtɜːnɪŋpɔɪnt; -s
turnip, -s ˈtɜːnɪp, -s
turnip-tops ˈtɜːnɪptɒps
turnkey, -s ˈtɜːnkiː [ˈtɜːŋk-], -z
Turnour ˈtɜːnə*
turn-out (assembly, equipage), -s ˈtɜːn-aʊt [also ˌ-ˈ- when preceded by a stress], -s
turnover, -s ˈtɜːnˌəʊvə*, -z
turnpike, -s ˈtɜːnpaɪk, -s
turn-round, -s ˈtɜːnraʊnd, -z
turnstile, -s ˈtɜːnstaɪl, -z
turnstone, -s ˈtɜːnstəʊn [-stən], -z
turntable, -s ˈtɜːnˌteɪbl, -z
turn-up, -s ˈtɜːnʌp, -s
turpentine ˈtɜːpəntaɪn [-pmt-]
Turpin ˈtɜːpɪn
turpitude ˈtɜːpɪtjuːd
turps tɜːps
turquoise, -s ˈtɜːkwɔɪz [-kwɑːz, -kwɔːz], -ɪz
turret, -s, -ed ˈtʌrɪt [-rət], -s, -ɪd
turtle, -s ˈtɜːtl, -z
turtle-dove, -s ˈtɜːtldʌv, -z
turves (plur. of turf) tɜːvz
Tuscan, -s, -y ˈtʌskən, -z, -ɪ
tush (s. interj.), -es tʌʃ, -ɪz
Tusitala ˌtuːsɪˈtɑːlə
tusk, -s, -ed, -y tʌsk, -s, -t, -ɪ
tusker, -s ˈtʌskə*, -z
Tussaud (surname) ˈtuːsəʊ
Tussaud's (exhibition) təˈsɔːdz [tʊˈs-, -ˈsəʊz]
tuss|le (s. v.), -les, -ling, -led ˈtʌs|l, -lz, -lɪŋ [-lɪŋ], -ld
tussock, -s, -y ˈtʌsək, -s, -ɪ
tussore ˈtʌsə* [-sɔː*, -sɔə*]
tut (s. v.), -s, -ting, -ted tʌt, -s, -ɪŋ, -ɪd

510

tut (*interj.*) ʇ [tʌt]

Tutankhamen ˌtuːtəŋˈkɑːmen [-tæŋ-, -mən] (*also, with* -mun, ˌtuːtəŋkɑː-ˈmuːn)

tutel|age, -ar, -ary ˈtjuːtɪl|ɪdʒ [-təl-], -əˣ, -ərɪ

Tuthill ˈtʌθɪl

tutor (*s. v.*), -s, -ing, -ed ; -age ˈtjuːtə*, -z, -rɪŋ, -d ; -rɪdʒ

tutorial, -ly tjuːˈtɔːrɪəl [tjʊˈt-], -ɪ

tutorship, -s ˈtjuːtəʃɪp, -s

tutti, -s ˈtʊti: [-tɪ], -z

tutti-frutti ˌtuːtɪˈfruːtɪ [ˌtʊ-, -ˈfrʊ-]

Tuttle ˈtʌtl

tutu (T.), -s ˈtuːtuː:, -z

tu-whit tʊˈwɪt [tʊˈhwɪt, tə-]

tu-whoo tʊˈwuː: [tʊˈhwuː:, tə-]

tuxedo (T.), -s tʌkˈsiːdəʊ, -z

TV ˌtiːˈviː

Twaddell ˈtwɒdl, twɒˈdel

twadd|le (*s. v.*), -les, -ling, -led, -ler/s, -ly ˈtwɒd|l, -lz, -lɪŋ [-lɪŋ], -ld, -lə*/z [-lə*/z], -lɪ

twain (T.) twem

twang (*s. v.*), -s, -ing, -ed twæŋ, -z, -ɪŋ, -d

twang|le, -les, -ling, -led ˈtwæŋg|l, -lz, -lɪŋ, -ld

'twas twɒz (*strong form*), twəz (*weak form*)

tweak, -s, -ing, -ed twiːk, -s, -ɪŋ, -t

tweed (T.), -s twiːd, -z

Tweeddale ˈtwiːddeɪl

Tweedie ˈtwiːdɪ

tweed|le (*s. v.*), -les, -ling, -led ˈtwiːd|l, -lz, -lɪŋ [-lɪŋ], -ld

Tweedle|dee, -dum ˌtwiːdl|ˈdiː:, -ˈdʌm

Tweedmouth ˈtwiːdməθ [-maʊθ]

Tweedsmuir ˈtwiːdzˌmjʊə* [-mjɔə*, -mjɔː*]

'tween twiːn

tween|y, -ies ˈtwiːn|ɪ, -ɪz

tweeny-maid, -s ˈtwiːnɪmeɪd, -z

tweet, -s, -ing, -ed, -er/s twiːt, -s, -ɪŋ, -ɪd, -ə*/z

tweezers ˈtwiːzəz

twelfth, -s, -ly twelfθ [-elθ], -s, -lɪ

twelve, -s twelv, -z

twelvemo [12mo] ˈtwelvməʊ

twelvemonth, -s ˈtwelvmʌnθ, -s

twelvish ˈtwelvɪʃ

twent|y, -ies, -ieth/s, -iethly, -yfold ˈtwent|ɪ, -ɪz, -ɪəθ/s [-jəθ/s, -ɪɪθ/s, -jɪθ/z], -ɪəθlɪ [-jəθlɪ, -ɪɪθlɪ, -jɪθlɪ], -ɪfəʊld

Twentyman ˈtwentɪmən

'twere twɜ:* (*strong form*), twə* (*weak form*)

twerp, -s twɜːp, -s

Twi twiː:

twice twaɪs

Twickenham ˈtwɪkn̩əm [-knəm, -kənəm]

twidd|le, -les, -ling, -led ˈtwɪd|l, -lz, -lɪŋ [-lɪŋ], -ld

twig (*s. v.*), -s, -ging, -ged twɪg, -z, -ɪŋ, -d

Twigg twɪg

twiggy ˈtwɪgɪ

twilight, -s ˈtwaɪlaɪt, -s

twill (*s. v.*), -s, -ing, -ed; -y twɪl, -z, -ɪŋ, -d; -ɪ

'twill twɪl (*normal form*), twəl, twl (*occasional weak forms*) ˑ

twin (*s. v.*), -s, -ning, -ned twɪn, -z, -ɪŋ, -d

twin|e, -es, -ing/ly, -ed, -er/s twaɪn, -z, -ɪŋ/lɪ, -d, -ə*/z

twing|e (*s. v.*), -es, -(e)ing, -ed twɪndʒ, -ɪz, -ɪŋ, -d

Twining ˈtwaɪnɪŋ

twink|le, -les, -ling, -led, -ler/s ˈtwɪŋk|l, -lz, -lɪŋ [-lɪŋ], -ld, -lə*/z [-lə*/z]

twirl, -s, -ing, -ed twɜːl, -z, -ɪŋ, -d

twirp, -s twɜːp, -s

twist (*s. v.*) (T.), -s, -ing, -ed, -er/s twɪst, -s, -ɪŋ, -ɪd, -ə*/z

Twistington ˈtwɪstɪŋtən

twist|y, -ier, -iest, -iness ˈtwɪst|ɪ, -ɪə* [-jə*], -ɪɪst [-jɪst], -ɪnɪs [-ɪnəs]

twit, -s, -ting/ly, -ted twɪt, -s, -ɪŋ/lɪ, -ɪd

twitch (*s. v.*), -es, -ing/s, -ed twɪtʃ, -ɪz, -ɪŋ/z, -t

twite, -s twaɪt, -s

twitt|er (*s. v.*), -ers, -ering, -ered ˈtwɪt|ə*, -əz, -ərɪŋ, -əd

'twixt twɪkst

two, twos tuː: [*also* tʊ *when the following word begins with* ə], tuːz

two-dimensional ˌtuːdɪˈmenʃənl [-daɪˈm-, -ʃnəl, -ʃn̩l, -ʃn̩l, -ʃənəl]

two-edged ˌtuːˈedʒd ['-- *when attributive*]

twofold ˈtuːfəʊld

two-ish ˈtuːɪʃ

two-legged ˌtuːˈlegd ['-- *when attributive*, ˌtuːˈlegɪd]

twopence, -s ˈtʌpəns [-pms], -ɪz (*see note under* penny)

twopenny ˈtʌpn̩ɪ [-pnɪ, -pənɪ]

twopenny-halfpenny ˌtʌpn̩ɪˈheɪpn̩ɪ [ˌtʌpnɪˈheɪpnɪ, ˌtʌpənɪˈheɪpənɪ]

twopennyworth, -s ˌtuːˈpenrwɜːθ [ˌtuː-ˈpenəθ, ˈtʌpn̩ɪwɜːθ, ˈtʌpnɪ-, ˈtʌpənɪ-, -wəθ], -s

two-ply ˈtuːplaɪ [ˌ-ˈ-]

511

two-seater, -s ˌtuːˈsiːtə*, -z
twosome, -s ˈtuːsəm, -z
two-step, -s ˈtuːstep, -s
two-stroke ˈtuːstrəʊk
two-time, -s, -ing, -ed ˈtuːtaɪm, -z, -ɪŋ, -d
two-tone ˌtuːˈtəʊn
two-way ˌtuːˈweɪ
two-year-old, -s ˈtuːjərəʊld, -z
Twyford ˈtwaɪfəd
Tyacke ˈtaɪək
Tyana ˈtaɪənə
Tybalt ˈtɪbəlt [-blt]
Tyburn ˈtaɪbɜːn
Tychicus ˈtɪkɪkəs
Tycho ˈtaɪkəʊ
tycoon, -s taɪˈkuːn, -z
Tydeus ˈtaɪdjuːs [-djəs, -dɪəs]
Tydfil ˈtɪdvɪl (*Welsh* ˈtɪdvil)
tying (*from* tie) ˈtaɪɪŋ
tyke, -s taɪk, -s
Tyldesley ˈtɪldzlɪ
Tyler ˈtaɪlə*
tympan|i, -ist/s ˈtɪmpən|ɪ, -ɪst/s
tympanic tɪmˈpænɪk
tympan|um, -ums, -a ˈtɪmpən|əm, -əmz, -ə
Tynan ˈtaɪnən
Tynd|ale, -all ˈtɪnd|l, -l
Tyndrum taɪnˈdrʌm
Tyne, -and Wear taɪn, -ənd ˈwɪə*
Tynemouth ˈtaɪnmaʊθ [-məθ, *old-fashioned* ˈtɪnməθ]
Tynwald ˈtɪnwəld
typ|e (*s. v.*), **-es, -ing, -ed** taɪp, -s, -ɪŋ, -t
type-bar, -s ˈtaɪpbɑː*, -z
typecast, -s, -ing ˈtaɪpkɑːst, -s, -ɪŋ
type-cutter, -s ˈtaɪpˌkʌtə*, -z
typeface, -s ˈtaɪpfeɪs, -ɪz
type-founder, -s ˈtaɪpˌfaʊndə*, -z
type-foundr|y, -ies ˈtaɪpˌfaʊndr|ɪ, -ɪz
typescript, -s ˈtaɪpskrɪpt, -s
type-set ˈtaɪpset
type-setter, -s ˈtaɪpˌsetə*, -z

typewrit|e, -es, -ing, typewrote, type-written, typewriter/s ˈtaɪpraɪt, -s, -ɪŋ, ˈtaɪprəʊt, ˈtaɪpˌrɪtn, ˈtaɪpˌraɪtə*/z
typhoid ˈtaɪfɔɪd
typhonic taɪˈfɒnɪk
typhoon, -s taɪˈfuːn, -z
typh|ous, -us ˈtaɪf|əs, -əs
typic|al, -ally, -alness ˈtɪpɪk|l, -əlɪ, -lnɪs [-nəs]
typi|fy, -fies, -fying, -fied ˈtɪpɪ|faɪ, -faɪz, -faɪɪŋ, -faɪd
typist, -s ˈtaɪpɪst, -s
typo, -s ˈtaɪpəʊ, -z
typograph|er/s, -y taɪˈpɒgrəf|ə*/z, -ɪ
typographic, -al, -ally ˌtaɪpəˈgræfɪk [-pəʊˈg-], -l, -əlɪ
typology taɪˈpɒlədʒɪ
typolog|ist/s, -y tɪpˈtɒlədʒ|ɪst/s, -ɪ
tyrannic|al, -ally, -alness tɪˈrænɪk|l [taɪˈr-], -əlɪ, -lnɪs [-nəs]
tyrannicide, -s tɪˈrænɪsaɪd [taɪˈr-], -z
tyranniz|e [-is|e], -es, -ing, -ed ˈtɪrənaɪz [ˈtɪrṇaɪz], -ɪz, -ɪŋ, -d
tyrannosaurus, -i tɪˌrænəˈsɔːr|əs, -aɪ
tyrannous, -ly ˈtɪrənəs [ˈtɪrṇəs], -lɪ
tyrann|y, -ies ˈtɪrən|ɪ [ˈtɪrṇ|ɪ], -ɪz
tyrant, -s ˈtaɪərənt, -s
tyre (T.), -s ˈtaɪə*, -z
Tyrian, -s ˈtɪrɪən, -z
tyro, -s ˈtaɪərəʊ, -z
Tyrol ˈtɪrəl [tɪˈrəʊl]
Tyrolean tɪˈrəʊlɪən [ˌtɪrəˈliːən, -ˈlɪən]
Tyrolese ˌtɪrəˈliːz [-rəʊˈl-]
Tyrolienne, -s tɪˌrəʊlɪˈen [ˌtɪrəʊlɪˈen], -z
Tyrone tɪˈrəʊn
Tyrrell ˈtɪrəl
Tyrrhenian, -s tɪˈriːnjən [-nɪən], -z
Tyrtaeus tɜːˈtiːəs
Tyrwhitt ˈtɪrɪt
Tyser ˈtaɪzə*
Tyson ˈtaɪsn
Tytler ˈtaɪtlə*
Tyzack ˈtaɪzæk [-zək], ˈtɪzæk [-zək]
tzigane, -s tsɪˈɡɑːn, -z

U

U (*the letter*), -'s juː, -z
Ubbelohde (*surname*) 'ʌbələud
ubiquitarian (U.), -s juːˌbɪkwɪ'teərɪən
[juˌb-], -z
ubiquitous juː'bɪkwɪtəs [juˈb-]
ubiquity juː'bɪkwətɪ [juˈb-, -ɪtɪ]
U-boat, -s 'juːbəut, -s
Uckfield 'ʌkfiːld
udal (U.) 'juːdl
Udall 'juːdəl
udder, -s 'ʌdə*, -z
U.D.I. ˌjuːdiːˈaɪ
Udolpho uːˈdɒlfəu [juː-]
udometer, -s juːˈdɒmɪtə* [-mətə*], -z
U.F.O. (*unidentified flying object*)
ˌjuːefˈəu
Uganda juːˈgændə [juˈg-]
ugh uːx, uːh, ʌx, uɸ, uh, ɜːh
Ughtred 'uːtrɪd [-red]
uglification ˌʌglɪfɪˈkeɪʃn
ugli|fy, -fies, -fying, -fied 'ʌglɪ|faɪ, -faɪz,
-faɪɪŋ, -faɪd
ugl|y, -ier, -iest, -iness 'ʌgl|ɪ, -ɪə*
[-jə*], -ɪɪst [-jɪst], -ɪnɪs [-məs]
Ugrian, -s 'uːgrɪən ['juːg-], -z
u(h)lan, -s uˈlaːn, -z
Uhland 'uːlənd [-lænd, -laːnd] ('uːlant)
Uig 'uːɪg ['juːɪg]
Uist 'juːɪst
Uitlander, -s 'eɪtlændə*, -z
ukase, -s juːˈkeɪz [-eɪs], -ɪz
ukelele, -s ˌjuːkəˈleɪlɪ, -z
Ukraine juːˈkreɪn [juˈk-]
Ukrainian juːˈkreɪmjən [juˈk-, -nɪən]
ulcer, -s, -ed 'ʌlsə*, -z, -d
ulcerat|e, -es, -ing, -ed 'ʌlsəreɪt, -s, -ɪŋ,
-ɪd
ulceration, -s ˌʌlsəˈreɪʃn, -z
ulcerous 'ʌlsərəs
ulema, -s 'uːlɪmə, -z
ulex 'juːleks
Ulfilas 'ulfɪlæs
Ulgham (*in Lincolnshire and Northumberland*) 'ʌfəm
Ulick 'juːlɪk
ullage 'ʌlɪdʒ
Ullswater 'ʌlzˌwɔːtə*
ulmus 'ʌlməs
uln|a, -ae, -ar 'ʌln|ə, -iː, -ə*

Ulrica (*English name*) 'ulrɪkə ['ʌl-]
Ulrich 'ulrɪk ('ulrɪç)
ulster (U.), -s, -ed 'ʌlstə*, -z, -d
Ulster|man, -men 'ʌlstə|mən, -mən
Ulster|woman, -women 'ʌlstə|wumən,
-wɪmɪn
ulterior, -ly ʌl'tɪərɪə*, -lɪ
ultim|ate, -ately 'ʌltɪm|ət [-mɪt], -ətlɪ
[-ɪtlɪ]
ultimatum, -s ˌʌltɪˈmeɪtəm, -z
ultimo 'ʌltɪməu
ultra (*s. adj.*), -s 'ʌltrə, -z
ultra (*in* ne plus ultra), *see* ne plus ultra
ultra- 'ʌltrə-
Note.—*Numerous compound adjectives may be formed by prefixing
ultra- to adjectives. These compounds have double stress, e.g.
ultra-fashionable ˌʌltrəˈfæʃənəbl
[-ʃnə-]; the pronunciation of all
such words may therefore be ascertained by reference to the simple
words. When such adjectives are
used as substantives they keep the
double stress.*
ultraism 'ʌltrəɪzəm
ultramarine ˌʌltrəməˈriːn
ultramontane ˌʌltrəˈmɒnteɪn
ultramontanism ˌʌltrəˈmɒntɪnɪzəm
[-tən-, -teɪn-]
ultrasonic ˌʌltrəˈsɒnɪk
ultra vires ˌʌltrəˈvaɪəriːz [ˌultraː-
ˈvɪəreɪz]
ululant 'juːljulənt
ululat|e, -es, -ing, -ed 'juːljuleɪt, -s, -ɪŋ,
-ɪd
ululation, -s ˌjuːljuˈleɪʃn, -z
Ulverston 'ʌlvəstən
Ulysses juːˈlɪsiːz [juˈl-, 'juːlɪsiːz]
umbel, -s 'ʌmbəl [-bel], -z
umbellifer|ae, -ous ˌʌmbeˈlɪfər|iː
[-bəˈl-], -əs
umber, -s, -y 'ʌmbə*, -z, -ɪ
umbilic, -s ʌmˈbɪlɪk, -s
umbilical (*mathematical term*) ʌmˈbɪlɪkl
[-lək-], (*medical term*) ˌʌmbɪˈlaɪkl
[-bəˈl-, ʌmˈbɪlɪkl, -lək-]
umbilicus, -es ʌmˈbɪlɪkəs [-lək-, ˌʌmbɪ-
ˈlaɪkəs, -bəˈl-], -ɪz

513

umble, -s ˈʌmbl, -z
umbo, -s, -nes ˈʌmbəʊ, -z, ʌmˈbəʊniːz
umbr|a, -as, -al ˈʌmbr|ə, -əz, -əl
umbrage ˈʌmbrɪdʒ
umbrageous, -ly, -ness ʌmˈbreɪdʒəs, -lɪ, -nɪs [-nəs]
umbrated ˈʌmbreɪtɪd
umbration, -s ʌmˈbreɪʃn, -z
umbrella, -s ʌmˈbrelə, -z
Umbria, -n/s ˈʌmbrɪə, -n/z
umbriferous ʌmˈbrɪfərəs
umbril, -s ˈʌmbrɪl, -z
Umfreville ˈʌmfrəvɪl
umiak, -s ˈuːmɪæk [-mjæk], -s
umlaut, -s ˈʊmlaʊt, -s
umph m̩m̩m̩ [ʌmf]
umpir|e (s. v.), -es, -ing, -ed ˈʌmpaɪə*, -z, -rɪŋ, -d
umpteen, -th ˌʌmpˈtiːn [ˈ--], -θ
umpty ˈʌmptɪ
un- ʌn-

Notes.—1. *The stressing of* un- *compounds depends on the meaning of the prefix, the commonness of the word, and other factors. Those not included in the following list are to be taken to have double stress. Thus* undetachable *is* ˌʌndɪˈtætʃəbl, un-countenanced *is* ˌʌnˈkaʊntənənst. 2. ʌn- *freq. assimilates before* p, b *to* ʌm- *(e.g. in* unpopular, unbroken*) and before* k, g *to* ʌŋ- *(e.g. in* unkind, ungrateful*).*

Una ˈjuːnə
unabashed ˌʌnəˈbæʃt
unabated ˌʌnəˈbeɪtɪd
unable ʌnˈeɪbl [ˌʌn-]
unabridged ˌʌnəˈbrɪdʒd
unaccented ˌʌnækˈsentɪd [-nək-, *also* ˈ--ˌ-- *when attributive*]
unacceptable ˌʌnəkˈseptəbl [-næk-]
unaccompanied ˌʌnəˈkʌmpənɪd [*also* ˈ--ˌ--- *when attributive*]
unaccountable ˌʌnəˈkaʊntəbl
unaccountab|ly, -leness ˌʌnəˈkaʊntəb|lɪ, -lnɪs [-nəs]
unaccustomed ˌʌnəˈkʌstər
unacknowledged ˌʌnəkˈnɒlɪdʒd
unacquainted ˌʌnəˈkweɪntɪd
unacted ˌʌnˈæktɪd
unadaptable ˌʌnəˈdæptəbl
unaddressed ˌʌnəˈdrest
unadorned ˌʌnəˈdɔːnd
unadulterated ˌʌnəˈdʌltəreɪtɪd
unadvisability ˈʌnədˌvaɪzəˈbɪlətɪ [-lɪt-]
unadvisable ˌʌnədˈvaɪzəbl
unadvisableness ˌʌnədˈvaɪzəblnɪs [-nəs]
unadvised ˌʌnədˈvaɪzd

unadvisedly ˌʌnədˈvaɪzɪdlɪ
unaffected (*not influenced*), ˌʌnəˈfektɪd
unaffected (*without affectation*), -ly, -ness ˌʌnəˈfektɪd, -lɪ, -nɪs [-nəs]
unafraid ˌʌnəˈfreɪd
unaided ˌʌnˈeɪdɪd [ʌn-]
unalienable ˌʌnˈeɪljənəbl [ʌn-, -lɪən-]
unalienably ʌnˈeɪljənəblɪ [-lɪən-]
unallotted ˌʌnəˈlɒtɪd
unallowable ˌʌnəˈlaʊəbl
unalloyed ˌʌnəˈlɔɪd
unalterability ʌnˌɔːltərəˈbɪlətɪ [ˈʌnˌɔːl-, -ˌɒl-, -lɪt-]
unalterab|le, -ly, -leness ʌnˈɔːltərəb|l [ˌʌnˈɔː-, -ˈɒl-], -lɪ, -nɪs [-nəs]
unaltered ˌʌnˈɔːltəd [ʌn-, -ˈɒl-]
unambiguous, -ly ˌʌnæmˈbɪgjʊəs [-gjwəs], -lɪ
unanalysable ˌʌnˈænəlaɪzəbl
unanimity ˌjuːnəˈnɪmətɪ [jʊn-, -næˈn-, -ɪtɪ]
unanimous, -ly, -ness juːˈnænɪməs [jʊˈn-, -nən-], -lɪ, -nɪs [-nəs]
unannounced ˌʌnəˈnaʊnst
unanswerable ˌʌnˈɑːnsərəbl [ʌnˈɑː-]
unanswered ˌʌnˈɑːnsəd [ʌnˈɑː-]
unappeas|able, -ed ˌʌnəˈpiːz|əbl, -d
unappetizing ˌʌnˈæpɪtaɪzɪŋ [ʌn-, -pət-]
unapplied ˌʌnəˈplaɪd
unappreciable ˌʌnəˈpriːʃəbl [-ʃjə-, -ʃɪə-]
unappreciated ˌʌnəˈpriːʃɪeɪtɪd
unapproachab|le, -ly, -leness ˌʌnəˈprəʊtʃəb|l, -lɪ, -lnɪs [-nəs]
unapproached ˌʌnəˈprəʊtʃt
unappropriate (*adj.*) ˌʌnəˈprəʊprɪət [-prɪɪt]
unappropriated ˌʌnəˈprəʊprɪeɪtɪd
unapproved ˌʌnəˈpruːvd
unarm, -s, -ing, -ed ˌʌnˈɑːm [ʌn-], -z, -ɪŋ, -d
unascertain|able, -ed ˌʌnæsəˈteɪn|əbl, -d
unashamed ˌʌnəˈʃeɪmd
unasked ˌʌnˈɑːskt [ʌn-]
unaspirated ˌʌnˈæspəreɪtɪd [ʌn-, -pɪr-]
unassailable ˌʌnəˈseɪləbl
unassignable ˌʌnəˈsaɪnəbl
unassimilated ˌʌnəˈsɪməleɪtɪd [-mɪl-]
unassisted ˌʌnəˈsɪstɪd
unassuming ˌʌnəˈsjuːmɪŋ [-ˈsuː-]
unattached ˌʌnəˈtætʃt
unattainable ˌʌnəˈteɪnəbl
unattempted ˌʌnəˈtemptɪd
unattended ˌʌnəˈtendɪd
unattested ˌʌnəˈtestɪd
unattractive, -ly, -ness ˌʌnəˈtræktɪv, -lɪ, -nɪs [-nəs]
unauthenticated ˌʌnɔːˈθentɪkeɪtɪd
unauthorized [-ised] ˌʌnˈɔːθəraɪzd [ʌn-]

unavailing ˌʌnə'veɪlɪŋ [also '—ˌ— when attributive]
unavailingly ˌʌnə'veɪlɪŋlɪ
unavenged ˌʌnə'vendʒd
unavoidab|le, -ly, -leness ˌʌnə'vɔɪdəb|l, -lɪ, -lnɪs [-nəs]
unaware, -s ˌʌnə'weə*, -z
unbalanc|e, -es, -ing, -ed ˌʌn'bæləns [ʌn-], -ɪz, -ɪŋ, -t
unbaptized ˌʌnbæp'taɪzd
unbar, -s, -ring, -red ˌʌn'bɑː:*, -z, -rɪŋ, -d
unbearab|le, -ly, -leness ʌn'beərəb|l [ˌʌn-], -lɪ, -lnɪs [-nəs]
unbeatable ˌʌn'biːtəbl
unbeaten ˌʌn'biːtn [ʌn-]
unbecoming, -ly, -ness ˌʌnbɪ'kʌmɪŋ [-bə'k-], -lɪ, -nɪs [-nəs]
unbefitting ˌʌnbɪ'fɪtɪŋ [-bə'f-]
unbegotten ˌʌnbɪ'gɒtn [-bə'g-]
unbeknown ˌʌnbɪ'nəʊn [-bə'n-]
unbelief ˌʌnbɪ'liːf [-bə'l-, '—-]
unbelievable ˌʌnbɪ'liːvəbl [-bə'l-]
unbeliever, -s ˌʌnbɪ'liːvə* [-bə'l-, '—ˌ—], -z
unbelieving ˌʌnbɪ'liːvɪŋ [-bə'l-, '—ˌ—]
unben|d, -ds, -ding, -ded, -t ˌʌn'ben|d, -dz, -dɪŋ, -dɪd, -t
unbeneficed ˌʌn'benɪfɪst
unbias(s)ed ˌʌn'baɪəst
unbidden ˌʌn'bɪdn
un|bind (undo binding), -binds, -binding, -bound ˌʌn|'baɪnd, -'baɪndz, -'baɪndɪŋ, -'baʊnd
unbleached ˌʌn'bliːtʃt [also '— when attributive]
unblemished ˌʌn'blemɪʃt [ʌn'b-]
unblushing, -ly ˌʌn'blʌʃɪŋ, -lɪ
unboiled ˌʌn'bɔɪld [also '— when attributive]
unbolt, -s, -ing, -ed ˌʌn'bəʊlt, -s, -ɪŋ, -ɪd
unborn ˌʌn'bɔ:n ['ʌnb- according to sentence-stress]
unbosom, -s, -ing, -ed ˌʌn'bʊzəm, -z, -ɪŋ, -d
unbought ˌʌn'bɔ:t [also 'ʌnb- when attributive]
unbound (not bound) ˌʌn'baʊnd [also 'ʌnb- when attributive]
unbounded ˌʌn'baʊndɪd [ʌn-]
unbridled ˌʌn'braɪdld [ʌn-]
unbroken ˌʌn'brəʊkən [ʌn-]
unbuck|le, -les, -ling, -led ˌʌn'bʌk|l [ʌn-], -lz, -lɪŋ [lɪŋ], -ld
unburd|en, -ens, -ening, -ened ˌʌn-'bɜ:d|n [ʌn-], -nz, -nɪŋ [-nɪŋ], -nd
unburied ˌʌn'berɪd [ʌn-]
unbusiness-like ˌʌn'bɪznɪslaɪk [ʌn'b-]

unbutt|on, -ons, -oning, -oned ˌʌn-'bʌt|n [ʌn-], -nz, -nɪŋ [-nɪŋ], -nd
uncalled for ˌʌn'kɔ:ldfɔ:* [ʌn'k-]
uncandid, -ly, -ness ˌʌn'kændɪd, -lɪ, -nɪs [-nəs]
uncann|y, -ier, -iest, -ily, -iness ʌn-'kæn|ɪ, -ɪə*, -ɪɪst, -ɪlɪ [-əlɪ], -ɪnɪs [-ɪnəs]
uncanonical ˌʌnkə'nɒnɪkl
uncared for ˌʌn'keədfɔ:* [ʌn-]
uncatalogued ˌʌn'kætəlɒgd
unceasing, -ly ʌn'si:sɪŋ [ˌʌn-], -lɪ
uncensored ˌʌn'sensəd [ʌn's-]
unceremonious, -ly, -ness 'ʌnˌserɪ-'məʊnjəs [-nɪəs], -lɪ, -nɪs [-nəs]
uncertain ʌn'sɜ:tn [ˌʌn's-, -tən, -tn]
uncertaint|y, -ies ʌn'sɜ:tnt|ɪ [-tən-, -tn-], -ɪz
unchain, -s, -ing, -ed ˌʌn'tʃeɪn, -z, -ɪŋ, -d
unchallenged ˌʌn'tʃæləndʒd [-lɪn-]
unchangeability 'ʌnˌtʃeɪndʒə'bɪlətɪ [ʌnˌtʃ-, -lɪt-]
unchangeable ˌʌn'tʃeɪndʒəbl [ʌn'tʃ-]
unchangeab|ly, -leness ˌʌn'tʃeɪndʒəb|lɪ [ʌn'tʃ-], -lnɪs [-nəs]
unchanged ˌʌn'tʃeɪndʒd [ʌn-]
unchanging ˌʌn'tʃeɪndʒɪŋ [ʌn'tʃ-]
uncharged ˌʌn'tʃɑ:dʒd
uncharitab|le, -ly, -leness ˌʌn'tʃærɪtəb|l [ʌn'tʃ-], -lɪ, -lnɪs [-nəs]
uncharted ˌʌn'tʃɑ:tɪd
unchartered ˌʌn'tʃɑ:təd
unchaste, -ly ˌʌn'tʃeɪst [ʌn-], -lɪ
unchastened ˌʌn'tʃeɪsnd [ʌn'tʃ-]
unchastity ˌʌn'tʃæstətɪ [-ɪtɪ]
uncheck|able, -ed ˌʌn'tʃek|əbl [ʌn-], -t
unchristian, -ly ˌʌn'krɪstʃən [ʌn-, -tjən], -lɪ
uncial (s. adj.), -s 'ʌnsɪəl [-nsjəl, -nʃɪəl, -nʃjəl, -nʃl], -z
unciform 'ʌnsɪfɔ:m
uncinate 'ʌnsɪneɪt [-nɪt]
uncircumcised ˌʌn'sɜ:kəmsaɪzd
uncircumcision 'ʌnˌsɜ:kəm'sɪʒn
unciv|il, -illy ˌʌn'sɪv|l [ʌn-, -ɪl], -əlɪ [-ɪlɪ]
unciviliz|ed [-is|ed], -able ˌʌn'sɪvjaɪz|d [ʌn-, -vəl-, -vɪlaɪ-], -əbl
unclaimed ˌʌn'kleɪmd [also '— when attributive]
unclasp, -s, -ing, -ed ˌʌn'klɑ:sp, -s, -ɪŋ, -t
unclassifiable ˌʌn'klæsɪfaɪəbl [-ˌ—'—-]
unclassified ˌʌn'klæsɪfaɪd [ʌn-]
uncle, -s 'ʌŋkl, -z
unclean, -ness ˌʌn'kli:n [ʌn-, also '— when attributive], -nɪs [-nəs]
uncleanl|y, -iness ˌʌn'klenl|ɪ [ʌn-], -ɪnɪs [-ɪnəs]

515

unclear ˌʌnˈklɪə*
unclos|e, -es, -ing, -ed ˌʌnˈkləʊz, -ɪz, -ɪŋ, -d
unclothed ˌʌnˈkləʊðd [also '– when attributive]
unclouded ˌʌnˈklaʊdɪd
uncluttered ˌʌnˈklʌtəd
uncoffined ˌʌnˈkɒfɪnd
uncoil, -s, -ing, -ed ˌʌnˈkɔɪl, -z, -ɪŋ, -d
uncollected ˌʌnkəˈlektɪd
uncoloured ˌʌnˈkʌləd
un-come-at-able ˌʌnkʌmˈætəbl
uncomely ˌʌnˈkʌmlɪ
uncomfortab|le, -ly, -leness ʌnˈkʌmfətəb|l, -lɪ, -lnɪs [-nəs]
uncommercial ˌʌnkəˈmɜːʃl [also 'ʌnkəˌm- when attributive]
uncommitted ˌʌnkəˈmɪtɪd
uncommon ʌnˈkɒmən [ˌʌnˈk-]
uncommon|ly, -ness ʌnˈkɒmən|lɪ, -nɪs [-nəs]
uncommunic|able, -ated ˌʌnkəˈmjuːnɪk|əbl [-ˈmjʊn-], -eɪtɪd
uncommunicative, -ness ˌʌnkəˈmjuːnɪkətɪv [-ˈmjʊn-, -keɪt-], -nɪs [-nəs]
uncomplaining, -ly ˌʌnkəmˈpleɪnɪŋ [also 'ʌnkəmˌp- when attributive], -lɪ
uncompleted ˌʌnkəmˈpliːtɪd
uncomplimentary 'ʌnˌkɒmplɪˈmentərɪ
uncompounded ˌʌnkəmˈpaʊndɪd
uncompromising, -ly, -ness ʌnˈkɒmprəmaɪzɪŋ [ˌʌn-, -prʊm-], -lɪ, -nɪs [-nəs]
unconcealed ˌʌnkənˈsiːld
unconcern, -ed, -edly, -edness ˌʌnkənˈsɜːn, -d, -ɪdlɪ, -ɪdnɪs [-nəs]
uncondi|tional, -tionally ˌʌnkənˈdɪ|ʃənl [-ʃnəl, -ʃn̩l, -ʃn̩l, -ʃənəl], -ʃn̩əlɪ [-ʃnəlɪ, -ʃn̩lɪ, -ʃənəlɪ]
unconditioned ˌʌnkənˈdɪʃnd
unconfined ˌʌnkənˈfaɪnd
unconfirmed ˌʌnkənˈfɜːmd
uncongenial ˌʌnkənˈdʒiːnjəl [-nɪəl]
unconnected ˌʌnkəˈnektɪd
unconquerable ʌnˈkɒŋkərəbl
unconquered ˌʌnˈkɒŋkəd [ʌn-]
unconscionab|le, -ly, -leness ʌnˈkɒnʃnəb|l [-ʃnə-, -ʃənə-], -lɪ, -lnɪs [-nəs]
unconscious, -ly, -ness ʌnˈkɒnʃəs [ˌʌnˈk-], -lɪ, -nɪs [-nəs]
unconsecrated ˌʌnˈkɒnsɪkreɪtɪd [ʌn-]
unconsidered ˌʌnkənˈsɪdəd [also '–ˌ– when attributive]
unconstitu|tional, -tionally 'ʌnˌkɒnstɪ-ˈtjuː|ʃənl [ˌʌn-, -ʃnəl, -ʃn̩l, -ʃn̩l, -ʃənəl], -ʃn̩əlɪ [-ʃnəlɪ, -ʃn̩lɪ, -ʃn̩lɪ, -ʃənəlɪ]

unconstrain|ed, -edly ˌʌnkənˈstreɪn|d, -ɪdlɪ
unconsumed ˌʌnkənˈsjuːmd [-ˈsuːmd]
uncontaminated ˌʌnkənˈtæmɪneɪtɪd
uncontestable ˌʌnkənˈtestəbl
uncontested ˌʌnkənˈtestɪd [also 'ʌnkənˌt- when attributive]
uncontradicted 'ʌnˌkɒntrəˈdɪktɪd
uncontrollable ˌʌnkənˈtrəʊləb|l
uncontrollab|ly, -leness ˌʌnkənˈtrəʊl-əb|lɪ, -lnɪs [-nəs]
uncontrolled ˌʌnkənˈtrəʊld
unconventional ˌʌnkənˈvenʃənl [-ʃnəl, -ʃn̩l, -ʃn̩l, -ʃənəl]
unconventionalit|y, -ies 'ʌnkənˌven-ʃəˈnælət|ɪ [-ʃn̩ˈæ-, -rt|ɪ], -ɪz
unconverted ˌʌnkənˈvɜːtɪd [also 'ʌn-kənˌv- when attributive]
unconvertible ˌʌnkənˈvɜːtəbl [-tɪb-]
unconvinced ˌʌnkənˈvɪnst
unconvincing ˌʌnkənˈvɪnsɪŋ
uncooked ˌʌnˈkʊkt ['ʌnk- according to sentence-stress]
uncooperative ˌʌnkəʊˈɒpərətɪv [-kʊˈɒ-]
uncord, -s, -ing, -ed ˌʌnˈkɔːd, -z, -ɪŋ, -ɪd
uncork, -s, -ing, -ed ˌʌnˈkɔːk, -s, -ɪŋ, -t
uncorrected ˌʌnkəˈrektɪd ['ʌnkəˌr- when attributive]
uncorroborated ˌʌnkəˈrɒbəreɪtɪd
uncorrupt, -ly, -ness ˌʌnkəˈrʌpt, -lɪ, -nɪs [-nəs]
uncountable ˌʌnˈkaʊntəbl
uncounted ˌʌnˈkaʊntɪd
uncoup|le, -les, -ling, -led ˌʌnˈkʌp|l, -lz, -lɪŋ [-lɪŋ], -ld
uncouth, -ly, -ness ʌnˈkuːθ, -lɪ, -nɪs [-nəs]
uncov|er, -ers, -ering, -ered ʌnˈkʌv|ə* [ˌʌnˈk-], -əz, -ərɪŋ, -əd
uncritical, -ally ˌʌnˈkrɪtɪk|l [ʌn-], -əlɪ
uncrossed ˌʌnˈkrɒst [old-fashioned -ˈkrɔːst, also 'ʌnkr- when attributive]
uncrowned ˌʌnˈkraʊnd [also 'ʌnkraʊnd when attributive]
unction, -s 'ʌŋkʃn, -z
unctuosity ˌʌŋktjuˈɒsətɪ [-rtɪ]
unctuous, -ly, -ness 'ʌŋktjʊəs [-tjwəs, -tʃʊəs, -tʃwəs], -lɪ, -nɪs [-nəs]
uncultivated ˌʌnˈkʌltɪveɪtɪd
uncultured ˌʌnˈkʌltʃəd
uncurbed ˌʌnˈkɜːbd
uncurl, -s, -ing, -ed ˌʌnˈkɜːl, -z, -ɪŋ, -d
uncut ˌʌnˈkʌt [also 'ʌnkʌt according to sentence-stress]
undamaged ˌʌnˈdæmɪdʒd
undate 'ʌndeɪt
undated (wavy) 'ʌndeɪtɪd
undated (not dated) ˌʌnˈdeɪtɪd

undaunted, -ly, -ness ˌʌnˈdɔːntɪd
[ʌnˈd-], -lɪ, -nɪs [-nəs]
undebated ˌʌndɪˈbeɪtɪd
undeceiv|e, -es, -ing, -ed ˌʌndɪˈsiːv, -z,
-ɪŋ, -d
undecennial ˌʌndɪˈsenjəl
undecided, -ly, -ness ˌʌndɪˈsaɪdɪd [also
'--,-- when attributive], -lɪ, -nɪs [-nəs]
undecipherable ˌʌndɪˈsaɪfərəbl
undecisive ˌʌndɪˈsaɪsɪv
undefended ˌʌndɪˈfendɪd [also '--,--
when attributive]
undefiled ˌʌndɪˈfaɪld
undefin|able, -ed ˌʌndɪˈfaɪn|əbl, -d
undelivered ˌʌndɪˈlɪvəd
undemonstrative ˌʌndɪˈmɒnstrətɪv
undeniable ˌʌndɪˈnaɪəbl
undeniably ˌʌndɪˈnaɪəblɪ
undenomina|tional, -tionalism 'ʌndɪ-
ˌnɒmɪˈneɪʃənl [-ʃnəl, -ʃṇḷ, -ʃnḷ,
-ʃənəl], -ʃṇəlɪzəm [-ʃnəl-, -ʃṇḷ-, -ʃnḷ-,
-ʃənəl-]
under (s. adj. adv. prep.), -s 'ʌndə*,
-z
Note.—Compounds with under- not
included in the following list are to
be taken to have double stress. Thus
under-masticate is ˌʌndəˈmæstɪkeɪt
underact, -s, -ing, -ed ˌʌndərˈækt
[-dəˈækt], -s, -ɪŋ, -ɪd
under-age ˌʌndərˈeɪdʒ [-dəˈeɪ-]
underarm 'ʌndərɑːm
underbid, -s, -ding ˌʌndəˈbɪd, -z, -ɪŋ
underbred ˌʌndəˈbred
underbrush 'ʌndəbrʌʃ
under|buy, -buys, -buying, -bought
ˌʌndəˈbaɪ, -ˈbaɪz, -ˈbaɪɪŋ, -ˈbɔːt
undercarriage, -s 'ʌndəˌkærɪdʒ, -ɪz
undercharge (s.), -s ˌʌndəˈtʃɑːdʒ
['ʌndətʃ-], -ɪz
undercharg|e (v.), -es, -ing, -ed ˌʌndə-
ˈtʃɑːdʒ, -ɪz, -ɪŋ, -d
underclay 'ʌndəkleɪ
under-clerk, -s 'ʌndəklɑːk, -s
undercliff, -s 'ʌndəklɪf, -s
underclothed ˌʌndəˈkləʊðd
underclothes 'ʌndəkləʊðz [old-fashioned
-kləʊz]
underclothing 'ʌndəˌkləʊðɪŋ
undercoat, -s 'ʌndəkəʊt, -s
under-colour, -s 'ʌndəˌkʌlə*, -z
under-cover 'ʌndəˌkʌvə*
undercroft, -s 'ʌndəkrɒft, -s
undercurrent, -s 'ʌndəˌkʌrənt, -s
undercut (s.), -s 'ʌndəkʌt, -s
undercut (adj. v.), -s, -ting ˌʌndəˈkʌt,
-s, -ɪŋ
under-developed ˌʌndədɪˈveləpt

under|do, -does, -doing, -did, -done
ˌʌndəˈduː, -ˈdʌz, -ˈduːɪŋ [-ˈdʊɪŋ],
-ˈdɪd, -ˈdʌn ['ʌndədʌn when attribu-
tive]
underdog, -s 'ʌndədɒg [ˌ--'-], -z
underdose, -s 'ʌndədəʊs, -ɪz
under|draw, -draws, -drawing, -drew,
-drawn ˌʌndəˈdrɔː, -ˈdrɔːz, -ˈdrɔːɪŋ
-ˈdruː, -ˈdrɔːn
under-dressed ˌʌndəˈdrest
underestimate (s.), -s ˌʌndərˈestɪmət
[-dəˈes-, -mɪt, -meɪt], -s
underestimat|e (v.), -es, -ing, -ed
ˌʌndərˈestɪmeɪt [-dəˈes-], -s, -ɪŋ, -ɪd
under-expo|se, -ses, -sing, -sed; -sure/s
ˌʌndərɪkˈspəʊ|z [-dəɪkˈs-, -dərekˈs-,
-dəekˈs-], -zɪz, -zɪŋ, -zd; -ʒə*/z
under|feed, -feeds, -feeding, -fed ˌʌndə|-
ˈfiːd, -ˈfiːdz, -ˈfiːdɪŋ, -ˈfed
under-felt, -s 'ʌndəfelt, -s
underfoot ˌʌndəˈfʊt
undergarment, -s 'ʌndəˌgɑːmənt, -s
under|go, -goes, -going, -went, -gone
ˌʌndəˈgəʊ, -ˈgəʊz, -ˈgəʊɪŋ, -ˈwent,
-ˈgɒn
undergraduate, -s ˌʌndəˈgrædʒʊət
[-ˈgrædjʊət, -dʒʊɪt, -djʊɪt], -s
underground (s. adj.) (U.) 'ʌndəgraʊnd
underground (adv.) ˌʌndəˈgraʊnd
undergrown ˌʌndəˈgrəʊn ['ʌndəgrəʊn]
undergrowth 'ʌndəgrəʊθ
underhand ˌʌndəˈhænd ['---]
underhanded, -ly, -ness ˌʌndəˈhændɪd
['ʌndəˌh-], -lɪ, -nɪs [-nəs]
Underhill 'ʌndəhɪl
underhung ˌʌndəˈhʌŋ [also 'ʌndəh-
when attributive]
underlay (s.), -s 'ʌndəleɪ, -z
under|lay (v.), -lays, -laying, -laid
ˌʌndəˈleɪ, -ˈleɪz, -ˈleɪɪŋ, -ˈleɪd
underlease, -s 'ʌndəliːs, -ɪz
underlet, -s, -ting ˌʌndəˈlet ['ʌndəl-], -s,
-ɪŋ
under|lie, -lies, -lying, -lay, -lain
ˌʌndəˈlaɪ, -ˈlaɪz, -ˈlaɪɪŋ, -ˈleɪ, -ˈleɪn
underline (s.), -s 'ʌndəlaɪn [ˌ--'-], -z
underlin|e (v.), -es, -ing, -ed ˌʌndəˈlaɪn,
-z, -ɪŋ, -d
underlinen 'ʌndəˌlɪnɪn
underling, -s 'ʌndəlɪŋ, -z
under|man (s.), -men 'ʌndə|mæn, -men
underman (v.), -s, -ning, -ned ˌʌndə-
ˈmæn, -z, -ɪŋ, -d
undermentioned ˌʌndəˈmenʃnd
['ʌndəˌm-]
undermin|e, -es, -ing, -ed, -er/s ˌʌndə-
ˈmaɪn, -z, -ɪŋ, -d, -ə*/z
undermost 'ʌndəməʊst

517

underneath ˌʌndəˈniːθ
underpants ˈʌndəpænts
underpass, -es ˈʌndəpɑːs, -ɪz
under|pay, -pays, -paying, -paid ˌʌndə|-ˈpeɪ, -ˈpeɪz, -ˈpeɪɪŋ, -ˈpeɪd [also ˈʌndəpeɪd when attributive]
underpayment, -s ˌʌndəˈpeɪmənt, -s
underpeopled ˌʌndəˈpiːpld
underpin, -s, -ning, -ned ˌʌndəˈpɪn, -z, -ɪŋ, -d
underplay (s.) ˈʌndəpleɪ
underplay (v.), -s, -ing, -ed ˌʌndəˈpleɪ, -z, -ɪŋ, -d
underplot, -s ˈʌndəplɒt, -s
underpopulated ˌʌndəˈpɒpjʊleɪtɪd [-pjəl-]
underprais|e, -es, -ing, -ed ˌʌndəˈpreɪz, -ɪz, -ɪŋ, -d
underprivileged ˌʌndəˈprɪvɪlɪdʒd [-vəl-]
underpriz|e, -es, -ing, -ed ˌʌndəˈpraɪz, -ɪz, -ɪŋ, -d
underproduction ˌʌndəprəˈdʌkʃn [-prʊˈd-, ˈ---ˌ--]
underprop, -s, -ping, -ped ˌʌndəˈprɒp, -s, -ɪŋ, -t
underrat|e, -es, -ing, -ed ˌʌndəˈreɪt, -s, -ɪŋ, -ɪd
under-ripe ˌʌndəˈraɪp [also ˈʌndər- according to sentence-stress]
under-roof, -s ˈʌndəruːf, -s
under|run, -runs, -running, -ran ˌʌndə|-ˈrʌn, -ˈrʌnz, -ˈrʌnɪŋ, -ˈræn
underscor|e, -es, -ing, -ed ˌʌndəˈskɔː* [-ˈskɔə*], -z, -ɪŋ, -d
undersea (adj.) ˈʌndəsiː
underseal (s. v.), -s, -ing, -ed ˈʌndəsiːl [ˌ--ˈ-], -z, -ɪŋ, -d
under-secretar|y, -ies; -yship/s ˌʌndə-ˈsekrətər|ɪ [-krɪt-, -ter|ɪ], -ɪz; -ɪʃɪp/s
under|sell, -sells, -selling, -sold ˌʌndə|-ˈsel, -ˈselz, -ˈselɪŋ, -ˈsəʊld
undersheriff, -s ˈʌndəˌʃerɪf [ˌ--ˈ--], -s
undershirt, -s ˈʌndəʃɜːt, -s
undershot ˈʌndəʃɒt
underside, -s ˈʌndəsaɪd, -z
undersign, -s, -ing, -ed ˌʌndəˈsaɪn, -z, -ɪŋ, -d
undersigned (s.) ˈʌndəsaɪnd [ˌ--ˈ-]
undersized ˌʌndəˈsaɪzd [ˈ---]
underskirt, -s ˈʌndəskɜːt, -s
understaffed ˌʌndəˈstɑːft
under|stand, -stands, -standing, -stood, -standed; -standable, -standably ˌʌndə|ˈstænd, -ˈstændz, -ˈstændɪŋ, -ˈstʊd, -ˈstændɪd; -ˈstændəbl, -ˈstændəblɪ
understat|e, -es, -ing, -ed ˌʌndəˈsteɪt, -s, -ɪŋ, -ɪd

understatement, -s ˌʌndəˈsteɪtmənt [ˈʌndəˌs-], -s
understocked ˌʌndəˈstɒkt
understood (from understand) ˌʌndə-ˈstʊd
understrapp|er/s, -ing ˈʌndəˌstræp|ə*/z, -ɪŋ
understrat|um, -a ˌʌndəˈstrɑːt|əm [ˈʌndəˌs-, -streɪt-], -ə
understud|y (s. v.), -ies, -ying, -ied ˈʌndəˌstʌd|ɪ, -ɪz, -ɪŋ [-jɪŋ], -ɪd
under|take (take upon oneself) -takes, -taking, -took, -taken ˌʌndə|ˈteɪk, -ˈteɪks, -ˈteɪkɪŋ, -ˈtʊk, -ˈteɪkən [-ˈteɪkɪŋ]
undertaker (one who agrees to perform), -s ˌʌndəˈteɪkə*, -z
undertaker (one who arranges funerals), -s ˈʌndəˌteɪkə*, -z
Undertaker (special historical sense), -s ˈʌndəˌteɪkə*, -z
undertaking (s.) (enterprise, promise), -s ˌʌndəˈteɪkɪŋ [ˈ--ˌ--], -z
undertaking (s.) (arranging funerals) ˈʌndəˌteɪkɪŋ
undertenan|cy, -cies, -t/s ˌʌndə-ˈtenən|sɪ [ˈʌndəˌt-], -sɪz, -t/s
under-the-counter ˌʌndəðəˈkaʊntə*
undertime ˈʌndətaɪm
under-timed ˌʌndəˈtaɪmd
undertint, -s ˈʌndətɪnt, -s
undertone, -s ˈʌndətəʊn, -z
undertook (from undertake) ˌʌndəˈtʊk
undertow, -s ˈʌndətəʊ, -z
undervaluation, -s ˈʌndəˌvæljʊˈeɪʃn, -z
underval|ue, -ues, -uing, -ued ˌʌndə-ˈvæl|juː [-jʊ], -juːz [-jʊz], -jʊɪŋ [-jwɪŋ], -juːd [-jʊd]
under|vest/s, -wear ˈʌndə|vest/s, -weə*
underwent (from undergo) ˌʌndəˈwent
underwing, -s ˈʌndəwɪŋ, -z
underwood (U.), -s ˈʌndəwʊd, -z
underwork (s.) ˈʌndəwɜːk
underwork (v.), -s, -ing, -ed ˌʌndə-ˈwɜːk, -s, -ɪŋ, -t
underworker (subordinate worker), -s ˈʌndəˌwɜːkə*, -z
underworld (U.) ˈʌndəwɜːld
underwrit|e, -es, -ing, underwrote, underwritten ˈʌndəraɪt [ˌʌndəˈr-], -s, -ɪŋ, ˈʌndərəʊt [ˌʌndəˈr-], ˈʌndəˌrɪtn [ˌʌndəˈr-]
underwriter, -s ˈʌndəˌraɪtə*, -z
undescribable ˌʌndɪˈskraɪbəbl
undeserv|ed, -edly, -edness ˌʌndɪˈzɜːv|d, -ɪdlɪ, -ɪdnɪs [-nəs]
undeserving, -ly ˌʌndɪˈzɜːvɪŋ, -lɪ

undesign|ed, -edly, -edness ˌʌndɪ'zaɪn|d, -ɪdlɪ, -ɪdnɪs [-nəs]
undesirability 'ʌndɪˌzaɪərə'bɪlətɪ [-lɪt-]
undesirab|le, -ly, -leness ˌʌndɪ'zaɪərəb|l, -lɪ, -lnɪs [-nəs]
undesirous ˌʌndɪ'zaɪərəs
undetected ˌʌndɪ'tektɪd
undeterminable ˌʌndɪ'tɜ:mɪnəbl
undeterminate, -ly, -ness ˌʌndɪ'tɜ:-mɪnət [-nɪt], -lɪ, -nɪs [-nəs]
undetermination 'ʌndɪˌtɜ:mɪ'neɪʃn
undetermined ˌʌndɪ'tɜ:mɪnd
undeterred ˌʌndɪ'tɜ:d
undeveloped ˌʌndɪ'veləpt
undeviating ʌn'di:vɪeɪtɪŋ [ˌʌn'd-, -vjeɪt-]
undeviatingly ʌn'di:vɪeɪtɪŋlɪ [-vjeɪt-]
undid (from undo) ˌʌn'dɪd [ʌn-]
undies 'ʌndɪz
undigested ˌʌndɪ'dʒestɪd [-daɪ'dʒ-]
undignified ʌn'dɪgnɪfaɪd [ˌʌn'd-]
undiluted ˌʌndaɪ'lju:tɪd [-dɪ'l-, -'lu:t-]
undiminished ˌʌndɪ'mɪnɪʃt [also '-ˌ- when attributive]
undimmed ˌʌn'dɪmd [ʌn-]
undine (U.), -s 'ʌndi:n [ʌn'd-, ʊn'd-], -z
undiplomatic ˌʌndɪplə'mætɪk [-pləʊ'm-, -plʊ'm-]
undiscerning ˌʌndɪ'sɜ:nɪŋ [-ɪ'zɜ:-]
undischarged ˌʌndɪs'tʃɑ:dʒd [also '-ˌ- when attributive]
undisciplined ʌn'dɪsɪplɪnd [ˌʌn'd-, -səp-]
undisclosed ˌʌndɪs'kləʊzd
undiscouraged ˌʌndɪ'skʌrɪdʒd
undiscoverab|le, -ly ˌʌndɪ'skʌvərəb|l, -lɪ
undiscovered ˌʌndɪ'skʌvəd [also 'ʌndɪˌsk- when attributive]
undiscussed ˌʌndɪ'skʌst
undisguised ˌʌndɪs'gaɪzd
undismayed ˌʌndɪs'meɪd
undisposed ˌʌndɪs'pəʊzd
undisputed ˌʌndɪ'spju:tɪd
undissolved ˌʌndɪ'zɒlvd
undistinctive ˌʌndɪ'stɪŋktɪv
undistinguishab|le, -ly, -leness ˌʌndɪ'stɪŋgwɪʃəb|l, -lɪ, -lnɪs [-nəs]
undistinguished ˌʌndɪ'stɪŋgwɪʃt
undistracted ˌʌndɪ'stræktɪd
undisturbed ˌʌndɪ'stɜ:bd
undivided, -ly, -ness ˌʌndɪ'vaɪdɪd, -lɪ, -nɪs [-nəs]
un|do, -does, -doing, -did, -done, -doer/s ˌʌn|'du: [ʌn-], -'dʌz, -'du:ɪŋ [-'dʊɪŋ], -'dɪd, -'dʌn, -'du:ə*/z [-'dʊə*/z]
undock, -s, -ing, -ed ˌʌn'dɒk, -s, -ɪŋ, -t
undomesticated ˌʌndə'mestɪkeɪtɪd [-dəʊ'm-]

undoubted, -ly ʌn'daʊtɪd, -lɪ
undraped ˌʌn'dreɪpt [also 'ʌndreɪpt when attributive]
undreamed of ʌn'dremtɒv [ˌʌn'd-, -'drempt-, -'dri:md-]
undreamt of ʌn'dremtɒv [ˌʌn'd-, -'drempt-]
undress (s.) ˌʌn'dres
undress (adj.) 'ʌndres
undress (v.), -es, -ing, -ed ˌʌn'dres [ʌn-], -ɪz, -ɪŋ, -t
undrinkable ˌʌn'drɪŋkəbl [ʌn-]
undue ˌʌn'dju: ['ʌnd-, ʌn'd-, according to sentence-stress]
undulat|e, -es, -ing/ly, -ed 'ʌndjʊleɪt, -s, -ɪŋ/lɪ, -ɪd
undulation, -s ˌʌndjʊ'leɪʃn, -z
undul|ant, -atory 'ʌndjʊl|ənt [-dʒʊl-], -ətrɪ [-leɪt-, ˌʌndjʊ'leɪtərɪ]
unduly ˌʌn'dju:lɪ [ʌn-]
unduti|ful, -fully, -fulness ˌʌn'dju:tɪ|fʊl [ʌn-], -fʊlɪ [-fəlɪ], -fʊlnɪs [-nəs]
undying, -ly ʌn'daɪɪŋ [ˌʌn-], -lɪ
unearned ˌʌn'ɜ:nd ['ʌnɜ:-, ʌn'ɜ:-, according to sentence-stress]
unearth, -s, -ing, -ed ˌʌn'ɜ:θ [ʌn'ɜ:θ], -s, -ɪŋ, -t
unearthl|y, -iness ʌn'ɜ:θl|ɪ, -mɪs [-məs]
uneas|y, -ier, -iest, -ily, -iness ʌn'i:z|ɪ [ˌʌn-], -ɪə* [-ɪə*], -ɪɪst [-jɪst], -ɪlɪ [-əlɪ], -mɪs [-məs]
uneatable, -ness ˌʌn'i:təbl [ʌn-], -nɪs [-nəs]
uneaten ˌʌn'i:tn [ʌn-]
uneconomic, -al 'ʌnˌi:kə'nɒmɪk [ˌʌni:k-, 'ʌnˌek-, ˌʌnek-], -l
unedifying ˌʌn'edɪfaɪɪŋ [ʌn-]
uneducated ˌʌn'edjʊkeɪtɪd [ʌn-, -dʒʊ-]
unelected ˌʌnɪ'lektɪd
unembarrassed ˌʌnɪm'bærəst [-nem-]
unemo|tional, -tionally ˌʌnɪ'məʊ|ʃənl [-ʃnəl, -ʃn̩l, -ʃnl, -ʃənəl], -ʃnəlɪ [-ʃnəlɪ, -ʃn̩lɪ, -ʃnlɪ, -ʃənəlɪ]
unemphatic ˌʌnɪm'fætɪk
unemployable ˌʌnɪm'plɔɪəbl [-nem-]
unemployed ˌʌnɪm'plɔɪd [-nem-]
unemployment ˌʌnɪm'plɔɪmənt [-nem-]
unenclosed ˌʌnɪn'kləʊzd [-nɪŋ'kl-, -nen'kl-]
unencumbered ˌʌnɪn'kʌmbəd [-nɪŋ'k-, -nen'k-]
unending ʌn'endɪŋ [ˌʌn'en-]
unendowed ˌʌnɪn'daʊd [-nen-]
unendurable ˌʌnɪn'djʊərəbl [-nen-, -'djɔər-, -'djɔ:r]
unengaged ˌʌnɪŋ'geɪdʒd
un-English ˌʌn'ɪŋglɪʃ [rarely -'eŋ-]
unenlightened ˌʌnɪn'laɪtnd [-nen-]

519

unenterprising ˌʌn'entəpraɪzɪŋ [ʌn-]
unenviable ˌʌn'envɪəbl [ʌn-, -vjə-]
unequ|al/s, -ally, -alness, -alled ˌʌn'i:-
kw|əl/z [ʌn-], -əlɪ, -əlnɪs [-nəs], -əld
unequitab|le, -ly ˌʌn'ekwɪtəb|l [ʌn-], -lɪ
unequivoc|al, -ally, -alness ˌʌnɪ'kwɪ-
vək|l [-vʊk-], -əlɪ, -lnɪs [-nəs]
unerring, -ly, -ness ˌʌn'ɜ:rɪŋ [ʌn-], -lɪ,
-nɪs [-nəs]
unescapable ˌʌnɪ'skeɪpəbl
U.N.E.S.C.O. ju:'neskəʊ [jʊ'n-]
unessential ˌʌnɪ'senʃl
uneven, -ly, -ness ˌʌn'i:vn [ʌn-], -lɪ,
-nɪs [-nəs]
unevent|ful, -fully, -fulness ˌʌnɪ'vent|-
fʊl, -fʊlɪ [-fəlɪ], -fʊlnɪs [-nəs]
unexampled ˌʌnɪg'zɑ:mpld [-neg-]
unexceptionab|le, -ly, -leness ˌʌnɪk'sep-
ʃnəb|l [-nek-, -ʃɲə-, -ʃənə-], -lɪ, -lnɪs
[-nəs]
unexcep|tional, -tionally ˌʌnɪk'sep|ʃənl
[-nek-, -ʃnəl, -ʃɲl, -ʃnl, -ʃənəl], -ʃɲəlɪ
[ʃnəlɪ, -ʃɲlɪ, -ʃnlɪ, -ʃənəlɪ]
unexhausted ˌʌnɪg'zɔ:stɪd [-neg-]
unexpected, -ly, -ness ˌʌnɪk'spektɪd
[-nek-], -lɪ, -nɪs [-nəs]
unexpired ˌʌnɪk'spaɪəd [-nek-]
unexplained ˌʌnɪk'spleɪnd [-nek-]
unexplored ˌʌnɪk'splɔ:d [-nek-, -'splɔəd]
unexposed ˌʌnɪk'spəʊzd [-nek-]
unexpressib|le, -ly ˌʌnɪk'spresəb|l
[-nek-, -sɪb-], -lɪ
unexpressive ˌʌnɪk'spresɪv [-nek-]
unexpurgated ˌʌn'ekspəgeɪtɪd [ʌn-]
unfading ʌn'feɪdɪŋ
unfailing, -ly, -ness ʌn'feɪlɪŋ, -lɪ, -nɪs
[-nəs]
unfair, -ly, -ness ˌʌn'feə* [ʌn-], -lɪ, -nɪs
[-nəs]
unfaith|ful, -fully, -fulness ʌn'feɪθ|fʊl
[ʌn-], -fʊlɪ [-fəlɪ], -fʊlnɪs [-nəs]
unfaltering, -ly ʌn'fɔ:ltərɪŋ [ˌʌn-, -'fɒl-],
-lɪ
unfamiliar, -ly ˌʌnfə'mɪljə* [-fm̩'ɪ-], -lɪ
unfamiliarity 'ʌnfəˌmɪlɪ'ærətɪ [-fm̩ˌɪ-,
-ɪtɪ]
unfashionable ˌʌn'fæʃnəbl [ʌn-, -ʃɲə-]
unfast|en, -ens, -ening, -ened ˌʌn-
'fɑ:s|n [ʌn-], -nz, -nɪŋ [-ɲ̩ɪŋ], -nd
unfathomab|le, -ly, -leness ʌn'fæðəm-
əb|l, -lɪ, -lnɪs [-nəs]
unfathomed ˌʌn'fæðəmd [ʌn-]
unfavourab|le, -ly, -leness ˌʌn'feɪvərəb|l
[ʌn-], -lɪ, -lnɪs [-nəs]
unfed ˌʌn'fed
unfeeling, -ly, -ness ʌn'fi:lɪŋ, -lɪ, -nɪs
[-nəs]
unfeigned ʌn'feɪnd [ˌʌn'f-]

unfeigned|ly, -ness ʌn'feɪnɪd|lɪ, -nɪs
[-nəs]
unfelt ˌʌn'felt
unfermented ˌʌnfə'mentɪd [-fɜ:'m-, also
'--,-- when attributive]
unfertilized [-ised] ˌʌn'fɜ:təlaɪzd [-tɪl-]
unfetter, -s, -ing, -ed ˌʌn'fetə*, -z, -rɪŋ,
-d
unfilial, -ly ˌʌn'fɪljəl [-lɪəl], -ɪ
unfinished ˌʌn'fɪnɪʃt [ʌn-, also '-,-- when
attributive]
unfit (adj.), -ly, -ness ˌʌn'fɪt [ʌn-], -lɪ,
-nɪs [-nəs]
unfit (v.), -s, -ting, -ted ˌʌn'fɪt [ʌn'f-],
-s, -ɪŋ, -ɪd
unfitting (adj.) ˌʌn'fɪtɪŋ [ʌn-]
unfittingly ʌn'fɪtɪŋlɪ
unfix, -es, -ing, -ed ˌʌn'fɪks, -ɪz, -ɪŋ, -t
unflagging ˌʌn'flægɪŋ [ʌn'f-]
unflappable ˌʌn'flæpəbl
unflattering, -ly ˌʌn'flætərɪŋ [ʌn-], -lɪ
unfledged ˌʌn'fledʒd [ʌn-, also '-- when
attributive]
unflinching ʌn'flɪntʃɪŋ [ˌʌn'f-]
unflinching|ly, -ness ʌn'flɪntʃɪŋ|lɪ, -nɪs
[-nəs]
unfold (open out folds, release sheep
from fold), -s, -ing, -ed ˌʌn'fəʊld
[ʌn-], -z, -ɪŋ, -ɪd
unfold (reveal), -s, -ing, -ed ʌn'fəʊld
[ˌʌn'f-], -z, -ɪŋ, -ɪd
unforeseeable ˌʌnfɔ:'si:əbl [-fɔ's-]
unforesee|ing, -n ˌʌnfɔ:'si:|ɪŋ, -n
unforgettable ˌʌnfə'getəbl
unforgiv|able, -en, -ing ˌʌnfə'gɪv|əbl,
-n, -ɪŋ
unforgotten ˌʌnfə'gɒtn
unformed ˌʌn'fɔ:md ['ʌnfɔ:md when
attributive]
unfortified ˌʌn'fɔ:tɪfaɪd [ʌn-]
unfortun|ate, -ately, -ateness ʌn'fɔ:-
tʃn|ət [-tʃɲ|ət, -tʃən|ət, -nɪt], -ətlɪ
[-ɪtlɪ], -ətnɪs [-nɪt-, -nəs]
unfounded ˌʌn'faʊndɪd [ʌn-]
unframed ˌʌn'freɪmd [also '-- when
attributive]
un|freeze, -freezes, -froze, -frozen
ˌʌn|'fri:z, -'fri:zɪz, -'frəʊz, -'frəʊzn
unfrequent, -ly ʌn'fri:kwənt, -lɪ
unfrequented ˌʌnfrɪ'kwentɪd
unfriend|ly, -liness ˌʌn'frend|lɪ [ʌn-],
-lnɪs [-nəs]
unfrock, -s, -ing, -ed ˌʌn'frɒk [ʌn-], -s,
-ɪŋ, -t
unfruit|ful, -fully, -fulness ˌʌn'fru:t|fʊl
[ʌn-], -fʊlɪ [-fəlɪ], -fʊlnɪs [-nəs]
unfulfilled ˌʌnfʊl'fɪld
unfurl, -s, -ing, -ed ˌʌn'fɜ:l, -z, -ɪŋ, -d

unfurnished ˌʌnˈfɜːnɪʃt [ʌn-, *also* ˈʌnˌf- *when attributive*]

ungainl|y, -iest, -iness ʌnˈgeɪnl|ɪ [ˌʌn-], -ɪɪst [-jɪst], -ɪnɪs [-ɪnəs]

ungarbled ˌʌnˈgɑːbld [ʌn-]

ungenerous, -ly ˌʌnˈdʒenərəs [ʌn-], -lɪ

ungenial ˌʌnˈdʒiːnjəl [ʌn-, -nɪəl]

ungent|le, -ly, -leness ˌʌnˈdʒent|l [ʌn-], -lɪ, -lnɪs [-nəs]

ungentleman|ly, -liness ʌnˈdʒentlmən|lɪ [ˌʌn-], -lɪnɪs [-ɪnəs]

un-get-at-able ˌʌngetˈætəbl

ungird, -s, -ing, -ed ˌʌnˈgɜːd, -z, -ɪŋ, -ɪd

unglazed ˌʌnˈgleɪzd [*also* ˈ-- *when attributive*]

unglorious ˌʌnˈglɔːrɪəs [ʌn-]

ungloved ˌʌnˈglʌvd [*also* ˈʌng- *when attributive*]

ungl|ue, -ues, -uing, -ued ˌʌnˈgl|uː, -uːz, -uːɪŋ [-ʊɪŋ], -uːd

ungodl|y, -ier, -iest, -iness ˌʌnˈgɒdl|ɪ [ʌn-], -ɪə* [-jə*], -ɪɪst [-jɪst], -ɪnɪs [-ɪnəs]

Ungoed ˈʌŋgɔɪd

ungotten ˌʌnˈgɒtn

ungovernab|le, -ly, -leness ˌʌnˈgʌvənəb|l [ʌn-, -vŋə-], -lɪ, -lnɪs [-nəs]

ungoverned ˌʌnˈgʌvənd

ungrace|ful, -fully, -fulness ˌʌnˈgreɪs|fʊl [ʌn-], -fʊlɪ [-fəlɪ], -fʊlnɪs [-nəs]

ungracious, -ly, -ness ˌʌnˈgreɪʃəs [ʌn-], -lɪ, -nɪs [-nəs]

ungrammatic|al, -ally ˌʌngrəˈmætɪk|l, -əlɪ

ungrateful ʌnˈgreɪtfʊl [ˌʌnˈg-]

ungrate|fully, -fulness ʌnˈgreɪt|fʊlɪ [-fəlɪ], -fʊlnɪs [-nəs]

ungrounded ˌʌnˈgraʊndɪd [ʌnˈg-]

ungrudging ˌʌnˈgrʌdʒɪŋ [ʌn-]

ungrudgingly ʌnˈgrʌdʒɪŋlɪ

unguarded ˌʌnˈgɑːdɪd [ʌn-]

unguarded|ly, -ness ʌnˈgɑːdɪd|lɪ, -nɪs [-nəs]

unguent, -s ˈʌŋgwənt [-gjʊənt], -s

unguided ˌʌnˈgaɪdɪd [ʌn-]

ungul|a, -ae ˈʌŋgjʊl|ə, -iː

ungulate (*s. adj.*), -s ˈʌŋgjʊleɪt [-lət, -lɪt], -s

unhallowed ˌʌnˈhæləʊd [ʌnˈh-]

unhampered ˌʌnˈhæmpəd [ʌn-]

unhand, -s, -ing, -ed ˌʌnˈhænd, -z, -ɪŋ, -ɪd

unhapp|y, -ier, -iest, -ily, -iness ʌnˈhæp|ɪ [ˌʌnˈh-], -ɪə*, -ɪɪst, -ɪlɪ [-əlɪ], -ɪnɪs [-nəs]

unharmed ˌʌnˈhɑːmd [ʌn-]

unharness, -es, -ing, -ed ˌʌnˈhɑːnɪs, -ɪz, -ɪŋ, -t

unhatched ˌʌnˈhætʃt

unhealth|y, -ier, -iest, -ily, -iness ʌnˈhelθ|ɪ [ˌʌnˈh-], -ɪə* [-jə*], -ɪɪst [-jɪst], -ɪlɪ [-əlɪ], -ɪnɪs [-nəs]

unheard (*not granted a hearing, etc.*) ˌʌnˈhɜːd

unheard of ˌʌnˈhɜːdɒv [ʌn-]

unheed|ed, -ing ˌʌnˈhiːd|ɪd [ʌn-], -ɪŋ

unhesitating, -ly ʌnˈhezɪteɪtɪŋ, -lɪ

unhing|e, -es, -ing, -ed ˌʌnˈhɪndʒ [ʌnˈh-], -ɪz, -ɪŋ, -d

unhistoric, -al ˌʌnhɪˈstɒrɪk [*occasionally* ˌʌnɪˈs-], -l

unhitch, -es, -ing, -ed ˌʌnˈhɪtʃ [ʌn-], -ɪz, -ɪŋ, -t

unhol|y, -iness ˌʌnˈhəʊl|ɪ [ʌn-], -ɪnɪs [-nəs]

unhook, -s, -ing, -ed ˌʌnˈhʊk [ʌn-], -s, -ɪŋ, -t

unhoped for ʌnˈhəʊptfɔː* [ˌʌn-]

unhors|e, -es, -ing, -ed ˌʌnˈhɔːs [ʌn-], -ɪz, -ɪŋ, -t

unhospitable ˌʌnhɒˈspɪtəbl [ˌʌnˈhɒspɪtəbl, ʌnˈhɒ-]

unhous|e, -es, -ing, -ed ˌʌnˈhaʊz, -ɪz, -ɪŋ, -d

unhuman ˌʌnˈhjuːmən [ʌn-]

unhung (*not hung*) ˌʌnˈhʌŋ

unhurt ˌʌnˈhɜːt

Uniat, -s ˈjuːnɪæt, -s

uniaxial, -ly ˌjuːnɪˈæksɪəl [-sjəl], -ɪ

U.N.I.C.E.F. ˈjuːnɪsef

unicorn, -s ˈjuːnɪkɔːn, -z

unicycle, -s ˈjuːnɪsaɪkl [ˌjuːnɪˈs-], -z

unideal ˌʌnaɪˈdɪəl [-ˈdiːəl, -ˈdiːl]

unidentified ˌʌnaɪˈdentɪfaɪd

unidiomatic ˈʌnˌɪdɪəˈmætɪk [-djəˈm-, -dɪʊˈm-, -djʊˈm-, -dɪəʊˈm-, -djəʊˈm-]

unifiable ˈjuːnɪfaɪəbl

unification, -s ˌjuːnɪfɪˈkeɪʃn [jʊn-], -z

†uniform (*s. adj.*), -s, -ed, -ly, -ness ˈjuːnɪfɔːm, -z, -d, -lɪ, -nɪs [-nəs]

uniformity ˌjuːnɪˈfɔːmətɪ [jʊn-, -ɪtɪ]

uni|fy, -fies, -fying, -fied ˈjuːnɪ|faɪ, -faɪz, -faɪɪŋ, -faɪd

unilateral, -ally ˌjuːnɪˈlætər|əl, -əlɪ

Unilever ˈjuːnɪliːvə*

uniliteral, -ally ˌjuːnɪˈlɪtər|əl, -əlɪ

unimaginab|le, -ly, -leness ˌʌnɪˈmædʒɪnəb|l [-dʒən-], -lɪ, -lnɪs [-nəs]

unimaginative, -ly, -ness ˌʌnɪˈmædʒɪnətɪv [-dʒən-], -lɪ, -nɪs [-nəs]

unimagined ˌʌnɪˈmædʒɪnd [-dʒənd]

unimpaired ˌʌnɪmˈpeəd

unimpeachable ˌʌnɪmˈpiːtʃəb|l

unimpeachab|ly, -leness ˌʌnɪmˈpiːtʃəb|lɪ, -lnɪs [-nəs]

unimpeded ˌʌnɪmˈpiːdɪd

521

unimportan|ce, -t ˌʌnɪm'pɔːtən|s, -t
unimpress|ive, -ed ˌʌnɪm'pres|ɪv, -t
uninflated ˌʌnɪn'fleɪtɪd
uninflected ˌʌnɪn'flektɪd
uninfluenced ˌʌn'ɪnflʊənst [ʌn-, -flwənst]
uninform|ative, -ed ˌʌnɪn'fɔːm|ətɪv, -d
uninhabitable, -ness ˌʌnɪn'hæbɪtəbl, -nɪs [-nəs]
uninhabited ˌʌnɪn'hæbɪtɪd
uninhibited ˌʌnɪn'hɪbɪtɪd
uninitiated ˌʌnɪ'nɪʃɪeɪtɪd [-ʃjeɪt-]
uninjured ˌʌn'ɪndʒəd [ʌn-]
uninspired ˌʌnɪn'spaɪəd
uninstructed ˌʌnɪn'strʌktɪd
uninsured ˌʌnɪn'ʃɔːd [-'ʃɔəd, -'ʃʊəd]
unintelligent, -ly ˌʌnɪn'telɪdʒənt, -lɪ
unintelligibility 'ʌnɪnˌtelɪdʒə'bɪlətɪ [-dʒɪ'b-, -lɪt-]
unintelligib|le, -ly ˌʌnɪn'telɪdʒəb|l [-lədʒ-, -dʒɪb-], -lɪ
uninten|tional, -tionally ˌʌnɪn'ten|ʃənl [-ʃnəl, -ʃn̩l, -ʃnl̩, -ʃənəl], -ʃnəlɪ [-ʃnəlɪ, -ʃn̩lɪ, -ʃnl̩ɪ, -ʃənəlɪ]
uninterest|ed, -ing ˌʌn'ɪntrəst|ɪd [ʌn-, -trɪs-, -təres-], -ɪŋ
unintermitting, -ly 'ʌnˌɪntə'mɪtɪŋ [ˌʌnɪ-], -lɪ
uninterrupted, -ly 'ʌnˌɪntə'rʌptɪd [ˌʌnɪ-], -lɪ
uninvit|ed, -ing ˌʌnɪn'vaɪt|ɪd, -ɪŋ
union (U.), -s 'juːnjən [-nɪən], -z
unioni|sm, -st/s 'juːnjənɪ|zəm [-nɪən-], -st/s
unipartite ˌjuːnɪ'pɑːtaɪt ['juːnɪˌp-]
unique, -ly, -ness juː'niːk [jʊ'n-], -lɪ, -nɪs [-nəs]
unisex 'juːnɪseks
unisexual ˌjuːnɪ'sekʃʊəl [-ksjʊəl, -ksjwəl, -ksjʊl, -kʃwəl, -kʃʊl, -kʃl]
unison, -s 'juːnɪzn [-ɪsn], -z
unissued ˌʌn'ɪʃjuːd [-'ɪʃjuːd, -'ɪsjuːd]
unit, -s 'juːnɪt, -s
unitable juː'naɪtəbl [jʊ'n-]
unitarian (U.), -s, -ism ˌjuːnɪ'teərɪən [jʊn-], -z, -ɪzəm
unitary 'juːnɪtərɪ
unit|e, -es, -ing, -ed/ly, -er/s juː'naɪt [jʊ'n-], -s, -ɪŋ, -ɪd/lɪ, -ə*/z
unit|y (U.), -ies 'juːnət|ɪ [-ɪt|ɪ], -ɪz
univalve, -s 'juːnɪvælv, -z
univers|al, -als, -ally, -alness, -alism, -alist/s ˌjuːnɪ'vɜːs|l [jʊn-], -lz, -əlɪ [-l̩ɪ], -lnɪs [-nəs], -əlɪzəm [-l̩ɪzəm], -əlɪst/s [-l̩ɪst/s]
universality ˌjuːnɪvɜː'sælətɪ [-ɪtɪ]
universaliz|e (-is|e), -es, -ing, -ed ˌjuːnɪ'vɜːsəlaɪz [jʊn-, -sl̩aɪz], -ɪz, -ɪŋ, -d

universe (U.), -s 'juːnɪvɜːs, -ɪz
universit|y, -ies ˌjuːnɪ'vɜːsət|ɪ [jʊn-, -sɪt|ɪ, -st|ɪ], -ɪz
univocal (s. adj.), -s ˌjuːnɪ'vəʊkl, -z
unjust, -ly, -ness ˌʌn'dʒʌst [ʌn-, also '-- when attributive], -lɪ, -nɪs [-nəs]
unjustifiab|le, -ly, -leness ʌn'dʒʌstɪfaɪəb|l [ˌʌn'dʒ-, ʌnˌdʒʌstɪ'f-, 'ʌnˌdʒʌstɪ'f-], -lɪ, -lnɪs [-nəs]
unkempt ˌʌn'kempt [ʌn-, also 'ʌnk- when attributive]
unkept ˌʌn'kept
unkin|d, -der, -dest, -dly, -dness ʌn'kaɪn|d [ˌʌn'k-], -də*, -dɪst, -dlɪ, -dnɪs [-nəs]
unknot, -s, -ting, -ted ˌʌn'nɒt, -s, -ɪŋ, -ɪd
unknowable ˌʌn'nəʊəbl [ʌn-]
unknowing, -ly, -ness ˌʌn'nəʊɪŋ [ʌn-], -lɪ, -nɪs [-nəs]
unknown ˌʌn'nəʊn [also 'ʌnn-, ʌn'n-, according to sentence-stress]
unlac|e, -es, -ing, -ed ˌʌn'leɪs, -ɪz, -ɪŋ, -t
unlad|e, -es, -ing, -ed ˌʌn'leɪd, -z, -ɪŋ, -ɪd
unladylike ˌʌn'leɪdɪlaɪk [ʌn-]
unlamented ˌʌnlə'mentɪd [also '-ˌ-- when attributive]
unlash, -es, -ing, -ed ˌʌn'læʃ, -ɪz, -ɪŋ, -t
unlatch, -es, -ing, -ed ˌʌn'lætʃ, -ɪz, -ɪŋ, -t
unlaw|ful, -fully, -fulness ˌʌn'lɔː|fʊl [ʌn-], -fʊlɪ [-fəlɪ], -fʊlnɪs [-nəs]
unleaded (without lead) ˌʌn'ledɪd [also '-ˌ-- when attributive]
unlearn, -s, -ing, -ed (p. tense, p. partic.), -t ˌʌn'lɜːn, -z, -ɪŋ, -t [-d], -t
unlearned (adj.), -ly, -ness ˌʌn'lɜːnɪd, -lɪ, -nɪs [-nəs]
unleavened ˌʌn'levnd [also 'ʌnˌl- when attributive]
unled ˌʌn'led
unless ən'les, [ˌʌn'les, n̩'les, also ˌʌn'les for special emphasis]
unlettered ˌʌn'letəd
Unley 'ʌnlɪ
unlicensed ˌʌn'laɪsənst [ʌn-]
unlike ˌʌn'laɪk ['ʌnl-, ʌn'l-]
unlikel|y, -ihood, -iness ʌn'laɪkl|ɪ [ˌʌn'l-], -ɪhʊd, -ɪnɪs [-ɪnəs]
unlikeness ˌʌn'laɪknɪs [ʌn-, -nəs]
unlimber, -s, -ing, -ed ˌʌn'lɪmbə*, -z, -rɪŋ, -d
unlimited ʌn'lɪmɪtɪd [ˌʌn'l-]
unlink, -s, -ing, -ed ˌʌn'lɪŋk, -s, -ɪŋ, -t [-'lɪŋt]
unliquidated ˌʌn'lɪkwɪdeɪtɪd [also 'ʌnˌlɪkwɪdeɪtɪd when attributive]

unlit ˌʌnˈlɪt [*also* ˈʌnlɪt *when attributive*]
unload, -s, -ing, -ed, -er/s ˌʌnˈləʊd [ʌn-], -z, -ɪŋ, -ɪd, -ə*/z
unlock, -s, -ing, -ed ˌʌnˈlɒk [ʌn-], -s, -ɪŋ, -t
unlooked for ʌnˈlʊktfɔː* [ˌʌn-]
unloos|e, -es, -ing, -ed ˌʌnˈluːs [ʌn-], -ɪz, -ɪŋ, -t
unloos|en, -ens, -ening, -ened ʌnˈluːs|n [ˌʌnˈl-], -nz, -ŋɪŋ [-nɪŋ], -nd
unlovel|y, -iness ˌʌnˈlʌvl|ɪ, -ɪnɪs [-ɪnəs]
unloving ˌʌnˈlʌvɪŋ
unluck|y, -ier, -iest, -ily, -iness ʌn-ˈlʌk|ɪ [ˌʌnˈl-], -ɪə*, -ɪɪst, -ɪlɪ [-əlɪ], -ɪnɪs [-ɪnəs]
un|make, -makes, -making, -made ˌʌn|ˈmeɪk, -ˈmeɪks, -ˈmeɪkɪŋ, -ˈmeɪd
unman, -s, -ning, -ned ˌʌnˈmæn, -z, -ɪŋ, -d
unmanageable ʌnˈmænɪdʒəbl [ˌʌnˈm-]
unmanageab|ly, -leness ʌnˈmænɪdʒ-əb|lɪ, -lnɪs [-nəs]
unmanl|y, -ier, -iest, -iness ˌʌn-ˈmænl|ɪ [ʌn-], -ɪə* [-jə*], -ɪɪst [-jɪst], -ɪnɪs [-ɪnəs]
unmanner|ly, -liness ʌnˈmænə|lɪ, -lɪnɪs [-nəs]
unmarked ˌʌnˈmɑːkt [*also* ˈ-- *according to sentence-stress*]
unmarriageable ˌʌnˈmærɪdʒəbl
unmarried ˌʌnˈmærɪd [*also* ˈʌnˌm- *according to sentence-stress*]
unmask, -s, -ing, -ed ˌʌnˈmɑːsk, -s, -ɪŋ, -t
unmatched ˌʌnˈmætʃt
unmeaning ˌʌnˈmiːnɪŋ
unmeaning|ly, -ness ʌnˈmiːnɪŋ|lɪ, -nɪs [-nəs]
unmeasurable ˌʌnˈmeʒərəbl
unmeasured ˌʌnˈmeʒəd
unmentionable, -s, -ness ʌnˈmenʃŋəbl [-ʃnə-, -ʃənə-], -z, -nɪs [-nəs]
unmentioned ˌʌnˈmenʃnd
unmerci|ful, -fully, -fulness ʌnˈmɜːsɪ|-fʊl [ˌʌn-], -fʊlɪ [-fəlɪ], -fʊlnɪs [-nəs]
unmerited ˌʌnˈmerɪtɪd [ʌn-]
unmethodical ˌʌnmɪˈθɒdɪkl [-meˈθ-, -məˈθ-]
unmind|ful, -fully, -fulness ʌnˈmaɪnd|-fʊl [ˌʌn-], -fʊlɪ [-fəlɪ], -fʊlnɪs [-nəs]
unmingled ˌʌnˈmɪŋgld
unmistak(e)ab|le, -ly, -leness ˌʌnmɪˈs-teɪkəb|l, -lɪ, -lnɪs [-nəs]
unmitigated ʌnˈmɪtɪgeɪtɪd
unmixed ˌʌnˈmɪkst [*also* ˈʌnm- *when attributive*]
unmodifiable ˌʌnˈmɒdɪfaɪəbl [ʌn-]
unmodified ˌʌnˈmɒdɪfaɪd [ʌn-]

unmolested ˌʌnməʊˈlestɪd
unmoor, -s, ing, -ed ˌʌnˈmɔː* [-ˈmɔə*, -ˈmʊə*], -z, -rɪŋ, -d
unmounted ˌʌnˈmaʊntɪd [*also* ˈʌnˌm- *when attributive*]
unmourned ˌʌnˈmɔːnd [-ˈmɔənd, *rarely* -ˈmʊənd]
unmov(e)able ˌʌnˈmuːvəbl [ʌn-]
unmoved ˌʌnˈmuːvd [ʌn-]
unmuff|le, -les, -ling, -led ˌʌnˈmʌf|l, -lz, -lɪŋ [-lɪŋ], -ld
unmusic|al, -ally ˌʌnˈmjuːzɪk|l, -əlɪ
unmuzz|le, -les, -ling, -led ˌʌnˈmʌz|l, -lz, -lɪŋ [-lɪŋ], -ld
unnamed ˌʌnˈneɪmd [*also* ˈʌnn- *when attributive*]
unnatur|al, -ally, -alness ʌnˈnætʃr|əl [ˌʌnˈn-, -tʃʊr-, -tʃər-], -əlɪ, -əlnɪs [-nəs]
unnavigable ˌʌnˈnævɪgəbl
unnecessarily ʌnˈnesəsərəlɪ [-sɪs-, -ser-, ˈʌnˌnesɪˈser-, ˈʌnˌnesəˈser-, -ɪlɪ]
unnecessar|y, -iness ʌnˈnesəsər|ɪ [ˌʌnˈn-, -sɪs-, -ser-], -ɪnɪs [-nəs]
unneighbourly ˌʌnˈneɪbəlɪ
unnerv|e, -es, -ing, -ed ˌʌnˈnɜːv, -z, -ɪŋ, -d
unnotice|able, -d ˌʌnˈnəʊtɪs|əbl [ʌn-], -t
U.N.N.R.A. ˈʌnrə
unnumbered ˌʌnˈnʌmbəd [*in contrast* ˈ-ˌ-]
U.N.O. ˈjuːnəʊ
unobjectionab|le, -ly ˌʌnəbˈdʒəkʃŋəb|l [-ʃnə-, -ʃənə-], -lɪ
unobliging ˌʌnəˈblaɪdʒɪŋ
unobliterated ˌʌnəˈblɪtəreɪtɪd [ˌʌnɒˈb-]
unobservan|ce, -t ˌʌnəbˈzɜːvən|s, -t
unobserv|ed, -edly ˌʌnəbˈzɜːv|d, -ɪdlɪ
unobstructed ˌʌnəbˈstrʌktɪd [*also* ˈʌnəbˌs- *when attributive*]
unobtainable ˌʌnəbˈteɪnəbl
unobtrusive, -ly, -ness ˌʌnəbˈtruːsɪv, -lɪ, -nɪs [-nəs]
unoccupied ˌʌnˈɒkjʊpaɪd [ʌn-]
unoffending ˌʌnəˈfendɪŋ [*also* ˈʌnəˌf- *when attributive*]
unoffensive ˌʌnəˈfensɪv
unofficial ˌʌnəˈfɪʃl [*also* ˈʌnəˌf- *when attributive*]
unopened ˌʌnˈəʊpənd [-pɪnd]
unopposed ˌʌnəˈpəʊzd
unordained ˌʌnɔːˈdeɪnd
unordered ˌʌnˈɔːdəd
unorganized ˌʌnˈɔːgənaɪzd [ʌn-, -gŋaɪ-]
unorthodox ˌʌnˈɔːθədɒks [ʌn-]
unorthodoxy ʌnˈɔːθədɒksɪ [ˌʌnˈɔː-]
unostentatious, -ly, -ness ˈʌnˌɒsten-ˈteɪʃəs [-tən-, ˌ---ˈ--], -lɪ, -nɪs [-nəs]

523

unowned ˌʌnˈəʊnd
unpack, -s, -ing, -ed, -er/s ˌʌnˈpæk, -s, -ɪŋ, -t, -əʳ/z
unpaid ˌʌnˈpeɪd [*also* ˈʌnp- *according to sentence-stress*]
unpaired ˌʌnˈpeəd
unpalatable ʌnˈpælətəbl [ˌʌnˈp-, -lɪt-]
unpalatableness ʌnˈpælətəblnɪs [-lɪt-, -nəs]
unparalleled ʌnˈpærəleld [ˌʌn-, -r]eld, -rələld, -r]əld]
unpardonable ʌnˈpɑːdṇəbl [ˌʌnˈp-, -dnə-]
unpardonab|ly, -leness ʌnˈpɑːdṇəb|lɪ [-dnə-], -lnɪs [-nəs]
unparliamentary ˈʌnˌpɑːləˈmentərɪ [-lɪˈm-, -ljə-]
unpatriotic ˈʌnˌpætrɪˈɒtɪk [-ˌpeɪt-]
unpaved ˌʌnˈpeɪvd [*also* ˈʌnp- *when attributive*]
unpeeled ˌʌnˈpiːld [*also* ˈʌnp- *when attributive*]
unperceiv|able, -ed ˌʌnpəˈsiːv|əbl, -d
unperforated ˌʌnˈpɜːfəreɪtɪd [ʌn-]
unperformed ˌʌnpəˈfɔːmd
unpersua|dable, -ded, -sive ˌʌnpəˈsweɪ|dəbl, -dɪd, -sɪv [-zɪv]
unperturb|able, -ed ˌʌnpəˈtɜːb|əbl, -d
unperverted ˌʌnpəˈvɜːtɪd
unphilosophic|al, -ally, -alness ʌn-ˌfɪləˈsɒfɪk|l [-əˈl-], -əlɪ, -lnɪs [-nəs]
unpick, -s, -ing, -ed ˌʌnˈpɪk, -s, -ɪŋ, -t
unpierced ˌʌnˈpɪəst
unpiloted ˌʌnˈpaɪlətɪd
unpin, -s, -ning, -ned ˌʌnˈpɪn, -z, -ɪŋ, -d
unpitied ˌʌnˈpɪtɪd
unpitying ˌʌnˈpɪtɪɪŋ [ʌnˈp-]
unpityingly ʌnˈpɪtɪɪŋlɪ
unplaced ˌʌnˈpleɪst
unplait, -s, -ing, -ed ˌʌnˈplæt, -s, -ɪŋ, -ɪd
unplayable ˌʌnˈpleɪəbl
unpleasant ʌnˈpleznt
unpleasant|ly, -ness ʌnˈpleznt|lɪ, -nɪs [-nəs]
unpleasing ˌʌnˈpliːzɪŋ
unpleasing|ly, -ness ˌʌnˈpliːzɪŋ|lɪ, -nɪs [-nəs]
unpliable ˌʌnˈplaɪəbl
unpoetic|al, -ally, -alness ˌʌnpəʊˈetɪk|l, -əlɪ, -lnɪs [-nəs]
unpolished ˌʌnˈpɒlɪʃt [*also* ˈʌnˌp- *according to sentence-stress*]
unpolitic ˌʌnˈpɒlətɪk [-lɪt-]
unpolluted ˌʌnpəˈluːtɪd [-ˈljuː-]
unpopular ˌʌnˈpɒpjʊlə* [ʌn-, -pjəl-]
unpopularity ˈʌnˌpɒpjʊˈlærətɪ [-pjəˈl-, -ɪtɪ]

unpractic|al, -ally ˌʌnˈpræktɪk|l [ʌn-], -əlɪ
unpracticality ˈʌnˌpræktɪˈkælətɪ [-ɪtɪ]
unpractised ʌnˈpræktɪst [ˌʌnˈp-]
unprecedented ʌnˈpresɪdəntɪd [ˌʌn-, -ˈpriːs-, -den-]
unpredictable ˌʌnprɪˈdɪktəbl [-prəˈd-]
unprejudiced ˌʌnˈpredʒʊdɪst [ʌnˈp-]
unpremeditated ˌʌnpriːˈmedɪteɪtɪd [-prɪ-]
unpreparation ˈʌnˌprepəˈreɪʃn
unprepar|ed, -edness ˌʌnprɪˈpeə|d [-prəˈp-], -rɪdlɪ [-dlɪ], -rɪdnɪs [-dnɪs, -nəs]
unprepossessing ˈʌnˌpriːpəˈzesɪŋ
unpresentable ˌʌnprɪˈzentəbl [-prəˈz-]
unpresuming ˌʌnprɪˈzjuːmɪŋ [-prəˈz-, -ˈzuː-]
unpretending, -ly ˌʌnprɪˈtendɪŋ [*also* ˈʌnprɪ,t- *when attributive*], -lɪ
unpretentious ˌʌnprɪˈtenʃəs [*also* ˈ--,-- *when attributive*]
unpretentious|ly, -ness ˌʌnprɪˈtenʃəs|lɪ, -nɪs [-nəs]
unpreventable ˌʌnprɪˈventəbl [-prəˈv-]
unpriced ˌʌnˈpraɪst
unprincipled ʌnˈprɪnsəpld [ˌʌnˈp-, -sɪp-]
unprintable ˌʌnˈprɪntəbl [ʌn-]
unprinted ˌʌnˈprɪntɪd
unproclaimed ˌʌnprəˈkleɪmd [-prəʊˈk-, -prʊˈk-]
unprocurable ˌʌnprəˈkjʊərəbl [-prʊˈk-, -ˈkjɔər-, -ˈkjɔːr-]
unproductive, -ly, -ness ˌʌnprəˈdʌktɪv [-prʊˈd-], -lɪ, -nɪs [-nəs]
unprofes|sional, -sionally ˌʌnprəˈfe|ʃənl [-prʊˈf-, -ʃnəl, -ʃṇ], -ʃnl, -ʃənəl], -ʃṇəlɪ [-ʃnəlɪ, -ʃṇlɪ, -ʃnlɪ, -ʃənəlɪ]
unprofitab|le, -ly, -leness ˌʌnˈprɒfɪtəb|l [ʌnˈp-], -lɪ, -lnɪs [-nəs]
unprohibited ˌʌnprəʊˈhɪbɪtɪd [-prʊˈh-]
unpromising ˌʌnˈprɒmɪsɪŋ [ʌn-]
unpronounceable ˌʌnprəˈnaʊnsəbl [-prʊˈn-, -prṇˈaʊ-]
unprop, -s, -ping, -ped ˌʌnˈprɒp, -s, -ɪŋ, -t
unpropitious, -ly, -ness ˌʌnprəˈpɪʃəs [-prʊˈp-], -lɪ, -nɪs [-nəs]
unprotected ˌʌnprəˈtektɪd [-prʊˈt-]
unprov|ed, -en ˌʌnˈpruːv|d, -n
unprovided ˌʌnprəˈvaɪdɪd [-prʊˈv-]
unprovok|ed, -edly ˌʌnprəˈvəʊk|t [-prʊˈv-], -ɪdlɪ [-tlɪ]
unpublished ˌʌnˈpʌblɪʃt [ˈʌnˌp- *according to sentence-stress*]
unpunctual, -ly ˌʌnˈpʌŋktʃʊəl [ʌn-, -tʃwəl, -tʃʊl, -tjʊəl, -tjwəl, -tjʊl], -ɪ
unpunctuality ˈʌnˌpʌŋktʃʊˈælətɪ [-tju-, -ɪtɪ]
unpunished ˌʌnˈpʌnɪʃt

unqualified (*without qualifications*) ˌʌn-
'kwɒlɪfaɪd [ʌn-], (*without reservation,
downright*) ʌn'kwɒlɪfaɪd
unquenchable ˌʌn'kwentʃəbl
unquestionab|le, -ly, -leness ʌn'kwes-
tʃənəb|l [ˌʌn-, -eʃtʃ-, -tʃnə-, -tʃnə-],
-lɪ, -lnɪs [-nəs]
unquesti|oned, -oning/ly ʌn'kwestʃ|ənd
[ˌʌn-, -eʃtʃ-], -ənɪŋ/lɪ [-n̩ɪŋ/lɪ]
unrav|el, -els, -elling, -elled, -eller/s
ʌn'ræv|l [ˌʌn-], -əlz, -|ɪŋ [-əlɪŋ], -ld,
-|ə*/z [-ələ*/z]
unread ˌʌn'red
unreadable, -ness ˌʌn'ri:dəbl [ʌn-], -nɪs
[-nəs]
unread|y, -ily, -iness ˌʌn'red|ɪ [ʌn-], -ɪlɪ
[-əlɪ], -ɪnɪs [-ɪnəs]
unreal ˌʌn'rɪəl [ʌn-, -'ri:əl]
unrealit|y, -ies ˌʌnrɪ'ælət|ɪ [-ri:'æ-, -ɪt|ɪ],
-ɪz
unreason ˌʌn'ri:zn [*in contrast* 'ʌnˌr-]
unreasonable ʌn'ri:znəbl [ˌʌn'r-, -znə-]
unreasonab|ly, -leness ʌn'ri:znəb|lɪ
[ˌʌn-, -znə-], -lnɪs [-nəs]
unreasoning ʌn'ri:znɪŋ [ˌʌn'r-, -znɪŋ]
unreceipted ˌʌnrɪ'si:tɪd [-rə's-, *also* '--ˌ--
when attributive]
unreceived ˌʌnrɪ'si:vd [-rə's-]
unreciprocated ˌʌnrɪ'sɪprəkeɪtɪd [-rə's-,
-prʊk-]
unreckoned ˌʌn'rekənd
unreclaimed ˌʌnrɪ'kleɪmd [*also* '--ˌ-
when attributive]
unrecognizable [-isa-] ˌʌn'rekəgnaɪzəbl
[ʌn'r-, 'ʌnˌrekəg'n-, -kɪg-]
unrecognized [-ised] ˌʌn'rekəgnaɪzd
[ʌn-, -kɪg-]
unreconcilable ˌʌn'rekənsaɪləbl [ʌn'r-,
'ʌnˌrekən's-, -kn-]
unreconciled ˌʌn'rekənsaɪld [ʌn-, -kn-]
unrecorded ˌʌnrɪ'kɔ:dɪd [-rə'k-]
unrecounted ˌʌnrɪ'kaʊntɪd [-rə'k-]
unredeemable ˌʌnrɪ'di:məbl [-rə'd-]
unredeemed ˌʌnrɪ'di:md [-rə'd-, *also* '--
when attributive]
unrefined ˌʌnrɪ'faɪnd [-rə'f-]
unreflecting ˌʌnrɪ'flektɪŋ [-rə'f-]
unreformed ˌʌnrɪ'fɔ:md [-rə'f-]
unrefuted ˌʌnrɪ'fju:tɪd [-rə'f-]
unregenerate ˌʌnrɪ'dʒenərət [-rə'dʒ-,
-rɪt]
unregistered ˌʌn'redʒɪstəd [ʌn-]
unrehearsed ˌʌnrɪ'hɜ:st [-rə'h-]
unrelated ˌʌnrɪ'leɪtɪd [-rə'l-]
unrelaxed ˌʌnrɪ'lækst [-rə'l-]
unrelenting ˌʌnrɪ'lentɪŋ [-rə'l-]
unrelenting|ly, -ness ˌʌnrɪ'lentɪŋ|lɪ
[-rə'l-], -nɪs [-nəs]

unreliability 'ʌnrɪˌlaɪə'bɪlətɪ [-rə,l-, -lɪt-]
unreliable, -ness ˌʌnrɪ'laɪəbl [-rə'l-],
-nɪs [-nəs]
unrelieved ˌʌnrɪ'li:vd [-rə'l-]
unremembered ˌʌnrɪ'membəd [-rə'm-]
unremitting ˌʌnrɪ'mɪtɪŋ [-rə'm-]
unremitting|ly, -ness ˌʌnrɪ'mɪtɪŋ|lɪ
[-rə'm-], -nɪs [-nəs]
unremonstrative ˌʌnrɪ'mɒnstrətɪv
[-rə'm-]
unremovable ˌʌnrɪ'mu:vəbl [-rə'm-]
unremunerative ˌʌnrɪ'mju:nərətɪv
[-rə'm-]
unrepaid ˌʌnrɪ'peɪd
unrepair, -able ˌʌnrɪ'peə* [-rə'p-], -rəbl
unrepealed ˌʌnrɪ'pi:ld [-rə'p-]
unrepeatable ˌʌnrɪ'pi:təbl [-rə'p-]
unrepentant ˌʌnrɪ'pentənt [-rə'p-]
unreported ˌʌnrɪ'pɔ:tɪd [-rə'p-]
unrepresented ˌʌnreprɪ'zentɪd
unrequested ˌʌnrɪ'kwestɪd [-rə'k-]
unrequited ˌʌnrɪ'kwaɪtɪd [-rə'k-]
unreserved ˌʌnrɪ'zɜ:vd [-rə'z-, *also* '---
when attributive]
unreservedly ˌʌnrɪ'zɜ:vɪdlɪ [-rə'z-]
unresisting, -ly ˌʌnrɪ'zɪstɪŋ [-rə'z-], -lɪ
unresolved ˌʌnrɪ'zɒlvd [-rə'z-]
unresponsive ˌʌnrɪ'spɒnsɪv [-rə's-]
unrest ʌn'rest [ʌn-]
unrest|ful, -fully, -fulness ʌn'rest|fʊl
[ʌn-], -fʊlɪ [-fəlɪ], -fʊlnɪs [-nəs]
unresting ʌn'restɪŋ [ʌn-]
unrestored ˌʌnrɪ'stɔ:d [-rə's-, -'stɔəd]
unrestrain|ed, -edly ˌʌnrɪ'streɪn|d
[-rə's-], -ɪdlɪ
unrestricted ˌʌnrɪ'strɪktɪd [-rə's-]
unretentive ˌʌnrɪ'tentɪv [-rə't-]
unreveal|ed, -ing ˌʌnrɪ'vi:l|d [-rə'v-], -ɪŋ
unrevoked ˌʌnrɪ'vəʊkt [-rə'v-]
unrewarded ˌʌnrɪ'wɔ:dɪd [-rə'w-]
unrighteous, -ly, -ness ʌn'raɪtʃəs [*rarely*
-tʃəs], -lɪ, -nɪs [-nəs]
unright|ful, -fully, -fulness ʌn'raɪt|fʊl
[ʌn-], -fʊlɪ [-fəlɪ], -fʊlnɪs [-nəs]
unripe ˌʌn'raɪp [*also* 'ʌnr-, ʌn'r-,
according to sentence-stress]
unripeness ˌʌn'raɪpnɪs [ʌn-, -nəs]
unrivalled ʌn'raɪvld [ˌʌn-]
unrob|e, -es, -ing, -ed ʌn'rəʊb [ʌn-], -z,
-ɪŋ, -d
unroll, -s, -ing, -ed ʌn'rəʊl [ʌn-], -z,
-ɪŋ, -d
unromantic, -ally ˌʌnrə'mæntɪk
[-rəʊ'm-], -əlɪ
unrop|e, -es, -ing, -ed ʌn'rəʊp, -s, -ɪŋ, -t
unruffled ˌʌn'rʌfld [ʌn-]
unrul|y, -ier, -iest, -iness ʌn'ru:l|ɪ, -ɪə*
[-jə*], -ɪɪst [-jɪst], -ɪnɪs [-ɪnəs]

525

unsadd|le, -les, -ling, -led ˌʌn'sæd|l [ʌn-], -lz, -lɪŋ [-lɪŋ], -ld
unsafe, -ly, -ness ˌʌn'seɪf [ʌn-], -lɪ, -nɪs [-nəs]
unsaid ˌʌn'sed [ʌn-]
unsal(e)able, -ness ˌʌn'seɪləbl [ʌn-], -nɪs [-nəs]
unsalted ˌʌn'sɔːltɪd [-'sɒl-]
unsanctified ˌʌn'sæŋktɪfaɪd
unsanitary ˌʌn'sænɪtərɪ [ʌn-, -ətərɪ]
unsatisfactor|y, -ily, -iness 'ʌnˌsætɪs-'fæktər|ɪ [ˌ---'---], -əlɪ [-ɪlɪ], -ɪnɪs [-ɪnəs]
unsatisf|ied, -y:ng ˌʌn'sætɪsf|aɪd, -aɪɪŋ
unsavour|y, -ily, -iness ˌʌn'seɪvər|ɪ [ʌn-], -əlɪ [-ɪlɪ], -ɪnɪs [-ɪnəs]
uns|ay, -ays, -aying, -aid ˌʌn's|eɪ ['ʌns|eɪ], -ez, -eɪɪŋ, -ed
unscalable ˌʌn'skeɪləbl
unscathed ˌʌn'skeɪðd [ʌn-]
unscented ˌʌn'sentɪd [in contrast 'ʌnˌs-]
†unscheduled ˌʌn'ʃedjuːld
unscholarly ˌʌn'skɒləlɪ
unschooled ˌʌn'skuːld
unscientific 'ʌnˌsaɪən'tɪfɪk [ˌ---'--]
unscr|ew, -ews, -ewing, -ewed ˌʌn-'skr|uː [ʌn-], -uːz, -uːɪŋ [-ʊɪŋ], -uːd
unscriptur|al, -ally ˌʌn'skrɪptʃər|əl [-tʃʊr-], -əlɪ
unscrupulous ʌn'skruːpjʊləs [ˌʌn's-, -pjəl-]
unscrupulous|ly, -ness ʌn'skruːpjʊləs|lɪ [-pjəl-], -nɪs [-nəs]
unseal, -s, -ing, -ed ˌʌn'siːl, -z, -ɪŋ, -d
unseasonab|le, -ly, -leness ʌn'siːznəb|l [ˌʌn's-, -znə-], -lɪ, -lnɪs [-nəs]
unseasoned ˌʌn'siːznd [also '-ˌ-- when attributive]
unseat, -s, -ing, -ed ˌʌn'siːt, -s, -ɪŋ, -ɪd
unseaworth|y, -iness ˌʌn'siːˌwɜːð|ɪ [ʌn-], -ɪnɪs [-ɪnəs]
unsectarian, -ism ˌʌnsek'teərɪən, -ɪzəm
unsecured ˌʌnsɪ'kjʊəd [-sə'k-, -'kjɔəd, -'kjɔːd]
unseeing ˌʌn'siːɪŋ
unseeml|y, -iness ʌn'siːml|ɪ, -ɪnɪs [-ɪnəs]
unseen ˌʌn'siːn [also 'ʌns-, ʌn's-, according to sentence-stress]
unselfish, -ly, -ness ˌʌn'selfɪʃ, -lɪ, -nɪs [-nəs]
unsensational ˌʌnsen'seɪʃənl [-sən-, -ʃnəl, -ʃn̩l, -ʃn̩l, -ʃənəl]
unsensitive ˌʌn'sensətɪv [ʌn's-, -sɪt-]
unsentimental ˌʌnˌsentɪ'mentl
unserviceable ˌʌn'sɜːvɪsəbl [ʌn-]
unsett|le, -les, -ling, -led ˌʌn'set|l [ʌn-], -lz, -lɪŋ [-lɪŋ], -ld
unsevered ˌʌn'sevəd [ʌn-]

unshack|le, -les, -ling, -led ˌʌn'ʃæk|l [ʌn-], -lz, -lɪŋ [-lɪŋ], -ld
unshakable ʌn'ʃeɪkəbl
unshaken ˌʌn'ʃeɪkən [ʌn-]
unshapely ˌʌn'ʃeɪplɪ [ʌn-]
unshaven ˌʌn'ʃeɪvn
unsheath|e, -es, -ing, -ed ˌʌn'ʃiːð [ʌn-], -z, -ɪŋ, -d
unship, -s, -ping, -ped ˌʌn'ʃɪp, -s, -ɪŋ, -t
un|shod, -shorn ˌʌn|'ʃɒd, -'ʃɔːn
unshrinkable ˌʌn'ʃrɪŋkəbl [ʌn-]
unshrinking, -ly ʌn'ʃrɪŋkɪŋ, -lɪ
unsighted ˌʌn'saɪtɪd [ʌn-]
unsightl|y, -ier, -iest, -iness ʌn'saɪtl|ɪ, -ɪə* [-ɪə*], -ɪɪst [-jɪst], -ɪnɪs [-nəs]
unsigned ˌʌn'saɪnd [also 'ʌnsaɪnd when attributive]
unskil|ful, -fully, -fulness ˌʌn'skɪl|fʊl [ʌn-], -fʊlɪ [-fəlɪ], -fʊlnɪs [-nəs]
unskilled ˌʌn'skɪld [also 'ʌnskɪld when attributive]
unslaked ˌʌn'sleɪkt
unsociability 'ʌnˌsəʊʃə'bɪlətɪ [-lɪt-]
unsociab|le, -ly, -leness ʌn'səʊʃəb|l [ˌʌn's-], -lɪ, -lnɪs [-nəs]
unsold ˌʌn'səʊld [also 'ʌnsəʊld when attributive]
unsolder, -s, -ing, -ed ˌʌn'sɒldə* [-'sɔːd-, -'sɒd-, -'səʊld-], -z, -rɪŋ, -d
unsolicited ˌʌnsə'lɪsɪtɪd
unsolved ˌʌn'sɒlvd [also 'ʌns- according to sentence-stress]
unsophisticated, -ly, -ness ˌʌnsə'fɪstɪkeɪtɪd [-tək-], -lɪ, -nɪs
unsophistication 'ʌnsəˌfɪstɪ'keɪʃn
unsorted ˌʌn'sɔːtɪd
unsought ˌʌn'sɔːt [ʌn's- in unsought for]
unsoun|d, -dly, -dness ˌʌn'saʊn|d, -dlɪ, -dnɪs [-nəs]
unsparing, -ly, -ness ʌn'speərɪŋ, -lɪ, -nɪs [-nəs]
unspeakab|le, -ly ʌn'spiːkəb|l, -lɪ
unspecified ˌʌn'spesɪfaɪd [ʌn-]
unspent ˌʌn'spent [also 'ʌnspent when attributive]
unspoiled ˌʌn'spɔɪlt [-ld]
unspoilt ˌʌn'spɔɪlt
unspoken ˌʌn'spəʊkən [ʌn-]
unsporting ˌʌn'spɔːtɪŋ
unsportsmanlike ˌʌn'spɔːtsmənlaɪk [ʌn-]
unspotted ˌʌn'spɒtɪd
unstable, -ness ˌʌn'steɪbl [ʌn-], -nɪs [-nəs]
unstack, -s, -ing, -ed ˌʌn'stæk, -s, -ɪŋ, -t
unstamped ˌʌn'stæmpt ['ʌnstæmpt when attributive]
unstarched ˌʌn'stɑːtʃt

unstatesmanlike ˌʌn'steɪtsmənlaɪk [ʌn-]
unsteadfast, -ly, -ness ˌʌn'stedfɑːst [ʌn-, -fəst], -lɪ, -nɪs [-nəs]
unstead|y, -ier, -iest, -ily, -iness ˌʌn-'sted|ɪ [ʌn-], -ɪə*, -ɪɪst, -ɪlɪ [-əlɪ], -ɪnɪs [-ɪnəs]
un|stick, -sticks, -sticking, -stuck ˌʌn|-'stɪk, -'stɪks, -'stɪkɪŋ, -'stʌk
unstinted ʌn'stɪntɪd
unstitch, -es, -ing, -ed ˌʌn'stɪtʃ, -ɪz, -ɪŋ, -t
unstop, -s, -ping, -ped ˌʌn'stɒp, -s, -ɪŋ, -t
unstrap, -s, -ping, -ped ˌʌn'stræp, -s, -ɪŋ, -t
unstressed ˌʌn'strest [also 'ʌnstrest when attributive]
unstrung ˌʌn'strʌŋ
unstudied ˌʌn'stʌdɪd [ʌn-]
unsub|duable, -dued ˌʌnsəb|'djuːəbl [-'djʊəbl], -'djuːd
unsubmissive, -ly, -ness ˌʌnsəb'mɪsɪv, -lɪ, -nɪs [-nəs]
unsubstantial ˌʌnsəb'stænʃl [-bz't-, -tɑːn-]
unsubstantiality 'ʌnsəbˌstænʃɪ'ælətɪ [-bzˌt-, -ɪtɪ]
unsuccess ˌʌnsək'ses ['ʌnsəkˌses]
unsuccess|ful, -fully, -fulness ˌʌnsək-'ses|fʊl, -fʊlɪ [-fəlɪ], -fʊlnɪs [-nəs]
unsuitability 'ʌnˌsuːtə'bɪlətɪ ['ʌnˌsjuː-, ˌʌnsuː-, ˌʌnsjuː-, -ɪtɪ]
unsuitab|le, -ly, -leness ˌʌn'suːtəb|l [ʌn-, -'sjuː-], -lɪ, -lnɪs [-nəs]
unsuited ˌʌn'suːtɪd [ʌn-, -'sjuː-]
unsullied ˌʌn'sʌlɪd
unsung ˌʌn'sʌŋ
unsupportab|le, -ly, -leness ˌʌnsə'pɔːt-əb|l, -lɪ, -lnɪs [-nəs]
unsupported ˌʌnsə'pɔːtɪd
unsure ˌʌn'ʃɔː* [ʌn-, -'ʃʊə*, -'ʃɔə*]
unsurmountable ˌʌnsə'maʊntəbl
unsurpass|able, -ed ˌʌnsə'pɑːs|əbl, -t
unsusceptibility 'ʌnsəˌseptə'bɪlətɪ [-tɪ'b-, -ɪtɪ]
unsusceptible ˌʌnsə'septəbl [-tɪb-]
unsuspected, -ly, -ness ˌʌnsə'spektɪd, -lɪ, -nɪs [-nəs]
unsuspecting, -ly, -ness ˌʌnsə'spektɪŋ, -lɪ, -nɪs [-nəs]
unsuspicious, -ly, -ness ˌʌnsə'spɪʃəs, -lɪ, -nɪs [-nəs]
unsweetened ˌʌn'swiːtnd [also 'ʌnˌs-when attributive]
unswerving, -ly ʌn'swɜːvɪŋ, -lɪ
unsymmetric, -al, -ally ˌʌnsɪ'metrɪk, -l, -əlɪ
un|symmetry ˌʌn'sɪmətrɪ [-ɪtrɪ]
unsympathetic, -ally 'ʌnˌsɪmpə'θetɪk, -əlɪ

unsystematic, -al, -ally ˌʌnsɪstə'mætɪk ['-ˌ--'--, -tɪm-], -l, -əlɪ
untainted ˌʌn'teɪntɪd [ʌn-]
untamable ˌʌn'teɪməbl
untang|le, -les, -ling, -led ˌʌn'tæŋg|l [ʌn-], -lz, -lɪŋ [-lŋ̩], -ld
untapped ˌʌn'tæpt
untarnished ˌʌn'tɑːnɪʃt [ʌn-]
untasted ˌʌn'teɪstɪd
untaught ˌʌn'tɔːt [also 'ʌntɔːt when attributive]
untaxed ˌʌn'tækst [also 'ʌntækst when attributive]
unteachable ˌʌn'tiːtʃəbl [ʌn-]
untempered ˌʌn'tempəd [also 'ʌnˌt-when attributive]
untenable ˌʌn'tenəbl [ʌn-, -'tiːn-]
untenanted ˌʌn'tenəntɪd
unthank|ful, -fully, -fulness ˌʌn'θæŋk|-fʊl [ʌn-], -fʊlɪ [-fəlɪ], -fʊlnɪs [-nəs]
unthinkable ʌn'θɪŋkəbl
unthinking, -ly ˌʌn'θɪŋkɪŋ [ʌn-]
unthinkingly ʌn'θɪŋkɪŋlɪ
unthought|ful, -fully, -fulness ˌʌn-'θɔːt|fʊl [ʌn-], -fʊlɪ [-fəlɪ], -fʊlnɪs [-nəs]
unthought of ʌn'θɔːtɒv
unthread, -s, -ing, -ed ˌʌn'θred, -z, -ɪŋ, -ɪd
unthrift|y, -ily, -iness ˌʌn'θrɪft|ɪ [ʌn-], -ɪlɪ [-əlɪ], -ɪnɪs [-ɪnəs]
untid|y (adj. v.), -ier, -iest, -ily, -iness, -ies, -ying, -ied ʌn'taɪd|ɪ [ˌʌn't-], -ɪə* [-jə*], -ɪɪst [-jɪst], -ɪlɪ [-əlɪ], -ɪnɪs [-ɪnəs] ; -ɪz, -ɪŋ [-jɪŋ], -ɪd
un|tie, -ties, -tying, -tied ˌʌn|'taɪ, -'taɪz, -'taɪɪŋ, -'taɪd
until ən'tɪl [ʌn'tɪl, n'tɪl, also occasionally 'ʌntɪl, 'ʌntl when followed by a stress]
untimel|y, -iness ʌn'taɪml|ɪ [ˌʌn-], -ɪnɪs [-ɪnəs]
untinged ˌʌn'tɪndʒd
untiring, -ly ʌn'taɪərɪŋ, -lɪ
unto 'ʌntʊ [-tuː, -tə]
Note.—The form 'ʌntu occurs chiefly in final position; the form 'ʌntə occurs only before consonants.
untold ˌʌn'təʊld [ʌn't-, also occasionally 'ʌntəʊld when attributive]
untouchable, -s ˌʌn'tʌtʃəbl [ˌʌn't-], -z
untouched ˌʌn'tʌtʃt [ʌn-]
untoward, -ly, -ness ˌʌntə'wɔːd [-tʊ'w-, ʌn'təʊəd, ˌʌn't-], -lɪ, -nɪs [-nəs]
untraceable ˌʌn'treɪsəbl
untrained ˌʌn'treɪnd [also 'ʌnt-, ʌn't-, according to sentence-stress]
untrammelled ʌn'træməld [ˌʌn-]

untransferable   ˌʌntræns'fɜːrəbl [-trɑːns-]

untranslat|able, -ed ˌʌntræns'leɪt|əbl [-trɑːns-, -trænz-, -trɑːnz-, -trənz-, -trəns-], -ɪd

untried ˌʌn'traɪd [also 'ʌntraɪd when attributive]

untrimmed ˌʌn'trɪmd [also 'ʌntrɪmd when attributive]

untrodden ˌʌn'trɒdn [also 'ʌnˌt- when attributive]

untroubled ˌʌn'trʌbld [ʌn-]

un|true, -trueness ˌʌn|'truː [ʌn-], -'truːnɪs [-nəs]

untruly ˌʌn'truːlɪ [ʌn-]

untrustworth|y, -ily, -iness ˌʌn'trʌst-ˌwɜːðɪ [ʌn-], -ɪlɪ [-əlɪ], -ɪnɪs [-ɪnəs]

untru|th, -ths ˌʌn'truː|θ [ʌn-], -ðz [-θs]

untruth|ful, -fully, -fulness ˌʌn'truːθ|-fʊl [ʌn-], -fʊlɪ [-fəlɪ], -fʊlnɪs [-nəs]

untuck, -s, -ing, -ed ˌʌn'tʌk, -s, -ɪŋ, -t

unturned ˌʌn'tɜːnd

untutored ˌʌn'tjuːtəd

untwist, -s, -ing, -ed ˌʌn'twɪst [ʌn-], -s, -ɪŋ, -ɪd

unused (not made use of) ˌʌn'juːzd [ʌn-]

unused (not accustomed) ˌʌn'juːst [ʌn-], rarely -'juːzd]

unu|sual, -sually, -sualness ʌn'juː|ʒl [ˌʌn'j-, -ʒwəl, -ʒʊl, -ʒʊəl], -ʒəlɪ [-ʒwəlɪ, -ʒlɪ, -ʒʊlɪ, -ʒʊəlɪ], -ʒlnɪs [-ʒwəlnɪs, -ʒʊlnɪs, -ʒʊəlnɪs, -nəs]

unutterab|le, -ly, -leness ʌn'ʌtərəb|l, -lɪ, -lnɪs [-nəs]

unuttered ˌʌn'ʌtəd

unvaccinated ˌʌn'væksɪneɪtɪd

unvariable ʌn'veərɪəbl [ˌʌn'v-]

unvaried ʌn'veərɪd

unvarnished (not varnished) ˌʌn'vɑːnɪʃt [ʌn-], (simple) ʌn'vɑːnɪʃt

unvarying ʌn'veərɪŋ

unveil, -s, -ing, -ed, -er/s ˌʌn'veɪl [ʌn'v-], -z, -ɪŋ, -d, -ə*/z

unventilated ˌʌn'ventɪleɪtɪd [ʌn-, -təl-]

unversed ˌʌn'vɜːst [ʌn-]

unvoic|e, -es, -ing, -ed ˌʌn'vɔɪs, -ɪz, -ɪŋ, -t [also 'ʌnvɔɪst when attributive]

unwanted ˌʌn'wɒntɪd [also 'ʌnˌw- when attributive]

unwar|ily, -iness ʌn'weər|əlɪ [-ɪlɪ], -ɪnɪs [-məs]

unwarlike ˌʌn'wɔːlaɪk [ʌn-]

unwarmed ˌʌn'wɔːmd [also 'ʌnw- when attributive]

unwarned ˌʌn'wɔːnd

unwarrantab|le, -ly, -leness ʌn'wɒrənt-əb|l, -lɪ, -lnɪs [-nəs]

unwarranted (not guaranteed) ˌʌn-'wɒrəntɪd

unwarranted (unjustified) ʌn'wɒrəntɪd

unwary ʌn'weərɪ [ˌʌn'w-]

unwashed ˌʌn'wɒʃt [also 'ʌnw- when attributive]

unwavering, -ly ʌn'weɪvərɪŋ, -lɪ

unwearable ˌʌn'weərəbl [ʌn-]

unwearied ʌn'wɪərɪd

unwearying ʌn'wɪərɪŋ

unwed ˌʌn'wed

unwelcome ˌʌn'welkəm [ˌʌn'w-]

unwell ˌʌn'wel [ʌn-]

unwholesome, -ly, -ness ˌʌn'həʊlsəm [ʌn-], -lɪ, -nɪs [-nəs]

unwield|y, -ier, -iest, -ily, -iness ʌn-'wiːld|ɪ, -ɪə* [-jə*], -ɪɪst [-jɪst], -ɪlɪ [-əlɪ], -ɪnɪs [-ɪnəs]

unwilling ˌʌn'wɪlɪŋ [ʌn-]

unwilling|ly, -ness ʌn'wɪlɪŋ|lɪ, -nɪs [-nəs]

Unwin 'ʌnwɪn

un|wind, -winds, -winding, -wound ˌʌn|'waɪnd [ʌn-], -'waɪndz, -'waɪndɪŋ, -'waʊnd

unwiped ˌʌn'waɪpt

unwisdom ˌʌn'wɪzdəm

unwise ˌʌn'waɪz [also 'ʌnw-, ʌn'w-, according to sentence-stress]

unwisely ˌʌn'waɪzlɪ [ʌn-]

unwished for ʌn'wɪʃtfɔː* [ˌʌn'w-]

unwitting, -ly ʌn'wɪtɪŋ, -lɪ

unwoman|ly, -liness ʌn'wʊmən|lɪ [ˌʌn'w-], -lɪnɪs [-ɪnəs]

unwonted, -ly, -ness ʌn'wəʊntɪd, -lɪ, -nɪs [-nəs]

unworkable ˌʌn'wɜːkəbl [ʌn-]

unworkmanlike ˌʌn'wɜːkmənlaɪk [ʌn-]

unworld|ly, -liness ˌʌn'wɜːld|lɪ [ʌn-], -lnɪs [-nəs]

unworn ˌʌn'wɔːn ['ʌnw- when attributive]

unworth|y, -ily, -iness ʌn'wɜːð|ɪ [ˌʌn'w-], -ɪlɪ [-əlɪ], -ɪnɪs [-ɪnəs]

unwound (from unwind) ˌʌn'waʊnd [ʌn-]

unwounded ˌʌn'wuːndɪd

unwrap, -s, -ping, -ped ˌʌn'ræp [ʌn-], -s, -ɪŋ, -t

unwritten ˌʌn'rɪtn [also 'ʌnˌr- when attributive]

unwrought ˌʌn'rɔːt

unyielding, -ly, -ness ʌn'jiːldɪŋ [ˌʌn'j-], -lɪ, -nɪs [-nəs]

unyok|e, -es, -ing, -ed ˌʌn'jəʊk [ʌn-], -s, -ɪŋ, -t

up ʌp

up-and-down ˌʌpən'daʊn

upas, -es 'juːpəs, -ɪz
upbraid, -s, -ing, -ed ʌp'breɪd, -z, -ɪŋ, -ɪd
upbringing 'ʌp,brɪŋɪŋ
upcast, -s 'ʌpkɑːst, -s
Upcott 'ʌpkət [-kɒt]
upcountry (s. adj.) ,ʌp'kʌntrɪ, (adv.) ʌp'kʌntrɪ
Updike 'ʌpdaɪk
Upham 'ʌpəm
upharsin juː'fɑːsɪn [uː-]
upheav|e, -es, -ing, -ed; -al/s ʌp'hiːv, -z, -ɪŋ, -d; -l/z
upheld (from uphold) ʌp'held
uphill ,ʌp'hɪl ['ʌph-, ʌp'h-, according to sentence-stress]
up|hold, -holds, -holding, -held, -holder/s ʌp|'həʊld, -'həʊldz, -'həʊldɪŋ, -'held, -'həʊldə*/s
upholst|er, -ers, -ering, -ered, -erer/s; -ery ʌp'həʊlst|ə* [əp-], -əz, -ərɪŋ, -əd, -ərə*/z; -ərɪ
Upjohn 'ʌpdʒɒn
upkeep 'ʌpkiːp
upland, -s; -er/s 'ʌplənd, -z; -ə*/z
uplift (s.) 'ʌplɪft
uplift (v.), -s, -ing, -ed ʌp'lɪft, -s, -ɪŋ, -ɪd
Upminster 'ʌp,mɪnstə*
upmost 'ʌpməʊst
upon ə'pɒn (strong form), əpən (occasional weak form)
upper (s. adj.), -s; -most 'ʌpə*, -z; -məʊst [-məst]
uppercut, -s 'ʌpəkʌt, -s
Uppingham 'ʌpɪŋəm
uppish, -ly, -ness 'ʌpɪʃ, -lɪ, -nɪs [-nəs]
Uppsala 'ʌpsɑːlə ['ʊp-, ʌp's-, ʊp's-]
uprais|e, -es, -ing, -ed ʌp'reɪz, -ɪz, -ɪŋ, -d ['ʌpreɪzd when attributive]
uprear, -s, -ing, -ed ʌp'rɪə*, -z, -rɪŋ, -d
Uprichard juː'prɪtʃɑːd [-tʃəd], ʌp'rɪtʃəd
upright (s.), -s 'ʌpraɪt, -s
upright (adj.) (honest) 'ʌpraɪt [,ʌp'r-]
upright (adj. adv.) (erect) ,ʌp'raɪt [also 'ʌpr-, ʌp'r-, according to sentence-stress]
upright|ly, -ness 'ʌp,raɪt|lɪ [ʌp'r-], -nɪs [-nəs]
uprising, -s 'ʌp,raɪzɪŋ [,-'--], -z
uproar, -s 'ʌprɔː* [-rɔə*], -z
uproarious, -ly, -ness ʌp'rɔːrɪəs [-'rɔər-], -lɪ, -nɪs [-nəs]
uproot, -s, -ing, -ed ʌp'ruːt, -s, -ɪŋ, -ɪd
Upsala 'ʌpsɑːlə ['ʊp-, ʌp's-, ʊp's-]
upset (s.), -s ʌp'set ['ʌpset], -s
upset (adj.) ʌp'set ['-- when attributive]
upset (v.), -s, -ting, -ter/s ʌp'set, -s, -ɪŋ, -ə*/z

Upsher 'ʌpʃə*
upshot 'ʌpʃɒt
upside, -s 'ʌpsaɪd, -z
upside-down ,ʌpsaɪd'daʊn
upsilon, -s juː'psaɪlən [ʊp's-, 'juːpsɪlən], -z
up-stag|e, -es, -ing, -ed ,ʌp'steɪdʒ, -ɪz, -ɪŋ, -d
upstairs ,ʌp'steəz ['ʌps-, ʌp's-, according to sentence-stress]
upstart, -s 'ʌpstɑːt, -s
upstream ,ʌp'striːm ['ʌpstriːm]
upstroke, -s 'ʌpstrəʊk, -s
upsurge (s.), -s 'ʌpsɜːdʒ, -ɪz
upsurg|e (v.), -es, -ing, -ed ʌp'sɜːdʒ, -ɪz, -ɪŋ, -d
uptake, -s 'ʌpteɪk, -s
upthrust, -s 'ʌpθrʌst [,ʌp'θrʌst], -s
uptight 'ʌptaɪt [,-'-]
uptilt, -s, -ing, -ed ʌp'tɪlt, -s, -ɪŋ, -ɪd
Upton 'ʌptən
uptown ,ʌp'taʊn [ʌp't- when preceded by a stress]
upturn, -s, -ing, -ed ʌp'tɜːn, -z, -ɪŋ, -d
upturned (adj.) ,ʌp'tɜːnd ['ʌpt-, ʌp't-, according to sentence-stress]
upward, -ly, -s 'ʌpwəd, -lɪ, -z
Upwey 'ʌpweɪ
ur (interj.), ʌː, ɜː
Ur ɜː* [ʊə*]
uraemia ,jʊə'riːmjə [jʊ'r-, jə'r-, jʊə'r-, jɔː'r-, -mɪə]
Ural 'jʊərəl ['jɔər-, 'jɔːr-]
uralite 'jʊərəlaɪt ['jɔər-, 'jɔːr-]
Urania, -n ,jʊə'reɪnjə [jʊ'r-, jə'r-, jʊə'r-, jɔː'r-, -nɪə]
uranium jʊ'reɪnɪəm [,jʊə'r-, jə'r-, jʊə'r-, jɔː'r-, -njəm]
Uranus 'jʊərənəs ['jɔər-, 'jɔːr-, jʊə-'reɪnəs]
urate, -s 'jʊəreɪt ['jɔər-, 'jɔːr-, -rɪt], -s
urban (U.), -ite/s 'ɜːbən, -aɪt/s
Urbana ɜː'bænə [-'bɑː-n-]
urbane (U.), -ly ɜː'beɪn, -lɪ
urbanity ɜː'bænətɪ [-ɪtɪ]
urbanization ,ɜːbənaɪ'zeɪʃn
urbaniz|e, -es, -ing, -ed 'ɜːbənaɪz, -ɪz, -ɪŋ, -d
Urbevilles 'ɜːbəvɪlz
urchin, -s 'ɜːtʃɪn, -z
Urdu 'ʊəduː ['ɜːd-, ,-'-, -'-) (Hindi wrdu)
Ure jʊə*
urea, -l jʊə'rɪə ['jʊərɪə, 'jɔər-, 'jɔːr-], -l
ureter, -s ,jʊə'riːtə*, -z
urethra, -s ,jʊə'riːθrə [jʊ'r-], -z
uretic (s. adj.), -s ,jʊə'retɪk [jʊ'r-, jə'r-], -s

urg|e (s. v.), **-es, -ing, -ed, -er/s** ɜːdʒ, -ɪz, -ɪŋ, -d, -ə*/z

urgen|cy, **-t/ly** 'ɜːdʒən|sɪ, -t/lɪ

Uriah ˌjʊə'raɪə [jʊ'r-, jə'r-]

uric 'jʊərɪk ['jɔər-, 'jɔːr-]

Uriel 'jʊərɪəl ['jɔər-, 'jɔːr-]

Urim 'jʊərɪm ['jɔər-, 'jɔːr-, 'ʊər-]

urin|al, **-als, -ary** 'jʊərɪn|l ['jɔər-, 'jɔːr-, ˌjʊə'raɪnl, jə'r-], -lz, -ərɪ

urinat|e, **-es, -ing, -ed** 'jʊərɪneɪt ['jɔər-, 'jɔːr-, -rən-], -s, -ɪŋ, -ɪd

urination ˌjʊərɪ'neɪʃn [ˌjɔər-, ˌjɔːr-]

urine, **-s** 'jʊərɪn ['jɔər-, 'jɔːr-], -z

Urmia 'ɜːmjə ['ʊəm-, -mɪə]

urn, **-s** ɜːn, -z

urolog|ist/s, **-y** jʊə'rɒlədʒ|ɪst/s, -ɪ

Urquhart 'ɜːkət

Ursa (constellation) 'ɜːsə

ursine 'ɜːsaɪn

Ursula 'ɜːsjʊlə ['ɜːʃjʊ-, 'ɜːʃʊ-]

Ursuline 'ɜːsjʊlaɪn ['ɜːʃ-, -lɪn]

urtica 'ɜːtɪkə

urticaria ˌɜːtɪ'keərɪə

Uruguay 'jʊərʊgwaɪ ['jʊr-, 'ʊr-, -rəg-, ˌ--'-, -weɪ]

Uruguayan, **-s** ˌjʊərʊ'gwaɪən [ˌjʊr-, ˌʊr-, -rə'g, -'gwerən], -z

Urumiah ʊ'ruːmjə [-mɪə]

urus 'jʊərəs ['jɔər-, 'jɔːr-]

us ʌs (strong form), əs, s (weak forms)

U.S.A. ˌjuːes'eɪ

usable 'juːzəbl

usage, **-s** 'juːzɪdʒ ['juːsɪ-], **-ɪz**

usance, **-s** 'juːzns, -ɪz

use (s.), **-s** juːs, -ɪz

us|e (v.) (make use of), **-es, -ing, -ed, -er/s** juːz, -ɪz, -ɪŋ, -d, -ə*/z

used (adj.) (accustomed) juːst [rarely juːzd]

used (from use v.) juːzd

used (v.) (was or were accustomed) juːst (when followed by to), juːst (when not followed by to) [rarely juːzd]

use(d)n't 'juːsnt (when followed by to), 'juːsnt (when not followed by to)

use|ful, **-fully, -fulness** 'juːs|fʊl, -fʊlɪ [-fəlɪ], -fʊlnɪs [-nəs]

useless, **-ly, -ness** 'juːslɪs [-ləs], -lɪ, -nɪs [-nəs]

usen't 'juːsnt (when followed by to), 'juːsnt (when not followed by to)

user, **-s** 'juːzə*, -z

uses (plur. of use s.) 'juːsɪz

uses (from use v.) 'juːzɪz

Ushant 'ʌʃənt

usher (s. v.) (U.), **-s, -ing, -ed** 'ʌʃə*, -z, -rɪŋ, -d

usherette, **-s** ˌʌʃə'ret, -s

usquebaugh, **-s** 'ʌskwɪbɔː, -z

U.S.S.R. ˌjuːeses'ɑː*

Ustinov 'juːstɪnɒf [-ɒv]

u|sual, **-sually, -sualness** 'juː|ʒl [-ʒwəl, -ʒʊl, -ʒʊəl], -ʒəlɪ [-ʒwəlɪ, -ʒ|ɪ, -ʒʊlɪ, -ʒʊəlɪ], -ʒlnɪs [-ʒwəlnɪs, -ʒʊlnɪs, -ʒʊəlnɪs, -nəs]

usufruct, **-s** 'juːsjuːfrʌkt [-sjʊ-, 'juːzj-], -s

usurer, **-s** 'juːʒərə*, -z

usurious, **-ly, -ness** juː'zjʊərɪəs [jʊ'z-, -'zjɔər-, -'zjɔːr-, juː'ʒʊə-, jʊ'ʒ-], -lɪ, -nɪs [-nəs]

usurp, **-s, -ing, -ed, -er/s** juː'zɜːp [jʊ'-], -s, -ɪŋ, -t, -ə*/z

usurpation, **-s** ˌjuːzɜː'peɪʃn, -z

usury 'juːʒʊrɪ [-ʒərɪ, -ʒʊərɪ]

Utah 'juːtɑː [or -tɔː: as in U.S.A.]

utensil, **-s** juː'tensl [jʊ't-, -sɪl], -z

uterine 'juːtəraɪn

uter|us, **-i, -uses** 'juːtər|əs, -aɪ, -əsɪz

Uther 'juːθə*

Uthwatt 'ʌθwɒt

Utica 'juːtɪkə

utilitarian (s. adj.), **-s, -ism** ˌjuːtɪlɪ-'teərɪən [juːˌtɪlɪ't-, jʊˌt-, -lə't-], -z, -ɪzəm

utility juː'tɪlətɪ [jʊ't-, -ɪtɪ]

utilization [-isa-] ˌjuːtəlaɪ'zeɪʃn [-tɪl-, -lɪ'z-]

utiliz|e [-is|e], **-es, -ing, -ed, -er/s; -able** 'juːtəlaɪz [-tɪl-], -ɪz, -ɪŋ, -d, -ə*/z; -əbl

utmost 'ʌtməʊst [-məst]

Utopia, **-n/s** juː'təʊpjə [jʊ't-, -pɪə], -n/z

Utrecht 'juːtrekt [-trext, -'-] ('ytrext)

utricle, **-s** 'juːtrɪkl, -z

utter (adj. v.), **-ly, -ness; -s, -ing, -ed, -er/s; -able** 'ʌtə*, -lɪ, -nɪs [-nəs]; -z, -rɪŋ, -d, -rə*/z; -rəbl

utterance, **-s** 'ʌtərəns, -ɪz

uttermost 'ʌtəməʊst [-məst]

Uttoxeter juː'tɒksɪtə* [ʌ'tɒksɪtə*, 'ʌksɪtə*]

Note.—The common pronunciation is juː'tɒksɪtə or ʌ'tɒksɪtə*. The former is more freq., and is the pronunciation of most outsiders.*

U-turn, **-s** 'juːtɜːn, -z

uvula, **-s** 'juːvjʊlə [-jəl-], **-z**

uvular 'juːvjʊlə* [-jəl-]

Uxbridge 'ʌksbrɪdʒ

uxorious ʌk'sɔːrɪəs

Uzbek, **-s** 'uzbek ['ʌz-], -s

Uzbekistan uzˌbekɪ'stɑːn [ʌz-]

Uzzah 'ʌzə

Uzzell 'ʌzl

Uzziah ʌ'zaɪə

V

V (*the letter*), **-'s** viː, **-z**

v. (*versus*) viː [ˈvɜːsəs], (*vide*) viː [siː, ˈvɪdeɪ, ˈvaɪdɪ]

vac, -s væk, -s

vacanc|y, -ies ˈveɪkəns|ɪ, -ɪz

vacant, -ly ˈveɪkənt, -lɪ

vacat|e, -es, -ing, -ed vəˈkeɪt [veɪˈk-], -s, -ɪŋ, -ɪd

vacation, -s vəˈkeɪʃn, -z

vaccinat|e, -es, -ing, -ed, -or/s ˈvæksmeɪt [-ksn̩eɪt], -s, -ɪŋ, -ɪd, -ə*/z

vaccination, -s ˌvæksɪˈneɪʃn [-ksn̩ˈeɪ-], -z

vaccine ˈvæksiːn [-sɪn]

Vachel(l) ˈveɪtʃəl

Vacher ˈvæʃə*, ˈveɪtʃə*

vacillat|e, -es, -ing/ly, -ed, -or/s ˈvæsəleɪt [-sɪl-, -sl̩-], -s, -ɪŋ/lɪ, -ɪd, -ə*/z

vacillation ˌvæsəˈleɪʃn [-sɪˈl-]

vacuity væˈkjuːətɪ [vəˈk-, -ˈkjʊətɪ, -ɪtɪ]

vacuo (*in* in vacuo) ˈvækjʊəʊ

vacuous, -ness ˈvækjʊəs [-kjwəs], -nɪs [-nəs]
-z

vacuum, -s ˈvækjʊəm [-kjwəm, -kjʊm],

vacuum-cleaner, -s ˈvækjʊəmˌkliːnə* [-kjwəm-, -kjʊm-], -z

vade-mecum, -s ˌvɑːdɪˈmeɪkəm [-kʊm, ˌveɪdɪˈmiːkəm, -kʌm], -z

vagabond (*s. adj.*), **-s** ˈvægəbɒnd [-bənd], -z

vagabondage ˈvægəbɒndɪdʒ

vagar|y, -ies ˈveɪgər|ɪ [vəˈgeər-], -ɪz

vagin|a/s, -al vəˈdʒaɪn|ə/z, -l

vagrancy ˈveɪgrənsɪ

vagrant (*s. adj.*), **-s, -ly** ˈveɪgrənt, -s, -lɪ

vague, -r, -st, -ly, -ness veɪg, -ə*, -ɪst, -lɪ, -nɪs [-nəs]

vail (**V.**), **-s, -ing, -ed** veɪl, -z, -ɪŋ, -d

Vaile veɪl

vain, -er, -est, -ly, -ness veɪn, -ə*, -ɪst, -lɪ, -nɪs [-nəs]

vainglorious, -ly, -ness ˌveɪnˈɡlɔːrɪəs, -lɪ, -nɪs [-nəs]

vainglory ˌveɪnˈɡlɔːrɪ

Valais ˈvæleɪ (valɛ)

valance, -s, -d ˈvæləns, -ɪz, -t

vale (*s.*) (**V.**), **-s** veɪl, -z

vale (*goodbye*) ˈveɪlɪ [ˈvæleɪ, ˈvɑː-]

valediction, -s ˌvælɪˈdɪkʃn, -z

valedictory ˌvælɪˈdɪktˈərɪ

valence (*damask, short curtain*), **-s, -d** ˈvæləns, -ɪz, -t

valence (*in chemistry*) ˈveɪləns

Valencia, -s vəˈlenˌɪə [-ʃjə, -ʃə, -sɪə, -sjə], -z

Valenciennes ˌvælənsɪˈen [-lɑ̃ːns-, -lɑːns-, -sɪˈenz, -ˈsjen, -ˈsjenz] (valɑ̃sjen)

Note.—There was formerly a pronunciation ˌvælənˈsiːnz.

valenc|y, -ies ˈveɪləns|ɪ, -ɪz

valentine, -s ˈvæləntaɪn, -z

Valentine (*Christian name*) ˈvæləntam, -tm, (*surname*) ˈvæləntm, -tam

Valentinian ˌvælənˈtɪnɪən [-njən]

Valera vəˈleərə

valerian (**V.**), **-s** vəˈlɪərɪən [ˈleə-], -z

Valerius vəˈlɪərɪəs

Valery(-rie) ˈvælərɪ

valet (*s.*), **-s** ˈvælɪt, -s [ˈvælɪ, ˈvæleɪ, -z]

valet (*v.*), **-s, -ing, -ed** ˈvælɪt, -s, -ɪŋ, -ɪd

valetudinarian, -s, -ism ˌvælɪtjuːdɪˈneərɪən, -z, -ɪzəm

Valhalla vælˈhælə

valiant, -ly, -ness ˈvæljənt, -lɪ, -nɪs [-nəs]

valid, -ly, -ness ˈvælɪd, -lɪ, -nɪs [-nəs]

validat|e, -es, -ing, -ed ˈvælɪdeɪt, -s, -ɪŋ, -ɪd

validation ˌvælɪˈdeɪʃn

validit|y, -ies vəˈlɪdət|ɪ [væˈl-, -ɪt|ɪ], -ɪz

valise, -s vəˈliːz [væˈl-, -iːsˌ, -ɪz

Valium ˈvælɪəm [ˈveɪ-, -ljəm]

Valkyrie, -s vælˈkɪərɪ [ˈvælkɪrɪ], -z

Valladolid ˌvælədəʊˈlɪd [-dɒˈl-] (baʎadoˈli)

Valletta vəˈletə

valley, -s ˈvælɪ, -z

Valois ˈvælwɑː [-lwɔː] (valwa)

valorous, -ly ˈvælərəs, -lɪ

valour ˈvælə*

Valparaiso ˌvælpəˈraɪzəʊ [-ˈreɪzəʊ] (balparaˈiso)

Valpy ˈvælpɪ

valse, -s vɑːls [væls, vɔːls], -ɪz

valuable, -s, -ness ˈvæljʊəbl [-ljwəb-, -ljʊb-], -z, -nɪs [-nəs]

valuation, -s ˌvæljʊˈeɪʃn, -z

531

val|ue (*s. v.*), -ues, -uing, -ued, -uer/s
  'væl|juː [-jʊ], -juːz [-jʊz], -jʊɪŋ
  [-jwɪŋ], -juːd [-jʊd], -jʊə*/z [-jwə*/z]
valueless 'væljʊlɪs [-ləs]
valve, -s vælv, -z
valvular 'vælvjʊlə*
vamoos|e, -es, -ing, -ed və'muːs [-uːz],
  -ɪz, -ɪŋ, və'muːst [-uːzd]
vamp (*s. v.*), -s, -ing, -ed, -er/s væmp,
  -s, -ɪŋ, -t [væmt], -ə*/z
vampire, -s 'væmpaɪə*, -z
van (*s. v.*), -s, -ning, -ned væn, -z, -ɪŋ, -d
vanadium və'neɪdɪəm [-djəm]
Vanbrugh 'vænbrə
  Note.—Sir John Vanbrugh, *the seven-
  teenth-century dramatist and architect, is sometimes referred to as*
  væn'bruː:.
Vancouver væn'kuːvə* [væŋ'k-]
vandal (V.), -s 'vændl, -z
†vandalism 'vændəlɪzəm
Vanderb|ilt, -yl 'vændəb|ɪlt, -aɪl
Van Diemen ˌvæn'diːmən
Vandyke [Van Dyck] (*name of artist,
  picture by him*), -s ˌvæn'daɪk, -s
vandyke (*adj.*) (*brown, etc.*) 'vændaɪk
vane (V.), -s, -d veɪn, -z, -d
Vanessa və'nesə
Van Eyck, -s ˌvæn'aɪk, -s
Vange vændʒ
van Gogh ˌvæn'gɒf [-'gɒk, -'gɒx]
vanguard, -s 'vængɑːd ['væŋg-], -z
van Homrigh ˌvæn'hɒmrɪg
vanilla və'nɪlə [vn̩'ɪlə]
vanish, -es, -ing, -ed 'vænɪʃ, -ɪz, -ɪŋ, -t
vanit|y, -ies 'vænət|ɪ [-ɪt|ɪ], -ɪz
vanquish, -es, -ing, -ed, -er/s; -able
  'væŋkwɪʃ, -ɪz, -ɪŋ, -t, -ə*/z; -əbl
Vansittart væn'sɪtət [-tɑːt]
van Straubenzee (*English surname*)
  ˌvænstrɔː'benzɪ
vantage, -s 'vɑːntɪdʒ, -ɪz
vapid, -ly, -ness 'væpɪd, -lɪ, -nɪs [-nəs]
vapidity væ'pɪdətɪ [və'p-, -ɪtɪ]
vaporization [-isa-], -s ˌveɪpəraɪ'zeɪʃn
  [-rɪ'z-], -z
vaporiz|e [-is|e], -es, -ing, -ed, -er/s
  'veɪpəraɪz, -ɪz, -ɪŋ, -d, -ə*/z
vaporosity ˌveɪpə'rɒsətɪ [-ɪtɪ]
vaporous, -ly, -ness 'veɪpərəs, -lɪ, -nɪs
  [-nəs]
vapour (*s. v.*), -s, -ing/s, -ed; -y 'veɪpə*,
  -z, -rɪŋ/z, -d; -rɪ
vapour-ba|th, -ths 'veɪpəbɑː|θ, -ðz
varec 'værek [-rɪk]
variability ˌveərɪə'bɪlətɪ [-ɪtɪ]
variab|le, -ly, -leness 'veərɪəb|l, -lɪ,
  -lnɪs [-nəs]

varian|ce, -t/s 'veərɪən|s, -t/s
variation, -s ˌveərɪ'eɪʃn [*rarely* ˌvær-], -z
varicella ˌværɪ'selə
varices (*plur. of* varix) 'værɪsiːz ['veər-]
varicose 'værɪkəʊs
varied 'veərɪd
variegat|e, -es, -ing, -ed 'veərɪgeɪt
  [*rarely* -rɪəg-, -rɪɪg-], -s, -ɪŋ, -ɪd
variegation, -s ˌveərɪ'geɪʃn [*rarely*
  -rɪə'g-, -rɪɪ'g-], -z
variet|y, -ies və'raɪət|ɪ, -ɪz
variform 'veərɪfɔːm
variola və'raɪələ
variole, -s 'veərɪəʊl, -z
varioloid 'veərɪəlɔɪd
variorum ˌveərɪ'ɔːrəm [ˌvær-]
various, -ly, -ness 'veərɪəs, -lɪ, -nɪs
  [-nəs]
variphone, -s 'veərɪfəʊn, -z
varix, varices 'veərɪks, 'værɪsiːz ['veər-]
varlet, -s 'vɑːlɪt, -s
Varley 'vɑːlɪ
varmint, -s 'vɑːmɪnt, -s
Varney 'vɑːnɪ
varnish (*s. v.*), -es, -ing, -ed, -er/s
  'vɑːnɪʃ, -ɪz, -ɪŋ, -t, -ə*/z
Varro 'værəʊ
varsit|y, -ies 'vɑːsət|ɪ [-ɪt|ɪ], -ɪz
varsovienne, -s ˌvɑːsəʊvɪ'en, -z
var|y, -ies, -ying, -ied 'veər|ɪ, -ɪz, -ɪɪŋ,
  -ɪd
Vasco da Gama ˌvæskəʊdə'gɑːmə
  [-dɑː'g-]
vascular 'væskjʊlə* [-kjə-]
vascularity ˌvæskjʊ'lærətɪ [-kjə-, -ɪtɪ]
vascul|um, -a 'væskjʊl|əm, -ə
vase, -s vɑːz, -ɪz
vasectom|y, -ies və'sektəm|ɪ [væ's-], -ɪz
vaseline 'væsəliːn [-æsl-, -æsɪl-, -æzɪl-,
  -æzl-, ˌvæsə'liːn]
vaso-motor ˌveɪzəʊ'məʊtə* [ˌveɪsəʊ-]
vassal, -s 'væsl, -z
vassalage 'væsəlɪdʒ [-sl̩-]
vast, -er, -est, -ly, -ness vɑːst, -ə*, -ɪst,
  -lɪ, -nɪs [-nəs]
vasty 'vɑːstɪ
vat (*s. v.*), -s, -ting, -ted væt, -s, -ɪŋ, -ɪd
V.A.T. ˌviːeɪ'tiː [væt]
vatful, -s 'vætfʊl, -z
Vathek 'væθek
Vatican 'vætɪkən
vaticinat|e, -es, -ing, -ed væ'tɪsɪneɪt, -s,
  -ɪŋ, -ɪd
vaticination, -s ˌvætɪsɪ'neɪʃn [væˌt-], -z
Vaud vəʊ (vo)
vaudeville (V.), -s 'vɔːdəvɪl ['vəʊd-,
  -viːl], -z
Vaudin (*surname*) 'vəʊdɪn

Vaudois (*sing.*) 'vəʊdwɑ: [-dwɔ:] (vodwa), (*plur.*) -z
Vaughan vɔ:n
vault (*s. v.*), -s, -ing/s, -ed, -er/s vɔ:lt [vɒlt], -s, -ɪŋ/z, -ɪd, -ə*/z
vaunt (*s. v.*), -s, -ing/ly, -ed, -er/s vɔ:nt, -s, -ɪŋ/lɪ, -ɪd, -ə*/z
Vaux (*English surname*) vɔ:z, vɒks, vɔ:ks, vəʊks, (*in de Vaux*) vəʊ
Note.—**Brougham and Vaux** *is* ˌbrʊmən'vɔ:ks
Vauxhall ˌvɒks'hɔ:l [ˌvɒk'sɔ:l, *also* '— *according to sentence-stress*]
vavasour (V.), -s 'vævəˌsʊə*, -z
V.C., -'s ˌviː'si:, -z
V-day 'vi:deɪ
veal (V.), -y vi:l, -ɪ
vector (*s.*), -s 'vektə* [-tɔ:*], -z
vector (*v.*), -s, -ing, -ed 'vektə*, -z, -rɪŋ, -d
vectorial vek'tɔ:rɪəl
Veda, -s 'veɪdə ['vi:d-], -z
Vedanta ve'dɑ:ntə [vɪ'd-, və'd-, -'dæn-] (*Hindi* vedanta)
vedette, -s vɪ'det [və'd-], -s
Vedic 'veɪdɪk ['vi:d-]
veer, -s, -ing/ly, -ed vɪə*, -z, -rɪŋ/lɪ, -d
Vega (*star*) 'vi:gə, (*foreign surname*) 'veɪgə
vegetable (*s. adj.*), -s 'vedʒtəbl [-dʒə-, -dʒɪ-], -z
vegetal 'vedʒɪtl
vegetarian (*s. adj.*), -s, -ism ˌvedʒɪ-'teərɪən [-dʒə't-], -z, -ɪzəm
vegetat|e, -es, -ing, -ed 'vedʒɪteɪt [-dʒə-], -s, -ɪŋ, -ɪd
vegetation, -s ˌvedʒɪ'teɪʃn [-dʒə't-], -z
vegetative, -ly 'vedʒɪtətɪv [-dʒə-, -teɪt-], -lɪ
vehemen|ce, -t/ly 'vi:əmən|s ['vi:ɪm-, 'vɪəm-, 'vi:hɪm-, 'vi:həm-], -t/lɪ
vehicle, -s 'vɪəkl ['vi:ɪk-], -z
vehicular vɪ'hɪkjʊlə* [və'h-, -kjəl-]
veil (*s. v.*), -s, -ing/s, -ed veɪl, -z, -ɪŋ/z, -d
vein, -s, -ed; -less, -like veɪn, -z, -d; -lɪs [-ləs], -laɪk
vein|y, -ier, -iest 'veɪn|ɪ, -ɪə*, -ɪɪst
Veitch vi:tʃ
velar (*s. adj.*), -s 'vi:lə*, -z
velaric vi:'lærɪk [vɪ'l-]
velarization [-isa-], -s ˌvi:ləraɪ'zeɪʃn [-rɪ'z-], -z
velariz|e [-is|e], -es, -ing, -ed 'vi:ləraɪz, -ɪz, -ɪŋ, -d
Velasquez (*artist*) vɪ'læskwɪz [ve'l-, -kɪz, -kez, -kwɪθ]
veldt (V.) velt
velic 'vi:lɪk

velleity ve'li:ətɪ [-ɪtɪ]
vellum, -s 'veləm, -z
veloce vɪ'ləʊtʃɪ [ve'l-, və'l-]
velocipede, -s vɪ'lɒsɪpi:d [və'l-, -səp-], -z
velocit|y, -ies vɪ'lɒsət|ɪ [və'l-, -ɪt|ɪ], -ɪz
velours və'lʊə*
velum, -s 'vi:ləm, -z
velvet, -s, -ed 'velvɪt, -s, -ɪd
velveteen, -s ˌvelvɪ'ti:n [-və't-, '—],-z
velvety 'velvɪtɪ [-vətɪ]
Venables 'venəblz
ven|al, -ally 'vi:n|l, -əlɪ
venality vi:'nælətɪ [vɪ'n-, -ɪtɪ]
vend, -s, -ing, -ed vend, -z, -ɪŋ, -ɪd
vendee, -s ˌven'di:, -z
vendetta, -s ven'detə, -z
vendible 'vendəbl [-dɪb-]
vendor, -s 'vendɔ:* [-də*], -z
veneer (*s. v.*), -s, -ing, -ed və'nɪə* [vɪ'n-], -z, -rɪŋ, -d
venerab|le, -ly, -ness 'venərəb|l, -lɪ, -lnɪs [-nəs]
venerat|e, -es, -ing, -ed, -or/s 'venəreɪt, -s, -ɪŋ, -ɪd, -ə*/z
veneration ˌvenə'reɪʃn
venereal və'nɪərɪəl [vɪ'n-, vi:'n-]
venery 'venərɪ
Venetian (*s. adj.*), -s və'ni:ʃn [vɪ'n-, -ʃjən, -ʃɪən], -z
Venezuela, -n/s ˌvenɪ'zweɪlə [ˌvene'z-, ˌvenə'z-], -n/z
veng|e, -es, -ing, -ed vendʒ, -ɪz, -ɪŋ, -d
vengeance 'vendʒəns
venge|ful, -fully, -fulness 'vendʒ|fʊl, -fʊlɪ [-fəlɪ], -fʊlnɪs [-nəs]
venial, -ly, -ness 'vi:njəl [-nɪəl], -ɪ, -nɪs [-nəs]
veniality ˌvi:nɪ'ælətɪ [-ɪtɪ]
Venice 'venɪs
venison 'venɪzn [-nɪsn, -nzn]
Venite, -s vɪ'naɪtɪ [ve'n-, -'ni:tɪ], -z
veni, vidi, vici 'veɪnɪ:ˌvi:di:'vi:ki: [*also with* w *for* v]
Venn, -er ven, -ə*
venom, -s, -ed 'venəm, -z, -d
venomous, -ly, -ness 'venəməs, -lɪ, -nɪs [-nəs]
venous 'vi:nəs
vent (*s. v.*), -s, -ing, -ed vent, -s, -ɪŋ, -ɪd
ventilat|e, -es, -ing, -ed 'ventɪleɪt [-təl-], -s, -ɪŋ, -ɪd
ventilation ˌventɪ'leɪʃn [-tə'l-]
ventilator, -s 'ventɪleɪtə* [-təl-], -z
Ventnor 'ventnə*
ventricle, -s 'ventrɪkl, -z
ventricular ven'trɪkjʊlə* [-kjə-]
ventriloquial, -ly ˌventrɪ'ləʊkwɪəl [-kwjəl], -ɪ

533

ventriloqui|sm, -st/s ven'trɪləkwɪ|zəm, -st/s

ventriloquiz|e [-is|e], -es, -ing, -ed ven'trɪləkwaɪz, -ɪz, -ɪŋ, -d

ventriloquy ven'trɪləkwɪ

vent|ure (*s. v.*), **-ures, -uring, -ured, -urer/s** 'ventʃ|ə*, -əz, -ərɪŋ, -əd, -ərə*/z

venturesome, -ly, -ness 'ventʃəsəm, -lɪ, -nɪs [-nəs]

venturous, -ly, -ness 'ventʃərəs, -lɪ, -nɪs [-nəs]

venue, -s 'venju:, -z

Venue (*in* Ben Venue) və'nju: [vɪ'n-]

Venus, -es 'vi:nəs, -ɪz

Venusian, -s vɪ'nju:sɪən [və'n-, -sjən, -zɪən, -zjən], -z

Vera 'vɪərə

Vera Cruz ˌvɪərə'kru:z [ˌve-, ˌveə-]

veracious, -ly və'reɪʃəs [vɪ'r-, ve'r-], -lɪ

veracity və'ræsətɪ [vɪ'r-, ve'r-, -ɪtɪ]

veranda(h), -s və'rændə, -z

verb, -s vɜ:b, -z

verb|al, -ally 'vɜ:b|l, -əlɪ

verbali|sm, -st/s 'vɜ:bəlɪ|zəm [-bl̩ɪ-], -st/s

verbaliz|e [is|e], -es, -ing, -ed 'vɜ:bəlaɪz [-bl̩aɪz], -ɪz, -ɪŋ, -d

verbatim vɜ:'bertɪm [-'bɑ:t-]

verbena, -s vɜ:'bi:nə [və'b-], -z

verbiage 'vɜ:bɪɪdʒ [-bjɪdʒ]

verbose, -ly, -ness vɜ:'bəʊs, -lɪ, -nɪs [-nəs]

verbosity vɜ:'bɒsətɪ [-ɪtɪ]

Vercingetorix ˌvɜ:sɪn'dʒetərɪks

verdan|cy, -t/ly 'vɜ:dən|sɪ, -t/lɪ

verd-antique ˌvɜ:dæn'ti:k

Verde vɜ:d

Verdi 'veədi: [-dɪ] ('verdi)

verdict, -s 'vɜ:dɪkt, -s

verdigris 'vɜ:dɪgrɪs [-gri:s]

verditer 'vɜ:dɪtə*

Verdun (*in France and Canada*) vɜ:'dʌn ['--] (vɛrdœ̃)

verdure 'vɜ:dʒə* [-djə*, -ˌdjʊə*]

Vere vɪə*

verg|e (*s. v.*), **-es, -ing, -ed** vɜ:dʒ, -ɪz, -ɪŋ, -d

verger, -s 'vɜ:dʒə*, -z

Vergil, -s 'vɜ:dʒɪl, -z

veridical ve'rɪdɪkl [vɪ'r-, və'r-]

verifiable 'verɪfaɪəbl [ˌ--'---]

verification, -s ˌverɪfɪ'keɪʃn, -z

veri|fy, -fies, -fying, -fied, -fier/s 'verɪ|faɪ, -faɪz, -faɪɪŋ, -faɪd, -faɪə*/z

verily 'verəlɪ [-lɪ]

verisimilitude ˌverɪsɪ'mɪlɪtju:d

veritab|le, -ly 'verɪtəb|l, -lɪ

verit|y (**V.**), **-ies** 'verət|ɪ [-ɪt|ɪ], -ɪz

verjuice 'vɜ:dʒu:s

Vermeer, -s və'mɪə* [vɜ:'m-, -'meə*], -z

vermeil 'vɜ:meɪl [-mɪl]

vermicelli ˌvɜ:mɪ'selɪ [-'tʃelɪ]

vermicide, -s 'vɜ:mɪsaɪd, -z

vermicular vɜ:'mɪkjʊlə* [-kjə-]

vermiform 'vɜ:mɪfɔ:m

vermilion, -s və'mɪljən [vɜ:'m-], -z

vermin, -ous 'vɜ:mɪn, -əs

Vermont vɜ:'mɒnt

vermouth, -s 'vɜ:məθ [-mu:θ, vɜ:'mu:θ, və'mu:θ], -s

vernacular (*s. adj.*), **-s, -ly** və'nækjʊlə* [-kjələ*], -z, -lɪ

vern|al, -ally 'vɜ:n|l, -əlɪ

Verne (*French author*) vɜ:n [veən] (vɛrn)

Verner (*English surname*) 'vɜ:nə*, (*Danish grammarian*) 'vɜ:nə* ['veənə*] ('vɛrnər)

Verney 'vɜ:nɪ

vernier, -s 'vɜ:njə* [-nɪə*], -z

Vernon 'vɜ:nən

Verona və'rəʊnə [vɪ'r-, ve'r-]

veronal 'verənl

Veronese (*artist*) ˌverəʊ'neɪzɪ (vero-'ne:ze)

veronese (*adj.*) ˌverə'ni:z [-rəʊ'n-, '---]

veronica (**V.**), **-s** və'rɒnɪkə [vɪ'r-, ve'r-], -z

Verrall 'verɔ:l, 'verəl

Verrey 'verɪ

verruca, -s və'ru:kə [vɪ'r-, ve'r-], -z

verrucose ve'ru:kəʊs [vɪ'r-, və'r-]

Versailles veə'saɪ [vɜ:'s-] (vɛrsɑ:j)

versant, -s 'vɜ:sənt, -s

versatile, -ly, -ness 'vɜ:sətaɪl, -lɪ, -nɪs [-nəs]

versatility ˌvɜ:sə'tɪlətɪ [-ɪtɪ]

Verschoyle 'vɜ:skɔɪl

verse, -s vɜ:s, -ɪz

versed vɜ:st

verset, -s 'vɜ:set [-sɪt], -s

versicle, -s 'vɜ:sɪkl, -z

versification ˌvɜ:sɪfɪ'keɪʃn

versificator, -s 'vɜ:sɪfɪˌkertə*, -z

versi|fy, -fies, -fying, -fied, -fier/s 'vɜ:sɪ|faɪ, -faɪz, -faɪɪŋ, -faɪd, -faɪə*/z

version, -s 'vɜ:ʃn [-ʒn], -z

verso 'vɜ:səʊ

verst, -s vɜ:st, -s

Verstegan vɜ:'sti:gən

Verstone 'vɜ:stən

versus 'vɜ:səs

vert (*s. adj.*) (**V.**), **-s** vɜ:t, -s

vertebr|a, -ae 'vɜ:tɪbr|ə, -i: [-aɪ, -eɪ]

vertebr|al, -ally 'vɜ:tɪbr|əl, -əlɪ

vertebrata ˌvɜːtɪˈbrɑːtə [-ˈbreɪtə]
vertebrate (s. adj.), **-s** ˈvɜːtɪbreɪt [-brət, -brɪt], -s
vertebrated ˈvɜːtɪbreɪtɪd
vertebration ˌvɜːtɪˈbreɪʃn
vert|ex, -ices, -exes ˈvɜːt|eks, -ɪsiːz, -eksɪz
vertic|al, -ally, -alness ˈvɜːtɪk|l, -əlɪ, -lnɪs [-nəs]
vertiginous vɜːˈtɪdʒɪnəs
vertigo ˈvɜːtɪɡəʊ [vɜːˈtaɪɡ-, less commonly vɜːˈtiːɡ-]
vertu vɜːˈtuː
Verulam ˈverʊləm
Verulami|an, -um ˌverʊˈleɪmj|ən [-mɪ|ən], -əm
vervain ˈvɜːveɪn
verve vɜːv [veəv]
very ˈverɪ
Very ˈvɪərɪ, ˈverɪ
Vesey ˈviːzɪ
Vesian ˈveziən [-zjən]
vesica, -s ˈvesɪkə [vɪˈsaɪkə, ˈviːsɪkə], -z
vesicle, -s ˈvesɪkl, -z
Vespa ˈvespə
Vespasian veˈspeɪʒjən [-ʒɪən, -ʒn, -zjən, -zɪən]
vesper, -s ˈvespə*, -z
vespertine ˈvespətaɪn [-pɜːt-]
vespiar|y, -ies ˈvespɪər|ɪ [-pjə-], -ɪz
vessel, -s ˈvesl, -z
vest (s. v.), **-s, -ing, -ed** vest, -s, -ɪŋ, -ɪd
vesta (V.), **-s** ˈvestə, -z
vestal (s. adj.), **-s** ˈvestl, -z
vestibular veˈstɪbjʊlə*
vestibule, -s, -d ˈvestɪbjuːl, -z, -d
vestige, -s ˈvestɪdʒ, -ɪz
vestigial veˈstɪdʒɪəl [-dʒjəl]
vestiture ˈvestɪtʃə*
vestment, -s ˈvestmənt, -s
vest-pocket, -s ˌvestˈpɒkɪt [ˈ-ˌ--], -s
Vestris ˈvestrɪs
vestr|y, -ies ˈvestr|ɪ, -ɪz
vesture, -s ˈvestʃə*, -z
vesuvian (V.), **-s; -ite** vɪˈsuːvjən [və's-, -ˈsjuː-, -vɪən], -aɪt
Vesuvius vɪˈsuːvjəs [vəˈs-, -ˈsjuː-, -vɪəs]
vet (s. v.), **-s, -ting, -ted** vet, -s, -ɪŋ, -ɪd
vetch, -es vetʃ, -ɪz
veteran (s. adj.), **-s** ˈvetərən, -z
veterinar|y (s. adj.), **-ies** ˈvetərɪnər|ɪ [ˈvetrɪ, ˈvetnr|ɪ], -ɪz
veto (s.), **-(e)s** ˈviːtəʊ, -z
veto (v.), **-es, -ing, -ed** ˈviːtəʊ, -z, -ɪŋ, -d
Vevey ˈveveɪ [ˈvevɪ] (in Switzerland vəvɛ)
vex, -es, -ing, -ed veks, -ɪz, -ɪŋ, -t
vexation, -s vekˈseɪʃn, -z

vexatious, -ly, -ness vekˈseɪʃəs, -lɪ, -nɪs [-nəs]
Vezian ˈveziən [-zjən]
V.H.F. ˌviːeɪtʃˈef
via ˈvaɪə
viability ˌvaɪəˈbɪlətɪ [-lɪt-]
viable ˈvaɪəbl
viaduct, -s ˈvaɪədʌkt [-dəkt], -s
vial, -s ˈvaɪəl [vaɪl], -z
Vialls ˈvaɪəlz, ˈvaɪɔːlz
Via Mala ˌvɪəˈmɑːlə [ˌviːə-]
viand, -s ˈvaɪənd, -z
viaticum, -s vaɪˈætɪkəm [vɪˈæ-], -z
vibes vaɪbz
vibrant (s. adj.), **-s** ˈvaɪbrənt, -s
vibraphone, -s ˈvaɪbrəfəʊn, -z
vibrat|e, -es, -ing, -ed vaɪˈbreɪt, -s, -ɪŋ, -ɪd
vibration, -s vaɪˈbreɪʃn, -z
vibrational vaɪˈbreɪʃənl [-ʃnəl, -ʃn̩l, -ʃn̩, -ʃənəl]
vibrative vaɪˈbreɪtɪv
vibrato, -s vɪˈbrɑːtəʊ, -z
vibrator, -s vaɪˈbreɪtə*, -z
vibratory ˈvaɪbrətərɪ [vaɪˈbreɪtərɪ]
viburnum, -s vaɪˈbɜːnəm, -z
vic (V.), **-s** vɪk, -s
vicar, -s; -age/s ˈvɪkə*, -z; -rɪdʒ/ɪz
vicarial vɪˈkeərɪəl [vaɪˈk-]
vicarious, -ly, -ness vɪˈkeərɪəs [vaɪˈk-], -lɪ, -nɪs [-nəs]
Vicary ˈvɪkərɪ
vice (s.), **-s** vaɪs, -ɪz
vice (prep.) ˈvaɪsɪ
vice- (prefix) ˌvaɪs-
Note.—Compounds with **vice-** have, as a rule, double stress, and the pronunciation of those not entered below may be ascertained by referring to the simple words.
vice-admiral, -s ˌvaɪsˈædmərəl, -z
vice-chair|man, -men ˌvaɪsˈtʃeə|mən, -mən
vice-chancellor, -s ˌvaɪsˈtʃɑːnsələ* [-slə*], -z
vice-consul, -s ˌvaɪsˈkɒnsl, -z
vice-consulate, -s ˌvaɪsˈkɒnsjʊlət [-sjə-, -səl-, -sʊl-, -lɪt], -s
vicegerent, -s ˌvaɪsˈdʒerənt [-ˈdʒɪər-], -s
vice-president, -s ˌvaɪsˈprezɪdənt, -s
vice-principal, -s ˌvaɪsˈprɪnsəpl [-sɪp-], -z
viceregal ˌvaɪsˈriːgl [also ˈ-ˌ-- when attributive]
vicereine, -s ˌvaɪsˈreɪn [ˈ--], -z
viceroy, -s ˈvaɪsrɔɪ, -z
viceroyship, -s ˈvaɪsrɔɪʃɪp, -s
vice versa ˌvaɪsɪˈvɜːsə

535

Vichy 'vi:ʃi: ['vi:ʃɪ, 'vɪ-] (viʃi)
vicinage 'vɪsɪnɪdʒ
vicinity vɪ'sɪnətɪ [və-, vaɪ's-, -ɪtɪ]
vicious, -ly, -ness 'vɪʃəs, -lɪ, -nɪs [-nəs]
vicissitude, -s vɪ'sɪsɪtju:d [vaɪ's-], -z
Vicker|s, -y 'vɪkə|z, -rɪ
Vicky 'vɪkɪ
victim, -s 'vɪktɪm, -z
victimization [-isa-] ˌvɪktɪmaɪ'zeɪʃn
victimiz|e [-is|e], -es, -ing, -ed 'vɪktɪm-aɪz, -ɪz, -ɪŋ, -d
victor (V.), -s 'vɪktə*, -z
victoria (V.), -s, -n/s vɪk'tɔːrɪə, -z, -n/z
victorine, -s 'vɪktəri:n [ˌvɪktə'ri:n], -z
Victorine 'vɪktəri:n
victorious, -ly, -ness vɪk'tɔːrɪəs, -lɪ, -nɪs [-nəs]
victor|y (V.), -ies 'vɪktər|ɪ, -ɪz
victu|al (s. v.), -als, -alling, -alled, -aller/s 'vɪt|l, -lz, -lɪŋ, -ld, -lə*/z
vicuna vɪ'kju:nə [vaɪ'k-]
vide 'vaɪdi: [-dɪ, 'vɪdeɪ]
videlicet vɪ'di:lɪset [vaɪ'd-, vɪ'deɪlɪket]
video, -tape/s 'vɪdɪəʊ, -teɪp/s
video-cassette, -s ˌvɪdɪəʊkə'set [-kæ's-], -s
video-recording, -s 'vɪdɪəʊrɪˌkɔ:dɪŋ [-rəˌk-], -z
vie, vies, vying, vied vaɪ, vaɪz, 'vaɪɪŋ, vaɪd
Vienna vɪ'enə
Viennese ˌvɪə'ni:z [vɪə'n-]
Viet-cong ˌvjet'kɒŋ
Viet-minh ˌvjet'mɪn
Viet-nam ˌvjet'næm [-'nɑ:m]
Vietnamese ˌvjetnə'mi:z
view (s. v.), -s, -ing, -ed, -er/s; -able vju:, -z, -ɪŋ ['vjʊɪŋ], -d, -ə*/z [vjʊə*/z]; -əbl
Vieweg 'fi:veg
view-finder, -s 'vju:ˌfaɪndə*, -z
view|less, -point/s 'vju:|lɪs [-ləs], -pɔɪnt/s
Vigar 'vaɪgə*
Vigers 'vaɪgəz
vigil, -s 'vɪdʒɪl [-dʒəl], -z
vigilan|ce, -t/ly 'vɪdʒɪlən|s [-dʒəl-, -dʒlən-], -t/lɪ
vigilante, -s ˌvɪdʒɪ'læntɪ, -z
vignett|e (s. v.), -es, -ing, -ed vɪ'njet [-'net], -s, -ɪŋ, -ɪd
Vignoles 'vɪnjəʊlz ['vi:-, -jəʊl, -jɒlz], vɪn'jɒlz [-'jəʊlz]
Vigo (in Spain) 'vi:gəʊ [old-fashioned 'vaɪgəʊ] ('bigo), (as name of ship) 'vi:gəʊ, (English placename) 'vaɪgəʊ, (in Indiana) 'vaɪgəʊ ['vi:gəʊ]

vigorous, -ly, -ness 'vɪgərəs, -lɪ, -nɪs [-nəs]
vigour 'vɪgə*
viking (V.), -s 'vaɪkɪŋ ['vi:k-], -z
vilayet, -s vɪ'lɑ:jet [vɪ'lɑ:jət, vɪ'laɪet, ˌvɪlɑ:'jet], -s
vile, -r, -st, -ly, -ness vaɪl, -ə*, -ɪst, -lɪ, -nɪs [-nəs]
vilification ˌvɪlɪfɪ'keɪʃn
vili|fy, -fies, -fying, -fied, -fier/s 'vɪlɪ|faɪ, -faɪz, -faɪɪŋ, -faɪd, -faɪə*/z
villa (V.), -s 'vɪlə, -z
village, -s 'vɪlɪdʒ, -ɪz
villager, -s 'vɪlɪdʒə*, -z
villain, -s 'vɪlən [in historical sense also -lɪn, -leɪn], -z
villainage 'vɪlɪnɪdʒ [-lən-]
villainous, -ly, -ness 'vɪlənəs, -lɪ, -nɪs [-nəs]
villain|y, -ies 'vɪlən|ɪ, -ɪz
villeg(g)iatura vɪˌledʒɪə'tʊərə [-dʒjə't-, -dʒə't-, -'tjʊər-, -'tjɔər-, -'tjɔ:r-]
villein, -s; -age 'vɪlɪn [-leɪn], -z; -ɪdʒ
Villette vɪ'let
Villiers 'vɪləz, 'vɪljəz [-lɪəz]
Vilna 'vɪlnə
vim vɪm
vinaigrette, -s ˌvɪnɪ'gret [-neɪ'g-], -s
Vincennes væn'sen [væn's-] (vɛ̃sɛn)
Vincent 'vɪnsənt
Vinci 'vɪntʃi: [-tʃɪ]
vincul|um, -a, -ums 'vɪŋkjʊl|əm, -ə, -əmz
vindicability ˌvɪndɪkə'bɪlətɪ [-lɪt-]
vindicable 'vɪndɪkəbl
vindicat|e, -es, -ing, -ed, -or/s 'vɪndɪ-keɪt, -s, -ɪŋ, -ɪd, -ə*/z
vindication ˌvɪndɪ'keɪʃn
vindicative 'vɪndɪkətɪv ['vɪndɪkeɪtɪv, ˌvɪn'dɪkətɪv]
vindictive, -ly, -ness vɪn'dɪktɪv, -lɪ, -nɪs [-nəs]
vine, -s vaɪn, -z
vine-dresser, -s 'vaɪnˌdresə*, -z
vinegar, -s, -y 'vɪnɪgə* [-nəg-], -z, -rɪ
viner|y, -ies 'vaɪnər|ɪ, -ɪz
Viney 'vaɪnɪ
vineyard, -s 'vɪnjəd [-jɑːd], -z
vingt-et-un ˌvænteɪ'ɜ:ŋ [ˌvæ̃nt-, -'ɜ:n, -'u:n] (vɛ̃teœ̃)
viniculture 'vɪnɪkʌltʃə* [ˌ--'--]
viniculturist, -s ˌvɪnɪ'kʌltʃərɪst ['-----], -s
vinous 'vaɪnəs
vint, -s, -ing, -ed vɪnt, -s, -ɪŋ, -ɪd
vintage, -s 'vɪntɪdʒ, -ɪz
Vinter 'vɪntə*
vintner, -s 'vɪntnə*, -z

viny 'vaɪnɪ
vinyl 'vaɪnɪl [-nl]
viol, -s 'vaɪəl [vaɪl, vɪəl], -z
viola (flower), -s 'vaɪələ ['vɪələ, 'vaɪəʊlə, 'vɪəʊlə, vaɪ'əʊlə, vɪ'əʊlə], -z
viola (musical instrument), -s vɪ'əʊlə ['vɪəʊlə], -z
Viola (Christian name) 'vaɪələ ['vaɪəʊlə], 'vɪəʊlə
violable 'vaɪələbl
violat|e, -es, -ing, -ed, -or/s 'vaɪəleɪt ['vaɪəʊl-], -s, -ɪŋ, -ɪd, -ə*/z
violation, -s ˌvaɪə'leɪʃn [ˌvaɪəʊ'l-], -z
violen|ce, -t/ly 'vaɪələn|s, -t/lɪ
violet (V.), -s 'vaɪələt [-lɪt], -s
violin (musical instrument), -s ˌvaɪə'lɪn, -z
violin (chemical substance) 'vaɪəlɪn
violinist, -s ˌvaɪə'lɪnɪst ['----], -s
violin-string, -s ˌvaɪə'lɪnstrɪŋ, -z
violist, -s (viola player) vɪ'əʊlɪst [viol player) 'vaɪəlɪst, -s
violoncell|ist/s, -o/s ˌvaɪələn't ʃel|ɪst/s [rarely ˌvɪəl-, -lɪn-], -əʊ/z
violone, -s 'vaɪələʊn ['vɪəl-], -z
V.I.P., -'s ˌviː'aɪ'piː, -z
Vipan 'vaɪpæn
viper, -s; -ish, -ous 'vaɪpə*, -z; -rɪʃ, -rəs
virago, -(e)s vɪ'rɑːgəʊ [-'reɪg-], -z
vires 'vaɪəriːz
Virgil, -s 'vɜːdʒɪl, -z
Virgili|an, -us vɜː'dʒɪlɪ|ən [və'dʒ-, -lj|ən], -əs
virgin, -s 'vɜːdʒɪn, -z
virginal (s. adj.), -s 'vɜːdʒɪnl, -z
Virginia, -s, -n/s və'dʒɪnjə [vɜː'dʒ-, -nɪə], -z, -n/z
virginibus puerisque vɜːˌgɪnɪbəs-puə'rɪskwɪ [vɜːˌdʒɪn-, -pjuə-]
virginity və'dʒɪnətɪ [vɜː'dʒ-, -ɪtɪ]
Virgo (constellation) 'vɜːgəʊ ['vɪəg-]
virgule, -s 'vɜːgjuːl, -z
viridescen|ce, -t ˌvɪrɪ'desn|s, -t
viridity vɪ'rɪdətɪ [-ɪtɪ]
virile 'vɪraɪl
virility vɪ'rɪlətɪ [və'r-, -ɪtɪ]
virology ˌvaɪə'rɒlədʒɪ
virtu vɜː'tuː
virtual, -ly 'vɜːtʃʊəl [-tʃwəl, -tʃʊl, -tjʊəl, -tjwəl, -tjʊl], -ɪ
virtue, -s 'vɜːtjuː, 'vɜːtʃuː, -z
virtuosity ˌvɜːtjʊ'ɒsətɪ [-tʃʊ-, -ɪtɪ]
virtuoso, -s ˌvɜːtjʊ'əʊzəʊ [-tʃʊ-, -'əʊsəʊ], -z
virtuous, -ly, -ness 'vɜːtʃʊəs [-tʃwəs, -tjʊəs, -tjwəs], -lɪ, -nɪs [-nəs]
virulen|ce, -t/ly 'vɪrʊlən|s [-rjʊ-], -t/lɪ
virus, -es 'vaɪərəs, -ɪz

ris vɪs
visa (s. v.), -s, -ing, -ed 'viːzə, -z, -ɪŋ ['viːzərɪŋ], -d
visage, -s 'vɪzɪdʒ, -ɪz
vis-à-vis ˌviːzɑː'viː [ˌvɪz-, -zɒv-, -zæv-, '---] (vizavi)
viscer|a, -al 'vɪsər|ə, -əl
viscid 'vɪsɪd
viscidity vɪ'sɪdətɪ [-ɪtɪ]
viscosity vɪ'skɒsətɪ [-ɪtɪ]
viscount, -s; -ess/es, -y, -ies 'vaɪkaʊnt, -s; -ɪs/ɪz, -ɪ, -ɪz
viscountc|y, -ies 'vaɪkaʊnts|ɪ, -ɪz
viscous, -ness 'vɪskəs, -nɪs [-nəs]
visé (s. v.), -s, -ing, -d 'viːzeɪ, -z, -ɪŋ, -d
visibility ˌvɪzə'bɪlətɪ [-zɪ'b-, -lɪt-]
visib|le, -ly, -leness 'vɪzəb|l [-zɪb-], -lɪ, -lnɪs [-nəs]
Visigoth, -s 'vɪzɪgɒθ ['vɪsɪ-], -s
vision, -s 'vɪʒn, -z
vi|sional, -sionally 'vɪ|ʒənl [-ʒnəl, -ʒn̩l, -ʒnl, -ʒənəl], -ʒnəlɪ [-ʒnəlɪ, -ʒn̩lɪ, -ʒnl̩ɪ, -ʒənəlɪ]
visionar|y (s. adj.), -ies 'vɪʒn̩r|ɪ [-ʒənə-, -ʒn̩ər-], -ɪz
visit (s. v.), -s, -ing, -ed, -or/s 'vɪzɪt, -s, -ɪŋ, -ɪd, -ə*/z
visitant (s. adj.), -s 'vɪzɪtənt, -s
visitation, -s ˌvɪzɪ'teɪʃn, -z
visite, -s vɪ'ziːt [viː'z-], -s
visor, -s 'vaɪzə*, -z
vista, -s 'vɪstə, -z
Vistula 'vɪstjʊlə
visual, -ly 'vɪʒʊəl [-zjʊəl, -zjwəl, -zjʊl, -ʒwəl, -ʒʊl, -ʒjʊəl, -ʒjwəl], -ɪ
visualization [-isa-] ˌvɪʒʊəlaɪ'zeɪʃn [-zjʊəl-, -zjwəl-, -zjʊl-, -ʒwəl-, -ʒʊl-, -ʒjʊəl-, -ʒjwəl-, -lɪ'z-]
visualiz|e [-is|e], -es, -ing, -ed, -er/s 'vɪʒʊəlaɪz [-zjʊəl-, -zjwəl-, -zjʊl-, -ʒwəl-, -ʒʊl-, -ʒjʊəl-, -ʒjwəl-], -ɪz, -ɪŋ, -d, -ə*/z
vita (glass) 'vaɪtə, (aqua) 'viːtə
vitae (curriculum) 'viːtaɪ ['vaɪtiː]
vit|al, -ally 'vaɪt|l, -əlɪ [-l̩ɪ]
vitality vaɪ'tælətɪ [-ɪtɪ]
vitalization [-isa-] ˌvaɪtəlaɪ'zeɪʃn [-tl̩aɪ-]
vitaliz|e [-is|e], -es, -ing, -ed 'vaɪtəlaɪz [-tl̩aɪz], -ɪz, -ɪŋ, -d
vitals 'vaɪtlz
vitamin, -s 'vɪtəmɪn ['vaɪt-], -z
vitamine, -s 'vɪtəmɪn ['vaɪt-, -miːn], -z
vitiat|e, -es, -ing, -ed, -or/s 'vɪʃɪeɪt, -s, -ɪŋ, -ɪd, -ə*/z
vitiation ˌvɪʃɪ'eɪʃn
viticulture 'vɪtɪkʌltʃə* ['vaɪt-]
vitreosity ˌvɪtrɪ'ɒsətɪ [-ɪtɪ]
vitreous, -ness 'vɪtrɪəs, -nɪs [-nəs]

537

vitrescen|ce, -t vɪ'tresn|s, -t
vitrifaction ˌvɪtrɪ'fækʃn
vitrification ˌvɪtrɪfɪ'keɪʃn
vitri|fy, -fies, -fying, -fied; -fiable
'vɪtrɪ|faɪ, -faɪz, -faɪɪŋ, -faɪd; -faɪəbl
vitriol 'vɪtrɪəl [-rɪɒl]
vitriolic ˌvɪtrɪ'ɒlɪk
Vitruvi|an, -us vɪ'tru:vj|ən [-vɪ|ən], -əs
vituperat|e, -es, -ing, -ed, -or/s
vɪ'tju:pəreɪt [vaɪ't-], -s, -ɪŋ, -ɪd, -ə*/z
vituperation, -s vɪˌtju:pə'reɪʃn [vaɪˌt-],
-z
vituperative, -ly vɪ'tju:pərətɪv [vaɪ't-,
-pəreɪt-], -lɪ
viva (interj.) (long live), -s 'vi:və, -z
viva (viva voce), -s 'vaɪvə, -z
vivace, -s vɪ'vɑ:tʃɪ, -z
vivacious, -ly, -ness vɪ'veɪʃəs [vaɪ'v-],
-lɪ, -nɪs [-nəs]
vivacity vɪ'væsətɪ [vaɪ'v-, -ɪtɪ]
vivarium, -s vaɪ'veərɪəm [vɪ'v-], -z
vivat (s.), -s 'vaɪvæt ['vi:v-], -s
viva voce ˌvaɪvə'vəʊsɪ [-'vəʊtʃɪ]
vive vi:v
Vivian 'vɪvɪən [-vjən]
vivid, -est, -ly, -ness 'vɪvɪd, -ɪst, -lɪ, -nɪs
[-nəs]
Vivien 'vɪvɪən [-vjən]
Vivienne 'vɪvɪən [-vjən], ˌvɪvɪ'en
vivification ˌvɪvɪfɪ'keɪʃn
vivi|fy, -fies, -fying, -fied 'vɪvɪ|faɪ, -faɪz,
-faɪɪŋ, -faɪd
viviparity ˌvɪvɪ'pærətɪ [-ɪtɪ]
viviparous, -ly, -ness vɪ'vɪpərəs [vaɪ'v-],
-lɪ, -nɪs [-nəs]
vivisect, -s, -ing, -ed, -or/s ˌvɪvɪ'sekt
['---], -s, -ɪŋ, -ɪd, -ə*/z
vivisection ˌvɪvɪ'sekʃn
vivisectionist, -s ˌvɪvɪ'sekʃn̩ɪst [-ʃənɪ-],
-s
vixen, -s 'vɪksn, -z
vixenish 'vɪksn̩ɪʃ [-sənɪʃ]
Viyella vaɪ'elə
viz. vɪz [vɪ'di:lɪset, vaɪ'd-, vɪ'deɪlɪket]
Note.—Many people in reading aloud
substitute namely 'neɪmlɪ for this
word.
Vizard 'vɪzɑ:d
Vizetelly ˌvɪzɪ'telɪ
vizier, -s vɪ'zɪə* ['vɪˌzɪə*], -z
Vladimir 'vlædɪˌmɪə* [-mə*], (Russian
vla'djimjir, Czech 'vladimir)
Vladivostok ˌvlædɪ'vɒstɒk (vladjivas-
'tok)
vocable, -s 'vəʊkəbl, -z
vocabular|y, -ies vəʊ'kæbjʊlər|ɪ [vʊ'k-,
-bjəl-], -ɪz
voc|al, -ally 'vəʊk|l, -əlɪ

vocalic vəʊ'kælɪk
vocalism 'vəʊkəlɪzəm [-kl̩ɪ-]
vocalist, -s 'vəʊkəlɪst [-kl̩ɪ-], -s
vocality vəʊ'kælətɪ [-ɪtɪ]
vocalization [-isa-], -s ˌvəʊkəlaɪ'zeɪʃn
[-kl̩aɪ'z-, -kəlɪ'z-, -kl̩ɪ'z-], -z
vocaliz|e [-is|e], -es, -ing, -ed 'vəʊkəlaɪz
[-kl̩aɪz], -ɪz, -ɪŋ, -d
vocation, -s vəʊ'keɪʃn [vʊ'k-], -z
voca|tional, -tionally vəʊ'keɪ|ʃənl
[vʊ'k-, -ʃnəl, -ʃn̩l, -ʃnl, -ʃənəl], -ʃn̩əlɪ
[-ʃnəlɪ, -ʃn̩lɪ, -ʃnlɪ, -ʃənəlɪ]
vocative (s. adj.), -s 'vɒkətɪv, -z
voce (in viva voce) 'vəʊsɪ [-tʃɪ], (in
sotto voce) 'vəʊtʃɪ
vociferat|e, -es, -ing, -ed, -or/s vəʊ'sɪ-
fəreɪt, -s, -ɪŋ, -ɪd, -ə*/z
vociferation, -s vəʊˌsɪfə'reɪʃn, -z
vociferous, -ly, -ness vəʊ'sɪfərəs, -lɪ,
-nɪs [-nəs]
vocoid, -s 'vəʊkɔɪd, -z
vodka, -s 'vɒdkə, -z
Vogt (English surname) vəʊkt
vogue vəʊg
voic|e (s. v.), -es, -ing, -ed vɔɪs, -ɪz, -ɪŋ,
-t
voiceover, -s 'vɔɪsˌəʊvə*, -z
voiceless, -ly, -ness 'vɔɪslɪs [-ləs], -lɪ,
-nɪs [-nəs]
void (s. adj. v.), -ness; -s, -ing, -ed;
-able, -ance vɔɪd, -nɪs [-nəs]; -z, -ɪŋ,
-ɪd; -əbl, -əns
voile vɔɪl
vol vɒl
volant 'vəʊlənt
Volapuk 'vɒləpʊk ['vəʊl-]
volatile (adj.), -ness 'vɒlətaɪl, -nɪs [-nəs]
volatile (in sal volatile) və'lætəlɪ [vəʊ'l-,
vʊ'l-, -tl̩ɪ]
volatility ˌvɒlə'tɪlətɪ [-ɪtɪ]
volatilization [-isa-] vɒˌlætɪlaɪ'zeɪʃn
[vəʊˌlæt-, vəˌlæt-, ˌvɒlət-, -təl-, -lɪ'z-]
volatiliz|e [-is|e], -es, -ing, -ed
vɒ'lætɪlaɪz [vəʊ'læt-, və'læt-, 'vɒlət-,
-təl-], -ɪz, -ɪŋ, -d
vol-au-vent, -s 'vɒləʊvɑ̃:ŋ [-vɔ̃:ŋ,
-vɑ:ŋ, -vɒŋ, ˌ-'-] (volovɑ̃)
volcanic, -ally vɒl'kænɪk, -əlɪ
volcanist, -s 'vɒlkənɪst, -s
volcano, -(e)s vɒl'keɪnəʊ, -z
vol|e (s. v.), -es, -ing, -ed vəʊl, -z, -ɪŋ, -d
volet, -s 'vɒleɪ (vɔlɛ), -z
Volga 'vɒlgə
Volhynia vɒl'hɪnɪə [-njə]
volition vəʊ'lɪʃn
volitive 'vɒlɪtɪv
volks|lied, -lieder 'fɒlks|li:d ['vɒl-]
('fɔlksli:t), -ˌli:də* ('fɔlksˌli:dər)

Volkswagen *(car),* **-s** 'fɒlks‚vɑːgən ['vɒlks-], -z
voll|ey *(s. v.),* **-eys, -eying, -eyed, -eyer/s** 'vɒl|ɪ, -ɪz, -ɪɪŋ, -ɪd, -ɪə*/z
volley-ball 'vɒlɪbɔːl
volplan|e *(s. v.),* **-es, -ing, -ed** 'vɒlpleɪn, -z, -ɪŋ, -d
Volpone vɒl'pəʊnɪ
Volsci 'vɒlskiː ['vɒlsaɪ]
Vol|scian, -s 'vɒl|skɪən [-skjən, -ʃɪən, -ʃjən, -sɪən, -sjən], -z
Volstead 'vɒlsted
volt *(electric unit),* **-s** vəʊlt [vɒlt], -s
volt *(movement of horse, movement in fencing),* **-s** vɒlt, -s
volta (V.) 'vɒltə
voltage, -s 'vəʊltɪdʒ ['vɒl-], -ɪz
voltaic vɒl'teɪk
Voltaire 'vɒlteə* [-'-] (vɔltɛːr)
voltameter, -s vɒl'tæmɪtə* [-mətə*], -z
volte 'vɒltɪ
volte-face,-s ‚vɒlt'fɑːs [-'fæs] (vɔltəfas), -ɪz
voltmeter, -s 'vəʊlt‚miːtə* ['vɒlt-], -z
volubility ‚vɒljʊ'bɪlətɪ [-lɪt-]
volub|le, -ly, -leness 'vɒljʊb|l, -lɪ, -lnɪs [-nəs]
volume, -s 'vɒljuːm [-ljʊm, -ljəm], -z
volumeter, -s vɒ'ljuːmɪtə* [və'l-, -'luː-, -mətə*], -z
volumetric, -al, -ally ‚vɒljʊ'metrɪk, -l, **voluminous, -ly, -ness** və'luːmɪnəs [vɒ'l-, -'ljuː-], -lɪ, -nɪs [-nəs]
voluntar|y *(s. adj.),* **-ies, -ily, -iness** 'vɒləntər|ɪ [-lɪt-], -ɪz, -əlɪ [-ɪlɪ], -ɪnɪs [-məs]
volunteer *(s. v.),* **-s, -ing, -ed** ‚vɒlən'tɪə* [-lɪ̩t-], -z, -rɪŋ, -d
voluptuar|y *(s. adj.),* **-ies** və'lʌptjʊər|ɪ [-tjwər-, -tjʊr-, -tʃʊər-, -tʃwər-, -tʃər-], -ɪz
voluptuous, -ly, -ness və'lʌptʃʊəs [-tʃwəs, -tjʊəs, -tjwəs], -lɪ, -nɪs [-nəs]
volute, -s, -d və'luːt [vɒ'l-, vəʊ'l-, -'ljuːt], -s, -ɪd
volution, -s və'luːʃn [vɒ'l-, vəʊ'l-, -'ljuː-], -z
Volvo *(car),* **-s** 'vɒlvəʊ, -z
Volze vəʊlz
vomit *(s. v.),* **-s, -ing, -ed** 'vɒmɪt, -s, -ɪŋ, -ɪd
vomitor|y *(s. adj.),* **-ies** 'vɒmɪtər|ɪ, -ɪz
Vondy 'vɒndɪ
voodoo 'vuːduː
Vooght *(surname)* vuːt
voracious, -ly, -ness və'reɪʃəs [vɔː'r-, vɒ'r-], -lɪ, -nɪs [-nəs]
voracity və'ræsətɪ [vɔː'r-, vɒ'r-, -ɪtɪ]

vort|ex, -ices, -exes 'vɔːt|eks, -ɪsiːz, -eksɪz
vortic|al, -ally 'vɔːtɪk|l, -əlɪ
vortices *(plur. of* **vortex)** 'vɔːtɪsiːz
Vosges vəʊʒ
votaress, -es 'vəʊtərɪs [-res], -ɪz
votar|y, -ies 'vəʊtər|ɪ, -ɪz
vot|e *(s. v.),* **-es, -ing, -ed, -er/s** vəʊt, -s, -ɪŋ, -ɪd, -ə*/z
voteless 'vəʊtlɪs [-ləs]
votive 'vəʊtɪv
vouch, -es, -ing, -ed vaʊtʃ, -ɪz, -ɪŋ, -t
voucher, -s 'vaʊtʃə*, -z
vouchsaf|e, -es, -ing, -ed vaʊtʃ'seɪf, -s, -ɪŋ, -t
Voules vəʊlz
vow *(s. v.),* **-s, -ing, -ed** vaʊ, -z, -ɪŋ, -d
vow|el *(s. v.),* **-els, -elling, -elled** 'vaʊ|əl, -əlz, -əlɪŋ, -əld
vowel-like 'vaʊəllaɪk
Vowles vəʊlz, vaʊlz
vox (V.) vɒks
vox celeste, -s ‚vɒkssɪ'lest, -s
vox humana, -s ‚vɒkshjuː'mɑːnə [-hjʊ'm-], -z
voyag|e *(s. v.),* **-es, -ing, -ed** 'vɔɪdʒ [vɔɪdʒ], -ɪz, -ɪŋ, -d
voyager, -s 'vɔɪədʒə* ['vɒɪdʒ-], -z
†**voyeur, -s** vwɑː'jɜː* [vɔɪ'ɜː*], -z
Voynich 'vɔɪnɪk
vraisemblance ‚vreɪsɑ̃:*m*'blɑ̃:*n*s [-sɔ̃:*m*-'blɔ̃:*n*s, -sɑːm'blɑːns, -sɒm'blɒns, '---] (vrɛsɑ̃blɑ̃:s)
Vryburg 'vraɪbɑːg
vulcan (V.) 'vʌlkən
vulcanite 'vʌlkənaɪt [-kn̩aɪt]
vulcanization [-isa-] ‚vʌlkənaɪ'zeɪʃn [-kn̩aɪ'z-, -kənɪ'z-, -kn̩ɪ'z-]
vulcaniz|e [-is|e], **-es, -ing, -ed** 'vʌlkənaɪz [-kn̩aɪz], -ɪz, -ɪŋ, -d [-lɪ
vulgar, -er, -est, -ly 'vʌlgə*, -rə*, -rɪst,
vulgarism, -s 'vʌlgərɪzəm, -z
vulgarit|y, -ies vʌl'gærət|ɪ [-ɪt|ɪ], -ɪz
vulgarization [-isa-] ‚vʌlgəraɪ'zeɪʃn [-rɪ'z-]
vulgariz|e [-is|e], **-es, -ing, -ed, -er/s** 'vʌlgəraɪz, -ɪz, -ɪŋ, -d, -ə*/z
Vulgate 'vʌlgeɪt [-gɪt, -gət]
Vulliamy 'vʌljəmɪ
vulnerability ‚vʌlnərə'bɪlətɪ [-lɪt-]
vulnerable, -ness 'vʌlnərəbl, -nɪs [-nəs]
Vulpecula vʌl'pekjʊlə
vulpine 'vʌlpaɪn
vulture, -s 'vʌltʃə*, -z
vultur|ine, -ous 'vʌltʃʊr|aɪn [-tʃər-, -tjʊr-], -əs
vulva 'vʌlvə
vying *(from* **vie)** 'vaɪɪŋ

539

W

W (*the letter*), **-'s** 'dʌbḷju: [-jʊ], -z
Waaf, -s wæf, -s
Wabash 'wɔːbæʃ
wabble, *etc.* = **wobble,** *etc.*
Wace weɪs
Wacey 'weɪsɪ
wad (*s. v.*), **-s, -ding, -ded** wɒd, -z, -ɪŋ, -ɪd
Waddell wɒ'del, 'wɒdl
wadding 'wɒdɪŋ
Waddington 'wɒdɪŋtən
wadd|le, -les, -ling, -led, -ler/s 'wɒd|l̩, -lz, -l̩ɪŋ [-lɪŋ], -ld, -l̩ə*/z [lə*/z]
wadd|y (*water-course*), **-ies** 'wɒd|ɪ, ['wæd-], -ɪz
wadd|y (*war-club*), **-ies** 'wɒd|ɪ, -ɪz
Waddy 'wɒdɪ
wad|e (*s. v.*) (**W.**), **-es, -ing, -ed** weɪd, -z, -ɪŋ, -ɪd
wader, -s 'weɪdə*, -z
Wadey 'weɪdɪ
Wadham 'wɒdəm
Wadhurst 'wɒdhɜːst
wadi, -s 'wɒdɪ ['wæd-, 'wɑːd-], -z
Wadi Halfa ˌwɒdɪ'hælfə [ˌwæd-, ˌwɑːd-]
Wadman 'wɒdmən
Wadsworth 'wɒdzwɜːθ [-wəθ]
Wady 'weɪdɪ
W.A.F., -'s wæf, -s
Wafd wɒft [wæft, wɑːft]
Wafdist, -s 'wɒfdɪst ['wæf-, 'wɑːf-], -s
wafer, -s; -y 'weɪfə*, -z; -rɪ
waff|le (*s. v.*), **-les, -ling, -led** 'wɒf|l̩, -lz, -l̩ɪŋ [-lɪŋ], -ld
waffle-iron, -s 'wɒfl̩ˌaɪən, -z
waft, -s, -ing, -ed wɑːft [wɒft, wɔːft], -s, -ɪŋ, -ɪd
wag (*s. v.*), **-s, -ging, -ged** wæg, -z, -ɪŋ, -d
wag|e (*s. v.*), **-es, -ing, -ed** weɪdʒ, -ɪz, -ɪŋ, -d
wage-earner, -s 'weɪdʒˌɜːnə*, -z
wag|er (*s. v.*), **-ers, -ering, -ered, -erer/s** 'weɪdʒ|ə*, -əz, -ərɪŋ, -əd, -ərə*/z
waggish, -ly, -ness 'wægɪʃ, -lɪ, -nɪs [-nəs]
wagg|le, -les, -ling, -led 'wæg|l̩, -lz, -l̩ɪŋ [-lɪŋ], -ld
waggon, -s 'wægən, -z

waggoner, -s 'wægənə*, -z
waggonette, -s ˌwægə'net, -s
Waghorn 'wæghɔːn
Wagnall 'wægnl̩ [-nəl]
Wagner (*English name*) 'wægnə*, (*German composer*) 'vɑːgnə* ('vɑːgnər)
Wagnerian, -s vɑːg'nɪərɪən, -z
Wagneriana ˌvɑːgnɪərɪ'ɑːnə [vɑːgˌnɪə-]
wagon, -s 'wægən, -z
wagoner, -s 'wægənə*, -z
wagonette, -s ˌwægə'net, -s
wagon-lit, -s ˌvægɔ̃ːn'liː [ˌvɑːg-, -gɒn-, '—] (vagɔ̃li), -z
Wagstaff 'wægstɑːf
wagtail, -s 'wægteɪl, -z
Wahabi, -s wə'hɑːbɪ [wɑː'h-], -z
waif, -s weɪf, -s
wail (*s. v.*), **-s, -ing/ly, -ed** weɪl, -z, -ɪŋ/lɪ, -d
wain, -s weɪn, -z
wainscot, -s, -ing, -ed 'weɪnskət ['wen-, -skɒt], -s, -ɪŋ, -ɪd
Wainwright 'weɪnraɪt
waist, -s weɪst, -s
waistband, -s 'weɪstbænd, -z
waistcoat, -s 'weɪskəʊt [-stk-, *old-fashioned* 'weskət, -ˈkɪt], -s
waist-deep ˌweɪst'diːp ['—]
waist-high ˌweɪst'haɪ ['—]
waistline 'weɪstlaɪn
wait (*s. v.*), **-s, -ing, -ed, -er/s** weɪt, -s, -ɪŋ, -ɪd, -ə*/z
waiting-maid, -s 'weɪtɪŋmeɪd, -z
waiting-room, -s 'weɪtɪŋrʊm [-ruːm], -z
waitress, -es 'weɪtrɪs [-trəs], -ɪz
Waitrose 'weɪtrəʊz
waiv|e, -es, -ing, -ed weɪv, -z, -ɪŋ, -d
waiver, -s 'weɪvə*, -z
wak|e (*s. v.*), **-es, -ing, -ed, woke, woken** weɪk, -s, -ɪŋ, -t, wəʊk, 'wəʊkən
Wakefield 'weɪkfiːld
wake|ful, -fully, -fulness 'weɪk|fʊl, -fʊlɪ [-fəlɪ], -fʊlnɪs [-nəs]
wak|en, -ens, -ening, -ened 'weɪk|ən, -ənz, -ənɪŋ [-ənɪŋ, -nɪŋ], -ənd
Wal (*personal name*) wɒl [wɔːl]
Walachia, -n/s wɒ'leɪkjə [wə-, -kɪə], -n/z
Walbrook 'wɔːlbrʊk ['wɒl-]

540

Walcheren 'vɑːlkərən ['vɑːlxə-, 'wɔːl-kərən, *old-fashioned* 'wɔːlʃərən, 'wɒlʃərən]
Walcott 'wɔːlkət ['wɒl-, -kɒt]
Waldeck 'wɔːldek ['wɒl-] ('valdɛk)
Waldegrave 'wɔːlgreɪv ['wɒl-], 'wɔːldəgreɪv ['wɒl-]
Note.—*Earl Waldegrave is* 'wɔːlgreɪv ['wɒl-].
Waldemar 'væeldəmɑː* ['vɑː l-, 'wɔː l-, -dɪm-]
Walden 'wɔːldən ['wɒl-]
Waldo 'wɔːldəʊ ['wɒl-]
Waldorf 'wɔːldɔːf ['wɒl-]
Waldstein (*American name*) 'wɔːldstam ['wɒl-], (*German name*) 'væeldstam ['vɑː l-, 'vɔː l-, 'vɒl-, 'wɔː l-, 'wɒl-, -dʃtam] ('valtʃtain)
wale, -s weɪl, -z
Waler, -s 'weɪlə*, -z
Waleran (*Baron*) 'wɔːlrən ['wɒl-], (*Buildings in Borough High Street, London*) 'wɒlərən
Wales weɪlz
Waley 'weɪlɪ
Walfish 'wɔːlfɪʃ ['wɒl-]
Walford 'wɔːlfəd ['wɒl-]
Walhalla væl'hæelə
Walham 'wɒləm
walk (*s. v.*), -s, -ing, -ed, -er/s wɔːk, -s, -ɪŋ, -t, -ə*/z
Walker 'wɔːkə*
Walkern 'wɔːlkɜːn [-kən]
Walkiden 'wɔːkɪdn
walkie-talkie, -s ˌwɔːkɪ'tɔːkɪ, -z
walking-stick, -s 'wɔːkɪŋstɪk, -s
walking-tour, -s 'wɔːkɪŋˌtʊə* [-tɔə*, -tɔː*], -z
walk-out, -s 'wɔːkaʊt, -s
walk-over, -s 'wɔːkˌəʊvə*, -z
Walkyrie, -s væl'kɪərɪ ['væelkɪrɪ], -z
wall (*s. v.*) (W.), -s, -ing, -ed wɔːl, -z, -ɪŋ, -d
wallab|y (W.), -ies 'wɒləb|ɪ, -ɪz
Wallace 'wɒlɪs [-ləs]
Wallach, -s 'wɒlək, -s
Wallachia, -n/s wɒ'leɪkjə [wə'l-, -kɪə], -n/z
walla(h), -s 'wɒlə, -z
Wallasey 'wɒləsɪ
Waller 'wɒlə*
wallet, -s 'wɒlɪt, -s
wall-eye, -s, -d 'wɔːlaɪ, -z, -d
wallflower, -s 'wɔːlˌflaʊə*, -z
wall-fruit 'wɔːlfruːt
Wallingford 'wɒlɪŋfəd
Wallis 'wɒlɪs
Walloon, -s wɒ'luːn [wə'l-], -z

wallop, -s, -ing/s, -ed 'wɒləp, -s, -ɪŋ/z, -t
wall|ow (*s. v.*), -ows, -owing, -owed, -ower/s 'wɒl|əʊ, -əʊz, -əʊɪŋ, -əʊd, -əʊə*/z
wall-paper, -s 'wɔːlˌpeɪpə*, -z
Wallsend 'wɔːlzend
Wallwork 'wɔːlwɜːk ['wɒl-]
Walmer 'wɔːlmə* ['wɒl-]
Walm(e)sley 'wɔːmzlɪ
Walmisley 'wɔːmzlɪ
Walney 'wɔːlnɪ ['wɒl-]
walnut, -s 'wɔːlnʌt [-nət], -s
Walpole 'wɔːlpəʊl ['wɒl-]
Walpurgis væl'pʊəgɪs [vɑː l-, -'pɜːg-] (val'purgis)
walrus, -es 'wɔːlrəs ['wɒl-, -rʌs], -ɪz
Walsall 'wɔːlsɔːl ['wɒl-, -sl]
Walsh wɔːlʃ [wɒlʃ]
Walsham 'wɔːlʃəm [*locally* 'wɔːlsəm]
Walsingham (*surname*) 'wɔːlsɪŋəm ['wɒl-], (*place*) 'wɔːlzɪŋəm ['wɒl-, -lsɪŋ-]
Walt wɔːlt [wɒlt]
Walter (*English name*) 'wɔːltə* ['wɒl-], (*German name*) 'vɑː ltə* ('valtər)
Walters 'wɔːltəz ['wɒl-]
Waltham 'wɔːltəm, 'wɔːlθəm ['wɒl-]
Note.—*The traditional local pronunciation at Great Waltham and Little Waltham in Essex is* 'wɔːltəm, *and this is the pronunciation used by those who have lived there for a long time. Some new residents pronounce* -lθəm. *In the case of Waltham Abbey and other places, the more common form is* 'wɔːlθəm.
Walthamstow 'wɔːlθəmstəʊ ['wɒl-, *old-fashioned* -ltəm-]
Walther (*German name*) 'vɑː ltə* ('valtər)
Walthew 'wɔːlθju: ['wɒl-]
Walton 'wɔːltən ['wɒl-]
waltz (*s. v.*), -es, -ing, -ed, -er/s wɔːls [wɒls, wɔːlts, wɒlts], -ɪz, -ɪŋ, -t, -ə*/z
Walworth 'wɔːlwəθ ['wɒl-, -wɜːθ]
wampum, -s 'wɒmpəm, -z
†wan, -ner, -nest, -ly, -ness wɒn, -ə*, -ɪst, -lɪ, -nɪs [-nəs]
Wanamaker 'wɒnəmeɪkə*
wand (W.), -s wɒnd, -z
wand|er, -ers, -ering, -ered, -erer/s 'wɒnd|ə*, -əz, -ərɪŋ, -əd, -ərə*/z
wanderlust 'wɒndəlʌst ['vɑː ndəlʊst]
Wandle 'wɒndl
Wandsworth 'wɒndzwəθ [-wɜːθ]
wan|e (*s. v.*), -es, -ing, -ed weɪn, -z, -ɪŋ, -d

541

Wanganui (*in New Zealand*) ˌwɒŋə'nuɪ
[-ŋgə-]
*Note.—The first is the form always
used by those of Polynesian descent.*
wang|le (*s. v.*), **-les, -ling, -led** 'wæŋg|l,
-lz, -lɪŋ, -ld
Wann wɒn
Wanstall 'wɒnstɔ:l
Wanstead 'wɒnstɪd [-sted]
want (*s. v.*), **-s, -ing, -ed** wɒnt, -s, -ɪŋ,
-ɪd
Wantage 'wɒntɪdʒ
wanting 'wɒntɪŋ
wanton, -ly, -ness 'wɒntən, -lɪ, -nɪs
[-nəs]
wapentake, -s 'wæpənteɪk ['wɒp-], -s
wapiti, -s 'wɒpɪtɪ, -z
Wapping 'wɒpɪŋ
Wappinger 'wɒpɪndʒə*
war (*s. v.*), **-s, -ring, -red** wɔ:*, -z, -rɪŋ,
-d
Warbeck 'wɔ:bek
warb|le, -les, -ling, -led 'wɔ:b|l, -lz, -lɪŋ
[-lɪŋ], -ld
warbler, -s 'wɔ:blə*, -z
Warburg (*Institute*) 'wɔ:bɜ:g
Warburton 'wɔ:bətn [-bə:tn]
war-cloud, -s 'wɔ:klaʊd, -z
war-club, -s 'wɔ:klʌb, -z
war-cr|y, -ies 'wɔ:kr|aɪ, -aɪz
ward (*s. v.*) (**W.**), **-s, -ing, -ed** wɔ:d, -z,
-ɪŋ, -ɪd
war-dance, -s 'wɔ:dɑ:ns, -ɪz
warden (**W.**), **-s** 'wɔ:dn, -z
warder (**W.**), **-s** 'wɔ:də*, -z
Wardlaw 'wɔ:dlɔ:
Wardle 'wɔ:dl
Wardour (*street in London*) 'wɔ:də*
wardress (*fem. warder*), **-es** 'wɔ:drɪs
[-dres], -ɪz
war-dress (*war costume*), **-es** 'wɔ:dres,
-ɪz
wardrobe, -s 'wɔ:drəʊb, -z
wardroom, -s 'wɔ:drʊm [-ru:m], -z
wardship 'wɔ:dʃɪp
ware (*s. interj.*) (**W.**), **-s** weə*, -z
Wareham 'weərəm
warehou|se (*s.*), **-ses** 'weəhaʊ|s, -zɪz
warehou|se (*v.*), **-ses, -sing, -sed** 'weə-
haʊ|z [-s], -zɪz [-sɪz], -zɪŋ [-sɪŋ], -zd
[-st]
warehouse|man, -men 'weəhaʊs|mən,
-mən
warfare 'wɔ:feə*
war-god, -s 'wɔ:gɒd, -z
war-grave, -s 'wɔ:greɪv, -z
Wargrave 'wɔ:greɪv
Warham 'wɔ:rəm

warhead, -s 'wɔ:hed, -z
war-horse, -s 'wɔ:hɔ:s, -ɪz
war|ily, -iness 'weər|əlɪ [-ɪlɪ], -mɪs
[-ɪnəs]
Waring 'weərɪŋ
warlike 'wɔ:laɪk
warlock (**W.**), **-s** 'wɔ:lɒk, -s
war-lord, -s 'wɔ:lɔ:d, -z
warm (*s. adj. v.*), **-er, -est, -ly, -ness;
-s, -ing, -ed** wɔ:m, -ə*, -ɪst, -lɪ, -nɪs
[-nəs]; -z, -ɪŋ, -d
war-maker, -s 'wɔ:ˌmeɪkə*, -z
warm-blooded ˌwɔ:m'blʌdɪd [*also* '-ˌ—
when attributive]
warmer (*s.*), **-s** 'wɔ:mə*, -z
warm-hearted ˌwɔ:m'hɑ:tɪd [*also* '-ˌ—
when attributive]
warming-pan, -s 'wɔ:mɪŋpæn, -z
Warmington 'wɔ:mɪŋtən
Warminster 'wɔ:mɪnstə*
warmish 'wɔ:mɪʃ
war-monger, -s 'wɔ:ˌmʌŋgə*, -z
warmth wɔ:mθ [-mpθ]
warn, -s, -ing/ly, -ed wɔ:n, -z, -ɪŋ/lɪ, -d
Warn|e, -er wɔ:n, -ə*
warning, -s 'wɔ:nɪŋ, -z
warp (*s. v.*), **-s, -ing, -ed** wɔ:p, -s, -ɪŋ, -t
war|-paint, -path 'wɔ:peɪnt, -pɑ:θ
warrant (*s. v.*), **-s, -ing, -ed, -er/s**
'wɒrənt, -s, -ɪŋ, -ɪd, -ə*/z
warrantab|le, -ly, -leness 'wɒrəntəb|l,
-lɪ, -lnɪs [-nəs]
warrantee, -s ˌwɒrən'ti:, -z
warrantor, -s 'wɒrəntɔ:* [-tə*, ˌwɒrən-
'tɔ:*], -z
warrant|y, -ies 'wɒrənt|ɪ, -ɪz
Warre wɔ:*
warren (**W.**), **-s** 'wɒrən [-rɪn], -z
Warrender 'wɒrəndə* [-rɪn-]
Warrington 'wɒrɪŋtən
warrior (**W.**), **-s** 'wɒrɪə*, -z
Warsaw 'wɔ:sɔ:
warship, -s 'wɔ:ʃɪp, -s
Warsop 'wɔ:səp
Warspite 'wɔ:spaɪt
wart, -s; -y wɔ:t, -s; -ɪ
wart-hog, -s 'wɔ:thɒg, -z
Warton 'wɔ:tn
war-wearied 'wɔ:ˌwɪərɪd
Warwick, -shire 'wɒrɪk, -ʃə* [-ˌʃɪə*]
war-worn 'wɔ:wɔ:n
war|y, -ier, -iest, -ily, -iness 'weər|ɪ,
-ɪə*, -ɪɪst, -əlɪ [-ɪlɪ], -mɪs [-ɪnəs]
was (*from* **be**) wɒz (*strong form*), wəz,
wz (*weak forms*)
Wasbrough 'wɒzbrə
wash (*s. v.*) (**W.**), **-es, -ing, -ed, -er/s;
-able** wɒʃ, -ɪz, -ɪŋ, -t, -ə*/z; -əbl

wash-basin, -s 'wɒʃˌbeɪsn, -z
washday, -s 'wɒʃdeɪ, -z
washer, -s 'wɒʃə*, -z
washer|woman, -women 'wɒʃə|ˌwʊmən, -ˌwɪmɪn
wash-hou|se, -ses 'wɒʃhaʊ|s, -zɪz
washing 'wɒʃɪŋ
washing-day, -s 'wɒʃɪŋdeɪ, -z
washing-machine, -s 'wɒʃɪŋməˌʃiːn, -z
washing-stand, -s 'wɒʃɪŋstænd, -z
Washington 'wɒʃɪŋtən
washing-up ˌwɒʃɪŋˈʌp
wash-out, -s 'wɒʃaʊt [ˌ-ˈ-], -s
wash-pot, -s 'wɒʃpɒt, -s
wash-stand, -s 'wɒʃstænd, -z
wash-tub, -s 'wɒʃtʌb, -z
wash|y, -ier, -iest, -iness 'wɒʃ|ɪ, -ɪə*, -ɪɪst, -ɪɪs [-məs]
wasn't 'wɒznt [also occasionally 'wɒzn when not final]
wasp, -s wɒsp, -s
waspish, -ly, -ness 'wɒspɪʃ, -lɪ, -nɪs [-nəs]
wasplike 'wɒsplaɪk
wassail, -s 'wɒseɪl ['wæs-, -sl], -z
wassailing 'wɒsəlɪŋ ['wæs-, -slɪŋ, -seɪlɪŋ]
Wassell 'wæsl
Wasson 'wɒsn
wast (from be) wɒst (strong form), wəst (weak form)
Wast, -water wɒst, -ˌwɔːtə*
wast|e (s. adj. v.), -es, -ing, -ed, -er/s; -age weɪst, -s, -ɪŋ, -ɪd, -ə*/z; -ɪdʒ
waste|ful, -fully, -fulness 'weɪst|fʊl, -fʊlɪ [-fəlɪ], -fʊlnɪs [-nəs]
waste-paper-basket, -s ˌweɪstˈpeɪpəˌbɑːskɪt, -s
waste-pipe, -s 'weɪstpaɪp, -s
wastrel, -s 'weɪstrəl, -z
Wat wɒt
watch (s. v.), -es, -ing, -ed, -er/s wɒtʃ, -ɪz, -ɪŋ, -t, -ə*/z
watch-case, -s 'wɒtʃkeɪs, -ɪz
watch-chain, -s 'wɒtʃtʃeɪn, -z
watch-dog, -s 'wɒtʃdɒg, -z
watch|ful, -fully, -fulness 'wɒtʃ|fʊl, -fʊlɪ [-fəlɪ], -fʊlnɪs [-nəs]
watch-glass, -es 'wɒtʃglɑːs, -ɪz
watch-key, -s 'wɒtʃkiː, -z
watch-maker, -s 'wɒtʃˌmeɪkə*, -z
watch|man, -men 'wɒtʃ|mən, -mən [-men]
watch-pocket, -s 'wɒtʃˌpɒkɪt, -s
watch-spring, -s 'wɒtʃsprɪŋ, -z
watch-stand, -s 'wɒtʃstænd, -z
watch-tower, -s 'wɒtʃˌtaʊə*, -z
watchword, -s 'wɒtʃwɜːd, -z
wat|er (s. v.), -ers, -ering, -ered 'wɔːt|ə*, -əz, -ərɪŋ, -əd

water-bed, -s 'wɔːtəbed, -z
water-borne 'wɔːtəbɔːn
water-bottle, -s 'wɔːtəˌbɒtl, -z
water-buck 'wɔːtəbʌk
Waterbur|y, -ies 'wɔːtəbər|ɪ, -ɪz
water-butt, -s 'wɔːtəbʌt, -s
water-carrier, -s 'wɔːtəˌkærɪə*, -z
watercart, -s 'wɔːtəkɑːt, -s
water-chute, -s 'wɔːtəʃuːt, -s
water-closet, -s 'wɔːtəˌklɒzɪt, -s
water-colour, -s 'wɔːtəˌkʌlə*, -z
water-cooled 'wɔːtəkuːld [ˌ-ˈ-]
watercourse, -s 'wɔːtəkɔːs [-kɔəs], -ɪz
watercress, -es 'wɔːtəkres, -ɪz
water-diviner/s 'wɔːtədɪˌvaɪnə*/z
water-divining 'wɔːtədɪˌvaɪnɪŋ
waterfall, -s 'wɔːtəfɔːl, -z
water-finder, -s 'wɔːtəˌfaɪndə*, -z
Waterford 'wɔːtəfəd
waterfowl 'wɔːtəfaʊl
waterfront, -s 'wɔːtəfrʌnt, -s
water-gas 'wɔːtəgæs [ˌ-ˈ-]
water-gate, -s 'wɔːtəgeɪt, -s
Watergate 'wɔːtəgeɪt
water-gauge, -s 'wɔːtəgeɪdʒ, -ɪz
waterglass 'wɔːtəglɑːs
water-glass, -es 'wɔːtəglɑːs, -ɪz
Waterhouse 'wɔːtəhaʊs
water-ice, -s 'wɔːtəraɪs, -ɪz
wateriness 'wɔːtərɪnɪs [-nəs]
watering-can, -s 'wɔːtərɪŋkæn, -z
watering-cart, -s 'wɔːtərɪŋkɑːt, -s
watering-place, -s 'wɔːtərɪŋpleɪs, -ɪz
waterless 'wɔːtəlɪs [-ləs]
water-level, -s 'wɔːtəˌlevl, -z
water-lil|y, -ies 'wɔːtəˌlɪl|ɪ, -ɪz
water-line, -s 'wɔːtəlaɪn, -z
waterlogged 'wɔːtəlɒgd
Waterloo ˌwɔːtəˈluː [ˈ---]
    Note.—The stressing '--- is that regularly used when the word is attributive (as in Waterloo Road).
water-main, -s 'wɔːtəmeɪn, -s
water|man (W.), -men 'wɔːtə|mən, -mən [-men]
watermark (s. v.), -s, -ing, -ed 'wɔːtəmɑːk, -s, -ɪŋ, -t
water-nymph, -s 'wɔːtənɪmf, -s
water-pipe, -s 'wɔːtəpaɪp, -s
water-power 'wɔːtəˌpaʊə*
waterproof (s. v.), -s, -ing, -ed 'wɔːtəpruːf, -s, -ɪŋ, -t
Waters 'wɔːtəz
watershed, -s 'wɔːtəʃed, -z
water-ski (s. v.), -s, -ing, -ed, -er/s 'wɔːtəskiː, -z, -ɪŋ, -d, -ˌskiːə*/z [-ˌskɪə*/z]
waterspout, -s 'wɔːtəspaʊt, -s

water-sprite, -s 'wɔːtəspraɪt, -s
water-suppl|y, -ies 'wɔːtəsə‚pl|aɪ, -aɪz
watertight 'wɔːtətaɪt
water-tower, -s 'wɔːtə‚tauə, -z
waterway, -s 'wɔːtəweɪ, -z
water-wheel, -s 'wɔːtəwiːl [-təhw-], -z
water-wings 'wɔːtəwɪŋz
waterworks 'wɔːtəwɜːks
water-worn 'wɔːtəwɔːn
watery 'wɔːtərɪ
Wat|ford, -kin/s, -son 'wɒt|fəd, -kɪn/z,
  -sn
Wathen 'wɒθən
Watling (Street) 'wɒtlɪŋ
watt (W.), -s wɒt, -s
wattage 'wɒtɪdʒ
Watteau, -s 'wɒtəu, -z
wattle, -s, -d 'wɒtl, -z, -d
wattmeter, -s 'wɒt‚miːtə*, -z
Watton 'wɒtn
Wauchope (surname, place in Scotland)
  'wɔːkəp [in Scotland 'wɔxəp]
Waugh wɔː [in Scotland wɔx]
waught, -s wɔːt [in Scotland wɔxt],
  -s
waul, -s wɔːl, -z
wav|e (s. v.), -es, -ing, -ed; -eless,
  -elet/s weɪv, -z, -ɪŋ, -d; -lɪs [-ləs],
  -lɪt/s [-lət/z]
waveband, -s 'weɪvbænd, -z
waveform, -s 'weɪvfɔːm, -z
wave-length, -s 'weɪvleŋkθ, -s
Wavell 'weɪvl
wav|er, -ers, -ering/ly, -ered, -erer/s
  'weɪv|ə*, -əz, -ərɪŋ/lɪ, -əd, -ərə*/z
Waverley 'weɪvəlɪ
wav|y, -ier, -iest, -ily, -iness 'weɪv|ɪ,
  -ɪə* [-jə*], -ɪɪst [-jɪst], -ɪlɪ [-əlɪ], -ɪnɪs
  [-məs]
wax (s. v.), -es, -ing, -ed; -en wæks, -ɪz,
  -ɪŋ, -t; -ən
waxwing, -s 'wækswɪŋ, -z
waxwork, -s 'wækswɜːk, -s
wax|y, -ier, -iest, -iness 'wæks|ɪ, -ɪə*
  [-jə*], -ɪɪst [-jɪst], -ɪnɪs [-məs]
way (W.), -s weɪ, -z
wayfar|er/s, -ing 'weɪ‚feər|ə*/z, -ɪŋ
Wayland 'weɪlənd
way|lay, -lays, -laying, -laid, -layer/s
  ‚weɪ'leɪ, -'leɪz, -'leɪɪŋ, -'leɪd, -'leɪə*/z
Wayn|e, -flete weɪn, -fliːt
wayside 'weɪsaɪd
wayward, -ly, -ness 'weɪwəd, -lɪ, -nɪs
  [-nəs]
W.C., -'s ‚dʌblju:'si: [-ju-], -z
we wiː (normal form), wɪ (freq. weak
  form)
  Note.—wɪ also occurs as a strong form

in the single expression we are
when are has its weak form ə*. We
are in this case is also written we're.

weak, -er, -est, -ly, -ness wiːk, -ə*, -ɪst,
  -lɪ, -nɪs [-nəs]
weak|en, -ens, -ening, -ened 'wiːk|ən,
  -ənz, -ŋɪŋ [-nɪŋ, -ənɪŋ], -ənd
weakening (s. adj.), -s 'wiːknɪŋ, -z
weakish 'wiːkɪʃ
weak-kneed ‚wiːk'niːd ['--]
weakling, -s 'wiːklɪŋ, -z
weak-minded ‚wiːk'maɪndɪd [also '-‚--
  when attributive]
weal, -s wiːl, -z
weald (W.), -s wiːld, -z
wealden (W.) 'wiːldən
wealth, -s welθ, -s
wealth|y, -ier, -iest, -ily, -iness 'welθ|ɪ,
  -ɪə* [-jə*], -ɪɪst [-jɪst], -ɪlɪ [-əlɪ], -ɪnɪs
  [-məs]
wean (s.), -s weɪn, -z
wean, -s, -ing, -ed wiːn, -z, -ɪŋ, -d
weaner, -s 'wiːnə*, -z
weanling, -s 'wiːnlɪŋ, -z
weapon, -s; -less 'wepən, -z; -lɪs [-ləs]
wear (s.) (corresponding to wear v.)
  weə*
wear (s.) (=weir), -s wɪə*, -z
Wear (river) wɪə*
wear (v.), -s, -ing, wore, worn, wearer/s
  weə*, -z, -ɪŋ, wɔː* [wɔə*], wɔːn,
  'weərə*/z
wearable 'weərəbl
Wearing 'weərɪŋ
wearisome, -ly, -ness 'wɪərɪsəm, -lɪ, -nɪs
  [-nəs]
Wearmouth 'wɪəməθ [-mauθ]
Wearn wɜːn
wear|y (adj. v.), -ier, -iest, -ily, -iness;
  -ies, -ying, -ied 'wɪər|ɪ, -ɪə*, -ɪɪst,
  -əlɪ [-ɪlɪ], -ɪnɪs [-məs]; -ɪz, -ɪɪŋ, -ɪd
weasand, -s 'wiːzənd ['wɪz-, -znd], -z
weasel, -s 'wiːzl, -z
weather (s. v.), -s, -ing, -ed; -beaten
  'weðə*, -z, -rɪŋ, -d; -‚biːtn
weatherboard, -s, -ing 'weðəbɔːd
  [-bəəd], -z, -ɪŋ
weather-bound 'weðəbaund
weathercock, -s 'weðəkɒk, -s
weather-eye, -s 'weðəraɪ [‚--'-], -z
weather-glass, -es 'weðəglɑːs, -ɪz
Weatherhead 'weðəhed
weatherly (W.) 'weðəlɪ
weather|man,   -men   'weðə|mæn,
  -men
weatherproof 'weðəpruːf
weathership, -s 'weðəʃɪp, -s
weathervane, -s 'weðəveɪn, -z

weather-wise 'weðəwaɪz
weather-worn 'weðəwɔ:n
weav|e, -es, -ing, wove, woven
  weaver/s wi:v, -z, -ɪŋ, wəʊv, 'wəʊvən,
  'wi:və*/z
weazened 'wi:znd
web, -s, -bed web, -z, -d
Webb(e) web
webb|ing, -y 'web|ɪŋ, -ɪ
Weber (English name) 'wi:bə*, (German
  composer) 'veɪbə* ('ve:bər)
webfooted 'web,fʊtɪd [,-'—]
Webster, -s 'webstə*, -z
wed, -s, -ding/s, -ded wed, -z, -ɪŋ/z, -ɪd
Weddell (surname) wə'del, 'wedl, (Sea)
  'wedl
Wedderburn 'wedəbə:n
wedding-cake, -s 'wedɪŋkeɪk, -s
wedding-day, -s 'wedɪŋdeɪ, -z
wedding-ring, -s 'wedɪŋrɪŋ, -z
wedg|e (s. v.), -es, -ing, -ed; -ewise
  wedʒ, -ɪz, -ɪŋ, -d; -waɪz
wedge-shaped 'wedʒʃeɪpt
Wedgwood 'wedʒwʊd
wedlock 'wedlɒk
Wednesbury 'wenzbərɪ [locally also
  'wedʒbərɪ]
Wednesday, -s 'wenzdɪ ['wedn-, -deɪ],
  -z
wee wi:
weed (s. v.), -s, -ing, -ed wi:d, -z, -ɪŋ, -ɪd
Weedon 'wi:dn
weed|y, -ier, -iest, -iness 'wi:d|ɪ, -ɪə*
  [-jə*], -ɪst [-jɪst], -ɪnɪs [-məs]
week, -s wi:k, -s
weekday, -s 'wi:kdeɪ, -z
week-end, -s ,wi:k'end ['—], -z
week-ender, -s ,wi:k'endə*, -z
Weekes wi:ks
Weekl(e)y 'wi:klɪ
weekl|y (s. adv.), -ies 'wi:kl|ɪ, -ɪz
Weeks wi:ks
Weelkes wi:lks
Weems wi:mz
ween, -s, -ing, -ed wi:n, -z, -ɪŋ, -d
weep, -s, -ing/ly, wept wi:p, -s, -ɪŋ/lɪ,
  wept
weeper, -s 'wi:pə*, -z
weever, -s 'wi:və*, -z
weevil, -s 'wi:vl [-vɪl], -z
weewee, -s, -ing, -d 'wi:wi:, -z, -ɪŋ, -d
weft weft
Weguelin 'wegəlɪn
Weigall 'waɪgɔ:l
weigh, -s, -ing, -ed; -able weɪ, -z, -ɪŋ,
  -d; -əbl ['weəbl]
weight (s. v.), -s, -ing, -ed weɪt, -s, -ɪŋ,
  -ɪd

weightless, -ness 'weɪtlɪs [-ləs], -nɪs
  [-nəs]
Weighton (in Market Weighton, Hum-
  berside) 'wi:tn
weight|y, -ier, -iest, -ily, -iness 'weɪt|ɪ,
  -ɪə* [-jə*], -ɪst [-jɪst], -ɪlɪ [-əlɪ], -ɪnɪs
  [-məs]
Wei-hai-wei ,weɪhaɪ'weɪ
Weimar 'vaɪmɑ:* ('vaimar)
weir (W.), -s wɪə*, -z
†weird, -er, -est, -ly, -ness wɪəd, -ə*, -ɪst,
  -lɪ, -nɪs [-nəs]
Weisshorn 'vaɪshɔ:n
Weland 'weɪlənd, 'wi:lənd
Welbeck 'welbek
Welch welʃ
Welcombe 'welkəm
welcom|e (s. adj. v. interj.), -es, -ing, -ed
  'welkəm, -z, -ɪŋ, -d
weld (s. v.), -s, -ing, -ed, -er/s weld, -z,
  -ɪŋ, -ɪd, -ə*/z
weldment 'weldmənt
Weldon 'weldɑn
welfare 'welfeə*
Welford 'welfəd
welkin 'welkɪn
well (s. adj. v. interj.), -s, -ing, -ed wel,
  -z, -ɪŋ, -d
welladay ,welə'deɪ ['—]
well-advised ,weləd'vaɪzd
Welland 'welənd
well-appointed ,welə'pɔɪntɪd
well-balanced ,wel'bælənst [also '-,--
  when attributive]
well-behaved ,welbɪ'heɪvd [also '--,-
  when attributive]
well-being ,wel'bi:ɪŋ ['-,—]
well-born ,wel'bɔ:n
well-bred ,wel'bred [also '-- according
  to sentence-stress]
Wellby 'welbɪ
well-chosen ,wel'tʃəʊzn [also '-,-- when
  attributive]
Wellcome 'welkəm
well-conducted ,welkən'dʌktɪd [also
  '--,-- when attributive]
well-connected ,welkə'nektɪd [also '-,--
  when attributive]
well-cooked ,wel'kʊkt [also '-- when
  attributive]
well-directed ,weldɪ'rektɪd [-də'r-,
  -daɪ'r-, also '--,-- when attributive]
well-disposed ,weldɪ'spəʊzd
well-do|er/s, -ing 'wel,du:|ə*/z
  [-,dʊə*/z, ,-' —], -ɪŋ
Welldon 'weldɑn
well-done ,wel'dʌn ['-- when attributive]
Weller 'welə*

Wellesley 'welzlı
well-found ,wel'faʊnd [also '– when attributive]
well-groomed ,wel'gru:md ['– when attributive]
well-grounded ,wel'graʊndıd
well-informed ,welın'fɔ:md
Wellingborough 'welıŋbərə
Wellington, -s 'welıŋtən, -z
wellingtonia, -s ,welıŋ'təʊnjə [-nıə], -z
well-intentioned ,welın'tenʃnd [also '–,– when attributive]
well-judged ,wel'dʒʌdʒd [also '– when attributive]
well-known ,wel'nəʊn [also '– according to sentence-stress]
well-made ,wel'meıd [also '– according to sentence-stress]
well-marked ,wel'mɑ:kt [also '– when attributive]
well-meaning ,wel'mi:nıŋ
well-meant ,wel'ment [also '– according to sentence-stress]
well-nigh 'welnaı
well-off ,wel'ɒf [old-fashioned -'ɔ:f, also '– according to sentence-stress]
well-ordered ,wel'ɔ:dəd [also '-,– when attributive]
well-proportioned ,welprə'pɔ:ʃnd [-prʊ'p-, also '–,– when attributive]
well-read ,wel'red [also '– according to sentence-stress]
well-rounded ,wel'raʊndıd
Wells welz
well-spoken ,wel'spəʊkən [also '-,– when attributive]
well-timed ,wel'taımd [also '– when attributive]
well-to-do ,weltə'du: [also '–– when attributive]
well-wisher, -s 'wel,wıʃə* [,-'––], -z
welsh, -es, -ing, -ed, -er/s welʃ, -ız, -ıŋ, -t, -ə*/z
Welsh, -man, -men welʃ, -mən, -mən [-men]
Welshpool 'welʃpu:l (Welsh ,welʃ'pu:l)
welt (s. v.), -s, -ing, -ed welt, -s, -ıŋ, -ıd
welt|er, -ers, -ering, -ered 'welt|ə*, -əz, -ərıŋ, -əd
welterweight, -s 'weltəweıt, -s
Welwyn 'welın
Wembley 'wemblı
Wemyss wi:mz
wen, -s wen, -z
Wenceslas 'wensısləs [-səs-, -læs]
wench, -es wenʧ, -ız
wend, -s, -ing, -ed wend, -z, -ıŋ, -ıd

Wend, -s, -ic, -ish wend [vend], -z, -ık, -ıʃ
Wendell 'wendl
Wendover 'wendəʊvə*
Wengen 'veŋən
Wengern Alp ,veŋən'ælp
Wenham 'wenəm
Wenish 'wenıʃ
Wenlock 'wenlɒk
Wensleydale 'wenzlıdeıl
went (from go) went
Wentworth 'wentwəθ [-wɜ:θ]
wept (from weep) wept
we're (=we are) wıə*
were (from be) wɜ:* (strong form; rarely weə*), wə* (weak form)
weren't wɜ:nt (rarely weənt)
werewol|f, -ves 'wıəwʊl|f ['wɜ:-], -vz
Wernher 'wɜ:nə*
wert (from be) wɜ:t (strong form), wət (weak form)
Weser (German river) 'veızə* ('ve:zər)
    Note.—'wi:zə* is necessary for rhyme in Browning's 'Pied Piper', but this pronunciation is exceptional.
Wesley 'wezlı, 'weslı
    Note.—Most people bearing the name Wesley pronounce 'weslı, but they are commonly called 'wezlı by others.
Wesleyan, -s; -ism 'wezlıən ['wesl-, -ljən], -z; -ızəm
    Note.—'wesl- appears to be the more usual pronunciation among Wesleyans; with those who are not Wesleyans 'wezl- is probably the commoner form. There exists also an old-fashioned pronunciation wes'li:ən.
Wessex 'wesıks
west (s. adj. v.) (W.) west
Westbourne 'westbɔ:n [-bɔən, -bən, esp. when attributive, as in W. Terrace]
West|brook, -bury 'west|brʊk, -bərı
Westcott 'westkət
Westenra 'westənrə
Westerham 'westərəm
westering 'westərıŋ
wester|ly, -n, -ner/s 'westə|lı, -n, -nə*/z
westerniz|e [-is|e], -es, -ing, -ed 'westənaız, -ız, -ıŋ, -d
westernmost 'westənməʊst
Westfield 'westfi:ld
Westgate 'westgeıt [-gıt]
Westlake 'westleık
Westmeath west'mi:ð
Westminster 'westmınstə* [-'––]
Westmor(e)land 'westmələnd ['wes-mlənd]

west-north-west ˌwestnɔːθ'west [*nautical pronunciation* -nɔː'west]

Weston 'westən

Weston - super - Mare 'westən ˌsuːpə-'meə* [-n ˌsjuːpə-, -nsjʊpə-, ˌ--'---, *rarely* -'meərɪ]

Westphalia, -n/s west'feɪljə [-lɪə], -n/z

west-south-west ˌwestsaʊθ'west [*nautical pronunciation* -saʊ'west]

westward, -s, -ly 'westwəd, -z, -lɪ

Westward Ho ˌwestwəd'həʊ

wet, -ter, -test, -ness wet, -ə*, -ɪst, -nɪs [-nəs]

wether, -s 'weðə*, -z

Wetherby 'weðəbɪ

wet-nurse, -s 'wetnɜːs, -ɪz

Wetterhorn 'vetəhɔːn

wettish 'wetɪʃ

Wexford 'weksfəd

wey (W.), -s weɪ, -z

Wey|bridge, -man, -mouth 'weɪ|brɪdʒ, -mən, -məθ

whack (s. v.), -s, -ing/s, -ed, -er/s wæk [hw-], -s, -ɪŋ/z, -t, -ə*/z

Whait weɪt [hw-]

whal|e, -es, -ing, -er/s weɪl [hw-], -z, -ɪŋ, -ə*/z

whalebone 'weɪlbəʊn ['hw-]

whale-fisher|y, -ies 'weɪlˌfɪʃər|ɪ ['hw-], -ɪz

whale-oil 'weɪlɔɪl ['hw-]

Whaley (*place near Buxton*) 'weɪlɪ ['hw-]

Whalley (*surname*) 'weɪlɪ ['hw-], 'wɔːlɪ ['hw-], (*abbey near Blackburn*) 'wɔːlɪ ['hw-]

whang (s. v.), -s, -in;, -ed wæŋ [hw-], -z, -ɪŋ, -d

whangee wæŋ'giː [hw-]

Wharam 'weərəm ['hw-]

whar|f, -ves, -fs wɔː|f [hw-], -vz, -fs

wharfage 'wɔːfɪdʒ ['hw-]

wharfinger, -s 'wɔːfɪndʒə* ['hw-], -z

Wharton 'wɔːtn [ˈˌɪw-]

what wɒt [hw-]

what-d'you-call-it 'wɒtdjʊˌkɔːlɪt ['hw-, -dʒʊ-]

whate'er wɒt'eə* [hw-]

Whateley 'weɪtlɪ ['hw-]

whatever wɒt'evə* [hw-, *rarely* wət-, hwət-]

What|ley, -man 'wɒt|lɪ ['hw-], -mən

Whatmough 'wɒtməʊ ['hw-]

whatnot, -s 'wɒtnɒt ['hw-], -s

what's-her-name 'wɒtsəneɪm ['hw-, -sn̩eɪm]

what's-his-name 'wɒtsɪzneɪm ['hw-]

whatsoe'er ˌwɒtsəʊ'eə* [ˌhw-]

whatsoever ˌwɒtsəʊ'evə* [ˌhw-]

what-you-may-call-it 'wɒtʃəməˌkɔːlɪt ['hw-]

wheat, -en wiːt [hw-], -n

wheat-ear, -s 'wiːtˌɪə* ['hw-], -z

Wheathampstead (*in Hertfordshire*) 'wiːtəmpsted ['wet-, 'hw-]

Wheat|ley, -on 'wiːt|lɪ ['hw-], -n

Wheatstone 'wiːtstən [ˈhw-, -stəʊn]

wheed|le, -les, -ling, -led, -ler/s 'wiːd|l ['hw-], -lz, -lɪŋ [-l̩ɪŋ], -ld, -lə*/z [-lə*/z]

wheel (s. v.), -s, -ing, -ed wiːl [hw-], -z, -ɪŋ, -d

wheelbarrow, -s 'wiːlˌbærəʊ ['hw-], -z

wheel-chair, -s ˌwiːl'tʃeə* [ˌhw-, '--], -z

wheeler (W.), -s 'wiːlə* ['hw-], -z

wheelwright (W.), -s 'wiːlraɪt ['hw-], -s

Wheen wiːn [hw-]

wheez|e (s. v.), -es, -ing, -ed; -y, -ier, -iest, -iness wiːz [hw-], -ɪz, -ɪŋ, -d; -ɪ, -ɪə* [-jə*], -ɪɪst [-jɪst], -ɪnɪs [-ɪnəs]

Whelan 'wiːlən ['hw-]

whelk, -s welk, -s

Note.—Not hwelk.

whelm, -s, -ing, -ed welm [hw-], -z, -ɪŋ, -d

whelp (s. v.), -s, -ing, -ed welp [hw-], -s, -ɪŋ, -t

when wen [hw-]

whence wens [hw-]

whene'er wen'eə* [hw-]

whenever wen'evə* [wən-, hw-]

whensoever ˌwensəʊ'evə* [ˌhw-]

where weə* [hw-]

whereabouts (s.) 'weərəbaʊts ['hw-]

whereabouts (*interrogation*) ˌweərə'baʊts [ˌhw-, *occasionally* '--- *when followed by a stress*]

whereas weər'æz [wər-, hw-]

whereat weər'æt [wər-, hw-]

whereby weə'baɪ [hw-]

where'er weər'eə* [wər-, hw-]

wherefore 'weəfɔː* ['hw-, -fɔə*]

where|in, -of, -on weər|'ɪn [hw-], -'ɒv [-'ɒf], -'ɒn

whereso|e'er, -ever ˌweəsəʊ'eə* [ˌhw-], -'evə*

whereto weə'tuː [hw-]

whereunder weər'ʌndə* [hw-]

whereunto ˌweərʌn'tuː [ˌhw-]

whereupon ˌweərə'pɒn [ˌhw-, '---]

wherever weər'evə* [wə'r-, hw-]

wherewith weə'wɪθ [hw-, -'wɪð]

wherewithal (s.) 'weəwɪðɔːl ['hw-]

wherewithal (adv.) ˌweəwɪ'ðɔːl [ˌhw-, '---]

wherr|y, -ies 'wer|ɪ ['hw-], -ɪz

whet (s. v.), **-s, -ting, -ted** wet [hw-], -s, -ɪŋ, -ɪd

whether 'weðə* ['hw-]

whetstone (**W.**), **-s** 'wetstəʊn ['hw-], -z

whew ŷ: [ŷ:, ŷ:u:, hwu:]

Whewell 'hju:əl [-ʋəl, -el, -ɪl]

whey weɪ [hw-]

Whibley 'wɪblɪ ['hw-]

which wɪtʃ [hw-]

whichever wɪtʃ'evə* [hw-]

Whickham 'wɪkəm ['hw-]

whiff (s. v.), **-s, -ing, -ed** wɪf [hw-], -s, -ɪŋ, -t

Whiffen 'wɪfɪn ['hw-]

whig (**W.**), **-s** wɪg [hw-], **-z**

whigg|ery, -ism 'wɪg|ərɪ ['hw-], -ɪzəm

whiggish, -ly, -ness 'wɪgɪʃ ['hw-], -lɪ, -nɪs [-nəs]

Whigham 'wɪgəm ['hw-]

whil|e (s. v. conj.), **-es, -ing, -ed** waɪl [hw-], -z, -ɪŋ, -d

whilom 'waɪləm ['hw-]

whilst waɪlst [hw-]

whim, **-s** wɪm [hw-], -z

whimbrel, **-s** 'wɪmbrəl ['hw-], -z

whimper, **-s, -ing/ly, -ed, -er/s** 'wɪmpə* ['hw-], -z, -rɪŋ/lɪ, -d, -rə*/z

whimsic|al, -ally, -alness 'wɪmzɪkl ['hw-, -msɪ-], -əlɪ, -lnɪs [-nəs]

whimsicality ˌwɪmzɪ'kælətɪ [ˌhw-, -msɪ-, -ɪtɪ]

whims|y, -ies 'wɪmz|ɪ ['hw-], -ɪz

whin, **-s** wɪn [hw-], -z

whinchat, **-s** 'wɪntʃæt ['hw-], -s

whin|e (s. v.), **-es, -ing/ly, -ed** waɪn [hw-], -z, -ɪŋ/lɪ, -d

whinger, **-s** 'wɪŋə* [hw-], -z

whinn|y (s. v.), **-ies, -ying, -ied** 'wɪn|ɪ ['hw-], -ɪz, -ɪɪŋ, -ɪd

whin|y, -ier, -iest, -iness 'waɪn|ɪ ['hw-], -ɪə*, -ɪɪst, -ɪnɪs [-məs]

whip (s. v.), **-s, -ping/s, -ped** wɪp [hw-], -s, -ɪŋ/z, -t

whip-cord 'wɪpkɔːd ['hw-]

whip-hand ˌwɪp'hænd [ˌhw-, '—]

whiplash 'wɪplæʃ ['hw-]

whipp|er-in, -ers-in ˌwɪp|ər'ɪn [ˌhw-], -əz'ɪn

whippersnapper, -s 'wɪpəˌsnæpə* ['hw-], -z

whippet, **-s** 'wɪpɪt ['hw-], -s

whipping-boy, **-s** 'wɪpɪŋbɔɪ ['hw-], -z

Whippingham 'wɪpɪŋəm ['hw-]

whipping-top, **-s** 'wɪpɪŋtɒp ['hw-], -s

Whipple 'wɪpl ['hw-]

whippoorwill, **-s** 'wɪpˌpʊəˌwɪl ['hw-, -pɔəˌw-, -pɔːˌw-], -z

Whipsnade 'wɪpsneɪd ['hw-]

whir (s. v.), **-s, -ring/s, -red** wɜː* [hw-], -z, -rɪŋ/z, -d

whirl (s. v.), **-s, -ing, -ed** wɜːl [hw-], -z, -ɪŋ, -d

whirligig, **-s** 'wɜːlɪgɪg ['hw-], -z

whirlpool, **-s** 'wɜːlpuːl ['hw-], -z

whirlwind, **-s** 'wɜːlwɪnd ['hw-], -z

whirr (s. v.), **-s, -ing/s, -ed** wɜː* [hw-], -z, -rɪŋ/z, -d

whisk (s. v.), **-s, -ing, -ed** wɪsk [hw-], **-s**, -ɪŋ, -t

whisker, **-s, -ed** 'wɪskə* ['hw-], -z, -d

whiskey, **-s** 'wɪskɪ ['hw-], -z

whisk|y, -ies 'wɪsk|ɪ ['hw-], -ɪz

whisp|er (s. v.), **-ers, -ering/s, -ered, -erer/s** 'wɪsp|ə* ['hw-], -əz, -ərɪŋ/z, -əd, -ərə*/z

whist wɪst [hw-]

whist-drive, **-s** 'wɪstdraɪv ['hw-], -z

whist|le (s. v.), **-les, -ling, -led** 'wɪs|l ['hw-], -lz, -lɪŋ [-lɪŋ], -ld

whistler (**W.**), **-s** 'wɪslə* ['hw-], -z

whit (**W.**) wɪt [hw-]

Whitaker 'wɪtəkə* ['hw-, -tɪk-]

Whit|bread, -by, -church 'wɪt|bred ['hw-], -bɪ, -tʃɜːtʃ

whit|e (s. adj. v.) (**W.**), **-es; -er, -est, -ely, -eness; -ing, -ed** waɪt [hw-], -s; -ə*, -ɪst, -lɪ, -nɪs [-nəs]; -ɪŋ, -ɪd

whitebait 'waɪtbeɪt ['hw-]

whitebeard, **-s, -ed** 'waɪtˌbɪəd ['hw-], -ɪd

whitecap, **-s** 'waɪtkæp ['hw-], -s

Whitechapel 'waɪtˌtʃæpl ['hw-]

Whitefield 'waɪtfiːld ['hw-], 'wɪt- ['hw-]

Whitefriars 'waɪtˌfraɪəz ['hw-, ˌ-'—]

Whitehall 'waɪthɔːl ['hw-, ˌ-'-]

Whitehaven 'waɪtˌheɪvn ['hw-]

whitehead (**W.**), **-s** 'waɪthed ['hw-], -z

white-heat ˌwaɪt'hiːt [ˌhw-]

white-hot ˌwaɪt'hɒt [ˌhw-, also '— when attributive]

Whiteley 'waɪtlɪ ['hw-]

white-livered 'waɪtˌlɪvəd ['hw-]

whit|en, -ens, -ening, -ened 'waɪt|n ['hw-], -nz, -nɪŋ [-n̩ɪŋ], -nd

whitening (s.) 'waɪtnɪŋ ['hw-]

whitethorn, **-s** 'waɪtθɔːn ['hw-], -z

whitethroat, **-s** 'waɪtθrəʊt ['hw-], -s

whitewash (s. v.), **-es, -ing, -ed, -er/s** 'waɪtwɒʃ ['hw-], -ɪz, -ɪŋ, -t, -ə*/z

whitewood 'waɪtwʊd ['hw-]

Whit|field, -gift 'wɪt|fiːld ['hw-], -gɪft

whither 'wɪðə* ['hw-]

whithersoever ˌwɪðəsəʊ'evə* [ˌhw-]

whiting (**W.**), **-s** 'waɪtɪŋ ['hw-], -z

whitish, **-ness** 'waɪtɪʃ ['hw-], -nɪs [-nəs]

whitleather 'wɪt‚leðə* ['hw-]
Whitley 'wɪtlɪ ['hw-]
whitlow, -s 'wɪtləʊ ['hw-], -z
Whit|man, -marsh, -ney, -stable, -stone
  'wɪt|mən ['hw-], -mɑːʃ, -nɪ, -stəbl,
  -stəʊn
Whitsun 'wɪtsn ['hw-]
Whitsunday, -s ‚wɪt'sʌndɪ [‚hw-,
  -'sʌndeɪ, -sn'deɪ], -z
Whitsuntide, -s 'wɪtsntaɪd ['hw-], -z
Whittaker 'wɪtəkə* ['hw-, -tɪk-]
Whittier 'wɪtɪə* ['hw-]
Whittingeham(e) 'wɪtɪndʒəm ['hw-]
Whittington 'wɪtɪŋtən ['hw-]
whitt|le (W.), -les, -ling, -led 'wɪt|l
  ['hw-], -lz, -lɪŋ [-lɪŋ], -ld
Whitworth 'wɪtwɜːθ ['hw-, -wəθ]
whit|y, -iness 'waɪt|ɪ ['hw-], -ɪnɪs [-nəs]
whiz, -zes, -zing, -zed wɪz [hw-], -ɪz,
  -ɪŋ, -d
whizz (s. v.), -es, -ing, -ed wɪz [hw-],
  -ɪz, -ɪŋ, -d
who (interrogative) huː [also hʊ when
  followed by a word beginning with ə or
  unstressed ɪ]
who (relative) huː (normal form), hʊ
  (freq. weak form), uː, ʊ (occasional
  weak forms)
whoa wəʊ
who-dun-it, -s ‚huː'dʌnɪt, -s
whoe'er 'wɪtəkə* [hʊ'eə*]
whoever huː'evə* [hʊ'e-, occasionally
  uː-, ʊ- when closely connected to
  preceding word in the sentence]
whole, -ness həʊl, -nɪs [-nəs]
whole-hearted ‚həʊl'hɑːtɪd
whole-hog, -ger/s ‚həʊl'hɒg, -ə*/z
whole-meal 'həʊlmiːl
wholesale 'həʊlseɪl
wholesaler, -s 'həʊl‚seɪlə*, -z
wholesome, -st, -ly, -ness 'həʊlsəm, -ɪst,
  -lɪ, -nɪs [-nəs]
wholly 'həʊllɪ ['həʊlɪ]
whom huːm (normal form), hʊm
  (occasional weak form)
whomsoever ‚huːmsəʊ'evə*
whoop (s. v.), -s, -ing, -ed huːp, -s, -ɪŋ, -t
whoopee (s.) 'wʊpiː [-pɪ], (interj.)
  wʊ'piː
whooping-cough 'huːpɪŋkɒf [old-
  fashioned -kɔːf]
whop, -s, -ping/s, -ped wɒp [hw-], -s,
  -ɪŋ/z, -t
whopper, -s 'wɒpə* ['hw-], -z
whor|e (s. v.), -es, -ing, -ed; -edom/s
  hɔː* [hɔə*], -z, -rɪŋ, -d; -dəm/z
whoreson, -s 'hɔːsn ['hɔəsn], -z
whorl, -s, -ed wɜːl [hw-], -z, -d

whortle, -s 'wɜːtl ['hw-], -z
whortleberr|y, -ies 'wɜːtl‚ber|ɪ ['hw-,
  -bər|ɪ], -ɪz
whose (interrogative) huːz
whose (relative) huːz (normal form), uːz
  (occasional weak form)
whoso 'huːsəʊ
whosoever ‚huːsəʊ'evə*
why waɪ [hw-]
Whyle (surname) 'waɪlɪ ['hw-]
Whymper 'wɪmpə* ['hw-]
Whyte waɪt [hw-]
Whytt waɪt [hw-]
wick (W.), -s wɪk, -s
wicked, -est, -ly, -ness/es 'wɪkɪd, -ɪst,
  -lɪ, -nɪs/ɪz [-nəs/ɪz]
Wickens 'wɪkɪnz
wicker, -work 'wɪkə*, -wɜːk
wicket, -s 'wɪkɪt, -s
wicket-gate, -s 'wɪkɪtgeɪt, -s
wicket-keeper, -s 'wɪkɪt‚kiːpə*, -z
Wickham 'wɪkəm
Wickliffe 'wɪklɪf
Wicklow 'wɪkləʊ
wide (s. adj.), -s, -r, -st, -ly, -ness waɪd,
  -z, -ə*, -ɪst, -lɪ, -nɪs [-nəs]
wide-awake (s.), -s 'waɪdəweɪk, -s
wide-awake (adj.) ‚waɪdə'weɪk
Widecombe 'wɪdɪkəm
Widemouth 'wɪdməθ
wid|en, -ens, -ening, -ened 'waɪd|n, -nz,
  -nɪŋ [-nɪŋ], -nd
widespread 'waɪdspred [‚-'-]
widgeon, -s 'wɪdʒən [-dʒɪn], -z
widish 'waɪdɪʃ
Widnes 'wɪdnɪs
widow, -s, -ed 'wɪdəʊ, -z, -d
widower, -s 'wɪdəʊə*, -z
widowhood 'wɪdəʊhʊd
width, -s wɪtθ [wɪdθ], -s
wield, -s, -ing, -ed wiːld, -z, -ɪŋ, -ɪd
Wiesbaden 'viːs‚bɑːdn ['viːz‚b-, viːs'b-,
  viːz'b-] ('viːs‚baːdən, locally vis-
  'baːdən)
wi|fe, -ves waɪ|f, -vz
wife|hood, -less 'waɪf|hʊd, -lɪs [-ləs]
wife|like, -ly 'waɪf|laɪk, -lɪ
Wiffen 'wɪfn
wig (s. v.), -s, -ging, -ged wɪg, -z, -ɪŋ, -d
Wigan 'wɪgən
wigging (s.), -s 'wɪgɪŋ, -z
Wiggins 'wɪgɪnz
wigg|le (s. v.), -les, -ling, -led 'wɪg|l, -lz,
  -lɪŋ [-lɪŋ], -ld
wiggle-waggle 'wɪgl‚wægl
wiggly 'wɪglɪ [-glɪ]
wight (W.), -s waɪt, -s
wig-maker, -s 'wɪg‚meɪkə*, -z

Wigmore 'wɪgmɔː* [-mɔə*]
Wigram 'wɪgrəm
Wig|ton, -town 'wɪg|tən, -tən
wigwam, -s 'wɪgwæm, -z
Wilberforce 'wɪlbəfɔːs
Wilbraham 'wɪlbrəhæm [-brəm, -brɪəm]
Wil|bur, -bye 'wɪl|bə*, -bɪ
Wilcox 'wɪlkɒks
wild (s. adj. adv.) (W.), -s, -er, -est, -ly,
   -ness waɪld, -z, -ə*, -ɪst, -lɪ, -nɪs [-nəs]
Wilde waɪld
wildebeest, -s 'wɪldɪbiːst ['vɪldə-], -s
Wilder 'waɪldə*
wilderness, -es 'wɪldənɪs [-nəs], -ɪz
wildfire 'waɪld,faɪə*
wilding (W.), -s 'waɪldɪŋ, -z
wildish 'waɪldɪʃ
wil|e (s. v.) (W.), -es, -ing, -ed waɪl, -z,
   -ɪŋ, -d
Wilfred [-rid] 'wɪlfrɪd ['wʊl-]
wil|ful, -fullest, -fully, -fulness 'wɪl|fʊl,
   -fʊlɪst [-fəlɪst], -fʊlɪ [-fəlɪ], -fʊlnɪs
   [-nəs]
Wilhelmina (English name) ,wɪlhel-
   'miːnə, ,wɪlə'miːnə
Wilk|es, -ie, -ins wɪlk|s, -ɪ, -ɪnz
Wilkinson 'wɪlkɪnsn
Wilks wɪlks
will (s.) (W.), -s wɪl, -z
will (transitive v.), -s, -ing, -ed wɪl, -z,
   -ɪŋ, -d
will (auxil. v.) wɪl (strong form), l
   (normal weak form), wəl, əl (occasional weak forms)
Willard 'wɪlɑːd [-ləd]
Willcocks [-cox] 'wɪlkɒks
Willes wɪlz
Willesden 'wɪlzdən
William, -s, -son 'wɪljəm, -z, -sn
Willie 'wɪlɪ
willing (adj.) (W.), -ly, -ness 'wɪlɪŋ, -lɪ,
   -nɪs [-nəs]
Willing|don, -ton 'wɪlɪŋ|dən, -tən
Willis 'wɪlɪs
will-o'-the-wisp, -s ,wɪləðə'wɪsp [-əð'w-,
   '----], -s
Willoughby 'wɪləbɪ
will|ow (s. v.), -ows, -owing, -owed;
   -owy 'wɪl|əʊ, -əʊz, -əʊɪŋ, -əʊd; -əʊɪ
willowherb 'wɪləʊhɜːb
willow-pattern 'wɪləʊ,pætən
willow-wren, -s 'wɪləʊren, -z
will-power, -s 'wɪl,paʊə*, -z
Wills wɪlz
Will|steed, -y 'wɪl|stiːd, -ɪ
willy-nilly ,wɪlɪ'nɪlɪ
Wilma 'wɪlmə
Wilmcote 'wɪlmkəʊt

Wilmington 'wɪlmɪŋtən
Wilmot(t) 'wɪlmət [-mɒt]
Wilmslow 'wɪlmzləʊ [locally 'wɪmzləʊ]
Wilna 'vɪlnə
Wilno (in Ontario) 'wɪlnəʊ
Wilsden 'wɪlzdən
Wilshire 'wɪlʃə* [-,ʃɪə*]
Wilson 'wɪlsn
wilt (from will, auxil. v.) wɪlt (normal
   form), əlt, lt (occasional weak forms)
wilt (v.), -s, -ing, -ed wɪlt, -s, -ɪŋ, -ɪd
Wilton, -s 'wɪltən, -z
Wilts. wɪlts
Wiltshire 'wɪlt-ʃə* [-,ʃɪə*]
wil|y, -ier, -iest, -iness 'waɪl|ɪ, -ɪə*, -ɪɪst,
   -ɪnɪs [-ɪnəs]
wimble (W.), -don 'wɪmbl, -dən
Wimborne 'wɪmbɔːn [-bɔən]
Wimms wɪmz
Wimperis 'wɪmpərɪs
wimple, -s 'wɪmpl, -z
Wimpole 'wɪmpəʊl
win (s. v.), -s, -ning, won, winner/s
   wɪn, -z, -ɪŋ, wʌn, 'wɪnə*/z
winc|e, -es, -ing, -ed wɪns, -ɪz, -ɪŋ, -t
wincey 'wɪnsɪ
winceyette ,wɪnsɪ'et
winch, -es wɪntʃ, -ɪz
Win|chelsea, -chester 'wɪn|tʃlsɪ [-siː],
   -tʃɪstə*
Winch|field, -ilsea, -more 'wɪntʃ|fiːld,
   -lsɪ [-siː], -mɔː* [-mɔə*]
wind (s.) (air blowing), -s wɪnd [in
   poetry sometimes waɪnd], -z
wind (v.) (go round, roll round), -s, -ing,
   wound waɪnd, -z, -ɪŋ, waʊnd
wind (v.) (blow horn), -s, -ing, -ed
   waɪnd, -z, -ɪŋ, -ɪd
wind (v.) (detect by scent, exhaust
   breath), -s, -ing, -ed wɪnd, -z, -ɪŋ, -ɪd
windage 'wɪndɪdʒ
windbag, -s 'wɪndbæg, -z
windbreak, -s, -er/s 'wɪndbreɪk, -s,
   -ə*/z
windcheater, -s 'wɪnd,tʃiːtə*, -z
wind-chest, -s 'wɪndtʃest, -s
wind-cone, -s 'wɪndkəʊn, -z
Winder, -mere 'wɪndə*, -,mɪə*
windfall, -s 'wɪndfɔːl, -z
Windham 'wɪndəm
   Note.—The place in Vermont, U.S.A.,
   is called locally 'wɪndhæm.
windhover, -s 'wɪnd,hɒvə*, -z
winding (in furnaces) 'wɪndɪŋ
winding (s. adj.), -s, -ly 'waɪndɪŋ, -z,
   -lɪ
winding-sheet, -s 'waɪndɪŋʃiːt, -s
winding-up ,waɪndɪŋ'ʌp

wind-instrument, -s 'wɪndˌɪnstrʊmənt
[-trəm-], -s
wind-jammer, -s 'wɪndˌdʒæmə*, -z
windlass, -es 'wɪndləs, -ɪz
Windley 'wɪndlɪ
windmill, -s 'wɪnmɪl [-ndm-], -z
window, -s 'wɪndəʊ, -z
window-box, -es 'wɪndəʊbɒks, -ɪz
window-cleaner, -s 'wɪndəʊˌkliːnə*, -z
window-dressing 'wɪndəʊˌdresɪŋ
window-pane, -s 'wɪndəʊpeɪn, -z
window-seat, -s 'wɪndəʊsiːt, -s
windpipe, -s 'wɪndpaɪp, -s
windrow, -s 'wɪndrəʊ, -z
wind-screen, -s, -wiper/s 'wɪndskriːn,
-z, -ˌwaɪpə*/z
Windsor 'wɪnzə*
wind-swept 'wɪndswept
Windus 'wɪndəs
windward (W.) 'wɪndwəd
wind|y, -ier, -iest, -ily, -iness 'wɪnd|ɪ,
-ɪə* [-jə*], -ɪɪst [-jɪst], -ɪlɪ [-əlɪ], -ɪnɪs
[-ɪnəs]
wine, -s waɪn, -z
wine-bibber, -s 'waɪnˌbɪbə*, -z
wine-bottle, -s 'waɪnˌbɒtl, -z
wine-cellar, -s 'waɪnˌselə*, -z
wineglass, -es 'waɪnglɑːs, -ɪz
wineglassful, -s 'waɪnglɑːsˌfʊl, -z
wine-press, -es 'waɪnpres, -ɪz
wine-skin, -s 'waɪnskɪn, -z
wing (s. v.) (W.), -s, -ing, -ed, -er/s
wɪŋ, -z, -ɪŋ, -d, -ə*/z
wing-commander, -s 'wɪŋkəˌmɑːndə*, -z
wing-covert, -s ˌwɪŋ'kʌvət, -s
winged (adj.) wɪŋd
-winged -wɪŋd
Wingfield 'wɪŋfiːld
wingspan 'wɪŋspæn
Winifred 'wɪnɪfrɪd
wink (s. v.) (W.), -s, -ing, -ed, -er/s
wɪŋk, -s, -ɪŋ, -t [wɪŋt], -ə*/z
Winkfield 'wɪŋkfiːld
Winkie 'wɪŋkɪ
winkle (W.), -s 'wɪŋkl, -z
Winnepesaukee ˌwɪnəpə'sɔːkɪ
winner, -s 'wɪnə*, -z
Winnie 'wɪnɪ
winning (s. adj.) (W.), -s, -ly 'wɪnɪŋ, -z,
-lɪ
winning-post, -s 'wɪnɪŋpəʊst, -s
Winnipeg 'wɪnɪpeg
winn|ow, -ows, -owing, -owed, -ower/s
'wɪn|əʊ, -əʊz, -əʊɪŋ, -əʊd, -əʊə*/z
winnowing-fan, -s 'wɪnəʊɪŋfæn, -z
Winslow 'wɪnzləʊ
winsome, -ly, -ness 'wɪnsəm, -lɪ, -nɪs
[-nəs]

Winstanley (in Greater Manchester)
'wɪnstənlɪ [wɪn'stænlɪ, esp. by new-
comers], (surname) 'wɪnstənlɪ, wɪn-
'stænlɪ
Winston 'wɪnstən
wint|er (s. v.) (W.), -ers, -ering, -ered
'wɪnt|ə*, -əz, -ərɪŋ, -əd
Winterbourne 'wɪntəbɔːn [-bɔən,
-ˌbʊən]
wintertime 'wɪntətaɪm
Winterton 'wɪntətən
Winton 'wɪntən
Wintour 'wɪntə*
wintr|y, -iness 'wɪntr|ɪ, -ɪnɪs [-ɪnəs]
winy 'waɪnɪ
wip|e (s. v.), -es, -ing, -ed, -er/s waɪp,
-s, -ɪŋ, -t, -ə*/z
wir|e (s. v.), -es, -ing, -ed 'waɪə*, -z,
-rɪŋ, -d
wire-cutter, -s 'waɪəˌkʌtə*, -z
wire|draw, -draws, -drawing, -drew,
-drawn, -drawer/s 'waɪədrɔː, -drɔːz,
-ˌdrɔːɪŋ, -druː, -drɔːn, -ˌdrɔːə*/z
wire-haired 'waɪəheəd
wireless (s. adj.), -es 'waɪəlɪs [-ləs], -ɪz
wire-pull|er/s, -ing 'waɪəˌpʊl|ə*/z, -ɪŋ
wire-worm, -s 'waɪəwɜːm, -z
wiring 'waɪərɪŋ
wir|y, -ier, -iest, -iness 'waɪər|ɪ, -ɪə*,
-ɪɪst, -ɪnɪs [-ɪnəs]
wis wɪs
Wisbech 'wɪzbiːtʃ
Wisconsin wɪs'kɒnsɪn
wisdom 'wɪzdəm
wise (s. adj.) (W.), -r, -st, -ly, -ness
waɪz, -ə*, -ɪst, -lɪ, -nɪs [-nəs]
wiseacre, -s 'waɪzˌeɪkə*, -z
wisecrack, -s 'waɪzkræk, -s
Wiseman 'waɪzmən
wish (s. v.), -es, -ing, -ed, -er/s wɪʃ, -ɪz,
-ɪŋ, -t, -ə*/z
wishbone, -s 'wɪʃbəʊn, -z
wish|ful, -fully, -fulness 'wɪʃ|fʊl, -fʊlɪ
[-fəlɪ], -fʊlnɪs [-nəs]
wishing-bone, -s 'wɪʃɪŋbəʊn, -z
wish-wash 'wɪʃwɒʃ
wishy-washy 'wɪʃɪˌwɒʃɪ [ˌ--'--]
wisp, -s wɪsp, -s
wist wɪst
Wist|ar, -er 'wɪst|ə*, -ə*
wistaria, -s wɪ'steərɪə, -z
wisteria, -s wɪ'stɪərɪə, -z
wist|ful, -fully, -fulness 'wɪst|fʊl, -fʊlɪ
[-fəlɪ], -fʊlnɪs [-nəs]
wit (s. v.), -s wɪt, -s
witch (s. v.), -es, -ing/ly, -ed wɪtʃ, -ɪz,
-ɪŋ/lɪ, -t
witchcraft 'wɪtʃkrɑːft

551

witch-doctor, -s 'wɪtʃˌdɒktə*, -z
witch-elm, -s 'wɪtʃelm [ˌ-'-], -z
witcher|y, -ies 'wɪtʃər|ɪ, -ɪz
witch-hazel, -s ˈwɪtʃˌheɪzl [ˌ-'--], -z
witch-hunt, -s 'wɪtʃhʌnt, -s
witching 'wɪtʃɪŋ
witena gemot, -s ˌwɪtɪnəgɪ'məʊt
 [-tən-, -gə'm-], -s
with wɪð [occasionally also wɪθ, esp.
 before words beginning with voiceless
 consonants]
 Note.—In the N. of England the word
 is generally pronounced wɪθ in all
 positions.
withal wɪ'ðɔ:l
Witham (surname) 'wɪðəm, (river in
 Lincolnshire) 'wɪðəm, (town in Essex)
 'wɪtəm
with|draw, -draws, -drawing, -drew,
 -drawn wɪð|'drɔ: [wɪθ|'d-], -'drɔ:z,
 -'drɔ:ŋ, -'dru:, -'drɔ:n
withdrawal, -s wɪð'drɔ:əl [wɪθ'd-], -z
withe, -s wɪθ, -s [wɪð, waɪð, -z]
with|er (W.), -ers, -ering/ly, -ered
 'wɪð|ə*, -əz, -ərɪŋ/lɪ, -əd
withers (s.) (W.) 'wɪðəz
with|hold, -holds, -holding, -held,
 -holden, -holder/s wɪð|'həʊld
 [wɪθ|'h-], -'həʊldz, -'həʊldɪŋ, -'held,
 -'həʊldən, -'həʊldə*/z
within wɪ'ðɪn [wɪð'ɪn]
without wɪ'ðaʊt [wɪð'aʊt]
with|-stand, -stands, -standing, -stood
 wɪð|'stænd [wɪθ|'s-], -'stændz,
 -'stændɪŋ, -'stʊd
with|y, -ies 'wɪð|ɪ, -ɪz
witless, -ly, -ness 'wɪtlɪs [-ləs], -lɪ, -nɪs
 [-nəs]
Witley 'wɪtlɪ
witness (s. v.), -es, -ing, -ed 'wɪtnɪs
 [-nəs], -ɪz, -ɪŋ, -t
witney (W.) 'wɪtnɪ
-witted -'wɪtɪd [-ˌwɪtɪd]
Wittenberg 'vɪtnbɜ:g [-beəg, old-
 fashioned 'wɪtnbɜ:g] ['vɪtənberk)
witticism, -s 'wɪtɪsɪzəm, -z
wittingly 'wɪtɪŋlɪ
witt|y, -ier, -iest, -ily, -iness 'wɪt|ɪ, -ɪə*,
 -ɪɪst, -ɪlɪ [-əlɪ], -ɪnɪs [-ɪnəs]
Witwatersrand (usual pronunciation in
 England) wɪt'wɔ:təzrænd ['wɪtˌw-],
 (pronunciations of English-speaking
 South Africans) 'wɪtˌwɑ:təz'rɑ:nd
 [-'rɑ:nt, 'vɪtˌvɑ:təz'rɒnt, '-ˌ--ˌ-]
 (Afrikaans 'vɪtˌvɑtərs'rɑnt)
wiv|e, -es, -ing, -ed waɪv, -z, -ɪŋ, -d
Wiveliscombe 'wɪvəlɪskəm [locally also
 'wɪlskəm]

Wivelsfield 'wɪvəlzfi:ld
wivern, -s 'waɪvən [-vɜ:n], -z
wives (plur. of wife, and from v. wive)
 waɪvz
wizard (s. adj.), -s, -ry 'wɪzəd, -z, -rɪ
wizen, -ed 'wɪzn, -d
w-ness 'dʌblju:nɪs [-jʊ-, -nəs]
wo wəʊ
woad wəʊd
wo-back ˌwəʊ'bæk
wobb|le (s. v.), -les, -ling, -led, -ler/s
 'wɒb|l, -lz, -lɪŋ [-lɪŋ], -ld, -lə*/z
 [-lə*/z]
wobb|ly, -liness 'wɒb|lɪ [-lɪ], -lɪnɪs
 [-lɪnɪs, -nəs]
Woburn (Abbey) 'wu:bɜ:n [-bən], (street
 and square in London) 'wəʊbən [-bɜ:n]
 (village) 'wəʊbən, 'wu:-
Wodehouse 'wʊdhaʊs
Woden 'wəʊdn
woe, -s wəʊ, -z
woebegone 'wəʊbɪˌgɒn
woe|ful, -fully, -fulness 'wəʊ|fʊl, -fʊlɪ
 [-fəlɪ], -fʊlnɪs [-nəs]
woke, -n (from wake) wəʊk, -ən
Woking, -ham 'wəʊkɪŋ, -əm
Wolborough 'wɒlbərə
Wolcot(t) 'wʊlkət
wold, -s wəʊld, -z
Woldingham 'wəʊldɪŋəm
Woledge 'wʊlɪdʒ
wol|f (s.) (W.), -ves wʊl|f, -vz
wolf (v.), -s, -ing, -ed wʊlf, -s, -ɪŋ, -t
wolf-cub, -s 'wʊlfkʌb, -z
Wolfe wʊlf
Wolfenden 'wʊlfəndən
Wolff wʊlf, vɒlf
wolf-hound, -s 'wʊlfhaʊnd, -z
wolfish, -ly, -ness 'wʊlfɪʃ, -lɪ, -nɪs [-nəs]
wolfram (W.), -ite 'wʊlfrəm, -aɪt
wolf-skin, -s 'wʊlfskɪn, -z
Wollaston 'wʊləstən
Wollaton (Nottinghamshire) 'wʊlətn
Wollstonecraft 'wʊlstənkrɑ:ft
Wolmer 'wʊlmə*
Wolseley, -s 'wʊlzlɪ, -z
Wolsey 'wʊlzɪ
Wolsingham 'wɒlsɪŋəm
Wolstanton 'wʊlstæntən [locally 'wʊl-
 stən]
Wolstenholme 'wʊlstənhəʊm
Wolverhampton 'wʊlvəˌhæmptən
 [ˌwʊlvə'h-]
wolverine, -s 'wʊlvəri:n, -z
Wolverton 'wʊlvətn [-tən]
wolves (plur. of wolf) wʊlvz
woman, women 'wʊmən, 'wɪmɪn
woman-hater, -s 'wʊmənˌheɪtə*, -z

womanhood 'wʊmənhʊd
womanish, -ly, -ness 'wʊmənɪʃ, -lɪ, -nɪs [-nəs]
womaniz|e [-is|e], -es, -ing, -ed, -er/s 'wʊmənaɪz, -ɪz, -ɪŋ, -d, -ə*/z
womankind ˌwʊmən'kaɪnd ['---]
womanlike 'wʊmənlaɪk
womanl|y, -iness 'wʊmənl|ɪ, -ɪnɪs [-məs]
womb, -s wuːm, -z
wombat, -s 'wɒmbæt [-bət], -s
Wombwell (*place in South Yorkshire*) 'wʊmwel [-wəl], (*surname*) 'wʊmwəl, 'wʌm-, 'wɒm-
women (*plur. of* **woman**) 'wɪmɪn
womenfolk 'wɪmɪnfəʊk
won (*from* **win**) wʌn
wond|er, -ers, -ering|ly, -ered, -erer/s 'wʌnd|ə*, -əz, -ərɪŋ/lɪ, -əd, -ərə*/z
wonder|ful, -fully, -fulness 'wʌndə|fʊl, -flɪ [-fʊlɪ, -fəlɪ], -fʊlnɪs [-nəs]
Wonderland 'wʌndəlænd
wonderment 'wʌndəmənt
wonder-worker, -s 'wʌndəˌwɜːkə*, -z
wondrous, -ly, -ness 'wʌndrəs, -lɪ, -nɪs [-nəs]
wonk|y, -ier, -iest, -ily, -iness 'wɒŋk|ɪ, -ɪə*, -ɪɪst, -ɪlɪ [-əlɪ], -ɪnɪs [-məs]
wont (*s. adj.*), **-ed** wəʊnt, -ɪd
won't (*s. adj.*), **-ed** wəʊnt [*also* wəʊn *when not final, also* wəʊmp *before the sounds* p, b, m, *and* wəʊŋk *before* k, g]
woo, -s, -ing, -ed, -er/s wuː, -z, -ɪŋ ['wʊɪŋ], -d, -ə*/z [wʊə*/z]
Wooburn 'wuːbɜːn
wood (**W.**), **-s, -ed** wʊd, -z, -ɪd
woodbind 'wʊdbaɪnd
woodbine (**W.**), **-s** 'wʊdbaɪn, -z
woodblock, -s 'wʊdblɒk, -s
Woodbridge 'wʊdbrɪdʒ
Woodbury 'wʊdbərɪ
wood-carv|er/s, -ing 'wʊdˌkɑːv|ə*/z, -ɪŋ
woodchuck, -s 'wʊdtʃʌk, -s
woodcock (**W.**), **-s** 'wʊdkɒk, -s
woodcut, -s 'wʊdkʌt, -s
wood-cutter, -s 'wʊdˌkʌtə*, -z
wooden, -ly, -ness 'wʊdn, -lɪ, -nɪs [-nəs]
wooden-headed 'wʊdnˌhedɪd [ˌ--'--]
Wood|ford, -house 'wʊd|fəd, -haʊs
woodland, -s 'wʊdlənd, -z
wood-|louse, -lice 'wʊd|laʊs, -laɪs
wood|man (**W.**), **-men** 'wʊd|mən, -mən
wood-nymph, -s 'wʊdnɪmf, -s
wood-pavement ˌwʊd'peɪvmənt ['-ˌ--]
woodpecker, -s 'wʊdˌpekə*, -z
wood-pigeon, -s 'wʊdˌpɪdʒɪn [-dʒən], -z
Woodroffe 'wʊdrɒf, -rʌf
Woodrow 'wʊdrəʊ

woodruff (**W.**), **-s** 'wʊdrʌf, -s
Woods wʊdz
Woodside ˌwʊd'saɪd ['--]
Wood|stock, -ward 'wʊd|stɒk, -wəd
wood-wind, -s 'wʊdwɪnd, -z
woodwork 'wʊdwɜːk
wood|y, -ier, -iest, -iness 'wʊd|ɪ, -ɪə*, -ɪɪst, -ɪnɪs [-məs]
woof, -s (*weaving*) wuːf, -s (*dog's bark*) wʊf
Woof (*surname*) wʊf
Wookey 'wʊkɪ
wool, -s wʊl, -z
Wooldridge 'wʊldrɪdʒ
Woolf wʊlf
Woolfardisworthy (*near Bideford, Devon*) 'wʊlzərɪ [wʊl'fɑːdɪsˌwɜːðɪ], (*near Crediton, Devon*) wʊl'fɑːdɪsˌwɜːðɪ
wool-gathering 'wʊlˌgæðərɪŋ
Woollard 'wʊlɑːd
woollen 'wʊlən [-lɪn]
Woolley 'wʊlɪ
Woolliams 'wʊljəmz
wooll|y (*s. adj.*), **-ies, -ier, -iest, -iness** 'wʊl|ɪ, -ɪz, -ɪə*, -ɪɪst, -ɪnɪs [-məs]
woolly-headed 'wʊlɪˌhedɪd [ˌ--'--]
Wooln|er, -ough 'wʊln|ə*, -əʊ
woolsack 'wʊlsæk
woolsey (**W.**) 'wʊlzɪ
Woolwich 'wʊlɪdʒ [-ɪtʃ]
woolwork 'wʊlwɜːk
Woolworth 'wʊlwəθ [-wɜːθ]
Woomera 'wʊmərə ['wuː-]
Woorstead 'wʊstɪd [-təd]
Woosley 'wuːzlɪ
Wooster 'wʊstə*
Wootton 'wʊtn
Worcester, -shire 'wʊstə*, -ʃə* [-ˌʃɪə*]
Worcs. wɜːks
word (*s. v.*), **-s, -ing/s, -ed; -less** wɜːd, -z, -ɪŋ/z, -ɪd; -lɪs [-ləs]
word-book, -s 'wɜːdbʊk, -s
word-formation 'wɜːdfɔːˌmeɪʃn
word-painting 'wɜːdˌpeɪntɪŋ
word-perfect ˌwɜːd'pɜːfɪkt
word-picture, -s 'wɜːdˌpɪktʃə*, -z
word-splitting 'wɜːdˌsplɪtɪŋ
Wordsworth 'wɜːdzwəθ [-wɜːθ]
Wordsworthian wɜːdz'wɜːðjən [-ðɪən]
word|y, -ier, -iest, -ily, -iness 'wɜːd|ɪ, -ɪə* [-jə*], -ɪɪst [-jɪst], -ɪlɪ [-əlɪ], -ɪnɪs [-məs]
wore (*from* **wear**) wɔː* [wɔə*]
work, -s, -ing/s, -ed, -er/s; -able/ness wɜːk, -s, -ɪŋ/z, -t, -ə*/z; -əbl/nɪs [-nəs]
workaday 'wɜːkədeɪ

work-bag, -s 'wɜːkbæg, -z
work-basket, -s 'wɜːkˌbɑːskɪt, -s
workbook, -s 'wɜːkbʊk, -s
work-box, -es 'wɜːkbɒks, -ɪz
work-day, -s 'wɜːkdeɪ, -z
workhou|se, -ses 'wɜːkhaʊ|s, -zɪz
Workington 'wɜːkɪŋtən
workless 'wɜːklɪs [-ləs]
work|man (W.), -men; -manlike
  'wɜːk|mən, -mən; -mənlaɪk
workman|ly, -ship 'wɜːkmən|lɪ, -ʃɪp
work-people 'wɜːkˌpiːpl
work-room, -s 'wɜːkrʊm [-ruːm], -z
workshop, -s 'wɜːkʃɒp, -s
work-shy 'wɜːkʃaɪ
Worksop 'wɜːksɒp [-səp]
work-table, -s 'wɜːkˌteɪbl, -z
world, -s wɜːld, -z
worldling, -s 'wɜːldlɪŋ, -z
worldl|y, -ier, -iest, -iness 'wɜːldl|ɪ, -ɪə*
  [-jə*], -ɪst [-jɪst], -ɪnɪs [-ɪnəs]
worldly-minded ˌwɜːldlɪˈmaɪndɪd ['--ˌ--]
worldly-wise ˌwɜːldlɪˈwaɪz
world-wide 'wɜːldwaɪd [also ˌ-'- when
  not attributive]
worm (s. v.), -s, -ing, -ed wɜːm, -z, -ɪŋ,
  -d
Worman 'wɔːmən
worm-cast, -s 'wɜːmkɑːst, -s
worm-eaten 'wɜːmˌiːtn
worm-gear, -s 'wɜːmˌgɪə*, -z
worm-hole, -s 'wɜːmhəʊl, -z
Worms (German city) vɔːmz [wɜːmz]
  (vɔrms)
wormwood (W.) 'wɜːmwʊd
worm|y, -iness 'wɜːm|ɪ, -ɪnɪs [-ɪnəs]
worn (from wear) wɔːn
worn-out ˌwɔːn'aʊt ['-- when attribu-
  tive]
Worple, -sdon 'wɔːpl, -zdən
Worrall 'wʌrəl, wɒrəl
worr|y (s. v.), -ies, -ying/ly, -ied, -ier/s
  'wʌr|ɪ, -ɪz, -ɪŋ/lɪ, -ɪd, -ɪə*/z
Worsborough 'wɜːzbərə
worse wɜːs
wors|en, -ens, -ening, -ened 'wɜːs|n,
  -nz, -nɪŋ [-ņɪŋ], -nd
Worsfold 'wɜːsfəʊld, 'wɔːzfəʊld
worship (s. v.) (W.), -s, -ping, -ped,
  -per/s 'wɜːʃɪp, -s, -ɪŋ, -t, -ə*/z
worship|ful, -fully, -fulness 'wɜːʃɪp|fʊl,
  -fʊlɪ [-fəlɪ], -fʊlnɪs [-nəs]
Worsley (surname) 'wɜːslɪ, 'wɜːzlɪ,
  (place near Manchester) 'wɜːslɪ
Worsnop 'wɜːznəp
worst (s. adj. v.), -s, -ing, -ed wɜːst, -s,
  -ɪŋ, -ɪd
Worstead 'wʊstɪd [-təd]

worsted (s.) (yarn, cloth) 'wʊstɪd [-təd]
worsted (v.) (from worst) 'wɜːstɪd
Worswick (surname) 'wɜːsɪk
wort, -s wɜːt, -s
worth (W.), -s wɜːθ, -s
Worthing, -ton 'wɜːðɪŋ, -tən
worthless, -ly, -ness 'wɜːθlɪs [-ləs], -lɪ,
  -nɪs [-nəs]
worth|y (s. adj.), -ies, -ier, -iest, -ily,
  -iness 'wɜːð|ɪ, -ɪz, -ɪə* [-jə*], -ɪɪst
  [-jɪst], -ɪlɪ [-əlɪ], -ɪnɪs [-ɪnəs]
Wortley 'wɜːtlɪ
wot wɒt
Wotherspoon 'wɒðəspuːn
Wotton 'wɒtn, 'wʊtn
  *Note.—The place in Buckingham-
  shire is called 'wʊtn.*
would (from will) wʊd **(strong form),**
  wəd, əd, d **(weak forms)**
would-be 'wʊdbiː [-bɪ]
wouldn't 'wʊdnt
wound (s. v.), -s, -ing, -ed wuːnd, -z, -ɪŋ,
  -ɪd
wound (from wind, v.) waʊnd
wove (from weave), -n wəʊv, -ən
wow, -s waʊ, -z
wrack, -s ræk, -s
wraith, -s reɪθ, -s
wrang|le, -les, -ling, -led, -ler/s 'ræŋg|l,
  -lz, -lɪŋ [-lɪŋ], -ld, -lə*/z [-lə*/z]
wrangler (candidate obtaining first class
  in mathematical tripos), -s 'ræŋglə*,
  -z
wrap (s. v.), -s, -ping/s, -ped ræp, -s,
  -ɪŋ/z, -t
wrapper, -s 'ræpə*, -z
wrasse, -s ræs, -ɪz
wrath rɒθ [rɔːθ]
Wrath (Cape) rɔːθ [in Scotland raθ, also
  rɑːθ, ræθ]
wrath|ful, -fully, -fulness 'rɒθ|fʊl
  ['rɔː-], -fʊlɪ [-fəlɪ], -fʊlnɪs [-nəs]
Wratislaw (English surname) 'rætɪslɔː
Wraxall 'ræksɔːl
Wray reɪ
wreak, -s, -ing, -ed, -er/s riːk, -s, -ɪŋ, -t,
  -ə*/z
wrea|th, -ths riː|θ, -ðz [-θs]
wreath|e, -es, -ing, -ed riːð, -z, -ɪŋ, -d
Wreay (in Cumbria) reɪ [locally rɪə]
wreck (s. v.), -s, -ing, -ed, -er/s; -age/s
  rek, -s, -ɪŋ, -t, -ə*/z; -ɪdʒ/ɪz
Wrekin 'riːkɪn
wren (W.), -s ren, -z
wrench (s. v.), -es, -ing, -ed rentʃ, -ɪz,
  -ɪŋ, -t
Wrenn ren

wrest, -s, -ing, -ed rest, -s, -ɪŋ, -ɪd
wrest|le, -les, -ling, -led, -ler/s 'res|l,
  -lz, -lɪŋ [-lɪŋ], -ld, -lə*/z [-lə*/z]
wretch, -es retʃ, -ɪz
wretched, -ly, -ness 'retʃɪd, -lɪ, -nɪs
  [-nəs]
Wrexham 'reksəm
wrigg|le, -les, -ling, -led, -ler/s 'rɪg|l,
  -lz, -lɪŋ [-lɪŋ], -ld, -lə*/z [-lə*/z]
wright (W.), -s raɪt, -s
Wrigley 'rɪglɪ
wring, -s, -ing, wrung rɪŋ, -z, -ɪŋ, rʌŋ
wrink|le, -les, -ling, -led 'rɪŋk|l, -lz, -lɪŋ
  [-lɪŋ], -ld
wrinkly 'rɪŋklɪ
Wriothesley 'raɪəθslɪ
wrist, -s rɪst, -s
wristband, -s 'rɪstbænd, -z
wristlet, -s 'rɪstlɪt [-lət], -s
wrist-watch, -es 'rɪstwɒtʃ, -ɪz
writ (s.), -s rɪt, -s
writ (=written) rɪt
writ|e, -es, -ing/s, wrote, written,
  writer/s raɪt, -s, -ɪŋ/z, rəʊt, 'rɪtn,
  'raɪtə*/z
writh|e, -es, -ing, -ed raɪð, -z, -ɪŋ, -d
writing (s.), -s 'raɪtɪŋ, -z
writing-case, -s 'raɪtɪŋkeɪs, -ɪz
writing-desk, -s 'raɪtɪŋdesk, -s
writing-paper 'raɪtɪŋˌpeɪpə*
writing-table, -s 'raɪtɪŋˌteɪbl, -z
written-off ˌrɪtn'ɒf [old-fashioned -'ɔːf]
Wroclaw (formerly Breslau) 'vrɒtslɑːf
  [-æf, -tswɑːf]
wrong (s. adj. v.) (W.), -s; -ly, -ness;
  -ing, -ed rɒŋ, -z; -lɪ, -nɪs [-nəs]; -ɪŋ, -d
wrong-doer, -s ˌrɒŋ'duə* [-'duːə*,
  'rɒŋˌduə*, 'rɒŋˌduːə*], -z
wrong-doing ˌrɒŋ'duːɪŋ [-'duɪŋ, 'rɒŋ-
  ˌduːɪŋ, -ˌduɪŋ]
wrong|ful, -fully, -fulness 'rɒŋ|fʊl, -fʊlɪ
  [-fəlɪ], -fʊlnɪs [-nəs]
wrongheaded, -ly, -ness ˌrɒŋ'hedɪd, -lɪ,
  -nɪs [-nəs]
Wrose rəʊz, rəʊs
wrote (from write) rəʊt
wroth rəʊθ [rɔːθ, rɒθ]

Wrotham (in Kent) 'ruːtəm
Wrottesley 'rɒtslɪ
wrought rɔːt
wrought-|iron, -up ˌrɔːt|'aɪən, -'ʌp
Wroxham 'rɒksəm
wrung (from wring) rʌŋ
W.R.V.S. ˌdʌbljuːɑːviː'es [-jʊɑː-]
wr|y, -ier [-yer], -iest [-yest], -yly,
  -yness r|aɪ, -aɪə*, -aɪɪst, -aɪlɪ, -aɪnɪs
  [-aɪnəs]
wryneck, -s 'raɪnek, -s
Wrythe raɪð
Wulf wʊlf
Wulfila 'wʊlfɪlə
Wulfstan 'wʊlfstən
Wurlitzer, -s 'wɜːlɪtsə*, -z
Württemberg 'vɜːtəmbeəg ['wɜːtəm-
  bɜːg] ('vʏrtəmberk)
Wuthering 'wʌðərɪŋ
W.V.S. ˌdʌbljuːviː'es [-jʊ-]
Wyandotte, -s 'waɪəndɒt, -s
Wyat(t) 'waɪət
Wych waɪtʃ, wɪtʃ
wych-elm, -s ˌwɪtʃ'elm ['—], -z
Wycherley 'wɪtʃəlɪ
wych-hazel, -s 'wɪtʃheɪzl [ˌ-'—], -z
Wyclif(fe) 'wɪklɪf
Wyclif(f)ite, -s 'wɪklɪfaɪt, -s
Wycombe 'wɪkəm
Wye waɪ
Wygram 'waɪgrəm
Wykeham, -ist/s 'wɪkəm, -ɪst/s
Wyld(e) waɪld
Wyl(l)ie 'waɪlɪ
Wylly 'waɪlɪ
Wyman 'waɪmən
Wymondham (in Norfolk) 'wɪməndəm
  [locally 'wɪndəm], (in Leicestershire)
  'waɪməndəm
Wyndham 'wɪndəm
Wynn(e) wɪn
Wynyard 'wɪnjəd [-jɑːd]
Wyoming waɪ'əʊmɪŋ
Wysard 'waɪzɑːd
Wytham 'waɪtəm
Wythenshawe 'wɪðənʃɔː
wyvern (W.), -s 'waɪvən [-vɜːn], -z

X

X (*the letter*), **-'s** eks, -ız
Xanadu 'zænədu:
Xanthipp|e, -us zæn'θɪp|ɪ [gz-, -n'tɪ-],
-əs
Xanthus 'zænθəs ['gz-]
Xavier 'zævɪə* ['zeɪv-, -vjə*] (xa'bjer)
xebec, -s 'zi:bek, -s
Xenia 'zenɪə [gz-, ks-, -eɪn-, -njə]
xenogamy zi:'nɒgəmɪ [gz-, zɪ-]
xenon 'zi:nɒn ['gz-]
xenophobe, -s 'zenəfəʊb ['gz-, -nəʊf-],
-z
xenophobia ˌzenə'fəʊbjə [ˌgz-, -nəʊ'f-,
-bɪə]
Xenophon 'zenəfən ['gz-]
xerography ˌzɪə'rɒgrəfɪ [ze'r-]

xerox (*s. v.*), **-es, -ing, -ed** 'zɪərɒks, -ız,
-ɪŋ, -t
Xerxes 'zɜ:ksi:z ['gz-]
Xhosa 'kɔ:sə ['kəʊsə, kl-] (˥hɔ:sa)
xi (*Greek letter*), **-'s** saɪ [gzaɪ, zaɪ], -z
Xmas 'krɪsməs [-stm-]
X-ray (*s. v.*), **-s, -ing, -ed** ˌeks'reɪ ['--],
-z, -ɪŋ, -d
xylem 'zaɪləm [-lem]
xylograph, -s 'zaɪləgrɑ:f ['gz-, -ləʊg-,
-græf], -s
xylograph|er/s, -y zaɪ'lɒgrəf|ə*/z [gz-],
-ɪ
xylonite 'zaɪlənaɪt ['gz-, -ləʊn-]
xylophone, -s 'zaɪləfəʊn ['gz-, 'zɪl-], -z
xylose 'zaɪləʊs [-ləʊz]

556

Y

Y *(the letter)*, **-'s** waɪ, -z
yacht *(s. v.)*, **-s, -ing, -ed** jɒt, -s, -ɪŋ, -ɪd
yachts|man, -men 'jɒts|mən, -mən
yah jɑ:
yahoo, **-s** jə'hu: [jɑ:'h-], -z
Yahveh 'jɑ:veɪ [jɑ:'veɪ, 'jɑ:və]
yak, **-s** jæk, -s
Yakutsk jæ'kʊtsk [jɑ:'k-, jə'k-]
  (ji'kutsk)
Yalding *(surname)* 'jældɪŋ, *(place name)*
  'jɔ:ldɪŋ
Yale jeɪl
Yalta 'jæltə
yam, **-s** jæm, -z
Yangtse-Kiang ˌjæŋtsɪ'kjæŋ [-kɪ'æŋ]
yank **(Y.), -s, -ing, -ed** jæŋk, -s, -ɪŋ, -t
  [-jæŋt]
Yankee, **-s** 'jæŋkɪ, -z
yap, **-s, -ping, -ped** jæp, -s, -ɪŋ, -t
yappy 'jæpɪ
yard, **-s** jɑ:d, -z
yardarm, **-s** 'jɑ:dɑ:m, -z
Yardley 'jɑ:dlɪ
yard-stick, **-s** 'jɑ:dstɪk, -s
Yare *(in Norfolk)* jeə*, *(in the Isle of
  Wight)* jɑ:*
Yarico 'jærɪkəʊ
Yarmouth 'jɑ:məθ
yarn *(s. v.)*, **-s, -ing, -ed** jɑ:n, -z, -ɪŋ, -d
yarrow **(Y.)** 'jærəʊ
yashmak, **-s** 'jæʃmæk, -s
yataghan, **-s** 'jætəgən, -z
Yate, **-s** jeɪt, -s
Yatman 'jætmən
yaw *(s. v.)*, **-s, -ing, -ed** jɔ:, -z, -ɪŋ, -d
yawl, **-s** jɔ:l, -z
yawn *(s. v.)*, **-s, -ing/ly, -ed** jɔ:n, -z,
  -ɪŋ/lɪ, -d
yaws jɔ:z
yclept ɪ'klept
ye *(you)* ji: *(normal form)*, jɪ *(occasional
  weak form)*
ye *(the)* ji: [*or as* the, *q.v.*]
yea jeɪ
Yeading 'jedɪŋ
yeah jeə
Yealm jæm
Yealmpton 'jæmptən
Yeames ji:mz

yean, **-s, -ing, -ed** ji:n, -z, -ɪŋ, -d
yeanling, **-s** 'ji:nlɪŋ, -z
year, **-s, -ly** jɪə* [jɜ:*], -z, -lɪ
year-book, **-s** 'jɪəbʊk ['jɜ:b-], -s
yearling, **-s** 'jɪəlɪŋ ['jɜ:l-], -z
yearn, **-s, -ing/s, -ed** jɜ:n, -z, -ɪŋ/z, -d
yeast, **-y, -iness** ji:st, -ɪ, -ɪnɪs [-ɪnəs]
Yeat(e)s jeɪts
Yeatman 'ji:tmən, 'jeɪtmən, 'jetmən
Yeddo *(old name of Tokyo)* 'jedəʊ
Yehudi je'hu:dɪ [jɪ'h-, jə'h-]
yelk jelk
yell *(s. v.)* **(Y.), -s, -ing, -ed** jel, -z, -ɪŋ,
  -d
yellow, **-s, -ed** 'jeləʊ, -z, -d
yellow-ammer, **-s** 'jeləʊˌæmə*, -z
yellow-band 'jeləʊbænd
yellow-hammer, **-s** 'jeləʊˌhæmə*, -z
yellowish, **-ness** 'jeləʊɪʃ, -nɪs [-nəs]
yellowness 'jeləʊnɪs [-nəs]
yellowplush 'jeləʊplʌʃ
Yellowstone 'jeləʊstəʊn [-stən]
yellowy 'jeləʊɪ
yelp *(s. v.)*, **-s, -ing, -ed** jelp, -s, -ɪŋ, -t
Yemen, **-i, -is** 'jemən, -ɪ, -ɪz
yen, **-s** jen, -z
Yeo jəʊ
Yeoburgh 'jɑ:bərə
yeo|man, -men 'jəʊ|mən, -mən
yeoman|ly, -ry 'jəʊmən|lɪ, -rɪ
Yeomans 'jəʊmənz
Yeovil 'jəʊvɪl
Yerkes *(American name)* 'jɜ:ki:z
yes jes [jeə]
yes|-man, -men 'jes|mæn, -men
yesterday 'jestədɪ [-deɪ, ˌjestə'deɪ]
yet jet
Yetholm 'jetəm
yeti, **-s** 'jetɪ, -z
yew, **-s** ju:, -z
Yg(g)drasil 'ɪgdræsl ['ɪgdrəsɪl]
Y-fronts 'waɪfrʌnts
Y-gun, **-s** 'waɪgʌn, -z
Yiddish 'jɪdɪʃ
yield *(s. v.)*, **-s, -ing/ly, -ed** ji:ld, -z,
  -ɪŋ/lɪ, -ɪd
y-ness 'waɪnɪs [-nəs]
yobo, **-s** 'jɒbəʊ, -z
yod, **-s** jɒd, -z

yod|el (*s. v.*), **-els, -el(l)ing, -el(l)ed** 'jəʊd|l ['jɒd-], -lz, -lɪŋ [-əlɪŋ], -ld

yog, -a, -i/s, -ism 'jəʊg, -ə, -ɪ/z, -ɪzəm

yogh(o)urt 'jɒgət ['jəʊg-, -gɜ:t, -gʊət]

yo-ho jəʊ'həʊ

yoick, -s, -ing, -ed jɔɪk, -s, -ɪŋ, -t

yoicks (*interj.*) jɔɪks

yok|e (*s. v.*), **-es, -ing, -ed** jəʊk, -s, -ɪŋ, -t

yokel, -s 'jəʊkl, -z

Yokohama ˌjəʊkəʊ'hɑ:mə

yolk, -s, -y jəʊk, -s, -ɪ

Yom Kippur ˌjɒm'kɪpə* [-kɪ'pʊə*]

yon(d) jɒn(d)

yonder 'jɒndə*

Yonge jʌŋ

yore jɔ:* [jɔə*]

Yorick 'jɒrɪk

York, -shire jɔ:k, -ʃə* [-ˌʃɪə*]

Yorke jɔ:k

yorker, -s 'jɔ:kə*, -z

Yorkist, -s 'jɔ:kɪst, -s

Yorks. jɔ:ks

Yorkshire|man, -men 'jɔ:kʃə|mən, -mən [-men]

Yoruba 'jɒrʊbə ['jəʊ-]

Yosemite jəʊ'semɪtɪ

Yost, -s jəʊst, -s

yotization [-isa-], -s ˌjəʊtaɪ'zeɪʃn [ˌjɒt-, -tɪ'z-], -z

yotiz|e [-is|e], **-es, -ing, -ed** 'jəʊtaɪz ['jɒt-], -ɪz, -ɪŋ, -d

you ju: (*normal form*), jʊ (*freq. weak form*), jə (*occasional weak form*)

Note 1.—*Sometimes when* **you** *is weakly stressed and is preceded by a word normally ending in* d, *the two words are joined closely together as if they formed a single word with the 'affricate' sound* dʒ *linking the two parts. Thus* did you *is often pronounced* 'dɪdʒu: (*or* 'dɪdʒʊ), *and* **behind you** bɪ'haɪndʒu: [-dʒʊ]

Similarly when the preceding word normally ends in t; *i.e.* hurt you *is sometimes pronounced* 'hɜ:tʃu: *or* 'hɜ:tʃʊ, *and* don't you know *as* ˌdəʊntʃu:'nəʊ [-tʃʊ-] *or* ˌdəʊntʃə'nəʊ. *See also* what-you-may-call-it.

Note 2.—jʊ *occurs as a strong form in the expression* you are *when* are *has its weak form* ə*. You are *in this case is also written* you're. *For*

other variants used in this case see you're.

Youghal (*near Cork*) jɔ:l, (*on Lake Derg*) 'jɒkəl ['jɒxəl]

Youmans 'ju:mənz

young (*s. adj.*) (**Y.**), **-er, -est** jʌŋ, -gə*, -gɪst

Younger 'jʌŋə*, 'jʌŋgə*

Younghusband 'jʌŋˌhʌzbənd

youngish 'jʌŋɪʃ [-ŋgɪ-]

Youngman 'jʌŋmən

youngster, -s 'jʌŋstə* [-ŋks-], -z

younker, -s 'jʌŋkə*, -z

your jɔ:* [jɔə*, *rarely* jʊə*] (*normal forms*), jə* (*occasional weak form*)

you're (=you are) jʊə* [jɔə*, jɔ:*]

yours jɔ:z [jɔəz, *rarely* jʊəz]

yoursel|f, -ves jɔ:'sel|f, [jɔə's-, *rarely* ˌjʊə's-, jə's-], -vz

you|th, -ths ju:|θ, -ðz

youth|ful, -fully, -fulness 'ju:θ|fʊl, -fʊlɪ [-fəlɪ], -fʊlnɪs [-nəs]

you've (=you have) ju:v (*normal form*), jʊv, jəv (*occasional weak forms*)

yo-yo, -s 'jəʊjəʊ, -z

Ypres (*in Belgium*) 'i:prə ['i:pəz, *sometimes facetiously* 'aɪpəz, 'waɪpəz] (ipr)

Ypres (*tower at Rye*) 'i:prə ['i:preɪ, 'waɪpəz]

Note.—*The* 'Ypres Castle', *a public house near by, is called locally the* 'waɪpəz.

Ysaye ɪ'zaɪɪ [ɪ'zaɪ]

Yser (*in Belgium*) 'i:zə* (izɛ:r)

Ysolde ɪ'zɒldə

Ystradgynlais ˌɪstræd'gɪnlaɪs [ˌʌstræd-'gʌnlaɪs] (*Welsh* əstrad'gənlais)

Ythan 'aɪθən

ytterbium ɪ'tɜ:bɪəm [-bjəm]

yttrium 'ɪtrɪəm

Y-tube, -s 'waɪtju:b, -z

Yucatan ˌju:kə'tɑ:n [jʊk-, -'tæn]

yucca, -s 'jʌkə, -z

Yugoslav, -s ˌju:gəʊ'slɑ:v ['---], -z

Yugoslavia, -n ˌju:gəʊ'slɑ:vjə [-vɪə], -n

Yuill 'ju:ɪl ['jʊɪl]

yuk, -ky jʌk, -ɪ

Yukon 'ju:kɒn

Yule ju:l

yulery 'ju:lərɪ

Yuletide 'ju:ltaɪd

Yum-Yum ˌjʌm'jʌm

yupp|y, -ies 'jʌp|ɪ, -ɪz

Yussuf 'jʊsʊf [-səf]

Z

Z (the letter), -'s zed, -z
Zabulon 'zæbjʊlən [zə'bju:lən, zæ'bju:-]
Zacchaeus zæ'ki:əs [zə'k-, -'kɪəs]
Zachariah ˌzækə'raɪə
Zacharias ˌzækə'raɪəs [-'raɪæs]
Zachary 'zækərɪ
Zadok 'zeɪdɒk
Zagreb 'zɑ:greb ['zæ-]
Zair|e, -ean zɑ:'ɪə* [-'i:ə*], -ɪən
Zalmunna zæl'mʌnə
Zama 'zɑ:mə
Zambez|i, -ia zæm'bi:z|ɪ, -jə [-ɪə]
Zambia, -n 'zæmbɪə [-bjə], -n
Zambra 'zæmbrə
Zangwill 'zæŋgwɪl
zan|y, -ies 'zeɪn|ɪ, -ɪz
Zanzibar ˌzænzɪ'bɑ:*
Zarathustra ˌzærə'θu:strə [ˌzɑ:r-]
zareba, -s zə'ri:bə, -z
Zarephath 'zærɪfæθ [-ref-, -rəf-]
Zaria 'zɑ:rɪə
zeal zi:l
Zealand, -er/s 'zi:lənd, -ə*/z
zealot, -s, -ry 'zelət, -s, -rɪ
zealous, -ly, -ness 'zeləs, -lɪ, -nɪs [-nəs]
Zebah 'zi:bə
Zebedee 'zebɪdi:
zebra, -s 'zebrə ['zi:b-], -z
zebu, -s 'zi:bu:, -z
Zebub 'zi:bʌb [-bəb, rarely zɪ'bʌb]
Zebulon 'zebjʊlən [ze'bju:lən]
zed, -s zed, -z
Zedekiah ˌzedɪ'kaɪə
Zeeb 'zi:eb [zi:b]
Zeeland 'zeɪlənd ['zi:l-]
Zeiss, -es zaɪs, -ɪz
Zeitgeist 'tsaɪtgaɪst ['zaɪt-] ('tsaitgaist)
Zeller (wine) 'zelə*
Zelotes zi:'ləʊti:z [zɪ'l-]
zemindar, -s 'zemɪndɑ:*, -z
zemstvo, -s 'zemstvəʊ ('zjemstvə), -z
Zen zen
Zena 'zi:nə
zenana, -s ze'nɑ:nə [zɪ'n-], -z
Zend zend
zenith, -s 'zenɪθ ['zi:n-], -s
Zeno 'zi:nəʊ

Zenobia zɪ'nəʊbjə [ze'n-, -bɪə]
Zephaniah ˌzefə'naɪə
zephyr (Z.), -s 'zefə*, -z
zeppelin (Z.), -s 'zepəlɪn [-p|ɪn], -z
Zermatt 'zɜ:mæt
zero, -s 'zɪərəʊ, -z
zerography ˌzɪə'rɒgrəfɪ [ze'r-]
Zerubbabel zɪ'rʌbəbl [zə'r-, in Jewish usage also zɪ'ru:ˌbɑ:-, zə'ru:ˌbɑ:-]
Zeruiah ˌzerʊ'aɪə [-rjʊ-]
zest zest
zeta, -s 'zi:tə, -z
Zetland 'zetlənd
zeugma, -s 'zju:gmə ['zu:-], -z
Zeus zju:s
Zidon 'zaɪdn [-dɒn]
zigzag (s. v.), -s, -ging, -ged 'zɪgzæg, -z, -ɪŋ, -d
Ziklag 'zɪklæg
Zilliacus ˌzɪlɪ'ɑ:kəs, -'eɪkəs
Zimbabwe zɪm'bɑ:bwɪ [-'bæ-, -bweɪ]
Zimri 'zɪmraɪ
zinc (s. v.), -s, -king, -ked zɪŋk, -s, -ɪŋ, -t
zin(c)ky 'zɪŋkɪ
zinco, -s 'zɪŋkəʊ, -z
zincograph, -s 'zɪŋkəʊgrɑ:f [-græf], -s
zingar|o, -i 'zɪŋgər|əʊ, -i:
zinnia, -s 'zɪnjə [-nɪə], -z
Zion, -ism, -ist/s, -ward/s 'zaɪən, -ɪzəm, -ɪst/s, -wəd/z
zip, -s zɪp, -s
zip-fastener, -s 'zɪpˌfɑ:snə* [ˌ-'--], -z
zipper, -s 'zɪpə*, -z
Zippor 'zɪpɔ:* [zɪ'pɔ:*]
Zipporah zɪ'pɔ:rə [rarely 'zɪpərə]
zirconium zɜ:'kəʊnɪəm [zə'k-, -njəm]
zither, -s 'zɪðə* ['zɪθə*], -z
zloty, -s 'zlɒtɪ, -z
Zoar 'zəʊɑ:* ['zəʊə*]
zodiac 'zəʊdɪæk [-djæk]
zodiacal zəʊ'daɪəkl
Zoe 'zəʊɪ
zoetrope, -s 'zəʊɪtrəʊp, -s
zoic 'zəʊɪk
Zola 'zəʊlə
zollverein, -s 'tsɒlfəraɪn ['zɒlvəraɪn] ('tsɔlfər'ain), -z
zombie, -s 'zɒmbɪ, -z
zon|al, -ally 'zəʊn|l [-əl], -əlɪ

559

zon|e (*s. v.*), **-es, -ing, -ed; -eless** zəʊn,
-z, -ɪŋ, -d; -lɪs [-ləs]
zonked zɒŋkt
Zoo, **-s** zu:, -z
zoograph|er/s, **-y** zəʊ'ɒgrəf|ə*/z, -ɪ
zooks zu:ks
zoolite, **-s** 'zəʊəlaɪt ['zəʊəʊl-], -s
zoologic|al, **-ally** ˌzəʊə'lɒdʒɪk|l [zʊə'l-,
zʊ'l-], -əlɪ
Zoological Garden, **-s** zʊˌlɒdʒɪkl'gɑːdn
[zəʊəˌl-, zʊəˌl-, zəˌl-, zlˌɒdʒ-, ˌzlɒdʒ-,
-ɒdʒk-], -z
zoolog|ist/s, **-y** zəʊ'ɒlədʒ|ɪst/s [zʊ'ɒ-], -ɪ
zoom, **-s, -ing, -ed** zu:m, -z, -ɪŋ, -d
zoomorphic ˌzəʊə'mɔːfɪk
zo|on, **-a** 'zəʊ|ɒn, -ə
zoophyte, **-s** 'zəʊəfaɪt, -s
zoot, **-s** zu:t, -s
zootom|ist/s, **-y** zəʊ'ɒtəm|ɪst/s, -ɪ
Zophar 'zəʊfɑ:* [-fə*]
zoril, **-s** 'zɒrɪl, -z

Zoroaster ˌzɒrəʊ'æstə*
Zoroastrian, **-s, -ism** ˌzɒrəʊ'æstrɪən, -z,
-ɪzəm
zouave (Z.), **-s** zu:'ɑːv [zʊ'ɑːv, zwɑːv,
'zu:ɑːv], -z
Zouch(e) zu:ʃ
zounds zaʊndz [zu:ndz]
zucchini zʊ'ki:nɪ
Zuleika (*Persian name*) zu:'leɪkə [zʊ'l-,
-'laɪkə], (*as English personal name*)
zu:'leɪkə [zʊ'l-]
Zulu, **-s** 'zu:lu:, -z
Zululand 'zu:lu:lænd
Zürich 'zjʊərɪk ['zʊə-] ('tsy:riç)
Zutphen 'zʌtfən
Zuyder Zee ˌzaɪdə'zeɪ [-'zi:]
zwieback, **-s** 'zwi:bæk [-bɑːk]
('tsvi:bak), -s
zygoma, **-ta** zaɪ'gəʊmə [zɪ'g-], -tə
zymosis zaɪ'məʊsɪs [zɪ'm-]
zymotic zaɪ'mɒtɪk [zɪ'm-]

SUPPLEMENT

Abidjan ˌæbiːˈdʒɑːn
A-bomb, -s ˈeɪbɒm, -z
abseil, -s, -ing, -ed ˈæbseɪl [-saɪl], -z, -ɪŋ, -d
A.B.T.A. ˈæbtə
academe ˈækədiːm
A.C.A.S ˈeɪkæs
accidie ˈæksɪdɪ
actinism ˈæktɪnɪzəm
acupuncture ˈækjʊpʌŋktʃə*
adversarial ˌædvəˈseərɪəl [-vɜːˈs-]
advocaat ˈædvəkɑː [-kɑːt, ˌ--ˈ-]
aerobic, -s eəˈrəʊbɪk, -s
affect (*s.*) (*psychology*), **-s** ˈæfekt, -s
Afro ˈæfrəʊ
ag(e)ǁism, -ist/s ˈeɪdʒǀɪzəm, -ɪst/s
aggro ˈægrəʊ
agitprop ˈædʒɪtprɒp
aleatoric, -ally ˌælɪəˈtɒrɪk, -lɪ
allegedly əˈledʒɪdlɪ
allotrope, -s ˈælətrəʊp, -s
alopecia ˌæləˈpiːʃə [-ʃjə, -ʃɪə]
alphabeticizǀe [-isǀe], -es, -ing, -ed ˌælfəˈbetɪsaɪz, -ɪz, -ɪŋ, -d
alphanumeric ˌælfənjuːˈmerɪk [-njʊ-]
also-ran ˈɔːlsəʊræn
alternator, -s ˈɔːltəneɪtə*, -z
alveolate ælˈvɪələt [-lɪt, -leɪt]
Amadeus ˌæməˈdeɪəs
amalgamate, -s, -ing, -ed əˈmælgəmeɪt, -s, -ɪŋ, -ɪd
amino əˈmiːnəʊ
amniocentesis ˌæmnɪəʊsenˈtiːsɪs [-sən-]
amniotic ˌæmnɪˈɒtɪk
amoebiasis ˌæmɪˈbaɪəsɪs [ˌæmiː-]
amphetamine æmˈfetəmiːn [-mɪn]
anabolic ˌænəˈbɒlɪk
anaerobic ˌæneəˈrəʊbɪk
anaglyph, -s ˈænəglɪf, -s
androgen, -s ˈændrəʊdʒən, -z
androgenic ˌændrəʊˈdʒenɪk
anecdotage ˈænɪkˈdəʊtɪdʒ [-nek-]
anglophone (*adj.*) ˈæŋgləʊfəʊn
anorectic (*s.*), **-s** ˌænəˈrektɪk, -s

anosmia æˈnɒzmɪə [eɪ-, -ˈnɒs-]
anoxia æˈnɒksɪə [eɪ-]
anthologizǀe [-isǀe], -es, -ing, -ed ænˈθɒlədʒaɪz, -ɪz, -ɪŋ, -d
antibiosis ˌæntɪbaɪˈəʊsɪs
antigen, -s ˈæntɪdʒən [-dʒen], -z
antihero, -es ˈæntɪˌhɪərəʊ, -z
antimatter ˈæntɪˌmætə*
antinomian, -s ˌæntɪˈnəʊmɪən, -z
antinovel, -s ˈæntɪˌnɒvl, -z
antiperspirant, -s ˌæntɪˈpɜːspərənt, -s
anuresis ˌænjʊəˈriːsɪs [-jɔər-, -jɔːr-]
anuria ˌænjʊəˈrɪə [-jɔər-, -jɔːr-]
aperiodic ˌeɪpɪərɪˈɒdɪk [-ˌ--ˈ--]
aperiodicity ˌeɪpɪərɪəˈdɪsətɪ [-rɪɒˈd-, -ɪtɪ, -ˌ---ˈ---]
apéritif, -s əˌperəˈtiːf [-rɪˈt-, -ˈ---, -tɪf], -s
apolitical ˌeɪpəˈlɪtɪkl [-pʊˈl-, -tək-]
appeasement, -s əˈpiːzmənt, -s
applicator, -s ˈæplɪkeɪtə*, -z
après-ski ˌæpreɪˈskiː
arcane ɑːˈkeɪn
archetypal ˌɑːkɪˈtaɪpl [ˈ----]
Armagnac ˈɑːmənjæk
Art Deco ˌɑːt ˈdekəʊ
arthropod, -s ˈɑːθrəpɒd, -z
Art Nouveau ˌɑːt ˈnuːvəʊ [ˌɑːˈn-, ˌ--ˈ-]
ashram, -s ˈæʃrəm [-ræm], -z
assay (*s.*), **-s** əˈseɪ [ˈæseɪ], -z
assimilable əˈsɪmɪləbl [-məl-]
astrobiology ˌæstrəʊbaɪˈɒlədʒɪ
astronauticǀal, -s ˌæstrəʊˈnɔːtɪkǀl, -s
Athlestaneford (*Lothian*) ˈelʃənfəd
atonality ˌeɪtəʊˈnælətɪ [-ɪtɪ]
audiologǀist/s, -y ˌɔːdɪˈɒlədʒǀɪst/s, -ɪ
Auschwitz ˈaʊʃvɪts
autarchǀy, -ies ˈɔːtɑːkǀɪ, -ɪz
autoclavǀe (*s. v.*), **-es, -ing, -ed** ˈɔːtəʊkleɪv, -z, -ɪŋ, -d
autocross ˈɔːtəʊkrɒs
autocue, -s ˈɔːtəʊkjuː, -z
automatǀe, -es, -ing, -ed ˈɔːtəʊmeɪt, -s, -ɪŋ, -ɪd
avionic, -s ˌeɪvɪˈɒnɪk, -s
A.W.A.C.S. ˈeɪwæks

561

ayatollah, -s ˌaɪəˈtɒlə, -z
azodye, -s ˈeɪzəʊdaɪ [ˈæz-], -z

back|cloth/s,   -drop/s   ˈbækklɒθ/s,
-drɒp/s
backcomb, -s, -ing, -ed ˈbækkəʊm, -z,
-ɪŋ, -d
backspac|e, -es, -ing, -ed ˈbækspeɪs,
-ɪz, -ɪŋ, -t
Baha|i/s, -ism bəˈhaɪ/z, -ɪzəm
ballot-paper, -s ˈbælətˌpeɪpə*, -z
barcode, -s ˈbɑːkəʊd, -z
bargraph, -s ˈbɑːgrɑːf [-græf], -s
bar mitzvah ˌbɑːˈmɪtsvə
barre, -s ˈbɑː*, -z
beaux-arts ˌbəʊˈzɑː*
becquerel, -s ˌbekəˈrel [ˈ---, ˈbekərəl],
-z
beetling (adj.) ˈbiːtlɪŋ
Beijing ˌbeɪˈdʒɪŋ
bel canto ˌbelˈkæntəʊ
Belorussi|a, -an/s ˌbjeləʊˈrʌʃ|ə, -n/z
Bernoulli bɜːˈnuːlɪ [bə-]
beta-blocker, -s ˈbiːtəˌblɒkə*, -z
bicameral ˌbaɪˈkæmərəl
biker, -s ˈbaɪkə*, -z
bilharzia bɪlˈhɑːtsɪə [-hɑːz-]
bimetallic ˌbaɪmɪˈtælɪk [-meˈt-, -məˈt-]
biodegradable   ˌbaɪəʊdɪˈgreɪdəbl
[-diːˈg-]
bioengineering ˈbaɪəʊˌendʒɪˈnɪərɪŋ
bionic baɪˈɒnɪk
biops|y, -ies ˈbaɪˌɒps|ɪ, -ɪz
biorhythm, -s ˈbaɪəʊˌrɪðəm [ˌrɪθəm], -z
birdwatch|er/s,   -ing   ˈbɜːdˌwɒtʃ|ə*/z,
-ɪŋ
blackbox, -es ˌblækˈbɒks, -ɪz
Boolean ˈbuːlɪən [-ljən]
Bophuthatswana ˌbəʊpuːtɑːˈtswɑːnə
Borges ˈbɔːges (ˈborxes)
boules buːl
Boulez ˈbuːlez
bouquet(s) garni(s) ˌbuːkeɪ ˈgɑːniː
[ˌbʊk-, ---ˈ-]
bouzouki buːˈzuːkɪ
bowdlerism, -s ˈbaʊdlərɪzəm, -z
bradycardia ˌbrædɪˈkɑːdɪə
brassica, -s ˈbræsɪkə, -z
breadline ˈbredlaɪn
Brecht brekt (breçt)
breviary also ˈbrevjərɪ [-vɪə-]
burger, -s ˈbɜːgə*, -z

busbar, -s ˈbʌsbɑː*, -z
butterfat ˈbʌtəfæt
buzzword, -s ˈbʌzwɜːd, -z
Byelorussi|a, -an/s ˌbjeləʊˈrʌʃ|ə, -n/z
byte, -s baɪt, -s

cabriolet, -s ˌkæbrɪəʊˈleɪ, -z
cack-handed ˌkækˈhændɪd [ˈ---]
caftan, -s ˈkæftæn, -z
cagoule, -s kəˈguːl, -z
calash, -es kəˈlæʃ, -ɪz
calabrese ˈkæləbriːs
calendula, -s kəˈlendjʊlə [kæ-, -jəl-,
-dʒʊl-, -dʒəl-], -z
californium ˌkælɪˈfɔːnɪəm [-njəm]
call-up (s.) ˈkɔːlʌp
calypso (C.), -s kəˈlɪpsəʊ, -z
campsite, -s ˈkæmpsaɪt, -s
camshaft, -s ˈkæmʃɑːft, -s
candela, -s kænˈdelə, -z
cantilena ˌkæntɪˈleɪnə
capacit|ance,   -or/s   kəˈpæsɪt|əns,
-ə*/z
caravel, -s ˈkærəvel [ˌ--ˈ-], -z
carbonade, -s ˌkɑːbəˈnɑːd, -z
carburation ˌkɑːbəˈreɪʃn [-bjʊr-]
carcinogen, -s kɑːˈsɪnədʒən [-dʒen], -z
carcinogenic ˌkɑːsɪnəʊˈdʒenɪk
cardiogram, -s ˈkɑːdɪəʊ græm, -z
cardiograph, -s ˈkɑːdɪəʊ grɑːf [-græf], -s
cardiovascular   ˌkɑːdɪəʊˈvæskjʊlə*
[-kjə-]
carnet, -s ˈkɑːneɪ, -z
carob, -s ˈkærəb, -z
cash-dispenser, -s ˈkæʃdɪˌspensə*, -z
cashflow ˈkæʃfləʊ
cash-register, -s ˈkæʃˌredʒɪstə*, -z
cassis ˈkæsiːs [-ˈ-]
casuarina, -s ˌkæʒʊəˈriːnə [ˌkæzjʊə-],
-z
catatonia ˌkætəˈtəʊnɪə [-njə]
catatonic ˌkætəˈtɒnɪk
catchment, -s ˈkætʃmənt, -s
catchphrase, -s ˈkætʃfreɪz, -ɪz
catenative kəˈtiːnətɪv
catwalk, -s ˈkætwɔːk, -s
Ceefax ˈsiːfæks
cellphone, -s ˈselfəʊn, -z
centavo, -s senˈtɑːvəʊ, -z
centrifug|e, -es, -ing, -ed ˈsentrɪ-
fjuːdʒ, -ɪz, -ɪŋ, -d
cerium ˈsɪərɪəm

chainsaw, -s 'tʃeɪnsɔː, -z
changeover (s.), -s 'tʃeɪndʒəʊvə*, -z
chapatti, -s tʃə'pɑːtɪ [-'pæ-], -z (Hindi
 cəpati)
Charolais 'ʃærəleɪ
chatshow, -s 'tʃæt-ʃəʊ, -z
check-in (s.), -s 'tʃekɪn, -z
check-out (s.), -s 'tʃekaʊt, -s
checkpoint, -s 'tʃekpɔɪnt, -s
check-up (s.), -s 'tʃekʌp, -s
chef d'équipe ˌʃefdə'kiːp
chemotherapy ˌkiːməʊ'θerəpɪ [ˌkem-]
cheong-sam, -s ˌtʃɒŋ'sæm, -z
chiasma, -ta kaɪ'æzmə, -tə
chickpea, -s 'tʃɪkpiː, -z
chiropractic ˌkaɪrəʊ'præktɪk
chiropractor, -s 'kaɪrəʊˌpræktə*, -z
chutzpah 'hʊtspə
clinician, -s klɪ'nɪʃn, -z
clipboard, -s 'klɪpbɔːd, -z
clitic, -s 'klɪtɪk, -s
cloisonné klwɑː'zɒneɪ [ˌklɔɪzə'neɪ]
clon|e (s. v.), -es, -ing, -ed kləʊn, -z,
 -ɪŋ, -d
cloud-cuckoo-land ˌklaʊd'kʊkuːlænd
Clydesdale, -s 'klaɪdzdeɪl, -z
COBOL 'kəʊbɒl
coda, -s 'kəʊdə, -z
cod|e (v.), -es, -ing, -ed, -er/s kəʊd, -z,
 -ɪŋ, -ɪd, -ə*/z
Cogenhoe (N'hants.) 'kʊknəʊ
collectivity ˌkɒlek'tɪvətɪ [-ɪtɪ]
colosto|my, -mies kə'lɒstə|mɪ [kɒ'l-],
 -mɪz
colostrum kə'lɒstrəm
Comecon 'kɒmɪkɒn
come-uppance kʌm'ʌpəns [-pns, -pms]
commedia dell'arte kə ˌmeɪdɪə del'ɑːteɪ
commendatory alsoˌkɒmen'deɪtərɪ
commensal kə'mensl
commis-chef, -s 'kɒmɪʃef, -s
compact-disc, -s ˌkɒmpækt'dɪsk [kəm-
 ˌpæ-], -s
complex (adj.) 'kɒmpleks [kəm'pleks]
compos mentis ˌkɒmpəs'mentɪs [-pɒs-]
comsat (satellite), -s 'kɒmsæt, -s
concelebrat|e, -es, -ing, -ed kɒn'selɪ-
 breɪt, -s, -ɪŋ, -ɪd
concelebration, -s ˌkɒnselɪ'breɪʃn, -z
conceptualis|e, -es, -ing, -ed kən'sept-
 ʃʊəlaɪz [-tjʊəl-, -tjwəl-], -ɪz, -ɪŋ, -d
conceptualization [-isa-] kənˌseptʃʊə-
 laɪ'zeɪʃn [-tjʊəl-, -tjwəl-, -lɪ'z-]
conceptually kən'septʃʊəlɪ [-tjʊəl-,

 -tjwəl-]
conjunct (s.), -s 'kɒndʒʌŋkt, -s
conservationist, -s ˌkɒnsə'veɪʃnɪst
 [-ʃənɪst, -ʃnɪst], -s
construct (s.), -s 'kɒnstrʌkt, -s
consultan|cy, -cies kən'sʌltən|sɪ, -sɪz
contraflow (s. adj.) 'kɒntrəfləʊ [ˌ--'-]
co-set, -s 'kəʊset, -s
CoSIRA kə'saɪərə
co-star (s.), -s 'kəʊstɑː*, -z
co-star (v.), -s, -ring, -red, 'kəʊstɑː*, -z,
 -rɪŋ, -d [-'-]
Coughlan also 'kəʊlən
crouton, -s 'kruːtɒn [-tɔ̃ːŋ], -z
Crundale (Kent) 'krʌndl
curlicue, -s 'kɜːlɪkjuː, -z
cutback (s.), -s 'kʌtbæk, -s

Dacca 'dækə
dacha, -s 'dætʃə, -z
Dachau 'dæxaʊ ['dæk-] ('daxau)
dahl dɑːl
daiquiri 'daɪkɪrɪ ['dæk-]
Dali 'dɑːlɪ
data|bank, -base 'deɪtə|bæŋk, -beɪs
day-dream (v.), -s, -ing, -ed, -t 'deɪdriːm, -z, -ɪŋ, -dremt [-drempt, rarely
 -driːmd], -dremt [-drempt]
deactivat|e, -es, -ing, -ed di:'æktɪveɪt,
 -s, -ɪŋ, -ɪd
death-wish, -es 'deθwɪʃ, -ɪz
de-brief, -s, -ing, -ed ˌdi:'briːf, -s, -ɪŋ, -t
de-bug, -s, -ging, -ged ˌdi:'bʌg, -z, -ɪŋ,
 -d
decaffeinate, -d di:'kæfɪneɪt, -ɪd
decahedr|on, -ons, -a, -al ˌdekə'hi:-
 dr|ən [-'hed-, 'dekə̩ h-], -ənz, -ə, -l
declassi|fy, -fies, -fying, -fied ˌdi:-
 'klæsɪ|faɪ, -faɪz, -faɪɪŋ, -faɪd
decok|e, -es, -ing, -ed ˌdi:'kəʊk, -s, -ɪŋ,
 -t
decongestant, -s ˌdi:kən'dʒestənt, -s
deconstruction, -ism, -ist/s ˌdi:kən-
 'strʌkʃn, -ɪzəm, -ɪst/s
deepfr|y, -ies, -ying, -ied ˌdi:p'fr|aɪ,
 -aɪz, -aɪɪŋ, -aɪd
defecat|e, -es, -ing, -ed 'defəkeɪt ['di:-],
 -s, -ɪŋ, -ɪd
déjà vu ˌdeʒɑː'vjuː
demythologis|e, -es, -ing, -ed ˌdi:mɪ-
 'θɒlədʒaɪz [-maɪ'θ-], -ɪz, -ɪŋ, -d
deregulat|e, -es, -ing, -ed ˌdi:'regjʊleɪt
 [-gjəl-], -s, -ɪŋ, -ɪd

563

deregulation ˌdiːregjʊ'leɪʃn [-gjə'l-]
dermatosis ˌdɜːmə'təʊsɪs
desalinat|e, -es, -ing, -ed ˌdiː'sælmeɪt,
-s, -ɪŋ, -ɪd
desalination ˌdiːsælɪ'neɪʃn
destruct, -s, -ing, -ed dɪ'strʌkt, -s, -ɪŋ,
-ɪd
detumescence ˌdiːtju:'mesns [-tjʊ'm-]
deus ex machina ˌdeɪəseks'mækɪnə,
[ˌdeɪʊs-]
diastalsis ˌdaɪə'stælsɪs
dichromate, -s ˌdaɪ'krəʊmeɪt [daɪ'k-], -s
dinette, -s daɪ'net, -s
dip-stick, -s 'dɪpstɪk, -s
disassociat|e, -es, -ing, -ed ˌdɪsə'səʊ-
ʃɪeɪt [-əʊsɪ-, -əʊsj-, -ʃjeɪt], -s, -ɪŋ, -ɪd
discommod|e, -es, -ing, -ed
ˌdɪskə'məʊd, -z, -ɪŋ, -ɪd
disforest, -s, -ing, -ed ˌdɪs'fɒrɪst, -s, -ɪŋ,
-ɪd
disincentive, -s ˌdɪsɪn'sentɪv, -z
disunity dɪs'junətɪ [dɪs-, -ɪtɪ]
D.J., -s ˌdiː'dʒeɪ, -z
doberman (pinscher), -s 'dəʊbəmən
('pɪnʃə*), -z
doctoral 'dɒktərəl
doña 'dɒnjə
door|man, -men 'dɔː|mən, -mən
double-glazing ˌdʌbl'gleɪzɪŋ
double-jointed ˌdʌbl'dʒɔɪntɪd
dreadlocks 'dredlɒks
Dubonnet du:'bɒneɪ [dju:-]
Dubrovnik du:'brɒvnɪk
dunnage 'dʌnɪdʒ
dust-bowl, -s 'dʌsɪbəʊl, -z
dustsheet, -s 'dʌsɪ-ʃi:t, -s

earful 'ɪəfʊl
easeful 'i:zfʊl
eau de nil ˌəʊdə'ni:l
eboniz|e [-is|e], -es, -ing, -ed 'ebənaɪz,
-ɪz, -ɪŋ, -d
eccrine 'ekraɪn [-rɪn]
echolalia ˌekəʊ'leɪlɪə [-ljə]
econometric, -s ɪˌkɒnə'metrɪk, -s
ecosphere 'i:kəʊˌsfɪə* ['ekəʊ-]
ecosystem, -s 'i:kəʊˌsɪstəm [-tɪm], -z
ectomorph, -s 'ektəʊmɔ:f, -s
ectomorph|ic, -ism ˌektəʊ'mɔ:f|ɪk,
-ɪzəm
edentate i:'denteɪt
E.F.L. ˌi:ef'el

egomania ˌegəʊ'meɪnɪə [ˌi:g-, -njə]
egomaniac, -s ˌegəʊ'meɪnɪæk [ˌi:g-,
-njæk], -s
ego-trip, -s 'egəʊtrɪp ['i:g-], -s
einsteinium ˌeɪn'staɪnɪəm [-njəm]
electroencephalogram, -s ɪˌlektrəʊen-
'sefələʊgræm [-ɪn's-, -en'k-, -eŋ'k-,
-ɪn'k-, -ɪŋ'k-], -z
electroencephalograph, -s ɪˌlektrəʊen-
'sefələʊgrɑːf [-ɪn's-, -en'k-, -eŋ'k-,
-ɪn'k-, -ɪŋ'k-, -græf], -s
electropalatogram, -s ɪˌlektrəʊ'pæl-
ətəʊgræm, -z
electropalatography ɪ'lektrəʊˌpæl-
ə'tɒgrəfɪ
El Salvador el'sælvədɔ:*
eminence grise ˌemmɒns'gri:z
empathiz|e [is|e], -es, -ing, -ed
'empəθaɪz, -ɪz, -ɪŋ, -d
en bloc ˌɑ̃:m'blɒk [ˌɔ̃:m'blɒk, ˌɑ:m'blɒk,
ˌɒm'blɒk] (ɑ̃blɔk)
encapsulat|e, -es, -ing, -ed ɪn'kæpsjʊ-
leɪt [ɪŋ-, en-], -s, -ɪŋ, -ɪd
endogenous ɪn'dɒdʒənəs [en-]
endomorph, -s 'endəʊmɔ:f, -s
endomorph|ic, -ism ˌendəʊ'mɔ:f|ɪk,
-ɪzəm
en famille ˌɑ̃:nfæ'mi: [ˌɔ̃:n-, ˌɑ:n-, ˌɒn-]
(ɑ̃famij)
enfant terrible ˌɑ̃:nfɑ̃:nte'ri:bl [ˌɔ̃:n-,
ˌɑ:n-, ˌɒn-] (ɑ̃fɑ̃tɛribl)
en suite ˌɑ̃:n'swi:t [ˌɔ̃:n-, ˌɑ:n-, ˌɒn-]
(ɑ̃sɥit)
entrechat, -s 'ɑ̃:ntrəʃɑ: ['ɔ̃:n-, 'ɑ:n-,
'ɒn-], -z
environmentalist, -s ɪnˌvaɪərən'ment-
əlɪst [en-, -tlɪst], -s
ephedrine 'efədrɪn [-fɪd-, -ri:n, ɪ'fedrɪn]
epidural, -s ˌepɪ'djʊərəl, -z
epiphyte, -s 'epɪfaɪt, -s
epoxy ɪ'pɒksɪ ['epɒksɪ]
erbium 'ɜ:bɪəm [-bjəm]
escalope, -s e'skælɒp [ɪ's-, -ləp], -s
escargot, -s ɪ'skɑ:gəʊ [e's-], -z
espadrille, -s 'espədrɪl [ˌ--'-], -z
ethane 'i:θeɪn ['eθ-]
ethnocentr|ic, -ism ˌeθnəʊ'sentr|ɪk,
-ɪzəm
eupnœa ju:p'ni:ə [-nɪə]
Eurocrat, -s 'jʊərəʊkræt, -s
europium jʊə'rəʊpɪəm [-pjəm]
event (v.), -s, -ing, -ed, -er/s ɪ'vent, -s,
-ɪŋ, -ɪd, -ə*/z
exclave, -s 'ekskleɪv, -z

exclusivity ˌeksklu:'sɪvətɪ [-ɪtɪ]
exhibitionist, -s ˌeksɪ'bɪʃn̩ɪst [-ʃənɪ-, -ʃnɪ-], -s
exocrine 'eksəʊkraɪn
exogenous ɪk'sɒdʒənəs [ek-]
extragalactic ˌekstrəgə'læktɪk
extraterrestrial, -s ˌekstrətə'restrɪəl [-te'r-, -tɪ'r-], -z

fabliau, -x 'fæblɪəʊ, -z
face-sav|er, -ing 'feɪsˌseɪv|ə*, -ɪŋ
factoriz|e [is|e], -es, -ing, -ed 'fæktəraɪz, -ɪz, -ɪŋ, -d
failsafe 'feɪlseɪf
Falang|e, -ist/s fə'lændʒ, -ɪst/s
Falla 'fɑ:ljə ['fæ-], ('faʎa)
fall-guy, -s 'fɔ:lgaɪ, -z
fantasiz|e [-is|e], -es, -ing, -ed 'fæntəsaɪz, -ɪz, -ɪŋ, -d
Fauré 'fɔ:reɪ ['fɒr-]
Fauv|ism, -ist/s 'fəʊv|ɪzəm, -ɪst/s
fedora, -s fɪ'dɔ:rə, -z
fellatio fə'leɪʃɪəʊ [fe-, fɪ-]
fennec, -s 'fenek, -s
fenugreek 'fenu:gri:k
fermium 'fɜ:mɪəm [-mjəm]
Ferrari fə'rɑ:rɪ [fe-]
festschrift, -s 'fest-ʃrɪft ['feʃʃrɪft], -s
feta (cheese) 'fetə
fibreoptic, -s ˌfaɪbər'ɒptɪk [-bə'ɒp-], -s
fibrillation ˌfaɪbrɪ'leɪʃn [ˌfɪb-]
fibrin, -ous 'fɪbrɪn, -əs
fibrinogen fɪ'brɪnəʊdʒən [-dʒen]
fibroma, -ta faɪ'brəʊmə, -tə
fibrositis ˌfaɪbrə'saɪtɪs
fiesta, -s fɪ'estə, -z
filing-clerk, -s 'faɪlɪŋklɑ:k, -s
filmset, -s, -ting 'fɪlmset, -s, -ɪŋ
Filofax 'faɪləʊfæks
finagl|e, -es, -ing, -ed, -er/s fɪ'neɪgl, -z, -ɪŋ [-lɪŋ], -d, -|ə*/z [-lə*/z]
fin-de-siècle ˌfændə'sjekl [ˌfændə] (fɛ̃dəsjɛkl)
fixat|e, -es, -ing, -ed fɪk'seɪt, -s, -ɪŋ, -ɪd
flambé 'flɑ:mbeɪ (flɑ̃be)
flammable 'flæməbl
flash-bulb, -s 'flæʃbʌlb, -z
flat-mate, -s 'flætmeɪt, -s
flavin(e) 'fleɪvɪn
flexitime 'fleksɪtaɪm
flooz|y, -ies 'flu:z|ɪ, -ɪz

floribunda ˌflɒrɪ'bʌndə
flowchart, -s 'fləʊtʃɑ:t, -s
fluorinated 'flɔ:rɪneɪtɪd ['flɒr-, 'fluər-]
flyingsaucer, -s ˌflaɪŋ'sɔ:sə*, -z
flying squad, -s 'flaɪŋ skwɒd, -z
fly-past, -s 'flaɪpɑ:st, -s
flyweight, -s 'flaɪweɪt, -s
folic (acid) 'fɒlɪk
fondant, -s 'fɒndənt, -s
fondue, -s 'fɒndju: [-du:]
fontanel(le), -s ˌfɒntə'nel, -z
footage 'fʊtɪdʒ
foram|en, -ina fɒ'reɪm|en, -ɪnə
force|feed, -feeds, -feeding, -fed 'fɔ:sfi:d [ˌ-'-], -fi:dz, -fi:dɪŋ, -fed
forename, -s 'fɔ:neɪm, -z
foreplay 'fɔ:pleɪ
forint, -s 'fɒrɪnt, -s
forklift, -s 'fɔ:klɪft, -s
formaliz|e [-is|e], -es, -ing, -ed 'fɔ:məlaɪz [-m̩laɪ-], -ɪz, -ɪŋ, -d
formulaic ˌfɔ:mju'leɪɪk [-mjə'l-]
forthright 'fɔ:θraɪt
francium 'frænsɪəm [-sjəm]
francophone 'fræŋkəʊfəʊn
franglais 'frɑ̃:ŋgleɪ ['frɑ:ŋ-, 'frɒŋ-]
free-range ˌfri:'reɪndʒ ['--']
freestyle 'fri:staɪl
freight-liner, -s 'freɪtˌlaɪnə*, -z
frisson, -s 'fri:sɒn [-sɔ̃:n], -z
frontbencher, -s ˌfrʌnt'bentʃə*, -z
fructose 'frʌktəʊs [-təʊz]
full-scale ˌfʊl'skeɪl
funerary (adj.) 'fju:nərərɪ

gadolinium ˌgædəʊ'lmɪəm [-njəm]
galactose gə'læktəʊs [-təʊz]
gallium 'gælɪəm [-ljəm]
gamelan 'gæmələn
gamete, -s 'gæmi:t, -s
gangling 'gæŋglɪŋ
gas-chamber, -s 'gæsˌtʃeɪmbə*, -z
gas-holder, -s 'gæsˌhəʊldə*, -z
gastro-enteritis 'gæstrəʊˌentə'raɪtɪs
Gauguin 'gəʊgæn[-gæn] (gogɛ̃)
Gaulli|sm -ist/s 'gəʊlɪ|zəm, -st/s
gazpacho gə'spɑ:tʃəʊ
gem|ma, -mae 'dʒem|ə, -i:
gemmule, -s 'dʒemju:l, -z
gemstone, -s 'dʒemstəʊn, -z
geomagnetic ˌdʒi:əʊmæg'netɪk [ˌdʒɪ-, -məg-]

geomagnetism ˌdʒiːəʊˈmægnɪtɪzəm [ˌdʒɪ-, -nət-]
geopolitics ˌdʒiːəʊˈpɒlətɪks [ˌdʒɪ-, -lɪt-]
geoscience ˌdʒiːəʊˈsaɪəns [ˌdʒɪ-]
geotropic ˌdʒiːəʊˈtrɒpɪk [ˌdʒɪ-]
geotropism ˌdʒiːəʊˈtrəʊpɪzəm [ˌdʒɪ-]
gerbil, -s ˈdʒɜːbɪl [-bl], -z
germanium dʒɜːˈmeɪnɪəm [dʒɜˈm-, -njəm]
germicidal ˌdʒɜːmɪˈsaɪdl [ˈ----]
gerontocracy ˌdʒerənˈtɒkrəsɪ
glabrous ˈgleɪbrəs
glinch, -es glɪntʃ, -ɪz
glissand|o, -i, -os glɪˈsænd|əʊ, -iː, -əʊz
gloss|ectomy, -itis glɒ|ˈsektəmɪ, -ˈsaɪtɪs
glossolalia ˌglɒsəʊˈleɪlɪə [-ljə]
gnocchi ˈnɒkɪ
gluesniff|er/s, -ing ˈgluːsnɪfə*/z, -ɪŋ
glutamate ˈgluːtəmeɪt
goatskin, -s ˈgəʊtskɪn, -z
Goidelic gɔɪˈdelɪk
grammaticality grəˌmætɪˈkælətɪ [-ɪtɪ]
granny-flat, -s ˈgrænɪflæt, -s
Granta ˈgræntə [ˈgrɑː-]
grapheme, -s ˈgræfiːm, -z
graticule, -s ˈgrætɪkjuːl, -z
grommet, -s ˈgrɒmɪt [ˈgrʌ-], -s
Gromyko grəˈmiːkəʊ
grosgrain ˈgrəʊgreɪn
groundsheet, -s ˈgraʊndʃiːt, -s
groundspeed, -s ˈgraʊndspiːd, -z
grout, -s graʊt, -s
G-string, -s ˈdʒiːstrɪŋ, -z
guesstimate (s.), **-s** ˈgestɪmət [-mɪt, -meɪt], -s
guesstimat|e (v.), **-es, -ing, -ed** ˈgestɪmeɪt, -s, -ɪŋ, -d
guideline, -s ˈgaɪdlaɪn, -z
Gurkhali gɜːˈkɑːliː [gʊəˈk-]
Guyanese ˌgaɪəˈniːz

habit-forming ˈhæbɪtˌfɔːmɪŋ
haecceity hekˈsiːətɪ [-ɪtɪ]
haematolog|ist/s, -y ˌhiːməˈtɒlədʒ|-ɪst/s, -ɪ
haematoma, -s, -ta ˌhiːməˈtəʊmə, -əz, -tə
haemostasis ˌhiːməʊˈsteɪsɪs
haiku ˈhaɪkuː
hakim hɑːˈkiːm [ˈ--]

halal həˈlɑːl
half-cock ˌhɑːfˈkɒk
half-li|fe, -ves ˈhɑːflaɪ|f, -vz
half-wit, -s ˈhɑːfwɪt, -s
hallucinat|e, -es, -ing, -ed həˈluːsmeɪt, [-ljuː-], -s, -ɪŋ, -ɪd
hallucinogen, -s ˌhæluːˈsmədʒən [-dʒen, -ˈ----], -z
hallucinogenic həˌluːsməʊˈdʒenɪk
halogen ˈhælədʒen
hang-glid|er/s, -ing ˈhæŋˌglaɪdə*/z, -ɪŋ
hang-up, -s ˈhæŋʌp, -s
Hanuk(k)ah ˈhænuːkə [-nək-]
Harare həˈrɑːrɪ
hardback, -s ˈhɑːdbæk, -s
hardcore ˈhɑːdkɔː
hard-working ˌhɑːdˈwɜːkɪŋ
has-been, -s ˈhæzbiːn [-bɪn], -z
hassl|e, -es, -ing, -ed ˈhæsl, -z, -lɪŋ [-l̩ŋ], -d
hatch-back, -s ˈhætʃbæk, -s
hatcher|y, -ies ˈhætʃər|ɪ, -ɪz
hautboy (organ stop) ˈhɔːtbɔɪ
hearing-aid, -s ˈhɪərɪŋeɪd, -z
heart-attack, -s ˈhɑːtəˌtæk, -s
heartland, -s ˈhɑːtlænd, -z
heliotropic ˌhiːlɪəʊˈtrɒpɪk
heliotropism ˌhiːlɪəʊˈtrəʊpɪzəm
heliport, -s ˈhelɪpɔːt, -s
helminthiasis ˌhelmɪnˈθaɪəsɪs
hemiplegi|a, -c ˌhemɪˈpliːdʒɪ|ə, -k
Hepplewhite ˈheplwaɪt [-hwaɪt]
heptameter, -s hepˈtæmɪtə* [-mətə*], -z
herbalism ˈhɜːbəlɪzəm [-bl̩-]
herbicide, -s ˈhɜːbɪsaɪd, -z
herbivore, -s ˈhɜːbɪvɔː*, -z
hermeneutic, -s ˌhɜːməˈnjuːtɪk, -s
heteronym, -s ˈhetərəʊnɪm, -z
heteronymous ˌhetəˈrɒnɪməs [-nəm-]
Hinayana ˌhiːnəˈjɑːnə
hire-purchase ˌhaɪəˈpɜːtʃəs [-tʃɪs]
histogram, -s ˈhɪstəgræm, -z
historicism hɪˈstɒrɪsɪzəm
historicity ˌhɪstɒˈrɪsətɪ [-təˈr-, -ɪtɪ]
holism ˈhəʊlɪzəm [ˈhɒl-]
holistic həʊˈlɪstɪk [hɒˈl-]
holmium ˈhəʊlmɪəm [-mjəm]
hologram, -s ˈhɒləgræm, -z
holography hɒˈlɒgrəfɪ
holophrastic ˌhɒləˈfræstɪk
Hooray Henr|y, -ies ˌhuːreɪˈhenr|ɪ, -ɪz
hormonal hɔːˈməʊnl [-nəl]
horrendous, -ly hɒˈrendəs [həˈr-], -lɪ

hospitaliz|e [-is|e], **-es**, **-ing**, **-ed**
'hɒspɪtḷaɪz [-təl-], -ɪz, -ɪŋ, -d
hospitalisation ˌhɒspɪtḷaɪ'zeɪʃn [-təl-]
hostel|ler/s, **-ling** 'hɒstə|lə*/z, -lɪŋ
[-tḷɪŋ]
hotline, -s 'hɒtlaɪn, -z
housebound 'haʊsbaʊnd
houseplant, -s 'haʊsplɑ:nt, -s
hoverport, -s 'hɒvəpɔ:t, -s
hubris 'hju:brɪs
humanoid, -s 'hju:mənɔɪd, -z
humidif|y, **-ies**, **-ying**, **-ied**, **-ier/s**
hju:'mɪdɪfaɪ [hjʊ-], -z, -ɪŋ, -d, -ə*/z
hydroelectric ˌhaɪdrəʊ'lektrɪk
hyp|e, -es, -ing, -ed 'haɪp, -s, -ɪŋ, -t
hyperactive ˌhaɪpər'æktɪv [-pə'æk-]
hypercorrect ˌhaɪpəkə'rekt
hyperglycaem|ia, **-ic** ˌhaɪpəglaɪ-
'si:m|ɪə [-mjə], -ɪk
hypericum, -s haɪ'perɪkəm, -z
hypermarket, -s 'haɪpəˌmɑ:kɪt, -s
hypnotherap|ist/s, **-y** ˌhɪpnəʊ'θer-
əp|ɪst/s, -ɪ

IATA aɪ'ɑ:tə [i:'ɑ:tə]
icebox, -es 'aɪsbɒks, -ɪz
icepick, -s 'aɪspɪk, -s
iceskat|e, -es, -ing, -ed, -er/s 'aɪsskeɪt,
-s, -ɪŋ, -ɪd, -ə*/z
idée(s) fixe(s) ˌi:deɪ'fɪks (idefiks)
identikit, -s aɪ'dentɪkɪt, -s
ileostom|y, -ies, ˌɪlɪ'ɒstəm|ɪ. -ɪz
ileum, -s 'ɪlɪəm, -z
ill-founded ˌɪl'faʊndɪd
impala, -s ɪm'pɑ:lə, -z
impasse, -es 'æmpɑ:s [æm-, ɪm-, -pæs]
(ɛ̃pɑs)
imperfective ˌɪmpə'fektɪv
impermanent ˌɪm'pɜ:mənənt [ɪm'p-]
impermissible ˌɪmpə'mɪsəbl [-sɪb-]
implausib|le, -ly ˌɪm'plɔ:zəb|l [-zɪb-],
-lɪ
implausibility ɪmˌplɔ:zə'bɪlətɪ [-zɪb-,
-ɪtɪ, ˌ---'---]
imprecise ˌɪmprɪ'saɪs [-prə-]
imprecision ˌɪmprɪ'sɪʒn [-prə-]
improvisatory ˌɪmprə'vaɪzətərɪ [-'vɪz-,
ˌɪmprəvaɪ'zeɪtərɪ]
in-built ˌɪm'bɪlt ['--]
incognizan|ce, -t ɪm'kɒgnɪzən|s, -t
inconsonant ɪm'kɒnsənənt
index-linked ˌɪndeks'lɪŋkt [-'lɪŋt]

Indic 'ɪndɪk
indium 'ɪndɪəm [-djəm]
individuation 'ɪndɪˌvɪdʒʊ'eɪʃn [-ˌvɪdjʊ-]
in-filling 'ɪnˌfɪlɪŋ
in-flight ˌɪn'flaɪt
inflorescence ˌɪnflɔ:'resəns [-flɒ'r-,
-flə'r-]
info (s.) 'ɪnfəʊ
infra dig ˌɪnfrə'dɪg
ingroup, -s 'ɪngru:p ['ɪŋg-], -s
in-house 'ɪnhaʊs [-'-]
in-law, -s 'ɪnlɔ:, -z
innards 'ɪnədz
innovative 'ɪnəvətɪv [-veɪt-]
innumer|acy, -ate ɪ'nju:mər|əsɪ, -ət
[-rɪt]
inquiline, -s 'ɪnkwɪlaɪn ['ɪŋk-], -z
insecticidal ɪnˌsektɪ'saɪdl
insentient ˌɪn'senʃnt [-ʃɪənt, -ʃjənt]
in-service 'ɪnsɜ:vɪs
in situ ˌɪn'sɪtju:
insole, -s 'ɪnsəʊl, -z
institutionaliz|e [-is|e], **-es**, **-ing**, **-ed**
ˌɪnstɪ'tju:ʃən|aɪz [-ʃŋəl-, -ʃŋl-,
-ʃənəl-] -ɪz, -ɪŋ, -d
interdisciplinary ˌɪntə'dɪsɪplɪnərɪ [-sə-,
ˌ--ˈ--'---]
interface, -s 'ɪntəfeɪs, -ɪz
interstitial ˌɪntə'stɪʃl
intrauterine ˌɪntrə'ju:təraɪn
investigative ɪn'vestɪgətɪv [-geɪt-]
in vitro ɪn'vi:trəʊ

jacuzzi, -s dʒə'ku:zɪ [dʒæ'k-]
jaywalk, -s, -ing, -ed, -er/s 'dʒeɪwɔ:k,
-s, -ɪŋ, -t, -ə*/z
jellaba(h), -s 'dʒeləbə, -z
jet-lag, -ged 'dʒetlæg, -d
job-shar|e, -es, -ing, -ed 'dʒɒbʃeə*, -z,
-rɪŋ, -d
joie de vivre ˌʒwɑ:də'vi:vrə (ʒwa-
dəvivr)
Jordanian, -s dʒɔ:'deɪnjən [-nɪən], -z
jump-jet, -s 'dʒʌmpdʒet, -s
jump-leads 'dʒʌmpli:dz
jump-off (s.), **-s** 'dʒʌmpɒf, -s
jump-suit, -s 'dʒʌmpsu:t, [-sju:t], -s
jump|y, -ier, -iest 'dʒʌmp|ɪ, -ɪə*, -ɪɪst
juvenilia ˌdʒu:və'nɪlɪə [-vɪ'n-]

kabuki kə'buːkɪ
kaftan, -s 'kæftæn, -z
kagoule, -s kə'guːl, -z
kamikaze ˌkæmɪ'kɑːzɪ
Kampuchea, -n/s ˌkæmpʊ'tʃɪə [-puː-], -n/z
kapellmeister, -s kə'pelmaɪstə*, -z
kan-ji 'kændʒɪ ['kɑːn-]
kebab, -s kɪ'bæb [kə-], -z
kepi, -s 'keɪpɪ, -z
Khruschev krʊs'tʃʃf ['--]
kilovolt, -s 'kɪləʊvəʊlt [-vɒlt], -s
kilohertz 'kɪləʊhɜːts [-heəts]
kink|y, -ier, -iest 'kɪŋk|ɪ, -ɪə*, -ɪɪst
kitsch 'kɪtʃ
kiwifruit, -s 'kiːwiːfruːt [-wɪf-], -s
know-all, -s 'nəʊɔːl, -z
Koestler 'kɜːslə*
Kosygin kə'siːgɪn

lactose 'læktəʊs [-təʊz]
lamé 'lɑːmeɪ
lan (information technology) læn
Lancia, -s 'lɑːnsjə [-sɪə], -z
langue de chat ˌlɑːŋdə'ʃɑː [ˌlɒŋ-] (lãgdəʃa)
langur, -s 'læŋgə* [læŋ'gʊə*], -z
lanthanum 'lænθənəm
larynges læ'rɪndʒiːz [lə'r-]
lasagna [-ne] lə'zænjə [-'sæn-, -'sɑːn-]
laterite 'lætəraɪt
lawrencium lə'rensɪəm [-sjəm]
leather-jacket, -s 'leðəˌdʒækɪt, -s
leave-taking 'liːvˌteɪkɪŋ
le Carré lə 'kæreɪ
lecithin 'lesɪθɪn
legionnaire, -s ˌliːdʒə'neə* [-dʒŋ'eə*], -z
legroom 'legrʊm [-ruːm]
lehr, -s lɪə*, -z
length|man, -men 'leŋθ|mən [-ŋkθ-], -mən
Lenin|ism, -ist/s 'lenɪn|ɪzəm, -ɪst/s
lenticel, -s 'lentɪsel, -z
lexeme, -s 'leksiːm, -z
lexis 'leksɪs
libertarian, -s, -ism, ˌlɪbə'teərɪən, -z, -ɪzəm
lichee, -s 'laɪtʃi: [ˌ-'-, 'lɪtʃiː, 'liː-], -z
lifestyle, -s 'laɪfstaɪl, -s
life-support 'laɪfsəˌpɔːt [ˌ--'-]
light-bulb, -s 'laɪtbʌlb, -z

lighting-up-time ˌlaɪtɪŋ'ʌptaɪm
lilies-of-the-valley ˌlɪlɪzəvðə'vælɪ
lilo, -s 'laɪləʊ, -z
lily-of-the-valley ˌlɪlɪəvðə'vælɪ
linctus, -es 'lɪŋktəs ['lɪŋtəs], -ɪz
line-out, -s 'laɪnaʊt, -s
line-up, -s 'laɪnʌp, -s
lingam 'lɪŋgəm
lipase, -es 'laɪpeɪz, -ɪz
lipid, -s 'lɪpɪd, -z
lipoid 'lɪpɔɪd
Lippizaner, -s ˌlɪpɪ'zeɪnə*, -z (lɪpɪtsɑːnər)
liverwort, -s 'lɪvəwɜːt, -s
Llandaff also ˌlæn'dæf
logo, -s 'ləʊgəʊ, -z
longueur lɔ̃ːŋ'gɜː* [lɔːŋ-, lɒŋ-] (lɔ̃gœr)
lonicera, -s lɒ'nɪsərə, -z
lookalike, -s 'lʊkəˌlaɪk, -s
looseleaf ˌluːs'liːf ['--]
loosestrife 'luːsstraɪf
loquat, -s 'ləʊkwɒt ['lɒk-, -kwæt], -s
lovage 'lʌvɪdʒ
lowkey ˌləʊ'kiː
low-loader, -s ˌləʊ'ləʊdə*, -z
Luanda lʊ'ændə [luː'æ-]
Lucinda luː'sɪndə
Luddite, -s 'lʌdaɪt, -s
lutetium luː'tiːʃɪəm

macaque, -s mə'kɑːk [-'kæk], -s
macedoine 'mæsədwɑːn [-sɪd-]
machismo mə'tʃɪzməʊ [mə'kɪ-]
macho 'mætʃəʊ ['mækəʊ]
macrame mə'krɑːmɪ
macrobiotic, -s ˌmækrəʊbaɪ'ɒtɪk, -s
Mahabharata məˌhɑː'bɑːrətə
Mahayana məhɑː'jɑːnə
mahonia mə'həʊnɪə [mɑː-, -njə]
Mailer 'meɪlə*
mamba, -s 'mæmbə, -z
mandala, -s 'mændələ [mən'dɑːlə]
mangetout, -s ˌmɑ̃ːʒ'tuː [ˌmɒndʒ-], -z
manmade ˌmæn'meɪd
mansard, -s 'mænsɑːd, -z
mantissa, -s mæn'tɪsə, -z
Marcuse mɑː'kjuːz, mɑː'kuːzə
marimba, -s mə'rɪmbə, -z
marinat|e, -es, -ing, -ed 'mærɪneɪt, [-rən-], -s, -ɪŋ, -ɪd
mark-up, -s 'mɑːkʌp, -s
marmoreal mɑː'mɔːrɪəl

marshmallow, -s ˌmɑːʃˈmæləʊ, -z
martingale, -s ˈmɑːtɪŋgeɪl, -z
Maserati, -s ˌmæzəˈrɑːtɪ, -z
mastectom|y, -ies mæˈstektəm|ɪ, -ɪz
master-mind, -s, -ing, -ed ˈmɑːstə-
maɪnd, -z, -ɪŋ, -ɪd
masturbat|e, -es, -ing, -ed ˈmæstəbeɪt,
-s, -ɪŋ, -ɪd
masturbation ˌmæstəˈbeɪʃn
matrilineal ˌmætrɪˈlɪnɪəl
maximiz|e [-is|e], -es, -ing, -ed
ˈmæksɪmaɪz, -ɪz, -ɪŋ, -d
maximisation ˌmæksɪmaɪˈzeɪʃn
May|a, -an/s ˈmaɪ|ə, -ən/z
mechanistic ˌmekəˈnɪstɪk
Medawar ˈmedəwə*
melamine ˈmeləmiːn [-mɪn]
Melchior ˈmelkɪɔː*
meninges məˈnɪndʒiːz [mɪ-]
meniscus, -es məˈnɪskəs [mɪ-], -ɪz
mescalin(e) ˈmeskəlɪn
metastasis məˈtæstəsɪs
metro, -s ˈmetrəʊ, -z
microbiolog|ist/s, -y ˌmaɪkrəʊbaɪ-
ˈɒlədʒɪst/s, -ɪ
microcomputer, -s ˈmaɪkrəʊkəm-
ˌpjuːtə*, -z
microdot, -s ˈmaɪkrəʊdɒt, -s
microelectronics ˈmaɪkrəʊˌlek-
ˈtrɒnɪks [ˌel-, ˌiː-]
microfiche, -es ˈmaɪkrəʊfiːʃ, -ɪz
Microne|sia, -sian/s ˌmaɪkrəʊˈniː|zjə
[-zɪə, -ʒjə, -ʒɪə, -ʒə, -sjə, -sɪə, -ʃjə, -ʃɪə,
-ʃə], -zjən/z [-zɪən/z, -ʒjən/z, -ʒɪən/z,
-ʒn/z, -sjən/z, -sɪən/z, -ʃjən/z, -ʃɪən/z,
-ʃn/z]
microprocessor, -s ˈmaɪkrəʊˌprəʊ-
sesə*, -z
microwave, -s ˈmaɪkrəweɪv [-krəʊ-], -z
millisecond, -s ˈmɪlɪˌsekənd, -z
mimesis mɪˈmiːsɪs [maɪˈmiːsɪs]
mistrial, -s ˈmɪsˈtraɪəl, -z
mock-up, -s ˈmɒkʌp, -s
mod, -s mɒd, -z
monetar|ist, -ism ˈmʌnɪtər|ɪst, -ɪzəm
mononucleosis ˈmɒnəʊˌnjuːklɪˈəʊsɪs
monosaccharide, -s ˌmɒnəʊˈsækəraɪd, -z
monosodium ˌmɒnəˈsəʊdjəm [ˌmɒnəʊ-,
-dɪəm]
moray (eel), -s ˈmɒreɪ, -z
mornay ˈmɔːneɪ
mortician, -s mɔːˈtɪʃn, -z
motocross ˈməʊtəʊkrɒs
motoriz|e [-is|e], -es, -ing, -ed

ˈməʊtəraɪz, -ɪz, -ɪŋ, -d
multi-coloured ˈmʌltɪˌkʌləd
multi-media ˌmʌltɪˈmiːdjə [-dɪə]
multi-national ˌmʌltɪˈnæʃənl [-ʃnəl,
-ʃnl̩, -ʃnl, -ʃənəl]
multi-racial ˌmʌltɪˈreɪʃl [-ʃɪəl, -ʃjəl]
multi-storey ˌmʌltɪˈstɔːrɪ
mung (beans) mʌŋ
musculature ˈmʌskjʊlətʃə* [-kjəl-,
-ˌtjʊə*, -ˌtʃʊə*]
mustachio, -s məˈstɑːʃɪəʊ, -z
muzak ˈmjuːzæk
myelitis ˌmaɪəˈlaɪtɪs [maɪˈl-, maɪˈl-]
myoelastic ˌmaɪəʊɪˈlæstɪk [-ˈlɑːs-]

naevus, -es ˈniːvəs, -ɪz
Namibia, -n/s nəˈmɪbɪə [-bjə], -n/z
nares ˈneəriːz
naso-pharynx ˌneɪzəʊˈfærɪŋks [-ˈfeər-]
Nauru ˈnaʊru:
Nauruan, -s ˌnaʊˈruːən [-ˈrʊən], -z
navarin, -s ˈnævərɪn, -z
navicular nəˈvɪkjʊlə* [-kjəl-]
necrophil|ia, -iac/s ˌnekrəʊˈfɪl|ɪə,
-ɪæk/s
needlecord ˈniːdlkɔːd
needlepoint ˈniːdlpɔɪnt
negat|e, -es, -ing, -ed nɪˈgeɪt [ne-], -s,
-ɪŋ, -ɪd
negritude ˈnegrɪtjuːd
Nembutal ˈnembjʊtəl
neo-classical ˌniːəʊˈklæsɪkl [ˌnɪəʊ-]
neo-classicism ˌniːəʊˈklæsɪsɪzəm [ˌnɪəʊ-]
neodymium ˌniːəʊˈdɪmɪəm [ˌnɪəʊ-,
-mjəm]
neonate, -s ˈniːəʊneɪt [ˈnɪəʊ-, ˈniːən-], -s
netsuke ˈnetsʊkɪ [-suːkɪ, ˈnetskɪ]
neutralism ˈnjuːtrəlɪzəm [-tr.l-]
neutralist, -s ˈnjuːtrəlɪst [-trl̩ɪst], -s
neutrino, -s njuːˈtriːnəʊ, -z
newspeak ˈnjuːspiːk
newsreader, -s ˈnjuːzˌriːdə*, -z
nightlife ˈnaɪtlaɪf
niobium naɪˈəʊbɪəm [-bjəm]
Nissan ˈnɪsæn
nitrochalk ˈnaɪtrəʊtʃɔːk [ˌ--ˈ-]
nobelium nəʊˈbiːlɪəm [-ljəm]
Noh nəʊ
non-aggression ˌnɒnəˈgreʃn
non-alcoholic ˌhɒnælkəˈhɒlɪk
nonalign|ed, -ment ˌnɒnəˈlaɪn|d,
-mənt

569

non-commercial ˌnɒnkə'mɜːʃl
non-competitive ˌnɒnkəm'petətɪv [-tɪt-]
non-contentious ˌnɒnkən'tenʃəs
non-contiguous ˌnɒnkən'tɪgʊəs [-kɒn-, -gjwəs]
non-contributory ˌnɒnkən'trɪbjʊtərɪ
non-co-operation ˌnɒnkəʊɒpə'reɪʃn ['--ˌ--'--, '-ˌ---'--]
non-driver, -s ˌnɒn'draɪvə*, -z
nonet, -s nəʊ'net, -s
non-event, -s ˌnɒnɪ'vent ['--ˌ-], -s
nonfiction ˌnɒn'fɪkʃn
non-flammable ˌnɒn'flæməbl
non-linear ˌnɒn'lɪnɪə* [-njə*]
non-occurrence ˌnɒnə'kʌrəns
non-operational ˌnɒnɒpə'reɪʃənl [-ʃnəl, -ʃn̩l, -ʃn̩l, -ʃənəl, '-ˌ--'-- (-)]
non-playing 'nɒnˌpleɪɪŋ
non-profit-making ˌnɒn'prɒfɪtˌmeɪkɪŋ
non-proliferation 'nɒnprəˌlɪfə'reɪʃn
non-restrictive ˌnɒnrɪ'strɪktɪv [-rə's-]
non-returnable ˌnɒnrɪ'tɜːnəbl [-rə't-]
non-skid ˌnɒn'skɪd
non-slip ˌnɒn'slɪp
non-smok|er/s, -ing ˌnɒn'sməʊkə*/z, -ɪŋ
non-starter, -s ˌnɒn'stɑːtə*, -z
non-stick ˌnɒn'stɪk
non-swimmer, -s ˌnɒn'swɪmə*, -z
non-U ˌnɒn'juː
normative 'nɔːmətɪv
nosh, -es, -ing, -ed nɒʃ, -ɪz, -ɪŋ, -t
novella, -s nəʊ'velə, -z
novena, -s nəʊ'viːnə, -z
nth *(degree)* enθ [entθ]
numinous 'njuːmɪnəs
numnah, -s 'nʌmnə, -z

oeuvre 'ɜːvrə (œːvr)
off-chance 'ɒftʃɑːns
off-cuts 'ɒfkʌts
officiant, -s ə'fɪʃɪənt, -s
off-line ˌɒf'laɪn
offset *(v. compensate)*, **-s, -ting** ɒf'set, -s, -ɪŋ
okra 'əʊkrə ['ɒkrə]
Om əʊm
oncolog|ist/s, -y ɒŋ'kɒlədʒ|ɪst/s, -ɪ
oncological ˌɒŋkə'lɒdʒɪkl
on-line ˌɒn'laɪn
O.P.E.C. [Opec] 'əʊpek
open-plan ˌəʊpm'plæn [ˌəʊpən'plæn]

optometrist/s, -y ˌɒptəʊ'metrɪst/s [-mɪt-], -ɪ
oregano ˌɒrɪ'gɑːnəʊ [ˌɒrə'g-]
orfe ɔːf
orgasmic ɔː'gæzmɪk
orienteering ˌɔːrɪən'tɪərɪŋ [ˌɒr-, -rɪen-]
origami ˌɒrɪ'gɑːmɪ [-gæmɪ]
Oriya ɒ'riːə
osteitis ˌɒstɪ'aɪtɪs
osteoarthritis ˌɒstɪəʊɑː'θraɪtɪs [-tjəʊ-]
out-dated ˌaʊt'deɪtɪd
out-of-date ˌaʊtəv'deɪt
over-compensat|e, -es, -ing, -ed ˌəʊvə-'kɒmpenseɪt [-pən-], -s, -ɪŋ, -ɪd
over-emphasis|e, -es, -ing, -ed ˌəʊvər-'emfəsaɪz [ˌəʊvə'e-], -ɪz, -ɪŋ, -d
over-fl|y, -ies, -ying, -flew, -flown ˌəʊvə'fl|aɪ, -aɪz, -aɪɪŋ, -fluː, -fləʊn
over-man, -s, -ning, -ned ˌəʊvə'mæn, -z, -ɪŋ, -d
over-protect, -s, -ing, -ed ˌəʊvəprə'tekt, [-prʊ't-], -s, -ɪŋ, -ɪd
over-protective ˌəʊvəprə'tektɪv [-prʊ't-]
over-qualified ˌəʊvə'kwɒlɪfaɪd
over-react, -s, -ing, -ed ˌəʊvərɪ'ækt [-riː'ækt], -s, -ɪŋ, -ɪd
over-sensitive ˌəʊvə'sensɪtɪv [-sət-]
over-sensitivity 'əʊvəˌsensɪ'tɪvətɪ [-sə't-, -ɪtɪ]
oversew, -s, -ing, -ed, -n 'əʊvəsəʊ, -z, -ɪŋ, -d, -n
over-sexed ˌəʊvə'sekst
overshoe, -s 'əʊvəʃuː, -z
overside *(adv.)* 'əʊvəsaɪd
over-simplification 'əʊvəˌsɪmplɪfɪ-'keɪʃn
overspill 'əʊvəspɪl
over-staff, -s, -ing, -ed ˌəʊvə'stɑːf, -s, -ɪŋ, -t
over-stimulat|e, -es, -ing, -ed ˌəʊvə'stɪmjʊleɪt [-mjəl-], -s, -ɪŋ, -ɪd
over-tax, -es, -ing, -ed ˌəʊvə'tæks, -ɪz, -ɪŋ, -t
over-us|e, -es, -ing, -ed ˌəʊvə'juːz, -ɪz, -ɪŋ, -d
over-zealous ˌəʊvə'zeləs

paedophile, -s 'piːdəʊfaɪl, -z
paedophil|ia, -iac/s ˌpiːdəʊ'fɪl|ɪə, -ɪæk/s
paella paɪ'elə
painkiller, -s 'peɪnkɪlə*, -z

Palaeocene 'pælɪəʊsiːn
palomino, -s ˌpælə'miːnəʊ, -z
panellist, -s 'pænəlɪst ['pænlɪst], -s
panga, -s 'pæŋgə, -z
pangolin, -s 'pæŋgəʊlɪn, -z
panicle, -s 'pænɪkl, -z
panlectal ˌpæn'lektəl [-tl]
paparazzi 'pæpərætsɪ [ˌ--'--]
paperwork 'peɪpəwɜːk
papillote, -s 'pæpɪlɒt, -s
para (paratrooper), -s 'pærə, -z
paracetamol ˌpærə'siːtəmɒl [-'set-]
paramedic, -al ˌpærə'medɪk, -l
parametric ˌpærə'metrɪk
paramilitary ˌpærə'mɪlɪtərɪ [-lət-]
paranormal ˌpærə'nɔːml
parapraxis ˌpærə'præksɪs
paraquat 'pærəkwɒt
parenting 'peərəntɪŋ
paresis pə'riːsɪs
paretic pə'retɪk
parfait 'pɑːfeɪ [-'-]
parka, -s 'pɑːkə, -z
paronomazia [-sia] ˌpærənə'meɪzɪə
[-zɪə, -sjə, -sɪə]
part-time ˌpɑː't'taɪm
patrilineal ˌpætrɪ'lɪnɪəl
patrolcar, -s pə'trəʊlkɑː:*, -z
payday, -s 'peɪdeɪ, -z
payload, -s 'peɪləʊd, -z
pay-train, -s 'peɪtreɪn, -z
pazazz pə'zæz
peacetime 'piːstaɪm
pectic, -in 'pektɪk, -ɪn
pee, -s, -ing, -d piː, -z, -ɪŋ, -d
peepal, -s 'piːpəl, -z
peergroup, -s 'pɪəgruːp, -s
pellagra pə'lægrə
pellitory 'pelɪtərɪ [-lət-]
penile 'piːnaɪl
performative pə'fɔːmətɪv
perilune, -s 'perɪluːn [-ljuːn], -z
perinatal ˌperɪ'neɪtl
periscopic ˌperɪ'skɒpɪk
permafrost 'pɜːməfrɒst [old-fashioned
-frɔːst]
petiole, -s 'piːtɪəʊl ['pet-], -z
petit bourgeois ˌpetɪ'bɔːʒwɑː [-'bʊəʒ-]
petit bourgeoisie 'petɪˌbɔːʒwɑː:'ziː
[-ˌbʊəʒ-]
petit four ˌpetɪ'fɔː:* [-'fʊə*]
petits fours ˌpetɪ'fɔːz [-'fʊəz]
petit mal ˌpetɪ'mæl
petit point ˌpetɪ'pɔɪnt

petrochemical ˌpetrəʊ'kemɪkl
phenomenological fəˌnɒmmə'lɒdʒɪkl
[fɪ-]
phenomenology fəˌnɒmɪ'nɒlədʒɪ [fɪ-]
phonaesthesia ˌfəʊnɪs'θiːzjə [-niːs-,
-nəs-, -zɪə, -ʒjə, -ʒɪə, -ʒə]
photocall, -s 'fəʊtəʊkɔːl, -z
photocell, -s 'fəʊtəʊsel, -z
photogrammetr|ist/s, -y ˌfəʊtə'græm-
ətr|ɪst/s, -ɪ
photon, -s 'fəʊtɒn, -z
photosensitive ˌfəʊtəʊ'sensɪtɪv [-sət-]
photosensitivity 'fəʊtəʊˌsensɪ'tɪvətɪ
[-səˈt-, -ɪtɪ]
photosynthesis ˌfəʊtəʊ'sɪnθəsɪs [-θɪs-]
photosynthesiz|e [-is|e], -es, -ing, -ed
ˌfəʊtəʊ'sɪnθəsaɪz [-θɪs-], -ɪz, -ɪŋ, -d
phototropic ˌfəʊtəʊ'trɒpɪk
phototropism ˌfəʊtəʊ'trəʊpɪzəm
phyl|um, -a 'faɪl|əm, -ə
picador, -s 'pɪkədɔː:* [-dɔə*], -z
piddling (adj.) 'pɪdlɪŋ
pièce(s) de resistance ˌpjesdəre'zɪst-
ɑː:ns [-rə'z-, -rɪ'z-, -təns, '--,--'-]
(pjɛsdərezistɑ̃s)
piggy-bank, -s 'pɪgɪbæŋk, -s
pinetum paɪ'niːtəm
pipal, -s 'piːpəl, -z
pipistrelle, -s 'pɪpɪstrel, -z
piranha, -s pɪ'rɑːnjə, -z
pitta (bread) 'pɪtə(bred)
piz(z)azz pə'zæz
pizzeria, -s ˌpiːtsə'riːə [ˌpɪt-, -'rɪə], -z
Planck plæŋk
plasterboard 'plɑːstəbɔːd [bɔəd]
platelet, -s 'pleɪtlɪt [-lət], -s
playschool 'pleɪskuːl
plonk (s. v.), -s, -ing, -ed plɒŋk, -s, -ɪŋ,
-t
plumule, -s 'pluːmjuːl, -z
polonium pə'ləʊnɪəm [-njəm]
polybag, -s 'pɒlɪbæg [ˌ--'-], -z
polymer, -s 'pɒlɪmə*, -z
polymeric ˌpɒlɪ'merɪk
polysyndeton ˌpɒlɪ'sɪndətən [-dɪt-]
polyunsaturated ˌpɒlʌn'sætʃəreɪtɪd
[-tʃʊr-, -tjur-]
polyvalent ˌpɒlɪ'veɪlənt
pop(p)adom, -s 'pɒpədəm, -z
porphyria pɔː'fɪrɪə
porterhou|se, -ses 'pɔːtəhaʊ|s, -zɪz
portière, -s pɔːtɪ'eə*, -z
postcode, -s 'pəʊsˈkəʊd, -z
post-doctoral ˌpəʊst'dɒktərəl

571

post-glacial ˌpəʊst'gleɪsjəl [-sɪəl, -ʃjəl,
   -ʃɪəl, -ʃl, -glæsɪəl, -glæsjəl]
postpositive ˌpəʊst'pɒzətɪv [-zɪt-]
postpositional ˌpəʊstpə'zɪʃənl [-ʃnəl,
   -ʃn̩l, -ʃn̩l, -ʃənəl]
potbound (*adj.*) 'pɒtbaʊnd
poussin (P.), -s 'pu:sæn, -z (pusɛ̃)
powerpack, -s 'paʊəpæk, -s
powerpoint, -s 'paʊəpɔɪnt, -s
praseodymium ˌpreɪzɪəʊ'dɪmɪəm
   [ˌpraɪzəʊ-, -mjəm]
preamplifier,   -s   pri:'æmplɪfaɪə*
   [prɪ'æ-], -z
precast ˌpri:'kɑːst
preclassical ˌpri:'klæsɪkl
precognition ˌpri:kɒg'nɪʃn
pre-dat|e, -es, -ing, -ed pri:'deɪt, -s,
   -ɪŋ, -ɪd
preheat, -s, -ing, -ed ˌpri:'hi:t, -s, -ɪŋ,
   -ɪd
premarital ˌpri:'mærɪtl
premedical ˌpri:'medɪkl
premedication ˌpri:medɪ'keɪʃn
premolar, -s ˌpri:'məʊlə*, -z
preschool ˌpri:'sku:l
Presley 'prezlɪ
press-stud, -s 'prestʌd ['presstʌd], -s
press-up, -s 'presʌp, -s
prestressed ˌpri:'strest
pretzel, -s 'pretsl, -z
Prinknash 'prɪmɪdʒ
privatisation ˌpraɪvɪtaɪ'zeɪʃn [-vət-]
privatiz|e [-is|e], -es, -ing, -ed
   'praɪvɪtaɪz, -ɪz, -ɪŋ, -d
profiterole, -s prɒ'fɪtərəʊl [prə'f-], -z
progesterone prə'dʒestərəʊn [prəʊ-]
programmatic ˌprəʊgrə'mætɪk
prole, -s prəʊl, -z
promethium prə'mi:θɪəm [prəʊ'm-,
   -θjəm]
proponent, -s prəʊ'pəʊnənt, -s
propylene 'prɒpɪli:n [-pəl-]
prosciutto prəʊ'ʃu:təʊ
protactinium ˌprəʊtæk'tɪnɪəm [-njəm]
Przewalski's (*horse*) prəʒə'vælskɪz
   [ˌprɪʒ-]
pseud, -s sju:d [su:d], -z
psych(e), -s, -ing, -ed saɪk, -s, -ɪŋ, -t
psycholinguistic, -s ˌsaɪkəʊlɪŋ'gwɪstɪk,
   -s
psychosexual ˌsaɪkəʊ'sekʃʊəl [-ksjʊəl,
   -ksjwəl, -ksjʊl, -kʃwəl, -kʃʊl]
Pulteney (Sir John de) 'pʊltnɪ
punchball, -s 'pʌntʃbɔ:l, -z

punchline, -s 'pʌntʃlaɪn, -z
punk, -s, -y, -ier, -iest pʌŋk, -s, -ɪ, -ɪə*,
   -ɪɪst

Qatar 'kʌtɑː*
quantiz|e [-is|e], -es, -ing, -ed
   'kwɒntaɪz, -ɪz, -ɪŋ, -d
quark, -s 'kwɑːk, -s
Quechua, -n/s 'ketʃʊə ['ketʃwə], -n/z
quiche, -s ki:ʃ, -ɪz
quiddity 'kwɪdɪtɪ [-ətɪ]
Qur'an kɒ'rɑːn [kɔː'r-, kʊ'r-, kə'r-]

raceme, -s 'ræsi:m ['reɪsi:m, rə'si:m]
R.A.D.A. 'rɑːdə
radicle, -s 'rædɪkl, -z
radiocarbon ˌreɪdɪəʊ'kɑːbən [-djəʊ-,
   -bn, -bɒn]
radioisotope,   -s   ˌreɪdɪəʊ'aɪsəʊtəʊp
   [-djəʊ-], -s
radiopag|e, -es, -ing, -ed, -er/s ˌreɪd-
   ɪəʊ'peɪdʒ [-djəʊ-], -ɪz, -ɪŋ, -d, -ə*/z
radon 'reɪdɒn
raga, -s 'rɑːgə [rɑːg], -z
rang|y, -ier, -iest 'reɪndʒ|ɪ, -ɪə*, -ɪɪst
raring (*adj.*) 'reərɪŋ
Rasta 'ræstə
Rastafarian, -s ˌræstə'feərɪən, -z
ratatouille ˌrætə'twi: [-'tu:i:] (ratatuj)
ravioli ˌrævɪ'əʊlɪ
razzamattazz 'ræzəmətæz [ˌ---'-]
reactivat|e, -es, -ing, -ed ˌri:'æktɪv-
   eɪt, -s, -ɪŋ, -ɪd
reafforest, -s, -ing, -ed ˌri:ə'fɒrɪst [ˌrɪə-,
   rɪə-], -s, -ɪŋ, -ɪd
reafforestation 'ri:əˌfɒrɪ'steɪʃn [-æˌf-,
   -re's-]
Reagan 'reɪgən
realign, -s, -ing, -ed, -ment/s ˌri:ə'laɪn
   [ˌrɪə-, rɪə-], -z, -ɪŋ, -d, -mənt/s
reallocat|e, -es, -ing, -ed ˌri:'æləʊkeɪt
   [rɪ'æ-], -s, -ɪŋ, -ɪd
reallocation ˌri:ælə'keɪʃn [-ˌ--'--]
reassess, -es, -ing, -ed, -ment/s ˌri:ə'ses
   [ˌrɪə-, rɪə-], -ɪz, -ɪŋ, -t, -mənt/s
reassign, -s, -ing, -ed ˌri:ə'saɪn [ˌrɪə-,
   rɪə-], -z, -ɪŋ, -d
reawak|en,   -ens,   -ening,   -ened
   ˌri:ə'weɪk|ən [ˌrɪə-, rɪə-], -ənz, -nɪŋ
   [-n̩ɪŋ, -ənɪŋ], -ənd

recap (s.), **-s** 'riːkæp, -s
recap (v.), **-s**, **-ping**, **-ped** 'riːkæp [ˌ-'-],
-s, -ɪŋ, -t
receptor, **-s** rɪ'septə* [rə's-], -z
recharg|e, **-es**, **-ing**, **-ed**, **-able** ˌriː-
'tʃɑːdʒ, -ɪz, -ɪŋ, -d, -əbl
recuperative rɪ'kuːpərətɪv [rə'k-,
-kjuː-]
re-enforc|e, **-es**, **-ing**, **-ed** ˌriːm'fɔːs, -ɪz,
-ɪŋ, -t
reflationary riː'fleɪʃn̩ərɪ [-ʃnərɪ,
-ʃn̩rɪ, -ʃənərɪ]
reggae 'regeɪ
regulatory 'regjʊlətərɪ [ˌregʊ'leɪtərɪ,
-gjəl-]
relational rɪ'leɪʃənl [rə'l-, -ʃnəl,
-ʃn̩l, -ʃnl, -ʃənəl]
relativ|ism, **-ist/s** 'relətɪv|ɪzəm,
-ɪst/s
relocat|e, **-es**, **-ing**, **-ed** ˌriːləʊ'keɪt, -s,
-ɪŋ, -ɪd
relocation ˌriːləʊ'keɪʃn
reluctivity ˌrelʌk'tɪvətɪ [-ɪtɪ]
remanence 'remənəns
remediation rɪˌmiːdɪ'eɪʃn [rəˌm-]
repetiteur, **-s** rɪˌpetɪ'tɜː* [rəˌp-], -z
replicable 'replɪkəbl
replicat|e, **-es**, **-ing**, **-ed** 'replɪkeɪt, -s,
-ɪŋ, -ɪd
replication, **-s** ˌreplɪ'keɪʃn, -z
repossess, **-es**, **-ing**, **-ed** ˌriːpə'zes
[-pʊ'z-], -ɪz, -ɪŋ, -t
repossession ˌriːpə'zeʃn [-pʊ'z-]
representational ˌreprɪzen'teɪʃənl
[-ʃnəl, -ʃn̩l, -ʃnl, -ʃənəl]
repris|e (s. v.), **-es**, **-ing**, **-ed** rɪ'priːz
[rə'p-], -ɪz, -ɪŋ, -d
reprographic, **-s** ˌriːprəʊ'græfɪk [ˌrep-],
-s
reshuffle (s.), **-s** 'riːʃʌfl [ˌ-'--], -z
re-sit (s.), **-s** 'riːsɪt, -s
re|sit (v.), **-sits**, **-sitting**, **-sat** ˌriː'sɪt,
-'sɪts, -'sɪtɪŋ, -'sæt
resorb, **-s**, **-ing**, **-ed** rɪ'sɔːb [rə'sɔːb,
rɪ'zɔːb, rə'zɔːb], -z, -ɪŋ, -d
resorp|tion, **-tive** rɪ'sɔːp|ʃn [rə'sɔːp-,
rɪ'zɔːp-, rə'zɔːp-], -tɪv
respray (s.), **-s** 'riːspreɪ, -z
respray (v.), **-s**, **-ing**, **-ed** ˌriː'spreɪ, -z,
-ɪŋ, -d
resurgen|ce, **-t** rɪ'sɜːdʒən|s [rə's-],
-t
retsina ret'siːnə
rev-counter, **-s** 'revˌkaʊntə*, -z

re-wir|e, **-es**, **-ing**, **-ed** ˌriː'waɪə*, -z,
-rɪŋ, -d
rhenium 'riːnɪəm [-njəm]
riesling 'riːslɪŋ
rightangle, **-s** 'raɪtˌæŋgl, -z
ripcord, **-s** 'rɪpkɔːd, -z
ritornello ˌrɪtə'neləʊ
ritualiz|e [**-is|e**], **-es**, **-ing**, **-ed**
'rɪtʃʊəlaɪz [-tʃwəl-, -tʃʊl-, -tʃəl-,
-tjʊəl-, -tjwəl-, -tjʊl-], -ɪz, -ɪŋ, -d
Ritz rɪts
ritz|y, **-ier**, **-iest** 'rɪts|ɪ, -ɪə*, -ɪɪst
riyal, **-s** riː'ɑːl, -z
rock-climb|er/s, **-ing** 'rɒkˌklaɪm|ə*/z,
-ɪŋ
rocket-base, **-s** 'rɒkɪt beɪs, -ɪz
rocket-range, **-s** 'rɒkɪtreɪndʒ, -ɪz
Rodin 'rəʊdæn (rɔdɛ̃)
rollmop, **-s** 'rəʊlmɒp, -s
roll-on, **-s** 'rəʊlɒn, -z
room-mate, **-s** 'rʊmmeɪt ['ruːm-], -s
rootstock, **-s** 'ruːtstɒk, -s
Rorschach 'rɔːʃɑːk
rosé 'rəʊzeɪ
rosehip, **-s** 'rəʊzhɪp, -s
Rosh Hashana ˌrɒʃhæ'ʃɑːnə
rotisserie, **-s** rəʊ'tiːsərɪ, -z
rotovator, **-s** 'rəʊtəveɪtə*, -z
rough|en, **-ens**, **-ening**, **-ened** 'rʌf|n,
-nz, -nɪŋ [-n̩ɪŋ], -nd
roux 'ruː
Rubik 'ruːbɪk
runcible 'rʌnsɪbl
rupiah, **-s** ruː'piːə, -z
rutilant 'ruːtɪlənt
rutile 'ruːtaɪl

sackcloth 'sækklɒθ [old-fashioned-klɔːθ]
sadhu, **-s** 'sɑːduː, -z
Sahel sɑː'hel
salestalk 'seɪlztɔːk
Salvadorian, **-s** ˌsælvə'dɔːrɪən, -z
samarium sə'meərɪəm
sangria 'sæŋgrɪə
sanitiz|e [**-is|e**], **-es**, **-ing**, **-ed**
'sænɪtaɪz, -ɪz, -ɪŋ, -d
Sartre 'sɑːtrə (sartr)
scandium 'skændɪəm [-djəm]
scatolog|ist/s, **-y** skæ'tɒlədʒ|ɪst/s, -ɪ
scatological ˌskætə'lɒdʒɪkl
schematiz|e [**-is|e**], **-es**, **-ing**, **-ed**
'skiːmətaɪz, -ɪz, -ɪŋ, -d

573

schmaltz ʃmɒlts
schnitzel, -s 'ʃnɪtsl, -z
schnorkel, -s 'ʃnɔːkl, -z
Schrödinger 'ʃrɜːdɪŋə*
Scouse skaʊs
scuba 'skuːbə ['skjuːbə]
sedat|e (v.), -es, -ing, -ed sɪ'deɪt, -s, -ɪŋ, -ɪd
sedation sɪ'deɪʃn
see-through (adj.) 'siːθruː
segmentation ˌsegmen'teɪʃn [-mən-]
self-image, -s ˌself'ɪmɪdʒ, -ɪz
sememe, -s 'siːmiːm, -z
sensor, -s 'sensə*, -z
serializ|e [-is|e], -es, -ing, -ed
  'sɪərɪəlaɪz, -ɪz, -ɪŋ, -d
serialisation, -s ˌsɪərɪəlaɪ'zeɪʃn [-lɪ'z-], -z
server|y, -ies 'sɜːvər|ɪ, -ɪz
servo-mechanism, -s 'sɜːvəʊˌmek-
  ənɪzəm, -z
Sesotho se'suːtuː
sex|ism, -ist/s 'seks|ɪzəm, -ɪst/s
sextuplet, -s 'sekstjʊplet [sek'stjuː-
  plet, -plɒt, -plɪt], -s
shebang ʃɪ'bæŋ [ʃə'b-]
Shelta 'ʃeltə
Sherpa, -s 'ʃɜːpə, -z
Shia(h) 'ʃiːə
Shi'ite, -s 'ʃiːaɪt, -s
shirtwaister, -s ˌʃɜːt'weɪstə*, -z
shish-kebab, -s 'ʃiːʃkɪˌbæb [-kəˌb-, ˌ--'-], -z
shockproof 'ʃɒkpruːf
shoestring 'ʃuːstrɪŋ
shortlist (s. v.), -s, -ing, -ed 'ʃɔːtlɪst, -s, -ɪŋ, -ɪd
shove-halfpenny ˌʃʌv'heɪpnɪ
showbiz 'ʃəʊbɪz
sideburn, -s 'saɪdbɜːn, -z
sidedish, -es 'saɪddɪʃ, -ɪz
sightscreen, -s 'saɪtskriːn, -z
simplistic sɪm'plɪstɪk
sinfonia, -s sɪn'fəʊnɪə [ˌsɪnfə'nɪə], -z
sinfonietta, -s ˌsɪnfəʊnɪ'etə [-fɒn-, -'njetə], -z
Sinitic saɪ'nɪtɪk [sɪ'n-]
sitcom, -s 'sɪtkɒm, -z
skateboard, -er/s, -ing 'skeɪtbɔːd [-bɔəd], -ə*/z, -ɪŋ
skewbald 'skjuːbɔːld
skew-whiff ˌskjuː'wɪf
skilift, -s 'skiːlɪft, -s
sleaz|y, -ier, -iest, -ily, -iness 'sliːz|ɪ,

-ɪə*, -ɪɪst, -ɪlɪ [-əlɪ], -ɪnɪs [-məs]
small-scale ˌsmɔːl'skeɪl
snazz|y, -ier, -iest, -ily 'snæz|ɪ, -ɪə*, -ɪɪst, -ɪlɪ [-əlɪ]
SNOBOL 'snəʊbɒl
snowblower, -s 'snəʊˌbləʊə*, -z
soapbox, -es 'səʊpbɒks, -ɪz
soap-opera, -s 'səʊpˌɒpərə, -z
socio-biolog|ist/s, -y ˌsəʊsɪəʊbaɪ-
  'ɒlədʒ|ɪst/s [-sɪəʊ-, -ʃjəʊ-, -ʃɪəʊ-], -ɪ
socioeconomic 'səʊsɪəʊˌiːkə'nɒmɪk
  [-sɪəʊ-, -ʃjəʊ-, -ʃɪəʊ-, -ˌek-]
sociolinguistic, -s ˌsəʊsɪəʊlɪŋ'gwɪstɪk
  [-sɪəʊ-, -ʃjəʊ-, -ʃɪəʊ-], -s
software 'sɒftweə* [old-fashioned'sɔːf-]
soigné(e) 'swɑːnjeɪ [-'-]
solid-state ˌsɒlɪd'steɪt
son et lumière ˌsɒneɪluː'mjeə* [ˌsɔːn-, ˌ--'--]
sorghum 'sɔːgəm
Sotho 'suːtuː
soul-destroying 'səʊldɪˌstrɔɪɪŋ
soul-searching 'səʊlˌsɜːtʃɪŋ
space-shuttle, -s 'speɪʃˌʃʌtl, -z
space-station, -s 'speɪsˌsteɪʃn, -z
spermicide, -s 'spɜːmɪsaɪd, -z
spermicidal ˌspɜːmɪ'saɪdl
sphragistics sfrə'dʒɪstɪks
sphygmomanometer, -s ˌsfɪgməʊmə-
  'nɒmɪtə* [-mətə*], -z
spiel ʃpiːl [spiːl]
splash-down, -s 'splæʃdaʊn, -z
split-level ˌsplɪt'levl
spokesperson, -s 'spəʊksˌpɜːsn, -z
sprechgesang 'ʃprekgəzʌŋ ['ʃprexg-, -zæŋ] (ʃprɛçgəzaŋ)
starch-reduced 'stɑːtʃrɪˌdjuːst [-rəˌd-]
stasis 'steɪsɪs
step-parent, -s 'stepˌpeərənt, -s
streetwise 'striːtwaɪz
stroganoff, -s 'strɒgənɒf, -s
strudel, -s 'struːdl, -z
stupa, -s 'stuːpə, -z
subaqua ˌsʌb'ækwə
Subaru, -s ˌsuːbə'ruː, -z
subatomic ˌsʌbə'tɒmɪk
subclinical ˌsʌb'klɪnɪkl
subculture, -s 'sʌbkʌltʃə*, -z
submariner, -s sʌb'mærɪnə* [-rən-], -z, -z
subnuclear ˌsʌb'njuːklɪə* [-ljə*]
suborbital ˌsʌb'ɔːbɪtl
subroutine, -s 'sʌbruːtiːn, -z
subset, -s 'sʌbset, -s
subsonic ˌsʌb'sɒnɪk

substandard ˌsʌb'stændəd
subsystem, -s 'sʌbsɪstəm [-tɪm], -z
subzero ˌsʌb'zɪərəʊ
sucrose 'su:krəʊs ['sju:-, -rəʊz]
Sunn|i, -ite/s 'sʊn|ɪ, -aɪt/s
supernov|a, -ae, -as ˌsu:pə'nəʊv|ə
[ˌsju:-], -i:, -əz
superpower, -s 'su:pəˌpaʊə* ['sju:-], -z
superstar, -s 'su:pəstɑ:* ['sju:-], -z
surrealistic səˌrɪə'lɪstɪk [sjʊ-, sʊ-]
sursum corda ˌsɜ:səm 'kɔ:də [-sʊm-]
Swapo 'swɒpəʊ
sweatshirt, -s 'swet-ʃɜ:t, -s
sweatshop, -s 'swet-ʃɒp, -s
sweetcorn 'swi:tkɔ:n
swing-wing ˌswɪŋ'wɪŋ
syllep|sis, -tic sɪ'lep|sɪs, -tɪk
symbolist, -s 'sɪmbəlɪst [-bʊl-, -bl̩-],
-s

Tabasco tə'bæskəʊ
tabla, -s 'tæblə, -z (*Hindi* təbla)
tamboura, -s tæm'bʊərə, -z
tandoori tæn'dʊərɪ
tanktop, -s 'tæŋktɒp, -s
tape-deck, -s 'teɪpdek, -s
taramasalata ˌtærəməsə'lɑ:tə
task force, -s 'tɑ:skfɔ:s, -ɪz
taxhaven, -s 'tæksˌheɪvn, -z
teabag, -s 'ti:bæg, -z
tear-jerker, -s 'tɪəˌdʒɜ:kə*, -z
tectonic, -s tek'tɒnɪk, -s
T.E.F.L. 'tefl
Telecom 'telɪkɒm
teletext, -s 'telɪtekst, -s
tellurian, -s te'lʊərɪən [tə'l-, tɪ'l-,
-ljʊə-], -z
temp (*s. v.*), **-s, -ing, -ed** temp, -s, -ɪŋ, -t
template, -s 'templeɪt [-plɪt], -s
tenderiz|e [-is|e], -es, -ing, -ed
'tendəraɪz, -ɪz, -ɪŋ, -d
tequila, -s tə'ki:lə [tɪ'k-], -z
terrari|um, -a tə'reərɪ|əm [te'r-,
tɪ'r-], -ə
terrine, -s 'teri:n [-'-]
tetrathlon te'træθlɒn [tɪ-, tə-, -lən]
theorbo, -s θɪ'ɔ:bəʊ, [θi:'ɔ:-], -z
thermonuclear ˌθɜ:məʊ'nju:klɪə* [-ljə*]
thermosetting 'θɜ:məʊˌsetɪŋ
thinktank, -s 'θɪŋktæŋk, -s
thuja, -s 'θu:jə, -z
thymine 'θaɪmi:n

Tobagonian, -s ˌtəʊbə'gəʊnjən [-nɪən],
-z
toluene 'tɒlju:i:n [-jʊi:n]
tonka-bean, -s 'tɒŋkəbi:n, -z
tonne, -s tʌn, -z
top-level ˌtɒp'levl
topologic, -al, -ally ˌtɒpə'lɒdʒɪk, -l, -əlɪ
topolog|ist/s, -y tɒ'pɒlədʒ|ɪst/s [tə'p-],
-ɪ
topside 'tɒpsaɪd
topsoil 'tɒpsɔɪl
tourism 'tʊərɪzəm ['tɔə-, 'tɔ:-]
towbar, -s 'təʊbɑ:*, -z
tracksuit, -s 'træksu:t [-sju:t], -s
trade-off (*s.*), **-s** 'treɪdɒf (*old-fashioned*
-ɔ:f], -s
Tradescant trə'deskənt
tradescantia ˌtrædɪ'skæntɪə
transfinite træns'faɪnaɪt [trɑ:n-]
transformational ˌtrænsfə'meɪʃənl
[ˌtrɑ:ns-, -ʃnəl, -ʃn̩l, -ʃnl̩, -ʃənəl]
transhumance ˌtrænshju:'mæns
[ˌtrɑ:n-, -'hju:məns]
transsexual trænz'sekʃʊəl [trɑ:n-,
-ksjʊəl, -ksjwəl, -ksjʊl, -kʃwəl,
-kʃʊl]
trattoria, -s ˌtrætə'rɪə, -z
trendsett|er/s, -ing 'trendˌset|ə*/z,
-ɪŋ
triage 'tri:ɑ:ʒ ['traɪdʒ]
triathlon traɪ'æθlɒn [-lən]
Triffid, -s 'trɪfɪd, -z
trinitroglycerin(e) 'traɪˌnaɪtrəʊ'glɪsərɪn [-ri:n, ˌ---'---]
trioxide, -s traɪ'ɒksaɪd [ˌ-'--], -z
triton 'traɪtɒn
troublemaker, -s 'trʌblˌmeɪkə*, -z
troubleshoot|er/s, -ing 'trʌblˌʃu:tə*/z,
-ɪŋ
T-shirt, -s 'ti:ʃɜ:t, -s
Tswana 'tswɑ:nə
tuberculin tu:'bɜ:kjʊlɪn [tjʊ-, -kjəl-]

U.C.C.A. 'ʌkə
ultrasound 'ʌltrəsaʊnd
ultraviolet ˌʌltrə'vaɪələt [-lɪt]
uncompetitive ˌʌnkəm'petətɪv [-tɪt-]
under-achiev|e, -es, -ing, -ed, -er/s
ˌʌndərə'tʃi:v [-dəə'tʃ-], -z, -ɪŋ, -d,
-ə*/z
underfloor (*adj.*) ˌʌndə'flɔ:* [-'flɔə*]
undernourished ˌʌndə'nʌrɪʃt

undersexed ˌʌndə'sekst
underwater ˌʌndə'wɔːtə*
unicameral ˌjuːnɪ'kæmərəl [-mrəl]
unicellular ˌjuːnɪ'seljʊlə*
uniformly 'juːnɪfɔːmlɪ [ˌ--'--]
univalent ˌjuːnɪ'veɪlənt
unliberated ˌʌn'lɪbəreɪtɪd
unrounded ˌʌn'raʊndɪd [-'--]
unsaturated ˌʌn'sætʃəreɪtɪd [-tʃʊr-, -tjʊr-, -'----]
unscheduled [also ˌʌn'ʃedʒuːld, ˌʌn'ske-, -dʒld]
unscripted ˌʌn'skrɪptɪd [ʌn-]
unshockable ˌʌn'ʃɒkəbl [-'----]
unsubstantiated ˌʌnsəb'stænʃɪeɪtɪd [-bz't-, -staːnʃ-, -ʃjeɪt-, -nsɪ-]
up-and-coming ˌʌpən'kʌmɪŋ
Upanishad, -s ʊ'pʌnɪʃəd, -z
update (s.), **-s** 'ʌpdeɪt, -s
updat|e, -es, -ing, -ed ʌp'deɪt [ˌ-'-], -s, -ɪŋ, -ɪd
upgrad|e, -es, -ing, -ed ʌp'greɪd [ˌ-'-], -z, -ɪŋ, -ɪd
upmarket (adj.) ˌʌp'maːkɪt ['---]
upswing (s.), **-s** 'ʌpswɪŋ, -z

vacuum-packed ˌvækjʊm'pækt [-kjuːm-, -kjʊəm-, -kjwəm-]
vandaliz|e [-is|e], -es, -ing, -ed 'vændəlaɪz [-dḷ-], -ɪz, -ɪŋ, -d
variate (s.), **-s** 'veərɪət [-rɪɪt], -s
V.D.U., -s ˌviːdiː'juː, -z
vegan, -s 'viːgən, -z
velcro 'velkrəʊ
vichyssoise ˌviːʃɪ'swaːz [ˌvɪʃɪ-]
Victoriana ˌvɪktɔːrɪ'aːnə [-ˌ--'--]
video text, -s 'vɪdɪəʊtekst, -s
viola da gamba, -s vɪˌəʊlədə'gæmbə, -z
viola d'amore vɪˌəʊlədæ'mɔːreɪ
Vishnu 'vɪʃnuː
vox populi vɒks 'pɒpjʊliː
voyeurism vwaː'jɜːrɪzəm [vɔɪ'ɜːrɪzəm, '----]
voyeuristic ˌvɔɪə'rɪstɪk
V.T.O.L. 'viːtɒl

wack|y, -ier, -iest 'wæk|ɪ, -ɪə*, -ɪɪst
walkabout, -s 'wɔːkəˌbaʊt, -s

walkway, -s 'wɔːkweɪ, -z
wan (information technology) wæn
warfarin 'wɔːfərɪn
wasteland 'weɪstlænd
watercannon 'wɔːtəˌkænən
waterhole, -s 'wɔːtəhəʊl, -z
watermeadow, -s 'wɔːtəˌmedəʊ, -z
watermelon, -s 'wɔːtəˌmelən, -z
watermill, -s 'wɔːtəmɪl, -z
waterpolo 'wɔːtəˌpəʊləʊ
weedkiller, -s 'wiːdˌkɪlə*, -z
weigela waɪ'dʒiːlə
weightlift|er/s, -ing 'weɪtˌlɪft|ə*/z, -ɪŋ
weightwatch|er/s, -ing 'weɪtˌwɒtʃ|ə*/z, -ɪŋ
weirdo, -s 'wɪədəʊ, -z
well-formed ˌwel'fɔːmd
wellie, -s 'welɪ, -z
weltanschauung 'veltənˌʃaʊʊŋ
wetsuit, -s 'wetsuːt [-sjuːt], -s
wheatgerm 'wiːtdʒɜːm ['hw-]
wheatmeal 'wiːtmiːl ['hw-]
wholefood, -s 'həʊlfuːd, -z
wildfowl 'waɪldfaʊl
wildlife 'waɪldlaɪf
wimp, -s, -ish wɪmp, -s, -ɪʃ
Wimpy, -bar/s 'wɪmpɪ, -baː*/z
window-shop, -s, -ing, -ed 'wɪndəʊ ʃɒp, -s, -ɪŋ, -t
wind-surf, -s, -ing, -t 'wɪndsɜːf. -s, -ɪŋ, -t
wine-bar, -s 'waɪnbaː*, -z
wok, -s wɒk, -s
woofer (electronics), **-s** 'wʊfə*, -z
word-processor, -s 'wɜːdˌprəʊsesə*, -z
word-processing 'wɜːdˌprəʊsesɪŋ
workaholic, -s ˌwɜːkə'hɒlɪk, -s
work-to-rule, -s ˌwɜːktə'ruːl, -z
worldview, -s 'wɜːldvjuː [ˌ-'-], -z

yarmulke, -z 'jʌmʊlkə, -z
ylang-ylang ˌiːlæŋ'iːlæŋ

zap, -s, -ping, -ed zæp, -s, -ɪŋ, -t
ziggurat, -s 'zɪgəræt, -s
zircon 'zɜːkɒn